BLOOMSBURY
ESSENTIAL
DICTIONARY

D1386646

A BLOOMSBURY REFERENCE BOOK
Created from the Bloomsbury Database of World English
www.bloomsbury.com/reference

First published in 2002
Reprinted 2004

Bloomsbury Publishing Plc, 38 Soho Square, London W1D 3HB

A CIP record for this title is available from the British Library

ISBN 0 7475 7615 7

10 9 8 7 6 5 4 3 2 1

Typeset by Selwood Systems, Midsomer Norton, Bath, United Kingdom
Printed in Great Britain by Clays Ltd, St Ives plc

Contents

Using Your Dictionary

Entry word

> **abbot** /ábbət/ n the head of a monastery
> —**abbotship** n

Inflected form

> **abide** /ə bíd/ (**abiding**, **abode** /ə bód/ or **abided**) v
> 1 vt tolerate o *I can't abide disobedient children.*
> 2 vi dwell (archaic)
> □ **abide by** vt follow or accept a rule or decision

Phrasal (two-word) verb

Definition number — Definition

> **ability** /ə bílləti/ n 1 the state of being able to do
> something 2 skill, talent, or intelligence

> **SYNONYMS** ability, skill, competence, aptitude, talent, capacity, capability core
> meaning: the necessary skill, knowledge, or
> experience to do something

Synonyms note

Inflected form

> **able** /áyb'l/ (**abler**, **ablest**) adj 1 in a position to
> do something 2 capable or talented —**ably**
> adv ◊ See note at **intelligent**

Cross-reference to boxed note

Incorrect spelling

> ~~abreviation~~ incorrect spelling of **abbreviation**

Geographical entry

> **Abuja** /ə bòò jaa/ official capital of Nigeria. Pop.
> 339,100 (1995).

Usage label

> **ac** abbr academic organization (in Internet
> addresses)

Alternative form of entry word

> **academia** /ákə deemi ə/, **academe** /ákə deem/ n
> academic life

Pronunciation

Example of use

> **access** /ák sess/ n 1 a means of entry or approach o *gained access via an upstairs window*
> 2 the right or opportunity to use something
> or meet somebody 3 an outburst (literary)
> ■ vt 1 enter a place 2 retrieve data from a
> computer
>
> **SPELLCHECK** Do not confuse the spelling of
> **access** and **excess** ('a surplus'), which sound
> similar.

New part of speech   Spellcheck note

Regional label

> **achcha** /úchə/ interj S Asia 1 all right 2 is that
> so?

Biographical entry

> **Adcock** /ád kok/, **Fleur** (b. 1934) New Zealand
> poet

Set phrase   Style label

> **aegis** /ée jiss/ ◊ **under the aegis of** with the
> support or protection of (fml)
>
> **ORIGIN** The Greek word from which **aegis** comes
> was used for the goatskin shield of the god
> Zeus, a symbol of his traditional function as a
> protector. The English form comes from Latin.

Word origins note

Cross-reference to more common spelling

> **aether** n = ether 2

Triangle warning of disputed usage

> **aggravate** /ággrə vayt/ (**-vating**, **-vated**) vt 1 △
> irritate or anger (infml) 2 make worse
> —**aggravating** adj —**aggravatingly** adv
> —**aggravation** /ággrə váysh'n/ n
>
> **USAGE** Many people still dislike the use of
> **aggravate** to mean 'irritate or anger somebody',
> despite a history of usage dating back to the
> 17C: *Their bad behaviour has been very aggravating.* Except in informal conversation, it
> is usually better to use an alternative word such
> as *annoy, exasperate,* or *irritate.*

Derived word   Usage note

Improving Your Spelling

Introduction
Spelling can be difficult. To use a dictionary effectively, you need to be able to make a good guess at how a word might be spelt in order to find a likely place to look it up – and this is not always easy.

How to look up a word whose spelling you do not know
The main alternative spellings for consonant and vowel sounds are given below. If you cannot find the word you want in the first place you look for it, look at the examples below to find different possible spellings that you could try.

Consonants
Consonants are all the letters of the alphabet except **a, e, i, o, u**, and sometimes **y**. Consonants in English can generally be doubled except for **h, j, k, q**, and **x**. If you cannot find the word with a doubled consonant, try a single one.

ALTERNATIVE SPELLINGS FOR CONSONANTS

Sound	Alternative spellings			
ch arch chin	**tch** kitchen patch	**tu** puncture statue		
f defend fair	**ph** dolphin phone	**gh** rough		
j cajole jam	**g** (before e, i, or y) gem logic edgy	**dg** badge judge		
k kitten	**c** crowd	**ck** chicken	**qu** opaque	**ch** chaos technique
n now done	**gn** gnaw campaign	**kn** kneel acknowledge		
qu liquid quick	**cqu** acquire	**kw** awkward		
s send base	**c** (before e, i, or y) centre acid juicy	**sc** scent ascend	**ss** professor confess	
sh shop cash	**ss** passion procession	**ti** patience cautious		
w forward	**u** (before vowel) persuade			

| x
taxi | ks
thanks | xc
except | cs
physics | |
| z
daze
marzipan | s (before
vowel)
please
easy | x
anxiety
xylophone | | |

There is also a sound somewhere between z and sh for which there is no consonant. It is usually spelt **su**, as in **pleasure** or **casual**, but can also be spelt **si**, as in **vision** or **precision**. In the Dictionary this sound is represented by /zh/.

Vowels
The vowels in the alphabet are **a, e, i, o, u,** and sometimes **y**. All the vowels have a 'long' vowel sound and a 'short' vowel sound. The 'long' sound is the sound of the letter as it would be pronounced if you were reciting the alphabet. The 'short' sounds are those in b**a**d, b**e**d, b**i**d, b**o**dy, and b**u**d. The letter **y** has the long and short sound of **i**, as in c**y**cle and bicycle.

A vowel on its own (between two consonants or at the beginning of a word) can have either the long or short sound. A vowel before a double consonant will have the short sound, as in **latter** (compare **later**) or **hopping** (compare **hoping**).

Long vowels
In general a vowel followed by a single consonant and then an **e** (with the **e** not pronounced) is a long vowel, eg

spade, these, bite, phone, prune, style

ALTERNATIVE SPELLINGS FOR THE LONG VOWELS A, E, I, O, AND U

Sound	Alternative spellings			
a make amiable	ai complaint aim	ay day	ea great	ei rein eight
e lethal even	ee sheep	ea peace eat	ie believe	ei ceiling
i Friday ice	igh light	ie pie	y cry	
o ghost over	oa roast oats	ow show own	oe hoe	ou although
u rude union	ew grew few	ue glue due	oo goose	ou group

ALTERNATIVE SPELLINGS FOR THE SHORT VOWELS E, I, AND U

Sound	Alternative spellings			
e bed elephant	ea ready			
i him ink	y gym			
u hundred under	o dozen	oo blood	ou touch	

ALTERNATIVE SPELLINGS FOR OTHER VOWEL SOUNDS

Sound	Alternative spellings					
aw straw awful	al alter fall	or fork order	au fraud author	oo door	ore shore	ough bought ought

aii pair	ar care various		
ar harm artist	al calm almond	a father	oir boudoir memoir
ier fierce	eer beer eerie	ear eardrum	ere severe
oor poor	ur cure	eur euro	
ow cow shower	ou round sour		
oy toy	oi voice oil		
u push	oo foot		
ur curve urgent	er merge	ir birth	ear pearl earn

The 'uh' sound

The vowel sound 'uh' is so short it is almost not pronounced at all. It can be written as e, a, i, o, or u, as in barrel, miserable, referee, about, turban, definite, responsible, common, pursue, and circus.

WORD ENDINGS

Sounds like	Possible spellings				
el	le cattle	al dental			
er	er driver	or actor	re lustre	ar burglar	eur chauffeur
i	y happy	ie calorie	ey money		
idj/ij	age manage	ege privilege	idge cartridge		
ius	ious delirious	eous hideous			
jus	geous courageous	gious prestigious			
shul	tial substantial	cial commercial			
shun	tion position	sion mansion	cion coercion		
shus	tious cautious	cious precious	scious conscious		
sul	stle castle	sle tussle	sel mussel		
ul	el barrel	le cattle	al dental		
us	ous jealous				

- Endings sounding like **ent** may also be spelt **ant**
- Endings sounding like **ence** may also be spelt **ance**

Some spelling rules to follow

Why does English have so many words that are difficult to spell? The main reason is that the 26 letters of the alphabet have to represent 44 different sounds. And confusingly, the same combination of letters can be used to represent quite distinct sounds. There are, however, a few rules that can guide you through the known pitfalls.

1. Adding -s or -es for plurals and verbs
The regular plural ending for nouns and the 3rd person singular ending for verbs is an added -s. Words ending in -ch, -s, -sh, -x, and -z add -es in the plural and 3rd person singular:

cat, cats	bush, bushes
beech, beeches	fox, foxes
batch, batches	waltz, waltzes
boss, bosses	

Words ending in -f or -fe sometimes add -s and sometimes change to -ves:

scarf, scarves

Exceptions: the plurals of **hero**, **potato**, and **tomato** end in -es rather than -s.

2. Changing y to ie
Words that end in -y keep the -y before -ing but change to -ies and -ied for the noun plural, the 3rd person present singular and the past tense of verbs, and before the -er and -est form of adjectives:

worry, worries, worried, worrying
try, tries, tried, trying
happy, happier, happiest

Names of people and places that end in -y keep the -y and just add -s in the plural, eg Mr and Mrs **Perry**, the **Perrys**.

Exceptions: words that end in a vowel and -y keep the -y before -s, -ed, -er, -est, and -ing:

play, plays, played, playing, player
key, keys, keyed, keying, keyer
greyer, greyest

3. Verbs ending in ie
Verbs like **lie**, **tie**, and **die** replace -ie with -y in the present participle:

lie, lies, lied, lying
die, dies, died, dying

Note the difference between **die** above and **dye, dyes, dyed, dyeing**.

4. Dropping e before ing
Words that end in a consonant and -e generally lose the -e before -s, -ed, -er, -ing, and also before -ise or -ize:

hike, hikes, hiked, hiking, hiker

Exceptions are the present participles of **singe** (= burn), which is **singeing** (to avoid confusion with 'singing'), and **age**, which can be spelt **ageing** or **aging**. Note also **swingeing** (= large), spelt with an -e- to avoid confusion with 'swinging'.

5. Words ending in c
Words ending in -c add -k before -ed and -ing:

panic, panics, panicked, panicking

An exception is **arc**, for which the participles are **arced** and **arcing**.

6. Doubling the consonant before -ed, -ing, and -er
Single-syllable words that end in a single vowel and a consonant usually double the consonant before -ed, -ing, -er, and -est:

pot, pots, potted, potting, potter
fit, fitter, fittest

Words of more than one syllable that end in a single vowel and a consonant and are stressed on the last syllable usually double the consonant before -ed and -ing:

regret, regrets, regretted, regretting
omit, omits, omitted, omitting

Compare these examples with **benefit** and **target**, which are stressed on the first syllable:

benefit, benefits, benefited, benefiting
target, targets, targeted, targeting

Exceptions: words ending in a single vowel and -l that are stressed on the first syllable double the -l before -ed and -ing:

> cancel, cancels, cancelled, cancelling
> travel, travels, travelled, travelling

7. ie, ei
The well-known rule 'i before e except after c' applies when the vowel rhymes with 'sheep':

> shriek, niece, 'i before e'
> ceiling, deceit, 'except after c'

There are some exceptions such as **caffeine, protein, seize, weird**, and the names **Sheila** and **Keith**.

8. Verbs ending in -ise or -ize
Although the traditional spelling of verbs like **characterise** is usually -ise, many publications, including this Dictionary, use the American -ize spelling. However, the following verbs are only ever spelt -ise:

advertise	comprise	exercise	supervise
advise	compromise	improvise	surmise
apprise	despise	merchandise	surprise
arise	devise	prise (open)	televise
chastise	enfranchise	revise	
circumcise	excise	rise	

Capsize, prize ('an award for a winner'), and **size** are only ever spelt -ize. **Apprize** and **prize** (open) may be spelt with a -z- in Australian English. Note also that **analyse** is spelt -yse, not -yze.

Alternative spellings
This list gives possible alternative spellings for some common word beginnings:

acs try acc:	accelerate	pel try pol:	polite
air try aer:	aerial	per try pur:	purple, pursue
ca try cha:	character	pre try pro:	provide
ce try che:	chemical	quo try qua:	qualification, quarrel
clor try chlor:	chlorine	ra try wra:	wrap
co try cho:	cholera	re try wre:	wreck
cr try chr:	Christmas	ri try wri:	wriggle, write
ecs try ex:	exercise	ro try wro:	wrong, wrote
ef try af:	affection, afraid	se try sce:	scene, scent
egs try exh:	exhaust	si try sci:	science, scissors
fer try fur:	furry	sic try psych:	psychology
fol try fal:	false	sosh try soci:	social
for try four:	fourteen	spesh try speci:	special, species
gi try gui:	guilt	squo try squa:	squabble, squad
hi try high:	higher	uf try euph:	euphoria
ho try who:	whole	uph try euph:	euphoria
meca try mecha:	mechanic	ur try eur:	Europe
na try kna:	knack, knave	vial try viol:	violin
ne try kne:	knee, knell	wa try wha:	whack, whale
ni try kni:	knife, knit	we try whe:	when, wheel
no try kno:	knob, know	wi try whi:	which, while
nur try neur:	neurosis	wo try wa:	wander, wash
nut try neut:	neutral	wor try wa:	water
ocs try ox:	oxygen	wur try wor:	work

Abbreviations, Symbols, and Labels

Abbreviations used in the Dictionary

abbr	abbreviation	*Info Sci*	information science
adj	adjective	*interj*	interjection
adv	adverb	*Lang*	language
Altern Med	alternative medicine	*Ling*	linguistics
Anat	anatomy	*Literat*	literature
Ancient Hist	ancient history	*Measure*	measurements
ANZ	Australian/New Zealand	*Med*	medicine
	English	*Microbiol*	microbiology
Archit	architecture	*modal v*	modal verb
Astron	astronomy	*n*	noun
Aus	Australian English	*Naut*	nautical
aux v	auxiliary verb	*npl*	plural noun
Biochem	biochemistry	*NZ*	New Zealand
Can	Canadian English	*Pharm*	pharmacology
Carib	Caribbean English	*Phys*	physics
Chem	chemistry	*Physiol*	physiology
Chem elem	chemical element	*pl*	plural
Chr	Christianity	*Plant Sci*	plant science
Comput	computing	*Pol*	politics
conj	conjunction	*prep*	preposition
Constr	construction industry	*pron*	pronoun
contr	contraction	*pronunc.*	pronunciation
Cook	cookery	*Psychiat*	psychiatry
Dent	dentistry	*Psychol*	psychology
det	determiner	*sing*	singular
Educ	education	*tdmk*	trademark
Eng	engineering	*v*	verb
Fin	finance	*Vet*	veterinary medicine
fml	formal	*vi*	intransitive verb
Geog	geography	*vr*	reflexive verb
Geol	geology	*vt*	transitive verb
Hist	history	*vti*	transitive/intransitive verb
Indust	industry	*Zool*	zoology
infml	informal		

Symbols used in the Dictionary

□	marks phrasal (two- or three-word) verbs
■	marks new part of speech
○	marks examples of use
◇	marks set phrases
=	cross-refers to more common spelling
◊	cross-refers to related entry or boxed note
♦	cross-refers to name of person or place
⚠	marks a disputed usage

Style and Register

The following labels mark the stylistic restrictions on the use of a word:

archaic	not used since pre-WWII
dated	no longer current, but still used by older speakers or authors
fml	formal: suitable in formal situations and formal writing
humorous	pompous or inflated language used for comic effect
infml	informal: used in relaxed conversation or writing
insult	used for deliberately insulting terms
literary	used in literature, poetry, and quality journalism
nonstandard	not considered part of correct or educated usage
offensive	likely to cause offence, intentionally or unintentionally
regional	used in the dialect of a particular variety of English
slang	used only in very relaxed conversation or writing
taboo	used for highly offensive, obscene, or vulgar terms
technical	used for specialist terms with an everyday equivalent

Pronunciation Key

Symbol	Example	Symbol	Example
a	at	n, nn	not, funny
aa	father	ng	song
aw	all	o	odd
ay	day	ō	open
air	hair	ŏŏ	good
b, bb	but, ribbon	oo	school
ch	chin	ow	owl
d, dd	do, ladder	oy	oil
ə	about, edible, item,	p, pp	pen, happy
	common, circus	r, rr	road, carry, hard
e	egg	s, ss	say, lesson
ee	eel	sh	sheep
f, ff	fond, differ	th	thin
g, gg	go, giggle	<u>th</u>	this
h	hot	t, tt	tell, butter
hw	when	u	up
i	it, happy, medium	ur	urge
ī	ice	v, vv	very, savvy
j, jj	juice, pigeon	w	wet
k	key, thick	y	yes
l, ll	let, silly	z, zz	zoo, blizzard
m, mm	mother, hammer	<u>zh</u>	vision

Foreign pronunciations

/hl/ as in Welsh Llangollen
/<u>kh</u>/ as in German Bach, Spanish Gijón
/N/ to show nasalization of the preceding vowel as in the French pronunciation
of un bon vin blanc /öN boN vaN blaaN/
/ö/ as in French boeuf, German schön
/ü/ as in French rue, German gemütlich

Stress

´ over a vowel indicates the syllable that has the strongest (primary) stress, or the
syllable before this that has medium (secondary) stress.
' before /l/, /m/, or /n/ shows that the consonant is syllabic (functions as a whole
syllable).

This Dictionary uses double consonants to show many sounds in the middle of
words because English spelling normally doubles letters in these positions.
Consonants are doubled when they are preceded by the stressed vowels /á, é, í, ó,
ú, ŏ́o/ and followed by either a vowel or a syllabic consonant, or by /l/, /r/, /y/,
or /w/. The consonant /k/ is not doubled.

The Dictionary shows pronunciations at all entry words apart from the following:
those that are made up of separate or hyphenated words given pronunciations elsewhere in the Dictionary; single-syllable entry words whose pronunciation is entirely predictable; and capitalized forms of the latter. At entries for people and places
where a name is repeated, the first occurrence only is given a pronunciation.

A

a[1] (*pl* **a's**), **A** (*pl* **A's** *or* **As**) *n* the 1st letter of the English alphabet

a[2] *abbr* are[2]

a[3] (*stressed*) /ay/ (*unstressed*) /ə/ *det* **1** refers to one person or thing not previously specified **2** indicates a type of person or thing ○ *He's a genius.* **3** one ○ *a thousand people* **4** per ○ *twice a day* **5** indicates somebody not known personally ○ *There's a Mr O'Flynn here to see you.* ◊ See note at **an**

A[1] *symbol* **1** ampere **2** *also* **Å** angstrom

A[2] /ay/ *n* **1** the 6th note in the musical scale of C major **2** the highest grade of a student's work **3** a human blood type containing a specific antigen ◊ **from A to B** from one place to another

AA *abbr* Alcoholics Anonymous

AAA *abbr* **1** /thrée áyz/ Amateur Athletic Association **2** /trípp'l áy/ *US, Can* American Automobile Association

A & E *abbr* accident and emergency

aardvark /aàrd vaark/ *n* a burrowing African mammal with a long snout

ORIGIN Aardvark comes from an Afrikaans word that literally means 'earth pig'.

Ab, Av *n* the 5th month of the year in the Jewish calendar

AB *n* a human blood type containing two specific antigens

ABA *abbr* Amateur Boxing Association

aback /ə bák/ ◊ **taken aback** surprised and upset or shocked

abacus /ábbəkəss/ (*pl* **-cuses** *or* **-ci** /-sī/) *n* a counting device consisting of a frame with beads or balls on rods

ORIGIN Abacus ultimately comes from a Hebrew word meaning 'dust'. It was used in Greek for a sand-covered board for drawing and writing on, and later meant 'table for arithmetical calculations'. The exact form **abacus** came into English via Latin. The first recorded use of it in English to mean 'counting device' was in the late 17C.

Abadan /ábbə daàn/ city in SW Iran. Pop. 296,081 (1996).

abalone /ábbə lố ni/ *n* a shellfish that has a shell with a line of holes and a pearly interior

abandon /ə bándən/ *v* **1** *vt* leave a person or animal behind for others to take care of **2** *vt* leave a place because of danger **3** *vt* renounce something previously done **4** *vt* give up control of something ○ *As troops closed in the town was abandoned to its fate.* **5** *vt* halt something in progress **6** *vr* give in to emotion ■ *n* lack of inhibition or self-restraint —**abandoned** *adj* —**abandonment** *n*

abase /ə báyss/ (**abasing, abased**) *v* **1** *vt* belittle or degrade **2** *vr* behave in a way that lowers your sense of dignity —**abasement** *n*

abash /ə básh/ *vt* make ashamed —**abashedly** /-idli/ *adv*

abate /ə báyt/ (**abating, abated**) *vti* gradually make or become less (*fml or literary*) —**abatement** *n*

abattoir /ábbə twaar/ *n* a place for killing animals for meat

Abbas /ábbəss/ (566?–653) Arabian merchant ~~abbatoir~~ incorrect spelling of **abattoir**

abbess /ábbess/ *n* the head of a convent

abbey /ábbi/ (*pl* **-beys**) *n* **1** a monastery or convent **2** a church used by monks or nuns

abbot /ábbət/ *n* the head of a monastery —**abbotship** *n*

abbr., abbrev. *abbr* abbreviation

abbreviate /ə brée vi ayt/ (**-ating, -ated**) *vt* shorten a word or text

abbreviation /ə brèevi áysh'n/ *n* **1** a reduced form of a word or phrase **2** the reduction of the full form of a word or phrase

ABC[1] *n* **1** the alphabet **2** the essentials of a particular subject

ABC[2] *abbr* Australian Broadcasting Corporation

abdicate /ábdi kayt/ (**-cating, -cated**) *v* **1** *vti* resign a position, especially the throne **2** *vt* neglect a duty or responsibility —**abdication** /ábdi káysh'n/ *n*

abdomen /ábdəmən/ *n* **1** the part of the body containing the stomach and intestines **2** the rear part of an insect —**abdominal** /ab dómmin'l/ *adj*

abduct /əb dúkt/ *vt* take somebody away by force —**abduction** *n* —**abductor** *n*

Abdullah II /ab dúllə/ (b. 1962) king of Jordan (1999–)

Abdul Rahman /ab doöl raàmən/, **Tunku** (1903–90) first prime minister of the Federation of Malaya (1957–63) and of Malaysia (1963–70)

Abelard /ábbə laard/, **Peter** (1079–1142) French philosopher and theologian

ABEND /áb end/ *n* **1** *also* **abend** a sudden computer program failure. Full form **abnormal end 2** warns e-mail correspondents of an imminent loss of Internet access. Full form **absent by enforced Net deprivation**

Aberdeen /ábbər deèn/ **1** port and industrial centre in NE Scotland. Pop. 227,430 (1996). **2** council area in NE Scotland. Pop. 218,220 (1993). —**Aberdonian** /ábbər dôni ən/ *n, adj*

Aberdeenshire /ábbər deènshər/ county in NE Scotland

Aberfan /ábbər ván/ coalmining village in S Wales, where in 1966 a landslide killed 144 people

aberrant /ə bérrənt/ *adj* not typical —**aberrance** *n*

aberration /ábbə ráysh'n/ *n* **1** a deviation from what is usual **2** a lapse

abet /ə bét/ (**abetting, abetted**) *vt* give help, especially in committing a crime —**abettor** *n*

abeyance /ə báy ənss/ *n* suspension of activity or operation o *a law that has fallen into abeyance* —**abeyant** *adj*

abhor /əb háwr/ (**-horring, -horred**) *vt* detest

abhorrent /əb hórrənt/ *adj* arousing feelings of repugnance —**abhorrence** *n*

abide /ə bíd/ (**abiding, abode** /ə bód/ *or* **abided**) *v* 1 *vt* tolerate o *I can't abide disobedient children.* 2 *vi* dwell (*archaic*)
□ **abide by** *vt* follow or accept a rule or decision

abiding /ə bídïng/ *adj* enduring

Abidjan /ábbi jaán/ cultural and commercial capital of the Côte d'Ivoire. Pop. 1,929,079 (1988).

Abilene /ábbə leen/ city in central Texas. Pop. 108,257 (1998).

ability /ə billəti/ *n* 1 the state of being able to do something 2 skill, talent, or intelligence

SYNONYMS ability, skill, competence, aptitude, talent, capacity, capability CORE MEANING: the necessary skill, knowledge, or experience to do something

abject /áb jekt/ *adj* 1 extremely bad or unpleasant o *abject poverty* 2 humble o *an abject apology* —**abjection** /ab jéksh'n/ *n* —**abjectly** *adv*

abjure /əb joór/ (**-juring, -jured**) *vt* 1 formally renounce a belief 2 abstain from something (*literary*) —**abjuration** /áb joor ráysh'n/ *n*

Abkhazia /ab kaázi ə/ autonomous republic in NW Georgia. Pop. 537,500 (1990).

ablative /ább lətiv/ *n* a grammatical case identifying the source, agent, or instrument of the action of the verb —**ablative** *adj*

ablaze /ə bláyz/ *adj* 1 on fire 2 brightly lit

able /áyb'l/ (**abler, ablest**) *adj* 1 in a position to do something 2 capable or talented —**ably** *adv* ◊ See note at **intelligent**

-able *suffix* 1 capable of or fit for o *readable* 2 tending to o *changeable* —**-ability** *suffix*

able-bodied /áyb'l bóddid/ *adj* fit and healthy

able seaman *n* a sailor with basic training

ablution /ə blóosh'n/ *n* ritual washing or cleansing of the body ■ **ablutions** *npl* 1 washing yourself (*fml or humorous*) 2 washing facilities

abnegate /ábni gayt/ (**-gating, -gated**) *vt* renounce (*fml*) —**abnegation** /ábni gáysh'n/ *n*

abnormal /ab náwrm'l/ *adj* unusual or not as expected —**abnormality** /áb nawr málləti/ *n* —**abnormally** *adv*

aboard /ə báwrd/ *adv, prep* onto a ship or vehicle

abode[1] /ə bód/ *n* somebody's home (*literary*)

abode[2] /ə bód/ past participle, past tense of **abide**

abolish /ə bóllish/ *vt* put an end to

abolition /ábbə lísh'n/ *n* 1 the process of abolishing something 2 *also* **Abolition** the ending of slavery in the United States

abolitionist /abə lísh'nist/ *n* 1 *also* **Abolitionist** an opponent of slavery 2 somebody who seeks to ban something —**abolitionism** *n*

A-bomb *n* an atom bomb

abominable /ə bómminəb'l/ *adj* loathsome or extremely unpleasant —**abominably** *adv*

Abominable Snowman *n* a yeti

abominate /ə bómmi nayt/ (**-nating, -nated**) *vt* loathe (*fml*)

abomination /ə bómmi náysh'n/ *n* 1 something horrible, disgusting, or shameful 2 intense dislike (*literary*)

aboriginal /ábbə ríjjinəl/ *adj* 1 existing in a place from the earliest known times 2 **Aboriginal** of the earliest inhabitants of Australia ■ *n* 1 an original inhabitant 2 **Aboriginal** an original inhabitant of Australia ◊ See note at **native**

aborigine /ábbə ríjjini/ *n* 1 an original inhabitant of a place (*often offensive*) 2 an animal or plant that has existed in a place since earliest times 3 **Aborigine** an original inhabitant of Australia

abort /ə báwrt/ *v* 1 *vti* remove a foetus to end a pregnancy 2 *vi* have a miscarriage (*technical*) 3 *vti* end something, or come to an end, prematurely

abortifacient /ə báwrti fáysh'nt/ *adj* causing a foetal abortion —**abortifacient** *n*

abortion /ə báwrsh'n/ *n* 1 an operation to end a pregnancy 2 a miscarriage (*technical*) —**abortionist** *n*

abortive /ə báwr tiv/ *adj* 1 not successfully completed 2 disrupted in development —**abortively** *adv*

ABO system *n* a system that classifies human blood by dividing it into the four groups A, B, AB, and O

abound /ə bównd/ *vi* 1 be plentiful 2 be well supplied

about /ə bówt/ *prep* 1 in connection with 2 approximately ■ *adv, prep* 1 in various places 2 in different directions ■ *adv* 1 in circulation 2 into a reversed position ◊ **be about** have something as an essential characteristic ◊ **be about to** be on the point of ◊ **what something or somebody is (all) about** what something or somebody involves or has as a purpose (*infml*)

about-turn *vi* turn around (*usually a command*) ■ *n* 1 a reversal of an opinion or policy 2 a turn to face in the opposite direction

above /ə búv/ *prep* over, higher than, or on top of ■ *prep, adv* 1 more than 2 superior to ■ *prep* beyond o *above criticism* ■ *adv, adj* in a previous place in writing (*often in combination*) o *using the information from the table above* o *the above-cited graph* ■ *adv* overhead, in a higher position, or on top ◊ **above all** as the most important thing

aboveboard /ə búv báwrd/ *adj* honest and legal —**aboveboard** *adv*

ORIGIN Aboveboard was originally a gambling term indicating that a player's hands were above the gaming table, or 'board', and concealed nothing.

abracadabra /ábbrəkə dábbrə/ *interj* supposedly ensures the success of a magic trick

abrade /ə bráyd/ (**abrading, abraded**) vti wear away

abrasion /ə bráy<u>zh</u>'n/ n **1** the process of wearing away **2** a scraped area of skin

abrasive /ə bráyssiv/ adj **1** using friction and roughness to smooth or clean **2** harsh in manner ■ n a smoothing substance —**abrasively** adv —**abrasiveness** n

abreast /ə brést/ adv side by side ■ adj well-informed

~~abreviation~~ incorrect spelling of **abbreviation**

abridge /ə bríj/ (**abridging, abridged**) vt shorten something such as text —**abridged** adj —**abridgment** n

abroad /ə bráwd/ adv **1** away from your own country **2** in circulation **3** everywhere ■ n foreign countries (infml)

~~abroard~~ incorrect spelling of **abroad**

abrogate /ábbrə gayt/ (**-gating, -gated**) vt repeal or abolish formally (fml) —**abrogation** /ábbrə gáysh'n/ n ◊ See note at **nullify**

abrupt /ə brúpt/ adj **1** sudden **2** brusque **3** steep —**abruptly** adv —**abruptness** n

Abruzzi /ə bróotsi/ agricultural region of central S Italy. Pop. 1,277,330 (1998).

ABS n a system of electronically controlled brakes that prevents a vehicle's wheels locking if the driver brakes suddenly. Full form **anti-lock braking system**

abscess /áb sess/ n a pus-filled cavity —**abscessed** adj

abscond /əb skónd, ab-/ vi **1** run away secretly **2** escape from a place of detention

abseil /áb sayl/ vi descend a steep or vertical face by rope —**abseil** n

absence /ábs'nss/ n **1** the state of not being present **2** time spent away

~~absense~~ incorrect spelling of **absence**

absent[1] /ábs'nt/ adj **1** not present ○ absent from school **2** inattentive —**absently** adv

absent[2] /ab sént/ vr leave or stay away ○ absented themselves from the meeting

absentee /ábs'n teé/ n somebody not present

absenteeism /ábs'n teé izəm/ n frequent absence, especially from work

absentee landlord n a landlord living elsewhere

absent-minded adj habitually inattentive or forgetful —**absent-mindedly** adv —**absent-mindedness** n

absinthe /ábssinth/, **absinth** n an alcoholic drink made from wormwood

absolute /ábssə loot/ adj **1** complete and un-mitigated ○ an absolute fool **2** having total power or authority **3** not dependent on or qualified by anything else **4** measured relative to absolute zero ■ n also **Absolute** in philosophy, ultimate reality —**absolutely** adv

absolute majority n a winning number of votes that is more than half of the total

absolute zero n the lowest possible temperature

absolution /ábssə loósh'n/ n forgiveness for sin

absolutism /ábssə lootizəm/ n **1** a political system in which a ruler's power is absolute **2** a philosophical theory regarding values as objective —**absolutist** n, adj

absolve /əb zólv/ (**-solving, -solved**) vt **1** state publicly or officially that somebody is blameless **2** relieve of obligation **3** forgive

absorb /əb sáwrb, -záwrb/ vt **1** soak up or take in something such as a liquid or nutrients **2** not transmit or pass on light, noise, or energy **3** incorporate something into a larger entity **4** use up or require something in quantity **5** engross somebody —**absorbed** adj —**absorber** n —**absorbing** adj

absorbent /əb sáwrbənt, -záwrb-/ adj able to absorb liquid —**absorbency** n

~~absorbtion~~ incorrect spelling of **absorption**

absorption /əb sáwrpsh'n, -záwrp-/ n **1** total mental concentration **2** the soaking up of a liquid **3** incorporation into something larger —**absorptive** adj

abstain /əb stáyn/ vi **1** not vote **2** choose not to do something

abstemious /ab steémi əss/ adj moderate or restrained in eating and drinking

abstention /əb sténsh'n/ n **1** a vote neither for nor against **2** the process of abstaining

abstinence /ábstinənss/ n self-denial —**abstinent** adj —**abstinently** adv

abstract adj /áb strakt/ **1** not physical or concrete **2** theoretical rather than applied **3** describes art that emphasizes form over realism ■ n /áb strakt/ **1** a printed summary **2** an intellectual concept **3** an abstract artwork ■ vt /əb strákt/ summarize —**abstractly** adv —**abstractness** n

abstracted /əb stráktid/ adj preoccupied

abstraction /əb stráksh'n/ n **1** preoccupation **2** a generalized concept **3** the process of abstracting

abstract noun n a noun that signifies a concept or quality, e.g. 'truth'

abstruse /əb stroóss/ adj difficult to understand —**abstrusely** adv ◊ See note at **obscure**

absurd /əb súrd/ adj **1** ludicrous **2** meaningless ■ n also **Absurd** the state of living in a meaningless universe —**absurdity** n —**absurdly** adv

ABTA abbr Association of British Travel Agents

Abu Dhabi /ábboo daábi/ capital of the United Arab Emirates, on an island in the Persian Gulf. Pop. 605,000 (1990).

Abuja /ə boò jaa/ official capital of Nigeria. Pop. 339,100 (1995).

abundant /ə búndənt/ adj **1** plentiful **2** well-supplied ○ abundant in natural resources —**abundance** n —**abundantly** adv

~~abundent~~ incorrect spelling of **abundant**

abuse n /ə byóoss/ **1** maltreatment **2** improper use **3** insulting or offensive language ■ vt /ə byóoz/ (**abusing, abused**) **1** treat somebody badly **2** misuse something **3** insult somebody ◊ See note at **misuse**

abusive /ə hyróoŝiv/ *adj* **1** insulting or offensive **2** involving illegal, improper, or harmful activities —**abusively** *adv*

abut /ə bút/ (**abutting, abutted**) *vti* be adjacent to something

abutment /ə bútmənt/ *n* **1** the state of being adjacent **2** the point at which two things abut

abysmal /ə bízm'l/ *adj* **1** appallingly bad **2** very deep —**abysmally** *adv*

abyss /ə bíss/ *n* **1** a very deep chasm **2** endless space

Abyssinia /ábbə sínni ə/ *n* former name for **Ethiopia** —**Abyssinian** *adj, n*

ac *abbr* academic organization *(in Internet addresses)*

Ac *symbol* actinium

AC *abbr* **1** alternating current **2** Athletic Club *(in club names)*

a/c, A/C *abbr* account

acacia /ə káyshə/ (*pl* -**cias** *or same*) *n* **1** a bush or tree with small fluffy yellow flowers **2** gum arabic

academia /ákə deémi ə/, **academe** /ákə deem/ *n* academic life

academic /ákə démmik/ *adj* **1** of education **2** scholarly and intellectual **3** irrelevant in practice ■ *n* **1** a university teacher **2** a scholarly person —**academically** *adv*

academician /ə káddə mísh'n/ *n* **1** an academic **2** a member of a scholarly society

academy /ə káddəmi/ (*pl* -**mies**) *n* **1** a society promoting knowledge or culture **2** a specialized educational institution **3** a secondary school, often a private one *(usually in school names)*

ORIGIN The original **Academy** was the school that the Greek philosopher Plato founded in the 4C BC. It was named after a park on the outskirts of Athens, where he taught his philosophy. The word came into English via Latin and French.

Academy Award *n* a film award given by the Academy of Motion Picture Arts and Sciences

a cappella /áakə péllə, ákə-/ *adv, adj* by singers without instrumental accompaniment

Acapulco /ákə poõlkõ/ seaport and resort in S Mexico. Pop. 687,292 (1995).

ACAS /áy kass/, **Acas** *n* an organization that mediates in industrial disputes. Full form **Advisory, Conciliation, and Arbitration Service**

acc. *abbr* **1** account **2** accusative

accademic incorrect spelling of **academic**

accede /ək seéd/ (-**ceding, -ceded**) *vi* **1** agree to something, especially unwillingly **2** come to power

SPELLCHECK Do not confuse the spelling of **accede** and **exceed** ('be greater than'), which sound similar.

accelerate /ək séllə rayt/ (-**ating, -ated**) *vti* **1** go or cause to go faster **2** happen or cause to

happen sooner than planned or expected —**acceleration** /ək séllə ráysh'n/ *n*

accelerated graphics port *n* a computer interface that allows the display of three-dimensional graphics

accelerator /ək séllə raytər/ *n* **1** a control mechanism that makes a vehicle go faster **2** a chemical that speeds up a reaction

accelerator card, accelerator board *n* a circuit board added to a computer to make it operate faster

accent *n* /áks'nt/ **1** a manner of pronunciation **2** a stress on a syllable or musical note **3** a mark on a letter indicating stress or pronunciation **4** the main emphasis ○ *The accent is on safety.* ■ *vt* /ak sént/ **1** emphasize or stress **2** mark with an accent

accentuate /ək sénchoo ayt/ (-**ating, -ated**) *vt* **1** draw attention to something **2** stress a syllable or musical note —**accentuation** /ək sénchoo áysh'n/ *n*

accept /ək sépt/ *v* **1** *vt* take something offered **2** *vti* say yes to something such as an invitation **3** *vt* endure or tolerate something **4** *vt* believe something **5** *vt* acknowledge and come to terms with something **6** *vt* admit something to be true **7** *vt* allow somebody to become a member **8** *vt* regard somebody or something with approval —**acceptance** *n* —**accepted** *adj*

acceptable /ək séptəb'l/ *adj* **1** adequate **2** approved of —**acceptability** /ək séptə bílləti/ *n* —**acceptably** *adv*

access /ák sess/ *n* **1** a means of entry or approach ○ *gained access via an upstairs window* **2** the right or opportunity to use something or meet somebody **3** an outburst *(literary)* ■ *vt* **1** enter a place **2** retrieve data from a computer

SPELLCHECK Do not confuse the spelling of **access** and **excess** ('a surplus'), which sound similar.

accessable incorrect spelling of **accessible**

accessible /ək séssəb'l/ *adj* **1** easy to enter or reach physically **2** easily understood **3** readily available **4** allowing wheelchair access —**accessibility** /ək séssə bílləti/ *n* —**accessibly** *adv*

accession /ək sésh'n/ *n* **1** the process of coming to power **2** the acceptance by a state of a treaty **3** agreement, especially when given unwillingly **4** an addition to a collection

accessorize /ək séssə rīz/ (-**izing, -ized**), **accessorise** *v* **1** *vt* provide something with accessories **2** *vti* complete an outfit with accessories

accessory /ək séssəri/ *n* (*pl* -**ries**) **1** an optional part **2** a fashion item such as a hat or handbag **3** somebody who helps a criminal ■ *adj* **1** additional **2** assisting in a crime

access profile *n* a description of the pattern of Internet use of a specific user

access time *n* the speed of a computer in accessing data

accident /áksidənt/ n 1 chance o *I met him by accident.* 2 a collision involving a moving vehicle 3 a chance happening 4 a mishap, or an unplanned, unfortunate event

accidental /áksi dént'l/ adj 1 happening by chance 2 incidental ■ n a musical note marked with a sharp, flat, or natural sign that is not in the key signature —**accidentally** adv

accident and emergency n a hospital's emergency department

~~accidently~~ incorrect spelling of **accidentally**

acclaim /ə kláym/ vt 1 praise publicly and enthusiastically 2 pronounce to be something deserving praise o *was acclaimed as the winner* ■ n public and enthusiastic praise —**acclamation** /áklə máysh'n/ n

acclimatize /ə klímə tíz/ (-tizing, -tized), **acclimatise** vti adapt or become adapted to a new environment —**acclimatization** /ə klímə tī záysh'n/ n

accolade /ákə layd, -laad/ n 1 a sign or expression of praise 2 public recognition

ORIGIN The root of **accolade** is Latin *collum* 'neck', which is also the source of English *collar*. The underlying idea is of putting your arm around somebody's neck as a sign of congratulations.

accommodate /ə kómmə dayt/ (-dating, -dated) v 1 vt provide lodging for 2 vt have room for 3 vt allow for 4 vt adjust actions in response to the needs of 5 vi adapt to a new situation

accommodating /ə kómmə dayting/ adj obliging somebody's wishes —**accommodatingly** adv

accommodation /ə kómmə dáysh'n/ n 1 lodging 2 room or space 3 willingness to oblige 4 an agreement or compromise 5 adjustment or adaptation

~~accomodate~~ incorrect spelling of **accommodate**

~~accomodation~~ incorrect spelling of **accommodation**

accompaniment /ə kúmpənimənt, -pni-/ n 1 a musical part that supports a soloist or more prominent performers 2 a simultaneous occurrence 3 an item that goes with another

accompanist /ə kúmpənist, -pnist/ n a musician who plays an accompaniment

accompany /ə kúmpəni, -pni/ (-nies, -nied) v 1 vt escort 2 vt be present or occur with 3 vt supplement 4 vti provide the musical accompaniment for

accomplice /ə kúmpliss, ə kóm-/ n somebody who helps a wrongdoer or criminal

accomplish /ə kúmplish, ə kóm-/ vt succeed in doing

SYNONYMS accomplish, achieve, attain, realize, carry out, pull off CORE MEANING: bring to a successful conclusion

accomplished /ə kúmplisht, ə kóm-/ adj 1 talented or skilled 2 complete and definite o *an accomplished fact*

accomplishment /ə kúmplishmənt, ə kóm-/ n

1 the achieving of something 2 something achieved 3 a talent or skill

accord /ə káwrd/ v 1 vt give or grant o *was accorded the same privileges as her predecessor* 2 vi agree o *accords with my own view* ■ n 1 an agreement 2 consensus or harmony

accordance /ə káwrd'nss/ n conformity with what is required o *in accordance with official guidelines*

according as conj depending on whether

accordingly /ə káwrdingli/ adv 1 correspondingly 2 in consequence

according to prep 1 in proportion to 2 as stated or determined by

accordion /ə káwrdi ən/ n a musical instrument with a bellows in the middle that forces air through metal reeds

accost /ə kóst/ vt approach and stop somebody aggressively or suggestively

account /ə kównt/ n 1 a report 2 an explanation 3 an arrangement for keeping money in a bank 4 an arrangement for obtaining goods or services on credit 5 a contract providing Internet access 6 a customer ■ **accounts** npl the financial records of a person or organization ■ vt consider or regard as *(fml)* o *We would account it a privilege to serve you.* ◇ **call somebody to account** demand an explanation of somebody's actions ◇ **on account of** because of ◇ **on no account** not ever ◇ **on somebody's account** out of concern for somebody's wellbeing ◇ **take account of, take into account** consider when making a decision

□ **account for** vt 1 explain 2 be responsible for

accountable /ə kówntəb'l/ adj 1 responsible for something 2 responsible to somebody —**accountability** /ə kówntə bílləti/ n

accountant /ə kówntənt/ n somebody who maintains and checks financial accounts —**accountancy** n

account executive n somebody handling an individual client's accounts

accounting /ə kównting/ n maintenance and checking of financial records

accounts payable npl a record of money owed by a company

accounts receivable npl a record of money owed to a company

~~accoustic~~ incorrect spelling of **acoustic**

accoutre /ə koótər/ (-tring, -tred) vt equip

accoutrement /ə koótrəmənt/ n 1 an accessory or associated piece of equipment 2 a piece of military equipment

Accra /ə kráá/ capital of Ghana. Pop. 953,500 (1990 estimate).

accredit /ə kréddit/ vt 1 give official recognition to 2 give authority to 3 *NZ* pass for university entrance —**accreditation** /ə kréddi táysh'n/ n

accretion /ə kréesh'n/ n an increase resulting from accumulation or addition

~~accross~~ incorrect spelling of **across**

accrue /ə kroó/ (-cruing, -crued) v 1 vi come into somebody's possession 2 vi increase 3 vt gather over a period of time ○ *investments accruing interest* —**accrual** *n*

acculturate /ə kúlchə rayt/ (-**ating**, -**ated**) *v* **1** *vi* take on another culture **2** *vt* change the culture of —**acculturation** /ə kúlchə ráysh'n/ *n*

accumulate /ə kyoómyŏŏ layt/ (-**lating**, -**lated**) *vti* collect over a period of time —**accumulation** /ə kyoómyŏŏ láysh'n/ *n* —**accumulative** /-lətiv/ *adj* ◊ See note at **collect**

accumulator /ə kyoómyŏŏ laytər/ *n* **1** a rechargeable battery **2** a section of computer memory for short-term storage **3** a bet on several races

accurate /ákyŏŏrət/ *adj* **1** representing the truth **2** free from errors —**accuracy** *n* —**accurately** *adv*

accursed /ə kúrssid, ə kúrst/, **accurst** /ə kúrst/ *adj* (*literary*) **1** doomed **2** horrible —**accursedly** /ə kúrssidli/ *adv*

accusation /ákyŏŏ záysh'n/ *n* **1** an allegation of wrongdoing **2** the accusing of somebody, or the state of being accused

accusative /ə kyoózətiv/ *n* a grammatical case identifying the direct object of a verb or the object of a preposition —**accusative** *adj*

accuse /ə kyooz/ (-**cusing**, -**cused**) *v* **1** *vti* confront and blame somebody **2** *vt* charge with a crime —**accused** *n*

accustom /ə kústəm/ *vt* make used to something

accustomed /ə kústəmd/ *adj* habitual

AC/DC *adj* powered by a battery or mains. Full form **alternating current/direct current**

ace *n* **1** a playing card with a single mark **2** in tennis, a serve that the opponent cannot return **3** in golf, a hole in one **4** a successful fighter pilot **5** somebody with an exceptional skill (*infml*) ■ *vt* (**acing**, **aced**) in tennis, serve an ace ■ *adj* excellent (*infml*) ◊ **within an ace of** very close to

acerbic /ə súrbik/ *adj* bitter ○ *an acerbic remark* —**acerbically** *adv* —**acerbity** *n*

~~accessory~~ incorrect spelling of **accessory**

acetate /ássi tayt/ *n* **1** a derivative of acetic acid **2** cellulose acetate

acetic acid /ə seétik-/ *n* CH_3COOH the main component of vinegar. Use: manufacture of drugs, dyes, plastics, fibres.

acetone /ássitōn/ *n* C_3H_6O a colourless flammable liquid. Use: paint and nail polish solvent.

acetylene /ə sétti leen/ *n* C_2H_2 a flammable gas. Use: in welding.

ACH *n* an interbank payment network. Full form **automated clearing house**

achcha /úchə/ *interj* S Asia **1** all right **2** is that so?

ache /ayk/ *vi* (**aching**, **ached**) **1** feel or be the site of a dull constant pain **2** yearn for the presence of somebody or something **3** want something badly (*infml*) ■ *n* a dull constant pain —**achingly** *adv* —**achy** *adj*

Achebe /ə cháybi/, **Chinua** (*b.* 1930) Nigerian novelist

~~acheive~~ incorrect spelling of **achieve**

achene /ə keén/, **akene** *n* a dry single-seeded fruit that does not open to release its seed

achieve /ə cheév/ (**achieving**, **achieved**) *vt* succeed in doing or gaining —**achievable** *adj* —**achievement** *n* ◊ See note at **accomplish**

Achilles /ə kílleez/ *n* in Greek mythology, a hero of the Trojan War

Achilles' heel *n* a small but fatal weakness

ORIGIN In Greek mythology, Achilles' mother dipped him in the river Styx as a baby to make him invulnerable, but the heel she held him by remained dry and became his only point of weakness. He died when struck in the heel by an arrow.

Achilles tendon *n* the tendon that connects the heel to the calf muscles

achromatic /áykrō máttik/ *adj* **1** white, grey, or black **2** able to reflect or refract light without spectral colour separation —**achromatically** *adv* —**achromatism** /ə krōmətizəm/ *n*

acid /ássid/ *n* **1** a corrosive chemical compound with a sour taste **2** LSD (*slang*) ■ *adj* **1** of an acid **2** sour-tasting **3** sharp, bitter, or sarcastic —**acidic** /ə síddik/ *adj* —**acidity** /ə síddəti/ *n*

acid house *n* a type of 1980s dance music

acidify /ə síddi fī/ (-**fies**, -**fied**) *vti* make or become acid

acid rain *n* polluted rain containing dilute acid

acid reflux *n* the return of stomach contents to the oesophagus

acid rock *n* rock music suggesting the influence of psychedelic drugs

acid test *n* a decisive test

acknowledge /ək nóllij/ (-**edging**, -**edged**) *v* **1** *vt* admit the truth or validity of **2** *vti* respond to a greeting or message **3** *vt* show appreciation of —**acknowledged** *adj* —**acknowledgment** *n*

~~acclaim~~ incorrect spelling of **acclaim**

acme /ákmi/ *n* the highest point

acne /ákni/ *n* a skin disease causing pimples

ORIGIN Acne has its origin in a mistake. The Greek word meaning 'highest point', from which English *acme* comes, could also mean 'pimple'. It was wrongly copied in this sense with *n* rather than *m*.

acolyte /ákə līt/ *n* **1** a cleric's assistant in performing liturgical rites **2** a follower or assistant

~~accommodate~~ incorrect spelling of **accommodate**

~~accommodation~~ incorrect spelling of **accommodation**

~~accompany~~ incorrect spelling of **accompany**

Aconcagua /ákən kágwə/ highest mountain in the Andes and in the western hemisphere, in W Argentina. Height 6,960 m/22,834 ft.

aconite /ákə nīt/ n 1 an extract from a dried poisonous root. Use: homeopathic remedy. 2 a plant with purple, blue, or white hooded flowers and poisonous roots

~~acording~~ incorrect spelling of **according**

acorn /áy kawrn/ n an oval-shaped fruit of an oak tree, in a cup-shaped base

acoustic /ə koóstik/, **acoustical** /-stik'l/ adj 1 of sound 2 designed to control or carry sound 3 not amplified electronically o *an acoustic guitar* ■ n 1 a musical instrument without amplification (infml) 2 the acoustics of a room —**acoustically** adv

acoustics /ə koóstiks/ n the study of sound (+ sing verb) ■ npl the sound-carrying ability of a room (+ pl verb) —**acoustician** /ákoo stísh'n/ n

acquaint /ə kwáynt/ vt make aware —**acquainted** adj

acquaintance /ə kwáyntənss/ n 1 somebody slightly known 2 slight knowledge o *only a basic acquaintance with French theatre*

acquiesce /ákwi éss/ (-escing, -esced) vi agree to something passively —**acquiescence** n —**acquiescent** adj ◊ See note at **agree**

acquire /ə kwír/ (-quiring, -quired) vt 1 obtain 2 learn or develop o *a habit I acquired in the army* —**acquired** adj ◊ See note at **get**

acquired immune deficiency syndrome, acquired immunodeficiency syndrome n full form of **Aids**

acquired taste n a liking for something that only develops gradually

acquisition /ákwi zísh'n/ n 1 the acquiring of something 2 a new possession

acquisitions /ákwi zísh'nz/ n a company department responsible for taking over other businesses (+ sing verb)

acquisitive /ə kwízzətiv/ adj eager to acquire things —**acquisitively** adv —**acquisitiveness** n

acquit /ə kwít/ (-quitting, -quitted) v 1 vt declare innocent 2 vr behave or perform o *acquitted themselves admirably*

acquittal /ə kwítt'l/ n a not-guilty verdict

acre /áykər/ n a unit of area equal to 4,046.86 sq. m/4,840 sq. yd ■ **acres** npl land

acreage /áykərij/ n land measured in acres

acrid /ákrid/ adj 1 unpleasantly pungent 2 bitter in tone or character —**acridity** /ə kríddəti/ n —**acridly** adv

~~acrilic~~ incorrect spelling of **acrylic**

acrimonious /ákri mốni əss/ adj resentful and angry —**acrimoniously** adv —**acrimony** /ákriməni/ n

acrobat /ákrə bat/ n a gymnastic entertainer —**acrobatic** /ákrə báttik/ adj

acrobatics /ákrə báttiks/ n (+ sing or pl verb) 1 gymnastic feats performed as entertainment 2 great skill or complexity o *verbal acrobatics*

acronym /ákrənim/ n a word formed from the initials of other words, e.g. 'NATO'

acropolis /ə króppəliss/ n 1 the fortified citadel of a city in ancient Greece 2 **Acropolis** the ancient citadel of Athens in Greece that was the religious focus of the city

across /ə króss/ prep 1 on the opposite side of 2 from one side to the other of ■ adj, adv so as to cross ■ adv 1 at or to the other side 2 measured in width

across-the-board adj, adv affecting everyone or everything equally

acrostic /ə króstik/ n a set of written lines containing letters that form a word when read downwards

acrylic /ə kríllik/ n 1 a synthetic fibre 2 a type of paint containing resin made from acrylic acid —**acrylic** adj

acrylic acid n $C_3H_4O_2$ a corrosive liquid. Use: manufacture of resins.

act n 1 something done 2 the process of doing something 3 a main part of a play 4 a performance in a show 5 a performer 6 a pretence 7 a record of a decision of a lawmaking body ■ v 1 vi take action o *need to act at once* 2 vti behave in a particular way 3 vi behave in a way intended to impress or deceive 4 vi function o *acts as a barrier* 5 vi be a substitute o *acting for the manager in her absence* 6 vi have an effect o *The painkiller starts to act immediately.* 7 vti play a role 8 vi be an actor ◊ **get your act together** become more organized (infml)

☐ **act out** vt misbehave to express feeling

☐ **act up** vi be troublesome

ACT abbr Australian Capital Territory

acting /ákting/ n the art, profession, or performance of an actor ■ adj carrying out particular duties or doing somebody else's job temporarily

actinide /ákti nīd/ n any element in the series of radioactive elements beginning with actinium and ending with lawrencium

actinium /ak tínni əm/ n (symbol **Ac**) a radioactive metallic chemical element

action /áksh'n/ n 1 the process of doing something 2 something done 3 a movement o *the action of a piston* 4 energetic activity 5 legal proceedings 6 the main events of a film or novel 7 function or influence o *the action of water on stone* 8 fighting during a war 9 an operating mechanism ■ interj tells film actors to start performing ■ vt put a plan into operation

actionable /áksh'nəb'l/ adj giving cause for legal action

action replay n a reshowing of a part of a sports broadcast

action stations npl posts for combat ■ interj orders people to go to their combat posts

activate /ákti vayt/ (-vating, -vated) v 1 vti make or become active 2 vt make radioactive —**activation** /ákti váysh'n/ n

active /áktiv/ adj 1 moving around 2 busy o *an active life* 3 having a chemical effect o *an active ingredient* 4 showing involvement o *an active role* 5 needing and using energy

6 describes a volcano that is not extinct **7** describes a verb or the voice of a verb in which the subject performs the action described by the verb ■ *n* the active voice of a verb —**actively** *adv*

active cell *n* an open spreadsheet cell

active-matrix display *n* a flat liquid-crystal screen with high colour resolution

active server page *n* an HTML page processed on a server

active service *n* military service in an operational area

activism /áktivizəm/ *n* vigorous organized action in pursuing a political or social end —**activist** *n, adj*

activity /ak tívvəti/ (*pl* -ties) *n* **1** something that somebody does (*often pl*) ○ *leisure activities* **2** physical exercise **3** the state of being active

act of God *n* an event beyond human control

actor /áktər/ *n* a performer in plays or films

actress /áktrəss/ *n* a female performer in plays or films

> **USAGE** Many actresses now prefer to refer to themselves as actors.

actual /ákchoo əl, ákchəl/ *adj* **1** real **2** existing now

actuality /ákchoo álləti/ (*pl* -ties) *n* **1** something that is real **2** everything that really exists or happens

actualize /ákchoo ə līz/ (-izing, -ized), **actualise** *vt* **1** make real or actual **2** portray or represent realistically —**actualization** /ákchoo ə lī záysh'n/ *n*

actually /ákchoo əli, ákchəli/ *adv* **1** in fact ○ *I've never actually been there.* **2** expresses a contradictory opinion or fact ○ *Actually, she's my sister.*

actuary /ákchoo əri/ (*pl* -ies) *n* a statistician who calculates insurance risks —**actuarial** /ákchoo áiri əl/ *adj*

actuate /ákchoo ayt/ (-ating, -ated) *vt* **1** cause somebody to act in a particular way **2** cause a mechanism to start working (*fml*)

acuity /ə kyoo əti/ *n* keenness of hearing, sight, or intellect

acumen /ákyoomən/ *n* sharpness of mind

~~acumulate~~ incorrect spelling of **accumulate**

acupressure /ákyoo preshər/ *n* a therapeutic treatment using manual pressure on specific parts of the body

acupuncture /ákyoo pungkchər/ *n* a therapeutic treatment using needles inserted in the skin at specific points —**acupuncturist** *n*

~~acurate~~ incorrect spelling of **accurate**

acute /ə kyoot/ *adj* **1** very great or bad ○ *an acute financial crisis* **2** perceptive ○ *an acute grasp of foreign affairs* **3** powerful and sensitive ○ *acute eyesight* **4** describes an angle of less than 90° **5** describes a disease that is severe and of short duration ■ *n also* **acute accent** a specific mark above a letter, as in 'á' or 'ó' —**acutely** *adv* —**acuteness** *n*

ad *n* an advertisement (*infml*)

AD *adv* indicates a date after the birth of Jesus Christ. Full form **anno Domini**

> **USAGE** AD is traditionally put before the numeral to which it relates (AD *1453*), but after if the century is spelt out: *the 5th century* AD. Some writers use PE (Present Era) or CE (Common Era) to avoid the association with Christianity.

A/D *abbr* analog to digital

Ada /áydə/ *n* a high-level computer language that is easy to read

> **ORIGIN Ada** is named after the English mathematician Augusta Ada Byron, Countess of Lovelace (1815–52).

adage /áddij/ *n* a saying

adagio /ə daáji ō/ *adv* slowly (*musical direction*) —**adagio** *n, adj*

Adam /áddəm/ *n* in the Bible, the first man ◇ **not know from Adam** have never met or seen before

adamant /áddəmənt/ *adj* firmly set in your opinion —**adamantly** *adv*

Adams /áddəmz/, **Gerry** (*b.* 1948) Northern Ireland politician

Adam's apple *n* the lump at the front of the throat, visible in men

Adana /áddənə/ city in S Turkey and capital of **Adana Province**. Pop. 1,131,198 (1997).

adapt /ə dápt/ *vti* **1** change to meet different requirements **2** adjust to new conditions —**adaptation** /áddap táysh'n, -əp-/

adaptable /ə dáptəb'l/ *adj* **1** changing easily **2** adjustable —**adaptability** /ə dáptə bílləti/ *n* —**adaptably** *adv*

adapter /ə dáptər/, **adaptor** *n* **1** a device for connecting an electric appliance to an otherwise incompatible power source **2** a device for connecting otherwise incompatible parts

adaptive /ə dáptiv/ *adj* usable in different conditions —**adaptively** *adv*

Adar /ə daár/ *n* the 12th month of the year in the Jewish calendar

Adar Rishon /-ríshon/ *n* the name given to the month of Adar during a leap year in the Jewish calendar

Adar Sheni /-sháyni/ *n* a 13th month added to the Jewish calendar after Adar in leap years

ADC *abbr* analogue-to-digital converter

Adcock /ád kok/, **Fleur** (*b.* 1934) New Zealand poet

add *v* **1** *vt* put something into or join something onto something else **2** *vti* calculate a total **3** *vi* increase the effect of something ○ *This adds to our problems.*

□ **add up** *v* **1** *vti* calculate or reach a total **2** *vi* make sense

□ **add up to** *vt* amount to or result in

ADD *abbr* attention deficit disorder

addendum /ə déndəm/ (*pl* -**da** /-də/) *n* **1** something added **2** a supplement to a book

adder[1] /áddər/ *n* somebody or something that adds

adder[2] /áddər/ *n* a small venomous European snake

ORIGIN An **adder** was originally *a nadder*: the *n* was lost when this common combination of words was misinterpreted.

---

addict /áddikt/ *n* **1** somebody dependent on something such as a drug **2** an enthusiast

addiction /ə díksh'n/ *n* **1** dependence on something such as a drug **2** great interest or devotion —**addicted** *adj*

addictive /ə díktiv/ *adj* causing addiction

add-in *n* COMPUT = **add-on**

Addis Ababa /áddiss ábbəbə/ capital of Ethiopia. Pop. 1,047,300 (1994).

Addison /áddiss'n/, **Joseph** (1672–1719) English essayist and politician

addition /ə dísh'n/ *n* **1** the process of adding **2** something added **3** the calculation of a total

additional /ə dísh'nəl/ *adj* extra —**additionally** *adv*

additive /áddətiv/ *n* something added, e.g. to food ■ *adj* involving adding something *(fml)*

addle /ádd'l/ (**-dling, -dled**) *vti* **1** confuse **2** rot or spoil

add-on, add-in *n* a piece of extra equipment for a computer

address /ə dréss/ *n* **1** the words or numbers identifying the location of a building, organization, or person **2** a formal talk **3** a number specifying a location in a computer's memory ■ *vt* **1** write an address on an item of mail **2** speak or make a speech to somebody **3** deal with a problem or issue

addressee /áddre seé, ə dréss eé/ *n* somebody to whom an item of mail is addressed

address harvester *n* a computer program that collects e-mail addresses from the Internet

adduce /ə dyóoss/ (**-ducing, -duced**) *vt* offer as evidence *(fml)* —**adducible** *adj*

Adelaide /ádd'l ayd/ state capital and main port of South Australia. Pop. 1,088,400 (1998).

Aden /áyd'n/ **1** port and second largest city in Yemen. Pop. 400,783 (1993 estimate). **2** former British protectorate that is now part of Yemen

Adenauer /áddə now ər/, **Konrad** (1876–1967) German chancellor of West Germany (1949–63)

adenoids /áddi noydz/ *npl* a mass of tissue at the back of the throat —**adenoidal** /áddi nóyd'l/ *adj*

adept *adj* /ə dépt/ skilful ■ *n* /ádd ept/ a skilled person —**adeptly** *adv* —**adeptness** *n*

adequate /áddikwət/ *adj* **1** sufficient to meet a need **2** just barely sufficient to meet a need —**adequacy** *n* —**adequately** *adv*

~~adequatly~~ incorrect spelling of **adequately**

adhere /əd heér/ (**-hering, -hered**) *vi* **1** act in accordance with ○ *adhere to the rules* **2** stick or hold firmly ○ *adhering to their beliefs* —**adherence** *n*

adherent /əd heérənt/ *n* a supporter ■ *adj* sticky *(fml)*

adhesion /əd heézh'n/ *n* **1** ability to stick or hold firmly **2** support for a cause or leader **3** the joining of normally unconnected body parts by bands of fibrous tissue

adhesive /əd heéssiv, -ziv/ *n* a substance used to stick things together ■ *adj* sticky

ad hoc /ad hók/ *adj, adv* just for a specific purpose

adhocracy /ad hókrəssi/ (*pl* **-cies**) *n* an organization that can alter to suit changing circumstances

~~adict~~ incorrect spelling of **addict**

adieu /ə dyóo/ *interj, n* (*pl* **adieux** /ə dyóoz/ *or* **adieus** /ə dyóoz/) goodbye, or an utterance of this *(literary)*

ad infinitum /ád infi nítəm/ *adv* endlessly

adipose /áddi póss/ *adj* fatty ■ *n* fat —**adiposity** /áddi póssəti/ *n*

Adirondack Mountains /áddə rón dak-/, **Adirondacks** /-daks/ mountain chain in NE New York State. Highest peak Mt Marcy 1,629 m/5,344 ft.

adj. *abbr* **1** adjective **2** adjunct

Adj. *abbr* adjutant

adjacent /ə jáyss'nt/ *adj* neighbouring or adjoining —**adjacency** *n*

adjective /ájjiktiv/ *n* a word qualifying or describing a noun, e.g. 'blue' in 'blue eyes' —**adjectival** /ájjik tív'l/ *adj*

adjoin /ə jóyn/ *vti* be next to or share a border with something —**adjoining** *adj*

adjourn /ə júrn/ *v* **1** *vti* postpone or defer **2** *vi* move as a group ○ *We adjourned to the lounge.* —**adjournment** *n*

adjudge /ə júj/ (**-judging, -judged**) *vt* make a judgment or declaration about

adjudicate /ə jóodi kayt/ (**-cating, -cated**) *vti* **1** make an official or judicial decision about something **2** judge a competition —**adjudication** /ə jóodi káysh'n/ *n* —**adjudicator** *n*

adjunct /ájjungkt/ *n* **1** something extra added on **2** an assistant —**adjunction** /ə júngksh'n/ *n* —**adjunctive** *adj*

adjure /ə jóor/ (**-juring, -jured**) *vt* **1** command solemnly **2** make an appeal to —**adjuration** /ájjoo ráysh'n/ *n*

adjust /ə júst/ *v* **1** *vt* change something slightly to make it fit or function better **2** *vti* adapt yourself to new circumstances —**adjustable** *adj* —**adjustment** *n*

adjutant /ájjootənt/ *n* a commanding officer's administrative assistant

Adler /áddlər/, **Alfred** (1870–1937) Austrian psychiatrist

ad lib /ád líb/ *adv* without advance preparation

ad-lib /ád líb/ *vti* (**ad-libbing, ad-libbed**) improvise a speech or performance ■ *adj* unplanned ■ *n* an improvised remark in a performance —**ad-libber** *n*

admin /ád min/ *n* administration *(infml)*

administer /əd mínnistər/ *vt* 1 be in charge of 2 dispense o *administer justice* 3 give as medication —**administrable** *adj*

administration /əd mínni stráysh'n/ *n* 1 the management of business or government 2 management or government staff 3 a term of office 4 the executive branch of a government 5 the process of administering something —**administrative** /əd mínnistrətiv/ —**administrator** /əd mínni straytər/ *n*

admirable /ádmərəb'l/ *adj* deserving approval —**admirably** *adv*

admiral /ádmərəl/ *n* 1 a naval commander 2 a brightly coloured butterfly —**admiralty** *n*

ORIGIN The Arabic word from which **admiral** comes meant 'commander' – in fact it is the same word that gave us *emir*. The *-al* ending comes from an Arabic element meaning 'of', and it was the familiarity of titles like 'commander of the sea' and 'commander of the faithful' that led Europeans to misunderstand the two Arabic forms, *amir-al*, as one. The word meant 'commander, emir' when first adopted into English, but as naval power became significant throughout Europe in the 15C **admiral** became firmly associated with the sea.

Admiralty /ádmərəlti/ *n* the former UK government department for the Navy

Admiralty Board *n* the UK government department for the Navy

admire /əd mír/ (-**miring**, -**mired**) *vt* 1 be impressed by 2 respect —**admiration** /ádmə ráysh'n/ *n* —**admirer** *n*

~~admision~~ incorrect spelling of **admission**

~~admissable~~ incorrect spelling of **admissible**

admissible /əd míssəb'l/ *adj* 1 allowable 2 allowed to enter 3 describes evidence acceptable in court —**admissibility** /əd míssə bílləti/ *n*

admission /əd mísh'n/ *n* 1 right of entry 2 the fee for entry 3 a confession or declaration

admit /əd mít/ (-**mitting**, -**mitted**) *v* 1 *vti* confess to a fault or error 2 *vti* acknowledge that something is true or possible 3 *vt* allow somebody to enter

admittance /əd mítt'nss/ *n* 1 permission to enter 2 entry to a place

admittedly /əd míttidli/ *adv* as must be acknowledged

admixture /əd míkschər/ *n* 1 a product of mixing 2 an ingredient 3 the process of mixing ingredients

admonish /əd mónnish/ *vt* 1 rebuke or reprimand 2 advise or warn —**admonishment** *n* —**admonition** /ádmə nísh'n/

ad nauseam /ad náwzi am/ *adv* to an extreme or annoying degree

~~ad nauseum~~ incorrect spelling of **ad nauseam**

ado /ə doo/ *n* bustle

adobe /ə dóbi/ *n* 1 earthen brick 2 a building made of adobe

adolescent /áddə léssn't/ *n* somebody between childhood and adulthood —**adolescence** *n* —**adolescent** *adj*

~~adolesent~~ incorrect spelling of **adolescent**

Adonis /ə dóniss/ *n* a handsome young man

ORIGIN The original **Adonis** was a handsome young man in Greek mythology.

adopt /ə dópt/ *vt* 1 legally raise another's child 2 choose to act in accordance with an idea, belief, or plan 3 assume a position or attitude 4 start using a new name or title —**adoptable** *adj* —**adopted** *adj* —**adoptee** /ə dóp teé/ *n* —**adoption** *n*

USAGE **adopted** or **adoptive**? Parents who adopt a child have an **adopted** child, and the child has **adoptive** parents. Any children related to the parents by birth have an **adopted** brother or sister; the **adopted** child has **adoptive** siblings.

adoptive /ə dóptiv/ *adj* related by adoption o *her adoptive parents*

adorable /ə dáwrəb'l/ *adj* delightful or lovable —**adorably** *adv*

adore /ə dáwr/ (**adoring**, **adored**) *vt* 1 love deeply 2 worship 3 like very much *(infml)* —**adoration** /áddə ráysh'n/ *n* —**adorer** *n*

adorn /ə dáwrn/ *vt* 1 add decoration to 2 enhance —**adornment** *n*

ADP *abbr* automatic data processing

adrenal /ə dreén'l/ *adj* 1 of or on the kidneys 2 of the adrenal glands ■ *n* ANAT = **adrenal gland**

adrenal gland *n* an organ secreting hormones, situated above each kidney

adrenalin /ə drénnəlin/, **adrenaline** *n* a hormone that increases blood pressure and heart rate at times of stress or danger

USAGE **adrenalin** or **adrenaline**? In British English, the usual spelling is **adrenalin**, but **adrenaline** is also used. In American usage, **adrenaline** is the more usual spelling, and **Adrenalin** (with a capital initial letter) is a trademark for a commercial drug.

~~adress~~ incorrect spelling of **address**

Adriatic Sea /áydri áttik-/ *n* arm of the Mediterranean Sea, between Italy and the Balkan Peninsula

adrift /ə dríft/ *adj*, *adv* 1 floating without control or direction 2 living without a goal or purpose

adroit /ə dróyt/ *adj* 1 skilful 2 quick-witted —**adroitly** *adv* —**adroitness** *n*

ADSL *abbr* asymmetrical digital subscriber line

adsorb /ad sáwrb, -záwrb/ *vti* undergo or cause to undergo adsorption

adsorption /ad sáwrpsh'n, -záwrp-/ *n* the adhesion of a thin layer of molecules of a substance to the surface of a solid or liquid —**adsorptive** *adj*

adspend /ád spend/ *n* an advertising budget

aduki bean *n* PLANTS, FOOD = **adzuki bean**

adulation /áddyoö láysh'n/ *n* excessive admiration —**adulate** /áddyoö layt/ *vt*

adult /áddult, ə dúlt/ *adj* **1** fully developed and mature ○ *an adult male* ○ *adult life* **2** unsuitable for children ■ *n* an adult person or other organism —**adulthood** *n*

adulterate /ə dúltə rayt/ (**-ating, -ated**) *vt* make impure —**adulteration** /ə dúltə ráysh'n/ *n* —**adulterator** *n*

adultery /ə dúltəri/ *n* extramarital sex —**adulterer** *n* —**adulterous** *adj*

~~adultry~~ incorrect spelling of **adultery**

adumbrate /áddum brayt/ (**-brating, -brated**) *vt* **1** indicate sketchily **2** foreshadow

adv. *abbr* adverb

advance /əd vaánss/ *v* (**-vancing, -vanced**) **1** *vti* move ahead **2** *vt* put forward as a proposal **3** *vt* lend or give beforehand **4** *vti* raise or rise in status **5** *vt* bring forward in time **6** *vti* further the progress or improvement of, or undergo progress or improvement ■ *n* **1** a development or improvement **2** a payment ahead of time **3** a movement ahead **4** a friendly, sometimes suggestive, approach made to somebody (*often pl*) ■ *adj* **1** ahead of time **2** going in front —**advancement** *n* —**advancer** *n*

advanced /əd vaánst/ *adj* **1** more highly developed **2** far along in progress

Advanced Higher *n* a Scottish school examination above and in addition to a Higher

advantage /əd vaántij/ *n* **1** a superior position **2** a favourable factor **3** a benefit or gain **4** in tennis, the point after deuce ■ *vt* (**-taging, -taged**) benefit ◊ **take advantage of 1** make use of **2** use in a selfish way

advantageous /ádvən táyjəss/ *adj* **1** giving an advantage **2** useful

advent /ád vent/ *n* **1** the arrival of something important **2 Advent** the four weeks before Christmas

adventitious /ádvən tíshəss/ *adj* **1** from an outside or unexpected source **2** developing in an unusual position ○ *adventitious roots*

adventure /əd vénchər/ *n* **1** an exciting, often risky, experience **2** a bold undertaking **3** involvement in adventures ■ *vi* (**-turing, -tured**) engage in a risky activity (*dated*)

adventure playground *n* an outdoor play area with climbing frames and similar equipment

adventurer /əd vénchərər/ *n* somebody in search of adventure

adventuresome /əd vénchərsəm/ *adj* daring

adventurous /əd vénchərəss/ *adj* **1** daring **2** risky —**adventurously** *adv* —**adventurousness** *n*

adverb /ád vurb/ *n* a word modifying a verb or adjective, e.g. 'slowly' in 'walked slowly' —**adverbial** /ad vúrbi əl/ *adj*

adversary /ádvərsəri/ (*pl* **-ies**) *n* an opponent —**adversarial** /ad vur sáiri əl/ *adj*

adverse /ád vurss, ad vúrss/ *adj* unfavourable or difficult —**adversely** *adv*

adversity /əd vúrssəti/ *n* misfortune

advert /ád vurt/ *n* an advertisement (*infml*)

advertise /ádvər tīz/ (**-tising, -tised**) *v* **1** *vti* publicize a commercial product or service **2** *vti* publicly announce something such as a job vacancy **3** *vt* tell others about something —**advertiser** *n* —**advertising** *n*

advertisement /əd vúrtissmənt/ *n* **1** advertising **2** a public announcement advertising something

~~advertisment~~ incorrect spelling of **advertisement**

advertorial /ádvər táwri əl/ *n* an advertisement presented as editorial comment

advice /əd víss/ *n* **1** recommendation about a course of action **2** official information

advice note *n* a notification of goods sent

advisable /əd vízəb'l/ *adj* worth doing and sensible —**advisability** /əd vízə bílləti/ *n*

advise /əd víz/ (**-vising, -vised**) *v* **1** *vti* offer advice to somebody **2** *vt* recommend something **3** *vt* inform somebody ◊ See note at **recommend**

advisedly /əd vízidli/ *adv* after consideration

adviser /əd vízər/, **advisor** *n* somebody who gives advice

---

USAGE adviser or **advisor**? Both spellings are used for 'somebody who gives advice'. **Adviser** is often regarded as more correct because *-er* is the more usual suffix for words formed directly from other English words. **Advisor** is common in American English and is probably influenced by the form of the adjective **advisory** or the spelling of Latin *advisor*.

---

advisory /əd vízəri/ *adj* giving advice

advocate *vt* /ádvə kayt/ (**-cating, -cated**) recommend or support ■ *n* /ádvəkət, -kayt/ **1** a supporter who speaks in favour of something **2** a legal representative **3** a Scottish barrister —**advocacy** /-kəssi/ *n* ◊ See note at **recommend**

adze, adz *n* a tool with an arched blade set at right angles to the handle. Use: trimming and shaping wood.

adzuki bean /ad zóoki-/, **aduki bean** /ə dóoki-/, **azuki bean** /ə zóoki-/ *n* **1** a bean used in vegetarian or sweet dishes **2** a plant that produces adzuki beans

Aegean Sea /i jee ən-/ arm of the Mediterranean Sea, between Greece and Turkey

aegis /éejiss/ ◊ **under the aegis of** with the support or protection of (*fml*)

ORIGIN The Greek word from which **aegis** comes was used for the goatskin shield of the god Zeus, a symbol of his traditional function as a protector. The English form comes from Latin.

Aeneas /i nee əss/ *n* in Greek and Roman mythology, a Trojan who spent many years travelling after the fall of Troy

Aeolis /ee ə liss/, **Aeolia** /ee óli ə/ ancient region on the northwestern coast of Asia Minor —**Aeolian** *adj*

aeon /ee ən, -on/, **eon** *n* **1** the longest unit of geological time **2** a vast amount of time (*infml; usually pl*) ○ *take aeons to finish*

aerate /áir rayt/ (**-ating, -ated**) vt introduce air into —**aeration** /air ráysh'n/ n

aerial /áiri əl/ adj **1** of or in the air **2** involving aircraft **3** light and insubstantial ■ n a metal rod for radio waves

aero abbr aviation industry (in Internet addresses)

aero-, aeri-, aer- prefix **1** air, atmosphere, gas ○ aerodynamic **2** aviation ○ aerospace

aerobatics /áirō báttiks/ n stunt flying (+ sing or pl verb) —**aerobatic** adj

aerobic /air rṓbik/ adj **1** of aerobics **2** needing oxygen **3** giving oxygen **4** increasing respiration —**aerobically** adv

aerobics /air rṓbiks/ n (+ sing or pl verb) **1** fitness exercises done to music **2** activities that increase respiration

aerodrome /áirō drṓm/ n a small airfield

aerodynamic /áirō dī námmik/ adj **1** of aerodynamics **2** designed to reduce air resistance —**aerodynamically** adv

aerodynamics /áirō dī námmiks/ n the study of objects moving through air (+ sing verb) ■ npl aerodynamic properties (+ pl verb) —**aerodynamicist** /-issist/ n

aerofoil /áirō foyl/ n a part of an aircraft that moves to provide lift or control

aerogram /áirə gram/, **aerogramme** n an airmail letter

aerolization /áirō ī záysh'n/ n the airborne transmission of a substance in a vaporized form

aeronautics /áirə náwtiks/ n the science of flight (+ sing verb)

aeroplane /áirə playn/ n a flying vehicle with wings and an engine

aerosol /áirə sol/ n **1** a container holding a substance that can be dispensed under pressure as a spray **2** a substance sprayed from an aerosol **3** a suspension of particles in a gas

aerosolize /áirəsə īīz/ (**-izing, -ized**), **aerosolise** vt convert a substance into a spray

aerospace /áirō spayss/ n the atmosphere and outer space ■ adj of aircraft and spacecraft

Aeschylus /ééskələss/ (525?–426 BC) Greek dramatist

Aesop /ééssəp/ (620?–560? BC) Greek writer of fables

AEST abbr Australian Eastern Standard Time

aesthete /éés theet/ n a lover of beauty

aesthetic /eess théttik, iss-/ adj **1** of aesthetics **2** appreciating beauty **3** pleasing in appearance ■ n a set of principles about art —**aesthetically** adv

aestheticism /eess théttisizəm, iss-/ n **1** the philosophical doctrine that all moral principles are derived from beauty **2** devotion to beauty

aesthetics /eess théttiks, iss-/ n **1** the philosophical study of beauty (+ sing verb) **2** the idea of beauty (+ sing or pl verb) —**aesthetician** /ééssthə tísh'n, éss-/ n

aether n = ether 2

aetiology /éeti óllə ji/, **etiology** n **1** the study of causes **2** the cause of a disease —**aetiologist** n

afar /ə faár/ adv far away (literary)

affable /áffəb'l/ adj friendly and good-natured —**affability** /áffə bílləti/ n —**affably** adv

affair /ə fáir/ n **1** a business matter **2** an incident, especially a scandalous one ○ that odd affair at work last year **3** a responsibility or concern ○ What he does with the information is his own affair. **4** a social event **5** an object of a particular kind ○ The house is a ramshackle affair. **6** a sexual relationship between two people who are not married to each other ■ **affairs** npl **1** business matters **2** matters of public interest ○ foreign affairs

affect[1] /ə fékt/ vt **1** cause a change in or influence **2** move emotionally

USAGE **affect** or **effect**? The verb **affect** means 'cause a change in': The floods affected the whole region. The noun **effect** describes the changes that result from this: The effects of the flooding were widespread. The verb **effect**, used in formal contexts, means 'make something happen': He effected a cure/a withdrawal/major changes.

affect[2] /ə fékt/ vt **1** pretend to have or be something **2** adopt a style or manner

affectation /áffek táysh'n/ n behaviour intended to impress

affected /ə féktid/ adj unnatural and intending or intended to impress —**affectedly** adv —**affectedness** n

affecting /ə fékting/ adj emotionally moving ■

affection /ə féksh'n/ n fondness or liking ■ npl **affections** npl feelings of fondness ⟡ See note at **love**

affectionate /ə féksh'nət/ adj loving —**affectionately** adv

affective /ə féktiv/ adj **1** of emotional expression **2** emotionally moving —**affectively** adv

affidavit /áffi dáyvit/ n a written version of a sworn statement

affiliate vti /ə filli ayt/ (**-ating, -ated**) combine with another person or organization ■ n /ə filli ət, -ayt/ an affiliated member —**affiliation** /ə filli áysh'n/ n

affinity /ə fínnəti/ (pl **-ties**) n **1** a natural liking or identification **2** a similarity or connection **3** relationship by marriage

affirm /ə fúrm/ vt **1** declare positively and publicly **2** declare support or admiration for —**affirmation** /áffər máysh'n/ n

affirmative /ə fúrmətiv/ adj indicating agreement ■ n **1** a positive assertion **2** a word or statement conveying agreement ■ interj yes —**affirmatively** adv

affirmative action n US, Can = **positive discrimination**

affix vt /ə fíks/ **1** fasten or attach **2** add on ■ n /áffiks/ **1** a part added to a word to modify its meaning or part of speech or to form an inflection **2** something attached

afflict /ə flíkt/ *vt* cause distress to

affliction /ə flíksh'n/ *n* **1** distress **2** a cause of distress

affluent /áffloo ənt/ *adj* wealthy —**affluence** *n* —**affluently** *adv*

> **ORIGIN Affluent** originally meant 'flowing', and later 'flowing freely' or 'abundant'. The association with wealth did not develop until the 18C.

afford /ə fáwrd/ *vt* **1** be able to buy **2** be able to do or provide without bad consequences ○ *We can't afford to be late.* **3** be able to spare **4** provide *(fml)* —**affordable** *adj*

afforest /ə fórrist/ *vt* plant trees on —**afforestation** /ə fórri stáysh'n/ *n*

affray /ə fráy/ *n* a fight in a public place

affront /ə frúnt/ *n* an open insult —**affront** *vt*

Afghan /áf gan, áfgən/ *n* **1** somebody from Afghanistan **2** *also* **Afghan hound** a tall dog with a long silky coat —**Afghan** *adj*

afghani /af gánni, -gaáni/ *(pl* -**is***)* *n* the main unit of Afghan currency

Afghanistan /af gánni staan, -stan/ landlocked country in SW Asia. Cap. Kabul. Pop. 26,813,057 (2001).

aficionado /ə físhə naàdō, ə físsi ə-/ *(pl* -**dos***)* *n* a knowledgeable enthusiast

afield /ə feeld/ *adv, adj* away from home or customary surroundings ○ *wandered far afield*

AFL *abbr* Australian Football League

aflame /ə fláym/ *adj* **1** on fire **2** impassioned

afloat /ə flót/ *adj, adv* **1** floating on water **2** on board a ship **3** financially solvent

afoot /ə foŏt/ *adj, adv* **1** happening, often secretly or subtly **2** on foot

aforementioned /ə fáwr mensh'nd/ *(fml)* *adj* mentioned earlier ■ *n* the person or thing previously mentioned

aforesaid /ə fáwr sed/ *adj* named earlier *(fml)*

a fortiori /ay fáwrti áwr ī, aa fáwrti áwree/ *adv* with more reason

AFP *abbr* Australian Federal Police

Afr. *abbr* **1** Africa **2** African

afraid /ə fráyd/ *adj* **1** frightened **2** reluctant **3** regretful

afresh /ə frésh/ *adv* again

Africa /áffrikə/ second largest continent, lying south of Europe with the Atlantic Ocean to the west and the Indian Ocean to the east. Pop. 797,148,044 (2000).

African /áffrikən/ *adj* of Africa ■ *n* **1** somebody from Africa **2** somebody of African descent

African American, Afro-American *n* an American of African descent —**African American** *adj* —**Afro-American** *adj*

Afrikaans /áffri kaánss/ *n* a South African language descended from Dutch ■ *adj* of Afrikaans or Afrikaners

Afrikaner /áffri kaánər/ *n* an Afrikaans-speaking South African —**Afrikaner** *adj*

Afro /áffrō/ *n (pl* -**ros***)* a hairstyle with tight curls ■ *adj* of Africa

aft *adv, adj* at the back of a ship or aircraft

after /aáftər/ *prep* **1** later than **2** behind **3** in pursuit of **4** regarding **5** following from **6** similar to or imitating **7** in conformity to **8** with the same name as ■ *adv* **1** later **2** farther back ■ *conj* following a time when ■ *adj* subsequent ◊ **after all 1** in spite of other appearances or considerations ○ *After all, she's only a beginner.* **2** in the end ○ *She decided to stay after all.*

afterbirth /aáftər burth/ *n* the placenta expelled after delivery of a foetus

aftercare /aáftər kair/ *n* **1** care provided after leaving a hospital, prison, or other institution **2** upkeep or support after purchase

aftereffect /aáftər i fekt/ *n* a delayed result, effect, or reaction

afterglow /aáftər glō/ *n* **1** a glow from a light no longer directly visible **2** a good feeling after something

after-hours *adj* occurring after closing time

afterlife /aáftər līf/ *n* **1** life after death **2** a later stage of life

aftermarket /aáftər maarkit/ *n* a market for replacement parts

aftermath /aáftə math, -maath/ *n* the consequences of or period following a bad event

> **ORIGIN** *Math* was a word meaning 'mowing', now obsolete. The **aftermath** was the grass that springs up after mowing, as a second crop.

afternoon /aáftər noón/ *n* the time between midday and evening

afters /aáftərz/ *n* dessert *(infml;* + *sing* or *pl verb)*

aftershave /aáftər shayv/ *n* a soothing scented liquid for men's faces after shaving

aftershock /aáftər shok/ *n* **1** a small earthquake following a larger one **2** a delayed reaction

aftertaste /aáftər tayst/ *n* **1** a persisting taste **2** an unpleasant feeling after something

afterthought /aáftər thawt/ *n* something added later

afterwards /aáftəwərdz/ *adv* at a later time

afterworld /aáftər wurld/ *n* the world of the dead

Ag *symbol* silver

aga /aágə/ *n* in an Islamic country, a military commander

Aga /aágə/ *tdmk* a trademark for a large iron stove

again /ə gén, ə gáyn/ *adv* **1** once more at another time **2** as before **3** in addition

against /ə génst, ə gáynst/ *prep* **1** in competition with **2** in contact with by leaning **3** in collision with **4** in the opposite direction to **5** in contrast with **6** as protection from **7** compared with **8** contrary to

Aga Khan IV /aágə kaán/ *(b.* 1936) Swiss-born Muslim leader

Agamemnon /ággə mém non/ *n* in Greek mythology, the leader of the Greek army in the Trojan War

agape[1] /ə gáyp/ adv, adj (literary) **1** wide open **2** open-mouthed

agape[2] /ággəpi/ n **1** nonsexual love **2** Christian love

agar /áygər, -gaar/, **agar-agar** n a powdered seaweed extract. Use: setting agent, thickener, culture medium for microorganisms.

Agassi /ágəssi/, **Andre** (b. 1970) US tennis player

agate /ággət/ n a typically striped form of chalcedony. Use: gems.

agave /ə gáyvi, ə gaávi, ággayv/ (pl **-ves** or same) n a spiny-leaved plant. Use: fibre, alcoholic drinks, especially tequila.

age n **1** how old somebody or something is **2** a stage of life **3** legal adulthood **4** the state of being old **5** also **Age** a historical era **6** also **Age** a relatively short division of recent geological time ■ **ages** npl **1** a long time (infml) **2** the progress of history ■ vti (**ageing** or **aging, aged**) **1** grow or cause somebody to grow old **2** improve or cause something to improve over time ◊ **come of age** reach the age of legal adulthood ◊ **of a certain age** no longer young (humorous)

-age suffix **1** action, or result of an action ○ coinage **2** housing ○ orphanage **3** condition, office ○ peerage **4** charge ○ postage

aged adj **1** /áyjid/ old or elderly **2** /ayjd/ of a particular age **3** /ayjd/ improved with time ■ /áyjid/ npl senior citizens (fml)

age group npl people of a similar age

ageism /áyjizəm/, **agism** n discrimination based on age —**ageist** adj

ageless /áyjləss/ adj **1** never seeming to grow older **2** of all generations —**agelessness** n

agency /áyjənssi/ (pl **-cies**) n **1** a company acting as an agent **2** a government organization **3** the office of an agency **4** action or operation

agenda /ə jéndə/ n **1** a list of business matters to be discussed or done **2** somebody's underlying motive

agent /áyjənt/ n **1** somebody representing another **2** somebody providing a particular service for another ○ a travel agent **3** something, e.g. a chemical substance, organism, or natural force, that causes an effect **4** a means effecting a result **5** a spy (infml)

agent provocateur /àzhoN prə vókə túr/ (pl **agents provocateurs** /pronunc. same/) n an undercover agent

age of consent n the legal age for marriage or sex

age-old adj having existed for a long time

agglomerate /ə glómmə rayt/ (**-ating, -ated**) vti collect together in a mass, or form something into a mass —**agglomeration** /ə glómmə ráysh'n/ n

agglutinate /ə glooti nayt/ (**-nating, -nated**) vti **1** adhere or cause something to adhere **2** form a compound word —**agglutination** /ə glooti náysh'n/ n

~~aggragate~~ incorrect spelling of **aggregate**

aggrandize /ə grán dīz, ággrən-/ (**-dizing, -dized**), **aggrandise** vt improve the status of —**aggrandizement** /ə grán dīzmənt, -dízmənt/ n

aggravate /ággrə vayt/ (**-vating, -vated**) vt **1** ⚠ irritate or anger (infml) **2** make worse —**aggravating** adj —**aggravatingly** adv —**aggravation** /ággrə váysh'n/ n

---

USAGE Many people still dislike the use of **aggravate** to mean 'irritate or anger somebody', despite a history of usage dating back to the 17C: *Their bad behaviour has been very aggravating.* Except in informal conversation, it is usually better to use an alternative word such as *annoy, exasperate,* or *irritate.*

---

aggregate adj /ággrigət, -gayt/ **1** forming a total or whole (fml) **2** describes a mixture of minerals resembling rock ■ n /ággrigət, -gayt/ **1** a total or whole (fml) **2** mixed stone, gravel, and sand ■ vti /ággri gayt/ (**-gating, -gated**) unite to form a total or whole —**aggregation** /ággri gáysh'n/ n

aggression /ə grésh'n/ n hostile actions, attitudes, or behaviour

aggressive /ə gréssiv/ adj **1** showing aggression **2** assertive or forceful ○ aggressive sales tactics —**aggressively** adv

aggressor /ə gréssər/ n a person or country that starts a war, fight, or argument

aggrieve /ə greev/ (**-grieving, -grieved**) vt cause distress to (fml) —**aggrieved** adj —**aggrievedly** /-idli/ adv

aggro /ággrō/ n threatening behaviour (slang)

aghast /ə gaást/ adj horrified

agile /ájjīl/ adj **1** nimble **2** mentally quick —**agilely** adv —**agility** /ə jílləti/ n

agitate /ájji tayt/ (**-tating, -tated**) v **1** vt make anxious **2** vi arouse public feeling or support **3** vt cause to move vigorously or violently —**agitated** adj —**agitatedly** adv —**agitation** /ájji táysh'n/ n —**agitator** n

aglow /ə glō/ adj glowing

AGM abbr annual general meeting

agnostic /ag nóstik/ n **1** somebody who denies that God's existence is provable **2** somebody who doubts something ○ I'm an agnostic concerning space aliens. —**agnostic** adj —**agnosticism** /-sizzəm/ n

ago /ə gó/ adv, adj before now

agog /ə góg/ adj very interested

ORIGIN Agog probably comes from the old French phrase *en gogues* 'enjoying yourself' (en was replaced with a-, as in asleep). The origin of the old French word gogue, 'merriment', is not known.

---

agonize /ággə nīz/ (**-nizing, -nized**), **agonise** v **1** vi spend much time worrying **2** vti suffer, or cause somebody to suffer —**agonizing** adj —**agonizingly** adv

agony /ággəni/ (pl **-nies**) n **1** great physical pain or mental anguish **2** an intense emotion ○ an agony of indecision

agony aunt n an advice columnist

agony column *n* a personal advice column

agora /ǽggərə/ (*pl* **-rae** /ǽggərī/ *or* **-ras**) *n* a marketplace, especially in ancient Greece

agoraphobia /ǽggərə fóbi ə/ *n* fear of open spaces or public places —**agoraphobic** *adj, n*

AGP *abbr* accelerated graphics port

Agra /áːgrə/ city in N India, site of the Taj Mahal. Pop. 891,790 (1991).

~~agragate~~ incorrect spelling of **aggregate**

Agrahayana /ágrəhī aːnə/ *n* HINDUISM, CALENDAR = **Margasirsa**

agrarian /ə gráiri ən/ *adj* **1** of land **2** of rural life **3** promoting farmers' interests ■ *n* a land reformer —**agrarianism** *n*

agree /ə greé/ (**agreed**) *v* **1** *vi* be in accord **2** *vi* consent to something **3** *vti* reach consensus or a decision about something ○ *agree on a plan* **4** *vi* be consistent ○ *The witnesses' stories don't agree.* **5** *vi* be suitable or good for somebody ○ *The climate doesn't agree with me.* **6** *vi* match grammatically

SYNONYMS **agree**, **concur**, **acquiesce**, **consent**, **assent** CORE MEANING: accept an idea, plan, or course of action that has been put forward

agreeable /ə greé əb'l/ *adj* **1** pleasing **2** friendly **3** willing to comply —**agreeableness** *n* —**agreeably** *adv*

agreement /ə greémənt/ *n* **1** a formal contract **2** consensus **3** grammatical correspondence

~~agression~~ incorrect spelling of **aggression**

~~agressive~~ incorrect spelling of **aggressive**

~~agressor~~ incorrect spelling of **aggressor**

agribusiness /ǽgri biznəss/ *n* farming as an industry

Agricola /ə gríkələ/, **Gnaeus Julius** (40–93 AD) Roman colonial administrator

agriculture /ǽgri kulchər/ *n* farming —**agricultural** /ǽgri kúlchərəl/ *adj* —**agriculturalist** *n* —**agriculturist** /ǽgri kúlchərist/ *n*

Agrippina (the Elder) /ǽgrə peénə/ (13? BC–AD 33) Roman noblewoman, mother of Caligula

Agrippina (the Younger) (15–59 AD) Roman noblewoman, sister of Caligula and mother of Nero

agrochemical /ǽgrō kémmik'l/, **agrichemical** /ǽggri-/ *n* a chemical used in farming

agronomy /ə grónnəmi/ *n* the science of soils and plants —**agronomist** *n*

aground /ə grównd/ *adj, adv* on ground, especially on the bottom of shallow water

AH *adv* indicates a date in the Islamic calendar. Full form **anno Hegirae**

ahead /ə héd/ *adv, adj* **1** in front **2** forwards **3** to the future **4** earlier ◊ **get ahead** succeed or advance financially (*infml*)

Ahern /ə húrn/, **Bertie** (*b.* 1951) Irish Taoiseach (prime minister) (1997–)

-aholic *suffix* dependent on or having an extreme fondness for ○ *workaholic*

ahoy /ə hóy/ *interj* attracts the attention of other sailors

AI *abbr* **1** artificial insemination **2** artificial intelligence

aid *vti* give help ■ *n* **1** money or supplies given to those in need **2** assistance ○ *A passer-by came to my aid.* **3** somebody or something helpful ○ *visual aids such as maps*

aide *n* **1** an assistant **2** an aide-de-camp ◊ See note at **assistant**

aide-de-camp /áyd də kaàN/ (*pl* **aides-de-camp** /*pronunc. same*/) *n* a military officer acting as confidential assistant to a general or senior officer

aide-mémoire /áyd mem waàr/ (*pl* **aide-mémoires** /*pronunc. same*/ *or* **aides-mémoire** /*pronunc. same*/) *n* (*fml*) **1** a brief written summary of decisions made in a meeting **2** a memory aid

Aids, AIDS *n* a serious disease of the immune system. Full form **acquired immune deficiency syndrome**

aikido /ī keédō, íki-/ *n* a martial art that uses blows made with the hands and feet

ail /ayl/ *vt* cause to suffer or have problems (*literary*)

SPELLCHECK Do not confuse the spelling of **ail** and **ale** ('beer'), which sound similar.

aileron /áylə ron/ *n* a flap on an aircraft wing

ailing /áyling/ *adj* **1** in poor condition ○ *the nation's ailing steel industry* **2** ill (*dated*)

ailment /áylmənt/ *n* an illness

aim *v* **1** *vi* plan to do something **2** *vt* direct a message, product, action, or blow **3** *vti* point a weapon ■ *n* **1** an intention **2** the aiming of a weapon ○ *Take aim and fire.* **3** skill in aiming

aimless /áymləss/ *adj* without purpose —**aimlessly** *adv*

ain't *contr* a contraction of 'am not', 'is not', 'are not', 'have not', or 'has not' (*nonstandard*)

air /air/ *n* **1** the gases forming the atmosphere **2** the atmosphere of an open space **3** the sky **4** transportation in an aircraft ○ *send it by air* ○ *an air terminal* **5** a distinctive quality ○ *an air of indifference* **6** a melody ■ **airs** *npl US* affected manners or conduct meant to impress others ■ *v* **1** *vti* broadcast, or be broadcast **2** *vt* make known **3** *vti* expose or be exposed to a fresh or warm atmosphere ◊ **clear the air** remove the tension or misunderstanding from a situation ◊ **in the air** happening or about to happen ◊ **on (the) air** being broadcast on radio or television ◊ **up in the air** undecided or uncertain ◊ **walk** *or* **tread on air** be extremely happy

SPELLCHECK Do not confuse the spelling of **air**, **ere** ('before'), **err** ('make a mistake'), or **heir** ('legal inheritor'), which sound similar.

AIR *abbr* All India Radio

air bag *n* a bag that inflates as a safety device in a car

air base *n* a military airport

airborne /áir bawrn/ *adj* **1** carried by air **2** in flight

air brake *n* **1** an air-operated brake **2** an aircraft brake

airbrush /áir brush/ *n* a paint-spraying device —**airbrush** *vt*

air chief marshal *n* an air force officer of a rank above air marshal

air commodore *n* an air force officer of a rank above group captain

air conditioning *n* an air-cooling system in a building or vehicle —**air conditioned** *adj* —**air conditioner** *n*

aircraft /áir kraaft/ (*pl same*) *n* a flying vehicle

aircraft carrier *n* a large warship with a deck designed to allow aircraft to take off and land

aircrew /áir kroo/ *n* the crew of an aircraft

airer /áirər/ *n* a frame on which to hang clothes to dry indoors

airfield /áir feeld/ *n* an area where aircraft can take off and land

airflow /áir flṓ/ *n* a flow of air

air force *n* a branch of the armed services using aircraft

air gun *n* a gun fired by compressed air

airhead /áir hed/ *n* a person regarded as unintelligent and superficial (*slang insult*)

air hostess *n* a woman flight attendant (*dated*)

airless /áirləss/ *adj* without air, fresh air, or movement of air ○ *an airless room* ○ *an airless night* —**airlessness** *n*

airlift /áir lift/ *n* the transport of people, supplies, or equipment by air, especially in an emergency —**airlift** *vt*

airline /áir līn/ *n* **1** a company operating commercial flights **2** a tube supplying air

airliner /áir līnər/ *n* a large passenger aircraft

airlock /áir lok/ *n* **1** an obstruction in the flow of a liquid caused by an air bubble **2** an airtight chamber

airmail /áir mayl/ *n* **1** the sending of mail by air **2** mail sent by air —**airmail** *adj, vt*

airman /áirmən/ (*pl* **-men** /-mən/) *n* a pilot, especially of a military aircraft

air marshal *n* **1** an officer in the air force of a rank above air vice-marshal **2** a sky marshal

airplay /áir play/ *n* the broadcasting of a recording

airport /áir pawrt/ *n* an area where civil aircraft may take off and land

air pump *n* a device for compressing or moving air

air rage *n* disruptive or aggressive behaviour by passengers aboard an aircraft

air raid *n* an attack by aircraft on a ground target

air rifle *n* a rifle fired by compressed air

airship /áir ship/ *n* a powered lighter-than-air aircraft

airspace /áir spayss/ *n* **1** the space above an area of land claimed by a government **2** the space occupied by a flying aircraft

air speed *n* an aircraft's speed in relation to the air

airstrip /áir strip/ *n* a runway with no airport facilities

air terminal *n* a departure point in a city for passengers to an airport

airtight /áir tīt/ *adj* **1** preventing the passage of air **2** without weak points ○ *an airtight alibi*

airtime /áir tīm/ *n* the time during which a programme or subject is broadcast

air vice-marshal *n* an air force officer of a rank above air commodore

airwaves /áir wayvz/ *npl* radio waves used in broadcasting

airway /áir way/ *n* **1** a route for aircraft (*often pl*) **2** a passage for air from the nose or mouth to the lungs **3** a tube to assist breathing

Airways /áir wayz/ *n* an air transport company (*in company names; + sing or pl verb*)

airworthy /áir wurthi/ *adj* in good enough condition to be safe to fly —**airworthiness** *n*

airy /áiri/ (**-ier, -iest**) *adj* **1** roomy **2** well ventilated **3** carefree or unconcerned ○ *an airy wave of her hand* **4** ethereal —**airily** *adv*

airy-fairy *adj* fanciful (*infml*)

Aisha /aá ee shaa, ai eéshaa/, **Ayeshah** (614?–678) wife of the prophet Muhammad

aisle /īl/ *n* a passageway between seating areas or displays of goods ◊ **rolling in the aisles** laughing very heartily (*infml*)

SPELLCHECK Do not confuse the spelling of **aisle** and **isle** ('an island'), which sound similar.

---

aitch /aych/ *n* the letter 'h'

Aix-en-Provence /éks aaN pro vaáNss/ city in SE France. Pop. 134,222 (1999).

Ajaccio /ə jáksi ṓ/ capital and main port of Corse-du-Sud Department, W Corsica, France. Pop. 52,880 (1999).

ajar /ə jaár/ *adj, adv* partially open

a.k.a., AKA *abbr* also known as

Akbar /ák baar/ (1542–1605) emperor of India (1556–1605)

Akhenaton /aákə naát'n, aák-/, **Ikhnaton** /ik-/ (*fl* 14C BC) Egyptian pharaoh

Akhmatova /ákmə tṓvə/, **Anna** (1889–1966) Russian poet

Akihito /áki heétṓ/ (*b.* 1933) emperor of Japan (1989–)

akimbo /ə kímbṓ/ *adj, adv* with the hands on the hips and elbows outwards

akin /ə kín/ *adj* **1** similar **2** related by blood

~~acknowledge~~ incorrect spelling of **acknowledge**

Al *symbol* aluminium

al. *abbr* **1** alcohol **2** alcoholic

-al *suffix* **1** of or characterized by ○ *delusional* **2** action, process ○ *disposal*

à la /aá laa, állə/, **a la** *prep* in the style of

alabaster /állə baastər, -bastər/ *n* a white or translucent gypsum. Use: decorative carving. ■ *adj* of or like alabaster

à la carte /aa laa kaárt, állə-/, **a la carte** *adj, adv* with each dish separately priced

alacrity /ə lákrəti/ *n* eager readiness

Alain-Fournier /állaN fŏŏr nyay/ (1886–1914) French writer and journalist

Alamein, El ♦ El 'Alamein

Alamogordo /államə gáwrdō/ city in S New Mexico, northeast of White Sands Missile Range, site of the first atom bomb explosion, on 16 July 1945. Pop. 28,312 (1998).

alarm /ə laárm/ *n* **1** fear **2** a warning sound, signal, or device **3** a security device fitted to property, or the sound it makes **4** an alarm clock ■ *vt* **1** frighten **2** warn **3** fit with a security device **—alarmed** *adj* **—alarming** *adj* **—alarmingly** *adv*

alarm clock *n* a clock that can be set to sound an alarm to wake somebody

alarmist /ə laármist/ *n* somebody who spreads unnecessary fear **—alarmism** *n* **—alarmist** *adj*

alas /ə láss/ *interj* expresses sorrow or regret ■ *adv* unfortunately

Alaska /ə láskə/ US state in NW North America. Cap. Juneau. Pop. 626,932 (2000). **—Alaskan** *adj, n*

Albania /al báyni ə/ country in SE Europe, bordering the Adriatic Sea. Cap. Tirana. Pop. 3,510,484 (2001).

Albanian /al báyni ən/ *n* **1** the official language of Albania **2** somebody from Albania **—Albanian** *adj*

Albany /áwlbəni/ **1** capital of New York State. Pop. 94,305 (1998). **2** coastal town in SW Western Australia. Pop. 20,493 (1996).

albatross /álbə tross/ (*pl* **-trosses** *or* **same**) *n* **1** a large seabird **2** a golf score of three under par

Albee /álbi/, **Edward** (*b.* 1928) US playwright

albeit /áwl bée it/ *conj* even though

Albert /álbərt/, **Prince** (1819–61) German-born prince consort to Queen Victoria

Albert, Lake lake in east-central Africa, on the border between Uganda and Democratic Republic of the Congo. Length 160 km/99 mi.

Alberti /al báirti/, **Leon Battista** (1404–72) Italian architect and writer

albino /al béenō/ (*pl* **-nos**) *n* a person, animal, or plant lacking the usual pigmentation **—albinism** /álbinizzəm/ *n*

album /álbəm/ *n* **1** a book with blank pages for keeping photographs, stamps, or other collected items **2** a music recording

ORIGIN The Latin word *album* means 'blank tablet', and comes from *albus* 'white'. It came into English through a German use of *album amicorum*, 'album of friends', an autograph book in which scholars collected signatures and greetings from colleagues.

albumen /álbyŏŏmin, al byŏŏmin/ *n* **1** the white of an egg (*technical*) **2** the protein component of egg white

albumin /álbyŏŏmin, al byŏŏmin/ *n* a water-soluble protein coagulated by heat **—albuminous** /al byŏŏminəss/ *adj*

Alcatraz /álkə traz/ island in San Francisco Bay, California, site of a federal prison from 1933 to 1963

alchemy /álkəmi/ *n* **1** an early form of chemistry that sought to change base metals into gold **2** a transforming or enchanting power **—alchemical** /al kémmik'l/ *adj* **—alchemist** *n*

~~alchol~~ incorrect spelling of **alcohol**

Alcock /áwl kok/, **Sir John William** (1892–1919) British aviator

alcohol /álkə hol/ *n* **1** C_2H_5OH a liquid found in intoxicating drinks or used as a solvent **2** drinks containing alcohol

alcoholic /álkə hóllik/ *adj* **1** of or containing alcohol **2** addicted to alcohol ■ *n* somebody addicted to alcohol

Alcoholics Anonymous *n* an organization for alcoholics

alcoholism /álkə holizəm/ *n* **1** addiction to alcohol **2** alcohol poisoning

alcopop /álkō pòp/ *n* a carbonated alcoholic drink

alcove /álkōv/ *n* a recess in a wall

al dente /al dén tay, -dénti/ *adj* cooked just long enough to be still firm and not soft

alder /áwldər/ *n* a deciduous tree of northern temperate regions

alderman /áwldərmən/ (*pl* **-men** /-mən/) *n* a member of a local council or legislative body

alderwoman /áwldər wŏŏmən/ (*pl* **-en** /-wimin/) *n* a woman member of a local council or legislative body

Aldrin /áwldrin/, **Buzz** (*b.* 1930) US astronaut

ale /ayl/ *n* **1** a type of beer brewed without hops **2** beer ◊ See note at **ail**

~~alein~~ incorrect spelling of **alien**

Aleppo /ə léppō/ city in NW Syria. Pop. 1,582,930 (1994).

alert /ə lúrt/ *adj* **1** watchful **2** mentally sharp and responsive ■ *n* **1** a warning of danger **2** a time during which an alert is in effect ■ *vt* warn of danger or difficulties **—alertly** *adv* **—alertness** *n* ◊ **on the alert** watchful and ready to act

Aleutian Islands /ə lŏŏsh'n-/ island chain off SW Alaska

A level *n* a school examination for 17 to 18 year-olds in a subject at advanced level

Alexander II /állig zaándər/ (1818–81) tsar of Russia (1855–81)

Alexander technique *n* a method of improving posture by developing awareness of it

ORIGIN The technique is named after the Australian physiotherapist Frederick Alexander (1869–1955), who developed it.

Alexander the Great (356–323 BC) king of Macedonia (336–323 BC)

Alexandra /állig zaándrə/ (1872–1918) German-born empress of Russia. ◊ **Nicholas II**

Alexandria /állig zaándri ə/ port in N Egypt. Pop. 3,328,000 (1998). —**Alexandrian** *adj*

~~alfabet~~ incorrect spelling of **alphabet**

Alfred (the Great) /álfrid/ (849–901) king of Wessex (871–901)

alfresco /al fréskō/ *adv, adj* outdoors

alga /álgə/ (*pl* **-gae** /-jee, -gee/) *n* a photo-synthesizing water organism such as seaweed

algebra /áljibrə/ *n* the branch of mathematics using letters to represent unknown numbers —**algebraic** /álji bráyik/ *adj* —**algebraically** *adv*

ORIGIN **Algebra** came via Italian and medieval Latin from an Arabic form meaning literally 'the reuniting of broken parts'. It was used in the title of a seminal work, 'The Science of Reunion and Equation', by the Arab mathematician al-Khwarizmi (780?-850?), whose translated works introduced Arabic numerals to Europe.

Algeria /al jeéri ə/ country in NW Africa. Cap. Algiers. Pop. 31,736,053 (2001). —**Algerian** *adj, n*

Algiers /al jeérz/ capital of Algeria. Pop. 2,561,992 (1998).

ALGOL /ál gol/, **Algol** *n* a high-level computer language. Full form **algorithm-oriented language**

algorithm /álgə rithəm/ *n* a problem-solving mathematical procedure or computer program —**algorithmic** /álgə ríthmik/ *adj*

Alhambra /al hámbrə/ *n* a citadel and palace in Granada, Spain, built for Moorish kings in the 12C and 13C

Muhammad Ali

Ali /aa lí/, **Muhammad** (b. 1942) US boxer

alias /áyli əss/ *n* 1 an assumed name 2 a name assigned to a computer file or directory ■ *adv* also known as

alibi /álli bī/ (*pl* **-bis**) *n* 1 an accused person's claim of having been somewhere other than at the scene of a crime 2 an excuse (*infml*)

alien /áyli ən/ *n* 1 an extraterrestrial being 2 a foreign resident of a country 3 an outsider ■ *adj* 1 outside somebody's previous experience, or not part of somebody's usual behaviour o *an alien practice* 2 foreign 3 extraterrestrial o *an alien spacecraft*

alienate /áyli ə nayt/ (**-ating, -ated**) *vt* 1 make somebody unsympathetic or hostile 2 cause somebody to feel dissatisfied 3 cause something, especially somebody's affection, to be

directed elsewhere —**alienation** /áyli ə náysh'n/ *n*

alight[1] /ə lít/ (**alighted** *or* **alit** /ə lít/) *vi* 1 get out of a vehicle 2 land after a flight

alight[2] /ə lít/ *adj* 1 on fire 2 full of light

align /ə lín/, **aline** (**alining, alined**) *vti* 1 bring or come into line or a correct position 2 ally yourself with a particular side o *The issue has aligned many citizens behind the candidate.* —**alignment** *n*

alike /ə lík/ *adj* similar in appearance or character ■ *adv* 1 in a similar or the same way 2 both —**alikeness** *n*

alimentary canal /álli méntəri-/ *n* the tubular passage between the mouth and the anus through which food passes for digestion and elimination as waste

alimony /álliməni/ *n* financial support to a former spouse

alit past tense and past participle of **alight**[1]

alive /ə lív/ *adj* 1 living 2 still in existence o *keeping their hopes alive* 3 full of energy or activity o *The town came alive at midnight.* 4 swarming o *alive with ants* 5 aware o *alive to the danger* —**aliveness** *n* ◊ See note at **living**

alkali /álkə lī/ (*pl* **-lis** *or* **same**) *n* 1 a chemical substance that neutralizes acids 2 a soluble salt harmful to crops —**alkaline** /-līn/ *adj* —**alkalinity** *n* /-línnəti/

alkaloid /álkə loyd/ *n* a chemical compound containing nitrogen, found in many plants

all /awl/ *det* 1 *also* **all of** the whole of o *All Europe was cold this winter.* o *All of the nation is affected.* 2 *also* **all of** every one of o *all employees over 30* o *All of the children were tired.* 3 any (*after an implicit negative word*) o *She denied all knowledge of it.* ■ *adv* very or totally (*infml*) o *I'm all confused.* ■ *pron* 1 the whole number or amount (+ *pl verb*) o *All of us are going to the match.* 2 everything or everyone o *All that glitters is not gold.* ■ *n* somebody's best effort o *I gave it my all.* ◊ **all along** for the whole time ◊ **all but** almost ◊ **(all) in all** when everything has been taken into account ◊ **all the same** 1 nevertheless 2 a matter of indifference o *I'd rather go by train, if it's all the same to you.* ◊ **be all over somebody** be extremely or excessively friendly or effusive towards somebody (*infml*)

SPELLCHECK Do not confuse the spelling of **all** and **awl** ('a sharp-pointed tool'), which sound similar.

Allah /álla/ *n* in Islam, the name of God

Allahabad /álləhə bad/ city in N India. Pop. 858,213 (1991).

allay /ə láy/ *vt* 1 calm an emotion or worry 2 relieve pain

all clear *n* 1 a signal that danger is over 2 a signal to proceed

~~alledged~~ incorrect spelling of **alleged**

allege /ə léj/ (**-leging, -leged**) *vt* assert without proof —**allegation** /álli gáysh'n/ *n*

alleged /ə léjd/ adj claimed but not proved —**allegedly** /ə léjjidli/ adv

allegiance /ə leèjənss/ n loyalty or devoted support

allegience incorrect spelling of **allegiance**

allegory /álligəri/ (pl -ries) n 1 a work of literature or art that uses symbolism to express meaning 2 the use of symbolism to express meaning —**allegorical** /álli górrik'l/ adj —**allegorist** n

allegro /ə láygrō, ə léggrō/ adv quickly (musical direction) —**allegro** adj, n

alleluia interj, n = **hallelujah**

Allen /állən/ ♦ **Van Allen, James**

Allen, Woody (b. 1935) US film director, actor, screenwriter, playwright, and humorous essayist

Allenby /állənbi/, **Edmund Henry Hynman, 1st Viscount** (1861–1936) British soldier

Allende /aa yén day/, **Isabel** (b. 1942) Chilean author

allergen /állər jen, -jən/ n a substance that causes an allergic reaction —**allergenic** /állər jénnik/ adj

allergic /ə lúrjik/ adj 1 having an allergy 2 of or caused by an allergy

allergy /állərji/ (pl -gies) n a hypersensitivity to a substance —**allergist** n

alleviate /ə leèvi ayt/ (-ating, -ated) vt lessen something unpleasant —**alleviation** /ə leèvi áysh'n/ n

alley /álli/ (pl -leys) n 1 a small street 2 a narrow passage between buildings 3 a bowling alley

all fours ◊ **on all fours** crawling along or crouched down on the hands and knees

alliance /ə lí ənss/ n 1 an association of people or groups with a common aim 2 the formation of a close relationship

allied /állīd, ə líd/ adj 1 joined in an alliance 2 similar or related ○ sociology and allied studies

alligator /álli gaytər/ n 1 (pl **alligators** or same) a large reptile with powerful jaws 2 leather made from alligator skin

ORIGIN **Alligator** is an alteration of Spanish el lagarto, literally 'the lizard'. Spanish explorers gave this name to the animal when they encountered it in the Americas.

all in adj 1 with everything included 2 extremely tired (infml)

Allingham /állingəm/, **Margery** (1904–66) British writer

alliteration /ə líttə ráysh'n/ n the repetition of the same consonants at the beginning of words

allmost incorrect spelling of **almost**

allocate /állə kayt/ (-cating, -cated) vt 1 give to or set aside for a specific person or purpose 2 share out or divide up —**allocable** adj —**allocation** /állə káysh'n/ n

All-Ordinaries Index n an index of Australian share prices

allot /ə lót/ (-lotting, -lotted) vt 1 give as a share 2 earmark or reserve

allotment /ə lótmənt/ n 1 a plot of land rented for growing vegetables or flowers 2 the allotting of something 3 something allotted

all out adv with maximum effort

all-out adj 1 greatest possible 2 describes a strike involving the whole workforce

all over adv (infml) 1 everywhere 2 stresses that something is characteristic of somebody ○ That's Jackie all over.

allow /ə lów/ v 1 vt let somebody do something 2 vt let something happen 3 vt let somebody or yourself have something, especially a benefit or pleasure ○ Allow her time to recover. 4 vi make provision for something 5 vt accept something to be true or valid (fml) —**allowable** adj —**allowed** adj

□ **allow for** vt allocate an amount for

allowance /ə lów ənss/ n 1 an amount of money given for a particular purpose 2 pocket money, especially for older children 3 a discount 4 an amount of income that is not taxable 5 a salary supplement 6 an amount allowed 7 the allowing of something

alloy n /álloy/ 1 a mixture of metals 2 something that debases what it is added to ■ vt /ə lóy/ 1 mix metals 2 debase something pure by adding ingredients ◊ See note at **mixture**

allready incorrect spelling of **already**

all right adj 1 generally good, satisfactory, or pleasant 2 just adequate 3 uninjured ■ interj yes ■ adv 1 in a satisfactory way 2 without any doubt ○ It's raining all right.

USAGE **all right** or **alright**? **Alright** is generally regarded as nonstandard. Use **all right** instead.

all round adv 1 in every respect 2 involving everyone

all-round adj 1 versatile 2 all-inclusive —**all-rounder** n

allspice /áwl spīss/ n a spice made from the ground dried berries of a tropical tree

allthough incorrect spelling of **although**

all-time adj best ever (infml)

allude /ə loōd/ (-luding, -luded) vi refer indirectly

SPELLCHECK Do not confuse the spelling of **allude** and **elude** ('escape from', 'avoid'), which sound similar.

allure /ə lyoōr, ə loōr/ n a highly attractive and tempting quality ○ the allure of the big city ■ vti (-luring, -lured) attract powerfully —**allurement** n —**alluring** adj

allusion /ə loōzh'n/ n 1 an indirect reference 2 the process of alluding to somebody or something —**allusive** /ə loōssiv/ adj

alluvium /ə loōvi əm/ (pl -**ums** or -**a** /-vi ə/) n soil deposited by water —**alluvial** adj

allways incorrect spelling of **always**

ally /ə lí, állī/ vti (-lies, -lied) 1 join in mutually supportive association 2 connect or be connected through marriage ■ *n* (*pl* -lies) a member of an alliance

alma mater /álmə maátər, -máytər/, **Alma Mater** *n* the institution where somebody was educated

almanac /áwlmə nak, álmə-/ *n* 1 an annual publication that includes a calendar, astronomical information, and details of anniversaries and events 2 a book of data published annually about a particular subject

Alma-Tadema /álmə táddimə/, **Sir Lawrence** (1836–1912) Dutch-born British painter

Almaty /al maáti/ former capital of Kazakhstan. Pop. 1,064,300 (1997).

almighty /awl míti/ *adj* all-powerful ■ *n* **Almighty** God

almond /áamənd, áalmənd/ *n* 1 an edible oval-shaped nut 2 a small tree that produces almonds

almost /áwlmōst, awl mốst/ *adv* nearly

alms /áamz/ *npl* charitable donations

almshouse /áamz howss/ (*pl* -houses /-howziz/) *n* a house provided by a charity for poor people or senior citizens

aloe /állō/ *n* a plant with fleshy toothed leaves

aloe vera /-veérə/ *n* 1 a soothing plant extract. Use: cosmetics, drugs. 2 a species of aloe with leaves that yield aloe vera

aloft /ə lóft/ *adv* high up in the air

alone /ə lốn/ *adv* without help from others ■ *adj* unique in some respect ○ *Am I alone in thinking this?* ■ *adv, adj* without company ○ *She returned alone.* —**aloneness** *n*

along /ə lóng/ *prep* 1 over the length of ○ *walked along the path* 2 parallel with ○ *sailed along the coast* ■ *adv* 1 forwards ○ *Move along, please.* 2 with somebody ○ *brought her friends along* 3 at or to a place ○ *There'll be a bus along in a minute.*

alongside /ə lóng síd, ə lóng sīd/ *prep* by the side of ○ *drew up alongside their car* ■ *adv* by the side ○ *anchored alongside*

aloof /ə loof/ *adj* 1 remote in manner 2 physically distant or apart —**aloofly** *adv*

aloud /ə lówd/ *adv* 1 audibly 2 loudly

alp *n* 1 a high mountain 2 a Swiss mountain pasture

ALP *abbr* Australian Labor Party

alpaca /al pákə/ *n* 1 (*pl* **alpacas** *or same*) a mammal related to the llama 2 wool cloth made from alpaca hair

alpha /álfə/ *n* 1 the 1st letter of the Greek alphabet 2 **Alpha** a communications code word for the letter 'A' 3 the highest category of mark given to a student's work

alphabet /álfə bet/ *n* a set of letters used to represent language

ORIGIN **Alphabet** comes from the names of the first two letters of the Greek alphabet, *alpha* and *beta*. The idea is the same as that in 'learning your ABC'.

alphabetical /álfə béttik'l/, **alphabetic** /-béttik/ *adj* 1 in the order of the letters of the alphabet 2 of an alphabet —**alphabetically** *adv*

alphabetize /álfə bet īz/ (-izing, -ized), **alphabetise** *vt* put in alphabetical order —**alphabetization** /álfə bet ī záysh'n/ *n*

alpha male *n* a dominant male animal

alphanumeric /álfənyoo mérrik/, **alphameric** /álfə mérrik/ *adj* combining letters and numbers —**alphanumerically** *adv*

alpha test *n* a first test of computer software or hardware by its publisher or manufacturer —**alpha-test** *vt*

alpine /álp īn/ *adj* 1 of high mountains 2 **Alpine** of the Alps 3 used in or involving mountain climbing 4 of downhill or slalom skiing ■ *n* a mountain plant

Alps mountain range in S Europe, stretching from SE France to Austria. Highest peak Mont Blanc 4,807 m/15,771 ft.

al-Qaeda /al kī eédə/, **al-Qaida** /al káydə/ *n* an international Islamic organization associated with several terrorist incidents, including the attack on the World Trade Center, New York (2001)

al-Quds /al koódz/ *n* Arabic name for **Jerusalem**

already /awl réddi, áwl redi/ *adv* 1 unexpectedly early ○ *Have you finished already?* 2 before now, or before a particular time in the past ○ *She had already left when I arrived.*

alright /awl rít, áwl rīt/ *adj* generally good, satisfactory, or pleasant *(nonstandard)* ◊ See note at **all right**

Alsace /al sáss/ *region in E France. Cap. Strasbourg. Pop. 1,734,145 (1999).

Alsatian /al sáysh'n/ *n* 1 a large powerful dog with short hair and erect ears 2 somebody from Alsace ■ *adj* from Alsace

also /áwlsō/ *adv* 1 in addition 2 likewise or similarly

also-ran *n* 1 a losing competitor, especially in a race 2 somebody regarded as unimportant

Altai Mountains /al tí-/ mountain range in central Asia, on the Kazakhstan-Mongolia border. Highest peak Mt Belukha 4,620 m/15,157 ft.

altar /áwltər/ *n* a raised surface in front of or on which religious ceremonies are performed

SPELLCHECK Do not confuse the spelling of **altar** and **alter** ('change'), which sound similar.

altarpiece /áwltər peess/ *n* a painting behind an altar

alter /áwltər/ *v* 1 *vti* change 2 *vt* adjust a garment to fit —**alterable** *adj* —**alteration** /áwltə ráysh'n/ *n* ◊ See note at **altar, change**

altercation /áwltər káysh'n/ *n* a heated argument —**altercate** /áwltər kayt/ *vi*

alter ego /áwltər eégō/ (*pl* **alter egos**) *n* 1 a second side to somebody's personality 2 a very close friend

alternate *vi* /áwltər nayt/ (-nating, -nated) 1 follow in an interchanging pattern ○ *as night alternates with day* 2 fluctuate ■ *adj* /awl túrnət/ **1** arranged in an alternating pattern **2** every other **3** *US, Can* able to be substituted —**alternately** /awl túrnətli/ *adv* —**alternation** /áwltər náysh'n/ *n*

alternating current *n* an electric current that regularly reverses direction

alternative /awl túrnətiv/ *n* **1** another possibility **2** the possibility of choosing **3** an option ○ *I can't decide which of the two alternatives is worse.* ■ *adj* **1** able to be substituted ○ *an alternative course of action* **2** mutually exclusive **3** unconventional ○ *alternative methods of painting* —**alternatively** *adv*

alternative medicine *n* nonorthodox medical treatment or remedies

alternator /áwltər naytər/ *n* a generator of alternating current

~~alternitive~~ incorrect spelling of **alternative**

although /awl thó/ *conj* in spite of the fact that

altimeter /al tímmitər, álti meetər/ *n* an instrument indicating altitude —**altimetric** /álti méttrik/ *adj* —**altimetry** /al tímmətri/ *n*

altitude /álti tyood/ *n* **1** height above sea level **2** a high place *(often pl)* **3** the angle of an astronomical object above the horizon —**altitudinal** /álti tyoodin'l/ *adj*

Alt key /áwlt-/ *n* a function-changing computer key

Altman /áwltmən/, **Robert** (*b.* 1925) US film director and screenwriter

alto /áltō/ (*pl* **-tos**) *n* **1** a contralto voice **2** the highest singing voice for a man **3** an alto singer

altogether /áwltə géthər, -geth-/ *adv* **1** with everything included **2** totally ○ *I'm not altogether satisfied.* **3** on the whole ○ *Altogether, it's been a success.*

altruism /áltroo izəm/ *n* selflessness —**altruist** *n* —**altruistic** /áltroo ístik/ *adj* —**altruistically** *adv*

alum /álləm/ *n* a colourless or white solid. Use: dyes, water purification, leather dressing.

aluminium /állə mínni əm/ *n* (*symbol* **Al**) a metallic chemical element. Use: lightweight construction, corrosion-resistant materials.

aluminum /ə loominəm/ *n* US = **aluminium**

alumna /ə lúmnə/ (*pl* **-nae** /-nī, -nee/) *n* a female graduate of a particular institution

alumnus /ə lúmnəss/ (*pl* **-ni** /-nī, -nee/) *n* a male graduate of a particular institution

always /áwl wayz, -wiz/ *adv* **1** every time or continuously **2** through all past or future time **3** if necessary ○ *You can always catch a later train.*

always-on *adj* **1** describes a home or business where Internet access is not restricted to a specific time **2** continuously connected

Alzheimer's disease /álts hīmərz-/, **Alzheimer's** *n* a degenerative medical disorder of the brain causing dementia

---

ORIGIN The disease is named after the German neurologist Alois Alzheimer (1864–1915), who described it in 1907.

---

am 1st person present singular of **be**

Am *symbol* americium

AM *abbr* amplitude modulation

a.m., AM, A.M. *adj, adv* before noon. Full form **ante meridiem**

amalgam /ə málgəm/ *n* **1** a mixture of elements or characteristics **2** a substance used as filling for tooth cavities ◊ See note at **mixture**

amalgamate /ə málgə mayt/ (**-mating, -mated**) *vti* combine into a unified whole —**amalgamation** /ə málgə máysh'n/ *n*

amanuensis /ə mánnyoo énssiss/ (*pl* **-ses** /-seez/) *n* (*literary*) **1** a scribe **2** a writer's assistant

---

ORIGIN Amanuensis goes back to a Latin phrase *a manu*, literally 'by hand'. It was used in *servus a manu*, a slave (*servus*) with secretarial duties.

---

amaryllis /ámmə rílliss/ (*pl* **-lises** *or* **same**) *n* a plant with large trumpet-shaped flowers on a single stalk

amass /ə máss/ *vti* gather together or collect over time ○ *amassed a fortune in the 1950s* ◊ See note at **collect**

amateur /ámmətər, -choor/ *n* **1** somebody doing something for pleasure rather than for pay **2** somebody considered unskilled ■ *adj* **1** for or by amateurs **2** unskilful or unprofessional —**amateurism** *n*

amateurish /ámmətərish, -choor-/ *adj* unskilled or unskilfully done —**amateurishly** *adv* —**amateurishness** *n*

Amati /ə máati/ family of Italian violin makers including **Andrea** (*d.* 1578), his son **Girolamo** (1556?–1630?), and grandson **Nicolò** (1596–1684)

amatory /ámmətəri/, **amatorial** /ámmə táwri əl/ *adj* of love, especially physical love *(fml)*

~~amatuer~~ incorrect spelling of **amateur**

amaze /ə máyz/ *vt* fill with wonder or astonishment —**amazed** *adj* —**amazement** *n* —**amazing** *adj* —**amazingly** *adv*

Amazon[1] /ámməz'n/ *n* **1** a mythological woman warrior **2** *also* **amazon** a strong woman —**Amazonian** /ámmə zóni ən/ *adj*

Amazon[2] /ámməz'n/ world's second longest river. It flows east from N Peru, through N South America and into the Atlantic Ocean in Brazil. Length 6,400 km/4,000 mi. —**Amazonian** /ámmə zóni ən/ *adj*

ambassador /am bássədər/ *n* **1** a diplomatic representative sent to a foreign country **2** a representative ○ *a goodwill ambassador for the charity* —**ambassadorial** /am bássə dáwri əl/ *adj* —**ambassadorship** *n*

amber /ámbər/ *n* **1** a yellow fossil resin. Use: jewellery, ornaments. **2** a brownish-yellow colour —**amber** *adj*

ambidextrous /ámbi dékstrəss/ *adj* **1** using either hand with equal skill **2** skilled in many ways —**ambidexterity** /ámbi dek stérrəti/ *n* —**ambidextrously** *adv*

ORIGIN Ambidextrous, literally 'right-handed on

both sides', comes from the Latin prefix *ambi-* 'both' and the adjective *dexter* 'right-handed'. The right hand has traditionally been associated with skill.

ambience /ámbi ɔnss, -onss/, **ambiance** *n* the atmosphere or mood of a place

ambient /ámbi ɔnt/ *adj* in the surrounding area o *ambient temperature*

ambient music *n* background music

ambiguous /am bíggyoo ɔss/ *adj* 1 having more than one meaning 2 causing uncertainty —**ambiguity** /ámbi gyoö ɔti/ *n* —**ambiguously** *adv* —**ambiguousness** *n*

ambit /ámbit/ *n* the scope, extent, or limits of something or somebody

ambition /am bísh'n/ *n* 1 desire for success in life o *She lacks ambition.* 2 an objective or goal

ambitious /am bíshəss/ *adj* 1 having ambition 2 impressive but difficult to achieve o *an ambitious plan* —**ambitiously** *adv*

ambivalence /am bívvələnss/ *n* 1 the presence of conflicting ideas or feelings 2 uncertainty —**ambivalent** *adj*

amble /ámb'l/ *vi* (**-bling, -bled**) walk slowly ■ *n* a slow walk

ambrosia /am brózi ə/ *n* 1 the food of the mythological deities 2 something delicious (*literary*)

ambulance /ámbyŏölənss/ *n* a vehicle for carrying people to hospital

ORIGIN **Ambulance** was adopted in the early 19C from French, with the meaning 'field hospital', a movable hospital facility set up near a battle site. The French word was formed from *hôpital ambulant*, literally 'walking hospital'. English **ambulance** later began to be used for a vehicle transporting the wounded and sick.

ambulatory /ámbyŏö láytəri/ *adj* of walking or moving (*fml*) ■ *n* (*pl* **-ries**) a walkway in a church or cloister

ambush /ámbŏŏsh/ *n* 1 a surprise attack 2 concealment before attacking o *waiting in ambush* ■ *vt* attack from a concealed position —**ambusher** *n*

ameliorate /ə meéli ə rayt/ (**-rating, -rated**) *vti* improve (*fml*) —**amelioration** /ə meéli ə ráysh'n/ *n* —**ameliorative** /-rətiv/ *adj*

amen /aá mén, áy-/ *interj* 1 affirms the content of a prayer or hymn 2 expresses strong agreement

amenable /ə meénəb'l/ *adj* 1 responsive to suggestion and willing to cooperate 2 susceptible to being affected in a particular way o *The tumour is not amenable to treatment.* —**amenability** /ə meénə bíllэti/ *n* —**amenably** *adv*

amend /ə ménd/ *vt* change something in order to improve or correct it

amendment /ə méndmənt/ *n* a change, correction, or improvement to something

amends /ə méndz/ *n* restitution of a wrong (*+ sing or pl verb*) o *a desire to make amends*

Amenhotep III /aá men hŏ tep/ (1411–1379 BC) king of Egypt (1417–1379 BC)

Amenhotep IV ♦ Akhenaton

amenity /ə meénəti/ (*pl* **-ties**) *n* 1 an attractive feature, service, or facility (*often pl*) o *the amenities of a luxury hotel* 2 pleasantness or attractiveness

amenorrhoea /áy menə reé ə/, **amenorrhea** *n* the unusual absence of menstruation —**amenorrhoeic** *adj*

America /ə mérrikə/ 1 the United States 2 *also* **Americas** North, South, and Central America 3 North America (*infml*)

ORIGIN **America** is first recorded in English in the early 16C. It comes from a Latinized form of the first name of the Italian navigator Amerigo Vespucci (1454–1512).

American /ə mérrikən/ *n* somebody from the United States ■ *adj* of America

American dream *n* the idea that everyone in the United States can succeed and prosper

American football *n* a US team game played with an oval ball

American Indian *n* a Native American (*sometimes offensive*) —**American Indian** *adj* ◊ See note at **Indian**

Americanism /ə mérrikənizəm/ *n* a US expression or custom

Americanize /ə mérrikə nīz/ (**-izing, -ized**), **Americanise** *vti* take on or give the qualities associated with the United States —**Americanization** /ə mérrikə nī záysh'n/ *n*

American Samoa US territory consisting of a group of islands in the South Pacific. Pop. 67,084 (2001).

Americas /ə mérrikəz/ ♦ **America** 2

americium /ámmə ríssi əm/ *n* (*symbol* **Am**) a radioactive metallic chemical element

Amerindian /ámmə ríndi ən/ *n* a member of an indigenous people of North, South, or Central America (*sometimes offensive*) —**Amerindian** *adj* ◊ See note at **Indian**

amethyst /ámmэthist/ *n* 1 a violet form of quartz. Use: gems. 2 a purple sapphire. Use: gems.

amiable /áymi əb'l/ *adj* friendly and pleasant —**amiability** /áymi ə bíllэti/ *n* —**amiably** *adv*

amicable /ámmikəb'l/ *adj* friendly and without bad feelings —**amicability** /ámmikə bíllэti/ *n* —**amicably** *adv*

amid /ə míd/, **amidst** /ə mídst/ *prep* 1 within or among 2 while something is happening

amidships /ə mídships/ *adv*, *adj* near the centre of a vessel

Amin /aa meén/, **Idi** (*b.* 1925) Ugandan head of state (1971–79)

amino acid /ə meénō-/ *n* a constituent of protein

Amis /áymiss/, **Sir Kingsley** (1922–95) British novelist

amiss /ə míss/ *adj* wrong o *Something is amiss.* ■ *adv* incorrectly o *Things began to go amiss.*

amity /ámməti/ *n* friendliness (*fml*)

Amman /ə maán/ capital of the Kingdom of Jordan. Pop. 1,187,000 (1995).

ammendment incorrect spelling of **amendment**

ammeter /ámmeetər/ n an instrument measuring electric current

ammo /ámmō/ n ammunition (infml)

ammonia /ə móni ə/ n 1 a pungent gas. Use: fertilizers, explosives, plastics. 2 a solution of ammonia. Use: household cleaners.

ammonite /ámmə nīt/ n the fossilized flat spiral shell of an extinct marine organism —**ammonitic** /ámmə níttik/ adj

ammunition /ámmyoō nísh'n/ n 1 bullets and missiles 2 explosive material 3 facts used to support an argument

amnesia /am neézi ə/ n memory loss —**amnesiac** n, adj

amnesty /ámnəsti/ (pl -ties) n 1 a pardon 2 a prosecution-free period

Amnesty International n a human rights organization

amniocentesis /ámni ō sen teéssiss/ (pl -ses /-seez/) n a test to determine the genetic constitution of a foetus

amoeba /ə meébə/ (pl -bae /-bee/ or -bas) n a single-celled organism —**amoebic** adj —**amoeboid** adj

amok /ə mók/, **amuck** /ə múk/ adv, adj out of control

among /ə múng/, **amongst** /-múngst/ prep 1 surrounded by o among friends 2 of or in a group o among the world's finest 3 between group members o divided among six of us

amoral /ay mórrəl/ adj 1 outside the scope of morality 2 without moral standards (disapproving) —**amorality** /áymo rálləti/ n —**amorally** adv

amorous /ámmərəss/ adj showing or feeling sexual desire —**amorously** adv —**amorousness** n

amorphous /ə máwrfəss/ adj 1 without any clear shape 2 not classifiable as a particular category or type 3 without a crystalline structure —**amorphousness** n

amortize /ə máwr tīz/ (-tizing, -tized), **amortise** vt 1 reduce a debt by instalments 2 write off the cost of an asset —**amortization** /ə máwr tī záysh'n/ n

amount /ə mównt/ n a quantity
☐ **amount to** vt 1 add up to 2 be equivalent to o Their action amounts to fraud.

amour-propre /ámmoor própprə/ n self-esteem (fml)

amp n 1 an ampere 2 an amplifier (infml)

amperage /ámpərij/ n the number of amperes measured in an electric current

ampere /ám pair/ n (symbol A) the SI unit of electric current

ORIGIN The **ampere** is named after the French physicist André-Marie Ampère (1775–1836), who was the first person to distinguish between electric current and voltage.

ampersand /ámpər sand/ n the symbol '&', meaning 'and'

ORIGIN **Ampersand** is a contraction of & per se and, literally '& by itself (means) and', an old name for the character whose significance is not entirely clear. The character itself is a printed version of a manuscript abbreviation for Latin et 'and'.

amphetamine /am féttə meen/ n a stimulant drug

amphibian /am fíbbi ən/ n 1 a land organism that breeds in water 2 an aircraft or vehicle operating on land and in water ■ adj living on land and in water

amphibious /am fíbbi əss/ adj 1 living on land and in water 2 operating on land and in water

amphitheatre /ámfi theertər/ n a circular building, room, or arena with tiered seats for spectators

amphora /ámfərə/ (pl -rae /-ree/ or -ras) n a narrow-necked jar with two handles used in the ancient world

ample /ámp'l/ (-pler, -plest) adj 1 more than enough 2 large in body size (often euphemistic) —**ampleness** n —**amply** adv

amplifier /ámpli fī ər/ n 1 a device that makes sounds louder 2 a device that increases the magnitude of a signal, voltage, or current

amplify /ámpli fī/ (-fies, -fied) vti 1 increase in magnitude 2 make or become louder 3 add detail to something —**amplification** /ámpli fi káysh'n/ n ◊ See note at **increase**

amplitude /ámpli tyood/ n 1 largeness in size, volume, or extent 2 breadth of range

ampoule /ám pool, -pyool/, **ampule** n a sealed container of medication

amputate /ámpyoō tayt/ (-tating, -tated) vti cut off part of the body surgically —**amputation** /ámpyoō táysh'n/ n

amputee /ámpyoō teé/ n somebody who has had a limb amputated

amrita /am reétə/, **amreeta** n 1 in Hindu mythology, a drink bestowing immortality 2 in Hindu mythology, immortality gained by drinking amrita

Amritsar /əm rítsər/ city in NW India, site of the Sikh Golden Temple. Pop. 708,835 (1991).

Amsterdam /ámstər dam/ capital of and commercial centre in the Netherlands. Pop. 731,200 (2000).

amuck adv, adj = **amok**

Amu Darya /aà moo daàryə/ longest river in Central Asia. Length 1,415 km/879 mi.

amulet /ámmyoōlət/ n an object or a piece of jewellery considered lucky

Amundsen /ámmənds'n/, **Roald** (1872–1928) Norwegian explorer

Amur /ə múr/ river in east-central Asia. Length 4,345 km/2,700 mi. (total river system).

amuse /ə myoóz/ (amusing, amused) vt 1 make smile or laugh 2 keep happily occupied —**amused** adj —**amusing** adj —**amusingly** adv

amusement /ə myoózmənt/ n 1 the feeling that something is funny 2 a recreational activity 3 a ride, game, or similar attraction

amusement arcade *n* an indoor place of recreation with coin operated machines

an *(stressed)* /an/ *(unstressed)* /ən/ *det* the form of 'a' used before an initial vowel sound

USAGE The practice of using **an** before words beginning with *h* and an unstressed syllable (e.g. *an hotel*) is falling out of use, and it is much more usual now to hear *a hotel*, with the *h* sounded.

-an, -ian *suffix* **1** of or relating to ○ *American* ○ *European* ○ *Christian* **2** a person with a particular expertise ○ *librarian*

-ana, -iana *suffix* a collection of objects or information about a topic, person, or place ○ *Victoriana*

Anabaptist /ánnə báptist/ *n* a member of a 16C Protestant movement advocating adult baptism —**Anabaptist** *adj*

anabolic steroid /ánnə bóllik-/ *n* a synthetic hormone. Use: developing muscle mass and strength.

anachronism /ə nákrənizəm/ *n* **1** something from an earlier or later historical period than other things in the same context **2** somebody or something that seems to belong to a different historical period —**anachronistic** /ə nákrə nístik/ *adj* —**anachronistically** *adv* —**anachronous** *adj* —**anachronously** *adv*

anaconda /ánnə kóndə/ *n* a nonpoisonous snake, the largest in the boa family

anaemia /ə neémi ə/, **anemia** *n* a deficiency of red blood cells —**anaemic** *adj*

anaemic /ə neèmik/, **anemic** *adj* **1** having anaemia **2** sick-looking —**anaemically** *adv*

anaerobic /ánnə róbik, án air-/ *adj* **1** not needing oxygen **2** lacking oxygen —**anaerobically** *adv*

anaesthesia /ánnəss theézi ə/, **anesthesia** *n* medically induced loss of sensation or unconsciousness

anaesthetic /ánnəss théttik/, **anesthetic** *n* a substance that causes anaesthesia —**anaesthetic** *adj*

anaesthetist /ə neésthətist/, **anesthetist** *n* somebody who is qualified to administer anaesthetics, especially a nurse or technician

anaesthetize /ə neésthə tīz/ (**-tizing, -tized**), **anesthetize, anaesthetise** /ə neésthətīz/ *vt* administer an anaesthetic to —**anaesthetization** /ə neésthə tī záysh'n/ *n*

anagram /ánnə gram/ *n* a word or phrase containing all the letters of another ○ *The word 'carthorse' is an anagram of 'orchestra'.* —**anagrammatic** /ánnəgrə máttik/ *adj* —**anagrammatically** *adv*

anal /áyn'l/ *adj* **1** of the anus **2** obsessively methodical or self-controlled —**anally** *adv*

analgesia /ánn'l jeèzi ə/ *n* **1** insensitivity to pain **2** pain control or relief —**analgesic** *adj, n*

analog *adj* US, Can COMPUT = **analogue**

analogous /ə nálləgəss/ *adj* similar in some respects —**analogously** *adv*

analogue /ánnə log/ *n* a corresponding thing ■ *adj* describes a clock or watch with a dial

analogue computer *n* a computer that uses a variable physical quantity to represent data

analogy /ə nálləji/ (*pl* **-gies**) *n* **1** a comparison between similar things **2** a similarity in some respects

analyse /ánnə līz/ (**-lysing, -lysed**), **analyze** (**-lyzing, -lyzed**) *vt* **1** break down into components **2** examine the structure of **3** examine in detail —**analysable** *adj* —**analyst** /-list/ *n*

analysis /ə nállississ/ (*pl* **-ses** /-seez/) *n* **1** separation into components for examination **2** a list of constituent elements **3** an examination of something in detail **4** an assessment based on examination

~~analysys~~ incorrect spelling of **analysis**

analytic /ánnə líttik/, **analytical** /-líttik'l/ *adj* of or using analysis —**analytically** *adv*

anaphylactic shock /ánnəfi láktik-/ *n* a sudden severe allergic reaction

anarchism /ánnər kizəm/ *n* **1** ideology rejecting all forms of government **2** the actions of anarchists

anarchist /ánnərkist/ *n* **1** a supporter of anarchism **2** a lawless person

anarchy /ánnərki/ *n* **1** lack of government **2** a state of chaos —**anarchic** /ə naárkik, ə n-/ *adj* —**anarchically** *adv*

anathema /ə náthəmə/ *n* **1** an object of loathing **2** a curse

Anatolia /ánnə tóli ə/ Asian part of Turkey —**Anatolian** *n, adj*

anatomy /ə náttəmi/ (*pl* **-mies**) *n* **1** the study of the structure of the human body **2** the physical structure of an organism **3** the shape of somebody's body *(infml)* —**anatomical** /ánnə tómmik'l/ *adj* —**anatomist** *n*

ANC *abbr* African National Congress

-ance *suffix* **1** action ○ *utterance* **2** *also* **-ancy** state or condition ○ *elegance*

ancestor /án sestər, ánsəstər/ *n* **1** a person from a distant generation whom somebody is descended from **2** a forerunner **3** an earlier species from which a plant or animal evolved

ancestry /án sestri, ánsəs-/ *n* the family or group that makes up somebody's ancestors —**ancestral** /ən séstrəl/ *adj*

anchor /ángkər/ *n* **1** a device that holds a ship in place **2** any device that keeps somebody or something in place **3** *also* **anchorman** /-man/, **anchorperson** /-purss'n/, **anchorwoman** /-wōomən/ a presenter on a news programme **4** somebody or something that provides a sense of stability *(literary)* ■ *v* **1** *vt* hold something securely in place **2** *vti* put down a ship's anchor **3** *vt* be a presenter on a news programme

anchorage /ángkərij/ *n* **1** a place where a ship is anchored **2** something holding somebody or something in place

anchorite /ángkə rīt/ *n* a religious recluse

anchovy /ánchəvi, an chóvi/ (*pl* **-vies** *or same*) *n* a small fish usually salted and canned

ancien régime /aàN syaN ray zheèm/ (*pl* **anciens régimes** /*pronunc. same*/) *n* **1** French society before the Revolution **2** a former system of government or management

ancient /áynshənt/ *adj* **1** of the distant past **2** very old ■ *n* **1** somebody from a civilization in the distant past **2** somebody of advanced years ■ **ancients** *npl* **1** the people of ancient Western civilizations **2** the ancient Greek and Roman authors

ancient history *n* the study of old civilizations

ancillary /an sílləri/ *adj* **1** providing support **2** subordinate ■ *n* (*pl* **-ries**) **1** a subordinate part **2** a nontechnical support employee

and *conj* **1** introduces something additional **2** links two verbs or statements and shows that the second follows the first ○ *Just add water and stir.* **3** introduces a result of something just mentioned ○ *Their work was excellent and won several awards.* **4** stresses repetition or continuity ○ *better and better* **5** plus ○ *One and one are two.* **6** but ○ *Eat a lot of fruit and avoid refined sugar.* **7** moreover ○ *The kids needed clothes, and I hadn't been paid in weeks.* **8** connects ideas and add emphasis ○ *We are courageous. And we will win this battle.* **9** used instead of 'to' with infinitives following some verbs (*infml*) ○ *I try and visit her once a week.*

> **USAGE** Using **and** at the beginning of a sentence is not incorrect, and can often be an effective way of drawing attention to what follows: *'You can't get away with this', he threatened. And we knew he meant it.*

AND *n* **1** in computing, an operator that links items that must occur together for a specific result to be achieved **2** *also* **AND circuit** a logic circuit used in computers that gives an output value of 1 if the values of all inputs are 1 and an output value of 0 otherwise

Andalusia /ándə loòssi ə/ autonomous region of S Spain. Pop. 7,236,459 (1998). Spanish **Andalucía** —**Andalusian** *adj, n*

Andaman Islands /ándəmən-/ island group of E India, between the Bay of Bengal and the **Andaman Sea**. Pop. 240,089 (1991).

andante /an dánti, -tay/ *adj, adv* to be played slowly (*musical direction*) —**andante** *n*

Andersen /ándərss'n/, **Hans Christian** (1805–75) Danish writer

Anderson /ándərss'n/, **Elizabeth Garrett** (1836–1917) British doctor

Anderson, Marian (1897–1993) US contralto

Andes /án deez/ South American mountain system extending along the western coast from Panama to Tierra del Fuego. Highest peak Aconcagua 6,960 m/22,835 ft. —**Andean** /ándi ən/ *adj, n*

andiron /ánd ī ərn/ *n* a metal holder for logs in a fireplace

Andorra /an dáwrə/ principality in SW Europe between France and Spain. Cap. Andorra la Vella. Pop. 67,627 (2001). —**Andorran** *adj, n*

Andorra la Vella /-lə véllə/ capital of Andorra. Pop. 21,513 (1998).

Andrea del Sarto /an dráy ə del saàrtō/ (1486–1530) Italian painter

Andreessen /an dráyss'n/, **Marc** (*b.* 1971) US computer scientist and technology executive

Andrew /ándroo/, **St** (*d.* AD 60) one of the 12 apostles of Jesus Christ

androgynous /an drójjənəss/ *adj* **1** giving an impression of ambiguous sexual identity ○ *androgynous looks* **2** having both male and female physical characteristics —**androgyny** *n*

android /án droyd/ *n* a human-looking robot

anecdote /ánnik dōt/ *n* a short account of something interesting or amusing —**anecdotal** /ánnik dōt'l/ *adj*

anemia etc. = **anaemia etc.**

anemone /ə némməni/ (*pl* **-nes** *or same*) *n* **1** a perennial flowering plant of the buttercup family with wild and cultivated types **2** a sea anemone

~~anenome~~ incorrect spelling of **anemone**

anesthesia etc. = **anaesthesia etc.**

aneurysm /ánnyŏŏrizəm/, **aneurism** *n* a fluid-filled bulge in an artery that can weaken the wall —**aneurysmal** /ánnyŏŏ rízm'l/ *adj*

anew /ə nyóo/ *adv* **1** again **2** in a new way

angel /áynjəl/ *n* **1** in some religions, a heavenly being who acts as God's messenger **2** a kind person (*infml*) **3** a spirit that is believed to protect and guide somebody **4** a financial backer (*infml*) ◊ See note at **backer**

angel cake *n* a light cake made without egg yolks

Angel Falls world's highest waterfall, in SE Venezuela. Height 979 m/3,212 ft.

angelic /an jéllik/ *adj* **1** kind or beautiful **2** well behaved **3** of angels —**angelically** *adv*

angelica /an jéllikə/ (*pl* **-cas** *or same*) *n* **1** candied plant stems used for decorating cakes and biscuits **2** a tall hollow-stemmed flowering plant whose stems are used for angelica

Angelico /an jéllikō/, **Fra** (1400?–55) Italian painter

Marian Anderson

Barnaby's

Maya Angelou

Angelou /ánjəloo/, **Maya** (b. 1928) US writer

Angelus /ánjiləss/, **angelus** n 1 a set of Roman Catholic prayers commemorating the Annunciation and Incarnation 2 a bell announcing the Angelus

anger /áng gər/ n a feeling of strong displeasure ■ vti become or make greatly displeased

---

SYNONYMS **anger, annoyance, irritation, indignation, fury, rage, ire, wrath** CORE MEANING: a feeling of strong displeasure in response to an assumed injury

---

Angers /aaN zhay/ capital of Maine-et-Loire Department, W France. Pop. 151,279 (1999).

angina /an jínə/, **angina pectoris** /-péktəriss/ n severe chest pains caused by a lack of blood flowing to the heart

angioplasty /ánji ō plasti/ (pl -ties) n surgery to clear a narrowed artery using an inflatable instrument

angiosperm /ánji ō spurm/ n a plant in which the sex organs are within flowers and the seeds are in a fruit

Angkor /áng kawr/ ancient capital of the early Khmer civilization in NW Cambodia, noted for its temples and monuments

angle[1] /áng g'l/ n 1 a space between diverging lines or surfaces, or a measure of the space 2 a figure formed by diverging lines 3 a projecting part 4 a position for viewing something ○ seen from various angles 5 a way of considering something ○ Look at the problem from another angle. ■ v (-gling, -gled) 1 vt direct or place something at an angle 2 vt present an idea, topic, or opinion with a particular audience in mind or in a biased way 3 vi change direction sharply

angle[2] /áng g'l/ (-gling, -gled) vi 1 fish with a rod 2 attempt to get something for yourself (infml) —**angler** n —**angling** n

Angle /áng g'l/ n a member of a Germanic people who settled in England in the 5C —**Anglian** /áng gli ən/ adj, n

Anglesey /áng g'lssi/ island off the coast of NW Wales. Pop. 67,200 (1995).

Anglican /áng glikən/ adj of the Anglican Church ■ n a member of the Anglican Church

Anglican Church, Anglican Communion n a group of Christian churches including the Churches of England, Ireland, and Wales, and the Episcopal Church of Scotland

Anglicism /áng gli sizəm/, **anglicism** n 1 a word used in British English 2 an English word used in a foreign language

anglicize /áng gli sīz/ (-cizing, -cized), **Anglicize, anglicise, Anglicise** vti make or become more English —**anglicization** /áng gli sī záysh'n/ n

Anglo /áng glō/ (pl -glos), **anglo** n Aus an offensive term for an Australian of British, Irish, or American origin (insult)

Anglo- prefix England, English, British ○ Anglophile ○ Anglo-Irish

Anglo-Indian adj introduced into English from a South Asian language ■ n 1 somebody with British and South Asian ancestry 2 a British person residing in South Asia, especially during colonial times

Anglo-Irish npl Irish people with English ancestry —**Anglo-Irish** adj

Anglophile /áng glō fīl/ n somebody who likes England and English people —**Anglophilia** /áng glō fílli ə/ n —**Anglophilic** /ánglō fillik/ adj

Anglophobe /áng glō fōb/ n somebody who dislikes England and English people —**Anglophobia** /áng glō fōbi ə/ n —**Anglophobic** /ánglō fōbik/ adj

anglophone /áng glə fōn/ n a speaker of English ■ adj describes a country where English is the native language of most people

Anglo-Saxon n 1 a member of any of the Germanic peoples who settled in England in the 5C 2 the Old English language —**Anglo-Saxon** adj

Angola /ang gṓlə/ country in west-central Africa. Cap. Luanda. Pop. 10,548,000 (1997). —**Angolan** adj, n

angora /ang gáwrə/ n 1 silky wool from a goat 2 a silky-haired goat, cat, or rabbit

angostura /áng gə styoórə/, **angostura bark** n the bark of a South American tree. Use: flavouring in bitters.

ORIGIN **Angostura** is named after a city in Venezuela whose modern name is Ciudad Bolívar.

---

angry /áng gri/ (-grier, -griest) adj 1 feeling very annoyed 2 expressing annoyance 3 stormy-looking 4 inflamed and painful-looking ○ an angry bruise —**angrily** adv

angst n 1 in existentialist philosophy, the feeling of dread that comes from an awareness of free will 2 anxiety about personal shortcomings or circumstances ◊ See note at **worry**

angstrom /ángstrəm, -strom/ n also **angstrom unit** (symbol Å) a unit used to measure electromagnetic radiation

Anguilla /ang gwíllə/ one of the Leeward Islands, in the E Caribbean. Pop. 7,300 (1990).

anguish /áng gwish/ n extreme anxiety ■ vti feel or cause to feel anguish —**anguished** adj

angular /áng gyŏŏlər/ adj 1 with sharp edges and corners 2 thin and bony —**angularly** adv

anhydrous /an hídrǝss/ *adj* with no water in its composition

anicca /ánnikǝ/ *n* in Buddhism, the cycle of birth, life, and death

~~anihilation~~ incorrect spelling of **annihilation**

aniline /ánnilin, -leen/ *n* a colourless poisonous liquid. Use: manufacture of dyes, resins, pharmaceuticals, explosives.

animadvert /ánni mad vúrt, -mǝd-/ *vi* comment critically

animal /ánnim'l/ *n* 1 a living organism with independent movement 2 a mammal 3 a person regarded as brutish *(infml)* 4 a person or thing *(infml)* ○ *The laser printer is a completely different animal.* ■ *adj* 1 derived from animals ○ *animal fats* 2 instinctive ○ *animal urges*

animal husbandry *n* the breeding and care of farm animals

animality /ánni mállǝti/ *n* animal characteristics

animal rights *npl* rights for animals that are similar to human rights

animate *vt* /ánni mayt/ (**-mating, -mated**) 1 make lively 2 inspire action or feelings in 3 create using animation techniques ■ *adj* /ánnimǝt/ physically alive —**animated** *adj* —**animatedly** *adv* —**animator** *n* ◊ See note at **living**

animation /ánni máysh'n/ *n* 1 films made by photographing a sequence of slightly varying pictures or models so that they appear to move 2 liveliness or activity

animatronics /ánnimǝ trónniks/ *n* the electronic manipulation of puppets or other models (+ *sing verb*) —**animatronic** *adj*

anime /ánni may, -mǝ/ *n* a Japanese style of animated cartoon, often with violent or sexually explicit content

animism /ánnimizǝm/ *n* 1 the belief that things in nature have souls 2 the belief in an organizing force in the universe —**animist** *adj, n* —**animistic** /ánni místik/ *adj*

animosity /ánni móssǝti/ (*pl* **-ties**) *n* hostility or resentment ◊ See note at **dislike**

animus /ánnimǝss/ *n* 1 hostility 2 a feeling that motivates somebody's actions

anion /án ī ǝn/ *n* a negative ion —**anionic** /án ī ónnik/ *adj*

anise /ánniss/ *n* 1 aniseed 2 the plant from which aniseed comes

aniseed /ánni seed/ *n* the liquorice-flavoured seeds of the anise plant. Use: flavouring.

Anjou /oN zhoó/ former province in W France

Ankara /ángkǝrǝ/ capital of Turkey. Pop. 2,937,524 (1997).

ankle /ángk'l/ *n* 1 the joint that connects the foot and the leg 2 the slim part of the leg above the ankle

anklet /ángklǝt/ *n* a chain or band worn round the ankle

annals /ánn'lz/ *npl* 1 recorded history 2 a historical record arranged chronologically

~~annalysis~~ incorrect spelling of **analysis**

Annam /a nám/ region in east-central Vietnam —**Annamese** /ánnǝ meéz/ *adj, n*

Annan /a nán, ánnǝn/, **Kofi** (*b.* 1938) Ghanaian Secretary General of the United Nations (1996–), awarded the Nobel Peace Prize (2001)

Annapolis /ǝ náppǝliss/ capital of Maryland. Pop. 33,585 (1998).

Annapurna /ánnǝ púrnǝ/ mountain in the Himalaya range, in Nepal. Height 8,078 m/26,504 ft.

Ann Arbor /an aárbǝr/ city in SE Michigan. Pop. 109,967 (1998).

Anne /an/ (1665–1714) queen of Great Britain and Ireland (1702–14)

Anne (of Cleves) /-kleevz/ (1515–57) German-born queen of England (1540) as the fourth wife of Henry VIII

anneal /ǝ neél/ *vti* make material stronger through heating

annex /ǝ néks/ *vt* 1 attach one thing to another 2 take over a territory and make it part of another country 3 attach a quality or condition to something else ■ *n* an annexe to a document —**annexation** /ánnek sáysh'n/ *n*

annexe /ánneks/ *n* 1 a building attached to another to extend its space 2 a document attached to another to provide further information

annihilate /ǝ nī ǝ layt/ (**-lating, -lated**) *vt* 1 destroy completely 2 defeat easily and convincingly *(infml)*

annihilation /ǝ nī ǝ láysh'n/ *n* complete destruction

anniversary /ánni vúrssǝri/ (*pl* **-ries**) *n* 1 the date of an important past event 2 a celebration or commemoration of an important past event

anno Domini /ánnō dómmi nī/ *adv* full form of **AD**

anno Hegirae /ánnō hǝ jīri/ *adv* full form of **AH**

~~annoint~~ incorrect spelling of **anoint**

~~annonymous~~ incorrect spelling of **anonymous**

annotate /ánnǝ tayt/ (**-tating, -tated**) *vt* add explanatory notes to

announce /ǝ nównss/ (**-nouncing, -nounced**) *vt* 1 tell or report publicly 2 say in a formal or forceful way 3 tell people formally of the arrival of 4 be a sign of the existence or imminence of —**announcement** *n*

announcer /ǝ nównssǝr/ *n* 1 somebody who makes public announcements 2 a TV or radio commentator

annoy /ǝ nóy/ *vt* 1 make somebody feel impatient or mildly angry 2 harass or bother somebody repeatedly —**annoyance** *n* —**annoying** *adj* —**annoyingly** *adv*

SYNONYMS annoy, irritate, exasperate, vex, irk CORE MEANING: cause a mild degree of anger in somebody

annual /ánnyoo ǝl/ *adj* 1 happening once a year 2 for a period of one year 3 describes a plant that dies after one season ■ *n* 1 an annual plant 2 a book or magazine published once a year —**annually** /ánnyoo ǝli/ *adv*

annual general meeting *n* a yearly meeting of members of an organization to deal with administrative matters

annuity /ə nyoö əti/ (*pl* **-ties**) *n* **1** a sum of money paid at regular intervals **2** an investment paying a fixed annual sum

annul /ə núl/ (**-nulling**, **-nulled**) *vt* **1** make a document or agreement invalid **2** declare a marriage invalid —**annulment** *n* ◊ See note at **nullify**

annular /ánnyoölər/ *adj* shaped like a ring

Annunciation /ə núnssi áysh'n/ *n* **1** in Christianity, the archangel Gabriel's visit to Mary to tell her that she would be the mother of Jesus Christ **2** the Christian festival that commemorates this visit. Date: 25 March.

anode /ánnōd/ *n* **1** the negative terminal of a battery **2** the positive electrode in an electrolytic cell

anodize /ánnō dīz/ (**-dizing**, **-dized**), **anodise** *vt* coat metal with an oxide —**anodization** /ánnō dī záysh'n/ *n*

anodyne /ánnō dīn/ *adj* **1** bland ○ *an anodyne speech* **2** soothing (*literary*) **3** giving relief from pain

anoint /ə nóynt/ *vt* **1** bless somebody with oil **2** ordain a cleric

anomaly /ə nómməli/ (*pl* **-lies**) *n* **1** an irregularity ○ *looking for anomalies in the blood tests* **2** a strange object or quality —**anomalous** *adj*

anon. /ə nón/ *abbr* anonymous

anonymizer /ə nónnə mīzər/ *n* a website enabling a user to browse the Internet without leaving any identity traces

anonymous /ə nónniməss/ *adj* **1** unnamed or unknown ○ *the anonymous author* **2** with the writer's or creator's name withheld ○ *an anonymous letter* **3** lacking distinctive features ○ *an anonymous shopping mall* —**anonymity** /ánnə nímməti/ *n*

anonymous FTP *n* an Internet file transfer in which no password is needed

anorak /ánnə rak/ *n* **1** a hooded waterproof jacket **2** an obsessive enthusiast (*humorous*) **3** a boring unfashionable person (*humorous*)

anorexia /ánnə réksi ə/ *n* **1** *also* **anorexia nervosa** an eating disorder deriving from an extreme fear of becoming overweight and marked by excessive dieting to the point of ill health **2** persistent loss of appetite —**anorexic** *n*, *adj*

another /ə núthər/ *det*, *pron* **1** one more ○ *need another person to help* ○ *May I have another?* **2** one that is different from some other ○ *another way of approaching the problem* ○ *This towel's wet: can you pass me another?*

Anouilh /ánnoo ee/, **Jean** (1910–87) French dramatist

Ansett /ánssət/, **Sir Reginald Myles** (1909–81) Australian aviator and business executive

answer /aánssər/ *n* **1** a response to a question **2** a way of solving something **3** a response to something that somebody says or does ■ *vti* **1** reply or respond to something **2** respond to something such as a ringing

telephone or a doorbell **3** match or correspond to something ○ *nobody who answers to that description* **4** fulfil a need, wish, or purpose

SYNONYMS answer, reply, response, rejoinder, retort, riposte CORE MEANING: something said, written, or done in acknowledgment of a question or remark, or in reaction to a situation

☐ **answer back** *vti* reply to somebody impudently
☐ **answer for** *vt* explain a mistake or fault
☐ **answer to** *vt* be accountable to somebody

answerable /aánssərəb'l/ *adj* **1** obliged to explain your actions to somebody **2** solvable

answering machine, answer machine *n* a device that records incoming phone messages

answering service *n* a business that takes phone messages on behalf of customers

ant *n* an insect that lives in complex colonies

-ant *suffix* **1** performing a particular action ○ *coolant* **2** being in a particular condition ○ *hesitant*

antacid /an tássid/ *adj* neutralizing acidity in the stomach ■ *n* an antacid drug

antagonism /an tággənizəm/ *n* **1** hostility **2** opposition between forces or substances

antagonist /an tággənist/ *n* **1** an opponent **2** a character in conflict with the hero in a story —**antagonistic** /an tággə nístik/ *adj* —**antagonistically** *adv*

antagonize /an tággə nīz/ (**-nizing**, **-nized**), **antagonise** *vt* arouse hostility in

Antananarivo /ántə nánnə rée vō/ capital of Madagascar. Pop. 1,052,835 (1993).

Antarctic /an taártktik/ region south of the Antarctic Circle —**Antarctic** *adj*

Antarctica /an taártkikə/ uninhabited continent surrounding the South Pole

Antarctic Circle *n* the parallel of latitude at 66°30′S, encircling Antarctica and its surrounding seas

Antarctic Ocean area of the S Atlantic, Indian, and Pacific oceans that surrounds Antarctica

~~Antartic~~ incorrect spelling of **Antarctic**

ante /ánti/ *n* a gambler's stake in a card game —**ante** *vti* ◊ **up the ante** demand more in a situation (*infml*)

ante- *prefix* before, in front ○ *anteroom*

anteater /ánt eetər/ *n* **1** a tropical mammal with a long nose and tongue that feeds on ants **2** a pangolin **3** an aardvark

antecedent /ánti seéd'nt/ *n* **1** something that existed or happened before something else **2** a word that a subsequent word refers back to ■ **antecedents** *npl* **1** ancestors **2** somebody's history ■ *adj* occurring earlier in time (*fml*) —**antecedence** *n*

antechamber /ánti chaymbər/ *n* a room leading to a larger room

antedate /ánti dáyt/ (**-dating, -dated**) vt **1** occur earlier than **2** put an earlier date on

antediluvian /ánti di loóvi ən/ adj **1** from a time before the biblical Flood **2** outdated

antelope /ántəlōp/ (pl **-lopes** or same) n a horned mammal of a large family that includes gazelles and impalas

antenatal /ánti náyt'l/ adj before childbirth —**antenatally** adv

antenna /an ténnə/ (pl **-nae** /-nee/ or **-nas**) n a thin sensor on the head of insects and some other organisms

antepenultimate /ánti pi núltimət/ adj third from last

anterior /an teéri ər/ adj (fml) **1** at the front of something **2** earlier than something else

anteroom /ánti room, -rōōm/ n a room that leads onto a larger room

anthem /ánthəm/ n **1** a song of allegiance and national identity **2** a rousing popular song o rock anthems **3** a short hymn sung by the choir during a religious service

anther /ánthər/ n a male flower part containing pollen

anthill /ánt hil/ n a mound of earth made by ants during the construction of their nest

anthology /an thólləji/ (pl **-gies**) n a collection of different writers' works —**anthologist** n

ORIGIN The Greek word from which **anthology** derives literally means 'a collection of flowers'. The original anthologies contained epigrams and short poems by various authors, chosen as being especially fine.

anthracite /ánthrə sīt/ n a hard slow-burning coal

anthrax /án thraks/ n an infectious disease of sheep and cattle transmittable to humans, causing skin ulcers (**cutaneous anthrax**) or a form of pneumonia (**pulmonary anthrax**)

anthropo- prefix human being o anthropomorphism

anthropoid /ánthrə poyd/ adj **1** of apes **2** like human beings ■ n **1** a primate **2** an ape of the family that includes chimpanzees and gorillas —**anthropoidal** /ánthrə póyd'l/ adj

anthropology /ánthrə pólləji/ n the study of human culture and development —**anthropologist** n

anthropomorphism /ánthrəpō máwrfizəm/ n the attribution of human characteristics to animals —**anthropomorphic** adj —**anthropomorphically** adv

anti- prefix **1** against or preventing o anticlerical o anticoagulant o anti-Communism **2** opposite o anticlimax o antiparticle

antiabortion /ánti ə báwrsh'n/ adj opposed to abortion —**antiabortionist** n

antiaircraft /ánti áir kraaft/ adj for attacking aeroplanes

antialiasing /ánti áyli əssing/ n the smoothing of the jagged edges of diagonal lines in computer images

antibacterial /ánti bak teéri əl/ adj preventing, killing, or reducing the growth of bacteria

antiballistic missile /ánti bə lístik-/ n a missile used to destroy a ballistic missile in flight

antibiotic /ánti bī óttik/ n a medication that destroys bacteria —**antibiotic** adj

antibody /ánti bodi/ (pl **-ies**) n a protein produced in the body in response to the presence of an antigen, e.g. a bacterium or virus

anti-choice adj opposed to abortion

Antichrist /ánti krīst/ n **1** an antagonist of Jesus Christ expected by the early Christian Church **2** also **antichrist** any opponent of Jesus Christ

anticipate /an tíssi payt/ (**-pating, -pated**) vt **1** act beforehand to prepare for or prevent something **2** expect something o We're anticipating trouble. —**anticipation** /an tíssi páysh'n/ n

anticlerical /ánti klérrik'l/ adj opposed to the involvement of the clergy in political affairs

anticlimax /ánti klí maks/ n **1** a disappointing end after a big buildup **2** a sudden change of tone from the serious to the trivial or dull —**anticlimactic** /ánti klī máktik/ adj —**anticlimactically** adv

anticlockwise /ánti klók wīz/ adj, adv in the opposite direction to the movement of a clock's hands

anticoagulant /ánti kō ággyóōlənt/ adj preventing normal blood clotting —**anticoagulant** n

anticompetitive /ántikəm péttətiv/ adj likely or certain to discourage competition

anticonvulsant /ántikən vúlssənt/ adj controlling convulsions —**anticonvulsant** n —**anticonvulsive** n, adj

anticorrosive /ánti kə róssiv/ adj controlling corrosion

anticrime /ánti krím/ adj designed to prevent or reduce crime

antics /ántiks/ npl silly pranks

anticyclone /ánti síklōn/ n an area of atmospheric high pressure that brings generally settled weather —**anticyclonic** /ánti sī klónnik/ adj

antidemocratic /ánti demmə kráttik/ adj opposed to democracy

antidepressant /ánti di préss'nt/ n a drug that controls depression —**antidepressant** adj —**antidepressive** adj

antidote /ántidōt/ n **1** a substance that counteracts a poison **2** something that brings welcome relief from something unpleasant o an antidote to boredom

antifreeze /ánti freez/ n a liquid that lowers the freezing point of another liquid, especially the water in a vehicle's radiator

antifungal /ánti fúng g'l/ adj preventing or reducing the growth of fungi

antigen /ántijən/ n a protein that stimulates the production of an antibody —**antigenic** /ánti jénnik/ adj —**antigenically** adv

Antigua and Barbuda /an teˈego ənd baar bóodə/ island nation in the Leeward Islands in the Caribbean Sea. Cap. St John's. Pop. 66,970 (2001). —**Antiguan** adj, n

antihero /ánti heerõ/ (pl **-roes**) n an unheroic central character —**antiheroic** /ánti hə rõ ik/ adj —**antiheroism** /ánti hérrõ izəm/ n

antihistamine /ánti hístə meen/ n a drug that controls allergies

antiknock /ánti nók/ n a chemical added to petrol. Use: prevents knocking in engines.

Antilles ⬥ **Greater Antilles, Lesser Antilles**

antilock brake /ánti lók-/ n an electronically controlled braking or braking system to prevent a vehicle's wheels from locking under sudden braking

antimacassar /ánti mə kássər/ n a small cloth cover put on the back of a chair to protect the upholstery

antimatter /ánti matər/ n hypothetical matter composed of particles of the same mass as ordinary particles but having opposite properties

antimony /ántiməni, an tímməni/ n (symbol **Sb**) a brittle metallic chemical element. Use: alloys, electronics.

antinuclear /ánti nyóokli ər/ adj opposed to nuclear weapons or power

antioxidant /ánti óksidənt/ n a substance that inhibits oxidation

antiparticle /ánti paartik'l/ n an elementary particle with the same mass as the corresponding particle but other properties opposite to it

antipasto /ánti pastõ/ (pl **-ti** /-pasti/ or **-tos**) n an appetizer

antipathy /an típpəthi/ n a strongly negative feeling —**antipathetic** /ántipə théttik/ adj —**antipathetically** adv ◊ See note at **dislike**

antiperspirant /ánti púrspərənt/ n a substance that controls sweating —**antiperspirant** adj

antipodes /an típpə deez/ npl **1** places at opposite sides of the Earth **2** opposites of any kind n **3 Antipodes** Australia and New Zealand viewed in relation to Britain (infml) —**antipodal** adj —**Antipodean** /an típpə deˈe ən/ adj

antipsychotic /ánti sī kóttik/ adj relieving the symptoms of psychosis

antiquarian /ánti kwáiri ən/ adj of or dealing in antiques or rare books ▪ n also **antiquary** a collector of or dealer in antiques or antiquities —**antiquarianism** n

antiquated /ánti kwaytid/ adj ancient or old-fashioned ◊ See note at **old-fashioned**

antique /an teèk/ n **1** an old item collected or highly valued because of its age **2** the artistic styles of the classical period (fml) ▪ adj **1** dealing in antiques **2** old and valuable or collectible **3** from classical times (fml) **4** very old or old-fashioned (infml) ▪ vt (**-tiquing, -tiqued**) give an old and worn appearance to

antiquity /an tíkwəti/ (pl **-ties**) n **1** ancient

history **2** the state of being very old **3** an ancient object

antiracism /ánti ráyssizəm/ n opposition to racial discrimination —**antiracist** adj, n

antirejection /ánti ri jéksh'n/ adj preventing rejection of a transplanted organ or tissue

antisatellite /ánti sátt'l īt/ adj for use against enemy satellites

anti-Semitism /ántee sémmətizəm/ n hatred of or discrimination against Jews (disapproving) —**anti-Semite** /ánti seè mīt, ánti sémmīt/ n —**anti-Semitic** /ánti sə míttik/ adj

antiseptic /ánti séptik/ adj **1** controlling infection **2** unexciting and unimaginative ▪ n a substance that controls infection

antiserum /ánti seerəm/ (pl **-rums** or **-ra** /-rə/) n serum containing specific antibodies providing immunity against a disease or venom

antismoking /ánti smõking/ adj opposed to tobacco smoking, or designed to stop people smoking

antisocial /ánti sõsh'l/ adj **1** not conforming to a society's accepted standards of behaviour **2** not sociable —**antisocially** adv

antistatic /ánti státtik/, **antistat** /ánti stat/ adj controlling static electricity

antisubmarine /ánti súbmə reen/ adj for use against enemy submarines

antitank /ánti tánk/ adj for use against armoured tanks

antitheft /ánti théft/ adj preventing theft

antithesis /an títhəssiss/ (pl **-ses** /-seez/) n **1** the direct opposite of something **2** a use of words or phrases that contrast with each other —**antithetical** /ánti théttik'l/ adj

antitoxin /ánti tóksin/ n an antibody produced in response to a poison

antitrust /ánti trúst/ adj US intended to oppose business monopolies

antiviral /ánti vírəl/ adj describes medication for use against viruses

antivirus /ánti vírəss/ adj describes software that identifies and removes computer viruses

antler /ántlər/ n one of a pair of branched horns that grow on a deer's head

Antonioni /án tõni õni/, **Michelangelo** (b. 1912) Italian film director

Antony /ántəni/, **Mark** (83?–30 BC) Roman politician and general

antonym /ántənim/ n a word that means the opposite of another word —**antonymous** /an tónnəməss/ adj —**antonymy** /an tónnə mi/ n

Antrim /ántrim/ **1** town in NE Northern Ireland. Pop. 20,878 (1991). **2** former county in NE Northern Ireland

Antwerp /án twurp/ city in Belgium. Pop. 447,632 (1999).

ANU abbr Australian National University

anual incorrect spelling of **annual**

Anubis /ə nyóobiss/ n an ancient Egyptian god of the dead, represented with the head of a jackal

anus /áynəss/ n the opening at the end of the alimentary canal through which the body's solid waste matter is released

anvil /ánvil/ n 1 a metalworker's hammering block 2 ANAT = **incus**

anxiety /ang zí əti/ (pl **-ties**) n 1 a feeling or cause of worry 2 a cause of worry 3 a strong wish to do something ◦ his anxiety to please ◊ See note at **worry**

anxious /ángkshəss/ adj 1 nervous or worried 2 eager 3 producing anxiety ◦ a few anxious moments —**anxiously** adv —**anxiousness** n

any /énni/ det, pron 1 even one or a little ◦ I don't want any dessert. ◦ I didn't see any. 2 every ◦ Any financial adviser would agree. ■ det without limit ◦ any number of foods ■ adv 1 to some degree (before adjectives and adverbs) ◦ Are you feeling any better? 2 US at all (infml) ◦ Her manners haven't improved any.

anybody /énni bodi, -bədi/ pron anyone

anyhow /énni how/ adv 1 in any case 2 in a careless way ◦ ideas produced anyhow 3 nevertheless

any more adv (in negative statements and questions) 1 now ◦ They don't make them like this any more! 2 from now on ◦ I'm not tolerating this any more.

anyone /énni wun/ pron 1 every person 2 even one person 3 an unimportant person

anything /énni thing/ pron something unspecified or unknown ■ adv at all (in negative statements and questions) ◦ He isn't anything like his brother. ◊ **anything but** not at all

anyway /énni way/ adv 1 in any case 2 regardless of something 3 in a careless way

anywhere /énni wair/ pron an unidentified place ■ adv 1 to any place 2 at or in any place

Anzac /án zak/ n 1 ANZ a World War I soldier 2 Aus an Australian soldier 3 Aus a typical Australian man

Anzac Day n an Australian and New Zealand public holiday. Date: 25 April.

AO abbr Officer of the Order of Australia

AOC n a certification for French wine that guarantees its origin. Full form **appellation d'origine contrôlée**

AONB n countryside protected from development. Full form **Area of Outstanding Natural Beauty**

aorta /ay áwrtə/ (pl **-tas** or **-tae** /-tee/) n the main artery leaving the heart —**aortic** adj

Aouita /ow eétə/, **Said** (b. 1960) Moroccan runner

a.p. abbr additional premium

apace /ə páyss/ adv 1 quickly 2 US, Can abreast

Apache /ə páchi/ (pl same or **-es**) n a member of a Native North American people who now live in Arizona, New Mexico, and Oklahoma —**Apache** adj —**Apachean** adj

apalling incorrect spelling of **appalling**

aparatus incorrect spelling of **apparatus**

aparent incorrect spelling of **apparent**

aparently incorrect spelling of **apparently**

apart /ə paart/ adv 1 not together ◦ scheduled appointments a month apart 2 into pieces 3 moving away after being together 4 removed from consideration ◦ The bad food apart, it was a pleasant party. 5 into a poor state or difficult situation ◦ ripped the peace process apart ◊ **apart from** 1 with the exception of 2 in addition to

apartheid /ə paart hayt, -hīt/ n a political system that segregates peoples and favours one group over the others

apartment /ə paartmənt/ n US, Can a flat ■ **apartments** npl a suite of adjoining rooms (fml)

apathy /áppəthi/ n 1 lack of enthusiasm or energy 2 emotional emptiness —**apathetic** /áppə théttik/ adj —**apathetically** adv

apatosaurus /ə páttə sáwrəss/, **apatosaur** /ə páttə sawr/ n a large plant-eating dinosaur

ape n a tailless primate ■ vt (**aping, aped**) imitate ◊ See note at **imitate**

apear incorrect spelling of **appear**

Apennines /áppə nīnz/ mountain range that forms the backbone of peninsular Italy. Highest peak Monte Corno 2,912 m/9,554 ft.

aperitif /ə pérrə teéf/ n a drink before a meal

aperture /áppər tyoor/ n 1 a narrow opening 2 an opening that lets light in, e.g. into a camera

apetite incorrect spelling of **appetite**

apex /áy peks/ (pl **apexes** or **apices** /áypi seez, áp-/) n 1 the highest point or tip 2 the most successful point ◦ at the apex of his career

Apex /áy peks/, **APEX** n a discounted ticket for a journey bought in advance. Full form **advance-purchase excursion**

aphasia /ə fáyzi ə, -zhə/ n loss of language abilities caused by brain damage —**aphasic** adj

aphid /áy fid/ n an insect that feeds on plants

aphorism /áffəriz(ə)m/ n a short statement expressing a general truth —**aphoristic** /áffə rístik/ adj —**aphoristically** adv

aphrodisiac /áffrə dízzi ak/ n something that arouses sexual desire —**aphrodisiac** adj

ORIGIN The Greek word from which **aphrodisiac** comes is formed from the name of Aphrodite, the goddess of love and beauty in Greek mythology.

Aphrodite /áffrə díti/ n in Greek mythology, the goddess of love and beauty. Roman equivalent **Venus**

apiary /áypi əri/ (pl **-ies**) n a place where bees are raised for their honey

apiece /ə peéss/ adv for each

aplomb /ə plóm/ n confident poise

ORIGIN **Aplomb** derives from the French phrase à plomb 'perpendicular', literally 'according to the plumb line', and originally had the meaning 'the state of being perpendicular'.

apocalypse /ə pókə lips/ n 1 total destruction 2 a revelation of the future

apocalyptic /ə pókə líptik/ *adj* **1** predicting disaster **2** involving destruction

Apocrypha /ə pókrifə/ *n* **1** early Christian writings of disputed authenticity that are included in only some versions of the Bible (+ *sing or pl verb*) **2** **apocrypha** writings or reports that are not regarded as authentic

apocryphal /ə pókrif'l/ *adj* widely believed or retold but probably not true

apogee /áppə jee/ *n* **1** the best point of something **2** the point in its orbit when the Moon or a satellite is farthest from Earth —**apogean** /áppə jee ən/ *adj*

apolitical /áypə líttik'l/ *adj* uninterested in politics —**apolitically** *adv*

Apollo /ə póllō/ *n* **1** in Greek mythology, the god of prophecy **2** *also* **apollo** a handsome man (*literary*) —**Apollonian** /áppə lốni ən/ *adj*

apologetic /ə póllə jéttik/ *adj* **1** expressing an apology **2** defending something in speech or writing —**apologetically** *adv*

apologia /áppə lṓji ə/ *n* a formal written defence of a belief or theory (*fml*)

apologist /ə póllǝjist/ *n* somebody who defends a belief or theory

apologize /ə póllǝ jīz/ (**-gizing, -gized**), **apologise** *vi* express remorse or regret

apology /ə póllǝji/ (*pl* **-gies**) *n* **1** a statement expressing remorse or regret **2** a notification of nonattendance at a meeting (*fml*) **3** an inferior example (*humorous*) ○ *an apology for a hotel*

apophthegm /áppə them/, **apothegm** *n* a maxim —**apophthegmatic** /áppə theg máttik/ *adj*

apoplectic /áppə pléktik/ *adj* **1** furiously angry **2** exhibiting symptoms of a stroke (*archaic*)

apoplexy /áppə pleksi/ *n* **1** a fit of anger **2** a stroke caused by a brain haemorrhage (*archaic*)

apostasy /ə póstəssi/ *n* renunciation of a religious or political belief

apostate /ə pó stayt/ *n* somebody who renounces a belief

a posteriori /áy pos térri áw rī, aà-, -teeri-/ *adj, adv* reasoning from observed facts back to causes or from details back to generalities

apostle /ə póss'l/ *n* **1** a strong promoter of an idea or cause **2** *also* **Apostle** one of Jesus Christ's disciples —**apostleship** *n*

apostolic /áppə stóllik/ *adj* **1** of the pope **2** of the Apostles

apostrophe[1] /ə póstrəfi/ *n* the punctuation symbol (')

USAGE The **apostrophe** is used in contractions (e.g. *we've, it's, hadn't, 'em*) and some literary words (e.g. *e'en, ne'er*) to show that a letter or letters have been omitted. When used to mark the possessive form of nouns, the apostrophe is followed by *s* unless the noun is plural and already ends in *s*: *the cat's tail; my children's computer; the companies' accounts;*. For singular nouns ending in *s* it is often acceptable to use either ' or 's: *Dickens' best-loved novel* or *Dickens's best-loved novel*. An apostrophe

may also be used to indicate relationships of description (*a summer's day*) or measurement (*ton days' absence*).

apostrophe[2] /ə póstrəfi/ *n* a speech addressing an absent or imaginary person —**apostrophic** /áppə stróffik/ *adj*

apothegm *n* = **apophthegm**

apotheosis /ə pốthi ốssiss/ *n* **1** the highest level of glory or power **2** the best example ○ *the apotheosis of Romantic music*

app *n* a computer application (*infml*)

appal /ə páwl/ (**-palling, -palled**) *vt* cause shock or disgust —**appalling** *adj*

Appalachian Mountains /áppə láychi ən-/, **Appalachians** North American mountain system, stretching from SE Canada to central Alabama. Highest peak Mt Mitchell 2,037 m/6,684 ft.

Appalachian Trail *n* a long-distance footpath in the E United States

appall *vt* US = **appal**

appalling /ə páwling/ *adj* **1** shocking or horrifying **2** very bad —**appallingly** *adv*

~~apparently~~ incorrect spelling of **apparently**

apparatus /áppə ráytəss/ (*pl* **-tuses** *or same*) *n* **1** a piece of equipment **2** a system that allows something to function

apparel /ə párrəl/ *n* clothing (*fml*)

apparent /ə párrənt/ *adj* **1** obvious **2** seeming ○ *her apparent indifference* —**apparently** *adv*

apparition /áppə rísh'n/ *n* **1** an appearance of something ghostly **2** an appearance of something unexpected or strange (*humorous*)

~~appartment~~ incorrect spelling of **apartment**

appeal /ə peél/ *n* **1** an earnest or urgent request ○ *an emotional appeal for forgiveness* **2** a campaign to raise money **3** attractive qualities **4** a formal request to a higher authority requesting a review of a decision **5** in cricket, a request for an umpire to dismiss a batsman ■ *vi* **1** engage in a campaign to raise money **2** make an earnest request **3** make a formal request to a higher authority for a review of a decision **4** be interesting or attractive

appealing /ə peéling/ *adj* **1** attractive or pleasing **2** requesting help or sympathy ○ *an appealing glance* —**appealingly** *adv*

appear /ə peér/ *v* **1** *vi* come into view **2** *vi* begin to exist **3** *vi* become available for sale ○ *Cheaper printers have appeared on the market.* **4** *vti* seem likely **5** *vi* come before the public, especially to perform a duty or to act **6** *vi* be present in a law court and involved in legal proceedings

appearance /ə peérənss/ *n* **1** the fact of appearing ○ *the appearance of the first spring flowers* **2** the way somebody or something looks ○ *a youthful appearance* **3** an outward aspect that creates a particular impression (*often pl*) **4** a performance or attendance at a public occasion

~~appearence~~ incorrect spelling of **appearance**

appease /ə peéz/ (**-peasing, -peased**) *vt* **1** pacify somebody by agreeing to demands **2** satisfy a need —**appeasement** *n*

appellation /áppə láysh'n/ *n* a name or title *(fml)*

append /ə pénd/ *vt* add or attach something to the end of a document

appendage /ə péndij/ *n* **1** something small or secondary attached to something else **2** a projecting body part

appendectomy /áppən déktəmi/ *(pl* -**mies**), **appendicectomy** /áppəndi séktəmi/ *n* a surgical operation to remove an inflamed or burst appendix

appendicitis /ə péndi sítiss/ *n* inflammation of the appendix

appendix /ə péndiks/ *(pl* -**dixes** *or* -**dices** /-di seez/) *n* **1** a blind-ended tube leading from the large intestine, near its junction with the small intestine **2** a collection of additional information at the end of a book

appertain /áppər táyn/ *vi* belong or relate to *(fml)*

appetite /áppi tīt/ *n* **1** a desire for food **2** a craving

appetizer /áppi tīzər/, **appetiser** *n* **1** a small dish of food served before the main course of a meal **2** a sample of something designed to stimulate interest

appetizing /áppi tīzing/, **appetising** *adj* stimulating the appetite —**appetizingly** *adv*

applaud /ə pláwd/ *v* **1** *vti* clap hands in approval of **2** *vt* express approval of —**applaudable** *adj*

applause /ə pláwz/ *n* the clapping of hands in approval

apple /áp'l/ *n* **1** a firm round fruit with a central core **2** a fruit tree that produces apples ◊ **the apple of somebody's eye** somebody who is much loved and favoured by another person

applecart /áp'l kaart/ ◊ **upset the applecart** spoil a plan or arrangement

applet /ápplit/ *n* a simple computer program that performs a single task within a larger application **2** a computer program that is transferred over the Internet and executed by the recipient's computer

appliance /ə plī ənss/ *n* **1** a domestic electrical device **2** a fire engine

applicable /ə plíkəb'l, ápplikəb'l/ *adj* relevant or appropriate —**applicability** /ə plíkə bílləti, ápplikə-/ *n* —**applicably** *adv*

applicant /ápplikənt/ *n* somebody who formally applies for something ◊ See note at **candidate**

application /áppli káysh'n/ *n* **1** a formal request for something **2** the use of something or the process of putting something to use **3** a use or value for a specific purpose **4** hard work **5** a computer program or piece of software designed to enable the end user to perform a specific task

application service provider *n* a company that provides one or more program functions, e.g. accounting, on behalf of another enterprise

applicator /áppli kaytər/ *n* a device for applying a substance

applied /ə plíd/ *adj* put to practical use

appliqué /ə plee kay/ *n* fabric pieces sewn on fabric to form a design —**appliqué** *vt*

apply /ə plí/ *(-plies, -plied)* *v* **1** *vi* make a formal request **2** *vt* make use of something to achieve a result ○ *apply pressure to stop the bleeding* **3** *vi* be relevant **4** *vt* spread something over a surface **5** *vr* give more effort to something ○ *I could have applied myself more.*

appoint /ə póynt/ *vt* select for a position or job —**appointee** /ə póyn tee/ *n*

appointed /ə póyntid/ *adj* **1** previously agreed on ○ *met at the appointed time* **2** furnished *(usually in combination)* ○ *a well-appointed flat*

appointment /ə póyntmənt/ *n* **1** an arrangement to meet somebody **2** selection of somebody for a job or position **3** a job or position ■ **appointments** *npl* furniture and fittings

appologize incorrect spelling of **apologize**

appology incorrect spelling of **apology**

apportion /ə páwrsh'n/ *vt* divide among several people

apportionment /ə páwrsh'nmənt/ *n* the division and allocation of something

apposite /áppəzit/ *adj* particularly appropriate —**appositely** *adv* —**appositeness** *n*

apposition /áppə zísh'n/ *n* **1** the positioning of one thing next to another **2** the relationship between adjacent noun phrases that refer to the same person or thing, as in 'my son, the actor' —**appositional** *adj*

appraise /ə práyz/ *(-praising, -praised)* *vt* **1** estimate the monetary value of **2** assess the merits or quality of —**appraisal** *n*

appreciable /ə preeshəb'l/ *adj* large enough to be noticed —**appreciably** *adv*

appreciate /ə preeshi ayt/ *(-ating, -ated)* *v* **1** *vt* be grateful for **2** *vt* value highly **3** *vi* gain in value —**appreciation** /ə preeshi áysh'n/ *n*

appreciative /ə preeshi ətiv, -shətiv/ *adj* grateful or approving —**appreciatively** *adv*

apprehend /áppri hénd/ *vt* **1** put under arrest **2** understand or perceive the importance or existence of

apprehension /áppri hénsh'n/ *n* **1** dread **2** an idea formed by observation **3** the arrest of somebody *(fml)* **4** the fact of grasping the importance or existence of something *(fml)*

apprehensive /áppri hénssiv/ *adj* worried that something bad will happen —**apprehensively** *adv* —**apprehensiveness** *n*

apprentice /ə préntiss/ *n* **1** somebody who is learning a trade or craft by working with a skilled professional **2** a novice ■ *vt* (**-ticing**, **-ticed**) give or take work as an apprentice ○ *apprenticed himself to an electrician* —**apprenticeship** *n* ◊ See note at **beginner**

apprise /ə príz/ *(-prising, -prised)* *vt* inform *(fml)*

approach /ə próch/ *v* **1** *vti* move closer to somebody or something **2** *vt* speak to in order to ask for something **3** *vt* deal with in a particular way ○ *approached the problem carefully*

4 *vt* come close to being ○ *statements approaching libel* **5** *vti* come closer to something in time **6** *vi* in golf, hit a ball from the fairway towards the green ■ *n* **1** a coming nearer in space or time **2** a method **3** an informal request or proposal *(often pl)* **4** something that is almost or close to being something else ○ *an approach to an apology* **5** a path or course leading to something **6** in golf, a shot from the fairway towards the green

approachable /ə prốchəb'l/ *adj* **1** invitingly friendly **2** easily accessible —**approachability** /ə prôchə bílləti/ *n* —**approachably** *adv*

approbation /áprə báysh'n/ *n* approval or consent —**approbatory** *adj*

~~approch~~ incorrect spelling of **approach**

appropriate *adj* /ə prôpri ət/ suitable for the occasion or circumstances ■ *vt* /ə prôpri ayt/ **(-ating, -ated)** **1** take something for your own use **2** set money aside for a particular purpose —**appropriately** *adv* —**appropriateness** *n*

appropriation /ə prôpri áysh'n/ *n* **1** the taking of something for your own use **2** a sum of money set aside for a particular purpose *(often pl)*

approval /ə proõv'l/ *n* **1** a favourable opinion **2** official agreement or permission ◇ **on approval** with the chance to try something before you buy it

approve /ə proõv/ **(-proving, -proved)** *v* **1** *vi* consider to be satisfactory or good **2** *vt* officially agree to or accept as satisfactory —**approved** *adj* —**approving** *adj* —**approvingly** *adv*

approx. *abbr* **1** approximate **2** approximately

approximate *adj* /ə prôksimət/ **1** nearly exact in number or quantity **2** similar ■ *vti* /ə prôksi mayt/ **(-mating, -mated)** be similar to something else —**approximately** *adv* —**approximation** /ə prôksi máysh'n/ *n*

~~approximately~~ incorrect spelling of **approximately**

appurtenance /ə púrtinəns/ *(fml)* *n* an accessory *(often pl)* ■ **appurtenances** *npl* equipment —**appurtenant** *adj*

APR *abbr* annual percentage rate

Apr. *abbr* April

~~apreciate~~ incorrect spelling of **appreciate**

après-ski /ápray skee/ *n* social activities after skiing —**après-ski** *adj*

apricot /áypri kot/ *n* **1** a small round fruit with a furry yellowish-orange skin **2** a fruit tree that produces apricots

April /áyprəl/ *n* the 4th month of the year in the Gregorian calendar

> **ORIGIN** The Latin word from which **April** comes probably goes back to the name of the Greek goddess Aphrodite. It came into Latin by way of Etruscan, an extinct language spoken in parts of Italy before Roman times.

April Fools' Day *n* traditionally, a day on which practical jokes are played. Date: 1 April.

a priori /áy prī áwrī, aá pri áwri/ *adj* **1** based on something that is already known **2** assumed or conceived beforehand —**a priori** *adv*

apron /áyprən/ *n* **1** a protective garment tied over clothes **2** a projecting edge of a platform **3** the parking area for planes at an airport

> **ORIGIN** 'An apron' was originally 'a napron': the *n* was lost when this common combination of words was misinterpreted. The earlier form *napron* comes from an old French word related to English *napkin*.

apropos /áprə pố/ *(fml)* *prep* in regard to ■ *adj* just right ■ *adv* incidentally

~~apropriate~~ incorrect spelling of **appropriate**

~~aproximately~~ incorrect spelling of **approximately**

apse *n* a rounded projecting part of a building, especially the end of a church where the altar is

apt *adj* **1** very appropriate **2** having a tendency to do something ○ *apt to get angry* **3** quick to learn —**aptly** *adv* —**aptness** *n*

aptitude /ápti tyood/ *n* **1** a natural ability **2** quickness in learning ◊ See note at **ability, talent**

Aqaba, Gulf of /ákəbə/ northeastern arm of the Red Sea, bordered by Egypt, Israel, Jordan, and Saudi Arabia. Length 160 km/99 mi.

aqua /ákwə/ *n* water used as a solvent *(technical)*

aqua- *prefix* water ○ *aquatint*

~~aquaduct~~ incorrect spelling of **aqueduct**

~~aquaint~~ incorrect spelling of **acquaint**

~~aquaintance~~ incorrect spelling of **acquaintance**

aqualung /ákwə lung/ *n* an underwater breathing apparatus used by divers

aquamarine /ákwə mə reén/ *n* **1** a greenish-blue form of beryl. Use: gems. **2** a greenish-blue colour —**aquamarine** *adj*

aquaplane /ákwə playn/ *n* a board on which a rider stands while being pulled by a motorboat ■ *vi* **(-planing, -planed)** **1** ride on an aquaplane **2** skid out of control on a wet road

aquarium /ə kwáiri əm/ *(pl* **-ums** *or* **-a** /-ri ə/*)* *n* **1** a container for fish **2** a building containing fish and other water organisms for study and display

Aquarius /ə kwáiri əss/ *n* **1** a zodiacal constellation in the southern hemisphere **2** the 11th sign of the zodiac —**Aquarius** *adj*

aquatic /ə kwáttik/ *adj* **1** of, in, or on water **2** living in water —**aquatically** *adv*

aquatint /ákwə tint/ *n* **1** an etching method producing colours like watercolours **2** an etched picture made using the aquatint method

Aqueduct: ancient Roman aqueduct in Tarragona, Spain

Yasir Arafat

aqueduct /ákwi dukt/ *n* **1** a bridge carrying a canal across a valley **2** a pipe or channel for moving water to a lower level, often across a great distance

aqueous /áykwi əss, ákwi-/ *adj* watery

aquiline /ákwi līn/ *adj* **1** describes a nose that is thin and curved like an eagle's beak or a face with such a nose **2** of eagles

Aquinas /ə kwínəss/, **Thomas, St** (1225–74) Italian philosopher and theologian

~~aquire~~ incorrect spelling of **acquire**

~~aquit~~ incorrect spelling of **acquit**

Aquitaine /ákwi tayn/ region of SW France. Pop. 2,908,359 (1999).

~~aquittal~~ incorrect spelling of **acquittal**

Ar *symbol* argon

Arab /árrəb/ *n* a member of an Arabic-speaking Semitic people who live throughout SW Asia and North Africa —**Arab** *adj*

arabesque /árrə bésk/ *n* **1** an ornate design that combines curves and natural shapes such as leaves and flowers **2** a ballet position in which the dancer stands on one leg and has the other raised and stretched out behind **3** a piece of classical music with an ornate melody

Arabia /ə ráybi ə/, **Arabian Peninsula** peninsula of SW Asia, bordering the Persian Gulf, the Arabian Sea, and the Red Sea

Arabian /ə ráybi ən/ *adj* of Arabia ■ *n* somebody from Arabia

Arabian Sea arm of the Indian Ocean between the Arabian Peninsula and South Asia

Arabic /árrəbik/ *n* a Semitic language that is the official language of several countries of SW Asia and North Africa ■ *adj* **1** of Arabia **2** of Arabic

Arabic numeral *n* any of the standard numbers 0, 1, 2, 3, 4, 5, 6, 7, 8, and 9

arable /árrəb'l/ *adj* describes land suitable for growing crops ■ *n* land suitable for cultivation

arachnid /ə ráknid/ *n* an eight-legged organism of the class that includes spiders and scorpions

arachnophobia /ə ráknə fóbi ə/ *n* fear of spiders —**arachnophobe** /ə ráknəfób/ *n* —**arachnophobic** *adj*

Arafat /árrə fat/, **Yasir** (*b.* 1929) chairman of the Palestinian Liberation Organization (1968–) and president of the Palestinian National Authority (1996–)

Aral Sea /árrəl-/ inland sea in SW Kazakhstan and NW Uzbekistan

Aramaic /árrə máy ik/ *n* a Semitic language of the ancient Near East, still spoken in the region —**Aramaic** *adj*

Aran /árrən/ *adj* describes traditional knitwear of the Aran Islands usually using cable stitch and diamond patterns

Aran Islands group of three islands, Inishmoor, Inishmaan, and Inisheer, situated at the mouth of Galway Bay in W Ireland. Pop. 803 (1981).

Ararat, Mt /árrə rat/ mountain in E Turkey, the landing place of Noah's Ark according to the Bible. Height 5,137 m / 16,854 ft.

arbiter /aárbitər/ *n* **1** somebody with the authority to settle a dispute **2** somebody with influence over what people say, think, or do

arbitrage /aárbitrij, -traazh/ *n* the simultaneous buying and selling of the same securities or commodities in different markets in order to make a quick profit —**arbitrageur** /aárbi traa zhúr/ *n*

arbitrary /aárbitrəri/ *adj* **1** based on wishes or feelings, not on facts or observations **2** randomly chosen —**arbitrarily** /aárbitrərəli, aárbi tráirəli/ *adv* —**arbitrariness** /-/ *n*

arbitrate /aárbi trayt/ (-**trating**, -**trated**) *v* **1** *vti* settle a dispute between others **2** *vt* submit a dispute to a third party for settlement —**arbitration** /aárbi tráysh'n/ *n* —**arbitrator** *n*

arbor¹ /aárbər/ *n* an axle on a machine or power tool

arbor² *n US* = **arbour**

arboreal /aar báwri əl/ *adj* **1** of trees **2** living in trees

arboretum /aárbə reétəm/ (*pl* -**tums** *or* -**ta** /-tə/) *n* a place where trees are planted for study and display

arbour /aárbər/ *n* **1** a place in a garden where plants are trained to give shade **2** a three-sided trellis for training plants, often incorporating a seat

arc *n* **1** a curved line or direction of movement **2** a section of a circle **3** an electrical discharge that flows across a gap ■ *vi* (**arcing** *or* **arcking**, **arced** *or* **arcked**) form or move in an arc

arcade /aar káyd/ *n* **1** a series of arches **2** a passageway with arches **3** an avenue of shops **4** an enclosed area with games machines —**arcaded** *adj*

Arcadia[1] /aar káydi ə/, **arcadia** *n* an imagined place of rural bliss —**Arcadian** *adj*

Arcadia[2] /aar káydi ə/ mountainous region of the central Peloponnese, SW Greece —**Arcadian** *adj, n*

arcane /aar káyn/ *adj* **1** mysteriously obscure **2** difficult or impossible to understand —**arcanely** *adv* —**arcaneness** *n* ◊ See note at obscure

arch[1] *n* **1** a curved structure forming the top of a window, doorway, or other space **2** something shaped like an arch ○ *the arch of his eyebrows* ■ *v* **1** *vt* form into an arch shape **2** *vi* move in a curving line —**arched** *adj*

arch[2] *adj* **1** greatest, especially most hostile **2** knowingly playful or mischievous —**archly** *adv* —**archness** *n*

arch- *prefix* **1** chief, most important ○ *archbishop* **2** extreme or very great ○ *archenemy*

-arch *suffix* leader, ruler ○ *matriarch* —**-archic** *suffix* —**-archy** *suffix*

Archaean /aar kée ən/, **Archean** *n* an aeon of geological time 3,800–2,500 million years ago —**Archaean** *adj*

archaeology /aarki ólləji/ *n* the study of ancient cultures through the remains of their buildings and artefacts —**archaeological** *adj* —**archaeologist** *n*

archaeopteryx /aarki óptəriks/ *n* a prehistoric bird

archaic /aar káyik/ *adj* **1** belonging to a much earlier time **2** describes a word that is no longer used in ordinary language **3** outmoded —**archaically** *adv*

archaism /aar kay izəm, -ki-/ *n* a word, expression, practice, or method from an earlier time that is no longer used —**archaist** *n*

archangel /aark aynjəl/ *n* a chief or principal angel —**archangelic** *adj*

archbishop /aarch bíshəp/ *n* a bishop of the highest rank

archbishopric /aarch bíshəprik/ *n* **1** an archdiocese **2** the status or term of office of an archbishop

archdeacon /aarch deékən/ *n* a member of the clergy of a rank below bishop who acts as a bishop's assistant —**archdeaconate** *n* —**archdeaconship** *n*

archdiocese /aarch dí əssiss/ *n* the area under an archbishop's control —**archdiocesan** /aarch dī óssəss'n/ *adj*

archduchess /aarch dúchiss/ *n* **1** an archduke's wife **2** a princess, especially in imperial Austria

archduke /aarch dyóok/ *n* a prince, especially in imperial Austria

archenemy /aarch énnəmi/ (*pl* -**mies**) *n* **1** a worst enemy **2** *also* **Archenemy** Satan

archeology etc. = **archaeology etc.**

archer /aarchər/ *n* somebody who uses a bow and arrow —**archery** *n*

archetype /aarki tīp/ *n* **1** something that all other things of the type are based on **2** a typical example **3** a recurring symbol in art or literature —**archetypal** /aarki tīp'l, -tīp'l/ *adj*

Archimedes /aarki meé deez/ (287–212 BC) Greek mathematician

archipelago /aarki péllə gō/ (*pl* -**gos** *or* -**goes**) *n* **1** a group of islands (*often in placenames*) **2** an area of sea with many islands —**archipelagic** /aarkipə lájjik/ *adj*

architect /aarki tekt/ *n* **1** somebody who designs buildings and advises on their construction **2** a creator of something ○ *the architect of economic reform* **3** a developer of the structure of a computer system or program

architectonic /aarki tek tónnik/ *adj* **1** of architecture or architectural qualities **2** of the classification of knowledge —**architectonically** *adv*

architecture /aarki tekchər/ *n* **1** the art and science of designing buildings **2** a particular building style —**architectural** /aarki tékchərəl/ *adj*

architrave /aarki trayv/ *n* **1** the part of a classical building that sits directly on top of the columns **2** a decorative moulding around a door or window surround

archive /aar kīv/ *n* **1** a collection of documents (*often pl*) **2** a place where archives are held **3** a copy of computer files stored, often in compressed form, on tape or disk **4** a computer file containing other compressed files **5** a directory of files that Internet users can access using anonymous FTP ■ *vt* (-**chiving**, -**chived**) **1** put a document in an archive **2** transfer computer data from a hard disk to an external storage medium **3** combine and compress computer files for storage —**archival** /aar kīv'l/ *adj*

archivist /aarkivist/ *n* somebody who looks after a document archive

archway /aarch way/ *n* an arched entrance

arc lamp, arc light *n* a bright electric light

arctic /aarktik/ *adj* very cold (*infml*)

Arctic /aarktik/ region north of the Arctic Circle —**Arctic** *adj*

Arctic Circle *n* the parallel of latitude at 66°30′N that marks the boundary of the Arctic

Arctic Ocean world's smallest ocean, mostly ice-covered, situated north of the Arctic Circle. Depth 5,500 m/17,880 ft.

Arden /aard'n/, **John** (*b.* 1930) British playwright

Ardennes /aar dén/ forested plateau in SE Belgium, Luxembourg, and NE France, site of the Battle of the Bulge in 1944

ardent /aard'nt/ *adj* passionate —**ardently** *adv*

ardour /aardər/ *n* intense emotion

arduous /aardyoo əss/ *adj* **1** difficult to achieve or endure **2** difficult to climb or cross —**arduously** *adv* —**arduousness** *n* ◊ See note at hard

are[1] *(stressed)* /aar/ *(unstressed)* /ər/ *v* the plural and 2nd person present singular tense of 'be'

are[2] /aar/ *n* a metric unit of area equal to 100 sq. m

area /áiri ə/ *n* 1 the extent of part of a surface enclosed within a boundary 2 a part of a whole ○ *this area of the brain* 3 a region or district 4 a subject, field of knowledge, or sphere of activity

arena /ə reénə/ *n* 1 a stadium 2 a place or situation where there is intense activity

aren't /aarnt/ *contr (infml)* 1 am not *(in questions)* 2 are not

Ares /aà reez/ *n* the Greek god of war. Roman equivalent **Mars**

Argentina /aàrjən teénə/, **Argentine, the** /aàrjən teen, -tin/ country in S South America. Cap. Buenos Aires. Pop. 37,384,816 (2001). —**Argentine** *adj, n* —**Argentinian** /aàrjən tínni ən/ *adj, n*

argon /aàr gon/ *n* *(symbol* **Ar***)* a chemical element that is an inert gas. Use: electric lights, gas shield in welding.

argot /aàrgō, -gət/ *n* jargon

arguable /aàrgyoo əb'l/ *adj* 1 plausible or possible 2 open to dispute —**arguably** *adv*

argue /aàrgyoo/ **(-guing, -gued)** *v* 1 have a disagreement or quarrel 2 *vti* give reasons for something ○ *argued that they should stay* ○ *argued for more days off* 3 *vti* provide evidence for something ○ *The decrease in crime may argue for a happier society.* ◊ See note at **disagree**

argueing *incorrect spelling of* **arguing**

arguement *incorrect spelling of* **argument**

argument /aàrgyōomənt/ *n* 1 a disagreement or quarrel 2 a reason put forward 3 the main point of view expressed in a book, report, or speech 4 a debate about whether something is correct

argumentation /aàrgyōomən táysh'n/ *n* 1 a debate 2 logical reasoning

argumentative /aàrgyōo méntətiv/ *adj* 1 inclined to disagree 2 characterized by disagreement —**argumentatively** *adv* —**argumentativeness** *n*

argyle /aar gíl/ *adj* knitted with a pattern of coloured diamonds ■ *n* a sock or sweater with an argyle diamond pattern

ORIGIN The **argyle** pattern is based on the tartan of the branch of the Campbell clan who lived in Argyll in Scotland.

Argyll and Bute /aar gíl ənd byoot/ administrative area in W Scotland

aria /aàri ə/ *n* a song in an opera sung solo or as a duet

arid /árrid/ *adj* 1 describes a region with an annual rainfall of less than 25 cm/10 in 2 completely lacking in interest or excitement —**aridity** /ə ríddəti/ *n* —**aridness** *n* ◊ See note at **dry**

Aries /áireez/ *n* 1 a zodiacal constellation in the northern hemisphere 2 the 1st sign of the zodiac —**Aries** *adj*

arise /ə ríz/ **(arising, arose** /ə róz/, **arisen** /ə rízz'n/**)** *vi* 1 occur or come to notice 2 stand up *(literary)*

aristocracy /árri stókrəssi/ *(pl* **-cies***)* *n* 1 people of a hereditary nobility or of the highest social class 2 any group regarded as superior to all others 3 government by an elite group, especially a hereditary nobility

aristocrat /árristə krat/ *n* a member of an aristocracy —**aristocratic** /árristə kráttik/ *adj*

Aristophanes /árri stóffə neez/ (448?–385 BC) Greek dramatist

Aristotle /árri stótt'l/ (384–322 BC) Greek philosopher and scientist

arithmetic *n* /ə ríthmətik/ 1 the branch of mathematics that deals with addition, subtraction, multiplication, and division 2 calculations using basic mathematics ■ *adj* /árrith méttik/ of arithmetic —**arithmetical** /árrith méttik'l/ *adj* —**arithmetically** *adv* —**arithmetician** /ə ríthmə tísh'n/ *n*

arithmetic logic unit *n* the circuit in a computer's central processing unit that makes calculations based on the results of calculations

arithmetic progression *n* a sequence of numbers in which a constant figure is added to each term to give the next

Arizona /árri zónə/ state in the SW United States. Cap: Phoenix. Pop: 5,130,632 (2000).

Arjuna /aàrjoónə/ *n* in Hindu mythology, a prince to whom Krishna explains Hindu doctrine

ark *n* 1 in the Bible, Noah's ship in the story of the Flood 2 *also* **Ark, Ark of the Covenant** the chest into which, in biblical accounts, Moses placed the Ten Commandments 3 *also* **Ark** a cabinet in a synagogue containing the Torah scrolls

Arkansas /aàrkən saw/ state in the south-central United States. Cap: Little Rock. Pop: 2,673,400 (2000).

Arkwright /aàrk rít/, **Sir Richard** (1732–92) British inventor of the cotton spinning frame

Arlington /aàrlingtən/ 1 city in NE Virginia. Pop. 177,275 (1998). 2 city in NE Texas. Pop. 306,497 (1998).

arm[1] *n* 1 a limb attached to the shoulder of the human body 2 a part of a chair that supports the human arm 3 a projecting part ○ *an arm of the sea* 4 a division of a larger group ○ *infantry as a combat arm* —**armful** *n* ◊ **an arm and a leg** a lot of money *(infml)* ◊ **with open arms** in a welcoming way

arm[2] *v* 1 *vti* equip somebody or something with weapons 2 *vt* activate a bomb or other weapon 3 *vt* provide somebody with something useful, e.g. information ■ *n* a weapon *(often pl)* ■ **arms** *npl* 1 warfare 2 a coat of arms ◊ **be up in arms** protest or complain angrily

armada /aar maáda/ n a large fleet of ships

armadillo /aàrmə dílló/ (pl **-los** or **same**) n a burrowing mammal with a hard plated body

Armageddon /aàrmə gédd'n/ n an all-destroying war

> **ORIGIN** The original **Armageddon**, in the Bible, is a battle between the forces of good and evil that is predicted to mark the end of the world and precede the Day of Judgment (Revelation 16:16).

Armagh /aar maá/ **1** town in S Northern Ireland. Pop. 14,640 (1991). **2** former county in S Northern Ireland

armature /aàrmachər/ n **1** the moving part in an electromagnetic device **2** a keeper for a magnet **3** a framework for a sculpture

armchair /aàrm chair/ n a chair with rests for the arms ■ adj with no first-hand experience o an armchair tourist

armed forces npl the troops of a country who fight on land, at sea, or in the air, taken as a whole

Armenia /aar meéni ə/ country in W Asia, between the Black and Caspian seas. Cap. Yerevan.　Pop.　3,336,100　(2001). —**Armenian** n, adj

armhole /aàrm hól/ n a hole in a garment for the arm to fit through

armistice /aàrmistiss/ n a truce in a war

Armistice Day n the anniversary of the end of World War I. Date: 11 November.

armour /aàrmər/ n **1** protective clothing of metal or leather worn by soldiers in the past **2** also **armour plate** a protective layer of metal covering a military vehicle **3** a protective covering on a plant or animal

armoured /aàrmərd/ adj **1** with protective armour **2** equipped with armoured vehicles

armourer /aàrmərər/ n **1** a maker of weapons and armour **2** a soldier who repairs small arms

armoury /aàrməri/ (pl **-ies**) n **1** a building for storing weapons **2** a collection of weapons **3** a building for military training **4** resources of any kind

armpit /aàrm pit/ n a hollow under the arm where it joins the body

arm's-length adj without a close relationship o an arms-length business transaction

Armstrong /aàrm strong/, **Louis** (1901–71) US jazz trumpeter, singer, and bandleader

Armstrong, Neil (b. 1930) US astronaut

Barnaby's

Neil Armstrong

army /aàrmi/ (pl **-mies**) n **1** the branch of the armed forces trained to fight on land **2** any trained or armed fighting force **3** a large organized group o an army of volunteers

Arne /aarn/, **Thomas** (1710–78) British composer

Arnhem Land /aàrnəm-/ region in N Australia, site of one of Australia's largest Aboriginal reserves

Arno /aàrnō/ river in Tuscany, central Italy. Length 240 km/150 mi.

Arnold /aàrn'ld/, **Matthew** (1822–88) British poet and critic

A-road n a primary route other than a motorway

aroma /ə rómə/ n **1** a smell or odour **2** a subtle quality o an aroma of scandal ◊ See note at **smell**

aromatherapy /ə rómə thérrəpi/ n treatment of physical and psychological disorders using plant oils —**aromatherapist** n

aromatic /árrə máttik/ adj having a pleasant smell ■ n a fragrant substance or plant —**aromatically** adv

arose past tense of **arise**

around /ə równd/ prep **1** to or on another side of o around the corner **2** surrounding or on all sides of **3** regarding o felt anxiety around the process of globalization ■ adv **1** on all sides **2** in an opposite direction o turned around **3** present or existing o since computers have been around ■ adv, prep **1** from place to place **2** in the vicinity **3** approximately ◊ **have been around** have had enough experience of life not to be easily deceived (infml)

arouse /ə rówz/ (**arousing, aroused**) vt **1** stimulate a response o aroused their interest **2** stimulate sexual desire in somebody —**arousal** n

Arp /aarp/, **Jean** (1887–1966) French sculptor

arpeggio /aar péjji ō/ (pl **-os**) n a series of musical notes in a chord

arr. abbr **1** arranged **2** arrival **3** arrives

arraign /ə ráyn/ vt **1** charge with an offence in court **2** accuse —**arraignment** n

arrange /ə ráynj/ (**-ranging, -ranged**) v **1** vt plan or prepare for something **2** vt make an agreement for an event to happen **3** vt put somebody or something in order or position **4** vti adapt music —**arrangement** n —**arranger** n

arrant /árrənt/ adj utter or extreme (disapproving) o arrant nonsense —**arrantly** adv

array /ə ráy/ n **1** a collection **2** a striking or orderly arrangement **3** fine clothes (literary) **4** an ordered arrangement of numbers or data ■ vt **1** arrange in an orderly way (fml) **2** put clothes or ornaments on somebody (literary) o was arrayed in ermine and diamonds

arrears /ə reérz/ npl unpaid debts

arrest /ə rést/ vt **1** take into custody **2** stop or slow (fml) **3** capture or hold (fml) o arrested *our attention* ■ *n* 1 the taking of somebody into custody 2 legal custody ○ *under arrest* 3 a sudden stopping of the movement or operation of something —**arresting** *adj* —**arrestingly** *adv*

Arrhenius /ə reénee əss/, **Svante August** (1859–1927) Swedish chemist. He developed a theory of ions carrying electrical charges.

arrival /ə rív'l/ *n* 1 the process, result, or time of arriving 2 somebody or something that arrives

arrive /ə rív/ (-**riving**, -**rived**) *vi* 1 reach a place 2 come, begin, or happen ○ *The moment of departure had arrived.* 3 reach after consideration or discussion ○ *arrive at a decision* 4 become successful or famous (*infml*)

arrogant /árrəgənt/ *adj* proudly contemptuous or self-important —**arrogance** *n* —**arrogantly** *adv* ◊ See note at **proud**

arrogate /árrə gayt/ (-**gating**, -**gated**) *vt* claim or take without right (*fml*) —**arrogation** /árrə gáysh'n/ *n*

arrow /árrō/ *n* 1 a pointed missile shot from a bow 2 an arrow-shaped direction sign

arrowhead /árrō hed/ *n* the point of an arrow

arrow key *n* a computer key that moves the cursor

arrowroot /árrō root/ *n* a starch derived from the rhizome of a tropical plant. Use: cookery.

> **ORIGIN Arrowroot** is altered from *aru-aru*, the name for the plant in a Native South American language of Guyana and neighbouring countries. It literally means 'meal of meals', but because the root of the plant was used to treat wounds caused by poisoned arrows, English-speakers changed it to **arrowroot**.

Arroyo /ə róy ō/, **Gloria** (*b.* 1947) president of the Philippines (2001–)

arse *n* a taboo term for the buttocks or anus (*offensive*)

arsenal /áarss'nəl/ *n* 1 a place where weapons are stored 2 a stockpile of weapons 3 a supply of resources

arsenic /áarssnik/ *n* (*symbol* **As**) 1 a poisonous solid chemical element. Use: alloys. 2 a compound of arsenic. Use: pesticide.

arson /áarss'n/ *n* the crime of setting fire to property —**arsonist** *n*

art *n* 1 the creation of beautiful or thought-provoking things 2 the works produced by art 3 a branch of art, such as painting or sculpture 4 creation by human beings rather than nature 5 technique or craft 6 skill or ability 7 cunning (*literary*) ■ **arts** *npl* 1 creative activities such as painting, music, and literature 2 nonscientific subjects

art. *abbr* 1 article 2 artificial 3 artillery 4 artist

Art deco: Chrysler Building, New York City (1930), designed by William van Alen

art deco /-dékō/, **Art Deco** *n* a 1930s design style using geometrical shapes and bold colours

artefact /áarti fakt/, **artifact** *n* an object made by a human being

Artemis /áartəmiss/ *n* in Greek mythology, the goddess of hunting. Roman equivalent **Diana**

arteriosclerosis /aar teéri ō sklə róssiss/ *n* the arterial disease atherosclerosis

artery /áartəri/ (*pl* -**ies**) *n* 1 a major blood vessel carrying blood away from the heart 2 a main route —**arterial** /aar teéri əl/ *adj*

artesian well /aar teézi ən-/ *n* a well supplying water by natural pressure

> **ORIGIN** The **artesian well** is named after the region of Artois (formerly *Arteis*) in NE France. The first artesian wells were drilled in Artois in the 18C.

artful /áartf'l/ *adj* 1 cunning and subtle 2 skilful and adroit —**artfully** *adv* —**artfulness** *n*

art gallery *n* a place that exhibits and sells works of art

arthritis /aar thrítiss/ *n* a condition causing stiff and painful joints —**arthritic** /aar thríttik/ *adj*, *n* —**arthritically** *adv*

arthropod /áarthrə pod/ *n* an invertebrate animal such as an insect, arachnid, centipede, or crustacean —**arthropod** *adj*

Arthur /áarthər/ *n* in medieval legend, a king of the Britons whose court was based at Camelot —**Arthurian** /aar thyoóri ən/ *adj*

~~artic~~ incorrect spelling of **arctic**

~~artical~~ incorrect spelling of **article**

artichoke /áartichōk/ (*pl* -**chokes** *or same*) *n* 1 a large scaly flower bud eaten as a vegetable 2 a plant that produces artichokes 3 a Jerusalem artichoke

article /áartik'l/ *n* 1 a piece of nonfiction writing such as one in a newspaper 2 an object or item 3 the word 'a', 'an', or 'the' used before a noun ■ *vt* (-**cling**, -**cled**) bind by contract, especially for professional training

articles of association *npl* company regulations

articulate *adj* /aar tíkyoōlət/ 1 able to express thoughts, ideas, and feelings coherently in speech 2 expressed coherently ■ *v* /aar tíkyoō layt/ (-**lating**, -**lated**) 1 *vt* express or communicate 2 *vti* speak or say distinctly 3 *vti* join in a way that allows movement —**articulacy** *n* —**articulated** /-laytid/ *adj*

—**articulately** adv —**articulateness** n
—**articulation** /-láysh'n/ n

artifact n — artefact

artifice /aártifiss/ n (fml) 1 a clever trick 2 insincere behaviour

artificial /aárti físh'l/ adj 1 made by human beings 2 made in imitation of something natural 3 insincere —**artificiality** /aártifishi álləti/ n —**artificially** adv

artificial insemination n a method of inducing pregnancy without sexual intercourse

artificial intelligence n the ability of computers to perform functions that normally require human intelligence

artificial life n the use of computer systems to simulate various aspects of natural human behaviour, such as learning and reproduction

artificial respiration n any method of forcing air into the lungs of somebody who has stopped breathing

artillery /aar tílləri/ n 1 powerful guns used by armed forces 2 soldiers using powerful guns

artisan /aárti zan, -zán/ n a skilled craftsperson —**artisanship** /aártiz'n ship/ n

artist /aártist/ n 1 a creator of art, especially a painter or sculptor 2 a performer or entertainer 3 a skilled person

artiste /aar teést/ n a performer or entertainer

artistic /aar tístik/ adj 1 good at or appreciative of art 2 of art —**artistically** adv

artistry /aártistri/ n 1 artistic ability 2 great skill

artless /aártləss/ adj 1 without deception 2 totally natural 3 lacking skill, knowledge, or elegance —**artlessly** adv —**artlessness** n

art nouveau /aárt noo vô, aàr-/, **Art Nouveau** n a late 19C design style using flowing lines

arts and crafts n the creative design of everyday objects (+ sing or pl verb)

artwork /aárt wurk/ n 1 a work of art 2 illustrative material for use in a publication

arty /aárti/ (**-ier, -iest**) adj affectedly artistic (infml)

Aruba /ə roóbə/ island off the N Venezuela coast, a self-governing part of the Netherlands. Pop. 70,007 (2001).

arum lily /áirəm-/ n a white ornamental lily

Aryan /áiri ən, árri-/ n 1 an Indo-European ancestor or descendant (dated) 2 in Nazi ideology, a person regarded as racially superior —**Aryan** adj

as (stressed) /az/ (unstressed) /əz/ conj 1 at the time that o fell down as I was running downstairs 2 what o Do as you like! 3 because o As we are very late we must hurry up. 4 introduces a comparison o as white as snow 5 introduces a clause referring to a previous statement o As I said, it's not easy. 6 in the way that o Everything went as planned. ■ prep 1 at the time when o As a child I was very mischievous. 2 in the capacity of o As a manager I am supposed to think strategically. ◇ **as far as** the extent to which a situation holds or is relevant o As far as I know, they are still living in Australia. ◇ **as is** in the present condition ◇ **as long as** provided that ◇ **as such** in the precise sense (often with a negative) o She had no experience as such. ◇ **as yet** up to the present time

USAGE Avoid false linkages when using **as** to mean 'in the capacity of': As a judge, you know I do not like being asked such questions (which one is the judge?).

As symbol arsenic

Asadha /aásədə/ n the 4th month of the year in the Hindu calendar

asafoetida /ássə féttidə, -feè-/ n a strong-smelling plant extract. Use: South Asian cooking.

asbestos /ass béss toss, əz béstəss/ n a fibrous carcinogenic mineral. Use: formerly, heat-resistant materials.

ascend /ə sénd/ v 1 vi move upwards 2 vti climb something 3 vt succeed to an important position (fml) o ascend the throne

ascendant /ə séndənt/, **ascendent** adj 1 moving upwards (literary) 2 dominant (fml) —**ascendancy** n

ascension /ə sénsh'n/ n 1 the process of ascending (fml) 2 **Ascension** in Christianity, Jesus Christ's rising to heaven

ascent /ə sént/ n 1 a climb 2 an upward movement 3 a rise to importance

SPELLCHECK Do not confuse the spelling of **ascent** and **assent** ('agree to something'), which sound similar.

ascertain /ássər táyn/ vt find out with certainty (fml) —**ascertainable** adj —**ascertainment** n

ascetic /ə séttik/ adj of or choosing an austere life of self-denial —**ascetic** n —**ascetically** adv —**asceticism** /ə séttisizəm/ n

Ascham /áskəm/, **Roger** (1515–68) English humanist and scholar

ASCII /áski/ n a computer data exchange standard. Full form **American Standard Code for Information Interchange**

ASCII file n a computer text file

ascorbic acid /ə skáwrbik-/ n vitamin C

ascribe /ə skríb/ (**-cribing, -cribed**) vt (fml) 1 give something as the cause of o ascribed his success to good luck 2 name somebody as the author of o a poem ascribed to Burns —**ascribable** adj —**ascription** /ə skrípsh'n/ n

ASEAN /ássi an/ abbr Association of Southeast Asian Nations

aseptic /ay séptik, ə-/ adj 1 without disease-causing microorganisms 2 preventing infection o aseptic techniques —**aseptically** adv

asexual /ay sékshoo əl/ adj without sex, sex organs, or sexual desire —**asexuality** /áy sekshoo álləti/ n —**asexually** adv

ash[1] n 1 the remains of something burnt (often pl) 2 volcanic dust

ash[2] (pl **ashes** or same) n 1 a deciduous tree

with winged fruits **2** the hard wood of an ash tree. Use: furniture, tool handles.

ashamed /ə sháymd/ *adj* full of shame and often embarrassment —**ashamedly** /-mədli/ *adv*

Ashanti /ə shánti/ administrative area and former kingdom in central Ghana

A share *n* a share without voting rights

Ashcroft /ásh kroft/, **Dame Peggy** (1907–91) British actor

Ashe /ash/, **Arthur** (1943–93) US tennis player

ashen /ásh'n/ *adj* **1** very pale **2** like ashes

Ashes /áshiz/ *n* a cricket trophy awarded to the winner of a series of matches between Australia and England

Ashgabat /áshgə bat/ capital of Turkmenistan. Pop. 462,000 (1995).

Ashora /ə sháwrə/, **Ashura** /ə shoorə/ *n* an Islamic festival associated by Sunni Muslims with the death of Muhammad's grandson Husain. Date: 10th day of Muharram.

ashore /ə sháwr/ *adv* to or on land

~~ashphalt~~ incorrect spelling of **asphalt**

ashram /áshrəm, aásh-/ *n* **1** in Hinduism, a retreat for the practice of yoga and other disciplines **2** a spiritual community

Ashton /áshtən/, **Sir Frederick** (1904–88) British dancer and choreographer

Ashton-Warner /-wáwrnər/, **Sylvia** (1905–84) New Zealand novelist and teacher

ashtray /ásh tray/ *n* a container for cigarette, cigar, or pipe ash

Ashurbanipal /áshoor bánni pal/ (668–627 BC) king of Assyria

Ash Wednesday *n* in Christianity, the first day of Lent

ashy /áshi/ (**-ier, -iest**) *adj* **1** extremely pale (*literary*) **2** like ash

Asia /áyshə, áyzhə/ the world's largest continent, bordered by the Ural and Caucasus mountains and the Arctic, Pacific, and Indian oceans. Pop. estimated 3.46 billion (1995).

Asia Minor historic region in W Asia, roughly corresponding to Asian Turkey

Asian /áysh'n, áyzh'n/ *adj* of Asia ■ *n* **1** somebody from Asia **2** somebody from South Asia

USAGE Asian has largely replaced *Asiatic*, both as a noun and as an adjective. When the reference is to people, *Asiatic* is now regarded as derogatory and should be strictly avoided. In British English, **Asian** is also used to refer to people from South Asia (the Indian subcontinent), or their descendants now living in Britain. In US English, **Asian** usually refers to people of East Asian origin or ancestry, for example from China, Japan, or Korea.

Asiatic /áyshi áttik, áyzi-/ *adj* describes things in or from Asia ○ *a semitropical Asiatic shrub* ○ *an Asiatic port* ■ *n* an offensive term for an Asian person

aside /ə síd/ *adv* **1** away or to one side **2** not under consideration ○ *Budget constraints*

aside, is it feasible? ■ *n* **1** an actor's comment to the audience **2** a comment made in an undertone

Asimov /ázzi mof/, **Isaac** (1920–92) Russian-born US scientist and writer

asinine /ássi nīn/ *adj* ridiculous —**asininely** *adv* —**asininity** /ássi nínnəti/ *n*

ask *v* **1** *vti* put a question to somebody **2** *vti* request something **3** *vt* invite **4** *vt* require **5** *vt* name as a price ◇ **for the asking** at no cost

□ **ask after** *vt* enquire about the welfare of

askance /ə skánss, ə skaánss/ *adv* with suspicion

askew /ə skyóo/ *adj, adv* at an angle or off centre

asking price *n* the price quoted

aslant /ə slaánt/ *adv* slanting

asleep /ə sleep/ *adj* **1** not awake or alert **2** numb through poor blood circulation

A/S level *n* a school examination between GCSE and A level. Full form **Advanced Supplementary level**

Asmara /ass maárə/ capital of Eritrea. Pop. 431,000 (1995).

asocial /ay sṓsh'l/ *adj* **1** unwilling or unable to interact socially **2** inconsiderate or indifferent to other members of society

~~association~~ incorrect spelling of **association**

asp *n* **1** a snake that killed Cleopatra **2** a S European viper

ASP *abbr* **1** active server page **2** application service provider

asparagus /ə spárrəgəss/ *n* **1** spear-shaped plant shoots eaten as a vegetable **2** a plant cultivated for its edible shoots

aspect /áss pekt/ *n* **1** one side or part of something **2** appearance **3** the direction towards which something faces **4** a grammatical category of verbs that is independent of tense

aspen /áspən/ (*pl* **-pens** *or* same) *n* a poplar tree with leaves that flutter in the breeze

Asperger's syndrome /áspurjərz-/, **Asperger syndrome** /áspurjər-/ *n* a severe developmental disorder akin to autism

asperity /ə spérrəti/ *n* **1** harshness or severity (*fml*) **2** roughness (*literary*)

aspersion /ə spúrsh'n/ *n* a defamatory remark (*often pl*)

asphalt /áss falt, -fawlt/ *n* a semisolid bituminous substance. Use: road surfacing, waterproofing, fungicides. ■ *vt* cover with asphalt

asphyxia /ass fíksi ə, əss-/ *n* suffocation

asphyxiate /ass fíksi ayt, əss-/ (**-ating, -ated**) *vti* suffocate —**asphyxiation** /ass fíksi áysh'n, əss-/ *n*

aspic /áspik/ *n* a savoury jelly

aspidistra /áspi dístrə/ *n* a leafy houseplant

aspirate (**-rating, -rated**) *vt* /áspi rayt/ **1** pronounce a sound, such as the letter 'h', while breathing out **2** remove liquid or gas by suction, especially from a body cavity (*technical*) —**aspirate** /áspərət/ *adj*

aspiration /áspi ráysh'n/ *n* **1** an ambition **2** the process of aspirating

aspirational /áspi ráysh'nəl/ *adj* ambitious for material success or self-improvement

aspire /ə spír/ (**-piring, -pired**) *vi* have a particular ambition —**aspirant** /áspirənt, ə spírənt/ *n*, *adj* —**aspiring** *adj*

aspirin /ásprin/ (*pl* **-rins** *or same*) *n* **1** a pain-relieving drug **2** a tablet containing aspirin

> **ORIGIN** The word **aspirin** was originally coined in German, where it was a contraction of *acetylierte Spirsäure*. This translates as 'acetylated spiraeic acid', a former name for salicylic acid, from which aspirin is derived.

~~asprin~~ incorrect spelling of **aspirin**

Asquith /áskwith/, **Herbert Henry, 1st Earl of Oxford and Asquith** (1852–1928) British prime minister (1908–16)

ass[1] *n* a mammal like a small horse with long ears

ass[2] *n US, Can* a taboo term for the buttocks or anus (*offensive*)

Assad /ə sád/, **Bashar al-** (*b*. 1965) president of Syria (2000–)

Assad, Hafez al- (1928–2000) president of Syria (1971–2000)

assail /ə sáyl/ *vt* **1** attack somebody with words or actions **2** overwhelm somebody's senses —**assailant** *n*

~~assasin~~ incorrect spelling of **assassin**

assassin /ə sássin/ *n* a murderer, especially one with a political motive

> **ORIGIN Assassin** comes from an Arabic word that literally means 'users of hashish (cannabis)'. The name originally applied to a group of 11C Muslims, who took hashish before going on assassination missions.

assassinate /ə sássi nayt/ (**-nating, -nated**) *vt* **1** murder somebody, especially a public figure, for political reasons **2** ruin or destroy something such as somebody's reputation —**assassination** /ə sássi náysh'n/ *n* ◊ See note at **kill**

assault /ə sáwlt/ *n* a physical or verbal attack ■ *vt* attack

assault course *n* a military training ground with obstacles

assay /ə sáy, ássay/ *n* **1** examination and analysis **2** the chemical analysis of a substance ■ *vt* **1** examine or analyse **2** attempt (*fml*) —**assayer** *n*

assemblage /ə sémblij/ *n* **1** the process of gathering people or things together **2** a collection **3** a work of art made from a collection of different objects

assemble /ə sémb'l/ (**-bling, -bled**) *v* **1** *vti* gather together **2** *vt* put components together to make something ◊ See note at **collect**

assembler /ə sémblər/ *n* **1** somebody who puts components together **2** a computer program that converts assembly language into machine language **3** *also* **assembly language** a low-level computer language

assembly /ə sémbli/ (*pl* **-blies**) *n* **1** a gathering together of people **2** a school meeting before classes **3** *also* **Assembly** a consultative or legislative body **4** the putting together of components **5** the translation of assembly language into machine language

assembly line *n* a series of work stations in a manufacturing system

assent /ə sént/ *vi* agree to something ■ *n* an expression of agreement —**assenter** *n* ◊ See note at **ascent, agree**

assert /ə súrt/ *v* **1** *vt* claim or state something emphatically **2** *vt* insist on or exercise a right **3** *vr* behave forcefully —**asserter** *n* —**assertion** /ə súrsh'n/ *n*

assertive /ə súrtiv/ *adj* acting confidently —**assertively** *adv* —**assertiveness** *n*

assess /ə séss/ *vt* **1** judge or evaluate **2** determine the amount or value of —**assessable** *adj* —**assessment** *n* —**assessor** *n*

asset /ásset/ *n* somebody or something useful or valuable ■ **assets** *npl* **1** the property of a person or organization **2** items constituting the value of an organization

> **ORIGIN Asset** derives from the French word for 'enough' (modern French *assez*). In the French formerly used in English law courts, 'having enough' meant 'having enough money or property to settle your debts', and from there **assets** came to mean property or financial resources. For 400 years only the form **assets** was used, as a singular noun ('my assets is...'). Later the -s was interpreted as the English plural ending, and the singular form **asset** appeared in the 19C.

asset-stripping *n* the selling of company assets individually for profit —**asset-stripper** *n*

assiduous /ə síddyoo əss/ *adj* very careful and diligent —**assiduously** *adv* ◊ See note at **careful**

assign /ə sín/ *vt* **1** give somebody a task or duty **2** send somebody to work somewhere **3** transfer property or rights **4** designate something for a particular use —**assignable** *adj* —**assigner** *n* —**assignor** *n*

assignation /ássig náysh'n/ *n* a lovers' secret meeting

assignment /ə sínmənt/ *n* **1** a task **2** an appointment **3** a legal transfer

assimilate /ə símmi layt/ (**-lating, -lated**) *v* **1** *vti* integrate **2** *vt* absorb information **3** *vt* absorb nutrients into the tissues of the body —**assimilable** *adj* —**assimilation** /ə símmi láysh'n/ *n*

assist /ə síst/ *vti* help ■ *n* a helpful act by a team player

assistance /ə sístənss/ *n* help made available

assistant /ə sístənt/ *n* **1** a helper **2** a shop employee ■ *adj* serving as a deputy ○ *an assistant operating room supervisor*

SYNONYMS assistant, helper, deputy, aide

CORE MEANING: somebody who helps another person in carrying out a task

assizes /ə síziz/ *npl* periodic courts in England and Wales before 1971

associate *v* /ə sóshi ayt, ə sóssi-/ (**-ating, -ated**) 1 *vt* connect one thing with another in the mind 2 *vi* spend time with somebody ■ *n* /ə sóshi ət, -ayt, ə sóssi-, -/ 1 a partner 2 a person with whom somebody has a social or business relationship ○ *couldn't identify any of his associates* 3 a member without full status ■ *adj* /ə sóshi ət, -ayt, ə sóssi-, -/ 1 allied 2 without full status as a member —**associable** *adj* —**associated** *adj* —**associateship** *n*

association /ə sóssi áysh'n, ə sóshi-/ *n* 1 a group of people or organizations 2 a linking or joining of people or things ○ *hasn't profited from her association with him* 3 social interaction ○ *freedom of association* 4 a linked idea

association football *n* soccer *(fml)*

associative /ə sóshi ətiv, ə sóssi-/ *adj* of psychological connections —**associatively** *adv*

associative memory *n* computer memory accessed by content

assonance /ássənənss/ *n* similarity of sound —**assonant** *adj*

assorted /ə sáwrtid/ *adj* 1 various 2 arranged in groups

assortment /ə sáwrtmənt/ *n* a collection of various similar things

asst *abbr* assistant

assuage /ə swáyj/ (**-suaging, -suaged**) *vt* relieve something unpleasant *(fml)*

assume /ə syoom/ (**-suming, -sumed**) *vt* 1 suppose something to be true 2 take responsibility for something 3 take on a quality ○ *The task assumed Herculean proportions.* —**assumable** *adj* —**assumed** *adj* ◊ See note at **deduce**

assuming /ə syooming/ *conj* if it is assumed that —**assumingly** *adv*

assumption /ə súmpsh'n/ *n* 1 something assumed or taken for granted 2 the assuming of something 3 **Assumption** a Christian festival marking the Virgin Mary's ascent to heaven. Date: 15 August.

assurance /ə sháwrənss, ə shóorənss/ *n* 1 a pledge or promise 2 self-confidence 3 certainty 4 insurance against a certainty such as death

assure /ə sháwr, ə shóor/ (**-suring, -sured**) *vt* 1 make confident 2 convince 3 make certain —**assurable** *adj*

assured /ə sháwrd, ə shóord/ *adj* 1 guaranteed 2 self-confident ■ *n* (*pl* **assured**) somebody with life assurance —**assuredly** /ə sháwridli, ə shóor-/ *adv* —**assuredness** /ə sháwridnəss, ə shóor-/ *n*

Assyria /ə sírri ə/ ancient kingdom in present-day N Iraq —**Assyrian** *adj*

Astaire /ə stáir/, **Fred** (1899–1987) US dancer and actor

Astana /ə stáanə/ capital of Kazakhstan. Pop. 270,400 (1997).

astatine /ástə teen/ *n* (*symbol* **At**) a radioactive chemical element. Use: in medicine as a tracer element.

aster /ástər/ *n* a garden plant with flowers like daisies

~~asterick~~ incorrect spelling of **asterisk**

asterisk /ástərisk/ *n* a star-shaped symbol used in printing ■ *vt* mark with an asterisk

USAGE The **asterisk** is usually placed at the beginning or end of a word. One or more asterisks may be used to mark a word or phrase in running text that is explained or expanded on elsewhere, usually in a footnote. A string of asterisks is sometimes used when part of a word is omitted, usually part of a swearword: *She was obviously p***ed off.*

astern /ə stúrn/ *adv* in or to the stern of a ship or boat

asteroid /ástə royd/ *n* a rocky object orbiting the Sun

asthma /ásmə/ *n* a respiratory disease, sometimes caused by allergies —**asthmatic** /ass máttik/ *adj, n*

astigmatism /ə stígmətizəm/ *n* 1 an unequal curving of the eye surface, producing blurred vision 2 a defect in a lens or mirror that prevents light rays from meeting at a single point —**astigmatic** /ástig máttik/ *adj*

astir /ə stúr/ *adj* 1 up and about 2 moving

astonish /ə stónnish/ *vt* amaze greatly —**astonishing** *adj* —**astonishingly** *adv* —**astonishment** *n*

Astor /ástər/, **Nancy, Viscountess** (1879–1964) US-born British politician

astound /ə stównd/ *vt* surprise greatly —**astounding** *adj* —**astoundingly** *adv*

astrakhan /ástrə kán, -káan/ *n* a fur fabric with a curly black or grey pile. Use: hats, trimming coats.

astral /ástrəl/ *adj* 1 of stars 2 in theosophical belief, above the material world —**astrally** *adv*

astray /ə stráy/ *adv* 1 off the right path 2 into error or sin ○ *led astray by unsuitable companions*

astride /ə stríd/ *prep* with one leg on each side of ■ *adv* with the legs apart

astringent /ə strínjənt/ *n* a substance that draws skin tissues together ■ *adj* sharp and acidic in tone —**astringency** *n* —**astringently** *adv*

astro-, astr- *prefix* star, the stars, outer space ○ *astronomy*

astrology /ə strólləji/ *n* the study of the way planets are thought to affect human affairs —**astrologer** /ə stróll-/ —**astrological** /ástrə lójjik'l/ *adj* —**astrologically** *adv*

astronaut /ástrə nawt/ *n* somebody trained to travel in space

astronomical /ástrə nómmik'l/, **astronomic** /-nómmik/ *adj* 1 of astronomy 2 immeasurably great *(infml)*

astronomical unit *n* a distance in space equal

to the mean distance between the Earth and the Sun

astronomy /ə strónnami/ n the scientific study of the universe —**astronomer** n

astrophysics /ástrō fízziks/ n the physics of astronomical objects (+ sing verb) —**astrophysical** adj —**astrophysicist** n

AstroTurf /ástrō turf/ tdmk a trademark for synthetic turf resembling grass

astute /ə styóot/ adj shrewd and perceptive —**astutely** adv —**astuteness** n

Asunción /a soónssi ón/ capital of Paraguay. Pop. 550,060 (1997).

asunder /ə súndər/ adv into separate parts or pieces (literary)

Asvina /áshvinə/ n the 7th month of the year in the Hindu calendar

Aswan /a swaán/ city in S Egypt. Pop. 220,000 (1992).

ASX abbr Aus Australian Stock Exchange

asylum /ə síləm/ n 1 shelter and protection from danger 2 protection and immunity from extradition 3 an offensive term for a hospital for people with psychiatric disorders (dated)

asymmetrical /ássi méttrik'l/, **asymmetric** /-méttrik/ adj not symmetrical or equal ○ an asymmetrical flower arrangement —**asymmetrically** adv —**asymmetry** /a símmətri, ay-/ n

asymmetrical digital subscriber line n a high-speed telephone line

asymmetric warfare n highly decentralized, unconventional warfare and attacks perpetrated on nation-states and civilians by paramilitaries, guerrillas, and terrorists

asymptomatic /áyssimptə máttik/ adj showing or producing no obvious symptoms —**asymptomatically** adv

asynchronous communication /ay síngkrənəss-/ n the sending of electronic data in one direction one character at a time

at prep 1 on or near a specific location or position ○ a face at the window 2 attending ○ at school 3 indicates when something happens ○ at midnight 4 indicates a rate or price ○ at 60 miles per hour 5 towards ○ She glanced at me. 6 as a reaction to ○ was amazed at that 7 in a particular activity or state ○ an expert at windsurfing ○ at risk 8 in a particular condition or state ○ at risk of infection ◇ **at all** in any way, to any extent, or under any conditions ◇ **where it's at** where all the action and excitement is happening (slang)

At symbol astatine

at. abbr 1 atmosphere 2 atomic

Atacama Desert /áttə kaámə-/ dry plateau in N Chile

Atahualpa /áttə waálpə/ (1500?–33) last ruler of the Inca Empire (1532–33)

Atanasoff /ə tánnə sof/, **John V.** (1903–95) US mathematical physicist. He developed many of the basic techniques later used in the design of the first electronic digital computer.

AKG London

Mustafa Kemal Atatürk

Atatürk /áttə turk/, **Mustafa Kemal** (1881–1938) founder and first president of the republic of Turkey (1923–38)

atavistic /áttə vístik/ adj 1 of the recurrence of a genetic feature after an absence lasting generations 2 primitive and instinctive —**atavism** n —**atavistically** adv

ate past tense of **eat**

-ate suffix 1 having, characterized by ○ duplicate 2 office, rank ○ archdeaconate 3 act on in a particular way ○ fluoridate 4 a chemical compound derived from a particular element or compound ○ nitrate

atempt incorrect spelling of **attempt**

atheist /áythi ist/ n somebody who does not believe in God or deities —**atheism** n —**atheistic** /áythi ístik/ adj

athelete incorrect spelling of **athlete**

Athelstan /áthəlstən/ (895?–939) king of Wessex and Mercia (926?–939)

Athena /ə theénə/, **Athene** /ə theéni/ n in Greek mythology, the goddess of wisdom. Roman equivalent **Minerva**

Athens /áthənz/ capital of Greece. Pop. 772,072 (1991). —**Athenian** /ə theéni ən/ adj, n

atherosclerosis /áthərōsklə róssiss/ n an arterial disease obstructing blood flow —**atherosclerotic** /-sklə róttik/ adj

athiest incorrect spelling of **atheist**

athlete /áth leet/ n 1 somebody with ability in athletics or sports activities 2 a competitor in athletics

ORIGIN The root of **athlete** is the Greek word for 'prize'. A Greek athlete could in theory be competing for any prize, but the word came to refer only to the physical exercises performed at public games, such as running, discus-throwing, or boxing.

athlete's foot n a fungal infection of the feet

athletic /ath léttik/ adj 1 of athletes, athletics, or sports activities in general 2 muscular and strong —**athletically** adv —**athleticism** /ath léttissizəm/ n

athletics /ath léttiks/ n 1 track-and-field events such as running, discus, and high jump (+ sing or pl verb) 2 US, Can sports activities (+ sing or pl verb)

-ation suffix an action or process, or the result of it ○ alienation ○ presentation

atitude incorrect spelling of **attitude**

Atlanta /at lánta/ capital of Georgia, United States. Pop. 403,819 (1998).

Atlantic /at lántik/ adj of the Atlantic Ocean ■ n also **Atlantic Ocean** world's second largest ocean, separating Europe and Africa from North and South America

Atlantic Rim n the regions bordering the Atlantic Ocean

Atlantis /at lántiss, at-/ n in Greek mythology, an island that sank into the sea

atlas /átlass/ n a book of maps

ORIGIN Collections of maps were published in the 17C with a picture of the mythological Titan, Atlas, at the front, holding up the world, so they came to be known as **atlases**. In the mythological story, Atlas held up the heavens, not the world.

Atlas Mountains /átlass-/ system of mountain ranges in Morocco, Algeria, and Tunisia. Highest peak Jebel Toubkal 4,165 m/13,665 ft.

~~atlass~~ incorrect spelling of **atlas**

ATM n a cashpoint. Full form **automated teller machine**

atmosphere /átmass feer/ n 1 the gases around an astronomical object 2 the air or climate of a place 3 a mood or tone 4 a unit of pressure —**atmospheric** /átmass férrik/ adj —**atmospherical** adj —**atmospherically** adv

atmospheric pressure n the downward pressure exerted by the weight of the overlying atmosphere

atmospherics /átmass férriks/ n 1 the study of electromagnetic radiation in the atmosphere (+ sing verb) 2 interference with electronic signals caused by electromagnetic radiation in the atmosphere (+ sing or pl verb) 3 the prevailing mood of a situation (+ pl verb)

at. no. abbr atomic number

ATOL abbr Air Travel Organizers' Licence

atoll /áttol, a tól/ n a coral island surrounding a lagoon

ORIGIN **Atoll** derives from the language of the Maldives in South Asia.

atom /áttam/ n 1 the smallest portion into which an element can be divided and still retain its properties 2 a very small amount o not an atom of truth

atom bomb n a highly destructive nuclear weapon

atomic /a tómmik/ adj 1 based on nuclear energy 2 of an atom or atoms —**atomically** adv

atomic energy n nuclear energy

atomize /átta mīz/ (-izing, -ized), **atomise** v 1 vt separate into atoms 2 vti change into spray 3 vt destroy

atomizer /átta mīzer/, **atomiser** n a spray device

atonal /ay tốn'l/ adj without a musical key —**atonality** /áy tō nállati/ n —**atonally** adv

atone /a tốn/ (**atoning, atoned**) vi make amends (fml) o atoned for his misdeeds —**atonement** n

atop /a tóp/ prep, adv on or to the top of something

atrium /áytri am/ (pl -**ums** or -**a** /-a/) n 1 a central hall with a glass roof 2 a Roman courtyard

atrocious /a trṓshass/ adj 1 very bad 2 very cruel —**atrociously** adv

atrocity /a trṓssati/ (pl -**ties**) n 1 a shockingly cruel act 2 extreme cruelty o an act of atrocity

atrophy /áttrafi/ n 1 a wasting away in size or strength o muscle atrophy 2 a lessening of an ability ■ vi (-**phies, -phying, -phied**) weaken —**atrophic** /a trṓffik/ adj

attach /a tách/ v 1 vt fasten or secure to something else 2 vt add or append to something else 3 vt ascribe or assign 4 vi be associated with 5 vt place on temporary duty —**attachable** adj

attaché /a tásh ay/ n a diplomat with a particular role o a military attaché

attaché case n a slender rigid briefcase

attached /a tácht/ adj 1 fastened to or enclosed with something else 2 devoted to or fond of somebody or something

~~attachement~~ incorrect spelling of **attachment**

attachment /a táchmant/ n 1 something attached 2 a means of attaching 3 an emotional bond 4 the process of attaching

attack /a ták/ v 1 vti try to harm somebody or something 2 vt criticize somebody 3 vti cause damage to somebody or something o The disease can attack at any age. 4 vt make a vigorous start on 5 vt try to score against an opposing team ■ n 1 an act of attacking 2 a bout of an illness —**attacker** n

attain /a táyn/ vt 1 accomplish 2 reach a particular state —**attainable** adj ◊ See note at **accomplish**

attainment /a táynmant/ n 1 the accomplishment of a goal 2 something achieved through effort (often pl)

attempt /a témpt/ vti try to do ■ n 1 a try or effort 2 an attack o an attempt on her life ◊ See note at **try**

attend /a ténd/ v 1 vti be present at an event 2 vti regularly go to a particular place 3 vi listen or watch carefully 4 vt accompany or be associated with —**attendee** /a tén dée, á ten-/ n —**attender** n

☐ **attend to** vti deal with

attendance /a téndanss/ n 1 presence at an event or place 2 the number of people attending an event

attendant /a téndant/ n 1 somebody serving in a public place 2 a servant or escort ■ adj accompanying or associated o drought and attendant forest fires

~~attendence~~ incorrect spelling of **attendance**

attention /a ténsh'n/ n 1 mental concentration o pay attention 2 notice or interest o media attention 3 appropriate or affectionate treatment 4 a formal military posture ■ interj orders military personnel to stand up straight —**attentive** adj —**attentively** adv —**attentiveness** n

attention deficit disorder, attention deficit hyperactivity disorder *n* in children, a condition marked by hyperactivity and inability to concentrate

attention line *n* a line in a letter with the recipient's name on it

attenuate /ə ténnyoo ayt/ (**-ating, -ated**) *vti* make or become weaker or thinner —**attenuation** /ə ténnyoo áysh'n/ *n*

attest /ə tést/ *vti* **1** be evidence of **2** confirm the validity of —**attestation** /átte stáysh'n/ *n* —**attestor** *n*

attic /áttik/ *n* a room or an area immediately under a roof

ORIGIN **Attic** was originally an adjective, adopted from French, describing an upper part of a façade that had a row of smaller columns above a main row below. This was the 'Attic' style, named after Attica in ancient Greece. The name *attic storey* was easily interpreted as meaning 'upper storey under the beams of a roof', and from there **attic** came to be used as a noun for a storey like this, or a room in one.

Attic /áttik/ *adj* of Attica ■ *n* an ancient Greek dialect

Attica /áttikə/ region of ancient Greece around Athens

Attila /ə tíllə/ (406?–453?) Hunnish warrior king

attire /ə tír/ (*fml*) *n* clothing ■ *vt* (**-tiring, -tired**) put clothes on somebody

attitude /átti tyood/ *n* **1** a personal feeling about something **2** body posture **3** an aggressive and challenging manner (*infml*) ○ *teenagers with attitude* **4** the orientation of an aircraft or spacecraft

Attlee /átti/, **Clement, 1st Earl Attlee** (1883–1967) British prime minister (1945–51)

attn *abbr* attention

attorney /ə túrni/ (*pl* **-neys**) *n* **1** somebody given legal power **2** *US* a lawyer —**attorneyship** *n*

attorney general (*pl* **attorney generals** *or* **attorneys general**) *n* the chief legal officer of a country or state

attract /ə trákt/ *vt* **1** cause somebody or something to come closer, e.g. by magnetism or temptation **2** elicit a response such as support, interest, or attention **3** appeal or be attractive to somebody

attraction /ə tráksh'n/ *n* **1** the power of attracting **2** a quality, feature, or site that attracts people

attractive /ə tráktiv/ *adj* **1** pleasant in appearance or manner **2** good-looking **3** interesting or appealing ○ *an attractive proposition* —**attractively** *adv* —**attractiveness** *n*

attribute *vt* /ə tríbbyoot/ (**-uting, -uted**) **1** say or think that something was caused or produced by somebody or something **2** assign a particular quality to something ■ *n* /áttri byoot/ a quality or property —**attributable** *adj* —**attribution** /áttri byoosh'n/ *n*

attributive /ə tríbbyōotiv/ *adj* preceding the noun in a noun phrase —**attributively** *adv*

attrition /ə trísh'n/ *n.* **1** the wearing away of a surface **2** a weakening caused by persistent attack **3** gradual reduction of staff

ATV *abbr* all-terrain vehicle

Margaret Atwood

Atwood /át woòd/, **Margaret** (*b.* 1939) Canadian writer

at. wt. *abbr* atomic weight

atypical /ay típpik'l/ *adj* not typical —**atypically** *adv*

Au *symbol* gold

aubergine /óbər zheen/ *n* **1** a long oval fleshy vegetable with a purple skin **2** a plant that produces aubergines

auburn /áwbən, áw burn/ *adj* reddish-brown —**auburn** *n*

Auckland /áwklənd/ **1** administrative region of New Zealand, in the northwest of the North Island. Pop. 1,159,400 (1998). **2** largest city and port in New Zealand. Pop. 1,076,100 (1998).

auction /áwksh'n/ *n* a sale by bidding, or this method of selling ■ *vti* sell goods by inviting bids —**auctionable** *adj*

auctioneer /áwkshə neér/ *n* somebody conducting an auction

AUD *abbr* Australian dollar

audacious /aw dáyshəss/ *adj* bold or daring —**audaciously** *adv* —**audacity** /aw dássəti/ *n*

W. H. Auden

Auden /áwd'n/, **W. H.** (1907–73) British-born US poet and dramatist

~~audience~~ incorrect spelling of **audience**

audible /áwdəb'l/ *adj* capable of being heard —**audibility** /áwdə bílləti/ *n* —**audibly** *adv*

audience /áwdi ənss/ *n* **1** the people watching or listening to a performance or broadcast **2** the readership of a particular author or publication **3** a formal interview

audio /áwdi ō/ *n* the recording and reproduction of sound

audio-, audi- *prefix* sound, hearing ○ *audiovisual*

audio book *n* a recorded book

audiology /áwdi óllaji/ *n* the diagnosis and treatment of hearing loss —**audiological** /áwdi ə lójjik'l/ *adj* —**audiologist** *n*

audiotape /áwdi ō tayp/ *n* 1 magnetic tape for recording sound 2 a sound recording on tape

audiotyping /áwdi ō tīping/ *n* the activity of typing recorded dictation —**audiotypist** *n*

audiovisual /áwdi ō vízhoo əl/ *adj* 1 of sound and vision 2 of hearing and sight ■ *n US* an audiovisual aid

audiovisual aid *n* a teaching aid using sound and vision

audit /áwdit/ *n* 1 a check of financial accounts 2 an efficiency check ■ *vt* carry out an audit of

audition /aw dísh'n/ *n* 1 a test performance by an actor or musician for a job 2 the sense or process of hearing ■ *vti* do or give somebody an audition

auditor /áwditər/ *n* 1 somebody who conducts an audit 2 a hearer or listener *(fml)*

auditorium /áwdi táwri əm/ (*pl* -**ums** *or* -**a** /-ri ə/) *n* 1 the part of a theatre where the audience sits 2 a hall or lecture room

auditory /áwditəri/ *adj* of hearing

audit trail *n* a record of operations or transactions

au fait /ō fáy/ *adj* knowledgeable about recent developments

> **ORIGIN** The literal meaning of **au fait** in French, from which it was borrowed, is 'to the fact'.

auf Wiedersehen /ówf véédər zayn, zay ən/ *interj* goodbye

Aug. *abbr* August

auger /áwgər/ *n* a hand tool for boring holes

> **SPELLCHECK** Do not confuse the spelling of **auger** and **augur** ('a foreteller of the future', 'predict the future'), which sound similar.

augment /awg mént/ *vti* increase or add to something *(fml)* —**augmentation** /áwg men táysh'n, -mən-/ *n* ◊ See note at **increase**

au gratin /ō gráttaN/ *adj* with a browned cooked crust

Augsburg /ówgz burg/ city in S Germany. Pop. 262,110 (1997).

augur /áwgər/ *n* 1 in ancient Rome, an interpreter of messages from deities 2 a foreteller of the future ■ *vti* indicate what will happen in the future ◊ See note at **auger**

augury /áwgyōōri/ (*pl* -**ries**) *n* 1 divination 2 a portent or omen

august /aw gúst/ *adj* dignified and splendid *(fml)*

August /áwgəst/ *n* the 8th month of the year in the Gregorian calendar

> **ORIGIN August** is named after the Roman emperor Augustus.

Augusta /ə gústə/ capital of Maine. Pop. 19,978 (1998).

Augustine /aw gústin/, **St** (AD 354–430) Roman priest and theologian

Augustus /aw gústəss/ (63 BC–AD 14) Roman emperor (27 BC–AD 14)

auk /awk/ *n* a black-and-white sea bird

auld lang syne /áwld lang zín/ *n Scotland* times long past *(archaic)*

Popperfoto

Aung San Suu Kyi

Aung San Suu Kyi /áwng san soo keé/, **Daw** (b. 1945) Burmese human rights activist

aunt /aant/ *n* somebody's father's or mother's sister or sister-in-law —**aunthood** *n*

au pair /ō páir/ *n* a young person from abroad working as a domestic helper

aura /áwrə/ (*pl* -**ras** *or* -**rae** /-reé/) *n* 1 a distinctive quality 2 a force emanating from somebody or something

aural /áwrəl/ *adj* of hearing or sound —**aurally** *adv*

> **USAGE aural** or **oral**? **Aural** is to do with hearing whereas **oral** is to do with speaking or the mouth. An *aural test* is an examination testing comprehension by listening, whereas in an *oral test* the answers are spoken rather than written.

Aurelian /aw reéli ən/ (AD 215?–275) Roman emperor (270–275)

Aurelius /aw reéli əss/, **Marcus** (121–180) Roman emperor (161–180) and philosopher

aureole /áw ri ōl/, **aureola** /aw reé ələ, áw ri ōlə/ *n* 1 a halo 2 the corona of the Sun

au revoir /ō rə vwáar/ *interj* goodbye

auricle /áwrik'l/ *n* 1 the visible part of the ear 2 an ear-shaped part of the heart

aurora /ə ráwrə/ *n* (*pl* -**ras** *or* -**rae** /-reé/) 1 coloured lights in the skies around the North or South poles 2 *also* **Aurora** dawn 3 **Aurora** in Roman mythology, the goddess of the dawn —**auroral** *adj*

aurora australis /aw ráwrə ə stráyliss/ *n* coloured lights in the skies around the South Pole

aurora borealis /-bawri áyliss/ *n* coloured lights in the skies around the North Pole

Aus. *abbr* 1 Australia 2 Australian

auspice /áwspiss/ ◊ **under the auspices of** with the help or support of a person or organization

auspicious /aw spíshəss/ *adj* promising well for the future —**auspiciously** *adv* —**auspiciousness** *n*

Aussie /ózzi/ *n* an Australian *(infml)* —**Aussie** *adj*

Aust. *abbr* 1 Australia 2 Australian

Austen /óstin/, **Jane** (1775–1817) British novelist

austere /aw steér, o-/ *adj* 1 involving physical hardship 2 strict and severe 3 plain and without luxury or adornment —**austerely** *adv* —**austereness** *n*

austerity /aw stérrəti, o-/ (*pl* **-ties**) *n* 1 severity or plainness 2 an economy measure, or such measures imposed as government policy

Austerlitz /áwsterlits, ów-/ town in the present-day E Czech Republic, near the site of a major battle in 1805 when Napoleon defeated Russian and Austrian forces

Austin /áwstin/ capital of Texas. Pop. 552,434 (1998).

Austral. *abbr* 1 Australasia 2 Australia 3 Australian

Australasia /áwstrə láyzhə/ Australia, New Zealand, New Guinea, and neighbouring islands of the S Pacific Ocean —**Australasian** *adj, n*

Australia /o stráyli ə/ country southeast of Asia comprising the continent of Australia and the island of Tasmania. Cap. Canberra. Pop. 19,357,594 (2001).

Australia Day *n* an Australian national holiday. Date: 1st Monday after 26 January.

Australian /o stráyli ən/ *adj* 1 of Australia 2 of the Aboriginal languages of Australia ■ *n* 1 somebody from Australia 2 English as it is used in Australia

Australian Alps mountain range in SE Australia. Highest peak Mt Kosciuszko 2,228 m/7,310 ft.

Australian Capital Territory federal district in SE Australia incorporating Canberra, the national capital. Pop. 308,700 (1998).

Austria /óstri ə/ country in central Europe. Cap. Vienna. Pop. 8,150,835 (2001). —**Austrian** *adj, n*

Austronesia /óströ neézhə, -neésha/ region consisting of Indonesia, Melanesia, Micronesia, Polynesia, and neighbouring islands in the Pacific Ocean

authentic /aw théntik/ *adj* 1 genuine and original 2 true and trustworthy —**authentically** *adv* —**authenticity** /áw then tíssəti, áwthən-/ *n*

authenticate /aw thénti kayt/ (**-cating, -cated**) *vt* confirm the genuineness or truth of

authentication /aw thénti káysh'n/ *n* 1 the process of authenticating 2 a computer user's identification

author /áwthər/ *n* 1 a writer 2 the creator or source of something ■ *vt* 1 be the author of 2 cause —**authorial** /aw tháwri əl/ *adj* —**authorship** *n*

authoring /áwthəring/ *n* the creation of content for viewing on a computer

authoritarian /aw thórri táiri ən/ *adj* strict and demanding obedience to authority —**authoritarian** *n* —**authoritarianism** *n*

authoritative /aw thórritətiv/ *adj* 1 backed by evidence, knowledge, or authority 2 showing authority —**authoritatively** *adv* —**authoritativeness** *n*

authority /aw thórrəti/ (*pl* **-ties**) *n* 1 the right to command 2 a holder of power 3 power given to somebody 4 a source of reliable information 5 an administrative body o *the local port authority* 6 justification 7 the ability to command respect

authorize /áwthə rīz/ (**-izing, -ized**), **authorise** *vt* give power or permission to somebody or for something —**authorization** /áwthə rī záysh'n/ *n*

Authorized Version *n* the English Bible of 1611

autism /áwtizəm/ *n* a psychological condition that disturbs perceptions and relationships —**autistic** /aw tístik/ *adj* —**autistically** *adv*

auto- *prefix* 1 self o *autobiography* 2 automatic o *autopilot*

autobiography /áwtō bī óggrəfi/ (*pl* **-phies**) *n* somebody's life story written by that person —**autobiographer** *n* —**autobiographical** /-bī ə gráffik'l/ *adj*

autochthonous /aw tókthənəss/ *adj* originating in the same area in which it is now found ◊ See note at **native**

autocracy /aw tókrəssi/ (*pl* **-cies**) *n* 1 rule by one person 2 a place ruled by one person

autocrat /áwtə krat/ *n* 1 a ruler with absolute authority 2 a bossy person —**autocratic** /áwtə kráttik/ *adj* —**autocratically** *adv*

autocross /áwtō kross/ *n* motor racing on rough ground

Autocue /áwtō kyoo/ *tdmk* a trademark for a device that displays text on a television screen to a speaker

autograph /áwtə graaf, -graf/ *n* somebody's signature, especially a famous person's ■ *vt* write your signature on o *autographing pictures of the band*

autoimmune /áwtō i myoòn/ *adj* caused by an allergy to substances occurring naturally in the body o *autoimmune diseases* —**autoimmunity** *n*

automate /áwtə mayt/ (**-mating, -mated**) *vti* make automatic

automated teller machine *n* full form of **ATM**

automatic /áwtə máttik/ *adj* 1 functioning without human intervention 2 done by prior arrangement 3 done without thought ■ *n* 1 a motor vehicle with an automatic gear-changing system 2 gun that fires continuously —**automatically** *adv*

automatic pilot *n* 1 an automatic steering system 2 autopilot (*infml*)

automation /áwtə máysh'n/ *n* replacement of human workers by machines

automaton /aw tómmətən, -ton/ (*pl* **-tons** *or* **-ta** /-mətə/) *n* 1 an independent and complex machine 2 somebody who acts like a machine —**automatous** *adj*

automobile /áwtə mə beel/ *n* a passenger-carrying motor vehicle with an engine

automotive /áwtō mótiv/ *adj* 1 of motor vehicles 2 self-propelled

autonomous /aw tónnəməss/ *adj* **1** self-governing **2** free to choose and act —**autonomy** /aw tónnəmi/ *n*

autonomous republic *n* a division of the Russian Federation

autopilot /áwtō pīlət/ *n* **1** an automatic pilot **2** unthinking or instinctive behaviour *(infml)* ○ *spent the day on autopilot handing out brochures*

autopsy /áwt opsi/ *n (pl* **-sies**) **1** a medical examination to find a cause of death **2** an exhaustive critical examination ■ *vt* (**-sies, -sying, -sied**) perform an autopsy on

autosave /áwtō sayv/ *n* the automatic saving of computer data

autosuggestion /áwtō sə jéschən/ *n* the influencing of somebody by that person's own power of suggestion

~~autum~~ incorrect spelling of **autumn**

autumn /áwtəm/ *n* **1** the season after summer and before winter **2** a period between success and decline ○ *in the autumn of his career as a cellist* —**autumnal** /aw túmn'l/ *adj*

auxiliary /awg zíllyəri, -zílləri/ *adj* **1** supporting or supplementary **2** held in reserve **3** secondary ■ *n (pl* **-ries**) **1** a supporting or reserve person or thing **2** *also* **auxiliary verb** a verb used with another verb, e.g. 'have' in 'we have met' **3** a member of a supporting military troop *(often pl)*

~~auxillary~~ incorrect spelling of **auxiliary**

Av *n* JUDAISM = **Ab**

AV *abbr* audiovisual

av. *abbr* **1** avenue **2** average

Av. *abbr* avenue

avail /ə váyl/ *v* **1** *vr* make use of ○ *avail yourself of the facilities* **2** *vti* be helpful to somebody else, or help somebody to do something *(fml)* ○ *Negotiation could not avail the deadlocked diplomats.* ■ *n* help or usefulness ○ *His protests were to no avail.*

available /ə váyləb'l/ *adj* able to be used, obtained, or spoken to —**availability** /ə váylə bílləti/ *n*

~~availible~~ incorrect spelling of **available**

avalanche /ávvə laanch/ *n* **1** a rapid fall of dislodged snow down a mountainside **2** an overwhelming quantity

avant-garde /ávong ga`ard/ *n* artists with new and experimental ideas and methods *(+ sing or pl verb)* ■ *adj* artistically new, experimental, or unconventional

avarice /ávvəriss/ *n* greed for wealth —**avaricious** /ávvə ríshəss/ *adj*

avatar /ávvə taar/ *n* **1** an incarnation of a Hindu deity in human or animal form **2** an embodiment of an idea or concept **3** an image of somebody in virtual reality

Ave. *abbr* avenue

avenge /ə vénj/ (**avenging, avenged**) *vt* act in retaliation for or on behalf of

avenue /ávvə nyoo/ *n* **1** a wide street **2** a means of approach

aver /ə vúr/ (**averring, averred**) *vt* assert confidently *(fml)* —**averment** *n*

average /ávvərij/ *n* **1** a typical level or amount **2** a figure calculated by dividing a total by the number of items ■ *adj* **1** typical **2** calculated as an average **3** not very good ■ *vt* (**-aging, -aged**) **1** calculate the average of **2** have or do as an average

averse /ə vúrss/ *adj* opposed to or disliking something *(fml)* —**aversely** *adv*

aversion /ə vúrsh'n/ *n* **1** a strong dislike **2** somebody or something disliked ◊ See note at **dislike**

aversion therapy *n* **1** therapy to eliminate undesirable behaviour by associating it with unpleasant consequences **2** therapy to overcome fears or dislikes

avert /ə vúrt/ *vt* **1** prevent something from happening **2** turn your eyes away —**avertible** *adj*

Avery /áyvəri/, **Oswald** (1877–1955) Canadian-born US bacteriologist and geneticist. He discovered that genetic information was transferred through DNA.

aviary /áyvi əri/ *(pl* **-ies**) *n* a large enclosure for birds

aviation /áyvi áysh'n/ *n* the development and use of aircraft

aviator /áyvi aytər/ *n* an aircraft pilot

avid /ávvid/ *adj* enthusiastic or eager —**avidly** *adv*

Avignon /ávvee nyoN/ city in SE France. Pop. 85,935 (1999).

avionics /áyvi ónniks/ *n* **1** technology applied to aircraft and spacecraft *(+ sing verb)* **2** the technological devices of aircraft and spacecraft *(+ pl verb)* —**avionic** *adj*

avocado /ávvə ka`adō/ *(pl* **-dos**) *n* **1** *also* **avocado pear** a green-fleshed edible fruit **2** a tree that produces avocados

ORIGIN **Avocado** came through Spanish from a Native South American word meaning literally 'testicle' (because of the shape of the fruit). The original Spanish form was altered under the influence of the more familiar word *avocado* 'advocate'.

avocation /ávvə káysh'n/ *n (fml)* **1** an occupation **2** a hobby —**avocational** *adj*

Avogadro /ávvə ga`adrō/, **Amedeo, Conte di Quaregna e Ceretto** (1776–1856) Italian physicist and chemist

avoid /ə vóyd/ *v* **1** *vt* keep away from **2** *vti* not do or prevent from happening —**avoidable** *adj* —**avoidance** *n*

avoirdupois /ávv waar dyoo pwaá, ávvərdə poyz/, **avoirdupois weight** *n* a system for measuring weights based on the pound

Avon /áyvən/ **1** river in central England, rising in Northamptonshire and flowing through Stratford to join the River Severn. Length 154 km/96 mi. **2** river in SW England, rising in Gloucestershire and flowing through Bristol to the Bristol Channel. Length 120 km/75 mi. **3** river in S England, rising in Wiltshire and flowing through Salisbury to the English Channel. Length 96 km/60 mi.

avow /ə vów/ *vt* **affirm** *(fml)* —**avowal** *n* —**avowedly** /ə vówidli/ *adv*

avuncular /ə vúngkyŏŏlər/ *adj* of or like an uncle —**avuncularity** /ə vúngkyŏŏ lárrəti/ *n* —**avuncularly** *adv*

AWACS /áy waks/ *n* an airborne military surveillance system. Full form **Airborne Warning and Control System**

await /ə wáyt/ *v* **1** *vti* wait for somebody or something **2** *vt* be going to happen or be given to somebody

awake /ə wáyk/ *adj* **1** not asleep **2** alert or aware ■ *vti* (**awaking, awoke** /ə wŏk/ *or* **awaked, awoken** /ə wŏkən/ *or* **awaked**) **1** rouse or emerge from sleep **2** make or become alert or aware

awaken /ə wáykən/ *vti* wake up —**awakening** *n*

award /ə wáwrd/ *n* **1** something given for merit or achievement **2** something granted by a law court or by arbitration ■ *vt* **1** give for merit or achievement ○ *awarded the prize to the whole class* **2** bestow by judicial decision or by arbitration

award wage, award rate *n ANZ* a statutory minimum wage

aware /ə wáir/ *adj* **1** having knowledge **2** noticing or realizing —**awareness** *n*

SYNONYMS **aware, conscious, mindful, cognizant, sensible** CORE MEANING: having knowledge of the existence of something

awash /ə wósh/ *adj* **1** covered in water **2** oversupplied

away /ə wáy/ *adv* **1** uninvolved ○ *stays away from trouble* **2** in a different direction ○ *turning his face away* **3** into or in the distance ○ *clouds away over there* ○ *walked away* **4** in the future ○ *only a week away* **5** into storage or safekeeping ○ *put the winter clothes away* **6** off (*follows a verb*) ○ *chipped the paint away* **7** to or from somebody's possession ○ *gave the old car away* **8** until something is used up ○ *frittered away his inheritance* **9** gradually ○ *The thunder died away.* **10** so as to show a change ○ *a gradual shift away from fossil fuels* **11** without stopping ○ *hammered away on the nails* ■ *adv, adj* **1** in another place ○ *will be away until next week* ○ *works away from the office* **2** in distance or time ○ *is located about 10 minutes away* ○ *works in a place not far away* ■ *adj* in golf, farthest from the hole

awe *n* great respect or wonder mixed with fear ■ *vt* (**awing, awed**) cause to feel awe

~~aweful~~ incorrect spelling of **awful**

awesome /áwsəm/ *adj* **1** impressive and frightening **2** excellent (*slang*) —**awesomely** *adv* —**awesomeness** *n*

awestruck /áw struk/, **awestricken** /-strikən/ *adj* full of awe

awful /áwf'l/ *adj* **1** extremely bad, unpleasant, or distressing **2** ill **3** very great (*infml*) —**awfulness** *n*

awfully /áwfli, -fəli/ *adv* **1** very **2** badly or unpleasantly

awhile /ə wíl/ *adv* for a brief period

awkward /áwkwərd/ *adj* **1** embarrassing or inconvenient **2** difficult or uncomfortable to use **3** without grace or coordination **4** shyly uncomfortable or embarrassed —**awkwardly** *adv* —**awkwardness** *n*

ORIGIN **Awkward** was originally an adverb meaning 'in the wrong direction', used in Scotland and N England. The adjective **awkward** meant 'back-handed' before it developed its modern senses.

awl /awl/ *n* a sharp-pointed tool for punching small holes ◊ See note at **all**

awning /áwning/ *n* an extendable canvas or metal roof

awoke past tense of **awake**

awoken past participle of **awake**

AWOL /áy wol/ *adj* away from a post without permission. Full form **absent without leave**

awry /ə rí/ *adj* **1** crooked **2** amiss

axe *n* **1** a tool with a flat heavy blade for cutting wood **2** dismissal from a job (*slang*) **3** closure or discontinuation (*slang*) ■ *vt* (**axing, axed**) (*slang*) **1** terminate **2** dismiss from a job ◊ **have an axe to grind** be motivated by some personal consideration

axiom /áksi əm/ *n* **1** a generally accepted truth **2** a basic proposition assumed to be true in a logical system —**axiomatic** /áksi ə máttik/ *adj*

axis /áksiss/ (*pl* **-es** /ák seez/) *n* **1** a line around which something rotates or is symmetrical **2** a line at the edge of a graph **3** an alliance

axle /áks'l/ *n* a shaft or spindle on which a wheel turns

ayatollah /í ə tóllə/ *n* a Shiite religious leader

Ayckbourn /áyk bawrn/, **Alan** (*b.* 1939) British dramatist

aye /ī/, **ay** *adv, interj* yes ■ *n* (*pl* **ayes**) a vote or voter in favour of a motion

Ayer /air/, **A. J.** (1910–89) British philosopher

Ayers Rock /áirz-/ former name for **Uluru**

Ayeshah ♦ **Aisha**

Ayurvedic medicine /aə yoor váydik-, -veedik-/ *n* an ancient Hindu system of healing

azalea /ə záyli ə/ (*pl* **-eas** *or* same) *n* a flowering bush

azan /aa zaán/ *n* the Islamic call to prayer

Azerbaijan /ázzər bī jaán/ country in W Asia. Cap. Baku. Pop. 7,771,092 (2001). —**Azerbaijani** *n, adj*

azimuth /ázziməth/ *n* **1** the eastward angle from north **2** the angular distance along the horizon between a point of reference and another object

Aznar /ath naár, ass naár/, **José María** (*b.* 1953) prime minister of Spain (1996–)

Azores /ə záwrz/ archipelago in the N Atlantic Ocean, an autonomous region of Portugal. Pop. 237,800 (1993).

in SW Russia

Aztec /áz tek/ *n* a member of a Native Central American people whose empire dominated central Mexico during the 14C and 15C —**Aztec** *adj*

azuki bean *n* cook = adzuki bean

azure /ázhər, áy-/ (*literary*) *adj* deep blue ■ *n* 1 the blue sky 2 a deep blue colour

B

b¹ (*pl* **b's**), **B** (*pl* **B's** *or* **Bs**) *n* the 2nd letter of the English alphabet

b² *abbr* 1 billion 2 born 3 bowled

B¹ (*pl* **B's** *or* **Bs**) *n* 1 the 7th note in the musical key of C major 2 the 2nd highest grade of a student's work 3 a human blood type containing a specific antigen

B² *symbol* boron

b. *abbr* born

B2B *abbr* business-to-business

B2C *abbr* business-to-consumer

B4 *abbr* before (*in e-mails*)

Ba *symbol* barium

BA *abbr* 1 Bachelor of Arts 2 British Airways

baa (**baas, baaing, baaed**) *vi* make the bleat of a sheep —**baa** *n*

baas /baass/ *n* S Africa boss

baba /baá baa, -bə/ *n* a rum-flavoured cake

Babbage /bábbij/, **Charles** (1791–1871) British mathematician and inventor of mechanical calculating machines that were forerunners of the computer

babble /bább'l/ (**-bling, -bled**) *v* 1 *vti* speak or say something incoherently 2 *vi* talk at length about irrelevant things 3 *vi* make a continuous murmuring sound (*refers to flowing water*) —**babble** *n*

babe *n* 1 a sexually attractive young woman or man (*slang*) 2 a baby

babel /báyb'l/ *n* a confused noise (*literary*)

ORIGIN Babel derives from the Tower of Babel, where, according to the Bible, God showed his anger at its construction by causing the people to speak different languages and become unintelligible to one another.

baboon /bə boʻon/ *n* 1 a large monkey with a prominent snout and bare pink patches on its buttocks 2 a person regarded as rude and clumsy (*insult*)

baby /báybi/ *n* (*pl* **-bies**) 1 a very young or unborn child or animal 2 a person who behaves childishly (*disapproving*) 3 the youngest member of a family or group 4 used as a term of endearment (*slang; sometimes offensive*) ■ *adj* describes small young vegetables ○ *baby carrots* ■ *vt* (**-bies, -bied**) treat with excessive care —**babyhood** *n* —**babyish** *adj*

ORIGIN Before the 11C, the term for what we now call a **baby** was *child*, and it was only after the 11C that *child* began to extend to the slightly more mature age that it now covers. **Baby** appeared in the 14C. It appears to be imitative of sounds made by infants before they can talk.

baby bond *n* a tax-free savings scheme for children and young people

baby boom *n* a large increase in birthrate

baby boomer *n* somebody born in a baby boom such as the one following World War II

baby grand *n* a small grand piano

Babylon /bábbilən, -lon/ capital of ancient Babylonia

Babylonia /bábbi lóni ə/ ancient empire in Mesopotamia, in present-day Iraq

babysit /báybisit/ (**-sitting, -sat** /-sat/) *vti* look after a child while the parents are away —**babysitter** *n*

baby talk, babytalk /bábi tawk/ *n* the simplified language often used by adults when talking to small children

baccalaureate /bákə láwri ət/ *n* 1 a school-leaving exam in France 2 a bachelor's degree (*fml*)

baccarat /bákə raa, -raá/ *n* a card game in which players bet against the bank

Bacchus /bákəss/ *n* in classical mythology, the god of wine

Bach /baak, baakh/, **Johann Sebastian** (1685–1750) German composer and organist

bachelor /báchələr/ *n* 1 an unmarried man 2 an unmarried young male seal —**bachelorhood** *n*

Bachelor of Arts *n* a university degree in a humanities subject

Bachelor of Science *n* a university degree in a science subject

Bach flower remedies /bách-/ *npl* a healing method using flower extracts

ORIGIN The remedies are named after their inventor, the British physician Edward Bach (1886–1936).

bacillus /bə sílləss/ (*pl* **-li** /-sīl ī/) *n* a rod-shaped bacterium

back *n* 1 the part of the human body nearest the spine, between the neck and the pelvis 2 the spine, or the area around an organism's spine 3 the rear of an object 4 the part of a seat that supports your back 5 a defensive player in a team ■ *adv* 1 in a reverse direction in space or time 2 at a distance ○ *Stay back.* 3 into a reclining position ○ *sit back* 4 to the original owner ○ *handed it back* 5 in response ○ *hit him back* 6 to a former condition or topic ○ *get back to the point* ■ *adj* 1 located at the back 2 situated in a remote location, e.g. away from main roads ■ *v* 1 *vti* move backwards 2 *vt* support a person, cause, or statement 3 *vt* bet on a person, team, or horse to win a race **4** *vt* reinforce by adding a physical support ◇ *back it with cardboard* **5** *vt* provide musical accompaniment for **6** *vi* change to an anticlockwise direction *(refers to winds)* —**backless** *adj* ◇ **get off somebody's back** stop criticizing or pressurizing somebody *(slang)* ◇ **have your back to the wall** be in a difficult situation with no obvious means of escape ◇ **put somebody's back up** annoy or antagonize somebody *(infml)* ◇ **the back of beyond** a remote place

USAGE Back can refer either to a change to an earlier time or to a later time. This possibility becomes particularly confusing when the subject is, for example, a decision, now in the past, about what was at the time the future: *Last month she told me she wanted to move my appointment back.* In a context like this, *make earlier* or *make later* is clearer.

☐ **back down** *or* **off** *vi* abandon a claim, commitment, or position

☐ **back out** *vi* withdraw from a prior commitment

☐ **back up** *v* **1** *vt* support somebody or something **2** *vt* copy computer files **3** *vi* form a long queue along a road

backache /bák ayk/ *n* pain in the back

back-and-forth *n US* a repeated exchange of ideas or information

back bench *n UK, ANZ, Can* in a parliament, a seating area for MPs who are not ministers or shadow ministers, or this group of MPs *(usually pl)* —**backbench** /bák bénch/ *adj*

backbencher /bák bénchər/ *n* **1** *UK, ANZ, Can* a junior member of a legislative assembly who is not a minister or shadow minister **2** *ANZ, US, Can* a member of a legislative assembly who has low seniority

backbite /bák bīt/ *(-biting, -bit* /-bit/, *-bitten* /-bitt'n/ *or* *-bit)* *vti* make spiteful remarks about somebody —**backbiter** *n*

backboard /bák bawrd/ *n* a board behind the basket in basketball

backbone /bák bōn/ *n* **1** an animal's spinal column **2** something similar in shape or position to a spinal column **3** any central supporting part **4** strength of character **5** a high-speed relay in a computer network

backbreaking /bák brayking/ *adj* physically exhausting

backchat /bák chat/ *n* insolent replies

backcloth /bák kloth/ *n* a theatre backdrop

backcomb /bák kōm/ *vt* comb hair towards the roots to create an appearance of thickness

back country *n ANZ, US, Can* a remote rural area

backdate /bák dayt/ *(-dating, -dated)* *vt* **1** put an earlier date on **2** make effective from an earlier date

back door *n* **1** a rear door **2** an underhand opportunity that gives somebody a dishonest advantage

backdoor /bák dawr/ *adj* indirect or underhand

backdrop /bák drop/ *n* **1** a painted cloth at the back of a theatre stage **2** a setting for something

back end *n* **1** a main computer **2** a piece of software controlling routine tasks

backer /bákər/ *n* **1** somebody who gives moral or financial support **2** somebody who lays bets

SYNONYMS backer, angel, guarantor, patron, sponsor CORE MEANING: somebody who provides financial support

backfire /bák fīr/ *(-firing, -fired)* *vi* **1** have the opposite effect to the one intended **2** produce an explosion of unburnt exhaust gases in the exhaust pipe of a motor vehicle —**backfire** *n*

back-formation *n* **1** the process of forming a new word by removing a real or imagined affix **2** a new word formed by removing an affix, e.g. 'televise' from 'television'

backgammon /bák gamən/ *n* **1** a board game in which counters are moved on the throw of a pair of dice **2** in backgammon, a complete victory

background /bák grownd/ *n* **1** personal circumstances and experiences **2** the circumstances that cause an event **3** the scenery behind something **4** the part of a picture that appears to be behind the main subject **5** information that explains something **6** a position of inconspicuousness **7** constant low level radiation ■ *adj* **1** forming part of the background **2** accompanying

background music *n* music to create atmosphere

background processing *n* execution of a subsidiary operation by a computer while the user works with another application

backhand /bák hand/ *n* **1** in racket games, a stroke played with the back of the hand towards the ball **2** the side of a court or a tennis player's body on which the player naturally plays a backhand **3** a style of handwriting in which the characters slope leftwards

backhanded /bák hándid/ *adj* **1** backhand **2** describes a comment with a double meaning, especially an apparent compliment that can also be understood as an insult —**backhandedly** *adv* —**backhandedness** *n*

backhander /bák handər/ *n* a bribe *(infml)*

backing /báking/ *n* **1** support or help **2** the rear surface of something, providing support or protection **3** musical accompaniment

backlash /bák lash/ *n* **1** a strong widespread adverse reaction **2** a violent backward movement

backlist /bák list/ *n* a publisher's range of earlier books that are still in print

backlog /bák log/ *n* a number of things still to be done before progress can be made

back number *n* an earlier issue of a publication

back office *n* a secure area of software ■ *adj* of internal matters

backpack /bák pak/ n 1 a rucksack 2 a set of equipment carried on a person's or an animal's back ■ vi hike or travel with a backpack —**backpacker** n

back pay n pay owed for work done earlier

backpedal /bák ped'l/ (-alling, -alled) v 1 vi pedal backwards 2 retract or tone down an earlier statement

backroom /bák room, -room/ n also **back room** a place where secret research or planning is carried out ■ adj unobtrusive or clandestine

back seat n a seat in the back of a vehicle

backside /bák síd, bák síd/ n the buttocks (infml)

backslash /bák slash/ n a keyboard character in the form of a left-leaning diagonal line

backslide /bák slíd/ (-sliding, -slid /-slid/) vi relapse into a former bad or immoral condition —**backslider** n

backspin /bák spin/ n the backward spinning motion of a ball that is moving forwards

backstage /bák stáyj/ adv 1 behind the scenes in a theatre 2 in private —**backstage** adj

backstop /bák stop/ n a screen to stop a ball

backstreet /bák street/ n a minor street ■ adj 1 in a minor street 2 illicit

backstroke /bák strōk/ n 1 a method of swimming on the back 2 a return stroke or movement in a mechanical system —**backstroke** vi

back-to-back adj 1 with backs facing or touching each other 2 consecutive —**back to back** adv

back to front adv the wrong way round

backtrack /bák trak/ vi 1 go back 2 distance yourself from a previous action, opinion, or statement

backup /bák up/ n 1 support or assistance 2 a substitute or reserve used when something fails 3 a copy of computer data made for safekeeping 4 the process of copying computer data 5 an excess quantity of something that builds up when the normal flow is obstructed —**backup** adj

backward /bákwərd/ adj 1 to or towards the rear 2 positioned the opposite way round or in the opposite order 3 not progressing or developing in the usual way (sometimes offensive) 4 retrograde ○ a backward step 5 towards the past ■ adv backwards —**backwardness** n ◊ **not be backward in coming forward** be quick and eager to claim something or advertise your accomplishments (infml)

backwards /bákwərdz/ adv 1 with the back facing the direction of movement 2 towards the rear 3 in the reverse order or direction 4 towards the past ◊ **bend** or **lean over backwards** make an exceptional effort ◊ **know something backwards** know something very well

backwash /bák wosh/ n 1 a backward movement of water from a broken wave 2 unpleasant consequences

backwater /bák wawtər/ n 1 a small stagnant branch of a river 2 a remote, uneventful place

backwoods /bák woodz/ npl 1 remote wooded areas 2 a remote unsophisticated area —**backwoods** adj —**backwoodsman** n

back yard n 1 a yard behind a house 2 somebody's neighbourhood —**backyard** adj

bacon /báykən/ n salted and dried meat from the back and sides of a pig ◊ **bring home the bacon** earn the money to support a family (infml) ◊ **save somebody's bacon** save somebody from serious trouble or harm (infml)

Bacon /báykn/, **Sir Francis, 1st Baron Verulam and Viscount St Albans** (1561–1626) English philosopher, lawyer, and politician

Bacon, Francis (1909–92) Irish-born British painter

bacteria plural of **bacterium**

bacterial /bak teeri əl/ adj of or caused by bacteria

bacteriology /bak teeri ólləji/ n the scientific study of bacteria —**bacteriological** /bak teeri ə lójjik'l/ adj —**bacteriologist** n

bacteriophage /bak teeri ə fayj/ n a virus that infects bacteria

bacterium /bak teeri əm/ (pl **-a** /-ri ə/) n a single-celled microorganism without distinct nuclei or organized cell structures, sometimes a cause of disease —**bacteroid** /báktə royd/ adj

Bactrian camel /báktri ən-/ n a two-humped camel

bad adj (**worse, worst**) 1 of unacceptably poor quality 2 unskilled or incompetent ○ a bad rendition of the piano solo 3 wicked 4 misbehaving and disobedient 5 angry and unpleasant ○ in a bad mood 6 offensive ○ bad language 7 harmful ○ a bad influence 8 rotten ○ a bad peach 9 injured or diseased ○ a bad tooth 10 unwell 11 ashamed, sorrowful, or disappointed ○ feel bad about it 12 more severe or unpleasant than usual ○ a bad headache 13 distressing ○ bad news 14 unfavourable ○ a bad report 15 (comparative **badder**, superlative **baddest**) very good (slang) ■ n unsatisfactory or unpleasant things ○ take the bad with the good —**badness** n

SYNONYMS **bad, criminal, delinquent, mischievous, naughty** CORE MEANING: indicating wrongdoing

bad blood n ill feeling

bad cheque n a cheque that is not honoured because of insufficient funds

bad debt n an amount of money owed but not paid

baddie /báddi/, **baddy** (pl **-dies**) n a villain in a film or book (infml)

bade past tense of **bid**

Baden-Powell /báyd'n pố əl, -pów əl/, **Agnes** (1858–1945) British founder of the Girl Guides Association

Baden-Powell, Robert, 1st Baron Baden-Powell of Gilwell (1857–1941) British soldier and founder of the Scout Movement

Bader /baˈadər/, **Sir Douglas** (1910–82) British fighter pilot

bad faith *n* insincerity, especially as shown in a failure to carry out a stated intention

badge *n* 1 an object worn as a sign of rank, membership, or support 2 an identifying feature ■ *vt* (**badging**, **badged**) put a badge or identifying mark on

badger /bájjər/ *n* a black-and-white nocturnal burrowing mammal ■ *vt* pester

badinage /báddi naazh, -naaj, báddi naˈazh/ *n* playful talk *(fml)*

badlands /bád landz/ *npl* a barren area with peaks and gullies formed by erosion

badly /báddli/ (**worse**, **worst**) *adv* 1 in an unsatisfactory or incompetent way 2 in a way that causes disappointment or suffering 3 to a severe degree 4 very much 5 in an annoying or immoral way

badly off (**worse off**, **worst off**) *adj* 1 not having much money 2 lacking in what is needed or required

badminton /bádmintən/ *n* 1 a game in which players hit a shuttlecock with rackets over a high net 2 a cocktail based on claret

ORIGIN The game of **badminton** takes its name from Badminton House, the country seat of the dukes of Beaufort in Avon, SW England. It was apparently first played there in its modern form, being developed from earlier informal games with a bat and shuttlecock.

badmouth /bád mowth, -mowth/ *vt* criticize *(slang)*

bad-tempered *adj* irritable —**bad-temperedly** *adv* —**bad-temperedness** *n*

Baffin Bay /báffin-/ large bay separating Greenland and Canada

Baffin Island large island in Nunavut Territory, NE Canada

baffle /báff'l/ *vt* (**-fling**, **-fled**) 1 puzzle somebody 2 control a flow ■ *n* 1 a device that prevents or controls a flow 2 a partition in a loudspeaker that separates sounds of different frequencies —**bafflement** *n* —**baffling** *adj* —**bafflingly** *adv*

BAFTA /báftə/ *abbr* British Academy of Film and Television Arts

bag *n* 1 a container made of a nonrigid material 2 the amount contained in a bag 3 a portable container for equipment or belongings 4 an item of baggage *(often pl)* 5 a handbag 6 a number of animals shot by a hunter 7 an offensive term deliberately insulting a woman's age and appearance *(slang insult)* 8 something that somebody is interested in or good at *(slang)* ■ **bags** *npl* loose skin under the eyes ■ *v* (**bagging**, **bagged**) 1 put something into a bag 2 *vti* bulge or make something bulge 3 *vt* shoot or capture an animal —**bagful** *n* ◇ **in the bag** certain to be achieved or obtained *(infml)*

bagatelle /bágga tél/ *n* 1 something unimportant *(fml)* 2 a board game in which

balls are rolled past obstacles into numbered holes 3 a short playful piece of music

Bagehot /bájjət/, **Walter** (1826–77) British economist and journalist

bagel /báyg'l/ *n* a ring-shaped bread roll with a chewy texture

baggage /bággij/ *n* 1 suitcases and bags carried by travellers 2 ideas, opinions, or feelings derived from past experiences, especially when regarded as an emotional encumbrance *(infml)*

baggy /bággi/ (**-gier**, **-giest**) *adj* hanging loose on the body —**baggily** *adv* —**bagginess** *n*

Baghdad /bág dád/, **Bagdad** capital of Iraq. Pop. 4,336,000 (1995).

bag lady *n* a homeless woman who carries her possessions around in bags *(infml)*

bagpipe /bág pīp/ *n* a pair of bagpipes ■ **bagpipes** *npl* a wind instrument consisting of an inflatable bag with several pipes through which air is forced to produce the notes —**bagpiper** *n*

baguette /ba gét/ *n* 1 a stick-shaped loaf of bread 2 a rectangular gemstone

Baguio /bággi ō/ summer capital of the Philippines. Pop. 268,772 (1999).

bah *interj* expresses disgust

Bahamas /bə haˈaməz/ island nation in the Atlantic Ocean southeast of Florida. Cap. Nassau. Pop. 297,852 (2001). —**Bahamian** /bə háymi ən/ *n, adj*

Bahrain /baa ráyn/, **Bahrein** island state in the Persian Gulf off the coast of Saudi Arabia. Cap. Manama. Pop. 645,361 (2001). —**Bahraini** *n, adj*

baht /baat/ (*pl* **bahts** *or same*) *n* the main unit of Thai currency

Baikal, Lake /bī kaál/ world's deepest lake, in S Siberia, Russia. Depth 1,637 m/5,371 ft.

bail¹ /bayl/ *n* 1 money paid to secure somebody's temporary release from legal custody and guarantee the person's future appearance in court 2 temporary release from custody ■ *vt* free somebody by paying bail

bail² /bayl/, **bale** (**baling**, **baled**) *vti* empty water from a boat
□ **bail** *or* **bale out** *v* 1 *vi* parachute from a plane *(infml)* 2 *vi* escape from a difficult situation *(infml)* 3 *vt* help somebody out of trouble

bail³ /bayl/ *n* each of the two short crosspieces of a wicket in cricket

bail⁴ /bayl/, **bale** *n* a semicircular handle or support

bailey /báyli/ *n* 1 the outer wall of a castle 2 a courtyard inside a castle wall

Bailey bridge /báyli-/ *n* a temporary bridge made of prefabricated parts

ORIGIN The bridge is named after the British engineer Sir D. Coleman Bailey (1901–85), who designed it.

bailiff /báylif/ *n* 1 a landowner's steward 2 a sheriff's officer empowered to take possession of a debtor's property **3** a district official with largely symbolic powers

bailiwick /báyliwik/ n somebody's sphere of specialized knowledge

bain-marie /báN mə ree/ (pl **bain-maries**) n a double container used to cook food gently or keep it warm

ORIGIN The original **bain-marie** was not a cooking utensil but an alchemist's apparatus, used in attempts to turn base metal into gold. In Greek the corresponding word meant literally 'furnace of Mary'. It was translated into Latin as 'bath of Mary', and this is also what the French form, which was adopted into English, means. The Mary in question is the sister of Moses (usually known as Miriam), who was reputed to be an expert alchemist.

Bairam /bī raàm/ n each of two Islamic festivals, the Lesser Bairam, marking the end of Ramadan, or the Greater Bairam, marking the end of the Islamic year

Baird /baird/, **John Logie** (1888–1946) British inventor. He demonstrated an electro-mechanical television system in 1926.

bairn /bairn/ n N England, Scotland a child

bait /bayt/ n **1** a piece of food used to lure an animal **2** an enticement of any kind ■ vt **1** put food on a hook to catch a fish **2** tease or taunt **3** attack an animal with dogs ◇ **rise to the bait** react to temptation or provocation in the desired way

haize /bayz/ n green woollen cloth. Use: to cover snooker and card tables.

Baja California /baà haa-/ peninsula in NW Mexico. Length 1,200 km/760 mi.

bak abbr a file extension indicating a backup file

bake v (**baking**, **baked**) **1** vti cook food in an oven without fat or oil **2** vti harden something by heating **3** vi be very hot (infml) ■ n a batch of baked food

baked beans npl haricot beans in tomato sauce

baker /báykər/ n somebody who makes bread and cakes

baker's dozen n thirteen

ORIGIN Retailers of bread formerly received an extra loaf with each dozen from the baker, which they were entitled to keep as profit. This is why the **baker's dozen** is 13 rather than 12.

bakery /báykəri/ (pl **-ies**) n **1** a place where food is baked **2** a shop selling baked foods

baking powder n a mixture containing sodium bicarbonate, starch, and acids. Use: making cakes rise.

baking soda n bicarbonate of soda. Use: making cakes rise.

bakkie /báki/ n S Africa **1** a pick-up truck **2** a bowl

baklava /baàklə vaa, bákləvə/ n a dessert made with thin layers of filo pastry, nuts, and syrup or honey

baksheesh /bák sheesh, bák sheesh/ n a tip or bribe

Baku /baa koó/ capital of Azerbaijan. Pop. 1,708,000 (1999).

Bakunin /bə koónnin/, **Mikhail** (1814–76) Russian anarchist

balaclava /bállə klaàvə/ n a knitted helmet that covers the head and part of the face

balalaika /bállə líkə/ n a Russian stringed instrument with a triangular body

balance /bállənss/ n **1** the condition of remaining steady on a relatively small base **2** the stability that results when opposite forces have equal strength **3** a state in which various elements form a harmonious whole **4** emotional stability **5** a weighing machine **6** a counterweight **7** the greater part of something **8** the remainder **9** a position of equal debit and credit **10** a difference between debit and credit **11 Balance** the constellation and zodiacal sign Libra ■ v (**-ancing, -anced**) **1** vti remain in or give something equilibrium **2** vti be or place something in a precarious position **3** vt assess something **4** vt weigh something **5** vti be equal or cancel something out **6** vt bring elements into harmony **7** vt make the elements of a chemical or mathematical equation equal **8** vt assess a financial account ◇ **hang in the balance** be in a situation in which success and failure seem equally likely ◇ **on balance** taking all the relevant factors into consideration ◇ **redress the balance** make the situation fairer by assisting somebody who was previously at a disadvantage

balanced /bállənst/ adj **1** even-handed **2** combining elements in a healthy way **3** mentally stable

balance of payments n a nation's debits and credits

balance of power n **1** equilibrium of power between nations **2** the power to affect a situation decisively

balance of trade n the difference between a nation's imports and exports

balance sheet n a statement of debits and credits

Balanchine /bállən cheen, bállən cheén/, **George** (1904–83) Russian-born US dancer and choreographer

balboa /bal bó ə/ n the main unit of Panamanian currency

Balboa /bal bó ə/, **Vasco Núñez de** (1475?–1519) Spanish explorer

balcony /bálkəni/ (pl **-nies**) n **1** a platform on the wall of a building, usually enclosed by a rail or parapet **2** in a theatre, a raised area of seating

bald /bawld/ adj **1** with little or no hair on the head **2** with no fur, grass, trees, or other natural covering **3** worn in texture o bald tyres **4** not explained or elaborated on o the bald truth —**baldness** n

bald eagle n a North American bird of prey with a white head and tail

balderdash /báwldər dash/ *n* nonsense

balding /báwlding/ *adj* going bald

Bob Adelman

James Baldwin

Baldwin /báwldwin/, **James** (1924–87) US writer

Baldwin, Stanley, 1st Earl Baldwin of Bewdley (1867–1947) British prime minister (1923–24, 1924–29, 1935–37)

bale[1] *n* a large bundle of hay or other raw material ■ *vti* (**baling, baled**) make something into bales

bale[2] *vti* = **bail**[2]

bale[3] *n* = **bail**[4]

Balearic Islands /bálli árrik-/ island group in the W Mediterranean including Majorca, Menorca, and Ibiza. It is an autonomous region of Spain. Pop. 736,865 (1991).

baleful /báylf'l/ *adj* 1 threatening 2 harmful —**balefully** *adv* —**balefulness** *n*

~~balence~~ incorrect spelling of **balance**

Balfour /bálfər, -fawr/, **Arthur James, 1st Earl of Balfour** (1848–1930) British prime minister (1902–05)

Bali /ba'ali/ island east of Java, S Indonesia. Pop. 2,895,600 (1995).

balk *v, n* = **baulk**

Balkan Mountains /báwlkən-/ mountain range in Yugoslavia and Bulgaria. Highest peak Botev Peak 2,376 m/7,795 ft.

Balkan Peninsula peninsula in SE Europe

Balkan States, Balkans /báwlkənz/ the countries on the Balkan Peninsula —**Balkan** *adj*

ball[1] *n* 1 a round object that is thrown, hit, or kicked in many games and sports 2 a rounded object or mass 3 any game played with a ball 4 a ball played in a particular way ○ *a long ball into the penalty area* 5 in cricket, a delivery by a bowler 6 in rugby, possession of the ball after a set piece 7 a round solid projectile 8 a rounded body part, e.g. at the base of the thumb or just behind the toes ○ *the ball of the foot* ■ *vti* make into or form a ball ◇ **get** *or* **set** *or* **start the ball rolling** start something off (*infml*) ◇ **on the ball** aware of what is going on and quick to respond (*infml*) ◇ **play ball** cooperate (*infml*)

ball[2] *n* a formal dance ◇ **have a ball** enjoy yourself very much (*infml*)

ballad /bálləd/ *n* 1 a narrative song 2 a slow romantic song —**balladist** *n* —**balladry** *n*

ballast /bálləst/ *n* 1 heavy material carried in a ship's hold to give stability 2 anything that gives extra bulk or stability 3 gravel used as the foundation for a road or railway track, or in making concrete ■ *vt* 1 load with ballast 2 stabilize

ball bearing *n* a bearing that uses small metal balls to reduce friction between moving metal parts

ball boy *n* in tennis, a boy who retrieves balls during a game

ballcock /báwl kok/ *n* a rod with a floating ball at one end that regulates the level of water in a tank

ballerina /bállə reenə/ *n* a woman ballet dancer

ballet /bállay/ *n* 1 a form of dramatic dance characterized by conventional steps and movements 2 a story performed by ballet dancers 3 a group of ballet dancers —**balletic** /ba léttik/ *adj*

ball game *n* 1 any game played with a ball 2 *US, Can* a baseball game

ball girl *n* in tennis, a girl who retrieves balls during a game

ballistic /bə lístik/ *adj* of projectiles

ballistic missile *n* a large missile that has no guidance system on board

ballistics /bə lístiks/ *n* (+ *sing verb*) 1 the study of projectiles 2 the study of firearms

balloon /bə loon/ *n* 1 a toy consisting of a small rubber bag filled with air 2 a large gas-filled bag with a gondola, used as a form of air transport 3 a rounded device encircling a character's speech in a cartoon ■ *vi* 1 form a large rounded shape 2 increase in amount ◇ **go over** *or* **down like a lead balloon** be completely unsuccessful (*infml*)

ballooning /bə looning/ *n* travelling in a balloon

balloon mortgage *n* a mortgage with a large final payment

ballot /bállət/ *n* 1 a voting system in which votes are cast in secret 2 a secret vote 3 *also* **ballot paper** a paper or other device by which to cast a vote ■ *v* 1 *vt* cast ballots or a ballot in voting 2 *vi* ask for a vote

ballot box *n* 1 a box for completed ballots 2 election by ballot

ballpark /báwl paark/ *US, Can n* 1 a park for playing ball games 2 a touchdown area for spacecraft ■ *adj* approximate (*infml*)

ballpoint /báwl poynt/, **ballpoint pen** *n* a pen with a rotating ball at its tip

ballroom /báwl room, -room/ *n* a room used for dancing

ballroom dancing *n* a style of formal dancing with set patterns of steps for couples

balls (*offensive*) *npl* a taboo term for the testicles ■ *n* 1 a taboo term meaning courage and determination 2 a taboo term meaning nonsense

balls up *vt* a taboo term meaning to botch something (*offensive*)

balls-up *n* a taboo term for something failed or messed up (*offensive*)

ballyhoo /bálli hoo/ *n* 1 an uproar 2 sensational advertising ■ *vt* (**-hooing, -hooed**) publicize something loudly

balm /baam/ n 1 an oily plant extract used in soothing ointments 2 something that soothes

balmy /báami/ (-ier, -iest) adj describes pleasantly mild weather —**balminess** n

baloney /bə lóni/ n nonsense (infml)

~~baloon~~ incorrect spelling of **balloon**

balsa /báwlssə/, **balsa wood** n a lightweight wood. Use: insulation, making models.

balsam /báwlssəm/ n 1 an oily resinous plant substance. Use: in perfumes, medicines. 2 a preparation containing balsam 3 any flowering plant of the Busy Lizzie family —**balsamic** /bawl sámmik/ adj

balsamic vinegar n a dark-coloured, sweet Italian vinegar

balti /báwlti, bál-/ n a spicy Pakistani dish traditionally served in the rounded pan it is cooked in

Baltic Sea /báwltik-/ sea in N Europe between Sweden, Finland, Russia, Estonia, Latvia, Lithuania, Poland, Germany, and Denmark

Baltic States Estonia, Latvia, and Lithuania, considered as a group

Baltimore /báwltə mawr/ port and largest city in Maryland. Pop. 645,593 (1998).

Baluchistan /bə lóochi staán/ mountainous dry region in SW Pakistan and SE Iran

baluster /bálləstər/ n a post supporting a handrail

balustrade /bállə stráyd/ n a decorative railing along the edge of a balcony or bridge

Balzac /bál zak/, **Honoré de** (1799–1850) French novelist —**Balzacian** /bal záki ən/ adj

Bamako /bámməkō/ capital of Mali. · Pop. 1,016,167 (1998).

bamboo /bam boó/ (pl -boos) n 1 the strong hollow stems of a tropical plant. Use: furniture, cane supports. 2 a tropical plant with tall, stiff, woody stems that produces bamboo

---

ORIGIN **Bamboo** comes ultimately from Malay. The earliest English forms ended in -s, because the direct source was Dutch *bamboes*, but this was later taken to be the English plural ending and a new singular form came into use.

---

bamboozle /ham hóóz'l/ vt trick or deceive somebody (infml)

ban /ban/ vt (banning, banned) 1 forbid something officially or legally 2 stop somebody doing something ■ n an official or legal order forbidding something

banal /bə naál/ adj dull and unoriginal —**banality** n —**banally** adv

banana /bə naánə/ n 1 a long curved yellow fruit 2 the tropical plant that produces bananas

banana republic n a small dictatorship with an economy dependent on the export of a single product (disapproving)

banana split n a sundae made of a banana, ice cream, and toppings

~~bancrupcy~~ incorrect spelling of **bankruptcy**

band[1] n 1 a group of musicians playing together, e.g. a group playing pop music 2 a group of people with the same beliefs or purpose o *a growing band of supporters*
□ **band together** vi unite as a group

band[2] n 1 a strip or loop of fabric, elastic, or other material 2 a strip of material whose colour or texture contrasts with the other material it is attached to 3 a plain ring worn on a finger 4 a range or group within a larger one

Banda /bándə/, **Hastings** (1906?–97) Malawi prime minister (1964–66) and president (1966–94)

bandage /bándij/ n a cloth strip for covering an injury —**bandage** vt

bandanna /ban dánnə/, **bandana** n a bright cotton scarf worn around the head or neck

Bandaranaike /bándərə nī́ əkə/ family of Sri Lankan politicians including **S.W.R.D.** (1899–1959) prime minister (1956–59) and his wife **Sirimavo** (1916–2000) prime minister (1960–65, 1970–77, 1994–2000). She was the world's first woman prime minister. ◊ **Kumaratunga**

Bandar Seri Begawan /bán daar sérri bə gáawon/ capital of Brunei. Pop. 50,000 (1995 estimate).

B & B abbr bed and breakfast (infml)

bandeau /bándō/ (pl -deaux /-dōz/) n 1 a band of material worn over the breasts 2 US, Can a ribbon or band for the hair

bandh, bundh n S Asia a general strike

bandicoot /bándi koot/ n an Australasian marsupial with a long pointed nose

bandit /bándit/ n an armed robber —**banditry** n

Bandler /bándlər/, **Faith** (b. 1918) Australian writer and activist

B and S Ball n a dance in the Australian outback for young people. Full form **Bachelor and Spinsters Ball**

bandstand /bánd stand/ n a public platform for a brass band to play on

Bandung /bán dŏong/ city in W Java, Indonesia. Pop. 3,557,665 (1997).

bandwagon /bánd wagən/ n an increasingly popular movement or cause

bandwidth /bánd width/ n 1 a range of radio frequencies 2 the capacity of an Internet connection or other communication channel

bandy /bándi/ vt (-dies, -died) casually exchange words ■ adj (-dier, -diest) describes legs that curve outwards so the knees cannot meet

bane n 1 a cause of continual misery 2 a cause of death, destruction, or ruin (literary) —**baneful** adj —**banefully** adv —**banefulness** n

bang n 1 a sudden loud noise 2 a sharp hit ■ v 1 vti hit hard or noisily 2 vti hit accidentally o *bang into the furniture* 3 vti close hard and noisily 4 vi make a loud noise ■ adv 1 exactly or precisely 2 suddenly ◊ **bang on** UK, Can exactly right (infml) ◊ **go out with a bang** end or finish something in a dramatic way (infml)
□ **bang on** vi keep talking (infml)

□ **bang up** vt lock up a prisoner (infml)

Bangalore /báng gə láwr/ capital of Karnataka State, India. Pop. 2,660,088 (1991).

banger /báng gər/ n (infml) **1** a sausage **2** an old car in poor condition

Bangkok /báng kók, báng kok/ capital and main port of Thailand. Pop. 5,882,000 (1990).

Bangla¹ /báng glə/ n LANG = **Bengali** 2 —**Bangla** adj

Bangla² /báng glə/ state in NE India consisting of the western part of the former Indian state of Bengal. Cap. Kolkata. Pop. 80,221,171 (2001).

Bangladesh /báng glə désh/ country in South Asia, on the Bay of Bengal, east of India. Cap. Dhaka. Pop. 131,269,860 (2001). —**Bangladeshi** n, adj

bangle /báng g'l/ n **1** a rigid bracelet **2** a disc or other decoration that hangs from a bracelet

Bangor /báng gər/ **1** coastal town in E Northern Ireland. Pop. 52,437 (1991). **2** city on the Menai Strait, N Wales. Pop. 12,330 (1991).

Bangui /baang geé/ capital of the Central African Republic. Pop. 524,000 (1996).

banish /bánnish/ vt **1** send away from a place as a punishment **2** get rid of —**banishment** n

banister /bánnistər/, **bannister** n **1** a handrail on a staircase (often pl) **2** a post supporting a handrail

banjo /bánjō/ (pl **-jos** or **-joes**) n a five-stringed instrument with a flat circular body

Banjul /ban jóol/ capital of the Gambia. Pop. 44,200 (1994).

bank¹ n **1** a financial institution offering current accounts and other financial services, or its local office **2** a fund of money or tokens for use in gambling games **3** a source of resources, e.g. of blood **4** a large container for waste items that are to be recycled o *a bottle bank* ■ v **1** vt deposit money in a bank **2** vi have an account with a particular financial institution

ORIGIN The three English words **bank** all come ultimately from the same ancient Germanic root, which is also the source of **bench**. The 'bank of a river' form arrived in the 12C from a Scandinavian language. The 'bank of oars' form was adopted in the 13C from a French word meaning 'bench'. The financial institution form came in the 15C from Italian, possibly via French: the sense developed in Italian from the table (or 'bench') on which banking was transacted.

□ **bank on** vt rely on

bank² n **1** the side of a waterway **2** a ridge of sand below the surface of water **3** a pile of earth or snow with sloping sides **4** a mass of clouds **5** a slope at a bend in a racetrack **6** the angle of an aircraft as it turns in the sky ■ v **1** vti pile up, or form something into a pile **2** vt cover a fire with coal to make it burn slowly **3** vti tilt an aircraft in the air or a motorcycle on a bend, or become tilted **4** vt build a slope into a road or racetrack at a bend

bank³ n **1** a row of similar things **2** a bench on which rowers sit, or a row of oars in a galley ■ vt put into rows

bankable /bángkəb'l/ adj **1** likely to bring in money **2** acceptable to a bank

bank account n an arrangement with a bank by which a customer can deposit and withdraw money

bank balance n the amount of money in a bank account

bankbook /bángk bŏŏk/ n a passbook for a savings account

bank card n UK a cheque card

banker /bángkər/ n **1** somebody who owns or manages a bank **2** in a gambling game, the player in charge of the bank

banker's order n a standing order

bank holiday n a public holiday

banknote /bángk nōt/ n a piece of paper money

bank rate n an interest rate used by banks as a base rate

bankroll /bángk rōl/ n **1** a fund of money **2** US, Can a roll of paper money ■ vt provide financing for (infml)

bankrupt /bángk rupt/ adj **1** judged legally unable to pay debts **2** completely lacking in a particular good quality —**bankrupt** n, vt —**bankruptcy** n

bank statement n a statement showing the transactions in a bank account over a specific period

banner /bánnər/ n **1** a cloth with a design or message on it, usually carried on two poles **2** a guiding principle **3** a flag **4** also **banner headline** a newspaper headline in large letters that runs the entire width of a page **5** a website advert

bannister n ARCHIT = **banister**

Bannister /bánnistər/, **Sir Roger** (b. 1929) British athlete. He was the first person to run the mile in under four minutes (1954).

bannock /bánnək/ n a round flat griddle cake

banns npl the announcement of a forthcoming marriage in a church (fml)

banoffee /bə nóffi/, **banoffi** n a creamy filling made from banana and soft toffee

banquet /bángkwit/ n an elaborate ceremonial meal —**banquet** vi

banshee /bán shee/ n **1** a supposed female spirit who wails to warn of impending death **2** Ireland a female fairy

ORIGIN Banshee comes from Irish, and means literally 'woman from the fairy world'.

bantam /bántəm/ n a small domestic fowl

bantamweight /bántəm wayt/ n **1** the weight category for boxers between flyweight and featherweight **2** a boxer who competes at bantamweight

banter /bántər/ n lighthearted teasing remarks ■ vi exchange teasing remarks

Banting /bánting/, **Sir Frederick Grant** (1891–1941) Canadian physician

Bantu /bán too/ (*pl same or* **-tus**) *n* (*sometimes offensive*) **1** the group of African languages that includes Xhosa and Zulu **2** a member of a large group of peoples from equatorial and southern Africa —**Bantu** *adj*

USAGE In South Africa after the apartheid era, **Bantu** is considered highly offensive when used with reference to Black people, especially in the singular to refer to one person, and *Black* or *African* are the normally accepted terms. In technical contexts outside South Africa, for example academic discussions of anthropology and language, **Bantu** continues in use.

banyan /bánnyən, -yan/ *n* **1** a tropical tree with roots that grow down from the branches to form secondary trunks **2** a loose jacket or shirt worn by men in parts of South Asia

baobab /báy ō bab/ *n* a tropical tree with a thick short trunk and edible fruit

Baotou /bów tố/ city on the Huang He, Inner Mongolia, N China. Pop. 1,340,000 (1995).

bap *n* a large soft bread roll

baptism /báptizəm/ *n* **1** a religious ceremony symbolizing purification or marking acceptance into a religious faith **2** an initiation —**baptismal** /bap tízm'l/ *adj*

baptism of fire *n* **1** a difficult or dangerous first experience in a new situation **2** a soldier's first battle

Baptist /báptist/ *n* a member of a Protestant denomination that baptizes people by total immersion when they are old enough to understand and declare their faith —**Baptist** *adj*

baptize /bap tíz/ (**-tizing, -tized**), **baptise** *v* *vti* perform the ceremony of baptism on **2** *vt* name during a baptism **3** *vt* initiate into a new experience or situation

bar[1] *n* **1** a relatively long straight piece of a solid material **2** a small block of a solid substance ○ *a gold bar* **3** something that blocks or hinders progress **4** a place where alcoholic drinks can be bought and drunk **5** a counter where drinks are served **6** a place providing a particular product or service ○ *a heel bar* **7** in a law court, the railing that separates the area for the judge, jury, and barristers from the rest of the court **8 Bar** barristers or their profession **9** in music, a unit of time **10** a vertical line separating musical units **11** a ridge of sand on the seabed or a river bed ■ *vt* (**barring, barred**) **1** fasten with a bar **2** block **3** refuse entry to ■ *prep* excluding ○ *It was our team's finest hour, bar none.*

bar[2] *n* a unit of pressure equal to 14.5 lb per sq. in.

Barak /baá rak/, **Ehud** (*b.* 1942) Israeli prime minister (1999–2001)

barb *n* **1** a reverse point on an arrow or hook that makes it difficult to remove **2** a wounding remark **3** a thick filament of a feather that sticks out from the main shaft **4** a bristle on a plant ■ *vt* put a reverse point on an arrow or hook —**barbed** *adj*

Barbados /baar báy doss/ island nation of the Windward Islands in the E Caribbean. Cap. Bridgetown. Pop. 275,330 (2001). —**Barbadian** *n, adj*

barbarian /baar báiri ən/ *n* **1** a member of a people regarded as uncivilized (*sometimes offensive*) **2** a person regarded as uncultured or highly aggressive —**barbarianism** *n*

barbaric /baar bárrik/ *adj* **1** cruel **2** uncivilized or unsophisticated (*sometimes offensive*) —**barbarically** *adv*

barbarism /baárbərizəm/ *n* **1** a cruel act **2** the nature of a civilization when regarded as primitive (*sometimes offensive*) **3** an ungrammatical word or expression

barbarity /baar bárrəti/ (*pl* **-ties**) *n* **1** a cruel act **2** an uncivilized condition

Barbarossa /baárbər róssə/ (1483?–1546) Greek-born Ottoman admiral and pirate

barbarous /baárbərəss/ *adj* **1** extremely cruel **2** uncivilized (*sometimes offensive*) **3** ungrammatical —**barbarously** *adv* —**barbarousness** *n*

Barbary ape /baárbəri-/ *n* a tailless monkey with greenish-brown hair

barbecue /baárbi kyoo/ *n* **1** an apparatus for cooking outdoors **2** an outdoor party with food cooked outdoors —**barbecue** *vt*

ORIGIN **Barbecue** came through Spanish into English in the 17C, from a Native South American language. It originally meant simply 'wooden framework', but the use of a framework for outdoor cooking gave rise to the sense 'an animal or meat cooked outdoors'. Later the word came also to refer to a gathering at which such meat was eaten. The original 'framework' sense died out in the 17C, but **barbecue** came again to refer to an apparatus for cooking outdoors in the late 19C.

barbed wire *n* wire with spikes along its length, used for keeping out intruders or attackers

barbel /baárb'l/ *n* a slender feeler like a whisker on the mouth of a fish

barbell /baár bel/ *n* a long metal bar with weights at each end, used in weightlifting

barber /baárbər/ *n* somebody who cuts men's hair ■ *vti* cut a man's hair

barbershop /baárbər shop/ *n* music for men singing in harmony

barbican /baárbikən/ *n* a strong defensive tower at the entrance to a town or fortress

barbie /baárbi/ *n* a barbecue (*infml*)

bar billiards *n* a billiards-style game formerly popular in pubs

Barbirolli /baárbə rólli/, **Sir John** (1899–1970) British conductor

barbiturate /baar bíchoorət/ *n* a sedative drug

Barbuda /baar boodə/ ♦ **Antigua and Barbuda** —**Barbudan** *n, adj*

Barcelona /baärssə lṓnə/ city and port in NE Spain. Pop. 1,505,581 (1998).

bar chart n a bar graph

bar code n a computer code on goods sold in shops, read by an optical scanner at the checkout

bard n **1** an ancient Celtic poet **2** a poet who wins a prize at a modern eisteddfod **3** any poet (literary or humorous) —**bardic** adj

Bardeen /baar deen/, **John** (1908–91) US physicist

Bardot /baar dṓ/, **Brigitte** (b. 1934) French actor and activist

bare /bair/ adj (**barer, barest**) **1** not covered by clothing **2** without the usual furnishings or decorations **3** without plants **4** basic ○ the bare facts **5** only just sufficient ○ the bare essentials ■ vt (**baring, bared**) expose ○ an investigative report that bared the details of the conspiracy —**bareness** n ◊ See note at **naked**

SPELLCHECK Do not confuse the spelling of **bare** and **bear** (the animal), which sound similar.

bareback /báir bak/ adv, adj on an unsaddled horse

barebones /báir bṓnz/ adj basic

barefaced /báir fáyst/ adj **1** shamelessly undisguised **2** with an uncovered or clean-shaven face —**barefacedly** /báir fáystli, -fáysidli/ adv —**barefacedness** /-fáystnəss, -fáysidnəss/ n

barefoot /báir fŏot/ adj, adv without shoes

barehanded /báir hándid/ adj, adv without weapons or gloves

bareheaded /báir héddid/ adj, adv with the head uncovered

barely /báirli/ adv **1** to a very limited extent ○ barely conscious **2** simply and without decoration ○ a barely furnished office

Barenboim /bárrən boym/, **Daniel** (b. 1942) Argentine-born Israeli pianist and conductor

Barents Sea /bárrənts-/ part of the Arctic Ocean, north of Norway, Finland, and Russia and south of Franz Josef Land

bargain /baärgin/ n **1** something offered or bought at less than the normal price **2** an agreement that gives each side obligations ■ v **1** vi negotiate with somebody **2** vt exchange something —**bargainer** n ◊ **into the bargain** as well

☐ **bargain for** vt be prepared for

☐ **bargain on** vt expect

bargaining chip, bargaining counter n something that can be used as an asset in negotiations

barge n **1** a long narrow flat-bottomed boat used for transporting freight **2** an open boat used on ceremonial occasions **3** a small motor launch used by a high-ranking naval officer ■ vti (**barging, barged**) move or push people roughly

☐ **barge in** vi intrude

bargin incorrect spelling of **bargain**

bar graph n a graph with bars representing values

Bari /baäri/ port in SE Italy. Pop. 331,568 (1999).

barista /ba rístə/ n somebody employed to make coffee

baritone /bárritōn/ n a man's singing voice between bass and tenor in range, or a man with this voice

barium /báiri əm/ n (symbol **Ba**) a silver-white chemical element. Use: alloys, radiography.

bark¹ n the abrupt sound made by a dog ■ v **1** vi make a dog's sound **2** vti speak or say abruptly and aggressively

bark² n the outer layer of a tree ■ vt **1** graze the skin on a part of your body **2** strip the bark from a tree

bark³ n SAILING = **barque**

barley /baärli/ n **1** the edible seeds of a cereal plant. Use: foods, malt production, livestock feed. **2** the cereal crop that the grain barley comes from

barley sugar n a clear hard sweet made from boiled sugar

barley water n a sweet cordial made with water, barley, and sugar

barmaid /baär mayd/ n a woman serving in a bar

barman /baärmən/ (pl **-men** /-mən/) n a man serving in a bar

barmbrack /baärm brak/ n Ireland currant bread

bar mitzvah /baar mítsvə/ n **1** the ceremony that marks a Jewish boy's 13th birthday **2** a Jewish boy as he reaches the age of 13

barmy /baärmi/ (**-ier, -iest**) adj (infml) **1** slightly irrational **2** nonsensical

barn n **1** a large farm outbuilding used as a grain store or livestock shelter **2** any large plain functional building

barnacle /baärnək'l/ n a hard-shelled organism that clings to rocks and ships

barnacle goose n a European wild goose with grey wings and a black-and-white head and body

Barnard /baär naard/, **Christiaan** (1922–2001) South African surgeon. He performed the world's first successful human heart transplant operation (1967).

Barnardo /bər naärdō/, **Thomas** (1845–1905) Irish-born British doctor and philanthropist

barn dance n **1** a party with country dancing **2** any of various country dances

barney /baärni/ n a noisy argument (infml)

barn owl n a whitish owl that nests in barns

barnstorm /baärn stawrm/ vti travel from place to place giving performances (infml) —**barnstormer** n —**barnstorming** adj

barnyard /baärn yaard/ n the area of a farm around a barn

barograph /bárrə graaf, -graf/ n a barometer supplying a continuous printed record —**barographic** /bárrə gráffik/ adj

barometer /bə rómmitər/ n 1 an instrument that measures changes in atmospheric pressure for weather forecasting 2 an indicator of the public mood —**barometric** /bárrə méttrik/ adj —**barometrically** adv —**barometry** n

baron /bárrən/ n 1 a nobleman of low rank 2 a powerful person ◦ an oil baron 3 a medieval nobleman

SPELLCHECK Do not confuse the spelling of **baron** and **barren** ('not productive'), which sound similar.

baroness /bárrənəss/ n 1 a noblewoman of low rank 2 a baron's wife or widow

baronet /bárrənət/ n a British nobleman of the lowest hereditary rank —**baronetcy** /bárrənətsi/ n

baronial /bə róni əl/ adj 1 of barons 2 large and impressive

baroque /bə rók/, **Baroque** n 1 a flamboyant style of European architecture and art popular from the 16C to the 18C 2 17C classical music —**baroque** adj

barque /baark/, **bark** n 1 a small ship with sails set breadthways 2 a small boat

Barquisimeto /baar kissi métto/ capital of Lara State, NW Venezuela. Pop. 602,622 (1991).

barrack[1] /bárrək/ n a barracks ■ vt put soldiers in barracks

barrack[2] /bárrək/ vti (infml) 1 shout at somebody in protest 2 Aus shout in support of

barracks /bárrəks/ n soldiers' quarters (+ sing or pl verb)

barracuda /bárrə kyoódə/ (pl **-das** or same) n a predatory sea fish with a long body and protruding teeth

barrage /bárraazh, -j/ n 1 a military bombardment 2 an overwhelming amount ◦ a barrage of criticism ■ vt (**-raging**, **-raged**) 1 fire continuously on an enemy 2 attack somebody continuously, e.g. with complaints

barrage balloon n a military balloon anchored to the ground to deter enemy aircraft

Barranquilla /bárran keé yə/ capital of Atlántico Department, N Colombia. Pop. 1,226,000 (1999).

barre /baar/ n a hip-high rod on a dance studio's wall, used for support by dancers while exercising

barrel /bárrəl/ n 1 a cylindrical container with a flat top and bottom for storing liquids 2 the amount held by a barrel 3 a unit of volume in the oil, brewing, and other industries, of varying amount 4 the tube-shaped part of a gun —**barrelful** n ◊ **over a barrel** in a situation of powerlessness ◊ **scrape the bottom of the barrel** use something of very poor quality

barrel organ n a mechanical organ operated by hand

barren /bárrən/ adj 1 without trees or plants 2 not producing fruit 3 unable to have children (literary) 4 not yielding useful results —**barrenly** adv —**barrenness** n ◊ See note at **baron**

barricade /bárri káyd, -kayd/ n a defensive barrier ■ vt (**-cading**, **-caded**) obstruct something or protect yourself with barricades

Barrie /bárri/, **Sir J. M.** (1860–1937) British playwright and author

barrier /bárri ər/ n 1 a structure that blocks access to or demarcates an area 2 an obstruction 3 a limit or threshold ◦ the sound barrier

barrier reef n a ridge of coral running parallel to a coastline

barring /baaring/ prep except for

Barrington /bárringtən/, **Jonah** (b. 1940) British squash player

barrister /bárristər/ n in England and Wales, a lawyer qualified to represent clients in the higher courts

barrow[1] /bárro/ n 1 a hand cart 2 a wheelbarrow

barrow[2] /bárro/ n an ancient burial mound

Barrymore /bárri mawr/ family of US actors including **Lionel** (1878–1954), his sister **Ethel** (1879–1959), and his brother **John** (1882–1942)

bartender /baar tendər/ n US somebody serving in a bar

barter /baártər/ v 1 vti exchange goods or services 2 vi negotiate the terms of an agreement ■ n 1 the process of bartering 2 things bartered

Barth /baarth/, **John** (b. 1930) US writer

Barthes /baart/, **Roland** (1915–80) French philosopher and writer

Bartholomew /baar thólləmyoo/, **St** (fl AD 1C) one of the 12 apostles of Jesus Christ

Bartók /baár tok/, **Béla** (1881–1945) Hungarian composer

Barton /baárt'n/, **Sir Edmund** (1849–1920) first prime minister of Australia (1901–03)

baryon /bárri on/ n a subatomic particle belonging to a group that undergoes strong interactions —**baryonic** /bárri ónnik/ adj

Popperfoto

Mikhail Baryshnikov

Baryshnikov /bə ríshnikof/, **Mikhail** (b. 1948) Russian-born US ballet dancer and choreographer

basalt /bássawlt/ n 1 a black shiny volcanic rock 2 black unglazed pottery —**basaltic** /bə sáwltik/ adj

bascule /báss kyool/ n 1 a counterbalanced device that pivots on a central axis 2 also **bascule bridge** a bridge with a lifting roadway

base[1] /bayss/ *n* **1** the lowest, bottom, or supporting part **2** a fundamental principle **3** a place from which activities start or are coordinated **4** a main ingredient to which others are added **5** the part of a body organ by which it is attached to another structure **6** the number on which a counting system is founded **7** a number that is multiplied a particular number of times **8** a baseline for a calculation **9** a chemical compound that reacts with an acid to form a salt **10** in baseball, any of the corners of the infield that a batter must touch while running ■ *vt* (**basing, based**) **1** make a base for **2** station in or assign to a base ◊ **touch base (with somebody)** communicate briefly

SPELLCHECK Do not confuse the spelling of **base** and **bass** ('low in musical pitch'), which sound similar.

base[2] /bayss/ (**baser, basest**) *adj* **1** lacking morals **2** of poor quality **3** describes a coin that contains a higher proportion of inexpensive metals than usual —**basely** *adv* —**baseness** *n*

baseball /báyss bawl/ *n* **1** a bat-and-ball game in which the batter runs round a diamond-shaped field to score a run **2** a ball used in baseball

baseball cap *n* a close-fitting cap with a long peak

base hit *n* in baseball, a hit allowing a batter to reach base

base jumping *n* parachuting from tall buildings and cliffs

Basel /baáz'l/, **Basle** /baal/ city in NW Switzerland. Pop. 168,735 (1998).

baseless /báyssləss/ *adj* **1** not based on fact or supported by evidence **2** without a base or foundation —**baselessly** *adv* —**baselessness** *n*

baseline /báyss līn/ *n* **1** a line used as the basis for a calculation, e.g. in navigation **2** a standard or reference **3** in tennis, badminton, or basketball, a boundary line at the end of a court

basement /báyssmənt/ *n* **1** an underground storey of a building **2** the foundation of a wall or building

base metal *n* any common inexpensive metal

base rate *n* an interest rate used by central banks as a basis for calculating their lending rates

bases plural of **basis**

bash (*infml*) *vt* strike with a heavy blow ■ *n* **1** a heavy blow **2** a big party

bashful /báshf'l/ *adj* shy —**bashfully** *adv* —**bashfulness** *n*

Bashir /bə sheér/, **Omar Hassan al-** (b. 1943) president of Sudan (1989–)

basic /báyssik/ *adj* **1** most important **2** elementary **3** without extra parts ◦ *a basic salary* **4** containing or consisting of a chemical base **5** alkaline **6** describes a chemical salt that contains hydroxide or oxide groups ■

basics *npl* the most important or elementary things relating to a sphere of activity —**basicity** /bay sissiti/ *n*

BASIC /báyssik/, **Basic** *n* a computer programming language that uses common English terms and algebra. Full form **Beginners All-purpose Symbolic Instruction Code**

basically /báyssikli/ *adv* **1** introduces the most important reason or a simplified explanation **2** in general

~~basiely~~ incorrect spelling of **basically**

basic rate *n* **1** the standard rate of pay, without bonuses **2** the standard rate of income tax

Basie /báyzi/, **Count** (1904–84) US composer and bandleader

basil /bázz'l/ *n* **1** the aromatic leaves of a herb. Use: flavouring. **2** a plant with aromatic leaves

basilica /bə zíllikə, -síllikə/ *n* **1** a Roman Catholic church given special privileges by the Pope **2** an ancient Roman building with a long central nave and a semicircular apse —**basilican** *adj*

basilisk /bázzə lisk/ *n* **1** a mythical reptile whose breath or look was fatal **2** a small lizard that can run on its long hind legs

basin /báyss'n/ *n* **1** an open container for washing **2** a bowl for preparing food **3** the contents of a basin **4** an area of land draining into a river or lake **5** a bowl-shaped depression in the Earth **6** a circular formation of sloping rock strata

basis /báyssiss/ (*pl* **-ses** /-seez/) *n* **1** the foundation of an argument or idea **2** a way of proceeding **3** a main component or ingredient

bask *vi* **1** lie in the pleasurable warmth of the sun **2** get pleasure from something

basket /baáskit/ *n* **1** a woven container, often with a handle **2** the contents of a basket **3** in basketball, a net or a goal scored —**basketful** *n*

basketball /baáskit bawl/ *n* **1** a ball game played by two teams of five players who pass the ball by hand on an indoor court **2** a ball used in basketball

basket of currencies *n* a group of currencies whose average value is used as a basis for calculating currency values

basketry /baáskitri/, **basketwork** /-wurk/ *n* **1** the craft of making baskets **2** baskets collectively

Basle ▸ Basel

bas mitzvah *n* JUDAISM = **bat mitzvah**

basque /bask, baask/ *n* a woman's tight-fitting corset

Basque /bask, baask/ *n* **1** a member of a European people of N Spain and SW France **2** the language of the Basque people —**Basque** *adj*

Basque Country autonomous region of N Spain. Pop. 2,098,628 (1998).

Basra /bázzrə/ port in SE Iraq. Pop. 406,296 (1987).

bas-relief /baá-/ *n* **1** flat sculpture in which

the design projects only slightly from the background surface **2** a piece of bas-relief

bass[1] /bayss/ *n* **1** a man's singing voice or the lowest range, or a man with that voice **2** the lowest musical or singing part in a harmony **3** the low-frequency element of audio reproduction ■ *adj* **1** deep in tone **2** low in pitch ◊ See note at **base**[1]

bass[2] /bass/ (*pl same or* **basses**) *n* **1** a spiny-finned fish **2** bass as food

bass clef *n* a musical symbol indicating that the top line of the music represents the A below middle C

Basseterre /bass táir/ capital of St Kitts and Nevis, on the southwestern coast of St Kitts island. Pop. 12,220 (1994).

bass guitar *n* a low-pitched guitar

bassinet /bássi nét/ *n* a baby's bed or pram shaped like a basket

bassist /báyssist/ *n* the player of a bass guitar or double bass

bassoon /bə soón/ *n* a low-pitched woodwind instrument of the oboe family —**bassoonist** *n*

Bass Strait /báss-/ channel between mainland Australia and Tasmania, approximately 225 km / 140 mi. wide

bastard /báastərd/ *n* **1** an offensive term for somebody regarded as obnoxious and disagreeable (*slang insult*) **2** an offensive term for somebody born to unmarried parents (*archaic or offensive*) **3** a very difficult task (*sometimes offensive*) **4** an inferior thing (*sometimes offensive*) ■ *adj* **1** not genuine and of lesser value o *bastard quartz* **2** an offensive term meaning born to unmarried parents

baste[1] (**basting, basted**) *vt* moisten during cooking

baste[2] (**basting, basted**) *vt* beat somebody severely

baste[3] (**basting, basted**) *vt* **1** sew loosely **2** sew with rows of diagonal stitches

bastion /básti ən/ *n* **1** a projecting part of a wall or fortification **2** a fortified place **3** a strong supporter or defender of something

bat[1] *n* **1** a club used in sports **2** a hand-held device for guiding landing aircraft **3** a heavy stick or club **4** a blow from a stick **5** in cricket, a batsman ■ *v* (**batting, batted**) **1** *vt* strike with a bat **2** *vi* in cricket or baseball, have a turn at batting ◊ **off your own bat** on your own initiative and without instructions or help from anyone (*infml*)

bat[2] *n* a small nocturnal flying mammal with leathery wings

ORIGIN The noun **bat** referring to an animal has a different origin from the verb **bat** as in 'batting your eyelids', and neither is related to the **bat** used in games. The original name of the flying mammal ended in a /k/ sound, not /t/, and came from a Scandinavian language. The verb **bat** 'blink' derives from the French verb that gave us *batter* 'hit repeatedly'. The sports **bat**

is the oldest of all these words, and its origin is not known for certain.

bat[3] (**batting, batted**) *vt* blink an eye

~~batallion~~ incorrect spelling of **battalion**

batch *n* **1** a quantity regarded as a group or unit **2** an amount of food baked at one time ■ *vt* arrange into batches, or process as a batch

~~batchelor~~ incorrect spelling of **bachelor**

batch file *n* a computer file containing a series of consecutive commands

batch processing *n* a method of processing data in which a computer gathers jobs and processes them until time becomes available

Bates /bayts/, **Daisy May** (1863–1951) Irish-born Australian journalist and anthropologist

Bates, H. E. (1905–74) British writer

Bates, H.W. (1825–92) British naturalist

bath /baath/ *n* (*pl* **baths** /baathz/) **1** a large container that people sit in to wash their bodies **2** an occasion when somebody washes the body in a bath **3** a treatment that involves immersing the body in a substance, e.g. mud **4** a liquid used for a particular purpose, e.g. developing photographs ■ **baths** *npl* **1** a bathhouse **2** a public swimming pool **3** a spa where patrons avail themselves of the water from natural mineral springs ■ *vti* wash yourself or somebody else in a bath

Bath /baath/ city in SW England, a spa since Roman times. Pop. 84,100 (1994).

bathe /bayth/ *v* (**bathing, bathed**) **1** *vi* swim or paddle in open water **2** *vt* cleanse a wound **3** *vt* dip something in a liquid **4** *vt* cover something, e.g. with light or colour **5** *vti US, Can* have a bath, or wash somebody in a bath ■ *n* an act of swimming or bathing (*dated*)

bather /báythər/ *n* a swimmer

bathers /báythərz/ *npl Aus* a swimsuit (*infml*)

bathetic /bə théttik/ *adj* **1** showing bathos **2** trite or absurdly sentimental —**bathetically** *adv*

bathhouse /báath howss/ (*pl* **-houses** /-howziz/) *n* a building equipped with baths

bathing costume /báything-/ *n* a swimming costume (*dated*)

bathing suit /báything-/ *n US, Can* a swimsuit

bath mitzvah *n* JUDAISM = **bat mitzvah**

bathos /báy thoss/ *n* **1** a sudden ludicrous change in speech or writing from an important or elevated subject to something commonplace **2** insincere, excessively sentimental pathos

bathrobe /báath rōb/ *n* a loose-fitting garment worn after or before bathing

bathroom /báath room, -rŏom/ *n* **1** a room containing a bath **2** a room with a toilet

bathysphere /báthi sfeer/ *n* a diving sphere that can be lowered to great depths

batik /báttik, bə teek/ *n* **1** a fabric printing technique that involves blanking out areas with wax **2** fabric dyed using this technique

Batista y Zaldívar /ba teèstə ee zal deé vaar/, **Fulgencio** (1901–73) Cuban soldier and head of state (1940–44, 1952 59)

batman /bátmən/ (pl **-men** /-mən/) n a military officer's personal servant

bat mitzvah /baat mítsvə/, **bath mitzvah, bas mitzvah** /baass-/ n 1 the ceremony that marks a Jewish girl's 13th birthday 2 a Jewish girl as she reaches the age of 13

baton /bátton, bátt'n/ n 1 a stick for conducting music 2 a police officer's stick used as a weapon 3 a relay runner's stick 4 a stick carried as a symbol of rank or office

Baton Rouge /bátt'n roózh/ capital of Louisiana. Pop. 211,551 (1998).

batsman /bátsmən/ (pl **-men** /-mən/) n in cricket, a player who is batting or who specializes in batting

battalion /bə tályən/ n 1 a large group of soldiers acting together 2 a military unit consisting of three or more companies 3 a large number of people or organisms (often pl)

~~battalion~~ incorrect spelling of **battalion**

batten /bátt'n/ n 1 a thin strip of wood used as a support in a building 2 a strip of wood or plastic used, e.g. to keep the edge of a sail in shape 3 a wooden slat used for fastening down the hatches on a ship ■ vt support or fasten with battens

Batten /bátt'n/, **Jean** (1909–82) New Zealand aviator

batter[1] /báttər/ vt 1 hit repeatedly 2 subject to persistent attack —**battered** adj

batter[2] /báttər/ n a mixture of flour, milk, and eggs used for making cakes and pancakes or for coating food before frying ■ vt coat food in batter

batter[3] /báttər/ n a player who is batting, especially in baseball

battering ram n 1 formerly, a heavy beam used to break down fortifications 2 a heavy implement used to break down doors

battery /báttəri/ (pl **-ies**) n 1 a portable source of electricity consisting of a number of electrical cells 2 the unlawful use of physical force on somebody 3 a grouping of artillery pieces or machine guns 4 an army artillery unit 5 a gun or artillery emplacement 6 a system of cages for the intensive rearing of poultry or livestock 7 a grouping of similar things used or considered together 8 the percussion section of an orchestra

battle /bátt'l/ n 1 a large-scale fight between armed forces 2 a struggle ■ v (**-tling, -tled**) 1 vi fight an enemy 2 vt struggle against ◊ See note at **fight**

USAGE The transitive use of **battle** (with a direct object, instead of *battle against* or *battle with*, as in *The people of South Carolina have been battling a hurricane*) is a feature of North American usage that has begun to enter other varieties of English also. This is partly a revival of an older use that died out in the 19C.

battleaxe /bátt'l aks/ n 1 a broad-headed axe 2 a woman who is regarded as fearsomely aggressive (insult)

battle cruiser n an armed warship lighter and faster than a battleship

battle cry n 1 a shout made by soldiers when going into battle 2 a supporters' slogan

battledress /bátt'l dress/ n a soldier's ordinary uniform

battlefield /bátt'l feeld/, **battleground** /-grownd/ n 1 the site of a battle 2 an area of conflict

battle line n the area along which a battle is fought

battlements /bátt'lmənts/ npl indentations on a parapet

battleship /bátt'l ship/ n a large, heavily armed and armoured warship, smaller than an aircraft carrier

batty /bátti/ (**-tier, -tiest**) adj slightly eccentric (infml) —**battiness** n

bauble /báwb'l/ n a trinket

baud /bawd/ n a unit of data transmission speed equal to one unit element per second

ORIGIN The **baud** is named after the French engineer J. M. E. Baudot (1845–1903), who invented a method of transmitting information using binary digits.

Baudelaire /bód lair/, **Charles** (1821–67) French poet and critic

Baudouin I /bó dwaN/ (1930–93) king of the Belgians (1951–93)

Bauhaus /bów howss/ n an early 20C German school of architecture and design

baulk /bawk, bawlk/, **balk** v 1 vi stop short 2 vi turn away 3 vti refuse to tackle ■ n 1 a large piece of wood 2 an unploughed ridge 3 in baseball, an illegal pitching move

baulk line n a dividing line on a billiards table

bauxite /báwk sīt/ n an ore that is the principal source of aluminium

Bavaria /bə váiri ə/ state in SE Germany. Cap. Munich. Pop. 12,086,548 (1998). —**Bavarian** n, adj

bawdy /báwdi/ (**-ier, -iest**) adj with a sexual content that is humorous or obscene —**bawdily** adv —**bawdiness** n

bawl vti 1 shout loudly 2 cry noisily (infml) ■ n a loud shout

□ **bawl out** vt scold loudly (infml)

Baxter /bákstər/, **James K.** (1926–72) New Zealand poet

bay[1] n a wide curved inlet of the sea

bay[2] n 1 a special area or compartment 2 a recessed part of a floor or room 3 a bay window

bay[3] n a small evergreen tree of the laurel family with aromatic leaves

bay[4] n 1 a horse with a reddish-brown coat 2 a reddish-brown colour —**bay** adj

bay[5] vi 1 howl plaintively 2 call noisily and aggressively for something to happen ■ n a position of no escape ◊ **keep somebody or**

something at bay keep somebody or something unpleasant at a distance

bay leaf *n* an aromatic leaf of a bay tree. Use: seasoning.

bayonet /báyənit/ *n* 1 a blade fitted to a rifle 2 a type of fitting with projecting pins that are twisted into slots ■ *vt* stab with a bayonet

Bayreuth /bī róyt/ city in S Germany, site of an annual Wagner opera festival. Pop. 72,840 (1997).

bay window *n* a rounded or three-sided window that projects from an outside wall

bazaar /bə zaár/ *n* 1 a sale of goods to raise money for charity 2 a street market in North Africa and Southwest Asia

~~bazar~~ incorrect spelling of **bazaar**

bazooka /bə zóokə/ *n* a portable anti-tank weapon fired from the shoulder

BB *symbol* double black (*describes pencils with very soft leads*)

BBC *abbr* British Broadcasting Corporation

BBQ *abbr* barbecue

BBS *abbr* bulletin board system

BC *adv* indicates a date before the birth of Jesus Christ (*after dates*) Full form **before Christ**

bcc, b.c.c. *abbr* blind carbon copy

BCE *adv* used as a non-Christian equivalent of BC in dates. Full form **before the Common Era**

BCG *n* anti-tuberculosis vaccine. Full form **bacillus Calmette-Guérin (vaccine)**

BCNZ *abbr* Broadcasting Corporation of New Zealand

be (*stressed*) /bee/ (*unstressed*) /bi/ (*1st person present sing* **am** (*stressed*) /am/ (*unstressed*) /əm/, *2nd person present sing* **are** (*stressed*) /aar/ (*unstressed*) /ər/, *3rd person present sing* **is** /iz/, *1st person present pl* **are**, *2nd person present pl* **are**, *3rd person present pl* **are**, *present subjunctive* **be**, *1st person sing past indicative* **was** (*stressed*) /woz/ (*unstressed*) /wəz/, *2nd person sing past indicative* **were** (*stressed*) /wur/ (*unstressed*) /wər/, *3rd person sing past indicative* **was**, *1st person pl past indicative* **were**, *2nd person pl past indicative* **were**, *3rd person pl past indicative* **were**, *past subjunctive* **were**, *past participle* **been** (*stressed*) /been/ (*unstressed*) /bin/) *vi* 1 used after 'it' to give a description or judgment of something o *It is a good thing that we left early.* 2 used after 'there' to indicate that something exists or is true o *There are many problems with her essay.* 3 exist o *I think, therefore I am.* 4 happen or take place o *The meeting was at four o'clock.* 5 make a visit o *I was in Italy during the summer.* 6 have a particular quality o *This sentence is concise.* 7 remain as a fact or situation o *The facts are these: it is cold and unhealthy here.* ■ *aux v* 8 expresses continuation or future intention o *My legs are getting tired.* o *I am leaving on the next train.* 9 forms the passive o *She was sent on the mission.* 10 used with an infinitive to express the future o *The meeting is to take place tomorrow.*

Be *symbol* beryllium

beach /beech/ *n* a strip of sand or pebbles on a coast ■ *vti* 1 haul a boat ashore 2 strand or become stranded on shore o *a whale that had been beached during a storm*

SPELLCHECK Do not confuse the spelling of **beach** and **beech** (the tree), which sound similar.

beachcomber /beech kōmər/ *n* 1 somebody who salvages things from a beach 2 a big wave that crashes onto a beach

beachhead /beech hed/ *n* a captured enemy beach

Beachy Head /beechi-/ chalk headland on the English Channel, SE England. Height 171 m/570 ft.

beacon /beekən/ *n* 1 a flashing light as a warning and guide 2 a radio transmitter that broadcasts navigation signals 3 a signal fire formerly lit on a hill as a warning

bead /beed/ *n* 1 a small ball or round gemstone strung on a necklace 2 a drop of moisture 3 a decorative raised edge or rim, e.g. on furniture 4 a knob that forms the front part of the sight of a gun ■ **beads** *npl* 1 a rosary 2 a necklace ■ *v* 1 *vt* decorate with beads 2 *vi* form into beads —**beaded** *adj*

beading /beeding/ *n* material used for making a decorative trim, e.g. on furniture

beadle /beed'l/ *n* 1 a minor church official with varying duties, including ushering 2 the caretaker of a synagogue

beady /beedi/ (**-ier, -iest**) *adj* 1 like beads 2 covered with beads 3 describes eyes that are watchful, often intrusively so (*infml*) —**beadiness** *n*

beagle /beeg'l/ *n* a small smooth-haired dog

beak /beek/ *n* 1 a bird's mouth 2 the protruding part of the mouth of organisms other than birds —**beaked** *adj* —**beakless** *adj* —**beaklike** *adj*

beaker /beekər/ *n* 1 a wide-mouthed cup without a handle 2 a laboratory container

be-all ◊ **the be-all and end-all** the thing or person regarded as the most important

beam /beem/ *n* 1 a horizontal structural support 2 a line of light 3 a ship's breadth 4 a side of a ship 5 a narrow stream of radiation 6 a radar signal that guides ships or aircraft 7 a broad smile 8 a pivoted horizontal part of a balance 9 a main supporting shaft, e.g. of a plough 10 an elevated horizontal bar on which women gymnasts perform, or the event using this ■ *v* 1 *vti* smile broadly 2 *vt* send as a radio or TV signal 3 *vti* shine brightly

bean /been/ *n* 1 a long, thin, usually green seed pod eaten cooked whole as a vegetable 2 a small, rounded, often kidney-shaped seed eaten as a vegetable and often dried for preserving 3 a plant with edible pods and seeds ◊ **full of beans** bright and energetic (*infml*) ◊ **spill the beans** reveal secret information (*infml*)

beanbag /beén bag/ n 1 a bean-filled bag used in games 2 a large cushion used as a seat

bean counter n an accountant (slang; sometimes offensive)

bean curd n tofu

beanfeast /beén feest/ n a celebration (infml dated)

beanie /beéni/ n a tight-fitting hat like a skull-cap

beanpole /beén pōl/ n a stick supporting a bean plant

bean sprouts npl young crisp shoots of sprouted bean seeds eaten as food

bear[1] /bair/ n 1 a large strong mammal with thick shaggy fur and long claws 2 a medium-sized furry mammal similar but unrelated to true bears o a koala bear 3 somebody who sells shares in anticipation of falling prices ◊ See note at **bare**

bear[2] /bair/ (**bore, borne** /bawrn/) v 1 vti tolerate something o Can you bear this heat? No, I can't bear it. 2 vt support the weight of something 3 vti withstand being subjected to something o Will her theories bear scrutiny? 4 vt merit something o bear further investigation 5 vt accept something as a responsibility 6 vt be characterized by something o bears no relation to reality 7 vt show physical signs of something o bears a likeness to his uncle 8 vt carry something 9 vt produce something 10 vt give birth to a child 11 vt have a particular thought or feeling o I bore him no ill will. 12 vi head in a particular direction 13 vt behave in a particular way o bore himself well

☐ **bear on** or **upon** vt be relevant to

☐ **bear out** vt confirm as correct

☐ **bear up** vi stay cheerful in difficulties

bearable /báirəb'l/ adj tolerable

beard /beerd/ n 1 the hair growing on a man's chin 2 a growth of long hair on a plant or animal ■ vt oppose or confront confidently —**bearded** adj —**beardless** adj

bearded dragon n a large Australian lizard with a pouch under its chin

Beardsley /beérdzli/, **Aubrey** (1872–98) British artist and illustrator

bearer /báirər/ n 1 somebody who brings, carries, or holds something 2 the holder of a note redeemable for payment

bearer bond n a bond payable only to the holder

bear garden n a rowdy place

bear hug n 1 a tight embrace 2 a squeezing hold in wrestling

bearing /báiring/ n 1 relevance to something else o This has no bearing on the matter under discussion. 2 a way of moving or standing 3 a calculation of direction or geographical position 4 a support for a moving machine part

bearish /báirish/ adj 1 bad-tempered 2 clumsy 3 selling rather than buying in anticipation of falling share prices

bear market n a stock market characterized by bearish activity

béarnaise sauce /báyər nayz-/ n a sauce thickened with egg yolk and flavoured with tarragon

bearskin /báir skin/ n 1 a bear's pelt 2 a soldier's tall fur hat

beast /beest/ n 1 a large animal 2 the instinctive or aggressive side of somebody's personality 3 a brutal person

beastly /beéstli/ adj nasty or horrible (infml dated) —**beastliness** n

beat /beet/ v (**beat, beaten** /beét'n/) 1 vt defeat somebody 2 vt hit somebody or something repeatedly 3 vi knock against something repeatedly o waves beating against the rocks 4 vi pulsate (refers to the heart or pulse) 5 vt set a musical rhythm o beating time with her baton 6 vt stir a liquid mixture, cream, or eggs vigorously 7 vt arrive or finish ahead of somebody else or of a time limit 8 vt surpass something o beat the long jump record 9 vt make or shape something by hitting or trampling o a beaten path 10 vti flap so as to fly (refers to wings) 11 vti drive game animals from cover to be hunted or shot ■ n 1 a steady throbbing (often in combination) o a heartbeat 2 a striking of one thing against another 3 a set or dominant rhythm 4 the usual route, especially of a police officer ■ adj tired out (infml) —**beating** n ◊ See note at **defeat**

SPELLCHECK Do not confuse the spelling of **beat** and **beet** (the plant), which sound similar.

☐ **beat down** vi come down strongly (refers to sun or rain)

☐ **beat up** vt injure with blows (infml)

beatific /beé ə tíffik/ adj blissfully happy (literary) —**beatifically** adv

~~beatiful~~ incorrect spelling of **beautiful**

beatify /bi átti fī/ (**-fies, -fied**) vt 1 in the Roman Catholic Church, state officially that a dead person lived a holy life 2 make somebody extremely happy (literary) —**beatification** /bi áttifi káysh'n/ n

beatitude /bi átti tyood/ n (literary) 1 the perfect happiness and inner peace supposed to be enjoyed by the soul in heaven 2 great happiness and serenity

Beatles /beét'lz/ (1959–70) British pop music group including **Paul McCartney** (b. 1942), **John Lennon** (1940–80), **George Harrison** (1943–2001), and **Ringo Starr** (b. 1940)

beatnik /beétnik/ n a member of a group rejecting traditional values in the 1950s

Beaton /beét'n/, **Sir Cecil** (1904–80) British photographer and designer

Beatrix /beé ətriks/ (b. 1938) queen of the Netherlands (1980–)

beat-up adj dilapidated (infml)

beau /bō/ (pl **beaus** or **beaux** /bō, bōz/) n a boyfriend (dated)

Beaufort scale /bṓfərt-/ n a scale indicating wind speed

ORIGIN The scale is named after the Irish admiral Sir Francis Beaufort (1774–1857).

Beaufort Sea /bốfərt-/ section of the Arctic Ocean northwest of Canada and north of Alaska. Depth 4,682 m/15,360 ft.

Beauharnais /bố aar náy/, **Joséphine de ↓ Joséphine**

Beaujolais /bốzhə lay/ n a light French wine from the Beaujolais district of Burgundy

Beaumarchais /bố maar shay/, **Pierre Augustin Caron de** (1732–99) French dramatist

beau monde /bố mónd/ n high society

Beaumont /bố mont/, **Francis** (1584–1616) English dramatist

~~beaurocracy~~ incorrect spelling of **bureaucracy**

beauteous /byoóti əss/ adj beautiful (literary) —**beauteousness** n

beautician /byoo tísh'n/ n US, Can somebody giving beauty treatments

beautiful /byoótəf'l/ adj very pleasing, especially to look at —**beautifully** adv

beautify /byoóti fī/ (-fies, -fied) vt make something beautiful —**beautification** /byoótifi káysh'n/ n —**beautifier** n

beauty /byoóti/ (pl -ties) n 1 a pleasing and impressive quality, especially of appearance 2 a beautiful woman 3 a fine thing

beauty queen n the winner of a contest for beautiful women

beauty salon, beauty shop, beauty parlour n a place for beauty treatments

beauty spot n 1 a popular scenic place 2 a small natural mark on the face

Simone de Beauvoir

Beauvoir /bố vwaar/, **Simone de** (1908–86) French writer

beaux plural of **beau**

beaver /beévər/ n 1 (pl **beavers** or **same**) a furry flat-tailed water animal 2 fur from a beaver 3 **Beaver, Beaver Scout** a member of the branch of the Scouts for the youngest age group ■ vi work hard and continuously (infml)

Beaverbrook /beévər brook/, **Max Aitken, 1st Baron** (1879–1964) Canadian-born British newspaper owner and politician

bebop /beé bop/ n fast complex jazz music originating in the 1940s

becalm /bi kaám/ vt stop a sailing boat through lack of wind

became past tense of **become**

because /bi kóz, -kəz/ conj 1 for the reason that 2 seeing that ○ It must have been raining, because the path is wet. ◊ See note at **reason**

béchamel sauce /báyshə mel-/ n a sauce made with milk, flour, and butter

ORIGIN The sauce is named after its inventor, Louis, Marquis de Béchamel (1630–1703), steward to Louis XIV of France.

beck[1] n N England a brook

beck[2] n a nod (literary) ◇ **at somebody's beck and call** always available and ready to carry out somebody's wishes

Becker /békər/, **Boris** (b. 1967) German tennis player

Becket /békit/, **Thomas à, St** (1118?–70) English saint and martyr

John Haynes
Samuel Beckett

Beckett /békit/, **Samuel** (1906–89) Irish-born writer

beckon /békən/ vti 1 gesture to somebody to come 2 attract or tempt somebody (literary)

become /bi kúm/ (-coming, -came /-káym/, -come) v 1 vi come to be 2 vt suit the appearance or status of —**becoming** adj □ **become of** vt happen to

~~becouse~~ incorrect spelling of **because**

becquerel /békə rel/ n (symbol **Bq**) an SI unit of radioactivity

ORIGIN The unit is named after the French physicist Antoine Henri Becquerel (1852–1908).

bed n 1 a piece of furniture on which to sleep 2 sleep or rest in a bed ○ time for bed 3 a place for sleeping 4 a patch of soil for growing plants 5 the ground under a body of water 6 a surface on which something is built or laid 7 a layer of rock ■ vt (bedding, bedded) 1 fix into a surrounding mass or surface 2 have sexual intercourse with (infml) □ **bed down** vi 1 settle down for sleep, usually in a makeshift bed ○ I'll bed down on the sofa. 2 sink and settle into position

BEd abbr Bachelor of Education

bed and breakfast n 1 overnight accommodation and breakfast in a guest house or private dwelling 2 a guesthouse

bedaub /bi dáwb/ vt smear thickly or carelessly (literary)

bedazzle /bi dázz'l/ (-zling, -zled) vt astonish and impress greatly (literary)

bedbug /béd bug/ n a small insect found in bedding that sucks blood

bedclothes /béd klōthz, -klōz/ npl bed coverings

bedding /bédding/ n 1 the mattress, pillows,

and coverings of a bed **2** material for animals to sleep on **3** a foundation layer

bedding plant *n* an annual plant for a flower bed

Bede /beed/, **St** (673?–735) English theologian and historian

bedeck /bi dék/ *vt* make pretty by decorating ○ *trees bedecked with coloured lights*

bedevil /bi dévv'l/ (**-illing, -illed**) *vt* cause continual problems to —**bedevilment** *n*

bedfellow /béd felō/ *n* an associate

Bedfordshire /bédfərdshər/ county in central England. Pop. 543,100 (1994).

bedlam /bédləm/ *n* uproar and chaos

ORIGIN **Bedlam** is a contraction of *Bethlehem*. The original **bedlam** was the Hospital of St Mary of Bethlehem in London, which housed people with psychiatric disorders.

Bedouin /béddoo in/ (*pl* **-ins** *or same*), **Beduin** *n* a nomadic Arab —**Bedouin** *adj*

bedpan /béd pan/ *n* a shallow container for urination or defecation in bed

bedpost /béd pōst/ *n* a post at the corner of a bed

bedraggled /bi drágg'ld/ *adj* wet, dirty, and untidy

bedridden /béd rid'n/ *adj* confined to bed

bedrock /béd rok/ *n* **1** underlying rock **2** underlying facts or principles

bedroll /béd rōl/ *n* a traveller's rolled-up bedding

bedroom /béd room, -rōōm/ *n* a room for sleeping

bedside /béd sīd/ *n* the space beside a bed —**bedside** *adj*

bedside manner *n* a doctor's manner when dealing with patients

bedsitter /béd sitər, -síttər/, **bedsit** /béd sit, bed sít/, **bedsitting room** *n* a room for sleeping and living in, usually rented

bedsore /béd sawr/ *n* a skin ulcer resulting from long confinement to bed

bedspread /béd spred/ *n* a top cover for a bed

bedstead /béd sted/ *n* the frame of a bed

bedtime /béd tīm/ *n* time for bed

Beduin *n, adj* PEOPLES = **Bedouin**

bee *n* **1** a flying insect that makes honey **2** *US, Can* a gathering for activity and socializing ◊ **have a bee in your bonnet (about)** think or talk about something obsessively

beech *n* **1** a deciduous tree with smooth grey bark **2** the wood of a beech tree. Use: furniture. ◊ See note at **beach**

Beecham /beechəm/, **Sir Thomas** (1879–1961) British conductor and impresario

beef *n* **1** meat from cattle **2** (*pl* **beeves**) an animal giving beef **3** a complaint (*slang*)
□ **beef up** *vt* make stronger or more effective (*infml*) ○ *beef up the article with some statistics*

beefburger /beef burgər/ *n* a burger made with beef

beefcake /beef kayk/ *n* muscular men (*infml*)

beefeater /beef eetər/ *n* a guard at the Tower of London wearing a Tudor-style uniform

beefsteak fungus /beef stayk-/ *n* an edible fungus with a large reddish cap

beef tomato, beefsteak tomato /beef stayk-/ *n* a large tomato

beefy /beefi/ (**-ier, -iest**) *adj* **1** muscular **2** powerful (*infml*) —**beefiness** *n*

beehive /bee hīv/ *n* **1** a structure housing a colony of bees **2** a tall hairstyle for women in the 1960s

beekeeper /bee keepər/ *n* somebody who keeps bees —**beekeeping** *n*

beeline /bee līn/ *n* a direct path or course ○ *We made a beeline for the comfortable seats.*

Beelzebub /bi élzi bub/ *n* the devil

been past participle of **be**

beep *n* a short high noise made by a car horn or electronic device ■ *vti* make or cause to make a beep

beeper /beepər/ *n* a pager that emits beeps (*infml*)

beer /beer/ *n* **1** an alcoholic drink brewed from malt and hops **2** a carbonated or fermented nonalcoholic drink ○ *ginger beer*

SPELLCHECK Do not confuse the spelling of **beer** and **bier** ('a stand for a coffin'), which sound similar.

beeswax /beez waks/ *n* wax produced by bees or commercially processed. Use: polish, candles, crayons. ■ *vt* polish with beeswax

beet /beet/ *n* a plant with an edible swollen root. Use: cookery, animal feed, sugar production ◊ See note at **beat**

Beethoven /báyt hōvən/, **Ludwig van** (1770–1827) German composer

beetle[1] /beet'l/ *n* an insect with a pair of outer wings that form a hard covering for the inner wings

beetle[2] /beet'l/ (**-tling, -tled**) *vi* overhang or jut out (*literary*)

Beeton /beet'n/, **Isabella Mary** (1836–65) British cookery writer

beetroot /beet root/ *n* **1** a dark-red plant root eaten as a vegetable **2** a plant that produces beetroot

befall /bi fáwl/ (**-fell** /-fél/, **-fallen** /-fáwlən/) *vti* happen, or happen to (*literary*)

befit /bi fít/ (**-fitting, -fitted**) *vt* be appropriate for —**befitting** *adj* —**befittingly** *adv*

before /bi fáwr/ *prep, conj, adv* **1** earlier than **2** preceding in sequence ■ *prep* **1** in the presence of ○ *spoke before a huge crowd* **2** with more importance than ■ *adv* previously ■ *conj* rather than ○ *I'll die before I'll tell you anything about it.*

beforehand /bi fáwr hand/ *adv* in advance

befriend /bi frénd/ *vt* make friends with

befuddle /bi fúdd'l/ (**-dling, -dled**) *vt* make confused or perplexed —**befuddled** *adj* —**befuddlement** *n*

beg (**begging**, **begged**) *vti* **1** ask earnestly for something **2** ask for charity
□ **beg off** *vi* ask to be excused from doing something

began past tense of **begin**

beget /bi gét/ (**-getting**, **-got** /-gót/ *or* **-gat** /-gát/, **-gotten** /-gótt'n/ *or* **-got**) *vt* **1** father a child *(archaic)* **2** cause something to happen

beggar /béggər/ *n* **1** somebody who begs for charity **2** a person of a particular type *(infml)* ○ *You lucky beggar!* ■ *vt* **1** make somebody very poor *(literary)* **2** be beyond description or belief ○ *a catastrophe that beggars understanding*

beggarly /béggərli/ *adj* paltry —**beggarliness** *n*

beggary /béggəri/ *n* extreme poverty

~~begger~~ incorrect spelling of **beggar**

begin /bi gín/ (**-ginning**, **-gan** /-gán/, **-gun** /-gún/) *vti* **1** do something that was not being done before **2** come or bring into being

Begin /báygin/, **Menachem** (1913–92) Russian-born Israeli prime minister (1977–83)

~~begining~~ incorrect spelling of **beginning**

beginner /bi gínnər/ *n* somebody who has just started learning or doing something

SYNONYMS beginner, apprentice, greenhorn, novice, tyro CORE MEANING: a person who has not acquired the necessary experience or skills to do something

beginning /bi gínning/ *n* the start or first part of something ■ **beginnings** *npl* early conditions ■ *adj* new to a job or activity ○ *beginning teachers*

begone /bi gón/ *interj* go away *(archaic)*

begonia /bi gôni ə/ *n* an ornamental flowering plant

begot past tense, past participle of **beget**

begotten past participle of **beget**

begrime /bi grím/ (**-griming**, **-grimed**) *vt* cover with grime

begrudge /bi grúj/ (**-grudging**, **-grudged**) *vt* **1** resent something that somebody else has ○ *He's always begrudged me my success.* **2** not want to give something

beguile /bi gíl/ (**-guiling**, **-guiled**) *vt* charm —**beguilement** *n* —**beguiling** *adj*

begum /báygəm, bee-/ *n* **1** in some Muslim communities, a title of respect for a woman **2** a high-ranking Muslim woman

begun past participle of **begin**

behalf /bi haáf/ ◇ **on behalf of 1** as somebody's representative **2** for somebody's benefit or support

Behan /bee ən/, **Brendan** (1923–64) Irish playwright and author

behave /bi háyv/ (**-having**, **-haved**) *vi* **1** act or function in a particular way ○ *He's been behaving oddly.* **2** conduct yourself politely towards others ○ *children who won't behave*

ORIGIN The second part of **behave** is the ordinary English verb *have*, with an old stressed pronunciation. It was used in the sense 'hold', so that 'behaving yourself' was holding or conducting yourself in a particular way. The prefix *be-* added emphasis.

behaviour /bi háyvyər/ *n* the way somebody or something behaves —**behavioural** *adj*

behaviourism /bi háyvyərizəm/ *n* psychology concentrating on observation and modification of behaviour —**behaviourist** *adj, n* —**behaviouristic** /bi háyvyə rístik/ *adj*

behead /bi héd/ *vt* cut off the head of

behemoth /bi hee moth, bíhi məth/ *n* something huge or powerful

ORIGIN The original **Behemoth** is a huge beast referred to in the Bible, usually thought to be a hippopotamus (Job 40:15).

behest /bi hést/ *n* order or request *(literary)* ○ *at her behest*

behind /bi hínd/ *prep, adv* **1** at the back of or following **2** later than ○ *behind schedule* ■ *adv* **1** in arrears ○ *She's behind on her payments.* **2** remaining ○ *was left behind* ■ *prep* **1** causing ○ *The criminals are behind the robbery.* **2** supporting ○ *I'm behind you all the way!* ■ *n* somebody's buttocks *(infml)*

behindhand /bi hínd hand/ *adj* **1** behind schedule **2** lagging behind

Behn /ben/, **Aphra** (1640–89) English writer

behold /bi hôld/ (**-held** /-héld/) *vt* look at or see *(literary; often in commands)* —**beholder** *n*

beholden /bi hôld'n/ *adj* under an obligation

behove /bi hôv/ (**-hoving**, **-hoved**) *vt* be fitting for somebody *(fml)*

Beiderbecke /bídər bek/, **Bix** (1903–31) US jazz cornet player, pianist, and composer

beige /bayzh/ *n* a very pale brown colour —**beige** *adj*

Beijing /báy jíng/ capital of China. Pop. 11,300,000 (1995).

being /bee ing/ present participle of **be** ■ *n* **1** existence **2** somebody's essential nature ○ *loved the child with all her being* **3** a living thing regarded as supernatural or alien

Beirut /bay roōt/ capital of Lebanon. Pop. 1,500,000 (1998 estimate).

bejewel /bi joō əl/ (**-elling**, **-elled**) *vt* decorate with jewels —**bejewelled** *adj*

belabour /bi láybər/ *vt* **1** harp on **2** criticize *(literary)*

Belarus /béllə roôss, byéllə-/ country in E Europe. Cap. Minsk. Pop. 10,350,194 (2001).

belated /bi láytid/ *adj* overdue —**belatedly** *adv*

belay /bi láy/ *vti* **1** fasten a line to a ship **2** secure a rope attached to a climber

belch *vti* **1** release stomach gas from the mouth noisily **2** send or come out visibly ○ *chimneys belching smoke* —**belch** *n*

beleaguer /bi leegər/ *vt* **1** harass or pressurize **2** surround with an army —**beleaguerment** *n*

~~beleif~~ incorrect spelling of **belief**

~~beleive~~ incorrect spelling of **believe**

Belém /bə lém/ port and capital of Pará State, N Brazil. Pop. 1,144,312 (1996).

Belfast /bél faast, bel faást/ capital of Northern Ireland. Pop. 297,300 (1996).

belfry /bélfri/ (pl **-fries**) n 1 the part of a church where bells are hung 2 a bell tower

ORIGIN Belfry originally had no connection with bells. The earliest forms had *r* not *l*, just like the French word from which the English derives, and meant 'movable tower used as a siege engine'. The phonetic change from *r* to *l* was reinforced by popular association with the word *bell*, which brought about the restriction in meaning to a bell tower or a space where bells are hung.

Belgian /béljən/ n somebody from Belgium ■ adj 1 of Belgium

Belgium /béljəm/ country in NW Europe, bordering the North Sea. Cap. Brussels. Pop. 10,258,762 (2001).

Belgrade /bél grayd/ capital of the Federal Republic of Yugoslavia. Pop. 1,594,483 (1998).

belie /bi lí/ (**-lying**, **-lied**) vt 1 give a false impression of 2 show to be false

belief /bi leéf/ n 1 acceptance that something is true or real 2 confidence that something is good 3 something accepted as true 4 a firm opinion

believe /bi leév/ (**-lieving**, **-lieved**) v 1 vt accept as true 2 vt accept as truthful o *I don't believe you.* 3 vi think that something exists o *believe in ghosts* 4 vi have faith in somebody or something o *You have to believe in yourself.* 5 vi have religious faith —**believable** adj —**believer** n

~~beligerent~~ incorrect spelling of **belligerent**

belittle /bi lítt'l/ (**-tling**, **-tled**) vt make something seem less good or important o *I don't want to belittle her achievement.* —**belittlement** n

Belize /be leéz, bə-/ country in Central America on the Caribbean Sea. Cap. Belmopan. Pop. 256,062 (2001). —**Belizean** /be leézh'n, bə-/ adj

Belize City main port of Belize, on the Caribbean Sea. Pop. 53,915 (1997).

Belkic /bélkich/, **Beriz** (b. 1946) Bosniac representative of the presidency of Bosnia and Herzegovina (2001–) which rotates between a Serb, a Bosnian Muslim, and a Croat

bell n 1 an object or device that makes a ringing sound 2 something with the curved flared shape of a bell ◊ **ring a bell** evoke a vague memory (infml)

Bell, Alexander Graham (1847–1922) Scottish-born US inventor and educator. He made the first intelligible telephonic transmission (1876).

belladonna /béllə dónnə/ n 1 a drug made from the poisonous black berries of deadly nightshade 2 the deadly nightshade plant

bell-bottom trousers, bell-bottoms npl trousers with flared legs

belle /bel/ n a beautiful woman

belles-lettres /bél léttrə/ n literature valued for elegance rather than content (+ sing or pl verb)

bellicose /béllikōss/ adj warlike or ready to quarrel —**bellicosity** /bélli kóssəti/ n

belligerent /bə lijjərənt/ adj 1 hostile or aggressive 2 engaged in war ■ n a participant in a war —**belligerence** n —**belligerently** adv

Bellingshausen Sea /béllingz howz'n-/ part of the S Pacific Ocean off the coast of W Antarctica

Bellini /be leéni/ family of Italian painters including **Jacopo** (1400?–70?) and his sons **Gentile** (1429?–1507) and **Giovanni** (1430?–1516)

Bellini, Vincenzo (1801–35) Italian composer

bell jar n a bell-shaped glass cover for protecting or containing something

Belloc /béllok/, **Hilaire** (1870–1953) French-born British writer

bellow /béllō/ v 1 vi make the roaring sound of a bull 2 vti shout loudly —**bellow** n

Bellow /béllō/, **Saul** (b. 1915) Canadian-born US writer

bellows /béllōz/ (pl same) n a device with a compressible chamber for pumping air

belly /bélli/ n (pl **-lies**) 1 the abdomen 2 the stomach (infml) 3 a bulging part ■ vti (**-lies**, **-lied**) bulge ◊ **go** or **turn belly up** go bankrupt or fail

bellyache /bélli ayk/ (**-aching**, **-ached**) vi complain (infml)

bellybutton /béli butt'n/ n the navel (infml)

belly dance n a dance using movements of the hips and abdomen —**belly dancer** n —**belly dancing** n

belly flop n a dive in which the front of the body hits the water —**belly-flop** vi

belly laugh n a deep unrestrained laugh

Belmopan /bélmə pán/ capital of Belize. Pop. 6,785 (1997).

Belo Horizonte /béllō hori zón tay/ capital of Minas Gerais State, Brazil. Pop. 2,091,448 (1996).

belong /bi lóng/ vi 1 be somebody's property o *The car belongs to her sister.* 2 be a member or part of something o *plants belonging to the daisy family* 3 be in the right or usual place o *Where does this chair belong?*

belonging /bi lónging/ n the state of feeling comfortable or accepted in a place ■ **belongings** npl personal possessions

beloved /bi lúvvid/ (predicative adj) /-lúvd/ adj adored ■ n /bi lúvvid/ a loved person o *a letter from his beloved*

below /bi lố/ adv 1 under or beneath 2 further on in a text ■ prep, adv at or to a lower level, standard, or grade

belt n 1 a strip of leather or other material worn round the waist 2 a strip of something different 3 an area associated with a particular industry, product, or characteristic o *the commuter belt* 4 a seat belt or safety belt 5 a moving band of flexible material used in machinery o *a fan belt* ■ vt 1 fasten with a belt 2 hit with a belt 3 hit hard (infml)

◊ **below the belt** unfair ◊ **have something under your belt** have done something that will benefit you in the future ◊ **tighten your belt** reduce your spending

☐ **belt out** *vt* sing or play loudly *(infml)*

☐ **belt up** *vi* stop talking *(slang; usually a command)*

belt-tightening *n* a reduction in spending

beluga /bə lōōgə/ *(pl* -**gas** *or same) n* **1** a large white sturgeon whose eggs are eaten as caviar **2** a white whale

belvedere /bélvə deer/ *n* a building with a fine view

bemoan /bi mṓn/ *vt* lament or complain about

bemused /bi myōōzd/ *adj* bewildered —**bemusedly** /-idli/ *adv* —**bemusement** *n*

ben *n Ireland, Scotland* a mountain *(often in placenames)* ○ *Ben Nevis*

Benares /bi naàriz/ former name for **Varanasi**

Benaud /bénnṓ/, **Richie** *(b. 1930)* Australian cricketer and broadcaster

bench *n* **1** a long backless seat **2** a long worktable **3** the office or position of a judge **4** a seat for sports officials or nonplaying team members, or the people occupying it ■ *vt* provide a place with benches

bench mark *n* a surveyor's reference marker

benchmark /bénch maark/ *n* **1** a standard for measurement or assessment **2** a test of computer performance —**benchmark** *adj, vt*

bend *v* (**bent**) **1** *vti* make or become curved or angled **2** *vi* stoop down **3** *vti* yield, or force to yield **4** *vti* change or cause to change direction **5** *vt* distort for somebody's benefit ○ *bend the rules* ■ *n* **1** a curve **2** an act of bending or being bent **3** a knot joining two ropes —**bendable** *adj* —**bendy** *adj*

bender /béndər/ *n* a drinking spree *(slang)*

bends *n* decompression sickness *(infml; + sing or pl verb)*

beneath /bi neèth/ *prep* underneath *(fml)* ○ *beneath the bed* ○ *Beneath his veneer of politeness lay hostility.* ■ *prep, adv* at a lower level *(fml)* ○ *hills and the village beneath* ■ *prep* too low in character for ○ *Gossiping is beneath you.*

Benedictine /bénni díktin/ *n* a member of an order founded by St Benedict of Nursia —**Benedictine** *adj*

benediction /bénni díksh'n/ *n* **1** an expression of approval **2** a prayer asking for God's blessing

Benedict of Nursia /bénni dikt əv núrssi ə, -núrshə/, **St** *(480–547)* Italian monk considered to be the founder of Western monastic tradition

benefaction /bénni fáksh'n/ *n* a good deed or charitable gift

benefactor /bénni faktər/ *n* a financial supporter

benefice /bénnifiss/ *n* a church office providing a living through an endowment

beneficent /bə néffissənt/ *adj* **1** doing good deeds **2** producing benefit —**beneficence** *n*

beneficial /bénni físh'l/ *adj* having a good effect —**beneficially** *adv*

beneficiary /bénni físhəri/ *(pl* -**ies**) *n* somebody who gives or receives a benefit

benefit /bénnifit/ *n* **1** something good or advantageous **2** a government payment to somebody needing assistance **3** a performance for charity ■ *vti* give or receive help, an advantage, or some other benefit ◊ **give somebody the benefit of the doubt** assume that somebody is innocent or truthful

Benelux /bénni luks/ *n* Belgium, the Netherlands, and Luxembourg

benevolent /bə névvələnt/ *adj* **1** kind **2** charitable —**benevolence** *n* —**benevolently** *adv*

Bengal /ben gáwl, beng-/ former province of NE India, now divided into Bangladesh and the Indian state of Bangla —**Bengalese** /ben gáw leéz, béng-/ *n*

Bengal, Bay of northeastern arm of the Indian Ocean between India, Myanmar, and the Malay peninsula

Bengali /ben gáwli, beng gáwli/ *n* **1** somebody from Bangladesh or Bangla **2** the language of Bangladesh or Bangla —**Bengali** *adj*

Benghazi /ben gaàzi, beng-/, **Bengasi** port in NE Libya. Pop. 804,000 *(1995)*.

David Ben-Gurion

Ben-Gurion /ben goòri ən/, **David** *(1886–1973)* Polish-born Israeli prime minister *(1948–53, 1955–63)*

~~benificial~~ incorrect spelling of **beneficial**

~~benifit~~ incorrect spelling of **benefit**

benighted /bi nítid/ *adj* unenlightened *(fml)* —**benightedness** *n*

benign /bi nín/ *adj* **1** kindly **2** favourable **3** harmless **4** not malignant or life-threatening ○ *a benign tumour* —**benignly** *adv*

Benin /bə neèn/ country in West Africa between Togo and Nigeria. Cap. Porto-Novo. Pop. 6,590,782 *(2001)*. —**Beninese** /bénni neéz/ *adj, n*

Bennett /bénnit/, **Alan** *(b. 1934)* British playwright and actor

Bennett, Arnold *(1867–1931)* British novelist

Ben Nevis /-névviss/ highest mountain in the British Isles, in W Scotland. Height 1,343 m / 4,406 ft.

bent past tense, past participle of **bend** ■ *adj* **1** curved **2** determined ○ *bent on revenge* **3** an offensive term meaning gay *(slang)* **4** dishonest or corrupt *(slang)* ■ *n* a natural inclination or talent ◊ See note at **talent**

Bentham /bénthəm/, **Jeremy** (1748–1832) British philosopher, jurist, and social reformer

Bentley /béntli/, **E. C.** (1875–1956) British writer

Benz /benz/, **Karl** (1844–1929) German engineer and automobile manufacturer

benzene /bén zeen/ n C_6H_6 a toxic liquid derived from petroleum. Use: manufacture of dyes, polymers, and industrial chemicals.

benzine /bén zeen/, **benzin** /-zin/ n a mixture of liquids derived from crude oil. Use: industrial solvent.

bequeath /bi kweeth, -kweeth/ vt **1** leave something to somebody in a will **2** hand something down to posterity —**bequeathal** n —**bequeathment** n

bequest /bi kwést/ n **1** the bequeathing of something **2** something bequeathed

berate /bi ráyt/ (-**rating**, -**rated**) vt scold vigorously and at length

Berber /búrbər/ (pl -**bers** or same) n **1** a member of a North African people **2** a group of languages spoken across North Africa, especially in Algeria and Morocco —**Berber** adj

Berchtesgaden /báirktəss gaad'n, báirkhtəss-/ town in SE Bavaria, Germany, near the site of Adolf Hitler's fortified retreat. Pop. 7,966 (1997).

bereaved /bi reévd/ adj deprived of a loved one by death ■ n (pl same) somebody bereaved —**bereave** vt —**bereavement** n

bereft /bi réft/ adj **1** lacking or deprived of something ○ bereft of new ideas **2** feeling a sense of loss

beret /bérray/ n a flat round soft hat

Berg /bairg/, **Alban** (1885–1935) Austrian composer

Berg /burg/, **Paul** (b. 1926) US molecular biologist. He identified transfer RNA (1956).

Bergen /búrgən/ port in SW Norway. Pop. 225,439 (1998).

Bergman /búrgmən/, **Ingmar** (b. 1918) Swedish film director

Bergman, **Ingrid** (1915–82) Swedish-born US film actor

Bergson /búrgss'n/, **Henri** (1859–1941) French philosopher —**Bergsonian** /burg sóni ən/ n, adj

beriberi /bérri bérri/ n a disease caused by thiamine deficiency

Bering Sea /báiring-/ arm of the North Pacific Ocean between the Aleutian Islands, Siberia, and Alaska. Depth 4,773 m/15,659 ft.

Bering Strait narrow stretch of sea between Russia and Alaska. At its narrowest point it is 82 km/51 mi. wide.

berk, burk n a person regarded as foolish (slang insult)

Berkeley /búrkli/ city in W California. Pop. 108,101 (1998).

Berkeley /baárkli/, **George** (1685–1753) Irish Anglican bishop and philosopher

berkelium /bur keéli əm/ n (symbol **Bk**) a synthetic radioactive element

ORIGIN **Berkelium** is named after Berkeley, California, where it was first made.

Berlin /bur lín/ capital of Germany. Pop. 3,472,009 (1997). —**Berliner** n

Berlin, Sir Isaiah (1909–97) Latvian-born British philosopher and historian

Berlioz /báirli ōz/, **Hector** (1803–69) French composer

Berlusconi /báirloo skôni/, **Silvio** (b. 1936) prime minister of Italy (1994, 2001–)

Bermuda /bər myoódə/ group of islands in the W North Atlantic Ocean, a self-governing British dependency. Cap. Hamilton. Pop. 63,503 (2001). —**Bermudan** n, adj

Bermuda shorts, Bermudas npl knee-length shorts

Bern /burn/, **Berne** capital of Switzerland. Pop. 123,254 (1998).

Bernadette of Lourdes /búrnə dét-/, **St** (1844–79) French nun and visionary

Berners-Lee /búrnərz leé/, **Tim** (b. 1955) British computer scientist who designed and introduced the World Wide Web (1989)

Barnaby's

Sarah Bernhardt

Bernhardt /búrn haart/, **Sarah** (1844–1923) French actor

Bernini /bur neéni/, **Gianlorenzo** (1598–1680) Italian sculptor and architect

Bernoulli /bur noóli/ family of Swiss mathematicians including **Johann** or **Jean** (1667–1748), his brother **Jakob** (1654–1705), and his Dutch-born son **Daniel** (1700–82), who was also a physicist

Bernstein /búrn stīn/, **Leonard** (1918–90) US conductor, composer, and pianist

berry /bérri/ (pl -**ries**) n a small juicy or fleshy fruit

SPELLCHECK Do not confuse the spelling of **berry** and **bury** ('put in a hole'), which sound similar.

berserk /bə zúrk/ adj extremely angry or violent ○ She'll go berserk if she finds out.

ORIGIN **Berserk** was originally a name for a Viking warrior who fought with unrestrained aggression. The word is Scandinavian, and probably literally means 'bear shirt', either because these warriors wore bearskins or because they were fierce.

berth n 1 a bed on a ship or train 2 a place to moor a ship in dock 3 room to manoeuvre at sea 4 a parking place ■ v 1 vti dock or moor a ship 2 vt assign a berth to

beryl /bérral/ n a mineral occurring in many colours. Use: gems.

beryllium /bə rílli əm/ n (symbol Be) a lightweight metallic chemical element. Use: alloys.

Berzelius /bər zeéli əss/, **Jöns Jakob, Baron** (1799–1848) Swedish chemist. He drew up the table of atomic weights.

beseech /bi seéch/ (**-sought** /-sáwt/ or **-seeched**) vt (literary) 1 beg somebody to do something 2 beg for something —**beseeching** adj

~~beserk~~ incorrect spelling of **berserk**

beset /bi sét/ (**-setting, -set**) vt (fml) 1 harass or trouble continually o was beset with fears 2 attack on all sides

beside /bi síd/ prep 1 at the side of 2 compared with 3 in addition to ◊ **beside yourself** in a very excited or agitated state

besides /bi sídz/ prep, adv in addition to something or somebody ■ adv moreover

besiege /bi seéj/ (**-sieging, -sieged**) vt 1 surround with an army 2 crowd around 3 harass

besmear /bi smeér/ vt smear with mud, dirt, or a greasy or sticky substance

besmirch /bi smúrch/ vt 1 sully somebody's reputation 2 make something dirty (literary)

besotted /bi sóttid/ adj infatuated

besought past tense, past participle of **beseech**

bespatter /bi spáttər/ vt splash with mud, paint, or a dirty substance

bespeak /bi speék/ (**-spoke** /-spók/, **-spoken** /-spókən/) vt 1 be a sign of (actions that bespeak complicity) 2 order in advance

bespectacled /bi spéktək'ld/ adj wearing spectacles

bespoke past tense of **bespeak** ■ adj made to order o a bespoke suit

best adj 1 better than all others o the best player o the best solution 2 most intimate o my best friends ■ adv 1 more than all others 2 most successfully o It works best in cold weather. ■ n 1 what is best o want the best for their family 2 somebody or something better than all others o is the best at hockey 3 the highest possible quality or standard o do your best

Best, Charles H. (1899–1978) US-born Canadian physiologist

Best, Elsdon (1856–1931) New Zealand ethnologist

bestial /bésti əl/ adj 1 inhuman or depraved o bestial cruelty 2 sexually depraved

bestiality /bésti álləti/ n 1 sexual activity between a human being and an animal 2 inhuman behaviour

bestir /bi stúr/ (**-stirring, -stirred**) vr start doing something (fml) o bestirred themselves

best man n the bridegroom's attendant at a wedding

bestow /bi stów/ vt give or present (fml) —**bestowal** n ◊ See note at **give**

bestride /bi stríd/ (**-striding, -strode** /-stród/ or **-strid** /-strid/, **-stridden** /-strídd'n/) vt stand across with one foot on each side of something

bestseller /bést séllər/ n a product that is commercially very successful —**bestselling** adj

bet vti (**betting, bet** or **betted**) 1 agree with somebody to give or receive something of value in predicting a result or making a challenge o I bet you £10 you can't lift that rock. 2 express certainty that something is true (infml) o I bet he's forgotten. ■ n 1 an agreement, prediction, or challenge made in betting 2 what somebody expects or thinks o My bet is that they'll drop the idea. 3 somebody or something likely to succeed o a safe bet for the presidency —**betting** n

beta /beétə/ n 1 the 2nd letter of the Greek alphabet 2 the 2nd highest grade of a student's work ■ adj 1 of electrons produced by splitting of neutrons during radioactive decay o beta particles o beta rays 2 describes software ready for beta tests o beta version

beta-blocker n a drug regulating heart activity. Use: treatment of high blood pressure.

beta test n a test of new computer software by customers —**beta-test** vt

betaware /beétə wair/ n software ready for beta tests

betel /beét'l/ (pl **-tels** or same) n the leaves of an Asian climbing plant chewed as a digestive aid

betel nut n a dark red seed wrapped in betel leaves with lime and chewed as a mild stimulant

bete noire /bét nwaár/ (pl **betes noires** /pronunc. same/) n somebody or something you particularly dislike

Bethlehem /béthli hem/ town in the West Bank near Jerusalem, the traditional birthplace of King David and Jesus Christ. Part of Israel since 1967, it has been administered by the Palestinian Authority since 1995. Pop. 21,947 (1997).

betide /bi tíd/ vti happen (literary)

Betjeman /béchəmən/, **Sir John** (1906–84) British poet

betoken /bi tókən/ vt be a sign of (literary)

betray /bi tráy/ vt 1 harm a person or country by helping or giving information to an enemy 2 reveal an emotion or quality, often unintentionally —**betrayal** n

betrothal /bi tróthəl/ n engagement to marry somebody (fml)

betrothed /bi tróthd/ (pl **-trotheds** or same) n the person somebody is engaged to marry (fml) —**betrothed** adj

Bettelheim /bétt'l hīm/, **Bruno** (1903–90) Austrian-born US psychologist

better[1] /béttər/ adj 1 more pleasing or acceptable than others of the same class, set, or kind 2 of higher quality or greater usefulness than others 3 improved in health ■ adv 1 to a greater degree or higher standard than others or than before **2** preferably ○ *Such things are better left unsaid.* ■ *vt* **1** surpass **2** improve *(fml)* ■ *n* a superior person *(often pl)* ◇ **get the better of** defeat ◇ **go one better** surpass something or outdo somebody ◇ **had better** ought to

better[2] /béttar/ *n* somebody who bets

better half *n* somebody's spouse *(infml)*

betterment /béttarmant/ *n* improvement, especially affecting somebody's financial or social standing *(fml)*

bettong /be tóng/ *n* a small nocturnal kangaroo with rounded ears and a bushy tail

between /bi tweén/ *prep, adv* in an intermediate position with respect to somebody or something ○ *between the wars* ○ *houses with fields between* ■ *prep* **1** to and from ○ *travelling between London and Oxford* **2** by the joint action of ○ *We managed to solve it between us.* **3** indicates comparison, choice, or relationship ○ *the difference between them* ○ *arguing between themselves* **4** by or to each in a group

betwixt /bi twíkst/ *adv, prep* between *(literary)*

~~beutiful~~ incorrect spelling of **beautiful**

Bevan /bév'n/, **Nye** (1897–1960) British politician

bevel /bév'l/ *n* **1** a slanting edge **2** a tool used to mark or measure angles ■ *vt* (**-elling**, **-elled**) make a slanting edge on ○ *a mirror with edges that had been bevelled*

beverage /bévvarij/ *n* a drink other than water

Beveridge /bévvarij/, **William, 1st Baron Beveridge of Tuggal** (1879–1963) Indian-born British economist

Bevin /bévvin/, **Ernest** (1881–1951) British trade union leader and politician

bevy /bévvi/ (*pl* **-ies**) *n* a group of people or animals

bewail /bi wáyl/ *vt* lament *(fml)*

beware /bi wáir/ *vti* be on guard against somebody or something *(only as a command and in the infinitive)*

bewhiskered /bi wískard/ *adj* with whiskers or a beard

Bewick /byoó ik/, **Thomas** (1753–1828) British wood engraver

bewilder /bi wíldar/ *vt* confuse —**bewilderment** *n*

bewitch /bi wích/ *vt* **1** enchant or captivate ○ *was bewitched by his charm* **2** cast a magic spell on —**bewitching** *adj*—**bewitchment** *n*

beyond /bi yónd/ *prep, adv* **1** on the other side of something **2** after a particular time ○ *in the next decade and beyond* ■ *prep* **1** past ○ *lived beyond their means* **2** except ○ *no information beyond what we know* **3** impossible for ○ *tasks that are beyond them*

bezique /bi zeék/ *n* a card game like whist

Bezos /báyzōss/, **Jeff** (*b.* 1964) US Internet entrepreneur

Bhadrapada /baàdra paada/, **Bhadra** *n* the 6th month of the year in the Hindu calendar

bhaji /baàji/ (*pl* **-jis**), **bhajee** *n* a deep-fried South Asian vegetable dish

bhang /bang/, **bang** *n* cannabis

bhangra /báng gra/ *n* popular music mixing Punjabi folk music with western pop music

Bhopal /bō paàl/ capital of Madhya Pradesh State, India. Pop. 1,062,771 (1991).

Bhumibol Adulyadej /poòmi pōn aa doòn la dayt/ ↦ **Rama IX**

Bhutan /boo taàn/ country in the eastern part of the Himalayan range between India and the Tibet region of China. Cap. Thimphu. Pop. 2,049,412 (2001). —**Bhutanese** /boóta néez/ *n, adj*

Bhutto /boòtō/, **Benazir** (*b.* 1953) prime minister of Pakistan (1988–90, 1993–96)

bi /bī/ *adj* bisexual *(slang)*

Bi *symbol* bismuth

bi- *prefix* two, twice, both ○ *bisexual* ◊ See note at **buy**

Biafra /bi áffra/ region of E Nigeria that was declared a secessionist state between 1967 and 1970 —**Biafran** *n, adj*

biannual /bī ánnyoo al/ *adj* twice-yearly ◊ See note at **biweekly**

USAGE biannual or **biennial**? **Biannual** means 'twice a year', whereas **biennial** means 'every two years'. To avoid confusion use the expressions *twice-yearly* and *two-yearly*.

Biarritz /beer ríts/ resort town on the Bay of Biscay in SW France. Pop. 30,055 (1999).

bias /bí ass/ *n* (*pl* **-ases** *or* **-asses**) **1** an unfair preference **2** a diagonal line across the weave of a fabric ○ *fabric cut on the bias* ■ *vt* (**-ases** *or* **-asses**, **-asing** *or* **-assing**, **-ased** *or* **-assed**) cause to have a bias ■ *adj* diagonal —**biased** *adj*

bias binding *n* a thin strip of fabric cut on the bias and used to bind raw edges

biathlon /bī áth lón/ *n* a competition that combines cross-country skiing with rifle shooting at targets along the course —**biathlete** *n*

bib *n* **1** a piece of material protecting a child's clothing under the chin **2** a flap of clothing covering the chest

Bible /bíb'l/ *n* **1** the Christian holy book **2** the Jewish holy book **3** *also* **bible** an authoritative or essential book on a subject

ORIGIN Bible comes from a Greek word that means simply 'book' and was originally a diminutive of the word for 'papyrus, scroll'. It reached English through ecclesiastical Latin and French.

biblical /bíbblik'l/, **Biblical** *adj* of or like the Bible —**biblically** *adv*

bibliography /bíbbli óggrafi/ (*pl* **-phies**) *n* **1** a list of books or articles used as sources **2** a list of publications by a particular author, on a particular subject, or issued by a particular publisher **3** the history, classification, or description of books —**bibliographer** *n* —**bibliographic** /bíbbli a gráffik/ *adj* —**bibliographical** *adj*

bibliophile /bíbbli ə fīl/ n a collector of books

bibulous /bíbbyōōləss/ adj tending to drink too much alcohol (fml)

bicameral /bī kámmərəl/ adj with two legislative chambers

bicarbonate of soda /bī kaárbənət-, -nayt-/ n sodium bicarbonate. Use: raising agent, antacid.

bicentenary /bí sen teénəri, -ténn-/ (pl -ries) n a 200th anniversary —**bicentenary** adj

biceps /bí seps/ (pl same) n a large muscle of the upper arm

bicker /bíkər/ vi argue about something unimportant

bicuspid /bī kúspid/ adj with two points ■ n a premolar tooth

bicycle /bí ssik'l/ n a two-wheeled vehicle moved by pedalling ■ vi (-cling, -cled) ride a bicycle —**bicyclist** n

bid v (bidding, bad archaic or bade /bad, bayd/ or bid, bidden /bídd'n/ or bid) 1 (past and past participle bid) vti offer money for something at an auction 2 (past and past participle bid) vi offer to do work for a specific price ◇ bidding for the contract 3 vt say something to somebody ◇ bade her farewell ■ n 1 an amount of money or a price offered 2 an attempt 3 in cards, a statement of the number of tricks to be taken —**bidder** n

biddable /bíddəb'l/ adj obedient

bidding /bídding/ n 1 the making of bids 2 somebody's orders ◇ They were eager to do our bidding.

bide (biding, bided or bode, bided) vi stay or remain (archaic)

bidet /beé day/ n a low basin for washing the genital and anal areas

Bielefeld /beélə felt/ city in NW Germany. Pop. 324,067 (1997).

biennial /bī énni əl/ adj 1 happening every two years 2 describes a plant that flowers in its second year —**biennial** n —**biennially** adv ◊ See note at **biannual**

bier /beer/ n 1 a stand for a coffin 2 a frame for carrying a coffin (literary) ◊ See note at **beer**

biff vt hit (infml) —**biff** n

bifocal /bī fók'l/ adj describes lenses with two focal lengths ■ **bifocals** npl a pair of glasses with bifocal lenses

bifurcate /bí fur kayt/ (-cating, -cated) vti divide or branch into two parts —**bifurcation** /bí fur káysh'n/ n

big adj (bigger, biggest) 1 of great size 2 powerful 3 significant 4 older ◇ my big sister 5 magnanimous ◇ She's a woman with a big heart. ■ adv ambitiously ◇ think big —**bigness** n ◊ **big on** enthusiastic about (infml) ◊ big on equality of opportunity ◊ **make it big** be extremely successful (infml)

bigamy /bíggəmi/ n the crime of being simultaneously married to two people —**bigamist** n —**bigamous** adj

Big Apple n New York City (infml)

big bang n the explosion that is said to have started the universe

Big Ben n the clock above the Houses of Parliament, the tower in which it stands, or the bell that chimes its hours

Big Brother n an authority exerting dictatorial control and maintaining a constant watch

ORIGIN The original **Big Brother** featured in George Orwell's novel Nineteen Eighty-Four (1949).

big business n large commercial organizations collectively

big dipper n a roller coaster

biger incorrect spelling of **bigger**

Bigfoot /bíg foot/, **bigfoot** n a legendary humanoid creature of NW North America

big game n large animals hunted for sport

bigheaded /bíg héddid/ adj conceited (infml)

big-hearted adj kind and generous —**big-heartedly** adv —**big-heartedness** n

bight /bīt/ n 1 a curve of the coastline forming a wide bay 2 a loop in a rope

bigmouth /bíg mowth/ n a person regarded as indiscreet or boastful (infml)

big name n somebody or something famous —**big-name** adj

bigot /bíggət/ n a person regarded as intolerant, opinionated, and, typically, racist —**bigoted** adj —**bigotry** n

big screen n the cinema

big shot n an important person (infml)

big-ticket adj expensive (infml)

big time (slang) n the highest level of success in a profession or other activity ■ adv on a grand scale or at the highest level —**big timer** n

big top n 1 a circus tent 2 the circus

big wheel n a Ferris wheel

bigwig /bíg wig/ n an important person (infml)

bijou /beé zhoo, beé zhoó/ adj small but fashionable and elegant (humorous) ◇ a bijou apartment ■ n (pl -jous /-zhooz/ or -joux /-zhoo/) a delicate jewel or ornament

bike (infml) n a bicycle or motorcycle ■ vi (biking, biked) go by bike

hiker /bíkər/ n a motorcyclist or bicycle rider

bikini /bi keéni/ n a woman's two-piece swimming costume

ORIGIN The **bikini** appeared on beaches not long after the United States had tested an atom bomb on Bikini Atoll in the Marshall Islands in the Pacific Ocean in 1946. The impact of the swimwear was presumably considered to be equally explosive.

Biko /beékō/, **Steve** (1946–77) South African political activist

bilateral /bī láttərəl/ adj 1 involving two groups of people 2 of or on both sides ◇ bilateral symmetry —**bilaterally** adv

Bilbao /bil baá ō/ port in N Spain. Pop. 358,467 (1998).

bilberry /bílbəri/ (*pl* -ries) *n* 1 an edible blue-black berry 2 a shrub that produces bilberries

bilby /bílbi/ (*pl* -bies) *n* a burrowing marsupial resembling a rat

bile *n* 1 digestive fluid produced in the liver and stored in the gallbladder 2 feelings of bitterness and irritability (*literary*)

bilge *n* 1 the lower part of a boat's hull, or the area inside it 2 dirty water that collects in the bilge 3 nonsense (*infml*)

bilingual /bī líng gwəl/ *adj* 1 speaking two languages 2 in two languages

bilious /bíli əss/ *adj* 1 feeling nauseated 2 nauseatingly unpleasant —**biliously** *adv* —**biliousness** *n*

bilk *vt* cheat or defraud (*infml*)

bill[1] *n* 1 a statement of money owed 2 an amount to be paid 3 a legislative proposal 4 an advertising poster 5 a list of items, especially a programme of entertainment 6 *US, Can* a banknote ■ *vt* 1 send a request for payment to 2 advertise ◊ **fill** *or* **fit the bill** be suitable for a specific purpose

bill[2] *n* 1 a bird's beak 2 the mouthparts of an animal such as a platypus, which resemble a beak

billabong /bílə bong/ *n Aus* a pool linked to river

billboard /bíl bawrd/ *n* a large board, typically on a roadside, for displaying advertisements

billet /bíllət/ *n* temporary accommodation for members of the armed forces ■ *v* 1 *vti* assign to or have temporary accommodation 2 *vt* provide temporary accommodation for

billet-doux /bíli doo/ (*pl* **billets-doux** /bíli dooz/) *n* a love letter

billfold /bíl fōld/ *n US, Can* a wallet

billhook /bíl hook/ *n* a tool with a broad curved blade. Use: pruning branches off trees.

billiards /bílyərdz/ *n* a game that involves hitting balls on a table with a cue (+ *sing verb*)

billing /bílling/ *n* a position on an entertainment programme or advertisement ◊ *top billing*

billion /bílyən/ (*pl* -**lions** *or* same) *n* 1 one thousand million 2 one million million (*dated*) 3 a very large number (*infml; often pl*) —**billionth** *n, adj*

billionaire /bílyə nair/ *n* somebody who has money and property worth more than a billion pounds

bill of exchange *n* a written instruction to pay a sum of money

bill of fare *n* a menu

bill of rights *n* a list of human rights guaranteed by law

billow /bílō/ *v* 1 *vti* swell or fill with air ◊ *billowing sails* 2 *vi* flow in a curling mass ◊ *smoke that billowed from the room* —**billow** *n* —**billowy** *adj*

billposter /bíl pōstər/, **billsticker** /-stikər/ *n* somebody who sticks up advertising posters

billycan /bíli kan/ *n* a light metal cooking pot used on a campfire

billy goat /bílli-/, **billy** *n* a male goat

Billy the Kid /bílli-/ (1859–81) US outlaw

biltong /bíll tong/ *n S Africa* sun-dried meat

bimbo /bímbō/ (*pl* -**bos** *or* -**boes**) *n* an offensive term for a woman considered attractive but unintelligent (*slang*)

bimetallic /bī me tállik/ *adj* made up of two metals

bimonthly /bī múnthli/ *adj* 1 happening or issued every two months 2 happening or issued twice a month ■ *n* (*pl* -**lies**) a bimonthly publication —**bimonthly** *adv* ◊ See note at **biweekly**

bin *n* 1 a container for rubbish (*often in combination*) ◊ *a waste-paper bin* 2 a large storage container 3 a set of shelves for storing wine ■ *vt* (**binning, binned**) 1 throw away 2 store in a bin

binary /bínəri/ *adj* 1 consisting of two parts or elements 2 describes a number system with two rather than ten as its base ◊ *binary notation* ■ *n* (*pl* -**ries**) 1 the binary number system 2 a binary digit

binary code *n* a computer code using the binary number system

binary coded decimal *n* a system using binary numbers for decimals

binary digit *n* either of the digits 0 and 1

binary file *n* a computer file containing characters that only a computer can read

binary star *n* a pair of stars with mutual gravitational attraction

bind /bīnd/ *v* (**bound** /bownd/, **bound**) 1 *vt* fasten something firmly to something else by winding a cord round both 2 *vt* wrap a bandage, tape, or cord around something, especially for protection 3 *vt* tie somebody's hands or feet together 4 *vt* protect or decorate the edge of fabric with tape, ribbon, or stitching 5 *vti* cause feelings of loyalty or closeness between people 6 *vt* oblige somebody to do something 7 *vt* fix the pages and cover of a book together, or cause surfaces to stick together ■ *n* something annoying or inconvenient ◊ **in a bind** in a difficult or unpleasant situation

binder /bíndər/ *n* 1 a hard cover for holding loose papers or magazines 2 a person or machine that binds something

bindery /bíndəri/ (*pl* -**ies**) *n* a bookbinding workshop

binding /bínding/ *n* 1 a book cover 2 something holding a book's pages together 3 tape used to bind the edge of fabric 4 a ski fastening ■ *adj* obliging somebody to do something ◊ *a binding agreement*

bindweed /bínd weed/ *n* a weed with twining stems

binge *n* 1 a heavy drinking or eating session 2 a session of self-indulgent activity ■ *vi* (**bingeing** *or* **binging, binged**) eat or drink too much

bingo /bíng gō/ *n* a lottery game played with numbered cards ■ *interj* 1 indicates a win in bingo 2 expresses triumph at success

Bin Laden /bin laàdən/, **Osama** (*b.* 1957) Saudi-born leader of the militant Islamic al-Qaeda organization

binnacle /bínnək'l/ *n* a housing for a ship's compass

binocular /bi nókyŏŏlər, bi-/ *adj* of or using both eyes

binoculars /bi nókyŏŏlərz, bi-/ *npl* a pair of small telescopes linked by one focusing device

binomial /bi nómi əl/ *n* **1** a mathematical expression with two terms **2** a two-part name for an organism, giving its genus and species —**binomial** *adj*

bio- *prefix* **1** life, biology o *biography* o *biochemistry* **2** biological warfare o *bioweapon* **3** involving the use of biological or chemical weapons o *bioterrorism*

biochemistry /bí ō kémmistri/ *n* **1** the chemistry of living organisms **2** the chemical nature of an organism or system —**biochemical** *adj* —**biochemist** *n*

biocomputer /bí ō kəm pyóotər/ *a* very fast computer whose calculations are made using biological processes

biodegradable /bí ō di gráydəb'l/ *adj* able to decompose naturally —**biodegradation** /bí ō déggrə dáysh'n/ —**biodegrade** *vti*

biodiversity /bí ō dī vúrssəti/ *n* the range of organisms present in an environment

bioethics /bí ō éthiks/ *n* the ethics of medical research and treatment (+ *sing verb*) —**bioethical** *adj* —**bioethicist** *n*

biogas /bí ō gass/ *n* a mixture of carbon dioxide and methane. Use: fuel.

biography /bī óggrəfi/ (*pl* -**phies**) *n* **1** an account of somebody's life **2** biographies in general —**biographer** *n* —**biographical** /bí ə gráffik'l/ *adj*

biohazard /bí ō hazərd/ *n* a toxic or infectious agent, or the potential harm such an agent can do to an organism —**biohazardous** /bí ō házzərdəss/ *adj*

Bioko /bi ŏkŏ/ island in the Gulf of Guinea, part of Equatorial Guinea. Pop. 57,190 (1983).

biological /bí ə lójik'l/ *adj* **1** of living things **2** of biology **3** describes detergents containing enzymes intended to digest stains **4** genetically related o *her biological parents* —**biologically** *adv*

biological clock *n* the set of mechanisms that link physiological processes with periodic cycles or with stages of development and ageing

biological control *n* pest control by introducing predators

biological warfare *n* the use of microorganisms to cause disease or death in war

biology /bī óllǝji/ *n* **1** the science of life **2** the life forms found in a particular place —**biologist** *n*

biomass /bí ō mass/ *n* plant and animal material used as fuel

biomedicine /bí ō médss'n/ *n* biological science applied to medicine —**biomedical** *adj*

bionic /bī ónnik/ *adj* **1** of or having electronically operated replacement body parts **2** of bionics

bionics /bī ónniks/ *n* (+ *sing verb*) **1** the application of biological information to machine design **2** the use of bionic body parts

biophysics /bí ō fízziks/ *n* the application of physics to biological studies (+ *sing verb*) —**biophysical** *adj* —**biophysicist** *n*

biopsy /bí opsi/ (*pl* -**sies**) *n* the removal of living tissue for examination

bioremediation /bí ō ri meédi áysh'n/ *n* the use of biological agents such as bacteria to clean up contaminated land

biorhythm /bí ō rithəm/ *n* a natural cyclical physiological change (*often pl*) —**biorhythmic** /bí ō ríthmik/ *adj*

BIOS *abbr* basic input-output system

biosatellite /bí ō satt'l īt/ *n* a satellite that can be lived in

bioscience /bí ō sī ənss/ *n* a science that studies living organisms

biosphere /bí ə sfeer/ *n* the whole area of the Earth's surface, atmosphere, and sea that is inhabited by living organisms

biotech /bí ō tek/ *n* biotechnology (*infml*)

biotechnology /bí ō tek nólləji/ *n* the use of biological processes in industrial production —**biotechnological** /bí ō teknə lójjik'l/ *adj* —**biotechnologist** *n*

bioterrorism /bí ō térrərizəm/, **bioterror** /bí ō terrər/ *n* terrorist acts involving the use of biological or chemical weapons —**bioterrorist** *adj*, *n*

biothreat /bí ō thret/ *n* a real or perceived threat of the use of biological or chemical weapons

biotin /bí ətin/ *n* a B vitamin found in egg yolk and liver

bioweapon /bí ō wepən/ *n* a biological or chemical weapon

bipartisan /bí paarti zán, bī páarti zan/ *adj* involving two political parties —**bipartisanism** *n*

bipartite /bī paàr tīt/ *adj* involving two groups of people

biped /bí ped/ *n* a two-legged animal

biplane /bí playn/ *n* an aeroplane with two sets of wings, one above the other

bipolar /bī pŏlər/ *adj* **1** of or having two poles **2** having two opposite opinions, attitudes, or natures —**bipolarity** /bí pō lárrəti/ *n*

bipolar disorder *n* a psychiatric disorder characterized by extreme mood swings

BIPS *abbr* bank Internet payment system

birch *n* **1** a tall tree with light coloured peeling bark **2** the wood of a birch tree **3** a birch rod for flogging

bird *n* **1** a two-legged feathered winged animal **2** a person of a particular type (*infml*) o *He's a wise old bird.* **3** an offensive term for a girl or woman (*dated infml*) —**birdlike** *adj* ◊ **kill two birds with one stone** achieve two aims with one action ◊ **the birds and the bees** the facts about sexual reproduction in human beings *(infml humorous)*

ORIGIN Originally **bird** was applied only to a young bird or nestling. The general word was *fowl*, and this use continued alongside **bird** long after the latter word had lost its restriction. *Fowl* is ultimately from the same ancient root as the verb *fly*, and related forms appear in other languages, but **bird** is unique to English and its origins are completely unknown.

birdbath /búrd baath/ (*pl* **-baths** /-baathz/) *n* a shallow basin for garden birds to bath in

birdbrain /búrd brayn/ *n* a person regarded as unintelligent *(infml insult)* —**birdbrained** *adj*

birdie /búrdi/ *n* **1** a golf score of one under par **2** a bird *(babytalk)*

birdlime /búrd līm/ *n* a sticky substance for trapping birds

bird of paradise *n* **1** a bird with bright feathers **2** a plant with flowers like a bird's crested head

bird of passage *n* a migratory bird

bird of prey *n* a bird that kills for food

bird's-eye view *n* **1** a view from high up **2** a general impression

birdsong /búrd song/ *n* the sounds made by birds

bird table *n* a table on which food for garden birds is placed

birdwatcher /búrd wochər/ *n* somebody who watches birds as a hobby —**birdwatching** *n*

biretta /bə réttə/ *n* a cleric's stiff hat

biriani *n* FOOD = **biryani**

Birkenhead /búrkən hed/ port in NW England. Pop. 93,087 (1991).

Birmingham /búrmingəm/ city and industrial centre in central England. Pop. 1,020,589 (1996).

birr *n* the main unit of Ethiopian currency

birth *n* **1** the time, event, or process of being born or begun **2** somebody's social or national heritage ○ *of noble birth* ■ *adj* biologically related as a parent ○ *his birth mother* ◇ **give birth** produce a child or young from the womb

birth canal *n* the passageway including the cervix and vagina through which a foetus emerges from the womb

birth certificate *n* a document recording somebody's birth

birth control *n* the deliberate prevention of pregnancy

birthday /búrth day, -di/ *n* **1** the anniversary of the day of somebody's birth **2** the day of somebody's birth

birthing /búrthing/ *n* the process of giving birth ■ *adj* facilitating childbirth

birthmark /búrth maark/ *n* a permanent blemish on the skin, present from birth

birthplace /búrth playss/ *n* the place where somebody was born or where something originated

birthrate /búrth rayt/ *n* the number of children born per year ○ *a declining birthrate*

birthright /búrth rīt/ *n* **1** a basic entitlement **2** property or money somebody expects to inherit

birthstone /búrth stōn/ *n* a stone popularly associated with the month in which somebody was born

biryani /bírri aáni/, **biriani** *n* a South Asian dish of spicy rice mixed with meat, fish, or vegetables

Biscay, Bay of /bíss kay/ arm of the North Atlantic Ocean between W France and N Spain

biscuit /bískit/ *n* **1** a small flat hard cake **2** unglazed pottery

ORIGIN Biscuit comes from French and means literally 'twice cooked'. Biscuits are returned to the oven to become dry and crisp after they have gone through an initial cooking process.

bise /beez/ *n* a northerly wind that blows in Switzerland and neighbouring parts of Italy and France

bisect /bī sékt/ *vt* **1** split into two **2** halve —**bisection** *n*

bisexual /bī sékshoo əl/ *adj* **1** attracted to both sexes **2** having both male and female characteristics —**bisexual** *n* —**bisexuality** /bī sékshoo álləti/ *n* —**bisexually** *adv*

Bishkek /bish kék/ capital of Kyrgyzstan. Pop. 585,800 (1996).

bishop /bíshəp/ *n* **1** a senior Christian cleric **2** a chess piece that moves diagonally

ORIGIN The Greek word from which **bishop** derives meant 'overseer', and had no particular religious connection. It later developed the more specific sense of 'church official', which was adopted into ecclesiastical Latin. The Greek form is the direct ancestor of *episcopal* and similar words. The initial *b* in **bishop** comes from a popular Latin variant that had lost the *e-*.

bishopric /bíshəprik/ *n* **1** a bishop's diocese **2** the rank of a bishop

Bismarck /bíz maark/ capital of North Dakota. Pop. 54,040 (1998).

Bismarck, Otto Edward Leopold von, Prince (1815–98) chancellor of the new German Empire (1871–90)

Bismarck Archipelago island group in the W Pacific Ocean, part of Papua New Guinea

Bismarck Sea arm of the SW Pacific Ocean northeast of New Guinea

bismuth /bízməth/ *n* (*symbol* **Bi**) a metallic chemical element. Use: alloys, medicines.

bison /bíss'n/ (*pl* same) *n* a large humped animal resembling an ox

bisque /bisk/ *n* shellfish soup

Bissau /bi sów/ capital and main port of Guinea-Bissau. Pop. 233,000 (1995).

bistro /beéstrō/ (*pl* **-tros**) *n* a small informal restaurant

bit[1] *n* **1** a piece or part ◊ *bits of paper* **2** a small amount **3** a short time ◊ *wait a bit* ◊ **a bit** somewhat *(infml)* ◊ **bit by bit** gradually ◊ **bits and pieces, bits and bobs** *(infml)* **1** personal belongings **2** miscellaneous small objects ◊ **do your bit** contribute your share of work ◊ **every bit** in every way ◊ **to bits** very much *(infml)* ◊ *I love them to bits.*

bit[2] *n* **1** the mouthpiece of a horse's bridle **2** a detachable cutting part of a drill

bit[3] *n* **1** a digit in binary notation **2** the smallest unit of information that can be stored in a computer

ORIGIN Bit here is a blend of *binary* and *digit*.

bit[4] past tense, past participle of **bite**

bitch *n* **1** a female dog **2** an offensive term for a woman regarded as spiteful or bad-tempered *(slang)* **3** something difficult *(slang; often offensive)* ■ *vi* talk spitefully about somebody *(slang; often offensive)*

bitchy /bíchi/ *(-ier, -iest) adj* malicious or unpleasant in speech or actions *(slang; often offensive)* —**bitchily** *adv* —**bitchiness** *n*

bite /bīt/ *v* (**biting, bit, bitten** /bítt'n/) **1** *vti* grip or cut something with the teeth **2** *vt* injure with the fangs or mouthparts **3** *vti* make firm contact with something **4** *vi* corrode something ◊ *The acid bites into the metal.* **5** *vi* take or rise to bait ◊ *no fish biting today* **6** *vt* annoy or upset somebody ◊ *What's biting you today?* ■ *n* **1** an act of biting **2** a mouthful **3** an injury produced by biting **4** a pleasantly sharp taste

biting /bíting/ *adj* **1** very cold **2** cleverly sarcastic —**bitingly** *adv*

bit map *n* a computer image represented as a pattern of dots corresponding to pixels

bit-map (**bit-mapping, bit-mapped**) *vt* represent as a bit map ◊ *a bit-mapped font*

bit stream *n* a simple unstructured sequence of bits transmitting data

bitten past participle of **bite**

bitter /bíttər/ *adj* **1** strong and sharp in taste **2** angry and resentful **3** difficult to accept ◊ *a bitter blow* **4** extremely hostile ◊ *bitter enemies* **5** very cold ■ *n UK* a sharp-tasting beer —**bitterly** *adv* —**bitterness** *n*

bitter end *n* the very end, however unpleasant ◊ *They held out to the bitter end.*

bittern /bíttərn/ *n* a wading bird with a booming call

bitter pill *n* something unavoidable and unpleasant

bitters /bíttərz/ *n* a flavoured alcoholic ingredient in some cocktails (+ *sing verb*) ■ *npl* a digestive tonic (+ *pl verb*)

bittersweet /bíttər sweet/ *adj* **1** both bitter and sweet in taste **2** both happy and sad

bitty /bítti/ *(-tier, -tiest) adj* made up of seemingly unconnected parts ◊ *a rather bitty documentary*

bitumen /bíttyŏoman/ *n* **1** a road-surfacing material **2** *Aus* a surfaced road —**bituminous** /bi tyŏominəss/ *adj*

~~**biulding**~~ incorrect spelling of **building**

bivalve /bī valv/ *n* a mollusc with a hinged shell

bivouac /bívvoo ak/ *n* **1** a military or mountaineering camp **2** a brief overnight stay ■ *vi* (**-acking, -acked**) make a simple temporary camp

biweekly /bī weékli/ *adj* **1** happening or issued every two weeks **2** happening or issued twice a week ■ *n* (*pl* **-lies**) a biweekly publication —**biweekly** *adv*

USAGE Confusion is caused by the fact that **biweekly** and *bimonthly* can mean either 'once every two weeks or months' or 'twice a week or month'. To avoid possible confusion, reword the sentence: *The talks are held twice a week at the local school. The talks are held every two weeks at the local school.*

biz[1] *n* *(slang)* **1** something wonderful **2** business

biz[2] *abbr* business (in Internet addresses)

~~**bizarre**~~ incorrect spelling of **bizarre**

bizarre /bi zaár/ *adj* grotesquely odd —**bizarrely** *adv* —**bizarreness** *n*

Bizet /beé zay/, **Georges** (1838–75) French composer

Bk *symbol* berkelium

blab (**blabbing, blabbed**) *vi* *(infml)* **1** tell secrets **2** chatter

blabber /blábbər/ *vi* chatter incoherently about something ■ *n* **1** somebody who cannot keep a secret **2** chatter

blabbermouth /blábbər mowth/ (*pl* **-mouths** /-mowthz/) *n* somebody who cannot keep a secret *(infml)*

black *adj* **1** of the colour of coal **2** without any light **3** *also* **Black** dark-skinned **4** served without milk ◊ *black coffee* **5** funny and macabre ◊ *black humour* **6** hopeless ◊ *The future is looking black.* **7** dirty **8** very bad or unfortunate ◊ *a black day for the industry* **9** evil ■ *n* **1** the colour of coal **2** total darkness **3** a black object or area, e.g. a ball in snooker or part of a roulette wheel ■ *vt* **1** make something black **2** use black polish on footwear **3** bruise somebody's eye **4** boycott goods —**blackly** *adv* —**blackness** *n* ❑ **black out** *v* **1** *vi* lose consciousness **2** *vt* cause a place to lose its electricity supply

Black, Shirley Temple (*b.* 1928) US actor and ambassador

black-and-blue *adj* bruised

black-and-white *adj* **1** representing or reproducing images not in colour **2** clear-cut and straightforward

blackball /blák bawl/ *vt* **1** prevent from becoming a member **2** exclude or ostracize ■ *n* a vote against somebody wanting to become a member

black bean *n* **1** a small dried black seed used in cooking **2** a fermented soya bean

black bear *n* **1** a bear that lives in North American forests **2** an Asian bear with black or dark brown fur marked with white

black belt n somebody who has achieved the highest level of skill in a martial art, or the belt symbolizing this achievement

blackberry /blákbəri/ (pl **-ries**) n **1** a small purple fruit composed of a cluster of parts **2** a thorny bush that produces blackberries

blackbird /blák burd/ n a common bird with predominantly black feathers

blackboard /blák bawrd/ n a board on which teachers write in classrooms

black box n **1** an aircraft's flight recorder **2** an electronic component of unknown construction

black bread n dark rye bread

blackcap /blák kap/ n a small songbird with a black-topped head

black comedy n comedy dealing with unpleasant subjects

Black Country region of the West Midlands, England

blackcurrant /blák kúrrənt/ n **1** a small edible dark-purple berry **2** a bush that produces blackcurrants

Black Death n a 14C epidemic of bubonic plague affecting Europe and Asia

black economy n the part of an economy consisting of unofficial or illegal earnings

blacken /blákən/ v **1** vti make or become black **2** vt harm somebody's reputation by slander

black eye n a bruised area round the eye

black-eyed bean n **1** a small bean with a black spot **2** a plant that produces black-eyed beans

blackfly /blák flï/ (pl **-flies** or same) n a black aphid that infests plants

Black Forest wooded highland region in SW Germany

Black Forest gateau, Black Forest cake n a rich chocolate cake topped and filled with cherries and whipped cream

blackguard /blággərd, blággaard/ n a dishonest or unprincipled person (dated)

black hat hacker n a hacker who accesses a computer system for malicious purposes

blackhead /blák hed/ n a small plug of dark fatty matter blocking a pore

black hole n **1** an object in space that pulls all surrounding matter into itself, thought to be formed when a star collapses **2** an imaginary place where things get lost (humorous)

black ice n thin ice on roads that is difficult to see

blackjack /blák jak/ n **1** the card game pontoon **2** US, Can a weapon in the form of a short leather-covered club **3** S Africa a weed with barbed seeds that stick to clothes

black knight n a company that makes a hostile takeover bid

blackleg /blák leg/ n somebody who betrays striking colleagues by working during a strike (slang)

blacklist /blák list/ n a list of people who are excluded or disapproved of ■ vt put on a blacklist

black magic n magic that invokes evil forces

blackmail /blák mayl/ n **1** the act of forcing somebody to do something by threatening to reveal secret information about them **2** coercion of any kind —**blackmail** vt

black mark n something that gives people a bad opinion of somebody or something

black market n illegal trading —**black marketeer** n

black mass n a service of devil-worship that imitates the Christian Mass

Blackmore /blák mawr/, **R. D.** (1825–1900) British writer

Black Muslim n a member of the Nation of Islam, an African American Islamic group based in the United States

blackout /blák owt/ n **1** a loss of electric power, e.g. because of strikes or fuel shortages **2** a temporary loss of consciousness **3** a refusal to broadcast radio or television programmes during a strike **4** the withholding of information, especially by official sources **5** a loss of radio communication **6** a period of extinguishing or hiding lights during a raid by enemy aircraft

black pepper n pepper made by grinding peppercorns with their dark husks still attached

Black Power n a US political movement formed to engender social and economic equality for Black people

black pudding n UK, Southern US a sausage made with pig's blood

Black Sea inland sea between SE Europe and Asia

black sheep n somebody regarded with shame by other members of a group

Blackshirt /blák shurt/ n a European fascist in World War II, especially a member of the Italian Fascist Party

blacksmith /blák smith/ n somebody who makes and repairs objects made of metal

blacksnake /blák snayk/ n a dark poisonous Australian snake

black spot n a place where something bad exists or happens

blackthorn /blák thawrn/ n **1** a thorny bush with blue-black berries **2** a walking stick made from the hard wood of a blackthorn

black tie n **1** a black bow tie **2** a formal style of dress for men that includes a black dinner jacket —**black-tie** adj

blacktop /blák top/ n US, Can **1** road-surfacing material **2** a road or other area with a blacktop surface

black widow n a highly poisonous black spider

ORIGIN The name **black widow** comes from the female's habit of eating her mate.

bladder /bláddər/ n a body organ that stores liquid or gas, especially the organ that stores urine

bladder wrack n a brown seaweed with bulbous air bladders on its fronds

blade *n* **1** the cutting part of a tool or weapon **2** a long thin flat part, e.g. of a propeller **3** a thin leaf **4** the flat striking part of something such as an oar or a golf club **5** the metal part of an ice skate that glides over the ice **6** a dashing man *(dated infml)* ■ **blades** *npl ANZ* hand-operated sheep shears ■ *vi* (**blading, bladed**) *US, Can* skate on in-line roller skates *(infml)*

blag (**blagging, blagged**) *vt* obtain or achieve something in an underhand way, e.g. by lying *(slang)*

Tony Blair

Blair /blair/, **Tony** (*b.* 1953) British prime minister (1997–)

Blairism /bláirizəm/ *n* the political policies and style of government of Tony Blair, typified by moderate and gradual social reform, financial prudence, and tight control over policy presentation —**Blairite** *n, adj*

Blake /blayk/, **William** (1757–1827) British poet, painter, and engraver —**Blakeian** *adj*

Blakey /bláyki/, **Art** (1919–90) US jazz drummer and band leader

blame *vt* (**blaming, blamed**) consider somebody responsible for something bad that happens ■ *n* responsibility —**blameless** *adj* —**blameworthy** *adj*

Blamey /bláymi/, **Sir Thomas Albert** (1884–1951) Australian soldier

blanch, blench *v* **1** *vi* turn pale **2** *vt* put food briefly in boiling water **3** *vti* remove colour from, or lose colour

blancmange /blə máanj, -máanzh/ *n* a cold milk-based dessert with a texture similar to that of jelly

bland *adj* **1** lacking flavour, character, or interest **2** free from anything annoying or upsetting —**blandly** *adv* —**blandness** *n*

blandishment /blándishmənt/ *n* **1** a piece of flattery *(fml; often pl)* **2** the use of flattery

blank *adj* **1** not written on, drawn on, recorded on, or printed on **2** without any images ○ *a blank screen* **3** showing no interest, understanding, or awareness ○ *a blank expression* **4** uneventful or unproductive **5** complete ○ *in blank amazement* ■ *n* **1** a space in which to write something on a form or other document **2** a mark indicating a missing word **3** a complete absence of awareness or memory ○ *My mind was a complete blank.* **4** a period about which nothing is known **5** *also* **blank cartridge** a gun cartridge without a bullet **6** a piece of a substance from which something is made ■ *v* **1** *vt* delete or block out **2** *vi* forget something suddenly and temporarily ○ *I just blanked.* **3** *vt* ignore *(infml)* —**blankly** *adv* —**blankness** *n* ◇ **draw a blank** be unable to think of or remember

blank cheque *n* **1** a cheque without a stated amount **2** complete freedom to act or decide *(infml)*

blanket /blángkit/ *n* **1** a large piece of thick cloth used as a cover for a bed **2** a covering layer of a substance ■ *adj* applying to all areas or situations ○ *a blanket instruction* ■ *vt* cover something completely

blank verse *n* unrhymed poetry with a regular rhythm and line length

Blantyre-Limbe /blán tīr lím bay/ largest city in Malawi. Pop. 2,000,000 (1998).

blare /blair/ (**blaring, blared**) *v* **1** *vti* make a loud harsh sound **2** *vt* announce —**blare** *n*

blarney /bláarni/ *n* nonsense *(infml)*

ORIGIN **Blarney** derives from the Blarney Stone, a stone in Blarney Castle near Cork, Ireland, that is said to give the power of persuasive talk to those who kiss it.

blasé /bláa zay/ *adj* not impressed or concerned

blaspheme /blass feém, blaass-/ (**-pheming, -phemed**) *v* swear or behave in a way that insults God or a religion —**blasphemer** *n*

blasphemy /blássfəmi/ *n* disrespect for God or a religion, or an action that shows such disrespect —**blasphemous** *adj*

blast *n* **1** a sudden strong current of air or gas **2** an explosion, or a sudden rush of air caused by an explosion **3** the loud sound of an explosion **4** the short loud sound of a whistle, horn, or instrument **5** a loud or angry outburst ■ *v* **1** *vti* blow up with explosives **2** *vti* come out or push out with great force and noise *(infml)* **3** *vt* hit hard *(infml)* **4** *vt* criticize *(infml)* ■ *interj* expresses annoyance *(infml)* —**blaster** *n* ◇ **(at) full blast** at maximum volume or speed ◇ See note at **criticize**

□ **blast off** *vi* be launched into space

blasted /bláastid/ *adj, adv* expresses annoyance *(infml)*

blast furnace *n* a metal-smelting furnace that uses a current of air to raise the temperature

blastoff /bláast of/ *n* the launch of a spacecraft

blatant /bláyt'nt/ *adj* obtrusive and conspicuous —**blatantly** *adv*

USAGE **blatant** or **flagrant**? A **blatant** lie is one so bare-faced that no one can miss it, whereas **flagrant** disregard for human life is unforgivably shameless or outrageous. Avoid using **blatant** to mean merely 'obvious' in such sentences as *There seems to be a blatant contradiction.* Here, substitute *obvious, clear*, or *glaring* for **blatant**.

blather /bláthər/ *vi* talk in a boring or un-intelligent way *(infml)* —**blather** *n*

blaze[1] *vi* (**blazing, blazed**) burn or shine

brightly ■ *n* 1 a large bright fire 2 an impressive display ○ *a blaze of publicity*

blaze² *n* a white mark on an animal's face ■ *vt* (**blazing, blazed**) 1 mark a new path 2 lead the way in doing something new

blaze³ (**blazing, blazed**) *vt* spread news or information loudly and clearly ○ *blazed the scandal all over the front page*

ORIGIN Blaze 'spread news' comes from an early Dutch or German verb meaning 'blow', and is unrelated to the other **blaze** words.

---

blazer /bláyzər/ *n* a jacket, especially one bearing the badge of a club or institution

blazon /bláyz'n/ *vt* 1 announce widely or ostentatiously 2 create or describe a coat of arms ■ *n* a coat of arms

bleach *n* a chemical solution. Use: removing colour, cleansing, disinfecting. ■ *v* 1 *vt* use bleach on 2 *vti* lighten, or become light, in colour

bleak *adj* 1 without hope or expectation of success 2 providing little comfort or shelter 3 cold and cloudy —**bleakly** *adv* —**bleakness** *n*

bleary /bléeri/ (**-ier, -iest**) *adj* not seeing clearly, usually because of sleepiness —**blearily** *adv* —**bleariness** *n*

bleat *v* 1 *vi* make the typical noise of a sheep or goat 2 *vti* complain annoyingly *(infml)* —**bleat** *n*

bleed (**bled**) *v* 1 *vi* lose blood from the body through a wound 2 *vt* take blood from somebody as a way of treating illness 3 *vi* feel sadness or pity *(often ironic)* ○ *My heart bleeds for you.* 4 *vi* exude sap 5 *vt* take money or resources from somebody, especially dishonestly *(infml)* 6 *vt* draw off a liquid or gas 7 *vi* release colour

bleeding /bléeding/ *adj, adv* adds emphasis *(slang)*

bleep *n* 1 a short high-pitched electronic signal 2 a pager ■ *v* 1 *vi* make a short high-pitched electronic sound 2 *vt* call somebody on a pager

bleeper /bléepər/ *n* a pager

blemish /blémmish/ *n* 1 a mark or flaw that spoils the appearance of something 2 something that spoils somebody's reputation —**blemish** *vt* ◊ See note at **flaw**

blench *vi* flinch or recoil in fear

blend *v* 1 *vti* mix one substance thoroughly with another 2 *vt* create by mixing together different types ○ *blended tea* 3 *vti* mix with other people or things so as not to be conspicuous 4 *vti* make a pleasing combination ■ *n* 1 a mixture or combination 2 a food or drink created from different types of the same substance ○ *a coffee blend* ◊ See note at **mixture**

blender /bléndər/ *n* 1 an electrical appliance used for mixing or liquidizing food 2 somebody or something that blends foods or drinks

Blériot /blérri ó/, **Louis** (1872–1936) French aviator

bless (**blessed** *or* **blest**) *vt* 1 make holy in a religious ceremony 2 invoke divine protection on ○ *bless this family* 3 declare approval and support for 4 give a desirable quality to ○ *was blessed with good looks*

ORIGIN Bless derives from the same ancient root as *blood*, and probably originally meant 'mark with blood as a religious rite'.

---

blessed /bléssid/ *adj* 1 holy 2 declared holy by the pope as the first stage towards being declared a saint ■ *adj, adv* adds emphasis *(infml)* —**blessedly** *adv* —**blessedness** *n*

blessing /bléssing/ *n* 1 help from God or another deity 2 a priest's act of invoking divine help or protection 3 a prayer said before a meal 4 something fortunate ○ *It's a blessing that you came so quickly.*

blether /bléthər/ *n Scotland* somebody who talks nonsense

blew 1 past tense of **blow**¹ 2 past tense of **blow**³

blight /blīt/ *n* 1 a destructive force or influence 2 a ruined state 3 a plant disease ■ *vt* 1 blight 2 affect a plant with blight

blighter /blītər/ *n* somebody who is envied or sympathized with *(dated infml)* ○ *He's a lucky blighter.*

Blighty /blīti/, **blighty** *n UK* Britain *(slang dated humorous)*

ORIGIN Blighty is an alteration of a Hindi word meaning 'foreign, European'. It was first used for 'home' by soldiers serving in British India.

---

blimey /blīmi/ *interj* expresses amazement or shock *(infml)*

blimp¹ *n* a small airship used in World War II

blimp², **Colonel Blimp** *n* a pompous person *(humorous)*

blind /blīnd/ *adj* 1 unable to see, permanently or temporarily 2 unable to recognize or understand something ○ *blind to the consequences* 3 uncontrollable and irrational ○ *blind rage* 4 unquestioning ○ *blind prejudice* 5 marked by lack of awareness ○ *a blind stupor* 6 not giving a clear view ○ *a blind corner* 7 closed at one end ○ *a blind tunnel* 8 done without looking ○ *a blind tasting* ■ *adv* 1 without prior examination or preparation ○ *You shouldn't buy livestock blind.* 2 using an aircraft's instruments only ○ *flying blind* 3 totally *(infml)* ○ *robbed his partner blind* ■ *vt* 1 make permanently blind 2 make unable to judge properly ■ *n* 1 a window covering that can be raised or lowered 2 something that conceals the true nature of somebody's activities —**blindly** *adv* —**blindness** *n*

blind alley *n* 1 a passage that is closed off at one end 2 something that will not produce worthwhile results

blind date *n* 1 a date with somebody you have not met before 2 somebody met on a blind date

blinder /blíndər/ n an outstanding performance (*infml*)

blindfold /blínd fōld/ n a bandage tied over somebody's eyes ■ vt 1 put a blindfold on 2 prevent from understanding ■ adj wearing a blindfold ■ adv 1 while blindfolded 2 unprepared

blinding /blínding/ adj 1 impairing vision 2 outstanding (*infml*) —**blindingly** adv

blind man's buff n a children's game in which a blindfolded player tries to catch and identify others

blind side n 1 the area that is out of your field of vision 2 in rugby, the side of the pitch nearest a touchline

blind spot n 1 a small area on the retina that lacks visual receptors 2 an area of knowledge about which somebody is ignorant 3 a direction in which vision is obscured

blini /blínni, blééni/ (pl **blinis** or same) n a small buckwheat pancake

blink v 1 vti close and reopen both eyes rapidly 2 vti look at somebody or something while blinking 3 vt remove something by blinking ○ *blinked away his tears* 4 vi flash on and off —**blink** n ◊ **on the blink** not working properly (*infml*)

blinker /blíngkər/ n a flashing light ■ **blinkers** npl 1 a pair of flaps attached to a horse's bridle to keep the horse looking straight ahead 2 a mental attitude that prevents somebody from considering a situation rationally ■ vt 1 fit a horse with blinkers 2 hinder somebody's judgment —**blinkered** adj

blinkered /blíngkərd/ adj narrow-minded ○ *took a very blinkered attitude*

blinking /blíngking/ adj adds emphasis (*slang*) —**blinking** adv

blip n 1 a spot of light that indicates the position of something on a display screen 2 a bleep 3 a sudden temporary problem —**blip** vi

bliss n 1 perfect happiness 2 spiritual joy —**blissful** /blíssf'l/ adj —**blissfully** adv

blister /blístər/ n 1 a painful, fluid-filled swelling on the skin 2 a bubble, e.g. on paintwork —**blister** vti

blistering /blístəring/ adj 1 very hot 2 scornful —**blisteringly** adv

blister pack n a type of packet in which a manufactured item is covered in a clear dome of plastic stuck to a cardboard backing

blithe /blīth/ adj cheerful and carefree —**blithely** adv —**blitheness** n

blithering /blíthəring/ adj useless (*infml*)

blitz /blits/ n 1 a sustained aerial attack 2 a blitzkrieg 3 a concerted effort to get something done (*infml*) 4 **Blitz** the bombing of British cities in World War II ■ vt 1 destroy by aerial bombing 2 deal with energetically (*infml*) 3 subject somebody to an overwhelming amount of something (*infml*)

blitzkrieg /blíts kreeg/ n a swift military offensive

Blixen /blíks'n/, **Karen, Baroness** (1885–1962) Danish writer. Pseudonym **Dinesen, Isak**

~~blizzard~~ incorrect spelling of **blizzard**

blizzard /blízzərd/ n a heavy snowstorm

bloated /blṓtid/ adj 1 swollen with liquid, air, or gas 2 too full after overeating —**bloat** vti —**bloatedness** n

bloater /blṓtər/ n a large herring that has been soaked in brine and smoked

blob n 1 a soft mass of a liquid or semiliquid substance 2 a small spot of colour ■ vt (**blobbing, blobbed**) put on in blobs

blok /blok/ n a united group of countries

SPELLCHECK Do not confuse the spelling of **bloc** and **block** ('square object', 'obstruction'), which sound similar.

---

block /blok/ n 1 a piece of solid material, e.g. concrete 2 a stand for displaying items at an auction 3 a large building divided into offices or flats 4 a group of buildings bounded on each side by a street 5 US, Can the section of a street between two parallel streets 6 a unit of space ○ *a block of text* 7 something that obstructs or prevents progress 8 a deliberate physical obstruction of play 9 a psychological inability to deal with something ■ v 1 vt obstruct or hinder 2 vti physically obstruct a player or ball 3 vti fail to remember something for psychological reasons 4 vt make into a block 5 vt support with a block ◊ **knock somebody's block off** punch somebody in the head (*slang*) ◊ See note at **bloc, hinder**

□ **block out** vt 1 put something out of your mind 2 describe something in a general way

blockade /blo káyd/ n 1 an organized attempt to prevent the movement of people or goods 2 the people or vehicles forming a blockade ■ vt (**-ading, -aded**) subject a place to a blockade

blockage /blókij/ n something that obstructs movement through a pipe or channel

block and tackle (pl **blocks and tackles**) n a system of pulleys through which rope is threaded, used for lifting or pulling things

block booking n a booking of a large number of tickets for the people in a group

blockbuster /blók bustər/ n something such as a book or film that achieves widespread popular success (*infml*)

blockbusting /blók busting/ adj commercially successful

block diagram n a diagram of a process or system in which parts are represented by labelled rectangles connected by lines

blockhead /blók hed/ n somebody considered unintelligent (*insult*)

block vote n a vote cast for an individual on behalf of an organization

Bloemfontein /blṓom fon tayn/ capital of Free State Province, South Africa. Pop. 126,867 (1991).

bloke n a man (*infml*) —**blokeish** adj

blond, blonde adj 1 describes hair that is yellowish or golden 2 fair-haired and light-skinned 3 light coloured ○ *blond wood* ■ n a fair-haired person —**blondness** n

USAGE **blond** or **blonde**? When describing hair, **blond** is normally used of a person of either sex: *Jane has blond hair.* When describing somebody directly, **blond** is often used of a man or boy and **blonde** of a woman or girl: *He is blond. Jane is blonde/is a blonde.*

Blondin /blON dáN/, **Charles** (1824–97) French acrobat

blood /blud/ n 1 the red fluid that circulates in the bodies of humans and other vertebrates 2 the body fluid of invertebrates 3 bloodshed or killing 4 blood considered as a vital life force 5 family or ancestry 6 pure breeding in animals, especially horses ■ vt 1 subject troops to their first experience of battle 2 let a dog taste the blood of a newly killed animal for the first time ◊ **have blood on your hands** be responsible for somebody's death ◊ **in cold blood** in a way that shows a complete lack of emotion

blood bank n a supply of blood or blood plasma for use in hospitals

bloodbath /blúd baath/ (pl **-baths** /-baathz/) n indiscriminate killing

blood brother n either one of two men or boys who are sworn friends

blood count n the number of cells and platelets in a given volume of blood, or the act of counting them

bloodcurdling /blúd kurd'ling/, **blood-curdling** adj arousing extreme fear

blood donor n somebody who gives their own blood for use in transfusions

blood group n any class into which human blood is divided for transfusion purposes

bloodhound /blúd hownd/ n a large tracking dog with drooping ears and sagging jowls

bloodless /blúdləss/ adj 1 without killing or violence 2 pale and anaemic-looking

bloodletting /blúd leting/ n 1 the removal of blood from the body as a treatment for disease or a method of diagnosis 2 bitter quarrelling

bloodline /blúd līn/ n a line of descent from a particular human or animal ancestor

blood money n 1 compensation paid to the relatives of somebody who has been killed 2 a fee paid to a hired killer

blood orange n an orange with red flesh

blood poisoning n an infection of the blood

blood pressure n the pressure exerted by blood against the walls of the blood vessels

blood relation, blood relative n a relative by birth

bloodshed /blúd shed/ n killings or injuries

bloodshot /blúd shot/ adj describes an eye that is inflamed and red

bloodstain /blúd stayn/ n a stain made by blood —**bloodstained** adj

bloodstock /blúd stok/ n horses bred for racing

bloodstone /blúd stōn/ n a green variety of chalcedony with small red spots or streaks. Use: gems.

bloodstream /blúd streem/ n the flow of blood around the body

bloodsucker /blúd sukər/ n 1 a parasite that sucks blood 2 somebody who exploits somebody else, especially by demanding money

blood sugar n the level of glucose in the blood

bloodthirsty /blúd thursti/ (**-ier, -iest**) adj 1 eager for violence 2 full of violence or killing

blood type n a blood group

blood vessel n an artery, capillary, or vein

bloody /blúddi/ adj (**-ier, -iest**) 1 bloodstained 2 involving a great deal of violence or killing 3 adds emphasis to a noun (slang; sometimes offensive) ■ adv adds emphasis to an adjective (slang; sometimes offensive) ■ vt (**-ies, -ied**) stain with blood

bloody mary, Bloody Mary n a cocktail consisting of vodka, tomato juice, and spices

bloody-minded adj intentionally uncooperative and obstructive (infml) —**bloody-mindedly** adv —**bloody-mindedness** n

bloom n 1 a flower 2 the mass of flowers on a single plant 3 the condition of being in flower ○ *in full bloom* 4 the condition of greatest freshness or health (literary) ○ *in the bloom of youth* 5 a fresh, healthy appearance or complexion ■ vi 1 come into flower 2 produce plants 3 prosper or flourish (literary) 4 appear healthy (literary)

bloomers /blóomərz/ npl (dated) 1 baggy knickers for women 2 loose trousers for women, gathered at the ankle and worn under a shorter skirt

ORIGIN **Bloomers** are named after the US feminist Amelia Jenks Bloomer (1818–94), who advocated the loose trousers that were the original **bloomers** as sensible and liberated dress for women.

blooming /blóoming/ adj flourishing ■ adj, adv adds emphasis (dated infml)

blossom /blóssəm/ n 1 a mass of flowers on a tree 2 a flower or mass of flowers ■ vi 1 come into flower 2 develop well 3 also **blossom out** stop being shy

blot n 1 a stain caused by a drop of liquid 2 an eyesore ○ *a blot on the landscape* 3 a blemish, e.g. on somebody's reputation ■ vt (**blotting, blotted**) 1 bring dishonour on the reputation of 2 dry with absorbent material

□ **blot out** vt 1 cover and obscure 2 obliterate from memory

blotch n an irregular spot or mark, especially on skin —**blotch** vti —**blotchy** adj

blotter /blóttər/ n a piece of blotting paper

blotting paper n paper that is used to absorb ink

blotto /blóttō/ adj very drunk (slang)

blouse /blowz/ n a woman's shirt

blouson /bloó zon/ *n* a short jacket that fits closely at the waist and more loosely over the upper body

blow[1] /bló/ *v* (**blew** /bloo/, **blown** /blōn/) **1** *vi* move as or with a current of air **2** *vti* send a stream of air out through the mouth **3** *vt* make something, e.g. glass or bubbles, by blowing **4** *vt* clear the nose by forcing air out through it **5** *vti* make a sound by blowing air through a musical instrument **6** *vi* expel moist air through a blowhole *(refers to whales and other marine mammals)* **7** *vi* breathe hard **8** *vti* destroy, open, or move something by the force of an explosion **9** *vti* cause or experience a blowout in a tyre *(infml)* **10** *vti* burn out or cause a fuse to burn out **11** *vt* squander money *(slang)* ■ *n* **1** an act of blowing **2** a strong wind *(infml)*
☐ **blow out** *v* **1** *vti* extinguish with a blast of air **2** *vi* puncture *(refers to tyres)*
☐ **blow over** *vi* **1** die down *(refers to storms)* **2** be forgotten *(infml)*
☐ **blow up** *v* **1** *vti* destroy or be destroyed by an explosion **2** *vti* inflate **3** *vt* enlarge using photographic techniques

blow[2] /blō/ *n* **1** a hard hit **2** an important action that helps a cause **3** a setback

blow[3] /blō/ (**blew** /bloo/, **blown** /blōn/) *vti* be in flower *(literary)*

blowback /bló bak/ *n* **1** the reverse flow of gases in a system **2** the powdery residue from a fired weapon **3** a reaction, often negative, to a situation *(infml)* ○ *the blowback from the press revelations*

blow-dry *vt* style hair with a hair dryer —**blow-dry** *n*

blower /bló ər/ *n* any machine that produces a current of air

blowfly /bló flī/ *(pl* **-flies**) *n* a fly that lays its eggs in rotting meat or in wounds

blowhole /bló hōl/ *n* **1** a nostril in the top of the head of a whale or similar mammal **2** a hole in ice where marine mammals come to the surface to breathe **3** *NZ* a volcanic vent

blow job *n* an offensive term meaning fellatio *(slang)*

blowlamp /bló lamp/ *n* a blowtorch

blown 1 past participle of **blow**[1] **2** past participle of **blow**[3]

blowout /bló owt/ *n* **1** a puncture in a tyre **2** a big party *(slang)*

blowpipe /bló pīp/ *n* a tube for shooting darts by blowing air

blowtorch /bló tawrch/, **blowlamp** /bló lamp/ *n* a small portable gas burner

blowup /bló up/, **blow-up** *n* **1** a photographic enlargement **2** an outburst of temper *(infml)* ■ *adj* inflatable

blowy /bló i/ (**-ier, -iest**) *adj* windy *(infml)*

blowzy /blówzi/ (**-zier, -ziest**), **blowsy** (**-sier, -siest**) *adj* **1** with a red face and a coarse complexion **2** dishevelled and unkempt in appearance

BLT *n* a bacon, lettuce, and tomato sandwich

blub (**blubbing, blubbed**) *vi* sob loudly *(infml)*

blubber /blúbbər/ *vi* sob loudly *(infml)* ■ *n* **1** the fat that insulates the body of whales and other marine mammals **2** unsightly fat *(infml; sometimes offensive)* —**blubberer** *n*

bludge (**bludging, bludged**) *vi* *ANZ (infml)* **1** live off somebody else's earnings or on state benefits **2** avoid work or responsibilities

bludgeon /blújjən/ *n* a short club ■ *vt* **1** hit repeatedly with a heavy object **2** coerce or bully

blue *adj* (**bluer, bluest**) **1** of the colour of the sky on a cloudless day **2** slightly purple in skin colour **3** depressed *(infml)* **4** referring to sex in an explicit or offensive way *(infml)* ○ *blue jokes* **5** Conservative in politics ■ *n* **1** the colour of the sky **2** a blue pigment **3** *also* **Blue** an Oxbridge athlete who has competed in matches between Oxford and Cambridge universities **4** a blue ring on an archery target **5** the blue ball in snooker **6** *ANZ* a fight *(slang)* ■ *vti* (**blues, blueing** *or* **bluing, blued**) make or become blue —**blueish** *adj* —**blueness** *n* —**bluish** *adj* ◇ **out of the blue** unexpectedly

blue baby *n* a baby with bluish skin colour caused by insufficient oxygen in the blood as a result of a congenital heart defect

bluebell /bloó bel/ *n* a woodland plant with small blue bell-shaped flowers

blueberry /bloóbəri/ *(pl* **-ries**) *n* **1** an edible dark blue berry **2** the bush that produces blueberries

bluebird /bloó burd/ *n* a North American songbird with bright blue plumage

blue blood *n* noble descent —**blue-blooded** *adj*

blue book *n* in the UK or Canada, a government report

bluebottle /bloó bott'l/ *n* a large buzzing fly with a metallic blue body

blue cheese *n* any whitish cheese with veins of blue mould

blue chip *n* **1** a valuable stock in a reliable company **2** a valuable asset or company —**blue-chip** *adj*

blue collar *adj* of manual workers

blue-eyed boy *n* a favourite or popular man or boy *(infml)*

bluegrass /bloó graass/ *n* **1** a style of country music that features close harmony **2** a blue-green grass. Use: fodder, lawns.

Blue Mountains plateau region in E New South Wales, Australia, part of the Great Dividing Range. Highest peak Bird Rock, 1,134 m/3,871 ft.

Blue Nile river in Ethiopia and Sudan that joins the White Nile to form the Nile at Khartoum. Length 1,370 km/850 mi.

blueprint /bloó print/ *n* **1** a print of a technical drawing, used as a reference during construction **2** a plan or an action that serves as a model

blue riband *n* the highest distinction in a particular field **blue-riband** *adj*

blue ribbon *n* a badge made of blue ribbon, awarded for first prize —**blue-ribbon** *adj*

blues *n* 1 a style of music marked by slow sad songs with a repetitive rhythm *(+sing or pl verb)* 2 *(pl same)* a song or instrumental piece in the style of the blues 3 a feeling of sadness *(infml; + pl verb)*

blue-sky *adj* purely theoretical *(infml)* —**blue-sky** *vi*

bluestocking /bloō stoking/ *n* an offensive term for a highly educated woman with scholarly interests

ORIGIN At the literary gatherings held at the houses of fashionable mid-18C hostesses, it became the custom to wear casual rather than formal dress. In the case of gentlemen's stockings, this meant grey worsted (called 'blue' at that time) rather than black silk. This lack of decorum was disapproved of in some quarters, and the participants were dubbed the 'Blue Stocking Society'. Women who attended the gatherings thus became known as 'Blue Stocking Ladies' (even though it was men who had worn the stockings).

bluetit /bloō tit/ *(pl* -**tits** *or same) n* a common bird with a blue cap and a yellow breast

bluff[1] *v* 1 *vti* pretend to be confident or knowledgeable 2 *vti* deceive other players in a card game about the value of your hand 3 *vt Malaysia, Singapore* deceive somebody in a minor way *(infml)* —**bluff** *n*

bluff[2] *n* a cliff with a broad face ■ *adj* blunt but kind in manner —**bluffly** *adv* —**bluffness** *n*

Blume /bloom/, **Judy** (b. 1938) US writer

blunder /blúndər/ *n* a stupid mistake ■ *vi* 1 make a serious mistake 2 move or act clumsily —**blunderingly** *adv*◊ See note at **mistake**

blunderbuss /blúndər buss/ *n* a 17C wide-mouthed gun

ORIGIN Blunderbuss is an alteration of Dutch *donderbus*, literally 'thunder gun', by association with *blunder*.

blunt *adj* 1 with a cutting edge that is not sharp 2 frank or honest but without sensitivity ■ *v* 1 *vti* become or make something less sharp 2 *vt* lessen or weaken a sense or emotion —**bluntly** *adv* —**bluntness** *n*

blur *n* 1 a fuzzy or indistinct image 2 a smear or smeared area ■ *vti* (**blurring, blurred**) 1 make or become vague ◦ *blurred the line between right and wrong* 2 make or become indistinct in shape or detail —**blurry** *adj*

blurb *n* a paragraph promoting a product, especially on a book jacket *(slang)* —**blurb** *vt*

ORIGIN The word **blurb** was coined by the US humorist Gelett Burgess. The noun, first found in print in 1914, is said to have been foreshadowed by a drawing of a young woman on a comic-book jacket of 1907, whose name was given as Miss Blinda Blurb.

blurt *vti* say something impulsively

blush *vi* 1 become red in the face because of embarrassment 2 feel embarrassed *(fml)* ■ *n* 1 a reddening of the face through embarrassment 2 a red or pink glow —**blushing** *adj*

blusher /blúshər/ *n* pink makeup for the cheeks

bluster /blústər/ *vti* 1 speak or say something loudly or arrogantly 2 behave in a bullying way towards somebody —**bluster** *n* —**blusteringly** *adv* —**blustery** *adj*

Blyth /blīth/, **Chay** (b. 1940) British yachtsman

Blyton /blīt'n/, **Enid** (1897–1968) British writer

BMA *abbr* British Medical Association

B movie *n* a low-budget film formerly shown before the main feature —**B-movie** *adj*

bmp, BMP *abbr* a file extension indicating a bit map file

BMX *n* the riding of bicycles over rough terrain. Full form **bicycle motocross**

boa /bố ə/ *n* 1 a tropical snake belonging to the family that kills by winding round its prey 2 a long fluffy scarf of feathers

boa constrictor *n* a large boa that kills by winding round its prey

boar /bawr/ *(pl* **boars** *or same) n* 1 an uncastrated pig 2 the male of various mammals

SPELLCHECK Do not confuse the spelling of **boar** and **bore** ('make somebody uninterested', 'make a hole'), which sound similar.

board /bawrd/ *n* 1 a plank of wood 2 a flat sheet of wood or plastic or other hard material 3 a flat surface on which to play a game, usually marked with coloured areas 4 a panel on which the controls of items of electrical equipment are mounted 5 a circuit board 6 a group of people chosen to make administrative decisions *(+ sing or pl verb)* 7 daily meals provided at the place where somebody lives ■ **boards** *npl* 1 the stage in a theatre 2 the wooden wall that encloses an ice hockey rink ■ *v* 1 *vti* get onto a vehicle as a passenger 2 *vti* take passengers on for a journey 3 *vt* go onto a ship in order to attack or inspect it 4 *also* **board up** *vti* cover something with boards 5 *vti* be provided with room and meals ◊ **go by the board** be neglected, no longer used, or cast aside ◊ **on board** 1 into or on a vehicle 2 into or in an existing group or project *(infml)* ◊ **take on board** 1 understand or realize something fully 2 accept or include something, e.g. a suggestion or new idea

SPELLCHECK Do not confuse the spelling of **board** and **bored** ('tired and impatient'), which sound similar.

boarder /báwrdər/ *n* 1 somebody paying for food and a room in a private home or boarding house 2 a pupil who lives at school during term time

board game *n* any game played on a board

boarding house *n* a private house providing rooms and meals to long-term paying guests

boarding pass, boarding card *n* an additional ticket that passengers need to show before they are allowed to board a vehicle

boarding school *n* a school that provides accommodation for pupils during term time

boardwalk /báwrd wawk/ *n* a raised walkway made of boards, built across marshy ground or sand

boast /bōst/ *v* 1 *vti* speak proudly about possessions or accomplishments 2 *vt* possess something desirable ○ *Our town boasts the world's biggest roller coaster.* ■ *n* 1 an excessively proud statement 2 a desirable possession —**boastful** *adj* —**boastfulness** *n*

boat /bōt/ *n* 1 a small vessel for travelling on water 2 any vessel used on water, e.g. a ship or submarine 3 a container shaped like a boat ■ *vti* travel or transport by boat ◇ **in the same boat** in the same situation *(infml)* ◇ **miss the boat** fail to take advantage of an opportunity *(infml)* ◇ **push the boat out** spend a lot of money when celebrating something or entertaining *(infml)* ◇ **rock the boat** cause trouble *(infml)*

boater /bótǝr/ *n* a straw hat with a flat top

boathook /bót hook/ *n* a pole for pulling or pushing small boats

Boat Race *n* 1 the annual race between the rowing teams Oxford and Cambridge universities 2 *also* **boat race** *Cockney* a face *(rhyming slang)*

boatswain /bóss'n/, **bo's'n** *n* a bosun

boat train *n* a train that takes people to and from docks

bob[1] (**bobbing, bobbed**) *vi* 1 bounce quickly, especially on the surface of water 2 make a curtsy, bow, or nod —**bob** *n*

bob[2] *n* a woman's short haircut ■ *vt* (**bobbing, bobbed**) cut hair short

bob[3] (*pl* same) *n* a shilling *(infml)*

Bob ◇ **Bob's your uncle** emphasises that something will be easy or simple to do *(infml)*

bobbin /bóbbin/ *n* a cylinder or spool onto which thread or wire is wound

bobble /bóbb'l/ *n* 1 a woollen ball used as a decoration, especially on a hat 2 an up-and-down movement ■ *vti* (**-bling, -bled**) move up and down

bobby /bóbbi/ (*pl* **-bies**) *n* a police officer *(infml dated)*

ORIGIN Bobby is a familiar form of the name *Robert*, and the Robert after whom police officers are named was Sir Robert Peel, who as home secretary introduced the 1828 Police Act and organized the London police force.

bobotie /bǝ bóti, bǝ bóoti/ *n* S Africa a curried minced meat dish

bobsleigh /bób slay/ *n* 1 a racing sledge 2 a long sledge made of two short sledges attached one behind the other ■ *vi* ride in a bobsleigh

Boccaccio /bo káchi ō/, **Giovanni** (1313–75) Italian writer and humanist

bod *n* (*slang*) 1 somebody's body 2 a person

bode[1] /bōd/ (**boding, boded**) *vti* be a sign that something is about to happen

bode[2] past tense of **bide**

bodega /bō dáygǝ/ *n* a wine shop in a Spanish-speaking country

bodge (**bodging**) *vti* make or fix something badly *(infml)*

bodice /bóddiss/ *n* the upper part of a dress

ORIGIN Bodice was originally *bodies*, the plural of *body*. It represents *body* in the sense 'upper part of a garment'. The plural form was used because the upper part of women's dresses was often in two parts, fastening down the middle.

bodily /bóddili/ *adj* of the body ■ *adv* 1 physically 2 using physical force

bodkin /bódkin/ *n* 1 a large blunt needle 2 a hole-punching tool

body /bóddi/ (*pl* **-ies**) *n* 1 the physical form of a human being or organism 2 the physical remains of a dead human being or organism 3 a torso 4 somebody's figure with regard to shape and muscle tone 5 a group of people 6 a collection ○ *a body of evidence* 7 a mass ○ *a body of water* 8 the outer shell of a vehicle 9 the main part of something 10 fullness of flavour in wine 11 the thickness of a liquid 12 fullness of texture, e.g. of hair 13 a woman's one-piece undergarment that covers the torso and fastens at the crotch 14 a person *(infml)*

body blow *n* a serious setback or disappointment

body building *n* the practice of muscle-developing —**body builder** *n*

body clock *n* somebody's physiological timing mechanism

body double *n* somebody whose body is filmed instead of that of an actor, especially in a nude scene

bodyguard /bóddi gaard/ *n* somebody hired to protect somebody from physical attack

body language *n* bodily mannerisms, postures, and facial expressions regarded as communicating unspoken feelings

body politic *n* the people of a nation regarded as a political whole

body search *n* a thorough search of the body of a person suspected of hiding something such as weapons or illegal drugs

body snatcher *n* formerly, somebody who stole corpses, usually in order to sell them for medical research —**body snatching** *n*

body stocking *n* a close-fitting one-piece garment that covers the body from the neck to the toes

bodywork /bóddi wurk/ *n* 1 the outer shell of a vehicle 2 the repair of vehicle bodies

Boer /boor, bawr/ *n* somebody of Dutch descent who settled in South Africa —**Boer** *adj*

boerewors /bóòrə vawrss/ n S Africa an Afrikaner sausage

boffin /bóffin/ n a scientific expert (infml)

bog n 1 an area of marshy ground 2 UK a toilet (slang) —**boggy** adj

□ **bog down** vt slow the progress of (infml) ○ got bogged down in unimportant details

Bogart /bó gaart/, **Humphrey** (1899–1957) US film actor

bogey /bógi/ n 1 a cause of trouble, annoyance, or fear 2 in golf, a score of one over par 3 a piece of nasal mucus (slang) ■ vt in golf, score one over par for a hole

bogeyman /bógi man/ (pl **bogeymen** /-men/) n an imaginary person or monster that frightens children

boggle /bógg'l/ (-**gling**) vi become baffled (infml)

bogie /bógi/ n 1 a framework with wheels on the undercarriage of a vehicle 2 also **bogy** (pl -**gies**) a small railway truck

Bogor /bó gawr/ city in Indonesia, on W Java. Pop. 3,696,848 (1997).

Bogotá /bóggə taá/ capital of Colombia. Pop. 6,276,000 (1999).

bog-standard adj ordinary and unexceptional (infml)

bogus /bógəss/ adj 1 fake or deceitful 2 US bad or useless (slang)

ORIGIN **Bogus** is first recorded in American usage in the 1820s, referring to a machine for producing counterfeit money. Its ultimate origins remain unclear.

bogy n RAIL = **bogie** 2

Bohemia /bō heémi ə/ historic region in the present-day W Czech Republic —**Bohemian** adj, n

bohemian /bō heémi ən/ n somebody with an unconventional lifestyle, especially somebody involved in the arts —**bohemian** adj —**bohemianism** n

Bohr /bawr/, **Niels** (1885–1962) Danish physicist. He participated in US atomic bomb development during World War II.

bohrium /báwri əm/ n (symbol Bh) a synthetic radioactive chemical element

boil[1] v 1 vti reach or cause to reach the point at which liquid turns into gas 2 vti contain or cause to contain boiling liquid 3 vti cook in boiling water or at the temperature at which surface bubbles form ○ Boil the spaghetti for about eight minutes. 4 vt clean or sterilize in boiling water 5 vi bubble on the surface ■ n the state of bubbling at a high temperature

□ **boil down** v 1 vti make or become a thicker liquid by boiling to remove water 2 vt summarize (infml)

□ **boil down to** vt amount to in essence (infml)

□ **boil over** v 1 vti froth up and overflow 2 vi overflow with an emotion

boil[2] n a pus-filled abscess on skin

boiler /bóylər/ n a water-heating tank used as a source of heat or power

boilerplate /bóylər playt/ n a reusable unit of computer code

boiler suit n a one-piece work suit

boiling point n 1 the temperature at which liquid boils 2 the point at which a situation becomes critical

Boise /bóyssi, bóyzi/ 1 capital of Idaho. Pop. 157,452 (1998). 2 river in SW Idaho. Length 150 km/95 mi.

boisterous /bóystərəss/ adj noisy, energetic, and rowdy —**boisterously** adv —**boisterousness** n ◊ See note at unruly

boistrous incorrect spelling of **boisterous**

bold /bōld/ adj 1 fearless and adventurous 2 requiring a daring personality 3 impudent or presumptuous 4 clear and conspicuous 5 also **boldface** with thicker or darker lines than standard print ■ n also **boldface** /bōld fayss/ bold printing type —**boldly** adv —**boldness** n

bole /bōl/ n a tree trunk

SPELLCHECK Do not confuse the spelling of **bole** and **bowl** ('a container'), which sound similar.

bolero /bə láirō/ (pl -**ros**) n 1 a Spanish dance that involves stamping and posturing 2 the music for a bolero 3 a short open jacket

Boleyn /bōò lín/, **Anne** (1507?–36) queen of England (1533–36) as the second wife of Henry VIII

Bolger /bóljər/, **Jim** (b. 1935) prime minister of New Zealand (1990–97)

bolivar /bólli vaar/, **bolivares** /bō leevaáress/ n the main unit of Venezuelan currency

Bolívar /bólli vaar/, **Simón** (1783–1830) South American revolutionary

Bolivia /bə lívvi ə/ landlocked country in west-central South America. Cap. La Paz. Pop. 8,300,463 (2001). —**Bolivian** n, adj

boliviano /bə lívvi aánō/ (pl -**nos**) n the main unit of Bolivian currency

boll /bōl/ n a rounded seed pod, especially of cotton

bollard /bóllaard/ n 1 a post for keeping traffic off an area of pavement 2 a post on a quay for mooring ships

bollocks /bólləks/ (offensive) npl a taboo term for the testicles ■ n a taboo term meaning nonsense

Bollywood /bólli wòòd/ n a nickname for the Indian film industry

Bolshevik /bólshəvik/ n 1 a member of the radical wing of the Russian Socialist party that became the Communist Party in 1918 2 also **bolshevik** a Communist or somebody sympathetic to Communism

ORIGIN The Russian form of **Bolshevik** is a derivative of a word meaning 'bigger' or 'more'. The members of the Russian Social Democratic Party, to whom the term was first applied, wanted 'big' reforms and were also in the majority, so the name was doubly apt.

bolshie /bólshi/, **bolshy** adj UK, Can argumentative or uncooperative (infml) —**bolshily** adv —**bolshiness** n

bolster /bólstər/ n a long cylindrical pillow ∎ vt encourage through support

bolt /bōlt/ n 1 a sliding metal bar for fastening a door 2 a metal bar with a screw thread and a flat end, used with a nut for fastening things 3 an arrow for a crossbow 4 a sliding part of a gun that ejects a used cartridge 5 a lightning flash 6 a large roll of fabric ∎ v 1 vt lock something with a bolt 2 vi rush away, especially out of fear 3 vt devour food hurriedly

bolthole /bólt hōl/ n a place of refuge

bolt-on adj attachable as an extra

bomb /bom/ n 1 an explosive device or projectile, often timed to explode at a specific time 2 also **Bomb** an atom bomb regarded as the absolute weapon of mass destruction 3 a lot of money (infml) 4 an artistic failure (infml) ∎ v 1 vti attack people and places with bombs 2 vi move very fast (infml) 3 vi be poor as a performance (infml)

bombard /bom baïd/ vt 1 attack an enemy with missiles 2 overwhelm with something, e.g. questions 3 hit with high-energy particles —**bombardment** n

bombardier /bómbə deér/ n 1 somebody who releases bombs 2 in the Royal Artillery, a noncommissioned officer of a rank below sergeant

bombast /bóm bast/ n pompous language —**bombastic** /bom bástik/ adj —**bombastically** adv

Bombay /bom báy/ former name for **Mumbai**

bombay mix n a spicy mixture of dried ingredients, eaten as a snack

bomber /bómmər/ n 1 an aircraft that drops bombs 2 somebody who plants bombs

bomber jacket n a short jacket with an elasticated waist

bombshell /bóm shel/ n 1 a surprising piece of news (infml) 2 an artillery shell or bomb

bomb site n an area destroyed by bombs

bona fide /bṓnə fī́di/ adj 1 authentic 2 sincere and honest

bonanza /bə nánzə/ n a source of great wealth

Bonaparte /bṓnə paàrt/, ♦ **Napoleon I**

bonbon /bón bon/ n a sweet

bonce n somebody's head (infml)

bond n 1 an object such as a rope, band, or chain that binds things together 2 a solemn promise 3 a document that legally obliges somebody to pay money 4 a certificate issued by a government or company promising to repay borrowed money at a fixed rate of interest on a specified date 5 the way in which one surface sticks to another 6 an adhesive substance 7 a force that binds atoms and ions in a molecule 8 a technique for overlapping bricks 9 a link between people, especially an emotional link 10 something that limits behaviour 11 secure storage of goods before payment of duty ∎ v 1 vti adhere or make surfaces adhere 2 vi become linked emotionally 3 vt store securely 4 vti convert or be converted into a debt with a bond as security 5 vi link atoms or ions with a chemical bond

bondage /bóndij/ n 1 slavery 2 the practice of being tied up during sex

bonded warehouse n a warehouse for storing goods before duty has been paid on them

bondholder /bónd hōldər/ n somebody who owns bonds

bone /bōn/ n 1 any one of the hard parts that form the skeleton in vertebrates 2 the material of which a vertebrate skeleton consists 3 any substance resembling bone, e.g. ivory ∎ vt (**boning, boned**) remove the bones from ∎ adv very ◦ bone idle —**boneless** adj ◇ **have a bone to pick with somebody** have a cause for disagreement with somebody ◇ **make no bones about** say something frankly □ **bone up** vi study intensely (infml)

bone china n 1 fine white porcelain 2 articles made of bone china

bone dry adj extremely dry

bone marrow n a soft substance inside bones that is involved in the production of red blood cells

bone meal n ground bones used as a fertilizer or animal feed

boneshaker /bṓn shaykər/ n an early type of bicycle with solid tyres and no springs

bonfire /bón fīr/ n a large outdoor fire

ORIGIN A **bonfire** was originally a bone fire, a large outdoor fire on which bones were burnt.

Bonfire Night n an annual celebration of the defeat of a 17C plot to blow up the English parliament. Date: 5 November.

Bonhoeffer /bón hōfər/, **Dietrich** (1906–45) German pastor and theologian

bonhomie /bónnə mee/ n good-humoured friendliness

Bonington /bónningtən/, **Sir Chris** (b. 1934) British mountaineer

bonk v 1 vt hit (infml) 2 vti an offensive term meaning to have sexual intercourse with somebody (slang) —**bonk** n

bonkers /bóngkərz/ adj an offensive term meaning irrational (infml)

bon mot /bón mṓ/ (pl **bons mots** /pronunc. same/) n a witty remark

Bonn /bon/ city in west-central Germany. Pop. 293,072 (1997).

Bonnard /bónnaar, bo naàr/, **Pierre** (1867–1947) French painter

Bonner /bónnər/, **Neville Thomas** (1922–99) Australian politician

bonnet /bónnit/ n 1 a woman's hat that frames the face and ties under the chin 2 the hinged cover of car's engine 3 Scotland a soft brimless man's hat

Bonneville Salt Flats /bónnəvil-/ barren salt

plain in NW Utah, used for setting world land speed records

Bonnie Prince Charlie /bónni prinss cha'arli/ ♦ Stuart, Charles Edward

bonny /bónni/ (**-nier, -niest**), **bonnie** *adj N England, Scotland* **1** attractive **2** plump and healthy-looking

Bono /bónô/, **Edward de** (*b.* 1933) Maltese-born British psychologist

bonsai /bón sī/ (*pl same or* **-sais**) *n* **1** the art of growing miniature trees by rigorous pruning of roots and branches **2** a miniaturized tree

bonus /bónəss/ *n* **1** an unexpected extra **2** an extra amount of money

bon vivant /bóN vee vóN/ (*pl* **bons vivants** /*pronunc. same*/), **bon viveur** /-vee vúr/ (*pl* **bons viveurs** /bóN vee vúr/) *n* somebody who enjoys good food, wine, and other luxuries

bon voyage /bóN waa yaa'zh, bón voy aa'zh/ *interj* expresses a wish for a good journey

bony /bóni/ (**-ier, -iest**) *adj* **1** very thin and with prominent bones **2** containing many bones **3** of or like bone —**boniness** *n*

boo *interj* **1** expresses disapproval **2** used to startle somebody ■ *vti* express disapproval of somebody ◇ *booed the speaker* —**boo** *n* ◇ **would not say boo to a goose** be extremely timid and shy (*infml*)

boob[1], **booby** /bóóbi/ (*pl* **-bies**) *n* a woman's breast (*slang; often offensive*)

boob[2] *n* **1** an unfortunate mistake (*infml*) **2** somebody considered unintelligent ■ *vi UK, Can* make an unfortunate mistake (*infml*)

booby /bóóbi/ (*pl* **-bies**) *n* a large tropical seabird

booby prize *n* the loser's prize

booby trap *n* **1** a trap set as a practical joke **2** a hidden explosive device —**booby-trap** *vt*

boogie /bóógi/ (**-ieing, -ied**) *vi* dance to pop music (*infml*)

boogie-woogie /bóógi wóógi/ *n* a jazz piano style derived from the blues

boohoo /boo hoo/ *n, interj* the sound of copious weeping

book /bóòk/ *n* **1** a collection of pages bound together **2** a published work of literature or reference **3** a set of things bound together, e.g. matches or fabric samples **4** a division of a long literary work **5** a bookmaker's record **6** in card games, a number of tricks needed in scoring **7** a set of rules ■ **books** *npl* financial accounts ■ *v* **1** *vti* make a reservation **2** *vt* reserve a place for somebody **3** *vt* engage as a performer **4** *vt* charge with a criminal offence **5** *vt* take the name of a player who breaks the rules —**bookable** *adj* ◇ **bring to book** make somebody account for their behaviour ◇ **in somebody's book** in somebody's opinion ◇ **throw the book at** impose the maximum penalty on

□ **book in** *vti* reserve accommodation for yourself or somebody else

bookbinder /bóòk bīndər/ *n* somebody who binds books professionally —**bookbinding** *n*

bookcase /bóòk kayss/ *n* a cabinet with shelves for storing books

book club *n* a firm selling books by post at reduced prices

~~bookeeping~~ incorrect spelling of **bookkeeping**

bookend /bóòk end/ *n* a support for a row of books

bookie /bóòki/ *n* a bookmaker (*infml*)

booking /bóòking/ *n* **1** an arrangement by which something such as a hotel room is kept for somebody's future use **2** an arrangement for somebody to perform somewhere

bookish /bóòkish/ *adj* fond of reading and studying to the exclusion of other activities —**bookishly** *adv* —**bookishness** *n*

bookkeeping /bóòk keeping/ *n* the process of recording financial transactions —**bookkeeper** *n*

booklet /bóòklət/ *n* a small paper-covered book

bookmaker /bóòk maykər/ *n* somebody who receives bets and pays out money to people who win —**bookmaking** *n*

bookmark /bóòk maark/ *n* **1** a marker put in a book to show the place where you stopped reading **2** the address of an Internet site, stored for easy access —**bookmark** *vt*

Book of Common Prayer *n* the official book giving the order and content of Anglican church services

bookplate /bóòk playt/ *n* a label in a book on which the owner's name is listed

bookshop /bóòk shop/ *n* a shop selling books

bookstall /bóòk stawl/ *n* a stand selling books and newspapers

book token *n* a voucher of a specific value that can be exchanged for books

book value *n* **1** the value of something according to the accounting records of the owner **2** the net value of a business

bookworm /bóòk wurm/ *n* **1** an enthusiastic reader (*infml*) **2** any insect whose larvae eat books

Boole /bool/, **George** (1815–64) British mathematician and logician. His system of algebra is of importance in designing and programming computers. —**Boolean** /bóòli ən/ *adj*

Boolean operator *n* a connecting word or symbol that allows a computer user to include or exclude items in a text search

boom[1] *n* **1** *vi* make a loud deep sound **2** *vt* say with a loud deep sound ■ *n* **1** a loud deep sound **2** a significant increase ◇ *a boom in sales*

boom[2] *n* **1** a pivoting beam attached to the bottom edge of a sail **2** an extendable overhead pole, especially one carrying the microphone on a film set **3** a floating barrier

boom and bust, boom or bust *n* a period of alternate economic growth and recession

boomerang /bóòmə rang/ *n* **1** a curved piece of wood that returns to the thrower **2** something that harms the person who does it ■ *vi* backfire and cause harm to the initiator

boom town *n* a town that quickly becomes prosperous on the back of a new and profitable industry

boon *n* a great benefit

boon companion *n* an inseparable friend

boor /boor/ *n* an ill-mannered person —**boorish** *adj*

boost *vt* **1** improve, strengthen, or increase something **2** vigorously promote **3** assist somebody by pushing or lifting from below —**boost** *n*

booster /boostar/ *n* **1** a radio-frequency amplifier **2** somebody or something that encourages something *(usually in combination)* **3** a supplementary dose of a vaccine given to maintain immunity

booster seat *n* an extra seat for a child fixed over a car seat or a chair

boot[1] *n* **1** a strong shoe that covers part of the lower leg *(often in combination)* **2** a luggage compartment in a car **3** a hard kick **4** dismissal from a job *(infml)* ○ *was given the boot* **5** a protective covering for a horse's lower leg ■ *vt* kick somebody or something hard ◇ **put the boot in** attack somebody, often somebody who is vulnerable or already hurt *(infml)*

□ **boot out** *vt* force somebody to leave *(infml)*

boot[2] *n* the process of starting or restarting a computer

ORIGIN Boot is a shortening of *bootstrap* in *bootstrap loader*, a simple program that enables a computer to start up and load its operating system.

□ **boot up** *vt* start a computer

boot[3] ◇ **to boot** in addition or also

boot camp *n* a training session or training course

bootee /boo tee/, **bootie** *n* **1** a baby's knitted boot **2** a woman's boot that extends as far as the ankle

booth /booth/ *(pl* **booths** /boothz/*) n* **1** a tent or stall **2** a small enclosed or partitioned compartment

Booth /booth/, **William** (1829–1912) British religious leader

Boothia Peninsula /boothi ə-/ northernmost tip of mainland North America, in the Northwest Territories, Canada

Boothroyd /booth royd/, **Betty** (*b.* 1929) British politician

bootleg /boot leg/ (**-legging**, **-legged**) *vti* deal in illegal goods —**bootleg** *adj* —**bootlegger** *n*

bootstrap /boot strap/ ◇ **pull yourself up by your (own) bootstraps** improve your situation in life by your own efforts

booty /booti/ *n* seized or stolen valuables

booze *(slang) vi* (**boozing**, **boozed**) overindulge in alcohol ■ *n* alcohol —**boozer** *n* —**boozily** *adv* —**boozy** *adj*

booze-up *n* a bout of excessive drinking *(slang)*

bop[1] *vi* (**bopping**, **bopped**) dance to pop music *(infml)* ■ *n* bebop

bop[2] *(infml) vt* (**bopping**, **bopped**) hit, especially in the face ■ *n* a punch in the face

boquet incorrect spelling of **bouquet**

borage /bórrij/ *n* a plant with blue flowers and thick hairy leaves

borax /báw raks/ *n* a white crystalline solid. Use: cleaning agent, water softener, preservative.

Bordeaux[1] /bawr dố/ capital of Gironde Department, SW France. Pop. 215,363 (1999).

Bordeaux[2] /bawr dố/ *n* wine from the Bordeaux region of France

border /báwrdar/ *n* **1** a line dividing two areas of land, or the area around the line **2** a strip around the edge of something **3** a narrow flowerbed ■ *vti* **1** form the boundary between two places **2** be next to

□ **border on** *vt* come close to being ○ *an admissions policy bordering on the ridiculous*

borderland /báwrdar land/ *n* the area at a territory's edge

borderline /báwrdar līn/ *n* the unclear line between similar states or qualities ■ *adj* **1** not clearly belonging to one category or another **2** describes a physiologically unstable condition **3** describes a medical condition that will develop if no preventive measures are taken

bore[1] /bawr/ *vt* (**boring**, **bored**) make somebody uninterested, tired, or annoyed ■ *n* somebody or something that bores —**boring** *adj* ◇ See note at **boar**

bore[2] /bawr/ *vti* (**boring**, **bored**) **1** make a deep hole in something **2** penetrate ■ *n* the internal diameter of a pipe or similar object

bore[3] /bawr/ *n* a tidal wave in a river

bore[4] /bawr/ past participle of **bear**[2]

boredom /báwrdam/ *n* the condition of feeling bored

borehole /báwr hōl/ *n* a hole drilled in the ground, often to extract water or oil

boreing incorrect spelling of **boring**

Borg /bawrg/, **Björn** (*b.* 1956) Swedish tennis player

Borges /báwr hess/, **Jorge Luis** (1899–1986) Argentine writer

Borgia /báwrjə/, **Cesare, Duke of the Romagna** (1476?–1507) Italian soldier

Borgia, Lucrezia (1480–1519) Italian art patron

Bormann /báwrmən, -man/, **Martin** (1900–45?) German Nazi official

born past participle of **bear**[2] ■ *adj* **1** brought into life **2** developed from a particular source or root cause ○ *a realization born of long experience* **3** naturally predisposed ○ *a born leader*

born-again *adj* **1** describes a Christian who has made a commitment as an adult to Jesus Christ **2** of evangelical Christianity **3** enthusiastic and committed

borne past participle of **bear**[2]

Borneo /báwrni ō/ island of the Malay Archipelago in the W Pacific Ocean, divided between Malaysia, Brunei, and Indonesia. Pop. 10,470,800 (1995). —**Bornean** *n*, *adj*

Borodin /bórrədin/, **Aleksander Porfiryevich** (1833–07) Russian composer and chemist

boron /báw ron/ n (symbol **B**) a yellow-brown element. Use: alloys, glass, ceramics, in nuclear reactors to absorb radiation.

borough /búrrə/ n 1 an administrative division of a city 2 an English town with historical privileges

borrow /bórrə/ v 1 vt use somebody else's property 2 vti receive money as a loan 3 vt take a book from a library 4 vt adopt a word from another language —**borrower** n —**borrowing** n

borscht /bawrsht/ n beetroot soup

borstal /báwrst'l/ n formerly, a prison for young offenders

Bosch /bosh/, **Hieronymus** (1450?–1516) Dutch painter

Bose /bṓss/, **Sir Jagadis Chandra** (1858–1937) Indian physicist and botanist

Bosnia and Herzegovina /bózni ə ənd húrtsə gṓ veènə/ country in SE Europe, between Croatia and the Federal Republic of Yugoslavia. Cap. Sarajevo. Pop. 3,922,205 (2001). —**Bosnian** adj, n

Bosniac /bózni ak/ n a Muslim inhabitant of Bosnia and Herzegovina —**Bosniac** adj

bosom /bóʊzzəm/ n 1 a woman's breasts 2 the part of a garment that covers the breasts 3 a protective place (literary) ○ back in the bosom of her family ■ adj close in friendship (infml) ○ a bosom buddy

Bosporus /bóspərəss/, **Bosphorus** /bósfərəss/ strait linking the Black Sea and the Sea of Marmara that separates European and Asian Turkey. Length 31 km/19 mi.

boss[1] n somebody in charge of others, especially at work ■ vt also **boss around** give orders to others ○ The big kids try to boss the little ones.

boss[2] n 1 a round raised part on a surface, e.g. in the centre of a shield 2 a ceiling decoration

bossa nova /bóssə nṓvə/ n 1 a lively ballroom dance that originated in Brazil 2 the music for the bossa nova

boss-eyed adj cross-eyed (infml)

bossy /bóssi/ (-ier, -iest) adj fond of giving people orders —**bossily** adv —**bossiness** n

Boston /bóstən/ 1 port in E England. Pop. 34,606 (1991). 2 capital of Massachusetts. Pop. 555,447 (1998). —**Bostonian** /bo stṓni ən/ n, adj

bosun /bṓss'n/ n a ship's officer responsible for maintaining equipment

Boswell /bóz wel, -wəl/, **James** (1740–95) Scottish lawyer and biographer

bot n a computer program performing routine or time-consuming tasks (usually in combination)

botanical /bə tánnik'l/, **botanic** /bə tánnik/ adj of plants

botanical garden, botanic garden n a garden where plants are grown and studied (often pl)

botanist /bóttə nist/ n a scientist who studies plants

botany /bóttəni/ n the scientific study of plants

botch (infml) vt also **botch up** do something badly because of clumsiness or carelessness ■ n also **botch-up** a badly done job

both /bōth/ det describes two people or things together ○ I liked both candidates. ■ conj not just one ○ Truancy is both a policing and an educational issue.

bother /bóthər/ v 1 vi make the effort to do something 2 vti make somebody feel worried 3 vt make somebody annoyed ■ n 1 the effort of doing something 2 a source of annoyance ■ interj expresses mild annoyance

---

SYNONYMS **bother**, **annoy**, **bug**, **disturb**, **trouble**, **worry** CORE MEANING: interfere with somebody's composure

---

bothersome /bóthərsəm/ adj annoying

Bothnia, Gulf of /bóthni ə/ northern arm of the Baltic Sea, between Finland and Sweden

bothy /bóthi/ (pl -ies) n 1 Scotland a hut providing shelter for hill walkers 2 formerly, a simple house for farmworkers

Botox /bṓ toks/ tdmk a trademark for an anti-wrinkle beauty treatment in which botulinum toxin is injected into the skin

Botswana /bot swaánə/ landlocked country in central-southern Africa. Cap. Gaborone. Pop. 1,586,119 (2001). —**Botswanan** n, adj

Sandro Botticelli: *The Birth of Venus* (after 1482)

Botticelli /bótti chélli/, **Sandro** (1445–1510) Italian painter

bottle /bótt'l/ n 1 a container for liquids with a narrow neck and without a handle 2 the amount of liquid contained in a bottle 3 a container for a baby's milk 4 courage (infml) ■ vt (-tling, -tled) 1 put in a bottle 2 preserve in jars

□ **bottle out** vi lose courage (infml)

□ **bottle up** vt contain feelings, especially feelings that would be better expressed

bottle bank n a container for used recyclable glass

bottle-feed vt feed a baby or animal with milk from a bottle

bottle-green adj dark-green —**bottle green** n

bottleneck /bótt'l nek/ n 1 a narrow section of road that slows down traffic 2 something that causes a delay in progress

bottom /bóttəm/ n 1 the lowest or deepest part of something 2 the underside of something

3 the farthest point of something ◊ *at the bottom of the road* **4** the ground under water **5** the end of a list **6** the root cause of something **7** the lowest level in a hierarchy **8** somebody's buttocks ■ *adj* **1** lowest ◊ *the bottom shelf* **2** in the position of least excellence ◊ *the bottom five teams* —**bottommost** *adj* ◊ **at bottom** in reality

□ **bottom out** *vi* reach the end of a period of decline

bottom drawer *n* a young woman's collection of household items gathered together in preparation for marriage

bottomless /bóttəmləss/ *adj* **1** very deep **2** plentiful ◊ *a bottomless fund*

bottom line *n* **1** the most important factor that must be accepted, however unpleasant **2** a company's final profit or loss at the end of an accounting period **3** the lowest acceptable amount, especially of money

botulism /bóttyŏŏlizəm/ *n* a type of food poisoning caused by eating contaminated preserved food

Boucher /boo shay/, **François** (1703–70) French painter

Boudicca /boodikə/, **Boadicea** /bố ədi seé ə/ (*d.* AD 62) English tribal queen

boudoir /boo dwaar/ *n* a woman's bedroom or private dressing room

bouffant /boo foN/ *adj* describes hair that is backcombed into a full shape —**bouffant** *n*

bougainvillea /boogən villi ə/, **bougainvillaea** *n* a brightly coloured ornamental climbing plant

bough /bow/ *n* a large main branch of a tree

SPELLCHECK Do not confuse the spelling of **bough, bow** ('bend over'), or **bow** ('front part of a vessel'), which sound similar.

bought past tense, past participle of **buy**

bouillabaisse /booyə béss, -báyss/ *n* a rich soup made from fish and shellfish

bouillon /boo yoN/ *n* cooking stock

boulder /bốldər/ *n* a large round rock

boules /bool/ *n* an outdoor game of French origin similar to bowling (+ *sing verb*)

boulevard /boōl vaar, boōlə vaard/, **Boulevard** *n* a wide street (*often in placenames*)

ORIGIN Boulevard is adopted from French, where its original meaning was 'rampart'. It later also came to refer to a promenade or walkway built on the top of a disused fortification. The French word comes from the same German and Dutch forms that gave us *bulwark* in English.

Boulez /boo lez/, **Pierre** (*b.* 1925) French composer and conductor

~~bouillon~~ incorrect spelling of **bouillon**

bounce *v* (**bouncing, bounced**) **1** *vti* spring or make something spring away from a surface **2** *vi* jump up and down **3** *vti* reflect or make something reflect from a surface **4** *vi* move in an up-and-down motion **5** *vti* return a cheque because of insufficient funds, or be

returned for this reason ■ *n* **1** the act of rebounding from a surface **2** springiness **3** energy —**bouncily** *adv* —**bounciness** *n* —**bouncy** *adj*

□ **bounce back** *vi* recover quickly

bouncer /bównssər/ *n* **1** a guard at the door of a bar or nightclub who ejects troublemakers **2** in cricket, a ball bouncing head high

bouncing /bównssing/ *adj* describes a healthy and active baby

bound[1] past participle, past tense of **bind** ■ *adj* **1** certain to do something **2** obliged

bound[2] *vi* go somewhere energetically with long strides —**bound** *n*

bound[3] *adj* **1** on the way somewhere (*often in combination*) **2** destined to achieve something

bound[4] *vt* **1** form the boundary of **2** impose limits on

boundary /bówndəri/ (*pl* **-ries**) *n* **1** a border dividing territories **2** a limit **3** the edge of a cricket pitch **4** in cricket, a shot that crosses the boundary

bounden /bówndən/ *v* past participle of **bind** (*literary*) ■ *adj* obligatory

bounder /bówndər/ *n* a dishonourable person (*dated; insult*)

boundless /bówndləss/ *adj* seeming to have no limit —**boundlessly** *adv* —**boundlessness** *n*

~~boundry~~ incorrect spelling of **boundary**

bounds ◊ **know no bounds** be very great, strong, or intense ◊ **out of bounds 1** outside the area where somebody is allowed to go **2** beyond what is acceptable

bounteous /bównti əss/ *adj* generous (*literary*)

bountiful /bówntif'l/ *adj* (*literary*) **1** generous **2** in plentiful supply ◊ See note at **generous**

bounty /bównti/ (*pl* **-ties**) *n* **1** a reward of money offered for finding a criminal **2** generosity (*literary*)

Bounty Islands /bównti-/ uninhabited island group in the SW Pacific Ocean, part of New Zealand

bouquet /boo káy, bō-/ *n* **1** a bunch of flowers **2** the scent of wine ◊ See note at **smell**

bouquet garni /boo kay gaárni/ (*pl* **bouquets garnis** /*pronunc. same*/) *n* a bunch of bag of mixed herbs used to flavour food

bourbon[1] /búrbən/ *n* a type of American whisky made from maize

bourbon[2] /boórbən/, **Bourbon** *n* a chocolate-flavoured biscuit

Bourbon /boórbən/ *adj* of the former French royal family —**Bourbon** *n*

bourgeois /boor zhwaá, boōr zhwaa/ *adj* **1** politically conservative and socially conventional, as the affluent middle classes are often depicted **2** in Marxist political theory, of the capitalist middle class, regarded as exploiters of the working class —**bourgeois** *n* —**bourgeoisie** /boōr zhwaa zeé/ *n*

Bournemouth /báwrnməth/ coastal town in SW England. Pop. 160,749 (1996).

bout /bowt/ *n* **1** an attack of an illness **2** a short period of activity **3** a boxing or wrestling match

boutique /booˈteèk/ n **1** a small clothes shop **2** a small specialist shop

boutique hotel n an upmarket, often stylish hotel with an individual character and decor

Boutros-Ghali /booˈtross gaàli/, **Boutros** (b. 1922) Egyptian diplomat and secretary-general of the United Nations (1992–96)

~~bouy~~ incorrect spelling of **buoy**

~~bouyant~~ incorrect spelling of **buoyant**

bovine /bō vīn/ adj **1** of cattle **2** slow (literary)

bovine spongiform encephalopathy /-spùnjə fawrm en sèffə lóppə thee/ n full form of **BSE**

bow[1] /bō/ n **1** a knot in which the loops remain visible **2** a weapon for firing arrows **3** a rod for playing stringed instruments **4** a curved shape or part, e.g. a bend in a river ■ vti **1** bend, or bend something, into a bow shape **2** draw a bow across the strings of an instrument

bow[2] /bow/ v **1** vti bend the head or body forward as a greeting or submission **2** vt bend because of heaviness **3** vi yield or submit —**bow** n

bow[3] /bow/ n the front part of a vessel ◊ See note at **bough**

bowdlerize /bówdlə rīz/ (**-izing**, **-ized**), **bowdlerise** vti remove parts of a literary work regarded as indecent ■ —**bowdlerism** n

ORIGIN **Bowdlerize** comes from the name of the British editor Dr Thomas Bowdler (1754–1825), who in 1818 published an expurgated edition of the works of Shakespeare, omitting words, expressions, and scenes that he considered unsuitable for family reading.

bowel /bów əl/ n **1** the intestine (often pl) **2** the part of the intestine that connects to the anus ■ **bowels** npl the innermost parts of something ◊ the bowels of the ship

Bowen /bō in/, **Elizabeth** (1899–1973) Irish writer

bower /bów ər/ n a shady area of a garden

bowl[1] /bōl/ n **1** a round container typically used for food or liquid **2** the amount contained in a bowl **3** a part shaped like a bowl —**bowlful** n ◊ See note at **bole**

bowl[2] /bōl/ v **1** vti roll, or roll something, smoothly along **2** vti in cricket, send a ball to a person batting **3** vt in cricket, dismiss a batsman or batswoman by hitting the stumps with a bowled ball **4** vi take part in a game of bowls or bowling **5** vt score a given number of points in bowling **6** vi move quickly ■ n **1** a wooden ball used in bowls **2** a ball used in tenpin bowling **3** a roll of the ball in bowls or bowling

□ **bowl over** vt **1** astonish **2** knock down accidentally

bowlegged /bō léggid, bō légd/ adj with outwards-curving legs

bowler /bólər/ n **1** in cricket, a player who bowls the ball **2** a player in bowling or bowls

bowler hat, bowler n a hard felt hat with a round crown and narrow brim

ORIGIN The **bowler hat** was designed in 1850 by the English hatter William Bowler.

bowling /bóling/ n **1** the game of bowls or tenpin bowling **2** in cricket, the throwing of the ball to the person batting

bowling alley n **1** a building for tenpin bowling **2** any of the smooth lanes used in tenpin bowling

bowling green n an area of grass where bowls is played

bowls /bōlz/ n a game in which heavy wooden balls are rolled towards a smaller target (+ sing verb)

bowsprit /bō sprit/ n a spar projecting from the front of a ship

bow tie /bō tī/ n a tie tied in a bow at the front of the neck

bow window /bō-/ n a window that curves out from a wall

bow-wow /bów wów, bów wow/ interj an imitation of a dog's barking ■ n a dog (babytalk)

box[1] n **1** a container, usually rectangular and with a lid **2** the amount that a box holds **3** a rectangular shape marked on a surface **4** a separated area of a theatre, courtroom, or stadium **5** a small building used as a shelter (usually in combination) ◊ a sentry box **6** television (slang) **7** NZ a wheeled container for coal ■ vt **1** pack in boxes **2** draw a box around **3** ANZ mix flocks or herds —**boxful** n

□ **box in** vt surround and restrict in movement

box[2] vti fight somebody using fists and the techniques of boxing

box[3] (pl same or **boxes**) n a dense evergreen shrub. Use: hedging.

boxer[1] /bóksər/ n a fighter in the sport of boxing

boxer[2] /bóksər/ n **1** a medium-sized smooth-haired dog with a flat face **2** **Boxer** a member of an early-20C Chinese secret society dedicated to removing all foreign influences from Chinese life

boxer shorts npl loose-fitting underpants

boxing /bóksing/ n the sport of fighting with fists wearing large padded gloves

Boxing Day n in the UK, a public holiday on the day after Christmas day. Date: 26 December.

ORIGIN **Boxing Day** was traditionally the day on which 'Christmas boxes', small presents or gifts of money, were given to people who had provided a regular service throughout the year.

box junction n a road junction with yellow markings that drivers are not allowed to block

box number n a number assigned to an anonymous address for mail

box office n a place where tickets are bought

for entertainments such as plays and concerts

boxroom /bóks room, -rôom/ n a small room used for storage

boy n 1 a young male person 2 a son 3 a male person from a particular area ○ *a local boy* ■ **boys** npl a group of male friends ■ *interj* expresses pleasure or annoyance —**boyhood** n ◊ See note at **buoy**

boycott /bóy kot/ vt refuse to buy or deal with something as a way of protesting against it —**boycott** n

ORIGIN **Boycotting** began in 1880 when Captain Charles Cunningham Boycott (1832–97), a British estate manager in County Mayo, Ireland, refused to reduce rents, with the result that workers and traders stopped dealing with him.

Boyd /boyd/, **Arthur Merric Bloomfield** (1920–99) Australian artist

Boyer /bóy ər/, **Herbert W.** (b. 1936) US biochemist. He codeveloped the recombinant DNA techniques that became the basis of genetic engineering.

boyfriend /bóy frend/ n a boy or man with whom somebody has a romantic or sexual relationship

boyish /bóyish/ adj with youthful male looks or behaviour —**boyishly** adv —**boyishness** n

Boyle /boyl/, **Robert** (1627–91) Irish-born English scientist, regarded as one of the founders of modern scientific method and the science of chemistry

bps n a measurement of computer data transfer speed. Full form **bits per second**

Bq symbol becquerel

Br symbol bromine

Br. abbr 1 Britain 2 British

bra n an undergarment supporting a woman's breasts

braaivleis /brí flayss/ (pl same) n S Africa an outdoor meal where meat is grilled

Brabham /brábbəm/, **Sir Jack** (b. 1926) Australian racing driver

brace n 1 a support for an injured part of the body 2 a clamp 3 a support for a part of a building under construction 4 DENT = **braces** npl ι 5 (pl same) a pair of similar things 6 a hand-operated tool for holding a drill bit 7 either of the symbols { } ■ **braces** npl 1 a dental appliance tightened to straighten teeth 2 straps for holding up trousers ■ v (**bracing, braced**) 1 vt support or strengthen something 2 vr prepare yourself

bracelet /bráysslət/ n a piece of jewellery worn around the wrist or arm

bracing /bráyssing/ adj refreshingly invigorating

bracken /brákən/ (pl same or -ens) n a large species of fern

bracket /brákit/ n 1 either of the symbols ( ) or [ ], used in pairs for enclosing and separating text (often pl) 2 an L-shaped structure fixed to a wall as a support for something, e.g. a shelf 3 a section of the population that falls within particular limits ○ *in a higher tax bracket* ■ vt 1 put inside brackets 2 support with brackets 3 group together because of similarities

brackish /brákish/ adj describes water that is slightly salty

brad n a thin nail with a small head

bradawl /brád awl/ n a hand tool for making holes in wood to prepare for nails or screws to be inserted

Bradbury /brádbəri/, **Malcolm Stanley** (1932–2000) British novelist, critic, and scholar

Bradbury, Ray Douglas (b. 1920) US science-fiction writer

Bradford /brádfərd/ city in N England. Pop. 289,376 (1992).

Sir Don Bradman

Bradman /brádmən/, **Sir Don** (1908–2001) Australian cricketer

brae /bray/ n Scotland a hillside (often in placenames)

brag (**bragging, bragged**) vi talk with too much pride —**brag** n —**bragging** n, adj —**braggingly** adv

Bragg, Sir William Henry (1862–1942) British physicist

braggadocio /brággə dốchi ō/ (pl **-os**) n 1 empty boasting and swaggering self-aggrandizement 2 a braggart

ORIGIN **Braggadocio** is an alteration of the name *Braggadocchio*, the personification of boastfulness in *The Faerie Queene* (1590–96) by Edmund Spenser.

braggart /brággərt/ n a boastful person

Brahe /braa, braa ə, braáhi/, **Tycho** (1546–1601) Danish astronomer

Brahma /braámə/ n 1 the Hindu god of knowledge and understanding, later called the Creator 2 also **Brahman** in Hinduism, the ultimate impersonal reality underlying everything in the universe

Brahmaputra /braámə pōōtrə/ river in Tibet and NE India, emptying into the Ganges delta in Bangladesh. Length 2,900 km/1,800 mi.

Brahmin /braámin/ (pl **-mins** or same), **brahmin** n a member of the highest Hindu caste —**Brahminic** /braa mínnik/ adj

AKG London

Johannes Brahms

Brahms /braamz/, **Johannes** (1833–97) German composer

braid n 1 silky cord or interwoven thread used for decorative edging 2 strands of hair interwoven ■ vt 1 interweave strands of something, e.g. hair 2 create something by braiding 3 decorate with braid

Braille /brayl/ n a writing system for visually impaired people consisting of patterns of raised dots that are read by touch

ORIGIN Braille is named after Louis Braille (1809–52), a French educator who invented it in 1828.

brain n 1 in vertebrates, the organ of thought and feeling that controls the nervous system 2 in invertebrates, a similar centre for controlling the nervous system 3 intellect or intellectual abilities 4 somebody considered very intelligent *(infml)* ■ vt hit on the head *(slang)* ◊ **have on the brain** be unable to stop thinking about *(infml)* ◊ **pick somebody's brains** ask somebody questions in order to get information or ideas ◊ **rack your brains** try very hard to solve a problem

brainchild /bráyn chīld/ n an original idea that is attributed to somebody

brain death n the end of all brain function —**brain dead** adj

brain drain n the emigration of highly skilled personnel such as scientists to a country offering better opportunities

brainless /bráynləss/ adj regarded as unintelligent —**brainlessness** n

brainpower /bráyn pow ər/ n intellectual ability

brainstorm /bráyn stawrm/ vti generate new ideas or solutions to problems quickly and spontaneously in a group discussion —**brainstorming** n

brains trust n 1 a group of experts who discuss issues of public interest on television or radio 2 a group of high-level advisers

brainteaser /bráyn teezər/ n a difficult problem or puzzle

brainwash /bráyn wosh/ vt induce to believe or do something by constant repetition

brain wave n 1 a wave of voltage resulting from electrical activity in the brain 2 a sudden inspired idea *(infml)*

brainy /bráyni/ (-ier, -iest) adj extremely intelligent *(infml)* —**braininess** n

braise /brayz/ (braising, braised) vt cook by browning in fat, adding a little liquid, and simmering in a covered pot

SPELLCHECK Do not confuse the spelling of **braise** and **braze** ('solder'), which sound similar.

brake¹ /brayk/ n 1 a device in a machine or vehicle that slows it down or stops it *(often pl)* 2 something that slows or halts something such as expenditure or development ■ v (braking, braked) 1 vti reduce the speed of a vehicle, or slow down or stop 2 vt slow down or halt the progress or development of ◊ See note at **break**

brake² /brayk/ n an area of dense bushes

brake light n a rear light on a motor vehicle that indicates braking

brake pad n a block of material that presses against a disc brake

brake shoe n a curved block that presses against a wheel to slow it down

bramble /brámb'l/ n a wild blackberry *(often pl)* ■ vi (-bling, -bled) collect berries from brambles

brambling /brámbling/ n a finch with a speckled head and back and a rusty-brown breast

bran n the husks of cereal grain removed during milling. Use: supplementary source of dietary fibre.

branch n 1 a part of a tree growing from the trunk 2 a part of a plant stem, root, or flower cluster 3 something that is like a tree branch in structure 4 a shop, bank, or another organization belonging to a larger group ○ *branches in every major city* 5 a subdivision of a large organization with a specific function or purpose 6 a part of a larger area of study ○ *a branch of medicine* 7 one line of a family descended from a common ancestor 8 a tributary of a river or stream ○ *a branch of the Colorado River* ■ v 1 vti divide into smaller parts ○ *The track branches off towards the river.* 2 vi grow branches —**branched off** adj

□ **branch out** vi expand activities or interests into a new or different area

branch line n a minor railway line serving smaller towns

Brancusi /bran koózi/, **Constantin** (1876–1957) Romanian sculptor

brand n 1 a product made by a company and identified by a specific name 2 a particular type or kind ○ *his brand of humour* 3 an owner's mark burnt on an animal's hide ■ vt 1 burn an owner's mark on the hide of 2 describe as bad or undesirable ○ *was branded a cheat* —**branded** adj

brandish /brándish/ vt wave about menacingly, theatrically, or triumphantly

brand leader n the best-selling product in a specific category

brand loyalty n the tendency to buy a specific brand of goods repeatedly

brand name *n* a trade name for a product made by a specific company —**brand-named** *adj*

brand-new *adj* completely new

Brando /brándō/, **Marlon** (*b.* 1924) US actor

Brandt /brant/, **Willy** (1913–92) chancellor of West Germany (1969–74)

brandy /brándi/ *n* an alcoholic spirit distilled from the fermented juice of grapes or other fruit

ORIGIN The earlier form of **brandy** was *brandy wine*, which came from a Dutch word meaning 'distilled (literally, burnt) wine'.

brandy snap *n* a sweet thin crisp cylindrical biscuit

Braque /braak, brak/, **Georges** (1882–1963) French painter

brash *adj* aggressively self-assertive —**brashly** *adv* —**brashness** *n*

Brasília /brə zílyə/ capital of Brazil. Pop. 1,821,946 (1996).

brass /braass/ *n* 1 a yellow alloy of zinc and copper 2 items made of brass ○ *clean the brass* 3 an item made of brass (*usually pl*) ○ *horse brasses* 4 an engraved plaque or tablet made of brass 5 brass musical instruments collectively 6 the players of brass instruments as a section of an orchestra 7 high-ranking military or police officers (*infml*) 8 *N England* money (*infml*) 9 excessive self-assurance (*infml*) ○ *had the brass to lie about it* —**brass** *adj* —**brassy** *adj*

brass band *n* a band consisting of brass instruments

brasserie /brássəri/ *n* a bar serving food and drink

brassica /brássikə/ *n* a plant of the family that includes cabbage, broccoli, and cauliflower

brassiere /brássi ər, brázzi ər/ *n* a bra

brass rubbing *n* 1 a copy of a brass engraving made by covering it with paper and rubbing it with graphite or chalk 2 the process of making a brass rubbing

brat *n* an annoyingly demanding and selfish child or young person —**brattish** *adj* —**bratty** *adj*

Bratislava /brátti slaávə/ capital of Slovakia. Pop. 449,547 (1999).

Braun /brown/, ◆ **von Braun, Wernher**

bravado /brə vaádō/ *n* real or pretended boldness or courage

brave /brayv/ *adj* (**braver**, **bravest**) having or showing courage ■ *n* a Native North American warrior ■ *vt* (**braving**, **braved**) 1 face something dangerous or unpleasant with courage and resolution 2 defy something against the odds —**bravely** *adv* —**braveness** *n* —**bravery** *n*

bravo /braávō, braa vố/ *interj* expresses approval of a performer or performance ■ *n* (*pl* **-vos**) 1 a cry of 'bravo' 2 **Bravo** a communications code word for the letter 'B'

bravura /brə vyoorə/ *n* 1 dazzling artistic flair 2 showy style or behaviour

brawl *n* a rough and noisy fight ■ *vi* 1 fight noisily 2 make a deep loud sound —**brawling** *n*

brawn *n* 1 strong muscles 2 physical strength

brawny /bráwni/ (**-ier**, **-iest**) *adj* muscular and strong-looking —**brawnily** *adv* —**brawniness** *n*

bray *v* 1 *vi* make the characteristic sound of a donkey 2 *vti* speak or say with a harsh rasping voice —**bray** *n*

braze /brayz/ (**brazing**, **brazed**) *vt* join metal with solder ◊ See note at **braise**

brazen /bráyz'n/ *adj* 1 bold and unashamed 2 harsh-sounding —**brazenly** *adv* —**brazenness** *n*

brazier /bráyzi ər/ *n* a metal container used outdoors for burning coal or charcoal

Brazil /brə zíl/ country in E South America Cap. Brasília. Pop. 174,468,580 (2001). —**Brazilian** *n*, *adj*

Brazil nut *n* 1 an edible seed with a hard triangular shell 2 an evergreen tree that produces Brazil nuts

Brazzaville /brázzə vil/ capital of the Republic of the Congo. Pop. 1,009,000 (1995 estimate).

breach /breech/ *v* 1 *vt* break through an obstruction 2 *vt* surpass a target or limit 3 *vt* break a law or promise 4 *vti* rise above the surface of the water (*refers to whales*) ■ *n* 1 an opening produced by force 2 a gap left when somebody or something leaves 3 a failure to keep or preserve something, e.g. a law or friendship ○ *a breach of confidentiality*

SPELLCHECK Do not confuse the spelling of **breach** and **breech** ('rear part of a gun barrel'), which sound similar.

bread /bred/ *n* 1 a food made by baking a mixture of flour, water, and yeast 2 a means of sustenance or survival 3 money (*slang dated*)

SPELLCHECK Do not confuse the spelling of **bread** and **bred** (past tense of *breed*), which sound similar.

bread and butter *n* 1 a dependable source of income 2 the mainstay of something

bread-and-butter *adj* 1 involving the basics 2 generating somebody's main income

breadboard /bréd bawrd/ *n* 1 a board on which to cut bread 2 a test version of an electrical or electronic circuit

breadfruit /bréd froot/ (*pl same or* **-fruits**) *n* 1 a large round seedless tropical fruit 2 an evergreen tree that produces breadfruit

breadline /bréd līn/ *n* a low standard of living guaranteeing only basic survival ○ *living on the breadline*

breadth /bredth, bretth/ *n* 1 the distance from one side of something to the other 2 the extent of something ○ *the breadth of her knowledge* 3 broad-mindedness ○ *breadth of vision*

—**breadthways** *adj, adv* —**breadthwise** *adj, adv*

breadwinner /bréd winǝr/ *n* somebody whose earnings are a family's main income

break /brayk/ *v* (**broke** /brōk/, **broken** /brṓkǝn/) 1 *vti* separate into pieces because of damage 2 *vti* fracture a bone in part of the body, or sustain a fracture 3 *vti* damage a part of a machine so that it stops working, or is damaged 4 *vti* make or develop a tear or hole, e.g. in a surface 5 *vt* disobey a rule or law 6 *vt* go back on a promise or agreement ○ *broke his word* 7 *vt* end a situation, relationship, or association ○ *break the deadlock* 8 *vt* stop or interrupt an activity or practice 9 *vt* destroy the career, resolve, or hope of somebody ○ *a role that could make or break her* 10 *vti* escape from a restraint ○ *break free* 11 *vti* take a rest period 12 *vt* reduce the effect or force of something ○ *break a fall* 13 *vt* beat a record 14 *vt* exceed a limit 15 *vti* reveal or be revealed ○ *broke it to me gently* 16 *vi* become deeper at puberty *(refers to a boy's voice)* 17 *vi* become unsteady because of emotion *(refers to voices)* 18 *vi* become light at sunrise 19 *vi* change after a settled period *(refers to the weather)* 20 *vi* suddenly start to rain, snow, or hail ○ *before the storm broke* 21 *vi* turn into surf upon reaching the shore *(refers to waves)* 22 *vt* decipher a code 23 *vt* forcibly open a safe 24 *vt* train a horse to accept a rider 25 *vt* exchange a banknote for coins or smaller notes 26 *vi* flow out during the first stage of labour *(refers to amniotic fluid)* ○ *Her waters have broken.* 27 *vt* impoverish or bankrupt somebody 28 *vti* emerge above the surface of the water 29 *vi* in boxing or wrestling, separate after being in a clinch ■ *n* 1 a rest period 2 a brief holiday 3 a temporary period away from a usual activity ○ *a career break* 4 a short period of time off from classes during the school day for play or rest 5 an end to a relationship, activity, practice, or association 6 a commercial broadcasting pause for, e.g. advertising 7 an interval in a sports match 8 a pause in speech ○ *a break in the conversation* 9 a bone fracture 10 a weather change 11 an unexpected opportunity to achieve success *(infml)* ○ *his big break* 12 a piece of good or bad luck 13 an advantageous financial situation in which somebody is repaid or makes a reduced payment ○ *a tax break* 14 a sudden escape attempt ○ *make a break for it* 15 sunrise *(literary)* ○ *at the break of day* —**breakable** *adj* ◇ **break even** make neither a profit nor a loss ◇ **give somebody a break** stop nagging or criticizing somebody *(infml)*

SPELLCHECK Do not confuse the spelling of **break** and **brake** ('of a vehicle'), which sound similar.

□ **break down** *v* 1 *vi* stop functioning properly 2 *vti* become upset emotionally 3 *vt* experience a physical or psychological collapse 4 *vti* weaken 5 *vt* divide into component parts

□ **break in** *vi* 1 enter a place forcibly or illegally 2 interrupt a conversation

□ **break off** *vti* end a relationship or association

□ **break out** *vi* 1 develop a skin rash 2 escape from something such as a prison

□ **break up** *v* 1 *vt* divide up or interrupt the continuity of 2 *vi* disperse 3 *vti* end something such as a romantic or professional relationship

breakage /bráykij/ *n* something broken by accident *(usually pl)* ○ *All breakages must be paid for.*

breakaway /bráykǝ way/ *n* somebody or something that has broken away from a person or group —**breakaway** *adj*

breakdancing /bráyk daanssing/ *n* acrobatic dancing to rap music —**breakdance** *n, vi* —**breakdancer** *n*

breakdown /bráyk down/ *n* 1 a failure to function properly 2 a disruption in communications between people or groups 3 a sudden physical or psychological collapse 4 a summary, explanation, or analysis of data

breaker /bráykǝr/ *n* 1 a large white-capped wave 2 a device that automatically stops the flow of electricity in a circuit

breakeven /bráyk eev'n/, **breakeven point** *n* the point at which expenditure is equalled by income

breakfast /brékfǝst/ *n* the first meal of the day —**breakfast** *vi*

ORIGIN Breakfast is literally the meal with which you 'break your fast' after the night. It is first recorded in the 15C.

breakfast television *n* informal magazine-style television programmes broadcast in the morning

break-in *n* a forcible or illegal entry

breaking point *n* the point at which somebody can no longer cope with a situation or at which a situation reaches a crisis

breakneck /bráyk nek/ *adj* dangerously fast ○ *at breakneck speed*

breakout /bráyk owt/ *n* an escape from imprisonment

break point *n* in tennis, a point that, if won, results in the player who is not serving winning the game

breakpoint /bráyk poynt/ *n* 1 a pause inserted in a computer program to enable correction of errors 2 a point where something stops, changes, or breaks apart

breakthrough /bráyk throo/ *n* 1 an important discovery with far-reaching consequences 2 the removal of a barrier to progress —**breakthrough** *adj*

breakup /bráyk up/ *n* 1 the separation of something such as a company or country into separate units ○ *the breakup of the Soviet Union* 2 the end of a relationship

breakwater /bráyk wawtǝr/ *n* a barrier protecting the shore from waves

Bream /breem/, **Julian** (b. 1933) British guitarist and lutenist

breast /brest/ n **1** one of the two organs on either side of the human chest, which in women are especially prominent and produce milk after childbirth **2** a milk-producing gland in mammals corresponding to the human breast **3** somebody's chest **4** the chest regarded as the seat of emotions *(literary)* ○ *with pride filling my breast* **5** a bird or mammal's chest **6** meat from a bird or mammal's chest **7** a projecting point ○ *the breast of a hill* ■ vt **1** push something with the chest **2** reach the top of a hill **3** face something boldly and deal with it in a determined way

breastbone /brést bōn/ n a long bone running down the centre of the chest

breast-feed (**breast-fed**) vti feed a baby by holding it so that it can suck milk from the breast

breastplate /brést playt/ n a piece of armour covering the chest

breaststroke /brést strōk/ n a swimming stroke in which both arms are extended and pulled back in a circular motion while both legs are thrust out and pulled back together —**breaststroke** vi

breath /breth/ n **1** air that is inhaled and exhaled **2** exhaled air that can be felt or smelt **3** an inhalation or exhalation of air ○ *take a deep breath* **4** a slight hint of something ○ *a breath of scandal* **5** the vital force or spirit of a person or animal **6** a slight movement of air ○ *not a breath of wind* —**breathy** adj ◊ **a breath of fresh air** somebody or something refreshingly new and exciting ◊ **in the same breath** at almost the same moment ◊ **out of breath** breathing heavily because of physical exertion ◊ **under your breath** in a whispering or muttering voice

USAGE breath or breathe? The noun is **breath** (*not a breath of air moving*), and the verb is **breathe** (*hard to breathe in the sultry air*).

breathalyse /brétha līz/ (-lysing, -lysed) vt test a driver for drunkenness with a Breathalyzer™

Breathalyzer /brétha līzər/ tdmk a trademark for an apparatus that measures a driver's blood alcohol level

breathe /breeth/ (**breathing, breathed**) v **1** vti take in and blow out air repeatedly in order to stay alive **2** vt exhale something ○ *a dragon breathing fire* **3** vi allow air and moisture out *(refers to fabrics)* **4** vt say something quietly or secretively **5** vi be alive **6** vti allow a person or animal a pause to rest —**breathable** adj ◊ **breathe easy** or **easily** relax and stop worrying ◊ See note at **breath**

breather /breethər/ n **1** a pause for a rest *(infml)* **2** somebody who breathes in a particular way *(in combination)* ○ *a heavy breather*

breathing space, breathing room n the opportunity to rest or think

breathless /bréthləss/ adj unable to breathe properly because of exertion, illness, or emotion —**breathlessly** adv —**breathlessness** n

breathtaking /bréth tayking/ adj extremely exciting or shocking

breath test n a test for measuring a driver's blood alcohol level

Brecht /brekht/, **Bertolt** (1898–1956) German playwright and director

Brecon Beacons National Park /brékən beékənz-/ national park in SE Wales

bred /bred/ past tense, past participle of **breed** ◊ See note at **bread**

breech /breech/ n **1** the rear part of the barrel of a rifle or shotgun **2** a part of a pulley, to which the rope or chain is attached **3** the buttocks ◊ See note at **breach**

breech birth n a delivery of a baby in which its buttocks or feet emerge first

breeches /bríchiz/, **britches** npl knee-length trousers

breed n **1** a distinct strain of an animal or plant within a species **2** a particular type of person or thing ○ *a new breed of manager* ■ v (**bred**) **1** vti mate and produce young **2** vt raise domestic animals or plants for commercial purposes or for competitions **3** vt produce or create something ○ *Experience breeds confidence.*

breeder /breédər/ n **1** somebody who breeds animals or plants **2** also **breeder reactor** a nuclear reactor that produces more fuel than it consumes

breeding /breéding/ n **1** somebody's ancestry **2** the mating and producing of young ○ *prime breeding stock* **3** the development of improved types of animals and plants **4** somebody's upbringing and training in manners and social skills

breeding ground n **1** an area where animals go to mate and produce young **2** an environment that encourages the development of something ○ *a breeding ground for new talent*

breeze n **1** a light to moderate wind **2** something easily achieved *(infml)* ■ vi (**breezing, breezed**) move briskly

☐ **breeze through** vti accomplish a task easily

breeze block n a lightweight block made from cement and coal or coke ashes. Use: building.

breezy /breézi/ (-ier, -iest) adj **1** with a light to moderate wind **2** relaxed and confident —**breezily** adv —**breeziness** n

Bremen /bráymən/ port in NW Germany. Pop. 549,182 (1997).

Brendan /bréndən/, **St.** (486?–578?) Irish saint and traveller

Brenner /brénnər/, **Sydney** (b. 1927) South African molecular biologist. He worked on molecular genetics and the DNA code.

Brenner Pass /brénnər-/ mountain pass between SW Austria and NE Italy

Brescia /brésha/ capital of **Brescia Province**, N Italy. Pop. 190,909 (1999).

brethren /bréthrən/ plural of **brother** n 2–3 ■ npl members of a group, family, or community *(literary or humorous)*

Breton /bréttoN/, **André** (1896–1966) French poet and essayist

Breughel ♦ **Brueghel**

breve /breev/ n 1 a mark, ˘, over a short vowel or short or unstressed syllable 2 a musical note equal in length to two semibreves

breviary /bréevi əri, brévvi-/ (pl -ies) n in the Roman Catholic Church, a book containing the hymns, psalms, and prayers prescribed for each day

brevity /brévvəti/ n 1 briefness in time 2 economical use of words

brew /broo/ vti 1 make beer 2 make tea or coffee 3 develop threateningly ◇ *A scandal was brewing.* —**brew** n —**brewer** n —**brewing** n

brewery /broo əri/ (pl -ies) n a building or company that brews beer

Brezhnev /brézh nef/, **Leonid Ilyich** (1906–82) leader of the Communist Party (1964–82) and president (1977–82) of the former Soviet Union

Brian Bórú /brí ən bə roo/ (941?–1014) king of Ireland (1002–14)

briar /brí ər/ (pl -ars or same), **brier** (pl -ers or same) n 1 a tobacco pipe 2 a bush of the heather family with hard woody roots. Use: tobacco pipes.

bribe vti (**bribing**, **bribed**) give somebody money or another incentive to do you a favour, especially an illegal or dishonest one ■ n money or another incentive given to persuade somebody to do something, especially something illegal or dishonest —**bribable** adj —**bribery** n

bric-a-brac /bríkə brak/ n small inexpensive ornaments

ORIGIN Bric-a-brac was adopted in the mid-19C, formed from an obsolete French phrase *à bric et à brac*, meaning 'at random'.

brick n 1 a small hard block of clay. Use: building or paving material. 2 a rectangular block of something, e.g. ice cream 3 a helpful or supportive person (dated infml) ■ vt 1 make with bricks 2 close up or wall off with bricks

brickbat /brík bat/ n a harsh criticism

bricklayer /brík lay ər/ n a skilled worker who constructs buildings and other permanent structures with bricks —**bricklaying** n

bricks-and-mortar, **brick-and-mortar** adj of physical business premises

brickwork /brík wurk/ n 1 a structure built from bricks 2 the technique or skill of laying bricks

bridal /bríd'l/ adj of brides or weddings

SPELLCHECK Do not confuse the spelling of **bridal** and **bridle** ('a harness for a horse's head'), which sound similar.

bride n a woman who is about to marry or has just married

bridegroom /bríd groom, -groóm/ n a man who is about to marry or has just married

bridesmaid /brídz mayd/ n a bride's attendant at a wedding

bridge[1] n 1 a structure allowing passage over an obstacle such as a river or road 2 a link or means of approach to something 3 a ship's control room or platform 4 a set of one or more false teeth attached to adjoining teeth 5 the top bony part of the nose 6 the part of a stringed instrument that keeps the strings away from its body ■ vt (**bridging**, **bridged**) 1 build a bridge over an obstacle 2 create understanding between people ◇ **burn your bridges** do something that makes it impossible to return to your former position

bridge[2] n a card game for two pairs of players

bridgehead /bríj hed/ n a forward position seized in enemy territory and used as a base for further advances

Bridgend /bri jénd/ county in S Wales

Bridges /bríjjiz/, **Robert** (1844–1930) British poet

Bridget, St /bríjjit/ ♦ **Brigid of Ireland**

Bridgetown /bríj town/ capital of Barbados. Pop. 123,000 (1995).

bridging loan n a short-term loan to finance the purchase of property while another is being sold

bridle /bríd'l/ n 1 a harness for a horse's head 2 a restraint ■ v (**-dling**, **-dled**) 1 vt put a bridle on 2 vi react angrily or indignantly 3 vt restrain, control, or curb ◇ See note at **bridal**

bridle path, **bridleway** /bríd'l way/ n a track for horse riding

Brie /bree/ n soft cheese with a whitish rind

brief /breef/ adj 1 lasting only a short time 2 concise 3 short in extent ■ n 1 a synopsis of a document or documents 2 a briefing 3 a description of what a job or task involves 4 a summary of a legal case for a barrister 5 a barrister or solicitor (infml) ■ **briefs** npl a piece of close-fitting underwear for the lower body ■ vt give a briefing to —**briefly** adv —**briefness** n

briefcase /breef kayss/ n a case with a handle for carrying books and papers

briefing /breefing/ n a meeting held to provide information, or the information provided

brier n = **briar**

brig[1] n a square-rigged two-masted sailing ship

brig[2] n N England, Scotland a bridge

Brig. abbr 1 brigade 2 brigadier

brigade /bri gáyd/ n 1 a military unit consisting of two or more battalions or regiments 2 a group with a shared goal or characteristic

brigadier /bríggə deér/ n an officer in the British Army or Royal Marines of a rank above colonel

brigand /bríggənd/ n a bandit (literary) —**brigandry** n

brigantine /bríggən teen, -tín/ n a two-masted sailing ship with square-rigged sails on the foremast and fore-and-aft sails on the mainmast

bright /brīt/ adj 1 reflecting or emitting light o *a bright moonlit night* 2 intensely coloured o *bright blue* 3 intelligent 4 cheerful and lively 5 likely to be successful o *a bright future for the company* —**bright** adv —**brightly** adv —**brightness** n ◊ See note at **intelligent**

brighten /brīt'n/ v 1 vi become cheerful or lively 2 vt add colour or interest to 3 vi become less overcast or rainy 4 vti fill or become filled with more light 5 vti make or become more promising

Brighton /brīt'n/ coastal city in S England. Pop. 156,124 (1996).

Brigid of Ireland /brījit-/, **St** (453?–524?) Irish abbess

~~brilliant~~ incorrect spelling of **brilliant**

brill (pl same or **brills**) n a flatfish closely related to a turbot

brilliant /brīlyənt/ adj 1 extremely bright or radiant o *brilliant sunshine* 2 intelligent or talented —**brilliance** n —**brilliantly** adv

brilliantine /brīlyən teen/ n an oily hair cream for men

brim n 1 the projecting rim around the edge of a hat 2 the top edge of a container ■ v (**brimming, brimmed**) 1 vti fill or be full to the top o *a cup brimming with hot coffee* 2 vi overflow o *eyes brimming with tears* —**brimless** adj

brimful /brīmfŏol/ adj 1 full to the top 2 richly supplied with something o *brimful of ideas*

brimstone /brīm stōn/ n 1 sulphur (archaic) 2 also **brimstone butterfly** a butterfly, the male of which is yellow and the female greenish-white

brindled /brīnd'ld/ adj brown or grey with darker streaks or patches

brine n 1 salt water for curing, preserving, or developing flavour in food 2 the sea (literary)

bring (**brought** /brawt/) v 1 vt have somebody or something with you when you come to a place o *Please bring me a glass of water.* 2 vt attract something o *a charm supposed to bring luck* 3 vt make something happen o *Heavy rain brought flooding.* 4 vt cause somebody or something to be in a particular state o *brought the meeting to a close* 5 vt cause something to enter the mind o *brought memories of good times* 6 vr make yourself do something o *She can't bring herself to think about it.* 7 vt be sold for a particular price —**bringer** n

☐ **bring about** vt make happen

☐ **bring down** vt 1 overthrow 2 kill or wound 3 ANZ, Can present a parliamentary bill

☐ **bring forth** vt 1 give birth to young 2 produce fruit or flowers

☐ **bring forward** vt suggest something for discussion or consideration

☐ **bring in** vt earn money o *barely bringing in enough to live on*

☐ **bring off** vt succeed in doing something difficult

☐ **bring on** vt cause o *exhaustion brought on by overwork*

☐ **bring out** vt 1 make known 2 emphasize a quality in o *That outfit brings out the red in your hair.*

☐ **bring round** or **around** vt 1 revive somebody from unconsciousness 2 alter somebody's opinion o *We eventually brought him round to our view.*

☐ **bring up** vt 1 raise a subject 2 rear a child 3 vomit something

bring-and-buy sale n a fundraising or charity sale in which people bring things to sell and buy things others have brought

brink n 1 the very edge 2 the onset of an action, event, or situation, especially an unpleasant one

brinkmanship /brīngkmən ship/ n the practice of taking a dispute to dangerous limits in order to force concessions

briny /brīni/ (**-ier, -iest**) adj of sea water

brio /bree ō/ n vigour

brioche /bri ósh/ n a sweet French bread

briquette /bri két/, **briquet** n a small block of compressed material used as fuel ■ vt (**-quetting, -quetted**) form into briquettes

Brisbane /brīzbən/ capital and main port of Queensland. Pop. 1,574,600 (1998).

brisk adj 1 quick and energetic o *a brisk walk* 2 busy o *Business was brisk.* 3 refreshingly cool o *brisk autumn days* —**briskly** adv —**briskness** n

bristle /brīss'l/ n one of a number of short stiff hairs on a mammal, plant, or a man's face ■ v (**-tling, -tled**) 1 vti make hair or fur stiffen because of fear or anger, or show such a response 2 vi take offence o *bristled at the suggestion* 3 vi be thickly covered o *a battleship bristling with guns* —**bristly** adj

Bristol /brīst'l/ port in SW England. Pop. 399,633 (1996).

Bristol Channel arm of the Atlantic Ocean between S Wales and SW England. Length 140 km/85 mi.

Brit n a British person (infml)

Brit. abbr 1 Britain 2 British

Britain /brītt'n/ ◆ **Great Britain**

Britannia /bri tánnyə/ n the symbol of Britain, shown as a seated helmeted woman holding a trident

~~Brittany~~ incorrect spelling of **Brittany**

~~Britian~~ incorrect spelling of **Britain**

British /brītish/ npl the people of the United Kingdom —**British** adj

British Asian n a British person of South Asian origin

British Columbia westernmost province of Canada, on the Pacific coast. Cap. Victoria. Pop. 4,063,760 (2000).

British Council n an organization that promotes the English language and British culture abroad

British Empire n a former empire controlled by Great Britain

British English n English as used in the United Kingdom

British Isles group of islands in the Atlantic Ocean off NW Europe, including Britain, Ireland, and many smaller islands

British Legion *n* a British military charity for members of the armed forces

British Summer Time *n* the time used in the United Kingdom from April to October

British West Indies British dependent territories in the Caribbean, including Anguilla, the British Virgin Islands, the Cayman Islands, Montserrat, and the Turks and Caicos

Briton /brítt'n/ *n* 1 a British person 2 a member of an ancient Celtic people of S Britain

Brittain /brítt'n/, **Vera** (1893–1970) British writer

Brittany /brítt əni/ peninsular region in NW France. Pop. 2,906,197 (1999).

Britten /brítt'n/, **Benjamin, Lord Britten of Aldeburgh** (1913–76) British composer

brittle /brítt'l/ *adj* hard and easily broken ■ *n* a crunchy sweet made from caramel and nuts —**brittleness** *n*

brittle-bone disease *n* osteoporosis

Brno /búrnō/ city in the Czech Republic. Pop. 384,727 (1999).

broach /brōch/ *vt* 1 bring up an awkward subject 2 pierce a cask to draw off liquid ■ *n* a tool for piercing casks

---

SPELLCHECK Do not confuse the spelling of **broach** and **brooch** ('a dress ornament'), which sound similar.

---

broad /brawd/ *adj* 1 wide ○ *a broad forehead* ○ *six inches broad* 2 large and spacious ○ *the broad steppes* 3 full and clear to see ○ *a broad grin* 4 covering a wide range ○ *has broad interests* 5 not detailed ○ *a broad outline of the project* 6 meant to be easily understood ○ *a broad hint* 7 describes a strongly regional accent ■ *n* a river that expands to cover low-lying land —**broadly** *adv* —**broadness** *n*

B-road *n* a secondary road

broadband /bráwd band/ *adj* 1 using many electromagnetic frequencies 2 able to transfer large amounts of data quickly

broad bean *n* 1 a large flat green seed eaten as a vegetable 2 a plant that produces broad beans

broad-brush *adj* attempting to cover all conditions and instances

broadcast /bráwd kaast/ *v* (**-cast** *or* **-casted**) 1 *vti* transmit a programme or information on television or radio 2 *vi* perform on television or radio 3 *vt* make something widely known ■ *n* 1 a television or radio programme 2 a transmission of television or radio signals —**broadcast** *adj* —**broadcaster** *n* —**broadcasting** *n*

broaden /bráwd'n/ *vti* 1 widen 2 enlarge the range of, or become more wide-ranging

broad gauge *n* railway track that is wider than the standard gauge

broad-leaved /-leevd/, **broadleaf** /bráwd leef/ *adj* describes trees that are not conifers and have broad rather than needle-shaped leaves

broadloom /bráwd loom/ *adj* describes a carpet woven on a wide loom —**broadloom** *n*

broad-minded *adj* tolerating a wide range of views and behaviour —**broad-mindedly** *adv* —**broad-mindedness** *n*

broadsheet /bráwd sheet/ *n* a large-format serious newspaper

broadside /bráwd sīd/ *n* 1 all the guns on one side of a ship, or the simultaneous firing of them 2 a strong verbal or written attack ■ *adv* 1 with the side facing towards something ○ *hit the rocks broadside on* 2 generally and indiscriminately ○ *Her proposals were attacked broadside.*

broad-spectrum *adj* describes antibiotics effective against a wide range of harmful organisms

Broadway /bráwd way/ *n* 1 a long avenue in New York City that runs through the theatre district 2 the US commercial theatre business

Broadwood /bráwd wood/, **John** (1732–1812) British piano manufacturer

brocade /brō káyd, brə-/ *n* a heavy fabric with a raised design —**brocade** *vt* —**brocaded** *adj*

broccoli /brókəli/ *n* 1 heads of tight green, purple, or white flower buds eaten as a vegetable 2 a plant that produces broccoli

brochure /brōshər, bro shóor/ *n* a booklet containing information or advertising

brochure site *n* a simple website advertising a company's products and giving contact details

~~broccoli~~ incorrect spelling of **broccoli**

Broglie /broy/, **Louis Victor, Prince de** (1892–1987) French physicist. He worked on electron waves and particles.

brogue[1] /brōg/ *n* a regional accent, especially an Irish one

brogue[2] /brōg/ *n* a leather shoe with decorative perforations

broil /broyl/ *v* 1 *vti* be or make very hot 2 *vt US, Can* cook using direct heat

broiler /bróylər/ *n* a roasting chicken

broke[1] past tense of **break**

broke[2] *adj* having no money (*infml*) ◊ **go for broke** risk everything to achieve a goal (*infml*)

broke[3] *vt* broker

broken /brṓkən/ past participle of **break** ■ *adj* 1 having been broken 2 out of order ○ *The CD player is broken.* 3 not continuous 4 split apart by divorce, separation, or desertion ○ *from a broken home* 5 imperfectly spoken ○ *in broken English* —**brokenly** *adv* —**brokenness** *n*

broken-down *adj* 1 damaged or not working 2 dilapidated

brokenhearted /brṓkən haártid/ *adj* grief-stricken —**brokenheartedly** *adv*

Broken Hill city in W New South Wales, Australia. Pop. 20,963 (1996).

broker /brókər/ n 1 a commercial agent or negotiator 2 a stockbroker ■ vt arrange a deal, sale, or other agreement

brokerage /brókərij/ n 1 a payment to a broker 2 the business of a broker

brolly /brólli/ (pl -lies) n an umbrella (infml)

bromide /bró mīd/ n a bromine compound

bromine /bró meen, -min/ n (symbol Br) a liquid nonmetallic element. Use: sedatives, photographic materials, drugs.

Bromley /brómmli/ borough of London. Pop. 293,400 (1995).

Bromsgrove /brómz grōv/ town in west-central England. Pop. 26,366 (1991).

bronchial /bróngki əl/ adj of the tubes that carry air from the windpipe to the lungs

bronchitis /brong kítiss/ n inflammation of the membrane lining the airways to the lungs —**bronchitic** /brong kíttik/ adj

bronchus /bróngkəss/ (pl -chi /-kī, -kee/) n an air passage to the lungs

bronco /bróng kō/, **broncho** n a wild horse of the W United States

Charlotte Brontë

Brontë /brónti/ family of British writers including **Charlotte** (1816–55) and her sisters **Emily** (1818–48) and **Anne** (1820–49)

brontosaurus /bróntə sáwrəss/, **brontosaur** /bróntə sawr/ n an apatosaurus (dated)

Bronx /brongks/ borough of New York City. Pop. 1,203,789 (1990).

bronze n 1 a yellowish-brown alloy of copper and tin or another substance 2 a bronze object, especially a work of art 3 a deep yellowish-brown colour ■ v (**bronzing, bronzed**) 1 vt make something look like bronze 2 vti tan the skin (infml) **bronze** adj —**bronzed** adj

Bronze Age n the historical period characterized by the use of bronze tools, between 3500 and 1500 BC

bronze medal n a medal for third place in a competition —**bronze medallist** n

brooch /brōch/ n an ornament pinned to clothing ◊ See note at **broach**

brood n 1 the young of a bird or other animal 2 the children of a family (infml humorous) ■ adj kept for breeding ◊ a brood mare ■ v 1 worry 2 vi think resentful or dark thoughts 3 vti sit on eggs, or cover chicks —**brooder** n —**brooding** adj

broody /bróodi/ (-ier, -iest) adj 1 ready to incubate eggs 2 eager to have a baby (infml) —**broodily** adv —**broodiness** n

brook[1] n a small stream

brook[2] vt tolerate (literary)

Brooke, Rupert (1887–1915) British poet

Brooklyn /brooklin/ borough of New York City. Pop. 2,300,664 (1990).

Brookner /brooknər/, **Anita** (b. 1928) British writer

broom /broom, broom/ n 1 a long-handled brush with a head of twigs or bristles 2 a bush with bright yellow flowers

broomstick /broom stik, broom-/ n 1 the long handle of a broom 2 a long-handled broom with a head of twigs

bros., Bros. abbr brothers

broth n 1 a nourishing soup made with poultry, meat, or vegetables 2 a clear soup made by cooking meat, poultry, seafood, or vegetables in water and then removing them

brothel /bróth'l/ n a house where prostitutes work

brother /brúthər/ n 1 a male sibling 2 (pl **brothers** or **brethren**) a member of the same group as another 3 (pl **brothers** or **brethren**) a member of a religious order for men

brotherhood /brúthər hood/ n 1 a group or organization of men with a common purpose 2 all the members of a specific profession or trade 3 a feeling of fellowship 4 the relationship or feeling of brothers

brother-in-law (pl **brothers-in-law**) n 1 a sister's or spouse's sister's husband 2 a spouse's brother

brotherly /brúthərli/ adj showing the affection of a brother —**brotherliness** n

brougham /broom, broo əm/ n a one-horse carriage with an open driver's seat and a closed passenger compartment

ORIGIN The **brougham** is named after the British politician Henry Peter Brougham, first Baron Brougham and Vaux (1778–1867), who designed it in 1838.

brought past tense, past participle of **bring**

brouhaha /broo haa haa/ n a noisy commotion (infml)

brow n 1 somebody's forehead 2 an eyebrow 3 the top of a hill

browbeat /brów beet/ (-beat, -beaten /-beet'n/) vt bully or intimidate

brown /brown/ n a colour between red and yellow, e.g. the colour of wood or soil ■ adj 1 brown in colour 2 suntanned ■ vti make or become brown —**brownness** n

brownfield site /brówn feeld-/ n an urban development site that has been previously built on but is currently unused

brown goods npl electrical household goods other than kitchen appliances

brownie /brówni/ n 1 a piece of rich flat chocolate cake 2 a helpful elf or goblin 3 **Brownie, Brownie Guide** a junior Guide aged between seven and ten

Browning /brówning/, **Elizabeth Barrett** (1806–61) British poet

Browning, Robert (1812–89) British poet

brown sauce *n* **1** a sauce made from meat stock and flour browned in fat **2** a cold spicy sauce made from fruit, vinegar, sugar, and spices

browse (**browsing, browsed**) *v* **1** *vti* read through casually **2** *vi* look through or over a collection of something casually **3** *vti* feed on tender vegetation *(refers to animals)* **4** *vti* scan and view computer files, especially on the World Wide Web —**browse** *n*

browser /brówzər/ *n* **1** a piece of software for searching the World Wide Web **2** a person or animal that browses

Broxbourne /bróks bawrn/ town in SE England. Pop. 82,200 (1995).

BRS *n* the on-off switch on a personal computer when used to power down after a sudden program failure. Full form **big red switch**

Brubeck /broo bek/, **Dave** (*b.* 1920) US jazz pianist and composer

Bruch /brookh/, **Max** (1838–1920) German composer

Bruckner /brookknər/, **Anton** (1824–96) Austrian composer

Brueghel /bróyg'l/, **Bruegel, Breughel** family of Flemish painters including **Pieter** (1520–69) and his son **Jan** (1568–1625)

Bruges /broozh/ capital of West Flanders Province, W Belgium. Pop. 115,991 (1999).

bruise /brooz/ *n* **1** a discoloration of skin or tissue caused by pressure or impact **2** a discoloration of plant tissue caused by pressure or impact ■ *vti* cause a bruise to develop on somebody or something, or develop a bruise

bruiser /broozər/ *n* a big strong man *(infml)*

Brummell /brúmm'l/, **Beau** (1778–1840) British dandy

Brummie /brúmmi/, **Brummy** (*pl* **-mies**) *n* somebody from Birmingham *(infml)* —**Brummie** *adj*

brunch *n* a mid-morning meal combining breakfast and lunch

Brunei /broo ní/ country in NW Borneo. Cap. Bandar Seri Begawan. Pop. 343,653 (2001).

Isambard Kingdom Brunel

Brunel /broo nél/, **Isambard Kingdom** (1806–59) British engineer

Brunelleschi /broonə léski/, **Filippo** (1377–1446) Italian architect and sculptor

brunette /broo nét/ *n* a woman with dark brown hair —**brunette** *adj*

brunt *n* the main impact of something ○ *had to bear the brunt of her anger*

bruschetta /broo skéttə, -shéttə/ *n* Italian bread toasted and drizzled with olive oil

brush¹ *n* **1** a tool consisting of bristles or hair **2** an act of brushing **3** a light stroke or contact **4** a short unpleasant encounter ○ *a brush with danger* **5** a bushy tail, especially a fox's kept as a hunting trophy **6** an electrical conductor in a generator or motor ■ *v* **1** *vti* use a brush on somebody or something **2** *vt* apply something with a brush to a surface **3** *vt* remove something with a brush or a brushing motion **4** *vt* reject somebody or something ○ *brushed aside the suggestion* **5** *vti* move lightly against something

□ **brush up** *vt* refresh your knowledge of or skill in

brush² *n* **1** thick undergrowth **2** land covered with thick undergrowth **3** brushwood

brushed *adj* **1** describes a fabric with a soft raised surface produced by brushing **2** describes a metallic surface with a non-reflective sheen

brushoff /brúsh of/ *n* an abrupt dismissal *(infml)*

brushwood /brúsh wŏod/ *n* **1** cut or broken twigs and branches **2** thick undergrowth

brusque /broosk/ *adj* abrupt in speech or manner —**brusquely** *adv* —**brusqueness** *n*

Brussels /brúss'lz/ capital of Belgium. Pop. 954,460 (1999).

Brussels sprout *n* **1** a green vegetable like a miniature cabbage **2** a plant that produces Brussels sprouts

brutal /broot'l/ *adj* **1** cruel and violent **2** harsh and severe —**brutality** /broo tálləti/ *n* —**brutally** *adv*

brutalism /broot'lizəm/ *n* a harsh massive modern architectural style —**brutalist** *n, adj*

brutalize /broot'l Iz/ (**-izing, -ized**), **brutalise** *vt* **1** make brutal **2** treat brutally —**brutalization** /broot'l I záysh'n/ *n*

brute *n* somebody brutal ■ *adj* **1** purely physical or instinctive **2** cruel or savage —**brutish** *adj*

Brutus /brootəss/, **Lucius Junius** (*fl* late 6C BC) Roman consul

Brutus, Marcus Junius (85?–42 BC) Roman general

BSc *abbr* Bachelor of Science

BSE *n* a disease affecting the nervous system of cattle. Full form **bovine spongiform encephalopathy**

BSI *abbr* British Standards Institution

BST *abbr* British Summer Time

Bt *abbr* baronet

BTEC /bee tek/ *abbr* Business and Technology Education Council

BTW, btw *abbr* by the way *(in e-mails)*

bubble /búbb'l/ *n* **1** a thin spherical film containing air or a gas **2** a globule of air or a gas within a liquid or solid **3** a transparent glass or plastic dome **4** a false feeling of confidence, especially in a business venture

○ *suffered when the dot.com bubble burst* ■ *vi* (**-bling, -bled**) **1** effervesce or boil up **2** be full of a lively emotion or enthusiasm ○ *bubbling with mirth*

bubble and squeak *n* a fried dish of leftover potatoes and cabbage

bubble bath *n* **1** a bath preparation that produces foam **2** a bath containing a foamy preparation

bubblegum /búbb'l gum/ *n* chewing gum that can be blown into bubbles

bubble-jet printer *n* a printer in which heated ink forms bubbles that burst on the paper

bubble memory *n* computer memory in which data is stored as binary digits represented by the presence or absence of minute areas of magnetization in a semiconductor

bubbly /búbb'li/ *adj* (**-blier, -bliest**) foamy or effervescent ■ *n* champagne (*infml*) —**bubbliness** *n*

Buber /bóobər/, **Martin** (1878–1965) Austrian-born Israeli theologian and philosopher

bubonic plague /byoo bónnik-/ *n* an infectious fatal epidemic disease transmitted by fleas

buccaneer /búkə neèr/ *n* **1** a pirate on the high seas **2** an unscrupulous businessperson or politician —**buccaneering** *adj, n*

> **ORIGIN Buccaneer** was adopted from a French word that means 'somebody who cooks or dries meat on a wooden frame over an open fire'. It is formed from a Native South American term for the frame. The hunters who regularly prepared meat in this way were independent and lawless, and became identified with the pirates of the Spanish-American coasts.

Buchan /búkən/, **John, 1st Baron Tweedsmuir** (1875–1940) British writer and administrator

Bucharest /bóokə rést/ capital of Romania. Pop. 2,037,000 (1997).

buck[1] *n* **1** a male animal of some species such as deer, goats, rabbits, and kangaroos **2** (*pl same or* **bucks**) *S Africa* a male or female antelope or deer

□ **buck up** *vti* make or become more cheerful (*infml*)

buck[2] *v* **1** *vi* jump with the back arched and the legs stiff (*refers to horses*) **2** *vt* throw a rider by bucking **3** *vti* oppose or resist something obstinately (*infml*) **4** *vt* take a risk against something ○ *buck the odds* —**buck** *n*

buck[3] *n ANZ, US, Can* a dollar (*infml*)

> **ORIGIN Buck** meaning 'dollar' is a shortening of *buckskin*. Buckskins were used as a unit of exchange with Native Americans in early frontier days.

buck[4] *n* a marker formerly used in poker to indicate somebody's turn to deal ◇ **pass the buck** shift responsibility to somebody else (*infml*)

Buck, Sir Peter (1880–1951) New Zealand anthropologist and politician

bucket /búkit/ *n* **1** a cylindrical container with an open top and a curved handle **2** *also*

bucketful the contents of a bucket, or the amount it holds **3** a bucket-shaped object, especially a scoop on a mechanical shovel ■ *vi* pour with rain (*infml*) ◇ **kick the bucket** die (*slang*)

bucket shop *n* an unreliable or unlicensed small business, especially a travel agency

Buckingham /búkingəm/, **George Villiers, 2nd Duke of** (1628–87) English courtier

Buckingham Palace *n* the official London residence of the British monarch

Buckinghamshire /búkingəmshər/ county in S England. Pop. 473,000 (1995).

buckle /búk'l/ *n* a fastener for a belt, shoe, or strap consisting of a metal frame with a hinged prong ■ *v* (**-ling, -led**) **1** *vti* fasten with a buckle **2** *vti* bend out of shape **3** *vi* collapse

□ **buckle down** *vi* start to work hard (*infml*)

□ **buckle up** *vti* fasten a seat belt

buckram /búkrəm/ *n* a stiff cotton or linen fabric. Use: bookbinding, stiffening clothes. —**buckram** *adj*

Bucks. /buks/ *abbr* Buckinghamshire

buck's fizz, Buck's fizz *n* a cocktail of champagne and orange juice

> **ORIGIN** The cocktail is named after *Buck's Club* in London.

buckshot /búk shot/ *n* lead shot for hunting game

buckskin /búk skin/ *n* **1** deerskin **2** soft greyish-yellow leather

bucktooth /búk tóoth/ (*pl* **-teeth** /-teèth/) *n* a protruding upper front tooth (*infml*) —**bucktoothed** *adj*

buckwheat /búk weet/ *n* **1** an edible triangular seed. Use: cereal, flour, animal fodder. **2** a plant that produces buckwheat

bucolic /byoo kóllik/ *adj* **1** of the countryside **2** of shepherds —**bucolically** *adv*

bud *n* **1** an outgrowth on a plant stem or branch consisting of a shortened stem and immature leaves or flowers **2** an unopened flower **3** an asexual reproductive outgrowth of a simple organism that separates and develops independently ■ *vi* (**budding, budded**) **1** produce plant buds **2** start to grow from a plant bud **3** begin to develop and increase ◇ **nip something in the bud** stop something at the very beginning (*infml*)

Budapest /bóodə pést/ capital of Hungary. Pop. 1,838,753 (1999).

buddha /bóoddə/, **Buddha** *n* **1** in Buddhism,

Buddha: Daibutsu (Great Buddha), Kamakura, Japan

somebody who has attained enlightenment **2** an image of Buddha

Buddha /bóodda/ (563?–483? BC) Nepalese-born Indian philosopher

Buddhism /bóoddizəm/ n a world religion based on the teachings of Buddha —**Buddhist** n, adj

budding /búdding/ adj promising ○ a budding actor

buddy /búddi/ (pl **-dies**) n US, Can a friend (infml) —**buddy** vi

budge (**budging**, **budged**) vti **1** move or change the position of something **2** change your opinion or the opinion of somebody else

budgerigar /bújjəri gaar/ n a small parrot often kept in a cage

ORIGIN **Budgerigar** comes from an Aboriginal language of SE Australia, where it meant literally 'good cockatoo'.

budget /bújjit/ n **1** a summary of income and spending **2** a plan for allocating resources **3** an amount of money allocated or needed for a specific purpose or period **4 Budget** a statement of the United Kingdom's financial position for the financial year with proposals for spending and taxation, presented by the Chancellor of the Exchequer ■ adj cheap or economical ■ v **1** vti plan the use of money or time ○ budget £20 a head ○ budget for growth **2** vi live according to a budget —**budgetary** adj

ORIGIN **Budget** comes from a French word that originally referred to a pouch or wallet. It began to refer to a statement or estimate of revenue and expenditure in the mid-18C.

budget account n an account with a department store allowing a customer to pay in regular instalments

budgie /bújji/ n a budgerigar (infml)

Buenos Aires /bwáy noss írriz/ capital of Argentina. Pop. 2,965,403 (1991).

buff[1] n **1** a pale yellowish-brown colour **2** a soft pale yellow leather made from buffalo, elk, or ox skin **3** a soft cloth for polishing ■ adj **1** pale yellowish-brown in colour **2** made of buff leather ■ vt polish

buff[2] n an enthusiast or fan

buff[3] adj US physically fit and strong (infml)

buffalo /búffalō/ (pl **-loes** or **-los** or same) n **1** a type of horned cattle **2** US, Can a North American bison

buffer /búffər/ n **1** a protection against impact or harm **2** a device on a train or track that stops the train running off the end of the track **3** a substance that maintains the pH of a solution **4** a temporary storage area for data being transmitted between two devices that function at different speeds —**buffer** vt

buffer zone n a neutral area that lies between hostile groups or territories

buffet[1] /bóo fay/ n **1** a self-service meal **2** a counter or table on which food and drink is displayed **3** also **buffet car** a railway carriage serving food and drink **4** a piece of

dining-room furniture for storing tableware

buffet[2] /búffit/ n **1** a blow or battering **2** a heavy or repeated blow – **buffet** vt

buffoon /bə fóon/ n a person regarded as foolish or bumbling —**buffoonery** n

bug n **1** an insect with thickened forewings and mouthparts adapted for piercing or sucking **2** US, Can any insect or similar organism considered to be a pest **3** an infectious microorganism, or an illness caused by one (infml) **4** a craze or obsession (infml) **5** a defect or error in something (infml) **6** a hidden listening device (infml) ■ vt (**bugging**, **bugged**) **1** pester (infml) **2** hide a listening device in order to hear ◊ See note at **bother**

bugbear /búg bair/ n **1** a source of unreasonable fear **2** a continuing nuisance or problem

bug-eyed adj with bulging eyes (infml)

bugger /búggər/ n **1** a taboo term for somebody who practises anal intercourse (offensive) **2** a taboo term for a person or thing regarded as unpleasant or difficult (slang offensive) **3** a person of a particular type (slang; often offensive) ■ v **1** vti a taboo term meaning to practise anal intercourse with somebody (offensive) **2** vt an offensive term meaning to damage or spoil something (slang) ■ interj an offensive term expressing annoyance or frustration (slang)

□ **bugger about** or **around** (offensive) vi a taboo term meaning to waste time ■ vt a taboo term meaning to cause difficulties for somebody

□ **bugger off** vi a taboo term meaning to go away (offensive)

□ **bugger up** vt a taboo term meaning to spoil or ruin something (offensive)

buggery /búggəri/ n a taboo term for anal intercourse (offensive)

buggy /búggi/ (pl **-gies**) n **1** a lightweight horse-drawn vehicle **2** a small battery-powered vehicle ○ a golf buggy **3** a pushchair

bugle /byóog'l/ n a brass instrument like a short valveless trumpet, used for military signals —**bugle** vi —**bugler** n

ORIGIN The fuller form buglehorn gives a clue to the original meaning of **bugle**, which was 'buffalo, wild ox'. The word came via French from Latin, and is related to bucolic.

build /bild/ v (**built** /bilt/, **built**) **1** vt make a structure by joining its parts together ○ built a wall **2** vt have something built ○ The emperor built these pavilions. **3** vti form or develop something ○ building a solid business reputation ○ vi increase ○ Tension was building. ■ n the physical structure of somebody's body ○ his heavy build —**builder** n

□ **build in** vt **1** incorporate in something's structure **2** include

□ **build up** v **1** vti develop **2** vt praise excessively **3** vt make stronger and healthier

building /bílding/ n **1** a walled roofed structure **2** the business or job of constructing houses or other large structures (often before a noun) ○ building materials

building block n 1 a large block of concrete or similar material used in the construction industry 2 a component regarded as contributing to the growth of something

building society n a financial organization, providing savings accounts, mortgages, and loans

buildup /bíld up/ n 1 an accumulation of something 2 an impressive description of somebody or something

built-in adj 1 designed or fitted as an integral part 2 forming a natural feature or characteristic

built-up adj 1 containing many buildings 2 made higher or thicker o built-up heels

~~buisness~~ incorrect spelling of **business**

Bujumbura /bōōjəm bōōrə/ capital of Burundi. Pop. 634,479 (1991 estimate).

Bukharin /boo kaárin, -khaárin/, **Nicolay Ivanovich** (1888–1938) Russian revolutionary and political theorist

Bulawayo /bōōllə wáy ō/ city in SW Zimbabwe. Pop. 620,936 (1992).

bulb n 1 an underground plant storage organ from which a new plant grows annually 2 a plant that grows from a bulb 3 a rounded part 4 a light bulb

bulbous /búlbəss/ adj 1 rounded and swollen-looking 2 growing from a bulb

Bulgakov /bōōl gaá kof/, **Mikhail** (1891–1940) Ukrainian writer

Bulgaria /bul gáiri ə/ country in SE Europe, on the Black Sea. Cap. Sofia. Pop. 7,707,495 (2001). —**Bulgarian** n, adj

bulge vi (**bulging**, **bulged**) swell up or out ■ n 1 a part that has expanded outwards 2 a sudden temporary increase —**bulging** adj

bulgur /búlgər/ n dried cracked wheat

bulimia /byoo límmi ə/ n an eating disorder in which bouts of overeating are followed by self-induced vomiting —**bulimic** adj, n

bulk n 1 large size 2 the greater part of something 3 a large or overweight person's body o eased his bulk through the narrow passageway 4 fibre in food ■ adj in or of a large quantity

bulkhead /búlk hed/ n a partition inside a ship, aircraft, or large vehicle

bulky /búlki/ (-**ier**, -**iest**) adj 1 awkwardly large 2 heavily built —**bulkily** adv —**bulkiness** n

bull[1] n 1 an uncastrated adult male of dairy or beef cattle 2 an adult male of large mammals including whales and elephants 3 an investor who buys securities in anticipation of rising prices 4 a bull's eye ◊ **take the bull by the horns** deal with a difficult situation (infml)

bull[2] n a pope's formal written statement

bulldog /bōōl dog/ n a smooth-haired muscular dog

bulldoze /bōōl dōz/ (-**dozing**) vt 1 demolish or remove with a bulldozer 2 force into action (infml)

bulldozer /bōōl dōzər/ n a construction vehicle used for moving earth or debris

Bullen /bōōllən/, **Keith** (1906–76) New Zealand geophysicist and mathematician

bullet /bōōllit/ n 1 a piece of ammunition used in a firearm 2 also **bullet point** a large dot highlighting items in a list ◊ **bite the bullet** deal with an unpleasant but unavoidable situation (infml)

bulletin /bōōllətin/ n 1 a news broadcast of a single news item 2 an official announcement 3 a newsletter

bulletin board n an online forum for exchanging e-mails or information, or for accessing software

bulletproof /bōōllit proof/ adj able to resist bullets

~~bullettin~~ incorrect spelling of **bulletin**

bullfight /bōōl fīt/ n a public entertainment in which a bull is baited and usually killed —**bullfighter** n —**bullfighting** n

bullfinch /bōōl finch/ n a small bird with a stubby beak, black head, and pink breast

bullfrog /bōōl frog/ n a large frog with a deep croak

bullion /bōōlli ən/ n bars of gold or silver

bullish /bōōllish/ adj 1 expecting rising stock market prices 2 optimistic (infml) —**bullishly** adv —**bullishness** n

bull market n a stock market in which prices are rising

bullock /bōōllək/ n 1 a young bull 2 a castrated bull

bullring /bōōl ring/ n an arena for bullfights

bull's eye n 1 the centre of a target, which usually carries the highest score 2 a shot that hits the bull's eye 3 a successful manoeuvre (infml)

bullshit /bōōl shit/ n an offensive term for talk considered foolish or inaccurate (slang) —**bullshit** vti —**bullshitter** n

bull terrier n a smooth-haired dog that is a cross between a bulldog and a terrier

bullwhip /bōōl wip/ n a long heavy plaited hide whip, knotted at the end

bully[1] /bōōlli/ (pl -**lies**) n somebody who intimidates or mistreats weaker people —**bully** vt —**bullying** n

bully[2] /bōōlli/ (pl -**lies**) n a small New Zealand river fish

bulrush /bōōl rush/ n 1 a tall marsh plant with brown flower spikes 2 a plant that grows in wet conditions with leaves resembling grass 3 in the Bible, a papyrus plant

bulwark /bōōlwərk/ n 1 a wall built to keep out attackers 2 somebody or something that gives protection or support —**bulwark** vt

bum[1] n the buttocks (infml)

bum[2] (infml) n 1 a good-for-nothing 2 US, Can a vagrant (sometimes offensive) ■ vt (**bumming**, **bummed**) get by begging ■ adj useless

bum bag n a small bag for valuables attached to a belt

bumble /búmb'l/ (-**bling**, -**bled**) v 1 vti speak in a hesitant or muddled way 2 vt move or proceed clumsily —**bumbling** adj

bumblebee /búmb'l bee/ *n* a large hairy bee

bumf, bumph *n* unwanted or uninteresting printed material *(infml)*

bump *vti* **1** hit or knock something **2** move in a jolting or bouncing way ○ *bumped along the dirt track* ■ *n* **1** an accidental knock **2** a swelling on the body caused by an impact **3** a lump on a surface ○ *a bump in the road*

□ **bump into** *vt* meet by chance

□ **bump off** *vt* murder *(slang)*

bumper /búmpər/ *n* a protective projecting rim on the front or back of a vehicle ■ *adj* unusually large or successful ○ *a bumper year for apples*

bumper car *n* a small electric fairground car

bumpkin /búmpkin/ *n* a country person seen as unsophisticated *(infml)*

bumptious /búmpshəss/ *adj* self-important

bumpy /búmpi/ (**-ier, -iest**) *adj* **1** having an uneven surface ○ *a bumpy road* **2** uncomfortably bouncy ○ *a bumpy ride* —**bumpily** *adv* —**bumpiness** *n*

bun *n* **1** a small round bread roll, sometimes sweetened **2** a small round sweet cake **3** a hairstyle in which the hair is coiled at the back of the head

bunch *n* **1** a collection or group **2** a cluster of fruits on a stem **3** a group of people *(infml)* ■ *vti* gather into a close group

bundle /búnd'l/ *n* **1** a collection of things held together **2** a lot of money *(slang)* ■ *vt* (**-dling, -dled**) **1** tie things together **2** shove or send somebody or something roughly and hurriedly *(infml)* ○ *bundled the suspect into the police car* **3** package computer hardware and software at an inclusive price

□ **bundle up** *vti* dress warmly *(infml)*

bundy /búndi/ (**-dies, -died**) *vi ANZ* clock on or off work

bung *n* **1** a plug or stopper **2** a bribe or payoff *(slang)* ■ *vt* **1** plug a hole in **2** place carelessly *(infml)*

□ **bung up** *vt* block a hole or passage *(infml)*

bungalow /búngg gəlō/ *n* a one-storey house

ORIGIN **Bungalow** comes from a Hindi word that means simply 'of Bengal' (the region that is now Bangladesh and the Indian state of Bangla).

bungee jump /búnji-/ *n* a dive from a high place using an elastic cord tied to the ankles —**bungee jumping** *n*

bungle /búng g'l/ (**-gling, -gled**) *vt* make fail through carelessness or clumsiness *(infml)* ○ *bungled the job* —**bungle** *n* —**bungling** *adj* —**bunglingly** *adv*

bunion /búnnyən/ *n* a swelling of the joint of the big toe

bunk[1] *n* **1** a simple bed built on a shelf or in a recess **2** *also* **bunk bed** one of a pair of single beds fitted one on top of the other

bunk[2] *vi* depart hurriedly

bunker /búngkər/ *n* **1** a large outdoor container **2** an underground shelter **3** a sand hazard on a golf course

bunker buster *n* a powerful laser-guided bomb designed to penetrate a reinforced target and explode

Bunker Hill /búngkər-/ hill in Boston, Massachusetts, near the site of the first battle of the War of American Independence in 1775. Height 34 m/110 ft.

bunkum /búngkəm/ *n* nonsense *(infml)*

ORIGIN **Bunkum** derives from the name of Buncombe County, North Carolina, in the United States. In a debate in the US Congress in about 1820 its representative made a long, dull, and irrelevant speech that he refused to cut short because he had to speak 'for Buncombe'. Buncombe quickly became a byword for long-windedness and nonsense.

bunny /búnni/ (*pl* **-nies**) *n* a child's word for a rabbit

Bunsen /búnss'n/, **Robert Wilhelm** (1811–99) German chemist and physicist. He popularized a safe laboratory gas burner.

Bunsen burner *n* a laboratory gas burner

bunting[1] /búnting/ *n* a small brown or grey songbird

bunting[2] /búnting/ *n* strings of cloth or paper used as outdoor decorations

Buñuel /boon wél/, **Luis** (1900–83) Spanish film director

Bunyan /búnnyən/, **John** (1628–88) English preacher and writer

bunyip /búnnyip/ *n Aus* a legendary monster inhabiting swamps and water holes

Buonarroti /bwónnə rótti/, **Michelangelo** ♦ **Michelangelo**

buoy /boy/ *n* **1** an anchored float that acts as a guide or warning for ships **2** a life buoy ■ *vt* **1** mark with a buoy **2** keep from falling or sinking

SPELLCHECK Do not confuse the spelling of **buoy** and **boy** ('a young male'), which sound similar.

buoyant /bóy ənt/ *adj* **1** causing objects to float **2** tending to float **3** quick to recover emotionally **4** cheerful —**buoyancy** *n* —**buoyantly** *adv*

bur *n* ENG, PLANT SCI = **burr**[1]

burble /búrb'l/ (**-bling, -bled**) *v* **1** *vi* make a bubbling sound **2** *vti* speak or say excitedly *(infml)* —**burble** *n*

burden[1] /búrd'n/ *n* **1** a load being carried **2** a worrying responsibility ■ *vt* give a difficult or worrying responsibility to —**burdensome** *adj*

burden[2] /búrd'n/ *n* **1** a chorus in a song **2** a main or recurring theme in music or literature *(literary)* ◊ See note at **subject**

burden of proof *n* legal responsibility to prove a charge or allegation

burdock /búr dok/ *n* a tall wild plant with prickly flowers

bureau /byoor rō/ (*pl* **-reaus** *or* **-reaux** /-rōz/) *n* **1** an organization, or a branch of an organization **2** a government department **3** a writing desk

bureaucracy /byoor rókrəssi/ (*pl* **-cies**) *n* **1** administrative officials considered collectively **2** complex, rigidly applied rules within an organization **3** a state or organization operated by officials

bureaucrat /byoorə krat/ *n* **1** an administrative or government official **2** an inflexible official

bureaucratic /byoor rə kráttik/ *adj* **1** administrative **2** rigidly applying complex rules —**bureaucratically** *adv*

bureau de change /byoor rō də shónNzh/ (*pl* **bureaus de change** /byoor rō-/ *or* **bureaux de change** /byoor rō-/) *n* a place for exchanging foreign currency

Buren /búrrən/ ♦ **Van Buren, Martin**

burgeon /búrjən/ *vi* (*literary*) **1** produce new growth (*refers to plants*) **2** develop rapidly —**burgeoning** *adj*

burger /búrgər/ *n* **1** a hamburger **2** a round flat cake made of chicken, fish, vegetables, or nuts, usually served in a bun

Burgess /búrjiss/, **Anthony** (1917–93) British writer and critic

Burgess, Guy (1911–63) British Soviet spy

burgh /búrrə/ *n* Scotland a town incorporated by royal charter

burgher /búrgər/ *n* **1** a medieval European merchant **2** a prosperous member of the middle class (*humorous*)

Burghley /búrli/, **Sir William Cecil, 1st Baron** (1520–98) English politician

burglar /búrglər/ *n* an illegal intruder and thief

burglary /búrglэri/ (*pl* **-ries**) *n* **1** the crime of entering a building illegally in order to steal something **2** an act of entering a building illegally to commit theft

burgle /búrg'l/ (**-gling, -gled**) *vt* enter a building illegally in order to steal something

~~burgler~~ incorrect spelling of **burglar**

burgundy /búrgəndi/ *n* **1** *also* **Burgundy** a red or white wine from the Burgundy region of France **2** a deep red colour —**burgundy** *adj*

burial /bérri əl/ *n* interment of a corpse

burka /búrkə/, **burqa** *n* a garment with veiled eye holes covering the entire body, worn in public by some Muslim women

Burke /burk/, **Edmund** (1729–97) Irish-born British writer, political philosopher, and politician

Burke, Robert O'Hara (1820–61) Irish-born Australian explorer

Burke, William (1792–1829) Irish murderer and grave robber

Burkina Faso /bur keenə fássō/ landlocked country in W Africa. Cap. Ouagadougou. Pop. 12,272,289 (2001).

burl *n* a knot on a tree

burlap /búr lap/ *n* coarse cloth woven from jute or hemp

burlesque /bur lésk/ *n* mockery of a serious matter by ludicrous imitation ■ *vt* (**-lesquing, -lesqued**) mock by ludicrous imitation

burly /búrli/ (**-lier, -liest**) *adj* sturdy and strong —**burliness** *n*

Burma /búrmə/ former name for **Myanmar**

Burmese /búr meéz/ (*pl same*) *n* **1** somebody from Myanmar **2** the official language of Myanmar —**Burmese** *adj*

burn[1] *v* (**burnt** *or* **burned**) **1** *vti* be or set something on fire **2** *vti* destroy something, or be destroyed by fire ○ *The house was burnt to the ground.* **3** *vt* damage something by fire or heat ○ *burnt his hand on the iron* **4** *vti* overcook something, or be overcooked **5** *vt* use something up ○ *burn calories* **6** *vt* use something as fuel **7** *vi* feel or look feverish ○ *Her cheeks were burning.* **8** *vti* cause or experience a hot stinging sensation ○ *That hot coffee will burn your throat.* **9** *vt* make a mark or hole as a result of intense heat ○ *burnt a hole in my shirt* **10** *vti* become sunburnt, or make somebody or a part of the body sunburnt **11** *vi* emit heat or light ○ *a light burning in the front room* **12** *vi* feel a strong emotion ○ *burning with shame* ■ *n* **1** an injury caused by fire, heat, radiation, a chemical, electricity, or friction **2** a mark or hole produced by burning **3** a firing of a rocket engine **4** a stinging or hot sensation **5** sunburn or windburn **6** a strong physical sensation produced by strenuous exercise, especially aerobics ○ *go for the burn*

□ **burn off** *vti* dissipate as a result of the sun's heat

□ **burn out** *vti* **1** wear out through heat or friction **2** make or become exhausted through overwork or stress (*infml*)

□ **burn up** *v* **1** *vti* destroy or be destroyed by fire **2** *vt* use up fuel

burn[2] *n* N England, Scotland a stream

Burne-Jones /búrn-/, **Sir Edward** (1833–98) British painter and designer

burner /búrnər/ *n* **1** a ring or plate on a cooker that heats up **2** the part of a stove that produces a flame when lit **3** an incinerator or furnace

Burnet /bər nét, búrnit/, **Sir Macfarlane** (1899–1985) Australian biologist

Burney /búrni/, **Fanny** (1752–1840) British novelist and diarist

burn-in *n* a test of an electronic device or piece of software in which it is run continuously for a period of time

burning /búrning/ *adj* **1** ardent ○ *a burning passion* **2** of urgent importance ○ *a burning issue*

burnish /búrnish/ *vt* **1** polish metal **2** make something shiny

burnout /búrn owt/ *n* **1** psychological exhaustion resulting from overwork or stress **2** a mechanical failure caused by overuse, excessive heat or friction, or failure of fuel supply

Burns, Robert (1759–96) Scottish poet

burnt past tense, past participle of **burn**[1]

burp *n* a belch ■ *v* **1** *vi* bring up wind **2** *vt* make a baby bring up wind

burr[1], **bur** *n* **1** a prickly husk of a seed **2** a rough edge on cut or drilled metal **3** a woody outgrowth on a tree

burr[2] *n* **1** a whirring sound **2** a rolled 'r' in some regional accents of English —**burr** *vti*

burrito /bə reétō/ (*pl* **-tos**) *n* a filled tortilla

Burroughs /búrrōz/, **William S.** (1914–97) US writer

burrow /búrrō/ *n* a hole or tunnel dug for use as a home by a small animal ■ *v* **1** *vti* dig or live in a burrow **2** *vi* force a way into something by creating a hole ○ *burrowed deeper into the bedclothes*

Bursa /búrssə/ city in NW Turkey. Pop. 1,095,842 (1997).

bursar /búrssər/ *n* a treasurer in an educational or religious institution —**bursarship** *n*

bursary /búrssəri/ (*pl* **-ries**) *n* **1** a grant or scholarship awarded to a student **2** a bursar's office

burst *v*(**burst**) **1** *vi* split apart because of internal pressure ○ *The suitcase had burst open.* **2** *vt* pierce, rupture, or split something open **3** *vi* be extremely full **4** *vt* overflow ○ *The river burst its banks.* **5** *vi* move, start, or appear suddenly and energetically ○ *burst in on the meeting* **6** *vi* be overwhelmed emotionally ○ *bursting with excitement* **7** *vi* suddenly start to express an emotion ○ *burst into tears* ■ *n* **1** a rupture or explosion **2** a short intense period of something ○ *a burst of activity* **3** a short sudden volley of gunfire

bursty /búrsti/ *adj* moving, transferred, or transmitted in spurts, as data is in a computer network

burton /búrt'n/ ◊ **go for a burton** be destroyed, ruined, or dead (*infml*)

Burton /búrt'n/, **Sir Richard Francis** (1821–90) British explorer and linguist

Burundi /bŏŏ rŏŏndi/ country in east-central Africa. Cap. Bujumbura. Pop. 6,223,897 (2001). —**Burundian** *n*, *adj*

bury /bérri/ (**-ies**, **-ied**) *v* **1** *vt* put something in a hole and cover it **2** *vt* put a corpse in a grave **3** *vt* cover somebody or something up completely ○ *was buried under the rubble* **4** *vt* make something hard to find ○ *The apology was buried in fine print.* **5** *vr* concentrate intensely on something ○ *buried herself in her family* **6** *vt* suppress or forget something ○ *an attempt to bury the past* ◊ See note at **berry**

bus /buss/ *n* (*pl* **buses** *or* **busses**) **1** a motor vehicle that carries passengers on one or two decks **2** a channel for transferring computer data ■ *vti* (**buses** *or* **busses**, **busing** *or* **bussing**, **bused** *or* **bussed**) travel or carry passengers by bus

ORIGIN Bus is a shortening of *omnibus*. It is recorded within a few years of the adoption of *omnibus* from French in the early 19C. The *omnibus* is a vehicle 'for everybody', which is what the word means in Latin.

busby /búzbi/ (*pl* **-bies**) *n* a soldier's tall fur hat

bush /bŏŏsh/ *n* **1** a woody plant with many branches that is smaller than a tree **2** a dense group of bushes **3** uncultivated and unsettled land, especially in Africa and Australia **4** a dense mass of something such as hair or beard **5** *NZ* the forest of New Zealand ■ *vi* branch out, spread, or grow thick like a bush ◊ **beat about the bush** discuss a subject without coming to the point

Bush /bŏŏsh/, **George** (*b.* 1924) 41st president of the United States (1989–93)

George W. Bush

Bush, George W. (*b.* 1946) 43rd president of the United States (2001–)

bushbaby /bŏŏsh baybi/ *n* a small tree-dwelling nocturnal primate with large eyes and a long tail

bushed /bŏŏsht/ *adj* exhausted from overwork or lack of sleep (*infml*)

bushel /bŏŏsh'l/ *n* a former unit of dry or liquid measure in the British Imperial system, equal to 8 imperial gallons (36.37 litres)

bushman /bŏŏshmən/ (*pl* **-men** /-mən/) *n* ANZ somebody who lives or travels in remote areas

bushranger /bŏŏsh raynjər/ *n* **1** *US*, *Can* somebody who lives in the wilderness **2** *ANZ* formerly, a criminal or escaped convict living on the run in the bush

bush telegraph *n* the spreading of information by word of mouth (*infml*)

bushwhack /bŏŏsh wak/ *vi* **1** *Aus*, *US*, *Can* cut through or travel through woods **2** *NZ* fell timber for a living —**bushwhacker** *n*

bushy /bŏŏshi/ (**-ier**, **-iest**) *adj* **1** describes hair that is thick and full ○ *bushy eyebrows* **2** describes a plant that is dense and woody —**bushiness** *n*

~~busines~~ incorrect spelling of **business**

business /bíznəss/ *n* **1** a line of work **2** a commercial organization **3** commercial activity or practice ○ *It's bad business to neglect smaller clients.* ○ *I threatened to take my business elsewhere.* **4** personal or private matters ○ *other people's business* **5** a difficult or unpleasant affair ○ *that business about the tickets* **6** unspecified activities **7** something excellent (*infml*) ■ *adj* of commerce

business card *n* a card with a person's name and business details on it

businesslike /bíznəss līk/ *adj* **1** efficient and practical **2** unemotional

businessman /bíznəss man/ (*pl* **-men** /-mən/,

-men/) *n* a man who works in business, especially at a senior level

business park *n* an area of businesses and light industry

businessperson /bíznəss purss'n/ (*pl* **-people** /-peep'l/) *n* somebody who works in business

business plan *n* a plan of the future strategy and development of a business

businesswoman /bíznəss woòmən/ (*pl* **-women** /-wimmin/) *n* a woman who works in business, especially at a senior level

busk *vi* entertain in the street —**busker** *n*

bus lane *n* a part of the road for buses only

busman's holiday /bússmənz-/ *n* a holiday doing something similar to your normal work (*infml*)

bus mouse *n* a mouse attached to a computer bus

bus network *n* a computer network in which all nodes are connected to a single bus

bust[1] *n* 1 a woman's breasts 2 a sculpture of the head and shoulders of a person

bust[2] *v* (**busted** *or* **bust**) 1 *vti* burst something 2 *vt* raid a place, or arrest a person (*slang*) ■ *n* economic failure or difficulty (*infml*) o **boom and bust** —**bust** *adj*

bustier /bústi ay/ *n* a woman's strapless bodice

bustle[1] /búss'l/ *vi* (**-tling**, **-tled**) work or go hurriedly or busily ■ *n* energetic activity

bustle[2] /búss'l/ *n* a pad formerly worn under the back of a woman's skirt

bust-up *n* a fight (*infml*)

busty /bústi/ (**-ier**, **-iest**) *adj* with large breasts (*infml*)

busy /bízzi/ *adj* (**-ier**, **-iest**) 1 engaged in work or other activity 2 full of activity 3 too elaborate o *a very busy painting* 4 describes a telephone line that is in use ■ *vr* (**-ies**, **-ied**) occupy or make busy o *busied himself with the wedding arrangements* —**busily** *adv* —**busyness** *n*

busybody /bízzi bodi/ (*pl* **-ies**) *n* a person regarded as prying or interfering (*infml*)

Busy Lizzie /-lízzi/ (*pl same or* **Busy Lizzies**) *n* a small house and garden plant with bright flowers and seed pods that burst when ripe

but *conj* 1 introduces an apparent contradiction o *It looks difficult, but it's actually quite easy.* 2 introduces a protest or expression of surprise o *'It's time to leave.' 'But we just got here!'* 3 introduces further information o *I've forgotten the map, but we probably won't need it.* 4 except that o *I should have phoned, but I don't have your number.* 5 without something else happening (*fml*) o *It never rains but it pours.* ■ *conj, prep* except o *nothing but water to drink* ■ *adv* only (*fml*) o *We can but try.* ■ **buts** *npl* objections (*infml*)

butane /byoó tayn/ *n* a colourless flammable gas. Use: lighter fluid, fuel.

butch /boóch/ *adj* masculine and strong in appearance

butcher /boóchər/ *n* 1 a seller of meat 2 somebody who slaughters animals for

meat 3 a brutal killer ■ *vt* 1 slaughter an animal for food 2 kill people brutally 3 botch something (*infml*) —**butchery** *n*

Buthelezi /boòtə láyzi/, **Mangosuthu Gatsha** (*b.* 1928) South African politician

butler /búttlər/ *n* the chief manservant of a household

Butlin /búttlin/, **Sir Billy** (1899–1980) British holiday camp organizer

butt[1] *v* 1 *vt* hit with the head or horns 2 *vi* jut out —**butt** *n*

□ **butt in** *vi* interrupt

butt[2] *n* an object of ridicule or contempt ■ *vti* abut

butt[3] *n* 1 the thicker or larger end of something, e.g. a rifle 2 the remains of a smoked cigarette 3 *US, Can* the buttocks (*infml; sometimes offensive*)

butt[4] *n* a cask

butte /byoot/ *n* a flat-topped hill

butter /búttər/ *n* a soft pale yellow dairy product ■ *vt* spread butter on —**buttery** *adj*

□ **butter up** *vt* flatter

butter bean *n* a flat cream-coloured bean

buttercup /búttər kup/ *n* a wild plant with yellow flowers

butterfat /búttər fat/ *n* the fat in dairy products

butterfingers /búttər fing gərz/ (*pl same*) *n* somebody who tends to drop things (*infml*) —**butterfingered** *adj*

butterfly /búttər flī/ *n* (*pl* **-flies**) 1 an insect with large colourful wings 2 a person lacking concentration 3 *also* **butterfly stroke** a swimming stroke in which both arms are lifted simultaneously ■ **butterflies** *npl* a nervous feeling in the stomach

buttermilk /búttər milk/ *n* a sour-tasting liquid remaining after butter-making

butterscotch /búttər skoch/ *n* a brittle sweet or flavouring made from butter and brown sugar

buttock /búttək/ *n* each of the fleshy mounds above a person's legs and below the hollow of the back (*often pl*)

button /bútt'n/ *n* 1 a small disc put through a hole or loop to fasten clothing 2 a switch that is pressed to activate an electrical device 3 *Aus, US, Can* a small round badge 4 an image on a computer screen that is clicked to activate a task 5 a part of a computer mouse that is pressed or clicked ■ *vti* fasten with buttons ◊ **on the button** exactly right (*infml*) ◊ **push somebody's buttons** provoke a reaction in somebody deliberately

button-down *adj* fastened down at the ends with buttons

buttonhole /bútt'n hōl/ *n* 1 a hole for a button in clothing 2 a flower worn on a lapel ■ *vt* (**-holing**, **-holed**) compel to stay and listen (*infml*)

button mushroom *n* a mushroom with a small unopened cap

buttress /búttrəss/ *n* 1 a supporting structure built against a wall 2 somebody or something that gives support ■ *vt* **1** support a wall with a buttress **2** support or reinforce an argument or opinion

buxom /búksəm/ *adj* describes a woman with large breasts *(humorous)* —**buxomness** *n*

Buxtehude /boõksta hoõda/, **Dietrich** (1637?–1707) Danish-born German organist and composer

buy /bī/ *v* (**bought** /bawt/) **1** *vti* acquire something by payment **2** *vt* bribe somebody **3** *vt* gain time by strategic action **4** *vt* obtain something by sacrifice **5** *vt* believe in or accept something *(infml)* ○ *I don't buy his excuses.* ■ *n* something bought

SPELLCHECK Do not confuse the spelling of **buy**, **bi-** ('two'), **by** ('beside, past, through', etc.), or **bye** ('automatic advance in a competition', 'goodbye'), which sound similar.

□ **buy in** *vti* buy something in quantity
□ **buy off** *vt* bribe
□ **buy out** *vt* **1** purchase all the shares of a company **2** pay somebody to relinquish part-ownership ○ *She was bought out by her partners.*
□ **buy up** *vt* buy all of

buy-back *n* the purchase of shares or goods that you previously sold, according to a contract

buyer /bī ər/ *n* **1** somebody who buys something **2** somebody whose job is buying goods for a company

buyout /bī owt/ *n* the purchase of a controlling interest in a company

buzz *n* **1** a low humming or vibrating sound made by an insect or an electronic device **2** a hum of talk **3** a telephone call *(infml)* **4** a feeling of excitement or intoxication *(infml)* ■ *v* **1** *vi* make a low humming or vibrating sound **2** *vi* be full of activity **3** *vti* activate a buzzer **4** *vt* fly low over *(infml)*
□ **buzz off** *vi* go away *(infml)*

buzzard /búzzərd/ (*pl* -**zards** *or same*) *n* **1** a large hawk **2** *US, Can* a vulture

buzzer /búzzər/ *n* an electronic device that buzzes

buzzword /búz wurd/ *n* a fashionable word *(infml)*

bw *abbr* black-and-white

BWI *abbr* British West Indies

by /bī/ *prep, adv* **1** past in space *(after a verb of movement)* **2** at a place for a short visit ○ *Drop by any time.* ■ *prep* **1** next to or along **2** through **3** no later than ○ *get there by midnight* **4** during ○ *By day he worked in a canning factory.* **5** in measures of ○ *sold by weight* **6** indicates a quantity in multiplication or division ○ *What is 144 divided by 12?* **7** indicates a dimension ○ *2 metres by 3* **8** indicates an amount of difference ○ *increased by 10%* **9** in amounts of a particular size **10** indicates progression ○ *One by one we told our stories.* **11** indicates the person or thing that does or causes something *(after a passive verb)* ○ *was loved by her parents* ○ *was melted by the sun*

12 indicates a creator ○ *a play by Shakespeare* **13** indicates a method, medium, or means ○ *by pressing this button* ○ *travelling by train* ■ *adv* **1** indicates the passage of time ○ *as the weeks go by* **2** away or aside ○ *put some of the money by* ◇ **by and by** after a while *(literary)* ◇ **by the by, by the bye** incidentally ◊ See note at **buy**

by- *prefix* **1** secondary, subsidiary, extra ○ *by-product* **2** past ○ *bygone*

Byatt /bī ət/, **Dame A. S.** (*b.* 1936) British novelist and academic

~~**byciele**~~ incorrect spelling of **bicycle**

bye[1] /bī/ *n* **1** an automatic advance to the next round of a competition without playing **2** in cricket, a run scored without hitting the ball ◊ See note at **buy**

bye[2] /bī/, **bye-bye** *interj* goodbye *(infml)* ◊ See note at **buy**

by-election, bye-election *n* a mid-term election

bygone /bī gon/ *adj* of long ago

bylaw /bī law/ *n* **1** a local law **2** a rule governing the internal affairs of an organization **3** a secondary law

ORIGIN The first part of **bylaw** probably comes from an old Scandinavian word for 'town, village', and is not the *by-* meaning 'subsidiary' or 'extra' that is found in such words as *by-election* and *by-product.*

byline /bī līn/ *n* a reporter's name printed at the head of an article

bypass /bī paass/ *n* **1** a road round a town **2** an operation to redirect the blood ○ *a heart bypass* ■ *vt* avoid an obstacle or problem by using an alternative route or method

by-product *n* **1** an incidental product in the manufacture of something else **2** a secondary result

Byrd /burd/, **William** (1543–1623) English composer

byre /bīr/ *n regional* a cowshed

Byron /bīrən/, **George Gordon Noel, 6th Baron Byron** (1788–1824) British poet

bystander /bī standər/ *n* somebody who observes but is not involved in something

byte /bīt/ *n* **1** a unit of computer information comprising eight bits **2** a unit of computer memory for storing a single character

ORIGIN Although it is a fairly recent word, the exact origin of **byte** is not certain. It may be an alteration of *bit* as a unit of computer information, influenced by *bite* (of food); or it may be based on 'binary digit eight'.

byway /bī way/ *n* **1** a side road **2** a minor aspect

byword /bī wurd/ *n* **1** somebody or something well-known for embodying a particular quality **2** a word or phrase in common use

Byzantine /bī zán tīn, -teen, bízz'n tīn, -teen/ *adj* **1** of Byzantium **2** of the Eastern Orthodox Church **3 byzantine** very complex ■ *n* somebody from Byzantium

Byzantium /bī zánti əm, bi-, bī zánshi əm, bi-/ ancient Greek city on the site of modern Istanbul

C

C[1] (*pl* **c's**), **C** (*pl* **C's** *or* **Cs**) *n* **1** the 3rd letter of the English alphabet **2** the Roman numeral for 100

C[2] *abbr* **1** carat **2** centimetre **3** century **4** circa **5** circumference **6** copyright

C[1] (*pl* **C's** *or* **Cs**) *n* **1** the 1st note in the musical scale of C major **2** the 3rd highest grade of a student's work

C[2] *symbol* **1** capacitance **2** carbon

C[3] *abbr* **1** Catholic **2** Celsius **3** century **4** Conservative

c., C. *abbr* circa *(before dates)*

C2B *abbr* consumer-to-business

C2C *abbr* consumer-to-consumer

Ca *symbol* calcium

CA *abbr* **1** California **2** certificate authority *(in e-mails)*

ca. *abbr* circa *(before dates)*

c/a *abbr* current account

CAA *abbr* Civil Aviation Authority

cab *n* **1** a taxi **2** the driver's compartment in a large vehicle or machine

CAB *abbr* Citizens' Advice Bureau

cabal /kə bál/ *n* **1** a group of conspirators **2** a secret plot

Caballé /kə bál yay, káb ə yáy/, **Montserrat** (*b.* 1933) Spanish operatic soprano

cabaret /kábbə ray/ *n* a floor show performed in a restaurant, club, or bar

cabbage /kábbij/ *n* **1** a large round head of green or purple leaves eaten as a vegetable **2** a plant that produces cabbages

caber /káybər/ *n* a long thick pole thrown in a competition in Scotland

cabin /kábbin/ *n* **1** a wooden hut **2** a room on a ship **3** the part of an aircraft or spacecraft for the crew or passengers

cabin class *n* an intermediate class on passenger ships —**cabin class** *adj, adv*

cabin crew *n* the staff of an aircraft who attend to the passengers

cabin cruiser *n* a luxurious motor boat

cabinet /kábbinət/ *n* **1** *also* **Cabinet** a group of senior government ministers (+ *sing or pl verb*) **2** a piece of furniture used for storage or display

cabinetmaker /kábbinət maykər/ *n* a woodworker who makes fine furniture —**cabinetmaking** *n*

cabinet minister *n* a senior government minister

cable /káyb'l/ *n* **1** a strong rope or wire **2** a bundle of electrical wires enclosed in a casing **3** *also* **cablegram** an overseas telegram **4** *also* **cable television** a television system in which signals are transmitted by cable ■ *v* (**-bling, -bled**) **1** *vti* send a telegram **2** *vt* supply a place with cable TV

cable car *n* a compartment suspended or moved by a cable, used for transport up and down steep hills

cable railway *n* a hillside railway using a moving cable

caboodle /kə bood'l/ ◊ **the whole (kit and) caboodle** the whole lot *(infml)*

Cabot, **John** (1450?–99?) Italian explorer

Cabot, **Sebastian** (1476?–1557) Italian-born English navigator and cartographer

cabriolet /kábbri ə lay/ *n* a two-door convertible car

cacao /kə káy ō, -kaà ō/ (*pl* **-os** *or* same) *n* **1** a seed from which cocoa products are derived **2** a tree that produces cacao seeds

cache /kash/ *n* **1** a hidden store, e.g. of weapons **2** a secret place for hiding things **3** an area of computer memory for temporary storage

> **SPELLCHECK** Do not confuse the spelling of **cache** and **cash** ('coins and banknotes'), which sound similar.

cachet /kásh ay/ *n* prestige or respect

cack-handed /kák hándid/ *adj* clumsy *(infml)* —**cack-handedness** *n*

cackle /kák'l/ (**-ling, -led**) *vi* **1** laugh harshly and shrilly **2** make a squawking noise *(refers to hens)* —**cackle** *n*

cacophony /kə kóffəni/ (*pl* **-nies**) *n* an unpleasant combination of loud or jarring sounds —**cacophonous** *adj*

cactus /káktəs/ (*pl* **-ti** /-tī/ *or* **-tuses** *or* same) *n* a spiny fleshy desert plant

cad *n* a man who behaves dishonourably *(dated)* —**caddish** *adj*

cadaver /kə daàvər, -dáy-/ *n* a corpse

cadaverous /kə dávvərəss/ *adj* like a corpse in being extremely thin or pale

caddie /káddi/, **caddy** (*pl* **-dies**) *n* a golfer's assistant —**caddie** *vi*

caddy /káddi/ (*pl* **-dies**) *n* **1** a small container for tea **2** a CD-ROM case

> **ORIGIN Caddy** comes from a Malay word that referred to a standard measure for tea set by the East India Company. A tea **caddy** was therefore a container for one 'caddy' of tea. A golfer's *caddie* or **caddy** is from a different source. It is an alteration of *cadet*.

Cade /kayd/, **Jack** (?–1450) Irish-born English rebel leader

cadence /káyd'nss/ *n* **1** rhythm or rhythmic flow **2** the rise and fall of the voice **3** a closing sequence of musical notes

cadenza /kə dénzə/ *n* a virtuoso solo passage near the end of a section or piece of music

cadet /kə dét/ n 1 a trainee in the armed forces or police 2 a member of a military organization for young people —**cadetship** n

cadge (**cadging**, **cadged**) vti scrounge or beg something from somebody (infml)

Cádiz /kə díz/ capital of **Cádiz Province**, SW Spain. Pop. 143,129 (1998).

cadmium /kádmi əm/ n (symbol **Cd**) a soft metallic chemical element. Use: alloys, electroplating, nuclear reactors, pigments, electronics.

cadre /kaádər, káy-/ n 1 a group of experienced military professionals 2 a tightly knit or highly trained group 3 a member of a cadre

CAE abbr computer-aided engineering

caecum /séekəm/ (pl **-ca** /-kə/) n the first part of the large intestine —**caecal** adj

Caen /koN/ capital of Calvados Department, NW France. Pop. 113,987 (1999).

Caesar /séezər/ n 1 a title of Roman emperors 2 also **caesar** a tyrant

Caesar /séezər/, **Gaius Julius** (100–44 BC) Roman general and political leader

Caesarea /séezə rée ə/ ancient port in present-day NW Israel

Caesarean /si záiri ən/ adj of or like Caesar or Caesars ■ n also **Caesarean section** a delivery of a baby by cutting through the mother's abdominal wall and womb

> **ORIGIN** A **Caesarean** is so called because Julius Caesar is reputed to have been born in this way.

caesium /séezi əm/ n (symbol **Cs**) a silver-white metallic element. Use: photoelectric cells.

café /káffay/ n an informal restaurant serving drinks and light meals

café latte /káffay láttay/, **caffè latte** n an espresso coffee with steamed milk

cafeteria /káffə teéri ə/ n a self-service restaurant

cafetière /káffə tyáir, -teér/ n a coffee pot with a plunger

caffeine /káffeen/ n a stimulant found in coffee and tea. Use: in soft drinks and medicine.

~~caffiene~~ incorrect spelling of **caffeine**

caftan n CLOTHING = **kaftan**

cage n a wire or barred enclosure ■ vt (**caging**, **caged**) put or keep in a cage or confined conditions —**caged** adj

Cage, John (1912–92) US composer

cagey /káyji/ (**-gier**, **-giest**), **cagy** adj cautious and secretive (infml) —**cagily** adv —**caginess** n

Cagney /kágni/, **James** (1899–1986) US film actor

cagoule /kə goól, ka-/ n a lightweight hooded waterproof jacket

cahoots /kə hoóts/ ◇ **be in cahoots (with)** have a secret agreement with, especially to do something dishonest or illegal (infml)

CAI abbr computer-aided instruction

Cain /kayn/ ◇ **raise Cain** cause a noisy disturbance (infml)

> **ORIGIN** In the Bible, **Cain** was the elder son of Adam and Eve, who killed his brother Abel (Genesis 4).

cairn /kairn/ n a pile of stones used as a marker

Cairn, Cairn terrier n a small Scottish terrier with a shaggy coat

Cairngorm Mountains /káirn gawrm-/, **Cairngorms** range of the Grampian Mountains in NE Scotland. Highest peak Ben Macdhui, 1,309 m/4,296 ft.

Cairo /kírō/ capital of Egypt and Africa's largest city. Pop. 6,789,000 (1998).

Caitra /káytrə/ n the 1st month of the year in the Hindu calendar

cajole /kə jól/ (**-joling**, **-joled**) vti persuade somebody gently —**cajolery** n

Cajun /káyjən/ n 1 in Louisiana, a descendant of French colonists exiled in the 18C from Canada 2 a dialect of French spoken in Louisiana —**Cajun** adj

> **ORIGIN Cajun** is an alteration of Acadian. Acadia was a French colony in Canada (now New Brunswick, Nova Scotia, and Prince Edward Island), whose inhabitants, the original **Cajuns**, moved to the S United States in the 18C, driven out by the British.

cake n 1 a baked sweet food containing flour and eggs 2 a shaped portion of savoury food 3 a block of something such as soap or ice ■ vti (**caking**, **caked**) form a thick layer or crust on something

CAL /kal/ abbr computer-assisted learning

Cal. abbr California

calabash /kállə bash/ n 1 a large round fruit or gourd 2 a plant that produces calabashes

calabrese /kállə bráyzi, -breez/ n a type of broccoli

Calabria /kə lábbri ə/ region in S Italy forming the 'toe' of the Italian peninsula. Pop. 2,064,718 (1998).

Calais /kállay/ port in N France, on the English Channel. Pop. 77,333 (1999).

calamity /kə lámməti/ (pl **-ties**) n a disaster —**calamitous** adj

Calamity Jane

Calamity Jane /kə lámməti jáyn/ (1852?–1903) US frontierswoman

calcify /kálssi fī/ (**-fies**, **-fied**) vti 1 turn into a calcium compound 2 become hard as a result

of calcium deposition *(refers to a body part)*
—**calcification** /kálssifi káysh'n/ *n*

calcium /kálssi əm/ *n (symbol* **Ca**) a silver-white metallic chemical element found in bone and limestone

calculate /kálkyoō layt/ (**-lating, -lated**) *v* **1** *vti* work something out mathematically **2** *vti* consider and decide o *calculating how to tackle the problem* **3** *vt* intend to have a particular effect o *methods calculated to please* —**calculable** *adj*

ORIGIN The root of **calculate** is Latin *calculus* 'pebble' (pebbles were used in counting with an abacus). *Calculus* itself is thought to come from the Latin word for 'limestone' from which English *chalk* developed. Sir Humphry Davy also used it as a basis for the word *calcium*, which he coined in 1808.

calculating /kálkyoō layting/ *adj* shrewd or scheming —**calculatingly** *adv*

calculation /kálkyoō láysh'n/ *n* **1** the process of calculating **2** something calculated **3** consideration of something, especially when thinking of personal advantage

calculator /kálkyoō laytər/ *n* an electronic device for arithmetical operations

calculus /kálkyoōləss/ (*pl* **-li** /-lī/ *or* **-luses**) *n* **1** a branch of mathematics dealing with relationships affected by changing variables **2** a kidney or bladder stone *(technical)*

Calcutta /kal kúttə/ former name for **Kolkata**

Calder /káwldər, kóld-/, **Alexander** (1898–1976) US painter and sculptor

caldron *n* = **cauldron**

calendar /kálindər/ *n* **1** a system of calculating the days and months of the year **2** a chart showing the days of a year, often with a separate page for each month **3** a timetable of events during a year

calendar month *n* any of the 12 named divisions of the year

calendar year *n* the period from 1 January to 31 December

calf[1] /kaaf/ (*pl* **calves** /kaavz/) *n* **1** a young cow or bull **2** a young elephant, giraffe, or whale

calf[2] /kaaf/ (*pl* **calves** /kaavz/) *n* the fleshy part of the lower leg

calf love *n* love felt by adolescents *(literary)*

Calgary /kálgəri/ city in S Alberta, Canada. Pop. 768,082 (1996).

Cali /kaáli/ capital of Valle de Cauca Department, W Colombia. Pop. 2,111,000 (1999).

caliber *n* US = **calibre**

calibrate /káli brayt/ (**-brating, -brated**) *vt* **1** mark the scale on a measuring instrument **2** test and adjust the accuracy of a measuring instrument —**calibration** /káli bráysh'n/ *n*

calibre /kállibər/ *n* **1** ability, intelligence, or character **2** the diameter of a gun barrel or bullet

calico /kállikō/ *n* an unbleached cotton cloth

ORIGIN Calico is named after the port of Calicut

(now called Kozhikode) in SE India, from which the cloth was exported.

California /kálli fáwrnyə/ state in the W United States, on the Pacific Ocean. Cap. Sacramento. Pop. 33,871,648 (2000). —**Californian** *n, adj*

californium /kálli fáwrni əm/ *n (symbol* **Cf**) a synthetic metallic element. Use: neutron source.

Caligula /kə líggyoōlə/ (AD 12–41) Roman emperor (AD 37–41)

caliph /káylif, kállif/ *n* a title taken by Islamic rulers —**caliphate** /kálli fayt, káyli-, -fit/ *n*

calk *vt, n* = **caulk**

call /kawl/ *v* **1** *vt* give a name to **2** *vt* describe or refer to in a particular way **3** *vti* shout or say loudly o *calling for help* **4** *vt* summon **5** *vti* telephone **6** *vi* visit **7** *vi* stop briefly somewhere o *Does this bus call at the cathedral?* **8** *vti* request or arrange for something to happen o *call a meeting* **9** *vt* US predict, especially in politics o *a hard election to call* **10** *vt* in a sport, declare as an official decision **11** *vt* demand repayment of o *call a loan* ■ *n* **1** a shout **2** a bird or animal cry **3** a telephone communication **4** a short visit o *make calls on the way home* **5** a demand o *There have been calls for him to resign.* **6** the strong appeal of a place or lifestyle **7** a declared choice or decision —**caller** *n* ◇ **be on call** be available to be summoned for work

☐ **call for** *vt* **1** ask for or require **2** stop briefly to collect somebody

☐ **call in** *v* **1** *vt* summon for help or advice **2** *vi* pay a quick visit **3** *vt* request repayment or the return of

☐ **call off** *vt* **1** cancel an event **2** stop an animal from attacking

☐ **call on** *vt* **1** ask somebody to do something **2** pay somebody a brief visit

☐ **call up** *vt* **1** recruit to the armed forces **2** evoke

☐ **call upon** *vt* **1** ask formally **2** make demands on

Callaghan /kálləhən, -han/, **James, Baron Callaghan of Cardiff** (*b.* 1912) British prime minister (1976–79)

Callao /kə yów/ chief port of Peru. Pop. 424,294 (1998).

Maria Callas

Callas /kálləss/, **Maria** (1923–77) US-born operatic soprano

call box *n* UK a telephone box

call centre n a business dealing with customer phone calls

caller /káwlər/ n 1 somebody who telephones or visits 2 an announcer, e.g. of square dance moves 3 Aus a sports commentator

caller ID n a device or service for identifying telephone callers

call girl n a prostitute contacted by telephone

calligraphy /kə líggrəfi/ n 1 the art of beautiful handwriting 2 beautiful handwriting —**calligrapher** n —**calligraphic** /kálli gráffik/ adj

calling /káwling/ n 1 a strong urge to follow a particular career 2 a job or profession

calling card n US, Can a visiting card

callipers /kállipərz/ npl a device with two hinged legs for measuring diameters

callisthenics /kálliss thénniks/ npl physical exercises for improving fitness and muscle tone (+ pl verb) ■ n the performance of callisthenics (+ sing verb) —**callisthenic** adj

callous /kálləss/ adj hardhearted —**callously** adv —**callousness** n

> **SPELLCHECK** Do not confuse the spelling of **callous** and **callus** ('thickened skin'), which sound similar.

calloused /kálləst/ adj having hard thickened skin

callow /kállō/ adj young and inexperienced

call-up n the order to join the armed forces in wartime

callus /kálləss/ n a patch of hard thickened skin ◊ See note at **callous**

calm /kaam/ adj 1 not anxious 2 not windy, stormy, or rough ■ n 1 peace and quiet 2 an absence of wind ■ vt make less anxious or upset —**calmative** adj —**calmly** adv —**calmness** n

calorie /kálləri/ n 1 a unit of energy equal to 4.1855 joules 2 a unit of energy often used to measure the energy-producing potential of food

calorific /kállə riffik/ adj of heat

calumny /kálləmni/ (pl -nies) n (fml) 1 defamation 2 a defamatory statement

Calvary /kálvəri/ hill outside ancient Jerusalem where the Crucifixion of Jesus Christ took place, according to the Bible

calve /kaav/ (**calving, calved**) vti give birth to a calf

calves 1 plural of **calf**[1] 2 plural of **calf**[2]

Calvin /kálvin/, **John** (1509–64) French-born Swiss Protestant theologian and reformer

Calvinism /kálvinizəm/ n John Calvin's religious doctrine of predestination and of salvation through faith —**Calvinist** n, adj

Calvino /kal veenō/, **Italo** (1923–85) Cuban-born Italian novelist

calypso /kə lípsō/ (pl -sos) n 1 a Caribbean song 2 Caribbean dance music

calyx /káyliks, kálliks/ (pl **calyxes** or **calyces** /-li seez/) n the sepals enclosing a flower bud

cam n a machine part that transfers motion

CAM abbr computer-aided manufacturing

camaraderie /kámmə raádəri, -ráddəri/ n friendship and trust among a group of people

camber /kámbər/ n 1 a convex curve across a road surface 2 the slant of a vehicle's wheels —**camber** vti

Cambodia /kam bōdi ə/ country in Southeast Asia. Cap. Phnom Penh. Pop. 12,491,501 (2001). —**Cambodian** n, adj

Cambrian /kámbri ən/ n a period of geological time 545–495 million years ago ■ adj 1 of the Cambrian 2 Welsh

cambric /káymbrik/ n a thin cotton fabric

> **ORIGIN Cambric** is named after the town of Cambrai (*Kamerijk* in Flemish) in N France, where the fabric was originally made.

Cambridge /káym brij/ 1 city in E England. Pop. 116,701 (1996). 2 city in E Massachusetts. Pop. 93,352 (1998).

Cambridgeshire /káym brijshər/ county of E England

camcorder /kám kawrdər/ n a portable video camera and recorder

Camden /kámdən/ borough in N London. Pop. 275,257 (1991).

came past tense of **come**

camel /kámm'l/ n (pl **camels** or **same**) a large desert animal with one or two humps

camel hair, camel's hair n 1 the hair of a camel. Use: clothing, rugs. 2 a fabric containing camel hair. Use: coats.

~~camelia~~ incorrect spelling of **camellia**

camellia /kə meéli ə/ (pl **-lias** or **same**) n an evergreen shrub with rose-shaped flowers

Camelot /kámmə lot/ n the legendary city of King Arthur

Camembert /kámməm bair/ n a soft French cheese with an edible rind

cameo /kámmi ō/ n 1 a stone carved in a raised design against a contrasting background 2 a brief appearance by a famous actor in a film or play

camera /kámmərə/ n 1 a device for taking photographs 2 a device used in producing film, video, or television images

> **ORIGIN** The Latin word *camera* meant 'room', originally 'vaulted room': it travelled through French to become English *chamber*. From the early 18C, a mid-17C invention, a small closed box with an aperture through which light from outside could be focused by a lens to produce images of external objects, came to be known as a *camera obscura*, literally 'dark room', because the box, or the room it was used in, had to be dark for the image to be seen clearly. By the mid-18C this was shortened to **camera**, and when similar devices began to be used for fixing photographic images in the 19C it was natural that they too should be called **cameras**.

~~cameraderie~~ incorrect spelling of **camaraderie**

camera-shy *adj* with a dislike of being photographed or filmed

Cameron /kámmərən/, **Julia Margaret** (1815–79) British photographer

Cameroon[1] /kámmə roón/ country in west-central Africa. Cap. Yaoundé. Pop. 15,803,220 (2001).

Cameroon[2] active volcano in SW Cameroon, highest mountain in West Africa. Height 4,095 m/13,435 ft.

camisole /kámmi sól/ *n* a woman's sleeveless undergarment covering the upper torso

~~camoflage~~ incorrect spelling of **camouflage**

camomile /kámmə míl/, **chamomile** *n* **1** the leaves and flowers of an aromatic plant. Use: medicine, herbal tea. **2** a plant from which camomile is obtained

camouflage /kámmə fláazh, -fláaj/ *n* protective concealment by resembling the surrounding environment ■ *vt* (**-flaging, -flaged**) **1** conceal by camouflage **2** disguise ○ *camouflaged his true intentions*

camp[1] *n* **1** a place with removable accommodation such as tents **2** a place with permanent buildings for a temporary stay ○ *a prison camp* **3** a group of people with the same ideas or aims ■ *vi* stay temporarily in a tent or similar accommodation

camp[2] *adj* **1** exaggeratedly or affectedly feminine, especially in a man **2** deliberately and exaggeratedly brash or vulgar —**camp** *n* —**campy** *adj*

campaign /kam páyn/ *n* **1** an organized series of actions or events to achieve a particular goal ○ *an advertising campaign* ○ *an electoral campaign* **2** a series of military operations ■ *vi* engage in a campaign —**campaigner** *n*

~~campain~~ incorrect spelling of **campaign**

campanile /kámpə neéli/ (*pl* **-les** *or* **-li** /-li/) *n* a bell tower, especially a freestanding one

campanology /kámpə nólləji/ *n* bell-ringing —**campanologist** *n*

camp bed *n* a small temporary bed

Campbell /kámb'l/, **Keith** (*b.* 1954) British microbiologist. With Ian Wilmut he was responsible for the first successful cloning of a mammal from adult cells.

Campbell, Kim (*b.* 1947) first woman prime minister of Canada (1993)

Campbell, Sir Malcolm (1885–1948) British motor-racing driver

Campbell, Roy (1901–57) South African-born British poet, translator, and journalist

Camp David /-dáyvid/ US presidential retreat in Catoctin Mountain Park, central Maryland

camper /kámpər/ *n* **1** somebody who camps **2** a motor vehicle equipped as a travelling home

camp follower *n* **1** somebody unofficially selling products or services, especially prostitution, to the military **2** an uncommitted or temporary supporter of a group

camphor /kámfər/ *n* a strong-smelling chemical compound. Use: in medicinal creams, manufacture of celluloid, plastics, and explosives.

Campinas /kam peénəss/ city in SE Brazil. Pop. 908,906 (1996).

Campion /kámpi ən/, **Thomas** (1567–1620) English poet

Campo Grande /kámpō grándi/ capital of Mato Grosso do Sul State, SW Brazil. Pop. 565,943 (1993).

Campos /kám poss/ city in SE Brazil. Pop. 389,547 (1996).

campsite /kámp sít/ *n* an area for camping, often with facilities such as toilets and showers

campus /kámpəss/ *n* the site of an organization or institution, especially a university, containing its main buildings and grounds

camshaft /kám shaaft/ *n* a shaft with cams attached, especially in an internal combustion engine

AKG London

Albert Camus

Camus /ka moó/, **Albert** (1913–60) Algerian-born French novelist, essayist, and dramatist

can[1] *n* **1** a sealed metal container holding food or drink **2** a metal container for liquids such as oil or paint **3** the contents of a can **4** a pressurized container holding liquid to be sprayed ■ *vt* (**canning, canned**) seal food or drink in a can —**canful** *n*

can[2] *modal v* **1** be able to ○ *Can you swim?* **2** indicates possibility or likelihood ○ *It can be dangerous.* **3** be allowed to ○ *Can I go?* **4** introduces a polite request or offer ○ *Can I make a suggestion?*

USAGE **can** or **may**? Many people draw a distinction between **can**, meaning 'be able to', and **may**, meaning 'be allowed to', but in everyday conversation *Can I go?* is as likely to be used as *May I go?* In more formal situations, it is wise to maintain the distinction.

Can. *abbr* **1** Canada **2** Canadian

Canada /kánnədə/ federation occupying the northern half of North America and the second largest country in the world. Cap. Ottawa. Pop. 31,592,805 (2001). —**Canadian** /kə náydi ən/ *adj, n*

canal /kə nál/ *n* **1** an artificial waterway for ships or boats **2** a tube-shaped passage in the body

canal boat *n* a long boat for canals

Canaletto /kánnə léttō/, **Antonio** (1697–1768) Italian artist

canalize /kánn'l īz/ (**-lizing, -lized**), **canalise** *v* **1** *vt* build canals in **2** *vi* flow into or form a channel

canapé /kánnə pay/ *n* a bite-sized piece of bread or pastry with a savoury topping, served as an appetizer

canard /kánnaard, ka naàrd/ *n* a false report or rumour (*literary*)

canary /kə náiri/ (*pl* **-ies**) *n* a yellow finch often kept in cages

ORIGIN The **canary** is named after the Canary Islands, the native habitat of the green finch from which the modern yellow pet bird developed. The birds were first imported to Britain in numbers in the 16C. The name of the islands themselves derives from the Latin word for 'dog' that gave us *canine*, because one of them was famous for its large dogs in Roman times.

Canary Islands /kə náiri-/, **Canaries** /kə náiriz/ island group in the Atlantic Ocean, off NW Africa, an autonomous region of Spain. Pop. 1,631,498 (1995).

canasta /kə nástə/ *n* a variation of rummy played with two packs of cards

Canaveral, Cape /kə návvərəl/ cape in east-central Florida, the launching site of US crewed space flights

Canberra /kánbərə/ capital of Australia, in Australian Capital Territory, SE Australia. Pop. 308,197 (1998).

cancan /kán kan/ *n* a high-kicking dance performed by women

cancel /kánss'l/ (**-celling, -celled**) *v* **1** *vti* stop something previously arranged from happening **2** *vti* end a contract **3** *vt* reverse an instruction to a machine **4** *vt* mark a postage stamp as used **5** *vt* delete something by crossing it out **6** *vti* remove a common factor or term from both parts of a fraction or equation —**cancellable** *adj* —**cancellation** /kánssə láysh'n/ *n*

□ **cancel out** *vt* neutralize the effect of something equal or opposite

cancelbot /kánss'l bot/ *n* a computer program that cancels unwanted Internet articles

cancer /kánssər/ *n* **1** a malignant tumour **2** an illness caused by a malignant tumour **3** something that is fast-spreading and undesirable or destructive **4** **Cancer** a constellation in the northern hemisphere **5** **Cancer** the 4th sign of the zodiac —**Cancerian** /kan seèri ən, -sáiri ən/ *n*, *adj* —**cancerous** *adj*

ORIGIN **Cancer** is adopted from a Latin word that literally means 'crab'. The ancient Greek physician Galen applied the equivalent Greek term to the disease, because the blood vessels around a cancer suggested a crab. Until the 17C the usual English term was *canker*, which came from Latin *cancer* via northern French. Before that **Cancer** usually referred to the constellation, so called because of its sideways movement across the sky.

Cancún /kan koòn/ island on the NE Yucatán peninsula, SE Mexico. Pop. 311,696 (1995).

candelabrum /kándə laàbrəm/ (*pl* **-bra** /-brə/ or **-brums**) *n* a branched candlestick or light fitting

candid /kándid/ *adj* **1** honest and direct **2** filmed or photographed informally or without the subject's knowledge —**candidly** *adv* —**candidness** *n*

ORIGIN **Candid** comes from the Latin word for 'white', and this was its first English meaning. Later senses 'innocent', 'pure', and 'fair', suggested by associations with whiteness, developed into the modern meaning 'honest and direct'. The Latin root of **candid** is also the source of *candidate*. Candidates for office in ancient Rome wore white togas.

candidate /kándi dayt, -dət/ *n* a seeker of or suitable person for a political office, job, or prize —**candidacy** *n*

SYNONYMS **candidate, contender, contestant, aspirant, applicant, entrant** CORE MEANING: somebody who is seeking to be chosen for something or to win something

candle /kánd'l/ *n* a wax shape, usually cylindrical, with a central wick that can be lit

candlelight /kánd'l līt/ *n* light from candles —**candlelit** *adj*

candlestick /kánd'l stik/ *n* a tall thin holder for a candle

candlewick /kánd'l wik/ *n* tufted cotton fabric. Use: bedspreads, dressing gowns.

candour /kándər/ *n* candidness

candy /kándi/ *n* US, Can a sweet or sweets ■ *vt* (**-dies, -died**) impregnate or coat with sugar

candyfloss /kándi floss/ *n* sugar spun into fine strands, usually onto a stick

candy-striped *adj* with thin coloured stripes on a white background

cane *n* **1** a walking stick **2** a stick for beating somebody as a punishment **3** a woody stem of a plant such as bamboo **4** flexible plant stems used to make baskets or furniture ■ *vt* (**caning, caned**) beat with a cane

Canetti /ka nétti/, **Elias** (1905–94) Bulgarian-born British writer

canine /káy nīn, kánn-/ *adj* of dogs ■ *n* also **canine tooth** a pointed tooth between the incisor and the bicuspid

canister /kánnistər/ *n* **1** a pressurized or sealed container **2** a metal container with a lid for storing dry foods

canker /kángkər/ *n* **1** a disease of trees affecting the trunk and branches **2** a spreading evil influence —**cankerous** *adj*

cannabis /kánnəbiss/ *n* **1** a drug derived from the hemp plant **2** the hemp plant

canned *adj* **1** sealed in a can **2** prerecorded o *canned laughter*

cannelloni /kánnə lóni/ *n* pasta tubes that are stuffed with a filling

cannery /kánnəri/ (*pl* **-ies**) *n* a food-canning factory

Cannes /kan, kanz/ city in SE France. Pop. 67,304 (1999).

cannibal /kánnib'l/ n 1 somebody who eats human flesh 2 an animal that eats its own species —**cannibalism** n

cannibalize /kánnibə līz/ (**-izing**, **-ized**), **cannibalise** vt take parts from something for use elsewhere —**cannibalization** /kánnibə līzáysh'n/ n

cannon /kánnən/ n 1 (pl **cannons** or same) a historical weapon that fired large iron balls 2 a modern heavy artillery weapon ■ vi collide with or bounce off something

SPELLCHECK Do not confuse the spelling of **cannon** and **canon** ('a rule', 'a decree', 'a collection', 'a musical technique', 'one of a cathedral's clergy'), which sound similar.

cannonball /kánnən bawl/ n a ball fired from a cannon in former times

cannot /kánnot, -ət, kə nót/ contr can not

canny /kánni/ (**-nier**, **-niest**) adj shrewd —**cannily** adv —**canniness** n

canoe /kə noó/ n a light narrow boat with pointed ends —**canoe** vi

canon[1] /kánnən/ n 1 a general rule 2 a religious decree 3 a body of religious writings 4 a set of artistic works such as the writings of a particular author 5 a musical technique in which different parts of the same piece are simultaneously sung or played ◊ See note at **cannon**

canon[2] /kánnən/ n a member of the Christian clergy attached to a cathedral

canonical /kə nónnik'l/, **canonic** /kə nónnik/ adj 1 following canon law 2 conforming to general principles —**canonically** adv

canonize /kánnə nīz/ (**-izing**, **-ized**), **canonise** vt 1 declare as a saint 2 glorify —**canonization** /kánnə nīz záysh'n/ n

canon law n Christian religious law

canoodle /kə noód'l/ (**-noodling**, **-noodled**) vti kiss and cuddle (infml)

can opener n a tin-opener

canopy /kánnəpi/ (pl **-pies**) n 1 a covering above something for shelter or decoration 2 the layer formed by the treetops in a forest 3 the part of a parachute that opens

~~canot~~ incorrect spelling of **cannot**

Canova /ka nóvə/, **Antonio, Marquis of Ischia** (1757–1822) Italian sculptor

cant[1] n 1 talk filled with platitudes 2 hypocritical talk 3 jargon —**cant** vi

cant[2] n 1 slope, or a sloping surface 2 a jolt that makes something slope ■ vti put or be at an angle

can't /kaant/ contr cannot

Cantab /kán tab/ adj of Cambridge University (after titles of academic awards)

cantaloupe /kántə loop/, **cantaloup** n a small orange-fleshed melon

cantankerous /kan tángkərəss/ adj bad-tempered —**cantankerously** adv —**cantankerousness** n

cantata /kan taátə/ n a musical work for voices and instruments, usually on a religious theme

canteen /kan teén/ n 1 a place where food is served in a school or workplace 2 a cutlery box 3 a portable drinking flask

~~canteloupe~~ incorrect spelling of **cantaloupe**

canter /kántər/ n a horse's pace between a gallop and a trot —**canter** vi

ORIGIN A **canter** was originally a Canterbury gallop, the pace at which medieval pilgrims rode to the shrine of St Thomas à Becket at Canterbury in SE England.

Canterbury /kántərbəri/ 1 city in SE England. Pop. 136,481 (1996). 2 administrative region of New Zealand, in the east of the South Island. Pop. 478,912 (1996).

cantilever /kánti leevər/ n a projecting load-bearing structure supported at only one end

cantina /kan teénə/ n a bar in a Spanish-speaking country or region

canto /kántō/ (pl **-tos**) n a part of a long poem

canton /kán ton, kan tón/ n a division or subdivision of a country such as Switzerland or France —**cantonal** /kántən'l/ adj

Canton /kan tón/ ♦ **Guangzhou**

Cantonese /kántə neéz/ (pl same) n 1 a Chinese language spoken in Guangdong in S China and widely elsewhere 2 somebody from Guangdong —**Cantonese** adj

cantonment /kan toónmənt/ n 1 a military camp 2 temporary accommodation for troops 3 assignment to temporary quarters

Canute /kə nyoót/ (994?–1035) king of England (1016–35), Denmark (1018–35), and Norway (1028–35)

canvas /kánvəss/ n 1 a strong heavy fabric. Use: sails, tents. 2 a piece of fabric for painting on 3 a vessel's sails 4 the floor of a boxing or wrestling ring

SPELLCHECK Do not confuse the spelling of **canvas** and **canvass** ('solicit orders, opinions, or votes'), which sound similar.

canvass /kánvəss/ v 1 vti visit people or a place to solicit orders, opinions, or votes 2 vt discuss a proposal or issue thoroughly ■ n an opinion poll —**canvasser** n ◊ See note at **canvas**

canyon /kánnyən/, **cañon** n a deep narrow valley

cap n 1 a close-fitting hat 2 a hat awarded to a player selected for a special team 3 a player awarded a cap 4 a cover for the end of something such as a pen or bottle 5 a covering at the top of something 6 the top or upper part of something 7 an upper limit 8 a detonator that explodes when struck 9 an explosive paper disc for a toy gun 10 a covering for a tooth 11 a patch on a bird's head ■ vt (**capping**, **capped**) 1 cover with a cap 2 lie on top of 3 surpass 4 add the finishing touch to 5 impose an upper limit on 6 select for a national sports team —**capful** n ◊ **cap in hand** with a humble attitude

CAP *abbr* 1 Common Agricultural Policy 2 /kap/ computer-aided production

cap. *abbr* capital

capability /káypə bílləti/ (*pl* **-ties**) *n* 1 the ability necessary to do something 2 an ability or characteristic that has potential for development ◊ See note at **ability**

capable /káypəb'l/ *adj* 1 competent or skilled 2 able to do a particular thing ○ *not capable of murder* 3 susceptible to or permitting something ○ *a remark capable of misinterpretation* —**capably** *adv*

capacious /kə páyshəss/ *adj* big enough to contain a large quantity

capacitance /kə pássitənss/ *n* 1 the ability to store an electrical charge 2 a measure of capacitance equal to the surface charge divided by the electrical potential

capacitor /kə pássitər/ *n* an electrical component used to store a charge

capacity /kə pássəti/ (*pl* **-ties**) *n* 1 mental or physical ability 2 the maximum amount that something can contain ○ *was filled to capacity* ○ *a capacity crowd* 3 maximum productivity ○ *The factory is working to capacity.* 4 an official role ○ *in my capacity as team captain* 5 a measure of electrical output 6 the storage space of a computer device ◊ See note at **ability**

cape[1] *n* a long sleeveless outer garment that is shorter than a cloak

cape[2] *n* a large headland

Cape Breton Island /-brétt'n-/ island in NE Nova Scotia, Canada

Cape Dutch *n* 1 an 18C South African style of architecture or furniture 2 the form of Dutch that developed into Afrikaans —**Cape Dutch** *adj*

caper[1] /káypər/ *n* 1 a playful jump 2 a playful act or trick 3 a dangerous or illegal activity (*infml*) ■ *vi* prance happily

caper[2] /káypər/ *n* 1 a small pickled flower bud used for flavouring (*often pl*) 2 a bush that produces capers

Capernaum /kə púrni əm/ city of ancient Palestine, on the northwestern shore of the Sea of Galilee

Cape Town legislative capital of South Africa and capital of **Western Cape Province**. Pop. 2,727,000 (1995).

Cape Verde /-vúrd/ island country in the Atlantic Ocean, west of Senegal. Cap. Praia. Pop. 405,163 (2001).

Cape York Peninsula peninsula in N Queensland, Australia, the most northerly point on the Australian mainland

capillary /kə pílləri/ *n* (*pl* **-ies**) a thin blood vessel ■ *adj* 1 of a phenomenon in which the surface of a liquid rises, falls, or distorts when in contact with a solid ○ *capillary action* 2 of or like blood capillaries

capital[1] /káppit'l/ *n* 1 a city that is a seat of government 2 a centre of a particular activity 3 material wealth 4 cash for investment 5 advantage derived from or useful in a particular situation ○ *making political capital out of the dispute* 6 a letter in its larger form, e.g. A, B, or C (*often pl*) ■ *adj* 1 of or involving the death penalty 2 very serious 3 principal 4 describes a letter in its larger form ○ *a capital D* 5 functioning as a seat of government ○ *a capital city* 6 of financial capital 7 excellent (*dated*)

capital[2] /káppit'l/ *n* the upper part of an architectural column

capital asset *n* a fixed asset of a business

capital expenditure *n* expenditure on fixed assets

capital gain *n* a profit from selling assets (*often pl*)

capital gains tax *n* a tax on the sale of assets

capital goods *npl* goods used in the production of other goods

capital-intensive *adj* having high financial cost relative to labour

capitalism /káppit'lizəm/ *n* an economic system based on private ownership of profit-making companies in a free market

capitalist /káppit'list/ *n* 1 an investor of money in business for profit 2 a supporter of capitalism ■ *adj* of capitalism

capitalize /káppit'l îz/ (**-izing**, **-ized**), **capitalise** *v* 1 *vti* write or key in capital letters or with an initial capital letter 2 *vi* take advantage of something ○ *to capitalize on an opponent's mistake* 3 *vt* use debt or budgeted expenditure as financial capital 4 *vt* finance 5 *vt* treat an expenditure as an asset rather than an expense —**capitalization** /káppit'l ī záysh'n/ *n*

capital punishment *n* the death penalty

capitation /káppi táysh'n/ *n* a fixed tax or payment per person

capitulate /kə píttyoo layt/ (**-lating**, **-lated**) *vi* 1 surrender 2 consent or yield —**capitulation** /kə píttyoo láysh'n/ *n* ◊ See note at **yield**

capon /káypən, -pon/ *n* a male chicken castrated to improve its flesh for eating

Al Capone

Library of Congress

Capone /kə pốn/, **Al** (1899–1947) Italian-born US gangster and racketeer

Capote /kə pốti/, **Truman** (1924–84) US writer

cappuccino /káppoo cheénō/ (*pl* **-nos**) *n* frothy milky coffee

ORIGIN The coffee was so called in Italian because it suggested the colour of the habit of a *Cappuccino*, a member of an order of friars who wore a cloak with a sharp-pointed hood or *cappuccio.*

cappucino incorrect spelling of **cappuccino**

Capri /kə preě, káppri/ island in the Bay of Naples, S Italy. Pop. 7,075 (1996).

caprice /kə preéss/ *n* 1 a whim 2 a sudden change or action 3 an impulsive tendency

capricious /kə príshəss/ *adj* given to sudden changes —**capriciously** *adv* —**capriciousness** *n*

Capricorn /káppri kawrn/ *n* 1 the 10th sign of the zodiac 2 *also* **Capricornus** a zodiacal constellation in the southern hemisphere

capri pants /kə preé-/, **Capri pants** *npl* women's trousers ending just below the knee

capsicum /kápsikəm/ *n* 1 a hot red pepper fruit 2 a plant that produces capsicums

capsize /kap síz/ (**-sizing, -sized**) *vti* overturn in water *(refers to boats)*

caps lock *n* a computer key that capitalizes all letters subsequently typed

capstan /kápstən/ *n* 1 a vertical rotating cylinder. Use: moving heavy weights, hauling in ropes. 2 a rotating shaft in a tape recorder

capsule /káp syool/ *n* 1 a small soluble container of medicine to be swallowed like a pill 2 a seed case 3 a membrane or sac enclosing an organ or body part 4 a vehicle or cabin for space travel 5 a seal on a container 6 a short summary ■ *adj* 1 very brief 2 compact ■ *vt* (**-suled, -suling**) summarize —**capsular** *adj*

capsule hotel *n* in Japan, a hotel in which the rooms are lockable cubicles

Capt. *abbr* Captain

captain /káptin/ *n* 1 somebody in command of a ship or aircraft 2 a naval officer of a rank above commander 3 *also* **Captain** an officer in the British Army or Royal Marines of a rank above lieutenant 4 a team leader 5 an important or influential person o *captains of industry* ■ *vt* be the captain of —**captaincy** *n*

caption /kápsh'n/ *n* 1 a description of an illustration 2 a film or television subtitle 3 a heading or subheading —**caption** *vt*

captious /kápshəss/ *adj* 1 excessively critical 2 intended to confuse or entrap an opponent in an argument

captivate /kápti vayt/ (**-vating, -vated**) *vt* enchant with pleasing or irresistible features —**captivating** *adj* —**captivation** /kápti váysh'n/ *n*

captive /káptiv/ *n* 1 a prisoner 2 somebody dominated by an emotion ■ *adj* 1 unable to escape 2 forced to buy, accept, or pay attention to something o *a captive audience* 3 irresistibly attracted —**captivity** /kap tívvəti/ *n*

captor /káptər/ *n* somebody who holds another person prisoner

capture /kápchər/ *vt* (**-turing, -tured**) 1 take a person or animal into captivity 2 seize or take control of something 3 dominate somebody's mind o *captured her imagination* 4 represent something accurately o *a picture*

capturing the innocence of childhood 5 record and store data on a computer ■ *n* 1 an act of capturing or being captured 2 somebody or something captured 3 the recording of data on a computer

capuccino incorrect spelling of **cappuccino**

capybara /káppi baáarə/ (*pl* **-ras** *or same*) *n* a large rodent of Central and South America

car *n* 1 a small passenger-carrying road vehicle 2 a railway vehicle for passengers 3 a compartment for passengers or cargo, e.g. in an airship

car. *abbr* carat

Caracas /kə rákəss/ capital of Venezuela. Pop. 1,964,846 (1992).

carafe /kə ráf, kə raáf/ *n* a container like a bottle with a flared open top for serving cold drinks such as wine or water

caramel /kárrə mel, -m'l/ *n* 1 melted or dissolved sugar heated until it turns brown 2 a chewy sweet

caramelize /kárrəmə líz/ (**-izing, -ized**), **caramelise** *vti* change into caramel —**caramelization** /kárrəmə lí záysh'n/ *n*

carapace /kárrə payss/ *n* an animal shell such as that on a turtle's back

carat /kárrət/ *n* 1 a unit of mass used for gems 2 a unit expressing the proportion of gold in an alloy

SPELLCHECK Do not confuse the spelling of **carat** and **carrot** (the vegetable), which sound similar.

Caravaggio /kárrə vájji ō/, **Michelangelo Merisi da** (1573–1610) Italian painter

caravan /kárrə van/ *n* 1 a vehicle for living in that is moved by towing 2 a group of desert merchants with camels 3 a group of travellers ■ *vi* (**-vanning, -vanned**) holiday or travel in a caravan —**caravanner** *n*

caravanserai /kárrə vánssə rī/, **caravansary** *n* 1 a large inn, especially for desert travellers 2 a group of travellers

caraway /kárrə way/ *n* 1 *also* **caraway seed** the dried seeds of a flowering plant, used as a spice 2 the plant that produces caraway

carbine /kaár bīn/ *n* a short lightweight rifle

carbohydrate /kaárbō hī drayt/ *n* 1 a naturally occurring compound that is an important source of energy in food 2 a food containing carbohydrates

carbolic acid /kaar bóllik-/ *n* CHEM = **phenol**

car bomb *n* a bomb concealed in or under a car —**car-bomb** *vt*

carbon /kaárbən/ *n* (*symbol* **C**) a nonmetallic chemical element that forms large numbers of organic compound —**carbonous** *adj*

carbon 14 *n* a naturally radioactive carbon isotope. Use: in carbon dating.

carbonate /kaárbə nayt/ (**-ating, -ated**) *vt* add carbon dioxide to a liquid

carbon copy *n* 1 a duplicate made with waxy paper 2 somebody or something identical to somebody or something else *(infml)*

carbon dating *n* a method of dating organic remains based on their content of carbon 14

carbon dioxide *n* a colourless odourless atmospheric gas. Use: in refrigeration, carbonated drinks, fire extinguishers.

carbon fibre *n* a strong synthetic fibre. Use: reinforcing resins, metals, and ceramics, making turbine blades.

Carboniferous /kaˈərbə níffərəss/ *n* a period of geological time 354–290 million years ago —**Carboniferous** *adj*

carbonize /kaˈərbə nīz/ (**-izing, -ized**), **carbonise** *v* **1** *vti* turn into carbon **2** *vt* cover or coat with carbon —**carbonization** /kaˈərbən ī záysh'n/ *n*

carbon monoxide *n* a colourless odourless toxic gas released when carbon-based fuels are burnt

car boot sale *n* an open-air sale of goods from the boots of people's cars

carbuncle /kaˈär bungk'l/ *n* **1** an inflamed swelling **2** a red gemstone

carburetor *n* US = **carburettor**

carburettor /kaˈär byoō réttər, kaˈärbə réttər/ *n* a device in an internal combustion engine that mixes the air and fuel

carcass /kaˈärkəss/, **carcase** *n* **1** the dead body of an animal **2** all that is left of something decayed or destroyed

carcinogen /kaar sínnəjən, kaˈärssinə jen/ *n* a cancer-causing substance or agent —**carcinogenic** /kaˈärssinō jénnik/ *adj*

carcinoma /kaˈärssi nōmə/ *n* a malignant tumour —**carcinomatous** *adj*

card[1] *n* **1** a folded piece of stiff paper, used to send greetings **2** a small piece of stiff paper printed with symbols or figures, used as part of a set for playing games **3** a piece of stiff paper, cardboard, or plastic showing something such as somebody's identity, business affiliation, or membership of a club **4** a small piece of plastic used for buying goods on credit or getting cash **5** a postcard **6** an amusing person *(dated infml)* **7** a piece of coloured stiff paper shown to a footballer who has violated a rule ◊ **a card up your sleeve** a secret plan ready to be used if necessary *(infml)* ◊ **on the cards** likely to happen *(infml)* ◊ **play your cards close to your chest** be secretive *(infml)* ◊ **put** *or* **lay your cards on the table** openly reveal your plans *(infml)*

card[2] *vt* comb and clean wool, cotton, or other fibres ■ *n* a tool or machine for carding fibre —**carder** *n*

cardamom /kaˈärdəməm/, **cardamon** /-mən/ *n* **1** the aromatic seeds and pods of a tropical plant, used as a spice **2** the plant that produces cardamom

cardboard /kaˈärd bawrd/ *n* lightweight paper board ■ *adj* two-dimensional or lacking in depth ○ *a cardboard portrayal of the hero*

card-carrying *adj* **1** officially listed as a member of an organization **2** deeply committed to a cause *(infml)*

cardholder /kaˈärd hōldər/ *n* an owner of a credit, debit, or other card

cardiac /kaˈärdi ak/ *adj* of the heart

cardiac arrest *n* the sudden stopping of the heartbeat

Cardiff /kaˈärdif/ capital and largest city of Wales. Pop. 315,040 (1996). Welsh **Caerdydd**

cardigan /kaˈärdigən/ *n* a long-sleeved knitted jacket that fastens at the front

---

ORIGIN The **cardigan** is named after James Thomas Brudenell, 7th earl of Cardigan (1797–1868), who was one of the first to wear it.

---

cardinal /kaˈärdinəl, -d'nəl/ *n* **1** a high-ranking member of the Roman Catholic clergy who is one of those from whom the next pope is elected **2** a deep red colour **3** *also* **cardinal number** a number denoting a quantity, not an order, e.g. 2 or 8 ■ *adj* **1** fundamentally important **2** bright red in colour

cardinal point *n* any of the four principal points of the compass

cardinal virtue *n* a traditionally important virtue

card index *n* an alphabetical listing on separate cards

cardio- *prefix* heart ○ *cardiovascular*

cardiology /kaˈärdi óllҙji/ *n* the branch of medicine dealing with disorders of the heart —**cardiological** /kaˈärdi ə lójjik'l/ *adj* —**cardiologist** *n*

cardiopulmonary /kaˈärdi ō púlmənəri, -pōōl-/ *adj* of the heart and lungs

cardiovascular /kaˈärdi ō váskyōōlər/ *adj* of the heart and blood vessels

Cardoso /kaar dōssō/, **Fernando Henrique** (*b.* 1931) president of Brazil (1995–)

cards *n* a game using a set of cards (+ *sing verb*)

cardsharp /kaˈärd shaarp/, **cardsharper** /-shaarpər/ *n* somebody who cheats regularly at cards

card table *n* a lightweight table for playing cards on

care *v* (**caring, cared**) **1** *vti* be interested in or concerned about something ○ *I don't care whether you come or not.* **2** *vi* feel affection **3** *vi* look after somebody or something ■ *n* **1** the keeping of something in good condition ○ *skin care* **2** careful attention to avoid damage or error **3** a worry **4** attention to somebody's wellbeing **5** a local authority's custody and maintenance of a child ◊ See note at **worry**

careen /kə reˈen/ *v* **1** *vi* move forwards at high speed, swaying or swerving **2** *vt* turn a boat on its side for cleaning or repair

career /kə reˈer/ *n* **1** a long-term or lifelong job **2** somebody's progress in their chosen profession **3** the general progress of something ■ *adj* expecting to work in a profession for life ■ *vi* lurch rapidly onwards

careers officer *n* an adviser on school pupils' careers

carefree /káir free/ *adj* without worries or responsibilities —**carefreeness** *n*

careful /káirf'l/ *adj* 1 acting with caution 2 showing close attention to detail 3 not overspending or being wasteful 4 watchful —**carefully** *adv* —**carefulness** *n*

SYNONYMS careful, conscientious, scrupulous, thorough, meticulous, painstaking, assiduous, punctilious, finicky, fussy CORE MEANING: exercising care and attention in doing something

~~carefull~~ incorrect spelling of **careful**

~~careing~~ incorrect spelling of **caring**

care in the community *n* a policy of integrating patients with disabilities into the local community

careless /káirləss/ *adj* 1 not attentive enough to details 2 showing no concern or consideration 3 done or displayed naturally and without effort o *a careless charm* —**carelessly** *adv* —**carelessness** *n*

carer /káirər/ *n* somebody who cares for a child or dependent adult full-time

caress /kə réss/ *vt* 1 touch or stroke affectionately 2 touch or affect in a soothing way ■ *n* a gentle touch

caretaker /káir taykər/ *n* 1 somebody who looks after a building and its contents 2 a temporary holder of an office or position

caretaker government *n* a government established temporarily until the next election

careworn /káir wawrn/ *adj* exhausted from worry

Carey /káiri/, **George** (*b*. 1935) British cleric and archbishop of Canterbury (1991–2002)

Carey, Peter Philip (*b*. 1943) Australian writer

cargo /káargō/ (*pl* -**goes**) *n* 1 goods carried as freight 2 a load

~~cariage~~ incorrect spelling of **carriage**

Caribbean /kárri bee ən/ region of island groups from the southeastern tip of Florida to the coast of Venezuela, separating the Caribbean Sea from the Atlantic Ocean —**Caribbean** *adj*, *n*

Caribbean Sea arm of the Atlantic Ocean, surrounded by the Greater and Lesser Antilles, N South America, and E Central America. Depth (Cayman Trench) 7,535 m/24,720 ft.

caribou /kárri boo/ (*pl* -**bous** or **same**) *n* a large deer with branched antlers

caricature /kárrika choor/ *n* 1 a drawing, description, or performance that exaggerates characteristics for comic effect 2 a ridiculously inappropriate or poor version of something —**caricature** *vt* —**caricaturist** *n*

caries /káir eez, kaíri eez/ *n* tooth decay —**carious** *adj*

carillon /kə rílyən, kárrillyən/ *n* 1 a set of stationary bells hung in a tower and played from a keyboard 2 a tune played on a carillon —**carillon** *vi*

caring /káiring/ *adj* 1 showing concern 2 of a profession such as nursing that involves looking after people ■ *n* the provision of medical or other care —**caringly** *adv*

carjacking /kaár jaking/ *n* the hijacking of a car —**carjack** *vti* —**carjacker** *n*

Carlow /kaárlō/ county in SE Republic of Ireland

Carl XVI Gustaf /kaárl gŏŏst af/ (*b*. 1946) king of Sweden (1973–)

Carlyle /kaar líl/, **Thomas** (1795–1881) Scottish historian and essayist

Carmarthenshire /kər maárth'nshər/ county in S Wales. Pop. 169,500 (1995).

carmine /kaár mīn, -min/ *n* 1 a deep purplish-red colour 2 a bright red pigment made from cochineal —**carmine** *adj*

carnage /kaárnij/ *n* 1 the widespread slaughter of people 2 serious injury to a great many people, e.g. in a major accident

carnal /kaárn'l/ *adj* 1 of physical needs, not spiritual needs (*fml*) 2 sensual or sexual —**carnality** /kaar nálləti/ *n* —**carnally** *adv*

carnation /kaar náysh'n/ *n* a perennial plant of the pink family, with white, pink, or red clove-scented flowers

carnauba /kaar nówbə, -náwbə/ *n* wax from a palm tree. Use: polish, candles.

Carnegie /kaar néggi, -náygi, -neégi, kaárnəgi/, **Andrew** (1835–1919) Scottish-born US industrialist and philanthropist

carnet /kaár nay/ *n* 1 a book of tickets for use on public transport 2 a customs document for a car

carnival /kaárniv'l/ *n* 1 a large public festival 2 *US, Can* a fair with amusements 3 the period before Lent celebrated with a carnival in many countries

ORIGIN Carnival comes from Italian, and is based on Latin words meaning 'meat, flesh' and 'raise, lift'. It refers to the Christian practice of giving up meat-eating for Lent, the 40 days before Easter. The **carnival** was originally a period of feasting and merry-making before the self-denial and abstinence of Lent.

carnivore /kaárni vawr/ *n* 1 a flesh-eating animal 2 a carnivorous plant

carnivorous /kaar nívvərəss/ *adj* 1 meat-eating 2 describes a plant that can digest insects and small invertebrates

carob /kárrəb/ (*pl* -**obs** or **same**) *n* 1 an edible powder with a taste like chocolate, made from pods 2 the evergreen Mediterranean tree that produces the pods from which carob is made

carol /kárrəl/ *n* a joyful song, especially one sung by Christians celebrating Christmas ■ *vi* (-**olling**, -**olled**) sing Christmas songs

Caroline Islands /kárrə līn-, -lin-/ archipelago in the W Pacific Ocean, east of the Philippines, comprising the Federated States of Micronesia and the Republic of Palau

Caroline of Brunswick /kárrə līn əv brúnzwik/

(1768–1821) German-born British titular queen consort of George IV

carouse /kə rówz/ (**-rousing**, **-roused**) vi drink alcohol and become noisy (literary) **—carouser** n

carousel /kárrə sél, -zél/ n 1 a circular conveyor belt for luggage at an airport 2 US, Can a merry-go-round at an amusement park or fairground 3 a rotating holder that loads photographic slides into a projector

carp[1] vi keep complaining or finding fault ◊ See note at **complain**

carp[2] (pl same or **carps**) n 1 a large freshwater fish with a single fin on its back 2 any fish of the family that includes carp, goldfish, and koi

car park n an enclosure or building where cars can be left temporarily

Carpathian Mountains /kaar páythi ən-/ mountain system in E Europe between Slovakia and Poland, extending southwards into E Romania. Highest peak Gerlachovka 2,655 m/8,711 ft.

carpel /ka̱arp'l/ n a female reproductive organ in a flower

Carpentaria, Gulf of /ka̱arpən táiri ə/ large gulf on the coast of N Australia

carpenter /ka̱arpintər/ n a builder and repairer of wooden structures or objects

carpentry /ka̱arpəntri/ n 1 the work or occupation of a carpenter 2 structures or objects produced by a carpenter

carpet /ka̱arpit/ n 1 thick heavy fabric for covering a floor 2 a piece of carpet ■ vt 1 cover a floor with a carpet 2 reprimand somebody severely (infml)

carpetbagger /ka̱arpit bagər/ n 1 after the American Civil War, a Northerner who moved to the South seeking political or commercial advantage 2 an outsider who only comes to a place to win a political seat

carpet-bomb vt destroy an area with intensive aerial bombing

carpeting /ka̱arpiting/ n 1 thick heavy fabric used for carpets 2 carpets collectively

carpet sweeper n a hand-operated carpet-cleaning device

car phone n a mobile phone for a car

car pool n a group of people who use their own cars in turn to transport the group

car-pool vi share driving responsibilities with other people in a group

carport /ka̱ar pawrt/ n an open-sided shelter for a car, attached to a building

carpus /ka̱arpəss/ (pl **-pi** /-pī/) n any of the eight bones in the wrist joint **—carpal** adj

carrageenan /kárrə geenən, kárrə geenən/, **carrageenin** n a complex carbohydrate obtained from seaweed. Use: commercial preparation of food and drink.

~~carraige~~ incorrect spelling of **carriage**

~~carreer~~ incorrect spelling of **career**

carrel /kárrəl/, **carrell** n a cubicle or small room for individual study

Carreras /kə ráirəss/, **José** (b. 1946) Spanish operatic tenor

~~carress~~ incorrect spelling of **caress**

carriage /kárrij/ n 1 a large four-wheeled horse-drawn vehicle 2 a railway coach 3 a wheeled platform for carrying or supporting something 4 somebody's posture while walking (fml) 5 the transporting and delivering of goods 6 a charge for transporting and delivering goods 7 a moving part of a machine, especially the sliding cylinder on a typewriter

carriage clock n a clock with a handle on top, originally used as a travel clock

carriageway /kárrij way/ n one side of a large road that is divided down the middle

~~Carribean~~ incorrect spelling of **Caribbean**

carrier /kárri ər/ n 1 a person or organization that transports people or goods 2 a person or organism infected with a disease or carrying a particular gene and able to spread it without showing symptoms of being affected by it 3 something that carries or moves something 4 an aircraft carrier 5 also **carrier bag** a large paper or plastic bag with handles, for carrying shopping

carrier pigeon n a domestic pigeon trained to deliver messages and then return home

carrion /kárri ən/ n 1 the rotting flesh of a dead animal 2 something decaying or disgusting (literary)

Carroll /kárrəl/, **Lewis** (1832–98) British writer

carrot /kárrət/ n 1 a thin tapering orange root used as a vegetable 2 the biennial plant that produces carrots 3 something offered as an inducement or incentive ◊ See note at **carat**

carrot-and-stick adj combining reward and punishment

carroty /kárrəti/ adj describes hair that is a reddish colour

carry /kárri/ v (**-ries**, **-ried**) 1 vt hold, move, and take somebody or something along or to another place 2 vt be a channel or route o pipelines carrying oil 3 vt have a transmissible disease 4 vt have something with you, e.g. in a pocket 5 vt publish or broadcast something 6 vt have something as a factor, consequence, or penalty 7 vti be pregnant with a child 8 vt develop an idea o carry an argument to its conclusion 9 vt move or behave in a particular way 10 vt stock something as merchandise 11 vi be heard at a distance 12 vti accept a proposal by voting for it, or be so accepted 13 vt transfer an item to the next column in a calculation ■ n (pl **-ries**) in American football, a sprint with the ball

☐ **carry forward** vt transfer an item to the next column in an account or calculation

☐ **carry off** vt do successfully or well

☐ **carry on** 1 vti continue doing something o She carried on after we left. 2 vt be involved in 3 vi behave foolishly or improperly (infml) 4 vi be sexually involved with somebody (infml disapproving)

☐ **carry out** vt 1 perform or accomplish an idea o carry out research 2 do what is ordered, planned, or instructed ◊ See note at **accomplish, perform**

□ **carry over** v 1 vt transfer an item to the next column in an account or calculation 2 vt defer something to the next tax year 3 vi continue to produce an effect in changed circumstances

□ **carry through** vt 1 do what was planned 2 help somebody survive a difficult experience

carrycot /kárri kot/ n a lightweight portable bed for a baby

carrying charge n 1 a delivery or storage charge 2 the cost to a business of holding assets that produce no income

carryon /kárri on/ n an airline passenger's hand luggage —**carryon** adj

carry-on n an incident involving annoying or foolish behaviour (infml)

carryout /kárri owt/ n 1 US, Scotland an item or batch of takeaway food 2 Scotland a place that sells takeaway food

carryover /kárri övər/ n 1 something deferred or continued with at a later time 2 an item transferred to the next column in an account or calculation

carsick /káar sik/ adj feeling sick because of the motion of a vehicle —**carsickness** n

UPI/Corbis-Bettmann

Rachel Carson

Carson /káarss'n/, **Rachel** (1907–64) US ecologist

Carson City capital of Nevada. Pop. 49,301 (1998).

cart n 1 an open horse-drawn vehicle for carrying goods 2 a lightweight horse-drawn carriage with two wheels 3 a light vehicle or barrow pushed by hand 4 US, Can a trolley for shopping or baggage 5 US a food or drinks trolley ■ vt 1 carry roughly or with difficulty (infml) 2 transport from one location to another

Cartagena /kaàrtə jeènə/ 1 port in NW Colombia. Pop. 877,000 (1999). 2 city and port in SE Spain. Pop. 175,628 (1998 estimate).

carte blanche /kaàrt blaànsh/ n complete freedom to act

cartel /kaar tél/ n 1 a group of businesses that unfairly or illegally fix prices to control a market 2 an alliance of like-minded political groups

Carter /kaàrtər/, **Angela** (1940–92) British writer

Carter, Howard (1873–1939) British archaeologist and draughtsman

Carter, Jimmy (b. 1924) 39th president of the United States (1977–81)

Carthage /kaàrthij/ ancient city on the coast of N Africa, near present-day Tunis —**Carthaginian** /kaàrthə jínni ən/ n, adj

carthorse /kaàrt hawrss/ n a large strong horse used for heavy farm work

Cartier /kaàrti ay/, **Jacques** (1491–1557) French navigator

Cartier-Bresson /kaàrti ay bréss oN/, **Henri** (b. 1908) French photographer

cartilage /kaàrtəlij, kaàrt'lij/ n strong elastic tissue around the joints in the body

cartography /kaar tógrəfi/ n the science or activity of making maps —**cartographer** n

carton /kaàrt'n/ n 1 a cardboard box 2 a plastic or card container for food or drinks 3 the contents of a food or drink carton

cartoon /kaar toòn/ n 1 an animated film, especially a humorous film for children 2 a comic strip 3 a humorous or satirical drawing published in a newspaper or magazine 4 a preliminary drawing of a work of art —**cartoonist** n

cartridge /kaàrtrij/ n 1 a cylindrical case holding a bullet or shot and an explosive charge 2 a container of liquid or powder used in a device such as a computer printer 3 a sealed plastic case containing film or tape

cartridge paper n thick, good-quality drawing paper with a grained surface

cartwheel /kaàrt weel/ n 1 a wooden wheel of a cart 2 an acrobatic movement in which the body is turned sideways onto the hands and then onto the feet again ■ vi do a cartwheel

Cartwright /kaàrt rīt/, **Edmund** (1743–1823) British inventor and clergyman

Caruso /kə roòssō/, **Enrico** (1873–1921) Italian operatic tenor

carve (**carving, carved**) vti cut cooked meat into slices

□ **carve out** vt make or achieve through hard work

□ **carve up** vt divide among several people (infml)

carver /kaàrvər/ n a knife for slicing cooked meats

carvery /kaàrvəri/ (pl **-ies**) n a restaurant or buffet where meat is carved to order

carving /kaàrving/ n 1 an object or design made by cutting wood 2 an act of carving

carving knife n a large knife for slicing cooked meat

car wash n a place for washing vehicles automatically with revolving brushes and jets of water

caryatid /kárri áttid/ (pl **-ids** or **-ides** /-átti deez/) n in classical architecture, a column in the shape of a female figure

Casablanca /kássə blángkə, kázzə-/ largest city in Morocco, on the Atlantic coast. Pop. 2,940,623 (1994).

Casals /kə sálz/, **Pablo** (1876–1973) Spanish cellist and composer

Casanova /kássə nóvə/ *n* a promiscuous seducer of women

Casanova /kássə nóvə/, **Giovanni Jacopo, Chevalier de Seingalt** (1725–98) Italian adventurer and author

cascade /ka skáyd/ *n* **1** a small waterfall or series of waterfalls **2** a downward flow of something **3** a succession of things, each affecting the next ■ *v* (**-cading, -caded**) **1** *vti* flow, or make something flow, fast and in large amounts **2** *vi* hang or lie in a flowing mass *(literary)* **3** *vt* arrange the windows on a computer screen so that they overlap, with the title bar of each visible

cascading menu *n* a menu in a computer program that opens when you select an option from an earlier menu

case¹ *n* **1** a situation or set of circumstances ○ *a case of mistaken identity* **2** an instance of something **3** a subject of investigation or scrutiny **4** a matter or issue in question **5** something examined in a law court **6** an argument for or against something ○ *make a good case for selling the business* **7** a grammatical form of a word that indicates its relationship to other words in a sentence **8** a particular kind of person *(infml)* ○ *a hopeless case* ■ *vt* (**casing, cased**) inspect a place, especially with a view to robbing it *(slang)* ◊ **in any case** taking into account everything said or done before

case² *n* **1** a holder, container, or outer covering **2** a container and its contents ○ *a case of wine* **3** a piece of luggage, especially a suitcase **4** the function of a printed character as either a capital or small letter ■ *vt* (**casing, cased**) put a covering round

casebook /káyss bŏok/ *n* a record of legal or medical cases

case history *n* a record of somebody's treatment kept by a doctor or social worker

caseload /káyss lōd/ *n* the number of cases being handled at a particular time

casement /káyssmənt/ *n* a hinged window

case study *n* an analysis of a particular situation used for drawing conclusions in similar situations

casework /káyss wurk/ *n* the system of assigning clients to social workers —**caseworker** *n*

cash /kash/ *n* **1** coins and banknotes **2** money in any form *(infml)* ○ *earn some cash* ■ *vt* exchange a cheque for ready money —**cashable** *adj* ◊ See note at **cache**

□ **cash in** *v* **1** *vt* convert something such as an insurance policy into cash **2** *vi* make a lot of money *(slang)*

□ **cash up** *vi* add up the day's takings in a business

cash and carry *n* (*pl* **cash and carries**) **1** an inexpensive wholesale store **2** the policy of selling goods without a delivery service ■ *adj* cash-only and without delivery

cashbook /kásh bŏok/ *n* a record of money spent and received

cash card *n* a plastic card for accessing a bank account

cash cow *n* a source of steady profit *(slang)*

cash crop *n* a crop grown to sell

cash desk *n* a counter where purchases are paid for

cash dispenser *n* a cash machine

cashew /káshoo, ka shoo/ *n* **1** *also* **cashew nut** a kidney-shaped edible nut **2** the tropical tree that produces cashews

cash flow *n* **1** the movement of money received and spent and its influence on the amount of money available **2** an assessment of a company's income and expenditure

cashier¹ /ka sheer/ *n* **1** a bank worker who deals with customers' routine transactions **2** somebody responsible for an organization's financial transactions ■ *vi* work as a cashier

cashier² /ka sheer/ *vt* dismiss from the armed forces for misconduct

cashier's cheque *n* a cleared cheque issued by a bank

cashless /káshləss/ *adj* using an electronic method of payment

cash machine *n* a machine for accessing a bank account by means of a plastic card

cashmere /kásh meer/ *n* **1** a soft luxurious wool fabric **2** a Himalayan goat from whose coat cashmere is made

cash on delivery *adv* requiring payment on delivery of goods

cashpoint /kásh poynt/ *n UK* a cash machine

cash register *n* a machine in a shop for recording sales and holding takings

casing /káyssing/ *n* an outer covering or frame

casino /kə seénō/ (*pl* **-nos**) *n* **1** a gambling establishment **2** a point-scoring card game in which the player's hand and an exposed hand can be combined

cask *n* **1** a barrel, especially one containing alcohol **2** the contents of a barrel

casket /ka'askit/ *n* **1** a decorative box for valuables **2** *US, Can* a coffin

Caspian Sea /káspi ən-/ world's largest inland body of water, between SE Europe and Asia

Cassandra /kə sándrə/ *n* somebody whose warnings of impending disaster are ignored

ORIGIN The original **Cassandra** in Greek mythology was the daughter of Priam, king of Troy.

Cassatt /kə sát/, **Mary** (1845–1926) US artist

cassava /kə saavə/ *n* **1** an edible tuber of a tropical plant. Use: as a vegetable, source of tapioca. **2** the plant that produces cassava tubers

casserole /kássərōl/ *n* **1** a heavy cooking pot for use in an oven **2** a dish of food cooked in liquid in a heavy pot in an oven

cassette /kə sét/ *n* a sealed plastic case containing tape or film

cassette deck *n* a tape deck that plays or records audio cassettes

cassette player *n* a machine that plays but does not record audio cassettes

cassette recorder *n* a machine that plays and records audio cassettes

Cassius /kássi əss/ (*fl* 53–42 BC) Roman general and conspirator

cassock /kássək/ *n* a priest's full-length robe

Casson /káss'n/, **Sir Hugh** (1910–99) British architect

cast *v* (**cast**) **1** *vt* throw or fling **2** *vt* register or deposit a vote **3** *vt* cause the appearance of ○ *cast a shadow* **4** *vt* introduce a negative effect ○ *cast doubt on his capability* **5** *vt* direct a look at **6** *vti* select for a performance or role **7** *vt* form using a mould **8** *vt* shed ○ *a snake that had cast its skin* ■ *n* **1** a throw, or the process of throwing **2** the performers in a production (*+ sing or pl verb*) **3** a mould for an object or the object moulded **4** a plaster cast **5** the nature of somebody's appearance ○ *a sly cast to his face* **6** a tinge of colour **7** skin or horns shed by an animal ◊ See note at **throw**

☐ **cast off** *vti* **1** untie mooring lines **2** finish knitting

☐ **cast on** *vti* begin knitting

☐ **cast out** *vt* eject, reject, or abandon (*fml*)

castanet /kástə nét/ *n* a rhythm instrument consisting of two small concave pieces of hard material clicked together by the fingers

castaway /káastə way/ *n* a survivor of a shipwreck —**castaway** *adj*

caste /kaast/ *n* **1** a Hindu hereditary social class **2** a group of people identified according to their rank, wealth, descent, or profession

castellated /kástə laytid/ *adj* with battlements or a serrated top edge

caster *n* FURNITURE, HOUSEHOLD = **castor**[1]

caster sugar /káastər-/ *n* fine white sugar used in baking

castigate /kásti gayt/ (*-gating, -gated*) *vt* criticize or punish (*fml*) —**castigation** /kásti gáysh'n/ *n* ◊ See note at **criticize**

Castile /ka stéel/ central region of Spain

casting /káasting/ *n* **1** the making of objects using moulds **2** an object made with a mould

casting vote *n* a deciding vote to break a tie

cast iron *n* hard brittle iron that is shaped in a mould

cast-iron *adj* **1** made of cast iron **2** very strong

castle /káass'l/ *n* **1** a large fortified building with tall solid walls, built during the Middle Ages **2** a large country house built to resemble a castle **3** in chess, a rook

Castlereagh /káass'l ray/, **Robert Stewart, 2nd Marquis of Londonderry** (1769–1822) Irish-born British politician and diplomat

castoff /káast of/ *n* something or somebody rejected as no longer useful (*often pl*)

castor[1] /káastər/, **caster** *n* **1** a small wheel under furniture that allows it to be moved easily **2** a small container with a perforated top for sprinkling sugar or salt

castor[2] /káastər/ *n* an aromatic oil secreted by beavers. Use: in medicine, perfumes.

Castor /káastər/ *n* a bright star in the constellation Gemini

castor oil *n* yellowish oil extracted from the seeds of a tropical plant. Use: laxative, lubricant.

castrate /ka stráyt/ (*-trating, -trated*) *vt* **1** remove the testicles of **2** take away the strength or power of —**castration** /ka stráysh'n/ *n*

Castries /ka stréess/ capital of St Lucia. Pop. 60,934 (1998).

Popperfoto

Fidel Castro

Castro /kástrō/, **Fidel** (*b.* 1927) Cuban prime minister (1959–76) and president (1976–)

casual /kázhyoo əl/ *adj* **1** done by chance or without a plan **2** of or taking on seasonal or temporary work **3** known only slightly ○ *a casual acquaintance* **4** not serious, rigorous, or emotionally committed **5** calm or nonchalant **6** informal or suitable for informal occasions ■ **casuals** *npl* informal clothes or footwear —**casually** *adv* —**casualness** *n*

casualty /kázhyoo əlti/ (*pl* **-ties**) *n* **1** a victim, especially of an accident or military action **2** a hospital's emergency department

casuist /kázzyoo ist/ *n* **1** somebody who deals with moral and ethical questions **2** somebody using misleadingly subtle reasoning (*disapproving*) —**casuistic** /kázzyoo ístik/ *adj* —**casuistry** *n*

casus belli /káassōōss béll ee/ (*pl same*) *n* a situation or event that leads to war (*fml*)

cat *n* **1** a small furry domestic animal that purrs and miaows **2** a large wild animal related to the domestic cat, e.g. a lion or tiger ◊ **let the cat out of the bag** disclose a secret or confidential information ◊ **put** *or* **set the cat among the pigeons** cause trouble

CAT *abbr* computerized axial tomography

cataclysm /káttəklizəm/ *n* **1** a disaster causing great changes in society **2** a devastating flood —**cataclysmic** *adj* —**cataclysmically** *adv*

catacomb /káttə koom, -kōm/ *n* an underground cemetery consisting of passages with burial chambers leading off them (*often pl*)

catafalque /káttə falk/ *n* a decorated platform on which a coffin rests in a public place

catagory incorrect spelling of **category**

Catalan /káttə lan/ *n* **1** a Romance language spoken in Catalonia, the Balearic Islands, and parts of S France **2** somebody from Catalonia —**Catalan** *adj*

catalepsy /káttə lepsi/ *n* a state of uncon-

…sciousness resembling a trance —**cataleptic** /káttə léptik/ adj

catalog n, v US = **catalogue**

catalogue /káttə log/ n 1 a list of items for sale or on exhibition 2 a list of the holdings in a library 3 a list of related things or events ○ a catalogue of disasters ■ v (-loguing, -logued) 1 vti make a catalogue of something 2 vt enter an item in a catalogue —**cataloguer** n

Catalonia /káttə lốni ə/, **Catalunya** /-loốnyə/, **Cataluña** autonomous region in NE Spain. Cap. Barcelona. Pop. 6,147,610 (1998). —**Catalonian** adj, n

catalyst /káttəlist/ n 1 a chemical substance that accelerates a chemical reaction without undergoing change 2 a stimulus to a change or event —**catalytic** /káttə líttik/ adj

catalytic converter n a chamber in the exhaust system of a vehicle that oxidizes exhaust fumes

catamaran /káttəmə rán/ n a double-hulled boat

> **ORIGIN Catamaran** comes from a language of S India and N Sri Lanka, and literally means 'tied wood'.

cat-and-mouse adj cruelly exploiting or compounding somebody else's fear

catapult /káttə pult/ n 1 a child's Y-shaped hand-held device with elastic stretched across it for firing stones 2 a mechanism for launching planes or missiles 3 a medieval weapon used for hurling stones ■ v 1 vti throw or be thrown with great force 2 vt abruptly change the circumstances of ○ was catapulted to fame

cataract /káttə rakt/ n 1 an opaque eye lens, or a disease causing it 2 a waterfall (literary)

catarrh /kə taár/ n inflammation of a mucous membrane, especially of the nose or throat —**catarrhal** adj —**catarrhous** adj

catastrophe /kə tástrəfi/ n a disaster

catastrophic /káttə stróffik/ adj 1 causing widespread damage or death 2 very bad or unsuccessful —**catastrophically** adv

catatonic /káttə tónnik/ adj in a state of inertia or apparent stupor characterized by rigid muscles

cat burglar n a stealthy agile burglar

catcall /kát kawl/ n a jeer

catch /kach/ v (**caught** /kawt/) 1 vti stop something with the hands or a container 2 vt grasp somebody or something suddenly 3 vt capture an animal or criminal 4 vt reach or get alongside somebody moving ahead 5 vt arrive in time to board, e.g. a plane 6 vti become infected with a disease 7 vt surprise somebody while engaged in an act or in a particular situation ○ caught me reading her diary ○ was caught in the rain 8 vt attract somebody's attention 9 vti manage to hear something 10 vt manage to see, e.g. a performance (infml) 11 vti entangle or trap, or become entangled or trapped 12 vt record something on film 13 vi begin to burn 14 vt in cricket, dismiss a batsman by catching a ball he or she has hit ■ n 1 an instance of catching something 2 somebody who can catch 3 a number of fish or other things caught at one time 4 an ideal romantic partner (infml) 5 a device that closes or fastens something 6 a hidden or unexpected disadvantage (infml) 7 a break in somebody's voice —**catchable** adj

□ **catch on** vi (infml) 1 become popular 2 understand something

□ **catch out** vt discover somebody doing something wrong (infml)

□ **catch up** v 1 vti reach somebody or something travelling ahead 2 vt pick something up 3 vi get or be brought up to date 4 vt engross somebody

□ **catch up with** vt 1 find a criminal or wrongdoer 2 finally affect somebody

catch-22 /-twenti toő/ n a situation that is impossible to deal with or escape from because of illogical rules

> **ORIGIN Catch-22** is taken from the title (and central idea) of a 1961 novel by the US writer Joseph Heller.

catchall /kách awl/ n something encompassing a range of possibilities

catcher /káchər/ n 1 something or somebody that catches 2 in baseball, a player positioned behind the batter

catching /káching/ adj infectious or contagious

catchment area /káchmənt-/ n 1 an area from which rainwater drains into a reservoir 2 the area of a community from which a particular school or hospital accepts pupils or patients

catch phrase n a phrase that becomes identified with a specific person

catchword /kách wurd/ n 1 a word that becomes identified with a specific person, period, or activity 2 a word marking the beginning or end of the range of material covered on a page, printed at the top or bottom of the page

catchy /káchi/ (**-ier, -iest**) adj 1 easy to remember 2 attracting interest or attention —**catchiness** n

catechism /káttəkizəm/ n a set of questions and answers used to test Christian religious knowledge —**catechismal** /káttə kízm'l/ adj

categorical /káttə górrik'l/, **categoric** /káttə górrik/ adj 1 absolute and explicit 2 involving categories —**categorically** adv

categorize /káttigə rīz/ (**-rizing, -rized**), **categorise** vt put into a category —**categorization** /káttigə rī záysh'n/ n

category /káttəgəri/ (pl **-ries**) n a set of people or things classified together ◊ See note at **type**

cater /káytər/ vi 1 provide what is wanted 2 prepare and supply food and drink —**caterer** n

catering /káytəring/ n the act or business of providing food and drinks to people

caterpillar /káttər pilər/ n a butterfly larva with a long soft body and many legs

ORIGIN **Caterpillar** probably goes back to Latin words that literally mean 'hairy cat'.

Caterpillar /káttər pilər/ tdmk a trademark for a continuous metal loop or belt made up of hinged links, fitted instead of wheels on tanks, bulldozers, and similar vehicles

~~caterpiller~~ incorrect spelling of **caterpillar**

caterwaul /káttər wawl/ vi **1** make a loud howling noise **2** argue loudly —**caterwaul** n

catfish /kát fish/ (pl same or -**fishes**) n a fish with sensitive organs like whiskers around its mouth

cat flap n a swinging flap over an opening in a door made for a cat

catgut /kát gut/ n tough thin cord made from animal intestines. Use: stringing musical instruments, surgical thread.

catharsis /kə tháarssiss/ (pl -**ses** /-seez/) n an emotional release brought about by an intense experience

cathartic /kə tháartik/ adj inducing catharsis —**cathartically** adv

cathedral /kə theédrəl/ n the most important church in a diocese

ORIGIN A **cathedral** was originally a cathedral church, with **cathedral** an adjective derived from Latin cathedra 'chair, bishop's seat'. A **cathedral** is thus a church that houses the bishop's throne. The English word chair also comes from Latin cathedra, via French.

Cather /káthər/, **Willa** (1873–1947) US writer

Catherine (of Aragon) /káth'rin əv árrəgən/ (1485–1536) Spanish-born queen of England (1509–33) as the first wife of Henry VIII

Catherine the Great

Catherine (the Great) (1729–96) empress of Russia (1762–96)

Catherine de Médicis /-də méddi chee, -me deéchi/, **Catherine de Medici** (1519–89) Italian-born queen of France (1560–63)

Catherine wheel n a firework that forms a multicoloured spinning wheel

catheter /káthitər/ n a thin tube inserted into the body to drain off liquid or keep a passage open

catheterize /káthitə rīz/ (-**izing**, -**ized**), **catheterise** vt put a catheter into —**catheterization** /káthitə rī záysh'n/ n

cathode /káthōd/ n **1** the negative electrode in

an electrolytic cell or electronic valve **2** the positive terminal in a battery

cathode ray tube n a vacuum tube in which a stream of electrons is directed onto a screen to produce an image, e.g. inside a television set

Catholic /káthlik, káthəlik/ adj **1** of the Roman Catholic Church **2** belonging to the community of all Christian churches **3 catholic** all-inclusive or all-embracing ■ n a member of the Roman Catholic Church

Catholicism /kə thóllisizəm/ n the beliefs and practices of the Roman Catholic Church

Catiline /káttə līn/ (108?–62 BC) Roman conspirator

catkin /kátkin/ n the hanging furry flower clusters on trees such as the willow and birch

cat litter n absorbent material in which a cat can urinate and defecate indoors

catmint /kátmint/, **catnip** /kátnip/ n a plant of the mint family whose smell attracts cats

catnap /kát nap/ n a short sleep —**catnap** vi

cat-o'-nine-tails (pl same) n a whip made of strands of knotted rope, formerly used for giving beatings

Cato the Elder /káytō-/, **Marcus Porcius** (234–149 BC) Roman general and politician

cat's cradle n a game in which a loop of string is threaded between the fingers in elaborate patterns

cat's eye n a gemstone cut to reflect a narrow band of light

Catseye /káts ī/ tdmk a trademark for a small reflecting device set into a road surface as a marker for drivers at night

Catskill Mountains /kátskil-/ group of mountains in the Appalachian system in SE New York State. Highest peak Slide Mountain, 1,281 m/4,204 ft.

catsuit /kát soot, -syoot/ n a woman's tight one-piece trouser suit

cat's whiskers n an excellent person or thing (dated slang)

cattery /káttəri/ (pl -**ies**) n a place where cats are bred or boarded

cattle /kátt'l/ npl **1** cows and other farm animals of the ox family **2** people regarded as lacking individuality

ORIGIN Originally **cattle** meant 'property, goods, wealth'. It comes from a northern variant of the French word that gave us chattel. Since wealth often derived from livestock, it commonly referred to domestic animals regarded as property, and after 1500 this was practically its sole meaning. From the 16C it has primarily implied cows and oxen.

cattle grid n a grid of metal bars over a shallow pit in a road, to stop cattle passing

cattleman /kátt'l man, -mən/ (pl -**men** /-men/) n somebody who owns, raises, or works with cattle

cattle prod n an electrified rod used for driving cattle

cattle truck *n* a railway wagon for cattle

catty /kátti/ (**-tier, -tiest**) *adj* spiteful or malicious —**cattily** *adv* —**cattiness** *n*

Catullus /kə túlləss/, **Gaius Valerius** (84?–54? BC) Roman poet —**Catullan** *adj*

catwalk /kát wawk/ *n* **1** a raised platform along which models walk at a fashion show **2** a high walkway

Caucasia /kaw káyzi ə, -zhə/ region of SE Europe and SW Asia between the Black Sea and the Caspian Sea, comprising Georgia, Armenia, Azerbaijan, and SW Russia

Caucasian /kaw káyzi ən, -zh'n/ *adj* **1** describes people who are white-skinned **2** of Caucasia —**Caucasian** *n*

Caucasus Mountains /káwkəssəss-/ mountain range extending through Georgia, Armenia, Azerbaijan, and SW Russia, considered a boundary between Europe and Asia. Highest peak El'brus 5,642 m/18,510 ft.

caucus /káwkəss/ *n* **1** a closed political meeting **2** a special-interest group ■ *vi* form or hold a caucus

ORIGIN **Caucus** probably comes from a Native North American language. It was first recorded in the United States in the mid-18C.

caught past tense, past participle of **catch**

cauldron /káwldrən/, **caldron** *n* a large pot in which liquids are boiled

cauliflower /kólli flow ər/ *n* **1** a head of hard white florets eaten as a vegetable **2** a plant related to cabbage that produces cauliflower

cauliflower cheese *n* a dish of cooked cauliflower served with a cheese sauce

cauliflower ear *n* an ear that has been permanently misshapen by being hit repeatedly

caulk /kawk/, **calk** *vt* **1** make a boat watertight by sealing the seams between the planks **2** stop up a gap or crack ■ *n* a substance used to fill gaps

causal /káwz'l/ *adj* **1** being or involving the cause of something **2** expressing a relationship of cause and effect —**causally** *adv*

causality /kaw zálləti/ *n* the principle that everything has a cause

causation /kaw záysh'n/ *n* **1** the process or fact of causing an effect **2** a cause-and-effect relationship

causative /káwzətiv/ *adj* involving a cause and its effect

cause /kawz/ *n* **1** something that makes something else happen or be so **2** a principle or aim that people believe in **3** a lawsuit, or the reason for a lawsuit ■ *vt* (**causing, caused**) be the reason for

cause célèbre /kóz sə lébbrə, káwz-/ (*pl* **causes célèbres** /kóz sə lébbrəz, káwz-/) *n* a famous legal case or public controversy

causeway /káwz way/ *n* a raised road across marshy land

ORIGIN **Causeway** has no connection with *cause*. It is formed from an earlier word, *causey*,

that had the same meaning. Its ultimate root is the Latin word for 'limestone'.

caustic /káwstik/ *adj* **1** corrosive **2** sarcastic ■ *n* a corrosive substance —**caustically** *adv* —**causticity** /kaw stíssəti/ *n* ◊ See note at **sarcastic**

cauterize /káwtə rīz/ (**-izing, -ized**), **cauterise** *vt* seal a wound with heat, a laser, or an electric current —**cauterization** /káwtə rī záysh'n/ *n*

caution /káwsh'n/ *n* **1** carefulness and lack of haste **2** a warning **3** a warning given by a police officer that a suspect's words may be used as evidence ■ *vt* warn ◊ **throw caution to the wind(s)** be reckless

cautionary /káwsh'nəri/ *adj* giving or involving a warning

cautious /káwshəss/ *adj* showing care and lack of haste —**cautiously** *adv* —**cautiousness** *n*

SYNONYMS **cautious, careful, chary, circumspect, prudent, vigilant, wary, guarded, cagey** CORE MEANING: showing care or awareness of possibilities

cavalcade /kávv'l káyd/ *n* **1** a procession of people on horses or in cars **2** a spectacular or dramatic series of people or things

cavalier /kávvə leйr/ *adj* showing an arrogant or careless disregard for something or somebody ■ *n* **1** a gentleman (*fml*) **2 Cavalier** a supporter of King Charles I —**cavalierly** *adv*

cavalry /kávv'lri/ (*pl* **-ries**) *n* **1** formerly, soldiers on horseback **2** soldiers equipped with tanks and other vehicles —**cavalryman** *n*

Cavan /kávv'n/ county in north-central Ireland. Pop. 53,000 (1996).

cave *n* a large natural hollow in a rock face or under the ground
□ **cave in** *v* **1** *vti* collapse **2** *vi* yield to persuasion or threats

caveat /kávvi at, káy-/ *n* a warning or proviso

caveat emptor /-émp tawr/ *n* the principle that the buyer is responsible for making sure purchases are of good quality

ORIGIN The origin is a Latin phrase, 'let the buyer beware'.

cave-in *n* the collapse of something, or the place where something collapses

Cavell /kávv'l/, **Edith** (1865–1915) British nurse, who was executed by the Germans during World War I for helping Allied soldiers escape from occupied Belgium

caveman /káyv man/ (*pl* **-men** /-men/) *n* **1** a Stone Age man **2** a brutish or uncivilized man (*infml*)

Cavendish /kávv'ndish/, **Henry** (1731–1810) British chemist and physicist. He identified hydrogen, discovered that water is a compound, and measured the earth's density.

cavern /kávvərn/ *n* a large cave

cavernous /kávvərnəss/ *adj* **1** large, dark, or deep **2** hollow-sounding

caviar /kávvi aar, -áàr/, **caviare** *n* the salted roe of a large fish, especially the sturgeon

cavil /kávv'l, kávvil/ *vi* (**-illing, -illed**) object for no good reason ■ *n* a trivial and carping criticism

caving /káyving/ *n* the activity of exploring underground caves —**caver** *n*

cavity /kávvəti/ (*pl* **-ties**) *n* 1 a hollow space in something 2 a hole in a tooth

cavity wall *n* a wall of a building consisting of two separate walls with a space between them

cavort /kə váwrt/ *vi* behave in a lively or un- inhibited way

Cavour /kə voòr, -váwr/, **Camillo Benso, Conte di** (1810–61) Italian politician and chief archi- tect of the unification of Italy (1861)

caw *vi* make the cry of a crow

Cawdor /káwdər/ parish in N Scotland, best known for its castle

Cawley /káwli/, **Evonne Fay** (*b.* 1951) Australian tennis player

Caxton /kákstən/, **William** (1422?–91) English printer

cayenne /kay én, kī-/, **cayenne pepper** *n* a red hot-tasting powder made from the dried ground fruit and seeds of various chillies

Cayenne /kay én, kī én/ capital of French Guiana. Pop. 41,000 (1990).

Cayman Islands /káymən-/ group of three islands in the NW Caribbean Sea, south of Cuba, a British dependency. Cap. George Town. Pop. 35,527 (2001).

Cazaly /kázz'li/, **Roy** (1893–1963) Australian Rules footballer

CB *abbr* 1 citizens band 2 Companion of the (Order of the) Bath

CBI *abbr* Confederation of British Industry

CBW *abbr* 1 chemical and biological warfare 2 chemical and biological weapon

cc *abbr* 1 (carbon) copy 2 cubic centimetre

CC *abbr* 1 City Council 2 County Council 3 Cricket Club

cc. *abbr* chapters

CCTV *abbr* closed-circuit television

Cd *symbol* cadmium

CD *abbr* 1 compact disc 2 Corps Diplomatique (*often displayed on the backs of cars that belong to embassies*)

CDE *n* a reusable compact disc. Full form **compact disc erasable**

CDI, CD-I *n* an interactive compact disc con- taining text, video, and audio. Full form **compact disc interactive**

Cdr *abbr* Commander

CDR[1] *n* a compact disc that can be recorded on once but not erased. Full form **compact disc recordable**

CDR[2] *abbr* Commander

CD-ROM /seé dee róm/ *n* a compact disc with a content that can be viewed on a computer but not changed. Full form **compact disc read- only memory**

CD-RW *abbr* CD rewritable

CDV *abbr* CD-video

CD-video *n* 1 a compact disc with video images 2 a player for CD-videos

Ce *symbol* cerium

CE *adv* used as a non-Christian equivalent of AD in dates. Full form **Common Era**

Geasar incorrect spelling of **Caesar**

cease /seess/ (**ceasing, ceased**) *vti* come or bring to an end

ceasefire /seéss fīr/ *n* 1 an agreement to stop fighting 2 an order to stop firing

ceaseless /seéssləss/ *adj* continuous or un- ending —**ceaselessly** *adv*

Ceauşescu /chow shéskoo/, **Nicolae** (1918–89) Romanian head of state (1967–89)

Cecil /séss'l/, **William ♦ Burghley**

cedar /seédər/ *n* 1 a tall evergreen tree with needles and rounded cones 2 wood from a cedar

cede /seed/ (**ceding, ceded**) *vt* surrender or give up something to another country, group, or person

---

SPELLCHECK Do not confuse the spelling of **cede** and **seed** (of a plant), which sound similar.

---

cedi /seédi/ (*pl same*) *n* the main unit of Gha- naian currency

cedilla /sə dillə/ (*pl* **-las**) *n* a mark placed beneath the letters c (ç) and s (ş) in some languages

ceilidh /káyli/ *n* a party with Scottish or Irish folk dancing

ceiling /seéling/ *n* 1 the overhead surface of a room 2 an upper limit 3 the level of the lowest clouds in the sky

Celebes /séllə beez, se leé beez/ ♦ **Sulawesi**

Celebes Sea arm of the W Pacific Ocean sur- rounded by the Philippines, Borneo, and Sulawesi

celebrant /sélləbrənt/ *n* 1 a participant in a religious ceremony 2 in some Christian churches, an officiating priest at Com- munion 3 ANZ somebody who officiates at civil ceremonies

celebrate /séllə brayt/ (**-brating, -brated**) *v* 1 *vt* mark an occasion with festivities 2 *vti* perform a religious ceremony 3 *vt* praise somebody or something publicly —**celebration** /séllə bráysh'n/ *n* —**celebratory** /sélləbrətəri, séllə bráytəri/ *adj*

celebrated /séllə braytid/ *adj* famous

celebrity /sə lébbrəti/ (*pl* **-ties**) *n* 1 a famous person 2 fame

celerity /sə lérrəti/ *n* quickness (*literary*)

celery /sélləri/ *n* 1 long greenish-white plant stems eaten as a vegetable 2 the plant that produces celery 3 the seeds of the celery plant. Use: as seasoning.

celestial /sə lésti əl/ *adj* 1 of heaven 2 of the sky —**celestially** *adv*

celibate /séllibət/ *adj* 1 abstaining from sex 2 unmarried because of a religious vow —**celibacy** *n* —**celibate** *n* —**celibately** *adv*

cell /sel/ n 1 a room for holding a prisoner 2 a small simple room, e.g. in a monastery 3 the smallest unit in the structure of an organism 4 a small enclosed structure, e.g. a compartment in a honeycomb 5 a device that produces electricity by chemical action 6 a small group of activists within a larger organization who work together secretly 7 an area covered by one radio transmitter in a mobile telephone system 8 a space for information in a table

cellar /séllər/ n 1 an underground room used for storage 2 a stock of wine

cellarage /séllərij/ n 1 a fee charged for storing something in a cellar 2 cellar space

cellblock /sél blok/ n a group of prison cells forming a unit

Cellini /che leéni/, **Benvenuto** (1500–71) Italian sculptor and goldsmith

cellist /chéllist/ n a cello player

cello /chéllō/ (pl **-los**) n a large stringed instrument held upright between a seated player's knees

---

ORIGIN Cello is shortened from *violoncello*, an Italian diminutive of *violone* 'double-bass viol'.

Cellophane /séllə fayn/ tdmk a trademark for a thin transparent material, used for wrapping and covering things

cellphone /sél fōn/, **cellular phone** n a mobile phone operated through a network of radio transmitters

cellular /séllyŏolər/ adj 1 involving living cells 2 consisting of small parts or groups 3 organized into cells for radio communication 4 porous or open in texture

cellulite /séllyŏo līt/ n fatty deposits beneath the skin that give a lumpy appearance

celluloid /séllyŏo loyd/ n a type of transparent plastic. Use: photographic film. **—celluloid** adj

cellulose /séllyŏo lōss, -lōz/ n the main component of plant cell walls. Use: plastics, lacquers, explosives, synthetic fibres. **—cellulosic** /séllyŏo lóssik, -lōzik/ adj

cellulose acetate n a chemical compound produced by the action of acid on cellulose. Use: photographic film, plastics, textile fibres, varnishes.

Celsius /sélssi əss/ adj measured on a metric temperature scale in which water freezes at 0° and boils at 100° (generally not in scientific contexts apart from meteorology)

ORIGIN The scale is named after the Swedish astronomer Anders Celsius (1701–44), who devised it.

---

celt /selt/ n a prehistoric cutting tool

Celt /kelt, selt/ n 1 somebody who speaks a Celtic language 2 a member of an ancient people who lived in central and W Europe

Celtic /kéltik, sélt-/ adj of the Celts or their language or culture ■ n a language group that includes Scottish Gaelic, Irish, and Breton **—Celticist** /kéltissist, sélt-/ n

cement mixer n 1 a portable machine for making concrete 2 a truck with a large rotating drum for making concrete

cemetary, cemetry incorrect spelling of **cemetery**

cemetery /sémmətri/ (pl **-ies**) n a burial place

cenotaph /sénnə taaf, -taf/ n a monument to people killed during a war

Cenozoic /seénō zō ik/ n the present era of geological time, which began 65 million years ago **—Cenozoic** adj

censor /sénssər/ n 1 an official who examines films, plays, and other works with a view to removing objectionable material 2 somebody or something exercising a suppressing control ■ vt 1 remove offensive parts from 2 exercise control over **—censorial** /sen sáwri əl/ adj

censorious /sen sáwri əss/ adj tending to be highly critical

censorship /sénssər ship/ n 1 the suppression of published or broadcast material 2 any form of suppression

censure /sénshər/ n 1 disapproval 2 official condemnation ■ vt (**-suring, -sured**) 1 criticize 2 condemn officially **—censurable** adj **—censurer** n ◊ See note at **criticize, disapprove**

census /sénssəss/ (pl **-suses**) n 1 an official count or survey of a population 2 any systematic count

cent /sent/ n a subunit of currency in the United States, Canada, Australia, New Zealand, South Africa, the European Union, and several other countries

cent. abbr centigrade

Centaur

centaur /sén tawr/ n in Greek mythology, a creature that is half man, half horse

centenarian /séntə náiri ən/ n a 100-year-old person ■ adj 100 years old

centenary /sen teénəri, -ténnə-/ n (pl **-ries**) a 100-year anniversary ■ adj 1 marking 100 years 2 happening once a century

centennial /sen ténni əl/ adj 1 involving a period of 100 years 2 happening once a century **—centennially** adv

center n, vti US = **centre**

centi- prefix 1 hundredth ○ centilitre 2 hundred ○ centipede

centigrade /sénti grayd/ adj Celsius

centilitre /sénti leetər/ n (symbol **cl**) a unit of volume equal to 1/100th of a litre

centimetre /sénti meetər/ *n* (*symbol* **cm**) a unit of length equal to 1/100th of a metre

centipede /sénti peed/ *n* an invertebrate organism with a segmented body and many legs

Central African Republic landlocked country in central Africa. Cap. Bangui. Pop. 3,576,884 (2001).

Central America southern part of North America, comprising Guatemala, Belize, Honduras, El Salvador, Nicaragua, Costa Rica, and Panama. Pop. 31,300,000 (1993).

Central Asia region comprising the countries of Kazakhstan, Kyrgyzstan, Tajikistan, Turkmenistan, and Uzbekistan

central bank *n* the main bank of a nation

Central European Time *n* the standard time adopted by most Western European countries, one hour ahead of Greenwich Mean Time

central government *n* the part of government that is concerned with national issues

central heating *n* a system for heating a whole building from one source —**centrally heated** *adj*

centralism /séntrəlizəm/ *n* the concentration of political power in a single authority —**centralist** *n, adj*

centralize /séntrə līz/ (**-izing, -ized**), **centralise** *vti* **1** concentrate political power in a single authority **2** group things in a single place —**centralization** /séntrə lī záysh'n/ *n*

central locking *n* automatic simultaneous operation of all the locks in a vehicle when a single door is locked

central nervous system *n* the brain and the spinal cord

central processing unit, central processor *n* the part of a computer that performs operations and executes software commands

central reservation *n UK* a strip of land between the carriageways of a major road

Central Standard Time, Central Time *n* **1** the local standard time in central North America **2** the local standard time in central Australia

centre /séntər/ *n* **1** the middle point, part, or area of something **2** a place for a particular activity o *a sports centre* **3** the focus or attention, activity, or influence o *the issue at the centre of the controversy* **4** a place or part where something is concentrated **5** *also* **Centre** politicians or political parties that are neither left-wing nor right-wing **6** a pivotal point or axis **7** in some sports, an attacking player in the middle of the field ■ *v* (**-tring, -tred**) **1** *vt* put something in or send something into the centre **2** *vti* focus or be focused on a particular theme

centre back *n* in some sports, a defensive player in the middle of the back line

centreboard /séntər bawrd/ *n* a retractable keel in a sailing boat

centred /séntərd/ *adj* **1** placed in the middle **2** *US* psychologically or emotionally well-balanced —**centredness** *n*

centrefold /séntər fōld/ *n* **1** a picture or feature that covers the middle two pages of a magazine **2** somebody posing naked or nearly naked in a centrefold

centre forward *n* in some sports, a player in the middle of the attacking line

centre half (*pl* **centre halfs**) *n* a player who plays in the middle of the field

centre of excellence *n* a place where the highest standards are aimed for in a specific activity

centre of gravity *n* **1** the focus of gravitational forces **2** *also* **centre of mass** the point at which the total mass of a body is assumed to be centred

centre spread *n* **1** the facing middle pages of a newspaper or magazine **2** an article on a centre spread

centre stage *n* **1** the middle of a theatre stage **2** the focus of people's interest —**centre stage** *adv*

centrifugal force /séntri fyoog'l-, sen tríffyōog'l-/ *n* the force that pulls a rotating object away from the centre of rotation

centrifuge /séntri fyooj, -fyoozh/ *n* **1** a device that rotates rapidly to separate substances of different densities **2** a device that simulates the effects of gravity or acceleration —**centrifuge** *vt*

centripetal force /sen tríppit'l-, séntri peet'l-/ *n* the force that pulls a rotating object towards the centre of rotation

centrism /séntrizəm/ *n* the holding of moderate views —**centrist** *n, adj*

~~centry~~ incorrect spelling of **century**

centurion /sen tyoóri ən, -choór-/ *n* in ancient Rome, an army officer in charge of a unit of foot soldiers —**centurial** *adj*

century /sénchəri/ (*pl* **-ries**) *n* **1** a period of 100 years **2** a 100-year period in a dating system, counted from year 00 or year 01 **3** in cricket, 100 runs scored by an individual batsman **4** in ancient Rome, a unit of soldiers originally comprising 100 men

CEO *abbr* chief executive officer

ceramic /sə rámmik/ *n* **1** a hard brittle heat-resistant material made from clay fired at a high temperature **2** a ceramic object —**ceramic** *adj*

ceramics /sə rámmiks/ *n* the art or industry of making ceramic objects (+ *sing verb*)

cereal /seéri əl/ *n* **1** a grain used as food **2** a grass cultivated for its edible grain **3** a breakfast food made from cereal grain

---

ORIGIN Cereal came through French from Latin, where it was based on the name of Ceres, the Roman goddess of agriculture.

SPELLCHECK Do not confuse the spelling of **cereal** and **serial** ('a story in parts'), which sound similar.

---

cerebellum /sérrə bélləm/ (*pl* **-lums** *or* **-la** /-lə/) *n* the rear part of the brain, divided into two hemispheres —**cerebellar** *adj*

cerebral /sérrəbrəl, sə reé-/ *adj* of the brain or intellect

cerebral palsy *n* a brain disorder that results in loss of muscle control —**cerebral-palsied** *adj*

cerebrovascular accident /sérrəbrō váskyōō-lər-/, **cerebral vascular accident** *n* any physical event, e.g. cerebral haemorrhage, that may lead to a stroke *(technical)*

cerebrum /sə reébrəm, sérrə-/ (*pl* -**brums** *or* -**bra** /-brə/) *n* the front part of the brain

Ceredigion /kérrə díggi on/ county and local council in Wales. Pop. 70,200 (1995).

ceremonial /sérrə mṓni əl/ *adj* 1 of formal occasions 2 involving a ceremony ■ *n* 1 formal etiquette 2 a ritual or ceremony —**ceremonialism** —**ceremonially** *adv*

ceremonious /sérrə mṓni əss/ *adj* 1 formal and careful to observe the rules of correct behaviour 2 involving ceremony

ceremony /sérrəməni/ (*pl* -**nies**) *n* 1 a ritual marking a formal occasion 2 formal etiquette

Ceres /seér eez/ *n* in Roman mythology, the goddess of agriculture. Greek equivalent **Demeter**

cerise /sə reéz, -reéss/ *n* a vivid pinkish-red colour —**cerise** *adj*

cerium /seéri əm/ *n* (*symbol* **Ce**) a grey metallic element. Use: glassmaking, ceramics, cigarette-lighter flints.

cert /surt/ *n* (*infml*) 1 somebody who is certain to do something 2 something that is certain to happen

CERT /surt/ *abbr* computer emergency response team *(in e-mails)*

cert. *abbr* certificate

certain /súrt'n/ *adj* 1 having no doubts ○ *I'm certain he's the man I saw.* 2 known or set 3 inevitable ○ *It's certain they'll lose.* 4 reliable 5 undeniably present but difficult to define ○ *a certain hesitation in his voice* 6 not named

certainly /súrt'nli/ *adv* 1 definitely or without doubt 2 yes

certainty /súrt'nti/ (*pl* -**ties**) *n* 1 complete confidence in the truth of something 2 something inevitable 3 somebody or something that is certain of success

certifiable /súrti fī əb'l/ *adj* 1 good enough to be given a certificate 2 needing to be reported to an appropriate authority *(infml)* 3 requiring psychiatric treatment *(dated)* —**certifiably** *adv*

certificate *n* /sər tíffikət/ 1 a document providing official evidence, information, or approval 2 an electronic identification document used in e-commerce ■ *vt* /sər tíffi kayt/ (-**cating**, -**cated**) 1 award a certificate to 2 authorize or prove with a certificate —**certification** /súrtifi káysh'n, sər tíffi-/ *n*

certify /súrti fī/ (-**fies**, -**fied**) *v* 1 *vti* confirm the truth or accuracy of 2 *vt* prove the quality of 3 *vt* issue a certificate to 4 *vt* declare somebody to have a psychiatric disorder *(dated)*

~~certin~~ incorrect spelling of **certain**

certitude /súrti tyood/ *n* 1 a feeling of certainty 2 the undeniable truth of something

Cervantes /sur vánt eez/, **Miguel de** (1547–1616) Spanish novelist and dramatist

cervical /sər vík'l, súrvik'l/ *adj* of a cervix

cervical smear *n* a test for cancer of the neck of the womb

cervix /súrviks/ (*pl* -**vixes** *or* -**vices** /-vi seez/) *n* the neck of the womb

cessation /se sáysh'n/ *n* a stop, pause, or interruption in something

cesspit /séss pit/ *n* 1 a pit where sewage or other waste matter is collected 2 a filthy or immoral place

cesspool /séss pool/ *n* 1 an underground container for sewage or other waste matter 2 a filthy or immoral place

CET *abbr* Central European Time

Ceylon /si lón/ former name for **Sri Lanka** —**Ceylonese** /séllə neéz/ *adj, n*

Cézanne /si zán, say-/, **Paul** (1839–1906) French painter

Cf *symbol* californium

cf. *abbr* compare

c/f *abbr* carried forward

CFC *n* a gas used in refrigerants and aerosols. Full form **chlorofluorocarbon**

CGI *abbr* computer-generated imagery

CGT *abbr* capital gains tax

Chablis /shábbli/, **chablis** *n* a dry white wine from central France

cha-cha /chaá chaa/, **cha-cha-cha** /chaá chaa chaá/ *n* 1 a rhythmic Latin American dance 2 the music for a cha-cha

chad *n* a fragment of paper such as that punched from a ballot to register a vote

Chad landlocked country in north-central Africa. Cap. Ndjamena. Pop. 8,707,078 (2001). —**Chadian** *adj, n*

Chad, Lake lake in central Africa, at the junction of Nigeria, Niger, and Chad

chador /chúddər/, **chadar, chuddar** *n* a dark cloak worn by Muslim women in public that covers the head and most of the body

chafe *vti* (**chafing, chafed**) 1 make or become worn 2 rub something, causing friction or warmth 3 annoy, or become annoyed ■ *n* 1 soreness or wear 2 a feeling of irritation

chaff[1] *n* 1 seed coverings removed by threshing 2 something worthless 3 glass or nylon filaments dispersed into the air to obstruct radar

chaff[2] *v* 1 *vt* tease light-heartedly 2 *vi* banter ■ *n* joking or teasing behaviour

chaffinch /cháffinch/ *n* a small European songbird with reddish-brown wings and a blue head

Chagall /sha gál/, **Marc** (1887–1985) Russian-born French painter and designer

chagrin /shággrin, shə grín/ *n* a feeling of irritation or humiliation —**chagrin** *vt*

chai /chī/ *n* S Asia tea

chain *n* **1** a series of joined metal rings used like a rope or as a decorative accessory **2** a chain worn as a badge of office **3** a series of connected things resembling a chain **4** a number of businesses under one management or ownership **5** a sequence of related events or facts **6** a unit of length equal to 66 ft **7** a series of atoms within a molecule **8** a series of geographical formations, e.g. mountains ■ **chains** *npl* restraining circumstances *(literary)* ■ *vt* **1** fasten with a chain **2** restrict the mobility or independence of —**chained** *adj*

Chain, Sir Ernst Boris (1906–79) German-born British biochemist. He shared a Nobel Prize in physiology or medicine (1945) with Alexander Fleming and Howard Walter Florey for the development of the first antibiotic, penicillin.

chain gang *n* a number of prisoners who work shackled together

chain letter *n* a letter requesting that copies be forwarded to others

chainlink fence /cháynlingk-/ *n* a fence made of strong interwoven wire —**chainlink fencing** *n*

chain mail *n* armour for a knight made of interlinked rings of metal

chain of command *n* a hierarchy of authority

chain reaction *n* **1** a connected sequence of events **2** a self-sustaining nuclear reaction **3** a series of chemical reactions in which the product of one helps to create the next

chain saw *n* a portable motor-driven saw with teeth that form a circular chain

chain-smoke *vti* smoke cigarettes continuously —**chain-smoker** *n*

chain stitch *n* a looped stitch resembling a chain —**chain-stitch** *vti*

chain store *n* one of a series of shops owned by the same company

chair *n* **1** a seat with a back and sometimes armrests for one person **2** a chairperson, or the position of a chairperson **3** a professor or professorship ■ *vt* preside over a committee or meeting

chair lift *n* a series of seats suspended from a moving cable, used for carrying people up or down a mountain

chairman /cháirmən/ (*pl* -**men** /-mən/) *n* **1** somebody who presides over a committee or meeting **2** the chief presiding officer of a company —**chairmanship** *n*

chairperson /cháir purs'n/ (*pl* -**sons**) *n* somebody who presides over a committee or meeting

chairwoman /cháir woomən/ (*pl* -**women** /-wimmin/) *n* a woman who presides over a committee or meeting

chaise /shayz/ (*pl* **chaises** /pronunc. same/) *n* a light two-wheeled carriage with a hood drawn by one horse

chaise longue /shayz lóng/ (*pl* **chaise longues** or **chaises longues** /pronunc. same/) *n* a chair with an elongated seat and one armrest, for lying on

~~chaise lounge~~ incorrect spelling of **chaise longue**

chalcedony /kal sédd'ni/ *n* a form of quartz. Use: gems, ornaments. —**chalcedonic** /kálssi dónnik/ *adj*

Chaldea /kal dée ə/ ancient region of Mesopotamia, between the Euphrates and the Persian Gulf, in modern-day S Iraq

~~chalenge~~ incorrect spelling of **challenge**

chalet /shállay/ *n* **1** a house or cottage traditionally made of wood with wide overhanging eaves **2** a small simple house used as holiday accommodation

chalice /chálliss/ *n* **1** a metal cup *(literary)* **2** a cup used at Communion or Mass

chalk /chawk/ *n* **1** a soft white rock consisting of calcium carbonate **2** a piece of chalk used for writing or drawing, especially on a blackboard ■ *vti* draw, write, or mark something with chalk —**chalky** *adj* ◊ **by a long chalk** by a large margin

□ **chalk up** *vt (infml)* **1** achieve something significant **2** attribute something to a person or thing

challenge /chállənj/ (-**lenging**, -**lenged**) *vt* **1** invite somebody to take part in a fight or contest **2** dare somebody to do something **3** call something into question **4** stimulate somebody by making demands on his or her intellect or abilities **5** order somebody to produce identification —**challenge** *n*

challenged /chállənjd/ *adj* **1** having a particular physical or mental disability ○ *physically challenged* **2** lacking in a particular quality *(humorous; sometimes offensive)*

challenger /chállənjər/ *n* **1** somebody who seeks a fight **2** somebody who opposes a champion

challenging /chállənjing/ *adj* demanding physical or psychological effort of a stimulating kind —**challengingly** *adv*

chamber /cháymbər/ *n* **1** a bedroom or other room *(literary)* **2** an official reception room **3** a room with a particular function ○ *in the council chamber* **4** an official assembly, or the place where it meets **5** a body of people organized into a group for a specific purpose **6** a compartment or cavity **7** a compartment for ammunition in a weapon ■ **chambers** *npl* **1** a judge's private office **2** a suite of offices used by lawyers ■ *adj* of chamber music —**chambered** *adj*

chamberlain /cháymbərlin/ *n* the manager of a royal or noble household

Chamberlain /cháymbərlin/, **Joseph** (1836–1914) British politician

Chamberlain /cháymbərlin/, **Neville** (1869–1940) British prime minister (1937–40)

chambermaid /cháymbər mayd/ *n* a woman who cleans hotel rooms

chamber music *n* classical instrumental music performed by a small group

chamber of commerce *n* an association of local business people who work together to promote their common interests

chamber orchestra *n* a small orchestra that performs classical music

chamber pot *n* a large bowl formerly kept in a bedroom and used as a toilet

chameleon /kə méeli ən/ *n* 1 a lizard that can change colour 2 somebody who often changes his or her appearance, opinions, or personality

ORIGIN According to the Greek elements from which it is formed, a **chameleon** is a 'ground lion'. The name came into English from Greek via Latin, and is first recorded in the 14C.

chamois /shám waa/ (*pl* **-ois** /-waa/ *or* **-oix** /-waa/) *n* 1 a mountain-dwelling goat antelope 2 *also* **chamois leather** soft pliable leather. Use: cleaning, polishing. 3 a chamois leather cloth

chamomile *n* PLANTS = **camomile**

champ[1] *n* 1 an Irish dish of mashed potatoes with spring onions 2 the process or sound of biting or chewing something vigorously ■ *vti* bite or chew something vigorously

champ[2] *n* a champion (*infml*)

champagne /sham páyn/ *n* a white sparkling wine, properly from the Champagne region of NE France

champion /chámpi ən/ *n* 1 the winner of a contest or show 2 a defender of a person or cause ■ *vt* defend a person or cause

ORIGIN A **champion** was originally just a 'fighting man'. The word entered English from French in this sense in the 13C. A more specific sense, 'somebody who fights on behalf of another, or for a cause', coexisted with it from the 14C, as did the figurative extension involving defence by argument rather than physical combat. The meaning 'winner' appeared in the early 18C. The French word from which **champion** derives goes back to Latin *campus* 'field, arena', which is also the source of English *camp*.

championship /chámpi ənship/ *n* 1 a contest to decide a champion 2 the title or time of being a champion

Champlain /sham pláyn/, **Samuel de** (1567?–1635) French explorer

chance *n* 1 the likelihood that something will happen (*often pl*) ○ *There's a good chance we'll win.* 2 an opportunity or opportune time for doing something ○ *I was given no chance to explain.* 3 the supposed force that makes things happen with no apparent cause 4 an unexpected happening 5 something caused by luck ■ *v* (**chancing, chanced**) 1 *vt* do something risky 2 *vi* do something or happen without a cause or plan

□ **chance on** *or* **upon** *vt* come across unexpectedly

chancel /cha͞anssəl/ *n* an area of a church near the altar

chancellery /cha͞anssələri, cha͞anssləri/ (*pl* **-ies**), **chancellory** *n* a chancellor's residence

chancellor /cha͞anssələr, cha͞ansslər/, **Chancellor** *n* 1 the head of the government in some parliamentary democracies 2 **Chancellor, Chancellor of the Exchequer** the British finance minister 3 *UK, Can* the honorary head of a university —**chancellorship** *n*

chancer /cha͞anssər/ *n* a risk-taking opportunist (*infml*)

chancery /cha͞anssəri/ (*pl* **-ies**), **Chancery** *n* 1 a court of equity ruling on matters not covered by common law 2 an office attached to an embassy

chancy /cha͞anssi/ (**-ier, -iest**), **chancey** *adj* 1 risky 2 random or haphazard —**chancily** *adv* —**chanciness** *n*

chandelier /shándə léer/ *n* a decorative hanging light with several branched parts

chandler /cha͞andlər/ *n* a seller of particular goods ○ *a ship's chandler*

Chandler /cha͞andlər/, **Raymond** (1888–1959) US writer

Chanel /shə nél/, **Coco** (1883–1971) French couturier

~~changable~~ incorrect spelling of **changeable**

Changchun /cháng cho͞on/ capital of **Jilin Province**, NE China. Pop. 4,150,000 (1995).

change /chaynj/ *v* (**changing, changed**) 1 *vti* become or make somebody or something different 2 *vt* exchange, substitute, or replace somebody or something 3 *vti* pass, or make something pass, from one state to another ○ *Water changes to ice on freezing.* 4 *vt* convert one currency into another 5 *vt* exchange money for smaller units of money 6 *vti* move from one vehicle to another on a journey 7 *vti* remove clothes and put on others 8 *vt* remove and replace something dirty or used ■ *n* 1 an alteration, variation, or modification 2 an exchange, substitution, or replacement of somebody or something 3 the balance of money given back to a customer paying for something with a larger coin or banknote than the marked price 4 coins 5 a sum of money exchanged for a coin or banknote of a higher denomination 6 a transition from one state to another ○ *a change in attitude* 7 a variation from a routine ○ *I could do with a change.* 8 a fresh set of something, especially clothes 9 the menopause (*infml dated*)

SYNONYMS change, **alter, modify, convert, vary, shift, transform, transmute** CORE MEANING: make or become different

changeable /cháynjəb'l/ *adj* liable to change or vary —**changeability** /cháynjə bílləti/ *n* —**changeably** *adv*

~~changeing~~ incorrect spelling of **changing**

changeless /cháynjləss/ *adj* unchanging —**changelessly** *adv* —**changelessness** *n*

changeling /cháynjling/ *n* in folklore, a child believed to have been exchanged for another by fairies

changeover /cháynj ōvər/ *n* **1** a complete change from one thing to another **2** the handing over of a baton in a relay race

change ringing *n* the ringing of bells in a changing order

Chang Jiang /cháng ji áng/ ♦ **Yangtze**

Changsha /cháng shää/ capital of **Hunan Province**, SE China. Pop. 1,520,000 (1995).

channel /chánn'l/ *n* **1** a strip of water separating an island from a mainland **2** a navigable passage in a river or harbour **3** the course of a river or canal **4** a tube or passage for a liquid to flow along ○ *a drainage channel* **5** a means of communication *(often pl)* ○ *go through the proper channels* **6** the part of a frequency spectrum used in TV or radio transmission **7** a TV or radio station **8** a groove or furrow **9** a supposed spirit medium ■ *v* (**-nelling, -nelled**) **1** *vt* direct something along a specific route **2** *vti* act as a medium for a supposed spirit **3** *vt* make a channel in land or water **4** *vt* make a groove or furrow in a surface

Channel /chánn'l/ ♦ **English Channel**

Channel-hop *vi* cross the English Channel for a day trip —**Channel-hopper** *n*

Channel Islands group of islands in the English Channel near the French coast, dependencies of the British crown. Pop. 143,534 (1991).

Channel Tunnel *n* a railway tunnel under the English Channel

chant *n* **1** a slogan spoken repeatedly by a crowd in a singsong intonation **2** a musical passage or text sung on the same note or series of notes —**chant** *vti*

chanteuse /shaan túrz/ *(pl* **-teuses** /pronunc. same/) *n* a woman singer

chantry /chaäntri/ *(pl* **-tries**), **chantry chapel** *n* a chapel endowed for performing masses

Chanukah, Chanukkah *n* JUDAISM = **Hanukkah**

chaos /káy oss/ *n* **1** disorder **2** *also* **Chaos** the condition supposed to have existed before the creation of the universe

chaos theory *n* the theory that natural systems are so sensitive that small changes can have far-reaching effects that appear random

chaotic /kay óttik/ *adj* **1** disordered **2** apparently random —**chaotically** *adv*

chap¹ *vti* (**chapping, chapped**) become or make sore and cracked by exposure to wind or cold *(refers to skin)* ■ *n* an area of sore cracked skin caused by exposure to wind or cold —**chapped** *adj*

chap² *n* a man *(infml)*

chap³ *n* the lower half of the jaw

chapati /chə paäti, -pátti/ *(pl* **-tis** *or* **-ties**), **chapatti** *n* a South Asian flat unleavened bread

chapel /cháppʼl/ *n* **1** a room for religious worship in an institution or large house **2** a separate area of a Christian church for private prayer **3** a service in a chapel

ORIGIN The original **chapel** was the shrine in which the cloak of the 4C Roman monk St Martin of Tours was kept. *Cappella*, a diminutive of the Latin word for 'cloak', is the source of the French word that was adopted as **chapel**. The meaning moved from the cloak, to the building housing it, to any similar place of worship.

chaperone /sháppərōn/, **chaperon** *n* **1** an older or married woman who supervises a young single woman at social events **2** a supervisor accompanying a group of young people —**chaperone** *vti*

chaplain /chápplin/ *n* a member of the clergy employed by an institution or a branch of the armed forces to give religious guidance —**chaplaincy** *n*

chaplet /chápplət/ *n* **1** a circle of beads or flowers worn on the head **2** a string of Roman Catholic prayer beads

Chaplin /chápplin/, **Charlie** (1889–1977) British-born US film actor, director, and producer

Chapman /chápmən/, **George** (1559?–1634) English dramatist and translator

chaps *npl* protective leather leggings

chapter /cháptər/ *n* **1** a section of a book with a number or title **2** a period in the development of something **3** a group of canons in a cathedral or knights in an order *(+ sing or pl verb)* **4** a branch of an organization *(+ sing or pl verb)* ◊ **give** *or* **quote chapter and verse** give exact information

chapter house *n* a building where a religious chapter meets

char¹ (**charring, charred**) *v* **1** *vti* blacken by burning **2** *vt* make into charcoal

char² *(pl* same *or* **chars**), **charr** *(pl* same *or* **charrs**) *n* a trout with light-coloured spots

char³ *n* a charwoman

charabanc /shárrə bang/ *n* a sightseeing bus

ORIGIN **Charabanc** is from a French word that literally means 'carriage with benches'.

character /kárrəktər/ *n* **1** the set of qualities that make somebody or something distinctive **2** positive qualities **3** somebody's reputation **4** somebody in a book, play, or film **5** an unusual person **6** somebody considered in terms of personality, behaviour, or appearance **7** a letter, number, or symbol **8** a written testimonial **9** somebody's role or position *(fml)* ○ *speaking in her character as chairperson* —**characterful** *adj* ◊ **in character, out of character** typical or untypical of the behaviour of a particular person

character actor *n* an actor who plays unusual or distinctive roles

character assassination *n* an attack on somebody's reputation

characteristic /kárrəktə rístik/ *n* **1** a defining feature **2** the whole number in a logarithm ■ *adj* typical —**characteristically** *adv*

characterization /kárrəktə ī záysh'n/, **characterisation** *n* **1** the portrayal of fictional characters in a book, play, or film **2** a description

characterize /kárrəktə rīz/ (**-izing, -ized**), **characterise** vt **1** describe **2** be representative of —**characterizable** adj

characterless /kárrəktərləss/ adj not interesting

charade /shə raàd, -ráyd/ n **1** a ridiculous pretence **2** a clue in charades

charades /shə raàdz, -ráydz/ n a guessing game involving visual or acted clues for a word or phrase (+ sing verb)

charcoal /cha̱árkōl/ n a form of carbon. Use: fuel, absorbent in extractors, drawing medium.

chard n a plant with large edible leaves and stems eaten as a vegetable

~~charecter~~ incorrect spelling of **character**

charge v (**charging, charged**) **1** vti ask somebody for money for goods or services **2** vt allow and record a deferred payment for something **3** vt formally accuse somebody of a crime **4** vt criticize somebody **5** vt order somebody to do something **6** vti attack somebody or something by rushing forwards **7** vti restore the power in a battery using electricity **8** vt load or fill something (fml) ■ n **1** the price or fee asked **2** the responsibility for looking after somebody or something **3** a person for whom somebody else is responsible **4** an accusation or indictment **5** a rush forwards to attack **6** the power in an electric battery **7** the positive and negative electric property of matter **8** an amount needed to cause detonation, fill a container, or operate a mechanism **9** an order or command

chargeable /chaàrjəb'l/ adj **1** liable to be reimbursed **2** liable to result in a criminal charge

charge card n a deferred payment card

charge-coupled device n a semiconductor device that converts light patterns into digital signals for a computer

chargé d'affaires /shaàr zhay da fáir/ (pl **chargés d'affaires** /shaàr zhay da fáir, shaàr zhayz-/) n a diplomat ranking below an ambassador or heading a minor diplomatic mission

charge hand n a worker with supervisory responsibilities ranking below a foreman

charge nurse n a nurse in charge of a ward

charger[1] /chaàrjər/ n **1** a device for restoring power to electrical batteries **2** a large cavalry horse

charger[2] /chaàrjər/ n a large flat serving dish, or a dish that is placed below a diner's plate

charge sheet n a police document recording criminal charges

charge-sheet vt S Asia charge formally with a crime

chargrill /cha̱ár gril/ vt grill food on a barbecue or a ridged pan

~~charicature~~ incorrect spelling of **caricature**

chariot /chárri ət/ n **1** an ancient two-wheeled horse-drawn vehicle **2** a four-wheeled horse-drawn ceremonial carriage —**charioteer** /chárri ə teèr/ n

charisma /kə rízmə/ n **1** personal magnetism **2** (pl **charismata**) a gift or power believed to be divinely bestowed

charismatic /kárriz máttik/ adj **1** having charisma **2** describes Christians who seek direct spiritual experiences in worship —**charismatic** n —**charismatically** adv

charitable /chárritəb'l/ adj **1** generous to people in need **2** sympathetic or tolerant in judging **3** of or providing charity —**charitably** adv

charity /chárrəti/ (pl **-ties**) n **1** voluntary provision of help to people in need, or the help provided **2** an organization providing charity **3** sympathy or tolerance in judging **4** impartial love of other people

charity shop n a shop raising money for charity

charlady /cha̱ár laydi/ (pl **-dies**) n a charwoman

charlatan /shaàrlətən/ n a false claimant of special skill or expertise —**charlatanism** n —**charlatanry** n

Charlemagne /shaàrlə mayn/ (742–814) Frankish king and emperor of the West (800–814)

Charles /chaarlz/, **Prince of Wales** (b. 1948) British heir apparent

Charles I (1600–49) king of England, Scotland, and Ireland (1625–49)

Charles II (1630–85) king of England, Scotland, and Ireland (1660–85)

Charles V (1500–58) Holy Roman Emperor (1519–58) and, as Charles I, king of Spain (1516–56)

Charleston[1] /chaàrlstən/ n a vigorous 1920s dance

Charleston[2] /chaàrlstən/ port in SE South Carolina. Pop. 87,044 (1998).

charlie /chaàrli/ n **1** cocaine (slang) **2** somebody regarded as unintelligent or silly (infml) **3 Charlie** a communications code word for the letter 'C'

Charlotte Amalie /shaàrlət ə maályə/ capital and main port of the US Virgin Islands, on S St Thomas. Pop. 12,000 (1990).

charm n **1** the power to delight or attract people **2** a feature that delights or attracts people (often pl) **3** something carried or worn because it is supposed to bring luck **4** a trinket worn on a bracelet or necklace **5** a magic spell ■ v **1** vti delight or attract somebody **2** vt influence somebody by charm or a charm —**charmer** n —**charmless** adj

charmed adj extremely lucky

charming /chaàrming/ adj able to delight or attract people ■ interj expresses displeasure (infml) —**charmingly** adv

charnel house /chaàrn'l-/ n a building for bones or dead bodies

charr n FISH = **char**[2]

chart n **1** a diagram or table of information **2** a map ■ **charts** npl a list of the best-selling musical recordings in a specific period ■ vt **1** make a chart of something **2** record or describe a plan or progress

charter /chaártər/ n 1 a formal document incorporating an organization 2 the written constitution of an organization 3 a document authorizing the setting up of a new branch of an organization 4 the hire or lease of a vehicle 5 a hired or leased vehicle ■ vt hire or lease a vehicle —**chartered** adj

charter flight n a nonscheduled flight

Chartres /shaártrə/ capital of Eure-et-Loire Department, north-central France. Pop. 40,361 (1999).

Chartreuse /shaar trúrz/ tdmk a trademark for a yellow or green aromatic liqueur

chart-topping adj reaching the top of the music charts —**chart-topper** n

charwoman /chaár wōomən/ (pl -**women** /-wimmin/) n a woman employed to clean a house or office

chary /cháiri/ (-**ier**, -**iest**) adj 1 wary 2 reluctant to share, give, or use something —**charily** adv —**chariness** n ◊ See note at **cautious**

Charybdis /kə ríbdiss/ n in Greek mythology, a monster in the form of a dangerous whirlpool at the mouth of the cave of the sea monster Scylla

chase¹ v (**chasing**, **chased**) 1 vti try to catch or overtake somebody or something 2 vt make a person or animal run away ○ chased the cat out of the garden 3 vi rush about ○ I chased about all day. 4 vt follow up or investigate something left undone or somebody who has not done something 5 vti try hard to get something 6 vti try persistently to start a sexual or romantic relationship with somebody ■ n 1 an attempt to catch or overtake somebody or something 2 the hunting of animals for sport 3 a steeplechase 4 a jazz duet ◊ **cut to the chase** address immediately what needs to be dealt with (infml) ◊ See note at **follow**

chase² n 1 the external part of a gun barrel behind the muzzle 2 a groove into which something fits ■ vt (**chasing**, **chased**) 1 decorate metal or glass by engraving or embossing 2 cut a thread in a screw

chaser /cháyssər/ n 1 somebody or something that chases 2 a second drink taken with or after one of a different kind (infml)

chasm /kázzəm/ n 1 a deep hole in the ground 2 a wide break or difference

chassis /shássi/ (pl -**sis** /-siz/) n 1 the main frame and the wheels of a vehicle 2 a mounting for an electric or electronic device 3 the landing gear of an aircraft

chaste adj 1 abstaining from sex on moral grounds 2 pure in thought and deed 3 plain in style —**chastely** adv —**chasteness** n

chasten /cháyss'n/ vt 1 make somebody less self-satisfied and more subdued 2 discipline somebody 3 moderate the intensity of something —**chastened** adj —**chastening** adj

chastise /cha stíz/ (-**tising**, -**tised**) vt punish or scold —**chastisement** n

chastity /chástəti/ n 1 sexual abstinence 2 plainness of style

chastity belt n a medieval device worn by a woman to prevent her from having sexual intercourse

chasuble /cházyŏob'l/ n a Christian priest's loose outer garment

chat vi (**chatting**, **chatted**) 1 converse informally 2 exchange messages in real time by computer ■ n 1 an act or period of chatting 2 a songbird with a chattering cry

chateau /sháttō/ (pl -**teaux** /-tōz, -tō/ or -**teaus** /-tō, -tōz/), **château** (pl -**teaux** /-tō, -tōz/) n a French castle

chatelaine /shátta layn/ n 1 formerly, the woman in charge of a castle or large house 2 formerly, a chain to which keys were attached, worn by a woman around her waist

chat group n a group that exchanges messages in real time by computer

chatline /chát līn/ n a telephone service allowing several people to phone the same number and have a conversation

chat room n a facility in a computer network for exchanging messages in real time

Chattanooga /cháttə nŏogə, chátt'n ŏogə/ port in SE Tennessee. Pop. 147,790 (1998).

chattel /chátt'l/ n an item of movable property ■ **chattels** npl personal possessions (fml)

chatter /cháttər/ vi 1 talk rapidly and informally about trivial matters 2 make high-pitched sounds resembling speech (refers to animals or machinery) 3 click together because of fear or cold (refers to teeth) —**chatter** n

chatterbox /cháttər boks/ n a talkative person (infml)

chattering classes npl articulate opinionated middle-class people (disapproving)

Chatterton /cháttərtən/, **Thomas** (1752–70) British poet and playwright

chatty /chátti/ (-**tier**, -**tiest**) adj 1 fond of chatting 2 friendly and informal in tone —**chattily** adv —**chattiness** n ◊ See note at **talkative**

Chatwin /cháttwin/, **Bruce** (1940–89) British writer

Chaucer /cháwssər/, **Geoffrey** (1343?–1400) English poet —**Chaucerian** /chaw seéri ən/ n, adj

Chaudhuri /chówdəri/, **Nirad Chandra** (1897–1999) Indian writer

chauffeur /shōfər/ n a hired driver ■ vti drive somebody from place to place, especially as a job

ORIGIN Chauffeur dates from the late 19C. It comes from French, where it meant 'stoker, fireman' and was used also for the stoker, and sometimes the driver, of a steam car. In English it was first used simply for 'motorist', but the modern meaning took over at the beginning of the 20C.

chauvinism /shóvənizəm/ n 1 aggressive patriotism 2 aggressive loyalty to a particular gender, group, or cause —**chauvinist** n —**chauvinistic** /shóvə nístik/ adj

ORIGIN Chauvinism comes from a Nicholas

Chauvin of Rochefort, a veteran of the Napoleonic wars noted for blind patriotism. The name and character became widely known through a popular play of 1831.

cheap /cheep/ adj **1** costing or charging little **2** poor in quality or low in value **3** undeserving of respect —**cheap** adv —**cheaply** adv —**cheapness** n ◊ **on the cheap** at very low cost (infml)

SPELLCHECK Do not confuse the spelling of **cheap** and **cheep** (of a bird), which sound similar.

cheapen /cheepən/ vti **1** make or become less expensive **2** degrade, or become degraded

cheapjack /cheep jak/ n a seller of inferior goods ■ adj inferior in value or quality

cheapskate /cheep skayt/ n a mean person (infml)

cheat /cheet/ v **1** vt deceive somebody to gain an advantage **2** vi break rules to gain an advantage **3** vi be sexually unfaithful **4** vt escape harm or injury by luck or cunning ■ n **1** somebody who cheats **2** a dishonest trick —**cheater** n

Chechen /ché chen/ n **1** somebody from Chechnya **2** the majority language in Chechnya —**Chechen** adj

Chechnya /chéchni ə/ autonomous republic in SW Russia. Cap. Grozny. Pop. 862,000 (1997).

check v **1** vti examine something to establish its state ◊ checked the door to make sure it was locked **2** vti confirm the truth or accuracy of something ◊ checking with the insurance company to find out whether he's covered **3** vt halt or slow something ◊ efforts to check inflation **4** vt make somebody or something stop suddenly ■ n **1** an examination of something to establish its state **2** something that tests the truth or accuracy of something else **3** a means of control or restraint **4** US, Can a cheque **5** US, Can a tick to show something's status or correctness **6** a pattern of squares in different colours **7** a square in a check pattern **8** in chess, move putting an opponent's king in checkmate ■ interj in chess, warns that an opponent's king is in check —**checkable** adj

□ **check in** vti register at a hotel or airport
□ **check out** v **1** vi pay the bill and leave a hotel **2** vt investigate somebody or something (infml) **3** vi be proved true

check box n a square on a computer screen that is clicked on to select an option

check digit n in computing, an extra digit used for validation

checked adj patterned with squares

check-in n **1** registration at a hotel or airport **2** a registration desk

checklist /chék list/ n a list of items for consideration or action

checkmate /chék mayt/ n **1** in chess, a winning position or move in which an opponent's king is in check **2** in chess, a move that produces checkmate ■ vt (-mating, -mated) **1** in

chess, put an opponent's king in checkmate **2** thwart somebody

ORIGIN **Checkmate** comes ultimately from a Persian phrase meaning 'the king is defeated or left helpless'. It entered English through French in the Middle Ages.

checkout /chék owt/ n **1** a supermarket till **2** a departure from a hotel

checkpoint /chék poynt/ n a place where police or soldiers stop and check vehicles

checksum /chék sum/ n a value used to check for transmission errors in data

checkup /chék up/ n a medical or dental examination

cheddar /chéddər/ n a hard yellow cheese

cheek n **1** the soft side area of the face between the nose and the ear **2** the side of a buttock (infml) **3** impertinence (infml) ◊ **cheek by jowl** side by side or very close together ◊ **turn the other cheek** accept injury or insults without retaliating

cheekbone /cheek bōn/ n a bone in the face below the eye and above the cheeks

cheeky /cheeki/ (-ier, -iest) adj impertinent —**cheekily** adv —**cheekiness** n

cheep /cheep/ n a shrill sound made by young bird —**cheep** v ◊ See note at **cheap**

cheer n **1** a shout of encouragement or support **2** a sense of wellbeing and optimism ■ v **1** vti shout encouragement or support to somebody ◊ cheered them on **2** also **cheer up** vt make somebody feel cheerful —**cheeringly** adv

cheerful /cheerf'l/ adj **1** happy and optimistic **2** bright and pleasant —**cheerfully** adv —**cheerfulness** n

cheerio /cheeri ó/ interj goodbye (infml)

cheerleader /cheer leedər/ n a performer who exhorts a crowd to cheer at a sports event

cheerless /cheerləss/ adj depressing —**cheerlessly** adv —**cheerlessness** n

cheers interj **1** expresses good wishes before drinking an alcoholic drink (infml) **2** goodbye **3** thanks

cheery /cheeri/ (-ier, -iest) adj cheerful —**cheerily** adv —**cheeriness** n

cheese /cheez/ n **1** a solid food made from milk curds **2** a block of cheese

cheeseburger /cheez burgər/ n a hamburger covered with melted cheese, served in a bun

cheesecake /cheez kayk/ n **1** a dessert of sweetened soft cheese on a biscuit or pastry base **2** photographs of attractive women (slang)

cheesecloth /cheez kloth/ n a light woven cotton material. Use: lightweight clothes, straining cheese.

cheesed off adj annoyed or bored (infml)

cheeseparing /cheez pairing/ adj stingy —**cheeseparing** n

cheesy /cheezi/ (-ier, -iest) adj **1** like cheese **2** cheap and tawdry (infml) —**cheesiness** n

cheetah /cheetə/ (pl -tahs or same) n a large wild cat with a yellowish-brown black-spotted coat that is the fastest land mammal

Cheever /chéevar/, **John** (1912–82) US writer

chef /shef/ n a professional cook

chef-d'oeuvre /sháy dúrvra/ (pl **chefs-d'oeuvre** /pronunc. same/) n a masterpiece

~~cheif~~ incorrect spelling of **chief**

Chekhov /chék of/, **Anton Pavlovich** (1860–1904) Russian writer —**Chekhovian** /che kóvi an/ n, adj

Chelsea bun /chélssi bún/ n a round currant bun

Chelyabinsk /chel yaábinsk/ city in W Russia. Pop. 1,393,608 (1995).

chemical /kémmik'l/ adj 1 of chemistry 2 composed of chemical substances ■ n a substance used in or made by chemistry —**chemically** adv

chemical dependency n drug addiction

chemical engineering n a branch of engineering dealing with the industrial applications of chemistry —**chemical engineer** n

chemical reaction n a process that changes the molecular composition of a substance

chemical warfare n warfare using chemical weapons

chemical weapon n a weapon containing a life-threatening or disabling chemical

chemise /sha meéz/ n 1 a long loose dress 2 a long loose undergarment

chemist /kémmist/ n 1 a shop selling medicines and toiletries 2 somebody who prepares and dispenses medicines 3 a scientist specializing in chemistry

chemistry /kémmistri/ n 1 the study of the structure, composition, properties, and reactive characteristics of substances 2 the chemical structure, composition, and properties of a substance 3 the spontaneous reaction of two people to each other

chemo- prefix chemical, chemistry o chemotherapy

chemoreceptor /keémō ri séptar/ n an organ responsive to chemical stimulus

chemotherapy /keémō thérrapi/, **chemo** n the treatment of diseases, especially cancer, with drugs —**chemotherapeutic** /keémō therra pyóotik/ adj —**chemotherapist** n

Cheney /cháyni/, **Dick** (b. 1941) vice president of the United States (2001–)

Chengdu /chéng dóo/ capital of Sichuan Province, south-central China. Pop. 4,320,000 (1995).

chenille /sha neél/ n 1 a soft thick cotton or silk fabric with a raised pile. Use: furnishings, clothes. 2 a thick silk, cotton, or worsted cord. Use: embroidery, fringes, trimmings.

Chennai /cha ní/ capital of Tamil Nadu State, SE India. Pop. 3,841,396 (1991).

Chen Shui-Bian /chan shwáy bi án/ (b. 1951) president of Taiwan (2000–)

Cheops /keé ops/ (2549?–2526 BC) Egyptian pharaoh

cheque /chek/ n a small printed form that is filled in and signed to instruct a bank to pay money to the person or firm named on it

chequebook journalism n payment for news

cheque card, **cheque guarantee card** n UK a plastic bank card that guarantees payment of a cheque

chequer /chékar/ n 1 a check pattern 2 a piece used in Chinese chequers ■ vt 1 mark with a check pattern 2 affect adversely from time to time o regrettable incidents that chequer his career

chequered /chékard/ adj 1 checked 2 characterized by periods of trouble or controversy o her chequered past

Chequers /chékarz/ n the British prime minister's country house

cherish /chérrish/ vt 1 love and care for 2 retain in mind fondly or hopefully —**cherishingly** adv

Chernobyl /char nőb'l, -nóbb'l/ n the site of a nuclear power plant disaster in 1986 near Kiev, Ukraine

Cherokee /chérra keé/ (pl same or **-kees**) n a member of a Native North American people who now live mainly in Oklahoma and North Carolina —**Cherokee** adj

cheroot /sha róot/ n a cigar with square-cut ends

cherry /chérri/ (pl **-ries**) n 1 a small round fruit with a hard stone 2 a tree that produces cherries 3 the wood of the tree that produces cherries. Use: furniture-making. 4 also **cherry red** a deep red colour —**cherry** adj

cherry-pick vti select only the best of something

cherry picker n a mobile crane with a platform for working off the ground

cherry tomato n a small tomato

cherub /chérrab/ n a depiction of an angel as a chubby child with wings —**cherubic** /cha róobik/ adj

Chesapeake Bay /chéssa peek-/ inlet of the Atlantic Ocean separating Virginia and Maryland

Cheshire /chéshar/ county in NW England. Pop. 975,000 (1994).

Cheshire cat n the cat from Lewis Carroll's Alice's Adventures in Wonderland, whose broad grin remained after it disappeared

chess[1] n a game played on a chequered board by two players, each with 16 pieces, whose object is to capture the opponent's king

chess[2] n a deck board or floorboard of a pontoon bridge

chessboard /chéss bawrd/ n a chequered board used for playing chess

chessman /chéss man/ (pl **-men** /-men/), **chesspiece** /chéss peess/ n a piece used in playing chess

chest n 1 the upper part or front of the human body below the neck and above the stomach 2 a strong rectangular box ◊ **get something**

off your chest talk openly about something upsetting

chesterfield /chéstərfeeld/ *n* a large leather sofa

ORIGIN **Chesterfields** are named after a 19C earl of Chesterfield (in Derbyshire).

Chesterfield /chéstərfeeld/, **Philip Dormer Stanhope, 4th Earl of Chesterfield** (1694–1773) British politician and writer

Chesterton /chéstərtən/, **G. K.** (1874–1936) British writer

chestnut /chéss nut/ *n* **1** an edible glossy brown nut **2** (*pl* **chestnuts** *or same*) a tree that bears chestnuts **3** a reddish-brown horse **4** a deep reddish-brown colour **5** an overused joke or story (*infml*) —**chestnut** *adj*

chest of drawers *n* a cabinet containing drawers for storing clothes

chesty /chésti/ (**-ier, -iest**) *adj* having phlegm in the lungs

cheval glass /shə vál-/ *n* a long mirror that tilts on a frame

chevalier /shə válli ər/ *n* **1** a French title of honour **2** a French knight or nobleman of the lowest rank

chevron /shévrən/ *n* a V-shaped symbol indicating rank on uniforms ■ **chevrons** *npl* a road sign with V-shapes indicating a sharp bend

chevy *vt* = **chivvy**

chew *vti* **1** bite food repeatedly in the mouth before swallowing **2** damage something by gnawing ○ *chewing her nails* ■ *n* **1** the process of chewing **2** a sweet that has to be chewed —**chewable** *adj*

□ **chew over** *vt* think about or discuss

chewing gum /choò ing-/ *n* a sweet flavoured substance that is chewed but not swallowed

chewy /choò i/ (**-ier, -iest**) *adj* requiring chewing —**chewiness** *n*

Cheyenne[1] /shī án/ (*pl same or* **-ennes**) *n* a member of a Native North American people who once lived in the W Great Plains —**Cheyenne** *adj*

Cheyenne[2] /shī án/ **1** river in E Wyoming and South Dakota. Length 848 km/527 mi. **2** capital of Wyoming. Pop. 53,640 (1998).

chi /kī/ (*pl* **chis**), **khi** (*pl* **khis**) *n* the 22nd letter of the Greek alphabet

Chiang Kai-shek

Chiang Kai-shek /cháng kī shék/ (1887–1975) Chinese military leader and president of Taiwan (1949–75)

Chianti /ki ánti/, **chianti** *n* a light Italian red wine

chiaroscuro /ki aarə skuúrrō/ *n* the artistic use of light and shade —**chiaroscurism** *n* —**chiaroscurist** *n*

Chiba /cheébə/ capital of **Chiba Prefecture**, E Honshu, Japan. Pop. 867,289 (2000).

chic /sheek/ *adj* stylish ■ *n* style and elegance —**chicness** *n*

Chicago /shi kaàgō/ city in NE Illinois. Pop. 2,802,079 (1998). —**Chicagoan** *n, adj*

chicane /shi káyn/ *n* **1** a sharp double bend on a motor-racing circuit **2** in bridge or whist, a hand with no trumps or no cards of one suit ■ *vi* (**-caning, -caned**) engaged in cheating

chicanery /shi káynəri/ *n* trickery or deception

Chichester /chíchistər/, **Sir Francis Charles** (1901–72) British aviator and sailor

chichi /sheé shee/ *adj* self-consciously stylish (*disapproving*) —**chichi** *n*

chick *n* **1** a baby bird **2** US, Can a young woman (*slang; sometimes offensive*)

chickadee /chíkə dee/ (*pl* **-dees** *or same*) *n* a North American grey tit with a dark crown on its head and a distinctive call

chicken /chíkin/ *n* **1** a common domestic fowl kept for its meat and eggs **2** the meat from a chicken as food **3** a person regarded as cowardly (*infml*) ■ *adj* cowardly (*infml*) ◊ See note at **cowardly**

□ **chicken out** *vi* lack the nerve to continue (*slang*)

chicken-and-egg situation *n* a situation in which it is impossible to know which of two related circumstances occurred first and caused the other

chicken feed *n* an insignificant amount of money (*infml*)

chicken-hearted, chicken-livered *adj* cowardly

chickenpox /chíkin poks/ *n* a viral disease usually affecting children and characterized by a rash and fever

chicken wire *n* wire netting

chickpea /chík pee/ *n* **1** a yellow edible seed **2** a plant that produces chickpeas

chickweed /chík weed/ *n* a common weed with small white flowers

chicle /chík'l/ *n* a gummy substance from the latex of a tropical evergreen tree. Use: making chewing gum.

chicory /chíkəri/ (*pl* **-ries**) *n* **1** pale, slightly bitter leaves eaten cooked or used in salad **2** a ground roasted root used as a coffee additive or substitute **3** a plant that produces chicory leaves and roots

chide /chīd/ (**chiding, chided** *or* **chid** /chid/, **chided** *or* **chid** *or* **chidden** /chídd'n/) *vti* reproach —**chidingly** *adv*

chief /cheef/ *n* **1** the leader of a group or organization **2** a chieftain **3** a ship's principal engineer ■ *adj* **1** most important, basic, or common **2** highest in authority or rank —**chiefdom** *n* —**chiefship** *n*

chief constable *n* in the UK, the police officer in charge of a regional police force

chief executive *n* 1 the head of an executive body 2 *also* **chief executive officer** the highest-ranking executive of a business or organization

chief justice *n* 1 the presiding justice of the US Supreme Court 2 the senior judge in the High Courts of Australia and other Commonwealth countries

chiefly /cheéflii/ *adv* 1 above all 2 in the main ■ *adj* of chiefs

chief minister *n* the leader of a national or provincial government in various countries with a parliamentary system, or a ruler's chief executive official

chief of staff *n* the person in charge of a military or administrative staff

chief petty officer *n* a noncommissioned officer in the US Navy or Coast Guard of a rank above petty officer

Chief Rabbi *n* the senior religious leader in some Jewish communities

chieftain /cheéftən/ *n* a leader of a people or similar ethnic group —**chieftaincy** *n* —**chieftainship** *n*

chiffon /shíffon/ *n* a very light sheer nylon, rayon, or silk fabric ■ *adj* 1 made of chiffon 2 fluffy because of added whipped egg whites or gelatin

Chifley /chíffli/, **Ben** (1885–1951) prime minister of Australia (1945–49)

chignon /sheén yon, -yoN/ *n* a knot of hair worn at the nape of the neck

chihuahua /chi waáwa/ *n* a very small dog originating in Mexico

Chihuahua /chi waá waa/ *n* capital of **Chihuahua State**, N Mexico. Pop. 627,662 (1995).

chilblain /chíl blayn/ *n* a red itchy swelling on the fingers or toes caused by the cold (*often pl*)

child /chīld/ (*pl* **children** /chíldrən/) *n* 1 a young human being between birth and puberty 2 a son or daughter of human parents 3 a baby or an infant 4 an immature person 5 a product or result of a particular environment, period, or influence ○ *a child of the 1960s* ◊ **with child** pregnant (*literary*) ◊ See note at **youth**

child abuse *n* mistreatment of a child —**child abuser** *n*

childbearing /chíld bairing/ *n* the process of carrying a child in the womb and giving birth to it ○ *Her years of childbearing are over.*

child benefit *n* in the UK and New Zealand, a state payment to the parents of a child to help pay for its maintenance

childbirth /chíld burth/ *n* the process of giving birth to a child

childcare /chíld kair/ *n* 1 the paid care and supervision of children by an adult 2 the care and supervision of children by a local authority in place of their parents

child-free /chíld free/ *adj* describes people who have no children, or a place in which children are not allowed ○ *child-free dining areas*

childhood /chíld hŏod/ *n* 1 the state of being a child, or the time when somebody is a child 2 an early stage

childish /chíldish/ *adj* 1 like a child 2 immature —**childishly** *adv* —**childishness** *n*

childless /chíldləss/ *adj* having no children

childlike /chíld līk/ *adj* having the positive qualities of a child ○ *childlike innocence*

child minder *n* somebody who looks after somebody else's children as a job —**child minding** *n*

child prodigy *n* an exceptionally talented child

childproof /chíld proof/ *adj* 1 hard for a child to open or operate 2 made safe for children ■ *vt* make safe for children or hard for children to open or operate

child restraint *n* a child's safety seat

child's play *n* a straightforward task

Child Support Agency *n* in the UK, the government agency responsible for ensuring that absent parents pay child maintenance

Chile /chílli/ country in SW South America. Cap. Santiago. Pop. 15,328,467 (2001). —**Chilean** *n*, *adj*

chili *n* US = **chilli**

chill *n* 1 a moderate coldness 2 a sudden short fever 3 a coldness caused by fever or fear 4 a depressing effect ■ *adj* moderately cold ■ *v* 1 *vt* make cold 2 *vti* refrigerate, or be refrigerated 3 *vt* make somebody afraid 4 *also* **chill out** *vi* calm down or relax (*infml*) —**chillness** *n*

chiller /chíllər/ *n* a refrigerated compartment

chilli /chílli/ (*pl* **-lies**) *n* 1 a red or green capsicum pepper pod with a strong flavour 2 *also* **chilli powder** a hot-tasting spice made from ground chillies 3 *also* **chilli con carne** a spicy dish of meat and beans

SPELLCHECK Do not confuse the spelling of **chilli** and **chilly** ('cold'), which sound similar.

chilling /chílling/ *adj* frightening —**chillingly** *adv*

chillum /chíllem/ *n* 1 a short straight pipe for smoking cannabis or tobacco 2 a quantity of cannabis or tobacco

chilly /chílli/ (**-ier, -iest**) *adj* 1 moderately cold 2 feeling rather cold 3 unfriendly —**chillily** *adv* —**chilliness** *n* ◊ See note at **chilli**

chimaera /kī meérə, ki-/ *n* 1 (*pl* **chimaeras** or *same*) a deep-sea fish with a skeleton of cartilage and a long thin tail 2 = **chimera**

Chimborazo /chímbə raázō/ mountain peak in central Ecuador. Height 6,310 m/20,702 ft.

chime[1] /chīm/ *n* 1 the sound of a bell 2 a device for striking a bell (*often pl*) 3 a series of notes sounded by a clock before striking 4 a percussion instrument consisting of hanging bells, metal bars, or tubes (*often pl*) 5 a decoration that moves and makes a pleasant sound in the wind ■ *v* (**chiming, chimed**) 1 *vi* ring harmoniously **2** *vt* indicate something by chiming **3** *vt* produce musical sound by striking a bell **4** *vi* agree or harmonize **5** *vti* say something or speak in a musical way

□ **chime in** *vi* interrupt other people's conversation

chime[2] /chīm/, **chimb** *n* a rim of a barrel

chimera /kī méerə, ki-/, **chimaera** *n* something totally unrealistic or impractical

ORIGIN In Greek mythology, Chimera was a monster with a lion's head, goat's body, and serpent's tail.

chimerical /kī mérrik'l, ki-/ *adj* imaginary

chimney /chímni/ (*pl* **-neys**) *n* **1** a structure for venting smoke, gas, or steam **2** the part of a chimney rising above a roof **3** a passage inside a chimney for venting smoke, gas, or steam **4** the funnel of a steam engine or steamship **5** a glass tube protecting a lamp flame **6** a cleft in a rock face through which a climber can ascend **7** *UK*, *regional* a fireplace

chimney breast *n* a projecting section of a wall surrounding a chimney or fireplace in a room

chimneypiece /chímni peess/ *n* a mantelpiece

chimney pot *n* a pipe placed on the top of a chimney to increase the draught

chimney stack *n* **1** a tall chimney on the roof of a factory **2** a tall industrial chimney

chimney sweep *n* somebody whose job is to remove soot from chimneys

chimpanzee /chím pan zeé/, **chimp** *n* a medium-sized ape

chin *n* the part of the face below the lips ■ *vti* (**chinning**, **chinned**) pull yourself up until your chin is level with a bar you are holding

china /chínə/ *n* **1** porcelain **2** articles made of china

China /chínə/ country in East Asia. Cap. Beijing. Pop. 1,273,111,300 (2001).

china clay *n* kaolin

China Sea part of the Pacific Ocean extending from Japan to the southern end of the Malay Peninsula. Depth 2,717 m/8,913 ft.

Chinatown /chínə town/ *n* an area of a city where many Chinese people live

chinchilla /chin chíllə/ *n* **1** (*pl* **chinchillas** or same) a bushy-tailed rodent kept for its fur **2** chinchilla fur

Chindwin /chín dwín/ river flowing from N Myanmar southwards into the River Irrawaddy. Length 1,200 km/720 mi.

Chinese /chī neéz/ *n* **1** somebody from China **2** the group of languages spoken in China **3** the official language of China —**Chinese** *adj*

Chinese cabbage *n* **1** *also* **Chinese leaves** a vegetable with wrinkled leaves **2** a plant with long white fleshy stems topped with dark green leaves, used as a vegetable in Asian cooking

Chinese calendar *n* the traditional calendar used in China that divides the year into 24 fifteen-day periods and is based on both the lunar and solar cycles

Chinese chequers *n* a board game played with marbles (+ *sing verb*)

Chinese lantern *n* **1** a paper lantern **2** a plant with orange fruit in papery orange cases

Chinese New Year *n* a festival day marking the new year. Date: between 21 January and 19 February.

Chinese whispers *n* a game for a group of people in which a message is whispered from one person to another to see how much it is changed in the process (+ *sing verb*)

chink[1] *n* a narrow opening

chink[2] *n* a sharp ringing sound ■ *vti* make or cause to make a sharp ringing sound

chinless /chínləss/ *adj* **1** having a receding chin **2** weak and ineffectual

chino /cheénō/ *n* cotton twill fabric. Use: military uniforms, casual trousers. ■ **chinos** *npl* chino trousers

chinook /chi noók/ *n* **1** a warm moist sea wind blowing onto the NE US coast **2** a dry warm wind blowing off the Rocky Mountains

chinstrap /chín strap/ *n* a hat or helmet strap passing under the chin

chintz *n* patterned glazed cotton fabric

chintzy /chíntsi/ (**-ier**, **-iest**) *adj* **1** brightly coloured and patterned **2** describes decor regarded as fussy or quaint (*infml*)

chinwag /chín wag/ *n* a long chat (*infml*) —**chinwagging** *n*

~~chior~~ incorrect spelling of **choir**

chip *n* **1** a small piece that has been broken or cut off something hard **2** a space left in something hard after a small piece has been broken off or out of it **3** a long piece of fried potato **4** a piece of thin crisp snack food ○ *corn chips* **5** a counter used as money in gambling **6** a wafer of semiconductor material **7** a short hit or kick of a ball over an obstacle or opponent ■ *v* (**chipping**, **chipped**) **1** *vt* break off a small piece from something **2** *vi* lose small pieces ○ *paint that will not chip easily* **3** *vt* produce a short hit or kick of a ball over an obstacle or opponent ○ *chipped the ball over the water and onto the green* **4** *vt* carve something by removing small pieces **5** *vt* chop something into chips ◇ **a chip off the old block** a person resembling his or her parents (*infml*) ◇ **have a chip on your shoulder** behave in a resentful manner (*infml*) ◇ **when the chips are down** at a time of crisis (*infml*)

□ **chip in** *v* (*infml*) **1** *vti* contribute something **2** *vi* interrupt

chipboard /chíp bawrd/ *n* board made of wood chips

chipmunk /chíp mungk/ (*pl* **-munks** or same) *n* a small striped rodent of the squirrel family

chipolata /chíppə laátə/ *n* a small thin pork sausage

Chippendale /chíppən dayl/ *adj* made in an 18C English furniture style —**Chippendale** *n*

Chippendale /chíppən dayl/, **Thomas** (1718–79) British furniture designer

chipper /chíppər/ adj cheerful (infml)

chippy /chíppi/ (pl **-pies**), **chippie** n (infml) **1** a fish and chip shop **2** a carpenter

chipset /chíp set/ n a group of microchips functioning as a unit

Chirac /sheér ak/, **Jacques** (b. 1932) prime minister (1974–76, 1986–88) and president (1995–) of France

Chirico /kírrikó/, **Giorgio de** (1888–1978) Greek-born Italian painter

chiromancy /kírō manssi/ n palmistry —**chiromancer** n

chiropody /ki róppədi, shi-/ n the branch of medicine concerned with the care and treatment of feet —**chiropodist** n

chiropractic /kírō práktik/ n a medical system in which disease and disorders are considered to be caused by misalignment of the bones —**chiropractor** /kírō praktər/ n

chirp n a short high-pitched sound made by a bird ■ v **1** vi make a chirp **2** vti say or speak in a cheerful manner

chirpy /chúrpi/ (**-ier**, **-iest**) adj cheerful (infml) —**chirpily** adv —**chirpiness** n

chisel /chízz'l/ n a tool with a flat bevelled blade for cutting and shaping wood or stone ■ vti (**-elling**, **-elled**) carve with a chisel

chiselled /chízzəl'd/ adj sharply-defined in shape or profile o a finely chiselled face

Chişinău /kíshi nố/ capital of Moldova. Pop. 770,000 (1995).

chit[1] n an official note or document

chit[2] n a girl regarded as saucily impudent (dated)

chitchat /chit chat/ n small talk (infml) —**chitchat** vi

chitin /kítin/ n a protective outer covering on some insects and arthropods and in cell walls —**chitinous** adj

Chittagong /chíttə gong/ port in SE Bangladesh. Pop. 1,566,070 (1991).

chitterlings /chíttərlingz/, **chitlins** /chíttlinz/, **chitlings** npl pig intestines cooked and eaten as food

chivalric /shív'lrik/ adj of knights and the knights' code

chivalry /shív'lri/ n **1** considerate behaviour, especially towards women **2** the medieval concept of knighthood —**chivalrous** adj

ORIGIN **Chivalry** was originally a collective noun for knights or horseman equipped for battle. It was adopted from French, and derives from the Latin word for 'horse', which is also the source (via Italian) of *cavalry*. **Chivalry** was also used from the 13C for the status and character of a knight. It began to refer specifically to the qualities of an ideal knight only in the late 18C.

chive /chīv/ n **1** a long narrow tubular leaf with an onion flavour. Use: seasoning food. (usually pl) **2** a plant that produces chives

chivvy /chívvi/ (**-vies**, **-vied**), **chevy** /chévvi/ vt urge or harass

chlamydia /klə míddi ə/ (pl **-as** or same or **-ae** /-ee/) n **1** a pathogenic bacterium **2** a sexually transmitted disease caused by chlamydia

chloride /kláwr īd/ n a compound containing chlorine and one other element

chlorinate /kláwri nayt/ (**-nating, -nated**) vt combine or treat with chlorine —**chlorinated** adj —**chlorination** /kláwri náysh'n/ n

chlorine /kláwr een/ n (symbol **Cl**) a gaseous poisonous greenish-yellow chemical element. Use: water purification, disinfectant.

ORIGIN **Chlorine** was coined by Sir Humphry Davy in 1810. He formed it from a Greek word meaning 'green', with reference to the greenish-yellow colour of the gas. The same Greek word appears in *chloroform* and *chlorophyll*.

chloroform /kláwrə fawrm/ n a colourless sweet-smelling toxic liquid that rapidly becomes a gas, causing unconsciousness if inhaled. Use: solvent, cleaning agent, formerly, anaesthetic. ■ vt render unconscious with chloroform

chlorophyll /klórrəfil/ n the green plant pigment involved in photosynthesis

chloroplast /kláwrə plast, -plaast/ n a component of a plant cell containing chlorophyll and involved in photosynthesis —**chloroplastic** /kláwrə plástik/ adj

~~chocalate~~ incorrect spelling of **chocolate**

choc ice n a chocolate-covered bar of ice cream

chock n **1** a block to stop something moving **2** a metal anchor used in climbing ■ vt stop something moving by securing it with a chock

chock-a-block adj packed full (infml)

chock-full adj completely full (infml)

chocoholic /chókə hóllik/, **chocaholic** n a lover of chocolate (humorous)

chocolate /chóklit/ n **1** a smooth sweet brown food made from cacao seeds, cocoa butter, milk, and sugar **2** a sweet covered in chocolate **3** a drink made from sweetened powdered chocolate and milk —**chocolatey** adj

ORIGIN In its earliest use **chocolate** meant only a drink, not the solid food. It came into English from Spanish from a Native South American word meaning literally 'bitter water'.

chocolate-box adj stereotypically and sentimentally pretty

Choctaw /chók taw/ (pl same or **-taws**) n **1** a member of a Native North American people who now live mainly in Oklahoma and S Mississippi **2** the language of the Choctaw people —**Choctaw** adj

choice /choyss/ n **1** a decision to choose somebody or something **2** the power or freedom to choose o They gave us no choice. **3** a selection to choose from o a wide choice of styles **4** a selected person or thing ■ adj (**choicer**,

choicest) 1 high-quality 2 rude or emphatic *(euphemistic)* ○ *a few choice words* ◇ **of choioo** the best or most suitable

choir /kwīr/ *n* 1 a group of singers performing together *(+ sing or pl verb)* 2 the area in a church where a choir sings

choirboy /kwír boy/ *n* a boy singer in a church choir

choirgirl /kwír gurl/ *n* a girl singer in a church choir

choir loft *n* an upstairs part of a church where a choir sings

choirmaster /kwír maastər/ *n* the trainer and conductor of a choir

choke[1] *v* (**choking, choked**) 1 *vi* stop breathing because of a blockage in the throat 2 *vt* prevent somebody from breathing by squeezing his or her throat 3 *vt* block a road, passage, or channel 4 *vt* prevent plants from growing by growing around and over them 5 *vi* lose your nerve and falter *(infml)* ■ *n* 1 a noise of somebody choking 2 a fuel mixture regulator for an engine —**choking** *adj*
□ **choke back** *vt* not let an emotion out

choke[2] *n* the inedible central part of an artichoke

choke chain, choke collar *n* a chain collar that tightens easily, used for training a dog

choke point *n* a narrow strait through which shipping must go

choker /chōkər/ *n* a close-fitting necklace or similar ornament

choko /chōkō/ *(pl* **-kos)** *n* ANZ a tropical fruit

cholera /kóllərə/ *n* an acute intestinal disease

choleric /kóllərik/ *adj* bad-tempered *(literary)* —**choler** *n*

cholesterol /kə léstə rol/ *n* a steroid alcohol produced in the liver and present in all animal cells but considered a health risk if found in high levels in the blood

chomp, chump *vti* bite or chew noisily *(infml)* —**chomp** *n*

Chomsky /chómski/, **Noam** *(b.* 1928) US linguist

Chongqing /chŏng kíng/, **Chungking, Ch'ung-ch'ing** city in SW China. Pop. 3,470,000 (1995).

chook *n* ANZ a chicken *(infml)*

choose /chooz/ (**choosing, chose** /chōz/, **chosen** /chōz'n/) *vti* 1 select ○ *chose a partner* 2 make a deliberate decision to do something

SPELLCHECK Do not confuse the spelling of **choose** and **chose** (past tense of *choose*).

choosy /choozi/ (**-ier, -iest**) *adj* fussy in making choices *(infml)* —**choosily** *adv* —**choosiness** *n*

Cho Oyu /chố ố yoo/ mountain in the Himalaya range. Height 8,201 m/26,906 ft.

chop[1] *v* (**chopping, chopped**) 1 *vt* cut something up with downward strokes of a sharp tool 2 *vt* sever or fell something 3 *vi* make chopping movements 4 *vt* form a hole or passage by chopping ○ *chopped his way through the undergrowth* 5 *vt* hit somebody or something

with a sharp downward movement 6 *vi* move in a different direction, or change your mind ■ *n* 1 a small piece of red meat with the bone attached 2 a sharp downward stroke or hit 3 dismissal from a job *(infml)* ○ *was given the chop* 4 the cancellation, closedown, or stoppage of something *(infml)* 5 irregular wave motions ○ *a lot of chop on the bay this morning*

chop[2] (**chopping, chopped**) ◇ **chop and change** have frequent abrupt, disconcerting, or irritating changes of mind

chop[3] *n* 1 a trademark, official stamp, or mark of quality, especially in East Asia 2 *Malaysia* a printing stamp ■ *vt* (**chopping, chopped**) *Malaysia* stamp with an official mark

chop[4] *n* W Africa food

chop-chop *interj, adv* quickly *(infml)*

Chopin /shóp aN, shŏp-/, **Frédéric François** (1810–49) Polish composer and pianist

chopper /chóppər/ *n* 1 a small axe 2 a cleaver 3 a helicopter *(infml)* 4 a motorcycle or bicycle with high handlebars and a long front fork 5 a device for producing a pulsing flow or beam of electricity, light, or radiation ■ **choppers** *npl* teeth *(slang)*

chopping board /chópping-/ *n* a board for chopping food

choppy /chóppi/ (**-pier, -piest**) *adj* rough, with many small waves —**choppily** *adv* —**choppiness** *n*

chops *npl* the jaws *(infml)*

chopstick /chóp stik/ *n* one of a pair of narrow sticks used for eating or preparing East Asian food

ORIGIN The first part of **chopstick** meant 'quick' in the pidgin English formerly used between Chinese people and Europeans in conducting trade and business. It is an alteration of a Cantonese word meaning 'urgent'.

chop suey /chop sóo i/ *n* a dish of shredded meat and mixed vegetables

choral /káwrəl/ *adj* 1 performed by a choir 2 of a chorus or choir —**chorally** *adv*

chorale /ko raàl/ *n* 1 a Lutheran hymn tune 2 a piece of music based on a chorale 3 *US* a group of singers specializing in church music

chord[1] /kawrd/ *n* a group of notes played or sung together —**chordal** *adj* ◇ **strike** or **touch a chord** produce an emotional response

USAGE chord or **cord**? In musical contexts the spelling is **chord**, in anatomical contexts (*spinal cord, umbilical cord, vocal cords*), **cord** is more usual. **Cord** is also used for a thick, strong string, and as a measurement of cut wood.

chord[2] /kawrd/ *n* 1 a straight line connecting two points on an arc or circle 2 a cord of the body 3 the horizontal part of a truss designed to absorb tension in a roof

chore /chawr/ *n* 1 a routine task *(often pl)* 2 an unenjoyable task

choreograph /kórri ə graaf/ *v* **1** *vti* devise dance movements for a piece of music **2** *vt* organize and coordinate —**choreographer** /kórri óggrəfər/ *n*

choreography /kórri óggrəfi/ (*pl* **-phies**) *n* **1** the devising of dance movements for a piece of music **2** the dance movements for a piece of music —**choreographic** /kórri ə gráffik/ *adj* —**choreographically** *adv*

chorister /kórristər/ *n* a singer in a chorus or choir

chorizo /chə reé zō/ (*pl* **-zos**) *n* a spicy sausage

chortle /cháwrt'l/ *n* a gleeful laugh —**chortle** *vi*

> **ORIGIN Chortle** is a blend of *chuckle* and *snort*, coined by Lewis Carroll in *Through the Looking-Glass* (1872).

chorus /káwrəss/ *n* **1** a part of a song repeated after each verse **2** a large group of singers performing choral or operatic music together (*+ sing or pl verb*) **3** a group of performers singing and dancing together in a musical or variety show (*+ sing or pl verb*) **4** a group of actors in a Greek drama speaking or singing together **5** a piece of music for a large group of singers **6** an expression of feeling by many people together ○ *a chorus of disapproval* ■ *vt* say together

chorus girl *n* a woman who sings and dances in a group in a stage or film production

chorus line *n* a chorus of singers and dancers in a musical or variety show

chose past tense of **choose** ◊ see note at **choose**

chosen /chōz'n/ past participle of **choose** ■ *adj* select ○ *one of the chosen few*

chow[1] *n* food (*slang*)

chow[2], **chow chow** *n* a stocky thick-coated dog of a breed originating in China

chowder /chówdər/ *n* a thick seafood or fish soup

chowk *n* S Asia a marketplace

chow mein /chów máyn/ *n* a dish of noodles, chopped meat, and vegetables

Chrétien /krétti əN/, **Jean** (*b.* 1934) prime minister (1993–) of Canada

Christ /krīst/ *n* **1** Jesus Christ **2** the Messiah in Jewish belief —**Christly** *adj*

> **ORIGIN Christ** came through Latin from Greek, and literally meant 'anointed'. The Greek was a direct translation of the Hebrew word that came separately into English as *Messiah*.

Christchurch /krīst church/ **1** town in S England. Pop. 40,500 (1991). **2** city in the east of the South Island, New Zealand. Pop. 339,500 (1998).

christen /kríss'n/ *vt* **1** baptize and name **2** give a name to **3** use for the first time (*infml*)

Christendom /kríss'ndəm/ *n* **1** Christian countries **2** Christians as a group (*fml*)

christening /kríss'ning/ *n* a Christian church ceremony to baptize and name a baby

Christian /krísschən/ *n* **1** a believer in the teachings of Jesus Christ **2** Malaysia a Protestant ■ *adj* **1** of the teachings of Jesus Christ **2** of Christianity

Christian Era *n* the period of history dating from the year Jesus Christ is believed to have been born

Christianity /krísti ánnəti/ *n* **1** the religion that follows Jesus Christ's teachings **2** the holding of Christian beliefs

Christian name *n* a first name, especially one given at a christening

Christian Science *n* a religious denomination whose members believe that faith can overcome illness —**Christian Scientist** *n*

Dame Agatha Christie

Christie /krísti/, **Dame Agatha** (1890–1976) British novelist and playwright

Christina /kri steénə/ (1626–89) queen of Sweden (1632–54)

Christmas /kríssməss/, **Christmas Day** *n* a festival celebrating the birth of Jesus Christ. Date: 25 December. —**Christmassy** *adj*

Christmas box *n* money traditionally given to tradespeople at Christmas

Christmas cake *n* a fruitcake made for Christmas

Christmas card *n* a greetings card sent at Christmas

Christmas carol *n* a song celebrating Christmas

Christmas cracker *n* a cracker pulled at Christmas

Christmas Eve *n* the day or evening before Christmas

Christmas Island /kríssməss-/ Australian island in the Indian Ocean, south of Java. Pop. 1,906 (1996).

Christmas pudding *n* a rich steamed fruit pudding eaten on Christmas Day

Christmas stocking *n* a stocking filled with presents for children at Christmas

Christmastime /kríssməss tīm/ *n* the period around Christmas

Christmas tree *n* a tree decorated with lights and ornaments at Christmas

Christopher /krístəfər/, **St** (*fl* 3C) patron saint of travellers

chromatic /krō máttik/ *adj* **1** describes a musical scale encompassing all the semitones in an octave **2** of colour —**chromatically** *adv*

chrome /krōm/ *n* **1** chromium **2** a compound containing chromium **3** a shiny chromium-plated metal. Use: formerly, car trim. ■ *vt* (**ohroming, chromed**) **1** coat with chromium **2** treat with a chromium compound

ORIGIN Chrome comes from a Greek word meaning 'colour'. It was coined in French as a name for chromium, the compounds of which are brightly coloured.

-chrome *suffix* colour, pigment o *monochrome*

chrome yellow *n* a yellow pigment

chromium /krṓ mi əm/ *n* (*symbol* **Cr**) a hard bluish-white metallic element. Use: alloys, electroplating.

chromosome /krṓmə sṓm/ *n* a rod-shaped structure in a cell nucleus that carries genes controlling inherited characteristics —**chromosomal** /krṓmə sṓm'l/ *adj*

chronic /krónnik/ *adj* **1** describes a long-lasting illness or condition **2** always present **3** habitual o *a chronic liar* **4** dire (*infml*) —**chronically** *adv* —**chronicity** /krə níssəti/ *n*

chronic fatigue syndrome *n* an illness characterized by exhaustion and weakness

chronicle /krónnik'l/ *n* **1** a chronological account **2** a fictional narrative ■ *vt* (**-cling, -cled**) make a chronological record of —**chronicler** *n*

chrono- *prefix* time o *chronology*

chronological /krónnə lójjik'l, krṓnə-/ *adj* **1** arranged in the order in which events occur **2** of chronology —**chronologically** *adv*

chronology /krə nólləji/ (*pl* **-gies**) *n* **1** the order in which events occur **2** a list of events in the order they occur —**chronologist** *n*

chronometer /krə nómmitər/ *n* a precision time-measuring instrument

chrysalis /kríssəliss/ *n* an insect in a cocoon at the stage between larva and adult

chrysanthemum /krə sánthiməm, -zán-/ *n* a garden plant whose large flowers have dense petal clusters

Chrysostom /kríssəstəm/, **John, St** (349?–407) Syrian theologian and orator

chub (*pl* **chubs** *or* **same**) *n* a minnow with a thick rounded body

chubby /chúbbi/ (**-bier, -biest**) *adj* plump in physique —**chubbily** *adv* —**chubbiness** *n*

chuck¹ *vt* **1** throw carelessly (*infml*) **2** get rid of (*infml*) **3** tickle affectionately under the chin —**chuck** *n* ◊ See note at **throw**
□ **chuck in** *vt* give up (*infml*)

chuck² *n* **1** a clamp on a lathe or drill **2** a cut of beef from the neck or shoulder

chuck³ *n* N England, regional an affectionate way of addressing somebody

chuckle /chúk'l/ (**-ling, -led**) *vti* laugh quietly —**chuckle** *n*

chuffed *adj* pleased (*infml*)

chug (**chugging, chugged**) *vi* **1** make or move with a repeated thudding sound like that of a small engine **2** continue steadily doing the usual things (*infml*) —**chug** *n*

Chukchi Sea /chúkchi-, chŏŏk-/ part of the Arctic Ocean north of the Bering Strait between Asia and North America

chum¹ *n* a friend (*dated infml*) ■ *vi* (**chumming, chummed**) be friends

chum² *n* fish bait scattered on the water ■ *vti* (**chumming, chummed**) engage in fishing using chum as bait

chum³ (*pl* **chums** *or* **same**), **chum salmon** *n* a salmon with wavy green streaks and blotches

chummy /chúmmi/ (**-mier, -miest**) *adj* friendly (*infml*) —**chummily** *adv* —**chumminess** *n*

chump¹ *n* **1** a person regarded as unwise (*infml* *dated*) **2** a thick end of a piece of meat o *a chump chop* **3** a thick piece of wood

chump² *vti, n* = chomp

chunder /chúndər/ *vti* vomit (*slang*) —**chunder** *n*

Chungking, Ch'ung-ch'ing ♦ Chongqing

chunk *n* **1** a thick square-shaped piece **2** a large amount or portion

chunky /chúngki/ (**-ier, -iest**) *adj* **1** containing lumps or bits **2** solid and square-shaped —**chunkiness** *n*

church *n* **1** a building for public worship, especially in the Christian religion **2** *also* **Church** the followers of a religion, especially Christianity, considered as group **3** a religious service o *go to church* **4** *also* **Church** religious leadership, especially when contrasted with state leadership **5** *also* **Church** a branch of the Christian religion —**churchy** *adj*

churchgoer /chúrch gō ər/ *n* somebody who attends church regularly —**churchgoing** *n, adj*

Churchill /chúrchil/, **Randolph, Lord** (1849–95) British politician

Sir Winston Churchill

Churchill, Sir Winston (1874–1965) British politician, writer, and prime minister (1940–45, 1951–55)

Church of England *n* the established Christian church in England, governed by bishops with the monarch as its titular head

Church of Scotland *n* the established Christian church in Scotland, which is Presbyterian

church school *n* a school founded or supported by the Church of England

churchwarden /chúrch wáwrd'n/ *n* **1** an Anglican layperson with church-related, usually business duties **2** a long-stemmed clay tobacco pipe

churchyard /chúrch yaard/ *n* a church cemetery

churlish /chúrlish/ *adj* 1 crass 2 unkind and grumpy —**churlishly** *adv* —**churlishness** *n*

churn *n* 1 a large milk can 2 a container for making butter ■ *v* 1 *vt* stir milk to make butter 2 *vt* make butter 3 *vti* splash violently 4 *vi* feel unsettled o *My stomach was churning.* □ **churn out** *vt* rapidly produce large quantities of

chute /shoot/ *n* 1 a sloping channel or passage to slide things down 2 a children's slide 3 a parachute (*infml*)

SPELLCHECK Do not confuse the spelling of **chute** and **shoot** ('fire a weapon', 'move fast', 'take a photograph', 'attempt to score a goal'), which sound similar.

chutney /chútni/ (*pl* **-neys**) *n* 1 a sweet and spicy fruit relish 2 *Carib* a Caribbean song similar to a calypso

chutzpah /hóotspə, kh-/, **hutzpah**, **chutzpa** *n* self-confidence (*infml*)

CIA *n* a US intelligence and counterintelligence organization operating outside the United States. Full form **Central Intelligence Agency**

ciabatta /chə báttə/ *n* a flat Italian bread made with olive oil

ciao /chow/ *interj* expresses a greeting (*infml*)

cicada /si kaádə/ (*pl* **-das** *or* **-dae** /-dee/) *n* a large winged insect living in trees and grass, the male of which makes a shrill sound

cicatrix /síkətriks/ (*pl* **-trices** /síkə trí seez/) *n* a scar (*technical*)

Cicero /síssərō/, **Marcus Tullius** (106–43 BC) Roman philosopher, writer, and politician —**Ciceronian** /sissə róni ən/ *adj*

Cid /sid/, **El** (1040?–99) Spanish military leader

CID *n* the detective branch of the UK police. Full form **Criminal Investigation Department**

cider /sídər/ *n* 1 an alcoholic drink made from apples 2 *US, Can* a nonalcoholic fresh apple drink

ORIGIN In English **cider** has always been made from apples. However, it goes back to a Hebrew word that meant strong drink in general.

~~cieling~~ incorrect spelling of **ceiling**

cigar /si gaár/ *n* a roll of tobacco leaves for smoking

~~cigaret~~ incorrect spelling of **cigarette**

cigarette /síggə rét/ *n* 1 a roll of shredded tobacco with a thin white paper cover 2 a roll of shredded leaves for smoking o *a marijuana cigarette*

~~cigarette~~ incorrect spelling of **cigarette**

~~cilinder~~ incorrect spelling of **cylinder**

~~cinamon~~ incorrect spelling of **cinnamon**

C in C, C-in-C *abbr* Commander in Chief

cinch *n* something easily done (*infml*)

Cincinnati /sínssi nátti/ city in SW Ohio. Pop. 336,400 (1998).

cinder /síndər/ *n* a small piece of charred wood or coal ■ **cinders** *npl* 1 ashes 2 fragments of solidified lava

cinder block *n US, Can* a breeze block

Cinderella /síndə réllə/ *n* a neglected person or thing ■ *adj* rags-to-riches

ORIGIN The original **Cinderella** is a fairy-tale character who is neglected by her sisters and set to drudge in the kitchen but is enabled by her fairy godmother to attend a ball and meet a prince. The story was popularized by a 1697 collection of traditional tales set down by Charles Perrault.

cine camera /sínni-/ *n* a camera for making moving pictures

cine film *n* film for making moving pictures

cinema /sínnəmə, sínni maa/ *n* 1 the film industry 2 films collectively 3 a building or room where films are shown 4 cinemas collectively

ORIGIN **Cinema** derives from a Greek word meaning 'movement', which was the basis of French *cinématographe*, the name given to the first film projector by its inventors, Auguste and Louis Lumière, in 1896. This was quickly shortened to *cinéma*, and borrowed into English.

cinematic /sínnə máttik/ *adj* 1 appropriate to film 2 of films —**cinematically** *adv*

cinematography /sínnəmə tóggrəfi/ *n* the photographing of films —**cinematographer** *n* —**cinematographic** /sínnə mətə gráffik/ *adj*

cinéma vérité /sínnəmə vérri tay/ *n* a documentary style of film-making

cinephile /sínni fīl/ *n* an enthusiast for film

cinnamon /sínnəmən/ *n* 1 a spice obtained from tree bark 2 a tree with bark from which cinnamon is obtained

cipher /sífər/, **cypher** *n* 1 a written code 2 the key to a cipher 3 a text in cipher ■ *vt* write in code

circa /súrkə/ *prep* on or in approximately a particular date

circadian /sur káydi ən/ *adj* occurring in a 24-hour cycle

~~circiut~~ incorrect spelling of **circuit**

circle /súrk'l/ *n* 1 a continuous round line, every point of which is equidistant from the centre 2 the area inside a circle 3 a circle-shaped area, object, or arrangement 4 a group of people with a common interest 5 a section of tiered seating in an upper level of a theatre ■ *v* (**-cling, -cled**) 1 *vti* move or move round something along a curving route 2 *vt* mark a ring round something

circlet /súrklət/ *n* a ring-like decoration, especially for a person's head

circuit /súrkit/ *n* 1 a circular path finishing where it began 2 an area bounded by a circular path 3 a single journey round a circular path 4 a regular journey round an area 5 a round of regularly attended or visited events or places 6 a route round which an electrical current can flow 7 a race track for motorsports ■ *vti* move along a circular path (*fml*)

circuit board *n* a board constituting a printed circuit

circuit breaker *n* a safety shut-off in an electrical circuit

circuit judge *n* a judge travelling from one court to another within a circuit

circuitous /sur kyoō itəss/ *adj* indirect and lengthy —**circuitously** *adv*

circuitry /súrkitri/ *n* 1 the components of an electrical circuit 2 the system of circuits in an electrical device

circuit training *n* sports training in which different exercises are performed in rotation

circular /súrkyoōlər/ *adj* 1 like a circle 2 following a curved path that ends where it began 3 not logical because of assuming as true something that needs to be proved 4 circuitous ■ *n* a widely distributed leaflet or notice —**circularity** /súrkyoō lárrəti/ *n* —**circularly** *adv*

circularize /súrkyoōlə rīz/ (-izing, -ized), **circularise** *vt* 1 publicize with leaflets or notices 2 canvass or poll

circular saw *n* a power saw with a rotating blade

circulate /súrkyoō layt/ (-lating, -lated) *v* 1 *vi* move round a circular system 2 *vti* pass or be passed round 3 *vi* flow freely in an enclosed space 4 *vi* mingle at a social event (*infml*) —**circulatory** *adj*

circulation /súrkyoō láysh'n/ *n* 1 the movement of blood round the body 2 free flow, e.g. of air or water 3 the distribution or communication of something 4 the number of copies of something sold or distributed 5 valid use as money

circum- *prefix* around ○ *circumnavigate*

circumcise /súrkəm sīz/ (-cising, -cised) *vt* 1 remove the foreskin of the penis of 2 remove the clitoris or the skin of the clitoris of —**circumcision** /súrkəm sízh'n/ *n*

circumference /sər kúmfrənss/ *n* 1 the distance around the edge of a circle or a circular object 2 the edge of a circle or a circular object

circumflex /súrkəm fleks/, **circumflex accent** *n* the pronunciation mark ^ placed above some vowels in some languages

circumlocution /súrkəm lə kyoōsh'n/ *n* the use of more words than necessary to avoid saying something directly —**circumlocutory** /-lókyoōtəri/ *adj*

circumnavigate /súrkəm návvi gayt/ (-gating, -gated) *vt* travel all the way around ○ *circumnavigate the globe* —**circumnavigation** /-navi gáysh'n/ *n*

circumpolar /súrkəm pólər/ *adj* in or near the polar regions (*technical*)

circumscribe /súrkəm skrīb/ (-scribing, -scribed) *v* 1 *vt* restrict the power or independence of somebody or something (*fml*) 2 draw one geometrical figure around another so that points touch

circumspect /súrkəm spekt/ *adj* careful to weigh up risks or consequences before acting —**circumspection** /súrkəm spéksh'n/ *n* —**circumspectly** *adv* ◊ See note at **cautious**

circumstance /súrkəmstənss, -staans/ *n* 1 a condition that affects a situation (*usually pl*) 2 events or conditions beyond somebody's control ■ **circumstances** *npl* prevailing financial, social, or material conditions ◊ **under** *or* **in no circumstances** no matter what the situation might be ◊ **under** *or* **in the circumstances** taking everything into account

circumstantial /súrkəm stánsh'l/ *adj* 1 based on inference, not proof 2 of or contingent on particular circumstances

circumvent /súrkəm vént/ *vt* 1 avoid the restrictions of a law without breaking it 2 outwit somebody —**circumvention** *n*

circus /súrkəss/ *n* 1 a group of travelling entertainers 2 a show performed by travelling entertainers 3 a noisy and confused scene or event (*infml*) ○ *a media circus* 4 a Roman stadium where gladiator fights and chariot races were held 5 a show in a Roman circus 6 a round open space where streets meet —**circusy** *adj*

cirque /surk/ *n* a semicircular hollow with steep walls formed by glacial erosion on mountains

cirrhosis /sə róssiss/ *n* a chronic liver disease —**cirrhotic** /sə róttik/ *adj*

cirrocumulus /sírrō kyoòmyoōləss/ (*pl* **-li** /-lī/) *n* a high-altitude cloud forming a broken layer

cirrus /sírrəss/ (*pl* **-ri** /-rī/) *n* a high-altitude wispy cloud —**cirrate** /sírrayt/ *adj*

cis /siss/ *adj* having two atoms on the same side of a double bond

CIS *abbr* Commonwealth of Independent States

cistern /sístərn/ *n* 1 a water tank, especially one providing water for a toilet 2 an underground tank for storing rainwater

citadel /síttəd'l, -del/ *n* 1 a fortified building used as a refuge 2 a defender of a principle

citation /sī táysh'n/ *n* 1 an official document or speech praising a person or group 2 a quotation from an authoritative source used as corroboration 3 an act or the process of citing something —**citational** *adj*

cite /sīt/ (**citing, cited**) *vt* 1 quote as an authority (*fml*) 2 officially praise

SPELLCHECK Do not confuse the spelling of **cite**, **site** ('a place', 'locate something'), and **sight** ('seeing', 'see something'), which sound similar.

citify /sítti fī/ (-fies, -fied) *vt* (*disapproving*) 1 turn into a city, or make more urban 2 make too like a city dweller —**citification** /síttifi káysh'n/ *n*

citizen /síttiz'n/ *n* 1 somebody who has the legal right to live in a country either by birth or naturalization 2 a permanent resident of a city or town —**citizenly** *adj*

citizenry /síttiz'nri/ (*pl* **-ries**) *n* citizens collectively (*fml; + sing or pl verb*)

citizen's arrest *n* an arrest made by an ordinary citizen

citizens band *n* radio frequencies used by the public

citizenship /síttiz'nship/ *n* 1 the legal status of being a citizen of a country 2 the rights and duties of a citizen

citric acid *n* acid from citrus fruits. Use: flavourings.

citron /síttrən/ *n* 1 a citrus fruit like a large lemon, whose rind is often candied 2 the small thorny tree that produces citrons

citronella /síttrə néllə/ *n* 1 *also* **citronella oil** a pale aromatic oil. Use: perfumery, soapmaking, insect repellents. 2 *also* **citronella grass** a lemon-scented grass of tropical Asia

citrus /síttrəss/ *n* fruits such as oranges and lemons collectively

city /sítti/ (*pl* **-ies**) *n* 1 a very large municipality 2 the people in a very large municipality 3 a large British town that formally has the title city, usually because it is the seat of a bishop and has a cathedral 4 **City** the important financial institutions of London 5 **City, City of London** the oldest part of London and its business and financial heart

---

SYNONYMS **city, conurbation, metropolis, town, municipality** CORE MEANING: an urban area where a large number of people live

---

city council *n* the governing body of a city

city father *n* an important public official in a city

city hall *n* 1 US, Can the officials and administrators who run a city 2 *also* **City Hall** a city council building

cityscape /sítti skayp/ *n* 1 a view of a city, especially of its skyline 2 a photograph or painting of a city

city slicker *n* a person from a city regarded as oversophisticated or self-important (*infml disapproving*)

city-state *n* an independent state consisting of a sovereign city and its surrounding territory

citywide /sítti wíd/ *adj* involving an entire city ■ *adv* all over a city

civet /sívvit/ *n* 1 a musky greasy substance. Use: perfume. 2 *also* **civet cat** a wild animal that looks like a cat and secretes civet

civic /sívvik/ *adj* 1 of a city's government 2 of the duties and responsibilities expected of a community member —**civically** *adv*

civic centre *n* 1 a complex containing the major public buildings in a town 2 US, Can a municipal entertainment centre

civics /sívviks/ *n* the study of citizenship (+ *sing verb*)

civil /sívv'l/ *adj* 1 of citizens 2 not military 3 performed by a state or city official ○ *a civil marriage* 4 describes a legal action that does not involve criminal proceedings 5 of a community 6 polite —**civilly** *adv*

civil defence *n* 1 the organizing and training of civilian volunteers to help in times of war

or emergency 2 civilian volunteers who participate in civil defence

civil disobedience *n* the refusal to obey a law as a form of nonviolent protest

civil engineering *n* the building of roads, bridges, and other large structures —**civil engineer** *n*

civilian /sə vílli ən/ *n* somebody who is not a member of the armed forces or of a police or fire and rescue department —**civilian** *adj*

civility /sə vílləti/ (*pl* **-ties**) *n* 1 politeness 2 a polite act

civilization /sívvə lī záysh'n/, **civilisation** *n* 1 a society with a high level of culture and social organization 2 an advanced level of development in society 3 advanced societies in general 4 populated areas

civilize /sívvə līz/ (**-lizing, -lized**), **civilise** *vt* 1 create a high level of culture and social organization in a place 2 make somebody more socially and culturally refined —**civilizing** *adj*

civilized /sívvə līzd/, **civilised** *adj* 1 having advanced cultural and social development 2 refined in tastes or morality

civil law *n* the branch of law that deals with the rights of citizens

civil liberties *npl* an individual's basic rights, guaranteed by law —**civil libertarian** *n*

civil list *n* the money paid by the state to support the royal family

civil rights *npl* the basic rights that all citizens in a free nation are supposed to have

civil servant *n* a government employee

civil service *n* all the government departments and the people who work in them

civil war *n* 1 a war between opposing groups within a country 2 **Civil War** the 17C English war between the Royalists and the Parliamentarians 3 **Civil War** the 19C US war between the North and the South

civvies /sívviz/ *npl* ordinary clothes, as opposed to a military uniform (*infml*)

CJD *abbr* Creutzfeldt-Jakob disease

cl *abbr* 1 centilitre 2 class

Cl *symbol* chlorine

clack *vti* make or cause to make a short loud noise —**clack** *n*

Clackmannanshire /klak mánnənshər/ local government unitary council in Scotland

clad[1] past tense, past participle of **clothe** ■ *adj* 1 dressed ○ *clad in blue* 2 covered (*literary; often in combination*) ○ *ivy-clad walls*

clad[2] (**cladding, clad**) *vt* 1 cover a wall with cladding 2 cover metal with a protective layer of material

cladding /kládding/ *n* 1 an outer layer of stone, tiles, or wood on an outer wall 2 a protective metal coating bonded to another metal

claim *vt* 1 say that something is true without providing evidence 2 demand something you are entitled to 3 require or demand attention ■ *n* 1 an assertion that something is true 2 the basis for demanding or getting something **3** a demand or request for something you are or feel entitled to **4** a sum of money requested

claimant /kláymənt/ *n* **1** somebody making a claim **2** somebody who brings a civil action in a court of law

clairvoyant /klair vóy ənt/ *n* somebody who is supposedly psychic **—clairvoyance** *n* **—clairvoyant** *adj*

clam *n* **1** a burrowing shellfish **2** the soft edible flesh of a clam

□ **clam up** *vi* refuse to talk *(infml)*

clambake /klám bayk/ *n* a picnic at which seafood such as clams is cooked and eaten

clamber /klámbər/ *vi* climb awkwardly **—clamber** *n*

clammy /klámmi/ (**-mier, -miest**) *adj* unpleasantly cold and damp **—clamminess** *n*

clamour /klámmər/ *vi* **1** make desperate and noisy demands **2** shout loudly ■ *n* **1** a persistent demand **2** a loud noise **—clamorous** *adj*

clamp *n* a device with jaws for holding things firmly ■ *vt* **1** fasten or immobilize with a clamp **2** hold firmly in position

□ **clamp down** *vi* take firm action to control or stop something

clampdown /klámp down/ *n* firm action taken to control or stop something

clan *n* (+ *sing* or *pl verb*) **1** a group of related families **2** a group of related Scottish families with a common surname and a single chief **3** a group with a shared aim *(infml)*

clandestine /klan déstin, klán de stín/ *adj* secret or furtive **—clandestinely** *adv* ◊ See note at **secret**

clang *vti* make or cause to make a loud ringing noise **—clang** *n*

clanger /klángər/ *n* an embarrassing mistake *(infml)*

clank *vti* make or cause to make a short loud metallic noise **—clank** *n*

clannish /klánnish/ *adj* inclined to stick together and exclude others **—clannishly** *adv* **—clannishness** *n*

clap[1] *v* (**clapping, clapped**) **1** *vti* hit your hands together loudly **2** *vt* put something or somebody somewhere quickly ○ *clapped him in jail* ■ *n* **1** a sudden loud sound made by hitting the hands together **2** an expression of approval through applause

clap[2] *n* gonorrhoea *(slang)*

clapboard /kláp bawrd/ *n* a long narrow wooden board. Use: surface siding of buildings.

clapped-out /klapt ówt/ *adj* worn out *(infml)*

clapper /kláppər/ *n* a moving part that strikes the inside of a bell to make it ring

clapperboard /kláppər bawrd/ *n* a pair of hinged boards clapped together at the start of each take in a film to help synchronize picture and sound

claptrap /kláp trap/ *n* nonsense *(infml)*

claque /klak/ *n* (+ *sing* or *pl verb*) **1** a group of people hired to applaud or jeer a performance **2** a person's entourage *(disapproving)*

Clare 1 island off the coast of W Ireland **2** river in the northeast of the South Island, New Zealand. Length 209 km/130 mi.

Clare (of Assisi) /-ə seéssi/, **St** (1194–1253) Italian nun, and one of the founders of the order of the Poor Ladies of Damiano, or Poor Clares

Clare, John (1793–1864) British poet and naturalist

claret /klárrət/ *n* a red wine from the Bordeaux region of France

clarify /klárri fī/ (**-fies, -fied**) *v* **1** *vt* make easier to understand by explanation **2** *vti* make or become clear or pure by heating or filtering **—clarification** /klárrifi káysh'n/ *n*

clarinet /klárrə nét/ *n* a woodwind instrument with a single reed

clarion call /klárri ən-/ *n* a call to action

clarity /klárrəti/ *n* the quality of being clear

Clark, Helen Elizabeth (b. 1950) New Zealand prime minister (1999–)

Clarke, Sir Arthur C. (b. 1917) British writer and scientist

Clarke, Marcus Andrew Hislop (1846–81) British-born Australian writer

clash *v* **1** *vi* fight or argue **2** *vi* be incompatible ○ *Her testimony clashes with the evidence.* **3** *vti* make or cause to make a loud harsh metallic noise **4** *vi* look unpleasant together ○ *His shirt and tie clash.* **5** *vi* conflict with something else in terms of timing or appropriateness *(refers to events)* **—clash** *n* ◊ See note at **fight**

clasp *vt* **1** hold tightly with your hands or arms **2** fasten with a device ■ *n* **1** a small buckle or fastening **2** a tight arm or hand hold

clasp knife *n* a pocket knife with a blade that folds into the handle

class *n* **1** a group of students taught together **2** a period during which students meet and are taught **3** a specific subject taught **4** a group within a society who share the same social or economic status **5** the structure of a society into classes **6** elegance and refinement *(infml)* **7** a categorization according to quality **8** a group of similar items or related organisms ■ *vt* assign to a group ◊ See note at **type**

class action *n* a legal action brought by several plaintiffs together

class-conscious *adj* aware of your own social class **—class-consciousness** *n*

classic /klássik/ *adj* **1** of the highest quality or lasting value, especially in the arts **2** definitive as an example of its kind **3** extremely and usually comically typical or fitting *(infml)* ■ *n* **1** a work or created object of lasting value and high quality ○ *a design classic* **2** something that is an outstanding or typical example of its kind ○ *Last night's show was a classic.*

classical /klássik'l/ *adj* 1 of ancient Greece or Rome 2 in the ancient Greek or Roman style 3 describes music considered to be serious or intellectual 4 of 18C and 19C European music 5 orthodox or conservative —**classicality** /klássi kálləti/ *n* —**classically** *adv* —**classicalness** *n*

classicism /klássissizəm/, **classicalism** /klássi'lizəm/ *n* 1 a restrained style in art and architecture based on that of ancient Greece and Rome 2 the study of Greek and Roman culture

classicist /klássissist/ *n* 1 a scholar of ancient Greek and Latin 2 an advocate of artistic classicism

classics /klássiks/ *n* the study of the language, literature, and history of ancient Greece and Rome (+ *sing verb*) ■ *npl* the literature of ancient Greece or Rome (+ *pl verb*)

classification /klássifi káysh'n/ *n* 1 the organization of things into groups 2 a category within an organized system —**classificatory** *adj*

classified /klássi fīd/ *adj* 1 available only to authorized people for reasons of national security 2 grouped by type

classified advertisement, classified ad *n* a small advertisement in a newspaper

classify /klássi fī/ (-fies, -fied) *vt* 1 categorize things or people 2 designate information as being classified for security —**classifiable** *adj*

classism /klaássizəm/ *n* discrimination based on social class —**classist** *adj*, *n*

classless /klaássləss/ *adj* 1 not organized into social classes 2 not belonging to a social class

classmate /klaáss mayt/ *n* somebody in the same class at school

classroom /klaáss room, -room/ *n* a room in a school where people are taught

class struggle *n* a struggle for power between social classes

classy /klaássi/ (-ier, -iest) *adj* very stylish and elegant (*infml*) —**classily** *adv* —**classiness** *n*

clatter /kláttər/ *vti* make or cause to make a harsh rattling or banging noise

Claudius I /kláwdi əss/ (10 BC–AD 54) Roman emperor (AD 41 54)

clause *n* 1 a group of words that contains a subject and predicate and can sometimes stand as a sentence 2 a section of a legal document —**clausal** *adj*

claustrophobia /kláwstrə fốbi ə, klóstrə-/ *n* fear of being in a confined space

claustrophobic /kláwstrə fốbik, klóstrə-/ *adj* 1 confined or cramped 2 of or affected by claustrophobia ■ *n* somebody who is affected by claustrophobia —**claustrophobically** *adv*

clave past tense of **cleave**²

clavichord /klávvi kawrd/ *n* an early keyboard instrument like a piano —**clavichordist** *n*

clavicle /klávvik'l/ *n* a collarbone —**clavicular** /klə víkyóolər, klə-/ *adj*

claw *n* 1 an animal's sharp nail 2 each of the pincers on a crab or similar organism 3 something resembling a claw ■ *v* 1 *vti* scratch or dig with claws or fingernails 2 *vt* make by scratching or digging with claws or fingernails —**clawed** *adj*

☐ **claw back** *vt* 1 get something back with effort 2 recover money paid out earlier, especially through taxation

clawback /kláw bak/ *n* the recovery of money, especially through taxation

claw hammer *n* a hammer with two prongs at one end of its head for removing nails

clay *n* 1 a fine-grained material that occurs naturally in soil, can be moulded when wet, and is hard when baked. Use: making bricks, ceramics, and cement. 2 heavy sticky earth 3 *also* **clay pigeon** a target launched into the air for shooting —**clayey** *adj*

Clay, Cassius ♦ Ali, Muhammad

claymore /kláy mawr/ *n* a large double-edged sword formerly used by Scottish Highlanders

clean /kleen/ *adj* 1 free of dirt 2 not polluted or adulterated 3 free of infection 4 freshly washed 5 morally upright 6 not obscene 7 blank o *a clean blackboard* 8 with no record of crime or infection 9 streamlined 10 complete o *a clean break with the past* 11 producing the least possible pollution ■ *vti* make or become clean ■ *n* a session of cleaning ■ *adv* 1 so as to make something clean 2 in a clean way 3 completely (*infml*) o *I clean forgot.* —**cleanly** *adv* —**cleanness** *n* ◇ **come clean** confess or tell the truth (*infml*)

☐ **clean out** *vt* take all the money or belongings of (*infml*)

☐ **clean up** *vti* make a place clean or tidy

clean-cut *adj* 1 with a sharp outline 2 neat-looking 3 unambiguously clear

cleaner /kleénər/ *n* 1 somebody employed to clean the interior of a building 2 a substance or machine used in cleaning

cleaners /kleénərz/ *n* a shop providing a dry-cleaning service ◇ **take to the cleaners** deprive of money or possessions (*slang*)

clean-limbed /-límd/ *adj* youthfully well-proportioned

cleanliness /klénnlinəss/ *n* the degree to which somebody or something is clean

clean-living *adj* living a morally upright life

clean room *n* a dirt-free room for special purposes

cleanse /klenz/ (**cleansing, cleansed**) *vt* 1 make thoroughly clean 2 make free from corruption, sin, or guilt —**cleansing** *n*

cleanser /klénzər/ *n* 1 a cleaning substance 2 a cosmetic product for cleaning the face

clean-shaven *adj* with facial hair shaved off

cleanup /kleén up/ *n* 1 a thorough cleaning 2 the elimination of something bad

clear /kleer/ *adj* 1 free from anything that darkens or obscures 2 transparent o *clear glass* 3 free from clouds 4 pure in hue 5 perfect and unblemished 6 easily heard or

clear 7 unambiguous, obvious, and allowing no doubt ○ *clear evidence of guilt* ○ *clear instructions* **8** mentally sharp and discerning **9** free from feelings of guilt ○ *a clear conscience* **10** unobstructed ○ *keep the aisles clear* **11** with all contents removed **12** not connected or touching **13** net of deductions or charges **14** debt-free ■ *adv* **1** out of the way **2** all the way *(infml)* ○ *They moved clear across the country.* ■ *v* **1** *vi* dissipate and disperse ○ *when the mist had cleared* **2** *vi* brighten and become free of clouds or fog **3** *vti* make or become transparent **4** *vt* rid something of extraneous or obstructive matter **5** *vt* remove confusion from the mind **6** *vt* make the mind free, or become free of the dulling effects of, e.g. sleep **7** *vt* prove somebody innocent **8** *vt* open a route by removing obstacles **9** *vt* remove people from a place **10** *vt* disentangle something, e.g. an anchor **11** *vt* move past something without touching it **12** *vti* authorize somebody or something, or be authorized ○ *The plane has been cleared for landing.* **13** *vt* acquire money as a profit *(infml)* **14** *vt* pay off a debt **15** *vi* be authorized and credited to the payee's account ○ *Cheques take three days to clear.* **16** *vti* settle banking accounts through a clearing house **17** *vt* in some sports, get the ball or puck out of your own defence area **18** *vt* delete computer data —**clearly** *adv* —**clearness** *n* ◇ **in the clear** free from suspicion or blame

□ **clear off** *vi* go away *(infml; often a command)*
□ **clear out** *vi* leave fast *(infml)*
□ **clear up** *v* **1** *vi* become less cloudy **2** *vti* get or make better **3** *vt* solve a mystery or explain a misunderstanding

clearance /klééranss/ *n* **1** the removal of obstructions or unwanted objects **2** permission for something to happen **3** the width or height of an opening **4** a sale of goods at reduced prices to get rid of stock **5** the forcible removal of people from land **6** the passage of commercial documents through a clearing house **7** in some sports, the process of clearing the ball or puck from the defence area

clear-cut *adj* **1** unambiguous **2** distinctly outlined

clear-headed *adj* able to think clearly, especially in difficult situations —**clear-headedly** *adv* —**clear-headedness** *n*

clearing /kléering/ *n* an open space in a wood

clearing bank *n* a bank that uses a central clearing house

clearing house *n* **1** an institution that coordinates transactions between banks **2** an agency that collects and distributes information

clear-out *n* a session of getting rid of unwanted items

clear-sighted *adj* **1** having good perception or judgment **2** with keen eyesight

clear-up *n* a tidying session

clearway /kléer way/ *n* a road where stopping is usually forbidden

cleat /kleet/ *n* **1** a device on a boat that a rope can be secured to **2** a piece of metal or hard plastic attached to the sole of a shoe

cleavage /kléevij/ *n* **1** the division or splitting of something **2** a split, division, or separation **3** the hollow visible between the breasts of a woman wearing a low-cut garment

cleave[1] /kleev/ **(cleaving, cleaved** or **clove** /klōv/ or **cleft, cleaved** or **cloven** /klóv'n/ or **cleft)** *vti* **1** split along a line of natural weakness **2** cut a path through something *(literary)*

cleave[2] /kleev/ **(cleaving, cleaved** or **clave** /klayv/, **cleaved)** *vi* cling faithfully to somebody or something *(fml)*

cleaver /kléevar/ *n* a heavy knife used by butchers

clef *n* in written or printed music, a symbol indicating pitch

cleft *vti* past tense, past participle of **cleave**[1] ■ *n* **1** a small indentation **2** a gap or split *(fml)* ■ *adj* split in half or fissured

cleft palate *n* a congenital fissure in the roof of the mouth

clematis /klémmatiss, klə máytiss/ *(pl* -**tises** or *same) n* a climbing plant with large flowers

clemency /klémmənssi/ *n* **1** mercy, or an act of mercy **2** mildness in weather

Clemens /klémmənz/, **Samuel Langhorne** ♦ **Twain, Mark**

clement /klémmənt/ *adj* **1** describes weather that is mild or not extreme **2** merciful —**clemently** *adv*

clementine /klémmən tīn, -teen/ *n* a small orange citrus fruit

clench *vt* **1** close your teeth or fist tightly **2** clutch something —**clench** *n* —**clenched** *adj*

Cleopatra /kleé ə páttra/ (69–30 BC) Egyptian queen (51–30 BC)

clerestory /kléer stawri, -stəri/ *(pl* -**ries)** *n* the upper part of a wall that contains windows

clergy /klúrji/ *n* people ordained for service in an organized religion *(+ sing or pl verb)*

cleric /klérrik/ *n* a member of the clergy

clerical /klérrik'l/ *adj* **1** of office work **2** of the clergy —**clerically** *adv*

clerk /klaark/ *n* **1** a general office worker **2** a government worker who keeps records **3** an administrator in a court of law —**clerk** *vi*

ORIGIN **Clerk** is essentially an older form of *cleric.* It derives from ecclesiastical Latin *clericus* 'of the Christian ministry'. **Clerks** were originally members of the clergy who, as literate members of medieval society, took on many of the administrative and secretarial functions that later fell to lay people. From the early 16C **clerk** began to be used for various officials, record-keepers, copyists, and the like. *Cleric* was introduced from Latin in the early 17C and replaced **clerk** in its original sense.

Cleveland /kléevlənd/ port in NE Ohio. Pop. 495,817 (1998).

clever /klévvər/ adj 1 intelligent or ingenious 2 pretentiously or superficially intelligent 3 highly skilled in using the hands —**cleverly** adv —**cleverness** n ◊ See note at **intelligent**

cliché /klee shay/ n 1 an overused expression that has lost its original force 2 an overused idea —**clichéd** adj

click n 1 a short sharp sound 2 a speech sound produced by sucking in air 3 a press and release of a computer mouse button ■ v 1 vti make or cause to make a short sharp sound 2 vti press and release a computer mouse button 3 vi suddenly become clearly understood (infml) ◊ It finally clicked where I'd seen him before. 4 vi communicate or work together easily (infml) ◊ The partners never clicked.

click art n computer clip art

click rate n the number of times an Internet site in an advertisement is visited, as a percentage of the number of times the advertisement itself is viewed

clicks-and-mortar, click-and-mortar adj combining online and traditional sales

clickstream /klík streem/ n the path of mouse clicks that somebody makes in navigating the World Wide Web

clickthrough /klík throo/ n a measure of the effectiveness of an Internet advertisement based on the number of times it is viewed

client /klí ənt/ n 1 somebody using a professional service 2 a customer 3 a computer program that obtains data from another computer in a network

clientele /klee on tél, -ən-/ n clients or customers as a group

client-server, client/server adj used on a computer network in which processing is divided between a client program on a user's machine and a network server program

cliff n a high steep rock face —**cliffy** adj

cliffhanger /klíf hangər/ n 1 an unresolved ending in a serialized drama 2 a tense situation —**cliffhanging** adj

climacteric /klī máktərik, klī mak térrik/ n 1 a period of important change 2 the menopause (technical) —**climacteric** adj

climactic /klī máktik/ adj 1 exciting 2 of a climax —**climactically** adv

climate /klímət/ n 1 the typical weather in a region 2 a place with weather of a particular type 3 a situation or atmosphere that prevails at a particular time or place —**climatic** /klī máttik/ adj —**climatically** adv

climatology /klímə tólləji/ n the study of climates —**climatologist** n

climax /klí maks/ n 1 the most exciting or important point 2 an orgasm 3 an ever-intensifying sequence of phrases, or the conclusion of such a sequence ■ v 1 vti reach or bring to the most exciting or important point 2 vi have an orgasm

ORIGIN **Climax** derives from a Greek word lit-

erally meaning 'ladder'. From its first use in English in the mid-18C it applied, as in Greek and Latin, to a rhetorical device in which ideas are expressed in order of increasing importance. The sense jumped from the steps towards the high point to the high point itself in the late 18C.

climb /klīm/ v 1 vti move towards the top of something, especially using the hands and feet 2 vi move with some effort ◊ climbed out of bed 3 vi rise steeply in amount 4 vi engage in mountaineering 5 vti grow upward, clinging to other plants or a support ■ n 1 the process or an act of climbing 2 a hill, mountain, or rock, or the route used to climb it

SPELLCHECK Do not confuse the spelling of **climb** and **clime** ('place with a particular climate'), which sound similar.

climb-down n a retreat from an argument or position

climber /klímər/ n 1 somebody who climbs 2 a plant that clings to another plant or support

climbing /klíming/ n the activity of climbing mountains

climbing frame n a structure for children to climb on

clime /klīm/ n a place with a particular type of climate (fml; often pl) ◊ See note at **climb**

~~climing~~ incorrect spelling of **climbing**

clinch v 1 vt resolve something decisively 2 vi in boxing or wrestling, put your arms around your opponent 3 vt flatten the protruding end of a nail ■ n 1 a passionate embrace (infml) 2 in boxing or wrestling, a tactic of pinning an opponent's arms down to the side of the body

clincher /klínchər/ n a deciding factor (infml)

cling (**clung**) vi 1 hold onto somebody or something tightly 2 stick to something 3 refuse to give up an idea, belief, or custom 4 need somebody emotionally —**clinging** adj

cling film n a clear plastic film used for wrapping food

clingstone /klíng stōn/ n a fruit with flesh that sticks to its stone

clingy /klíngi/ (**-ier, -iest**) adj (infml) 1 emotionally dependent 2 sticking to the body —**clinginess** n

clinic /klínnik/ n 1 a medical centre for outpatients, often attached to a hospital 2 a specialized medical centre 3 a group medical practice 4 a private hospital 5 a teaching session for student doctors at the patients' bedsides

ORIGIN **Clinic** derives ultimately from the Greek word for 'bed'. It was at first an adjective, acquired through Latin and referring especially to the sickbed. The modern noun came through French or German.

clinical /klínnik'l/ adj 1 based on medical treatment or observation 2 unemotional —**clinically** adv

clinician /kli nísh'n/ *n* a doctor who works directly with patients

clink[1] *vti* make or cause to make a light ringing sound —**clink** *n*

clink[2] *n* a prison *(slang dated)*

ORIGIN 'The Clink' was a prison in Southwark, London. The use of **clink** for a prison generally appears to have been extended from this. The name is recorded from the early 16C, but its origin is unknown.

clinker /klíngkər/ *n* **1** a hard mass of coal residue in a fire **2** a brick that has been fired too long

Hillary Rodham Clinton and Bill Clinton

Clinton /klíntən/, **Bill** (*b.* 1946) 42nd president of the United States (1993–2001)

Clinton, Hillary Rodham (*b.* 1947) US lawyer, first lady (1993–2001), and senator

clip[1] *vt* (**clipping, clipped**) **1** cut or trim something **2** remove something by cutting **3** shorten the time taken for something **4** shorten a speech sound **5** abbreviate a word **6** reduce power or influence **7** hit somebody with a glancing blow *(infml)* ■ *n* **1** a film or TV extract **2** an extract from a newspaper or magazine **3** a glancing blow **4** a particular rate of speed *(infml)*

clip[2] *n* **1** a gripping device *(often in combination)* **2** a piece of jewellery that attaches to clothing **3** a bullet-holder for an automatic weapon ■ *vti* (**clipping, clipped**) hold or be held with a clip

clip art *n* prepared artwork for use in computer documents

clipboard /klíp bawrd/ *n* **1** a board with a clip for securing papers **2** a part of computer memory where cut or copied data is stored temporarily

clip-clop *n* the sound of horses' hooves on a hard surface ■ *vi* (**clip-clopping, clip-clopped**) go clip-clop

clip-on *adj* attaching by means of a clip ■ *n* an accessory that attaches with a clip

clipped *adj* **1** neatly trimmed **2** with each word spoken clearly

clipper /klíppər/ *n* a fast sailing ship ■ **clippers** *npl* a tool similar to scissors, used for cutting or clipping something

clipping /klípping/ *n* a cutting from a newspaper or magazine ■ **clippings** *npl* pieces of hair or grass that have been cut off

clique /kleek/ *n* an exclusive group —**cliquey** *adj* —**cliquish** *adj* —**cliquishness** *n*

clitoris /klíttəriss/ *n* a sensitive female sex organ at the top of the vulva —**clitoral** *adj*

Clive /klīv/, **Robert, Baron Clive of Plassey** (1725–74) British soldier and colonial administrator

Cllr *abbr* Councillor

cloaca /klō áykə/ (*pl* -**cae** /-kee/) *n* the terminal part of the gut in reptiles, amphibians, birds, many fishes, and some invertebrates —**cloacal** *adj*

cloak *n* **1** a long sleeveless outer garment that fastens at the neck **2** something that conceals *(literary)* ○ *left under a cloak of secrecy* ■ *vt* conceal something

cloak-and-dagger *adj* full of secrecy

cloakroom /klōk room, -rōōm/ *n* **1** a place for leaving coats **2** a lavatory

clobber /klóbbər/ *(infml)* *vt* **1** hit with great force **2** defeat utterly ■ *n* somebody's belongings or clothes

cloche /klosh/ *n* **1** a protective glass or clear plastic cover for plants **2** a woman's close-fitting hat with a narrow brim

clock *n* **1** a device for displaying the time **2** a measuring instrument with a dial or digital display **3** the seed head of a dandelion ■ *vt* measure the time or speed of *(infml)* ○ *a car that was clocked at 95 mph* ◇ **around** *or* **round the clock** day and night, without stopping

clock radio *n* a combination clock and radio

clockwise /klók wīz/ *adv, adj* in the direction that a clock's hands move

clockwork /klók wurk/ *n* a system of cogs and springs used to drive a clock or moving toy ◇ **like clockwork** with efficiency or predictability

clod *n* **1** a lump of earth **2** a person regarded as unintelligent *(insult)* —**cloddish** *adj*

clodhopper /klód hopər/ *n* a person regarded as awkward and unsophisticated *(infml insult)* ■ **clodhoppers** *npl* big heavy shoes or boots *(infml)*

clog *v* (**clogging, clogged**) **1** *vti* block or become blocked gradually **2** *vt* hinder movement on or in ■ *n* **1** a heavy shoe made of wood or with a wooden sole **2** an obstruction

cloisonné /klwaa zónn ay/ *adj* decorated with a pattern of enamel pieces —**cloisonné** *n*

cloister /klóystər/ *n* **1** a covered walkway round a courtyard **2** a monastery or convent ■ *vr* find a quiet secluded place to go —**cloistral** *adj*

cloistered /klóystərd/ *adj* **1** secluded **2** in a monastery

clomp *n, vti* = **clump**[2]

clone /klōn/ *n* **1** a genetically identical organism produced asexually **2** a piece of hardware or software that is a functional copy of a more expensive product ■ *vt* (**cloning, cloned**) **1** produce a genetically identical copy of an organism asexually

2 make a copy of an object or product —**clonal** adj ◊ See note at **copy**

ORIGIN **Clone** is from a Greek word meaning 'twig'.

clonk n a dull hollow sound ■ vi make a dull hollow sound

clop n the sound of horses' hooves on a hard surface —**clop** vi

close[1] /klōss/ adj (**closer, closest**) **1** near in space, time, or relationship **2** about to happen **3** in a very friendly or affectionate relationship ○ a close friend **4** thorough ○ a close inspection **5** decided by a small margin ○ a close contest **6** allowing little space between parts **7** very similar ○ a close copy **8** nearly correct or exact, but not quite **9** secretively silent ○ was close about the cause of the disaster **10** cut very short **11** stingy **12** stuffy and airless ■ adv (**closer, closest**) so as to be close —**closely** adv—**closeness** n

close[2] /klōz/ v (**closing, closed**) **1** vti move to cover an opening **2** vti bring together the edges of something **3** vti stop operating, or shut down a business temporarily or permanently **4** vt block access to something such as a road **5** vti come or bring to an end **6** vti reduce the distance between two people or things **7** vt bring a deal to closure **8** vt deactivate and store a computer file or program ■ n the end of an activity or period of time

□ **close down** vi stop broadcasting at the end of the day

□ **close in** vi approach and surround somebody or something

□ **close up** vti **1** lock a building at the end of a working day **2** come or bring things closer together

close[3] /klōss/ n **1** a cul-de-sac (often in street names) **2** an area round a cathedral

close-cropped adj cut short

closed adj **1** no longer doing business **2** denying access **3** no longer to be discussed or investigated **4** rigidly excluding the ideas of others **5** not admitting outsiders

closed-circuit television, closed-circuit TV n a television transmission system in which cameras transmit pictures by cable to connected monitors

closed-door adj not open to the public or the media

closed-end fund n an investment company with a fixed number of shares

closedown /klōz down/ n **1** a temporary or permanent stopping of work or operations **2** the end of a broadcasting day

closed shop n a workplace that employs union members only

close-fisted adj reluctant to spend money —**close-fistedness** n

close-grained adj describes wood with a dense texture and a smooth surface

close-knit adj mutually supportive

closemouthed /klōss mówthd, -mówtht/ adj reticent

close-run adj decided by a small margin

close season n **1** the period of the year when no hunting is allowed **2** the period between seasonal sports competitions

closet /klózzit/ n US, Can a large cupboard ■ vt put in a room with privacy ○ He closeted himself in the study all morning. ◊ **come out of the closet** acknowledge openly something previously kept secret

close-up n **1** a photograph or a film or television shot taken at close range **2** a detailed look at something ■ adj at close range

closing /klōzing/ adj final ○ the closing stages ■ n a fastening

closing time n the time when a business closes for the day

closure /klōzhər/ n **1** the permanent ending of a business activity **2** an act or the process of blocking access to something **3** something that closes an opening **4** a procedure for cutting a parliamentary debate short ■ vt (**-suring, -sured**) apply closure to a debate or speaker in parliament

clot n **1** a thick sticky mass, especially of blood **2** an offensive term for somebody regarded as unintelligent (infml) ■ vti (**clotting, clotted**) thicken into a mass

cloth /kloth/ n **1** fabric made from thread or fibres **2** a piece of fabric used for a specific purpose (often in combination)

clothe /klōth/ (**clothing, clothed** or **clad**) vt **1** put clothes on **2** provide with clothing **3** cover ○ a field that was clothed in leaves **4** conceal or obscure

clothes /klōthz/ npl garments for covering the body

clotheshorse /klōthz hawrss/ n **1** a frame for drying clothes on indoors **2** somebody who dresses fashionably (infml)

clothesline /klōthz līn/ n a line on which to hang laundry to dry

clothier /klōthi ər/ n a retailer of clothes or cloth

clothing /klōthing/ n **1** clothes **2** a covering for something

cloud n **1** a visible mass of water or ice particles in the sky **2** a mass of particles in the air, e.g. dust or smoke **3** a flying mass of insects or birds **4** something that causes worry or gloom ■ v **1** vti make or become cloudy **2** vt make more confused ○ cloud the issue **3** vt make appear less good ○ It will cloud her reputation. **4** vti make or become troubled or gloomy ○ His face clouded with disappointment. ◊ **on cloud nine** extremely happy (infml) ◊ **under a cloud** in disgrace

ORIGIN **Cloud** originally meant 'a mass of earth, a hill'. A resemblance between cumulus clouds and hills presumably accounts for the transferred meaning. **Cloud** replaced the earlier word for massed water vapour in the 13C, though that word continued as welkin, a poetic name for the sky.

cloudburst /klówd burst/ n a sudden heavy rain shower

cloud-cuckoo-land n an imaginary problem-free place

clouded /klówdid/ adj 1 troubled 2 opaque

cloudless /klówdləss/ adj 1 bright and clear 2 without problems —**cloudlessness** n

cloudy /klówdi/ (-ier, -iest) adj 1 with clouds 2 opaque —**cloudiness** n

clout n (infml) 1 power and influence 2 a blow with the hand or fist ■ vt hit with the hand or fist

clove[1] /klōv/ n 1 a dried aromatic flower bud used as a spice 2 a tree that produces cloves

ORIGIN The name of the spice **clove** comes ultimately from the Latin word for 'nail' (the type that is hammered), from the appearance of the single clove-tree bud and its stalk. The garlic **clove** is from an ancient root that also gave rise to cleave 'split'.

clove[2] /klōv/ n a segment of a compound plant bulb, e.g. garlic

clove[3] /klōv/ past tense of **cleave**[1]

clove[4] /klōv/ past tense of **cleave**[2]

cloven /klóv'n/ past participle of **cleave**[1] ■ adj split in two (literary)

cloven hoof n 1 the divided hoof of a sheep, pig, or similar mammal 2 in Christianity, a mark traditionally indicating the presence of the devil —**cloven-hoofed** adj

clover /klóvər/ n a low-growing plant with rounded three-part leaves. Use: forage. ◇ **in clover** financially well off (infml)

cloverleaf /klóvər leef/ (pl **cloverleaves** /-leevz/) n 1 a three-lobed leaf of a clover 2 a road junction with a layout that resembles a four-leafed clover

clown /klown/ n 1 a comic circus performer 2 somebody who is funny 3 a prankster 4 somebody regarded as ill-mannered or ineffectual (infml) ■ vi perform as a clown —**clownish** adj

cloy vti sicken or disgust somebody with too much of something initially thought pleasant —**cloying** adj

club n 1 a thick stick used as a weapon 2 in golf, a long thin implement for hitting the ball 3 an association of people with a common interest 4 an organization for the pursuit of a sport 5 the premises of an association of people 6 a building providing recreational facilities for its members 7 an organization giving discounts to members in return for regular purchases 8 a savings scheme 9 a nightclub 10 a black symbol like a three-leafed clover on a playing card ■ vt (**clubbing, clubbed**) hit with a club

□ **club together** vi collaborate as a group

clubbable /klúbbəb'l/, **clubable** adj sociable

clubbing /klúbbing/ n 1 the activity of going to nightclubs 2 a medical condition in which the base of the fingers and toes become thickened

club class n an intermediate class of airline travel

club foot n 1 a congenital condition in which one foot is twisted inward 2 a foot affected by clubfoot —**club-footed** adj

clubhouse /klúb howss/ n the premises of a sports club

clubs n the suit of cards with a club as its symbol (+ sing or pl verb)

club sandwich n a sandwich with two layers of fillings between three slices of bread

club soda n US, Can carbonated water drunk alone or mixed with alcohol

cluck v 1 vi make short low clicking sounds (refers to hens) 2 vti express disapproval or concern with a clicking sound ■ n a hen's low clicking sound

clue n 1 an aid in solving a mystery or crime 2 a piece of information used in solving a crossword puzzle

□ **clue in** vt give necessary information to

clued-up /klood úp/ adj well-informed (infml)

clueless /klóoləss/ adj uninformed and incompetent (infml) —**cluelessness** n

clump[1] n 1 a cluster of growing things 2 a mass of similar things ■ vti combine into a mass

clump[2], **clomp** n a thumping sound ■ vi move with a clump

clumsy /klúmzi/ (-sier, -siest) adj awkward or badly coordinated —**clumsily** adv —**clumsiness** n

clung past tense, past participle of **cling**

clunk n a dull metallic sound —**clunk** vti

clunky /klúngki/ (-ier, -iest) adj 1 heavy and awkward 2 US, Can awkwardly designed (infml)

cluster /klústər/ n a dense bunch or group ■ vti form into a cluster

cluster bomb n an aerial bomb dispersing smaller bombs as it falls

cluster controller n a central computer in a network

clutch[1] v 1 vt grip tightly 2 vi make a grabbing movement ■ n 1 a mechanism that connects rotating shafts in a motor vehicle 2 the pedal activating the clutch in a motor vehicle 3 a grip on something ■ controlling power (often pl) ○ was caught in the clutches of terror

clutch[2] n a group of eggs laid together at one time

clutter /klúttər/ n 1 an untidy collection of objects 2 a disorganized mess ■ vt fill with clutter

Clyde /klīd/ river in SW Scotland, flowing through Glasgow to the Firth of Clyde. Length 171 km/106 mi.

cm symbol centimetre

Cm symbol curium

Cmdr abbr Commander

CND abbr Campaign for Nuclear Disarmament

Co symbol cobalt

CO[1] abbr 1 Colorado 2 Commanding Officer

CO[2], **C.O.** abbr commanding officer

Co. abbr 1 Colorado 2 Company (in names of businesses) 3 County (in placenames)

co- *prefix* **1** together, jointly o *coeducation* **2** associate, alternate o *copilot* **3** to the same degree o *coextensive* **4** the complement of an angle o *cotangent*

c/o *abbr* care of

coach *n* **1** a long-distance bus **2** a horse-drawn carriage **3** a railway carriage **4** somebody who trains sports players or performers **5** a tutor **6** *US, Can* an inexpensive class of travel ■ *v* **1** *vt* train an athlete or performer **2** *vt* give a student private instruction **3** *vti* transport people or travel in a coach ◊ See note at **teach**

ORIGIN Coach came through French and German from Hungarian, where it was formed from the name of Kocs, a village where carriages and carts were built. The 'training' uses arose in 19C university slang, from a tutor carrying a student through an examination as though in a coach.

coaching /kṓching/ *n* **1** the training of athletes or performers **2** training in overcoming emotional problems

coaching inn *n* a roadside inn for coach passengers

coachman /kṓchmən/ (*pl* **-men** /-mən/) *n* the driver of a horse-drawn coach

coachwork /kṓch wurk/ *n* the painted bodywork of a road vehicle or railway carriage

coagulate /kō ággyŏŏ layt/ (**-lating, -lated**) *vti* turn into a semisolid mass —**coagulation** /kō ággyŏŏ láysh'n/ *n*

coal *n* a black rock formed by the decomposition of plant material. Use: fuel. —**coaly** *adj*

coalesce /kṓ ə léss/ (**-lescing, -lesced**) *vti* merge into a single group —**coalescence** *n*

coalface /kṓl fayss/ *n* **1** a seam of coal being worked **2** a situation in which hard or practical work gets done

coalfield /kṓl feeld/ *n* an area with coal deposits

coal gas *n* **1** a methane and hydrogen mixture. Use: fuel. **2** the gas produced when coal is burned

coalition /kṓ ə lísh'n/ *n* **1** a temporary political or military alliance **2** Coalition in Australia, a long standing political coalition between the Liberal Party and the National Party —**coalitionist** *n*

coalmine /kṓl mīn/ *n* a mine where coal is dug —**coalminer** *n* —**coalmining** *n*

coal scuttle *n* a metal container for holding coal for a domestic fire

coal tar *n* a thick black liquid that is a byproduct of coke production. Use: making dyes, drugs, and soap.

coarse /kawrss/ (**coarser, coarsest**) *adj* **1** rough to the touch **2** consisting of large grains or thick strands **3** lacking good taste, refinement, or propriety —**coarsely** *adv* —**coarsen** *vti* —**coarseness** *n*

SPELLCHECK Do not confuse the spelling of **coarse** and **course** ('a sequence of events', 'a route', 'a programme of study'), which sound similar.

coarse fishing *n* freshwater fishing for fish other than salmon and related fish

coast *n* **1** the land next to the sea **2** the seaside ■ *vi* **1** move by momentum alone, without applying power **2** succeed effortlessly —**coastal** *adj*

coaster /kṓstər/ *n* a small mat for a glass

coastguard /kṓst gaard/ *n* **1** an emergency service that rescues people in trouble at sea **2** a member of a coastguard

coastline /kṓst līn/ *n* the outline of a coast as viewed from the sea or on a map

coast-to-coast *adj* across a whole island or continent

coat *n* **1** a warm long outer garment with sleeves **2** the fur, wool, or hair covering a mammal **3** a thin covering, e.g., of paint ■ *vt* cover a surface with a thin layer of something

coat hanger *n* a frame on which to hang an article of clothing

coating /kṓting/ *n* a thin layer covering something

coat of arms *n* a design on a shield that signifies a specific institution or family

coax /kōks/ *v* **1** *vti* persuade gently, or use gentle persuasion **2** *vt* obtain by gentle persuasion —**coaxingly** *adv*

coaxial cable /kō áksi əl-/ *n* a two-layer cable used for high-speed transmission, e.g. of television or telephone signals

cob *n* **1** the core to which individual maize kernels are attached **2** a rounded loaf of bread **3** a hazelnut **4** a male swan **5** a short-legged riding horse

cobalt /kṓ bawlt, -bolt/ *n* (*symbol* **Co**) a silvery-white chemical element. Use: colouring ceramics, alloys.

ORIGIN Cobalt comes from a German word meaning 'goblin, demon'. The element often occurs as an impurity in silver ore, and German silver miners attributed its presence to goblins' mischief.

cobber /kóbbər/ *n* ANZ a friend (*infml dated*)

Cobbett /kóbbit/, **William** (1763–1835) British writer, journalist, and reformer

cobble[1] /kóbb'l/ *n* **1** a cobblestone **2** a naturally rounded rock fragment ■ *vt* (**-bling, -bled**) pave a road with cobblestones —**cobbled** *adj*

□ **cobble together** *vt* make roughly from what is available

cobble[2] /kóbb'l/ (**-bling, -bled**) *vt* make or repair shoes

cobbler[1] /kóbblər/ *n* a maker or mender of shoes

cobbler[2] /kóbblər/ *n* **1** a baked fruit dessert with a soft thick crust **2** an iced drink made with alcohol and sugar

cobblers /kóbblərz/ *n* an offensive term for something perceived as nonsense (*slang*)

cobblestone /kóbb'l stōn/ n a small rounded paving stone —**cobblestoned** adj

cobnut /kób nut/ n a hazelnut

COBOL /kố bol/, **Cobol** n a computer programming language designed for business applications

cobra /kóbra/ n a venomous snake with a flap of skin resembling a hood on its head

cobweb /kób web/ n a spider's dusty web ■ **cobwebs** npl a sluggish mental state

coca /kóka/ (pl same) n 1 the dried leaves of a South American bush. Use: stimulants, cocaine, other alkaloids. 2 a bush whose leaves yield coca

cocaine /kō káyn/ n an addictive drug processed from coca leaves

coccus /kókass/· (pl -ci /kóksī/) n a rounded bacterium

coccyx /kók siks/ (pl -cyges /-sī jeez/ or -cyxes) n a small bone at the base of the human spine —**coccygeal** /kok sījji al/ adj

Cochin /kố chin/ major port in Kerala State, SW India. Pop. 564,589 (1991).

cochineal /kóchi neël/ n a red dye and food colouring obtained from dried insect bodies

cochlea /kókli a/ (pl -ae /-ee/ or -as) n a spiral structure in the inner ear —**cochlear** adj

cock n 1 an adult male chicken 2 any adult male bird 3 the hammer of a gun 4 the raised position of the hammer of gun 5 a taboo term for the penis (offensive) 6 a stopcock 7 the tilted position of a hat ■ vt 1 prepare a gun for firing 2 turn your ears or eyes to listen or look 3 tilt something at an angle

cockade /ko káyd/ n an ornamental ribbon on a hat or livery

cock-a-doodle-doo /-doò/ n a cock's call —**cock-a-doodle-doo** vi

cock-a-hoop adj 1 elated 2 boastful

cock-a-leekie /-leéki/ n chicken and leek soup

cock-and-bull story, **cock-and-bull** n an absurd tale or excuse

cockatoo /kóka toò/ (pl -toos) n 1 a parrot with a prominent crest 2 Aus a small-scale farmer

ORIGIN **Cockatoo** came through Dutch from a Malay word. Its actual form has been influenced by English cock.

cockchafer /kók chayfar/ n a destructive European beetle

cockcrow /kók krō/ n daybreak (literary)

cocked hat n a two- or three-cornered hat worn in the 18C

cockerel /kókaral/ n a young domestic cock

Cockerell /kókaral/, **Sir Christopher** (1910–99) British radio and marine engineer. His experiments (1953–59) led to the invention of the hovercraft.

cocker spaniel n a medium-sized spaniel with long ears

cockeyed /kók īd/ adj 1 foolish (infml) 2 not aligned

cockfight /kók fīt/ n an illegal fight between cocks —**cockfighting** n

cockle¹ /kók'l/ n 1 a mollusc with a heart-shaped two-part shell 2 also **cockleshell** the shell of a cockle

cockle² /kók'l/ n a weed of the pink family

cockney /kókni/ (pl -neys) n 1 also **Cockney** somebody born in the East End of London 2 also **Cockney** the dialect of native Londoners from the East End 3 Aus a young Australian snapper —**cockneyism** n

ORIGIN **Cockney** comes from old forms that literally mean 'cock's egg'. This was a small misshapen egg, in medieval times popularly said to be laid by a cock. The term came to be used for a 'pampered child', and then for a 'town dweller', considered less hardy than somebody from the countryside. From around 1600 it referred specifically to 'a person born in the city of London'. A traditional definition says that a true cockney is born within the sound of Bow bells, and this was reported as early as 1617.

cockpit /kók pit/ n 1 the part of an aircraft where the pilot sits 2 a space for the driver in a racing car 3 an enclosed area containing the wheel or tiller of a small ship

cockroach /kók rōch/ n a nocturnal oval-bodied insect that is a household pest

ORIGIN **Cockroach** came in the early 17C from Spanish cucaracha. A variety of early spellings reflect this, but by the 19C it had been assimilated to the English forms cock and roach.

cockscomb /kóks kōm/ n 1 a fleshy crest on the head of a domestic cock 2 a plant with a crest of red flowers

cocksure /kok shoòr, -sháwr/ adj overconfident —**cocksureness** n

cocktail /kók tayl/ n 1 a drink consisting of a mixture of other drinks, usually alcohol and a soft drink 2 a light food served as an appetizer (usually in combination) o a prawn cocktail 3 a mixture or combination

cocktail lounge n a bar serving cocktails, especially in a hotel

cocktail party n an early evening party where cocktails are served

cocktail stick n a stick on which hors d'oeuvres are served

cockup /kók up/ n something that is bungled (infml)

cocky /kóki/ (-ier, -iest) adj arrogantly overconfident (infml) —**cockily** adv —**cockiness** n

cocoa /kốkō/ n 1 a brown powder made from ground roasted cocoa beans. Use: chocolate, cooking, hot drink. 2 a hot drink made with cocoa powder

cocoa bean n a bean-shaped seed of the cacao tree

cocoa butter n a fatty substance obtained from cocoa beans. Use: chocolate, cosmetics, suntan oils.

coconut /kốka nut/ (pl same or -nuts) n 1 a fruit with a hard fibrous shell, firm white flesh, and sweet juice **2** the edible white flesh of a coconut fruit **3** *also* **coconut palm** a tropical palm tree that produces coconuts

coconut oil *n* oil obtained from the flesh of the coconut. Use: in foods, cosmetics.

cocoon /kə koòn/ *n* **1** the silky cover for a caterpillar or other larva during its pupal stage **2** something that resembles a cocoon in the way that it provides protection or a sense of safety ■ *vt* **1** wrap for warmth or protection **2** keep safe from unpleasantness or danger —**cocooned** *adj*

Cocos Islands /kókəss-/ dependency of Australia consisting of 27 small islands in the E Indian Ocean. Pop. 595 (1993).

Cocteau /kóktō/, **Jean** (1889–1963) French writer and film director

cod[1] /(*pl same or* cods) *n* **1** a large sea fish with three dorsal fins **2** cod as food **3** *ANZ* any of various Australian fish similar to cod

cod[2] *Ireland n* a person regarded as mildly unintelligent ■ *vti* (**codding, codded**) fool around or trick

Cod, Cape peninsula in SE Massachusetts

COD *abbr* cash on delivery

coda /kódə/ *n* **1** the final section of a musical piece **2** a section at the end of a text giving added information

coddle /kódd'l/ *vt* **1** be overprotective of somebody **2** cook an egg gently in water

code *n* **1** a system of letters, numbers, or symbols into which ordinary language is converted for secret transmission **2** a system of letters or numbers that gives information, e.g. a postal area **3** a system of symbols, numbers, or signals that conveys information to a computer **4** a set of rules and regulations o *the penal code* **5** standards concerning acceptable behaviour o *her moral code* ■ *vt* (**coding, coded**) put in code —**coder** *n*

codeine /kó deen/ *n* a derivative of morphine used as a painkiller

code name *n* a name used to disguise the identity of somebody or something —**code-name** *vt*

codex /kó deks/ (*pl* **-dices** /di seez/) *n* a collection of old manuscript texts in book form

codfish /kód fish/ (*pl same or* **-fishes**) *n* a cod

codger /kójjər/ *n* a man, especially a man of advanced years regarded as eccentric *(infml insult)*

codicil /kódissil/ *n* **1** an addition to a will that modifies it **2** an appendix to a text *(fml)*

codify /kódi fī/ (**-fies, -fied**) *vt* arrange into an organized system —**codification** /kódifi káysh'n/ *n*

cod-liver oil *n* a vitamin-rich oil from the liver of a cod. Use: food supplement.

coeducation /kó eddyoō káysh'n/ *n* the education of both sexes together —**coeducational** *adj*

coefficient /kó i físh'nt/ *n* **1** the numerical part

of an algebraic term **2** a constant that is a measure of a property of a substance

coeliac disease /seéli ak-/ *n* a disease caused by sensitivity to gluten that makes the digestive system unable to absorb fat

coerce /kō úrss/ (**-ercing, -erced**) *vt* force to do something —**coercible** *adj* —**coercion** *n*

coercive /kō úrssiv/ *adj* using force —**coercively** *adv*

Coetzee /kúrt zee/, **J. M.** (*b.* 1940) South African novelist

coeval /kō eév'l/ *adj* equal in age or duration *(fml)*

coexist /kó ig zíst/ *vi* **1** exist at the same time and in the same place **2** live together peacefully —**coexistence** *n* —**coexistent** *adj*

coextensive /kó ik sténssiv/ *adj* with the same range or limits —**coextensively** *adv*

C of E *abbr* Church of England

coffee /kóffi/ *n* **1** a drink made from ground or processed beans **2** beans for making coffee **3** the bush that produces coffee beans **4** a pale brown colour —**coffee** *adj*

coffee bar *n* a small café

coffee bean *n* a bean-shaped seed of the coffee bush

coffee cake *n* **1** a coffee-flavoured cake **2** *US, Can* a cake eaten with coffee

coffeehouse /kóffi howss/ (*pl* **-houses** /-howziz/) *n* a café

coffee morning *n* an informal gathering where coffee and snacks are served, often with the proceeds going to charity

coffeepot /kóffi pot/ *n* a jug for serving coffee

coffee table *n* a low living-room table

coffee-table book *n* a large illustrated book for display or casual perusal

coffer /kóffər/ *n* a strongbox ■ **coffers** *npl* funds

coffin /kóffin/ *n* a box in which a corpse is buried or cremated

cog *n* **1** a tooth on a cogwheel **2** a cogwheel —**cogged** *adj*

cogent /kójənt/ *adj* rational and convincing —**cogency** *n* —**cogently** *adv* ◊ See note at **valid**

cogitate /kójji tayt/ (**-tating, -tated**) *vti* think deeply and carefully about something *(fml)* —**cogitation** /kójji táysh'n/ *n* —**cogitative** *adj*

cognac /kón yak/ *n* high-quality French brandy

cognate /kóg nayt/ *adj* related in some way *(fml)*

~~cognative~~ incorrect spelling of **cognitive**

cognition /kog nísh'n/ *n* **1** acquisition of knowledge through reasoning or perception **2** knowledge acquired via reasoning or perception

cognitive /kógnitiv/ *adj* **1** of the acquisition of knowledge by cognition **2** of thought processes —**cognitively** *adv*

cognizance /kógnizənss/, **cognisance** *n* *(fml)* **1** a state or degree of awareness **2** the extent of somebody's knowledge

cognizant /kógnizənt/, **cognisant** *adj* aware of something *(fml)* ◊ See note at **aware**

cognomen /kog nṓ men/ (*, pl* **-nomens** *or* **-nomina** /-nómminə/) *n* 1 a nickname *(fml)* 2 a family name given as the third name to a citizen of ancient Rome —**cognominal** /kog nómmin'l/ *adj*

cognoscenti /kónnyō shénti, kógnə-/ (*sing* **-te** /-tay/) *npl* connoisseurs or experts

cogwheel /kóg weel/ *n* a toothed wheel that fits into another to transmit motion

cohabit /kō hábbit/ *vi* 1 live together in a relationship 2 coexist —**cohabitation** /kō habi táysh'n/ *n*

Cohen /kố in/, **Stanley** (*b.* 1935) US biochemist. He jointly developed the recombinant DNA techniques that became the basis of genetic engineering.

cohere /kō heèr/ (**-hering, -hered**) *vi (fml)* 1 stick together 2 be logically consistent

coherent /kō heèrənt/ *adj* 1 logically or aesthetically consistent 2 able to speak clearly and logically —**coherence** *n* —**coherently** *adv*

cohesion /kō heèzh'n/ *n* the state of joining or working together —**cohesive** /kō heèssiv/ *adj* —**cohesively** *adv*

cohort /kō hawrt/ *n* 1 in ancient Rome, a unit of the army that was one tenth of a legion 2 a group of people 3 *US* a supporter or associate *(disapproving)* 4 a group of soldiers 5 a group of people with statistical similarities

ORIGIN Cohort derives from a Latin word that literally means 'enclosed space'. It was then used of 'people within an enclosed space', and specifically 'an infantry unit of the Roman army'. After its adoption into English, it began to be used generally for 'a group of people' in the early 18C, and for an 'associate' in the United States in the mid-20C.

coiffure /kwaa fyoòr/ *n* a person's hairstyle, especially a woman's *(fml or humorous)* —**coiffure** *vt* —**coiffured** *adj*

coil *n* 1 a series of connected loops 2 a single loop in a series 3 a spiral 4 a wire spiral through which an electric current is passed, e.g. to create magnetism ■ *v* 1 *vti* curl or wind into loops 2 *vi* curve or bend

coin *n* 1 a piece of metal money 2 metal money in general ■ *vt* 1 mint coins 2 invent a new word or phrase

coinage /kóynij/ *n* a new word or phrase

coincide /kố in síd/ (**-ciding, -cided**) *vi* 1 happen at the same time 2 be in the same position or form

coincidence /kō ínssidənss/ *n* 1 a chance happening 2 the fact of happening by chance or at the same time —**coincidental** /kō ínssi dént'l/ *adj* —**coincidentally** *adv*

coir /kóyər/ *n* coconut fibre. Use: matting, rope.

coitus /kố itəss/ *n* sexual intercourse *(fml or technical)* —**coital** *adj*

coke[1] *n* a solid carbon residue produced from coal. Use: fuel.

coke[2] *n* cocaine *(slang)*

Coke *tdmk* a trademark for a cola-flavoured soft drink

col *n* 1 a low point in a mountain ridge 2 a region of low atmospheric pressure

COL /kol/ *abbr* computer-oriented language

col. *abbr* 1 college 2 colour

Col. *abbr* Colonel

cola[1] /kốlə/ *n* 1 a sweet fizzy drink flavoured with cola nuts 2 a tropical evergreen tree that produces cola nuts

cola[2] plural of **colon**[2]

~~colaborate~~ incorrect spelling of **collaborate**

colander /kúlləndər/ *n* a strainer for draining water from food

cola nut *n* a seed of the cola tree. Use: carbonated drinks, medicines.

~~colateral~~ incorrect spelling of **collateral**

Colbert /kốl bair/, **Jean-Baptiste** (1619–83) French politician

cold *adj* 1 at a low temperature 2 making a place seem cooler 3 cooked hot then cooled 4 taciturn and emotionless 5 unfriendly and uncaring 6 no longer recent or fresh and therefore hard to follow ○ *a cold trail* ■ *n* 1 a viral infection of the nose and throat 2 cold weather or conditions ■ *adv* without any preparation ○ *sang the part cold* —**coldly** *adv* —**coldness** *n* ◇ **blow hot and cold** be alternately enthusiastic and indifferent ◇ **leave cold** fail to impress or excite ◇ **out cold** unconscious or in a deep sleep *(infml)*

cold-blooded /-blúddid/ *adj* 1 with a body temperature that varies according to the temperature of the surroundings 2 lacking pity or friendliness —**cold-bloodedly** *adv* —**cold-bloodedness** *n*

coldboot /kóld boot/ *vt* restart a computer by switching it off and on again

cold call *n* a telephone call or visit made to an unknown prospective customer —**cold-call** *vt*

cold comfort *n* something that does not help

cold cream *n* a thick paste used for cleansing and softening the skin on the face

cold cuts *npl* slices of cold cooked meat

cold feet *npl* a loss of nerve

cold frame *n* a glass structure for protecting young plants

cold-hearted /-haártid/ *adj* lacking sympathy —**cold-heartedly** *adv* —**cold-heartedness** *n*

cold-pressed *adj* describes oil obtained from olives without heating

cold shoulder *n* an instance of unfriendliness —**coldshoulder** /kóld shốldər/ *vt*

cold snap *n* a sudden short period of cold weather

cold sore *n* a blister near the lips caused by a virus

cold storage *n* chilled conditions in which food is preserved

cold sweat *n* a nervous or frightened state

cold turkey *n* 1 the abrupt withdrawal of addictive drugs with no other treatment to ease the symptoms **2** withdrawal symptoms

cold war *n* **1** a state of enmity between nations without open hostilities **2 Cold War** the hostile but nonviolent Communist-Western relations that existed between 1946 and 1989

Coleridge /kólərij/, **Samuel Taylor** (1772–1834) British poet

coleslaw /kól slaw/ *n* a cabbage and carrot salad in a mayonnaise dressing

Colette

Colette /ko lét/ (1873–1954) French novelist

colic /kóllik/ *n* **1** a pain in the abdomen, often caused by inflammation or an obstruction **2** crying in babies caused by intestinal discomfort

colitis /kə lítiss, ko-/ *n* inflammation of the colon —**colitic** /kə líttik, ko-/ *adj*

collaborate /kə lábbə rayt/ (**-rating, -rated**) *vi* **1** work with another person or group **2** betray others by working with an enemy —**collaboration** /kə lábbə ráysh'n/ *n* —**collaborative** *adj* —**collaborator** *n*

collage /ko laazh, kóllaazh/ *n* **1** a picture made by sticking pieces of things on a surface **2** the art of making collages

collagen /kólləjən/ *n* a protein found in skin and other connective tissue —**collagenous** /kə lájjənəss/ *adj*

collapse /kə láps/ *v* (**-lapsing, -lapsed**) **1** *vi* fall down as a result of structural weakness or a lack of support **2** *vi* fail abruptly **3** *vi* fall, sit, or lie down suddenly **4** *vi* suddenly sit or lie down **5** *vti* fold for easy storage ■ *n* **1** an abrupt failure or end **2** an act of falling down suddenly **3** a sudden decrease in value —**collapsible** *adj*

collar /kóllər/ *n* **1** the part of a garment round the neck **2** a band round the neck of an animal to identify it or tie it to a lead **3** a band of colour round a mammal's or bird's neck **4** a ring-shaped device or part ■ *vt* arrest a criminal suspect *(slang)* —**collared** *adj* ◇ **hot under the collar** angry, irritated, or agitated *(infml)*

collarbone /kóllər bōn/ *n* each of the two curved bones that connect the human breastbone to the shoulder

collate /kə láyt, ko-/ (**-lating, -lated**) *vt* **1** put pages in the correct order **2** bring pieces of information together and compare them —**collator** *n*

collateral /kə láttərəl/ *n* property or goods used as security against a loan ■ *adj* **1** parallel or corresponding **2** descended from the same ancestor but through a different line **3** additional to and in support of something **4** accompanying but secondary

collateral damage *n* unintended damage to civilian life or property during a military operation

collation /kə láysh'n/ *n* **1** the collating of something **2** a light meal

colleague /kólleeg/ *n* a person somebody works with —**colleagueship** *n*

collect /kə lékt/ *v* **1** *vt* gather and bring things together **2** *vt* obtain and keep objects of the same type **3** *vt* fetch people or things and take them somewhere **4** *vt* take the money or a prize you are entitled to **5** *vti* gather and accumulate in a place **6** *vi* gradually assemble in a place **7** *vr* get control of yourself

---

SYNONYMS collect, accumulate, gather, amass, assemble, stockpile, hoard CORE MEANING: bring dispersed things together

---

collectable /kə léktəb'l/, **collectible** *n* an object valued by collectors ■ *adj* of interest to collectors

collected /kə léktid/ *adj* **1** calm and composed **2** brought together as a whole

collection /kə léksh'n/ *n* **1** a group of people or things **2** the objects owned by a particular collector or held in a museum **3** the process or an act of collecting something

collective /kə léktiv/ *adj* **1** shared by or applying to everyone in a group **2** collected to form a whole **3** run by workers, sometimes under state supervision ■ *n* **1** a collective enterprise run by workers **2** the members of a collective —**collectively** *adv* —**collectiveness** *n*

collective bargaining *n* negotiations between a union and management

collective farm *n* a state-supervised farm run by workers

collective noun *n* a noun that refers to a group of people or things as a unit

collectivism /kə léktivizəm/ *n* the ownership and management of factories and farms by the people of a nation —**collectivist** *n*

collectivize /kə lékti vīz/ (**-izing, -ized**), **collectivise** *vt* organize an enterprise on collective principles —**collectivization** /kə lékti vī záysh'n/ *n*

collector /kə léktər/ *n* **1** somebody who collects objects **2** somebody whose job is collecting things, e.g. tickets on a train **3** a container where things collect

collector's item *n* an object desired by collectors

colleen /kə leén, kólleen/ *n* **1** *Ireland* a girl **2** an Irish girl

college /kóllij/ *n* **1** an institution of higher or further education, especially one offering courses in specialized or practical subjects **2** a division of some British universities, e.g. Oxford or Cambridge **3** a school, especially a British public school **4** the staff and students of a college **5** a group of people of the same profession

collegial /kə leeji əl/ *adj* **1** of a college or university **2** with power shared equally between colleagues

collegiate /kə leeji ət/ *adj* **1** of a college **2** describes a university consisting of separate colleges

~~college~~ incorrect spelling of **colleague**

collide /kə líd/ (**-liding, -lided**) *vi* **1** crash into somebody or something **2** come into conflict with somebody

collie /kólli/ *n* a dog bred to herd sheep

~~collieflour, collieflower~~ incorrect spelling of **cauliflower**

colliery /kóllyəri/ (*pl* **-ies**) *n* a coal mine

Collins /kóllinz/, **Michael** (1890–1922) Irish politician

Collins, Wilkie (1824–89) British novelist

collision /kə lízh'n/ *n* **1** a crash between two moving vehicles, objects, or people **2** a conflict

collocate *v* /kóllə kayt/ (**-cating, -cated**) **1** *vi* occur frequently with another word **2** *vt* put something next to something else *(fml)* ■ *n* /kólləkət/ a word that frequently occurs with another **—collocation** /kóllə káysh'n/ *n* **—collocational** *adj*

colloid /kólloyd/ *n* a suspension of small particles dispersed in another substance **—colloid** *adj* **—colloidal** /kə lóyd'l/ *adj*

~~colloquail~~ incorrect spelling of **colloquial**

colloquial /kə lókwi əl/ *adj* describes language used in informal speech, rather than in writing **—colloquially** *adv*

colloquialism /kə lókwi əlizəm/ *n* an informal word or phrase

colloquium /kə lókwi əm/ (*pl* **-ums** *or* **-a** /-ə/) *n* **1** an academic seminar **2** a meeting to discuss something

colloquy /kólləkwi/ (*pl* **-quies**) *n* **1** a discussion *(fml)* **2** a written dialogue

~~collosal~~ incorrect spelling of **colossal**

collude /kə lóod/ (**-luding, -luded**) *vi* work secretly with somebody to do something wrong or illegal

collusion /kə lóozh'n/ *n* secret cooperation between people who do something wrong or illegal **—collusive** *adj*

colocation /kó lō káysh'n/ *n* the sharing of the facilities of a hosting centre with other Internet clients

cologne /kə lốn/ *n* a scented liquid that is lighter than perfume

Cologne /kə lốn/ port in W Germany. Pop. 963,817 (1997).

Colombia /kə lúmbi ə, -lóm-/ country in NW South America. Cap. Bogotá. Pop. 40,349,388 (2001). **—Colombian** *n, adj*

Colombo /kə lúmbō/ commercial capital, largest city, and port of Sri Lanka. Pop. 615,000 (1995).

colon[1] /kốlən, -lon/ *n* **1** the punctuation mark (:) used to divide distinct but related elements of a sentence **2** a mark (:) used in phonetics after a vowel to show that it is long ◊ See note at **semicolon**

USAGE The **colon** is used to divide a sentence when the second part explains or elaborates on what has gone before: *They have put forward a different theory: the phenomenon may be caused by global warming.* It is also used to introduce a list or a quotation: *You will need the following equipment: waterproof clothing, strong walking boots, and a map. Martin Luther King wrote in* Chaos or Community *(1967): 'A riot is at bottom the language of the unheard'.*

colon[2] /kốlən, -lon/ (*pl* **-lons** *or* **-la** /-lə/) *n* the part of the large intestine between the caecum and the rectum

colón /ko lốn/ (*pl* **-lóns** *or* **-lones** /-lốness/) *n* the main unit of currency in Costa Rica and El Salvador

colonel /kúrn'l/, **Colonel** *n* a military rank in the British Army or Royal Marines above lieutenant colonel **—colonelcy** *n* **—colonelship** *n*

SPELLCHECK Do not confuse the spelling of **colonel** and **kernel** ('the edible part of a nut'), which sound similar.

Colonel Blimp *n* = **blimp**[2]

colonial /kə lốni əl/ *adj* **1** of a colony **2** *also* **Colonial** of the British Empire or the British colonies in North America before independence **3** living in colonies ■ *n* somebody who lives in a colony

colonialism /kə lốni əlizəm/ *n* the policy of ruling nations as colonies **—colonialist** *n* **—colonialistic** /kə lốni ə lístik/ *adj*

colonic /kō lónnik/ *adj* of the colon

colonic irrigation, colonic hydrotherapy *n* the cleansing of the colon by injecting water into the anus

colonist /kóllənist/ *n* somebody living in a new colony

colonize /kóllə nīz/ (**-nizing, -nized**), **colonise** *vti* **1** establish a colony in another country or place **2** establish an organism in a new ecosystem, or become established in a new ecosystem **—colonization** /kóllə nī záysh'n/ *n*

colonnade /kóllə náyd/ *n* a row of columns supporting a roof or arches

colony /kólləni/ (*pl* **-nies**) *n* **1** a country or region ruled by another distant power **2** a group of organisms living together

colophon /kóllə fon/ *n* **1** a publisher's emblem on a book **2** the publication details given at the end of a book

color *n, vti* US = **colour**

Colorado /kóllə ráadō/ **1** state in the W United States. Cap. Denver. Pop. 4,301,261 (2000). **2** major North American river, rising in N Colorado and flowing southwest through the Grand Canyon. Length 2,330 km/1,450 mi.

Colorado Desert desert area of SE California

coloration /kúllə ráysh'n/, **colouration** n the pattern of colour on an object or an organism

coloratura /kóllərə toórə/ n a demanding and florid passage or piece of vocal music

colossal /kə lóss'l/ adj enormous in size or extent ○ a colossal high-rise office building —**colossally** adv

colossus /kə lóssəss/ (pl -**si** /-sī/ or -**suses**) n 1 a huge statue 2 an enormously large or powerful person or thing

colostomy /kə lóstəmi/ (pl -**mies**) n an operation to create an artificial anus in the abdomen

colour /kúllər/ n 1 the property of objects that depends on reflected light and is perceived as red, blue, green, or other shades 2 a pigment or dye 3 a hue other than black or white ○ printed in colour 4 the shade of somebody's skin 5 a healthy look to the skin 6 brightness and variety in hues 7 a quality that adds interest ○ The story lacks colour. ■ **colours** npl the flag of a national or military unit ■ v 1 vt change the colour of or add colour to 2 vi take on or change hue 3 vi blush 4 vt skew an opinion or judgment ◊ **nail your colours to the mast** make your opinions or intentions obvious ◊ **with flying colours** to an excellent standard

colourant /kúllərənt/ n a colouring agent such as a dye

colouration n = coloration

colour bar n legal or social barriers between ethnic groups with different skin colours

colour-blind adj 1 unable to distinguish between some colours 2 not discriminating on the grounds of ethnic group or skin colour —**colour blindness** n

colour-code vt identify or distinguish between colours by using colours

coloured /kúllərd/ adj 1 having a particular colour or colours (often in combination) 2 an offensive term for a member of an ethnic group whose members are dark-skinned (dated) 3 **Coloured** S Africa of mixed ethnic origin —**Coloured** n

colourfast /kúllər faast/ adj containing a dye that will not wash out

colourful /kúllərf'l/ adj 1 brightly coloured ○ colourful costumes 2 interesting and exciting ○ a colourful period of history —**colourfully** adv —**colourfulness** n

colouring /kúlləring/ n 1 a substance that gives a hue to something 2 appearance with regard to colour 3 the characteristic colours of a bird or animal

colourize /kúllər īz/ (-**izing**, -**ized**), **colourise** vt add colour to a black-and-white film

colourless /kúllərləss/ adj 1 lacking colour 2 characterless ○ a colourless personality —**colourlessly** adv —**colourlessness** n

colour supplement n a magazine with colour photographs accompanying a newspaper

colourway /kúllər way/ n one of a range of colours available

colt n a young male horse

coltish /kṓltish/ adj lively and energetic —**coltishly** adv —**coltishness** n

Coltrane /kol tráyn/, **John** (1926–67) US jazz saxophonist and composer

Columba /kə lúmbə/, **St** (521–597) Irish missionary

Columbia /kə lúmbi ə/ capital of South Carolina. Pop. 110,840 (1998).

columbine /kólləm bīn/ (pl -**bines** or same) n a plant with five-petalled flowers with long spurs

Columbus /kə lúmbəss/ capital and largest city of Ohio. Pop. 670,234 (1998).

Columbus, Christopher (1451–1506) Italian explorer

column /kólləm/ n 1 a long cylindrical upright support 2 something with a long cylindrical upright shape ○ a column of smoke 3 a line of people or things 4 a vertical section of print on a page 5 a regularly appearing article in a newspaper or magazine 6 a vertical arrangement of numbers —**columnar** /kə lúmnər/ adj

columnist /kólləmnist/ n somebody who writes a newspaper or magazine column

com abbr commercial organization (in Internet addresses)

COM n the conversion of computer output to microfilm. Full form **computer output microfilm**

com. abbr commerce

coma[1] /kṓmə/ n a long period of unconsciousness

coma[2] /kṓmə/ (pl -**mae** /-mee/) n a cloud around the head of a comet

~~comand~~ incorrect spelling of **command**

comatose /kṓmətōss/ adj in a coma

comb /kṓm/ n 1 a toothed instrument for tidying or arranging the hair 2 a tool for cleaning wool 3 a cock's fleshy crest ■ vt 1 tidy the hair or clean wool with a comb 2 search a place thoroughly

combat /kóm bat/ n 1 the process of fighting ○ unarmed combat 2 a struggle for or against something, or between two forces ○ a combat between good and evil ■ vt 1 try to destroy or control something dangerous or undesirable ○ measures to combat pollution 2 resist somebody or something

combatant /kómbətənt/ n somebody taking part in a war, fight, struggle, or argument

combat fatigue n a psychological disorder resulting from the stress of battle

combative /kómbətiv/ adj eager to fight or argue —**combativeness** n

combination /kómbi náysh'n/ n 1 a mixture or combined set 2 the process or result of combining 3 a set of numbers that open a lock ◊ See note at **mixture**

combine vti /kəm bīn/ (-**bining**, -**bined**) 1 join or mix together 2 unite chemically to form a single substance ■ n /kóm bīn/ 1 an association of business or political organizations 2 *also* **combine harvester** a machine that reaps and threshes grain

combo /kómbō/ (*pl* **-bos**) *n* a jazz group

combust /kəm búst/ *vti* burn with a flame

combustible /kəm bústəb'l/ *adj* able or likely to catch fire and burn —**combustibility** /kəm bústə billəti/ *n* —**combustibly** *adv*

combustion /kəm búschən/ *n* 1 the burning of fuel in an engine 2 a chemical reaction producing heat and light —**combustive** *adj*

come /kum/ *v* (**came, come**) 1 *vi* approach or reach a place 2 *vi* reach a state o *came to pieces in my hands* 3 *vi* happen or exist 4 *vi* occur in the mind o *The idea came to me in the bath.* 5 *vi* originate o *comes from China* 6 *vi* result o *comes from eating too much chocolate* 7 *vi* amount or add up to o *comes to £14.50* 8 *vi* have an orgasm (*slang; sometimes offensive*) 9 *vt* adopt a particular attitude or behaviour (*infml*) o *Don't come the innocent – I saw you do it!* ◼ *prep* by a particular time in the future o *It should be finished come Wednesday.* ◇ **come what may** whatever happens

☐ **come about** *vi* happen
☐ **come across** *v* 1 *vt* find 2 *vi* be communicated
☐ **come along** *vi* progress o *How's the new recruit coming along?*
☐ **come before** *vt* be judged or considered by
☐ **come by** *vt* obtain
☐ **come down** *vi* 1 decrease, e.g. in cost or altitude 2 reach a decision o *came down on the side of common sense* 3 be handed down
☐ **come in** *vi* prove to have a particular quality o *come in handy*
☐ **come in for** *vt* be subjected to
☐ **come into** *vt* inherit money
☐ **come of** *vt* result from o *This situation comes of greed.*
☐ **come off** *v* 1 *vt* become detached from something 2 *vi* happen as planned (*infml*) 3 *vi* succeed (*infml*)
☐ **come on** *vi* 1 automatically start to operate 2 hurry up (*usually as a command*) 3 progress or advance 4 begin at a particular time (*refers to radio or television programmes*)
☐ **come out** *vi* 1 be revealed 2 be published 3 reveal something secret about yourself, especially your sexual preferences 4 become visible in the sky o *if the sun comes out*
☐ **come out with** *vt* say
☐ **come over** *v* 1 *vi* be communicated 2 *vi* give a particular impression o *He comes over as sincere.* 3 *vt* affect o *A feeling of dizziness came over me.*
☐ **come round** *vi* 1 regain consciousness 2 change your opinion
☐ **come through** *vti* survive something unpleasant or dangerous
☐ **come to** *vi* regain consciousness
☐ **come up** *vi* 1 be mentioned 2 occur unexpectedly
☐ **come upon** *vt* find accidentally
☐ **come up to** *vt* match or equal
☐ **come up with** *vt* produce or devise

comeback /kúm bak/ *n* 1 a return to success, fame, or popularity 2 a sharp reply 3 a complaint or claim for compensation

comedian /kə meedi ən/ *n* an entertainer who tells jokes or performs comic acts

comedienne /kə meedi én/ *n* 1 a female comedian 2 a comic actress

comedown /kúm down/ *n* a decline in status (*infml*)

comedy /kómmədi/ (*pl* **-dies**) *n* 1 a funny play, film, or book 2 comedies as a genre 3 humorous entertainment —**comedic** /kə meedik/ *adj*

~~comeing~~ incorrect spelling of **coming**

comely /kúmmli/ (**-lier, -liest**) *adj* good-looking (*literary*) —**comeliness** *n*

ORIGIN Comely is probably a shortening of obsolete *becomely* 'fitting', formed from *become* in the sense surviving in *becoming*.

come-on *n* 1 an enticement or inducement (*infml*) 2 an indication of sexual interest

comestible /kə méstəb'l/ (*fml*) *n* an item of food ◼ *adj* edible

comet /kómmit/ *n* an astronomical object composed of a mass of ice and dust with a long luminous tail

ORIGIN Comet comes from a Greek word that literally means 'long-haired'. The tail of a comet was seen as hair streaming in the wind. The word arrived in English in the 12C, via Latin and French.

comeuppance /kum úppənss/ *n* something unpleasant regarded as fair punishment (*infml*) o *He got his comeuppance in the end.*

~~comfertable~~ incorrect spelling of **comfortable**

comfort /kúmfərt/ *n* 1 conditions in which somebody feels physically relaxed o *in the comfort of your own home* 2 a source of comfort o *It's a comfort to know that she's safe.* 3 relief from pain or anxiety ◼ *vt* bring comfort to somebody in pain or distress

comfortable /kúmftəb'l, -fərtəb'l/ *adj* 1 feeling comfort or ease 2 providing comfort 3 adequate or large o *won by a comfortable majority* —**comfortably** *adv*

comforter /kúmfərtər/ *n* 1 somebody who gives comfort 2 *US, Can* a quilt

comfrey /kúmfri/ *n* a plant with hairy leaves and stems. Use: in herbal medicine.

comfy /kúmfi/ (**-fier, -fiest**) *adj* comfortable (*infml*)

comic /kómmik/ *adj* 1 funny 2 of comedy o *a great comic routine* ◼ *n* 1 a comedian o *a nightclub comic* 2 a magazine with stories told in coloured cartoons

comical /kómmik'l/ *adj* causing smiles or laughter —**comically** *adv*

comic strip *n* a series of cartoons telling a story or joke

coming /kúmming/ *adj* 1 happening or starting soon 2 likely to be successful o *She's the coming power in this company.* ◼ *n* the arrival of a person or event

coming of age *n* the reaching of the official age of adulthood

comings and goings *npl* busy activity involving frequent arrivals and departures

~~commission~~ incorrect spelling of **commission**

~~comitee~~ incorrect spelling of **committee**

comma /kómmə/ *n* a punctuation mark (,) that represents a pause or separates items in a list

command /kə maánd/ *n* 1 an order to do something ○ *obey their every command* 2 control or authority ○ *take command* ○ *in command* 3 a thorough knowledge of something ○ *a command of French* 4 an operating instruction to a computer ■ *v* 1 *vt* give a command to 2 *vti* have authority or control over 3 *vt* deserve or be entitled to ○ *command respect* 4 *vt* be in a position that has a wide view over ○ *The balcony commands a view of the bay.*

commandant /kómmən dant/ *n* an officer in charge of a military establishment

command economy *n* a government-controlled economy

commandeer /kómmən deér/ *vt* 1 seize for official or military purposes 2 take and use, often by force

commander /kə maándər/ *n* somebody who commands, especially a military officer

commander in chief (*pl* **commanders in chief**) *n* a supreme commander

commanding /kə maánding/ *adj* 1 impressive or authoritative ○ *a commanding presence* 2 showing clear superiority ○ *a commanding lead* —**commandingly** *adv*

commanding officer *n* an officer in command

command key *n* a key that gives an instruction to a computer

commandment /kə maándmənt/ *n* a divine command

command module *n* the part of a spacecraft where the crew live and operate the controls

commando /kə maándō/ (*pl* **-dos** *or* **-does**) *n* a soldier specially trained for dangerous raids

commemorate /kə mémmə rayt/ *vt* 1 honour the memory of in a ceremony 2 be a memorial to —**commemoration** /kə mémmə ráysh'n/ *n* —**commemorative** /-rətiv/ *adj*, *n*

commence /kə ménss/ (**-mencing**, **-menced**) *vti* begin —**commencement** *n*

commend /kə ménd/ *vt* 1 praise formally or officially 2 cause to be accepted ○ *The plan has little to commend it.* —**commendable** *adj* —**commendably** *adv* —**commendation** /kómmen dáysh'n/ *n*

commensurate /kə ménshərət/ *adj* 1 equal in size 2 proportionate ○ *rewards commensurate with the efforts made* —**commensurately** *adv* —**commensuration** /kə ménshə ráysh'n/ *n*

comment /kómment/ *n* 1 a remark or observation 2 an explanatory note ■ *vti* make a comment about somebody or something

commentary /kómməntəri/ (*pl* **-ies**) *n* 1 a spoken description of an event, especially a sporting event 2 a series of explanatory notes or an explanatory essay

commentator /kómmən taytər/ *n* 1 somebody providing a broadcast commentary 2 a reporter who analyses events —**commentate** *vi*

commerce /kómmurss/ *n* trade in goods and services

commercial /kə múrsh'l/ *adj* 1 of or for commerce 2 done primarily for profit ■ *n* a radio or television advertisement —**commercially** *adv*

commercial bank *n* a bank dealing with businesses

commercial break *n* an interruption of a programme for advertisements

commercialism /kə múrsh'lizəm/ *n* 1 the principles and methods of commerce 2 excessive emphasis on profit —**commercialist** *n* —**commercialistic** /kə múrsh'l ístik/ *adj*

commercialize /kə múrsh'l iz/ (**-izing**, **-ized**), **commercialise** *vt* 1 apply commercial principles or methods to 2 exploit for profit —**commercialization** /kə múrsh'l ī záysh'n/ *n*

commie /kómmi/, **commy** (*pl* **-mies**) *n* a communist (*infml disapproving*) —**commie** *adj*

commingle /ko míng g'l/ (**-gling**, **-gled**) *v* 1 *vti* mix (*literary*) 2 *vt* combine funds or properties

commiserate /kə mízzə rayt/ (**-ating**, **-ated**) *vi* express sympathy

commiseration /kə mízzə ráysh'n/ *n* sympathy ■ **commiserations** *npl* expressions of sympathy

commissariat /kómmi sáiri ət/ *n* 1 an army supply department 2 a government department in the former Soviet Union before 1946

commissary /kómmissəri/ (*pl* **-ies**) *n* a deputy or representative

commission /kə mísh'n/ *n* 1 a fee paid to an agent 2 a task, especially an order to produce a piece of work 3 a government agency 4 a group with a specific task 5 an appointment as a military officer 6 the authority to act as an agent ■ *vt* 1 assign a task to somebody 2 order something to be produced by somebody 3 make somebody a military officer ◇ **on commission** receiving a percentage of the value of sales made ◇ **out of commission** not in operational use or working order

commissionaire /kə míshə náir/ *n* a uniformed attendant at a cinema, hotel, or theatre

commissioned officer *n* a military officer appointed by commission

commissioner /kə mísh'nər/ *n* 1 somebody belonging to or working for a commission 2 a government representative in an administrative area —**commissionership** *n*

commissioner for oaths *n* a solicitor authorized to authenticate oaths

commit /kə mít/ (**-mitting**, **-mitted**) *v* 1 *vi* promise devotion or dedication 2 *vt* promise or devote resources, time, or money 3 *vt* do something wrong or illegal 4 *vt* entrust something for protection 5 *vt* consign or record something ○ *committed the numbers to memory*

6 *vt* confine somebody to an institution —**committable** *adj*

~~commitee~~ incorrect spelling of **committee**

commitment /kə mítmənt/ *n* **1** a responsibility or obligation ○ *family commitments* **2** dedication to a cause, person, or relationship **3** a previously planned engagement

committee /kə mítti/ *n* a group appointed to perform a function on behalf of a larger group

~~committment~~ incorrect spelling of **commitment**

commode /kə mṓd/ *n* **1** a chair holding a chamber pot **2** a decorated cabinet

commodious /kə mṓdi əss/ *adj* roomy

commodity /kə mṓddəti/ (*pl* -**ties**) *n* **1** an item bought and sold **2** a useful thing

commodore /kómmə dawr/ *n* **1** a naval officer of a rank above captain **2** a merchant navy captain

common /kómmən/ *adj* **1** shared ○ *a common goal* **2** of or for all ○ *for the common good* **3** often occurring or seen **4** used or done by most people ○ *in common parlance* **5** without special privilege, rank, or status ○ *the common people* **6** ill-bred or vulgar ■ *n* a piece of public land —**commonly** *adv* —**commonness** *n*

common carrier *n* a transportation company

common denominator *n* **1** a number divisible by the lower numbers of two or more fractions **2** a shared belief or characteristic

commoner /kómmənər/ *n* an ordinary person who does not belong to the nobility

Common Era *n* the Christian Era, especially as used in reckoning dates

common ground *n* an area of agreement between people or groups

common knowledge *n* something generally known

common law *n* law that has evolved, as distinct from law established by legislation

common-law *adj* describes an unofficial marriage or a partner in such a marriage

Common Market *n* the European Union (*dated*)

common noun *n* a noun designating any member of a class, e.g. 'city', as distinct from a proper noun such as 'Paris'

common or garden *adj* ordinary

commonplace /kómmən playss/ *adj* **1** often occurring or encountered **2** unoriginal and uninteresting ■ *n* something commonplace, especially an unoriginal remark —**commonplaceness** *n*

common room *n* a room where residents, staff, or students can relax

commons /kómmənz/ *n* **1** a college or university dining hall (+ *sing verb*) **2 Commons** the House of Commons (+ *sing or pl verb*) **3** people without special privilege, rank, or status (+ *sing or pl verb*)

common sense *n* sound practical judgment derived from experience —**commonsense** /kómmən senss/ *adj* —**commonsensical** /-sénssik'l/ *adj*

commonwealth /kómmən welth/ *n* **1** a nation or its people **2** *also* **Commonwealth** a republic or self-governing territory **3** *also* **Commonwealth** an association of states **4 Commonwealth, Commonwealth of Nations** an association of sovereign states with the British monarch as its head

Commonwealth of Independent States *n* an association of former Soviet republics

commotion /kə mṓsh'n/ *n* a scene of noisy confusion or activity

communal /kómmyoon'l, kə myṓn'l/ *adj* **1** shared **2** of or belonging to a community or commune —**communally** *adv*

commune[1] /kóm yoon/ *n* **1** a community with shared possessions and responsibilities **2** the smallest administrative district in some countries

commune[2] /kə myṓn, kóm yoon/ (-**muning**, -**muned**) *vi* relate spiritually to something ○ *communing with nature*

communicable /kə myṓnikəb'l/ *adj* able to be transmitted or communicated ○ *a communicable disease* —**communicability** /kə myṓnikə bílləti/ *n*

communicant /kə myṓnikənt/ *n* a recipient of the Christian sacrament of Communion

communicate /kə myṓni kayt/ (-**cating**, -**cated**) *v* **1** *vti* give or exchange information **2** *vi* be connected or have common access **3** *vi* give or receive Communion —**communicator** *n*

communication /kə myṓni káysh'n/ *n* **1** giving or exchange of information **2** a written or spoken message **3** rapport ■ **communications** *npl* the technology used for sending and receiving messages (+ *pl verb*) —**communicational** *adj*

communication cord *n* a cord pulled by a railway passenger for an emergency stop

communications /kəmyoóni káysh'nz/ *npl* (+ *pl verb*) **1** the technology used for sending and receiving messages **2** the routes used for sending messages or moving troops and supplies ■ *n* (+ *sing or pl verb*) **1** effective use of words **2** the study of methods of communicating

communicative /kə myṓnikətiv/ *adj* **1** talkative **2** of communication

communion /kə myṓni ən/ *n* **1** a feeling of intimacy **2** a religious group with its own set of beliefs **3** a sense of fellowship between religious groups **4 Communion** a Christian sacrament commemorating Jesus Christ's last meal with his disciples **5 Communion** the consecrated bread and wine consumed at Communion

communiqué /kə myṓni kay/ *n* an official announcement

communism /kómmyoŏnizəm/ *n* **1** a classless political system in which all property and wealth are owned by everybody **2** *also* **Communism** the Marxist-Leninist version of communism **3** *also* **Communism** a totalitarian system of government with a state-controlled economy —**communist** *n*, *adj*

—Communist *n, adj* **—communistic** /kómmyoŏ nístik/ *adj*

community /kə myoŏnəti/ (*pl* **-ties**) *n* **1** a group of people living in the same area **2** a particular group of people within a society ○ *the financial community* **3** a group of nations **4** the plants and animals living together in an area

community centre *n* a building used for community activities

community service *n* work beneficial to the community, required of an offender as punishment

commute /kə myoŏt/ (**-muting, -muted**) *v* **1** *vi* travel regularly between places, especially between home and work **2** *vt* reduce the severity of a penalty **3** *vti* replace something with something else, or be a replacement —**commutation** /kómmyoŏ táysh'n/ *n* —**commuter** *n*

commuter belt *n* a residential area where many commuters live

Como /kṓmō/ capital of **Como Province**, N Italy, on the southwestern shore of **Lake Como**. Pop. 83,871 (1997).

Comoros /kómmərōz, kə máwrōz/ independent state consisting of a group of islands in the Indian Ocean, off the coast of Mozambique. Cap. Moroni. Pop. 596,202 (2001). —**Comorian** /kə máwri ən/ *n, adj*

compact[1] *adj* /kəm pákt/ **1** closely packed together **2** small and efficiently arranged ■ *vti* /kəm pákt/ make or become more dense or firmly packed ■ *n* /kóm pakt/ a case for makeup, especially face powder —**compactly** *adv* —**compactness** *n*

compact[2] /kóm pakt/ *n* an agreement

compact disc *n* a plastic disc on which music or computer data is digitally recorded

companion /kəm pánnyən/ *n* **1** a friend who accompanies or spends time with another **2** a matching article —**companion** *vt*

companionable /kəm pánnyənəb'l/ *adj* providing or enjoying pleasant company ○ *a companionable silence*

companionship /kəm pánnyən ship/ *n* the company of friends, or the relationship between friends

company /kúmpəni/ (*pl* **-nies**) *n* **1** a business enterprise **2** the state or fact of being with other people ○ *feel at ease in company* **3** a group of people, e.g. actors or soldiers **4** somebody's companions **5** a guest or guests ○ *having company for dinner*

comparable /kómpərəb'l/ *adj* **1** capable of being compared **2** similar —**comparability** /kómpərə bílləti/ *n* —**comparably** *adv*

comparative /kəm párrətiv/ *adj* **1** of or expressing comparison **2** relative ○ *He passed with comparative ease.* **3** describes an adjective or adverb in a form expressing increase, e.g. 'slower' or 'more importantly' ■ *n* the comparative degree, or a comparative form of a word —**comparatively** *adv*

compare /kəm páir/ *vt* (**-paring, -pared**) **1** examine for similarities and differences **2** consider or represent as similar ■ *n* comparison (*literary*) ○ *beautiful beyond compare*

comparison /kəm párriss'n/ *n* **1** the process or result of comparing **2** similarity

~~comparitive~~ incorrect spelling of **comparative**

compartment /kəm páartmənt/ *n* **1** a partitioned space **2** a section of a railway carriage —**compartmental** /kóm paart ment'l/ *adj*

compartmentalize /kóm paart ment'l īz/ (**-izing, -ized**), **compartmentalise** *vt* divide into separate areas or categories —**compartmentalization** /kóm paart ment'l ī záysh'n/ *n*

compass /kúmpəss/ *n* **1** a device for finding or indicating direction relative to magnetic north **2** the scope of something such as a subject ■ **compasses** *npl* a hinged device for drawing circles ■ *vt* **1** understand (*fml*) **2** surround or encircle **3** achieve (*literary*)

compassion /kəm pásh'n/ *n* sympathy for the suffering of others

compassionate /kəm pásh'nət/ *adj* showing compassion —**compassionately** *adv*

compassionate leave *n* special leave granted for personal reasons, e.g. the death of a close relative

~~compatable~~ incorrect spelling of **compatible**

compatible /kəm páttəb'l/ *adj* **1** able to exist, live, or work together without conflict **2** consistent ○ *not compatible with the facts* **3** in computing, able to be used with or substituted for something else —**compatibility** /kəm páttə bílləti/ *n* —**compatibly** *adv*

compatriot /kəm páttri ət/ *n* a fellow citizen

compel /kəm pél/ (**-pelling, -pelled**) *vt* force

compelling /kəm pélling/ *adj* **1** holding the attention or interest ○ *a compelling account* **2** making somebody do something ○ *a compelling need*

compendium /kəm péndi əm/ (*pl* **-ums** *or* **-a** / ə/) *n* **1** a short but comprehensive account **2** a collection of items, e.g. board games or books, brought together in a single unit

compensate /kómpən sayt/ (**-sating, -sated**) *v* **1** *vt* pay compensation to **2** *vti* counterbalance or make up for something —**compensatory** /kómpən sáytəri/ *adj*

compensation /kómpən sáysh'n/ *n* **1** money paid to make up for loss or damage, or in return for work done **2** payment of compensation **3** something that makes up for something else ○ *one of the compensations of living abroad*

compere /kóm pair/ *n* the host of an entertainment show —**compere** *vti*

~~competant~~ incorrect spelling of **competent**

compete /kəm peét/ (**-peting, -peted**) *vi* try to win or do better than others

competence /kómpitənss/, **competency** /-tənssi/ *n* **1** the quality of being competent **2** a specific skill or ability ◊ See note at **ability**

competent /kómpitənt/ *adj* **1** having enough skill or ability **2** good enough **3** legally capable or qualified —**competently** *adv*

competition /kómpə tísh'n/ n **1** the process of trying to win something or do better than others **2** an activity in which people try to win something **3** the opposition in a competitive situation ○ *keep one step ahead of the competition*

competitive /kəm péttitiv/ *adj* **1** involving an attempt to win something or to do better than others **2** inclined to want to do better than others **3** as good as or slightly better than that offered by others ○ *a highly competitive salary* —**competitively** *adv* —**competitiveness** *n*

competitor /kəm péttitər/ *n* **1** a participant in a competition **2** a rival or opponent in a competitive situation

compile /kəm pil/ (**-piling, -piled**) *vt* **1** gather together or create from various sources **2** convert into a high-level computer language into an intermediate one —**compilation** /kómpi láysh'n/ *n*

compiler /kəm pilər/ *n* **1** somebody who compiles something, e.g. lists or other items **2** a computer program that converts another program from a high-level language into an intermediate language

complacent /kəm pláyss'nt/ *adj* self-satisfied and unaware of possible dangers —**complacency** *n* —**complacently** *adv*

complain /kəm playn/ *vi* **1** express unhappiness or dissatisfaction **2** describe symptoms that are being experienced ○ *complained of chest pains* —**complainer** *n*

SYNONYMS complain, object, protest, grumble, grouse, carp, gripe, whine, nag CORE MEANING: indicate dissatisfaction with something

---

complainant /kəm pláynənt/ *n* somebody who makes a legal complaint

complaint /kəm playnt/ *n* **1** a statement or cause of unhappiness or dissatisfaction **2** an ailment

complaisant /kəm pláyz'nt/ *adj* seeking to please —**complaisance** *n* —**complaisantly** *adv*

complement *n* /kómplimənt/ **1** something that completes or perfects something else **2** the quantity required for completeness ○ *a full complement of staff* ■ *vt* /kómpli ment/ complete or perfect something

---

USAGE complement or compliment? A **complement** is something added to make a thing complete, whereas a **compliment** is an expression of praise: *This wine is the perfect complement to the meal. My compliments to the chef.* A **complimentary** copy of a book is one given without charge, whereas a **complementary** copy is one that completes a set of books.

---

complementary /kómpli méntəri/ *adj* **1** completing or perfecting **2** describes each of two angles that together make a right angle ◊ See note at **complement**

complementary medicine *n* medical treatment that addresses the causes rather than the symptoms of disease

complete /kəm pleet/ *adj* **1** whole **2** finished **3** utter or unmitigated ○ *a complete waste of time* ■ *vt* (**-pleting, -pleted**) **1** make whole **2** finish **3** accomplish —**completely** *adv* —**completeness** *n* —**completion** *n*

complex *adj* /kóm pleks, kəm pléks/ **1** difficult to analyse, understand, or solve **2** having many parts ■ *n* /kóm pleks/ **1** a set of interconnected buildings **2** an unreasonable or obsessive set of feelings that influence behaviour —**complexity** /kəm pléksəti/ *n*

complexion /kəm pléksh'n/ *n* **1** the quality and colour of somebody's skin **2** the character or appearance of something ○ *puts an entirely new complexion on the matter*

compliant /kəm plí ənt/ *adj* **1** ready to obey and conform **2** conforming to requirements (*often in combination*) ○ *industry-compliant* —**compliance** *n*

complicate /kómpli kayt/ (**-cating, -cated**) *vt* make more complex

complicated /kómpli kaytid/ *adj* having many interrelated parts or elements and therefore difficult to understand or deal with

complication /kómpli káysh'n/ *n* **1** a difficult or confused state **2** something that increases difficulty or complexity

complicity /kəm plíssəti/ *n* involvement in wrongdoing —**complicit** *adj*

compliment *n* /kómplimənt/ **1** an expression of praise **2** a gesture of respect ■ **compliments** *npl* expressions of respect and good wishes ■ *vt* /kómpli ment/ praise or congratulate ◊ See note at **complement**

complimentary /kómpli méntəri/ *adj* **1** expressing praise **2** given free as a courtesy or favour ○ *complimentary tickets* —**complimentarily** *adv* ◊ See note at **complement**

comply /kəm plí/ (**-plies, -plied**) *vi* obey or conform

component /kəm pónənt/ *n* **1** a part, element, or constituent **2** an electrical or mechanical part ■ *adj* forming part of a whole —**componential** /kómpə nénsh'l/ *adj*

comport /kəm páwrt/ *v* (*fml*) **1** *vr* behave **2** *vi* agree or be consistent —**comportment** *n*

compose /kəm póz/ (**-posing, -posed**) *v* **1** *vt* make by combining parts **2** *vt* put together to form a whole **3** *vti* create a piece of music or writing **4** *vt* make calm in manner **5** *vti* set type for printing —**composer** *n*

composed /kəm pózd/ *adj* calm and self-possessed —**composedly** /-zidli/ *adv*

composite /kómpazit/ *adj* **1** made up of different parts **2** with flower heads made up of many small flowers —**composite** *n*

composition /kómpə zísh'n/ *n* **1** the way in which something is made or in which its parts are arranged **2** the process of composing **3** a piece of music **4** a short essay —**compositional** *adj*

compositor /kəm pózzitər/ *n* a typesetter

compos mentis /kómpəss méntiss/ *adj* sane

compost /kóm post/ *n* 1 decayed organic matter used to enrich soil 2 a soil mixture for pot plants ■ *v* 1 *vti* turn into compost 2 *vt* treat with compost

composure /kəm pṓzhər/ *n* calmness and self-possession

compote /kóm pōt/ *n* a stewed fruit dessert

compound[1] *n* /kóm pownd/ 1 a combination or mixture 2 a substance formed by the chemical combination of elements in fixed proportions 3 a word made up of other words ■ *adj* /kóm pownd/ having two or more different parts ■ *v* /kəm pównd, kom-/ 1 *vti* combine 2 *vt* make by combining parts 3 *vt* intensify ◊ See note at **mixture**

compound[2] /kóm pownd/ *n* an enclosed group of buildings

compound fracture *n* a fracture in which a broken bone pierces the skin

compound interest *n* interest calculated on the total of the original sum and interest already accrued

comprehend /kómpri hénd/ *v* 1 *vti* understand 2 *vt* include (*fml*)

comprehensible /kómpri hénssəb'l/ *adj* intelligible —**comprehensibility** /kómpri hénssə bílləti/ *n* —**comprehensibly** *adv*

comprehension /kómpri hénsh'n/ *n* 1 the understanding of something 2 the ability to understand ○ *beyond my comprehension*

comprehensive /kómpri hénssiv/ *adj* 1 including or covering many things 2 including or covering everything ■ *n also* **comprehensive school** a secondary school for pupils of all abilities —**comprehensively** *adv* —**comprehensiveness** *n*

compress *v* /kəm préss/ 1 *vti* make or become smaller or shorter 2 *vt* press things together ■ *n* /kóm pres/ a pad pressed firmly against a part of the body, e.g. to stop bleeding —**compressible** *adj* —**compression** /kəm présh'n/ *n*

compressor /kəm préssər/ *n* a machine that compresses gas

~~comprimise~~ incorrect spelling of **compromise**

comprise /kəm prī́z/ (**-prising, -prised**) *vt* 1 include 2 consist of 3 △ constitute

USAGE Comprise is concerned with a whole having a number of parts: *The house comprises three bedrooms, a bathroom, a kitchen, and a living room.* Use of **comprise** in the sense 'constitute' is controversial. Avoid constructions like this if you wish to steer clear of criticism: *The house is comprised of three bedrooms, a bathroom, a kitchen, and a living room; Three bedrooms, a bathroom, a kitchen, and a living room comprise the house.*

compromise /kómprə mīz/ *n* 1 an agreement involving concessions on both sides 2 something accepted when what is wanted is unattainable ■ *v* (**-mising, -mised**) 1 *vi* agree by conceding 2 *vt* undermine or devalue ○ *compromised his integrity* 3 *vt* put at risk ○ *compromising our chances of success*

Compton /kómptən, kúmp-/, **Sir Denis** (1918–97) British cricketer and footballer

Compton-Burnett /kómptən bər nét/, **Ivy, Dame** (1884–1969) British novelist

comptroller /kən trṓlər/ *n* a financial supervisor —**comptrollership** *n*

compulsion /kəm púlsh'n/ *n* 1 an act of compelling, or the state of being compelled 2 an impulse or urge

compulsive /kəm púlssiv/ *adj* 1 unable to resist doing something ○ *a compulsive liar* 2 powerfully interesting —**compulsively** *adv* —**compulsiveness** *n*

compulsory /kəm púlssəri/ *adj* 1 required by authority 2 caused by force —**compulsorily** *adv*

compunction /kəm púngksh'n/ *n* shame and regret about wrongdoing

computation /kómpyoo táysh'n/ *n* 1 the use of a computer or computers 2 mathematical or arithmetical calculation —**computational** *adj*

compute /kəm pyoot/ (**-puting, -puted**) *v* 1 *vt* calculate, using numbers 2 *vi* use a computer

computed tomography, computerized tomography *n* a technique for producing images of cross sections of the body

computer /kəm pyootər/ *n* an electronic device for processing and storing data

computer-aided design *n* the use of computer software for design

computer-aided engineering *n* automated engineering analysis using computer simulations

computer conferencing *n* the use of computers to exchange information as if at a meeting

computer dating *n* the business of matching apparently compatible couples by computer

computerese /kəm pyootə reéz/ *n* computer jargon (*humorous*)

computer game *n* a game played on a computer

computer graphics *n* generation of pictures on a computer (+ *sing verb*) ■ *npl* computer-generated images (+ *pl verb*)

computerize /kəm pyootə rī́z/ (**-izing, -ized**), **computerise** *vt* 1 convert to or provide a computer-based system 2 store on a computer —**computerization** /kəm pyootə rī záysh'n/ *n*

computerized tomography *n* MED = **computed tomography**

computer language *n* a language used for writing computer programs

computer-literate *adj* able to use computers —**computer literacy** *n*

computerphobe /kəm pyootərfṓb/ *n* somebody who dislikes or fears computers (*infml*) —**computerphobia** /kəm pyootər fṓbi ə/ *n* —**computerphobic** /-fṓbik/ *adj*

computer science *n* the study of computers

computer virus *n* a computer program that

copies itself into other programs, often causing damage

computing /kəm pyóoting/ *n* the use of computers

comrade /kóm rayd, -rid/ *n* **1** a friend or companion **2** another member of the same group, especially a soldier —**comradely** *adj* —**comradeship** *n*

con[1] *vt* (**conning, conned**) trick by lying ■ *n* a dishonest trick or a swindle

con[2] *n* an argument against doing something o *the pros and cons*

Con. *abbr* Conservative

Conakry /kónnə kri, kónnə krée/ capital and main port of Guinea. Pop. 705,280 (1983 estimate).

concatenate /kon káttə nayt, kən-/ *vt* (**-nating, -nated**) **1** connect into a linked system **2** in computing, link together to form a single unit ■ *adj* linked together —**concatenation** /kon káttə náysh'n, kən-/ *n*

concave /kón kayv, kon káyv/ *adj* curved inwards —**concavity** /kon kávvəti/ *n*

conceal /kən seél/ *vt* hide something or somebody —**concealable** *adj* —**concealment** *n*

concede /kən seéd/ (**-ceding, -ceded**) *v* **1** *vt* reluctantly accept something to be true **2** *vti* acknowledge defeat in a contest or debate, often before the end **3** *vt* give a goal or point away **4** *vt* grant or yield a right or privilege ~~conceed~~ incorrect spelling of **concede**

conceit /kən seét/ *n* **1** excessive pride in yourself **2** an exaggerated comparison in literature

conceited /kən seétid/ *adj* having an excessively high opinion of yourself —**conceitedly** *adv* —**conceitedness** *n* ◊ See note at **proud**

conceive /kən seév/ (**-ceiving, -ceived**) *v* **1** *vti* think of or imagine something **2** *vt* invent, devise, or originate **3** *vti* become pregnant with a child or with young —**conceivable** *adj* —**conceivably** *adv*

concentrate /kónss trayt/ *v* (**-trating, -trated**) **1** *vti* silently focus your thoughts and attention on something **2** *vti* devote all efforts and resources to one thing **3** *vti* cluster together **4** *vt* make a substance purer, thicker, or stronger, especially by removing water ■ *n* a concentrated substance

concentration /kónss'n tráysh'n/ *n* **1** the devotion of all thoughts or efforts and resources to one thing **2** a cluster of things in a single area **3** the strength of a solution

concentration camp *n* **1** a Nazi prison camp in World War II **2** a prison camp for civilians in war

concentrator /kónss'n traytər/ *n* a telecommunications device that combines outgoing messages

concentric /kən séntrik, kon-/ *adj* describes circles and spheres of different sizes with the same centre —**concentrically** *adv* —**concentricity** /kónss'n tríssəti/ *n*

Concepción /kən sépsi ón/ capital of Con-

cepción **Department**, central Paraguay. Pop. 35,276 (1992).

concept /kón sept/ *n* **1** something thought or imagined **2** a broad abstract idea or principle o *the concept of time* **3** the most basic understanding of something o *has little concept of what is involved* —**conceptual** /kən séptyoo əl/ *adj* —**conceptually** *adv*

conception /kən sépsh'n/ *n* **1** a broad understanding of something **2** something being conceived in the mind **3** fertilization of an egg by a sperm **4** the origin or beginnings of something **5** formulation of an idea —**conceptional** *adj*

concept product *n* an innovative commercial product not yet in production

conceptual art, concept art *n* art designed to present ideas

conceptualize /kən séptyoo ə līz/ (**-izing, -ized**), **conceptualise** *vti* form a concept of something —**conceptualization** /kən séptyoo ə lī záysh'n/ *n*

concern /kən súrn/ *vt* **1** make worried **2** involve **3** be of interest or importance to **4** relate to or be about ■ *n* **1** worry or a cause of worry **2** a matter that affects somebody o *It's not my concern.* **3** caring feelings **4** a business enterprise

concerned /kən súrnd/ *adj* **1** anxious or worried **2** interested **3** involved —**concernedly** /-nidli/ *adv*

concerning /kən súrning/ *prep* about or to do with o *information concerning her disappearance*

concert /kónssərt/ *n* **1** a public musical performance **2** concerted action o *a concert of criticism* ■ *vti* do or plan cooperatively

concerted /kən súrtid/ *adj* planned or done together —**concertedly** *adv* —**concertedness** *n*

concertina /kónssər teénə/ *n* a musical instrument resembling a small accordion ■ *vi* collapse in folds —**concertinist** *n*

ORIGIN Concertina looks as though it ought to be from Italian, like so many other musical terms, but in fact it was formed in English from *concert*. (If it had been an Italian adoption it would have been pronounced with /ch/ like *concerto* rather than with /s/.) The first **concertina** was patented in Britain in 1829 by its inventor, Sir Charles Wheatstone.

concerto /kən cháirtō, -chúrtō/ (*pl* **-tos** *or* **-ti** /-ti/) *n* an instrumental musical composition for soloist and orchestra

concession /kən sésh'n/ *n* **1** a special privilege **2** a reduced price for some groups of people **3** the process or an instance of yielding reluctantly **4** something unwillingly admitted or acknowledged **5** a small business outlet inside another establishment **6** a licence to use land for a specific purpose —**concessionary** *adj*

concessionaire /kən sésh'n áir/, **concessionnaire, concessioner** /kən sésh'nər/ *n* a holder or operator of a concession

conch /kongk, konch/ (*pl* **conchs** /kongks/ *or* **conches** /kónchiz/) *n* **1** a tropical sea animal with a large spiral shell **2** the shell of a conch. Use: horn or trumpet, ornament, jewellery.

concierge /kónssi airzh, kóN-/ (*pl* **-cierges** /*pronunc. same*/) *n* an employee in a hotel or block of flats who helps guests or residents

~~concieve~~ incorrect spelling of **conceive**

conciliate /kən silli ayt/ (**-ating, -ated**) *vti* **1** bring opposing parties together **2** regain the support or friendship of —**conciliation** /kən silli áysh'n/ *n* —**conciliatory** /-ətəri/ *adj*

concise /kən síss/ *adj* short and clearly written or stated —**concisely** *adv* —**conciseness** *n*

conclave /kóng klayv/ *n* **1** a secret meeting **2** in the Roman Catholic Church, a meeting to elect a pope

conclude /kən klood/ (**-cluding, -cluded**) *v* **1** *vt* come to a conclusion about something **2** *vti* end or finish ○ *concluded the discussion* **3** *vt* settle a deal ◊ See note at **deduce**

conclusion /kən loozh'n/ *n* **1** a decision or opinion based on reasoning **2** the final part of something, *(fml)* **3** the settlement of a deal

conclusive /kən loossiv/ *adj* proving something beyond doubt —**conclusively** *adv* —**conclusiveness** *n*

concoct /kən kókt/ *vt* **1** create a new dish by mixing ingredients **2** think up a story, excuse, lie, or plan —**concoction** *n*

concomitant /kən kómmitənt/ *adj* happening at the same time —**concomitance** *n* —**concomitant** *n*

concord /kóng kawrd/ *n* **1** peaceful coexistence or agreement **2** a peace treaty

Concord /kóng kawrd/ capital of New Hampshire. Pop. 37,444 (1998).

concordance /kən káwrd'nss/ *n* **1** similarity or agreement **2** an index of all the words used by an author or in a text

concordant /kən káwrd'nt/ *adj* showing harmony or agreement *(fml)* —**concordantly** *adv*

concourse /kóng kawrss/ *n* **1** a large space where people gather and move about, e.g. in an airport terminal **2** a crowd

concrete /kóng kreet/ *n* a hard construction material containing cement ■ *adj* **1** solid and real **2** definite ○ *concrete proposals for reform* ■ *vt* (**-creting, -creted**) cover with concrete —**concretely** *adv* —**concreteness** *n*

concrete jungle *n* a place full of featureless buildings perceived as hostile

concrete noun *n* a word denoting a physical thing, e.g. 'clock' or 'elephant'

concubine /kóng kyōō bīn/ *n* **1** a female lover with the status of a subordinate wife **2** a woman cohabiting with her lover *(dated)* —**concubinage** /kon kyōōbinij, kən-/ *n*

concur /kən kúr/ (**-curring, -curred**) *v* **1** *vti* agree **2** *vi* coincide ◊ See note at **agree**

concurrent /kən kúrrənt/ *adj* happening together —**concurrence** *n* —**concurrently** *adv*

concussion /kən kúsh'n/ *n* **1** a brain injury caused by a blow that can result in temporary disorientation, memory loss, or unconsciousness **2** a sudden jolting or shaking —**concussive** /-kússiv/ *adj*

~~condem~~ incorrect spelling of **condemn**

condemn /kən dém/ *vt* **1** state to be bad or unacceptable **2** sentence to a severe punishment **3** force to experience something unpleasant **4** ban the use or consumption of —**condemnation** /kón dem náysh'n, kón dəm-/ *n* —**condemnatory** /kən démnətori, kón dem náytəri/ *adj* ◊ See note at **criticize, disapprove**

condemned cell *n* the room of a prisoner awaiting execution

condensation /kón den sáysh'n, kóndən sáysh'n/ *n* **1** the process of condensing **2** a film of water droplets on a cold surface

condense /kən dénss/ (**-densing, -densed**) *v* **1** *vti* change from gas to liquid **2** *vt* make a text shorter by removing unnecessary words **3** *vti* thicken by removing water —**condensability** /kən dénssə billəti/ *n*

condensed milk *n* thickened sweetened milk

condenser /kən dénssər/ *n* **1** a device that converts gas to liquid **2** a capacitor

condescend /kóndi sénd/ *vi* **1** behave in a superior way towards others **2** do something that would normally be beneath your dignity ○ *She condescended to travel with us.* —**condescension** /-sénsh'n/ *n*

condescending /kón di sénding/ *adj* arrogantly superior —**condescendingly** *adv*

~~condesending~~ incorrect spelling of **condescending**

condiment /kóndimənt/ *n* a seasoning such as salt or pepper used at the table

condition /kən dísh'n/ *n* **1** a particular state of repair or ability to function ○ *a car in poor condition* **2** one thing necessary for something else to happen ○ *a condition of the agreement* **3** a general state or way of being **4** position, rank, or social status *(fml)* **5** a state of fitness or health ○ *out of condition* **6** a physical disorder ■ **conditions** *npl* **1** influential factors or circumstances ○ *better working conditions* **2** the state of the weather ■ *vt* **1** train to react in a particular way **2** improve the quality or condition of by special treatment **3** adapt

conditional /kən dísh'nəl/ *adj* **1** dependent on something else **2** describes a verb form, word, or clause that states a condition or limitation ■ *n* a conditional verb form, word, or clause —**conditionally** *adv*

conditioner /kən dísh'nər/ *n* a substance for improving the condition or texture of hair or fabric

condole /kən dṓl/ (**-doling, -doled**) *vi* express sympathy

condolence /kən dṓlənss/ *n* a sympathetic word or message *(often pl)* —**condolent** *adj*

condom /kóndəm, -dom/ *n* a contraceptive worn on the penis

condominium /kɔ́ndə mínni əm/ *n* **1** *US, Can* an individually owned flat **2** *US, Can* a building containing condominiums **3** joint government of a country by two or more other countries

condone /kən dốn/ (**-doning, -doned**) *vt* consider wrongdoing acceptable o *condoning violence* —**condonable** *adj*

condor /kón dawr, kóndər/ *n* a large Andean vulture

conduce /kən dyóoss/ (**-ducing, -duced**) *vi* contribute to bringing something about *(fml)*

conducive /kən dyóossiv/ *adj* tending to bring about a good or intended result o *not conducive to a good working relationship*

conduct *v* /kən dúkt/ **1** *vti* direct the playing or singing of an instrumental or vocal group **2** *vt* carry out, manage, or control something o *conduct business* **3** *vr* behave in a particular manner **4** *vti* transmit heat, light, sound, or electricity **5** *vt* accompany and guide somebody ■ *n* /kón dukt/ **1** behaviour **2** the management or execution of something o *the conduct of the campaign* —**conduction** *n* —**conductive** *adj* —**conductivity** *n* ◊ See note at **guide**

conductor /kən dúktər/ *n* **1** the director of an orchestra or choir **2** somebody who collects fares on a bus **3** *US, Can* the guard on a railway train **4** a substance, body, or medium that conducts energy

conduit /kóndyoo it, kóndit/ *n* **1** a pipe or channel for liquid **2** a protective cover for a cable **3** a means of conveying information

cone *n* **1** an object with a round base that tapers to a point **2** a cone-shaped wafer for ice cream **3** a seed-bearing structure of pines and firs **4** a light-sensitive cell in the eye □ **cone off** *vt* close a road or part of a road with cones

~~conection~~ incorrect spelling of **connection**

coneflower /kón flowr/ *n* a plant of the daisy family with a cone-shaped centre

Coney Island /kốni-/ amusement area in S Brooklyn, New York City

confab /kón fab/ *n* a chat or discussion *(infml)*

confabulate /kən fábbyòo layt/ (**-lating, -lated**) *vi* have a chat or discussion *(fml)* —**confabulation** /kən fábbyòo láysh'n/ *n*

confection /kən féksh'n/ *n* **1** a sweet food made from sugar and other ingredients **2** an elaborate creation

confectioner /kən féksh'nər/ *n* a maker of sweets

confectionery /kən féksh'nəri/ *n* **1** sweets considered collectively **2** the making of sweets

confederacy /kən féddərəssi/ *n* **1** a political alliance **2 Confederacy** the confederation of the 11 states that seceded from the United States in 1861, starting the American Civil War

confederate *n* /kən féddərət/ **1** an ally **2** an accomplice **3 Confederate** a supporter or soldier of the Confederacy ■ *adj* /kən féddərət/ allied ■ *vti* /kən féddə rayt/ (**-ating, -ated**) unite in a confederacy

confederation /kən féddə ráysh'n/ *n* **1** a group of loosely allied states **2** the formation of or state of being a confederation

confer /kən fúr/ (**-ferring, -ferred**) *v* **1** *vi* discuss something with somebody **2** *vt* give an honour or title to *(fml)* o *conferred an honorary degree on the president* —**conferment** *n* —**conferral** *n* ◊ See note at **give**

~~conferred~~ incorrect spelling of **conferred**

conference /kónfərənss/ *n* **1** a meeting for lectures or discussions **2** a sports league

conference call *n* a group telephone conversation

conferencing /kónfərənssing/ *n* the holding of a meeting with participants linked by telephone, video, or computer

confess /kən féss/ *v* **1** *vti* admit wrongdoing **2** *vt* reluctantly acknowledge something to be true **3** *vti* admit sins and ask for God's forgiveness

confession /kən fésh'n/ *n* **1** an admission of wrongdoing or guilt **2** an open acknowledgment of feelings or beliefs **3** a formal declaration of sins

confessional /kən fésh'nəl/ *adj* of an intimate nature ■ *n* a place for confession in a Roman Catholic church

confessor /kən féssər/ *n* **1** a priest who hears confessions **2** somebody who confesses

confetti /kən fétti/ *n* pieces of coloured paper thrown over the bride and groom at a wedding

ORIGIN Confetti is from an Italian plural meaning 'small sweets'. Small sweets were traditionally thrown at carnivals. English took the word but substituted pieces of paper, and started throwing them at weddings. **Confetti** is from the same Latin source as *confection*.

confidant /kónfi dánt, kónfi dant/ *n* somebody to whom secrets are told

confidante /kónfi dánt, kónfi dant/ *n* a woman to whom secrets are told

confide /kən fíd/ (**-fiding, -fided**) *vti* tell somebody something secret

confidence /kónfidənss/ *n* **1** belief in your own abilities **2** faith in the ability of somebody or something to perform satisfactorily **3** a secret told to somebody **4** a relationship grounded in trust o *told you in confidence*

confidence trick *n* a swindle that involves first gaining the victim's trust —**confidence trickster** *n*

confident /kónfidənt/ *adj* **1** self-assured or certain of success **2** convinced o *confident of her opponent's skill* —**confidently** *adv*

confidential /kónfi dénsh'l/ *adj* **1** private and secret **2** dealing with private affairs —**confidentiality** /kónfi denshi álləti/ *n* —**confidentially** *adv*

configuration /kən fíggə ráysh'n, -fíggyə-/ *n* **1** the way in which parts are arranged **2** a shape or outline **3** the setup of the components of a computer system —**configurational** adj —**configurative** /kən fíggərətiv, -fíggyöö-/ adj

configure /kən fíggər/ (**-uring, -ured**) vt set up or arrange parts, e.g. of a computer, for a specific purpose

confine vt /kən fín/ (**-fining, -fined**) 1 keep within limits 2 keep from leaving a place o *was confined to her room* ■ **confines** /kón fínz/ npl boundaries

confined /kən fínd/ adj cramped, restricted, or completely enclosed o *a confined space*

confinement /kən fínmənt/ n 1 restriction or limitation within boundaries 2 the process or time of giving birth (dated)

confirm /kən fúrm/ v 1 vt prove to be true 2 vti make an arrangement definite o *confirm your booking* 3 vt ratify 4 vt in Judaism and Christianity, admit into a religious body —**confirmation** /kónfər máysh'n/ n

confirmed /kən fúrmd/ adj settled in a habit and unlikely to change

confiscate /kónfi skayt/ (**-cating, -cated**) vt take away by authority or as a penalty —**confiscation** /kónfi skáysh'n/ n

conflagration /kónflə gráysh'n/ n a large destructive fire

conflate /kən fláyt/ (**-flating, -flated**) vti merge into a unified whole —**conflation** n

conflict n /kón flikt/ 1 a continued battle 2 a disagreement or clash, e.g. between ideas or people ■ vi /kən flíkt/ differ or be incompatible ◊ See note at **fight**

confluence /kónfloo ənss/ n 1 a meeting of streams 2 a meeting of two or more things —**confluent** adj, n

conform /kən fáwrm/ v 1 vi behave acceptably 2 vi comply with a standard 3 vi fit in with an idea 4 vti be or make similar —**conformer** n

conformation /kón fawr máysh'n/ n 1 the structure or form of something 2 symmetry of parts

conformist /kən fáwrmist/ n 1 somebody who conforms 2 a member of an established national church —**conformism** n —**conformist** adj

conformity /kən fáwrməti/ n 1 the following of the behaviour or thinking of the majority of people 2 compliance, agreement, or similarity

confound /kən fównd/ vt 1 fail to distinguish between 2 bewilder 3 prove to be wrong

confounded /kən fówndid/ adj in a state of bewilderment —**confoundedly** adv

confrère /kón frair/ n a colleague (fml)

confront /kən frúnt/ vt 1 challenge or defy somebody or something face to face 2 bring somebody face to face with something o *confronted her with the evidence* 3 encounter a difficulty

confrontation /kón frun táysh'n/ n 1 a face-to-face encounter, especially a hostile one 2 a fight or battle 3 hostility or conflict 4 the process of confronting a difficulty —**confrontational** adj

Confucius /kən fyoôshəss/ (551?–479? BC) Chinese philosopher, administrator, and moralist

confuse /kən tyooz/ (**-fusing, -fused**) vt 1 make somebody unable to think clearly 2 mistake one person or thing for another 3 cause disorder in something —**confusable** adj —**confused** adj —**confusedly** /-fyoôzidli, -fyoôzdli/ adv —**confusing** adj —**confusingly** adv —**confusion** /-fyoôzh'n/ n

confute /kən fyoôt/ (**-futing, -futed**) vt prove wrong (fml) —**confutation** /kónfyoô táysh'n/ n

conga /kóng gə/ n a dance performed in a long line, each person holding the waist of the one ahead

congeal /kən jeél/ vti thicken or solidify a liquid, or become thickened or solidified —**congealment** n

congenial /kən jeéni əl/ adj 1 pleasant and suited to somebody's character and tastes o *a congenial atmosphere* 2 compatible in tastes or interests o *congenial companions* 3 friendly —**congeniality** /kən jeéni álləti/ n —**congenially** adv

congenital /kən jénnit'l/ adj 1 existing at somebody's birth o *a congenital disorder* 2 ingrained in somebody's character —**congenitally** adv

conger eel /kóng gər-/, **conger** n a large sea eel

congestion /kən jéschən/ n 1 excessive traffic or people, making movement difficult 2 excessive fluid in a body part such as the lungs —**congested** adj

congestion charging n an urban traffic-reduction scheme in which drivers pay a charge to drive in a city centre

conglomerate n /kən glómmərət/ 1 a business organization composed of a number of companies involved in different activities 2 something formed from different things gathered together 3 rock containing pieces of other rocks ■ vti /kən glómmə rayt/ (**-ating, -ated**) gather together to form a mass —**conglomerate** adj —**conglomeration** /kən glómmə ráysh'n/ n

Congo /kóng gō/ Africa's second longest river, rising in the south of the Democratic Republic of the Congo and emptying into the Atlantic Ocean. Length 4,374 km/2,718 mi. ■ 1 also **Congo, Democratic Republic of the** large equatorial country of Central Africa with a coastline on the Atlantic Ocean. Cap. Kinshasa. Pop. 53,624,718 (2001). 2 also **Congo, Republic of the** country in west-central Africa, on the Atlantic coast. Cap. Brazzaville. Pop. 2,894,336 (2001). —**Congolese** /kóng gə leéz/ adj, n

Congo franc n the main unit of currency in the Democratic Republic of the Congo

congratulate /kən gráttyoô layt, -gráchoô-/ (**-lating, -lated**) v 1 vt express pleasure to somebody for an achievement or good fortune 2 vr feel self-satisfied o *She congratulated herself upon winning.* —**congratulatory** adj

congratulation /kən gráttyoŏ láysh'n, -gráchoo-/ *n* the act of congratulating somebody ■ *npl*, *interj* **congratulations** an expression of pleasure at somebody's achievement or good fortune

congregate /kóng gri gayt/ (**-gating**, **-gated**) *vti* assemble or gather together, or gather people or animals together

congregation /kóng gri gáysh'n/ *n* **1** the worshippers at a religious service **2** the members of a church **3** a gathering of people or animals o *a congregation of geese*

congress /kóng gress/ *n* **1** a conference or meeting of delegates or representatives **2 Congress** the governing and law-making body of the United States and some other countries —**congressional** /kən grésh'nəl/ *adj* —**congressionally** *adv* —**congressman** *n* —**congressperson** *n* —**congresswoman** *n*

Congreve /kóng greev/, **William** (1670–1729) English playwright and poet

congruent /kóng groo ənt/ *adj* **1** corresponding or consistent *(fml)* **2** with identical geometric shapes —**congruence** *n* —**congruency** *n* —**congruently** *adv*

congruous /kóng groo əss/ *adj* **1** appropriate *(fml)* **2** corresponding or consistent

conical /kónnik'l/ *adj* **1** cone-shaped **2** of a cone

conifer /kónnifər, kónifər/ *n* a cone-bearing tree —**coniferous** /kə níffərəss/ *adj*

conj. *abbr* **1** conjugation **2** conjunction

conjecture /kən jékchər/ *n* **1** guesswork **2** a guess —**conjectural** *adj* —**conjecture** *vti*

conjoin /kən jóyn/ *vti* join together *(fml)*

conjoint /kən jóynt/ *adj* **1** involving two or more combined entities **2** joined together —**conjointly** *adv*

conjugal /kónjoŏg'l/ *adj* of marriage

conjugal rights *npl* the rights of a spouse to sexual intercourse

conjugate *v* /kónjoŏ gayt/ (**-gating**, **-gated**) **1** *vt* state the forms of a verb **2** *vi* have different grammatical forms *(refers to verbs)* ■ *adj* /kónjoŏgət, -gayt/ joined together in pairs *(fml)* —**conjugable** *adj* —**conjugative** *adj*

conjugation /kónjoŏ gáysh'n/ *n* **1** the inflections of a verb **2** reproduction in single-celled organisms —**conjugational** *adj*

conjunction /kən júngksh'n/ *n* **1** the combining of two or more things **2** a simultaneous occurrence **3** a connecting word such as 'and' or 'if' —**conjunctional** *adj*

conjunctiva /kón jungk tívə/ (*pl* **-vas** or **-vae** /-vee/) *n* a membrane under the eyelid —**conjunctival** *adj*

conjunctive /kən júngktiv/ *adj* **1** serving to connect **2** having been combined —**conjunctively** *adv*

conjunctivitis /kən júngkti vítiss/ *n* inflammation of the conjunctiva

conjure /kúnjər/ (**-juring**, **-jured**) *v* **1** *vi* perform magic tricks **2** *vti* invoke supposed supernatural forces —**conjuration** /kónjoŏ ráysh'n/ *n* —**conjurer** *n* —**conjuror** *n*

□ **conjure up** *vt* **1** create something in the mind **2** produce something as if by magic

conk[1] *n* the head or nose *(slang)*

conk[2] □ **conk out** *vi* *(infml)* **1** fail or break down **2** collapse or fall asleep

conker /kóngkər/ *n UK* a horse chestnut without its spiny casing

con man *n* a swindler *(infml)*

Connacht /kónnawt, -nət/, **Connaught** province on the coast of the W Republic of Ireland. Pop. 423,031 (1991).

connect /kə nékt/ *v* **1** *vti* link or join together **2** *vt* associate in the mind with somebody or something **3** *vt* link to a source of electricity, gas, or water **4** *vi* allow passengers to transfer from one vehicle to another o *Does this train connect with the one to Edinburgh?* —**connectible** *adj* —**connector** *n*

Connecticut /kə néttikət/ southernmost state in New England, NE United States. Pop. 3,405,565 (2000).

connection /kə néksh'n/ *n* **1** the linking or joining of parts, things, or people **2** something that links things o *check for a loose connection* **3** an association o *denied any connection with the organization* **4** a context o *in this connection* **5** an influential contact *(often pl)* o *has connections in the publishing world* **6** a relative *(often pl)* **7** a transport link, or a vehicle scheduled to provide such a link **8** a telecommunications link

connective /kə néktiv/ *adj* linking ■ *n* a linking word such as a conjunction —**connectively** *adv*

connective tissue *n* tissue that supports and connects body parts

connectivity /kónnek tívvəti/ *n* the ability to communicate with another piece of computer hardware or software

connect time *n* the period of time a computer user is logged on to a remote computer

connive /kə nív/ (**-niving**, **-nived**) *vi* **1** plot or scheme **2** give tacit consent or encouragement to wrongdoing —**connivance** *n* —**conniving** *adj*

~~connoiseur~~ incorrect spelling of **connoisseur**

connoisseur /kónnə súr/ *n* somebody with expert knowledge or discriminating taste

Connolly /kónn'li/, **Maureen** (1934–69) US tennis player

connotation /kónnə táysh'n/ *n* an implied additional meaning —**connotative** /kónnə taytiv, kə nótətiv/ *adj*

connote /kə nót/ (**-noting**, **-noted**) *vt* **1** have an implied additional meaning o *The word 'hearth' connotes cosiness and warmth.* **2** imply something else o *His reluctance connotes cowardice.*

connubial /kə nyoŏbi əl/ *adj* of marriage *(literary)* —**connubially** *adv*

conquer /kóngkər/ *vt* **1** seize an area or defeat a people by military force **2** overcome a difficulty or problem **3** make a difficult mountain ascent —**conqueror** *n* ◊ See note at **defeat**

conquest /kóng kwest/ n 1 the act of conquering 2 something acquired by conquering

conquistador /kon kwísta dawr/ (pl **-dors** or **-dores** /-dáwr ayz/) n a 16C Spanish conqueror in Mexico, Peru, or Central America

Conrad /kón rad/, **Joseph** (1857–1924) Polish-born British writer

conscience /kónsh'nss/ n 1 the sense of right and wrong that governs somebody's conduct 2 compliance with your conscience

conscience-stricken adj feeling guilty

~~consceiencious~~ incorrect spelling of **conscientious**

conscientious /kónshi énshəss/ adj 1 painstaking and diligent 2 in accordance with somebody's conscience —**conscientiously** adv —**conscientiousness** n ◊ See note at **careful**

conscientious objector n somebody whose religious or moral beliefs forbid military service

conscious /kónshəss/ adj 1 awake 2 aware 3 considered and deliberate ○ a conscious effort not to lose her temper 4 fully informed, concerned, or interested (often in combination) ○ safety-conscious 5 of the part of the mind that thinks and perceives —**consciously** adv ◊ See note at **aware**

consciousness /kónshəssnəss/ n 1 the state of being conscious 2 somebody's mind and thoughts 3 the feelings and beliefs shared by a group

consciousness-raising n 1 improving people's awareness and understanding of issues 2 the increasing of self-awareness —**consciousness-raiser** n

conscript vt /kən skrípt/ compel to do military service ■ n /kón skript/ a conscripted military recruit —**conscription** /kən skrípsh'n/ n

consecrate /kónssi krayt/ (-**crating**, **-crated**) vt 1 declare a place holy 2 bless bread and wine for the Christian sacrament of Communion 3 ordain a Christian priest as a bishop 4 dedicate something to a specific purpose —**consecration** /kónssi kráysh'n/ n

consecutive /kən sékyóótiv/ adj successive —**consecutively** adv

consensual /kən sénssyóó əl/ adj by mutual consent —**consensually** adv

consensus /kən sénssəss/ n general agreement among all or most members of a group

USAGE The word **consensus** is often misspelt concensus, probably from the erroneous influence of the word census.

consent /kən sént/ vi 1 give permission for something 2 agree to do something ■ n 1 permission 2 general agreement ◊ See note at **agree**

~~consentrate~~ incorrect spelling of **concentrate**

consequence /kónssikwənss/ n 1 something that follows as a result 2 importance (fml)

consequent /kónssikwənt/ adj following as a consequence

consequential /kónssi kwénsh'l/ adj 1 arising as an indirect cost 2 important —**consequentially** adv

consequently /kónssikwəntli/ adv as a result

~~consern~~ incorrect spelling of **concern**

conservancy /kən súrv'nssi/ (pl **-cies**) n a commission or board responsible for the protection of both the land and wildlife of an area

conservation /kónssər váysh'n/ n 1 protection from loss, change, or damage 2 the preservation and care of natural and cultural resources —**conservational** adj —**conservationist** n, adj

conservatism /kən súrvətizəm/ n 1 reluctance to accept change 2 a right-wing political viewpoint

conservative /kən súrvətiv/ adj 1 reluctant to accept change 2 having a right-wing political viewpoint 3 cautiously moderate ○ a conservative estimate 4 conventional in appearance 5 **Conservative** of the Conservative Party ■ n 1 a traditionalist 2 somebody with a right-wing political viewpoint —**conservatively** adv —**conservativeness** n

Conservative Party n the main British right-wing political party (+ sing or pl verb)

conservator /kən súrvətər/ n 1 a restorer of works of art 2 a protector of the interests of a legally incompetent person

conservatory /kən súrvətəri/ (pl **-ries**) n 1 a glass-walled room for growing plants or relaxing 2 an advanced music or drama school

conserve vt /kən súrv/ (-**serving**, **-served**) 1 protect something from harm or decay 2 use resources sparingly ■ n /kón surv, kən súrv/ a fruit preparation resembling jam

~~consession~~ incorrect spelling of **concession**

consider /kən síddər/ v 1 vti think carefully about something ○ time to consider whether this is what you really want 2 vt have as an opinion 3 vt show respect for 4 vt discuss formally

considerable /kən síddərəb'l/ adj 1 large 2 significant —**considerably** adv

considerate /kən síddərət/ adj mindful of the needs of others —**considerately** adv —**considerateness** n

consideration /kən síddə ráysh'n/ n 1 careful thought or deliberation 2 thoughtfulness or sensitivity toward others 3 a relevant factor in assessing something 4 a payment (fml)

considering /kən síddəring/ prep, conj taking something into account ■ adv taking everything into account (usually at the end of a phrase or sentence) ○ We've done a good job, considering.

~~consience~~ incorrect spelling of **conscience**

consign /kən sín/ vt 1 entrust to the care of another 2 put or send somewhere for disposal 3 deliver for sale

consignment /kən sínmənt/ n 1 a quantity or package delivered or to be delivered 2 the entrusting of somebody to another's care

~~conscious~~ incorrect spelling of **conscious**

consist /kən síst/ vi **1** be made up of diverse parts or things o *The dressing consists of olive oil and vinegar.* **2** be based on or defined by something o *Its attractiveness consists in its simplicity.*

~~consistant~~ incorrect spelling of **consistent**

consistency /kən sístənssi/, **consistence** /-ənss/ n **1** the ability to be reliable, constant, or uniform **2** reasonable or logical harmony between parts **3** the degree of thickness or smoothness of a mixture

consistent /kən sístənt/ adj **1** logically harmonious o *consistent with the evidence* **2** reliable, constant, or uniform —**consistently** adv

consolation /kónssə láysh'n/ n **1** a source of comfort to somebody upset or disappointed **2** comfort given to somebody in distress o *words of consolation*

consolation prize n a prize for the loser in a game or competition

console[1] /kən sốl/ (-**soling**, -**soled**) vt comfort somebody in grief —**consolatory** /-lə tərí/ adj —**consolingly** adv

console[2] /kón sõl/ n **1** a cabinet for a television or musical sound system **2** a control panel **3** the part of an organ that houses the keyboards or manuals, pedals, and stops

consolidate /kən sólli dayt/ (-**dating**, -**dated**) vti **1** unite, or be united **2** strengthen your position —**consolidation** /kən sólli dáysh'n/ n

consols /kón solz, kən sólz/ npl government bonds with a fixed interest rate

consommé /kon sómmay/ n a thin clear soup

consonant /kónss'nənt/ n a speech sound produced by partly or totally blocking the path of air through the mouth, or the corresponding letter of the alphabet ■ adj **1** in agreement (fml) **2** containing pleasant chords or harmonies —**consonance** n —**consonantal** /kónssə nánt'l/ adj

consort vi /kən sáwrt/ associate with undesirable people (fml) ■ n /kón sawrt/ **1** also **Consort** the spouse of a monarch **2** a partner (fml)

consortium /kən sáwrti əm/ (pl -**a** /-ə/) n an association of organizations set up for a common purpose

conspicuous /kən spíkyŏŏ əss/ adj **1** easily visible **2** attracting attention —**conspicuously** adv

conspicuous consumption n extravagant spending to impress others

conspiracy /kən spírrəssi/ (pl -**cies**) n **1** a secret plan or agreement between two or more people to commit an illegal act **2** a group of conspirators

conspiracy of silence n an agreement to keep silent about a matter of public interest

conspiracy theory n a belief that a particular event is the result of a secret plot —**conspiracy theorist** n

conspirator /kən spírrətər/ n a member of a group secretly planning an illegal act

conspiratorial /kən spírrə táwri əl/ adj indicating or suggesting involvement in a secret plot o *a conspiratorial whisper* —**conspiratorially** adv

conspire /kən spír/ (-**spiring**, -**spired**) vi **1** plan secretly to act illegally together **2** combine with an unpleasant result o *Bad weather and transport strikes conspired to ruin our trip.*

constable /kúnstəb'l, kón-/ n a police officer of the lowest rank

Constable /kúnstəb'l/, **John** (1776–1837) British painter

constabulary /kən stábbyŏŏlərí/ (pl -**ies**) n a police force

Constance, Lake /kónstənss/ lake on the borders of Austria, Germany, and Switzerland. Depth 252 m/827 ft. Length 74 km/46 mi.

constant /kónstənt/ adj **1** always present **2** happening or done repeatedly **3** not changing or varying **4** faithful ■ n **1** an unvarying thing or quality **2** a quantity with a fixed value —**constancy** n —**constantly** adv

Constantine II /kónstən tīn, -teen/ (b. 1940) king of Greece (1964–73)

Constantine (the Great) (274–337) Roman emperor (306–37)

Constantinople /kón stanti nṓp'l/ former name for Istanbul

constellation /kónstə láysh'n/ n **1** a group of stars forming a distinctive pattern **2** a gathering of celebrities **3** a group of related things

consternation /kónstər náysh'n/ n shocked dismay

constipation /kónsti páysh'n/ n difficulty in defecation —**constipated** /kónsti paytid/ adj

constituency /kən stíttyoo ənssi, -stíchyoo-/ (pl -**cies**) n **1** an electoral district **2** the voters in a district

constituent /kən stíttyoo ənt, -stíchyoo-/ n **1** a resident of an electoral district **2** a part of a whole ■ adj **1** forming a part (fml) **2** having the power to draw up or alter a constitution

constitute /kónsti tyoot/ (-**tuting**, -**tuted**) vt **1** be or amount to o *This letter does not constitute an offer of employment.* **2** be all or a particular part of **3** formally establish (fml)

constitution /kónsti tyóosh'n/ n **1** a statement of the laws of a country or organization **2** somebody's general health and physical resilience **3** the parts, ingredients, or members of something **4** the formal creation or establishment of something

constitutional /kónsti tyóosh'nəl/ adj of, involving, or in accordance with a constitution ■ n a walk taken for health reasons —**constitutionality** /kónsti tyóosh'n állətí/ n —**constitutionally** adv

constrain /kən stráyn/ vt **1** force to do something **2** limit or restrict —**constrainable** adj

constrained /kən stráynd/ *adj* reserved or inhibited

constraint /kən stráynt/ *n* **1** a limiting factor **2** a lack of warmth or spontaneity **3** restriction of freedom of action

constrict /kən stríkt/ *v* **1** *vti* make or become narrower **2** *vt* limit or restrict **3** *vt* suffocate prey by squeezing —**constriction** /kən stríksh'n/ *n* —**constrictive** *adj* —**constrictor** *n*

construct *vt* /kən strúkt/ **1** build or assemble **2** create in the mind ■ *n* /kónstrukt/ something created in the mind —**constructible** *adj* —**constructor** *n*

construction /kən strúksh'n/ *n* **1** the building of something such as a large structure **2** a structure or other thing that is built **3** the way something is built **4** an interpretation (*fml*) **5** a grammatical arrangement of words —**constructional** *adj*

constructive /kən strúktiv/ *adj* **1** useful or helpful ○ *constructive criticism* **2** structural —**constructively** *adv* —**constructiveness** *n*

constructive dismissal *n* an action that forces an employee to resign

construe /kən stroó/ (**-struing, -strued**) *v* **1** *vt* interpret **2** *vti* analyse the grammar of a piece of text —**construal** *n*

consul /kónss'l/ *n* **1** a government official living in a foreign city as a diplomat **2** either of the chief magistrates in ancient Rome —**consular** /kónssyoŏlər/ *adj*

consulate /kónssyoŏlət/ *n* **1** a consul's office or residence **2** the position or jurisdiction of a consul

consult /kən súlt/ *v* **1** *vti* ask somebody for specialist advice or information, or for permission **2** *vt* look at something such as a book or watch for information —**consultation** /kónss'l táysh'n, kónsul-/ *n* —**consultative** *adj*

consultant /kən súltant/ *n* **1** an expert or professional adviser **2** a senior doctor or surgeon —**consultancy** *n* —**consultantship** *n*

consulting room *n* a room in which a doctor sees patients

consumables /kən syoómab'lz/ *npl* goods that have to be bought regularly because they are used up or worn out —**consumable** *adj*

~~consumate~~ incorrect spelling of **consummate**

consume /kən syoóm/ (**-suming, -sumed**) *vt* **1** eat or drink **2** use up **3** absorb totally ○ *consumed by jealousy* **4** destroy completely ○ *consumed by fire*

consumer /kən syoómər/ *n* **1** a buyer of goods or services **2** somebody or something that consumes something —**consumership** *n*

consumer durables *npl* long-lasting household items

consumer goods *npl* items bought by consumers rather than used to produce other goods

consumerism /kən syoómərizəm/ *n* **1** the belief that trade in consumer goods is good for the economy **2** the protection of consumers' rights **3** a materialistic attitude (*disapproving*) —**consumerist** *n*, *adj*

consuming /kən syoóming/ *adj* extremely intense or absorbing

consummate *v* /kónssə mayt, kónssyoŏ-/ (**-mating, -mated**) **1** *vt* complete a marriage or relationship by having sexual intercourse **2** *vti* conclude (*fml*) ■ *adj* /kónssəmət, kən súmmət/ **1** supreme or perfect **2** utter or total —**consummately** *adv* —**consummation** /kónssə máysh'n, kónsyoŏ-/ *n*

consumption /kən súmpsh'n/ *n* **1** the eating or drinking of something, or the amount eaten or drunk **2** the use of natural resources or fuels, or the amount used **3** consumer use of goods and services **4** a wasting disease such as tuberculosis (*dated*)

consumptive /kən súmptiv/ *adj* **1** engaged in or encouraging consumption, especially in a wasteful or destructive way **2** affected by tuberculosis (*dated*)

cont. *abbr* **1** containing **2** continued

contact /kón takt/ *n* **1** communication ○ *in contact with his family* **2** physical connection by touch **3** interaction ○ *came into contact with some interesting people and new ideas* **4** a useful acquaintance **5** a possible carrier of a disease **6** a device making an electrical connection **7** a contact lens (*infml*) ■ *vt* communicate with by telephone, letter, or e-mail ■ *adj* **1** used for communicating with somebody ○ *a contact address* **2** caused by touch —**contactable** /kon táktəb'l/ *adj*

contact lens *n* a glass or plastic lens worn in the eye

contagion /kən táyjən/ *n* **1** the spread of disease by physical contact **2** a disease spread by physical contact **3** a harmful influence that spreads

contagious /kən táyjəss/ *adj* **1** describes a disease that can be transmitted by contact **2** having a disease that can be transmitted by contact **3** quickly spread from one person to another ○ *Laughter is contagious.* —**contagiously** *adv* —**contagiousness** *n*

contain /kən táyn/ *vt* **1** have or hold inside **2** include or consist of **3** control or hold back ○ *contained the riot* ○ *couldn't contain my excitement* —**containable** *adj*

container /kən táynər/ *n* an object used to hold something, especially for storage or transport

containerize /kən táynə rīz/ (**-izing, -ized**), **containerise** *vt* **1** pack large in large containers for transporting **2** modernize a port, system, or industry to handle standard cargo containers —**containerization** /kən táynə rī záysh'n/ *n*

containment /kən táynmənt/ *n* action to stop the spread of something undesirable

contaminate /kən támmi nayt/ (**-nating, -nated**) *vt* make impure or polluted —**contaminant** *n* —**contamination** /kən támmi náysh'n/ *n* —**contaminative** /-nətiv/ *adj*

contemplate /kóntəm playt, -tem-/ (**-plating**, **-plated**) vt 1 look at thoughtfully 2 consider seriously 3 have as a possible intention —**contemplation** /kóntəm pláysh'n, -tem-/ n

contemplative /kən témplətiv/ adj calm and thoughtful —**contemplatively** adv —**contemplativeness** n

contemporaneous /kən témpə ráyni əss, kon-/ adj happening or existing at the same time —**contemporaneity** /kən témpərə neé əti, kon-/ n —**contemporaneously** adv

contemporary /kən témprəri/ adj 1 existing or dating from the same period 2 existing now 3 modern in style ■ n (pl **-ies**) 1 somebody or something from the same period 2 somebody of the same age as another

~~contempory~~ incorrect spelling of **contemporary**

contempt /kən témpt/ n 1 an attitude of utter disgust or hatred 2 also **contempt of court** the crime of wilfully disobeying the rules or decisions of a court of law

contemptible /kən témptəb'l/ adj deserving contempt —**contemptibility** /kən témptə bílləti/ n —**contemptibleness** n —**contemptibly** adv

contemptuous /kən témptyoo əss/ adj showing or feeling contempt —**contemptuously** adv —**contemptuousness** n

contend /kən ténd/ v 1 vi state or argue that something is true 2 vti compete for something 3 vi deal with something difficult —**contender** n

content[1] /kón tent/ n 1 the amount of material contained in a whole 2 subject matter 3 the meaning or message of a creative work ■ **contents** npl 1 everything in a container 2 a list of subject or chapter headings

content[2] /kən tént/ adj 1 also **contented** quietly satisfied and happy 2 ready to accept something ■ v 1 vt cause to feel content 2 vr accept or make do with something ○ We contented ourselves with a light supper. —**contentedly** adv —**contentedness** n —**contently** adv —**contentment** n

contention /kən ténsh'n/ n 1 an assertion in an argument 2 disagreement

contentious /kən ténshəss/ adj 1 creating disagreement 2 argumentative

contest n /kón test/ 1 a competition to find the best 2 a struggle for control ■ vt /kən tést/ 1 challenge or question something 2 take part in a contest to win something —**contestable** adj

ORIGIN Contest has its origins in legal language. It derives from a Latin verb that meant 'call to witness, begin a lawsuit by calling witnesses'. That meaning is based on the same word that gave testify and testimony to English. The element of competition involved in legal battles formed the basis for the more general senses that later developed.

contestant /kən téstənt/ n somebody competing in a contest ◊ See note at **candidate**

context /kón tekst/ n 1 the text surrounding a word or passage 2 a set of surrounding conditions —**contextual** /kən tékstyoo əl/ adj

contextualize /kən tékstyoo ə līz/ (**-izing**, **-ized**), **contextualise** vt place in context —**contextualization** /kən tékstyoo ə īī záysh'n/ n

contiguous /kən tíggyoo əss/ adj (fml) 1 adjoining something else 2 neighbouring another property —**contiguity** /kónti gyoó əti/ n —**contiguously** adv —**contiguousness** n

continent[1] /kóntinənt/ n 1 any of the seven large land masses that constitute most of the Earth's dry surfaces 2 **Continent** mainland Europe ○ travelled on the Continent

continent[2] /kóntinənt/ adj 1 able to control urination and defecation 2 celibate —**continence** n

continental /kónti nént'l/ adj 1 of the Earth's continents 2 **Continental** of mainland Europe ■ n also **Continental** a person from mainland Europe (infml) —**continentalism** n —**continentalist** n

continental breakfast n a breakfast of bread and coffee

Continental Divide series of mountain ridges, running from Alaska to Mexico and including the Rocky Mountains, that forms the main watershed of North America

continental drift n the theory explaining the movement of continents across the Earth's crust

continental shelf n the sea bed around a continent

contingency /kən tínjənssi/ (pl **-cies**) n 1 also **contingence** something that may happen 2 something set aside for unforeseen emergencies 3 dependence upon chance

contingency fee n a payment for professional services that is conditional upon success

contingency plan n a plan to deal with a possible problem

contingent /kən tínjənt/ adj 1 dependent on what may happen or be the case 2 possible but not certain 3 happening by chance ■ n 1 a group of people 2 a group of military personnel —**contingently** adv

~~continous~~ incorrect spelling of **continuous**

continual /kən tínnyoo əl/ adj 1 recurring very frequently 2 without stopping —**continually** adv —**continualness** n

USAGE continual or **continuous**? A **continual** noise is one that is constantly repeated, like a dog's barking, and a **continuous** noise is one that continues without stopping, like the roar of a waterfall. The same distinction applies to the adverbs **continually** and **continuously**: Hecklers continually interrupted the speaker. She drove continuously for two hours. In popular usage, however, **continual** and **continuously** are now frequently used to mean 'without stopping'.

continuance /kən tínnyoo ənss/ n 1 the continuation of something 2 the length of time that something lasts

continuation /kən tínnyoo áysh'n/ *n* **1** the process of continuing **2** an addition or extension

continue /kən tinnyoo/ (**-ues, -uing, -ued**) *v* **1** *vti* keep going **2** *vti* last, or cause to last, throughout a particular period **3** *vti* start again after a break **4** *vti* say something else **5** *vti* extend beyond a particular point **6** *vi* move further —**continued** *adj*

continuing /kən tínnyoo ing/ *adj* existing and likely to continue existing

continuing education *n* classes for adult students

continuity /kónti nyoó əti/ (*pl* **-ties**) *n* **1** the fact of being the same or of not stopping **2** a consistent whole **3** consistency between scenes or shots in a film or broadcast

continuous /kən tínnyoo əss/ *adj* **1** unchanged or uninterrupted **2** without gaps or breaks **3** describes the progressive aspect of a verb —**continuously** *adv* —**continuousness** *n* ◊ See note at **continual**

continuum /kən tínnyoo əm/ (*pl* **-a** /-ə/ *or* **-ums**) *n* a continuous series of things that blend into one another

contort /kən táwrt/ *v* **1** *vti* twist or be twisted out of its natural shape **2** *vt* make unrecognizable —**contorted** *adj* —**contortedly** *adv* —**contortedness** *n* —**contortive** *adj*

contortion /kən táwrsh'n/ *n* **1** a twisted shape or position **2** a complex manoeuvre

contortionist /kən táwrsh'nist/ *n* **1** somebody such as an acrobat who performs bending feats with the body **2** a skilful manipulator or manoeuvrer

contour /kón toor/ *n* **1** a shape's outline (*often pl*) **2** the general nature or character of something ■ *adj* **1** shaped to fit something **2** following the shape of the land ■ *vt* **1** shape to fit **2** put contour lines on

contour line *n* a line on a map connecting points on a land surface that are the same height above sea level

contra- *prefix* against, opposite, contrasting ○ *contraband* ○ *contradistinction*

contraband /kóntrə band/ *n* goods traded or supplied illegally —**contraband** *adj* —**contrabandage** *n* —**contrabandist** *n*

contraception /kóntrə sépsh'n/ *n* **1** prevention of pregnancy **2** methods or devices used to prevent pregnancy

contraceptive /kóntrə séptiv/ *n* a device or drug designed to prevent pregnancy —**contraceptive** *adj*

contraceptive ring *n* a plastic ring inserted into the vagina that releases a constant flow of a contraceptive drug

contract *n* /kón trakt/ **1** a formal or legally binding agreement, or the document that records it **2** a paid assassin's assignment (*infml*) ○ *a contract killing* **3** in the game of bridge, a winning bid in a single hand ■ *v* /kən trákt/ **1** *vti* shrink or lessen **2** *vti* tighten or draw together **3** *vt* formally or legally agree to do something **4** *vt* get an illness **5** *vt* shorten a word or phrase —**contractible** *adj*

□ **contract out** *v* **1** *vti* give work to outsiders **2** *vi* withdraw formally

contract bridge *n* the most common version of bridge, in which points are awarded only for tricks bid and won

contraction /kən tráksh'n/ *n* **1** reduction in size **2** a tightening or narrowing of a muscle, organ, or other body part **3** a tightening of the womb muscles that occurs before childbirth **4** a shortened word —**contractional** *adj* —**contractive** *adj*

contractor /kən tráktər/ *n* **1** a company or person under contract to do a particular job, especially a builder **2** something that contracts, e.g. a muscle

contractual /kən trákchoo əl/ *adj* involving a formal agreement —**contractually** *adv*

contradict /kóntrə díkt/ *vt* **1** disagree with **2** show to be not true —**contradictive** *adj* —**contradictively** *adv* —**contradictiveness** *n* ◊ See note at **disagree**

contradiction /kóntrə díksh'n/ *n* **1** something with illogical or inconsistent parts **2** a statement that opposes somebody or something

contradictory /kóntrə díktəri/ *adj* **1** illogical or inconsistent **2** opposing somebody —**contradictorily** *adv* —**contradictoriness** *n*

contradistinction /kóntrədi stíngksh'n/ *n* a distinction made by pointing out contrasting qualities —**contradistinctive** *adj*

contraflow /kóntrəflō/ *n* a temporary two-way traffic system on one carriageway

contrail /kón trayl/ *n* a vapour trail made by a high-flying aircraft

contralto /kən traáltō/ (*pl* **-tos**) *n* **1** the lowest female vocal range **2** somebody with a contralto voice

contraption /kən trápsh'n/ *n* a device or machine (*infml*)

contrapuntal /kóntrə púnt'l/ *adj* of counterpoint —**contrapuntally** *adv*

contrarian /kən tráiri ən/ *n* **1** somebody who always takes an opposing position in a discussion **2** a maverick investor

contrariwise /kən tráiri wíz/ *adv* **1** in the opposite way **2** on the other hand

contrary /kóntrəri/ *adj* **1** conflicting with something ○ *orders that are contrary to ethics* **2** opposite in direction ○ *flew in a direction contrary to the rest of the aeroplanes* **3** obstructing or hindering progress ○ *slowed by contrary winds* **4** /kən tráiri/ deliberately disobedient ■ *n* the opposite ○ *argued the contrary instead of agreeing* —**contrarily** *adv* /kən tráirəli/ *adv* —**contrariness** /kən tráirinəss/ *n*

contrast *n* /kón traast/ **1** a marked difference **2** a juxtaposition of different things **3** the degree of lightness and darkness in something such as a painting or television image ■ *vti* /kən traást/ be or show to be different —**contrastable** *adj* —**contrasting** *adj*

contravene /kóntrə veén/ (**-vening, -vened**) *vt* **1** violate a rule or law **2** contradict somebody —**contravention** /-vénsh'n/ *n*

~~contraversial~~ incorrect spelling of **controversial**

contretemps /kóntrə ton/ n (fml) **1** a quarrel **2** a mishap

contribute /kóntri byoot, kən tríbbyoot/ (-**uting**, -**uted**) v **1** vti give money for a specific purpose **2** vi be a partial cause of something **3** vti offer an opinion or remark —**contributive** adj —**contributor** n

contribution /kóntri byoosh'n/ n **1** something given for a specific purpose **2** a role played in achieving something

contributory /kən tríbbyōōtəri/ adj **1** helping something to happen **2** given along with other things ■ n (pl -**ries**) somebody who gives money or time

con trick n a confidence trick (infml)

contrite /kón trīt, kən trít/ adj **1** deeply sorry for a wrong **2** arising from a sense of guilt —**contritely** adv —**contriteness** n —**contrition** /kən trísh'n/ n

contrivance /kən trív'nss/ n (fml) **1** a gadget **2** a devious plot **3** the devising of a clever scheme

contrive /kən trív/ (-**triving**, -**trived**) v **1** vt do something by being clever and creative **2** make something ingenious **3** manage to do something

contrived /kən trívd/ adj **1** not natural and spontaneous **2** unlike reality

control /kən tról/ vt (-**trolling**, -**trolled**) **1** operate a machine **2** restrain or limit something **3** manage something such as a business ■ n **1** the ability or authority to manage something **2** an operating switch **3** a skill (often in combination) ○ good ball control **4** a set of limits and restrictions **5** a place where something is checked or inspected (usually in combination) ○ passport control **6** a subject used as a comparative standard in an experiment or survey **7** a supervising person or group **8** also **control key** a special computer keyboard key pressed with others to perform specific functions ■ **controls** npl **1** the system used for controlling something such as a machine or vehicle **2** regulations —**controllable** adj

~~controll~~ incorrect spelling of **control**

controlled substance n a substance, usually a drug, whose use is regulated by law

controller /kən trólər/ n **1** somebody who controls or organizes something **2** a financial supervisor

controlling interest n ownership of enough of a business to allow ultimate control

control tower n a building from which aircraft are directed

controversial /kóntrə vúrsh'l/ adj causing strong disagreement —**controversially** adv

controversy /kóntrə vurssi, kən tróvvərsi/ (pl -**sies**) n a dispute about a contentious topic

USAGE The traditional pronunciation of **controversy** is with the stress on the first syllable (on the analogy of words such as acrimony and matrimony); however stress on the second syllable is increasingly heard

contumacious /kóntyōō máyshəss/ adj flagrantly insubordinate or rebellious

contumely /kón tyoomli/ n contempt (literary)

contusion /kən tyoozh'n/ n a bruise (technical) —**contuse** vt

conundrum /kə núndrəm/ n **1** a word puzzle **2** something confusing or puzzling ◊ See note at **problem**

conurbation /kón ur báysh'n/ n a large urban area created when neighbouring towns merge into each other ◊ See note at **city**

convalesce /kónvə léss/ (-**lescing**, -**lesced**) vi undergo a period of recovery from an illness

convalescent /kónvə léss'nt/ n a patient recovering from an illness —**convalescence** n —**convalescent** adj

convection /kən véksh'n/ n **1** a circulatory motion in a liquid or gas **2** the upward movement of hot air in the atmosphere that leads to cloud formation —**convectional** adj —**convective** adj

convector /kən véktər/ n a heater that releases heat from a heating element by means of convection

convene /kən veen/ (-**vening**, -**vened**) vti gather for a meeting

~~conveniant~~ incorrect spelling of **convenient**

convenience /kən veeni ənss/ n **1** the quality of being convenient **2** personal comfort **3** something providing ease or comfort

convenience food n quickly prepared food

convenience store n a small shop with long opening hours

convenient /kən veeni ənt/ adj involving little trouble or effort —**conveniently** adv

convent /kónvənt/ n **1** a religious community of women **2** the buildings occupied by a convent

convention /kən vénsh'n/ n **1** a gathering of people with a common interest **2** the people attending a formal meeting **3** a formal agreement **4** the usual way of doing things **5** a familiar device or method

conventional /kən vénsh'nəl/ adj **1** socially accepted **2** usual, established, or traditional **3** of a large or formal gathering of people **4** not using nuclear weapons or nuclear energy —**conventionalism** n —**conventionalist** n —**conventionality** /kən vénshənálləti/ n —**conventionalize** vt —**conventionally** adv

converge /kən vúrj/ (-**verging**, -**verged**) vi **1** reach the same point from different directions ○ roads that converged at an intersection **2** become the same ○ rapidly converging political parties **3** arrive in a large group at the same destination —**convergence** n —**convergency** n —**convergent** adj

conversant /kən vúrss'nt/ adj having knowledge or experience ○ conversant with politics —**conversance** n —**conversantly** adv

conversation /kónvər sáysh'n/ *n* **1** a casual talk **2** the activity of talking, especially informally **3** a real-time interaction with a computer

conversational /kónvər sáysh'nəl/ *adj* **1** of a conversation **2** informal in language —**conversationally** *adv*

conversationalist /kónvər sáysh'nəlist/, **conversationist** /-sáysh'nist/ *n* somebody who talks with ease

conversation piece *n* **1** an object that interests people and gets them talking **2** a group portrait

converse[1] *vi* /kən vúrss/ (**-versing, -versed**) **1** talk with another or others **2** interact with a computer ■ *n* /kón vurss/ conversation *(archaic)*

converse[2] /kón vurss/ *n* the opposite of something —**converse** *adj* —**conversely** *adv*

conversion /kən vúrsh'n/ *n* **1** a change in nature, form, or function **2** something altered **3** a change from one measuring or calculating system to another **4** adoption of new beliefs **5** in rugby and American football, a successful kick of the ball over the crossbar following a try or touchdown —**conversional** *adj*

convert *v* /kən vúrt/ **1** *vti* change something, or be changed, in character, form, or function **2** *vt* change an amount or quantity from one measuring or calculating system to another **3** *vti* change your own or somebody else's beliefs **4** *vti* in rugby and American football, kick the ball over the crossbar to score additional points ◊ See note at **change**

converter /kən vúrtər/, **convertor** *n* a device that converts one thing into another

convertible /kən vúrtəb'l/ *adj* **1** capable of being converted **2** exchangeable for gold or another currency ■ *n* a car with a removable roof

convex /kón veks, kon véks/ *adj* curving outwards —**convexity** /kon véksəti/ *n*

convey /kən váy/ (**-veys, -veying, -veyed**) *vt* **1** take a person, people, or things somewhere *(fml)* **2** communicate something **3** have something as a meaning —**conveyable** *adj*

conveyance /kən váy ənss/ *n* **1** the conveying of people or things **2** a vehicle *(fml)* **3** a transfer of ownership

conveyor /kən váy ər/, **conveyer** *n* **1** *also* **conveyor belt** a moving belt that transports objects from one point to another within a building **2** a means of transmitting something

convict *vt* /kən víkt/ **1** declare a person charged of a crime guilty **2** show somebody to be at fault ■ *n* /kón vikt/ somebody in prison —**convictable** *adj*

conviction /kən víksh'n/ *n* **1** a firmly held belief **2** firmness of belief **3** a guilty verdict —**convictional** *adj*

convince /kən vínss/ (**-vincing, -vinced**) *vt* **1** make somebody certain **2** persuade somebody to do something —**convincible** *adj*

convincing /kən vínssing/ *adj* **1** persuasive **2** beyond doubt —**convincingly** *adv* ◊ See note at **valid**

convivial /kən vívvi əl/ *adj* **1** pleasant because of its friendliness **2** enjoying the company of others —**conviviality** /kən vívvi álləti/ *n* —**convivially** *adv*

convocation /kónvə káysh'n/ *n* **1** a formal assembly **2** the act of calling a meeting

convoke /kən vốk/ (**-voking, -voked**) *vt* call a formal meeting

convoluted /kónvə lootid/ *adj* **1** extremely intricate **2** having many twists or whorls —**convolutedly** *adv* —**convolutedness** *n*

convolution /kónvə loosh'n/ *n* **1** a curve, coil, or twist **2** a complex or intricate matter —**convolutional** *adj*

convolvulus /kən vólvyооbləss/ (*pl* **-luses** *or* **-li** /-lī/) *n* a climbing plant with a twining growth pattern

convoy /kón voy/ *n* **1** a group of vehicles or ships travelling together **2** an escort for vehicles or ships —**convoy** *vt*

convulse /kən vúlss/ (**-vulsing, -vulsed**) *v* **1** *vti* shake uncontrollably **2** *vt* disrupt or disturb —**convulsive** *adj* —**convulsively** *adv* —**convulsiveness** *n*

convulsion /kən vúlsh'n/ *n* an uncontrollable shaking of the body *(often pl)* ■ **convulsions** *npl* fits of laughter

Conwy /kónwi/ town and local government district in North Wales. Pop. 3,627 (1991); district 111,200 (1995).

coo *v* (**coos, cooing, cooed**) **1** *vi* make the deep hooting sound of a pigeon **2** *vti* say something very tenderly ■ *n* a pigeon's deep hooting sound

cook *v* **1** *vti* prepare food **2** *vti* make or become hot **3** *vt* tamper with information in order to deceive people *(slang)* ■ *n* somebody who prepares food —**cookable** *adj*

☐ **cook up** *vt* invent something, e.g. an excuse *(infml)*

Cook, James, Captain (1728–79) British explorer and cartographer

Cook, Thomas (1808–92) British travel agent considered by many to be the father of modern tourism

cook-chill *adj* describes food that has been precooked and refrigerated ■ *n* the precooking and packaging of food

cooker /koókər/ *n* **1** *UK* an appliance for cooking that usually includes a hob, oven, and grill **2** a device that cooks food in a particular way

cookery /koókəri/ *n* the preparation of food

cookery book, cookbook /koók boók/ *n* a book of recipes

cookie /koóki/, **cooky** (*pl* **-ies**) *n* **1** *US, Can* a biscuit **2** a person regarded as being of a particular type or disposition *(infml)* ○ *a tough cookie* **3** a computer file containing user information, automatically sent to a central computer when the user logs on

cooking /kŏoking/ *n* **1** the preparation of food **2** prepared food ■ *adj* used in cooking

Cook Islands self-governing island group in free association with New Zealand, in the South Pacific Ocean. Pop. 20,611 (2001).

Cook Strait area of ocean separating the North Island and the South Island of New Zealand. At its narrowest, it is 22 km/14 mi. wide.

cookware /kŏok wair/ *n* utensils used in cooking

cool *adj* **1** fairly cold, usually pleasantly so **2** giving an impression of coldness ○ *a cool mint green* **3** *also* **cool-headed** staying calm under pressure **4** unfriendly **5** fashionable *(infml)* **6** indicates approval or admiration *(slang)* **7** describes a style of jazz with a relaxed rhythm ■ *vti* **1** make or become less warm ○ *Wait until the mixture cools.* **2** make or become less intense ■ *n* **1** comparative coldness, especially pleasant coldness **2** calmness under pressure *(infml)* —**coolness** *n* ◊ **keep your cool** remain calm *(infml)* ◊ **lose your cool** become angry and excitable *(infml)*

☐ **cool off** *vi* become cool again

coolant /kŏolənt/ *n* a substance that prevents overheating, especially in vehicle engines

cool bag *n* an insulated food or drink container

cooler /kŏolər/ *n* **1** a large cool room for food storage **2** a cold drink

coolie /kŏoli/ *n* an offensive term for a local man hired cheaply to do manual labour in parts of Southeast Asia

cooling-off period *n* **1** a negotiated break in a dispute **2** a time to reconsider before making a legally binding agreement

cooling tower *n* a chimney for condensing the steam produced by an industrial process

coolly /kŏol li/ *adv* **1** in a calm manner **2** in an unfriendly manner

Coombs /koomz/, **Nuggett** (1906–97) Australian economist

coop *n* an enclosure for poultry
☐ **coop up** *vt* keep in a small place

co-op /kŏ op/, **coop** *n* a cooperative *(infml)*

cooper /kŏopər/ *n* a barrel-maker —**cooperage** *n*

Cooper /kŏopər/, **Gary** (1901–61) US film actor

Cooper, James Fenimore (1789–1851) US writer

cooperate /kō óppə rayt/ *(-ating, -ated)* *v* **1** *vi* work together **2** do what is asked —**cooperation** /kō óppə ráysh'n/ *n*

cooperative /kō óppərətiv/ *adj* **1** willing to help **2** working together **3** operated collectively ■ *n* a business owned by the workers, with profits shared equally —**cooperatively** *adv* —**cooperativeness** *n*

co-opt /kō ópt/ *vt* **1** appoint somebody as a member of a group **2** neutralize the power of a faction by inviting and taking it into a larger group **3** adopt or appropriate something —**co-optation** /kō op táysh'n/ *n*

coordinate *v* /kō áwrdi nayt/ *(-nating, -nated)* **1** *vt* organize and bring together the parts of a complex enterprise **2** *vti* move or work together smoothly **3** *vt* put or class things together **4** *vti* combine to make a pleasing set or match ■ *n* /kō áwrdinət/ **1** a number specifying the exact position of something **2** somebody or something equal in importance ■ **coordinates** *npl* matching clothes ■ *adj* /kō áwrdinət/ **1** equal in rank or importance **2** involving the use of co-ordinates —**coordinated** *adj* —**coordination** /kō áwrdi náysh'n/ *n* —**coordinative** *adj* —**coordinator** *n*

Coordinated Universal Time *n* = Greenwich Mean Time

coot *(pl* **coots** *or same) n* a black water bird with a white beak and long toes

cootie /kŏoti/ *n NZ, US, Can* a louse *(infml)*

cop *n* a police officer *(infml)* ■ *vt* (**copping, copped**) grab *(slang)*
☐ **cop out** *vi* avoid doing something out of fear *(slang)*

cope[1] (**coping, coped**) *vi* handle something successfully

cope[2] *n* a priest's cloak

cope[3] (**coping, coped**) *vt* provide a wall with a coping

Copenhagen /kópən háygən, -háəgən/ capital and largest city of Denmark. Pop. 491,082 (1999).

Nicolaus Copernicus

Copernicus /kə púrnikəss/, **Nicolaus** (1473–1543) Polish astronomer —**Copernican** *adj*

copier /kóppi ər/ *n* a photocopier

copilot /kó pīlət/ *n* an assistant pilot

coping /kóping/ *n* the top course of brick or stone that caps a wall

copious /kópi əss/ *adj* abundant —**copiously** *adv* —**copiousness** *n*

Aaron Copland

Copland /kóplənd/, **Aaron** (1900–90) US composer

cop-out *n* an evasion of responsibility *(slang)*

copper[1] /kóppər/ *n* **1** *(symbol* **Cu)** a reddish-brown metal. Use: wiring, coatings, alloys. **2** a reddish-brown colour **3** a small coin *(infml)* **4** a pot for boiling water ■ *vt* cover with copper —**copper** *adj* —**coppery** *adj*

copper[2] /kóppər/ *n* a police officer *(dated infml)*

copper-bottomed *adj* reliable, especially financially

copperhead /kóppər hed/ *(pl* **-heads** *or same) n* **1** a poisonous reddish-brown North American snake **2** a poisonous Australian snake with a copper-coloured band round its head

copperplate /kóppər playt/ *n* **1** a style of elaborate clear handwriting **2** a copper printing plate **3** a print made from a copperplate

coppice /kóppiss/, **copse** *n* an area of densely growing small trees, especially one in which the trees are cut regularly to encourage young growth

copra /kóprə/ *n* dried coconut flesh

coprocessor /kó pró sessər/ *n* a second processor in a computer that improves performance

copula /kóppyòolə/ *(pl* **-las** *or* **-lae** /-lee/) *n* a verb such as 'be' or 'seem' that links a subject and an adjective or noun phrase *(technical)* —**copular** *adj*

copulate /kóppyòo layt/ (**-lating, -lated**) *vi* have sex —**copulation** /kóppyòo láysh'n/ *n*

copy /kóppi/ *n* (*pl* **-ies**) **1** something that is made exactly like something else **2** one of many identical specimens of something, e.g. a book **3** the written text of something such as a book or newspaper, as distinct from the graphics ■ *vt* (**-ies, -ied**) **1** make an identical version of **2** do the same as **3** send a copy of a document to somebody —**copyable** *adj*

SYNONYMS copy, reproduce, duplicate, clone, replicate, re-create CORE MEANING: make something that resembles something else to a greater or lesser degree

copybook /kóppi bŏŏk/ *n* a book of handwriting specimens ■ *adj* **1** excellent **2** unoriginal

copycat /kóppi kat/ *(infml) n* somebody who imitates somebody else ■ *adj* done in imitation

copy editor *n* somebody who corrects written material before its publication

copyist /kóppi ist/ *n* somebody who makes written copies of handwritten documents

copy protection *n* a way to prevent software from unauthorized copying —**copy-protected** *adj*

copyright /kóppi rīt/ *n* a creative artist's legal right to control the use and reproduction of his or her original work —**copyright** *vt*

~~copywrite~~ incorrect spelling of **copyright**

copywriter /kóppi rītər/ *n* a writer of advertisements —**copywriting** *n*

coq au vin /kók ō váN, -ván/ *n* a French dish of chicken cooked in red wine

coquette /ko két/ *n* a woman who flirts —**coquettish** *adj*

coracle /kórrək'l/ *n* a small round boat made of animal skins stretched across a wooden frame

ORIGIN **Coracle** was adopted from Welsh.

Barnaby's

Coral

coral /kórrəl/ *n* **1** a marine organism that lives in colonies and has an external skeleton **2** a hard deposit consisting of the skeletons of corals, often forming marine reefs **3** a deep reddish-orange colour —**coral** *adj*

coral reef *n* a marine ridge of coral skeletons

Coral Sea arm of the SW Pacific Ocean bounded by Australia, New Guinea, the Solomon Islands, and Vanuatu

cor anglais /káwr óng glay/ *(pl same or* **cors anglais** /káwrz-/) *n* a woodwind instrument like an oboe but with a lower pitch

Corbusier ♦ Le Corbusier

cord *n* **1** thick strong string or rope **2** a length of material used as a fastening or belt **3** an electrical cable **4** a body part resembling rope, e.g. the spinal cord **5** ribbed fabric, especially corduroy ■ **cords** *npl* corduroy trousers *(infml)* ■ *vt* tie with a cord ◊ See note at **chord**

Corday /káwrd ay/, **Charlotte** (1768–93) French assassin of Jean-Paul Marat during the French Revolution

cordial /káwrdi əl/ *adj* **1** friendly and hospitable **2** deeply felt *(literary)* ◊ has a *cordial* dislike for *dogs* ■ *n* **1** a fruit drink in concentrated form for diluting with water **2** a medicinal drink —**cordiality** /káwrdi álleti/ *n* —**cordially** *adv*

cordite /káwrd īt/ *n* a smokeless explosive made using gun cotton

cordless /káwrdləss/ *adj* not needing mains electricity

córdoba /káwrdəbə/ *n* the main unit of Nicaraguan currency

Cordoba /káwrdəbə/, **Córdoba** capital of **Córdoba Province**, S Spain. Pop. 309,961 (1998).

cordon /káwrd'n/ *n* **1** a line of people or vehicles or a temporary crowd-control fence encircling an area **2** a ribbon worn as a decoration or as a sign of rank

□ **cordon off** *vt* seal off an area with people, vehicles, or barriers

cordon bleu /káwr don blúr/ *adj* describes cooking of the highest class

corduroy /káwdə roy, -lyñ́-/ n ribbed cotton fabric ■ **corduroys** npl trousers made of corduroy

ORIGIN Corduroy is probably a compound made up of *cord* and *duroy*, which was a lightweight worsted material formerly used for men's clothing. The origins of this name are unknown. A popular explanation of **corduroy** is that it comes from French *corde du roi* 'cord of the king', but there is no real evidence for this.

core n **1** the essential part of something ○ *the core of the argument* **2** the central hard part of a piece of fruit **3** the centre of the Earth **4** the central part of a nuclear reactor **5** a sample obtained by drilling **6** formerly, the main memory in a computer before the introduction of semiconductors ■ adj essential ■ vt (**coring, cored**) take the core out of a piece of fruit

CORE abbr Congress of Racial Equality

core curriculum n a set of compulsory school subjects

core dump n a transfer of data from a computer's main memory to an external source

~~corelate~~ incorrect spelling of **correlate**

~~corespondence~~ incorrect spelling of **correspondence**

co-respondent /kố ri spóndənt/, **corespondent** n an alleged adulterous sexual partner in divorce proceedings —**co-respondency** n

core time n the part of the working day during which flexitime workers must be at work

Corfu /kawr foō, -fyoō/ most northerly of the Ionian Islands, west of Greece. Pop. 107,592 (1991).

corgi /káwrgi/ (pl -**gis**) n a small dog with smooth hair and short legs

CORGI /káwrgi/ abbr Council for Registered Gas Installers

coriander /kórri ándər/ n **1** leaves or seeds used as a food flavouring **2** the aromatic plant from which coriander is taken

Corinth /kórrinth/ ancient city and modern town in S Greece. Pop. 27,412 (1991).

Corinthian /kə rínthi ən/ adj **1** of Corinth **2** describes an architectural column that is slender and ornate at its top —**Corinthian** n

cork n **1** the outer bark of a Mediterranean evergreen oak. Use: bottle stoppers, insulation. **2** a bottle stopper made of cork or plastic **3** an angling float ■ vt seal a container with a top —**corky** adj

Cork port in SW Ireland. Pop. 180,000 (1996).

corkage /káwrkij/ n a fee charged in unlicensed restaurants for serving the wine that customers bring for themselves

corked adj **1** sealed with a cork **2** describes wine given an unpleasant flavour by a tainted cork

corker /káwrkər/ n a particularly remarkable or astounding person or thing (infml)

corkscrew /káwrk skroō/ n a device for removing corks from bottles ■ vi move in a spiral path ■ adj shaped like a spiral

cormorant /káwrmərənt/ n a large diving sea bird with a long neck

corn[1] n **1** UK, Ireland any cereal crop, especially wheat, barley, or oats **2** UK, Ireland grain produced by cereal plants **3** maize

corn[2] n a hard thick patch of skin on the foot

Corn. abbr Cornwall

cornball /káwrn bawl/ n US an overly sentimental person —**cornball** adj

corn bread n US, Can bread made from maize flour

corn chip n a piece of fried cornmeal batter eaten as a snack

corncob /káwrn kob/ n **1** an ear of sweetcorn or maize **2** the core of an ear of maize

corncrake /káwrn krayk/ n a speckled bird with a harsh call

corn dog n US, Can a hot dog fried in maizeflour batter

corn dolly n a straw ornament

cornea /káwrni ə, kawr neé ə/ (pl -**as** or -**ae** /-eé/) n a transparent membrane covering the front of the eye —**corneal** adj

corned beef n cooked and salted beef

Corneille /kawr náy/, **Pierre** (1606–84) French playwright

corner /káwrnər/ n **1** the angle formed where two lines, boundaries, or surfaces meet **2** an area enclosed by converging lines or boundaries **3** a projecting part **4** a place where two roads meet **5** a difficult situation **6** a quiet or remote place **7** an object fitted over a corner **8** a monopoly of a particular market **9** a kick or shot from the corner of a sports field ■ adj **1** located on a corner **2** intended for a corner ■ v **1** vt force into a difficult position **2** vt acquire a monopoly of **3** vi turn a corner (refers to vehicles or their drivers) ◇ **cut corners** do something in a quick, cheap, or careless way ◇ **turn the corner** get past the worst part of a difficult situation

corner shop n a shop on a street corner

cornerstone /káwrnər stōn/ n **1** a fundamentally important person or thing **2** a stone at the corner of two walls

cornet /káwrnit/ n **1** a brass instrument like a small trumpet **2** a conical wafer for ice cream **3** a paper cone for holding sweets

corn-fed adj fed on maize

cornflakes /káwrn flayks/ npl a breakfast cereal made from maize

cornflour /káwrn flow ər/ n flour made from maize

cornflower /káwrn flow ər/ n a blue-flowered plant found in cultivated fields

cornice /káwrniss/ n **1** a projecting moulding along the top of an external wall **2** a decorative plaster moulding around a room where the walls and ceiling meet **3** the part of a classical building that is supported by columns

Cornish /káwrnish/ *adj* of Cornwall ■ *npl* the people of Cornwall ■ *n* an extinct Celtic language of Cornwall

Cornish pasty *n* a pastry with edges pinched together over a filling of meat and vegetables

cornmeal /káwrn meel/ *n* flour made from maize

corn on the cob *n* an ear of maize cooked whole

cornrow /káwrn rō/ *n* a braided row of hair lying flat against the scalp —**cornrow** *vt*

cornstarch /káwrn staarch/ *n US, Can* cornflour

cornucopia /káwrnyōō kṓpi ə/ *n* **1** an abundance **2** a goat's horn overflowing with produce, symbolizing prosperity —**cornucopian** *adj*

Cornwall /káwrnwəl, -wawl/ county in the extreme southwest of England. Pop. 482,000 (1995).

corny /káwrni/ (**-ier, -iest**) *adj* sentimental in an annoying, unsophisticated way —**cornily** *adv* —**corniness** *n*

corollary /kə rólləri/ (*pl* **-ies**) *n* **1** a natural consequence of something **2** a fact that must be true when another related statement is proved true

corona /kə rṓnə/ (*pl* **-nas** *or* **-nae** /-nee/) *n* **1** a ring of light around the Moon **2** the outermost part of the Sun's atmosphere **3** the lip of the trumpet of a daffodil or similar flower **4** a long cigar with a blunt rounded end —**coronal** /kórrən'l/ *adj*

coronary /kórrənəri/ *n* (*pl* **-ies**) a heart attack (*infml*) ■ *adj* **1** supplying or draining blood from the heart **2** of the coronary arteries and veins

coronary thrombosis *n* blockage of an artery by a blood clot, often resulting in a heart attack

coronation /kórrə náysh'n/ *n* the ceremony or act of crowning a monarch

coroner /kórrənər/ *n* an official who investigates suspicious deaths —**coronership** *n*

coronet /kórrənit/ *n* **1** a small crown **2** a woman's head decoration shaped like a slender crown

Corot /kórrō/, **Jean-Baptiste Camille** (1796–1875) French painter

corp. *abbr* corporation

Corp. *abbr* corporal[2]

~~corperation~~ incorrect spelling of **corporation**

corpora plural of **corpus**

corporal[1] /káwrpərəl/ *adj* of the body —**corporality** /káwrpə rálləti/ *n* —**corporally** *adv*

corporal[2] /káwrpərəl/ *n* **1** a noncommissioned officer in various armed forces, ranking above a private **2** a petty officer in the Royal Navy —**corporalcy** *n* —**corporalship** *n*

corporal[3] /káwrpərəl/, **corporale** /káwrpə ráyli/ *n* a white cloth on which the bread and wine are placed during the Christian service of Communion

corporal punishment *n* the act of striking somebody as a punishment

corporate /káwrpərət/ *adj* **1** involving businesses or their employees, often as distinct from private individuals **2** having been incorporated **3** of a group as a whole (*fml*) —**corporately** *adv*

corporate disaster recovery *n* computer data recovery operations for businesses

corporate raider *n* somebody who buys shares in order to seize control of a company

corporation /káwrpə ráysh'n/ *n* **1** a group regarded as an individual by law **2** the governing authority of a municipality

corporation tax *n* a tax on the profits of a company

corporatism /káwrpərətizəm/ *n* the running of a state by large organizations —**corporatist** *adj, n*

corporeal /kawr páwri əl/ *adj* **1** of the physical body **2** material or physical, rather than spiritual —**corporeality** /kawr páwri álləti/ *n* —**corporeally** *adv*

corps /kawr/ (*pl* **corps** /kawrz/) *n* **1** a specialized military force **2** a tactical military unit made up of two or more divisions **3** a group of associated people o *the press corps*

corps de ballet /kawr də bállay/ (*pl same*) *n* the dancers in a ballet company who do not perform individually

corpse *n* a dead body

corpulent /káwrpyōōlənt/ *adj* overweight —**corpulence** *n*

corpus /káwrpəss/ (*pl* **-pora** /-pərə/) *n* **1** a body of writings **2** the main part

corpuscle /káwr puss'l/ *n* a cell in blood or lymph —**corpuscular** /kawr púskyōōlər/ *adj*

corral /kə raál/ *US, Can* *n* a fenced area for keeping livestock in ■ *vt* (**-ralling, -ralled**) **1** drive animals into a corral **2** gather and control people or things (*infml*)

correct /kə rékt/ *vt* **1** remove errors from something **2** point out errors in something **3** rectify an imperfection in something, e.g. eyesight ■ *adj* **1** accurate or without errors **2** acceptable or meeting a required standard —**corrective** *adj* —**correctly** *adv* —**correctness** *n*

correction /kə réksh'n/ *n* **1** an alteration that removes errors **2** a written comment correcting an error in a text **3** removal of errors —**correctional** *adj*

correctional facility *n US* a prison

Corregidor /kə réggi dawr/ island at the entrance to Manila Bay in the Philippines

correlate /kórrə layt/ *v* (**-lating, -lated**) **1** *vi* have a mutual or complementary relationship, or show things to have one **2** *vt* gather and compare things ■ *adj* having a mutual or complementary relationship ■ *n* **1** a thing having a mutual or complementary relationship with another **2** one variable related to another variable

correlation /kórrə láysh'n/ *n* **1** a mutual or complementary relationship **2** the act of correlating things —**correlational** *adj*

correlative /kə réllətiv/ adj 1 in a mutual or complementary relationship 2 describes words used together in a grammatical construction but not adjacent —**correlative** n —**correlatively** adv —**correlativeness** n —**correlativity** /kə réllə tívvəti/ n

correspond /kórri spónd/ vi 1 conform or be consistent 2 be similar or equivalent 3 write to one another —**corresponding** adj —**correspondingly** adv

correspondence /kórri spóndənss/ n 1 communication by writing 2 letters or other written messages 3 the state or fact of corresponding to something

correspondence course n an educational course followed by post

correspondent /kórri spóndənt/ n 1 somebody communicating by writing 2 somebody providing news reports on a particular place or subject ■ adj corresponding

corridor /kórri dawr/ n 1 a passage inside a building 2 a passageway in a railway carriage 3 a strip of land belonging to one country and extending through another 4 a specific region of airspace for air traffic

corrie /kórri/ n GEOG = **cirque**

corroborate /kə róbbə rayt/ (**-rating, -rated**) vt show or confirm the truth of —**corroboration** /kə róbbə ráysh'n/ n —**corroborative** /-ətiv/ adj —**corroboratively** adv —**corroborator** n

corroboree /kə róbbəri/ n Aus an Aboriginal gathering

corrode /kə ród/ (**-roding, -roded**) v 1 vti destroy or be destroyed progressively by chemical action 2 vt undermine gradually —**corrodible** adj

~~correlary~~ incorrect spelling of **corollary**

corrosion /kə rózh'n/ n 1 gradual destruction by chemical action, or the resulting damage 2 rust or other material produced by corrosion —**corrosible** /kə róssəb'l/ adj

corrosive /kə róssiv/ adj 1 progressively destructive owing to chemical action 2 destroying something gradually ■ n a destructive substance —**corrosively** adv —**corrosiveness** n

corrugated /kórrə gaytid/ adj having ridges and troughs —**corrugate** vti

corrupt /kə rúpt/ adj 1 immoral or dishonest 2 depraved 3 describes computer data or software containing errors ■ v 1 vti make or become dishonest, immoral, or depraved 2 vt introduce errors into computer data —**corruptible** adj —**corruptly** adv —**corruptness** n

corruption /kə rúpsh'n/ n 1 dishonest behaviour engaged in for personal gain 2 depravity 3 a word or phrase altered from its original form

corsage /kawr saázh, káwrss aazh/ n a small bouquet of flowers worn on a dress

corsair /káwrss air, kawr sáir/ n 1 a pirate, especially on the North African coast between the 16C and 19C 2 a pirate ship or its owner

corset /káwrssit/ n a stiff undergarment formerly worn by women to shape the waist and breasts or by men to pull in the waist

Corsica /káwrssikə/ island in the Mediterranean Sea, an administrative region of France. Pop. 249,737 (1990). —**Corsican** adj, n

cortege /kawr táyzh, -tézh/, **cortège** n 1 a funeral procession 2 a retinue of attendants

Cortés /káwr tez/, **Hernán** (1485–1547) Spanish explorer

cortex /káwr teks/ (pl **-tices** /-ti seez/ or **-texes**) n 1 the outer layer of a body part 2 a layer of plant tissue beneath the epidermis —**cortical** /káwrtik'l/ adj

cortisone /káwrti zōn/ n a hormone secreted by the adrenal cortex

corundum /kə rúndəm/ n a hard mineral form of aluminium oxide. Use: gems, abrasives.

corvette /kawr vét/ n 1 a naval escort ship 2 a small wooden sailing ship with one tier of guns

cos[1] /koss/ (pl **coses** or same) n a crisp lettuce with long leaves

cos[2] abbr cosine

Cos /koss/ second largest of the Greek Dodecanese Islands, off the coast of Turkey. Pop. 20,350 (1981).

Cosa Nostra /kōssə nóstrə, kózə-/ n an organized crime group in the United States with links to the Sicilian Mafia

ORIGIN Cosa Nostra literally means 'our concern' in Italian.

Cosgrave /kóz grayv/, **William Thomas** (1880–1965) president of the Irish Free State (1922–32)

cosh n a blunt weapon made of solid rubber —**cosh** vt

cosign /kố sīn, kō sĩn/ vt 1 sign something jointly 2 sign something as guarantor —**cosignatory** /kō sígnətəri/ n

cosine /kố sīn/ n a ratio of the length of the adjacent side of a right-angled triangle to the length of the hypotenuse

cosmeceutical /kózmə syoōtik'l/ n a cosmetic product claiming pharmaceutical properties, e.g. an anti-ageing cream

cosmetic /koz méttik/ n a substance applied to the face or body to make it more attractive (often pl) ■ adj 1 intended to improve appearance 2 done only for appearances —**cosmetically** adv

cosmetic surgery n plastic surgery to improve appearance

cosmic /kózmik/ adj 1 of the whole universe 2 great or enormous —**cosmically** adv

cosmic radiation n cosmic rays

cosmic ray n a stream of high-energy radiation from space

cosmo- prefix the universe, space o cosmology

cosmogony /koz móggəni/ n the study of the origin of the universe —**cosmogonist** n

cosmology /koz móllaji/ n 1 the study of the nature of the universe 2 the scientific study of the structure of the universe

—**cosmological** /kózmə lójjik'l/ adj —**cosmologist** n

cosmonaut /kózmə nawt/ n a Russian astronaut

cosmopolitan /kózmə póllitən/ adj 1 containing features of or people from different countries 2 well travelled 3 sophisticated and well educated ■ n a well-travelled person —**cosmopolitanism** n

cosmos[1] /kóz moss/ n 1 the whole universe 2 an ordered system

cosmos[2] /kóz moss/ (pl **-moses** or same) n a plant with flowers like daisies

cosset /kóssit/ vt give excessive care and protection to

cost vt (**cost**) 1 be priced at 2 cause the loss of ■ n 1 the amount of money paid for or spent doing something 2 the loss of something, or the effort involved in doing something ■ **costs** npl 1 legal expenses 2 the calculated amount of money needed for something ◇ housing costs

cost accounting n accounting concerned with a business's production costs

co-star n a performer who shares equal prominence with another ■ v (**co-starring, co-starred**) 1 vi star jointly with another performer 2 vt feature as a joint star

Costa Rica /kóstə reékə/ country in S Central America between the Caribbean Sea and the Pacific Ocean. Cap. San José. Pop. 3,773,057 (2001). —**Costa Rican** n, adj

cost-effective adj economically worthwhile —**cost-effectively** adv —**cost-effectiveness** n

costermonger /kóstər mung gər/, **coster** /kóstər/ n a fruit and vegetable seller (archaic)

costly /kóstli/ (**-lier, -liest**) adj 1 expensive 2 luxurious 3 involving great time or effort —**costliness** n

cost of living n living expenses

cost-plus n a pricing system that calculates the selling price of something by adding a fixed percentage as profit

cost price n the price that a seller paid for something

cost-push, cost-push inflation n inflation caused by rising production costs

costume /kós tyoom/ n 1 special clothes worn by a performer 2 the clothes traditionally worn during a particular period in the past 3 the clothes worn for a particular activity ■ vt (**-tuming, -tumed**) dress in a costume

ORIGIN **Costume** comes from the same Latin word as *custom*, which has remained closer to the original meaning. *Custom* entered English through French in the early Middle Ages. **Costume** came from French via Italian in the early 18C. At first **costume** was a term of art criticism and referred to the fashion, furniture, and other features of a painting in relation to their historical accuracy. Current senses did not develop until the 19C.

costume drama n a drama set in a previous historical period

costume jewellery n decorative but cheap jewels

costumier /ko styoómi ər, -i ay/, **costumer** /kós tyoomər/ n a maker of costumes

cosy /kózi/ adj (**cosier, cosiest**) 1 snug 2 friendly and intimate ■ n (pl **cosies**) a knitted or padded covering to keep something warm —**cosily** adv —**cosiness** n ◇ **cosy up** 1 cuddle up 2 ingratiate yourself (slang)

cot[1] n 1 a baby's bed with high sides 2 US, Can a camp bed

cot[2] abbr cotangent

cotangent /kō tánjənt/ n a ratio of the length of the side of a right-angled triangle that is adjacent to the angle divided by the opposite side —**cotangential** /kō tan jénsh'l/ adj

cot death n the sudden and unexplained death of a sleeping baby

Côte d'Azur /kōt da zyoór/ part of the French Riviera near the Italian border

Côte d'Ivoire /-dee vwaàr/ country in West Africa, situated north of the Gulf of Guinea. Cap. Yamoussoukro. Pop. 16,393,221 (2001).

coterie /kótəri/ n a small exclusive group

cotillion /kə tíllyən, kō-/ n 1 a complex 18C French dance 2 US a dance like a quadrille 3 the music for a cotillion

Cotopaxi /kótə páksi/ volcano in the Andes, in central Ecuador. It is the highest active volcano in the world. Height 5,897 m/19,347 ft.

Cotswolds /kóts wōldz/ range of limestone hills in SW England

cottage /kóttij/ n 1 a small house, especially in the country 2 Can a holiday home —**cottager** n —**cottagey** adj

cottage cheese n a soft white semisolid cheese with a lumpy texture

cottage hospital n a small rural hospital

cottage industry n a small home-based business

cottage pie n a dish of minced beef topped with mashed potato

cotton /kótt'n/ n 1 a soft white fibre that grows in the seed pods of a bush. Use: textiles. 2 fabric made from cotton 3 yarn or thread made from cotton or a synthetic substitute 4 something made of cotton fabric (often pl) 5 the tropical and subtropical bush that produces cotton fibre —**cottony** adj □ **cotton on** vi begin to understand (infml)

Cotton Belt n the cotton-growing region of the United States

cotton bud n a cotton-tipped stick used, e.g., for cleaning ears

cotton candy n US, Can candyfloss

cottonwood /kótt'n wōod/ (pl **-woods** or same) n a poplar tree with seeds that have cottony tufts

cotton wool n 1 soft fluffy cotton fibre. Use: cleaning skin, removing makeup. 2 unprocessed cotton

couch /kowch/ n 1 a long comfortable seat for two or more people 2 a psychiatrist's long seat on which a patient may lie ■ *vt phrase* in a certain way

couchette /koo shét/ *n* a seat on a train that is convertible to a bed

couch grass /kówch-, koóch-/ *n* a grass with rapidly spreading underground roots

couch potato *n* an inactive person who watches television constantly *(slang disapproving)*

cougar /koógər, -aar/ *(pl* **-gars** *or* same*)* *n* a puma

cough /kof/ *v* 1 *vi* expel air from the lungs noisily 2 *vt* expel something by coughing ■ *n* 1 an act or sound of coughing 2 an illness causing coughing

□ **cough up** *vti* hand over very reluctantly *(slang)*

cough drop *n* a sweet that soothes a cough

cough mixture *n* a syrup for soothing coughs

~~cought~~ incorrect spelling of **caught**

co.uk *abbr* UK commercial organization *(in Internet addresses)*

could /koŏd/ *modal v* 1 past tense of **can**² 2 expresses possibility o *You could go tomorrow.* o *We could have gone.* 3 expresses a request o *Could you close the window please?* 4 expresses a polite offer o *You could stay at my place.* ◊ See note at **would**

couldn't /koŏdd'nt/ *contr* could not

coulis /koóli/ *(pl* same*)* *n* a thin purée of fruit or vegetables used as a garnish

coulomb /koŏ lom/ *n* *(symbol* **C***)* a unit of electric charge equal to the amount of charge transported by a current of one ampere in one second

ORIGIN The **coulomb** is named after the French physicist Charles-Augustin de Coulomb (1736–1806), who pioneered research into electricity.

~~counceler~~ incorrect spelling of **counsellor**

council /kównss'l/ *n* 1 a group of people who run the administrative affairs of a town or district 2 any committee of appointed people

USAGE **council** or **counsel**? **Council** means a body of people, especially in an advisory or administrative context. **Counsel** most often means a lawyer or lawyers, whereas a *counsellor* gives some other kind of professional advice. The verb **counsel** describes the activity of such advisers: *Financial analysts counselled caution.*

council area *n* the geographical or administrative area under the control of a particular council

councillor /kównsələr/ *n* 1 a member of an advisory council 2 an elected member of a local council —**councillorship** *n*

council of war *n* a meeting of senior military officers to discuss strategy in wartime

council tax *n* in the United Kingdom, a local tax based on property values

counsel /kównss'l/ *n* 1 a lawyer conducting a case in court 2 somebody who gives advice *(+ sing or pl verb)* 3 advice *(fml; often pl)* ■ *vt*

(**-selling, -selled**) 1 advise to do something *(fml)* 2 advise on personal problems ◊ See note at **council**

counseling *n* US = **counselling**

counselling /kównss'ling/ *n* professional help with personal problems

counsellor /kównss'lər/ *n* 1 somebody who gives advice 2 a professional adviser 3 *also* **counsellor-at-law** *(pl* **counsellors-at-law***) Ireland* an advisory barrister 4 a senior officer in the diplomatic service —**counsellorship** *n*

count¹ /kownt/ *v* 1 *vti* say numbers in order 2 *vti* add things up to see how many there are 3 *vt* include in a calculation o *Did you count time as well as expenses?* 4 *vti* consider or be considered 5 *vi* be of importance 6 *vi* have a particular value ■ *n* 1 an act of saying numbers in order 2 an act of adding things up to find a total 3 a total 4 a charge against a defendant on trial 5 in boxing and wrestling, a referee's count after which a fight or point is decided ◊ **out for the count** unconscious or deeply asleep *(slang)*

□ **count in** *vt* include

□ **count on** *vt* 1 rely on 2 be sure of

□ **count out** *vt* 1 count things one by one 2 exclude somebody or something

count² /kownt/ *n* a nobleman in some European countries, of a rank equal to that of a British earl

countable /kówntəb'l/ *adj* 1 able to be counted 2 describes a noun that is able to form a plural —**countably** *adv*

countdown /kównt down/ *n* 1 a backwards count that signals the approach of a major event, e.g. a rocket launch 2 the activities or period immediately before an event

countenance /kówntənənss/ *(fml)* *n* 1 a face or expression 2 composure ■ *vt* (**-nancing, -nanced**) tolerate or approve of

counter¹ /kówntər/ *n* 1 a flat surface in a shop or other business where goods are displayed, served, or paid for 2 a flat surface in a kitchen 3 a small marker in games, usually a disc ◊ **under the counter** secretly

counter² /kówntər/ *vti* 1 contradict or oppose somebody 2 do something in opposition ■ *adj* contradicting ■ *n* 1 a response in retaliation 2 something done that is the opposite of something else 3 a returning punch

counter³ /kówntər/ *n* 1 a device that counts or measures something 2 somebody whose job is counting something

counter- *prefix* 1 contrary, opposing o *counterclockwise* 2 complementary, corresponding o *counterpart*

counteract /kówntər ákt/ *vt* lessen the effect of —**counteraction** *n* —**counteractive** *adj*

counterattack /kówntər ə tak/ *n* a response to an attack

counterbalance /kówntər ball ənss/ *vt* (**-ancing, -anced**) 1 have an equal and opposing effect on 2 balance with an equal weight ■ *n* 1 a counterbalancing person or thing 2 a weight that balances another

counterclockwise /kówntər klók wīz/ adv, adj US, Can anticlockwise

counterculture /kówntər kulchər/ n a culture with values that are deliberately in opposition to those of mainstream society —**countercultural** /kówntər kúlchərəl/ adj

counterfeit /kówntərfit/ adj 1 forged and therefore not real or legal 2 insincere ■ v 1 vti forge something, e.g. a signature or money 2 vt pretend to feel an emotion ■ n a forgery —**counterfeiter** n

~~counterfit~~ incorrect spelling of **counterfeit**

counterfoil /kówntər foyl/ n the part of a cheque kept by the issuer

counterinsurgency /kówntər in súrjənssi/ n action taken by a government to quash a rebellion —**counterinsurgent** n

counterintelligence /kówntər in téllijənss/ n activities designed to thwart the activities of enemy spies

counterintuitive /kówntər in tyoo itiv/ adj contrary to natural expectations —**counterintuitively** adv

countermand /kówntər maànd, kówntər maand/ vt 1 cancel a command 2 recall somebody or something previously sent somewhere ■ n an order cancelling another

countermeasure /kówntər mezhər/ n a defensive reaction

counteroffensive /kówntər ə fenssiv/ n an offensive launched in response to an enemy offensive

counterpane /kówntər payn/ n a bedspread (dated)

counterpart /kówntər paart/ n 1 a person or thing that corresponds to another 2 a complementary part or thing

counterpoint /kówntər poynt/ n 1 the combination of two or more separate melodies so that each remains distinct 2 a contrasting element ■ vt 1 contrast with something else 2 arrange music in counterpoint

counterproductive /kówntər prə dúktiv/ adj producing problems —**counterproductively** adv

counter-revolution n a revolution that aims to reverse a previous revolution —**counter-revolutionary** n, adj **counter-revolutionist** n

countersign /kówntər sīn/ vt sign a document already signed, e.g. as a witness to the earlier signature ■ n a secret password

countertenor /kówntər tenər/ n 1 a high male singing voice 2 a man with a high singing voice

countertop /kówntər top/ n US, Can the upper surface of a worktop

counterweight /kówntər wayt/ n 1 a counterbalancing weight 2 something with a compensatory effect —**counterweighted** adj

countess /kówntiss, -ess, kown téss/ n 1 the wife of a count or earl 2 a European noblewoman with the rank of count in her own right

countless /kówntləss/ adj too many to count —**countlessly** adv

count noun n a noun that has a plural form and can be used with 'a' or 'an'

countrified /kúntri fīd/, **countryfied** adj 1 in a style appropriate to the countryside 2 unsophisticated

country /kúntri/ n (pl -tries) 1 a separate nation 2 somebody's homeland 3 a geographically distinct area 4 areas that are farmed and remain relatively undeveloped 5 a region with a special character o *mountainous country* 6 a nation's people o *the support of the whole country* ■ adj 1 characteristic of rural areas 2 of country music ◇ **go to the country** hold a general election

country club n a private sports and social club

country house n a large house in the countryside

countryman /kúntrimən/ (pl -men /-mən/) n 1 somebody from the countryside 2 somebody from the same nation as you

country music, country and western n a style of popular music based on the folk music of the US South and the cowboy music of the US West —**country musician** n

countryside /kúntri sīd/ n 1 rural land, usually farmed 2 country people

countrywide /kúntri wīd/ adj, adv throughout a nation

countrywoman /kúntri woomən/ (pl -en /-wimin/) n 1 a woman from the countryside 2 a woman from the same nation as you

county /kównti/ (pl -ties) n 1 a unit of local government in some countries and federal states 2 the people of a county

county court n a local court in England and Wales with the power to decide some civil cases

county town n a town that is the seat of local government in a county

coup /koo/ n 1 a skilful and successful action 2 a seizure of political power, especially by an army

coup de grâce /koò də graàss/ (pl **coups de grâce** /pronunc. same/), **coup de grace** (pl **coups de grace**) n 1 the final blow or shot that kills a person or animal 2 an act that assures victory

coup d'état /koò day taà/ (pl **coups d'état** /pronunc. same/) n a political coup

coupe[1] /koop/ n 1 a dessert of ice cream with fruit 2 a shallow glass dish or wine glass

coupe[2] /koop, koò pay/ n US, Can a coupé

coupé /koò pay/ n a car with two doors, a sloping back, and a fixed roof

Couperin /koòpə ran, -raN/, **François** (1668–1733) French composer and organist

couple /kúpp'l/ n 1 two similar things considered together 2 a few things of the same kind 3 two people who are romantic, sexual, or married partners 4 two people doing something together 5 something that joins two parts ■ vt (-pling, -pled) 1 associate or combine two things 2 join two things

couplet /kúpplət/ n two lines of verse that form a unit

coupling /kúppling/ n 1 something that joins two things 2 the act of joining two things together

coupon /koo pon/ n 1 a voucher redeemed by a shop or company 2 an order form 3 a certificate of interest on a bond 4 a ticket issued in a rationing system

courage /kúrrij/ n the quality of being brave —**courageous** /kə ráyjəss/ adj —**courageously** adv

---

SYNONYMS **courage, bravery, fearlessness, nerve, guts, pluck, mettle** CORE MEANING: personal resoluteness in the face of danger or difficulties

---

~~courageus~~ incorrect spelling of **courageous**

Courbet /koor bay/, **Gustave** (1819–77) French painter

courgette /kawr zhét/ n UK a small vegetable marrow

courier /koorri ər/ n 1 a person or firm providing a delivery service 2 an official messenger 3 a secret messenger 4 a holidaymakers' guide employed by a holiday company ■ vt send by courier

course /kawrss/ n 1 the way events develop or progress 2 the progression of a period of time ○ in the course of the afternoon 3 a direction travelled 4 an action chosen 5 a programme of study 6 a unit in an educational programme 7 a part of a meal served at one time 8 the path of a river 9 a swift onward movement 10 an established sequence of medical treatment 11 a place where a particular sporting activity is carried on ○ a golf course 12 a layer of bricks ■ v (**coursing, coursed**) 1 vi run fast 2 vti hunt animals with greyhounds ◇ **in due course** after an appropriate period of time ◊ See note at **coarse**

course book n a book used as the basis of a course of study

courseware /káwrss wair/ n educational software

coursework /káwrss wurk/ n work assigned to students during an academic course

court[1] /kawrt/ n 1 a session of an official body with the authority to decide legal cases 2 the room or building where a court is constituted 3 the judge or people in a court 4 an open space within a walled area 5 an area on which a particular ball game is played 6 a monarch's attendants 7 an important person's followers 8 used in the names of places or groups of buildings ◇ **be laughed out of court** be ridiculed severely (infml) ◇ **pay court to** try to win influence with or the favour of somebody through flattery or attentiveness

court[2] /kawrt/ v 1 vt be attentive to somebody in order to win favour or influence 2 vt try to gain something, e.g. somebody's attention 3 vt behave in a way that makes a bad experience likely ○ courted disaster 4 vt try to

win somebody's love (dated) 5 vi be sweethearts (dated)

Court /kawrt/, **Margaret Jean** (b. 1942) Australian tennis player

courtesan /káwrti zán, káwrti zan/ n a high-class prostitute

courtesy /kúrtəssi/ n (pl -sies) 1 polite or considerate behaviour 2 a polite or considerate action ■ adj 1 done for the sake of politeness 2 provided free —**courteous** /-ti əss/ adj —**courteously** adv —**courteousness** n

courthouse /káwrt howss/ n a building where a law court is based

courtier /káwrti ər/ n 1 a member of a royal court 2 somebody who flatters an important person

~~courtieus~~ incorrect spelling of **courteous**

courtly /káwrtli/ (-lier, -liest) adj having refined manners —**courtliness** n

court martial (pl **courts martial** or **court martials**) n a military court

court-martial (**court-martialling, court-martialled**) vt try an accused person in a military court

Court of Appeal n a court in England and Wales that hears appeals

court of law n a court that hears legal cases

court order n an order issued by a judge

courtroom /káwrt room, -room/ n a hall or room in which a court of law is held

courtship /káwrt ship/ n 1 the process of trying to gain somebody's love 2 a romantic relationship that is a prelude to marriage 3 ingratiating behaviour

court shoe n a woman's shoe with a plain low-cut front and a moderately high heel

courtyard /káwrt yaard/ n an open space surrounded by walls

couscous /kooss kooss/ n 1 a food made of small grains of semolina 2 a dish of stew and couscous

cousin /kúzz'n/ n 1 an uncle's or aunt's child 2 a relative descended from a common ancestor 3 somebody with whom you have something in common —**cousinly** adj

---

ORIGIN Cousin derives from a Latin word that applied only to a cousin on your mother's side. It meant literally 'mother's sister's child'. By the time it entered English from French, a father's nephews and nieces were included in its scope. Early English use became wider still, allowing any relative outside the immediate family to be referred to as a **cousin**.

Cousteau /koóstō/, **Jacques** (1910–97) French underwater explorer

couture /koo tyoor/ n 1 fashion design 2 high-fashion clothing

couturier /koo tyoóri ay/ n a fashion designer

cove /kōv/ n 1 a small bay enclosed by cliffs 2 a nook in a cliff ■ vti (**coving, coved**) make or have an inward curve

coven /kúw'n/ n a group of witches

covenant /kúvvənənt/ n 1 a contract, especially one making payments to a charity 2 **Covenant** a 17C Scottish pact to defend Presbyterianism ■ vt promise solemnly or legally to do something —**covenantal** /kúvvə nánt'l/ adj

Coventry /kóvvəntri/ city in central England. Pop. 306,503 (1996). ◊ **send to Coventry** refuse to speak or associate with somebody as a punishment or mark of disapproval

co-venture /kō vénchər/ vti undertake a business venture in partnership with another person or firm ■ n a business partnership

cover /kúvvər/ v 1 vt put one thing over the whole or top of something else 2 vt be all over something 3 vt be wrapped around something 4 vt put clothing on a part of the body 5 vt be worn on a part of the body 6 vt put a lid on something 7 vt talk or write about, e.g. an event 8 vt provide news of something 9 vt take something into account 10 vt extend over an area 11 vt hide something 12 vt insure something or insure against something 13 vt be enough to pay for a purchase 14 vt protect somebody from attack, e.g. by aiming a weapon at an enemy 15 vi do somebody else's job 16 vi tell lies for somebody 17 vt copulate with a female (refers to male animals, especially stallions) 18 vt in card games, to play a card of a higher value than another card already played 19 vt in sport, defend an area against an opponent 20 vt sit on eggs (refers to female birds) ■ n 1 something that covers 2 a lid 3 a book or magazine binding 4 a cloth that covers furniture 5 a shelter from the weather 6 a hiding place 7 plants that cover an area of ground 8 defence against attack 9 an assumed identity or pretext that protects, e.g. a spy, from detection 10 a cover charge 11 insurance protection 12 an understudy 13 an envelope ■ **covers** npl coverings on a bed —**coverable** adj ◊ **blow somebody's cover** expose somebody's disguise, lie, or pretence ◊ **under cover of** hidden or protected by ◊ **under separate cover** in another envelope or package

□ **cover up** vt 1 cover something completely 2 conceal something bad

coverage /kúvvərij/ n 1 media attention 2 the audience for a television or radio programme or the readership of a newspaper or magazine 3 the degree to which something is covered by something else

coveralls /kúvvər awlz/ npl US overalls

cover charge n an extra charge for service in a restaurant or nightclub, added to the cost of food or drinks

cover girl n a female model who appears on the front cover of a magazine

covering /kúvvəring/ n something that covers

covering letter n an accompanying explanatory letter

coverlet /kúvvərlət/ n a decorative cover for a bed

cover note n a temporary insurance certificate

cover page, cover sheet n the top sheet of a fax transmission that bears the sender's name and other details

cover story n 1 the main feature in a magazine, illustrated on the front cover 2 a false story, e.g. to protect a spy's identity

covert /kúvvərt, kóvurt/ adj secret ■ n 1 a mass of undergrowth providing cover for game birds 2 a shelter —**covertly** adv —**covertness** n ◊ See note at **secret**

cover-up n the concealment of something illegal or immoral

covet /kúvvət/ v 1 vti greedily desire to have somebody else's property 2 vt desire something very much (fml) —**coveter** n —**covetous** adj ◊ See note at **want**

covey /kúvvi/ (pl -eys) n a group of game birds

cow[1] /kow/ n 1 a large female mammal kept for its milk and meat 2 a male or female of any breed of domestic cattle 3 a large female mammal, e.g. a female whale 4 an offensive term for a woman (slang)

cow[2] /kow/ vt make submissive

coward /ków ərd/ n somebody who lacks courage

Coward /ków ərd/, **Sir Noel** (1899–1973) British dramatist, actor, and songwriter

cowardice /ków ərdiss/ n lack of courage

cowardly /ków ərdli/ adj lacking courage —**cowardliness** n —**cowardly** adv

> SYNONYMS **cowardly, faint-hearted, spineless, gutless, pusillanimous, craven, chicken** CORE MEANING: lacking in courage

cowboy /ków boy/ n 1 a man who looks after cattle in the W United States 2 a male character in Westerns 3 an unreliable or unqualified person (infml)

cowboy hat n a hat with a high crown and a wide brim

Cowdrey /kówdri/, **Colin, Baron Cowdrey of Tonbridge** (1932–2000) Indian-born British cricketer

cower /ków ər/ vi cringe in fear

cowgirl /ków gurl/ n 1 US, Can a woman who looks after cattle in the W United States 2 a woman character in Westerns who rides with cowboys

cowhand /ków hand/ n US, Can a cowboy or cowgirl in the W United States

cowhide /ków hīd/ n 1 the processed skin of a cow 2 leather made from cowhide

cowl /kowl/ n 1 a monk's hood 2 a hood for a chimney or air vent

cowlick /ków lik/ n a tuft of hair on somebody's head that habitually sticks up

cowling /kówling/ n a removable covering for an aircraft engine or fuselage

coworker /kō wurkər/ n a fellow worker

cowpat /ków pat/ n a mass of cow dung

cowpox /ków poks/ n a viral skin disease of cattle

cowrie /kówri/, **cowry** (pl **-ries**) n 1 a brightly coloured mollusc 2 a cowrie shell, formerly used as money in some parts of Africa and Asia

cowshed /ków shed/ n a building for cattle

cowslip /kówslip/ n a small flowering plant of the primrose family

cox n somebody who directs a team of rowers and steers the boat ■ vti steer a rowing boat

coxcomb /kóks kōm/ n a fashionable, conceited man (archaic) —**coxcombry** n

coxswain /kóks'n, -swayn/ n 1 in rowing, a cox 2 somebody in charge of a lifeboat

coy adj 1 pretending in a teasing or flirtatious way to be shy 2 annoyingly uncommunicative —**coyly** adv —**coyness** n

ORIGIN **Coy** comes from the same Latin word as *quiet*, and originally meant 'quiet, still'. This quickly developed to 'shy'. Both **coy** and *quiet* entered English directly from French.

Coy. abbr company

coyote /kóy ōt, koy ōti/ (pl **-tes** or same) n a North American mammal like a small wolf

coypu /kóy poo/ (pl **-pus** or same) n a very large South American rodent

cozy adj, n US = **cosy**

CPR abbr Canadian Pacific Railway

cps abbr 1 characters per second 2 cycles per second

CPS abbr Crown Prosecution Service

CPU abbr central processing unit

Cr symbol chromium

cr. abbr credit

crab n 1 a crustacean with a broad flat shell and a pair of large pincers at the front 2 the flesh of a crab as food 3 **Crab** the constellation and zodiacal sign Cancer ■ v (**crabbing**, **crabbed**) 1 vti scurry sideways 2 vi catch crabs

crab apple n 1 a small sour apple. Use: preserves. 2 the tree on which crab apples grow

Crabbe /krab/, **George** (1754–1832) British poet and clergyman

crabbed /krábbd, krábbid/ adj 1 bad-tempered 2 describes handwriting that is small, untidy, and hard to read

crabby /krábbi/ (**-bier**, **-biest**) adj bad-tempered —**crabbily** adv —**crabbiness** n

crabmeat /kráb meet/ n edible crab flesh

crabwise /kráb wīz/ adv, adj 1 sideways 2 by indirect means

crack v 1 vti break without coming or making something come fully apart 2 vti break with a sharp noise 3 vti make or cause something to make a loud sharp noise 4 vt hit something or somebody hard 5 vti fail or break down, or make something fail or break down 6 vti break down psychologically 7 vi become hoarse or change in pitch (refers to voices) 8 vt decode or solve a code or puzzle (infml) 9 vt force your way into something, especially a safe (infml) 10 vt break a molecule into smaller molecules or radicals ■ n 1 a thin

break ○ *cracks in the ice* 2 a long narrow opening 3 a sharp noise 4 a sharp blow (infml) ○ *a crack over the head* 5 an attempt (infml) 6 Ireland, Scotland conversation 7 a purified form of cocaine (slang) ■ adj excellent ○ *She's a crack shot.* ◇ **be not all he's** or **she's** or **it's cracked up to be** be not as good as promised or reputed ◇ **crack it** achieve something or be successful (infml) ◇ **get cracking** start moving or doing something quickly or more quickly (infml)

☐ **crack down** vi take strong action against something or somebody undesirable (infml)

☐ **crack on** vi work hard (infml)

☐ **crack up** v (infml) 1 vi have a nervous breakdown 2 vti laugh or cause to laugh uncontrollably

crackbrained /krák braynd/ adj irrational ○ *a crackbrained idea*

crackdown /krák down/ n firm action taken to control something

cracked adj 1 having cracks 2 irrational (infml) 3 coarsely crushed ○ *cracked wheat*

cracker /krákər/ n 1 a decorated tube that opens with an explosive noise when both ends are pulled 2 a flat crisp unsweetened biscuit 3 an excellent person or thing (infml)

crackers /krákərz/ adj mildly eccentric (infml)

cracking /kráking/ adj (infml) 1 very quick 2 excellent

crackle /krák'l/ vi (**-ling**, **-led**) 1 make a series of snapping noises like the noises that wood makes when it burns 2 be lively, energetic, or scintillating ■ n 1 a series of snapping noises 2 fine decorative cracks in pottery

crackling /krákling/ n 1 snapping or popping noises 2 crisply cooked pork skin

crackly /krákli/ (**-lier**, **-liest**) adj 1 brittle in texture 2 making a series of snapping noises

crackpot /krák pot/ adj unrealistically imaginative or bizarre (infml) ○ *a crackpot scheme* —**crackpot** n

crack-up n a nervous breakdown (infml)

cradle /kráyd'l/ n 1 a baby's bed with rockers 2 the place from which something starts or develops 3 a supporting framework for something being built 4 a support for a telephone handset ■ vt (**-dling**, **-dled**) 1 hold carefully and closely 2 put into a cradle

craft /kraaft/ n 1 a skilful creative activity 2 an object produced by skilful handwork (often pl) 3 a skilled profession or activity (often in combination) ○ *the craft of film-making* 4 resourceful devious cunning 5 (pl same) a boat, ship, aeroplane, or space vehicle (often in combination) ■ vt create something with skill, especially using the hands

craftsman /kraaftsmən/ (pl **-men** /-mən/) n 1 a skilled worker 2 a skilful man —**craftsmanlike** adj —**craftsmanship** n

craftsperson /kraafts purss'n/ (pl **-people** /-peep'l/) n somebody skilled in making things by hand

craftswoman /kraafts woomən/ (pl **-en** /-wimin/) n 1 a skilled woman worker 2 a skilful woman

crafty /kráafti/ (**-ier, -iest**) *adj* using cunning to deceive people —**craftily** *adv* —**craftiness** *n*

crag *n* a protruding rocky part of a mountainside

craggy /krággi/ (**-gier**) (**-giest**) *adj* **1** rocky and steep **2** with rugged facial features —**cragginess** *n*

cram (**cramming, crammed**) *v* **1** *vt* force something into a small space **2** *vt* eat food greedily **3** *vti* study intensively (*infml*)

crammer /krámmər/ *n* a school or tutor that prepares students intensively for an examination

cramp[1] *n* **1** a painful involuntary muscle contraction **2** temporary muscle paralysis ■ **cramps** *npl* abdominal pain ■ *vi* be affected with cramp

cramp[2] *n* **1** a device for holding things together **2** a confined place or situation

cramped *adj* **1** lacking space **2** packed into too small a space

crampon /krám pon, krámpən/ *n* a set of spikes fitted on a climbing boot (*usually pl*)

Cranach /kráa nakh/, **Lucas, the Elder** (1472–1553) German painter and engraver

cranberry /kránbəri/ (*pl* **-ries**) *n* **1** a sour red berry. Use: juice, sauces. **2** the evergreen plant that yields cranberries

crane *n* **1** a machine that lifts heavy objects by means of a movable beam **2** a moving support for a film or television camera **3** a long-necked, long-legged bird that lives near water ■ *v* (**craning, craned**) **1** *vti* stretch your neck in order to get a better view **2** *vt* move something by use of a crane

Crane, Stephen (1871–1900) US writer

crane fly *n* a daddy longlegs

cranium /kráyni əm/ (*pl* **-ums** *or* **-a** /-ə/) *n* the skull —**cranial** *adj*

crank *n* **1** a mechanical device for transmitting motion **2** a person regarded as eccentric (*infml insult*) ■ *vti* use a crank on

□ **crank out** *vt* produce in large quantities (*infml*)

□ **crank up** *vt* increase the force, volume, or intensity of (*infml*)

crankshaft /krángk ohaaft/ *n* a shaft driving or driven by a crank

cranky /krángki/ (**-ier, -iest**) *adj* **1** not in good working order **2** *US, Can* easily irritated (*infml*) —**crankily** *adv* —**crankiness** *n*

Cranmer /kránmər/, **Thomas** (1489–1556) English archbishop

cranny /kránni/ (*pl* **-nies**) *n* a narrow hole —**crannied** *adj*

crap[1] (*slang*) *n* **1** an offensive term for junk or something worthless or annoying **2** an offensive term for excrement ■ *vti* (**crapping, crapped**) an offensive term meaning to defecate —**crappy** *adj*

crap[2] *n US, Can* a losing throw at craps

crape *n* **1** light crinkled crêpe fabric **2** a black band worn when in mourning

craps *n US, Can* a gambling game played with dice (+ *sing verb*)

crapshoot /kráp shoot/ *n US* a craps game

crash *n* **1** a vehicle collision **2** a loud noise **3** a computer breakdown **4** a stock market collapse ■ *v* **1** *vti* collide or make something collide violently **2** *vti* make or cause something to make a loud noise **3** *vti* break into pieces noisily **4** *vti* move noisily **5** *vti* have or cause a complete computer failure **6** *vi* collapse financially **7** *vi* drop sharply in value **8** *vti* attend uninvited (*infml*) **9** *vi* sleep in a different place from usual (*slang*) ■ *adj* rapid and intensive

□ **crash out** *vi* fall asleep suddenly (*infml*)

crash barrier *n* a safety barrier along a road

crash course *n* a rapid and intensive study programme

crash diet *n* a severe diet in order to lose weight quickly

crash dive *n* a rapid dive by a submarine

crash-dive *vti* **1** descend or make an aircraft descend rapidly and crash **2** make or cause a submarine to make a rapid dive

crash helmet *n* a safety helmet for a cyclist, motorcyclist, or racing driver

crash landing *n* an emergency aircraft landing —**crashland** /krásh land/ *vti*

crass *adj* **1** thoughtless and vulgar **2** extreme —**crassly** *adv* —**crassness** *n*

crate *n* a large box or basket ■ *vti* (**crating, crated**) put in a crate

crater /kráytər/ *n* **1** a circular hole at a volcano summit **2** a hole left by a meteorite or an explosion **3** an ancient Greek wine bowl **4 Crater** a constellation of the southern hemisphere ■ *vti* form or make something form craters

cravat /krə vát/ *n* a man's neckerchief tied in front

ORIGIN Cravat is an adoption of a French word meaning literally 'Croatian'. Croatian mercenaries in French military service wore linen scarfs or neckbands tied at the front. In the 1650s the style became fashionable and the name **cravat** was born.

crave /kráyv/ (**craving, craved**) *v* **1** *vti* desire something strongly **2** *vt* beg somebody for something (*archaic*) —**cravingly** *adv* ◊ See note at **want**

craven /kráyv'n/ *adj* cowardly —**cravenly** *adv* —**cravenness** *n* ◊ See note at **cowardly**

craving /kráyving/ *n* a strong desire for something

craw *n* a bird or insect's crop

crawl *vi* **1** move along on the hands and knees **2** move slowly with the body close to the surface **3** move forwards very slowly **4** be servile (*infml*) **5** be overrun **6** have a feeling of being covered by moving insects ◊ *made his skin crawl* ■ *n* **1** a very slow speed **2** an overarm swimming stroke

crawler /kráwlər/ *n* **1** an insect or animal that crawls **2** a vehicle with tracks instead of wheels **3** a computer program collecting online documents

crayfish /kráyfish/ (pl same or **-fishes**), **crawfish** /kráwfish/ n **1** a freshwater crustacean resembling a lobster **2** crayfish as food

crayon /kráy on/ n **1** a coloured wax stick for drawing **2** a drawing done using crayons —**crayon** vti

craze n **1** a fad **2** a personal obsession ■ vti (**crazing, crazed**) **1** make or become irrational (often offensive) **2** produce or have cracks in pottery glaze —**crazed** adj

crazy /kráyzi/ (**-zier, -ziest**) adj (infml) **1** an offensive term meaning affected by a psychiatric disorder **2** ridiculous **3** excessively fond of ○ crazy about tennis —**crazily** adv —**craziness** n

crazy paving n a decorative pavement of irregularly shaped stones

creak /kreek/ vi make or move with a prolonged squeaking sound —**creak** n —**creaking** adj

SPELLCHECK Do not confuse the spelling of **creak** and **creek** ('a narrow tidal inlet'), which sound similar.

creaky /kreéki/ (**-ier, -iest**) adj making a prolonged squeaking noise —**creakily** adv —**creakiness** n

cream /kreem/ n **1** the fatty part of milk **2** a creamy lotion **3** a food with a soft texture **4** a soft-centred chocolate **5** the best part of something **6** a yellowish-white colour ■ vt mix until creamy —**cream** adj

cream cheese n soft white unmatured cheese

cream cracker n a crisp unsweetened biscuit eaten with cheese

creamer /kreémər/ n a substitute for cream, used in coffee or tea

creamery /kreémɔri/ (pl **-ies**) n a business selling dairy products

cream of tartar n an ingredient of baking powder

cream puff n a cream-filled pastry

cream soda n a vanilla-flavoured carbonated soft drink

cream tea n an afternoon meal of tea and scones with jam and cream

creamy /kreémi/ (**-ier, -iest**) adj **1** smooth or tasting like cream **2** containing cream —**creamily** adv —**creaminess** n

crease /kreess/ n **1** a fold put in fabric by pressing or crushing **2** a wrinkle in the skin **3** in cricket, a line near the wicket ■ vti (**creasing, creased**) make creases in, or acquire creases —**creased** adj —**creasy** adj

□ **crease up** vti laugh or make somebody laugh uncontrollably (infml)

create /kri áyt/ (**-ating, -ated**) v **1** vt make exist **2** vt give rise to **3** vti produce a work of art or invent something **4** vt give somebody a new title, role, or position **5** vi make a fuss (infml)

creation /kri áysh'n/ n **1** the process of making somebody or something exist **2** the Earth and its inhabitants **3** something created by human imagination or invention **4 Creation** the making of the universe by God according to the Bible **5 Creation** the universe as made by God according to the Bible —**creational** adj

creationism /kri áysh'nizəm/ n the belief that God created the universe as described in the Bible —**creationist** adj, n

creative /kri áytiv/ adj **1** new and original in conception **2** able to create things **3** using resources imaginatively —**creatively** adv —**creativeness** n —**creativity** /kreé ay tívvəti/ n

creative writing n the writing of stories, poems, and other works of the imagination

creator /kri áytər/ n **1** somebody who creates something **2** also **Creator** God

creature /kreéchər/ n **1** a living being **2** an unpleasant living being **3** somebody or something created ○ a creature of your imagination **4** a particular type of person ○ He's a harmless creature.

creature comforts npl necessities for a comfortable life

crèche /kresh, kraysh/ n a childcare facility

credence /kreéd'nss/ n **1** belief in the truth of something **2** trustworthiness

credential /krə dénsh'l/ n **1** proof of ability or trustworthiness **2** authentication ■ **credentials** npl official identification

credibility /kréddə bílləti/ n **1** believableness **2** a willingness to believe something

credible /kréddəb'l/ adj **1** believable **2** trustworthy —**credibly** adv

credit /kréddit/ n **1** an arrangement for delayed payment of something **2** money a customer is owed by a shop and can spend there **3** the balance in an account **4** an amount of money paid into an account or against an amount owed **5** somebody's financial status **6** recognition or an acknowledgment for something **7** a source of pride **8** the column in which account payments are recorded **9** a completed unit of an educational course ■ **credits** npl a list of everyone involved in a film or TV programme ■ vt **1** believe **2** recognize as responsible for an achievement **3** attribute **4** add or record as a credit to a bank account ◇ **to somebody's credit** a source of commendation for somebody

creditable /kréddítəb'l/ adj praiseworthy —**creditability** /kréddítə bílləti/ n

credit card n a bank card for buying goods or services on credit

credit note n a written acknowledgment of the money a customer is owed by a shop and can spend there

creditor /kréddítər/ n somebody who is owed money

credit rating n an estimate of somebody's financial creditworthiness

credit transfer n a transfer of money between bank accounts

credit union *n* a cooperative lending association

creditworthy /kréddit wurthi/ *adj* sufficiently reliable to be given financial credit —**creditworthiness** *n*

credo /kráydō/ (*pl* **-dos**) *n* **1** a statement of beliefs **2 Credo** the statement of Christian beliefs

credulity /krə dyŏólǝti/ *n* willingness to believe things too readily

credulous /kréddyŏólǝss/ *adj* ready to believe anything —**credulously** *adv* —**credulousness** *n*

creed *n* **1** a statement of beliefs **2** a religion

creek /kreek/ *n* **1** a narrow tidal inlet **2** *ANZ, US, Can* a stream ◊ **up the creek (without a paddle)** in a difficult situation, or in trouble (*infml*) ◊ See note at **creak**

creel *n* **1** a wicker basket for fish **2** a wicker fish trap

creep *vi* (**crept** *or* **creeped**) **1** move slowly and quietly **2** move near the ground **3** proceed or develop slowly **4** shiver with disgust **5** spread over a surface by sending out tendrils, suckers, or roots **6** be displaced slightly ■ *n* **1** a slow quiet movement **2** a person regarded as repellent or obsequious (*infml*) **3** a slight displacement ■ **creeps** *npl* an uneasy feeling of fear or disgust (*infml*) —**creeping** *adj*

creeper /kreepǝr/ *n* **1** a plant that spreads over a surface by sending out tendrils, suckers, or roots **2** a small climbing plant

creepy /kreepi/ (**-ier, -iest**) *adj* (*infml*) **1** frighteningly or disgustingly unnerving **2** repellent —**creepily** *adv* —**creepiness** *n*

creepy-crawly (*pl* **creepy-crawlies**) *n* a crawling insect (*infml*)

cremate /krə máyt/ (**-mating, -mated**) *vt* incinerate a corpse —**cremation** *n*

crematorium /krémmǝ táwri ǝm/ (*pl* **-ums** *or* **-a** /-ǝ/) *n* a place used for cremation

crème caramel /krém kárrǝ mél/ (*pl* **crème caramels** *or* **crèmes caramel** /pronunc. same/) *n* a cold custard dessert with a caramel sauce

crème de la crème /krém dǝ la krém/ *n* the elite of a group

crème de menthe /krém dǝ máanth/ (*pl* **crème de menthes** *or* **crèmes de menthe** /pronunc. same/) *n* a mint-flavoured liqueur

crème fraîche /krém frésh/ *n* thickened soured cream

creole /kreè ōl/ *n* **1** a language of mixed origin **2 Creole** somebody of French ancestry in the S United States **3 Creole** the French-based language of Louisiana **4 Creole** a group of languages spoken in some Caribbean islands **5 Creole** a Caribbean person of European ancestry **6 Creole** a Creole speaker ■ *adj* **1** cooked as in New Orleans **2** *also* **Creole** of a creole

creosote /kreè ǝ sōt/ *n* a wood preservative made from coal tar —**creosote** *vt*

crêpe /krayp/ *n* **1** a light crinkled fabric **2** a thin pancake **3** *also* **crêpe paper** crinkly decorative paper **4** *also* **crêpe rubber** rubber in the form of thin crinkled sheets, used for making the soles of shoes

crept past tense, past participle of **creep**

crescendo /krǝ shéndō/ (*pl* **-dos** *or* **-does** *or* **-di** /-dee/) *n* **1** an increase in loudness in music **2** a passage of music of increasing loudness **3** an intensification of something —**crescendo** *adj, adv*

crescent /kréss'nt, krézz'nt/ *n* **1** an arc shape **2** an arc-shaped object **3** *also* **Crescent** the symbol of Islam or Turkey —**crescent** *adj*

cress (*pl* **same** *or* **cresses**) *n* a plant with pungent-tasting leaves used in salads and as a garnish

crest *n* **1** the top of a curve or slope **2** a culmination **3** a tuft on a bird or animal's head **4** an ornament on the top of a helmet **5** a heraldic symbol of a family or office ■ *v* **1** *vi* rise to a crest **2** *vt* reach or be at the top of —**crested** *adj*

crestfallen /krést fawlǝn/ *adj* downcast

Cretaceous /kri táyshǝss/ *n* a period of geological time 142–65 million years ago —**Cretaceous** *adj*

Crete /kreet/ largest Greek island, in the S Aegean Sea. Pop. 540,054 (1991). —**Cretan** *adj, n*

cretin /kréttin/ *n* **1** an offensive term for somebody considered unintelligent (*insult*) **2** somebody with a thyroid hormone deficiency (*dated; sometimes offensive*) —**cretinism** *n* —**cretinous** *adj*

Creutzfeldt-Jakob disease /króyts felt yák ob-/ *n* a slow developing fatal brain disease

crevasse /krǝ váss/ *n* a deep crack, especially in a glacier ■ *vti* (**-vassing, -vassed**) form or cause to form crevasses

crevice /krévviss/ *n* a fissure, especially in a rock —**creviced** *adj*

crew[1] *n* **1** the staff of a ship, aircraft, or spacecraft **2** a ship's staff excluding its officers **3** a group working together on a task **4** a group of friends or associates (*infml*) **5** the rowers and cox of a racing boat ■ *v* **1** *vi* be a crew member **2** *vt* help to operate

crew[2] past tense of **crow**[2]

crew cut *n* a very short hairstyle

crew neck *n* a round neckline —**crew-neck** *adj*

crib *n* **1** a container for hay from which livestock feed **2** a model of the manger in which Jesus Christ slept after his birth **3** a horse or cattle stall **4** *US, Can* a cot **5** *also* **crib sheet** a sheet containing information used for cheating in an examination **6** an act of plagiarism **7** *ANZ* a snack (*infml*) ■ *v* (**cribbing, cribbed**) **1** *vti* plagiarize (*infml*) **2** *vt* put in a crib —**cribber** *n*

cribbage /kríbbij/ *n* a card game with a board and pegs for keeping score

cribbage board *n* a board with pegs for keeping score in cribbage

crick *n* a painful stiffness in the neck or back —**crick** *vt*

Crick, Francis H. C. (*b.* 1916) British biophysicist. With James D. Watson and Maurice Wilkins he discovered the structure of DNA (1953).

cricket¹ /kríkit/ *n* an outdoor game for two teams of 11 players using a flat bat, a small hard ball, and wickets —**cricket** *vi* —**cricketer** *n*

cricket² /kríkit/ *n* a leaping chirping insect

crier /krí ər/ *n* 1 somebody or something that cries 2 a town crier

crime *n* 1 an illegal act 2 illegal activity ○ *measures to combat crime* 3 any act considered morally wrong 4 an undesirable act (*infml*)

Crimea /krī meé ə/ peninsula in SE Ukraine between the Black Sea and the Sea of Azov —**Crimean** *n, adj*

crime wave *n* a period when an unusually high number of crimes occur

criminal /krímminəl/ *n* somebody acting illegally ■ *adj* 1 punishable as a crime 2 of criminals 3 wrong or unacceptable —**criminally** *adv*

criminalize /krímminə līz/ (-**izing, -ized**), **criminalise** *vt* 1 make illegal 2 make into a criminal —**criminalization** /krímminə līz áysh'n/ *n*

criminology /krímmi nóllaji/ *n* the study of crime and criminals —**criminological** /krímminə lójjik'l/ *adj* —**criminologist** *n*

crimp *vt* 1 fold or press the ends or edges of something together 2 pleat something ■ *n* 1 a crimping action 2 a tight artificial hair wave 3 a crease formed by crimping

crimson /krímz'n/ *n* a deep, rich red colour ■ *v* 1 *vti* make or become crimson 2 *vi* blush —**crimson** *adj*

ORIGIN **Crimson** derives from the name of a small plant-sucking insect (the 'kermes'). The bodies of the adult females are dried to be the source of a red dye. The name comes from Arabic, via Spanish, French, and other Romance forms.

cringe (**cringing, cringed**) *vi* 1 retract the head and body in a frightened or servile way 2 react in an embarrassed or uncomfortable way (*infml*) —**cringe** *n* —**cringer** *n*

crinkle /kríngk'l/ *vti* 1 crease up 2 make or cause to make a rustling sound ■ *n* a tiny crease or wave

crinkly /kríngkli/ (-**klier, -kliest**) *adj* 1 wavy or creased up tightly 2 making a rustling sound —**crinkliness** *n*

crinoline /krínnəlin/ *n* a stiff or hooped petticoat worn to expand a skirt —**crinolined** *adj*

Crippen /kríppin/, **Hawley Harvey** (1862–1910) US-born British dentist and murderer

cripple /krípp'l/ *n* an offensive term for a person with physical disabilities ■ *vt* (-**pling, -pled**) 1 an offensive term meaning to cause to have a physical disability 2 an offensive

term meaning to damage —**crippled** *adj* —**crippling** *adj*

crisis /krí siss/ (*pl* -**ses** /-seez/) *n* 1 a dangerous or worrying time 2 a critical moment or turning point

crisis management *n* the process of dealing with problems as they arise

crisp *adj* 1 hard but easily broken 2 fresh and crunchy ○ *a crisp apple* 3 smooth, firm, and clean ○ *crisp fabric* 4 distinct and clear ○ *crisp lines* 5 sharp and concise ○ *a crisp reply* 6 invigorating ■ *n* a thin slice of fried potato eaten as a snack —**crisp** *vti* —**crisply** *adv* —**crispness** *n*

crispbread /krísp bred/ *n* a flat rye, wheat, or corn biscuit

crispy /kríspi/ (-**ier, -iest**) *adj* light and crunchy —**crispily** *adv* —**crispiness** *n*

crisscross /kríss kross/ *n* a pattern of lines that cross each other ■ *adj* with crossed vertical and horizontal lines ■ *adv* back and forth ■ *v* 1 *vti* make a pattern of crossed lines on something 2 *vt* go to and fro across something

ORIGIN **Crisscross** was originally *Christ's cross.* In early use this referred not to a crucifix, but to any mark or figure of a cross.

criterion /krī teéri ən/ (*pl* -**a** /-ə/) *n* a standard by which to judge things (*often pl*)

USAGE **criterion** or **criteria**? **Criterion** is singular, and **criteria** is plural; it is generally regarded as incorrect to use **criteria** as a singular noun (with **criterias** as a bogus plural).

critic /kríttik/ *n* 1 a reviewer of films, plays, publications, or arts events 2 a fault-finder

critical /kríttik'l/ *adj* 1 finding fault 2 giving comments, analyses, or judgments 3 crucial 4 essential 5 life-threatening —**critically** *adv* —**criticalness** *n*

critical mass *n* 1 the amount of fissionable material required for a nuclear chain reaction 2 the required size or amount

criticism /kríttissizəm/ *n* 1 an opinion criticizing somebody or something 2 disapproval 3 assessment of a creative work

criticize /krítti sīz/ (-**cizing, -cized**), **criticise** *vti* 1 express disapproval of the faults of somebody or something 2 give a considered assessment of something

SYNONYMS **criticize, censure, castigate, blast, condemn, nitpick** CORE MEANING: express disapproval or dissatisfaction with somebody or something

critique /kri teék/ *n* 1 a review of somebody's work 2 criticism of a creative work —**critique** *vt*

~~**criticism**~~ incorrect spelling of **criticism**

critter /kríttər/ *n* US, Can a living thing, often a child or an animal (*infml or regional*)

croak *n* a rough low vibrating sound made by a frog, crow, or a person with a sore throat

■ **v 1** *vi* produce a croak **2** *vti* say or speak in a croak **3** *vi* die *(slang)* —**croaky** *adj*

Croatia /krō áyshə/ country in SE Europe, on the Balkan Peninsula, bordering the Adriatic Sea. Cap. Zagreb. Pop. 4,334,142 (2001). —**Croatian** *n*, *adj*

crochet /krō shay/ *n* needlework using a hook to loop wool or thread ■ *vti* (**-cheting** /-shaying/, **-cheted** /-shayd/) make using crochet —**crocheter** /krō shayər/ *n*

crock¹ *n* a clay pot

crock² *n* a worn-out person or thing *(infml)*

crockery /krókəri/ *n* china or pottery dishes

Crockett /krókit/, **Davy** (1786–1836) US frontiersman

crocodile /krókə dīl/ (*pl* **-diles** *or* same) *n* **1** a large reptile with a long thick-skinned body and strong jaws that lives near water **2** leather from crocodile skin **3** a line of children walking in pairs *(infml)*

crocodile tears *npl* pretended or hypocritical tears

crocus /krókəss/ (*pl* **-cuses** *or* **-ci** /-kī, -kee/) *n* a spring flower with white, purple, or yellow petals

Croesus /kreéssəss/ *n* a very wealthy man

Croesus /kreéssəss/ (*fl* 6C BC) king of Lydia (560–546 BC) who was proverbially wealthy

croft *n* a small Scottish farm —**crofter** *n* —**crofting** *n*

croissant /krwáss oN/ *n* a crescent-shaped roll

Crompton /krómptən/, **Samuel** (1753–1827) British inventor

Cromwell /króm wel/, **Oliver** (1599–1658) English soldier and Lord Protector of England (1653–58)

crone *n* an offensive term for a woman of advanced years who is regarded as bad-tempered or malicious *(insult)*

cronie incorrect spelling of **chronic**

Cronin /krónin/, **A. J.** (1896–1981) Scottish novelist and physician

cronology incorrect spelling of **chronology**

Cronus /krónəss/, **Cronos, Kronos** *n* in Greek mythology, the god of the sky. Roman equivalent **Saturn**

crony /króni/ (*pl* **-nies**) *n* a close friend, especially one granted special favours *(disapproving)*

cronyism /króni izəm/ *n* the practice of doing favours for friends *(disapproving)*

crook /krook/ *n* **1** a criminal or dishonest person *(infml)* **2** a bend in something **3** a hook-shaped device **4** a shepherd's hooked stick ■ *vti* form into a bend ■ *adj* ANZ *(infml)* **1** unwell **2** unpleasant or unsatisfactory

ORIGIN A **crook** 'criminal' is literally a 'bent person.' The use is first recorded in the late 19C, but the word itself dates from the early medieval period and derives from an old Scandinavian form meaning 'hook.'

crooked /krookid/ *adj* **1** bent or twisted **2** set at an angle **3** illegal or dishonest *(infml)* —**crookedly** *adv* —**crookedness** *n*

croon *vti* **1** sing or murmur gently **2** sing smoothly and sentimentally —**croon** *n* —**crooner** *n*

crop *n* **1** a plant grown for food or other use **2** an amount produced by a plant or area in a particular period **3** a group of people or things in relation to a particular period of time **4** a whip handle **5** a short hairstyle **6** a storage pouch in the gullet of many birds ■ *vt* (**cropping, cropped**) **1** cut something very short **2** cut off part of a photo

☐ **crop up** *vi* happen or appear unexpectedly *(infml)*

crop circle *n* a mysterious flat circle in a field planted with crops

crop-dusting *n* the spraying of crops with chemicals from the air

cropper /króppər/ *n* a plant giving a particular yield ○ *a heavy cropper*

crop rotation *n* the growing of different crops in succession on a piece of land

crop top *n* a women's top exposing the midriff

croquet /krō kay, -ki/ *n* **1** a lawn game with balls and mallets **2** a stroke in croquet ■ *vti* (**-queting** /-kay ing, -ki ing/, **-queted** /-kayd, -kid/) knock somebody's croquet ball away

croquette /kro két/ *n* a small fried savoury cake

crore (*pl* **crores** *or* same) *n* S Asia ten million

crosier /krőzi ər, -zhər/, **crozier** *n* a hooked rod carried by bishop

cross *n* **1** a mark (X) consisting of two lines that bisect each other, used to mark or cancel something, or in place of a signature by somebody who cannot write **2** a Christian symbol consisting of a vertical line intersected at right angles by a shorter line **3** *also* **Cross** the wooden structure on which, according to the Bible, Jesus Christ died **4** a cross-shaped object or structure **5** a difficulty that has to be borne **6** a hybrid **7** in football or hockey, a pass sent across the pitch ■ *v* **1** *vt* draw a line across **2** *vti* move across **3** *vti* meet at one point **4** *vt* place things one across the other **5** *vi* be en route at the same time in the reverse direction *(refers to letters and other forms of communication)* **6** *vti* connect telephone lines wrongly, or be connected wrongly **7** *vt* interbreed plants or animals **8** *vt* make the Christian sign of the cross over somebody or something **9** *vt* in football or hockey, pass a ball across a pitch **10** *vt* go against somebody ■ *adj* annoyed or angry —**crossable** *adj* —**crossly** *adv* —**crossness** *n*

☐ **cross off** *vt* no longer include in a list

☐ **cross out** *vt* delete with a line

cross- *prefix* **1** crossing ○ *crosspiece* **2** opposing, opposite ○ *crosscurrent* **3** reciprocal, mutual ○ *cross-fertilization*

crossbar /króss baar/ *n* **1** a horizontal pole between two verticals **2** the horizontal bar connecting the handlebars to the saddle in a bicycle frame

crossbones /króss hōnz/ *npl* a symbol of two crossed bones

crossbow /króss bō/ *n* a weapon that fires bolts —**crossbowman** *n*

crossbreed /króss breed/ *vti* (-**bred**) breed new strains from genetically different individuals ■ *n* a product of crossbreeding —**crossbred** *adj, n*

crosscheck /króss chék/ *vt* 1 verify something in another way 2 in hockey, ice hockey, or lacrosse, obstruct an opponent by using your stick —**crosscheck** *n*

cross-country *adj* 1 done over fields or hills, or through woods 2 from one side of a country to the other ■ *n* races or racing over fields or hills, or through woods

cross-country skiing *n* skiing on flat ground

cross-cultural *adj* including or comparing different cultures —**cross-culturally** *adv*

crosscurrent /króss kurrənt/ *n* 1 a contrary flow 2 an opposite tendency

cross-examine *vt* 1 question a witness for the opposing side in a law court 2 question somebody relentlessly (*infml*) —**cross-examination** *n* —**cross-examiner** *n*

cross-eyed *adj* an offensive term meaning having one or both eyes turned in towards the nose

cross-fertilization *n* 1 the fertilization of a female sex cell by a male sex cell from a different individual, usually of the same species 2 a mutually beneficial exchange of ideas —**cross-fertilize** *vti*

crossfire /króss fīr/ *n* 1 gunfire from different directions 2 a fierce clash of opinions

cross-grained *adj* with the grain running across the length

crossing /króssing/ *n* 1 a point where somebody can cross a barrier such as a road, water, or a border 2 a point where routes cross 3 a trip across water

cross-legged /-légd, -léggid/ *adj* with knees apart and ankles crossed

crossover /króss ōvər/ *n* 1 a crossing place or transfer point 2 the extension of the popularity of an artistic work to a different audience 3 somebody or something whose popularity now extends to a different audience ■ *adj* mixing two different styles

crosspiece /króss peess/ *n* a part that crosses a structure

cross-platform *adj* available for different computer systems

cross-purpose *n* a conflicting purpose ◊ **at cross-purposes** not understanding each other, usually through failing to realize that the other person means or intends something different

cross-question *vt* cross-examine ■ *n* a question to a witness under cross-examination

cross-reference *n* a direction to a reader to look elsewhere for information ■ *v* 1 *vt* put cross-references into a text 2 *also* **cross-refer**

vti direct a reader to look elsewhere for information

crossroads /króss rōdz/ *n* (+ *sing verb*) 1 a road junction 2 a decisive moment

cross section *n* 1 a plane formed by cutting through an object at right angles to an axis 2 something cut in cross section 3 a representative sample —**cross-sectional** *adj*

cross-stitch *n* 1 a cross-shaped embroidery stitch 2 embroidery using cross-stitches —**cross-stitch** *vti*

cross-town *adj* going across town —**crosstown** /króss town/ *adv*

crosstrainer /króss traynər/ *n* 1 somebody training for different sports 2 a sports shoe for use in different sports —**cross-train** *vi*

crosswind /króss wind/ *n* a wind blowing across a route

crosswise /króss wīz/ *adv* 1 so as to cross or be positioned across 2 in a cross shape —**crosswise** *adj*

crossword /króss wurd/, **crossword puzzle** *n* a word puzzle on a square grid, with clues for filling in lines

crotch *n* 1 the place where the legs join the body 2 a place where a tree divides into two branches —**crotched** *adj*

crotchet /króchit/ *n* a musical note equivalent to a quarter of a semibreve in length, shown as a black dot with a stem

crotchety /króchəti/ *adj* irritable (*infml*) —**crotchetiness** *n*

crouch /krowch/ *vi* 1 squat 2 bend in preparation to pounce (*refers to animals*) —**crouch** *n*

croup[1] /kroop/ *n* a childhood throat inflammation producing breathing difficulties —**croupy** *adj*

croup[2] /kroop/, **croupe** *n* the hindquarters of a four-legged animal

croupier /kroópi ay, -ər/ *n* somebody in charge of a gambling table in a casino

crouton /kroo ton/ *n* a crunchy cube of fried bread used as a garnish (*usually pl*)

crow[1] /krō/ *n* a large black bird related to the rook and raven ◊ **as the crow flies** in a straight line

crow[2] /krō/ *vi* 1 cry like a cock 2 cry out happily (*refers to babies*) 3 boast —**crow** *n*

crowbar /krō baar/ *n* a strong metal bar used as a lever

crowd /krowd/ *n* 1 a large group of people gathered together 2 a set of people with some thing in common 3 the mass or majority of people ■ *v* 1 *vi* throng together 2 *vt* fill or pack something 3 *vti* press near to somebody or something 4 *vti* herd or cram a group into a place 5 *vti* advance or pass somebody or something by shoving —**crowded** *adj*

☐ **crowd out** *vt* push out by force of numbers

crown /krown/ *n* 1 a headdress symbolizing royalty 2 a headdress or title symbolizing achievement or victory 3 a reigning monarch

4 also **Crown** a monarch's power **5** an emblem resembling a crown **6** the top part of something **7** the top of the head **8** the visible part of a tooth **9** an artificial tooth ■ *vt* **1** confer royal status on somebody **2** reward somebody with a crown **3** be the summit of something **4** put the finishing touch to something **5** fit a crown on a tooth **6** top one thing with something else

Crown Colony *n* a British colony governed by the Crown

Crown Court *n* a criminal court in England and Wales

crowned head *n* a monarch

crowning /krówning/ *n* **1** a coronation **2** a stage in labour when the baby's head appears ■ *adj* **1** representing supreme achievement **2** forming a summit

crown prince *n* a male heir to a throne

crown princess *n* a female heir to a throne, or the wife of a crown prince

Crown Prosecution Service *n* in England and Wales, the official body that decides whether a case should be brought to trial

crow's feet *npl* wrinkles near the eyes

crow's-nest *n* **1** a lookout point at the top of a ship's mast **2** a high lookout point on land

crozier *n* CHR = **crosier**

CRT *n* a computer monitor containing a cathode ray tube

crucial /króosh'l/ *adj* **1** vital in determining an outcome **2** very important (*infml*)

crucible /króossib'l/ *n* **1** a container for melting ores or metals **2** a set of testing circumstances

~~crucifiction~~ incorrect spelling of **crucifixion**

crucifix /króossifiks/ *n* a representation of the crucified Jesus Christ

crucifixion /króossi fíksh'n/ *n* **1** a form of execution in which somebody is fixed on an upright cross to die **2** an execution by crucifixion **3** **Crucifixion** the crucifixion of Jesus Christ, according to the Bible

cruciform /króossi fawrm/ *adj* cross-shaped

crucify /króossi fī/ (*-fies, -fied*) *vt* **1** execute somebody by crucifixion **2** treat somebody cruelly

crud *n* filth (*slang*) —**cruddy** *adj*

crude *adj* (*cruder, crudest*) **1** unprocessed ○ *crude ore* **2** unskilful ○ *a crude model of a ship* **3** vulgar ○ *a crude gesture* ■ *n* unrefined petroleum —**crudely** *adv* —**crudeness** *n* —**crudity** *n*

crudités /króodi tay/ *npl* raw vegetable pieces eaten as an appetizer

cruel /króo əl/ (*-eller, -ellest*) *adj* **1** deliberately causing pain or distress **2** painful or distressing —**cruelly** *adv* —**cruelness** *n*

cruelty /króo əlti/ (*pl* -**ties**) *n* **1** a deliberately cruel act **2** the condition of being cruel

cruet /króo it/ *n* **1** a container for a condiment **2** a condiment set

Cruikshank /króok shangk/, **George** (1792–1878) British caricaturist and illustrator

cruise /krooz/ *v* (**cruising, cruised**) **1** *vti* travel over a sea **2** *vi* move at a steady fast rate **3** *vti* go out to seek a sexual partner (*slang*) **4** *vi* proceed in a casual way ■ *n* a journey by sea

cruise control *n* a device in a vehicle for maintaining a uniform speed

cruise missile *n* a long-range low-flying guided missile

cruiser /króozər/ *n* **1** a small warship **2** a cabin cruiser

cruller /krúllər/ *n* US, Can a small ring-shaped or twisted piece of deep-fried sweet dough

crumb /krum/ *n* **1** a small fragment of bread, cake, or biscuit **2** a small amount **3** the inner part of a loaf of bread ■ *v* **1** *vt* put crumbs on or in food **2** *vti* crumble

crumble /krúmb'l/ *v* (**-bling, -bled**) **1** *vti* reduce or be reduced to tiny bits **2** *vi* disintegrate ■ *n* a baked fruit pudding with a crumb topping

crumbly /krúmbli/ (**crumblier, crumbliest**) *adj* **1** tending to crumble **2** containing or covered with many crumbs —**crumbliness** *n*

crummy /krúmmi/ (**-mier, -miest**) *adj* (*infml*) **1** of little value **2** unwell or unhappy

crumpet /krúmpit/ *n* **1** a flat cake with an elastic texture and small holes, eaten toasted **2** *Scotland* a large thin pancake

crumple /krúmp'l/ (**-pling, -pled**) *vti* **1** crease and wrinkle **2** collapse, or make collapse —**crumple** *n* —**crumply** *adj*

crumple zone *n* a part of a motor vehicle that absorbs the force of an impact by collapsing

crunch *v* **1** *vt* munch noisily **2** *vti* make or cause something to make a crushing sound **3** *vt* rapidly process numbers or data (*infml*) ■ *n* **1** a crushing sound **2** also **crunch time** a decisive moment

crunchy /krúnchi/ (**-ier, -iest**) *adj* crisp and making a crunching sound when eaten or walked on —**crunchily** *adv* —**crunchiness** *n*

crusade /kroo sáyd/ *n* **1** also **Crusade** a medieval military expedition by European Christians to take back areas of the Holy Land from Muslim control **2** a religiously motivated war or campaign ■ *vi* (**-sading, -saded**) **1** campaign vigorously **2** fight in a medieval crusade

crusader /kroo sáydər/ *n* **1** also **Crusader** a soldier in one of the medieval crusades **2** a vigorous campaigner for or against something

cruse /krooz/ *n* a small earthenware container for holding liquids (*archaic*)

crush *v* **1** *vti* compress so as to cause injury or damage **2** *vti* crease **3** *vti* grind **4** *vt* quell a protest by force **5** *vt* overwhelm somebody or something **6** *vt* pulp fruit or vegetables **7** *vt* squash somebody **8** *vt* oppress somebody **9** *vt* humiliate somebody with a remark ■ *n* **1** a crowd of people **2** a crowded situation **3** a fruit drink **4** an infatuation (*infml*) —**crushing** *adj* ◊ See note at **love**

crush barrier *n* a barrier for restraining crowds

crushed *adj* describes fabric made to look crumpled

crust *n* 1 the hard outer part of a loaf of bread 2 a piece of crust or hard bread 3 the pastry cover or case for a pie 4 a hard outer layer on something 5 a scab 6 the solid outer layer of the Earth ■ *vti* 1 form a crust on something 2 make or become encrusted

crustacean /kru stáysh'n/ *n* a hard-shelled invertebrate animal with several pairs of legs, antennae, and eyes on stalks —**crustacean** *adj*

crusty /krústi/ (-ier, -iest) *adj* 1 with a crust 2 curt —**crustily** *adv* —**crustiness** *n*

crutch *n* 1 a walking aid consisting of a stick with a forearm or armpit rest 2 something providing help or support 3 a crotch ■ *vt* support with a crutch

crux (*pl* **cruxes** *or* **cruces** /króo seez/) *n* 1 a crucial point 2 a puzzling problem

Crux *n* the Southern Cross

cry *v* (**cries, cried**) 1 *vti* weep 2 *vti* shout 3 *vi* make a distinctive sound *(refers to birds or mammals)* ■ *n* (*pl* **cries**) 1 a loud inarticulate expression of rage, pain, or surprise 2 a shout 3 the distinctive call of a bird or animal 4 a period of weeping 5 a public demand for something ◊ **in full cry** in enthusiastic pursuit

☐ **cry off** *vi* cancel an arrangement *(infml)*

☐ **cry out** *v* 1 *vt* shout loudly 2 *vi* be in need

crybaby /krī baybi/ (*pl* **-bies**) *n* a person regarded as easily made to cry *(insult)*

crying /krī ing/ *adj* desperate or deplorable and demanding a remedy

cryogenics /krī ō jénniks/ *n* the study of extremely low temperatures *(+ sing verb)* —**cryogenic** *adj*

crypt /kript/ *n* an underground chamber *adj*

cryptic /kríptik/ *adj* 1 ambiguous or obscure 2 secret or hidden 3 indicating a crossword solution indirectly 4 using codes —**cryptically** *adv* —**crypticness** *n* ◊ See note at **obscure**

crypto- *prefix* secret, hidden ○ *cryptogram*

cryptogram /kríptə gram/ *n* 1 a coded message 2 a symbol with a secret meaning

cryptographic key *n* a parameter that determines the transformation of data to encrypted format

cryptography /krip tóggrəfi/ *n* 1 the study of codes 2 coded writing —**cryptographer** *n* —**cryptographic** /kríptə gráffik/ *adj* —**cryptographical** *adj*

crystal /kríst'l/ *n* 1 a clear colourless mineral, especially quartz 2 a piece of crystal 3 a solid with a patterned internal structure 4 something like a crystal ○ *snow crystals* ○ *crystals of salt* 5 heavy sparkling glass 6 crystal glass objects 7 a covering for a watch face ■ *adj* very clear and sparkling

crystal ball *n* 1 a fortune teller's globe 2 a means of predicting the future

crystal clear *adj* 1 very clear and sparkling 2 obvious or easily understood

crystalline /krístə līn/ *adj* 1 of or like crystal 2 very clear and sparkling

crystallize /krístə līz/ (-lizing, -lized), **crystallise** *vti* 1 make or become well defined 2 form crystals —**crystallization** /krístə lī záysh'n/ *n*

Cs *symbol* caesium

CS *abbr* 1 chief of staff 2 Christian Science 3 civil service 4 Court of Session

CSA *abbr* Child Support Agency

CSE *n* a former school-leaving certificate in England and Wales. Full form **Certificate of Secondary Education**

CS gas *n* a powerful tear gas

ORIGIN *CS* is from the initial letters of the surnames of the US chemists who developed the gas, B. B. Corson (1896–?) and R. W. Stoughton (1906–57).

CST *abbr* Central Standard Time

CT *abbr* computed tomography

Ct. *abbr* Count *(in titles)*

C to C /seè tə seé/, **C2C** *adj* of an Internet transaction between two consumers. Full form **consumer-to-consumer**

CTRL, Ctrl *abbr* control (key)

CTRL-ALT-DEL *n* the keystroke combination for rebooting a computer

CT scan *n* a diagnostic radiological scan of parts of the body using computed tomography

Cu *symbol* copper[1]

cu. *abbr* cubic

cub *n* 1 an offspring of a carnivorous mammal such as a bear or lion 2 a **Cub** a Cub Scout ■ *vi* (**cubbing, cubbed**) produce cubs

Cuba /kyoóbə/ country in the Caribbean Sea composed of two main islands and over 1,000 islets. Cap. Havana. Pop. 11,184,023 (2001). —**Cuban** *adj, n*

cubbyhole /kúbbi hōl/, **cubby** (*pl* **-bies**) *n* 1 a small space or room 2 a small storage compartment

cube[1] /kyoob/ *n* 1 a solid figure of six equal sides 2 a cube-shaped object 3 the product of a number multiplied by itself twice ■ *vt* (**cubing, cubed**) 1 dice food 2 multiply a number by itself twice

cube[2] /kyoó bay, koó-/, **cubé** *n* a plant with poisonous roots

cube root *n* a number that, when multiplied by itself twice, equals a given number

cubic /kyoóbik/, **cubical** *adj* 1 cube-shaped 2 three-dimensional 3 with a volume equal to that of a particular cube 4 of or containing a cubed variable 5 (*symbol* **c**) with three equal axes ■ *n* a cubic expression, equation, or curve

cubicle /kyoóbik'l/ *n* a partitioned area of a room

cubism /kyoóbizəm/ *n* an artistic style based on

geometric shapes —**cubist** n —**cubistic** /kyoo bístik/ adj

cubit /kyóobit/ n an ancient unit of length based on the distance from the elbow to the tip of the middle finger

cub reporter n a novice reporter

Cub Scout n a member of the junior branch of the Scouts

cuckold /kúkōld/ n a man whose wife is unfaithful ■ vt make a cuckold of —**cuckoldry** n

ORIGIN Cuckold is related to *cuckoo*. The underlying idea is probably of a man taking over another man's wife in the same way as a cuckoo uses another bird's nest. The word was adopted from French.

cuckoo /kóŏkoo/ n (pl **-oos**) **1** a bird that lays its eggs in other birds' nests **2** a cuckoo's call ■ adj bizarre (infml) ■ vi (**-oos, -ooed**) give the call of the cuckoo

cuckoo clock n a clock with a mechanical cuckoo that indicates the hour

cucumber /kyóŏ kumbər/ n **1** a long green fruit with white flesh used as a vegetable chiefly in salads **2** a plant that produces cucumbers

cud n partly digested food chewed a second time by a ruminant such as a cow

cuddle /kúdd'l/ (**-dling, -dled**) v **1** vti tenderly hug **2** vi assume a comfortable position —**cuddle** n

cuddly /kúdd'li/ (**-dlier, -dliest**) adj **1** pleasant to hold because of being soft, warm, or endearingly attractive **2** fond of cuddling

cudgel /kújjəl/ n a short heavy club —**cudgel** vt

cue[1] /kyoo/ n **1** a signal to somebody to do something, especially to a performer to come on stage or start performing **2** a prompt or reminder ■ vt (**cued**) give a signal or prompt to

SPELLCHECK Do not confuse the spelling of **cue** and **queue** ('a line of waiting people'), which sound similar.

□ **cue in** vt instruct or remind

cue[2] /kyoo/ n a stick used to strike the cue ball in billiards, snooker, or pool ■ vt (**cued**) strike with a cue

cue ball n the white ball struck in order to hit another ball in billiards, snooker, or pool

cue card n a large card from which somebody speaking on television reads

cuff[1] n **1** the part of a sleeve at the wrist **2** ANZ, US, Can the fold at the bottom of a trouser leg

cuff[2] vt hit with an open hand —**cuff** n

cuff link n a fastener for a shirt cuff (often pl)

cuirass /kwi ráss/ n a piece of armour for the upper body

cuisine /kwi zeén/ n **1** a cooking style **2** a range of food

cul-de-sac /kúl də sak, kóol-/ (pl **culs-de-sac**

/pronunc. same/ or **cul-de-sacs**) n **1** a street closed at one end **2** an impasse

culinary /kúllinəri/ adj of cooking

cull vt **1** remove an animal from a herd or flock **2** remove somebody or something from a group as worthless **3** select somebody or something **4** reduce a herd or group by killing members of it —**cull** n —**culler** n

culminate /kúlmi nayt/ (**-nating, -nated**) vti **1** come or bring to the highest point **2** finish spectacularly

culmination /kúlmi náysh'n/ n **1** the highest point of something **2** an act of reaching or bringing something to a climax

culottes /kyoo lóts/ npl women's shorts resembling a skirt

culpable /kúlpəb'l/ adj guilty —**culpability** /kúlpə bílləti/ n

culpable homicide n Scotland manslaughter

culprit /kúlprit/ n **1** a wrongdoer **2** an accused person

ORIGIN Culprit is thought to derive from a misinterpretation of a written abbreviation used in law courts. The earliest recorded examples, in the late 17C, are all of the formula 'Culprit, how will you be tried?', said by the clerk of a court to a person who has pleaded not guilty. It is surmised that this is a misunderstanding of a legal French abbreviation *cul. prist*, representing a longer expression meaning 'You are guilty; we are ready to prove it'. In 1700 **culprit** is recorded outside the legal formula and court records, meaning 'prisoner at the bar, the accused'. The modern sense of 'wrongdoer' is recorded in the middle of the 18C, and may be influenced by Latin *culpa* 'fault, blame'.

cult n **1** a minority religion regarded with disapproval by the majority **2** a group of adherents to a cult **3** idolization **4** an object of idolization **5** a fad **6** a system of supernatural beliefs —**cultish** adj —**cultist** n

cultivate /kúlti vayt/ (**-vating, -vated**) vt **1** prepare land for crops **2** grow plants **3** improve or develop something through study **4** become friends with somebody for personal advantage —**cultivable** adj —**cultivated** adj

cultivation /kúlti váysh'n/ n **1** the preparation of land for crops, or the growing of plants **2** improvement or development through education

cultivator /kúlti vaytər/ n a soil-breaking device

cultural /kúlchərəl/ adj **1** of a specific culture **2** of the arts —**culturally** adv

cultural cringe n Aus a feeling of national cultural inferiority

culture /kúlchər/ n **1** the arts **2** knowledge and sophistication **3** the shared beliefs and values of a group **4** a people with shared beliefs and values **5** the development of artefacts and symbols in the advancement of a society **6** the growing of biological material for scientific purposes **7** a biological material grown for scientific purposes **8** the cultivation of land ■ vt (-turing, -tured) 1 grow biological material for scientific purposes 2 cultivate plants

cultured /kúlchərd/ adj 1 educated and sophisticated 2 grown in a nutrient substance for scientific purposes

cultured pearl n an artificially created pearl

culture shock n a feeling of confusion resulting from sudden exposure to an unfamiliar culture

culvert /kúlvərt/ n 1 an underground duct 2 a structure covering a culvert

cum prep with (infml)

cumbersome /kúmbərsəm/ adj 1 heavy or bulky 2 complicated or problematic —**cumbersomely** adv —**cumbersomeness** n

Cumbria /kúmbri ə/ county in NW England. Pop. 490,300 (1995). —**Cumbrian** n, adj

cum dividend /kúm dívvidənd/ adv with a right to the current dividend when buying a security

cumin /kúmmin/, **cummin** n 1 aromatic seeds used as a spice 2 a plant that produces cumin

cummerbund /kúmmər bund/ n a broad band worn around the waist as part of a man's formal dress

cummings /kúmmingz/, **e. e.** (1894–1962) US poet

cum new adv with a right to new share offers when buying a security

cumulative /kyoómyóolətiv/ adj 1 gradually building up in strength or effect 2 resulting from successive additions —**cumulatively** adv

cumulonimbus /kyoómyóo lō nímbəss/ (pl -bi /-bī/ or -buses) n a tall dark thunder cloud

cumulus /kyoómyóoləss/ (pl -li /-lī/) n a large fluffy cloud —**cumulous** adj

AKG London

Cuneiform: Sumerian clay tablet (18C BC)

cuneiform /kyoóni fawrm/ adj 1 of an ancient writing system of SW Asia with wedge-shaped characters 2 wedge-shaped 3 of wedge-shaped ankle bones ■ n cuneiform script

cunnilingus /kúnni líng gəss/ n oral stimulation of a woman's genitals

cunning /kúnning/ adj 1 crafty and deceitful 2 cleverly thought out ■ n 1 craftiness and deceitfulness 2 skilful ingenuity or grace —**cunningly** adv —**cunningness** n

Cunningham /kúnningəm/, **Merce** (b. 1919) US dancer and choreographer

cunt n 1 a taboo term for a woman's genitals (offensive) 2 a taboo term for somebody seen as unpleasant or contemptible (insult)

cup n 1 a small drinking container with a handle 2 the contents of a cup 3 a volume measure used in cooking, equal to 227 ml/8 fl oz 4 an ornamental trophy awarded as a winner's prize 5 a sports competition to win a cup 6 a bowl-shaped object or part ■ vt (cupping, cupped) 1 form a hand or the hands into a cup shape 2 hold something in cupped hands —**cupful** n

cupbearer /kúp bairər/ n somebody who serves wine to royalty

cupboard /kúbbərd/ n a storage unit or recess with a door

cupboard love n a false show of affection to gain something

cupcake /kúp kayk/ n a small cake baked in a cup-shaped mould and usually iced

Cup Final n the final match in a knockout cup

cupid /kyoópid/ n 1 a representation of a young boy with wings and a bow and arrow, as a symbol of love 2 **Cupid** in Roman mythology, the god of love. Greek equivalent **Eros**

cupidity /kyoo píddəti/ n greed (fml)

cupola /kyoópələ/ n 1 a dome-shaped roof 2 a dome on a roof

cupric /kyoóprik/ adj containing copper with a valency of 2

cup tie n a match in a knockout cup

cur n a mongrel dog

curable /kyoórəb'l/ adj able to be cured

curaçao /kyoórə sō/ n an orange-flavoured liqueur

Curaçao /kyoórə sō/ largest island of the Netherlands Antilles, in the Caribbean Sea

curacy /kyoórəssi/ (pl -cies) n the position of a curate

curare /kyoo raári/, **curari** n 1 a dark resin from certain South American plants. Use: traditional arrow poison, muscle relaxant in medicine. 2 a vine from which curare is obtained

curate[1] /kyoórət/ n 1 a priest's assistant 2 a member of the clergy in charge of a parish

curate[2] /kyoo ráyt/ (-rating, -rated) v 1 vti look after a museum or gallery 2 vt organize an exhibition

curate's egg n something with good and bad parts

curative /kyoórətiv/ adj capable of curing ■ n a medicine or medical treatment

curator /kyoo ráytər/ n 1 the head of a museum or gallery 2 an exhibition organizer —**curatorial** /kyoórə táwri əl/ adj —**curatorship** n

curb n 1 an imposed limitation 2 a horse's bit and attached chain 3 a line of stones forming the edge of a lawn 4 a raised part surrounding a skylight or well 5 US, Can a kerb ■ vt restrain something

curd n 1 the solid part of sour milk used for

making cheese **2** a substance resembling milk curd ■ *vti* curdle —**curdy** *adj*

curdle /kúrd'l/ (**-dling, -dled**) *vti* separate into curds and whey

cure /kyuor/ *v* (**curing, cured**) **1** *vti* heal a person or animal **2** *vt* treat an illness successfully **3** *vt* resolve a problem **4** *vt* preserve food by drying, smoking, or salting **5** *vt* preserve or treat a substance or material by drying or adding chemicals ■ *n* **1** something that restores health **2** a recovery from ill health **3** a solution to a problem

curé /kyoor ay/ *n* a French priest

cure-all *n* a universal remedy

~~currency~~ incorrect spelling of **currency**

curettage /kyoóra taázh, kyoo réttij/, **curettement** /kyoo rétmant/ *n* the process of scraping inside a body cavity to remove unwanted tissue

curfew /kúr fyoo/ *n* **1** an official order for people to remain indoors after a specified time **2** a time or signal for a curfew **3** the length of a curfew

~~curiculum~~ incorrect spelling of **curriculum**

Marie Curie

Curie /kyoòri/, **Marie** (1867–1934) Polish-born French chemist and physicist. She pioneered research into radioactivity.

Curie, Pierre (1859–1906) French physicist. He shared the Nobel Prize in physics in 1903 with his wife, Marie Curie.

curio /kyoòri ō/ (*pl* **-os**) *n* an unusual artefact

curiosity /kyoòri óssəti/ (*pl* **-ties**) *n* **1** eagerness to know about something **2** inquisitiveness **3** somebody or something interesting and unusual

curious /kyoòri əss/ *adj* **1** eager to know **2** too inquisitive —**curiously** *adv* —**curiousness** *n*

~~curiousity~~ incorrect spelling of **curiosity**

Curitiba /koòri teéba/ capital of Paraná State, S Brazil. Pop. 1,476,253 (1996).

curium /kyoòri əm/ *n* (*symbol* **Cm**) a silvery-white metallic radioactive element

curl /v **1** *vti* put hair into waves, coils, or spirals, or be naturally like this **2** *vti* make or become curved or coiled **3** *vi* move in a curve or spiral ■ *n* **1** a lock of hair with a curved or coiled shape (*often pl*) **2** the tendency of hair to curl naturally **3** something curved or coiled **4** the adoption of a curved shape
□ **curl up** *vi* curve the body and draw up the legs

Curl, Robert Floyd (*b.* 1933) US chemist. He jointly discovered the molecular family of carbon called fullerenes.

curler /kúrlər/ *n* **1** a roller or device for curling hair **2** a player of the game of curling

curlew /kúr lyoo/ *n* a large brown shore bird with a curved bill

curlicue /kúrli kyoo/ *n* a curved decorative flourish —**curlicued** *adj*

curling /kúrling/ *n* a sport involving sliding stones on ice

curling tongs *npl* a heated rod for curling hair

curly /kúrli/ (**-ier, -iest**) *adj* **1** with curls **2** curved or coiled —**curliness** *n*

curmudgeon /kur mújjən/ *n* somebody irritable or stubborn —**curmudgeonly** *adj*

Curnow /kúr now/, **Allen** (1911–2001) New Zealand poet

currant /kúrrənt/ *n* **1** a small dried grape. Use: in cookery. **2** a small round fruit of a deciduous bush **3** a bush bearing currants

ORIGIN The **currant** originates in Corinth in Greece. Small dried grapes of high quality were exported from there in the Middle Ages, and were known in French, and then in English, as 'raisins of Corinth'. The actual early English form was *raisins of Corauntz*, abbreviated to *Corauntz* by the early 16C and **currant** by the end of the 16C. The term **currant** also came to be applied to northern fruits in the late 16C in the mistaken popular belief that these were the source of the E Mediterranean dried fruit.

SPELLCHECK Do not confuse the spelling of **currant** and **current** ('existing now'), which sound similar.

currency /kúrrənssi/ (*pl* **-cies**) *n* **1** a country's money **2** the acceptance of an idea or term **3** the circulation of something, especially money

current /kúrrənt/ *adj* **1** existing now **2** valid ■ *n* **1** a flow or stream of water or air **2** a flow of electricity **3** the rate of flow of electricity —**currently** *adv* —**currentness** *n* ◊ See note at **current**

current account *n* a bank account from which money may be withdrawn on demand

current affairs *npl* topical news items

curriculum /kə ríkyoòləm/ (*pl* **-la** /-lə/ *or* **-lums**) *n* the subjects taught in an educational institution, or the elements taught in a subject —**curricular** *adj*

curriculum vitae /kə ríkyoòləm vee tī, -ví tee/ (*pl* **curricula vitae** /kə ríkyoòlə-/) *n* a summary of somebody's qualifications and experience

curry[1] /kúrri/ *n* (*pl* **-ries**) **1** a dish of meat, fish, or vegetables in a highly spiced sauce **2** seasoning for curry ■ *vt* (**-ries, -ried**) cook in a highly spiced sauce

ORIGIN Curry comes from a language of S India and N Sri Lanka, and means literally 'sauce'.

curry[2] /kúrri/ (**-ries, -ried**) *vt* **1** groom a horse **2** give leather a flexible and waterproof finish

curry powder *n* a mixture of spices for making curry

curse *n* **1** a swearword **2** an appeal to a supernatural being for evil to happen **3** a source of harm ■ *v* (**cursing**, **cursed**) **1** *vi* use a swearword **2** *vt* swear at

cursed /kúrssid, kurst/ *adj* **1** supposedly made the victim of a curse **2** wicked or hateful **3** annoying or frustrating (*infml*) —**cursedly** *adv* —**cursedness** /kúrssidnəss/ *n*

cursive /kúrssiv/ *adj* written with the letters of a word joined together ■ *n* cursive writing —**cursively** *adv*

cursor /kúrssər/ *n* a moving marker on a computer screen indicating where a keystroke will appear ■ *vi* move a cursor

cursory /kúrssəri/ *adj* quick and superficial —**cursorily** *adv* —**cursoriness** *n*

curt *adj* **1** rudely brief **2** using few words —**curtly** *adv* —**curtness** *n*

curtail /kur táyl/ *vt* cut short —**curtailment** *n*

curtain /kúrt'n/ *n* **1** a piece of cloth hung to cover a window or door, or around a bed **2** a hanging cloth at the front of a stage in a theatre **3** the beginning or end of a performance, act, or scene in a theatre **4** a barrier or screen **5** something resembling a curtain ◇ *a curtain of water* ■ *vt* **1** cover or divide with a curtain **2** fit with curtains ◊ **bring down the curtain on** bring to an end (*infml*)

curtain call *n* an appearance by a performer to receive applause at the end of a performance

curtain raiser *n* **1** a short performance before the main one **2** a minor event before a major one

~~curtesy~~ incorrect spelling of **courtesy**

Curtin /kúrtin/, **John Joseph** (1885–1945) prime minister of Australia (1941–45)

~~curtious~~ incorrect spelling of **courteous**

curtsy /kúrtsi/ (**-sies, -sied**), **curtsey** *vi* bend the knees with one foot behind the other in respect (*refers to women*) —**curtsy** *n*

ORIGIN **Curtsy** is a contracted form of *courtesy*, used from the beginning of the 16C. It is found in a variety of *courtesy*'s meanings until the mid-17C, but in the late 16C began to specialize as a 'respectful gesture', and now is further restricted to a woman's bending of the knees.

curvaceous /kur váyshəss/ *adj* describes a woman with shapely curves —**curvaceousness** *n*

curvature /kúrvəchər/ *n* **1** the quality of being curved **2** degree of curve

curve *n* **1** a line with a regular smooth bend **2** something shaped in a curve ■ *vti* (**curving, curved**) **1** form or cause to form a curve **2** move in a curve —**curved** *adj* —**curviness** *n* —**curvy** *adj*

cushion /kóosh'n/ *n* **1** a soft filled bag for sitting on **2** a soft supportive or protective pad **3** something limiting the unpleasant effect of a situation ■ *vt* **1** protect against impact **2** reduce the unpleasant effect of **3** support or place on a cushion —**cushiony** *adj*

cushy /kóoshi/ (**-ier, -iest**) *adj* well-paid and easy (*infml*) —**cushily** *adv* —**cushiness** *n*

ORIGIN **Cushy** comes from a Hindi word meaning 'pleasant'. It is recorded from the 1st decade of the 20C.

cusp *n* **1** the border between two signs of the zodiac **2** either of the pointed ends of a crescent moon **3** a ridge on a molar tooth **4** a point of intersection of two arcs

cuss (*infml*) *vti* swear at somebody or something ■ *n* **1** somebody regarded as annoying **2** a swearword

custard /kústərd/ *n* **1** a sweet sauce made from eggs, milk, and sugar, or from milk and a special powder **2** a sweet dish of eggs, milk, and sugar —**custardy** *adj*

ORIGIN A **custard** was originally an open pie of meat or fruit (the name referred to the pie's pastry shell or crust). The filling included stock or milk, often thickened with eggs. By around 1600 the term indicated a dish in its own right made of eggs beaten into milk and cooked.

custard pie *n* a pie thrown in slapstick comedy

Custer /kústər/, **George Armstrong** (1839–76) US soldier

custodial /ku stódi əl/ *adj* **1** involving detention in prison **2** of legal custody of a child **3** of a custodian

custodian /ku stódi ən/ *n* **1** somebody responsible for looking after something valuable for somebody else **2** a protector or upholder of something valuable **3** a building caretaker —**custodianship** *n*

custody /kústədi/ *n* **1** detention by the police or the authorities **2** the legal right to look after a child **3** the state of being under somebody's protection

custom /kústəm/ *n* **1** a tradition **2** usual behaviour **3** the regular purchase of goods from a particular shop **4** a particular shop's customers ■ *adj* **1** made or changed to order **2** making goods to order ◊ See note at **habit**

customary /kústəməri/ *adj* usual or characteristic —**customarily** *adv* ◊ See note at **usual**

custom-built, custom-made *adj* built specially for one customer —**custom-build** *vt*

customer /kústəmər/ *n* **1** a buyer of goods or services **2** a particular type of person (*infml*) ◇ *a cool customer*

custom house, customs house *n* a place for collecting customs

customize /kústə mīz/ (**-izing, -ized**), **customise** *vt* change according to a specific requirement —**customization** /kústə mī záysh'n/ *n*

customs /kústəmz/ *n* (+ *sing or pl verb*) **1** *also* **Customs** a place where goods entering a country are examined to see what duty is payable on them **2** *also* **Customs** the government agency responsible for collecting duties on imported goods **3** duties payable on imports and exports

cut v(**cutting, cut**) 1 vti divide or separate something into pieces with a sharp tool 2 vti pierce or make a hole in something with a sharp tool 3 vi be sharp enough to cut something 4 vt injure somebody with a sharp object and cause bleeding 5 vt shorten something with a sharp tool 6 vt fashion a garment by cutting 7 vi take or be a short cut o *This path cuts through the woods.* 8 vt reduce or remove a quantity o *cut a budget* 9 vt shorten something by editing 10 vti delete computer data ♦ **paste** 11 vti edit a film, video, or TV programme 12 vi stop filming *(usually a command)* 13 vi change a scene suddenly when filming 14 vt stop providing something o *cut the supply of food to the refugee camps* 15 vt switch something off o *cut the engine* 16 vti divide a pack of cards in two after shuffling them 17 vt make a recording of a song or songs *(infml)* 18 vti remove grime from something in cleaning it 19 vti intersect 20 vi change direction sharply o *cut to the right* 21 vt grow a tooth through the gums 22 vt snub somebody 23 vti hurt somebody's feelings 24 vt dilute a liquid ■ n 1 a wound in the skin made by a sharp instrument 2 an incision 3 a reduction 4 a haircut 5 a garment style 6 a removal of a section of text or film, or a section removed 7 an edited version of a film o *the director's cut* 8 a share of money *(infml)* 9 a stopping of a supply 10 a piece of meat for cooking 11 a track on a musical recording 12 a dividing of a pack of cards in two after shuffling them 13 a block with a design cut in it used for printing *(often in combination)* 14 hurtful words or behaviour ■ adj 1 injured with something sharp 2 separated with a knife —**cuttable** adj ◊ **a cut above** superior to somebody or something else ◊ **cut and run** leave a place quickly to avoid being caught or detained ◊ **cut both ways** have both advantages and disadvantages ◊ **cut it fine** allow barely enough time for something ◊ **cut loose** behave in an unrestrained way *(infml)*

□ **cut back** v 1 vti reduce something 2 vt remove the top of a plant to encourage new growth

□ **cut down** v 1 vti reduce something 2 vt fell a tree 3 vt kill somebody

□ **cut in** v 1 vi interrupt somebody or something 2 vi join traffic dangerously 3 vti join the middle of a queue

□ **cut off** vt 1 stop supplying something 2 isolate somebody or something 3 stop somebody talking

□ **cut out** vi stop functioning o *The engine cut out.* ■ adj naturally suited for something

□ **cut up** vt pull in too soon in front of another vehicle when overtaking ■ adj upset *(infml)*

cut-and-dried adj 1 decided and fixed 2 predictable

cut-and-paste n a computer facility for deleting data from one place and inserting it in another —**cut-and-paste** vt

cutaway /kúttə way/ n a model from which a part is removed to show the inside ■ adj giving a view of the inside

cutback /kút bak/ n a reduction

cute /kyoot/ (**cuter, cutest**) adj 1 attractive in a childlike or endearing way 2 *US* shrewd —**cutely** adv —**cuteness** n

ORIGIN Cute is a shortened form of *acute*. It is first recorded in the early 18C, in the sense 'shrewd'; 'attractive' followed in the early 19C.

cutesy /kyoótsi/ (**-sier, -siest**) adj trying too hard to be charming —**cutesiness** n

cut glass n glass with a pattern cut in its surface

cut-glass adj 1 made of cut glass 2 sounding extremely upper-class

Cuthbert /kúthbərt/, **St** (630?–687) English missionary

Cuthbert, Betty (b. 1938) Australian sprinter

cuticle /kyoótik'l/ n 1 an edge of hard skin at the base of a fingernail or toenail 2 the epidermis 3 the protective outer layer of a plant or animal —**cuticular** /kyoo tíkyoŏlər/ adj

cutin /kyoótin/ n a waxy mixture forming the cuticle of a plant

cut-in n a camera shot that focuses on a smaller portion of a scene already established

cutlass /kúttləss/ n a short sword formerly used by sailors

cutler /kúttlər/ n a maker of cutlery

cutlery /kúttləri/ n 1 knives, forks, and spoons for eating 2 knives and other instruments with blades

cutlet /kúttlət/ n 1 a neck cut of lamb or veal 2 a flat cake of chopped food covered in breadcrumbs and fried

cutoff /kút of/ n 1 the limit or date when something stops 2 an end to the supply of something 3 a valve controlling the flow of fluid or gas ■ **cutoffs** npl shorts made by cutting off the legs of trousers

cutout /kút owt/ n 1 a silhouette shape 2 something cut out 3 a safety device for switching off an electric circuit

cutover /kút ōvər/ n the transfer from one computer system to a new system

cut-price, cut-rate adj 1 cheaper than usual 2 selling cheap goods

cutter /kúttər/ n 1 a sharp tool *(often pl)* 2 somebody who cuts something 3 a single-masted sailing boat

cutthroat /kút thrót/ adj aggressive and merciless ■ n 1 a murderer or other dangerous person 2 *also* **cutthroat razor** an old-fashioned razor with a long blade that folds into the handle

cutting /kútting/ n 1 a part of a plant removed for propagation 2 an article cut from a newspaper or magazine 3 an open trench cut through high ground for a railway, road, or canal ■ adj 1 abrasive and hurtful 2 very cold —**cuttingly** adv

cutting edge n the most advanced stage of something —**cutting-edge** adj

cutting room *n* a room where film is edited

cuttlefish /kútt'l fish/ (*pl* same *or* **-fishes**) *n* an invertebrate animal with ten arms and an internal shell that lives on the seabed

CV *abbr* curriculum vitae

CWO *abbr* chief Web officer

cwt *abbr* hundredweight

cyan /sí ən, -an-/ *n* a greenish-blue colour —**cyan** *adj*

cyanide /sí ə nīd/ *n* a poisonous inorganic salt

cyber- *prefix* **1** computers and information systems ○ *cybernetics* **2** virtual reality ○ *cyberspace* **3** the Internet ○ *cybercafé*

cybercafé /síbər kaffay/ *n* a café offering Internet access

cybercast /síbər kaast/ *n* a broadcast of an event transmitted on the Internet —**cybercast** *vti*

cybermediary /síbər meédi əri/ (*pl* **-ies**) *n* an organization that facilitates or collects fees for online transactions without owning the products or services

cybernate /síbər nayt/ (**-nating, -nated**) *vt* control a manufacturing process by computer —**cybernation** /síbər náysh'n/ *n*

cybernetics /síbər néttiks/ *n* (+ *sing verb*) **1** the study of communication in organisms, organic processes, and mechanical or electronic systems **2** the replication of biological control systems using technology —**cybernetic** *adj* —**cybernetician** /síbərni tísh'n/ *n*

cyberself /síbər self/ (*pl* **-selves** /-selvz/) *n* a false identity taken on by an Internet user

cybersex /síbər seks/ *n* sexual stimulation involving virtual reality or the Internet

cyberspace /síbər spayss/ *n* **1** the imagined place where electronic data goes **2** virtual reality

cybersquatting /síbər skwoting/ *n* the registration of a trademarked domain name in order to sell it to the trademark owner

cyberterrorism /síbər térrərizəm/ *n* the sabotage of computer systems by using the Internet —**cyberterrorist** *n, adj*

cyberwar /síbər wawr/ *n* warfare conducted with and against computer systems

cyborg /sí bawrg/ *n* a part-human, part-robot fictional being

cybrary /síbrəri/ (*pl* **-ies**) *n* an Internet library —**cybrarian** /síbráiri ən/ *n*

Cyclades /síklə deez/ large group of Greek islands in the S Aegean Sea. Pop. 88,485 (1981).

cyclamen /síkləmən/ *n* a flowering plant with heart-shaped leaves

cycle /sík'l/ *n* **1** a repeated sequence of events **2** a period of time between repeated events **3** a complete mechanical or electronic process **4** a bicycle **5** a bicycle ride **6** a series of linked literary or musical works ■ *v* (**-cling, -cled**) **1** *vi* ride a bicycle **2** *vti* put or go through a cycle

cyclic /síklik, sík-/, **cyclical** /-lik'l/ *adj* **1** occurring in cycles **2** composed of a closed ring of atoms —**cyclically** *adv* —**cyclicity** /sī klíssətl, si-/ *n*

cyclist /síklist/ *n* a rider of a bicycle

cyclone /síklōn/ *n* **1** a large-scale storm system with rotating winds **2** a violent rotating storm —**cyclonic** /sī klónnik/ *adj*

cyclops /sí klops/ (*pl* **-clopes** /sī klō peez/ *or* same) *n* **1** a one-eyed crustacean **2 Cyclops** in Greek mythology, a one-eyed giant

cyder /sídər/ *n* cider (*archaic*)

cygnet /sígnət/ *n* a young swan

cylinder /síllindər/ *n* **1** a tube shape **2** a tube-shaped geometrical solid or surface **3** a tube-shaped object **4** a chamber for a piston in an engine **5** a rotating part of a revolver containing cartridge chambers —**cylindered** *adj*

cylinder head *n* the closed detachable end of an engine cylinder

cylindrical /si líndrik'l/, **cylindric** /-drik/ *adj* cylinder-shaped —**cylindrically** *adv*

cymbal /símb'l/ *n* a circular brass percussion instrument

SPELLCHECK Do not confuse the spelling of **cymbal** and **symbol** ('a representation'), which sound similar.

cynic /sínnik/ *n* **1** somebody believing that people are insincere and motivated by self-interest **2** somebody sarcastic **3 Cynic** an ancient Greek philosopher who believed in virtue through self-control —**Cynic** *adj* —**cynicism** /sínnissizəm/ *n*

cynical /sínnik'l/ *adj* **1** distrustful of human nature **2** sarcastic **3** ignoring accepted standards of behaviour ○ *a cynical disregard for the welfare of employees* —**cynically** *adv*

cynosure /sínə syoor, sínnə-, -zyoor/ *n* the centre of attention (*fml*) —**cynosural** /sínə syóorəl, sínnə-, -zyóorəl/ *adj*

cypher *n* = cipher

cypress /síprəss/ *n* **1** a conifer with hard wood and leaves like scales **2** the hard wood of the cypress tree

Cypriot /síppri ət/, **Cypriote** *n* somebody from Cyprus ■ *adj* of Cyprus

Cyprus /síprəss/ island country in the E Mediterranean Sea, partitioned between the Greek Cypriot south and the officially unrecognized Turkish Republic of Northern Cyprus. Cap. Nicosia. Pop. 762,887 (2001).

Cyrano de Bergerac /sírrənō də búrzhə rak/, **Savinien** (1619–55) French poet and dramatist

Cyrillic /si ríllik/ *adj* of the alphabet used in the Slavic languages ■ *n* the Slavic alphabet

cyst /sist/ *n* **1** a spherical swelling containing fluid in human or animal tissue **2** a thin-walled bladder or sac in or enclosing an organism —**cystoid** /sís toyd/ *adj, n*

cystic /sístik/ *adj* **1** of a cyst **2** containing a cyst

cystic fibrosis /-fī bróssiss/ *n* a hereditary glandular disease affecting respiratory function

cystitis /si stítiss/ *n* inflammation of the bladder

cytology /sī tólləji/ *n* **1** the scientific study of cell structures and functions **2** the testing of cells from body tissue, especially for cancer diagnosis —**cytological** *adj* —**cytologist** *n*

cytoplasm /sítō plazəm/ *n* the contents of a cell excluding the nucleus —**cytoplasmic** /sítō plázmik/ *adj* —**cytoplasmically** *adv*

czar *n* = **tsar**

czarina *n* = **tsarina**

Czech /chek/ *n* **1** somebody from the Czech Republic **2** somebody from Czechoslovakia **3** the official language of the Czech Republic —**Czech** *adj*

Czechoslovakia /chékəslə vaáki ə, -vák-, chékō slō váki ə/ former country in central Europe, now divided into the Czech Republic and Slovakia

Czech Republic country in central Europe. Cap. Prague. Pop. 10,264,212 (2001).

D

d[1] (*pl* **d's**), **D** (*pl* **D's** *or* **Ds**) *n* **1** the 4th letter of the English alphabet **2** the Roman numeral for 500

d[2] *abbr* **1** date **2** daughter **3** day **4** degree **5** departs **6** depth **7** died

'd *contr* **1** did **2** had **3** should **4** would

d', D' see also under surname

D[1] (*pl* **D's** *or* **Ds**) *n* **1** the second note in the musical scale of C major **2** the 4th highest grade of a student's work

D[2] *symbol* **1** dispersion **2** drag

D[3] *abbr* **1** democratic **2** Department

DA *abbr* district attorney

d.a. *abbr* deposit account

dab[1] *vt* (**dabbing, dabbed**) **1** tap gently **2** apply gently to a surface ■ *n* **1** a small quantity **2** a gentle tap

dab[2] (*pl* **dabs** *or* **same**) *n* **1** a small brown European flatfish **2** a dab as food

dabble /dább'l/ (**-bling, -bled**) *v* **1** *vti* splash in water, or dip something in water **2** *vi* become involved superficially **3** *vi* move under water for food (*refers to ducks*) —**dabbler** *n*

dab hand *n* an expert (*infml*)

Dacca ♦ **Dhaka**

dace (*pl* same *or* **daces**) *n* **1** a small freshwater European fish with a slim olive-green body **2** a small North American freshwater fish

dacha /dácha/ *n* a Russian country home

dachshund /dáksənd, dásh-, -hoönd/ *n* a short long-bodied dog

ORIGIN **Dachshund** is an adoption of a German word that means literally 'badger dog'. The

breed was originally used to hunt badgers by burrowing into their setts.

~~dachsund~~ incorrect spelling of **dachshund**

dactyl /dáktil/ *n* **1** a metrical foot of three syllables, one long followed by two short **2** a finger or toe

dad, daddy /dáddi/ *n* a father (*infml*)

Dada /daà daa/, **dada, Dadaism** /-izəm/, **dadaism** *n* a European movement in literature and art of the early 20C

daddy longlegs /-lóng legz/ (*pl* same) *n* a long-legged fly

dado /dáydō/ *n* (*pl* **-does** *or* **-dos**) **1** the lower part of an interior wall, decorated differently from the upper part **2** a rectangular groove cut in a board to form part of a joint ■ *vt* (**-does, -doing, -doed**) **1** cut a dado in **2** insert into a dado

dado rail *n* a decorative rail fitted round an interior wall, usually at middle height

Daedalus /deéd aləs/ *n* in Greek mythology, a craftsman who built the Labyrinth to house the Minotaur and made wings to escape with his son Icarus

daemon /deémən, dī-, dáy-/, **daimon** /dí mōn/ *n* **1** a guardian spirit **2** a piece of software that carries out background tasks —**daemonic** /di mónnik/ *adj*

daffodil /dáffədil/ *n* a plant with yellow trumpet-shaped flowers

daffy /dáffi/ (**-fier, -fiest**) *adj* silly (*infml*)

daft *adj* not sensible (*infml*) ◊ a daft idea . —**daftly** *adv* —**daftness** *n*

Dafydd ap Gwilym /dávvith ap gwílllim/ (1320?–80?) Welsh poet

da Gama /də gaámə/ ♦ **Gama, Vasco da**

dagga /dúkhə, daágə/ *n* S Africa hemp used for smoking

dagger /dággər/ *n* **1** a short pointed knife used as a weapon **2** a sign resembling the shape of a dagger, used as a reference mark in a text ■ *vt* mark text with a dagger ◊ **look daggers at** look at in an angry or hostile way

daggy /dággi/ (**-gier, -giest**) *adj* ANZ (*infml*) **1** unfashionable **2** messy and untidy

Daguerre /də gáir/, **Louis Jacques** (1789–1851) French painter and pioneer photographer

Dahl /daal/, **Roald** (1916–90) British writer

dahlia /dáyli ə/ *n* a perennial plant with showy flowers

ORIGIN The **dahlia** is named after the Swedish botanist Andreas Dahl (1751–89), who discovered the plant in Mexico in 1788.

daily /dáyli/ *adj* done every day **2** for each day ■ *adv* on every day ■ *n* (*pl* **-lies**) a newspaper published every day (*often pl*)

Daimler /dáymlər/, **Gottlieb** (1834–1900) German engineer and inventor

daimon *n* = **daemon**

Daintree /dáyn tree/ river in N Queensland, Australia. Length 108 km/67 mi.

dainty /dáynti/ *adj* (**-lier**, **-tioct**) **1** delicate and pretty **2** tasty **3** refined in taste ■ *n* (*pl* **-ties**) a delicacy or titbit —**daintily** *adv* —**daintiness** *n*

ORIGIN **Dainty** first appears in English as a noun. It comes from a Latin word that is also the source of *dignity*. Both words entered English through French. The French word from which **dainty** derives showed the natural long development of the Latin word, but the French source of *dignity* had been consciously altered to conform to its Latin original. The adjective **dainty** developed from the noun. The idea of a delicacy or titbit, already present in French, gave rise to the sense 'choice, tasty' and then 'delicate and pretty'.

daiquiri /díkəri, dák-/ (*pl* **-ris**) *n* a cocktail made with rum and lemon or lime juice

dairy /dáiri/ (*pl* **-ies**) *n* **1** an establishment that sells, processes, or produces milk **2** *NZ* a grocery store —**dairy** *adj* —**dairyman** *n* —**dairywoman** *n*

SPELLCHECK Do not confuse the spelling of **dairy** and **diary** ('a personal record of events', 'a book for recording appointments').

dais /dáy iss, dayss/ *n* a raised platform in a hall

daisy /dáyzi/ (*pl* **-sies**) *n* **1** a low-growing wild flowering plant **2** a tall plant with large petals

ORIGIN **Daisy** is a contraction of *day's eye*. The flowers open and reveal a yellow disc in the morning, and close again at night.

daisy chain *n* a garland of daisies

daisycutter /dáyzi kutər/ *n* **1** in cricket, a ball that skims the ground **2** a bomb that detonates just above ground level to clear an area

Dakar /dák aar, -ər/ capital of Senegal. Pop. 1,708,000 (1995).

daks, dacks *npl ANZ* trousers (*infml*)

dal *n* FOOD = **dhal**

Dalai Lama /dállī laámə/ *n* the traditional secular and spiritual ruler of Tibet

dalasi /də laássi/ (*pl* **-sis**) *n* the main unit of Gambian currency

dale *n* **1** a lowland valley **2 dales, Dales** an area of wild moorland divided by valleys in N England

Dalek /dáa lek/, **dalek** *n* a malevolent robot

AKG London
Salvador Dali

Dali /daáli/, **Dalí, Salvador** (1904–89) Spanish painter —**Daliesque** /daáli ésk/ *adj*

dalia incorrect spelling of **dahlia**

Dalian /daá ll áːi/ port in NE China. Pop. 2,560,000 (1995).

Dalit /daálit/ *n* a member of the lowest caste in the Indian caste system

Dallas /dálləs/ city in NE Texas. Pop. 1,075,894 (1998).

dally /dálli/ (**-lies**, **-lied**) *vi* **1** act in a flirtatious manner **2** dawdle or waste time —**dalliance** *n*

Dalmatia /dal máyshə/ coastal region of Croatia bordering the Adriatic Sea

Dalmatian /dal máysh'n/ *n* **1** *also* **dalmatian** a spotted dog **2** somebody from Dalmatia —**Dalmatian** *adj*

Dalton /dáwltən/, **John** (1766–1844) British physicist and meteorologist. He laid the foundations of modern atomic theory and also first described colour blindness.

dam[1] *n* **1** a concrete barrier built across a river or lake to control the flow of water **2** a reservoir confined by a dam ■ *vt* (**damming**, **dammed**) **1** confine or restrain with a dam **2** obstruct

dam[2] *n* the female parent of an animal, especially of four-legged domestic livestock

damage /dámmij/ *n* **1** harm or injury **2** adverse effect **3** cost (*infml*) ■ **damages** *npl* money paid as compensation ■ *vt* (**-aging**, **-aged**) cause harm or injury to —**damaging** *adj*

Damascus /də máskəss, -maáskəss/ capital of Syria. Pop. 2,036,000 (1995). —**Damascene** /dámmə seen, -seén/ *n, adj*

damask /dámməsk/ *n* fabric with a pattern woven into it. Use: table linen.

damask rose *n* a rose with greyish-pink flowers. Use: essential oil.

dame *n* **1** *US, Can* a woman or girl (*often offensive*) **2** a married woman, especially one in charge of a household (*archaic*) **3 Dame** a title given to a woman awarded an order of chivalry **4 Dame** the wife of a baronet or knight

damn /dam/ *interj, adj, adv* expresses annoyance (*infml; sometimes offensive*) ■ *vt* **1** declare to be bad **2** doom to failure **3** condemn to hell

damnable /dámnəb'l/ *adj* detestable (*dated*) —**damnably** *adv*

damnation /dam náysh'n/ *n* **1** condemnation to hell or eternal punishment in hell **2** a sin ■ *interj* expresses anger (*dated*)

damned /damd/ *adj* **1** condemned to hell **2** expresses annoyance (*infml*) ■ *adv* very (*infml*) ■ *npl* people who have been condemned to hell

damnedest /dámdist/ *n* everything somebody can possibly do (*infml*)

damning /dámming/ *adj* **1** highly critical **2** proving that somebody or something is guilty, wrong, or bad —**damningly** *adv*

damp *adj* **1** moist **2** half-hearted ■ *n* **1** slight wetness **2** a harmful gas found in coalmines

■ *vt* **1** dampen **2** *also* **damp down** extinguish or make burn slowly —**dampness** *n*

dampcourse /dámp kawrss/ *n* a waterproof layer in a brick wall designed to stop damp rising

dampen /dámpən/ *vt* **1** moisten **2** deaden or stifle —**dampener** *n*

damper /dámpər/ *n* **1** a discouraging person or thing **2** a metal plate in a chimney that controls a fire **3** *Aus* unleavened bread **4** a device to control or stop vibration

Dampier /dámpi ər/, **William** (1652–1715) English explorer

damp squib *n* a letdown *(infml)*

damsel /dámz'l/ *n* a girl or young woman *(literary)*

damson /dámz'n/ *n* **1** a small purple plum **2** a fruit tree that produces damsons

dan, Dan *n* **1** any of the numbered black-belt proficiency levels in martial arts **2** somebody proficient in a martial art

dance *v* (**dancing, danced**) **1** *vti* move rhythmically to music **2** *vi* jump up and down in an emotional manner **3** *vi* move quickly or nimbly ■ *n* **1** a set of rhythmical body movements performed to music **2** a period of dancing **3** an occasion for dancing **4** the art of dancing **5** a piece of music for dancing —**danceable** *adj* —**dancer** *n* —**dancing** *n*

dance band *n* a band that plays music for dancing

dance floor *n* an area of a room for dancing

dance hall *n* a place where dances are held

D and C *n* a gynaecological procedure in which some of the lining of the uterus is removed. Full form **dilatation and curettage**

dandelion /dándi lī ən/ *n* a weed with yellow flowers

ORIGIN Dandelion was adopted from a French word meaning literally 'lion's tooth'. The name probably refers to the tooth-shaped edges of its leaves.

dander[1] /dándər/ *n* **1** particles shed from the hair or feathers of an animal **2** *Ireland* dandruff

dander[2] /dándər/, **daunder** /dáwndər/ *N England, Scotland n* a casual walk ■ *vi* saunter

dandle /dánd'l/ *vt* **1** move gently up and down **2** fondle or pet

dandruff /dándrəf, -druf/ *n* scales of dead skin on the scalp —**dandruffy** *adj*

dandy /dándi/ *n* (*pl* -**dies**) a fashionable man who is too concerned with his appearance *(dated)* ■ *adj* (-**dier, -diest**) *US, Can* excellent *(infml dated)* —**dandify** *vt* —**dandily** *adv* —**dandyish** *adj*

Dane *n* somebody from Denmark

danger /dáynjər/ *n* **1** exposure to harm **2** somebody or something that causes harm *(often pl)* ○ *the dangers of smoking*

danger money *n* extra money paid for dangerous work

dangerous /dáynjərəss/ *adj* **1** likely to cause harm **2** involving risk —**dangerously** *adv* —**dangerousness** *n*

dangle /dáng g'l/ (-**gling, -gled**) *v* **1** *vti* hang or cause to hang loosely **2** *vt* offer as an inducement —**dangly** *adj*

dangling participle *n* a participle not grammatically linked to the word it modifies

USAGE Dangling participles typically occur at the beginning of sentences and modify either the wrong thing or nothing in particular: *Startled by the noise, her book fell to the floor* (but it was she, not her book, who was startled). *Lying in the sun, it was hard to think of home* (who was lying in the sun?). Correct such mismatches by changing the wording: *Startled by the noise, she dropped her book* and *Lying in the sun, he found it hard to think of home.*

Danish /dáynish/ *adj* of Denmark ■ *n* **1** the official language of Denmark **2** *also* **danish** a Danish pastry ■ *npl* people from Denmark

Danish blue *n* a blue-veined cheese with a strong taste

Danish pastry *n* a puff pastry with a sweet filling

dank *adj* damp and cold —**dankly** *adv* —**dankness** *n*

D'Annunzio /da noónssi ō/, **Gabriele** (1863–1938) Italian novelist, poet, and playwright

Dante Alighieri /dánti alli gyálrī/ (1265–1321) Italian poet —**Dantean** /dánti ən, dan tee ən/ *adj, n*

Danton /dántən, daáN toN/, **Georges Jacques** (1759–94) French lawyer and revolutionary

Danube /dán yoob/ longest river in W Europe, flowing southeastwards from SW Germany into the Black Sea. Length 2,850 km/1,770 mi.

Danzig /dánssig/ ♦ **Gdansk**

Da Ponte /da pónti/, **Lorenzo** (1749–1838) Italian librettist and poet

dapper /dápər/ *adj* describes a man who is neat and elegant —**dapperly** *adv* —**dapperness** *n*

dappled /dápp'ld/, **dapple** *adj* spotted with a different colour

dapple-grey *adj* describes a horse of a light-grey colour with darker spots —**dapple-grey** *n*

Darby and Joan /daárbi ən jṓn/ *n* a contented and devoted couple who have been together for a long time

Dardanelles /daárdə nélz/ strait in NW Turkey linking the Aegean Sea with the Sea of Marmara. Length 70 km/43 mi.

dare /dair/ *modal v* (**daring, dared**) **1** have enough courage for ○ *I dared not ask.* ■ *vt* **2** have the audacity to do **3** issue a challenge to ■ *n* a challenge

daredevil /dáir dev'l/ *n* a risk-taker ■ *adj* **1** with carefree disregard of danger **2** dangerous

daresay /dáir sáy/ ◇ **I daresay, I dare say 1** expresses disbelief or scepticism **2** dismisses something that is true but considered irrelevant

Dar es Salaam /daár ess sə laám/ largest city in Tanzania. Pop. 1,747,000 (1995).

daring /dáiring/ adj 1 brave and adventurous 2 risky ■ n boldness —**daringly** adv —**daringness** n

Darius I /də rí əss/ (558–486 BC) king of Persia (521–486 BC)

dark adj 1 not light or lit 2 not light in colour 3 brownish or blackish 4 miserable ○ the dark days of the war 5 suggesting anger 6 nasty 7 mysterious 8 unenlightened or unsophisticated (fml) ■ n 1 a place or situation where there is little light 2 night or nightfall —**darkness** n ◇ **in the dark** unaware of something

Dark Ages npl the period before the Middle Ages

dark chocolate n chocolate to which milk has not been added

darken /daárkən/ vti 1 get darker, or make something darker 2 become unhappy, or make somebody unhappy

dark fibre n fibre optic cable that is not transmitting a signal

dark glasses npl sunglasses

dark horse n 1 a little-known person 2 an unexpectedly successful contestant or candidate

darkly /daárkli/ adv 1 threateningly 2 in black or a dark colour

dark matter n matter that astronomers claim makes up most of the universe

darkroom /daárk room, -rōom/ n a room for developing photographs

darling /daárling/ n 1 used as an affectionate term of address 2 a considerate person 3 a favourite ■ adj 1 dearly loved 2 shows approval (infml)

Darling /daárling/ river in S Queensland and New South Wales, Australia. Length 2,739 km/1,702 mi.

darn[1] vti repair fabric with a network of thread —**darning** n

darn[2] interj, adj, adv, vt damn (infml; euphemistic)

Darnley /daárnli/, **Henry Stewart, Lord** (1545–67) Scottish nobleman and second husband of Mary, Queen of Scots

dart n 1 a short weighted arrow used in the game of darts 2 a short arrow used as a weapon 3 a sudden fast movement 4 a stitched tapering fold in clothing ■ vti move or send swiftly

dartboard /daárt bawrd/ n a round target used in the game of darts

darts n an indoor game in which small weighted arrows are thrown at a target (+ sing verb)

Darwin /daárwin/ capital of Northern Territory, Australia. Pop. 86,600 (1998).

Darwin, Charles (1809–82) British naturalist.

He laid the foundation of modern evolutionary theory.

Darwinian /daar wínni ən/ adj of Darwin or his evolutionary theories —**Darwinian** n

Darwinism /daárwinizəm/ n the theory that living things originate, evolve, and survive in response to environmental forces —**Darwinist** n, adj

dash n 1 a short horizontal line used as a punctuation mark, often in place of a comma or colon 2 a horizontal line representing a long sound or flash of light in Morse code 3 a rush 4 a sprint race 5 a small quantity of one thing added to another 6 vigour and verve ■ v 1 vi hurry 2 vti knock or throw something violently, or be knocked or violently thrown (fml) 3 vt ruin something 4 vt discourage somebody

□ **dash off** vt create quickly (infml)

dashboard /dáshbawrd/ n a panel of controls and dials in front of the driver of a vehicle

dashing /dáshing/ adj 1 stylish 2 spirited (dated) —**dashingly** adv

dastardly /dástərdli/ adj treacherous or cowardly —**dastardliness** n

data /dáytə, daátə/ n (+ sing or pl verb) 1 factual information 2 information processed by a computer ■ plural of **datum**

USAGE Data is, strictly speaking, the plural of the noun datum. Its use as a singular noun is, however, extremely common, especially in computing contexts, and few perceive it as wrong these days.

data bank n 1 a store of information, especially when kept on a computer 2 a database

database /dáytə bayss/ n a large and structured collection of data on computer that can be accessed quickly

data capture n the collecting and entering of computer data

data centre n a place at which large amounts of data or information relating to a particular field of knowledge are stored

data element n the smallest piece of information in an electronic business transaction

dataglove /dáytə gluv/ n a glove used in a virtual reality system to allow the user to explore and feed information into the virtual environment

data mining n the search for hidden information in a database

dataport /dáytə pawrt/ n a socket for connecting a laptop to the Internet

data processing n operations performed on computer data

data protection n 1 the prevention of the misuse of computer data 2 the installation of safeguards for computer data

data warehouse n a database for commercial analysis

date[1] n 1 a string of numbers denoting a particular day, month, and year 2 a time that locates a past or future event 3 a period during which something was made **4** an appointment to meet somebody ○ *a dinner date* **5** a romantic appointment ○ *go out on a date* **6** a partner on a romantic date ■ *v* (**dating, dated**) **1** *vt* put a date on a document **2** *vt* assign a date to something **3** *vi* originate **4** *vi* go out of style **5** *vti* go on romantic dates with somebody ◊ **to date** up to the present time

date² *n* **1** a small oval fruit with a single hard narrow seed **2** *also* **date palm** a tall palm tree that produces dates

dated /dáytid/ *adj* **1** old-fashioned **2** showing a date

dateline /dáyt lin/ *n* a line at the head of a newspaper article giving the date and place of writing

date rape *n* rape committed during or after a romantic engagement —**date-rape** *vt*

date stamp *n* a stamp used for marking the date on documents —**date-stamp** *vt*

dating agency *n* an agency that finds potential romantic partners for people

dative /dáytiv/ *n* **1** in some languages, a grammatical word form that expresses an indirect object **2** a word in the dative form —**dative** *adj*

datum /dáytəm, dáa-/ (*pl* **-ta** /-tə/) *n* an item of information ◊ See note at **data**

daub *v* **1** *vt* apply blotchily **2** *vti* paint pictures crudely ■ *n* **1** a blotch **2** a bad painting

daughter /dáwtər/ *n* **1** a female child **2** a woman who is the product of something (*literary*) ○ *a true daughter of the revolution*

daughterboard /dáwtər bawrd/ *n* an auxiliary printed circuit board that connects to a computer's motherboard

daughter-in-law (*pl* **daughters-in-law**) *n* a son's wife

Daughters of the American Revolution *npl* a women's patriotic society in the United States

Daumier /dó mi ay/, **Honoré** (1808–79) French painter and caricaturist

daunt *vt* frighten or intimidate

dauntless /dáwntləss/ *adj* not usually frightened —**dauntlessly** *adv* —**dauntlessness** *n*

dauphin /dáwfin, dō-/ *n* formerly, a crown prince of France

ORIGIN Dauphin is essentially the same word as *dolphin*. Both come from Latin via French, but *dolphin* represents an earlier French form than **dauphin**. The title **dauphin** originally belonged to the lords of the Viennois, an area in SE France, whose coat of arms incorporated three dolphins. After the Viennois province of Dauphiné was sold to the French crown in 1343, the king gave it to his eldest son. From then on all eldest sons of the French monarch inherited it, along with the title **dauphin**.

Davao /də vów/ city on Mindanao island in the S Philippines. Pop. 1,191,000 (1995).

davenport /dáv'n pawrt/ *n* **1** a writing desk **2** *US, Can* a large sofa

David /dáyvid/, **St** (520?–589?) patron saint of Wales

David (*d.* 962 BC) king of Judah (1000–962 BC)

David, Sir Edgeworth (1858–1934) Welsh-born Australian geologist and explorer

David /da veed/, **Jacques-Louis** (1748–1825) French painter

David-and-Goliath *adj* describes a situation in which a much smaller and apparently weaker person or organization is pitted against one that is very large and powerful

ORIGIN The reference is to the biblical story of the killing of the Philistine giant Goliath by the young David using just a sling and a stone (1 Samuel 17).

Davies /dáyviss/, **Robertson** (1913–95) Canadian novelist, essayist, and playwright

Davies, W. H. (1871–1940) British poet

da Vinci ♦ **Leonardo da Vinci**

Davis /dáyviss/, **Bette** (1908–89) US film actor

Davis, Miles (1926–91) US jazz trumpeter and composer

Davis Cup *n* **1** an international men's tennis competition **2** the trophy awarded in the Davis Cup

Davy /dáyvi/, **Sir Humphry** (1778–1829) British chemist. He invented the miner's safety lamp.

dawdle /dáwd'l/ (**-dling, -dled**) *vi* **1** move annoyingly slowly **2** waste time —**dawdler** *n* —**dawdling** *n*, *adj*

Dawkins /dáwkinz/, **Richard** (*b.* 1941) British evolutionary biologist. He is best known for his book *The Selfish Gene* (1976), which describes the gene's strategy for survival.

dawn *n* **1** the first appearance of light in the sky as the Sun rises **2** the beginning of something ■ *vi* **1** begin (*refers to a new day*) ○ *The day dawned cloudy and wet.* **2** become apparent ○ *It finally dawned on me that few would survive.* **3** start to exist (*literary*)

dawn chorus *n* birdsong at daybreak

dawning /dáwning/ *n* the beginning of a day or period of time ■ *adj* developing

dawn raid *n* **1** a surprise military attack carried out at dawn **2** a corporate takeover strategy that involves buying up shares at the start of a day's financial trading

day *n* **1** a period of 24 hours **2** the period from sunrise to sunset **3** the part of a 24-hour period when somebody is working or active **4** an indefinite period or point in time **5** a period of fame or popularity **6** the period in somebody's life when he or she is active or involved in something ◊ **call it a day** finish work ◊ **carry** *or* **win the day** gain a victory ◊ **day after day** for days in a row ◊ **day by day** progressively ◊ **day in, day out** every day and all day long ◊ **have seen better days** be in a less prosperous or less good condition than previously ◊ **make somebody's day** make somebody very happy ◊ **save the day** prevent defeat or disaster

Dayan /dī án/, **Moshe** (1915–81) Israeli general and politician

daybook /dáy bŏŏk/ n an accounts book for daily records

dayboy /dáy boy/ n a male boarding-school pupil who lives at home

daybreak /dáy brayk/ n dawn

daycare /dáy kair/ n supervision or treatment given during the day to dependent people

daydream /dáy dreem/ n 1 a dream experienced while awake 2 an unrealizable hope or fantasy ■ vi (**-dreamt** /-dremt/ or **-dreamed**) think distracting thoughts —**daydreamer** n —**daydreaming** n

daygirl /dáy gurl/ n a female boarding-school pupil who lives at home

Day-Glo /dáy glō/ tdmk a trademark for fluorescent dyes and colouring agents

day job n the job somebody does to earn an income while trying to be successful in another field

Day-Lewis /day lŏŏ iss/, **Cecil** (1904–72) Irishborn British poet and novelist

daylight /dáy līt/ n 1 sunlight 2 daytime 3 dawn 4 public awareness or scrutiny

daylight robbery n overcharging (infml)

daylight-saving time n an adjustment of clock time to allow more hours of daylight at a particular time of year

daylong /dáy long/ adj, adv all day

day nursery n a nursery for preschool children

Day of Atonement n Yom Kippur

day release n days off from work for education

day return n a ticket or fare for a journey to a place and back in one day

day room n a communal recreation room in an institution

day school n 1 a private school without boarding facilities 2 a school with daytime classes only

days of grace npl extra days allowed for payment

daytime /dáy tīm/ n the sunlit part of the day ■ adj of or for daytime

day-to-day adj 1 everyday 2 one day at a time

day trading n the quick buying and subsequent selling of securities on the same day to make a profit on price movements —**day trader** n

day trip n a trip completed within a day —**day tripper** n

daze n a confused state ■ vt (**dazing, dazed**) 1 stun 2 bewilder —**dazed** adj —**dazedly** /dáyzidli/ adv

dazzle /dázz'l/ vti (**-zling, -zled**) 1 make somebody temporarily unable to see 2 greatly amaze and impress somebody ■ n light that dazzles

dazzling /dázzling/ adj 1 very bright 2 spectacularly impressive —**dazzlingly** adv

dB symbol decibel

Db symbol dubnium

DBA abbr doing business as (in e mails)

DBMS abbr database management system

DBS abbr direct broadcasting by satellite

DC abbr 1 Detective Constable 2 direct current

D-day n 1 the beginning of the Allied military operation to liberate Europe from Nazi occupation during World War II 2 the day when any activity is to begin

DDT n a powerful insecticide that has been widely banned since 1974. Full form **dichlorodiphenyltrichloroethane**

de, De see also under surname

de- prefix 1 opposite, reverse ○ deactivate 2 remove ○ decaffeinate 3 reduce ○ degrade 4 get off ○ deplane

deacon /deékən/ n 1 in some Christian churches, an ordained person ranking below a priest 2 in some Protestant churches, a lay person assisting a minister

deaconess /deékənəss/ n in some Christian churches, an ordained woman who ranks below a priest

deactivate /dee ákti vayt/ (**-vating, -vated**) vt 1 make something inactive 2 stop an active compound from working —**deactivation** /dee ákti váysh'n/ n

dead /ded/ adj 1 no longer alive 2 inanimate 3 without living things 4 without physical sensation 5 unwilling or unable to respond 6 lacking any signs of life 7 lacking activity or interest 8 no longer current or relevant 9 no longer operating 10 not burning 11 not resonant 12 totally quiet 13 sudden, abrupt, and complete 14 exact ■ npl dead people ■ adv 1 precisely 2 entirely 3 abruptly or immediately 4 very (infml) —**deadness** n

SYNONYMS dead, deceased, departed, late, lifeless, defunct, extinct CORE MEANING: no longer living, functioning, or in existence

dead beat adj exhausted (infml)

deadbeat /déd beet/ n somebody regarded as irresponsible and lazy (slang insult)

dead bolt, deadbolt /déd bōlt/ n a bolt without a spring, operated by a key or knob

dead duck n something or somebody with no chance of success or survival (slang)

deaden /dédd'n/ vt 1 make something less intense or resonant 2 desensitize somebody or something

dead end n 1 a point at which something ends abruptly 2 a passage that ends abruptly 3 a situation that leads nowhere

dead-end adj 1 with a closed end 2 without any prospect of progress or improvement

dead hand n an oppressive influence

deadhead /déd hed/ vt remove dead flowers from a plant

dead heat n a race or other contest in which two or more contestants finish together or have the same score —**dead-heat** vi

dead letter n 1 a letter that a postal service cannot deliver, e.g. because the address is incomplete **2** an unenforced or ineffective rule

deadline /déd līn/ *n* the time by which something must be done or completed

---

ORIGIN A **deadline** was originally a line marked around the boundary of a prison, beyond which prisoners were forbidden to stray on pain of death.

---

deadlock /déd lok/ *n* **1** a situation in which a negotiation is stalled because of an unwillingness to compromise **2** in sport, a draw **3** a lock that can only be opened with a key —**deadlock** *vti*

dead loss *n* **1** a person or thing regarded as completely useless (*infml*) **2** a complete loss for which no compensation is available

deadly /déddli/ *adj* (-**lier**, -**liest**) **1** causing death **2** very precise ○ *deadly aim* **3** extremely hostile ○ *deadly enemies* **4** dull (*infml*) ■ *adv* **1** like a dead person ○ *deadly pale* **2** completely

---

SYNONYMS deadly, fatal, mortal, lethal, terminal CORE MEANING: causing death

---

deadly nightshade *n* a plant with poisonous black berries

deadpan /déd pan/ *adj* purposely impassive ■ *adv* without expression ■ *n* an expressionless face or performer —**deadpan** *vi*

dead reckoning *n* a method of determining the position of a ship or aircraft by charting its course and speed from a known position

dead ringer *n* a person who looks very much like another (*infml*)

Dead Sea salt lake on the Israel-Jordan border that is 400 m/1,312 ft below sea level, the lowest point on Earth

dead shot *n* an expert shot

deadstart /déd staart/ *vti* coldboot a computer

dead time *n* a time lapse between the responses of an electrical component

dead weight *n* **1** a heavy weight **2** an oppressive burden

deadwood /déd wòòd/ *n* **1** dead trees and branches **2** a person or thing regarded as useless or superfluous

deaf /def/ *adj* **1** completely or partially unable to hear **2** unresponsive or indifferent ○ *deaf to our plea* ■ *npl* people who are deaf —**deafness** *n*

deaf aid *n* a hearing aid

deafen /déff'n/ *vt* **1** make somebody unable to hear **2** soundproof a room or building

deafening /déff'ning/ *adj* very loud —**deafeningly** *adv*

deaf-mute *adj* ⚠ an offensive term meaning unable to hear or speak (*dated*) —**deaf-mute** *n*

USAGE Deaf-mute and mute in reference to people who are unable to hear or speak are highly offensive and should be avoided. Preferred substitutes are *hearing-impaired* or *hearing-and-speech-impaired.*

Deakin /deekin/, **Alfred** (1856–1919) prime minister of Australia (1903–04, 1905–08, and 1909–10)

deal[1] /deel/ *n* **1** a business transaction **2** a bargain (*infml*) **3** a particular kind of treatment received from somebody (*infml*) ○ *a raw deal* **4** in a card game, a distribution of the cards ■ *v* (**dealt** /delt/) **1** *vti* in a card game, distribute the cards **2** *vti* sell illegal drugs **3** *vt* make somebody experience or suffer something ◇ **make a big deal out of** treat something as more important than it is (*infml*)

□ **deal in** *vt* trade in something
□ **deal out** *vt* distribute
□ **deal with** *vt* **1** take action to achieve or solve **2** have as a subject

deal[2] /deel/ *n* **1** softwood timber **2** a board of softwood

dealer /déelər/ *n* **1** a seller or trader **2** a seller of illegal drugs **3** somebody who deals cards

dealership /déelərship/ *n* **1** a franchise to sell a particular product **2** a dealer's premises

dealing /déeling/ *n* conduct or treatment, especially in business ■ **dealings** *npl* transactions and relations

dealmaker /déel maykər/ *n* a negotiator of business or political deals —**dealmaking** *n*

dealt past tense, past participle of **deal**[1]

dean /deen/ *n* **1** a senior academic administrator who manages a faculty **2** a senior member of the clergy in some churches —**deanship** *n*

ORIGIN Dean derives ultimately from Latin *decem* 'ten'. From this a compound meaning 'person in charge of ten others' was formed and developed into the French form that was the immediate source of **dean**. A variant of that French word was separately adopted into English as *doyen*.

---

deanery /déenəri/ (*pl* -**ies**) *n* **1** the position or residence of an academic dean **2** a group of parishes administered by a dean

dear /deer/ *adj* **1** beloved **2** costly **3** charging a lot **4 Dear** used before a name to begin a letter ■ *n* a person who is regarded fondly ■ *interj* expresses shock or regret ○ *Oh dear!* ■ *adv* dearly —**dearness** *n*

SPELLCHECK Do not confuse the spelling of **dear** and **deer** (the animal), which sound similar.

Dear John letter, Dear John *n* a letter from a woman terminating a relationship with a man

dearly /déerli/ *adv* **1** with strong feelings **2** at great cost

dearth /durth/ *n* a scarcity or lack ◊ See note at **lack**

death /deth/ *n* **1** the end of being alive **2** a way of dying **3** the fact that a particular person dies **4** the end of something —**deathless** *adj* —**death-like** *adj* ◇ **to death** very much ○ *bored to death*

deathbed /déth bed/ n a bed where somebody dies ■ adj while dying

deathblow /déth blō/ n 1 an action or event that destroys something 2 a killing blow

death camp n a camp where prisoners are systematically killed

death certificate n a document recording somebody's death

death-dealing adj fatal

death duty n a former name for the tax paid on inherited property

deathly /déthli/ adj 1 like death 2 extreme ■ adv extremely —**deathliness** n

death mask n a cast of a dead person's face

death penalty n capital punishment

death rate n the proportion of deaths to the population of a particular area

death rattle n a sound made in the throat while dying

death row /-rō/ n a set of cells for prisoners awaiting execution

death sentence n 1 the punishment of death, received in a court of law 2 something that has a fatal result

death's head n a human skull or its image

death squad n an organized group of people who murder their enemies or political opponents

deathtrap /déth trap/ n a dangerous building or vehicle (infml)

death warrant n 1 a legal order to execute somebody 2 something that is fatal

death wish n a desire to die

debacle /day baʼakʼl, di-/ n 1 a chaotic failure 2 a sudden breakup of river ice in spring

debar /di baʼar/ (-barring, -barred) vti exclude somebody from taking part in or belonging to something —**debarment** n

debark /di baʼark/ vi disembark —**debarkation** /deé baar kaysh'n/ n

debase /di báyss/ (-basing, -based) vt 1 reduce the quality or purity of 2 reduce the value or importance of —**debasement** n

debate /di báyt/ vti (-bating, -bated) 1 talk or argue about something 2 think about opposing aspects of something ■ n 1 an organized discussion of an issue 2 argument or prolonged discussion —**debatable** adj —**debatably** adv —**debater** n

debauch /di báwch/ (fml) vt 1 lead into immoral behaviour 2 seduce sexually ■ n an episode of immoral behaviour —**debaucher** n —**debaucherly** n

de Beauvoir, Simone ♦ Beauvoir, Simone de

debenture /di bénchər/ n 1 also **debenture bond** a bond backed only by the credit rating of the issuer 2 a certificate of debt —**debentured** adj

debilitate /di bílli tayt/ (-tating, -tated) vt sap the strength of —**debilitating** adj —**debilitation** /di bílli táysh'n/ n —**debilitative** adj

debility /di bílləti/ n general lack of energy or strength

debit /débbit/ n 1 a recorded debt or expense in accounts 2 a sum of money taken out of a bank account 3 a column for recording debts or expenses in an account ■ vt 1 record a debit in an account 2 take money from somebody's account as payment for something

debit card n a card used for shopping without cash, with the money transferred directly from the buyer's account to the seller's

debonair /débbə náir/ adj sophisticated and elegant —**debonairly** adv

debouch /di bówch, di boósh, dee-/ vi 1 move into more open terrain 2 emerge into a wider place (refers to a valley or a flow of water)

debrief /dee breéf/ vt question somebody after an event in order to find out information about it —**debriefing** n

debris /déb ree, dáy bree/, **débris** n fragments of something destroyed

debt /det/ n 1 something that is owed 2 the state of owing something

debtor /déttər/ n somebody who owes another person something

debug /dee búg/ (-bugging, -bugged) vt 1 find and remove errors in something, especially a computer program 2 remove secret listening devices from a place —**debugger** n

debunk /dee búngk/ vt show to be wrong or false

Debussy /də byoóssi/, **Claude** (1862–1918) French composer

debut /dáybyoo, débb-/ n 1 the first public appearance of a player or performer 2 a young woman's first formal social engagement, marking her entry into fashionable society ■ vti make, or cause to make, a first formal public appearance

debutante /débbyoo taant/ n a young woman being introduced into fashionable society

Dec. abbr December

decade /dék ayd, di káyd/ n a period of ten years

USAGE The pronunciation of **decade** with a stress on the second syllable is increasingly heard, but the traditional pronunciation puts the stress on the first syllable.

decadence /dékədənss/ n 1 a process or state of moral decline in society 2 uninhibited self-indulgence

decadent /dékədənt/ adj 1 in decline, especially morally 2 uninhibitedly self-indulgent —**decadent** n —**decadently** adv

decaf /deé kaf/ (infml) n a decaffeinated drink ■ adj decaffeinated

decaffeinated /dee káffi naytid, di-/ adj with the caffeine removed ■ n a drink from which the caffeine has been removed —**decaffeinate** vt

decamp /di kámp/ vi 1 suddenly or secretly leave 2 leave a camp —**decampment** n

decant /di kánt/ vt 1 pour a liquid gently into

another container so as not to disturb the sediment **2** move people temporarily

decanter /di kántər/ *n* a decorative bottle for serving drinks

decapitate /di káppi tayt/ (**-tating, -tated**) *vt* behead —**decapitation** /di káppi táysh'n/ *n*

decathlon /di káth lon, -lən/ *n* a contest involving ten athletic events —**decathlete** *n*

decay /di káy/ *v* **1** *vti* decompose, or cause to decompose **2** *vti* decline, or cause to decline **3** *vi* undergo radioactive disintegration ■ *n* **1** a state or process of decline or decomposition **2** a rotten or spoiled part **3** the disintegration of radioactive material **4** a gradual decrease in something

decease /di seéss/ *n* death *(literary)* ■ *vi* (**-ceasing, -ceased**) die *(fml)*

deceased /di seést/ *(fml) n* a person who has recently died ■ *adj* recently dead ◊ See note at **dead**

deceit /di seét/ *n* **1** the act or practice of misleading somebody **2** something done to mislead

deceitful /di seétf'l/ *adj* deliberately misleading —**deceitfully** *adv* —**deceitfulness** *n*

deceive /di seév/ (**-ceiving, -ceived**) *v* **1** *vt* intentionally mislead somebody **2** *vr* fool yourself

decelerate /dee séllə rayt/ (**-ating, -ated**) *vi* slow down —**deceleration** /dee séllə ráysh'n/ *n*

December /di sémbər/ *n* the 12th month of the year in the Gregorian calendar

ORIGIN December derives from the name of the tenth month of the Roman year, formed from Latin *decem* 'ten'.

decency /deéss'nssi/ *n* **1** conformity with moral standards **2** modesty or propriety ■ **decencies** *npl* the commonly accepted standards of good behaviour *(fml)*

decent /deéss'nt/ *adj* **1** conforming to accepted standards of moral behaviour **2** above average **3** satisfactory **4** wearing enough clothes to avoid embarrassment *(infml)* **5** kind —**decently** *adv* —**decentness** *n*

decentralize /dee séntrə līz/ (**-izing, -ized**), **decentralise** *vti* reorganize something in order to distribute power more widely —**decentralization** /dee séntrə lī záysh'n/ *n*

deception /di sépsh'n/ *n* **1** the practice of misleading somebody **2** something intended to mislead

deceptive /di séptiv/ *adj* **1** intended to mislead **2** able to be mistaken for something else —**deceptiveness** *n*

deceptively /di séptivli/ *adv* misleadingly

USAGE Is a **deceptively** large house surprisingly large or surprisingly small? Unless the context makes the meaning clear, **deceptively** is best avoided.

decibel /déssi bel, déssib'l/ *n (symbol* **dB**) a unit of relative loudness

decide /di sīd/ (**-ciding, -cided**) *v* **1** *vti* make a choice or come to a conclusion about some-

thing **2** *vt* end something in a definite way —**decidable** *adj*

decided /di sīdid/ *adj* **1** obvious ○ *a decided slant* **2** firm or certain

decidedly /di sīdidli/ *adv* unmistakably —**decidedness** *n*

decider /di sīdər/ *n* something that settles a contest or argument

deciduous /di síddyoo əss/ *adj* **1** describes a plant or tree that sheds its leaves in autumn **2** consisting of deciduous trees

~~decieve~~ incorrect spelling of **deceive**

decimal /déssim'l/ *adj* using the number 10 as a base ■ *n* a number in the decimal system —**decimally** *adv*

decimalize /déssimə līz/ (**-izing, -ized**), **decimalise** *vti* convert a country's currency or measuring system to a decimal system —**decimalization** /déssimə lī záysh'n/ *n*

decimal place *n* a position after the decimal point

decimal point *n* a dot in a decimal number that divides the whole numbers from the smaller divisions

decimate /déssi mayt/ (**-mating, -mated**) *vt* **1** kill or remove a large proportion of **2** almost destroy completely —**decimation** /déssi máysh'n/ *n*

decipher /di sīfər/ *vt* **1** make out what a piece of writing says **2** work out the meaning of something —**decipherable** *adj* —**decipherment** *n*

decision /di sízh'n/ *n* **1** a choice or conclusion arrived at after thinking **2** firmness in choosing **3** the process of choosing

decisive /di síssiv/ *adj* **1** settling something **2** able to make definite decisions —**decisively** *adv* —**decisiveness** *n*

deck *n* **1** a floor on a ship **2** a section of a passenger vehicle on one level **3** an audio unit for playing a particular type of recording **4** *US, Can* a level of a building or other structure **5** *US, Can* a pack of cards ■ *vt* decorate or adorn something or somebody *(literary)* ○ *all decked out for the party* —**decked** *adj* ◊ **clear the deck** *or* **decks** get rid of all obstacles prior to beginning a new task ◊ **hit the deck** fall on the floor or ground *(infml)*

deck chair *n* a folding wood and canvas chair

decking /déking/ *n* material forming a deck or seating platform in a garden

declaim /di kláym/ *vti* speak, or say formally and dramatically

declamation /déklə máysh'n/ *n* **1** a formal dramatic speech **2** the process of declaiming

declamatory /di klámmətəri/ *adj* **1** formal and dramatic in speech **2** loud and impressive but with little meaning —**declamatorily** *adv*

declaration /déklə ráysh'n/ *n* **1** a formal statement **2** an official proclamation **3** the process of making a declaration

declaration of independence *n* a formal statement asserting freedom

declarative /di klárrətiv/ *adj* in the form of a statement —**declaratively** *adv*

declare /di kláir/ (**-claring, -clared**) *v* 1 *vti* announce something clearly or loudly 2 *vt* state something formally or officially 3 *vt* reveal goods to customs officials as dutiable or taxable 4 *vt* announce that a particular condition exists 5 *vti* in bridge, say which suit is trumps 6 *vi* in cricket, choose to end an innings

déclassé /day kláss ay, -kláass-, dáy kla sáy/ *adj* reduced to a lower class or status in society

declassify /dee klássi fī/ (**-fies, -fied**) *vt* remove from an official list of confidential or top-secret material —**declassification** /dee klássifi káysh'n/ *n*

declension /di klénsh'n/ *n* 1 a set of nouns, adjectives, or pronouns that take the same inflections 2 the process by which sets of nouns, adjectives, or pronouns form inflections 3 the process of worsening or falling away (*fml*) —**declensional** *adj*

decline /di klín/ *v* (**-clining, -clined**) 1 *vti* refuse an invitation 2 *vt* refuse to participate in something 3 *vi* diminish 4 *vi* get weaker 5 *vti* form inflections, or list all the inflections of a noun, adjective, or pronoun ■ *n* 1 deterioration 2 a period near the end of something —**declination** /dékli náysh'n/ *n*

declivity /di klívvəti/ (*pl* **-ties**) *n* 1 a sloping surface 2 the fact that something slopes downwards

decoction /di kóksh'n/ *n* 1 the process of extracting something by boiling a substance 2 a concentrated substance extracted by boiling

decode /dee kốd/ (**-coding, -coded**) *vt* 1 decipher a coded message 2 establish the meaning of something expressed indirectly —**decodable** *adj* —**decoder** *n*

décolletage /dáy kol taa*zh*, day kóllə taa*zh*/ *n* a low neckline

décolleté /day kól tay, -kóllə tay/ *n* a woman's upper chest, visible above a low neckline ■ *adj* 1 with a low neckline 2 wearing a low-cut garment

decolonize /dee kóllə nīz/ (**-nizing, -nized**), **decolonise** *vt* grant independence to a colony —**decolonization** /dee kóllə nī záysh'n/ *n*

decommission /deèkə mísh'n/ *vt* remove from service

decompiler /deèkəm pílər/ *n* a computer program that translates basic machine code into high-level code

decompose /deèkəm pốz/ (**-posing, -posed**) *vti* 1 rot, or cause organic matter to rot 2 break down, or cause something to break down, into smaller or simpler pieces —**decomposable** *adj* —**decomposition** /deè kompə zísh'n/ *n*

decompress /deèkəm préss/ *vt* 1 reduce the atmospheric pressure in an enclosed space 2 expand computer data stored in a compressed form —**decompression** *n*

decompression chamber *n* a sealed room where decompression is carried out

decompression sickness, decompression illness *n* a condition experienced by divers who come to the surface of water too quickly, causing nitrogen to form in the blood and tissues

decongestant /deèkən jéstənt/ *n* a medicine that relieves nasal congestion —**decongestant** *adj* —**decongestive** *adj*

deconstruct /deèkən strúkt/ *vt* analyse a text using the theories of deconstruction

deconstruction /deèkən strúksh'n/ *n* critical analysis in which no single meaning is assumed and the apparent unity of a symbol, text, or film is questioned —**deconstructionist** *n, adj*

decontaminate /deèkən támmi nayt/ (**-nating, -nated**) *vt* remove contamination from —**decontamination** /deèkən támmi náysh'n/ *n* —**decontaminative** *adj*

decontrol /deèkən trốl/ (**-trolling, -trolled**) *vt* remove official restraints or regulations from

decor /dáy kawr, dék-/, **décor** *n* 1 the style of interior furnishings 2 stage scenery

decorate /dékə rayt/ (**-rating, -rated**) *v* 1 *vt* make something attractive by adding ornamental elements 2 *vti* paint or wallpaper a building or room 3 *vt* award somebody a medal

decoration /dékə ráysh'n/ *n* 1 an attractive item 2 ornamentation 3 the painting and wallpapering in a room 4 an award or honour

decorative /dékərətiv/ *adj* 1 attractive but not functional 2 of the decoration in a room 3 ornamental —**decoratively** *adv* —**decorativeness** *n*

decorator /dékə raytər/ *n* somebody whose job is decorating rooms

decorous /dékərəss/ *adj* 1 socially acceptable in a formal or solemn setting 2 dignified —**decorously** *adv* —**decorousness** *n*

decorum /di káwrəm/ *n* 1 dignity or decorous behaviour 2 the appropriateness of an artistic element to the work as a whole

decouple /dee kúpp'l/ (**-pling, -pled**) *vt* separate or disengage one thing from another

decoy /deè koy, di kóy/ *n* 1 something used by hunters to attract the animal they are hunting, often a model of the animal itself 2 anything that lures somebody into a trap ■ *vt* deceive by a decoy

ORIGIN Decoy probably represents Dutch *de kooi*, where *de* is the definite article, 'the', and *kooi* is the word for 'decoy'.

decrease *vti* /di kreéss/ (**-creasing, -creased**) lessen, or cause something to lessen, in size or degree ■ *n* /deè kreéss/ 1 a process of decreasing 2 a reduction —**decreasing** *adj* —**decreasingly** *adv*

decree /di kreé/ *n* 1 an official order 2 a court ruling —**decree** *vt*

decree absolute (*pl* **decrees absolute**) *n* a final divorce ruling

decree nisi /-nī sī/ (*pl* **decrees nisi**) *n* an interim divorce ruling

decrepit /di kréppit/ *adj* **1** old and in poor condition **2** not young or strong *(infml)* —**decrepitly** *adv* —**decrepitude** *n* ◊ See note at **weak**

decrescendo /deékrə shéndō/ *adv* with a gradual decrease in volume ■ *n* (*pl* **-dos**) a piece or passage of music played decrescendo —**decrescendo** *adj*

decriminalize /dee krímminə līz/ (**-izing, -ized**), **decriminalise** *vt* legalize something that was formerly illegal —**decriminalization** /deè krímminə līzáysh'n/ *n*

decry /di krí/ (**-cries, -cried**) *vt* criticize strongly —**decrial** *n* —**decrier** *n*

decrypt /dee krípt/ *vt* decode —**decryption** *n*

dedicate /déddi kayt/ (**-cating, -cated**) *vt* **1** devote attention or energy to something **2** set something aside as special **3** address a work of art to somebody **4** set something apart as holy **5** play a piece of music to somebody on the radio, as a tribute —**dedicative** /-kətiv, -kaytiv/ *adj* —**dedicatory** /-kətəri, -kaytəri/ *adj*

dedicated /déddi kaytid/ *adj* **1** devoted to a particular cause or job **2** intended only for one purpose

dedication /déddi káysh'n/ *n* **1** the quality of being dedicated **2** an inscription in a book **3** a piece of music played on the radio as a tribute to somebody **4** the setting aside of something for a particular purpose —**dedicational** *adj*

deduce /di dyoóss/ (**-ducing, -duced**) *vt* **1** reach a particular conclusion by using information logically **2** infer something from a general principle —**deducible** *adj*

SYNONYMS **deduce, infer, assume, reason, conclude, work out, figure out** CORE MEANING: reach a logical conclusion on the basis of information

deduct /di dúkt/ *vt* subtract an amount

deductible /di dúktəb'l/ *adj* liable to be deducted —**deductibility** /di dúktə bílləti/ *n*

deduction /di dúksh'n/ *n* **1** a conclusion drawn from available information **2** the drawing of a conclusion **3** an amount deducted **4** the subtraction of an amount **5** the process of reasoning logically

deductive /di dúktiv/ *adj* of deduction —**deductively** *adv*

deed *n* **1** something done **2** a legal document, especially one enshrining ownership

deed of covenant *n* a signed agreement to make payments to a charity or other organization over a particular period

deed poll *n* a document signed by one party only, especially a document by which somebody legally changes his or her name

ORIGIN **Deed poll** does not follow the usual rules of English word formation, which would dictate that the first word, **deed**, modifies and describes the second word, **poll**. It is usually pronounced like that now, too, with the heavier stress on **deed**. In fact a **deed poll** is a kind of

deed, one that is cut cleanly at the edge rather than indented, as it would be if two copies that needed to be matched up were being produced. **Poll** is an adjective, a shortened form of *polled* 'cut cleanly'.

deejay /deé jay/ *n* a DJ *(infml)* —**deejay** *vi*

deem *vt* consider to be *(fml)*

deep *adj* **1** extending down from a surface **2** far from top to bottom or front to back **3** far from the edge or top **4** made up of a particular number of rows **5** coming from or reaching inside the body **6** low in pitch **7** dark in colour **8** extreme or intense **9** intellectually profound ■ *adj, adv* **1** relatively near your own goal **2** in cricket, relatively near the boundary ■ *adv* far ■ *n* **1** the sea **2** in cricket, a fielding position far from the batsman —**deeply** *adv* —**deepness** *n* ◊ **in deep** very involved

deep-dish *adj* describes food baked in a deep container

deepen /deépən/ *vti* **1** make or become deep or deeper **2** make or become more intense

deep end *n* the part of a swimming pool where the water is deepest ◊ **be thrown in at the deep end** have to do something new or difficult with very little experience ◊ **go off (at) the deep end** fly into a rage

deep-freeze *vt* **1** freeze something quickly **2** keep something very cold —**deep-frozen** *adj*

deep-fry *vt* cook food in deep oil —**deep-fried** *adj*

deep-pan *adj* describes a pizza with a thick base

deep-rooted, deep-seated *adj* firmly held or believed in

deep-sea *adj* of the deep waters far from the coast

deep-set *adj* describes eyes having deep sockets

Deep South region in the SE United States, usually considered to consist of Alabama, Georgia, Louisiana, Mississippi, and South Carolina, and regarded as the heartland of traditional Southern culture

deer /deer/ (*pl same*) *n* any of various ruminant mammals the males of which have antlers ◊ See note at **dear**

ORIGIN The original meaning of **deer** was simply 'animal'. It goes back to an ancient root that apparently signified 'breathing creature'. The modern more restricted sense had superseded 'animal' by the 15C.

deerskin /deér skin/ *n* a deer's hide

deerstalker /deér stawkər/ *n* a tweed hat with earflaps that can be tied back

de-escalate /dee éskə layt/ (**de-escalating, de-escalated**) *vt* reduce the level or intensity of a difficult or dangerous situation —**de-escalation** /deé eskə láysh'n/ *n*

deface /di fáyss/ (**-facing, -faced**) *vt* spoil the appearance of —**defacement** *n*

de facto /day láktō/ *adv* in fact ■ *adj* existing in fact but without legal sanctions ■ *n* (*pl* **de factos**) *ANZ* a partner with whom somebody lives (*infml*)

defalcate /deé fal kayt, -fawl-/ (**-cating, -cated**) *vt* embezzle assets —**defalcation** /deé fal káysh'n, -fawl-/ *n*

defame /di fáym/ (**-faming, -famed**) *vt* harm the reputation of —**defamation** /déffa máysh'n/ *n* —**defamatory** /di fámmətəri/ *adj* ◊ See note at **malign**

default /di fáwlt/ *n* **1** an option that will be automatically selected by a computer if the user chooses no other **2** a failure to do something, especially to meet a financial obligation, appear in court, or take part in a competition ■ *vi* **1** fail to pay a debt, appear in court, or take part in a competition **2** use a computer's preset option

defeat /di feét/ *vt* **1** win a victory over an enemy or competitor **2** cause the failure of something **3** baffle somebody ■ *n* **1** an instance of losing to an opponent **2** failure

SYNONYMS defeat, beat, **conquer**, **vanquish**, **overcome**, **triumph over**, **thrash**, **trounce** CORE MEANING: win a victory

defeatist /di feétist/ *adj* expecting failure ■ *n* somebody who expects failure —**defeatism** *n*

defecate /déffə kayt/ (**-cating, -cated**) *v* **1** *vi* expel faeces (*fml or technical*) **2** *vt* remove impurities from a solution —**defecation** /déffə káysh'n/ *n*

defect *n* /deé fekt/ **1** a personal failing or weakness **2** a feature that prevents something from being perfect ■ *vi* /di fékt/ **1** leave your native country for political reasons **2** abandon an allegiance —**defection** /di fékshən/ *n* —**defector** /di féktər/ *n* ◊ See note at **flaw**

defective /di féktiv/ *adj* **1** faulty **2** incomplete —**defectively** *adv* —**defectiveness** *n*

defence /di fénss/ *n* **1** protection, especially from enemy attack **2** something that gives protection **3** justification **4** a defendant and his or her lawyer in court **5** in sports, defensive play or players —**defenceless** *adj* —**defencelessness** *n*

defence mechanism *n* **1** a frame of mind that avoids emotional distress **2** a natural protective response

defend /di fénd/ *v* **1** *vt* protect somebody or something from attack by an enemy **2** *vti* represent an accused person in court **3** *vt* support a position or belief **4** *vi* in sports, resist an opponent **5** *vt* try to keep a title, especially in sports **6** *vt* in sports, protect your goal —**defendable** *adj* ◊ See note at **safeguard**

defendant /di féndənt/ *n* the accused person in legal proceedings

~~defendent~~ incorrect spelling of **defendant**

defender /di féndər/ *n* **1** a protector **2** a supporter **3** in sports, a defensive player **4** the holder of a title that is challenged

Defender of the Faith *n* a title held by British monarchs since Henry VIII

defense *n* US = **defence**

defensible /di fénssəb'l/ *adj* **1** able to be protected **2** justifiable —**defensibly** *adv*

defensive /di fénssiv/ *adj* **1** quick to deflect perceived criticism **2** designed to give protection **3** in sports, favouring defence as a playing strategy —**defensively** *adv* —**defensiveness** *n* ◊ **on the defensive** expecting criticism or aggression

defer¹ /di fúr/ (**-ferring, -ferred**) *vti* postpone something —**deferment** *n* —**deferral** *n*

defer² /di fúr/ (**-ferring, -ferred**) *vi* submit to somebody else's judgment or wishes

~~defered~~ incorrect spelling of **deferred**

deference /déffərənss/ *n* **1** respect, especially in putting another person's interests first **2** submission

deferential /déffə rénsh'l/ *adj* showing respect, often to the point of obsequiousness —**deferentially** *adv*

deferred annuity *n* an investment that pays out some time after the final premium has been paid

~~deffered~~ incorrect spelling of **deferred**

defiance /di fí anss/ *n* open disobedience

defiant /di fí ənt/ *adj* **1** challenging somebody or something aggressively **2** openly disobedient —**defiantly** *adv*

deficiency /di físh'nssi/ (*pl* **-cies**) *n* **1** a shortage, especially of a nutrient **2** an amount by which something falls short ◊ See note at **lack**

deficiency disease *n* a disease resulting from a lack of required nutrients

deficient /di físh'nt/ *adj* **1** lacking in something, especially something necessary **2** inadequate —**deficiently** *adv*

deficit /déffəsit/ *n* a shortfall ◊ See note at **lack**

defile¹ /di fíl/ (**-filing, -filed**) *vt* **1** damage the reputation of **2** destroy the sanctity of **3** make dirty (*fml*) —**defilement** *n* —**defiler** *n*

defile² /di fíl/ *n* **1** a narrow mountain pass **2** a narrow passage ■ *vi* (**-filing, -filed**) march in single file

~~definate~~ incorrect spelling of **definite**

~~definately~~ incorrect spelling of **definitely**

define /di fín/ (**-fining, -fined**) *v* **1** *vti* give the meaning of a word **2** *vt* state something exactly **3** *vt* characterize somebody or something **4** *vt* show something clearly —**definable** *adj* —**definably** *adv*

definite /déffənət/ *adj* **1** with clear limits ○ *set a definite age range for membership* **2** fixed and not to be altered ○ *Is there a definite date for the meeting?* **3** certain and unlikely to have a change of mind ○ *I'm definite about this.* **4** obvious or unquestionable ○ *a definite turn for the better* —**definiteness** *n*

USAGE **definite** or **definitive**? **Definite** describes something as being clearly defined or precise without making any strong judgment about it: *He has definite ideas on the subject.* **Definitive** means conclusive, decisive, or authoritative and is a more evaluative word: *It's the definitive book on the subject.*

definite article *n* the word 'the' in English, or a word with a similar function in another language

definitely /déffənətli/ *adv* **1** certainly **2** finally and unchangeably ○ *Has she definitely decided to go?* **3** clearly and unmistakably

definition /déffə nísh'n/ *n* **1** a statement of the meaning of a word, e.g. in a dictionary **2** the act of defining a word **3** clarification **4** the clarity of an image or sound, or the sharpness of an edge —**definitional** *adj*

definitive /di fínnətiv/ *adj* **1** conclusive and final **2** most authoritative —**definitively** *adv* —**definitiveness** *n* ◊ See note at **definite**

~~definitly~~ incorrect spelling of **definitely**

deflate /di fláyt/ (-**flating, -flated**) *v* **1** *vti* let the air out of something, or lose the air inside and become flat **2** *vt* make somebody less confident or hopeful **3** *vt* cause deflation in an economy —**deflated** *adj*

deflation /di fláysh'n/ *n* **1** collapse because of air loss **2** loss of confidence or hope **3** reduced economic activity —**deflationary** *adj*

deflect /di flékt/ *v* **1** *vti* change course as a result of hitting something, or cause to change course **2** *vt* direct attention away from something —**deflective** *adj* —**deflector** *n*

deflection /di fléksh'n/ *n* **1** a change of course **2** the amount by which something is deflected **3** the act of diverting attention from something

deflower /dee flówər/ *vt* **1** have sex with a virgin (*literary*) **2** strip a plant of flowers

Defoe /di fó/, **Daniel** (1660?–1731) English novelist and journalist

defoliant /dee fóli ənt/ *n* a chemical that removes leaves

defoliate /dee fóli ayt/ (-**ating, -ated**) *vt* strip the leaves from —**defoliation** /dee fóli áysh'n/ *n*

deforest /dee fórrist/ *vt* remove all or most of the trees from —**deforestation** /dee fórri stáysh'n/ *n*

deform /di fáwrm/ *v* **1** *vt* make distorted or twisted **2** *vti* spoil —**deformation** /dée tawr máysh'n/ *n* —**deformed** *adj*

deformity /di fáwrməti/ (*pl* **-ties**) *n* **1** the condition of being badly formed or disfigured **2** something with a shape that is far from the norm

DEFRA /déffrə/ *abbr UK* Department of the Environment, Food, and Rural Affairs

defragment /dée frag mént/, **defrag** /dée frag/ (-**fragging, -fragged**) *vt* reorganize the storage space on a computer's hard disk

defraud /di fráwd/ *vt* cheat somebody out of money

defray /di fráy/ *vt* pay some or all of the cost of —**defrayal** *n* —**defrayment** *n*

defrock /dee frók/ *vt* remove a priest from the clergy

defrost /di fróst, dee-/ *v* **1** *vt* remove ice from something **2** *vti* thaw frozen food, or become thawed —**defroster** *n*

deft *adj* **1** quick and skilful **2** clever —**deftly** *adv* —**deftness** *n*

defunct /di fúngkt/ *adj* **1** no longer operating **2** dead (*humorous*) —**defunctness** *n* ◊ See note at **dead**

defuse /dee fyóoz/ (-**fusing, -fused**) *vt* **1** make a bomb harmless **2** ease a tense or violent situation

SPELLCHECK Do not confuse the spelling of **defuse** and **diffuse** ('spread widely'), which sound similar.

defy /di fí/ (-**fies, -fied**) *vt* **1** openly resist the authority of **2** challenge to do something **3** not be explained or clarified by ○ *defies all logic*

Degas /dáy gaa/, **Edgar** (1834–1917) French painter and sculptor

Charles de Gaulle

de Gaulle /də gól/, **Charles, General** (1890–1970) president of France (1959–69)

degenerate *vi* /di jénnə rayt/ (-**ating, -ated**) become worse ■ *adj* /di jénnə rət/ **1** in a worsened condition **2** inferior ■ *n* /di jénnə rət/ a person regarded as immoral or corrupt —**degeneracy** *n* —**degenerately** *adv* —**degeneration** /di jénnə ráysh'n/ *n*

degenerative /di jénnərətiv/ *adj* gradually worsening

degradation /déggrə dáysh'n/ *n* **1** great humiliation brought about by loss of status or self-esteem **2** the act of humiliating somebody **3** a decline in quality **4** the process of decline or breakdown —**degrade** /di gráyd/ *vti* —**degraded** *adj* —**degrading** *adj*

degree /di grée/ *n* **1** extent or amount **2** an educational qualification awarded by universities and higher-education colleges **3** (*symbol* °) a unit of temperature measurement ○ *degrees Celsius* **4** (*symbol* °) a unit for measuring angles **5** (*symbol* °) a unit of latitude or longitude **6** a classification of the severity of burns on a body **7** (*symbol* °) a unit of measurement on some scales, e.g. alcohol content of spirits **8** in grammar the state of an adjective or adverb in the positive, comparative, or superlative form **9** an indication of the closeness of a family relationship **10** social status (*fml or literary*) ○ *a family of high degree*

degression /di grésh'n/ *n* a gradual decrease (*fml*) —**degressive** *adj*

De Havilland /də hávvilənd/, **Sir Geoffrey** (1882–1965) British aviation pioneer and aircraft designer

dehumanize /dee hyóomə níz/ (-**izing**, -**ized**), **dehumanise** vt **1** make somebody less human **2** take away the people-friendly features of something —**dehumanization** /dee hyóomə nī záysh'n/ n —**dehumanizing** adj

dehumidifier /dee hyoo míddi fīr ər/ n a device for removing moisture from the air in a room or building —**dehumidification** /dee hyoo míddifi káysh'n/ n —**dehumidify** vt

dehydrate /dee hī dráyt/ (-**drating**, -**drated**) v **1** vt remove water from **2** vti lose, or cause somebody to lose, body fluids —**dehydrated** adj —**dehydration** n

de-ice /dee íss/ (**de-icing, de-iced**) vt remove or keep ice from

deify /dee i fī, dáy-/ (-**fies, -fied**) vt **1** make into a god **2** honour or adore —**deification** /dee ifi káysh'n, dáy-/ n

deign /dayn/ vi do something in a manner that shows you think it is beneath you

deism /dee izəm, dáy-/ n belief in God that argues a basis in reason and that holds that God made the world but does not interfere in it —**deist** n —**deistic** /dee ístik, day-/ adj

deity /dee iti, dáy-/ (pl -**ties**) n **1** a god or goddess **2** divine status

déjà vu /dáy zhaa voó, -vyoó/ n **1** the feeling of having experienced something before when you know that this is not true **2** boring familiarity

dejected /di jéktid/ adj very unhappy or unhopeful —**dejectedly** adv

dejection /di jéksh'n/ n great unhappiness or lack of hope

de jure /dee joóri, day yoó ray/ adv, adj by law

Dekker /dékər/, **Thomas** (1572?–1632) English dramatist and pamphleteer

de Klerk /də klúrk/, **F. W.** (b. 1936) president of South Africa (1989–94)

de Kooning /də koóning/, **Willem** (1904–97) Dutch-born US artist

del. abbr delete

de la see also under surname

Delacroix /déllə krwaa/, **Eugène** (1798–1863) French painter and lithographer

de la Mare /də la máir/, **Walter** (1873–1956) British poet, anthologist, and novelist

~~delapidated~~ incorrect spelling of **dilapidated**

de la Tour, Georges ♦ La Tour, Georges de

Delaware /déllə wair/ state of the E United States. Cap. Dover. Pop. 783,600 (2000). —**Delawarean** /déllə wáiri ən/ n, adj

delay /di láy/ v **1** vti put something off until later **2** vt make somebody or something late ○ I was delayed at the office. ■ n **1** lateness **2** the extent of lateness

delayed action n the activation of a mechanism a short time after it has been set

delectable /di léktəb'l/ adj **1** good to eat **2** delightful ■ n something very tasty

—delectability /di léktə bílləti/ n —**delectably** adv

delectation /dee lek táysh'n/ n delight (fml)

delegate n /délligət, délli gayt/ somebody chosen to represent or given the authority to act on behalf of another ■ vti /délli gayt/ (-**gating, -gated**) **1** give a task to **2** give power or authority to somebody —**delegator** n

delegation /déllə gáysh'n/ n **1** a group representing others at a meeting or conference **2** the act of giving responsibility to somebody else

~~delemma~~ incorrect spelling of **dilemma**

delete /di leét/ vt (-**leting, -leted**) remove or erase something printed, written, or stored in a computer ■ n also **delete key** a computer key that is pressed to remove data

deleterious /délli teéri əss/ adj harmful —**deleteriously** adv —**deleteriousness** n

deletion /di leésh'n/ n **1** the removal of something written, printed, or stored in a computer **2** something removed or crossed out

delft, Delft n white pottery with blue designs

ORIGIN The pottery takes its name from Delft, a city in the W Netherlands.

Delhi /délli/ city in N India and capital of the Union Territory of Delhi. Pop. 7,206,704 (1991).

deli /délli/ (pl -**is**) n a delicatessen (infml)

deliberate adj /di líbbərət/ **1** intentional **2** careful ■ vti /di líbbə rayt/ (-**ating, -ated**) think about something carefully —**deliberately** adv —**deliberateness** n —**deliberative** adj

deliberation /di líbbə ráysh'n/ n (fml) **1** careful thought **2** discussion

delicacy /déllikəssi/ (pl -**cies**) n **1** a delicious or highly prized food **2** sensitivity to the feelings of others **3** the need for tact **4** subtlety and refinement **5** fragility **6** lack of strength

delicate /déllikət/ adj **1** having a fine structure that is easily damaged or broken **2** physically weak or unwell **3** subtle ○ a delicate shade of blue **4** with fine details **5** skilful **6** needing tact **7** with a refined and sensitive taste **8** easily offended **9** measuring accurately —**delicately** adv —**delicateness** n ◊ See note at **fragile**

delicatessen /déllikə téss'n/ n **1** a specialized food shop **2** prepared food sold in a delicatessen

delicious /di líshəss/ adj **1** good to eat **2** delightful —**deliciously** adv —**deliciousness** n

delight /di líit/ n **1** joy or pleasure **2** somebody or something that brings joy or pleasure ■ v **1** vti give joy or pleasure to somebody **2** vi gain enjoyment from ○ delights in outwitting her brother —**delighted** adj —**delightedly** adv

delightful /di líitf'l/ adj very pleasing —**delightfully** adv —**delightfulness** n

delimit /di límmit/ vt establish or mark the limits of something —**delimitation** /di límmi táysh'n/ n

delimiter /di límmitər/ *n* in computing, a character marking the end or beginning of a data element

delineate /di línni ayt/ (**-ating**, **-ated**) *vt* 1 describe or explain in detail (*fml*) 2 draw or portray 3 demarcate —**delineable** *adj* —**delineation** /di línni áysh'n/ *n* —**delineative** *adj*

delinquent /di língkwənt/ *n* a lawbreaker, especially a young offender ■ *adj* 1 antisocial or unlawful 2 ignoring a duty (*fml*) —**delinquency** *n*

deliquesce /délli kwéss/ (**-quescing**, **-quesced**) *vi* 1 dissolve gradually by absorbing moisture from the air 2 form many branches without a main stem —**deliquescent** *adj*

delirious /di lírri əss/ *adj* affected by delirium —**deliriously** *adv* —**deliriousness** *n*

delirium /di lírri əm/ (*pl* **-ums** *or* **-a** /-ri ə/) *n* 1 a temporary mental disturbance marked by extreme confusion and sometimes hallucinations, caused by fever, poisoning, or brain injury 2 great excitement

delirium tremens /-trémmenz, -treé menz/ *n* a condition caused by alcoholism, marked by agitation, tremors, and hallucinations

Delius /deéli əss/, **Frederick** (1862–1934) British composer

deliver /di lívvər/ *v* 1 carry something to a person or address 2 *vt* assist during the birth of a baby 3 *vt* give birth to a baby 4 *vt* make a speech or announcement 5 *vt* throw a ball or punch 6 *vi* do as you promised 7 *vt* provide or produce something —**deliverance** *n*

delivery /di lívvəri/ (*pl* **-ies**) *n* 1 the act of delivering something 2 a regular visit by a postal service or vendor's vehicle 3 an item brought to a person or address 4 the act of giving birth 5 a manner of speaking 6 a rescue from captivity, harm, or evil

dell *n* a small valley (*literary*)

Delors /də láwr/, **Jacques** (*b*. 1925) French president of the European Commission (1985–94)

Delos /deé loss/ smallest of the Greek Cyclades islands —**Delian** *adj*, *n*

delouse /deé lowss/ (**-lousing**, **-loused**) *vt* remove the lice from the skin of a person or animal

Delphi /délfi/ ancient Greek town in central Greece, the site of the Temple of Apollo and an oracle

delphinium /del fínni əm/ (*pl* **-ums** *or* **-a** /-ni ə/) *n* a tall plant with flowers that grow on spikes

ORIGIN **Delphinium** derives from a Greek word for 'larkspur' that literally means 'little dolphin'. The name refers to the shape of the flowers.

delta /déltə/ *n* 1 a triangular area of land at the mouth of a river 2 *also* **Delta** the area around a river delta 3 the 4th letter of the Greek alphabet 4 **Delta** a communications code word for the letter 'D'

deltoid /dél toyd/ *n* a thick triangular muscle that covers the shoulder joint ■ *adj* triangular (*technical*)

delts *npl* the deltoid muscles (*infml*)

delude /di loód/ (**-luding**, **-luded**) *vt* lead into a false belief —**deluded** *adj*

deluge /déllyooj/ *n* 1 a sudden heavy downpour 2 a vast quantity 3 **Deluge** the biblical Flood ■ *vt* (**-uging**, **-uged**) 1 overwhelm somebody with something 2 flood a place

delusion /di loózh'n/ *n* 1 a false belief 2 a mistaken notion —**delusional** *adj* —**delusive** *adj*

deluxe /də lúks/, **de luxe** *adj* of a luxurious standard

delve (**delving**, **delved**) *vi* 1 dig into something and search around 2 search for information

Dem. *abbr* Democrat

demagnetize /dee mágnə tīz/ (**-izing**, **-ized**), **demagnetise** *vt* stop something being magnetic —**demagnetization** /dee mágnə tī záysh'n/ *n*

demagogic /démmə góggik/, **demagogical** /-ik'l/ *adj* appealing to emotions in a way considered politically dangerous —**demagogically** *adv*

demagogue /démmə gog/ *n* 1 an emotive dictator 2 a popular leader in ancient times —**demagoguery** *n*

ORIGIN **Demagogue** comes from a Greek word that means literally 'leader of the people'. The original **demagogues** were unofficial leaders in ancient Athens in the 4C BC who exerted influence in the name of the ordinary people.

demand /di maánd/ *n* 1 a forceful request 2 customer interest in buying particular goods or services 3 a need for resources or action ■ *v* 1 *vt* request or ask something forcefully 2 *vti* require resources in order to function or succeed ◇ **on demand** whenever a request is received

demand deposit *n* an immediately withdrawable deposit of money

demanding /di maánding/ *adj* requiring a lot of time or effort

demarcate /deé maar kayt/ (**-cating**, **-cated**) *vt* 1 determine and set the official borders of a territory 2 set down clearly the bounds of an activity or situation —**demarcation** /deé maar káysh'n/ *n*

De Maria /də ma reé ə/, **Walter** (*b*. 1935) US artist

dematerialize /deémə teéri ə līz/ (**-izing**, **-ized**), **dematerialise** *vti* disappear or cause to disappear physically or apparently —**dematerialization** /deémə teéri ə lī záysh'n/ *n*

demean /di meén/ *vt* humiliate and degrade —**demeaning** *adj*

demeanour /di meénər/ *n* outward behaviour

demented /di méntid/ *adj* 1 regarded as entirely irrational (*infml*) 2 affected by dementia —**dementedly** *adv* —**dementedness** *n*

dementia /di ménshə/ *n* a progressive deterioration of intellectual functions such as memory

demerit /dee mérrit/ n 1 a negative feature (often pl) 2 US, Can a mark against somebody for deficiency or misconduct —**demeritorious** /dee mérri táwri əss/ adj

demesne /di máyn/ n 1 possession and use of your own land, as opposed to tenancy (fml) 2 the lands attached to a large house (archaic)

Demeter /di meétər/ n in Greek mythology, the goddess of corn. Roman equivalent **Ceres**

demi- prefix half, partly o demigod

demigod /démmi god/ n 1 somebody treated like a god 2 in mythology, a human being with the powers of a god

demijohn /démmi jon/ n a large bottle with a short narrow neck

> **ORIGIN Demijohn** is an alteration of French dame-jeanne, literally 'Lady Jane', the popular name of the bottle in France. When the word was adopted into English in the mid-18C, its form was closer to the original French. By the 19C it had been assimilated to the more familiar demi- 'half' and the man's name John.

demilitarize /dee millitə rīz/ (-rizing, -rized), de- **militarise** vt remove troops and military equipment from —**demilitarization** /dee millitə rī záysh'n/ n

DeMille /də míl/, **Cecil B.** (1881–1959) US film director and producer

demise /di míz/ n (fml) 1 somebody's death 2 the end of something

demister /dee místər/ n a device in a car that clears condensation from the inside of the windscreen

demo /démmō/ (pl demos) n (infml) 1 a public protest, especially a match in the street 2 a trial version of a piece of software 3 a music sample sent to a recording company 4 a demonstration of a product

demob /dee mób/ (-mobbing, -mobbed) vti demobilize members of the armed forces, or be demobilized (infml)

demobilize /di mōbə līz/ (-izing, -ized), de- **mobilise** vti release members of the armed forces from active duty, or be released from such duty —**demobilization** /di mōbə lī záysh'n/ n

democracy /di mókrəssi/ (pl -cies) n 1 a form of government in which all people are represented by elected representatives 2 a nation that operates a democracy 3 the control of any organization or institution by its members

democrat /démmə krat/ n 1 a supporter of democracy 2 **Democrat** a member of the US Democratic Party or the Australian Democratic party

democratic /démmə kráttik/ adj 1 of or characterized by democracy 2 **Democratic** of the US Democratic Party or the Australian Democratic party —**democratically** adv

Democratic Party n a major US political party

democratize /di mókrə tīz/ (-tizing, -tized), de- **mocratise** vt 1 make a country into a democracy 2 introduce democracy to —**democratization** /di mókrə ti záysh'n/ n

Democritus /di mókritəss/ (460?–370? BC) Greek philosopher

démodé /day mōd ay/ adj out of style

demodulate /dee móddyoō layt/ (-lating, -lated) vt extract a signal carrying information from a radio wave —**demodulation** /dee modyoo láysh'n/ n —**demodulator** n

demographic /démmə gráffik/ adj of human populations —**demographically** adv

demographics /démmə gráffiks/ npl the characteristics and statistics of a human population

demography /di móggrəfi/ n 1 the study of human populations 2 the makeup of a particular human population —**demographer** n

demolish /di móllish/ vt 1 destroy a building or structure completely 2 damage something irreparably 3 beat an opponent convincingly (infml) 4 eat food fast and greedily (infml)

demolition /démmə lísh'n/ n 1 the deliberate destruction of a building or other structure 2 the destruction or annihilation of something ■ **demolitions** npl explosives

demon /deémən/ n 1 an evil spirit 2 a personal fear or anxiety 3 an expert at something (infml)

demonic /di mónnik/ adj 1 of or resembling a demon 2 intense or frantic —**demonically** adv

demonize /deémə nīz/ (-izing, -ized), **demonise** vt cause to appear evil in the eyes of others —**demonization** /deémə nī záysh'n/ n

demonology /deémə nóllaji/ n the study of demons in folklore —**demonological** /deémənə lójjik'l/ adj —**demonologist** n

demonstrable /di mónstrəb'l/ adj 1 so obvious as to be readily provable 2 capable of being shown to exist or be true —**demonstrably** adv

demonstrate /démmən strayt/ (-strating, -strated) v 1 vt explain or show how something works 2 vt show something convincingly 3 vi protest or express support publicly —**demonstrator** n

demonstration /démmən stráysh'n/ n 1 a display showing how to do something 2 conclusive proof 3 a public protest or show of support —**demonstrational** adj

demonstrative /di mónstrətiv/ adj 1 obviously affectionate 2 proving something 3 in grammar, describes a word such as 'this' or 'those' specifying which person or thing is being referred to —**demonstratively** adv —**demonstrativeness** n

demoralize /di mórrə līz/ (-izing, -ized), de- **moralise** vt erode the morale of —**demoralization** /di mórrə lī záysh'n/ n —**demoralizingly** adv

demote /dee mōt/ (-moting, -moted) vt reduce the rank or status of —**demotion** /dee mōsh'n/ n

demotic /di móttik/ adj 1 of ordinary people (fml) 2 **Demotic** of modern spoken Greek ■ n **Demotic** modern spoken Greek

demotivate /dee móti vayt/ (**-vating, -vated**) *vt* make feel less enthusiastic about doing something —**demotivation** /dee móti váysh'n/ *n*

Dempsey /démpsi/, **Jack** (1895–1983) US boxer

demur /di múr/ (**-murring, -murred**) *vi* **1** express reluctance **2** object mildly —**demurral** *n* ◊ See note at **object**

demure /di myoór/ (**-murer, -murest**) *adj* **1** looking shyly modest **2** affectedly shy or modest —**demurely** *adv* —**demureness** *n*

demutualize /dee myoóchoo ə líz/ (**-izing, -ized**), **demutualise** *vti* convert from a mutual organization to a public company —**demutualization** /dee myoóchoo ə lī záysh'n/ *n*

demystify /dee místi fī/ (**-fies, -fied**) *vt* make less mysterious —**demystification** /dee místifi káysh'n/ *n*

den *n* **1** a wild animal's lair **2** a place where illegal activities take place **3** a children's hideout **1** *US*, *Can* a room for relaxing

denar /deènər/ *n* the main unit of currency in the Former Yugoslav Republic of Macedonia

denationalize /dee násh'nə līz/ (**-izing, -ized**), **denationalise** *vt* **1** sell a state-owned industry or company to private owners **2** deprive a people of national rights or characteristics —**denationalization** /dee násh'nə lī záysh'n/ *n*

Denbighshire /dénbishər/ county in NE Wales. Pop. 91,600 (1995).

Deng Xiaoping /dúng shów píng/ (1904–97) Chinese political leader and national leader of China (1976–97)

deniable /di nī əb'l/ *adj* able to be denied —**deniably** *adv*

denial /di nī əl/ *n* **1** a statement saying that something is not true **2** refusal to grant something **3** refusal to acknowledge or face something

denier /dénni ər/ *n* a measure of the fineness of a fibre

denigrate /dénni grayt/ (**-grating, -grated**) *vt* **1** defame the character or reputation of **2** disparage and belittle —**denigration** /dénni gráysh'n/ *n* —**denigrator** *n*

denim /dénnim/ *n* hard-wearing cotton cloth. Use: clothing, especially jeans. ■ **denims** *npl* denim garments

ORIGIN **Denim** is named after the city of Nîmes in S France where the original cloth, *serge denim*, from French *serge de Nîmes*, was primarily manufactured. It is first recorded in English in the late 17C. The modern word and fabric belong to the 19C.

denizen /dénniz'n/ *n* a resident of a place

Denmark /dén maark/ southernmost country in Scandinavia. Cap. Copenhagen. Pop. 5,352,815 (2001).

denominate /di nómmi nayt/ (**-nating, -nated**) *vt* give a name to (*fml*)

denomination /di nómmi náysh'n/ *n* **1** a religious grouping within a faith **2** a unit of value or measure, especially of currency —**denominational** *adj*

denominator /di nómmi naytər/ *n* **1** the number below the line in a fraction **2** a common characteristic

denote /di nót/ (**-noting, -noted**) *vt* **1** have as a particular meaning **2** refer to —**denotation** /deènō táysh'n/ *n* —**denotative** /deè nōtaytiv/ *adj*

denouement /day noò moN/ *n* **1** the final stage of a story, when everything is revealed or solved **2** the final stage or climax of a series of events

ORIGIN **Denouement** comes from a French word that means literally 'the untying of a knot'. It is first recorded in the mid-18C.

denounce /di nównss/ (**-nouncing, -nounced**) *vt* criticize or accuse publicly and harshly —**denouncement** *n* —**denouncer** *n* ◊ See note at **disapprove**

dense (**denser, densest**) *adj* **1** with parts tightly packed together **2** very thick and difficult to see through or get through **3** with a high mass **4** hard to penetrate intellectually **5** regarded as slow to learn or understand (*infml disapproving*) —**densely** *adv* —**denseness** *n*

density /dénssəti/ (*pl* **-ties**) *n* **1** how full an area is **2** (*symbol* ρ) relative mass

dent *v* **1** *vti* make or suffer a depression in the surface by hitting **2** *vt* harm or spoil ■ *n* **1** a depression in a surface **2** damage, e.g. to somebody's reputation

dental /dént'l/ *adj* of dentistry or teeth

dental floss *n* thread for cleaning between the teeth

dental hygienist *n* somebody whose job is to clean teeth

dentine /dén teen/, **dentin** /-tin/ *n* the calcium-containing part of teeth, beneath the enamel —**dentinal** /-tin'l/ *adj*

dentist /déntist/ *n* somebody whose job is treating and preventing tooth and gum disorders —**dentistry** *n*

denture /dénchər/ *n* a partial or complete set of false teeth

denude /di nyoód/ (**-nuding, -nuded**) *vt* remove all covering from somebody or something —**denudation** /deè nyoo dáysh'n/ *n*

denunciation /di núnssi áysh'n/ *n* a public condemnation

Denver /dénvər/ capital of Colorado. Pop. 499,055 (1998).

deny /di nī/ (**-nies, -nied**) *vt* **1** say that something is not true **2** refuse to let somebody have something **3** refuse to acknowledge something

deodorant /dee ódərənt/ *n* **1** a substance applied to the body, especially under the arms, to mask or prevent body odour **2** any substance that disguises smells

deodorize /dee ódə rīz/ (**-izing, -ized**), **deodorise** *vt* disguise and eliminate the unpleasant smells of —**deodorizer** *n*

dep. *abbr* **1** department **2** departs

depart /di paàrt/ *vi* **1** leave a place, especially at the start of a journey **2** be different

departed /di paàrtid/ *adj* dead *(literary)* ■ *n* the person who has died *(fml or literary)* ◊ See note at **dead**

department /di paàrtmənt/ *n* **1** a section of a large organization **2** a major division of a government **3** somebody's speciality *(infml)* —**departmental** /deè paart mént'l/ *adj*

departmentalize /deè paart mént'l īz/ *(-izing, -ized)*, **departmentalise** *vt* divide into departments —**departmentalization** /deè paart mént'l ī záysh'n/ *n*

department store *n* a large store that sells a wide range of goods

departure /di paàrchər/ *n* **1** the action of setting off on a journey **2** a change from what is usual

departure lounge *n* a waiting area for passengers in an airport

depend /di pénd/ *vi* **1** be affected or decided by other factors **2** vary according to circumstances

□ **depend on** *or* **upon** *vt* **1** require something in order to exist **2** rely on somebody

dependable /di péndəb'l/ *adj* reliable —**dependability** /di péndə bíllati/ *n* —**dependably** *adv*

dependant /di péndənt/ *n* a person supported financially by another

dependence /di péndənss/ *n* **1** a need for something in order to survive **2** a physical or psychological need

dependency /di péndənssi/ *(pl -cies)* *n* **1** a territory under the jurisdiction of another country **2** dependence

dependent /di péndənt/ *adj* **1** not able to live without support from others **2** needing a particular thing *(usually in combination)* **3** affected or decided by other factors *(often in combination)* ○ *age-dependent* —**dependently** *adv*

depersonalize /deè púrss'nəl īz/ *(-izing, -ized)*, **depersonalise** *vt* make impersonal —**depersonalization** /deè púrss'nəl ī záysh'n/ *n*

depict /di píkt/ *vt* **1** describe in words **2** show in an art form —**depiction** *n* —**depictive** *adj*

depilatory /di píllətəri/ *adj* removing hair —**depilatory** *n*

deplane /dee pláyn/ *(-planing, -planed)* *vi* US, Can disembark from an aeroplane

deplete /di pleèt/ *(-pleting, -pleted)* *vt* **1** use up or reduce **2** empty out —**depletion** *n*

deplorable /di pláwrəb'l/ *adj* deserving strong condemnation —**deplorability** /di pláwrə bíllati/ *n* —**deplorably** *adv*

deplore /di pláwr/ *(-ploring, -plored)* *vt* **1** condemn as unacceptable **2** regret —**deploringly** *adv* ◊ See note at **disapprove**

deploy /di plóy/ *v* **1** *vti* position forces in preparation for military action **2** *vt* use something —**deployment** *n*

depopulate /dee póppyoò layt/ *(-lating, -lated)* *vt* reduce the population of —**depopulation** /dee póppyoò láysh'n/ *n*

deport[1] /di páwrt/ *vt* **1** forcibly repatriate a foreign national **2** banish somebody from his or her country —**deportation** /deè pawr táysh'n/ *n*

deport[2] /di páwrt/ *vr* behave ○ *how she deports herself*

deportee /deè pawr teè/ *n* a deported person

deportment /di páwrtmənt/ *n* the way in which somebody stands, sits, or moves

depose /di pôz/ *(-posing, -posed)* *v* **1** *vt* remove from office or power **2** *vti* give evidence to a court —**deposal** *n*

deposit /di pózzit/ *v* **1** *vt* put or leave something somewhere **2** *vti* leave a substance somewhere as part of a natural process **3** *vt* put money in a bank **4** *vt* give a sum of money as security ■ *n* **1** an act of putting money in a bank **2** an amount of money paid as security or partial payment **3** an accumulation of a substance **4** a coating **5** something put or left somewhere —**depositor** *n*

deposit account *n* an interest-earning bank account

deposition /déppə zísh'n, deèpə-/ *n* **1** a witness's testimony given under oath, especially a written statement read out in court **2** the ousting of somebody from office or power **3** a building-up of deposits —**depositional** *adj*

depository /di pózzitəri/ *(pl -ries)* *n* a storehouse

depot /déppō/ *n* **1** a warehouse **2** a building where vehicles are based and serviced **3** US, Can a railway or bus station **4** a military store facility

deprave /di práyv/ *(-praving, -praved)* *vt* make morally corrupt —**depraved** *adj* —**depravedly** /-práyvidli, -práyvd-/ *adv* —**depravity** /di právvəti/ *n*

deprecate /déppri kayt/ *(-cating, -cated)* *vt* **1** condemn as unacceptable **2** belittle —**deprecating** *adj* —**deprecation** /déppri káysh'n/ *n* —**deprecatory** /-kaytəri, -kətəri/ *adj*

depreciate /di preèshi ayt/ *(-ating, -ated)* *v* **1** *vti* lose value, or cause to lose value **2** *vt* belittle —**depreciation** /di preèshi áysh'n/ *n* —**depreciatory** /-ətəri/ *adj*

depredation /dépprə dáysh'n/ *n* a plundering attack

depress /di préss/ *vt* **1** make to feel sad or hopeless **2** press down —**depressible** *adj* —**depressing** *adj* —**depressingly** *adv*

depressant /di préss'nt/ *n* a drug or agent that slows the body's vital functions —**depressant** *adj*

depressed /di prést/ *adj* **1** feeling very unhappy or hopeless **2** affected by clinical depression **3** lacking economic resources ○ *a depressed area* **4** not active ○ *the depressed dollar* ○ *depressed markets* **5** lower than the surrounding area

depression /di présh'n/ *n* **1** unhappiness **2** a psychiatric disorder with symptoms possibly including feelings of acute hope-lessness, lack of energy, and suicidal tendencies **3** an economic slump **4** a hollow **5** a mass of low atmospheric pressure

depressive /di préssiv/ *adj* **1** causing depression **2** affected by depression ■ *n* a habitually depressed person —**depressively** *adv* —**depressiveness** *n*

deprivation /déppri váysh'n/ *n* **1** a state of poverty **2** the act of taking something away

deprive /di prív/ (**-priving, -prived**) *vt* **1** not allow somebody to have something **2** take something away from something

deprived /di prívd/ *adj* lacking the things needed for a comfortable or successful life

deprogramme /dee pró gram/ (**-gramming, -grammed**) *vt* remove the effect of indoctrination from

dept *abbr* department

depth *n* **1** how deep something is **2** the fact of being deep **3** intensity of colour **4** complexity of character **5** breadth of scope ■ **depths** *npl* **1** the lowest point or moment **2** the deep part of something ○ *the ocean depths* ○ *She wandered into the depths of the forest.* **3** the middle part of a long process ○ *in the depths of tedious research*

depth charge, depth bomb *n* an underwater bomb

deputation /déppyŏŏ táysh'n/ *n* **1** a group of representatives **2** the appointment of a deputy

depute /di pyóŏt/ (*fml*) *vt* (**-puting, -puted**) choose somebody as a representative ■ *adj* Scotland deputy

deputize /déppyŏŏ tīz/ (**-tizing, -tized**), **deputise** *v* **1** *vi* be a deputy **2** *vt* select as a deputy —**deputization** /déppyŏŏ tī záysh'n/ *n*

deputy /déppyŏŏti/ (*pl* **-ties**) *n* **1** somebody's representative **2** a second-in-command **3** a member of parliament in some countries, e.g. France and Germany

de Quincey /də kwínssi/, **Thomas** (1785–1859) British essayist and critic

derail /dee ráyl/ *vti* **1** cause a train to come off the rails **2** cause something to go off course or fail —**derailment** *n*

derailleur /di ráylyər/ *n* a device for changing gears on a bicycle that lifts the chain from one sprocket wheel to another

derange /di ráynj/ (**-ranging, -ranged**) *vt* **1** make irrational **2** throw into disorder —**deranged** *adj* —**derangement** *n*

derby /dáarbi/ (*pl* **-bies**) *n* **1** a race open to all qualified competitors **2** an important contest, especially between local teams **3** Derby one of two classic horse races for three-year-olds, one run at Epsom, the other in Kentucky **4** US, Can a bowler hat

ORIGIN All the uses of **derby** derive from the classic English horse race known as the *Derby*, named after Edward Stanley, 12th earl of Derby (1752–1834), who founded the race in 1780.

Derby[1] /dáarbi/ *n* a pale cheese sometimes flavoured with sage

Derby[2] /dáarbi/ **1** city in north-central England. Pop. 225,400 (1997). **2** port in NW Australia. Pop. 11,942 (1998 estimate).

Derbyshire /dáarbishər/ county in north-central England. Pop. 726,000 (1995).

deregulate /dee réggyŏŏ layt/ (**-lating, -lated**) *vt* free an organization or industry from regulation —**deregulation** /dee réggyŏŏ láysh'n/ *n* —**deregulator** *n* —**deregulatory** *adj*

derelict /dérrəlikt/ *adj* **1** no longer lived in **2** in poor condition because of neglect ■ *n* **1** a homeless person **2** a piece of abandoned property, especially a ship

dereliction /dérrə líksh'n/ *n* **1** neglect of duty **2** the act of abandoning something

deride /di ríd/ (**-riding, -rided**) *vt* ridicule

~~de rigeur~~ incorrect spelling of **de rigueur**

de rigueur /də ri gúr/ *adj* required by etiquette or current fashion

derision /di rízh'n/ *n* mocking scorn —**derisible** /di rízzəb'l/ *adj*

derisive /di ríssiv, -ziv/ *adj* mockingly scornful —**derisively** *adv*

USAGE derisive or **derisory**? **Derisive** means 'showing contempt or ridicule': *a derisive laugh.* **Derisory** means 'deserving contempt or ridicule': *a derisory offer.*

derisory /di ríssəri, -ríz-/ *adj* ridiculously small

derivation /dérri váysh'n/ *n* **1** the source of something, e.g. a word **2** the formation or development of a word —**derivational** *adj* ◊ See note at **origin**

derivative /di rívvətiv/ *adj* based on something else and therefore unoriginal ■ *n* **1** a thing derived from another **2** a word formed from another **3** a chemical product produced from a related substance ○ *an opium derivative*

derive /di rív/ (**-riving, -rived**) *v* **1** *vti* get something from a source, or come from a source **2** *vt* deduce something **3** *vt* make a chemical compound from another **4** *vti* form one word from another, or be formed from another word —**derivable** *adj*

dermatitis /dúrmə títiss/ *n* skin inflammation

dermatology /dúrmə tólləji/ *n* the branch of medicine dealing with the skin —**dermatological** /dúrmətə lójjik'l/ *adj* —**dermatologist** *n*

dermis /dúrmiss/ *n* a thick layer of skin beneath the epidermis —**dermal** *adj*

derogate /dérrə gayt/ (**-gating, -gated**) *v* **1** *vi* deviate from a norm, rule, or set conditions **2** *vi* detract (*fml*) **3** *vt* criticize or disparage —**derogation** /dérrə gáysh'n/ *n* —**derogative** *adj*

derogatory /di róggətəri/ *adj* disparaging —**derogatorily** *adv*

derrick /dérrik/ *n* **1** a crane for loading things onto a ship **2** a platform that holds the drilling equipment over an oil well

ORIGIN A **derrick** was originally a 'gallows'.

The name comes from the surname of a noted London hangman active around 1600. However, from the middle of the 18C **derrick** referred to various types of hoisting apparatus.

Derrida /de reèda/, **Jacques** (*b.* 1930) Algerian-born French philosopher

derrière /dérri air, dérri áir/ *n* somebody's bottom (*humorous*)

derring-do /dérring doó/ *n* brave adventurous behaviour (*dated*)

ORIGIN Derring-do derives from various misunderstandings and misuses. The phrase *dorring do* 'daring to do' occurs in the late 14C in a poem by Geoffrey Chaucer, and was copied in the 15C by the poet John Lydgate. 16C editions of Lydgate misprinted this as *derring do*. The poet Edmund Spenser took this up, but misunderstood the grammatical construction and treated it as a noun meaning 'brave adventurous behaviour'. Spenser's use was revived in the early 19C by Sir Walter Scott.

derringer /dérrinjər/ *n* a pocket-sized short-barrelled pistol

ORIGIN The **derringer** is named after the US gunsmith Henry Deringer (1786–1868), who designed it.

derv *n* diesel oil as fuel for road vehicles

dervish /dúrvish/ *n* a member of any of various Muslim religious groups, especially one known for energetic dancing

DES *abbr* data encryption standard

desalinate /dee sálli nayt/ (**-nating, -nated**) *vt* remove salt from —**desalination** /dee sálli náysh'n/ *n*

descale /dee skáyl/ (**-scaling, -scaled**) *vt* remove limescale from a kettle or other appliance

descant /déss kant, díss-/ *n* a high melody played or sung above the basic melody

Descartes /dáy kaart/, **René** (1596–1650) French philosopher and mathematician

descend /di sénd/ *v* **1** *vti* go down a staircase, hill, or other downward incline **2** *vi* come nearer the ground **3** *vi* slope downwards **4** *vti* be related to an ancestor **5** *vi* be inherited from parents or ancestors **6** *vi* behave in a way that is below your normal standards **7** *vi* arrive suddenly and in numbers

descendant /di séndənt/ *n* somebody related to a particular person who lived in the past

descent /di sént/ *n* **1** the act of descending **2** a way down **3** a change from better to worse **4** ancestral background **5** a sudden arrival or attack

SPELLCHECK Do not confuse the spelling of **descent** and **dissent** ('disagree'), which sound similar.

describe /di skríb/ (**-scribing, -scribed**) *vt* **1** give an account of what somebody or something is like **2** label or typify something **3** draw the outline of a shape (*fml*) —**describable** *adj*

description /di skrípsh'n/ *n* **1** an account of

what somebody or something is like **2** the process of describing **3** a variety or type ○ *cakes of every description*

descriptive /di skríptiv/ *adj* describing what somebody or something is like —**descriptively** *adv* —**descriptiveness** *n*

descriptor /di skríptər/ *n* in a database, a word used to categorize records of a particular type

descry /di skrí/ (**-scries, -scried**) *vt* catch sight of (*literary*) —**descrier** *n*

~~desease~~ incorrect spelling of **disease**

desecrate /déssi krayt/ (**-crating, -crated**) *vt* damage or insult something holy —**desecration** /déssi kráysh'n/ *n*

desegregate /dee séggri gayt/ (**-gating, -gated**) *vti* end the enforced separation of racial or social groups —**desegregation** /dee séggri gáysh'n/ *n* —**desegregationist** *n*

deselect /deè si lékt/ *vt* **1** reject an MP for selection as a candidate for election **2** in computing, remove an option from a menu or list —**deselection** *n*

~~desend~~ incorrect spelling of **descend**

desensitize /dee sénssə tíz/ (**-tizing, -tized**), **desensitise** *vt* **1** make somebody or something less sensitive **2** make somebody less allergic —**desensitization** /dee sénssə tī záysh'n/ *n*

~~desent~~[1] incorrect spelling of **decent**

~~desent~~[2] incorrect spelling of **descent**

desert[1] /dézzərt/ *n* **1** an area of land with no permanent bodies of water and erratic rainfall **2** a deprived place

desert[2] /di zúrt/ *v* **1** *vt* abandon a place or person **2** *vti* leave a branch of the armed forces without permission —**deserted** *adj* —**deserter** *n* —**desertion** /di zúrsh'n/ *n*

USAGE desert or dessert? **Dessert**, pronounced with the stress on the second syllable, means 'a sweet course eaten at the end of a meal'. **Desert**, pronounced with the stress on the first syllable, means 'an area with little rainfall', and with the stress on the second syllable means 'something deserved', as in *just deserts*, or is a verb meaning 'abandon' or 'leave without permission'.

desert[3] /di zúrt/ *n* a deserved punishment or reward (*usually pl*)

desertification /di zúrtifi káysh'n/ *n* the process of becoming a desert

desert island *n* an isolated tropical island

deserve /di zúrv/ (**-serving, -served**) *vt* have earned or be worthy of —**deserved** *adj* —**deservedly** /di zúrvidli/ *adv*

deserving /di zúrving/ *adj* worthy of receiving something —**deservingly** *adv*

desexualize /dee sékshoo ə líz/ (**-izing, -ized**), **desexualise** *vt* suppress the sexual characteristics of —**desexualization** /dee sékshoo ə lī záysh'n/ *n*

deshabille /dáyssə beèl/, **dishabille** /díssə-/ *n* a state in which somebody is partially or casually dressed (*fml*)

desiccate /déssi kayt/ (**-cating, -cated**) *vt* remove the moisture from —**desiccated** *adj* —**desiccation** /déssi káysh'n/ *n* —**desiccative** *adj*

desideratum /di zíddə ráatəm, -síddə-/ (*pl* **-ta** /-tə/) *n* something desired or necessary *(fml)*

design /di zín/ *v* **1** *vti* create a detailed plan of the form and structure of something **2** *vti* plan and make something skilfully **3** *vt* intend something for a particular use ■ *n* **1** a picture of the form and structure of an object **2** the way something is made **3** a decorative pattern **4** the process of designing ■ **designs** *npl* a selfish or dishonest plan

designate /dézzig nayt/ *vt* (**-nating, -nated**) **1** give a name or descriptive label to **2** choose for a particular purpose or position **3** mark or indicate ■ *adj* chosen for a future post —**designative** *adj* —**designatory** /dézzig náytəri, -nətəri/ *adj*

designated driver *n* a member of a group who agrees not to drink alcohol in order to drive the others home

designation /dézzig náysh'n/ *n* **1** a name, label, or description **2** the fact of being designated

designer /di zínər/ *n* somebody who designs things, especially clothes ■ *adj* **1** fashionable **2** designed by somebody famous

designer drug *n* a drug with effects similar to those of an illegal drug but made legally

designing /di zíning/ *adj* scheming

desirable /di zírəb'l/ *adj* **1** worth having **2** sexually attractive —**desirability** /di zírə billəti/ *n* —**desirably** *adv*

desire /di zír/ *vt* (**-siring, -sired**) **1** wish for **2** find sexually attractive ■ *n* **1** a craving **2** something wished for *(fml)* ◊ See note at **want**

~~desireable~~ incorrect spelling of **desirable**

desirous /di zírəss/ *adj* wanting to have something *(fml)*

desist /di síst, -zíst/ *vi* cease doing something —**desistance** *n*

desk *n* **1** a table used for writing or other work **2** a counter where a service is provided

ORIGIN **Desk** derives from the same Latin and Greek words as *dish, disc,* and *discus*. The key point in the development of **desk** seems to be when the round dish or tray was set on legs and became a table, then a writing table, a sense already acquired in medieval Latin, from which English adopted the word in the 14C.

deskill /dee skíl/ *vt* automate a job further and remove the need for human skill or initiative

desktop /désk top/ *n* **1** the surface of a desk **2** a display on a computer screen that shows icons representing equipment, programs, and files ■ *adj* usable on top of a desk

desktop publishing *n* the production of professional-looking publications using personal computers

Des Moines /di móyn/ capital of Iowa. Pop. 191,293 (1998).

desolate *adj* /déssələt/ **1** uninhabited and bleak **2** sad and without hope **3** dismal ■ *vt* /déssə layt/ (**-lating, -lated**) make desolate —**desolately** *adv* —**desolation** /déssə láysh'n/ *n*

de Soto /də sótō/, **Hernando** (1500?–42?) Spanish explorer

despair /di spáir/ *n* **1** a feeling of hopelessness **2** a cause of hopelessness ■ *vi* lose hope

despairing /di spáiring/ *adj* feeling or showing loss of hope —**despairingly** *adv*

~~desparate~~ incorrect spelling of **desperate**

despatch *vti, n* = dispatch

desperado /déspə ráadō/ (*pl* **-does** or **-dos**) *n* a bold violent criminal

desperate /désspərət/ *adj* **1** feeling or expressing a complete lack of hope **2** as a last resort ○ *desperate measures* **3** very serious or bad ○ *desperate hunger* **4** in great need ○ *desperate for money* —**desperately** *adv* —**desperation** /déspə ráysh'n/ *n*

~~desperatly~~ incorrect spelling of **desperately**

despicable /di spíkəb'l/ *adj* worthy of contempt —**despicably** *adv*

despise /di spíz/ (**-spising, -spised**) *vt* regard with contempt

despite /di spít/ *prep* **1** regardless of **2** contrary to

despoil /di spóyl/ *vt* plunder —**despoiler** *n* —**despoilment** *n* —**despoliation** /di spóli áysh'n/ *n*

despondent /di spóndənt/ *adj* completely lacking in hope or confidence —**despondence** *n* —**despondency** *n* —**despondently** *adv*

despot /déss pot, -pət/ *n* **1** a ruler with absolute power **2** a tyrannical person —**despotic** /di spóttik/ *adj* —**despotism** /déspətizəm/ *n*

dessert /di zúrt/ *n* a sweet dish concluding a meal ◊ See note at **desert**²

dessertspoon /di zúrt spoon/ *n* **1** a medium-sized spoon for eating a dessert **2** *also* **dessertspoonful** an amount held by a dessertspoon

dessert wine *n* a sweet wine served with a dessert

~~dessicated~~ incorrect spelling of **desiccated**

destabilize /dee stáybə līz/ (**-lizing, -lized**), **destabilise** *vt* undermine and make unstable —**destabilization** /dee stáybə lī záysh'n/ *n*

destination /désti náysh'n/ *n* **1** the place to which somebody is travelling **2** an intended or destined purpose or end

destined /déstind/ *adj* **1** sure to achieve or have something **2** heading towards a place

destiny /déstini/ (*pl* **-nies**) *n* **1** somebody's future regarded as preordained **2** *also* **Destiny** a force that supposedly predetermines events

destitute /désti tyoot/ *adj* **1** lacking the necessities of life **2** completely lacking something —**destitution** /désti tyóosh'n/ *n*

destroy /di stróy/ *v* **1** *vti* demolish, ruin, or abolish something **2** *vt* defeat somebody convincingly **3** *vt* kill an animal mercifully

destroyer /di stróy ər/ *n* **1** a small fast warship **2** somebody or something that causes destruction

destruction /di strúksh'n/ *n* **1** the process of destroying something or somebody **2** severe damage caused by something

destructive /di strúktiv/ *adj* **1** destroying **2** meant to cause damage —**destructively** *adv* —**destructiveness** *n*

desultory /déss'ltəri/ *adj* **1** aimlessly passing from one thing to another **2** random —**desultorily** *adv*

ORIGIN Desultory comes from a Latin word meaning literally 'leaping from one thing to another'. It referred particularly to the circus trick of jumping between galloping horses.

detach /di tách/ *v* **1** *vti* separate or disconnect **2** *vt* send on a special assignment —**detachable** *adj*

detached /di tácht/ *adj* **1** not attached **2** free from emotional involvement —**detachedly** /di táchidli, di táchtli/ *adv*

detachment /di táchmənt/ *n* **1** aloofness **2** lack of bias or personal involvement **3** separation or disconnection **4** a military unit chosen for special duties

detail /deé tayl/ *n* **1** an individual part, especially one of several items of information **2** the inclusion or description of all elements ◦ *attention to detail* **3** an insignificant part **4** a group, especially a military unit, with a special task ■ **details** *npl* personal facts ■ *vt* **1** list items **2** add refinements to something **3** give a specialized assignment to military personnel

detailed /deé tayld/ *adj* containing or emphasizing details

detain /di táyn/ *vt* **1** delay the progress of **2** hold in custody —**detainee** /deé tay neé, di-/ *n* —**detainment** *n*

detect /di tékt/ *vt* perceive the existence of —**detectable** *adj* —**detectably** *adv*

detection /di téksh'n/ *n* **1** the act of noticing or discovering the existence of something **2** detective work

detective /di téktiv/ *n* somebody who investigates and gathers evidence about possible crimes or wrongdoing —**detective** *adj*

detector /di téktor/ *n* **1** a sensing device **2** somebody or something that detects

détente /day tónt, -taánt/ *n* an easing of tension between nations

detention /di ténsh'n/ *n* **1** the process or state of being held in custody **2** punishment by being detained after school

detention centre *n* a place where young offenders are detained as a punishment

deter /di túr/ (**-terring, -terred**) *vti* discourage from taking action —**determent** *n*

detergent /di túrjənt/ *n* a chemical cleansing substance —**detergent** *adj*

deteriorate /di teéri ə rayt/ (**-rating, -rated**) *vti* become or make worse —**deterioration** /di teéri ə ráysh'n/ *n*

determinant /di túrminənt/ *n* a cause or determining factor —**determinant** *adj*

determinate /di túrminət/ *adj* with exact and definite limits —**determinacy** *n*

determination /di túrmi náysh'n/ *n* **1** firmness of purpose **2** a fixed purpose **3** the act of discovering or ascertaining something *(fml)* **4** a decision on a course of action *(fml)* **5** the settlement of a dispute or contest

determine /di túrmin/ (**-mining, -mined**) *v* **1** *vt* decide or settle conclusively **2** *vt* find out **3** *vt* influence or give form to **4** *vt* fix the limits of **5** *vti* adopt or cause to adopt a purpose —**determining** *adj*

determined /di túrmind/ *adj* with a firmness of purpose —**determinedly** *adv* —**determinedness** *n*

determiner /di túrminər/ *n* **1** a word that comes before a noun and specifies or identifies what it refers to **2** somebody or something that determines

determinism /di túrminizəm/ *n* the belief that everything has a cause and that there is no free will —**determinist** *n*

deterrent /di térrənt/ *adj* acting to deter ■ *n* something that deters or is intended to deter —**deterrence** *n*

detest /di tést/ *vt* hate —**detestation** /deé te stáysh'n/ *n*

detestable /di téstəb'l/ *adj* deserving hatred —**detestably** *adv*

dethrone /dee thrôn/ (**-throning, -throned**) *vt* remove from a throne or position of power —**dethronement** *n*

detonate /déttə nayt/ (**-nating, -nated**) *vti* explode —**detonation** /déttə náysh'n/ *n* —**detonator** *n*

detour /deé toor, day toòr/ *n* a deviation from a chosen or more direct route —**detour** *vti*

detoxify /dee tóksi fī/ (**-fies, -fied**), **detox** /deé toks/ *v* **1** *vt* remove or transform a toxic substance **2** *vti* rid somebody or yourself of toxic, especially addictive, substances —**detox** *n* —**detoxification** /dee tóksifi káysh'n/ *n*

detract /di trákt/ *vi* take away something that gives quality or value —**detraction** *n* —**detractive** *adj* —**detractor** *n*

detrain /dee tráyn/ *vi* disembark from a train —**detrainment** *n*

detriment /déttrimənt/ *n* damage or disadvantage —**detrimental** /déttri mént'l/ *adj* —**detrimentally** *adv*

detritus /di trítəss/ *n* **1** debris **2** rock fragments —**detrital** *adj*

Detroit /di tróyt/ *city* in SE Michigan. Pop. 970,196 (1998).

de trop /də trô/ *adj* superfluous or excessive *(literary)*

deuce /dyooss/ *n* **1** in racket games, a tied score requiring an extra margin to win **2** a playing card or dice throw with the value of two

Deutschmark /dóych maark/, **Deutsche Mark** /dóychə-/ *n* the main unit of the former German currency

De Valera /dévvə láirə/, Eamon (1882–1975) US-born prime minister (1932–48, 1951–54, and 1957–59) and president (1959–73) of Ireland

devalue /dee vállyoo/ (**-uing**, **-ued**) vti 1 lower a currency's value 2 make or become less valuable —**devaluation** /dèe valyoo áysh'n/ n —**devaluationist** n

devastate /dévvə stayt/ (**-tating**, **-tated**) vt 1 damage severely 2 upset enormously —**devastation** /dévvə stáysh'n/ n

devastating /dévvə stayting/ adj 1 severely damaging 2 very upsetting 3 sharply critical —**devastatingly** adv

develop /di vélləp/ v 1 vti change and grow, increase, or become more advanced, or cause to do this 2 vi arise and increase ○ tension was developing 3 vt acquire a feature, habit, or illness 4 vt enlarge on a plan or idea 5 vt turn photographic film into negatives or prints

~~develope~~ incorrect spelling of **develop**

developed /di vélləpt/ adj wealthy and industrialized

~~develepement~~ incorrect spelling of **development**

developer /di vélləpər/ n 1 somebody who develops something 2 a buyer of land for building 3 chemical for making exposed film into negatives or prints

developing /di vélləping/ adj describes a country or society that is not industrialized

development /di vélləpmənt/ n 1 an event causing or reflecting change (often pl) 2 the act of developing something 3 the fact of being developed 4 a group of buildings built as a single construction project —**developmental** /di vélləp mént'l/ adj —**developmentally** adv

Devi /dáyvi/ n the supreme Hindu goddess, wife of Shiva, manifested in the forms Durga, Kali, Parvati, and Sati

deviant /déevi ənt/ adj different from the norm or from an accepted standard ■ n somebody regarded as behaving differently or unacceptably —**deviance** n

deviate /déevi ayt/ (**-ating**, **-ated**) vi 1 be different 2 turn from a course

deviation /dèevi áysh'n/ n 1 a change or difference from what is usual or planned 2 unacceptable behaviour or attitudes 3 a difference from a statistical average

device /di víss/ n 1 a tool or machine 2 a ploy or trick 3 a bomb or other explosive 4 a literary or dramatic technique to produce an effect 5 an emblem or motto ◇ **leave somebody to his or her own devices** let somebody do as he or she wishes

~~devide~~ incorrect spelling of **divide**

devil /dévv'l/ n 1 also **Devil** in some religions, the personification of the spirit of evil 2 a subordinate spirit 3 an evil person 4 a mischievous person or animal 5 a person of a particular kind ○ a lucky devil ■ vt (**-illing**, **-illed**) make food spicy

devilish /dévv'lish/ adj 1 sinister or cruel

2 mischievous ■ adv very (infml dated) —**devilishly** adv

devil-may-care adj 1 reckless 2 cheerfully unconcerned

devilment /dévv'lmənt/ n mischievous behaviour

devilry /dévv'lri/ n 1 evil behaviour 2 acts supposedly performed with the help of spirits

devil's advocate n 1 somebody who argues for the sake of provoking discussion or conflict 2 formerly, a Roman Catholic official opposing canonization

devil's food cake n a dark chocolate cake

Devil's Island rocky islet in the Atlantic Ocean off the coast of French Guiana, formerly the site of a penal colony

devious /déevi əss/ adj 1 unfair or underhand 2 roundabout ○ a devious route —**deviously** adv —**deviousness** n

devise /di víz/ (**-vising**, **-vised**) vt 1 think up a plan 2 pass on property through a will —**devisable** adj

devoid /di vóyd/ adj lacking in or without something

devolution /dèevə loósh'n/ n 1 the act of delegating responsibilities 2 the delegating of power from a central to a regional or local level —**devolutionary** adj

devolutionist /dèevə loósh'nist/ n somebody supporting a decentralizing of political power —**devolutionist** adj

devolve /di vólv/ (**-volving**, **-volved**) vti transfer or be transferred to another person or organization —**devolvement** n

Devon /dévv'n/ county in SW England. Pop. 378,900 (1995).

Devonian /de vóni ən/ n a period of geological time 417–354 million years ago —**Devonian** adj

devote /di vót/ (**-voting**, **-voted**) vt commit or allot to a particular purpose

devoted /di vótid/ adj 1 loving and committed 2 dedicated —**devotedly** adv —**devotedness** n

devotee /dévvə tée/ n 1 a keen enthusiast 2 a religious person

devotion /di vósh'n/ n 1 committed love 2 dedication 3 religious fervour ■ **devotions** npl prayers —**devotional** adj

devour /di vówr/ vt 1 eat quickly 2 take in eagerly 3 destroy (literary) —**devouring** adj

devout /di vówt/ adj 1 very religious 2 very sincere (fml) —**devoutly** adv —**devoutness** n

dew /dyoo/ n moisture from the air condensed as water droplets on cool outdoor surfaces during the night —**dewy** adj

---

SPELLCHECK Do not confuse the spelling of **dew** and **due** ('expected', 'ready', 'appropriate'), which sound similar.

Dewar /dyoó ər/, Donald (1937–2000) Scottish politician and first First Minister of Scotland (1999–2000)

dewdrop /dyoo drop/ n a drop of dew

Dewey /dyoo i/, **Melvil** (1851–1931) US librarian and educationist

dewfall /dyoo fawl/ n 1 the time at which dew forms 2 the amount of dew that forms

dewlap /dyoo lap/ n a hanging flap of skin on an animal's neck —**dewlapped** adj

dew point n the air temperature at which dew begins to form

dewy-eyed adj naive and innocent

dexterous /dékstərəss/, **dextrous** /dékstrəss/ adj 1 physically skilful, especially with the hands 2 quick-witted —**dexterity** /dek stérrəti/ n —**dexterously** adv

ORIGIN **Dexterous** comes from a Latin word that means literally 'right-handed'.

dextrose /dékstrōz/ n a form of glucose found in tissue and also manufactured from starch

DFES abbr Department for Education and Skills

DG abbr director-general

dhaba /daàbə/ n S Asia a roadside food stall

Dhaka /dákə/, **Dacca** capital of Bangladesh. Pop. 3,368,940 (1991).

dhal /daal/, **dal** n a South Asian stew made from pulses

dharma /daàrmə/ n 1 in Hinduism, somebody's duty to behave according to religious codes 2 in Buddhism, the eternal truths about life and the universe —**dharmic** adj

Dhaulagiri /dówlə geèri/ one of the world's highest mountains, in the Himalayan range in N Nepal. Height 8,172 m/26,811 ft.

dhobi /dóbi/ n in South Asia, somebody who washes clothes

dhow /dow/ n an Arab sailing ship with low sides, one or two masts, and triangular curving sails

Dhu al-Hijjah /doo əl hijjaa/ n the 12th month of the year in the Islamic calendar

Dhu al-Qa'dah /doo əl kaà daa/ n the 11th month of the year in the Islamic calendar

di- prefix 1 two, twice, double o dilemma 2 containing two atoms, radicals, or groups o dioxide

diabetes /dí ə beè teez/ n a medical disorder causing high levels of sugar in the blood —**diabetic** /dí ə béttik/ adj, n

diabolical /dí ə bóllik'l/ adj 1 relating to the devil 2 evil 3 very bad (infml) —**diabolically** adv

diachronic /dí ə krónnik/ adj relating to or showing development through time —**diachronically** adv

diacritic /dí ə kríttik/ adj marking a change ■ n also **diacritical mark** a mark added above or below a letter to show a change from the normal pronunciation —**diacritically** adv

diadem /dí ə dem/ n a jewelled headband or crown

ORIGIN **Diadem** came via French and Latin from Greek, where it referred to the regal headband

of the Persian kings, which was adopted by Alexander the Great. It was formed from a verb meaning 'bind'.

diaeresis /dī eérəssiss/ (pl -ses /-seez/), **dieresis** n the mark (¨) added above a vowel to show that it is pronounced as a separate syllable or has a particular pronunciation

Diaghilev /di ággə lef/, **Sergei** (1872–1929) Russian ballet impresario

diagnosis /dí əg nṓssiss/ (pl -ses /-seez/) n 1 the identification of an illness 2 the identification of a problem or fault 3 decision reached by diagnosis —**diagnose** /dí əgnṓz/ vt —**diagnostic** /dí əg nóstik/ adj —**diagnostician** /dí əg no stísh'n/ n

SPELLCHECK Do not confuse the spelling of **diagnosis** and **diagnoses** (plural of diagnosis), which sound similar.

diagonal /dí ággənəl/ adj 1 slanting or oblique 2 with slanting lines or markings ■ n 1 a slanting line 2 a line joining angles —**diagonally** adv

diagram /dí ə gram/ n 1 a simple explanatory drawing 2 a chart presenting information graphically —**diagrammatic** /dí əgrə máttik/ adj —**diagrammatically** adv

dial /dí əl/ n 1 an indicator with a movable pointer 2 a control knob 3 a station indicator on a radio 4 a clock face 5 on some telephones, a disc with holes in it used for calling a number ■ vti (-alling, -alled) call a number on a telephone —**dialler** n

dialect /dí ə lekt/ n 1 a regional variety of a language 2 a language regarded as a member of a family of related languages —**dialectal** /dí ə lékt'l/ adj

dialectic /dí ə léktik/ n 1 a tension that exists between conflicting ideas 2 the investigation of truth through discussion 3 also **dialectics** a method of resolving apparent conflict between ideas by establishing truths on both sides —**dialectical** adj —**dialectician** /dí ə lek tísh'n/ n

dialling code n a telephone number prefix indicating area or country

dialling tone n a continuous sound on a telephone indicating that a number can be called

dialog box /dí ə log-/ n a small box on a computer screen that presents the user with a choice

dialogue /dí ə log/ n 1 the characters' words in a play, film, or book 2 a formal discussion or negotiation (fml) 3 a conversation (fml) ■ vi (-loguing, -logued) take part in a dialogue

dial-up adj describes a connection between computers that is achieved by means of a modem and a telephone line

dialysis /dī álləssiss/ n 1 the process of filtering waste from the blood of a patient with malfunctioning kidneys 2 the separation of substances from a solution —**dialytic** /dí ə líttik/ adj

diamanté /deè ə mónt ay, dí ə-/ adj decorated

with imitation diamonds ■ *n* imitation diamonds

diameter /dī ámmitər/ *n* **1** a line through the centre of a circle **2** the width of a circle or of something circular —**diametral** /-itrəl/ *adj* —**diametrally** *adv*

diametrical /dī ə méttrik'l/ *adj* completely opposite or different —**diametrically** *adv*

diamond /dī əmənd/ *n* **1** a hard colourless mineral that is a form of carbon. Use: gems, abrasives, cutting tools. **2** a shape like a square resting on a corner **3** a playing card with a diamond-shaped symbol **4** in baseball, the area bounded by the bases, or the whole field of play ■ *adj* 60th ■ *vt* decorate with diamonds

ORIGIN Diamond comes ultimately from the Greek word that is also the source of *adamant*. It meant 'diamond, hardest iron or steel'. The Greek word passed into Latin, after which it took two separate courses. Largely unchanged, it came via French into English as *adamant*. In medieval Latin it was also altered to a *dia*- form, and came via French into English as *diamond*.

diamond anniversary *n* a 60th anniversary, especially a wedding anniversary

diamond jubilee *n* a 60th anniversary, especially of a monarch's rule

Diana /dī ánnə/ *n* in Roman mythology, the goddess of hunting. Greek equivalent **Artemis**

Diana, Princess of Wales

Diana /dī ánnə/, **Princess of Wales** (1961–97) British princess

diaper /dī əpər/ *n US, Can* a baby's nappy

ORIGIN Babies' **diapers** or nappies were originally made of the fabric **diaper**, a linen or cotton material woven with a pattern of diamonds. The ultimate root is a Greek word meaning 'white'.

diaphanous /dī áffənəss/ *adj* **1** transparent **2** insubstantial (*literary*) —**diaphaneity** /dī əfə née əti/ *n*

diaphragm /dī ə fram/ *n* **1** a muscular wall below the rib cage **2** a dome-shaped contraceptive placed inside the vagina **3** a camera's mechanism controlling the opening for light **4** a vibrating disc in sound equipment —**diaphragmatic** /dī ə frag máttik/ *adj*

diaphram incorrect spelling of **diaphragm**

diarhea, diarrea incorrect spelling of **diarrhoea**

diarist /dī ərist/ *n* a diary writer

diarrhoea /dī ə reé ə/, **diarrhea** *n* **1** frequent and excessive bowel movements **2** watery stools

diary /dī əri/ (*pl* -ries) *n* **1** a personal record of events in somebody's life, written daily or regularly **2** a blank book for recording personal events **3** a book with dated pages for recording appointments ◊ See note at **dairy**

Dias /deé ass/, **Diáz, Bartolomeu** (1450?–1500) Portuguese navigator and explorer

diaspora /dī áspərə/ *n* **1** a dispersion of a language, culture, or people **2 Diaspora** the exile of the Jews from Israel **3 Diaspora** all Jews living outside Israel

diatonic /dī ə tónnik/ *adj* of a simple musical scale with seven tones ■ *n* an interval in a diatonic scale —**diatonically** *adv* —**diatonicism** /-tónnisizəm/ *n*

diatribe /dī ə trīb/ *n* a bitter verbal criticism

dibs *npl* **1** the game jacks **2** a claim to something (*infml*)

dice /dīss/ *n* **1** (*pl same*) a numbered cube used in games **2** a gambling game played with dice (*+ sing or pl verb*) ■ *npl* small cubes of food (*+ pl verb*) ■ *v* (**dicing, diced**) **1** *vt* cut food into small cubes **2** *vti* gamble with dice **3** *vi* take risks ◊ **load the dice** manipulate a situation unfairly in order to obtain a desired result

dicey /dīssi/ (-**ier**, -**iest**), **dicy** *adj* risky (*infml*)

dichotomy /dī kóttəmi/ (*pl* -**mies**) *n* a separation into different or contradictory things —**dichotomous** *adj*

dicision incorrect spelling of **decision**

dick *n* an offensive term for the penis (*slang*)

dickens /díkinz/ *n* adds emphasis (*infml*) ○ *What the dickens are you doing?*

Dickens /díkinz/, **Charles** (1812–70) British novelist

Dickensian /di kénzi ən/ *adj* **1** of or reminiscent of Charles Dickens or his books and their characters or settings **2** full of twists and amazing coincidences **3** reminiscent of poverty-stricken Victorian Britain

dicker /díkər/ *vi* haggle (*infml*)

Dickinson /díkinss'n/, **Emily** (1830–86) US poet

dicky[1] /díki/ (*pl* -**ies**), **dickey** *n* a false shirt front or neck

dicky[2] /díki/ (-**ier**, -**iest**) *adj* (*infml*) **1** unwell **2** not reliable

dicky bird, **dickeybird** /díki burd/ *n* a small bird (*babytalk*)

dicotyledon /dī kotti leéd'n/ *n* a plant belonging to the group that has two leaves in the seed —**dicotyledonous** *adj*

dicta plural of **dictum**

Dictaphone /díktəfōn/ *tdmk* a trademark for a small hand-held tape recorder used for dictation

dictate *v* /dik táyt/ (-**tating**, -**tated**) **1** *vti* speak aloud words that are to be written down **2** *vti* give orders or make decisions authoritatively **3** *vt* control or influence ○ *action*

dictated by the weather conditions ■ *n* /dík tayt/
1 a command given 2 a governing principle

dictation /dik táysh'n/ *n* 1 the act of speaking
aloud words that are written down or of
writing down what is said 2 words written
down

dictator /dik táytər/ *n* 1 an absolute ruler 2 an
autocratic or domineering person

dictatorial /díktə táwri əl/ *adj* 1 tending to give
orders or make decisions for others 2 of dic-
tators —**dictatorially** *adv*

dictatorship /dik táytər ship/ *n* 1 a dictator's
power or rule 2 government by a dictator
3 a country ruled by a dictator

diction /díksh'n/ *n* 1 clarity of speech 2 the
choice of words to fit a specific context
—**dictional** *adj*

dictionary /díksh'nəri/ (*pl* -**ies**) *n* 1 a book giving
meanings or translations of words 2 a book
listing other types of information alphabetically 3 an alphabetical list of computer
codes used in a program

dictum /díktəm/ (*pl* -**tums** *or* -**ta** /-tə/) *n* 1 a
pronouncement (*fml*) 2 a saying

dicy *adj* = **dicey**

did past tense of **do**[1]

didactic /dī dáktik, di-/ *adj* 1 containing a moral
or political message 2 fond of instructing or
advising others —**didactically** *adv*

diddle /dídd'l/ (-**dling**, -**dled**) *vt* cheat somebody
(*infml*) —**diddler** *n*

didnt incorrect spelling of **didn't**

Diderot /deedərṓ/, **Denis** (1713–84) French en-
cyclopedist and philosopher

didgeridoo /díjjəri doó/ (*pl* -**doos**), **didjeridoo** *n*
an Aboriginal wind instrument with a long
thick wooden pipe

didi /deè dee/ *n S Asia* 1 an older sister (*often a
form of address*) 2 a form of address for an
older woman

didn't /díd'nt/ *contr* did not

Dido /dīdṓ/ *n* in Roman mythology, queen of
Carthage

die[1] /dī/ (**dies**, **dying**, **died**) *v* 1 *vi* stop living 2 *vi*
stop existing, especially gradually ○ *feelings I
thought had died long ago* 3 *vi* stop functioning
○ *The engine suddenly died.* 4 *vt* die in a particular way ○ *died a gruesome death* 5 *vi* be
very eager for something ○ *dying to see them*
◇ **to die for** highly desirable

SPELLCHECK Do not confuse the spelling of **die**
and **dye** ('cause to change colour', 'a colouring
agent'), which sound similar.

☐ **die away** *vi* grow faint
☐ **die down** *vi* fade in strength or intensity
☐ **die off** *vi* die one by one
☐ **die out** *vi* 1 cease gradually to exist 2 disappear gradually

die[2] /dī/ *n* 1 (*pl* **dice** /dīss/) a numbered cube
used in games (*fml*) 2 a cutting, stamping, or
pressing tool 3 a moulding tool

dieback /dī bak/ *n* the gradual death of a plant

Diefenbaker /deéfən baykər/, **John George**
(1895–1979) prime minister of Canada
(1957–63)

diegn incorrect spelling of **deign**

diehard /dī haard/ *adj* stubbornly resistant to
change —**diehard** *n* —**diehardism** *n*

dieing incorrect spelling of **dying**

dieresis *n* LING = **diaeresis**

diesel /deéz'l/ *n* 1 *also* **diesel engine** an engine
that heats diesel oil by compression alone
2 a vehicle with a diesel engine 3 *also* **diesel
oil** a thick oily fuel distilled from petroleum

diet[1] /dī ət/ *n* 1 what a person or animal eats
2 a controlled intake of food ■ *adj* designed
or promoted for weight loss ■ *vi* eat less in
order to lose weight —**dietary** *adj* —**dieter** *n*

diet[2] /dī ət/ *n* 1 a parliament in some countries
2 a court session in Scotland

dietetic /dī ə téttik/ *adj* 1 of people's diets
2 prepared with special diets in mind

dietetics /dī ə téttiks/ *n* the study of food and
nutrition (+ *sing verb*)

dieties incorrect spelling of **deities**

dietitian /dī ə tísh'n/, **dietician** *n* a nutrition
specialist

diferent incorrect spelling of **different**

differ /díffər/ *vi* 1 be unlike 2 disagree ◊ See
note at **disagree**

difference /díffrənss/ *n* 1 the state of being
unlike somebody or something 2 a distinguishing feature 3 a significant change 4 a
disagreement 5 an answer to a subtraction
equation ◇ **split the difference** take the
average of two amounts, or agree on something that is halfway between two extremes

different /díffrənt/ *adj* 1 unlike somebody or
something else 2 distinct —**differently** *adv*

USAGE different from or **different than**? No one
objects to **different from** (on the analogy of
differ from: *His attitude towards women was
quite different from that of his
contemporaries*). *Different to* is not so generally
accepted, although it is commonly used in
British English. *Different than* is also seen and
heard, especially in US English. Although some
object to it as a matter of principle and it
should be avoided in formal writing, it can at
times serve as a useful short cut. Compare *The
book has a title different from the one that I
thought it had* with *The book has a different
title than I thought*.

differential /díffə rénsh'l/ *n* a difference
between points on a scale ■ *adj* of differences

differentiate /díffə rénshi ayt/ (-**ating**, -**ated**) *vti*
1 see or establish differences between things
2 treat people differently, e.g. because of differences in ability —**differentiable** *adj*
—**differentiation** /díffə renshi áysh'n/ *n*

difficult /díffik'lt/ *adj* 1 hard to do, understand,
or deal with 2 full of problems 3 hard to
please or persuade —**difficultness** *n* ◊ See
note at **hard**

difficulty /dífflk'ltı/ n (pl **-ties**) **1** the quality of being difficult **2** something difficult **3** effort ■ **difficulties** npl **1** trouble **2** objections

diffident /díffidənt/ adj **1** lacking self-confidence **2** reserved or restrained —**diffidence** n —**diffidently** adv

diffraction /di fráksh'n/ n the bending or spreading out of waves, e.g. of light or sound

diffrent incorrect spelling of **different**

diffuse[1] /di fyooz/ (**-fusing, -fused**) vti **1** spread through something **2** scatter or become scattered **3** undergo or subject to diffusion —**diffusible** adj ◊ See note at **defuse**

diffuse[2] /di fyooss/ adj **1** spread throughout an area **2** lacking organization and conciseness —**diffusely** adv —**diffuseness** n ◊ See note at **wordy**

diffusion /di fyoozh'n/ n **1** the process or result of diffusing **2** the spread of cultural features **3** the scattering of light as a result of reflection **4** the random movement of atoms, molecules, or ions —**diffusional** adj

difficult incorrect spelling of **difficult**

dig v (**digging, dug**) **1** vti break up or remove earth **2** vt create by digging **3** vti obtain, uncover, or free by digging **4** vt discover by research **5** vi search carefully **6** vti prod or poke **7** vt like or enjoy (slang dated) ■ n **1** a prod or poke **2** a cutting remark **3** an archaeological excavation

□ **dig in** v **1** vti take up military positions **2** vi fight stubbornly **3** vi start eating (infml)

□ **dig out** vt retrieve (infml)

□ **dig up** vt **1** take out of the ground **2** find out through investigation (infml)

digerati /díjjə raáti/ npl computer experts (infml)

digest vt /dī jést, di-/ **1** process food in the body **2** absorb something mentally **3** organize something systematically to extract essential information **4** abridge something ■ n /dī'jest/ **1** a summary **2** a collection of abridged pieces of writing

digestible /dī jéstəb'l, di-/ adj easily digested —**digestibility** /dī jéstə bílləti, di-/ n

digestion /dī jéschən, di-/ n **1** the processing of food in the body **2** the ability to digest food **3** the ability to absorb ideas —**digestional** adj

digestive /dī jéstiv, di-/ adj of digestion ■ n **1** something that aids digestion **2** a digestive biscuit

digestive biscuit n a semisweet biscuit made from wholemeal flour

digger /díggər/ n **1** somebody or something that digs **2** a tool or machine for digging **3** also **Digger** somebody from Australia or New Zealand (infml)

diggings /díggingz/ n a place where something is mined ■ npl material excavated

digit /díjjit/ n **1** a numeral **2** a finger or toe

digital /díjjit'l/ adj **1** representing data as numbers **2** representing sound or light waves as numbers **3** like a finger or toe **4** done with or operated by the fingers or toes —**digitally** adv

digital audio tape n tape used for recording sound digitally

digital cash n credits used to buy things online

digital coins npl small denominations of online currency

digital computer n a computer processing data in binary form

digital encryption standard n a standard for data encryption

digital imagery, digital imaging n the transformation of a digital image by a computer

digital signature n a digital signal that identifies a user

Digital Subscriber Line n full form of **DSL**

digital television n a television system or set using digital transmission

digital video disc, digital versatile disc n full form of **DVD**

digitize /díjji tīz/ (**-tizing, -tized**), **digitise** vt convert to digital form —**digitization** /díjji tī záysh'n/ n —**digitizer** n

dignified /dígni fīd/ adj calm and serious

dignify /dígni fī/ (**-fies, -fied**) vt **1** give distinction to **2** give undeserved attention to

dignitary /dígnitəri/ (pl **-ies**) n a person of high rank

dignity /dígnəti/ n **1** pride and self-respect **2** seriousness in behaviour **3** worthiness **4** due respect

digress /dī gréss/ vi move off a central topic —**digression** n

Dijon /deé zhoN/ capital of Côte d'Or Department, east-central France. Pop. 149,867 (1999).

diktat /dík taat/ n **1** a dictatorial statement **2** a harsh settlement imposed on a defeated enemy

dilapidated /di láppi daytid/ adj in disrepair —**dilapidation** /dī láppi dáysh'n/ n

dilate /dī láyt, di-/ (**-lating, -lated**) v **1** vti become or make larger or wider **2** vi talk or write at length —**dilatation** /dílə táysh'n, díllə-/ —**dilation** /dī láysh'n, di-/ n

dilatory /díllətəri/ adj **1** slow to do something **2** intended to delay

dildo /díldō/ (pl **-dos**), **dildoe** (pl **-does**) n a sexual aid shaped like a penis

dilema incorrect spelling of **dilemma**

dilemma /di lémmə, dī-/ n a situation with unsatisfactory choices

dilettante /dílli tánti, -taánti/ (pl **-tantes** or **-tanti** /-ti/) n somebody whose interest is only superficial —**dilettante** adj —**dilettantism** n

diligent /díllijənt/ adj persistent and hardworking —**diligence** n —**diligently** adv

dill n **1** the feathery leaves or the seeds of an aromatic plant. Use: flavouring, garnish. **2** the plant that produces dill

dill pickle n a pickled cucumber flavoured with dill

dilly bag /dílli-/ n Aus a bag made of plaited grass or reeds

dilly-dally /dílli / (**dilly-dallies**, **dilly-dallied**) *vi* waste time in indecision

dilute /dī loot, -lyoot/ *v* (**-luting**, **-luted**) 1 *vt* make thinner or weaker by adding water or other liquid 2 *vti* lessen in the strength or effect ■ *adj* thinned by liquid —**diluteness** *n* —**dilution** *n*

dim *adj* (**dimmer**, **dimmest**) 1 not well lit 2 producing little light 3 dull in colour 4 not clearly visible 5 not easy to perceive or understand 6 not clearly remembered 7 not seeing clearly 8 unlikely to be successful 9 regarded as unintelligent *(infml insult)* ■ *v* (**dimming**, **dimmed**) 1 *vti* make or become dim 2 *vt US, Can* dip headlights —**dimly** *adv* —**dimness** *n*

dime *n US, Can* a coin worth ten cents

ORIGIN **Dime** originally meant 'tenth part, tithe'. It was adopted from French in this sense in the 14C. The use of a coin worth ten cents dates from the late 18C.

dimension /di ménsh'n, dī-/ *n* 1 a measurement of the extent of something in one or more directions 2 an aspect or feature 3 a coordinate used with others to locate something in space and time ■ **dimensions** *npl* size or scope —**dimensional** *adj* —**dimensionally** *adv*

diminish /di mínnish/ *vti* 1 make or become smaller 2 appear or cause to appear smaller —**diminished** *adj* —**diminishingly** *adv* —**diminishment** *n*

diminished responsibility *n* the legal defence that a psychiatric disorder partially reduces culpability for a crime

diminuendo /di mínnyoo éndō/ *adv* gradually decreasing in volume *(musical direction)* ■ *n* (*pl* **-dos**) a piece of music played or sung diminuendo —**diminuendo** *adj*

diminution /dímmi nyóosh'n/ *n* reduction

diminutive /di mínnyŏŏtiv/ *adj* 1 very small 2 describes a word or suffix indicating smallness or fondness —**diminutive** *n* —**diminutively** *adv* —**diminutiveness** *n*

DIMM /dim/ *n* a module adding RAM to a computer. Full form **dual in-line memory module**

dimmer /dímmər/ *n* 1 *also* **dimmer switch** a device for varying a light's brightness 2 *US* a dip switch for headlights

dimple /dímp'l/ *n* an indented area in the skin or another surface ■ *v* (**-pling**, **-pled**) 1 *vi* form a dimple 2 *vt* produce dimples in —**dimply** *adj*

dim sum /dím súm/ *n* dumplings and other Chinese dishes served in small portions as part of a meal (+ *sing or pl verb*)

dimwit /dím wit/ *n* a person regarded as unintelligent *(infml insult)* —**dimwitted** /dím wíttid/ *adj*

din *n* a loud persistent noise ■ *v* (**dinning**, **dinned**) 1 *vi* make a loud noise 2 *vt* fix something in somebody's mind through repetition

DIN /din/ *n* 1 a measurement of the speed of photographic film 2 a standard electrical connection system used with television and audio equipment

ORIGIN **DIN** is a German acronym formed from the initial letters of *Deutsche Industrie-Norm* 'German industry standard'.

dinar /deé naar/ *n* a currency unit in some North African, SW Asian, and SE European countries

Dinaric Alps /di nárrik-, dī-/ range of the Eastern Alps, extending from NE Italy southeastwards along the Adriatic coast of the Balkan Peninsula. Highest peak Bobotov Kuk 2,522 m/8,274 ft.

dine (**dining**, **dined**) *v* 1 *vi* eat dinner 2 *vi* eat a meal 3 *vt* provide dinner for *(infml)*

diner /dínər/ *n* 1 a person who eats 2 *US, Can* an inexpensive restaurant

Dinesen /dínniss'n/, **Isak** (1885–1962) Danish writer

dinette /dī nét/ *n* a small dining area in or near a kitchen

ding *vti* ring with a high-pitched sound —**ding** *n*

ding-a-ling *n* a tinkle of a bell

dingbat /díng bat/ *n* a printer's symbol

ding-dong *n* 1 the sound of a bell 2 a fierce argument *(infml)*

dinghy /díngi, díng gi/ (*pl* **-ghies**) *n* 1 a small boat 2 an inflatable life raft

dingo /díng gō/ (*pl* **-goes**) *n* an Australian wild dog

dingy /dínji/ (**-gier**, **-giest**) *adj* 1 dirty or faded 2 shabby —**dingily** *adv* —**dinginess** *n*

dining room *n* a room where meals are served

dinkum /díngkəm/ *adj ANZ* genuine *(infml)*

dinky /díngki/ (**-kier**, **-kiest**) *adj* small and compact *(infml)*

dinner /dínnər/ *n* 1 a main meal 2 a banquet

dinner jacket *n* a man's formal jacket without tails

dinner party *n* a party at which a dinner is served

dinner service, dinner set *n* a set of matching crockery for a meal

dinnertime /dínnər tīm/ *n* the time when dinner is eaten

dinosaur /dínə sawr/ *n* 1 an extinct reptile that lived in the Mesozoic era 2 an outmoded person or thing —**dinosaurian** /dínə sáwri ən/ *adj*

ORIGIN The scientific name of the **dinosaur** was formed in modern Latin in the mid-19C from Greek words that mean literally 'terrible lizard'.

dint *n* a dent —**dint** *vt*

diocese /dī əssiss/ *n* all the churches or the district under a bishop's authority —**diocesan** /dī óssiss'n/ *adj*

Diocletian /dī ə kleésh'n/ (245–313) emperor of Rome (284–305)

diode /dī ōd/ *n* a device that converts alternating electrical current to direct current

Diogenes /dī ójjə neez/ (412?–323 BC) Greek philosopher

Dionysus /dī ə nīssəss/ *n* in Greek mythology, Bacchus

diorama /dī ə raámə/ *n* a miniature three-dimensional replica of a scene —**dioramic** /dī ə rámmik/ *adj*

dioxide /dī ók sīd/ *n* a chemical compound with two oxygen atoms

dioxin /dī óksin/ *n* any derivative of dibenzo-*p*-dioxin, a carcinogen and toxic environmental pollutant

dip *v* (**dipping, dipped**) **1** *vt* put something briefly in liquid **2** *vi* suddenly move downwards ○ *The plane dipped and then flew on.* **3** *vt* lower something ○ *The horse dipped its head.* **4** *vi* become less ○ *Prices dipped sharply.* **5** *vti* put your hand into something in order to remove something **6** *vt* lower headlights **7** *vt* disinfect an animal by total immersion **8** *vi* slope downwards ○ *The road dipped towards the river.* ■ *n* **1** an act or instance of dipping **2** a short swim **3** a hollow in the ground **4** a mixture for dipping something into

□ **dip into** *vt* **1** read only parts of a book **2** use money from savings

dip., Dip. *abbr* diploma

diphtheria /dif theéri ə, dip-/ *n* an infectious bacterial disease that attacks the membranes of the throat and releases a dangerous toxin —**diphtherial** *adj* —**diphtheritic** /dífthə ríttik, díp-/ *adj*

diphthong /díf thong, díp-/ *n* **1** a speech sound consisting of two vowels pronounced as one syllable **2** a character formed by joining two letters —**diphthongal** /dif thóng g'l, dip-/ *adj*

diploma /di plṓmə/ *n* **1** an educational certificate **2** an official paper describing rights and privileges

ORIGIN **Diploma** came via Latin from a Greek word that means literally 'folded paper'. Because official papers were often folded, the Latin word came to mean 'official document, state paper'. This sense is recorded in English alongside 'document conferring an honour or privilege' from the mid-17C. By the early 18C it referred also to a university qualification.

diplomacy /di plṓməssi/ *n* **1** international relations **2** skill in international dealings **3** tact

diplomat /díplə mat/ *n* **1** a government representative abroad **2** a tactful person

diplomatic /díplə máttik/ *adj* **1** involving diplomacy **2** tactful —**diplomatically** *adv*

diplomatic bag *n* a bag in which diplomats' mail is sent

diplomatic corps *n* all the foreign diplomats of a country

diplomatic immunity *n* a diplomat's freedom from taxation, customs inspections, and other legal restraints

diplomatist /di plṓmətist/ *n* a professional diplomat

dipper /díppər/ *n* **1** a scoop or ladle **2** a small water bird

dippy /díppi/ (**-pier, -piest**) *adj* regarded as foolish or eccentric (*infml*)

dipsomaniac /dípsō máyni ak/ *n* an alcoholic (*dated*)

dipstick /díp stik/ *n* a measuring rod for liquid

dip switch *n* a switch for dimming headlights

~~diptheria~~ incorrect spelling of **diphtheria**

~~dipthong~~ incorrect spelling of **diphthong**

diptych /díptik/ *n* a painting consisting of two parts joined together

dire (**direr, direst**) *adj* **1** very bad **2** threatening disaster —**direly** *adv* —**direness** *n*

direct /di rékt, dī-/ *v* **1** *vt* supervise or manage something **2** *vt* instruct somebody (*fml*) **3** *vt* focus attention or concentrate activities **4** *vt* aim or address something **5** *vt* tell somebody how to get somewhere **6** *vti* provide instructions or guidance to actors or the makers of a film or play ■ *adj* **1** not stopping or deviating ○ *a direct flight* **2** without intervention ○ *a direct contact* **3** straightforward ○ *a direct appeal to our emotions* **4** precise or exact ○ *a direct quotation* **5** related in an unbroken line ○ *a direct descendant* **6** complete or utter ○ *in direct contradiction to our conclusions* ■ *adv* **1** straight, without diversion **2** with nothing or nobody intervening —**directness** *n*

direct action *n* strikes or boycotts intended to influence a government or employer at first hand

direct current *n* electrical current that flows in only one direction

direct debit *n* payment of a creditor from a bank account by prior arrangement, in amounts that can be varied by the creditor

direction /di réksh'n, dī-/ *n* **1** the management or supervision of something **2** the way in which something moves, travels, or develops ○ *takes a new direction* **3** the art or practice of directing a film or play **4** a sense of purpose **5** an instruction in music ■ **directions** *npl* instructions —**directionless** *adj*

directional /di réksh'nəl, dī-/ *adj* **1** of direction **2** more efficient in one direction ○ *a directional aerial* **3** indicating a trend —**directionality** /di rékshə nálləti, dī-/ *n*

directive /di réktiv, dī-/ *n* an order or official instruction ■ *adj* **1** providing guidance **2** showing direction

directly /di réktli, dī-/ *adv* **1** straight, with no deviations **2** with nothing or nobody intervening **3** completely **4** clearly **5** without delay (*dated*) ■ *conj* immediately after

direct mail *n* advertising by mail addressed to individual customers

direct marketing, direct selling *n* a way of selling in which a company deals with individual customers, e.g. through mail order catalogues

direct object *n* a word or phrase representing the person or thing affected directly by the action of the verb in a sentence

director /di rḗktər, dī-/ n 1 a manager of an organized group or activity 2 a member of the board that runs a business 3 somebody who directs a film or play —**directorial** /dī rek tɔ́wri əl, di rḗk-/ adj —**directorship** n

directorate /di rḗktərət, dī-/ n a group of directors, or those in a business or a government

director-general (pl **directors-general**) n a chief director of a large public organization

Director of Public Prosecutions n 1 the head of the Crown Prosecution Service 2 in Australia, a state or federal official responsible for prosecutions

directory /di rḗktəri, dī-/ (pl **-ries**) n 1 a book listing names, addresses, and telephone numbers 2 an index of computer files

directory enquiries n a service providing telephone numbers

direct selling n MARKETING = **direct marketing**

direct speech n the actual words that somebody speaks, printed in quotation marks

direct tax n a tax on income

dirge n 1 a funeral hymn 2 a piece of mournful music

ORIGIN **Dirge** is a contraction of Latin *dirige* 'guide, direct'. *Dirige, Domine, Deus meus, in conspectu tuo viam meam* 'Direct, Lord, my God, my way in thy sight' (Psalm 5:8) was formerly part of the funeral service in the Roman Catholic Church.

dirham /deér ram, deérrəm/ n a unit of currency in some North African and Middle Eastern countries

dirigible /dírrijəb'l/ n an airship ■ adj steerable

dirk n a dagger with a long straight handle

dirndl /dúrnd'l/, **dirndl skirt** n a full skirt gathered at the waist

dirt n 1 a substance that soils or stains 2 earth, soil, or mud 3 scandalous information about somebody or something

dirt bike n an off-road motorcycle

dirt-cheap adj, adv very cheap (infml)

dirt-poor adj very poor

dirt track n 1 an unsurfaced track 2 a race track of earth mixed with gravel and cinders

dirty /dúrti/ adj (**-ier, -iest**) 1 soiled or stained 2 causing pollution o a dirty engine 3 making somebody grimy o a dirty job 4 not honest or legal 5 malicious 6 sexually suggestive 7 expressing anger o a dirty look 8 despicable (infml) o a dirty trick 9 lacking brightness or clarity 10 stormy o dirty weather ■ adv (**-ier, -iest**) 1 unfairly 2 suggestively ■ vti (**-ies, -ied**) make or become dirty —**dirtily** adv —**dirtiness** n ◇ **get your hands dirty** perform a degrading or unpleasant act

SYNONYMS **dirty, filthy, grubby, grimy, soiled, squalid, unclean** CORE MEANING: not clean

dirty bomb n a bomb containing radioactive nuclear waste dispersed by means of conventional explosives

Dis /diss/ n 1 in Roman mythology, Pluto 2 in Roman mythology, the underworld. Greek equivalent **Hades**

dis- prefix 1 undo, do the opposite o disapprove 2 the opposite or absence of o discourtesy 3 deprive of, remove from o dishonour 4 not o disobedient

disability /díssə bílləti/ (pl **-ties**) n 1 a condition that restricts somebody's ability to perform some or all of the tasks of daily life 2 a factor that prevents or disqualifies somebody from doing something

disable /diss áyb'l/ (**-bling, -bled**) vt 1 restrict somebody in everyday activities 2 stop something from functioning —**disablement** n

disabled /diss áyb'ld/ adj 1 affected by a disability 2 unable to operate or function ■ npl people with disabilities

USAGE Although the adjective **disabled** has a long history of use by those so affected, *people with disabilities* is preferred over the adjectival and noun forms of **disabled**.

disabuse /díssə byōoz/ (**-busing, -bused**) vt make somebody realize that something is untrue

disadvantage /díssəd vaántij/ n 1 a factor that makes something less good or valuable 2 an unfavourable situation ■ vt (**-taging, -taged**) put in an unfavourable situation

disadvantaged /díssəd vaántijd/ adj 1 in a worse position than other people 2 in an unfair position competitively

disadvantageous /díss advən táyjəss, diss ádvən-/ adj unhelpful or unfavourable —**disadvantageously** adv —**disadvantageousness** n

disaffected /díssə féktid/ adj dissatisfied, especially with somebody to whom loyalty and respect are owed

disagree /díssə greé/ vi 1 not agree 2 not correspond 3 have a bad effect

SYNONYMS **disagree, differ, argue, dispute, take issue with, contradict, agree to differ, be at odds** CORE MEANING: have or express a difference of opinion with somebody

disagreeable /díssə greé əb'l/ adj 1 unpleasant 2 rude or quarrelsome —**disagreeableness** n —**disagreeably** adv

disagreement /díssə greémənt/ n 1 failure to agree 2 a minor argument

disallow /díssə lów/ vt 1 reject something 2 cancel something previously allowed —**disallowance** n

disallusion incorrect spelling of **disillusion**

disambiguate /díss am bíggyoo ayt/ (**-ating, -ated**) vt make unambiguous —**disambiguation** /díss am bíggyoo áysh'n/ n

disapear incorrect spelling of **disappear**

disapoint incorrect spelling of **disappoint**

disappear /díssə peér/ vi 1 vanish from sight 2 no longer be in a place 3 cease to exist —**disappearance** n

disappoint /díssə póynt/ v 1 vi be less good than expected 2 vt fail somebody by not doing as expected —**disappointed** adj —**disappointedly** adv —**disappointing** adj —**disappointingly** adv

disappointment /díssə póyntmənt/ n 1 the feeling of being let down 2 something disappointing

disapprobation /diss ápprə báysh'n/ n condemnation (fml)

disapproval /díssə proov'l/ n an attitude of dislike or condemnation

disapprove /díssə proov/ (-proving, -proved) v 1 vi judge somebody or something negatively 2 vt refuse to sanction (fml) —**disapproving** adj —**disapprovingly** adv

SYNONYMS **disapprove, frown on, object, criticize, condemn, deplore, denounce, censure** CORE MEANING: have an unfavourable opinion of

disarm /diss aárm/ v 1 vti give up or force to give up weapons 2 vt defuse a bomb 3 vt make somebody feel less hostile —**disarming** adj —**disarmingly** adv

disarmament /diss aármǝmǝnt/ n 1 a reduction in arms 2 the state of having given up arms

disarrange /díssə ráynj/ (-ranging, -ranged) vt make untidy —**disarrangement** n

disarray /díssə ráy/ n 1 a disorganized state 2 untidiness ■ vt 1 make disorganized 2 make somebody feel less hostile (archaic)

disassemble /díssə sémb'l/ (-bling, -bled) vt take apart —**disassembly** n

disassociate /díssə sŏshi ayt, -sŏssi-/ (-ating, -ated) v 1 vt end somebody's association with something 2 vr distance yourself from somebody or something

disaster /di zaàstər/ n a very damaging or destructive event

ORIGIN Disasters get their name from astrology. The word was adopted in the late 16C from an Italian word that means literally 'ill-starred'. In astrology disasters are attributed to the adverse influence of the stars. The Italian word derives from the Latin for 'star', the source of astrology itself, as well as astral, astronomy, and other words beginning astro-.

disaster area n a place that is in a state of emergency after a natural disaster

disaster movie n a film about a disastrous event

~~disasterous~~ incorrect spelling of **disastrous**

disastrous /di zaàstrəss/ adj 1 having very damaging or destructive results 2 completely unsuccessful —**disastrously** adv —**disastrousness** n

~~disatisfied~~ incorrect spelling of **dissatisfied**

disavow /díssə vów/ vt deny any knowledge of or association with —**disavowal** n —**disavowedly** /-idli/ adv

disband /diss bánd/ vti break up as a group, or break up a group —**disbandment** n

disbar /diss baár/ (-barring, -barred) vt bar a barrister from practising law —**disbarment** n

disbelief /díss bi leéf/ n a feeling of not believing

disbelieve /díss bi leév/ (-lieving, -lieved) v 1 vt not believe 2 vi have no religious faith —**disbeliever** n —**disbelieving** adj —**disbelievingly** adv

disburse /diss búrss/ (-bursing, -bursed) vt pay out —**disbursement** n

SPELLCHECK Do not confuse the spelling of **disburse** and **disperse** ('scatter'), which sound similar.

disc, disk n 1 a round flat object 2 a circular piece of metal on a vehicle's wheel that a pad presses against 3 a circular blade on a plough 4 a flat round part between the bones of the spine 5 the centre of a flower head 6 a gramophone record

discard /diss kaárd/ vt 1 throw something away 2 in card games, reject a card from a hand ■ n 1 /díss kaard/ the act of discarding a playing card 2 something discarded

discern /di súrn, -zúrn/ vt 1 see or notice something that is not obvious 2 understand something —**discernible** adj —**discernibly** adv —**discernment** n

discerning /di súrning, -zúrning/ adj showing good judgment and taste —**discerningly** adv

discharge v /diss chaárj/ (-charging, -charged) 1 vti emit or dispose of a liquid or gas 2 vt dismiss or release somebody from something such as a hospital or other institution, employment, or the armed forces 3 vt carry out a duty (fml) 4 vt pay a debt (fml) 5 vti shoot a bullet, or be shot from a gun (fml) 6 vti offload a cargo or empty something of its contents 7 vti lose an electric charge 8 vti drain electricity from a device, or be drained ■ n /díss chaárj/ 1 an act of discharging somebody 2 a flow of liquid, especially mucus, from the body 3 emission or rate of emission 4 the performance of a duty (fml) 5 the payment of a debt (fml) 6 the firing of a gun (fml) 7 a continuous flow of electricity through the air 8 the discharging of cargo or contents

disciple /di síp'l/ n 1 a follower of a person or idea 2 also **Disciple** one of the 12 original followers of Jesus Christ —**discipleship** n

disciplinarian /díssəpli náiri ən/ n an enforcer of discipline

disciplinary /díssəplinəri/ adj 1 of enforcement and punishment 2 of an academic subject

discipline /díssəplin/ n 1 the act of making people obey rules 2 a controlled and orderly state, especially among school students 3 calm controlled behaviour 4 a field of activity or subject of study 5 punishment ■ v (-plining, -plined) 1 vr make yourself do something regularly 2 vt punish somebody 3 vt teach obedience or order to somebody —**disciplined** adj

disc jockey n a DJ

disclaim /diss kláym/ *vt* **1** deny a connection with **2** deny the validity of

disclaimer /diss kláymər/ *n* **1** a refusal to accept responsibility **2** a statement renouncing a legal right

disclose /diss klóz/ (**-closing, -closed**) *vt* **1** tell something previously secret **2** show something previously covered —**disclosable** *adj*

disclosure /diss klózhər/ *n* the revealing of information that was previously secret

disco /dískō/ (*pl* **-cos**) *n* **1** a club or party with dancing to pop music **2** pop music with a steady beat for dancing to **3** a style of dancing to disco music

discography /di skóggrəfi/ (*pl* **-phies**) *n* a list of musical recordings —**discographer** *n* —**discographic** /dískə gráffik/ *adj*

discolour /diss kúllər/ *vti* make something take on a faded, darkened, or dirty appearance —**discoloration** /diss kúllə ráysh'n/ *n* —**discoloured** *adj*

discomfit /diss kúmfit/ *vt* **1** make somebody unsettled or confused **2** thwart plans *(fml)* —**discomfiture** *n*

discomfort /diss kúmfərt/ *n* **1** a state of physical unease **2** embarrassment **3** a cause of unease ■ *vt* make uncomfortable —**discomforting** *adj*

discomposure /dískəm pózhər/ *n* loss of mental or physical composure —**discompose** *vt*

disconcert /dískən súrt/ *vt* make somebody feel uneasy —**disconcerted** *adj* —**disconcerting** *adj*

disconnect /dískə nékt/ *v* **1** *vti* detach an appliance from a power source **2** *vt* shut off the supply of a public utility **3** *vt* break a telephone connection between two people **4** *vt* detach one part from another —**disconnection** *n*

disconnected /dískə néktid/ *adj* lacking any logical connection —**disconnectedly** *adv* —**disconnectedness** *n*

disconsolate /diss kónssələt/ *adj* extremely sad and disappointed —**disconsolately** *adv*

discontent /dískən tént/ *n* dissatisfied unhappiness

discontented /dískən téntid/ *adj* dissatisfied and unhappy about something —**discontentedly** *adv* —**discontentedness** *n*

discontinue /dískən tínnyoo/ (**-uing, -ued**) *v* **1** *vti* stop doing something **2** *vt* stop manufacturing a product —**discontinuance** *n* —**discontinuation** /dískən tínnyoo áysh'n/ *n* —**discontinued** *adj*

discontinuity /díss konti nyóo əti/ (*pl* **-ties**) *n* a break in an otherwise continuous process

discontinuous /dískən tínnyoo əss/ *adj* having gaps or breaks

discord /díss kawrd/ *n* **1** a lack of agreement **2** an inharmonious combination of musical sounds

discordant /diss káwrd'nt/ *adj* **1** disagreeing **2** lacking in musical harmony —**discordance** *n* —**discordantly** *adv*

discotheque /dískə tek/ *n* a disco

discount *n* /díss kownt/ **1** a reduction in the usual price **2** *also* **discount rate** the rate at which expected cash returns from a security are converted into its market price **3** the interest deducted from the value of a promissory note before a sale or loan is completed ■ *v* /diss kównt/ **1** *vt* reject something as untrue or trivial **2** *vt* reduce a product in price **3** *vti* make a loan at a reduced rate ■ *adj* /diss kównt/ reduced in price —**discountable** /diss kówntəb'l, díss kowntəb'l/ *adj*

discountenance /diss kówntinənss/ (**-nancing, -nanced**) *vt* embarrass *(fml)*

discount store, discounter /diss kówntər, díss kowntər/ *n* a shop selling discounted goods

discourage /diss kúrrij/ (**-aging, -aged**) *vt* **1** try to stop somebody from doing something **2** tend to stop something by making it difficult or unpleasant **3** make somebody lose hope or enthusiasm —**discouragement** *n* —**discouraging** *adj*

discourse *n* /díss kawrss/ **1** a serious speech or piece of writing **2** a serious conversation **3** the language used in a particular context o *political discourse* ■ *vi* /diss káwrss/ (**-coursing, -coursed**) **1** speak or write seriously on a topic **2** converse *(fml)*

discourtesy /diss kúrtəssi/ (*pl* **-sies**) *n* a rude action or rude behaviour —**discourteous** *adj* —**discourteously** *adv*

discover /diss kúvvər/ *vt* **1** find something out o *soon discovered my mistake* **2** be the first to find or learn something **3** find somebody or something by chance or by searching o *was discovered living in Florida* **4** first notice an interest in or a talent for something —**discoverer** *n*

discovery /diss kúvvəri/ (*pl* **-ies**) *n* **1** something learnt or found **2** the process of finding out something previously unknown **3** the process of finding somebody or something by chance or by searching

discredit /diss kréddit/ *vt* **1** damage the reputation or standing of **2** cast doubt on ■ *n* loss of reputation or standing o *brought the game into discredit* —**discreditable** *adj*

discreet /di skreet/ *adj* **1** careful to avoid causing upset or embarrassment to others **2** good at keeping secrets **3** subtle and tasteful o *wearing discreet makeup* **4** not ostentatious —**discreetly** *adv* —**discreetness** *n*

SPELLCHECK Do not confuse the spelling of **discreet** and **discrete** ('completely separate'), which sound similar.

---

discrepancy /di skréppənssi/ (*pl* **-cies**) *n* a difference between two things that should match or correspond o *found a discrepancy in the figures* —**discrepant** *adj*

discrete /di skreet/ *adj* completely separate —**discretely** *adv* —**discreteness** *n* ◊ See note at **discreet**

discretion /di krésh'n/ *n* **1** the ability to avoid causing upset or embarrassment to others

2 the freedom to decide about something
3 the ability to keep secrets

discretionary /di skrésh'nəri/ *adj* 1 giving somebody the freedom to decide about something 2 given or refused according to circumstances

discriminate /di skrími nayt/ (-nating, -nated) *v* 1 *vi* treat somebody unfairly because of prejudice 2 *vti* discern differences between things

discriminating /di skrími nayting/ *adj* showing an ability to recognize superior quality —**discriminatingly** *adv*

discrimination /di skrími náysh'n/ *n* 1 unfair treatment of people, e.g. on grounds of race, ethnicity, or gender 2 the ability to recognize superior quality

discriminatory /di skríminətəri/ *adj* treating somebody unfairly, e.g. on grounds of race, ethnicity, or gender —**discriminatorily** *adv*

~~discription~~ incorrect spelling of **description**

discursive /diss kúrssiv/ *adj* lengthy and containing digressions

discus /dískəss/ (*pl* -**cuses** *or* -**ci** /-kī/) *n* 1 a disc thrown in athletics 2 the sporting event of throwing the discus

discuss /di skúss/ *vt* 1 talk about a subject with somebody in order to explore it or reach a decision 2 write or speak about a topic formally —**discussant** *n*

discussion /di skúsh'n/ *n* 1 a talk among people about a topic or an issue 2 a spoken or written examination of a topic

disdain /diss dáyn/ *n* complete lack of respect ■ *vt* regard with contempt —**disdainful** *adj* —**disdainfully** *adv*

disease /di zeéz/ *n* 1 a condition with pathological symptoms in humans, plants, or animals 2 a disorder with recognizable signs —**diseased** *adj*

disembark /díssim báark/ *vi* get off a passenger vehicle —**disembarkation** /diss ém baar káysh'n, díss im-/ *n*

disembodied /díssim bóddid/ *adj* lacking physical presence ○ *the eerie sound of a disembodied voice in the passageway*

disembowel /díssim bów əl/ (-**elling**, -**elled**) *vt* remove the internal organs of —**disembowelment** *n*

disempower /díssim pów ər/ *vt* remove authority or confidence from —**disempowerment** *n*

disenchant /díssin chaànt/ *vt* create dissatisfaction with somebody or something previously regarded as good —**disenchanted** *adj* —**disenchantment** *n*

disenfranchise /díssin fránch īz/ (-**chising**, -**chised**) *vt* deprive of a right, especially the right to vote —**disenfranchisement** /-fránchizmənt/ *n*

disengage /díssin gáyj/ (-**gaging**, -**gaged**) *v* 1 *vti* disconnect one thing from another, or become disconnected 2 *vt* detach yourself mentally 3 *vti* end involvement in a war or combat —**disengagement** *n*

disentangle /díssin táng g'l/ (-**gling**, -**gled**) *vt* 1 untangle things that are tied or knotted together 2 clarify something confusing 3 free somebody else or yourself from a complicated situation —**disentanglement** *n*

disequilibrium /díss eekwi líbbri əm/ *n* a lack of stability or balance

disestablish /díssi stáblish/ *vt* 1 stop an established custom 2 end the connection between a state and its official church —**disestablishment** *n*

disfavour /diss fáyvər/ *n* 1 the state of being disapproved of 2 a feeling of disapproval

disfigure /diss fíggər/ (-**uring**, -**ured**) *vt* spoil the appearance of —**disfigurement** *n* — *adj*

disfranchise /dis fránch īz/ (-**chising**, -**chised**) *vt* disenfranchise somebody —**disfranchisement** /dis fránchizmənt/ *n*

disgorge /diss gáwrj/ (-**gorging**, -**gorged**) *vt* 1 pour out in a stream ○ *disgorged the contents of her purse* 2 let out in large numbers ○ *the factory disgorging workers* 3 regurgitate or vomit

disgrace /diss gráyss/ *n* 1 shame or loss of the respect of others 2 something shameful or unacceptable ■ *vt* (-**gracing**, -**graced**) bring shame or loss of respect or status to

disgraceful /diss gráyssf'l/ *adj* shamefully bad or unacceptable —**disgracefully** *adv*

disguise /diss gíz/ *vt* (-**guising**, -**guised**) 1 change somebody's appearance to prevent recognition 2 hide feelings or facts ○ *could barely disguise her delight* ■ *n* 1 a change of appearance made to prevent recognition 2 the state of being changed in appearance ○ *went to the ball in disguise* —**disguised** *adj*

disgruntled /diss grúntl'd/ *adj* dissatisfied and irritated

disgust /diss gúst/ *n* 1 strong disapproval or distaste 2 impatient irritation ■ *vt* make somebody feel revolted —**disgusted** *adj* —**disgusting** *adj* ◊ See note at **dislike**

dish *n* 1 a single serving of food 2 food prepared according to a particular recipe or style 3 a radio or television receiver 4 somebody good-looking (*slang*) ■ **dishes** *npl* dirty plates, cutlery, and pans
□ **dish out** *vt* 1 hand out freely (*infml*) 2 serve food

dishabille *n* = deshabille

disharmony /diss háarməni/ *n* 1 conflict between people 2 lack of musical harmony —**disharmonious** /díss haar mōni əss/ *adj*

dishcloth /dísh kloth/ *n* a cloth for washing or drying dishes

dishearten /diss háart'n/ *vt* make somebody lose confidence or enthusiasm —**disheartening** *adj*

dishevel /di shévv'l/ (-**elling**, -**elled**) *vt* cause somebody's hair or clothes to look untidy —**dishevelment** *n*

dishonest /diss ónnist/ *adj* deceitful or lying —**dishonestly** *adv*

dishonesty /diss ónnisti/ *n* deceitful behaviour

dishonour /diss ónnər/ n 1 loss of other people's respect 2 failure or refusal by a bank to pay a cheque (fml) ■ vt 1 bring shame on somebody or something 2 break a promise or agreement 3 fail or refuse to pay a cheque

dishonourable /diss ónnərəb'l/ adj shameful and bringing a loss of respect or reputation —**dishonourably** adv

dishonourable discharge n dismissal from the armed forces for misconduct

dishrag /dísh rag/ n a dishcloth

dishwasher /dísh woshər/ n 1 a machine for washing dishes 2 somebody employed to wash dishes

dishwater /dísh wawtər/ n water used for washing dishes

dishy /díshi/ (-ier, -iest) adj good-looking (infml)

disign incorrect spelling of **design**

disillusion /dissi loozh'n/ vt show somebody that an ideal or belief is mistaken ■ n also **disillusionment** disappointment caused by realizing that an ideal or belief is mistaken —**disillusioned** adj

disincentive /díssin séntiv/ n a deterrent or discouragement

disinclination /díssinkli náysh'n/ n a reluctance to do something —**disinclined** /díssin klínd/ adj

disinfect /díssin fékt/ vt rid of bacteria using a chemical liquid —**disinfection** n

disinfectant /díssin féktənt/ n a chemical for killing bacteria

disinformation /díssinfər máysh'n/ n deliberately misleading information

ORIGIN **Disinformation** is modelled on a Russian word, *dezinformatsiya*.

disingenuous /díssin jénnyoo əss/ adj slyly insincere —**disingenuously** adv

disinherit /díssin hérrit/ vt deprive of an inheritance —**disinheritance** n

disintegrate /diss ínti grayt/ (-grating, -grated) vti 1 break into fragments 2 lose or cause to lose unity 3 undergo or cause to undergo atomic fission —**disintegration** /diss ínti gráysh'n/ n

disinter /díssin túr/ (-terring, -terred) vt 1 dig up a buried corpse 2 expose something hidden (fml) —**disinterment** n

disinterest /diss íntrəst/ vt cause to lose interest or partiality ■ n 1 impartiality 2 a lack of interest ◊ See note at **disinterested**

disinterested /diss íntrəstid/ adj 1 impartial 2 ⚠ not interested —**disinterestedly** adv

USAGE **disinterested** or **uninterested**? **Disinterested** means 'impartial' and also has a widely used but much criticized meaning, 'not interested'.

disinvest /díssin vést/ vti withdraw investment in something —**disinvestment** n

disipline incorrect spelling of **discipline**

disjointed /diss jóyntid/ adj not connected in

an easily understandable way —**disjointedly** adv

disjunction /diss júngksh'n/ n a disconnection of joined parts

disjunctive /diss júngktiv/ adj dividing or separating (technical) —**disjunctively** adv

disk n 1 an information storage device used in a computer 2 = **disc**

disk drive n a device for reading data from and writing data to computer disks

diskette /di skét/ n COMPUT = **floppy disk**

disk operating system n a computer operating system

dislike /diss lík/ vt (-liking, -liked) have no liking for somebody or something ■ n 1 a feeling of disapproval or distaste 2 something considered disagreeable —**dislikable** adj

SYNONYMS **dislike**, **distaste**, **hatred**, **hate**, **disgust**, **loathing**, **repugnance**, **abhorrence**, **animosity**, **antipathy**, **aversion**, **revulsion** CORE MEANING: a feeling of not liking somebody or something

dislocate /dísslə kayt/ (-cating, -cated) vt 1 put something out of its usual place 2 move a body part from its normal position —**dislocation** /dísslə káysh'n/ n

dislodge /diss lój/ (-lodging, -lodged) v remove from a fixed position —**dislodgment** n

disloyal /diss lóy əl/ adj failing to support or be true to somebody or something —**disloyally** adv —**disloyalty** n

dismal /dízm'l/ adj 1 depressing 2 of a poor standard or quality —**dismally** adv

ORIGIN **Dismal** comes ultimately from Latin *dies mali*, literally 'evil days', referring to the 24 days in the year that were unlucky according to ancient and medieval belief. The word is first recorded in English as a noun in the early medieval period, in *the dismal*, meaning these days. As an adjective it occurs earliest in *dismal day*, but from the late 16C begins to be associated with things other than 'day'.

dismantle /diss mánt'l/ (-tling, -tled) v 1 vti take or come apart 2 vt destroy by removing key elements 3 vt remove equipment or furniture from —**dismantlement** n

dismay /diss máy/ vt discourage or alarm ■ n a feeling of anxious discouragement —**dismayingly** adv

dismember /diss mémbər/ vt 1 remove the limbs from a body 2 divide something up —**dismemberment** n

dismiss /diss míss/ vt 1 end somebody's employment 2 send somebody away 3 refuse to consider something 4 refuse to give a legal case further hearing in court 5 put a player or team out of a match or competition —**dismissal** n —**dismissible** adj

dismissive /diss míssiv/ adj contemptuously ignoring or refusing to consider something —**dismissively** adv

dismount /diss mównt/ vi 1 get off an animal's

back **2** get off a bicycle or motorcycle —**dismount** n

CORBIS/Bettmann

Walt Disney

Disney /dízni/, **Walt** (1901–66) US animator and producer

disobedient /díssə beédi ənt/ adj refusing to obey —**disobedience** n —**disobediently** adv

disobey /díssə báy/ (**-beys, -beying, -beyed**) vti refuse to obey

disobliging /díssə blíjing/ adj unwilling to help

~~disolve~~ incorrect spelling of **dissolve**

disorder /diss áwrdər/ n **1** an illness **2** a lack of order or organization **3** public violence or rioting

disordered /diss áwrdərd/ adj **1** untidy or confused **2** not functioning normally —**disorderedness** n

disorderly /diss áwrdərli/ adj **1** lacking order **2** unruly **3** disturbing the public order —**disorderliness** n

disorderly conduct n behaviour likely to cause a breach of the peace

disorganization /diss áwrgə nī záysh'n/, **disorganisation** n lack of organization or method —**disorganize** vt

disorientate /diss áwri ən tayt/ (**-tating, -tated**), **disorient** /diss áwri ənt/ vt make somebody lose his or her bearings —**disorientated** adj —**disorientation** /diss áwri ən táysh'n/ n

disown /diss ốn/ vt deny a relationship with —**disownment** n

~~dispair~~ incorrect spelling of **despair**

disparage /di spárrij/ (**-aging, -aged**) vt express contempt or disapproval for —**disparagement** n —**disparaging** adj —**disparagingly** adv

disparate /díspərət/ adj very different —**disparately** adv —**disparateness** n

~~disparity~~ incorrect spelling of **disparity**

disparity /di spárrəti/ (pl **-ties**) n **1** a lack of equality **2** a lack of similarity

dispassionate /diss pásh'nət/ adj calmly objective —**dispassionately** adv

dispatch /di spách/, **despatch** vt **1** send something off **2** deal with quickly **3** kill a person or an animal ■ n **1** an act of dispatching somebody or something **2** speed in doing or going **3** an official message **4** a news report —**dispatcher** n

dispatch box n **1** a red case for documents used by a British government minister **2 Dispatch Box** a lectern in the British Parliament from which a minister speaks

dispel /di spél/ (**-pelling, -pelled**) vt rid somebody's mind of something, e.g. a mistaken idea

dispensable /di spénssəb'l/ adj not essential

dispensary /di spénssəri/ (pl **-ries**) n **1** a place where a pharmacist prepares and supplies medicines to patients **2** a medical centre on a naval vessel or a military installation

dispensation /díspən sáysh'n/ n **1** an exemption **2** a document giving an exemption **3** in Christian belief, a divinely ordained system —**dispensational** adj

dispense /di spénss/ (**-pensing, -pensed**) vt **1** distribute something to a number of people **2** supply a product **3** prepare and supply medicines

□ **dispense with** vt manage without

dispenser /di spénssər/ n **1** a device for dispensing goods (usually in combination) **2** a distributor of something

~~dispensible~~ incorrect spelling of **dispensable**

dispersal /di spúrss'l/ n distribution of people or things over an area

disperse /di spúrss/ (**-persing, -persed**) vti **1** scatter in different directions **2** distribute over a wide area **3** disappear or cause to disappear

dispersion /di spúrsh'n/ n **1** the scattering or distribution of something over an area **2** the state of being scattered or distributed over an area

dispirited /di spírritid/ adj discouraged —**dispiritedly** adv

dispiriting /di spírriting/ adj causing discouragement —**dispiritingly** adv

displace /diss pláyss/ (**-placing, -placed**) vt **1** move from the usual place **2** force to leave home because of war **3** replace —**displaceable** adj

displaced person n a refugee

displacement /diss pláyssmənt/ n **1** movement of something from its usual place **2** the fluid displaced by an object such as a ship **3** the amount of movement of an object in a particular direction

display /di spláy/ v **1** vt make visible or evident **2** vti show data or appear on a monitor ■ n **1** a set of things arranged or done for others to see (often in combination) **2** the state of being visible or arranged for viewing **3** an act of showing a feeling or quality ○ a display of courage **4** an electronic device presenting visual information

displease /diss pleéz/ (**-pleasing, -pleased**) vti annoy —**displeased** adj —**displeasure** /diss plézhər/ n

disport /di spáwrt/ vi behave playfully (archaic or humorous)

disposable /di spózəb'l/ adj **1** throwaway **2** available for use —**disposability** /di spózə bílləti/ n —**disposableness** n

disposable income n income after obligations have been met

disposal /di spóz'l/ n **1** the process of getting

rid of something **2** the orderly arrangement of something **3** the transfer of something to somebody else's ownership ◊ **at somebody's disposal** available for somebody's use or to do somebody's bidding

dispose /di spóz/ (**-posing, -posed**) v **1** vt put people or things into a particular order or place (fml) ○ a commander who disposed his forces along the coast **2** vti settle something (fml) ○ an outcome to be disposed by the court **3** vt incline somebody to do something □ **dispose of** vt **1** get rid of **2** transfer to somebody else's ownership

disposed /di spózd/ adj **1** inclined or tending to something **2** with a particular attitude towards ○ favourably disposed to us

disposition /díspə zísh'n/ n **1** temperament **2** a behavioural tendency **3** the settlement of something (fml)—**dispositional** adj

dispossess /díspə zéss/ vt take away property from (fml)—**dispossession** n—**dispossessor** n

dispossessed /díspə zést/ adj deprived of property or rights ■ npl dispossessed people

disproportion /díspra páwrsh'n/ n a state of being out of proportion

disproportionate /díspra páwrsh'nat/, **disproportional** /-sh'nal/ adj out of proportion—**disproportionately** adv

disprove /diss próov/ (**-proving, -proved**) vt prove something wrong—**disproof** /diss próof/ n—**disprovable** adj—**disproval** n

disputable /di spyóotab'l/ adj open to argument—**disputably** adv

disputation /díspyóo táysh'n/ n (fml) **1** argument **2** a formal academic debate

disputatious /díspyóo táyshəss/ adj argumentative

dispute /di spyóot/ v (**-puting, -puted**) **1** vti question the truth of **2** vi disagree or argue **3** vt contest or fight for (fml) ○ disputed territory ■ n **1** /di spyóot, díss pyoot/ an argument **2** a disagreement between workers and management ○ a labour dispute ◊ See note at **disagree**

disqualify /diss kwólli fí/ (**-fies, -fied**) vt **1** make ineligible **2** take away a legal right from—**disqualification** /diss kwóllifi káysh'n/ n—**disqualified** adj

disquiet /diss kwí ət/ n a state of inner unease ■ vt make anxious (literary)—**disquieting** adj

disquisition /dískwi zísh'n/ n a long essay or speech—**disquisitional** adj

Disraeli /diz ráyli/, **Benjamin, 1st Earl of Beac-**

Benjamin Disraeli

onsfield (1804–81) British prime minister (1868, 1874–80)

disregard /díssri gaárd/ vt ignore ■ n lack of attention or respect—**disregardful** adj

disrepair /díssri páir/ n poor condition

disreputable /diss réppyōotab'l/ adj not respectable—**disreputableness** n—**disreputably** adv

disrepute /díssri pyóot/ n lack of a good reputation

disrespect /díssri spékt/ n a lack of respect ■ vt show no respect for—**disrespectful** adj—**disrespectfully** adv

disrobe /diss rób/ (**-robing, -robed**) vti undress—**disrobement** n

disrupt /diss rúpt/ vt interrupt the normal course or functioning of—**disruption** /diss rúpsh'n/ n—**disruptive** adj—**disruptively** adv—**disruptiveness** n

~~dissapear~~ incorrect spelling of **disappear**

~~dissapoint~~ incorrect spelling of **disappoint**

dissatisfaction /díss satiss fáksh'n, di sáttiss-/ n discontent

dissatisfy /díss sáttiss fí/ (**-fies, -fied**) vt fail to satisfy—**dissatisfied** adj

dissect /dī sékt, di-/ v **1** vti cut up a dead organism and examine it scientifically **2** vt examine something in detail ○ dissected the speech—**dissection** /dī séksh'n, di-/ n

dissemble /di sémb'l/ (**-bling, -bled**) vi pretend in order to conceal information or feelings—**dissemblance** n

disseminate /di sémmi nayt/ (**-nating, -nated**) vti spread something far and wide—**dissemination** /di sémmi náysh'n/ n ◊ See note at **scatter**

dissension /di sénsh'n/ n disagreement

dissent /di sént/ vi **1** disagree with a majority or official view **2** reject the doctrine of an established church ■ n **1** disagreement from a generally held opinion **2** rejection of the doctrine of an established church **3** refusal to accept a political regime—**dissenting** adj ◊ See note at **descent**

dissenter /di séntər/ n **1** somebody who disagrees **2 Dissenter** a Protestant opposed to the Church of England's authority in the 17C and 18C

dissertation /díssər táysh'n/ n a long essay, especially one written for a university degree—**dissertational** adj

disservice /diss súrviss/ n an action that causes harm

dissident /díssidənt/ n somebody who disagrees publicly with a political or religious system—**dissidence** n—**dissident** adj

dissimilar /di símmilər/ adj different—**dissimilarity** /díssimi lárrəti/ n—**dissimilarly** adv

dissimulate /di símmyōo layt/ (**-lating, -lated**) vti hide your true feelings—**dissimulation** /di símmyōo láysh'n/ n

dissipate /díssi payt/ (**-pating, -pated**) v **1** vti disappear or cause to disappear gradually

○ *storm clouds dissipating* **2** *vt* spend wastefully —**dissipation** /díssi páysh'n/ *n*

dissipated /díssi paytid/ *adj* overindulging in physical pleasure

dissociate /di sṓshi ayt, -sṓssi-/ (**-ating, -ated**) *vt* **1** regard as distinct **2** = **disassociate** —**dissociable** *adj* —**dissociative** *adj*

dissolution /díssə loósh'n/ *n* **1** the breaking down of something into parts **2** the dissolving of an organization, assembly, or relationship **3** the formal closing of an assembly or parliament **4** the ending of a legal relationship

dissolve /di zólv/ *v* (**-solving, -solved**) **1** *vti* become or make something become absorbed in a liquid **2** *vti* break up an organization **3** *vi* suddenly express an emotion such as laughter or tears ○ *He dissolved into tears.* **4** *vt* formally close an assembly or parliament **5** *vt* end a legal relationship such as a marriage ■ *n* the fading out of one film scene and the fading in of the next —**dissolvable** *adj*

dissonance /díssənənss/ *n* **1** an unpleasant combination of sounds or musical notes **2** inconsistency between ideas —**dissonant** *adj*

dissuade /di swáyd/ (**-suading, -suaded**) *vt* talk somebody out of doing something —**dissuadable** *adj* —**dissuasion** /di swáyzh'n/ *n* —**dissuasive** *adj*

distaff /dí staaf/ (*pl* **-taffs** *or* **-taves** /-stayvz/) *n* a rod on which wool is wound for use in spinning ◇ **on the distaff side** regarding the women or the female side of a family

distance /dístənss/ *n* **1** length in space, time, or attitude, especially between two things ○ *the distance between Paris and New York* **2** a place or position at a distinct remove ○ *seen from a distance* **3** closeness allowing an activity ○ *within hailing distance* **4** the state of being aloof **5** an interval of time ○ *at a distance of 20 years* ■ *v* (**-tancing, -tanced**) **1** *vr* put at a distance from ○ *distanced herself from the family argument* **2** *vt* say or show that you do not support somebody or something ○ *distanced himself from the disgraced politician* ◇ **go the distance** continue to the end of a task or project

distance learning *n* study by mail or electronic means

distant /dístənt/ *adj* far away in space, time, or attitude —**distantly** *adv* —**distantness** *n*

distaste /diss táyst/ *n* disapproval or dislike ◇ See note at **dislike**

distasteful /diss táystf'l/ *adj* unpleasant and eliciting dislike or disapproval —**distastefully** *adv* —**distastefulness** *n*

distemper[1] /di stémpər/ *n* a viral disease of domestic animals

distemper[2] /di stémpər/ *n* paint containing glue or size instead of oil —**distemper** *vt*

distend /di sténd/ *vti* swell or inflate —**distensible** /-sténssəb'l/ *adj* —**distension** /-sténsh'n/ *n*

distil /di stíl/ (**-tilling, -tilled**) *v* **1** *vt* make alcoholic spirits **2** *vti* purify liquid by heating it and then condensing its vapour **3** *vt* create something from essential elements —**distillation** /dístə láysh'n/ *n*

distill *vti* US = **distil**

distillate /dístələt, -ayt/ *n* liquid produced by distillation

distiller /di stíllər/ *n* a manufacturer of alcoholic spirits —**distillery** *n*

distinct /di stíngkt/ *adj* **1** clearly separate **2** apparent to the senses **3** certain or definite ○ *a distinct possibility* —**distinctly** *adv* —**distinctness** *n*

distinction /di stíngksh'n/ *n* **1** a difference **2** high quality ○ *research of distinction* **3** something to be proud of **4** a high mark in an examination

distinctive /di stíngktiv/ *adj* uniquely characteristic of somebody or something —**distinctively** *adv* —**distinctiveness** *n*

distinguish /di stíng gwish/ *v* **1** *vti* recognize differences between people or things ○ *distinguish between virtue and vice* **2** *vt* be the difference between people or things ○ *What distinguishes dogs from wolves?* **3** *vt* recognize or identify something ○ *distinguished a flaw in the crystal* **4** *vr* do something well —**distinguishable** *adj* —**distinguishing** *adj*

distinguished /di stíng gwisht/ *adj* **1** recognized for excellence **2** authoritative and dignified

distort /di stáwrt/ *v* **1** *vti* alter or cause to alter in shape, form, or appearance **2** *vt* describe inaccurately —**distorted** *adj* —**distortedness** *n* —**distortion** *n*

distract /di strákt/ *vt* **1** divert somebody's attention from something **2** amuse or entertain somebody —**distracted** *adj* —**distracting** *adj* —**distractingly** *adv* —**distractor** *n*

distraction /di stráksh'n/ *n* **1** a thing that diverts attention from something else **2** an amusement **3** a state of emotional upset

distrait /di stráy, dí stray/ *adj* distracted and inattentive (*literary*)

distraught /di stráwt/ *adj* extremely upset

distress /di stréss/ *n* **1** mental suffering **2** hardship or difficulty **3** severe physical pain ■ *vt* upset somebody —**distressing** *adj* —**distressingly** *adv*

distressed /di strést/ *adj* **1** very upset **2** lacking money (*dated*) **3** describes furniture or fabric made to look old

distress signal *n* a signal requesting help sent by a ship or aircraft in trouble

distribute /di stríbbyoot/ (**-uting, -uted**) *vt* **1** give or share things out **2** spread or scatter things about **3** US sell and deliver goods —**distributable** *adj* —**distribution** /dístri byoósh'n/ *n* —**distributional** *adj* ◇ See note at **scatter**

distributive /di stríbbyootiv/ *adj* **1** involving distribution **2** producing equal results —**distributively** *adv*

distributor /di stríbbyootər/, **distributer** *n* **1** a person, group, or firm that distributes something **2** a wholesaler **3** a device in an engine for conveying electricity to the spark plugs

district /dístrikt/ n **1** an area of a town or country **2** the area surrounding a particular place

district attorney n in the US, the official prosecutor for a specific urban jurisdiction

district court n **1** in Scotland, a magistrates' court **2** in Australia, a court for minor offences

district nurse n a community nurse

District of Columbia federal district of the E United States, coextensive with the city of Washington, D.C.

~~distroy~~ incorrect spelling of **destroy**

distrust /diss trúst/ n a lack of trust —**distrust** vt —**distrustful** adj —**distrustfully** adv

disturb /di stúrb/ vt **1** interrupt somebody busy **2** make somebody feel anxious or uneasy **3** change the shape or position of something **4** spoil the peace and quiet of something —**disturbing** adj —**disturbingly** adv ◊ See note at **bother**

disturbance /di stúrbənss/ n **1** disruption **2** a commotion **3** psychological or emotional difficulties

disturbed /di stúrbd/ adj **1** anxious or uneasy **2** affected by a psychological disorder

disuse /diss yóoss/ n the state of not being in use —**disused** /-yóozd/ adj

ditch n a narrow drainage or irrigation channel ■ v (infml) **1** vt abandon or throw away **2** vti make or cause to make an emergency landing on water

ditchwater /dích wawtər/ n stagnant water in ditches ◊ as dull as ditchwater

dither /díthər/ vi be agitated and indecisive ■ n an agitated or indecisive state

dithering /díthəring/ n **1** nervous indecisiveness **2** the mixing of pixels of different colours on a computer screen to create new colours

ditsy /dítsi/ (-sier, -siest), **ditzy** (-zier, -ziest) adj US, Can seeming silly or scatterbrained (slang)

ditto /díttō/ interj indicates that the same thing applies to you (infml) ■ adv indicates that the same thing applies ■ n (pl -tos) a pair of symbols (") representing text repeated exactly from what appears above

ORIGIN Ditto derives from a northern form of Italian detto, literally 'said', used in much the same way as English said meaning 'previously mentioned' (The said car was later found abandoned). In Italian, and originally in English in the 17C, it referred only to the month just mentioned. After the 17C, however, it extended its range to mean 'the same, similar(ly)'.

ditty /dítti/ (pl -ties) n a short simple song

diuretic /díyoo réttik/ adj causing increased urine output —**diuretic** n —**diuretically** adv

diurnal /dī úrn'l/ adj **1** happening or active in the daytime **2** happening every day —**diurnally** adv

div. abbr division

diva /déevə/ (pl **vas** or **-ve** /-vay/) n **1** a well-known woman opera singer **2** a successful woman performer

divan /di ván/ n **1** a bed with no headboard or footboard **2** a backless sofa

ORIGIN Divan came into English via French and Italian from Turkish and Persian. It was first adopted in the late 16C as the Ottoman council of state and the room in which it was held. The long seats against the wall that were characteristic of Eastern courts and council chambers had also come to have the Persian name for **divan**, and this appears in English in the early 18C. The modern 'sofa' developed from there.

dive /dīv/ vi (**diving, dived**) **1** jump headfirst into water **2** swim or submerge under water **3** descend or make an aircraft descend steeply and rapidly **4** move suddenly and rapidly ◊ dive for the door **5** put a hand quickly into something to remove something ◊ dived into the drawer to retrieve her ID card **6** drop in value ■ n **1** an act or instance of diving **2** a disreputable establishment (infml) —**diver** n —**diving** n

dive-bomb vt descend steeply and drop bombs on —**dive-bomber** n —**dive-bombing** n

diverge /dī vúrj/ (**-verging, -verged**) vi **1** move apart **2** differ —**diverging** adj

divergence /dī vúrjənss/, **divergency** /-jənssi/ (pl **-cies**) n **1** a difference or disparity **2** the process of moving apart **3** the amount by which one thing differs from something else —**divergent** adj

divers /dívərz/ adj several or many (literary)

diverse /dī vúrss, dī vurss/ adj **1** consisting of different things ◊ culturally diverse **2** differing from one another

diversify /dī vúrssi fī/ (**-fies, -fied**) vti **1** make or become varied **2** expand into new areas of business —**diversification** /dī vúrssifi káysh'n/ n —**diversified** adj

diversion /dī vúrsh'n/ n **1** an enjoyable activity **2** an alternative route for traffic **3** a change in the purpose or direction of something **4** a mock attack —**diversionary** adj

diversity /dī vúrssəti/ n **1** variety **2** social inclusiveness

divert /dī vúrt/ vt **1** change the route of **2** draw attention from **3** change the purpose or use of **4** amuse —**diverting** adj —**divertingly** adv

diverticulitis /dívər tikyoō lítiss/ n inflammation of pockets in the intestine

divertimento /di vúrti méntō/ (pl **-ti** /-ti/) n a piece of light classical instrumental music

divest /dī vést/ vt **1** take something away from somebody or something **2** take something off somebody (fml or humorous) **3** get rid of something —**divestment** n

divestiture /dī véstichər/ n US the sale by a company of one or more of its assets

divide /di víd/ v (**-viding, -vided**) **1** vti split into parts, or be split **2** vti share ◊ divide the spoils *of war* **3** *vi* move apart in different directions **4** *vi* be a boundary between two places **5** *vt* cause disagreement between **6** *vti* calculate how many times one number contains another **7** *vt* mark off in sections ■ *n* 1 a boundary or gap **2** *US, Can* a watershed

dividend /dívvi dend/ *n* 1 a bonus 2 a share-holder's share of a company's profits 3 a number to be divided by another

divider /di vídər/ *n* a device separating some-thing into sections ■ **dividers** *npl* a meas-uring instrument with two hinged legs

dividing line *n* something acting as a bound-ary

divination /dívvi náysh'n/ *n* 1 a search for know-ledge of the future by supernatural means 2 a prophecy —**divinatory** /di vínnətəri/ *adj*

divine /di vín/ *adj* 1 being God or a deity 2 of God or a deity 3 relating to worship 4 ex-presses approval *(infml)* ■ *vt* (**-vining, -vined**) discover by guesswork or intuition ■ *n* 1 a theologian **2** *also* **Divine** God —**divinable** *adj* —**divinely** *adv*

divine right *n* a monarch's supposed God-given right to rule

diving bell *n* a bell-shaped diving apparatus

diving board *n* a raised board beside a swim-ming pool for diving

diving suit *n* a waterproof suit worn for diving

divining rod *n* a forked stick for detecting water or minerals

divinity /di vínnəti/ *n* (*pl* **-ties**) *n* 1 theology 2 the quality of being God or a deity 3 *also* **Divinity** God or a deity

divisible /di vízzəb'l/ *adj* 1 able to be divided 2 able to be separated —**divisibility** /di vízzə bílləti/ *n*

division /di vízh'n/ *n* 1 the splitting of some-thing into parts 2 the sharing out of something 3 the dividing of one number by another 4 a disagreement 5 a separate part, section, or unit of something 6 a self-contained unit of an army —**divisional** *adj*

division sign *n* a mathematical sign indicating division

divisive /di víssiv/ *adj* causing disagreement —**divisively** *adv* —**divisiveness** *n*

divisor /di vízər/ *n* a number divided into another number

divorce /di váwrss/ *n* 1 the legal ending of a marriage 2 a separation or split *o a divorce between theory and practice* ■ *v* (**-vorcing, -vorced**) 1 *vti* legally end a marriage to some-body 2 *vt* separate *o divorced truth from specu-lation* —**divorced** *adj*

divorcé /di váwr seé, -váwrss ay/ *n US* a divorced man

divorcée /di váwr seé/ *n* a divorced person

divot /dívvət/ *n* in golf, a lump of grass and earth dug out accidentally

divulge /dī vúlj/ (**-vulging, -vulged**) *vt* reveal information —**divulgence** *n*

ORIGIN Divulge comes from a Latin word formed from the word meaning 'common people' that

is also the source of *vulgar*. When first adopted in the 15C it meant simply 'make publicly known'. It was not until the 17C that it began to imply publishing what had previously been secret.

divvy /dívvi/ (**-vies, -vied**) *vt* divide something up *(infml)*

Diwali /di waáli/, **Divali** *n* a Hindu festival in honour of Lakshmi. Date: autumn.

Dixieland /díksi land/, **dixieland** *n* jazz ori-ginating in New Orleans, with a two-beat rhythm and improvisation

ORIGIN Dixieland takes its name from the *Ori-ginal Dixieland Jazz Band*, the first jazz band to record commercially.

DIY, d.i.y. *n* the activity of making or repairing things yourself in your home. Full form **do-it-yourself**

dizzy /dízzi/ (**-zier, -ziest**) *adj* 1 unsteady and giddy 2 causing an unsteady and giddy feeling *o the dizzy height of the tower* 3 con-sidered foolish or thoughtless *(infml)* —**dizzily** *adv* —**dizziness** *n* —**dizzy** *vt*

DJ *n* 1 somebody whose job is to play recorded music 2 a dinner jacket *(infml)*

Djibouti /ji booti/ 1 country in NE Africa, on the Gulf of Aden. Cap. Djibouti. Pop. 460,700 (2001). 2 capital of the Republic of Djibouti. Pop. 383,000 (1995 estimate).

DNA *n* a nucleic acid molecule that is the major component of chromosomes and carries genetic information. Full form **de-oxyribonucleic acid**

DNA fingerprinting *n* identification of some-body from his or her DNA

Dnieper /neépər, dnee-/ river flowing through W Russia, Belarus, and Ukraine into the Black Sea. Length 2,290 km/1,420 mi.

Dniester /neéstər, dnee-/ river flowing through Ukraine and Moldova into the Black Sea. Length 1,400 km/870 mi.

D-notice *n* an official ban on the publication of something for security reasons

DNS *abbr* domain name system

do[1] /doo/ *v* (**does** (*strooced*) /duz/ (*unstressed*) /dəz/, **doing, did** /did/, **done** /dun/) 1 *vt* perform an action, activity, or task *o did the cleaning* 2 *vt* use something in a particular way *o did nothing with the money* 3 *vt* have an effect or result *o These disputes do little to help the peace process.* 4 *vti* work at something *o What do you do for a living?* 5 *vt* behave in a particular way *o always does what he wants* 6 *vi* progress or get along *o The firm is doing well.* 7 *vt* provide something *o We don't do a lunch menu.* 8 *vt* achieve a speed or rate *o doing 100 mph* 9 *vt* put on a performance of something *o going to do 'Macbeth'* 10 *vti* be adequate *o £10 will do.* 11 *vt* serve time in prison *(slang)* *o do 10 to 20 years* 12 *vt* cheat somebody *(infml)* *o did her out of her inheritance* 13 *vt* take an illegal drug *(slang)* ■ *aux v* 14 forms questions and negatives *o What did she want? o Do not sit here.* 15 gives emphasis *o Do be* *quiet!* **1C** replaces a verb to avoid repetition ○ *I ate less than you did.* ■ *n UK, NZ, US* a social gathering *(infml)* ○ *attended a big do at the White House* ◇ **could do with** need or would like something

☐ **do away with** *vt* **1** abolish **2** kill *(infml)*

☐ **do down** *vt* cheat

☐ **do in** *vt (infml)* **1** kill **2** tire out

☐ **do up** *vt* **1** fasten ○ *did up the buttons* **2** repair or redecorate **3** cover with a decorative wrapping **4** dress smartly *(infml)*

☐ **do without** *vti* manage without

DO *n* a certification for Spanish wine that guarantees its origin. Full form **denominación de origen**

DOA *abbr* dead on arrival

doable /dóō əb'l/ *adj* able to be done

DOB, d.o.b. *abbr* date of birth

dobra /dóbrə/ *n* the main unit of currency in São Tomé and Príncipe

doc *abbr* a file extension indicating a document file

DOC *n* a certification for Italian wine that guarantees its origin. Full form **denominazione di origine controllata**

docent /dóss'nt/ *n* **1** *US* a lecturer in some US universities **2** *US, Can* a tourist guide, e.g. at a cathedral or museum —**docentship** *n*

docile /dó sīl/ *adj* quiet and easy to control —**docilely** *adv* —**docility** /dō síllati/ *n*

dock[1] *n* **1** a place for ships to moor **2** *US, Can* a pier or wharf **3** a dry dock ■ *vti* **1** moor a vessel **2** link one spacecraft up with another

dock[2] *n* the place in a courtroom where an accused person sits

dock[3] *(pl* **docks** *or* same*) n* **1** a broad-leafed plant with a long taproot **2** a broad-leafed weed

dock[4] *vt* **1** remove the tail of an animal **2** reduce the wages of somebody as a punishment

docker /dókər/ *n* somebody who loads and unloads ships

docket /dókit/ *n* a document listing the contents of a parcel ■ *vt* list the contents of a package

docking station *n* a piece of hardware for recharging a portable computer

dockland /dók land/ *n* the area surrounding a city's docks *(often pl)*

dockyard /dók yaard/ *n* a dock for ships

doctor /dóktər/ *n* **1** somebody qualified and licensed to give medical treatment **2** *US, Can* a dentist, vet, or osteopath **3** somebody with the highest university degree *(infml)* ■ *v* **1** *vt* change something in order to deceive **2** *vt* add a drug, alcohol, or poison to food or drink **3** *vt* remove the sex organs of an animal to prevent reproduction **4** *vti* treat people who are ill —**doctoral** *adj*

ORIGIN **Doctor** came via French from Latin, where it meant 'teacher'. In English it was first used for any learned person. Its use in regard to the medical profession was at first just one of many applications of the general sense, and did not become firmly established until the later part of the 16C.

doctorate /dóktərət/ *n* the highest university degree

Doctor of Philosophy *n* **1** the highest university degree **2** somebody with a Doctor of Philosophy degree

doctrinaire /dóktri náir/ *adj* rigidly adhering to a specified theory —**doctrinaire** *n* —**doctrinairism** *n* —**doctrinarian** *n*

doctrine /dóktrin/ *n* **1** a rule or principle forming the basis of a belief or theory **2** a set of religious ideas taught as being truthful or correct —**doctrinal** *adj* —**doctrinally** *adv*

docudrama /dókyōō draamə/ *n* a dramatization of a true story

document *n* /dókyōōmənt/ **1** a formal piece of writing providing information or a record **2** a film, photograph, or other recording containing information and usable as evidence **3** a computer file such as a database, spreadsheet, or text file ■ *vt* /dókyōō ment/ **1** record in a document **2** support with evidence —**documentable** /dókyōō méntəb'l/ *adj* —**documental** /dókyōō mént'l/ *adj*

documentary /dókyōō méntəri/ *n (pl* **-ries**) a factual film or TV programme on a specific subject ■ *adj* consisting of documents

documentation /dókyōō men táysh'n/ *n* **1** documents used as evidence or for reference **2** information and instructions for using a piece of computer software

dodder /dóddər/ *vi* tremble or walk unsteadily —**doddering** *adj*

doddle /dódd'l/ *n* something easy *(infml)*

dodecahedron /dó dekə heédrən/ *(pl* **-drons** *or* **-dra** /-drə/) *n* a solid figure with 12 faces

Dodecanese /dó dekə neéz/ group of islands in the SE Aegean Sea that form a department of Greece. Cap. Rhodes. Pop. 145,071 (1981).

dodge *v* (**dodging, dodged**) **1** *vti* move quickly to avoid somebody or something **2** *vt* avoid doing something unpleasant ■ *n* **1** a trick to avoid doing something unpleasant **2** a quick movement to avoid somebody or something

Dodgem /dójjəm/ *tdmk* a trademark for a bumper car

dodger /dójjər/ *n* **1** somebody who avoids a duty or responsibility **2** somebody dishonest and untrustworthy

dodgy /dójji/ (**-ier, -iest**) *adj (infml)* **1** suspect or dishonest **2** risky —**dodgily** *adv*

dodo /dódō/ *(pl* **-dos** *or* **-does**) *n* an extinct flightless bird

ORIGIN **Dodo** was adopted in the early 17C from Portuguese. Its literal meaning was 'simpleton, fool'. The phrase *as dead as a dodo* is first recorded in the first decade of the 20C, over 200 years after the bird's extinction.

Dodoma /dódəmə/ capital of Tanzania. Pop. 189,000 (1995).

doe /dṓ/ *n* a female mammal such as a deer, rabbit, or goat

SPELLCHECK Do not confuse the spelling of **doe** and **dough** ('of bread'), which sound similar.

doer /dṓo ər/ *n* **1** somebody who does a particular thing *(often in combination)* ○ *a wrong-doer* **2** somebody who takes action rather than just thinking or talking about it

does 3rd person present singular of **do**

doesn't /dúzz'nt/ *contr* does not

~~does'nt~~ incorrect spelling of **doesn't**

doff *vt* take off your hat

ORIGIN Doff is a contraction of *do off* in its archaic sense 'put or take off'. The verb *don* is similarly formed.

dog *n* **1** a domestic carnivorous animal whose characteristic call is a bark **2** a male dog **3** a wild animal such as a wolf or fox that is related to domestic dogs **4** a woman regarded as not good-looking *(insult)* **5** a person of a particular type *(infml)* ○ *You lucky dog!* ■ *vt* (**dogging, dogged**) **1** bother somebody persistently **2** follow somebody closely ◇ **dog in the manger** preventing others from having what you cannot use yourself ◇ **a dog's breakfast** *or* **dinner** something messy, disorganized, or badly done *(infml)* ◇ **a dog's life** a wretched existence ◇ **go to the dogs** deteriorate *(infml)*

dog biscuit *n* a hard biscuit for dogs

dog collar *n* **1** a collar for a dog **2** a clerical collar *(infml)*

dog days *npl* **1** the hottest period of the summer **2** a lazy or unsuccessful period

ORIGIN The name **dog days** alludes to the 'Dog Star' or Sirius, the brightest star in the sky. In ancient times it was noted that the hottest period of the year began when Sirius and the Sun rose at the same time.

doge /dṓj, dṓzh/ *n* the chief magistrate in Renaissance Venice and Genoa

dog-eared *adj* with worn and well-thumbed pages

dog-end *n* the discarded end of a smoked cigarette *(infml)*

dogfight /dóg fīt/ *n* aerial combat between fighter planes —**dogfighting** *n*

dogfish /dóg fish/ (*pl* -**fishes** *or same*) *n* a small long-tailed shark

dogged /dóggid/ *adj* obstinately determined —**doggedly** *adv* —**doggedness** *n*

doggerel /dóggərəl/ *n* humorous poetry with an irregular rhythm

doggy /dóggi/ (*pl* -**gies**), **doggie** *n* a dog *(babytalk)* ■ *adj* resembling a dog

doggy bag *n* a bag in which a restaurant customer takes home leftover food

doggy paddle *n* a swimming stroke involving rapid downward movements with the arms and legs

dog handler *n* a police officer working with a trained dog

doghouse /dóg howss/ (*pl* -**houses** / howziz/) *n* US, Can a kennel for a dog ◇ **in the doghouse** in disgrace *(infml)*

dogie /dṓgi/, **dogy** (*pl* -**gies**), **dogey** (*pl* -**geys**) *n* US, Can a motherless calf

dogleg /dóg leg/ *n* **1** a sharp bend in a road **2** in golf, a sharp bend in a fairway —**dogleg** *vi* —**doglegged** /dóg léggid, dóg légd/ *adj*

dogma /dógmə/ (*pl* -**mas** *or* -**mata** /-mətə/) *n* a set of firmly held religious, political, or philosophical beliefs

dogmatic /dog máttik/ *adj* expressing or adhering to strong beliefs —**dogmatically** *adv* —**dogmatism** /dógmətizəm/ *n* —**dogmatist** *n*

do-gooder /-gŏoddər/ *n* somebody who tries to help others, but whose actions may be unwelcome *(infml; disapproving)*

dogsbody /dógz bodi/ (*pl* -**ies**) *n* somebody given menial jobs *(infml)*

dogsled /dóg sled/ *n* a sledge pulled by dogs

dog-tired *adj* exhausted *(infml)*

dog warden *n* somebody whose job is to catch stray dogs

dogwood /dóg wŏod/ (*pl* -**woods** *or same*) *n* a tree or bush with white flowers and red stems

dogy *n* US, Can ZOOL = **dogie**

doh¹ *n* a syllable used in singing the 1st note of a scale

doh² /dṓ/ *interj* humorously acknowledges having done or said something stupid *(slang)*

DoH, DOH *abbr* Department of Health

Doha /dṓ haa, dṓ ə/ capital and largest city of Qatar, on the Persian Gulf. Pop. 392,384 (1995).

doily /dóyli/ (*pl* **doilies** *or* **doylies**) *n* a lacy mat for a plate

ORIGIN The **doily** is named after a 17C London cloth merchant. The word originally signified a woollen material. The simple noun is short for *doily napkin*, and is recorded from the early 18C.

doing /dṓo ing/ present participle of **do¹** ■ *n* the performing or carrying out of something ■ **doings** *npl* somebody's achievements or social activities

do-it-yourself *n* the activity of making or repairing things yourself in your home —**do-it-yourselfer** *n*

doldrums /dóldrəmz, dốl-/ *npl* **1** stagnation **2** gloominess **3** an area without wind north of the equator

dole (**doled, doling**) □ **dole out** *vt* distribute *(infml)*

doleful /dṓlf'l/ *adj* sad —**dolefully** *adv* —**dolefulness** *n*

doll /dol/ *n* **1** a child's toy in the shape of a person **2** a woman regarded as good-looking *(infml; sometimes offensive)*

ORIGIN Doll is from a familiar form of the

woman's name *Dorothy*. It is first recorded in the mid-16C, as a term for a man's mistress or lover, but this use died out during the 17C. As a toy it is found from the late 17C. From the early 18C it was used again for a woman, though this time one regarded as pretty if unintelligent or frivolous, a use that later extended to include any attractive woman.

□ **doll up** *vt* dress smartly (*infml*)

dollar /dóllər/ *n* a unit of currency used in the United States, Canada, New Zealand, and several other countries

ORIGIN **Dollar** represents a northern form of German *taler*, a former silver coin. This was a shortening of *Joachimstaler*, literally 'of Joachim's valley', named after Joachimstal (now Jachymov in the Czech Republic), where the silver used for the coins was mined. The name **dollar** was formally adopted for the currency of the United States in 1785.

dollar sign *n* the symbol ($) that represents a dollar

dollop /dóllap/ *n* a spoon-sized amount of something soft, especially food (*infml*)

doll's house *n* a toy house

dolly /dólli/ (*pl* **-lies**) *n* 1 a toy doll (*babytalk*) 2 a moving platform for filming moving shots

dolmen /dólmən/ *n* a prehistoric stone structure believed to have been a tomb

Dolomites /dóllə mīts/ mountain group in the NE Italian Alps. Highest peak Marmolada, 3,342 km/10,964 ft.

dolour /dóllər/ *n* sadness (*literary*) —**dolorous** /dóllərəss/ *adj*

dolphin /dólfin/ (*pl* **-phins** *or same*) *n* 1 an intelligent sea mammal resembling a large fish, with a beak-shaped snout 2 a large sea game fish

dolt *n* a person regarded as unintelligent (*dated infml insult*)

domain /dō máyn, də-/ *n* 1 a sphere of influence 2 somebody's territory 3 the set of possible values specified for a given mathematical function 4 *ANZ* a public recreation area 5 *also* **domain name** an Internet address

domain name, domain *n* the Internet address of a computer or network

dome /dōm/ *n* 1 a hemispheric-shaped roof or other structure 2 the hemispheric-shaped top of something —**domed** *adj*

Domesday Book /dóomz day book/, **Doomsday Book** *n* an English land survey commissioned by William the Conqueror in 1085

domestic /də méstik/ *adj* 1 of or used in the home 2 of a family 3 kept as a farm animal or pet 4 not foreign 5 of a nation's internal affairs 6 enjoying home and family life ■ *n* a household servant —**domestically** *adv*

domesticate /də mésti kayt/ (**-cating, -cated**) *vt* 1 tame a wild animal 2 accustom somebody to home life or housework (*humorous*) —**domesticated** *adj* —**domestication** /də mésti káysh'n/ *n*

domesticity /dóm e stíssəti, dóm-/ *n* 1 home life 2 a fondness for home life

domestic partner *n US* a person with whom somebody cohabits who is not a spouse

domicile /dómmi sīl/ *n* somebody's legal place of residence

domiciled /dómmi sīld/ *adj* resident in a particular place

dominant /dómminənt/ *adj* 1 exerting power over others 2 more important, effective, or prominent than others 3 describes a gene that causes a parental characteristic to occur in any offspring 4 describes a characteristic determined by a dominant gene 5 describes the 5th note of a musical scale —**dominance** *n* —**dominantly** *adv*

dominate /dómmi nayt/ (**-nating, -nated**) *vti* 1 exert power over 2 be the most important aspect of 3 have a prevailing influence on —**domination** /dómmi náysh'n/ *n*

dominatrix /dómmi náytriks/ (*pl* **-trices** /-tri seez/) *n* a dominant woman partner in a sadomasochistic relationship

domineering /dómmi neéring/ *adj* tyrannical or overbearing

~~doment~~ incorrect spelling of **dominant**

Domingo /də ming gō/, **Plácido** (*b.* 1941) Spanish-born operatic tenor

Dominic /dómminik/, **St** (1170?–1221) Spanish priest and theologian

Dominica /dómmi neékə, də mínnikə/ island country in the Windward Islands, in the E Caribbean Sea. Cap. Roseau. Pop. 70,786 (2001). Length 47 km/29 mi. —**Dominican** *n*, *adj*

Dominican /də mínnikən/ *n* a member of the religious order founded by St Dominic —**Dominican** *adj*

Dominican Republic /də mínnikən-/ country on Hispaniola Island in the N Caribbean Sea. Cap. Santo Domingo. Pop. 8,581,477 (2001). Length 380 km/235 mi. —**Dominican** *n*, *adj*

dominion /də mínnyən/ *n* 1 ruling power 2 a sphere of influence 3 a land governed by a ruler (*often pl*) 4 *also* **Dominion** a self-governing part of the British Commonwealth

domino /dómminō/ (*pl* **-noes**) *n* a small playing tile, one of 28 that are covered with up to six dots

domino effect *n* a succession of related events, each caused by the preceding one

dominoes /dómminōz/ *n* a game played using dominoes (*+ sing verb*)

Domitian /də mísh'n/, **Marcus** (AD 51–96) Roman emperor (81–96)

don[1] *n* 1 a university or college teacher, especially at Oxford or Cambridge 2 a Spanish gentleman or aristocrat 3 a leader of an organized crime family 4 **Don** a title used before a man's name in a Spanish-speaking country

don[2] (**donning, donned**) *vt* put on a garment

ORIGIN **Don** is a contraction of *do on* in its

archaic sense 'put on'. The verb *doff* is similarly formed.

Don river in W Russia, flowing into the Sea of Azov. Length 1,870 km/1,160 mi.

Doña /dónnyə/ n a title used before a married woman's name in a Spanish-speaking country

donate /dō náyt/ (**-nating, -nated**) vt 1 give or present something, especially to a charity 2 give blood, reproductive material, or a body part for another person —**donation** /dō náysh'n/ n ◊ See note at **give**

Donatello /dónnə téllō/ (1386?–1466) Italian sculptor

done /dun/ past participle of **do**[1] ■ adj 1 completed or finished 2 cooked through 3 socially acceptable ○ *It's just not done.* ■ interj confirms acceptance of a deal ◊ **have done with** be finished with something

done for adj facing ruin or destruction (infml)

Donegal /dónni gawl/ county in NW Ireland. Pop. 129,000 (1996).

doner kebab /dónnər-/ n a piece of pitta bread filled with spiced grilled meat

Donets /də néts, -nyéts/ river in SW Russia and SE Ukraine. Length 1,020 km/631 mi.

Donets'k /də nyétsk/ city in SE Ukraine. Pop. 1,065,000 (1998).

dong[1] n a deep toll of a bell —**dong** vi

dong[2] n the main unit of Vietnamese currency

donga /dóng gə/ n ANZ, S Africa a ravine caused by erosion

dongle /dóng g'l/ n a device plugged into a computer to allow protected software to be used

Donizetti /dónni zétti/, **Gaetano** (1797–1848) Italian composer

Don Juan /dón joo ən, dón waàn/ n a man who has casual sex with many women

donkey /dóngki/ (pl **-keys**) n a domesticated grey or brown mammal resembling a small long-eared horse ◊ **donkey's years** a very long time (infml)

donkey derby n a donkey race for amusement

donkey jacket n UK a thick heavy dark jacket

donkeywork /dóngki wurk/ n 1 hard work (infml) 2 groundwork

Donne /dun/, **John** (1572–1631) English poet, prose writer, and cleric

donnish /dónnish/ adj like a stereotypical professor

donor /dốnər/ n 1 somebody who gives something, especially money 2 somebody who gives blood, reproductive material, or a body part for another person —**donorship** n

donor card n a card authorizing medical use of the carrier's body parts after death

Don Quixote /dón kwíksət, -kee hốti/ n an impractical idealist who champions hopeless causes

ORIGIN The original **Don Quixote** was the hero of a romance (1605–15) by the Spanish writer Miguel de Cervantes.

don't /dōnt/ contr do not

doodle /doōd'l/ (**-dling, -dled**) vti scribble drawings or designs absent-mindedly — **doodle** n

doolally /doo lálli/ adj an offensive term meaning irrational or in poor mental health (infml)

doom n 1 a dreadful fate 2 an official judgment on somebody (fml) ■ vt condemn to a dreadful fate —**doomed** adj

doomsayer /doōm say ər/ n a predictor of disaster

doomsday /doōmz day/ n 1 also **Doomsday** the day of the Last Judgment 2 the end of the world

door /dawr/ n 1 a movable panel for opening or closing an entrance 2 a gap forming an entrance ◊ **close** or **shut the door on something** disallow the possibility of something happening ◊ **lay something at somebody's door** blame something on somebody ◊ **out of doors** in the open air ◊ **show somebody the door** tell somebody to leave

doorbell /dawr bel/ n an electric bell on or beside a door for the convenience of visitors

do-or-die adj performed or done in utter recklessness

doorjamb /dawr jam/ n a doorpost

doorkeeper /dáwr keepər/ n somebody on duty at a door

doorknob /dáwr nob/ n a round handle on a door used to open and close it

doorman /dáwrmən/ (pl **-men** /-mən/) n an attendant at the entrance to a building

doormat /dáwr mat/ n 1 a mat on which to wipe your shoes 2 somebody who submits to inconsiderate treatment (infml; disapproving)

~~doormouse~~ incorrect spelling of **dormouse**

doornail /dáwr nayl/ n a stud formerly used on doors

doorplate /dáwr playt/ n a sign attached to a door

doorpost /dáwr pōst/ n a vertical side piece of the frame of a door

doorsill /dáwr sil/ n the bottom part of the frame of a door

doorstep /dáwr step/ n a step in front of a door ■ v (**-stepping, -stepped**) 1 vti canvass all the houses in an area 2 vt wait at the door of a famous person to interview or photograph him or her —**doorstepping** n ◊ **on somebody's (own) doorstep** very near where somebody lives

doorstop /dáwr stop/ n 1 something used to keep a door open 2 a rubber projection that prevents damage to a wall when a door is opened

door to door adv 1 going from one house to the next, usually to solicit or sell something 2 from the start to the finish of a journey —**door-to-door** adj

doorway /dáwr way/ n 1 an entrance to a building 2 an opportunity to achieve or escape from something

doo-wop /dóò wɒp/ *n* harmonized rhythm-and-blues singing of nonsense words

dopamine /dópə meen/ *n* a chemical compound occurring in the brain

dope *n* 1 an illegal drug, especially cannabis *(slang)* 2 an illegal drug affecting the performance of an athlete or racehorse 3 a person regarded as unintelligent *(infml insult)* ■ *vt* (**doping, doped**) add an illegal drug to food or drink

dopey /dópi/ (**-ier, -iest**), **dopy** (**-ier, -iest**) *adj* 1 half-asleep or drowsy 2 considered unintelligent *(infml)*

doppelgänger /dópp'l gangər, -geng-/ *n* 1 somebody similar to another person 2 a ghost identical to a living person

Doppler effect /dópplər-/, **Doppler shift** *n* an apparent change in the frequency of a sound or light wave because of motion

Doric /dórrik/ *n* 1 an ancient Greek dialect 2 a dialect of Scots ■ *adj* 1 in a simple classical Greek architectural style 2 of Doric

dork *n* a person regarded as unintelligent or unfashionable *(slang insult)* —**dorky** *adj*

dorm *n* a dormitory *(infml)*

dormant /dáwrmənt/ *adj* 1 not actively growing in order to survive adverse environmental conditions 2 temporarily inactive or not in use 3 not erupting, but not extinct *(refers to volcanoes)* —**dormancy** *n*

dormer /dáwrmər/, **dormer window** *n* a window projecting from a roof

dormitory /dáwrmitəri/ (*pl* **-ries**) *n* 1 a large room with many beds 2 *US, Can* a university hall of residence

dormitory town *n* a town where commuters live

Dormobile /dáwrmō beel/ *tdmk* a trademark for a motor vehicle equipped for living and sleeping in as well as travelling

dormouse /dáwr mowss/ (*pl* **-mice** /-mīss/) *n* a small nocturnal reddish-brown rodent

dorsal /dáwrss'l/ *adj* of or on the back —**dorsally** *adv*

Dorset /dáwrssit/ county on southern coast of England. Pop. 673,000 (1994).

Dortmund /dáwrtmənd, -mŏŏnd/ inland port in NW Germany. Pop. 600,918 (1997).

dory[1] /dáwri/ (*pl* **-ries**) *n* a small boat

dory[2] /dáwri/ (*pl* **-ries**) *n* a bottom-dwelling sea fish with an extendable mouth

DOS *abbr* 1 denial-of-service 2 disk operating system

dosage /dóssij/ *n* the amount and frequency prescribed for a medicine

dose /dōss/ *n* 1 a prescribed amount of medicine 2 an amount of radiation to which somebody has been exposed ■ *vt* (**dosing, dosed**) give medicine to

dosh *n* money *(infml)*

doss, doss down *vi* sleep on an improvised bed *(slang)*

dosshouse /dóss howss/ *n* a cheap lodging house *(infml)*

dossier /dóssi ay, -ər/ *n* a set of papers containing information on somebody or something

Fyodor Dostoyevsky

Dostoyevsky /dóst oy éfski/, **Fyodor** (1821–81) Russian novelist

dot *n* 1 a written or printed point, especially one above an 'i' or 'j' or used as a punctuation mark 2 a punctuation mark in an Internet address 3 a spot or speck ○ *The ship was a dot on the horizon.* 4 a small amount ○ *a dot of butter* 5 the shorter of the two symbols used in Morse code 6 a symbol placed after a musical note to increase its value by half ■ *vt* (**dotting, dotted**) 1 mark something with a dot 2 sprinkle something with small amounts of something ○ *Dot the surface with butter.* ◇ **on the dot (of)** exactly at a particular time

dotage /dótij/ *n* physical and mental weakening sometimes experienced in old age *(offensive)*

dot.com, dot-com *n* an Internet business —**dot-com** *adj* —**dot-comer** /dot kómmər/ *n*

dote (**doting, doted**) *vi* show extreme fondness for somebody —**doting** *adj* —**dotingly** *adv*

dot matrix *n* an array of dots displaying information

dot pitch *n* a measure of the clarity of a computer image

dotted /dóttid/ *adj* 1 marked with dots 2 describes musical notes increased in value by a half 3 covered with specks ○ *a sky dotted with stars*

dotted line *n* a printed line of dots or dashes

dotty /dótti/ (**-tier, -tiest**) *adj* endearingly irrational or impractical *(infml)* —**dottiness** *n*

Douala /doo aálə/, **Duala** largest port in Cameroon. Pop. 1,500,000 (1997).

double /dúbb'l/ *adj* 1 being twice as much or many 2 having two equal or similar parts 3 meant for two people 4 folded in two 5 having extra flower petals ■ *adv* 1 twice as much 2 so as to form two layers or folds ■ *n* 1 twice the usual amount 2 a person or thing identical to somebody else or something else 3 a hotel room for two people 4 a stand-in for a film actor 5 in the game of bridge, a call that increases the score for success or failure in a contract ■ *v* (**-bling, -bled**) 1 *vti* increase twofold 2 *vt* fold something in two 3 *vi* have a second function or role 4 *vi* act as a stand-in 5 *vi* in the game of bridge, announce a double —**doubly** *adv* ◇ **at** or **on the double** straightaway and as quickly as possible *(infml)*

□ **double back** *vi* go back along the same route

□ **double over** *vi* bend deeply from the waist

□ **double up** *vi* **1** share with somebody else **2** bend the body sharply

double act *n* a pair of entertainers who perform together

double agent *n* a spy working for two nations simultaneously

double-barrelled *adj* **1** describes guns with two barrels **2** formed from two names, usually hyphenated

double bass *n* the largest instrument in the violin family

double bed *n* a bed wide enough for two sleepers

double bill *n* a programme of entertainment with two main elements

double bind *n* **1** a dilemma with two undesirable alternative courses **2** a dilemma caused by contradictory demands

double-blind *adj* describes an experiment with neither the scientists nor the subjects knowing which treatment is genuine and which is a control procedure

double boiler *n* a pan that heats the contents of another pan fitted on top of it

double-book *vti* promise the same booking to two people

double-breasted *adj* describes a coat or jacket with a large overlap at the front and two rows of buttons

double-check *vti* verify by checking twice

double chin *n* a fold of loose flesh under the chin —**double-chinned** *adj*

double-click *vti* press a mouse button twice quickly, e.g. to activate a command

double cream *n UK* high-fat cream that thickens when whipped

double-cross *vt* betray an associate —**double-crossing** *adj*

double date *n* a situation in which two couples go out socially together —**double-date** *vti*

double-dealing *n* deceit involving betrayal of an associate —**double-dealer** *n* —**double-dealing** *adj*

double-decker *n* **1** a bus or train with two levels **2** something with two layers

double density *adj* with double the storage capacity of a standard computer disk

double-digit *adj* between 10 and 99

double Dutch *n* incomprehensible talk or writing *(infml)*

double-edged *adj* **1** ambiguous **2** having two purposes or effects

double entendre /doòb'l on tóndra/ (*pl* **double entendres** /*pronunc. same*/) *n* an ambiguous remark with a sexually suggestive meaning

double fault *n* in tennis, two consecutive incorrect serves —**double-fault** *vi*

double figures *npl* the numbers from 10 to 99

double first *n* a first-class degree in two subjects

double glazing *n* windows with two layers of glass separated by a space for insulation —**double-glaze** *vt*

double helix *n* the double-spiral molecular structure of DNA

double jeopardy *n* a second prosecution of somebody for the same crime

double-jointed *adj* able to bend in the opposite direction to that in which joints normally bend —**double-jointedness** *n*

double life *n* a life in which somebody has two identities

double negative *n* a phrase containing two negatives

double-park *vti* park alongside another parked vehicle —**double-parking** *n*

doubles /dúbb'lz/ (*pl same*) *n* a racket game between pairs of players

double-sided *adj* having two usable sides

double standard *n* a standard applied unfairly to different groups

doublet /dúbblət/ *n* a man's close-fitting jacket popular between the 15C and 17C

double take *n* a delayed reaction of surprise *(infml)*

double talk, doublespeak /dúbb'l speek/ *n* talk intended to confuse or deceive

doublethink /dúbb'l thingk/ *n* acceptance of opposing beliefs and falsehoods as a way of deceiving yourself

double time *n* **1** double the usual rate of pay **2** a musical tempo twice as fast as the basic tempo

double vision *n* a condition in which the eyes see two of everything

double whammy *n* a pair of unpleasant things happening together *(slang)*

doubloon /du blòon/ *n* a former Spanish coin

doubt /dowt/ *vt* **1** think something unlikely ○ *I doubt if he'll come.* **2** mistrust ○ *no reason to doubt her* ■ *n* mistrustful uncertainty —**doubter** *n* ◇ **beyond (the shadow of a) doubt** completely certain ◇ **in doubt 1** feeling uncertain **2** unlikely or improbable ◇ See note at **doubtful**

doubtful /dówtf'l/ *adj* **1** unsure **2** unlikely —**doubtfully** *adv* —**doubtfulness** *n*

SYNONYMS **doubtful, uncertain, unsure, in doubt, dubious, sceptical** CORE MEANING: feeling doubt or uncertainty

doubting Thomas *n* somebody insisting on proof

ORIGIN The original **doubting Thomas** was the apostle of Jesus Christ in the Bible who would not accept the Resurrection until he had seen and touched Jesus Christ's wounds (John 14:1–7, 20:19–29).

doubtless /dówtləss/ *adv* **1** for sure or certain **2** in all probability

douche /doosh/ *n* **1** the cleaning of a body part with a water jet **2** a piece of equipment producing a cleansing water jet ■ *vti* (**douching, douched**) clean a body part with a water jet

dough /dṓ/ n 1 a mixture of flour and water, often with other ingredients such as yeast, for baking bread or pastry 2 money (slang) ◊ See note at **doe**

doughnut /dṓ nut/ n a sugar-coated cake of deep-fried dough, either ring-shaped or round

~~doughter~~ incorrect spelling of **daughter**

doughty /dówti/ (**-tier, -tiest**) adj resolute (dated) —**doughtily** adv —**doughtiness** n

doughy /dṓ i/ (**-ier, -iest**) adj 1 resembling dough in consistency 2 pale and flabby

Douglas-Home /dúgglass hyoóm/, **Sir Alec, 14th Earl of Home** (1903–95) British prime minister (1963–64)

doula /doóla/ n a woman who assists in childbirth

dour /door/ adj severe, morose, or unfriendly —**dourly** adv —**dourness** n

Douro /doóro/, **Duero** /dwáiro/ river in N Spain and N Portugal. Length 895 km/556 mi.

douse /dowss/ (**dousing, doused**), **dowse** (**dowsing, dowsed**) vt 1 immerse in water 2 put water or other liquid on —**douse** n —**douser** n

dove /duv/ n 1 a small bird of the pigeon family, with a cooing call 2 also **Dove** a supporter of peace

dovecote /dúvkōt/, **dovecot** /-kot/ n a home for domestic pigeons

Dover /dóvər/ 1 city in SE England, England's busiest port and the one nearest to France. Pop. 39,200 (1994). 2 capital of Delaware. Pop. 30,369 (1998).

Dover, Strait of narrowest part of the English Channel, between Dover, England, and Calais, France. Length 34 km/21 mi.

dovetail /dúv tayl/ v 1 vti fit neatly together 2 vt fasten pieces of wood with interlocking V-shaped joints ■ n also **dovetail joint** a joint made using V-shaped projecting pieces of wood

dowager /dów əjər/ n a widow with her husband's title or property

dowdy /dówdi/ (**-dier, -diest**) adj plain and unfashionable —**dowdily** adv —**dowdiness** n

dowel /dów əl/ n also **dowel pin** a peg for joining pieces of wood or metal ■ vt (**-elling, -elled**) join pieces of wood or metal with dowels

dower /dów ər/ n a dowry (archaic)

Dow Jones Average /dów-/ tdmk a trademark for an index of the prices of selected stocks, based on a formula developed and revised periodically by Dow Jones & Company, Inc.

down[1] /down/ prep 1 to or at a lower level on or in something ◦ ran down the stairs 2 to or at a position farther along ◦ halfway down the street ■ adv 1 at or to a lower level or position ◦ down in the basement ◦ get interest rates down 2 away from the present or a more important location ◦ go down to the beach 3 to a more southerly place ◦ drive down to Atlanta

4 short or losing by a particular amount ◦ two goals down at half time 5 having only a particular amount left ◦ I'm down to my last pound. 6 in part payment or as a deposit ◦ put 5% down 7 from an earlier to a later period or person ◦ jewels that had been handed down to him 8 on paper as a record ◦ wrote it down 9 chosen or scheduled for something ◦ We're down for both sessions. 10 away from a university ◦ down from Cambridge ■ adj 1 unhappy 2 not in operation (refers to computer systems) 3 given in part payment or as a deposit ◦ a down payment on the car ■ vt 1 eat or drink quickly 2 make fall to the ground ◊ **be down to** be the result of ◊ **down under** to or in Australia or New Zealand (infml)

ORIGIN The adverb **down** is a very early shortening of archaic adown, literally 'of a hill', used in the same sense. The noun **down** 'hill' now mainly occurs in placenames and in the Downs, chalk uplands in S England. It may be of Celtic origin, and ultimately related to town.

down[2] /down/ n 1 soft fluffy feathers or hairs 2 a covering of soft hairs

down[3] /down/ n a grassy treeless hill (often in placenames) ■ **downs** npl rolling grassland

Down /down/ former county in SE Northern Ireland

down-and-out adj jobless and poor (infml) —**down-and-out** n

down-at-heel adj shabbily dressed

downbeat /dówn beet/ adj pessimistic ■ n 1 the first beat in a bar of music 2 a conductor's downward gesture indicating a downbeat

downburst /dówn burst/ n a powerful downward wind associated with thunderstorms, of special danger to aircraft

downcast /dówn kaast/ adj 1 sad 2 looking down

downer /dównər/ n 1 a sedative drug (slang) 2 somebody or something regarded as depressing (infml)

downfall /dówn fawl/ n failure or ruin negating prior success, or a cause of this

downgrade /dówn grayd/ (**-grading, -graded**) vt lower the status or value of

downhearted /dówn haártid/ adj discouraged

downhill adv /down híl/ towards the bottom of a hill ■ adj /dówn híl/ sloping down ■ n /dówn híl/ a skiing race down a long mountain slope ◊ **go downhill** decline or deteriorate

Downing Street /dówning-/ n 1 the London street containing the official residence of the British prime minister 2 the British prime minister or government

download /down lṓd/ vti transfer data between computers or be transferred by computer ■ n 1 a downloading of data 2 downloaded data

downmarket /dówn maarkit/ adj cheap and of low quality

down payment n a partial payment made on a purchase

downpipe /dówn pīp/ *n* a pipe carrying rain-water from the roof

downplay /dówn pláy/ *vt* make something seem less important or serious

downpour /dówn pawr/ *n* a heavy fall of rain

downright /dówn rīt/ *adj* complete and utter ■ *adv* completely and utterly

downriver /dówn rívvər/ *adv, adj* towards the mouth of a river

downshift /dówn shíft/ *vi* change a highly paid but stressful job for a lower paid but less stressful one —**downshift** *n*

downside /dówn sīd/ *n* a negative side to something positive

downsize /dówn sīz/ (-**sizing**, -**sized**) *vti* make a business smaller by cutting employees' jobs

Down's syndrome /dównz-/ *n* a genetic disorder characterized by unique facial features and some learning disabilities

downstage /dówn stáyj/ *adv, adj* to or at the front of a stage

downstairs /dówn stáirz/ *adv* to a lower floor ■ *adj* on a lower floor ■ *n* the lower floor of a building

downstream /dówn streém/ *adj* **1** situated towards the mouth of a river **2** occurring in the later stages of production ■ *adv* towards the mouth of a river

downswing /dówn swing/ *n* **1** a downward trend **2** the downward part of a golfer's swing

downtime /dówn tīm/ *n* the time when work or production is stopped, e.g. because machinery is not working

down-to-earth *adj* practical and realistic

downtown /dówn tówn/ *adj, adv NZ, US, Can* in or to the centre of a city, especially its business centre ■ *n US, Can* a city centre

downtrend /dówn trend/ *n* a downward trend

downtrodden /dówn tród'n/ *adj* oppressed

downturn /dówn turn/ *n* a reduction in economic activity

downward /dównwərd/ *adj* **1** moving to a lower place, level, or condition **2** coming from an origin or source

downwardly mobile *adj* moving to a lower status, social class, or income bracket —**downward mobility** *n*

downwards /dównwərdz/, **downward** /-wərd/ *adv* **1** towards a lower place, level, or condition **2** to a later time or generation —**downwardly** *adv*

downwind /dówn wínd/ *adv, adj* in the direction of the wind

downy /dówni/ (-**ier**, -**iest**) *adj* **1** soft and fluffy **2** covered with soft hairs

dowry /dówri/ (*pl* -**ries**) *n* a bride's family's gift to her bridegroom

dowse[1] /dowz/ (**dowsing**, **dowsed**) *vi* use a divining rod —**dowser** *n*

dowse[2] *vt, n* = **douse**

dowsing rod *n* a divining rod

doyen /dóy ən/ *n* the most senior and respected man in a sphere of activity

doyenne /doy énn/ *n* the most senior and respected woman in a sphere of activity

Doyle /doyl/, **Sir Arthur Conan** (1859–1930) Scottish-born British writer and physician

D'Oyly Carte /dóyli kaárt/, **Richard** (1844–1901) British theatre agent, manager, and producer

doz. *abbr* dozen

doze /dōz/ (**dozing**, **dozed**) *vi* **1** have a short light sleep **2** laze or daydream —**doze** *n*
□ **doze off** *vi* fall into a light sleep

dozen /dúzz'n/ *n* (*pl same*), *det* a group of 12 objects or people ■ *npl, adv* **dozens** a large number (*infml*) ○ *has dozens of friends* ○ *gave away dozens more*

ORIGIN **Dozen** comes through French from Latin *duodecim* 'twelve', which was formed from *duo* 'two' and *decem* 'ten'.

dozy /dózi/ (-**zier**, -**ziest**) *adj* **1** drowsy **2** slow in understanding (*infml*) —**dozily** *adv* —**doziness** *n*

DP *abbr* displaced person

DPhil, DPh *abbr* Doctor of Philosophy

dpi *n* a measure of the density of a computer or printer image. Full form **dots per inch**

DPP *abbr* Director of Public Prosecutions

DPT *abbr* diphtheria, pertussis, tetanus (vaccine)

Dr *abbr* doctor

drab *adj* (**drabber, drabbest**) **1** lacking colour or brightness **2** boring **3** pale greyish-brown in colour ■ *n* a pale greyish-brown colour —**drably** *adv* —**drabness** *n*

Drabble /dráb'l/, **Margaret** (*b.* 1939) British novelist, editor, and critic

drachma /drákmə/ (*pl* -**mas** *or* -**mae** /-mī/) *n* the main unit of the former Greek currency

Draco /dráykō/ (*fl* 7C BC) Athenian political leader and legislator

draconian /drə kóni ən/ *adj* excessively harsh

ORIGIN The first person to introduce **draconian** laws was Draco.

draft *n* **1** a preliminary version of a text, picture, or plan **2** a bank cheque **3** *US* military conscription ■ *n, adj US* = **draught** ■ *vt* **1** make a draft of something **2** transfer somebody somewhere for work or a task **3** *US* call up somebody for military service **4** *ANZ* sort livestock into smaller groups —**drafter** *n*

draftsman *n US* = **draughtsman**

drafty *adj US* = **draughty**

drag *v* (**dragging, dragged**) **1** *vt* pull something heavy along with effort **2** *vt* move or remove somebody or something by pulling with force **3** *vti* trail along the ground **4** *vi* pass or proceed slowly and boringly **5** *vt* move a computer icon with a mouse **6** *vt* search a body of water with a net or hook **7** *vi* puff on a cigarette, pipe, or cigar (*infml*) ■ *n* **1** a hindrance **2** (*symbol* **D**) the resistance experienced by a moving object **3** somebody or something boring (*infml*) **4** clothing characteristic of one sex worn by somebody of the other sex *(slang)* ◊ **drag your feet** or **heels** do something slowly and reluctantly ◊ See note at **pull**

□ **drag down** *vt* **1** bring to a lower level or status **2** make listless or tired

□ **drag in** *vt* involve inappropriately

□ **drag out** *vt* prolong

drag and drop *vt* move a computer icon somewhere with a mouse

dragnet /drág net/ *n* **1** a weighted net for fishing or for dragging a body of water **2** a police hunt for a criminal

dragon /drággən/ *n* **1** a large fire-breathing mythical monster with wings and a long tail **2** a large lizard

dragonfly /drággən flī/ (*pl* **-flies**) *n* a long thin flying insect with transparent wings and a shimmering body

dragoon /drə góon/ *n* **1** a 17–18C mounted infantryman **2** an 18–19C cavalryman ■ *vt* **1** force into doing something **2** subjugate using military troops

drag queen *n* a male performer dressed as a woman for comic effect

drag race *n* a short race between cars to discover which has the fastest acceleration —**drag racer** *n* —**drag racing** *n*

dragster /drágstər/ *n* **1** a car specially designed for drag racing **2** the driver of a dragster

drain *n* **1** a pipe that takes sewage or waste water away from a building **2** something that uses up resources **3** the gradual loss or diminishing of an important resource ■ *v* **1** *vti* flow out or away, or allow to flow out or away **2** *vti* empty or become empty by causing a liquid to flow out **3** *vt* make land drier by leading water away from it **4** *vt* drink all the contents of a container **5** *vt* use something up gradually ○ *draining the company's financial resources* **6** *vi* disappear gradually ○ *The colour drained from her face.* **7** *vt* leave somebody feeling exhausted ◊ **down the drain** wasted or squandered *(infml)*

drainage /dráynij/ *n* **1** the process of draining something **2** a sewage system

drainer /dráynər/ *n* a rack or container for draining things

draining board *n* a drying area next to a sink

drainpipe /dráyn pīp/ *n* a pipe for draining rainwater away from a roof ■ **drainpipes, drainpipe trousers** *npl* narrow trousers

drake *n* a male duck

Drake, Sir Francis (1540?–96) English navigator and admiral

dram[1] *n* a unit of weight equal to 1/16 of an ounce

ORIGIN Dram derives through Latin from a Greek word that is thought to have originally signified the number of coins that can be held in one hand. The same Greek word is also the source of *drachma*, a unit of Greek currency.

---

dram[2] *n* the main unit of Armenian currency

DRAM /dée ram/ *abbr* dynamic random access memory

drama /draamə/ *n* **1** a serious play written for the stage, television, or radio **2** plays as a genre or subject of study

drama documentary *n* a documentary in which real events are re-enacted by actors

dramatic /drə máttik/ *adj* **1** of or for the theatre **2** exciting and intense **3** sudden and marked **4** very impressive in appearance, colour, or effect —**dramatically** *adv*

dramatic irony *n* a situation in which a character in a play is unaware of something that the audience knows

dramatics /drə máttiks/ *n* the production of plays (+ *sing or pl verb*) ■ *npl* melodramatic behaviour (+ *pl verb*)

dramatis personae /drámmətiss pər só nī/ *npl* **1** a list of the characters in a play **2** the characters in a play *(fml)*

dramatist /drámmətist/ *n* a playwright

dramatize /drámmə tīz/ (**-tizing, -tized**), **dramatise** *v* **1** *vt* adapt material for the stage **2** *vti* exaggerate the importance or seriousness of a situation —**dramatization** /drámmə tī záysh'n/ *n* —**dramatizer** *n*

drank past tense of **drink**

drape *v* (**draping, draped**) **1** *vt* place fabric over something so that it falls in loose folds **2** *vi* hang in loose folds **3** *vt* rest part of the body casually on or over something ■ *n* **1** US, Can a curtain hung, e.g., at a window (*usually pl*) **2** a piece of fabric draped over something **3** the way fabric hangs

drapery /dráypəri/ *n* **1** cloth or a piece of cloth arranged to hang in folds **2** fabrics and sewing materials

drastic /drástik/ *adj* having a powerful effect or far-reaching consequences —**drastically** *adv*

drat *interj* expresses annoyance *(infml)*

draught[1] /draaft/ *n* **1** a current of air **2** the act of pulling something along or drawing something in **3** a mouthful of air, liquid, or smoke **4** beer in barrels **5** the depth needed by a ship to float **6** a piece used in draughts ■ *adj* **1** served from the barrel **2** used to pull heavy loads

draughts /draafts/ *n* a game played on a chequered board with pieces that move diagonally (+ *sing verb*)

draughtsman /draaftsmən/ (*pl* **-men** /-mən/) *n* **1** a technical designer **2** a man with a particular skill in drawing ○ *He's an excellent draughtsman.* **3** a piece used in draughts —**draughtsmanship** *n*

draughtsperson /draafts purss'n/ *n* a technical designer

draughty /draafti/ (**-tier, -tiest**) *adj* windy and cold —**draughtiness** *n*

Drava /draavə/ river flowing through N Italy, Austria, and Slovenia, and forming part of Croatia's frontier with Hungary before joining the Danube. Length 719 km/447 mi.

Dravidian /drə víddi ən/ n 1 a family of languages spoken in S India and NE Sri Lanka 2 a member of an aboriginal Indian people —**Dravidian** adj

draw v (**drew, drawn**) 1 vti make a picture using, e.g., a pencil 2 vi move in a particular direction with a smooth motion ○ *Another car drew alongside ours.* 3 vi approach a particular point in time 4 vt pull something towards or away from something else 5 vt pull a vehicle ○ *a carriage drawn by six horses* 6 vt open or close a curtain 7 vt pull on a string, rope, or cord 8 vt pull back the string of an archery bow 9 vt take something out of its packaging or enclosure ○ *drew the letter out of the envelope* 10 vti pull a weapon from, e.g. a holster 11 vt remove liquid from a container using a tap 12 vt elicit a response 13 vt find a physical or a moral resource in, e.g. a person ○ *drew courage from her example* 14 vt obtain information from somebody 15 vt cause attention to be directed in a particular direction ○ *draw admiring glances* 16 vt attract people wanting to see something ○ *The performance always drew crowds.* 17 vti suck something such as air or smoke in 18 vi allow a current of air through 19 vt receive money 20 vt write out a cheque or a legal document 21 vt arrive at a conclusion or inference 22 vt formulate a distinction or parallel ○ *drew a distinction between the causes of the two events* 23 vt choose something at random 24 vt in card games, take a card or make a player play a certain suit 25 vti finish equal in a sport or game 26 vt disembowel a victim ■ n 1 the act of pulling 2 a lottery or raffle, or the selection of a lottery winner 3 a usually random selection of contestants 4 a random choice 5 a popular attraction 6 a contest that neither side wins 7 a pulling of a gun ◊ See note at **pull**

ORIGIN The picture-making sense of **draw** arose from the idea of 'drawing' or 'pulling' a pen or brush across a surface.

☐ **draw back** vi pull back suddenly, e.g. in fear
☐ **draw in** vt entice an unwilling participant into an act
☐ **draw on** v 1 vt make use of a resource 2 vi move to or enter a later stage ○ *as the day drew on*
☐ **draw out** v 1 vt prolong 2 vi grow longer (*refers to days*) 3 vt encourage to talk freely
☐ **draw up** v 1 vt write out a legal document 2 vti come or bring something to a stop ○ *saw the bus draw up*

drawback /dráw bak/ n a disadvantage

drawbridge /dráw brij/ n a bridge that can be raised

drawdown /dráw down/ n a lowering of the water level in a reservoir

drawer /drawr/ n 1 a box-shaped storage compartment that slides in and out of a piece of furniture 2 somebody who writes a cheque 3 somebody or something that draws

drawers /drawrz/ npl underpants, especially large old-fashioned underpants for women

drawing /dráw ing/ n 1 a picture made with a pencil, pen, or similar instrument 2 the art of making pictures while not using paint

drawing board n a board on which to draw ◊ **back to the drawing board** indicates a need to redesign a failed operation or project (*infml*)

drawing pin n a short pin with a flat head for pinning a piece of paper or card to a surface

drawing room n a formal room in a house used for entertaining guests

ORIGIN A **drawing room** was originally a *withdrawing room*. It referred to a private room off a more public one, and later to a room to which guests could withdraw after dinner.

drawl vti speak or say slowly ■ n a slow way of speaking —**drawler** n —**drawlingly** adv

drawn past tense of **draw** ■ adj tired-looking and haggard

drawn-out adj continuing longer than necessary or desirable

drawstring /dráw string/ n a cord that can be drawn tight to close an opening around a bag or in a garment

dray n a cart without sides

dread /dred/ vti 1 feel extremely frightened by the prospect of something 2 be reluctant to deal with something ■ n 1 terror 2 a source of fear ■ adj causing fear or awe (*literary*)

dreaded /dréddid/ adj feared

dreadful /dréddf'l/ adj 1 extremely bad 2 extreme —**dreadfully** adv —**dreadfulness** n

dreadlocks /dréd loks/ npl a hairstyle in which long strands are twisted from the scalp to the tips

dreadnought /dréd nawt/, **dreadnaught** n a battleship with guns all of the same calibre

dream /dreem/ n 1 a sequence of images that appear in the mind during sleep 2 a daydream 3 something hoped or wished for 4 an unrealizable hope 5 a state of inattention ○ *in a dream* 6 something beautiful ■ v (**dreamt** /dremt/ *or* **dreamed**) 1 vti have a dream while sleeping 2 vi engage in daydreaming 3 vi wish for something ○ *dreamt of living abroad* 4 vi consider ○ *How could you even dream of doing such a thing?* ■ adj ideal ○ *dream holiday* —**dreamer** n —**dreamless** adj —**dream-like** adj

☐ **dream up** vt devise or invent

dreamland /dreem land/ n 1 a fantasy world 2 a state of sleep (*infml*)

dream ticket n US an ideal joint candidacy (*infml*)

Dreamtime /dreem tīm/ n in the mythology of Australian Aboriginals, the time of the creation of the world

dream world n a fantasy world

dreamy /dreemi/ (**-ier, -iest**) adj 1 strange, vague, or ethereal 2 given to daydreaming —**dreamily** adv —**dreaminess** n

dreary /dreeri/ (**-rier, -riest**) adj dull and gloomy —**drearily** adv —**dreariness** n

dredge[1] n also **dredger** 1 a machine for digging underwater 2 a boat or barge with a dredge on it ■ v (**dredging**, **dredged**) 1 vt remove material with a dredge 2 vti clear a channel with a dredge

□ **dredge up** vt find hidden information or mention forgotten incidents

dredge[2] (**dredging**, **dredged**) vt sprinkle with a coating of flour or sugar —**dredger** n

dregs npl 1 gritty particles at the bottom of a container of liquid 2 the least valuable part of something

drench vt make somebody or something completely wet

Dresden /drézdən/ capital of the state of Saxony, Germany. Pop. 474,443 (1997).

dress v 1 vti put clothes on yourself or somebody else 2 vi wear particular clothing o usually dresses in black 3 vt decorate a room or object 4 vt arrange goods in a window display 5 vt bandage or cover a wound 6 vt put a sauce on a salad 7 vt clean and prepare fish and game for cooking or selling 8 vt arrange hair ■ n 1 a woman's one-piece garment combining a top and skirt 2 the type of clothes somebody is wearing 3 clothes ■ adj formal, or requiring formal attire ◇ **dressed to kill** dressed in very glamorous clothes (infml)

□ **dress down** v 1 vi wear casual clothes (infml) 2 vt reprimand somebody

□ **dress up** v 1 vi dress formally 2 vi put on costumes 3 vt disguise something to make it look more pleasant

dressage /dréss aazh/ n 1 the process of training a horse to execute precise movements 2 an event in which horses and riders execute precise movements

dress circle n the first-floor gallery in an auditorium

dress code n an obligatory or recommended way to dress for something

dresser /dréssər/ n 1 a piece of furniture combining shelves and a cupboard 2 US, Can a bedroom chest of drawers 3 somebody who dresses in a specific way 4 an actor's assistant who deals with costumes 5 a personal grooming assistant

dressing /dréssing/ n 1 a bandage or covering for a wound 2 a sauce for a salad 3 US, Can stuffing for a piece of meat

dressing-down n a severe reprimand

dressing gown n a coat of soft light material worn indoors

dressing room n 1 a room in which an actor puts on makeup and costumes 2 a room in which to change clothes

dressing table n a bedroom table with drawers and a mirror

dressmaker /dréss maykər/ n somebody who makes dresses —**dressmaking** n

dress rehearsal n 1 a final rehearsal in costume 2 a full-scale practice before an event

dress sense n good taste in clothes

dress shirt n a man's formal shirt

dress uniform n a ceremonial military uniform

dressy /dréssi/ (-ier, -iest) adj 1 elegant in dress 2 requiring guests to dress formally —**dressily** adv —**dressiness** n

drew past tense of **draw**

Dreyfus /dráyfəss/, **Alfred** (1859–1935) French soldier falsely accused of treason by anti-Semites

drib n a small, negligible amount of something ◇ **in dribs and drabs** in very small amounts

dribble /dríbb'l/ v (-bling, -bled) 1 vi let saliva spill from the mouth 2 vti spill or be spilled in drops 3 vti in football and other ball games, move the ball around skilfully to keep possession ■ n 1 a tiny amount of liquid 2 an act of dribbling a ball —**dribbler** n —**dribbly** adj

drier[1] comparative of **dry**

drier[2] n = **dryer**[2]

driest superlative of **dry**

drift v 1 vi be carried along by the flow of water or air 2 vi move or wander aimlessly 3 vi deviate from a set course or position 4 vti form or cause to form heaps as a result of wind or water currents ■ n 1 a heap or bank of something such as snow or leaves 2 a drifting movement 3 a gradual change 4 the general meaning of something —**drifty** adj

drifter /dríftər/ n somebody who never settles in one place for long

drift ice n floating ice

drift net n a large fishing net supported by floats

driftwood /dríft wood/ n broken pieces of wood found washed ashore or floating in water

drill[1] n 1 an implement that rotates at high speed to bore holes 2 training by repetition 3 a repeated exercise 4 a routine for doing something (infml) ■ v 1 vti bore a hole with a drill 2 vti practise marching, or instruct soldiers in marching 3 vt teach somebody by rote —**driller** n ◇ See note at **teach**

drill[2] n 1 a furrow for seeds 2 a seed-planting machine 3 a planted row of seeds —**drill** vt

drill[3] n thick cotton fabric. Use: working clothes, uniforms.

drill[4] n a baboon with brown fur and a black face

drilling platform n a structure supporting an oil rig

drill sergeant, drillmaster /dríll maastər/ n a noncommissioned officer who drills soldiers

drily /dríli/, **dryly** adv with subtle irony or humour

drink vti (**drank**, **drunk**) 1 swallow a liquid 2 imbibe alcohol ■ n 1 drinkable liquid 2 an amount of liquid that somebody drinks 3 an alcoholic beverage 4 excessive consumption of alcohol

□ **drink in** vt 1 absorb liquid 2 absorb something with the mind and senses

drinkable /dríngkəb'l/ *adj* 1 safe to drink 2 pleasant or enjoyable to drink

drink-driving *n* the offence of driving after having drunk too much alcohol —**drink-driver** *n*

drinker /dríngkər/ *n* 1 somebody who drinks a particular beverage *(in combination)* 2 somebody who drinks alcoholic beverages

drinking fountain *n* a device supplying a jet of drinkable water

drinking song *n* a song sung by people drinking alcohol

drinking-up time *n* a time when people in a pub must finish their drinks

drinking water *n* water that is safe for human consumption

drip *v* (**dripping, dripped**) 1 *vti* fall or let fall in drops 2 *vt* let out in a great quantity ○ *a voice dripping malice* ■ *n* 1 a small amount of liquid 2 an instance of a liquid falling in drops 3 the sound of falling drops 4 a medical procedure for injecting a liquid 5 a person regarded as socially inept *(slang insult)*

drip-dry *adj* requiring no ironing after washing ■ *vti* (**drip-dries, drip-dried**) dry naturally without using a dryer

drip-feed (**drip-fed**) *vt* provide plants with a continuous water supply

dripping /drípping/ *n* fat from cooking meat ■ **drippings** *npl US* juices from cooking meat ■ *adj also* **dripping wet** thoroughly wet

drive /drīv/ *v* (**driving, drove** /drōv/, **driven** /drív'n/) 1 *vti* operate, travel in, or take somebody in a vehicle 2 *vt* provide the power or momentum for 3 *vt* force to do, experience, or be something ○ *was driven to despair* ○ *Fear drove the elephants to stampede.* 4 *vti* move or propel with force 5 *vt NZ* fell trees by cutting one down in such a way that it knocks others down ■ *n* 1 a ride taken in a vehicle 2 a road linking a house to a street 3 *also* **Drive** a wide road *(often in placenames)* 4 the means of converting power into motion in a machine *(often in combination)* 5 a computer device with data on a spinning disk 6 a hard hit of a ball 7 a fast direct movement 8 focused energy and determination 9 a powerful motivating force 10 a major organized effort 11 a sustained military attack

drive-by, drive-by shooting *n* the firing of a gun at somebody from a moving vehicle *(infml)*

drive-in *n* a business serving customers who stay in their parked cars

drivel /drív'l/ *n* 1 silly talk 2 drooled saliva ■ *vi* (**-elling, -elled**) 1 talk nonsense 2 drool —**drivelling** *n*

driven /drív'n/ past participle of **drive** ■ *adj* 1 compelled by need or ambition 2 caused by a particular thing *(in combination)* ○ *a demand-driven economy*

driver /drívər/ *n* 1 somebody who drives or is able to drive a vehicle 2 a golf club used for hitting the ball a long way 3 a tool that applies pressure 4 a strong force, e.g. in an organization

drive shaft *n* a rotating shaft transmitting power from the engine to wheels or a propeller

drive-through, drive-up *n US* a business that serves people who wait by a special window in their cars

drive time *n* weekday commuting hours

driveway /drív way/ *n* a road linking a house to a street

driving /dríving/ *adj* 1 falling or being blown hard ○ *a driving rain* 2 having the ability or influence to make something happen ■ *n* the operating of a vehicle by somebody —**drivingly** *adv*

driving test *n* a test to determine driving skill that people must pass before driving without supervision on public roads

drizzle /drízz'l/ *n* light rain ■ *v* (**-zling, -zled**) 1 *vi* rain lightly 2 *vt* dribble liquid over food —**drizzly** *adj*

drogue parachute /drōg-/ *n* a small parachute released before a larger one

droll /drōl/ *adj* oddly amusing —**drollness** *n* —**drolly** *adv*

drollery /dróləri/ *n* 1 quirky humour 2 amusing talk or behaviour

dromedary /drómmədəri, drúmmə-/ (*pl* **-ies**) *n* a one-humped camel

drone[1] /drōn/ (**droning, droned**) *v* 1 *vi* make a low humming sound 2 *vti* talk or say in a slow boring voice —**drone** *n* —**droningly** *adv*

drone[2] /drōn/ *n* 1 a male bee whose only function is mating 2 a person regarded as lazy *(insult)*

drongo /dróng gō/ (*pl* **-gos**) *n* a black tropical bird with a long forked tail

drool *v* 1 *vi* show exaggerated appreciation 2 *vi* dribble saliva 3 *vti* talk nonsense ■ *n* saliva dribbling from the mouth —**droolingly** *adv*

droop *v* 1 *vti* hang or bend down limply 2 *vi* be dispirited ■ *n* a sagging position —**droopily** *adv* —**droopingly** *adv* —**droopy** *adj*

drop *v* (**dropping, dropped**) 1 *vt* let go of something and cause it to fall 2 *vi* fall from a higher to a lower place 3 *vti* move or decrease to a lower position or level 4 *vti* fall or cause to fall in small round portions of liquid 5 *vi* slope down 6 *vti* lower the voice 7 *vt* let somebody out of a vehicle 8 *vt* stop doing, planning, or talking about something 9 *vt* remove somebody from membership in an organization 10 *vt* omit something, e.g. a word 11 *vi* collapse from exhaustion ■ *n* 1 a small amount or round portion of liquid 2 a very small amount ○ *not a drop of sympathy* 3 a decrease 4 the distance between a high point and the ground 5 a steep slope or incline 6 a descent or delivery of goods by parachute ■ **drops** *npl* liquid medicine applied to the ear, nose, or eye in small quantities ◇ **a drop in the ocean** an insignificant part of the full quantity required ◇ **at the**

drop of a hat without needing persuasion or prompting

□ **drop behind** vi gradually get farther behind

□ **drop by** or **in** or **over** vi visit somebody casually

□ **drop off** vi (infml) **1** doze off **2** undergo a gradual decrease ○ Sales have dropped off.

□ **drop out** vi **1** leave without finishing an activity **2** reject society (infml)

drop curtain, drop cloth n **1** in a theatre, a cloth with scenery painted on it, lowered from the flies **2** a theatre curtain that is lowered and raised from above, not opened and closed from the sides

drop goal n in rugby, a goal scored by a drop kick

drop-in centre n a place that people can visit without an appointment

drop kick n **1** in rugby or American football, a method of kicking a ball on the half-volley by dropping it from the hands **2** in amateur wrestling, an illegal move in which a wrestler leaps into the air and strikes an opponent with both feet —**drop-kick** vti

drop leaf n a folding extension on a table

droplet /dróplət/ n a tiny drop

drop-off n a gradual decrease

dropout /dróp owt/ n **1** a student who leaves university or college without graduating **2** somebody who chooses an unconventional lifestyle (infml) **3** in rugby, a drop kick by the defending team to restart the game

dropper /dróppər/ n a tube for dispensing drops (often in combination)

droppings /dróppingz/ npl animal dung

drop scone n a small thick pancake

drop shot n in racket games, a soft shot intended to bounce so low that the opponent cannot hit it back

dropsy /drópsi/ n the medical condition oedema (dated) —**dropsied** adj

dross n **1** something worthless **2** Scotland small coals —**drossy** adj

drought /drowt/ n **1** a long period of extremely dry weather producing a water shortage **2** a serious lack of something necessary —**droughty** adj

drove[1] /drōv/ past tense of **drive**

drove[2] /drōv/ n a group of animals moving together ■ **droves** npl crowds of people ■ vti (**droving, droved**) move animals along —**drover** n

drown /drown/ v **1** vti die or kill by immersion in water **2** also **drown out** vt prevent from being heard by making a louder sound **3** vt cover with too much liquid —**drowned** adj

drowse /drowz/ (**drowsing, drowsed**) vi be partway between sleeping and waking —**drowse** n

drowsy /drówzi/ (**-ier, -iest**) adj **1** almost asleep **2** causing sleepiness —**drowsily** adv —**drowsiness** n

drub vt (**drubbing, drubbed**) **1** beat with a heavy

stick **2** defeat comprehensively ■ n a blow with a stick —**drubbing** n

drudge n somebody who does menial work —**drudge** vi —**drudgingly** adv

drudgery /drújjəri/ n boring or exhausting work

drug n **1** a substance given as a medicine **2** an illegal substance taken for the pleasurable effects it produces ■ vt (**drugging, drugged**) **1** give a drug to **2** add a drug to

drugged adj **1** affected by drugs **2** tired and stupefied

druggist /drúggist/ n US, Can a pharmaceutical chemist

drug runner n somebody who transports illegal drugs

drugstore /drúg stawr/ n US, Can a chemist's shop

Druid /dróo id/, **druid** n **1** a priest of an ancient Celtic religion **2** a modern follower of an ancient Celtic religion —**druidic** /droo íddik/ adj —**druidical** adj

drum n **1** a percussion instrument consisting of a membrane stretched over a frame **2** a tapping sound **3** a large cylindrical container, spool, or part **4** an eardrum ■ vi (**drumming, drummed**) **1** play a drum **2** tap repeatedly on a surface —**drumming** n ◇ **bang** or **beat the drum (for)** try to attract favourable attention for (infml)

□ **drum into** vt tell somebody something repeatedly

□ **drum up** vt **1** try to elicit support **2** invent an explanation

drumbeat /drúm beet/ n a tap or rhythmic series of taps on a drum

drum kit n a set of drums used for playing music in a band

drum major n the leader of a marching band

drummer /drúmmər/ n **1** a drum player **2** US, Can a travelling salesperson

drum roll n a continuous drumming, often heralding an important arrival or event

drumstick /drúm stik/ n **1** a stick for beating a drum **2** the lower half of the leg of a bird such as a chicken when prepared for eating

drunk past participle of **drink** ■ adj **1** intoxicated with alcohol **2** emotionally intoxicated ■ n also **drunkard** /drúngkərd/ somebody who is habitually drunk

drunk-driver n somebody who drives a car when too drunk to drive

drunken /drúngkən/ adj **1** involving alcohol **2** intoxicated by or as if by alcohol **3** drunk or frequently drunk —**drunkenly** adv —**drunkenness** n

~~drunkeness~~ incorrect spelling of **drunkenness**

drupe n a fruit with a large stone inside

dry adj (**drier** or **dryer, driest** or **dryest**) **1** not wet or moist **2** lacking rain or moisture in the air **3** lacking in desired levels of moisture or moistness ○ dry skin **4** without flesh attached ○ dry bones **5** thirsty **6** lacking sweetness ○ dry sherry **7** shrewdly amusing **8** boring and academic **9** matter-of-fact ■ v (**dries,**

dried 1 *vti* make or become dry 2 *vi* forget your lines during a performance —**dryness** *n*

SYNONYMS dry, dehydrated, desiccated, arid, parched, shrivelled, sere CORE MEANING: lacking moisture

☐ **dry out** *vti* make or become completely dry
☐ **dry up** v 1 *vti* lose or cause to lose moisture 2 *vi* stop being available as a resource
dryad /drī ad, -əd/ (*pl* -**ads** *or* -**ades** /-ə deez/) *n* in Greek mythology, a wood nymph
dry-clean *vt* clean with chemicals, not with water —**dry-cleaner** *n* —**dry-cleaning** *n*
Dryden /drīd'n/, **John** (1631–1700) English poet, dramatist, and critic
dry dock *n* a waterless area for ship repairs —**dry-dock** *vti*
dryer[1] /drī ər/ comparative of **dry**
dryer[2] /drī ər/, **drier** *n* a drying device or machine, especially one for laundry
dryest superlative of **dry**
dry-eyed *adj* not crying or weeping
dry ice *n* a solid form of carbon dioxide. Use: refrigeration, production of artificial fog.
dry land *n* land, not the sea
dryland /drī land/ *n* areas of little rainfall, collectively (*often pl*) —**dryland** *adj*
dryly *adv* = **drily**
dry rot *n* crumbling decay in wood, caused by various fungi
dry run *n* a rehearsal of a future planned action
Drysdale /drīz dayl/, **Sir Russell** (1912–81) British-born Australian landscape painter
DTI *abbr* Department of Trade and Industry
DTLR, DTLGR *abbr* Department of Transport, Local Government, and the Regions
DTP *abbr* desktop publishing
DTs *npl* delirium tremens (*infml*)
DTV *abbr* digital television
du, Du see also under surname
dual /dyoo əl/ *adj* having two parts, functions, aspects, or items ○ *dual citizenship* ○ *serving a dual purpose* —**dually** *adv*

SPELLCHECK Do not confuse the spelling of **dual** and **duel** ('a contest'), which sound similar.

dual carriageway *n* a road with a barrier between traffic flows
dualism /dyoo əlizəm/ *n* 1 a state in which something has two distinct parts or aspects 2 the philosophical theory that human beings are made up of independent constituents, the body and the mind or soul 3 the religious doctrine that the antagonistic forces of good and evil determine the course of events —**dualist** *n* —**dualistic** /dyoo ə lístik/ *adj*
duality /dyoo álləti/ (*pl* -**ties**) *n* a situation or nature with two complementary or opposing parts
dub[1] (**dubbing, dubbed**) *vt* 1 give a descriptive nickname to 2 confer a knighthood on

dub[2] (**dubbing, dubbed**) *vt* 1 add a soundtrack in a different language to a film or television show 2 copy a recording onto a different recording medium 3 add sounds to a film —**dub** *n*

ORIGIN **Dub** in sound recording is a shortening of *double*.

Dubai /doo bí/, **Dubayy** capital of **Dubai state** in the NE United Arab Emirates. Pop. 674,100 (1995).
Du Barry /doo bárri, dyoo-/, **Marie Jeanne Bécu, Comtesse** (1743?–93) French courtier and mistress of Louis XV
dubbin /dúbbin/ *n* a greasy cream for polishing leather
Dubček /doop chek, doob-/, **Alexander** (1921–92) Czech political leader (1968)
dubiety /dyoo bí əti/ (*pl* -**ties**) *n* (*fml*) 1 uncertainty about something 2 something doubtful
dubious /dyoóbi əss/ *adj* 1 unsure about an outcome 2 of doubtful character or quality —**dubiously** *adv* —**dubiousness** *n* ◊ See note at **doubtful**
Dublin /dúbblin/ capital of the Republic of Ireland. Pop. 953,000 (1996). —**Dubliner** *n*
dubnium /dúbni əm/ *n* (*symbol* **Db**) a rare unstable chemical element

ORIGIN **Dubnium** was named in 1967 after Dubna in Russia, site of the Joint Nuclear Institute.

ducal /dyoók'l/ *adj* of a duke or dukedom
ducat /dúkət/ *n* a coin formerly used in some European countries ■ **ducats** *npl* cash (*infml dated*)
Duchamp /dyoo shaáN/, **Marcel** (1887–1968) French-born US artist
duchess /dúchəss/ *n* 1 a high-ranking noblewoman 2 the wife or widow of a duke
duchy /dúchi/ (*pl* -**ies**) *n* a duke or duchess's territory
duck[1] (*pl* **ducks** *or* same) *n* 1 a common water bird with webbed feet and a broad flat bill 2 a female duck 3 a duck as food

ORIGIN Although the verb **duck** is recorded later than the noun **duck**, it is assumed that it comes from an ancient root and that a **duck** is literally a 'bird that ducks'. No related language uses its form of the word as a name for a bird.

duck[2] *v* 1 *vti* move your head down quickly 2 *vi* move somewhere quickly to avoid being seen 3 *vti* plunge under water 4 *vt* avoid dealing with something that ought to be dealt with —**duck** *n*
duck[3] *n* strong cotton or canvas cloth. Use: clothing, furnishings. ■ **ducks** *npl* white trousers
duck[4] *n* a score of zero

ORIGIN **Duck** 'zero' is a shortening of *duck's egg*, which the figure was thought to resemble.

duck-billed platypus *n* a platypus

duckling /dúkling/ *n* a young duck

ducks and drakes *n* the activity of bouncing stones across water (*+ sing verb*)

duckweed /dúk weed/ *n* a floating aquatic plant

duct *n* **1** a tube, pipe, or channel for something such as electrical cables or heated air **2** a tube in a body organ **3** a tube containing electrical cables ■ *vt* cause to pass through a channel —**ductless** *adj*

ductile /dúk tīl/ *adj* **1** malleable enough to be worked **2** easily influenced —**ductility** /duk tíllati/ *n* ◊ See note at **pliable**

dud *n* **1** a failure (*infml*) **2** a shell that does not explode ■ *adj* (**dudder**, **duddest**) useless (*infml*)

dude /dyood, dood/ *n US, Can* a man (*slang*)

dude ranch *n US, Can* a holiday complex in the W United States offering outdoor activities

dudgeon /dújjən/ *n* a fit of pique

Dudley /dúddli/, ♦ **Leicester, Earl of**

duds *npl* clothes (*infml*)

due /dyoo/ *adj* **1** expected to arrive **2** awaiting something that is part of a normal progression of events **3** proper and appropriate **4** owed as a debt **5** payable at once or on demand **6** attributable ○ *a delay due to weather* ■ *n* somebody's right ■ **dues** *npl* membership fees ■ *adv* directly and exactly ○ *due west* ◊ See note at **dew**

duel /dyoo əl/ *n* **1** a formal fight over a matter of honour **2** a struggle between two parties —**duel** *vi* —**dueller** *n* —**duellist** *n* ◊ See note at **dual**

~~duely~~ incorrect spelling of **duly**

Duero ♦ **Douro**

duet /dyoo ét/ *n* **1** a composition for two performers **2** a pair —**duettist** *n*

duff[1] *adj* useless (*infml*)

duff[2] □ **duff up** *vt* beat somebody up (*slang*)

duff[3] *n* a steamed pudding

duffel /dúff'l/, **duffle** *n* **1** thick woollen fabric with a nap on both sides **2** *US* camping and hiking gear

> **ORIGIN** The fabric **duffel** is named after the Belgian town of Duffel, where it was first made.

duffel bag *n* a cylindrical bag with a drawstring

duffel coat *n* a thick woollen coat with a hood and toggles

duffer /dúffər/ *n* somebody considered unintelligent or incompetent (*infml dated insult*)

Dufy /dyoofi/, **Raoul** (1877–53) French painter, illustrator, and designer

dug[1] past participle, past tense of **dig**

dug[2] *n* an animal's milk-producing gland

dugout /dúg owt/ *n* **1** a soldiers' shelter dug into the ground **2** a canoe made from a hollowed log

duh *interj US* expresses an ironic response to being told something obvious or that you already know (*slang*)

Duisburg /dyoóssburg/ inland port in NW Germany. Pop. 536,106 (1997).

du jour /dyoo zhoór/ *adj* **1** offered or served on the current day **2** latest

duke /dyook/ *n* **1** a high-ranking nobleman **2** the ruler of a principality or a duchy —**dukedom** *n*

> **ORIGIN Duke** was an early adoption from French, referring to a sovereign prince in some Continental European countries. It was not used as a title of English noblemen until introduced as a rank of the peerage in the 14C by Edward III. The French term derives from a Latin word meaning 'leader'.

dulcet /dúlssit/ *adj* pleasant to hear

dulcimer /dúlssimər/ *n* a zither

dull *adj* **1** boring **2** overcast **3** not bright or vivid **4** not intensely felt **5** muffled in sound **6** blunt and not sharp **7** regarded as unintelligent **8** slow to respond ○ *dull reflexes* **9** not busy **10** listless ■ *vti* **1** make or become less acute **2** reduce in loudness **3** make or become blunt **4** make or become less bright or intense **5** make or become less busy —**dullness** *n* —**dully** *adv*

dullard /dúllərd/ *n* a person regarded as unintelligent or slow to learn (*literary*)

Duluth /də loóth/ major port in NE Minnesota. Pop. 81,228 (1998).

duly /dyoóli/ *adv* **1** properly and suitably ○ *duly grateful* **2** at the proper or expected time ○ *At the signal the train duly departed.*

Dumas /dyoo maa/, **Alexandre** (1802–70) and his son **Alexandre** (1824–95) French novelists and dramatists

du Maurier /dyoo mórri ay/, **Dame Daphne** (1907–89) British novelist

dumb /dum/ *adj* **1** an offensive term meaning unable to speak **2** temporarily speechless **3** done without speech **4** intentionally silent **5** lacking human speech **6** producing no sound **7** regarded as unintelligent (*infml insult*) **8** not able to process data —**dumbly** *adv* —**dumbness** *n*

□ **dumb down** *vti* make something condescendingly simplistic (*infml*)

dumbbell /dúm bel/ *n* a piece of exercise equipment consisting of a short metal bar with a weight at each end

dumb bomb *n* an unguided bomb or missile

~~dumbell~~ incorrect spelling of **dumbbell**

dumbfound /dúm fównd/, **dumfound** *vti* make somebody speechless with astonishment

dumb show *n* **1** wordless communication by actors using gestures or facial expressions **2** a play in mime

dumbstruck /dúm struk/ *adj* speechless with shock or astonishment

dumbwaiter /dúm wáytər/ *n* **1** a small lift for moving kitchen items between the floors of a building **2** a movable food stand placed near the table during a meal **3** a revolving tray for holding a selection of foods

Dumfries /dum freess/ town in S Scotland. Pop. 38,000 (1996).

Dumfries and Galloway /-gállə way/ council area in SW Scotland. Pop. 145,000 (1996).

dummy /dúmmi/ n (pl **-mies**) **1** a mannequin in a shop **2** a model used by a ventriloquist **3** an imitation of something **4** a small object for a baby to suck **5** in team games such as soccer or rugby, a feigned pass **6** a person or organization acting as a front for somebody else **7** somebody regarded as unintelligent or naive (infml insult) **8** a nonexplosive form of munition **9** a facsimile page or book showing what the final product will look like **10** in the game of bridge, an exposed hand ■ vt (**-mies, -mied**) make into a facsimile page or book

dummy run n a practice or try-out of a process

dump vt **1** deposit something on a surface carelessly **2** throw something out as unwanted **3** get rid of waste at a waste disposal site **4** end a relationship with somebody (infml) **5** flood a market with cheap merchandise **6** get rid of stocks **7** leave somebody to be cared for by others (infml disapproving) **8** transfer unprocessed computer data from one place to another ■ n **1** a waste disposal site **2** an unpleasant or dirty place (infml) **3** a munitions and supply area **4** an act of discarding something **5** a transfer of unprocessed computer data from one place to another

dumpbin /dúmp bin/ n a display container in a shop

dumper /dúmpər/ n Aus a powerful ocean wave

dumper truck n a heavy lorry with an open bed that tilts up to unload

dumpling /dúmpling/ n **1** a small ball of dough cooked and served with soup or stew **2** a pastry dessert

dumps npl a gloomy state of mind (infml)

dumpy /dúmpi/ (**-ier, -iest**) adj regarded as being short and plump (infml disapproving) —**dumpiness** n

dun[1] n **1** a brownish-grey colour **2** a brownish-grey horse ■ adj (**dunner, dunnest**) brownish-grey

dun[2] (**dunning, dunned**) vt harass for the payment of a debt —**dun** n

AKG London

Isadora Duncan

Duncan /dúngkən/, **Isadora** (1877–1927) US dancer

dunce n a person regarded as unintelligent or slow-witted (insult)

ORIGIN Dunce is from the middle name of the

Scottish philosopher and theologian John Duns Scotus (?1266–1308). His system of learning was highly influential in the late Middle Ages, but in the 16C his ideas were discredited and ridiculed, so that eventually his name became an insult.

dunce's cap, dunce cap n a pointed hat formerly worn as a punishment by a pupil regarded as unintelligent

Dundee /dun deé/ **1** city in E Scotland. Pop. 150,250 (1996). **2** City of Dundee council area in E Scotland —**Dundonian** /dun dóni ən/ n, adj

Dundee cake n a rich fruitcake with almonds on the top

dunderhead /dúndər hed/ n a person regarded as unintelligent or slow to learn (infml insult) —**dunderheaded** adj

dune /dyoon/ n a hill of sand

dune buggy n a motorized vehicle for use on sand

Dunedin /dun eédin/ city and port on the southeastern coast of the South Island, New Zealand. Pop. 112,400 (1998).

dung n animal excrement or manure —**dungy** adj

dungarees /dúng gə reéz/ npl a casual one-piece garment consisting of trousers and a bib with shoulder straps

dungeon /dúnjən/ n a prison cell, especially one underground

dunk vt **1** dip food in a liquid **2** quickly submerge something in a liquid ■ n also **dunk shot** in basketball, a shot in which the ball is slammed through the hoop from above —**dunker** n

Dunkirk /dun kúrk/ port in NE France. In World War II over 330,000 Allied troops were evacuated from the town by sea, under constant enemy fire. Pop. 70,850 (1999).

Dunlop /dún lop/, **John Boyd** (1840–1921) British inventor. He invented the pneumatic tyre in about 1887.

Dunlop, Weary (1907–93) Australian surgeon and war hero

dunt regional n **1** an injury from a blow **2** an act of hitting somebody or something ■ vt hit

duo /dyoó ō/ (pl **-os**) n **1** a composition for two performers **2** a pair of musicians who play together **3** a pair of closely associated people **4** a set of two closely related things

duo- prefix two ○ *duopoly*

duodecimal /dyoò ō déssim'l/ adj based on the number 12 ■ n **1** a duodecimal number **2** a 12th part —**duodecimally** adv

duodenum /dyoò ō deénəm/ (pl **-na** /-nə/ or **-nums**) n the first section of the small intestine immediately beyond the stomach —**duodenal** adj

duopoly /dyoo óppəli/ (pl **-lies**) n a concentration of economic power in two organizations or companies —**duopolistic** /dyoo óppə lístik/ adj

dupatta /doò pútta/ n S Asia a woman's scarf

dupe /dyoōp/ *vt* (**duping, duped**) trick ■ *n* a victim of deceit

duple /dyoōp'l/ *adj* having two beats to the musical bar

duplex /dyoō pleks/ *n* **1** *Aus, US, Can* a house divided into two separate flats **2** the transmission of signals over a communications channel in both directions at the same time ■ *adj* **1** twofold **2** having two parts performing the same function independently

duplicate *vt* /dyoōpli kayt/ (**-cating, -cated**) **1** make an exact copy of **2** repeat ■ *n* /-kət/ **1** an exact copy **2** a spare object of the same kind **3** a repeat of an earlier action or achievement ■ *adj* /dyoōpli kət/ **1** copied exactly **2** having two corresponding parts —**duplicable** *adj* —**duplicative** /-kətiv/ *adj* ◊ See note at **copy**

duplication /dyoōpli káysh'n/ *n* **1** the act of repeating or copying something **2** an exact copy

duplicator /dyoōpli kaytər/ *n* a machine for copying printed matter

duplicity /dyoo plíssəti/ *n* **1** deceitfulness **2** the state of being double (*fml*) —**duplicitous** *adj*

du Pré /dyoo práy/, **Jacqueline** (1945–87) British cellist and teacher

durable /dyoōrəb'l/ *adj* lasting for a long time without sustaining damage or wear —**durability** /dyoōrə bílləti/ *n* —**durably** *adv*

duration /dyoo ráysh'n/ *n* the time that something lasts —**durational** *adj*

Durban /dúrbən/ port in E South Africa. Pop. 1,264,000 (1995).

Dürer /dyoōrər/, **Albrecht** (1471–1528) German painter and engraver

duress /dyoō réss/ *n* **1** the use of force or threats **2** illegal force or coercion, e.g. against a criminal suspect

Durex /dyoōr eks/ *tdmk* **1** *UK* a trademark for a condom **2** *Aus* a trademark for a transparent adhesive tape

Durham /dúrrəm/ **1** city in NE England. Pop. 153,513 (1998). **2** county in NE England. Pop. 507,100 (1995).

during /dyoōring/ *prep* **1** throughout the period of **2** at some point in the period of

Durkheim /dúrk hīm/, **Émile** (1858–1917) French social theorist

Durrell /dúrrəl/, **Gerald** (1925–95) British naturalist and writer

Durrell, Lawrence (1912–90) British novelist, poet, and travel writer

Dushanbe /doo shaánbi/ capital of Tajikistan. Pop. 664,000 (1995).

dusk *n* **1** the period after the Sun goes below the horizon but before the sky is dark **2** partial or almost complete darkness (*literary*)

dusky /dúski/ (**-ier, -iest**) *adj* **1** dark-coloured **2** having little or insufficient light —**duskily** *adv* —**duskiness** *n*

Düsseldorf /dooss'l dawrf/ capital of North

Rhine-Westphalia, west-central Germany. Pop. 572,638 (1997).

dust *n* **1** small dry particles of matter **2** an act of removing household dust ■ *v* **1** *vti* remove household dust from a surface **2** *vt* sprinkle a powdery substance over something ◊ **bite the dust** suffer a total failure (*infml*) ◊ **gather dust** remain unused

□ **dust down** *vt* **1** *also* **dust off** recycle something old **2** clean something by wiping or brushing

dustbin /dúst bin/ *n* a large outdoor container for household rubbish

dustbin man *n* *UK* a dustman

dust bowl *n* **1** an area in which the dry topsoil is exposed and dust storms occur **2 Dust Bowl** a large area in the south-central United States that suffered badly from wind erosion during the 1930s

dustcart /dúst kaart/ *n* *UK* a vehicle for collecting and compacting household waste

dust cover *n* **1** a cover for protecting equipment or furniture **2** *also* **dust jacket** a paper cover that protects a hardback book

dust devil *n* a small dust-laden whirlwind

duster /dústər/ *n* **1** a cloth used for removing household dust from furniture **2** a woman's long loose coat **3** a device for spreading agrochemicals

dustman /dústmən/ (*pl* **-men** /-mən/) *n* *UK* somebody who removes household rubbish

dustpan /dúst pan/ *n* a container into which dirt can be swept

dust storm *n* a dust-carrying windstorm

dust-up *n* an argument or fight (*slang*)

dusty /dústi/ (**-ier, -iest**) *adj* **1** full of dust **2** boring

Dutch *n* the official language of the Netherlands ■ *npl* the people of the Netherlands —**Dutch** *adj* ◊ **go Dutch** pay for your own part of a meal or entertainment

Dutch auction *n* an auction with gradually decreasing prices

Dutch barn *n* a barn with a curved roof and open sides

Dutch courage *n* alcohol-induced courage (*infml*)

ORIGIN Derogatory expressions like this containing *Dutch* stem from the rivalry between the Dutch and the English in the 17C and 18C. The novelist and poet Sir Walter Scott refers to **Dutch courage** in the early 19C.

Dutch elm disease *n* a serious fungal disease of elm trees

ORIGIN The disease is 'Dutch' because it was identified by Dutch scientists.

Dutchman /dúchmən/ (*pl* **-men** /-mən/) *n* a man from the Netherlands

Dutch oven *n* **1** a heavy cooking pot **2** an open-fronted metal box for cooking food on an open fire

Dutchwoman /dúch woŏmən/ (pl **-women** /-wimin/) n a woman from the Netherlands

duteous /dyoóti əss/ adj obediently dutiful (archaic) —**duteously** adv —**duteousness** n

dutiable /dyoóti əb'l/ adj subject to customs duty

dutiful /dyoótif'l/ adj 1 done to fulfil obligations 2 careful to fulfil obligations —**dutifully** adv —**dutifulness** n

duty /dyoóti/ (pl **-ties**) n 1 an obligation 2 a task allocated to somebody 3 the urge to fulfil obligations 4 an import or export tax 5 suitability for a particular grade of use (usually in combination) ○ heavy-duty carpet ◇ **off duty** not at work

duty-free adj exempted from customs or excise duties —**duty-free** adv

duty officer n an officer on duty at a specific time

Duvalier /dyoŏ válli ay/, **François** (1907–71) Haitian national leader (1957–71)

duvet /doŏ vay, dyoŏ-/ n a thick warm quilt for a bed

duvet day n any one of an agreed number of days that some employees can take as leave at short notice in addition to their official holiday allowance

DVD n a large-capacity CD used for storing video and audio data. Full form **digital video disc**

DVD-A n an audio DVD

DVD-ROM n a video CD-ROM

DVI abbr digital video imaging

Dvina /dveénə/ river in W Russia, W Belarus, and Latvia. Length 1,020 km/634 mi.

DVLA abbr Driving and Vehicle Licensing Agency

Dvořák /dváwr zhak/, **Antonín** (1841–1904) Bohemian Czech composer

Dvorak keyboard /dváwr zhak-/ n a keyboard arranged for quicker typing

ORIGIN The keyboard is named after August Dvorak, who devised it in the first part of the 20C.

DVT abbr deep-vein thrombosis

dwarf n (pl **dwarves** or **dwarfs**) 1 an imaginary being resembling a small human 2 a person who is atypically small for medical reasons 3 a plant or animal that is smaller than others of its species ■ vt 1 cause to seem small by comparison 2 stunt the growth of —**dwarfish** adj —**dwarfism** n

dwell (**dwelt** or **dwelled**) vi reside in a particular place (literary) —**dweller** n

□ **dwell on** or **upon** vt think, write, or talk about at length

dwelling /dwélling/ n a home (fml) ■ adj living in a particular place (usually in combination) ○ bottom-dwelling fishes

dwindle /dwínd'l/ (**-dling**, **-dled**) vti decrease gradually in size, number, or intensity

DWP abbr Department for Work and Pensions

Dy symbol dysprosium

Dyck /dīk/, **Sir Anthony van** (1599–1641) Flemish painter

dye /dī/ v 1 vt colour by soaking in a solution 2 vi respond to colouring in a particular way ■ n 1 a colouring agent or solution 2 the colour produced by a dye —**dyable** adj —**dyer** n ◊ See note at **die**

dyed-in-the-wool adj 1 wholeheartedly and stubbornly attached to a viewpoint 2 dyed before weaving

dying /dī ing/ adj 1 about to die 2 occurring just before death 3 occurring as something is about to end

dyke[1] /dīk/, **dike** n 1 an embankment built to prevent floods 2 a barrier 3 a causeway 4 a ditch 5 Scotland a dry-stone wall —**dyke** vt

dyke[2] /dīk/, **dike** n an offensive term for a lesbian (slang)

Bob Dylan

Dylan /díllən/, **Bob** (b. 1941) US singer and songwriter

dynamic /dī námmik/ adj 1 full of energy and enthusiasm 2 characterized by vigorous activity and change 3 of energy 4 of dynamics ■ n a driving force —**dynamically** adv

dynamics /dī námmiks/ npl 1 the forces that produce activity and change in any situation or sphere of existence (+ pl verb) 2 the different levels of loudness and softness in a musical piece (+ pl verb) ■ n the study of motion (+ sing verb)

dynamism /dínəmizəm/ n 1 vigorousness and forcefulness 2 the philosophical or scientific theory that explains an event as the expression of forces residing in the object or person involved —**dynamist** n

dynamite /dínə mīt/ n 1 a powerful explosive. Use: blasting. 2 a very exciting or dangerous person or thing (slang) ■ vt (**-miting, -mited**) blast with dynamite

ORIGIN Dynamite was given its name by its inventor, Alfred Nobel, in 1867. It comes from the Greek word for 'strength, force' that is also the base of dynamism, dynamo, and similar words.

dynamo /dínəmō/ (pl **-mos**) n 1 a generator of electricity from mechanical energy 2 an energetic person (infml)

dynasty /dínnəsti/ (pl **-ties**) n 1 a succession of hereditary rulers 2 a prominent, powerful family —**dynastic** /di nástik/ adj

dysentery /díss'ntəri/ *n* a disease of the lower intestine that causes severe diarrhoea and the passage of blood and mucus —**dysenteric** /díss'n térrik/ *adj*

~~dysentry~~ incorrect spelling of **dysentery**

dysfunction /diss fúngksh'n/ *n* a medical problem in the functioning of a part of the body

dysfunctional /diss fúngksh'nəl/ *adj* 1 failing to function properly 2 unable to relate emotionally and socially

dyslexia /diss léksi ə/ *n* a learning disability marked by difficulty in recognizing and understanding written language —**dyslexic** *adj, n*

dyspepsia /diss pépsi ə/ *n* indigestion (*technical*)

dyspeptic /diss péptik/ *adj* 1 having indigestion 2 bad-tempered —**dyspeptic** *n*

dysprosium /diss prózi əm/ *n* (*symbol* Dy) a soft silvery chemical element. Use: laser materials, nuclear research.

dystopia /diss tốpi ə/ *n* an imaginary place where everything is very bad —**dystopian** *adj*

dystrophy /dístrəfi/ (*pl* **-phies**), **dystrophia** /diss trốfi ə/ *n* a progressive degeneration of body tissue

E

e[1] (*pl* **e's**), **E** (*pl* **E's** *or* **Es**) *n* the 5th letter of the English alphabet

e[2] *symbol* 1 electron 2 the transcendental number 2.718 282...

E[1] (*pl* **E's** *or* **Es**) *n* 1 the 3rd note in the musical scale of C major 2 the 5th highest grade of a student's work 3 the illegal drug ecstasy (*slang*)

E[2] *abbr* 1 east 2 eastern

e- *prefix* 1 electronic ○ *e-mail* 2 electronic data transfer via the Internet ○ *e-commerce*

E- *prefix* a food additive that conforms to an EU standard, specified by a number

each /eech/ *det, pron* every one of two or more people or things ○ *Each person was given a gift.* ○ *Each of them is to receive a gift.* ■ *adv* to or for every one of two or more people or things ○ *Give them two each.*

each other *pron* each of two or more people in a group, having the same relationship

each way for a win or place in a race, as the condition of a bet —**each-way** *adj*

eager /eégər/ *adj* enthusiastic and excited about doing something ○ *eager to set out* ○ *eager faces* —**eagerly** *adv* —**eagerness** *n*

eagle /eég'l/ *n* 1 a large bird of prey with a soaring flight 2 a golf score of two under par —**eaglet** *n*

eagle eye *n* keen eyesight or attention —**eagle-eyed** *adj*

Eames /eemz/, **Charles** (1907–78) US designer and architect

ear[1] /eer/ *n* 1 the organ of hearing in mammals and other vertebrates 2 the external part of a vertebrate's ear 3 an invertebrate sensory organ like an ear 4 an ability to tell sounds apart ○ *has a good ear* 5 a person's attention ○ *lend an ear* ◇ **all ears** listening attentively or enthusiastically (*infml*) ◇ **have somebody's ear** be a trusted adviser to somebody ◇ **have** *or* **keep your ear to the ground** pay attention to new developments or information ◇ **out on your ear** unceremoniously thrown out or dismissed (*infml*) ◇ **wet behind the ears** very inexperienced or naive

ORIGIN The **ear** that you hear with comes from an ancient word that probably meant 'perception'; an **ear** of corn comes from a word that meant 'be pointed or sharp'.

ear[2] /eer/ *n* a plant part containing grain

earache /eér ayk/ *n* a pain in the ear

eardrum /eér drum/ *n* a sound-transmitting membrane in the ear

earful /eér fŏol/ *n* a scolding or tirade of abuse (*infml*)

Barnaby's

Amelia Earhart

Earhart /áir haart/, **Amelia** (1898–1937) US aviator

earhole /eér hōl/ *n* the opening leading into the ear (*infml*)

earl /url/ *n* a middle-ranking British nobleman —**earldom** *n*

earlobe /eér lōb/ *n* the lower part of the outer ear

early /úrli/ *adv* (**-lier, -liest**) 1 before the expected time 2 near the beginning ○ *started talking early* ■ *adj* (**-lier, -liest**) 1 occurring near the beginning 2 occurring before the expected time —**earliness** *n*

earmark /eér maark/ *vt* 1 designate something for a particular purpose ○ *funds earmarked for research* 2 put an identification mark on an animal's ear ■ *n* an identification mark on an animal's ear

earn /urn/ *v* 1 *vti* make money by working 2 *vt* acquire something as a reward or result

earner /úrnər/ *n* 1 somebody who earns an income ○ *earners of wages* 2 a source of profit ○ *a nice little earner*

earnest /úrnist/ *adj* intensely serious and sincere **—earnestly** *adv* **—earnestness** *n*

earnings /úrningz/ *npl* money earned

EAROM /ee rom/ *abbr* electrically alterable read-only memory

earphone /eer fōn/ *n* a device that converts electricity to sound and is held to the ear (often pl)

earpiece /eer peess/ *n* **1** the part of a device that people hear through **2** the part of a glasses frame that goes around the ear

ear-piercing *adj* very loud

earplug /eer plug/ *n* a soft plug inserted in the ear to keep out noise, water, or cold (often pl)

earring /eer ring/ *n* a piece of jewellery worn on the ear (often pl)

earset /eer set/ *n* a piece of equipment attached to a computer or mobile phone that enables the user to make telephone calls without using the hands

earshot /eer shot/ *n* the distance in which sound is audible ○ out of earshot

earsplitting /eer spliting/ *adj* very loud

earth /urth/ *n* **1** *also* **Earth** the 3rd planet from the Sun, on which human beings live **2** dry land **3** soil in which plants grow **4** a fox's burrow **5** an electrical connection to the ground for safety ■ *vt* connect an electrical appliance to the ground for safety **—earthward** *adj, adv* **—earthwards** *adv* ◇ **come back (down) to earth** come back to reality

earthbound /úrth bownd/ *adj* **1** heading towards Earth **2** mundane and unimaginative

earthen /úrth'n/ *adj* made of earth

earthenware /úrth'n wair/ *n* pottery made of baked clay

earthling /úrthling/ *n* a human being as contrasted with an extraterrestrial or supernatural being

earthly /úrthli/ (**-lier, -liest**) *adj* **1** characteristic of this world **2** possible or imaginable ○ no earthly use

earth mother *n* a sensual and motherly woman

earthmover /úrth moovar/ *n* a bulldozer or mechanical digger **—earthmoving** *adj*

earthquake /úrth kwayk/ *n* **1** a shaking of the Earth's crust resulting from release of stress along a fault line or from volcanic activity **2** a severely disruptive event

earth science *n* geology or a similar Earth-related science

earthshattering /úrth shàttaring/, **earthshaking** /úrth shayking/ *adj* extremely great or important

earthwork /úrth wurk/ *n* an earth fortification (often pl)

earthworm /úrth wurm/ *n* a worm that burrows in the soil

earthy /úrthi/ (**-ier, -iest**) *adj* **1** like soil **2** not squeamish or pretentious **3** rather indecent **—earthily** *adv* **—earthiness** *n*

earwax /eer waks/ *n* a waxy substance secreted by glands in the ear

earwig /eer wig/ *n* a slender insect with pincers at the end of its abdomen ■ *vi* eavesdrop (humorous)

ORIGIN The *wig* of **earwig** is an ancient word that meant 'insect', and is probably related to *wiggle*. There is a common myth that earwigs crawl into people's ears.

ease /eez/ *n* **1** lack of difficulty **2** lack of awkwardness **3** comfort and affluence **4** relaxation ■ *v* (**easing, eased**) **1** *vt* make less unpleasant **2** *vt* relieve from pain **3** *also* **ease off** *vi* become less strong or intense **4** *vti* manoeuvre gently

easel /eez'l/ *n* a support for an artist's canvas or blackboard

ORIGIN The Dutch word that **easel** derives from meant 'donkey' (because the easel, like the donkey, carries a load), and is related to English *ass*.

easement /eezmant/ *n* a limited legal right to use something

easily /eezili/ *adv* **1** without difficulty **2** quickly or soon **3** by far ○ easily the best **4** as a likelihood ○ could easily have forgotten

east /eest/ *n* **1** the direction in which the sun rises **2** the compass point opposite west **3** *also* **East** the part of an area or country that is in the east, or the part of the world to the east of Europe and the west of America ■ *adj* **1** in the east **2** describes a wind that blows from the east ■ *adv* towards the east **—eastbound** *adj*

East Africa region in east-central Africa, usually including Burundi, Kenya, Rwanda, Somalia, Tanzania, and Uganda **—East African** *n, adj*

East Anglia /-áng gli ə/ mainly agricultural region in E England **—East Anglian** *n, adj*

East Asia the countries, territories, and regions of China, Hong Kong, Japan, North Korea, South Korea, Macau, Mongolia, parts of Russia, and Taiwan **—East Asian** *adj*

East Ayrshire /-áirshar/ council area in west-central Scotland

Eastbourne /eest bawrn/ seaside resort in SE England. Pop. 94,793 (1991).

East Dunbartonshire /-dun baart'nshar/ council area in central Scotland

Easter /eestar/ *n* **1** a Christian festival marking the resurrection of Jesus Christ. Date: the Sunday following the full moon on or after 21 March. **2** the period from Good Friday to Easter Monday

ORIGIN Easter comes from the name of a Germanic goddess of the dawn, and is related to *east*. Both come from an ancient word meaning 'shine'.

Easter egg *n* **1** a chocolate egg given as an Easter gift **2** a hidden element of a computer program

Barnaby's

Easter Island

Easter Island /eestər-/ island in the South Pacific Ocean belonging to Chile. Pop. 2,095 (1989). —**Easter Islander** n

easterly /eestərli/ adj 1 in the east 2 describes a wind that blows from the east ∎ n a wind from the east —**easterly** adv

Easter Monday n the Monday after the Christian festival of Easter

eastern /eestərn/ adj 1 in the east 2 facing east 3 blowing from the east —**easternmost** adj

Eastern Cape province in SE South Africa. Cap. Bisho. Pop. 6,519,300 (1998).

easterner /eestərnər/ n a person from the east of a country or region

Eastern Europe region comprising the countries of east and central Europe that had close ties with the former Soviet Union, including Poland, the Czech Republic, Slovakia, Hungary, Romania, Bulgaria, Albania, and the former Yugoslavia

eastern hemisphere n the part of the Earth that contains Asia, Australasia, and most of Europe and Africa

Eastern Orthodox Church n the Orthodox Christian churches of E Europe

Eastern Standard Time, Eastern Time n 1 the local standard time in E North America 2 the standard time in E Australia, ten hours ahead of Greenwich Mean Time

East Germany former republic of central Europe, now the eastern part of Germany —**East German** n, adj

East Indies /-in deez/ formerly, India, Southeast Asia, and the Malay Archipelago, especially Indonesia —**East Indian** adj, n

East Kilbride /-kil bríd/ town in south-central Scotland. Pop. 70,422 (1991).

East Lothian /-lóthi ən/ council area in SE Scotland

Eastman /eestmən/, **George** (1854–1932) US inventor and philanthropist

east-northeast n the compass point between east and northeast —**east-northeast** adj, adv

East Renfrewshire council area in central Scotland

East Riding of Yorkshire /-ríding-/ 1 historic division of Yorkshire in NE England 2 council area in NE England

east-southeast n the compass point between east and southeast —**east-southeast** adj, adv

East Sussex /-sússiks/ county in SE England

East Timor disputed territory on the eastern half of the island of Timor in Southeast Asia Cap. Dili. Pop. 839,700 (1995).

eastward /eestwərd/ adj in the east ∎ n a direction towards or point in the east ∎ adv also **eastwards** towards the east —**eastwardly** adj, adv

easy /eezi/ (**-ier, -iest**) adj 1 not difficult 2 inappropriately effortless ○ always taking the easy way out 3 relaxed and informal ○ had an easy manner 4 good-natured 5 financially prosperous 6 not severe 7 unhurried ○ an easy pace 8 not steep ○ an easy climb 9 pleasant to experience ○ easy on the eyes 10 lacking preferences (infml) ○ You decide. I'm easy. —**easiness** n ◇ **go easy on** treat gently or leniently (infml) ◇ **take it easy** 1 relax or not work too hard 2 avoid becoming upset

~~easyer~~ incorrect spelling of **easier**

easygoing /eezi gó ing/ adj 1 relaxed, informal, and tolerant 2 unhurried

easy listening n soothing popular music

~~easyly~~ incorrect spelling of **easily**

eat /eet/ (**ate** /et, ayt/, **eaten** /eet'n/) v 1 vti consume food as sustenance 2 vt have as a usual food 3 vi have a meal 4 vt use a lot of (slang) 5 vti penetrate a surface by corrosive or mechanical action —**eater** n

☐ **eat into** vt use up part of

☐ **eat up** v 1 vti eat completely 2 vt obsess ○ was eaten up by remorse 3 vt consume quickly (infml) ○ a job that eats up my time

eatable /eetəb'l/ adj usable or enjoyable as food

eatery /eetəri/ (pl **-ies**) n a restaurant (infml)

eating disorder n an emotional disorder manifesting as an obsessive attitude to food

eats /eets/ npl food (slang)

eau de cologne /ó də kə lón/ n scented liquid that is lighter than perfume

eaves /eevz/ npl the part of a roof that projects beyond the supporting wall

eavesdrop /eevz drop/ (**-dropping, -dropped**) vi listen secretly —**eavesdropper** n

ORIGIN The obsolete noun **eavesdrop** referred to the ground below the roof of a building onto which rainwater fell from the eaves. It was a place where somebody could stand close enough to hear conversations going on inside.

Eban /eé ban/, **Abba** (b. 1915) South African-born Israeli politician and diplomat

ebb vi 1 recede from the shore (refers to the sea or tide) 2 diminish ∎ n 1 a tidal movement away from the land 2 a diminution

Ebola /i bólə/, **Ebola virus** n a usually lethal virus transmitted by blood and body fluids

ebony /ébbəni/ n 1 a dark, very hard wood 2 an Asian tree that produces ebony

e-book n a hand-held electronic device for reading text, or the text itself

ebullient /i búliyənt, i bóoll-/ adj lively and enthusiastic —**ebullience** n

e-business n 1 business conducted on the

Internet **2** a company using Internet technology

EC *abbr* European Commission

ECB *abbr* European Central Bank

eccentric /ik séntrik, ek-/ *adj* **1** unconventional **2** off-centre **3** not concentric ■ *n* a person regarded as unconventional —**eccentrically** *adv* —**eccentricity** /ék sen tríssəti/ *n*

Eccles /ék'lz/, **Sir John** (1903–97) Australian physiologist who worked on the transmission of impulses between nerve cells

ecclesiastic /i kleézi ástik/ *n* a member of the Christian clergy

ecclesiastical /i kleézi ástik'l/ *adj* of the Christian Church

Ecevit /échavit/, **Bülent** (b. 1925) prime minister of Turkey (1974, 1978–79, 1999–)

ECG *abbr* electrocardiogram

echelon /ésha lon/ *n* **1** a level in a hierarchy **2** a formation with each position to the side of the one in front

ORIGIN **Echelon** derives from French, and comes from the same Latin word as English *scale*.

echidna /i kídna/ *n* a spiny insect-eating mammal with a long snout

echinacea /éki náyssi a/ *n* **1** a herbal remedy prepared from coneflowers **2** a coneflower

echinoderm /i kína durm/ *n* a sea animal with a symmetrical body, e.g. a starfish

echo /ékō/ *n* (*pl* **-oes**) **1** a repetition of a sound caused by the reflection of the sound waves from a surface **2** a repetition of another person's opinion **3** something that reminds you of something earlier **4 Echo** a communications code word for the letter 'E' ■ *v* (**-oing, -oed**) **1** *vt* repeat something by the reflection of sound waves **2** *vt* repeat another person's opinion **3** *vt* imitate or have elements of something earlier **4** *vi* resound by the reflection of sound waves —**echoic** /e kō ik/ *adj*

ORIGIN **Echo** derives from a Greek word relating to sound. In Greek mythology, Echo was a nymph who pined away for love of a youth, Narcissus, until only her voice could be heard.

echo chamber *n* a room with walls that reflect sound

echolocation /ékō lō káysh'n/ *n* the location of objects using reflection of emitted sounds

Eckert /ékart/, **John Presper** (1919–95) US electronics engineer. He worked with John Mauchly on the ENIAC project (1943–46) that developed the first general-purpose electronic digital computer.

éclair /ay kláir, i-/ *n* **1** a finger-shaped cake of light pastry filled with cream and usually iced **2** a hard sweet with a soft filling

eclampsia /i klámpsi a/ *n* high blood pressure and convulsions in late pregnancy

éclat /ay klaá, áy klaa/ *n* **1** great success **2** ostentatious display

eclectic /i kléktik/ *adj* **1** made up of elements from various sources **2** choosing from various sources —**eclectically** *adv* —**eclecticism** /-sizəm/ *n*

eclipse /i klíps/ *n* **1** an obscuring of one astronomical object by another **2** a decline in status or power ■ *vt* (**eclipsing, eclipsed**) **1** obscure another astronomical object **2** outdo or overshadow somebody or something

ecliptic /i klíptik/ *n* the circular path of the Sun's annual motion relative to the stars

Eco /ékō/, **Umberto** (b. 1932) Italian novelist and academic

eco- *prefix* environment, ecology ○ *ecofriendly*

ecocide /ékō sīd, eékō-/ *n* destruction of the environment

ecofriendly /eékō frendli, ékō-/ *adj* not harmful to the environment

E. coli /ee kố lī/ *n* a bacterium in the colon, *Escherichia coli*, that causes food poisoning

ecology /i kóllaji/ *n* the study of the relationship between organisms and their environment —**ecological** /eékə lójjik'l, ékə-/ *adj* —**ecologically** *adv* —**ecologist** *n*

ORIGIN **Ecology** was coined by the German scientist Ernst Haeckel from a Greek word meaning 'house'. The same Greek word gave rise to *economy*.

e-commerce *n* business transacted online, especially over the Internet

economic /ékə nómmik, eékə-/ *adj* **1** of economics or a country's economy **2** making profits **3** of material goods and resources **4** = **economical** 3

economical /ékə nómmik'l, eékə-/ *adj* **1** resourcefully frugal **2** inexpensive **3** efficient and not wasteful of time or energy —**economically** *adv*

economic migrant *n* a travelling worker, especially one who goes to another country for better prospects

economics /ékə nómmiks, eékə-/ *n* the study of the production, distribution, and consumption of goods and services (+ *sing verb*) ■ *npl* financial aspects (+ *pl verb*) —**economist** /i kónnəmist/ *n*

economize /i kónnə mīz/ (**-mizing, -mized**), **economise** *vi* reduce expenditure

economy /i kónnəmi/ *n* (*pl* **-mies**) **1** a way of organizing the financial affairs of a country or community **2** thrift **3** a saving **4** a sparing use of something **5** *also* **economy class** a cheaper category of travel, especially on airlines ■ *adj* cheaper

economy drive *n* an organized attempt to make savings

ecosphere /eékō sfeer, ékō-/ *n* the biosphere

ecosystem /eékō sistəm, ékō-/ *n* a group of interdependent organisms and their environment

ecoterrorism /eékō térrərizəm, ékō-/ *n* **1** sabotage carried out in the name of protecting the environment **2** deliberate destruction of the environment —**eco-terrorist** *n*

ecotourism /eēkō toŏrizəm, ékō-/ *n* tourism that seeks to avoid ecological damage to places visited —**ecotourist** *n*

ecowarrior /eēkō worri ər, ékō-/ *n* an environmental activist

ecru /ékroo, áy-/ *adj* of a pale yellowish-brown colour —**ecru** *n*

~~ecstacy~~ incorrect spelling of **ecstasy**

ecstasy /ékstəssi/ (*pl* -**sies**) *n* 1 intense delight 2 loss of self-control during an intense experience 3 *also* Ecstasy an illegal synthetic drug used as a stimulant and to relax inhibitions

ecstatic /ik státtik, ek-/ *adj* 1 greatly delighted 2 dominated by an intense emotion —**ecstatically** *adv*

ECT *abbr* electroconvulsive therapy

ectomorph /éktə mawrf/ *n* a person with long lean limbs

-ectomy *suffix* surgical removal of a body part o *appendectomy*

ectopic pregnancy /ek tóppik-/ *n* an egg developing outside the womb

Ecuador /ékwə dawr/ country in NW South America bordering the Pacific Ocean. Cap. Quito. Pop. 13,183,978 (2001). —**Ecuadorian** /ékwə dáwri ən/ *n, adj*

ecumenical /eékyōō ménnik'l/, **ecumenic** /-ménnik/ *adj* 1 of Christian Church unity 2 universal —**ecumenism** /i kyóoménnizzəm/ *n*

eczema /éksəmə/ *n* a skin condition with reddening, itching, and scaly patches

ed. *abbr* 1 edited 2 edition 3 editor

-ed *suffix* 1 forms the past participle and past tense of regular verbs o *passed* 2 having, characterized by, like o *redheaded* o *bigoted* o *hinged*

Edam /eé dam/ *n* a Dutch cheese usually sold covered with red wax

eddy /éddi/ *n* (*pl* -**dies**) a small whirl in flowing liquid or gas ■ *vi* (-**dies, -died**) flow contrary to the main current

edelweiss /áyd'l vīss/ *n* a small alpine plant with white woolly leaves

Eden /eéd'n/ *n* 1 in the Bible, the garden where the first man and woman lived 2 a perfect place —**Edenic** /ee dénnik/ *adj*

Eden /eéd'n/, **Anthony, 1st Earl of Avon** (1897–1977) British prime minister (1955–57)

edge *n* 1 a border forming the outermost part of something 2 an area or position above a steep drop 3 a point just before a marked change or event o *on the edge of tears* 4 a line where two surfaces meet 5 the cutting side of a blade 6 a sharp quality o *an edge to her remarks* 7 an advantage (*infml*) ■ *v* (**edging, edged**) 1 *vt* add a border to 2 *vi* move gradually sideways ◇ **live on the edge** be habitually in highly stressful situations ◇ **on edge** irritated or nervous ◇ **take the edge off** reduce the intensity of

edgeways /éj wayz/, **edgewise** /-wīz/ *adv, adj* with the edge first

Edgeworth /éj wurth/, **Maria** (1767–1849) British novelist

edging /éjjing/ *n* a decorative or protective border

edgy /éjji/ (-**ier, -iest**) *adj* 1 nervous 2 trend-setting —**edgily** *adv* —**edginess** *n*

edible /éddəb'l/ *adj* able to be eaten by human beings, or enjoyable to eat

edict /eédikt/ *n* an authoritative decree or command

edifice /éddifiss/ *n* a large building

edify /éddifī/ (-**fies, -fied**) *vt* give useful or improving information to —**edification** /éddifi káysh'n/ *n*

Edinburgh /éddinbərə/ 1 capital of Scotland. Pop. 448,850 (1996). 2 **City of Edinburgh** council area in Central Scotland

Edinburgh, Duke of ♦ Philip, Prince

Thomas Alva Edison

Edison /éddiss'n/, **Thomas Alva** (1847–1931) US inventor

edit /éddit/ *vt* 1 prepare a text for publication 2 decide the content of a newspaper, magazine, or broadcast programme 3 cut a film or tape to give it its final order and content

edition /i dísh'n/ *n* 1 a particular version or instalment of a publication or programme 2 a batch of copies of a publication printed at the same time

editor /éddtər/ *n* 1 the person in overall charge of a publication 2 a journalist in charge of a specific part of a newspaper or magazine 3 a person who prepares a text for publication 4 in broadcasting, a controller of programme content 5 somebody who edits film or tape —**editorship** *n*

editorial /éddi táwri əl/ *adj* of editing ■ *n* a newspaper article expressing the editor's opinion

editorialize /éddi táwri ə līz/ (-**izing, -ized**), **editorialise** *vi* 1 write editorials 2 write subjectively, especially when inappropriate

Edmonton /édmantən/ capital of Alberta, Canada. Pop. 616,306 (1996).

EDP *abbr* electronic data processing

edu *abbr* US educational organization (*in Internet addresses*)

educate /éddyōō kayt/ (-**cating, -cated**) *v* 1 *vti* impart knowledge to somebody by classroom or electronic instruction 2 *vt* arrange schooling for somebody —**educable** /-kəb'l/

adj —**educative** /-kətiv/ *adj* —**educator** *n* ◊
See note at **teach**

educated /éddyŏŏ kaytid/ *adj* 1 well-taught
2 showing good taste, knowledge, or cultivation 3 based on knowledge o *an educated
guess*

education /éddyŏŏ káysh'n/ *n* 1 the process of
teaching or learning 2 knowledge acquired
through teaching 3 the study of teaching and
learning 4 the system for educating people
5 a learning experience —**educational** *adj*

educationist /éddyŏŏ káysh'nist/, **educationalist**
/-káysh'nəlist/ *n* an expert in education

edutainment /éddyŏŏ táynmənt/ *n* material, e.g.
software, that educates and entertains at the
same time

Edward I /éddwərd/ (1239–1307) king of
England (1272–1307)

Edward II (1284–1327) king of England (1307–
27)

Edward III (1312–77) king of England (1327–
77)

Edward IV (1442–83) king of England (1461–
83)

Edward V (1470–83?) king of England (1483)

Edward VI (1537–53) king of England (1547–
53)

Edward VII (1841–1910) king of the United
Kingdom (1901–10)

Edward VIII (1894–1972) king of the United
Kingdom (January–December 1936), later
Duke of Windsor after he abdicated

Edward (the Black Prince) (1330–76) prince
of Wales and father of Richard II

Edward (the Confessor) (1002?–66) saint and
king of the English (1042–66)

Edwardian /ed wáwrdi ən/ *adj* of the reign of
Edward VII of the United Kingdom ■ *n*
somebody who lived in the era of Edward
VII

eel (*pl* **eels** *or* same) *n* a long thin fish with a
smooth skin and reduced fins

-eer *suffix* 1 a person engaged in or concerned
with o *charioteer* 2 a contemptible person or
act o *profiteer*

eerie /éeri/ *adj* unnerving and suggesting the
supernatural —**eerily** *adv* —**eeriness** *n*

ORIGIN Eerie was originally a Scottish and N
English word meaning 'fearful'. The focus
shifted towards the end of the 18C to the
supposedly supernatural cause of the uneasy
feeling.

~~eery~~ incorrect spelling of **eerie**

efface /i fáyss/ (**-facing**, **-faced**) *vt* rub out or
erase —**effacement** *n*

effect /i fékt/ *n* 1 a change resulting from an
action 2 success in bringing about change
o *I pleaded with them, but to no effect.* 3 the
state of being in force or operation o *come
into effect* 4 a feeling or impression in the
mind o *The overall effect was light and spacious.*
5 a device that adds to the perceived realism
of a film, play, or broadcast (*often pl*) 6 the

essential meaning of a statement o *or words
to that effect* ■ **effects** *npl* belongings (*fml*) ■
vt achieve or make (*fml*) o *effected an escape
through a window* ◊ **in effect** actually ◊ See
note at **affect**

effective /i féktiv/ *adj* 1 producing a result
2 producing a favourable impression o *effective use of imagery* 3 officially in force
—**effectively** *adv* —**effectiveness** *n*

SYNONYMS effective, efficient, effectual,
efficacious CORE MEANING: producing a result

effectual /i fékchoo əl/ *adj* (*fml*) 1 potentially
successful in producing a desired or intended result 2 in force or valid —**effectually**
adv ◊ See note at **effective**

effeminate /i fémminət/ *adj* describes a man
considered to be like a girl or woman
(*disapproving*) —**effeminacy** *n* —**effeminately**
adv

effervesce /éffər véss/ (**-vescing**, **-vesced**) *vi*
produce tiny gas bubbles (*refers to liquids*)
—**effervescence** *n* —**effervescent** *adj*

effete /i feét/ *adj* decadent and lacking vitality
—**effetely** *adv* —**effeteness** *n*

efficacious /éffi káyshəss/ *adj* able to produce a
desired result (*fml*) —**efficacy** /éffikəssi/ *n* ◊
See note at **effective**

efficient /i físh'nt/ *adj* 1 well-organized 2 able
to function without waste —**efficiency** *n*
—**efficiently** *adv* ◊ See note at **effective**

effigy /éffiji/ (*pl* **-gies**) *n* a model or carving of
a person

efflorescence /éfflə réss'nss/ *n* a process or time
of developing and flourishing (*literary*)
—**efflorescent** *adj*

effluence /éffloo ənss/ *n* a flowing out, e.g. from
a sewer

effluent /éffloo ənt/ *n* 1 liquid waste 2 a stream
or river that flows out of a larger body of
water

effluvium /i floóvi əm, e-/ (*pl* **-a** /-ə/) *n* an outflow
of something unpleasant or harmful (*often
pl*)

effort /éffərt/ *n* 1 energy exerted to achieve a
purpose 2 activity directed towards a specific end o *the peacekeeping effort* 3 a serious
attempt o *made an effort to listen* 4 the result
of an attempt o *not a bad effort*

effortless /éffərtləss/ *adj* done with no effort
—**effortlessly** *adv* —**effortlessness** *n*

effrontery /i frúntəri/ *n* shameless cheek

effusion /i fyŏŏzh'n/ *n* 1 an unrestrained outpouring of feelings 2 a pouring out of something such as liquid or light

effusive /i fyoóssiv/ *adj* unrestrained in expressing feelings —**effusively** *adv*

~~eficient~~ incorrect spelling of **efficient**

E-FIT *tdmk* a trademark for a computer
program that creates a likeness of the face of
a police suspect, based on a witness's description

EFL *abbr* English as a foreign language

EFRA /ˈeftrə/ abbr electronic forms routing and approval

EFTA /ˈeftə/ abbr European Free Trade Association

EFTS /efts/ abbr electronic funds transfer system

e.g., eg, eg. abbr for or as an example

USAGE **e.g.** or **i.e.**? Use **e.g.**, 'for or as an example' (from Latin *exempli gratia*), to list a few items out of many: *I have the laboratory equipment, e.g.* [not *i.e.*] *beakers, thermometers, and test tubes.* Use **i.e.**, 'that is, that is to say' (from Latin *id est*), to specify one thing only: *The tribunal, i.e.* [not *e.g.*] *the industrial tribunal, is set for noon on Friday.*

EGA abbr enhanced graphics adapter

egalitarian /i ˌgálli táiri ən/ adj believing in equality —**egalitarian** n —**egalitarianism** n

egg[1] n **1** a reproductive structure in a protective covering that allows embryo development outside the mother's body **2** a hard-shelled object laid by a hen **3** something shaped like a hen's egg **4** a female reproductive cell **5** a person (infml dated) —**eggy** adj

ORIGIN **Egg** came into English from an early Scandinavian language. It was used side by side for 200 years with the older native English word, which had a soft -y- sound rather than a hard -g-. **Egg** took over completely during the 16C. **Egging somebody on**, also from a Scandinavian language, is related to English *edge*.

egg[2] □ **egg on** vt encourage, especially to do something foolish or wrong

eggcup /ég kup/ n a small cup for a boiled egg

egghead /ég hed/ n an intellectual (infml)

eggplant /ég plaant/ n ANZ, US, Can **1** a large oval fleshy fruit with a purple skin **2** a plant that produces eggplants

eggshell /ég shel/ n the hard covering of an egg ■ adj describes a slightly glossy paint finish

ego /ˈeegō, éggō/ (pl **egos**) n **1** a person's sense of self-esteem o *fragile egos* **2** an inflated sense of self-importance **3** in psychoanalysis, the part of the mind containing consciousness

egocentric /ˌeegō séntrik, éggō-/ adj self-centred —**egocentrism** n

egoism /ˈeegō izəm, éggō-/ n **1** the condition of being self-centred **2** morality derived from self-interest —**egoist** n —**egoistic** /ˌeegō ístik, éggō-/ adj —**egoistical** adj

egotism /ˈeegōtizəm, éggō-/ n **1** an inflated sense of self-importance **2** the condition of being self-centred —**egotist** n —**egotistic** /ˌeegō tístik, éggō-/ adj —**egotistical** adj

ego trip n an action or experience boosting somebody's own ego (slang)

egregious /i greejəss, -ji əss/ adj outrageously bad (fml) —**egregiously** adv —**egregiousness** n

egress /ée gress/ n (fml) **1** a coming or going out **2** an exit

egret /ˈeegrət/ n a heron with long ornamental feathers

Egypt /ˈeejipt/ country in NE Africa bordering the Mediterranean and the Red seas. Cap. Cairo. Pop. 69,536,644 (2001).

Egyptian /i jípsh'n/ n **1** somebody from Egypt **2** the language of ancient Egypt —**Egyptian** adj

Eichmann /ˈíkmən, íkh-/, **Adolf** (1906–62) German Nazi official

Eid al-Adha /ˈeéd ōōl aadə/, **Eid ul-Adha**, **Eid** n an Islamic festival to end a Mecca pilgrimage

Eid al-Fitr /ˈeéd ōōl feetər/, **Eid ul-Fitr**, **Eid** n an Islamic festival at the end of Ramadan

eider /ˈídər/ (pl **-ders** or same), **eider duck** n a large sea duck

eiderdown /ˈídər down/ n **1** a bed covering stuffed with soft material **2** eider ducks' feathers. Use: stuffing pillows and bed coverings.

Eiffel /ˈíf'l/, **Gustave** (1832–1923) French engineer, best known as the designer of the Eiffel Tower (1889)

eight /ayt/ n **1** the number 8 **2** a rowing crew of eight rowers —**eight** adj, pron —**eighth** n, adj, adv

eighteen /ay teén, áyt een/ n **1** the number 18 **2** Aus an Australian football team —**eighteen** adj, pron —**eighteenth** n, adj, adv

eighty /ˈáyti/ n the number 80 ■ **eighties** npl **1** the numbers 80 to 89, especially as a range of temperatures **2** the years from 80 to 89 in a century or somebody's life —**eightieth** n, adj, adv —**eighty** adj, pron

eigth incorrect spelling of **eight**

Eilat /ay laát/, **Elat** seaport in S Israel. Pop. 38,200 (1999).

eina /áy naa/ interj S Africa expresses pain

Einstein /ˈín stīn/, **Albert** (1879–1955) German-born US physicist. His theory of general relativity revolutionized scientific thought.

einsteinium /ˈín stíni əm/ n (symbol **Es**) a synthetic radioactive chemical element

Eire /áirə/ Ireland

Dwight D. Eisenhower

Eisenhower /ˈíz'n how ər/, **Dwight D.** (1890–1969) 34th president of the United States (1953–61)

eisteddfod /ī stédfəd, ī stéth vod/ (pl **-fods** or **-fodau** /i stéth vóddī/) n a Welsh festival of music and poetry

either /íthər, eéthər/ *det*, *pron* **1** one or the other of two o *with either hand* o *either of them* **2** indicates a negative o *cannot send e-mails to either address* ■ *det* both o *either side of the street* ■ *conj* indicates alternatives o *Either you go or you stay.* ■ *adv* indicates connection or partial agreement o *You won't find poverty but you won't find luxury either.*

ejaculate *v* /i jákyoŏ layt/ (**-lating**, **-lated**) **1** *vti* eject semen during orgasm **2** *vt* exclaim suddenly *(literary)* ■ *n* /-lət/ ejaculated semen —**ejaculation** /i jákyoŏ láysh'n/ *n*

eject /i jékt/ *v* **1** *vt* push out with force **2** *vt* remove from a place or position o *was ejected from the meeting* **3** *vi* leave an aircraft in an escape device —**ejection** *n*

ejector seat /i jéktər-/ *n* a seat in an aircraft that can be ejected with its occupant in an in-flight emergency

eke /eek/ (**eking**, **eked**) □ **eke out** *vt* **1** make something last with sparing use **2** supplement something insufficient or inadequate

elaborate *adj* /i lábbərət/ **1** finely or richly decorated **2** detailed and thorough o *made elaborate preparations* ■ *v* /-rayt/ (**-rating**, **-rated**) **1** *vi* give more detail **2** *vt* work out in detail —**elaborately** *adv* —**elaborateness** *n* —**elaboration** /i lábbə ráysh'n/ *n*

El 'Alamein /el állə mayn/ town in N Egypt, site of two World War II battles in 1942 between British and German forces

élan /ay lóN, ay lán/, **elan** *n* vigour and enthusiasm

eland /eéland/ (*pl* **elands** or **same**) *n* a large African antelope with humped shoulders and spiralling horns

elapse /i láps/ (**elapsing**, **elapsed**) *vi* go by gradually in time

elastic /i lástik/ *n* **1** a stretchy material **2** *US*, *Can* a rubber band ■ *adj* **1** of or like elastic **2** easily changed **3** returning to its original shape —**elasticate** *vt* —**elasticity** /eé lass tíssəti/ *n* ◊ See note at **pliable**

elastic band *n* a rubber band

Elastoplast /i lástə plaast/ *tdmk* a trademark for a range of plasters, bandages, and dressings

Elat ◆ **Eilat**

elation /i láysh'n/ *n* great happiness and excitement —**elate** *vt* —**elated** *adj*

Elba /élbə/ island off the coast of W Italy, the place of Napoleon's first period of exile (1814–15)

Elbe /elb/ river in central Europe. Length 1,170 km/724 mi.

elbow /élbō/ *n* **1** the joint in the arm **2** a joint in an animal leg ■ *vti* push somebody with the elbow

elbow grease *n* hard physical effort *(infml)*

elbowroom /élbō room, -rŏŏm/ *n* space to move around in comfortably *(infml)*

Elbrus, Mt /el broóss/, **El'brus** highest mountain in Europe, in the Caucasus Mountains in S Russia. Height 5,642 m/18,510 ft.

Elburz Mountains /el boŏrz-/ mountain range in N Iran. Highest peak Damavand, 5,604 m/18,386 ft.

elder[1] /éldər/ *adj* **1** born earlier **2** superior in rank or experience ■ *n* **1** a person born earlier **2** a senior member of a church or community

elder[2] /éldər/ *n* a tree with purplish-black berries

elderberry /éldər berri, -bəri/ (*pl* **-ries**) *n* **1** a fruit of the elder tree **2** an elder tree

elderly /éldərli/ *adj* past middle age *(sometimes offensive)* —**elderliness** *n*

elder statesman *n* a respected retired official

eldest /éldist/ *adj* born first

El Dorado /élda raádō/ *n* **1** a legendary place of fabulous wealth **2** a place of riches

Eleanor of Aquitaine /éllinər əv ákwi tayn/ (1122?–1204) French-born queen of France (1137–52) and England (1154–89)

elect /i lékt/ *v* **1** *vt* choose by vote **2** *vt* decide to do **3** *vti* *US* choose ■ *adj* chosen but not yet in office *(after the noun)* o *president elect*

election /i léksh'n/ *n* **1** an event for choosing a winning candidate by vote **2** a choosing or being chosen by vote o *stood for election*

electioneer /i lékshə neér/ *vi* engage in an election campaign

elective /i léktiv/ *adj* **1** not compulsory o *elective surgery* **2** requiring election o *elective office* **3** of voting ■ *n* an optional subject of study

elector /i léktər/ *n* **1** somebody who votes **2** *also* **Elector** a German ruler who elected the Holy Roman Emperor *(often as a title)*

electoral /i léktərəl/ *adj* of elections

electoral roll, electoral register *n* a list of people entitled to vote

electorate /i léktərət/ *n* **1** a complete body of voters **2** *ANZ* an area represented by an MP

electric /i léktrik/ *adj* **1** involving, using, conveying, or caused by electricity **2** tense or excited o *an electric atmosphere* ■ **electrics** *npl* electrical equipment or parts

electrical /i léktrik'l/ *adj* **1** involving the application of electricity in technology **2** of electric cables, circuits, or functioning o *You'll need an electrician for the electrical work.* —**electrically** *adv*

electric blanket *n* a blanket heated by electricity

electric chair *n* a chair for executing criminals by electricity

electric eel *n* a fish producing an electric charge

electric eye *n* an electric control device using light

electric field *n* an area of electric forces

electrician /i lek trísh'n, éllek-/ *n* somebody who works with electrical wiring or apparatus

electricity /i lek tríssəti, éllek-/ *n* **1** energy created by moving charged particles

2 electric current, especially as a source of power

electric shock *n* a sudden painful reaction caused by an electric current flowing through the body

electric storm *n* a storm with thunder and lightning

electrify /i léktri fī/ (**-fies, -fied**) *vt* **1** convert to the use of electricity **2** charge electrically **3** be thrilling to —**electrification** /i léktrifi káysh'n/ *n*

electrocardiograph /i léktrō kaˊardi ə graaf, -graf/ *n* a device to record heart activity via electrodes placed on the chest —**electrocardiogram** *n* —**electrocardiography** /-kaˊardi ˊóggrəfi/ *n*

electroconvulsive therapy /i léktrō kən vúlssiv-/ *n* a treatment for severe psychiatric disorders involving electric shocks

electrocute /i léktrə kyoot/ (**-cuting, -cuted**) *vt* **1** injure or kill with an electric shock **2** execute in an electric chair —**electrocution** /i léktrə kyoˊosh'n/ *n*

electrode /i lék trōd/ *n* a conductor through which electricity flows

electroencephalograph /i léktrō in séffələ graaf, -graf/ *n* a device producing a record of brain activity via electrodes placed on the scalp —**electroencephalogram** *n* —**electroencephalography** /-in séffə lóggrəfi/ *n*

electrolysis /i lek trólləssiss, éllek-/ *n* **1** chemical separation into components using electricity **2** a technique of removing body hair or a growth by applying electricity through a needle

electrolyte /i léktrō līt/ *n* **1** a compound that is able to conduct electricity **2** an ion in an electrolyte **3** an ion in cells, blood, or other organic material

electrolytic /i léktrō líttik/ *adj* **1** of electrolysis **2** of electrolytes

electromagnet /i léktrō mágnit/ *n* a magnetized iron core

electromagnetism /i léktrō mágnə tizəm/ *n* magnetism from electric currents —**electromagnetic** /i léktrō mag néttik/ *adj* —**electromagnetically** *adv*

electromotive force /i léktrō móˊtiv-/ *n* **1** a force that causes the flow of electricity from one point to another **2** (*symbol E*) energy in a source such as a battery that is convertible into electricity

electron /i lék tron/ *n* an elementary particle that orbits the nucleus of an atom

electronic /i lek trónnik, éllek-/ *adj* **1** involving a controlled flow of electrons **2** using valves, transistors, or silicon chips **3** using or controlled by computer —**electronically** *adv*

electronic data processing *n* computer-based tasks involving the input and manipulation of data

electronic mail *n* full form of **e-mail**

electronic point of sale *n* a computerized checkout system in shops

electronic publishing *n* publishing on computer network or CD-ROM

electronic purse *n* a method of prepayment used in e-commerce, in which cash is stored electronically on a microchip

electronics /i lek trónniks, éllek-/ *n* the technology of electronic devices (*+ sing verb*) ■ *npl* electronic parts (*+ pl verb*)

electronic signature *n* an encoded attachment to an electronic message, verifying the identity of its sender

electron microscope *n* a powerful microscope that uses electron beams —**electron microscopy** *n*

electroplate /i léktrō playt/ (**-plating, -plated**) *vt* coat a surface with metal by electrolysis

electroshock therapy /i léktrō shok-/ *n* PSYCHIAT = **electroconvulsive therapy**

elegant /élligənt/ *adj* **1** stylish and graceful **2** pleasingly concise —**elegance** *n* —**elegantly** *adv*

elegiac /élli jī ək/, **elegiacal** /-jī ək'l/ *adj* expressing sorrow or regret (*literary*) —**elegiacally** *adv*

~~elegible~~ incorrect spelling of **eligible**

elegy /élləji/ (*pl* **-gies**) *n* an elegiac poem

ORIGIN The Greek word from which **elegy** derives was originally applied to any song, but by the time it passed from Latin and French into English, it always had overtones of sadness.

element /éllimənt/ *n* **1** a separate part or group within a larger whole ○ *criminal elements* **2** a small amount ○ *an element of risk* **3** a factor leading to something ○ *a key element in its success* **4** *also* **chemical element** a substance that cannot be broken down into a simpler one by chemical reaction **5** each of four former supposed basic units of matter, earth, water, air, and fire **6** the heating part of an electrical appliance ■ **elements** *npl* **1** the forces of the weather, especially when harsh or damaging **2** basic principles **3** the bread and wine in the Christian Communion ceremony

elemental /élli mént'l/ *adj* **1** fundamental **2** of natural forces

elementary /élli méntəri/ *adj* **1** involving only the most basic facts or principles **2** simple to do or understand

elementary particle *n* a basic indivisible constituent of matter

elephant /éllifant/ (*pl* **-phants** *or same*) *n* a large greyish animal with a long trunk and pointed tusks

elephantiasis /éllifən tī əssiss/ *n* a disfiguring illness causing swelling

elephantine /élli fán tīn/ *adj* **1** slow and heavy **2** enormous

elevate /élli vayt/ (**-vating, -vated**) *vt* **1** raise to a higher level or place **2** raise to a higher rank

elevation /élli váysh'n/ *n* **1** a height above a reference point, especially sea level **2** a raising of something, or the fact of being raised **3** a degree or amount by which something is raised **4** an architectural drawing of a side of a building —**elevational** *adj*

elevator /élli vaytər/ *n* **1** *ANZ, US, Can* a platform or compartment for taking things or people to a higher or lower level in a building **2** *US, Can* a grain storehouse with a mechanism for moving the grain

eleven /i lévv'n/ *n* **1** the number 11 **2** a team of 11, e.g. a football team —**eleven** *adj, pron* —**eleventh** *n, adj, adv*

eleven-plus *n* an examination in a school student's last primary year to determine his or her next stage of education

elevenses /i lévv'nziz/ *n* a mid-morning snack (+ *sing or pl verb*)

elf (*pl* **elves**) *n* a small imaginary being often considered to be a mischief-maker

elfin /élfin/ *adj* **1** of or like an elf **2** delicate ○ *elfin features*

Elgar /él gaar/, **Sir Edward** (1857–1934) British composer

El Greco ♦ **Greco, El**

elicit /i líssit/ *vt* provoke by way of reaction ○ *elicited a smile*

> **SPELLCHECK** Do not confuse the spelling of **elicit** and **illicit** ('illegal'), which sound similar.

elide /i líd/ (**eliding, elided**) *vt* omit an element of a word or phrase

eligible /éllijab'l/ *adj* **1** qualified to do, be, or get something **2** marriageable —**eligibility** /éllijə billəti/ *n*

eliminate /i límmi nayt/ (**-nating, -nated**) *vt* **1** take away from a list or group, or from consideration **2** put an end to ○ *seek to eliminate poverty* **3** put out of a competition —**elimination** /i límmi náysh'n/ *n*

ELINT /éllint/, **elint** *n* the gathering of information by electronic means. Full form **electronic intelligence**

George Eliot

Eliot /élli ət/, **George** (1819–80) British novelist
Eliot, T. S. (1888–1965) US-born British poet, critic, and dramatist

elision /i lízh'n/ *n* omission of an element of a word or phrase

elite /i leet, ay-/ *n* **1** a privileged minority (+ *sing or pl verb*) **2** a size of printing type, 12 characters per inch —**elite** *adj*

elitism /i leetizəm, ay-/ *n* belief in the existence of or domination by an elite group —**elitist** *n, adj*

elixir /i líksər/ *n* **1** a sweetened liquid drug **2** a remedy to cure all ills

> **ORIGIN** An **elixir** is thought of as a liquid, but it seems to come from a Greek word meaning 'dry', and probably referred to a powder for treating wounds.

Elizabeth I /i lízzəbəth/ (1533–1603) queen of England and Ireland (1558–1603)
Elizabeth II (*b.* 1926) queen of the United Kingdom (1952–)
Elizabethan /i lízzə beeth'n/ *adj* of the reign of Elizabeth I

elk (*pl same or* **elks**) *n* a deer with large antlers

Duke Ellington

Ellington /éllingtən/, **Duke** (1899–1974) US jazz pianist, composer, and band leader

ellipse /i líps/ *n* a shape resembling an oval

ellipsis /i lípsiss/ (*pl* **-ses** /-seez/) *n* **1** omission of an implied word **2** a mark indicating omitted text, usually in the form of three dots

> **USAGE** The **ellipsis** in the form of three dots is used when text is omitted from the beginning, middle, or end of a quotation: *Shakespeare wrote, 'When sorrows come, they come...in battalions'*. (The full quotation is *When sorrows come, they come not single spies,/But in battalions*). When the ellipsis comes at the end of a sentence, it is usually followed by a full stop.

elliptical /i líptik'l/, **elliptic** /i líptik/ *adj* **1** of or like an ellipse **2** highly economical in speech or writing —**elliptically** *adv*

Ellis Island /élliss-/ island in upper New York Bay near Manhattan, from 1892 to 1954 the chief entry point for immigrants to the United States

elm *n* **1** a large deciduous tree **2** the wood of the elm tree. Use: fuel, furniture, boats, construction.

El Niño /el neènyō/ *n* a periodic change in Pacific currents, causing weather disruption

elocution /éllə kyoósh'n/ *n* the art of clear speaking —**elocutionary** *adj*

elongate /ee long gayt/ (**-gating, -gated**) *vti* lengthen or become longer —**elongated** *adj*

elope /i lóp/ (**eloping, eloped**) *vi* leave secretly to get married —**elopement** *n*

eloquent /éllakwənt/ *adj* **1** speaking or spoken forcefully and with grace **2** expressing emotion clearly —**eloquence** *n* —**eloquently** *adv*

El Salvador /el sálvə dawl/ country on the Pacific coast of Central America. Cap. San Salvador. Pop. 6,237,662 (2001).

else /elss/ adj, adv 1 in addition ○ *There's something else I'd like to say.* 2 different ○ *go somewhere else*

elsewhere /élss wáir/ adv to or at an unnamed other place

ELT n the teaching of English to non-native speakers. Full form **English language teaching**

elucidate /i loóssi dayt/ (**-dating, -dated**) vt explain or clarify —**elucidation** /i loóssi dáysh'n/ n

elude /i loód/ (**eluding, eluded**) vt 1 escape from or avoid 2 be beyond the understanding or memory of ○ *Her name eludes me.* ◊ See note at **allude**

Elul /e loól/ n the 6th month of the year in the Jewish calendar

elusive /i loóssiv/ adj 1 hard to find or catch 2 hard to define, identify, or remember —**elusively** adv —**elusiveness** n

SPELLCHECK Do not confuse the spelling of **elusive** and **allusive** ('making an allusion'), which sound similar.

elver /élvər/ n a young eel

elves plural of **elf**

Elysian Fields npl Elysium

Elysium /i lízzi əm/ n 1 in Greek mythology, heaven 2 an ideal place or condition —**Elysian** adj

em /em/ n a variable measure of printing width, equal to the point size of the type and corresponding to the width of the letter M

'em /əm/ contr them (infml)

em- prefix = **en-** (before m, b, or p) ○ *émbark*

emaciated /i máyssi aytid/ adj very thin because of starvation or illness —**emaciation** /i máyssi áysh'n/ n ◊ See note at **thin**

e-mail /ée mayl/, **email** n 1 a system that allows text-based messages to be exchanged electronically, e.g. between computers or mobile phones 2 an e-mail message ■ vt communicate with or send by e-mail —**e-mailable** adj

emalangeni plural of **lilangeni**

emanate /émmə nayt/ (**-nating, -nated**) v 1 vi come out from a source 2 vt send out (fml) —**emanation** /émmə náysh'n/ n

emancipate /i mánssi payt/ (**-pating, -pated**) vt 1 set free from slavery or imprisonment 2 free from restrictions —**emancipation** /i mánssi páysh'n/ n —**emancipatory** adj

emasculate /i máskyoō layt/ (**-lating, -lated**) vt 1 castrate (literary) 2 weaken the effectiveness of (fml; sometimes offensive) —**emasculation** /i máskyoō láysh'n/ n

embalm /im baám, em-/ vt preserve a corpse from decay after death —**embalmer** n —**embalmment** n

embankment /im bángkmənt/ n a confining or supporting ridge of earth

embarass incorrect spelling of **embarrass**

embargo /em baárgō/ n (pl **-goes**) 1 an order stopping trade or another activity 2 an order halting movement of ships ■ vt (**-going, -goed**) place an embargo on

embark /em baárk/ vti go or put on board a ship or aircraft —**embarkation** /ém baar káysh'n/ n □ **embark on** vti begin doing

embarass incorrect spelling of **embarrass**

embarrass /im bárrəss, em-/ vti make or become self-conscious ○ *He's easily embarrassed.* —**embarrassing** adj —**embarrassingly** adv —**embarrassment** n

embassy /émbəssi/ (pl **-sies**) n 1 an ambassador's headquarters 2 an ambassador's staff

embattled /im bátt'ld/ adj 1 under assault or pressure 2 fighting or ready to fight

embed /im béd/ (**-bedding, -bedded**), **imbed** vti 1 place or be placed solidly in a surrounding mass 2 fix or be fixed in the mind or memory

embellish /im béllish/ vt 1 beautify or ornament 2 add fictitious or exaggerated details to —**embellishment** n

ember /émbər/ n a burning fragment from a dying fire

embezzle /im bézz'l/ (**-zling, -zled**) vti misuse entrusted money or property —**embezzlement** n —**embezzler** n ◊ See note at **steal**

embitter /im bíttər/ vt arouse bitter or aggrieved feelings in

emblazon /im bláyz'n/ vt decorate with a coat of arms or vivid design

emblem /émbləm/ n a symbol or image that represents something

emblematic /émblə máttik/, **emblematical** /-máttik'l/ adj serving as an emblem of something

embody /im bóddi/ (**-ies, -ied**) vt 1 make tangible or visible 2 incorporate into an organized whole —**embodiment** n

embolden /im bṓld'n/ vt give courage to

embolism /émbəlizəm/ n a blockage of an artery, usually caused by a blood clot

emboss /im bóss/ vt decorate with a raised pattern —**embossment** n

embouchure /ómboō shoór/ n the position of lips and tongue when playing a wind instrument

embrace /im bráyss/ v (**-bracing, -braced**) 1 vti hug somebody or each other 2 vt take advantage of eagerly ○ *embrace an opportunity* 3 vt adopt as a belief or practice 4 vt include or encompass ■ n a hug

embrasure /im bráyzhər/ n 1 a slanted opening in a fortification 2 a tapered opening in a wall, wider on the inside than outside

embrocation /émbrə káysh'n/ n a lotion to relieve muscle or joint pain

embroider /im bróydər/ vti 1 sew a pattern into fabric 2 embellish a story —**embroiderer** n

embroidery /im bróydəri/ (pl **-ies**) n 1 the

making of decorative needlework **2** something with decorative needlework

embroil /im bróyl/ *vt* involve in conflict

embryo /émbri ó/ (*pl* -os) *n* an offspring of a human or other animal, or of a plant, in the initial stage of development after fertilization

embryology /émbri óllǝji/ *n* the study of embryos —**embryological** /émbri ǝ lójjik'l/ *adj* —**embryologist** *n*

embryonic /émbri ónnik/ *adj* **1** of an embryo **2** in an early developmental stage

emend /i ménd/ *vt* change the wording of to make more correct —**emendation** /éē men dáysh'n/ *n*

emerald /émmǝrǝld/ *n* **1** a green precious stone, a form of beryl. Use: gems. **2** a bright green colour —**emerald** *adj*

ORIGIN Emerald comes ultimately from a Semitic word meaning 'shine' that gave rise to a noun meaning 'green gem' in ancient Greek. From there it passed into English via Latin and French.

emerge /i múrj/ (**emerging, emerged**) *v* **1** *vi* come out of or from behind something **2** *vi* survive after a difficult experience **3** *vti* become known or apparent ○ *It emerged that I had been wrong all along.* —**emergence** *n* —**emergent** *adj*

emergency /i múrjǝnssi/ *n* (*pl* -**cies**) **1** a sudden crisis requiring action **2** *ANZ* a reserve player ■ *adj* **1** acting or used in an emergency **2** requiring or involving immediate medical treatment ○ *emergency admissions*

emergency room *n US, Can* the casualty department of a hospital

emerita /i mérritǝ/ *adj* retired but retaining a professional title (*of women*)

emeritus /i mérritǝss/ *adj* retired but retaining a professional title (*of men*)

Emerson /émmǝrss'n/, **Ralph Waldo** (1803–82) US essayist, lecturer, and poet —**Emersonian** /émmǝr sóni ǝn/ *adj*

emery /émmǝri/ *n* a variety of the mineral corundum. Use: abrasives.

emetic /i móttik/ *adj* causing vomiting —**emetic** *n*

emf *abbr* electromotive force

emigrant /émmigrǝnt/ *n* somebody who moves to another country —**emigrant** *adj*

emigrate /émmi grayt/ (-**grating, -grated**) *vi* leave to live in another country —**emigration** /émmi gráysh'n/ *n*

émigré /émmi gray, áymi-/ *n* a political refugee

eminence /émminǝnss/ *n* **1** high position or status **2** a hill (*fml*) **3 Eminence** the title of a Catholic cardinal

eminent /émminǝnt/ *adj* **1** of high standing or reputation **2** conspicuously high

eminently /émminǝntli/ *adv* very ○ *eminently qualified*

emir /e mǝǝr/ *n* in some Islamic countries, an independent ruler

emirate /émmirǝt, e mǝǝrǝt/ *n* a territory under an emir's rule

emissary /émmissǝri/ (*pl* -**ies**) *n* a representative sent on a diplomatic mission

emission /i mísh'n/ *n* **1** the letting out of something, especially into the atmosphere **2** something given out, especially into the atmosphere ○ *harmful exhaust emissions*

emit /i mít/ (**emitting, emitted**) *vt* **1** let out, especially into the atmosphere **2** utter ○ *emitted a giggle* —**emitter** *n*

Emmy /émmi/ (*pl* -**mys**) *n* an award given by the American Academy of Television Arts and Sciences

emollient /i mólli ǝnt/ *adj* **1** soothing to the skin **2** calming in manner (*fml*) —**emollient** *n*

emolument /i móllyōomǝnt/ *n* a payment (*fml*) ◊ See note at **wage**

emote /i mót/ (**emoting, emoted**) *vi* display exaggerated emotions

emoticon /i móti kon/ *n* a symbolic picture representing an emotion, made from computer keyboard characters and usually to be viewed sideways

emotion /i mósh'n/ *n* **1** a heightened feeling such as anger or grief **2** agitation caused by strong feelings —**emotionless** *adj*

emotional /i mósh'nǝl/ *adj* **1** relating to emotions **2** easily affected by emotions **3** expressing or stirring emotions ○ *an emotional tribute* —**emotionally** *adv*

emotive /i mótiv/ *adj* causing or involving emotion —**emotively** *adv* —**emotiveness** *n*

empanada /émpǝ naàdǝ/ *n* a spicy or sweet turnover in Spanish or Latin American cookery

empathize /émpǝ thīz/ (-**thizing, -thized**), **empathise** *vi* feel empathy ○ *empathized with them in their grief*

empathy /émpǝthi/ *n* understanding of and identification with another's feelings —**empathetic** /émpǝ théttik/ *adj* —**empathic** /em páthik/ *adj*

~~emperer~~ incorrect spelling of **emperor**

emperor /émpǝrǝr/ *n* a man or boy ruling an empire

emperor penguin *n* a very large Antarctic penguin

emphasis /émfǝssiss/ (*pl* -**ses** /-seez/) *n* **1** special importance ○ *puts emphasis on exercise* **2** extra spoken stress on an important word or phrase

emphasize /émfǝ sīz/ (-**sizing, -sized**), **emphasise** *vt* put emphasis on

emphatic /im fáttik/ *adj* **1** expressed or done with emphasis **2** forcible and definite ○ *an emphatic refusal* —**emphatically** *adv*

emphysema /émfǝ seèmǝ, -zeèmǝ/ *n* a lung condition causing breathing impairment

empire /ém pīr/ *n* **1** a group of territories ruled by a single supreme authority **2** a large far-flung business **3** a part of an organization that somebody personally controls

empire-building *n* a tendency to enlarge a sphere of authority —**empire-builder** *n*

empirical /em pírrik'l/ *adj* based on observation and experiment rather than theory —**empirically** *adv*

empiricism /em pírrissízəm/ *n* **1** the philosophical belief that all knowledge is derived from the experience of the senses **2** the application of observation and experiment —**empiricist** *n*

emplacement /im pláyssmənt/ *n* a position for large weaponry

employ /im plóy/ *vt* **1** give paid work to **2** keep busy **3** utilize ■ *n* the state of employing a worker *(fml)* o *in her employ* —**employable** *adj* ◊ See note at **use**

employee /im plóy ee, ém ploy eé/ *n* a paid worker

employer /im plóy ər/ *n* a person or organization that engages workers

employment /im plóymənt/ *n* **1** the condition of working for pay **2** work or the job done by somebody **3** the number of paid workers in a population **4** the using of something

emporium /em páwri əm/ *(pl* -ums *or* -a /-ri ə/) *n* a shop offering a wide selection of goods

empower /im pów ər/ *vt* **1** give authority to **2** make more confident or assertive —**empowerment** *n*

empress /émprəss/ *n* **1** a woman or girl ruling an empire **2** an emperor's wife

empty /émpti/ *adj* (-tier, -tiest) **1** containing nothing **2** unoccupied o *an empty chair* **3** with no passengers or load **4** insincere o *empty promises* **5** without meaning or purpose o *an empty life* ■ *v* (-ties, -tied) **1** *vt* remove the contents o *emptied his pockets* **2** *vti* discharge or transfer, or be discharged or transferred o *The stream empties into the lake.* ■ *n* (*pl* -ties) a container without contents —**emptily** *adv* —**emptiness** *n* ◊ See note at **vacant, vain**

empty-handed *adj* **1** with nothing in the hands **2** having gained nothing o *came back from the negotiations empty-handed*

empty-headed *adj* regarded as silly and unintelligent *(insult)*

EMS *abbr* European Monetary System

emu /ee myoo/ *n* (*pl* **emus** *or* **same**) a large Australian flightless bird

EMU *abbr* European Monetary Union

emulate /émyoo layt/ *vt* **1** try to equal **2** compete successfully with **3** behave like a different computer system —**emulation** /émyoo láysh'n/ *n* —**emulator** *n* ◊ See note at **imitate**

emulsifier /i múlssi fī ər/ *n* a chemical agent that stops substances separating

emulsify /i múlssi fī/ (-fies, -fied) *vti* convert into an emulsion —**emulsification** /i múlssifi káysh'n/ *n*

emulsion /i múlsh'n/ *n* **1** a suspension of liquid within another liquid **2** a light-sensitive photographic coating **3** a water-based paint for walls

en *n* a measure of printing width, half that of an em

en- *prefix* **1** put or go into, or cover with o *entomb* **2** cause to be o *enthral* **3** thoroughly o *enmesh*

-en *suffix* **1** cause or come to be or have o *loosen* **2** made of or resembling o *earthen*

enable /in áyb'l/ (-bling, -bled) *vt* **1** provide with means to do something **2** make possible o *enabling legislation* —**enablement** *n*

-enabled *suffix* made capable of using or operating with o *Web-enabled*

enact /in ákt/ *vt* **1** act out **2** make into law —**enactment** *n*

~~enamal~~ incorrect spelling of **enamel**

enamel /i námm'l/ *n* **1** a glassy decorative or protective coating **2** a paint with a hard shiny finish **3** a hard calcium-containing layer on a tooth crown ■ *vt* (-elling, -elled) coat with enamel —**enameller** *n*

enamoured /in ámmərd/ *adj* captivated by or in love with somebody

en bloc /oN blók, on-/ *adv* all together

encamp /in kámp/ *vi* set up a camp —**encampment** *n*

encapsulate /in kápsyoō layt/ (-lating, -lated) *v* **1** *vt* express in a concise form **2** *vti* enclose or be enclosed completely —**encapsulation** /in kápsyoō láysh'n/ *n*

encase /in káyss/ (-casing, -cased) *vt* surround closely with a case or cover —**encasement** *n*

encash /in kásh/ *vt* convert into cash —**encashment** *n*

encephalitis /en séffə lítiss, -kéffə-/ *n* a brain inflammation —**encephalitic** /-líttik/ *adj*

enchant /in cháant/ *vt* **1** delight **2** put under a spell —**enchanter** *n* —**enchanting** *adj* —**enchantingly** *adv* —**enchantment** *n* —**enchantress** *n*

enchilada /én chi laádə/ *n* a rolled tortilla with a savoury filling

encircle /in súrk'l/ (-cling, -cled) *vt* **1** surround **2** make a circuit of

encl. *abbr* enclosed

enclave /én klayv, ón-/ *n* **1** a region surrounded by foreign territory **2** a distinct group in a larger community

enclose /in klóz/ (-closing, -closed) *vt* **1** surround **2** put a boundary around **3** insert in an envelope or package

enclosure /in klózhər/ *n* **1** a piece of land surrounded by a boundary **2** a boundary fence **3** something enclosed in a letter or package **4** a reserved area at a sports event **5** the act or fact of enclosing something

encode /in kód/ (-coding, -coded) *vt* **1** convert to code **2** convert into digital form for processing by computer

encomium /en kómi əm/ (*pl* -ums *or* -a /-mi ə/) *n* an expression of high praise *(fml)*

encompass /in kúmpəss/ *vt* **1** include in its entirety **2** encircle

encore /óng kawr/ *n* an extra or repeated performance of something ■ *interj* demands a repeat performance ■ *vt* give an encore of

encounter /in kówntər/ *vt* **1** meet unexpectedly **2** meet in conflict **3** come up against ■ *n* **1** an unexpected meeting **2** a confrontation

encourage /in kúrrij/ (**-aging, -aged**) *vt* **1** give hope, confidence, or support to **2** foster the growth or development of —**encouragement** *n* —**encouraging** *adj* —**encouragingly** *adv*

encroach /in króch/ *vi* **1** intrude gradually or stealthily ○ *encroaching on civil liberties* **2** exceed proper limits —**encroachment** *n*

encrustation /in krust áysh'n/, **incrustation** /in krust áysh'n/ *n* **1** the covering of something with a hard coating or a layer of jewels **2** a hard coating or decorative layer —**encrust** /in krúst/ *vt* —**encrusted** *adj*

encrypt /in krípt/ *vt* **1** convert into code or cipher **2** encode in a digital form using a key —**encryption** /-krípsh'n/ *n*

encumber /in kúmbər/ *vt* **1** hinder **2** load down

encumbrance /in kúmbrənss/ *n* a burden or hindrance

encyclical /en síklik'l/ *n* a papal statement on church doctrine sent to Roman Catholic bishops

encyclopedia /in síklə peédi ə/, **encyclopaedia** *n* a comprehensive reference work

encyclopedic /in síklə peédik/, **encyclopaedic** *adj* embracing a broadly inclusive range of knowledge

end *n* **1** the final part of something that has consumed time ○ *the end of the lesson* **2** the extremity of an object **3** a limit or boundary **4** a stopping ○ *an end to hostilities* **5** an extremity of a scale **6** a goal or purpose ○ *an end in itself* **7** a part of a communications link ○ *on the other end of the phone* **8** death or destruction ○ *met an untimely end* **9** a leftover piece **10** a share of joint responsibility ○ *your end of the bargain* **11** half of a playing field or court, defended by one side **12** in American football, a player positioned at the end of a line ■ *v* **1** *vti* come or bring to a stop **2** *vi* result ○ *ended in an uproar* **3** *vi* reach a limit at a place **4** *vi* reach a tip ◇ **get (hold of) the wrong end of the stick** misunderstand what somebody is saying ◇ **in the end** finally ◇ **make ends meet** be able to pay for the expenses of daily living ◇ **on end** for an uninterrupted period ○ *rained for days on end* □ **end up** *vi* **1** become something eventually **2** arrive at a destination at long last

endanger /in dáynjər/ *vt* put at risk —**endangerment** *n*

endangered species *n* a species threatened by extinction

endear /in deér/ *vt* cause to be liked ○ *didn't endear herself to us*

endearing /in deéring/ *adj* causing fond feelings —**endearingly** *adv*

endearment /in deérmənt/ *n* an expression of affection

endeavour /in dévvər/ *vt* try hard ■ *n* **1** an earnest effort to achieve something **2** an enterprise

endemic /en démmik/ *adj* commonly occurring in or restricted to a particular place or group of people ○ *a disease endemic in the tropics* —**endemically** *adv*

~~endevour~~ incorrect spelling of **endeavour**

endgame /énd gaym/ *n* **1** in chess, the last stage of a game **2** the last stage of a process or contest

ending /énding/ *n* the final part or tip of something ○ *a sad ending* ○ *nerve endings*

endive /én dīv, éndiv, óN deev/ *n* **1** a leafy plant used in salads and as a garnish **2** US chicory

endless /éndləss/ *adj* **1** seeming without end or unlimited ○ *endless patience* **2** forming one piece ○ *an endless belt* —**endlessly** *adv*

endocrine gland /éndō krīn-, -krin-/ *n* a gland that secretes hormones directly into the blood or lymph

endogenous /en dójjənəss/ *adj* **1** without an external cause **2** produced inside an organism

endorphin /en dáwrfin/ *n* a natural painkiller released from the brain

endorse /in dáwrss/ (**-dorsing, -dorsed**) *vt* **1** give approval or public support to ○ *refuses to endorse either candidate* ○ *endorses various cosmetics* **2** sign a cheque on the back to obtain cash or specify a payee —**endorsement** *n*

endoscope /éndə skōp/ *n* a long tube with a camera on the end, inserted in the body for diagnosis or minor surgery —**endoscopy** /en dóskəpi/ *n*

endow /in dów/ *vt* **1** provide with income or property **2** provide with something desirable ○ *endowed with a perfect climate*

endowment /in dówmənt/ *n* an amount of income or property provided to a person or institution

endurance /in dyoórənss/ *n* **1** an ability to bear prolonged hardship **2** persistence over time

endure /in dyoór/ (**-during, -dured**) *v* **1** *vti* bear hardship **2** *vt* tolerate *(fml)* **3** *vi* survive or last —**endurable** *adj* —**enduring** *adj*

end user *n* any of the ultimate users that a product is designed for

endways /énd wayz/, **endwise** /-wīz/ *adv* **1** with the end up or forward **2** with ends touching

end zone *n* in American football, each of two scoring areas at the ends of the field

enema /énnəmə/ *n* an insertion of liquid into the rectum to flush out the bowels

enemy /énnəmi/ (*pl* **-mies**) *n* **1** somebody who is actively unfriendly towards another **2** a military opponent **3** something harmful or obstructive

energetic /énnər jéttik/ *adj* **1** forceful **2** requiring stamina —**energetically** *adv*

energize /énnər jīz/ (**-gizing, -gized**), **energise** *vt* **1** give energy to **2** supply with electrical power

energy /énnərji/ (*pl* -**gies**) *n* 1 vigour 2 a forceful effort ○ *concentrate our energies on success* 3 a power supply or source 4 (*symbol E*) the capacity of a body or system to do work

enervate /énnər vayt/ (-**vating**, -**vated**) *vt* lessen the vitality of —**enervation** /énnər váysh'n/ *n*

enfant terrible /óN foN te reéblə/ *n* 1 somebody whose unconventional behaviour is shocking 2 an avant-garde young artist

enfeeble /in feéb'l/ (-**bling**, -**bled**) *vt* make weak

enfilade /énfi layd/ *n* a burst of gunfire aimed along the entire length of a body of troops —**enfilade** *vt*

enflict incorrect spelling of **inflict**

enfold /in fóld/ *vt* 1 envelop 2 take in an embrace

enforceable incorrect spelling of **enforceable**

enforce /in fáwrss/ (-**forcing**, -**forced**) *vt* compel obedience to a law or rule —**enforceable** *adj* —**enforcement** *n*

enforcer /in fáwrssər/ *n* somebody who enforces a law

enfranchise /in frán chīz/ (-**chising**, -**chised**) *vt* 1 give the right to vote to 2 set free —**enfranchisement** /-chiz-/ *n*

Eng. *abbr* 1 England 2 English

engage /in gáyj/ (-**gaging**, -**gaged**) *v* 1 *vti* involve or become involved in something 2 *vt* require the use of something ○ *Her writing engages most of her time.* 3 *vt* hold the attention of somebody 4 *vt* attract somebody by being pleasant 5 *vti* make a promise 6 *vti* fight an enemy 7 *vt* hire somebody 8 *vti* interlock one thing with another, or become interlocked ○ *engaged the gears* 9 *vti* activate, or become activated

engagé /óng ga zháy/ *adj* politically committed

engaged /in gáyjd/ *adj* 1 having agreed to marry 2 occupied or in use 3 currently being used for a telephone call 4 fighting a battle 5 with parts interlocked 6 *US* actively involved

engagement /in gáyjmənt/ *n* 1 an agreement to marry 2 a commitment to go somewhere 3 a brief job, especially one for a performer 4 a battle ◊ See note at **fight**

engagement ring *n* a ring given by a man to his fiancée

engaging /in gáyjing/ *adj* attractive or charming —**engagingly** *adv*

Engels /éng g'lz/, **Friedrich** (1820–95) German political thinker and revolutionary

engender /in jéndər/ *vt* 1 cause to exist ○ *Secrecy engenders suspicion.* 2 produce offspring (*fml*)

engine /énjin/ *n* 1 a machine that converts energy into mechanical power 2 a railway locomotive —**engined** *adj*

engine driver *n* a train driver

engineer /énji neér/ *n* 1 an engineering professional 2 *US, Can* a train driver 3 somebody who operates or services machines 4 a soldier belonging to a unit specializing in building things ■ *vt* 1 plan or bring about,

especially with ingenuity or secretiveness 2 use engineering skill to design or create

engineering /énji neéring/ *n* 1 the application of science to the design, construction, and maintenance of buildings and manufactured things 2 a branch of engineering pursued as a profession ○ *mechanical engineering*

England /íng glənd/ country forming the southern and largest part of Great Britain and of the United Kingdom. Cap. London. Pop. 49,495,000 (1998).

English /íng glish/ *n* 1 the Germanic language of the United Kingdom, the United States, and many other countries 2 the study of English or literature in English 3 understandable or grammatically correct English ■ *npl* the people of England ■ *adj* 1 of the English language 2 of England or the people of England —**Englishness** *n*

ORIGIN England and the **English** are named after the Angles, the Germanic people who invaded and settled in England in the 5C and 6C AD. They came from Angul (now Angeln) in N Germany, which got its name from its shape, somewhat resembling a fishhook. **English** has been spelt with *e* since the earliest records.

English breakfast *n* a substantial cooked breakfast

English Channel area of water between England and France linking the North Sea with the Atlantic Ocean. Length 565 km/351 mi.

English horn *n* MUSIC = **cor anglais**

Englishman /íng glishmən/ (*pl* -**men** /-mən/) *n* a man from England

Englishwoman /íng glish woomən/ (*pl* -**women** /-wimin/) *n* a woman from England

engorge /in gáwrj/ (-**gorging**, -**gorged**) *vti* fill with blood —**engorgement** *n*

engrave /in gráyv/ (-**graving**, -**graved**) *vt* 1 carve or etch a surface 2 carve or etch a design onto a surface 3 impress something deeply on the mind —**engraver** *n*

engraving /in gráyving/ *n* 1 an engraved print or design 2 the act of carving or etching images

engross /in gróss/ *vt* 1 occupy the whole attention of somebody 2 buy enough of a commodity to control the market —**engrossing** *adj* —**engrossingly** *adv*

engulf /in gúlf/ *vt* 1 surround, cover, and swallow up 2 overwhelm —**engulfment** *n*

enhance /in haánss/ (-**hancing**, -**hanced**) *vt* 1 improve or add a desirable quality to something 2 increase the clarity of an electronic image using a computer program —**enhancement** *n*

enigma /i nígmə/ *n* somebody or something not easily explained or understood —**enigmatic** /énnig máttik/ *adj* —**enigmatically** *adv*

enjoin /in jóyn/ *vt* 1 command or impose with authority (*fml*) ○ *were enjoined to be silent* ○ *enjoined secrecy upon us* 2 forbid or command by legal injunction —**enjoinment** n

enjoy /in jóy/ v 1 vt find pleasing 2 vt have the use or benefit of 3 vt have as a good feature 4 vr have a good experience

enjoyable /in jóy əb'l/ adj providing pleasure —**enjoyably** adv

enjoyment /in jóymənt/ n 1 pleasure 2 the experiencing of something that provides pleasure 3 a source of pleasure 4 use or benefit of something, especially as a legal right

enlarge /in laárj/ (-**larging**, -**larged**) v 1 vti make or become larger 2 vti broaden in scope 3 vi give more detail 4 vt make a photograph larger —**enlargement** n —**enlarger** n ◊ See note at **increase**

enlighten /in líťn/ vt 1 give clarifying information to 2 free from ignorance, prejudice, or superstition —**enlightening** adj

enlightened /in líťnd/ adj 1 free of ignorance, prejudice, or superstition 2 well-informed

enlightenment /in líťnmənt/ n 1 the process of enlightening somebody 2 an enlightened state 3 a spiritual state that transcends desire and suffering 4 **Enlightenment** an 18C intellectual movement that emphasized reason and science

enlist /in líst/ vti 1 enrol in the armed forces 2 gain the support of, or become actively involved in an effort —**enlistment** n

enlisted person n US a low-ranking member of the US armed forces

enliven /in lív'n/ vt 1 invigorate 2 make brighter or more cheerful —**enlivenment** n

en masse /óN máss/ adv in a group

enmesh /in mésh/ vt 1 entangle 2 catch in a net

enmity /énmiti/ (pl -**ties**) n hostility or hatred between enemies

~~enmety~~ incorrect spelling of **enemy**

ennoble /i nốb'l/ (-**bling**, -**bled**) vt 1 make noble or more dignified (fml) 2 elevate to membership of the nobility —**ennoblement** n

ennui /ón wee/ n general weariness and dissatisfaction with life

enormity /i náwrməti/ (pl -**ties**) n 1 extreme evil 2 an extremely evil act 3 △ enormous size or degree 4 great significance

USAGE **enormity** or **enormousness**? **Enormity** strictly means 'evil' or 'an evil act': the enormity of the crime. **Enormousness** refers to significant size or scale: the enormousness of the task.

enormous /i náwrməss/ adj unusually large —**enormously** adv —**enormousness** n

enough /i núf/ adj as much of as is needed or bearable ○ enough time to shop ○ in enough trouble already ■ adv 1 as much as is needed ○ run fast enough 2 adds emphasis ○ Oddly enough, we'd met before. 3 to a degree that can be tolerated ○ She was arrogant enough before the promotion. ■ pron the needed or tolerated amount ○ Bring more money; we never have enough.

en passant /ón páss ont, óN pa soN/ adv in passing (fml)

enquire /in kwír/ (-**quiring**, -**quired**), **inquire** v 1 vti ask something 2 vi try to find out the facts —**enquirer** n —**enquiring** adj —**enquiringly** adv

USAGE **inquire** or **enquire**? For many users, the two spellings are interchangeable, as with enquiry and inquiry. A useful distinction that some people maintain, however, is to use **enquire** and enquiry in contexts of casual requests for information, and to reserve **inquire** and inquiry for contexts of formal, official, or academic investigation: He enquired after her health. Try directory enquiries. The police are inquiring into the circumstances that led up to his disappearance. There will have to be a public inquiry into the allegations.

enrage /in ráyj/ (-**raging**, -**raged**) vt make very angry

enrapture /in rápchər/ (-**turing**, -**tured**) vt delight

enrich /in rích/ vt 1 improve the quality of 2 make wealthier —**enrichment** n

enrol /in rốl/ (-**rolling**, -**rolled**) vti enter the name of yourself or somebody else on a register or list ○ enrol the children in school —**enrollee** /in rố leé/ n

enrolment /in rốlmənt/ n 1 an instance of signing up formally for something 2 the number of people registered ○ a decline in enrolment

en route /ón roòt, oN-/ adv on the way

ensconce /in skónss/ (-**sconcing**, -**sconced**) vt settle somewhere comfortably

ensemble /on sómb'l/ n 1 a group of performers (+ sing or pl verb) 2 an outfit of clothes 3 something created by putting separate parts together 4 a section of a play or ballet in which the whole cast is involved ■ adj collaborative

enshrine /in shrín/ (-**shrining**, -**shrined**) vt 1 protect from change, especially in law 2 keep in a shrine —**enshrinement** n

enshroud /in shrówd/ vt 1 obscure 2 wrap in a shroud

ensign /én sīn, énss'n/ n 1 a flag indicating a ship's nationality 2 a US Navy or Coast Guard commissioned officer of the lowest rank 3 a badge of office

enslave /in sláyv/ (-**slaving**, -**slaved**) vt 1 subject to a controlling influence that takes away freedom 2 make into a slave —**enslavement** n

ensnare /in snáir/ (-**snaring**, -**snared**) vt 1 trap in an unpleasant situation 2 catch in a trap —**ensnarement** n

ensue /in syoò/ (-**suing**, -**sued**) vi happen after or as a result something —**ensuing** adj

en suite /ón sweét, oN-/ adj, adv adjoining and forming part of the same unit

ensure /in shoòr, in shawr/ (-**suring**, -**sured**) vt make certain or sure of

entablature /en tábbləchər/ n in classical architecture, the section of a structure that lies between the columns and the roof

entail /in táyl/ *vt* **1** have something as a consequence **2** restrict the future ownership of property to specified descendants through a will ■ *n* **1** the restriction of future ownership of property to specified descendants **2** an entailed property —**entailment** *n*

entangle /in táng g'l/ (**-gling, -gled**) *vt* **1** tangle up **2** put into a difficult situation —**entanglement** *n*

entente /on tónt/ *n* a friendly understanding between countries

enter /éntər/ *v* **1** *vti* go or come into a place **2** *vt* write or type in a book or on a computer **3** *vt* submit for formal consideration **4** *vti* register as a competitor **5** *vti* join or become involved in something ○ *enter the race for President* **6** *vi* walk on stage as a performer **7** *vti* force a way into something, e.g. the body ○ *The bullet entered here.*

□ **enter into** *vt* **1** take part in something **2** be relevant to something **3** sign up to a contract

enteritis /éntə rítiss/ *n* inflammation of the intestines

enter key *n* the return key on a computer keyboard

enterprise /éntər prīz/ *n* **1** a commercial business **2** a daring new venture **3** readiness to put effort into new ventures and activities **4** organized business activities aimed at growth and profit

enterprising /éntər prīzing/ *adj* showing initiative —**enterprisingly** *adv*

entertain /éntər táyn/ *v* **1** *vti* amuse or interest somebody or an audience **2** *vti* offer hospitality to a guest, especially in the form of food and drink **3** *vt* consider

entertainer /éntər táynər/ *n* somebody who performs, especially professionally

entertaining /éntər táyning/ *adj* amusing or interesting —**entertainingly** *adv*

entertainment /éntər táynmənt/ *n* **1** the various ways of amusing people, especially by performing for them **2** the amount of enjoyment people get from something **3** a performance or exhibition

enthral /in thráwl/ (**-thralling, -thralled**) *vt* **1** hold the attention of in delight or fascination **2** enslave (*literary*) —**enthralment** *n*

enthrone /in thrón/ (**-throning, -throned**) *vt* **1** put on a throne as a monarch (*fml*) **2** regard as important (*literary*) —**enthronement** *n*

enthuse /in thyóoz/ (**-thusing, -thused**) *vti* **1** be or make enthusiastic **2** speak or say with enthusiasm

enthusiasm /in thyóozi azəm/ *n* **1** excited interest **2** something somebody is passionately interested in

ORIGIN Enthusiasm was not always approved of. The word originally meant 'possession by a god' (its root is the Greek word for 'god' that gave us *theology* and related words). The frenzy associated with this led to its disapproving use

as 'extravagant religious emotion' in the mid-17C. More positive uses of the word did not appear until the early 18C.

enthusiast /in thyóozi ast/ *n* somebody who is passionately interested and involved in something

enthusiastic /in thyóozi ástik/ *adj* showing passionate interest —**enthusiastically** *adv*

entice /in tíss/ (**-ticing, -ticed**) *vt* tempt by offering something attractive —**enticement** *n* —**enticing** *adj* —**enticingly** *adv*

entire /in tír/ *adj* **1** from beginning to end, or including everything ○ *rained the entire night* **2** absolute or without doubt or question ○ *The day was an entire fiasco.* —**entirely** *adv* —**entirety** /in tírəti/ *n*

~~entirly~~ incorrect spelling of **entirely**

entitle /in tít'l/ (**-tling, -tled**) *vt* **1** allow to claim something **2** give a title to —**entitlement** *n*

entity /éntəti/ (*pl* **-ties**) *n* something that exists as a separate object

entomb /in tóom/ *vt* **1** put a corpse in a tomb **2** put something in a deep or hidden place ○ *treasures entombed in secret vaults* —**entombment** *n*

entomology /éntə mólləji/ *n* the scientific study of insects —**entomological** /éntəmə lójjik'l/ *adj* —**entomologist** *n*

entourage /ón too raazh/ *n* a group of people accompanying a famous or important person

entrails /én traylz/ *npl* **1** internal organs **2** the inner workings of something complex

entrance¹ /éntrənss/ *n* **1** a door or gate by which to enter **2** an act of entering a room

entrance² /in traánss/ (**-trancing, -tranced**) *vt* **1** fascinate **2** put a spell on —**entrancingly** *adv*

entrant /éntrənt/ *n* a competitor ◊ See note at **candidate**

entrap /in tráp/ (**-trapping, -trapped**) *vt* **1** trick into doing something wrong **2** catch in a trap —**entrapment** *n*

entreat /in tréet/ *vti* beg desperately —**entreatingly** *adv*

entreaty /in tréeti/ (*pl* **-ies**) *n* a desperate plea

entrée /ón tray/ *n* **1** the main course of a meal **2** a dish served before the main course of a formal meal

entrench /in trénch/ *vt* **1** dig a defensive ditch round **2** protect —**entrenchment** *n*

entrenched /in tréncht/ *adj* **1** firmly held ○ *deeply entrenched political views* **2** firmly established

entre nous /óntrə nóo/ *adv* between ourselves

entrepreneur /óntrəprə núr/ *n* an initiator or a financial backer of new businesses —**entrepreneurial** *adj* —**entrepreneurialism** *n* —**entrepreneurism** *n*

entropy /éntrəpi/ *n* **1** a measure of the disorder that exists in a system **2** (*symbol* **S**) a measure of the energy in a system that is unavailable to do work —**entropic** /en tróppik/ adj —**entropically** adv

ORIGIN The German original of **entropy** was coined in 1865 by the German physicist Rudolph Clausius (1822–88), who developed the concept. He based it on *energy*, using the Greek word for 'turning, transformation'. The English form of the word appeared just a few years after the German.

entrust /in trúst/ vt give somebody responsibility for something —**entrustment** n

entry /éntri/ (pl -tries) n 1 an act of coming or going into a place 2 the right to go into a place or become a member of an organization 3 a single written item, e.g. in a diary or on a list 4 a way into a place 5 somebody or something entered in a contest 6 an actor's appearance on stage 7 in some card games, a winning card

entry-level adj suitable for somebody who is new to a job, field, or subject

Entryphone /éntri fōn/ tdmk a trademark for an intercom system that links each flat in a building with the main door and allows the occupant to open the door remotely

entwine /in twín/ (**entwining, entwined**) vti twist together

E number n an identification code for a food additive, consisting of the letter E followed by a number

enumerate /i nyóomə rayt/ (-ating, -ated) vt 1 list a number of things individually 2 count how many things there are in something —**enumerable** adj —**enumeration** /i nyóomə ráysh'n/ n

enunciate /i núnssi ayt/ (-ating, -ated) v 1 vti speak or say clearly 2 vt state or explain clearly —**enunciation** /i núnssi áysh'n/ n

envelop /in véllǝp/ vt 1 wrap something up completely 2 conceal something —**envelopment** n ◊ See note at **envelope**

envelope /énvǝ lōp, ónvǝ-/ n 1 a paper container for a letter 2 something that surrounds or encloses something else ○ *seafood sauce in filo pastry envelopes* 3 the part of an airship or hot-air balloon that contains the gas

SPELLCHECK Do not confuse the spelling of **envelope** and **envelop** ('wrap up'), which are spelt similarly but are not pronounced alike.

enviable /énvi əb'l/ adj causing feelings of envy —**enviably** adv

envious /énvi əss/ adj wanting what somebody else has —**enviously** adv —**enviousness** n

~~enviroment~~ incorrect spelling of **environment**

environment /in vírǝnmǝnt/ n 1 the natural world as the habitat of living things 2 a set of social and physical conditions that surround and influence the way somebody lives ○ *a nurturing environment* —**environmental** /in vírǝn mént'l/ adj —**environmentally** adv

environmentalist /in vírǝn mént'list/ n 1 somebody working to protect the environment 2 somebody who believes that environment is more important than heredity to a person's development —**environmentalism** n

environmentally friendly, environment-friendly adj minimizing harm to the natural world

environs /in vírǝnz/ npl the surrounding area

envisage /in vízzij/ (-aging, -aged) vt 1 *also* **envision** /in vízh'n/ picture in the mind, especially as a future possibility 2 regard in a particular way

envoy /én voy/ n 1 an official representative of a national government 2 *also* **envoi** the concluding part of a poem

envy /énvi/ n the feeling of wanting what somebody else has ■ vt (-vies, -vied) want what somebody else has

enzyme /én zīm/ n a protein controlling biochemical reactions —**enzymatic** /én zī máttik, énzi-/ adj

Eocene /eé ō seen/ n an epoch of geological time 55–34 million years ago —**Eocene** adj

eon n = **aeon**

Eos /eé oss/ n in Greek mythology, the goddess of the dawn. Roman equivalent **Aurora**

EP n an extended-play gramophone record

EPA n a fatty acid in fish oil. Full form **eicosapentaenoic acid**

epaulette /éppə lét/ n a decoration on the shoulder of a garment, especially a uniform jacket

épée /éppay/ (pl **épées**) n a fencing sword heavier than a foil

ephemera /i fémmərə, i feé-/ n (pl -**ae** /-ee/ or -**as**) 1 something transitory 2 a mayfly ■ npl collectable items originally expected to be short-lived

ephemeral /i fémmərəl, i feé-/ adj transitory —**ephemerality** /i fémmə rálləti, i feémə-/ n —**ephemerally** adv ◊ See note at **temporary**

Ephesus /éffəsəss/ ancient Greek city on the coast of W Asia Minor, in present-day Turkey

epic /éppik/ n 1 a long narrative poem 2 epic poetry as a genre 3 a large-scale production of a work of literature, cinema, television, or theatre ■ adj 1 of or like an epic 2 very large or heroic —**epical** adj

epicentre /éppi sentər/ n 1 the point on the Earth's surface above the focus of an earthquake 2 a focal point —**epicentral** /éppi séntrəl/ adj

epicure /éppi kyoor/ n 1 a gourmet 2 somebody who loves luxury and sensual pleasures —**epicurism** n

ORIGIN Epicures get their name from the Greek philosopher Epicurus. He taught that the greatest good is freedom from pain and emotional disturbance, but his thought came to be associated with the pursuit of pleasure, and one of the earlier senses in English was 'glutton'.

epicurean /éppi kyoo reé ən/ adj 1 devoted to sensual pleasure, especially good food

2 pleasing to an epicure —**epicurean** n —**epicureanism** n

Epicurus /éppi kyoŏráss/ (341–270 BC) Greek philosopher

epidemic /éppi démmik/ n **1** a fast-spreading disease **2** a rapid development, especially of something bad ■ adj spreading unusually quickly and extensively —**epidemically** adv ◊ See note at **widespread**

epidemiology /éppi deèmi óllǝji/ n **1** the study of the origin and spread of diseases **2** the origin and development of a particular disease —**epidemiological** /-deèmi ǝ lójjik'l/ adj —**epidemiologically** adv —**epidemiologist** n

epidermis /éppi dúrmiss/ n the outer layer of the skin —**epidermal** adj

epidural /éppi dyoŏrǝl/ n an anaesthetic injection into the spine

epiglottis /éppi glóttiss/ (pl **-tises** or **-tides** /-tideez/) n a flap of cartilage at the base of the tongue that covers the air passages during eating or drinking —**epiglottal** adj

epigram /éppi gram/ n **1** a witty saying **2** a short poem

epigrammatic /éppigrǝ máttik/, **epigrammatical** /-máttik'l/ adj **1** in the form of an epigram **2** tending to use epigrams —**epigrammatically** adv

epigraph /éppi graaf, -graf/ n **1** an introductory quotation in a book **2** an inscription on a monument —**epigraphic** /éppi gráffik/ adj —**epigraphical** adj —**epigraphically** adv

epilepsy /éppi lepsi/ n a medical disorder of the brain that periodically causes a sudden loss of consciousness, often with convulsions

epileptic /éppi léptik/ adj of or affected by epilepsy ■ n an offensive term for somebody who has epilepsy —**epileptically** adv

epilogue /éppi log/ n **1** an actor's short concluding speech, delivered directly to the audience **2** an actor who delivers an epilogue **3** a short section at the end of a book, sometimes detailing the fate of the characters **4** formerly, a programme shown at the end of the day's broadcasting

epinephrine /éppi néf reen/, **epinephrin** /-frin/ n synthetic adrenaline. Use: to relax the airways, constrict blood vessels.

epiphany /i piffǝni/ (pl **-nies**) n **1** an appearance of a god **2** a sudden realization **3 Epiphany** the Christian festival celebrating Jesus Christ's divinity as revealed by the Three Wise Men. Date: 6 January.

epiphyte /éppi fīt/ n a plant that grows on another —**epiphytic** /-fíttik/ adj

episcopacy /i pískǝpǝssi/ n church government by bishops

episcopal /i pískǝp'l/ adj **1** of bishops **2** governed by bishops

Episcopal Church n a Protestant denomination that is in communion with the Anglican Church —**Episcopal** adj

episcopalian /i pískǝ páyli ǝn/ adj **1** believing in church government by bishops **2** Epis-

copalian belonging to the Episcopal Church —**episcopalian** n —**Episcopalian** n —**episcopalianism** n —**Episcopalianism** n

episcopate /i-pískǝpǝt/ n **1** the office or position of a bishop **2** a diocese

episode /éppis sōd/ n **1** a significant incident **2** an individual part of a serialized work **3** an event in a narrative

episodic /éppi sóddik/, **episodical** /-sóddik'l/ adj **1** divided into episodes **2** sporadic —**episodically** adv

epistle /i píss'l/ n **1** a letter (fml) **2** a book in letter form **3 Epistle** a letter from the apostle Paul or another early Christian writer, included as a book of the Bible

epistolary /i pístǝlǝri/ adj in the form of a letter or letters

epitaph /éppi taaf, -taf/ n **1** an inscription on a tombstone **2** a speech or a piece of writing commemorating a dead person —**epitaphic** /eppi taáffik, -táffik/ adj

epithet /éppi thet/ n **1** a descriptive word added to somebody's name **2** an insult —**epithetical** /-théttik'l/ adj

epitome /i píttǝmi/ n **1** a perfect example **2** a summary of a written work (fml)

epitomize /i píttǝ mīz/ (**-mizing, -mized**), **epitomise** vt **1** exemplify perfectly **2** summarize (fml) —**epitomization** /i píttǝ mī záysh'n/ n

~~epitomy~~ incorrect spelling of **epitome**

epoch /eè pok/ n **1** a significant period in history or in somebody's life **2** the beginning of a long and historically significant period **3** a unit of geological time —**epochal** /éppok'l, eè pok'l/ adj

epoch-making adj having momentous significance

eponymous /i pónnimǝss/ adj having the same name as the title or name of something else, e.g. the title of a book ◦ the eponymous hero —**eponymously** adv

epoxy /i póksi/, **epoxy resin** n a tough synthetic resin. Use: adhesives, surface coatings.

epsilon /ep sílon, épsilon/ n the 5th letter of the Greek alphabet

Epsom salts /épsǝm-/ n a bitter-tasting medicine. Use: to reduce swelling. (+ sing verb)

Epstein /ép stīn/, **Sir Jacob** (1880–1959) US-born British sculptor

Epstein-Barr virus /ép stīn baár-/ n a virus believed to cause glandular fever, also associated with other diseases

EQ n a ratio of educational attainment to chronological age. Full form **educational quotient**

equable /ékwǝb'l/ adj **1** calm and not easily disturbed **2** free from marked variation and extremes —**equability** /ékwǝ bíllǝti/ n —**equably** adv

equal /eèkwǝl/ adj **1** identical in size, quantity, value, or standard **2** having the same rights, opportunities, and privileges as others **3** evenly balanced between opposing sides ◦ hoping for an equal match in the next game

4 equipped with the necessary qualities or means to succeed ○ *was equal to the task* ■ *n* somebody or something equal in quality to another ■ *vt* (**equalling, equalled**) **1** have the same value as ○ *Two plus two equals four.* **2** do, produce, or achieve something to the same standard as ○ *equalled the world record*

equality /i kwólləti/ (*pl* **-ties**) *n* **1** the state of being equal **2** an equation with equal quantities on each side of the equal sign

equalize /eékwə līz/ (**-izing, -ized**), **equalise** *v* **1** *vt* make uniform or equal **2** *vi* achieve the same score —**equalization** /eékwə lī záysh'n/ *n*

equalizer /eékwə līzər/, **equaliser** *n* **1** somebody or something that equalizes things **2** an electronic device that reduces distortion in a sound system

equally /eékwəli/ *adv* **1** in the same way **2** to the same extent **3** in the same-sized amounts

equal opportunity *n* equal treatment for all people (*often pl*)

equal sign, equals sign *n* a mathematical symbol (=) showing equality

equanimity /ékwə nímməti, eékwə-/ *n* evenness of temper even under stress —**equanimous** /i kwánniməss, i kwónni-/ *adj*

equate /i kwáyt, ee-/ (**equating, equated**) *vt* be, or consider something to be, equivalent to something else —**equatable** *adj*

equation /i kwáyzh'n/ *n* **1** a mathematical statement of equality **2** a situation involving variable elements —**equational** *adj*

equator /i kwáytər/ *n* **1** an imaginary circle around the middle of the Earth **2** an imaginary circle around the middle of an astronomical object

ORIGIN The fuller form of the medieval Latin term from which **equator** derives was *circulus aequator diei et noctis* 'circle equalizing day and night'.

equatorial /ékwə táwri əl, eékwə-/ *adj* **1** of or around the equator **2** situated in the plane of an equator

Equatorial Guinea country in W Africa bordering the Atlantic Ocean and comprising a mainland section, Río Muni, and several islands. Cap. Malabo. Pop. 486,060 (2001).

equerry /i kwérri, ékwəri/ (*pl* **-ries**) *n* **1** a personal attendant of a member of the British royal family **2** formerly, an officer responsible for the royal horses

equestrian /i kwéstri ən/ *adj* of horses or riding ■ *n* a skilled rider —**equestrianism** *n*

equidistant /eékwi dístənt, ékwi-/ *adj* equally distant —**equidistantly** *adv*

equilateral /eékwi láttərəl, ékwi-/ *adj* with sides of equal length ■ *n* **1** an equilateral figure **2** a side of an equilateral figure

equilibrium /eékwi líbbri əm, ékwi-/ (*pl* **-ums** *or* **-a** /-ə/) *n* **1** a state or sense of being able to maintain bodily balance **2** emotional stability **3** a balance between forces

equine /é kwīn, ee-/ *adj* **1** of horses **2** resembling a horse ■ *n* a horse or other member of the horse family

equinoctial /eékwi nóksh'l, ékwi nóksh'l/ *adj* occurring at an equinox ■ *n* a storm that occurs during an equinox

equinox /eékwi noks, ékwi-/ *n* either of the times of year when the Sun crosses the equator and day and night are of equal length everywhere on Earth

equip /i kwíp/ (**equipping, equipped**) *vt* **1** provide with the necessary tools, supplies, or clothing for a specific activity **2** provide with the necessary training or experience to succeed —**equipper** *n*

~~equiped~~ incorrect spelling of **equipped**

equipment /i kwípmənt/ *n* **1** the necessary tools, supplies, or clothing for a specific activity **2** the process of providing somebody with equipment **3** the personal resources that enable a person to succeed

equitable /ékwitəb'l/ *adj* **1** fair and just (*fml*) **2** of the law of equity —**equitably** *adv*

equity /ékwiti/ *n* **1** fairness and lack of bias (*fml*) **2** a system of jurisprudence that modifies common and statute law to take into account fairness **3** the value of a piece of property over and above the mortgage on it ■ **equities** *npl* shares entitling the holder to a share in profits

equivalent /i kwívvələnt/ *adj* equal in effect, value, or meaning ■ *n* something considered to be equal or to have an equal effect, value or meaning —**equivalence** *n* —**equivalently** *adv*

~~equivelent~~ incorrect spelling of **equivalent**

equivocal /i kwívvək'l/ *adj* **1** ambiguous, often deliberately so **2** difficult to interpret or understand —**equivocality** /i kwívvə kálləti/ *n* —**equivocally** *adv*

equivocate /i kwívvə kayt/ (**-cating, -cated**) *vi* be deliberately unclear and evasive —**equivocatingly** *adv* —**equivocation** /i kwívvə káysh'n/ *n*

er *interj* expresses hesitation

Er *symbol* erbium

ER *abbr* **1** Elizabetha Regina **2** US emergency room

-er[1] *suffix* **1** somebody or something that performs or undergoes a particular action ○ *adjuster* ○ *fryer* **2** somebody connected with something, often as an occupation ○ *trucker* **3** somebody or something with a particular characteristic, quality, or form ○ *ten-pounder* **4** somebody from a particular place ○ *Londoner*

-er[2] *suffix* more

era /eérə/ *n* **1** a period of time made distinctive, e.g., by a significant development ○ *the Elizabethan era* **2** a time period with a numbering system that begins at a particular significant event ○ *the Christian era* **3** a division of geological time composed of several periods

ORIGIN **Era** is based on a Latin word that came

tn mean a 'number used as a basis for counting'. In this sense it was used as a prefix before dates, and from there developed 'system of numbering years from a noteworthy event', which is the sense in which **era** appeared in English in the mid-17C. As a 'period of time' it is recorded from the mid-18C.

ERA *abbr US* Equal Rights Amendment

eradicate /i ráddi kayt/ (**-cating, -cated**) *vt* get rid of completely —**eradicable** *adj* —**eradicably** *adv* —**eradication** /i ráddi káysh'n/ *n*

erase /i ráyz/ (**erasing, erased**) *vt* **1** remove written or typed material with a rubber or correction fluid **2** remove or destroy something —**erasable** *adj*

eraser /i ráyzər/ *n* a rubber used for removing pencil marks

Erasmus /i rázməss/, **Desiderius** (1466?–1536) Dutch scholar and writer

erasure /i ráyzhər/ *n* **1** removal or destruction of something **2** an erased thing, e.g. a mark

erbium /úrbi əm/ *n* (*symbol* **Er**) a soft silvery metallic chemical element. Use: alloys, pigment.

ORIGIN **Erbium** is named after the town of Ytterby in Sweden, where the first mineral of the series of elements to which it belongs was discovered.

ere /air/ *prep, conj* before (*literary*) ◊ See note at **air**

erect /i rékt/ *adj* **1** in an upright position ○ *an erect plant stem* **2** firm and swollen as a result of being filled with blood, e.g. when sexually aroused ■ *vt* **1** construct something in place from basic parts and materials **2** set something upright —**erectly** *adv* —**erectness** *n*

erectile /i rék tíl/ *adj* capable of swelling with blood and becoming stiff —**erectility** /i rék tílləti/ *n*

erection /i réksh'n/ *n* **1** the process of constructing something or putting something up **2** a swollen stiffened state of tissue, especially of the penis **3** a building or other large structure (*fml*)

ergo /úrgō/ *adv, conj* therefore or so

ergonomics /úrgə nómmiks/ *n* the study of workplace design (*+ sing verb*) —**ergonomic** *adj* —**ergonomically** *adv*

Ericson /érriks'n/, **Leif** (975–1020) Icelandic explorer

Eric the Red /érrik-/ (950?–1000?) Norwegian explorer

Erie, Lake /eéri/ southernmost and fourth largest of the Great Lakes

Erikson /érrikss'n/, **Erik** (1902–94) German-born US psychoanalyst

Eritrea /érri tráy ə/ country on the Red Sea coast in NE Africa. Cap. Asmara. Pop. 4,298,269 (2001). —**Eritrean** *n, adj*

ermine /úrmin/ (*pl* **-mines** *or* same) *n* **1** a stoat,

especially in its white winter coat **2** the white fur of a stoat

ORIGIN **Ermine** probably ultimately derives from a medieval Latin name meaning 'Armenian mouse'. It entered English from French in the early medieval period.

Erne /urn/ river in the Republic of Ireland and Northern Ireland, emptying into Donegal Bay. Along its route it broadens into two large lakes, Upper and Lower Lough Erne.

Ernst /airnst, urnst/, **Max** (1891–1976) German-born French artist

erode /i ród/ (**eroding, eroded**) *vti* **1** wear away land, or be worn away, by wind or water **2** break down gradually ○ *Deceit will erode any friendship.* —**erodible** *adj*

erogenous /i rójjənəss/ *adj* sensitive and arousing sexual feelings when touched or stroked

erogenous zone *n* a sexually sensitive area of the body

Eros /eér oss/ *n* in Greek mythology, the god of love. Roman equivalent **Cupid**

erosion /i rózh'n/ *n* **1** the process of wearing away or being worn away **2** a gradual breaking down of something —**erosional** *adj*

erotic /i róttik/ *adj* **1** arousing sexual feelings **2** marked by sexual desire —**erotically** *adv*

ORIGIN **Erotic** was adopted from French in the mid-17C. It comes from the Greek word for 'sensual love', represented in mythology by the god Eros.

erotica /i róttika/ *n* sexually explicit material

eroticism /i rótti sizəm/, **erotism** /érrə tizəm/ *n* **1** an erotic quality **2** sexual desire —**eroticist** *n*

err /ur, air/ *vi* (*fml*) **1** make a mistake **2** behave badly ◊ See note at **air**

errand /érrənd/ *n* **1** a short trip to do something for somebody else **2** the purpose of an errand

errant /érrənt/ *adj* **1** behaving badly **2** straying from an intended course **3** looking for adventure (*literary*) —**errantly** *adv*

erratic /i ráttik/ *adj* **1** not regular or consistent and often below standard **2** often changing direction —**erratically** *adv*

erratum /e ráatəm/ (*pl* **-ta** /-tə/) *n* a printing error

erroneous /i róni əss/ *adj* incorrect —**erroneously** *adv* —**erroneousness** *n*

error /érrər/ *n* **1** a mistake **2** a wrong belief **3** the state of believing or acting wrongly **4** the fact of being wrong **5** a problem detected by a computer program ◊ See note at **mistake**

error message *n* a message alerting a computer user to a problem

ersatz /áir zats/ *adj* artificial or presented as a substitute (*disapproving*)

Erse /urss/ *n* the Gaelic language —**Erse** *adj*

erstwhile /úrst wíl/ *adj* former ■ *adv* formerly (*archaic*)

erudite /érrŏŏ dīt/ *adj* knowledgeable as a result of study —**eruditely** *adv* —**erudition** ||

ORIGIN **Erudite** comes from a Latin word

meaning 'trained, instructed', which was its original English use. The Latin source is based on the word from which *rude* derives, combined with a prefix meaning 'out of', so an **erudite** person has literally been trained out of rudeness.

erudition /érròö dísh'n/ n knowledge acquired by study

erupt /i rúpt/ v **1** vti violently release material such as gas, steam, or lava **2** vi burst out **3** vi appear as a rash on the skin —**eruption** n —**eruptive** adj —**eruptively** adv

Es symbol einsteinium

-es suffix used for '-s' in words ending in -s, -ss, -x, -sh, or -ch (pronounced 'ch') o *buses* o *birches*

Esc abbr escape (key)

escalate /éska layt/ (**-lating, -lated**) vti become or make greater or more intense —**escalation** /éska láysh'n/ n

escalator /éska laytər/ n a set of moving steps that carry people between the floors of a building

escalope /éska lop, e skóllap/ n a thin slice of meat

escapade /éska payd/ n a rash action or activity

escape /i skáyp/ v (**-caping, -caped**) **1** vti break free from captivity **2** vt avoid a bad situation **3** vi leak out **4** vt fail to be remembered or understood by somebody o *a little village whose name escapes me* **5** vi exit a computer procedure ■ n **1** an instance of breaking free from captivity **2** an act of avoiding a bad situation **3** a means of getting away **4** a pleasant and welcome distraction **5** a computer key for exiting a program or cancelling a command —**escapable** adj

escape artist n a performer who is skilled at escaping from restraints

escape clause n a legal way out of a contract

escapee /i skáy peè, éskay-/ n somebody who has escaped

escapism /i skáypizəm/ n **1** things that provide escape from unpleasant everyday realities **2** indulgence in fantasies to escape reality —**escapist** adj, n

escapologist /éska póllajist/ n a performer who is skilled at escaping from restraints

escarole /éskəròl/ n US, Can a curly endive

escarpment /i skaárpmənt/ n **1** a steep slope at the edge of a plateau **2** a slope built in front of a fortification

Escher /éshər/, **M. C.** (1898–1972) Dutch graphic artist

eschew /iss chóö/ vt avoid doing or using —**eschewal** n

Escoffier /i skóffi ay/, **Auguste** (1846–1935) French chef and cookery author

escort n /éss kawrt/ **1** a person accompanying somebody or something as a guard or as a mark of honour **2** an accompanying military vessel or aircraft **3** a man or woman hired as a social partner —**escort** /i skáwrt/ vt

escritoire /éskri twaár/ n a writing desk

escudo /i skoódô/ n (pl **-dos**) the main unit of the former currency of Portugal

escutcheon /i skúchən/ n **1** a heraldic shield **2** a protective plate or shield, especially one fitted round a keyhole —**escutcheoned** adj

-ese suffix **1** from, of, native to, or inhabiting a particular place o *Taiwanese* **2** the language of a particular place o *Chinese* **3** style or jargon o *officialese*

~~esential~~ incorrect spelling of **essential**

Eshkol /ésh kol/, **Levi** (1895–1969) Russian-born Israeli prime minister (1963–69)

Eskimo /éskimô/ (pl **-mos** or same) n **1** a member of a people indigenous to N Canada, Alaska, Greenland, and Siberia, comprising the Inuit and Yupik (sometimes offensive) **2** the language group comprising Inuit and Yupik —**Eskimo** adj

Esky /éski/ tdmk Aus a trademark for an insulated portable container for keeping food and beverages cool

ESL abbr English as a second language

ESOL abbr English for speakers of other languages

esophagus n US = oesophagus

esoteric /éssô térrik, eèssô-/ adj **1** intended for or understood only by an initiated few **2** difficult to understand —**esoterically** adv

ESP abbr **1** English for special purposes **2** extrasensory perception

esp. abbr especially

espadrille /éspə dríl, éspədril/ n a canvas shoe with a rope sole

espalier /i spálli ay, -li ər/ n a tree trained to grow flat against a wall with its branches in a near horizontal position

esparto /e spaár tô/ (pl **-tos**), **esparto grass** n a coarse fibrous grass. Use: paper, ropes, mats.

especial /i spésh'l/ adj (fml) **1** notable **2** particular

especially /i spésh'li/ adv **1** exceptionally **2** in particular o *They're a helpful group, especially Mark.*

> **USAGE especially** or **specially**? **Especially** means 'exceptionally': *The buildings are not especially large.* **Specially** means 'for a special purpose': *specially designed ramps for wheelchair access.* In rapid conversation, the first syllable of **especially** tends to be slurred or omitted, and this can affect the correct choice when the words are written.

~~especialy~~ incorrect spelling of **especially**

Esperanto /éspə rántô/ n an artificial language based on root forms of words common to major European languages —**Esperantist** n

espionage /éspi ə naazh, éspi ə naázh/ n the activity of spying

esplanade /ésplə náyd, -naàd, ésplə nayd/ n a long wide walkway, especially by the sea

espousal /i spówz'l/ n **1** the adoption of something as a belief or cause **2** a marriage (fml; often pl)

espouse /i spówz/ (**-pousing**, **-poused**) vt **1** adopt as a belief or cause **2** marry, or give in marriage *(archaic)* —**espouser** n

espresso /es préssó/, **expresso** /iks-/ n **1** very strong coffee made in a machine that forces steam through finely ground beans **2** a cup of espresso

ORIGIN **Espresso** is from Italian, and means literally 'squeezed, pressed out'. It goes back to the Latin word that also gave us *express*.

esprit de corps /e spreé də káwr/ n a pride in belonging to something

espy /i spí/ (**-pies**, **-pied**) vt suddenly see *(literary)*

Esq. *abbr* Esquire *(in correspondence)*

-esque *suffix* in the style of, like o *statuesque* o *Pythonesque*

esquire /i skwír/ n **1** a knight's attendant **2 Esquire** a man's courtesy title, especially on documents

-ess *suffix* woman or girl o *heiress*

USAGE In recent times, the **-ess** ending has come to be regarded as sexist and old-fashioned. Words such as *authoress* and *manageress* are dropping out of use and the base term is used for both sexes.

essay /éssay/ n **1** a piece of nonfiction writing on a particular subject **2** a piece of written work set as an assignment for a student **3** an attempt *(fml)* **4** a test of something *(fml)* ■ vt **1** attempt *(fml)* **2** test

essayist /éssayist/ n a writer of essays

Essen /éss'n/ n city in west-central Germany. Pop. 617,955 (1997).

essence /éss'nss/ n **1** the most basic element or feature of something **2** the perfect embodiment of something o *She is the essence of tact.* **3** a concentrated plant extract ◊ **of the essence** of the highest importance

ORIGIN **Essence** comes ultimately from the Latin verb *esse* 'be'.

essential /i sénsh'l/ adj **1** required or necessary o *It's essential that we arrive on time.* **2** constituting the character or feature that makes something what it is o *Being three-sided is essential to being a triangle.* ■ n something essential —**essentially** adv ◊ See note at **necessary**

essential oil n a concentrated oil extracted from a plant

Essex /éssiks/ county in E England

Essex, Robert Devereux, 2nd Earl of (1566–1601) English soldier and courtier

EST *abbr* Eastern Standard Time

-est *suffix* most o *hardest* o *sloppiest*

establish /i stábblish/ vt **1** start or set up something intended to continue for some time **2** prove the truth or validity of something **3** cause somebody or something to be accepted or recognized

established /i stábblisht/ adj **1** accepted as true

or valid **2** successful and recognized publicly as such

establishment /i stábblishmənt/ n **1** the act of establishing something **2** something established as a business, institution, or undertaking **3** *also* **Establishment** the people in power in a society —**establishmentarian** /i stábblishmən táiri ən/ n

estate /i stáyt/ n **1** a piece of privately owned rural land with a large house on it **2** a commercial or industrial area **3** all of somebody's property, especially that of a dead person **4** an estate car **5** somebody's overall situation **6** a sector of society, traditionally the clergy, the nobility, or the middle class **7** any of the three divisions of parliament, the Lords Temporal, the Lords Spiritual, and the Commons **8** any of the three sectors of constitutional government, the Crown, the Lords, and the Commons **9** a plantation

estate agent n **1** somebody who sells houses for clients **2** a manager of landed property —**estate agency** n

estate car n *UK* a large car with extra carrying space

esteem /i steém/ vt **1** value highly **2** regard in a particular way ■ n **1** high regard **2** estimation of worth ◊ See note at **regard**

ester /éstər/ n a compound produced by an acid reacting with an alcohol

esthetic, esthetics etc *US* = aesthetic etc

estimable /éstiməb'l/ adj admirable

estimate vt /ésti mayt/ (**-mating**, **-mated**) **1** calculate roughly **2** assess the cost of and submit a price ■ n /ésti mət/ **1** a rough calculation **2** an approximate price —**estimation** /ésti máysh'n/ n —**estimator** n

Estonia /e stóni ə/ country in NE Europe on the Gulf of Finland that gained its independence from the former Soviet Union in 1991. Cap. Tallinn. Pop. 1,423,316 (2001). —**Estonian** n, adj

estranged /i stráynjd/ adj separated from a spouse —**estrangement** n

estrogen n *US* = oestrogen

estuary /éstyŏori/ (*pl* **-ies**) n the wide lower section of a river where it meets the sea —**estuarial** /éstyŏŏ áiri əl/ adj

-et *suffix* **1** small one o *islet* **2** something worn on o *anklet*

eta /eétə/ n the 7th letter of the Greek alphabet

ETA[1] *abbr* estimated time of arrival

ETA[2] /éttə/, **Eta** n a Basque nationalist guerrilla group

e-tail /ee tayl/ n Internet retail —**e-tailer** n —**e-tailing** n

et al.[1] /et ál/ and others *(of joint authors of a book or article)*

ORIGIN This is an abbreviation of Latin *et alii*.

et al.[2] /et ál/ and elsewhere

ORIGIN This is an abbreviation of Latin *et alibi*.

etc. *abbr* et cetera

et cetera /it séttərə/, **etcetera** *adv* and so on ■ *n* something or somebody unspecified

etch *v* **1** *vti* cut a design into a surface or printing plate with acid, a sharp tool, or a laser beam **2** *vt* make something clearly visible —**etcher** *n*

etching /éching/ *n* **1** a print made from an etched plate **2** the art of making etched designs

eternal /i túrn'l/ *adj* **1** existing through all time **2** unchanging ○ *eternal truths* **3** seemingly everlasting *(infml)* ○ *an eternal student* ■ *n* **Eternal** God —**eternally** *adv*

eternal triangle *n* a sexual or romantic relationship among three persons that involves emotional conflicts

eternity /i túrnəti/ *n* **1** infinite time **2** a timeless state conceived as being experienced after death **3** a very long time *(infml)* ○ *took an eternity*

ethanol /éethənol, éthə-/ *n* the alcohol in alcoholic beverages, also used as a solvent and in the manufacture of other chemicals

Ethelred II /éth'l red/ (968–1016) king of the English (978–1016)

ether /éethər/ *n* **1** a colourless liquid with a pleasant smell. Use: solvent. **2** *also* **aether** the sky or the air *(literary)*

ethereal /i théeri əl/ *adj* **1** very delicate or highly refined **2** light or insubstantial **3** belonging to the heavens —**ethereally** *adv* —**etherealness** *n*

ethic /éthik/ *n* a set of moral principles ■ *adj* of ethics

ethical /éthik'l/ *adj* **1** conforming to accepted standards of moral behaviour **2** of ethics —**ethically** *adv*

ethics /éthiks/ *n* the study of moral standards and their effect on conduct *(+ sing verb)* ■ *npl* a code of morality *(+ pl verb)*

Ethiopia /éethi ópi ə/ landlocked country in NE Africa. Cap. Addis Ababa. Pop. 65,891,874 (2001). —**Ethiopian** *adj, n*

ethnic /éthnik/ *adj* **1** of or classified according to distinctive social characteristics, e.g. of race, culture, or language **2** belonging to a particular social group, especially a minority group ○ *ethnic Albanians* **3** of non-Western cultures ○ *ethnic clothing* ■ *n* US, Can a member of an ethnic minority —**ethnically** *adv*

ethnic cleansing *n* the violent elimination of an ethnic group

ethnicity /eth níssəti/ *(pl* -**ties***)* *n* ethnic affiliation or distinctiveness

ethnic minority *n* an ethnic group that is a minority population in a country

ethnography /eth nóggrəfi/ *n* the description of ethnic groups —**ethnographer** *n* —**ethnographic** /éthnə gráffik/ *adj*

ethnology /eth nóllaji/ *n* **1** the study of ethnic groups **2** the scientific study of human cultures —**ethnologist** *n*

ethos /ée thoss/ *n* the distinctive character of a group or period of time

etiolated /éeti ə laytid/ *adj* describes a plant that is pale and spindly from having been grown in poor light conditions —**etiolation** /éeti ə láysh'n/ *n*

etiology *n* = aetiology

etiquette /étti ket/ *n* the rules of acceptable behaviour

> **ORIGIN Etiquette** is adopted from a French word that originally and literally meant 'ticket'. *Ticket* is, in fact, an earlier adoption of the same word. The transfer to 'rules of behaviour' seems to have derived from a custom of writing details of the formalities of court on small pieces of card for reference.

Etna, Mt /étnə/ volcano in E Sicily, Italy. Height 3,323 m/10,902 ft.

Etruria /e tróori ə/ ancient region on the coast of NW Italy, where the Etruscan civilization flourished in the 1st millennium BC —**Etrurian** *n, adj*

Etruscan /i trúskən/ *n* a member of an ancient people who lived in Etruria —**Etruscan** *adj*

-ette *suffix* **1** small ○ *diskette* **2** female ○ *suffragette* ○ *usherette* **3** imitation ○ *leatherette*

étude /áy tyood/ *n* a short musical composition for a solo instrument intended to develop technique or display skill

etymology /étti móllaji/ *(pl* -**gies***)* *n* **1** the study of word origins **2** the history of a word —**etymological** /éttimə lójjik'l/ *adj* —**etymologically** *adv* —**etymologist** *n*

> **ORIGIN Etymology** derives ultimately from a Greek word meaning 'real', and so means etymologically 'the study of the real meanings of words'. Its scope was later extended to include establishing the root word from which another word derives.

eu *abbr* Europe *(in Internet addresses)*

Eu *symbol* europium

EU *abbr* European Union

eucalyptus /yóokə líptəss/ *(pl* -**tuses** *or* -**ti** /-tī/*)*, **eucalypt** /yóokə lipt/ *n* an Australian evergreen tree with aromatic leaves

Eucharist /yóokərist/ *n* **1** the Christian ceremony of communion **2** the bread and wine used during Communion —**Eucharistic** /yóokə rístik/ *adj*

> **ORIGIN Eucharist** came through French and ecclesiastical Latin from a Greek word that meant 'giving of thanks', and earlier 'gratitude'.

euchre /yóokər/ *n* **1** a card game played with the highest 32 cards **2** an instance of preventing an opponent from taking tricks in euchre ■ *vt* (-**chring**, -**chred**) **1** prevent an opponent from taking tricks in euchre **2** ANZ, US, Can trick somebody

Euclid /yóoklid/ *(fl* 300 BC) Greek mathematician

eugenics /yoo jénniks/ *n* selective breeding as a proposed method of human improvement

(+ sing verb) —**eugenic** *adj* —**eugenically** *adv* —**eugenicist** /yoo jénnissist/ *n*

Eugénie /yoo jeéni, ŏ zhay neé/ (1826–1920) Spanish-born empress of France (1853–71)

eulogize /yoólə jīz/ (**-gizing, -gized**), **eulogise** *vti* praise somebody or something highly —**eulogizer** *n*

eulogy /yoóləji/ (*pl* **-gies**) *n* **1** a spoken or written tribute **2** high praise *(fml)* —**eulogist** *n*

Eumenides /yoo ménni deez/ *n* in Greek mythology, three fertility goddesses later identified with the Furies

eunuch /yoónək/ *n* a castrated human male

> **ORIGIN Eunuch** derives from a Greek word meaning literally 'keeper of the bed'. Because men attendants in the harems of Eastern courts were formerly castrated, the concept of castration became a dominant and then essential part of the meaning of the word.

euphemism /yoófəmizəm/ *n* **1** a less offensive synonym **2** the use of inoffensive words —**euphemistic** /yoófə místik/ *adj* —**euphemistically** *adv*

euphonious /yoo fṓni əss/ *adj* **1** pleasant-sounding **2** made easier to pronounce by a change in speech sounds —**euphoniously** *adv* —**euphony** /yoófəni/ *n*

euphonium /yoo fṓni əm/ *n* a brass-band instrument like a small tuba

euphoria /yoo fáwri ə/ *n* extreme happiness —**euphoric** /yoo fórrik/ *adj* —**euphorically** *adv*

Euphrates /yoo fráy teez/ river in SW Asia, rising in Turkey and flowing through Syria and Iraq before joining the River Tigris near the Persian Gulf. Length 2,700 km / 1,700 mi.

Eurasia /yoor áyshə, -áyzhə/ *n* the land mass consisting of the continents of Europe and Asia

Eurasian /yoor áyzh'n, -áysh'n/ *adj* of Europe and Asia ■ *n* **1** formerly, somebody with a European and an Asian parent **2** an offensive term for somebody with a white American and a Southeast Asian parent

eureka /yoo reékə/ *interj* expresses triumph

> **ORIGIN Eureka** comes from a Greek word meaning literally 'I have found'. It is the exclamation traditionally said to have been uttered by the Greek mathematician Archimedes when he discovered the principle of water displacement that provided a method for establishing the purity of gold.

Euripides /yoo ríppi deez/ (480?–406? BC) Greek dramatist

euro[1] /yoórō/ (*pl* **-ros** or same) *n* the currency unit of the European Union, which in 2002 replaced local currency in some member states

euro[2] /yoórō/ (*pl* **-ros** or same) *n* Aus a wallaroo

Euro- *prefix* Europe, European ○ *Eurodollar*

eurocent /yoórō sent/ *n* the cent used in the European Union

Eurocentric /yoórō séntrik/ *adj* focusing on Europe, often in a way that is arrogantly dismissive of other cultures *(disapproving)* —**Eurocentrism** *n*

Eurocrat /yoórə krat/, **eurocrat** *n* a bureaucrat in the European Union

Euro-MP *n* a member of the European Parliament

Europa /yoo rṓpə/ *n* in Greek mythology, a Phoenician princess abducted by Zeus

Europe /yoórəp/ the second smallest continent after Australia, lying west of Asia, north of Africa, and east of the Atlantic Ocean. Pop. 725,962,762 (2000).

European /yoórə peé ən/ *adj* **1** of Europe **2** of the European Union ■ *n* **1** somebody from Europe **2** an advocate of European union

European Commission *n* an executive arm of the European Union

European Union *n* an economic and political alliance of 15 European nations

europium /yoo rṓpi əm/ *n* (*symbol* **Eu**) a soft silvery-white metallic element. Use: lasers.

Eurosceptic /yoórō skeptik/ *n* a British politician opposed to closer links between the United Kingdom and mainland Europe —**Euroscepticism** /yoórō sképtisizəm/ *n*

Eurovision song contest /yoórō vizh'n-/ *n* an annual televised song competition

Eurozone /yoórō zōn/ *n* the geographic area comprising the European Union countries using the euro as a monetary unit

Eurydice /yoo ríddissi/ *n* in Greek mythology, the wife of Orpheus

Eustachian tube /yoo stáysh'n-/ *n* a passage in the ear that equalizes air pressure on both sides of the eardrum

> **ORIGIN** The passage is named after the Italian anatomist Bartolomeo Eustachio (1520–74), who was known for his descriptions of the human ear and heart.

euthanasia /yoóthə náyzi ə, -náyzhə/ *n* the painless killing of somebody to relieve suffering

evacuate /i vákyoo ayt/ (**-ating, -ated**) *v* **1** *vt* make everyone leave a place **2** *vti* empty the bowels or bladder *(technical)* **3** *vt* empty something *(fml)* —**evacuation** /i vákyoo ásh'n/ *n*

evacuee /i vákyoo eè/ *n* somebody moved to a safer place to live

evade /i váyd/ (**evading, evaded**) *vt* **1** escape or avoid somebody or something cleverly **2** avoid something difficult or unpleasant **3** be difficult for somebody to find or achieve *(fml)* ○ *Success evaded him.* —**evader** *n*

evaluate /i vállyoo ayt/ (**-ating, -ated**) *vt* **1** examine and judge the value or importance of something **2** put a value on an item —**evaluation** /i vállyoo áysh'n/ *n* —**evaluative** *adj* —**evaluator** *n*

evanescent /évvə néss'nt/ *adj* disappearing after only a short time —**evanescence** *n*

evangelical /eè van jéllik'l/ *adj* **1** *also* **Evangelical** of a Protestant denomination whose followers believe in the authority of the

Bible **2** with strong beliefs and enthusiastic about encouraging people to share them ■ *n also* **Evangelical** a member of an evangelical Christian church

evangelism /i vánjəlizəm/ *n* **1** the spreading of Christianity **2** enthusiastic promotion of a cause

evangelist /i vánjəlist/ *n* **1** a Christian who tries to convert people to Christianity **2** *also* **Evangelist** any of the writers of the Christian Gospels —**evangelistic** /i vánjə lístik/ *adj*

evangelize /i vánjə līz/ (**-izing, -ized**), **evangelise** *vti* **1** try to convert people to Christianity **2** be an enthusiastic advocate for a cause —**evangelization** /i vánjə līz záysh'n/ *n*

Evans /évv'nz/, **Sir Arthur John** (1851–1941) British archaeologist

Evans, Dame Edith (1888–1976) British actor

evaporate /i váppə rayt/ (**-rating, -rated**) *v* **1** *vti* change liquid to vapour by heating, or be changed to vapour in this way **2** *vi* disappear gradually —**evaporation** /i váppə ráysh'n/ *n*

evaporated milk *n* concentrated milk thickened by heating

evasion /i váyzh'n/ *n* **1** the avoidance of something **2** an act of avoiding a question or an issue by giving an indirect answer

evasive /i váyssiv/ *adj* **1** avoiding a question or an issue **2** intended to avoid trouble o *took evasive action* —**evasively** *adv* —**evasiveness** *n*

eve /eev/ *n* **1** the period immediately before an event **2** *also* **Eve** the day, evening, or night before a religious festival or public holiday

Eve /eev/ *n* in the Bible, the first woman

Evelyn /eevlin/, **John** (1620–1706) English writer and government official

even[1] /eev'n/ *adj* **1** not sloping, rough, or irregular **2** at the same height **3** aligned **4** not changing or fluctuating **5** the same throughout **6** equal in amount, number, or extent **7** well-balanced **8** exactly divisible by two o with an even number o *the even pages* **10** calm and steady ■ *vti* make or become level or equal —**evenly** *adv* —**evenness** *n* ◇ **get even** take revenge

even[2] /eev'n/ *n* evening (*literary*)

even[3] /eev'n/ *adv* **1** so much as **2** to a greater extent ◇ **even so** regardless of anything else

evenhanded /eev'n hándid/ *adj* fair and impartial —**evenhandedly** *adv* —**evenhandedness** *n*

evening /eevning/ *n* **1** the part of the day from late afternoon to early night **2** *regional* an afternoon

evening class *n* an education session held in the evening

evening dress *n* **1** formal clothing **2** a woman's formal dress

evening star *n* a planet seen in the west at sunset

even money *n* betting odds in which the winnings are the same as the stakes ■ *adj* as likely as not

evens /eev'nz/ *adj, adv* with an equal chance of winning or losing a bet

event /i vént/ *n* **1** an important incident **2** an organized occasion **3** an individual sporting contest ■ *vi* compete in eventing

even-tempered *adj* not easily angered or upset —**even-temperedly** *adv* —**even-temperedness** *n*

eventful /i véntf'l/ *adj* **1** interesting or exciting **2** having a major effect on somebody's life —**eventfully** *adv*

eventide /eev'n tīd/ *n* an evening (*literary*)

eventing /i vénting/ *n* a horse-riding competition that includes dressage, cross-country riding, and show jumping

eventual /i vénchoo əl/ *adj* happening at some, usually relatively distant, point in the future —**eventually** *adv*

eventuality /i vénchoo álləti/ (*pl* **-ties**) *n* a possibility that may happen

eventuate /i vénchoo ayt/ (**-ating, -ated**) *vi* happen as a final result (*fml*)

ever /évvər/ *adv* **1** at any time **2** indicates surprise o *How ever did she do it?* **3** increasingly (*fml*) **4** adds emphasis (*infml*) o *ever so handsome*

Mt Everest: western shoulder of the mountain

Everest, Mt /évvərist/ mountain in the Himalaya range on the border between Nepal and China. It is the highest mountain in the world. Height 8,850 m/29,035 ft.

Everglades /évvər glaydz/ subtropical swamp covering much of S Florida

evergreen /évvər green/ *adj* with leaves throughout the year ■ *n* an evergreen tree

everlasting /évvər laásting/ *adj* **1** lasting forever **2** lasting a long time ■ *n* infinity —**everlastingly** *adv*

evermore /évvər máwr/ *adv* forever (*literary*)

every /évvri/ *det* **1** each member of a group, without exception o *Every life is precious.* **2** the utmost o *every intention of succeeding* **3** each, occurring intermittently or proportionately o *meet every two weeks* ◇ **every other** each alternate thing, person, or occasion

everyday /évvree day/ *adj* **1** ordinary and unremarkable **2** happening or done each day

Everyman /évvri man/, **everyman** *n* an ordinary person

everyone /évvri wun/, **everybody** /-bodi/ *pron* every person

everything /évvri thing/ *pron* **1** all things

2 something all-important ○ *Family is everything.*

everywhere /évvri wair/ *adv* in all places

evict /i víkt/ *vt* **1** eject a tenant from a property by legal means **2** throw somebody out of a place —**evictee** /i vík tee/ *n* —**eviction** *n*

evidence /évvidənss/ *n* **1** something that is a sign or proof of the existence or truth of something **2** objects or information considered in relation to proof of guilt ■ *vt* (-**dencing, -denced**) demonstrate or prove

evident /évvidənt/ *adj* clear or obvious —**evidently** *adv*

evil /eev'l/ *adj* **1** morally bad or wrong **2** deliberately causing harm or misfortune ■ *n* **1** *also* **Évil** the force regarded as causing harmful or unpleasant effects **2** something unpleasant or morally wrong ○ *the social evil of alcoholism* —**evilly** *adv* —**evilness** *n*

evildoer /eev'l doo ər, eev'l doŏ ər/ *n* somebody who does something evil —**evildoing** *n*

evil eye *n* **1** a look of strong dislike **2** a supposed harmful magical power

evince /i vínss/ (**evincing, evinced**) *vt* **1** show clearly **2** reveal by action or implication —**evincible** *adj*

eviscerate /i víssə rayt/ (-**ating, -ated**) *vt* **1** disembowel a person or animal **2** remove the important part of something —**evisceration** /i víssə ráysh'n/ *n*

Evita /i veétə/ ♦ **Perón, Eva**

evocative /i vókətiv/ *adj* prompting vivid memories or images, often of the past —**evocatively** *adv* —**evocativeness** *n*

evoke /i vók/ (**evoking, evoked**) *vt* **1** bring something to mind, often from the past **2** cause a particular reaction or feeling —**evocation** /eevō káysh'n, évvō-/ *n*

evolution /eevə loósh'n, évvə-/ *n* **1** the theoretical process by which living things develop from earlier forms **2** any developmental process —**evolutional** *adj* —**evolutionary** *adj*

evolve /i vólv/ (**evolving, evolved**) *vti* **1** develop or cause to develop gradually **2** develop or cause to develop via evolutionary change —**evolvement** *n*

every incorrect spelling of **every**

ewe /yoo/ *n* a female sheep

ewer /yoŏ ər/ *n* a large jug with a wide spout

ex[1] *n* a former spouse (*infml*)

ex[2] *prep* **1** excluding ○ *ex dividend* **2** sold from ○ *ex works*

ex- *prefix* **1** out, outside, away ○ *exclude* **2** former ○ *ex-husband*

exacerbate /ig zássər bayt/ (-**bating, -bated**) *vt* make worse —**exacerbation** /ig zássər báysh'n/ *n*

exact /ig zákt/ *adj* **1** correct in all details **2** precise and not allowing for variation ○ *the exact amount* **3** emphasizes the significance of the thing being referred to ○ *on this the exact spot* **4** rigorous and thorough ○ *an exact argument* ■ *vt* **1** demand and obtain **2** inflict as suffering (*fml*) —**exactness** *n*

exacting /ig zákting/ *adj* **1** insisting on hard work **2** requiring attention to detail —**exactingly** *adv*

exactitude /ig zákti tyood/ *n* precision and accuracy

exactly /ig záktli/ *adv* **1** no more or less ○ *exactly two miles away* **2** in all details, or to the greatest degree ○ *did exactly as he was told* **3** expresses agreement

exagerate incorrect spelling of **exaggerate**

exaggerate /ig zájjə rayt/ (-**ating, -ated**) *v* **1** overstate something **2** *vt* make something more extreme or noticeable —**exaggeratedly** *adv* —**exaggeration** /ig zájjə ráysh'n/ *n*

exalt /ig záwlt, -zólt/ *vt* (*fml*) **1** promote in rank or status **2** praise highly —**exaltation** /ég zawl táysh'n, ég zol-/ *n*

exalted /ig záwltid, -zóltid/ *adj* (*fml*) **1** high in rank or status **2** noble in character —**exaltedly** *adv* —**exaltedness** *n*

exam /ig zám/ *n* **1** a test of knowledge or ability **2** *US* a medical examination

examination /ig zámmi náysh'n/ *n* **1** the process of looking at something and considering it carefully **2** a test of knowledge or ability **3** a medical inspection of a patient

examine /ig zámmin/ (-**ining, -ined**) *vt* **1** inspect something in detail **2** analyse something to understand or expose it ○ *examine your conscience* **3** test the knowledge or ability of somebody **4** inspect the condition of a patient —**examinable** *adj* —**examinee** /ig zámmi neé/ *n* —**examiner** *n*

exam paper, examination paper *n* a set of questions for students to answer

example /ig zaámp'l/ *n* **1** something that is representative because it has typical qualities **2** somebody or something that serves as a model to be copied **3** an illustration that provides evidence ○ *several examples of mismanagement*

exasperate /ig záspə rayt, -zaáspə-/ (-**ating, -ated**) *vt* make frustrated or annoyed —**exasperatedly** *adv* —**exasperating** *adj* —**exasperation** /ig záspə ráysh'n, -zaáspə-/ *n* ▷ See note at **annoy**

exaust incorrect spelling of **exhaust**

Excalibur /ek skállibər/ *n* King Arthur's sword

excavate /ékskə vayt/ (-**vating, -vated**) *v* **1** *vti* remove earth by digging **2** *vt* form a shape or hole by digging or hollowing **3** *vti* dig a site for artefacts **4** *vti* uncover something with difficulty

excavation /ékskə váysh'n/ *n* **1** the process of digging **2** a site where digging is taking place

excavator /ékskə vaytər/ *n* **1** a mechanical digger **2** a person or animal that excavates something

exceede incorrect spelling of **exceed**

exceed /ik seéd/ *vt* **1** be greater than something **2** go beyond limits ▷ See note at **accede**

exceeding /ik seéding/ *adj* very great (*literary*)

exceedingly /ik seédingli/ *adv* extremely

excel /ik sél/ (-**celling**, -**celled**) v 1 vti do better than before or than expected 2 vi be very good

excellence /éksələnss/ n the quality of being outstandingly good

Excellency /éksələnssi/ (pl -**cies**), **Excellence** /-lənss/ n a term of address for some high officials

excellent /éksələnt/ adj outstandingly good ■ interj agreed —**excellently** adv

except /ik sépt/ prep other than ○ every house except ours ■ conj but not or other than ○ He dislikes the game except when he wins. ■ vt exclude (fml) ◇ **except for** apart from

excepted /ik séptid/ adj excluded as an exception ○ present company excepted

excepting /ik sépting/ prep, conj except for (fml)

exception /ik sépsh'n/ n somebody or something excluded from or not fitting into a general pattern

exceptionable /ik sépsh'nəb'l/ adj open to objection (fml)

exceptional /ik sépsh'nəl/ adj 1 unusual 2 outstanding —**exceptionally** adv

excerpt n /éks urpt/ an extracted section or passage of a longer work ■ vt /ek súrpt/ take a section or passage from a longer work

excess n /ik séss, éks ess/ 1 an amount beyond what is required 2 behaviour that goes beyond what is socially or morally acceptable 3 UK, Carib a fixed amount of money that a policy-holder must pay towards an insurance claim ■ adj /éks ess, ek séss/ more than what is required or wanted ◊ See note at **access**

excessive /ik séssiv/ adj more than is considered usual, sufficient, or healthy —**excessively** adv —**excessiveness** n

exchange /iks cháynj/ vt (-**changing**, -**changed**) 1 give something and get something else in return ○ exchange land for peace 2 give or do something and receive the same in return ○ exchange glances 3 replace something ○ exchanged the coat for a smaller size ■ n 1 the process of an instance of giving and receiving 2 a short conversation or argument 3 something given or received 4 an arrangement between families, schools, or organizations to visit each other's country 5 a building used for trading in commodities, securities, or other assets 6 a centre with equipment for interconnecting telephone lines 7 the transferring of money between two currencies 8 a system of payments in which commercial documents are used instead of money —**exchangeable** adj

exchange rate n the value of one currency if exchanged for another

Exchange Rate Mechanism n a former system controlling the exchange rate between some countries in the European Union

exchequer /iks chékər/, **Exchequer** n 1 the treasury of a government or organization 2 a government's assets

ORIGIN Exchequer came via French from a Latin word meaning 'chessboard', and this is in fact the earliest sense in English. The connection with revenue derives from the practice of making calculations using counters on a chequered cloth. The word then came to apply to the department of state for collecting revenues set up by the Norman kings in England. In other senses, **exchequer** was shortened to chequer, and chequer was shortened to check.

excise[1] /ék sīz/ a tax on goods manufactured or sold within a country ■ vt /ik síz/ (-**cising**, -**cised**) impose a tax on

excise[2] /ik síz/ (-**cising**, -**cised**) vt 1 delete (fml) 2 remove surgically —**excision** /ik sízh'n/ n

excitable /ik sítəb'l/ adj easily excited —**excitability** /ik sítə billəti/ n —**excitableness** n —**excitably** adv

excite /ik sít/ (-**citing**, -**cited**) vt 1 cause somebody to feel enjoyment or pleasurable anticipation 2 put somebody in an unpleasant state of heightened emotion 3 arouse a particular emotion 4 evoke a thought 5 arouse somebody sexually —**excited** adj —**excitedly** adv —**exciting** adj —**excitingly** adv

excitement /ik sítmənt/ n 1 the state of being excited 2 an exciting event 3 the act of stimulating something

exclaim /ik skláym/ vti say something loudly and suddenly

exclaimation incorrect spelling of **exclamation**

exclamation /éksklə máysh'n/ n 1 a word, phrase, or sentence that is suddenly shouted out 2 the act of exclaiming —**exclamational** adj

exclamation mark n a punctuation mark (!) used for exclamations

exclude /ik sklood/ (-**cluding**, -**cluded**) vt 1 keep somebody or something from entering or participating 2 not consider something 3 omit something 4 ban a schoolchild on disciplinary grounds

exclusion /ik skloozh'n/ n 1 the act of excluding somebody or something 2 the fact of being excluded —**exclusionary** adj

exclusion zone n an area that is out of bounds

exclusive /ik skloossiv/ adj 1 high-class ○ an exclusive nightclub 2 restricted in use or access ○ exclusive use of the pool 3 published or broadcast in only one place ○ exclusive coverage 4 confined to one thing ■ n a report printed in only one publication or broadcast in only one programme —**exclusively** adv —**exclusiveness** n

excommunicate vt /ékskə myooni kayt/ (-**cating**, -**cated**) exclude somebody from the Christian community because of doctrinal differences or for morally offensive behaviour ■ adj /ékskə myooonikət, -kayt/ excommunicated ■ n /ékskə myooonikət, -kayt/ an excommunicated person —**excommunication** /ékskə myooóni káysh'n/ n

excoriate /ik skáwri ayt, -skórri-/ (-**ating**, -**ated**) vt (fml) 1 criticize very strongly 2 tear the skin off —**excoriation** /ik skáwri áysh'n, -skórri-/ n

excrement /ékskrimənt/ n waste material expelled from the body (technical) —**excremental** /ékskri mént'l/ adj

excrescence /ik skréss'nss/ n 1 an outgrowth, especially an unusual or undesirable one 2 an unsightly addition

excreta /ik skreeta/ npl waste matter expelled from the body (technical) —**excretal** adj

excrete /ik skreet/ (-creting, -creted) vt 1 expel waste from the body (fml) 2 eliminate waste from leaves and roots —**excretion** n —**excretory** adj

excruciating /ik skrooshi ayting/ adj 1 extremely painful 2 hard to bear —**excruciatingly** adv

exculpate /éks kul payt, iks kúl payt/ (-pating, -pated) vt prove somebody innocent (fml) —**exculpation** /éks kul páysh'n/ n

excursion /ik skúrsh'n, -skúrzh'n/ n 1 a short trip to a place and back 2 a group on an excursion

excuse vt /ik skyooz/ (-cusing, -cused) 1 forgive for a mistake or wrongdoing 2 make allowances for 3 release from an obligation 4 provide justification for 5 allow to leave ■ n /ik skyooss/ 1 a justification 2 a false reason 3 a bad example (infml) —**excusable** adj —**excusably** adv

exe abbr a file extension indicating a program file. Full form **executable**

exec /ig zék/ n an executive (infml)

execrable /éksikrəb'l/ adj 1 very bad 2 detestable —**execrably** adv

execrate /éksi krayt/ (-crating, -crated) vt (literary or fml) 1 feel loathing for 2 criticize severely —**execration** /éksi kráysh'n/ n

executable /éksi kyootəb'l/ adj able to run as a computer program —**executable** n

execute /éksi kyoot/ (-cuting, -cuted) v 1 vt carry out an instruction or plan 2 vt perform an action or movement 3 vt create something ○ execute a drawing 4 vt kill somebody, especially as a punishment for a crime. 5 vti run a computer file or program 6 vt sign a legal document before witnesses 7 vt carry out the terms of a legal document —**executer** n —**execution** /éksi kyoósh'n/ n ◊ See note at **kill, perform**

executioner /éksi kyoósh'nər/ n 1 the official who carries out the execution of a criminal 2 an assassin

executive /ig zékyoŏtiv/ n 1 a senior manager 2 the section of a government responsible for implementing laws ■ adj 1 of policymaking 2 for businesspeople 3 very expensive ○ executive homes

executor /ig zékyoŏtər/ n 1 somebody implementing the terms of a will 2 somebody who carries something out

exegesis /éksi jeéssiss/ (pl -ses /-seez/) n the analysis or interpretation of texts, especially biblical texts —**exegetic** adj

exellent incorrect spelling of **excellent**

exemplar /ig zém plaar, -plər/ n an ideal example worth copying or imitating (literary)

exemplary /ig zémpləri/ adj setting a good example —**exemplarily** adv

exemplify /ig zémpli fi/ (-fies, -fied) vt 1 show something by being an example of it 2 give an example of something —**exemplification** /ig zémplifi káysh'n/ n

exempt /ig zémpt/ adj not subject to something that others have to do or pay ■ vt 1 free somebody from an obligation 2 release something from a rule that applies to others —**exemptible** adj

exemption /ig zémpsh'n/ n 1 freedom from an obligation 2 an exempt person or thing

exept incorrect spelling of **except**

exercise /éksər sīz/ n 1 physical activity designed to keep you fit 2 a series of physical movements designed to keep you fit (often pl) 3 the practising of a skill or procedure (often pl) 4 a piece of work intended as a test 5 a set of military training operations or manoeuvres 6 an activity intended to achieve a particular purpose 7 the carrying out or using of something (fml) ■ v (-cising, -cised) 1 vi take exercise in order to stay fit 2 vt subject a person, a part of the body, or an animal to physical exertion 3 vt put something to practical use 4 vt show a particular type of behaviour ○ exercise caution 5 vt occupy or worry somebody (fml) ○ The problem has exercised me greatly. —**exercisable** adj

exercize incorrect spelling of **exercise**

exerpt incorrect spelling of **excerpt**

exert /ig zúrt/ v 1 vt bring influence, pressure, or authority to bear on a situation 2 vr make an effort —**exertion** n

exeunt /éksi unt, -ay ənt/ vi exit from the stage together (as a stage direction)

exfoliate /eks fóli ayt/ (-ating, -ated) v 1 vt remove a thin outer layer from something, or shed such a layer 2 vti scrub the skin to remove the dead outer layer —**exfoliation** /eks fóli áysh'n/ n —**exfoliative** adj

ex gratia /eks gráysha/ adj, adv given voluntarily

exhale /eks háyl, eg záyl/ (-haling, -haled) v 1 vti breathe out 2 vt give off a smell or vapour (literary) —**exhalation** /éks hə láysh'n/ n

exhaust /ig záwst/ vt 1 tire somebody out 2 use something up 3 try out all possibilities 4 say everything there is to say about something ■ n 1 a discharge of waste gases 2 an escape system for waste gases —**exhausted** adj —**exhaustedly** adv —**exhaustible** adj —**exhaustion** n

exhaustive /ig záwstiv/ adj complete and detailed —**exhaustively** adv —**exhaustiveness** n

exhibit /ig zíbbit/ v 1 vti display works of art 2 vt show something to others 3 vt show signs of something (fml) ○ beginning to exhibit signs of metal fatigue ■ n 1 an object on display 2 a piece of evidence shown in court

exhibition /éksi bísh'n/ n 1 a public display of works of art 2 a demonstration of a skill

3 a display of a particular type of behaviour ◇ **make an exhibition of yourself** behave embarrassingly in public and attract attention to yourself

exhibitionism /éksi bísh'nizəm/ *n* **1** attention-seeking behaviour **2** the psychological disorder that prompts somebody to expose their genitals in public —**exhibitionist** *n*

exhilarate /ig zíllə rayt/ (-**rating**, -**rated**) *vt* make somebody feel happy and alive —**exhilarating** *adj* —**exhilaratingly** *adv* —**exhilaration** /ig zíllə ráysh'n/ *n*

exhilerating incorrect spelling of **exhilarating**

exhileration incorrect spelling of **exhilaration**

exhort /ig záwrt/ *v* (*fml*) **1** *vt* urge strongly to do something **2** *vi* give somebody earnest advice —**exhortation** /égz awr táysh'n/ *n* —**exhortative** /ig záwrtətiv/ *adj*

exhume /eks hyoóm, ig zyoóm/ (-**huming**, -**humed**) *vt* **1** dig up a body from a grave **2** re-introduce something neglected or forgotten —**exhumation** /éks hyoo máysh'n, ég zyoo-/ *n*

exibition incorrect spelling of **exhibition**

exigency /éksijənssi, ig zíjjənssi/ (*pl* -**cies**), **exigence** /éksijənss/ *n* (*fml*) **1** an urgent need (*often pl*) **2** something needing immediate action —**exigent** *adj*

exiguous /ig zíggyoo əss, ik sígg-/ *adj* meagre (*fml*) —**exiguity** /éksi gyóō əti/ *n*

exile /égz īl, éks-/ *n* **1** unwilling absence from your own country, whether enforced by a government or made necessary by the political situation **2** somebody living unwillingly outside his or her own country ■ *vt* (-**iling**, -**iled**) banish somebody from his or her region or country —**exilic** /eg zíllik, ek síllik/ *adj*

exist /ig zíst/ *vi* **1** be real or actual **2** be able to continue living ◇ *We need food to exist.* **3** occur in a particular place or situation

existance incorrect spelling of **existence**

existence /ig zístənss/ *n* **1** the state of being real or actual **2** presence in a place or situation **3** a way of living, especially a life of hardship

existent /ig zístənt/ *adj* (*fml*) **1** real or actual **2** currently existing or in operation

existential /égzi sténsh'l, éksi-/ *adj* **1** of human existence **2** crucial in shaping individual destiny **3** of existentialism —**existentially** *adv*

existentialism /égzi sténsh'lizəm, éksi-/ *n* a philosophical movement centred on individual free will and personal responsibility and denying any meaning or structure in the universe —**existentialist** *adj, n*

existing /ig zísting/ *adj* currently present, in operation, or available

exit /éksit, égzit/ *n* **1** a door or other means of leaving a room or building **2** a departure from a room, building, or gathering **3** an act of terminating a computer operation ■ *v* **1** *vti* leave a place **2** *vi* go offstage (*refers to actors*) **3** *vti* terminate a computer program

exit poll *n* a survey of people's votes as they leave the voting place

exodus /éksədəss/ *n* **1** a departure by large numbers of people **2 Exodus** in the Bible, the flight of the Israelites from Egypt

ex officio /éks ə físhi ō/ *adv, adj* as a consequence of the holding of a specific official position

exonerate /ig zónnə rayt/ (-**ating**, -**ated**) *vt* **1** free from blame or guilt **2** free from an obligation —**exoneration** /ig zónnə ráysh'n/ *n*

exorbitant /ig záwrbitənt/ *adj* unreasonably high or large —**exorbitance** *n* —**exorbitantly** *adv*

exorcism /éks awrsizəm/ *n* **1** the driving out of evil spirits **2** a ceremony conducted to drive out evil spirits —**exorcist** *n*

exorcize /éks awr síz, éksər-/ (-**cizing**, -**cized**), **exorcise** *vt* **1** use prayers and religious rituals with the intention of freeing a person or place from evil **2** get rid of an oppressive feeling or memory

exoskeleton /éksō skéllitən/ *n* the hard protective covering of many organisms, e.g. crustaceans —**exoskeletal** *adj*

exosphere /éksō sfeer/ *n* the outermost region of the atmosphere —**exospheric** /éksō sférrik/ *adj*

exotic /ig zóttik/ *adj* **1** strikingly different and exciting and suggesting distant countries and cultures **2** introduced from elsewhere ◇ *exotic species* ■ *n* an exotic person or thing —**exotically** *adv* —**exoticness** *n*

exotica /ig zóttikə/ *npl* highly unusual things

exotic dancer *n* a stripper

expand /ik spánd/ *v* **1** *vti* increase in scope, number, or size **2** *vti* open out after being folded **3** *vi* describe something more fully **4** *vt* give the full form of something, e.g. an abbreviation —**expandable** *adj* —**expansible** /ik spánssəb'l/ *adj* ◇ See note at **increase**

expanse /ik spánss/ *n* a wide area or surface

expansion /ik spánsh'n/ *n* **1** the process of becoming enlarged **2** an increase in scope, extent, or size **3** a fuller treatment or form —**expansionary** *adj*

expansionism /ik spánsh'nizəm/ *n* a policy of expanding, especially territorially or economically —**expansionist** *n, adj* —**expansionistic** /ik spánshə nístik/ *adj*

expansive /ik spánssiv/ *adj* **1** talkative **2** covering a wide area, or broad in scope (*fml*) **3** lavish ◇ *an expansive lifestyle* —**expansively** *adv* —**expansiveness** *n*

expat /éks pát/ *n* an expatriate (*infml*)

expatiate /ek spáyshi ayt/ (-**ating**, -**ated**) *vi* speak or write at length —**expatiation** /ek spáyshi áysh'n/ *n*

expatriate *n* /eks páttri ət, -páytri-, -ayt/ somebody who lives abroad ■ *adj* of people living abroad ■ *vi* /eks páttri ayt, -páytri-/ (-**ating**, -**ated**) settle abroad —**expatriation** /éks páttri áysh'n, -páytri-/ *n*

expatriot incorrect spelling of **expatriate**

expect /ik spékt/ v 1 vt confidently believe that something will happen 2 vt wait for an anticipated thing 3 vt demand something as a right or duty 4 vti be pregnant with or look forward to the birth of a baby (infml; only in progressive tenses) —**expectedly** adv —**expectedness** n

expectancy /ik spéktənssi/ (pl -**cies**), **expectance** /ik spéktənss/ n 1 excited anticipation 2 something expected

expectant /ik spéktənt/ adj 1 excitedly anticipating something 2 expecting a baby —**expectantly** adv

expectation /éks pek táysh'n/ n 1 a confident belief or strong hope that something will happen 2 a notion of what something will be like (often pl) 3 an expected standard (often pl) 4 excited anticipation

expectorant /ik spéktərənt/ n a medicine that stimulates the production of phlegm, as a treatment for coughs —**expectorant** adj

expectorate /ik spéktə rayt/ (-**rating**, -**rated**) vti cough up and spit out phlegm —**expectoration** /ik spéktə ráysh'n/ n

ORIGIN Expectorate comes from a Latin verb meaning literally 'get out of the chest'. **Expect** and related words also derive from Latin, but from a verb meaning 'look'. Both words are formed with the prefix ex- 'out'.

expediency /ik speédi ənssi/, **expedience** /-ənss/ n 1 the use of fast and effective but often morally questionable methods 2 appropriateness or usefulness

expedient /ik speédi ənt/ adj 1 appropriate or advisable 2 advantageous for practical rather than moral reasons ■ n something that achieves an aim quickly —**expediently** adv

expedite /ékspə dīt/ (-**diting**, -**dited**) vt (fml) 1 speed up the progress of 2 deal with quickly and efficiently

expedition /ékspə dísh'n/ n 1 an organized journey made by a group for a specific purpose 2 the people making an expedition 3 an outing

expeditious /ékspə díshəss/ adj prompt

expel /ik spél/ (-**pelling**, -**pelled**) vt 1 dismiss from an institution such as a school, political party, or club 2 force out

~~expence~~ incorrect spelling of **expense**

expend /ik spénd/ vt 1 use up time, energy, or another resource 2 spend money (fml)

expendable /ik spéndəb'l/ adj 1 not worth preserving 2 dispensable —**expendable** n

expenditure /ik spéndichər/ n money spent

expense /ik spénss/ n 1 an amount of money spent on something 2 the value of a resource that has been used and that can be charged against revenues ■ **expenses** npl money spent in the pursuit of business

~~expensiv~~ incorrect spelling of **expensive**

expensive /ik spénssiv/ adj 1 costing a lot of money 2 charging a lot of money —**expensively** adv

~~experiance~~ incorrect spelling of **experience**

experience /ik speéri ənss/ n 1 lengthy involvement in something, leading to knowledge and skill 2 knowledge and skill acquired over a period of time 3 something that happens to somebody ■ vt (-**encing**, -**enced**) 1 undergo or be involved in something 2 feel a sensation or emotion

experienced /ik speéri ənst/ adj having knowledge and skill gained from experience

experiential /ik speéri énsh'l/ adj based on experience —**experientially** adv

experiment n /ik spérrimənt/ 1 a scientific test 2 an instance of doing something new o switch to decaffeinated coffee as an experiment ■ vi /ik spérri ment/ 1 try new things 2 carry out a scientific test —**experimentation** /ik spérri men táysh'n/ n

experimental /ik spérri mént'l/ adj 1 using ideas or methods that are new and untried 2 of scientific experiments —**experimentally** adv

expert /éks purt/ n a skilled or knowledgeable person ■ adj 1 skilled or knowledgeable 2 given or done by an expert —**expertly** adv —**expertness** n

expertise /éks pur teéz/ n expert skill or knowledge

expert system n a computer program that solves problems

expiate /ékspi ayt/ (-**ating**, -**ated**) vt atone for wrongdoing —**expiation** /ékspi áysh'n/ n —**expiatory** /ékspi ətəri, ékspi áytəri/ adj

~~expidition~~ incorrect spelling of **expedition**

expire /ik spīr/ (-**piring**, -**pired**) vi 1 come to an end or be no longer valid 2 breathe out (technical) 3 die (fml or literary) —**expiration** /ékspi ráysh'n/ n

expiry /ik spīri/ n the fact of ending or ceasing to be valid

explain /ik spláyn/ v 1 vti give details about something 2 vt clarify the meaning of something —**explainable** adj

~~explaination~~ incorrect spelling of **explanation**

explanation /éksplə náysh'n/ n 1 a statement explaining something 2 the act of giving details or reasons

explanatory /ik splánnətəri/, **explanative** /ik splánnətiv/ adj explaining something

expletive /ik spleétiv/ n a swearword

explicable /ik splíkəb'l, éksplik-/ adj explainable —**explicably** adv

explicate /ékspli kayt/ (-**cating**, -**cated**) vt 1 explain something, especially a text, in a detailed way 2 develop a theory —**explication** /ékspli káysh'n/ n —**explicative** /ik splíkətiv/ adj

explicit /ik splíssit/ adj 1 clear and obvious 2 definite 3 showing or describing sex openly —**explicitly** adv —**explicitness** n

USAGE explicit or **implicit**? **Explicit** means 'clear, obvious, and definite': gave explicit directions. **Implicit** means 'implied or unstated but understood': implicit trust.

explode /ik splṓd/ (**-ploding, -ploded**) v 1 vti burst with a sudden release of energy and a loud noise 2 vti burst or shatter suddenly 3 vi express an emotion suddenly and forcefully 4 vi increase dramatically ○ *The growth rate in home ownership exploded.* 5 vi appear suddenly ○ *a new band that has suddenly exploded onto the scene*

exploded /ik splṓdid/ adj showing the parts of something separately but in their relative positions

exploit vt /ik splóyt/ 1 take advantage of somebody 2 use something in order to gain a benefit ○ *fully exploit natural gas reserves* ■ n /éks ployt/ an exciting or daring act —**exploitable** adj —**exploitation** /éks ploy táysh'n/ n —**exploitative** adj —**exploiter** n

explore /ik spláwr/ (**-ploring, -plored**) vti 1 travel to places for the purpose of discovery 2 investigate or study something 3 search a place for natural resources —**exploration** /éksplə ráysh'n/ n —**exploratory** /ik splórrətəri, -splǻwrə-/ adj —**explorer** n

explosion /ik splṓzh'n/ n 1 a sudden noisy release of energy 2 the bursting or shattering of something 3 a sudden burst of emotion 4 a dramatic increase ○ *an explosion in e-mail subscriptions* 5 the sudden appearance of something

explosive /ik splṓssiv, -splṓz-/ adj 1 liable to explode 2 operated by exploding 3 tending towards violent anger ○ *an explosive temperament* ■ n 1 a substance that can explode (often pl) 2 a bomb —**explosively** adv —**explosiveness** n

expo /ékspṓ/ n a large exhibition or trade fair

exponent /ik spṓnənt/ n 1 a supporter or promoter of a cause 2 a practitioner of an art or skill 3 a number or variable indicating the number of times the number it is attached to is to be multiplied by itself

exponential /ékspə nénsh'l, ékspō-/ adj involving numbers multiplied by themselves 2 using a base of natural logarithms 3 rapidly developing or increasing ○ *an exponential increase in sales* —**exponentially** adv

export v /ik spáwrt, éks pawrt/ 1 vti send goods abroad for sale or exchange 2 vt spread one society's culture to another 3 vt transfer computer data from one program to another ■ n /éks pawrt/ 1 the selling or exchange of goods abroad 2 a product sold or exchanged abroad —**exportation** /éks pawr táysh'n/ n —**exporter** n

expose /ik spṓz/ (**-posing, -posed**) v 1 vt allow something to be seen 2 vt put somebody in an unprotected situation 3 vt make somebody experience something 4 vt reveal somebody's wrongdoings 5 vr reveal the genitals indecently in public 6 vt allow light onto a film

exposé /ek spṓz ay/ (pl **-sés**) n 1 a book or article revealing wrongdoing 2 a declaration of facts

exposed /ik spṓzd/ adj 1 visible or unprotected 2 with no shelter

exposition /ékspə zísh'n/ n 1 a detailed description or discussion 2 the act of describing or discussing something 3 a large exhibition or trade fair —**expositive** /ik spózzitiv/ adj —**expository** /-təri/ adj

expostulate /ik spóstyoō layt/ (**-lating, -lated**) vi express disagreement or disapproval —**expostulation** /ik spóstyoō láysh'n/ n —**expostulatory** adj ◊ See note at **object**

exposure /ik spṓzhər/ n 1 contact with or experience of something 2 the harmful effects of extreme weather conditions 3 publicity 4 the revelation of a scandal or of somebody's identity 5 the amount of time that light is allowed into a camera 6 a single section of film exposed for a photograph 7 the direction a room or building faces ○ *a southern exposure*

expound /ik spównd/ vti describe and explain something —**expounder** n

express /ik spréss/ v 1 vt state thoughts or feelings in words 2 vt show meaning symbolically 3 vr reveal your thoughts or feelings to others ○ *expresses herself through her music* 4 vt represent something as a symbol ○ *Express the fractions as decimal numbers.* 5 vt squeeze something out (fml) 6 vt send something by special fast delivery ■ adj 1 done or travelling very quickly 2 for brief transactions or a few transactions only ○ *use the express checkout* 3 stated clearly ○ *his express wish* 4 specific ○ *formed for the express purpose of making a profit* ■ n 1 a fast train or bus 2 a fast delivery service —**expressible** adj

expression /ik présh'n/ n 1 a look on somebody's face 2 a word or phrase that communicates an idea 3 the conveying of thoughts or feelings 4 a way of communicating something 5 a mathematical representation of numbers or quantities —**expressional** adj

expressionism /ik présh'nizəm/ n 1 an art movement concentrating on expressing feelings and moods rather than objective reality 2 a literary movement presenting stylized reality —**expressionist** n, adj —**expressionistic** /ik présh'n níctik'/ adj

expressionless /ik présh'nləss/ adj showing no emotion

expressive /ik spréssiv/ adj 1 full of feelings and meanings 2 conveying a particular meaning —**expressively** adv —**expressiveness** n

expressly /ik spréssli/ adv 1 specifically 2 unambiguously

expressway /ik spréss way/ n Aus, US, Can a motorway

expropriate /ik spṓpri ayt/ (**-ating, -ated**) vt take away something belonging to another person —**expropriation** /ik spṓpri áysh'n/ n

expulsion /ik spúlsh'n/ n 1 dismissal from a place or from membership of a group 2 the act of forcing somebody or something out —**expulsive** adj

expunge /ik spúnj/ (**-punging, -punged**) vt 1 delete something unwanted 2 put an end to something —**expunction** /ik spúngksh'n/ n

expurgate /ékspər gayt/ (-gating, -gated) vt edit by removing offensive parts —**expurgation** /ékspər gáysh'n/ n

exquisite /ik skwízzit, ékskwizit/ adj 1 beautiful and delicate 2 excellent and delightful 3 sensitive and discriminating —**exquisitely** adv —**exquisiteness** n

ex-service adj 1 formerly in the armed forces 2 of former armed forces personnel

extant /ek stánt, ékstənt/ adj still in existence ◊ See note at **living**

~~extasy~~ incorrect spelling of **ecstasy**

extemporaneous /ik stémpə ráyni əss/, **extemporary** /ik stémpərəri/ adj 1 done unrehearsed 2 prepared but said without notes —**extemporaneity** /ik stémpərə neé əti, -náy əti/ n —**extemporaneously** adv

extempore /ik stémpəri/ adj, adv without rehearsing

extemporize /ik stémpə ríz/ (-rizing, -rized), **temporise** vti 1 perform something without preparation 2 handle something in a makeshift way —**extemporization** /ik stémpə rí záysh'n/ n

extend /ik sténd/ v 1 vi occupy distance or space 2 vi continue for a time 3 vi be applicable to somebody or something ◊ The offer extends to new readers too. 4 vt increase the size or limits of something 5 vt increase a time span 6 vt increase an amount by adding something 7 vt offer or give something —**extendable** adj —**extensible** adj ◊ See note at **increase**

extended /ik sténdid/ adj 1 lasting longer than usual or expected 2 made longer or larger

extended family n a family unit consisting of parents, children, and all other relatives

extension /ik sténsh'n/ n 1 an addition to a building 2 an additional piece 3 an additional telephone line or telephone 4 the telephone number of an additional telephone line 5 also **extension cable, extension lead** an electrical cable with a socket at one end and a plug at the other, used for plugging something into a distant power source 6 an additional period of time 7 an extended drinks licence 8 in computing, a file extension ■ **extensions** npl extra hair attached to somebody's own hair —**extensional** adj

extensive /ik sténssiv/ adj 1 covering a large area 2 broad in scope 3 large in amount —**extensively** adv —**extensiveness** n

extent /ik stént/ n 1 the range or scope of something 2 the size of something

extenuate /ik sténnyoo ayt/ (-ating, -ated) vt diminish the seriousness of —**extenuating** adj —**extenuation** /ik sténnyoo áysh'n/ n

exterior /ik steéri ər/ adj 1 on or for the outside of something 2 coming from outside ◊ an exterior cause ■ n 1 the outside surface, appearance, or coating of something 2 somebody's outward appearance ◊ her calm exterior

exterminate /ik stúrmi nayt/ (-nating, -nated) vt completely kill or destroy —**extermination** /ik stúrmi náysh'n/ n —**exterminator** n

external /ik stúrn'l/ adj 1 situated on, happening on, or coming from the outside ◊ external forces 2 for use on the outside of something 3 conveyed by outward appearance 4 outside an organization ■ n Aus an extramural student ■ **externals** npl outward appearances —**externally** adv

externalize /ik stúrnə líz/ (-izing, -ized), **externalise** vt express feelings in a visible or perceptible way —**externalization** /ik stúrnə lí záysh'n/ n

extinct /ik stíngkt/ adj 1 having no members of a species or family still living 2 no longer in existence ◊ an extinct civilization 3 describes a volcano that no longer erupts —**extinction** n ◊ See note at **dead**

extinguish /ik stíng gwish/ vt 1 put out a fire or light 2 put an end to or destroy somebody or something (literary) —**extinguisher** n

extirpate /ék stur payt/ (-pating, -pated) vt completely remove or destroy something undesirable (fml) —**extirpation** /ék stur páysh'n/ n —**extirpative** adj

extol /ik stól/ (-tolling, -tolled) vt praise enthusiastically (literary) —**extolment** n

extort /ik stáwrt/ vt obtain by force or threats —**extortive** adj

extortion /ik stáwrsh'n/ n 1 the act of obtaining something by force or threats 2 the charging of unfairly high prices (infml) —**extortionate** adj —**extortioner** n

extra /ékstrə/ adj 1 added over and above the usual or necessary amount or number 2 more and better ■ adv exceptionally ■ pron more ■ n 1 something additional 2 an actor with a minor nonspeaking part in a film 3 a special edition of a newspaper 4 in cricket, a run scored without hitting the ball

extra- prefix beyond or outside something ◊ extraterrestrial ◊ extracurricular

extract vt /ik strákt/ 1 pull something out 2 obtain something from a source 3 get something by force 4 copy or remove a passage from a text or film 5 derive pleasure from something 6 obtain a substance by an industrial or chemical process ■ n /ék strakt/ 1 a passage taken from a text or film 2 a purified concentrated substance ◊ vanilla extract —**extractor** n

extraction /ik stráksh'n/ n 1 the process of extracting something 2 the removal of a tooth 3 ethnic origin

extracurricular /ékstrə kə ríkyoŏlər/ adj 1 happening or done outside the normal school curriculum 2 with somebody other than a spouse or partner (infml)

extradite /ékstrə dít/ (-diting, -dited) vt hand over somebody accused of a crime to a different legal authority —**extradition** /ékstrə dísh'n/ n

extrajudicial /ékstrə joo dísh'l/ adj 1 outside normal legal proceedings 2 outside a court's jurisdiction

extramarital /ékstrə márrit'l/ adj outside marriage

extramural /ékstrə myóórəl/ *adj* **1** outside the usual course of study **2** outside the walls or boundaries of a place or organization

extraneous /ik stráyni əss/ *adj* **1** not relevant or essential **2** coming from outside —**extraneously** *adv* —**extraneousness** *n*

extraordinaire /ik stráwdi náir/ *adj* outstanding *(after nouns)* ○ *a piano player extraordinaire*

extraordinary /ik stráwrd'nəri, ékstrə áwrd'nəri/ *adj* **1** unusually excellent or strange **2** additional and having a special purpose —**extraordinarily** *adv* —**extraordinariness** *n*

extrapolate /ik stráppə layt/ (**-lating, -lated**) *vti* infer information from known facts —**extrapolation** /ik stráppə láysh'n/ *n*

extrasensory perception /ékstrə sénssəri-/ *n* an awareness beyond the normal senses

extraterrestrial /ékstrətə réstri əl/ *adj* existing outside the Earth ■ *n* an alien from space

extraterritorial /ékstrə térri táwri əl/ *adj* outside a territorial boundary —**extraterritorially** *adv*

extra time *n* an extra period of play added on to allow a decisive point or goal to be scored

extravagance /ik strávvəgənss/, **extravagancy** /-gənssi/ (*pl* **-cies**) *n* **1** wasteful spending **2** an expensive thing

extravagant /ik strávvəgənt/ *adj* **1** spending too much **2** beyond what is reasonable ○ *an extravagant claim* **3** unreasonably high in price —**extravagantly** *adv* —**extravagantness** *n*

ORIGIN Extravagant derives from a medieval Latin word formed from Latin elements meaning 'outside, beyond' and 'wander'. The second element is also the source of English *vagabond* and *vagrant*. At first **extravagant** meant 'divergent, irrelevant' and 'strange, unsuitable'. The connection with expenditure did not develop until the early 18C.

extravaganza /ik strávvə gánzə/ *n* **1** a lavish entertainment **2** a spectacular display

~~extravagent~~ incorrect spelling of **extravagant**

extravert *n, adj* PSYCHOL = **extrovert**

extreme /ik stréem/ *adj* **1** highest in degree or intensity **2** beyond what is reasonable **3** farthest out **4** very strict or severe **5** describes an activity in which participants seek out dangerous experiences ■ *n* **1** the furthest limit or highest degree **2** somebody or something that represents either of the two ends of a scale ■ **extremes** *npl* drastic measures —**extremeness** *n*

extremely /ik streémli/ *adv* very

extremist /ik streémist/ *n* somebody who holds extreme opinions or supports extreme measures —**extremism** *n* —**extremist** *adj*

extremity /ik strémməti/ (*pl* **-ties**) *n* **1** the farthest point **2** the highest degree or greatest intensity of something **3** a condition of great danger or distress **4** a hand or foot *(often pl)*

~~extremly~~ incorrect spelling of **extremely**

extricate /ékstri kayt/ (**-cating, -cated**) *vt* release with difficulty from a place or situation —**extrication** /ékstri káysh'n/ *n*

extrinsic /ek strínssik, -zik/ *adj* **1** not essential **2** coming from outside ○ *extrinsic influences* —**extrinsically** *adv*

~~extrordinary~~ incorrect spelling of **extraordinary**

extrovert /ékstrə vurt/, **extravert** *n* an outgoing person —**extroversion** /ékstrə vúrsh'n/ *n* —**extroverted** *adj*

extrude /ik stróód/ (**-truding, -truded**) *vt* **1** force something out **2** make something by forcing a substance through a mould or nozzle —**extrusion** *n*

exuberant /ig zyóób'rənt/ *adj* **1** full of enthusiasm **2** flamboyant —**exuberance** *n* —**exuberantly** *adv*

exude /ig zyóód/ (**-uding, -uded**) *v* **1** *vt* display a particular quality in manner **2** *vti* release or be released slowly

exult /ig zúlt/ *vi* **1** be very happy **2** be triumphant —**exultant** *adj* —**exultantly** *adv* —**exultation** /ég zul táysh'n, ék sul-/ *n*

-ey *suffix* = **-y** 1

eyas /í əss/ *n* a young hawk or falcon

Eyck /ík/, **Jan van** (1390?–1441) Flemish painter

eye /í/ *n* **1** the organ of vision **2** the visible part of the eye **3** the power of sight *(often pl)* **4** somebody's gaze or attention **5** a look or facial expression **6** the ability to judge or appreciate something **7** a point of view ○ *was lovely in her eyes* **8** a new shoot on a potato **9** a hole in a needle ■ *vt* (**eyeing** *or* **eying**, **eyed**) **1** look at inquisitively **2** ogle *(infml)* ◇ **make eyes at** to look at somebody in a flirtatious way *(infml)* ◇ **see eye to eye (with)** have a similar outlook or viewpoint (to) ◇ **turn a blind eye (to)** pretend not to be aware (of) ◇ **with an eye to** having as a purpose or objective ◇ **with your eyes (wide) open** fully aware of all that is involved

eyeball /í bawl/ *n* the round mass of the eye

eyebrow /í brow/ *n* **1** a line of hair above the eye socket **2** a bony ridge above the eye

eye candy *n* something visually attractive but intellectually undemanding *(slang)*

eye-catching *adj* attracting attention —**eye-catcher** *n* —**eye-catchingly** *adv*

eye contact *n* the act of looking directly into somebody's eyes

eyeful /í fööl/ *n* **1** a good look at something or somebody *(infml)* **2** an offensive term for somebody regarded as good-looking *(slang)*

eyeglass /í glaass/ *n* **1** a single lens for correcting vision **2** an eyepiece of an optical instrument ■ **eyeglasses** *npl US, Can* sight-correcting or protective glasses *(fml)*

eyelash /í lash/ *n* a hair at the edge of the eyelid

eyelet /í lət/ *n* **1** a hole for a cord to fit through **2** a metal reinforcement for an eyelet

eyelevel /í lev'l/ *adj* at the height of a person's eyes

eyelid /í lid/ *n* a fold of skin over the eye

eyeliner /í línər/ *n* a cosmetic used to darken the edges of the eyelids

eye opener *n* something revealing or surprising —**eye-opening** *adj*

eye patch *n* a covering worn over one eye

eyepiece /í peess/ *n* the lens that the user looks through in an optical instrument

eye shadow *n* a cosmetic used to colour the eyelids

eyesight /í sīt/ *n* the ability to see

eye socket *n* the part of the skull containing the eye

eyesore /í sawr/ *n* an ugly sight

eyestrain /í strayn/ *n* tiredness or irritation in the eyes

eyetooth /í tooth/ (*pl* **-teeth** /-teeth/) *n* a canine tooth

eyewash /í wosh/ *n* a cleansing liquid for sore eyes

eyewear /í wair/ *n* glasses and contact lenses

eyewitness /í witnəss, T witnəss/ *n* somebody who sees something happen

Eyre, Lake /air/ largest salt lake in Australia, in central South Australia

Eyre, Edward John (1815–1901) British explorer and colonial official

eyrie /eeri, áiri, íri/ *n* 1 an eagle's nest 2 a high inaccessible place

Eysenck /í zengk/, **H. J.** (1916–97) German-born British psychologist

e-zine /ee zeen/ *n* a website with magazine-style content and layout

F

f¹ (*pl* **f's**), **F** (*pl* **F's** *or* **Fs**) *n* the 6th letter of the English alphabet

f² *symbol* 1 focal length 2 function

f³ *abbr* 1 folio 2 forte² *adv* (*musical direction*)

F¹ *abbr* 1 Fahrenheit 2 fail (*as a grade on a piece of work*) 3 farad 4 female 5 feminine

F² (*pl* **F's** *or* **Fs**) *n* the 4th note in the musical scale of C major

F. *abbr* Fahrenheit

F2F *abbr* face-to-face (*in e-mails*)

fa *n* MUSIC = fah

FA *abbr* Football Association

fab *adj* fabulous (*infml*)

Fabergé /fábbər zhay/, **Peter Carl** (1846–1920) Russian goldsmith and jeweller

fable /fáyb'l/ *n* 1 a story that teaches a lesson, especially with animals as characters 2 a false account 3 a legend 4 myths and legends collectively ■ *vt* (**-bling, -bled**) tell in fable

fabled /fáyb'ld/ *adj* 1 legendary 2 fictitious

fabric /fábbrik/ *n* 1 cloth 2 the fundamental structure or nature of something

fabricate /fábbri kayt/ (**-cating, -cated**) *vt* 1 make up something untrue 2 construct something

from different parts 3 forge a signature or document —**fabrication** /fábbri káysh'n/ *n*

fabulous /fábbyŏŏlass/ *adj* 1 excellent (*infml*) 2 amazing 3 typical of or described in a fable —**fabulously** *adv* —**fabulousness** *n*

façade /fə saàd/, **facade** *n* 1 the front surface of a building 2 a deceptive appearance

face *n* 1 the front of the human head 2 a person being looked at (*infml*) ○ *familiar faces in the audience* 3 a facial expression or look ○ *Why the long face?* 4 an unpleasant facial expression ○ *pulling faces at people* 5 the way something looks 6 the outward appearance of somebody or something ○ *put on a brave face* ○ *the Internet changing the face of business* 7 personal reputation ○ *lose face* 8 a surface of an object presented in a particular direction ○ *the faces of a gem* 9 a visible or exposed surface of something such as a building or cliff 10 a dial on a clock or instrument ■ *v* (**facing, faced**) 1 *vti* turn towards a particular person, thing, or direction 2 *vt* be in a position opposite 3 *vt* meet or confront directly ○ *forced to face the enemy* 4 *vt* accept the unpleasant facts about 5 *vt* have to contend with 6 *vt* be encountered by ○ *the problems facing them* 7 *vt* have the prospect of experiencing something unpleasant ○ *could face a jail sentence* —**faceable** *adj* ◇ **fly in the face of** defy ◇ **in (the) face of** when confronted by or in spite of something (*slang*)

□ **face down** *vt* confront and prevail against

□ **face off** *vti* in some games, begin play by dropping the puck or ball between two opposing players

□ **face up to** *vt* 1 accept the unpleasant truth of 2 confront bravely

facecloth /fáyss kloth/, **face flannel** *n* a cloth for washing the face

facedown /fáyss down/ *n* a determined confrontation between adversaries

faceless /fáysslass/ *adj* anonymous and characterless —**facelessness** *n*

facelift /fáyss lift/ *n* 1 a surgical operation to tighten the skin of the face 2 a smartening up

face mask *n* 1 *also* **face pack** a cosmetic preparation for cleansing the pores of the face 2 a covering for the face to protect or disguise it

face-off *n* 1 in some games, a beginning of play in which the referee drops the puck or ball between two opposing players 2 a confrontation

face powder *n* cosmetic powder for the face

face-saving *adj* intended to preserve somebody's reputation or dignity —**face-saver** *n*

facet /fássit/ *n* 1 an aspect of something 2 any surface of a cut gemstone —**faceted** *adj*

face time *n* 1 time spent on television 2 extra time at a place of employment

facetious /fə seéshəss/ *adj* 1 supposed to be funny but silly or inappropriate 2 not in earnest or to be taken seriously —**facetiously** *adv* —**facetiousness** *n*

face-to-face *adj, adv* **1** in each other's presence **2** directly confronting something unpleasant

face value *n* **1** the value that is stated on something such as a note or coin **2** the seeming worth or meaning of something

facia *n* = fascia

facial /fáysh'l/ *adj* on or of the face ■ *n* a beauty treatment for the face —**facially** *adv*

facile /fáss īl/ *adj* **1** superficial in thought or feeling **2** fluent but insincere **3** easy to do **4** working easily —**facilely** *adv* —**facileness** *n*

facilitate /fə síllə tayt/ (**-tating, -tated**) *vt* make easy or easier to do —**facilitation** /fə síllə táysh'n/ *n* —**facilitator** *n*

facility /fə sílləti/ *n* (*pl* **-ties**) **1** skill **2** something designed to provide a particular service or meet a particular need (*often pl*) ◇ **facilities** ■ **facilities** *npl* a toilet

facing /fáyssing/ *n* a piece of fabric sewn inside a garment to neaten the edges

~~facism~~ incorrect spelling of **fascism**

facsimile /fak símməli/ *n* **1** an exact copy **2** a fax (*dated*)

fact *n* something known to be true ◇ **in (actual) fact** in reality

fact-finding *adj* for gathering information —**fact-finder** *n*

faction[1] /fáksh'n/ *n* **1** a dissenting minority within a larger group **2** conflict within a group —**factional** *adj*

faction[2] /fáksh'n/ *n* **1** writing or film-making that dramatizes history **2** a dramatized work based on real life

-faction *suffix* production ◇ *putrefaction*

factious /fákshəss/ *adj* of or causing conflict within a group —**factiously** *adv* —**factiousness** *n*

factitious /fak tíshəss/ *adj* **1** contrived and insincere **2** artificial or invented (*fml*)

factoid /fákt oyd/ *n* **1** an unreliable piece of information **2** a single fact

factor /fáktər/ *n* **1** something that influences or contributes to a result **2** an amount by which something is multiplied ◇ *increased by a factor of three* **3** one of two or more quantities that when multiplied together give a particular quantity ◇ *3 and 5 are factors of 15.* **4** somebody who acts as an agent **5** *Scotland* a manager of an estate ■ *v* **1** *vi* act as a factor **2** *vt* calculate the factors of a given quantity ◇ **factor in** *vt* take into account

factorage /fáktərij/ *n* **1** money charged by a factor **2** the work of a factor

factorial /fak táwri əl/ *n* (*symbol* !) the result of multiplying a number by every whole number between itself and 1 inclusive

factorize /fáktə rīz/ (**-izing, -ized**), **factorise** *vti* calculate the factors of an integer —**factorization** /fáktə rī záysh'n/ *n*

factory /fáktəri/ (*pl* **-ries**) *n* a building where goods are manufactured

factory floor *n* an area of a factory where manufacturing takes place

factory ship *n* a fishing vessel equipped to process its catch

factotum /fak tótəm/ *n* somebody who does many jobs

> **ORIGIN Factotum** derives from a Latin instruction 'do everything!'. In medieval Latin this was used in stereotypical names such as *Magister Factotum* 'Mr Do-Everything' and *Johannes Factotum* 'John Do-Everything', and it is in these forms that **factotum** first appears in English in the mid-16C. The first ordinary noun use is recorded in the early 17C.

fact sheet *n* a document giving information

factual /fákchoo əl/ *adj* **1** containing facts **2** truthful —**factually** *adv*

faculty /fák'lti/ (*pl* **-ties**) *n* **1** a mental power **2** an ability **3** a division of a university dealing with a particular subject **4** the teaching staff at a school, college, or university

FA Cup *n* **1** an annual knockout football competition organized by the Football Association **2** the FA Cup trophy

fad *n* **1** a short-lived fashion **2** a personal idiosyncrasy

faddish /fáddish/ *adj* US faddy

faddy /fáddi/ (**-dier, -diest**) *adj* given to fads

fade (**fading, faded**) *v* **1** *vti* lose or make lose brightness, colour, or loudness gradually **2** *vi* become tired **3** *vi* disappear slowly

fade-in *n* a gradual introduction of sound or an image

fade-out *n* **1** a gradual decrease in loudness or brightness **2** a weakening of a TV or radio signal

faeces /feesseez/ *npl* the body's solid waste —**faecal** /feek'l/ *adj*

faerie /fáy əri, fáiri/, **faery** (*pl* **-ies**) *n* (*literary*) **1** fairyland **2** a fairy

Faeroe Islands ♦ **Faroe Islands**

faff □ **faff about** *or* **around** *vi* waste time by fussing or dithering (*infml*)

fag[1] *n* something boring or wearisome to do (*infml*) ■ *vti* (**fagging, fagged**) *US* exhaust through work

fag[2] *n* a cigarette (*infml*)

fag[3] *n US, Can* an offensive term for a gay man (*slang offensive insult*) —**faggy** *adj*

fag end *n* a cigarette stub (*infml*)

fagged, fagged out *adj* very tired or worn out (*infml*)

faggot[1] /fággət/ *n* **1** a bundle of sticks for firewood **2** a meatball made of offal

faggot[2] /fággət/ *n US, Can* an offensive term for a gay man (*slang offensive insult*) —**faggoty** *adj*

fah /faa/, **fa** *n* a syllable used in singing the 4th note of a scale

Fahd /faad/ (*b.* 1923) king of Saudi Arabia (1982–)

Fahrenheit /fárrən hīt/ *adj* (*symbol* **F**) of a temperature scale at which water freezes at 32°F and boils at 212°F under normal atmospheric conditions. ◊ **Celsius**

ORIGIN The **Fahrenheit** scale is named after the German physicist Gabriel Fahrenheit (1686–1736), who devised it.

faience /fī ónss, -aánss/, **faïence** *n* pottery with a coloured opaque metallic glaze

ORIGIN Faience derives from the French name for the town of Faenza in N Italy.

fail /fayl/ *v* **1** *vi* be unsuccessful **2** *vi* be unable or unwilling to do something ○ *failed to see what all the fuss was about* **3** *vti* not pass an exam or course **4** *vt* judge a student not good enough to pass an exam or course **5** *vi* stop functioning or growing **6** *vi* collapse financially **7** *vt* let somebody down by not doing what is expected or needed ■ *n* a failure to reach the required standard ◊ **without fail** for certain

failing /fáyling/ *n* a shortcoming ■ *prep* without the occurrence of ◊ See note at **flaw**

fail-safe *adj* **1** designed to switch to a safe condition if there is a fault or failure **2** sure to succeed

failure /fáylyər/ *n* **1** lack of success, or an unsuccessful attempt **2** somebody or something that fails **3** the breakdown of something ○ *engine failure*

fain /fayn/ *(archaic) adv* happily or eagerly ■ *adj* **1** eager **2** compelled

faint /faynt/ *adj* **1** dim to the sight or hearing **2** unenthusiastic ○ *damn with faint praise* **3** dizzy and weak **4** slight or remote ○ *a faint chance* ■ *vi* lose consciousness briefly ■ *n* a sudden loss of consciousness —**faintly** *adv* —**faintness** *n*

SPELLCHECK Do not confuse the spelling of **faint** and **feint** ('a deceptive action'), which sound similar.

faint-hearted *adj* timid or cowardly —**faint-heartedly** *adv* —**faint-heartedness** *n* ◊ See note at **cowardly**

fair[1] /fair/ *adj* **1** reasonable or unbiased **2** according to the rules ○ *fair and free elections* **3** describes light-coloured hair or skin, or somebody with this **4** sizeable ○ *a fair number of responses* **5** better than acceptable ○ *a fair understanding of the problems* **6** no more than average **7** pleasing to look at **8** not stormy or cloudy **9** not blocked ○ *a fair view of the mountains* **10** unsullied ■ *adv* **1** properly **2** directly —**fairness** *n* ◊ **fair and square** justly, fairly, or according to the rules

SPELLCHECK Do not confuse the spelling of **fair** and **fare** ('the cost of travel'), which sound similar.

fair[2] /fair/ *n* **1** an outdoor event with amusements **2** a large market for buying and selling goods **3** a commercial exhibition **4** a sale to raise money **5** *Scotland* a trades holiday

fair copy *n* an unmarked corrected version of a document

fair dinkum *(infml) adj Aus* genuine ■ *adv Aus* really ■ *n ANZ* fair play

Fairfax /fáir faks/, **John** (1804–77) British-born Australian newspaper proprietor

fair game *n* a legitimate target

fairground /fáir grownd/ *n* a place where a fair is held

fair-haired *adj* with light-coloured hair

fairly /fáirli/ *adv* **1** honestly or justly **2** moderately **3** considerably

fair-minded *adj* impartial —**fair-mindedly** *adv* —**fair-mindedness** *n*

fairness /fáirnəss/ *n* **1** the quality of being fair **2** beauty

fair play *n* **1** playing a game by the rules **2** proper conduct

fair sex *n* women *(literary)*

fairway /fáir way/ *n* a stretch of grass between a golf tee and the green

fairy /fáiri/ *(pl -ies) n* **1** a small imaginary being with magical powers **2** an offensive term for a gay man *(slang offensive insult)*

fairyfloss /fáiri floss/ *n Aus* candyfloss

fairy godmother *n* **1** a fairy who gives help to a specific person **2** somebody very helpful to another

fairyland /fáiri land/ *n* **1** the imaginary land of fairies **2** an enchanting place

fairy lights *npl* small electric lights used as decoration

fairy tale, fairy story *n* **1** a story about fairies or imaginary happenings **2** an unlikely explanation

fairy-tale *adj* **1** from a fairy tale **2** very fortunate, happy, or beautiful

Faisal /físs'l/ (1905–75) king of Saudi Arabia (1964–75)

Faisal II (1935–58) king of Iraq (1939–58)

Faisalabad /físsələ bad/ city in NE Pakistan. Pop. 1,977,246 (1998).

fait accompli /fáyt ə kóm plee/ *(pl **faits accomplis** /pronunc. same/) n* something already done or decided and unalterable

faith *n* **1** belief or trust **2** a religion or religious group **3** trust in God **4** a set of beliefs ◊ **on faith** without proof

faithful /fáythf'l/ *adj* **1** consistently loyal **2** not adulterous or promiscuous **3** conscientious **4** in accordance with the truth ○ *a faithful account of the events* **5** with unwavering belief ■ *npl* **1** *also* **Faithful** religious believers **2** loyal supporters —**faithfully** *adv* —**faithfulness** *n*

faithless /fáythləss/ *adj* **1** disloyal **2** untrustworthy —**faithlessly** *adv* —**faithlessness** *n*

faith school *n* a school run by a religious organization

fajitas /fə héetəss/ *npl* a Mexican dish of strips of grilled meat in a soft flour tortilla

fake *n* somebody or something that is not genuine ■ *adj* not genuine ■ *v* (**faking, faked**) **1** *vt* falsely present as genuine **2** *vti* pretend feeling or knowledge —**fakery** *n*

fakir /fáy keer, fə keér/ *n* a religious Muslim, especially a Sufi, who lives by begging

~~falacy~~ incorrect spelling of **fallacy**

falafel /fə laáf'l/, **felafel** *n* a deep-fried ball of ground chickpeas

falcon /fáwlkən/ *n* **1** a fast-flying bird of prey **2** a hawk trained to hunt

falconry /fáwlkənri/ *n* the training and use of falcons for hunting —**falconer** *n*

Falkirk /fáwl kurk/ **1** town in central Scotland. Pop. 35,968 (1991). **2** council area in central Scotland

Falkland Islands /fáwlklənd-/ group of islands and British dependency in the South Atlantic Ocean. Pop. 2,317 (1995).

fall /fawl/ *vi* (**fell, fallen** /fáwlən/) **1** move downwards by the force of gravity **2** drop or be lowered ○ *when the curtain falls* **3** come down suddenly from an upright position, especially by accident **4** become less or lower ○ *prices fell* **5** lose or be defeated militarily or politically **6** hang down **7** take place as if falling and enveloping something ○ *Night fell.* **8** display disappointment ○ *Her face fell.* **9** come to rest by chance ○ *His gaze fell on a book.* **10** enter a particular state or condition ○ *fell silent* **11** sin *(archaic)* ■ *n* **1** an act of falling down **2** something that has fallen ○ *a heavy fall of snow* **3** a distance down **4** *US, Can* the season of autumn **5** a waterfall *(often pl, often in placenames)* ◊ **fall flat** fail to have the intended effect ◊ **fall foul** *or* **afoul of** come into conflict with ◊ **fall short** be less than is needed ◊ **fall short of** fail to meet a desired standard

□ **fall back** *vi* retreat
□ **fall back on** *or* **upon** *vt* have recourse to
□ **fall behind** *vi* fail to keep up
□ **fall for** *vt* **1** fall in love with **2** be duped by
□ **fall in** *vi* **1** form ranks **2** cave in
□ **fall in with** *vt* meet and join
□ **fall off** *vi* decline in number or quantity
□ **fall on** *or* **upon** *vt* **1** attack *(literary)* **2** begin eagerly
□ **fall out** *vi* quarrel
□ **fall through** *vi* fail to work out successfully
□ **fall to** *vt* be the duty or responsibility of

Falla /fí ə/, **Manuel de** (1876–1946) Spanish composer and pianist

fallacious /fə láyshəss/ *adj* **1** containing a mistaken belief **2** deceptive —**fallaciously** *adv* —**fallaciousness** *n*

fallacy /fálləssi/ (*pl* -**cies**) *n* **1** a mistaken belief or idea **2** an invalid argument

fallback /fáwl bak/ *n* **1** a replacement or alternative **2** a retreat or withdrawal —**fallback** *adj*

fallen woman *n* a woman who has had extra-marital sex *(literary)*

fall guy *n* a scapegoat *(infml)*

fallible /fálləb'l/ *adj* tending to make mistakes —**fallibility** /fállə bílləti/ *n*

falling-out (*pl* **fallings-out**) *n* a quarrel

falling star *n* a brief streak of light in the night sky created by a meteor

fall line *n* **1** an imaginary line between highland and lowland regions **2** a natural route of descent between two points on a hill

falloff /fáwl of/ *n* a decrease, as in prices or demand

fallopian tube /fə lópi ən-/, **Fallopian tube** *n* each of two tubes through which a mammal's eggs pass from an ovary to the womb

ORIGIN The **fallopian tubes** are named after the Italian anatomist Gabriele Fallopio (1523–62), who is reputed to have discovered them.

fallout /fáwl owt/ *n* **1** radioactive particles that settle to Earth after a nuclear explosion or leak **2** incidental consequences, especially undesirable ones

fallout shelter *n* a shelter from nuclear war

fallow[1] /fálló/ *adj* **1** left unseeded after ploughing **2** currently inactive

fallow[2] /fálló/ *adj* yellowish-brown —**fallow** *n*

fallow deer *n* a deer of Europe and Asia, the male of which has broad flattened antlers and a spotted coat in summer

false /fawlss, folss/ (**falser, falsest**) *adj* **1** not true or factual **2** mistaken **3** artificial **4** deliberately deceptive ○ *false promises* —**falsely** *adv* —**falseness** *n*

false alarm *n* **1** a needless alarm **2** something causing needless worry

false dawn *n* **1** the light that occurs just before sunrise **2** a favourable sign whose expectations are unfulfilled

falsehood /fáwlss hŏŏd, fólss-/ *n* **1** a lie **2** the telling of lies ◊ See note at **lie**

false imprisonment *n* illegal imprisonment

false move *n* an action showing an error of timing or judgment

false pretences *npl* deception in order to gain something

false start *n* **1** an abandoned start of a race **2** an unsuccessful start

falsetto /fawl séttō, fol-/ (*pl* -**tos**) *n* **1** a high singing voice used by men **2** a singer who uses falsetto —**falsetto** *adv*

falsify /fáwlssi fī, fólss-/ (-**fies, -fied**) *vt* **1** alter fraudulently **2** misrepresent —**falsification** /fáwlssifi káysh'n, fólssi-/ *n*

falsity /fáwlssəti, fólss-/ (*pl* -**ties**) *n* **1** the fact or state of being untrue **2** something untrue

falter /fáwltər, fól-/ *v* **1** *vi* lose confidence and become hesitant **2** *vi* begin to fail **3** *vi* stumble **4** *vti* speak or say hesitantly —**faltering** *adj* ◊ See note at **hesitate**

fame *n* the condition of being very well known **famed** *adj* famous

familial /fə mílli əl/ *adj* of a family or families

familiar /fə mílli ər/ *adj* **1** often encountered **2** thoroughly acquainted with something **3** friendly, often to the point of impertinence

■ *n* an intimate friend *(fml)* —**familiarly** *adv* —**familiarness** *n*

ORIGIN Familiar came through French from a Latin word meaning 'of the family', and early uses retain this or contain a mixture of it.

familiarity /fə mílli árrəti/ *n* **1** thorough knowledge **2** intimacy **3** familiar quality **4** (*pl* **familiarities**) an unwelcome intimacy *(dated)*

familiarize /fə mílli ə rīz/ (**-izing, -ized**), **familiarise** *vt* provide with the necessary information or experience —**familiarization** /fə mílli ə rī záysh'n/ *n*

~~familier~~ incorrect spelling of **familiar**

family /fámmli/ *n* (*pl* **-lies**) **1** a group of relatives **2** a group of people who live together, usually consisting of parents and children **3** the other members of somebody's family ○ *spending time with her family* **4** a child or set of children born to somebody ○ *thinking of starting a family* **5** a group with something in common **6** a group of related languages **7** a group of related organisms ■ *adj* **1** used by a family **2** appropriate for children ○ *family viewing*

family court *n* a court dealing with families

family credit *n* a former UK state allowance paid to families

family doctor *n* a GP

family man *n* a man fond of family life

family name *n* a surname

family planning *n* birth control

family room *n* a room for the use of adults accompanied by children

family tree *n* a chart showing the generations of a family

famine /fámmin/ *n* **1** a severe food shortage resulting in widespread hunger or starvation **2** a severe shortage

famish /fámmish/ *vti* be or make extremely hungry —**famished** *adj*

famous /fáyməss/ *adj* **1** very well known **2** excellent *(dated)* —**famously** *adv*

fan[1] *n* **1** an electrical device with rotating blades for moving air **2** a hand-held device waved to cool the face **3** something shaped like an open hand-held fan ■ *vt* (**fanning, fanned**) **1** blow a current of air across something **2** stir up emotions

ORIGIN The cooling **fan** is recorded from the mid-16C. Before that a **fan** was always a device for winnowing grain, which is the meaning of the Latin word from which it derives. **Fan** 'enthusiast' is completely unrelated. It is a shortening of *fanatic*.

□ **fan out** *vti* spread in a fan shape

fan[2] *n* an enthusiast for a particular person or activity

fanatic /fə náttik/ *n* **1** somebody with extreme or irrational beliefs **2** somebody with an obsessive interest in something ■ *adj* also **fanatical** holding extreme or irrational beliefs

or enthusiasms —**fanatically** *adv* —**fanaticism** /fə náttisizəm/ *n*

ORIGIN Fanatic came via French from a Latin word meaning 'inspired by a god, frenzied' and literally 'of a temple'.

fan belt *n* a belt that turns the cooling fan on a motor vehicle's engine

fanciable /fánssi əb'l/ *adj* desirable *(infml)*

fancier /fánssi ər/ *n* somebody with an interest in breeding a particular plant or animal ○ *a pigeon fancier*

fanciful /fánssif'l/ *adj* **1** imaginary **2** imaginative and impractical —**fancifully** *adv*

fan club *n* an organization for fans of a celebrity or performer

fancy /fánssi/ *adj* (**-cier, -ciest**) **1** elaborate and ornate **2** intricately and skilfully performed ○ *fancy footwork* **3** aiming to impress ○ *bought a fancy car* **4** expensive ○ *fancy prices* ■ *v* (**-cies, -cied**) **1** *vt* wish for **2** *vt* find sexually attractive *(infml)* **3** *vr* flatter yourself **4** *vt* suppose **5** *vt* imagine **6** *vt* identify as a potential winner ■ *n* (*pl* **-cies**) **1** a sudden liking **2** an unfounded belief **3** something imaginary **4** a likely winner **5** playful imaginativeness —**fancily** *adv* —**fanciness** *n*

fancy dress *n* clothing depicting a famous person, character, or period, worn as a costume to a party

ORIGIN Fancy dress is not 'fancy' because it is elaborate, but because it is chosen and arranged according to the wearer's fancy.

fancy-free *adj* carefree

fancywork /fánssi wurk/ *n* decorative needlework

fandango /fan dáng gō/ (*pl* **-gos**) *n* **1** a Spanish or Latin American dance for a couple, in triple time **2** the music for a fandango

fanfare /fán fair/ *n* **1** a trumpet flourish **2** a showy display to announce or publicize something

fang *n* **1** a canine tooth **2** a snake's tooth

fan heater *n* an electric heater blowing out warm air

fanlight /fán līt/ *n* a window above a door, traditionally semicircular

fan mail *n* letters from fans

fanny /fánni/ (*pl* **-nies**) *n* US, Can the buttocks *(slang)*

fantabulous /fan tábbyŏŏləss/ *adj* excellent *(humorous)*

fantasia /fan táyzi ə, fántə zeé ə/ *n* a musical composition in a free and improvisatory style

fantasize /fántə sīz/ (**-sizing, -sized**), **fantasise** *vti* imagine something pleasurable —**fantasist** *n*

fantastic /fan tástik/, **fantastical** /-ik'l/ *adj* **1** excellent **2** bizarre in appearance **3** incredible but real or true **4** enormous **5** imaginary ■ *interj* expresses pleasure *(infml)* —**fantastically** *adv*

fantasy /fántəssi/ (*pl* **-sies**) *n* **1** a creation of the imagination **2** an impractical idea **3** the creative power of the imagination **4** a genre of fiction with imaginary worlds and super-natural events **5** a fantasia

ORIGIN Fantasy goes back to a Greek word meaning 'appearance, imagination', formed from a verb meaning 'show, make visible'. It entered English through French in the 14C. By the 15C a contracted form appeared, and this developed a different range of meanings as *fancy*.

fanzine /fán zeen/ *n* a fan club magazine

FAO *abbr* Food and Agriculture Organization (of the UN)

f.a.o. *abbr* for the attention of

FAQ, FAQs *abbr* frequently asked questions

far *adv* (**farther** /fáàrthər/ *or* **further** /fúrthər/, **far-thest** /fáàrthist/ *or* **furthest** /fúrthist/) **1** a long way off **2** a long time off **3** much or many ○ *far more difficult* ■ *adj* (**farther** *or* **further**, **farthest** *or* **furthest**) **1** remote in space or time ○ *the far distance* **2** more distant ○ *in the far corner* **3** extreme ◊ **far and away** without a doubt and by a large margin ◊ **far and wide** covering a great distance ◊ **far from** by no means ○ *far from over*

farad /fárrəd, fá rad/ *n* (*symbol* **F**) a unit of electrical capacitance

ORIGIN Farad is shortened from the name of Michael Faraday.

Popperfoto

Michael Faraday

Faraday /fárrə day/, **Michael** (1791–1867) British physicist and chemist

faraway /fáàrə wáy/ *adj* **1** remote **2** appearing dreamy or absent-minded

farce *n* **1** a comic play or style of drama with absurd events **2** an absurd situation

ORIGIN Farce comes from a French word meaning literally 'stuffing, forcemeat', which was adopted into English with this sense in the late medieval period. The French word had already developed a metaphorical use 'comic interlude', and this was separately taken into English in the early 16C. This sense arose through the practice of introducing comic inter-ludes into religious plays in the Middle Ages.

farcical /fáàrsikl/ *adj* **1** absurd and confused **2** in the style of farce —**farcically** *adv*

fare /fair/ *n* **1** an amount paid for somebody to travel **2** a paying passenger **3** food provided ■ *vi* (**faring**, **fared**) **1** manage in doing some-

thing ○ *How did she fare in the exam?* **2** turn out in a specified way **3** go on a journey ◊ See note at **fair**

Far East the countries of East Asia, sometimes also of Southeast Asia *(dated)* —**Far-Eastern** *adj*

~~Farenheit~~ incorrect spelling of **Fahrenheit**

fare stage *n* **1** a section of a bus route that determines the fare **2** a bus stop at the end of a fare stage

farewell /fair wél/ *n* an expression of parting good wishes ■ *interj* goodbye *(literary)* —**farewell** *adj*

far-fetched *adj* unconvincing

far-flung *adj* **1** widespread **2** remote

Fargo /fáàrgō/ city in SE North Dakota. Pop. 86,718 (1998).

farina /fə reénə/ *n* **1** flour or meal **2** starch

farinaceous /fárri náyshəss/ *adj* containing starch

farm *n* **1** an area of agricultural land with its buildings **2** a place where particular animals or crops are raised commercially *(usually in combination)* ○ *a trout farm* ■ *v* **1** *vti* use land for agriculture **2** *vt* rear animals, birds, or fish commercially —**farming** *n*

farmer /fáàrmər/ *n* an owner or operator of a farm

farmers' market *n* a market for farm produce

farmhouse /fáàrm howss/ *n* (*pl* **-houses** /-howziz/) **1** a farmer's house **2** *also* **farmhouse loaf** a rectangular loaf of white bread with a rounded top ■ *adj* made on a farm

farmland /fáàrm land/ *n* land suitable or used for farming

farmstay /fáàrm stay/ *n ANZ, Can* a holiday on farm

farmstead /fáàrm sted/ *n* a farm and its build-ings

farmyard /fáàrm yaard/ *n* a yard beside farm buildings

Faroe Islands /fáirō-/, **Faeroe Islands** group of islands and Danish territory in the North Atlantic Ocean. Cap. Tórshavn. Pop. 45,661 (2001).

far-off *adj* remote

Farouk I /fə roòk/ (1920–65) king of Egypt (1936–52)

far-out *adj* unusual *(slang)* —**far-outness** *n*

Farquhar /fáàrkər/, **George** (1678–1707) Irish dramatist

farrago /fə raàgō/ (*pl* **-gos** *or* **-goes**) *n* a jumble

Farrakhan /fárrə kaàn/, **Louis Abdul** (*b.* 1933) US religious leader, leader of the Nation of Islam

far-reaching *adj* extensive in effect

farrier /fárri ər/ *n* somebody who shoes horses

farrow /fárrō/ *vi* give birth to piglets ■ *n* a litter of pigs

Farsi /fáàrssi/ *n* the official language of Iran —**Farsi** *adj*

farsighted /fáàr sítid/ *adj* **1** *also* **farseeing** able to make sound judgments regarding the future **2** *US, Can* long-sighted **3** *also* **far-**

seeing able to see a long way —**farsightedly** *adv* —**farsightedness** *n*

fart *(slang)* *vti* an offensive term meaning to release intestinal gases through the anus ■ *n* an offensive term for a discharge of intestinal gas from the anus

farther /faárthər/ *adv* to a greater distance or extent ■ *adj* more distant —**farthermost** *adj*

farthest /faárthist/ *adv* to the greatest distance or extent ■ *adj* most distant

farthing /faárthing/ *n* a former British coin worth one quarter of the old penny

farthingale /faárthing gayl/ *n* a structure worn to hold out a skirt in the late 16C and early 17C

fascia /fáyshə, fáyshi ə, fáshə, fáyssi ə/ *(pl -ciae /-shi ee/ or -cias)*, **facia** *(pl -ciae or -cias)* *n* 1 a flat horizontal surface just below the edge of the roof of a building 2 a vehicle's dashboard

fascinate /fássi nayt/ *(-nating, -nated)* *v* 1 *vti* captivate 2 *vt* immobilize, especially through fear —**fascinating** *adj* —**fascinatingly** *adv* —**fascination** /fássi náysh'n/ *n*

fascism /fáshizəm/, **Fascism** *n* dictatorial government, especially combined with extreme nationalism —**fascist** *n, adj*

ORIGIN Fascism was adopted from Italian *fascismo*, the principles and organization of the *fascisti*. These were members of the *Partita Nazionale Fascista* 'National Fascist Party', an Italian nationalist organization formed in 1919 by Benito Mussolini (1883–1945), initially to oppose communism. The party controlled Italy from 1922 to 1943, with Mussolini as dictator from 1925. The name was formed from *fascio* meaning 'bundle' and also 'group', which came from Latin *fascis* 'bundle'. In ancient Rome, bundles (*fasces*) of rods tied to an axe with a red string were a symbol of the total power of senior magistrates; the *fasces* were adopted as an emblem by the Italian Fascists.

fashion /fásh'n/ *n* 1 style in clothing or appearance 2 the current style in clothing, furnishings, or appearance o *no longer in fashion* 3 a manner of behaving or doing something ■ *vt* 1 give shape or form to 2 form by influence or training o *attitudes fashioned by his grandparents* ◊ **after a fashion** in some way but not very well

fashionable /fásh'nəb'l/ *adj* 1 currently popular o *fashionable ideas* 2 associated with rich, famous, or glamorous people o *a fashionable nightspot* —**fashionably** *adv*

fashion house *n* a business that designs, makes, and sells fashionable clothes

~~fashon~~ incorrect spelling of **fashion**

~~fasinating~~ incorrect spelling of **fascinating**

fast[1] *adj* 1 acting or moving rapidly 2 done quickly 3 running ahead of time o *My watch is ten minutes fast.* 4 conducive to great speed o *a fast road* 5 describes photographic film or equipment with a short exposure 6 pursuing excitement and pleasure *(infml)* o *in with a*

fast crowd 7 not liable to fade or change colour 8 strong, close, and loyal *(literary)* o *fast friends* 9 firmly fastened or shut ■ *adv* 1 rapidly 2 immediately or in quick succession 3 ahead of the correct time 4 soundly o *fast asleep* 5 firmly so as to prevent movement o *hold fast*

fast[2] *vi* abstain from food ■ *n* a period of fasting —**faster** *n*

fast-acting *adj* soon taking effect

fastback /faást bak/ *n* a car with a back that forms a continuous curve down from the roof edge

fast-breeder reactor *n* a nuclear reactor that produces more fissionable material than it consumes

fasten /faáss'n/ *vti* 1 attach or become attached securely 2 shut or be shut tightly

fastener /faáss'nər/, **fastening** /faáss'ning/ *n* a device for fastening something

fast food *n* processed food prepared quickly

fast-forward *n* a function on a tape recorder or player for winding tape forwards quickly ■ *vti* advance a tape rapidly

fastidious /fa stídi əss/ *adj* 1 demanding about detail 2 sensitive about cleanliness

fast lane *n* 1 a passing lane of a motorway 2 the hectic lifestyle of people pursuing excitement and pleasure *(infml)* —**fast-lane** *adj*

fastness /faástnəss/ *n* 1 the state or quality of being fixed, firm, or secure 2 a fortress *(literary)*

fast track *n* a rapid route to progress or advancement *(infml)* —**fast-track** *adj, vt*

fat *n* 1 a water-insoluble chemical belonging to a group that is a main constituent of the body 2 tissue containing fat 3 solidified oil or fat used in cooking 4 quantity in excess of what is needed *(infml)* o *a budget with no fat* ■ *adj* *(fatter, fattest)* 1 overweight 2 containing fat 3 thick o *a fat book* 4 profitable o *fat contracts* 5 very wealthy 6 with abundant contents or supplies o *a fat savings account* 7 minimal *(infml)* o *Fat chance!* —**fatness** *n*

FAT /fat/ *n* a table of computer information about the structure of stored files on a disk. Full form **file allocation table**

fatal /fáyt'l/ *adj* 1 leading to death 2 ruinous 3 decisive —**fatally** *adv* —**fatalness** *n* ◊ See note at **deadly**

fatalism /fáyt'lizəm/ *n* 1 the philosophical doctrine that all events are fated to happen 2 belief in fate —**fatalist** *n* —**fatalistic** /fáyt'l ístik/ *adj*

fatality /fə tálləti, fay-/ *(pl -ties)* *n* a death resulting from an accident or disaster

fat cat *n* somebody rich *(slang insult)*

fate *n* 1 a force believed to predetermine events 2 an outcome or final result 3 something determined by fate ■ **Fates** *npl* in Greek mythology, the goddesses of destiny. Roman equivalent **Parcae** ■ *vt* *(fating, fated)* make inevitable —**fated** *adj* ◊ **tempt fate** take a risk

fateful /fáytf'l/ *adj* **1** making a dire outcome inevitable **2** decided by fate

fathead /fát hed/ *n* a person regarded as unintelligent and thoughtless *(slang insult)* —**fatheaded** /fát héddid/ *adj*

father /faäthər/ *n* **1** a man who is a parent or acts as a parent **2** a male ancestor, founder, or civic leader **3 Father** God **4 Father** used as a title for a clergyman in some Christian churches ■ *vt* beget as a father —**fatherhood** *n* —**fatherless** *adj*

Father Christmas *n* an imaginary old man who brings Christmas presents

father figure *n* an older man whom others look to for advice and protection

father-in-law (*pl* **fathers-in-law**) *n* a spouse's father

fatherland /faäthər land/ *n* **1** somebody's homeland **2** the homeland of somebody's ancestors

fatherly /faäthərli/ *adj* like a father —**fatherliness** *n*

Father's Day *n* a day honouring fathers. Date: 3rd Sunday in June.

fathom /fáthəm/ *n* a measure of water depth equal to 1.83 m/6 ft ■ *vt* **1** measure water depth using a sounding line **2** comprehend something —**fathomable** *adj*

fathomless /fáthəmləss/ *adj* **1** endlessly deep **2** mystifying —**fathomlessness** *n*

fatigue /fə teeg/ *n* **1** mental or physical exhaustion **2** the weakening of material under stress ○ *metal fatigue* ■ **fatigues** *npl* informal military uniforms worn day to day and in battle ■ *vti* make or become tired —**fatigued** *adj*

Fatima /fáttimə/ (606?–632 BC) youngest daughter of Muhammad

fat suit *n* a naturalistic costume designed to make an actor appear overweight

fatten /fátt'n/ *vti* make or become fat or plump —**fattening** *adj*

fatty /fátti/ (**-tier, -tiest**) *adj* **1** containing fat **2** derived from fat —**fattiness** *n*

fatty acid *n* an organic acid belonging to a group occurring as fats, waxes, and oils

fatuous /fáttyoo əss/ *adj* showing lack of intelligence and awareness —**fatuity** /fə tyoo əti/ *n* —**fatuously** *adv*

fatwa /fát waa/, **fatwah** *n* a legal opinion or religious decree issued by an Islamic leader

faucet /fáwssit/ *n* US, Can a tap on a pipe, for drawing off liquid

Faulkner /fáwknər/, **William** (1897–1962) US writer —**Faulknerian** /fawk neeri ən/ *adj*

fault /fawlt, folt/ *n* **1** responsibility for a mistake, failure, or wrongdoing **2** a personal shortcoming **3** a defect in something **4** an error, especially in calculation **5** a misdemeanour **6** a displacement in the Earth's crust, with a break in the continuity of rocks **7** in some racket games, an invalid serve ■ *vt* blame or find fault with —**faultless** *adj* —**faultlessly**

adv ◊ **find fault with** criticize ◊ **to a fault** excessively ◊ See note at **flaw**

faultfinding /fáwlt fīnding, fólt-/ *n* **1** criticism, especially when constant and petty **2** the tracing of faults —**faultfinder** *n* —**faultfinding** *adj*

fault line *n* a linear feature on the Earth's surface, occurring where displaced rock layers have broken through

faulty /fáwlti, fólti/ (**-ier, -iest**) *adj* containing defects —**faultily** *adv* —**faultiness** *n*

faun /fawn/ *n* in Roman mythology, a rural god depicted as part man and part goat

> **SPELLCHECK** Do not confuse the spelling of **faun** and **fawn** ('a young deer', 'a yellowish-brown colour'), which sound similar.

fauna /fáwnə/ *n* the animal life of a particular area or period —**faunal** *adj*

> **ORIGIN Fauna** derives from the name of an ancient Roman rural goddess. The Swedish naturalist Carolus Linnaeus (1707–78) named his catalogue of the animals of Sweden after her: *Fauna suecica* 'Swedish Fauna' (1746). The use paralleled that of *flora* and quickly caught on. It is first recorded in English in 1771.

Faunus /fáwnəss/ *n* in Roman mythology, the god of nature. Greek equivalent **Pan**

Fauré /fáwr ay/, **Gabriel** (1845–1924) French composer and organist

Faust /fowst/ (b. 1480?) German fortune-teller and magician reputed to have sold his soul to the devil —**Faustian** *adj*

fauvism /fóvizəm/, **Fauvism** *n* a 20C artistic movement characterized by simple forms and bright colours

faux /fō/ *adj* imitation ○ *faux marble*

faux pas /fó paa/ (*pl* **faux pas** /fó paáz/) *n* a social blunder ◊ See note at **mistake**

fava bean /faävə-/ *n* US a broad bean

fave /fayv/ *adj* favourite *(slang)*

favor *n, v* US = **favour**

favorite *adj, n* US = **favourite**

favour /fáyvər/ *n* **1** a kind act **2** an approving attitude **3** preferential treatment **4** a token of loyalty or affection **5** a small gift given to guests at a party ■ **favours** *npl* sexual intimacy, especially as consented to by a woman *(dated)* ■ *vt* **1** prefer **2** treat with particular kindness **3** express support for **4** be advantageous to ○ *tax cuts that favour the rich* **5** show preferential treatment to **6** be careful with **7** resemble in appearance ○ *favours her uncle* ◊ See note at **regard**

favourable /fáyvərəb'l/ *adj* **1** advantageous **2** suggesting a promising future ○ *a favourable outlook* **3** expressing or winning approval ○ *a favourable reaction* **4** winning approval ○ *make a favourable impression* —**favourably** *adv*

favourite /fáyvərit/ *adj* most liked ■ *n* **1** a person or thing liked most **2** somebody favoured by a superior **3** a competitor considered most likely to win

favouritism /fáyvərətizəm/ n the unfair favouring of a person or group

Fawkes /fawks/, (1570–1606) English conspirator, executed for his part in the Gunpowder Plot

fawn[1] /fawn/ n **1** a young deer **2** a yellowish-brown colour —**fawn** adj ◊ See note at **faun**

fawn[2] /fawn/ vi **1** seek favour by flattery **2** try to please by showing enthusiastic affection —**fawner** n —**fawning** adj

fax n **1** a document or image sent electronically over telephone lines and reproduced in its original form **2** also **fax machine** a machine for sending faxes ■ vt send by fax

fay n a fairy (literary)

faze /fayz/ (**fazing, fazed**) v **1** vt disconcert or fluster **2** vi Ireland have an effect

SPELLCHECK Do not confuse the spelling of **faze** and **phase** ('a stage of development'), which sound similar.

FBI n an arm of the US Justice Department that deals with national security and interstate crime. Full form **Federal Bureau of Investigation**

FCO abbr Foreign and Commonwealth Office

fealty /fée əlti/ (pl -**ties**) n allegiance to a feudal lord

fear /feer/ n **1** a feeling of anxiety that something bad will happen **2** a frightening thought **3** reverence and awe ■ v **1** vti be afraid of something **2** vt express regretfully (fml)

□ **fear for** vt worry about the risk or danger to

fearful /féerf'l/ adj **1** feeling or showing fear o fearful for their safety **2** frightening o a fearful storm **3** very bad (infml) o a fearful headache —**fearfully** adv —**fearfulness** n

fearless /féerləss/ adj courageous —**fearlessly** adv —**fearlessness** n ◊ See note at **courage**

fearsome /féersəm/ adj **1** frightening **2** inspiring reverence and awe —**fearsomely** adv —**fearsomeness** n

~~feasable~~ incorrect spelling of **feasible**

feasible /féezəb'l/ adj **1** possible **2** plausible —**feasibility** /féezə bíllati/ n —**feasibly** adv

feast /feest/ n **1** a large meal, especially a celebratory meal for a large number of people **2** something that gives pleasure **3** a religious celebration ■ vi **1** attend a celebratory meal **2** eat with enjoyment o feasting on strawberries **3** take delight o feasting on the view

feat /feet/ n a notable act

feather /féthər/ n **1** an individual part of a bird's plumage, consisting of a hollow central shaft with interlocking fine strands on both sides **2** something resembling a bird's feather ■ v **1** vt fit or cover with feathers **2** vti turn an oar blade horizontally to decrease wind resistance **3** vt alter the position of an aircraft's propeller blades to decrease wind resistance **4** vt cut hair to form layers —**feathered** adj ◊ **a feather in somebody's cap** an act or

achievement that gives somebody cause to be proud

feather duster n a brush made of feathers attached to a stick

featherweight /féthər wayt/ n **1** the weight category for boxers between bantamweight and lightweight **2** a boxer who competes at featherweight

feathery /féthəri/ adj **1** resembling feathers **2** consisting of feathers

feature /féechər/ n **1** a part of the face that makes it distinctive **2** a distinctive part o a geographical feature **3** a full-length film **4** a regular article in a newspaper, magazine, or broadcast programme **5** a prominent story in a newspaper, magazine, or broadcast programme ■ v (-turing, -tured) **1** vt contain as an important element **2** vti give or have prominence in a performance **3** vi figure in something —**featured** adj

feature film n a full-length film

feature-length adj as long as a full-length film

featureless /féechərləss/ adj lacking distinctiveness

Feb. abbr February

febrile /féeb ríl/ adj of fever

February /fébbroo əri, fébbyoo-/ (pl -**ies**) n the 2nd month of the year in the Gregorian calendar

ORIGIN February came through French from Latin, where the month was named after a Roman festival of purification that was held on the 15th.

~~Febuary~~ incorrect spelling of **February**

feces npl US = faeces

feckless /fékləss/ adj **1** good-for-nothing **2** unlikely to be successful —**fecklessly** adv —**fecklessness** n

fecund /fékənd, féek-/ adj **1** fertile (fml) **2** highly productive —**fecundity** /fi kúndəti/ n

fed past participle, past tense of **feed**

federal /féddərəl/ adj **1** of a form of government with some central powers and some powers retained by individual states or regions **2** of the central government in a federal system

Federal Bureau of Investigation n full form of **FBI**

federalism /féddərəlizəm/ n **1** the system of federal government **2** support for the principle of federal government —**federalist** n, adj

federate /féddə rayt/ (-**ating, -ated**) vti unite in a federation

Federated States of Micronesia ◆ Micronesia, Federated States of

federation /féddə ráysh'n/ n **1** a federal union, political system, or alliance for a common goal **2** **Federation** the union of Australian states

fed up adj having reached the limits of tolerance or patience (infml)

fee n **1** a payment for professional services **2** a fixed charge made by an institution for membership, access, or participation **3** an inherited or heritable interest in land ◊ See note at **wage**

ORIGIN Fee and its close relatives *feudal* and *fief* take us back to the beginnings of European feudal society, when the ownership of cattle symbolized wealth. The ancient source of **fee**, denoting 'livestock', is also the source of the German word *Vieh* 'cattle'.

feeble /féeb'l/ (**-bler, -blest**) *adj* **1** physically or mentally weak **2** unconvincing —**feebleness** *n* —**feebly** *adv* ◊ See note at **weak**

feeble-minded *adj* an offensive term meaning below average in intelligence *(dated)* —**feeble-mindedly** *adv* —**feeble-mindedness** *n*

feed *v* (**fed**) **1** *vt* give food to a person or an animal **2** *vt* give something as food to a person or an animal o *fed the horse carrots* **3** *vt* be sufficient food for a person or animal o *This loaf won't feed us all.* **4** *vi* eat **5** *vt* sustain or support a belief or behaviour o *Compliments feed vanity.* **6** *vt* provide something with the necessary material for operation **7** *vti* move or pass something gradually ■ *n* **1** an act or occasion of feeding **2** food, especially for animals or babies **3** a large meal *(infml dated)*
□ **feed up** *vt* fatten

feedback /féed bak/ *n* **1** noise in a loudspeaker caused by a return of part of the output **2** a response intended to provide useful information for future decisions

feeder /féedər/ *n* **1** a container for food for animals or birds **2** a machine part that controls input o *a document feeder* **3** a tributary of a river **4** a road, railway, or airline that connects with a larger one

feeding bottle *n* a bottle for feeding a baby

feeding frenzy *n* a violent period of feeding by a large number of animals converging on the same food source

feeding ground *n* an area where wildlife regularly feeds

feedstuff /féed stuf/ *n* livestock feed

feel *v* (**felt**) **1** *vi* seem to yourself to be in a particular emotional state o *Don't feel sad.* **2** *vi* cause a particular sensation o *The water feels cold.* **3** *vt* think that something is so o *I feel you're lying to me.* **4** *vti* experience an emotion or sensation o *felt no regret* **5** *vt* perceive something by touch **6** *vt* examine something by touching **7** *vt* make your way hesitantly **8** *vi* use touch in searching o *feeling around for her keys* **9** *vt* have a sensation in a body part **10** *vt* be aware of something not visible or apparent ■ *n* **1** an act of touching **2** an impression gained from touch **3** an impression sensed from something o *a hotel with a more traditional feel* **4** an instinct for something
□ **feel for** *vt* have sympathy for

feeler /féelər/ *n* **1** an organ of touch such as

an insect's antenna **2** an attempt to test the reaction of others

feel-good *adj* causing or involving a sense of wellbeing

feeling /féeling/ *n* **1** the sense of touch **2** the ability to have physical sensation **3** something experienced physically or mentally **4** affection **5** the ability to experience or express emotion ■ **feelings** *npl* sensibilities ■ *adj* **1** sensitive to touch **2** expressive —**feelingly** *adv*

feet plural of **foot**

feign /fayn/ *vt* **1** pretend **2** invent or make up

feind incorrect spelling of **fiend**

feint[1] /faynt/ *n* **1** a deliberately deceptive move or action **2** a mock attack to distract attention from the main attack ■ *vti* make a feint ◊ See note at **faint**

feint[2] /faynt/ *adj* printed with faint lines as a guide for writing

feisty /físti/ (**-ier, -iest**) *adj* spirited *(infml)* —**feistily** *adv* —**feistiness** *n*

ORIGIN Feisty means literally 'like a feist', that is, a small aggressive dog. *Feist* is still used in some parts of the United States. It is a variant of *fist*, a shortening of *fisting cur*, literally 'dog that breaks wind', used as a term of contempt.

felafel *n* COOK = **falafel**

feldspar /féld spaar/, **felspar** /fél-/ *n* a common silicate mineral containing calcium, sodium, potassium, and other minerals —**feldspathic** /feld spáthik/ *adj*

felicitation /fə líssi táysh'n/ *n* a congratulating of somebody *(fml; often pl)*

felicitous /fə líssitəss/ *adj* appropriate or fortunate

felicity /fə líssəti/ (*pl* **-ties**) *n* **1** happiness **2** something producing happiness **3** appropriateness

feline /fée lín/ *adj* **1** of the cat family **2** resembling a cat ■ *n* a member of the cat family —**felinity** /fə línnəti/ *n*

fell[1] past tense of **fall**

fell[2] *vt* **1** chop a tree down **2** knock somebody down

fell[3] *adj* fierce *(literary)*

fell[4] *n* an open hillside

fell[5] *n* an animal hide

fellatio /fe láyshi ō/ *n* oral sex performed on a man

Fellini /fe léeni/, **Federico** (1920–93) Italian film director

felloe /féllō/, **felly** /félli/ (*pl* **-lies**) *n* a wheel rim

fellow /féllō/ *n* **1** a man or boy *(dated)* **2** one of a pair **3** *also* **Fellow** a member of a learned society **4** a graduate student supported by a university department ■ *adj* being in the same group

ORIGIN Fellow comes from an ancient Scandinavian word that literally meant 'somebody who lays money'. Sharing costs or financial risks implies 'partner, associate', and this was the original sense in English. The first element of the word is related to *fee*.

fellow feeling *n* sympathy

fellowship /félō ship/ *n* **1** the sharing of common interests, goals, experiences, or views **2** a society of like-minded people **3** companionship **4** a graduate post supported by a university department

fellow traveller *n* **1** somebody on the same journey **2** a Communist sympathizer

felon /féllən/ *n* somebody guilty of a felony

felony /félləni/ (*pl* -**nies**) *n* a serious crime such as murder —**felonious** /fə lṓni əss/ *adj*

felspar *n* MINERALS = **feldspar**

felt[1] past tense, past participle of **feel**

felt[2] *n* **1** compressed wool or animal-hair fabric **2** a synthetic fabric made by the process of matting ○ *roofing felt* —**felt** *vti*

felt tip *n* **1** a pen point made from compressed fibre **2** a pen with a felt tip

fem. *abbr* **1** female **2** feminine

female /fée mayl/ *adj* **1** of the sex that produces offspring **2** of women **3** describes flowers that have carpels but no stamens ■ *n* a female person or animal —**femaleness** *n*

ORIGIN Female is not etymologically related to **male**. **Female** came via French from Latin *femella*, a diminutive of *femina* 'woman' (from which English gets *feminine*). *Femina* derives from a verb meaning 'suck', so originates in the idea of 'somebody from whom milk is sucked'. *Male* developed from Latin *masculus* 'man'.

feminine /fémmənin/ *adj* **1** conventionally characteristic of or attributed to women **2** classified grammatically in the gender that includes the majority of words referring to females ■ *n* a feminine word or form —**femininely** *adv* —**femininity** /fémmə nínnəti/ *n*

~~femininity~~ incorrect spelling of **femininity**

feminism /fémmənizəm/ *n* **1** belief in the need to secure rights and opportunities for women equal to those of men **2** the movement dedicated to securing women's rights —**feminist** *n*, *adj*

feminize /fémmə nīz/ (-**nizing**, -**nized**), **feminise** *vt* make characteristic of or suitable for women —**feminization** /fémmə nī záysh'n/ *n*

femme fatale /fám fə taál/ (*pl* **femmes fatales** /*pronunc. same*/) *n* a woman regarded as very attractive and dangerous (*disapproving*)

femur /féemər/ (*pl* **femurs** *or* **femora** /fémmərə/) *n* **1** the main bone in the human thigh **2** a large bone in the upper leg of vertebrates that live on land

fen *n* an inland marsh

fence *n* **1** a structure erected to enclose an area or create a barrier **2** an obstacle for horses to jump over **3** a buyer of stolen goods (*slang*) ■ *v* (**fencing**, **fenced**) **1** *vt* enclose with a fence **2** *vti* deal in stolen goods (*slang*) **3** *vi* fight with a sword **4** *vi* avoid answering a question —**fencer** *n* ◇ **mend fences** restore good re-

lations with somebody after a disagreement ◇ **sit** *or* **be on the fence** be unwilling or unable to choose

Fencing: As one fencer lunges forwards the other prepares to parry

Popperfoto

fencing /fénssing/ *n* **1** fighting with slender swords **2** material for making fences **3** fences collectively **4** evasiveness under questioning

fend *vt* defend from harm (*archaic*) ◇ **fend for yourself** support or provide for yourself

□ **fend off** *vt* repulse

fender /féndər/ *n* **1** a metal guard for the front of a fireplace **2** *US, Can* the wing of a motor vehicle

feng shui /fúng shwáy/ *n* a Chinese system aiming at achieving harmony between people and the places they live and work in

fenland /fén land/ *n* inland marshland

fennel /fénn'l/ *n* an aromatic plant with seeds and feathery leaves or with bulbous stalks that have an aniseed flavour

fenugreek /fénnyoō greek/ *n* **1** the aromatic seeds of a leguminous plant. Use: in medicine, food flavouring. **2** the plant that produces fenugreek

FEP *abbr* front-end processor

feral /férrəl, féerəl/ *adj* **1** gone wild after formerly being domesticated or cultivated ○ *feral cats* **2** savage

Ferdinand I /fúrdi nand/ (1503–64) Holy Roman Emperor (1558–64), king of Bohemia (1526–64), and king of Germany (1531–64)

Ferdinand V (1452–1516) king of Castile (1474–1504); as Ferdinand II, king of Sicily (1468–1516) and of Aragon (1479–1516); as Ferdinand III, king of Naples (1503–16)

Fermanagh /fər mánnə/ county in SW Northern Ireland

Fermat /fər mát, fúr maa/, **Pierre de** (1601–65) French mathematician

ferment *vti* /fər mént/ **1** subject to or undergo fermentation **2** cause or be in a state of commotion or agitation ■ *n* /fúr ment/ a state of commotion or agitation

SPELLCHECK Do not confuse the spelling of **ferment** and **foment** ('cause trouble'), which sound similar.

fermentation /fúr men táysh'n/ *n* the breakdown of carbohydrates by microorganisms

Fermi /fúrmi/, **Enrico** (1901–54) Italian-born US physicist

fermium /fúrmi əm/ n (*symbol* **Fm**) an artificial radioactive element. Use: tracer.

fern n a plant that has no flowers and reproduces by means of spores —**ferny** adj

ferocious /fə róshəss/ adj 1 very fierce or savage 2 extreme —**ferociously** adv —**ferocity** /fə róssəti/ n

ferret /férrit/ n a domesticated polecat bred for hunting rabbits or rats ■ vti hunt using a ferret

---

ORIGIN Ferret comes ultimately from Latin *fur* 'thief', which is also the source of *furtive*. It entered English from French.

□ **ferret out** vt locate or discover something by persistent searching

ferric /férrik/ adj containing iron, especially with a valency of 3

Ferris wheel /férriss-/, **ferris wheel** n an amusement ride consisting of a giant revolving wheel with seats hanging down from it

---

ORIGIN The **Ferris wheel** is named after the US engineer G. W. G. Ferris (1859–96), who invented it.

---

ferrous /férrəss/ adj containing iron, especially with a valency of 2

ferrule /férrool, férrəl/ n a protective cap on or around a shaft or pole

ferry /férri/ n (pl **-ries**) 1 *also* **ferryboat** a boat for transporting passengers, vehicles, or goods 2 a place where a ferry berths ■ vt (**-ries, -ried**) 1 transport passengers, vehicles, or goods by ferry 2 transport passengers back and forth

ferryman /férri man, -mən/ (pl **-men** /-mən/) n an owner or operator of a ferry

fertile /fúr til/ adj 1 able to produce offspring 2 able to produce fruits or seeds 3 describes an egg or seed that is able to develop 4 producing good crops 5 creative or productive —**fertility** /fur tílləti/ n

Fertile Crescent n a fertile area in SW Asia

fertility drug n a drug for treating infertility in women

fertilize /fúrti līz/ (**-lizing, -lized**), **fertilise** vt 1 unite a male reproductive cell with a female cell and begin the process of reproduction 2 apply fertilizer to soil or plants —**fertilization** /fúrti lī záysh'n/ n

fertilizer /fúrti līzər/, **fertiliser** n a substance added to soil to aid plant growth

fervent /fúrvənt/, **fervid** /-vid/ adj showing passionate enthusiasm —**fervency** n —**fervently** adv —**fervidly** adv —**fervidness** n

fervour /fúrvər/ n intensity of emotion

fescue /fés kyoo/, **fescue grass** n a grass with narrow spiky leaves. Use: lawns, pasture.

fest n a social gathering for a particular activity (*infml*) o *a music fest*

fester /féstər/ vi 1 produce pus 2 become rotten 3 rankle

festival /féstiv'l/ n 1 a time of celebration 2 a programme of cultural events —**festival** adj

festive /féstiv/ adj 1 of celebration 2 cheerful o *in a festive mood* —**festively** adv —**festiveness** n

festivity /fe stívvəti/ n (pl **-ties**) 1 the merrymaking typical of a celebration 2 a celebration ■ **festivities** npl celebrations or merrymaking

festoon /fe stoon/ n a garland hanging in a loop or curve between two points ■ vt hang festoons on —**festooned** adj

feta /fétta/ n a crumbly cheese used especially in Greek dishes

fetal adj = **foetal** (*technical*)

fetch vt 1 go and get 2 cause to come 3 bring as a sale price

□ **fetch up** vi arrive (*infml*)

fetching /féching/ adj 1 good-looking 2 having or giving an attractive quality o *a fetching hat* —**fetchingly** adv

fête /fayt/, **fete** n 1 a bazaar, sale, or similar charity event 2 a holiday or day of celebration 3 a religious festival ■ vt (**fêting, fêted; feting, feted**) honour lavishly ◊ See note at **fate**

fetid /féttid, feétid/, **foetid** adj nauseating —**fetidly** adv —**fetidness** n

fetish /féttish/, **fetich** n 1 an object of obsession o *make a fetish of neatness* 2 an object arousing sexual desire 3 an object believed to have magical powers —**fetishism** n —**fetishist** n —**fetishistic** /fétti shístik/ adj

---

ORIGIN Fetish and *factitious* 'insincere, artificial' both have their origin in a Latin adjective meaning 'made by art'. While *factitious* came directly from Latin, **fetish** came through French and Portuguese, and the Portuguese descendant of the Latin source came to be used as a noun meaning 'sorcery, charm'. This entered English via French in the early 17C, referring specifically to a magical object used by West African peoples.

---

fetlock /fét lok/ n a projection on the lower part of the leg of a horse or related animal

---

ORIGIN Fetlock probably means literally 'lock of hair on the foot'.

---

fetter /féttər/ n (*often pl*) 1 a shackle for the ankles 2 a means of restraint ■ vt 1 put fetters on 2 restrain

fettle /fétt'l/ ◊ **in fine** or **good fettle** in good health, condition, or spirits

fettuccine /féttə cheéni/, **fettuccini** n 1 narrow flat pasta (*+ sing or pl verb*) 2 a dish made with fettuccine

fetus n = **foetus** (*technical*)

feud /fyood/ n a long violent dispute ■ vi participate in a feud

feudal /fyood'l/ adj of feudalism —**feudally** adv

feudalism /fyood'lizəm/ n the medieval social system in which vassals held land from lords in exchange for military service —**feudalistic** /fyood'l ístik/ adj

fever /feévər/ n 1 an unusually high body temperature 2 a disease with fever 3 a state of high excitement *(often in combination)* **4** a craze

fevered /feevərd/ *adj* **1** affected by fever **2** highly excited

feverish /feevərish/ *adj* **1** having a fever **2** agitated —**feverishly** *adv* —**feverishness** *n*

fever pitch *n* a highly agitated state

few /fyoo/ (**fewer, fewest**) *npl, pron, det* a limited number o *A fortunate few escaped.* o *Few will ever know.* o *Few people came.* ■ *det, pron* **a few** some, though not many o *a few books* o *A few escaped.* —**fewness** *n*

USAGE **fewer** or **less**? **Fewer** is used with things you can count: *fewer meetings, fewer people.* **Less** is used with things you cannot count: *less time, less prestige.* The same rule applies to **fewer than** and **less than**: *fewer than 20 people, less than a majority.* In an exception to the rule, **less** and **less than** are often used with nouns that indicate distance, weights and measurements, sums of money, and units of time, because they are thought of as collective amounts: *gifts for 50 pounds or less, arrived in less than four hours.* In addition, plural nouns can precede the set phrase *or less: eight items or less.*

fey /fay/ *adj* **1** giving an impression of other-worldliness or unworldliness **2** clairvoyant

fez (*pl* **fezzes**) *n* a flat-topped conical hat

ORIGIN The **fez** is probably named after the city of Fez in Morocco. The word entered English in the early 19C from French and Turkish.

ff *symbol* fortissimo

fiancé /fi ón say/ *n* the man to whom a woman is engaged to be married

fiancée /fi ón say/ *n* the woman to whom a man is engaged to be married

Fianna Fáil /feè ənə fóyl, -fàəl/ *n* an Irish political party, founded in 1926

ORIGIN **Fianna Fáil** means literally 'warriors of Ireland'.

fiasco /fi áskō/ (*pl* **-cos**) *n* a humiliating failure

ORIGIN **Fiasco** comes from an Italian word that literally means 'bottle'. The origin of the English use is Italian theatrical slang, where *far fiasco*, literally 'make a bottle', meant 'have a complete failure in a performance'. The reason for this is not clear.

fiat /feè at, fí at/ *n* **1** an official authorization **2** an arbitrary order

fiat money *n* money decreed to be legal tender by a government but not convertible into coin

fib *(infml)* *n* an insignificant lie ■ *vi* (**fibbing, fibbed**) tell insignificant lies —**fibber** *n* ◊ See note at **lie**

fiber *n* US = **fibre**

fibre /fíbər/ *n* **1** a thin thread **2** thread for yarn **3** cloth made from fibres **4** the essential character of something **5** strength of character o *the moral fibre of this nation* **6** coarse fibrous substances in food **7** strands from the stems or leaves of some plants used for making rope and textiles **8** a long thin structure of the body tissues, e.g. muscle cells and nerve cells —**fibred** *adj*

fibreboard /fíbər bawrd/ *n* compressed wood fibre. Use: building materials.

fibreglass /fíbər glaass/ *n* **1** compressed glass fibres. Use: insulation. **2** material made from fibreglass. Use: boat hulls, car bodies.

fibre optics *n* the use of light transmitted through fibres to transmit information *(+ sing verb)* —**fibre-optic** *adj*

fibrillate /fíbri layt, fíbbri-/ (**-lating, -lated**) *vti* beat or contract rapidly and irregularly

fibrillation /fíbri láysh'n, fíbbri-/ *n* rapid irregular beating of the heart

fibrin /fíbrin, fíbb-/ *n* a protein that helps blood to clot

fibrinogen /fi brínnəjən, fi-/ *n* a protein present in the blood that is converted to fibrin

fibroid /fí broyd/ *adj* like fibres ■ *n* a benign growth of fibrous and muscle tissue

fibrous /fíbrəss/ *adj* **1** consisting of fibres **2** in elongated threads —**fibrousness** *n*

fibula /fíbbyoolə/ (*pl* **-lae** /-lee/ *or* **-las**) *n* the outer and narrower bone in the lower leg of humans and other land-dwelling vertebrates

fiche /feesh/ *n* a microfiche *(infml)*

fickle /fík'l/ (**-ler, -lest**) *adj* changeable in affections or intentions —**fickleness** *n*

~~ficticious~~ incorrect spelling of **fictitious**

fiction /fíksh'n/ *n* **1** novels and stories describing imaginary people and events **2** a work of fiction **3** an untrue statement meant to deceive —**fictional** *adj*

fictionalize /fíksh'nə līz/ (**-izing, -ized**), **fictionalise** *vt* make into fiction —**fictionalization** /fíksh'nə līz záysh'n/ *n*

fictitious /fik tíshəss/ *adj* **1** false and intended to deceive o *gave a fictitious name* **2** fictional —**fictitiously** *adv* —**fictitiousness** *n*

fictive /fíktiv/ *adj* **1** of fiction **2** not real or true —**fictively** *adv*

fiddle /fídd'l/ *n* a violin ■ *v* (**-dling, -dled**) **1** *vi* play the violin **2** *vt* swindle *(infml)* **3** *vt* falsify *(infml)* **4** *vi* toy nervously with something **5** *vti* waste time **6** *vi* tamper with something *(infml)* **7** *vi* tinker with something to fix it —**fiddler** *n*

ORIGIN The ultimate source of both **fiddle** and **violin** is Latin *Vitula*, the name of a Roman goddess of joy and victory. From it was formed the verb *vitulari*, source of *vitula*, which in turn gave rise to *violin* and *viola* in the Romance languages and to English *fiddle* and German *Fiedel* in the Germanic languages.

fiddlesticks /fídd'l stiks/ *interj* expresses annoyance or disagreement *(infml dated)*

fiddling /fídd'ling/ *adj* insignificant

fiddly /fíddli/ (**-dlier, -dliest**) *adj* tricky to do *(infml)*

fidelity /fi délləti/ n 1 loyalty 2 sexual faithfulness 3 factual accuracy or reproductive precision 4 precision of reproduction of sound or images

fidget /fíjjit/ vi move about nervously ■ n somebody who fidgets ■ **fidgets** npl uneasiness and restlessness

fidgety /fíjjəti/ adj 1 inclined to fidget 2 uneasy and restless —**fidgetiness** n

fiduciary /fi dyóoshi əri/ adj relating to trusts or the relationship between a trustee and the person acted for ■ n (pl -ies) a trustee

fief /feef/ n 1 a piece of land granted by a feudal lord 2 a fiefdom

fiefdom /feéfdəm/ n 1 the lands of a feudal lord 2 something under somebody's influence or authority

field /feeld/ n 1 an area of agricultural land 2 a playing area for a sport 3 an area rich in a natural resource ○ a gas field 4 a broad area of something ○ an ice field 5 a sphere of activity 6 a place outside an institution or workplace where practical work is undertaken 7 a battlefield 8 a group of contestants in a race or similar event 9 in physics, an area within which a force exerts an influence at every point 10 also **field of view** an area in the eyepiece of an optical instrument in which the image is visible 11 an area in a computer memory or screen where information can be entered and manipulated ■ v 1 vt retrieve a ball that is in play 2 vi be a fielder 3 vt deploy a group, especially for military action 4 vt deal with a question or complaint ◇ **play the field** date many people

field day n 1 a time of unrestrained activity or pleasure 2 US, Can a day for amateur sports or competitions

fielder /feéldər/ n in cricket, baseball, or rounders, somebody who catches or retrieves the ball when it is struck

field event n a throwing or jumping competition

field glasses npl binoculars

field goal n 1 in American football, a goal made with a kick 2 in basketball, a goal made in normal play

field hockey n US hockey played on a field as opposed to ice hockey

Fielding /feélding/, **Henry** (1707–54) British novelist and dramatist

field marshal n the highest-ranking officer in the British army and some other armies

fieldmouse /feéld mowss/ n a small mouse that lives in fields or gardens

fieldsman /feéldzmən/ (pl -men /-mən/) n a cricket fielder

field sports npl outdoor country sports involving catching or killing animals

field test n a test of a product under normal conditions of use —**field-test** vt

field trip n an excursion to study something firsthand

fieldwork /feéld wurk/ n work done outside the normal place of work or study to gain firsthand experience —**fieldworker** n

fiend /feend/ n 1 a devil or evil spirit 2 somebody who is exceedingly evil 3 an enthusiast for a subject or activity

fiendish /feéndish/ adj 1 diabolical 2 cunning and malicious 3 extremely difficult to solve or analyse —**fiendishly** adv —**fiendishness** n

fient incorrect spelling of **feint**

fierce /feerss/ (**fiercer, fiercest**) adj 1 aggressive 2 violent or intense ○ a fierce battle 3 deeply and intensely felt ○ fierce loyalty —**fiercely** adv —**fierceness** n

fiery /fíri/ (-ier, -iest) adj 1 glowing hot 2 bright red 3 prone to intense emotion 4 spicy —**fierily** adv —**fieriness** n

fiesta /fi éstə/ n 1 a religious festival, especially one in a Spanish-speaking country 2 a festival

FIFA /feéfə/ n the international football governing body

ORIGIN **FIFA** is a French acronym formed from the initial letters of 'Fédération Internationale de Football Association'.

fife n a small flute without keys —**fifer** n

Fife council area in east-central Scotland

fifteen /fif teén/ n 1 the number 15 2 a team of 15 players —**fifteen** adj, pron —**fifteenth** adj, adv, n

fifth n 1 one of five parts of something 2 a five note interval in a diatonic musical scale 3 5th gear in a motor vehicle —**fifth** adj, adv

fifth column n a secret or subversive group —**fifth columnist** n

ORIGIN The original **fifth column** was the group of supporters that General Emilio Mola claimed to have inside Madrid when he was besieging it during the Spanish Civil War (1936–39), in addition to the four columns encircling the city.

fifth-generation adj describes a highly advanced but as yet undeveloped level of computer technology

fifty /fífti/ n (pl -ties) 1 the number 50 2 a £50 note ■ **fifties** npl 1 the numbers 50 to 59, particularly as a range of temperatures 2 the years from 50 to 59 in a century or somebody's life —**fiftieth** adj, adv, n —**fifty** adj, pron

fifty-fifty adj, adv in exactly equal shares

fig n 1 a sweet-tasting pear-shaped fruit with many seeds 2 a fruit tree that produces figs

fig. abbr 1 figurative 2 figure

fight /fit/ v (**fought** /fawt/) 1 vti use violence against somebody who resists 2 vti go to war with another country or group 3 vt carry on a contest such as an election or court case 4 vi struggle determinedly 5 vti oppose something vigorously ○ fight injustice 6 vi quarrel ■ n 1 a violent encounter 2 a determined effort to achieve or resist something 3 a verbal confrontation 4 the ability or willingness to continue a battle or struggle **5** a boxing match

SYNONYMS **fight**, **battle**, **war**, **conflict**, **engagement**, **skirmish**, **clash** CORE MEANING: a struggle between opposing armed forces

☐ **fight back** *vt* restrain tears or emotion

☐ **fight off** *vt* **1** fend off an attacker **2** avoid succumbing to an illness or emotion

fighter /fitər/ *n* **1** a fast military aircraft designed for attack **2** a very determined person **3** a soldier **4** a boxer

fig leaf *n* **1** a stylized representation of a leaf of the fig tree, covering the genitals in art **2** something meant to hide something else

figment /figmənt/ *n* a purely imaginary thing

figurative /figgərətiv, figgyoō-/ *adj* **1** not literal **2** describes art using human and animal figures —**figuratively** *adv* —**figurativeness** *n*

figure /figgər/ *n* **1** a symbol representing a number **2** an amount expressed numerically **3** somebody's body shape **4** a representation of a person in art **5** a human shape seen indistinctly **6** somebody within a particular context ○ *a prominent figure in her community* **7** somebody embodying a particular role ○ *a father figure* **8** an illustrative drawing or diagram in a book or article **9** a geometric form ■ **figures** *npl* mathematical calculations *(infml)* ■ *v* (**-uring**, **-ured**) **1** *vi* be included in something ○ *did not figure in the outcome* **2** *vt* imagine or guess

☐ **figure out** *vt* **1** find a solution or explanation for **2** decide

figurehead /figgər hed/ *n* **1** a carved figure on the bow of a ship **2** somebody nominally in charge

figure of eight *n* an outline of a number eight

figure of speech *n* a nonliteral expression or use of language

figure skating *n* ice skating in which the skaters move in patterns —**figure skater** *n*

figurine /figgə reen/ *n* a small ornamental figure or statuette

Fiji /feeji/ island nation in the S Pacific Ocean north of New Zealand. Cap. Suva. Pop. 844,330 (2001).

~~filagree~~ incorrect spelling of **filigree**

filament /filləmənt/ *n* **1** a slender strand or fibre **2** a thin wire that produces light in a light bulb

filbert /filbərt/ *n* **1** a hazelnut **2** a hazel tree

ORIGIN The **filbert** is named after the 7C abbot St Philibert, whose feast day is towards the end of August, when hazelnuts begin to ripen.

filch *vt* steal furtively *(infml)* —**filcher** *n* ◊ See note at **steal**

file[1] *n* **1** a folder, cabinet, or other container for storing papers **2** an ordered collection of documents **3** a uniquely named collection of computer instructions or data **4** a line of people or things one behind the other ■ *v* (**filing**, **filed**) **1** *vt* put something in order in a file **2** *vt* submit a claim or complaint to the

appropriate authority **3** *vi* move in a line one behind the other

file[2] *n* a metal tool with sharpened ridges for smoothing an edge or surface ■ *vti* (**filing**, **filed**) make something smooth using a file

file extension *n* a sequence of characters following the dot in a computer file name, identifying the file type

file format *n* the pattern and convention by which a computer program stores information in a file

file manager *n* a computer program to manage files

filename /fil naym/ *n* a title for a computer file

file server *n* a computer in a network that other computers access

filet /fillay/ *n* a fillet of fish or meat ■ *vt* cut into fillets

filial /filli əl/ *adj* of the relationship of children to their parents —**filially** *adv*

filibuster /filli bustər/ *n* a tactic such as a long-winded speech used to delay or prevent the passage of legislation —**filibuster** *vi*

ORIGIN A **filibuster** was a pirate who pillaged Spanish colonies in the Caribbean in the 17C. In the mid-19C the term was used in connection with a band of Americans who fomented revolution in Latin America. It readily transferred to obstruction at home, and was used of preventing legislation in the United States in the late 19C. The word **filibuster** itself came through Spanish and French from the Dutch word that was adopted into English as *freebooter*.

filigree /filli gree/ *n* lacy metal ornamentation ■ *vt* (**-greeing**, **-greed**) form into a delicate pattern —**filigree** *adj*

ORIGIN **Filigree** is an alteration of *filigrane* and was adopted from a French word that itself came from Italian *filigrano*. The elements making up the Italian original represent Latin *filum* 'thread' and *granum* 'seed'.

filing cabinet *n* a storage cabinet for files

Filipino /filli peenō/ *adj* of the Philippines ■ *n* (*pl* **-nos**) **1** the official language of the Philippines **2** somebody from the Philippines

fill *v* **1** *vti* make something full, or become full **2** *vt* take up all the space inside something or all the surface of something ○ *The room was filled with light.* **3** *vt* cover a blank area with writing or drawing **4** *vt* become present or very noticeable throughout something ○ *The scent of spring filled the air.* **5** *vt* make somebody feel a strong emotion ○ *were filled with joy* **6** *vt* close up a hole **7** *vt* meet a need **8** *vt* occupy free time **9** *vt* choose somebody for or hold a job or office ■ *n* enough or plenty of something ○ *I've had my fill of his complaints.*

☐ **fill in** *v* **1** *vt* complete the blank spaces in something **2** *vi* be a substitute for somebody **3** *vt* give somebody information

☐ **fill out** *v* **1** *vt* complete the blank spaces in a form or document **2** *vti* become or make something bigger

☐ **fill up** *v* **1** *vti* become or make something full **2** *vt* satisfy somebody's hunger

filler /fíllər/ *n* **1** a substance for plugging a crack or smoothing a surface **2** an item of less important material added to take up time or space in a broadcast or publication

filler cap *n* cap sealing the pipe to the petrol tank of a motor vehicle

fillet /fíllit/ *n* **1** a boneless portion of fish or meat **2** a ribbon worn around the head **3** a flat narrow architectural moulding ■ *vt* cut into fillets

fill-in *n* somebody who takes another person's place temporarily

filling /fílling/ *n* **1** a plug for the cavity in a decayed tooth **2** something used to fill the space inside something, e.g. a pillow or quilt **3** a food mixture put inside something such as a pie ■ *adj* satisfying hunger

filling station *n* a petrol station

fillip /fíllip/ *n* **1** something that gives you a feeling of encouragement **2** a snapping movement of the fingers —**fillip** *vt*

filly /fíli/ (*pl* **-lies**) *n* a young female horse

film *n* **1** a series of moving pictures on a screen, either telling a story or recording real events **2** films collectively **3** the coated strip of cellulose on which still or moving pictures are captured **4** a thin layer ■ *v* **1** *vt* capture somebody or something on film **2** *vti* make a film

☐ **film over** *vi* become covered with a thin layer of something

filmic /fílmik/ *adj* characteristic of a cinema film

filmmaker /fílm maykər/ *n* a film director or producer —**filmmaking** *n*

film noir /film nwaár/ (*pl* **films noirs** /*pronunc. same*/) *n* a cinematic genre featuring shadowy images, cynical antiheroes, and urban settings

film star *n* a well-known film actor

filmstrip /film strip/ *n* a strip of photographs that can be projected on a screen

filmy /fílmi/ (**-ier, -iest**) *adj* **1** light and transparent **2** covered with a film —**filminess** *n*

filo /féelō/, **filo pastry** *n* fine-layered Greek pastry

filter /fíltər/ *n* **1** a straining device **2** a porous material used for straining **3** a tinted screen placed over a lens to reduce light intensity **4** a device that blocks some sound frequencies and lets others through **5** a traffic signal that allows vehicles to turn left or right while stopping the main flow of traffic ahead ■ *v* **1** *vti* pass through a filter **2** *vi* trickle ○ *People filtered into the auditorium.* —**filterless** *adj*

filter tip *n* **1** a filtering device on a cigarette through which the smoke passes **2** a cigarette with a filter tip —**filter-tipped** *adj*

filthy /fílthi/ *adj* (**-ier, -iest**) **1** extremely dirty **2** despicable or morally objectionable **3** unpleasant (*infml*) ■ *adv* very (*infml*) ○ *filthy rich*

—**filth** *n* —**filthily** *adv* —**filthiness** *n* ◊ See note at **dirty**

filtration /fil tráysh'n/ *n* the process of filtering something

fin *n* **1** an organ extending from the body of a fish or aquatic animal that helps in balance and propulsion **2** a similar part attached to the hull of a submarine **3** the upright part of an aircraft's tail **4** a stabilizing structure on a rocket or missile **5** a rib on a heating device —**finned** *adj*

fin. *abbr* finance

finagle /fi náyg'l/ (**-gling, -gled**) *vti* get something by trickery (*infml*)

final /fín'l/ *adj* **1** last in a series ○ *final reminder* **2** allowing no change ○ *My decision is final.* ■ *n* the last of a series of contests ■ **finals** *npl* **1** the last decisive rounds of a tournament **2** university or college exams at the end of a course —**finally** *adv*

finale /fi naáli/ *n* **1** a final theatrical number **2** a final musical movement

finalist /fín'list/ *n* a competitor in the finals of a competition

finality /fī nálləti/ *n* the quality of being final

finalize /fín'ə līz/ (**-izing, -ized**), **finalise** *vt* **1** put something into its final form **2** complete a transaction —**finalization** /fín'ə līzáysh'n/ *n*

Final Solution, final solution *n* the Nazis' systematic killing of Jews

~~finaly~~ incorrect spelling of **finally**

finance /fī nanss, fi nánss/ *n* **1** the business of controlling money **2** money required to fund something ■ **finances** *npl* the money at the disposal of a person, organization, or country ■ *vt* (**-nancing, -nanced**) provide the money for

---

ORIGIN The original idea underlying modern senses of **finance** is 'finally settling a debt'. The French word from which it derives is ultimately from Latin *finis* 'end'.

---

finance company, finance house *n* a business that loans money

financial /fī nánsh'l, fi-/ *adj* **1** connected with money **2** *ANZ* well off (*infml*) —**financially** *adv*

financial year *n* a 12-month accounting period

financier /fī nánssi ər, fi-/ *n* a wealthy investor who is skilled in finance

~~finantial~~ incorrect spelling of **financial**

finch *n* a small songbird with a short broad bill

find /fīnd/ *v* (**found, found** /fownd/) **1** *vt* discover something after searching **2** *vt* get something back after losing it **3** *vt* discover something for the first time **4** *vt* discover somebody or something accidentally **5** *vt* experience something ○ *found them easy to get along with* **6** *vt* manage to get something ○ *couldn't find the money to buy it* **7** *vti* reach a verdict about a defendant **8** *vr* become conscious of your own condition or situation ■ *n* a new discovery

□**find out** v 1 vti discover the details about something 2 vt detect somebody's wrongdoing

finder /fíndər/ n 1 somebody who finds things 2 a small telescope attached to a larger telescope

fin de siècle /fáN də syéklə/ n the last years of the 19C

fine[1] adj (**finer**, **finest**) 1 quite well or satisfactory (infml) 2 not coarse 3 sunny 4 thin, sharp, or delicate 5 much better than average ○ a fine wine 6 delicately formed 7 very subtle ○ a fine distinction ■ adv 1 well (infml) ○ It works just fine. 2 into tiny pieces —**finely** adv —**fineness** n

fine[2] n a sum of money paid as a punishment ■ vt (**fining**, **fined**) punish by imposing a payment —**finable** adj

fine art n 1 the creation of beautiful objects for their own sake 2 a college course in art (often pl) 3 any art form regarded as having purely aesthetic value (often pl)

fine print n details printed in small characters

finery /fínəri/ n showy clothes

fines herbes /feenz áirb/ npl mixed fresh herbs

finesse /fi néss/ n 1 elegant ability and dexterity 2 tactful treatment of a difficult situation 3 in bridge, an attempt to win a trick with a card that is not the best in the player's hand ■ vti (**-nessing**, **-nessed**) 1 in bridge, try to win a trick with a card that is not the best in the hand 2 achieve or handle something tactfully (literary)

fine-tooth comb, **fine-toothed comb** n 1 a tool with narrow tight-set teeth for combing thoroughly 2 a detailed approach to an investigation or enquiry

fine-tune v 1 vt adjust and improve an engine's performance 2 vti get something just right —**fine-tuning** n

finger /fíng gər/ n 1 one of the digits of the hand, sometimes excluding the thumb 2 the part of a glove that covers a finger 3 a narrow strip 4 a long narrow portion of food ■ v 1 vt touch something gently 2 vti play an instrument using the fingers ◇ **put your finger on** identify ◇ **twist somebody round your little finger** succeed in getting somebody to do exactly as you wish

ORIGIN Finger goes back to an ancient form that meant 'five'.

finger bowl n a bowl for rinsing the fingers after eating

fingering /fíng gəring/ n the use of fingers to play a musical instrument

fingermark /fíng gər maark/ n a dirty mark made by a finger

fingernail /fíng gər nayl/ n the hard layer of keratin that covers the fingertip

fingerprint /fíng gər print/ n 1 a unique pattern on the inside of every fingertip 2 a distinguishing characteristic ■ vt record the fingerprints of

fingertip /fíng gər tip/ n a finger's end ■ adj using the fingertips ◇ **have at your fingertips** know all the details of

finicky /fínniki/ (**-ier**, **-iest**), **finicking** /-king/ adj 1 too concerned with details 2 too detailed —**finickiness** n ◊ See note at **careful**

finish /fínnish/ v 1 vti come or bring to an end 2 vt use up 3 vt destroy (infml) 4 vt give a desired effect to a surface such as wood ■ n 1 the end part of something 2 a special top layer 3 a spurt of speed at the end of a race 4 quality of workmanship —**finisher** n

□**finish off** vt 1 complete 2 ruin or exhaust (infml)

□**finish up** v 1 vt use up 2 vi arrive finally

□**finish with** vt 1 no longer want to have a relationship with (infml) 2 not need any longer

finished /fínnisht/ adj 1 done skilfully 2 having no further prospect of success

finishing school n a fee-paying school for girls that emphasizes social skills

finite /fín īt/ adj 1 limited 2 countable or measurable 3 in a verb form that expresses person, number, and tense —**finitely** adv —**finiteness** n

Finland /fínnlənd/ country in N Europe on the Baltic Sea. Cap. Helsinki. Pop. 5,175,783 (2001). Finnish **Suomi**

Finn n somebody from Finland

~~finnish~~ incorrect spelling of **finish**

Finnish /fínnish/ n the official language of Finland —**Finnish** adj

fiord n GEOG = **fjord**

fir (pl **firs** or **same**) n an evergreen tree with needle-shaped leaves

fire n 1 the rapid production of light, heat, and flames from something that is burning 2 the light, heat, and flames from something that is burning 3 a pile of burning fuel 4 a heating device 5 the destructive burning of something ○ fire damage 6 the discharge from guns 7 a gem's brilliance 8 eagerness and passion ■ v (**firing**, **fired**) 1 vti discharge a bullet 2 vt launch something forcefully 3 vt dismiss somebody from work (infml) 4 vi begin to burn fuel and start working 5 vt stoke or fill with fuel 6 vt bake in a kiln 7 vt strike with force 8 vt excite ■ interj 1 warns people of a fire 2 commands somebody to shoot a weapon —**fired** adj ◇ **on fire** full of eagerness or passion ◇ **play with fire** do something dangerous or risky ◇ **under fire** 1 being shot at 2 subject to severe criticism

□**fire off** vt direct things such as questions in sharp bursts

□**fire up** vti make somebody very enthusiastic

fire alarm n a bell or siren warning of a fire

fire ant n an ant with a painful sting

firearm /fír aarm/ n a portable gun

fireball /fír bawl/ n 1 the centre of a nuclear explosion 2 a bright meteor 3 a ball of lightning

firebomb /fír bom/ n a bomb designed to start a fire —**firebomb** vti —**firebombing** n

firebrand /fír brand/ *n* **1** a burning stick carried as a torch or weapon **2** an agitator who tries to stir up others

firebreak /fír brayk/ *n* an area cleared to halt a forest fire

firebrick /fír brik/ *n* a strong heat-resistant brick. Use: fireplaces, furnaces.

fire brigade *n* an organization of firefighters

firecracker /fír krakər/ *n* an explosive paper cartridge

fire door *n* **1** a fireproof door **2** an emergency exit

fire drill *n* a rehearsal for evacuating a building in an emergency

fire-eater *n* an entertainer who appears to swallow fire —**fire-eating** *n*

fire engine *n* a large truck equipped to fight fires and rescue people

fire escape *n* an exterior stairway that serves as an emergency exit from a building

fire extinguisher *n* a hand-held device containing chemicals for putting out small fires

firefighter /fír fìtər/ *n* somebody whose job is putting out fires and rescuing people —**firefighting** *n*

firefly /fír flī/ (*pl* **-flies**) *n* a nocturnal beetle that produces light

fireguard /fír gaard/ *n* a screen that protects people from sparks from an open fire

fire hydrant *n* a water connection in the street for firefighters' emergency use

fire irons *npl* tools for tending a fire in a fireplace

firelight /fír līt/ *n* the light from an open fire

firelighter /fír lìtər/ *n* a block of an inflammable substance used to start a fire in a fireplace

fireman /fírmən/ (*pl* **-men** /-mən/) *n* a man who is a firefighter

fireplace /fír playss/ *n* a low recess in a wall for an open fire

firepower /fír pow ər/ *n* destructive military power

fire practice *n* a fire drill

fireproof /fír proof/ *adj* unburnable or very resistant to fire —**fireproof** *vt*

fire raiser *n* an arsonist

fire-retardant *adj* inhibiting the spread of fire

fire sale *n* a sell-off of fire-damaged goods

fire screen *n* **1** a fireguard **2** a decorative screen to cover a fireplace that is not in use

fireside /fír sīd/ *n* the part of a room by the fireplace ■ *adj* safe and comfortable

fire station *n* the headquarters of a team of firefighters

firestorm /fír stawrm/ *n* **1** a large uncontrollable blaze **2** *US* an intense disturbance

fire trail *n Aus* a firefighters' road through a forest

firetrap /fír trap/ *n* a building that is unsafe in the event of fire

firewall /fír wawl/ *n* **1** a fireproof wall that confines a fire to one area **2** a piece of software that prevents unauthorized access

fire watcher *n* a lookout for fires

firewood /fír wŏŏd/ *n* wood burned as fuel

firework /fír wurk/ *n* an explosive object designed to make a brilliant display when lit ■ **fireworks** *npl* **1** a display of fireworks **2** an angry outburst (*infml*) **3** a spectacular display (*infml*)

~~firey~~ incorrect spelling of **fiery**

firing line *n* **1** the front position in battle **2** the forefront of a movement or action

firing squad *n* a group of soldiers who execute somebody by gunfire

firm[1] *adj* **1** not yielding to touch **2** securely fixed **3** determined **4** trustworthy ■ *adv* in a determined way ■ *vti* make or become firm —**firmly** *adv* —**firmness** *n*

☐ **firm up** *v* **1** *vt* make more definite ○ *firmed up the date for the meeting* **2** *vi* stabilize

firm[2] *n* a commercial organization

firmament /fúrməmənt/ *n* the sky (*literary*)

firmware /fúrm wair/ *n* software stored on a memory chip rather than as part of a program

ORIGIN **Firmware** is 'firm' in that the instructions will not be lost when power is shut off.

first *adj* **1** before the rest in numerical order or position **2** earlier than the rest **3** most important **4** fundamental **5** best ■ *n* **1** something that has not been done before or has never existed before **2** the person or thing that is number one in a series **3** the lowest gear in a motor vehicle **4** a first-class honours degree ■ *adv* **1** before others **2** originally **3** initially **4** more willingly

first aid *n* emergency medical help

first base *n* in baseball, the initial base that a player attempts to reach after hitting the ball ◇ **get to first base** *US, Can* succeed in the initial phase of an activity (*infml*)

first-born *n* the eldest offspring ■ *adj* first in birth order

first class *n* **1** the highest rank or standard **2** the best accommodation offered on a plane, ship, or train **3** the postal service that offers the most speedy delivery —**first-class** *adj, adv*

first cousin *n* a child of an uncle or aunt

first edition *n* **1** a copy of a book in its original printed form **2** the first copy of a newspaper subsequently changed during the day

first-footing *n Scotland* the making of goodwill visits to friends and neighbours in the early hours of the New Year

first fruits *npl* **1** the first crop harvested **2** the first benefits of something

first-generation *adj* **1** being the children of immigrant parents **2** describes the earliest form of a technology

firsthand /fúrst hánd/ *adj, adv* from the original source

first language *n* **1** somebody's native language **2** a country's main language

first lieutenant *n* **1** a naval officer responsible for maintaining a ship **2** *US* a US Army, Marine, or Air Force commissioned officer of a rank above second lieutenant

first light *n* dawn

firstly /fúrstli/ *adv* to start with

first mate *n* a merchant-ship captain's second-in-command

first name *n* a name that comes before a family name

first night *n* the first public production of a play or show

first offender *n* a criminal convicted for the first time

first officer *n* **1** a ship's first mate **2** the captain of a commercial aircraft

first person *n* **1** the form of a verb or pronoun used to refer to the speaker or writer **2** a style of writing in the first person

first principle *n* something on which beliefs are based

first-rate *adj* excellent

first reading *n* the introductory stage in a legislature for a new bill

first refusal *n* the first chance to buy something before it is offered to others

first school *n* a school for young children

first strike *n* a nuclear attack that thwarts an enemy that has nuclear capabilities

First World *n* the main industrialized nations

First World War *n* World War I

firth *n* *Scotland* an estuary (*often in placenames*)

fiscal /físk'l/ *adj* **1** of the public treasury **2** financial —**fiscally** *adv*

> ORIGIN **Fiscal** comes ultimately from a Latin word that literally meant 'rush basket'. The senses 'purse' and 'treasury' developed within Latin. The adjective formed from it passed into English in the mid-16C.

Fischer /físhər/, **Bobby** (*b.* 1943) US chess player

fish *n* (*pl same or* **fishes**) **1** a vertebrate with gills that lives in water **2** fish as food **3 Fish, Fishes** the zodiacal sign Pisces ■ *v* **1** *vti* try to catch fish **2** *vt* try to catch fish in a particular place **3** *vi* search (*infml*)
□ **fish out** *vt* find or take out after feeling round with the hands (*infml*)

fish and chips *n* fried fish with chips (+ *sing or pl verb*)

fishbowl /físh bōl/ *n* **1** a round glass bowl in which fish are kept **2** a place or lifestyle that is highly visible to the public

fish cake *n* an individual savoury fish-based patty

Fisher /físhər/, **Andrew** (1862–1928) Scottish-born prime minister of Australia (1908–09, 1910–13, and 1914–15)

fisherman /físhərmən/ (*pl* -**men** /-mən/) *n* somebody who catches fish

fishery /físhəri/ (*pl* -**ies**) *n* **1** a region of water where commercial fishing is carried on **2** the fishing industry **3** a business that catches or processes fish **4** a place for rearing fish

fisheye lens /físh ī-/ *n* a very wide-angle lens on a camera

fish farm *n* a place for rearing fish commercially —**fish farmer** *n* —**fish farming** *n*

fish finger *n* a rectangular-shaped piece of filleted or minced fish covered in breadcrumbs or batter

fishhook /físh hŏŏk/ *n* a hook for catching fish

fishing /físhing/ *n* the activity of catching fish

fishing rod *n* a flexible pole to fish with

fish knife *n* a broad-bladed knife for eating fish

fishmeal /físh meel/ *n* an animal feed or garden fertilizer made from fish

fishmonger /físh mung gər/ *n* **1** somebody whose job is selling fish **2** *also* **fishmonger's** (*pl same*) a shop selling fish

fishnet /físh net/ *n* a fabric similar to netting. Use: stockings, tights.

fish slice *n* a kitchen utensil with a slotted blade for lifting cooked food

fishtail /físh tayl/ *vi* swing an aeroplane's tail from side to side to reduce speed

fishwife /físh wīf/ *n* **1** a woman regarded as coarse and loud (*insult*) **2** a woman whose job is selling fish (*archaic*)

fishy /físhi/ (**-ier, -iest**) *adj* **1** like fish in smell, taste, or feel **2** dubious (*infml*) —**fishily** *adv*

fission /físh'n/ *n* **1** the act or process of breaking up into parts **2** the splitting of an atomic nucleus, with release of energy —**fissionable** *adj*

fissure /físhər/ *n* **1** a crack, especially in rock **2** the process of splitting **3** a split in a body part **4** a division in a group ■ *vi* (**-suring, -sured**) split

fist *n* a clenched hand ■ *vt* hit with the fist —**fistful** *n*

fistfight /físt fīt/ *n* a fight with fists

fisticuffs /físti kufs/ *npl* fighting with fists (*archaic or humorous*)

fit[1] *v* (**fitting, fitted**) **1** *vti* be the right size or shape for something or somebody **2** *vti* be appropriate for or compatible with something **3** *vt* try clothing on somebody and make necessary adjustments to its size and shape ■ *adj* (**fitter, fittest**) **1** appropriate **2** worthy **3** physically strong and healthy **4** appearing likely to do something (*infml*) ○ *looked fit to drop* ■ *n* the way that something fits
□ **fit in** *v* **1** *vi* conform well **2** *vt* find time for
□ **fit out** *vt* equip with the required items
□ **fit up** *vt* **1** equip something **2** make somebody appear guilty (*slang*)

fit[2] *n* a sudden outburst or series of convulsions ◇ **by fits and starts** starting and stopping repeatedly

fitful /fítf'l/ *adj* happening in bursts —**fitfully** *adv* —**fitfulness** *n*

fitment /fítmənt/ *n* something fitted in a particular place, especially a piece of fitted furniture

fitness /fítnəss/ n 1 the state of being physically fit 2 suitability

fitness centre n a place with facilities for people to improve or maintain their physical fitness

fitted /fíttid/ adj 1 built for and fixed into a designated space 2 with fitted furniture

fitted sheet n a sheet for a bed with an elastic edge or corners

fitter /fíttər/ n 1 somebody who maintains or assembles machinery 2 somebody who alters clothes

fitting /fítting/ adj suitable ■ n 1 a detachable part 2 an instance of trying on clothes to see if they fit 3 a clothes size ■ **fittings** npl furniture and accessories —**fittingly** adv —**fittingness** n

Ella Fitzgerald

Fitzgerald /fits jérrəld/, **Ella** (1917–96) US jazz singer

Fitzgerald, F. Scott (1896–1940) US writer

five /fīv/ n the number 5 —**five** adj, pron

five-a-side n football with five players per team

five o'clock shadow n a beard growth noticeable several hours after a man shaves

fiver /fívər/ n a five-pound note (infml)

fives /fīvz/ n a game resembling squash in which the ball is hit with the hand (+ sing verb)

five-star adj top-quality

five stones n the game of jacks (+ sing verb)

fix v 1 vt mend or correct something 2 vt agree to or arrange something 3 vt fasten something in place 4 vt attribute blame 5 vti make or become secure 6 vt direct the eyes or attention 7 vt hold the attention of somebody 8 vt influence something dishonestly (infml) 9 vt convert nitrogen to a stable biologically available form 10 vt make a photographic image permanent ■ n 1 a predicament (infml) 2 a superficial solution (infml) 3 a calculation of the position of something, e.g. using radar 4 an act of influencing something dishonestly (infml) 5 an illegal drug injection (slang) —**fixable** adj

□ **fix on** vt choose

□ **fix up** vt 1 arrange something such as a meeting 2 arrange a date for somebody with a prospective romantic partner

fixation /fik sáysh'n/ n 1 an obsession 2 a childhood attachment that results in immature psychosexual behaviour —**fixated** adj

fixative /fíksətiv/ n 1 a liquid sprayed onto something, e.g. a drawing, for protection 2 glue ■ adj tending to fix something

fixed adj 1 securely in position 2 not subject to change 3 unchanging in expression 4 agreed on 5 firmly or dogmatically held in the mind 6 dishonestly arranged (slang) —**fixedly** /-idli/ adv —**fixedness** /fíksidnəss/ n

fixed asset n a business asset that is not traded (usually pl)

fixed cost n a business expense that does not vary according to the amount of business, e.g. rent (usually pl)

fixer /fíksər/ n 1 somebody who solves problems 2 a chemical used in photography to stop the development of an image

fixity /fíksəti/ n the state of being fixed and unchanging

fixture /fíkschər/ n 1 an object in a fixed position 2 a person permanently established in a place or position 3 a sports event 4 a social event

fizz vi 1 produce gas bubbles 2 hiss ■ n 1 effervescence 2 a hissing sound 3 liveliness

fizzle /fízz'l/ vi (**-zling, -zled**) 1 make a hissing sound 2 peter out after a good start ■ n a hissing sound

fizzy /fízzi/ (**-ier, -iest**) adj producing or containing gas bubbles —**fizziness** n

fjord /feé awrd/, **fiord** n a narrow, steep-sided inlet of the sea in Scandinavia

flab n unwanted body fat (infml)

flabbergast /flábbər gaast/ vt astonish greatly (infml)

flabby /flábbi/ (**-bier, -biest**) adj having unwanted body fat (infml) —**flabbily** adv —**flabbiness** n

flaccid /fláksid, flássid/ adj 1 limp 2 lacking vitality – **flaccidity** /flak síddəti, fla-/ n —**flaccidly** adv

flacid incorrect spelling of **flaccid**

flack n = flak

flag[1] n 1 a coloured cloth flown as an emblem, especially of national identity 2 a decoration similar to a flag 3 national identity symbolized by a flag 4 a marking device, e.g. a tag attached to something 5 in American football, an official's flag thrown to the ground as a sign of illegal play 6 an indicator generated by a computer program of a condition such as an error ■ vt (**flagging, flagged**) 1 mark something in order to draw attention to it 2 draw attention to something 3 send information using a flag or flags 4 stop a vehicle by waving at the driver 5 in American football, indicate illegal play with a flag

flag[2] (**flagging, flagged**) vi 1 become weak or tired 2 hang limply

flag[3] n a flagstone ■ vt (**flagging, flagged**) pave with flagstones —**flagged** adj

ORIGIN The **flag** found also in *flagstone* is probably from a Scandinavian language. Nothing is known for certain about the origin of the other **flag** words.

flag[4] *n* an iris plant

flag day *n* a day when money is collected for charity

flagellant /flájjələnt/, **flagellator** /-laytər/ *n* 1 a religious person who whips himself or herself as a punishment for sin 2 somebody who is sexually stimulated by whipping —**flagellation** /flájjə láysh'n/ *n*

flagellum /flə jélləm/ (*pl* **-la** /-lə/ *or* **-lums**) *n* 1 a slender appendage of many micro-organisms, used for movement 2 a part of an insect's antenna —**flagellate** /flájjələt, -layt/ *adj*

flagging /flágging/ *adj* becoming weak or tired —**flaggingly** *adv*

flag of convenience *n* the flag of a country under which a ship is registered because of its favourable regulations

flagon /flággən/ *n* 1 a large wide bottle with a short neck, for alcoholic drink 2 a flagon's contents

flagpole /flág pōl/, **flagstaff** /flág staaf/ *n* a pole on which a flag is flown

flagrant /fláygrənt/ *adj* very obvious and objectionable —**flagrance** *n* —**flagrancy** *n* —**flagrantly** *adv* ◊ See note at **blatant**

flagship /flág ship/ *n* 1 the main or best ship in a fleet of ships 2 the most important or impressive thing in a group

flagstone /flág stōn/ *n* 1 a paving stone 2 rock that splits into slabs

flag-waving *n* excessive patriotism —**flag-waver** *n*

flail /flayl/ *v* 1 *vti* thrash around, or move something around violently 2 *vt* hit with a whip ■ *n* 1 a manual threshing implement, consisting of a handle attached to a free swinging blade 2 a weapon shaped like a threshing flail

flair /flair/ *n* 1 talent 2 elegance ◊ See note at **flare**, **talent**

flak, **flack** *n* 1 anti-aircraft fire directed from the ground 2 criticism (*infml*)

ORIGIN Flak is a German acronym formed from letters of *Fliegerabwehrkanonen*, literally 'aviator defence cannons'. It dates from World War II.

flake *n* 1 a small flat piece of something 2 a small individual piece of a manufactured substance ■ *v* (**flaking**, **flaked**) 1 *vi* fall off in flakes 2 *vt* break into flakes
□ **flake out** *vi* collapse from exhaustion

flak jacket *n* a bullet-proof garment

flaky /fláyki/ (**-ier**, **-iest**) *adj* 1 like flakes 2 tending to break off in flakes —**flakily** *adv* —**flakiness** *n*

flaky pastry *n* a rich type of pastry

flambé /flóm bay/, **flambée** *vt* (**-bés**, **-béed**; **-bées**, **-béed**) flavour food by pouring an alcoholic spirit on it, then burning it off ■ *adj* served in ignited spirit

flamboyant /flam bóy ənt/ *adj* 1 showy in a self-promoting way 2 brightly coloured or elaborately decorated —**flamboyance** *n* —**flamboyantly** *adv*

flame *n* 1 a hot glowing body of burning gas 2 a strong feeling 3 a lover (*infml*) 4 an angry or abusive e-mail message ■ *v* (**flaming**, **flamed**) 1 *vi* burn producing a flame 2 *vi* have a fiery glow 3 *vi* feel a strong emotion 4 *vti* criticize or abuse somebody by e-mail —**flamer** *n* ◊ **fan the flames** make a tense or difficult situation worse

flamenco /flə méngkō/ (*pl* **-cos**) *n* 1 a vigorous Spanish dance with hand clapping 2 music for a flamenco

ORIGIN Flamenco comes from a Spanish word meaning 'Flemish person'. In the Middle Ages the people of Flanders had a reputation for bright flamboyant dress.

flameproof /fláym proof/ *adj* 1 describes textiles resistant to fire 2 describes cookware for use on direct heat

flame-retardant, **flame-resistant** *adj* resistant to catching fire

flame-thrower *n* a weapon that projects a stream of burning liquid

flame war *n* an exchange of abusive e-mails

flaming /fláyming/ *adj* 1 producing flames 2 angry or intense 3 glowing 4 vivid in colour 5 expresses anger (*infml*)

flamingo /flə míng gō/ (*pl* **-gos** *or* **-goes** *or* **same**) *n* a large pink tropical wading bird

ORIGIN Flamingo is first recorded in English in the mid-16C, and comes via Portuguese from obsolete Spanish *flamengo*. The Spanish may come from Dutch *Vlaming* 'Flemish person', or ultimately from Latin *flamma* 'flame'. Whether its ultimate source is Dutch or Latin, the motivation behind the bird's name is its bright appearance. The Latin derivation would make it the 'flame'-coloured bird; the Dutch derivation would refer to the bright flamboyant dress of the people of Flanders (whence the Spanish dance, the *flamenco*).

flammable /flámməb'l/ *adj* able to catch fire

flan *n* an open pastry case with a filling

Flanders /flaándərz/ historical region of NW Europe comprising parts of present-day W Belgium, N France, and SW Netherlands

flange /flanj/ *n* a projecting collar or rim —**flanged** *adj*

flank *n* 1 a side of the lower torso 2 a cut of meat from an animal's flank 3 a side of something, e.g. a sports field or a military formation ■ *vt* be on or at the side of

flannel /flánn'l/ *n* 1 soft cotton cloth. Use: clothing, sleepwear, sheets. 2 soft woollen cloth. Use: clothing. 3 a facecloth 4 insincere or evasive talk (*infml*) ■ **flannels** *npl* trousers made of flannel ■ *vi* (**flannelling**, **flanelled**) talk in an evasive or insincere way

flannelette /flánnə lét/ *n* light cotton flannel

flap *v* (**flapping**, **flapped**) 1 *vti* move something such as wings or arms up and down 2 *vi* fly by moving the wings 3 *vi* move or sway repeatedly ○ *flags flapping in the breeze* **4** *vi* be panicky *(infml)* **5** *vt* hit something with a broad object ■ *n* **1** a flat thin piece of something, attached at one edge, used as a cover **2** the part of a book's dust jacket that folds inside the cover **3** an act or sound of flapping **4** a panicked state *(infml)* **5** a movable surface on the back of an aircraft's wing used to create lift and drag —**flappy** *adj*

flapjack /fláp jak/ *n* **1** a chewy cake made with oats **2** *US, Can* a thin flat cake cooked on a hot greased flat pan

flapper /fláppər/ *n* a young unconventional woman of the 1920s

flare /flair/ *v* (**flaring, flared**) **1** *vi* burn suddenly and brightly **2** *vi* recur or intensify suddenly **3** *vi* become suddenly angry **4** *vti* widen out **5** *vt* burn off unwanted gas in the open air ■ *n* **1** a sudden or unsteady blaze of light or fire **2** a device for producing a light as a distress signal **3** a widening shape **4** an outburst of emotion **5** unwanted light in an optical device **6** a flame for burning off waste gas **7** an area of inflammation ■ **flares** *npl* trousers with wide legs below the knee —**flared** *adj*

SPELLCHECK Do not confuse the spelling of **flare** and **flair** ('talent'), which sound similar.

flare-up *n* **1** a sudden outburst of aggression *(infml)* **2** a recurrence of something

flash *v* **1** *vti* emit light suddenly, or be emitted as light suddenly **2** *vti* reflect light from another source, or be reflected in this way **3** *vti* catch or cause to catch fire suddenly **4** *vti* signal to somebody with lights **5** *vi* move quickly **6** *vti* appear or cause to appear for a moment **7** *vi* expose the genitals indecently in public *(infml)* **8** *vt* display something ostentatiously *(infml)* ■ *n* **1** a sudden burst of light **2** a sudden burst of something, e.g. inspiration **3** a brief moment **4** a device used to light a photographic subject, or the light it produces *(infml)* **5** a short news broadcast *(infml)* **6** a badge on a uniform or vehicle ■ *adj* showy *(infml)* ◊ **a flash in the pan** a sudden brief success that is not, or not likely to be, repeated

flashback /flásh bak/ *n* **1** a recurring memory of a traumatic experience **2** an event or scene from the past inserted into a narrative

flashbulb /flásh bulb/ *n* a bulb producing a bright light for photography

flash burn *n* a burn caused by brief intense heat

flashcard /flásh kaard/ *n* a card that displays words or numbers, used as a learning aid

flasher /fláshər/ *n* a flashing light

flash flood *n* a sudden and destructive rush of water caused by heavy rainfall

flashgun /flásh gun/ *n* a device producing a flash when a camera's shutter opens

flashlight /flásh līt/ *n US* an electric torch

flash memory *n* a read-only computer memory chip that can be erased and re-programmed in blocks

flashpoint /flásh poynt/ *n* **1** the temperature at which a vapour ignites **2** a trouble spot

flashy /fláshi/ (**-ier, -iest**) *adj* **1** ostentatiously smart **2** momentarily brilliant —**flashily** *adv* —**flashiness** *n*

flask *n* **1** a small bottle used in a laboratory **2** a small flat container for alcohol **3** a vacuum flask

flat[1] *adj* (**flatter, flattest**) **1** level and horizontal **2** even and smooth **3** lying horizontally **4** no longer fizzy **5** not inflated **6** in music, below the correct pitch **7** in music, one semitone below natural **8** lacking excitement **9** emphatically absolute ○ *a flat lie* ■ *adv* (**flatter, flattest**) **1** below the correct musical pitch **2** very *(infml)* ○ *flat broke* **3** exactly ■ *n* **1** a level surface **2** a note lowered by a semitone **3** a deflated tyre *(infml)* —**flatly** *adv* —**flatness** *n*

flat[2] *n* **1** a set of rooms on one floor **2** *NZ* a shared house ■ *vi ANZ* share a flat *(infml)*

flatbed /flát bed/ *n* a truck or trailer with an open flat area for freight

flat-chested /-chéstid/ *adj* with small breasts

flatfish /flát fish/ (*pl same* or **-fishes**) *n* any sea fish with a flat body and both eyes on the upper side

flat-footed *adj* **1** having feet with low arches **2** unprepared

flatiron /flát ī ərn/ *n* an iron used to press clothes

flatland /flát land/ *n* a large stretch of level land

flatlet /flátlət/ *n* a small flat with only a few rooms

flatmate /flát mayt/ *n* somebody sharing a flat

flatpack /flát pak/ *n* a piece of furniture packed flat for home assembly

flat race *n* a horse race without jumps —**flat racing** *n*

flatten /flátt'n/ *v* **1** *vti* make or become flat **2** *vt* stand flat against something

flatter /fláttər/ *v* **1** *vt* compliment somebody in order to win favour **2** *vt* appeal to somebody's vanity **3** *vt* make somebody or something look good **4** *vr* feel unjustifiably satisfied with yourself or something you have done —**flatterer** *n* —**flattering** *adj* —**flatteringly** *adv*

flattery /fláttəri/ *n* **1** the paying of compliments to win favour **2** compliments

flattop /flát top/ *n* a haircut that is flat on top

flatulent /fláttyŏŏlənt/ *adj* **1** full of or causing wind in the digestive system **2** pompous or self-important —**flatulence** *n* —**flatulently** *adv*

Flaubert /flṓ bair/, **Gustave** (1821–80) French novelist —**Flaubertian** /flṓ báirti ən/ *adj*

flaunt /flawnt/ *v* **1** *vt* show off something **2** *vr* parade yourself shamelessly

USAGE flaunt or **flout**? **Flaunt** expresses the idea of shameless or ostentatious display: *He flaunted his wealth.* **Flout** expresses the idea of openly disobeying or defying a law or convention: *drivers who flout the law.*

flautist /fláwtist/ *n* a flute player

flavour /fláyvor/ *n* 1 the characteristic taste of something 2 a representative idea of something ◇ *gives a flavour of the book* 3 a unique characteristic ■ *vt* 1 give flavour to food 2 give uniqueness to something —**flavourful** *adj* —**flavourless** *adj*

> **ORIGIN Flavour** when it was first used in English meant 'smell' not 'taste'. Smell contributes to taste, and a shift in meaning might be seen as natural, but it is not until 300 years later, in the late 17C, that the use 'characteristic taste' appears.

flavouring /fláyvoring/ *n* something that adds flavour to food

flaw[1] *n* 1 a blemish that makes something imperfect 2 any imperfection —**flawed** *adj*

> **SYNONYMS flaw, imperfection, fault, defect, failing, blemish** CORE MEANING: something that detracts from perfection

flaw[2] *n* 1 a gust of wind 2 a squall

flawless /fláwləss/ *adj* perfect —**flawlessly** *adv* —**flawlessness** *n*

flax *n* a fine light-coloured plant fibre. Use: linen textiles.

flaxen /fláks'n/ *adj* 1 of a pale yellow colour 2 made from flax

flay *vt* 1 whip severely 2 strip the skin off

flea /flee/ *n* 1 a small leaping bloodsucking insect 2 a small beetle or crustacean that jumps like a flea

> **SPELLCHECK** Do not confuse the spelling of **flea** and **flee** ('run away'), which sound similar.

flea-bitten *adj* covered with fleas or their bites

flea collar *n* a pet's collar containing flea repellent

flea market *n* a market selling cheap or used goods

fleapit /flee pit/ *n* a run-down entertainment venue

fleck *n* a small mark or streak ■ *vt* streak or spot

fledgling /fléjling/, **fledgeling** *n* 1 a young bird with new flight feathers 2 somebody inexperienced ■ *adj* inexperienced

> **ORIGIN Fledgling** is a relatively late (mid-19C) formation from a verb *fledge*, on the model of *nestling*. Fledge is now found mainly in *fully-fledged*. It means 'develop feathers that are large enough for flight', and ultimately comes from an ancient root meaning 'fly'.

flee /flee/ (**fled**) *vi* 1 run away 2 disappear quickly (*literary*) ◇ See note at **flea**

fleece *n* 1 the woolly coat of a sheep 2 a mass of wool shorn from a sheep 3 soft fabric with a nap or pile. Use: outer garments, lining. 4 a soft warm jacket ■ *vt* (**fleecing, fleeced**)

1 swindle somebody out of money (*infml*) 2 shear sheep —**fleecer** *n*

fleecy /fleessi/ (-**ier**, -**iest**) *adj* made of or resembling fleece —**fleeciness** *n*

fleet[1] *n* 1 a group of naval ships 2 a number of vehicles or craft under single ownership

fleet[2] *adj* (*literary*) 1 moving quickly 2 passing or fading quickly

Fleet Air Arm *n* the aviation section of the Royal Navy

fleeting /fleeting/ *adj* passing or fading quickly —**fleetingly** *adv* —**fleetingness** *n* ◇ See note at **temporary**

Fleet Street *n* the British newspaper industry

Fleming /flémming/, **Sir Alexander** (1881–1955) British microbiologist. He shared a Nobel Prize in physiology or medicine (1945) with E. B. Chain and H. W. Florey for his discovery of the first antibiotic, penicillin.

Flemish /flémmish/ *adj* of Flanders ■ *n* one of the official languages of Belgium, closely related to Dutch ■ *npl* the people of Flanders

flesh *n* 1 the soft tissues that cover the bones of the body 2 the meat of animals 3 the pulp of fruits and vegetables 4 the physical aspect of humanity ◇ **in the flesh** in person ◇ **press the flesh** greet and shake the hands of many people in public (*infml*)

□ **flesh out** *vt* amplify and add details to

flesh and blood *n* 1 relatives 2 human nature

fleshly /fléshli/ (-**lier**, -**liest**) *adj* 1 bodily 2 of physical pleasure 3 not spiritual —**fleshliness** *n*

flesh wound *n* a superficial wound

fleshy /fléshi/ (-**ier**, -**iest**) *adj* 1 plump 2 with more flesh than other parts of the body —**fleshiness** *n*

Fletcher /fléchər/, **John** (1579–1625) English dramatist

fleur-de-lis /flúr də lee/ (*pl* **fleurs-de-lis** /flúr də leez/), **fleur-de-lys** (*pl* **fleurs-de-lys**) *n* a heraldic symbol in the form of three tapering petals tied by a surrounding band

flew /floo/ past tense of **fly**[1] ◇ See note at **flu**

flex[1] *vti* 1 bend something or be able to be bent easily 2 bend or contract a body part

flex[2] *n* a wire connecting electrical equipment to the main electricity supply

flexable incorrect spelling of **flexible**

flexible /fléksəb'l/ *adj* 1 able to bend without breaking 2 able to adapt to new situations —**flexibility** /fléksə bílləti/ *n* —**flexibly** *adv*

flexitime /fléksi tīm/ *n* a system giving employees adaptable working hours

flick[1] *n* 1 a quick jerking movement 2 a quick blow ■ *v* 1 *vt* hit with a quick jerking movement 2 *vti* move jerkily 3 *vt* move or propel with a quick blow ◇ *flick a switch*

□ **flick through** *vt* read superficially while turning the pages quickly

flick[2] *n* a film (*infml; in combination*) ■ **flicks** *npl* the cinema (*infml dated*)

flicker /flíkər/ *vi* 1 shine unsteadily 2 flutter or move jerkily ■ *n* 1 a fluctuating light 2 a short-lived feeling or expression ○ *a flicker of joy* —**flickeringly** *adv*

flick knife *n* a penknife with a blade that flicks open

flier /flí ər/, **flyer** *n* **1** an aircraft pilot **2** an aircraft passenger **3** a printed sheet, usually an advertisement, that is widely distributed

flight[1] /flít/ *n* **1** the process or act of flying **2** an air journey **3** the ability to fly **4** a series of steps between floors **5** a group of birds or planes flying together **6** an instance of imagining something strange or unreasonable ○ *a flight of the imagination*

flight[2] /flít/ *n* the act of running away

flight attendant *n* somebody who attends to airline passengers during a flight

flight bag *n* a small suitcase

flight deck *n* **1** the runway on an aircraft carrier **2** the part of an aeroplane where the pilot sits and where the controls are

flightless /flítləss/ *adj* unable to fly

flight lieutenant *n* a Royal Air Force officer of a rank above flying officer

flight path *n* the course taken by an aircraft

flight plan *n* information on a proposed flight

flight recorder *n* an instrument built into a plane that records details of its flight

flight sergeant *n* a Royal Air Force non-commissioned officer of a rank above sergeant

flight simulator *n* a training device for pilots that mimics the conditions in a plane

flight-test *vt* test a new aircraft's performance —**flight test** *n*

flighty /flíti/ (**-ier, -iest**) *adj* changeable and capricious —**flightily** *adv* —**flightiness** *n*

flimsy /flímzi/ (**-sier, -siest**) *adj* **1** fragile **2** easily torn **3** unconvincing and difficult to believe ○ *a flimsy excuse* —**flimsily** *adv* —**flimsiness** *n* ◊ See note at **fragile**

flinch *vi* **1** react involuntarily to pain or fear with a small backwards movement **2** avoid confronting somebody or doing something —**flinchingly** *adv* ◊ See note at **recoil**

fling *v* (**flung**) **1** *vt* throw something violently **2** *vt* move forcefully **3** *vt* move your head or arms suddenly and dramatically ■ *n* (*infml*) **1** a short romantic affair **2** a period of carefree enjoyment ◊ See note at **throw**

flint *n* **1** a very hard quartz that makes sparks **2** the part of a cigarette lighter that makes the spark

flintlock /flint lok/ *n* **1** a type of early firearm with a flint in the hammer **2** the firing mechanism of a flintlock

Flintshire /flíntshər/ county in NE Wales. Pop. 145,700 (1995).

flinty /flínti/ (**-ier, -iest**) *adj* **1** stern and unemotional **2** containing flint —**flintiness** *n*

flip *v* (**flipping, flipped**) **1** *vti* turn something over quickly, or turn quickly **2** *vt* move something with a quick light motion **3** *vti* turn the pages of a book or magazine **4** *vti* spin a coin in the air to decide something **5** *vi* suddenly

become angry (*slang*) ■ *adj* (**flipper, flippest**) flippant (*infml*) ■ *n* **1** the spinning of a coin in the air **2** a complete turn of the body in the air

flip chart *n* a large pad of paper mounted on an easel

flip-flop *n* **1** a backless sandal (*infml*) **2** a backwards flip

flippant /flíppənt/ *adj* not taking something seriously enough —**flippancy** *n* —**flippantly** *adv*

flipper /flíppər/ *n* **1** an aquatic animal's broad flat limb, used for swimming **2** a broad flat rubber extension for a swimmer's or diver's foot

flip side *n* **1** the disadvantages (*slang*) **2** the less popular song on a record (*dated*)

flirt /flurt/ *vi* **1** express a playful sexual interest in somebody **2** consider something only casually ○ *flirt with the idea of moving to Chicago* ■ *n* somebody who behaves in a playfully alluring way —**flirtingly** *adv*

flirtation /flur táysh'n/ *n* **1** a playful display of sexual interest **2** a period of casual interest in something

flirtatious /flur táyshəss/ *adj* tending to flirt with people —**flirtatiously** *adv* —**flirtatiousness** *n*

flit (**flitting, flitted**) *vi* move quickly from place to place without stopping for long —**flitter** *n*

float /flṓt/ *v* **1** *vi* rest on the surface of a liquid **2** *vt* place or move something on the surface of a liquid **3** *vi* stay up in the air **4** *vi* be heard or smelt faintly ○ *The scent of her perfume floated across the lawn.* **5** *vi* move gracefully (*literary*) **6** *vt* propose something as a plan (*infml*) **7** *vi* live or act without a fixed purpose or plan ○ *He floated from job to job.* **8** *vt* finance a company by selling shares in it to the public ■ *n* **1** a floating object that keeps another object buoyant **2** a small amount of money kept for giving change **3** an elaborately decorated vehicle in a carnival parade **4** *UK* an electrically powered delivery vehicle

floater /flṓtər/ *n* a moving spot on the eye that interferes with vision

floating voter *n* a voter with no fixed political allegiance

flock *n* **1** a group of birds or sheep **2** a crowd of people ■ *vi* go in large numbers

floe /flṓ/ *n* a mass of ice on the ocean

SPELLCHECK Do not confuse the spelling of **floe** and **flow** ('move freely'), which sound similar.

flog (**flogging, flogged**) *vt* **1** beat very hard **2** sell (*infml*)

flood /flud/ *n* **1** a large amount of water covering a previously dry area **2** high tide **3** a huge number of people or things ○ *a flood of complaints* **4** a floodlight **5** **Flood** in the Bible, a devastating flood that covered the Earth ■ *v* **1** *vti* cover an area with water, or be completely covered with water **2** *vi* overflow **3** *vt* supply or produce to excess —**flooded** *adj*

□ **flood out** *vt* force to leave because of flooding

floodgate /flúd gayt/ *n* **1** a gate in a sluice that controls the flow of water **2** something that serves to contain the potentially destructive spread of something

floodlight /flúd lìt/ *n* a powerful lamp that shines over a wide area ■ *vt* (-**lit** /-lìt/, -**lit**) light with floodlights

floodplain /flúd playn/ *n* an area of low-lying flat land next to a river

flood tide *n* **1** a rising tide **2** an irresistible force

floor /flawr/ *n* **1** the part of a room on which you walk **2** one level of a building **3** the ground at the bottom of a natural feature such as a lake or forest **4** the part of a legislature where members sit **5** the part of a stock exchange where securities are traded **6** the lowest limit ■ *vt* **1** astonish somebody **2** knock somebody down

floorboard /fláwr bawrd/ *n* a wooden board joined to others to form a floor

flooring /fláwring/ *n* materials used to make a floor

floor plan *n* a plan of a room seen from above

floorshow /fláwr shò/ *n* an entertainment at a nightclub

flop *vi* (**flopping, flopped**) **1** sit or lie down heavily **2** move or hang limply **3** fail completely (*infml*) ■ *n* a total failure (*infml*)

floppy /flóppi/ *adj* (-**pier, -piest**) hanging limply ■ *n* (*pl* -**pies**) a floppy disk (*infml*) —**floppily** *adv* —**floppiness** *n*

floppy disk *n* a small data storage disk used in computers

> **ORIGIN** A **floppy disk** is 'floppy' only in comparison with a *hard disk*. The magnetic disk itself is flexible but the outer casing is now more rigid than it was in the earlier days of computers.

flops, FLOPS *abbr* floating-point operations per second (*indicates the speed of a computer*)

floptical /flóptik'l/ *adj* describes a system for storing computer data on a disk that combines magnetic and optical technology

flora /fláwrə/ (*pl* -**ras** *or* -**rae** /-ree/) *n* **1** all plants, especially all those found in a particular area (*fml*) **2** a book that describes plants

> **ORIGIN** The name of the Roman goddess of flowers, Flora, was used in the Latin titles of descriptive catalogues of plants from the mid-17C. The word first appears in English use in the late 18C. *Flora* was formed from the Latin word for 'flower', from which *flower* itself derives.

floral /fláwrəl/ *adj* of, decorated with, or containing flowers —**florally** *adv*

Florence /flórrənss/ city in central Italy on the River Arno. Pop. 376,760 (1999). Italian **Firenze**

~~florescent~~ incorrect spelling of **fluorescent**

floret /flórrət/ *n* **1** a small flower, especially one in a flower head made up of many flowers

2 one of the parts into which a head of cauliflower or broccoli can be separated

Florey /fláwri/, **Sir Howard Walter, Baron Florey of Adelaide and Marston** (1898–1968) Australian scientist. He shared a Nobel Prize in physiology or medicine (1945) with Alexander Fleming and E. B. Chain for the development of the first antibiotic, penicillin.

florid /flórrid/ *adj* **1** having an unhealthy red complexion **2** ornate in wording and style —**floridly** *adv* —**floridness** *n*

Florida /flórridə/ state in the SE United States. Cap. Tallahassee. Pop. 15,982,378 (2000). —**Floridian** /flə ríddi ən/ *adj, n*

Florida Keys /-keèz/ chain of islands and reefs in S Florida, extending into the Gulf of Mexico. Length 309 km/192 mi.

florist /flórrist/ *n* **1** somebody who sells flowers **2** *also* **florist's** (*pl* same) a shop that sells flowers and plants

floss *vti* clean between your teeth with special thread ■ *n* **1** dental floss **2** short silkworm fibres

flotation /flō táysh'n/ *n* **1** the selling of shares in a company to finance it **2** the process or condition of floating

flotation tank *n* a tank of salt water and minerals in which somebody floats to relax

flotilla /flō tíllə/ *n* a fleet of small ships

flotsam /flótsəm/ *n* **1** wreckage floating in the sea **2** people who live on the margins of society (*sometimes offensive*)

flounce¹ /flownss/ (**flouncing, flounced**) *vi* move with an angry swagger —**flounce** *n*

flounce² /flownss/ *n* a decorative strip of gathered cloth on a garment or curtain

flounder¹ /flówndər/ *vi* **1** move in a clumsy uncontrolled way **2** hesitate in confusion

flounder² /flówndər/ (*pl* same *or* -**ders**) *n* **1** a flatfish of shallow coastal waters **2** a flounder as food

flour /flów ər/ *n* **1** finely ground cereal grains **2** ground powder made from any dried edible plant ■ *vt* cover with flour —**floury** *adj*

> **SPELLCHECK** Do not confuse the spelling of **flour** and **flower** (of a plant), which sound similar.

~~flourescent~~ incorrect spelling of **fluorescent**
~~flouride~~ incorrect spelling of **fluoride**
~~flourine~~ incorrect spelling of **fluorine**

flourish /flúrrish/ *vi* **1** be healthy or grow well **2** do well or succeed ■ *n* **1** a dramatic hand or body movement **2** an embellishment to something handwritten

flout /flowt/ *vt* openly ignore a law or convention —**floutingly** *adv* ◊ See note at **flaunt**

flow /flō/ *vi* **1** move freely from place to place **2** circulate in the body (*refers especially to blood*) **3** be said fluently **4** be available in large quantities (*refers to alcoholic drinks*) **5** be experienced as an emotion intensely and often visibly **6** derive from something *(literary)* **7** hang loosely and gracefully *(refers to clothes or hair)* ■ *n* **1** the movement of a fluid or an electrical charge **2** a mass or quantity that is flowing **3** a steady stream of people or things —**flowingly** *adv* ◊ **go with the flow** fall in with the mood or thinking of others ◊ See note at **floe**

flow chart, flow diagram *n* a diagram showing a sequence of operations in a process

flower /flów ər/ *n* **1** the coloured part of a plant, containing its sexual organs **2** a single stem with a flower on it **3** a plant grown for its flowers **4** the period during which a plant is in bloom **5** the best part of something ■ *vi* **1** produce blooms **2** develop to maturity —**flowered** *adj* ◊ See note at **flour**

flowerbed /flów ər bed/ *n* an area of ground planted with flowers

flowering /flów əring/ *adj* able to produce blooms ■ *n* a period of success

flowerpot /flów ər pot/ *n* a container for growing plants

flowery /flów əri/ *(-ier, -iest) adj* **1** full of overly elaborate expressions **2** of or decorated with flowers —**floweriness** *n*

flown past participle of **fly**[1]

flow sheet *n* a flow chart

flu /floo/ *n* a viral illness producing a high fever, respiratory inflammation, and muscle pain

ORIGIN Flu is a shortening of *influenza*, first recorded in the mid-19C. *Influenza* itself originally referred specifically to a severe epidemic of 1743, which began in Italy.

SPELLCHECK Do not confuse the spelling of **flu, flue** ('a smoke or heat outlet'), and **flew** (past tense of *fly*), which sound similar.

fluctuate /flúkchoo ayt/ *(-ating, -ated) vi* vary in level, degree, or value —**fluctuation** /flúkchoo áysh'n/ *n*

flue /floo/ *n* a smoke or heat outlet ◊ See note at **flu**

fluent /flóo ənt/ *adj* **1** having or showing a good command of a language **2** elegantly and effortlessly expressed —**fluency** *n* —**fluently** *adv*

fluff *n* **1** light balls of fibre that collect on fabric **2** downy fuzz on some birds or seeds ■ *vt* **1** perform something badly *(infml)* **2** shake or pat something to get air into it

fluffy /flúffi/ *(-ier, -iest) adj* soft and light in texture **2** downy or feathery —**fluffily** *adv* —**fluffiness** *n*

fluid /flóo id/ *n* **1** anything liquid **2** in scientific usage, a liquid or gas ■ *adj* **1** smooth and graceful in movement or performance **2** likely to change ○ *The situation remains fluid.* —**fluidity** /floo íddəti/ *n* —**fluidly** *adv*

fluid ounce *n* **1** a UK unit of liquid measurement equal to $\frac{1}{20}$ of an imperial pint or 28.41 ml **2** a US unit of liquid measurement equal to $\frac{1}{16}$ of a US pint or 29.57 ml

fluke[1] *n* an accidental success *(infml)* —**fluky** *adj*

fluke[2] *n* a parasitic worm with a flattened body

fluke[3] *n* **1** either of the blades at the ends of an anchor **2** either of the lobes of a whale's tail

flume *n* an artificial water channel for transporting logs or for swimmers to slide down

flummox /flúmməks/ *vt* baffle and confuse *(infml)*

flung past participle, past tense of **fling**

flunk *vti* fail an exam or course *(infml)*

flunky /flúngki/ *(pl -kies),* **flunkey** *(pl -keys) n* **1** a servile assistant *(infml)* **2** a manservant in livery —**flunkyism** *n*

fluoresce /floor réss/ *(-rescing, -resced) vi* experience or show fluorescence

fluorescence /floor réss'nss/ *n* **1** the emission of light by an object exposed to radiation **2** glowing light produced by fluorescence

fluorescent /floor réss'nt/ *adj* **1** capable of producing or undergoing fluorescence **2** bright and dazzling in colour

fluorescent lamp, fluorescent light *n* an electric lamp containing a low pressure vapour in a glass tube

fluoridate /flóori dayt/ *(-dating, -dated) vt* treat water by adding small amounts of fluoride salts —**fluoridation** /flóori dáysh'n/ *n*

fluoride /flóor īd/ *n* any chemical compound consisting of fluorine and another element or group

fluorine /flóor een/ *n (symbol* F) a toxic reactive gaseous chemical element. Use: water treatment, making fluorides and fluorocarbons.

fluorocarbon /flóorō káarbən/ *n* an inert chemical containing carbon and fluorine. Use: nonstick coatings, lubricants, refrigerants, solvents.

flurry /flúrri/ *n (pl -ries)* **1** a burst of activity **2** a short period of rainfall, snowfall, or wind ■ *v (-ries, -ried)* **1** *vt* agitate or confuse **2** *vi* snow lightly

flush[1] *v* **1** *vi* go red in the face **2** *vti* make water flow through a toilet to clean it after use **3** *vt* dispose of in a toilet **4** *vt* clean with water ■ *n* **1** a sudden intense feeling **2** the beginning of an exciting or pleasurable period **3** a sudden rush of things **4** reddishness

flush[2] *adj* **1** level with something **2** beside or against something **3** temporarily rich *(infml)* ■ *adv* **1** completely level **2** directly or squarely ■ *vt* fit things so that they form a level surface —**flushness** *n*

flush[3] *vt* drive out of hiding ■ *n* birds frightened out of hiding

flush[4] *n* in poker, a hand of cards of one suit

flushed *adj* **1** red-faced **2** excited

fluster /flústər/ *vti* make or become nervous ■ *n* a nervous or agitated state —**flustered** *adj*

flute *n* **1** a wind instrument with a high-pitched sound **2** a decorative groove, especially in an architectural column **3** a tall glass for sparkling wine ■ *vt* **(fluting, fluted)** make rounded grooves in —**fluted** *adj*

flutist /flóotist/ *n* a flautist

flutter /flúttər/ v 1 vi move with a gentle waving motion 2 vti move quickly up and down or side to side 3 vti flap the wings rapidly 4 vi fly lightly or noiselessly 5 vi beat rapidly, either because of a disorder or from excitement *(refers to the heart)* 6 vi have a quivering nervous or excited feeling ■ n 1 a quick movement 2 agitation or excitement 3 a rapid heartbeat 4 a small bet *(infml)* —**flutteringly** adv —**fluttery** adj

fluvial /flóõvi əl/ adj of rivers

flux n 1 constant change 2 a substance that aids flowing, e.g. in soldering, welding, or ceramic glazes 3 flow or a rate of flow 4 the strength of a magnetic or electrical field in a particular area

fly[1] v **(flies, flew** /floo/**, flown** /flōn/**) 1** vi move through the air **2** vi travel in an aircraft **3** vt take or send something by air **4** vti be the pilot of a plane **5** vt travel over an area by air **6** vti display a flag, or be displayed, on a pole **7** vi move freely in the air ○ *with her hair flying* **8** vi go at top speed ○ *I must fly!* **9** vi move quickly and with explosive force ○ *sent debris flying everywhere* **10** vi pass quickly ○ *The time flew by.* **11** vi rush to do something ○ *He flew to our aid.* ■ n (pl **flies**) **1** the front opening of a pair of trousers *(usually pl)* **2** the entrance flap of a tent **3** US a fly sheet ■ **flies** npl the area above a stage in a theatre ◇ **fly high** enjoy a period of great success or happiness ◇ **let fly** speak angrily ◇ **on the fly** while a computer program is running *(infml)*

□ **fly at** vt attack physically or verbally

fly[2] (pl **flies**) n 1 a two-winged insect, many of which are pests **2** any flying insect *(usually in combination)* ◇ **a fly in the ointment** a problem that spoils a good situation

fly[3] adj clever and sharp *(infml)*

flyaway /flí ə way/ adj fine and light

flyblown /flí blōn/ adj 1 maggot-ridden and contaminated 2 dirty

flyby /flí bī/ n a flight close to something, especially a space flight close to an astronomical object

fly-by-night adj 1 unscrupulous in business 2 not lasting long

flycatcher /flí kachər/ n an insect-eating songbird

flyer n = flier

fly half n in rugby, a player who plays behind the forwards and the scrum half

flying /flí ing/ adj 1 able to fly 2 moving fast ■ n air travel

flying buttress n a prop-like support built out from an outside wall

flying doctor n ANZ a doctor who reaches patients in remote locations by air

flying fish n a fish that leaps using its large fins like wings

flying fox n an Australasian fruit bat

flying mouse n a computer mouse that can be lifted and used as a pointer

flying officer n an RAF officer of a rank above pilot officer

flying picket n a picket who travels to various workplaces to support other strikes

flying saucer n a disc-shaped UFO

flying squad n a police or military unit that can be deployed quickly

flying squirrel n a nocturnal squirrel that uses a flap of skin between its front and back limbs to glide between trees

flyleaf /flí leef/ (pl **-leaves** /-leevz/) n the first page in a hardback book, attached to the inside cover page

Flynn /flin/, **Errol** (1909–59) Australian-born US actor

Flynn, John (1880–1951) Australian missionary

fly-on-the-wall adj filmed in a way that shows something as it really is

flyover /flí ōvər/ n a main road on a bridge crossing another main road

flypaper /flí paypər/ n sticky paper on which to catch flies

fly-past n a ceremonial flight past people on the ground

flyposting /flí pōsting/ n the activity of putting up posters illegally

fly sheet n the outer shell of a tent, or an outer tarpaulin fitted over a tent

flysheet /flí sheet/ n a small advertising poster

fly spray n a spray that kills flying insects

fly swatter n a tool for swatting insects

fly-tipping n the illegal dumping of rubbish

flyweight /flí wayt/ n 1 the lightest weight category for a boxer 2 a boxer who competes at this weight

flywheel /flí weel/ n a heavy wheel that maintains a constant speed of rotation in a machine

fm abbr 1 fathom 2 also FM frequency modulation

Fm symbol fermium

FO abbr Foreign Office

foal /fōl/ n a young horse ■ vi give birth to a foal

foam /fōm/ n 1 a mass of bubbles on a liquid 2 any thick frothy substance ○ *shaving foam* 3 a fire-extinguishing substance 4 rubber, plastic, or similar material containing bubbles of air ■ vi produce bubbles —**foaminess** n —**foamy** adj

foam rubber n a spongy form of rubber. Use: mattresses, padding, insulation.

fob n 1 a chain for a pocket watch 2 an ornament or electronic device on a key ring or chain

□ **fob off** vt 1 mislead so as to forestall questioning 2 give something inferior or unwanted to

focaccia /fə káchə, fō-/ n flat Italian bread made with yeast and olive oil and sprinkled with a topping

focal /fók'l/ adj 1 principal 2 of the focusing of an image —**focally** adv

focal length *n* (*symbol* **f**) the distance from a lens to a focal point

focal point *n* **1** the point at which rays of light meeting a lens converge or appear to diverge **2** a centre of attention

fo'c's'le *n* NAUT = **forecastle**

focus /fṓkəss/ *n* (*pl* **-cuses** *or* **-ci** /-sī/) **1** the main emphasis of something **2** an area of concern ○ *Our investigation has a narrow focus.* **3** a concentrated quality ○ *bring focus to the problem* **4** the sharpness of an image **5** the condition of seeing sharply **6** (*pl* **foci**) a focal point **7** a device on a camera for adjusting the lens ■ *vti* (**-cuses** *or* **-cusses**, **-cusing** *or* **-cussing**, **-cused** *or* **-cussed**) **1** direct your attention to somebody or something **2** adjust vision to see something clearly **3** adjust a lens for a clear image

focused /fṓkəst/, **focussed** *adj* **1** concentrated **2** single-minded

focus group *n* a representative group of people who are questioned about their opinions as part of political or market research

fodder /fóddər/ *n* food for livestock

foe *n* an enemy *(fml)*

FOE, FoE *abbr* Friends of the Earth

foetal /féet'l/, **fetal** *adj* of a foetus

foetid *adj* = **fetid**

foetus /féetəss/, **fetus** *n* an unborn child

fog *n* **1** condensed water vapour in the air at or near ground level **2** something that reduces visibility **3** a state of muddle ■ *v* (**fogging**, **fogged**) **1** *vti* make or become obscured with condensation **2** *vt* make confused —**fogged** *adj*

fog bank *n* a mass of thick fog

fogbound /fóg bownd/ *adj* **1** prevented by fog from travelling **2** shrouded in fog

foggy /fóggi/ (**-gier**, **-giest**) *adj* **1** filled with or obscured by fog **2** vague ○ *only a foggy idea* —**foggily** *adv* —**fogginess** *n*

foghorn /fóg hawrn/ *n* a horn sounded to warn of fog

foglamp /fóg lamp/, **fog light** *n* a car light with a beam designed to penetrate fog

fogy /fṓgi/ (*pl* **-gies**), **fogey** (*pl* **-geys**) *n* a person regarded as old-fashioned —**fogyish** *adj* —**fogyism** *n*

foible /fóyb'l/ *n* a personal weakness or quirk *(usually pl)*

ORIGIN Foible is from a later form of the French word that entered English much earlier as *feeble*. It was originally used as an adjective meaning 'weak', between the late 16C and early 18C. The earliest use of the noun (mid-17C) was a technical term in fencing. The usual modern sense is recorded from the late 17C.

---

foie gras /fwaa graa/ *n* a fattened goose liver, or pâté made from it

foil[1] *n* **1** metal in thin sheets **2** a good contrast to something **3** a wing-shaped blade attached to the bottom of a hydrofoil

foil[2] *vt* thwart somebody's success

foil[3] *n* a long thin sword used in fencing

foist *vt* **1** force somebody to accept something undesirable **2** give somebody something inferior on the pretence that it is genuine

fold[1] /fōld/ *v* **1** *vt* bend something flat over on itself **2** *vt* make something smaller by folding it or parts of it **3** *vt* draw the arms, legs, or hands together or towards the body **4** *vt* bring the wings together or next to the body **5** *vt* put your arms round and hold somebody **6** *vi* go out of business **7** *vi* in card games, give up your hand ■ *n* **1** a folded part **2** a crease caused by folding **3** a part of something that hangs in a folded shape —**foldable** *adj* —**folding** *adj*

☐ **fold in** *vt* add a food ingredient to a mixture carefully and lightly

fold[2] /fōld/ *n* **1** an enclosed area for livestock, especially sheep **2** livestock in a fold **3** a group with interests or traits in common ○ *We welcomed them back to the fold.*

-fold *suffix* **1** divided into parts ○ *manifold* **2** times ○ *tenfold*

foldaway /fṓld ə way/ *adj* made to be folded and stored

folder /fṓldər/ *n* **1** a piece of card folded to make a file in which papers can be held **2** a conceptual container for the storage of computer files in some operating systems

foldout /fṓld owt/ *n* an extra-large page in a publication, folded to fit —**foldout** *adj*

foldup /fṓld up/ *adj* designed to be folded

foliage /fṓli ij/ *n* **1** leaves **2** leafy decoration

folio /fṓli ō/ *n* (*pl* **-os**) **1** a large book or manuscript **2** a large sheet of paper folded to make four pages for a book **3** a page numbered on the front ■ *adj* printed in a large format

folk /fōk/ *npl* people in general (*+ pl verb*) ■ *n* folk music (*+ sing verb*) ■ *adj* **1** traditional, especially passed down orally **2** from the ideas of ordinary people

folk dance *n* **1** a traditional dance **2** music for a traditional dance

folk hero *n* somebody who is admired by the public

folklore /fṓk lawr/ *n* **1** traditional stories, usually passed down orally **2** local stories and gossip that become legends —**folklorist** *n*

folk music *n* **1** traditional songs and music **2** modern music in a traditional style

folk song *n* **1** a traditional song **2** a modern song in a traditional style —**folk singer** *n* —**folk singing** *n*

folksy /fṓksi/ (**-sier**, **-siest**) *adj* **1** in the style of folk traditions **2** affectedly traditional or informal —**folksiness** *n*

folktale /fṓk tayl/ *n* a traditional story

follicle /fóllik'l/ *n* a small gland, cavity, or sac —**follicular** /fo likyōolər/ *adj*

follow /fóllō/ *v* **1** *vti* come after somebody or something ○ *the main course followed by dessert* **2** *vt* add to something already done ○ *She* *followed her lecture with a demonstration.* **3** *vti* go after or behind somebody, moving in the same direction **4** *vt* keep under surveillance **5** *vt* pay close attention to **6** *vt* go along the course of ◦ *follow the path* **7** *vt* go in the direction indicated by ◦ *Follow that sign ahead.* **8** *vt* act or develop in accordance with **9** *vti* do the same as ◦ *She followed her father into medicine.* **10** *vti* understand something **11** *vt* engage in as a career or profession **12** *vt* keep up to date with **13** *vi* result from something

SYNONYMS follow, chase, pursue, tail, shadow, stalk, trail CORE MEANING: go after or behind

☐ **follow on** in cricket, be forced to bat again after a low-scoring first innings
☐ **follow through** *v* **1** *vti* take further action to complete something **2** *vi* continue the motion of a swing or throw
☐ **follow up** *vt* **1** act on information **2** do after or in addition to something ◦ *will follow up the phone call with a letter*

follower /fóllō ər/ *n* **1** somebody who comes or travels after somebody or something else **2** a supporter or admirer of a person, cause, or activity

following /fóllō ing/ *adj* **1** next in order **2** about to be mentioned ■ *n* **1** a group of followers **2** the things about to be mentioned *(+ pl verb)* ■ *prep* after

follow-my-leader *n* a game in which players copy another's actions

follow-on *adj* continuing or resulting ■ *n* **1** a continuation or consequence of a previous event **2** in cricket, an act of following on after a low score

follow-through *n* **1** a continuation and completion of something **2** in a sport, the concluding part of a movement

follow-up *n* **1** further action intended to supplement something **2** something that gives more information —**follow-up** *adj*

folly /fólli/ *(pl* **-lies)** *n* **1** thoughtless or reckless behaviour **2** a thoughtless or reckless act or idea *(often pl)* **3** an impractical building of eccentric design

foment /fō mént, fə mént/ *vt* stir up trouble or rebellion —**fomentation** /fṓ men táysh'n, fṓmən-/ *n* ◊ See note at **ferment**

fond *adj* **1** feeling or showing love or affection for somebody **2** liking or enjoying something **3** overly doting **4** overoptimistic ◦ *fond hopes* —**fondly** *adv* —**fondness** *n* ◊ See note at **love**

Fonda /fóndə/, **Henry** (1905–82) US film and stage actor

fondant /fóndənt/ *n* **1** sugar paste. Use: filling for chocolates, coating for cakes and confectionery. **2** a soft sweet made with fondant

fondle /fónd'l/ (**-dling, -dled**) *v* **1** *vt* stroke lovingly or sexually **2** touch sexually in an unwelcome way

fondue /fón dyoo, -doo/ *n* a dish eaten by dipping

small pieces of food into melted cheese or hot oil

font[1] *n* **1** a receptacle for baptismal water or holy water **2** an abundant source *(literary)*

font[2], **fount** /fownt/ *n* a set of type or characters of the same style and size

fontanelle /fóntə nél/ *n* a soft, membrane-covered space between bones at the front and back of a young baby's skull

Fonteyn /fon táyn/, **Dame Margot** (1919–91) British ballet dancer

food *n* **1** substances that people, plants, and animals eat or absorb to obtain the nutrients they need **2** solid nourishment, not drinks **3** a mental stimulus

food chain *n* a hierarchy of feeding relationships among organisms

foodie /fóodi/, **foody** *(pl* **-ies)** *n* somebody who enjoys good food *(infml)*

food poisoning *n* inflammation of the stomach and intestines caused by eating contaminated food

food processor *n* an appliance that chops and blends foods

foodstuff /fóod stuf/ *n* any edible substance *(usually pl)*

food web *n* the various food chains that exist within a particular ecological community

fool *n* **1** a person considered to lack good sense or judgment **2** a person considered to be or made to appear ridiculous **3** formerly, a court entertainer **4** a creamy fruit dessert ■ *v* **1** *vt* deceive or trick **2** *vi* say something jokingly ◊ **be nobody's fool** be wise enough not to be easily deceived

☐ **fool around** *or* **about** *vi* **1** behave in a silly or comical way **2** waste time
☐ **fool with** *vt* play or tinker with

foolhardy /fóol haardi/ *adj* bold but reckless —**foolhardiness** *n*

foolish /fóolish/ *adj* **1** not sensible **2** feeling or appearing ridiculous ◦ *a foolish grin* **3** unimportant ◦ *a foolish worry* —**foolishly** *adv* —**foolishness** *n*

foolproof /fóol proof/ *adj* **1** designed to function despite human error **2** infallible

fool's cap *n* a jester's hat

foolscap /fóol skap, fóolz kap/ *n* a large paper size

ORIGIN The original **foolscap** paper had a fool's cap as its watermark.

fool's gold *n* any mineral with a gold lustre, especially pyrites

fool's paradise *n* a state of happiness based on unrealistic hopes ◦ *living in a fool's paradise*

foot *n* *(pl* **feet** /feet/) **1** the part of the leg below the ankle **2** an organ of an invertebrate animal that is used to grip or move **3** *(symbol* ' *)* a unit of length equal to .3048 m/12 in **4** the lowest part of something **5** the part of a sock or boot that covers the foot **6** something that gives support like a foot, e.g. a shaped part at the end of the leg of a chair **7** a unit of poetic

metre ■ *vt* pay the full cost of —**footed** *adj*
◇ **drag your feet** move or do something slowly and reluctantly (*infml*) ◇ **fall or land on your feet** end up in a good position ◇ **find your feet** become adjusted to a new situation ◇ **get off on the wrong foot** begin something badly ◇ **get on or to your feet** return to a healthy or financially stable condition ◇ **have at your feet** be the object of enormous admiration and devotion from ◇ **have feet of clay** have a weakness or flaw that is not obvious at first ◇ **have or keep both or your feet on the ground** act and think sensibly ◇ **on foot** walking ◇ **put your best foot forward** try as hard as you can to impress or please ◇ **put your feet up** stop working and relax ◇ **put your foot down 1** insist firmly on an opinion or decision **2** make a motor vehicle travel faster by depressing the accelerator ◇ **put your foot in it** make a tactless or embarrassing mistake (*infml*) ◇ **shoot yourself in the foot** do something that harms your own interests ◇ **sweep somebody off his or her feet** charm somebody completely

footage /fŏottij/ *n* **1** a filmed sequence showing an event **2** size measured in feet

foot-and-mouth disease *n* a viral disease of animals with divided hoofs

football /fŏot bawl/ *n* **1** a game in which two teams of 11 players try to kick or head a ball into the opposing team's goal **2** any team game in which a ball is kicked or carried **3** a ball used in football **4** a problem that is often discussed, without any real attempt at finding a solution ○ *a political football* —**footballer** *n*

football pools *npl* an organized form of gambling involving the prediction of football results

footboard /fŏot bawrd/ *n* **1** a board at the bottom of a bed **2** a support for the feet in a vehicle

footbridge /fŏot brij/ *n* a bridge for pedestrians

footer /fŏottər/ *n* a piece of text below the main text of a page, especially text inserted on each page by word-processing software

footfall /fŏot fawl/ *n* **1** the sound of footsteps **2** the number of potential customers who visit a shop or business in a given period

foothill /fŏot hil/ *n* a hill that forms the approach to a mountain (*often pl*)

foothold /fŏot hōld/ *n* **1** a place where a climber's foot can get support **2** a firm base for progress

footie /fŏotti/ *n* football (*infml*)

footing /fŏotting/ *n* **1** the secure placement of the feet when standing, walking, or running **2** a base for progress **3** a particular status, condition, or relationship ○ *put the discussion on a more scientific footing*

footle /fŏot'l/ *n* nonsense

footlights /fŏot līts/ *npl* **1** lights along the front of a stage **2** the theatre as a profession

footling /fŏotling/ *adj* unimportant (*infml*)

footloose /fŏot looss/ *adj* free to do anything or go anywhere

footman /fŏotmən/ (*pl* **-men** /-mən/) *n* a male servant in uniform

footmark /fŏot maark/ *n* a mark made on a surface by somebody's foot

footnote /fŏot nōt/ *n* **1** a piece of information at the bottom of a page **2** an additional detail

foot passenger *n* a ferry passenger without a car

footpath /fŏot paath/ (*pl* **-paths** /-paathz/) *n* a path for walkers

footprint /fŏot print/ *n* **1** a mark made on a surface by somebody's foot **2** the desk space occupied by a computer or other machine

footrest /fŏot rest/ *n* something on which to rest your feet

footsie /fŏotsi/ *n* flirtatious play with the feet (*infml*) ◇ **play footsie** *US* collaborate (*infml*)

foot soldier *n* an infantry soldier

footsore /fŏot sawr/ *adj* having aching feet

footstep /fŏot step/ *n* **1** the sound of somebody's foot hitting the ground **2** a mark made by a foot ◇ **follow in somebody's footsteps** emulate another person's life or work

footstool /fŏot stool/ *n* a piece of furniture that supports the feet

footwear /fŏot wair/ *n* shoes and boots

footwork /fŏot wurk/ *n* the movement of the feet in sport or dancing

fop *n* a man obsessed by fashion and his appearance —**foppery** *n* —**foppish** *adj*

for *prep* **1** intended to be received or used by ○ *a letter for you* **2** on behalf of ○ *acting for his client* **3** towards somebody or something ○ *heading for Paris* **4** indicates how long something lasts or extends ○ *was off work for a week* **5** because of ○ *did it for love* **6** with the purpose of ○ *That towel is for drying your hands on.* **7** in exchange for ○ *got it for a few pounds* **8** instead of ○ *found an understudy for him* **9** with reference to the normal characteristics of ○ *It's warm for April.* **10** in order to get ○ *hoping for promotion* **11** having the same meaning as ○ *the common term for rubella* ■ *adv, prep* in favour or support of somebody or something ○ *Ten voted for, and eleven against.* ■ *conj* because (*fml*)

forage /fŏrrij/ *n* **1** food for animals **2** a search, especially over a wide area or among a variety of things ■ *v* (**-aging, -aged**) **1** *vi* search an area for food and supplies **2** *vti* raid an area for food **3** *vi* engage in a search ○ *foraging in the attic for the lost papers* —**forager** *n*

foray /fŏrray/ *n* **1** a sudden military raid **2** an attempt at something unfamiliar

forbear[1] /fawr báir/ (**-bore** /-báwr/, **-borne** /-báwrn/) *v* (*fml*) **1** *vi* hold back from doing or saying something **2** *vti* be tolerant of something —**forbearance** *n* —**forbearing** *adj* —**forbearingly** *adv*

USAGE As a verb, **forbear** is the only spelling. As a noun, **forebear** ('an ancestor') is preferred.

---

forbear[2] /fáwr báir/ *n* = **forebear**

forbid /fər bíd/ (**-bidding**, **-bade** /-bád, -báyd/ or **-bad** /-bád/, **-bidden** /-bídd'n/ or **-bid**) vt **1** order somebody not to do something **2** not allow something —**forbiddance** n

forbidding /fər bídding/ adj **1** hostile or stern **2** coldly uninviting —**forbiddingly** adv —**forbiddingness** n

~~forbiding~~ incorrect spelling of **foreboding**

force n **1** strength ○ *toppled by the force of the storm* **2** physical power or violence used against somebody or something ○ *the use of force as a last resort* **3** the state of being in effect ○ *The regulations come into force next week.* **4** intellectual or moral power ○ *swayed by the force of his argument* **5** an influential person or thing ○ *a force for good* **6** a group of military personnel, ships, or aircraft organized to fight **7** a body of police officers **8** a group of people working together ○ *a sales force* **9** (*symbol F*) a physical influence that moves an object, equal to the rate of change in the object's momentum ■ **forces** npl the military organizations of a country ■ vt (**forcing, forced**) **1** compel somebody to do something **2** move using physical strength **3** create a way or passage using physical strength **4** obtain something by pressure ○ *trying to force a confrontation* **5** do something in a strained or unnatural way ○ *managed to force a smile* **6** make a plant mature early —**forceable** adj ◇ **in force 1** in a large group **2** valid

---

ORIGIN Force derives ultimately from Latin *fortis* 'strong', which is also seen in *comfort*, *fortify*, and numerous other words. It came into English through French.

☐ **force on** or **upon** vt impose something on somebody

~~forceably~~ incorrect spelling of **forcibly**

forced adj **1** not natural ○ *forced laughter* **2** done out of necessity ○ *a forced error* —**forcedness** /-sídnəss/ n

forced landing n an emergency landing

force-feed (**force-fed**) vt **1** compel to eat **2** compel to learn

force field n in science fiction, an invisible barrier

forceful /fáwrssf'l/ adj **1** powerful **2** impressive or persuasive —**forcefully** adv —**forcefulness** n

force majeure /fáwrss ma zhúr/ n **1** prevention from doing something by an unexpected event (*fml*) **2** superior power

forcemeat /fáwrss meet/ n finely chopped meat, fish, or vegetables, used for stuffing

forceps /fáwr seps, -səps/ npl a surgical instrument resembling tongs or tweezers

forcible /fáwrssəb'l/ adj **1** using strength ○ *forcible entry by a burglar* **2** intensely persuasive ○ *a forcible reminder* —**forcibly** adv

ford n a crossing place through shallow water —**ford** vt —**fordable** adj

Ford, Gerald R. (*b.* 1913) 38th president of the United States (1974–77)

Henry Ford

Ford, Henry (1863–1947) US industrialist

Ford, John (1895–1973) US film director

fore n the front of something (*literary*) ■ adj positioned at the front ■ adv towards the front ■ interj in golf, warns others that you have hit a golf ball in their direction

fore- prefix **1** before, earlier ○ *forebear* **2** front, in front ○ *forehead*

forearm[1] /fáwr aarm/ n the lower arm

forearm[2] /fawr aárm/ vt prepare or arm in advance of an expected conflict

forebear /fáwr bair/, **forbear** n an ancestor (*often pl*) ◊ See note at **forbear**[1]

foreboding /fawr bóding/ n **1** a premonition **2** a bad omen ■ adj ominous —**forbode** vti —**forebodingly** adv

forecast vt /fáwr kaast/ (**-cast** or **-casted**) **1** predict **2** be an early sign of ■ n **1** a weather prediction **2** a prediction of future developments —**forecaster** n

forecastle /fóks'l/, **fo'c's'le** n **1** a space in the bow of a ship for the crew's quarters **2** a raised deck at the bow of a ship

foreclose /fawr klóz/ (**-closing, -closed**) v **1** vti seize a property, usually for nonpayment of a mortgage **2** vt prevent (*fml*) —**foreclosure** /fawr klózhər/ n

forecourt /fáwr kawrt/ n **1** an open area at the front of a building used by the public **2** the front section of a tennis, badminton, or handball court

forefinger /fáwr fing gər/ n an index finger

forefoot /fáwr foot/ (*pl* **-feet** /-feet/) n an animal's front foot

forefront /fáwr frunt/ n **1** the leading or most important position **2** the foremost part

foregather /fawr gáthər/ vi = **forgather**

forego vt = **forgo**

foregoing /fawr gố ing, fáwr gō ing/ adj previously mentioned

foregone /fáwr gon/ adj already completed or determined ○ *a foregone conclusion*

foreground /fáwr grownd/ n **1** the part of a picture that appears nearest the viewer **2** the leading or most important position ■ adj currently receiving computer commands through the keyboard, while other programs are operating ■ vt highlight

forehand /fáwr hand/ n **1** in racket games, a stroke played with the palm facing forwards **2** the part of a horse in front of the rider

—**forehand** adj, adv, vt —**forehanded** adj, adv

forehead /fórrid, fáwr hed/ n the part of the face above the eyebrows

foreign /fórrin/ adj **1** of another country ○ foreign currency **2** dealing with another country ○ foreign policy **3** coming from outside ○ a foreign body in the eye **4** uncharacteristic ○ foreign to her nature —**foreignness** n

> **ORIGIN Foreign** goes back to a Latin word meaning 'out of doors', and this was an early meaning in English. The French word from which it immediately derived in the 13C was not spelt -gn, and neither was **foreign** until the 16C. The change seems to have come about by analogy with *sovereign*, which itself had been altered to conform to *reign*.

foreigner /fórrinər/ n **1** somebody from another country **2** an outsider

foreign exchange n **1** the currencies of foreign countries **2** dealings in foreign money

foreign legion n a section of an army consisting of foreign volunteers

Foreign Office n the UK government department responsible for relations with other countries. Full form **Foreign and Commonwealth Office**

Foreign Secretary n the UK cabinet minister responsible for relations with other countries

foreknowledge /fawr nóllij/ n prior knowledge

foreleg /fáwr leg/ n an animal's front leg

forelimb /fáwr lim/ n a front limb

forelock /fáwr lok/ n **1** a lock of hair growing over the human forehead **2** the front part of a horse's mane

foreman /fáwrmən/ (pl -men /-mən/) n **1** a man in charge of other workers **2** a male leader of a jury —**foremanship** n

foremast /fáwr mast/ n the mast nearest the front of a vessel

foremost /fáwr mōst/ adj **1** most notable **2** farthest forward ■ adv **1** in first position **2** to the front

forenoon /fáwr noon/ n the morning hours

forensic /fə rénssik, -rénzik/ adj **1** using science to solve crime **2** of debating —**forensically** adv —**forensics** n

foreperson /fáwr purss'n/ (pl -persons or -people /-peep'l/) n **1** a person in charge of other workers **2** the head of a jury

foreplay /fáwr play/ n sexual stimulation before intercourse

forerunner /fáwr runər/ n **1** a predecessor **2** somebody or something showing the future

foresee /fawr seé/ (-saw /-sáw/, -seen /-seén/) vti know or expect that something will happen before it does —**foreseeable** adj —**foreseeably** adv

foreshadow /fawr sháddō/ vt be a warning or indication of

foreshore /fáwr shawr/ n **1** the part of a shore between the high and low watermarks **2** the part of a shore between the high watermark and cultivated land

foreshorten /fawr sháwrt'n/ vt make something in a drawing or painting appear shorter than it actually is to create perspective

foresight /fáwr sīt/ n the ability to think ahead —**foresighted** /fawr sítid/ adj

foreskin /fáwr skin/ n the fold of skin covering the tip of the penis

forest /fórrist/ n a large dense growth of trees —**forested** adj

forestall /fawr stáwl/ vt prevent or hinder —**forestalment** n

forester /fórristər/ n **1** the manager of a forest **2** a forest dweller (archaic)

forestry /fórristri/ n **1** the planting and growing of trees **2** the science and profession of forest management

foretaste /fáwr tayst/ n a sample of what is to come ■ vt (-tasting, -tasted) have a foretaste of

foretell /fawr tél/ (-told /-tóld/) vt predict future events (literary) —**foreteller** n

forethought /fáwr thawt/ n careful thought about the future —**forethoughtful** /fawr tháwtf'l/ adj

forever /fər évvər/ adv also **for ever 1** for all time **2** for a very long time (infml)

forevermore /fər évvər máwr/, **for evermore** adv for all time (literary)

~~foreward~~ incorrect spelling of **forward**

forewarn /fawr wáwrn/ vt warn about something that is going to happen

forewoman /fáwr wŏŏmən/ (pl -en /-wimən/) n **1** a woman in charge of other workers **2** a woman leader of a jury

foreword /fáwr wurd/ n an introductory essay in a book

forex abbr foreign exchange

forfeit /fáwrfit/ n **1** a penalty for wrongdoing or breaking the law **2** the act of giving something up willingly so as to get something else **3** a penalty in a game ■ adj taken away as punishment ■ vt **1** lose something as punishment for a mistake or wrongdoing **2** give up something willingly so as to get something else **3** take something away from somebody as a penalty —**forfeitable** adj

forfeiture /fáwrfichər/ n **1** something forfeited **2** the act of willingly giving something up so as to get something else

~~forfiet~~ incorrect spelling of **forfeit**

forgather /fawr gáthər/, **foregather** vi assemble as a group (fml)

forgave past tense of **forgive**

forge[1] n **1** a metal-working shop **2** a furnace for heating metal ■ v (forging, forged) **1** vti make an illegal copy of something **2** vt establish something with effort ○ forge a durable relationship **3** vt shape metal by heating and hammering —**forger** n

> **ORIGIN Forge** 'make an illegal copy' came

through French from the Latin verb that also gave us *fabricate*. It is recorded from the beginning of the 13C. Like its sources, **forge** at first meant simply 'make, construct'. The sense 'shape metal' appears in the 14C. **Forge** as in *forge ahead* is unrelated and not as old, appearing in the mid-18C. Its origin is not certain, though it may be an alteration of *force*.

forge[2] **(forging, forged), forge ahead** *vi* **1** move forward with a surge of speed **2** move slowly and steadily

forgery /fáwrjəri/ (*pl* **-ies**) *n* **1** the illegal copying of something **2** an illegal copy

forget /fər gét/ (**-getting, -got** /-gót/, **-gotten** /-góttʼn/) *v* **1** *vti* not remember something **2** *vt* leave behind accidentally **3** *vti* neglect to give due attention to something **4** *vt* stop worrying about **5** *vti* not mention something **6** *vr* lose control of your manners or emotions ○ In his anger, he forgot himself. —**forgettable** *adj* ◊ See note at **neglect**

forgetful /fər gétfʼl/ *adj* **1** absent-minded **2** neglectful of duty or responsibility (*fml*) —**forgetfully** *adv* —**forgetfulness** *n*

forget-me-not *n* a small plant with small pale-blue flowers

ORIGIN **Forget-me-nots** were worn by lovers in the 15C. The English name is recorded in the mid-16C, and is a translation from French.

---

forgive /fər gív/ (**-giving, -gave** /-gáyv/, **-given** /-gívʼn/) *v* **1** *vti* stop being angry about something **2** *vt* pardon somebody or something —**forgivable** *adj* —**forgivably** *adv* —**forgiveness** *n*

forgiving /fər gívving/ *adj* **1** inclined to forgive **2** allowing for a degree of imperfection —**forgivingly** *adv*

forgo /fawr gṓ/ (**-goes, -went** /-wént/, **-gone** /-gón/), **forego** *vt* do without

forgot past tense of **forget**

forgotten past participle of **forget**

~~forhead~~ incorrect spelling of **forehead**

~~foriegn~~ incorrect spelling of **foreign**

forint /fórrint/ *n* the main unit of Hungarian currency

fork *n* **1** a metal eating or serving utensil with prongs **2** a pronged garden or agricultural tool **3** a point where something divides **4** a branch of a road or river **5** a pronged machine part **6** in chess, a position in which two pieces are under attack from one of the opponent's pieces ■ *v* **1** *vti* move something with a fork **2** *vi* divide into two —**forked** *adj* —**forkful** *n*

forked lightning *n* lightning that splits into two or more branches near the ground

forked tongue *n* untruthful or misleading speech (*literary or humorous*)

forklift /fáwrk lìft/ *n* **1** an industrial device with two long steel bars for lifting loads **2** *also* **forklift truck** a vehicle fitted with a forklift —**forklift** *vt*

forlorn /fər láwrn, fawr-/ *adj* **1** lonely and miserable **2** hopeless (*literary*) —**forlornly** *adv* —**forlornness** *n*

form *n* **1** basic structure or shape **2** the particular way that something is or appears to be ○ *bonuses in the form of extra days off* **3** a type or kind ○ *Friction is a form of energy.* **4** an indistinct shape ○ *a shadowy form in the distance* **5** a document with blank spaces for entering information **6** the condition of a person, group, or organization ○ *a violinist at the top of her form* **7** the track record of a horse, athlete, or team **8** the structure of an artistic work as opposed to its content **9** a mould or frame **10** a class or year in a school **11** behaviour or manners ○ *It's considered bad form to cheat at games.* **12** a long backless wooden bench **13** a hare's lair ■ *v* **1** *vti* give a shape to, or take shape **2** *vti* start to exist, or make exist **3** *vt* construct or establish **4** *vt* develop in the mind **5** *vt* influence and mould somebody or something **6** *vt* constitute or serve as ○ *mountains forming a natural boundary*

formal /fáwrmʼl/ *adj* **1** in accordance with accepted conventions ○ *He's terribly formal.* **2** official ○ *a formal invitation to Buckingham Palace* **3** methodical **4** used in serious, official, or public communications ○ *a formal word* **5** systematically ordered or arranged ○ *a formal garden* —**formally** *adv* —**formalness** *n*

formaldehyde /fawr máldi hīd/ *n* a pungent gas. Use: manufacture of resins and fertilizers, preservation of organic specimens.

formalin /fáwrməlin/ *n* a solution of formaldehyde. Use: disinfectant, preservation of organic specimens.

formalism /fáwrm'lizəm/ *n* emphasis on outward appearance or form rather than content or meaning —**formalistic** /fáwrmə lístik/ *adj*

formality /fawr málləti/ (*pl* **-ties**) *n* **1** the quality of being formal **2** an official procedure that is part of a longer procedure (*often pl*) **3** a necessary but insignificant procedure

formalize /fáwrmə līz/ (**-izing, -ized**), **formalise** *v* **1** *vt* make official or formal **2** *vt* give a specific shape or pattern to something, e.g. thoughts or plans **3** *vti* become or make formal —**formalization** /fáwrmə līzáysh'n/ *n*

format /fáwr mat/ *n* **1** the way something is presented, organized, or arranged **2** the layout of a publication **3** the structure or organization of digital data ○ *files in ASCII format* ■ *vt* (**-matting, -matted**) **1** arrange the layout or organization of something **2** organize a disk for data storage

---

ORIGIN **Format** came through French from German in the mid-19C. It derives from the past participle of the Latin verb that gave us *form*, used in *liber formatus* 'shaped book'.

---

formation /fawr máysh'n/ *n* **1** the development of something **2** the creation of something **3** shape or structure **4** a formal pattern —**formational** *adj*

formative /fáwrmətiv/ *adj* influential in shaping or developing something

former[1] /fáwrmər/ *adj* **1** previous ○ *met her on a former occasion* **2** having previously had a particular name or status ○ *the former Soviet Union* **3** being the first of two things or people mentioned ■ *n* the first of two

former[2] /fáwrmər/ *n* **1** a member of a form in a school *(in combination)* ○ *a sixth former* **2** somebody or something that shapes something

formerly /fáwrmərli/ *adv* in the past, but no longer

Formica /fawr míkə/ *tdmk* a trademark for a strong plastic laminate sheeting often used to cover surfaces

formic acid /fáwrmik-/ *n* an acid that occurs naturally in ants. Use: paper, textiles, insecticides, refrigerants.

formidable /fáwrmidəb'l, fər míddəb'l/ *adj* **1** difficult to deal with **2** inspiring awe —**formidably** *adv*

formless /fáwrmləss/ *adj* having no distinctive shape —**formlessly** *adv* —**formlessness** *n*

form letter *n* a letter with the same wording that is sent to many recipients

formula /fáwrmyoolə/ (*pl* -**las** *or* -**lae** /-lee/) *n* **1** a plan **2** a prescribed method of doing something **3** an established form of words **4** a set of symbols representing the chemical composition of a compound **5** a rule expressed in symbols **6** *also* **Formula** a category of racing car *(usually in combination)* —**formulaic** /fáwrmyoo láy ik/ *adj* —**formulaically** *adv*

formulate /fáwrmyoo layt/ (-**lating**, -**lated**) *vt* **1** devise carefully **2** say or write carefully —**formulation** /fáwrmyoo láysh'n/ *n*

fornicate /fáwrni kayt/ (-**cating**, -**cated**) *vi* have sex outside marriage *(fml)* —**fornication** /fáwrni káysh'n/ *n* —**fornicator** *n*

Forrest /fórrist/, **Sir John, 1st Baron Forrest of Bunbury** (1847–1918) Australian explorer and politician

forsake /fər sáyk/ (-**saking**, -**sook** /-soŏk/, -**saken** /-sáykən/) *vt* **1** abandon somebody or something **2** give up something that gives pleasure —**forsaken** *adj*

forsee incorrect spelling of **foresee**

forsooth /fər soŏth/ *adv* indeed *(archaic)*

Forster /fáwrstər/, **E. M.** (1879–1970) British novelist

forswear /fawr swáir/ (-**swore** /-swáwr/, -**sworn** /-swáwrn/) *v* *(literary)* **1** *vt* reject strongly **2** *vi* perjure yourself

forsythia /fawr síthiə/ *n* a yellow-flowered bush

fort *n* a building or group of buildings with strong defences ◇ **hold the fort** take charge of something in the absence of the person usually responsible *(infml)*

Fortaleza /fórtə létsə/ port in NE Brazil, on the Atlantic Ocean. Pop. 1,965,513 (1996).

forte[1] /fáwr tay, fawrt/ *n* somebody's strong point

forte[2] /fáwr tay, fáwrti/ *adv* in a loud manner *(musical direction)* ■ *n* a loud musical note or passage —**forte** *adj*

forteen incorrect spelling of **fourteen**

forth /fawrth/ *adv* **1** onward **2** out into view ◇ **and so forth** et cetera

> **SPELLCHECK** Do not confuse the spelling of **forth** and **fourth** ('one of four parts'), which sound similar.

Forth, Firth of estuary of the River Forth in SE Scotland. Length 77 km/48 mi.

FORTH /fawrth/ *n* a high-level computer programming language used in scientific and industrial control applications

forthcoming /fawrth kúmming/ *adj* **1** future ○ *a forthcoming book* **2** available when wanted ○ *Help is forthcoming.* **3** willing to give information ○ *a press secretary who is less than forthcoming*

forthright /fáwrth rīt/ *adj* candid and outspoken —**forthrightly** *adv* —**forthrightness** *n*

forthwith /fáwrth with, -wíth/ *adv* immediately

fortification /fáwrtifi káysh'n/ *n* **1** a strong structure for defending a place *(often pl)* **2** the building of defences

fortified wine *n* a drink such as sherry or port made from wine to which strong alcohol has been added

fortify /fáwrti fī/ (-**fies**, -**fied**) *vt* **1** make a place safer with defensive structures **2** make a structure stronger **3** add extra ingredients to something **4** strengthen or encourage somebody —**fortifiable** *adj*

fortissimo /fawr tíssimō/ *adv* very loudly *(musical direction)* ■ *n* (*pl* -**mos** *or* -**mi** /-mee/) a very loud musical note or passage —**fortissimo** *adj*

fortitude /fáwrti tyood/ *n* brave determination —**fortitudinous** /fáwrti tyoŏdinəss/ *adj*

Fort Lauderdale /-láwdər dayl/ city in SE Florida, on the Atlantic Ocean. Pop. 153,728 (1998).

fortnight /fáwrt nīt/ *n* a period of two weeks

fortnightly /fáwrt nītli/ *adj, adv* every two weeks ■ *n* (*pl* -**lies**) a publication appearing every other week

FORTRAN /fáwr tran/ *n* an early computer programming language

> **ORIGIN Fortran** is a blend and contraction of *formula* and *translation*.

fortress /fáwrtrəss/ *n* **1** a fortified place or town with a long-term military presence **2** a place that is impossible to get into

fortuitous /fawr tyoŏ itəss/ *adj* **1** accidental or unplanned **2** happening by lucky chance —**fortuitously** *adv*

fortunate /fáwrchənət/ *adj* **1** enjoying good luck **2** resulting from good luck —**fortunateness** *n* ◇ See note at **lucky**

fortunately /fáwrchənətli/ *adv* **1** by lucky chance **2** indicates happiness or relief ○ *Fortunately, the lion was caught.*

~~fortunatly~~ incorrect spelling of **fortunately**

fortune /fáwrchən/ *n* **1** great wealth or property **2** a large sum of money *(infml)* **3** *also* **Fortune** fate **4** luck ■ **fortunes** *npl* life's ups and downs

fortune cookie *n* a Chinese biscuit containing a message

fortune hunter *n* somebody who tries to obtain wealth by marrying somebody rich *(disapproving)* —**fortune hunting** *n*

fortune teller *n* somebody who claims to foretell the future —**fortune-telling** *n*

Fort Worth /-wúrth/ city in NE Texas. Pop. 491,801 (1998).

forty /fáwrti/ *n* the number 40 ■ **forties** *npl* **1** the numbers 40 to 49, particularly as a range of temperature **2** the years from 40 to 49 in a century or in somebody's life —**fortieth** *adj, adv, n* —**forty** *adj, pron*

forty-five *n* **1** a small gramophone record **2** *US, Can* a .45-calibre pistol

forty winks *n* a nap *(infml; + sing or pl verb)*

forum /fáwrəm/ *(pl* **-rums** *or* **-ra** /-rə/*) n* **1** a medium for expressing an opinion or debating an issue **2** a meeting for a discussion **3** an Internet discussion group **4** a public square in an ancient Roman city

forward /fáwrwərd, *in UK nautical use also* fórrəd/ *adv also* **forwards 1** ahead **2** as progress towards a goal ○ *a step forward in employee safety* **3** to the front of a ship or an aircraft ○ *prefer a berth farther forward* ■ *adj* **1** directed ahead **2** directed to a future goal **3** situated at the front of a ship or an aircraft **4** unrestrained or impertinent in behaviour ■ *n* in some team sports, an attacking player ■ *vt* **1** redirect a letter **2** advance or promote something —**forwardly** *adv* —**forwardness** *n*

forwarding address *n* a new address to which letters are to be redirected

forward-looking *adj* planning for or looking towards the future

forward market *n* a market in financial futures

fossick /fóssik/ *vi ANZ* **1** rummage **2** look for gold or gems in locations that have already been worked

Barnaby's

Fossil: Trilobite

fossil /fóss'l/ *n* **1** the preserved remains of an animal or plant **2** somebody regarded as old-fashioned and unwilling to change *(infml insult)* **3** something outdated

ORIGIN Fossil was adopted from French, where it was formed from a Latin adjective meaning 'dug up'.

fossil fuel *n* a fuel derived from prehistoric organisms

fossilize /fóssə līz/ *(-izing, -ized),* **fossilise** *vti* **1** make or become a fossil **2** make or be unable to change —**fossilization** /fóssə līzáysh'n/ *n* —**fossilized** *adj*

foster /fóstər/ *v* **1** *vti* rear a child who is not yours in exchange for payment from a local authority **2** *vt* arrange care for a child with adults who are not its parents **3** *vt* look after and bring up a child **4** *vt* encourage and develop something **5** *vt* keep alive a feeling or thought ■ *adj* providing care as or receiving care from adults who are not the birth parents

~~fotograph~~ incorrect spelling of **photograph**

Foucault /fookṓ/, **Jean-Bernard Léon** (1819–68) French physicist

Foucault, Michel (1926–84) French philosopher

fought past tense, past participle of **fight**

foul /fowl/ *adj* **1** disgusting to the senses ○ *a foul smell* **2** clogged with dirt **3** contaminated **4** unpleasant *(infml)* **5** vulgar or obscene **6** in sports, illegal according to the rules **7** unfair or dishonest **8** stormy or wet and unpleasant **9** decaying and rotten **10** evil **11** entangled and unable to move ○ *a foul anchor line* ■ *n* **1** in sports, an illegal action **2** an entanglement preventing movement ■ *v* **1** *vti* in sports, act illegally against an opponent **2** *vti* entangle and prevent from moving, or become entangled and unable to move **3** *vti* obstruct, or become obstructed **4** *vt* make dirty —**foully** *adv* —**foulness** *n*

SPELLCHECK Do not confuse the spelling of **foul** and **fowl** ('any edible or game bird'), which sound similar.

□ **foul up** *vti* bungle, or be bungled *(infml)*

foul line *n* in basketball, a line from which a free throw is taken after a foul

foul-mouthed *adj* using obscene language

foul play *n* **1** unfair behaviour **2** treachery or criminal violence

foul-up *n* a blunder *(infml)*

found[1] /fownd/ *vt* **1** set up something such as an institution or organization **2** support something such as a conclusion with evidence or reasoning

found[2] /fownd/ *vt* **1** cast metal or glass **2** produce from a mould by casting

found[3] /fownd/ past tense, past participle of **find**

foundation /fown dáysh'n/ *n* **1** an underground support for a building *(often pl)* **2** the basis of a theory or idea **3** a base layer of make-up **4** the establishing of an institution **5** a charitable or educational institution **6** a fund supporting an institution —**foundational** *adj*

foundation course *n* an introductory course of study

foundation stone n 1 a stone laid to mark the start of construction of a building 2 a basis for something

founder /fówndər/ v 1 vti sink, or cause to sink 2 vi collapse and fail 3 vi become stuck in soft ground or snow

founder member n one of first members of an organization

founding father n a founder of an institution, movement, or organization

foundling /fówndling/ n an abandoned baby (dated)

foundry /fówndri/ (pl -ries) n a place for casting metal or glass

fount[1] /fownt/ n (literary) 1 a source 2 a fountain or spring of water

fount[2] /fownt/ n PRINTING = font[2]

fountain /fówntin/ n 1 an ornamental water jet 2 a natural spring 3 a device producing a jet of water for drinking 4 a jet of liquid 5 a source of something abstract

fountainhead /fówntin hed/ n 1 a spring that is the source of a stream 2 a primary source of something abstract

fountain pen n a refillable pen with a nib and an ink reservoir

four /fawr/ n 1 the number 4 2 a cricket shot scoring four runs 3 a four-oared racing boat 4 a four-member rowing crew —**four** adj, pron

four-by-four n a four-wheel-drive vehicle

four-colour adj using cyan, magenta, yellow, and black to print full-coloured pictures

four-flush vi in poker, bet boldly though holding a bad hand

4GL abbr fourth-generation language

four-leaf clover, four-leaved clover, four-leafed clover n a clover leaf with four parts that is considered lucky

four-letter word n a short vulgar word

four-poster, four-poster bed n a bed with four vertical posts at each corner for a canopy or curtains

fourscore /fawr skáwr/ adj 80 in number (archaic)

foursome /fáwrsəm/ n 1 a group of four people 2 a golf game for two pairs

foursquare /fawr skwáir/ adj 1 showing determination (literary) 2 solid and strong —**foursquare** adv

four-star adj describes high-octane petrol —**fourstar** n

four-stroke adj describes an internal combustion engine requiring four strokes per cycle

fourteen /fawr teen/ n the number 14 —**fourteen** adj, pron —**fourteenth** adj, adv, n

fourth /fawrth/ n 1 one of four parts of something 2 a musical interval of four notes —**fourth** adj, adv ◊ See note at **forth**

fourth dimension n time when used with the three other dimensions to specify the location of an event

fourth estate, Fourth Estate n journalists as a group

ORIGIN From medieval times, society was analysed in terms of 'estates', groups of people participating in government, either directly or through representatives. Traditionally in England there were three, originally the clergy, the barons and knights, and the commons. Different divisions were made in other European countries. A number of people and groups have been dubbed the 'fourth estate', but the name has stuck to the press. The historian and essayist Thomas Carlyle attributed the first use to Edmund Burke, but it has also been claimed for the politician Lord Brougham, who is said to have used it in the House of Commons in 1823 or 1824.

fourth-generation language n an advanced computer language resembling human speech

~~fourty~~ incorrect spelling of **forty**

four-wheel drive n a system in which engine power is transmitted to all four wheels of a vehicle

fowl /fowl/ (pl **fowls** or same) n 1 a chicken or related bird 2 any edible or game bird ◊ See note at **foul**

fox n 1 a carnivorous wild mammal resembling a dog, with reddish-brown fur and a bushy tail 2 the fur of a fox 3 a trickster (infml) ■ vt 1 baffle somebody 2 deceive or outwit somebody —**foxiness** n —**foxy** adj

ORIGIN Fox probably derives from an ancient root meaning 'tail'.

Fox, Charles James (1749–1806) British politician

Fox, George (1624–91) English religious leader

Fox, Sir William (1812–93) British-born explorer, painter, and premier of New Zealand (1856, 1861–62, 1869–72, 1873)

foxglove /fóks gluv/ (pl same or **-gloves**) n a plant with purple and white thimble-shaped flowers. Use: source of digitalis.

foxhound /fóks hownd/ n a dog used for hunting foxes

foxhunting /fóks hunting/ n the hunting of foxes on horseback with dogs

fox terrier n a small white dog with dark markings

foxtrot /fóks trot/ n 1 a ballroom dance alternating long walking steps and short running steps 2 the music for a foxtrot 3 **Foxtrot** a communications code word for the letter 'F'

foyer /fóy ay, fwí ay/ n a reception area in a public building

Fr symbol francium

fracas /frák aa/ (pl same) n a noisy quarrel or fight

fractal /frákt'l/ n an irregular or fragmented geometrical shape that can be repeatedly subdivided into smaller copies of the whole, used in computer modelling —**fractal** adj

fraction /fráksh'n/ n 1 a number that is not a whole number 2 a small amount ○ *a fraction of the cost* 3 a part 4 a component of a mixture, separated by differences in chemical or physical properties —**fractional** *adj* —**fractionally** *adv*

fractious /frákshəss/ *adj* irritable and complaining —**fractiously** *adv* —**fractiousness** *n*

fracture /frákchər/ n 1 a break in a bone 2 an act of breaking something, especially a bone 3 a break or crack in an object or material 4 a split in a system or organization ■ *vti* (**-turing, -tured**) 1 break a bone, or be broken 2 damage something, or be damaged

fragile /frájj l/ *adj* 1 easily broken or destroyed 2 physically weak because of illness —**fragility** /frə jílləti/ n

SYNONYMS **fragile, delicate, frail, flimsy, frangible, friable** CORE MEANING: easily broken or damaged

fragment n /frágmənt/ 1 a broken piece 2 an incomplete part of a whole ■ *vti* /frag mént/ 1 break into small pieces 2 break up —**fragmented** /frag méntid/ *adj*

fragmentary /frágməntəri/ *adj* consisting only of fragments

fragmentation /frágmən táysh'n, -men-/ n 1 the breaking up of something 2 a loss of unity and cohesion 3 the shattering of an explosive device

Fragonard /frággə naar/, **Jean Honoré** (1732–1806) French painter and engraver

fragrance /fráygrənss/ n 1 a sweet smell 2 sweetness of smell 3 a perfume —**fragranced** *adj* ◊ See note at **smell**

fragrant /fráygrənt/ *adj* smelling sweet

frail (**frailer, frailest**) *adj* 1 physically weak 2 easy to break or damage 3 insubstantial —**frailness** n —**frailty** n ◊ See note at **fragile, weak**

frame n 1 an underlying, supporting, or surrounding structure ○ *a bike with a steel frame* ○ *a window frame* 2 the part of a pair of spectacles that holds the lenses and fits around the ears 3 a piece of equipment made of bars, used e.g. for helping somebody to walk 4 a person's body 5 a single picture on a strip of film or in a comic strip 6 one of the games making up a match in snooker, billiards, and pool 7 on a computer screen, a rectangular area that contains all or a portion of a web page ■ **frames** *npl* a frame for spectacles ■ *vt* (**framing, framed**) 1 mount a picture in a frame 2 form a surrounding framework for something 3 construct or express an idea or statement 4 cause somebody innocent to appear guilty (*slang*)

Janet Frame

Frame, Janet (*b.* 1924) New Zealand writer

frame of mind n somebody's psychological state at a specific time

frame of reference n 1 a set of standards used for judging or deciding something 2 a set of geometric axes for determining the location of a point in space

framework /fráym wurk/ n 1 a structure consisting of interconnecting bars 2 a set of underlying ideas 3 the context in which something happens

franc n 1 the main unit of currency in several French-speaking countries 2 the main unit of the former currency in France, Belgium, and Luxembourg

ORIGIN The name **franc** probably derives from Latin *Francorum rex* 'king of the Franks', which appeared on gold coins minted in the reign (1350–64) of Jean le Bon.

France largest country in W Europe. Cap. Paris. Pop. 59,551,227 (2001).

franchise /frán chīz/ n 1 a licence to sell a company's products exclusively in a particular area 2 the area in which somebody has a commercial franchise 3 a privilege granted by an authority 4 the right to vote —**franchise** *vt*

Francis I /fraánssiss/ (1494–1547) king of France (1515–47)

Francis (of Assisi), St (1182–1226) Italian mystic and preacher. He founded the Franciscan order.

Franciscan /fran sískən/ n a member of a Roman Catholic order of monks and nuns largely devoted to missionary and charitable work —**Franciscan** *adj*

francium /fránss i əm/ n (*symbol* **Fr**) an unstable radioactive element

Franck /frangk, fraaNk/, **César Auguste** (1822–90) Belgian-born French composer and organist

Franco /fráŋkō/, **Francisco** (1892–1975) authoritarian head of state of Spain (1939–75)

francophone /fráŋkō fōn/ n a speaker of French ■ *adj* 1 French-speaking 2 of a French-speaking area

frangible /fránjəb'l/ *adj* capable of being broken or easily damaged ◊ See note at **fragile**

Franglais /fróng glay/, **franglais** n a mixture of French and English words and idioms —**Franglais** *adj*

frank *adj* **1** open, honest, and sometimes blunt **2** pleasingly honest ■ *vt* print an official mark over a stamp or on a piece of mail without a stamp to show that postage has been paid ■ *n* an official mark on a piece of mail to show that postage has been paid —**frankly** *adv* —**frankness** *n*

ORIGIN Frank derives through French from Latin *francus* 'free, not enslaved or captive', and this was the first recorded sense in English. It was originally identical with the ethnic name *Frank*, because after the Franks conquered Gaul in the 6C only they and those under their protection had full political freedom. The modern senses of **frank** developed from the 16C.

Frank *n* a member of an ancient Germanic people —**Frankish** *adj*

AKG London

Anne Frank

Frank, Anne (1929–45) German Jewish diarist
Frankenstein /frángkən stīn/ *n* **1** a creator of something destructive **2** *also* **Frankenstein's monster** an invention that escapes its creator's control and threatens harm or destruction **3** a monster, usually represented as a large coarse-featured person
Frankfurt /frángk furt/ *also* **Frankfurt am Main** /-am mín/ city in west-central Germany. Pop. 652,412 (1997). ■ *also* **Frankfurt an der Oder** city in NE Germany, on the River Oder. Pop. 87,863 (1989).
frankfurter /frángk furtər/, **frankfurt** /-furt/ *n* a sausage of finely minced pork or beef

ORIGIN Frankfurter is a shortening of German *Frankfurter Wurst* 'sausage from Frankfurt'. It is first recorded in the late 19C.

frankincense /frángkin senss/ *n* an aromatic resin used as incense
franking machine *n* a machine for printing a postage mark on letters and parcels instead of using a stamp
Franklin /frángklin/, **Benjamin** (1706–90) American diplomat, printer, author, and scientist
Franklin, Miles (1879–1954) Australian writer and feminist
frantic /frántik/ *adj* **1** emotionally out of control **2** excited, hurried, and confused —**frantically** *adv*
~~frantiely~~ incorrect spelling of **frantically**
Franz Josef /fránts yṓssəf/ (1830–1916) emperor of Austria (1848–1916) and king of Hungary (1867–1916)

Franz Josef Land archipelago of small islands in the Arctic Ocean, in NW Russia
frappé /fráppay/ *adj* served chilled or poured over crushed ice ■ *n* a drink served chilled poured over crushed ice
Fraser /fráyzər/, **Dawn** (b. 1937) Australian swimmer
Fraser, Malcolm (b. 1930) prime minister of Australia (1975–83)
fraternal /frə túrn'l/ *adj* **1** of brothers **2** showing friendship and mutual support —**fraternally** *adv*
fraternity /frə túrnəti/ (*pl* -**ties**) *n* **1** a group of people with something in common **2** a society formed for a common purpose **3** brotherly love **4** US, Can a social society for men at a university or college
fraternize /fráttər nīz/ (-**nizing**, -**nized**), **fraternise** *v* **1** *vi* spend time with other people socially, especially people considered unsuitable **2** *vti* socialize with somebody against military regulations —**fraternization** /fráttər nī záysh'n/ *n*
fratricide /fráttri sīd, fráytri-/ *n* **1** the killing of a brother **2** a killer of a brother —**fratricidal** /fráttri sīd'l, fráytri-/ *adj*
fraud *n* **1** the crime of obtaining money or advantage by deception **2** somebody who deceives somebody else, usually for financial gain **3** something intended to deceive
fraud squad *n* the British police department for investigating fraud
fraudster /fráwdstər/ *n* somebody who commits fraud
fraudulent /fráwdyŏŏlənt/ *adj* designed to deceive —**fraudulently** *adv*
fraught /frawt/ *adj* **1** full of or accompanied by problems or dangers ○ *an evening fraught with hostility* **2** tense and anxious ○ *exhausted and fraught after the harrowing flight*

ORIGIN Fraught originally meant 'laden' and applied to ships. It is related to *freight*. *Fraught with* 'full of or accompanied by' dates from the mid-16C, but the unqualified sense 'tense and anxious' is recorded only from the mid-20C.

fray[1] *vti* **1** wear away and hang in threads, or make something do this **2** make or become strained ■ *n* a worn part on which loose threads are showing
fray[2] *n* **1** an argument or fight **2** an exciting or lively activity or situation
frazzle /frázz'l/ *n* **1** an exhausted state **2** US a frayed state ■ *vt* (-**zling**, -**zled**) exhaust —**frazzled** *adj*
freak /freek/ *n* **1** a person, animal, or plant regarded as strikingly unusual *(sometimes offensive)* **2** a highly unusual occurrence **3** somebody regarded as unconventional *(infml insult)* **4** a fanatic *(infml)* ○ *a fitness freak* ■ *adj* highly unusual or unlikely ■ *vti* become or make overexcited or overemotional *(infml)* ○ *a loud explosion that freaked*

the cattle —**freakish** *adj* —**freakishly** *adv* —**freaky** *adj*

□ **freak out** *vti* make or become extremely upset or agitated *(slang)*

freckle /frék'l/ *n* a small brown mark on the human skin ■ *vti* (**-ling, -led**) mark or become marked with freckles —**freckly** *adj*

Frederick I /fréddrik/ (1123?–90) Holy Roman Emperor and king of Germany (1152–90), and king of Italy (1155–90)

Frederick II (1712–86) king of Prussia (1740–86)

free *adj* (**freer, freest**) **1** not controlled, restricted, or regulated ○ *You are free to choose.* **2** not held as a prisoner **3** not restricted in rights ○ *It's a free country.* **4** not ruled by a foreign country or power **5** not subject to traditional conventions or limitations ○ *free verse* **6** not affected by a particular thing *(often in combination)* ○ *a trouble-free trip* **7** not containing a particular thing *(often in combination)* ○ *a salt-free diet* **8** costing nothing **9** not busy **10** not being used ○ *Is this seat free?* **11** not attached ○ *grabbed the free end of the rope* **12** giving something readily ○ *very free with her advice* **13** not exact ○ *a free translation* **14** not chemically combined ■ *adv* without cost ■ *vt* (**freed**) **1** release from captivity **2** rid of something ○ *freed the air of smoke* **3** make available or enable —**freely** *adv* —**freeness** *n*

free agent *n* somebody able to act freely

free association *n* **1** the process by which one thought is allowed to lead spontaneously to the next **2** a psychoanalytical technique for exploring somebody's unconscious by using free association —**free-associate** *vi*

freebase /frée bayss/ *v* (**-based, -based**) **1** *vt* prepare cocaine for smoking by heating it with water and a volatile liquid **2** *vti* smoke or inhale cocaine purified by burning it with ether *(slang)* ■ *n* freebased cocaine

freebie /frée bi/ *n* a promotional gift *(infml)*

freebooter /frée bootər/ *n* a pirate or plunderer —**freeboot** *vi*

ORIGIN Freebooter was adopted in the late 16C from Dutch *vrijbuiter*, whose elements correspond to English *free* and *booty* and the suffix *-er*. The same Dutch word came through Spanish and French as *filibuster* 'tactic to delay legislation'.

freeborn /frée bawrn/ *adj* **1** being a free citizen from birth **2** of people who were born as free citizens

freedom /frée dəm/ *n* **1** the state of being able to act and live freely **2** release from captivity or slavery **3** a country's right to self-rule **4** the right to act or speak freely **5** the state of not being affected by something unpleasant ○ *freedom from fear* **6** ease of movement **7** the right to treat a place as your own **8** the citizenship of a city awarded as an honour

freedom fighter *n* a fighter in an armed revolution against a regime regarded as unjust

free enterprise *n* freedom to trade without government control

free fall *n* **1** a descent with an unopened parachute for the first part of a parachute jump **2** an uncontrollable rapid decline —**free-fall** *vi*

free-floating *adj* not committed to one specific thing, especially a political party

Freefone /frée fōn/ *tdmk* a trademark for a phone system in which the holder of the phone number pays the cost of the call

free-for-all *n* a disorganized argument or fight in which all those present participate *(infml)*

free hand *n* complete freedom to act and decide

freehand /frée hand/ *adj, adv* drawn by hand without the aid of, e.g., a ruler or compass

freehold /frée hōld/ *n* **1** legal ownership of property granting unconditional rights **2** a freehold property —**freeholder** *n*

free house *n* a pub that is not owned by a particular brewery so that it can sell whatever beers it chooses

free kick *n* in football, a kick of a stationary ball granted as a result of an infringement by an opponent

freelance /frée laanss/ *n* **1** *also* **freelancer** /-laanssər/ a self-employed person who works for different clients **2** somebody, especially a politician, not committed to any group —**freelance** *adj, adv, vi*

freeloader /frée lōdər/ *n* somebody who exploits somebody else's generosity *(infml)* —**freeload** /frée lōd, free lōd/ *vi*

free love *n* sex without commitment

freeman /frée mən/ (*pl* -**men** /-mən/) *n* **1** a man who is not enslaved **2** a man awarded the freedom of a city as an honour

Freeman /frée mən/, **Cathy** (*b.* 1973) Australian sprinter

free market *n* trading without government control —**free-market** *adj* —**free-marketeer** *n*

Freemason /frée màyss'n/ *n* a member of a worldwide society of men that has secret rites and does charitable work —**Freemasonry** *n*

freenet /frée net/ *n* a free online computer information network

free port *n* **1** a port open to all shipping **2** a duty-free zone at a port or airport

free radical *n* a reactive atom or molecule with an unpaired electron

free-range *adj* **1** not caged or penned **2** produced by free-range poultry or livestock

free rein *n* complete freedom to act and decide

freesheet /frée sheet/ *n* a free newspaper

freesia /frée zhə, frée zi ə/ *n* a small plant with fragrant brightly coloured flowers

free speech *n* the right to express publicly all opinions

free spirit *n* somebody not afraid to flout convention —**free-spirited** *adj*

freestanding /freé stánding/ *adj* **1** not fixed to a support **2** grammatically independent

freestyle /freé stíl/ *adj* **1** describes a sports event that allows a free choice of style or manoeuvres **2** in swimming, using the front crawl stroke ■ *n* a freestyle race or event —**freestyler** *n*

freethinker /freé thíngkər/ *n* somebody who does not accept dogma —**freethinking** *adj, n*

Freetown /freé town/ capital, largest city, and chief port of Sierra Leone. Pop. 699,000 (1995).

free trade *n* international trade that is not subject to protective restrictions against imports —**free-trader** *n*

free verse *n* verse without a fixed metrical pattern

freeware /freé wair/ *n* computer software that is available without cost

freeway /freé way/ *n* **1** *Aus, US, Can* a motorway **2** *US, Can* a toll-free road

freewheel /freé weél/ *vi* **1** continue moving on a bicycle or in a vehicle without using power **2** live in a carefree way ■ *n* **1** a device on a bicycle that enables the rear wheel to keep rotating after pedalling has stopped **2** a device in a motor vehicle's transmission that disengages the drive shaft and allows it to rotate freely when revolving faster than the engine shaft —**freewheeling** *adj*

free will *n* the power of independent action and choice

freeze /freez/ *v* (**freezing**, **froze** /frōz/, **frozen** /frōz'n/) **1** *vti* turn to solid through cold **2** *vti* cover or become covered with ice **3** *vti* block or become blocked with ice **4** *vti* harden through cold **5** *vti* stick through cold **6** *vt* preserve with extreme cold **7** *vti* feel or cause to feel very cold **8** *vti* harm or kill, or be harmed or killed, by cold **9** *vi* drop to freezing point **10** *vti* stop moving **11** *vi* come to a standstill through shock **12** *vi* stop responding to commands *(refers to computers)* **13** *vt* halt before completion **14** *vt* keep at the present level ○ *freeze prices* **15** *vt* prevent the sale or liquidation of ○ *They froze her bank account.* **16** *vt* stop the manufacture of **17** *vt* stop at a specific frame and show a still image ■ *n* **1** *also* **freeze-up** a period of very cold weather **2** a restriction on something

---

SPELLCHECK Do not confuse the spelling of **freeze** and **frieze** ('a decorative band'), which sound similar.

☐ **freeze up** *vt* trap in ice

freeze-frame *n* **1** a single frame of film viewed as a static image **2** a device on a video recorder allowing the viewing of a single frame ■ *vt* present a single frame of film as a static image

freezer /freézər/ *n* a very cold refrigerated cabinet

freezing /freézing/ *adj* very cold ■ *n* *also* **freezing point** the temperature at which something freezes

freight /frayt/ *n* **1** goods for commercial transport **2** the standard class of commercial transport for goods **3** a charge for the transport of goods ■ *vt* transport goods by commercial carrier

freighter /fráytər/ *n* **1** a ship or aircraft for transporting freight **2** a freight shipper or charterer

freight train *n* a train for carrying freight

~~freind~~ incorrect spelling of **friend**

~~freize~~ incorrect spelling of **frieze**

French *n* the Romance language that is the official language of France and some other countries ■ *npl* the people of France —**French** *adj* —**Frenchman** *n* —**Frenchwoman** *n*

French bean *n* **1** a long green bean pod eaten whole as a vegetable **2** a plant producing French beans

French bread *n* crusty white bread in the form of a long slim cylindrical loaf

French Canadian *n* **1** a French-speaking Canadian **2** the Canadian form of the French language —**French-Canadian** *adj*

French dressing *n* **1** a salad dressing of oil, vinegar, and seasoning **2** *US, Can* a creamy tomato-flavoured commercial salad dressing

French fries *npl* deep-fried potato strips

French Guiana /-gī ánnə, -gi aánə/ overseas region of France, on the northeastern coast of South America. Cap. Cayenne. Pop. 114,808 (1990). —**French Guianan** *adj, n* —**French Guianese** /-gī ə neéz, -gi-/ *adj, n*

French horn *n* a brass musical instrument consisting of a coiled pipe ending in a wide bell

French kiss *n* a kiss in which the tongue is used

French polish *n* shellac dissolved in alcohol. Use. wood varnish. —**French polish** *vt*

French Polynesia overseas territory of France, consisting of several island groups in the S Pacific Ocean. Cap. Papeete. Pop. 188,814 (1988).

French stick *n* a thin loaf of French bread

French toast *n* sliced bread dipped in beaten egg and fried

frenetic /frə néttik/ *adj* characterized by feverish activity, confusion, and hurry ○ *frenetic activity* —**frenetically** *adv*

frenzy /frénzi/ *n* **1** uncontrolled agitated behaviour **2** a burst of energetic activity —**frenzied** *adj*

frequency /freékwənssi/ (*pl* -**cies**) *n* **1** *also* **frequence** /-kwənss/ the fact of occurring frequently **2** the rate of occurrence of something **3** a broadcasting wavelength **4** (*symbol* **v**) the rate of recurrence of an oscillation, waveform, or cycle

frequency modulation *n* radio transmission in which the frequency of the wave is varied in accordance with the particularities of the sound being broadcast

frequent *adj* /freekwənt/ **1** occurring often **2** habitual ■ *vt* /fri kwént/ go often to a particular place —**frequenter** /fri kwéntər/ *n* —**frequently** *adv*

fresco /fréskō/ *n* (*pl* -**coes** *or* -**cos**) **1** a wall or ceiling painting done on fresh plaster **2** the technique of painting on fresh plaster ■ *vt* (-**coes, -coing, -coed**) paint a wall or ceiling with a fresco

fresh *adj* **1** not stale or decaying ○ *fresh milk* **2** not preserved, matured, or processed ○ *fresh, frozen, or tinned peas* **3** additional or replacing something ○ *put in a fresh cartridge* **4** new or clean ○ *fresh towels* **5** not affected by time ○ *still fresh in her mind* **6** excitingly different ○ *fresh ideas* **7** alert and full of energy ○ *feeling fresh after a good night's sleep* **8** describes water that is not salty **9** blowing coolly and strongly ○ *a fresh wind from the west* **10** cool and windy ○ *It's rather fresh today.* **11** pleasantly clear and unpolluted ○ *fresh air* **12** healthy-looking ○ *a fresh complexion* **13** making unwanted sexual advances (*infml*) **14** overly familiar or impudent (*infml*) **15** having recently arrived ○ *fresh from his trip* ■ *adv* recently (*usually in combination*) ○ *fresh-cooked salmon* —**freshly** *adv* —**freshness** *n* ◊ See note at **new**

freshen /frésh'n/ *v* **1** *vti* make or become fresh **2** *vi* increase in strength (*refers to winds*) —**freshener** *n*

□ **freshen up** *v* **1** *vi* wash and improve your appearance **2** *vt* refill a drink

fresher /fréshər/ *n* a first-year college or university student (*infml*)

freshman /fréshmən/ (*pl* -**men** /-mən/) *n* **1** a fresher **2** *US* a beginner or newcomer to a post ○ *Senate freshmen*

freshwater /frésh wawtər/ *adj* **1** of water that does not contain salt **2** used on or accustomed only to inland waters

fret[1] *vti* (**fretting, fretted**) **1** worry **2** wear away ■ *n* a worried state

fret[2] *n* a ridge on the neck of a stringed instrument —**fretted** *adj*

fret[3] *n* an ornament or border with a geometrical pattern —**fret** *vt*

fretful /frétf'l/ *adj* irritable and easily worried —**fretfully** *adv* —**fretfulness** *n*

fretsaw /frét saw/ *n* a thin-bladed saw used to cut curves in wood

fretwork /frét wurk/ *n* **1** ornamental woodwork with an open pattern **2** decorative designs consisting of frets

Freud /froyd/, **Anna** (1895–1982) Austrian-born British psychoanalyst

Sigmund Freud

Freud, Sigmund (1856–1939) Austrian physician and founder of psychoanalysis

Freudian /fróydi ən/ *adj* of Sigmund Freud or his theories ■ *n* a follower of Freud —**Freudianism** *n*

Freudian slip *n* a psychologically significant slip of the tongue

Freya /fráy ə/ *n* in Norse mythology, the goddess of love, fertility, and beauty

Fri. *abbr* Friday

friable /frí əb'l/ *adj* brittle and crumbly —**friability** /frí ə bílləti/ *n* ◊ See note at **fragile**

friar /frí ər/ *n* a member of a Roman Catholic religious order for men —**friarly** *adj*

friary /frí əri/ (*pl* -**ies**) *n* **1** a community of friars **2** a building where friars live

fricassee /fríkə say, -sáy, -see, -seé/ *n* meat stewed in a white sauce —**fricassee** *vt*

fricative /fríkətiv/ *adj* describes a consonant made by forcing the breath through a narrow opening —**fricative** *n*

friction /fríksh'n/ *n* **1** the rubbing of two objects against each other **2** a disagreement between groups with different aims **3** the resistance encountered by an object moving relative to another object with which it is in contact —**frictional** *adj*

Friday /frí day, -di/ *n* the 5th day of the week

ORIGIN Friday is named after Frigg, the goddess of married love and the hearth in Scandinavian mythology.

fridge *n* a refrigerator (*infml*)

fridge-freezer *n* a refrigerator and freezer as separate compartments in a single unit

fried /frīd/ *adj* cooked by frying

Friedan /free dán/, **Betty** (*b*. 1921) US feminist and author

Friedman /freédmən/, **Milton** (*b*. 1912) US economist

~~frieght~~ incorrect spelling of **freight**

friend /frend/ *n* **1** a person who trusts and is fond of somebody else **2** a person on good terms with somebody else **3** an ally **4** an advocate of a cause **5** a patron of a charity or institution **6 Friend** a member of the Society of Friends, also called Quakers —**friendless** *adj*

friendly /fréndli/ *adj* (-**lier, -liest**) **1** affectionate and trusting **2** helpful **3** allied or on the same side **4** having a pleasant and welcoming atmosphere **5** played for practice or entertainment and not forming part of a competition **6** easy to use or understand *(usually in combination)* ○ *child-friendly materials* ■ *n (pl* **-lies)** a game played for practice or entertainment and not forming part of a competition ○ *a series of friendlies* —**friendliness** *n* —**friendly** *adv*

friendly fire *n* gunfire or artillery fire accidentally directed at military personnel from their own or their allies' forces

friendly society *n* an association providing insurance and pensions

friendship /frénd ship/ *n* **1** a relationship between friends **2** mutually friendly feelings between people

Friends of the Earth *n* an international environmental organization *(+ sing or pl verb)*

frier *n* = **fryer**

fries /frīz/ *npl* deep-fried potato strips

Friesian /frēezh'n, freézi ən/ *n* large black and white cow

frieze /freez/ *n* **1** a decorative band along the wall of a room just below the ceiling **2** a horizontal decorative band forming part of the entablature of a classical building ◊ See note at **freeze**

frigate /fríggət/ *n* **1** a British warship next in size below a destroyer **2** *US* a medium-sized US warship larger than a destroyer and used for escort duty **3** an 18C or 19C sailing ship equipped for war

fright /frīt/ *n* **1** a sudden feeling of fear **2** the state of being afraid **3** something very unpleasant-looking *(infml)* ○ *My hair's a fright this morning.*

frighten /frīt'n/ *v* **1** *vti* make or become afraid **2** *vt* scare into leaving ○ *frightened him off* —**frightened** *adj* —**frightening** *adj*

~~frightend~~ incorrect spelling of **frightened**

frightful /frīt'l/ *adj* **1** very serious or alarming ○ *the frightful prospect of losing the farm* **2** very bad or unpleasant ○ *a frightful smell* **3** very great ○ *a frightful bore* —**frightfully** *adv*

frigid /fríjjid/ *adj* **1** sexually unresponsive **2** lacking emotional warmth **3** very cold —**frigidity** /fri jíddəti/ *n* —**frigidly** *adv*

frill *n* **1** a decorative band of material with many folds **2** in cooking, a decorative paper band placed round a cake or a bone end **3** an unnecessary addition *(usually pl)* —**frilled** *adj* —**frilly** *adj*

fringe *n* **1** a decorative edging of strands **2** a border of hair cut to hang over the forehead **3** a border or edging **4** an outer limit *(often pl)* ○ *on the fringes of civilization* **5** an area or activity less important than another or others *(usually pl)* ○ *on the fringes of political life* **6** a faction with views unrepresentative of the rest of a group **7** the part of an arts festival devoted to experimental or low-budget works ■ *adj* **1** outlying **2** playing a minor role **3** outside the mainstream and regarded as unconventional **4** not belonging ideologically to the main part of a group ■

vt **(fringing, fringed) 1** form a fringe around **2** decorate with a fringe —**fringed** *adj*

fringe benefit *n* **1** an additional or incidental advantage derived from an activity **2** an additional advantage provided to an employee

frippery /fríppəri/ *(pl* **-ies)** *n* **1** an article worn for show **2** something trifling *(literary)* —**frippery** *adj*

Frisbee /frízbi/ *tdmk* a trademark for a plastic disc thrown from person to person in a game

frisk *v* **1** *vi* leap around playfully **2** *vt* search somebody quickly —**frisk** *n* —**frisking** *n*

frisky /fríski/ **(-ier, -iest)** *adj* feeling playful, or behaving in a playful way —**friskily** *adv* —**friskiness** *n*

frisson /freésson, frísson, free sóN/ *n* a thrilling feeling *(literary)*

frit *n* the basic materials for glass, pottery glazes, or enamels ■ *vt* **(fritting, fritted)** fuse in order to make frit

fritter[1] /fríttər/ *n* a piece of meat, fish, vegetable, or fruit dipped in batter and fried

ORIGIN Fritter as in 'fried cake' is, not unexpectedly, related to *fry*: they go back to the same Latin verb. **Fritter** as in *fritter away* comes from a noun *fritters* meaning 'scraps', whose origin is not certainly known.

fritter[2] /fríttər/ □ **fritter away** *vt* squander gradually

Friuli /free óoli/ *historic region of SE Europe comprising parts of present-day NE Italy and Slovenia*

frivolous /frívvələss/ *adj* **1** not worth taking seriously **2** silly —**frivolity** /fri vólləti/ *n* —**frivolously** *adv* —**frivolousness** *n*

frizz *vti* form into tight curls ■ *n* **1** frizzed hair **2** the act of frizzing hair

frizzle[1] /frízz'l/ **(-zling, -zled)** *vti* **1** burn or shrivel **2** fry and sizzle

frizzle[2] /frízz'l/ *vti* **(-zles, -zling, -zled)** form into tight curls ■ *n* a short tight curl

frizzy /frízzi/ **(-zier, -ziest), frizzly** /frízlee/ **(-zlier, -zliest)** *adj* in tight curls —**frizzlily** *adv* —**frizziness** *n*

fro *adv* ◊ **to and fro**

Frobisher /frṓbishər/, **Sir Martin** (1535?–94) *English navigator*

frock *n* **1** a woman's or girl's dress *(dated)* **2** a loose outer garment traditionally worn by artists and farm workers **3** a monk's cassock

frock coat *n* a 19C man's knee-length coat for formal day wear

frog[1] *n* **1** a small tailless amphibious animal with webbed feet and long back legs used for jumping **2** a nut used to secure the strings on a violin bow **3** a support for flowers in an arrangement ◊ **have a frog in your throat** be hoarse

frog[2] *n* an ornamental loop and button

frogman /frógmən/ *(pl* **-men** /-mən/) *n* an underwater swimmer with breathing equipment engaged in military, police, or rescue work

frogmarch /fróg maarch/ vt force somebody to walk somewhere with arms pinned behind the back —**frogmarch** n

frogspawn /fróg spawn/ n a mass of frogs' eggs in a transparent jelly

frolic /fróllik/ vi (-icking, -icked) play lightheartedly ■ n 1 something lively and carefree 2 lively carefree play —**frolicsome** adj

from prep 1 indicates the source or beginning of something o a passage from a novel 2 indicates a range o We are open from 2 to 4:30. 3 indicates the distance between two points o not far from here 4 indicates the material or substance used to make something o built from native pine 5 indicates the cause of something o low morale resulting from staff cuts 6 indicates that an action does not or should not happen o prevented from seeing her

fromage frais /frómmaazh fráy/ n a soft fresh cheese resembling thick yoghurt

Fromm /from/, **Erich** (1900–80) German-born US psychoanalyst

frond n 1 a large leaf divided into many thin sections, found on many nonflowering plants, especially ferns or palms 2 a seaweed resembling fern leaves

front /frunt/ n 1 a part or surface facing forward 2 the area at the forward part of something 3 the façade of a building facing a street 4 the side of a property adjoining a river, lake, or street 5 the direction straight ahead o Face the front. 6 a leading position o companies at the front of genetic research 7 an aspect o The situation looks bad on all fronts. 8 a battle zone 9 a particular area of activity o the work front 10 a line along which one mass of air meets another differing in temperature or density 11 a group with a common purpose 12 a way of behaving adopted to deal with a situation or conceal feelings o put on a brave front 13 a cover for illegal activities 14 a figurehead leader with no real power ■ adj situated at the front ■ vt 1 face towards something 2 be a front for 3 be the leader of a group, e.g. a band

frontage /frúntij/ n 1 the front of a building 2 the land between a building and a street 3 the length of the front of a building or piece of land adjoining a street, lake, or river

frontal[1] /frúnt'l/ adj 1 situated at or in the front 2 showing the front of somebody or something 3 direct and very forceful o made a frontal attack on her political opponent 4 of the forehead —**frontally** adv

frontal[2] /frúnt'l/ n 1 a cloth covering the front of an altar 2 the façade of a building

front bench n 1 in the British parliament, one of two benches reserved for Government ministers and their Opposition counterparts 2 the most important members of the Government or the Opposition —**frontbencher** n

front door n 1 the main entrance to a building 2 the usual approved means of doing something

front end n 1 the user interface of a computer system 2 a computer that performs preliminary processing on data before passing it to another computer for further processing

front-end adj 1 of the start of a process 2 of the user interface of a computer system

front-end load n a high initial payment made by an investor

frontier /frun teer/ n 1 a border between two countries 2 the edge of an area that is being settled by pioneers 3 the limit of knowledge in a specific field

frontispiece /frúntiss peess/ n a book illustration facing the title page

---

ORIGIN Frontispiece was assimilated to the word piece, but has no connection with it. Etymologically the word divides into two parts, fronti, a form of the Latin word for 'forehead', and spiece, a Latin root meaning 'see' (the same as in spectator). A frontispiece was at first the 'façade of a building'. It developed the sense 'title page of a book' (now obsolete) in the early 17C, and then the modern meaning 'illustration opposite the title page' in the late 17C.

---

front line /null/ n 1 the forward line of a battle, position, or formation 2 the most advanced, important, or conspicuous position

frontline /frúnt līn/ adj advanced or leading

frontline state n a nation situated on the border of a war-torn or war-threatened area

front-load vt assign the bulk of the costs of an insurance scheme or investment to an early stage

front man n a figurehead without real power (infml)

front matter n the preliminary pages of a book before the main text

front of house n 1 the area for the audience in a performance venue 2 the area for diners in a restaurant

front-page adj important enough to appear on the front page of a newspaper

front room n a sitting room at the front of a house

front-runner n a leader in a race or contest (infml)

front-wheel drive n a system in which engine power is transmitted to the front wheels of a motor vehicle

frost n 1 frozen water crystals on a cold surface 2 an outdoor temperature below freezing point 3 a cold, unfriendly attitude 4 the process of freezing ■ v 1 vti cover something or be covered with frost 2 vt give a roughened or dull surface to glass or metal 3 vt US, Can put icing on a cake

Frost, Robert (1874–1963) US poet

frostbite /fróst bīt/ n injury to body extremities caused by exposure to freezing temperatures ■ vt (-biting, -bit /-bit/, -bitten /-bitt'n/) injure by exposure to freezing temperatures

frosting /frósting/ n 1 soft icing made with whisked egg whites 2 a rough or dull surface given to glass or metal

frosty /frósti/ (**-ier, -iest**) adj **1** very cold in temperature **2** covered in frost **3** cold in manner —**frostily** adv —**frostiness** n

froth /froth/ n **1** foam **2** foamy saliva **3** something that lacks substance or seriousness ■ v **1** vt cause to foam **2** vi produce foam —**frothily** adv —**frothiness** n —**frothy** adj

frown /frown/ v **1** vi wrinkle the brow in a displeased expression **2** vt express by frowning —**frown** n —**frowningly** adv

☐ **frown on** or **upon** vt disapprove of.

frowzy /frówzi/ (**-ier, -iest**), **frowsy** adj **1** untidy or shabby **2** also **frowsty** stuffy or musty

froze past tense of **freeze**

frozen /fróz'n/ past participle of **freeze** ■ adj **1** covered by or made into ice **2** damaged or made inoperable by ice **3** extremely cold **4** preserved by freezing for eating at a later time **5** immobile **6** fixed at a particular level to avoid undesirable economic or social consequences —**frozenly** adv —**frozenness** n

fructose /frúk tōz, -tòss, fróok tōz/ n a sugar in fruits and honey

frugal /fróog'l/ adj **1** thrifty **2** meagre —**frugality** /froo gállati/ n —**frugally** adv

fruit /froot/ n **1** the edible part of a plant, usually fleshy and containing seeds **2** the ovary of a plant **3** a spore-producing part of a plant **4** the produce of a plant, grown or harvested by humans **5** a product or consequence ■ vti produce or cause to produce fruit

fruit bat n a large bat of a group including many fruit-eaters

fruitcake /fróot kayk/ n **1** a dense cake containing dried fruit **2** a person regarded as irrational (infml insult)

fruit cocktail n a salad of diced fruits in syrup, usually sold in tins

fruiterer /fróotərər/ n a dealer in fruit

fruit fly n **1** a small plant-eating insect **2** a small insect that eats decaying fruit

fruitful /fróotf'l/ adj **1** bearing much fruit **2** prolific **3** successful or beneficial —**fruitfully** adv —**fruitfulness** n

fruition /froo ísh'n/ n **1** completion **2** the enjoyment of a desired outcome

fruitless /fróotləss/ adj **1** unsuccessful **2** bearing no fruit —**fruitlessly** adv —**fruitlessness** n

fruit machine n UK a coin-operated gambling machine

fruit salad n a mixture of fruit pieces in juice or syrup, served as a dessert

fruity /fróoti/ (**-ier, -iest**) adj **1** of fruit **2** rich in tone **3** sexually suggestive (infml) —**fruitiness** n

frump n a woman regarded as unfashionably dressed (infml insult) —**frumpish** adj —**frumpy** adj

frustrate /fru stráyt/ (**-trating, -trated**) vt **1** thwart something or somebody **2** discourage or exasperate somebody —**frustrated** adj —**frustrating** adj —**frustratingly** adv —**frustration** /fru stráysh'n/ n

fry[1] /frī/ (**fries, fried**) vti cook quickly in very hot fat

fry[2] /frī/ npl young fishes

Fry /frī/, **Elizabeth** (1780–1845) British prison reformer

fryer /frí ər/, **frier** n **1** a container for frying food (usually in combination) **2** US, Can a young chicken for frying

frying pan n a shallow metal pan with a long handle for frying food

fry-up n a meal of various fried foods (infml)

ft abbr foot or feet

FT index n a share index compiled by the Financial Times newspaper

FTP n a standard procedure for transferring files over a network. Full form **file transfer protocol** ■ vt transfer using FTP

Fuchs /fooks/, **Sir Vivian Ernest** (1908–99) British geologist and explorer

fuchsia /fyóoshə/ n a plant with purplish-pink or white drooping flowers

---

ORIGIN The **fuchsia** is named after the German botanist Leonhard Fuchs (1501–66).

---

fuck (offensive) v **1** vti a taboo term meaning to have sexual intercourse **2** vt a taboo term meaning to destroy somebody or something ■ n a taboo term for an act of sexual intercourse ■ interj a taboo term expressing strong anger

☐ **fuck off** vi a taboo term meaning to go away (offensive)

☐ **fuck up** vt a taboo term meaning spoil or botch (offensive)

fuddle /fúdd'l/ (**-dling, -dled**) vt confuse, e.g. with alcohol —**fuddle** n

fuddy-duddy /fúddi dudi/ (pl **fuddy-duddies**) n a person regarded as old-fashioned and dull (infml; sometimes offensive)

fudge n a soft grainy toffee ■ vti (**fudging, fudged**) alter in order to deceive (infml)

fuel /fyoo əl/ n **1** something burned to provide power or heat **2** the fissionable material burned to create nuclear energy **3** something that stimulates or maintains an emotion ○ adding fuel to his anger ■ vt (**-elling, -elled**) **1** supply something with fuel **2** stimulate or maintain an emotion ○ fuelled her passion

fuel cell n a device that generates electricity by converting the energy of a fuel and an antioxidant into electricity

fuel injection n a system for running an internal combustion engine without a carburettor by forcing fuel directly into the combustion chamber —**fuel-injected** adj

fuel oil n a liquid petroleum product used to produce heat or power

Fuentes /fwént ayss/, **Carlos** (b. 1928) Mexican writer

fug n a stuffy atmosphere

fugitive /fyóojitiv/ n **1** somebody who runs away, especially from justice **2** something elusive ■ adj **1** running away **2** lasting only briefly ○ the fugitive hour of dawn **3** moving from place to place **4** written or composed for a specific occasion *(literary)* **5** hard to understand or retain *(fml)* ○ *the fugitive nature of astrophysics*

fugue /fyoog/ *n* **1** a musical form in which a theme is stated and varied contrapuntally **2** *also* **fugue state** a state in which somebody experiences temporary and selective memory loss —**fugal** *adj*

Mt Fuji

Fuji, Mt /fōoji/, **Fujiyama** /fōoji a'amə/ dormant volcano and the highest mountain in Japan. Height 3,776 m/12,387 ft.

Fukuoka /fōokoo ōka/ port on N Kyushu Island, Japan. Pop. 1,279,671 (2000).

Fulbright /fōol brīt/, **J. William** (1905–95) US politician and educator

fulcrum /fōolkrəm/ (*pl* **-crums** *or* **-cra** /-krə/) *n* **1** the pivot of a lever **2** a prop supporting something revolving about it or depending on it

fulfil /fōol fil/ (**-filling, -filled**) *vt* **1** achieve something expected, desired, or promised **2** carry out a request or order **3** satisfy a standard or requirement **4** complete something **5** supply goods ordered ○ *fulfil an order for new cars* —**fulfilment** *n* ◊ See note at **perform**

fulfill *vt* US = **fulfil**

fulfillment *n* US = **fulfilment**

full[1] /fōol/ *adj* **1** filled to capacity **2** having a large amount or number of something ○ *full of mischief* **3** greatest in degree or extent ○ *at full speed* **4** with nothing or no one missing ○ *a full complement of staff* **5** completely developed ○ *in full bloom* **6** having fulfilled all the requirements for something **7** having eaten enough **8** busy, active, and varied ○ *live a full life* **9** plump ○ *a full figure* **10** having the same parents ○ *my full brother* **11** sonorous ○ *chanted in full voice* ■ *adv* **1** completely ○ *turned full round* **2** exactly ○ *took a hit full on the chest* ■ *n* the greatest extent or fullest degree ○ *enjoyed himself to the full* —**fullness** *n* —**fully** *adv* ◊ **be full of yourself** be very conceited and arrogant

full[2] /fōol/ *vti* make cloth bulkier by dampening and beating it, or become bulkier in this way

fullback /fōol bak/ *n* **1** in sports such as football, rugby, or hockey, a defender **2** in American football, a player positioned behind the quarterback or a fullback's position

full-blooded *adj* **1** vigorous **2** thoroughbred

full-blown *adj* **1** complete **2** fully in bloom

full board *n* board at a hotel that includes accommodation and all meals

full dress *n* clothes for a ceremony or formal occasion

full-dress *adj* important and complete ○ *a full-dress investigation*

Fuller /fōolər/, **Buckminster** (1895–1983) US engineer, designer, architect, and writer

~~fullfill~~ incorrect spelling of **fulfil**

full-frontal *adj* showing the whole front of the nude body including the genitals

full house *n* in poker, a hand containing three cards of the same value and a pair of another value

full-length *adj* describes a mirror or portrait showing the whole body

full marks *npl* a perfect score in an assessment or examination

full monty /-mónti/ *n* everything needed or appropriate *(slang)*

full moon *n* **1** the Moon appearing as a complete circle **2** the time when the Moon appears as a full circle

full-scale *adj* **1** life-size **2** done with total commitment of effort and resources

full-size, full-sized *adj* of the usual size for something

full stop *n* **1** the punctuation mark (.) used at the end of a sentence or in abbreviations **2** a complete halt or end

USAGE A **full stop** is used at the end of a sentence that is not a question or exclamation: *It rained last Saturday.* It is also used after some abbreviations: *at 11 a.m. on 7 Aug. 2000.* The full stop is increasingly omitted in abbreviations, especially in contractions (e.g. *Dr, St, Ltd*) and after capital letters (e.g. *BBC, USA, VCR*). Shortened forms used as words in their own right (e.g. *gym, disco, pub*) and acronyms pronounced as words (e.g. *Aids, laser, NATO*) should not be written with full stops. The same mark is used in decimal notation (*2.5 children*), where it is read as 'point'. It is also used in Internet addresses, where it is read as 'dot' (*.com*).

full time *n* in football and other sports, the end of a match ■ *adv* during all of the time considered usual for an activity ○ *worked full time*

full-time *adj* **1** involving or using all the time usual or appropriate for an activity **2** occurring at or indicating the end of a match —**full-timer** *n*

fully-featured *adj* having the whole range of possible functions, capabilities, or options ○ *a fully-featured PC*

fully-fledged *adj* **1** completely developed **2** fully qualified

fully-grown *adj* mature or adult

fulminate /fōolmi nayt, fúl-/ (**-nating, -nated**) *v* **1** *vi* speak scathingly **2** *vti* explode violently —**fulmination** /fōolmi náysh'n, fúl-/ *n*

fulsome /foólsəm/ *adj* **1** excessively complimentary **2** lavish —**fulsomely** *adv*

fumble /fúmb'l/ (**-bling**, **-bled**) *v* **1** *vti* grope clumsily in searching for something **2** *vi* act clumsily, hesitantly, or unsuccessfully **3** *vt* bungle —**fumble** *n* —**fumblingly** *adv*

fume *v* (**fuming, fumed**) **1** *vi* be angry **2** *vi* emit gas or smoke **3** *vt* fumigate something ■ *n* (*often pl*) **1** smoke or gas **2** an acrid smell —**fumingly** *adv*

fumigate /fyoómi gayt/ (**-gating, -gated**) *vti* treat something with fumes to disinfect it or kill pests —**fumigant** *n* —**fumigation** /fyoómi gáysh'n/ *n* —**fumigator** *n*

fun *n* **1** amusement or enjoyment **2** something amusing or enjoyable ■ *adj* **1** amusing or enjoyable (*infml*) ○ *a fun movie* **2** cheap and flamboyant ○ *fun jewellery* ◇ **make fun of** tease ◇ **poke fun at** mock or ridicule

Funafuti /foónə foóti/ atoll and capital of Tuvalu, in the W Pacific Ocean. Pop. 3,432 (1990).

function /fúngksh'n/ *n* **1** the purpose of something **2** a role assigned to somebody or something **3** a social event **4** a variable quantity determined by other values **5** a quality or characteristic that depends on and varies with another ○ *Success is a function of determination and ability.* **6** (*symbol* **f**) a one-to-one correspondence between members of two mathematical sets **7** a single computer operation **8** a computer program's main purpose **9** the role of a word or phrase in a construction **10** practical usefulness, as opposed to aesthetic appeal ■ *vi* **1** serve a purpose or perform a role **2** be in working order

functional /fúngksh'nəl/ *adj* **1** practical or useful **2** operational —**functionally** *adv*

functionalism /fúngksh'nəlìzəm/ *n* **1** the belief that the intended function of something should determine its form **2** a philosophy emphasizing that the practical is more important than the aesthetic —**functionalist** *n*, *adj*

functionality /fúngkshə nálti/ *n* the range of functions, capabilities, and options a computer offers

functionary /fúngksh'nəri/ (*pl* **-ies**) *n* an unimportant official

function key *n* a keyboard button that instructs the computer to perform a specific action

function word *n* a word whose primary purpose is to perform a syntactic function in a sentence

fund *n* **1** a supply **2** a sum of money saved or invested for a purpose ■ **funds** *npl* money ■ *vt* provide money for something

fundamental /fúndə mént'l/ *adj* **1** basic **2** central or essential ■ *n* **1** a basic principle or element (*often pl*) **2** the principal musical tone in a chord **3** the lowest frequency in a vibration —**fundamentally** *adv*

fundamentalism /fúndə mént'lìzəm/ *n* **1** a religious or political movement with a strict view of doctrine **2** the belief that religious or political doctrine should be implemented strictly —**fundamentalist** *n*, *adj*

~~fundemental~~ incorrect spelling of **fundamental**

fundi /fúndi/ (*pl* **-dis**) *n S Africa* an expert

funding /fúnding/ *n* money to support a project

fundraiser /fúnd rayzər/ *n* **1** somebody who raises money for a nonprofitmaking organization **2** a money-raising activity or event for a nonprofitmaking organization —**fundraising** *n*

funeral /fyoónərəl/ *n* **1** a ceremony for somebody who has died **2** an end to something **3** a funeral procession

funeral director *n* a funeral director

funeral parlour, funeral home *n* a business establishment arranging or performing funerals

funerary /fyoónərəri/ *adj* of funerals

funereal /fyoo neéri əl/ *adj* **1** of or like a funeral **2** gloomy

funfair /fún fair/ *n* a fair with amusements

fungicide /fúnji sīd, fúng gi-/ *n* a chemical that kills fungi —**fungicidal** /fúnji sīd'l, fúng gi-/ *adj*

fungoid /fúng goyd/ *adj* of or like fungus ■ *n* a fungus

fungus /fúng gəss/ (*pl* **-gi** /-gī/ *or* **-guses**) *n* a spore-producing organism of a group including moulds and mushrooms —**fungal** *adj*

funicular /fyoo níkyŏŏlər/ *adj* **1** of a rope's tension **2** operated by a rope or cable wound or pulled by a machine ■ *n* a cable-operated railway

funk[1] *n* a musical style with a heavy rhythmic bass and beat

funk[2] (*infml dated*) *n* a state of fear ■ *vti* not do something out of fear

funky /fúngki/ (**-ier, -iest**) *adj* **1** like funk music **2** like blues music (*slang*) **3** unconventional (*infml*) **4** stylish and new (*slang*)

funnel /fúnn'l/ *n* **1** a cone-shaped utensil for pouring liquids into containers **2** a chimney on a steamship or steam train ■ *v* (**-nelling, -nelled**) **1** *vti* move into and through a narrow space **2** *vt* concentrate resources somewhere

funnel cloud *n* a funnel-shaped cloud projecting from the bottom of a thundercloud

funny /fúnni/ (**-nier, -niest**) *adj* **1** causing amusement or laughter **2** strange or puzzling **3** unconventional **4** unwell (*infml*) **5** tricky or dishonest (*infml*) —**funnily** *adv* —**funniness** *n*

SYNONYMS funny, comic, comical, droll, facetious, humorous, witty, hilarious, side-splitting CORE MEANING: causing or intended to cause amusement

funny bone *n* **1** the point at the outside of the elbow where a nerve is close to the longer arm bone (*infml*) **2** somebody's sense of humour

ORIGIN As well as a reference to the tingling sensation caused when the nerve at the point of the elbow is hit, the name may involve a pun on *humerus* 'arm bone' and *humorous*.

funny man *n* a man who is a comedian, clown, or humorist

fun run *n* a leisure run to promote fitness or raise money for charity

fur *n* **1** the soft dense coat of hair on a mammal **2** hairs from a mammal's coat **3** a dressed pelt from a mammal such as a mink. Use: garments; decoration. **4** a coat, jacket, or stole made of fur or of fake fur **5** something hairy **6** a whitish coating on the tongue (*infml*) **7** a lime deposit in a kettle or pipe —**furred** *adj*

□ **fur up** *vti* coat or become coated with lime

fur. *abbr* furlong

Furies /fyóoriz/ *npl* in Greek mythology, three avenging goddesses

furious /fyóori əss/ *adj* **1** very angry **2** very energetic —**furiously** *adv*

furl *vti* roll up and secure a flag or sail, or become rolled up and secure ■ *n* a furled section of a flag or sail

furlong /fúr long/ *n* a measure of distance equal to 220 yd (approximately 201 m)

ORIGIN **Furlong** means etymologically 'furrow long', and so was the length of a furrow ploughed across a field ten acres square.

furlough /fúrlō/ *n* a leave of absence, especially from military duty

furnace /fúrniss/ *n* **1** an enclosure producing great heat, e.g. to heat a building or smelt metal **2** a very hot place (*infml*)

furnish /fúrnish/ *vt* **1** put furniture in a place **2** supply something (*fml*) —**furnished** *adj* —**furnisher** *n*

furnishings /fúrnishingz/ *npl* furniture, carpets, and curtains

furniture /fúrnichər/ *n* movable items such as tables and chairs in a room, garden, or patio

furore /fyoō ráwri/ *n* **1** an angry public reaction **2** a state of excitement **3** a craze

furrier /fúrri ər/ *n* **1** a fur dealer **2** a maker or seller of fur garments and accessories

furrow /fúrrō/ *n* **1** a narrow trench in soil made by a plough **2** a groove **3** a wrinkle on the forehead ■ *vti* make furrows in or become marked with furrows —**furrowed** *adj*

furry /fúri/ (**-rier, -riest**) *adj* **1** covered in fur **2** looking or feeling like fur —**furriness** *n*

further /fúrthər/ *adj* additional ■ *adv* **1** to a greater degree or extent **2** to a greater distance **3** in addition ■ *vt* advance —**furthermost** *adj*

furtherance /fúrthərənss/ *n* advancement or progress

further education *n* post-school education that does not lead to a university degree

furthermore /fúrthər mawr, fúrthər máwr/ *adv* in addition

furthest /fúrthist/ *adj* most distant ■ *adv* **1** to the greatest degree or extent **2** to the greatest distance

furtive /fúrtiv/ *adj* **1** secretive **2** shifty —**furtively** *adv* —**furtiveness** *n* ◊ See note at **secret**

fury /fyóori/ (*pl* **-ries**) *n* **1** great rage **2** a burst of violent anger **3** a wild physical force ◊ *felt the fury of the hurricane* **4 Fury** in Greek mythology, one of the Furies ◊ See note at **anger**

furze *n* gorse

~~fuschia~~ incorrect spelling of **fuchsia**

fuse[1] /fyooz/ *n* an electrical circuit breaker containing a piece of metal that melts if the current is too strong ■ *vti* (**fusing, fused**) **1** stop working because of a damaged fuse **2** combine **3** liquefy —**fused** *adj*

fuse[2] /fyooz/ *n* **1** a cord or trail of a combustible substance ignited at one end to carry a flame to an explosive device **2** a mechanical or electrical detonator for a bomb or grenade ■ *vt* (**fusing, fused**) equip a bomb or grenade with a detonator

fuse box *n* a container for a building's electrical fuses

fuselage /fyóozə laazh, fyoōzəlij/ *n* an aeroplane body, excluding the wings

Fushun /foō shoōn/ city in NE China. Pop. 1,530,000 (1995).

fusilier /fyóozi leer/, **fusileer** *n* formerly, a British soldier in a regiment armed with lightweight muskets

fusillade /fyóozi layd, -laad/ *n* **1** a blast of gunfire from several guns at once **2** an onslaught ■ *vt* (**-lading, -laded**) fire at an enemy in a sustained burst from several guns at once

fusion /fyoōzh'n/ *n* **1** the heating and liquefying of a substance **2** the blending of two or more things **3** a combination of musical styles from different traditions

fusion bomb *n* a hydrogen bomb using nuclear fusion

fusion food, fusion cuisine *n* a style of cooking combining different international influences

fuss *n* **1** unnecessarily busy or excited activity **2** needless worry over trivialities **3** a protest or complaint about something trivial **4** a noisy argument **5** an excited display of affection or concern **6** excessive decoration ■ *vi* **1** worry too much about trivialities **2** make nervous or aimless fiddling movements ◦ *fussed with her hair*

fusspot /fúss pot/ *n* somebody who worries too much about trivialities (*infml*)

fussy /fússi/ (**-ier, -iest**) *adj* **1** worrying too much about trivialities **2** excessively choosy **3** overly elaborate, e.g. in design ◊ See note at **careful**

fustian /fústi ən/ *n* **1** a coarse cotton-linen cloth **2** bombast —**fustian** *adj*

fusty /fústi/ (**-tier, -tiest**) *adj* **1** smelling stale **2** outdated

futile /fyoō tíl/ *adj* **1** vain or pointless **2** frivolous —**futilely** *adv* —**futility** /fyoo tílləti/ *n*

futon /foō ton/ *n* **1** a Japanese-style mattress used as a bed **2** a sofa bed with a futon mattress

future /fyóochər/ n 1 a time yet to come 2 events yet to happen 3 an expected or projected state 4 the tense or verb forms used for referring to events that have not yet happened ■ **futures** npl commodities traded for later delivery ■ adj 1 yet to occur 2 of or in the tense used for referring to events that have not yet happened

future perfect n the form of a verb that expresses a completed action in the future, e.g. using 'will have' with the past participle

future shock n stress caused by rapid technological change

futurism /fyóochərizəm/ n 1 an early 20C artistic movement valuing the beauty of technology 2 belief in the need to look to the future for personal and social fulfilment —**futurist** n, adj

futuristic /fyóochə rístik/ adj 1 appearing to be ahead of the times in design or technology 2 showing life in a future time —**futuristically** adv

futurity /fyoo tyóorəti, -chóorəti/ (pl -ties) n 1 the future 2 a future event (fml)

futurology /fyóochə rólləji/ n the study and forecasting of the future on the basis of current trends —**futurological** /fyoóchərə lójjik'l/ adj —**futurologist** n

Fuzhou /foó zhó/ city in SE China. Pop. 1,590,000 (1995).

fuzz n 1 a mass of short fine hairs or fibres 2 an offensive term for the police (slang) ■ vti 1 cover or become covered with fuzz 2 blur or become blurred

fuzzy /fúzzi/ (-ier, -iest) adj 1 covered with fuzz 2 consisting of fuzz 3 frizzy 4 blurred ○ fuzzy vision —**fuzzily** adv —**fuzziness** n

fuzzy logic n logic allowing for imprecision in answers to questions used in computer programming designed to mimic human intelligence

fwd abbr forward

-fy suffix make, cause to become ○ modify

FYI abbr for your information (in e-mails and office memos)

G

g[1] (pl **g's**), **G** (pl **G's** or **Gs**) n the 7th letter of the English alphabet

g[2] symbol acceleration of free fall as a result of gravity

g[3] abbr 1 gauge 2 gram

G[1] (pl **G's** or **Gs**) n 1 the 5th note in the musical scale of C major 2 in the United States, Canada, Australia, and New Zealand, a general-audience film rating 3 US $1,000 (slang)

G[2] symbol gravitational constant

G8 n the eight most industrialized nations. Full form **Group of Eight**

Ga symbol gallium

gab (**gabbing, gabbed**) vi chat idly (infml) —**gab** n

gabardine /gábbər deèn/ n 1 a smooth twill fabric 2 a gabardine garment

gabble /gább'l/ (-bling, -bled) v 1 vti speak or say unintelligibly 2 vi make the throaty sound of a goose —**gabble** n

gable /gáyb'l/ n a triangular section of a building's wall where the roof slopes meet —**gabled** adj

Gable /gáyb'l/, **Clark** (1901–60) US film actor

Gabon /ga bón, gə bón/ country in west-central Africa on the Atlantic coast. Cap. Libreville. Pop. 1,221,175 (2001). —**Gabonese** /gábbə neéz/ n, adj

Gaborone /gábbə róni/ capital of Botswana. Pop. 133,468 (1991).

Gabriel /gáybri əl/ n in Christian, Islamic, and Jewish tradition, an archangel who acts as God's messenger

gad (**gadding, gadded**) vi be out having fun (humorous)

gadabout /gáddə bowt/ n somebody always in search of entertainment or activity (humorous)

Gaddafi /gə dáffi/, **Gadaffi, Qaddafi** /kə-/, **Muammar al-** (b. 1942) Libyan soldier and national leader (1969–)

gadfly /gád flī/ (pl -flies) n 1 a fly that bites livestock 2 somebody regarded as annoying

gadget /gájjit/ n 1 a small ingenious device 2 a device that is of no real use

gadgetry /gájjitri/ n gadgets collectively

gadolinium /gáddə línni əm/ n (symbol Gd) a silvery-white metallic element. Use: high-temperature alloys, neutron absorber in nuclear reactors and fuels.

Gaea n = Gaia

Gael /gayl/ n 1 somebody who speaks Gaelic 2 a Scottish Highlander

Gaelic /gáylik, gállik/ n a Celtic language spoken in Scotland and Ireland —**Gaelic** adj

Gaelic football n an Irish ball game between teams of ten players who can kick or punch the ball

gaff[1] n 1 a hooked pole used to hold and land fish 2 a pole used to support the upper edge of a ship's sail ■ vt hold fish with a hooked pole

gaff[2] n a house (slang)

gaffe /gaf/ n a social blunder

gaffer /gáffər/ n (infml) 1 UK somebody's boss 2 a chief lighting electrician on a television or film set 3 UK a man

gag n 1 something put over a person's mouth to prevent speech 2 a restraint of free speech 3 a comic remark or action 4 a trick or practical joke (infml) 5 a procedure to force closure of a parliamentary debate 6 a surgical device to keep a patient's mouth open ■ v (**gagging, gagged**) 1 vt put something over somebody's mouth to prevent speech **2** *vt* prevent somebody from saying or revealing something **3** *vti* choke or retch

gaga /gaà gaa/ *adj* an offensive term meaning mentally confused *(infml)*

Gagarin /gə gaàrin/, **Yuri** (1934–68) Soviet cosmonaut

gage[1] *(archaic)* *n* **1** a pledge left until a debt is paid or an obligation fulfilled **2** a token thrown down or offered as a challenge to fight ■ *vt* (**gaging, gaged**) offer as a pledge

gage[2] *n*, *vt* = **gauge**

gagging order *n* a court order that forbids somebody from saying or revealing something

gaggle /gágg'l/ *n* **1** a group of geese **2** a group of people ○ *a gaggle of children*

Gaia /gí ə/, **Gaea** /jée ə/, **Ge** /gay/ *n* in Greek mythology, the personification of the Earth

gaiety /gáy əti/ (*pl* -**ties**) *n* **1** joyfulness or light-heartedness **2** a spirited activity **3** the bright or colourful appearance of something such as clothing *(dated)*

gaijin /gí jin/ (*pl* same) *n* a foreigner in Japan

gaily /gáyli/ *adv* **1** joyfully or lightheartedly **2** showing a lack of concern **3** in bright colours *(dated)*

gain[1] *v* **1** *vt* acquire or arrive at through effort, skill, or merit ○ *gain a victory* ○ *gain access* **2** *vi* get an advantage ○ *No one stands to gain from this.* **3** *vti* get more of something gradually, or increase gradually ○ *gain in confidence* ○ *gain experience* **4** *vi* get closer to somebody being pursued or farther away from a pursuer **5** *vti* increase in or by a particular amount ○ *The pound had gained two points.* **6** *vti* run ahead of the correct time ○ *My watch gains ten minutes every day.* **7** *vt* reach *(literary)* ○ *gained the shore* ■ *n* **1** an achievement **2** an amount by which something has increased **3** a benefit or profit —**gainable** *adj* ◊ See note at **get**

gain[2] *n* a notch to fit something into ■ *vt* **1** cut a notch in **2** fit into a notch

gainful /gáynf'l/ *adj* profitable or advantageous —**gainfully** *adv*

gainsay /gáyn sáy/ (**-said** /-séd/) *vt* (*fml*) **1** deny **2** contradict —**gainsayer** *n*

Gainsborough /gáynzbərə/, **Thomas** (1727–88) British painter

gait /gayt/ *n* **1** a manner of walking **2** a horse's pace having a specific pattern of steps

SPELLCHECK Do not confuse the spelling of **gait** and **gate** ('a movable barrier'), which sound similar.

gaiter /gáytər/ *n* a covering for the leg from the instep to the ankle or knee *(usually pl)* —**gaitered** *adj*

gal *n* a girl or woman *(slang dated; sometimes offensive)*

gal. *abbr* gallon

gala /gaàlə/ *n* a lavish party with food and entertainment

galactic /gə láktik/ *adj* of galaxies or the Milky Way

galactose /gə láktōss/ *n* a sugar that is a constituent of lactose

Galahad /gállə had/ *n* **1** in Arthurian legend, one of the knights of the Round Table **2** somebody who acts nobly

Galápagos Islands /gə láppəgəss-/, **Galapagos Islands** group of islands off W Ecuador in the Pacific Ocean. Pop. 9,785 (1990).

galaxy /gálləksi/ (*pl* -**ies**) *n* **1** a large group of stars, gas, and dust forming a unit within the universe **2** a distinguished gathering **3 Galaxy** the Milky Way

ORIGIN Galaxy came via French and Latin from the Greek word for the 'Milky Way', which was formed from *gala* 'milk'. *Milky Way* itself is a translation from Latin. The names derive from the white appearance of massed stars in the night sky.

Galbraith /gal bráyth/, **John Kenneth** (*b.* 1908) Canadian-born US economist

gale *n* a strong wind, technically of force 8 or 9 ■ **gales** *npl* loud outbursts ○ *gales of laughter*

Galen /gáylən/ (129–199?) Greek physician and scholar

galilee /gálli lee/ *n* a porch or chapel of a medieval church

Galilee /gálli lee/ region of ancient Palestine between the River Jordan and the Sea of Galilee

Galilee, Sea of freshwater lake in NE Israel on the River Jordan

Galileo /gálli láy ō/ (1564–1642) Italian physicist and astronomer

gall[1] *n* **1** audacity **2** bitter feeling *(literary)*

ORIGIN Gall 'audacity, bitter feeling' comes from an ancient Scandinavian word meaning 'yellow' (it originally referred to bile, which is of a yellowish-green colour). **Gall** 'sore on an animal' is from an old German word, while **gall** 'swelling on a plant' came via French from Latin.

gall[2] *n* a sore on an animal caused by rubbing ■ *vt* **1** make angry or annoyed **2** break the surface of through rubbing

gall[3] *n* a swelling on a tree or plant

gall. *abbr* gallon

gallant /gállənt, gə lánt/ *adj* **1** courteous and attentive **2** brave *(literary)* ■ *n* **1** a man courteous to women *(dated)* **2** a male lover *(archaic)* —**gallantly** *adv*

gallantry /gálləntri/ (*pl* -**ries**) *n* **1** courage **2** courtesy and attentiveness **3** something gallant said or done *(dated)*

gallbladder /gáwl bladər/ *n* a sac on the right side of the liver where bile is stored

galleon /gálli ən/ *n* a large three-masted sailing ship

gallery /gálləri/ (*pl* -**ies**) *n* **1** a place for art exhibitions **2** a covered walkway that is open on one or both sides **3** an enclosed passageway inside a building **4** a long narrow space or room with a specific function **5** a balcony along the wall of a large building **6** an underground passage **7** a photographer's studio **8** a balcony in a theatre, especially the highest area, or the seats or audience in it **9** a group of spectators, especially at a tennis or squash match **10** an assorted collection —**galleried** adj

galley /gálli/ (pl **-leys**) n **1** a large ship used in ancient and medieval times, often with oars **2** a long rowing boat **3** a kitchen on a boat, train, or aircraft **4** also **galley proof** a first test copy of printed material for correction, usually not yet divided into pages

Gallic /gállik/ adj French

galling /gáwling/ adj exasperating —**gallingly** adv

gallium /gálli əm/ n (symbol Ga) a rare metallic element. Use: high-temperature thermometers, semiconductors, alloys.

gallivant /gálli vant/ vi travel around for pleasure (infml)

gallon /gállən/ n **1** a British unit of volume equal to eight imperial pints (approximately 4.55 litres) **2** a US unit of volume equal to eight US pints (approximately 3.79 litres)

gallop /gálləp/ n **1** the fastest pace of a horse, with all four feet off the ground at the same time **2** a fast pace ■ vti ride a horse fast

galloping /gálləping/ adj **1** fast-developing **2** like a gallop in speed or rhythm

gallows /gállōz/ (pl same) n a frame for hanging criminals

ORIGIN Gallows comes from an ancient word meaning 'pole'. It was originally singular, though it occurred frequently in pair of gallows, from the two uprights with a crosspiece from which it was constructed. From that **gallows** came to be treated as a singular itself.

gallows humour n macabre humour

gallstone /gáwl stōn/ n a solid mass formed in the gallbladder

galore /gə láwr/ adj in large quantities or numbers ○ food galore

ORIGIN Galore comes from an Irish phrase meaning literally 'to sufficiency'. It is first recorded in the early 17C.

galoshes /gə lóshiz/ npl waterproof overshoes

Galsworthy /gáwlz wurthi/, **John** (1867–1933) British novelist and playwright

galumph /gə lúmf/ vi move boisterously or clumsily (infml)

ORIGIN Galumph is a blend of gallop and triumph, coined by Lewis Carroll in Through the Looking-Glass (1872).

galvanic /gal vánnik/ adj **1** of chemically produced direct current **2** sudden or startling like an electric shock —**galvanically** adv

ORIGIN Galvanic, galvanize, and related words

are formed from the name of the Italian physiologist Luigi Galvani (1737–98), whose research led to the discovery that electricity can result from chemical action.

galvanize /gálvə nīz/ (**-nizing, -nized**), **galvanise** vt **1** stimulate somebody or something to activity **2** coat metal with zinc —**galvanization** /gálvə nī záysh'n/ n

galvanometer /gálvə nómmitər/ n an instrument for measuring electric current —**galvanometric** /gálvənə méttrik/ adj —**galvanometry** n

Galway /gáwl way/ **1** seaport in the W Republic of Ireland, on **Galway Bay**, an inlet of the Atlantic Ocean. Pop. 57,000 (1996). **2** county in Connacht Province, W Republic of Ireland

Gama /gaámə/, **Vasco da** (1469?–1524) Portuguese navigator and explorer

Gambia /gámbi ə/, **the Gambia** country on the coast of West Africa. Cap. Banjul. Pop. 1,411,205 (2001). —**Gambian** n, adj

gambit /gámbit/ n **1** a stratagem to secure an advantage **2** an opening move in chess

gamble /gámb'l/ v (**-bling, -bled**) **1** vi play games of chance **2** vt bet money **3** vi take a chance on something ○ gambling on nice weather **4** vi endanger somebody or something ○ gambled with the success of the show ■ n **1** a bet **2** something risky —**gambler** n —**gambling** n

ORIGIN Gamble is probably an alteration of an old word gamel 'play games, frolic', which was a derivative of game. Alternatively it could have been formed directly from game and the suffix -le. It is first recorded in the early 18C. **Gamble** has no direct connection with gambol, which is an alteration of earlier gambade 'horse's leap, caper'. This came via French from an Italian word formed from gamba 'leg'.

gambol /gámb'l/ (**-bolling, -bolled**) vi leap or skip about playfully —**gambol** n

game n **1** something played for fun **2** a competitive activity with rules **3** an occasion of a game **4** a part of a match that forms a scoring unit **5** an aspect of a game ○ Their defensive game was terrible. **6** a style or level of playing ○ raise your game **7** a stratagem or tactic **8** an occupation (infml) ○ the advertising game **9** something not taken seriously **10** wild animals hunted for sport, or their meat ■ **games** npl an event with many sporting contests ■ adj **1** ready and willing **2** brave ■ vi (**gaming, gamed**) gamble for money —**gamely** adv ◇ **ahead of the game** anticipating new developments ◇ **give the game away** reveal a secret ◇ **play the game** follow the rules of a given situation, even if they are unspoken

game bird n a bird that is hunted for sport

gamekeeper /gáym keepər/ n somebody who looks after game, as on an estate or game reserve —**gamekeeping** n

game plan n a strategy to win a competition or achieve an objective

game point *n* **1** in racket games, a situation with the potential to win the game on the next point **2** a point that wins the game

game reserve, game preserve *n* a protected area for wild animals

game show *n* a TV show with games and prizes

gamesmanship /gáymzmanship/ *n* **1** strategic behaviour to gain an advantage **2** play of questionable fairness to gain an advantage

gamete /gámmeet/ *n* a cell with half the usual number of chromosomes that unites with another cell of the opposite sex in the process of sexual reproduction —**gametic** /gə méttik/ *adj*

game warden *n* somebody looking after game on a game reserve

gamey *adj* = **gamy**

gamine /gámmeen/ *n* **1** a boyish girl or young woman **2** a girl street urchin ■ *adj* appealingly boyish

gaming /gáyming/ *n* gambling for money

gamma /gámmə/ *n* **1** the 3rd letter of the Greek alphabet **2** the 3rd highest category of mark given to a student's work

gamma globulin *n* a protein containing antibodies that is a component of blood serum

gamma ray *n* a high-energy photon emitted from a nucleus of a radioactive atom

gammon[1] /gámmən/ *n* **1** the lower part of a side of bacon **2** cured or smoked ham

gammon[2] /gámmən/ *n* a win at backgammon —**gammon** *vt*

gammy /gámmi/ (**-mier, -miest**) *adj* injured or impaired (*infml*)

Gamow /gám ov/, **George** (1904–68) Russian-born US theoretical physicist. He was a proponent of the theory that the universe was created in a gigantic explosion.

gamut /gámmət/ *n* the full range of something

> **ORIGIN Gamut** was originally *gamma-ut*. This was the name of a note in medieval musical notation, the lowest of a particular sequence. **Gamut** came to refer to the full range of notes that a voice or instrument can produce. The modern figurative sense is first recorded in the early 17C.

gamy /gáymi/ (**-ier, -iest**), **gamey** (**-ier, -iest**) *adj* **1** tasting of or like game **2** rank-smelling —**gaminess** *n*

gander /gándər/ *n* **1** a male goose **2** a look or glance (*infml*)

Gandhi /gándi/, **Indira** (1917–84) prime minister of India (1966–77, 1980–84)

Barnaby's

Mohandas Karamchand Gandhi

Gandhi, Mohandas Karamchand (1869–1948) Indian thinker and nationalist leader

G & T, g and t *abbr* gin and tonic

gang *n* **1** a group of trouble-making young people **2** a group of criminals **3** a group of workers **4** a group of people who enjoy each other's company

□ **gang up on** *vt* unite to attack or intimidate

Ganges /gán jeez/ river in N India and Bangladesh, emptying into the Bay of Bengal. Length 2,510 km/1,560 mi.

gangland /gáng land, -lənd/ *n* the world of organized crime —**gangland** *adj*

gangling /gáng gling/, **gangly** /-glee/ (**-glier, -gliest**) *adj* awkwardly tall and thin

ganglion /gáng gli ən/ (*pl* **-a** /-ə/ *or* **-ons**) *n* **1** a cluster of nerve cells **2** a swelling on a joint or tendon —**ganglionic** /gáng gli ónnik/ *adj*

gangplank /gáng plangk/ *n* a movable walkway for embarking and disembarking a ship

gangrene /gáng green/ *n* the death of an area of body tissue as a result of lack of blood ■ *vti* (**-grening, -grened**) affect or become affected with gangrene —**gangrenous** /gáng grinəss/ *adj*

gangsta rap /gángstə-/ *n* rap music with lyrics about violence and gangs

gangster /gángstər/ *n* a member of a criminal gang —**gangsterism** *n*

gangway /gáng way/ *n* **1** a narrow walkway **2** an entrance in a ship's side **3** a gangplank ■ *interj* make way

ganja /gánjə, gaàn-/ *n* marijuana (*slang*)

gannet /gánnit/ *n* a fish-eating seabird

gantry /gántri/ (*pl* **-tries**) *n* a supporting framework for signals or machinery

gaol *n, vt* = **jail**

gap *n* **1** an opening in a structure **2** something missing in a sequence or whole **3** an interval of time during which something stops happening ○ *after a gap of three years* **4** a disparity ○ *the gap between rich and poor* —**gappy** *adj*

gape *vi* (**gaping, gaped**) **1** stare with the mouth open **2** open into a gap ■ *n* **1** an open-mouthed stare **2** an opening of the mouth —**gaping** *adj* ◊ See note at **gaze**

gap-toothed *adj* with gaps between the teeth

garage /gárraazh, -rij/ *n* **1** a building for a motor vehicle or motor vehicles **2** an establishment repairing motor vehicles **3** *also* **garage music** a style of dance music influenced by disco and soul music ■ *vt* (**-raging, -raged**) put a vehicle in a garage

garage sale *n ANZ, US, Can* a sale of used or unwanted household items held in the garage of a house

Garagum Desert /gárrə gum-/ desert occupying a large portion of Turkmenistan

garam masala /gaàrəm mə saàlə/ *n* a spice mixture used in South Asian cookery

~~garantee~~ incorrect spelling of **guarantee**

garb *n* **1** a distinctive outfit of clothes **2** an outward appearance

garbage /gaàrbij/ *n* **1** nonsense **2** somebody or something worthless **3** *US* discarded food waste or unwanted material **4** worthless computer data

garbanzo /gaar bánzō/ (*pl* **-zos**), **garbanzo bean** *n* a chickpea

garble /gaárb'l/ (**-bling**, **-bled**) *vt* **1** confuse a message or information so that it is misleading or unintelligible **2** scramble the transmission of a message or signal —**garbled** *adj*

Garbo /gaárbō/, **Greta** (1905–90) Swedish-born US film actor

García Lorca /gaar seè ə-/ ♦ **Lorca**

García Márquez /gaar seè ɔ maár kez/, **Gabriel** (*b.* 1928) Colombian writer

garçon /gaár son, -soN/ *n* a French waiter

garda /gaárdə/ (*pl* **-daí** /gaar deè/) *n* **1** an Irish police officer **2 Garda** the Irish police force

garden /gaárd'n/ *n* **1** an area of ground where flowers, fruits, or vegetables are grown (*often pl* in street names) **2** a planted area of ground **3** a park with planted areas (*often pl*) **4** a fertile farming region **5** an outdoor eating and drinking establishment o *a beer garden* ■ *adj* **1** of gardens **2** of the common or ordinary kind ■ *vi* look after a garden —**gardener** *n*

ORIGIN **Garden** goes back to the same ancient root as *yard*, but it came to English through the Romance languages rather than by a direct Germanic route.

garden centre *n* an establishment selling plants and gardening equipment

garden city *n* a planned town with parks

garden flat *n* a flat with access to a garden

gardenia /gaar deèni ə/ *n* an evergreen tree with white flowers

ORIGIN The **gardenia** is named after the Scottish-American naturalist Alexander Garden (1730?-91).

garden party *n* a social gathering in a garden or in the grounds of a large house

~~gardian~~ incorrect spelling of **guardian**

gargantuan /gaar gántyoo ən/ *adj* huge

ORIGIN The description **gargantuan** derives from Gargantua, a giant with an enormous appetite in the satire of that name (1534) by François Rabelais.

gargle /gaárg'l/ *v* (**-gling**, **-gled**) **1** *vti* cleanse the mouth and throat by breathing air out through liquid held in the back of the mouth **2** *vi* make a guttural sound like that made when gargling ■ *n* **1** a mouthwash **2** a guttural sound like that made when gargling

ORIGIN **Gargle** belongs to a set of words from an ancient root representing a sound made in the throat. It was adopted in the early 16C from a French verb formed from *gargouille* 'throat'. French *gargouille* is also the source of **gargoyle** 'grotesque drainage spout', so called because the rainwater often ran off through a carved figure's mouth. **Gurgle** came from Latin *gurgulio* 'gullet', and is closely related.

gargoyle /gaár goyl/ *n* a drainage spout in the form of a grotesque figure

Garibaldi /gárri báwldi/, **Giuseppe** (1807–82) French-born Italian patriot

garish /gáirish/ *adj* overly bright or elaborate —**garishly** *adv* —**garishness** *n*

garland /gaárlənd/ *n* **1** a flower wreath **2** a hanging flower or paper decoration ■ *vt* decorate with a garland

Garland /gaárlənd/, **Judy** (1922–69) US film actor and singer

garlic /gaárlik/ *n* **1** a bulb that is divided into cloves and has a pungent odour and flavour. Use: in cooking, medicine. **2** the plant whose bulbs are garlic —**garlicky** *adj*

garment /gaármənt/ *n* a clothing item

garner /gaárnər/ *vt* **1** gather in for storage **2** win or gain by an effort

garnet /gaárnit/ *n* **1** a red semiprecious stone. Use: gems. **2** a dark red colour —**garnet** *adj*

garnish /gaárnish/ *vt* **1** add an accompaniment to food or drink to enhance its flavour or appearance **2** decorate something with an ornament ■ *n* an enhancement for food or drink —**garnishing** *n*

garret /gárrət/ *n* an attic

Garrick /gárrik/, **David** (1717–79) British actor, theatrical manager, and playwright

garrison /gárriss'n/ *n* **1** a body of stationed troops **2** a place for stationing troops ■ *vt* station troops at a place

garrotte /gə rót/, **garrote** *n* **1** a method of execution by strangulation using a metal band **2** a metal band used in executions —**garrotte** *vt*

garrulous /gárrələss, gárryōō-/ *adj* **1** talking too much **2** wordy —**garrulously** *adv* —**garrulousness** *n* ◊ See note at **talkative**

garter /gaártər/ *n* **1** a band for holding up stockings, socks, or a shirt sleeve **2 Garter** the badge of the highest order of British knighthood, the Order of the Garter —**garter** *vt*

garter snake *n* a harmless snake with stripes running the length of its body

Garvey /gaárvi/, **Marcus** (1887–1940) Jamaican-born US civil rights advocate

Gary /gárri/ city in NW Indiana, on Lake Michigan. Pop. 108,469 (1998).

gas *n* **1** a substance such as air that is neither solid nor liquid and can expand indefinitely **2** a combustible gaseous substance such as natural gas or propane, used as fuel **3** a gaseous substance for poisoning or asphyxiating somebody **4** a gaseous substance used as an anaesthetic **5** *US, Can* petrol **6** an explosive mixture of methane and air ■ *v* (**gases** *or* **gasses**, **gassing**, **gassed**) **1** *vt* attack, injure, or kill with gas **2** *vi* release gas **3** *vi* talk idly (*infml*)

ORIGIN **Gas** is based on the Greek form of *chaos*. The first letter in Greek was pronounced like the sound of the letter *g* in the dialect of Flemish chemist J. B. van Helmont (1577–1644), who coined the word for a supposed highly refined form of water. The modern use arose in the early 18C.

gasbag /gáss bag/ *n* a person regarded as an idle talker (*infml*)

gas chamber *n* a room where people are gassed

Gascoyne-Cecil /gáss koyn séss'l/, **Robert Arthur Talbot, 3rd Marquess of Salisbury** (1830–1903) British prime minister (1885–86, 1886–92, 1895–1902)

gaseous /gássi əss, gáyssi-/ *adj* 1 resembling gas 2 containing gas

gash *n* a deep cut —**gash** *vt*

gasholder /gáss hōldər/ *n* a storage tank for gas used as fuel

gasify /gássi fī/ (-**fies**, -**fied**) *vti* make into or become a gas

Gaskell /gáss'l/, **Elizabeth Cleghorn** (1810–65) British novelist

gasket /gáskit/ *n* 1 a rubber seal to make a joint impermeable to gas or liquid 2 a rope for securing a furled sail

gaslight /gáss lít/ *n* 1 illumination from burning gas 2 a lamp fuelled by gas

gasman /gáss man/ (*pl* -**men** /-men/) *n* a gas-meter reader

gas mask *n* a mask protecting the wearer against poisonous gas

gas meter *n* a device for measuring the amount of gas that has been consumed

gasoline /gássəleen/ *n US, Can* petrol

gasometer /ga sómmitər/ *n* 1 a gas-measuring apparatus 2 a gasholder

gasp *n* 1 a sudden audible intake of breath, e.g. in surprise or pain 2 a difficult intake of breath ■ *vi* 1 labour to breathe 2 breathe in sharply

gassy /gássi/ (-**sier**, -**siest**) *adj* 1 full of gas 2 like gas

gastric /gástrik/ *adj* of the stomach

gastric juice *n* an acidic digestive secretion in the stomach

gastritis /ga strítiss/ *n* inflammation of the stomach lining

gastroenteritis /gástrō entə rítiss/ *n* stomach and intestinal inflammation

gastroenterology /gástrō éntə róllэji/ *n* the study of disorders of the stomach and intestines

gastrointestinal /gástrō in téstinəl/ *adj* of the stomach and intestines

gastronomy /ga strónnəmi/ (*pl* -**mies**) *n* 1 gourmet eating 2 a cuisine typical of a particular region —**gastronomic** /gástrə nómmik/ *adj*

gas turbine *n* an internal-combustion engine operated by hot gases

gasworks /gáss wurks/ (*pl same*) *n* a factory where gas for fuel is produced

gate /gayt/ *n* 1 a movable barrier across a gap in a fence or wall 2 an opening in a fence, wall, or defensive structure 3 a point of access 4 an arrival or departure point for passengers at an airport 5 a sliding barrier or valve for regulating the passage of fluid 6 the total number of spectators admitted to a sporting event or an entertainment 7 the total amount of money from ticket sales to a sporting event or an entertainment 8 a path between poles in a slalom race 9 a logic circuit in a computer 10 an electronic switch regulating the flow of current —**gated** *adj* ◊ See note at **gait**

gateau /gáttō/ (*pl* -**teaux** /-tōz/), **gâteau** (*pl* -**teaux**) *n* a rich layered cake

gatecrasher /gáyt krashər/ *n* an uninvited guest, or a spectator without a ticket —**gatecrash** *vti*

gatefold /gáyt fōld/ *n* an oversize page that is folded to the size of other pages

gatehouse /gáyt howss/ (*pl* -**houses** /-howziz/) *n* a building at a gate

gatekeeper /gáyt keepər/ *n* 1 a guard at a gate 2 a controller of access to something or somebody

gateleg table /gáyt leg-/ *n* a folding table with movable legs that swing out to support the leaves

gatepost /gáyt pōst/ *n* a post supporting a gate

Gates /gayts/, **Bill** (*b*. 1955) US entrepreneur and technology executive

Gateshead /gáyts hed/ town in NE England. Pop. 200,968 (1996).

gateway /gáyt way/ *n* 1 an opening with a gate 2 an access point 3 a connection between two computer networks

gather /gáthər/ *v* 1 *vti* form into a group 2 *vt* harvest a crop 3 *vt* collect data from various sources 4 *vt* attract a group of people as a following or audience ○ *gathered quite a crowd* 5 *vti* accumulate 6 *vt* summon up energies or strength from within 7 *vt* surmise that something is so 8 *vt* bring somebody or something close 9 *vt* lift somebody or something up 10 *vt* pull a fabric together in a series of folds held by stitching ■ *n* each of a series of folds in fabric —**gatherer** *n* ◊ See note at **collect**

gathering /gáthəring/ *n* an assembly of people

GATT /gat/, **Gatt** *abbr* General Agreement on Tariffs and Trade

gauche /gōsh/ *adj* socially awkward —**gauchely** *adv* —**gaucheness** *n*

gaucho /gówchō/ (*pl* -**chos**) *n* a South American cowboy

Gaudí /gow deé/, **Antoni** (1852–1926) Spanish architect

gaudy[1] /gáwdi/ (-**ier**, -**iest**) *adj* brightly coloured or elaborately decorated to an unpleasant or vulgar degree —**gaudily** *adv* —**gaudiness** *n*

gaudy[2] /gáwdi/ (*pl* -**ies**) *n* a celebratory dinner at some universities and colleges

gauge /gayj/, **gage** *vt* (**gauging, gauged; gaging, gaged**) 1 calculate the amount or extent of something 2 form a judgment of something uncertain or variable ■ *n* 1 a standard measurement or scale of measurement 2 a device for measuring an amount or quantity or for testing accuracy **3** a criterion **4** the distance between the rails of a railway track or tramway **5** the distance between the wheels on the axle of a vehicle **6** the diameter of wire or a needle **7** the thickness of a thin material **8** a diameter inside a gun barrel

Gauguin /gŏ gaN/, **Paul** (1848–1903) French painter

Gaul /gawl/ *n* ancient region of W Europe that included large portions of modern-day France, Belgium, and neighbouring countries

Gaulle ♦ de Gaulle, Charles

gaunt *adj* **1** thin and bony **2** stark in outline or appearance —**gauntness** *n*

gauntlet¹ /gáwntlət/ *n* a long glove with a cuff that covers part of the forearm ◊ **throw down the gauntlet** issue a challenge

gauntlet² /gáwntlət/ *n* a former military punishment in which two lines of men with weapons beat somebody forced to run between them ◊ **run the gauntlet** endure attack or criticism from all sides

ORIGIN The glove the **gauntlet** has no part in *running the gauntlet*. It comes from a French word meaning 'little glove'. The **gauntlet** that you run was originally a *gantlope*, from Swedish *gantlopp* 'passageway'.

~~gaurd~~ incorrect spelling of **guard**

gauze /gawz/ *n* **1** a finely-woven fabric. Use: curtains, clothes. **2** a surgical dressing consisting of layers of loosely woven material —**gauzy** *adj*

ORIGIN Gauze was probably named after Gaza on the E Mediterranean coast, which was associated with its production in the Middle Ages. The word entered English through French.

gave past tense of **give**

gavel /gáv'l/ *n* an auctioneer's hammer ■ *vti* (**-elling, -elled**) use a gavel to bring an end to something

gavotte /ga vót/ *n* **1** a French country dance like a fast minuet **2** a piece of music for a gavotte

Gawain /gaáwayn/ *n* in Arthurian legend, a knight who was the enemy of Sir Lancelot

gawk, gawp *vi* stare stupidly (*infml*) ◊ See note at **gaze**

gawky /gáwki/ (**-ier, -iest**) *adj* ungainly (*infml*) —**gawkily** *adv* —**gawkiness** *n*

gay *adj* **1** homosexual **2** merry (*dated*) **3** bright in colour (*dated*) ■ *n* a homosexual man or woman —**gayness** *n*

USAGE Gay is preferred over *homosexual*. The adjective **gay** encompasses both men and women, but when there is a need to specify both genders, as in *gay and lesbian alliances*, **gay** means men. Avoid using **gay** as a noun, as in *He's a gay* and *Four gays walked in*, because it can be taken to be offensive. Preferred substitutes are *He is gay* and *Four gay people/men/women walked in*.

Gay, John (1685–1732) English poet and dramatist

Gaza /gaázə/ seaport and principal city of the Gaza Strip, on the Mediterranean. Pop. 353,632 (1997).

Gaza Strip region on the E Mediterranean coast bordering Egypt and Israel, under the control of the Palestinian National Authority. Pop. 1,178,119 (2001).

gaze *vi* (**gazing, gazed**) look fixedly ■ *n* a steady look

SYNONYMS gaze, gape, gawk, gawp, ogle, rubberneck, stare CORE MEANING: look at somebody or something steadily or at length

gazebo /gə zéeb ŏ/ (*pl* **-bos** *or* **-boes**) *n* a small building with a view

gazelle /gə zél/ (*pl* **-zelles** *or* same) *n* a small fast antelope with long ringed horns and black face markings

gazette /gə zét/ *n* a newspaper

gazetteer /gázzə teér/ *n* a geographical reference book

gazpacho /gəss paách-/ *n* a cold soup containing chopped raw tomatoes, cucumber, and other vegetables

gazump /gə zúmp/ *vt* charge more for a house after accepting a lower offer (*infml*) —**gazump** *n*

GB *abbr* Great Britain

GBH *abbr* grievous bodily harm

Gbyte *abbr* gigabyte

GCE *n* a secondary school examination in England and Wales, now only at advanced level. Full form **General Certificate of Education**

GCSE *n* a school examination in England and Wales at around age 16. Full form **General Certificate of Secondary Education**

Gd *symbol* gadolinium

Gdansk /gə dánsk/ city in N Poland, on the **Gulf of Gdansk**, an inlet of the Baltic Sea. Pop. 461,300 (1997). German **Danzig**

g'day /gə dáy/ *interj Aus* hello (*infml*)

Gdns *abbr* Gardens (*in addresses*)

GDP *abbr* gross domestic product

Ge¹ *n* = Gaia

Ge² *symbol* germanium

gear /geer/ *n* **1** a toothed part of a machine that transmits motion by engaging with another toothed part **2** one of the fixed transmission settings in a vehicle **3** the engaged state of a vehicle's gears ○ *Put the car in gear.* **4** equipment needed for a particular activity (*infml*) **5** clothes (*infml*) ■ *vt* **1** put gears in **2** engage the gears of

□ **gear up** *vti* get ready for something

gearbox /geér boks/ *n* **1** a casing round a set of gears **2** a set of gears in a vehicle or engine

gearing /geéring/ *n* **1** a set of mechanical gears, or their power **2** the providing of something with gears **3** the ratio of a company's debt capital to the value of its ordinary shares

gear lever, gear stick *n* a lever for changing gears

gecko /gékō/ (*pl* **-os** *or* **-oes**) *n* a small tropical lizard that can climb smooth vertical surfaces

gee /jee/ *interj US, Can* expresses enthusiasm or surprise ■ *vt* (**geed**) urge an animal to move faster

Gee /jee/, **Maurice Gough** (*b.* 1931) New Zealand novelist

geek /geek/ *n US, Can* somebody regarded as socially awkward (*insult*) —**geeky** *adj*

geese plural of **goose**

Geiger counter /gígər-/ *n* an instrument for detecting radiation

> **ORIGIN** The instrument is named after the German physicist Hans Geiger (1882–1945), who invented it.

geisha /gáyshə/ (*pl same or* **-shas**), **geisha girl** *n* **1** a Japanese woman educated as a hostess for men **2** a Japanese prostitute

gel /jel/ *n* a semisolid substance with the consistency of jelly ■ *vi* (**gelling**, **gelled**) **1** become a gel **2** take on a definite form (*infml*) **3** get on well together (*infml*)

gelatin /jéllətin/, **gelatine** /-teen/ *n* **1** a semisolid protein. Use: foods, medicine, glue, photography. **2** a substance with the consistency of jelly

gelatinous /ji láttinəss/ *adj* **1** semisolid **2** of gelatin

geld /geld/ (**gelded** *or* **gelt** /gelt/) *vt* castrate an animal, especially a horse

gelding /gélding/ *n* a castrated horse

gelignite /jéllig nīt/ *n* a form of dynamite made with gelled nitroglycerine

gem /jem/ *n* **1** a precious stone that has been cut and polished **2** somebody or something excellent (*infml*)

Gemini /jémmi nī/ *n* **1** a zodiacal constellation in the northern hemisphere **2** the 3rd sign of the zodiac —**Gemini** *adj*

gemstone /jém stōn/ *n* a stone used in jewellery

gen /jen/ *n* information (*infml*)

gen. *abbr* general

Gen. *abbr* General

gendarme /zhónd aarm, zha'aNd-/ *n* a French police officer

gender /jéndər/ *n* **1** somebody's sex **2** the categorization of nouns and pronouns in some languages according to the form taken by words that qualify them **3** a particular category of noun or pronoun

gene /jeen/ *n* the basic unit of heredity consisting of a specific sequence of DNA or RNA in a fixed position on a chromosome

genealogy /jeeèni álləji/ (*pl* **-gies**) *n* **1** the study of the history of families **2** a pedigree or line of family descent —**genealogical** /jeeèni ə lójjik'l/ *adj* —**genealogist** *n*

~~geneeology~~ incorrect spelling of **genealogy**

gene pool *n* all the genes of a population or species

genera plural of **genus**

general /jénnərəl/ *adj* **1** of or including nearly all the members of a category **2** usual ○ *as a general rule* **3** widespread ○ *a general sense of urgency* **4** with a varied content ○ *a general store* **5** not specialized in knowledge ○ *for the general reader* **6** not specific ○ *in general terms* ■ *n also* **General** an officer of a rank above lieutenant general ◇ **in general 1** as a whole **2** in most cases

general anaesthetic *n* an anaesthetic producing unconsciousness

general election *n* an election for political representatives for the entire country

General Headquarters *n* full form of **GHQ**

general hospital *n* a nonspecialist hospital

generalissimo /jénnərə líssimō/ (*pl* **-mos**) *n* a top military leader

generalist /jénnərəlist/ *n* a nonspecialist

generality /jénnə rálləti/ (*pl* **-ties**) *n* **1** the state of being general **2** a general statement

generalize /jénnərə līz/ (**-izing**, **-ized**), **generalise** *v* **1** *vti* express something general **2** *vi* make a sweeping statement **3** *vti* give wider use to something **4** *vt* make something generally known **5** *vti* make a general inference —**generalization** /jénnərə lī záysh'n/ *n*

generally /jénnərəli/ *adv* **1** usually **2** as a whole ○ *not meant for the public generally* **3** in general terms ○ *spoke generally*

general meeting *n* a meeting for all members of a group or organization

general practice *n* the work of a doctor who is not a specialist

general practitioner *n* full form of **GP**

general purpose *adj* all-purpose

generalship /jénnərəl ship/ *n* **1** the exercising of military command **2** a general's rank or period of service

general staff *n* the group of officers helping military commanders

generate /jénnə rayt/ (**-ating**, **-ated**) *vt* create or produce ○ *generate income* ○ *generate electricity*

generation /jénnə ráysh'n/ *n* **1** a group of contemporaries **2** a single stage in the descent from a common ancestor **3** a period of time taken to produce a new generation **4** a particular generation (*usually in combination*) ○ *first-generation immigrants* **5** a new type of product or technology, or a new stage in the development of a product or technology **6** the production of power or energy —**generational** *adj*

generation gap *n* a difference between generations in their attitudes and interests that inhibits understanding

generation X, Generation X *n* the generation of young adults who were born between about 1965 and 1980, especially in the United States and Canada —**generation Xer** *n*

> **ORIGIN** The term comes from the title of a novel by Douglas Coupland (*b.* 1961), *Generation X: Tales for an Accelerated Culture*.

generative /jénnərətiv/ *adj* **1** of reproduction **2** with a productive capability

generator /jénnə raytər/ *n* **1** a device for producing electricity or gas **2** an originator, e.g. of an idea or plan

generic /jə nérrik/ *adj* **1** applying generally **2** suitable in a variety of contexts **3** of a genus **4** describes pharmaceutical products without a brand name —**generically** *adv*

generous /jénnərəss/ *adj* **1** kind in giving or sharing **2** noble **3** substantial in size or quantity ○ *a generous portion* —**generosity** /jénnə róssəti/ *n* —**generously** *adv* —**generousness** *n*

SYNONYMS **generous, liberal, magnanimous, munificent, bountiful** CORE MEANING: giving readily to others

genesis /jénnəssiss/ (*pl* **-ses** /-seez/) *n* the time or circumstances of something's coming into being

Genet /zhə náy/, **Jean** (1910–86) French writer

gene therapy *n* the treatment of disease by replacing genes

genetic /jə néttik/ *adj* of genes or genetics —**genetically** *adv*

genetically modified *adj* with an altered genetic makeup

genetic code *n* an order of DNA or RNA sequences that is the basis of heredity

genetic fingerprinting *n* = **DNA fingerprinting**

genetic modification, genetic engineering *n* the alteration and recombination of genetic material by technological means, resulting in transgenic organisms —**genetic engineer** *n*

genetics /jə néttiks/ *n* **1** the study of heredity and genetic variation (*+ sing verb*) **2** the genetic makeup of an organism (*+ sing or pl verb*) —**geneticist** /jə néttissist/ *n*

Geneva /jə neévə/ city in W Switzerland. Pop. 172,809 (1998). French **Genève** —**Genevan** *adj, n* —**Genevese** /jénnə veéz/ *adj, n*

Geneva, Lake largest lake in central Europe, between Switzerland and SE France

Genghis Khan /géng giss kaàn, jéng-/ (1167?–1227) Mongol conqueror

genial /jeéni əl/ *adj* **1** kind and good-natured **2** mild and warm ○ *a genial climate* —**geniality** /jeéni álləti/ *n* —**genially** *adv*

genie /jeéni/ (*pl* **-nies** *or* **-nii** /-ni ī/) *n* a magical spirit in Arabian stories that will obey the person who summons it

genital /jénnit'l/ *adj* of the sex organs —**genitally** *adv*

genitals /jénnit'lz/, **genitalia** /-táyli ə/ *npl* the sex organs

genitive /jénnətiv/ *n* **1** a grammatical case in some languages that usually indicates possession **2** a word or form in the genitive —**genitive** *adj*

genius /jeéni əss/ *n* **1** somebody with outstanding talent **2** outstanding talent **3** somebody with a particular skill ○ *a genius with computers* **4** (*pl* **genii** /jeéni ī/) a special

quality of a place, period, or people ◊ See note at **talent**

Genoa /jénnō ə/ city in NW Italy, on the **Gulf of Genoa**, an inlet of the Ligurian Sea. Pop. 641,437 (1999). —**Genoese** /jénnō eéz/ *n, adj*

genocide /jénnə sīd/ *n* the murder or attempted murder of an entire ethnic group —**genocidal** /jénnə sīd'l/ *adj*

genome /jeé nōm/ *n* the full set of chromosomes and genes that an individual organism inherits —**genomic** /ji nómik/ *adj*

genomics /ji nómiks/ *n* the study and identification of gene sequences (*+ sing verb*)

genotype /jénnə tīp/ *n* **1** the genetic makeup of an organism **2** a group of organisms with similar genetic makeup —**genotypic** /jénnə típpik/ *adj*

~~genrally~~ incorrect spelling of **generally**

~~genration~~ incorrect spelling of **generation**

genre /zhónrə, zhóNrə/ *n* **1** a category of artistic works **2** a type of painting depicting household scenes ◊ See note at **type**

gent /jent/ *n* a gentleman (*infml dated*)

genteel /jen teél/ *adj* **1** well-mannered and well-bred **2** pretentiously well-mannered and respectable —**genteelly** *adv* —**genteelness** *n*

ORIGIN **Genteel** is a late 16C readoption of the French word that had earlier become *gentle*. It goes back to a Latin word meaning 'of the same family', then later 'of good family', which has also come into English as *gentile*, through a use of it in the 4C Latin version of the Bible, the Vulgate.

gentian /jénsh'n/ *n* **1** the dried root of a flowering plant. Use: digestive stimulant in herbal medicine. **2** a showy flowering plant whose roots are dried as gentian

gentile /jént īl/ *n* **1** a non-Jewish person **2** somebody Christian as opposed to Jewish —**gentile** *adj*

Gentileschi /jéntə léski/, **Artemisia** (1593?–1651) Italian painter

gentility /jen tílləti/ *n* **1** refinement and good manners **2** upper-class status **3** pretentiously refined manners and behaviour

gentle /jént'l/ (**-tler, -tlest**) *adj* **1** mild and kind **2** moderate and not severe ○ *a gentle reprimand* **3** using little force ○ *a gentle tap on the shoulder* **4** not steep ○ *a gentle slope* —**gentleness** *n* —**gently** *adv*

gentlefolk /jént'l fōk/, **gentlefolks** /-fōks/ *npl* upper-class people (*archaic*)

gentleman /jént'lmən/ (*pl* **-men** /-mən/) *n* **1** a polite and cultured man **2** any man ○ *ladies and gentlemen* **3** an upper-class man —**gentlemanly** *adj*

gentleman-farmer *n* **1** a farmer with independent means, who farms for pleasure **2** a farm owner who employs others to manage it

gentleman's agreement, gentlemen's agreement *n* an agreement based on trust

gentlewoman /jént'l wŏŏmən/ (*pl* **-women** /-wimin/) *n* **1** a polite and cultured woman **2** an upper-class woman

gentrify /jéntri fī/ (**-fies**, **-fied**) *vt* make a working-class area middle-class —**gentrification** /jéntrifi káysh'n/ *n*

gentry /jéntri/ *n* (+ *sing or pl verb*) **1** the upper classes **2** the English social class of people who do not belong to the nobility but who are entitled to a coat of arms

genuflect /jénnyŏŏ flekt/ *vi* **1** kneel as a gesture of respect **2** show excessive respect —**genuflection** /jénnyŏŏ fléksh'n/ *n*

genuine /jénnyoo in/ *adj* **1** having the qualities or value claimed **2** sincerely felt or expressed —**genuinely** *adv* —**genuineness** *n*

genus /jéènəss, jénn-/ (*pl* **genera** /jénnərə/) *n* **1** a set of closely related species **2** a group with common characteristics

geo- *prefix* **1** earth, soil ○ *geology* **2** geography, global ○ *geopolitics*

geocentric /jeè ō séntrik/ *adj* **1** describes the solar system regarded as having Earth at its centre **2** measured or considered from Earth's centre

geochemistry /jeè ō kémmistri/ *n* the chemistry of the Earth and other astronomical bodies —**geochemical** *adj* —**geochemist** *n*

geochronology /jeè ō krə nólləji/ *n* the study of the ages of geological events and rock formations —**geochronological** /jeè ō krónnə lójjik'l/ *adj* —**geochronologist** *n*

geode /jeè ōd/ *n* **1** a rock with a cavity lined or filled with crystals **2** a crystal-lined cavity within a geode

geodesic dome /jeè ō deèssik-/ *n* a dome made of flat sections

geodesy /jee óddəssi/ *n* the scientific measurement of the size and shape of the Earth's surface —**geodesist** *n*

Geoffrey of Monmouth /jéffri əv mónməth/ (1100?–54) English historian and cleric

geography /ji óggrəfi/ (*pl* **-phies**) *n* **1** the study of Earth's physical features **2** the physical features of a place or region —**geographer** *n* —**geographic** /jeè ə gráffik/ *adj* —**geographical** *adj* —**geographically** *adv*

geology /ji ólləji/ *n* the study of rocks and minerals —**geological** *adj* —**geologist** *n*

geometric /jeè ə méttrik/, **geometrical** /-ik'l/ *adj* **1** of geometry **2** using simple lines —**geometrically** *adv*

geometric progression *n* a series of numbers in which each number is separated by the same numerical step

geometry /ji ómmətri/ *n* the mathematics of shapes —**geometric** *adj* —**geometrically** *adv* —**geometrician** /jeè ə me trísh'n, jee ómmə-/ *n*

geophysics /jeè ō fízziks/ *n* the science of Earth's physical processes (+ *sing verb*) —**geophysical** *adj* —**geophysicist** *n*

geopolitics /jeè ō póllatiks/ *n* the study of the relationship between a country's geography and politics (+ *sing verb*) ■ *npl* the influences of geography on politics (+ *pl verb*) —**geopolitical** /jeè ō pə líttik'l/ *adj* —**geopolitician** /jeè ō póllə tísh'n/ *n*

Geordie /jáwrdi/ *n* **1** somebody from the area along the lower Tyne **2** the dialect spoken by Geordies —**Geordie** *adj*

George /jawrj/, **St** (*d.* 303?) patron saint of England

George I (1660–1727) king of Great Britain and Ireland (1714–27)

George II (1683–1760) king of Great Britain and Ireland (1727–60)

George III (1738–1820) king of Great Britain and Ireland (1760–1820)

George IV (1762–1830) king of Great Britain and Ireland (1820–30)

George V (1865–1936) king of Great Britain and Ireland (1910–22), then of Great Britain and Northern Ireland (1922–36)

George VI (1895–1952) king of Great Britain and Northern Ireland (1936–52)

Georgetown /jáwrj town/ **1** capital of Guyana. Pop. 254,000 (1995). **2** district of NW Washington, D.C.

George Town 1 capital of the Cayman Islands. Pop. 19,000 (1996). **2** town in N Tasmania, Australia. Pop. 5,045 (1991). **3** city of W Malaysia, on Penang Island. Pop. 219,380 (1991).

Georgia /jáwrjə/ **1** state in the SE United States. Cap. Atlanta. Pop. 8,186,453 (2000). **2** country in S Caucasia, on the coast of the E Black Sea. Cap. Tbilisi. Pop. 4,989,285 (2001).

Georgian[1] /jáwrjən/ *adj* of the period 1714 to 1830 in Britain, when George I, II, III, and IV reigned in succession

Georgian[2] /jáwrjən/ *n* **1** the language of the Republic of Georgia **2** somebody from the Republic of Georgia **3** somebody from the US state of Georgia —**Georgian** *adj*

Georgievski /jáwrji évski/, **Ljubco** (*b.* 1966) prime minister of the Former Yugoslav Republic of Macedonia (1998–)

geostationary /jeè ō stáysh'nəri/ *adj* appearing to remain stationary over a point on Earth

geothermal /jeè ō thúrm'l/ *adj* of Earth's internal heat —**geothermally** *adv*

geranium /jə ráyni əm/ *n* **1** a popular garden plant with brightly coloured flowers **2** a plant with saucer-shaped flowers

gerbil /júrb'l/ *n* a small rodent resembling a mouse with long back legs

geriatric /jérri áttrik/ *adj* of elderly people ■ *n* an elderly person (*technical*)

geriatrics /jérri áttriks/ *n* the medical treatment of the elderly (+ *sing verb*) —**geriatrician** /jérri ə trísh'n/ *n*

Géricault /zháyri kṓ/, **Théodore** (1791–1824) French painter

germ /jurm/ *n* **1** a microorganism, especially one causing disease **2** the smallest element in an organism that is capable of complete development **3** the beginning of something that will develop

ORIGIN Germ goes back to a Latin word meaning

'sprout, seed', which was the original sense of the word in English. It survives metaphorically in the sense 'beginning', and in some fixed contexts such as *wheat germ*. The modern use 'microorganism' dates from the late 19C, and springs from the idea of a **germ** as the source from which disease develops.

German /júrmən/ *n* **1** somebody from Germany **2** the language of Germany, Austria, and parts of Switzerland —**German** *n, adj*

germane /jur máyn/ *adj* relevant —**germanely** *adv* —**germaneness** *n*

Germanic /jur mánnik/ *n* **1** a NW European language group, including English, German, and the Scandinavian languages **2** the ancestor of modern Germanic languages ■ *adj* **1** of Germanic **2** of Germany

germanium /jur máyni əm/ *n* (*symbol* **Ge**) a brittle grey chemical element. Use: semiconductors, alloys.

German measles *n* a contagious childhood viral disease causing a reddish-pink rash

German shepherd *n* an Alsatian dog

Germany /júrməni/ country in central Europe. Cap. Berlin. Pop. 83,029,536 (2001).

germicide /júrmi síd/ *n* a substance that kills germs —**germicidal** /júrmi síd'l/ *adj*

germinate /júrmi nayt/ (**-nating, -nated**) *v* **1** *vti* start growing from seed **2** *vi* be created and start to develop —**germination** /júrmi náysh'n/ *n*

germ warfare *n* biological warfare

gerontocracy /jérron tókrəssi/ (*pl* **-cies**) *n* **1** government by elders **2** the elders forming a government (+ *sing or pl verb*) —**gerontocratic** /jə róntə kráttik/ *adj*

gerontology /jérron tólləji/ *n* the scientific study of ageing —**gerontological** /jə róntə lójjik'l/ *adj* —**gerontologist** *n*

gerrymander /jérri mandər/ *vti* try to get extra votes unfairly, especially by changing boundaries —**gerrymander** *n*

ORIGIN The name of Massachusetts governor Eldridge Gerry and *salamander* combined to create this word. In 1812 he changed the boundaries of electoral districts to favour his own Democratic Party. The outline of these on a map was thought to resemble a salamander.

Gershwin /gúrshwin/, **George** (1898–1937) US composer

gerund /jérrənd/ *n* a noun derived from a verb, e.g. in English by adding -ing —**gerundial** /jə rúndi əl/ *adj*

Gestalt /gə shtált/ (*pl* **-stalts** *or* **-stalten** /-shtáltən/), **gestalt** *n* a set of things regarded as more than the sum of its parts —**gestaltist** *n*

Gestalt psychology *n* a branch of psychology that treats behaviour and perception as an integrated whole

Gestapo /ge stáapō/ *n* the Nazi secret police

ORIGIN Gestapo is a German acronym formed

from *Geheime Staatspolizei* 'Secret State Police'.

gestation /je stáysh'n/ *n* **1** the carrying of offspring in the womb **2** the period of development of a foetus **3** the development of an idea or plan in the mind —**gestational** *adj* —**gestatory** *adj*

gesticulate /je stíkyoo layt/ (**-lating, -lated**) *vti* make or express by gestures —**gesticulation** /je stíkyoo láysh'n/ *n*

gesture /jéschər/ *n* **1** a body movement or an action that communicates something **2** the use of gestures ■ *vti* (**-turing, -tured**) communicate by a body movement —**gestural** *adj*

gesundheit /gə zoont hít/ *interj* expresses a wish for good health to somebody who has just sneezed (*humorous*)

get /get/ (**getting, got**) *v* **1** *vi* become or begin to have a particular quality o *getting hungry* **2** *vt* cause to be done o *got it cleaned* **3** *vt* fetch or bring o *went to get the coats* **4** *vt* become infected by or develop o *got chicken pox* **5** *vi* enter or leave a particular state o *get ready* **6** *vi* move or arrive somewhere o *got home late* **7** *vt* begin (*infml*) o *Let's get going.* **8** forms passives o *got burnt* **9** *vt* manage or contrive (*infml*) o *How did she get to be so famous?* **10** *vt* persuade o *tried to get her to go* **11** *vt* hear or understand (*infml*) **12** *vt* use as a form of transport o *get a plane* **13** *vt* receive as a signal o *gets six channels* **14** *vt* annoy or irritate (*infml*) **15** *vt* begin to have o *when I get the time* o *got the wrong idea* **16** *vt* manage to see **17** *vt* hit (*infml*) **18** *vt* have revenge on (*infml*) o *will get them in the end* —**getable** *adj* ◊ **get with it** become responsive to new styles and ideas (*infml*)

SYNONYMS get, acquire, obtain, gain, procure, secure CORE MEANING: come into possession of something

□ **get about** *vi* **1** move about in spite of a medical condition **2** become known **3** travel, especially against expectations **4** have a social life

□ **get across** *vti* make something understood

□ **get ahead** *vi* be successful

□ **get along** *vi* **1** be friendly **2** manage to make progress

□ **get around** *v* **1** *vi* have a social life **2** = **get round**

□ **get at** *vt* **1** reach **2** try to say **3** criticize repeatedly **4** find something out

□ **get away** *vi* **1** escape **2** leave a place ■ *interj* expresses disbelief

□ **get away with** *vt* experience no bad results from something that might have been expected to produce them

□ **get back** *vt* take revenge on

□ **get by** *vi* just manage to keep going

□ **get down to** *vt* start doing

□ **get into** *vt* get involved or interested in something

□ **get off** *v* **1** *vi* leave **2** *vt* send a communication or parcel **3** *vi* have a lucky escape o *got off* *lightly* **4** *vti* gain an acquittal in a court of law, or obtain an acquittal for somebody *(infml)*

□ **get on** *vi* **1** deal with and make progress in a situation **2** be friendly **3** become older

□ **get out** *v* **1** *vti* leave, or enable somebody to leave **2** *vi* become known

□ **get out of** *vt* avoid or enable somebody to avoid doing

□ **get over** *vt* recover from an illness or bad experience

□ **get round** *v* **1** *vt* deal successfully with an obstruction **2** *vt* persuade somebody reluctant **3** *vi* say or do something at last ◇ *finally got round to admitting it*

□ **get through** *v* **1** *vt* use or spend **2** *vti* make somebody understand

□ **get to** *vt* annoy

□ **get together** *vi* meet for social or business purposes ◇ **get it together** become organized so as to perform efficiently *(slang)*

□ **get up** *v* **1** *vti* get out of bed **2** *vt* rouse energy, strength, or similar qualities

getaway /géttə way/ *n* a quick departure, especially after committing a crime

Gethsemane, Garden of /geth sémmani/ *n* in the Bible, the olive grove just outside Jerusalem where Jesus Christ was betrayed after the Last Supper (Matthew 26:36)

get-out *n* a means of avoidance

get-together *n* a social gathering *(infml)*

Getty /gétti/, **J. Paul** (1892–1976) US oil executive

Gettysburg /géttiz burg/ borough in S Pennsylvania, site of a decisive Northern victory in 1863 during the American Civil War. Pop. 7,376 (1998).

getup /gét up/ *n* a costume or outfit *(infml)*

gewgaw /gyoò gaw/ *n* a trinket

geyser /geèzə, gízə/ *n* **1** a spring gushing hot water and steam **2** a water heater

GG *abbr* Girl Guides

Ghana /gaánə/ country in West Africa, on the northern coast of the Gulf of Guinea. Cap. Accra. Pop. 19,894,014 (2001). —**Ghanaian** /gaa náy ən/ *n, adj*

~~Ghandi~~ incorrect spelling of **Gandhi**

gharry /gárri/ *(pl* -ries*) n* S Asia a horse-drawn carriage

ghastly /gaàstli/ *(-lier, -liest) adj* **1** horrifying or very upsetting **2** very unpleasant ◇ *a ghastly smell* —**ghastliness** *n*

ORIGIN Ghastly comes from an obsolete verb *gast* that meant 'terrify'. The same element is seen in *aghast*. The *gh* spelling is modelled on *ghost*. It was used by the poet Edmund Spenser in the late 16C, and has since become established.

ghat /gaat/ *n* in South Asia, a place with steps down a river bank

ghee /gee/, **ghi** *n* clarified butter, especially as used in South Asian cookery

Ghent /gent/ city in W Belgium. Pop. 224,074 (1999).

gherao /gə rów/ *n* S Asia preventing somebody from leaving, e.g. a workplace, as a protest

gherkin /gúrkin/ *n* **1** a small cucumber. Use: pickling. **2** a prickly Caribbean fruit. Use: pickling.

ghetto /géttō/ *(pl* -tos *or* -toes*) n* **1** an area of a city lived in by a minority group **2** a Jewish quarter in a city

ORIGIN The first **ghettos** were in Italy. The origin of the word is not clear, however. It may be an alteration of Italian *getto* 'foundry', since the first ghetto established in Venice, in 1516, was on the site of a foundry; or it could be a shortening of Italian *borghetto*, literally 'small borough'.

ghetto blaster *n* a portable stereo system *(infml; often offensive)*

ghettoize /géttō īz/ *(-izing, -ized)*, **ghettoise** *vt* **1** segregate a minority group **2** limit the opportunities of a group of people *(sometimes offensive)* —**ghettoization** /géttō ī záysh'n/ *n*

ghost /gōst/ *n* **1** a supposed spirit of somebody who has died, remaining after death **2** a faint trace ◇ *the ghost of a smile* **3** a secondary image seen on a screen or through a telescope **4** a ghostwriter ■ *vt* be the ghostwriter of —**ghost-like** *adj* ◇ **give up the ghost** stop working or functioning for good *(infml)*

ghostly /gōstli/ *(-lier, -liest) adj* **1** pale or insubstantial like a ghost **2** reminiscent of ghosts —**ghostliness** *n*

ghost site *n* a viewable but obsolete website

ghost story *n* a story about ghosts

ghost town *n* **1** an abandoned town **2** a deserted place *(infml)*

ghost train *n* a fairground ride that takes passengers through a dark place with amusingly frightening sights and sounds

ghostwriter /gōst rītər/ *n* an author who writes a book to be published as the work of somebody else —**ghostwrite** *vti*

ghoul /gool/ *n* **1** somebody morbidly interested in repulsive things **2** in Islamic folklore, a body-snatching demon —**ghoulish** *adj*

GHQ *n* the headquarters of an organization, especially a military headquarters. Full form **General Headquarters**

GHz *abbr* gigahertz

gi /gee/, **gie** *n* a karate or judo outfit

GI *n* an enlisted US soldier or veteran

ORIGIN In the 1930s and 1940s, **GI** designated items of US army equipment, indicating 'government (or general) issue'. This was soon extended to the soldiers themselves.

-gi *suffix* S Asia a respectful form of address added to a name or title ◇ *doctorgi*

Giacometti /jákə métti/, **Alberto** (1901–66) Swiss sculptor and painter

giant /jī ənt/ *n* **1** an imaginary being who resembles a human but is much taller, larger, and stronger **2** somebody outstanding in a particular field of activity ■ *adj* very big

giantess /jí ən tess/ n in fairy tales, myths, and legends, a very large being similar to a woman

giant-killer n somebody who defeats a much stronger opponent

giant panda n a Chinese black-and-white panda

gibber /jíbbər/ vi be incoherent —**gibber** n

gibberish /jíbbərish/ n nonsensical or incoherent talk

gibbet /jíbbit/ n 1 a post for exhibiting the bodies of people who have been hanged 2 a gallows

gibbon /gíbbən/ n a small slender long-armed ape

gibe /jīb/, **jibe** n a mocking remark ■ vti (**gibing, gibed; jibing, jibed**) make mocking remarks about somebody —**gibingly** adv

giblets /jíbbləts/ n the liver, heart, gizzard, and neck of an edible fowl

Gibraltar /ji bráwltər, -brólt-/ British dependency at the western entrance to the Mediterranean Sea. Pop. 27,170 (1995). —**Gibraltarian** /jí brawl táiri ən, -brol-/ n, adj

Gibraltar, Rock of limestone and shale ridge near the tip of the S Iberian Peninsula. Height 426 m/1,398 ft.

Gibraltar, Strait of channel connecting the Mediterranean Sea to the Atlantic Ocean and separating North Africa from the Rock of Gibraltar. Length 60 km/40 mi.

Gibran /ji braán/, **Kahlil** (1883–1931) Lebanese-born US mystic, painter, and poet

giddy /gíddi/ (**-dier, -diest**) adj 1 dizzy 2 causing dizziness —**giddily** adv —**giddiness** n

Gide /zheed/, **André** (1869–1951) French writer

Gielgud /geel good/, **Sir John** (1904–2000) British actor

GIF /gif/ n a format for a graphics file widely used on the World Wide Web. Full form **graphic interchange format** ■ abbr a file extension for a graphic interchange format file

gift /gift/ n 1 something given to please the recipient or to show gratitude 2 a special talent 3 an act of giving ■ vt bestow as a gift ◊ See note at **talent**

GIFT n a method of aiding conception in which eggs and sperm are placed in a woman's fallopian tubes. Full form **gamete intrafallopian transfer**

gifted /gíftid/ adj having or showing exceptional talent or intelligence —**giftedness** n ◊ See note at **intelligent**

gift shop n a shop selling gifts

gift token, gift voucher n a slip of paper that can be bought to exchange for goods

giftwrap /gíft rap/, **giftwrapping** /-raping/ n decorated wrapping paper —**giftwrap** vt

gig[1] /gig/ n a two-wheeled one-horse carriage

gig[2] /gig/ n a booking or performance by a musician or group at a venue where they do not play regularly (infml)

giga- prefix a thousand million ◊ gigaton

ORIGIN Giga- is from the Greek word that is the source of **giant**.

gigabit /gíggəbit/ n a unit of computer network capacity equal to one megabyte of information

gigabyte /gíggə bīt/ n a unit of computer data or storage space equal to 1,024 megabytes

gigaflop /gíggə flop/ n a unit of computing speed equal to 1,000 million floating-point operations per second

gigahertz /gíggə hurts/ (pl same) n (symbol **GHz**) a unit of frequency equal to 1,000 million hertz, or cycles, per second

gigantic /jī gántik/ adj 1 very large, tall, or bulky 2 very great ◊ a gigantic task —**gigantically** adv

giggle /gígg'l/ vti (**-gling, -gled**) laugh lightly or nervously ■ n a light or nervous laugh ■ **giggles** npl a fit of light or nervous laughter (infml) —**giggling** adj —**giggly** adj

GIGO /gígō/ n the principle that a computer program or process is only as good as the ideas or data put into it. Full form **garbage in, garbage out**

gigolo /jíggəlō/ (pl -los) n 1 a man who receives payment for being a woman's sexual or social partner 2 a man who is a professional dancing partner or escort for women

Gila monster /heélə-, geélə-/ n a large brightly coloured venomous lizard of US and Mexican deserts

Gilbert /gílbərt/, **Sir W. S.** (1836–1911) British librettist and dramatist

gild /gild/ vt 1 cover with a thin layer of gold 2 colour gold (literary) ◊ See note at **guild**

gilded /gíldid/ adj 1 covered with a thin layer of gold 2 wealthy and privileged ◊ gilded youth

Giles /jīlz/, **Ernest** (1835–97) British-born Australian explorer

gill[1] /gil/ n 1 the breathing organ of fish 2 the spore-producing organ of mushrooms ◊ **green around the gills** looking on the point of being sick (infml)

gill[2] /jil/ n a liquid measure equal to a quarter of a pint

Gillespie /gi léspi/, **Dizzy** (1917–93) US jazz trumpeter

gillie /gílli/, **ghillie** n a hunter's attendant or guide in Scotland

Gillies /gílliss/, **Sir Harold** (1882–1960) New Zealand surgeon

gillyflower /jílli flow ər/ n 1 a clove-scented pink 2 a sweet-scented flower (archaic)

Gilmore /gíl mawr/, **Dame Mary Jean** (1865–1962) Australian poet and journalist

gilt[1] /gilt/ n 1 a thin layer of gold 2 a government bond with a guaranteed payment (often pl) —**gilt** adj ◊ See note at **guilt**

gilt[2] /gilt/ n a young female pig

gilt-edged adj 1 very safe, especially as an investment 2 with a gold edge

gimbal /jímb'l, gí-/ n a set of pivoted rings for holding an object such as a ship's compass horizontal ■ vt (-balling, -balled) support on gimbals

gimcrack /jím krak/ adj showy but shoddily made —**gimcrack** n

gimlet /gímmlət/ n 1 a tool for boring holes in wood 2 a cocktail made of vodka or gin with lime juice ■ adj piercing or penetrating o a gimlet eye

gimmick /gímmik/ n 1 something attention-grabbing 2 a dishonest trick 3 a gadget 4 US a hidden disadvantage to an offer or opportunity —**gimmickry** n —**gimmicky** adj

gin¹ /jin/ n 1 a colourless alcoholic spirit distilled from grain and flavoured with juniper berries 2 the card game gin rummy (infml)

ORIGIN Gin derives its name from its chief flavouring agent, juniper. It is an abbreviation of genever, the Dutch name for the drink, which in English was often written geneva, by association with the Swiss town Geneva. Both the abbreviated and the longer form are recorded from the early 18C. Gin 'hoist, trap' is much older, and is a shortening of the French word that gave us engine.

gin² /jin/ n 1 a hoist operated by hand 2 a trap or snare ■ vt (ginning, ginned) separate cotton from its seeds

ginger /jínjər/ n 1 a hot-tasting rhizome used as a spice 2 a plant whose rhizomes are ginger 3 a brownish-yellow colour —**ginger** adj —**gingery** adj

ORIGIN Ginger has a long and complex history. It ultimately derives from an ancient language of S India and N Sri Lanka. This word passed through Sanskrit and other South Asian languages into Greek and Latin, where its initial consonant was z. This became g in the medieval period. From medieval Latin the word passed into English, and also, in a slightly different form, into French. After the Norman Conquest the French word was adopted into English, and this combined with the earlier English form to produce modern ginger.

☐ **ginger up** vt make more lively

ginger ale n a ginger-flavoured soft drink

ginger beer n a mildly alcoholic ginger-flavoured drink

gingerbread /jínjər bred/ n 1 a ginger-flavoured cake or biscuit 2 elaborate decoration

ORIGIN Gingerbread was adopted from French gingembras 'preserved ginger' (the original sense in English), but was quickly assimilated to the more familiar ginger and bread. The form then influenced the application of the word, and from the 15C it was used to refer to a kind of cake.

gingerbread man n a gingerbread biscuit in the stylized shape of a person

gingerly /jínjərli/ adv very cautiously or tentatively —**gingerly** adj

ginger nut, ginger snap n a crisp ginger biscuit

gingham /gíngəm/ n a checked cotton fabric

gingivitis /jínji vítiss/ n gum inflammation

ginkgo /gíngkō/ (pl -goes), **gingko** (pl -koes) n a Chinese tree with fan-shaped leaves

ginkgo biloba /-bi lóbə/ n a herbal preparation made from the pulverized leaves of the ginkgo tree

ginormous /jī náwrməss/ adj huge (infml)

gin rummy n a form of the card game rummy for two players

Ginsberg /gínzbərg/, **Allen** (1926–97) US poet

ginseng /jín seng/ (pl -sengs or same) n 1 a tonic medicine prepared from an aromatic root 2 a plant whose roots are prepared as ginseng

gin sling n a cocktail of iced gin with water and lemon

Giotto /jóttō/ (1267?–1337) Italian painter

gipsy n, adj = gypsy

giraffe /jə raáf/ (pl -raffes or same) n a tall African mammal with a very long neck

gird /gurd/ (**girded** or **girt** /gurt/) v 1 vr get ready for conflict or vigorous activity 2 vt put a belt around, or fasten on with a belt (literary)

girder /gúrdər/ n a large supporting beam

girdle /gúrd'l/ n 1 a woman's elasticated foundation garment extending from the waist to the thigh 2 a narrow belt worn around the waist ■ vt (-dling, -dled) surround (literary)

girl /gurl/ n 1 a female child 2 a woman (often offensive) 3 a daughter (infml) 4 a girlfriend —**girlhood** n

ORIGIN The origin of girl is not really known. It appeared in the 13C, referring to a child of either sex. There are no clear examples of the modern use until the mid-16C.

girl Friday n a young woman acting as somebody's personal assistant (sometimes offensive)

ORIGIN Girl Friday is modelled on Man Friday, the castaway hero's all-round helper in Robinson Crusoe (1719) by Daniel Defoe.

girlfriend /gúrl frend/ n 1 a woman or girl sweetheart or lover 2 a woman friend

Girl Guide n a member of the Guides Association

girlie /gúrli/ adj 1 showing nude women (often offensive) 2 noticeably or deliberately feminine (often disapproving) ■ n a little girl (infml dated)

girlish /gúrlish/ adj 1 of girls 2 more appropriate for a girl than a woman —**girlishly** adv —**girlishness** n

giro /jírō/ n (pl -ros) 1 a bank system for transferring money 2 a state benefit cheque (infml) ■ vt (-ros, -roing, -roed) pay money by giro

girth /gurth/ n 1 the distance round something thick and cylindrical 2 a band fastened round a horse's belly to keep a saddle in place ■ vt fasten a girth on a horse

gismo *n* = gizmo

gist /jist/ *n* the main point or meaning of something

git /git/ *n* an offensive term for somebody regarded as contemptible *(infml insult)*

~~giutar~~ incorrect spelling of **guitar**

give /giv/ *v* (**giving, gave** /gayv/, **given** /gívv'n/) **1** *vt* pass something into the possession of somebody ○ *gave him a present* **2** *vt* deliver something to somebody in payment or exchange for something ○ *gave me £10 for it* **3** *vt* administer something to somebody ○ *gave her the medicine twice a day* **4** *vt* grant something such as power, a right, or time to somebody ○ *Give me half an hour and I'll be there.* **5** *vt* communicate information or an opinion to somebody ○ *Give them my love.* **6** *vt* convey an idea or impression to somebody **7** *vt* impart a particular feeling to somebody ○ *gives us a sense of security* **8** *vt* perform an action directed at somebody ○ *gave him a quick glance* **9** *vt* provide a service for somebody ○ *gave her a massage* **10** *vt* devote something such as time or effort to something or somebody ○ *gave their lives to helping others* **11** *vt* organize or do something as an entertainment ○ *gave a party* **12** *vt* emit or utter a sound ○ *gave a sigh* **13** *vt* cause somebody to believe something ○ *was given to understand that they had left* **14** *vi* yield or collapse under pressure ○ *The floor gave.* **15** *vt* concede that somebody has an advantage or a particular quality ■ *n* the ability or tendency to yield under pressure —**giver** *n*

SYNONYMS **give, present, confer, bestow, donate, grant** CORE MEANING: hand over something to somebody

---

□ **give away** *vt* **1** give something as a present **2** disclose information or a secret by mistake **3** betray somebody by providing information **4** present a bride to her husband at a wedding **5** let an opponent score a point through carelessness or illegal play

□ **give back** *vt* return something

□ **give in** *v* **1** *vi* admit defeat **2** *vi* accept conditions **3** *vt* hand over something such as schoolwork

□ **give of** *vt* contribute your time or energy

□ **give off** *vt* emit

□ **give on to** *vt* overlook or lead to

□ **give out** *v* **1** *vt* hand over or distribute **2** *vt* emit **3** *vi* be used up **4** *vi* stop working

□ **give up** *v* **1** *vi* surrender **2** *vt* hand something over **3** *vt* stop using or doing something **4** *vt* lose hope for a good outcome with regard to somebody or something ○ *given them up for lost*

□ **give up on** *vt* **1** abandon a plan **2** despair of somebody or something

give-and-take *n* cooperation and compromise *(infml)*

giveaway /gív ə way/ *n* **1** something that reveals or betrays something ○ *Her accent's a dead giveaway.* **2** a gift, especially something given away as a publicity gimmick or an incentive to buy something *(infml)*

given /gívv'n/ past participle of **give** ■ *adj* **1** of a particular person or thing **2** arranged earlier ■ *prep* **1** granted ○ *Given time, we'll solve the problem.* **2** in view of ○ *given the uncertainty of the situation* ■ *n* an accepted fact

given name *n* a chosen name or names as opposed to a family name

Giza /geezə/ city in N Egypt on the western bank of the River Nile, site of the Great Pyramids and the Sphinx. Pop. 4,779,000 (1998).

gizmo /gízmō/ (*pl* **-mos**), **gismo** *n* a complicated device or piece of equipment *(infml)*

gizzard /gízzərd/ *n* a part of a bird's digestive tract where food is broken down by the action of the muscles and small ingested stones

glacé /glássay/ *adj* **1** glazed with a sugar solution **2** made from icing sugar and water

glacial /gláysh'l/ *adj* **1** of a glacier or glaciers **2** icily cold **3** coldly hostile

glaciate /gláyssi ayt/ (**-ating, -ated**) *v* **1** *vti* cover or become covered with a glacier **2** *vt* subject to glacial action —**glaciation** /gláyssi áysh'n/ *n*

glacier /glássi ər/ *n* an ice mass formed in mountain valleys or at the poles that moves slowly

glad (**gladder, gladdest**) *adj* **1** delighted **2** cheerfully willing ○ *glad to help* **3** grateful ○ *glad of the chance to relax* —**gladly** *adv* —**gladness** *n*

gladden /glád'n/ *vti* be or make glad

glade *n* a clearing in a forest

glad hand *n* **1** an enthusiastic but insincere handshake **2** a friendly welcome

gladiator /gláddi aytər/ *n* a fighter in the ancient Roman arena —**gladiatorial** /gláddi ə táwri əl/ *adj*

gladiolus /gláddi ṓləss/ (*pl* **same** or **-li** /-lī/ or **-luses**), **gladiola** /-lə/ (*pl* **-las** or **same**) *n* a tall flowering garden plant with spikes of funnel-shaped flowers

glad rags *npl* somebody's finest articles of clothing *(infml)*

W. E. Gladstone

Gladstone /gládstən/, **W. E.** (1809–98) British prime minister (1868–74, 1880–85, 1886, and 1892–94)

glamorize /glámmə rīz/ (**-izing, -ized**), **glamorise** *vt* **1** make glamorous **2** romanticize —**glamorization** /glámmə rī záysh'n/ *n*

glamorous /glámmərəss/, **glamourous** *adj* **1** exciting and desirable **2** dressed or made up to be good-looking

glamour /glámmər/ n **1** exciting allure **2** expensive good looks —**glamour** adj

ORIGIN Few students would consider grammar glamorous, but **glamour** is an alteration of *grammar*. It appears in Scottish use in the early 18C meaning 'magic, enchantment'. The sense was taken from *gramarye*, an obsolete derivative of *grammar* that had moved from 'knowledge of grammar, learning' to 'knowledge of magic, occult learning'. The modern uses of **glamour** began in the mid-19C.

glance v (**glancing, glanced**) **1** vi look quickly **2** vi make a cursory examination **3** vi touch on a matter briefly **4** vi glint **5** vt strike at an angle ■ n **1** a quick look **2** a passing mention **3** a cursory examination **4** an oblique strike

glancing /gláanssing/ adj striking obliquely —**glancingly** adv

gland n a cell mass in the body that removes substances from the bloodstream and excretes or modifies them

glandular /glándyŏŏlər/ adj **1** of glands **2** resulting from gland dysfunction

glandular fever n an acute infectious viral disease marked by fever and swelling of the lymph nodes

glare vi (**glaring, glared**) **1** stare intently and angrily **2** be unpleasantly bright ■ n **1** an intent and angry look **2** excessive brightness

glaring /gláiring/ adj **1** very obvious **2** staring intently and angrily **3** unpleasantly bright —**glaringly** adv

Glasgow /gláazgō, glázgō/ **1** city in SW Scotland on the River Clyde. Pop. 616,430 (1996 estimate). **2 City of Glasgow** council area in west-central Scotland

glasnost /gláss nost/ n a policy of government openness and accountability, especially in the last years of the Soviet Union

glass n **1** a transparent solid substance made from sand melted in combination with other oxides. Use: making such objects as windows, bottles, lenses. **2** something made of glass, especially a container for a drink **3** an amount contained in a glass ■ **glasses** npl **1** a pair of sight-correcting lenses worn in a frame over the eyes **2** binoculars —**glass** adj —**glassful** n

Glass, Philip (b. 1937) US composer

glass ceiling n an unofficial barrier to career advancement because of gender, age, race, ethnicity, or sexual preference

glass fibre n fibreglass

glasshouse /gláass howss/ (pl **-houses** /-howziz/) n **1** a greenhouse **2** a situation that attracts media attention

glassware /gláass wair/ n glass objects

glass wool n a mass of glass fibres. Use: insulation, as air filters, in the manufacture of fibreglass.

glassy /gláassi/ (**-ier, -iest**) adj **1** smooth and slippery **2** blankly expressionless —**glassily** adv —**glassiness** n

glassy-eyed adj blankly staring

Glaswegian /glaaz wééjən/ n somebody from Glasgow in Scotland —**Glaswegian** adj

glaucoma /glaw kṓmə/ n an eye disorder that leads to optic nerve damage —**glaucomatous** adj

glaucous /gláwkəss/ adj **1** covered in a greyish powder **2** of a greyish-green or blue colour

glaze vt (**glazing, glazed**) **1** cover a ceramic object with a clear or coloured shiny finish **2** coat food with milk or egg to produce a shiny finish **3** coat an oil painting with a nearly transparent coating **4** fit a window or door with glass ■ n **1** a clear or coloured shiny coating for a ceramic object **2** a coating to produce a shiny finish on food **3** a coating for an oil painting —**glazer** n

glazier /gláyzi ər/ n a glass fitter

glazing /gláyzing/ n **1** a hard shiny coating **2** the covering of something with a glaze **3** the glass for a window or door

gleam /gleem/ vi **1** shine brightly **2** flash for a short time ■ n **1** a bright shining quality **2** a flash of light **3** a brief indication

gleaming /gléeming/ adj bright and clean-looking —**gleamingly** adv

glean /gleen/ v **1** vt obtain information gradually or in small amounts **2** vti gather any of the crop left behind in a harvested field

gleanings /gléeningz/ npl **1** things collected over a period of time **2** the useable parts of a crop left behind in a harvested field

glebe n **1** land as a source of abundant produce (literary) **2** an area of church land providing extra income for a member of the clergy

glee n **1** great delight **2** a gloatingly jubilant feeling —**gleeful** adj —**gleefully** adv

gleeming incorrect spelling of **gleaming**

glen n a long narrow valley, especially in Scotland

Glenn /glen/, **John** (b. 1921) US astronaut and senator

glib adj **1** fluent in an insincere way o *a glib talker* **2** lacking in thought or preparation o *a glib generalization* —**glibly** adv —**glibness** n

glide vti (**gliding, glided**) **1** move smoothly **2** fly or land without engine power ■ n a smooth movement

glider /glídər/ n an aircraft with no engine

glide time n NZ flexitime system

glimmer /glímmər/ vi **1** emit a dim glow **2** be present to a small extent ■ n **1** a faint flashing light **2** a faint sign or small amount —**glimmering** adj

glimpse n **1** a brief look or sighting **2** a small indication or appearance ■ v (**glimpsing, glimpsed**) **1** vt catch sight of **2** vi take a brief look

glint vi flash briefly ■ n **1** a brief flash **2** a slight indication

glissando /gli sándō/ (pl **-di** /-dee/ or **-dos**) n a sliding movement from one note to another on a musical instrument

glisten /glíss'n/ *vi* **1** reflect light from a wet surface **2** have a glossy sheen *(refers to hair or an animal's pelt)* —**glisten** *n*

glitch *n* **1** a small problem **2** an unwanted electronic signal —**glitchy** *adj*

glitter /glíttər/ *vi* **1** sparkle or shimmer brightly **2** shine with emotion *(refers to eyes)* **3** be vivacious ■ *n* **1** a sparkly decoration **2** sparkling light **3** glamour —**glittery** *adj*

glitterati /glíttə raáti/ *npl* glamorous people

ORIGIN Glitterati is a blend of *glitter* and *literati* (the literate, educated elite). It was coined by *Time* magazine in 1956.

---

glitz *n* superficial glamour —**glitzy** *adj*

gloaming /glóming/ *n* twilight *(literary)*

gloat /glót/ *vi* be smugly happy —**gloat** *n* —**gloater** *n* —**gloatingly** *adv*

glob *n* a small amount of something soft or semiliquid *(infml)*

global /glốb'l/ *adj* **1** worldwide **2** taking all aspects into account **3** affecting the whole of a computer system, program, or file **4** spherical —**globally** *adv*

globalize /glốbə lìz/ (**-izing, -ized**), **globalise** *vti* make or become global in application or operation —**globalization** /glốbə lĩ záysh'n/ *n*

global village *n* the whole world regarded as a single community

global warming *n* an increase in the world's temperatures

globe *n* **1** a map of the Earth on a sphere **2** the Earth **3** a hollow spherical object **4** *ANZ, Canada, S Africa* a light bulb

globe artichoke *n* an artichoke

globetrot /glốb trot/ (**-trotting, -trotted**) *vi* travel far and wide —**globetrotter** *n*

globular /glốbyòòlər/ *adj* **1** spherical **2** having globules

globule /glốbbyool/ *n* a drop of liquid or semiliquid

globulin /glốbbyòòlin/ *n* a simple globular protein

glockenspiel /glókən shpeel/ *n* a percussion instrument consisting of a set of metal bars mounted on a frame

glogg *n* mulled wine

gloom *n* **1** murky darkness **2** despondency —**gloom** *vti*

gloomy /glóomi/ (**-ier, -iest**) *adj* **1** dark and cheerless **2** offering little hope ○ *gloomy prospects* **3** despondent —**gloomily** *adv* —**gloominess** *n*

gloop *n* a sticky or messy substance *(infml)* —**gloopy** *adj*

glorify /gláwri fī/ (**-fies, -fied**) *vt* **1** make something appear better than it really is **2** extol somebody or something **3** praise a deity —**glorified** *adj*

glorious /gláwri əss/ *adj* **1** exceptionally lovely ○ *glorious summer weather* **2** outstanding ○ *a glorious career* **3** highly enjoyable —**gloriously** *adv*

glory /gláwri/ (*pl* **-ries**) *n* **1** fame and honour **2** an achievement that brings admiration **3** praise of a deity **4** awesome splendour **5** astounding beauty **6** the idealized bliss of heaven
□ **glory in** *vt* enjoy greatly

glory days *npl* a time of great success

Glos. *abbr* Gloucestershire

gloss[1] *n* **1** shininess **2** deceptive and superficial attractiveness **3** *also* **gloss paint** a paint that produces a shiny finish ■ *vt* **1** make shiny **2** use gloss paint on
□ **gloss over** *vt* address too lightly or omit entirely

gloss[2] *n* **1** a short definition or translation of a word or phrase **2** an interpretation or explanation ■ *vt* **1** give a gloss for a word or phrase **2** insert glosses in a text

glossary /glóssəri/ (*pl* **-ries**) *n* an alphabetical list of terms and their meanings

glossy /glóssi/ *adj* (**-ier, -iest**) **1** shiny and smooth **2** superficially stylish *(infml)* ■ *n* (*pl* **-ies**) **1** a photo with a shiny finish **2** a glossy magazine *(infml)* —**glossily** *adv* —**glossiness** *n*

glossy magazine *n* an expensive magazine with high-quality colour photographs

glottal stop /glótt'l-/ *n* a speech sound created by opening and closing the glottis and suddenly releasing air

glottis /glóttiss/ (*pl* **-tises** *or* **-tides** /-ti deez/) *n* **1** an opening between the vocal cords **2** the part of the larynx involved in producing speech

Gloucestershire /glóstərshər/ county in west-central England

glove /gluv/ *n* **1** a covering for the hand with separate sections for the fingers and thumb **2** a protective covering for the hand worn in some sports ■ *vt* (**gloving, gloved**) put a glove on

glove compartment *n* a storage space in the dashboard of a car

glove puppet *n* a hollow puppet fitting over the hand

glow /glố/ *n* **1** the light from something hot **2** a soft steady light without heat or flames **3** a soft reflected light **4** rosiness of complexion **5** a redness of the face caused by embarrassment ■ *vi* **1** emit light and heat **2** emit or reflect a soft light **3** shine with health **4** be flushed with embarrassment

glower /glốw ər/ *vi* glare silently or sullenly —**glower** *n* —**gloweringly** *adv*

glowing /glố ing/ *adj* **1** shining softly and steadily **2** rich, strong, or bright in colour **3** full of praise —**glowingly** *adv*

glowworm /glố wurm/ *n* a luminous larva of some types of firefly

gloxinia /glok sínni ə/ *n* a plant with large bell-shaped flowers

---

ORIGIN The **gloxinia** is named after the 18C German botanist Benjamin Gloxin, who first described it.

---

glucosamine /gloo kŏssəmin/ *n* an amino derivative of glucose. Use: food supplement, treatment for arthritis and other joint disorders.

glucose /glóŏkōz, -kōss/ *n* **1** a sugar produced in plants by photosynthesis and in animals by the metabolism of carbohydrates **2** a syrupy mixture. Use: food manufacture, alcoholic fermentation.

glue *n* **1** an adhesive substance obtained from boiling animal parts **2** any adhesive substance ■ *vt* (**gluing, glued**) **1** stick things together with glue **2** cause somebody, or somebody's gaze, to remain completely still (*infml*) ○ *have been glued to the TV* —**gluey** *adj* —**gluiness** *n*

glue ear *n* a condition affecting children's hearing resulting from poor drainage of the middle ear

glue-sniffing *n* the practice of inhaling glue fumes for their intoxicating effect —**glue-sniffer** *n*

glug *n* **1** the sound of liquid being poured **2** a quantity of liquid poured from a bottle —**glug** *vti*

glum (**glummer, glummest**) *adj* quietly miserable —**glumly** *adv* —**glumness** *n*

glut *n* an excess supply ■ *vt* (**glutting, glutted**) **1** supply a market with too much of a product **2** give somebody enough or too much

gluten /glóŏt'n/ *n* a mixture of two proteins found in some cereal grains, especially wheat

glutinous /glóŏtinəss/ *adj* sticky

glutton /glútt'n/ *n* an excessive eater or drinker —**gluttonous** *adj*

gluttony /glútt'ni/ *n* excessive eating or drinking

glycerin /glíssərin/, **glycerine, glycerol** /glíssə rol/ *n* a thick sweet liquid obtained from fats and oils. Use: solvent, antifreeze, manufacture of soaps, cosmetics, lubricants, and dynamite.

glycogen /glíkəjən/ *n* a complex carbohydrate found in the liver and muscles that is easily converted to glucose —**glycogenic** /glíkə jénnik/ *adj*

glyph /glif/ *n* a carved vertical groove, especially in an ancient Greek frieze —**glyphic** *adj*

gm *abbr* gram[1]

GM *abbr* **1** general manager **2** genetic modification **3** genetically modified

GMO *abbr* genetically modified organism

GMT *abbr* Greenwich Mean Time

gnarled /naarld/ *adj* **1** knotted and twisted **2** misshapen or weather-beaten

gnash /nash/ *vt* grind your teeth together

gnat /nat/ *n* a small biting fly

gnaw /naw/ (**gnawed** *or* **gnawn** *archaic*) **v 1** *vti* chew at something **2** *vt* make by chewing ○ *The mice had gnawed a hole in the box.* **3** *vt* erode **4** *vi* be a source of worry ○ *a question*

that had gnawed at her for years —**gnaw** *n* —**gnawing** *adj*

gneiss /nīss/ *n* a coarse rock with light and dark bands —**gneissic** *adj*

gnome[1] /nōm/ *n* **1** in folklore and fairy tales, a tiny being resembling a dwarf, living underground and guarding treasure **2** a model of a gnome used as a garden ornament —**gnome-like** *adj*

ORIGIN Gnome came through French from a Latin word coined by the 16C Swiss physician Paracelsus. He gave the name to a diminutive imaginary being living in the earth. It has no connection with **gnome** 'short saying', which is from Greek.

---

gnome[2] /nōm/ *n* a short saying

gnomic /nṓmik/ *adj* **1** expressing basic truths pithily **2** cryptic

Gnosticism /nóstissizəm/ *n* a pre-Christian and early Christian religious movement teaching that salvation comes by learning esoteric spiritual truths —**Gnostic** *n, adj*

GNP *abbr* gross national product

gnu /noo/ (*pl same or* **gnus**) *n* a large African antelope with a head resembling that of an ox

GNVQ *n* a post-secondary-school vocational qualification. Full form **General National Vocational Qualification**

go[1] /gō/ *vi* (**goes, went, gone** /gon/) **1** leave a place **2** move in order to do something ○ *went to live elsewhere* **3** attend ○ *go to evening classes* **4** lead, or have as a starting point or destination **5** elapse **6** be spent or used up **7** belong ○ *The towels go in the cupboard.* **8** function or operate ○ *The car won't go.* **9** get weaker, fail, or break down ○ *My eyesight is starting to go.* **10** become ○ *going nuts* **11** proceed or happen in a particular way ○ *went unchallenged* ○ *go barefoot* **12** continually remain in a particular situation ○ *go without food* **13** expresses future action or intent (*in progressive tenses*) ○ *What are you going to do?* ■ *n* (*pl* **gos**) **1** an attempt or chance to do something **2** a turn or move in a game **3** energy and vitality (*infml*) ◇ **anything goes** anything is to be tolerated ◇ **make a go of** make a success of ◇ **on the go** very active and busy

☐ **go about** *vt* tackle a problem or task

☐ **go after** *vt* try to get

☐ **go against** *vt* **1** oppose **2** be contrary to

☐ **go ahead** *vi* start or continue

☐ **go along** *vi* accompany somebody

☐ **go along with** *vt* accept doing something, or obey somebody

☐ **go around** *vti* be widely known or current in a particular place

☐ **go at** *vt* attempt with vigour

☐ **go back** *vi* originate from a particular time

☐ **go back on** *vt* change your mind about

☐ **go by** **v 1** *vi* pass in time **2** *vt* use as a source of information or guidance

☐ **go down** *vi* **1** sink beneath the surface or horizon **2** fall from the air and crash **3** be defeated in a competition *(infml)* **4** be relegated in a sports league **5** be remembered in a particular way **6** become ill *(infml)* ○ *went down with flu* **7** be sent to prison *(infml)* **8** leave university at the end of term

☐ **go for** *vt* **1** like a lot *(infml)* **2** choose *(infml)* **3** attack **4** command as a price **5** apply or be relevant to ○ *Be careful, and that goes for all of you.* ◇ **go for it** aggressively pursue a goal *(slang; often a command)* ◇ **have something going for you** be in a situation where something is useful or helpful to you *(infml)*

☐ **go in for** *vt* **1** enter as a competitor **2** enjoy doing

☐ **go into** *vt* **1** examine or look into something **2** be a factor of a number or amount

☐ **go in with** *vt* begin a joint venture

☐ **go off** *v* **1** *vi* become bad **2** *vi* explode or be fired **3** *vi* begin to ring or sound **4** *vi* be carried out **5** *vi* depart **6** *vti* leave a sports pitch, stage, or other public place **7** *vt* stop liking

☐ **go on** *v* **1** *vi* carry on **2** *vi* happen or occur **3** *vti* make an entrance on a stage, sports field, or other public place **4** *vi* talk too much **5** *vi* do something afterwards **6** *vt* use as reliable information

☐ **go out** *vi* **1** socialize or enjoy yourself away from home **2** finish your part in a game **3** be forced out of a game or a competition **4** go on a date **5** be broadcast

☐ **go over** *v* **1** *vi* change to a new system **2** *vi* change allegiance **3** *vt* examine or consider carefully

☐ **go through** *vt* **1** examine the parts or contents of something **2** undergo unpleasantness

☐ **go under** *vi* fail or close down

☐ **go up** *vi* **1** be built **2** be displayed **3** detonate or ignite

☐ **go with** *vt* be an accepted or usual part of something

☐ **go without** *vt* not have something needed

go² /gṓ/ *n* a Japanese board game played with stones

goad *vt* **1** provoke into action **2** prod with a stick ■ *n* **1** a pointed animal prod **2** a stimulus to action ◊ See note at **motive**

go-ahead *n* permission to proceed *(infml)* ■ *adj* enterprising

goal *n* **1** the target area in a sport **2** a score achieved by getting a ball or puck in the goal **3** a successful shot at a goal **4** an aim —**goalless** *adj*

goal difference *n* the difference between goals scored and goals conceded

goalkeeper /gṓl keepər/, **goalie** /gṓli/ *n* a player who protects the goal

goal kick *n* **1** in football, a free kick by the goalkeeper near the goal **2** in rugby, an attacker's free kick to convert a try

goal line *n* in games such as football and hockey, the line across which the ball must be passed or carried in order to score

goalmouth /gṓl mowth/ *(pl* -**mouths** /-mowthz/*) n* in games such as football and hockey, the area directly in front of the goal

goalpost /gṓl pōst/ *n* each of two posts marking a goal ◇ **move the goalposts** change the rules after a course of action has been embarked on

goat *n* **1** *(pl* **goats** *or same)* a horned animal related to sheep **2** a man regarded as lecherous *(insult)* **3** **Goat** the zodiacal sign Capricorn —**goatish** *adj* ◇ **get somebody's goat** annoy or irritate somebody *(infml)*

goatee /gṓ tee/ *n* a short pointed beard

goatherd /gṓt hurd/ *n* a herder of goats

goatskin /gṓt skin/ *n* the skin of a goat

gob¹ *(slang) n* a lump of a soft wet substance ○ *a gob of whipped cream* ■ *vi* (**gobbing, gobbed**) spit phlegm

gob² *n* a person's mouth *(slang disapproving)*

gob³ *n* mining waste

gobbet /góbbit/ *n* **1** a drop of liquid or semiliquid **2** an extract from a text

gobble¹ /góbb'l/ (**-bling, -bled**) *vt* **1** eat quickly and greedily **2** use up *(infml humorous)* ○ *watching the payphone gobble her money*

gobble² /góbb'l/ (**-bling, -bled**) *vi* make the sound of a male turkey —**gobble** *n*

gobbledegook /góbb'ldigook/, **gobbledygook** *n* nonsense or jargon *(infml)*

go-between *n* somebody who mediates or carries messages between people

Gobi Desert /góbi-/ desert in N China and S Mongolia

goblet /góbblət/ *n* **1** a stemmed glass **2** a large cup *(archaic)*

goblin /góbblin/ *n* in folklore and fairy tales, a tiny mischievous or evil being

gobsmacked /gób smakt/ *adj* extremely shocked *(slang)*

gobstopper /gób stopər/ *n* a large sweet

goby /gṓbi/ *(pl* -**bies**) *n* a small spiny-finned fish

go-cart, go-kart *n* a very small open-framed car with an engine, used for racing

god *n* **1** a supernatural being that is an object of worship **2** somebody who is widely admired *(infml)* **3** **God** the supreme being in some religions **4** **God** in Christianity, the supreme being worshipped as the trinity ■ **gods** *npl* fate —**godless** *adj* —**god-like** *adj*

Godard /góddaar/, **Jean-Luc** (b. 1930) French film director

godchild /gód chīld/ *(pl* -**children** /-children/*) n* a child with a godparent or godparents

goddaughter /gód dawtər/ *n* a female godchild

goddess /góddess/ *n* **1** a female supernatural being that is an object of worship **2** a woman who is widely admired *(infml)*

~~godess~~ incorrect spelling of **goddess**

godfather /gód faathər/ *n* **1** a man who is somebody's godparent **2** a man who heads a criminal organization *(infml)*

God-fearing *adj* deeply devout

godforsaken /gódfər sayk'n/ *adj* cheerless

God-given *adj* inherent ○ *God-given abilities*

godhead /gód hed/ *n* 1 the nature or essence of being divine 2 **Godhead** the Christian God

Godiva /gə dívə/, **Lady** (1040?–80?) English noblewoman said to have ridden naked to get taxes reduced

godly /gódli/ (**-lier, -liest**) *adj* 1 devout (*fml*) 2 divine —**godliness** *n*

godmother /gód muthər/ *n* a woman who is somebody's godparent

godown /gó down/ *n* a South Asian warehouse

godparent /gód pairənt/ *n* a sponsor of a baptized child who promises to take a special interest in him or her

godsend /gód send/ *n* 1 an unexpected benefit 2 something or somebody very useful

God's gift *n* an extremely valuable or gifted person (*often ironic*)

God slot *n* a scheduled time for the broadcasting of religious programmes (*sometimes offensive*)

godson /gód sun/ *n* a male godchild

Godthåb /gód hawb/ former name for **Nuuk**

Godunov /góddŏŏ nof/, **Boris Fyodorovich** (1551?–1605) tsar of Russia (1598–1605)

Godwin Austen, Mt /góddwin óstin/ ♦ **K2**

Goebbels /góbl'z/, **Joseph** (1897–1945) German Nazi leader

goer /gó ər/ *n* 1 a regular attender (*usually in combination*) 2 a person regarded as promiscuous (*slang; sometimes offensive*)

Goering /gúring, góring/, **Göring, Hermann** (1893–1946) German Nazi leader

Goethe /gótə/, **Johann Wolfgang von** (1749–1832) German writer and scientist

go-getter /gó géttər/ *n* an enterprising person (*infml*) —**go-getting** *adj, n*

gogga /khókhə/ *n* S Africa an insect (*infml*)

goggle /gógg'l/ *v* (**-gling, -gled**) 1 *vi* stare wide-eyed 2 *vti* roll the eyes ■ *adj* describes bulging eyes —**goggle** *n*

goggle-eyed *adj* with staring eyes

goggles /gógg'lz/ *npl* protective glasses

Gogh ♦ **van Gogh, Vincent**

Gogol /gó gol, -gəl/, **Nikolay Vasilyevich** (1809–52) Russian writer

Goh Chok Tong /gó chok tóng/ (*b.* 1941) prime minister of Singapore (1990–)

going /gó ing/ *n* 1 an act of leaving a place 2 the conditions for progress or movement ○ *The going gets tough when you reach the rocky terrain.* ■ *adj* 1 currently operating successfully ○ *a going business* 2 currently accepted as standard ○ *the going rate for platinum*

going-over (*pl* **goings-over**) *n* a thorough examination (*infml*)

goings-on *npl* happenings, especially of a suspicious or scandalous nature (*infml*)

goiter *n* US = **goitre**

goitre /góytər/ *n* enlargement of the thyroid gland —**goitrous** *adj*

go-kart *n* MOTOR SPORTS = **go-cart**

Golan Heights /gó lan-/ disputed upland region on the border between Israel and Syria, northeast of the Sea of Galilee. It was annexed by Israel in 1981.

gold /góld/ *n* 1 (*symbol* **Au**) a yellow metallic element. Use: jewellery, alloys. 2 a deep rich yellow colour 3 things made of gold 4 wealth —**gold** *adj*

gold brick *n* something that is only superficially valuable

gold digger *n* 1 a person regarded as courting somebody for money (*insult*) 2 a gold miner —**gold-digging** *n*

gold disc *n* 1 a top selling record 2 a master disc from which a CD is made

gold dust *n* particles of gold ◊ **like gold dust** very valuable or difficult to obtain

golden /góld'n/ *adj* 1 coloured like gold 2 made of gold 3 excellent ○ *a golden opportunity* 4 idyllic ○ *the golden years of their lives* 5 favoured ○ *her golden boy* 6 50th ○ *their golden wedding anniversary*

golden age *n* 1 a period of excellence 2 in classical mythology, the earliest and best age

golden eagle *n* a large brown eagle with golden brown feathers on its head

golden handshake *n* a large payment made to an employee to compensate for the loss of a job (*infml*)

golden jubilee *n* a 50th anniversary

golden mean *n* the middle course that avoids extremes

golden retriever *n* a medium-sized dog with golden fur

goldenrod /góld'n rod/ (*pl* **-rods** or same) *n* a tall yellow-flowered plant that blooms in late summer

golden rule *n* 1 a basic l rule that must be followed 2 a rule of conduct advising people to treat others as they would wish to be treated themselves

golden share *n* a controlling share in a company

golden syrup *n* a yellow syrup used for desserts

golden triangle *n* the part of Southeast Asia where Laos, Thailand, and Myanmar meet and where much opium is grown

goldfinch /góld finch/ *n* a small finch with yellow and black markings

goldfish /góldfish/ (*pl* same or **-fishes**) *n* a small aquarium fish

goldfish bowl *n* a place or situation open to public scrutiny

gold leaf *n* gold in thin sheets

gold medal *n* a medal given as a first prize —**gold medallist** *n*

gold mine *n* 1 a place where gold is mined 2 a rich source, especially of wealth —**gold-miner** *n* —**gold-mining** *n*

gold-plated *adj* coated with gold —**gold-plate** *vt*

gold rush *n* 1 a rush to an area where gold has

been discovered **2** a rush to make money from a new source or by a new means

goldsmith /góld smith/ *n* a maker of gold articles

Goldsmith /góld smith/, **Oliver** (1730–74) Irish-born British writer

gold standard *n* **1** a system of valuing currency in relation to the price of gold **2** the best example of its kind

Goldwyn /góldwin/, **Samuel** (1882–1974) Russian-born US film producer

golf *n* **1** an outdoor game in which a small ball is hit a long distance into a hole using a variety of clubs **2 Golf** a communications code word for the letter 'G' ■ *vi* play golf —**golfer** *n* —**golfing** *n*

golf ball *n* a ball used in golf

golf club *n* **1** a club with a long shaft and metal or wooden head used for hitting golf balls **2** a golfers' association or its premises

golf course *n* an area of land for playing golf

golf links *npl* a golf course by the sea

Golgotha /gólgothə/ ♦ **Calvary**

goliath /gə líˈəth/, **Goliath** *n* a gigantic or overpowering opponent

ORIGIN In the Bible, Goliath was a giant Philistine who was slain by David using a sling and a stone.

-gon *suffix* a figure having a particular number of angles o *hexagon*

gonad /gó nad, gónnad/ *n* an organ that produces reproductive cells

gondola /góndələ/ *n* **1** a Venetian canal boat **2** a cabin suspended below a balloon or airship **3** a cable car **4** a freestanding shelving unit in a shop

ORIGIN Gondola is, as might be expected, from Venetian Italian. It is an alteration of a verb meaning 'roll, rock' in a Romance dialect of the NE Alps.

gondolier /góndə leèr/ *n* somebody who guides a Venetian gondola

Condwanaland /gon dwaànə land/ ancient land mass, part of the supercontinent of Pangaea, comprising South America, Africa, peninsular India, Australia, and Antarctica

gone /gon/ past participle of **go**¹ ■ *adj* **1** absent after leaving somewhere **2** irrecoverable **3** used up **4** advanced in time **5** having been pregnant for a particular time **6** dead *(infml)* **7** infatuated *(infml)*

goner /gónnər/ *n* a person who is dead or about to die *(slang)*

gong *n* **1** a resonant bronze plate. Use: orchestral percussion instrument, to summon people to meals. **2** a round bell. Use: as an alarm. **3** a medal *(slang)*

gonorrhoea /gónnə reè ə/, **gonorrhea** *n* a sexually transmitted bacterial disease of the genitals —**gonorrhoeal** *adj*

goo *n* a soft sticky substance *(infml)*

good /goŏd/ *adj* (**better** /béttər/, **best**) **1** of high quality **2** suitable **3** skilled **4** virtuous

5 kindly **6** affording pleasure **7** not damaged or spoilt **8** ample o *a good income* **9** honourable **10** valid or allowable o *a good explanation* **11** beneficial to health **12** able to produce a desired result o *a joke that is always good for a laugh* **13** being at least o *a good 30 minutes* ■ *n* **1** a beneficial effect **2** a positive or useful aspect o *take the good with the bad* **3** something worth having or achieving o *the good of the nation* ◇ **for good** permanently ◇ **good and** completely *(infml)* o *I'll leave when I'm good and ready.* ◇ **make good** become successful

good afternoon *interj* says hello or goodbye in the afternoon

goodbye /goŏd bíˈ/ *interj* expresses good wishes upon parting or on ending a telephone conversation ■ *n* an act of leaving

ORIGIN Goodbye is a contraction of 'God be with you'.

good day *interj* says hello or goodbye during the day *(fml)*

good evening *interj* says hello or goodbye in the evening

good faith *n* honest intent

good-for-nothing *n* a person regarded as lazy *(insult)* —**good-for-nothing** *adj*

Good Friday *n* the Friday before Easter, when Christians remember Jesus Christ's death

goodhearted /goŏd haártid/ *adj* kindly and generous —**goodheartedly** *adv* —**goodheartedness** *n*

Good Hope, Cape of /goŏd hóp/ Cape in SW South Africa that divides the South Atlantic and Indian oceans

good-humoured *adj* cheerful —**good-humouredly** *adv*

goodie *n* = **goody**

goodish /goŏddish/ *adj* **1** rather good **2** rather large

good life *n* a comfortable existence

good looks *npl* a pleasant personal appearance, especially facial appearance —**good-looking** *adj*

goodly /goŏdli/ (**-lier**, **-liest**) *adj* **1** rather large **2** attractive *(archaic)* —**goodliness** *n*

Goodman /goŏdmən/, **Benny** (1909–86) US jazz clarinet player and band leader

good morning *interj* says hello or goodbye in the morning

good-natured *adj* pleasant and obliging —**good-naturedly** *adv*

goodness /goŏdnəss/ *n* **1** the quality of being good **2** the nutrition or other benefit to be derived from something ■ *interj* expresses surprise

goodnight /goŏd níˈt/ *interj* says goodbye at night —**goodnight** *adj*

goods /goŏdz/ *n* items that are bought, sold, or transported *(+ sing or pl verb)* ■ *npl* portable property

Good Samaritan *n* a person who helps somebody in trouble

ORIGIN The **Good Samaritan** is the subject of a parable in the Bible (Luke 10:30–37). He stopped and helped a man who had been attacked and left for dead by thieves on the road from Jerusalem to Jericho, after others had passed him by.

good-tempered *adj* of a placid disposition —**good-temperedly** *adv*

good-time girl *n* a young woman seeking pleasure *(disapproving)*

goodwill /góod wíl/ *n* 1 a friendly disposition ○ *a goodwill gesture* 2 willingness 3 the nontangible value of a business

goody /góoddi/, **goodie** *n (pl* **-ies)** 1 something sweet *(often pl)* 2 somebody who is good, especially the sympathetic character in a story ■ *interj* indicates delight *(infml)*

Goodyear /góod yeer/, **Charles** (1800–60) US inventor

goody-goody *adj* a person regarded as smugly virtuous *(infml)*

gooey /góo i/ **(-ier, -iest)** *adj* sticky and soft —**gooeyness** *n*

goofy /góofi/ **(-ier, -iest)** *adj* with teeth that stick out *(infml)* —**goofily** *adv* —**goofiness** *n*

googly /góogli/ *(pl* **-glies)** *n* in cricket, a deceptive ball

goon *n* 1 a person regarded as clumsy or uncouth *(insult)* 2 US, *Can* a thug

goose /gooss/ *n (pl* **geese** /geess/) 1 a large long-necked water bird with a honking call 2 a female goose 3 the flesh of a goose, cooked as food 4 a person regarded as silly ■ *vt* (**goosing, goosed**) prod in the buttocks *(slang)*

gooseberry /góozbəri/ *(pl* **-ries)** *n* 1 an edible green or red fruit, usually eaten cooked and sweetened 2 the spiny bush that gooseberries grow on 3 an unwanted extra person *(infml)*

gooseflesh /góoss flesh/ *n* skin affected by goose pimples

goose pimples, goose bumps *npl* temporary pimples on the skin brought on by cold, fear, or sudden excitement —**goose-pimply** *adj*

goose step *n* a high stiff marching step —**goose-step** *vi*

gopher /góofər/ *n* a burrowing rodent with fur-lined cheek pouches

Mikhail Gorbachev

Gorbachev /gáwrbə chof/, **Mikhail** (b. 1931) general secretary of the Soviet Communist Party (1985–91) and president of the former Soviet Union (1988–91)

Gordian knot /gáwrdi ən-/ *n* a complicated problem with no apparent solution

ORIGIN The original **Gordian knot** was in the possession of Gordius, king of Gordium in ancient Phrygia, Asia Minor. Prophecy had it that it could be untied only by the future ruler of Asia, but Alexander the Great sliced through it.

Gordimer /gáwrdimər/, **Nadine** (b. 1923) South African novelist

Gordon River /gáwrd'n-/ longest river in Tasmania, Australia, flowing west into the S Indian Ocean. Length 181 km/112 mi.

gore[1] (**goring, gored**) *vt* pierce the flesh with horns

ORIGIN The three English words **gore** are etymologically distinct. The origin of **gore** 'pierce', which appeared in the 14C, is obscure. **Gore** 'blood' is from an ancient root. It originally meant 'dung, dirt, slime', and then from the mid-16C 'coagulating blood'. **Gore** 'section of fabric' is of equally ancient origin, and in the earliest English sources meant 'corner of land'.

gore[2] *n* coagulating blood from a wound

gore[3] *n* a triangular section of fabric sewn together with others to form a wide skirt

gorge *n* 1 a deep narrow valley 2 the contents of the stomach 3 an obstruction in a passage ■ *v* (**gorging, gorged**) 1 *vti* eat greedily 2 *vt* fill with blood

gorgeous /gáwrjəss/ *adj* 1 outstandingly beautiful or richly coloured 2 very pleasant *(infml)* ○ *a gorgeous day* —**gorgeously** *adv* —**gorgeousness** *n*

Gorgon /gáwrgən/ *n* 1 in Greek mythology, a monstrous woman with snakes for hair, who turned those who looked at her into stone 2 *also* **gorgon** a woman regarded as frightening or ugly *(insult)* —**Gorgonian** /gawr góni ən/ *adj*

Gorgonzola /gáwrgən zólə/, **gorgonzola** *n* an Italian blue cheese

gorilla /gə ríllə/ *n* 1 the largest type of ape 2 a thug *(infml)*

ORIGIN The name was applied to the largest ape in 1847 by the US missionary and scientist Thomas Savage. It was taken from Greek, where it was used in an account of an expedition to West Africa, explained as the name given to the women of a tribe of wild hairy people.

SPELLCHECK Do not confuse the spelling of **gorilla** and **guerrilla** ('a paramilitary soldier'), which sound similar.

Göring ◆ Goering, Hermann

Gorky /gáwrki/, **Gorki** former name for **Nizhniy Novgorod**

Gorky, Arshile (1904–48) Armenian-born US painter

gormless /gáwrmləss/ *adj* unintelligent *(infml)*

gorilla incorrect spelling of **gorilla**

gorse *n* a spiny shrub with yellow flowers

gory /gáwri/ (**-rier, -riest**) *adj* **1** covered with blood **2** involving bloodshed **3** horrible o *the gory details* —**gorily** *adv* —**goriness** *n*

gosh *interj* expresses surprise *(infml)*

goshawk /góss hawk/ *n* a large hawk with broad rounded wings and a long tail

gosling /gózzling/ *n* an immature goose

go-slow *n* an industrial protest in which workers deliberately work slowly

gospel /gósp'l/ *n* **1** a set of beliefs **2** the absolute truth **3** *also* **gospel music** religious vocal music that originated among African American Christians in the S United States **4 Gospel** the teachings of Jesus Christ, especially as contained in the Bible

ORIGIN **Gospel** represents what is essentially a contraction of *good spell*, with *spell* in the obsolete sense 'news', and so is the 'good news' preached by Jesus Christ. The first element of **gospel** came to be associated with *God* rather than *good*.

gossamer /góssəmər/ *n* **1** a fine film of cobwebs **2** a delicate fabric

gossip /góssip/ *n* **1** conversation about the personal details of others' lives, especially when malicious **2** casual conversation about recent events **3** somebody who habitually discusses the personal details of others' lives ■ *vi* spread rumours —**gossipy** *adj*

gossip column *n* a press feature about people's private lives —**gossip columnist** *n*

got past participle, past tense of **get**

goth /goth/ *n* **1** *also* **Goth** a style of popular music that combines heavy metal with punk **2** *also* **Goth** a fashion style featuring dark clothes and makeup **3** *also* **Goth** somebody who follows goth music and fashion **4 Goth** a member of an ancient Germanic people

Gothenburg /góth'n burg/ principal port in SW Sweden. Pop. 459,593 (1998). Swedish **Göteborg**

Gothic: Interior of Cologne Cathedral, Germany (begun 1248)

gothic /góthik/ *adj* **1** *also* **Gothic** belonging to a genre of fiction characterized by gloom and darkness **2 Gothic** of a medieval architectural style characterized by high ceilings and arched windows **3 Gothic** of the ancient Goths **4** printed in heavy angular characters ■ *n* **1** the goth style of music or fashion

2 a simple typeface with strokes of uniform width

gotten /gótt'n/ *US, Can* past participle of **get**

Göttingen /gótingən/ university town in central Germany. Pop. 127,519 (1997).

gouache /gŏŏ aásh/ *n* **1** a painting technique in which opaque watercolours are mixed with gum **2** a gouache painting

Gouda /gówdə/ *n* a mild Dutch cheese

gouge /gowj/ *v* (**gouging, gouged**) **1** *vti* carve out a hole **2** *vti* form something roughly by cutting **3** *vt* injure or remove somebody's eye with the thumb ■ *n* a chisel with a concave blade. Use: cutting grooves and holes in wood. —**gouger** *n*

goulash /gŏŏl ash/ *n* a spicy Hungarian stew

Gould /gŏŏld/, **Shane** (*b.* 1956) Australian swimmer

Gounod /gŏŏnŏ/, **Charles François** (1818–93) French composer

gourd /gŏŏrd/ *n* **1** any of various hard-skinned fruits whose skin is hollowed out and used for making containers **2** a gourd-producing plant

gourde /gŏŏrd/ *n* the main unit of Haitian currency

gourmand /gŏŏrmənd/ *n* a food lover

gourmet /goor may/ *n* a food expert ■ *adj* describes special high-quality food

gout /gowt/ *n* **1** a disease causing swollen joints through deposits of excess uric acid **2** a large blob or clot

gov *abbr* government organization *(in Internet addresses)*

gov. *abbr* **1** government **2** governor

governor incorrect spelling of **governor**

goverment incorrect spelling of **government**

govern /gúvv'n/ *v* **1** *vti* have political authority over a country, state, or organization **2** *vt* control the actions or behaviour of **3** *vt* control by exercising restraint o *unable to govern her emotions* **4** *vt* have the controlling influence over o *issues that govern the final settlement*

ORIGIN **Govern** came through French and Latin from a Greek word that meant 'steer a ship'.

governance /gúvv'nənss/ *n* **1** the manner of government **2** the act or state of governing

governess /gúvvərnəss/ *n* a woman employed to teach children at home

governing body *n* a group that regulates an activity or institution

government /gúvv'nmənt/ *n* **1** a group of people who have political authority **2** a type of political system **3** the state viewed as a ruling political power **4** the control of something **5** political science as a subject of study —**government** *adj* —**governmental** /gúvv'n mént'l/ *adj*

Government House *n* the official residence of the governor-general of Australia

governor /gúvv'nər/ *n* **1** a member of a governing body **2** a governing official **3** a principal prison officer **4** a device for regulating the speed of an engine **5** the representative of the British crown in Australia at state level —**governorship** *n*

governor general (*pl* **governors general** *or* **governor generals**) *n* **1** a representative of the British Crown in some Commonwealth countries **2** a chief governor —**governor-generalship** *n*

govt *abbr* government

gown /gown/ *n* **1** an elegant dress **2** a long robe **3** a loose outer garment

Goya /góy əl/, **Francisco de** (1746–1828) Spanish painter

GP *n* a family doctor. Full form **general practitioner**

GPO *abbr* General Post Office

GPRS *n* a system that provides Internet access via mobile phones and other wireless systems. Full form **general packet radio service**

GPS *n* a satellite navigation system, or a device that makes use of it. Full form **Global Positioning System**

gr. *abbr* **1** grade **2** grain **3** gram[1] **4** gross

Gr. *abbr* **1** Greece **2** Greek

grab (**grabbing**, **grabbed**) *v* **1** *vt* pick up or take hold of quickly, suddenly, or forcefully **2** *vti* try to grasp something ○ *Stop grabbing or I won't give you any.* **3** *vt* seize violently or dishonestly **4** *vt* attract or impress and affect emotionally (*infml*) **5** *vt* hurriedly get (*infml*) ○ *grab a bite to eat* —**grab** *n* —**grabbable** *adj*

Gracchus /grákəss/, **Tiberius Sempronius** (163–133 BC) and his brother **Gaius Sempronius** (153–121 BC) Roman politicians and social reformers

grace *n* **1** elegance of form or movement **2** polite and decent behaviour **3** generosity of spirit **4** a short prayer said at mealtimes **5** *also* **grace period** an extra time allowed before paying a debt **6** a pleasing or admirable quality (*usually pl*) **7** in Christianity, the love, mercy, and goodwill that is God's gift to humankind ■ *vt* (**gracing**, **graced**) **1** contribute pleasingly to an event (*often ironic*) ○ *So good of you to grace us with your presence.* **2** add elegance to something ■ *n* **Grace** a form of address used for a duke, duchess, or archbishop ■ **Graces** *npl* in Greek mythology, three goddesses who had the power to grant charm, happiness, and beauty ◊ **fall from grace** lose a favoured or privileged position ◊ **with (a) bad grace** in a rude and bad-tempered way ◊ **with (a) good grace** in a polite and willing way

Grace, W. G. (1848–1915) British cricket player

graceful /gráyssf'l/ *adj* **1** elegant and beautiful **2** poised and dignified —**gracefully** *adv* —**gracefulness** *n*

graceless /gráyssləss/ *adj* **1** without elegance **2** lacking dignity —**gracelessly** *adv* —**gracelessness** *n*

grace note *n* an extra ornamental note added to a piece of music

gracious /gráyshəss/ *adj* **1** kind and polite **2** elegant ○ *gracious living* ■ *interj* expresses surprise —**graciously** *adv* —**graciousness** *n*

grackle /grák'l/ *n* **1** a starling with mostly black feathers **2** a North American blackbird

grad. *abbr* gradient

gradation /grə dáysh'n/ *n* **1** a series of degrees, steps, or stages **2** a single degree, step, or stage **3** the arrangement of things according to size, rank, or quality —**gradational** *adj*

grade *n* **1** a level in a scale of progression (*often in combination*) **2** a mark showing a stage in a process **3** a mark indicating the quality of a student's work **4** a year in school in the US and Canadian systems ○ *He's in the 9th grade.* **5** a rank, e.g. in the military **6** a group of people of the same rank ■ *vt* (**grading**, **graded**) **1** classify things or people by rank, quality, or level **2** make a road level —**gradable** *adj*

gradient /gráydi ənt/ *n* **1** the rate of slope **2** a slope ■ *adj* sloping

gradual /grájjoo əl/ *adj* proceeding, developing, or changing slowly —**gradually** *adv* —**gradualness** *n*

graduate *n* /grájjoo ət/ the holder of a first degree ■ *v* /grájjoo ayt/ (**-ating, -ated**) **1** *vi* receive a degree **2** *vi* move up in level or standard **3** *vt* mark with units of measurement ■ *adj* /grájjoo ət/ postgraduate

graduated /grájjoo aytid/ *adj* **1** in stages **2** marked with units of measurement

graduation /grájjoo áysh'n/ *n* **1** the completion of studies **2** a ceremony in which degrees are given **3** a unit of measurement marked on an instrument

Graeco-Roman /greèkō-/, **Greco-Roman** *adj* **1** of ancient Greece and Rome **2** describes a style of wrestling in which no holds are allowed below the waist

graffiti /grə feéti/ *n* drawings or writing on walls or other surfaces in public places (*+ sing or pl verb*)

USAGE graffito or **graffiti**? **Graffiti** comes from an Italian plural: the Italian singular is *graffito*. It is acceptable, however, to use **graffiti** as a singular when the meaning is 'inscriptions in general' or even 'an inscription'.

grafitti incorrect spelling of **graffiti**

graft[1] *n* **1** a piece of transplanted tissue **2** a piece of a plant shoot joined to the stem of another plant ■ *vt* **1** transplant living tissue **2** join part of one plant to another

graft[2] *n* **1** hard work (*infml*) **2** cheating for personal gain by somebody in a powerful or elected position ■ *vi* work hard (*infml*) —**grafter** *n*

Graham /gráy əm/, **Billy** (*b.* 1918) US evangelist

Martha Graham: Performing in *Judith* (1957)

Graham, Martha (1893–1991) US dancer, choreographer, and teacher

Grahame /gráy əm/, **Kenneth** (1859–1932) British writer

grail n 1 something that is eagerly sought after 2 **Grail** according to legend, the cup used by Jesus Christ at the Last Supper

grain n 1 cereal crops 2 a small seed 3 a tiny single piece 4 a small amount 5 the smallest unit of weight in various systems 6 any of the particles in a photographic emulsion that form an image 7 interference affecting a television image ■ v 1 *vti* form grains 2 *vt* give a grain or a grainy appearance to —**grained** adj ◇ **go against the grain** be contrary to somebody's natural tendencies, wishes, or feelings

Grainger /gráynjər/, **Percy** (1882–1961) Australian-born US pianist and composer

grainy /gráyni/ (-**ier**, -**iest**) adj 1 describes a photograph in which the image is not clear 2 resembling grains in size or texture —**graininess** n

gram[1], **gramme** n (*symbol* **g**) a metric unit of mass

gram[2] n an edible legume, e.g. green gram or black gram

-gram suffix 1 something written, drawn, or recorded ○ *mammogram* 2 a message delivered by a third party ○ *telegram*

grammar /grámmər/ n 1 the rules for forming words and putting them together 2 the rules that apply to words in a particular language 3 the quality of language used, in relation to standards of correctness ○ *bad grammar* 4 a book dealing with the grammar of a language

grammarian /grə máiri ən/ n a grammar expert

grammar school n a secondary school for children of high academic ability

grammatical /grə máttik'l/ adj 1 in or of the rules of grammar 2 correct in terms of grammar —**grammaticality** /grə mátti kálləti/ —**grammatically** adv

gramme n MEASURE = **gram**[1]

~~grammer~~ incorrect spelling of **grammar**

gramophone /grámmə fōn/ n a record player (*dated*)

Grampian Mountains /grámpi ən-/ mountain range in central Scotland that forms a natural division between the Highlands and Lowlands. Highest peak Ben Nevis 1,343 m/4,406 ft.

grampus /grámpəss/ (*pl same or* -**puses**) n a large dolphin with a blunt snout

gran n a grandmother (*infml*)

Granada /grə naádə/ city in S Spain, site of the Alhambra. Pop. 241,471 (1998).

granary /gránnəri/ (*pl* -**ries**) n a grain warehouse

Gran Chaco /gran chákō/ region in south-central South America, extending from S Bolivia through Paraguay to N Argentina

grand adj 1 impressive in appearance or style 2 ambitious and far-reaching 3 worthy of respect 4 haughty 5 very enjoyable ■ n (*infml*) 1 1,000 pounds in money 2 a grand piano —**grandly** adv —**grandness** n

grand- prefix one generation further removed ○ *granddaughter* ○ *grandfather*

grandad n = **granddad**

grandaddy n = **granddaddy**

~~granddaughter~~ incorrect spelling of **granddaughter**

Grand Canal main waterway of Venice, Italy. Length 3 km/2 mi.

Grand Canyon gorge in NW Arizona, carved by the Colorado River. Its width varies from 8 to 29 km/5 to 18 mi., and its depth can exceed 1.6 km/1 mi. Length 446 km/277 mi.

grandchild /grán chīld/ (*pl* -**children** /-children/) n a child's child

granddad /grán dad/, **grandad** n a grandfather (*infml*)

granddaddy /grán dadi/, **grandaddy** n the first or most impressive of its kind

granddaughter /grán dawtər/ n a child's daughter

grandee /gran dee/ n 1 a highly respected and influential person 2 a Spanish or Portuguese nobleman

grandeur /gránjər/ n impressive appearance or style

grandfather /gránd faathər/ n 1 a parent's father 2 a male ancestor —**grandfatherly** adj

grandfather clock n a tall clock that stands on the floor

grand finale n a final spectacular scene or performance

grandiloquence /gran dílləkwənss/ n a lofty way of speaking or writing —**grandiloquent** adj

grandiose /grándi ōss/ adj 1 pretentious and pompous 2 magnificent —**grandiosely** adv —**grandiosity** /grándi óssəti/ n

grand jury n in the United States and Canada, a jury called to decide if there are grounds for a criminal trial —**grand juror** n

grandma /grán maa/ n a grandmother (*infml*)

grand mal /graán mál/ n a form of epilepsy in which there is loss of consciousness and severe convulsions

grandmama /gránmə maa/ n a grandmother (*dated*)

grand master, grandmaster /grán maastər/ n

1 a top chess player 2 somebody who is outstanding in a particular field

grandmother /gránˈmuthər/ n 1 a parent's mother 2 a female ancestor —**grandmotherly** adj

Grand National n an annual British steeple-chase

grand opera n a serious opera in which all the words are sung

grandpa /gránˈpaa/ n a grandfather (infml)

grandparent /gránd pairənt/ n a parent's parent —**grandparental** /gránd pə rénťl/ adj

grand piano n a large harp-shaped piano with horizontal strings

Grand Prix /grón prée/ (pl same or **Grands Prix** /pronunc. same/) n 1 an important international car race 2 any important sports competition

grand slam n 1 the winning of all the major competitions in a series 2 any major sporting competition 3 in bridge and some other card games, an instance of winning all the tricks in a game

grandson /gránˈsun/ n a child's son

grandstand /gránd stand/ n 1 a structure, usually with a roof, containing rows of seats for spectators 2 the spectators in a grandstand ■ adj giving an unobstructed view ■ vi seek attention or admiration —**grandstander** n

grand total n a final total

grand tour n 1 a tour of several places or all the parts of a place 2 formerly, a tour of European cultural centres undertaken by young upper-class Englishmen as part of their education

~~grandure~~ incorrect spelling of **grandeur**

grange /graynj/ n 1 a large farmhouse 2 a granary or barn (archaic)

granite /gránnit/ n 1 a very hard coarse-grained rock. Use: building. 2 toughness of character

granny /gránni/ (pl -nies), **grannie** n a grandmother (infml)

granny flat n a flat in a family home for an elderly relative

granny knot n an incorrectly tied reef knot that slips

grant vt 1 comply with a request 2 allow something as a favour 3 acknowledge the truth of something ■ n a sum of money given by a government or organization for a specific purpose ◇ **take for granted** 1 fail to realize the value of 2 assume the truth of ◇ See note at **give**

Grant, Cary (1904–86) British-born US film actor

Grant, Ulysses S. (1822–85) Union army general and 18th president of the United States (1869–77)

granted /graàntid/ adv, conj although it is true

granular /gránnyōōlər/ adj 1 made up of granules 2 with the texture or appearance of granules —**granularity** /gránnyōō lárrəti/ n

granulate /gránnyōō layt/ (-lating, -lated) vti 1 form or make into granules 2 become or make grainy in texture or appearance —**granulation** /gránnyōō láysh'n/ n

granulated sugar n coarse white sugar

granule /gránˈyool/ n a small grain or particle

grape n 1 a small green or purple edible berry that grows in bunches on a vine 2 also **grapeshot** small iron balls fired simultaneously from a cannon

grapefruit /gráyp froot/ (pl same or -fruits) n 1 a large yellow or pink citrus fruit 2 the tree that produces grapefruit

grapevine /gráyp vīn/ n 1 a vine that bears grapes 2 the path along which information or rumour passes informally from person to person (infml)

graph n a diagram showing relationships between two or more variable quantities ■ vt put data on a graph

graph- prefix writing (before vowels) ○ graphology

-graph suffix 1 something written or drawn ○ digraph 2 an instrument for writing, drawing, or recording ○ seismograph

graphic /gráffik/ adj 1 vividly detailed 2 shown in writing 3 shown in pictures 4 also **graphical** of graphs 5 of drawing, printing, and the other graphic arts ■ n (often pl) 1 a picture produced by a computer 2 a book illustration —**graphically** adv —**graphicness** n

graphical user interface n a computer operating system that relies on the use of icons, menus, and a mouse

graphic arts npl artistic processes based on the use of lines rather than colour —**graphic artist** n

graphic design n the art or practice of designing books, magazines, or any medium that combines images and text —**graphic designer** n

graphic novel n a work of fiction for adults in the form of a comic strip

graphics /gráffiks/ n (+ sing verb) 1 the presentation of information in the form of diagrams and illustrations 2 the art of displaying, storing, and manipulating computer data as symbols, diagrams, or pictures

graphics card n a circuit board that enables a computer to display screen information

graphics tablet n an electronic drawing device used for entering designs into a computer

graphite /gráf īt/ n a soft black form of carbon. Use: lubricants, carbon fibres, pencil lead.

graphology /gra fóllaji/ n 1 the psychological study of handwriting 2 the linguistic study of writing —**graphological** /gráffa lójjik'l/ adj —**graphologist** n

graph paper n paper with a series of intersecting horizontal and vertical lines

-graphy suffix 1 a particular process or technique of writing or making an image ○ photo-

graphy **2** writing about or study of a particular subject ○ *biography*

grapnel /grápn'l/ n **1** *also* **grappling iron, grappling hook** a device with hooks on the end of a rope that can be thrown and attached to something **2** an anchor for a small boat

grapple /grápp'l/ v (-**pling**, -**pled**) **1** *vi* struggle with somebody physically **2** *vi* struggle to deal with something **3** *vt* grab hold of ■ *n* **1** a grapnel **2** a struggle

Grasmere /graáss meer/ village in NW England, on **Lake Grasmere**. Pop. 1,100 (1981).

grasp *vti* **1** take or try to take hold of somebody or something **2** take or try to take an opportunity **3** understand or try to understand something ■ *n* **1** a firm hold **2** understanding ○ *a poor grasp of the facts* **3** the ability to achieve something ○ *Success was within her grasp.* **4** control ○ *in the tyrant's grasp*

grasping /graásping/ adj greedy for money

grass n **1** (*pl* **grasses** *or* **same**) a low-growing green plant used to form lawns **2** a grass-covered area **3** (*pl* **grasses** *or* **same**) a hollow-stemmed green plant belonging to a group that includes many cereals **4** marijuana (*slang*) **6** an informer (*slang*) ■ v **1** *vti* cover an area with grass **2** *vi* be an informer (*slang*)

Grass, Günter (*b.* 1927) German writer and political activist

grasshopper /graáss hopər/ n a slender jumping insect with strong back legs

grassland /graáss land/ n **1** grass-covered land **2** pasture land

grass roots *npl* **1** the ordinary people of a community or organization **2** the origin or basis of something

grassroots /graáss roots/, **grass-roots** adj involving ordinary people

grass snake n a common nonpoisonous green snake

grassy /graássi/ (-**ier**, -**iest**) adj **1** grass-covered **2** like grass —**grassiness** n

grate[1] n **1** a framework of bars to keep solid fuel in a fireplace, stove, or furnace **2** a fireplace

grate[2] (**grating**, **grated**) v **1** *vti* make into small pieces using a grater **2** *vti* make or cause to make a harsh rubbing noise **3** *vi* be a source of irritation or annoyance **4** *vt* say in a harsh voice —**grated** adj

grateful /gráytf'l/ adj having a desire or reason to thank somebody —**gratefully** adv —**gratefulness** n

grater /gráytər/ n a device with sharp-edged holes on which something such as cheese can be rubbed to reduce it to small pieces

gratify /grátti fī/ (-**fies**, -**fied**) vt **1** make somebody feel pleased or satisfied **2** fulfil a desire —**gratification** /gráttifi káysh'n/ n —**gratifying** adj —**gratifyingly** adv

grating[1] /gráyting/ n a metal grille

grating[2] /gráyting/ adj **1** unpleasantly rough or harsh **2** irritating or annoying —**gratingly** adv

gratis /gráttiss, gráytiss, graáa-/ adj, adv received or given without cost or payment

gratitude /grátti tyood/ n a feeling of being grateful to somebody

gratuitous /grə tyóo itəss/ adj **1** unnecessary and unjustifiable **2** received or given without cost or payment —**gratuitously** adv —**gratuitousness** n

gratuity /grə tyóo əti/ (*pl* -**ties**) n **1** an extra sum of money given in appreciation **2** a sum of money given to somebody on retirement

grave[1] /grayv/ n a burial place in the ground

grave[2] /grayv/ (**graver**, **gravest**) adj solemn or serious in manner —**gravely** adv —**graveness** n

grave[3] /graav/ n the mark (') placed above a vowel to indicate a particular pronunciation ■ adj with a grave accent

gravedigger /gráyv digər/ n somebody who digs graves

gravel /grávv'l/ n small stones used for paths and in concrete ■ vt (-**elling**, -**elled**) cover with gravel

gravelly /gráov'li/ adj **1** sounding rough or harsh **2** like or covered with gravel

graven image n a carving of a god

Graves, Robert (1895–1985) British poet and novelist

graveside /gráyv sīd/ n the area around an open grave

gravestone /gráyv stōn/ n a stone that marks a grave

graveyard /gráyv yaard/ n **1** an area where people are buried **2** a dumping place for old and unwanted objects and equipment

graveyard shift n a period of work after midnight

gravid /grávvid/ adj pregnant with young or eggs (*technical*) —**gravidity** /grə víddəti/ n —**gravidly** adv

gravitas /grávvi tass, -taass/ n seriousness of tone or behaviour

gravitate /grávvi tayt/ (-**tating**, -**tated**) v **1** *vi* move gradually and steadily towards somebody or something **2** *vti* move or cause to move under the influence of gravity

gravitation /grávvi táysh'n/ n **1** gradual and steady movement in the direction of somebody or something **2** the mutual force of attraction between all things that have mass —**gravitational** adj —**gravitationally** adv

gravitational constant n a numerical factor relating force, mass, and distance

gravity /grávvəti/ n **1** the force of attraction that an astronomical object such as the Earth exerts on objects on or near its surface **2** gravitation **3** the seriousness of something considered in terms of its consequences **4** solemnity and seriousness in behaviour

gravy /gráyvi/ n a sauce made with meat juices

ORIGIN In the medieval period *gravy* was a kind of spiced white sauce. It came to be applied to meat juices in the late 16C. The form of the English word seems to be the result of misreading *n* for *u* (used for both *u* and *v* in the manuscripts of the time) in the French form *grané*.

gravy boat *n* a container for serving gravy

gravy train *n* a source of easy money *(infml)*

gray[1] *adj, n, vi* US = **grey**

gray[2] *n* (*symbol* **Gy**) a unit of absorbed radiation

ORIGIN The unit is named after the English radiologist L. H. Gray (1905–65).

Gray, Thomas (1716–71) British poet

gray scale *n* a scale for the shades of grey used in printing

Graz /graats/ city in SE Austria. Pop. 240,513 (1999).

graze[1] (**grazing, grazed**) *v* **1** *vti* eat grass in fields **2** *vt* allow animals to eat grass **3** *vt* use land for feeding animals **4** *vi* eat snacks throughout the day instead of regular meals *(slang)*

graze[2] *v* (**grazing, grazed**) **1** *vti* touch something lightly **2** *vt* break the skin slightly ■ *n* **1** a slight break in the skin **2** a light touch

grease *n* /greess/ **1** animal fat **2** a thick lubricant **3** oil for the hair ■ *vt* /greess, greez/ (**greasing, greased**) put grease on something ◇ **grease somebody's palm** *or* **hand** bribe somebody *(infml)*

grease gun *n* a device for forcing grease into machinery

greasepaint /gréess paynt/ *n* actors' makeup

greaseproof paper /gréess proof-/ *n* grease-resistant paper. Use: in cooking, preparing, or wrapping food.

greasy /gréessi, gréezi/ (**-ier, -iest**) *adj* **1** covered with, containing, or caused by grease **2** having excessive natural oils **3** slippery **4** unpleasantly friendly or flattering —**greasily** *adv* —**greasiness** *n*

great /grayt/ *adj* **1** impressively large **2** large in number ○ *a great crowd of well-wishers* **3** bigger than others of the same kind **4** much ○ *It gives me great pleasure to introduce our speaker tonight.* **5** lasting a long time **6** very significant or important **7** exceptionally talented ○ *a great artist* **8** powerful **9** able to deal with something well *(infml)* ○ *great with kids* **10** very good ○ *great food* **11** very suitable *(infml)* ○ *shoes great for walking* **12** showing much interest in something ○ *a great opera fan* ■ *n* somebody of lasting fame or influence —**greatly** *adv* —**greatness** *n*

great- *prefix* **1** being a parent of a grandparent ○ *great-grandmother* **2** being a grandchild's child ○ *great-grandson* **3** being a parent's aunt or uncle ○ *great-aunt* **4** being a nephew's or niece's child ○ *great-nephew*

great ape *n* a large ape such as a gorilla, chimpanzee, or orang-utan

Great Australian Bight inlet of the Indian Ocean stretching 1,100 km/685 mi. from Cape Pasley in Western Australia to Cape Carnot in South Australia

Great Barrier Reef chain of coral reefs in the Coral Sea, off the coast of Queensland, Australia. Length 2,010 km/1,250 mi.

Great Britain island of NW Europe, comprising England, Scotland, and Wales

great circle *n* a circle on the surface of a sphere that has the same radius and centre as the sphere

greatcoat /gráyt kōt/ *n* an overcoat

Great Dane *n* a very large dog with long legs, a square head, and a deep muzzle

Great Dividing Range system of mountain ranges and plateaus extending along the coast of E Australia. Highest peak Mt Kosciuzko 2,228 m/7,310 ft.

Greater Antilles /gráytər an tílleez/ island group in the N Caribbean Sea, comprising Cuba, Jamaica, Hispaniola, and Puerto Rico

Greater Sunda Islands /-súndə-/ island group of Indonesia that includes Sumatra, Java, Borneo, and Sulawesi

~~greatful~~ incorrect spelling of **grateful**

great-grandchild *n* a child of a grandchild

Great Lakes group of five freshwater lakes in north-central North America, comprising Lakes Superior, Michigan, Huron, Erie, and Ontario

Great Plains vast grassland region in central North America, stretching from central Canada to S Texas

Great Rift Valley depression of SW Asia and E Africa extending more than 4,830 km/3,000 mi. from the valley of the River Jordan in Syria to Mozambique

Great Salt Lake shallow body of salt water in NW Utah

Great Sandy Desert desert in NW Australia

Great Victoria Desert desert of Western Australia and South Australia

great white shark *n* a large grey-brown and white shark that feeds on large fish and marine mammals

grebe /greeb/ (*pl* **grebes** *or* **same**) *n* a freshwater diving bird with lobed toes

Grecian /greésh'n/ *adj* in the ancient Greek style of architecture or sculpture —**Grecianize** *vt*

Greco /grékō/, **El** (1541–1614) Greek-born Spanish painter

Greco-Roman *adj* ANCIENT HIST, ARTS, WRESTLING = **Graeco-Roman**

Greece /greess/ country in SE Europe, comprising the southernmost part of the Balkan Peninsula and numerous islands in the E Mediterranean. Cap. Athens. Pop. 10,623,835 (2001).

greed *n* **1** the habit of eating too much **2** a strong desire for more of something than is needed

greedy /greédi/ (**-ier, -iest**) *adj* **1** eating too much **2** wanting much more of something than is needed —**greedily** *adv* —**greediness** *n*

Greek *n* **1** somebody from Greece **2** the language of modern or ancient Greece ■ *adj*

1 of Greece or the Greeks **2** of the Greek language

green *adj* **1** of the colour of grass, between yellow and blue in the spectrum **2** having edible green leaves **3** grassy or leafy **4** *also* **Green** advocating protection of the environment **5** produced in a way that minimizes environmental harm **6** not ripe **7** raw and unsmoked **8** describes unseasoned wood **9** envious or jealous **10** sickly-looking **11** naive and lacking experience ■ *n* **1** the colour of grass **2** a grassy area, especially one surrounding a golf hole **3** *Scotland* a grassy area belonging to a house or block of flats **4** foliage **5** *also* **Green** an advocate of protection of the environment ■ **greens** *npl* vegetables with green leaves and stems ■ *v* **1** *vti* become or make green **2** *vt* plant trees in an urban area —**greenly** *adv* —**greenness** *n*

green bean *n* a bean with a green pod

green belt *n* **1** an area of undeveloped land around a city **2** an area of irrigated land bordering a desert

green card *n* **1** an identification card and work permit issued in the United States to nationals of other countries **2** a driving insurance document for use in Europe

Greene /green/, **Graham** (1904–91) British writer

greenery /greenəri/ *n* **1** green plants **2** leaves and branches used as decoration

green-eyed monster *n* jealousy

green fingers *npl* gardening skill —**green-fingered** *adj*

greenfly /green flī/ (*pl same or* **-flies**) *n* a small green aphid

greengage /green gayj/ *n* **1** a type of greenish plum **2** a tree that produces greengages

ORIGIN The **greengage** is named after Sir William Gage (1657–1727), who introduced it to England.

greengrocer /green grōssər/ *n* **1** a dealer in fresh fruit and vegetables **2** *also* **greengrocer's** (*pl same*) a greengrocer's shop

greenhorn /green hawrn/ *n* an inexperienced and unsophisticated person who is easily duped ◊ See note at **beginner**

greenhouse /green howss/ (*pl* **-houses** /-howziz/) *n* a glass or transparent structure in which to grow plants that need protection from the elements

greenhouse effect *n* the warming of the Earth's atmosphere as a result of atmospheric pollution

greenhouse gas *n* a gas that contributes to the warming of the Earth's atmosphere

greening /greening/ *n* **1** the process of planting trees and other vegetation in an area **2** the process of becoming more aware, or of increasing others' awareness, of environmental issues

green keeper *n* somebody who maintains a golf course

Greenland /greenland/ island of Denmark, in the North Atlantic and Arctic oceans, off NE Canada. Pop. 56,352 (2001). —**Greenlander** *n*

green light *n* **1** a green-coloured light that signals traffic to proceed **2** permission to begin doing something

green man *n* a symbol on a pedestrian crossing that indicates that it is safe to cross

Green Mountains mountain range in the Appalachian system, extending from E Canada to Vermont

green paper *n* in the United Kingdom and Canada, a policy document for discussion in parliament

Green Party *n* an environmentalist political party

Greenpeace /green peess/ *n* an international environmentalist pressure group

green pepper *n* an unripe sweet pepper

green pound *n* the British pound in EU agricultural trading

green revolution *n* the introduction of modern farming techniques to increase crop production

greenroom /green room, -rōōm/ *n* a lounge in a TV studio or concert hall where performers can relax

green tea *n* tea made from tea leaves that have been dried but not fermented

Greenway /green way/, **Francis Howard** (1777–1837) British-born Australian architect

Greenwich /grénnich, -ij/ borough of London, on the River Thames, site of the prime meridian, which passes through the Royal Greenwich Observatory. Pop. 211,141 (1991).

Greenwich Mean Time *n* the time in a zone that includes the prime meridian

Greer, Germaine (*b.* 1939) Australian writer and feminist

greet[1] *vt* **1** welcome **2** address courteously **3** address in a letter **4** respond or react to ○ *The news was greeted with dismay.* —**greeter** *n*

greet[2] *vi Scotland* (*nonstandard*) **1** weep **2** complain

greeting /greeting/ *n* **1** a friendly gesture **2** an act of welcoming somebody ■ **greetings** *npl* a message of good wishes

greetings card *n* a decorated card used to send greetings

gregarious /gri gáiri əss/ *adj* **1** friendly and sociable **2** describes organisms that live in groups —**gregariously** *adv* —**gregariousness** *n*

Gregg, Sir Norman McAlister (1892–1966) Australian ophthalmologist

Gregorian calendar /gri gáwri ən-/ *n* the calendar in general use worldwide

ORIGIN The **Gregorian calendar** is named after Pope Gregory XIII, who introduced it in 1582.

Gregorian chant *n* a Roman Catholic liturgical chant that is sung without accompaniment

ORIGIN The **Gregorian chant** is named after

Pope Gregory I (540?–604), who is credited with introducing it.

Gregory XIII /gréggəri/ (1502–85) pope (1572–85)

gremlin /grémmlin/ n an imaginary creature that damages machinery (infml)

Grenada /grə náydə/ island state in the SE Caribbean Sea, comprising the island of Grenada and some of the S **Grenadines**. Cap. St George's. Pop. 89,227 (2001). —**Grenadian** n, adj

grenade /gri náyd/ n 1 a small bomb that is thrown by hand or fired from a small weapon 2 a sealed glass projectile containing tear gas or another chemical

---

ORIGIN Grenade comes from a French word originally meaning 'pomegranate', which was its first sense in English, in the mid-16C. The use of the word for an explosive device is recorded from the late 16C. The name was suggested by the resemblance of the shape of early grenades to a pomegranate.

---

grenadier /grénnə deér/ (pl same or -diers) n 1 formerly, a grenade-carrying soldier 2 a type of sea fish with no tail fin

Grenadier, Grenadier guard n a soldier in the Guards ■ **Grenadiers** npl in the British army, the first regiment of the Guards division

grenadine /grénnə deen/ n a syrup made from pomegranates. Use: in cocktails.

Grenoble /grə nṓb'l/ city in SE France. Pop. 153,317 (1999).

grew past tense of **grow**

grey n 1 the colour of ash 2 something that is grey, especially an item of clothing ■ vi turn grey —**greyness** n

Grey, Lady Jane (1537–54) queen of England (1553)

grey area n an unclear situation or subject

greyhound /gráy hownd/ n a slim fast dog

ORIGIN Greyhounds do not get their name from the colour grey – it has never been a significant characteristic of the breed. The first element comes from an ancient root meaning 'bitch'.

---

greylag /gráy lag/, **greylag goose** n a common wild goose with light brownish-grey plumage and an orange or pink bill

grey literature n publications that have no commercial purpose

grey matter n 1 intelligence or brains (infml) 2 the brownish-grey tissue in the brain

grey squirrel n a tree squirrel with grey fur

grey whale n a baleen whale of the N Pacific

grid n 1 a network of reference lines on a map 2 any pattern of adjacent squares 3 a grating made of bars 4 a network for distributing electricity, gas, or water

griddle /grídd'l/ n 1 a flat metal cooking surface 2 a sieve used by miners ■ vt (-dling, -dled) cook on a griddle

griddlecake /grídd'l kayk/ n a cake similar to a scone, cooked on a griddle

gridiron /gríd ī ərn/ n 1 a grill on which food is cooked 2 a grating made of bars 3 an American football field 4 the game of American football (infml)

gridlock /gríd lok/ n 1 a traffic jam 2 a deadlock —**gridlocked** adj

grief /greef/ n 1 intense sorrow 2 a cause of intense sorrow 3 annoyance or trouble (infml)

grief-stricken adj deeply affected by grief

Grieg /greeg/, **Edvard** (1843–1907) Norwegian composer

grievance /greévənss/ n 1 something regarded as a reason to complain 2 resentment 3 a formal objection

grieve /greev/ (**grieving, grieved**) vti experience or cause somebody to experience intense sorrow —**griever** n

grievous /greévəss/ adj 1 very serious or significant 2 very bad or severe —**grievously** adv

grievous bodily harm n severe physical injury caused to somebody intentionally

griffin /gríffin/, **griffon** /gríffən/, **gryphon** n a mythical monster that is part eagle and part lion

Griffith /gríffith/, **D. W.** (1875–1948) US film director

grill /gril/ v 1 vti cook under or over direct heat 2 vt interrogate (infml) ■ n 1 a part of a cooker radiating heat downwards 2 a flat surface of metal bars used for grilling 3 food cooked on a grill ◊ See note at **question**

SPELLCHECK Do not confuse the spelling of **grill** and **grille** ('a lattice of bars'), which sound similar.

---

grille /gril/ n a pattern or lattice of bars, e.g. in the front of a window or the radiator of a vehicle ◊ See note at **grill**

grim (**grimmer, grimmest**) adj 1 depressingly gloomy 2 forbidding in appearance 3 sternly serious —**grimly** adv —**grimness** n

grimace /grímməss, gri máyss/ n a contorted facial expression indicating disgust or pain —**grimace** vi

grime n accumulated or ingrained dirt —**grimy** adj

Grimm, Jacob (1785–1863) and his brother **Wilhelm Karl** (1786–1859) German philologists and folklorists

Grim Reaper n death personified

grin (**grinning, grinned**) vi smile broadly —**grin** n

grind /grīnd/ v (**ground** /grownd/, **ground**) 1 vti crush into very small pieces 2 vti rub together with a grating noise ○ grinding her teeth 3 vt push something down with a twisting motion 4 vt US mince food 5 vt smooth or sharpen something by rubbing or friction ■ n 1 something boring and repetitive (infml) 2 the process of grinding something or the texture obtained from grinding ○ a fine grind of coffee 3 a grinding noise —**grindingly** adv

☐ **grind on** *vi* continue in an unrelenting way

☐ **grind out** *vt* produce mechanically as a result of boredom with routine ○ *grinding out articles for the local paper*

grindstone /grínd stōn/ *n* a stone or wheel used for grinding, sharpening, or polishing

grip *n* **1** a firm hold **2** a manner of holding something **3** a handle or other holding device **4** the capability of something not to slip ○ *shoes with grip* **5** control or power ○ *in the grip of fear* **6** a hairgrip **7** a small suitcase ■ *v* (**gripping, gripped**) **1** *vt* grasp or hold firmly **2** *vti* adhere to a surface **3** *vt* capture the interest or attention of —**gripping** *adj*

gripe (*infml*) *vi* (**griping, griped**) grumble constantly ■ *n* a minor complaint —**griping** *adj* ◊ See note at **complain**

gripe water *n* a medicine to relieve colic in babies

Gris /greess/, **Juan** (1887–1927) Spanish-born French artist

grisly /grízli/ (**-lier, -liest**) *adj* gruesomely unpleasant or horrible —**grisliness** *n*

SPELLCHECK Do not confuse the spelling of **grisly** and **grizzly** (a type of bear), which sound similar.

---

grist *n* grain that is ground into flour ◊ **grist to the** *or* **somebody's mill** a potential source of advantage

gristle /gríss'l/ *n* tough cartilage in meat —**gristly** *adj*

grit *n* **1** sand or stone particles **2** firmness of character ■ *vt* (**gritting, gritted**) **1** clench the teeth **2** cover a surface, e.g. an icy road, with grit

grits *n US* coarsely ground maize that is boiled and eaten (*+ sing or pl verb*)

gritty /grítti/ (**-tier, -tiest**) *adj* **1** courageous or resolute **2** starkly realistic **3** like or covered with grit —**grittily** *adv* —**grittiness** *n*

grizzle /grízz'l/ (**-zling, -zled**) *vi* cry and whine (*infml; refers to young children*)

grizzled /grízz'ld/ *adj* **1** streaked with grey hairs ○ *his grizzled beard* **2** grey-haired

grizzly bear /grízzli-/, **grizzly** (*pl* **-ies**) *n* a large brown North American bear ◊ See note at **grisly**

groan *n* **1** a long low cry of pain or misery **2** a loud creaking sound ■ *v* **1** *vt* utter or express with a groan **2** *vi* make a loud creaking sound ○ *The floorboards groaned under their weight.*

grocer /grṓssər/ *n* **1** a seller of food and other household goods **2** *also* **grocer's** (*pl* same), **grocery** a grocer's shop

---

ORIGIN A **grocer** was originally a 'wholesaler', literally somebody selling 'in gross'. The word goes back through French to Latin *grossus*.

---

groceries /grṓssəriz/ *npl* food and other household goods

grog *n* **1** a mixture of rum and water **2** *ANZ* alcoholic drink (*infml*)

ORIGIN Grog comes from the nickname (Old

Grogram) of Admiral Edward Vernon (1684–1757), the British admiral who introduced the practice of watering down the rum that was served to sailors in the Royal Navy. His nickname is said to come from his habit of wearing a 'grogram' cloak. Grogram was a coarse fabric whose name derives from French *gros grain* 'coarse grain'.

---

groggy /gróggi/ (**-gier, -giest**) *adj* weak or dizzy —**groggily** *adv* —**grogginess** *n*

groin *n* the area between the thighs and the abdomen

grommet /grómmit, grúmm-/, **grummet** /grúmm-/ *n* **1** a protective eyelet, or a ring that reinforces one **2** a tube for draining the middle ear

groom *n* **1** a bridegroom **2** somebody who cares for horses ■ *v* **1** *vti* clean the fur, skin, or feathers of an animal **2** *vt* neaten or care for the appearance of yourself or somebody else ○ *a well-groomed young man* **3** *vt* train or prepare for a particular position ○ *being groomed for the presidency*

groove *n* **1** a narrow channel in a surface **2** a settled routine (*infml*) —**groove** *vt* —**grooved** *adj*

groovy /grṓovi/ (**-ier, -iest**) *adj* fashionable or excellent (*slang dated*) —**groovily** *adv* —**grooviness** *n*

grope (**groping, groped**) *v* **1** *vi* search by feeling ○ *groping for the light switch* **2** *vi* strive blindly or uncertainly ○ *groping for inspiration* **3** *vt* feel your way, e.g. in the dark **4** *vt* fondle somebody, often roughly or awkwardly (*infml*) —**grope** *n*

Gropius /grṓpi əss/, **Walter** (1883–1969) German-born US architect and educator

gross /grōss/ *adj* **1** measured or counted prior to deductions ○ *the gross weight of the shipment* **2** flagrantly wrong ○ *gross misconduct* **3** vulgar or coarse **4** extremely overweight (*infml*) **5** disgusting (*infml*) ■ *n* **1** (*pl* same) a quantity of 144 **2** (*pl* **grosses**) a gross amount ■ *vt* earn before deductions ■ *adv* before or without deductions ○ *paid gross* —**grossly** *adv* —**grossness** *n*

gross domestic product *n* the value of goods and services produced by a country excluding foreign investment income

gross national product *n* the value of goods and services produced by a country including foreign investment income

grotesque /grō tésk/ *adj* **1** strangely distorted ○ *grotesque shadows* **2** bizarre or incongruous —**grotesque** *n* —**grotesquely** *adv* —**grotesqueness** *n*

ORIGIN Grotesque came through French from Italian *grottesca* 'like a grotto'. The Italian word was applied to wall paintings discovered in excavations of ancient buildings, many of which depicted fantastical human and animal forms interwoven with flowers and foliage.

---

grotto /gróttō/ (*pl* **-toes** *or* **-tos**) *n* a natural or imitation cave with interesting features

grotty /gróttí/ (**-tier, -tiest**) *adj* (*infml*) **1** generally unpleasant **2** unwell —**grottily** *adv* —**grottiness** *n*

grouch /growch/ (*infml*) *vi* complain ■ *n* **1** a complaint **2** a habitually complaining or bad-tempered person —**grouchy** *adj*

ground[1] /grownd/ *n* **1** the surface of the land **2** earth or soil **3** an area of land used for a specific purpose (*often pl*) o *burial ground* **4** an area of knowledge or discussion o *Most of the ground had been covered in an earlier lecture.* **5** a reason or foundation (*often pl*) o *grounds for believing his story* ■ **grounds** *npl* **1** land surrounding a building **2** dregs or sediment ■ *v* **1** *vt* teach somebody the basics (*usually passive*) o *was well grounded in machine operation* **2** *vt* base an idea, decision, or belief on a strong foundation o *a decision that was grounded in personal experience* **3** *vt* prevent a pilot or aircraft from flying **4** *vt* make a child stay at home as a punishment (*infml*) **5** *vti* go or run aground **6** *vt* put something on the ground ◊ **break fresh** *or* **new ground** do or discover something new ◊ **get off the ground** get started or operating ◊ **hit the ground running** begin to deal with a new situation without delay (*infml*)

ground[2] /grownd/ past participle, past tense of **grind**

groundbreaking /grównd brayking/ *adj* new and innovative —**groundbreaker** *n*

ground cover *n* dense low-growing plants

ground floor *n* the floor of a building at street level

ground glass *n* **1** glass with a roughened surface **2** glass particles. Use: abrasive.

groundless /grówndləss/ *adj* not justified or true —**groundlessly** *adv* —**groundlessness** *n*

groundnut /grównd nut/ *n* **1** a peanut **2** the edible tuber of a climbing vine **3** (*pl* **groundnuts** *or same*) a plant that produces groundnuts

ground plan *n* a plan of the floor of a building

ground rent *n* a sum paid to lease land

ground rule *n* (*often pl*) **1** a fundamental rule **2** in sport, a rule that is specific to a particular place of play

groundsheet /grównd sheet/ *n* a waterproof sheet placed on the ground, e.g. in a tent

groundsman /grówndzmən/ (*pl* **-men** /-mən/) *n* somebody maintaining a sports ground or the grounds of a building

ground squirrel *n* a ground-dwelling burrowing squirrel

groundswell /grównd swel/ *n* **1** a deep wide movement of the sea **2** a rising general feeling o *a groundswell of public opinion*

ground water *n* underground water

groundwork /grównd wurk/ *n* basic preparatory tasks

ground zero *n* **1** the point above or below a nuclear explosion **2** the most basic level or starting point o *learning programming from ground zero* **3 Ground Zero** the huge debris field resulting from the terrorist attacks on the World Trade Center towers in New York City on 11 September 2001

group /groop/ *n* **1** a number of people or things considered or placed together **2** a band of musicians **3** a number of companies under common control ■ *vti* form a group ■ *adj* of or in a group or groups o *a group practice* o *group activities* —**grouping** *n*

group captain *n* an officer in the Royal Air Force of a rank above wing commander

groupie /groópi/ *n* a highly, often excessively, enthusiastic fan, e.g. of a film star or a popular musician or band (*infml*)

group therapy *n* psychological treatment involving group sessions for discussing personal problems

groupware /groóp wair/ *n* computer software for use by groups

grouse[1] /growss/ (*pl same*) *n* a reddish-brown ground-dwelling game bird

grouse[2] /growss/ (**grousing, groused**) *vi* complain (*infml*) —**grouse** *n* ◊ See note at **complain**

grout /growt/ *n* mortar for filling gaps, especially between tiles ■ **grouts** *npl* dregs ■ *vt* apply grout to

grove /grōv/ *n* a group or plantation of trees

grovel /gróvv'l/ (**-elling, -elled**) *vi* **1** behave in a servile way **2** crawl or lie face down on the ground —**groveller** *n* —**grovellingly** *adv*

grow /grō/ (**grew** /groo/, **grown** /grōn/) *v* **1** *vi* become larger or greater **2** *vti* develop naturally o *Plants won't grow in this soil.* o *grow a moustache* **3** *vi* be a product of something o *Hatred grew out of mutual ignorance.* **4** *vi* become o *The night grew cold.* **5** *vt* develop and expand o *an attempt to grow the business* —**grower** *n*

□ **grow into** *vt* grow or develop to fit

□ **grow on** *vt* gradually become more pleasing to o *a song that grows on you*

□ **grow out of** *vt* become too big or mature for

□ **grow up** *vi* **1** become an adult **2** behave more maturely

growbag /grō bag/ *n* a bag for growing plants in

growing pains *npl* **1** pains in the limbs of a child or adolescent **2** early problems

growl /growl/ *vti* **1** make a low hostile sound in the throat **2** speak, say something, or communicate with a growling sound —**growl** *n*

grown-up *adj* **1** fully mature **2** for adults ■ *n* an adult, or somebody who is an adult and behaves like one

growth /grōth/ *n* **1** the process of growing **2** an increase **3** something that has grown o *three days' growth of beard* **4** a formation of tissue such as a tumour, with no physiological function ■ *adj* expanding or developing o *growth industries*

groyne /groyn/ *n* a sea wall preventing land erosion

Grozny /gróznī/, **Groznyy** capital of Chechnya. Pop. 372,742 (1995).

grub v (**grubbing, grubbed**) 1 vt dig something up, especially without proper tools 2 vt remove roots and stumps from the ground 3 vi engage in a search through or under things ■ n 1 a larva 2 food (infml)

grubby /grúbbi/ (**-bier, -biest**) adj 1 dirty 2 contemptible or sordid —**grubbily** adv —**grubbiness** n◊ See note at **dirty**

grubstake /grúb stayk/ US, Can n supplies or money given to a prospector or entrepreneur in return for a share in any future profits ■ vt (**-staking, -staked**) give a grubstake to —**grubstaker** n

grudge n a feeling of resentment ■ vt (**grudging, grudged**) 1 give something reluctantly 2 envy somebody or something —**grudging** adj —**grudgingly** adv

gruel /grooʊ əl/ n thin porridge

gruelling /grooʊ əling/ adj extremely arduous —**gruellingly** adv

gruesome /grooʊssəm/ adj sickening or horrifying ○ gruesome photographs of the accident —**gruesomely** adv—**gruesomeness** n

gruff adj 1 surly 2 sounding rough or harsh —**gruffly** adv—**gruffness** n

grumble /grúmb'l/ vi (**-bling, -bled**) vi complain or mutter discontentedly —**grumble** n —**grumbly** adj◊ See note at **complain**

grump n a bad-tempered or sullen person (infml)

grumpy /grúmpi/ (**-ier, -iest**) adj bad-tempered or sullen —**grumpily** adv—**grumpiness** n

grunge /grunj/ n 1 rock music with punk and heavy metal elements 2 a scruffy fashion style —**grungy** adj

grunt v 1 vi make the noise of a pig 2 vti speak, say something, or communicate in a gruff or inarticulate way ■ n 1 a grunting sound 2 a tropical sea fish that grunts

Gruyère /grooʊ yair/ n a hard mild Swiss cheese with holes in it

gryphon /gríff'n/ n LEGEND = **griffin**

gsoh abbr good sense of humour (in personal columns)

GST abbr goods and services tax

G-string n a piece of material covering the pubic area

guacamole /gwaʹakə móli/ n spiced mashed avocados and tomatoes

Guadalajara /gwaʹadələ haʹarə/ capital of Jalisco State, in west-central Mexico. Pop. 1,633,216 (1995).

Guadalcanal /gwaʹadəlkə nál/ largest of the Solomon Islands, in the SW Pacific Ocean

Guadeloupe /gwaʹadə loóp/ an overseas department of France consisting of a group of islands in the E Caribbean. Cap. Basse-Terre. Pop. 431,170 (2001).

~~guage~~ incorrect spelling of **gauge**

Guam /gwaam/ largest of the Mariana Islands, in the NW Pacific Ocean, an unincorporated territory of the United States. Cap. Agana. Pop. 157,557 (2001). —**Guamanian** /gwaa máyni ən/ n, adj

Guangzhou /gwáng jó/ capital and chief port of **Guangdong Province**, S China. Pop. 4,490,000 (1995).

guano /gwaʹanó/ n 1 the droppings of birds, bats, or seals 2 a fertilizer consisting of guano

Guantánamo Bay /gwan taʹanəmó-/ inlet of the Caribbean Sea in SE Cuba. It is the site of a major US naval base.

guaraní /gwaʹarə neʹe/ (pl **-nies** or **-nís**) n the main unit of Paraguayan currency

guarantee /gárrən teʹe/ n 1 an assurance that something will happen ○ no guarantee of success 2 a promise of quality stating that faulty goods or work will be replaced, repaired, or redone 3 a promise to be responsible for somebody else's debts or obligations ■ vt (**-teed**) 1 assure or promise something 2 give a guarantee for goods or work 3 accept responsibility for somebody else's debts or obligations

guarantor /gárrən táwr/ n somebody who gives a guarantee ◊ See note at **backer**

guaranty /gárrən teʹe/ (pl **-ties**) n 1 a guarantee of responsibility for debts or obligations 2 the giving of something as security for a promise, or something so given ◊ See note at **backer**

guard /gaard/ vt 1 watch over to protect somebody or something 2 watch over to prevent the escape of a captive 3 control passage through a means of access ○ sentries guarding the gates ■ n 1 somebody who guards 2 a ceremonial escort 3 also **Guard** a member of a regiment originally protecting a sovereign 4 the act or responsibility of guarding 5 a protective device or cover to prevent injury 6 a means of protection ○ as a guard against inflation 7 defence ○ while her guard was down ◊ See note at **safeguard**

☐ **guard against** vt take precautions against

guard dog n a dog used for protection

guarded /gaʹardid/ adj wary or noncommittal —**guardedly** adv—**guardedness** n◊ See note at **cautious**

guardhouse /gaard howss/ (pl **-houses** /-howziz/) n a military building housing guards and prisoners

guardian /gaʹardi ən/ n 1 a protector 2 somebody legally responsible for another, especially a minor —**guardianship** n

guardian angel n an angel supposed to look after a particular person

guard of honour n a body of troops acting as a ceremonial escort

guardrail /gaʹard rayl/ n a safety rail

guardroom /gaʹard room, -room/ n a room for military guards on duty or for military prisoners

Guarneri /gwaa nyérri/ family of Italian violin makers including **Andrea** (1626–98) and his grandson **Giuseppe Antonio** (1687–1745)

~~Guatamala~~ incorrect spelling of **Guatemala**

Guatemala /gwaʹatə maʹalə/ country in Central America, on the Gulf of Honduras. Cap.

Guatemala City. Pop. 12,974,361 (2001).
—**Guatemalan** *adj, n*

Guatemala City capital of Guatemala. Pop. 1,167,495 (1995).

guava /gwaávə/ *n* **1** a pear-shaped tropical fruit with red or yellow-green skin. Use: jam. **2** a tree that produces guavas

gubbins /gúbbinz/ *(infml) n* *(pl* **gubbinses)** a nameless gadget ■ *npl* oddments

gubernatorial /gòobərnə táwri əl/ *adj* of a governor

guck *n* an unpleasant substance *(infml)*

guernsey /gúrnzi/ *(pl* -**seys)** *n* **1** *also* **Guernsey** a brown-and-white dairy cow **2** a woollen sweater typically worn by sailors and fishermen **3** *Aus* a sleeveless sports shirt or jumper

Guernsey /gúrnzi/ second largest of the Channel Islands, in the English Channel off France. Pop. 64,342 (2001).

guerrilla /gə rílllə, ge-/, **guerilla** *n* a member of an irregular paramilitary unit, usually politically motivated ◊ See note at **gorilla**

guess /gess/ *v* **1** *vti* form an opinion about something without full information ○ *Guess where I've been.* **2** *vt* arrive at the correct answer or conclusion by guessing ○ *I guessed it would be you.* **3** *vt US, Can* think or suppose ○ *I guess I'll have the steak.* ■ *n* **1** an opinion formed by guessing **2** an act or result of guessing ○ *Have another guess.* —**guessable** *adj* ◊ **anybody's guess** something that cannot be reliably predicted *(infml)*

guesstimate /géstimət/ *n* an estimate based on guessing *(infml)* —**guesstimate** /-mayt/ *vti*

guesswork /géss wurk/ *n* the process or result of guessing

guest /gest/ *n* **1** a recipient of hospitality **2** a customer of a hotel or restaurant **3** somebody invited to join others **4** somebody making a special appearance on a show ■ *vi* make a special appearance on a show ■ *adj* **1** appearing as a guest ○ *a guest star* **2** for guests

guest beer *n* a beer available in a bar for a short time

guesthouse /gést howss/ *(pl* -**houses** /-howziz/) *n* **1** a small hotel **2** *US* a house for visitors

guest of honour *n* an important guest

guestroom /gést room, -rōom/ *n* a bedroom for guests

guest worker *n* a nonresident foreign worker

AKG London
Che Guevara

Guevara /gə vaárə/, **Che** (1928–67) Argentine-born South American revolutionary leader

guff *n* nonsense or empty talk *(infml)*

guffaw /gə fáw/ *vi* laugh loudly and raucously —**guffaw** *n*

GUI *abbr* graphical user interface

guidance /gíd'nss/ *n* **1** advice **2** leadership **3** electronic flight-control and targeting systems

guide /gīd/ *v* **(guiding, guided) 1** *vti* show somebody the way **2** *vt* direct or steer **3** *vt* advise or influence ○ *Be guided by your conscience.* ■ *n* **1** somebody or something that guides **2** somebody who leads or supervises a tour **3** *also* **guidebook** a tourist information book **4** a source of information ○ *a TV guide* **5** *also* **Guide** a member of the Guide Association

SYNONYMS **guide, conduct, direct, lead, steer, usher** CORE MEANING: show somebody the way to a place

Guide Association *n* a scouting organization for girls

guided missile *n* a self-propelled missile steered by an electronic guidance system

guide dog *n* a dog trained to lead a sightless person

guideline /gíd līn/ *n* **1** an official recommendation or instruction on the proper action to take **2** a line marking a correct position or route

~~guidence~~ incorrect spelling of **guidance**

guiding light *n* an example and inspiration

guild /gild/ *n* an association of people with a common trade or interests —**guildsman** *n* —**guildswoman** *n*

SPELLCHECK Do not confuse the spelling of **guild** and **gild** ('cover with gold'), which sound similar.

guilder /gíldər/ *n* **1** the main unit of the former currency of the Netherlands **2** the main unit of currency of Suriname

guildhall /gíld hawl/ *n* **1** a town hall **2** a guild's meeting place

guile /gīl/ *n* cunning and deceitfulness —**guileful** *adj* —**guileless** *adj*

guillemot /gílli mot/ *n* a black-and-white diving sea bird

guillotine /gíllə teen/ *n* **1** a machine for beheading people, consisting of a sliding blade in a vertical frame **2** an instrument for cutting sheet metal or paper —**guillotine** *vt*

ORIGIN The **guillotine** is named after the French physician Joseph-Ignace Guillotin (1738–1814), who suggested it as a more humane means of beheading in 1789, at the beginning of the French Revolution.

guilt /gilt/ *n* **1** the fact of having done wrong **2** awareness of wrongdoing **3** responsibility for wrongdoing **4** legal culpability —**guiltless** *adj*

SPELLCHECK Do not confuse the spelling of **guilt** and **gilt** ('a thin layer of gold'), which sound similar.

guilty /gílti/ (**-ier**, **-iest**) *adj* **1** responsible for a crime or wrongdoing **2** ashamed of wrongdoing **3** showing, suggesting, or causing guilt ○ *a guilty look* —**guiltily** *adv*

guinea /gínni/ *n* an old unit of British currency worth 21 shillings

Guinea /gínni/ country in West Africa, on the Atlantic coast. Cap. Conakry. Pop. 7,613,870 (2001). —**Guinean** *adj*, *n*

Guinea-Bissau /-bi sów/ country in West Africa, on the Atlantic coast. Cap. Bissau. Pop. 1,315,822 (2001).

guinea fowl *n* a plump short-tailed bird with speckled plumage. Use: food.

guinea pig *n* **1** a plump tailless rodent kept as a pet **2** somebody or something used as the subject of an experiment or test

Guinevere /gwínni veer/ *n* legendary English queen, wife of King Arthur

Guinness /gínniss/, **Sir Alec** (1914–2000) British actor

guise /gíz/ *n* **1** a deceptive outward appearance **2** a different form or appearance ○ *old ideas in a new guise*

guitar /gi taár/ *n* a stringed musical instrument with a long neck and flat body, played by plucking or strumming —**guitarist** *n*

Guiyang /gwáy yáng/ capital of **Guizhou Province**, S China. Pop. 1,930,000 (1995).

gulag /goól ag/ *n* a political prison or labour camp in the former Soviet Union, or a network of such prisons or camps

ORIGIN Gulag is a Russian acronym formed from letters of *Glavnoe upravlenie isprevitelnotrudovykh lagerie* 'Chief administration for corrective labour camps'.

gulch *n US*, *Can* a ravine

gulf *n* **1** a large inlet of a sea (*often in placenames*) **2** a deep wide hole **3** a vast difference dividing people or groups

Gulf States *n* **1** the oil-producing countries bordering the Persian Gulf **2** the US states bordering the Gulf of Mexico

Gulf Stream *n* a warm current of the Atlantic Ocean, flowing northeast from the Gulf of Mexico along the coast of North America, then east to the British Isles

Gulf War *n* **1** a war (1991) in the Persian Gulf between US-led coalition forces and Iraq, following Iraq's invasion (1990) of Kuwait **2** = **Iran-Iraq War**

Gulf War syndrome *n* varied symptoms including respiratory distress, rashes, and nausea experienced by some troops who served in the 1991 Gulf War

gull[1] *n* a common white-and-grey sea bird

gull[2] (*archaic*) *vt* deceive ■ *n* a gullible person

gullet /gúllit/ *n* the oesophagus or throat

gullible /gúllab'l/ *adj* easily deceived —**gullibility** /gúllə bílləti/ *n*

gully /gúlli/ (*pl* **-lies**) *n* **1** a deep narrow ditch cut by water **2** a narrow mountain passage **3** an artificial channel for water —**gully** *vti*

gulp *v* **1** *vt* swallow hurriedly or in large mouthfuls **2** *vi* make a swallowing motion or sound, e.g. in fear —**gulp** *n*

gum[1] *n* **1** a sticky plant substance, especially one that hardens **2** any sticky substance **3** a glue used for sticking paper **4** a tree that produces gum **5** chewing gum (*infml*) ■ *vt* (**gumming**, **gummed**) stick something to something else —**gummy** *adj*

□ **gum up** *vt* obstruct, seal, or immobilize with or as if with a sticky substance

gum[2] *n* the flesh around the teeth (*often pl*)

gum arabic *n* a sticky substance from some acacia trees. Use: adhesives, confectionery, medicine.

gumbo /gúmbō/ (*pl* **-bos**) *n* **1** okra **2** a stew thickened with okra **3 Gumbo** a French patois

gumboil /gúm boyl/ *n* a mouth abscess on the gum

gum boot *n* a heavy waterproof boot

gumdrop /gúm drop/ *n* a chewy fruit-flavoured sweet

gumption /gúmpsh'n/ *n* common sense (*infml*)

gum tree *n* a tree that produces gum

gun *n* **1** a weapon that fires bullets or other projectiles **2** a device that forces something out under pressure ○ *a paint gun* **3** a shot fired from a gun, e.g. as a signal ◇ **go great guns** do something at great speed or very effectively ◇ **jump the gun** act prematurely ◇ **stick to your guns** refuse to change your plans or opinions

ORIGIN Gun probably comes from a form of the Scandinavian woman's name *Gunnhildr*, which is a compound of *gunnr* 'battle' and *hildr* 'war'. It has not been uncommon throughout history for weapons to be given women's names.

□ **gun down** *vt* shoot and kill or severely injure (*infml*)

□ **gun for** *vt* set out to attack or criticize (*infml*)

gunboat /gún bōt/ *n* a small ship with guns mounted on it

gunboat diplomacy *n* diplomacy between nations, with one nation using the threat of attack

gun dog *n* a dog of a breed trained to retrieve shot game

gunfight /gún fīt/ *n* a fight between people with guns —**gunfighter** *n*

gunfire /gún fīr/ *n* shots from a gun or guns

gunge *n* an unpleasant substance (*infml*) —**gungy** *adj*

gung ho /gúng hṓ/ *adj* very keen (*infml*)

gunman /gúnmən/ (*pl* **-men** /-mən/) *n* **1** somebody armed with a gun, especially a criminal or assassin **2** a skilful shooter

gunmetal /gún met'l/ *n* **1** a dark grey bronze. Use: formerly, cannon manufacture. **2** a dark grey alloy. Use: formerly, household and industrial items, toys.

gunnel *n NAUT* = **gunwale**

Gunnell /gúnn'l/, **Sally** (*b*. 1966) British athlete

gunner /gúnnər/ *n* **1** a soldier who fires a large gun **2** a soldier in an artillery regiment

gunnery /gúnnəri/ *n* **1** the science of guns and their design, construction, and use **2** the use of guns

gunny /gúnni/ *n* coarse jute or hemp cloth. Use: sacks.

gunplay /gún play/ *n* the shooting of guns

gunpoint /gún poynt/ ◊ **at gunpoint** under the threat of being shot and killed if orders are not obeyed

gunpowder /gún powdər/ *n* an explosive powder. Use: fireworks and other explosives, charge in some firearms.

Gunpowder Plot *n* a plot, involving Guy Fawkes, to blow up Parliament in 1605

gunrunning /gún runing/ *n* the smuggling of guns —**gunrunner** *n*

gunship /gún ship/ *n* an aircraft with guns mounted on it

gunshot /gún shot/ *n* **1** the sound of a gun being fired **2** bullets or shot fired from a gun

gun-shy *adj* **1** timid or wary **2** afraid of guns or their noise

gunsmith /gún smith/ *n* a maker, seller, or repairer of guns

gunwale /gúnn'l/, **gunnel** *n* the top edge of a ship's sides above the deck (*often pl*)

ORIGIN The **gunwale** gets its name because it was used in the past to support guns. *Wales* are the timbers forming the outside of a wooden ship.

---

guppy /gúppi/ (*pl* **-pies**) *n* a small brightly coloured freshwater fish

---

ORIGIN The **guppy** is named after the Reverend R. J. Lechmere Guppy (1836–1916), who sent the first specimen from Trinidad to the British Museum.

---

gurgle /gúrg'l/ (**-gling, -gled**) *v* **1** *vi* make a bubbling noise (*refers to flowing liquid*) **2** *vti* make a noise or say something with a bubbling sound in the throat —**gurgle** *n*

guru /gŏŏ roo/ (*pl* **-rus**) *n* **1** a prominent or influential leader, founder, or teacher ○ *a management guru* **2** a spiritual leader or intellectual guide **3** a Hindu or Sikh religious teacher

Guru Nanak /gŏŏ roo naanək/ ♦ **Nanak**

Guru Nanak Jananti /-jə nánti/ *n* a Sikh festival marking the birthday of Guru Nanak. Date: November.

gush *vti* **1** flow or cause to flow out fast and in large quantities **2** speak, behave, or say something effusively —**gush** *n* —**gushing** *adj*

gusher /gúshər/ *n* **1** a free-flowing oil well **2** an effusive person

gushy /gúshi/ (**-ier, -iest**) *adj* overly enthusiastic or emotional —**gushily** *adv*

gusset /gússit/ *n* a piece of fabric inserted for reinforcement or expansion

gust *n* **1** a sudden rush of wind **2** an emotional outburst ■ *vi* blow in gusts —**gusty** *adj*

Gustav II Adolph /gŏŏst aav áddolf/ (1594–1632) king of Sweden (1611–32)

Gustav I Vasa /vaázə/ (1496–1560) king of Sweden (1523–60)

gusto /gústō/ *n* hearty enjoyment

gut *n* **1** the alimentary canal, or part of it **2** the place where instincts are felt ○ *a gut reaction* **3** a tough fine cord made from animal intestines or a similar material ■ **guts** *npl* **1** the intestines **2** courage (*slang*) **3** inner or central parts, e.g. the workings of a machine ■ *vt* (**gutting, gutted**) **1** remove the insides of an animal **2** destroy the interior of a building

Gutenberg /gŏŏt'n burg/**, Johannes** (1400?–68) German printer. He is credited with the invention of movable type.

gutless /gútləss/ *adj* lacking courage and determination ◊ See note at **cowardly**

gutsy /gútsi/ (**-ier, -iest**) *adj* courageous (*infml*) —**gutsily** *adv* —**gutsiness** *n*

gutted /gúttid/ *adj* very disappointed or upset (*infml*)

gutter /gúttər/ *n* **1** a drainage channel at the edge of a road **2** a rainwater channel on a roof **3** a poor or degraded way of life **4** a channel at the side of a ten-pin bowling lane ■ *vi* **1** melt quickly (*refers to candles*) **2** flicker on the point of being extinguished (*refers to burning flames*) **3** trickle

~~gutteral~~ incorrect spelling of **guttural**

gutter press *n* newspapers that deal primarily with scandal and gossip

guttersnipe /gúttər snīp/ *n* a dirty ragged child who lives on the streets (*dated insult*)

guttural /gúttərəl/ *adj* **1** characterized by harsh or throaty speech sounds **2** pronounced with the tongue near the soft palate

guv *n* a term of address for a man in a superior social position or a boss (*infml*)

guy[1] /gī/ *n* **1** a man (*infml*) **2** an effigy of Guy Fawkes burnt on a bonfire ■ **guys** *npl* people of either sex (*infml*) ○ *How long have you guys been waiting?* ■ *vt* poke fun at

---

ORIGIN **Guy** is from the name of Guy Fawkes (1570–1606), one of the Roman Catholic conspirators who planned to blow up the British Houses of Parliament in the Gunpowder Plot of 1605. He was hanged and effigies of him have traditionally been burnt on Bonfire Night. The name **guy** was originally applied to these effigies, in the early 19C. In the mid-19C the word is also recorded with the sense 'grotesquely dressed person'. As simply a term for a 'man' or 'person', **guy** began its life at the end of the 19C in the United States.

---

guy[2] /gī/ *n* a rope or wire tightened to support something such as a tent ■ *vt* support with guys

Guyana /gī aánə/ country in South America, on the North Atlantic coast. Cap. Georgetown. Pop. 697,181 (2001). —**Guyanese** /gī ə neéz/ *adj, n*

Guy Fawkes Night /gī fáwks-/ *n* CALENDAR = **Bonfire Night**

guzzle /gúzz'l/ (**-zling, -zled**) *vti* gobble something greedily *(infml)* —**guzzler** *n*

Gwynedd /gwínnath/ county in NW Wales

Gy *symbol* gray²

Gyanendra /gya néndrə/ (*b.* 1947) king of Nepal (2001–)

gym /jim/ *n* a gymnasium *(infml)*

gymkhana /jim kaánə/ *n* a horse-riding event

> **ORIGIN Gymkhana** comes from an Urdu word meaning 'racket court', literally 'ball court'. The first part of the English word has been assimilated to *gymnasium* and related forms. It began in British India in the mid-19C, referring to a public place with facilities for athletics, and later to an athletics display. The specific use 'horse-riding event' does not appear to have arisen until the 1930s.

gymnasium /jim náyzi əm/ (*pl* **-ums** *or* **-a** /-ə/) *n* a large hall equipped for physical exercise

> **ORIGIN Gymnasium** derives ultimately from Greek *gumnos* 'naked'. Exercising naked was the custom in ancient Greece. The English noun comes immediately from Latin, where it meant 'school'.

gymnastics /jim nástiks/ *n* (+ *sing verb*) **1** physical training intended to develop agility and strength using exercises and equipment **2** gymnastics performed as a competitive sport or for display ■ *npl* actions demonstrating agility and skill (+ *pl verb*) ○ *verbal gymnastics* —**gymnast** /jím nast/ *n* —**gymnastic** *adj* —**gymnastically** *adv*

gymnosperm /jímnə spurm/ *n* any woody cone-bearing plant —**gymnospermous** /jímnə spúrməss/ *adj*

gymslip /jím slip/ *n* a schoolgirl's sleeveless dress worn over a blouse

gynaecology /gíni kólləji/ *n* the branch of medicine that deals with women's health, especially with the health of women's reproductive organs —**gynaecological** /gínikə lójjik'l/ *adj* —**gynaecologist** *n*

gynecology *n* US **-** gynaecology

gyp, gip *n* pain *(infml)* ○ *My arthritis is giving me gyp.*

gypsophila /jip sóffilə/ *n* a flowering plant with tiny flowers

gypsum /jípsəm/ *n* a white mineral of hydrated calcium sulphate. Use: cement, plaster, fertilizers.

gypsy /jípsi/ (*pl* **-sies**) *n* **1** somebody with a nomadic lifestyle *(infml; sometimes offensive)* **2 Gypsy, Gipsy** an offensive term for a member of the Roma people

gyrate /jī ráyt/ (**-rating, -rated**) *vi* move in a circle or spiral, especially round a fixed central point —**gyration** *n*

gyroscope /jī́rə skōp/ *n* a self-stabilizing device consisting of a rotating wheel inside a circular frame. Use: compasses and other navigational aids, stabilizing mechanisms on ships and aircraft. —**gyroscopic** /jī́rə skóppik/ *adj*

H

h¹ (*pl* **h's**), **H** (*pl* **H's** *or* **Hs**) *n* the 8th letter of the English alphabet

h² *abbr* **1** height **2** high **3** hour **4** hundred

H¹ *abbr* **1** hard **2** height

H² *symbol* **1** henry **2** hydrogen

ha¹, hah *interj* **1** expresses various emotions such as surprise or triumph **2** indicates the sound of laughter

ha² *symbol* hectare

Haarlem /haárləm/ city in W Netherlands. Pop. 148,772 (2000).

habeas corpus /háybi əss káwrpəss/ *n* a writ ordering a detained person to be brought into court

> **ORIGIN Habeas corpus** means 'you may have the body' in Latin. These are the first words of the writ.

haberdasher /hábbər dashər/ *n* a dealer in small sewing articles such as thread and buttons

> **ORIGIN Haberdasher** seems to go back ultimately to an old French word *hapertas*, whose meaning is unclear. It could be the name of a fabric, or mean 'piece of cloth', or 'small goods'. A **haberdasher** was originally a dealer in any small household articles, then from the 16C to the 18C usually a dealer in hats and caps.

haberdashery /hábbər dashəri/ (*pl* **-ies**) *n* **1** goods sold by a haberdasher **2** a haberdasher's shop or department

~~habeus corpus~~ incorrect spelling of **habeas corpus**

habit /hábbit/ *n* **1** a behaviour pattern or regular repetitive action **2** an addiction *(slang)* **3** a long loose gown worn by monks and nuns **4** a characteristic appearance or growth pattern **5** an attitude or disposition

> **SYNONYMS habit, custom, tradition, practice, routine, wont** CORE MEANING: established pattern of behaviour

habitable /hábbitəb'l/ *adj* fit to live in —**habitability** /hábbitə bílləti/ *n*

habitat /hábbi tat/ *n* **1** the natural environment in which a plant or animal lives **2** the place where somebody or something is usually found

habitation /hábbi táysh'n/ *n* **1** the act of inhabiting a place, or the state of being inhabited **2** a place in which to live

habit-forming *adj* causing dependence and continued use ○ *habit-forming drugs*

habitual /hə bíchoo əl/ *adj* **1** done regularly or as a habit **2** persisting in doing something because of a tendency or desire ○ *a habitual criminal* **3** characteristic ○ *She tackled the*

problem with her habitual single-mindedness.
—**habitually** *adv* ◊ See note at **usual**

habituate /hə bíchoo ayt/ (-**ating**, -**ated**) *vt* make somebody used to something *(fml)* o *People living in cities become habituated to crowds.*

habitué /hə bíchoo ay/ (*pl* -**tués**) *n* a frequent visitor

hacienda /hássi éndə/ *n* **1** a large estate in a Spanish-speaking country **2** a house on a hacienda

hack¹ *v* **1** *vti* cut something using repeated rough or heavy blows **2** *vt* cut or divide something roughly or carelessly *(infml)* o *hacked a whole chunk off the article I wrote* **3** *vi* gain access to or manipulate a computer system, especially without authority **4** *vt* cope with a difficult or unpleasant situation *(infml)* **5** *vi* make a harsh dry coughing noise ■ *n* **1** a quick chop **2** a harsh dry coughing noise

hack² *n* **1** an old or worn-out horse **2** a horse ride at an unhurried pace **3** a mediocre worker *(disapproving)* **4** a hired writer *(disapproving)* **5** a loyal political party worker *(disapproving)* ■ *vti* ride a horse at an un-hurried pace ■ *adj* hackneyed

ORIGIN Hack here is a shortening of *hackney*. Hack 'cut' is of Germanic origin.

hacker /hákər/ *n* **1** somebody who gains un-authorized access to a computer system **2** a computer enthusiast

hackney /hákni/ *n* **1** a carriage or automobile for hire **2** a horse for riding or driving —**hackneyism** *n*

ORIGIN Hackney is recorded from the medieval period, and probably derives from the name of what was then a village on the outskirts of London, where horses were raised and pas-tured. (Hackney is now a borough of inner London.) A **hackney** was originally a horse for ordinary riding, often one kept for hire, and the common condition of such horses gave rise to the connotations of overuse seen in its deriv-ative *hackneyed*.

hackneyed /háknid/ *adj* trite or unoriginal o *a hackneyed sales pitch*

hacksaw /hák saw/ *n* a saw for cutting metal —**hacksaw** *vt*

hacktivism /háktivizəm/ *n* political activism in-volving the use or sabotage of computer net-works —**hacktivist** *n*, *adj*

had past tense, past participle of **have**

haddock /háddək/ (*pl same or* -**docks**) *n* **1** a sea fish related to but smaller than the cod **2** haddock as food

Hades /háy deez/ *n* **1** in Greek mythology, the underworld. Roman equivalent **Dis** **2** in Greek mythology, the god of the under-world. Roman equivalent **Pluto** **1** **3** *also* **hades** hell *(infml)* —**Hadean** *adj*

Hadith /háddith/, **hadith** *n* the collected tra-ditions, teachings, and stories of the prophet Muhammad

hadj *n* ISLAM = **hajj**

hadji *n* ISLAM = **hajji**

hadn't /hádd'nt/ *contr* had not

Hadrian /háydri ən/ (76–138) Roman emperor (117–138)

Hadrian's Wall *n* an ancient Roman wall across N England

hadron /háddron/ *n* an elementary particle that reacts strongly with other particles

hadrosaur /háddrə sawr/, **hadrosaurus** /-sáwrɔss/ (*pl* -**uses**) *n* an amphibious plant-eating dinosaur with a snout resembling a duck's bill, and strong hind legs

haematology /heèmə tólləji/ *n* the branch of medicine devoted to the study of blood and blood-producing tissues —**haematologic** /heèmətə lójjik/ *adj* —**haematologist** *n*

haemo- *prefix* blood o *haemophilia*

haemoglobin /heèmə glóbin/ *n* an oxygen-transporting substance in red blood cells

haemophilia /heèmə fílli ə/ *n* a disorder in which the blood fails to clot normally —**haemophiliac** *n* —**haemophilic** *adj*

~~haemorrage~~ incorrect spelling of **haemorrhage**

haemorrhage /hémmərij/ *n* **1** excessive bleed-ing **2** an uncontrolled loss o *a haemorrhage of cash that threatened the firm* —**haemorrhage** *vti*

haemorrhoids /hémmə roydz/ *npl* swollen anal veins —**haemorrhoidal** /hémmə róyd'l/ *adj*

haere mai /hírə mí/ *interj* NZ welcome

hafnium /háfni əm/ *n* (*symbol* **Hf**) a silvery metallic chemical element. Use: nuclear reactor rods, tungsten filaments.

hag *n* **1** an offensive term for a woman of advanced years considered unattractive or spiteful *(slang)* **2** a witch —**haggish** *adj*

haggard /hággərd/ *adj* showing on the face signs of fatigue, anxiety, or hunger —**haggardly** *adv* —**haggardness** *n*

haggis /hággiss/ (*pl* -**gises**) *n* a Scottish dish consisting of a seasoned mixture packed into a round skin

ORIGIN One possible source of haggis is an old verb *hag*, a northern variant of *hack* 'chop'. An alternative possibility is old French *agace* 'magpie'. This is supported by a parallel se-mantic development of English *pie*, which ori-ginally meant 'magpie' but became 'pastry case with a filling'. The miscellaneous assortment of ingredients in a haggis would represent the magpie's hoard of bright odds and ends.

haggle /hágg'l/ (-**gling**, -**gled**) *vi* bargain or argue over something such as a price or a contract —**haggle** *n* —**haggler** *n*

hagiography /hággi óggrəfi/ (*pl* -**phies**) *n* **1** bi-ography dealing with the lives of saints **2** a biography that shows undue reverence —**hagiographer** *n*

hah *interj* = **ha¹**

ha-ha /haà haa/ *interj* indicates the sound of laughter

Hahn /haan/, **Otto** (1879–1968) German physical chemist. He was awarded the Nobel Prize in chemistry in 1944 for his work on nuclear fission.

hahnium /háani əm/ n (*symbol* **Hn**) dubnium or hassium

Haifa /hífə/ chief seaport of Israel, in the north of the country. Pop. 265,700 (1999).

Haig /hayg/, **Douglas, 1st Earl Haig** (1861–1928) British field marshal

haiku /híkoo/ (*pl same*) n a 3-line Japanese poem containing 17 syllables altogether

hail¹ /hayl/ n **1** pellets of ice that fall like rain **2** a barrage of something unpleasant or harmful o *a hail of missiles* —**hail** vi

hail² /hayl/ vt **1** greet somebody **2** offer praise **3** call or signal something or somebody o *hail a taxi* ■ *interj* hello (*literary*) —**hail** n —**hailer** n

□ **hail from** vt come from a particular place

Haile Selassie I /híli sə lássi/ (1892–1975) emperor of Ethiopia (1930–36, 1942–74)

hail-fellow-well-met adj exuberantly or excessively friendly ■ n a very friendly person

Hail Mary (*pl* **Hail Marys**) n a Christian prayer invoking the Virgin Mary's intercession

hailstone /háyl stōn/ n a pellet of hail

hailstorm /háyl stawrm/ n a storm with hail

hair /hair/ n **1** the strands growing on the head or body **2** a single strand of hair **3** a growth on a plant resembling a hair **4** a tiny amount or degree o *won by a hair* —**hairless** adj ◇ **let your hair down** behave in a more relaxed way than usual (*infml*) ◇ **split hairs** argue about fine distinctions

SPELLCHECK Do not confuse the spelling of **hair** and **hare** (the animal), which sound similar.

~~hair-brained~~ incorrect spelling of **harebrained**

hairbrush /háir brush/ n a brush for the hair

haircut /háir kut/ n **1** a cutting of somebody's hair **2** the way somebody's hair is cut

hairdo /háir doo/ (*pl* **-dos**) n a hairstyle

hairdresser /háir dressər/ n **1** somebody whose work is cutting and styling hair **2** *also* **hairdresser's** a hairdresser's place of business —**hairdressing** n

hair dryer n an electrical appliance for drying hair with heated air

hairgrip /háir grip/ n a U-shaped piece of wire or plastic used to hold the hair in place

hairline /háir līn/ n **1** the line on the top of the forehead behind which hair grows **2** a very thin line

hairnet /háir net/ n a circle of netting worn to hold the hair in place

hairpiece /háir peess/ n a toupee or bunch of false hair

hairpin /háir pin/ n **1** a U-shaped wire used to hold the hair in place **2** a sharp bend in a road

hair-raising adj terrifying or thrilling —**hair-raiser** n

hair's-breadth n a very small margin

hair shirt n a shirt made from scratchy material, formerly worn by religious people as a means of self-punishment

hair slide n an ornamental clip for the hair

hairsplitting /háir spliting/ n excessive attention to unimportant details —**hairsplitting** adj

hair spray n a spray used to hold a hairstyle in place

hairstyle /háir stīl/ n the way somebody's hair is cut, styled, or arranged —**hairstyling** n —**hairstylist** n

hair trigger n **1** a very sensitive gun trigger **2** a very quick response —**hair-trigger** adj

hair weave n false hair interwoven with somebody's own hair —**hairweave** vt —**hairweaving** n

hairy /háiri/ (**-ier, -iest**) adj **1** covered with hair **2** made of or resembling hair **3** frightening (*infml*) —**hairiness** n

Haiti /háyti/ country in the N Caribbean, occupying the western third of the island of Hispaniola. Cap. Port-au-Prince. Pop. 6,964,549 (2001). —**Haitian** /háysh'n, haa eésh'n/ n, adj

Haitink /hítingk/, **Bernard** (b. 1929) Dutch conductor

hajj, hadj, haj n a pilgrimage to Mecca

hajji /hájji/, **hadji** n a Muslim who has made a pilgrimage to Mecca

hake (*pl same or* **hakes**) n **1** a sea fish resembling the cod, with two dorsal fins and an elongated body **2** hake as food

hakim /hə keém/, **hakeem** n **1** a Muslim doctor **2** a Muslim judge

Hakluyt /hák loot/, **Richard** (1552?–1616) English geographer

halal /hə laál, hállal/ adj describes meat from animals slaughtered according to Islamic law ■ n halal meat ■ vt (**-lalling, -lalled**) slaughter animals in the Islamic way

halcyon days /hálssi ən-/ npl a tranquil happy time (*literary*)

ORIGIN The first word of **halcyon days** derives from the Greek for 'kingfisher'. In Greek mythology, the halcyon was a bird resembling the kingfisher with the power to calm the waves at the time of the winter solstice when it nested at sea. **Halcyon days** originally referred to two weeks of calm weather around this time.

hale¹ (**haler, halest**) adj fit and strong —**haleness** n

hale² (**haling, haled**) vt make somebody go somewhere (*fml*)

half /haaf/ n (*pl* **halves** /haavz/), det, pron each of two equal parts into which a whole is or can be divided ■ n (*pl* **halves** /haavz/) **1** in some sports, each of two periods into which playing time is divided **2** a half fare **3** a half a pint, especially of beer ■ adj, adv **1** partial or partially o *a half-smile* **2** in equal parts o *He's half French and half Spanish.* ◇ **by half** to an excessive extent o *She's too friendly by* *half.* ◇ **not half** not at all ○ *Mmm! This cake's not half bad!*

half-and-half *adj* containing half each of two things ■ *adv* in two equal portions ■ *n* a mixture of two things in equal parts

halfback /haáf bak/ *n* **1** in some team sports, a player positioned in front of the last defensive line **2** in rugby, a player positioned behind the scrum

half-baked *adj* poorly thought out *(infml)*

half board *n* bed, breakfast, and evening meal at a hotel

half-breed, half-caste *n* an offensive term for a person of mixed racial parentage *(insult)*

half-brother *n* a brother with only one parent in common with another

half-cocked *adj* with inadequate planning or preparation

half-day *n* half a regular working day, especially when taken as a holiday

half-hearted *adj* feeling or showing little enthusiasm —**half-heartedly** *adv* —**half-heartedness** *n*

half-holiday *n* a holiday for half a working or school day

half-hour *n* **1** a period of 30 minutes **2** a point in time 30 minutes after the hour ○ *chiming on the hour and half-hour* —**half-hourly** *adv, adj*

half-life *n* **1** (*symbol* T$\frac{1}{2}$) the time it takes a substance to lose half its radioactivity through decay **2** the time it takes for half an amount of something such as a drug to be removed from living tissue

half-mast, half-staff *n* the position to which a flag is lowered as a sign of mourning

halfpenny /háypni, -pəni/ (*pl* same *or* -nies) *n* an old unit of British currency worth half a penny

half-price *adj, adv* at half the usual price

half-sister *n* a sister with only one parent in common with another

half term *n* a holiday halfway through a school term

half-time *n* a rest period halfway through a game

halftone /haáf tōn/ *n* **1** an intermediate shade of brightness or darkness, e.g. in a photograph **2** a process for reproducing shading in print

half-truth *n* a misleadingly incomplete statement

halfway /haáf wáy/ *adv, adj* **1** at or to the middle point between two things **2** only partial or partially

halfway house *n* **1** a compromise **2** a rehabilitation centre **3** a point or stopping place halfway through a long journey

halfwit /haáf wit/ *n* an offensive term for a person regarded as foolish or stupid *(insult)*

half-yearly *adv, adj* once every six months

halibut /hállibət/ (*pl* -buts *or* same) *n* **1** a large ocean flatfish **2** halibut as food

ORIGIN The **halibut** is literally a 'holy flatfish'. It was commonly eaten on holy days.

Halifax /hálli faks/ **1** town in N England. Pop. 91,069 (1991). **2** capital of Nova Scotia, Canada. Pop. 113,910 (1996).

halitosis /hálli tṓssiss/ *n* bad breath

hall *n* **1** an entrance room **2** a corridor **3** a building with a large public room **4** a large room where people gather, e.g. for dining **5** a large country house **6** a university hall of residence

hallelujah /hálli lōoyə/, **alleluia** /álli-/ *interj* **1** expresses praise to God **2** expresses relief —**hallelujah** *n*

Halley /hálli, háwli/, **Edmond** (1656–1742) British astronomer

Hall-Jones /háwl jṓnz/, **William** (1851–1936) British-born prime minister of New Zealand (1906)

hallmark /háwl maark/ *n* **1** a mark of quality, especially on an object made of a precious metal **2** a distinguishing mark —**hallmark** *vt*

ORIGIN The 'hall' in **hallmark** is Goldsmiths' Hall in London, where the Goldsmiths' Company assayed and stamped gold and silver articles.

hallo *interj, n* = hello

hall of residence *n* a university building providing accommodation for students

Halloween /hállō ee'n/, **Hallowe'en** *n* the night of 31 October, the eve of All Saints' Day

hallucinate /hə lōossi nayt/ (-nating, -nated) *vti* imagine seeing or hearing somebody or something —**hallucinative** /-ətiv/ *adj* —**hallucinatory** /-ətəri/ *adj*

hallucination /hə lōossi náysh'n/ *n* **1** the act of hallucinating **2** a false perception sometimes caused by a psychiatric disorder or by drugs *(often pl)*

hallucinogen /hə lōossinə jen/ *n* a drug that induces hallucinations —**hallucinogenic** /hə lōossinə jénnik/ *adj*

hallway /háwl way/ *n* an entrance hall or corridor

halo /háylō/ *n* (*pl* -loes *or* -los) **1** a circle of light around a saint's head in religious art **2** a circle of light around the Moon or Sun ■ *vt* (-los, -loed) surround with a halo

halogen /hálləjən/ *n* any of the five chemical elements, fluorine, chlorine, iodine, bromine, or astatine ■ *adj* describes a light or heat source containing halogen vapour ○ *a halogen bulb*

Hals /halss/, **Frans** (1580?–1666) Flemish-born Dutch painter

halt[1] /hawlt, holt/ *n* **1** a temporary stop **2** a small railway station ■ *interj* commands somebody to stop ■ *vti* stop

halt[2] *vi* act hesitantly

halter /háwltər, hólt-/ n **1** a rope or leather device put over an animal's head and used to lead it **2** a woman's top that leaves the back and shoulders bare —**halter** vt

halter neck n **1** a dress or top that is tied behind the neck **2** a garment with a halter neck —**halter-neck** adj

halting /háwlting, hólt-/ adj hesitant o halting speech —**haltingly** adv

halve /haav/ (**halving, halved**) v **1** vt divide into two equal parts **2** vti reduce or be reduced by half

halves plural of **half**

ham[1] n **1** cured meat from a pig's thigh **2** a pig's thigh **3** the back of somebody's upper leg

ham[2] n a performer who overacts ■ vti (**hamming, hammed**) overact —**ham** adj —**hammy** adj

> **ORIGIN** A **ham** actor was probably a hamfatter. This is a US slang term for an inexpert performer. Its origin is not certain, but it may represent an alteration of amateur, or it may have been inspired by a song, 'The Ham-fat Man'.

ham[3] n an amateur radio operator

Hamas /hámmass/ n a fundamentalist Islamic Palestinian organization supporting resistance to Israel in the Israeli-occupied territories

Hamburg /hám burg/ city in north-central Germany. Pop. 1,705,872 (1997).

hamburger /hám burgər/ n **1** a flat cake of minced meat **2** a grilled or fried hamburger served in a bun

> **ORIGIN** The **hamburger** was originally more fully a Hamburger steak (or Hamburg steak), and is named after Hamburg in Germany. It was first recorded in the 1880s in the United States.

ham-fisted, ham-handed adj clumsy with the hands (infml)

Hamilton /hámm'ltən/, **Emma, Lady** (1765–1815) British courtier. She was the mistress of Horatio Nelson.

hamlet /hámmlət/ n a small village or group of houses

Hammarskjöld /hámmər shoōld/, **Dag** (1905–61) Swedish diplomat, secretary-general of the United Nations (1953–61)

hammer /hámmər/ n **1** a hand tool with a heavy head for pounding or driving in nails **2** a powered mechanical striking tool **3** a part that strikes something else, e.g. in a piano or gun **4** a heavy metal ball thrown in athletics, or the field event in which it is thrown ■ v **1** vti pound or drive something in with or as if with a hammer **2** vt defeat by a large margin (infml)

□ **hammer away at** vt work hard at

□ **hammer out** vt agree on or establish after prolonged discussion

Hammer /hámmər/, **Armand** (1898–1990) US industrialist, art collector, and philanthropist

Hammett /hámmət/, **Dashiell** (1894–1961) US writer

hammock /hámmək/ n a simple hanging bed suspended at both ends

Hammond /hámmənd/, **Dame Joan Hood** (1912–96) New Zealand-born Australian opera singer

hamper[1] /hámpər/ vt prevent the free movement or action of ◊ See note at **hinder**

hamper[2] /hámpər/ n **1** a large basket for carrying food, e.g. for a picnic **2** US, Can a large basket for laundry

Hampshire /hámpshər/ county in S England, bordering the English Channel

hamster /hámstər/ n **1** a small rodent with cheek pouches and a short tail **2** a cordless computer mouse

hamstring /hám string/ n **1** either of two tendons at the back of the knee **2** a muscle at the back of the thigh ■ vt (**-strung** /-strung/) **1** cut the hamstring of **2** make powerless or ineffective o hamstrung by lack of funds

Hamsun /hámsoōn/, **Knut** (1859–1952) Norwegian author

Han ♦ Han Jiang

hand n **1** the part at the end of the human arm below the wrist **2** an animal part corresponding to the human hand **3** a pointer on a clock or dial **4** a player's cards **5** in a card game, a round **6** influence or directing action **7** a part in doing something o Who else had a hand in this? **8** help or assistance o Give me a hand. **9** a sign of agreement, especially to an offer of marriage **10** a round of applause **11** possession or power o Your future is in your own hands. **12** a member of a ship's crew **13** somebody with a particular level of competence or experience o I'm an old hand at this. **14** a manual worker o a farm hand **15** handwriting ■ vt **1** pass by hand **2** lead by the hand ◊ **at hand 1** nearby **2** about to happen ◊ **be hand in glove** cooperate, usually for a secret or illegal purpose ◊ **change hands** pass to a different owner ◊ **force somebody's hand** pressure somebody to do something against his or her will or earlier than planned ◊ **(from) hand to mouth** with barely enough to live on ◊ **in hand** under control ◊ **on hand** near and available ◊ **out of hand** immediately and without consideration ◊ **wash your hands of** refuse to continue being responsible for

□ **hand down** vt **1** bequeath something **2** US, Can pronounce a verdict or sentence

□ **hand in** vt submit something o handed in her notice

□ **hand out** vt distribute or administer

□ **hand over** vt surrender, give, or transfer to somebody else

handbag /hánd bag/ n a woman's small bag for personal items

handball /hánd bawl/ n **1** a game in which a ball is hit with the hands against a wall **2** a ball used in handball

handbill /hánd bil/ *n* a printed sheet of paper distributed by hand

handbook /hánd bŏŏk/ *n* a small reference book, manual, or travel guide

handbrake /hánd brayk/ *n* a hand-operated brake

handcart /hánd kaart/ *n* a cart pulled or pushed by hand

handcraft /hánd kraaft/ *n* skill in making things with the hands ■ *vt* make using manual skill

handcuff /hánd kuf/ *n* each of a pair of joined metal rings locked around somebody's wrists as a restraint *(usually pl)* ■ *vt* **1** put in handcuffs **2** make powerless or ineffective

Handel /hánd'l/, **George Frideric** (1685–1759) German-born British composer

handful /hánd fŏŏl/ *n* **1** an amount contained by the hand **2** a small amount or number **3** a troublesome person or thing *(infml)*

hand grenade *n* a small bomb thrown by hand

handgun /hánd gun/ *n* a gun held in one hand

hand-held *adj* operated while held in the hand ■ *n* a palmtop computer

handicap /hándi kap/ *n* **1** a hindrance **2** an added advantage or disadvantage given to a competitor to balance a contest, or a contest balanced in this way **3** a physical or mental disability *(often offensive)* ■ *vt* **(-capping, -capped) 1** hinder somebody or something **2** give a handicap to a competitor

---

ORIGIN Handicap is a contraction of *hand in cap*, originally a betting game between contestants who offered to exchange items of personal property, whose difference in value was adjudicated by an umpire. The contestants placed their hands in a hat, along with some forfeit money, and the way in which they withdrew their hands – full or empty – signified whether they accepted or rejected the umpire's adjudication. If they both either accepted or rejected it, the umpire took the forfeit money; if they disagreed, the one who accepted it got the money. The application to horseracing arose in the 18C from the notion of an umpire adjudicating on the weight disadvantage to be given to a particular horse.

---

handicapped /hándi kapt/ *adj* with a physical or mental disability *(often offensive)* ■ *npl* an offensive term for people who have a disability

---

USAGE Although **handicapped** has a long history of use by those so affected, *people with disabilities* is preferred over the adjective and noun uses of **handicapped**.

---

handicraft /hándi kraaft/ *n* **1** a craft or occupation requiring manual skill **2** something made by hand

handiwork /hándi wurk/ *n* **1** the result of somebody's action **2** work done by hand

handkerchief /hángkər chif, -cheef/ *(pl* **-chiefs** *or* **-chieves** /-cheevz/*) n* a square of cloth used especially for wiping the nose

handle /hánd'l/ *n* **1** a part for holding or operating something **2** a name *(slang)* ■ *v* **(-dling, -dled) 1** *vt* touch with the hands **2** *vt* operate **3** *vt* take charge of, deal with, or control **4** *vt* deal in ○ *handling stolen goods* **5** *vi* respond to control ○ *a yacht that handles well in bad weather* —**handling** *n* ◇ **fly off the handle** lose your temper *(infml)* ◇ **get a handle on** understand or be able to control

handlebars /hánd'l baarz/ *npl* the steering handles of a bicycle or motorcycle

handler /hándlər/ *n* **1** an animal trainer **2** a manager, e.g. of a performer or a national political candidate **3** somebody who works or deals with something ○ *a baggage handler*

handmade /hánd máyd/ *adj* made by hand

hand-me-down *n* **1** an outgrown or unwanted garment passed on to another person **2** something previously discarded by one person or group that is taken up by another

handout /hánd owt/ *n* **1** a charitable gift **2** a document distributed to a group

hand-pick /hánd pík/ *vt* **1** choose carefully ○ *handpicked the starting lineup* **2** pick or harvest by hand

handrail /hánd rayl/ *n* a rail to hold with the hand for support

handsaw /hánd saw/ *n* a small saw for use with one hand

hands down *adv* **1** with great ease **2** in a way that is not open to question

handset /hánd set/ *n* the part of a telephone that contains the receiver and transmitter

handshake /hánd shayk/ *n* **1** a gesture of gripping and shaking somebody's hand **2** an exchange of signals establishing a link between computers or other devices —**handshaking** *n*

hands-off *adj* with no active or personal involvement

handsome /hánssəm/ *adj* **1** good-looking **2** generous —**handsomely** *adv* —**handsomeness** *n*

hands-on *adj* **1** involving actual use ○ *a hands-on method of learning computer skills* **2** involving physical touching ○ *a museum with hands-on exhibits for children* **3** personally or actively involved ○ *a hands-on manager*

handspring /hánd spring/ *n* an acrobatic flipping over of the body using the hands

handstand /hánd stand/ *n* an act of balancing on the hands with the legs straight up in the air

hand-to-hand *adj* involving bodily contact between people ○ *hand-to-hand fighting* —**hand to hand** *adv*

hand-to-mouth *adj* with barely enough to live on —**hand to mouth** *adv*

handwork /hánd wurk/ *n* work done by hand —**handworker** *n*

handwriting /hánd ríting/ *n* **1** writing done by hand **2** a way of writing by hand —**handwritten** *adj*

handy /hándi/ (**-ier, -iest**) adj **1** conveniently accessible **2** useful **3** skilful at practical things —**handily** adv —**handiness** n

handyman /hándi man/ (pl **-men** /-men/) n somebody who is paid to do or skilled at doing small jobs such as household repairs

hang v (**hung**) **1** vti fasten or hold something so that it is not supported from below, or be fastened or held in this way **2** vt fix a door on its hinges **3** (past and past participle **hanged**) vti kill or be killed by putting a rope around the neck and removing any support for the body **4** vt decorate something by hanging things on it ○ trees hung with lights **5** vt put up wallpaper **6** vti display or be displayed by hanging (refers to pictures) **7** vt let your head droop **8** vt suspend meat from a rope or wire for a time to improve its quality **9** vi drape ○ The jacket hung badly on her. ■ n a way of hanging ◇ **get the hang of** learn how to do

□ **hang around** vi **1** loiter or waste time **2** associate regularly

□ **hang back** vi be reluctant

□ **hang on** v **1** vi hold on tightly **2** vi persist in an endeavour **3** vt depend on **4** vi wait ○ Hang on a minute while I find out.

□ **hang out** vi spend time casually somewhere or with somebody (infml)

□ **hang over** v **1** vt be imminent or threatening for **2** vi be postponed

□ **hang together** vi be consistent

□ **hang up** vi end a telephone call

hangar /hángər/ n a building housing aircraft

ORIGIN **Hangar** is an adoption of a French word meaning 'shed', whose origin is unknown. It is first recorded in English, with this more general meaning, in the late 17C. The first known use in the modern context of aircraft is from 1902, and refers to a **hangar** in France.

SPELLCHECK Do not confuse the spelling of **hangar** and **hanger** ('a support for hanging something'), which sound similar.

hangdog /háng dog/ adj looking guilty or sad

hanger /hángər/ n **1** a support for hanging something, especially a frame for hanging a garment **2** somebody who hangs something ◇ See note at **hangar**

hanger-on (pl **hangers-on**) n a sycophantic or parasitic follower

Barnaby's

Hang-glider

hang-glider n an unpowered aircraft with a wing-shaped frame from which the pilot hangs —**hang-glide** vi —**hang-gliding** n

hangi /húngi, hángi/ (pl same) n NZ **1** a pit for outdoor cooking on hot stones **2** a feast prepared in a hangi

hanging /hánging/ n **1** execution by putting a rope around the neck and removing any other support for the body **2** a decorative fabric hung on a wall (often pl)

hangman /hángmən/ (pl **-men** /-mən/) n **1** an executioner who hangs people **2** a game that involves guessing the letters of a word before the other player has drawn a stylized gallows, with one line for every wrong guess

hangnail /háng nayl/ n a partly detached piece of skin beside a fingernail

ORIGIN **Hangnail** is an alteration of earlier agnail. The first element of this word was unfamiliar and puzzling, and was altered by popular etymology in the late 17C. In fact it represents an ancient root meaning 'tight, painful'.

hangout /háng owt/ n a place frequented by a person or group (infml)

hangover /háng övər/ n **1** the unpleasant after effects of drinking too much alcohol **2** a remainder of the past

Hang Seng index /háng séng-/ n an index of relative prices on the Hong Kong Stock Exchange

hang-up n **1** a psychological problem or inhibition (infml) **2** a source of delay

Hangzhou /háng jó/ capital of **Zhejiang Province**, SE China, at the head of **Hangzhou Bay**, an inlet of the East China Sea. Pop. 4,210,000 (1995).

Han Jiang /hán jyáng/, **Han** river of central China. Length 1,532 km/952 mi.

hank n a loose ball or coil of material such as wool or rope

hanker /hángkər/ vi want something badly or persistently ○ hankers after something she can't have —**hankering** n

~~hankerchief~~ incorrect spelling of **handkerchief**

hankie /hángki/, **hanky** (pl **-kies**) n a handkerchief (infml)

hanky-panky /hángki pángki/ n **1** frivolous sexual behaviour **2** suspicious activity

Hannibal /hánnib'l/ (247–183 BC) Carthaginian general

Hanoi /ha nóy/ capital of Vietnam. Pop. 1,073,760 (1992).

Hanover /hánnōvər/ city in NW Germany. Pop. 525,763 (1997).

Hansard /hán saard/ n the official published reports of British parliamentary proceedings

hansom /hánssəm/, **hansom cab** n a two-wheeled covered horse-drawn carriage

ORIGIN The **hansom** is named after the British architect Joseph Aloysius Hansom (1803–82), who patented an improved design of cab in 1834.

Hanukkah /hánnəkə, haàn-, kháàn-/, **Hanukah**, **Chanukah** n a Jewish festival marking the rededication of the Temple in Jerusalem. Date: from 25th day of Kislev, in December, for eight days.

~~hapen~~ incorrect spelling of **happen**

haphazard /hap házzərd/ *adj* unplanned, sloppy, or random —**haphazardly** *adv* —**haphazardness** *n*

ORIGIN Haphazard is formed from archaic *hap* 'happening, occurrence' and *hazard* in the old sense 'chance'.

hapless /háppləss/ *adj* unlucky —**haplessly** *adv* —**haplessness** *n*

happen /háppən/ *v* **1** *vi* occur or take place o *How did it happen?* **2** *vt* do something by chance o *if you happen to find it* **3** *vi* affect, especially in an unpleasant way o *I hope nothing has happened to her.* **4** *vi* be by chance o *It happened to be the last one in the shop.*
□ **happen on** *or* **upon** *vt* discover or encounter something or somebody by chance

happening /háppəning/ *n* something that happens

happenstance /hápp'n stanss/, **happenchance** /háppən chaanss/ *n* a chance occurrence

happy /háppi/ (**-pier**, **-piest**) *adj* **1** feeling pleasure **2** causing pleasure o *happy news* **3** satisfied o *I am happy with my performance.* **4** willing o *happy to help* **5** fortunate o *a happy coincidence* —**happily** *adv* —**happiness** *n*

happy-go-lucky *adj* tending not to worry about the future

happy hour *n* a time when drinks are sold at reduced prices in bars or pubs

happy medium *n* a satisfying compromise

~~happyness~~ incorrect spelling of **happiness**

hapu /haápoo/ *n NZ* a unit of Maori society forming a division of a tribe

hara-kiri /hárrə kírri, -keêr ri/ *n* Japanese ritualistic suicide involving disembowelment

harangue /hə ráng/ (**-ranguing**, **-rangued**) *vti* address loudly, forcefully, or angrily, usually at length —**harangue** *n*

Harare /hə raári/ capital of Zimbabwe. Pop. 1,410,000 (1995).

harass /hárrəss, hə ráss/ *vt* **1** keep bothering or attacking somebody **2** exhaust an enemy with repeated attacks —**harassed** *adj* —**harassment** *n*

Harbin /haár bín/ capital of **Heilongjiang Province**, NE China. Pop. 4,470,000 (1995).

harbinger /haárbinjər/ *n* somebody or something that announces a future event

harbour /haárbər/ *n* **1** a sheltered place where ships can anchor or moor **2** a place of refuge ■ *vt* **1** keep in your mind for a long time o *harbouring a secret fear of the dark* **2** provide shelter or sanctuary for

hard *adj* **1** not easily cut or bent **2** difficult o *a hard decision* **3** involving much effort o *a hard climb* **4** using much force o *a hard tug on the rope* **5** demanding and strict o *a hard taskmaster* **6** unsympathetic **7** resentful or bitter o *no hard feelings* **8** real or true o *the hard facts*

9 tough, violent, or ruthless **10** radical o *the hard left* **11** harsh or severe o *a hard winter* **12** describes water that contains mineral salts **13** describes beverages high in alcohol content **14** describes dangerously addictive drugs **15** describes the consonants 'c' and 'g' pronounced as in 'come' and 'go' ■ *adv* **1** with force o *hit the ball hard* **2** to an extreme degree o *pulled the truck over hard* **3** with energetic strength o *worked hard* **4** with concentration o *studied hard* —**hardness** *n* ◇ **be hard on 1** treat severely **2** be unfortunate for ◇ **be hard put to** find it difficult to

SYNONYMS **hard, difficult, strenuous, tough, arduous, laborious** CORE MEANING: requiring effort or exertion

hard-and-fast *adj* rigidly enforced

hardback /haárd bak/, **hardcover** /haárd kuvvər/ *n* a book with a stiff cover

hard-bitten *adj* tough and experienced

hardboard /haárd bawrd/ *n* board made from compressed wood chips and sawdust

hard-boiled *adj* **1** describes an egg that is cooked until firm **2** tough, realistic, and unsentimental (*infml*) —**hard-boil** *vt*

hardbound /haárd bownd/ *adj* describes a book in a stiff cover

hard copy *n* printed-out computer data

hard core *n* **1** the committed nucleus of a group **2** fast rock music with repetitive rhythmic sounds

hard-core /haárd kawr/ *adj* **1** uncompromising and committed **2** describes explicit pornography

hardcover *n* PRINTING = **hardback**

hard disk, hard drive *n* a permanent information storage unit inside a computer

harden /haárd'n/ *vti* **1** make or become hard or harder **2** make or become more determined —**hardener** *n*

hardheaded /haárd héddid/ *adj* logical and realistic —**hardheadedly** *adv* —**hardheadedness** *n*

hardhearted /haárd haártid/ *adj* cruel or unsympathetic —**hardheartedly** *adv* —**hardheartedness** *n*

hard-hitting *adj* brutally honest o *a hard-hitting documentary*

Hardie /haárdi/, **Keir** (1856–1915) British politician. He founded the first labour party in Britain.

Hardie Boys /haárdi bóyz/, **Sir Michael** (*b.* 1931) lawyer and governor general of New Zealand (1996–)

hard labour *n* a prison sentence including physical work

hard line *n* an inflexible and uncompromising position

hardline /haárd lín/ *adj* inflexible —**hardliner** *n*

hardly /haárdli/ *adv* **1** almost not o *It's hardly likely.* o *There are hardly any left.* **2** only with difficulty o *I could hardly move.* **3** only just

○ *Hardly had I rung the bell when the door was opened.*

hard-nosed *adj* tough and shrewd *(infml)*

hard palate *n* the bony front part of the roof of the mouth

hardpan /haàrd pan/ *n* hard material in a layer below the soil

hard-pressed *adj* **1** lacking sufficient resources **2** having difficulty

hard rock *n* loud rock music with an insistent beat

hard sell *n* aggressive marketing or selling

hardship /haàrd ship/ *n* **1** difficulty or suffering caused by a lack of something **2** a cause of hardship

hard shoulder *n* a lane alongside a motorway for use in an emergency

hardtop /haàrd top/ *n* **1** US, Can a car with a fixed metal roof **2** a car with a detachable hard roof

hard up *adj* poor *(infml)*

hardware /haàrd wair/ *n* **1** tools and implements **2** computer equipment and peripherals **3** military weapons

hardwire /haàrd wīr/ (**-wiring, -wired**) *vt* build a function into a computer with hardware

hardwood /haàrd wood/ *n* **1** wood from a broad-leaved tree rather than a conifer **2** a tree that produces hardwood

hardy /haàrdi/ (**-dier, -diest**) *adj* **1** robust and able to withstand physical hardship **2** describes plants that are not sensitive to cold —**hardily** *adv* —**hardiness** *n*

Hardy /haàrdi/, **Thomas** (1840–1928) British novelist and poet

hare /hair/ *n* (*pl* same *or* **hares**) **1** a fast-running animal resembling a rabbit, with large hind legs **2** the flesh of a hare as food ■ *vi* (**haring, hared**) run fast ◊ See note at **hair**

harebrained /hair braynd/ *adj* foolish or impractical

Hare Krishna /hàrri-/ *n* **1** a Hindu religious group that worships the god Krishna **2** a member of Hare Krishna

harelip /hair lip/ *n* an offensive term for an upper lip congenitally divided into two parts that have been only partially reunited by surgery

harem /haà reem, haa reèm, háirəm/ *n* **1** the part of a Muslim house reserved for wives and concubines **2** the women living in a harem **3** any group of women admirers or followers *(humorous; sometimes offensive)*

ORIGIN Harem comes from an Arabic word that literally means 'forbidden place'. It came to be applied to the separate women's quarters in a Muslim house, and from there to the women themselves.

Hargrave /haàr grayv/, **Lawrence** (1850–1915) British-born Australian aviator and explorer

Hargreaves /haàr greevz/, **James** (1720–78) British inventor. He invented the spinning jenny in 1764.

haricot /hárrikō/ *n* **1** a white bean **2** a plant that produces haricots

Harijan /húrrijən/ *n* a Hindu of low caste

hark *vi* listen *(archaic)*

☐ **hark back** *vi* **1** think or speak again about something past **2** be similar to something past

Harlem /haàrləm/ *n* district of New York City, on N Manhattan Island

harlequin /haàrləkwin/ *n* **1** a clown **2 Harlequin** a comic character wearing diamond-patterned tights and a black mask ■ *adj* patterned with multicoloured diamond shapes

Harley Street /haàrli-/ *n* a London street containing many doctors' private practices

harlot /haàrlət/ *n* a female prostitute *(literary)*

ORIGIN A **harlot** was not originally a woman. At first it meant 'vagabond, rogue, beggar', as did the French word from which it was adopted.

harm *n* physical or mental damage or injury ■ *vt* cause harm to

SYNONYMS harm, damage, hurt, injure, wound CORE MEANING: weaken or impair something or somebody

harmful /haàrmf'l/ *adj* damaging —**harmfully** *adv* —**harmfulness** *n*

harmless /haàrmləss/ *adj* **1** not dangerous **2** unobjectionable or inoffensive —**harmlessly** *adv* —**harmlessness** *n*

harmonic /haar mónnik/ *adj* produced by harmony ■ *n* an overtone on a stringed instrument —**harmonically** *adv*

harmonica /haar mónnikə/ *n* a small rectangular wind instrument containing a set of metal reeds

ORIGIN The name **harmonica** was introduced by Benjamin Franklin for an instrument he devised in the early 1760s, a row of glasses turning on an axis and dipping into water, which were played by the finger. This was an improved and mechanized version of what were called 'musical glasses' (and would now be called a *glass harmonica*). As a name for the wind instrument **harmonica** is recorded from the 1890s.

harmonics /haar mónniks/ *n* the science of the physical properties of musical sound *(+ sing verb)*

harmonious /haar móni əss/ *adj* **1** of or in harmony **2** blending pleasantly —**harmoniously** *adv*

harmonium /haar móni əm/ *n* an organ with a foot-operated bellows

harmonize /haàrmə nīz/ (**-nizing, -nized**), **harmonise** *v* **1** *vti* blend pleasingly **2** *vt* make systems similar —**harmonization** /haàrmə nī záysh'n/ *n*

harmony /haárməni/ (pl **-nies**) n **1** a pleasing combination of musical sounds **2** a situation in which there is agreement **3** a pleasing effect in the arrangement of the parts of something **4** a combination of notes sung or played together

harness /haárnəss/ n **1** a set of leather straps for attaching an animal to a cart or carriage that it pulls **2** a set of straps for holding somebody in position ■ vt **1** fit an animal with a harness **2** get control of and use something —**harnesser** n

Harold II /hárrəld/ (1020?–66) king of the English (1066)

harp n a large triangular stringed instrument played by plucking —**harp** vi —**harper** n —**harpist** n

☐ **harp on** vti repeat something tiresomely

harpoon /haar poón/ n a weapon like a spear attached to a cord and thrown or fired at a whale or other sea animal —**harpoon** vt

harpsichord /haárpsi kawrd/ n a keyboard instrument played by plucking —**harpsichordist** n

harpy /haárpi/ (pl **-pies**) n **1** an offensive term for a woman regarded as unpleasant or greedy (insult) **2 Harpy** in Greek mythology, a monster that was half woman and half bird of prey

~~harrass~~ incorrect spelling of **harass**

harridan /hárridən/ n an offensive term for a woman regarded as domineering or bad-tempered (insult)

Harris /hárriss/, **Sir Arthur Travers** (1892–1984) British air marshal

Harrisburg /hárriss burg/ capital of Pennsylvania. Pop. 49,502 (1998).

harrow /hárrō/ n a farm machine for breaking up soil —**harrow** vti

harrowing /hárrō ing/ adj very distressing —**harrowingly** adv

harry /hárri/ (**-ries**, **-ried**) vt **1** distress by repeated attacks **2** raid or pillage

harsh /haársh/ adj **1** difficult to endure ○ harsh conditions **2** severe in judgment ○ harsh criticism **3** jarring or unpleasant ○ a harsh voice ○ a harsh light —**harshly** adv —**harshness** n

hart (pl **harts** or same) n a male deer

hartal /haar taál, hur taál, haár taal/ n S Asia a work shutdown in protest

Hartford /haártfərd/ capital of Connecticut. Pop. 131,523 (1998).

harum-scarum /háirəm skáirəm/ adj careless and disorganized

Harvard University /haárvərd-/ n the oldest university in the United States, founded in 1636 in Massachusetts

harvest /haárvist/ n **1** the quantity of a crop gathered in a season ○ a record harvest **2** the gathering of a mature crop ○ berries ripe for harvest **3** the season in which crops are gathered ■ vti gather a crop

ORIGIN Harvest was originally the name for the third season of the year, 'autumn'. It derives from an ancient root meaning 'gather', and so always had connections with fruit and crops. Uses more directly connected with crops are recorded from the medieval period.

harvester /haárvistər/ n **1** a machine that gathers crops **2** somebody who gathers crops

harvest festival n a Christian service of thanksgiving for a harvest

harvest moon n the full moon nearest to the autumnal equinox

Harvey /haárvi/, **William** (1578–1657) English physician. He discovered the circulation of the blood.

has 3rd person present singular of **have**

has-been n somebody who is no longer important (infml)

hash[1] n **1** also **hash mark** the symbol #, especially on a telephone keypad or computer keyboard **2** a fried dish of potatoes and meat ■ vt US chop meat or vegetables into tiny pieces

hash[2] n hashish (slang)

hash browns npl US, Can a fried dish of chopped potatoes

hashish /háshish, há sheesh, ha sheesh/, **hasheesh** /há sheesh, ha sheesh/ n cannabis resin used as an illegal drug

hasn't /házz'nt/ contr has not

hasp n a hinged metal fastening that fits over a staple and is secured by a pin, bolt, or padlock —**hasp** vt

Hassan II /hə saán/ (1929–99) king of Morocco (1961–99)

Hassan /ha sán/, **Abdiqasim Salad** (b. 1942) president of Somalia (2000–)

~~hassel~~ incorrect spelling of **hassle**

hassium /hássi əm/ n (symbol **Hs**) a rare, unstable chemical element

hassle /háss'l/ (infml) n aggravation, or a source of aggravation ■ vt (**-sling**, **-sled**) keep bothering or annoying

hassock /hássək/ n a cushion on which to kneel in a Christian church

haste n great speed (fml)

hasten /háyss'n/ v **1** vi do or say something immediately ○ 'And I agree', he hastened to add. **2** vt speed something up ○ would hasten his recovery **3** vi go somewhere quickly (literary) ○ hastened to her side

Hastings /háystingz/ town in S England, site of the Battle of Hastings in 1066. Pop. 81,139 (1991). ■ city in the east of the North Island, New Zealand. Pop. 59,900 (1998).

hasty /háysti/ (**-ier**, **-iest**) adj done or acting too quickly —**hastily** adv —**hastiness** n

hat n **1** a head covering **2** one of various areas of responsibility that somebody has ○ put on her accountant's hat —**hatted** adj —**hatter** n ◇ **keep under your hat** keep secret ◇ **take your hat off to** acknowledge admiration for

hatch[1] n **1** a door in the floor or ceiling of something **2** a small hole or door between two rooms **3** *also* **hatchback** a car with a rear door that is hinged from the roof

hatch[2] *v* **1** *vti* come or make a young organism come out of an egg **2** *vi* break open for the release of a young organism *(refers to eggs)* **3** *vt* secretly devise a plot

hatch[3] *vti* mark or be marked with parallel crossed lines to show shading —**hatching** *n*

hatchery /háchəri/ (*pl* -**ies**) *n* a place where fish or poultry eggs are hatched commercially

hatchet /háchit/ *n* a small short-handled axe ◇ **bury the hatchet** make peace after a disagreement ◇ **do a hatchet job on** criticize severely *(infml)*

hatchet man *n* (*infml*) **1** somebody brought in to make cuts in staff or funding **2** *US, Can* a hired killer

hate *v* (**hating, hated**) **1** *vt* dislike somebody intensely **2** *vti* have strong distaste or aversion for something o *I hate cleaning the windows.* ■ *n* **1** a feeling of intense dislike **2** something hated —**hated** *adj* —**hater** *n* ◇ See note at **dislike**

hate crime *n* a crime motivated by prejudice against a group

hateful /háytf'l/ *adj* **1** spitefully malevolent **2** evoking feelings of hatred —**hatefully** *adv* —**hatefulness** *n*

hate mail *n* mail expressing hatred of the recipient

Hathaway /háthə way/, **Anne** (1556–1623) wife of William Shakespeare

hatred /háytrid/ *n* intense dislike or hostility ◇ See note at **dislike**

Hatshepsut /hát shép soot/ (*fl* 15C BC) queen of Egypt (1479–57 BC)

Hatteras, Cape /háttərəss/ promontory in E North Carolina, renowned for treacherous weather conditions

hat trick *n* a series of three wins or successes, especially goals in a game

Haughey /háwhi/, **Charles** (*b.* 1925) prime minister of Ireland (1979–81, 1982, and 1987–92)

haughty /háwti/ (-**tier**, -**tiest**) *adj* superior and condescending —**haughtily** *adv* —**haughtiness** *n*

haul *vt* **1** pull or drag something with effort **2** transport something heavy and bulky ■ *n* **1** a group of stolen items **2** a single catch of fish **3** a distance over which something is transported or somebody travels —**hauler** *n* ◇ See note at **pull**

haulage /háwlij/ *n* **1** the transporting of goods by road or rail **2** the cost of transporting goods by road or rail

haulier /háwli ər/ *n* a transporter of goods by road or rail

haunch *n* **1** the hip, buttock, and upper thigh **2** an animal's back leg

haunt *vt* **1** visit as a ghost **2** be a constant source of unease or worry for ■ *n* a place somebody often visits

haunted /háwntid/ *adj* **1** believed to be frequented by a ghost **2** looking frightened or worried

haunting /háwnting/ *adj* evoking strong emotion —**hauntingly** *adv*

Hauraki Gulf /how raaki-/ inlet of Pacific Ocean in the northeast of the North Island, New Zealand

Haussmann /óss man/, **George-Eugène, Baron** (1809–91) French town planner

haute couture /ōt-/ *n* the business of designing and making exclusive clothing, or such clothing itself

haute cuisine /ōt-/ *n* classic French cooking

hauteur /ō túr/ *n* haughtiness

Havana[1] /hə vánnə/ capital, port, and largest city of Cuba. Pop. 2,184,990 (1996). —**Havanan** *adj, n*

Havana[2] /hə vánnə/, **Havana cigar** *n* a high-quality Cuban cigar

have (*stressed*) /hav/ (*unstressed*) /həv, əv/ *v* (**has, having, had**) **1** *vt* own or possess o *She has a small cottage in the country.* **2** *vt* possess as a quality or characteristic o *He had short dark hair.* ■ *aux v* **3** forms perfect tenses o *Have you finished? o I have lost my keys. o would have enjoyed it* ■ *v* **4** must o *We have to go now. o There has to be another way.* **5** *vt* receive or obtain o *I had a letter from him yesterday.* **6** *vt* eat or drink o *He had breakfast early.* **7** *vt* think of or remember o *I have an idea.* **8** *vt* experience or undergo o *We had a great time. o I had my car stolen.* **9** *vt* be affected by o *She has flu.* **10** *vt* engage in o *They had a long talk about cars.* **11** *vt* organize o *We had a party last week.* **12** *vt* arrange for something to be done for you o *I've just had my hair cut.* **13** *vt* tolerate o *I won't have such behaviour!* **14** *vt* provide accommodation or entertainment for o *We had a friend to stay for the weekend.* **15** *vt* be a prospective parent of o *We're having a baby.* **16** *vt* make something happen o *Have him phone me tomorrow.* ■ **haves** *npl* rich or privileged people ◇ **have (got) it in for** want to harm ◇ **have something on somebody** have unfavourable information about somebody's activities ◇ **have it out (with)** argue over an issue with ◇ **have to do with** be relevant to ◇ **have what it takes** have the necessary skills, personality, or attitude to be successful

☐ **have on** *vt* **1** be wearing **2** tease *(infml)*

Havel /haav'l, háv'l/, **Václav** (*b.* 1936) dramatist and president of Czechoslovakia (1989–92) and of the Czech Republic (1993–)

haven /háyv'n/ *n* **1** a place of rest, shelter, or safety **2** an anchorage *(literary)*

have-nots *npl* people who are not rich or privileged

haven't /hávv'nt/ *contr* have not

haversack /hávvər sak/ *n* a bag carried over one shoulder or on the back

ORIGIN Haversack comes via French from an obsolete German compound meaning literally 'oats bag', as carried by cavalry soldiers. It is first recorded in English—for human pro-visions—in the mid-18C.

Havilland ♦ De Havilland, Sir Geoffrey

havoc /hávvək/ n 1 destruction or devastation 2 chaos

haw[1] n 1 a hawthorn 2 the fruit of the haw-thorn

haw[2] vi make a sound expressing hesitation —**haw** n

Hawaii /hə wí i/ 1 state of the United States in the N Pacific Ocean, consisting of eight main islands and over 100 others. Cap. Honolulu. Pop. 1,211,537 (2000). 2 largest island in the state of Hawaii. Pop. 137,291 (1995). —**Hawaiian** n, adj

hawk[1] n 1 a bird of prey with broad wings, a long tail, and a short hooked bill 2 also **Hawk** somebody favouring the use of force in im-plementing foreign policy ■ v 1 vi hunt with hawks 2 vti attack while flying —**hawking** n —**hawkish** adj

hawk[2] v 1 vi clear the throat 2 vt cough up phlegm —**hawk** n

hawk[3] vti sell goods on the streets —**hawker** n

Hawke, Bob (b. 1929) Australian prime min-ister (1983–91)

hawk-eyed adj quick to see things

Hawking /háwking/, **Stephen** (b. 1942) British physicist and mathematician. He wrote *A Brief History of Time* (1988).

Hawksmoor /háwks mŏŏr, -mawr/, **Nicholas** (1661–1736) British architect

hawser /háwzər/ n a cable for mooring or towing a ship

hawthorn /háw thawrn/ n a thorny tree with white or pink flowers and reddish berries

Hawthorne /háw thawrn/, **Nathaniel** (1804–64) US writer

hay n cut and dried grass, often used as fodder

Haydn /híd'n/, **Joseph** (1732–1809) Austrian composer

hay fever n an allergic reaction to pollen

hayloft /háy loft/ n a loft for storing hay in a stable or a barn

haymaker /háy maykər/ n 1 a worker who cuts, bales, or stores hay 2 a machine for drying hay

hayseed /háy seed/ n 1 grass seed removed from hay 2 pieces of grass or straw that fall from hay

haystack /háy stak/, **hayrick** /háy rik/ n a large pile of hay in a field

haywire /háy wīr/ adj functioning erratically (infml)

hazard /házzərd/ n 1 a potential danger 2 a dangerous outcome 3 a dice game re-sembling craps 4 an obstacle on a golf course 5 in billiards, a scoring stroke ■ vt 1 suggest tentatively 2 risk the loss of

hazard light n a flashing light on a car for warning other drivers

hazardous /házzərdəss/ adj potentially dan-

gerous —**hazardously** adv —**hazard-ousness** n

hazardous waste n a toxic by-product of a manufacturing process or nuclear pro-cessing

haze n 1 mist, cloud, or smoke in the atmosphere obscuring the view 2 a vague obscuring factor 3 a disoriented mental or physical state ■ vi (**hazing, hazed**) become saturated with atmospheric particles

hazel /háyz'l/ (pl -**zels** or same) n 1 also **hazel-nut** an edible brown nut 2 a small tree pro-ducing hazels 3 the wood of the hazel tree. Use: baskets, hurdles. 4 a light-brown colour

Hazlitt /házlit/, **William** (1778–1830) British es-sayist

hazy /háyzi/ (-**ier, -iest**) adj 1 unclear because of mist, cloud, or smoke 2 imprecise or in-distinctly remembered —**hazily** adv —**haziness** n

H-bomb n a hydrogen bomb

HD abbr 1 hard disk 2 high density

he (stressed) /hee/ (unstressed) /hi, i/ pron refers to a male person or animal who has been previously mentioned or whose identity is known (as the subject of a verb) ■ n a male animal or a boy, especially a new baby

He symbol helium

head /hed/ n 1 the topmost part of a vertebrate body, containing the brain 2 the farthest forward section of an invertebrate body 3 the centre of the human intellect and emo-tions 4 a leader 5 a head teacher 6 a crisis point ○ *The dispute came to a head.* 7 the wider top of a long thin object ○ *the head of a nail* 8 a flower cluster, or a compact cluster of leaves and stalks 9 the source of a river 10 the obverse of a coin that shows a leader's head 11 the part of a machine that records, reads, or erases sounds, images, or data 12 a title above a section of text 13 the pressure exerted by a liquid or gas ○ *a head of steam* ■ adj chief ■ v 1 vt control a group or organization 2 vt be at the front or top of something 3 vi move in a particular direction 4 vt hit a ball with the head —**headed** adj —**headless** adj ◇ **above** or **over somebody's head** too difficult for somebody to under-stand ◇ **be** or **go off** or **out of your head** be or become psychologically disturbed ◇ **go to somebody's head** 1 make somebody con-ceited or overconfident 2 make somebody dizzy ◇ **head over heels** 1 rolling or turning upside down 2 completely ○ *head over heels in love* ◇ **keep your head** remain calm ◇ **knock something on the head** put an end to some-thing, or prevent something from de-veloping any further (infml) ◇ **lose your head** lose self-control

□ **head off** vt 1 intercept 2 forestall

headache /héd ayk/ n 1 a pain in the head 2 a source of worry (infml) —**headachy** adj

headband /héd band/ n a strip of fabric for keeping the hair in place

headboard /héd bawrd/ n a board at the head of a bed

head boy *n* a senior boy elected to represent his school

head-butt *vt* hit somebody with the head —**head-butt** *n*

headcam /héd kam/ *n* a video camera mounted on a person's head or on headgear

headcheese /héd cheez/ (*pl* -**cheeses** *or same*) *n* US, Can FOOD = **brawn**

head count *n* the process of counting the people in a group, or the number counted

headdress /héd dress/ *n* an elaborate head covering often worn as a sign of rank

header /héddər/ *n* 1 in football, a shot made with the head 2 a headlong fall 3 a heading on each page of a document 4 the part at the top of an e-mail for information about the message 5 a crosswise brick in a wall 6 somebody or something that makes, fits, or removes the tops of things

headfirst /héd fúrst/ *adv, adj* with the head leading ■ *adv* rashly and thoughtlessly

headgear /héd geer/ *n* something worn on the head

head girl *n* a senior girl elected to represent her school

headhunt /héd hunt/ *v* 1 *vt* attempt to recruit somebody from another company 2 *vi* cut off and collect the heads of enemies as trophies —**headhunter** *n* —**headhunting** *n*

heading /hédding/ *n* 1 the title for a section of text 2 a ship's or aircraft's course

headland /héddlənd/ *n* 1 a promontory jutting into the sea 2 an unploughed strip at the edge of a field

headlight /héd lít/, **headlamp** /-lamp/ *n* a strong light on the front of a vehicle

headline /héd lín/ *n* the title of a newspaper article, printed in larger, heavier type ■ **headlines** *npl* the main news items in a newspaper or news broadcast ■ *vt* (-**lining**, -**lined**) 1 give a prominent heading to 2 US present as the star of a show

headlock /héd lok/ *n* a wrestling hold in which an arm is placed around an opponent's head

headlong /héd long/ *adv, adj* 1 with the head foremost 2 moving fast and out of control

headman /hédmən, héd man/ (*pl* -**men** /-mən, -men/) *n* 1 a community or village chief 2 a leader or overseer

headmaster /hed maástər/ *n* a man in charge of a school —**headmasterly** *adj*

headmistress /hed místrəss/ *n* a woman in charge of a school —**headmistressy** *adj*

head of government *n* the person in charge of a country's government

head of state *n* the chief representative of a country

head-on *adv, adj* with the front facing forwards ■ *adv* without evasion or compromise ■ *adj* uncompromising

headphones /héd fōnz/ *npl* a device with earphones, worn on the head

headpiece /héd peess/ *n* 1 an ornamental design printed at the beginning of a text 2 a protective covering for the head

headquarter /hed kwáwrtər/ *vt* provide with headquarters

headquarters /hed kwáwrtərz, héd kwawrtərz/ *n* (+ *sing or pl verb*) 1 a military commander's operational base 2 a head office or centre of operations

headrest /héd rest/ *n* a support for the head on the back of a seat

headroom /héd room, -room/ *n* the overhead clearance in a room or vehicle, or under a bridge

headscarf /héd skaarf/ (*pl* -**scarves** /-skaarvz/) *n* a scarf for covering the head

headset /héd set/ *n* a set of headphones with a mouthpiece

headship /hédship/ *n* 1 the position of head teacher 2 the position of leader

headstand /héd stand/ *n* a position in which somebody balances on the head and hands

head start *n* a competitive advantage

headstone /héd stōn/ *n* 1 a gravestone 2 a keystone

headstrong /héd strong/ *adj* wilful and stubborn —**headstrongness** *n*

head teacher *n* the teacher in charge of a school

head-to-head *adv, adj* in or involving a direct encounter ■ *adv* with heads adjacent ■ *n* a direct encounter

head waiter *n* the chief waiter in a restaurant

headwaters /héd wawtərz/ *npl* the source waters of a river

headway /héd way/ *n* 1 progress 2 forward movement 3 headroom

headwind /héd wind/ *n* a wind coming from in front

headword /héd wurd/ *n* the key word at the start of a text, especially a main entry in a dictionary

heady /héddi/ (-**ier**, -**iest**) *adj* 1 exhilarating 2 intoxicating —**headily** *adv* —**headiness** *n*

heal /heel/ *v* 1 *vt* restore a person, body part, or injury to health 2 *vi* be repaired naturally ○ *The bone is healing nicely.* 3 *vt* correct something causing problems ○ *heal the rift in the party* —**healer** *n* —**healing** *adj, n*

> **SPELLCHECK** Do not confuse the spelling of **heal** and **heel** (of a foot), which sound similar.

health /helth/ *n* 1 the general condition of the body or mind in relation to the presence or absence of illness or injury 2 the general condition of something ■ *adj* 1 devoted to the wellbeing of the general public 2 promoting physical and mental wellbeing

health care *n* the provision of medical services to maintain health

health centre *n* 1 a local headquarters for health-care services 2 a place offering health care

health farm, health spa *n* a commercial establishment, usually rural, with facilities for improving health and fitness

health food *n* a food eaten to improve or maintain health

healthful /hélthf'l/ *adj* beneficial to health

health insurance *n* insurance against the costs incurred through ill health

health visitor *n* UK a nurse who makes home visits

healthy /hélthi/ (**-ier, -iest**) *adj* **1** in good physical or mental condition **2** beneficial to health **3** suggestive of good health **4** psychologically sound **5** functioning well **6** considerable *(infml)* o *a healthy profit* —**healthily** *adv* —**healthiness** *n*

Heaney /héeni/, **Seamus** (*b.* 1939) Irish poet

heap /heep/ *n* **1** a rounded pile **2** something old or battered, especially a building or car *(infml)* **3** a large amount *(infml; often pl)* ■ *vt* **1** put in a pile o *heaped vegetables on his plate* **2** fill with a pile **3** give in abundance o *heaped scorn on my suggestion*

☐ **heap up** *v* **1** *vti* form into a pile **2** *vt* collect in large amounts

heaped /heept/ *adj* filled with something that rises in a small heap

hear /heer/ (**heard** /hurd/) *v* **1** *vti* perceive a sound **2** *vti* be told or informed of something **3** *vt* listen to **4** *vti* understand by listening —**hearable** *adj* —**hearer** *n*

SPELLCHECK Do not confuse the spelling of **hear** and **here** ('in this place'), which sound similar.

☐ **hear from** *vt* receive news from
☐ **hear of** *vt* consider as a possibility o *wouldn't hear of him paying*

hearing /héering/ *n* **1** the ability to perceive sound **2** the distance within which something can be heard **3** a chance to be heard **4** a trial in a court of law **5** a preliminary examination of an accused person to decide whether to go to trial

hearing aid *n* a device worn in or behind the ear to improve hearing

hearing-impaired *adj* with reduced hearing

hearken /haárkən/ *vi* listen *(archaic)*

hearsay /héer say/ *n* information heard from somebody else —**hearsay** *adj*

hearse /hurss/ *n* a vehicle that transports corpses at funerals

---

ORIGIN Agricultural harrows in the Middle Ages were typically toothed triangular frames, so the word for a harrow came to be applied in French to a triangular toothed frame for holding candles, particularly those placed over a coffin at funeral services. This was the meaning of **hearse** when English acquired it, and it gradually developed via 'canopy placed over a coffin' and 'coffin, bier' to the modern sense of 'funeral vehicle'.

Hearst /hurst/, **William Randolph** (1863–1951) US publisher and politician

heart /haart/ *n* **1** the organ in the chest that pumps blood around the body **2** the human heart considered as the basis and centre of emotional life **3** somebody's essential character o *has a good heart* **4** compassion o *Have you no heart?* **5** affection o *won the hearts of the audience* **6** spirit and determination o *played with a lot of heart* **7** a mood, mental state, or frame of mind o *in good heart* **8** the distinctive and characteristic centre of something o *the heart of rural England* **9** the part of a vegetable around its core **10** an animal heart used as food **11** a depiction of a heart as a symbol of love **12** a playing card with one or more red heart symbols on it ◊ **at heart** in essence or reality ◊ **eat your heart out** be consumed with envy ◊ **heart and soul** completely ◊ **learn** *or* **know by heart** memorize *or* have memorized ◊ **lose heart** become discouraged ◊ **take heart** become encouraged ◊ **take to heart 1** take seriously **2** be upset by ◊ **with all your heart** sincerely

heartache /haárt ayk/ *n* emotional pain

heart attack *n* **1** a sudden interruption of the heart's normal function **2** a sudden severe shock *(infml)*

heartbeat /haárt beet/ *n* **1** a contraction of the heart that drives blood through the body **2** the continuous pulsation of the heart

heartbreak /haárt brayk/ *n* intense grief —**heartbreaking** *adj*

heartbreaker /haárt braykər/ *n* somebody with whom many people fall unhappily in love

heartbroken /haárt brókən/ *adj* feeling intense grief —**heartbrokenly** *adv*

heartburn /haárt burn/ *n* an unpleasant sensation in the lower chest caused by stomach acid

heart disease *n* a condition of the heart that impairs functioning

hearten /haárt'n/ *vt* encourage —**heartening** *adj* —**hearteningly** *adv*

heartfelt /haárt felt/ *adj* deeply felt

hearth /haarth/ *n* **1** the floor of a fireplace **2** the fireplace of a home, thought of as a symbol of the home and family life

hearth rug *n* a small rug placed in front of a fireplace

heartland /haárt land/ *n* **1** the central part of a country **2** an area of a country with special economic, political, military, or sentimental significance *(often pl)*

heartless /haártləss/ *adj* cruel and unfeeling —**heartlessly** *adv* —**heartlessness** *n*

heartrending /haárt rending/ *adj* causing extreme emotional distress ◊ See note at **moving**

hearts /haarts/ *n* **1** the suit of cards marked with red heart symbols *(+ sing or pl verb)* **2** a card game in which players try to win either all or no hearts cards and the queen of spades *(+ sing verb)*

heart-searching *n* mental self-examination

heartsick /haárt sik/ *adj* very disappointed or sad —**heartsickness** *n*

heartstrings /haàrt stringz/ *npl* somebody's deepest feelings

heartthrob /haàrt throb/ *n* somebody considered very attractive *(infml)*

heart-to-heart *adj* very frank and intimate ■ *n* a frank intimate talk

heartwarming /haàrt wawrming/ *adj* emotionally gratifying —**heartwarmingly** *adv*

hearty /haàrti/ (**-ier, -iest**) *adj* **1** sincere and enthusiastic **2** healthy **3** strongly felt **4** substantial and nourishing **5** overloud and overenthusiastic, especially about sport *(infml)* —**heartily** *adv* —**heartiness** *n*

heat /heet/ *n* **1** (*symbol* **Q**) energy perceived as temperature **2** the perceptible degree of hotness **3** a source of warmth, e.g. for cooking or keeping warm **4** intense emotion **5** the time of greatest activity ○ *in the heat of the campaign* **6** the spiciness of some foods **7** a sexually receptive stage in a female mammal's reproductive cycle **8** a preliminary round in a race or contest to eliminate some competitors or establish a starting order **9** psychological pressure *(infml)* ■ *vti* make or become warm or hot

□ **heat up** *vti* make or become hotter or more intense

heated /heetid/ *adj* **1** made hot or warm **2** intense or angry ○ *a heated argument* —**heatedly** *adv*

heater /heetər/ *n* **1** a heating device **2** a heating element in a valve

heat exhaustion *n* physical exhaustion caused by extreme heat

heath /heeth/ *n* **1** an area of uncultivated open land covered with rough grass and small bushes **2** a low bush commonly found on heaths

Heath /heeth/, **Sir Edward** (*b.* 1916) British prime minister (1970–74)

heathen /heeth'n/ *n* **1** an offensive term for a person who practices a religion other than Christianity, Judaism, or Islam **2** an offensive term for somebody viewed as irreligious or uncivilized —**heathen** *adj*

ORIGIN Etymologically a **heathen** is simply 'somebody who lives on a heath'. By implication such a person was savage and uncivilized. Its early association with religion may have been influenced by Latin *paganus*, which came to refer to a non-Christian but originally was also simply 'somebody who lives in the country'.

heather /héthər/ *n* a low-growing evergreen plant with spiky leaves and small flowers

Heath Robinson /heeth róbbinss'n/ *adj* flimsy and wildly contrived *(humorous)*

ORIGIN The adjective derives from the name of the British humorous artist W. Heath Robinson (1872–1944), whose illustrations featured wildly contrived devices.

heat-proof *adj* not affected by heat in an oven or from a flame

heat rash *n* prickly heat

heat-seeking *adj* able to follow infrared radiation from heat

heatstroke /heet strōk/ *n* a medical condition caused by exposure to extreme heat

heat wave *n* an unusually hot period of weather

heave /heev/ (**heaving, heaved**) *v* **1** *vt* move using great physical effort **2** *vi* exert physical effort in a rhythmic burst ○ *heave on a rope* **3** *vt* direct something heavy somewhere by tossing *(infml)* **4** *vi* rise and fall rhythmically ○ *His chest was heaving.* **5** *vti* vomit *(infml)* **6** *vt* laboriously utter a sigh **7** (*past* **hove** /hōv/) *vti* move or make a ship move in a particular direction —**heave** *n* ◊ See note at **throw**

heaven /hévv'n/ *n* **1** *also* **Heaven** a place or condition of perfect happiness where good people are believed to go after death, according to some religions **2** a blissful experience ■ **heavens** *npl* the sky above the Earth ◇ **move heaven and earth** do everything possible to make something happen

heavenly /hévv'nli/ (**-lier, -liest**) *adj* **1** of God and Heaven **2** in the sky or in space as seen from the Earth **3** lovely *(infml)*

heavenly body *n* an object that is permanently present in the sky, e.g. a star or planet

heaven-sent *adj* happening or coming at just the right time

heavenward /hévv'nwərd/ *adj* directed towards heaven or the sky ■ *adv also* **heavenwards** towards heaven or the sky

heavy /hévvi/ *adj* (**-ier, -iest**) **1** weighing a lot **2** occurring or produced in large amounts ○ *heavy rain* **3** needing strength ○ *heavy physical work* **4** difficult to fulfil or cope with **5** having great force ○ *a heavy blow* **6** affected by tiredness ○ *eyes heavy with sleep* **7** dully loud ○ *a heavy thud* **8** industrial-scale ○ *heavy industry* **9** sad ○ *a heavy heart* **10** requiring concentration to be understood ○ *a heavy novel* **11** hard to digest ○ *a heavy meal* ■ *n* (*pl* **-ies**) **1** a villain in a play, film, or opera *(infml)* **2** somebody hired to intimidate people with threats or violence *(slang)* **3** *US* somebody powerful or influential *(slang)* —**heavily** *adv* —**heaviness** *n*

heavy-duty *adj* tough and durable

heavy goods vehicle *n* a large road vehicle for transporting goods

heavy-handed *adj* **1** physically or socially clumsy **2** harsh and oppressive —**heavy-handedly** *adv* —**heavy-handedness** *n*

heavy-hearted *adj* feeling sad —**heavy-heartedly** *adv* —**heavy-heartedness** *n*

heavy metal *n* **1** a type of loud rock music with a very strong beat **2** a metal with a high relative density

heavyset /hévvi sét/ *adj* having a large or solid build

heavyweight /hévvi wayt/ *n* **1** the weight category in boxing between light heavyweight and superheavyweight **2** a boxer who competes at heavyweight **3** somebody or something heavy **4** somebody or something powerful or influential

Hebraic /hi bráy ik/, **Hebraical** /-ik'l/ *adj* of Hebrew or the Israelites —**Hebraically** *adv*

Hebrew /heébroo/ *n* **1** a Semitic language, the modern form of which is one of the official languages of Israel **2** an Israelite —**Hebrew** *adj*

Hebrides /hébbrə deez/ island group off W Scotland —**Hebridean** /hébbri deé ən/ *adj, n*

heck (*infml*) *interj* expresses irritation or emphasis ■ *n* emphasizes annoyance or disagreement ○ *What the heck is going on?*

heckle /hék'l/ (**-ling**, **-led**) *vti* interrupt somebody giving a speech or performance by shouting —**heckler** *n*

hectare /hék taar, -tair/ *n* a metric unit of area equal to 100 ares or 10,000 sq. m (2.471 acres)

hectic /héktik/ *adj* **1** constantly busy and hurried **2** hot and feverish ○ *a hectic flush* —**hectically** *adv*

hecto-, hect- *prefix* one hundred ○ *hectogram*

hector /héktər/ *vti* speak or address in an intimidating way

Hector /héktər/ *n* a mythological Trojan hero

he'd (*stressed*) /heed/ (*unstressed*) /hid, id/ *contr* **1** he had **2** he would

hedge *n* **1** a close-set row of bushes forming a barrier **2** a means of protection against something, especially financial loss ■ *v* (**hedging**, **hedged**) **1** *vt* put bushes around an area **2** *vi* be evasive **3** *vi* try to offset possible financial losses

hedgehog /héj hog/ *n* a small spiny mammal that rolls into a ball when attacked

hedgerow /héj rō/ *n* a row of bushes at a roadside or around a field

hedonism /heéd'nizəm, hédd'n-/ *n* **1** the self-indulgent pursuit of pleasure **2** the philosophy that regards pleasure as the highest good —**hedonist** *n* —**hedonistic** /heédə nístik, héddə-/ *adj*

heed *vti* pay attention to advice or an adviser ■ *n* serious attention to advice —**heedful** *adj* —**heedfully** *adv* —**heedless** *adj* —**heedlessly** *adv*

heehaw /heé haw/ *n* a donkey's bray —**heehaw** *vi*

heel[1] /heel/ *n* **1** the back of a foot below the ankle **2** the back part of a shoe or sock that covers the heel **3** the back of the underside of a shoe, which is thicker or taller than the rest of the shoe **4** the thicker part of the palm of the hand next to the wrist **5** a crusty end of a loaf of bread **6** the hard rind from a wedge of cheese **7** the part of a golf club head to which the shaft is attached **8** the end of a violin bow that is held when playing **9** a small piece of a plant stem left attached to a cutting to promote growth **10** a man regarded as behaving reprehensibly (*insult*) ■ *v* **1** *vt* fit or repair the heel of a shoe **2** *vi* follow by somebody's heels (*refers to dogs*) **3** *vt* dig heels into an animal that is being ridden **4** *vi* move the heels in dancing **5** *vt*

mishit a golf ball with the heel of a club **6** *vt* kick a ball with the heel —**heeled** *adj* ◊ **cool** *or* **kick your heels** wait or be kept waiting for a long time (*infml*) ◊ **dig in your heels** hold stubbornly to a position or attitude ◊ **(hard) on the heels of 1** close behind **2** soon after ◊ **take to your heels** run off ◊ **to heel** under control or discipline ◊ See note at **heal**

heel[2] /heel/ *vti* lean, or make a ship lean, to one side

Hefei /hó fáy/, **Hofei** capital of **Anhui Province**, E China. Pop. 1,320,000 (1995).

heft *vt* **1** lift something heavy **2** estimate the weight of something by lifting it ■ *n* great weight

hefty /héfti/ (**-ier, -iest**) *adj* **1** powerfully built **2** heavy, forceful, or strenuous **3** considerable ○ *a hefty sum* —**heftily** *adv* —**heftiness** *n*

Hegel /háyg'l/, **G. W. F.** (1770–1831) German philosopher —**Hegelian** /hi gáyli ən/ *adj, n*

hegemony /hi gémməni, -jémmən/ *n* dominance or control, especially by one country over others —**hegemonic** /héggə mónnik, héjjə-/ *adj*

hegira /héjjirə, hi jírə/ *n* **1** *also* **hejira** a flight or withdrawal from somewhere **2 Hegira, Hejira** Muhammad's withdrawal from Mecca to Medina to escape persecution **3 Hegira, Hejira** the Muslim era, dated from the first day of the lunar year of Muhammad's Hegira

Heidegger /hí degər/, **Martin** (1889–1976) German philosopher

Heidelberg /híd'l burg/ city in SW Germany, on the River Neckar. Pop. 138,964 (1997).

heifer /héffər/ *n* a young cow that has never had a calf

Heifetz /hífits/, **Jascha** (1901–87) Lithuanian-born US violinist

heigh-ho /hay-/ *interj* expresses boredom, disappointment, or resignation

height /hīt/ *n* **1** the distance between the lowest and highest point of somebody or something ○ *a cliff about 70 metres in height* **2** the distance that somebody or something is above a point **3** the condition of being noticeably tall or high in comparison with others **4** a high place or position (*often pl*) **5** the highest point of something **6** a high level of intensity or severity (*often pl*) **7** the time of greatest intensity, activity, or success ○ *at the height of her powers* **8** the most extreme example of something ○ *the height of folly* ■ **heights** *npl* hills or mountains (*often in placenames*)

heighten /hít'n/ *vti* **1** make or become greater or higher **2** appear or make brighter —**heightened** *adj*

~~heighth~~ incorrect spelling of **height**

Heimlich manoeuvre /hímlik-/ *n* an emergency treatment for choking that uses an upward thrust immediately below the breastbone

ORIGIN The treatment is named after Henry J. Heimlich (1920–), who devised it.

Heine /hínə/, **Heinrich** (1797–1856) German poet

heinous /háynəss/ adj utterly evil —**heinously** adv —**heinousness** n

heir /air/ n **1** the legal inheritor of something **2** a recipient of a tradition —**heirless** adj —**heirship** n ◊ See note at **air**

heir apparent (pl **heirs apparent**) n **1** somebody whose right to an inheritance cannot be altered by the birth of another heir **2** the expected successor of somebody's position

~~heirarchy~~ incorrect spelling of **hierarchy**

heiress /áirəss/ n a woman who is the legal inheritor of something

heirloom /air loom/ n **1** something valuable handed down from one generation of a family to another **2** something legally inherited by somebody

heir presumptive (pl **heirs presumptive**) n somebody whose right to an inheritance ceases on the birth of somebody with a stronger legal claim

Heisenberg /híz'n burg/, **Werner** (1901–76) German physicist

heist /híst/ n US, Can an armed robbery (slang) —**heist** vt

hejira n = **hegira**

Heke Pokai /hékay pókī/, **Hone** (1810?–50) Maori leader

held past tense, past participle of **hold**[1]

Helen /héllən/, **Helen of Troy** n in Greek mythology, the wife of Menelaus, a beautiful woman whose abduction by Paris was the cause of the Trojan War

Helena /héllənə/ capital of Montana. Pop. 28,306 (1998).

helical /héllik'l/ adj in the shape of a helix or spiral —**helically** adv

helicopter /hélli koptər/ n an aircraft with rotors instead of wings ■ vti fly in a helicopter

ORIGIN **Helicopter** is formed from Greek words that mean 'spiral' and 'wing'. The name was originally coined in French, and early examples in English sometimes have a French form. The usual modern spelling is recorded from the 1880s.

Heliopolis /heeli óppəliss/ city of ancient Egypt, in the Nile delta

Helios /heeli oss/ n in Greek mythology, the god of the sun. Roman equivalent **Sol**

heliotrope /heeli ə trōp/ (pl **-tropes** or same) n **1** a plant with purple flowers **2** a plant with flowers that turn towards the sun

helipad /hélli pad/ n a helicopter landing place

heliport /hélli pawrt/ n an airport for helicopters

helium /heeli əm/ n (symbol **He**) an inert gas. Use: inert atmospheres, cryogenic research, lasers, inflating balloons.

helix /heeliks/ (pl **helices** /hélli seez/ or **helixes**) n **1** something in the shape of a spiral or coil **2** a mathematical spiral curve

hell n **1** also **Hell** a place or condition of punishment where bad people are believed to go after death, according to many religions **2** also **Hell** Satan, or the powers of evil that are believed to live in hell, according to some religions **3** the place where everyone is believed to go after death, according to some religions **4** a situation in which there is great unpleasantness or suffering ■ interj expresses annoyance or surprise (sometimes offensive) ◊ **a** or **one hell of a** a particularly large, intense, or impressive example or amount of (infml) ◊ **come hell or high water** whatever difficulties there may be ◊ **from hell** of the worst sort imaginable (infml) ◊ **give somebody hell** scold somebody severely (infml) ◊ **(just) for the hell of it** just for amusement or excitement (infml) ◊ **like hell** very fast or very intensely (infml) ◊ **raise hell** (infml) **1** object strongly and loudly **2** cause a noisy disturbance

ORIGIN **Hell** goes back to an ancient form meaning 'hide, conceal', and is in fact related to the second part of **conceal**.

he'll (stressed) /heel/ (unstressed) /eel, il/ contr **1** he shall **2** he will

hell-bent adj determined to do something, regardless of the consequences

Hellene /hélleen/ n somebody from Greece (fml)

Hellenic /he leénik, -lénnik/ adj of Greece, or its people, languages, or culture

Heller /héllər/, **Joseph** (1923–99) US writer

Hellespont /héllispont/ ♦ **Dardanelles**

hellhole /hél hōl/ n a dreadful place

hellish /héllish/ adj **1** very wicked or cruel **2** of hell **3** very unpleasant or difficult (infml) —**hellishly** adv —**hellishness** n

hello /hə ló, he-/, **hallo** /hə ló, ha-/, **hullo** /hə ló, hu-/ interj, n (pl **-los**) **1** expresses a greeting **2** used to attract attention ○ Hello! Is there anyone in? **3** expresses surprise ○ Hello! What's this?

helm n **1** a ship's steering apparatus **2** a position of control or leadership in an organization or country ■ vt control and direct an organization or country

helmet /hélmit/ n a hard protective head covering —**helmeted** adj

helmsman /hélmzmən/ (pl **-men** /-mən/) n **1** somebody whose job it is to steer a ship **2** the leader of an organization or country

Héloïse /éllō eez/ (1098?–1164) French abbess and lover of Peter Abelard

help v **1** vti provide assistance to somebody **2** vti make something easier or more likely ○ More experience would help you get a better job. **3** vti bring about an improvement in an unpleasant situation ○ I took the medicine, but it didn't help. **4** vti provide somebody with something needed, especially money **5** vt give somebody or yourself a serving of food ○ Help yourself to some more. **6** vt keep somebody or yourself from doing something (usually in negative statements) ○ I couldn't help overhearing. ■ n **1** assistance **2** somebody or something that assists **3** somebody paid to clean somebody else's house ■ *interj* calls for assistance —**helper** *n* ◇ **help yourself** take something for your own use ◊ See note at **assistant**

□ **help out** *vti* give somebody some help

help desk *n* a service providing technical support for users of a computer system or network

helpful /hélpfʼl/ *adj* providing or willing to provide help —**helpfully** *adv* —**helpfulness** *n*

helping /hélping/ *n* an amount of food served to somebody

helpless /hélpləss/ *adj* **1** needing help **2** defenceless **3** unable to prevent something from happening —**helplessly** *adv* —**helplessness** *n*

helpline /hélp līn/ *n* a telephone advice or information service

helpmate /hélp mayt/ *n* a helpful companion, especially a spouse

ORIGIN **Helpmate** is first recorded in the early 18C, and was influenced by, if not actually based on, earlier (late 17C) *helpmeet*, with the same meaning. *Helpmeet* itself derives from a misunderstanding of a phrase in the Bible (Genesis 2:18, 20), 'an help meet for him', which actually means 'a helper suitable for him', with *meet* as an adjective, not a noun.

Helsinki /hel síngki/ capital and chief port of Finland. Pop. 551,123 (2000).

helter-skelter /héltər skéltər/ *adv, adj* **1** hurriedly **2** haphazardly ■ *n* **1** a spiral slide at a fairground **2** a hurried or confused state

~~helth~~ incorrect spelling of **health**

hem[1] *n* **1** a folded stitched edge on a piece of fabric **2** a hemline ■ *v* (**hemming, hemmed**) **1** *vti* make a hem on a fabric or garment **2** *also* **hem in** *vt* surround or confine

hem[2] (**hemming, hemmed**) *vi* hesitate in speech by making a noise in the throat —**hem** *interj, n* ◇ **hem and haw** hesitate while speaking or deciding about something

he-man *n* a muscular man (*infml*)

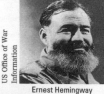

US Office of War Information

Ernest Hemingway

Hemingway /hémming way/, **Ernest** (1899–1961) US writer

hemisphere /hémmi sfeer/ *n* **1** one half of the Earth **2** one half of a sphere **3** each of the two halves of the front part of the brain —**hemispheric** /hémmi sférrik/ *adj* —**hemispherical** *adj*

hemline /hém līn/ *n* **1** the bottom edge of a skirt, dress, or coat **2** the height above or below the knee of the hem of a piece of women's clothing

hemlock /hém lok/ (*pl* **-locks** *or same*) *n* **1** a poison obtained from the fruit of a herbaceous plant **2** a herbaceous plant from which hemlock is obtained **3** an evergreen tree with short blunt needles and small cones

hemp *n* **1** a tough plant fibre. Use: canvas, rope, paper, cloth. **2** cannabis **3** (*pl same or* **hemps**) an Asian plant that produces hemp fibre or cannabis

hen *n* **1** an adult female domestic fowl **2** a female bird —**hennish** *adj*

hence *adv* (*fml*) **1** because of this **2** later than now

henceforth /hénss fáwrth/, **henceforward** /-fáwrwərd/, **henceforwards** /-fáwrwərdz/ *adv* from now on

henchman /hénchmən/ (*pl* **-men** /-mən/) *n* **1** a supporter or associate, especially of somebody involved in a criminal or dishonest cause (*disapproving*) **2** a loyal follower

ORIGIN The first part of **henchman** seems to represent *hengest*, an old form meaning 'stallion'. In the earliest records a **henchman** is a squire or page, but the connection with horses suggests that the word may originally have meant 'groom'. It fell out of use in the course of the 17C, but reappeared in the 18C for the personal attendant of a Scottish Highland chief. This was taken up by Sir Walter Scott in the early 19C, and he also appears to have been the first to extend the use to any trusty right-hand man.

henna /hénnə/ *n* **1** a red dye. Use: hair dye, cosmetics, fabric colourant. **2** a bush from whose leaves henna is obtained —**henna** *adj, vt*

hen night *n* a night out for a woman who is about to be married with her women friends (*sometimes offensive*)

hen party *n* a celebration for women only (*sometimes offensive*)

henpeck /hén pek/ *vt* subject a husband to continual nagging (*offensive*) —**henpecked** *adj*

Henrietta Maria /hénri éttə mə reé ə/ (1609–69) French-born queen consort of Charles I of England

henry /hénri/ (*pl* **-ries**) *n* (*symbol* **H**) the SI unit of electrical inductance

Henry I /hénri/ (1068–1135) king of the English (1100–35)

Henry II (1133–89) king of the English (1154–89)

Henry III (1207–72) king of England (1216–72)

Henry IV (1367–1413) king of England (1399–1413)

Henry IV (1553–1610) king of France (1589–1610)

Henry V (1387–1422) king of England (1413–22)

Henry VI (1421–71) king of England (1422–61, 1470–71)

Henry VII (1457–1509) king of England (1485–1509)

Henry VIII (1491–1547) king of England and Ireland (1509–47)

hepatitis /héppə títəss/ *n* inflammation of the liver

Hepburn /hép burn/, **Audrey** (1929–93) Belgian-born US actor

Hepburn, Katharine (*b.* 1907?) US actor

Hephaestus /hi féestəss/ *n* in Greek mythology, the god of fire. Roman equivalent **Vulcan**

Hepplewhite /hépp'l wīt/, **George** (*d.* 1786) British furniture designer

heptagon /héptəgən/ *n* a seven-sided figure —**heptagonal** /hep tággənəl/ *adj*

Hepworth /hép wurth/, **Dame Barbara** (1903–75) British sculptor

her *pron* (as the object or complement of a verb or preposition) **1** refers to a woman, girl, or female animal who has been previously mentioned or whose identity is known ○ *Ask her to wait.* **2** refers to a country that has been previously mentioned or whose identity is known (*fml*) ○ *Britain and those who trade with her* **3** refers to a car, machine, or ship ○ *Fill her up, please.* ■ *det* belonging to or associated with her ○ *That's her coat.* ○ *the Bismarck and her crew*

Hera /heérə/ *n* in Greek mythology, the queen of the gods. Roman equivalent **Juno** 1

Heraclitus /hérrə klítəss/ (*fl* 500? BC) Greek philosopher —**Heraclitean** /hérrə klíshi ən/ *adj*

Herakles *n* in Greek mythology, a son of Zeus noted for his strength. Roman equivalent **Hercules** 1

herald /hérrəld/ *n* **1** a bringer of news **2** a sign of what will happen (*literary*) **3** formerly, a king's official messenger ■ *vt* **1** give or be a sign of something that is going to happen **2** welcome or announce somebody or something enthusiastically

heraldic /hə ráldik, he-/ *adj* of heraldry or heralds —**heraldically** *adv*

heraldry /hérrəldri/ *n* **1** the study of coats of arms **2** coats of arms

Herat /hə rát/ city in NW Afghanistan. Pop. 177,300 (1988 estimate).

herb *n* **1** a low-growing aromatic plant used as a seasoning or for its medicinal properties **2** a plant that does not have woody stems and forms new stems each season

herbaceous /hər báyshəss/ *adj* of plants that do not have woody stems and form new stems each season

herbaceous border *n* a flower bed containing perennial plants

herbal /húrb'l/ *adj* of aromatic herbs ■ *n* a book listing herbs and their properties

herbalism /húrbə lizəm/ *n* alternative medicine based on herbs

herbalist /húrbəlist/ *n* **1** somebody who sells

medicinal herbs or treats people with them **2** *S Africa* a traditional doctor

herbicide /húrbi sīd/ *n* a chemical substance for killing weeds or unwanted plants —**herbicidal** /húrbi sīd'l/ *adj*

herbivore /húrbi vawr/ *n* an animal that eats only plants

herbivorous /hur bívvərəss/ *adj* describes an animal that eats only plants

Herculaneum /húrkyōo láyni əm/ ancient Roman town near modern Naples, destroyed with its neighbour Pompeii in the eruption of Vesuvius in AD 79

Herculean /húrkyoo leé ən, hur kyóoli ən/ *adj* **1** of or associated with Hercules **2** herculean needing great strength or effort

Hercules /húrkyōo leez/ *n* **1** in Roman mythology, a son of Zeus noted for his strength. Greek equivalent **Herakles 2** (*pl same or* **Herculeses**) a very strong man

herd *n* **1** a large group of domestic animals of the same kind, especially cattle **2** a large group of wild animals of the same kind **3** a large group of people with a common interest or purpose **4** ordinary people acting and thinking as a group (*disapproving*) ■ *vt* **1** control a group of animals **2** move or collect a group of people or animals somewhere —**herder** *n*

here /heer/ *adv* **1** in this place **2** at this point or stage **3** now **4** indicates an offer ○ *Here's my phone number.* **5** introduces a topic ○ *Now, here is a question for everybody.* ◇ **neither here nor there** irrelevant ◊ See note at **hear**

hereafter /heer áaftər/ (*fml*) *adv* **1** after the present time **2** in any following part of a text **3** after death ■ *n* life after death

hereby /heer bí, heér bī/ *adv* by this means (*fml*)

hereditary /hi rédditəri/ *adj* **1** passed on genetically **2** handed down through generations by inheritance **3** holding a right or property through inheritance

heredity /hi rédditi/ *n* **1** the passing on of genetic characteristics **2** ancestry

Herefordshire /hérrifərdshər/ county in W England

herein /heer ín/ *adv* (*fml*) **1** in this document **2** in this respect

hereinafter /heerin áaftər/ *adv* later in this document (*fml*)

hereof /heer óv/ *adv* of this (*fml*)

heresy /hérrəssi/ (*pl* -sies) *n* **1** an unorthodox religious belief **2** an unorthodox opinion in philosophy, science, or politics

heretic /hérrətik/ *n* **1** somebody who holds an unorthodox religious belief **2** somebody who holds an unorthodox opinion in philosophy, science, or politics —**heretical** /hə réttik'l/ *adj*

hereto /heer tóo/ *adv* to this document or matter (*fml*)

heretofore /heértoo fáwr/ *adv* up until now (*fml*)

hereupon /heèrə pón/ *adv* (*fml*) **1** at this **2** on this matter

Hereward the Wake /hérriwərd thə wáyk/ (*fl* 1060–71) Anglo-Saxon rebel

herewith /heer wíth, -wíth/ *adv* 1 with this communication 2 by this statement (*fml*)

heritable /hérritəb'l/ *adj* able to be inherited —**heritability** /hérritə bíllatí/ *n*

heritage /hérritij/ *n* 1 the status, conditions, or character acquired through birth into a particular family or social class 2 a country's history, historical buildings, and past culture considered as benefiting the present generation 3 something passing from generation to generation within a social group

hermaphrodite /hur máffrə dít/ *n* 1 a person, animal, or plant with both male and female sexual organs and characteristics 2 somebody or something combining contradictory elements —**hermaphroditic** /hur máffrə díttik/ *adj* —**hermaphroditism** *n*

ORIGIN Hermaphrodite derives from the name (combining the names of his parents) of Hermaphroditus, who was the son of Hermes, the messenger of the Greek gods, and Aphrodite, the Greek goddess of love. Myth has it that a nymph Salmacis desired, and achieved, complete union with him, their two bodies becoming one.

Hermes /húr meez/ *n* in Greek mythology, a god who was a messenger. Roman equivalent **Mercury** 1

hermetic /hur méttik/, **hermetical** /-ik'l/ *adj* 1 airtight 2 protected from outside influence 3 hard to understand —**hermetically** *adv*

hermit /húrmit/ *n* 1 somebody who chooses to live in isolation from society 2 an early Christian living apart from society —**hermitic** /hur míttik/ *adj*

hermitage /húrmitij/ *n* 1 a place where a hermit lives 2 an isolated place 3 **Hermitage** an art museum in St Petersburg, Russia

hermit crab *n* a crab that lives in an empty mollusc shell

hernia /húrni ə/ (*pl* -**as** *or* -**ae** /-ee/) *n* a medical condition in which an internal organ projects through the wall of the cavity that contains it —**hernial** *adj*

hero /heềrō/ (*pl* -**roes**) *n* 1 a very brave person 2 somebody admired 3 the main male character in a fictional plot

Hero /heềrō/ *n* in Greek mythology, a priestess of Aphrodite whose lover Leander swam the Hellespont every night to visit her

Herod (the Great) /hérrəd-/ (73–4 BC) king of Judea (37–4 BC)

Herod Antipas /-ánti pass/ (21 BC–AD 39) Galilean leader

Herodotus /hə róddətəss/ (484?–425? BC) Greek historian

heroic /hi rố ik/ *adj* 1 exceedingly courageous 2 of or for a hero 3 grand or extreme ■ **heroics** *npl* overdramatic behaviour or talk —**heroically** *adv*

heroic couplet *n* a pair of rhyming lines of iambic pentameter verse

heroin /hérrō in/ *n* a derivative of morphine that is an addictive illegal narcotic drug

SPELLCHECK Do not confuse the spelling of **heroin** and **heroine** ('a brave woman'), which sound similar.

heroine /hérrō in/ *n* 1 a very brave woman 2 an admired woman 3 the main woman character in a fictional plot ◊ See note at **heroin**

heroism /hérrō izəm/ *n* great courage

heron /hérrən/ *n* a long-necked freshwater wading bird

~~heros~~ incorrect spelling of **heroes**

hero worship *n* 1 great admiration for somebody 2 the ancient Greek or Roman practice of worshipping semidivine heroes —**hero-worship** *vt* —**hero-worshipper** *n*

herpes /húr peez/ *n* a viral infection causing small painful blisters on the mouth or genitals

Herrick /hérrik/, **Robert** (1591–1674) English poet

herring /hérring/ (*pl* -**rings** *or* same) *n* 1 a small sea fish with silvery scales 2 a herring as food

herringbone /hérring bōn/ *n* a pattern of interlocking V shapes

herring gull *n* a large common white gull with a grey back and grey wings tipped with black

hers *pron* 1 indicates that something belongs to or is associated with a woman, girl, or female animal who has been previously mentioned or whose identity is known ○ *an uncle of hers* 2 indicates that something belongs to or is associated with a country that has been previously mentioned or whose identity is known (*fml*)

Herschel /húrsh'l/ family of British astronomers including **Sir William** (1738–1822), his sister **Caroline** (1750–1848), and his son **Sir John Frederick William** (1792–1871)

herself (*stressed*) /hər sélf/ (*unstressed*) /ər sélf/ *pron* 1 refers to the same woman, girl, or female animal as the subject of the verb ○ *She decided to treat herself.* 2 emphasizes or clarifies which woman, girl, or female animal is being referred to ○ *a letter from the author herself* 3 shows that a woman, girl or female animal is alone or unaided ○ *sitting by herself* 4 her normal self ○ *She's not herself today.*

Hertfordshire /haártfərdshər/ county in SE England

Herts. *abbr* Hertfordshire

hertz (*pl* same) *n* (*symbol* **Hz**) the SI unit of frequency equal to one cycle per second

Hertz, Heinrich (1857–94) German physicist. His work on electromagnetic waves led to the development of the telegraph and radio. —**Hertzian** *adj*

Herzegovina /húrtsə gō veênə/ ♦ **Bosnia and Herzegovina**

he's *contr* 1 he has 2 he is

Heshvan /héshvən/, **Cheshvan** /khésh vaan, -vən/ *n* the 8th month of the year in the Jewish calendar

hesitant /hézzitənt/ *adj* slow or reluctant to act because of uncertainty or doubt —**hesitancy** *n* —**hesitantly** *adv* ◊ See note at **unwilling**

hesitate /hézzi tayt/ (**-tating**, **-tated**) *vi* 1 be slow to act, or break off from doing something, because of uncertainty or doubt 2 be reluctant to do something —**hesitatingly** *adv* —**hesitation** /hézzi táysh'n/ *n*

SYNONYMS **hesitate, pause, falter, stumble, waver, vacillate** CORE MEANING: show uncertainty or indecision

~~hesitent~~ incorrect spelling of **hesitant**

Hess, Rudolf (1894–1987) German Nazi deputy leader

Hesse /hess, héssə/, **Hermann** (1877–1962) German novelist and poet

hessian /héssi ən/ *n* a coarse strong jute or hemp fabric. Use: bags, upholstery.

Hestia /hésti ə/ *n* in Greek mythology, the goddess of the hearth. Roman equivalent **Vesta**

hetero- *prefix* different, other ○ *heterosexual*

heterodox /héttərə doks/ *adj* disagreeing with established opinions —**heterodoxy** *n*

heterogeneous /héttərō jeeni əss/, **heterogenous** /hétta rójjənəss/ *adj* 1 consisting of unrelated or dissimilar parts 2 unrelated or dissimilar —**heterogeneity** /héttərō jə nee əti, -náyəti/ *n* —**heterogeneously** *adv*

heterosexism /héttərō séksizəm/ *n* discrimination against homosexual men and women by heterosexuals —**heterosexist** *n, adj*

heterosexual /héttərō sékshoo əl/ *n* somebody sexually attracted to members of the opposite sex —**heterosexual** *adj* —**heterosexuality** /héttərō sékshoo álləti/ *n*

het up *adj* very agitated (*infml*)

heuristic /hyoó rístik/ *adj* 1 of a teaching method that encourages learners to discover solutions for themselves 2 involving trial and error 3 describes a computer program that is able to change in response to the user ■ *n* a helpful procedure for getting a solution —**heuristically** *adv*

heuristics /hyoo rístiks/ *n* problem-solving by trial and error (+ *sing verb*)

~~heven~~ incorrect spelling of **heaven**

hew /hyoo/ (**hewn** /hyoon/ or **hewed**) *v* 1 *vti* cut wood or stone with an axe 2 *vt* make by cutting wood or stone

SPELLCHECK Do not confuse the spelling of **hew** and **hue** ('a shade of colour'), which sound similar.

hex *n* 1 a curse or evil spell 2 a bringer of bad luck ■ *vt* 1 curse or bewitch 2 have a bad effect on

hexadecimal /héksə déssim'l/ *adj* based on the number 16 ■ *n* 1 a number with base 16 2 a notation for numbers with base 16

hexagon /héksəgən/ *n* a six-sided figure —**hexagonal** /hek sággən'l/ *adj*

hexagram /héksə gram/ *n* 1 a six-pointed star-shaped figure 2 a pattern of six lines used in divination

hexameter /hek sámmitər/ *n* a verse line of six metrical feet —**hexametric** /héksə méttrik/ *adj*

hey *interj* 1 demands somebody's attention (*infml*) 2 expresses surprise, irritation, or dismay

heyday /háy day/ *n* somebody's or something's prime

ORIGIN **Heyday** represents a use of an old exclamation of joy or surprise, the original form of which was *heyda*. It therefore has no etymological connection with *day*, or with 'making hay'.

Heyerdahl /háy ər daal, hí-/, **Thor** (*b.* 1914) Norwegian anthropologist

Hf *symbol* hafnium

Hg *symbol* mercury

HGV *abbr* heavy goods vehicle

hi *interj* hello (*infml*)

Hialeah /hí ə lee ə/ *city* in SE Florida. Pop. 211,392 (1998).

hiatus /hí áytəss, hi-/ (*pl* **-tuses** or same) *n* an unexpected gap or break in continuity

Hiawatha /hí ə wóthə/ (*fl* 1550) Native American leader

hibernate /híbər nayt/ (**-nating**, **-nated**) *vi* pass the winter in a dormant state resembling sleep —**hibernation** /híbər náysh'n/ *n*

Hibernia /hí búrni ə/ *n* Ireland (*literary*) —**Hibernian** *adj, n*

hibiscus /hi bískəss, hí-/ *n* a bush with large brightly coloured flowers

hiccup /híkup/, **hiccough** /híkup/ *n* 1 a convulsive gasp produced by an abrupt involuntary contraction of the diaphragm 2 a setback in arrangements (*infml*) ■ **hiccups** *npl* an attack of gulping intakes of breath **hiooup** *vti*

hick *n* a country person regarded as unsophisticated (*infml insult*)

Hickok /híkok/, **Wild Bill** (1837–76) US law enforcer, gunfighter, and scout

hickory /híkəri/ (*pl* **-ries**) *n* 1 a hard light-coloured wood. Use: tool handles, sports equipment, furniture. 2 a North American tree that produces nuts and hickory wood

hidden agenda *n* an undisclosed motive or aim

hide[1] *v* (**hiding, hid, hidden** /hídd'n/ or **hid**) 1 *vti* move deliberately out of sight 2 *vt* keep something secret 3 *vt* block the view of something ■ *n* a wildlife observation post
□ **hide out** *vi* be in or go into hiding

hide[2] *n* the skin of an animal such as a deer, cow, or buffalo (*often in combination*)

hide-and-seek *n* a children's game in which one player lets the others hide and then tries to find them

hideaway /hídə way/ n a secret hiding place or refuge

hidebound /híd bownd/ adj 1 narrow-minded and stubborn 2 with dry stiff skin

hideous /híddi əss/ adj 1 horrible to see or hear 2 morally repulsive —**hideously** adv —**hideousness** n ◊ See note at **unattractive**

hideout /híd owt/ n a place to hide in

hiding /híding/ n a beating (infml)

hie /hī/ (**hies**, **hieing** or **hying**, **hied**) vi hurry somewhere (archaic)

~~heifer~~ incorrect spelling of **heifer**

~~hieght~~ incorrect spelling of **height**

hierarchy /hír aarki/ (pl -**chies**) n 1 an organization or group divided into ranks 2 the controlling group in an organization or system —**hierarchical** adj —**hierarchically** adv

> **ORIGIN** Originally **hierarchy** referred to the divisions of angelic beings in early Christian theology, and for a long time after its first appearance in the 14C it is found primarily in religious and ecclesiastical contexts. This is in keeping with its Greek origins: its first element represents Greek **hieros** 'sacred, holy'. The general use of any group with members ranked one above the other did not develop until the 17C.

hieroglyphics /hírə glíffiks/ n a writing system that uses pictures or symbols (+ sing verb) ■ npl writing that is hard to decipher (infml; + pl verb)

hifalutin adj = **highfalutin**

hi-fi /hí fí/ (pl **hi-fis**) n 1 a set of high-quality audio equipment 2 high fidelity

higgledy-piggledy /hígg'ldi pígg'ldi/ adj disorganized and scattered ■ adv in a messy state

high /hī/ (**higher**, **highest**) adj 1 of great height ○ a high wall 2 reaching a particular height above a known or stated level ○ ten feet high 3 above average 4 raised in musical or sound pitch 5 blowing strongly (refers to wind) 6 important in rank 7 very favourable ○ high esteem 8 at a peak of activity or intensity ○ high summer 9 under the influence of drugs or alcohol (slang) 10 strong-smelling or strong-tasting ■ adv at, in, or into a high position ○ flew high into the sky ■ n 1 a higher than usual level or position ○ prices reaching all-time highs 2 a mass of high atmospheric pressure 3 a top temperature ○ today's high of 35 degrees 4 an elated or intoxicated state (infml) ◊ **high and dry** stranded and abandoned ◊ **high and low** in every conceivable place ◊ **high and mighty** arrogant and self-important

> **SPELLCHECK** Do not confuse the spelling of **higher** and **hire** ('employ', 'rent'), which sound similar.

highball /hí bawl/ n US, Can a tall drink of spirits mixed with water or a carbonated drink

highborn /hí bawrn/ adj born into a rich or noble family

highbrow /hí brow/ adj intellectual ■ n an intellectual person —**highbrowism** n

highchair /hí cháir/ n a baby's chair with long legs and often a detachable tray, used at mealtimes

High Church n a section of the Anglican Church in which elaborate rituals and ceremonies are used

high-class adj 1 for the rich 2 sophisticated

high command n 1 a group of senior officers who jointly control military operations 2 a military headquarters

High Commission n an embassy of one Commonwealth country in another

High Commissioner n 1 an ambassador for one Commonwealth country in another 2 the head of an international commission

High Court n 1 the most senior court in England, Wales, Scotland, and some other countries 2 the US Supreme Court

high-end adj 1 expensive ○ high-end consumers 2 having extensive and sophisticated capabilities and features

Higher /hí ər/ n a Scottish school examination taken after five or six years of secondary education

higher education n post-sixth form education

higher-up n somebody in a position of authority (infml)

high explosive n a chemical that causes a large explosion. Use: rock blasting, military applications.

highfalutin /hífə lóotin, -t'n/, **hifalutin**, **highfaluting** /-lóoting/ adj pretentious (infml)

high fidelity n very high-quality sound reproduction

high-five n a gesture of greeting consisting of a slapping of raised palms (slang) —**high-five** vti

high-flier, **high-flyer** n a high achiever

high-flown adj unconvincingly exalted ○ a high-flown prose style

high frequency n a radio frequency in the range 3–30 MHz or of a wavelength of 10–100 m

high-grade adj of a high quality

high ground n 1 a raised area 2 a position of moral superiority

high-handed adj dismissing the views of others —**high-handedness** n

High Holidays, **High Holy Days** npl the period of Jewish festivals from Rosh Hashanah to Yom Kippur

highjack v, n = **hijack**

high jinks, **hijinks** /hí jingks/ n fun and games (infml; + sing or pl verb)

high jump n an athletics event in which athletes jump over a high horizontal bar —**high jumper** n —**high jumping** n

highland /hílənd/ n an area of hilly land ■ **highlands** npl a hilly or mountainous area ■ adj

1 of highlands 2 **Highland** of the Scottish Highlands —**Highlander** n —**Highlander** n

Highland /híland/ a council area of N Scotland

Highland fling n an energetic Scottish solo dance

Highland Games n a meeting for Highland sports and dancing (+ sing or pl verb)

Highlands /hílandz/ mountainous area of northern mainland Scotland

high-level adj involving high-ranking people

high-level language n a computer programming language approximating to natural language

high life n the life of fashionable people (often ironic)

highlife /hí líf/ n a type of West African music with jazz elements

highlight /hí lít/ n 1 the best part of an event 2 a representative part ○ gave us highlights of the president's speech 3 a contrasting pale area, e.g. in a photograph ■ **highlights** npl light streaks in hair ■ vt 1 emphasize 2 mark with a highlighter 3 put light streaks in

highlighter /hí lítər/ n 1 a broad-tipped felt pen with brightly coloured transparent ink 2 a cosmetic for the face, used to emphasize features

highly /híli/ adv 1 to an extreme degree 2 favourably 3 in a high position or rank

highly-strung adj nervous

high-maintenance adj requiring excessive attention

High Mass n a fully ceremonial Roman Catholic Mass

high-minded adj with high moral principles —**high-mindedly** adv

highness /hínəss/ n 1 height 2 **Highness** a title and form of address for a royal person

high noon n 1 noon exactly 2 the peak of achievement or activity

high-octane adj with a high octane content

high-pitched adj 1 at the top of the sound range 2 with a steep slope

high point n the best part of an event

high-powered adj 1 dynamic 2 influential 3 also **high-power** giving a high magnification

high-pressure adj 1 operating at greater than normal pressure 2 stressful

high priest n 1 the main proponent of an ideology 2 a Jewish chief priest

high profile n a position of high public prominence

high resolution n the use of a large number of dots to create a detailed image

high-rise adj 1 multistorey 2 describes bicycles with high handlebars —**high-rise** n

high road n 1 a main road 2 the most direct route

high school n 1 a secondary school 2 an upper secondary school

high seas npl the open sea

high season n the peak time of year

high-spirited adj lively —**high-spiritedly** adv

high spot n the highlight of an experience or event

high street, High Street n 1 the main street in a town 2 retail trade (infml)

hieght incorrect spelling of **height**

high table n a dining table for senior people, especially in public schools and some university colleges

hightail /hí tayl/ vti leave quickly (slang)

high tea n an early evening meal of cooked food, cakes, and tea

high tech, hi-tech n 1 advanced technology 2 plain and simple design —**high-tech** adj

high tide, high water n the time or point when the tide is highest

high treason n treason against somebody's own country

high-water mark n 1 a mark showing the highest level reached by a body of water 2 the peak of something

highway /hí way/ n 1 a public road (fml) 2 US, Can a main road

Highway Code n a road-users' handbook or set of rules

highwayman /hí waymən/ (pl -men /-mən/) n formerly, a roadside robber

high wire n a tightrope used in a circus act

hijack /hí jak/, **highjack** vt 1 seize an aircraft, ship, or train with force 2 take control of something for your own ends (infml) ■ n an act of hijacking an aircraft, ship, train, or motor vehicle —**hijacker** n —**hijacking** n

hijinks n = high jinks

hike v (hiking, hiked) 1 vi take a long walk, especially for pleasure 2 vi go on a training march 3 vt raise an amount to an unreasonable level ○ have hiked petrol prices 4 vt pull something up ■ n 1 a pleasurable long walk 2 a sudden large increase in something —**hiker** n

hilarious /hi laíri əss/ adj very funny —**hilariously** adv

hilarity /hi lárrəti/ n laughter or amusement

Hildegard (of Bingen) /híldə gaard əv bíngən/, **St** (1098–1179) German writer and composer

hill n 1 an area of high land smaller than a mountain 2 a gradient in a road 3 a pile or mound ◇ **over the hill** at an age that is supposedly past the prime of life (infml)

Hillary /hílləri/, **Sir Edmund** (b. 1919) New Zealand mountaineer and explorer who was one of the first two climbers to reach the summit of Mount Everest (1953)

hillbilly /híl bili/ (pl -lies) n US, Can a country person regarded as unsophisticated (infml; sometimes offensive)

hillock /híllək/ n a small hill

hillside /híl síd/ n the side of a hill

hill station n in colonial India, a mountain retreat offering British officials respite from the heat

hilltop /híl top/ *n* the summit of a hill

hilly /hílli/ (**-ier**, **-iest**) *adj* **1** having many hills **2** having steep slopes —**hilliness** *n*

hilt *n* the handle of a sword or knife ◊ **(up) to the hilt** to the maximum

him *pron* refers to a man, boy, or male animal who has been previously mentioned or whose identity is known *(as the object or complement of a verb or preposition)*

Himalaya /hímmə láyə/, **Himalayas** mountain system in Asia, forming the northern boundary of the South Asian subcontinent. Highest peak Mt Everest 8,848 m/29,028 ft. —**Himalayan** *adj*

Himmler /hímmlər/, **Heinrich** (1900–45) German Nazi official

himself *(stressed)* /him sélf/ *(unstressed)* /im sélf/ *pron* **1** refers to the same man, boy, or male animal as the subject of the verb ○ *He decided to treat himself.* **2** emphasizes or clarifies which man, boy, or male animal is being referred to ○ *a letter from the author himself* **3** alone or without help ○ *sitting by himself* **4** his normal self ○ *He's not himself today.*

hind[1] /hīnd/ *adj* at the back

hind[2] /hīnd/ *n* a female deer

Hindemith /híndə mit/, **Paul** (1895–1963) German composer and viola player

hinder /híndər/ *vt* delay or obstruct

SYNONYMS **hinder**, **block**, **hamper**, **hold back**, **impede**, **obstruct** CORE MEANING: put difficulties in the way of progress

~~hinderance~~ incorrect spelling of **hindrance**

Hindi /híndi/ *n* one of the official languages of India —**Hindi** *adj*

hindmost /hínd mōst/ *adj* farthest back *(literary)*

hindquarter /hínd kwawrtər/ *n* a back part of a carcass consisting of one leg and one or two ribs ■ **hindquarters** *npl* the rear of a four-legged animal

hindrance /híndrənss/ *n* **1** something that is in the way **2** the obstructing of progress

hindsight /hínd sīt/ *n* understanding or knowledge after the fact

Hindu /hin dóò, hín doo/ *n* **1** a follower of Hinduism **2** somebody from Hindustan ■ *adj* **1** of Hinduism **2** of Hindus

Hinduism /híndoo izəm/ *n* the largest Indian religion, which believes in reincarnation and a large number of gods and goddesses

Hindu Kush /-kŏŏsh/ mountain system in central Asia, mainly in Afghanistan but extending into Jammu and Kashmir. Highest peak Tirich Mir 7,690 m/25,230 ft.

Hindustan /híndoo staán/ *n* formerly, the Hindi-speaking region of N India, or the wider Hindi-speaking area of South Asia —**Hindustani** *adj*

hinge *n* a movable joint that fastens two things together and allows one of them to pivot —**hinged** *adj*

□ **hinge on** *vt* depend on ○ *Our plans hinge on the weather.*

Hinkler /híngklər/, **Bert** (1892–1933) Australian aviator

hint *vti* suggest something indirectly ■ *n* **1** an indirect suggestion **2** a piece of advice **3** a very small amount

hinterland /híntər land/ *n* **1** the land adjacent to the sea or a river **2** the area surrounding a city **3** a remote country region

hip[1] *n* **1** the part of each side of the human body between the waist and the thigh **2** a hipbone

hip[2] *n* a rosehip

hip[3] (**hipper**, **hippest**) *adj* fashionable *(slang)* —**hiply** *adv* —**hipness** *n*

hipbone /híp bōn/ *n* either of the two large bones forming the sides of the pelvis

hip flask *n* a small flat flask for alcohol carried in a pocket

hip-hop *n* rap music *(slang)*

~~hipocrisy~~ incorrect spelling of **hypocrisy**

hippie /híppi/, **hippy** (*pl* **-pies**) *n* an unconventional young person, especially in the 1960s *(infml)* —**hippiedom** *n*

hippo /híppō/ (*pl* **-pos**) *n* a hippopotamus *(infml)*

Hippocrates /hi pókrə teez/ (460?–377? BC) Greek physician —**Hippocratic** /híppə kráttik/ *adj*

Hippocratic oath *n* a doctor's promise to uphold medical ethics and standards

ORIGIN The oath is 'Hippocratic' because Hippocrates reputedly formulated a similar one.

hippodrome /híppə drōm/ *n* a stadium used for horseracing and chariot racing in ancient Greece or Rome

hippopotamus /híppə póttəmэss/ (*pl* **-muses** or **-mi** /-mī/) *n* a large African amphibious mammal

ORIGIN **Hippopotamus** comes from a Greek word meaning literally 'horse of the river'.

hippy[1] *n* = **hippie**

hippy[2] /híppi/ (**-pier**, **-piest**) *adj* with wide hips

hipsters /hípstərz/ *npl* trousers that go up to the hips instead of the waist

hire /hīr/ *v* (**hiring**, **hired**) **1** *vti* employ somebody **2** *vt* pay for the use of something ○ *hired the village hall for the reception* ■ *n* the act of hiring something or somebody —**hirable** *adj* —**hirer** *n* ◊ See note at **high**

hired hand *n* a paid farm worker

hireling /hírling/ *n* somebody who works for money, especially somebody whose only motivation is money *(disapproving)*

hire purchase *n* payment in instalments for something bought

Hirohito /heérō heétō/ (1901–89) emperor of Japan (1926–89)

Hiroshima /hi róshimə, hírrə sheémə/ city on SW Honshu Island, Japan. It was devastated by the first atom bomb to be used in war, in August 1945. Pop. 1,106,922 (2000).

hirsute /húr syoot/ adj 1 with a lot of hair 2 covered with stiff hairs —**hirsuteness** n

his det, pron belonging to or associated with him

Hispanic /hi spánnik/ adj 1 of Spain 2 of Spanish-speaking people ■ n a Hispanic American ■ adj of people of Spanish descent

Hispanic American n a US citizen of Spanish descent —**Hispanic-American** adj

Hispaniola /híspən yólə/ island in the Caribbean southeast of Cuba, divided between Haiti and the Dominican Republic

hiss v 1 vi make a sound like a continuous 's' 2 vti show a negative opinion of somebody or something by making this sound ■ n 1 a sound like a continuous 's' 2 a sound expressing disapproval

histamine /hístə meen/ n a substance released by immune cells that produces allergic reactions —**histaminic** /hístə mínnik/ adj

histogram /hístə gram/ n a statistical bar graph

histology /hi stólləji/ n the study of the microscopic structures of animal and plant tissue —**histological** adj —**histologist** n

historian /hi stáwri ən/ n 1 a student or scholar of history 2 a recorder of events

historic /hi stórrik/ adj 1 significant to history and to the future ○ a historic decision 2 associated with history or events in history ○ visited the historic sites of Rome

historical /hi stórrik'l/ adj 1 based on past events ○ historical novels 2 used in the past ○ historical weaponry 3 supported by facts from history ○ historical analysis 4 of the study of history ○ a series of historical monographs —**historicalness** n

historically /hi stórrikli/ adv 1 with a view to or in terms of history 2 many times before

historiography /hi stórri óggrəfi/ n 1 the methods of historical research 2 the writing of history —**historiographical** adj

history /hístəri/ (pl -ries) n 1 events that happened in the past 2 the study of the past 3 a record of events 4 somebody's personal background 5 an interesting past 6 something or somebody no longer important

history list n a record of the input of previous users of a computer

histrionic /hístri ónnik/, **histrionical** /-ik'l/ adj 1 annoyingly overdramatic 2 of acting or actors in the theatre (fml) —**histrionically** adv

histrionics /hístri ónniks/ n overdone emotion (+ sing or pl verb) ■ npl dramatic performances (fml; + pl verb)

hit v (hitting, hit) 1 vti deliver a blow to something or somebody 2 vti come or bring into forceful contact ○ His van skidded and hit a parked car. 3 vt make a ball move with a bat or hand 4 vt strike a button or key, e.g. on a keyboard (infml) 5 vt score a particular number of points by striking a ball 6 vt reach a target 7 vt affect somebody badly ○ a law that will hit investors hard 8 vt arrive at a particular level (slang) ○ The temperature hit 36 today. ■ n 1 a hard blow 2 a collision

3 something that hits a target 4 a success 5 the effect of a drug (slang) 6 a professional killing (slang) 7 an instance of accessing a database or Internet file —**hitter** n ◇ **hit it off** get along very well (infml) □ **hit back** vi retaliate

hit-and-miss adj carelessly done

hit-and-run adj 1 not stopping after causing an accident ○ a hit-and-run driver 2 happening fast and without warning ○ a hit-and-run attack

hitch v 1 vti hitchhike (infml) 2 vt connect two things so that one can move the other ○ hitched the horse to the wagon 3 vt fasten something to stop it from moving ○ hitched the horse to a fence ■ n 1 an obstacle or problem that prevents progress 2 a means of connecting two things 3 a knot that unties easily 4 a sudden pull on something —**hitcher** n

Sir Alfred Hitchcock

Hitchcock /hích kok/, **Sir Alfred** (1899–1980) British film director

hitchhike /hích hīk/ (-hiking, -hiked) vi get a free ride by signalling to drivers from the side of the road —**hitchhiker** n

hi-tech n, adj = high tech

hither /híthər/ adv to this place (archaic)

hitherto /híthər toó, híthər toó/ adv up to now or the time in question

Hitler /hítlər/, **Adolf** (1889–1945) Austrian-born German Nazi dictator

hit list n a list of possible murder victims (infml)

hit man n a hired killer (slang)

hit-or-miss adj with variable success

hit out (pl hit outs or hits out) n in hockey, a hit that restarts the game from the 16-yard line

hit parade n a list of pop music's bestselling recordings for a specified week (dated)

HIV n a virus that disables the immune system and can lead to Aids. Full form **human immunodeficiency virus**

hive /hīv/ n 1 a home for bees 2 a colony of bees ■ v (hiving, hived) 1 vti put bees into a hive 2 vt keep something for use later □ **hive off** vt separate from the whole or a larger group

hives /hīvz/ n MED = urticaria (+ sing or pl verb)

HIV-positive adj shown by a test to be infected with the HIV virus

HLL abbr high-level language

HMG abbr Her Majesty's Government

HMI *abbr* Her Majesty's Inspector (of Schools)

HMS, H.M.S. *abbr* **1** Her Majesty's Service **2** Her Majesty's Ship

HMSO *abbr* Her Majesty's Stationery Office

Hn *symbol* hahnium

HNC *n* a formal technical qualification. Full form **Higher National Certificate**

HND *n* a vocational qualification approximately equivalent to a degree without honours. Full form **Higher National Diploma**

ho *interj* **1** expresses various emotions, from triumph to derision **2** attracts attention

Ho *symbol* holmium

hoard /hawrd/ *vt* store a supply of food or other resources —**hoard** *n* —**hoarder** *n* ◊ See note at **collect**

SPELLCHECK Do not confuse the spelling of **hoard** and **horde** ('a large group of people'), which sound similar.

hoarding /háwrding/ *n* **1** a billboard **2** a tall screen erected round a building site

hoar frost *n* dew turned to frost

hoarse /hawrss/ (**hoarser, hoarsest**) *adj* **1** sounding rough **2** with a harshly grating voice —**hoarsely** *adv* —**hoarseness** *n*

SPELLCHECK Do not confuse the spelling of **hoarse** and **horse** (the animal), which sound similar.

hoary /háwri/ (**-ier, -iest**) *adj* **1** stale from overuse ○ *hoary old jokes* **2** white with age —**hoarily** *adv* —**hoariness** *n*

hoax *n* a deception ■ *vt* deceive —**hoaxer** *n*

hob *n* **1** a cooking surface with rings, hot plates, or burners **2** an area in a fireplace to keep pans warm

Hobart /hó baart/ capital of Tasmania, Australia. Pop. 195,000 (1998).

Hobbes /hobz/, **Thomas** (1588–1679) English philosopher and political theorist —**Hobbesian** *adj, n*

hobble /hóbb'l/ *v* (**-bling, -bled**) **1** *vi* limp along **2** *vt* limit a horse's movement by tying its legs together **3** *vt* restrict somebody's actions ■ *n* **1** an unsteady walk **2** a rope or strap used for tying a horse's legs together

Hobbs, Jack (1882–1963) British cricketer

hobby /hóbbi/ (*pl* **-bies**) *n* an enjoyable activity done for pleasure

ORIGIN Hobby is a variant of *Robbie*, a familiar form of the man's name *Robert*. It first occurred in *hobbyhorse*, referring to a figure of a horse's head attached to a performer in folk dance, then as a child's toy consisting of a horse's head on a stick. In the late 17C it came to mean 'something pursued for pleasure', and was shortened to **hobby** in the early 19C.

hobbyhorse /hóbbi hawrss/ *n* **1** a toy consisting of an artificial horse's head on a long stick **2** a horse figure used in folk dances **3** a favourite topic

hobbyist /hóbbi ist/ *n* somebody with a hobby

hobgoblin /hób góbblin, hób goblin/ *n* **1** an imaginary mischievous or evil elf or goblin **2** a fear or worry

hobnail /hób nayl/ *n* a nail that protects the soles of boots —**hobnailed** *adj*

hobnob /hób nob/ (**-nobbing, -nobbed**) *vi* socialize with somebody informally (*disapproving*)

ORIGIN Hobnob comes from an old toast *hob and nob*, or *hob or nob*, used with a clinking of glasses before drinking. Literally the phrase means 'have and/or not have': the words are later variants of *hab*, an old form of *have*, and *nab*, its negative equivalent. The verb **hobnob** originally meant 'drink together'.

hobo /hóbō/ (*pl* **-boes**) *n* a poor homeless wanderer or traveller

Hobson's choice /hóbss'nz-/ *n* a choice between the thing offered and nothing at all

ORIGIN Hobson's choice is named after Thomas Hobson (1554–1631), who kept a livery stable in Cambridge. He gave his customers the choice of the next horse or none at all.

Ho Chi Minh /hó chee mín/ (1890–1969) resistance leader and president of North Vietnam (1954–69)

Ho Chi Minh City largest city in Vietnam. Pop. 3,015,743 (1992).

hock¹ *n* **1** an animal's lower leg joint **2** a joint of meat from an animal's lower leg

hock² *n* a type of German white wine

ORIGIN Hock is shortened from Hochheim, a town on the River Main, Germany.

hockey /hóki/ *n* **1** a team sport in which a small ball is hit with the curved end of a stick **2** *US, Can* ice hockey

David Hockney

Hockney /hókni/, **David** (*b.* 1937) British painter

hocus-pocus /hōkəss pókəss/ (*pl* **hocus-pocuses** *or* **hocus-pocusses**) *n* a conjurer's incantation

hod *n* a trough on a pole. Use: carrying heavy building materials.

hodgepodge /hój poj/ *n* a jumble

Hodgkin /hójkin/, **Dorothy Mary** (1910–94) Egyptian-born British chemist. She was awarded the Nobel Prize in chemistry (1964) for work on X-rays, molecular science, and penicillin.

Hodgkin's disease *n* a malignant tumour on the lymph nodes

ORIGIN The disease is named after the British

physician Thomas Hodgkin (1798–1866), who described it.

hoe *n* a weeding tool consisting of a blade on a long pole —**hoe** *vti*

hog *n* **1** a pig **2** *US* any mammal of the pig family **3** *also* **hogg** *UK regional, ANZ* a young sheep ■ *vt* (**hogging, hogged**) selfishly take more of something than you need, or keep something for an unfairly long time *(infml)* ◊ **go the whole hog** do something wholeheartedly *(slang)*

Hogarth /hŏ gaarth/, **William** (1697–1764) British painter and engraver —**Hogarthian** /hŏ gaárthi ən/ *adj*

Hogmanay /hógmə nay, -náy/ *n Scotland* New Year's Eve

hogshead /hógz hed/ *n* a unit of measure for alcohol equal to 54 imperial gallons or 63 US gallons

hogwash /hóg wosh/ *n* **1** nonsense *(infml)* **2** leftovers of food that are fed to pigs

Hohhot /hó hót/ capital of Inner Mongolia, NE China. Pop. 1,090,000 (1995).

hoick *vti* pull violently or suddenly *(infml)*

hoi polloi /hóypə lóy, hóy pólloy/ *n* the masses of the common people *(disapproving)*

hoist *vt* lift, especially using a mechanical device ■ *n* **1** a device for lifting **2** an act of lifting something

hoity-toity /hóyti tóyti/ *adj* pretentiously self-important and snobbish *(infml)*

Hokkaido /ho kídō/ second largest island of Japan, north of Honshu. Pop. 5,643,647 (1990).

hokum /hókəm/ *n US, Can* **1** nonsense or lies *(infml)* **2** unnecessary theatrics

Hokusai /hókoŏ sī/, **Katsushika** (1760–1849) Japanese painter and book illustrator

Holbein /hólbīn/, **Hans, the Younger** (1497–1543) and his father **Hans, the Elder** (1460?–1524) German painters

hold[1] *v* (**held**) **1** *vt* grasp and physically retain something **2** *vt* lift something and keep it in position **3** *vi* fix something in position **4** *vi* embrace somebody **5** *vt* contain something, usually a particular amount **6** *vt* retain or reserve something **7** *vt* stop somebody from leaving **8** *vt* keep possession of something by force **9** *vt* arrange or stage something **10** *vt* possess something **11** *vt* have a particular position and perform the duties of it ○ *held the office of treasurer* **12** *vti* keep a promise or ensure that another person keeps a promise ○ *held her to her agreement* **13** *vt* believe or feel something ○ *'We hold these truths to be self-evident'*. **14** *vt* regard somebody in a particular way ○ *holds her in high esteem* **15** *vr* have a particular way of standing or walking ○ *She holds herself well*. **16** *vt* engross somebody **17** *vt* decide something legally **18** *vi* persist ○ *a cold spell had been holding all week* **19** *vi* remain or stand firm ○ *The dam held throughout the flooding*. **20** *vi* remain valid **21** *vti* wait on a telephone line ■ *n* **1** an act of grasping and retaining the grasp **2** a

wrestling technique **3** a support **4** control over somebody **5** a delaying ◊ **hold good** be true or valid ◊ **hold something against somebody** bear a grudge against somebody ◊ **on hold 1** waiting to be connected or reconnected to somebody during a telephone call **2** suspended or postponed ◊ **no holds barred** with no restrictions

☐ **hold back** *v* **1** *vti* restrain somebody or yourself **2** *vt* keep something back

☐ **hold down** *vt* keep a job *(infml)*

☐ **hold forth** *vi* speak at length, often tediously

☐ **hold in** *vt* restrain emotions

☐ **hold off** *v* **1** *vti* refrain from doing something **2** *vt* resist an attacker

☐ **hold on** *vi* **1** wait **2** persist

☐ **hold out** *v* **1** *vt* extend or proffer **2** *vi* last ○ *Is the food holding out?* **3** *vi* endure

☐ **hold over** *vt* defer something

☐ **hold together** *vti* keep united

☐ **hold up** *v* **1** *vt* cause to be delayed **2** *vt* rob at gunpoint **3** *vt* display or present as an example ○ *The firefighter was held up as a hero.* **4** *vi* endure **5** *vi* remain the same ○ *Interest rates have not held up this quarter.* **6** *vi* stand up to scrutiny

☐ **hold with** *vt* approve of or agree with

hold[2] *n* a ship's or plane's cargo space

holdall /hóld awl/ *n* a large bag for carrying clothes and other items

holder /hóldər/ *n* **1** a container *(often in combination)* **2** somebody in possession of something such as a cheque, ticket, lease, or title *(often in combination)*

holding /hólding/ *n* **1** a piece of leased land **2** a piece of property *(often pl)*

holding company *n* a company with a controlling interest in another company or other companies

holding pattern *n* the path of a plane that is awaiting permission to land

holdover /hóld ōvər/ *n* a performer or performance given an extended run

holdup /hóld up/ *n* **1** an armed robbery **2** a delay

hole /hōl/ *n* **1** a cavity in an object or area **2** a gap, opening, or perforation ○ *a hole in his socks* **3** a burrow **4** an unpleasant place *(infml)* **5** a flaw, e.g. in an argument **6** an awkward situation *(infml)* **7** a mobile space in a semiconductor **8** in golf, a target in the ground **9** any of the areas that a golf course is divided into ■ *vt* (**holing, holed**) **1** make a hole or holes in **2** put in a hole —**holey** *adj* ◊ **pick holes in** find fault with, often over minor defects

> **SPELLCHECK** Do not confuse the spelling of **hole** and **whole** ('entire'), which sound similar.

☐ **hole up** *vi* shelter ○ *The bear holed up in a cave.*

hole-and-corner *adj* secret

hole in one *n* a golf shot that puts the ball in the hole from the tee

Holi /hóli/ *n* the Hindu festival of spring

holiday /hólli day, -di/ *n* **1** a day of leisure **2** a period of leisure **3** a legal day off ○ *a public holiday* ■ *vi* spend a holiday

Holiday /hólli day/, **Billie** (1915–59) US jazz singer

holiday camp *n* a purpose-built site with holiday accommodation and facilities

holidaymaker /hólli day maykər, -di-/ *n UK, ANZ* somebody on holiday

holier-than-thou *adj* self-righteous (*disapproving*)

holiness /hólinəss/ *n* **1** the state or quality of being holy **2 Holiness** a title given to the pope

holistic /hō lístik/ *adj* of the whole, especially taking into account all of somebody's mental, physical, and social conditions in the treatment of illness —**holism** /hólizəm/ *n* —**holistically** *adv*

Holland /hólland/ **1** the Netherlands (*infml*) **2** former administrative division of Lincolnshire, England, known as the Parts of Holland

holler /hóllər/ *vti US* shout loudly (*infml*) —**holler** *n*

hollow /hóllō/ *adj* **1** not solid **2** concave **3** echoing as if in an empty space (*refers to sounds*) ■ *n* **1** a cavity in an object or area **2** a valley ■ *v* **1** *vt* make a cavity in **2** *vti* make or become hollowed —**hollow** *adv* —**hollowly** *adv* —**hollowness** *n* ◊ See note at **vain**

Hollows /hóllōz/, **Fred** (1930–93) New Zealand-born Australian ophthalmologist

holly /hólli/ (*pl* **-lies**) *n* **1** an evergreen shrub with red berries **2** holly leaves and berries used as a decoration

hollyhock /hólli hok/ *n* a tall plant with showy flowers

Hollywood /hólliwŏod/ district of Los Angeles, California, a centre of the US film and television industry

holmium /hólmi əm/ *n* (*symbol* **Ho**) a soft silvery-white metallic element

holocaust /hóllə kawst/ *n* **1** complete destruction, especially by fire **2** wholesale destruction of any kind **3 Holocaust** the systematic extermination of European Jews and other ethnic groups by the Nazis during World War II

ORIGIN Holocaust came via French from a Greek word meaning 'burnt whole'. It was originally used in English for a 'burnt offering', a 'sacrifice completely consumed by fire'. John Milton is the first English writer recorded as using it in the wider sense 'complete destruction by fire', in the late 17C, and in the succeeding centuries several precedents were set for its modern application to 'nuclear destruction' and 'mass murder'. The specific application to the mass murder of the Jews by the Nazis during World War II was introduced by historians during the 1950s, probably as an equivalent to Hebrew *ḥurban* and *shoah* 'catastrophe' (used in the same sense).

Holocene /hóllō seen/ *n* the present epoch of geological time, which began 10,000 years ago —**Holocene** *adj*

hologram /hóllə gram/ *n* a three-dimensional photographic image

holograph /hóllə graaf, -graf/ *n* a manuscript handwritten by its author —**holograph** *adj*

holography /ho lóggrəfi/ *n* the process of making or using holograms —**holographic** /hóllə gráffik/ *adj*

Holst /hōlst/, **Gustav** (1874–1934) British composer

holster /hólstər/ *n* a gun holder, usually worn on the hip or shoulder —**holster** *vt*

holy /hóli/ (**-lier, -liest**) *adj* **1** sacred ○ *holy relics* **2** saintly **3** having been consecrated ○ *holy water* —**holily** *adv*

Holy Communion *n* Communion in the Christian church

Holy Family *n* the family of Jesus Christ, especially as represented in art

Holy Father *n* the pope

Holy Ghost *n* in Christianity, the Holy Spirit

Holy Grail *n* the legendary Grail

Holy Land region on the eastern shore of the Mediterranean Sea, equivalent to the historic region of Palestine

Holyoake /hóli ōk/, **Sir Keith** (1904–83) prime minister of New Zealand (1957, 1960–72)

holy of holies *n* **1** the inner chamber in the ancient Jewish Temple, where the Ark of the Covenant was kept **2** any sacred place

holy orders *npl* **1** the rite of ordination as a member of the Christian clergy **2** the rank of an ordained Christian minister or priest

Holy Roman Empire *n* a former European empire (800–1806) —**Holy Roman Emperor** *n*

Holy Spirit *n* in Christianity, the third person of the Trinity

holy war *n* a religious war

holy water *n* blessed water in a church

Holy Week *n* the week leading up to Easter

homage /hómmij/ *n* **1** deference **2** a vassal's public acknowledgment of allegiance to a feudal lord

homburg /hóm burg/ *n* a man's felt hat

home /hōm/ *n* **1** a place where somebody lives **2** a family group ○ *Theirs was a happy home, full of love.* **3** somebody's birthplace **4** an animal's native habitat **5** an establishment where full-time care is provided to people who are not wholly independent **6** in many games, the place or point that must be hit in order to score or reached in order to be safe from attack ■ *adj* **1** domestic ○ *home furnishings* **2** of a household ○ *home life* **3** of a sports team's own territory ○ *a home game* ■ *adv* **1** at or to somebody's domicile **2** effectively ○ *criticism that hit home* **3** to the centre of something or as far as possible into something ○ *drove the nail home* ■ *v* (**homing, homed**) **1** *vi* return to your domicile or operational base **2** *vt* be guided electronically to a target **3** *vi* move towards a place or point

—home-like adj ◇ **at home** 1 at ease or in a familiar and friendly place 2 having knowledge of or familiarity with a subject or activity ◇ **come** or **be brought home to** be fully understood and appreciated by

☐ **home in on** vt 1 proceed towards a target 2 direct attention to

home banking n computer banking from home

home-brew n homemade beer **—home-brewed** adj

homecoming /hốm kuming/ n a return home

home economics n the study in school of household management (+ sing verb)

home front n civilian activities during a war

homegrown /hốm grốn/ adj 1 grown in somebody's own garden 2 locally produced ◇ homegrown talent

home help n 1 a paid domestic helper 2 a domestic aid service provided by a local authority

homeland /hốm land/ n 1 somebody's native country 2 formerly in South Africa under apartheid, a self-governing territory for Black people ■ adj US of your own country ◇ homeland defence

homeless /hốmləss/ adj having no home ■ npl people with no home **—homelessness** n

homely /hốmli/ (-lier, -liest) adj 1 cosy 2 unpretentious in manner 3 US, Can regarded as not good-looking **—homeliness** n ◇ See note at **unattractive**

homemade /hốm máyd/ adj 1 made at home 2 makeshift

homemaker /hốm maykər/ n a manager of a household, especially a housewife or househusband

homeo- prefix similar, alike ◇ homeostasis

Home Office n the British government department responsible for domestic affairs

homeopathy /hốmi óppəthi/, **homoeopathy** n a complementary disease-treatment system that uses small doses of natural substances **homoopath** /hốmi ə pàth/ n **—homeopathic** /hốmi ə páthik/ adj **—homeopathically** adv **—homeopathist** n

homeostasis /hốmi ō stáyssiss/, **homoeostasis** n the body's ability to maintain its temperature and other physiological processes at a constant level **—homeostatic** /-státtik/ adj

homeowner /hốm ōnər/ n somebody who owns his or her home, as opposed to renting it

homepage /hốm payj/ n 1 a website's opening page 2 a personal site on the Internet

home plate n in baseball, the slab by which the batter stands when hitting and on which a base runner must land in order to score

homer /hốmər/ n a homing device

Homer /hốmər/ (fl 8C BC) Greek poet

home rule n self-government

home run n in baseball, a hit that allows the batter to make a circuit of all four bases and score a run

Home Secretary n the head of the Home Office

home shopping n shopping done via computer or television from home

homesick /hốm sik/ adj unhappy and longing for home **—homesickness** n

homespun /hốm spun/ adj 1 plain and simple 2 spun or woven by hand at home ■ n rough cloth woven from homespun thread

homestead /hốm sted/ n a house, outbuildings, and land **—homesteader** n

home straight n 1 the last section of a racecourse 2 the last stage of an undertaking

home town n the town or city of somebody's birth

home unit n ANZ a purpose-built flat

homeward /hốmwərd/ adv also **homewards** towards home ■ adj going home

homework /hốm wurk/ n 1 school work done at home 2 preparatory work (infml)

homey /hốmi/ (-ier, -iest), **homy** adj having the atmosphere of a comfortable home ◇ a homey little hotel **—homeyness** n

homicidal /hốmmi sîd'l/ adj intending or likely to commit murder

homicide /hốmmi sîd/ n the act or result of unlawfully killing somebody

homiletic /hốmmi léttik/ adj 1 of preaching sermons 2 of or like a homily

homily /hốmmili/ (pl -lies) n 1 a religious lecture 2 a moralizing speech (disapproving) **—homilist** n

homing /hốming/ adj 1 describes a bird that has the ability to return home 2 describes a missile or other device that is able to guide itself to a target

homing pigeon n a pigeon trained to return home

hominid /hốmminid/ n a member of a primate family including human beings **—hominid** adj

hominy /hốmmini/ n US puffed and dried maize kernels cooked and eaten as food

homo- prefix alike, same ◇ homograph

homoeopathy n ALTERN MED = homeopathy

homoeostasis n PHYSIOL = homeostasis

homogeneous /hốmə jéeni əss, hốmmə-/, **homogenous** /ho mójjənəss/ adj 1 of the same kind 2 having a uniform composition or structure throughout **—homogeneity** /hốmôjə neè əti, hốmmô-, -náyəti/ n **—homogeneously** adv

homogenize /ho mójjə nîz/ (-nizing, -nized), **homogenise** v 1 vt give milk or cream an even consistency 2 vti become or make homogeneous **—homogenization** /ho mójjə nî záysh'n/ n

homograph /hốmmə graaf, -graf/ n a word with the same spelling as another but a different meaning **—homographic** /hốmmə gráffik/ adj

homologous /ho mólləgəss/ adj sharing a similar or related structure, position, function, or value

homonym /hốmmənim/ n a word with the same spelling or pronunciation as another, but a different meaning —**homonymic** /hómmə nímmik/ adj —**homonymy** /ho mónnimi/ n

homophobia /hốmō fốbi ə, hómmō-/ n an irrational hatred or fear of homosexuality —**homophobe** /hốmō fōb, hómmə-/ n —**homophobic** adj

homophone /hómmə fōn/ n a word with the same pronunciation as another but a different meaning —**homophonous** /ho móffənəss/ adj

Homo sapiens /hốmō sáppi enz, -sáypi-/ n the species of modern human beings

homosexual /hốmō sékshoo əl, hómmə-/ n somebody who is sexually attracted to people of the same sex ■ adj 1 sexually attracted to people of the same sex 2 of homosexuality —**homosexuality** /hốmō sék shoo álləti, hómmə-/ adj ◊ See note at **gay**

ORIGIN Homosexual comes from Greek *homos* 'same', not, as is sometimes supposed, from Latin *homo* 'man'.

Homs /homs, homz/ city in W Syria, on the River Orontes. Pop. 540,133 (1994).

homy adj = homey

hon. abbr 1 honorary 2 honourable

Hon. abbr Honourable

Honduras /hon dyo͞orǎss/ country in Central America, with coastlines on the Caribbean Sea and the Pacific Ocean. Cap. Tegucigalpa. Pop. 6,406,052 (2001). —**Honduran** adj, n

hone /hōn/ vt (**honing, honed**) 1 improve with refinements o *honed the speech through re-writes* 2 sharpen on a whetstone ■ n 1 a whetstone 2 a machine tool with a rotating abrasive head

USAGE hone in or home in? Hone means 'sharpen' (*hone a blade*) or, in an extended figurative sense, 'improve, refine' (*I honed my ideas*). It is the verb **home**, meaning 'move towards', that makes sense with the particle *in*, as in *He homed in on his opponent's weaknesses.*

honest /ónnist/ adj 1 morally upright 2 truthful or true 3 impartial 4 reasonable in a particular situation o *an honest mistake* 5 modestly unpretentious o *honest country folk* —**honestly** adv —**honesty** n

honest broker n an arbitrator

honey /húnni/ n 1 a sweet substance made by bees. Use: spread, sweetener. 2 US, Can used as an affectionate term of address (infml) 3 US somebody very nice or very attractive (infml) 4 US something extremely good (infml)

honeybee /húnni bee/ n a bee that makes honey

honeycomb /húnni kōm/ n 1 a structure of six-sided cells constructed out of wax by bees for storing honey 2 a section of a honeycomb containing honey and eaten as food ■ vt provide with a network of holes or tunnels —**honeycombed** adj

honeydew melon /húnni dyoo-/ n a melon with sweet pale green flesh

honeyed /húnnid/, **honied** adj 1 ingratiating 2 pleasant-sounding

honeymoon /húnni moon/ n 1 a holiday for a newly married couple 2 an initial short-lived period of good feeling —**honeymoon** vi —**honeymooner** n

honeysuckle /húnni suk'l/ n a climbing shrub with fragrant flowers

hongi /hóngee/ n NZ a Maori greeting in which people rub noses

Hong Kong /hóng kóng/ special administrative region of China on the southeastern coast. Cap. Victoria. Pop. 7,210,505 (2001).

Honiara /hóni aárə/ capital of the Solomon Islands. Pop. 35,288 (1990).

honied adj = honeyed

honk n 1 the cry of a goose 2 the sound of a car horn 3 a sound resembling a goose or car horn ■ v 1 vi produce a honk 2 vti sound a car horn

honky-tonk /hóngki tongk/ n ragtime piano-playing

Honolulu /hónnə looˌloo/ capital of Hawaii. Pop. 395,789 (1998).

honorarium /ónnə ráiri əm/ (pl -**ums** or -**a** /-ə/) n a fee for a professional service ◊ See note at **wage**

honorary /ónnərəri/ adj 1 awarded as an honour 2 unpaid

honorific /ónnə ríffik/ adj conferring honour ■ n 1 a title of respect 2 a form of a word used as a sign of respect

honour /ónnər/ n 1 personal integrity o *It's a matter of honour.* 2 respect 3 a woman's virginity or reputation for chastity (dated) 4 a source of pride o *an honour to your parents and school* 5 a mark of distinction 6 **Honour** a form of address used to a judge or mayor o *Your Honour, may we approach the bench?* ■ **honours, Honours** npl an academic distinction ■ vt 1 have great respect for somebody or something 2 give somebody a special title or award 3 pay tribute to somebody 4 dignify an occasion by making an appearance 5 accept something as money o *The bank won't honour a cheque without a signature.* 6 keep a promise —**honourless** adj

honourable /ónnərəb'l/ adj 1 having personal integrity 2 deserving or gaining honour 3 **Honourable** used as a title of respect because of an official position held o *The Honourable Mr Smith, the presiding judge, is on the bench.* —**honourably** adv

honourable discharge n official dismissal from the armed forces, stipulating that all duties have been honourably fulfilled

Honours List n a list of the people who have been awarded honours by the British monarch

Honshu /hón shoo/ largest and most populous island of Japan. Pop. 99,254,194 (1990).

hooch n US, Can cheap or illegally made alcohol (slang)

hood[1] /hood/ n 1 a covering for the head attached to a coat 2 a cover for an appliance or machine 3 US, Can the bonnet of a car 4 a part of an academic robe that hangs down at the back **5** a folding roof on a vehicle ■ *vt* cover with a hood —**hooded** *adj* —**hoodless** *adj*

hood² /hood/ *n US, Can* a hoodlum *(slang)*

-hood *suffix* **1** quality, state, condition ○ *knighthood* **2** a group of people ○ *brotherhood*

hoodlum /hoodləm/ *n* **1** a gangster **2** a young vandal or criminal

hoodoo /hoodoo/ *n* **1** voodoo **2** bad luck ■ *vt* (**-doos, -dooing, -dooed**) seem to bring bad luck to —**hoodooism** *n*

hoodwink /hood wingk/ *vt* deceive or dupe —**hoodwinker** *n*

hooey /hoo i/ *n* nonsense *(infml)*

hoof /hoof, hoof/ *n* (*pl* **hooves** /hoovz, hoovz/ *or* **hoofs**) **1** the foot of a horse, deer, or similar animal **2** the horny material that a hoof consists of **3** an animal with hooves ■ *vt* **1** travel a particular distance on foot *(slang)* **2** kick something or somebody —**hooved** *adj*

hoo-hah /hoo haa/, **hoo-ha** *n* a big fuss *(slang)*

hook /hook/ *n* **1** a bent piece of metal used to attach, hang, or lift something **2** something resembling a hook **3** a fishhook **4** something used as a means of trapping somebody **5** something that attracts somebody, especially a potential customer *(infml)* **6** a short swinging blow **7** in golf, a shot that swerves in the direction of the swing ■ *v* **1** *vti* fasten with a hook **2** *vt* attach one thing to another **3** *vti* bend like a hook **4** *vt* ensnare something using a hook **5** *vt* catch somebody's attention **6** *vt* hit somebody with a curving blow **7** *vt* in golf, strike a ball so that it curves in the direction of the swing **8** *vt* in rugby, kick the ball backwards ◇ **by hook or by crook** by some means or other ◇ **hook, line, and sinker** completely *(infml)* ◇ **off the hook** free of a difficult situation *(infml)*

□ **hook up** *vt* connect electronic devices

hookah /hookə/ *n* a water pipe for smoking

hook and eye (*pl* **hooks and eyes**) *n* a clothes fastener consisting of a hook inserted into a loop

hooked /hookt/ *adj* **1** shaped like a hook **2** having a hook at the end **3** addicted *(slang)* **4** obsessed with something *(slang)*

hooker /hookər/ *n* an offensive term for a prostitute *(slang)*

hookup /hook up/ *n* **1** a connection to a utility such as electricity or gas ○ *a gas hookup* **2** a system of electronic equipment designed to operate together *(infml)*

hookworm /hook wurm/ *n* a parasitic worm with hooked mouthparts

hooligan /hooligən/ *n* a violent youth *(infml)*

ORIGIN The origin of **hooligan** is not known for certain. It first appeared in print in 1898. It may derive from a stereotypical Irish surname. The *Hooligans* were a fictional rowdy Irish family in a music hall song of the 1890s, and a comic Irish character in a cartoon of the time was also called *Hooligan*.

hoop *n* **1** a ring of metal or plastic, e.g. for holding a barrel together **2** a large ring-shaped toy **3** a paper-covered ring through which circus animals jump **4** a stiff support for a skirt **5** a ring-shaped earring —**hooped** *adj* ◇ **jump** *or* **go through hoops (for)** go to extreme lengths to please somebody *(infml)*

hoopla /hoop laa/ *n* a fairground game in which you throw hoops over prizes

hooray /hoo ráy/, **hurray** /hə ráy, hoo ráy/ *interj* used as a shout of joy ■ *n* a shout of joy

hoot *n* **1** an owl's cry **2** the sound made by a train whistle or car horn **3** a laughing sound **4** a hilarious person or thing *(slang)* ■ *v* **1** *vi* emit a hoot **2** *vi* laugh **3** sound a car horn ◇ **not care** *or* **give a hoot** be completely uninterested *(infml)*

hooter /hootər/ *n* a large nose *(slang humorous)*

Hoover /hoovər/ *tdmk* a trademark for a vacuum cleaner

Hoover /hoovər/, **J. Edgar** (1895–1972) US director of the FBI (1924–72)

hooves plural of **hoof**

hop¹ *v* (**hopping, hopped**) **1** *vi* jump lightly on one foot **2** *vi* jump lightly with both or all feet **3** *vt* leap over something **4** *vi* limp **5** *vi* get on or off a passenger vehicle *(infml)* ■ *n* **1** a small quick jump **2** a short flight *(infml)* **3** a dance *(infml)*

hop² *n* a climbing vine with flowers ■ **hops** *npl* dried hop flowers. Use: flavouring beer.

hope *vti* (**hoping, hoped**) want or expect something ■ *n* **1** the confidence that something good will happen **2** likelihood of success ○ *There's not much hope that things will improve.* **3** a wish or desire

hopeful /hópf'l/ *adj* **1** having hope **2** giving hope ■ *n* somebody who hopes or expects to be successful —**hopefulness** *n*

hopefully /hópfəli/ *adv* **1** in a hopeful way ○ *a hopefully worded apology* **2** △ indicates that something is hoped

USAGE Many people object when **hopefully** is used as a so-called sentence adverb, that is to say, as an introductory word that qualifies the entire sentence, as in *Hopefully, someone can resolve this.* The criticism arises from the fact that in this sentence no one is present who is meant to be doing the hoping. You can avoid the whole problem by saying *Let's hope, Let us hope,* or *It is to be hoped.*

~~hopeing~~ incorrect spelling of **hoping**

hopeless /hópləss/ *adj* **1** with no hope of success **2** feeling despair —**hopelessly** *adv* —**hopelessness** *n*

Hopkins /hópkinz/, **Gerard Manley** (1844–89) British poet

hopper /hóppər/ *n* **1** a large funnel-shaped industrial dispenser **2** a vehicle that discharges its load through an opening in the bottom

Hopper /hóppər/, **Edward** (1882–1967) US artist

hopscotch /hóp skoch/ *n* a children's game in

which players hop along squares marked on the ground

ORIGIN *Scotch* in **hopscotch** means 'scratched line'.

Horace /hórrəss/ (65–8 BC) Roman poet —**Horatian** /hə ráysh'n/ *adj*

horde /hawrd/ *n* **1** a large group of people *(often pl)* **2** a nomadic group ◊ See note at **hoard**

~~horizen~~ incorrect spelling of **horizon**

horizon /hə ríz'n/ *n* **1** the line where the land or sea meets the sky **2** a circle on the celestial sphere ■ **horizons** *npl* somebody's range of experience, knowledge, or interests —**horizonal** *adj*

horizontal /hórri zónt'l/ *adj* **1** parallel to the horizon and at right angles to the vertical **2** having the same importance and status ○ *a horizontal promotion* **3** applied equally to all members or parts ○ *a horizontal bonus* ■ *n* a horizontal line or surface —**horizontally** *adv*

hormone /háwrmōn/ *n* **1** a chemical produced in one part of the body that has an effect in another part **2** a chemical in plants or insects that regulates growth —**hormonal** /hawr môn'l/ *adj*

hormone replacement therapy *n* a treatment to offset menopausal symptoms

Hormuz, Strait of /hawr mooz, háwrmooz/ narrow waterway between Iran and the Arabian Peninsula, linking the Persian Gulf with the Arabian Sea

horn *n* **1** a device that makes a noise as a warning *(often in combination)* **2** a projection on an animal's head **3** any projection resembling a horn **4** a French horn **5** a simple wind instrument made from an animal's horn **6** the hard substance of horns **7** a horn-shaped area ■ *vt* attack somebody with horns *(refers to horned mammals)* —**horned** *adj* ◊ **draw in your horns** adopt a less active or less assertive position

Horn, Cape cape in S Chile, at the southern extremity of South America. Height 424 m/1,391 ft.

hornbill /háwrn bil/ *n* a tropical bird with a large curved bill

hornet /háwrnit/ *n* a large stinging wasp

hornpipe /háwrn pīp/ *n* **1** a British sailors' dance **2** the music for a hornpipe

horny /háwrni/ **(-ier, -iest)** *adj* sexually excited *(infml)* —**hornily** *adv* —**horniness** *n*

horology /ho rólləji/ *n* **1** the measurement of time **2** the making of clocks —**horological** *adj* —**horologist** *n*

horoscope /hórrə skōp/ *n* **1** an astrological forecast **2** a diagram of the positions of the stars and planets at a specific time —**horoscopic** /hórrə skóppik/ *adj*

Horowitz /hórrə wits/**, Vladimir** (1904–89) Russian-born US pianist

horrendous /ho réndəss, hə-/ *adj* dreadful —**horrendously** *adj* —**horrendousness** *n*

horrible /hórrəb'l/ *adj* **1** very unpleasant

2 causing horror **3** unkind or rude *(infml)* —**horribleness** *n* —**horribly** *adv*

ORIGIN Horrible and related words go back to a Latin verb *horrere* that described hair standing on end and so came to mean 'tremble, shudder'.

horrid /hórrid/ *adj* **1** nasty *(infml)* **2** causing disgust or horror —**horridly** *adv* —**horridness** *n*

horrific /ho ríffik, hə-/ *adj* very disturbing or frightening —**horrifically** *adv*

horrify /hórri fī/ **(-fies, -fied)** *vt* **1** cause to feel horror **2** shock or dismay —**horrified** *adj* —**horrifying** *adj* —**horrifyingly** *adv*

horror /hórrər/ *n* **1** intense fear or dislike **2** something that causes horror **3** something unpleasant *(infml)* **4** a badly behaved child *(infml)* ■ *adj* describes grotesque and terrifying films or literature

horror story *n* **1** a frightening fictional tale **2** a report of a horrifying experience

horror-struck, horror-stricken *adj* feeling horror

hors de combat /áwr də kóm baa/ *adj* no longer able to participate, usually because of an injury

hors d'oeuvre /awr dúrv/ **(***pl* **same** or **hors d'oeuvres** /-dúrv, -dúrvz/**)** *n* an appetizer

horse /hawrss/ *n* **1** a four-legged animal used for riding and pulling vehicles **2** a stallion or gelding **3** any animal of the horse family **4** a piece of gymnastic equipment for vaulting **5** a frame or support ◊ **flog a dead horse** pursue a topic or course of action likely to be totally unproductive ◊ **from the horse's mouth** from a well-informed and reliable source ◊ See note at **hoarse**

☐ **horse around** or **about** *vi* fool around

horseback /háwrss bak/ *adj, adv* on a horse's back

horsebox /háwrss boks/ *n* a vehicle for carrying horses

horse chestnut *n* **1** a shiny brown inedible seed **2** a large tree that produces horse chestnuts

horsedrawn /háwrss drawn/ *adj* pulled by horses

horseflesh /háwrss flesh/ *n* **1** a horse, or horses in general **2** the meat from a horse

horsefly /háwrss flī/ **(***pl* **-flies)** *n* a large biting fly

horsehair /háwrss hair/ *n* the long coarse hair from a horse. Use: upholstery, mattress filling, cloth.

horseman /háwrssmən/ **(***pl* **-men** /-mən/**)** *n* a man who rides horses —**horsemanship** *n*

horseplay /háwrss play/ *n* boisterous play

horsepower /háwrss pow ər/ *n* a unit of power equal to 550 foot-pounds per second

horseracing /háwss rayssing/ *n* organized racing for horses and their riders

horseradish /háwrss radish/ *n* **1** a long pungent root. Use: in cooking as a seasoning. **2** a tall flowering plant whose roots are eaten as horseradish

horse sense *n* common sense *(infml)*

horseshoe /háwrss shoo/ *n* **1** a U-shaped piece of metal nailed to a horse's hoof for protection **2** a good-luck token in the shape of a horseshoe

horseshoes /háwrss shooz/ *n US, Can* a game in which players throw horseshoes at a post and score points depending on how close they land to the post *(+ sing verb)*

horsewhip /háwrss wip/ *n* a whip for controlling a horse ■ *vt* (**-whipping, -whipped**) beat severely

horsewoman /háwrss wōomən/ *(pl* **-women** /-wimin/) *n* a woman who rides horses

horsey /háwrssi/ *(-ier, -iest)*, **horsy** *adj* **1** of horses **2** looking like a horse **3** interested in horses

hortatory /háwrtətəri/ *adj* urging a course of action *(fml)*

horticulture /háwrti kulchər/ *n* the science or activity of cultivating flowers, fruit, and salad vegetables in gardens or greenhouses —**horticultural** /háwrti kúlchərəl/ *adj* —**horticulturist** /háwrti kúlchərist/ *n*

Horus /háwrəss/ *n* the ancient Egyptian sun god

hosanna /hō zánnə/, **hosannah** *n, interj* a shout of praise

Hosay /hō sáy/, **Hosein** /-sáyn/ *n* an Islamic religious festival marking the martyrdom of Imam Hosein. Date: 10th day of Moharram.

hose /hōz/ *n* a flexible tube through which a liquid can flow ■ *npl US* stockings or tights ■ *vt* (**hosing, hosed**) spray or wash with water

hosepipe /hóz pīp/ *n* a flexible pipe for conveying water

hosiery /hózi əri/ *n* socks and stockings

hospice /hóspiss/ *n* a nursing home for terminally ill people

hospitable /ho spíttəb'l, hóspitəb'l/ *adj* **1** cordial and generous to visitors **2** agreeable ○ *a hospitable climate* —**hospitably** *adv*

hospital /hóspit'l/ *n* **1** an institution providing medical care **2** a place where items of a particular kind are repaired

ORIGIN **Hospital, hostel,** and **hotel** all go back to the same medieval Latin word meaning 'guesthouse, inn'. It was formed from the Latin *hospes* 'host, guest'. **Hospital** came into English from an early French form in the 13C, and was originally a hostel for pilgrims and travellers. It was not used explicitly for a place for treating the sick or wounded until the mid-16C.

hospitality /hóspi tálləti/ *n* kindness to visitors

hospitalize /hóspitə līz/ (**-izing, -ized**), **hospitalise** *vt* send somebody to hospital —**hospitalization** /hóspitə lī záysh'n/ *n*

host¹ /hōst/ *n* **1** somebody who entertains guests **2** somebody who introduces guests on a show **3** the organization providing facilities for an event **4** an organism infected

by a parasite **5** the landlord of an inn *(dated)* **6** *also* **host computer** the main computer controlling files in a network ■ *vt* **1** accommodate an event **2** introduce guests on a show **3** entertain guests at a social event **4** create a website for a client

host² /hōst/ *n* **1** a large number of people or things **2** an army *(archaic)*

Host /hōst/, **host** *n* the consecrated bread used during the Christian sacrament of Communion

hostage /hóstij/ *n* somebody held prisoner until specific demands are met

hostel /hóst'l/ *n* **1** an inexpensive lodging for young travellers **2** a supervised lodging for workers or young offenders **3** a place of accommodation for homeless people

hostelling /hóst'ling/ *n* the activity of staying at hostels while travelling

hostelry /hóst'lri/ *(pl* **-ries**) *n* an inn *(humorous or archaic)*

hostess /hóstiss, hō stéss/ *n* **1** a woman who entertains guests **2** a woman who introduces guests on a show **3** a woman who is employed to be a dance partner for customers in a nightclub —**hostess** *vti*

hostile /hóss tīl/ *adj* **1** very unfriendly **2** opposed to somebody or something **3** of an enemy ○ *hostile fire* **4** adverse ○ *a hostile environment* **5** describes a takeover bid that is opposed by the owners or managers of a company —**hostile** *n* —**hostilely** *adv*

hostility /ho stílləti/ *n* **1** intense aggression or anger **2** strong opposition ■ **hostilities** *npl* open acts of warfare

hot (**hotter, hottest**) *adj* **1** very warm, or too warm for comfort **2** very spicy **3** controversial ○ *a hot topic* **4** quickly angered ○ *a hot temper* **5** brightly vivid in hue ○ *hot pink* **6** following closely ○ *hot on the trail* **7** topical and interesting ○ *hot news* **8** exciting *(infml)* ○ *a hot new talent* **9** very popular *(infml)* ○ *one of the hottest items for sale* **10** knowledgeable or skilled *(infml)* ○ *not very hot at maths* **11** stolen *(slang)* **12** electrically charged ○ *a hot wire* **13** radioactive **14** in an elevated energy state as a result of nuclear processes —**hotly** *adv* —**hotness** *n*

☐ **hot up** *vti* intensify *(infml)*

hot air *n* empty statements or promises *(infml)*

hot-air balloon *n* a large balloon with a passenger compartment suspended from it

hotbed /hót bed/ *n* **1** an environment where something flourishes, especially something undesirable ○ *a hotbed of corruption* **2** a heated glass-covered planting bed

hot-blooded *adj* easily excited or aroused —**hot-bloodedness** *n*

hotcake /hót kayk/ ◇ **sell like hotcakes** sell very quickly *(infml)*

hotchpotch /hóch poch/ *n* a jumble

hot cross bun *n* a currant bun marked with a cross, traditionally eaten on Good Friday

hot-desking *n* the practice of using any available desk at work —**hot-desk** *vi*

hot dog *n* a sausage, typically served in a bread roll

hotel /hō tél/ *n* **1** a place where people pay for lodging, and where meals are often available **2** *S Asia* a restaurant **3 Hotel** a communications code word for the letter 'H'

hotelier /hō télli ay, -télli ər/ *n* a hotel proprietor

hotelling /hō télling/ *n* the act of providing temporary office desk space for somebody

hot flush *n* a sudden hot feeling experienced by some menopausal women

hotfoot /hót fŏot, hót fŏot/ *adv* quickly

hotheaded /hót héddid/ *adj* impetuous —**hothead** /hót hed/ *n* —**hotheadedly** *adv* —**hotheadedness** *n*

hothouse /hót howss/ (*pl* -**houses** /-howziz/) *n* **1** a heated greenhouse **2** a place where something flourishes and develops ○ *a hothouse of technological innovation*

hot key *n* a computer key or combination of keys that provides a short cut for a specific function

hotline /hót līn/ *n* **1** a direct telephone link to a service **2** a permanent communications link between political leaders

hotlink /hót lingk/ *n* a hyperlink

hotlist /hót list/ *n* a file of a computer user's most recent hypertext link connections

hot money *n* funds transferred from one currency to another for short-term gain

hot pants *npl* brief tight shorts

hot plate *n* **1** a heated cooking surface **2** a device for keeping food warm

hotpot /hót pot/ *n* a meat and vegetable stew

hot potato *n* a topic that is hard to handle

hot rod *n* a very powerful car (*slang*)

hot seat ◇ **in the hot seat** facing or liable to face criticism or difficult questioning

hotshot /hót shot/ *n* a self-assured expert (*infml disapproving*) —**hotshot** *adj*

hot spot *n* **1** a place of potential unrest **2** a small area of intense heat

hot spring *n* a spring of water heated geothermally

hot stuff *n* (*infml*) **1** a very good person or thing **2** a person who is regarded as very sexually attractive

hot toddy *n* a drink of alcohol and hot water, usually sweetened

hot tub *n* a large bath for more than one person to relax or socialize in

hot-water bottle *n* a warming water-filled container

hot-wire *vt* start a car without a key (*infml*)

Houdini /hŏo deeni/, **Harry** (1874–1926) Hungarian-born US magician

hound /hownd/ *n* **1** a dog bred for hunting **2** any dog (*infml*) ■ *vt* **1** pursue doggedly **2** urge or nag

hour /owr/ *n* **1** a period of 60 minutes **2** the point in time at the start of an hour ○ *There's a bus at 20 past the hour.* **3** time of day ○ *at this unearthly hour* **4** a regular time for something

○ *her lunch hour* **5** a significant period ○ *your hour of glory* **6** a time of success ○ *This is your hour.* **7** somebody's time of death ○ *The doctors thought his hour had finally come.* ■ **hours** *npl* **1** a long time ○ *I was waiting for hours.* **2** the times for doing particular things ○ *banking hours* ◇ **of the hour** currently relevant or popular ○ *She's the woman of the hour.*

hourglass /ówr glaass/ *n* a time-measuring device in which sand falls from one glass bulb into another

hour hand *n* the short hand on a timepiece

houri /hŏori/ *n* in Islamic belief, one of the beautiful young women who attend Muslim men in paradise

hourly /ówrli/ *adj* **1** happening each hour or very regularly ○ *hourly news* **2** calculated or paid by the hour ○ *hourly wages* —**hourly** *adv*

house *n* /howss/ (*pl* **houses** /hówziz/) **1** a building for people to live in **2** the occupants of a house **3** a building for animals **4** a restaurant or other eating establishment ○ *the speciality of the house* **5** a theatre **6** a business operation ○ *a publishing house* **7** a division of a school **8** *also* **House** a legislative group or the building in which it meets **9** *also* **House** a family line **10** a division of the zodiac ■ *vt* /howz/ (**housing, housed**) **1** give somebody a place to live **2** contain something ○ *a shed that houses our lawn mowers* ◇ **bring the house down** provoke a great deal of laughter or applause ◇ **on the house** given free by somebody who would normally charge ◇ **put your house in order** organize your life properly

house arrest *n* a form of legal confinement in which the prisoner is not allowed to leave his or her home

houseboat /hówss bōt/ *n* a large flat-bottomed boat equipped for use as a home

housebound /hówss bownd/ *adj* unable to go outside, e.g. because of illness or bad weather

housebreaking /hówss brayking/ *n* illegal forcible entry into a building in order to commit a crime —**housebreaker** *n*

housecoat /hówss kōt/ *n* a woman's casual outer garment, worn at home

housefly /hówss flī/ (*pl* -**flies**) *n* a common fly that lives in or around houses

house guest *n* a visitor to somebody's home

household /hówss hōld/ *n* the people who live together in a house ■ *adj* **1** belonging to a household **2** familiar to all ○ *a household word*

householder /hówss hōldər/ *n* somebody who owns, rents, or is in charge of a house

househusband /hówss huzbənd/ *n* a man who manages a household full time and does not go out to work

housekeeper /hówss keepər/ *n* somebody who

manages the running of somebody else's house

housekeeping /hówss keeping/ n 1 household maintenance 2 the money used for running a household 3 maintenance of a computer system

house lights npl lights that illuminate a theatre auditorium

housemaid /hówss mayd/ n a woman servant (dated)

houseman /hówssman/ (pl -men /-man/) n a junior hospital doctor (dated)

house martin n a small swallow

housemaster /hówss maastar/ n a man responsible for the boarders living in a house at a boarding school

housemistress /hówss mistrass/ n a woman responsible for the boarders living in a house at a boarding school

house music n a style of fast and repetitive electronic dance music

house of cards n a highly unstable situation or organization, liable to collapse

House of Commons n the lower house of the parliaments of the United Kingdom and Canada

house officer n UK a junior hospital doctor

house of ill fame, house of ill repute n a brothel

House of Lords n the upper house of the UK Parliament

House of Representatives n 1 the lower house of the US Congress 2 the lower house of the Australian federal parliament 3 the parliament of New Zealand

house party n 1 a large party with overnight guests at somebody's residence 2 the guests at a house party

houseplant /hówss plaant/ n a plant grown indoors

house-proud adj proud of your home and its state of cleanliness

house-sit vi take care of somebody's house while they are away

Houses of Parliament npl 1 the buildings of the UK Parliament 2 the House of Commons and the House of Lords considered together

house-to-house adj from one house to the next o a house-to-house search

housewarming /hówss wawrming/, **housewarming party** n a party in a new house

housewife /hówss wíf/ (pl -wives /-wívz/) n a woman who manages a household full time and does not go out to work

housework /hówss wurk/ n household chores

housing /hówzing/ n 1 living accommodation 2 the provision of living accommodation 3 a protective cover for a machine part

housing association n an organization providing affordable accommodation for people on low incomes

housing estate n a planned area of housing

Housman /hówssman/, **A. E.** (1859 1936) British poet and scholar

Houston /hyóóstan/ major port in SE Texas. Pop. 1,786,691 (1998).

hove past tense of **heave** v 7

hovel /hóv'l/ n a small, dirty, or poorly built house

hover /hóvvar/ vi 1 stay in the air without moving far from the same spot 2 wait nearby in a nervous or expectant way 3 stay around the same level o temperatures hovering in the low teens

hovercraft /hóvvar kraaft/ (pl same) n a vehicle that glides over water or land on a cushion of air

how /how/ adv in what way o How do I open the window? ■ conj that o Do you remember how we were ridiculed? ■ adv to what extent o How high is the roof? ■ conj in whatever way o Do it how you want. ■ adv 1 like what o How was the film? 2 used in exclamations o How nice to see you! ■ n the way and means of accomplishing something o I'm not interested in the hows or whys. ◇ **how about** introduces a suggestion (infml) o How about a cup of coffee?

Howard, Catherine (1520?–42) queen of England (1540–42) as the 5th wife of Henry VIII

Howard, John (b. 1939) prime minister of Australia (1996–)

howdah /hówda/ n a seat on an elephant

however /how évvar/ adv 1 to whatever degree 2 in whatever way 3 how

howitzer /hówitsar/ n a combat artillery cannon

howl /howl/ vi 1 make a long whining sound 2 cry out in pain or distress 3 roar with laughter (slang) ■ n 1 a long moaning cry 2 a loud cry of pain, distress, or disapproval □ **howl down** vt disapprovingly drown out the sound or speech of

howler /hówlar/ n 1 a ridiculous mistake (infml) 2 somebody or something that howls

howsoever /hówsō évvar/ adv however (fml)

Hoy and West Mainland National Scenic Area in NE Scotland. The Old Man of Hoy is a pillar-shaped rock just off the coast of the island of Hoy.

Hoyle /hoyl/, **Sir Fred** (1915–2001) British astronomer and writer

hp abbr horsepower

HP abbr hire purchase

HQ, h.q. abbr headquarters

hr abbr hour

HR abbr human resources

HRH abbr 1 Her Royal Highness 2 His Royal Highness

HRT abbr hormone replacement therapy

hryvnia /hrívni a/ (pl same or -as) n the main unit of Ukrainian currency

Hs symbol hassium

html, htm abbr a file extension for a HyperText Markup Language file

HTML *n* a system of tagging used to format a text document for the World Wide Web. Full form **HyperText Markup Language**

HTTP *abbr* HyperText Transfer Protocol

Huang He /hwáng hó/ second longest river in China, flowing through the north-central part of the country. Length 5,464 km/3,395 mi.

hub *n* **1** the central part of a wheel or other rotating device **2** a centre of activity or interest **3** *also* **hub airport** a central airport from which passengers fly to smaller local airports

Hubble /húbb'l/, **Edwin** (1889–1953) US astronomer

hubbub /húbbub/ *n* **1** a confused din, especially from a number of voices speaking at once **2** an excited fuss

hubby /húbbi/ (*pl* **-bies**) *n* a husband (*infml*)

hubcap /húb kap/ *n* a cover for the centre of a vehicle's wheel

hubris /hyóobriss, hoó-/ *n* **1** overweening pride and arrogance **2** excessive ambition —**hubristic** /hyoo brístik, hoo-/ *adj*

huckleberry /húk'lbəri/ (*pl* **-ries**) *n* **1** an edible dark-blue berry **2** the plant that produces huckleberries

huckster /húkstər/ *n* an aggressive salesperson —**huckster** *vti*

huddle /húdd'l/ *n* a tightly packed group ■ *vi* (**-dling, -dled**) **1** gather tightly together **2** crouch near the ground or in a corner

Hudson /húdss'n/ river in E New York State, emptying into Upper New York Bay at New York City. Length 492 km/306 mi.

Hudson Bay almost landlocked inland sea of east-central Canada. Depth 258 m/846 ft.

hue /hyoo/ *n* **1** a colour ○ *flowers of every hue* **2** a shade of a colour ○ *a pleasing hue of green* **3** a type in a particular range ○ *all hues of political opinion* ◊ See note at **hew**

hue and cry *n* an uproar

huff *n* a fit of anger or sulking ■ *vi* **1** make angry statements **2** blow or pant laboriously

hug *v* (**hugging, hugged**) **1** *vti* embrace somebody or something affectionately **2** *vt* put your arms round something **3** *vr* congratulate yourself ■ *n* an affectionate embrace

huge /hyooj/ (**huger, hugest**) *adj* **1** enormous **2** large in scope ○ *huge talent* —**hugely** *adv* —**hugeness** *n*

Hughes /hyooz/, **Howard** (1905–76) US industrialist

Hughes, Robert (*b.* 1938) Australian art critic and writer

Hughes, Ted (1930–98) British poet

Hughes, William Morris (1862–1952) British-born prime minister of Australia (1915–23)

Hugo /hyóogō/, **Victor** (1802–85) French poet, novelist, and dramatist

Huguenot /hyóogənō/ *n* a French Protestant —**Huguenot** *adj*

huh /hu/ *interj* **1** expresses surprise or disdain **2** expresses an invitation to agree ○ *Great shot, huh?*

hui /hoó ee/ (*pl same*) *n* *NZ* a Maori social gathering

hula /hoóla/ *n* a Polynesian dance involving swaying hips and hand gestures

hulk *n* **1** a big, often clumsy person **2** a wrecked ship's empty hull **3** an unwieldy ship

hulking /húlking/, **hulky** /-ki/ (**-ier, -iest**) *adj* huge

hull /hul/ *n* **1** the body of a ship **2** the body of a large vehicle **3** a rocket casing **4** the outer covering of a seed or fruit ■ *vt* remove the hull from a seed or fruit

hullabaloo /húlləbə loó/, **hullaballoo** *n* a din or fuss

hullo *interj*, *n* = **hello**

hum *v* (**humming, hummed**) **1** *vi* make a droning sound ○ *bees humming* **2** *vti* sing with the lips closed **3** *vi* give off a low steady sound ○ *a room that hummed with strange electronic equipment* **4** *vi* be extremely busy (*infml*) ○ *This place is really humming.* ■ *n* a humming noise

human /hyóomən/ *adj* **1** of people **2** made up of people ○ *a human chain* **3** compassionately kind ■ *n* a human being —**humanness** *n*

human being *n* a member of the human species

humane /hyoo máyn/ *adj* **1** compassionate **2** involving minimal pain —**humanely** *adv* —**humaneness** *n*

human ecology *n* the study of people within an environment

humane society *n* an organization promoting kindness to animals

Human Genome Project *n* an international research initiative to sequence and identify human genes and their positions on chromosomes

human interest *n* the power to appeal to public sympathy or curiosity —**human-interest** *adj*

humanism /hyóomənizəm/ *n* **1** a belief system based on the best of human nature rather than religious faith **2** *also* **Humanism** a Renaissance cultural movement deriving from the rediscovery of the arts and philosophy of ancient Greece and Rome —**humanist** *n*, *adj* —**humanistic** /hyóomə nístik/ *adj*

humanitarian /hyoo mánni táiri ən/ *adj* committed to improving the lives of other people —**humanitarian** *n* —**humanitarianism** *n*

humanity /hyoo mánnəti/ *n* **1** humankind **2** the qualities typical of a human being ■ **humanities, Humanities** *npl* **1** the liberal arts as subjects of study **2** classical studies

humanize /hyóomə nīz/ (**-izing, -ized**), **humanise** *vti* **1** make or become human **2** make or become humane —**humanization** /hyóomə nī záysh'n/ *n*

humankind /hyóomən kínd/ *n* human beings collectively

humanly /hyóomənli/ *adv* **1** within the limits of human ability ◇ *if humanly possible* **2** in a way characteristic of human beings **3** according to human experience

humanmade /hyóomən mayd/ *adj* made by human beings, not occurring naturally

human nature *n* the essential character of human beings

humanoid /hyóomə noyd/ *adj* resembling a human being —**humanoid** *n*

human resources *n* employee recruitment and management (+ *sing verb*) ■ *npl* the personnel of an organization (+ *pl verb*)

human rights *npl* rights such as freedom, justice, and equality that are considered to belong to everyone ■ *n* the protection or study of human rights (+ *sing verb*)

humble /húmb'l/ *adj* (**-bler**, **-blest**) **1** modest in attitude **2** respectful **3** lowly ◇ *of humble origins* ■ *vt* (**-bling**, **-bled**) cause to feel less important —**humbled** *adj* —**humbling** *adj* —**humbly** *adv*

Humboldt Current /húm bōlt-/ *n* cold current of the South Pacific Ocean that flows north along the coastline of South America

humbug /húm bug/ *n* **1** nonsense **2** a deception **3** somebody who deceives others as to his or her identity or history ■ *vti* (**-bugging**, **-bugged**) deceive

humdinger /húmdingər/ *n* somebody or something exceptional (*slang*)

humdrum /húm drum/ *adj* dull and ordinary

Hume /hyoom/, **David** (1711–76) Scottish philosopher and historian

humerus /hyóomərəss/ (*pl* **-i** /-rī/) *n* the long bone of the human upper arm or an animal's front limb —**humeral** *adj*

humid /hyóomid/ *adj* with relatively high moisture in the air

humidify /hyoo míddi fī/ (**-fies**, **-fied**) *vt* make more humid —**humidification** /hyoo míddifi káysh'n/ *n* —**humidifier** *n*

humidity /hyoo míddəti/ *n* **1** atmospheric moisture **2** a high moisture level in the air

humiliate /hyoo mílli ayt/ (**-ating**, **-ated**) *vt* damage the dignity or pride of, especially publicly —**humiliating** *adj* —**humiliation** /-mílli áysh'n/ *n*

humility /hyoo mílləti/ *n* modesty or respectfulness

~~huminist~~ incorrect spelling of **humanist**

humint /hyóomint/, **HUMINT** *n* intelligence information acquired from people in enemy territory. Full form **human intelligence**

hummingbird /húmming burd/ *n* a small brightly coloured bird that hovers by rapid beating of its wings

hummock /húmmək/ *n* a small hill

hummus /hóomməss/, **humus**, **hoummos** /hóomməss/ *n* a dip made with mashed chickpeas

humorist /hyóomərist/ *n* **1** a comic writer or performer **2** an amusing person

humorous /hyóomərəss/ *adj* amusing or witty —**humorously** *adv*

humour /hyóomər/ *n* **1** amusing quality ◇ *couldn't see the humour in it* **2** the ability to see that something is amusing **3** a mood or state of mind **4** a body fluid ■ *vt* do what somebody wants to keep him or her happy —**humourless** *adj* —**humourlessly** *adv*

~~humourous~~ incorrect spelling of **humorous**

hump *n* **1** a rounded protuberance on an animal's back **2** a pronounced outward curve of a person's upper back ■ *vt* move with effort (*infml*) —**humpy** *adj* ◇ **over the hump** past the worst or most difficult part ◇ **the hump** a mood of annoyance, resentment, or unhappiness (*infml*)

humpback /húmp bak/ *n* **1** somebody with a hump on his or her back **2** a humped back **3** *also* **humpback whale** a large dark-coloured whale with a humped back **4** *also* **humpback bridge**, **humpbacked bridge** a small curved bridge —**humpbacked** *adj*

humph *interj* expresses displeasure

Humphries /húmfriz/, **Barry** (*b.* 1934) Australian writer and performer

humus[1] /hyóoməss/ *n* the organic component of soil

humus[2] *n* FOOD = **hummus**

Hun *n* **1** member of an early Asian nomadic people **2** an offensive term for a German person or the German people (*dated slang*) —**Hunnish** *adj*

hunch *n* **1** an intuitive feeling about something **2** a stoop of the body ■ *v* **1** *vti* bend the upper body forwards **2** *vi* crouch

hunchback /húnch bak/ *n* **1** somebody with a hump on his or her back **2** a humped back —**hunchbacked** *adj*

hundred /húndrəd/ *n* **1** the number 100 **2** a large number ◇ *hundreds of people* **3** the third digit to the left of a decimal point **4** in cricket, 100 runs **5** a historical county subdivision ■ **hundreds** *npl* **1** the numbers 100 to 999 **2** large numbers —**hundred** *adj* —**hundredth** *n*, *adj*

hundreds-and-thousands *npl* tiny cake decorations made of coloured strands of sugar

hundredweight /húndrəd wayt/ *n* **1** a weight of 112 lb **2** *US* a weight of 100 lb

hung past participle, past tense of **hang**

Hungarian /hung gáiri ən/ *n* **1** somebody from Hungary **2** the official language of Hungary —**Hungarian** *adj*

Hungary /húng gəri/ country in central Europe. Cap. Budapest. Pop. 10,106,017 (2001).

hunger /húng gər/ *n* **1** the need or desire to eat **2** starvation **3** a strong desire for something ◇ *a hunger for knowledge* ■ *vi* have a strong desire for something

hunger strike *n* a refusal to eat as a protest —**hunger striker** *n*

hungover /hung óvər/ *adj* suffering from a hangover

hungry /húng gri/ (**-grier**, **-griest**) *adj* **1** needing or wanting to eat **2** wanting something greatly ○ *hungry for new experiences* —**hungrily** *adv*

hung up *adj* (*infml*) **1** obsessed **2** worried

hunk *n* **1** a large chunk of something **2** a man with a good physique (*infml*)

hunker /húngkər/ *vi* crouch

hunky /húngki/ (**-ier**, **-iest**) *adj* having a good male physique (*infml*)

hunky-dory /-dáwri/ *adj* fine or satisfactory (*infml*)

hunt *v* **1** *vti* pursue and kill an animal for sport or food **2** *vt* seek out and try to capture somebody **3** *vi* search for something difficult to find **4** *vt* harass somebody **5** *vi* chase animals with hounds **6** *vt* use an animal in a blood sport ■ *n* **1** a search for something **2** a search for prey **3** a hunting expedition —**hunted** *adj* —**hunting** *n*

Hunt, Holman (1827–1910) British painter

hunter /húntər/ *n* **1** a person or animal that hunts for food or sport **2** a horse or dog bred or used for hunting

hunter-gatherer *n* a member of a society that forages for food instead of raising crops or livestock

Hunter Valley agricultural and industrial region in E New South Wales, Australia

hunting ground *n* **1** an area for hunting **2** a source of something useful or desired ○ *a good hunting ground for antiques*

huntress /húntrəss/ *n* a woman or goddess who hunts (*literary*)

hunt saboteur *n* an anti-foxhunting activist

huntsman /húntsmən/ (*pl* **-men** /-mən/) *n* **1** a hunt official in charge of hounds **2** a man who goes hunting

hurdle /húrd'l/ *n* **1** a light barrier for runners to jump over in some races **2** a difficulty or obstacle ■ *v* (**-dling**, **-dled**) **1** *vi* race over hurdles **2** *vt* jump over a racing barrier —**hurdler** *n*

hurdles /húrd'lz/ *n* a footrace over light barriers (+ *sing verb*)

hurdy-gurdy /húrdi gúrdi, húrdi gurdi/ (*pl* **hurdy-gurdies**) *n* a barrel organ or similar instrument played by turning a handle

hurl *vt* **1** throw violently **2** yell ○ *hurling abuse* —**hurl** *n* ◊ See note at **throw**

hurling /húrling/ *n* an Irish team game played with broad sticks and a leather ball

hurly-burly /húrli búrli/ *n* noisy bustling activity

Huron, Lake /hyóorən/ second largest of the Great Lakes. Depth 229 m/751 ft.

hurray *interj*, *n* = **hooray**

hurricane /húrrikən, -kayn/ *n* **1** a severe tropical storm with very strong winds **2** somebody or something that acts with speed, force, and effectiveness

---

ORIGIN Hurricane came via Spanish from a Native Central American word meaning 'god of the storm'.

---

hurricane lamp *n* a lantern protected with glass from the weather

hurry /húrri/ *v* (**-ries**, **-ried**) **1** *vi* move or do something with great or excessive speed **2** *vt* encourage to speed up ■ *n* **1** haste **2** urgency —**hurried** *adj* —**hurriedly** *adv*

hurt *v* (**hurt**) **1** *vt* injure **2** *vti* cause pain to, or experience pain **3** *vti* upset somebody's feelings, or feel upset **4** *vti* have a detrimental effect on something ○ *hurt her chances* ■ *n* **1** pain **2** an injury —**hurt** *adj* ◊ See note at **harm**

hurtful /húrtf'l/ *adj* emotionally painful —**hurtfully** *adv* —**hurtfulness** *n*

hurtle /húrt'l/ (**-tling**, **-tled**) *vi* move at very high speed

husband /húzbənd/ *n* the man to whom a woman is married ■ *vt* be thrifty with

husbandman /húzbəndmən/ (*pl* **-men** /-mən/) *n* a farmer (*archaic*)

husbandry /húzbəndri/ *n* **1** farming **2** frugal management of resources

hush *vti* cause to be quiet, or become quiet ■ *n* silence

□ **hush up** *vt* prevent the disclosure of (*infml*)

hush-hush *adj* secret (*infml*)

hush money *n* money paid as a bribe not to disclose information (*infml*)

husk *n* **1** the outer covering of some fruits, nuts, and grains **2** a useless outer shell ■ *vt* remove husks from

husky[1] /húski/ (**-ier**, **-iest**) *adj* **1** throaty or hoarse **2** *US* burly and compact in physique —**huskily** *adv* —**huskiness** *n*

husky[2] /húski/ (*pl* **-kies**) *n* a large working dog with a thick coat

Huss, John (1372?–1415) Bohemian nationalist and religious reformer

hussar /hoŏ zaár/ *n* a European light cavalry soldier

Hussein I /hoŏ sáyn/ (1935–99) king of Jordan (1952–99)

Hussein, Saddam (*b.* 1937) Iraqi national leader

hussy /hússi/ (*pl* **-sies**) *n* an offensive term for a woman or girl whose behaviour is regarded as too forward (*dated*)

hustings /hústingz/ *n* the location or activities of a political campaign

hustle /húss'l/ *v* (**-tling**, **-tled**) **1** *vt* convey roughly or hurriedly from a place **2** *vi* hurry (*infml*) **3** *vt* deal with quickly **4** *vt* *US, Can* sell aggressively ■ *n* noisy activity —**hustler** *n*

Huston /hyoŏstən/, **John** (1906–87) US film director and actor

hut *n* a one-room building

hutch *n* a shelter for housing a small animal

Hutton /hútt'n/, **James** (1726–97) Scottish geologist

Huxley /húksli/, **Aldous** (1894–1963) British novelist and essayist

Huxley, Andrew (*b.* 1917) British physiologist

hyacinth /hí ə sinth/ *n* a plant grown from a bulb, with heads of pink, white, or blue flowers —**hyacinthine** /hí ə sín thīn/ *adj*

hyaena *n* ZOOL = **hyena**

hybrid /híbrid/ *n* **1** a plant or animal produced by crossing genetically different forms **2** something made up of a mixture of different elements —**hybrid** *adj*

hybridize /híbri dīz/ (**-izing, -ized**), **hybridise** *vti* crossbreed a plant or animal —**hybridization** /híbri dī záysh'n/ *n*

Hyderabad /hídərə bad/ **1** capital of Andhra Pradesh State, India. Pop. 2,964,638 (1991). **2** city in SE Pakistan, on the River Indus. Pop. 1,151,274 (1998).

hydra /hídrə/ (*pl* **-dras** *or* **-drae** /-dree/) *n* **1** a freshwater organism that has a cylindrical body with a mouth surrounded by tentacles at one end **2 Hydra** a large constellation near the celestial equator

hydrangea /hī dráynjə/ *n* a bush with large clusters of white, pink, or blue flowers

hydrant /hídrənt/ *n* a fire hydrant

hydrate /hí drayt, hī dráyt/ *vt* (**-drating, -drated**) **1** give water to somebody or something to regulate fluid balance **2** add water to a chemical compound to form different crystals ■ *n* a chemical compound containing water molecules —**hydration** /hīdráysh'n/ *n*

hydraulic /hī dróllik/ *adj* driven by fluid under pressure —**hydraulically** *adv*

hydraulics /hī drólliks/ *n* the study of fluids (+ *sing verb*)

hydro[1] /hídrō/ (*pl* **-dros**) *n* **1** a hydroelectric power plant **2** hydroelectric power

hydro[2] (*pl* **-dros**) *n* a place offering hydropathic treatment

hydro- *prefix* **1** water, liquid, moisture o *hydroelectric* **2** hydrogen o *hydrocarbon*

hydrocarbon /hídrō kaárbən/ *n* a chemical compound containing hydrogen and carbon

hydrocephalus /hídrō séffələss, -kéffələss/, **hydrocephaly** /hídrō séffəli, -kéffəli/ *n* increased fluid round the brain **hydrocephalic** /hídrō sə fállik, -kə-/ *adj*

hydrochloric acid /hídrə klórrik-/ *n* HCl a strong colourless acid. Use: industrial and laboratory processes.

hydrodynamics /hídrō dī námmiks/ *n* the area of fluid dynamics concerned with the study of liquids (+ *sing verb*) —**hydrodynamic** *adj* —**hydrodynamicist** /-námmissist/ *n*

hydroelectric /hídrō i léktrik/ *adj* **1** generated by converting water power to electricity **2** of hydroelectric power generation —**hydroelectrically** *adv* —**hydroelectricity** /hídrō i lek tríssəti/ *n*

hydrofoil /hídrə foyl/ *n* **1** a high-speed boat with wing-shaped blades under the hull that lift the boat out of the water **2** a wing-shaped blade on a hydrofoil

hydrogen /hídrəjən/ *n* (*symbol* **H**) a reactive gaseous element. Use: production of ammonia, reduction of metal ores to metals.

hydrogenate /hī drójjə nayt/ (**-ating, -ated**) *vt* add hydrogen to —**hydrogenation** /hī drójjə náysh'n/ *n*

hydrogen bomb *n* a nuclear weapon in which energy is released by the fusion of hydrogen nuclei

hydrogen chloride *n* HCl a colourless fuming corrosive gas. Use: manufacture of PVC.

hydrogen peroxide *n* H_2O_2 an unstable viscous liquid. Use: bleach, mild antiseptic, component in rocket fuel.

~~hydrolic~~ incorrect spelling of **hydraulic**

hydrolysis /hī drólləssiss/ *n* the reaction of a compound with water resulting in two or more new compounds —**hydrolytic** /hídrə líttik/ *adj*

hydrometer /hī drómmitər/ *n* an instrument that determines the specific gravity of liquids —**hydrometric** /hídrō méttrik/ *adj* —**hydrometry** *n*

hydropathy /hī dróppəthi/ *n* the internal and external application of water for healing —**hydropath** /hídrə path/ *n* —**hydropathic** /hídrō páthik/ *adj*

hydrophobia /hídrō fóbi ə/ *n* **1** rabies **2** fear of water —**hydrophobic** *adj*

hydroplane /hídrō playn/ *n* a fast boat that rises up out of the water at high speed ■ *vi* (**-planing, -planed**) **1** skim along the surface of water **2** skid on a wet road surface

hydroponics /hídrō pónniks/ *n* the growing of plants in a nutrient liquid (+ *sing verb*) —**hydroponic** *adj*

hydrostatics /hídrō státtiks/ *n* the scientific study of liquids at rest (+ *sing verb*) —**hydrostatic** *adj*

hydrotherapy /hídrō thérrəpi/ *n* the external use of water for healing, e.g. exercise in a pool —**hydrotherapist** *n*

hydroxide /hī drók sīd/ *n* a chemical compound containing the group -OH

hyena /hī eénə/, **hyaena** *n* a scavenging wild mammal resembling a dog, with a sloping back —**hyenic** *adj*

~~hygeine~~ incorrect spelling of **hygiene**

hygiene /hí jeen/ *n* **1** the science of the preservation of health **2** cleanliness —**hygienic** /hī jeénik/ *adj* —**hygienically** *adv*

hygienist /hí jeenist/ *n* somebody trained in hygiene

hymen /hí men/ *n* a thin mucous membrane covering the opening of the vagina

hymn /him/ *n* **1** a religious song of praise **2** a song of praise ■ *v* **1** *vt* sing in praise of **2** *vi* sing hymns

hymn book, hymnal /hímnəl/ *n* a book of church hymns

hype /hīp/ *n* excessive publicity or extravagant claims for somebody or something ■ *vt* (**hyping, hyped**) publicize excessively

hyped up *adj* highly stimulated (*slang*)

hyper /hípər/ *adj* (*infml*) **1** excessively active **2** very excitable

hyper- *prefix* **1** over, above, beyond ○ *hypertext* **2** excessive, unusually high ○ *hypertension*

hyperactive /hípər áktiv/ *adj* unusually active and unable to concentrate —**hyperactively** *adv* —**hyperactivity** /-ak tívvəti/ *n*

hyperbola /hī púrbələ/ (*pl* **-las** or **-lae** /-lee/) *n* a conic section formed by a point that moves in a plane so that the difference in its distance from two fixed points in the plane remains constant

hyperbole /hī púrbəli/ *n* exaggeration for effect

hyperbolic /hípər bóllik/, **hyperbolical** /-bóllik'l/ *adj* **1** of a hyperbola **2** of hyperbole —**hyperbolically** *adv*

hypercritical /hípər kríttik'l/ *adj* excessively critical —**hypercritically** *adv*

hyperglycaemia /hípər glī seémi ə/ *n* an excessively high level of blood sugar —**hyperglycaemic** *adj*

hyperinflation /hípərin fláysh'n/ *n* very high and rapid inflation —**hyperinflationary** *adj*

hyperlink /hípər lingk/ *n* a link in hypertext

hypermarket /hípər maarkit/ *n* a very large self-service shop selling products usually sold in supermarkets, hardware shops, and department stores

hypermedia /hípər meedi ə/ *n* a multi-media hypertext system

hypersensitive /hípər sénssətiv/ *adj* **1** very easily upset or offended **2** showing a strong reaction to a drug, allergen, or other agent —**hypersensitivity** /hípər sénssə tívvəti/ *n*

hypersonic /hípər sónnik/ *adj* moving at a speed at least five times the speed of sound —**hypersonically** *adv*

hypertension /hípər ténsh'n/ *n* **1** high blood pressure **2** arterial disease accompanied by high blood pressure

hypertext /hípər tekst/ *n* a system of storing images, text, and other computer files that allows direct links to related electronic data

HyperText Markup Language *n* full form of **HTML**

HyperText Transfer Protocol *n* the technical rules for formatting and transmitting messages on the World Wide Web

hypertrophy /hī púrtrəfi/ *n* (*pl* **-phies**) a growth in size of an organ through an increase in the size, rather than the number, of its cells ■ *vti* (**-phies, -phied**) grow larger by cell enlargement —**hypertrophic** /hípər trôffik/ *adj*

hyperventilate /hípər vénti layt/ (**-lating, -lated**) *vi* breathe unusually deeply or rapidly —**hyperventilation** /hípər venti láysh'n/ *n*

hyphen /híf'n/ *n* a dash in punctuation showing a break between syllables or parts of a compound word ■ *vt* hyphenate

USAGE A number of compound words and phrases are joined by hyphens: *thirty-seven; well-wisher; old-fashioned; mother-in-law.* For some the hyphens are optional, or inserted only when the word or phrase is used before a noun: *a coffee-table book; a well-timed attack* (but *the book on the coffee table; if the attack is well timed*). Most words with prefixes do not have a hyphen, exceptions being those where a capital letter follows the prefix (e.g. *pre-Christian*) and those where the word could be confused with another (e.g. *re-form* meaning 'form again' as distinct from *reform*). A hyphen is sometimes inserted when a prefix ending in a vowel is added to a word beginning with a vowel (e.g. *co-opt, de-ice*). See **dash**.

hyphenate /hífə nayt/ (**-ating, -ated**) *vt* use a hyphen in —**hyphenation** /hífə náysh'n/ *n*

hypnosis /hip nóssiss/ (*pl* **-ses** /-seez/) *n* **1** a state resembling sleep that can be artificially induced and that may increase suggestibility **2** the technique or practice of inducing hypnosis

hypnotherapy /híppnō thérrəpi/ *n* the use of hypnosis to treat illness or psychological disorders —**hypnotherapist** *n*

hypnotic /hip nóttik/ *adj* **1** of sleep or hypnosis **2** fascinating (*infml*) ■ *n* **1** something causing sleep or drowsiness **2** somebody easily hypnotized —**hypnotically** *adv*

hypnotism /hípnətizəm/ *n* **1** study or practice of inducing hypnosis **2** the state of hypnosis —**hypnotist** *n*

hypnotize /hípnə tīz/ (**-tizing, -tized**), **hypnotise** *vt* **1** put into a state of hypnosis **2** fascinate

hypo- *prefix* **1** under, below ○ *hypothalamus* **2** unusually low ○ *hypoglycaemia*

hypoallergenic /hípō állər jénnik/ *adj* unlikely to cause an allergic reaction

hypochondria /hípə kóndri ə/ *n* the deluded persistent conviction of being ill —**hypochondriac** *adj, n*

~~hypocrasy, hypocricy~~ incorrect spelling of **hypocrisy**

hypocrisy /hi pókrəssi/ (*pl* **-sies**) *n* **1** the pretence of having admirable principles, beliefs, or feelings **2** a hypocritical act

hypocrite /híppəkrit/ *n* somebody who pretends to have admirable principles, beliefs, or feelings —**hypocritical** /híppə kríttik'l/ *adj* —**hypocritically** *adv*

hypodermic /hípə dúrmik/ *adj* **1** of the area of tissue beneath the skin **2** injected or used to inject beneath the skin ■ *n* a hypodermic injection, needle, or syringe (*infml*) —**hypodermically** *adv*

hypoglycaemia /hípō glī seémi ə/ *n* an excessively low level of blood sugar —**hypoglycaemic** *adj*

hypotenuse /hī póttə nyooz/ *n* the longest side of a right-angled triangle

hypothalamus /hípō thálləmass/ (*pl* **-mi** /-mī/) *n* an area of the brain that controls involuntary functions —**hypothalamic** /hípōthə lámmik/ *adj*

hypothermia /hípō thúrmi ə/ *n* dangerously low body temperature —**hypothermic** *adj*

hypothesis /hī póthəssiss/ (*pl* **-ses** /-seez/) *n* **1** a theory used as a basis for further investigation **2** an assumption made for the sake of argument

hypothesize /hī póthə sīz/ (**-sizing**, **-sized**), **hypothesise** *vti* assume something as a hypothesis

hypothetical /hīpə théttik'l/, **hypothetic** /-théttik/ *adj* assumed as a basis for further investigation or for the sake of argument —**hypothetically** *adv*

hyrax /hī raks/ (*pl* **-raxes** *or* **-races** /-rə seez/) *n* a small Mediterranean mammal resembling a rabbit

hyssop /híssəp/ *n* an aromatic herb similar to mint. Use: in aromatherapy and alternative medicine.

hysterectomy /hístə réktəmi/ (*pl* **-mies**) *n* a surgical operation to remove the womb —**hysterectomize** *vt*

hysteria /hi steéri ə/ *n* **1** emotional instability caused by a trauma **2** a state of extreme emotion, especially among a large number of people

ORIGIN **Hysteria** derives ultimately from the Greek word for 'womb'. It was given that name in the early 19C, when the condition was often believed to be peculiar to women.

hysteric /hi stérrik/ *adj* hysterical ■ *n* somebody affected by hysteria (*dated; sometimes offensive*)

hysterical /hi stérrik'l/ *adj* **1** of or affected by hysteria **2** extremely funny (*infml*) —**hysterically** *adv*

hysterics /hi stérriks/ *n* (+ *sing or pl verb*) **1** uncontrollable laughter (*infml*) **2** a state of hysteria

Hz *symbol* hertz

I

i¹ (*pl* **i's**), **I** (*pl* **I's** *or* **Is**) *n* **1** the 9th letter of the English alphabet **2** the Roman numeral for 1 ◊ **dot the i's and cross the t's** pay careful attention to the details

i² *symbol* the imaginary number √-1

I¹ *pron* refers to the speaker or writer himself or herself (*as the subject of a verb*)

USAGE **I** or **me**? **I** is the subjective, or subject, form: *I agree*; *you and I* [not *you and me*] *know better than that*. **Me** is the objective, or object, form, coming after verbs and prepositions: *she agrees with me*; *a present for you and me*. After the verb *be* use *It is me* or *It's me*. *It is I*, technically correct, is used only in very formal speech or writing.

I² *symbol* **1** electric current **2** iodine

-i- joins word elements ○ *fossiliferous*

-ia *suffix* **1** placenames ○ *Australia* **2** plurals ○ *memorabilia*

-ial *suffix* connected with or belonging to ○ *secretarial*

iamb /í am, í amb/ *n* a metrical unit consisting of one short or unstressed syllable followed by one long or stressed one —**iambic** /ī ámbik/ *adj*

iambic pentameter *n* a poetic line consisting of five iambs

-ian *suffix* belonging to, coming from, being involved in, or being like ○ *Italian*

IATA *abbr* International Air Transport Association

Ibadan /i báddən/ capital of Oyo State, SW Nigeria. Pop. 1,365,000 (1995).

Iberian Peninsula /ī beéri ən-/, **Iberia** /ībéeri ə/ peninsula in SW Europe, divided into Spain, Portugal, and Gibraltar —**Iberian** *adj, n*

ibex /í beks/ (*pl* **ibexes** *or* **same**) *n* a wild mountain goat with long horns

ibid., ib. *abbr* ibidem

ibidem /íbbi dem/ *adv* cites the same publication, chapter, or page previously cited

ibis /íbiss/ (*pl* **ibises** *or* **same**) *n* a tropical wading bird with a downward-curving bill

Ibiza /i beétha/ third largest of the Balearic Islands, in the W Mediterranean Sea

-ible *suffix* **1** = **-able** ○ *audible* **2** causing ○ *horrible* —**-ibility** *suffix*

Ibn Saud /íbbən sówd/, **Abdul Aziz** (1880?–1953) king of Saudi Arabia (1932–53)

IBS *abbr* irritable bowel syndrome

Henrik Ibsen

Ibsen /íbss'n/, **Henrik** (1828–1906) Norwegian playwright

ibuprofen /í byoo pró fen/ *n* a pain-relieving and anti-inflammatory drug

-ic *suffix* **1** of or relating to, having the nature of ○ *anarchic* **2** with a valency that is higher than that of a related compound or ion ending in *-ous* ○ *ferric*

Icarus /íkərəss/ *n* in Greek mythology, the son of Daedalus who flew too close to the sun, which melted the wax of his artificial wings —**Icarian** /i káiri ən/ *adj*

ice /īss/ *n* **1** frozen water **2** an expanse of frozen water **3** a substance like ice ○ *dry ice* **4** pieces of frozen water used to cool food or drink **5** an ice cream **6** extreme unfriendliness ■ *adj* made of ice ■ *v* (**icing**, **iced**) **1** *vi* develop a thin surface coating of ice **2** *vt* put icing on a cake —**iced** *adj* ◊ **break the ice** overcome initial restraint on first meeting somebody ◊ **cut no ice** fail to impress or make a difference ◊ **on ice** in abeyance or postponed

ice age n **1** a period when much of the Earth is covered with ice sheets and glaciers **2 Ice Age** the most recent ice age

iceberg /íss burg/ n a mass of floating ice with the greater part submerged

icebound /íss bownd/ adj immobilized by ice

icebox /íss boks/ n **1** an insulated container that keeps food cool **2** a small freezer compartment inside a refrigerator **3** US, Can a refrigerator

icebreaker /íss braykər/ n **1** a talk or game that relaxes a group at a meeting or social gathering **2** a ship for breaking ice **3** a tool for breaking ice —**icebreaking** n, adj

ice bucket n a container for ice cubes

icecap /íss kap/ n a permanent covering of ice, e.g. on a mountain

ice-cold adj very cold

ice cream n **1** a frozen dessert made with cream and flavourings **2** a serving of ice cream

ice-cream soda n a fizzy drink with ice cream in it

ice floe n a sheet of ice floating in the sea

ice hockey n a team game played on ice by skaters using sticks and a rubber disc called a puck

Iceland /ísslənd/ island country in the North Atlantic Ocean. Cap. Reykjavik. Pop. 277,906 (2001). —**Icelander** n

Icelandic /íss lándik/ adj of Iceland ■ n the language of Iceland

ice lolly n a flavoured piece of ice on a stick

iceman /íss man/ (pl -**men** /-men/) n an explorer or mountaineer experienced in travelling on ice

ice pack n **1** an ice-filled cloth or bag for pressing against an injury **2** a large area of floating ice that has formed a solid mass

ice pick n a lightweight hand-held tool for chipping or breaking ice

ice rink n a frozen surface for skating

ice sheet n a long-lasting expanse of ice

ice skate n a boot fitted with a blade for skating on ice —**ice-skate** vi —**ice-skater** n —**ice skating** n

ice water n **1** melted ice **2** US chilled water as a drink

I Ching /ee chíng/ n **1** an ancient Chinese system of fortune-telling **2** the book that explains I Ching

ichneumon fly /ik nyoómən-/, **ichneumon wasp**, **ichneumon** n an insect resembling a wasp that is a parasite of other insects

ichthyology /íkthi ólləji/ n the scientific study of fish —**ichthyological** /íkthi ə lójjik'l/ adj —**ichthyologist** n

ichthyosaur /íkthi ə sawr/, **ichthyosaurus** /íkthi ə sáwrəss/ (pl -**ruses** or -**ri** /-sáwr ī/) n a prehistoric reptile with a long snout and paddle-shaped limbs

icicle /íssik'l/ n a hanging tapered rod of ice, formed when dripping water freezes

ORIGIN Icicle is a compound of *ice* and an old word *ickle* that itself meant 'icicle'.

icing /íssing/ n **1** glazing for cakes made from powdered sugar **2** the formation of ice on surfaces

icing sugar n powdered sugar

AKG London

Icon: Eastern Orthodox icon of *Christus Acheiropoietus* in the Cathedral of the Assumption, Moscow

icon /í kon/ n *also* **ikon** an image of a holy person, used in worship in Eastern Orthodox churches **2** somebody famous for and symbolizing something o *the all-time rock 'n' roll icon* **3** an image on a computer screen that represents something such as a program or device

iconic /ī kónnik/ adj **1** of somebody or something admired as an icon **2** of a religious icon —**iconically** adv

iconoclast /ī kónnə klast/ n **1** somebody who challenges tradition **2** a destroyer or opponent of religious images —**iconoclasm** n —**iconoclastic** /ī kónnə klástik/ adj

iconography /íkə nóggrəfi/ n a set of images or symbols recognized as having a specific meaning —**iconographer** n —**iconographical** adj

ICQ n a computer program for making online contact

-ics suffix **1** a science, art, or knowledge o *mathematics* **2** an activity or action o *callisthenics*

ICT abbr information and communications technology

ICU abbr intensive care unit

icy /íssi/ (-**ier**, -**iest**) adj **1** ice-covered **2** very cold **3** very unfriendly —**icily** adv —**iciness** n

id n in psychoanalytic theory, a part of the human psyche that is the source of instinctive impulses

I'd contr **1** I had **2** I would

ID n a proof of identity such as a card or document (infml)

id. abbr idem

Idaho /ídəhō/ state in the NW United States. Cap. Boise. Pop. 1,293,953 (2000). —**Idahoan** /ídə hō ən, ídə hō ən/ adj, n

idea /ī deé ə/ n **1** an opinion **2** a suggestion o *was his idea to go* **3** an impression or thought o *get the wrong idea* **4** a plan for doing something **5** the aim or purpose of something **6** the gist of something ◊ **get ideas** become ambitious, or begin thinking undesirable thoughts (*infml*)

ideal /ī deé əl/ *n* **1** a perfect example **2** a principle aspired to ■ *adj* **1** serving as the best example **2** perfect but imaginary —**ideally** *adv*

idealism /ī deé əlizəm/ *n* **1** belief in perfection **2** living by high ideals —**idealist** *n* —**idealistic** /ī deé ə lístik/ *adj* —**idealistically** *adv*

idealize /ī deé ə līz/ (**-izing, -ized**), **idealise** *vt* think of or represent as perfect —**idealization** /ī deé ə lī záysh'n/ *n* —**idealized** *adj*

~~ideally~~ incorrect spelling of **ideally**

idem /íddem, ī-/ *pron* the same one, especially the one just referred to

identical /ī déntik'l/ *adj* **1** alike in every way **2** one and the same —**identically** *adv*

identical twin *n* either of a pair of twins developed from a single fertilized egg

~~identicle~~ incorrect spelling of **identical**

identification /ī déntifi káysh'n/ *n* **1** recognition of the identity of somebody or something **2** a proof of identity **3** a strong feeling of affinity with another person or group

identification parade *n* a group of people shown to a witness of a crime for possible identification of the perpetrator

identifier /ī dénti fī ər/ *n* a symbol that identifies a body of data

identify /ī dénti fī/ (**-fies, -fied**) *vt* **1** recognize and name **2** consider as the same —**identifiable** *adj* —**identifiably** *adv*
□ **identify with** *vt* **1** feel affinity with somebody **2** associate one thing with another

Identikit /ī déntikit/ *tdmk* a trademark for a set of pictures showing varied facial features that can be combined to produce a human likeness

identity /ī déntəti/ (*pl* **-ties**) *n* **1** the name or essential character that identifies somebody or something **2** sameness **3** *ANZ* a celebrity (*infml*)

identity card *n* a card showing who the holder is

identity parade *n* CRIME = **identification parade**

identity theft *n* theft of personal information, e.g. somebody's credit card details

ideogram /íddi ə gram/, **ideograph** /íddi ə graaf, -graf/ *n* **1** a symbol in some writing systems that represents a thing or concept rather than the word for it **2** a graphical symbol that represents a word, e.g. '@' or '&' —**ideogrammatic** /íddi əgrə máttik/ *adj* —**ideographic** /íddi ə gráffik/ *adj*

ideologue /ī́di ə log/ *n* a zealous supporter of an ideology

ideology /ī́di óllaji/ (*pl* **-gies**) *n* a system of social, economic, or political beliefs —**ideological** /ī́di ə lójjik'l/ *adj* —**ideologically** *adv* —**ideologist** *n*

idiocy /íddi əssi/ *n* an offensive term for extreme lack of intelligence or foresight

idiolect /íddi ə lekt/ *n* the way an individual person uses language —**idiolectal** /íddi ə lékt'l/ *adj*

idiom /íddi əm/ *n* **1** a fixed expression with a nonliteral meaning **2** the natural way of using a language

idiomatic /íddi ə máttik/, **idiomatical** /-máttik'l/ *adj* **1** characteristic of the way native speakers use a language **2** of the nature of an idiom —**idiomatically** *adv*

~~idiosyncracy~~ incorrect spelling of **idiosyncrasy**

idiosyncrasy /íddi ō síngkrəssi/ (*pl* **-sies**) *n* a way of behaving that is peculiar to a person or group —**idiosyncratic** /íddi ō sing kráttik/ *adj*

idiot /íddi ət/ *n* a person regarded as extremely foolish (*insult*) —**idiotic** /íddi óttik/ *adj* —**idiotically** *adv*

ORIGIN Idiot goes back to a Greek word that meant 'private person', and deriving from that 'ordinary person', and then 'ignorant person'. It passed into Latin in the last sense, and from there into French and English.

idle /īd'l/ *adj* (**idler, idlest**) **1** habitually lazy **2** not working or in use **3** frivolous and a waste of time **4** unfounded ○ *idle gossip* **5** ineffective ○ *idle threats* ■ *n* the speed of an engine with the gear disengaged ■ *v* (**idling, idled**) **1** *vti* pass time aimlessly **2** *vi* move slowly and aimlessly **3** *vti* run with the gear disengaged —**idleness** *n* —**idler** *n* —**idly** *adv* ◊ See note at **vain**

SPELLCHECK Do not confuse the spelling of **idle** and **idol** ('an object of adoration'), which sound similar.

idol /īd'l/ *n* **1** an object of adoration **2** an object worshipped as a god ◊ See note at **idle**

idolatry /ī dóllətri/ *n* **1** idol worship (*disapproving*) **2** extreme admiration —**idolater** *n* —**idolatrous** *adj*

idolize /ī́də līz/ (**izing, ized**), **idolise** *vt* **1** admire fanatically **2** worship as an idol (*disapproving*) —**idolization** /ī́də lī záysh'n/ *n*

IDP *abbr* integrated data processing

idyll /ídd'l, īd'l/ *n* **1** an experience of serene happiness **2** a tranquil charming scene —**idyllic** /i díllik, ī-/ *adj*

i.e. *abbr* that is to say ◊ See note at **e.g.**

-ie *suffix* **1** one that is small or dear ○ *auntie* ○ *birdie* **2** one having a particular character ○ *sweetie*

~~iether~~ incorrect spelling of **either**

if *conj* **1** indicates the conditions required for something to happen ○ *If you give me the money, I'll buy one for you.* **2** indicates what may be the case ○ *If the car has broken down, we'll be late.* **3** introduces an indirect question ○ *asked if I would stay* **4** modifies a statement ○ *by Thursday, if not earlier* ■ *n* **1** a doubt **2** a condition or qualification ◊ **ifs and buts** excuses or protests

IFA *abbr* independent financial adviser

IFC *abbr* International Finance Corporation *(of the UN)*

iffy /íffi/ (**-fier, -fiest**) *adj* doubtful *(infml)* —**iffiness** *n*

igloo /ígglōō/ *n* a dome-shaped Inuit house built from packed snow

Ignatius Loyola /ig náyshəss loy ólə, -lóyələ/, **St** (1491–1556) Spanish priest and a founder of the Jesuits (Society of Jesus)

igneous /ígni əss/ *adj* **1** describes rock that was formerly molten **2** of fire *(fml)*

ignite /ig nít/ (**-niting, -nited**) *vti* **1** set fire to, or begin to burn **2** heat gas until it burns —**ignitable** *adj*

ignition /ig nísh'n/ *n* **1** the process of igniting **2** a mechanism for starting an internal-combustion engine

ignoble /ig nṓbl/ *adj* **1** dishonourable **2** not of the nobility *(fml)* —**ignobly** *adv*

ignominy /ígnəmini/ *n* **1** (*pl* **ignominies**) disgrace and dishonour **2** a disgraceful act *(fml)* —**ignominious** /ígnə mínni əss/ *adj* —**ignominiously** *adv*

ignoramus /ígnə ráyməss/ *n* a person regarded as lacking knowledge *(insult)*

ORIGIN **Ignoramus** comes from a Latin verbal form meaning 'we do not know', and in legal use 'we take no notice'. Originally it was the endorsement made by a grand jury when rejecting an indictment, occurring in phrases like *find an ignoramus* and *bring in an ignoramus*. The sense 'ignorant person' dates from the early 17C, and may be taken from the title of the play *Ignoramus* (1615) by George Ruggle, a comedy satirizing lawyers.

ignorant /ígnərənt/ *adj* **1** lacking knowledge or education **2** unaware ○ *ignorant of the danger* —**ignorance** *n* —**ignorantly** *adv*

ignore /ig náwr/ (**-noring, -nored**) *vt* refuse to notice somebody or something

~~ignorent~~ incorrect spelling of **ignorant**

Iguaçu Falls /i gwaa sōō-/ waterfall on the Iguaçu River, in S Brazil. Height 80 m/260 ft.

iguana /i gwaánə/ (*pl* **-nas** *or* **same**) *n* a large plant-eating tropical lizard

Ihimaera /íhi mírə/, **Witi** (*b.* 1944) New Zealand novelist

ihram /ee raám/ *n* **1** a white cotton robe worn by men when they are pilgrims to Mecca **2** the state of holiness conferred or symbolized by the wearing of the ihram

Ikhnaton ♦ **Akhenaton**

-ile *suffix* of, relating to, capable of ○ *volatile*

~~ilegal~~ incorrect spelling of **illegal**

ileum /ílli əm/ (*pl* **-a** /-ə/) *n* the lowest part of the small intestine —**ileitis** /ílli ítiss/ *n*

ilex /í leks/ *n* any tree or bush related to holly

ilium /ílli əm/ (*pl* **-a** /-ə/) *n* the wide flat upper portion of the pelvis

ilk /ilk/ *n* sort or type *(infml)* ○ *journalists and others of that ilk*

ill *adj* (**worse, worst** /wurst/) **1** unwell **2** resulting in harm, pain, or trouble **3** unkind and unfriendly ○ *ill feeling* **4** unfavourable ○ *an ill wind* **5** morally bad ○ *of ill repute* ■ *adv* (**worse, worst**) **1** badly ○ *ill treated* **2** unfavourably ○ *bodes ill* ■ *n* **1** harm or evil ○ *wished them ill* **2** an unfavourable opinion ○ *don't think ill of him*

I'll /īl/ *contr* I will

ill. *abbr* **1** illustrated **2** illustration

ill-advised *adj* not wise to do —**ill-advisedly** *adv*

ill-assorted *adj* not well matched

ill at ease *adj* uncomfortable and nervous

ill-bred *adj* rude or bad-mannered —**ill-breeding** *n*

ill-conceived *adj* not well planned or thought out

ill-considered *adj* unwise or not well thought out

ill-defined *adj* not clearly or sharply defined

ill-disposed *adj* unfriendly or hostile

illegal /i leeg'l/ *adj* **1** against the law or rules **2** not permitted by a computer program —**illegality** /íllee gálləti/ *n* —**illegally** *adv* ◊ See note at **unlawful**

illegible /i léjjəb'l/ *adj* impossible or hard to read —**illegibility** /i léjjə bílləti/ *n* —**illegibly** *adv*

illegitimate /íllə jíttəmət/ *adj* **1** against the law or rules **2** born out of wedlock —**illegitimacy** *n* —**illegitimately** *adv*

ill-fated *adj* ending in disaster

ill-favoured *adj* **1** unattractive to look at, especially facially **2** objectionable *(literary)*

ill feeling *n* animosity or resentment

ill-founded *adj* without a convincing basis

ill-gotten *adj* acquired dishonestly or illegally

ill health *n* a poor state of general health

ill humour *n* a bad mood or bad temper —**ill-humoured** *adj*

illiberal /i líbbərəl/ *adj* **1** narrow-minded **2** ungenerous *(fml)*

illicit /i líssit/ *adj* **1** illegal **2** unacceptable by prevailing social standards —**illicitly** *adv* —**illicitness** *n* ◊ See note at **elicit, unlawful**

Illinois state in the north-central United States. Cap. Springfield. Pop. 12,419,293 (2000). —**Illinoisan** *adj, n*

illiquid /i líkwid/ *adj* **1** hard to convert into cash **2** not having enough cash

illiterate /i líttərət/ *adj* **1** an offensive term describing somebody unable to read and write **2** uneducated in a particular subject —**illiteracy** *n* —**illiterately** *adv*

ill-judged *adj* imprudent or tactless

ill-mannered *adj* rude —**ill-manneredly** *adv*

ill-natured /-náychərd/ *adj* bad-tempered, especially by disposition —**ill-naturedly** *adv*

illness /ílnəss/ *n* **1** a disease or sickness **2** bad health

illogical /i lójjik'l/ *adj* **1** not following the rules of logic **2** unreasonable —**illogicality** /i lójji kálləti/ n —**illogically** adv

ill-omened /-ómənd/, **ill-starred** adj apparently fated to end badly

ill-tempered adj irritable —**ill-temperedly** adv

ill-timed adj done at an unsuitable time

ill-treat vt **1** behave unkindly or harshly towards **2** misuse —**ill-treatment** n ◊ See note at **misuse**

illuminate /i loómi nayt/ (**-nating, -nated**) v **1** vti light up or be lit up **2** vt decorate something with lights **3** vt make something easier to understand **4** vti enlighten somebody (literary) **5** vt add coloured letters or designs to a manuscript or page **6** vt cause somebody's face to look happy and animated —**illuminated** adj —**illuminating** adj —**illuminator** n

illumination /i loómi náysh'n/ n **1** the lighting up of something **2** available light in a place or for a purpose **3** clarification and explanation **4** intellectual or spiritual enlightenment **5** ornamentation of a manuscript or page with coloured letters or designs

illumine /i loómin/ (**-mining, -mined**) vt illuminate (fml)

ill-use vt treat harshly and cruelly —**ill-usage** n —**ill-use** n

illusion /i loózh'n/ n **1** something with a deceptive appearance **2** the ability to consider appearances to be deceptive, or of the mind to be deceived by them **3** a false idea —**illusionary** adj

illusionist /i loózh'nist, i lyoó-/ n **1** a magician **2** a painter of pictorial illusions —**illusionistic** /i loózh'n ístik, i lyoó-/ adj

illusory /i loózəri, i loóss-/, **illusive** /i loóssiv, i lyoó-/ adj imaginary —**illusively** adv —**illusorily** adv

illustrate /íllə strayt/ (**-trating, -trated**) v **1** vt accompany with pictures or graphics **2** vti clarify something with examples and comparisons **3** vt be characteristic and revealing of —**illustrator** n

illustration /íllə stráysh'n/ n **1** a picture or graphic that complements a text **2** the provision of pictures or graphics to accompany a text **3** something that helps explain or exemplify something else —**illustrational** adj

illustrative /ílləstrətiv, i lús-, íllə straytiv/ adj serving as an illustration

illustrious /i lústri əss/ adj extremely distinguished —**illustriously** adv —**illustriousness** n

ill will n hostility or dislike

~~illness~~ incorrect spelling of **illness**

I'm contr I am

image /ímmij/ n **1** an actual or mental picture **2** a likeness seen in a mirror, seen through a lens, or produced on a screen **3** somebody who closely resembles somebody else ○ She's the image of her father. **4** a typical or extreme example ○ the very image of greed **5** a metaphor or simile ■ vt (**-aging**) **1** produce or

reflect an image of **2** form a mental image of **3** describe in visual terms **4** typify —**imager** n

image compression n a technique for storing a visual image in a reduced electronic form

image map n an electronic graphic image with areas for hypertext links

imagery /ímmijəri/ n **1** metaphors, similes, and other figurative language **2** mental or pictorial images

imaginary /i májjinəri/ adj existing only in the mind

imaginary unit n the positive square root of –1

imagination /i májji náysh'n/ n **1** the ability to form images in the mind, especially of things not directly experienced **2** the creative part of the mind **3** resourcefulness

imaginative /i májjinətiv/ adj **1** skilled at forming images in the mind or thinking originally **2** new and original **3** of the imagination —**imaginatively** adv —**imaginativeness** n

imagine /i májjin/ (**-ining, -ined**) v **1** vti form an image of something in the mind **2** vt see or hear something unreal **3** vt assume or suppose something —**imaginable** adj —**imaginably** adv —**imagining** n

~~imaginery~~ incorrect spelling of **imaginary**

imago /i máygō, i maágō/ (pl **-goes** or **-gines** /i májjə neez/) n a sexually mature adult insect

imam /i maám, i mám/ n **1** a leader of prayers in a mosque **2** also **Imam** an Islamic religious leader regarded as a direct descendant of Muhammad or Ali —**imamate** /i maá mayt/ n

IMAX /í maks/ tdmk a trademark for a giant-screen large-format film and motion-simulation entertainment system

imbalance /im bállənss/ n a lack of balance, e.g. in emphasis or proportion —**imbalanced** adj

imbecile /ímbə seel, -sil/ n an offensive term for somebody regarded as very foolish or unintelligent (insult) —**imbecilic** /ímbə síllik/ adj —**imbecility** /-sílləti/ n

~~imbed~~ vt = **embed**

imbibe /im bíb/ (**-bibing, -bibed**) v **1** vti drink (fml or humorous) **2** vt take in mentally (literary) —**imbiber** n

imbroglio /im brôli ō/ (pl **-glios**) n a complicated situation

imbue /im byoó/ (**-buing, -bued**) vt **1** fill with a particular quality ○ poetry imbued with melancholy **2** soak with a stain or dye (fml)

~~imediately~~ incorrect spelling of **immediately**

IMF abbr International Monetary Fund

~~imformation~~ incorrect spelling of **information**

~~iminent~~ incorrect spelling of **imminent**

imitate /ímmi tayt/ (**-tating, -tated**) vt **1** follow the example or style of **2** mimic **3** be or look like ○ a case of life imitating art —**imitator** n

SYNONYMS imitate, copy, emulate, mimic, take off, ape CORE MEANING: adopt the behaviour of another person

imitation /immi táysh'n/ n **1** the imitating of somebody or something **2** a copy or fake ■ adj not genuine —**imitational** adj

imitative /ímmitətiv/ adj **1** attempting to copy something but usually inferior **2** involving imitation —**imitatively** adv

immaculate /i mákyŏŏlət/ adj **1** completely clean **2** faultless —**immaculately** adv —**immaculateness** n

Immaculate Conception n the Roman Catholic doctrine of the Virgin Mary's freedom from original sin from the moment of her conception

immanent /immənənt/ adj **1** existing within or inherent in something (fml) **2** existing in all parts of the universe —**immanence** n —**immanently** adv

SPELLCHECK Do not confuse the spelling of **immanent** and **imminent** ('about to occur'), which sound similar.

immaterial /immə teeri əl/ adj **1** not relevant **2** having no physical substance —**immateriality** /immə teeri álləti/ n

immature /immə tyŏŏr, -chŏŏr/ adj **1** not fully developed **2** childish —**immaturely** adv —**immaturity** n

immeasurable /i mézhərəb'l/ adj vast or huge —**immeasurability** /i mézhərə bílləti/ n —**immeasurably** adv

immediate /i meedi ət/ adj **1** happening or done without pause or delay **2** nearest o his immediate family **3** needing to be dealt with first o the immediate problem —**immediacy** n

immediately /i meedi ətli/ adv **1** without any delay **2** very closely in space or time ■ conj as soon as

immemorial /immi máwri əl/ adj so old that it seems always to have existed —**immemorially** adv

immense /i ménss/ adj **1** huge **2** unable to be measured —**immensely** adv —**immensity** n

immerse /i múrss/ (-mersing, -mersed) v **1** vt completely submerge in liquid **2** vr occupy yourself totally with something **3** vt baptize by submerging all or part of the body —**immersion** n

immersion heater n an electric water heater with a submerged heating element

immigrant /immigrənt/ n **1** somebody settling in a new country **2** a plant or animal established in a new place —**immigrant** adj

immigration /immi gráysh'n/ n **1** the arrival of settlers in a new country **2** the passport control point at an airport, seaport, or border —**immigrate** /immi grayt/ vi

imminent /imminənt/ adj about to occur —**imminence** n —**imminently** adv ◊ See note at immanent

immobile /i mŏ bīl/ adj **1** motionless **2** incapable of motion —**immobility** /immŏ bílləti/ n

immobilize /i mŏbi līz/ (-lizing, -lized), **immobilise** vt **1** prevent from moving **2** put a machine out of action —**immobilization** /i mŏbi līz záysh'n/ n

immoderate /i móddərət/ adj excessive —**immoderately** adv —**immoderation** /i móddə ráysh'n/ n

immodest /i móddist/ adj **1** boastful **2** indecent or offensive —**immodestly** adv —**immodesty** n

immolate /immə layt/ (-lating, -lated) vt kill or give up as a sacrifice (literary) —**immolation** /immə láysh'n/ n

immoral /i mórrəl/ adj contrary to accepted moral principles —**immorality** /immə rálləti/ n —**immorally** adv

immortal /i máwrt'l/ adj **1** able to have eternal life **2** famous and long remembered —**immortal** n —**immortality** /immawr tálləti/ n

immortalize /i máwrt'l līz/ (-izing, -ized), **mortalise** vt **1** make lastingly famous **2** give eternal life to —**immortalization** /i máwrt'l īz záysh'n/ n

immovable /i mŏŏvəb'l/, **immoveable** adj **1** unable to be moved **2** having a fixed opinion —**immovably** adv

immune /i myŏŏn/ adj **1** protected from getting a particular disease **2** of the body's resistance to disease **3** not subject to something or susceptible to something o immune from prosecution

immune response n the response of the immune system to a disease-causing agent

immune system n the bodily system that recognizes and fights disease

immunity /i myŏŏnəti/ (pl -ties) n **1** resistance to disease **2** freedom from responsibility or punishment

immunize /immyŏŏ nīz/ (-nizing, -nized), **immunise** vt make somebody resistant to a disease, especially by inoculation —**immunization** /immyŏŏ nī záysh'n/ n

immuno- prefix immune, immunity o immunodeficiency

immunodeficiency /immyŏŏnŏ di físh'nssi/ (pl -cies) n inability of the immune system to respond to and fight disease —**immunodeficient** adj

immunoglobulin /immyŏŏnŏ glóbbyŏŏlin/ n an antibody formed by the immune system and present in the blood

immunology /immyŏŏ nólləji/ n the scientific study of the immune system —**immunological** adj —**immunologist** n

immunosuppression /immyŏŏnŏ sə présh'n/ n inhibition of the ability of the immune system to fight disease —**immuno-suppressant** adj, n —**immunosuppressive** adj, n

immure /i myŏŏr/ (-muring, -mured) vt **1** imprison (literary) **2** shut away from other people (fml) —**immurement** n

immutable /i myŏŏtəb'l/ adj unchanging or unchangeable —**immutability** /i myŏŏtə bílləti/ n —**immutably** adv

imp n **1** a mischievous child **2** a small demon

ORIGIN An **imp** was originally a 'young plant shoot'. This was metaphorically extended to 'descendant of a noble family' and 'child'. From the 16C it could be used specifically for a 'child of the devil', and this sense weakened to imply just mischief in the 17C.

imp. *abbr* **1** imperative **2** imperfect

impact *n* /ím pakt/ **1** the hitting of one object by another **2** the force of a collision **3** a strong effect ■ *vt*/im pákt/ **1** strike something with force **2** have an effect on something —**impaction** /im páksh'n/ *n*

impacted /im páktid/ *adj* describes a tooth wedged sideways under the gum

impair /im páir/ *vt* weaken or damage —**impairment** *n*

impala /im paálə/ (*pl* -**las** *or same*) *n* an antelope with curving horns

impale /im páyl/ (-**paling**, -**paled**) *vt* pierce with a pointed object —**impalement** *n*

impalpable /im pálpəb'l/ *adj* (*fml*) **1** unable to be touched or sensed **2** hard to understand —**impalpably** *adv*

impanel /im pánn'l/ (-**elling**, -**elled**), **empanel** /em-/ (-**elling**, -**elled**) *vt* **1** list people as possible jurors **2** select a jury from a list

impart /im páart/ *vt* **1** communicate information or knowledge **2** give a particular quality

impartial /im paársh'l/ *adj* not biased in favour of one side or argument —**impartiality** /im paárshi álləti/ *n* —**impartially** *adv*

impassable /im paássəb'l/ *adj* **1** impossible to travel on or through **2** impossible to overcome —**impassably** *adv*

impasse /am paáss, ám paass, im paáss, ím paass/ *n* a block to progress or agreement

impassioned /im pásh'nd/ *adj* showing strong feelings

impassive /im pássiv/ *adj* **1** expressionless **2** devoid of all emotion —**impassively** *adv* —**impassivity** /ímpə sívvəti/ *n*

SYNONYMS impassive, apathetic, phlegmatic, stolid, stoic, unmoved CORE MEANING: showing no emotional response or interest

impatiens /im páyshi enz, -pálli-/ (*pl same*) *n* PLANTS = **Busy Lizzie**

impatient /im páysh'nt/ *adj* **1** annoyed at being kept waiting or being delayed **2** eager **3** easily annoyed —**impatience** *n* —**impatiently** *adv*

impeach /im peéch/ *vt* **1** *US, Can* accuse a serving government official with serious misconduct while in office **2** *US* remove somebody, especially a president, from public office because of having committed crimes (*fml*) **3** bring charges against somebody **4** question the good character of somebody (*fml*) —**impeachable** *adj* —**impeachment** *n*

impeccable /im pékəb'l/ *adj* **1** perfect **2** free from sin —**impeccably** *adv*

impecunious /ímpi kyoóni əss/ *adj* having little or no money

impedance /im peéd'nss/ *n* **1** something that delays or prevents progress (*fml*) **2** (*symbol* Z) the opposition in an electrical circuit to the flow of alternating current

impede /im peéd/ (-**peding**, -**peded**) *vt* hinder the movement or progress of ◊ See note at **hinder**

impediment /im péddimənt/ *n* **1** an impairment, especially in speech **2** an obstacle

impedimenta /im péddi méntə/ *npl* obstructions (*literary*)

impel /im pél/ (-**pelling**, -**pelled**) *vt* **1** force to do something **2** cause to move (*fml*)

impending /im pénding/ *adj* imminent or threatening

impenetrable /im pénnitrəb'l/ *adj* **1** impossible to get in or through **2** incomprehensible —**impenetrability** /im pénnitrə bílləti/ *n* —**impenetrably** *adv*

impenitent /im pénnit'nt/ *adj* not repentant —**impenitence** *n* —**impenitently** *adv*

imperative /im pérrətiv/ *adj* **1** necessary **2** describes a mood or form of a verb expressing a command ■ *n* **1** something that must be done **2** the form of a verb used to give an order —**imperatively** *adv*

imperceptible /ímpər séptəb'l/ *adj* too small or gradual to be noticed —**imperceptibly** *adv*

imperfect /im púrfikt/ *adj* **1** faulty or incomplete **2** describes a verb or tense that expresses incomplete action ■ *n* **1** the imperfect tense of a verb **2** a verb in the imperfect tense —**imperfectly** *adv*

imperfection /impər féksh'n/ *n* **1** a fault or defect **2** the possession of faults or defects ◊ See note at **flaw**

imperial /im peéri əl/ *adj* **1** belonging to an empire, emperor, or empress **2** of a country's authority over colonies or other countries **3** supremely powerful **4** grand or majestic **5** of the nonmetric measures used in the United Kingdom —**imperially** *adv*

imperialism /im peéri əlizəm/ *n* **1** belief in the extension of the authority of one country over colonies or other countries **2** the political, military, or economic domination of one country by another —**imperialist** *n, adj* —**imperialistic** /im peéri ə lístik/ *adj*

imperil /im pérrəl/ (-**illing**, -**illed**) *vt* endanger —**imperilment** *n*

imperious /im peéri əss/ *adj* haughty and domineering —**imperiously** *adv* —**imperiousness** *n*

imperishable /im pérrishəb'l/ *adj* not liable to become spoilt, weak, or damaged —**imperishably** *adv*

impermanent /im púrmənənt/ *adj* not lasting —**impermanence** *n*

impermeable /im púrmi əb'l/ *adj* not permitting liquid, gas, or other fluids to pass through —**impermeability** /im púrmi ə bílləti/ *n*

impermissible /impər míssəb'l/ *adj* not permitted or permissible

impersonal /im púrs'nəl/ *adj* **1** focusing on facts or events rather than people or personalities **2** not treating people as individuals ○ *an im-*

personal bureaucracy **3** cold and alienating o *brisk and impersonal service* —**impersonality** /im púrssə nálləti/ n —**impersonally** adv

impersonate /im púrssə nayt/ (**-ating, -ated**) vt **1** mimic the voice, appearance, and manners of somebody, especially in order to entertain **2** pretend to be somebody else in order to deceive —**impersonation** /im púrssə náysh'n/ n —**impersonator** n

impertinent /im púrtinənt/ adj (fml) **1** cheeky or disrespectful **2** irrelevant —**impertinence** n —**impertinently** adv

imperturbable /ímpər túrbəb'l/ adj consistently calm —**imperturbably** adv

impervious /im púrvi əss/ adj **1** not responsive to the suggestions or opinions of others **2** not allowing passage of something, especially a liquid o *impervious to damp* —**imperviously** adv —**imperviousness** n

impetigo /ímpi tígō/ n a contagious skin disease with blisters that form scabs

impetuous /im péttyoo əss/ adj **1** acting impulsively **2** done on impulse —**impetuously** adv —**impetuousness** n

impetus /ímpitəss/ n **1** the energy or motivation to do something **2** a force that maintains speed in spite of resistance

impiety /im pí əti/ (pl **-ties**) n **1** lack of religious respect **2** an act showing lack of religious respect

impinge /im pínj/ (**-pingeing, -pinged**) vi **1** strike or hit something **2** interfere with the usual course or extent of something (fml) o *impinges on our freedom* —**impingement** n

impious /ímpi əss, im pí əss/ adj showing lack of religious respect —**impiously** adv

impish /ímpish/ adj mischievous —**impishly** adv —**impishness** n

implacable /im plákəb'l/ adj impossible to pacify or reduce in strength —**implacability** /im pláke bílləti/ n —**implacably** adv

implant vt /im pláant/ **1** fix in the mind or consciousness **2** insert into something that encloses **3** fix in the ground to grow **4** embed in the body surgically ■ n /ím plaant/ something inserted into the body during surgery —**implantation** /im plaant táysh'n/ n

implausible /im pláwzəb'l/ adj hard to believe —**implausibility** /im pláwzə bílləti/ n —**implausibly** adv

implement n /ímplimənt/ a tool or utensil ■ vt /ímpli ment/ put into effect or action —**implementation** /ímpli men táysh'n/ n

implicate /ímpli kayt/ (**-cating, -cated**) vt **1** show or suggest that somebody or something is connected with something such as a crime **2** imply something (fml)

implication /ímpli káysh'n/ n **1** something involved as a consequence o *the wider implications of the decision* **2** the process of implying rather than stating —**implicational** adj

implicit /im plíssit/ adj **1** implied but not stated **2** not affected by doubt or uncertainty

o *implicit trust* **3** present as a necessary part —**implicitly** adv ⟩ See note at **explicit**

~~impliment~~ incorrect spelling of **implement**

implode /im plṓd/ (**-ploding, -ploded**) vti burst inwards

implore /im pláwr/ (**-ploring, -plored**) vt beg or plead with somebody to do something (fml) —**imploring** adj —**imploringly** adv

implosion /im plṓzh'n/ n a violent inward collapse

imply /im plí/ (**-plies, -plied**) vt **1** suggest without saying **2** involve as a necessary part or condition —**implied** adj ⟩ See note at **infer**

impolite /ímpə lít/ adj rude or discourteous —**impolitely** adv —**impoliteness** n

impolitic /im póllətik/ adj unwise because of possible disastrous consequences —**impoliticly** adv

imponderable /im póndərəb'l/ adj not measurable in terms of importance or effect ■ n something whose importance or effect is impossible to calculate (often pl) —**imponderability** /im póndərə bílləti/ n

import vt /im páwrt/ **1** bring in goods or materials from abroad to sell or use commercially **2** transfer computer data from one location to another **3** imply or signify something (fml) ■ n /ím pawrt/ **1** something imported for sale or commercial use **2** the importing of something **3** the true significance of something —**importation** /ím pawr táysh'n/ n —**importer** n

important /im páwrt'nt/ adj **1** having interest, value, or relevance **2** high-ranking or influential —**importance** n —**importantly** adv

~~importent~~ incorrect spelling of **important**

importunate /im páwrtyŏŏnət/ adj (fml) **1** demanding and persistent **2** urgent or pressing —**importunately** adv

importune /im páwr tyoon, ím pawr tyŏŏn/ (**-tuning, -tuned**) vt ask insistently for something (fml)

impose /im pṓz/ (**-posing, -posed**) v **1** vt levy or enforce something compulsory such as a tax or a punishment **2** vt make people comply with or agree to something o *changes that were imposed on us* **3** vti force yourself on others —**imposition** /ímpə zísh'n/ n

imposing /im pṓzing/ adj large and impressive —**imposingly** adv

impossible /im póssəb'l/ adj **1** not able to exist or be done **2** very difficult to deal with o *an impossible child* —**impossibility** /im póssə bílləti/ n —**impossibly** adv

impostor /im póstər/, **imposter** n somebody who uses another's name or identity —**imposture** /im póschər/ n

impotent /ímpətənt/ adj **1** unable to have or maintain an erection of the penis **2** powerless —**impotence** n —**impotently** adv

impound /im pównd/ vt **1** put something confiscated in a confined place o *impounded their car* **2** take goods into legal custody —**impoundment** n

impoverish /im póvvərish/ *vt (fml)* 1 make poor 2 spoil or reduce in quality —**impoverishment** *n*

impracticable /im práktikəb'l/ *adj* not possible to do or achieve effectively —**impracticably** *adv*

impractical /im práktik'l/ *adj* 1 not workable 2 not good at performing practical tasks or dealing with practical matters —**impracticality** /im prákti kálləti/ *n* —**impractically** *adv*

imprecation /impri káysh'n/ *n* a curse or oath *(fml)*

imprecise /impri síss/ *adj* not precise or accurate —**imprecisely** *adv* —**imprecision** /-sízh'n/ *n*

impregnable /im prégnəb'l/ *adj* 1 impossible to capture or break into 2 unable to be shaken by outside influence ○ *impregnable faith* —**impregnability** /im prégnə bílləti/ *n* —**impregnably** *adv*

impregnate (**-nating, -nated**) *vt* /im preg nayt/ 1 incorporate a chemical into, especially by soaking 2 make pregnant —**impregnation** /ím preg náysh'n/ *n*

impresario /impra saári ō/ (*pl* **-os**) *n* 1 a producer or promoter of commercial entertainment 2 the business head of an opera or ballet company

ORIGIN **Impresario** comes from an Italian word meaning literally 'somebody who undertakes something'. It has no connection with impressing people. The word is first recorded in English in the mid-18C.

impress[1] *v* /im préss/ 1 *vti* affect or please somebody greatly 2 *vt* make clearly understood ○ *impressed the seriousness of the situation on them* 3 *vt* press a pattern or mark onto —**impressible** *adj*

impress[2] /im préss/ *vt* 1 seize for public use 2 force to serve in an army or navy

impression /im présh'n/ *n* 1 an effect that stays in somebody's mind ○ *made a good impression* 2 a general idea ○ *got the impression he was serious* 3 a pressed-in shape 4 an entertaining imitation of somebody 5 all the copies of a book printed at one time

impressionable /im présh'nəb'l/ *adj* open to the opinions of others and easily influenced —**impressionably** *adv*

impressionism /im présh'nizəm/, **Impressionism** *n* 1 a style of painting that aims to capture the immediate general effect of a scene without the details 2 a style of music expressing impressions and feelings

impressionist /im présh'nist/ *n* 1 *also* **Impressionist** a practitioner of impressionism 2 an entertainer who does impressions of people ■ *adj also* **Impressionist** of impressionism

impressionistic /im présha nístik/ *adj* 1 giving a broad picture or general idea rather than detail 2 like impressionist art or music —**impressionistically** *adv*

impressive /im préssiv/ *adj* making a deep impression on the mind or senses —**impressively** *adv* —**impressiveness** *n*

imprimatur /impri maátər, -máytər/ *n* 1 official approval *(fml)* 2 an official licence to print or publish something

imprint *n* /ímprint/ 1 a pattern or mark pressed into a surface ○ *saw the imprint of a foot on the soil* 2 a publisher's name and other publication details printed in a book 3 a special mark printed or stamped on something 4 a lasting effect ■ *vt* /im print/ 1 produce a mark by printing or stamping 2 fix an image or thought in a vivid or lasting way —**imprinter** *n*

imprison /im prízz'n/ *vt* put in prison —**imprisonment** *n*

improbable /im próbbəb'l/ *adj* not likely to happen or to be true —**improbability** /im próbbə billəti/ *n* —**improbably** *adv*

impromptu /im prómptyoo/ *adj* done or said without prior thought or preparation —**impromptu** *adv*, *n*

improper /im próppər/ *adj* 1 unsuitable *(fml)* 2 rude —**improperly** *adv*

improper fraction *n* a fraction equalling or greater than one

impropriety /ímprə prí əti/ (*pl* **-ties**) *n* lack of propriety, or an inappropriate act

improve /im proov/ (**-proving, -proved**) *v* 1 *vti* make or become better 2 *vt* increase the value of property —**improvable** *adj*

□ **improve on** *or* **upon** *vt* surpass in quality or performance

improvement /im proovmant/ *n* 1 the process of getting better or making something better 2 a change or addition that makes something better 3 an increase in value, especially of property

improvident /im próvvidənt/ *adj* failing to prepare for the future —**improvidence** *n* —**improvidently** *adv*

improvise /ímprə vīz/ (**-vising, -vised**) *vti* 1 perform something not previously composed or written 2 make something out of whatever materials are available —**improvisation** /ímprə vī záysh'n/ *n* —**improvisational** *adj* —**improvisatory** *adj* —**improviser** *n*

imprudent /im prood'nt/ *adj* unwise and lacking in care or forethought —**imprudence** *n* —**imprudently** *adv*

impudent /ímpyoodənt/ *adj* rude and disrespectful —**impudence** *n* —**impudently** *adv*

impugn /im pyoon/ *vt* cast doubt on or criticize as unreliable or unworthy of respect —**impugnable** *adj*

impulse /ím pulss/ *n* 1 a force driving something forward 2 a forward motion 3 a sudden urge 4 an instinctive drive 5 a motive 6 a signal transmitted along a nerve fibre or muscle

impulsive /im púlssiv/ *adj* 1 inclined to act on sudden urges 2 motivated by a sudden urge —**impulsively** *adv* —**impulsiveness** *n*

impunity /im pyóonəti/ *n* freedom from punishment or unpleasant consequences

impure /im pyóor/ *adj* 1 contaminated 2 mixed with something of inferior quality 3 sinful

impurity /im pyóorəti/ (*pl* **-ties**) *n* 1 lack of purity 2 a contaminant

impute /im pyóot/ (**-puting, -puted**) *vt* 1 attribute a bad action or event to 2 attribute a quality to as a source or cause —**imputation** /impyóo táysh'n/ *n*

in *prep* 1 indicates a place o *He spent a year in Russia.* 2 indicates a state or condition being experienced o *The computer industry is in flux.* 3 after a period of time 4 during 5 indicates the means by which something is expressed o *The speech was in French.* 6 indicates a subject area o *a degree in biology* 7 as a consequence of 8 indicates that something is covered by something o *The package was in brown paper.* 9 indicates how somebody is dressed ■ *adv* 1 to or towards the inside o *Come in.* 2 to or towards a place 3 at or within a place o *staying in tonight* 4 alight o *keeping the fire in* ■ *adj* 1 fashionable 2 holding power or office ◇ **in for** about to experience ◇ **in on** having knowledge about or involvement in ◇ **in that** because ◇ **in with** associated or friendly with ◇ **the ins and outs** all the details of something

In *symbol* indium

in., in *abbr* 1 inch 2 inches

in- *prefix* 1 not, lack of o *inopportune* o *inability* 2 in, into, towards, within o *inculcate*

inability /ínnə bílləti/ *n* the state of not being able to do something

inable incorrect spelling of **enable**

inaccessible /ínnək séssəb'l/ *adj* 1 difficult to get to 2 hard to understand —**inaccessibility** /ínnək séssə bílləti/ *n* —**inaccessibly** *adv*

inaccurate /in ákyóorət/ *adj* not correct —**inaccuracy** *n* —**inaccurately** *adv*

inaction /in áksh'n/ *n* 1 failure to act 2 absence of activity

inactivate /in ákti vayt/ (**-vating, -vated**) *vt* make inactive —**inactivation** /in ákti váysh'n/ *n*

inactive /in áktiv/ *adj* 1 not taking action 2 not being used or operated 3 lazy or sedentary 4 describes a volcano that is dormant —**inactively** *adv* —**inactivity** /in ak tívvəti/ *n*

inadequate /in áddikwət/ *adj* not enough or not good enough —**inadequacy** *n* —**inadequately** *adv*

inadmissible /ínnəd míssəb'l/ *adj* not allowable or acceptable, especially in a court of law —**inadmissibility** /ínnəd missə bílləti/ *n*

inadvertently /ínnəd vúrt'ntli/ *adv* without intending to or realizing —**inadvertence** *n* —**inadvertent** *adj*

inadvisable /ínnəd vízəb'l/ *adj* not to be recommended —**inadvisability** /ínnəd vízə bílləti/ *n*

inalienable /in áyli ənəb'l/ *adj* impossible to take away or transfer to another —**inalienability** /in áyli ənə bílləti/ *n*

inamorata /in ámmə raátə/ (*pl* **-tas**) *n* a woman lover, or a woman whom somebody loves (*literary*)

inane /i náyn/ *adj* silly or time-wasting —**inanely** *adv* —**inaneness** *n* —**inanity** /i nánnəti/ *n*

inanimate /in ánnimət/ *adj* 1 not living 2 not lively —**inanimateness** *n*

inapplicable /ínnə plíkəb'l/ *adj* not applicable, suitable, or relevant —**inapplicability** /ínnə plikə bílləti/ *n*

inappropriate /ínnə própri ət/ *adj* not fitting, timely, or suitable —**inappropriately** *adv* —**inappropriateness** *n*

inapt /in ápt/ *adj* 1 not suitable 2 lacking skill or aptitude —**inaptly** *adv* —**inaptness** *n*

inarticulate /in aar tíkyóolət/ *adj* 1 not good at speaking effectively 2 not understandable as speech or language 3 not effectively expressed 4 not expressed or able to be expressed in words —**inarticulacy** *n* —**inarticulately** *adv*

inasmuch as /innəz múch əz/ *conj* 1 because 2 to the extent that

inattention /ínnə ténsh'n/ *n* failure to pay attention —**inattentive** *adj*

inaudible /in áwdəb'l/ *adj* impossible to hear —**inaudibility** /in áwdə bílləti/ *n* —**inaudibly** *adv*

inaugural /i náwgyóorəl/ *adj* 1 marking a beginning 2 first of several

inaugurate /i náwgyóo rayt/ (**-rating, -rated**) *vt* 1 install formally into office 2 open or begin ceremonially —**inauguration** /i náwg yóo ráysh'n/ *n* —**inaugurator** *n*

inauspicious /in aw spíshəss/ *adj* suggesting failure or an unpromising future —**inauspiciously** *adv* —**inauspiciousness** *n*

inauthentic /in aw théntik/ *adj* not authentic or genuine —**inauthenticity** /in aw then tíssəti/ *n*

in-between *adj, adv* falling between others

inboard /in bawrd/ *adj* located inside a boat's hull ■ *n* a boat with an inboard motor ■ *adv* away from the sides

inborn /in bawrn/ *adj* innate

inbound /in bownd/ *adj* incoming

inbred /in bred/ *adj* 1 innate 2 produced by inbreeding

inbreeding /ín breeding/ *n* the mating of closely related individuals of a species

in-built *adj* 1 innate 2 fitted inside

inc. *abbr* 1 included 2 *also* **Inc.** *US, Can* incorporated

Inca /íngkə/ (*pl same or* **-cas**) *n* member of a Native South American people —**Inca** *adj*

incalculable /in kálkyóoləb'l/ *adj* 1 too great to measure 2 impossible to foresee —**incalculability** /in kálkyóolə bílləti/ *n* —**incalculably** *adv*

incandescent /in kan déss'nt/ *adj* 1 glowing with heat 2 showing intense emotion, especially anger —**incandescence** *n*

incantation /in kan táysh'n/ *n* 1 the use of supposedly magic words **2** a set of supposedly magic words —**incantational** adj

incapable /in káypəb'l/ adj **1** lacking the necessary ability **2** unable to function or perform adequately **3** unable to look after yourself —**incapability** /in káypə billəti/ n —**incapably** adv

incapacitate /ínkə pássi tayt/ (-tating, -tated) vt **1** deprive of power, force, or effectiveness **2** disqualify or make legally ineligible —**incapacitation** /ínkə passi táysh'n/ n

incapacity /ínkə pássəti/ n **1** lack of ability, force, or effectiveness **2** a physical or mental challenge

in-car adj fitted or provided inside a car

incarcerate /in kaárssə rayt/ (-ating, -ated) vt (fml) **1** imprison somebody **2** confine somebody —**incarceration** /in kaárssə ráysh'n/ n

incarnate adj /in kaárnət/ **1** made human **2** personified ■ vt /in kaár nayt/ (-nating, -nated) **1** show in or give human form **2** personify

incarnation /in kaar náysh'n/ n **1** the personification of a quality or idea **2** in some religious beliefs, one life in a series of lives spent in a particular body **3 Incarnation** in Christianity, God in the form of Jesus Christ

incautious /in káwshəss/ adj careless or rash —**incautiously** adv —**incautiousness** n

incendiary /in séndi əri/ adj **1** containing chemicals that cause fire **2** likely to catch fire ■ n (pl -ies) a bomb designed to cause fire

incense[1] /in senss/ n **1** a substance burnt for its fragrant smell **2** smoke or fragrance from incense

incense[2] /in sénss/ (-censing, -censed) vt enrage —**incensed** adj

incentive /in séntiv/ n something that encourages somebody to do something ■ adj encouraging or motivating ◊ See note at **motive**

inception /in sépsh'n/ n the beginning of something (fml)

incertitude /in súrtityood/ n **1** doubt **2** lack of self-confidence

incessant /in séss'nt/ adj continuing uninterrupted —**incessancy** n —**incessantly** adv

incest /ín sest/ n sex between close relatives —**incestuous** adj —**incestuously** adv —**incestuousness** n

> **ORIGIN Incest** comes from a Latin word formed from the prefix in- 'not' and the adjective castus 'chaste', from which chaste also derives.

incestuous /in séstyoo əss/ adj **1** of or involving incest **2** guilty of incest **3** unhealthily exclusive of the influence or involvement of others —**incestuously** adv —**incestuousness** n

inch[1] /inch/ n **1** (symbol ") a unit of length equal to $\frac{1}{12}$ of a foot **2** a small amount ○ The committee won't budge an inch. ■ vti move slowly

inch[2] n a small island in Scotland or Ireland (often in placenames)

inchoate /in kó ət/ adj (fml) **1** just beginning to develop **2** only partly formed

Inchon /in chón/, **Inch'ŏn** port in NW South Korea. Pop. 2,307,618 (1995).

incidence /ínssidənss/ n **1** the frequency with which something occurs **2** an instance of something happening

incident /ínssidənt/ n **1** a single event **2** a violent public occurrence **3** an event with potentially serious consequences ■ adj **1** related to or occurring as a consequence of something (fml) **2** striking the surface of something

incidental /ínssi dént'l/ adj **1** related to or accompanying something more important **2** occurring by chance **3** occasional ■ n a minor item —**incidentally** adv

incidental music n the background music to a film or television programme

~~incidently~~ incorrect spelling of **incidentally**

incinerate /in sínnə rayt/ (-ating, -ated) vti burn something thoroughly —**incineration** /in sínnə ráysh'n/ n

incinerator /in sínnə raytər/ n a furnace for burning waste

incipient /in síppi ənt/ adj beginning to appear or develop —**incipience** n

incise /in síz/ (-cising, -cised) vt **1** engrave or carve a design into **2** cut into

incision /in sízh'n/ n a cut or the act of cutting, especially by a surgeon

incisive /in síssiv/ adj **1** quick to understand **2** expressed clearly —**incisively** adv —**incisiveness** n

incisor /in sízər/ n a flat sharp front tooth —**incisal** adj

incite /in sít/ (-citing, -cited) vt stir up feelings in or provoke action from somebody —**incitement** n —**inciter** n

incivility /ínssi villəti/ (pl -ties) n **1** rude behaviour or language **2** a rude act or remark

incl. abbr **1** including **2** inclusive

inclement /in klémmənt/ adj **1** describes weather that is not pleasant or mild **2** showing little mercy (fml) —**inclemency** n —**inclemently** adv

inclination /ínkli náysh'n/ n **1** a feeling that influences a choice or decision **2** a tendency towards something **3** deviation from a line or plane **4** a slope —**inclinational** adj

incline vti /in klín/ (-clining, -clined) **1** be or make somebody likely to take a particular course of action **2** angle, or be angled ■ n /ín klín/ a slope —**inclined** adj

include /in kloŏd/ (-cluding, -cluded) vt **1** contain or have as a constituent **2** bring into a group —**including** prep

inclusion /in kloŏzh'n/ n **1** the addition or presence of somebody or something in a group **2** somebody or something that is included

inclusive /in kloŏssiv/ adj **1** indicates a range within which a series of items is included **2** including many things or everything —**inclusively** adv —**inclusiveness** n

incognito /ín kog nee̊tō/ *adj*, *adv* in disguise

incoherent /ín kō hee̊rənt/ *adj* **1** lacking clarity or organization **2** unable to speak or express thoughts or feelings clearly —**incoherence** *n* —**incoherently** *adv*

incombustible /ínkəm bústəb'l/ *adj* not combustible —**incombustibility** /ínkəm bústə bíllətí/ *n*

income /ín kum/ *n* the amount of money received over a period of time as payment for something or as profit

incomer /ín kummər/ *n* a newcomer to a place

income support *n* state benefit for the unemployed and people on low incomes

income tax *n* tax on income from employment, business, or capital

incoming /ín kumming/ *adj* **1** arriving **2** taking up a new job

incommensurate /ínkə ménshərət/ *adj* not proportionate to or up to the level of something —**incommensurately** *adv*

incommode /ínkə mṓd/ (**-moding**, **-moded**) *vt* bother or inconvenience *(fml)*

incommodious /ínkə mṓdi əss/ *adj (fml)* **1** uncomfortably cramped **2** causing inconvenience —**incommodiously** *adv*

incommunicado /ínkə myō̌oni ka̋adō̌/ *adj*, *adv* with no means of communicating with others

incomparable /ín kómpərəb'l/ *adj* **1** unequalled in quality **2** so different that a valid comparison is not possible —**incomparability** /ín kómpərə bíllətí/ *n* —**incomparably** *adv*

incompatible /ínkəm páttəb'l/ *adj* **1** unable to cooperate or coexist **2** in computing, not able to be used with or substituted for something else —**incompatibility** /ínkəm páttə bíllətí/ *n* —**incompatibly** *adv*

incompetent /ín kómpitənt/ *adj* **1** bad at doing something **2** lacking the necessary legal status or power for the purpose in question —**incompetence** *n* —**incompetent** *n* —**incompetently** *adv*

incomplete /ínkəm pleet̊/ *adj* **1** lacking something that properly belongs with it **2** unfinished —**incompletely** *adv* —**incompleteness** *n*

incomprehensible /ín kómpri hénssəb'l/ *adj* impossible or very difficult to understand —**incomprehensibility** /ín kómpri hénssə bíllətí/ *n* —**incomprehensibly** *adv*

incomprehension /ín kómpri hénsh'n/ *n* an inability to understand

inconceivable /ínkən see̊vəb'l/ *adj* **1** unimaginable **2** extremely unlikely —**inconceivably** *adv*

inconclusive /ínkən kló̌ossiv/ *adj* not providing a clear result, firm conclusion, or definite proof —**inconclusively** *adv* —**inconclusiveness** *n*

incongruent /ín kóng groo ənt/ *adj* not corresponding in structure or content —**incongruence** *n* —**incongruently** *adv*

incongruous /ín kóng groo əss/ *adj* **1** unsuitable or odd **2** not in keeping or inconsistent with something —**incongruity** /ínkən gró̌o əti/ *n* —**incongruously** *adv* —**incongruousness** *n*

inconsequential /ín kónssi kwénsh'l/ *adj* unimportant —**inconsequentiality** /ín kónssi kwénshi állətí/ *n* —**inconsequentially** *adv*

inconsiderable /ínkən síddərəb'l/ *adj* **1** small *(often with 'not')* **2** unworthy of consideration *(fml)* —**inconsiderably** *adv*

inconsiderate /ínkən síddərət/ *adj* failing to consider other people's feelings or wishes —**inconsiderately** *adv* —**inconsiderateness** *n*

inconsistent /ínkən sístənt/ *adj* **1** containing conflicting or contradictory elements **2** varying and unpredictable —**inconsistency** *n* —**inconsistently** *adv*

inconsolable /ínkən sṓləb'l/ *adj* too distressed to be comforted —**inconsolably** *adv*

inconspicuous /ínkən spíkyoo əss/ *adj* not obvious or noticeable —**inconspicuously** *adv* —**inconspicuousness** *n*

inconstant /ín kónstənt/ *adj* **1** unfaithful *(literary)* **2** changeable —**inconstancy** *n* —**inconstantly** *adv*

incontestable /ínkən téstəb'l/ *adj* impossible to dispute —**incontestability** /ínkən téstə bíllətí/ *n* —**incontestably** *adv*

incontinent /ín kóntinənt/ *adj* **1** unable to control the bladder or bowels **2** lacking restraint in sexual matters —**incontinence** *n* —**incontinently** *adv*

incontrovertible /ín kontrə vúrtəb'l/ *adj* undeniable —**incontrovertibly** *adv*

inconvenience /ínkən vee̊ni ənss/ *n* **1** the fact of being annoying or bothersome **2** an annoyance ■ *vt* (**-iencing**, **-ienced**) cause bother or difficulty to

inconvenient /ínkən vee̊ni ənt/ *adj* causing bother or annoyance —**inconveniently** *adv*

inconvertible /ínkən vúrtəb'l/ *adj* not exchangeable for gold or foreign currency

incorporate *vti* /ín káwrpə rayt/ **1** combine something or include it within something already formed **2** form or become a corporation —**incorporated** *adj* —**incorporation** /ín káwrpə ráysh'n/ *n*

incorporeal /ín kawr páwri əl/ *adj* without physical being *(fml)* —**incorporeality** /-páwri állətí/ *n* —**incorporeally** *adv*

incorrect /ínkə rékt/ *adj* **1** wrong, false, or inaccurate **2** not appropriate or proper —**incorrectly** *adv* —**incorrectness** *n*

incorrigible /ín kórrijəb'l/ *adj* **1** impossible to improve or reform **2** unruly and unmanageable —**incorrigibility** /ín kórrijə bíllətí/ *n* —**incorrigibly** *adv*

incorruptible /ínkə rúptəb'l/ *adj* **1** incapable of being corrupted **2** not subject to decomposition —**incorruptibility** /ínkə rúptə bíllətí/ *n* —**incorruptibly** *adv*

increase *vti* /in kreèss, íng kreess/ (**-creasing**, **-creased**) make or become larger or greater ■ *n* /íng kreess, in kreèss/ **1** a rise to a greater number, quantity, or degree **2** the process of increasing in size —**increasing** *adj* —**increasingly** *adv*

SYNONYMS increase, expand, enlarge, extend, augment, intensify, amplify CORE MEANING: make larger or greater

~~incredable~~ incorrect spelling of **incredible**

incredible /in kréddəb'l/ *adj* **1** beyond belief **2** unexpectedly large or great (*infml*) —**incredibility** /in kréddə bílləti/ *n* —**incredibly** *adv*

incredulous /in kréddyŏŏləss/ *adj* **1** unwilling to believe **2** showing disbelief —**incredulity** /ínkrə dyŏŏlɒti/ *n* —**incredulously** *adv* —**incredulousness** *n*

increment /íngkrimənt/ *n* **1** an increase in something, especially one of a series of increases on a scale **2** the act of increasing something —**incremental** /íngkri mént'l/ *adj* —**incrementally** *adv*

incriminate /in krímmi nayt/ (-**nating**, -**nated**) *vt* **1** make appear guilty **2** accuse of wrongdoing —**incriminating** *adj* —**incrimination** /in krímmi náysh'n/ *n* —**incriminatory** *adj*

incrustation *n* = encrustation

incubate /íngkyŏŏ bayt/ (-**bating**, -**bated**) *v* **1** *vti* sit on newly laid eggs to keep them warm, or be kept warm in this way **2** *vt* keep a baby in an incubator **3** *vti* grow microorganisms in a controlled environment **4** *vi* develop to the point at which symptoms of a disease begin to appear —**incubation** /íngkyŏŏ báysh'n/ *n*

incubation period *n* an interval between being infected with a disease and the appearance of symptoms

incubator /íngkyŏŏ baytər/ *n* a hospital apparatus in which premature or sick babies are kept in a controlled environment

incubus /íngkyŏŏbəss/ (*pl* -**bi** /-bī/ *or* -**buses**) *n* in medieval times, a male demon who was believed to have sex with sleeping women

incudes plural of **incus**

inculcate /ín kul kayt/ (-**cating**, -**cated**) *vt* impress on somebody's mind —**inculcation** /ín kul káysh'n/ *n*

inculpate /ín kul payt/ (-**pating**, -**pated**) *vt* accuse of wrongdoing (*archaic*) —**inculpation** /ín kul páysh'n/ *n*

incumbency /in kúmbənssi/ *n* the period during which somebody occupies an official post (*fml*)

incumbent /in kúmbənt/ *adj* **1** necessary as a duty or obligation (*fml*) **2** currently holding a position or office ■ *n* somebody incumbent in a position or office —**incumbently** *adv*

incur /in kúr/ (-**curring**, -**curred**) *vt* **1** become burdened with something, especially a cost or debt **2** experience something unpleasant ○ *had incurred his anger* —**incurrable** *adj* —**incurrence** *n*

incurable /in kyŏŏrəb'l/ *adj* **1** impossible to cure **2** impossible to change —**incurability** /in kyŏŏrə bílləti/ *n* —**incurably** *adv*

incurious /in kyŏŏri əss/ *adj* not curious or inquisitive —**incuriosity** /in kyŏŏri óssəti/ *n* —**incuriously** *adv*

incursion /in kúrsh'n/ *n* **1** a raid **2** an unwelcome intrusion (*fml*) —**incursive** /in kúrssiv/ *adj*

incus /íngkəss/ (*pl* -**cudes** /in kyŏŏd eez/) *n* a small bone shaped like an anvil in the middle ear

ind., ind *abbr* **1** independent **2** index

Ind., Ind *abbr* Independent

indaba /in daábə/ *n* S Africa **1** a meeting or conference **2** a problem (*infml*)

indebted /in déttid/ *adj* **1** in debt **2** obligated —**indebtedness** *n*

indecent /in déess'nt/ *adj* **1** offending public standards, especially in sexual matters **2** improper under the circumstances ○ *with indecent haste* —**indecency** *n* —**indecently** *adv*

indecent assault *n* a sexual attack that falls short of rape

indecent exposure *n* the act of deliberately displaying the genitals in public

indecipherable /índi sífərəb'l/ *adj* impossible to read or understand —**indecipherably** *adv*

indecision /índi sízh'n/ *n* the inability to decide

indecisive /índi síssiv/ *adj* **1** unable to decide **2** without a clear outcome —**indecisively** *adv* —**indecisiveness** *n*

indecorous /in dékərəss/ *adj* impolite or socially unacceptable —**indecorously** *adv* —**indecorum** /índi káwrəm/ *n*

indeed /in déed/ *adv* **1** indicates agreement or confirmation **2** adds emphasis after a descriptive word or phrase ○ *I am willing, indeed eager, to help.*

indefatigable /índi fáttigəb'l/ *adj* never tiring or losing determination —**indefatigability** /índi fáttigə bílləti/ *n* —**indefatigably** *adv*

indefensible /índi fénssəb'l/ *adj* **1** too bad to be justified or excused **2** incapable of being defended **3** not based on fact —**indefensibility** /índi fénssə bílləti/ *n* —**indefensibly** *adv*

indefinable /índi fínəb'l/ *adj* impossible to define or describe —**indefinability** /índi fínə bílləti/ *n* —**indefinably** *adv*

indefinite /in déffənət/ *adj* **1** unlimited **2** not clearly defined **3** vague about plans or thoughts —**indefinitely** *adv* —**indefiniteness** *n*

indefinite article *n* in English, either of the words 'a' or 'an', referring to something simply as one of its kind

indelible /in déllib'l/ *adj* **1** impossible to remove or alter **2** containing indelible ink or lead ○ *an indelible pencil* **3** permanent —**indelibly** *adv*

indelicate /in déllikət/ *adj* **1** tactless or offensive **2** coarse in texture or appearance —**indelicacy** *n* —**indelicately** *adv* —**indelicateness** *n*

indemnify /in démni fī/ (-**fies**, -**fied**) *vt* **1** insure against loss **2** reimburse after loss —**indemnification** /in démnifi káysh'n/ *n*

indemnity /in démnəti/ (*pl* -**ties**) *n* **1** insurance against loss or damage **2** a compensation paid for loss or damage

indent[1] *v* /in dént/ **1** *vti* begin a line of writing or typing in from the margin **2** *vt* form a deep recess in something **3** *vt* make a jagged edge on something **4** *vt* order foreign goods through an agent ■ *n* /ín dent, in dént/ **1** a space set in from the margin of a page **2** an indenture *(archaic)* **3** an order of foreign goods **4** an official order for supplies —**indented** *adj*

ORIGIN Etymologically, English has two separate words **indent**, although they have converged to a considerable extent. The one meaning 'form a recess in' is simply a derivative of *dent*. **Indent** 'make a jagged edge on' owes its origin to Latin *dens* 'tooth'. This formed the basis of a verb *indentare* that denoted the drawing up of a contract between two parties on two identical documents that were cut along a matching line of notches or 'teeth' that could subsequently be rejoined to prove their authenticity.

indent[2] *vt* /in dént/ make a hole or depression in ■ *n* /ín dent, in dént/ a dent or depression in a surface

indentation /ín den táysh'n/ *n* **1** a notch or recess **2** a jagged edge **3** a space left at the beginning of a line **4** the act of indenting something

indenture /in dénchər/ *n* a contract between an apprentice and a master or employer *(often pl)* ■ *vt* commit somebody to work as an apprentice or servant —**indentureship** *n*

~~independant~~ incorrect spelling of **independent**

independence /índi péndənss/ *n* **1** freedom from control by or reliance on another person, organization, or state **2** the beginning of a state's political freedom

independent /índi péndənt/ *adj* **1** not controlled by another person, organization, or state **2** able to function by itself **3** self-supporting **4** capable of thinking and acting without the help of others **5** done without interference or outside influence **6** *also* **Independent** not affiliated to a political party ■ *n* **1** somebody or something not controlled by another **2** *also* **Independent** a politician or voter who does not belong to any political party —**independently** *adv*

independent clause *n* a clause that can be a sentence

in-depth *adj* carefully considering all aspects —**in depth** *adv*

indescribable /índi skríbəb'l/ *adj* **1** impossible to describe **2** so great as to defy description —**indescribability** /índi skríbə bílləti/ *n* —**indescribably** *adv*

~~indespensable~~ incorrect spelling of **indispensable**

~~indestructable~~ incorrect spelling of **indestructible**

indestructible /índi strúktəb'l/ *adj* impossible to destroy —**indestructibility** /índi strúktə bílləti/ *n* —**indestructibly** *adv*

indeterminable /índi túrminəb'l/ *adj* **1** impossible to find out definitely **2** impossible to answer or settle —**indeterminably** *adv*

indeterminate /índi túrminət/ *adj* **1** not known exactly **2** not precise or clear —**indeterminacy** *n* —**indeterminately** *adv*

index /ín deks/ *n* (*pl* -**dexes** *or* -**dices** /-di seez/) **1** an alphabetical list in a book giving the pages on which to find specific things **2** a catalogue, e.g. of books in a library **3** a publication giving a list of published works **4** series of labelled indentations in the pages of a book to help finding a section quickly **5** an indicator or sign **6** a pointer or needle on a piece of scientific equipment **7** a character ☞ in printing that draws attention to something **8** a mathematical exponent or other number given as a superscript or subscript in a mathematical expression **9** a data structure that enables quick access to data ■ *v* **1** *vti* make an index for something **2** *vt* put in an index **3** *vt* indicate *(fml)* **4** *vt* make index-linked —**indexer** *n*

indexation /ín dek sáysh'n/ *n* the linking of something to living costs

index finger *n* the finger next to the thumb

index fund *n* an investment fund composed of companies listed in a stock market index

index-linked *adj* linked to the cost-of-living index

India[1] /índi ə/ country in South Asia. Cap. New Delhi. Pop. 1,029,991,100 (2001).

India[2] /índi ə/ *n* a communications code word for the letter 'I'

Indian /índi ən/ *n* **1** somebody who comes from India **2** a Native North, South, or Central American *(sometimes offensive)* ■ *adj* of India, or its peoples, languages, or cultures

USAGE As a name applied in error by Columbus and early European explorers, **Indian** may well be regarded as insensitive or even offensive. Some of the people in question prefer to be called *American Indian(s)*, but others prefer the term *Native American(s)*, this last choice being the one least likely to cause offence.

Indiana /índi ánnə/ state in the north-central United States. Cap. Indianapolis. Pop. 6,080,485 (2000). —**Indianan** *n*, *adj*

Indianapolis /índi ə náppəliss/ capital of Indiana. Pop. 741,304 (1998).

Indian ink *n* **1** a black ink **2** the pigment used to make Indian ink

Indian Ocean ocean stretching from Asia in the north to Antarctica in the south and from Africa in the west to Australia in the east

Indian summer *n* **1** a period of mild autumn weather **2** a time of calm

indicate /índi kayt/ (-**cating**, -**cated**) *v* **1** *vt* point to something **2** *vt* show the existence or truth of something **3** *vt* register a measurement **4** *vt* show what somebody thinks or intends **5** *vti* give signals as a driver —**indication** /índi káysh'n/ *n*

indicative /in díkətiv/ *adj* 1 indicating the existence or truth of something 2 describes the basic mood of verbs used in ordinary objective statements ■ *n* the basic mood of a verb, or a verb in this mood —**indicatively** *adv*

indicator /índi kaytər/ *n* 1 a driver's signal 2 something that shows what conditions or trends exist 3 a measuring instrument 4 something such as a sign or pointer that gives information 5 a substance that shows the presence of something such as a chemical

indices plural of **index**

indict /in dít/ *vt* 1 formally charge with a crime 2 accuse of wrongdoing —**indictable** *adj*

indictment /in dítmənt/ *n* 1 a statement or indication that something is wrong ○ *a stinging indictment of our prison system* 2 the act of indicting somebody 3 a formal charge of criminal wrongdoing 4 an accusation of criminal conduct

indie /índi/ *(slang) n* an independent company ■ *adj* issued by or produced by a small company

indifferent /in díffrənt/ *adj* 1 showing no care or interest 2 favouring neither side —**indifference** *n* —**indifferently** *adv*

indigenous /in díjjinəss/ *adj* 1 belonging to and typical of a place 2 natural or inborn *(fml)* —**indigenously** *adv* ◊ See note at **native**

indigent /índijənt/ *adj* lacking the bare necessities of life *(fml)* —**indigence** *n* —**indigent** *n*

indigestible /índi jéstəb'l/ *adj* difficult or impossible to digest —**indigestibility** /índi jéstə bílləti/ *n*

indigestion /índi jéschən/ *n* discomfort after eating

indignant /in dígnənt/ *adj* angry at unfairness —**indignantly** *adv*

indignation /índig náysh'n/ *n* anger at unfairness ◊ See note at **anger**

indignity /indígnəti/ *(pl* **-ties**) *n* a situation that results in humiliation

indigo /índigō/ *(pl* **-gos** *or* **-goes**) *n* 1 a deep purplish-blue colour 2 a blue dye 3 a plant that yields indigo dye —**indigo** *adj*

> **ORIGIN Indigo** is etymologically 'from India', as indeed were supplies of the dye. It is first recorded in English in the mid-16C.

indirect /índi rékt, índī-/ *adj* 1 not in a straight line 2 not occurring as the immediate or intended effect 3 not obvious or straightforward —**indirectly** *adv* —**indirectness** *n*

indirect cost *n* a general business expense

indirect object *n* a person or thing indirectly affected by the action of the verb and the direct object

indirect question *n* a question in indirect speech

indirect speech *n* a report of something said that does not use the speaker's actual words

indirect tax *n* a tax on goods and services

indiscernible /índi súrnəb'l/ *adj* impossible to see or notice —**indiscernibly** *adv*

indiscipline /in díssəplin/ *n* lack of discipline

indiscreet /índi skreet/ *adj* carelessly tactless —**indiscreetly** *adv* —**indiscreetness** *n*

indiscretion /índi skrésh'n/ *n* 1 tactless lack of judgment 2 something that is tactless or unwise

indiscriminate /índi skrímminət/ *adj* 1 making no careful distinctions or choices 2 random —**indiscriminately** *adv* —**indiscriminateness** *n*

indispensable /índi spénssəb'l/ *adj* 1 essential 2 unavoidable ■ *n* an essential item —**indispensability** /índi spénssə bílləti/ *n* —**indispensably** *adv* ◊ See note at **necessary**

~~indispensible~~ incorrect spelling of **indispensable**

indisposed /índi spózd/ *adj (fml)* 1 too ill to do something 2 unwilling to say or do something

indisposition /índispə zísh'n/ *n (fml)* 1 a minor illness 2 reluctance

indisputable /índi spyóotəb'l/ *adj* not to be questioned or denied —**indisputably** *adv*

indissoluble /índi sóllyoob'l/ *adj* incapable of being dissolved, broken, or undone —**indissolubility** /índi sóllyoò bílləti/ *n*

indistinct /índi stíngkt/ *adj* 1 not clearly seen or heard 2 not clearly expressed or remembered —**indistinctly** *adv* —**indistinctness** *n*

indistinguishable /índi stíng gwíshəb'l/ *adj* 1 very like somebody or something else 2 very hard to see, hear, or understand —**indistinguishably** *adv*

indium /índi əm/ *n (symbol* **In***)* a soft silvery rare metallic element. Use: alloys, transistors, electroplating.

individual /índi víddyoo əl/ *n* 1 a particular person distinct from others in a group 2 a human being 3 a separate thing ■ *adj* 1 considered separately from others 2 of or for one person 3 very distinctive —**individually** *adv*

individualism /índi víddyoo əlizəm/ *n* 1 the pursuit of personal goals 2 a personal trait

individualist /índi víjjoo əlist/ *n* 1 an independent thinker 2 a believer in individualism —**individualistic** /índi vidyoo ə lístik/ *adj*

individuality /índi vidyoo álləti/ *(pl* **-ties**) *n* 1 a specific distinguishing trait or character 2 the state of being an individual

individualize /índi víddyoo ə līz/ *(***-izing, -ized***),* **individualise** *vt* 1 give an individual character to 2 treat individually —**individualization** /índi víddyoo ə īz záysh'n/ *n*

individuate /índi víddyoo ayt/ *(***-ating, -ated***) vt* make separate and distinct

indivisible /índi vízzəb'l/ *adj* 1 not separable 2 not capable of being divided by another number without a remainder —**indivisibility** /índi vizə bílləti/ n —**indivisibly** adv

Indo- prefix India ○ Indo-European

Indochina /índō chínə/ peninsula of Southeast Asia that comprises Myanmar, Thailand, Cambodia, Vietnam, Laos, and the Malay Peninsula —**Indochinese** /índō chī née′z/ adj, n

indoctrinate /in dóktri nayt/ (**-nating, -nated**) vt teach a belief with the aim of discouraging independent thought —**indoctrination** /in dóktri náysh′n/ n

Indo-European n 1 a family of European and Asian languages 2 the ancestor of modern Indo-European —**Indo-European** adj

indolent /índələnt/ adj lazy —**indolence** n —**indolently** adv

indomitable /in dómmitəb′l/ adj impossible to defeat or subdue —**indomitability** /in dómmitə bílləti/ n —**indomitably** adv

Indonesia /índə née′zi ə, -née′zhə/ country in Southeast Asia. Cap. Jakarta. Pop. 228,437,870 (2001). —**Indonesian** n, adj

indoor /ín dawr/ adj in a building

indoors /in dáwrz/ adv in or into a building

indrawn /ín dráwn/ adj 1 drawn or pulled in 2 unresponsive or reserved

indubitable /in dyóobitəb′l/ adj definitely true —**indubitably** adv

induce /in dyōóss/ (**-ducing, -duced**) vt 1 persuade or influence somebody to do something 2 produce a particular mental or physical state 3 hasten the birth of a baby by a medical intervention

inducement /in dyōóss mənt/ n 1 a reason or incentive that induces somebody to do something 2 the inducing of something ◊ See note at **motive**

induct /in dúkt/ vt 1 formally install in a position or office 2 introduce new ideas to —**inductee** /ín duk tée/ n

inductance /in dúktənss/ n the property of an electric circuit whereby an electromotive force is created by a change of current

induction /in dúksh′n/ n 1 the process of inducing a state, feeling, or idea 2 the process of hastening a baby's birth by a medical intervention 3 the act of inducting somebody into a position or office 4 in logic, the process of generalizing from specific observed instances 5 the creation of electric or magnetic forces by proximity to another electric or magnetic field —**inductional** adj

induction coil n an electrical transformer

inductive /in dúktiv/ adj 1 of electric or magnetic induction 2 reaching a conclusion based on observation —**inductively** adv —**inductiveness** n

indulge /in dúlj/ (**-dulging, -dulged**) v 1 vti allow yourself or somebody else to experience something enjoyable 2 vi drink alcohol 3 vt give somebody time to do something or the chance to do it

indulgence /in dúljənss/ n 1 the act of yielding to somebody's wish 2 something allowed as a luxury 3 a tolerant attitude

indulgent /in dúljənt/ adj permissive or kind —**indulgently** adv

Indus /índəss/ river in south-central Asia, rising in W Tibet and flowing into the Arabian Sea. Length 2,900 km/1,800 mi.

industrial /in dústri əl/ adj 1 of industry 2 with many developed industries —**industrially** adv

industrial action n a protest by workers

industrial archaeology n the study of past industries

industrial espionage n the theft of trade secrets

industrial estate n a special area for factories and businesses

industrialism /in dústri əlizəm/ n the organization of society around industry

industrialist /in dústri əlist/ n an owner or top manager in industry

industrialize /in dústri ə līz/ (**-izing, -ized**), **industrialise** vti adapt to industrial methods of production and manufacturing —**industrialization** /in dústri ə lī záysh′n/ n

industrial park n ANZ, US, Can a special area for factories and businesses

industrial relations npl the relationship between management and employees

Industrial Revolution n the industrialization of Great Britain, Europe, and the United States that began in the second half of the 18C

industrial tribunal n a court for disputes between management and employees

industrious /in dústri əss/ adj working diligently —**industriously** adv —**industriousness** n

industry /índəstri/ (pl **-tries**) n 1 activity connected with the large-scale production of a product 2 a particular branch of industry devoted to the production of a particular thing 3 a popular activity that has become commercialized ○ the fitness industry 4 hard work (fml or literary)

inebriate /i née′bri ayt/ vt (**-ating, -ated**) 1 make intoxicated 2 excite (fml) ■ n an intoxicated person (fml) —**inebriated** adj —**inebriation** /i née′bri áysh′n/ n

inedible /in éddəb′l/ adj unfit to eat —**inedibility** /in éddə bílləti/ n —**inedibly** adv

ineffable /in éffəb′l/ adj unable to be expressed in words —**ineffability** /in éffə bílləti/ n —**ineffably** adv

ineffective /ínni féktiv/ adj 1 not producing the desired result 2 lacking competence —**ineffectively** adv —**ineffectiveness** n

ineffectual /ínni fékchoo əl/ adj 1 incompetent or indecisive 2 incapable of producing the desired outcome —**ineffectually** adv

inefficient /ínni físh′nt/ adj not making the best use of time and resources —**inefficiency** n

inelegant /in élligənt/ adj 1 lacking grace,

sophistication, and style **2** unnecessarily complicated or long —**inelegance** *n*

ineligible /in élliyəb'l/ *adj* not eligible —**ineligibility** /in éllijə bíllətee/ *n*

ineluctable /ínni lúktəb'l/ *adj* unavoidable *(fml)* —**ineluctably** *adv*

inept /i népt/ *adj* **1** lacking in competence or skill **2** totally inappropriate —**ineptitude** *n* —**ineptly** *adv* —**ineptness** *n*

inequality /ínni kwóllǝti/ (*pl* **-ties**) *n* **1** difference in social or economic status **2** lack of equal treatment

inequitable /in ékwitǝb'l/ *adj* unfair *(fml)* —**inequitably** *adv*

inequity /in ékwǝti/ (*pl* **-ties**) *n* **1** unfair treatment *(fml)* **2** an unfair situation or action

ineradicable /ínni ráddikǝb'l/ *adj* impossible to remove —**ineradicably** *adv*

inert /i núrt/ *adj* **1** motionless **2** not readily changed by chemical or biological reaction —**inertly** *adv* —**inertness** *n*

> **ORIGIN Inert** comes from a Latin word that literally meant 'unskilled'. It was formed from *in-* 'not' and *art-*, the stem of *ars* 'art' (from which English *art* derives). The sense 'sluggish' developed in Latin.

inertia /i núrshǝ/ *n* **1** apathy **2** the property of a body by which it remains at rest or continues moving in a straight line unless acted upon by a directional force —**inertial** *adj* —**inertially** *adv*

inertia selling *n* a method of selling that involves sending unsolicited products to potential customers and demanding payment if they are not returned on time

inescapable /ínni skáypǝb'l/ *adj* inevitable —**inescapability** /ínni skaypǝ bíllǝti/ *n* —**inescapably** *adv*

inessential /ínni sénsh'l/ *adj* **1** not essential **2** without substance or being *(literary)* —**inessential** *n* —**inessentially** *adv*

inestimable /in éstimǝb'l/ *adj* extremely useful or valuable —**inestimability** /in éstimǝ bíllǝti/ *n* —**inestimably** *adv*

inevitable /in évvitǝb'l/ *adj* unavoidable ■ *n* something certain to happen —**inevitability** /in évvitǝ billǝti/ *n* —**inevitably** *adv*

~~inevitible~~ incorrect spelling of **inevitable**

inexact /ínnig zákt/ *adj* **1** not fully accurate **2** not thorough or careful —**inexactitude** /ínnig zákti tyood/ *n* —**inexactly** *adv* —**inexactness** *n*

inexcusable /ínnik skyoózǝb'l/ *adj* impossible to excuse or justify —**inexcusability** /ínnik skyoózǝ bíllǝti/ *n* —**inexcusably** *adv*

inexhaustible /ínnig záwstǝb'l/ *adj* **1** impossible to use up **2** never tiring —**inexhaustibility** /ínnig záwstǝ bíllǝti/ *n* —**inexhaustibly** *adv*

inexorable /in éksǝrǝb'l/ *adj* **1** unstoppable *(fml)* **2** not swayed by pleas or attempts to persuade —**inexorability** /in éksǝrǝ bíllǝti/ *n* —**inexorably** *adv*

inexpensive /ínnik sпénssiv/ *adj* cheap —**inexpensively** *adv* —**inexpensiveness** *n*

inexperience /ínnik speéri ǝnss/ *n* **1** lack of experience **2** lack of sophistication —**inexperienced** *adj*

inexpert /in ékspurt/ *adj* lacking skill or experience —**inexpertly** *adv* —**inexpertness** *n*

inexplicable /ínnik splíkǝb'l, in éksplikǝb'l/ *adj* impossible to explain or justify —**inexplicability** /ínnik splíkǝ bíllǝti, in éksplikǝ-/ *n* —**inexplicably** *adv*

inexpressible /ínnik spréssǝb'l/ *adj* impossible to put into words —**inexpressibly** *adv*

inexpressive /ínnik spréssiv/ *adj* showing no emotion —**inexpressively** *adv* —**inexpressiveness** *n*

inextinguishable /ínnik stíng gwishǝb'l/ *adj* impossible to extinguish or suppress

in extremis /in ik streémiss/ *adv* in desperate circumstances ■ *adj* near death

inextricable /ínnik stríkǝb'l, in ékstrikǝb'l/ *adj* **1** impossible to escape from **2** impossible to separate or disentangle —**inextricability** /ínnik stríkǝ bíllǝti, in ékstrikǝ-/ *n* —**inextricably** *adv*

infallible /in fállǝb'l/ *adj* **1** incapable of making mistakes **2** certain not to fail **3** incapable of being mistaken in matters of doctrine —**infallibility** /in fállǝ bíllǝti/ *n* —**infallibly** *adv*

infamous /ínfǝmǝss/ *adj* **1** notorious **2** so bad as to destroy somebody's reputation —**infamously** *adv*

infamy /ínfǝmi/ *n* **1** notoriety **2** shameful or criminal conduct

infancy /ínfǝnssi/ *n* **1** babyhood **2** the beginning or early stages of something

infant /ínfǝnt/ *n* **1** a baby **2** a young schoolchild ■ *adj* just beginning —**infanthood** *n*

> **ORIGIN** An **infant** is etymologically 'unable to speak'. The word comes via French from Latin.

infanticide /in fánti sīd/ *n* **1** the murder of an infant **2** a killer of an infant —**infanticidal** /in fánti sīd'l/ *adj*

infantile /ínfǝn tīl/ *adj* **1** showing a lack of maturity **2** of young children

infant mortality rate *n* the rate of deaths during the first year of life

infantry /ínfǝntri/ *n* soldiers who fight on foot, or a unit of them —**infantryman** *n*

infant school *n* a school for very young children

infatuation /in fáttyoo áysh'n/ *n* **1** a great but short-lived passion for somebody or something **2** the object of somebody's infatuation —**infatuated** /in fáttyoo aytid/ *adj* ◊ See note at **love**

infect /in fékt/ *vt* **1** cause disease or infection in **2** affect, usually adversely **3** communicate a feeling to —**infected** *adj* —**infective** *adj*

infection /in féksh'n/ *n* **1** the reproduction of disease-producing microorganisms in the body **2** the transmission of a disease **3** a communicable disease

infectious /in fékshəss/ adj 1 describes a disease that can be passed on 2 caused by bacteria or other microorganisms 3 causing infection 4 affecting the feelings of others o *infectious laughter* —**infectiously** adv —**infectiousness** n

infer /in fúr/ (-**ferring, -ferred**) v 1 vti conclude something from reasoning or evidence 2 vt lead to as a conclusion 3 vt imply —**inferable** adj

USAGE infer or **imply**? **Infer** is to conclude something on the basis of reasoning or evidence: *From her comments I inferred that she supported the legislation.* **Imply** is to make something understood without expressing it directly: *Her comments implied that she supported the legislation.*

inference /infərənss/ n 1 a conclusion drawn from reasoning or evidence 2 the process of reasoning from a premise to a conclusion —**inferential** /ínfə rénsh'l/ adj —**inferentially** adv

inferior /in feéri ər/ adj 1 lower in standing or rank 2 lower in quality, standard, or value 3 in a lower position than something else —**inferior** n —**inferiority** /in feéri órrəti/ n

inferiority complex n a sense of being inferior

infernal /in fúrn'l/ adj 1 of the underworld 2 diabolical in nature 3 very annoying —**infernally** adv

inferno /in fúrnō/ (pl -**nos**) n 1 a huge destructive fire 2 a hellish place

infertile /in fúr tīl/ adj 1 physically incapable of having offspring 2 not producing crops —**infertility** /ínfər tílləti/ n

infest /in fést/ vt overrun a place to an unpleasant or harmful degree o *lice infesting their clothing* —**infestation** /ín fe stáysh'n/ n —**infested** adj

infidel /ínfid'l/ n (disapproving) 1 somebody who does not believe in a particular religion 2 somebody with no religious beliefs

infidelity /ínfi délləti/ (pl -**ties**) n 1 unfaithfulness, especially to a sexual partner 2 an unfaithful act

infield /ín feeld/ n in cricket, the area near the wicket

infighting /ín fīting/ n 1 internal squabbling 2 fighting at close range —**infighter** n

infill /ín fil/ n the building of new buildings in the spaces between existing buildings —**infill** vt —**infilling** n

infiltrate /ínfil trayt/ (-**trating, -trated**) vti 1 cross or send somebody into enemy territory without the enemy's knowledge 2 pass through a substance by filtration —**infiltration** /ínfil tráysh'n/ n —**infiltrator** n

infinite /ínfinət/ adj 1 without measurable limits 2 exceedingly great 3 greater than any assigned value 4 extending in space indefinitely —**infinite** n —**infinitely** adv —**infiniteness** n

infinite loop n a series of instructions in a computer program that repeats endlessly

infinitesimal /ínfini téssim'l/ adj 1 tiny 2 able to assume values close to but greater than zero —**infinitesimally** adv

infinitive /in fínnitiv/ n the basic form of a verb, in English usually preceded by 'to'

infinitude /in fínni tyood/ n 1 boundlessness 2 a very large number, degree, or extent

infinity /in fínnəti/ (pl -**ties**) n 1 limitless time, space, or distance 2 an amount or number too great to count

infirm /in fúrm/ adj not strong or healthy ◊ See note at **weak**

infirmary /in fúrməri/ (pl -**ries**) n a hospital or other place where sick or injured people are cared for

infirmity /in fúrməti/ (pl -**ties**) n 1 lack of strength and vitality 2 a character flaw

in flagrante delicto /in flə gránti di líktō/, **in flagrante** adv 1 in the act of committing an offence 2 in the act of having sex

inflame /in fláym/ (-**flaming, -flamed**) vt 1 provoke a powerful response in 2 make more angry, violent, or intense —**inflamed** adj

inflammable /in flámmə́b'l/ adj 1 easily set on fire 2 easily made angry or violent —**inflammability** /in flámmə bílləti/ n —**inflammable** n —**inflammably** adv

inflammation /ínflə máysh'n/ n 1 swelling and redness produced by an infection 2 a heightening of emotion

inflammatory /in flámmətəri/ adj 1 likely to arouse anger or violence 2 of inflammation —**inflammatorily** adv

inflate /in fláyt/ (-**flating, -flated**) vti 1 expand by filling with air or a gas 2 appear or cause to appear greater —**inflatable** adj

inflated /in fláytid/ adj 1 exaggerated or greater than is justified o *a sense of inflated importance* 2 excessively high 3 filled with air or a gas —**inflatedly** adv —**inflatedness** n

inflation /in fláysh'n/ n 1 an increase in the money supply relative to the supply of goods and services, resulting in higher prices 2 the act of inflating or condition of being inflated —**inflationary** adj

inflect /in flékt/ v 1 vt vary the pitch or tone of the voice 2 vti change the form of a word to show grammatical changes such as tense, mood, gender, or number —**inflectable** adj —**inflected** adj

inflection /in fléksh'n/, **inflexion** n 1 a change in the pitch or tone of the voice 2 a change in the form of a word to show grammatical changes such as tense, mood, gender, or number —**inflectional** adj

inflexible /in fléksəb'l/ adj 1 adhering firmly to a viewpoint or principle 2 impossible to change o *an inflexible rule* 3 stiff and difficult to bend —**inflexibility** /in fléksə bílləti/ n —**inflexibly** adv

inflict /in flíkt/ vt 1 cause damage or harm to 2 force on somebody —**infliction** /in flíksh'n/ n

in-flight adj provided for passengers during a flight

inflow /ín flõ/ n **1** something that flows in **2** an instance or the process of flowing in —**inflowing** n

influence /ín floo ənss/ n **1** an effect on something **2** the power to affect other people's thinking or actions **3** a special advantage that comes from wealth or social status **4** somebody who can sway another person ■ vt (-**encing, -enced**) **1** persuade or sway **2** have the power to affect ◇ **under the influence** intoxicated by having drunk alcohol (infml)

~~influencial~~ incorrect spelling of **influential**

influential /ín floo énsh'l/ adj able to influence people —**influentially** adv

influenza /ín floo énzə/ n a viral illness producing high fever, respiratory inflammation, and muscle pain (technical) —**influenzal** adj

influx /ín fluks/ n **1** a sudden arrival in large numbers **2** an inflow

info[1] /ínfō/ n information (infml)

info[2] abbr general use (in Internet addresses)

~~infomation~~ incorrect spelling of **information**

infomediary /ínfō meédi əri/ n a website providing specialist information for producers of goods and customers

infomercial /ínfō múrsh'l/ n a television commercial made in the style of a documentary

inform /ín fáwrm/ v **1** vt communicate information to **2** vr familiarize yourself with something **3** vi tell the police about somebody's wrongdoings

informal /ín fáwrm'l/ adj **1** characterized by an absence of formality and ceremony **2** unofficial **3** casual and everyday —**informality** /ín fawr málləti/ n —**informally** adv

informant /ín fáwrmənt/ n **1** somebody who supplies information **2** a police informer

informatics /ínfər máttiks/ n INFO SCI = **information science** (+ sing verb)

information /ínfər máysh'n/ n **1** knowledge **2** gathered facts **3** the communication of facts and knowledge **4** computer data —**informational** adj

information retrieval n the systematic storage and retrieval of computer data

information science n the study of data collection, organization, and distribution, especially using computers

information technology n the use of computing, electronics, and telecommunications to process and distribute information

information theory n the mathematical analysis of data transmission, reception, storage, and retrieval

informative /ín fáwrmətiv/ adj providing useful information —**informatively** adv —**informativeness** n

informed /ín fáwrmd/ adj **1** showing, having, or based on knowledge **2** based on full awareness —**informedly** /ín fáwrmidli/ adv

informed consent n a patient's agreement to undergo an operation or treatment after being informed of the risks

informer /ín fáwrmər/ n somebody who provides information about a crime to the police

infotainment /ínfō táynmənt/ n information treated or presented as entertainment —**infotainer** n

infra /ínfrə/ adv refers a reader to a point later in a text (fml)

infra- prefix below, beneath, inferior ○ infrastructure

infraction /ín fráksh'n/ n a failure to obey a rule

infra dig /ínfrə díg/ adj beneath somebody's dignity (infml)

infrared /ínfrə réd/ n electromagnetic radiation that lies outside the visible spectrum —**infrared** adj

infrastructure /ínfrə strukchər/ n **1** the basic organizational structure of a company or organization **2** the public services or systems necessary to the economic activity of a country or region

infrequent /ín freékwənt/ adj not appearing, happening, or encountered often —**infrequency** n —**infrequently** adv

infringe /ín frínj/ (-**fringing, -fringed**) v **1** vt disobey or disregard a law or the terms of a agreement **2** vti encroach on somebody's rights or property —**infringement** n

infuriate /ín fyoóri ayt/ (-**ating, -ated**) vt make furious —**infuriated** adj —**infuriating** adj —**infuriatingly** adv

infuse /ín fyoóz/ (-**fusing, -fused**) v **1** vt fill with a strong emotion **2** vt fix firmly in somebody else's mind **3** vti steep in liquid —**infusion** n

-ing suffix **1** action or process ○ cooking **2** forms the present participle of verbs ○ raining **3** somebody or something that has a particular character ○ gelding

ingenious /ín jeéni əss/ adj **1** inventive **2** clever and effective —**ingeniously** adv —**ingeniousness** n

ingénue /ánzhə nyoo/ n **1** an unsophisticated girl or young woman **2** a character in a play who is a naive young woman

ingenuity /ínjə nyoó əti/ n inventiveness

ingenuous /ín jénnyoo əss/ adj **1** innocent and unworldly **2** seeming honest and direct —**ingenuously** adv —**ingenuousness** n

ingest /ín jést/ vt take into the body by swallowing or absorbing —**ingestion** n

Ingham /íngəm/ town in NE Queensland, Australia. Pop. 5,075 (1991).

inglenook /íng g'l noõk/ n **1** a recess beside a fireplace **2** a fireside seat

inglorious /ín gláwri əss/ adj bringing shame or dishonour —**ingloriously** adv

ingoing /ín gō ing/ adj arriving in a place or position

ingot /íng gət/ n a cast block of metal, typically oblong

ingrained /ín gráynd/ adj **1** worked deep into something ○ ingrained dirt **2** impressed on somebody's mind **3** long-established and confirmed ○ ingrained habits —**ingrain** vt —**ingrainedness** /-idnəss/ n

ingrate /ín grayt, in gráyt/ *n* an ungrateful person (*fml or literary*)

ingratiate /in gráyshi ayt/ (**-ating, -ated**) *vr* seek to please somebody, especially to gain an advantage —**ingratiating** *adj* —**ingratiation** /in gráyshi áysh'n/ *n*

ingratitude /in grátti tyood/ *n* lack of gratitude

~~ingrediant~~ incorrect spelling of **ingredient**

ingredient /in greédi ənt/ *n* 1 an item in a recipe 2 a required part o *the ingredients of a good marriage*

Ingres /áng grə/, **Jean-Auguste-Dominique** (1780–1867) French artist

ingress /ín gress/ *n* 1 entry 2 the right of entry

in-group *n* a group united by common values

ingrowing /ín grố ing/ *adj* growing inwards

ingrown /in grốn/ *adj* 1 grown into the flesh 2 having become a natural part of somebody's character

inhabit /in hábbit/ *vt* 1 live or reside in 2 be found or present in —**inhabitable** *adj* —**inhabited** *adj*

inhabitant /in hábbitənt/ *n* a person or animal that lives in a particular place

inhalant /in háylənt/ *adj* breathed in ■ *n* a medicine in the form of a vapour or gas that is inhaled

inhale /in háyl/ (**-haling, -haled**) *vti* breathe something into the lungs —**inhalation** /ínhə láysh'n/ *n*

inhaler /in háylər/ *n* a device for inhaling medicine

inharmonious /ín haar mốni əss/ *adj* 1 sounding unpleasant or out of harmony 2 characterized by disagreement or conflict

inherent /in hérrənt, -heérənt/ *adj* forming a basic and essential part of something —**inherency** *n* —**inherently** *adv*

inherit /in hérrit/ *v* 1 *vti* receive something when somebody dies under the terms of a will 2 *vt* receive a genetic characteristic from a parent 3 *vt* get something from a predecessor —**inheritor** *n*

inheritance /in hérritənss/ *n* 1 a sum of money, property, or a title that is inherited 2 ownership or succession by heredity 3 the right to inherit 4 something that is inherited from the past 5 the transmission of genetically controlled characteristics from parent to offspring

inheritance tax *n* a tax on inherited property

inhibit /in híbbit/ *vt* 1 prevent from continuing or developing 2 prevent from behaving freely or without self-consciousness —**inhibited** *adj* —**inhibitive** *adj*

inhibition /ín hi bísh'n/ *n* 1 a feeling that prevents somebody from behaving freely or without self-consciousness 2 something that inhibits, or the act of inhibiting

inhospitable /ín ho spíttəb'l, in hóspit-/ *adj* 1 not friendly or welcoming 2 harsh and difficult to live or work in o *an inhospitable climate* —**inhospitably** *adv* —**inhospitality** /in hóspi tálləti/ *n*

in-house *adj, adv* within a company or organization

inhuman /in hyoómən/ *adj* 1 very cruel 2 unfeeling —**inhumanly** *adv* —**inhumanness** *n*

inhumane /ín hyoo máyn/ *adj* not compassionate —**inhumanely** *adv* —**inhumaneness** *n*

inhumanity /ín hyoo mánnəti/ (*pl* **-ties**) *n* 1 great cruelty 2 an extremely cruel act

inimical /i nímmik'l/ *adj* (*fml*) 1 not favourable 2 hostile

inimitable /i nímmitəb'l/ *adj* unique and impossible to imitate —**inimitably** *adv*

iniquity /i níkwəti/ (*pl* **-ties**) *n* 1 injustice or immorality 2 an unjust or immoral act —**iniquitous** *adj*

initial /i nísh'l/ *adj* 1 coming at the start 2 describes the first letter in a word ■ *n* 1 the first letter of a name, used as an abbreviation 2 a large ornate first letter ■ **initials** *npl* the first letters of somebody's names, used as an abbreviation ■ *vt* (**-tialling, -tialled**) mark with initials —**initially** *adv*

initialize /i níshə lítz/ (**-izing, -ized**), **initialise** *vti* prepare a computer for use, often by resetting a memory location to its original position —**initialization** /i níshə IT záysh'n/ *n*

initiate *vt* /i níshi ayt/ (**-ating, -ated**) 1 cause an event, activity, or process to begin 2 introduce somebody to a new activity or interest 3 allow somebody to take part in a ceremony, in order to become a member of a group ■ *n* /i níshi ət/ 1 somebody initiated into a group 2 somebody newly introduced to something ■ *adj* /i níshi ət/ 1 recently initiated 2 having secret or special knowledge —**initiation** /i níshi áysh'n/ *n* —**initiator** *n*

initiative /i níshətiv, i níshi ətiv/ *n* 1 the ability to act and make decisions without help 2 the first step in a process 3 a plan or strategy 4 an advantageous position

inject /in jékt/ *v* 1 *vti* put fluid into the body with a syringe 2 *vt* force a liquid or gas into something 3 *vt* add something new to a situation o *inject a little levity* —**injection** *n*

in-joke *n* a joke understood only by a small group

injudicious /ínjoó díshəss/ *adj* unwise —**injudiciously** *adv* —**injudiciousness** *n*

injunction /in júngksh'n/ *n* 1 a court order prohibiting something 2 a command

injure /ínjər/ (**-juring, -jured**) *vt* 1 cause physical harm to 2 cause distress to by being unkind ◊ See note at **harm**

injury /ínjəri/ (*pl* **-ries**) *n* 1 physical damage to the body 2 a wound 3 harm done to somebody's reputation —**injurious** /in joóri əss/ *adj*

injury time *n* in sport, time added for injury stoppages

~~injust~~ incorrect spelling of **unjust**

injustice /in jústiss/ *n* unfair treatment, or an instance of this

ink *n* 1 liquid for writing, drawing, or printing

2 a dark liquid ejected by an octopus, squid, or related organism to deter predators ■ *vt* write something with ink —**inker** *n* —**inky** *adj*

inkblot /ingk blot/ *n* **1** a stain or spot of spilt ink **2** a pattern of blots or dots for analysis in a psychological test

ink-jet printer *n* a printer that prints using droplets of ink from a matrix of tiny ink jets

inkling /ingkling/ *n* **1** a faint idea **2** a hint

inkstand /ingk stand/ *n* a stand on a desk for ink, pens, and other writing materials

inkwell /ingk wel/ *n* a pot for holding ink, especially one that fits into a hole in a desk

inlaid /in láyd, ín layd/ *adj* **1** set into a surface **2** decorated with an inlaid pattern

inland /inland/ *adj* **1** not near a coast or border **2** within a country ■ *adv* in or into the interior of a country

Inland Revenue *n* the UK tax-collecting authority

Inland Sea arm of the Pacific Ocean in Japan, between the islands of Honshu, Shikoku, and Kyushu. Length 430 km/270 mi.

in-law *n* a relative by marriage *(infml)*

inlay *vt* /in láy, ín lay/ (-**laid**, -**laid** /in láyd, -layd/) **1** set into a surface **2** decorate with an inlaid design ■ *n* /in lay/ **1** pieces of material set into a surface **2** a decorative pattern formed by inlaying —**inlayer** *n*

inlet /ín let/ *n* **1** a narrow stretch of water extending inland from a coast **2** a stretch of water between two islands

in-line skates *npl* roller skates with wheels in a single line —**in-line skating** *n*

~~inlist~~ incorrect spelling of **enlist**

in loco parentis /in lōkō pə réntiss/ *adv* responsible as a parent for somebody else's child

inmate /ín mayt/ *n* somebody confined to an institution

in memoriam /ín mi máwri əm/ *prep*, *adv* in memory of somebody *(in epitaphs and obituaries)*

inmost *adj* = **innermost**

inn *n* **1** a pub *(often in pub names)* **2** a place providing lodging for travellers *(dated)* **3** formerly, a residence for law students

ORIGIN Inn is related to *in*, being etymologically a place you stay 'in'. In its earliest uses it could be a permanent lodging or home. The sense 'pub' began to develop in the 14C.

~~inaccurate~~ incorrect spelling of **inaccurate**

innards /ínnərdz/ *npl* *(infml)* **1** the internal organs of the body **2** the internal parts of a machine

innate /i náyt/ *adj* **1** present from birth **2** integral —**innately** *adv* —**innateness** *n*

inner /ínnər/ *adj* **1** near or closer to the centre **2** being or occurring inside **3** of the mind ■ *n* **1** a bull's-eye **2** a hit on a bull's-eye

inner city *n* the central area of a city —**inner-city** *adj*

innermost /ínnər mōst/, **inmost** /ín mōst/ *adj* **1** most private or personal **2** farthest from the outside

inner tube *n* a rubber tube inside a tyre

inning /ínning/ *n* a division of a baseball game in which each team bats until it makes three outs

innings /ínningz/ *(pl same)* *n* **1** in cricket, a team's turn at batting **2** a period of success

innkeeper /ín keepər/ *n* somebody in charge of an inn

innocent /ínnəss'nt/ *adj* **1** not guilty of a crime **2** harmless in intention **3** pure and uncorrupted by evil **4** naive ■ *n* a blameless or naive person —**innocence** *n* —**innocently** *adv*

Innocent III /ínnəss'nt/ (1160?–1216) pope (1198–1216)

~~inoculation~~ incorrect spelling of **inoculation**

innocuous /i nókyoo əss/ *adj* **1** unlikely to offend **2** harmless —**innocuously** *adv* —**innocuousness** *n*

innovate /ínnə vayt/ (-**vating**, -**vated**) *vi* try out new ideas —**innovative** /-vaytiv, -vətiv/ *adj* —**innovatively** *adv* —**innovativeness** *n* —**innovator** *n*

innovation /ínnə váysh'n/ *n* **1** the process of inventing or introducing new things **2** a new invention, idea, or method —**innovational** *adj*

Innsbruck /ínz brook/ capital of **Tirol Province**, W Austria. Pop. 110,997 (1999).

innuendo /ínnyoo éndō/ *(pl* -**does** *or* -**dos)** *n* a remark that hints at something improper

innumerable /i nyoómərəb'l/ *adj* countless —**innumerability** /i nyoómərə billəti/ *n* —**innumerably** *adv*

innumerate /i nyoómərət/ *adj* unable to do arithmetic

~~inocence~~ incorrect spelling of **innocence**

inoculate /i nókyoo layt/ (-**lating**, -**lated**) *vt* inject or introduce a substance that protects against a disease —**inoculation** /i nókyoo láysh'n/ *n*

inoffensive /ínnə fénssiv/ *adj* not harmful, annoying, or offensive —**inoffensively** *adv* —**inoffensiveness** *n*

inoperable /in óppərəb'l/ *adj* **1** too far advanced for effective surgery **2** not workable

inoperative /in óppərətiv/ *adj* **1** not functioning properly **2** ineffective or unenforceable —**inoperatively** *adv*

inopportune /in óppər tyoon/ *adj* happening at an inconvenient time —**inopportunely** *adv* —**inopportunity** /in óppər tyoonəti/ *n*

inordinate /in áwrdinət/ *adj* excessive in amount or degree —**inordinately** *adv*

inorganic /ín awr gánnik/ *adj* **1** composed of minerals rather than living material **2** describes a chemical compound that contains no carbon —**inorganically** *adv*

inorganic chemistry *n* the study of inorganic compounds

inpatient /ín paysh'nt/ n somebody receiving medical treatment that requires a hospital stay ■ adj for inpatients

input /ín poot/ n 1 comments or suggestions made 2 something that enters a process or situation from outside 3 the energy that operates a machine 4 data entered into a computer ■ v (-putting, -putted or -put) 1 vt contribute information (infml) 2 enter data into a computer

inquest /ín kwest/ n 1 a formal inquiry , usually before a jury 2 an investigation into what went wrong (literary)

inquietude /in kwî ə tyood/ n restlessness of mind (literary)

inquire, etc. vti = enquire, etc.

inquiry /in kwîri/ (pl -ies), **enquiry** n 1 a formal investigation 2 a request for information

inquisition /ingkwi zísh'n/ n 1 a period of intense questioning 2 a harsh or unfair investigation 3 **Inquisition** a former Roman Catholic tribunal for judging heretics —**inquisitional** adj

inquisitive /in kwízzətiv/ adj 1 eager for knowledge 2 too curious —**inquisitively** adv —**inquisitiveness** n

inquisitor /in kwízzitər/ n 1 a relentless interrogator 2 also **Inquisitor** a member of the Roman Catholic Inquisition —**inquisitorial** /in kwízzə tawri əl/ adj

inquorate /in kwáwrət, -rayt/ adj with too few people present to make official decisions

in re /in reè, -ráy/ prep with regard to

inroads /ín rōdz/ npl an encroachment

inrush /ín rush/ n an influx

ins. abbr insurance

insalubrious /ínssə loò bri əss/ adj unwholesome or unpleasant —**insalubrity** n

insane /in sáyn/ adj 1 legally incompetent or irresponsible because of a psychiatric disorder 2 wildly unreasonable or unwise (infml) —**insanely** adv —**insanity** n

insanitary /in sánnitəri/ adj dirty or unhygienic

insatiable /in sáyshəb'l/ adj always wanting more —**insatiability** /in sáyshə bíllətí/ n —**insatiably** adv

inscribe /in skríb/ (-scribing, -scribed) vt 1 put writing or engraving on a surface 2 write a dedication on a book or photograph

inscription /in skrípsh'n/ n 1 words or letters written or engraved on something 2 a dedication written in a book or on a photograph —**inscriptional** adj

inscrutable /in skrootab'l/ adj not expressing anything clearly and hard to interpret o an inscrutable expression —**inscrutability** /in skroota bíllətí/ n —**inscrutably** adv

insect /in sekt/ n 1 a small six-legged animal with a segmented body 2 any small organism that resembles an insect (not in technical use)

ORIGIN Insect derives from Latin insectum, which means literally 'something cut up or into'. The name refers to the segmented structure of an insect body. The Latin was itself a

direct translation from Greek entomon, which is seen in English entomology. Insect is first recorded in 1601.

insecticide /in sékti síd/ n a chemical substance used to kill insects —**insecticidal** /in sékti síd'l/ adj

insectivore /in sékti vawr/ n an insect-eating organism —**insectivorous** /in sek tívvərəss/ adj

insecure /ínssi kyoór/ adj 1 not confident 2 not safe —**insecurely** adv —**insecurity** /ínsi kyoórətee/ n

inseminate /in sémmi nayt/ (-nating, -nated) vt 1 put semen into the reproductive tract of a woman or female animal 2 introduce something such as a new idea or principle —**insemination** /in sémmi náysh'n/ n

insensate /in sén sayt, -sət/ adj 1 inanimate and thus unable to feel 2 irrational (fml)

insensible /in sénssəb'l/ adj 1 without feeling or consciousness 2 not aware or responsive —**insensibility** /in sénssə bíllətí/ n

insensitive /in sénssətiv/ adj 1 thoughtless of others 2 not responsive to physical stimulus —**insensitively** adv —**insensitivity** /in sénssə tívvətí/ n

insentient /in sénshənt/ adj without life, consciousness, or perception —**insentience** n

inseparable /in séppərəb'l/ adj 1 always together 2 unable to be separated —**inseparability** /in séppərə bíllətí/ n —**inseparably** adv

insert vt /in súrt/ 1 put inside or into something 2 add to something written ■ n /ín surt/ 1 an advertising supplement in a magazine 2 an added part —**insertion** n

in-service adj 1 happening during full-time employment o in-service training 2 working as a full-time employee

inset /in sét/ (-setting, -set) vt insert into a larger thing —**inset** /ín set/ n

inshallah /in shállə/, **insh'allah** interj an expression meaning 'if God wills', used to suggest that something in the future is uncertain

inshore /in shawr/ adj near a coast ■ adv towards a coast

inside /in síd, ín síd/ adj, prep happening or coming from within an organization o inside knowledge of the buyout ■ adv, prep within a place o I looked inside. o Everyone's inside the office. 2 within or into somebody's inner feelings ■ prep within a particular time (infml) ■ adj 1 inner or interior o an inside pocket 2 farthest from the centre of a road o an inside lane ■ adv in prison (infml) ■ n 1 an interior or inner part 2 the part of a road farthest from the centre 3 a position that gives access to information ■ **insides** npl internal organs of the body (infml) ◊ **inside out** with the part that is normally inside facing outwards ◊ **know something inside out** know something extremely well

inside information n something that only insiders know

inside job *n* a crime committed by or with the help of an employee of the person or organization affected *(infml)*

inside lane *n* the lane of a road nearest the roadside

inside leg *n* **1** an inside trouser leg seam **2** the measurement of the inside leg

insider /in sídər/ *n* a member of a group who has access to information about the group

insider dealing, insider trading *n* stock transactions made with inside information.

inside track *n* **1** the inner lane of a racetrack **2** a position of advantage

insidious /in síddi əss/ *adj* gradual and harmful —**insidiously** *adv* —**insidiousness** *n*

insight /in sít/ *n* **1** perceptiveness **2** a clear perception —**insightful** *adj* —**insightfully** *adv*

insignia /in sígni ə/ *(pl same or* **-as**) *n* **1** a badge of authority or membership **2** an identifying mark

insignificant /ínsig níffikənt/ *adj* **1** without importance **2** without meaning —**insignificance** *n* —**insignificantly** *adv*

insincere /ín sin seér/ *adj* not having or expressing genuine feelings —**insincerely** *adv* —**insincerity** /ín sin sérrəti/ *n*

insinuate /in sínnyoo ayt/ *(-ating, -ated)* *v* **1** *vti* hint or suggest something indirectly **2** *vr* worm your way in —**insinuatingly** *adv* —**insinuation** /in sínnyoo áysh'n/ *n*

insipid /in síppid/ *adj* **1** dull and unexciting **2** flavourless —**insipidity** /ínsi píddəti/ *n* —**insipidly** *adv*

insist /in síst/ *vti* **1** state or demand firmly despite opposition **2** be persistent in a demand ○ *insist on punctuality*

insistant incorrect spelling of **insistent**

insistent /in sístənt/ *adj* **1** persistent in demanding something **2** demanding attention ○ *insistent pleas* —**insistence** *n* —**insistently** *adv*

in situ /in síttyoo/ *adv, adj* in its natural or original place

insofar as /ín sō faár əz/ *conj* to the extent that

insole /ínsōl/ *n* **1** a shoe lining **2** a removable pad inside a shoe

insolent /ínssələnt/ *adj* openly disrespectful —**insolence** *n* —**insolently** *adv*

insoluble /in sóllyoob'l/ *adj* **1** not dissolvable **2** impossible to solve —**insolubility** /in sóllyoob billəti/ *n*

insolvable /in sólvəb'l/ *adj* impossible to solve —**insolvability** /in sólvə billəti/ *n*

insolvent /in sólvənt/ *adj* unable to pay debts —**insolvency** *n*

insomnia /in sómni ə/ *n* difficulty in sleeping —**insomniac** *adj, n*

insomuch as /ínssō múch az/ *conj* because

insouciance /in soóssi ənss/ *n* a carefree attitude —**insouciant** *adj*

inspect /in spékt/ *vt* **1** look at critically **2** survey

inspection /in spéksh'n/ *n* **1** a critical examination **2** an official examination

inspector /in spéktər/ *n* **1** an official examiner **2** a police officer of middle rank —**inspectorship** *n*

inspectorate /in spéktərət/ *n* a group of inspectors

inspiration /ínspi ráysh'n/ *n* **1** the stimulus to do creative work **2** a person or thing that inspires somebody **3** creativeness **4** a good idea **5** supposed divine influence —**inspirational** *adj*

inspire /in spír/ *(-spiring, -spired)* *vt* **1** stimulate somebody to greater effort, enthusiasm, or creativity **2** arouse a particular feeling —**inspired** *adj* —**inspiringly** *adv*

inst., Inst. *abbr* institute

instability /ínstə billəti/ *n* **1** the quality of being unstable or unpredictable **2** lack of steadiness or firmness

instalation incorrect spelling of **installation**

install /in stáwl/, **instal** *vt* *(-stalling, -stalled; -stalling, -stalled)* **1** fit or connect equipment and make it ready for use **2** load software onto a computer **3** place somebody in an official post ■ *n* the process of loading software onto a computer —**installer** *n*

installation /ínstə láysh'n/ *n* **1** the process of installing equipment **2** a place that houses equipment **3** something that has been installed **4** a military base

installment *n* US = **instalment**

instalment /in stáwlmənt/ *n* a part in a series

instance /ínstənss/ *n* **1** an example **2** an occurrence ■ *vt* *(-stancing, -stanced)* offer or serve as an example ◇ **for instance** as an example

instant /ínstənt/ *adj* **1** happening immediately, without delay ○ *an instant dislike* **2** in a form that is quickly and easily prepared ○ *instant coffee* **3** achieved suddenly and effortlessly ○ *an instant success* ■ *n* **1** a very short time **2** a moment in time

ORIGIN Instant goes back to a Latin verb meaning 'be present'. Its original sense in English was 'urgent', and it later also meant 'current' and 'imminent'. The modern sense 'happening immediately' did not develop until the late 16C.

instantaneous /ínstən táyni əss/ *adj* **1** happening immediately **2** indicating the value of a varying quantity at a given instant —**instantaneity** /in stántə náy əti, -neè əti/ *n* —**instantaneously** *adv*

instantly /ínstəntli/ *adv* **1** immediately **2** urgently *(archaic)* ■ *conj* as soon as

instant messaging *n* a system for electronic communication by means of live e-mail or chat rooms

instead /in stéd/ *adv* in somebody's or something's place ◇ **instead of** as an alternative to or substitute for

instep /in step/ *n* the upper part of the foot between the ankle and toes

instigate /ínsti gayt/ *(-gating, -gated)* *vt* **1** get a

process started **2** start trouble —**instigation**
/ínsti gáysh'n/ n —**instigator** n

instil /in stíl/ vt **1** introduce something such as
an idea or principle to somebody's mind by
repetition **2** pour a liquid into something
drop by drop —**instilment** n

instill vt US = **instil**

instinct /ín stingkt/ n **1** an inborn pattern of
behaviour **2** a strong natural impulse
—**instinctive** /in stíngktiv/ adj —**instinctively**
adv —**instinctiveness** n —**instinctual** /in
stíngktyoo əl/ adj

institute /ínsti tyoot/ vt (**-tuting, -tuted**) **1** start or
initiate formally **2** set up or establish ■ n
1 an organization for promoting something
such as an art or science **2** an educational
institution, especially for technical subjects

institution /ínsti tyóosh'n/ n **1** a large and influential organization **2** an established practice
○ the institution of marriage **3** the initiation
or establishment of something **4** a long-
established person or thing (infml) **5** a place
where people who are mentally or physically challenged are cared for —**institutional**
adj

institutionalize /ínsti tyóosh'nə līz/ (**-izing,
-ized**), **institutionalise** vt **1** put into an institution such as a hospital or prison **2** make
an accepted part of a large organization or
society —**institutionalization** /ínsti tyóosh'nə
līz áysh'n/ n

institutionalized /ínsti tyóosh'nə līzd/ adj
unable to think and act independently
outside an institution such as a prison

in-store adj within a store ○ an in-store deli

instruct /in strúkt/ vt **1** train or teach **2** give an
order to **3** give information to ◊ See note at
teach

instruction /in strúksh'n/ n **1** teaching, or the
facts and skills taught **2** an order or
command ■ **instructions** npl information on
how to use or make something
—**instructional** adj

instructive /in strúktiv/ adj providing useful
information or insight —**instructively** adv
—**instructiveness** n

instructor /in strúktər/ n a teacher or trainer
—**instructorship** n

instrument /ínstrōomənt/ n **1** a tool or mechanical device, especially one for precise work
2 an object used to produce music **3** a measuring device **4** a means of doing something
5 a legal document (fml)

instrumental /ínstrōo mént'l/ adj **1** for or played
by musical instruments, not voices **2** important in having achieved a result ■ n a
piece of music played by instruments
—**instrumentally** adv

instrumentalist /ínstrōo mént'list/ n somebody
who plays a musical instrument

instrumentation /ínstrōo men táysh'n, ínstrə
mən-/ n **1** the arrangement of music for instruments **2** equipment for the control or
operation of something

instrument panel n a mounted set of control
devices

insubordinate /ín sə báwrdinət/ adj disobedient
or rebellious —**insubordination** /ín sə báwrdə
náysh'n/ n

insubstantial /ín səb stánsh'l/ adj **1** not very
large, solid, or strong **2** not tangible or real

insufferable /in súffərəb'l/ adj unbearable
—**insufferably** adv

insufficient /ínsə físh'nt/ adj not adequate to
satisfy a purpose or standard —**insufficiency** n —**insufficiently** adv

insular /ínssyōolər/ adj **1** limited in outlook **2** of
islands —**insularism** n —**insularity** /ínssyōo
lárrəti/ n

insulate /ínssyōo layt/ (**-lating, -lated**) vt
1 protect or isolate somebody from something **2** prevent or reduce the flow of heat,
electricity, or sound from or through something —**insulator** n

insulating tape n strong waterproof tape used
to insulate electrical conductors

insulation /ínssyōo láysh'n/ n **1** material used to
insulate something **2** the process of insulating something

insulin /ínssyōolin/ n a hormone that regulates
the glucose level in blood

insult v /in súlt/ **1** vti do or say something rude
or insensitive to somebody **2** vt show a lack
of respect for ■ n /ín sult/ **1** n /ín sult/ a rude
or insensitive remark or action that offends
somebody **2** something that shows a lack or
respect —**insulting** adj —**insultingly** adv

insuperable /in sóopərəb'l/ adj impossible to
overcome —**insuperably** adv

insupportable /ínsə páwrtəb'l/ adj **1** impossible
to endure **2** unjustifiable —**insupportably**
adv

insurance /in shóorənss, -sháwr-/ n **1** financial
protection against loss or harm **2** a payment
made to obtain insurance **3** the insurance
business **4** a means of protection

insurance policy n a contract providing insurance

insure /in shóor, -sháwr/ (**-suring, -sured**) v **1** vti
cover something with insurance **2** vi protect
against risk **3** vt US, Can = **ensure** —**insurable**
adj —**insured** adj, n —**insurer** n

~~insurence~~ incorrect spelling of **insurance**

insurgent /in súrjənt/ n a rebel against authority,
especially one involved in an uprising
—**insurgence** n —**insurgent** adj

insurmountable /ín sər mówntəb'l/ adj too great
to overcome —**insurmountability** /ín sər
mówntə bílləti/ n —**insurmountably** adv

insurrection /ínssə réksh'n/ n rebellion against
a country's government or rulers
—**insurrectional** adj —**insurrectionism** n
—**insurrectionist** n, adj

int abbr international organization (in Internet
addresses)

int. abbr **1** interest **2** intransitive

intact /in tákt/ adj **1** whole and undamaged
2 with all the necessary parts —**intactness** n

intaglio /in taáli ō, -tálli ō/ (*pl* **-glios** *or* **-gli** /in taál ee/) *n* a design carved into stone or hard metal

intake /ín tayk/ *n* **1** an amount taken in **2** the act of taking something in

intangible /in tánjəb'l/ *adj* **1** not able to be touched or seen **2** hard to define or describe —**intangibility** /in tánjə bílləti/ *n* —**intangible** *n* —**intangibly** *adv*

intangible asset *n* a valuable but unquantifiable business asset such as goodwill

integer /íntijər/ *n* a positive or negative whole number

integral /íntigrəl, in téggrəl/ *adj* **1** necessary or constituent **2** composed of parts that together form a whole **3** with no parts missing —**integrally** *adv*

integrate /ínti grayt/ (**-grating, -grated**) *v* **1** *vti* fit in with a group and its activities **2** *vt* combine parts or objects into a functioning whole —**integrable** *adj* —**integrated** *adj* —**integration** /ínti gráysh'n/ *n*

integrated circuit *n* a tiny complex of electronic components on a wafer of semiconducting material —**integrated circuitry** *n*

integrator /ínti graytər/ *n* **1** a computer component that solves equations **2** somebody or something that integrates

integrity /in téggrəti/ *n* **1** the possession of high moral principles or professional standards **2** the state of being complete and undivided (*fml*)

integument /in téggyŏŏmənt/ *n* an outer protective layer of an organism

~~intelectual~~ incorrect spelling of **intellectual**

~~inteligence~~ incorrect spelling of **intelligence**

intellect /íntə lekt/ *n* **1** mental ability **2** an intelligent person

intellectual /íntə lékchoo əl/ *adj* **1** of thought and reasoning **2** intelligent and knowledgeable **3** for intelligent people ■ *n* an intellectual person —**intellectually** *adv*

intellectualize /íntə lékchoo ə līz/ (**-izing, -ized**), **intellectualise** *vti* consider or explain something using reasoning alone —**intellectualization** /íntə lékchoo ə lī záysh'n/ *n*

intellectual property *n* original creative work that can be protected by law

intelligence /in téllijənss/ *n* **1** the ability to think and learn **2** secret information, or its collection **3** an organization or the people involved in gathering secret information

intelligence quotient *n* full form of **IQ**

intelligent /in téllijənt/ *adj* **1** having a high level of intelligence **2** sensible or rational **3** able to store and process data electronically —**intelligently** *adv*

> SYNONYMS **intelligent, bright, quick, smart, clever, able, gifted** CORE MEANING: having the ability to learn and understand easily

intelligentsia /in télli jéntsi ə/ *n* the most intellectual or highly educated members of a society

intelligible /in téllijəb'l/ *adj* understandable —**intelligibility** /in téllijə bílləti/ *n* —**intelligibly** *adv*

intemperate /in témpərət/ *adj* **1** drinking alcohol to excess **2** lacking self-control —**intemperance** *n* —**intemperately** *adv*

intend /in ténd/ *vt* **1** mean to do **2** do, say, or produce for a particular purpose

intendant /in téndənt/ *n* an administrative official in some countries

intended /in téndid/ *adj* **1** aimed at or designed for **2** planned for the future **3** said or done deliberately ■ *n* a future husband or wife (*dated or humorous*)

intense /in ténss/ *adj* **1** extreme in a way that can be felt o *intense heat* **2** involving great effort or activity **3** narrowly focused o *an intense stare* **4** showing deep serious emotions o *an intense student* —**intensely** *adv* —**intenseness** *n* —**intensity** /in ténssəti/ *n*

intensify /in ténssi fī/ (**-fies, -fied**) *vti* make or become greater or more intense —**intensification** /in ténssifi káysh'n/ *n* ◊ See note at **increase**

intensive /in ténssiv/ *adj* **1** involving concentrated effort **2** of modern agricultural methods that increase production **3** making heavy use of something (*often in combination*) o *capital-intensive* ■ *n* also **intensifier** a word that intensifies another word —**intensively** *adv* —**intensiveness** *n*

intensive care *n* a hospital department for patients who need constant monitoring

intent /in tént/ *n* **1** a plan or purpose **2** somebody's state of mind when committing or planning a crime ■ *adj* **1** with fixed attention **2** determined —**intently** *adv* —**intentness** *n* ◊ **to all intents and purposes** in effect

intention /in ténsh'n/ *n* **1** an aim or objective **2** the quality of having a purpose in mind o *act without intention*

intentional /in ténsh'nəl/ *adj* done on purpose —**intentionality** /in ténshə nálləti/ *n* —**intentionally** *adv*

inter /in túr/ (**-terring, -terred**) *vt* bury in a grave or tomb

inter- *prefix* **1** between, among o *intercut* **2** mutual, reciprocal o *interchange* **3** involving two or more groups o *international*

interact /íntər ákt/ *vi* **1** act on each other **2** communicate or work with somebody else or together

interaction /íntər áksh'n/ *n* **1** the process of interacting **2** any of the forces that exist between elementary particles, namely gravitational, electromagnetic, strong, and weak —**interactional** *adj*

interactive /íntər áktiv/ *adj* **1** communicating or collaborating **2** allowing or involving user-machine communication —**interactively** *adv* —**interactivity** /íntər ak tívvətee/ *n*

inter alia /íntər áyli ə, -aáli-, -álli-/ *adv* among other things

interbreed /íntər breéd/ (**-bred** /-bréd/) *vti* **1** mate with a member of a different breed or species

2 breed or make something breed within a closed group or a narrow range of types

intercede /intər seéd/ (-ceding, -ceded) vi 1 plead or speak on somebody's behalf 2 mediate in a dispute

intercept /intər sépt/ v 1 vti prevent people or objects from reaching their destination or target 2 vt in sport, get possession of the ball when it was intended for an opponent —**intercept** /íntər sépt/ n —**interception** n

interceptor /intər séptər/, **intercepter** n a fast fighter plane or guided missile designed to intercept enemy aircraft or missiles

intercession /intər sésh'n/ n 1 the act of interceding on somebody's behalf 2 a prayer on another's behalf —**intercessional** adj —**intercessor** /intər séssər, -sessər/ n

interchange v /intər cháynj/ (-changing, -changed) 1 vti switch places or the places of two things 2 vti alternate with each other in a series 3 vt give and receive in return ■ n /íntər chaynj/ 1 an exchange of ideas or information 2 the act of alternating or changing places 3 a major road junction at which vehicles do not cross other traffic to change direction

interchangeable /intər cháynjəb'l/ adj usable instead of another or each other —**interchangeably** adv

interchange fee n a fee paid by one bank to another to cover cardholder costs until payment is made

intercity /intər sítti/ adj happening or travelling between cities

intercollegiate /intərkə leéjət/ adj happening between colleges

intercom /íntər kom/ n a communications system between parts of a building

intercommunicate /intərkə myoóni kayt/ (-cating, -cated) vi 1 talk to each other 2 connect and have access to each other ○ intercommunicating hotel rooms —**intercommunication** /-myoóni káysh'n/ n —**intercommunicative** /-kətiv/ adj

interconnect /intərkə nékt/ vti 1 join onto one another 2 relate two or more things —**interconnection** n

intercontinental /íntər konti nént'l/ adj happening or travelling between continents

intercourse /íntər kawrss/ n 1 penetration of a woman's vagina by a man's penis 2 mutual dealings

intercut /intər kút/ (-cutting, -cut) vt alternate scenes during editing of a film to show events occurring simultaneously

interdenominational /íntər di nómmi náysh'nəl/ adj involving different religious denominations

interdepartmental /íntər dee paart mént'l/ adj involving different departments

interdependent /íntərdi péndənt/ adj 1 depending on each other to exist 2 relying on mutual support or cooperation —**interdepend** vi —**interdependence** n —**interdependently** adv

interdict n /íntər dikt/ an official order prohibiting something ■ vt /intər díkt/ ban by law —**interdiction** n

interdisciplinary /íntər díssiplinəri, -dissi plínnəri/ adj involving different subjects or fields of study

interest /íntrəst/ n 1 curiosity or concern 2 a power, quality, or aspect that attracts attention 3 an enjoyable activity (often pl) 4 the good or advantage of something ○ in the interests of peace 5 somebody's involvement in something that makes its outcome important ○ took a personal interest in the project 6 a borrowing charge or payment for a loan 7 a share in something 8 a personal connection that influences something ■ **interests** npl a group of people, especially influential people, who share an aim ■ vt 1 get the attention of 2 cause to want to have something

interested /íntrəstid/ adj 1 curious or concerned 2 wanting something 3 affected by or involved in something —**interestedly** adv

interesting /íntrəsting/ adj 1 arousing curiosity or attention 2 not boring —**interestingly** adv

interface /íntər fayss/ n 1 a surface or point forming a common boundary 2 a point of interaction 3 a common boundary between devices, or a person and a device, across which data flows 4 a piece of software that allows communication between devices or between a computer and its operator ■ vti (-facing, -faced) 1 meet or join at a common boundary 2 interact —**interfacial** /intər fáysh'l/ adj

~~interferance~~ incorrect spelling of **interference**

interfere /intər feér/ (-fering, -fered) vi 1 meddle in the affairs of others 2 delay or obstruct the course of something 3 cause electronic interference 4 touch somebody sexually in an unwelcome or criminal way (euphemistic) —**interfering** adj —**interferingly** adv

interference /intər feéranss/ n 1 meddling in other people's affairs 2 the delay or obstruction of the course of something 3 a signal that disrupts radio, telephone, or television reception —**interferential** /íntərfə rénsh'l/ adj

interferon /intər feér on/ n a protein produced by cells in response to virus infection that inhibits viral replication

intergalactic /íntərgə láktik/ adj occurring, moving, or situated between galaxies

intergovernmental /íntər gúvvərn mént'l, -gúvvər-/ adj between two or more governments

interim /íntərim/ adj 1 having a temporary effect 2 holding office until a permanent replacement can be elected or appointed ■ n the intervening time between events

interior /in teéri ər/ n 1 the inside of something 2 the inside of a building or room 3 the part of a country that is farthest from the coast 4 **Interior** the internal affairs of a country ■ adj 1 located inside 2 central or inland

3 occurring in the mind **4 Interior** of the internal affairs of a country

interior decoration *n* **1** the decorations and furnishings of a room or building **2** interior design —**interior decorator** *n*

interior design *n* the planning of the decoration and furnishings of a room or building —**interior designer** *n*

interject /intər jékt/ *vti* interrupt with a comment —**interjectory** *adj*

interjection /intər jéksh'n/ *n* **1** an exclamation expressing an emotion **2** a comment made abruptly —**interjectional** *adj*

interlace /intər láyss/ (-**lacing**, -**laced**) *v* **1** *vti* weave together **2** *vt* break up the flow or monotony of something with something else —**interlacement** *n*

interlard /intər laárd/ *vt* vary or interrupt speech or writing by inserting contrasting material

interleave /intər leév/ (-**leaving**, -**leaved**) *vt* add extra pages between the pages of a book

interlink /intər língk/ *vti* connect in several ways

interlock /intər lók/ *vti* **1** fit together closely **2** operate or cause to operate as a unit

interlocutor /intər lókyŏotar/ *n* a participant in a discussion or conversation (*fml*)

interloper /intər lópər/ *n* **1** an intruder **2** somebody who interferes in other people's affairs —**interlope** *vi*

interlude /intər lood/ *n* **1** a period of time during which something different happens **2** a short piece of entertainment performed during a break

intermarry /intər márri/ (-**ries**, -**ried**) *vi* **1** marry a member of another group **2** marry within a group —**intermarriage** *n*

intermediary /intər meédi əri/ *n* (*pl* -**ies**) **1** a go-between or mediator **2** a means or medium for bringing something about ■ *adj* **1** mediating **2** lying in between

intermediate[1] /intər meédi ət/ *adj* being between two different states or extremes —**intermediate** *n* —**intermediately** *adv*

intermediate[2] /intər meédi ayt/ (-**ating**, -**ated**) *vi* act as a go-between or mediator

intermediate technology *n* low-cost technology introduced in developing countries

interment /in túrmənt/ *n* the burial of a corpse

intermezzo /intər métsō, -médzō/ (*pl* -**zos** *or* -**zi** /-métsi, -médzi/) *n* **1** a short movement in a longer musical work **2** a short piece of music

interminable /in túrminəb'l/ *adj* seemingly endless —**interminably** *adv*

intermingle /intər míng g'l/ (-**gling**, -**gled**), **intermix** /intər míks/ *vti* mix together

intermission /intər mísh'n/ *n* **1** *US* an interval in a performance **2** a pause in an activity

intermittent /intər mítt'nt/ *adj* happening from time to time —**intermittently** *adv* ◊ See note at **periodic**

intern *v* /in túrn/ **1** *vt* detain in confinement on grounds of national security **2** *vi US, Can* work as an intern ■ *n* /in turn/ *also* **interne** **1** *Aus, US, Can* a junior doctor in a hospital **2** *US, Can* a trainee —**internment** *n* —**internship** *n*

internal /in túrn'l/ *adj* **1** located inside o *internal organs* **2** intended for use inside **3** inherent or natural **4** occurring within a country **5** occurring within the mind —**internally** *adv*

internal-combustion engine *n* an engine that burns fuel in chambers within it

internalize /in túrnə līz/ (-**izing**, -**ized**), **internalise** *vt* **1** adopt others' beliefs or attitudes **2** keep a problem to yourself and not express it —**internalization** /in túrnə līzáysh'n/ *n*

internal medicine *n* the branch of medicine dealing with the internal organs

international /intər násh'nəl/ *adj* **1** involving several countries or people from several countries **2** crossing national boundaries ■ *n* **1** a contest between teams from different countries **2** a member of an international team **3 International** any of various international socialist organizations —**internationality** /intər násh'n álləti/ *n* —**internationally** *adv*

International Atomic Time *n* a precise system of measuring time in which a second is defined in terms of atomic events

International Date Line *n* an internationally agreed imaginary line where the date changes by one day

internationalism /intər násh'nəlizəm/ *n* **1** cooperation between countries **2** interest in and respect for other countries

internationalize /intər násh'nə līz/ (-**izing**, -**ized**), **internationalise** *vt* **1** make international **2** put under international control or protection —**internationalization** /intər násh'nə līz áysh'n/ *n*

international relations *npl* relations between countries ■ *n* the study of relations between countries (+ *sing verb*)

interne *n US* = **intern**

internecine /intər neé sín/ *adj* **1** occurring within a group or organization **2** mutually destructive

ORIGIN The original meaning of **internecine** is 'attended by great slaughter'. Its modern connotations of 'conflict within a group' arose from the standard interpretation of *inter-* as 'among, between', but in fact in the case of Latin *internecinus* it was being used simply to add emphasis.

internee /intər neé/ *n* a prisoner who has been interned

Internet /intər net/, **internet** *n* a global computer network giving access to services such as e-mail and the World Wide Web

Internet hotel *n* a place with many computers handling Internet traffic for businesses

Internet protocol *n* a data transmission standard for the Internet

Internet service provider *n* a business offering Internet access to subscribers

internist /ín turnist/ *n* a specialist in diseases affecting the internal organs

interpenetrate /íntər pénni trayt/ (**-trating**) *vti* mix or weave together thoroughly —**interpenetration** /íntər pénni tráysh'n/ *n*

interpersonal /íntər púrss'nəl/ *adj* of relationships between people —**interpersonally** *adv*

interplanetary /íntər plánnitəri/ *adj* between planets

interplay /íntər play/ *n* mutual effect and interaction

Interpol /íntər pol/ *n* an association of national police forces that promotes international co-operation in apprehending criminals. Full form **International Criminal Police Organization**

interpolate /in túrpə layt/ (**-lating**, **-lated**) *vt* 1 insert something into something else 2 add words to a text —**interpolation** /in túrpə láysh'n/ *n*

interpose /íntər pốz/ (**-posing**, **-posed**) *v* 1 *vti* interrupt by saying something when somebody else is speaking 2 *vt* place something or yourself between people or things —**interposition** /íntərpə zísh'n/ *n*

~~interpretation~~ incorrect spelling of **interpretation**

interpret /in túrprit/ *v* 1 *vt* establish or explain the meaning of something 2 *vt* ascribe a meaning to something ○ *interpreted her response as a rejection* 3 *vt* perform something in a way that reflects your understanding of it or feelings about it 4 *vti* translate what somebody is saying in another language —**interpretable** *adj* —**interpretative** *adj* —**interpreter** *n* —**interpretive** *n*

interpretation /in túrpri táysh'n/ *n* 1 the establishment of the meaning of something 2 an ascription of a particular meaning to something —**interpretational** *adj*

interracial /íntər ráysh'l/ *adj* occurring between or involving different races —**interracially** *adv*

interregnum /íntər régnəm/ (*pl* **-nums** *or* **-na** /-régnə/) *n* 1 a time between one reign and the next 2 a time without government or control —**interregnal** *adj*

interrelate /íntər ri láyt/ (**-lating**, **-lated**) *vti* have or bring into a relationship —**interrelation** *n*

interrogate /in térrə gayt/ (**-gating**, **-gated**) *vt* 1 question somebody thoroughly 2 request a response from a computer device or program —**interrogation** /in térrə gáysh'n/ *n* —**interrogator** *n* ◊ See note at **question**

interrogative /íntə róggətiv/ *adj* 1 questioning 2 consisting of or used in asking a question ○ *an interrogative pronoun* ■ *n* 1 a word used to form a question 2 the form of a sentence that is used to ask a question —**interrogatively** *adv*

interrupt /íntə rúpt/ *v* 1 *vti* stop a speaker or a speaker's utterance 2 *vti* disturb somebody or somebody's work 3 *vt* cause something to stop 4 *vt* take a break from doing something ■ *n* 1 a signal to a computer processor to

suspend an operation 2 a circuit that conveys an interrupt signal —**interruption** *n*

interscholastic /íntərskə lástik/ *adj* occurring between schools

intersect /íntər sékt/ *vti* 1 cross 2 overlap

intersection /íntər séksh'n/ *n* 1 the act of intersecting 2 a place where two roads or paths cross 3 a crossing point 4 a point or set of points common to intersecting geometric figures —**intersectional** *adj*

intersperse /íntər spúrss/ (**-spersing**, **-spersed**) *vt* 1 break the continuity of something with something else 2 put something here and there in or among something else —**interspersion** *n*

interstate *adj* /íntər stáyt/ occurring between or connecting states ■ *n* /íntər stayt/ a major motorway between US cities ■ *adv Aus* to or in another state

interstellar /íntər stéllər/ *adj* occurring between stars

interstice /in túrstiss/ *n* a small space between two things or parts

interstitial /íntər stísh'l/ *adj* of interstices ■ *n* an unsolicited advertisement on the World Wide Web that briefly precedes a selected page

intertwine /íntər twín/ (**-twining**, **-twined**) *vti* 1 twist together 2 link together —**intertwinement** *n*

~~interrupt~~ incorrect spelling of **interrupt**

interval /íntərv'l/ *n* 1 an intervening period of time 2 an intervening distance 3 a break in a performance 4 a difference in musical pitch between two notes

intervene /íntər veén/ (**-vening**, **-vened**) *vi* 1 act to change what is happening 2 prevent or delay something by happening 3 elapse before an event or time ○ *the intervening years* —**intervention** /íntər vénsh'n/ *n*

interventionism /íntər vénsh'nizəm/ *n* 1 involvement in another country's affairs 2 government interference in economic matters —**interventionist** *n*, *adj*

interview /íntər vyoo/ *n* a meeting for asking somebody questions ■ *v* 1 *vt* ask somebody questions in an interview 2 *vi* perform in an interview ○ *interviews well* —**interviewee** /íntər vyoo eé/ *n* —**interviewer** *n*

interwar /íntər wáwr/ *adj* occurring between wars

interweave /íntər weév/ (**-weaving**, **-wove** /-wṓv/, **-woven** /-wṓv'n/) *vti* 1 weave together 2 combine

intestate /in tést ayt/ *adj* leaving no legally valid will —**intestacy** /in téstəssi/ *n*

intestine /in téstin/ *n* a part of the digestive tract between the stomach and the anus or an equivalent structure (*often pl*) —**intestinal** *adj*

intifada /ínti faádə/ *n* the Palestinian uprising in the West Bank and Gaza Strip that started in 1987

intimate[1] /íntimət/ *adj* 1 of a close personal

relationship **2** cosy and private **3** private and personal **4** involving or having a sexual relationship *(euphemistic)* **5** thorough and based on personal experience ■ *n* a close friend —**intimacy** *n* —**intimately** *adv*

intimate² /ínti mayt/ (**-mating, -mated**) *vt* hint quietly or subtly —**intimation** /ínti máysh'n/ *n*

intimidate /in tímmi dayt/ (**-dating, -dated**) *vt* **1** persuade or dissuade by frightening **2** cause to feel overawed or inadequate —**intimidatingly** *adv* —**intimidation** /in tímmi dáysh'n/ *n*

into *(stressed)* /íntoo/ *(unstressed)* /íntə, íntŏŏ/ *prep* **1** indicates movement to the interior or inner part ○ *came into the house* **2** indicates movement to the midst of ○ *leapt into the water* **3** indicates beginning to do or be involved in ○ *burst into action* ○ *went into marketing* **4** indicates contact with ○ *bumped into them* **5** indicates the result of change ○ *turned into a frog* **6** indicates the result of influence or persuasion ○ *talked me into going* **7** indicates division ○ *9 into 63 equals 7.* ○ *divided the cake into six* **8** enthusiastic about *(infml)* ○ *really into tennis*

intolerable /in tóllərəb'l/ *adj* **1** impossible to bear **2** very unpleasant —**intolerably** *adv*

intolerant /in tóllərənt/ *adj* **1** easily annoyed **2** not willing to accept cultural or ethnic differences —**intolerance** *n* —**intolerantly** *adv*

~~intolerent~~ incorrect spelling of **intolerant**

intonation /íntə náysh'n/ *n* **1** the rising and falling pitch of the voice **2** an intoning —**intonational** *adj*

intone /in tốn/ (**-toning, -toned**) *vt* say something in a solemn or chanting way *(fml)* —**intonement** *n*

in toto /in tốtō/ *adv* as a whole

intoxicant /in tóksikənt/ *n* an intoxicating substance —**intoxicant** *adj*

intoxicate /in tóksi kayt/ (**-cating, -cated**) *vt* **1** make drunk or stupefied **2** make highly excited —**intoxicated** *adj* —**intoxicatedly** *adv* —**intoxicating** *adj* —**intoxication** /-káysh'n/ *n*

intra- prefix within or inside

intracompany /íntrə kúmpəni/ *adj* occurring within a company

intractable /in tráktəb'l/ *adj* **1** strong-willed and rebellious *(fml)* **2** difficult to deal with or solve —**intractably** *adv* ◊ See note at **unruly**

intramural /íntrə myŏŏrəl/ *adj* occurring within a college or other institution

intranet /íntrə net/ *n* a computer network within an organization

intransigent /in tránssijənt, -zijənt/ *adj* refusing to compromise —**intransigence** *n*

intransitive /in tránssitiv/ *adj* describes a verb that does not require a direct object to complete its meaning —**intransitive** *n* —**intransitively** *adv*

intrapreneur /íntrəprə núr/ *n* an entrepreneur within a company —**intrapreneurial** *adj*

intrauterine /íntrə yŏŏtə rín/ *adj* occurring or designed for use inside the womb

intrauterine device *n* a contraceptive device inserted into the womb

intravenous /íntrə veénəss/ *adj* **1** occurring within or administered into a vein **2** used in administering fluids or drugs into the veins —**intravenously** *adv*

in-tray *n* a tray for incoming paperwork

intrepid /in tréppid/ *adj* fearless and persistent *(literary or humorous)* —**intrepidity** /íntrə píddəti/ *n* —**intrepidly** *adv*

~~intrest~~ incorrect spelling of **interest**

intricate /íntrikət/ *adj* **1** with many small or detailed parts **2** complex and difficult to understand or resolve —**intricacy** *n* —**intricately** *adv*

intrigue *n* /ín treeg, in treég/ **1** secret plotting **2** a secret plot ■ *v* /in treég/ (**-triguing, -trigued**) **1** *vt* interest or arouse the curiosity of **2** *vi* scheme —**intriguer** *n* —**intriguingly** *adv*

intrinsic /in trínssik/, **intrinsical** /-trínssik'l/ *adj* **1** basic and essential to what something is **2** by or in itself —**intrinsically** *adv*

intro /íntrō/ *n* an introduction *(infml)*

intro- prefix **1** in, into ○ *introduce* **2** inward ○ *introvert*

introduce /íntrə dyóoss/ (**-ducing, -duced**) *vt* **1** present yourself or another person to a stranger **2** bring in something new **3** cause somebody to experience something new **4** preface something with something else **5** talk about something for the first time **6** insert one thing into another

introduction /íntrə dúksh'n/ *n* **1** an explanatory section at the beginning of a book or other text **2** something giving the basic facts about something **3** the act of introducing somebody or something **4** a first experience **5** the beginning of a piece of music

introductory /íntrə dúktəri/ *adj* **1** introducing what is to come **2** providing the basic facts or skills

introspection /íntrə spéksh'n/ *n* the examination of your own feelings —**introspective** *adj* —**introspectively** *adv*

introvert /íntrə vurt/ *n* **1** a reserved person **2** somebody focusing on his or her own self ■ *vt* turn something inwards —**introversion** /íntrə vúrsh'n/ *n* —**introverted** *adj*

intrude /in trŏŏd/ (**-truding, -truded**) *vi* **1** invade somebody's privacy **2** have an unpleasant effect

intruder /in trŏŏdər/ *n* **1** somebody who enters illegally **2** an unwelcome person

intrusion /in trŏŏzh'n/ *n* **1** a disturbance of somebody's peace or privacy **2** something unwelcome —**intrusive** /in trŏŏssiv/ *adj* —**intrusively** *adv*

intuit /in tyŏŏ it/ *vt* know instinctively

intuition /íntyoo ísh'n/ *n* **1** instinctive knowledge, or the ability to know things instinctively **2** something known instinctively —**intuitional** *adj* —**intuitive** /in tyŏŏ itiv/ *adj* —**intuitively** *adv* —**intuitiveness** *n*

~~inuendo~~ incorrect spelling of **innuendo**

Inuit /ínnóo it, -yōō-/ (*pl same or* **-its**), **Innuit** *n* 1 a member of a people of the Arctic or Greenland 2 the language of the Inuit people —**Inuit** *adj*

inundate /ín un dayt, ínnən-/ (**-dating, -dated**) *vt* 1 overwhelm with a huge quantity of things 2 flood with water *(fml)* —**inundation** /ín un dáysh'n, ínnən-/ *n*

invade /in váyd/ (**-vading, -vaded**) *v* 1 *vti* enter a country by military force 2 *vt* enter and spread through something, especially causing damage 3 *vt* go somewhere in large numbers o *has been invaded by tourists* 4 *vt* spoil something by interrupting or intruding on it o *invading our privacy* —**invader** *n*

invalid[1] /in vállid/ *adj* 1 not legal 2 based on a mistake —**invalidity** /ínvə líddəti/ *n* —**invalidly** *adv*

invalid[2] /ínvəlid, -leed/ *n* somebody with an incapacitating disease or medical condition ■ *vt* send away because of illness o *was invalided out of the army* —**invalid** *adj*

invalidate /in válli dayt/ (**-dating, -dated**) *vt* 1 make not legal 2 show to be wrong or worthless —**invalidation** /in válli dáysh'n/ *n* ◊ See note at **nullify**

invaluable /in vállyoo əb'l/ *adj* extremely useful or valuable —**invaluably** *adv*

invariable /in váiri əb'l/ *adj* never changing ■ *n* a constant quantity —**invariability** /in váiri ə bílləti/ *n* —**invariably** *adv*

invasion /in váyzh'n/ *n* 1 an entry into a country by military force 2 an arrival in large numbers 3 a spoiling of something by interrupting or intruding on it

invasive /in váyssiv/ *adj* 1 involving military invasion 2 intruding on somebody's privacy or rights 3 attacking adjacent tissue —**invasively** *adv*

invective /in véktiv/ *n* abusive language *(fml)*

inveigh /in váy/ *vi* speak out angrily

ORIGIN When first adopted in the late 15C, **inveigh** meant 'carry in, introduce'. This accords with the etymological meaning of Latin *invehere*, from which it derives. *Vehere* is also the source of *vehicle*. Latin *invehere* had also developed a form meaning 'attack, assault with words', and this was taken into English in the early 16C.

inveigle /in váyg'l, -vée-/ (**-gling, -gled**) *vt* 1 persuade or entice 2 obtain by persuasion —**inveiglement** *n*

invent /in vént/ *vt* 1 create something new 2 make up something false o *invented a reason for being late* —**inventor** *n*

invention /in vénsh'n/ *n* 1 a newly created thing 2 the creating of something new 3 a lie *(euphemistic)*

inventive /in véntiv/ *adj* 1 skilled at inventing 2 displaying creativity —**inventively** *adv* —**inventiveness** *n*

inventory /ínvəntəri/ *n* (*pl* **-ries**) 1 a list of items 2 a record of a business's assets, or the assets themselves 3 a stock of goods ■ *vt* (**-ries, -ried**) make an inventory of

Inverclyde /ínvər klíd/ council area in SW Scotland

Inverness /ínvər néss/ city in N Scotland. Pop. 63,850 (1993).

inverse /in vúrss, ín vurss/ *adj* opposite to or reversing something —**inverse** *n* —**inversely** *adv*

inversion /in vúrsh'n/ *n* a reversal of the order or position of the parts of something

invert /in vúrt/ *vt* 1 reverse the order or position of the parts of something 2 make something the opposite of what it was before —**inverted** *adj* —**invertible** *adj*

invertebrate /in vúrtibrət/ *n* an animal without a backbone —**invertebrate** *adj*

inverted comma *n* each of a pair of punctuation marks used to enclose direct speech and quotations

USAGE Inverted commas are used to enclose direct speech and quotations: *'Where are you?'* he called. Mae West said, *'A man in the house is worth two in the street'*. They are also used around some titles, e.g. those of poems, short stories, and articles: *Hilaire Belloc's poem 'On a Sundial'*, but titles of novels, plays, films, etc. are conventionally printed in italics instead. Inverted commas are often used to make a particular word or phrase stand out from the surrounding text, usually to draw attention to it or because the author is using it self-consciously or sceptically: *words such as 'toothbrush' and 'redcurrant'; a more 'family-friendly' environment.* Either single (' ') or double (" ") inverted commas may be used in all these cases. Where one piece of direct speech occurs within another, or within a quotation, use inverted commas of the opposite type: *She said, 'I told him to leave and he asked "Why should I?"'*

invest /in vést/ *v* 1 *vti* use money to buy shares or bonds 2 *vti* deposit money in an account that pays interest 3 *vti* spend money on a project 4 *vt* contribute time or effort to something 5 *vt* give something a particular quality 6 *vt* confer something such as authority on a person or group —**investor** *n*

investigate /in vésti gayt/ (**-gating, -gated**) *v* 1 *vti* carry out an official examination or enquiry into something 2 *vi* go and have a look —**investigation** /in vésti gáysh'n/ *n* —**investigative** *adj* —**investigator** *n*

investiture /in véstichər/ *n* the formal installation of somebody in an official position

investment /in véstmənt/ *n* 1 the use of money for future profit 2 an amount of money invested 3 something invested in 4 the contribution of time or effort to an activity

investment analyst *n* a stock exchange researcher

investment trust *n* a legally constituted group of investors

inveterate /in véttərət/ *adj* 1 doing something habitually 2 firmly established —**inveteracy** *n* —**inveterately** *adv*

invidious /in víddi əss/ *adj* 1 involving an unfair distinction 2 unpleasant and likely to cause resentment —**invidiously** *adv* —**invidiousness** *n*

invigilate /in víjji layt/ (**-lating, -lated**) *vti* supervise the taking of an exam —**invigilation** /in víjji láysh'n/ *n*

invigorate /in víggə rayt/ (**-ating, -ated**) *vt* fill with energy —**invigorating** *adj* —**invigoratingly** *adv* —**invigoration** /in víggə ráysh'n/ *n*

invincible /in vínssəb'l/ *adj* 1 unbeatable 2 too great or difficult to overcome —**invincibility** /in vínssə bílləti/ *n* —**invincibly** *adv*

inviolable /in ví aləb'l/ *adj* 1 secure from infringement 2 secure from attack —**inviolability** /in ví ələ bílləti/ *n* —**inviolably** *adv*

inviolate /in ví ələt/ *adj* not subject to detrimental change —**inviolately** *adv*

invisible /in vízzəb'l/ *adj* 1 impossible to see 2 hidden 3 not easily noticed —**invisibility** /in vízzə bílləti/ *n* —**invisibly** *adv*

invisible ink *n* a liquid used to write things that remain invisible until the paper is treated in some way

invitation /ínvi táysh'n/ *n* 1 a spoken or written message inviting somebody 2 the act of inviting ■ *adj* open only to those asked —**invitational** *adj, n*

invite *vt* /in vít/ (**-viting, -vited**) 1 ask to come somewhere or participate in something 2 welcome 3 provoke ■ *n* /in vít/ an invitation (*infml*)

inviting /in víting/ *adj* suggesting or offering pleasure o *an inviting smell* —**invitingly** *adv*

in vitro /in veétró/ *adj, adv* in an artificial environment such as a test tube

in vitro fertilization *n* fertilization achieved in laboratory conditions outside a living organism

invocation /ínvə káysh'n/ *n* 1 a calling upon a higher power 2 a prayer forming part of a service —**invocational** *adj*

invoice /in voyss/ *n* a written record of goods or services provided and a request for payment ■ *vt* (**-voicing, -voiced**) send an invoice to

invoke /in vók/ (**-voking, -voked**) *vt* 1 call upon a higher power 2 use something in support of an argument or case

involuntary /in vóllantəri/ *adj* 1 required or done against somebody's will 2 spontaneous and automatic —**involuntarily** *adv*

involve /in vólv/ (**-volving, -volved**) *vt* 1 contain as a necessary element 2 concern or have to do with 3 cause to participate 4 embroil or implicate 5 engross —**involved** *adj* —**involvement** *n* —**involving** *adj*

invulnerable /in vúlnərəb'l/ *adj* 1 unable to be hurt 2 safe from attack —**invulnerability** /in vúlnərə bílləti/ *n* —**invulnerably** *adv*

inward /ínnwərd/ *adj* 1 situated inside 2 of the mind or spirit ■ *adv also* **inwards** /ínnwərdz/ 1 towards the inside or centre 2 towards the mind or spirit —**inwardness** *n*

inward-looking *adj* preoccupied with your own concerns

inwardly /ínnwərdli/ *adv* 1 to or in yourself 2 on or to the inside

I/O *abbr* input/output

iodine /í ə deen/ *n* 1 (*symbol* I) a nonmetallic crystalline halogen element. Use: pharmaceuticals, dyes, isotopes in medicine and industry. 2 an antiseptic containing dissolved iodine

ORIGIN **Iodine** was coined by Sir Humphry Davy in 1814 as an extension of French *iode*, the name given to the element by the French physicist Joseph-Louis Gay-Lussac (1778–1850). He based it on Greek *iōdēs* 'violet-coloured', because heated iodine crystals produce a purple vapour.

iodize /í ə díz/ (**-dizing, -dized**), **iodise** *vt* treat with iodine —**iodization** /í ə dí záysh'n/ *n*

ion /í ən, í on/ *n* an electrically charged atom or atom group —**ionic** /ī ónnik/ *adj*

-ion *suffix* 1 action or process o *eruption* o *erosion* 2 result of an action or process o *abrasion*

Ionesco /eè ə nésk ó/, **Eugène** (1912–94) Romanian-born French dramatist

Ionia /ī óni ə/ ancient region of W Asia Minor, on the Aegean coast —**Ionian** *adj, n*

Ionian Islands /ī óni ən-/ group of seven Greek islands in the Ionian and Mediterranean seas. Pop. 191,003 (1991).

Ionian Sea arm of the Mediterranean Sea between SE Italy and W Greece

Ionic /ī ónnik/ *adj* of a classical architectural order characterized by columns with a scroll-like ornamentation at the top

ionize /í ə níz/ (**-izing, -ized**), **ionise** *vti* change into ions —**ionization** /í ə nī záysh'n/ *n*

ionosphere /ī ónnə sfeer/ *n* the ionized layers in the upper atmosphere —**ionospheric** /ī ónnə sférrik/ *adj*

iota /ī ótə/ *n* 1 the 9th letter of the Greek alphabet 2 a very small amount o *anyone with an iota of sense*

IOU *n* a written record of a debt

Iowa /í əwə/ state in the north-central United States. Cap. Des Moines. Pop. 2,926,324 (2000). —**Iowan** *adj, n*

IP *abbr* 1 image processing 2 Internet protocol

IPO *abbr* initial public offering

ipso facto /ípsō fáktō/ *adv* because of a particular fact

IQ *n* a measure of intelligence obtained through a series of aptitude tests. Full form **intelligence quotient**

Iqbal /ík bal/, **Sir Muhammad** (1875–1938) Indian philosopher, poet, and political leader

Ir *symbol* iridium

IR *abbr* **1** information retrieval **2** infrared (radiation) **3** Inland Revenue

IRA *n* an Irish nationalist organization. Full form **Irish Republican Army**

Iran /i ráàn, i rán/ country in SW Asia. Cap. Tehran. Pop. 66,128,965 (2001).

Iranian /i ráyni ən/ *n* **1** a large group of languages spoken in the region northeast of the Persian Gulf **2** somebody from Iran —**Iranian** *adj*

Iran-Iraq War *n* the war (1980–88) between Iran and Iraq, following Iraq's invasion of border territory in Iran

Iraq /i ráàk, i rák/ country in SW Asia. Cap. Baghdad. Pop. 23,331,985 (2001).

Iraqi /i ráàki, i ráki/ *n* **1** somebody from Iraq **2** the Arabic dialect of Iraq —**Iraqi** *adj*

irascible /i rássəb'l/ *adj* quick-tempered —**irascibility** /i rássə bílləti/ *n* —**irascibly** *adv*

irate /ī ráyt/ *adj* very angry —**irately** *adv* —**irateness** *n*

~~**irational**~~ incorrect spelling of **irrational**

IRC *abbr* Internet relay chat *(in e-mails)*

ire *n* great anger *(fml)* ◊ See note at **anger**

Ireland /írlənd/ **1** island of NW Europe, in the North Atlantic Ocean, comprising the Republic of Ireland and the British province of Northern Ireland **2** country occupying most of the island of Ireland. Cap. Dublin. Pop. 3,840,838 (2001).

Ireland, Northern ♦ Northern Ireland

iridescent /írri déss'nt/ *adj* having lustrous rainbow colours —**iridescence** *n*

iridium /i ríddi əm, ī-/ *n* (*symbol* **Ir**) a silver-white metallic element. Use: corrosion-resistant alloys.

iris /íriss/ *n* **1** the coloured part of an eye **2** a flowering plant with large sword-shaped leaves

Irish /írish/ *adj* **1** of Ireland **2** of the Gaelic language of Ireland **3** of the English dialect of Ireland ■ *npl* the people from Ireland ■ *n* the Gaelic language of Ireland —**Irishman** *n* —**Irishness** *n* —**Irishwoman** *n*

Irish coffee *n* coffee with Irish whiskey, topped with whipped cream

Irish Gaelic *n* an official language of the Republic of Ireland —**Irish Gaelic** *adj*

Irish moss *n* an edible seaweed

Irish Sea arm of the N Atlantic Ocean between Great Britain and Ireland

Irish setter *n* a large dog with a reddish coat

Irish stew *n* a lamb and potato stew

Irish whiskey *n* whisky made in Ireland

irk *vt* annoy slightly ◊ See note at **annoy, bother**

irksome /úrksəm/ *adj* slightly annoying —**irksomely** *adv* —**irksomeness** *n*

Irkutsk /ur kóotsk, eer-/ city in S Siberian Russia. Pop. 668,449 (1995).

IRO *abbr* international relief organization

iron /ī ərn/ *n* **1** (*symbol* **Fe**) a metallic element. Use: engineering and structural products.

2 a heated tool made of iron or steel ○ *a soldering iron* **3** an appliance with a flat metal base, used for pressing clothes **4** a metal-headed golf club **5** a hard, strong, or unyielding quality ○ *a will of iron* ■ **irons** *npl* manacles or fetters for the arms or legs ■ *adj* **1** made of iron **2** very strong or tough **3** determined or cruel ■ *vti* press clothes with an iron ◇ **pump iron** do weightlifting exercises *(slang)*

□ **iron out** *vt* settle a problem or resolve a dispute by removing difficulties

Iron Age *n* the archaeological period immediately after the Bronze Age, when iron was increasingly used

ironclad /ī ərn klad/ *adj* **1** covered or protected with iron plates **2** not liable to be contradicted or changed ○ *an ironclad agreement*

Iron Curtain *n* the militarized border and policy of isolation that prevented W and E Europeans from communicating freely during the Cold War

ironic /ī rónnik/, **ironical** /ī rónnik'l/ *adj* **1** involving irony **2** △ involving a surprising or apparently contradictory fact —**ironically** *adv* ◊ See note at **sarcastic**

USAGE Do not use **irony**, **ironic**, and **ironically** to refer to coincidental or improbable situations, as opposed to truly incongruous ones: *Coincidentally* [not *Ironically*] *both the defence counsel and the prosecutor graduated from the same university.*

ironing /ī ərning/ *n* **1** the act of pressing clothes **2** clothes for pressing

ironing board *n* a board for ironing clothes on

iron man *n* **1** a strong man **2** *also* **Iron Man** *ANZ*, *US* a men's sports competition held on a beach and including a variety of disciplines

ironmonger /ī ərn mung gər/ *n UK* a dealer in metal goods —**ironmongery** *n*

iron rations *npl* emergency food

ironstone /ī ərn stōn/ *n* **1** an iron-bearing sedimentary rock **2** a hard white pottery

ironware /ī ərn wair/ *n* iron goods

Iron Woman *n ANZ*, *US* a women's sports competition held on a beach and including a variety of disciplines

ironwork /ī ərn wurk/ *n* something made of iron, e.g. a decorative gate

ironworks /ī ərn wurks/ *n* (*pl same*) a factory where iron is smelted or heavy iron goods are made (+ *sing or pl verb*)

irony /írəni/ *n* (*pl* **-nies**) **1** humour based on words suggesting the opposite of their literal meaning **2** something humorous based on contradiction **3** incongruity between what actually happens and what might be expected ◊ See note at **ironic**

ORIGIN Irony has nothing to do with *iron*. It came through Latin from a Greek word that meant 'pretended ignorance'. It referred particularly to a device taught by the philosopher Socrates as a way of getting the better of an opponent in argument, and this was one of its earliest meanings in English.

irradiate /i ráydi ayt/ (**-ating, -ated**) *vt* **1** expose to radiation **2** light up —**irradiation** /i ráydi áysh'n/ *n*

irrational /i rásh'nəl/ *adj* **1** contrary to or lacking in reason or logic **2** unable to think clearly —**irrationality** /i rásh'n álləti/ *n* —**irrationally** *adv*

irrational number *n* a real number that is not rational

Irrawaddy /írrə wóddi/ principal river of Myanmar. Length 2,100 km/1,300 mi.

irreconcilable /i rékən síləb'l/ *adj* **1** incompatible **2** unresolvable —**irreconcilably** *adv*

irrecoverable /írri kúvvərəb'l/ *adj* incapable of being regained or repaired —**irrecoverably** *adv*

irredeemable /írri deémbəb'l/ *adj* **1** unable to be bought back or paid off **2** irrecoverable **3** not convertible into coins **4** incapable of reforming or being saved —**irredeemably** *adv*

irreducible /írri dyoóssəb'l/ *adj* **1** incapable of being decreased **2** incapable of simplification —**irreducibly** *adv*

irrefutable /írri fyoótəb'l, i réffyoótəb'l/ *adj* incapable of being refuted or disproved —**irrefutably** *adv*

irregardless /írri gaárdləss/ *adv* △ regardless (*nonstandard*)

USAGE Since the prefix *ir-* means 'not' (as it does in *irrespective*), and the suffix *-less* means 'without', **irregardless** is a double negative and regarded as nonstandard. Use instead *irrespective* or *regardless*.

irregular /i réggyoólər/ *adj* **1** not of uniform appearance **2** occurring at odd intervals **3** not conforming to accepted rules, standards, or practices **4** not forming part of an official military body **5** not following the usual rules of word formation o *an irregular verb* ■ *n* a soldier who is not part of the regular forces —**irregularity** /i réggyoó lárrəti/ *n* —**irregularly** *adv*

irrelevant /i rélləvənt/ *adj* not relevant —**irrelevance** *n* —**irrelevantly** *adv*

~~irrelevent~~ incorrect spelling of **irrelevant**

irreligious /írri líjjəss/ *adj* **1** lacking any religious faith **2** against religion —**irreligiously** *adv* —**irreligiousness** *n*

irremediable /írri meédi əb'l/ *adj* incapable of being remedied —**irremediably** *adv*

irreparable /i réppərəb'l/ *adj* not repairable or able to be put right —**irreparably** *adv*

irreplaceable /írri pláyssəb'l/ *adj* incapable of being replaced —**irreplaceably** *adv*

irrepressible /írri préssəb'l/ *adj* not able to be controlled —**irrepressibility** /írri préssə bílləti/ *n* —**irrepressibly** *adv*

irreproachable /írri próchəb'l/ *adj* beyond criticism —**irreproachably** *adv*

~~irresistable~~ incorrect spelling of **irresistible**

irresistible /írri zístəb'l/ *adj* **1** unable to be resisted or successfully opposed **2** very desirable —**irresistibility** /írri zístə bílləti/ *n* —**irresistibly** *adv*

irresolute /i rézzə loot/ *adj* incapable of deciding —**irresolutely** *adv* —**irresolution** /i rézzə loósh'n/ *n*

irrespective /írri spéktiv/ *adv* regardless (*infml*) —**irrespectively** *adv* ◊ **irrespective of** without taking into account ◊ See note at **irregardless**

irresponsible /írri spónssəb'l/ *adj* not caring about the consequences of personal actions —**irresponsibility** /írri spónssə bílləti/ *n* —**irresponsibly** *adv*

irretrievable /írri treévəb'l/ *adj* **1** not recoverable after being lost **2** irreparable —**irretrievability** /írri treévə bílləti/ *n* —**irretrievably** *adv*

~~irrevelant~~ incorrect spelling of **irrelevant**

~~irreverent~~ incorrect spelling of **irreverent**

irreverent /i révvərənt/ *adj* lacking in respect —**irreverence** *n* —**irreverently** *adv*

irreversible /írri vúrssəb'l/ *adj* incapable of reversal —**irreversibility** /írri vúrssə bílləti/ *n* —**irreversibly** *adv*

irrevocable /i révvəkəb'l/ *adj* impossible to revoke, undo, or change —**irrevocability** /i révvəkə bílləti/ *n* —**irrevocably** *adv*

irrigate /írri gayt/ (**-gating, -gated**) *vt* **1** supply a dry area with water for growing crops **2** make water or liquid medication flow through or over a body part or wound —**irrigable** *adj* —**irrigation** /írri gáysh'n/ *n*

irritable /írritəb'l/ *adj* **1** easily annoyed **2** sensitive, especially to inflammation —**irritability** /írritə bílləti/ *n* —**irritably** *adv*

irritable bowel syndrome *n* a bowel condition in which there is recurrent pain with constipation or diarrhoea

irritant /írritənt/ *adj* causing irritation —**irritant** *n*

irritate /írri tayt/ (**-tating, -tated**) *v* **1** *vti* annoy somebody **2** *vt* produce a painful reaction in —**irritating** *adj* —**irritatingly** *adv* —**irritation** /írri táysh'n/ *n* ◊ See note at **anger, annoy**

irrupt /i rúpt/ *vi* **1** enter abruptly **2** increase quickly —**irruption** *n*

Irtysh ♦ Ob'-Irtysh

Irving /úrving/, **Sir Henry** (1838–1905) British actor and theatrical manager

is /iz/ 3rd person present singular of **be**

IS *abbr* information services

is. *abbr* island

Is. *abbr* Island (*in placenames*)

ISA *abbr* individual savings account

Isabella I /ízzə béllə/ (1451–1504) queen of Castile and León (1474–1504)

ISBN *abbr* International Standard Book Number

ISDN *n* a digital telephone network that can transmit sound and data. Full form **Integrated Services Digital Network**

ISE *abbr* International Stock Exchange

-ise *suffix* = **-ize**

-ish *suffix* **1** characteristic of, like, tending to ○ *babyish* **2** of or relating to, from ○ *Polish* **3** somewhat, approximately ○ *brownish*

Isherwood /Íshərwŏŏd/, **Christopher** (1904–86) British-born US writer

isinglass /Ízing glaass/ *n* **1** a gelatin used as a clarifying agent and in adhesives and jellies **2** mica

Isis /Íssiss/ *n* Egyptian mother goddess

Islam /Íz laam, iss-/ *n* **1** a monotheistic religion based on the word of God as revealed to Muhammad and on his teachings **2** the Muslim world —**Islamic** /iz lámmik, iss-/ *adj*

Islamabad /iz lámmə bad/ capital of Pakistan. Pop. 791,085 (1998).

Islamism /Ízz-, Ísslə-/ *n* **1** a conservative Islamic political movement **2** the religion or principles of Islam —**Islamist** *adj, n*

Islamize /Ízzlə mīz, Íssla-/ (-izing, -ized), **Islamise** *vt* **1** convert to Islam **2** make subject to Islamic law —**Islamization** /Ízzlə mī záysh'n, Íssla-/ *n*

island /Íland/ *n* **1** a land mass surrounded by water *(often in placenames)* **2** something like an island in being isolated or surrounded by something different —**islander** *n*

ORIGIN Despite their similarity, **island** and *isle* have completely different origins. **Island** goes back to a compound formed from an ancient root meaning 'water' combined with the word *land*. *Isle* comes from Latin *insula*, meaning 'island'. The resemblance is due to a 16C change in the spelling of **island** under the influence of the semantically close *isle*.

isle /Íl/ *n* an island *(literary)* ◊ See note at **aisle**

Isle of Man island in the Irish Sea, a self-governing Crown dependency of the United Kingdom. Cap. Douglas. Pop. 69,788 (1991).

Isle of Wight /-wīt/ island off S England. Pop. 125,100 (1995).

islet /Ílət/ *n* a small island

-ism *suffix* **1** action, process ○ *mesmerism* **2** characteristic behaviour or manner ○ *despotism* **3** state, condition ○ *conservatism* **4** unusual or unhealthy state ○ *alcoholism* **5** doctrine, system of beliefs ○ *defeatism* **6** prejudice ○ *sexism*

Ismail Samani Peak /Íss mī eèl sə maàni-/ highest peak in Tajikistan. Height 7,495 m /24,590 ft.

isn't /Ízz'nt/ *contr* is not

isobar /Íssō baar/ *n* a line on a weather map connecting places with equal atmospheric pressure —**isobaric** /Íssō bárrik/ *adj*

isoceles incorrect spelling of **isosceles**

isolate /Íssə layt/ (-lating, -lated) *vt* **1** separate from others **2** put in quarantine —**isolation** /Íssō láysh'n/ *n*

isolated /Íssə laytid/ *adj* **1** far away from other inhabited areas **2** alone or lonely **3** rare and unlikely to recur ○ *an isolated incident*

isolationism /Íssə láysh'nizəm/ *n* a national policy of avoidance of international relations —**isolationist** *n, adj*

isomer /Íssəmər/ *n* **1** one of two or more molecules with the same number of atoms but different chemical structures **2** one of two or more nuclides with the same mass number but different energy states —**isomeric** /Íssō mérrik/ *adj*

isometric /Íssō méttrik/, **isometrical** /-méttrik'l/ *adj* **1** equal in dimension or measurement **2** involving pushing the muscles against something —**isometrically** *adv*

isometrics /Íssō méttriks/ *n* isometric exercise (+ *sing* or *pl verb*)

isosceles /Í sóssə leez/ *adj* describes a triangle with two sides of equal length ○ *an isosceles triangle*

isotherm /Íssō thurm/ *n* a line on a weather map connecting places with equal or constant temperature —**isothermal** *adj*

isotonic /Íssə tónnik/ *adj* **1** of muscle contraction under relatively constant tension **2** with equal osmotic pressure **3** containing the same concentration of salts and minerals as the body ○ *isotonic drinks* —**isotonically** *adv*

isotope /Íssətōp/ *n* each of two or more forms of an element with the same atomic number —**isotopic** /Íssə tóppik/ *adj*

ISP *abbr* Internet service provider

I-spy *n* a children's guessing game in which one player gives the initial letter of something visible and others try to identify it

Israel /Íz rayl/ country in SW Asia, on the eastern shore of the Mediterranean Sea. Cap. Jerusalem. Pop. 5,938,093 (2001). —**Israeli** /iz ráyli/ *n, adj*

Israelite /Ízzri ə līt, Ízzrə-/ *n* a member of an ancient Hebrew people descended from Jacob —**Israelitic** /Ízzri ə líttik, Ízzrə-/ *adj*

Isreal incorrect spelling of **Israel**

issue /Íssyoo, Íshoo/ *n* **1** a subject of concern **2** the main subject in a debate **3** a copy of a publication for a particular date **4** a set of things made available for sale at the same time **5** the official distribution of something ○ *the issue of parking permits* **6** something officially distributed ○ *government issue rations* **7** offspring ○ *died without issue* **8** △ a source of conflict, misgiving, or emotional distress *(infml)* ○ *had issues with some of her suggestions* ■ *v* (-suing, -sued) **1** *vt* supply or distribute officially **2** *vt* release as a public statement or warning **3** *vt* release for sale at a particular time **4** *vt* publish **5** *vi* come out from somewhere ○ *Smoke issued from the burning building.* —**issuer** *n* ◊ **at issue** under discussion or to be decided ◊ **take issue** disagree

USAGE Avoid using **issue** as a vague substitute for *problem*, *difficulty*, or *point of disagreement* or to denote intentionally unstated emotions, typically emotional or mental, as in *He's one of those people who always has issues.*

-ist *suffix* **1** somebody practising a particular skill or profession o *psychologist* **2** somebody following a particular belief or school of thought o *idealist* **3** somebody playing a particular instrument o *guitarist* **4** somebody prejudiced against a particular social group o *racist* —**-istic** *suffix*

Istanbul /íss tan bóol/ largest city in Turkey, on the Bosporus. Pop. 8,274,921 (1997).

isthmus /íssməss, ísth-/ (*pl* **-muses** *or* **-mi** /-mī/) **1** a narrow strip of land connecting two larger masses **2** a narrow connection or passage between body parts —**isthmian** *adj, n*

it *pron* **1** refers to an object, animal, or abstraction **2** indicates a particular situation or point of view o *won't talk about it* o *It's strange.* **3** indicates something reported o *it was said that* **4** indicates weather or temperature o *It's raining and cold.* **5** indicates time o *It's six o'clock.* **6** emphasizes a following clause o *It's you who's always complaining.* ■ *n* the player in children's games who must catch or find the others

IT *abbr* information technology

Italian /i tállyən/ *n* **1** somebody from Italy **2** the language of Italy —**Italian** *adj* —**Italianate** *adj*

italic /i tállik/ *adj* printed, written, or using letters sloping to the right ■ *n* **1** an italic letter (*often pl*) **2** **Italic** the language family that includes Latin

italicize /i tálli sīz/ (**-cizing, -cized**), **italicise** *vt* print in italic type —**italicization** /i tálli sī záysh'n/ *n*

Italy /íttəli/ country in S Europe. Cap. Rome. Pop. 57,679,825 (2001).

itch *v* **1** *vti* make somebody want to scratch the skin **2** *vi* be eager ■ *n* **1** a feeling of wanting to scratch **2** an eager longing for something —**itchiness** *n* —**itching** *n* —**itchy** *adj*

it'd *contr* **1** it had **2** it would

-ite *suffix* **1** mineral, rock, ore, soil, fossil o *graphite* **2** descendant or follower of o *Trotskyite* **3** native or resident of o *urbanite* **4** salt or ester of an acid with a name ending in *-ous* o *sulphite*

item /ítəm/ *n* **1** one thing in a collection **2** one thing in a list **3** a broadcast or published report **4** a couple in a relationship (*infml*)

ORIGIN **Item** comes from a Latin adverb meaning 'likewise'.

itemize /ítə mīz/ (**-izing, -ized**), **itemise** *vt* list the individual things in a set of related things o *an itemized bill* —**itemization** /ítə mī záysh'n/ *n*

iteration /íttə ráysh'n/ *n* a repetition —**iterate** /íttə rayt/ *vt* —**iterative** /íttərətiv/ *adj*

Ithaca /íthəkə/ city in south-central New York State. Pop. 28,172 (1998).

itinerant /ī tínnərənt/ *adj* travelling to find or perform work —**itinerant** *n*

itinerary /ī tínnərəri/ (*pl* **-ies**) *n* **1** a list of places to be visited **2** a record of a journey

-itis *suffix* inflammation, disease o *dermatitis*

it'll *contr* it will

its *det* of or belonging to it

USAGE **its** or **it's**? The possessive form of the pronoun *it* is **its**, even though it does not have an apostrophe before the *s*: *The cat is licking its* [not *it's*] *paws*. **It's** is a contraction for *it is* or *it has*: *It's* [not *Its*] *going to rain tonight*.

it's *contr* **1** it has **2** it is

itself /it sélf/ *pron* **1** refers back to something that is the subject of the verb o *His ignorance finally revealed itself.* **2** emphasizes something just mentioned o *The house itself was cheap.*

ITV *abbr* Independent Television

IUD *abbr* intrauterine device

IV *abbr* intravenous

Ivan IV /ívən/ (1530–84) tsar of Russia (1547–84)

I've *contr* I have

-ive *suffix* tending to or performing o *illustrative*

IVF *abbr* in vitro fertilization

ivory /ívəri/ *n* (*pl* **-ries**) **1** the material of the tusks of elephants and some other animals **2** something made of ivory **3** a creamy-white colour ■ **ivories** *npl* **1** piano keys (*infml*) **2** teeth (*slang*) —**ivory** *adj*

Ivory Coast former name for **Côte d'Ivoire**

ivory tower *n* a state or situation separated from real-life problems

ORIGIN **Ivory tower** is a translation of French *tour d'ivoire*, which was first used in 1837 by the writer Charles-Augustin Sainte-Beuve (1804–69) to refer to the aloofness from everyday realities of the poet Alfred de Vigny (1797–1863).

ivy /ívi/ (*pl* **ivies** *or same*) *n* an evergreen climbing plant —**ivied** *adj*

Ivy League *n* a group of prestigious US universities —**Ivy League** *adj* —**Ivy Leaguer** *n*

iwi /ēewi/ (*pl same*) *n* NZ a people or community

Iyar /ée yaar/ *n* the 2nd month of the year in the Jewish calendar

-ize *suffix* **1** cause to be, make o *formalize* **2** treat with or as o *lionize* **3** become, become like o *crystallize* — **-ization** *suffix*

Izmir /iz meer/ seaport in W Turkey. Pop. 2,130,359 (1997).

J

j (*pl* **j's**), **J** (*pl* **J's** *or* **Js**) *n* the 10th letter of the English alphabet

J¹ *symbol* joule

J² *abbr* Journal

ja /yaa/ *interj* S Africa yes (*infml*)

jab *vti* (**jabbing, jabbed**) **1** poke something sharply **2** make a short fast punch at an opponent ■ *n* **1** a sharp pushing or poking movement **2** a short sharp punch **3** an injection into the body *(infml)*

Jabalpur /júbb'l póor/ city in central India. Pop. 741,927 (1991).

jabber /jábbər/ *vti* talk or say something very fast —**jabber** *n*

jack *n* **1** a portable device for lifting heavy objects **2** a playing card with a picture of a young man on it, ranking between a ten and a queen **3** an electrical socket into which a plug is inserted **4** an object used in the game of jacks **5** the male of various animals ■ *vt* raise with a jack

ORIGIN The various uses of **jack** all come from the name *Jack*, a nickname for *John*. The term often implies 'ordinary' or 'small'.

☐ **jack in** *vt* stop doing *(infml)*
☐ **jack up** *vt* increase the amount of

jackal /ják awl, ják'l/ (*pl* **-als** *or* **same**) *n* a wild animal resembling a dog

jackass /ják ass/ *n* **1** a male ass **2** a person regarded as unintelligent *(slang insult)*

jackboot /ják boot/ *n* a military boot that comes up to or over the knee

jackdaw /ják daw/ *n* a large black bird

jacket /jákit/ *n* **1** a short coat **2** an outer covering or casing ■ *vt* put a jacket on

jacket potato *n* a potato baked in its skin

Jack Frost *n* frost personified

jackhammer /ják hammər/ *n* a hand-held pounding power tool

jack-in-the-box (*pl* **jacks-in-the-box** *or* **jack-in-the-boxes**) *n* a child's toy consisting of a puppet on a spring inside a box

jackknife /ják nīf/ *n* (*pl* **-knives**) **1** a folding knife **2** a dive in which the diver bends the body to touch the toes and then straightens out ■ *vi* (**-knifing, -knifed**) **1** lose control so that the trailer swings round to be at an angle to the cab *(refers to articulated lorries)* **2** do a jackknife dive

jack-of-all-trades (*pl* **jacks-of-all-trades**) *n* somebody who can do many types of work

jack-o'-lantern *n* a lantern made from a hollowed-out pumpkin

jackpot /ják pot/ *n* the most valuable cash prize, e.g. in a lottery

jack rabbit *n* a large hare

Jack Robinson ◇ **before you can** *or* **could say Jack Robinson** without the slightest delay or hesitation *(infml)*

jacks *n* a game that involves picking up small metal or plastic pieces between bouncing or throwing and catching a small ball (+ *sing verb*)

Jackson /jáks'n/ capital of Mississippi State. Pop. 188,419 (1998).

Jack the Ripper (*fl* 1880s) nickname of a notorious, unidentified 19C British serial murderer

Jacobean /jákə beé ən/ *adj* of the reign of James I of England and Ireland —**Jacobean** *n*

ORIGIN Jacobean and **Jacobite** are from the Latin form of 'James', *Jacobus.*

Jacobite /jákə bīt/ *n* a supporter of James II and his descendants in their claim to the British throne —**Jacobite** *adj* —**Jacobitism** *n*

Jacuzzi /jə kōozi/ *tdmk* a trademark for a whirlpool bath

jade[1] *n* a semiprecious stone. Use: ornaments, jewellery.

ORIGIN Despite the close association of **jade** with China and Japan, its name has no Asian connections. A derivative of Latin *ilia* 'flanks', the part of the body where the kidneys are situated, passed into Spanish as *ijada*. It was thought that jade could cure pain in the renal area, so the Spanish called it *piedra de ijada*, literally 'stone of the flanks', eventually reduced to *ijada*. In French it became *ejade*. Subsequently *l'ejade* 'the jade' became *le jade*, from which English **jade** is derived.

jade[2] (*archaic*) *n* a tired old horse ■ *vti* (**jading, jaded**) make or become exhausted

jaded /jáydid/ *adj* **1** bored through having or doing too much of something **2** exhausted —**jadedness** *n*

Jaffa /jáffə/, **Jaffa orange** *n* a variety of thick-skinned juicy orange

jag *n* a period of overindulgence or loss of control *(infml)*

jagged /jággid/ *adj* **1** with sharp points **2** uneven —**jaggedly** *adv* —**jaggedness** *n*

jaggery /jággəri/ *n* S Asia coarse brown sugar

jaguar /jággyoo ər/ *n* a big wild cat related to the leopard

jai alai /hī ə lī/ *n* a game derived from pelota

jail /jayl/, **gaol** *n* a secure place where criminals and suspects awaiting trial are kept ■ *vt* put in jail

ORIGIN Jail goes back to Latin *cavea* 'cave', and would literally have meant 'little cave'. The form **jail** came through mainstream French, and *gaol* from a northern variant. Originally *gaol* was pronounced with a hard /g/ (as in *go*), but from the 17C it became just a spelling variant.

jailbird /jáyl burd/ *n* a current or former prisoner in a jail *(slang)*

jailbreak /jáyl brayk/ *n* an escape from jail

jailer /jáylər/, **jailor, gaoler** *n* a prison guard

Jain /jīn, jayn/, **Jaina** /jīnə, jáynə/ *n* a believer in Jainism —**Jain** *adj*

Jainism /jīnizəm, jáyn-/ *n* an ancient branch of Hinduism that advocates deep respect for all living things —**Jainist** *adj*

Jaipur /jī póor/ capital of Rajasthan State, N India. Pop. 1,458,483 (1991).

Jakarta /jə kaártə/ capital and largest city of Indonesia. Pop. 7,764,764 (1997).

jalapeño /hálla páy nyố/ (*pl* **-ños**), **jalapeño pepper** *n* a small hot pepper

jalopy /jə lóppi/ (*pl* **-ies**) *n* an old or dilapidated car (*dated infml*)

jalousie /zhá'lloō zee/ *n* a slatted window covering

jam *v* (**jamming, jammed**) **1** *vt* push something forcibly into a tight space **2** *vt* fill something with people or things crushed together **3** *vti* stop or cause to stop working through sticking or locking ○ *The photocopier jammed.* **4** *vt* block something up and prevent passage **5** *vt* apply brakes hard ○ *jammed on the brakes* **6** *vt* interfere with broadcasting signals **7** *vt* overwhelm a switchboard with telephone calls **8** *vi* improvise music together ■ *n* **1** a spread made of fruit boiled with sugar **2** a difficult situation (*infml*) **3** a stoppage —**jammer** *n*

Jamaica /jə máykə/ island country in the N Caribbean Sea. Cap. Kingston. Pop. 2,665,636 (2001). —**Jamaican** *n, adj*

jamb /jam/ *n* an upright support of a door or window frame

jamboree /jámbə reè/ *n* **1** a big celebration **2** an international meeting of Scouts or Guides

ORIGIN The origin of **jamboree** is not known. It first appears in the United States in the 1860s. It was adopted as the title for the 1920 International Rally of Boy Scouts, and has been used by the Scout and Guide Associations ever since.

James¹, St, 'James the Great' (*fl* AD 1C) in the Bible, one of the 12 apostles of Jesus Christ

James², St, 'James the Less' (*d.* AD 62?) traditionally regarded as the brother of Jesus

James I (1566–1625) king of England and Ireland (1603–25), also James VI of Scotland (1567–1625)

James II (1633–1701) king of England, Scotland, and Ireland (1685–88)

James, Henry (1843–1916) US-born British novelist

James, Jesse (1847–82) US outlaw

James, P. D., Baroness James of Holland Park (*b.* 1920) British novelist

Jameson, Sir Leander (1853–1917) British-born South African politician

Jamestown /jáymz town/ **1** city in SW New York State. Pop. 32,166 (1998). **2** former village in SE Virginia, the first permanent English settlement in America

jam jar *n* a jar for jam

Jammu and Kashmir /júmmoo-/ state in N India, a section of the disputed territory of Kashmir. Cap. Srinagar. Pop. 7,720,000 (1991).

jammy /jámmi/ (**-mier, -miest**) *adj* **1** sticky with jam **2** lucky (*infml*)

jam session *n* a session of musical improvisation

Jan. *abbr* January

Janáček /yánnə chek/, **Leoš** (1854–1928) Czech composer

jangle /jáng g'l/ (**-gling, -gled**) *vti* **1** make or cause to make a harsh metallic sound **2** irritate somebody's nerves —**jangle** *n* —**jangly** *adj*

janitor /jánnitər/ *n* somebody employed to clean and maintain a building —**janitorial** /jánni táwri əl/ *adj*

January /jánnyoō əri, jánnyoōri/ (*pl* **-ys**) *n* the 1st month of the Gregorian calendar

ORIGIN January is named after *Janus*, a Roman god of beginnings and of gates and doors, who was represented with two faces looking in opposite directions (in the case of the month, behind to the old year and ahead to the new).

Japan /jə pán/ country in East Asia, comprising four large islands and more than 1,000 others. Cap. Tokyo. Pop. 126,771,660 (2001).

Japan, Sea of arm of the W Pacific Ocean between Korea and Japan

Japanese /jáppə neèz/ (*pl* same) *n* **1** somebody from Japan **2** the official language of Japan —**Japanese** *adj*

Japanize /jáppə nīz/ (**-nizing, -nized**), **Japanise** *vti* make or become Japanese in appearance or style —**Japanization** /jáppə nī záysh'n/ *n*

jape /jayp/ *n* a joke or playful act of mischief (*literary*) —**jape** *vi*

Japlish /jápplish/ *n* Japanese with a mixture of English words and phrases

japonica /jə pónnikə/ *n* a camellia

jar¹ *n* **1** a cylindrical storage container with a wide opening **2** *also* **jarful** a jar's contents **3** an alcoholic drink (*infml*)

jar² *v* (**jarring, jarred**) **1** *vti* irritate or disturb ○ *That constant drilling really jars my nerves.* **2** *vi* clash or conflict **3** *vti* make or cause to make a grating sound **4** *vti* shake abruptly **5** *vt* injure by jolting ■ *n* **1** a physical jolt **2** a grating sound —**jarring** *adj*

jardinière /zhaardini áir, -din yáir/ *n* a pot for house plants

jargon /jaárgon/ *n* **1** specialist or technical language **2** unintelligible language (*disapproving*) —**jargonistic** /jaárgə nístik/ *adj*

jasmine /jázmin, jássmin/ (*pl* **-mines** *or* same), **jessamine** /jéssəmin/ *n* a climbing plant with fragrant flowers

jasper /jáspər/ *n* a red iron-bearing form of quartz. Use: jewellery, ornaments.

jaundice /jáwndiss/ *n* an illness causing yellowing of the skin, tissues, and whites of the eyes ■ *vt* (**-dicing, -diced**) **1** make cynical, jealous, or prejudiced **2** affect with jaundice —**jaundiced** *adj*

jaunt *n* a short excursion —**jaunt** *vi*

jaunty /jáwnti/ (**-tier, -tiest**) *adj* **1** carefree **2** eye-catching in a casual way —**jauntily** *adv* —**jauntiness** *n*

Java /jaávə/ island in Southeast Asia, the most populous island in Indonesia. Pop. 114,733,500 (1995).

javelin /jávvəlin/ *n* **1** a light spear thrown as a weapon or in competitions **2** a throwing contest using a javelin

jaw *n* **1** either of two bones anchoring the teeth and forming the structural basis of the mouth in vertebrates **2** an invertebrate body part with a function or structure similar to a vertebrate jaw **3** a gripping part of a tool or machine **4** the lower, mobile part of the face ■ **jaws** *npl* **1** a natural entrance **2** a situation dangerously close to something horrible or frightening ■ *vi* talk at length *(slang)*

jawbone /jáw bōn/ *n* a bone in the jaw, especially the lower jaw

jay *n* a noisy brightly coloured bird of the crow family

jaywalk /jáy wawk/ *vi* cross a street anywhere other than at a designated crossing place —**jaywalker** *n* —**jaywalking** *n*

jazz *n* **1** a type of syncopated popular music of African American origin **2** unnamed things *(slang)* ○ *a new motorcycle and all the jazz that comes with it* ■ *vi* play or dance to jazz

---

ORIGIN The term **jazz** originated in the S United States (it is first recorded in 1909, applied to a type of ragtime dance), and it is tempting to speculate that its ancestor crossed the Atlantic in the slave-ships from Africa. In the absence of any certain origin, various colourful theories have been put forward – for example that **jazz** came from the nickname of a certain Jasbo Brown, an itinerant musician along the banks of the Mississippi ('Jasbo' perhaps being an alteration of 'Jasper').

☐ **jazz up** *vt* make more lively or interesting *(infml)*

jazzy /jázzi/ (**-ier**, **-iest**) *adj* showy *(infml)* —**jazziness** *n*

JCB *tdmk* a trademark for an excavating and earth-moving machine with a large shovel at the front and a digging arm at the back

JCL *n* a powerful computer language used for batch processing. Full form **Job Control Language**

jealous /jélləss/ *adj* **1** bitterly envious **2** suspicious of rivals **3** possessively watchful —**jealously** *adv* —**jealousness** *n* —**jealousy** *n*

jeans /jeenz/ *npl* hard-wearing casual trousers with raised seams, usually made of denim

---

ORIGIN Jeans were originally made of *jean*, a strong twill cotton. The name goes back to a French form of Genoa, the Italian city where the cloth was first made.

Jedda ♦ Jiddah

Jeep *tdmk* a trademark for a four-wheel-drive vehicle suitable for rough terrain

jeer *vti* express derision of somebody or something vocally —**jeer** *n* —**jeeringly** *adv*

Thomas Jefferson

Jefferson /jéffərss'n/, **Thomas** (1743–1826) 3rd president of the United States (1801–09)

Jefferson City capital of Missouri. Pop. 34,911 (1998).

Jeffreys /jéffriz/, **Sir Alec J.** (*b.* 1950) British geneticist. He developed the technique for establishing an individual's genetic identification, known as genetic fingerprinting.

Jehovah /ji hóvə/ *n* in the Bible, a form of the Hebrew name of God

Jehovah's Witness *n* a member of a religious group believing in the imminence of Jesus Christ's reign on Earth

jejune /ji joõn/ *adj* **1** boring and intellectually undemanding **2** childish

jejunum /ji joõnəm/ *n* the middle part of the small intestine —**jejunal** *adj*

Jekyll /jeék'l/, **Gertrude** (1843–1932) British landscape gardener and writer

Jekyll and Hyde /jék'l ənd híd/ *n* a person who has two distinct personalities, one good and the other evil

---

ORIGIN The term comes from *The Strange Case of Dr. Jekyll and Mr. Hyde* (1886), by Robert Louis Stevenson.

---

jell *vti* **1** solidify **2** take shape, or cause to take shape

jelly /jélli/ *n* **1** a wobbly dessert made from gelatin **2** a semisolid fruit preserve **3** a substance with the consistency of jelly ■ *vti* (**-lies, -lied**) set into a jelly —**jellied** *adj*

jelly baby *n* a sweet in the stylized shape of a baby

jellybean /jélli been/ *n* a bean-shaped sweet with a hard coating and a soft jelly centre

jellyfish /jélli fish/ (*pl* **-fishes** or **same**) *n* a stinging invertebrate marine animal

~~jelous~~ incorrect spelling of **jealous**

jemmy /jémmi/ *n* (*pl* **-mies**) a lever for prising something open ■ *vt* (**-mies, -mied**) open with a jemmy

je ne sais quoi /zhə nə say kwaá/ *n* an undefinable quality *(literary or humorous)*

ORIGIN Je ne sais quoi means literally 'I do not know what' in French.

Jenner /jénnər/, **Edward** (1749–1823) British physician. He discovered a vaccine against smallpox.

jenny /jénni/ *n* (*pl* **-nies**) *n* a female of various animals ○ *a jenny wren*

jeopardize /jéppər dīz/ (**-izing, -ized**), **jeopardise** vt endanger

jeopardy /jéppərdi/ n the risk of loss, harm, or death

ORIGIN **Jeopardy** derives from French *jeu parti* literally 'divided game', and so originally referred to chances being even or uncertain. Early on, however, the emphasis began to fall on the riskiness and danger of the uncertainty rather than the equal chance of a successful outcome.

~~jepardy~~ incorrect spelling of **jeopardy**

jerboa /jur bố ə/ (*pl* **-as**) n 1 a small rodent of Asia and Africa 2 a small marsupial of central Australia

jeremiad /jérri mí əd/ n a lengthy complaint (*fml*)

Jericho /jérrikō/ town in the Jordan Valley. According to the Bible, the ancient town was destroyed by Joshua after he led the Israelites back from captivity in Egypt. Pop. 14,744 (1997).

jerk[1] v 1 vt pull suddenly 2 vti move joltingly ■ n 1 a sudden pull 2 a jolting motion 3 a twitch 4 US, Can a person regarded as behaving foolishly (*slang insult*) 5 an overhead lift in weightlifting

jerk[2] vt preserve meat in strips by sun-drying or smoking

jerkin /júrkin/ n a close-fitting sleeveless jacket

jerky[1] /júrki/ (**-ier, -iest**) adj moving with sudden stops and starts —**jerkily** adv —**jerkiness** n

jerky[2] /júrki/ n strips of meat preserved by sun-drying or smoking

jeroboam /jérrə bố əm/ n a large wine bottle holding the equivalent of four standard bottles

ORIGIN In the Bible, Jeroboam was 'a mighty man of valour' (I Kings 11:28).

Jerome /jə rốm/, **St** (347?–419?) Croatian-born monk and scholar. He was the first translator of the Bible into Latin.

Jerome, Jerome K. (1859–1927) British novelist

jerry-built adj shoddily built

jerry can n a can for petrol or water

jersey /júrzi/ (*pl* **-seys**) n 1 a plain knitted fabric used for clothing 2 a sweater 3 a shirt for sports 4 **Jersey** a breed of pale brown dairy cattle

ORIGIN The fabric **jersey** was originally a woollen worsted made on the island of Jersey.

Jersey /júrzi/ largest and southernmost of the Channel Islands, in the English Channel. Pop. 89,361 (2001).

Jerusalem /jə roʻossələm/ historic city lying at the intersection of Israel and the West Bank. The whole of the city is claimed by Israel as its capital, but this is disputed internationally. Pop. 633,700 (1999).

Jerusalem artichoke n 1 an edible tuber with a knobbly skin and white flesh 2 a perennial plant that produces edible tubers

ORIGIN **Jerusalem artichokes** do not come from Jerusalem. The name is an alteration of Italian *girasole* 'sunflower', because the plant does belong to the sunflower family.

jessamine n = jasmine

jest n 1 a joke or playful act (*literary*) 2 something joked about (*archaic*) ■ vi be witty about something (*literary*) —**jestingly** adv

jester /jéstər/ n 1 an entertainer employed at a medieval court 2 somebody who jokes

Jesuit /jézzyoo it/ n a member of the Society of Jesus, a Roman Catholic religious order —**Jesuitic** /jézzyoo íttik/ adj —**Jesuitical** adj

Jesus Christ /jeézəss-/, **Jesus** n a religious teacher whose life and teachings form the basis of Christianity

jet[1] n 1 a pressurized stream of fluid 2 a hole through which fluid is forced 3 *also* **jet engine** an engine that produces forward thrust using discharged gases o *using jet technology* 4 an aircraft powered by a jet engine ■ v (**jetting, jetted**) 1 vi travel by jet aircraft 2 vti flow or send out forcefully in a thin stream

ORIGIN The verb **jet** was adopted from French *jeter* 'throw' in the late 16C. It originally meant 'protrude, stick out'. This sense is best preserved in related *jetty* 'projecting pier', while the underlying meaning 'throw' is still present in *jettison* 'throw something overboard'. **Jet** began to be used for 'spurt out in a forceful stream' in the 17C. The notion of using such a stream to create forward motion was first encapsulated in the term *jet propulsion* in the mid-19C, but it did not take concrete form until the term *jet engine* was recorded in 1943.

jet[2] n 1 a black mineral. Use: jewellery, ornaments. 2 *also* **jet black** a dark black colour —**jet** adj

jet lag n fatigue and disorientation following a long flight across different time zones —**jet-lagged** adj

jetsam /jétsəm/ n 1 cargo or equipment discarded by a ship in distress 2 discarded things

jet set n the social set of rich international travellers (*infml*) —**jet-setter** n

Jet Ski *tdmk* a trademark for a jet-propelled personal watercraft

jet stream n a permanent high-level wind current moving east

jettison /jéttiss'n/ vt 1 throw overboard 2 reject o *plans that had to be jettisoned*

jetty /jétti/ (*pl* **-ties**) n 1 a landing pier 2 a breakwater

Jew n 1 a believer in Judaism 2 a member of a Semitic people descended from the ancient Hebrews and following Judaism

jewel /joʻo əl/ n 1 a personal ornament made from a gemstone 2 a gemstone 3 a small crystal or gemstone used as a watch bearing

4 a prized example ■ *vt* (**-elling**, **-elled**) adorn with jewels

jewel box, jewel case *n* **1** a box for jewellery **2** a hinged plastic case for a CD

jeweler, etc. *n* US = jeweller, etc.

jeweller /joō əlɔr/ *n* a maker, seller, or repairer of jewellery

jewellery /joō əlri/ *n* ornaments for the body, e.g. necklaces, bracelets, earrings, and rings ○ *a jewellery box*

Jewess /joō iss/ *n* a taboo term for a Jewish woman or girl (*dated*)

Jewish /joō ish/ *adj* **1** of Judaism **2** of Jews —**Jewishly** *adv* —**Jewishness** *n*

Jewry /joōri/ *n* Judaism or its followers

jew's harp *n* a musical instrument held between the teeth and played by plucking a protruding metal tongue

Jezebel /jézzə bel/, **jezebel** *n* an offensive term for a woman regarded as sexually immoral (*insult*)

ORIGIN The original **Jezebel** was a Phoenician princess of the 9C BC who became the wife of Ahab, king of Israel, as related in the Bible (1 Kings 21:5–15, 2 Kings 9:30–37).

Jiang Qing /jyáng chíng/ (1914–91) Chinese political activist

Jiang Zemin /jyáng tsay mín/ (b. 1926) president of the People's Republic of China (1993–)

jib *n* **1** a small triangular sail in front of the main mast of a sailing vessel **2** a crane's projecting arm

jibe *n*, *vti* = gibe

Jiddah /jíddə/, **Jedda** /jéddə/ port in W Saudi Arabia, on the Red Sea. Pop. 1,490,000 (1995).

jiffy /jíffi/, **jiff** /jif/ *n* a brief moment (*infml*) ○ *I'll be ready in a jiffy*.

jig *n* **1** a lively dance in triple time **2** the music for a jig **3** a device for holding a piece of work in place and guiding a tool to cut or drill it ■ *v* (**jigging**, **jigged**) **1** *vti* jerk around quickly **2** *vi* dance a jig

jigger /jíggər/ *n* **1** a measure for alcoholic spirits, around 1.5 fl. oz **2** a jig operator **3** a small sail at the stern of a small sailing boat

jiggery-pokery /jíggəri pókəri/ *n* scheming or deceit (*infml*)

jiggle /jígg'l/ (**-gling**, **-gled**) *vti* shake with small repeated movements —**jiggle** *n* —**jiggly** *adj*

jigsaw /jíg saw/ *n* **1** *also* **jigsaw puzzle** a game consisting of a set of irregularly shaped interlocking pieces fitted together to make a picture **2** a power saw for cutting curves ■ *vt* cut with a jigsaw

jihad /ji hád/ *n* a holy war by Muslims against people or countries regarded as hostile to Islam

jilt *vt* reject a lover

Jinan /jeè nán/, **Chi-nan** capital of **Shandong Province**, E China. Pop. 3,470,000 (1995).

jingle /jíng g'l/ *n* **1** a metallic tinkle **2** a catchy tune used for advertising a product ■ *vti*

(**-gling**, **-gled**) make or cause to make a metallic tinkling sound —**jingly** *adj*

jingoism /jíng gō izəm/ *n* aggressive nationalism —**jingoist** *adj*, *n* —**jingoistic** /jíng gō ístik/ *adj*

ORIGIN The context of the coining of **jingoism** was British foreign policy of the late 1870s. The Prime Minister, Benjamin Disraeli, favoured sending gunboats to halt the advance of the Russian fleet out of its own waters into the Mediterranean. This gave rise to a music-hall song, written in 1878 by G.W. Hunt, the refrain of which went: 'We don't want to fight, yet by Jingo! if we do, We've got the ships, we've got the men, and got the money too'. Opponents of the policy picked up on the word *jingo* and used it as an icon of blind patriotism.

Jinnah /jínnə/, **Muhammad Ali** (1876–1948) president and governor-general of Pakistan (1947–48)

jinni /jínni/ (*pl* **jinn** /jin/), **djinni** (*pl* **djinn**) *n* an Islamic magic spirit

jinx *n* a supposed cause of misfortune ■ *vt* bring misfortune on —**jinxed** *adj*

jitterbug /jíttər bug/ *n* a fast 1940s dance for couples

jittery /jíttəri/ *adj* **1** nervous **2** jerky

jiujitsu *n* MARTIAL ARTS = jujitsu

jive /jīv/ *n* **1** jazz or swing music of the 1930s and 1940s **2** a lively jazz or rock and roll dancing style ■ *vi* (**jiving**, **jived**) dance the jive —**jiver** *n*

jnr, Jnr *abbr* junior

Joan of Arc /jón əv aárk/, **St** (1412–31) French patriot and saint

job /job/ *n* **1** a paid occupation **2** a task or piece of work **3** the function of somebody or something **4** a difficult time or experience ○ *had quite a job getting it to start* **5** a crime (*infml*) ○ *a bank job* ■ *vi* (**jobbing**, **jobbed**) take occasional or casual work —**jobless** *adj* —**joblessness** *n*

jobber /jóbbər/ *n* somebody taking occasional or casual work —**jobbing** *adj*

Jobcentre /jób sentər/ *n* a government office where jobs are advertised

job club *n* a club for helping unemployed people find jobs

job description *n* a written description of the responsibilities of a specific job

job lot *n* an assortment of articles

Jobs /jobz/, **Steve** (b. 1955) US entrepreneur and technology executive

Job's comforter /jóbz-/ *n* somebody who causes more misery in an attempt to offer comfort

job seeker *n* somebody looking for a job

Jobseeker's Allowance /jób seekərz-/ *n* a government allowance paid to an unemployed person

job-sharing *n* the dividing up of a full-time job between part-time workers —**job-share** *n*, *vi* —**job-sharer** *n*

jock *n* a disc jockey *(infml)*

jockey /jóki/ *n* (*pl* **-eys**) a racehorse rider ■ *v* (**-eying, -eyed**) **1** *vti* ride a racehorse **2** *vi* manoeuvre to try to gain an advantage

jockstrap /jók strap/ *n* a support for a sportsman's genitals

jocose /jə kṓss, jō-/ *adj* playful and humorous *(literary)* —**jocosely** *adv* —**jocosity** /jə kóssə ti, jō-/ *n*

jocular /jókyŏŏlər/ *adj* **1** playful and joking **2** intended to be humorous —**jocularity** /jókyŏŏ lárrəti/ *n* —**jocularly** *adv*

jocund /jókənd/ *adj* cheerful and good-humoured *(literary)* —**jocundity** /jə kúndəti/ *n*

jodhpurs /jódpərz/ *npl* riding breeches that are wide at the hip and narrow at the calves

Joe Bloggs *n* the average man in the street *(infml)*

joey /jṓ i/ *n Aus* a young kangaroo

jog (**jogging, jogged**) *v* **1** *vi* run at a slow steady pace **2** *vi* go slowly but steadily **3** *vt* nudge —**jog** *n* —**jogging** *n*

jogger /jóggər/ *n* somebody who jogs for exercise ■ **joggers** *npl* loose trousers for jogging

joggle /jógg'l/ (**-gling, -gled**) *vti* shake gently —**joggle** *n*

jog trot *n* **1** a slow running pace **2** a boring pace of life

Johannesburg /jō hánnəss burg/ capital of **Gauteng Province**, NE South Africa. Pop. 2,172,000 (1995).

John /jon/, **St** (*d*. 101?) in the Bible, one of the 12 apostles of Jesus Christ. By tradition he is considered to be the author of the fourth Gospel, three Epistles, and the Book of Revelations.

John (1167–1216) king of England (1199–1216)

John (of Gaunt) /-gáwnt/, **Duke of Lancaster** (1340–99) English soldier and politician

John (the Baptist), St (8? BC–AD 27?) Judaean prophet

John, Augustus (1878–1961) British painter

John, Gwen (1876–1939) British painter

John Bull *n* **1** the personification of England **2** an archetypal Englishman —**John Bullish** *adj* —**John Bullishness** *n* —**John Bullism** *n*

ORIGIN The original **John Bull** was a character representing the English nation in the satire *Law is a Bottomless Pit*, the first in a collection of pamphlets called *The History of John Bull* issued in 1712 by John Arbuthnot (1667–1735). These advocated ending the war with France in which Britain was engaged at the time.

John Paul II (*b*. 1920) pope (1978–)

Johns /jonz/, **Jasper** (*b*. 1930) US artist

Amy Johnson

Johnson /jónss'n/, **Amy** (1903–41) British aviator

Johnson, Lyndon Baines (1908–73) 36th president of the United States (1963–69)

Johnson, Samuel (1709–84) British critic, poet, and lexicographer —**Johnsonian** /jon sṓni ən/ *adj*

joie de vivre /zhwáa də veévrə/ *n* exuberance and love of life

join *v* **1** *vti* bring or come together **2** *vt* fix things together **3** *vt* connect two or more things ○ *join the dots* **4** *vti* become part of a group **5** *vt* agree to do the same as somebody **6** *vt* unite people in a partnership such as marriage **7** *vt* meet or share the company of somebody ○ *I'll join you for dinner.* —**joinable** *adj*

□ **join in** *vti* participate in an activity

□ **join up** *vi* **1** enlist in the armed forces **2** meet for a joint activity

joiner /jóynər/ *n* a construction carpenter, especially one who makes finished woodwork

joinery /jóynəri/ *n* **1** the finished woodwork in a building **2** the work of a joiner, or the techniques that a joiner uses

joint *adj* **1** owned in common **2** combined ○ *the joint ravages of the weather and pollution* **3** sharing the same role **4** done together ■ *n* **1** a junction between bones **2** a place where parts or things are joined **3** a large piece of roasted meat **4** a cannabis cigarette *(slang)* **5** a place on a plant stem from which leaves or branches grow ■ *vt* **1** fit parts or things together with a joint **2** divide a carcass into pieces for cooking —**jointed** *adj* —**jointly** *adv* ◊ **out of joint 1** dislocated or painfully displaced **2** disturbed or disrupted

joint stock *n* stock held jointly in a company

joint venture *n* a business enterprise jointly undertaken by two or more companies

joist *n* a beam supporting a floor, roof, or ceiling

joke *n* **1** a funny story **2** something said or done to amuse people **3** something laughably inadequate *(infml)* ■ *v* (**joking, joked**) **1** *vti* make jokes or say something to amuse people **2** *vi* try to be amusing —**jokingly** *adv*

joker /jṓkər/ *n* **1** a teller or player of jokes **2** a playing card bearing the picture of a jester, which can sometimes be substituted for any other card **3** an amusing eccentric person *(infml)* **4** a thoughtless or inconsiderate person *(infml)*

jokey /jṓki/ (**-ier, -iest**), **joky** adj good-humoured and amusing —**jokily** adv

jollification /jóllifí káysh'n/ n an enthusiastic celebration

jollity /jóllati/ n fun or cheerful celebration

jolly /jólli/ (**-lier, -liest**) adj 1 friendly and cheerful 2 happily festive (dated)
□ **jolly along** vt keep somebody happy (infml)

Jolly Roger /-rójjar/ n a pirates' black flag showing a white skull and crossbones

jolt /jṓlt/ v 1 vti shake or jerk violently 2 vi bump up and down or from side to side while moving 3 vt bring abruptly back to reality ■ n 1 a sudden violent movement 2 a shock or sudden reminder —**joltingly** adv —**jolty** adj

Jonah /jṓna/ n somebody thought to be a bringer of bad luck —**Jonahesque** /jṓna ésk/ adj

> **ORIGIN** In the Bible, Jonah was a Hebrew prophet of the 8C BC who disobeyed God and attempted to escape by sea. He was thrown overboard in a storm as a bringer of bad luck, but was swallowed by a great fish and vomited out three days later, unharmed.

Jones, Inigo (1573–1652) English architect and stage designer

Joneses /jṓnziz/ npl somebody's next-door neighbours ○ keeping up with the Joneses

jonquil /jóngkwil/ n a narcissus with small fragrant flowers

Jonson /jónss'n/, **Ben** (1572–1637) English playwright and poet

Corbis-Bettmann

Scott Joplin

Joplin /jópplin/, **Scott** (1868–1917) US composer

Jordan /jáwrd'n/ 1 country in SW Asia. Cap. Amman. Pop. 5,153,378 (2001). 2 river in SW Asia, rising in Syria and flowing south through the Sea of Galilee to the Dead Sea. Length 320 km/200 mi. —**Jordanian** /jawr dáyni an/ adj, n

Joseph, St (fl 1C BC) in the Bible, the husband of Mary, the mother of Jesus

Joséphine /jṓza feen/ (1763–1814) empress of the French (1804–09)

josh vti tease good-humouredly (infml) —**joshingly** adv

Jospin /zhóss paN/, **Lionel** (b. 1937) prime minister of France (1997–)

joss stick /jóss-/ n a stick of incense

jostle /jóss'l/ (**-tling, -tled**) vti knock against somebody deliberately

jot vt (**jotting, jotted**) write quickly ■ n a tiny bit

jotter /jóttar/, **jotter pad** n 1 a notepad 2 Scotland a school exercise book

joule /jool/ n (symbol J) the SI unit of energy or work

> **ORIGIN** The **joule** is named after the British physicist James Prescott Joule (1818–89).

journal /júrn'l/ n 1 a magazine or periodical 2 a detailed personal diary 3 an official record of proceedings

journalese /júrn'l eez/ n the writing style regarded as typical of journalists (disapproving)

journalism /júrn'lizam/ n 1 the job of gathering, editing, and publishing news in the media 2 writing or reporting for the media as a literary genre —**journalist** n —**journalistic** /júrn'l ístik/ adj —**journalistically** adv

~~journel~~ incorrect spelling of **journal**

journey /júrni/ n (pl **-neys**) 1 a trip or expedition from one place to another 2 a gradual passing from one state to a more advanced state ○ a spiritual journey ■ vi (**-neying, -neyed**) travel from one place to another —**journeyer** n

journeyman /júrniman/ (pl **-men** /-man/) n 1 a qualified artisan working for an employer 2 somebody with ordinary competence at something

> **ORIGIN** One of the strands in the history of **journey** is the meaning 'a day's work', which existed alongside 'a day's travel' in the French word from which it was adopted. A **journeyman** was originally one qualified to work for a daily wage rather than as an apprentice.

joust /jowst/ n a medieval tournament in which mounted knights charged each other with lances ■ vi 1 engage in a joust 2 engage in a contest

Jove /jṓv/ n the Roman god Jupiter —**Jovian** adj

jovial /jṓvi al/ adj cheerful in mood or disposition —**joviality** /jṓvi állati/ n —**jovially** adv

jowl[1] /jowl/ n 1 the lower jaw 2 a cheek

jowl[2] /jowl/ n 1 the hanging part of a double chin 2 a piece of hanging flesh under the chin of an animal or bird

joy n 1 great happiness 2 something that brings great happiness —**joyless** adj —**joylessly** adv —**joylessness** n

Joyce /joyss/, **James** (1882–1941) Irish novelist

Joyce, William (1900–46) British traitor

joyful /jóyf'l/ adj 1 feeling or showing joy 2 causing joy —**joyfully** adv —**joyfulness** n

joyous /jóy ass/ adj expressing, causing, or full of joy (literary) —**joyously** adv —**joyousness** n

joyriding /jóy rīding/ n the crime of high-speed driving in a stolen car —**joyride** n, vi —**joyrider** n

joystick /jóy stik/ n 1 a control lever of an aircraft or small vehicle 2 a hand-held lever for controlling cursor movement or a video game symbol

JP *abbr* Justice of the Peace

jpeg /jáy peg/, **jpg** *abbr* a file extension for a Joint Photographic Experts Group file

JPEG /jáy peg/ *n* a format for a compressed graphics file widely used on the World Wide Web. Full form **Joint Photographic Experts Group**

jr, Jr *abbr* junior

Juan Carlos /waán kaár loss/ (*b.* 1938) king of Spain (1975–)

jubilant /jóobilənt/ *adj* triumphantly joyful —**jubilantly** *adv*

jubilation /jóobi láysh'n/ *n* uninhibited rejoicing and celebration

jubilee /jóobilee, jòobi leé/ *n* 1 a special anniversary of an event 2 a time of celebration

ORIGIN **Jubilee** goes back to a Hebrew word meaning literally 'ram'. This derives from the ram's horn with which the Jewish year of jubilee was proclaimed every 50 years. There was originally no connection with words like *jubilant* and *jubilation*, to which **jubilee** might now appear to be related (they come from Latin *jubilare* 'call out, shout for joy'). Association with them did, however, reinforce the celebratory aspects of **jubilee**, so that the idea of a 50-year period has in many contexts been lost. We now refer to a 50th anniversary as a *golden jubilee*, but before the 19C **jubilee** alone would have meant just that.

Judaea /joo deé ə/, **Judah** /jóodə/ historic region in SW Asia, incorporating parts of present-day Israel and the West Bank —**Judaean** *adj, n*

Judaism /jóo day izəm/ *n* 1 the religion of the Jewish people 2 the Jewish way of life —**Judaistic** /jòo day ístik/ *adj*

Judas /jóodəss/ *n* 1 *also* **Judas Iscariot** /-iz kárree ət/ one of the 12 apostles of Jesus Christ, who betrayed him 2 a person regarded as a traitor (*literary*)

judder /júddər/ *vi* shake violently —**judder** *n*

Jude /jood/, **St** (*fl* AD 1C) one of the 12 apostles of Jesus Christ

judge *n* 1 a senior lawyer who supervises court trials 2 an adjudicator in a contest or competition ■ *v* (**judging, judged**) 1 *vt* act as a judge in a court case, contest, or competition 2 *vti* assess the quality or likelihood of something 3 *vt* form an opinion of 4 *vt* condemn on moral grounds

judgment /júyjmənt/, **judgement** *n* 1 the decision in a court case 2 the decision of a judge in a contest or competition 3 a decision on a disputed matter 4 discernment or good sense 5 an opinion formed after considering something 6 an estimate based on observation 7 the judging of a case, contest, or competition 8 a misfortune regarded as a divine punishment (*archaic or humorous*) 9 **Judgment, Judgment Day** in various re-

ligions, God's judgment on humanity at the end of the world

judgmental /juj mént'l/ *adj* tending to judge or criticize people —**judgmentally** *adv*

judicature /jóodikəchər, joo díkəchər/ *n* 1 the dispensation of justice 2 the position or authority of a judge

judicial /joo dísh'l/ *adj* 1 of judges, court judgments, or the justice system 2 enforced by a law court —**judicially** *adv*

judiciary /joo díshəri, -díshi əri/ *n* (*pl* -**ies**) 1 the branch of government that dispenses justice 2 the court system ■ *adj* of judges

judicious /joo díshəss/ *adj* sensible and wise —**judiciously** *adv* —**judiciousness** *n*

judo /jóodō/ *n* a Japanese martial art that makes use of balance and body weight —**judoist** *n*

jug *n* 1 a container with a handle and a lip in its rim for pouring 2 *also* **jugful** the liquid contained in a jug 3 prison (*humorous*)

jugged hare *n* hare stew

juggernaut /júggər nawt/ *n* 1 a huge lorry 2 an irresistible crushing force 3 **Juggernaut** a form of the Hindu god Krishna

ORIGIN **Juggernaut** is one of the forms taken by the Hindu god Krishna. Every year in Puri in NE India a statue of Juggernaut is pulled through the town on a huge chariot. It used to be said, fictitiously, that worshippers of Krishna threw themselves under the wheels of the Juggernaut wagon in an access of religious ecstasy, so **juggernaut** came to be used in English for an irresistible crushing force. The pejorative British application to large lorries did not become firmly established until the late 1960s.

juggle /júgg'l/ (**-gling, -gled**) *v* 1 *vti* keep several objects in the air at once by throwing and catching them in quick succession 2 *vt* arrange things to fit into a schedule —**juggler** *n*

jugular /júggyŏolər/ *adj* of the neck ■ *n* *also* **jugular vein** the vein returning blood from the head

juice /jooss/ *n* 1 the liquid from fruit or vegetables 2 a natural fluid or secretion of the body ○ *gastric juices* 3 the liquid from cooking meat 4 fuel for a vehicle or electricity (*infml*) ■ *vt* (**juicing, juiced**) extract juice from

juicer /jóossər/ *n* a kitchen appliance for extracting fruit or vegetable juice

juicy /jóossi/ (**-ier, -iest**) *adj* 1 containing a lot of juice 2 interesting or titillating —**juiciness** *n*

jujitsu /joo jítsoo/, **jiujitsu** *n* a Japanese system of unarmed fighting devised by the samurai

juju /jóojoo/ *n* 1 an object thought to possess magical powers 2 the supposed magic power of a juju —**jujuism** *n*

jukebox /jóok boks/ *n* a coin-operated machine that plays selected records or compact discs

ORIGIN The first element of **jukebox** is probably ultimately of West African origin. It seems to have come into English from a word meaning 'disorderly' or 'wicked' in a creole language spoken by people in the SE United States and on neighbouring islands. The first known written record of the word dates from 1935, and that for **jukebox** from 1939.

jukskei /yoõk skay/ *n S Africa* a game involving throwing pegs at stakes

Jul. *abbr* July

Julian (of Norwich) /joõli ən əv nórrich/ (1342–1416) English mystic

Julian date /joõli ən-/ *n* in computer programming, a date expressed as the number of days since 1 January of the current year

julienne /joõli én, zhoõli-/ *adj* describes food cut into long thin strips

Juliet /joõli ət/ *n* a communications code word for the letter 'J'

July /joõ líɪ/ (*pl* **-lies**) *n* the 7th month of the year in the Gregorian calendar

ORIGIN July is named after Julius Caesar, who was born in that month.

Jumada /joõ maádə/ *n* either the 5th or the 6th month of the year in the Islamic calendar

jumble /júmb'l/ *vti* (**-bling**, **-bled**) **1** put things out of order **2** muddle things up mentally ■ *n* **1** a muddled mass **2** articles for a jumble sale

jumble sale *n* a sale of second-hand articles for charity

jumbo /júmbō/ *n* **1** somebody or something larger than usual **2** *also* **jumbo jet** a large wide-bodied passenger jet aircraft

ORIGIN The word **jumbo** was popularized through Jumbo, a very large elephant at the zoo in London, who was sold to Barnum and Bailey's circus in 1882.

jump *v* **1** *vi* leave a surface with both feet **2** *vt* pass over an obstacle by jumping **3** *vi* move quickly in a particular direction ○ *Jump in and I'll drive you home.* **4** *vi* move abruptly or discontinuously ○ *jumping from one thing to another* **5** *vi* start in surprise or fright **6** *vi* rise suddenly by a large amount **7** *vti* leave the rails accidentally *(refers to trains)* **8** *vt* ambush somebody *(infml)* **9** *vt* leave a place, or abandon a commitment ○ *jumped bail* ○ *jump ship* ■ *n* **1** a jumping movement, or the distance jumped **2** an obstacle or apparatus used in jumping competitions or races

□ **jump at** *vt* accept eagerly

□ **jump on** *vt* attack somebody physically or verbally *(infml)*

□ **jump up** *vi* stand up quickly

jump ball *n* in basketball, a restarting of play in which a referee throws the ball up between two opponents who each try to tip it towards a team member

jumped-up *adj* undeservedly self-important *(infml disapproving)*

jumper[1] /júmpər/ *n* **1** a person or animal that jumps **2** a short wire for making an electrical connection

jumper[2] /júmpər/ *n* a knitted garment for the upper body, usually with sleeves, that is pulled on over the head

jumping jack *n* a firework consisting of a pleated tube that jumps along the ground as each pleat explodes

jumping-off point *n* **1** a place from which to start a journey **2** a basis for beginning something

jump jet *n* a jet aircraft that takes off and lands vertically

jump leads *npl* electric cables for recharging a flat battery

jump-off *n* **1** the start of a race or military attack **2** the deciding round of a show-jumping contest

jump shot *n* a basketball shot from mid air —**jump shooter** *n*

jump-start *vt* start a vehicle using jump leads —**jump-start** *n*

jumpsuit *n* **1** a woman's one-piece suit combining top and trousers **2** a parachutist's one-piece garment

jumpy /júmpi/ (**-ier**, **-iest**) *adj* very nervous or anxious —**jumpily** *adv* —**jumpiness** *n*

Jun. *abbr* June

junction /júngksh'n/ *n* **1** a place where things join **2** *UK* a motorway exit —**junctional** *adj*

junction box *n* an enclosed box containing electrical connections

juncture /júngkchər/ *n* **1** a point in time **2** a place where things join *(fml)*

June *n* the 6th month of the year in the Gregorian calendar

ORIGIN June is named after Juno, the queen of the gods in Roman mythology.

Juneau /joõnō/ port and capital of Alaska. Pop. 30,191 (1998).

Jung /yoõng/, **Carl Gustav** (1875–1961) Swiss psychiatrist —**Jungian** *adj, n*

jungle /júng g'l/ *n* **1** a tropical forest **2** an area thickly covered with vegetation **3** an impenetrably complex system **4** a fiercely competitive environment

junior /joõni ər/ *adj* **1** of or for youth or childhood **2** *also* **Junior** identifies the younger of two family members with the same name, e.g. father and son **3** of low rank or little experience **4** smaller than the standard size **5** for schoolchildren between 7 and 11 ■ *n* **1** somebody younger than another being referred to ○ *three years his junior* **2** a person of low rank or little experience **3** a student in a junior school **4** a child younger than a teenager **5** a third-year high-school or college student in the United States

junior school *n* a state school for children between 7 and 11

juniper /joõnipər/ *n* **1** the oil from small purple cones resembling berries. Use: to flavour gin.

2 an evergreen bush or tree whose cones produce juniper oil

junk[1] *(infml)* n 1 unwanted or worthless objects 2 cheap low-quality goods 3 nonsense ∎ vt discard —**junky** adj

junk[2] n a flat-bottomed Chinese sailing boat

junk bond n a high-risk investment bond with a possible high return

junket /júngkit/ n 1 an expenses-paid trip, especially one taken by a politician at public expense 2 a milk dessert set with rennet ∎ vi go on an expenses-paid trip

junk food n highly processed food lacking nutritional balance

junkie /júngki/, **junky** (pl -ies) n a drug addict *(slang)*

junk mail n unsolicited mail, especially advertisements

junk shop n a shop selling second-hand goods or low quality antiques

junkyard /júngk yaard/ n a place where junk is collected

Juno /jóonō/ n in Roman mythology, the queen of the gods. Greek equivalent **Hera** —**Junoesque** /jóonō ésk/ adj

junta /júnta, hŏónta, jŏónta/ n (+ sing or pl verb) 1 a group of military rulers in charge of a country after a coup 2 a group of people secretly working towards a common goal

Jupiter /jŏópitər/ n 1 in Roman mythology, the ruler of the gods. Greek equivalent **Zeus** 2 the largest planet in the solar system

Jura Mountains /jŏóra-/ mountain range between France and Switzerland. Highest peak Crêt de la Neige 1,718 m/5,636 ft.

Jurassic /jŏŏ rássik/ n a period of geological time 205–142 million years ago —**Jurassic** adj

juridical /jŏŏ ríddik'l/, **juridic** /-ríddik/ adj of the law or judges

jurisdiction /jŏŏriss díksh'n/ n 1 the authority to enforce laws or make legal judgments 2 the area over which legal authority extends 3 authority generally —**jurisdictional** adj

jurisprudence /jŏŏriss prŏŏd'nss/ n 1 the philosophy of law 2 the law as it applies in a particular place or situation —**jurisprudent** adj, n —**jurisprudential** /jŏŏrisprŏŏ dénsh'l/ adj

jurist /jŏŏrist/ n a legal expert —**juristic** /joor ístik/ adj —**juristical** adj

juror /jŏŏrər/ n a jury member

jury /jŏŏri/ (pl -ries) n 1 a group of people chosen to decide a legal case 2 a group of people judging a competition

jury box n the part of a court where the jury sits

jury-rig (jury-rigging, jury-rigged) vt build or fit out in a makeshift manner

jury service n service as a juror

just adv 1 a very short time ago o He's just left. 2 at this moment *(also with 'about to' and 'going to')* o I was just about to tell you. 3 only or merely o got off with just a warning 4 barely o arrived just in time 5 emphasizes a statement o It's just plain wrong. 6 exactly o just

what I need ∎ adj 1 fair and impartial 2 morally correct —**justly** adv —**justness** n ◊ **just about** almost ◊ **just like that** without effort or inconvenience ◊ **just now** 1 a very short time ago 2 at this very moment ◊ **just so** 1 that is right 2 done or arranged precisely

justice /jústiss/ n 1 fairness or reasonableness in treating people or making decisions 2 the legal system, or the application of law 3 legal validity 4 sound or good reason ◊ **do justice to** convey the true merits of

justice of the peace n a local magistrate

justifiable /jústi fī əb'l/ adj able to be justified —**justifiability** /jústi fī ə bílləti/ n —**justifiably** adv

justifiable homicide n lawful killing

justification /jústifi káysh'n/ n 1 something that justifies an action or attitude 2 the act of justifying something

justify /jústi fī/ (-fies, -fied) vt 1 give or serve as an acceptable reason or excuse for something 2 explain something 3 adjust the spacing of a line to align the margins of a text 4 in Christian belief, free somebody from sin through faith in Jesus Christ

Justinian I /ju stínni ən/ (483–565) Roman emperor (527–65)

just-in-time n a manufacturing system in which goods are produced and delivered as they are required

jut (jutting, jutted) vti stick out —**jut** n —**jutting** adj

jute n 1 a coarse plant fibre. Use: sacking, rope. 2 either of two plants that provide jute

Jute n a member of a Germanic people who invaded SE England in the 5C —**Jutish** adj

Jutland /júttlənd/ peninsula in N Europe, comprising all of mainland Denmark and part of N Germany. Length 338 km/210 mi.

Juvenal /jŏóvənəl/ (AD 65?–128?) Roman satirist

juvenile /jŏóvə nīl/ adj 1 youthful 2 of or for young people 3 childish ∎ n a young person —**juvenilely** adv —**juvenileness** n

juvenile delinquent n a young criminal —**juvenile delinquency** n

juxtapose /júkstə pōz/ (-posing, -posed) vt put side by side —**juxtaposition** /júkstəpə zísh'n/ n

Jyaistha /jī ástə/ n the 3rd month of the year in the Hindu calendar

K

k[1] (pl k's), **K** (pl K's or Ks) n the 11th letter of the English alphabet

k[2] abbr kilo-

K[1] symbol 1 kelvin 2 kinetic energy 3 one thousand 4 one thousand pounds 5 potassium

K² *abbr* **1** kilobyte **2** kilometre

K2 second highest mountain in the world, in the Karakorum Range in the W Himalayan range. Height 8,611 m/28,250 ft.

Kabul /ka'aboŏl/ capital of Afghanistan. Pop. 700,000 (1993).

Kaffir /káffər/, **Kafir** *n* **1** *S Africa* a taboo term for a Black African person *(offensive)* **2** the Xhosa language *(dated)*

Kafka /káfkə/, **Franz** (1883–1924) Austrian (Czech) novelist

Kafkaesque /káfkə ésk/ *adj* **1** of Kafka's work **2** impersonal and overcomplex

kaftan /káf tan/, **caftan** *n* **1** a full-length men's tunic worn chiefly in E Mediterranean countries **2** a Western imitation of the kaftan worn by men or women

~~kahki~~ incorrect spelling of **khaki**

AKG London

Frida Kahlo: Photographed in 1930 by Edward Weston

Kahlo /ka'al ō/, **Frida** (1907–54) Mexican painter

kaiser /kízər/ *n* a former German emperor

Kalahari Desert /kállə ha'ari-/ dry region in Botswana, Namibia, and South Africa

Kalashnikov /kə láshni kof/ *n* a Russian-made semi-automatic rifle used among terrorists and paramilitary groups

ORIGIN The **Kalashnikov** is named after its Russian developer M. T. Kalashnikov (1919–).

kale, kail *n* **1** a variety of cabbage with dark-green curly leaves **2** *Scotland* cabbage

kaleidoscope /kə lídəskōp/ *n* **1** a cylindrical optical toy with mirrors and shifting colours inside that create coloured patterns **2** a complex shifting scene or pattern —**kaleidoscopic** /kə lídə skóppik/ *adj*

ORIGIN The **kaleidoscope** was given its name in 1817 by its inventor, the British physicist Sir David Brewster. He formed it from the Greek word for 'beautiful' that is also seen in *calligraphy*, a Greek word meaning 'shape', and the ending *-scope* used for optical instruments.

~~kaliedoscope~~ incorrect spelling of **kaleidoscope**

Kamakura /ka'amə koŏrə/ city on SE Honshu Island, Japan. Pop. 169,945 (2000).

Kamchatka Peninsula /kam chátkə-/ peninsula of E Russia that separates the Sea of Okhotsk from the Bering Sea and the Pacific Ocean

kameez /kə meéz/ *(pl same or* **-meezes***)* *n* S Asia a long tunic worn over trousers

kamikaze /kámmi ka'azi/ *n* **1** a Japanese suicide pilot in World War II **2** an aircraft used by a kamikaze **3** somebody reckless and self-destructive *(infml)* —**kamikaze** *adj*

Kampala /kam pa'alə/ capital of Uganda. Pop. 773,463 (1991 estimate).

Kampuchea /kámpoŏ cheë ə/ former name for **Cambodia** —**Kampuchean** *n, adj*

Kanchenjunga /kánchən júng gə/ third highest mountain in the world, in the Himalaya range, on the border between Nepal and India. Height 8,598 m/28,209 ft.

Kandahar /kándə ha'ar/ capital of **Kandahar Province**, S Afghanistan. Pop. 225,500 (1988 estimate).

Kandinsky /kan dínski/, **Wassily** (1866–1944) Russian painter

kangaroo /káng gə roŏ/ *(pl* **-roos***)* *n* **1** a large long-tailed marsupial with powerful hindquarters **2** **Kangaroo** a member of the Australian national Rugby League team *(infml)*

kangaroo court *n* an unofficial or mock court delivering summary judgment

Kanpur /ka'an poŏr/ city in N India, on the River Ganges. Pop. 1,874,409 (1991).

Kansas /kánzəss/ state in the central United States. Cap. Topeka. Pop. 2,688,418 (2000). —**Kansan** *n, adj*

Kansas City 1 largest city in Missouri. Pop. 441,574 (1998). **2** city in NE Kansas, directly across the state line from Kansas City, Missouri. Pop. 141,297 (1998).

Kant, Immanuel (1724–1804) German philosopher —**Kantian** *adj* —**Kantianism** *n*

Kaohsiung /ków shyŏong/ city in SW Taiwan, on the Taiwan Strait. Pop. 1,462,302 (1999).

kaolin /káy əlin/, **kaoline** *n* a white clay. Use: porcelain, ceramics, medicines.

ORIGIN Kaolin comes ultimately from the name of a hill in Jiangxi province, N China, where fine white china clay is found. The name means literally 'high hill' in Chinese.

kapok /káy pok/ *n* a silky fibre obtained from the seed covering of a tropical tree. Use: stuffing, padding.

kappa /káppə/ *n* the 10th letter of the Greek alphabet

kaput /kə poŏt, ka-/ *adj* broken or out of order *(infml)*

ORIGIN Kaput came immediately from German in the late 19C, but the German itself was taken from a French term used in some card games, meaning 'without tricks'.

Karachi /kə ra'achi/ seaport and largest city of Pakistan. Pop. 9,269,265 (1998).

Karakorum Range /kárrə káwrəm-/ mountain range in south-central Asia, in the W Himalaya range. Highest peak K2 8,611 m/28,250 ft.

karaoke /ka'arə ŏki, kárri-/ *n* a form of entertainment in which amateurs sing to pre-recorded music

Kara Sea /kaa'ri-/ arm of the Arctic Sea, off the coast of N Siberian Russia

Barnaby's

Karate

karate /kə raáti/ n a Japanese martial art using fast kicks and blows

Karlsruhe /kaárlz roo ə/ city in SW Germany. Pop. 277,011 (1997).

karma /kaárma/ n the Hindu and Buddhist belief that the quality of people's current and future lives is determined by their behaviour in this and past lives —**karmic** adj

Karoo /kə roó/, **Karroo** semidesert plateau region of SW South Africa

Karttika /kaártika/, **Kartika** n the 8th month of the year in the Hindu calendar

Karzai /kaar zí/, **Hamid** (b. 1955?) chairman of the Interim Administration of Afghanistan (2001–2)

Kashmir /kash meér/ disputed territory in the northern part of South Asia

Kasparov /káspə rof/, **Garry** (b. 1963) Armenian chess player

Katmandu /kát man doó/, **Kathmandu** capital of Nepal. Pop. 533,000 (1995).

Katzav /kát zav/, **Qatzav, Moshe** (b. 1945) president of Israel (2000–)

Kauai /kaa wí/ fourth largest island in Hawaii. Pop. 55,983 (1995).

Kauffman /kówfmən/, **Angelica** (1741–1807) Swiss painter

kaumatua /kow maʿa too ə/ n a Maori elder or leader

Kaunas /kównəss/ city in central Lithuania. Pop. 412,610 (2000).

Kaunda /kaa o'ndə/, **Kenneth** (b. 1924) president of Zambia (1964–91)

Kawasaki /kaʿawə saáki/ city on east-central Honshu Island, Japan, beside Tokyo Bay. Pop. 1,218,233 (2000).

kayak /kí ak/ n 1 a sports canoe propelled by double-bladed paddles 2 a traditional Inuit animal-skin boat propelled by one or two people using double-bladed paddles —**kayak** vti —**kayaker** n

Kazakhstan /kázzak staán/ country in Central Asia, on the Caspian Sea. Cap. Astana. Pop. 16,731,303 (2001). —**Kazakh** n, adj

Kazantzakis /kázzan zaákiss/, **Nikos** (1883–1957) Greek writer

kazoo /kə zoó/ (pl -**zoos**) n a simple toy instrument that makes a buzzing sound when blown

KB abbr kilobyte

Keating /keéting/, **Paul** (b. 1944) prime minister of Australia (1991–96)

Keaton /keét'n/, **Buster** (1895–1966) US silent film comedian

Keats /keets/, **John** (1795–1821) British poet —**Keatsian** adj

kebab /ki báb, kə baáb/ n a selection of small pieces of food threaded onto a stick and grilled

kedgeree /kéjjə reé/ n 1 a dish of rice, smoked fish, and hard-boiled eggs 2 a dish of South Asian origin consisting of lentils, rice, and sometimes fish

keel n 1 the main structural member of a ship, stretching along the bottom from bow to stern 2 the main structural element of an aircraft's fuselage ◇ **on an even keel** in a stable condition

□ **keel over** vi collapse or fall over (infml)

keelhaul /keél hawl/ vt 1 drag somebody from one side to the other under the keel of a ship as a punishment 2 rebuke severely (infml)

keen[1] adj 1 enthusiastic 2 attracted to or fond of somebody or something 3 quick to understand things 4 sensitive or finely tuned ○ a keen sense of smell 5 intense ○ keen competition 6 with a sharp edge ○ a keen razor 7 cold and biting ○ a keen wind 8 competitively low ○ keen prices —**keenly** adv —**keenness** n

keen[2] vi lament loudly for the dead

~~keeness~~ incorrect spelling of **keenness**

keep v 1 vti hold or maintain in your possession ○ The sample is yours to keep. 2 vt maintain in a particular place or condition ○ Keep your arm up. 3 vt store somewhere when not in use ○ kept the keys in a drawer 4 vti continue, or cause to continue, in a particular way ○ kept working 5 vt not tell anybody about ○ keep a secret 6 vt adhere faithfully to ○ kept his word 7 vt fulfil as a religious duty ○ keep the Sabbath 8 vt create or maintain as a record ○ keep a diary 9 vi not spoil or decay 10 vi be in a particular condition or state of health ○ keeping well 11 vt have in stock available for sale ○ keep a large selection of scarves 12 vt detain or delay ○ I won't keep you a moment. 13 vt look after as an owner ○ keep pets ■ n 1 food and lodging ○ work for your keep 2 the innermost fortified part of a castle ◇ **for keeps** permanently or forever (infml) ◇ **keep something to yourself** refrain from revealing something

□ **keep back** vt 1 not reveal or tell somebody about 2 withhold for later use

□ **keep down** vt 1 maintain in a state of inferiority or oppression 2 maintain at a low level

□ **keep from** vt 1 refrain from disclosing something to 2 prevent somebody from doing something

□ **keep in with** vt maintain good relations with

□ **keep on** v 1 vi continue in an activity 2 vt continue to employ

□ **keep to** *vt* not deviate from

□ **keep up** *v* **1** *vt* maintain at the present level **2** *vi* go or progress at the same pace as somebody or something **3** *vt* maintain in good condition

keeper /kéepər/ *n* **1** somebody who oversees a museum, gallery, or exhibition **2** somebody whose job is to look after or protect animals **3** somebody in charge of a building *(usually in combination)* ○ *a lighthouse keeper* **4** a prison guard **5** a gamekeeper **6** somebody who maintains something ○ *a good record keeper* **7** a goalkeeper or wicketkeeper *(infml)* **8** a holding device **9** in American football, a move in which the quarterback runs towards the goal with the ball

keep fit *n* fitness exercises

keeping /kéeping/ *n* **1** looking after somebody or something **2** somebody's charge or possession ○ *in his keeping* ◊ **in keeping with** consistent with or suitable for ◊ **out of keeping with** not consistent with or suitable for

keepsake /kéep sayk/ *n* a small item kept as a memento

keg *n* **1** a small barrel **2** the contents of a keg **3** a beer barrel

keiretsu /kay rétsoo/ *(pl same)* *n* a Japanese business conglomerate

Kelly /kélli/, **Gene** (1912–96) US film actor, dancer, and director

Kelly, Grace (1929–82) US film actor

Kelly, Ned (1855–80) Australian bushranger and folk hero

kelp *n* **1** a brown seaweed with thick broad fronds **2** seaweed ash. Use: source of potash and iodine.

kelvin /kélvin/ *n* (*symbol* **K**) the SI unit of absolute temperature

Kelvin /kélvin/, **William Thomson, 1st Baron** (1824–1907) British physicist

ken *n* knowledge ■ *vti* (**kenning, kenned** or **kent**) *Scotland* know

Keneally /kə néeli, -nálli/, **Thomas** (*b.* 1935) Australian novelist

Kennedy, Cape /kénnədi/ former name for **Canaveral, Cape**

John F. Kennedy

Kennedy, John F. (1917–63) 35th president of the United States (1961–63)

kennel /kénn'l/ *n* a hut for a dog to sleep in ■ *vti* (**-nelling, -nelled**) put or stay in a kennels

ORIGIN Kennel derives ultimately from Latin *canis* 'dog', which also gave us *canine* and other words.

kennels /kénn'lz/ *(pl same)* *n* a place where dogs are boarded or bred

Kenny /kénni/, **Elizabeth** (1886–1952) Australian nurse and physical therapist

Kent county in SE England, and a former Anglo-Saxon kingdom

Kentucky /ken túki/ state in the east-central United States. Cap. Frankfort. Pop. 4,041,769 (2000). —**Kentuckian** *n, adj*

Kenya /kénnyə, kéenyə/ country in E Africa. Cap. Nairobi. Pop. 30,765,916 (2001). —**Kenyan** *n, adj*

Kenyatta /ken yáttə/, **Jomo** (1891–1978) prime minister (1963–64) and president of Kenya (1964–78)

Kepler /képplər/, **Johannes** (1571–1630) German astronomer

kept past tense, past participle of **keep**

kept woman *n* a woman supported by a lover *(often offensive)*

keratin /kérrətin/ *n* a fibrous protein that is the main constituent of nails, hair, and hooves

kerb *n* the edge of a pavement —**kerb** *vt*

kerb crawling *n* the act of driving slowly beside a pavement looking for prostitutes —**kerb crawler** *n*

kerbside /kúrb síd/ *n* the edge of a street or pavement bordered by a kerb

kerchief /kúrchif, -cheef/ *n* a square scarf

Kerensky /kərénski/, **Aleksandr Fyodorovich** (1881–1970) Russian revolutionary leader

kerfuffle /kər fúff'l/ *n* a commotion *(infml)*

kernel /kúrn'l/ *n* **1** the edible content of a nut or fruit stone **2** the grain of a cereal that contains a seed and husk **3** the central part ◊ See note at **colonel**

kerosene /kérrə seen/ *n* *ANZ, US, Can* a colourless flammable oil distilled from petroleum. Use: fuel.

Kerouac /kérrŏŏ ak/, **Jack** (1922–69) US novelist

Kerry /kérri/ county in Munster Province, SW Republic of Ireland

kestrel /késtrəl/ *n* a small falcon

ketch *n* a small two-masted sailing ship

ketchup /kéchəp, -up/ *n* a thick savoury cold tomato sauce

kettle /két'l/ *n* **1** a container with a handle, spout, and lid for boiling water **2** a metal cooking pot with a lid ○ *a fish kettle*

kettledrum /két'l drum/ *n* a percussion instrument consisting of a large metal drum with a parchment skin top —**kettledrummer** *n*

key[1] /kee/ *n* **1** a metal bar with notches or grooves that is turned to operate a lock's mechanism **2** a device such as a plastic card for opening a door or lock **3** a tool that is turned to wind, set, or calibrate a mechanism **4** a means of achieving, understanding, accessing, or controlling something ○ *the key to success* ○ *the key to the riddle* **5** an explanatory text or list **6** a lever or button on a musical instrument that is pressed to produce a sound **7** a system of related musical notes in a scale beginning on a particular note ○ *in the key of E* **8** a computer or typewriter keyboard button **9** a field in a database record that uniquely identifies that record **10** in cryptography, a sequence of symbols or characters for encoding or decoding **11** the pitch or quality of a voice or expressive sound ■ *adj* crucial ■ *v* (**keying, keyed**) **1** *vti* type characters using a computer keyboard **2** *vt* lock or adjust with a key **3** *vt* provide with an explanatory key **4** *vt* regulate the pitch of

key² /kee/ *n* a small low island of sand or coral in the Gulf of Mexico or the Caribbean

keyboard /kee bawrd/ *n* **1** a set of keys in a row or rows for a computer or musical instrument **2** a musical instrument with a keyboard ■ *vti* input data using a computer keyboard —**keyboarder** *n*

keyboardist /kee bawrdist/ *n* a keyboard instrument player

key card *n* a plastic card with an encoded metal strip giving access to a door or mechanism

key database *n* in e-commerce, a database that holds all keys used by a certificate authority

keyed up *adj* excited or tense (*infml*)

keyhole /kee hōl/ *n* the hole in a lock for a key

keyhole surgery *n* surgery performed using instruments inserted through a small incision in the body and manipulated externally

Key Largo /-laárgō/ one of the largest of the Florida Keys, off the tip of SE Florida. Length 48 km/30 mi.

Keynes /kaynz/, **John Maynard, 1st Baron Keynes of Tilton** (1883–1946) British economist —**Keynesian** *n, adj*

keynote /kee nōt/ *n* **1** the main theme of something **2** the tonic in a musical scale ■ *adj* containing the main theme ■ *v* (**-noting, -noted**) **1** *vti* deliver an important speech to a conference or meeting **2** *vt* outline an important policy in a speech or report

keypad /kee pad/ *n* **1** a small keyboard with numbers on the pad **2** the part of a computer keyboard containing the number and command keys

key ring *n* a metal ring for holding keys

key signature *n* a group of sharps or flats at the beginning of a piece of music showing what key it is in

keystone /kee stōn/ *n* **1** the central stone in an arch **2** something upon which other related things depend

keystroke /kee strōk/ *n* a single stroke of a keyboard key

key word *n* **1** a word used as a reference point for further information or as an indication of the contents of a document **2** a word used as a key to a code

kg *symbol* kilogram

KGB *n* the former Soviet secret police

Khabarovsk /kə baa rófsk/ city in SE Russia, near the border of China. Pop. 774,762 (1995).

khaki /ka'aki/ *n* **1** a brownish-yellow colour **2** a tough brownish-yellow cloth. Use: trousers, military uniforms. —**khaki** *adj*

Khamenei /kha'a me náy/, **Ali, Ayatollah** (*b.* 1939) supreme spiritual leader of Iran (1989–)

Imran Khan

Khan /kaan/, **Imran** (*b.* 1952) Pakistani cricketer

Kharkov /ka'ar kof/ city in E Ukraine. Pop. 1,521,000 (1998).

Khartoum /kaar toom/ capital of Sudan and of **Khartoum Province**. Pop. 924,505 (1993).

Khatami /ka'a taa mi/, **Mohammad** (*b.* 1943) president of Iran (1997–) and cleric

Khmer /kmair/ (*pl same or* **Khmers**) *n* **1** a member of a people of Cambodia **2** the official language of Cambodia —**Khmer** *adj*

Khomeini /khóm ay nee/, **Ruhollah, Ayatollah** (1900?–89) Iranian religious and political leader

Khrushchev /kroóss chof/, **Nikita** (1894–1971) premier of the former Soviet Union (1958–64)

Khulna /koolna/ river port in SW Bangladesh. Pop. 601,051 (1991).

Khyber Pass /kíbər-/ mountain pass in W Asia, the most important pass connecting Afghanistan and Pakistan

kHz *abbr* kilohertz

kibble¹ /kíbb'l/ *n* a large barrel used in wells or mines for lifting water, ore, or rubbish to the surface

kibble² /kíbb'l/ (**-bling, -bled**) *vt* grind into small pieces

kibbutz /ki boots/ (*pl* **-butzim** /-boot seem/) *n* a collective farm or factory in Israel

kiblah /kíbbla/, **kibla** *n* the direction of Mecca that Muslims must face when praying

kibosh /kí bosh/ *vt* put a stop to

kick *v* **1** *vti* strike somebody or something with the foot **2** *vti* move something by striking it with the foot **3** *vti* make a thrashing movement with the legs **4** *vti* raise the leg high quickly **5** *vi* recoil (*refers to firearms*) **6** *vr* be irritated with yourself (*infml*) ■ *n* **1** a blow with the foot **2** a thrashing leg movement **3** a swift raising of the leg **4** the act or an instance of kicking a ball **5** a pleasurable feeling (*infml*) **6** a sudden stimulant effect produced by something such as alcohol **7** a temporary strong interest *(infml)* ○ *on a health kick* **8** the recoil of a gun —**kicker** *n*

☐ **kick around** *v (infml)* **1** *vt* discuss casually **2** *vi* remain forgotten or neglected

☐ **kick in** *vi* take effect *(infml)*

☐ **kick off** *vi* **1** in football, start play by kicking the ball off the centre spot **2** begin *(infml)*

☐ **kick out** *vt* expel or send away *(infml)*

☐ **kick up** *vt* cause or instigate *(infml)* ○ *kicked up a fuss*

kickback /kík bak/ *n* a bribe paid to gain an advantage *(infml)*

kickboxing /kík boksing/ *n* a form of boxing with kicking as well as punching —**kickboxer** *n*

kickoff /kík of/ *n* **1** in football, the place kick that begins the match **2** the start of something, or the time at which something starts *(infml)* **3** the starting time of a football match **4** the start of a football match

kickstand /kík stand/ *n* a pivoting metal bar on a bicycle or motorcycle used to keep it upright when stationary

kick-start *vt* **1** start a motorcycle by stepping down on the starter **2** start a process or activity quickly and forcefully ■ *n also* **kick-starter** the pedal on a motorcycle that starts it when stepped on forcefully

kid[1] *n* **1** a child or young person *(infml)* **2** a young goat **3** soft leather from a young goat ■ *adj* younger *(infml)* ○ *my kid sister* ■ *vti* (**kidding, kidded**) give birth to a young goat ◊ See note at **youth**

kid[2] (**kidding, kidded**) *v* **1** *vti* say or speak in fun or teasing **2** *vt* deceive *(infml)* ○ *Don't kid yourself.*

kiddy /kíddi/ (*pl* **-dies**), **kiddie** *n* a small child *(infml)*

kid glove ◊ **handle with kid gloves** deal with using great care or delicacy

kidnap /kíd nap/ *vti* (**-napping, -napped**) abduct and hold somebody, usually for ransom ■ *n also* **kidnapping** a crime of abducting and holding somebody, usually for ransom —**kidnapper** *n*

kidney /kídni/ (*pl* **-neys**) *n* **1** either of two organs in the vertebrate abdomen for filtering waste liquid **2** an animal kidney used as food

kidney bean *n* **1** a small dark-red kidney-shaped edible bean **2** a plant producing kidney beans

Kiel /keel/ seaport and capital of Schleswig-Holstein State, in north-central Germany. Pop. 246,586 (1997).

Kierkegaard /kéerkə gaard/, **Søren** (1813–55) Danish philosopher

Kiev /keéy ef/ capital and largest city of Ukraine. Pop. 2,600,000 (1998).

Kigali /ki gaáli/ capital of Rwanda. Pop. 286,000 (1995).

Kildare /kil dáir/ county in the SE Republic of Ireland

Kilimanjaro, Mt /kílləmən jaárō/ highest mountain in Africa, in NE Tanzania. Height 5,895 m/19,341 ft.

Kilkenny /kil kénni/ county in the SE Republic of Ireland

kill *v* **1** *vti* cause a person or animal to die **2** *vt* ruin or end something **3** *vt* cause severe pain to somebody *(infml)* ○ *My feet are killing me!* **4** *vt* overpower something subtle ○ *Her perfume killed the scent of the roses.* **5** *vr* over-exert yourself *(infml; often ironic)* ○ *killed herself to finish on time* **6** *vt* use up spare time *(infml)* ○ *an hour to kill* **7** *vt* stop a plan or the passage of a bill **8** *vti* have an overpowering effect on somebody *(infml)* ○ *dressed to kill* ■ *n* **1** the moment or an act of killing a person or animal **2** the prey killed by a person or animal —**killing** *n, adj*

SYNONYMS kill, murder, assassinate, execute, put to death, slaughter, slay, put down, put to sleep CORE MEANING: deprive of life

killer /kíllər/ *n* **1** somebody or something that kills **2** something very difficult *(infml)* **3** a destructive force, person, or organism

killer instinct *n* **1** the urge to kill **2** a strong will to win at any cost

killer whale *n* a black-and-white toothed whale inhabiting colder seas

killing fields *npl* a place of carnage

killjoy /kíl joy/ *n* somebody who spoils the fun of others

kiln /kiln/ *n* an industrial oven ■ *vt* process in a kiln

kilo /keélō/ *n* **1** (*symbol* **k**) a kilogram **2** a communications code word for the letter 'K'

kilo- *prefix* **1** (*symbol* **k**) a thousand (10³) ○ *kilogram* **2** a binary thousand ○ *kilobyte*

kilobit /kílləbit/ *n* 1,024 bits

kilobyte /kíllə bīt/ *n* 1,024 bytes

kilogram /kíllə gram/, **kilogramme** *n* (*symbol* **kg**) 1,000 grams

kilohertz /kíllō hurts/ *n* 1,000 hertz

kilometre /kíllə meetər, ki lómmitər/ *n* 1,000 metres

kilowatt /kíllə wot/ *n* 1,000 watts

kilt *n* a Scottish tartan garment like a skirt, traditionally worn by men ■ *vt* pleat a skirt vertically —**kilted** *adj*

kilter /kíltər/ *n* good working order

Kim Dae Jung /kím dī jong/ (*b.* 1925) president of South Korea (1998–)

Kim Jong Il /kím jong íl/ (*b.* 1941) premier of North Korea (1994–)

kimono /ki mónō/ (*pl* **-nos**) *n* **1** a full-length loose traditional Japanese garment **2** a Western garment resembling a kimono, especially a dressing gown —**kimonoed** *adj*

kin *n* **1** somebody's family group (+ *pl verb*) **2** a member of a group that shares characteristics with another group **3** a blood relation ■ *adj* related

kina /keénə/ *n* the main unit of Papua New Guinean currency

kind[1] /kīnd/ *adj* **1** generous, warm, or compassionate ○ *You're very kind.* ○ *a kind act* **2** not harsh, unpleasant, or dangerous ○ *a detergent* *that is kind to the environment* ◊ See note at **generous**

kind² /kīnd/ *n* **1** a group of people or things that share features ○ *What kind of fruit is this?* **2** an example of something regarded as inferior or unsatisfactory ○ *a kind of apology* ◊ **in kind 1** with goods or services and not money **2** with something of the same sort ◊ **kind of** rather *(infml)* ◊ **of a kind 1** alike in only some respects **2** alike, or belonging to the same sort ◊ See note at **type**

kindergarten /kíndər gaart'n/ *n ANZ, US* a school or class for young children before they start formal education

kind-hearted /-haártid/ *adj* friendly, sympathetic, and generous by nature —**kind-heartedly** *adv* —**kind-heartedness** *n*

kindle /kínd'l/ (**-dling, -dled**) *vti* **1** start burning **2** glow or make glow **3** excite or interest, or become excited or interested

kindling /kíndling/ *n* material that burns easily, used for starting a fire

kindly /kíndli/ *adj* (**-lier, -liest**) **1** friendly, sympathetic, and generous **2** pleasant, mild, or comfortable ■ *adv* **1** please **2** in a kind way —**kindliness** *n*

kindness /kíndnəss/ *n* **1** generosity, warmth, and compassion **2** a generous, warm, or compassionate act

kindred /kíndrəd/ *adj* **1** close to somebody or something because of similar qualities or interests **2** related by blood *(fml)* ■ *n* **1** an affinity **2** a blood relationship **3** somebody's family group (*+ pl verb*) —**kindredship** *n*

kinetic /ki néttik, kī-/ *adj* of motion

kinetic energy *n* (*symbol* **T** or **Eₖ**) the energy that a body has because of its motion

kinetics /ki néttiks, kī-/ *n* (*+ sing verb*) **1** the study of motion **2** the branch of chemistry that studies rates of reactions

kinfolk /kín fōk/ *npl* somebody's relatives

king *n* **1** a man or boy who rules as monarch **2** a ruler of a group **3** an animal considered the best, strongest, or biggest of its kind **4** the foremost man in a particular field **5** a high-value playing card with a picture of a king on it **6** the principal chess piece **7** a crowned piece in draughts **8 King** in Christianity, God or Jesus Christ ■ *vt* **1** crown a playing piece in draughts **2** crown somebody king —**kingliness** *n* —**kingly** *adj* —**kingship** *n*

King, Billie Jean (*b.* 1943) US tennis player

AKG London

Martin Luther King, Jr.

King, Martin Luther, Jr. (1929–68) US civil rights leader and minister

kingdom /kíngdəm/ *n* **1** the territory or people ruled by a monarch **2** a sphere of activity in which somebody or something dominates **3** any of the three groups, animal, vegetable, and mineral, into which natural things are traditionally divided

kingfisher /kíng fishər/ *n* a brightly coloured bird that feeds on fish

King James Bible, King James Version *n* the Authorized Version of the Bible

kingmaker /kíng maykər/ *n* somebody with the power to appoint people to important positions

kingpin /kíng pin/ *n* **1** the most important person in a group or place *(infml)* **2** the crux of an argument

Kingsford Smith /kíngzfərd smíth/**, Sir Charles Edward** (1897–1935) Australian aviator

king-size, king-sized *adj* **1** larger than standard **2** very great *(infml)*

Kingston /kíngstən/ **1** chief seaport and capital of Jamaica. Pop. 538,100 (1995). **2** city in E New York State. Pop. 21,860 (1998).

Kingstown /kíngz town/ capital and principal port of St Vincent and the Grenadines, on St Vincent Island. Pop. 16,130 (1995).

kink *n* **1** a tight twist or coil in an otherwise straight section of something **2** an eccentricity in somebody's personality or behaviour ■ *vti* contain a kink, or give a kink to

kinky /kíngki/ (**-ier, -iest**) *adj* **1** tightly twisted or coiled **2** of or engaging in unusual sexual practices *(infml)* **3** sexually provocative *(infml dated)* —**kinkily** *adv* —**kinkiness** *n*

Kinsey /kínzi/**, Alfred** (1894–1956) US biologist, best known for his studies of male (1948) and female (1953) sexuality (the *Kinsey Reports*)

kinsfolk /kínz fōk/ *npl* somebody's relatives

Kinshasa /kin shaássa/ capital of the Democratic Republic of the Congo. Pop. 4,655,313 (1994).

kinship /kínship/ *n* **1** relationship by blood or marriage **2** relationship through common characteristics or a common origin

kinsman /kínzmən/ (*pl* **-men** /-mən/) *n* a male relative

kinswoman /-wŏŏmən/ (*pl* **-en** /-wimin/) *n* a female relative

kiosk /keé osk/ *n* **1** a small roofed street stall **2** a small cylindrical structure on a street for displaying advertising **3** a telephone booth *(dated)*

kip¹ *UK (infml) n* a sleep ■ *vi* (**kipping, kipped**) sleep or nap

kip² (*pl* **same**) *n* the main unit of currency of Laos

Kipling /kípling/**, Rudyard** (1865–1936) British writer and poet

kipper /kíppər/ *n* **1** a smoked herring **2** a male salmon in the spawning season ■ *vt* smoke herring

Kiribati /kírri baáti/ independent island state in

the west-central Pacific Ocean, part of Micronesia. Cap. Tarawa. Pop. 94,149 (2001).

kirk /kurk/ *n* **1** *Scotland* a church **2 Kirk** the Church of Scotland

kirsch /keersh/, **kirschwasser** /ke'ersh vassər/ *n* cherry brandy from Germany or France

Kisangani /ki'ssang gaàni/ capital of Orientale Region, in N Democratic Republic of the Congo. Pop. 417,517 (1994).

Kislev /kísslәf, kiss lév/ *n* the 9th month of the year in the Jewish calendar

kismet /kíz met, -mət/ *n* **1** Allah's will **2** fate

kiss *vti* touch with the lips —**kiss** *n* —**kissable** *adj*

kisser /kíssәr/ *n* **1** somebody who kisses **2** a mouth *(slang)*

kiss of death *n* somebody or something that will cause failure or disaster

kiss of life *n (infml)* **1** mouth-to-mouth resuscitation **2** something that revives an enterprise

kit *n* **1** a set of articles, tools, or equipment used for a particular purpose or activity **2** a set of parts to be assembled

□ **kit out** *vt* outfit somebody for a particular activity

Kitakyushu /keeta kyo'oshoo/ city in the north of Kyushu Island, Japan. Pop. 1,005,353 (2000).

kitbag /kít bag/ *n* a soft cylindrical shoulder bag

kitchen /kíchin/ *n* a room or area where food is prepared and cooked

kitchen cabinet *n* a political leader's unofficial advisers

Kitchener /kíchәnәr/, **Horatio Herbert, 1st Baron Kitchener of Khartoum and 1st Earl of Broome** (1850–1916) British field marshal and politician

kitchenette /kíchi nét/ *n* a small kitchen area

kitchen garden *n* a garden for growing vegetables, herbs, and sometimes fruit, for a household —**kitchen gardener** *n*

kitchen tea *n ANZ* a party at which women give kitchen equipment as gifts to a bride just before a wedding

kitchenware /kíchin wair/ *n* utensils for preparing and cooking food

kite *n* **1** a fabric- or paper-covered framework flown in the wind at the end of a string **2** a small slim hawk

Kitemark /kít maark/ *n* the official mark of approval of the British Standards Institution

kith /kith/ ◊ **kith and kin** somebody's friends and relatives

kitsch /kich/ *n* **1** artistic tastelessness **2** tasteless decorative objects —**kitschy** *adj*

kitten /kítt'n/ *n* a young cat ■ *vi* give birth to young cats ◊ **have kittens** become angry, excited, or nervous *(infml)*

kittenish /kítt'nish/ *adj* **1** frisky **2** flirtatious —**kittenishness** *n*

kitty[1] /kítti/ *(pl* -**ties**) *n* a cat *(infml)*

kitty[2] /kítti/ *(pl* -**ties**) *n* **1** a fund of money to

which people have contributed in order to buy something in common **2** a pool of bets

Kitty Hawk /kítti hawk/ town in NE North Carolina, on the Atlantic Ocean, site of the Wright brothers' successful glider and aeroplane experiments. Pop. 2,336 (1998).

kiwi /ke'ewi/ *(pl same or* -**wis**) *n* **1** a flightless New Zealand bird **2** *also* **Kiwi** somebody from New Zealand *(infml)* **3** *also* **kiwi fruit** a sweet green fruit with a brownish skin

Klansman /klánzmən/ *(pl* -**men** /-mən/) *n* a member of the Ku Klux Klan

klaxon /kláks'n/ *n* a loud electric horn

Klee /klay/, **Paul** (1879–1940) Swiss painter

Kleenex /kle'e neks/ *tdmk* a trademark for a soft facial tissue

Klein /klīn/, **Melanie** (1882–1960) Austrian psychoanalyst

kleptomania /kléptə máyni ə/ *n* an obsessive desire to steal —**kleptomaniac** *n*

Klerk ◆ de Klerk, F. W.

Klimt, Gustav (1862–1918) Austrian painter

Klondike /klón dīk/ region of NW Yukon Territory, Canada, named after the **Klondike River**, which traverses it

km *abbr* **1** kilometre **2** Comoros *(in Internet addresses)*

knack /nak/ *n* **1** an easy clever way of doing something **2** a natural ability or talent ◊ See note at **talent**

knacker /nákər/ *n* **1** somebody who slaughters old or injured horses for their body parts **2** a demolition merchant ■ *vt* tire out *(slang)* —**knackered** *adj*

knapsack /náp sak/ *n* a bag designed for carrying personal items on a hiker's back

knave /nayv/ *n* **1** a cunning untrustworthy man *(archaic)* **2** a jack in card games —**knavery** *n* —**knavish** *adj*

knead /need/ *v* **1** *vti* work dough or clay until it is smooth **2** *vt* massage a body part to relax the muscles —**kneader** *n* ◊ See note at **need**

knee /nee/ *n* **1** the joint of the human leg between the thigh and the lower leg **2** the area around the knee joint **3** the upper part of the thigh of somebody sitting down o *Come and sit on my knee.* **4** the middle joint of a four-legged animal's hind leg or of a bird's leg **5** a growth from a tree root protruding above the surface of water ■ *vt* (**kneed**) hit with the knee ◊ **bring somebody to his** *or* **her knees** make somebody weak or vulnerable

kneecap /nee kap/ *n* the flat bone at the front of the knee joint

knee-deep *adj* **1** standing in something as high as the knees o *knee-deep in water* **2** reaching as high as the knees

knee-high *adj* up to the knees

knee jerk *n* an involuntary contraction of the thigh muscle, producing a sudden extension of the leg below the knee

knee-jerk *adj* tending to react predictably and without thinking, or happening as a result of such a reaction *(infml)* ○ *a knee-jerk politician* ○ *a knee-jerk opinion*

kneel /neel/ *(knelt* /nelt/ *or kneeled) vi* rest on or get down on both knees

knees-up *(pl knees-ups) n UK* a lively party with dancing *(infml)*

knell /nel/ *n* **1** the sound of a bell rung slowly, especially in mourning **2** an ominous signal for somebody or something *(literary)*

knew past tense of **know**

knickerbocker glory /níkər bokər-/ *n* an ice-cream dessert in a tall conical glass

knickers /níkərz/ *npl* **1** woman's or girl's underpants **2** *also* **knickerbockers** *US, Can* loose short breeches gathered at the knee

---

ORIGIN Knickers is a shortening of *knickerbockers*. This was originally (in the 1850s) a US term for loose-fitting breeches for men, but in Britain in the 1870s *knickerbockers* came to be used of an undergarment for women. In the 1880s it was shortened to **knickers** in both senses. *Knickerbockers* is taken from the name Diedrich Knickerbocker, given by Washington Irving to the pretended author of his *History of New York* (1809). He presumably invented *Knickerbocker* as a typical Dutch-sounding name. The transfer to *knickerbockers* is said to derive from the breeches' resemblance to Dutchmen's knee breeches as depicted in William Cruikshank's original illustrations for the *History of New York*.

---

knick-knack /ník-/ *n* a small ornament

knife /nīf/ *n (pl knives* /nīvz/*)* **1** a tool consisting of a sharp blade with a handle for cutting **2** a knife designed as a stabbing weapon ■ *vt (knifing, knifed)* stab —**knifer** *n* ◇ **under the knife** undergoing surgery *(infml)*

knife-edge *n* a point in a situation at which it is balanced precariously between two possible outcomes

knifepoint /níf poynt/ ◇ **at knifepoint** while being threatened with a knife

knight /nīt/ *n* **1** a late-medieval mounted soldier of high social rank **2** an early-medieval mounted soldier of low social rank **3** a man with a nonhereditary title 'Sir' **4** a chesspiece shaped like a horse's head **5** a member of a religious or secret brotherhood **6** a champion of a cause **7** a protector of a woman ■ *vt* make a man a knight —**knightly** *adj*

SPELLCHECK Do not confuse the spelling of **knight** and **night** ('period of darkness'), which sound similar.

---

knight-errant *(pl knights-errant) n* a wandering medieval knight —**knight-errantry** *n*

knighthood /nít hood/ *n* **1** the rank or title of a knight **2** chivalry and honour

Knights of the Round Table *npl* the order of knights of Arthurian legend

Knight Templar /-témplər/ *(pl Knights Templar) n* a member of a medieval Christian military order

knit /nit/ *v* **(knitting, knitted** *or* **knit) 1** *vti* interlock wool loops to make a garment or fabric **2** *vti* use a plain stitch in knitting **3** *vti* unite **4** *vi* grow together again after fracture *(refers to bone)* **5** *vt* draw the brows together in a frown ■ *n* something made by knitting —**knitter** *n* —**knitting** *n*

SPELLCHECK Do not confuse the spelling of **knit** and **nit** ('an egg of a louse'), which sound similar.

---

knitwear /nít wair/ *n* knitted clothing

knives plural of **knife**

knob /nob/ *n* **1** a rounded handle or switch **2** a rounded projection **3** a small piece ○ *a knob of butter* —**knobbly** *adj* —**knobby** *adj*

knock /nok/ *v* **1** *vi* make a noise by hitting something, often repeatedly ○ *knock at the door* ○ *branches knocking against the window* **2** *vt* strike with a blow ○ *knocked the vase off the table* **3** *vti* collide, or cause to collide ○ *knocked my head on a low beam* **4** *vt* make with repeated blows ○ *knocked a hole in the partition* **5** *vt* criticize *(infml)* ■ *n* **1** a blow or collision **2** a sound of knocking **3** a setback or bad experience *(infml)*

□ **knock about** *or* **around** *v (infml)* **1** *vt* abuse somebody physically **2** *vi* travel around an area **3** *vi* habitually spend time with somebody **4** *vi* be in some uncertain place ○ *I'm sure it's knocking about somewhere in the office.*

□ **knock back** *vt* gulp a drink down *(infml)*

□ **knock down** *vt* **1** cause somebody to fall **2** hit somebody with a vehicle **3** demolish a building **4** cut the price of something *(infml)* **5** cause somebody to reduce a price ○ *He wanted £75 but I knocked him down to £60.*

□ **knock off** *v* **1** *vi* stop work for a break or at the end of a day *(infml)* **2** *vt* deduct from a price or score **3** *vt* produce with ease or speed *(infml)* **4** *vt* rob or steal *(slang)*

□ **knock out** *vt* **1** make unconscious **2** in boxing, defeat with a knockout **3** eliminate from a tournament **4** produce with ease or speed *(infml)* **5** please or impress greatly *(infml)*

□ **knock over** *vt* hit with a vehicle

knockabout /nókə bowt/ *n* comedy involving boisterous physical activity

knock-back *n NZ, Scotland* a rejection *(infml)*

knockdown /nók down/ *adj* **1** very powerful ○ *a knockdown blow* **2** easily disassembled **3** reduced or very cheap ○ *a knockdown price*

knocker /nókər/ *n* a fixture used for knocking on a door

knock-on *adj* progressively affecting other people or things ○ *the knock-on effect of the factory closure*

knockout /nók owt/ *n* **1** a punch that wins a boxing match **2** a boxing victory won by a knockout **3** an elimination competition **4** somebody or something stunning or excellent *(infml)*

knock-up *n* a practice period before a racket game

knoledge incorrect spelling of **knowledge**

knoll /nōl/ *n* a small rounded hill

Knossos /nósəss, knóssəss/ ruined city in N Crete, the centre of the Minoan civilization from about 3,000 BC to 1,100 BC

knot /not/ *n* **1** a lump-shaped object formed when a strand is interlaced with itself or another strand and pulled tight **2** a tangled mass of strands **3** a deep bond, especially marriage **4** a dark whorl in timber **5** a lump, e.g. on a tree trunk or in the body **6** a unit of speed equal to one nautical mile per hour **7** a tight group ○ *a knot of people* **8** a tense feeling ○ *a knot in my stomach* ■ *v* (**knotting, knotted**) **1** *vt* tie in a knot **2** *vti* tangle —**knotty** *adj* ◇ **tie (up) in knots** confuse utterly ◇ **tie the knot** get married (*infml*)

> **SPELLCHECK** Do not confuse the spelling of **knot** and **not** (indicating a negative), which sound similar.

know /nō/ (**knew** /nyoo/, **known** /nōn/) *v* **1** *vti* have information in the mind **2** *vti* be certain about something **3** *vt* have learned ○ *know how to operate a computer* **4** *vt* be acquainted or familiar with **5** *vt* be able to distinguish ○ *know right from wrong* —**knowable** *adj* ◇ **in the know** possessing information that is secret or restricted ◇ **know backwards** be completely familiar with

> **SPELLCHECK** Do not confuse the spelling of **know** and **no** (indicating a negative response), which sound similar.

know-all *n* somebody who claims to know everything (*infml*)

know-how *n* practical ability and knowledge (*infml*)

knowing /nō ing/ *adj* **1** indicating secret knowledge ○ *a knowing smile* **2** shrewd or clever **3** intentional —**knowingly** *adv*

knowledge /nóllij/ *n* **1** information in the mind **2** awareness **3** all that can be known

knowledgeable /nóllijəb'l/, **knowledgable** *adj* knowing a great deal —**knowledgeably** *adv*

knowledge base *n* data used for solving problems

knowledge management *n* the organization of intellectual resources and information systems within a company

knowlegable incorrect spelling of **knowledgeable**

known past participle of **know**

Knox /noks/, **John** (1513?–72) Scottish religious reformer

knuckle /núk'l/ *n* **1** a finger joint **2** the rounded projection of a knuckle when a fist is made (*often pl*) **3** a piece of meat from the lower joint of the hind leg ◇ **near the knuckle** rather indecent

□ **knuckle down** *vi* work hard (*infml*)

□ **knuckle under** *vi* submit

knuckle-duster *n* a weapon worn over the knuckles

KO (*infml*) *n* (*pl* **KO's**) a knockout ■ *vt* (**KO's, KO'ing, KO'd**) knock out, especially in boxing

koala /kō áalə/, **koala bear** *n* a grey furry marsupial resembling a bear

Kobe /kóbi/ seaport on S Honshu Island, Japan, on Osaka Bay. Pop. 1,461,678 (2000).

Kodály /kōd ī/, **Zoltán** (1882–1967) Hungarian composer

Kodiak Island /kódi ak-/ island of SW Alaska, in the Gulf of Alaska

koeksister /kóok sistər/ *n* S Africa a syrup-coated doughnut

kofta /kóftə/ (*pl* **kofta** or **koftas**) *n* a South Asian dish of meatballs

kohl /kōl/ *n* a preparation used as dark eye makeup

kohlrabi /kōl ráabi/ *n* **1** (*pl* **kohlrabies**) a turnip-shaped cabbage stem eaten as a vegetable **2** a plant that produces kohlrabies

koi (*pl* same), **koi carp** *n* a brightly-coloured carp kept as a pond fish

Koizumi /koy zóomi/, **Junichiro** (b. 1942) Japanese prime minister (2001–))

Kok, Wim (b. 1938) prime minister of the Netherlands (1994–)

Kokoschka /ko kóshkə/, **Oskar** (1886–1980) Austrian-born painter and writer

Kola Peninsula /kólə-/ peninsula in NW European Russia, between the Barents Sea and the White Sea

Kolkata /kol kúttə/ capital of Bangla state and port in NE India. Pop. 4,580,544 (2001).

Kolonia /kə lóni ə/ largest town in the Federated States of Micronesia, and capital of Pohnpei island state. Pop. 6,600 (1994).

kookaburra /kóokə burrə/ (*pl* **-ras** or same) *n* a large Australian kingfisher with a laughing call

koppie /kóppi/, **kopje** *n* S Africa a small hill

Koran /kaw ráan, kə-/, **Qur'an** *n* the sacred text of Islam —**Koranic** /-ránnik/ *adj*

Korean /kə reè ən/ *n* **1** somebody from North or South Korea **2** the language of North and South Korea —**Korean** *adj*

korma /káwrmə/ *n* a South Asian dish of meat or vegetables in a mildly spiced, creamy sauce

koruna /ko róonə/ *n* the main unit of Czech and Slovak currency

Kos ◆ **Cos**

Kosciuszko, Mt /kóssi úsk ō/ highest mountain in Australia, in the Snowy Mountains in SE New South Wales. Height 2,228 m /7,310 ft.

Kościuszko /kóssi úsk ō/, **Tadeusz** (1746–1817) Polish soldier and revolutionary

kosher /kṓshər/ *adj* **1** describes food prepared according to Jewish law **2** genuine (*infml*) **3** lawful or proper (*infml*) —**kosher** *vt*

Kosovo /kóssəvə, -vō/ former autonomous province in SW Serbia. Pop. 1,956,196 (1991). Albanian **Kosova** —**Kosovan** *n, adj* —**Kosovar** /-vaar/ *n, adj*

Kostunica /kosh tóonitsə/, **Vojislav** (b. 1944)

president of the Federal Republic of Yugoslavia (2000–)

Kowloon /kow loón/ peninsula in SE China, forming part of Hong Kong. Pop. 2,030,683 (1991).

kowtow /ków tów/ *vi* **1** kneel and touch the forehead to the ground to show respect **2** be servile —**kowtow** *n*

ORIGIN **Kowtow** comes from a Chinese compound word meaning literally 'strike head'. The Chinese custom was first described in English in the early 1800s, but it took only until the 1820s for it to become extended to any servile act and to be used as a verb.

---

kph *abbr* kilometres per hour

Kr *symbol* krypton

Krafft-Ebing /kráft ébbing/, **Richard, Freiherr von** (1840–1902) German neuropsychologist

kraft /kraaft/, **kraft paper** *n* thick brown paper. Use: bags, wrapping paper.

Krakatau /krákə tów/, **Krakatoa** /-tó ə/ **1** small volcanic island in SW Indonesia, in the Sunda Strait between Java and Sumatra **2** volcano on the island of Krakatau, Indonesia. Height 813 m/2,667 ft.

Kraków /krákow, -ō, -of/, **Cracow** city in S Poland. Pop. 740,500 (1997).

krans (*pl* **kranses**), **krantz** (*pl* **krantzes**) *n* S Africa a rock cliff

Krasnodar /krássnə daár/ port in SW Russia. Pop. 761,681 (1995).

Krasnoyarsk /krássnə yaásk/ city in S Siberian Russia. Pop. 1,122,874 (1995).

Kreisler /krísslər/, **Fritz** (1875–1962) Austrianborn US violinist and composer

Kremlin /krémmlin/ *n* **1** a walled compound in Moscow housing the Russian government **2** the former Soviet government

krill (*pl* same) *n* a tiny crustacean resembling a shrimp

Krishna /kríshnə/ *n* the Hindu god often depicted as a young man tending cattle, who is an incarnation of Vishnu —**Krishnaism** *n*

Krizanovic /kri zhánnəvich/, **Jozo** (*b*. 1944) Croat representative of the presidency of Bosnia and Herzegovina (2001–), which rotates between a Serb, a Bosnian Muslim, and a Croat

krona /krónə/ (*pl* **-nor** /-nawr/) *n* the main unit of Swedish currency

króna /krónə/ *n* the main unit of Icelandic currency

krone /krónə/ (*pl* **-ner** /-nər/) *n* the main unit of Danish and Norwegian currency

kroon /kroon/ (*pl* **kroons** or **krooni** /króoni/) *n* the main unit of Estonian currency

Kroto /krótō/, **Sir Harold Walter** (*b*. 1939) British chemist. He co-discovered the molecular family of carbon called fullerenes.

krypton /krípt on, kríptən/ *n* (*symbol* **Kr**) a gaseous chemical element. Use: fluorescent lamps, lasers.

Kuala Lumpur /kwaálə lóompoor/ capital of Malaysia. Pop. 1,145,342 (1996).

Kublai Khan /kóoblə kaán/ (1215–94) Mongol leader and emperor of China (1279–94)

Kubrick /kyoóbrik/, **Stanley** (1928–99) US film director

kudos /kyoó doss/ *n* praise or honour (*+ sing verb*)

Kufuor /koo fwáwr/, **John** (*b*. 1938) president of Ghana (2001–)

Ku Klux Klan /kóo kluks klán/ *n* a US white supremacist group

kulfi /koólfi/ (*pl* **-fis**) *n* South Asian ice cream

Kumaratunga /koo maárə tóongə/, **Chandrika** (*b*. 1945) Sri Lankan president (1994–)

kumquat *n* **1** a small orange edible fruit **2** a tree that produces kumquats

kuna /kónə/ (*pl* **-ne** /-ne/) *n* the main unit of Croatian currency

kung fu /kúng foó, kóong-/ *n* a Chinese martial art using circular movements of the arms and legs

Kunlun Mountains /koón lóon-/ mountain range in W China. Height 7,723 m/25,338 ft. Length 3,000 km/2,000 mi.

Kunming /koón míng/ capital of **Yunnan Province**, SW China. Pop. 1,740,000 (1995).

Kurd *n* a member of a people of SW Asia —**Kurdish** *adj*

Kurdistan /kúrdi staán/ region in SW Asia, encompassing parts of Turkey, Iraq, Iran, Armenia, and Syria, considered the homeland of the Kurdish people. Pop. 26,000,000 (early 1990s).

Kuril Islands /koó reel-/, **Kurile Islands** island chain in the Pacific Ocean extending from NE Hokkaido in Japan to S Kamchatka Peninsula in Russia. Pop. 25,000 (1990).

Kurosawa /koórə saáwə/, **Akira** (1910–98) Japanese film director

Kuwait /koö wáyt/ country in SW Asia, at the northwestern tip of the Persian Gulf. Cap. Kuwait City. Pop. 2,041,961 (2001). —**Kuwaiti** *n, adj*

Kuwait City capital of Kuwait. Pop. 28,259 (1995).

kW *abbr* kilowatt

kwacha /kwaáchə/ *n* the main unit of Malawian and Zambian currency

kwanza /kwánzə/ (*pl* **-zas** or same) *n* the main unit of Angolan currency

Kwasniewski /kvash nyéfski/, **Aleksander** (*b*. 1954) president of Poland (1995–)

kwela /kwáylə/ *n* a style of urban South African pop music

kyat /ki aát/ *n* the main unit of currency in Myanmar

Kyd /kid/, **Thomas** (1558–94) English playwright

Kyoto /ki ótō/ city on S Honshu Island, Japan. Pop. 1,388,267 (2000).

Kyrgyzstan /keérgi staan/ country in Central Asia. Cap. Bishkek. Pop. 4,753,003 (2001).

Kyushu /kyoˈo shoo/ southernmost of the four major islands of Japan. Pop. 13,269,000 (1990).

L

l[1] (*pl* **l's**), **L** (*pl* **L's** *or* **Ls**) *n* **1** the 12th letter of the English alphabet **2** the Roman numeral for 50

l[2] *abbr* **1** left **2** length **3** line **4** litre

L[1] *symbol* luminosity

L[2] *abbr* **1** large **2** learner

L8R *abbr* later *(in e-mails)*

La *symbol* lanthanum

LA *abbr* Los Angeles

lab *n* a laboratory *(infml)*

Lab. *abbr* Labour

label /láyb'l/ *n* **1** an informative piece of paper or fabric attached to something **2** a descriptive word or phrase **3** a name of a recording company ■ *vt* (**-belling, -belled**) **1** attach a label to **2** use a particular word to describe ○ *resents being labelled as a trouble-maker*

labial /láybi əl/ *adj* of the lips

labor *n*, *vti Aus*, *US* = labour

laboratory /lə bórrətəri/ (*pl* **-ries**) *n* **1** a place for scientific research and experimentation **2** a place for the manufacture of drugs or chemicals

laborious /lə báwri əss/ *adj* requiring or involving much effort —**laboriously** *adv* ◊ See note at **hard**

labour /láybər/ *n* **1** physical work **2** workers collectively **3** a supply of work or workers **4** a task, especially a difficult one *(often pl)* **5** the process of childbirth **6 Labour** the Labour Party (+ *sing or pl verb*) ■ *v* **1** *vi* work hard **2** *vi* do something with difficulty **3** *vt* overemphasize or repeat ○ *Don't labour the point.* ■ *adj* **Labour** of the Labour Party —**labourer** *n* ◊ See note at **work**

□ **labour under** *vt* be at a disadvantage because of believing something to be true that is not ○ *labouring under the misconception that the problem had been solved*

Labour Day *n* **1** a US and Canadian public holiday honouring working people. Date: 1st Monday in September. **2** a national holiday in some countries honouring working people. Date: 1 May.

laboured /láybərd/ *adj* showing obvious effort or difficulty

labour of love *n* something demanding or difficult done for pleasure rather than money

Labour Party *n* a British political party founded to support working people

labour-saving *adj* describes a device intended to save human effort

Labrador[1] /lábbrə dawr/ *n* a large dog with a short thick coat

Labrador[2] /lábbrə dawr/ mainland portion of Newfoundland, Canada, on the Labrador Sea

Labrador Current cold ocean current that flows south past Newfoundland, Canada, and W Greenland to join the Gulf Stream

Labrador Sea arm of the Atlantic Ocean that separates Canada from Greenland

laburnum /lə búrnəm/ *n* a tree with yellow drooping clusters of flowers

labyrinth /lábbərinth/ *n* **1** a confusing network of paths or passages **2** something very complicated **3 Labyrinth** in Greek mythology, the maze that confined the Minotaur —**labyrinthine** /lábbə rín thīn/ *adj*

Lacan /ləkaán/, **Jacques** (1901–81) French psychoanalyst

lace /layss/ *n* **1** a delicate fabric with a pattern of holes **2** a cord used to tie edges together, especially on footwear ■ *vt* (**lacing, laced**) **1** fasten something with a lace or laces **2** thread a lace through holes **3** add alcohol or drugs to a drink

lacerate /lássə rayt/ (**-ating, -ated**) *vt* **1** cut the flesh jaggedly **2** distress somebody deeply —**laceration** /lássə ráysh'n/ *n*

lachrymose /lákrimōss, -mōz/ *adj (literary)* **1** crying or tending to cry easily and often **2** so sad as to make people cry

lack *n* a shortage or absence ■ *v* **1** *vt* be without or in need of **2** *vi* have too little of something

---

SYNONYMS **lack, shortage, deficiency, deficit, want, dearth** CORE MEANING: an insufficiency or absence of something

---

lackadaisical /lákə dáyzik'l/ *adj* without enthusiasm or effort —**lackadaisically** *adv*

lackey /láki/ (*pl* **-eys**) *n* **1** a servile follower **2** a male servant *(archaic)* —**lackey** *vi*

ORIGIN **Lackey** goes back to an Arabic form meaning 'the judge'. It came to English through Catalan and French, where it had come to mean 'foot soldier' and then 'footman'.

lacking /láking/ *adj* **1** without something necessary ○ *lacking in good taste* **2** not present or available

lackluster *adj US* = lacklustre

lacklustre /lák lustər/ *adj* lacking energy or passion

laconic /lə kónnik/ *adj* using few words —**laconically** *adv*

La Coruña /la ko roónya/ port and capital of **La Coruña Province**, in the autonomous region of Galicia, NW Spain. Pop. 243,134 (1998).

lacquer /lákər/ *n* **1** a solution that dries to form a hard glossy decorative or protective coating **2** hair spray *(dated)* —**lacquer** *vt* —**lacquerer** *n*

Popperfoto

Lacrosse

lacrosse /lə króss/ *n* a team sport played with a netted stick and a small hard ball

ORIGIN **Lacrosse** was originated by Native North Americans. French-speakers in Canada gave it the name *jeu de la crosse* 'game of the hooked stick'. As an English word it is first recorded in the mid-19C.

lactate /lak táyt, lák tayt/ (**-tating**, **-tated**) *vi* produce milk in the body *(refers to female mammals)* —**lactation** /lak táysh'n/ *n*

lactic acid /láktik-/ *n* $C_3H_6O_3$ a colourless organic acid produced by muscles and found in sour milk

lactose /lák tōss, -tōz/ *n* 1 a sugar found in milk 2 a form of lactose derived from whey. Use: in food products, pharmaceuticals.

lacuna /lə kyoönə/ (*pl* **-nae** /-nee/ *or* **-nas**) *n* 1 a gap *(literary)* 2 a small cavity, e.g. in bone or cartilage —**lacunal** *adj*

lacy /láyssi/ (**-ier**, **-iest**) *adj* 1 made of lace 2 like lace in appearance ○ *lacy clouds* —**laciness** *n*

lad *n* 1 a boy or young man 2 a man *(infml)*

Ladakh /lə daák/ mountainous region of NW India, Pakistan, and China

ladder /láddər/ *n* 1 a portable device with parallel sides and rungs to climb up or down 2 a path to advancement 3 a vertical line of undone stitches in hosiery —**ladder** *vti*

~~ladel~~ incorrect spelling of **ladle**

laden /láyd'n/ *adj* 1 heavily loaded *(often in combination)* ○ *fruit-laden boughs* 2 oppressed or weighed down ○ *laden with guilt*

Laden ♦ bin Laden, Osama

la-di-da /laá dee daá/, **lah-di-dah**, **la-de-da** *adj* affectedly upper-class *(infml)*

ladies /láydiz/ *n* a women's public toilet *(infml; + sing verb)*

ladies' man, **lady's man** *n* a man who likes flirting with women

ladle /láyd'l/ *n* a long spoon with a deep bowl ■ *vt* (**-dling**, **-dled**) serve using a ladle

Ladoga, Lake /laádəgə/ largest lake in Europe, in NW Russia

lady /láydi/ (*pl* **-dies**) *n* 1 a woman 2 an aristocratic woman 3 **Lady** a title for some female members of the aristocracy

ORIGIN **Lady** means literally 'bread-kneader'. In origin it is a compound of *hlaf*, an early form of *loaf*, and *-dige*, which represents an ancient root meaning 'knead' that also gave us *dough*.

ladybird /láydi burd/ *n* a small red beetle with black spots

lady-in-waiting (*pl* **ladies-in-waiting**) *n* a female attendant for a queen or princess

lady-killer *n* a man who is very attractive to women

ladylike /láydi līk/ *adj* polite and dignified

Ladyship /láydi ship/ *n* a form of address for a woman with the title of 'Lady'

lady's maid *n* a woman's personal female servant

lady's man *n* = **ladies' man**

lag[1] *vi* (**lagging**, **lagged**) 1 fall behind compared with others 2 decrease in intensity ○ *Interest in the scandal has never lagged.* ■ *n* a period of time between events

lag[2] (**lagging**, **lagged**) *vt* insulate a water pipe or tank

lag[3] *n* a prisoner *(slang)*

lager /laágər/ *n* 1 light-coloured beer 2 a glass of lager

ORIGIN **Lager** was originally more fully *lager beer*. This was a partial translation of German *Lager-Bier*, literally 'storehouse beer', beer made for keeping. It is recorded in English from the 1850s.

laggard /lággərd/ *n* somebody or something who falls behind —**laggardly** *adv*, *adj*

lagging /lágging/ *n* insulating material for water pipes and tanks

lagoon /lə goón/ *n* a partly enclosed area of sea water

Lagos /láy goss/ largest city, chief port, and former capital of Nigeria. Pop. 1,484,000 (1995).

Lagos Escobar /laágoss éskō baar/, **Ricardo** (*b.* 1938) president of Chile (2000–)

lah, **la** *n* a syllable used in singing the 6th note of a scale

lah-di-dah *adj* = **la-di-da**

Lahore /lə háwr/ capital of Punjab Province, NE Pakistan. Pop. 5,063,499 (1998).

laid past tense, past participle of **lay**[1]

laid-back *adj* relaxed and easygoing *(infml)*

Lailat al-Miraj /láylat al mi ráj/ *n* an Islamic festival marking the ascent of Muhammad to heaven. Date: 27th of Rajab.

Lailat ul-Qadr /láy lat oŏl kaádər/ *n* an Islamic festival marking the sending down of the Koran to Muhammad. Date: 27th of Ramadan.

Laing /lang/, **R. D.** (1927–89) British psychiatrist

lair *n* 1 a wild animal's den 2 a retreat or hideaway *(infml)*

laird *n Scotland* a landowner

laissez-faire /léssay fáir, láy say-/, **laisser-faire** *n* 1 a principle of noninterference, especially lack of government regulation of private industry 2 letting people do as they please

laity /láy əti/ *npl* lay people, especially people who do not belong to the clergy

lake *n* 1 an inland body of water 2 a pool of liquid

Lake District region of mountains and lakes in NW England

lakh /laak/ (*pl* **lakhs** *or same*) *n S Asia* a hundred thousand, especially 100,000 rupees

Lakshmi /lákshmi/, **Laksmi** *n* the Hindu goddess of prosperity, the wife of Vishnu

lam¹ (**lamming, lammed**) *vi* hit somebody or something hard *(infml)* ○ *lammed into him with her fists*

lam² *n US, Can* a hasty escape

lama /la'amə/ *n* a Tibetan or Mongolian Buddhist monk

Lamaism /la'amə izəm/ *n* a form of Buddhism in Tibet and Mongolia, with elements from other religions —**Lamaist** *n, adj*

Lamarck /lə maárk/, **Jean-Baptiste Pierre Antoine de Monet, Chevalier de** (1744–1829) French naturalist and evolutionist. His theory that evolution proceeded by the inheritance of acquired characteristics was superseded by Darwin's theory of natural selection. —**Lamarckian** *adj, n*

lamb /lam/ *n* 1 a young sheep 2 the meat of a lamb ■ *vti* give birth to a lamb —**lambing** *n*

Lamb /lam/, **Charles** (1775–1834) British essayist. Pseudonym **Elia**

lambada /lam ba'adə/ *n* 1 a fast rhythmic Latin-American dance 2 the music for a lambada

lambaste /lam báyst/ (**-basting, -basted**), **lambast** /-bást/ *vt* criticize severely

lambda /lámdə/ *n* the 11th letter of the Greek alphabet

lambent /lámbənt/ *adj* 1 glowing or flickering *(literary)* 2 with a light but brilliant touch ○ *lambent wit* —**lambency** *n*

lambskin /lám skin/ *n* 1 a woolly lamb's pelt 2 leather from a lamb's hide

lame (**lamer, lamest**) *adj* 1 walking unevenly because of a leg injury or impairment *(offensive of a person)* 2 unconvincing *(sometimes offensive)* 3 ineffective *(sometimes offensive)* —**lame** *vt* —**lamely** *adv* —**lameness** *n*

lamé /la'a may/ *n* a fabric interwoven with metallic threads

lame duck *n* somebody or something regarded as weak or unfortunate *(offensive of a person)*

lament /lə mént/ *vti* express sadness or disappointed regret about something ■ *n* 1 an expression of sadness or regret 2 a song or poem of mourning —**lamentation** /lámmən táysh'n/ *n*

lamentable /láməntəb'l/ *adj* pitiful or deplorable —**lamentably** *adv*

laminate *vt* /lámmi nayt/ (**-nating, -nated**) 1 cover something with a thin protective sheet 2 bond layers together ■ *n* /lámminət/ material made up of bonded layers ■ *adj* /lámminət/ in layers —**lamination** /lámmi náysh'n/ *n*

lamp *n* 1 a device producing light, especially electric light 2 a device producing ultraviolet light or infrared heat radiation

lampblack /lámp blak/ *n* powdered carbon. Use: pigment, printing ink, in electrodes.

Lampedusa /lámpi dōozə/, **Giuseppe Tomasi di** (1896–1957) Italian author

lampoon /lam pōon/ *n* a satirical attack in writing or verse —**lampoon** *vt* —**lampooner** *n* —**lampoonist** *n*

ORIGIN Lampoon was adopted from French *lampon* in the mid-17C, but its origins in French are not altogether clear. It may come from *lampons* 'let us drink', used as a refrain in songs.

---

lamppost /lámp pōst/ *n* a post supporting a streetlight

lampshade /lámp shayd/ *n* a decorative cover for a lamp

LAN /lan/ *abbr* local area network

Lancashire /lángkəshər/ coastal county in NW England

lance /laanss/ *n* a long weapon with a metal point ■ *vt* (**lancing, lanced**) pierce with a sharp instrument ○ *lance a blister*

lance corporal *n* an Army or Royal Marines noncommissioned officer of a rank above private

Lancelot /la'anssə lot/ *n* in Arthurian legend, one of the knights of the Round Table

lancet /la'anssit/ *n* 1 a scalpel 2 a narrow pointed arch, or a window with this shape

land *n* 1 the dry solid part of the Earth's surface 2 a particular kind of ground ○ *low-lying land* 3 ground used for agriculture ○ *working on the land* 4 an area of owned ground ○ *Get off my land!* 5 a country ○ *her native land* ○ *foreign lands* 6 an imagined place ○ *the land of make-believe* ■ *v* 1 *vi* arrive by aircraft 2 *vti* come or bring down from the air onto water or solid ground 3 *vti* go or put ashore from a ship 4 *vt* catch and bring in a fish 5 *vt* obtain something desired ○ *landed a job in Hollywood* 6 *vt* strike a blow 7 *vi* appear or arrive unexpectedly or unwelcomely 8 *vti* end up or cause to end up somewhere unpleasant ○ *landed him in jail* —**lander** *n* —**landless** *adj*

☐ **land up** *vi UK, Can* end up somewhere *(infml)*

land agent *n* 1 an estate manager 2 an agent for the sale of land —**land agency** *n*

landed /lándid/ *adj* 1 owning land 2 consisting of land

landfall /lánd fawl/ *n* 1 arrival on or sighting of land after a sea journey 2 the first land reached after a journey

landfill /lánd fil/ *n* 1 the burial of waste material 2 an area where refuse is buried

landing /lánding/ *n* 1 the act of coming down to the ground or the ground 2 a level area between flights of stairs

landing gear *n* an aircraft's undercarriage

landing stage *n* a platform for loading and unloading passengers and goods from a boat

landing strip *n* an airstrip

landlady /lánd laydi/ (*pl* **-dies**) *n* 1 a woman who rents out property or lodgings 2 a woman who runs a pub

landline /lánd līn/ *n* a telecommunications cable on land

landlocked /lánd lokt/ *adj* surrounded by land

landlord /lánd lawrd/ *n* 1 somebody who rents out property or lodgings 2 a man who runs a pub

landlubber /lánd lubər/ *n* somebody who is clumsy aboard a ship due to lack of experience at sea —**landlubberly** *adj*

landmark /lánd maark/ *n* 1 a prominent structure or feature that identifies a location 2 a significant or historic event or development

landmass /lánd mass/ *n* a huge area of land

landmine /lánd mīn/ *n* a buried explosive device

landowner /lánd ōnər/ *n* an owner of land —**landowning** *n*, *adj*

land reform *n* the redistribution of land to the landless

Land Registry *n* a UK government department that registers the ownership of land

land rights *npl ANZ* the Aboriginal people's claim to land ownership

landscape /lánd skayp/ *n* 1 an expanse of scenery 2 a picture of scenery ■ *vt* (**-scaping, -scaped**) improve the appearance of an area of land by reshaping and planting

landslide /lánd slīd/ *n* 1 a sudden collapse of land on a mountainside or cliff 2 an overwhelming victory

landward /lándwərd/ *adj* facing land —**landwards** *adv*

lane *n* 1 a narrow road or path 2 a division of a road or motorway for a single line of vehicles or a particular type of vehicle 3 a track assigned to a single runner or swimmer in a race 4 a shipping route

Lang, Fritz (1890–1976) Austrian-born US film director

Lange /lóngi/, **David Russell** (*b.* 1942) prime minister of New Zealand (1984–89)

langoustine /lóng gōō steén/ *n* a large prawn or small lobster

language /láng gwij/ *n* 1 the system of words, sounds, and grammar used by a particular group of people for communication 2 communication with words 3 a specialist vocabulary 4 a style of verbal expression 5 a set of symbols and rules for writing computer programs ◊ **speak the same language** have values or interests in common

ORIGIN **Language** goes back to Latin *lingua* 'tongue'. The suffix *-age* was added in French, from which the word was adopted in the 13C.

SYNONYMS **language**, vocabulary, idiolect, tongue, dialect, slang, jargon, parlance, lingo CORE MEANING: communication by words

Languedoc /lóng gə dók/ historical region and former province in S France, stretching from the Pyrenees to the River Rhône

languid /láng gwid/ *adj* 1 without energy 2 slow-moving —**languidly** *adv*

languish /láng gwish/ *vi* 1 be neglected or deprived 2 become weaker or less successful

languor /láng gər/ *n* 1 a pleasant feeling of weariness 2 listlessness and indifference —**languorous** *adj*

laniard *n* = lanyard

lank *adj* 1 limp and straight ○ *lank hair* 2 long and slender —**lankly** *adv* —**lankness** *n*

lanky /lángki/ (**-ier, -iest**) *adj* tall and thin in an ungraceful way —**lankily** *adv* —**lankiness** *n*

lanolin /lánnəlin/, **lanoline** /-leen/ *n* fat from sheep's wool. Use: in skin creams and ointments.

Lansing /lánssing/ capital of Michigan. Pop. 127,825 (1998).

lantern /lántərn/ *n* a portable lamp with transparent sides

lanthanide /lánthə nīd/ *n* any of a group of rare-earth elements

lanthanum /lánthənəm/ *n* (*symbol* **La**) a rare-earth metallic element. Use: glass manufacture.

lanyard /lányərd/, **laniard** *n* 1 a cord worn round the neck for carrying something 2 a short rope used aboard a ship

Lanzhou /lán jṓ/, **Lan-chou, Lanchow** capital of **Gansu Province,** N China. Pop. 1,194,640 (1990).

Laos /lowss/ independent state of Southeast Asia. Cap. Vientiane. Pop. 5,635,967 (2001). —**Laotian** /lówsh'n, lay ṓsh'n/ *n*, *adj*

Lao-tzu /lów tsóō/ (570?–490? BC) Chinese philosopher

lap[1] *n* the top of a seated person's thighs

lap[2] *n* 1 a circuit of a racetrack 2 a stage, e.g. of a journey ■ *v* (**lapping, lapped**) 1 *vt* overtake a competitor by a complete lap 2 *vt* enfold or wrap (*literary*) 3 *vti* overlap (*literary*)

lap[3] (**lapping, lapped**) *vti* 1 drink liquid with the tongue (*refers to animals*) 2 wash gently against a surface

☐ **lap up** *v* 1 *vti* = lap[3] 1 2 *vt* enjoy something eagerly and uncritically

laparoscopy /láppə róskəpi/ (*pl* **-pies**) *n* an internal abdominal examination through a tube-shaped instrument —**laparoscope** /láppərə skōp/ *n* —**laparoscopic** /láppərə skóppik/ *adj*

La Paz /la páz/ capital of Bolivia. Pop. 758,141 (1997).

lapdog /láp dog/ *n* a small pet dog

lapel /lə pél/ *n* the folded-back front edge of a jacket

lapis lazuli /láppiss lázzyōō lī, -li/ *n* a deep blue semiprecious stone. Use: jewellery.

Lapland /láplənd/ Arctic region extending across the northern parts of Norway, Sweden, Finland, and the Kola Peninsula of Russia —**Laplander** *n*

lap of honour *n* an extra lap performed by a winner to acknowledge applause

Lapp *n* an offensive term for a member of the Sami people —**Lapp** *adj*

lapsang souchong /láp sang soo shóng/ *n* a variety of Chinese tea with a smoky flavour

lapse *n* **1** a momentary fault or failure in behaviour or morality **2** a gap in continuity **3** a passage of time **4** a failure to exercise a legal right in time ■ *vi* (**lapsing, lapsed**) **1** gradually end or stop doing something **2** decline in value, quality, or conduct **3** become null and void through disuse, negligence, or death —**lapsed** *adj*

Laptev Sea /láptef-/ arm of the Arctic Ocean off N Siberian Russia

laptop /láp top/ *n* a small portable computer

lapware /láp wair/ *n* computer software for children

lapwing /láp wing/ (*pl* **-wings** *or same*) *n* a bird of the plover family with a long crest

> **ORIGIN** Early forms of **lapwing** show it to be composed of *leap* and an ancient root related to *wink* that meant 'move from side to side'. Its name derives from the manner of its flight.

~~laquer~~ incorrect spelling of **lacquer**

~~larceney~~ incorrect spelling of **larceny**

larceny /laárss'ni/ *n* theft of personal property (*dated*) —**larcenist** *n* —**larcenous** *adj*

larch (*pl* **larches** *or same*) *n* **1** a deciduous tree of the pine family **2** the durable wood of a larch tree

lard *n* white pork fat used in cooking ■ *v* **1** *vti* add strips of fat to meat before cooking **2** *vt* add to speech or writing ○ *larded with quotations*

larder /laárdər/ *n* a room or cupboard for storing food

large (**larger, largest**) *adj* **1** big in size **2** general in scope ○ *a large view of the subject* —**largeness** *n* ◇ **at large 1** as a widely based and general group of people **2** escaped or free and possibly dangerous ◇ **by and large** speaking generally ◇ **large it, live large** live or celebrate in an extravagant way (*infml*)

large intestine *n* the last section of the alimentary canal

largely /laárjli/ *adv* **1** mainly **2** on a grand scale

larger-than-life *adj* impressive and flamboyant

large-scale *adj* **1** big and detailed **2** extensive

largesse /laar jéss/, **largess** *n* **1** generosity **2** gifts

largo /laárgō/ *adv* fairly slowly (*musical direction*) —**largo** *adj*, *n*

lari /laári/ (*pl* **same** *or* **-ris**) *n* the main unit of Georgian currency

lariat /lárri ət/ *n* US, Can **1** a lasso **2** a rope for tethering an animal

lark¹ *n* a small brownish songbird

lark² *n* **1** a piece of harmless mischief or adventurous fun ○ *did it for a lark* **2** an area of activity (*infml*) ○ *have a go at the catering lark*

■ *vi* **1** have fun **2** act mischievously —**larkish** *adj*

Larkin /laárkin/, **Philip** (1922–85) British poet and jazz critic

larkspur /laárk spur/ *n* a delphinium plant

larva /laárvə/ (*pl* **-vae** /-vee/) *n* the immature worm-shaped form of an insect —**larval** *adj*

laryngitis /lárrin jítiss/ *n* inflammation of the larynx —**laryngitic** /-jíttik/ *adj*

larynx /lárringks/ (*pl* **larynges** /lə rín jeez/ *or* **larynxes**) *n* the part of the respiratory tract containing the vocal cords

lasagne /lə zánnyə, -sánn-, -zaán-/ (*pl* **-gnes** *or same*), **lasagna** (*pl* **-gnas** *or* **-gne**) *n* **1** a dish of alternate layers of thin sheets of pasta and filling **2** pasta in the form of thin sheets

lascivious /lə sívvi əss/ *adj* **1** lewd **2** erotic —**lasciviously** *adv*

Lasdun /lázdən/, **Sir Denys** (1914–2001) British architect

laser /láyzər/ *n* a device emitting a highly focused beam of light

> **ORIGIN Laser** is an acronym formed from initial letters of 'light amplification by stimulated emission of radiation'. It was first reported in 1960.

laser printer *n* a computer printer that uses a laser beam to transfer the image

lash¹ *n* **1** a stroke with a whip **2** an eyelash ■ *v* **1** *vti* strike a surface with violence ○ *Heavy rain lashed the windows.* **2** *vti* criticize somebody severely ○ *lashing into her former colleagues* **3** *vt* strike with a whip **4** *vti* flick something to and fro, or move in this way □ **lash out** *vi* make a sudden verbal or physical attack

lash² *vt* tie something tightly or securely to something else

lashings /láshingz/ *npl* large quantities

Las Palmas /lass pálməss/ seaport and capital of **Las Palmas Province**, NE Grand Canary Island, Spain. Pop. 352,641 (1998).

lass *n* a girl or young woman (*sometimes offensive*)

lassie /lássi/ *n* N England, Scotland a girl or young woman (*infml; sometimes offensive*)

lassitude /lássi tyood/ *n* tiredness and apathy

lasso /lə soó, la-, lássō/ *n* (*pl* **-sos**) a rope with a sliding noose ■ *vt* (**-sos, -soing, -soed**) catch an animal with a lasso

last¹ *adj* **1** most recent **2** being or occurring after all the others **3** final or only remaining **4** least suitable, desirable, or likely ○ *the last thing I wanted to hear* ■ *adv* **1** most recently **2** after all the others ■ *n* **1** somebody or something that is last **2** the final moment ○ *cheerful to the last* —**lastly** *adv* ◇ **at last** finally ◇ **at long last** eventually ◇ **every last** every one

last² *vti* **1** continue for a period of time **2** be sufficient for or remain available to somebody for a period of time ○ *enough bread to last us a week* —**lastingly** *adv*

last[3] n a foot-shaped block used by a shoe maker or cobbler

last-ditch adj final and desperate

lasting /laásting/ adj permanent, or continuing for a long time

Last Judgment n in some beliefs, God's final judgment on humankind at the end of the world

last minute n the latest possible time —**last-minute** adj

last name n somebody's surname

last rites npl 1 a Roman Catholic ceremony for a dying person 2 religious burial rites

Last Supper n Jesus Christ's last meal with his disciples

last word n 1 the final remark in a discussion or argument 2 the ultimate decision 3 the best o the last word in luxury

Las Vegas /lass váygəss/ city in S Nevada. Pop. 404,288 (1998).

lat /laat/ (pl **lati** /látti/ or **lats**) n the main unit of Latvian currency

lat. abbr latitude

latch n 1 a device for keeping a door shut consisting of a movable bar that fits into a notch 2 a door lock that needs a key to be opened from the outside but not the inside ■ vt secure with a latch

□ **latch onto** vt 1 cling or stick to, especially in an unwelcome way 2 adopt something enthusiastically o latched onto the idea

latchkey /lách kee/ (pl **-keys**) n a door key

latchkey child n a child who returns to an empty home after school

late adj, adv (**later**, **latest**) 1 after the expected or usual time 2 near the end of a period of time o late morning 3 recent or recently ■ adj 1 dead o her late uncle 2 until recently o that reporter, late of the European bureau —**lateness** n ◊ **of late** recently ◊ See note at **dead**

latecomer /láyt kumər/ n 1 somebody who arrives late 2 somebody who has recently become involved with or interested in some thing

lately /láytli/ adv recently

latent /láyt'nt/ adj 1 present or existing, but in an undeveloped or unexpressed form 2 having the potential to develop —**latency** n

later /láytər/ comparative of **late** ■ adv after the present time or a specific period of time

lateral /láttərəl/ adj 1 of or at the side 2 sideways —**laterally** adv

lateral thinking n an unconventional approach to solving problems

latest /láytist/ superlative of **late** ■ adj newest, most recent, or most up-to-date —**latest** n

latex /láy teks/ (pl **-texes** or **-tices** /-ti seez/) n 1 a milky liquid produced by some plants 2 a mixture of rubber or plastic particles in water. Use: manufacture of emulsion paints, adhesives, and synthetic rubber products.

lath /laath, lath/ n a thin wooden strip used to support plaster or tiles —**lath** vt

lathe /layth/ n a machine that turns and cuts wood or metal

lather /laáthər, láthər/ n 1 foam produced by soap or detergent used with water 2 white foam produced during periods of heavy exercise, especially by horses 3 an agitated state (infml) ■ v 1 vti produce or cause to produce lather 2 vt cover with soapy lather —**lathery** adj

lathi /laáti/ n S Asia 1 a truncheon 2 a stick used as weapon

Latin /láttin/ n 1 the language of ancient Rome, adopted in medieval Europe as the language of education, culture, religion, and government 2 somebody who speaks a Romance language, especially somebody from S Europe or Latin America —**Latin** adj —**Latinize** vt

Latin America those countries of the Americas that developed from the colonies of Spain, Portugal, and France —**Latin-American** adj, n

latitude /látti tyood/ n 1 an imaginary line around the Earth parallel to the equator, or its angular distance from the equator 2 an area of the Earth's surface near a particular latitude (often pl) o the northern latitudes 3 scope for freedom of action o It's a very creative job, allowing me a great deal of latitude. —**latitudinal** /látti tyoòdin'l/ adj

latke /látkə/ n a fried grated potato cake

La Tour /la toòr/, **Georges de** (1593–1652) French painter

latrine /lə treén/ n a toilet, especially a communal one on a military base

latte /láttay/ n an espresso coffee with steamed milk

latter /láttər/ n, adj the second of two ■ adj coming relatively near the end o in the latter part of his life

latter-day adj resembling somebody or something from the past o a latter-day Churchill

latterly /láttərli/ adv recently

lattice /láttiss/ n 1 also **latticework** /láttiss wurk/ a crisscross framework of interwoven strips 2 a regular geometrical arrangement of points, e.g. the atoms in a crystal —**latticed** adj

Latvia /látvi ə/ country in NE Europe, bordering the Baltic Sea. Cap. Riga. Pop. 2,385,231 (2001). —**Latvian** n, adj

laud /lawd/ vt praise highly —**laudatory** /láwdətəri/ adj

SPELLCHECK Do not confuse the spelling of **laud** and **lord** ('an aristocrat'), which sound similar.

Laud /lawd/, **William, Archbishop of Canterbury** (1573–1645) English cleric

laudable /láwdəb'l/ adj praiseworthy —**laudably** adv

laudanum /láwd'nəm/ n a solution of opium in alcohol. Use: formerly, for pain relief.

laugh /laaf/ vi 1 make sounds in the throat expressing amusement 2 mock or show contempt for somebody or something ■ *n* 1 a sound made when laughing 2 somebody or something funny or entertaining *(infml)* —**laugher** *n* —**laughingly** *adv* ◊ **have the last laugh** be proved right or triumph in the end

□ **laugh off** *vt* treat something serious as trivial

laughable /láafəb'l/ *adj* ridiculously inadequate —**laughably** *adv*

laughing stock *n* an object of ridicule

laughter /láaftər/ *n* the sound or act of laughing

launch[1] /lawnch/ *vt* 1 fire a spacecraft or missile into the air 2 put a boat or ship into the water 3 begin or initiate a planned activity ○ *launched an investigation* 4 put a new product on sale 5 hurl yourself at something or somebody —**launch** *n* —**launcher** *n*

□ **launch into** *vt* begin suddenly and enthusiastically ○ *launched into a description of her new invention*

□ **launch out** *vi* start something new and untried

launch[2] /lawnch/ *n* a large motorboat

launch pad, launching pad *n* 1 a platform for launching rockets 2 a starting point for success

launder /láwndər/ *vt* 1 wash clothes or linen 2 pass money through a legitimate account to disguise its illegal origins

launderette /láwndə rét, -drét/, **laundrette** *n* an establishment with coin-operated washing machines

Laundromat /láwndrə mat/ *Aus, US, Can* a service mark for a self-service coin-operated commercial laundry

laundry /láwndri/ *(pl* -**dries***)* *n* 1 dirty washing 2 freshly laundered clothes 3 a place where clothes and linen are laundered

ORIGIN Laundry is a contraction of an obsolete word *lavendry*, which goes back to the Latin verb *lavare* 'wash'. **Laundry** is first recorded early in the 16C. It was based on, and reinforced by, the related *launder*, which is now a verb but was originally a noun, 'a person who washes linen'.

laureate /láwri ət, lórr-/ *n* 1 an award winner in the arts or sciences 2 a poet laureate —**laureate** *adj* —**laureateship** *n*

laurel /lórrəl/ *n* 1 the bay tree 2 an evergreen tree or bush with dark or spotted leaves and berries 3 a wreath of bay leaves awarded as an honour in classical times ■ **laurels** *npl* honour won for achievement ◊ **rest on your laurels** be satisfied with your success and do nothing to improve on it

Lausanne /lō zán/ city of W Switzerland, on Lake Geneva. Pop. 114,161 (1998).

lava /láavə/ *n* 1 molten rock flowing from a volcano 2 rock formed from solidified lava

Laval /lə vál/ city in W France. Pop. 50,473 (1990).

lavatorial /lávvə táwri əl/ *adj* containing references to excretion *(disapproving)* ○ *lavatorial humour*

lavatory /lávvətri/ *(pl* -**ries***)* *n* a toilet

lavender /lávvəndər/ *n* 1 a plant with fragrant leaves and flowers 2 dried lavender flowers and leaves. Use: essential oil, perfume for clothes, linen, or toiletries. 3 a pale purple colour

laver[1] /láyvər/ *n* a basin for ritual washing in synagogues

laver[2] /láavər/ *n* a dried edible seaweed

Laver /láyvər/, **Rod** (*b.* 1938) Australian tennis player

laver bread /láavər-/ *n* fried cakes of boiled seaweed

lavish /lávvish/ *adj* 1 abundant 2 generous or extravagant ■ *vt* give or spend lavishly ○ *lavished attention on the child* —**lavishly** *adv* —**lavishness** *n*

Lavoisier /lə vwáazi ay/, **Antoine Laurent** (1743–94) French chemist. He published the first proper table of the chemical elements.

law *n* 1 a binding or enforceable rule 2 a piece of legislation 3 the body of laws of a community 4 control or authority ○ *the rule of law* 5 the legal profession 6 the police 7 a statement of scientific truth ◊ **lay down the law** express an opinion in an overbearing or dogmatic way

law-abiding *adj* obeying the law

law and order *n* 1 enforcement of the law 2 social stability resulting from observance of the law

lawbreaker /láw braykər/ *n* somebody who breaks the law —**lawbreaking** *n, adj*

law centre *n* a publicly funded legal advice centre

lawful /láwf'l/ *adj* permitted or authorized by law —**lawfully** *adv* —**lawfulness** *n* ◊ See note at **legal**

lawless /láwləss/ *adj* 1 unregulated 2 having no laws —**lawlessly** *adv* —**lawlessness** *n*

Law Lords *npl* members of the House of Lords qualified to take part in judicial business

lawmaker /láw maykər/ *n* somebody who drafts and enacts laws —**lawmaking** *n, adj*

lawn[1] *n* an area of short cultivated grass

lawn[2] *n* a fine light fabric. Use: clothing, household linen.

USAGE The material **lawn** is probably named after Laon, a town in France that was noted for linen manufacture.

lawn mower *n* a machine for cutting grass

law of the jungle *n* aggressive or competitive behaviour motivated by self-interest or survival

D. H. Lawrence

Lawrence /lórrənss/, **D. H.** (1885–1930) British writer

Lawrence, T. E. (1888–1935) British soldier and author

lawrencium /lə rénssi əm/ n (*symbol* **Lr**) a radioactive metallic chemical element

ORIGIN Lawrencium is named after the US physicist Ernest O. Lawrence (1901–58).

Lawson /láwss'n/, **Henry Hertzberg** (1867–1922) Australian writer

Lawson, Louisa (1848–1920) Australian writer, publisher, and feminist

lawsuit /láw soot, -syoot/ n a court case between individuals

lawyer /láwyər, lóy ər/ n somebody qualified to practise law

lax adj 1 not strict or careful enough 2 not tight or tense —**laxity** n —**laxly** adv —**laxness** n

laxative /láksətiv/ n a drug used to promote bowel movements —**laxative** adj

lay[1] v (**laid**) 1 vt put something or somebody down in a horizontal position 2 vt put or place something ○ *laid emphasis on this fact* 3 vt place something over a surface 4 vt cause something to lie flat 5 vt prepare by setting out the required items ○ *lay the table for lunch* 6 vti produce eggs 7 vt devise or prepare something ○ *lay a trap* ■ n the way something lies ◇ **be laid low** become ill or incapacitated ◇ **lay it on (thick)** exaggerate greatly ◇ **lay yourself open to** put yourself in a position where you are vulnerable to

□ **lay by** vt set something aside for the future

□ **lay down** vt 1 surrender or sacrifice something 2 formulate a rule

□ **lay in** vt acquire and store for the future

□ **lay into** vt hit forcefully

□ **lay off** v 1 vt stop employing somebody when there is insufficient work 2 vti stop doing or using something (*infml*)

□ **lay on** vt 1 apply or use something to excess 2 provide something

□ **lay out** vt 1 spread something out for display 2 plan or design something 3 prepare somebody for burial 4 spend money

□ **lay up** vt 1 store something for future use 2 confine somebody with an injury or illness

lay[2] adj 1 not belonging to the clergy 2 without specialist knowledge or professional training

lay[3] n 1 a poem for singing 2 a song

lay[4] past tense of **lie**[1]

layabout /láy ə bowt/ n a person regarded as lazy or idle

lay-by (*pl* **lay-bys**) n 1 UK a stopping place at the edge of a road 2 ANZ paying for goods in instalments

layer /láy ər/ n 1 a flat covering or single thickness 2 somebody who lays something (*usually in combination*) ○ *a bricklayer* ■ v 1 vti arrange in or form into layers 2 vt cut hair in different lengths

layette /lay ét/ n a set of clothing and accessories for a baby

layman /láymən/ (*pl* -**men** /-mən/) n a layperson, especially a man

layoff /láy of/ n 1 the laying off of employees 2 a period of unemployment

layout /láy owt/ n 1 the way things are arranged, or a design showing this 2 the design or arrangement of printed matter on a page

layperson /láy purss'n/ (*pl* -**people** /-peep'l/) n 1 somebody without specialist knowledge or professional training 2 somebody who is not a member of the clergy

lay reader n a layperson who acts as a reader in church services

laywoman /láy wŏomən/ (*pl* -**en** /-wimin/) n a female layperson

laze (**lazing, lazed**) vi relax or be idle

lazy /láyzi/ (-**zier**, -**ziest**) adj 1 not wanting to work or make an effort 2 conducive to idleness —**lazily** adv —**laziness** n

lazybones /láyzi bōnz/ (*pl same*) n a person regarded as lazy (*infml*)

lazy Susan /-sŏoz'n/ n a revolving circular tray used on a dining table

lb abbr pound or pounds

lbw abbr leg before wicket

lc abbr lower case

LCD abbr 1 liquid-crystal display 2 lowest common denominator

lea /lee/ n a grassy field (*literary*)

LEA abbr Local Education Authority

leach /leech/ vti drain away from soil when dissolved in rainwater (*refers to minerals and chemicals*)

Leach, Bernard (1887–1979) British potter

Leacock /leé kok/, **Stephen** (1869–1944) British-born Canadian writer

lead[1] /leed/ v (**led** /led/) 1 vti show the way to others, usually by going ahead 2 vi be the way somewhere ○ *a path leading to the canal* 3 vt bring a person or animal by pulling 4 vti direct or command others 5 vt be in charge of something 6 vt cause somebody to do something 7 vi result in something ○ *leading to confusion* 8 vt live a particular kind of life 9 vti be at the beginning or front of something 10 vti be ahead of others ■ n 1 the front position, first place, or principal role 2 a distance between competitors 3 a starring role or actor 4 the role of somebody in command or in charge 5 an example or precedent 6 a tip or clue 7 a line used to control a dog when walking it **8** a wire conducting electricity ◊ See note at **guide**

☐ **lead off** *vi* begin first

☐ **lead on** *vt* entice with a false promise

☐ **lead up to** *vt* **1** prepare the way for something **2** approach a subject indirectly

lead² /led/ *n* **1** (*symbol* **Pb**) a heavy bluish-grey metallic chemical element. Use: car batteries, pipes, solder, radiation shields. **2** a weight on a line for measuring depth **3** a stick of graphite in a pencil ■ *vt* cover with lead

SPELLCHECK Do not confuse the spelling of **lead** (a noun meaning 'heavy metallic chemical element') and **led** (past tense and past participle of the verb **lead**), which sound similar.

lead balloon /led-/ *n* a complete failure

leaded /léddid/ *adj* **1** containing lead **2** with small glass panes secured by lead strips

leaden /lédd'n/ *adj* **1** of lead **2** dull and grey **3** tired and heavy —**leadenly** *adv*

leader /leédər/ *n* **1** somebody or something that leads **2** the principal musician of an orchestra **3** *also* **leading article** a newspaper article expressing the editor's opinion

leadership /leédər ship/ *n* **1** the office or position of the leader of a body of people **2** ability to lead or influence people **3** the guiding or directing of people

lead-in /leéd-/ *n* **1** an introductory remark **2** aerial wire

leading¹ /leéding/ *adj* **1** very important or well known **2** ahead

leading² /lédding/ *n* **1** lead strips around glass panes **2** the spacing around lines of type

leading edge /leéding-/ *n* **1** the forefront of development ◦ *at the leading edge of technology* **2** the forward edge of an aircraft wing, propeller, or aerofoil

leading lady /leéding-/ *n* somebody who plays the main female role in a play or film

leading light /leéding-/ *n* an outstanding or influential person

leading man /leéding-/ *n* somebody who plays the main male role in a play or film

leading question /leéding-/ *n* a question that prompts the desired answer

lead time /leéd-/ *n* the time needed to do something, e.g. between ordering and delivery of goods

leaf /leef/ (*pl* **leaves** /leevz/) *n* **1** a flat green part that grows from the stem or branch of a plant and whose main function is photosynthesis **2** leaves, or the state or time of having leaves ◦ *when the trees are in leaf* **3** a sheet of paper in a book **4** very thin metal foil **5** a hinged, sliding, or removable part of a table top, door, or shutter —**leafless** *adj* ◊ **turn over a new leaf** start to behave in a more acceptable way

☐ **leaf through** *vt* turn the pages of

leaflet /leéflət/ *n* **1** a piece of printed material distributed free **2** a small leaf ■ *vti* distribute leaflets in a place or to a group

leafy /leéfi/ (**-ier**, **-iest**) *adj* **1** with many leaves or trees **2** describes vegetables with edible leaves —**leafiness** *n*

~~**leag, leage**~~ incorrect spelling of **league**

league /leeg/ *n* **1** a group of states or organizations with common interests or goals **2** a group of sports clubs or teams that compete with each other —**league** *vti*

league table *n* **1** a list of members of a sports league **2** a list of ranking order based on performance

leak /leek/ *n* **1** a hole or crack through which something escapes or enters **2** an accidental escape or entry of gas, liquid, or electricity **3** a disclosure of confidential information **4** an act of urination *(slang)* ■ *vti* **1** let something in or out accidentally through a hole or crack, or escape or enter in this way **2** disclose confidential information unofficially or covertly, or be disclosed in this way —**leakage** *n* —**leakiness** *n* —**leakproof** *adj* —**leaky** *adj*

SPELLCHECK Do not confuse the spelling of **leak** and **leek** (the vegetable), which sound similar.

Leakey /leéki/ family of British archaeologists and palaeontologists including **Louis** (1903– 72), his wife **Mary** (1913–96), and their son **Richard** (*b.* 1944)

lean¹ /leen/ (**leant** /lent/ *or* **leaned**) *v* **1** *vi* bend or incline **2** *vti* rest against something for support **3** *vi* show a tendency or preference ◦ *leaning towards a more tolerant approach* —**lean** *n* —**leaning** *n*

☐ **lean on** *vt* be dependent on or supported by

lean² /leen/ *adj* **1** without excess body fat **2** not fatty ◦ *lean meat* **3** not productive or profitable **4** economical and efficient ■ *n* meat without fat —**leanly** *adv* —**leanness** *n* ◊ See note at **thin**

Lean /leen/, **Sir David** (1908–91) British film director

Leander /li ándər/ *n* in Greek mythology, the lover of Hero who drowned while swimming to visit her

lean-to (*pl* **lean-tos**) *n* a structure with a sloping roof built against a wall

leap /leep/ (**leapt** /lept/ *or* **leaped**) *vi* **1** jump high or a long distance **2** move, change, or increase abruptly or substantially —**leap** *n* ◊ **in** *or* **by leaps and bounds** extremely rapidly

leapfrog /leép frog/ *n* a game in which players vault over each other ■ *v* (**-frogging**, **-frogged**) **1** *vt* vault over somebody in leapfrog, or over something as if in leapfrog **2** *vi* advance quickly by passing others

leap year *n* a year with 366 days, occurring usually once every four years

Lear /leer/, **Edward** (1812–88) British writer and artist

learn /lurn/ (**learned** *or* **learnt** /lurnt/) *vti* **1** acquire knowledge of a subject or skill **2** find out something —**learner** *n*

learned /lúrnid/ *adj* having or showing much education and knowledge —**learnedness** *n*

learning /lúrning/ *n* **1** the acquisition of knowledge **2** acquired knowledge

learning curve *n* **1** the rate of learning something new **2** a graph plotting the rate of learning against the time spent

learning disability, learning difficulty *n* a condition that prevents or hinders somebody from learning basic skills such as reading and mathematics —**learning-disabled** *adj*

lease /leess/ *n* **1** a rental contract **2** the period of time covered by a lease ■ *vt* (**leasing, leased**) rent —**leasable** *adj* —**leaser** *n*

leaseback /leéss bak/ *n* an arrangement that involves selling property then renting it from the new owner

leasehold /leéss hōld/ *n* the holding of a property through a lease —**leaseholder** *n*

leash /leesh/ *n* **1** a dog's lead **2** a restraint ■ *vt* restrain

least /leest/ *pron* the smallest or lowest ■ *adj* smallest or lowest ■ *adv* to or in the smallest or lowest degree ◊ **at least 1** not less than **2** in any case ◊ *At least you still have a job.* ◊ **not (in) the least** not at all ◊ **not least** especially

leather /léthər/ *n* **1** the tanned and dressed hide of animals **2** a polishing cloth made of leather —**leather** *adj* —**leathery** *adj*

leave[1] /leev/ (**leaving, left**) *v* **1** *vti* go away from a person or place **2** *vt* cause something to remain **3** *vt* let something remain behind accidentally **4** *vt* give something in a will **5** *vt* not change the condition of something **6** *vt* have something remaining ◊ *6 minus 4 leaves 2.* **7** *vt* set something aside **8** *vt* abandon a person or place **9** *vt* have somebody as a survivor **10** *vti* give up your position in something **11** *vt* give a task to another person ◊ *Leave it to me.* ◊ **leave much to be desired** be highly unsatisfactory

☐ **leave behind** *vt* **1** progress faster than **2** forget about ◊ *leaving your cares behind you*

☐ **leave off** *v* **1** *vi* stop doing something **2** *vt* stop using or wearing

☐ **leave out** *vt* omit or exclude

leave[2] /leev/ *n* **1** a period of permitted absence **2** permission (*fml*)

leaven /lév'n/ *n* also **leavening** /lév'ning/ **1** a raising agent in dough **2** something that enlivens (*literary*) ■ *vt* **1** make bread or cake rise **2** enliven something (*literary*)

leave of absence *n* **1** permission to be absent **2** time away from work

leaves plural of **leaf**

leave-taking *n* a farewell (*literary*)

leavings /leévingz/ *npl* scraps

Leavis /leéviss/**, F. R.** (1895–1978) British literary critic

Lebanon /lébbənən/ country in SW Asia, on the Mediterranean Sea. Cap. Beirut. Pop. 3,627,774 (2001). —**Lebanese** /lébbə neéz/ *n, adj*

lecher /léchər/ *n* a man regarded as lustful (*disapproving*) —**lecherous** *adj* —**lecherously** *adv* —**lechery** *n*

ORIGIN **Lecher** comes from a French word meaning literally 'licker'. The verb from which it derives had come to mean 'live a life of debauchery or gluttony' as well as 'lick'.

Le Corbusier /lə káwr boózi ay/ (1887–1965) Swiss-born French architect and designer

lectern /léktərn/ *n* a reading stand

lecture /lékchər/ *n* **1** an instructional speech **2** a teaching session at which a lecture is given —**lecture** *vti*

lecturer /lékchərər/ *n* **1** a university teacher ranking below professor **2** a professional or experienced speaker about a specific topic

lecture theatre *n* a room in which speeches are made and lectures given

led /led/ past tense, past participle of **lead**[1] ◊ See note at **lead**[2]

LED *n* a semiconductor used for indicator lights on electronic equipment. Full form **light-emitting diode**

ledge /n/ **1** a narrow shelf fixed to a wall **2** a flat surface projecting from a rock face **3** a raised surface underwater, especially near a shore —**ledged** *adj*

ledger /léjjər/ *n* a financial record book with columns for debits and credits

lee *n* **1** the side of a ship that is away from the wind **2** shelter from the elements

Lee, Laurie (1914–97) British poet and writer

Lee, Robert E. (1807–70) US Confederate general

leech *n* **1** a blood-sucking worm **2** an exploiter of other people

Leeds city in N England. Pop. 726,939 (1996).

leek /leek/ *n* a slender edible plant with green leaves and a white stem and bulb ◊ See note at **leak**

Lee Kuan Yew /leé kwa'an yoó/ (*b.* 1923) prime minister of Singapore (1959–90)

leer /vi/ look lasciviously or maliciously —**leer** *n* —**leering** *adj*

leery /leéri/ (**-ier, -iest**) *adj* suspicious or wary (*infml*) —**leeriness** *n*

lees *npl* wine sediment

leeward /leéward/ *nautical* /loó ərd/ *adj, adv* away from the wind

Leeward Islands /leéward-/ group of islands in the NE Caribbean. The principal islands include Antigua and Barbuda, Guadeloupe, Montserrat, and St Kitts.

leeway /leé way/ *n* **1** a margin for variation **2** failure to make progress

left[1] *adj* **1** on or towards the west when somebody is facing north **2** also **Left** advocating liberal, socialist, or communist political and social changes or reform **3** on the river bank to the left when somebody is looking downstream ■ *adv* on or towards the left side ■ *n* **1** the left side of somebody or something **2** also **Left** people who support liberal, socialist, or communist political and social changes or reform **3** a position to the left of somebody or something, or a turn towards the left **4** a left-handed punch, or the ability to deliver such a punch —**leftism** *n* —**leftist** *n, adj*

ORIGIN The earliest meaning of **left** is 'weak'. It came to refer to the left, or 'weaker', side of the body around the beginning of the 13C.

left² past tense, past participle of **leave¹**

left-click *vti* click with the left mouse button

~~leftenant~~ incorrect spelling of **lieutenant**

left-hand *adj* **1** on or towards the left **2** intended for or done by the left hand

left-handed *adj, adv* using the left hand, rather than the right, for tasks such as writing ■ *adj* done with the left hand

left-hander /-hándər/ *n* somebody who uses his or her left hand for most things

leftover /léft óvər/ *adj* remaining unused ■ *n* something remaining ■ **leftovers** *npl* food saved from a previous meal

leftward /léftwərd/ *adj* moving towards or located on the left —**leftwards** *adv*

left wing *n* **1** the members of an organization who most favour change **2** the side of a field of play that is left of an opponent's goal —**left-wing** *adj* —**left-winger** *n*

lefty /léfti/ (*pl* **-ies**), **leftie** *n* somebody with left-wing beliefs (*infml*)

leg *n* **1** a lower limb that a person or animal uses for support or motion **2** a supporting pole **3** meat from the leg of an animal or bird **4** a part of a piece of clothing that covers the leg **5** a section of a journey or course **6** the part of a relay race completed by one athlete **7** a portion of a sports competition that has its own winner **8** one of two football games played as a unit in a competition **9** the left-hand side of a cricket field ◇ **a leg up 1** an upwards boost **2** something that helps somebody to make progress ◇ **leg it** (*infml*) **1** run away, especially in order to escape **2** walk or run ◇ **on your last legs** on the verge of collapse ◇ **pull somebody's leg** tell somebody something untrue as a tease (*infml*)

legacy /léggəssi/ *n* (*pl* **-cies**) **1** a bequest made in a will **2** something from the past that still exists or has an effect ■ *adj* still in use although technically superseded ○ *legacy software*

legal /léeg'l/ *adj* **1** of the law **2** of or for lawyers **3** established or permitted by law —**legally** *adv*

SYNONYMS legal, lawful, decriminalized, legalized, legitimate, licit CORE MEANING: describes something that is permitted, recognized, or required by law

legal aid *n* **1** free lawyers' services **2** government aid for legal costs

legalese /léegə léez/ *n* law jargon

legality /li gálləti/ *n* conformity to the law

legalize /léegə līz/ (**-izing, -ized**), **legalise** *vt* make lawful —**legalization** /léegə līzáysh'n/ *n*

legal tender *n* valid currency

legate /léggət/ *n* **1** a pope's representative **2** a government representative or diplomat —**legateship** *n*

legatee /léggə téé/ *n* a recipient of a legacy

legation /li gáysh'n/ *n* **1** a senior diplomat's residence **2** a group of diplomats on a mission

legato /li gaató/ *adv* smoothly (*musical direction*) —**legato** *adj, n*

legend /léjjənd/ *n* **1** an old story presented as history but unlikely to be true **2** old stories in general **3** a popular modern myth **4** a celebrity **5** an inscription on an object **6** a caption for an illustration **7** an explanation of symbols on a map —**legendary** *adj*

legerdemain /léjjərdə máyn/ *n* a show of skill or cleverness, especially with deceitful intent

-legged /léggid/ *suffix* **1** with a particular number of legs ○ *four-legged* **2** with a particular type or position of legs ○ *cross-legged*

legging /légging/ *n* a protective covering for the lower leg ■ **leggings** *npl* close-fitting trousers

leggy /léggi/ (**-gier, -giest**) *adj* with long or shapely legs

legible /léjjəb'l/ *adj* clear enough to be read —**legibility** /léjjə bílləti/ *n* —**legibly** *adv*

legion /léejən/ *n* **1** in ancient Rome, an army division **2** a large body of soldiers **3** an association of ex-military personnel **4** a multitude (*often pl*) ■ *adj* many (*literary*) —**legionary** *adj* —**legionnaire** /léejə náir/ *n*

legionnaires' disease *n* virulent bacterial pneumonia

ORIGIN Legionnaires' disease is so called because the first recognized outbreak was at an American Legion convention in Philadelphia in 1976.

legislate /léjji slayt/ (**-lating, -lated**) *v* **1** *vi* make laws **2** *vt* bring about by making laws —**legislator** *n*

legislation /léjji sláysh'n/ *n* **1** the process of making laws **2** a law or body of laws

legislative /léjjislətiv/ *adj* of law-making or a law-making body

legislature /léjjisləchər/ *n* a body of people authorized to make laws

~~legitamate~~ incorrect spelling of **legitimate**

legitimate *adj* /lə jíttimət/ **1** legal **2** conforming to acknowledged standards **3** well-founded ○ *legitimate concerns about water quality* **4** born of legally married parents ■ *vt* /lə jitti mayt/ LAW = **legitimize** —**legitimacy** *n* —**legitimately** *adv*

legitimize /lə jitti mīz/ (**-mizing, -mized**), **legitimise** *vt* **1** legalize **2** prove to be lawful —**legitimization** /lə jitti mī záysh'n/ *n*

legless /léggləss/ *adj* **1** with no legs **2** drunk (*infml*)

Lego /léggō/ *tdmk* a trademark for a toy consisting of plastic building blocks and other components

legroom /lég room, -rŏŏm/ *n* space for your legs to move

Le Guin /lə gwín/, **Ursula** (*b*. 1929) US science-fiction writer

legume /léggyoom/ *n* **1** an edible seed or pod such as a bean or pea **2** a plant that produces legumes —**leguminous** /li gyŏōminəss/ *adj*

legwork /lég wurk/ *n* basic research (*infml*)

Le Havre /lə haávrə/ seaport in N France, on the English Channel. Pop. 190,905 (1999).

lei[1] /lay/ (*pl* **leis**) *n* in Polynesia and Hawaii, a flower garland worn around the neck

lei[2] /lay/ plural of **leu**

Leibniz /líb nits/, **Leibnitz, Gottfried Wilhelm von, Baron** (1646–1716) German philosopher and mathematician —**Leibnizian** /líb nítsi ən/ *adj, n*

Leicester /léstər/ city in central England. Pop. 299,080 (1997).

Leicester, Robert Dudley, 1st Earl of (1532–88) English courtier

Leicestershire /léstərshər/ county in central England

Leichhardt /lík haart/, **Ludwig** (1813–48?) Prussian-born Australian naturalist and explorer

Leigh /lee/, **Mike** (*b*. 1943) British playwright and film director

Leipzig /lípsig/ city in east-central Germany. Pop. 481,526 (1997).

leisure /lézhər/ *n* free time —**leisured** *adj* ◇ **at your leisure** at a time and pace that suits you

leisure centre *n* a public building with space and equipment for recreational activities

leisurely /lézhərli/ *adj* slow and relaxed ■ *adv* in an unhurried way —**leisureliness** *n*

leisurewear /lézhər wair/ *n* comfortable clothing worn for relaxation or play

leitmotif /lítmō teef/, **leitmotiv** *n* **1** a thematic passage in a piece of music **2** a main recurring theme

Leitrim /leetrim/ county in Connacht Province, N Republic of Ireland

~~leiu~~ incorrect spelling of **lieu**

lek *n* the main unit of Albanian currency

lekker /lékər/ *adj* S Africa pleasant (*infml*)

Lemaître /lə méttrə/, **Georges-Henri** (1894–1966) Belgian astrophysicist and priest. He was a proponent of the 'big bang' theory of the universe.

lemming /lémming/ *n* **1** a rodent with a small thick furry body **2** a conformist mindlessly following a destructive course of action

lemon /lémmən/ *n* **1** an oval yellow citrus fruit with sour juicy flesh **2** a tree that produces lemons **3** a pale yellow colour **4** something that is defective or disappointing (*infml*) —**lemon** *adj* —**lemony** *adj*

lemonade /lémmə nayd/ *n* **1** a fizzy clear drink **2** a drink made from lemons

lemon curd, lemon cheese *n* a sweet yellow spread made with lemons

lemon grass *n* a type of grass that produces perfumed oil and is used in cookery

lemon sole *n* **1** an edible flatfish **2** lemon sole as food

lemon-squeezer *n* a kitchen gadget for squeezing the juice from citrus fruits

lempira /lem peérə/ *n* the main unit of Honduran currency

lemur /leémər/ *n* a primate that lives in Madagascar

Lena /leénə/ river in Siberian Russia, emptying into the Laptev Sea. Length 4,400 km/2,700 mi.

lend (**lent**) *v* **1** *vt* let somebody borrow something **2** *vti* give somebody money for a limited time **3** *vt* add a quality to something ○ *lend an air of intimacy* —**lender** *n* ◇ **lend itself to** be suitable for a particular purpose

length *n* **1** the distance from end to end **2** the quality of being long **3** the time something takes from beginning to end **4** a long piece of something narrow ○ *a length of copper piping* **5** a standard unit of measurement ○ *three lengths of fabric* **6** a swim from end to end in a swimming pool **7** a set distance **8** in a race, a unit of distance between two competitors, measured as the length of one competitor ○ *two lengths ahead* **9** the degree to which somebody pursues an action or a thought ○ *going to great lengths to win* ◇ **at length 1** in great detail and for a long time (*fml*) **2** after a long while or a delay

lengthen /léngth'n/ *vti* become or make longer

lengthways /léngth wayz/, **lengthwise** /-wīz/ *adv, adj* along or parallel to the longest side

lengthy /léngthi/ (-**ier**, -**iest**) *adj* long, or too long —**lengthily** *adv* —**lengthiness** *n*

lenient /leéni ənt/ *adj* not harsh —**lenience** *n* —**leniency** *n* —**leniently** *adv*

AKG London

Vladimir Ilyich Lenin

Lenin /lénnin/, **Vladimir Ilyich** (1870–1924) Russian revolutionary leader

Leningrad /lénnin grad/ former name for **St Petersburg**

Leninism /lénninizəm/ *n* Lenin's theories developed from Marxism —**Leninist** *n, adj*

Lenin Peak mountain on the border between Tajikistan and Kyrgyzstan, in the Trans-Alai Range of the Pamirs. Height 7,134 m/23,406 ft.

lens /lenz/ *n* **1** a piece of curved and polished glass or other transparent material that forms an image by focusing light **2** a system of lenses used in a camera or other optical instrument **3** a contact lens **4** the part of the eye that focuses light on the retina

lent past participle, past tense of **lend**

Lent *n* in the Christian calendar, the period of 40 weekdays before Easter

---

ORIGIN Lent, like earlier **Lenten**, of which it is a shortened form, was originally the name of the season of spring. It comes from the same ancient root as *long*, with reference to the lengthening of the days at that time of year. Because the ecclesiastical period of **Lent** fell within spring, however, it came increasingly to have that more restrictive sense.

~~lenth~~ incorrect spelling of **length**

lentil /lént'l/ *n* **1** an edible seed that is sold dried and split **2** a plant that produces lentils

lento /léntō/ *adv* slowly *(musical direction)* —**lento** *adj, n*

Leo /leé ō/ *n* **1** a zodiacal constellation in the northern hemisphere **2** the 5th sign of the zodiac —**Leo** *adj* —**Leonian** /lee ṓni ən/ *n*

Leo X /leé ō/ (1475–1521) pope (1513–21)

Leonardo da Vinci /leé ō naàrd ō də vínchi/ (1452–1519) Italian painter, sculptor, architect, engineer, and scientist

leone /lee ṓn/ *n* the main unit of Sierra Leonean currency

leonine /leé ə nīn/ *adj* of or like a lion

leopard /léppərd/ *n* a large slender wild cat with a brown to red coat with black spots

leotard /leé ə taard/ *n* a tight stretchy garment that covers the torso, worn especially by dancers, gymnasts, and athletes

---

ORIGIN The **leotard** is named after the French trapeze artist Jules Léotard (1830–70), who designed it.

---

leper /léppər/ *n* **1** somebody with leprosy **2** somebody whom other people avoid

leprechaun /léppri kawn/ *n* in Irish folklore, a mischievous elf

---

ORIGIN Leprechaun comes from an Irish word meaning literally 'little body'. It was first used in English in the early 17C.

---

leprosy /léprəssi/ *n* a tropical disease of the skin and nerves —**leprous** *adj*

lepton /lép ton/ *n* a subatomic particle that interacts only weakly with other particles —**leptonic** /lep tónnik/ *adj*

Lermontov /lyérməntəf/, **Mikhail Yuryevich** (1814–41) Russian poet and novelist

lesbian /lézbi ən/ *n* a woman who is sexually attracted to other women —**lesbian** *adj* —**lesbianism** *n*

Lesbos /léz boss/ island in E Greece, in the Aegean Sea. Pop. 103,700 (1991). —**Lesbian** *adj, n*

lesion /leèzh'n/ *n* a damaged area in part of the body, especially a skin wound

Lesotho /lə sṓtō/ country in southern Africa, bordered on all sides by South Africa. Cap. Maseru. Pop. 2,177,062 (2001).

less *det, pron* a smaller amount ◼ *adv* to a smaller degree ◼ *prep* with the subtraction of ◇ **less than** not o *has been less than pleasant*

-less *suffix* **1** without, lacking o *headless* o *restless* **2** unable to be o *fathomless*

lessee /le seé/ *n* somebody who holds a lease

lessen /léss'n/ *vti* make or become less

Lesseps /léssəps/, **Ferdinand Marie, Vicomte de** (1805–94) French diplomat and engineer

lesser /léssər/ *adj, adv* not as big or important

Lesser Antilles /-an tílleez/ island group in the Caribbean, stretching from Puerto Rico southeastwards to the coast of Venezuela and comprising the Virgin Islands, Leeward Islands, and Windward Islands

Lesser Sunda Islands ♦ Sunda Islands

Doris Lessing

Lessing /léssing/, **Doris** (*b.* 1919) British novelist, brought up in southern Africa

lesson /léss'n/ *n* **1** a period of time spent teaching or studying **2** the material taught in a lesson **3** a useful experience that teaches you something **4** new or better knowledge **5** *also* **Lesson** a Bible passage read during a church service **6** a rebuke o *gave her a lesson in manners*

ORIGIN Lesson came via French from a Latin word meaning 'reading'. This etymological sense survives in the **lesson** read in church. From 'something to be read' it came to mean 'something to be studied', and then a 'period of time spent teaching or studying'.

---

lessor /le sáwr, léssawr/ *n* somebody who grants a lease

lest *conj* in case

let[1] *vt* (**letting, let**) **1** not prevent **2** give permission to do something o *Dad won't let me.* **3** expresses a suggestion o *Let us pray.* **4** allow in or out o *let blood* **5** expresses resignation or indifference o *Let them try!* **6** rent out ◼ *n* a grant of a lease ◇ **let alone** even less o *a region barely explored, let alone mapped* ◇ **let go (of)** stop holding ◇ **let somebody go** dismiss somebody from his or her employment ◇ **let somebody have it** attack somebody physically or verbally ◇ **let yourself go 1** start acting in a much more relaxed way than usual **2** stop caring about your appearance

☐ **let down** *vt* **1** lower something **2** disappoint

somebody **3** make air come out of something **4** lengthen a garment

□ **let off** *vt* **1** excuse somebody from punishment **2** allow somebody to get off a vehicle

□ **let on** *v* **1** *vi* share a secret *(infml)* **2** *vi* pretend **3** *vt* allow somebody to get on a vehicle

□ **let out** *vt* **1** make a loud yell **2** release somebody or something **3** enlarge a garment

□ **let up** *vi* **1** become slower **2** relax

let² *n* in tennis or squash, a replayed service shot or point

-let *suffix* **1** small one ○ *droplet* **2** something worn on ○ *bracelet* ○ *necklet*

letdown /lét down/ *n* a disappointment

lethal /leeth'l/ *adj* **1** deadly **2** harmful —**lethality** /lee tháləti/ *n* —**lethally** *adv* ◊ See note at **deadly**

lethargy /léthərji/ *n* **1** sluggishness **2** lack of enthusiasm —**lethargic** /lə thaárjik/ *adj* —**lethargically** *adv*

let-out *n* a way out of an agreement

let's *contr* let us

letter /léttər/ *n* **1** a message sent by mail **2** a symbol representing a sound or sounds and used to spell words ■ *vt* write letters or words on

letter bomb *n* **1** a package containing explosives that is sent by mail **2** a destructive e-mail

letterbox /léttər boks/ *n* **1** a slot for delivering mail through a door **2** a postbox

lettered /léttərd/ *adj* **1** with letters written on it **2** educated

letterhead /léttər hed/ *n* **1** headed stationery for writing letters on **2** a printed name and address on stationery

lettering /léttəring/ *n* the act or a style of writing

letter of credit *n* an official bank document authorising somebody to draw money from another bank

letter-quality *adj* describes printing of high quality

letting /létting/ *n* a let property

lettuce /léttiss/ *n* a plant grown for its edible leaves, which are eaten raw in salads

---

ORIGIN Lettuce goes back to Latin *lac* 'milk', which is also the first element of *lactate*. The name refers to the milky sap of its stalk.

---

let-up *n* a pause *(infml)*

leu /láy oo/ *(pl* **lei** /lay/*)* *n* the main unit of Romanian and Moldovan currency

leukaemia /loo keémi ə/ *n* a cancer in which white blood cells displace normal blood —**leukaemic** *adj, n*

leukemia *n* US = leukaemia

lev /lev/ *(pl* **leva** /lévə/*)* *n* the main unit of Bulgarian currency

Levant /li vánt/ former name for the region in the E Mediterranean comprising modern-day Lebanon, Israel, and parts of Syria and Turkey —**Levantine** /lév'n tīn/ *n, adj*

levee /lévvi, lévvay/ *n* a natural or artificial embankment beside a river

level /lév'l/ *n* **1** a position from which height is measured ○ *10,000 feet above sea level* **2** height from a reference point ○ *the low level of the river* **3** a particular position relative to a rank or scale **4** an amount or concentration **5** the position of a particular floor in a structure ○ *ground level* **6** a horizontal surface **7** US a spirit level ■ *adj* **1** flat and horizontal, with an even surface **2** smooth or even **3** equal to or even with another person or group ○ *level at three games all* **4** next to or alongside **5** steady ○ *maintaining a level pressure* ■ *v* (**-elling**, **-elled**) **1** *vt* make something level **2** *vt* demolish and flatten a building **3** *vi* be honest with somebody *(infml)* **4** *vt* aim a gun **5** *vt* direct attention —**levelly** *adv*—**levelness** *n* ◊ **on the level** honest and trustworthy *(infml)*

□ **level off** *vti* **1** *also* **level out** start to fly level with the ground, or make an aircraft do this **2** make or become steady

level crossing *n* a place where a road crosses a railway line

level-headed *adj* calm and sensible —**level-headedly** *adv* —**level-headedness** *n*

leveller /lévvələr/ *n* **1** something that makes situations more equal **2** a believer in equality **3 Leveller** a 17C English radical dissenter

lever /leevər/ *n* **1** a rigid bar that pivots on a fulcrum and is used for moving a load at one end by means of force applied at the other end **2** a projecting part of a device or machine used for controlling it ■ *vt* move with a lever

Lever /leevər/, **William Hesketh, 1st Viscount Leverhulme** (1851–1925) British industrialist and philanthropist

leverage /leevərij/ *n* **1** the action of a lever **2** the mechanical advantage gained by using a lever **3** the power to get things done **4** the use of borrowed money to purchase an asset in the hope of increasing the return on the investment ■ *vti* (**-aging**, **-aged**) borrow money in order to buy a company

leveraged buyout *n* a way of buying a company using borrowed money secured by the assets of the target company

leveret /lévvərət/ *n* a young hare

Levi /lévvi/, **Primo** (1919–87) Italian novelist, poet, and scientist

leviathan /lə ví əth'n/ *n* **1** something huge **2** a whale *(literary)*

ORIGIN Leviathan was a sea monster in the Bible.

Levi-Strauss /lévvi strówss/, **Claude Gustave** (*b.* 1908) French social anthropologist

levitate /lévvi tayt/ (**-tating**, **-tated**) *vti* rise in the air, or cause to rise —**levitation** /lévvi táysh'n/ *n*

levity /lévvəti/ *n* flippancy

levy /lévvi/ *vt* (**-ies**, **-ied**) **1** officially demand tax payments **2** raise an army ■ *n* (*pl* **-ies**) **1** a tax **2** the raising of tax **3** an army —**leviable** *adj*

lewd /lood, lyood/ *adj* sexual in an offensive way —**lewdly** *adv* —**lewdness** *n*

Lewis /lóo iss/, **Carl** (*b.* 1961) US athlete

Lewis, C. S. (1898–1963) Irish-born British critic, scholar, and novelist

lexical /léksik'l/ *adj* **1** of words **2** of a lexicon —**lexically** *adv*

lexicography /léksi kóggrəfi/ *n* the process or activity of writing dictionaries —**lexicographer** *n* —**lexicographic** /léksikə gráffik/ *adj*

lexicology /léksi kólləji/ *n* the study of word meanings and origins —**lexicological** /léksikə lójjik'l/ *adj* —**lexicologist** *n*

lexicon /léksikən, -kon/ (*pl* **-cons** *or* **-ca** /-kə/) *n* **1** a dictionary **2** the vocabulary of a particular field of activity

Lexington /léksingtən/ town in NE Massachusetts, site of the first battle of the War of American Independence in 1775. Pop. 28,974 (1996).

lexis /léksiss/ *n* the entire vocabulary of a language

ley line /láy-, leé-/ *n* the line of an ancient path between landmarks, especially places of worship

Lhasa /laássə/ city and capital of the autonomous region of Tibet, SW China. Pop. 161,788 (1991).

Li *symbol* lithium

liability /lí̄ ə bílləti/ *n* (*pl* **-ties**) **1** obligation under the law **2** a debt **3** a disadvantage **4** somebody who is a burden ■ **liabilities** *npl* the debts and other financial obligations that appear on a balance sheet

liable /lí̄ əb'l/ *adj* **1** legally responsible **2** susceptible or likely to experience something

liaise /li áyz/ (**-aising**, **-aised**) *vi* cooperate closely

liaison /li áyz'n, -zon/ *n* **1** exchange of information or planning of joint efforts **2** a love affair between people who are not married to each other

Liao /lee ó/ river in NE China. Length 1,345 km/836 mi.

liar /lí̄ ər/ *n* somebody who tells lies

~~liase~~ incorrect spelling of **liaise**

~~liason~~ incorrect spelling of **liaison**

Lib. *abbr* Liberal

~~libary~~ incorrect spelling of **library**

libation /lī̄ báysh'n/ *n* **1** the pouring of a liquid as a religious offering, or the liquid poured **2** an alcoholic drink (*humorous*) —**libational** *adj*

Lib Dem *abbr* Liberal Democrat

libel /lí̄b'l/ *n* **1** a false public statement that damages somebody's reputation **2** the making of a libel ■ *vt* (**-belling**, **-belled**) defame —**libeller** *n* —**libellous** *adj* ◊ See note at **malign**

ORIGIN **Libel** came via French from a Latin word meaning literally 'little book'. A **libel** in English was originally a 'formal document' or 'written statement'. In the early 16C it also developed

the sense 'pamphlet, leaflet', and was applied especially to one defaming somebody's character. It is out of this that the modern sense 'false damaging statement' arose in the early 17C.

liberal /líbbərəl/ *adj* **1** broad-minded and tolerant **2** favouring gradual political or social reforms, especially those that extend democracy, distribute wealth more evenly, and protect individual freedom **3** generous with money, time, or another asset ○ *liberal in her bequests* **4** generous in quantity ○ *a liberal helping* **5** culturally oriented ○ *a liberal education* **6** of political liberalism **7 Liberal** of a Liberal Party ■ *n* **1** a liberal person **2 Liberal** a member of a Liberal Party —**liberally** *adv* ◊ See note at **generous**

liberal arts *npl* education in culturally rather than vocationally oriented subjects

Liberal Democrat *n* a member of a British centre-left political party

liberalism /líbbərəlizəm/ *n* **1** a belief in tolerance and gradual reform in moral, religious, or political matters **2** a political theory stressing individualism —**liberalistic** /líbbərə lístik/ *adj*

liberality /líbbə rálləti/, **liberalness** /líbbərəl nəss/ *n* **1** generosity with money, time, or another asset **2** largeness in size or amount

liberalize /líbbərə lī̄z/ (**-izing**, **-ized**), **liberalise** *vti* make or become less strict —**liberalization** /líbbərə lī̄ záysh'n/ *n*

Liberal Party *n* **1** a former UK political party **2** a major Canadian political party

liberal studies *n* a combined arts subject that provides general cultural knowledge (+ *sing verb*)

liberate /líbbə rayt/ (**-ating**, **-ated**) *vt* **1** set somebody free physically **2** release somebody from social constraints —**liberatingly** *adv* —**liberation** /líbbə ráysh'n/ *n* —**liberationist** *n* —**liberator** *n*

Liberia /lī̄ beéri ə/ country in West Africa, on the North Atlantic Ocean. Cap. Monrovia. Pop. 3,225,837 (2001). —**Liberian** *adj, n*

libertarian /líbbər táiri ən/ *n* an advocate of individual responsibility or freedom —**libertarianism** *n*

libertine /líbbər teen, -tī̄n/ *n* somebody who leads an immoral life —**libertine** *adj* —**libertinism** *n*

liberty /líbbərti/ *n* (*pl* **-ties**) *n* **1** freedom from constraint or force **2** freedom from captivity **3** a basic political, social, and economic right to choose how to think or act (*often pl*) **4** a breach of etiquette

libidinous /li bíddinəss/ *adj* having or expressing strong sexual desire

libido /li beédō/ (*pl* **-dos**) *n* **1** sex drive **2** in some theories, the psychic and emotional energy linked to sexuality —**libidinal** /li bíddin'l/ *adj*

Libra /leébrə/ *n* **1** a zodiacal constellation in the southern hemisphere **2** the 7th sign of the zodiac —**Libran** *n, adj*

librarian /ˈlī bráiri ən/ *n* a library worker

library /ˈlībrəri, lībri/ (*pl* **-ies**) *n* **1** a place where books or other research materials are kept **2** a collection of books, newspapers, records, tapes, or other research materials

~~libray~~ incorrect spelling of **library**

libretto /li bréttō/ (*pl* **-tos** *or* **-ti** /-ti/) *n* the words of an opera —**librettist** *n*

Libreville /leèbrə vil/ chief port and capital of Gabon. Pop. 365,650 (1993 estimate).

Libya /ˈlíbbi ə/ country in North Africa, on the Mediterranean Sea. Cap. Tripoli. Pop. 5,240,599 (2001). —**Libyan** *n, adj*

Libyan Desert arid region in NE Africa, in Libya, Egypt, and Sudan, the northeastern part of the Sahara Desert

lice plural of **louse**

licence /ˈlíss'nss/ *n* **1** a permit **2** legal authorization **3** a chance to do something **4** artistic freedom to bend the truth **5** lack of restraint

license /ˈlíss'nss/ *vt* (**-censing, -censed**) formally allow ■ US = **licence**

licensee /ˈlíss'n seè/ *n* somebody with an official licence to do something

licentiate /ˈlī sénshi ət/ *n* **1** somebody authorized to practice a profession **2** an academic degree awarded by some European Universities, or somebody with this qualification

licentious /ˈlī sénshəss/ *adj* sexually immoral

lichen /ˈlíkən, líchən/ *n* a complex organism consisting of fungi and algae growing together that often appears as grey, green, or yellow patches on rocks and trees —**lichenous** *adj*

Lichtenstein /ˈlíktən stīn/, **Roy** (1923–97) US painter, graphic artist, and sculptor

licit /ˈlíssit/ *adj* allowed by law ◊ See note at **legal**

lick *v* **1** *vt* pass the tongue over something **2** *vti* brush against something **3** *vt* defeat a competitor convincingly *(infml)* ■ *n* **1** a movement of the tongue over something **2** a quickly applied coating ○ *a lick of paint* —**licker** *n*

licking /ˈlíking/ *n* (*infml*) **1** a beating **2** a convincing defeat

licorice *n* US = **liquorice**

lid *n* **1** a top for a container **2** an eyelid **3** a restraint or control that keeps something within acceptable bounds *(infml)* —**lidded** *adj*

lido /leèdō, lídō/ (*pl* **-dos**) *n* a pool or beach

lie[1] /ˈlī/ *vi* (**lying** /ˈlī ing/, **lay, lain**) **1** stretch out on a surface **2** be placed flat on a surface ○ *A book lay open on the table.* **3** be located in a particular place ○ *lying due south of here* **4** be buried **5** be in a particular position in a competition **6** be in a particular condition or state ○ *lay hidden for years* **7** be still to come ○ *Years of work lie ahead of us.* **8** stay undisturbed ■ *n* **1** a place where an animal returns to rest or hide **2** in golf, the position of a hit ball that has come to rest

□ **lie back** *vi* recline and relax

□ **lie down** *vi* **1** lie on a surface **2** rest in bed

□ **lie with** *vi* be the responsibility of

lie[2] /ˈlī/ *vi* (**lying** /ˈlī ing/, **lied, lied** /ˈlīd/) **1** deliberately say something untrue in order to deceive **2** give a false impression ■ *n* **1** something said or written that is untrue **2** a false impression

SYNONYMS lie, untruth, falsehood, fabrication, fib, white lie CORE MEANING: something that is not true

Liechtenstein /ˈlíkhtən shtīn/ independent principality in central Europe. Cap. Vaduz. Pop. 32,528 (2001).

lie detector *n* a machine for sensing untruthfulness during questioning

lie-down *n* a short rest *(infml)*

lief /leef/ *adv* willingly *(archaic)*

liege /leej/ *n* **1** a feudal lord **2** a vassal ■ *adj* faithful or loyal *(archaic)* —**liegedom** *n*

Liège /li ézh/ capital of **Liège Province**, E Belgium. Pop. 187,538 (1999).

lie-in *n* a longer stay in bed than usual *(infml)*

lien /leen, leè ən/ *n* a legal claim on somebody's property

~~liesure~~ incorrect spelling of **leisure**

lieu /lyoo, loo/ ◊ **in lieu (of)** instead or in place of something else

Lieut *abbr* Lieutenant

lieutenant /lef ténnənt/ *n* **1** a deputy **2** an army officer of a rank above second lieutenant **3** a navy officer of a rank above sub lieutenant or lieutenant junior grade —**lieutenancy** *n*

ORIGIN A **lieutenant** is literally somebody 'holding the place', somebody deputizing for another. The French word from which it was adopted in the 14C was formed from *lieu* (as in *in lieu of* 'in place of') and *tenant* 'holding', from which English *tenant* derives. **Lieutenant** did not come to refer to a specific rank until the 16C.

lieutenant colonel *n* in some armed forces, an officer of a rank above major

lieutenant commander *n* an officer in the US, British, or Canadian navies, or in the US Coast Guard, of a rank above lieutenant

lieutenant general *n* in some armed forces, an officer of a rank above major general

lieutenant governor *n* **1** an elected official in a United States state government of a rank below governor **2** a Canadian provincial official representing the British monarch —**lieutenant governorship** *n*

life (*pl* **lives** /ˈlīvz/) *n* **1** the quality that distinguishes living organisms from dead ones or inanimate matter **2** a living being, especially a person *(usually pl)* ○ *dozens of lives lost* **3** living things considered together ○ *an expert on Amazonian plant life* **4** the whole time that somebody is alive **5** a time when something functions beyond some part of somebody's life ○ *social life* **7** human activity **8** life imprisonment *(infml)* **9** the character or conditions of somebody's existence ○ *had a hard* *life* **10** a characteristic way of living ○ *country life* **11** a biography **12** vitality ◇ **get a life** do something to make your existence less boring *(infml)*

life assurance *n* a financial plan for providing a legacy by making regular payments to a company

life belt *n* a belt or ring that keeps the wearer afloat

lifeblood /líf blud/ *n* **1** blood regarded as necessary for life *(literary)* **2** something vital to a whole

lifeboat /líf bōt/ *n* **1** a boat kept on a larger ship for use in emergencies **2** a rescue boat

life buoy *n* a buoyant float for keeping somebody's head and shoulders above water in an emergency

life cycle *n* **1** the stages of development of a living organism **2** all the stages in the development of something

life expectancy *n* somebody's expected length of life

life form *n* any living organism

lifeguard /líf gaard/ *n* a trained person who watches over swimmers and saves those in danger

life history *n* **1** all the stages of an organism's life **2** somebody's life story

life imprisonment *n* punishment requiring a convicted criminal to remain in prison until he or she dies

life jacket *n* a jacket that keeps the wearer afloat

lifeless /lífləss/ *adj* **1** dead **2** lacking animation —**lifelessly** *adv* —**lifelessness** *n* ◇ See note at **dead**

lifelike /líf līk/ *adj* true to life

lifeline /líf līn/ *n* **1** a safety cable attached to somebody performing a dangerous manoeuvre **2** a vital means of communication or support

lifelong /líf long/ *adj* lasting for life

life partner *n* a long-term romantic or sexual partner

life peer *n* a member of the House of Lords with a title that lasts only for his or her lifetime —**life peerage** *n*

life raft *n* an inflatable lifeboat

lifesaver /líf sayvər/ *n* **1** a provider of greatly needed help **2** *ANZ* a lifeguard

lifesaving /líf sayving/ *adj* rescuing or reviving ■ *n* **1** techniques or efforts to rescue people, especially from drowning **2** a multi-activity Australian water-based sport

life sentence *n* a judgment of life imprisonment

life-size *adj* as big as the real thing

life span *n* **1** an expected length of life **2** the length of time something is expected to last or function

lifestyle /líf stīl/ *n* a manner of living

life-support system, life support *n* **1** a piece of technical equipment that temporarily performs a vital body function, e.g. respiration **2** a piece of technical equipment that provides living conditions for people in environments in which these are unavailable —**life support** *adj*

life-threatening *adj* very dangerous

lifetime /líf tīm/ *n* **1** the length of time that somebody or something remains alive **2** the length of time that something remains useful or functional

LIFO /lífō/ *abbr* last in, first out

lift *v* **1** *vti* go or raise to a higher position **2** *vt* take and move something **3** *vt* revoke an order ○ *lift a ban* **4** *vti* make or become cheerful ○ *visibly lifted his spirits* **5** *vi* disappear or become less severe ○ *until the fog lifts* **6** *vt* make a sound louder ○ *lift their voices* **7** *vt* harvest crops **8** *vt* steal something *(infml)* ■ *n* **1** a cage that carries people or goods between the floors of a building **2** a ride to a destination in somebody else's vehicle *(infml)* **3** a rise in spirits **4** the process of raising something **5** the force needed to raise something **6** the degree to which something rises **7** the combination of upward forces acting on an aircraft —**liftable** *adj* —**lifter** *n*

□ **lift off** *vi* leave a launch pad *(refers to spacecraft)*

liftoff /líft of/ *n* **1** the moment when a rocket leaves a launch pad **2** the initial thrust that launches a rocket

ligament /líggəmənt/ *n* **1** a band of tough tissue connecting body parts **2** a connector —**ligamental** /líggə mént'l/ *adj*

ligature /líggəchər/ *n* **1** something used for tying **2** a character consisting of joined letters **3** a curved line in a musical score used for combining the duration of notes

Ligeti /lígəti, li gétti/, **György** (*b.* 1923) Hungarian composer

light[1] /līt/ *n* **1** electromagnetic radiation, particularly in the range visible to the human eye **2** an artificial source of light **3** a particular kind of light ○ *fading light* **4** somebody's share or access to light ○ *standing in my light* **5** daylight **6** dawn **7** a traffic signal **8** general notice ○ *came to light* **9** the way that something is viewed ○ *regarded in exceptionally bad light* **10** a source of fire, especially a match ■ **lights** *npl* a person's ideas or beliefs ■ *adj* **1** full of brightness **2** pale ○ *decorated in light green* ■ *v* (**lit** *or* **lighted**) **1** *vti* make or start to burn **2** *vt* illuminate something **3** *vt* give something an animated look ○ *A smile lit his face.* **4** *vt* lead somebody with a light —**lightness** *n* ◇ **bring to light** reveal ◇ **come to light** be revealed ◇ **in (the) light of** taking into consideration ◇ **see the light** suddenly understand or appreciate something ◇ **shed** *or* **throw** *or* **cast light on** help to clarify

□ **light up** *v* **1** *vti* light a cigarette or pipe **2** *vt* illuminate **3** *vi* begin shining **4** *vti* make or become cheerful

light[2] /līt/ *adj* **1** not heavy in weight **2** not dense **3** not forceful **4** easy to do **5** consuming small quantities of something **6** not severe

○ *a light sentence* **7** not intellectually demanding **8** lacking the usual or expected quantity of something, especially alcohol **9** not burdened by worry ○ *a light heart* **10** slightly dizzy ○ *a light head* **11** nimble **12** easily digested or not filling ○ *a light snack* **13** delicately flavoured **14** easily woken or disturbed ○ *a light sleeper* **15** carrying small weights **16** manufacturing small products without heavy machinery ■ *adv* **1** leniently **2** with little luggage ■ *vi* (**lighted** *or* **lit**) come to rest *(refers to birds)* —**lightly** *adv* —**lightness** *n* ◇ **make light of** treat as unimportant

light bulb *n* a glass sphere with a filament that produces light

lighten[1] /lít'n/ *vti* make or become less heavy or burdensome

lighten[2] /lít'n/ *v* **1** *vti* make or become pale **2** *vi* glow

lighter[1] /lítər/ *n* **1** a small device for lighting cigarettes **2** somebody or something that lights something *(usually in combination)*

lighter[2] /lítər/ *n* a flat-bottomed cargo boat

light-fingered *adj* **1** likely to steal things **2** nimble with the fingers

light-footed *adj* able to walk or run with agility —**light-footedly** *adv*

lightheaded /lít héddid/ *adj* **1** dizzy or euphoric **2** tending to behave in a silly way —**lightheadedly** *adv* —**lightheadedness** *n*

lighthearted /lít haártid/ *adj* **1** happy and relaxed **2** entertaining in a carefree way —**lightheartedly** *adv* —**lightheartedness** *n*

light heavyweight *n* **1** the weight category in boxing between middleweight and heavyweight **2** a boxer who competes at light heavyweight

lighthouse /lít howss/ (*pl* **-houses** /-howziz/) *n* a tall coastal building with a flashing light to guide sailors

lighting /líting/ *n* **1** a type or quality of light, or the equipment that produces it **2** equipment for providing light effects on a stage or film set **3** the effect produced by lights on a stage or film set

lighting-up time *n* a time of day when vehicles must use headlights

lightning /lítning/ *n* a discharge of atmospheric electricity appearing as flashes of light in the sky ■ *adj* very fast or sudden

lightning conductor *n* a device protecting a building from lightning by conducting it to the ground

lightning strike *n* **1** an industrial strike happening at short notice **2** an unexpected attack

light pen, light stylus *n* a pen-shaped computer device for manipulating information on a screen

light railway *n* a railway for light traffic

lights /líts/ *npl* the lungs of a domestic animal used as food

light show *n* **1** a display of moving lights, often at a rock or pop concert **2** an entertainment consisting of coloured lights synchronized with recorded music

lights out *n* **1** a time when people must sleep **2** a signal sounded at lights out

lightweight /lít wayt/ *adj* **1** not heavy in weight or texture **2** lacking intellectual depth ■ *n* **1** somebody or something regarded as insignificant ○ *a political lightweight* **2** the weight category in boxing between featherweight and welterweight **3** a boxer who competes at lightweight

light-year *n* the distance that light travels in a vacuum in one solar year, approximately 9.46 billion km/5.88 billion mi. ■ **light-years** *npl* a long way *(infml)*

ligneous /lígni əss/ *adj* of or like wood

lignite /líg nít/ *n* soft brown-black coal —**lignitic** /lig níttik/ *adj*

Ligurian Sea /li góöri ən-/ arm of the Mediterranean Sea between NW Italy and Corsica and Elba

likable /líkəb'l/, **likeable** *adj* pleasant and friendly —**likably** *adv*

like[1] *prep* **1** resembling **2** such as **3** indicates characteristics *(often in questions)* ○ *What's it like there at this time of year?* **4** typical of *(often negative)* **5** inclined towards ○ *felt like screaming* **6** with a suggestion of ○ *It looks like rain.* ■ *conj* **1** as **2** △ as if or as though *(nonstandard)* ■ *adv* **1** in a particular way *(infml)* ○ *looked like new* **2** △ used as filler or for emphasis *(nonstandard)* **3** △ introduces direct speech *(nonstandard)* ■ *n* **1** something similar **2** an exact counterpart ■ *adj* alike ◇ **the likes of** people or things of the particular sort

USAGE Avoid using the conjunction **like** to mean 'as' or 'as if' or 'as though' with a following verb: *It sounds like she may resign.* Say instead: *It sounds as if she may resign.* Avoid also using **like** as a meaningless filler: *'Once, when I was, like, 13 or 14...'*, or to introduce speech: *She was like, 'Don't worry'.*

like[2] *v* (**liking, liked**) **1** *vt* regard as enjoyable **2** *vt* consider to be pleasant ○ *I really like her.* **3** *vt* want to have or do ○ *Would you like a drink?* **4** *vt* regard in a positive way **5** *vi* have a preference ○ *if you like* ■ *n* a preference

-like *suffix* resembling or characteristic of ○ *workmanlike*

likelihood /líkli höōd/ *n* **1** a degree of probability **2** a probable event

likely /líkli/ *adj* (**-lier, -liest**) **1** probable **2** plausible *(often ironic)* **3** suitable ■ *adv* probably

~~likelyhood~~ incorrect spelling of **likelihood**

like-minded *adj* sharing the same opinions —**like-mindedness** *n*

liken /líkən/ *vt* compare to another, especially to point out similarities

likeness /líknəss/ *n* **1** similarity in appearance **2** a representation of somebody

likewise /lík wíz/ *adv* **1** in the same way **2** also

liking /líking/ n 1 fondness or enjoyment 2 preference ◊ See note at **love**

~~likly~~ incorrect spelling of **likely**

lilac /lílak/ (pl **-lacs** or same) n 1 a small tree with fragrant white or purple flowers 2 a pale purple colour tinged with blue —**lilac** adj

lilangeni /leé lang gáyni/ (pl **emalangeni** /émmo lang gáyni/) n the main unit of currency of Swaziland

Lilliputian /lílli pyoósh'n/, **lilliputian** n a very small person or thing ∎ adj 1 tiny 2 trivial or petty

ORIGIN Lilliputian originally referred to Lilliput, an imaginary country in Jonathan Swift's *Gulliver's Travels* (1726), whose inhabitants were only 6 in. (15 cm) tall.

Lilo /lílō/ tdmk a trademark for an inflatable bed for use in swimming-pools or on the sea

LILO /lílō/ n last in, last out data storage

Lilongwe /li lóng way/ capital and second largest city of Malawi. Pop. 1,000,000 (1998).

lilt n 1 a pleasant rising and falling variation in voice pitch 2 a cheerful piece of music (archaic) —**lilt** vti —**lilting** adj

lily /lílli/ (pl **-ies**) n 1 a perennial plant with large, sometimes trumpet-shaped, flowers 2 a plant resembling a lily ◊ **gild the lily** try to improve something that is already good or beautiful enough

lily-livered /-livərd/ adj cowardly (dated)

lily of the valley (pl **lilies of the valley** or same) n a small perennial plant with sweet-smelling, bell-shaped white or pink flówers on a single stem

lily pad n a leaf of a water lily

lily-white adj 1 pale and unblemished 2 blameless

Lima[1] /leémə/ n a communications code word for the letter 'L'

Lima[2] /leémə/ capital of Peru. Pop. 6,464,693 (1998).

lima bean /límə-, leémə-/ n a pale green flattish edible bean

limb /lim/ n 1 an arm, leg, wing, flipper, or similar appendage 2 a large tree branch ◊ **be out on a limb** in an isolated position, without support

limber /límbər/ adj 1 supple and agile 2 flexible —**limberness** n

☐ **limber up** vi do gentle physical exercises to loosen the muscles

limbo[1] /límbō/, **Limbo** n in Roman Catholic theology, a place for the souls of unbaptized children

limbo[2] /límbō/ (pl **-bos**) n a Caribbean dance that involves bending backwards and passing under a bar

lime[1] n 1 calcium oxide 2 a form of calcium used for improving soil ∎ vt (**liming**, **limed**) spread or treat with lime

lime[2] n 1 a round green citrus fruit with sour

juicy flesh 2 also **lime tree** an evergreen tree that produces limes

lime[3] n 1 also **lime tree** a deciduous tree with heart-shaped leaves 2 the wood of a lime tree

limeade /lím áyd/ n a carbonated drink made from or tasting of lime juice

limelight /lím līt/ n 1 the focus of attention 2 an early form of stage lighting in which quicklime was heated to produce a brilliant light, or the light so produced

limerick /límmərik/ n a five-line humorous poem with regular metre and rhyme patterns

ORIGIN The **limerick** is said to derive its name from a Victorian custom of singing nonsense songs with this rhyme scheme, with the refrain 'Will you come up to Limerick?' The first known use of the word dates from 1896.

Limerick /límmərik/ 1 chief city in the SW Republic of Ireland. Pop. 79,000 (1996). 2 county in Munster Province, SW Republic of Ireland

limescale /lím skayl/ n a deposit of lime on the inside of a kettle or boiler

limestone /lím stōn/ n a sedimentary rock that consists mainly of the skeletons of sea organisms

limey /lími/ n ANZ, US, Can an offensive term for a British person (slang)

ORIGIN Limey alludes to the lime juice formerly given to sailors in the British Navy to prevent scurvy.

limit /límmit/ n 1 the furthest point, degree, or amount 2 a maximum or minimum amount or number allowed 3 a boundary of an area (often pl) ○ the city limits ∎ vt 1 restrict 2 be a boundary to —**limitless** adj —**limitlessly** adv —**limitlessness** n ◊ **be the limit** be extremely bad or outrageous

limitation /límmi táysh'n/ n 1 an imposed restriction 2 a disadvantage or weakness (often pl) 3 the setting of a limit ○ damage limitation

limited /límmitid/ adj 1 existing within imposed limits or restrictions 2 lacking full scope, extent, or authority ○ limited powers 3 with less talent or skill than expected or required 4 also **Limited** with restricted shareholder liability —**limitedly** adv —**limitedness** n

limited company n a company with limited shareholder liability

limited edition n a limited edition of a book or art print produced in limited numbers

limited liability n an investor's liability for a company's debts that is limited to the value of his or her stake

limo /límmō/ (pl **-os**) n a limousine (infml)

limousine /límmə zeén, -zeen/ n 1 a large, luxurious, chauffeur-driven car 2 US, Can a vehicle transporting people to and from an airport

ORIGIN Limousine in French means literally

'woman from Limousin (a former province of central France)'. However it was also used as the name of a type of cloak with a cape worn by cart drivers in Limousin, and it is this that seems to have suggested the name **limousine**. The driver's separate compartment in early limousines, at the beginning of the 20C, was outside, though covered with a roof.

limp[1] *vi* **1** walk unevenly because of an injury or disability **2** proceed with difficulty ■ *n* an impaired gait *(sometimes offensive)*

limp[2] *adj* **1** not stiff or rigid **2** lacking strength, energy, or enthusiasm —**limply** *adv* —**limpness** *n*

limpet /límpit/ *(pl* -**pets** *or same) n* a marine organism with a rough conical shell that clings to rocks

limpid /límpid/ *adj* **1** transparent **2** lucid —**limpidly** *adv*

Limpopo /lim pṓpō/ river in SE Africa, rising in N South Africa and flowing through S Mozambique to the Indian Ocean. Length 1,800 km/1,100 mi.

linchpin /línch pin/, **lynchpin** *n* **1** a pin through an axle that stops a wheel from coming off **2** an essential element in the success of something

Lincoln /língkən/ **1** city in E England, noted for its cathedral. Pop. 84,600 (1994). **2** capital of Nebraska. Pop. 213,088 (1998).

Library of Congress

Abraham Lincoln

Lincoln, Abraham (1809–65) 16th president of the United States (1861–65)

Lincolnshire /língkənshər/ county in E England

linctus /língktəss/ *n* a cough syrup

Lindbergh /línd burg/, **Charles Augustus** (1902–74) US aviator and engineer

linden /líndən/ *(pl* -**dens** *or same) n* TREES = **lime**[3] **1**

Lindsay /líndzi/, **Norman Alfred William** (1879–1969) Australian artist and writer

line[1] *n* **1** a long narrow mark **2** a facial wrinkle *(often pl)* **3** in geometry, a one-dimensional path traced by a moving point or drawn between two fixed points **4** a border **5** a transport company **6** a rope, wire, or cable **7** a type of merchandise **8** a row of words on a page **9** a characteristic contour *(often pl)* o *the car's sleek lines* **10** a version of something o *uttered the official line* **11** a specialized area of work **12** a brief written message **13** *US, Can* a queue of people or vehicles ■ **lines** *npl* an actor's spoken words ■ *vt* (**lining, lined**) **1** mark a line on **2** arrange or be

arranged in a line or along an edge o *shrubs lining the driveway* ◇ **all along the line** throughout or at every stage ◇ **draw the line** set limits ◇ **in line for** likely to receive ◇ **lay it on the line** speak frankly *(infml)* ◇ **lay** or **put something on the line** risk the loss of something valuable *(infml)* ◇ **out of line** *US (infml)* **1** rude and disrespectful **2** unruly or out of control ◇ **read between the lines** deduce something that is not explicit *(infml)* ◇ **toe the line** comply with expectations

□ **line up** *v* **1** *vti* arrange in or form a row **2** *vi* form a queue **3** *vt* organize or provide o *lined up a keynote speaker*

line[2] (**lining, lined**) *vt* **1** cover or reinforce the inside surface of **2** cover the surface of o *walls were lined with books*

lineage /línni ij/ *n* **1** a line of descent **2** a related group of people

lineal /línni əl/ *adj* in a direct line from an ancestor —**lineally** *adv*

lineament /línni əmənt/ *n* a feature or contour *(literary)*

linear /línni ər/ *adj* **1** of lines **2** of a straight line **3** describes variables that change proportionally —**linearity** /línni árrəti/ *n* —**linearly** *adv*

linebacker /lín bakər/ *n* an American football player positioned behind the defensive line —**linebacking** *n*

line dancing *n* a dance performed in rows to country-and-western music —**line dance** *n*, *vi* —**line dancer** *n*

line drawing *n* a drawing made using only lines

line management *n* the group of managers in a company who are involved in production or the central part of the business —**line manager** *n*

linen /línnin/ *(pl* same *or* -**ens**) *n* **1** thread or fabric made from flax **2** clothes or household items made from linen *(often pl)*

line of credit *n* the limit of available credit

line-out *n* a restart of play in rugby union

liner[1] /línər/ *n* a passenger ship or plane

liner[2] /línər/ *n* a lining, or material used for making lining

linesman /línzmən/ *(pl* -**men** /-mən/) *n* an assistant referee

lineup /lín up/ *n* **1** in sports, a list of players and their positions **2** a television schedule

ling[1] *(pl* same *or* **lings**) *n* **1** an edible sea fish related to the cod **2** ling as food

ling[2] *n* heather

-ling *suffix* **1** one connected with or resembling o *sapling* **2** a small one o *gosling*

linger /líng gər/ *vi* **1** put off leaving because of reluctance to go **2** wait around or move about idly **3** remain alive while gradually dying —**lingering** *adj*

lingerie /lánzhəri, lónzhəri, láNzhəri/ *n* women's underwear

lingo /líng gō/ *(pl* -**goes**) *n (infml)* **1** a language that is not the speaker's native language **2** a set of specialized terms

lingua franca /líng gwə frángkə/ (pl **lingua francas** or **linguae francae** /-gwee-kee/) n **1** a language used in common by speakers of different languages **2** formerly, a traders' language that was a mixture of several Mediterranean languages

lingual /líng gwəl/ adj of the tongue —**lingually** adv

linguine /ling gwéeni/, **linguini** n pasta in long narrow flat strips

linguist /líng gwist/ n **1** a speaker of several languages **2** a student of linguistics

linguistic /ling gwístik/ adj **1** of language **2** of linguistics —**linguistically** adv

linguistics /ling gwístiks/ n the study of language (+ sing verb)

liniment /línnəmənt/ n a liquid rubbed into the skin to relieve pain

lining /líning/ n an interior covering, or the material from which it is made

link n **1** a ring or loop forming part of a chain **2** a connection **3** a hypertext connection allowing direct access to related electronic text, images, and other data **4** a part of a transport system **5** a broadcasting unit for relaying signals ■ vti connect, or be connected

linkage /língkij/ n **1** a connection, or the fact of being connected **2** a system of interconnected parts

links n (+ sing or pl verb) **1** a golf course, especially by the sea **2** Scotland an undulating sandy area

linkup /língk up/ n a connection

Linnaeus /li née əss, -náy-/, **Carolus** (1707–78) Swedish naturalist. He devised the standard system of binomial nomenclature for plants and animals. —**Linnaean** adj

linnet /línnit/ (pl -**nets** or same) n a small brown songbird of the finch family

lino /línō/ n linoleum (infml)

linocut /línō kut/ n a print from a design cut in linoleum

linoleum /li nóli əm/ n a tough washable floor covering

linseed /lín seed/ n **1** the seed of the flax plant, which yields oil **2** flax grown as a crop for oil

lint n **1** soft absorbent material used for medical dressings **2** small pieces of fibre or fluff —**linty** adj

lintel /línt'l/ n a supporting beam above a window or door

lion /lí ən/ n **1** a large wild cat with a tawny coat, the male of which has a shaggy mane **2** somebody who is brave and strong **3 Lion** the constellation Leo ◊ **the lion's share** the largest or best part

lioness /lí ə ness/ n a female lion

lionhearted /lí ən haártid/ adj courageous —**lionheartedness** n

lionize /lí ə nīz/ (-**izing**, -**ized**), **lionise** vt treat

somebody as a celebrity —**lionization** /lí ə nī záysh'n/ n

lip n **1** either of two fleshy folds around the mouth **2** something shaped like a lip **3** impertinence (slang) **4** any of two sets of folds of skin at the opening of the vulva ◊ **a stiff upper lip** a brave and unemotional bearing (infml) ◊ **bite your lip** restrain yourself from saying something (infml)

lip gloss n a shiny lip cosmetic

lipid /líppid/, **lipide** n a biological compound that is not soluble in water, e.g. a fat —**lipidic** /li píddik/ adj

liposuction /líppō suksh'n, lípō-/ n cosmetic surgery to remove body fat

Lippi /líppi/, **Fra Filippo** (1406?–69) Italian painter

Lipponen /líppənən/, **Paavo Tapio** (b. 1941) prime minister of Finland (1995–)

lip-read /-reed/ (**lip-read** /-red/) vti understand what is said by watching a speaker's lips move —**lip-reader** n

lip salve n ointment for the lips

lip service n insincere respect or agreement

lipstick /líp stik/ n a cosmetic for colouring the lips

lip-synch, lip-sync vti match lip movements to recorded sound

liquefy /líkwi fī/ (-**fies**, -**fied**) vti become or make liquid —**liquefaction** /líkwi fáksh'n/ n

~~liquer~~ incorrect spelling of **liqueur**

liqueur /li kyoór/ n a sweet alcoholic drink

liquid /líkwid/ n any flowing substance similar to water in consistency ■ adj **1** in the form of a liquid **2** describes assets easily converted into cash **3** clear and shining —**liquidly** adv

liquidate /líkwi dayt/ (-**dating**, -**dated**) v **1** vti pay a debt **2** vti wind up a business **3** vt turn assets into cash —**liquidation** /líkwi dáysh'n/ n —**liquidator** n

liquid-crystal display n a display of characters created by applying electricity to cells made of liquid crystal to make some of them change colour

liquidity /li kwíddəti/ n **1** the quality of being liquid **2** the quality of being easily converted into cash

liquidize /líkwi dīz/ (-**izing**, -**ized**), **liquidise** vti make or become liquid

liquidizer /líkwi dīzər/, **liquidiser** n a kitchen blender

liquor /líkər/ n **1** an alcoholic beverage produced by distillation rather than fermentation **2** the reduced liquid left after cooking food

liquorice /líkərish, -iss/ n **1** a dried black plant root. Use: laxative, confectionery, brewing. **2** a kind of soft black or red sweet

ORIGIN Liquorice comes ultimately from Greek *glukurrhiza*, literally 'sweet root'. Its first element is related to *glucose* and its second to *rhizome*.

lira /lćerə/ (*pl* **-re** /leerə, -r ay/) *n* **1** the main unit of currency of Turkey and Malta **2** the former unit of Italian currency

Lisbon /lízbən/ capital of Portugal. Pop. 601,180 (1995).

lisle /íl/ *n* fine smooth cotton thread. Use: stockings.

lisp *n* **1** a speech defect in which 's' sounds are pronounced as a soft 'th' **2** a speech sound made by somebody with a lisp —**lisp** *vti* —**lisping** *adj, n* —**lispingly** *adv*

LISP /lisp/ *n* a programming language used in artificial intelligence

ORIGIN LISP is a contraction of 'list processor'. It was coined in the 1950s.

lissom /líssəm/, **lissome** *adj* **1** gracefully slender and flexible **2** quick and graceful in moving —**lissomly** *adv* —**lissomness** *n*

list[1] *n* **1** a series of words, names, numbers, or other pieces of information written one after the other **2** an ordered set of data ■ *vt* **1** arrange items as an ordered series **2** include somebody or something in an ordered series **3** admit a security for trading on an exchange ○ *is listed on the New York Stock Exchange*

list[2] *vi* lean to one side ■ *n* a sideways tilt

listed building *n* a building that cannot be demolished or altered by law

listen /líss'n/ *vi* **1** make a conscious effort to hear **2** pay attention and take into account ■ *n* an act of hearing (*infml*) —**listenable** *adj* —**listener** *n*
□ **listen in** *vi* **1** eavesdrop **2** monitor telecommunications

Lister /lístər/, **Joseph, 1st Baron** (1827–1912) British surgeon. His development of antiseptic techniques greatly reduced surgical mortality.

listeria /li steeri ə/ *n* a rod-shaped disease-causing bacterium found in food

listing /lísting/ *n* **1** an entry in a list, catalogue, or directory **2** a list, catalogue, or directory **3** a printout of a computer file or program ■ **listings** *npl* published lists of cultural events

listless /lístləss/ *adj* weary or unwilling to make an effort —**listlessly** *adv* —**listlessness** *n*

Liston /lístən/, **Sonny** (1932–70) US boxer

list price *n* a published retail price that a seller may discount

listserv /líst surv/ *n* an Internet service allowing users to have online discussions

AKG London
Franz Liszt

Liszt /list/, **Franz** (1811–86) Hungarian pianist, composer, and conductor

lit past participle, past tense of **light**[1]

lit. *abbr* litre

litany /líttəni/ (*pl* **-nies**) *n* **1** a series of prayers including invocations from a priest or minister and responses from the congregation **2** a long repetitious list

litas /leè taass/ (*pl same*) *n* the main unit of Lithuanian currency

lite *adj* low in calories, sugar, fat, or alcohol (*in labelling or advertising foods and beverages*)

liter *n* US = **litre**

literacy /líttərəssi/ *n* **1** reading and writing ability **2** competence in a particular subject ○ *computer literacy*

literal /líttərəl/ *adj* **1** strictly adhering to the basic meaning of an original text ○ *a literal interpretation* **2** word for word ○ *a literal transcript* **3** taking things at face value **4** including or dealing only with the facts **5** using alphabetical letters —**literalness** *n*

literally /líttərəli/ *adv* **1** strictly adhering to basic meaning **2** △ adds emphasis (*infml*) ○ *I was literally freezing.*

USAGE In formal contexts, avoid using **literally** for emphasis, especially when combined with a colourful figure of speech: *The manager is literally hopping mad.* Say instead *The manager is absolutely furious* or *The manager is really livid.*

literary /líttərəri/ *adj* **1** of literature **2** formally expressed **3** professionally involved with or knowledgeable about literature —**literariness** *n*

literate /líttərət/ *adj* **1** able to read and write **2** competent in a particular subject ○ *computer-literate* **3** well-educated or cultured —**literate** *n* —**literately** *adv* —**literateness** *n*

literati /líttə raá tee/ *npl* (*fml*) **1** highly educated people **2** authors and others deeply involved in literature

literature /líttərəchər/ *n* **1** creative written works such as fiction, poetry, drama, and criticism **2** a body of written works of a language, culture, or period ○ *Russian literature* **3** writings on a specific subject ○ *scientific literature* **4** printed information ○ *the company's promotional literature*

lithe /líth/ (**lither, lithest**) *adj* flexible and supple —**lithely** *adv* —**litheness** *n* —**lithesome** *adj*

Lithgow /líthgō/ town in SE New South Wales, Australia. Pop. 11,989 (1991).

lithium /líthi əm/ *n* (*symbol* **Li**) a soft silver-white chemical element that is the lightest metal known. Use: alloys, ceramics, batteries, medical treatment for bipolar disorder.

lithography /li thógrəfi/ *n* a printing process using a plate on which only the image to be printed takes up ink —**lithograph** /lítha graaf, -graf/ *n, vti* —**lithographer** *n* —**lithographic** /lítha gráffik/ *adj*

Lithuania /líthyōō áyni ə/ country in NE Europe,

bordering the Baltic Sea. Cap. Vilnius. Pop. 3,610,535 (2001). —**Lithuanian** n, adj

litigate /lítti gayt/ (**-gating, -gated**) vi pursue or be involved in a lawsuit —**litigant** n, adj —**litigator** n

litigation /lítti gáysh'n/ n the process or state of bringing a lawsuit

litigious /li tíjjəss/ adj **1** inclined to take legal action **2** of legal action

litmus /lítməss/ n a powdery substance obtained from lichens. Use: indicator for acids or bases, turning red in acids and blue in bases.

litmus paper n paper treated with litmus.

litmus test n **1** a test using litmus paper to identify whether something is an acid or base **2** a test in which a single factor determines the outcome o *making the nominee's stand on trade a litmus test for their support*

litotes /lítō teez, lī tṓt eez/ (pl same) n understatement for effect, often involving a negative, or an example of this

~~litrature~~ incorrect spelling of **literature**

litre /léetər/ n a measure of volume equal to 1 cubic decimetre or 1.056 liquid quarts

litter /líttər/ n **1** scattered rubbish **2** a group of young animals born in a single birth **3** bedding for animals **4** material for a pet's toilet tray **5** a stretcher *(dated)* **6** formerly, a couch with poles for carrying somebody ■ v **1** vti make a place untidy by leaving litter **2** vt cover a place with scattered objects —**litterer** n

~~litterature~~ incorrect spelling of **literature**

little /lítt'l/ adj (**-tler, -tlest**) **1** small or of less than average size **2** young **3** describes a younger sister or brother o *my little sister* **4** small in a pleasant way o *his cute little habits* **5** short or quick o *gave a little smile* ■ det, pron **1** a small amount *(after 'a')* o *I only ate a little.* **2** not much o *had little or no effect* ■ adv **1** hardly o *little did they know* **2** not often o *visiting them little* —**littleness** n ◊ **little by little** gradually

Little Bighorn /-bíg hawrn/ river in S Montana. General George Armstrong Custer and his army were defeated and killed by Native Americans on its banks in June 1876. Length 145 km/90 mi.

little finger n the smallest finger of the human hand

Little Rock capital of Arkansas. Pop. 175,303 (1998).

little toe n the smallest toe of the human foot

littoral /líttərəl/ adj **1** on or near a shore **2** living on or near a shore ■ n a shore

liturgy /líttərji/ (pl **-gies**) n **1** a form of worship set down by a church **2** also **Liturgy** the form of service used for celebrating Communion in a Christian church —**liturgical** /li túrjik'l/ adj

livable /lívvəb'l/, **liveable** adj **1** comfortable to live in o *a livable town* **2** endurable and worthwhile

live[1] /liv/ (**living** /lívving/, **lived** /livd/) v **1** vi be alive **2** vi stay alive o *lived through a serious illness* **3** vi reside in a particular place or way o *lives alone* **4** vti have a particular kind of life o *live comfortably* **5** vi make a living in a particular way o *lives by waiting tables* **6** vti fully enjoy life o *really knew how to live* **7** vi persist o *Her fame lives on.* **8** vt experience or go through o *living a nightmare* ◊ **live it up** live or celebrate in an extravagant way *(infml)*

☐ **live down** vt cause something shameful to be forgotten by living in a commendable way

☐ **live in** vi live at your workplace

☐ **live off** vt rely on financially

☐ **live on** vt **1** live off somebody or something **2** eat a particular food to survive

☐ **live out** vt **1** do something previously imagined **2** live until the end of a particular period

☐ **live up to** vt meet expectations

☐ **live with** vt tolerate something

live[2] /līv/ adj **1** living **2** broadcast as it happens **3** appearing performing, or performed in person o *I'd rather dance to live music.* **4** recorded during a performance **5** relevant to current concerns o *a live issue* **6** connected to a power source **7** charged with an explosive o *live ammunition* **8** burning or glowing o *live coals* **9** containing living bacteria **10** describes a volcano that is still active ■ adv **1** in front of an audience **2** broadcast while the event happens

lived-in /lívd-/ adj **1** slightly untidy but homely **2** careworn

live-in /lív-/ adj **1** living at your place of work **2** sharing a home with a sexual partner

livelihood /lívlihŏŏd/ n a job or other source of income

livelong /lív long/ adj emphasizes how long a period of time seems to last *(literary)*

lively /lívli/ (**-lier, -liest**) adj **1** full of energy **2** animated, exciting, or stimulating **3** enthusiastic o *takes a lively interest in everything* **4** full of movement o *a lively dance* —**livelily** adv —**liveliness** n

~~livelyhood~~ incorrect spelling of **livelihood**

liven /lív'n/ vti make or become lively

liver /lívvər/ n **1** a large glandular organ in vertebrates that secretes bile and stores and filters blood **2** the liver of a mammal, fowl, or fish as food

Liverpool /lívvər pool/ port in NW England, on the River Mersey. Pop. 467,995 (1996).

Liverpudlian /lívvər púddli ən/ n somebody from Liverpool —**Liverpudlian** adj

liver spot n a brown spot on the skin

livery /lívvəri/ (pl **-ies**) n **1** a uniform, especially one worn by servants **2** an emblem or design **3** the professional care or renting of horses —**liveried** adj

livery company n a chartered London guild

liveryman /lívvərimən/ (pl **-men** /-mən/) n **1** a member of a livery company **2** an owner or employee of a livery stable

livery stable *n* **1** a stable that hires out horses **2** a place that stables horses

livestock /lív stok/ *n* animals raised for food or other products or kept for use, especially on a farm

live wire /lív-/ *n* **1** a wire connected to a power source **2** an energetic person *(infml)*

livid /lívvid/ *adj* **1** furious **2** with a bluish bruised colour **3** ashen —**lividity** /li víddəti/ *n* —**lividly** *adv*

living /lívving/ *adj* **1** alive **2** realistic or true to life ○ *the living image of her mother* **3** still in use ○ *a living language* ■ *n* **1** a means of earning money to live on, or the money somebody so earns ○ *What do you do for a living?* **2** the maintaining of life ○ *the cost of living* **3** quality or manner of life ○ *healthy living* ■ *npl* people who are alive

SYNONYMS living, alive, animate, extant CORE MEANING: having life or existence

living death *n* a period of unrelieved misery

living room *n* a room in a house for relaxing or entertaining

Livingstone /lívvingstən/, **David** (1813–73) British physician, missionary, and explorer

living wage *n* a wage that can support a family in reasonable comfort

living will *n* a document in which the signer declines to be kept alive artificially by life-support systems if he or she becomes terminally ill

Livy /lívvi/ (59 BC–AD 17) Roman historian

lizard /lízzərd/ *n* **1** a four-legged reptile with a long scaly body, movable eyelids, and a long tapering tail **2** a large reptile such as an alligator or crocodile that resembles a lizard

Lizard Island /lízzərd-/ island off the coast of Queensland, Australia

Ljubljana /lyŏŏ bli áənə/ capital of Slovenia. Pop. 330,000 (1997).

'll *contr* **1** shall **2** will

llama /laamə/ *n* a domesticated long-haired mammal related to camels

Llandaff /lándəf, hlan dáf/ suburb of Cardiff, SE Wales

Llandudno /hlan dúdnō/ town in N Wales. Pop. 14,576 (1991).

David Lloyd George

Lloyd George /lóyd jáwrj/, **David, 1st Earl of Dwyfor** (1863–1945) British prime minister (1916–22)

load *n* **1** something carried or transported **2** the amount that is carried or dealt with at one time *(often in combination)* ○ *a boat load of passengers* ○ *a small load of dirty shirts* **3** the amount of work that a person or machine is required to do ○ *my teaching load* **4** a mental burden **5** a single charge of ammunition for a gun **6** the total force and weight that a structure is designed to withstand **7** a charge added to the price of some unit trust shares ■ **loads** *npl* a large amount or a lot of *(infml)* ○ *loads of visitors* ■ *v* **1** *vti* put cargo or passengers on a vehicle, ship, or aircraft **2** *vt* put a load on an animal, or give a load to a person to carry **3** *vt* put something in a device for it to function or operate on ○ *load a camera with film* **4** *vti* put ammunition in a firearm **5** *vt* weight one side of a dice or a roulette wheel to prevent it from operating randomly ○ *He must have loaded the dice* **6** *vt* add surcharge to an insurance premium —**loader** *n*

loaded /lṓdid/ *adj* **1** carrying a full load **2** describes a weapon containing ammunition **3** with a hidden implication ○ *a loaded question* **4** rich *(slang)* **5** describes dice or a roulette wheel weighted unfairly

loading /lṓding/ *n* **1** a load or weight carried **2** material added to increase weight **3** an additional insurance premium **4** Aus an additional wage

loaf[1] /lṓf/ *(pl* **loaves)** *n* **1** a quantity of bread shaped and baked as a whole **2** a quantity of food shaped in a rectangular block *(in combination)* ○ *meatloaf*

loaf[2] /lṓf/ *vi* spend time lazily

ORIGIN Loafing has no connection with bread. The verb **loaf** was extracted from *loafer*, which was itself probably taken from German *Land-läufer* 'tramp' (literally 'land-runner'). **Loaf** is first recorded in the 1830s.

loafer /lṓfər/ *n* **1** a casual leather slip-on shoe **2** a lazy person

loam *n* **1** fertile workable soil **2** clay and sand mixed for building —**loamy** *adj*

loan *n* **1** an amount of money lent **2** the act of lending something ■ *vt* lend —**loaner** *n*

loanback /lṓn bak/ *n* the ability to borrow from a pension fund

loan shark *n* an unethical moneylender *(disapproving)*

loanword /lṓn wurd/ *n* a word borrowed from another language

loath /lṓth/, **loth** *adj* reluctant ◊ See note at **unwilling**

loathe /lṓth/ (**loathing, loathed**) *vt* dislike intensely —**loathingly** *adv*

~~loathesome~~ incorrect spelling of **loathsome**

loathing /lṓthing/ *n* intense dislike ◊ See note at **dislike**

loathsome /lṓthsəm/ *adj* repulsive —**loathsomeness** *n*

loaves plural of **loaf**[1]

lob *v* (**lobbing, lobbed**) **1** *vti* hit a ball in a high arc **2** *vt* throw casually ■ *n* a high arching shot

lobby /lóbbi/ *n* (*pl* **-bies**) **1** an entrance area in a public building **2** a public area in a legislative building **3** a voting corridor in Parliament **4** a group trying to influence political policy (*+ sing or pl verb*) **5** an attempt to influence policy ■ *v* (**-bies, -bied**) **1** *vti* petition politicians or influential people **2** *vt* campaign about legislation —**lobbyer** *n* —**lobbyism** *n* —**lobbyist** *n*

lobe *n* **1** an earlobe **2** any rounded body part

lobelia /lō beéli a/ *n* a plant with white or purple flowers

lobola /lo bṓla/, **lobolo** /lo bṓlō/ *n* a payment made by bridegroom's family to the bride's family in parts of Africa

lobotomy /la bóttəmi/ (*pl* **-mies**) *n* a surgical operation to sever the nerves connecting the front part of the brain to an area that sends information to the cortex —**lobotomize** *vt*

lobster /lóbstər/ *n* **1** a hard-shelled sea animal with a pair of large pincers **2** a crustacean related to the lobster **3** a lobster's flesh as food

lobster pot *n* a lobster trap

local /lṓk'l/ *adj* **1** in or for a nearby area **2** characteristic of a particular area **3** not widespread **4** of a comparatively small governmental region **5** affecting only a particular part of the body ■ *n* **1** somebody who comes from a particular area **2** a neighbourhood pub (*infml*) —**locally** *adv* —**localness** *n*

local anaesthetic *n* a drug that eliminates pain in a particular part of the body

local area network *n* a network of personal computers within a small area

local authority *n* an authority administering local affairs

local colour *n* interesting characteristic features of a particular place

locale /lō kaál/ *n* the location of an event or story

local government *n* the government of a city, county, or region

locality /lō kállati/ (*pl* **-ties**) *n* **1** a particular place **2** situation at a particular point in space or time

localize /lṓkə līz/ (**-izing, -ized**), **localise** *vt* **1** confine to a place **2** find the location of —**localization** /lṓkə līzáysh'n/ *n*

locate /lō káyt/ (**-cating, -cated**) *v* **1** *vt* find **2** *vti* establish a residence or business in a place **3** *vt* position or situate —**locater** *n*

location /lō káysh'n/ *n* **1** the site or position of something **2** a film setting **3** the discovery of something —**locational** *adj*

loch /lokh, lok/ *n* Scotland **1** a lake **2** a long narrow inlet

lock[1] *n* **1** a fastening mechanism usually operated by a key **2** a gated section of a waterway **3** the degree of turn of a vehicle's steering wheel **4** a wrestling hold **5** the part of a gun that causes the explosion ■ *v* *vti* **1** fasten using a lock **2** *vt* put something or somebody in a locked place **3** *vt* secure a place by fastening locks **4** *vt* prevent the unauthorized use of something, especially on a computer **5** *vti* fix or be fixed in place **6** *vt* hold somebody tightly **7** *vt* trap somebody in a difficult situation —**lockable** *adj*
◇ **lock, stock, and barrel** completely

☐ **lock away** *vt* **1** imprison **2** store in a locked place

☐ **lock out** *vt* prevent somebody from entering by locking a door

☐ **lock up** *vt* **1** imprison somebody **2** store something in a secure place

lock[2] *n* a piece of hair ■ **locks** *npl* human hair (*literary*)

Locke, John (1632–1704) English philosopher

locker room *n* a changing room with lockers

locket /lókit/ *n* a small decorative case for a picture or memento worn on a neck chain

lockjaw /lók jaw/ *n* a sustained spasm of the jaw muscles that is an early symptom of tetanus

lockkeeper /lók keepər/ *n* a person in charge of a waterway lock

lockout /lók owt/ *n* a refusal by management to allow workers into the workplace

locksmith /lók smith/ *n* somebody who installs and repairs locks —**locksmithing** *n*

lockup /lók up/ *n* **1** a place with prison cells **2** a rented garage **3** a small shop **4** the securing of a building, or the time when this is done

loco /lṓkō/ *adj* wildly irrational (*infml*)

locomotion /lṓkə mṓsh'n/ *n* movement from one place to another

locomotive /lṓkə mṓtiv/ *n* a railway engine ■ *adj* of locomotion

locum /lṓkəm/, **locum tenens** /-ténnenz/ (*pl* **locum tenentes** /-te nén teez/) *n* somebody who does the job of another person, e.g. a doctor, who is away

locus /lṓkəss/ (*pl* **-ci** /lṓ sī/) *n* **1** a place where something happens **2** a set of points, the positions of which satisfy a set of algebraic conditions

locust /lṓkəst/ *n* **1** a swarming grasshopper **2** a pod-bearing tree such as the carob

locution /la kyoósh'n/ *n* **1** a typical phrase **2** somebody's style of speech

lode *n* **1** a deposit of ore **2** a waterway that drains a fen

lodestar /lṓd staar/ *n* **1** the North Star **2** a guiding principle (*literary*)

lodestone /lṓd stōn/ *n* **1** magnetite **2** an attraction

lodge *n* **1** a small gatekeeper's house **2** a small building providing temporary accommodation in the country **3** an inn or hotel **4** a porter's room **5** a branch of a union or society **6** a meeting hall **7** a Native North American dwelling **8** a beaver's den ■ *v* (**lodging, lodged**) **1** *vt* make a complaint or appeal **2** *vt* deposit something in a safe place **3** *vti* stick or get stuck **4** *vi* live in somebody else's house *(dated)* **5** *vt* place somebody in temporary accommodation **6** *vt* give somebody the power to act

lodger /lójjər/ *n* a paying guest

lodging /lójjing/ *n* somewhere to stay, especially temporarily ■ **lodgings** *npl* a rented room or rooms in a boarding house or private home *(dated)*

Lodz /wooch/, **Łódź** /wooj/ city in central Poland. Pop. 812,300 (1997).

Loeb /lób/, **Jacques** (1859–1924) German-born US physiologist known for his pioneering work on tropism and animal instincts

loft *n* **1** the area between a ceiling and a roof **2** the upper floor of a barn **3** a gallery in a church **4** *US, Can* the upper floor of a warehouse or factory, converted to living space **5** the slanting angle on a golf club ■ *vt* hit a ball high

lofty /lófti/ **(-ier, -iest)** *adj* **1** haughty **2** exalted **3** high-ranking **4** very high

log[1] *n* **1** a piece cut from a tree **2** a record of a journey **3** a record of events ■ *v* **(logging, logged)** **1** *vt* record an event in a log **2** *vi* fell trees *vti* cut up a tree for logs —**logger** *n* —**logging** *n* ◊ **sleep like a log** sleep very soundly

☐ **log off** *or* **out** *vi* end a computer session

☐ **log on** *or* **in** *vti* enter a computer system

log[2] *n* a logarithm *(infml)*

Logan, Mt /lógən/ highest peak in Canada, in the St Elias Range in SW Yukon Territory. Height 5,959 m/19,551 ft.

loganberry /lógənbəri/ *(pl* **-ries)** *n* **1** a purplish-red fruit like a large raspberry **2** the plant that produces loganberries

ORIGIN The **loganberry** is named after the US horticulturist James H. Logan (1841–1928), who first cultivated it.

logarithm /lóggə rithəm/ *n* the power to which a base must be raised to equal a given number —**logarithmic** /lóggə ríthmik/ *adj* —**logarithmically** *adv*

ORIGIN The word **logarithm** was coined in the early 17C by the British mathematician John Napier. He formed it from Greek *logos* 'ratio' and *arithmos* 'number'.

logbook /lóg bòok/ *n* **1** a book containing a record of a journey **2** a vehicle registration document

log cabin *n* a simple house made of logs

loge /lózh/ *n* a box in a theatre

loggerhead /lóggər hed/ ◊ **at loggerheads** involved in a quarrel or feud

logic /lójjik/ *n* **1** the branch of philosophy that deals with the theory of reasoning **2** a system of reasoning **3** sensible argument and thought **4** the design of a computer's circuit

logical /lójjik'l/ *adj* **1** sensible and based on facts **2** able to think rationally —**logicality** /lójji kálləti/ *n* —**logically** *adv*

logic bomb *n* a piece of software that acts as a virus

logic circuit *n* a computer switching circuit that performs operations on input signals

logistics /lə jístiks/ *n* (+ *sing or pl verb*) **1** the organization of a complex task **2** the planning of an industrial process **3** the organization of troop movements

logjam /lóg jam/ *n* **1** a deadlock **2** *US, Can* a river blockage caused by floating logs

logo /lógō/ *(pl* **-gos)** *n* a design used as a symbol of an organization

logon /lóggon/, **login** /lóggin/ *n* **1** the act of logging on to a computer **2** a password used to log on

loin /loyn/ *n* **1** the part of the back between the ribs and the hips **2** meat cut from the loin of an animal ■ **loins** *npl* the area below the waist at the front of the body and above the thighs *(literary)* ◊ **gird (up) your loins** prepare yourself to do something difficult and challenging

loincloth /lóyn kloth/ *n* a cloth worn around the hips to cover the genitals

Loire /lwaar/ longest river in France, rising in the southeast and flowing to the Bay of Biscay in the northwest. Length 1,020 km/634 mi.

loiter /lóytər/ *vi* **1** stand around idly **2** proceed slowly —**loiterer** *n*

loll /lol/ *vi* **1** lounge in a relaxed way **2** droop

lollipop /lólli pop/ *n* hard sweet on a stick

lollipop lady *n* a woman who stops traffic for schoolchildren *(infml)*

lollipop man *n* a man who stops traffic for schoolchildren *(infml)*

lollop /lólləp/ *vi* move in a bouncy uncontrolled way

lolly /lólli/ *(pl* **-lies)** *n* **1** a lollipop *(infml)* **2** money *(infml)* **3** *Aus* a sweet

Lombardy /lómbərdi/ autonomous region in north-central Italy. Cap. Milan. Pop. 9,028,913 (1998). —**Lombardic** /lom baárdik/ *adj*

Lomé /ló may/ capital of Togo. Pop. 700,000 (1997).

London /lúndən/ capital of the United Kingdom, in SE England. Pop. 7,074,265 (1996). —**Londoner** *n*

London, Jack (1876–1916) US writer

Londonderry /lúndən deri/ city in NW Northern Ireland. Pop. 72,334 (1991).

lone /lón/ *adj* only one ○ *a lone survivor*

lonely /lónli/ **(-ier, -liest)** *adj* **1** feeling alone and sad **2** isolated **3** lacking support —**loneliness** *n*

lonely hearts *adj* of or for people who are looking for a romantic relationship

~~lonelyness~~ incorrect spelling of **loneliness**

loner /lónər/ *n* somebody who likes being alone

lone wolf *n* a loner

long[1] *adj* **1** extending a considerable distance **2** going on or back for a lengthy period **3** having many items **4** of a particular length **5** with a greater length than width **6** extending in time or space beyond what is usual or desirable **7** having plenty of a particular thing *(infml)* ○ *long on rhetoric* **8** drawn out in pronunciation ■ *adv* **1** for a long time **2** for a particular length of time ○ *all day long* **3** at a much earlier or later time ○ *long after he left* ■ *n* a long time ○ *Are you here for long?* ◇ **as** *or* **so long as 1** because of the fact that **2** on the condition that ◇ **before long** before much time passes ◇ **long since** a long time ago ◇ **no longer** not now ◇ **the long and the short of it** the basic idea or facts

long² *vi* have a strong desire or yearning for somebody or something ○ *She longed for summer.* ◊ See note at **want**

long. *abbr* longitude

long-awaited *adj* hoped for and expected for a long time

Long Beach 1 city in SW California. Pop. 430,905 (1998). **2** city in SE New York State, on an island off S Long Island. Pop. 34,244 (1998).

longboat /lóng bōt/ *n* a Viking ship

longbow /lóngbō/ *n* a large hand-drawn bow —**longbowman** *n*

long-distance *adj* **1** for a long way **2** between distant telephones **3** relating to foot races of over 1,500 m/one mile long ■ *adv* using a long-distance telephone line

long division *n* a method of division of large numbers that shows each step

long-drawn-out *adj* prolonged

longevity /lon jévvati/ *(pl* **-ties)** *n* **1** long life **2** the duration of life

long face *n* a sad expression —**long-faced** *adj*

Longfellow /lóng fel ō/, **Henry Wadsworth** (1807–82) US poet

Longford /lóngfərd/ county in the SE Republic of Ireland

longhand /lóng hand/ *n* handwriting as opposed to typing

long haul *n* a long distance *(infml)* —**long-haul** *adj*

longing /lónging/ *n* a steady strong desire ■ *adj* showing yearning —**longingly** *adv*

Long Island island in SE New York State. Queens and Brooklyn, two boroughs of New York City, are situated at its western end. Pop. 6,882,362 (1997).

Long Island Sound inlet of the Atlantic Ocean between N Long Island, New York, and S Connecticut

longitude /lónji tyood, lónggi-/ *n* the angular distance of a place from the prime meridian in Greenwich, England

longitudinal /lónji tyóōdin'l, lónggi-/ *adj* **1** going from top to bottom **2** of longitude —**longitudinally** *adv*

long johns /-jonz/ *npl* underwear with full-length legs

long jump *n* a competition in which athletes jump for distance rather than height

long-lasting *adj* lasting a long time

long-life *adj* specially treated to last longer

long-lived *adj* living or existing for a long time

long-lost *adj* not seen for a long time *(humorous)*

Longo /lóng ō/, **Robert** (*b.* 1953) US painter, sculptor, filmmaker, and performance artist

long-playing record *n* full form of **LP**

long-range *adj* **1** extending well into the future **2** travelling long distances **3** able to hit distant targets

Longreach /lóng reech/ town in central Queensland, Australia. Pop. 3,604 (1991).

longship /lóng ship/ *n* a Viking ship

longshoreman /lóng shawrmən/ *(pl* **-men** /-mən/) *n* US, Can a docker

long shot *n* **1** somebody or something unlikely to win or succeed **2** a camera shot of a distant object ◇ **(not) by a long shot** (not) in any way at all *(infml)*

long-sighted *adj* **1** able to see distant objects better than nearby ones **2** taking future needs into consideration —**long-sightedly** *adv* —**long-sightedness** *n*

long-standing *adj* having existed for a long time

long-suffering *adj* patiently enduring unpleasantness

long term *n* a time lasting from now far into the future

long-term *adj* **1** of or affecting the long term **2** long-lasting

longtime /lóng tīm/ *adj* having existed for years

longueur /long gúr/ *n* a period of boredom

long vacation *n* the long summer holiday enjoyed by British universities and law courts

long wave *n* a radio wave over 1,000m

long-winded /-wíndid/ *adj* **1** using too many words **2** not easily becoming short of breath —**long-windedness** *n* ◊ See note at **wordy**

loo *(pl* **loos)** *n* a toilet *(infml)*

ORIGIN The origin of **loo** is obscure. The most widely claimed source is *gardy loo* (based on pseudo-French *gare de l'eau* 'mind the water'), used in 18C Edinburgh to warn passers-by when a chamber pot was about to be emptied into the street below. However, this is chronologically unlikely, as there is no evidence of **loo** being used for 'lavatory' before the 1930s. Other possible candidates include *Waterloo* (the link with 'water' gives this some plausibility) and *louvre*, from the use of slatted screens for a makeshift lavatory. The likeliest source is perhaps French *lieux d'aisances*, literally 'places of ease', hence 'lavatory', possibly picked up by British service personnel in France during World War I.

look *v* **1** *vi* turn the eyes towards or on something **2** *vi* use the eyes to search **3** *vi* appear in a particular way **4** *vi* consider ○ *look at the problem* **5** *vt* fit something by appearance ○ *looks his age* **6** *vi* face a particular way ○ *The house looks over the lake.* ■ *n* **1** an act or instance of looking **2** the way somebody or something appears **3** a facial expression ■ **looks** *npl* outward appearance

☐ **look after** *vt* take care of

☐ **look ahead** *vi* think about the future

☐ **look back** *vi* think about the past

☐ **look down on** *or* **upon** *vt* treat as inferior

☐ **look for** *vt* **1** search for **2** expect

☐ **look forward to** *vt* await eagerly

☐ **look in on** *vt* pay a brief visit to *(infml)*

☐ **look into** *vt* investigate carefully

☐ **look on** *v* **1** *vi* be a spectator **2** *also* **look upon** *vt* regard

☐ **look out** *v* **1** *vi* be careful **2** *vt* search for and find

☐ **look out for** *vt* **1** watch for *(infml)* **2** take care of

☐ **look over** *vt* **1** visit and inspect **2** examine

☐ **look through** *vt* ignore or not notice ○ *I smiled at her, but she looked right through me.*

☐ **look to** *vt* rely on

☐ **look up** *v* **1** *vt* search for in a reference book **2** *vi* improve **3** *vt* visit

☐ **look up to** *vt* respect and admire

lookalike /lóokə lìk/ *n* somebody or something that looks very much like another *(infml)*

looker /lóokər/ *n* somebody who watches

looker-on *(pl* **lookers-on)** *n* an onlooker

look-in *n* a chance to participate *(infml)*

looking glass *n* a mirror *(archaic)*

lookout /lóok owt/ *n* **1** a careful watch **2** somebody watching for danger **3** a place that gives a good view **4** a problem *(infml)* ○ *That's your lookout.*

lookover /lóokòvər/ *n* a quick inspection

look-up *n* a computer procedure that matches a term against stored information

loom[1] *vi* **1** appear as a large shape **2** be about to happen

loom[2] *n* a weaving apparatus

loon *n* US, Can a diving water bird

loony /lóoni/ (**-ier, -iest**), **looney** *adj* **1** an offensive term meaning affected by a psychiatric disorder **2** considered silly or strange *(infml)* —**looniness** *n* —**loony** *n*

loop *n* **1** a circle or oval made by a line curving over itself **2** a loop of string or other material **3** a contraceptive device **4** a closed circuit **5** a set of commands in a computer program **6** a flight manoeuvre in which the plane flies through a vertical circle ■ *v* **1** *vti* be in or form into a loop **2** *vt* fasten, join, or arrange something using a loop ◊ **in** *or* **out of the loop** US, Can be or not be among the people who are decision-makers or are fully informed *(infml)*

loophole /lóop hòl/ *n* **1** a gap in a law **2** a slit in a wall

loopy /lóopi/ (**-ier, -iest**) *adj* **1** having loops **2** an offensive term meaning irrational

loose /looss/ *adj* (**looser, loosest**) **1** not firmly fixed **2** not fastened or pulled tight **3** not tight-fitting **4** free ○ *broke loose* **5** not packaged **6** not dense or compact **7** imprecise ○ *a loose translation* **8** considered sexually promiscuous *(dated; disapproving)* ■ *adv* (**looser,**

loosest) freely ■ *v* (**loosing, loosed**) **1** *vt* set a person or animal free **2** *vt* untie a knot **3** *vti* make or become less tight **4** *vt* fire a missile —**loosely** *adv* —**looseness** *n* ◊ **be on the loose** free from confinement

USAGE **loose** or **lose**? **Lose** is a verb only, as in *Don't lose* [not *loose*] *possession of the ball,* or *you'll lose the game.* **Loose** is an adjective, adverb, and verb, as in *loose* [not *lose*] *floorboards; dogs running loose* [not *lose*]; *loosed her grip.*

loose cannon *n* an indiscreet and unpredictable person *(slang)*

loose cover *n* a loose furniture cover that can be easily removed

loose end *n* an unfinished detail *(infml; often pl)* ◊ **at a loose end** restless and bored *(infml)*

loose-leaf *adj* having removable pages

loosen /lóoss'n/ *v* **1** *vti* make or become less tight **2** *vt* untie hair or a knot **3** *vt* relax control or strictness

☐ **loosen up** *v* **1** *vti* do exercises, or exercise muscles and joints **2** *vi* relax

loot /loot/ *n* **1** things taken during a war or riot **2** stolen goods **3** money *(infml)* ■ *vti* take things from a place during a war or riot —**looter** *n*

lop (**lopping, lopped**) *vt* **1** cut a branch off a tree **2** cut something off

lope *v* (**loping, loped**) **1** *vi* run with long easy strides **2** *vti* canter or make a horse canter ■ *n* a gait with long strides

lop-eared /-éerd/ *adj* with long hanging ears

Lope de Vega /lópay de váygə/ (1562–1635) Spanish playwright and poet

lopsided /lop sídid/ *adj* **1** leaning to one side **2** unevenly balanced

loquacious /lo kwáyshəss/ *adj* talkative —**loquaciously** *adv* —**loquacity** /lo kwássəti/ *n* ◊ See note at **talkative**

Federico García Lorca

Lorca /láwrkə/, **Federico García** (1898–1936) Spanish poet and playwright

lord /lawd/ *n* **1** an aristocrat **2** a feudal superior **3** any powerful man **4 Lord** the Christian or Jewish God **5 Lord** a title given to some noblemen **6 Lord** a title given to some high-ranking British officials ■ *interj* **Lord** expresses surprise ■ **Lords** *npl* the British House of Lords ◊ **lord it** act in a superior, masterful, or bullying way *(disapproving)* ◊ See note at **laud**

ORIGIN Lord means literally 'bread guardian'.

In origin it is a compound of *hlaf*, an early form of *loaf*, and *ward*.

Lord Chancellor *n* the head of the English and Welsh judiciary

Lord Howe Island /-hów-/ island off E New South Wales, Australia, in the south Pacific Ocean. Pop. 369 (1996).

lordly /láwrdli/ (**-lier, -liest**) *adj* **1** arrogant **2** impressive —**lordliness** *n*

Lord Mayor *n* the mayor of a large British city

lordship /láwrd ship/ *n* **1** the position, land, or tenure of a lord **2 Lordship** a respectful form of address used to a bishop or a judge

Lord's Prayer *n* the most important Christian prayer

Lords Spiritual *npl* the Anglican bishops entitled to sit in the House of Lords

Lords Temporal *npl* the members of the House of Lords excluding the Lords Spiritual

lore *n* **1** knowledge handed down verbally **2** knowledge acquired from teaching or experience

Lorrain /lə ráyn/, **Claude** (1600–82) French painter

lorry /lórri/ (*pl* **-ries**) *n* a large goods vehicle

Los Angeles /los ánjələss, -leez/ city in SW California, the second most populous city in the United States. Pop. 3,597,556 (1998).

lose /looz/ (**losing, lost**) *v* **1** *vti* fail to win **2** *vt* be unable to find something **3** *vt* fail to keep something **4** *vt* cease to have something **5** *vt* experience a reduction in something **6** *vt* make somebody fail to win something ○ *a mistake that lost us the game* **7** *vt* not use something such as time to your advantage **8** *vt* be unable to control something, e.g. your temper **9** *vt* have a loved one die **10** *vt* leave somebody behind **11** *vt* confuse somebody **12** *vt* no longer see or hear something **13** *vti* be or become slow by an amount of time *(refers to timepieces)* —**losable** *adj* ◊ **lose it** *(infml)* **1** become removed from reality **2** be unable to maintain emotional control or composure ◊ See note at **loose**
□ **lose out** *vi* fail to win or obtain something *(infml)*

~~loseing~~ incorrect spelling of **losing**

loser /loozər/ *n* **1** somebody who has not won **2** somebody who is habitually unsuccessful or unlucky *(insult)*

loss *n* **1** the fact of no longer having something **2** death **3** somebody or something lost **4** money spent in excess of income *(often pl)* **5** a sad feeling deriving from an absence **6** a reduction in level or amount **7** an instance of losing a contest **8** an insurance claim ◊ **at a loss** uncertain what to say or do ◊ **cut your losses** withdraw from a situation in which there is no possibility of winning

loss adjuster *n* somebody employed by an insurance company to asses losses and compensation

loss leader *n* an article deliberately sold at a loss to attract custom

lost *v* past tense, past participle of **lose** ■ *adj* **1** mislaid **2** unable to find the way **3** wasted **4** not understood or appreciated by somebody **5** no longer in existence **6** preoccupied **7** confused by something complicated

lost cause *n* something that cannot succeed

lost property *n* **1** things accidentally left behind **2** *also* **lost property office** a place where lost property is kept

lot *pron* a large number of people or things ■ *n* **1** a set of people or things **2** an item in an auction **3** a specific group of people *(infml)* **4** somebody's destiny ○ *our lot in life* **5** *US, Can* a piece of land ■ **lots** *npl* large numbers or a large amount *(infml)* ◊ **a lot** *(infml)* **1** a great extent or degree **2** often or much of the time

USAGE **a lot** or **alot**? The one-word spelling **alot** is nonstandard usage and should be avoided. In formal writing avoid **a lot** in favour of *much, many, a great deal of*, and the like.

loth *adj* = **loath**

loti /lóti/ (*pl* **maloti** /maa lóti/) *n* the main unit of currency in Lesotho

lotion /lósh'n/ *n* a liquid skin cream

lottery /lóttəri/ (*pl* **-ies**) *n* **1** a large-scale gambling game **2** a situation in which the outcome depends on chance

lotto /lóttô/ *n* **1** a game resembling bingo **2** *also* **Lotto** a state-run lottery in Australia and some US states

lotus /lótəss/ (*pl* **-tuses** *or same*) *n* **1** in Greek mythology, a fruit causing drowsiness **2** a water plant with large rounded leaves and pink flowers

lotus-eater *n* **1** a lazy and indulgent person **2** in Greek mythology, somebody who lived in a state of idle stupor after eating the lotus fruit

louche /loosh/ *adj* disreputable

loud /lowd/ *adj* **1** high in volume of sound **2** expressing something noisily ○ *loud protests* **3** shockingly bright in colour or bold in design ■ *adv* loudly —**loudly** *adv* —**loudness** *n*

loudhailer /lówd háylər/ *n* a hand-held device for amplifying the voice

loudmouth /lówd mowth/ (*pl* **-mouths** /-mowthz, -mowths/) *n* a loud boaster *(infml)* —**loudmouthed** /lówd mowthd, -mowtht/ *adj*

loudspeaker /lówd speekər/ *n* a device for converting electrical signals into sound

lough /lokh, lok/ *n Ireland* **1** a lake **2** a long narrow inlet

Louis XIV /lóô i/ (1638–1715) king of France (1643–1715)

Louis XV (1710–74) king of France (1715–74)

Louis XVI (1754–93) king of France (1774–93)

Louisiana /loo eézi aánnə/ state in the S United States, on the Gulf of Mexico. Cap. Baton Rouge. Pop. 4,468,976 (2000). —**Louisianan** *n, adj*

Louisiana Purchase territory of the W United States purchased from France in 1803. It extended from the Gulf of Mexico northwards to the Canadian border and from the Mississippi River westwards to the Rocky Mountains.

Louis Philippe /lóō i fee leèp/ (1773–1850) king of France (1830–50)

Louisville /lóō i vil/ largest city in Kentucky. Pop. 255,045 (1998).

lounge /lownj/ *n* **1** a sitting room in a house **2** a public room for relaxing **3** a period of lounging ■ *vi* (**lounging, lounged**) **1** lie or sit lazily **2** pass time lazily

lounge bar *n* a more comfortable area in a pub

lounger /lównjər/ *n* **1** a reclining chair or couch **2** somebody who lounges about

lounge suit *n* a man's suit of matching jacket and trousers

lour *vi, n =* **lower**²

Lourdes /loordz/ town in SW France, a major site of Roman Catholic pilgrimage. Pop. 15,203 (1999).

louse /lowss/ *n* (*pl* **lice** /līss/) **1** a parasitic insect **2** a small invertebrate animal (*often in combination*) ■ *vt* (**lousing, loused**) rid a person or animal of lice

lousy /lówzi/ (**-ier, -iest**) *adj* (*infml*) **1** inferior **2** unpleasant —**lousily** *adv* —**lousiness** *n*

lout /lowt/ *n* a person regarded as ill-mannered (*insult*)

Louth 1 /lowth/ county in the SE Republic of Ireland **2** /lowth/ town in E England. Pop. 14,248 (1991).

louvre /loovər/, **louver** *n* **1** a frame with angled horizontal slats **2** a slat in a louvre

Louvre /loovrə/ *n* the French national art museum

lovable /lúvvəb'l/, **loveable** *adj* worthy of love —**lovably** *adv*

love /luv/ *v* (**loving, loved**) **1** *vti* feel tender affection for a person or animal **2** *vti* feel romantic and sexual desire for somebody **3** *vt* like something very much **4** *vt* show kindness to somebody ○ *love your enemies* ■ *n* **1** very strong affection **2** passionate attraction and sexual desire **3** somebody who is loved **4** a romantic affair **5** a strong liking **6** something that you feel enthusiastic about **7** a score of zero —**loveless** *adj*

SYNONYMS **love, liking, affection, fondness, passion, infatuation, crush** CORE MEANING: a strong positive feeling towards somebody or something

love affair *n* **1** a sexual or romantic relationship **2** an intense liking

lovebird /lúv burd/ *n* **1** a small parrot **2** a lover (*usually pl*)

lovebite /lúv bīt/ *n* a bruised area of skin caused by sucking

love child *n* a child of unmarried parents

loved one *n* somebody who is dear to you

~~loveing~~ incorrect spelling of **loving**

love life *n* sexual and romantic relationships

lovelorn /lúv lawrn/ *adj* very unhappy because of romantic problems

lovely /lúvli/ *adj* (**-lier, -liest**) **1** beautiful and pleasing **2** delightful ■ *n* (*pl* **-lies**) a good-looking person (*often in the pl; sometimes offensive*) —**loveliness** *n*

lovemaking /lúv mayking/ *n* **1** sexual activity **2** courtship (*dated*)

love nest *n* a place where lovers can meet

lover /lúvvər/ *n* **1** a sexual partner **2** somebody who likes or is devoted to a particular thing (*often in combination*)

love seat *n* a small sofa

lovesick /lúv sik/ *adj* unhappy because of love —**lovesickness** *n*

loving /lúvving/ *adj* **1** showing affection **2** done with careful attention —**lovingly** *adv* —**lovingness** *n*

loving cup *n* a two-handled drinking or ornamental vessel

loving kindness *n* compassion

~~lovly~~ incorrect spelling of **lovely**

low¹ /lo/ *adj* **1** with relatively little height **2** close to the ground **3** below average or standard **4** small in value or importance **5** near depletion **6** turned down or dimmed **7** quiet **8** deep in pitch **9** near the bottom of a scale **10** dispirited **11** providing slow vehicular speed **12** lacking status ■ *adv* **1** in a low position **2** with a deep tone **3** quietly ■ *n* **1** a low position or degree **2** a region of low atmospheric pressure **3** an unhappy or unsuccessful period —**lowness** *n* ◇ **lay low** cause to feel overcome or helpless

low² /lo/ *n* the mooing sound of a cow ■ *vi* moo

lowborn /lo báwrn/ *adj* born to lower-class parents

lowbrow /lo brow/ *adj* unsophisticated (*disapproving*) ■ *n* an unsophisticated person

low-cal *adj* with relatively few calories

Low Church *n* a branch of the Church of England that favours less ritual and ceremony

Low Countries region in NW Europe, made up of Belgium, the Netherlands, and Luxembourg. Pop. 26,016,000 (1995).

lowdown /lo down/ *n* the inside information about somebody or something (*infml*)

low-down *adj* despicable (*infml*) ○ *a low-down trick*

Lowell /lo əl/, **Robert** (1917–77) US poet

lower¹ /lo ər/ *adj* **1** below another **2** reduced or less ○ *lower wages* **3** closer to the bottom ○ *the lower slopes* **4** of less importance **5** earlier in a geological period **6** describes organisms that are less advanced in terms of development or complexity ○ *a lower life form* ■ *v* **1** *vt* bring something to a lower level **2** *vti* reduce or be reduced **3** *vt* move your head or eyes downwards **4** *vr* humiliate yourself **5** *vt* reduce the volume or pitch of a sound ○ *lower your voice*

lower[2] /lów ər/, **lour** /lowr/ vi 1 be overcast 2 look angry ■ n a scowl —**lowering** adj

Lower California /ló ər-/ ♦ Baja California

lowercase /ló ər káyss/ n small letters, not capitals —**lowercase** adj, vt

lower class /ló ər-/ n the lowest social group (often pl) —**lower-class** adj

lower house /ló ər-/, **lower chamber** n one of the two branches of a legislature

Lower Hutt /ló ər hút/ city in the North Island, New Zealand. Pop. 98,000 (1998).

lowest common denominator n 1 the lowest multiple shared by a set of denominators 2 the mass of ordinary people regarded as undiscerning

lowest common multiple n the lowest number that is divisible by all the members of a set

low-fat adj describes food with relatively little fat

low frequency n a radio frequency ranging from 30 to 300 kilohertz

low-grade adj 1 inferior in quality 2 describes a medical condition that is mild and not serious

low-hanging fruit n a target that is easy to accomplish, or a problem that is easy to solve

low-key, low-keyed /-keed/ adj 1 restrained or understated 2 subdued in colour

lowland /lóland/ n an area of relatively low or flat land —**lowland** adj

Lowlands /lólandz/ region of Scotland lying south of the Highlands —**Lowlander** n

low-level adj 1 situated or done at lower than the usual level 2 low in status or intensity

low-level language n a computer programming language that is closer to machine language than to ordinary speech

lowlife /ló líf/ n criminal or immoral people (infml insult) —**lowlife** adj

lowlights /ló líts/ npl strands of hair dyed to a darker shade

lowly /lóli/ adj (-lier, -liest) 1 low in status 2 meek ■ adv (-lier, -liest) in a meek way —**lowliness** n

low-lying adj relatively close to sea level

low-maintenance adj needing little effort or expense to keep in good condition

low-pitched adj 1 low in tone 2 shallow in slope

low point n the least enjoyable or successful period

low-pressure adj 1 having or exerting little pressure 2 relaxed

low profile n behaviour that avoids public attention

low-resolution, low-res adj describes a computer screen or printer with ill-defined text or graphics

low rise n a building of few storeys —**low-rise** adj

Lowry /lówri/, **L. S.** (1887–1976) British painter

Lowry, Malcolm (1909–57) British writer and poet

low-slung adj close to the ground

low technology, low tech n simple technology, especially that used to make basic items or perform basic tasks —**low-tech** adj

low tide, low water n 1 the lowest tide level, or the time when the tide is at this level 2 the worst point in something

low-water mark n 1 a line marking low tide 2 the worst point in something

lox[1] n smoked salmon

lox[2] n liquid oxygen

loyal /lóyəl/ adj 1 faithful 2 showing a feeling of devotion or duty to somebody or something —**loyally** adv —**loyalness** n

loyalist /lóy əlist/ n 1 somebody who is loyal to his or her country or government 2 **Loyalist** a supporter of Northern Ireland's union with Britain 3 **Loyalist** an American who supported the British during the War of American Independence —**loyalism** n

loyalty /lóyəlti/ (pl -ties) n 1 the state of being loyal 2 a feeling of devotion or duty to somebody or something (often pl)

loyalty card n a card that gives regular customers rewards or discounts

lozenge /lózzinj/ n 1 a medicated sweet or tablet 2 a diamond shape

LP n a long-playing record

LPG abbr liquefied petroleum gas

L-plate n a sign on a car that shows that the driver is a learner

Lr symbol lawrencium

LSD n a hallucinogenic drug

> **ORIGIN LSD** is an acronym formed from letters of German Lysergsäure Diäthylamid 'lysergic acid diethylamide'.

LSE abbr London School of Economics

Ltd, ltd abbr limited (liability) (after the name of a British company)

Lu symbol lutetium

Luanda /loo ándə/ capital of Angola. Pop. 2,080,000 (1995).

lube Aus, US, Can (infml) n lubricant ■ vt (lubing, lubed) lubricate

lubricant /loóbrikənt/ n 1 a friction-reducing substance 2 an element that eases a difficult situation —**lubricant** adj

lubricate /loóbri kayt/ (-cating, -cated) vt 1 apply lubricant to 2 make slippery —**lubrication** /loóbri káysh'n/ n

lubricious /loo bríshəss/, **lubricous** /loóbrikəss/ adj (literary) 1 lewd or obscene 2 slippery —**lubricity** n

Lubumbashi /loobóom báshi/ capital of Shaba Administrative Region, SE Democratic Republic of the Congo. Pop. 851,381 (1994).

Lucas /loókəss/, **George** (b. 1944) US film director and producer

Lucerne /loo súrn/ city in central Switzerland. Pop. 57,193 (1998).

Lucerne, Lake of lake in central Switzerland

lucid /loóossid/ adj **1** easily understood **2** rational **3** shining —**lucidity** /loo síddəti/ n —**lucidly** adv —**lucidness** n

Lucifer /loóossifər/ n **1** Satan **2** the morning star

~~lucious~~ incorrect spelling of **luscious**

luck n **1** good fortune **2** a fortunate or unfortunate event, or a series of such events ○ *Our luck had changed.*

luckily /lúkili/ adv as the result of good luck

luckless /lúkləss/ adj unfortunate

Lucknow /lúk now/ capital of Uttar Pradesh State, N India. Pop. 1,619,115 (1991).

lucky /lúki/ (**-ier**, **-iest**) adj **1** having good luck **2** bringing good luck **3** resulting from good luck —**luckiness** n

SYNONYMS **lucky, fortunate, happy, providential, serendipitous** CORE MEANING: relating to advantage or good fortune

lucky dip n a game in which people pick mystery prizes out of a container

lucrative /loókrətiv/ adj producing profit or wealth —**lucratively** adv —**lucrativeness** n

lucre /loókər/ n money (*dated or humorous*)

Luddite /lúddīt/ n **1** an opponent of new technology **2** a 19C protester against technology —**Luddism** n —**Luddite** adj

ORIGIN According to tradition, the **Luddites** were named after Ned Ludd, an 18C farm worker from Leicestershire, who destroyed two machines in a fit of rage.

ludicrous /loódikrəss/ adj absurdly ridiculous —**ludicrously** adv —**ludicrousness** n

ludo /loódō/ n a board game played with counters and dice

lug[1] (**lugging**, **lugged**) vt pull something heavy or bulky with effort

lug[2] n **1** a projecting part used for grabbing or turning **2** a small projection on a boot or tyre improving traction **3** an ear (*infml*)

luge /loozh/ n a racing toboggan   **lugo** vi —**luger** n

luggage /lúggij/ n suitcases and bags

luggage rack n **1** US = **roof rack 2** an overhead frame in a train or bus for luggage

luggage van n a railway carriage for luggage

lugubrious /lə goóbri əss/ adj mournful or gloomy

Luhansk /loo hánsk/, **Luhans'k** city in E Ukraine. Pop. 475,000 (1998).

Lukács /loó kach/, **György** (1885–1971) Hungarian philosopher, critic, and politician

Luke, St (*fl* AD 1C) evangelist. By tradition he is considered to be the author of the biblical Acts of the Apostles and the third Gospel of the New Testament.

lukewarm /loók wáwrm/ adj **1** warm but not hot **2** showing little enthusiasm —**lukewarmly** adv —**lukewarmness** n

lull /lul/ vt **1** soothe or calm somebody or something **2** give somebody a false sense of security ■ n a period of calm

lullaby /lúllə bī/ (*pl* **-bies**) n **1** a gentle song for soothing a child to sleep **2** the music for a lullaby

lulu /loó loo/ n an outstanding person or thing (*slang*)

lumbago /lum báygō/ n pain in the lower back

lumbar /lúmbər/ adj of the lower back

SPELLCHECK Do not confuse the spelling of **lumbar** and **lumber** ('unwanted objects'), which sound similar.

lumbar puncture n the insertion of a needle into the spinal cord to draw out a sample of spinal fluid

lumber[1] /lúmbər/ n **1** US, Can timber **2** unwanted objects ■ vt **1** burden somebody with something or somebody unwanted (*infml*) **2** pile things together ◊ See note at **lumbar**

lumber[2] /lúmbər/ vi move clumsily

lumberjack /lúmbər jak/ n US, Can somebody who fells trees for timber

luminary /loóminəri/ (*pl* **-ies**) n **1** an eminent person **2** a sun, moon, or star (*literary*)

luminescence /loómi néss'nss/ n the emission of light without heat —**luminescent** adj

luminosity /loómi nóssəti/ n **1** the state of being luminous **2** (*symbol* **L**) the energy radiated by an astronomical object

luminous /loóminəss/ adj **1** emitting light **2** bright **3** illuminated —**luminously** adv

lump[1] n **1** a solid chunk **2** a tumour **3** a sugar cube ■ v **1** vt group people or things together, often without good reason **2** vi move heavily ■ adj in lumps

lump[2] vt put up with (*infml*)

lumpectomy /lum péktəmi/ (*pl* **-mies**) n the removal of a breast tumour

lumpen /lúmpən, loóm-/ adj (*disapproving*) **1** living on the margins of society **2** not educated or enlightened

lump sum n a single payment of a total amount

lumpy /lúmpi/ (**-ier**, **-iest**) adj with unwanted lumps —**lumpily** adv —**lumpiness** n

lunacy /loónəssi/ n behaviour regarded as irrational or misguided

lunar /loónər/ adj **1** of the Moon **2** used for travel to the Moon

lunar module n a spacecraft that lands on the Moon's surface

lunar month n **1** a period between new moons **2** a 28-day period

lunatic /loónətik/ adj **1** considered thoughtless or reckless **2** a former term, now offensive, meaning affected by a psychiatric disorder (*archaic offensive*) —**lunatic** n

lunatic fringe n members of a group or society whose views are regarded as extreme (*insult*)

lunch n **1** a midday meal **2** the food eaten at midday ■ vi eat lunch ◊ **out to lunch** regarded as being out of touch with reality *(insult)*

ORIGIN Lunch is an abbreviation of *luncheon*. The origin of the latter is not known for certain. It may be an alteration of *nuncheon* 'light refreshment, snack', the constituents of which are early forms of *noon* and obsolete *shench* 'drink, cupful'. *Luncheon* is recorded from the mid-17C, and **lunch** from the early 19C.

lunchbox /lúnch boks/ *n* a container used to carry food such as sandwiches to work or school

luncheon /lúnchən/ *n (fml)* **1** lunch **2** a midday gathering with food

luncheon meat *n* cold processed meat

luncheon voucher *n* a food voucher used to buy a lunchtime snack or meal

lunchtime /lúnch tīm/ *n* the time when lunch is usually eaten

lung *n* a respiratory organ, especially in vertebrates —**lungful** *n* ◊ **at the top of your lungs** extremely loudly *(infml)*

lunge[1] /lunj/ *n* **1** a sudden attacking forward movement **2** a quick thrust ■ *vi* **(lunging, lunged) 1** move suddenly forwards in a threatening way **2** make a quick thrust

lunge[2] /lunj/, **longe** /lunj, lonj/ *n* **1** a horse-training rope **2** a circular horse-training area ■ *vt* **(lunging, lunged; longing, longed)** train a horse using a lunge

lunkhead /lúngk hed/ *n* somebody regarded as unintelligent *(infml insult)*

Luoyang /ló yáng/ city in east-central China. Pop. 1,370,000 (1995).

lupin /loopin/ *n* a plant with tall flower spikes

lupine /loo pīn/ *adj* **1** of a wolf **2** ravenous

lurch[1] *vi* **1** pitch suddenly to one side **2** move unsteadily —**lurch** *n* —**lurchingly** *adv*

lurch[2] *n* a losing position in cribbage ◊ **leave in the lurch** abandon in a difficult or embarrassing situation

lure /lyoor, loor/ *vt* **(luring, lured) 1** entice somebody **2** recall a falcon ■ *n* **1** something enticing **2** attraction **3** a device that attracts a fish

lurid /lyoórid, loór-/ *adj* **1** horrifying or shocking **2** unattractively bright —**luridly** *adv* —**luridness** *n*

lurk *vi* **1** move or wait furtively **2** exist unsuspected **3** read messages in an online forum but make no contributions *(slang)* —**lurker** *n* —**lurking** *adj*

Lusaka /loo saåkə, -zaåka/ capital of Zambia. Pop. 1,317,000 (1995).

luscious /lúshəss/ *adj* **1** sweet and juicy **2** appealing to the senses **3** sexually desirable *(infml)* —**lusciously** *adv* —**lusciousness** *n*

lush[1] /lush/ *adj* **1** growing vigorously **2** sweet and juicy **3** luxurious —**lushly** *adv* —**lushness** *n*

lush[2] /lush/ *n US* a heavy drinker *(slang)*

lust *n* **1** strong sexual desire **2** eagerness ■ *vi* **1** feel strong sexual desire **2** feel a great eagerness —**lustful** *adj* —**lustfully** *adv*

luster *n, vt US* = **lustre**

lustre /lústər/ *n* **1** a soft sheen of reflected light **2** shininess **3** splendour

lustrous /lústrəss/ *adj* shining —**lustrously** *adv* —**lustrousness** *n*

lusty /lústi/ **(-ier, -iest)** *adj* **1** strong and healthy **2** energetic or enthusiastic —**lustily** *adv* —**lustiness** *n*

lute[1] /loot/ *n* a musical instrument resembling a guitar with a pear-shaped body

lute[2] /loot/ *n* paste or other substance used as a sealant ■ *vt* seal with lute

lutetium /loo teéshəm, -shi əm/ *n (symbol Lu)* a metallic element. Use: catalyst in the nuclear industries.

Luther /loóthər/, **Martin** (1483–1546) German theologian and religious reformer —**Lutheran** *n, adj*

Lutyens /lúttyənz/, **Sir Edwin Landseer** (1869–1944) British architect

luvvie /lúvvi/, **luvvy** *(pl* **-vies)** *n* an actor or theatrical person *(infml humorous or disapproving)* —**luvviness** *n*

Luxembourg /lúksəm burg/ **1** country in W Europe. Cap. Luxembourg (City). Pop. 442,972 (2001). **2** largest and southernmost province of Belgium. Cap. Arlon. Pop. 245,140 (1999). —**Luxembourger** *n*

Luxembourg City capital of Luxembourg, in the south-central part of the country. Pop. 79,500 (1994).

Luxemburg /lúksəm burg/, **Rosa** (1871–1919) Polish-born German political activist

~~**luxery**~~ incorrect spelling of **luxury**

luxuriant /lug zyoóri ənt, luk syoóri-, lug zhoóri-/ *adj* with a great deal of thick healthy growth —**luxuriance** *n* —**luxuriantly** *adv*

luxuriate /lug zyoóri ayt, luk syoóri-, lug zhoóri-/ **(-ating, -ated)** *vi* **1** derive great enjoyment **2** grow vigorously

luxurious /lug zyoóri əss, luk syoóri-, lug zhoóri-/ *adj* **1** comfortable and expensive **2** enjoying luxury —**luxuriously** *adv* —**luxuriousness** *n*

luxury /lúkshəri/ *(pl* **-ries)** *n* **1** pleasurable self-indulgent activity **2** a nonessential item **3** great comfort

Luzon /loo zón/ largest island in the Philippines. Pop. 30,759,000 (1990).

LW *abbr* long wave

lyceum /lī seé əm/ *n* a concert hall or theatre *(usually in names of buildings)*

lychee /lí chee, lí chee/, **litchi, lichee** *n* **1** a small round Chinese fruit **2** a Chinese tree that produces lychees

lych-gate /lich-/, **lich-gate** *n* a covered gateway into a churchyard

Lycra /líkrə/ *tdmk* a trademark for a lightweight stretchy polyurethane fabric. Use: clothing, particularly sportswear.

Lydia /líddi ə/ ancient country in present-day NW Turkey, on the Aegean Sea —**Lydian** *adj, n*

Lyme disease /lím-/ n a serious infectious disease transmitted by ticks

ORIGIN The disease is named after a town in Connecticut, USA, where an outbreak occurred.

Lymington /límmingtən/ town and seaport in SW England. Pop. 13,508 (1991).

lymph /limf/ n body fluid containing white cells

lymphatic /lim fáttik/ adj of lymph or the system that transports lymph ■ n a vessel that transports lymph

lymph node n an organ that filters microorganisms and other particles from lymph

lynch /linch/ vt put to death illegally without trial, usually by hanging —**lynching** n

ORIGIN Lynching derives its name from Captain William Lynch (1724–1820), a planter and justice of the peace who organized an illegal tribunal in Virginia, in the United States, in 1780.

lynch mob n a group of people who lynch somebody

lynchpin n FNG = linchpin

lynx /lingks/ n 1 (pl same or lynxes) a short-tailed medium-sized wild cat 2 Lynx a faint constellation of the northern hemisphere

Lyons /lee óN/, **Lyon** city in east-central France. Pop. 445,452 (1999).

Lyons /lī ənz/, **Joseph Aloysius** (1879–1939) prime minister of Australia (1932–39)

lyre /līr/ n a U-shaped stringed instrument of ancient Greece

lyric /lírrik/ adj 1 of poetry expressing personal feelings 2 singing with a lightness of voice ■ n 1 the words of a song (often pl) 2 a short personal poem —**lyricist** /-sist/ n

lyrical /lírrik'l/ adj 1 LITERAT, MUSIC = lyric 2 exceedingly complimentary —**lyrically** adv

lyricism /lírrissizəm/ n 1 a lyric style in poetry or music 2 enthusiastically emotional expression

Lysenko /li séngk ō/, **Trofim Denisovich** (1898–1976) Russian geneticist and agronomist. His erroneous belief that acquired characteristics can be inherited dominated Soviet agricultural policy (1940–65).

M

m[1] (pl **m's**), **M** (pl **M's** or **Ms**) n 1 the 13th letter of the English alphabet 2 the Roman numeral for 1,000

m[2] symbol 1 mass 2 metre 3 million 4 minute(s)

m[3] abbr 1 married 2 mile 3 minute(s)

M abbr 1 male 2 mass 3 medium (of clothes size) 4 million 5 motorway

M. abbr Monsieur

M8 abbr mate (in e-mails)

mA symbol milliampere(s)

MA, M.A. abbr Master of Arts

ma'am /mam, maam, məm/ n a formal or respectful form of address for a woman

Mabo /maábō/ n an Australian ruling relating to land rights

Mabo /maábō/, **Eddie** (1936–92) Australian land rights campaigner

mac, mack n a mackintosh (infml)

MAC /mak/ n a type of satellite television transmission system. Full form **multiplexed analogue component**

Mac- /mək/, **Mc-**, **M'-** /mə/ prefix son of (in proper names)

macabre /mə kaábrə, -bə/ adj horribly gruesome —**macabrely** adv

ORIGIN Macabre in its usual modern sense is recorded from the late 19C. Before then it appeared only in dance macabre (and earlier than that, dance of macabre), translating French danse macabre, the 'Dance of Death', in which a figure representing Death entices people to dance with him until they collapse and die. It is thought that macabre here is an alteration of Macabé and that the whole phrase translates medieval Latin chorea Machabaeorum 'dance of the Maccabees'. The Maccabees were a Jewish family involved in a religious revolt in biblical times, and their slaughter may have been represented in a medieval miracle play, giving rise to the idea of a deadly dance.

macadam /mə káddəm/ n a smooth hard road surface containing broken stones

ORIGIN Macadam is named after the Scottish civil engineer John Loudon McAdam (1756–1836), who developed the system of making such road surfaces.

macaroni /máka róni/ n small pasta tubes

macaroon /máka roón/ n a light biscuit containing ground almonds or coconut

MacArthur /mək aárthər/, **Douglas** (1880–1964) US general

Macau /mə ków/, **Macao** Special Administrative Region in SE China. Pop. 453,733 (2001).

macaw /mə káw/ (pl -caws or same) n a large tropical parrot

Macbeth /mək béth/ (c. 1005–57) king of Scotland (1040–57)

macchiato /máki aátō/ n an espresso coffee with a touch of milk

MacDiarmid /mək dúrmid/, **Hugh** (1892–1978) Scottish poet, editor, and critic

MacDonald /mək dónn'ld/, **Ramsay** (1866–1937) British prime minister (1924, 1929–35)

mace[1] n 1 a ceremonial staff of office 2 a spiked metal club

mace[2] n a spice made from the case of a nutmeg seed

Macedonia /mássə dóni ə/ 1 *also* **Macedon** /mássə don/ ancient kingdom in N Greece 2 country in SE Europe, formerly a constituent republic of Yugoslavia. Cap. Skopje. Pop. 2,046,209 (2001). Official name **Former Yugoslav Republic of Macedonia** 3 mountainous region of NE Greece. Cap. Thessaloniki. Pop. 1,710,513 (1991). 4 district in SW Bulgaria —**Macedonian** *n, adj*

macerate /mássə rayt/ (-**ating**, -**ated**) *vti* 1 soften or be softened by soaking 2 separate or become separated by soaking —**maceration** /mássə ráysh'n/ *n*

Mach /makh/, **Ernst** (1838–1916) Austrian physicist and philosopher

machete /mə shétti, -chétti/ *n* a large heavy knife

Machiavelli /máki ə vélli, mákyə-/, **Niccolò** (1469–1527) Italian historian, politician, and philosopher

Machiavellian /máki ə vélli ən/ *adj* 1 cunning and unscrupulous 2 of Machiavelli —**Machiavellian** *n* —**Machiavellianism** *n*

machine /mə sheen/ *n* 1 a mechanical device with moving parts, often powered by electricity 2 a simple unpowered device such as a lever or pulley 3 a powered form of transport 4 a group of people in political control ■ *vti* (-**chining**, -**chined**) cut or shape using a machine —**machine-like** *adj*

machine gun *n* an automatic weapon that fires a rapid series of shots —**machine-gun** *vt*

machine language, machine code *n* computer instructions written in binary code

machine-readable *adj* able to be used directly by a computer

machinery /mə sheenəri/ *n* 1 mechanical parts 2 machines 3 a set of processes or procedures

machine tool *n* a machine that shapes and finishes metals —**machine-tooled** *adj*

machine translation *n* computer translation

machinist /mə sheenist/ *n* somebody who cuts or shapes something using a machine

machismo /mə chízmō/ *n* stereotypical masculinity

Mach number /maak-, mák-/ *n* the speed of an object relative to the speed of sound

macho /máchō/ *adj* stereotypically masculine —**machoism** *n*

Machu Picchu

Machu Picchu /maáchoo peékchoó, -peéchoo/ ruined Inca city

macintosh *n* CLOTHING = **mackintosh**

mack *n* CLOTHING = **mac**

Mackay /mə kí/ coastal city in NE Queensland. Pop. 44,880 (1996).

Mackenzie /mə kénzi/ river in the Northwest Territories, Canada. Length 1,800 km/1,120 mi.

~~mackeral~~ incorrect spelling of **mackerel**

mackerel /mákrəl/ (*pl* -**els** *or same*) *n* 1 an oily fish of the N Atlantic 2 any fish related to the mackerel, especially the Spanish mackerel

Mackillop /mə killəp/, **Mary** (1842–1909) Australian nun who founded the Sisters of St Joseph of the Sacred Heart and became Australia's first saint

mackintosh /mákin tosh/, **macintosh** *n* a raincoat (*dated*)

ORIGIN The **mackintosh** is named after the Scottish inventor Charles Macintosh (1766–1843), who patented a waterproof rubberized cloth.

Mackintosh /mákin tosh/, **Charles Rennie** (1868–1928) British architect and interior designer

Harold Macmillan

Macmillan /mək míllən/, **Harold, 1st Earl of Stockton** (1894–1986) prime minister of the United Kingdom (1957–63)

MacNeice /mək neéss/, **Louis** (1907–63) British poet and playwright

Mâcon /maà koN/ city in east-central France. Pop. 34,469 (1999).

Macquarie /mə kwórri/, **Lachlan** (1762–1824) Australian colonial administrator

macramé /mə kraámi, -may/ *n* decorative work in knotted string

macro /mákrō/ (*pl* -**ros**), **macroinstruction** /mákrō in strúksh'n/ *n* a computer instruction that initiates several additional instructions

macro- *prefix* 1 large, inclusive ○ *macrocosm* 2 long ○ *macrobiotics*

macrobiotics /mákrō bī óttiks/ *n* a vegan diet said to prolong life (*+ sing verb*) —**macrobiotic** *adj*

macrocosm /mákrō kozəm/ *n* a complex system seen as a single unit —**macrocosmic** /mákrō kózmik/ *adj*

macroeconomics /mákrō eekə nómmiks, -ekə-/ *n* the study of large-scale economic systems (*+ sing verb*) —**macroeconomic** *adj* —**macroeconomist** /-i kónnəmist/ *n*

mad (**madder, maddest**) *adj* 1 very angry 2 an offensive term meaning affected by a psychiatric disorder 3 very unwise or rash (*sometimes offensive*) 4 frantic (*sometimes* *offensive)* **5** passionate about something *(often in combination, sometimes offensive)* **6** describes an animal with rabies —**madly** *adv* —**madness** *n*

MAD *abbr* major affective disorder

Madagascar /máddə gáskər/ island country in the Indian Ocean, off the coast of SE Africa. Cap. Antananarivo. Pop. 15,982,563 (2001). —**Madagascan** *adj, n*

Madam *(pl* **Mesdames** *or* **Madams)** *n* **1** addresses a woman in a letter *(fml)* **2** addresses a female official, used before the name of her position **3** a woman who runs a brothel **4** a petulant or wilful girl *(infml disapproving)* **5 madam** *(pl* **mesdames** /may daám/) a polite term of address for a woman *(fml)*

Madame /máddəm/ *(pl* **Mesdames** /may dam/) *n* the title of a Frenchwoman, used before her name or as a polite term of address

madcap /mád kap/ *adj* reckless —**madcap** *n*

mad cow disease *n* VET = **BSE**

madden /mádd'n/ *vt* **1** make very angry **2** make irrational —**maddening** *adj* —**maddeningly** *adv*

made past tense, past participle of **make**

Madeira /mə deérə/ *n* a fortified wine made on the Madeira Islands

Madeira cake *n* a fine-textured plain cake

Madeira Islands /mə deérə-/ group of islands in the E North Atlantic Ocean, an autonomous region of Portugal. Pop. 256,000 (1992).

mademoiselle /máddəmwə zél/ *(pl* **mesdemoiselles** /máydə-/ *or* **mademoiselles)** *n* **1** a young Frenchwoman **2 Mademoiselle** the title of a young Frenchwoman, used before her name or as a polite form of address *(sometimes offensive)*

made-to-order *adj* perfectly suitable

made-up *adj* **1** untrue **2** wearing cosmetics

madhouse /mád howss/ *(pl* **-houses** /-howziz/) *n* **1** an offensive term for a hospital for people with psychiatric disorders **2** a scene of chaos or confusion *(infml; sometimes offensive)*

madison /máddisən/ *n* a cycling relay race

Madison /máddisən/ **1** capital of Wisconsin. Pop. 209,306 (1998). **2** town in S Connecticut. Pop. 15,485 (1990). **3** city in N New Jersey. Pop. 15,828 (1998).

Madison, James (1751–1836) 4th president of the United States (1809–17)

Madison Avenue /máddiss'n-/ *n* the US advertising industry

ORIGIN **Madison Avenue** is the street in New York that is the centre of the advertising industry.

madman /mádmən/ *(pl* **-men** /-mən/) *n* an offensive term for a man with a psychiatric disorder

Madonna /mə dónnə/ *n* the Virgin Mary

madras /mə draáss, -dráss/ *n* **1** a type of strong fine cloth, often with a striped or checked design **2** a fairly hot curry

Madras /mə draáss/ former name for **Chennai**

madrasa /mə drássə/ *n* **1** a school for the study of Islamic religion and thought **2** an Islamic religious school for boys

Madrid /mə dríd/ capital of Spain. Pop. 2,881,506 (1998).

madrigal /máddrig'l/ *n* **1** an English part song for unaccompanied voices **2** a medieval Italian song —**madrigalist** *n*

ORIGIN **Madrigal** goes back ultimately to the Latin word for 'womb'. This formed a derivative meaning 'of a mother' and from that 'uncomplicated'. This passed into Italian, and then into English in the late 16C. A **madrigal** was originally a simple song, presumably of the kind a mother would sing to a child.

madwoman /mád wõõmən/ *(pl* **-en** /-wimin/) *n* an offensive term for a woman with a psychiatric disorder

maelstrom /máyl strom/ *n* **1** a whirlpool **2** a turbulent or violent situation

maestro /mÍstrõ/ *(pl* **-tros** *or* **-tri** /-tri/) *n* an expert, especially a musician, conductor, or composer

Mafia /máffi ə/ *n* **1** an international secret criminal organization **2** *also* **mafia** a mutually supportive clique

Mafioso /máffi õssõ, -õzõ/ *(pl* **-si** /-õsee, -ee/ *or* **-sos),** **mafioso** *n* a Mafia member

mag. *abbr* **1** magazine **2** magnesium

magazine /mággə zeén/ *n* **1** a periodical publication **2** a television or radio programme containing assorted items **3** a bullet or cartridge holder **4** a storehouse for military supplies **5** a photographic slide holder

ORIGIN **Magazine** came through French and Italian from an Arabic word meaning 'storehouse', which was also the original sense in English in the late 16C. The 'publication' sense derived from the idea of a storehouse of information. **Magazine** came to be used as a title for books providing information in the mid-17C, and developed its familiar modern use of 'periodical publication' in the mid-18C.

Magdeburg /mágdə burg/ capital of Saxony-Anhalt State, north-central Germany. Pop. 265,379 (1997).

Magellan, Strait of /mə géllən/ channel separating mainland South America and Tierra del Fuego, between the Atlantic and Pacific oceans. Length 560 km/350 mi.

Magellan, Ferdinand (1480?–1521) Portuguese explorer

magenta /mə jéntə/ *n* a purplish-pink colour —**magenta** *adj*

maggot /mággət/ *n* the larva of a fly

Magha /múggə/ *n* the 11th month in the Hindu calendar

Magi /máy jī/ *npl* in the Bible, the three wise men who came to celebrate the birth of Jesus Christ —**Magian** /-ji ən/ *adj, n* —**Magianism** *n*

magic /májjik/ *n* **1** a supposed supernatural power that makes impossible things happen

2 the practice of magic **3** conjuring tricks or illusions **4** a mysterious quality, talent, or skill ■ *adj* **1** of or for magic **2** particularly important **3** excellent *(infml)* ■ *vt* (**-icking, -icked**) cause to appear, disappear, change, or move by magic

magical /májjik'l/ *adj* **1** apparently produced by magic **2** wonderful —**magically** *adv*

magic bullet *n* **1** a drug that cures a serious disease with no undesirable side effects on the patient **2** an easy solution

magic carpet *n* an imaginary flying carpet

magic eye *n* a tuning aid in a radio receiver

magician /mə jísh'n/ *n* **1** an entertainer who performs conjuring tricks and illusions **2** somebody who supposedly has the supernatural power to use magic

magic wand *n* **1** a stick used by a magician **2** something that is able to work wonders

magisterial /májji steéri əl/ *adj* **1** dignified **2** domineering **3** authoritative

magistracy /májjistrəssi/ (*pl* **-cies**), **magistrature** /-strəchər/ *n* **1** the position of a magistrate **2** a magistrate's term of office

magistrate /májji strayt, -strət/ *n* **1** a judge in a lower court **2** a local law officer —**magistrateship** *n*

magistrates' court *n* a court for preliminary hearings or summary jurisdiction

magma /mágmə/ *n* molten rock —**magmatic** /mag máttik/ *adj*

Magna Carta /mágnə kaártə/, **Magna Charta** *n* **1** an important medieval social charter that established civil rights in England **2** any document that establishes rights

magnanimous /mag nánniməss/ *adj* very generous or forgiving —**magnanimity** /mágnə nímməti/ *n* —**magnanimously** *adv* ◊ See note at **generous**

magnate /mág nayt, -nət/ *n* **1** somebody who is rich and powerful **2** a senior noble —**magnateship** *n*

magnesia /mag neéshə, -neézhə/ *n* a white powder. Use: antacid, laxative.

magnesium /mag neézi əm/ *n* (*symbol* **Mg**) a light silver-white metallic element. Use: alloys, photography, fireworks.

magnet /mágnət/ *n* a piece of metal that attracts or clings to iron or steel objects

magnetic /mag néttik/ *adj* **1** having the power of a magnet **2** able to be magnetized **3** of or using magnetism **4** of the Earth's magnetism **5** powerfully charming —**magnetically** *adv*

magnetic bubble *n* a small magnetic region in a film of magnetic material. Use: to store data in computer memory.

magnetic disk *n* a computer disk

magnetic field *n* a region surrounding a magnetized body

magnetic north *n* the direction of the north magnetic pole

magnetic pole *n* **1** either of the two points at the end of a magnet **2** either of two regions near the Earth's geographic poles at which the Earth's magnetic field is strongest

magnetic recording *n* **1** the storing of data on a magnetized medium **2** a surface containing magnetically recorded information

magnetic resonance imaging *n* a medical imaging technique that uses electromagnetic radiation

magnetic stripe, magnetic strip *n* a strip of a magnetic medium encoded with information on a plastic card

magnetic tape *n* thin tape coated with iron oxide, used to record sounds, images, or data

magnetism /mágnətizəm/ *n* **1** the phenomenon of physical attraction for iron **2** the force exerted by a magnetic field **3** strong attractiveness, e.g. the power of somebody's personality to influence others

magnetize /mágnə tīz/ (**-izing, -ized**), **magnetise** *v* **1** *vti* make or become magnetic **2** *vt* attract somebody strongly —**magnetization** /mágnə tī záysh'n/ *n*

magnetite /mágnə tīt/ *n* a common black magnetic mineral

~~magnificent~~ incorrect spelling of **magnificent**

magnification /mágnifi káysh'n/ *n* **1** the process of making something appear physically larger **2** an increase of actual size

magnificent /mag níffiss'nt/ *adj* **1** beautiful and impressive **2** very good *(infml)* —**magnificence** *n* —**magnificently** *adv*

magnify /mágni fī/ (**-fies, -fied**) *vt* **1** increase the apparent size of something, especially by using a microscope or lens **2** increase the actual size of something **3** overstate the importance of something —**magnifier** *n*

magnifying glass *n* a hand-held lens used to make objects appear larger

magnitude /mágni tyood/ *n* **1** greatness of size, volume, or extent **2** importance **3** a measure of the energy of an earthquake **4** a number assigned to a mathematical quantity **5** the brightness of an astronomical object

magnolia /mag nóli ə/ (*pl* **-nolia** *or* **-nolias**) *n* **1** a small tree or bush with flowers of various colours **2** a creamy-white colour —**magnolia** *adj*

magnum[1] /mágnəm/ *n* **1** a wine bottle that holds the equivalent of two normal bottles **2** the contents of a magnum

magnum[2] /mágnəm/ *adj* describes a firearm cartridge with a more powerful charge than others of the same calibre ■ *n* a powerful gun

magnum opus *n* a great work of art or literature

magpie /mág pī/ *n* **1** a black-and-white bird of the crow family **2** a black-and-white Australian songbird **3** an avid but indiscriminate collector *(infml)*

ORIGIN A **magpie** was originally just a *pie*. The name came via French from Latin *pica*, which probably goes back to an ancient root meaning 'pointed' (with reference to a bird's beak). *Mag-*

was added in the late 16C. In origin it represents *Mag*, a shortened form of the name *Margaret*, but the reason for the addition is not known.

Magritte /ma greét/, **René** (1898–1967) Belgian painter

maharajah /maàhə raàjə/, **maharaja** *n* an Indian prince of a rank above a rajah

maharani /maàhə raàni/ *n* **1** a maharajah's wife **2** an Indian princess of a rank above a rani

maharishi /maàhə ríshi/ *n* in Hinduism, a religious instructor

Mahathir bin Muhammad /maa haà teer bin mə hámmid/ (*b.* 1925) prime minister of Malaysia (1981–)

mahatma /mə haàtmə, -hát-/ *n S Asia* a title bestowed on somebody deeply revered

Mahdi /maàdi/ *n* in Islamic belief, a prophet who is expected to appear before the world ends

Mahfouz /maa foòz/, **Naguib** (*b.* 1911) Egyptian novelist and screenwriter

mahjongg /maà jóng/, **mahjong** *n* a Chinese game using tiles marked with designs

Mahler /maàlər/, **Gustav** (1860–1911) Czechborn Austrian composer and conductor

mahogany /mə hóggəni/ (*pl* **-nies**) *n* **1** a reddish-brown hardwood. Use: construction, furniture-making. **2** a tropical tree that produces mahogany

mahout /mə hówt/ *n* an elephant driver

maid /mayd/ *n* **1** a female servant **2** a young unmarried woman (*literary; sometimes offensive*)

maiden /máyd'n/ *n* **1** a young unmarried woman (*sometimes offensive*) **2** a virgin (*literary*) ■ *adj* first (*sometimes offensive*) ○ *the ship's maiden voyage* —**maidenly** *adj*

maidenhead /máyd'n hed/ *n* (*literary*) **1** a hymen **2** a woman's virginity

maiden name *n* a married woman's surname at birth

maid of honour *n* **1** an unmarried attendant of a queen or princess **2** *US, Can* a chief bridesmaid

mail[1] *n* **1** items sent by post **2** the postal system **3** a particular collection or delivery of mail **4** a vehicle transporting mail **5** e-mail (*infml*) ■ *vt Aus, US, Can* send by post or email —**mailer** *n*

mail[2] *n* flexible armour

mailbag /máyl bag/ *n* **1** a sack for transporting mail **2** *US, Can* mail received on a particular subject

mailbox /máyl boks/ *n* **1** *ANZ, US* a box into which mail is delivered **2** *US* a postbox

Mailer /máylər/, **Norman** (*b.* 1923) US writer

mailing list *n* a list of names and addresses to which advertising material or information is sent

mail merge *n* a word-processing technique for creating a series of individualized documents

mail order *n* buying and selling by post

mailshot /máyl shot/ *n* **1** a sending of unsolicited items of mail **2** an item sent in a mailshot

maim *vt* wound or disable severely

main /mayn/ *adj* **1** greatest in size or importance **2** utmost ○ *main force* ■ *n* a large pipe or cable for distributing water, gas, or electricity ◇ **in the main** largely or in general

Main /mīn, mayn/ river in south-central Germany. Length 523 km/325 mi.

main course *n* the principal dish of a meal

Maine /mayn/ state in the NE United States. Cap. Augusta. Pop. 1,274,923 (2000).

mainframe /máyn fraym/ *n* a powerful computer accommodating several users simultaneously

mainland /máynlənd, -land/ *n* the principal landmass of a country or continent —**mainlander** *n*

main line *n* a major rail route

mainline /máyn līn/ *vti* (**-lining, -lined**) inject drugs intravenously (*slang*) ■ *adj* of a major rail route —**mainliner** *n*

mainly /máynli/ *adv* usually or mostly

mainmast /máyn maast/ *n* the principal mast on a sailing vessel

main memory *n* a computer's random access memory

mainsail /máyn sayl, máynss'l/ *n* a vessel's principal sail

mainspring /máyn spring/ *n* **1** the principal spring in a watch or clock **2** the chief reason for an action

mainstay /máyn stay/ *n* **1** the chief support ○ *the mainstay of the country's economy* **2** a line securing a mainmast

mainstream /máyn streem/ *n* the most widely accepted current of thought or behaviour ■ *vti* enrol students with physical or learning disabilities in general classes —**mainstream** *adj*

maintain /mayn táyn, mən-/ *vt* **1** cause something to continue **2** keep something in working order by regular checks and repairs **3** provide somebody with financial support **4** insist on the truth of something ○ *maintained that she knew nothing about it* **5** update a website or software package —**maintainable** *adj*

maintenance /máyntənənss/ *n* **1** regular repair work **2** continuation or preservation **3** the provision of financial support

~~maintenence~~ incorrect spelling of **maintenance**

Mainz /mīnts/ port in SW Germany. Pop. 184,627 (1997).

maisonette /máyzə nét/ *n* a self-contained flat on two floors

maître d'hôtel /méttrə dō tél/ (*pl* **maîtres d'hôtel** /pronunc. same/) *n* **1** a head-waiter **2** a senior male servant

maize *n* **1** a cereal crop that produces corncobs **2** grains of a maize plant

Maj. *abbr* Major

majesty /májjəsti/ *n* **1** great dignity **2** supreme power **3 Majesty** a title for a king or queen —**majestic** /mə jéstik/ *adj* —**majestically** *adv*

major /máyjər/ *n* **1** an army officer, or an officer of the US and Canadian air forces and the US Marine Corps, of a rank above captain **2** *ANZ, US, Can* a college or university student's main subject **3** *ANZ, US, Can* a student specializing in a particular subject ○ *a philosophy major* ■ *adj* **1** of high standing ○ *a major recording artist* **2** large or significant **3** serious ■ *vi ANZ, US, Can* study a particular main subject ○ *majoring in philosophy*

ORIGIN Major derives from the comparative (meaning 'larger, greater') of Latin *magnus*. As a military term it was adopted from French in the mid-17C. It represents a shortening of *sergent-major* 'sergeant major', a rank that was formerly more senior than it is now.

Major /máyjər/, **John** (*b.* 1943) British prime minister (1990–97)

Majorca /mə yáwrkə/, **Mallorca** largest of the Balearic Islands, in the W Mediterranean Sea. Pop. 736,885 (1994). —**Majorcan** *n, adj*

major-domo /-dṓmō/ (*pl* **major-domos**) *n* the chief male servant of a large household

majority /mə jórrəti/ (*pl* **-ties**) *n* **1** more than one-half of a group of people or things (+ *sing or pl verb*) **2** the number of votes by which a person or group wins **3** the age of legal responsibility

major scale *n* a musical scale with a semitone between the third and fourth notes and the seventh and eighth notes

Makalu /múkəloo/ mountain in the Himalaya range, on the Nepal-China border. Height 8,481 m/27,825 ft.

Makarios III /mə kaàri oss/ (1913–77) Cypriot archbishop (1950–74) and first president of Cyprus (1959–77)

make *vt* (**making, made**) **1** do or perform an action **2** produce, construct, or manufacture something **3** prepare or arrange something **4** create or form something **5** formulate something ○ *make a promise* **6** reckon or estimate something ○ *What time do you make it?* **7** cause somebody or something to be something particular ○ *made him unhappy* ○ *made it illegal to sell fireworks* **8** change something into something else ○ *making wood into charcoal* **9** appoint somebody to a particular position **10** cause somebody or something to do a particular thing ○ *made me lose my place* **11** force somebody to do something ○ *You can't make her stay.* **12** earn a sum of money **13** amount to a total ■ *n* **1** a brand of a product **2** the process of making something —**makable** *adj* —**maker** *n* ◇ **have it made** be in a position to succeed without serious problems *(infml)* ◇ **make do (with something)** use something as a substitute ◇ **make it 1** be successful *(infml)* **2** succeed in getting somewhere ◇ **on the make 1** trying

hard to succeed *(infml)* **2** trying to find a sexual partner *(slang)*

☐ **make away with** *or* **off with** *vt* steal
☐ **make for** *vt* **1** move towards **2** result in
☐ **make off** *vi* leave in haste
☐ **make out** *vt* **1** see or hear indistinctly **2** understand **3** complete in writing ○ *make out a cheque* **4** imply or claim ○ *made out that I was lying*
☐ **make over** *vt* **1** transfer the ownership of **2** change the appearance of
☐ **make up** *v* **1** prepare something by putting things together **2** *vt* constitute something **3** *vt* invent a story or excuse **4** *vti* apply cosmetics to the face **5** *vti* resolve a quarrel **6** *vi* compensate for something
☐ **make up to** *vt* **1** try to gain the favour of **2** flirt with

Makeba /mə káybə/, **Miriam** (*b.* 1932) South African-born US jazz and folk singer

make-believe *n* imaginary situations or events that somebody pretends are true

makeover /máyk ōvər/ *n* a change of physical appearance

makeshift /máyk shift/ *adj* providing a temporary substitute —**makeshift** *n*

makeup /máyk up/ *n* **1** facial cosmetics **2** the way parts or qualities are combined or arranged

making /máyking/ *n* **1** production or manufacture **2** the cause of somebody's success ■ **makings** *npl* **1** required ingredients **2** potential ○ *He has the makings of a great musician.*

mal- *prefix* bad, badly ○ *malpractice*

Malabar Coast /mállə baar-/ coastal region of SW India, extending from Goa southwards

Malabo /málləbō/ capital, port, and largest city of Equatorial Guinea, on N Bioko Island. Pop. 30,000 (1995).

Malacca, Strait of /mə lákə/ strait in Southeast Asia between the Malay Peninsula and Sumatra. Length 800 km/500 mi.

malachite /mállə kīt/ *n* a green mineral. Use: decorative stones, source of copper.

maladjusted /mállə jústid/ *adj* **1** unable to cope with everyday social situations **2** not properly adjusted —**maladjustment** *n*

maladministration /málləd mini stráysh'n/ *n* incompetent or dishonest management

maladroit /mállə dróyt/ *adj* clumsy or insensitive —**maladroitly** *adv* —**maladroitness** *n*

malady /mállədi/ (*pl* **-dies**) *n* **1** an illness *(dated or humorous)* **2** a problem

Málaga /málləgə/ port in S Spain. Pop. 528,079 (1998).

malaise /ma láyz/ *n* **1** a general feeling of illness **2** a general feeling of discontent

Malamud, Bernard (1914–86) US novelist and short-story writer

malapropism /mállə propizəm/ *n* the unintentional use of a wrong word that sounds similar

ORIGIN The original perpetrator of **mala-**

propisms was Mrs Malaprop, a character in Richard Sheridan's play *The Rivals* (1775). Her name is based on *malapropos* 'inappropriate(ly)', from French *mal à propos*, literally 'badly to the purpose'.

malaria /məˈláiri ə/ *n* a recurring illness transmitted by mosquitoes —**malarial** *adj*

ORIGIN Malaria was adopted in the mid-18C from Italian *mal' aria*, literally 'bad air'. Originally it was associated particularly with Rome, and referred to a condition of the air around marshes and swamps that was thought to cause fevers.

malarkey /məˈlaárki/, **malarky** *n* nonsense or insincere talk *(infml)*

Malawi /məˈlaáwi/ country in SE Africa. Cap. Lilongwe. Pop. 10,548,250 (2001). —**Malawian** *n, adj*

Malawi, Lake lake in southeast-central Africa, lying between Malawi, Mozambique, and Tanzania. Also called **Nyasa, Lake**

Malay /məˈláy/ *n* 1 a member of a Southeast Asian ethnic group 2 the language of Malaysia —**Malay** *adj*

Malay Archipelago largest system of island groups in the world, in the South Pacific Ocean southeast of Asia and north of Australia, and including Indonesia and the Philippines

Malay Peninsula peninsula in Southeast Asia between the South China Sea and the Strait of Malacca, including parts of Myanmar, Thailand, and Malaysia. Length 1,210 km/750 mi.

Malaysia /məˈláyzi ə, -zhə/ country in Southeast Asia. Cap. Kuala Lumpur. Pop. 22,229,040 (2001). —**Malaysian** *n, adj*

Malcolm III /málkəm/ (1031?–93) king of Scotland (1057–93)

Malcolm X (1925–65) US political activist

malcontent /mál kən tent/ *n* a person who is discontented with something, e.g. a political system —**malcontent** *adj*

Maldives /máwl deevz, -dīvz/ island country in the N Indian Ocean. Cap. Male. Pop. 310,764 (2001). —**Maldivian** /mawl dívvi ən, mal-/ *n, adj*

male *adj* 1 of the sex that produces sperm 2 of men or boys 3 capable of fertilizing a female sex cell 4 describes a flower or plant that bears only stamens and does not produce fruit —**male** *n* —**maleness** *n*

male chauvinist *n* a man who believes that men are superior to women *(disapproving)* —**male chauvinism** *n*

malediction /málli díksh'n/ *n (fml)* 1 a curse 2 slander

malefactor /málli faktər/ *n* a wrongdoer —**malefaction** /málli fáksh'n/ *n*

maleficent /mə léffiss'nt/ *adj* harmful or evil —**maleficence** *n*

male menopause *n* midlife anxiety in men

malevolent /mə lévvələnt/ *adj* 1 wanting to harm others 2 harmful or evil —**malevolence** *n* —**malevolently** *adv*

malfeasance /mal feéz'nss/ *n (fml)* 1 misconduct 2 an unlawful act

malformation /mál fawr máysh'n/ *n* an unusual shape or structure —**malformed** /mal fáwrmd/ *adj*

malfunction /mal fúngksh'n/ *vi* fail to work correctly —**malfunction** *n*

Mali /maáli/ country in West Africa. Cap. Bamako. Pop. 11,008,518 (2001).

malice /málliss/ *n* the desire or intention to do harm —**malicious** /mə líshəss/ *adj* —**maliciously** *adv* —**maliciousness** *n*

malign /mə lín/ *vt* say or write something bad about ■ *adj* harmful or evil —**malignity** /mə lígnəti/ *n* —**malignly** *adv*

SYNONYMS malign, defame, slander, libel, vilify CORE MEANING: say or write something damaging about somebody

malignant /mə lígnənt/ *adj* 1 showing a desire to harm others 2 likely to cause harm 3 likely to spread through the body ○ *a malignant tumour* —**malignancy** *n* —**malignantly** *adv*

malinger /mə líng gər/ *vi* feign illness

mall /mawl, mal/ *n* 1 US a large indoor shopping complex 2 a shady avenue

ORIGIN The *shopping mall* derives from **mall** as a name for the alley used in *pall-mall*, a game rather like croquet that was once highly fashionable in Britain. An alley in St James's Park, London, came to be used as a walk, and the name of *the Mall* was then transferred to any sheltered promenade. These 17C and 18C uses were invoked in the 20C with the introduction of the pedestrian or enclosed shopping area.

mallard /mállaard, -ərd/ *(pl* **-lards** *or same) n* a wild duck in which the male has a dark green head

Mallarmé /mál aar may/, **Stéphane** (1842–98) French poet

malleable /málli əb'l/ *adj* 1 able to be shaped and bent 2 easily persuaded or influenced —**malleability** /málli ə bílləti/ *n* ◊ See note at **pliable**

mallee /mállee/ *n* 1 a shrubby eucalyptus tree 2 *Aus* an area with many mallee trees

mallet /mállət/ *n* 1 a tool with a large cylindrical wooden or metal head 2 a stick with a cylindrical head used in croquet or polo

malleus /málli əss/ *(pl* **-i** /-lī/*) n* the outermost of the three small bones in the middle ear. ◊ **incus, stapes**

Mallorca ◗ **Majorca**

mallow /mállō/ *(pl* **-lows** *or same) n* a flowering plant with hairs on the stem and leaves

Malmö /málmo/ port in SW Sweden. Pop. 254,904 (1998).

malnourished /mal núrrisht/ *adj* having a diet that is inadequate or inappropriate —**malnourishment** *n*

malnutrition /mál nyoo trísh'n/ *n* unhealthy or inadequate nutrition

malodorous /mal ṓdərəss/ *adj* smelling bad

Malory /málləri/, **Sir Thomas** (*d.* 1471) English writer and translator

maloti plural of **loti**

malpractice /mal práktiss/ *n* wrong or negligent conduct of a professional or official —**malpractitioner** /mál prak tísh'nər/ *n*

Malraux /mal rṓ/, **André** (1901–76) French novelist, art theorist, archaeologist, and public servant

malt /mawlt, molt/ *n* **1** partly germinated grain. Use: brewing beer, distilling whisky. **2** *also* **malt liquor** beer or malt whisky ■ *v* **1** *vti* change grain into malt **2** *vt* make or mix something with malt —**malt** *adj*

Malta /máwltə, móltə/ island country in the central Mediterranean Sea. Cap. Valletta. Pop. 394,583 (2001).

Maltese /máwl teéz, mól-/ (*pl same*) *n* **1** somebody from Malta **2** the language of Malta —**Maltese** *adj*

Maltese cross *n* a cross with arms like inward-pointing arrowheads

Malthus /málthəss/, **Thomas Robert** (1766–1834) British economist —**Malthusian** /mal thyóozi ən/ *adj*, *n* —**Malthusianism** *n*

maltose /máwl tōz, -tōss, mól-/ *n* a white crystalline sugar

maltreat /mal treét/ *vt* treat badly —**maltreatment** *n* ◊ See note at **misuse**

malt whisky *n* whisky distilled from malted barley

mama /mə maá/, **mamma** *n* mother (*infml dated*)

mamba /mámbə/ *n* a large venomous snake of tropical Africa

mambo /mámbō/ (*pl* -**bos**) *n* **1** a dance resembling the rumba **2** the music for a mambo —**mambo** *vi*

Mamet /mámmit/, **David** (*b.* 1947) US playwright and film director

mammal /mámm'l/ *n* a class of warm-blooded vertebrate animals in which the female has milk-producing organs —**mammalian** /mə máyli ən/ *adj*

ORIGIN The taxonomic name *Mammalia* was coined in Latin by the Swedish naturalist Carolus Linnaeus. He based it on Latin *mamma* 'breast', as it refers to the class of animals that suckle their young. The word was anglicized as the plural **mammals** in the early 19C.

mammary /mámməri/ *adj* of a milk-producing organ such as a breast or udder

mammogram /mámmə gram/ *n* an X-ray of the breast

mammography /ma mṓgrəfi/ *n* X-ray examination of a breast

mammon /mámmən/, **Mammon** *n* wealth regarded as an evil influence

mammoth /mámməth/ *n* (*pl* -**moths** *or same*) **1** an extinct hairy elephant **2** something enormous ■ *adj* huge

ORIGIN Mammoth was adopted in the early 18C from Russian. It came ultimately from a Siberian word meaning literally 'earth, soil'. The first remains of **mammoths** to be found were dug out of the frozen soil of Siberia, and it came to be believed that the animals burrowed in the earth. The adjectival use of **mammoth** for 'huge' dates from the early 19C.

man *n* (*pl* **men**) **1** an adult male human being **2** a person (*often offensive if used of women*) **3** a man with a particular occupation or nationality (*usually in combination*) **4** the human race (*often offensive as excluding women*) **5** an employee or worker (*often offensive as excluding women*) **6** a husband or male companion (*slang*) **7** a piece used in board games ■ *vt* (**manning, manned**) (*often offensive*) **1** supply with workers or a crew **2** be ready to operate or defend —**man-like** *adj*

Man, Isle of ▶ **Isle of Man**

MAN /man/ *abbr* metropolitan area network

man about town (*pl* **men about town**) *n* a sophisticated man in fashionable society (*dated*)

manacle /mánnək'l/ *n* each of a pair of joined rings around a prisoner's wrist (*usually pl*) —**manacle** *vt*

manage /mánnij/ (**-aging, -aged**) *v* **1** *vti* administer or run a business, department, or project **2** *vti* achieve something with difficulty ○ *eventually managed to open the door* **3** *vi* cope in a difficult situation **4** *vt* deal with a situation or process that requires skilful control ○ *managing patient care* **5** *vt* discipline or control a person or animal —**manageable** *adj* —**manageably** *adv*

management /mánnijmənt/ *n* **1** administration **2** managers as a group **3** successful or skilful handling ○ *crisis management* —**managemental** /mánnij mént'l/ *adj*

management information system *n* a system that helps managers run a company, especially a computerized system

manager /mánnijər/ *n* **1** somebody who manages a business, department, or project **2** an organizer of somebody's business affairs **3** an organizer of training and other affairs for a sportsperson or team —**managerial** /mánni jeéri əl/ *adj* —**managership** *n*

managing director *n* a person in charge of a company

managment incorrect spelling of **management**

Managua /mə nágwə/ capital of Nicaragua. Pop. 1,200,000 (1995).

Manama /mə naámə/ capital of Bahrain. Pop. 148,000 (1995).

mañana /man yaánə/ *adv* **1** tomorrow **2** later

Manassas /mə nássəss/ city in NE Virginia, the site of the two US Civil War battles of Bull Run in 1861 and 1862. Pop. 35,300 (1998).

manat /mánnat/ *n* the main unit of currency in Azerbaijan and Turkmenistan

manatee /mánnə tée/ *n* a large aquatic plant-eating mammal with front flippers and a broad flattened tail

Manaus /mə nówss/ capital of Amazonas State, NW Brazil. Pop. 1,157,357 (1996).

manchester /mánchistər/ *n ANZ* household linen

Manchester city in NW England, connected by the **Manchester Ship Canal** with the Irish Sea. Pop. 430,818 (1996).

Manchuria /man chóöri ə/ historical name for a region of NE China comprising Heilongjiang, Jilin, and Liaoning provinces —**Manchurian** *n, adj*

Mancunian /man kyóöni ən/ *n* somebody from Manchester in NW England —**Mancunian** *adj*

mandala /mándələ, man dáalə/ *n* in Buddhism or Hinduism, a circular design representing the universe

Mandalay /mándə láy/ city in central Myanmar. Pop. 532,949 (1983).

mandarin /mándərin/ *n* **1** a high-ranking official in the Chinese Empire **2** a high-ranking civil servant **3 Mandarin, Mandarin Chinese** Modern Standard Chinese, the official language of the People's Republic of China **4** *also* **mandarin orange** a small orange citrus fruit with a loose skin **5** a tree that produces mandarins —**Mandarin** *adj* —**mandarinate** *n*

ORIGIN **Mandarin** is not ultimately from Chinese, as might have been expected. It goes back to a Sanskrit root meaning 'think', and entered English through Malay and Portuguese. The fruit is probably called a **mandarin** because of its colour. Chinese mandarins traditionally wore yellow robes.

mandate /mán dayt/ *n* **1** an authoritative order **2** authority bestowed by an electoral victory **3** an instruction for a regular transfer of funds **4** a territory placed by the League of Nations under the administration of a member state ■ *vt* (**-dating, -dated**) **1** delegate authority to somebody **2** *US* make something mandatory

mandatory /mándətəri/ *adj* **1** compulsory **2** with the power of a mandate —**mandatorily** *adv*

Nelson Mandela

Mandela /man déllə, -dáylə/, **Nelson** (*b.* 1918) president of South Africa (1994–99)

Mandelstam /mánd'l stam/, **Osip Yemilyevich** (1891?–1938?) Russian poet

mandible /mándib'l/ *n* **1** the lower jaw of a person or animal (*technical*) **2** each of the upper and lower parts of a bird's beak —**mandibular** /man díbbyŏōlər/ *adj*

mandir /mún deer/ *n S Asia* a Hindu temple

mandolin /mánda lín/ *n* a stringed instrument of the lute family with a pear-shaped body

mandrake /mán drayk/ *n* a plant with a forked root formerly believed to have magical powers

mandrill /mándril/ *n* a large baboon with a colourful muzzle in the male

mane *n* **1** long hair on an animal's neck **2** thick long hair on somebody's head (*literary or infml*) —**maned** *adj*

Manet /mán ay/, **Édouard** (1832–83) French painter

maneuver *n, vti* US = manoeuvre

manful /mánf'l/ *adj* brave and determined as a man is traditionally supposed to be **manfully** *adv* —**manfulness** *n*

manganese /máng gə neez/ *n* (*symbol* **Mn**) a brittle greyish-white metallic element. Use: alloys, strengthening steel.

mange /maynj/ *n* a skin disease of animals that causes itching and hair loss —**mangy** *adj*

manger /máynjər/ *n* an eating trough for animals

mangetout /mónj toò, móNzh-/, **mangetout pea** *n* a pea with an edible pod

mangle[1] /máng g'l/ (**-gling, -gled**) *vt* **1** mutilate by tearing or crushing **2** ruin by carelessness or incompetence

ORIGIN The two English words **mangle** are not related, though shared ideas of crushing could easily suggest that they are. The verb meaning 'mutilate by crushing or tearing' was adopted in the 14C from the French verb that also gave us *maim*. The 'clothes wringer' is considerably later, late 17C, and comes from Dutch *mangel*, a shortening of *mangelstok* 'crushing roller'. The second element is related to English *stock*. The first goes back to Greek *magganon* 'engine of war, axis of a pulley'.

mangle[2] /máng g'l/ *n* a machine with rotating cylinders to squeeze water out of wet washing —**mangle** *vt*

mango /máng gō/ (*pl* **-goes** *or* **-gos**) *n* **1** a juicy sweet red or green fruit **2** a tropical evergreen tree that produces mangoes

mangrove /máng grōv/ *n* a tropical evergreen tree of tidal coasts with exposed intertwined roots

manhandle /mán hand'l, man hánd'l/ (**-dling, -dled**) *vt* **1** handle somebody or something roughly **2** move something unwieldy by hand

Manhattan[1] /man hátt'n/, **manhattan** *n* a whisky and vermouth cocktail

Manhattan[2] borough of New York City, mainly on **Manhattan Island** at the northern end of New York Bay. Pop. 1,487,536 (1990).

manhole /mán hōl/ *n* a covered opening giving access to a sewer or drain

manhood /mán hŏŏd/ *n* 1 the state of being a man 2 manliness

man-hour *n* the work of one person per hour *(sometimes offensive)*

manhunt /mán hunt/ *n* a search for a criminal

mania /máyni ə/ *n* 1 an obsessive interest or enthusiasm 2 a psychiatric disorder involving excessive activity and impulsive behaviour

-mania *suffix* an excessive enthusiasm for ○ *pyromania*

maniac /máyni ak/ *n* 1 an offensive term for somebody regarded as irrational because of a psychiatric disorder 2 an obsessive enthusiast —**maniacal** /mə ní ək'l/ *adj* —**maniacally** *adv*

manic /mánnik/ *adj* 1 of mania 2 hectic *(infml; sometimes offensive)* —**manically** *adv*

manic-depressive *n* a person with bipolar disorder —**manic-depressive** *adj*

manicure /mánni kyoor/ *n* a cosmetic treatment of the hands and fingernails ■ *vt* (-**curing**, -**cured**) 1 treat with a manicure 2 cut and shape carefully ○ *a neatly manicured lawn* —**manicurist** *n*

manifest /mánni fest/ *adj* obvious ■ *v* 1 *vt* show clearly 2 *vi* appear ■ *n* a list of cargo or passengers —**manifestly** *adv*

manifestation /mánni fe stáysh'n/ *n* 1 a manifesting or being manifested 2 a sign of the presence or existence of something 3 a public demonstration

manifesto /mánni féstō/ (*pl* -**toes** *or* -**tos**) *n* a declaration of principles, policies, and objectives

manifold /mánni fōld/ *adj* 1 many and various 2 having many parts or forms ■ *n* a chamber or pipe with several openings

manikin /mánnikin/, **mannikin** *n* 1 a dummy for displaying clothes 2 an anatomical model of the human body

manila /mə nílla/, **Manila** *n* 1 a cigar made in Manila 2 *also* **Manila paper** strong pale-brown paper

Manila /mə nílla/ capital of the Philippines. Pop. 1,580,924 (1999).

man in the street *n* the average person *(sometimes offensive)*

manipulate /mə níppyoo layt/ (-**lating**, -**lated**) *vt* 1 operate or handle something skilfully 2 control somebody or something deviously 3 falsify something for personal advantage 4 work with data on a computer 5 examine or treat a body part by moving it with the hands —**manipulation** /mə níppyoo láysh'n/ *n* —**manipulative** /-lətiv/ *adj* —**manipulator** *n* —**manipulatory** *adj*

Manitoba /mánni tóbə/ province in south-central Canada. Cap. Winnipeg. Pop. 1,147,880 (2000). —**Manitoban** *adj*, *n*

mankind /man kínd/ *n* 1 all human beings *(often offensive)* 2 men as distinct from women *(dated)*

manky /mángki/ (-**kier**, -**kiest**) *adj* dirty or otherwise unpleasant *(infml)*

manly /mánnli/ (-**lier**, -**liest**) *adj* 1 conventionally typical of or appropriate to a man 2 having manly qualities —**manliness** *n*

man-made, manmade /mán máyd/ *adj* artificial or synthetic and not natural *(often offensive)*

Mann, Thomas (1875–1955) German-born US novelist and critic

manna /mánnə/ *n* 1 in the Bible, divinely provided sustenance 2 an unexpected benefit

mannequin /mánnikin/ *n* 1 a dummy for displaying clothes 2 a fashion model *(dated)*

manner /mánnər/ *n* 1 the way something is done 2 a way of behaving ■ **manners** *npl* 1 social behaviour 2 customs and practices ◇ **in a manner of speaking** in some ways ◇ **to the manner born** thoroughly adapted to something

mannered /mánnərd/ *adj* 1 affected 2 behaving in a particular way *(usually in combination)* ○ *an ill-mannered child*

mannerism /mánnərizəm/ *n* 1 an idiosyncrasy 2 affected behaviour 3 *also* **Mannerism** a late-16C style of art and architecture characterized by stylized and elongated forms

mannerly /mánnərli/ *adj* polite

Mannheim /mánn hīm/ city in SW Germany, on the River Rhine. Pop. 316,223 (1997).

mannikin *n* = manikin

Manning /mánning/, **Patrick Augustus Mervyn** (*b*. 1946) prime minister of Trinidad and Tobago (1991–95, 2001–)

mannish /mánnish/ *adj* 1 suitable for a man rather than a woman *(often offensive)* ○ *a mannish haircut* 2 like or typical of a man

manoeuvre /mə nóóvər/ *n* 1 a skilled movement or action 2 a military movement or exercise *(often pl)* ■ *v* (-**vring**, -**vred**) 1 *vti* move skilfully ○ *manoeuvred the boat into the berth* 2 *vti* do military exercises 3 *vt* manipulate for personal advantage —**manoeuvrability** /mə nóóvərə bílləti/ *n* —**manoeuvrable** *adj*

ORIGIN Manoeuvre was adopted in the late 18C from a French verb that had previously entered English in the 14C as *manure* 'manage, occupy, or till land'.

---

man of letters *n* a writer *(fml)*

man of the cloth *n* a clergyman

man-of-war (*pl* **men-of-war**) *n* a warship

manometer /mə nómmitər/ *n* an instrument for measuring gas pressure —**manometric** /mánnə méttrik/ *adj* —**manometry** *n*

manor /mánnər/ *n* 1 a large house and the land surrounding it, especially a feudal estate controlled by a lord 2 *also* **manor house** the residence of the lord or lady of a manor —**manorial** /mə náwri əl/ *adj*

manor house *n* a lord's or lady's house

~~manouvre~~ incorrect spelling of **manoeuvre**

manpower /mán pow ər/ n power in terms of the number of people available or needed *(sometimes offensive)*

manqué /móngk ay, maaN káy/ adj frustrated in your ambitions o *a poet manqué*

mansard roof /mán saard-, -ərd-/ n a roof with a double slope on all sides

manse /manss/ n a Christian minister's house

manservant /mán survənt/ (pl **menservants** /mén survənts/) n a male servant, especially a valet

Mansfield, Katherine (1888–1923) New Zealand-born British writer

mansion /mánsh'n/ n 1 a large and grand house 2 a division of the zodiac

man-sized, man-size adj 1 larger than the ordinary size 2 of the size of a man o *a man-sized hole*

manslaughter /mán slawtər/ n the unpremeditated killing of a human being

Mantegna /man ténnyə/, **Andrea** (1431–1506) Italian painter

mantel /mánt'l/ n an ornamental fireplace frame

mantelpiece /mánt'l peess/ n a mantel or its projecting top

mantelshelf /mánt'l shelf/ (pl **-shelves** /-shelvz/) n the projecting top of a mantel

mantilla /man tíllə/ n a lace scarf covering the head and shoulders

mantis /mántiss/ (pl **-tises** or **-tes** /-teez/) n a large predatory insect with grasping front legs

mantissa /man tíssə/ n a fractional part of a logarithm

mantle /mánt'l/ n 1 a sleeveless cloak 2 a covering *(literary)* 3 an incandescent circle of wire mesh around a lamp flame 4 the part of the Earth between the crust and the core 5 ARCHIT = **mantel** —**mantle** vt

man-to-man adj honest and intimate o *a man-to-man talk* —**man-to-man** adv

mantra /mántrə/ n 1 a sacred word repeated in meditation 2 an often repeated expression or idea

manual /mánnyoo əl/ adj 1 of or using the hands 2 involving physical rather than mental effort 3 operated by a person rather than a machine ■ n a small book that contains information and instructions —**manually** adv

manufacture /mánnyoō fákchər/ (**-turing, -tured**) v 1 vti make something, or produce something industrially 2 vt invent an excuse —**manufacture** n —**manufacturer** n —**manufacturing** n, adj

manuka /mə noōkə, maanəkə/ n a New Zealand tree with aromatic leaves

manure /mə nyoór/ n 1 fertilizer made from dung 2 any fertilizer or compost —**manure** vt

ORIGIN Manure came into English in the 14C as a verb, from a French word meaning 'manage,

occupy, or till land' (the same verb was re-adopted in a later form as *manoeuvre*). It had developed into Latin words meaning literally 'work with the hands'. The English noun that means 'dung as a fertilizer' was formed from the verb in the mid-16C.

manuscript /mánnyoōskript/ n 1 a handwritten book 2 an author's original text

Manx adj of the Isle of Man ■ n a Celtic language of the Isle of Man ■ npl the Manx people —**Manxman** n —**Manxwoman** n

many /ménni/ det, pron a considerable number

many-sided adj having many sides or aspects

Maoism /mów izəm/ n the doctrines and teachings of Mao Zedong —**Maoist** n, adj

Maori /mówri/ (pl same) n 1 a member of a New Zealand people 2 the language of the Maori people —**Maori** adj

AKG London

Mao Zedong

Mao Zedong /mów tsay toōng/, **Mao Tse-tung** (1893–1976) chairman of the People's Republic of China (1949–76)

map n 1 a geographical diagram showing locations 2 a diagram showing relative positions, e.g. of the stars ■ vt (**mapping, mapped**) create a map of —**mappable** adj ◇ **on the map** in a prominent position *(infml)* □ **map out** vt plan

maple /máyp'l/ n 1 a deciduous tree with winged seeds 2 the wood of the maple tree. Use: furniture, flooring.

maple syrup n a sweet syrup made from the sap of a particular maple

Maputo /mə poōtō/ capital of Mozambique. Pop. 1,098,000 (1991 estimate).

mar (**marring, marred**) vt spoil

mar. abbr 1 maritime 2 married

Mar. abbr March

marabou /márrəboo/ n 1 a large African stork 2 down from a marabou's tail. Use: trimming for clothes.

marabout /márrəboo/ n 1 a Muslim hermit or monk 2 the tomb of a marabout

maraca /mə rákə/ n a rattle usually used in pairs as a percussion instrument

Maracaibo, Lake /márrə kíbō/ largest lake in South America, in NW Venezuela

maraschino /márrə skeénō, -sheénō/ n a cherry liqueur

maraschino cherry n a cocktail cherry preserved in maraschino-flavoured syrup

Marat /má raa/, **Jean-Paul** (1743–93) French journalist and politician

marathon /márrəth'n, -thon/ n **1** a long-distance running or walking race **2** a lengthy and difficult task —**marathoner** n

ORIGIN According to tradition, when the Greek army defeated the Persians at Marathon, on the northeastern coast of Attica, in 490 BC, the runner Pheidippides was dispatched to bring the good news to Athens (in fact there is no contemporary evidence for the story, which is not recorded until 700 years after the event). When the modern Olympic Games were first held, in Athens in 1896, a long-distance race was introduced to commemorate the ancient feat, run over a course supposedly equal in distance to the journey from Marathon to Athens (about 35 km/22 mi.). The present distance was established at the 1948 London Olympics.

marauding /mə ráwding/ adj roving around attacking and looting —**marauder** n

marble /maárb'l/ n **1** a dense crystallized rock. Use: building, sculpture, and monuments. ■ **2** a small glass ball used in games ■ **marbles** npl mental abilities (infml) ○ lost his marbles ■ vt (-bling, -bled) colour paper with mottled streaks

marbling /maárbling/ n **1** colouring like marble **2** streaks of fat in meat

Marburg disease /maár burg-/ n a severe, often lethal, viral infection

ORIGIN The disease is named after the city of Marburg in Germany, where the first major outbreak occurred.

marcasite /maárkə sīt, -zeèt/ n **1** a yellow mineral. Use: jewellery. **2** a decorative piece of polished metal

march[1] v **1** vi walk in military fashion, with regular movements of the arms and legs at a steady rhythmic pace **2** vti move in military-style formation ○ marched the troops off to battle **3** vi walk with determination ○ marched into the shop and demanded to see the manager **4** vt force somebody to go somewhere ○ grabbed the boys and marched them into the house **5** vi walk with others in a protest or demonstration **6** vi pass steadily ○ Time marches on. ■ n **1** an act of marching ○ a four-hour march back to the camp ○ a protest march **2** a marching speed **3** a steady forwards movement ○ the march of time **4** a piece of music in marching rhythm ◇ **steal a march on somebody** do something before somebody else to your own advantage

march[2] n a border area between two countries

March n the 3rd month of the year in the Gregorian calendar

ORIGIN March is named after Mars, the Roman god of war.

marching orders npl orders to set off on a military expedition

marchioness /maárshə néss, -shənəss/ n a noblewoman ranking between a duchess and a countess

Marconi /maar kóni/, **Guglielmo, Marchese** (1874–1937) Italian electrical engineer. He pioneered the practical development of radio signalling.

Marcos /maárk oss/, **Ferdinand** (1917–89) Philippine national leader and president-dictator of the Philippines (1965–86)

Marcus Aurelius ♦ Aurelius, Marcus

Mardi Gras /maárdi graá/ (pl **Mardis Gras** /pronunc. same/) n **1** the Tuesday before Lent **2** a carnival before Lent

mare[1] /mair/ n an adult female horse

mare[2] /maá ray/ (pl **-ria** /-ri ə/) n a dark plain on the Moon or Mars

Mare ♦ de la Mare, Walter

Margaret /maárgrət, -ərət/, **St** (1046?–93) queen of Scotland (1070–93) as wife of Malcolm III

margarine /maárjə reèn, maárgə-/ n a yellow fatty substance used as a spread and in cooking

ORIGIN Margarine comes from French. The substance was originally made from clarified beef fat. The name is based on Greek margaron 'pearl', through the name (margaric acid in English) of a fatty acid that was believed to be a constituent of animal fats (including beef fat) and whose crystals had a pearly lustre.

margarita /maárgə reétə/ n a tequila cocktail

Margasirsa /maárgə seérsə/ n the 9th month of the year in the Hindu calendar. Also called **Agrahayana**

margin /maárjin/ n **1** a blank space at the side of a page **2** an outer edge **3** a part furthest from the centre (often pl) ○ on the margins of society **4** the difference between amounts or numbers ○ won by a small margin **5** an additional amount allowed as a precaution ○ no margin for error

marginal /maárjin'l/ adj **1** in or on a margin **2** small in scale or importance **3** on the fringes of a group **4** barely acceptable or viable **5** won by only a small majority in an election —**marginal** n —**marginally** adv

marginalize /maárjinə līz/ (-**izing**, -**ized**), **marginalise** vt prevent from having power or commanding attention —**marginalization** /maárjinə līz záysh'n/ n

marguerite /maárgə reét/ n a garden plant resembling a daisy

mariachi /maári aáchi, márri-/ (pl **-chis**) n **1** a Mexican street band **2** traditional Mexican folk music played by a mariachi

~~marriage~~ incorrect spelling of **marriage**

Mariana Islands /márri aánə-/ island group in the W North Pacific Ocean, east of the Philippines, comprising Guam and the Commonwealth of the Northern Mariana Islands. Pop. 226,500 (2000).

Maria Theresa /mə reè ə tə ráyzə/ (1717–80) archduchess of Austria and queen of Hungary and Bohemia (1740–80)

Marie Antoinette /márri antwə nét/ (1755–93) queen of France as the wife of Louis XVI

Marie de Médicis /mə rèè də méddi chee/ (1573–1642) queen and regent of France (1600–17)

marigold /márri gōld/ n a garden plant with yellow or orange flowers

marijuana /márri waànə, -hwaànə/, **marihuana** n 1 a drug derived from the hemp plant 2 the hemp plant

marimba /mə rímbə/ n a musical instrument like a xylophone with resonators beneath the bars

marina /mə rèènə/ n a harbour for pleasure boats

marinade /márri náyd, -nayd/ n a flavoured liquid in which food may be soaked before cooking ■ vti (-nading, -naded) marinate

ORIGIN The word **marinade** is related to *marine*. It came via French from a verb meaning 'pickle in brine' in Spanish and Italian and deriving from Latin *aqua marina* 'seawater, brine'. **Marinade** is first recorded in English in the early 18C; related *marinate* is a little older (mid-17C).

marinate /márri nayt/ (-nating, -nated) vti soak in a marinade before cooking —**marination** /márri náysh'n/ n

marine /mə rèèn/ adj 1 of the sea 2 of ships or sailing ■ n 1 also **Marine** a seagoing soldier 2 a fleet of ships (fml)

Marine Corps n a branch of the US armed forces operating on land and at sea

mariner /márrinər/ n a sailor

marionette /márri ə nét/ n a puppet worked by strings

marital /márrit'l/ adj of marriage —**maritally** adv

maritime /márri tīm/ adj of or close to the sea

Maritime Provinces, Maritimes collective name for the E Canadian provinces of New Brunswick, Nova Scotia, and Prince Edward Island —**Maritimer** n

marjoram /maàrjərəm/ n an aromatic herb used in cooking

mark[1] /maark/ n 1 a spot, line, patch, or impression on a surface 2 a symbol (often in combination) o a question mark 3 an indication o as a mark of respect 4 a sign of influence or involvement o left his mark on the company 5 an identifying feature or characteristic 6 a number or letter indicating somebody's assessment of correctness, quality, or performance 7 a target, aim, or goal 8 a guide to position or direction ■ v 1 vti make a mark or marks on something o The vase has marked the table. 2 vt make visible or identifiable with a mark 3 vt be an indicator of o marks the end of an era 4 vt celebrate or give prominence to o mark the occasion 5 vt assess and indicate the quality or correctness of 6 vt take notice of (often a command) o Mark my words, this will make a difference. —**marker** n ◇ **wide of the mark, off the mark** incorrect

SPELLCHECK Do not confuse the spelling of **mark** and **marque** ('a commercial brand'), which sound similar.

□ **mark down** vt lower the price of

□ **mark off** vt separate one area from another with a line or barrier

□ **mark out** vt indicate the boundaries and divisions of

□ **mark up** vt 1 increase the price of 2 insert corrections and instructions on

mark[2] /maark/ n a Deutschmark

Mark /maark/, **St** (fl 1C) evangelist. By tradition he is considered to be the author of the second Gospel in the Bible.

marka /múrkə/ the main unit of currency in Bosnia and Herzegovina

Mark Antony ♦ Antony, Mark

markdown /maàrk down/ n a price reduction

marked adj 1 noticeable 2 singled out for something unpleasant —**markedly** /maàrkidli/ adv

market /maàrkit/ n 1 a gathering for buying and selling 2 a place where a market is held 3 a collection of small shops or stalls 4 the area of economic activity involving buying and selling 5 the buying and selling of a particular commodity 6 a group of potential customers 7 demand for a particular product or service 8 the stock market ■ vt offer something for sale in a way that makes people want to buy it —**marketer** n —**marketing** n ◇ **in the market (for)** interested in buying something ◇ **on the market** available for customers to buy

marketable /maàrkitəb'l/ adj 1 fit to be sold o a highly marketable property 2 in demand o skills that are readily marketable

market economy n an economy regulated by the laws of supply and demand

marketeer /maàrki teèr/ n 1 somebody who trades at or in a market 2 a supporter of a particular type of market (usually in combination) o a free marketeer

market garden n a plot for growing produce for sale —**market gardener** n —**market gardening** n

market leader n a company with the largest market share

market maker n somebody who buys and sells securities

marketplace /maàrkit playss/ n 1 an open space for a market 2 the sphere of trading

market price n the current price of something

market research n the study of consumers' wants and purchases —**market researcher** n

market share n a share of the total sales of a product

market value n the amount for which something can be sold on the open market

marking /maàrking/ n 1 a mark or pattern of marks (often pl) 2 the assessment and grading of written work

markka /maàr kaa, -kə/ (pl -**kaa** /-kaa/) n the main unit of the former Finnish currency

marksman /maàrksmən/ (pl -**men** /-mən/) n 1 somebody skilled in shooting 2 a man considered a good or bad shot —**marksmanship** *n*

markswoman /maarks woomən/ (*pl* -**men** /-wimin/) *n* **1** a woman skilled in shooting **2** a woman considered a good or bad shot

markup /maark up/ *n* **1** an amount added to a price **2** the addition to a text of coding or instructions for layout and style

markup language *n* a computer coding system specifying the layout and style of a document

marl *n* a mixture of clay and lime. Use: fertilizer, water softener. —**marly** *adj*

Marlborough /maarlbərə/, **John Churchill, 1st Duke of** (1650–1722) English general

marlin /maarlin/ (*pl* -**lins** *or same*) *n* a game fish with an elongated upper jaw

Marlowe /maarlō/, **Christopher** (1564–93) English playwright

marmalade /maarmə layd/ *n* a preserve of citrus fruit containing shredded rind ■ *adj* describes a cat with orange fur

ORIGIN **Marmalade** was originally 'quince jam'. The word is first recorded in English in the late 15C. It came via French from Portuguese, where it was formed from *marmelo* 'quince'. This goes back to a Greek word that referred to a kind of apple grafted onto a quince.

Marmara, Sea of /maarmərə/, **Marmora, Sea of** inland sea in NW Turkey, connected with the Black Sea by the Bosporus and with the Aegean Sea by the Dardanelles

marmoreal /maar máwri əl/ *adj* of marble (*literary*)

marmoset /maarmə zét, -zet/ (*pl* -**sets** *or same*) *n* a small furry monkey with tufted ears and a long tail

marmot /maarmət/ (*pl* -**mots** *or same*) *n* a stout-bodied burrowing rodent

Marne /maarn/ river in NE France, flowing into the River Seine near Paris. Length 525 km/326 mi.

maroon[1] /mə roòn/ *n* a deep purplish-red colour —**maroon** *adj*

ORIGIN The two English words **maroon** are as unrelated as their meanings suggest. The colour came via French and Italian from a Greek word meaning 'chestnut'. The verb **maroon** was formed from a noun, a name given to descendants of runaway slaves in Suriname and the Caribbean islands. This came from a French shortening of American Spanish *cimarrón*, literally 'wild, untamed'.

maroon[2] /mə roòn/ *vt* leave isolated without any means of escape

marque /maark/ *n* a commercial brand, especially of a luxury or high-performance product ◊ See note at **mark**

marquee /maar keé/ *n* a large tent used for social gatherings

Marquesas Islands /maar káyssəss-/ group of volcanic islands in French Polynesia, in the South Pacific Ocean. Pop. 7,538 (1988).

marquess /maarkwiss/ *n* a nobleman ranking between a duke and an earl —**marquessate** *n*

marquetry /maarkitri/ *n* **1** decorative designs made of inlaid wood or other materials **2** the craft of making marquetry

Márquez /maar kez/ ♦ **García Márquez, Gabriel**

marquis /maarkwiss, maar keé/ (*pl* -**quises** *or* -**quis** /-keèz/) *n* **1** in various European countries, a nobleman ranking above a count **2** a marquess —**marquisate** /maarkwizit, -zayt/ *n*

marquise /maar keéz/ *n* in some European countries, a noblewoman ranking above a countess

~~marrage~~ incorrect spelling of **marriage**

Marrakesh /márrə késh/, **Marrakech** city in W Morocco. Pop. 745,541 (1994).

marriage /márrij/ *n* **1** a legal relationship between two people living together as sexual partners **2** a married relationship between two particular people ○ *They have a happy marriage.* **3** the joining of two people in marriage **4** a union of two things —**marriageability** /márrijə billəti/ *n* —**marriageable** *adj*

marriage bureau *n* an organization that introduces single people to each other

married /márrid/ *adj* **1** having a spouse **2** of marriage ■ **marrieds** *npl* married people

marrow /márrō/ *n* **1** a large cylindrical vegetable with a green rind **2** (*pl* **marrows** *or same*) a plant that produces marrows **3** a soft tissue in the central cavity of bones

marrowbone /márrō bōn/ *n* a bone that contains edible marrow

marry /márri/ (-**ries**, -**ried**) *v* **1** *vti* take somebody in marriage **2** *vt* join in marriage **3** *vt* give in marriage **4** *vt* acquire by marriage ○ *hoping to marry money* **5** *vti* match or combine successfully

□ **marry off** *vt* find a marriage partner for

Mars /maarz/ *n* **1** in Roman mythology, the god of war. Greek equivalent **Ares 2** the 4th planet from the Sun

Marsala /maar saálə/ *n* a Sicilian fortified wine

Marseillaise /maar say éz, -áyz, maarssə láyz/ *n* the French national anthem

Marseilles /maar sáy/, **Marseille** port in SE France. Pop. 798,430 (1999).

marsh *n* an area of soft wet ground —**marshy** *adj*

marshal /maarsh'l/ *n* **1** a high-ranking officer in some armed forces **2** somebody in charge of an event such as a parade or a race **3** a high official in a royal court **4** a US federal law enforcement officer **5** the head of a fire or police service in some US cities ■ *v* (-**shalling**, -**shalled**) **1** *vt* arrange in appropriate order ○ *marshal your thoughts* **2** *vt* gather and organize **3** *vt* guide or lead ceremoniously **4** *vti* act as a marshal at an event

SPELLCHECK Do not confuse the spelling of **marshal** and **martial** ('military', 'warlike'), which sound similar.

marshalling yard *n* a place where trains are made up

Marshall Islands /maàrsh'l-/ island country in the central N Pacific Ocean. Cap. Majuro. Pop. 70,822 (2001).

Marshal of the Royal Air Force *n* the highest-ranking officer of the Royal Air Force

marsh gas *n* methane formed by decomposing plant matter in the absence of air

marshland /maàrsh land, -lənd/ *n* marshy ground

marsh mallow *n* a medicinal herb with pink flowers

marshmallow /maarsh mállō/ *n* a soft spongy sweet —**marshmallowy** *adj*

ORIGIN **Marshmallow** was originally made from the root of the marsh mallow plant.

marsh marigold *n* a plant with yellow flowers that grows in marshy ground

marsupial /maar syoòpi əl, -soò-/ *n* an animal with a pouch in which the young develop

mart *n* a market

marten /maàrtin/ *n* (*pl* **-tens** *or* **same**) *n* a short-legged bushy-tailed mammal with a long slender body that lives in trees

Martha's Vineyard /maàrthəz-/ island in SE Massachusetts, in the Atlantic Ocean. Pop. 8,900 (1990).

martial /maàrsh'l/ *adj* **1** military **2** fierce or hostile —**martially** *adv* ◊ See note at **marshal**

martial art *n* a system of combat and self-defence such as judo or karate

martial law *n* control of civilians by armed forces

Martian /maàrsh'n/ *adj* of the planet Mars ■ *n* a supposed inhabitant of Mars

martin /maàrtin/ *n* a bird related to the swallow

martinet /maàrti nét/ *n* a rigid disciplinarian

ORIGIN The original **martinet** was the 17C French soldier Jean Martinet, who invented a system of military drill.

martini /maar teèni/ *n* a cocktail of gin or vodka with vermouth

Martinique /maàrti neèk/ island department of France in the E Caribbean Sea. Pop. 418,454 (2001).

Martinů /maàrti noo/, **Bohuslav Jan** (1890–1959) Czech composer

martyr /maàrtər/ *n* **1** somebody who chooses to die rather than deny a belief **2** somebody who makes sacrifices for a cause ■ *vt* kill somebody for a belief —**martyrdom** *n*

~~marvelous~~ incorrect spelling of **marvellous**

marvel /maàrv'l/ *n* **1** a wonderful thing **2** a very skilful person ■ *vi* (**-velling**, **-velled**) be amazed

Marvell /maàrvəl/, **Andrew** (1621–78) English poet and politician

marvellous /maàrvələss/ *adj* **1** amazingly impressive **2** extremely good —**marvellously** *adv*

marvelous *adj* US = **marvellous**

Karl Marx

Marx /maarks/, **Karl** (1818–83) German political philosopher —**Marxian** *adj*

Marx Brothers (*fl* early 20C) US comedians. **Chico** (born Leonard, 1891–1961), **Groucho** (born Julius Henry, 1895–1977), and **Harpo** (born Adolph, 1888–1964), the three most prominent of the brothers, appeared in comedy films such as *A Night at the Opera* (1935).

Marxism /maàrks izəm/ *n* Karl Marx's political and economic theories about class struggle leading to social change —**Marxist** *n, adj*

Marxism-Leninism *n* a further development of Marxism including the theories of Lenin —**Marxist-Leninist** *n, adj*

Mary /máiri/ *n* in the Bible, the mother of Jesus Christ

Mary /máiri/ (1867–1953) queen of the United Kingdom as wife of George V

Mary I (1516–58) queen of England and Ireland (1553–58)

Mary II (1662–94) queen of England, Scotland, and Ireland (1689–94)

Mary (Queen of Scots) (1542–87) queen of Scotland (1542–67)

Maryland /máirilənd/ state in the E United States. Cap. Annapolis. Pop. 5,296,486 (2000). —**Marylander** *n*

Mary Magdalene /máiri magdə léni, -mágdələn/ *n* follower of Jesus Christ

marzipan /maàrzi pan, -pán/ *n* a paste made from ground almonds and sugar

ORIGIN **Marzipan** goes back ultimately to Arabic *mawtabān*, literally 'enthroned king'. The Saracens used it as the name of a medieval Venetian coin that had a figure of the seated Jesus Christ on it. In the Italian dialect of Venice the word became *matapan*, and eventually, in general Italian, *marzapane*. Its meaning supposedly progressed from the 'coin' via 'measure of weight or capacity', 'box of such capacity', and 'such a box containing confectionery' to 'the contents of such a box'. English acquired the word and it became *marchpane*. Around the 19C **marzipan** was borrowed from German. This was an alteration of Italian *marzapane*, based on the misconception that it came from Latin *marci panis* 'St Mark's bread'.

Masaccio /mə saàchee ō/ (1401?–27) Italian painter

masc. *abbr* masculine

mascara /ma skaára, mə-/ *n* a cosmetic for eyelashes —**mascara** *vt*

mascarpone /maáskər pōni/ *n* a rich Italian cream cheese

mascot /máss kot, máskət/ *n* something or somebody believed to bring good luck

masculine /máskyōolin/ *adj* 1 of men and boys 2 traditionally associated with men rather than women 3 of a grammatical gender including the majority of words referring to males ■ *n* the masculine grammatical gender, or a word or form in this gender —**masculinely** *adv* —**masculinity** /máskyōo línnəti/ *n*

Masefield /máyss feeld/, **John** (1878–1967) British poet

Maseru /mə sáiroo/ capital of Lesotho. Pop. 297,000 (1995).

mash *n* 1 a mixture of grain and water used to make alcohol 2 ground animal food 3 a pulpy mass 4 mashed potatoes (*infml*) ■ *vt* 1 crush something to a pulp 2 soak grain

MASH /mash/, **M.A.S.H.** *abbr* mobile army surgical hospital

masint /mássint/, **MASINT** *n* intelligence data acquired, typically electronically, about possible attacks using weapons of mass destruction. Full form **materials intelligence**

mask *n* 1 a covering for the eyes or face 2 something that conceals or disguises something ○ *a mask for his true feelings* 3 a mould of a face 4 an animal's face markings ■ *vt* 1 conceal or disguise something 2 shield part of something, e.g. from paint or light —**masked** *adj*

masked ball *n* a dance at which the guests wear disguises

masking tape *n* adhesive tape used to shield parts of a surface when painting

masochism /mássəkizəm/ *n* 1 sexual pleasure derived from being hurt or humiliated 2 the tendency to seek and enjoy suffering —**masochist** *n* —**masochistic** /mássə kístik/ *adj*

ORIGIN **Masochism** was explored by the Austrian novelist Leopold von Sacher-Masoch (1835–95), whose name became permanently associated with it.

mason /máyss'n/ *n* 1 somebody who works with stone 2 **Mason** a Freemason —**Masonic** /mə sónnik/ *adj*

Mason-Dixon Line /máyss'n díks'n-/ *n* the boundary between free and slave states before the American Civil War

ORIGIN The **Mason-Dixon line** was surveyed in 1763–67 by Charles Mason and Jeremiah Dixon.

masonry /máyss'nri/ *n* 1 a mason's trade 2 stonework 3 **Masonry** Freemasonry

Masqat ◆ **Muscat**

masque /maask/ *n* a dramatic entertainment with masked performers

masquerade /maàskə ráyd/ *n* 1 a party where people wear masks and costumes 2 a disguise or pretence ■ *vi* (**-ading, -aded**) pretend to be somebody or something else

mass *n* 1 a lump of matter 2 a collection of things 3 a large unspecified quantity (*often pl*) ○ *masses of work to do* 4 the majority 5 the physical property of an object that is based on the amount of matter it contains ■ **masses** *npl* the ordinary people ■ *vti* gather in a mass ■ *adj* 1 involving a large number ○ *a mass demonstration* 2 general

Mass, mass *n* 1 in some Christian churches, the ceremony of Communion 2 a musical setting of a Roman Catholic Mass

Massachusetts /mássə chōossəts/ state in the NE United States. Cap. Boston. Pop. 6,349,097 (2000).

massacre /mássəkər/ *n* 1 the killing of many people 2 a bad defeat (*infml*) —**massacre** *vt*

massage /mássaazh, -aaj/ *n* a treatment that involves rubbing or kneading the muscles ■ *vt* (**-saging, -saged**) 1 rub or knead the muscles of 2 manipulate statistics or other information deceptively —**massager** *n*

Massenet /mássə nay/, **Jules Émile Frédéric** (1842–1912) French composer

masseur /ma súr/ *n* a man whose job is massaging

masseuse /ma sóz/ *n* a woman whose job is massaging

Massey /mássi/, **William Ferguson** (1856–1925) Irish-born prime minister of New Zealand (1912–25)

massif /mássif, ma seéf/ *n* a mountain range or large mountain mass

Massif Central /másseef son traál/ highland region in south-central France

massive /mássiv/ *adj* 1 bulky and heavy 2 extremely large in amount or degree —**massively** *adv* —**massiveness** *n*

mass-market *adj* appealing to a wide range of people

mass media *n* the communications media in general (+ *sing or pl verb*)

mass noun *n* a noun representing something that cannot be counted, e.g. 'water'

mass-produce *vt* make products in large quantities —**mass-producer** *n* —**mass production** *n*

mast[1] *n* 1 a vertical pole, especially one supporting a sail or flag 2 a tall broadcasting aerial

mast[2] *n* nuts used as pig food

mastectomy /ma stéktəmi/ (*pl* **-mies**) *n* the surgical removal of a breast

master /maástər/ *n* 1 somebody in authority or control (*sometimes offensive as excluding women*) 2 the owner of an animal 3 somebody highly skilled at something 4 a skilled worker qualified to teach apprentices (*usually in combination*) ○ *a master craftsman* 5 an original from which copies are made 6 a male teacher (*dated*) 7 the captain of a merchant ship ■ *adj (sometimes offensive)* **1** controlling o *the master switch* **2** principal o *the master bedroom* ■ *vt* **1** learn thoroughly or well **2** control or overcome *(sometimes offensive)* —**masterless** *adj*

master class *n* a class given by an expert *(sometimes offensive)*

masterful /máàstərf'l/ *adj* **1** expert *(sometimes offensive)* **2** able or tending to lead —**masterfully** *adv* —**masterfulness** *n*

master key *n* a key that will open all the locks in a place

masterly /máàstərli/ *adj* brilliantly skilled —**masterliness** *n*

mastermind /máàstər mīnd/ *n* somebody who plans and oversees a complex process —**mastermind** *vt*

Master of Arts *n* a usually postgraduate degree in a nonscience subject

master of ceremonies *n* the host of a formal event *(sometimes offensive)*

Master of Science *n* a usually postgraduate degree in a science subject

Master of the Rolls *n* a senior English judge

masterpiece /máàstər peess/, **masterwork** /-wurk/ *n* a great artistic work

Master's degree *n* a Master of Arts or Master of Science degree

masterstroke /máàstər strōk/ *n* a brilliant idea or tactic

mastery /máàstəri/ *n* **1** expert skill **2** complete control *(sometimes offensive)*

masthead /máàst hed/ *n* **1** the top of a mast **2** a newspaper's title as displayed on the front page

mastic /mástik/ *n* **1** an aromatic resin. Use: lacquer, varnish, adhesives, condiments. **2** a flexible cement. Use: filler, adhesive, sealant.

masticate /másti kayt/ *vti* chew food —**mastication** /másti káysh'n/ *n*

mastiff /mástif/ *n* a big smooth-haired dog

ORIGIN Mastiff goes back to a Latin word meaning 'tame', literally 'used to the hand'. It entered English through a French word that ended in *-in*. Where the *-iff* came from is not known.

mastitis /ma stítiss/ *n* inflammation of a woman's breast or a cow's udder

mastodon /mástə don, -dən/ *n* a large shaggy extinct mammal

mastoid process /mást oyd-/ *n* a bony protuberance on the skull behind the ear

masturbate /mástər bayt/ *(-bating, -bated)* *vi* stroke the genitals for sexual pleasure —**masturbation** /mástər báysh'n/ *n* —**masturbatory** *adj*

mat[1] *n* **1** a piece of material placed on the floor or other surface for decoration or protection **2** a thick mass ■ *vti* (**matting, matted**) form or form into a tangled mass —**matted** *adj*

mat[2] *n, adj* = matt

matador /máttə dawr/ *n* a bullfighter who kills the bull

Mata Hari /máàtə haári/ (1876–1917) Dutch dancer and spy

match[1] *n* **1** a contest **2** a close likeness of somebody or something **3** an equal or counterpart **4** one half of a pair **5** a marital partnership or partner ■ *v* **1** *vt* be similar or identical to **2** *vt* compete equally with o *I can match him for speed.* **3** *vti* make a pleasing combination with something **4** *vt* be or find a match for —**matchable** *adj*

ORIGIN The two words **match** are unrelated. The first is an ancient Germanic word, the earliest English sense of which was 'husband or wife, sexual partner'. The second was adopted in the 14C from French. It originally meant 'wick of a candle or lamp'. The modern **match** dates from the mid-19C.

match[2] *n* **1** a thin stick with a tip that ignites **2** an explosives fuse

matchbook /mách book/ *n* a cardboard folder containing matches

matchbox /mách boks/ *n* a box for matches

matchless /máchləss/ *adj* unrivalled

matchmaker /mách maykər/ *n* somebody who arranges relationships or marriages

match point *n* the final point of a match

matchstick /mách stik/ *n* the stem of a match —**matchstick** *adj*

mate[1] *n* **1** a friend **2** a breeding partner **3** a partner in sex or marriage *(infml or humorous)* **4** a skilled worker's helper **5** a deck officer **6** something that matches ■ *v* (**mating, mated**) **1** *vti* breed **2** *vi* have sex **3** *vt* connect two objects

mate[2] *n, vt* (**mating, mated**), *interj* checkmate

maté /máa tay, máttay/ *n* a tea-like drink made from the dried leaves of a South American tree

material /mə teéri əl/ *n* **1** a substance used to make things **2** information used in the making of a book, film, or similar work **3** cloth or fabric ■ **materials** *npl* equipment ■ *adj* **1** physical **2** worldly **3** relevant or important —**materially** *adv*

materialism /mə teéri əlizəm/ *n* **1** the theory that physical matter is the only reality **2** devotion to wealth and possessions —**materialist** *n* —**materialistic** /mə teéri ə lístik/ *adj*

materialize /mə teéri ə līz/ *(-izing, -ized)*, **materialise** *vi* **1** become real **2** assume a physical form —**materialization** /mə teéri ə lī záysh'n/ *n*

matériel /mə teéri él/, **materiel** *n* military supplies and equipment

maternal /mə túrn'l/ *adj* **1** of or like a mother **2** on or from the mother's side of a family o *my maternal grandfather* —**maternally** *adv*

maternity /mə túrnəti/ *n* **1** motherhood **2** the period during pregnancy or around the time of childbirth *(usually in combination)* o *maternity clothes*

maternity benefit, **maternity allowance** *n* payments made to a mother around the time of her child's birth

maternity leave *n* leave from work around the time of childbirth

matey /máyti/ (**-ier, -iest**), **maty** *adj* friendly —**matily** *adv* —**matiness** *n*

math /math/ *n US, Can* mathematics *(infml)*

math. *abbr* mathematics

mathematical /máthə máttik'l/ *adj* **1** of mathematics **2** very accurate —**mathematically** *adv*

mathematics /máthə máttiks/ *n* the study of relationships among numbers, shapes, and quantities (+ *sing verb*) ■ *npl* calculations (+ *pl verb*) —**mathematician** /máthəmə tísh'n/ *n*

> **ORIGIN** The central importance of mathematics is reflected in its origins. It goes back to a Greek root that meant simply 'learn'. In the Middle Ages **mathematics** referred to the four subjects that formed the basis of medieval scientific knowledge: geometry, arithmetic, astronomy, and music.

~~mathmatics~~ incorrect spelling of **mathematics**

maths /maths/ *n* mathematics *(infml)*

matinée /mátti nay/, **matinee** *n* an afternoon performance

matins /máttinz/, **mattins** *n* in some Christian churches, a morning ceremony or liturgy

Henri Matisse: Photographed in 1948 working on his paper cut-outs

Matisse /mə teéss/, **Henri** (1869–1954) French artist

~~matress~~ incorrect spelling of **mattress**

matriarch /máytri aark/ *n* **1** a female head of a family or community **2** a woman in a position of great power or respect —**matriarchal** /máytri aárk'l/ *adj*

matriarchy /máytri aarki/ *n* a social order, community, or organization in which women are in charge

matricide /máytri sīd, máttri-/ *n* **1** the killing of a mother by her child **2** somebody who commits matricide —**matricidal** /máytri síd'l, máttri-/ *adj*

matriculate /mə tríkyōo layt/ (**-lating, -lated**) *vti* admit or be admitted as a college or university student —**matriculation** /mə tríkyoo láysh'n/ *n*

matrimony /máttriməni/ *n* **1** the married state **2** the marriage ceremony —**matrimonial** /máttri mŏni əl/ *adj*

matrix /máytriks/ (*pl* **-trices** /-tri seéz/ *or* **-trixes**) *n* **1** a substance in which something is embedded **2** a situation in which something develops **3** a rectangular arrangement of mathematical elements

matron /máytrən/ *n* **1** a mature woman **2** a woman in charge of medical and housekeeping arrangements, e.g. in a boarding school **3** especially formerly, a woman who is head of a nursing staff

matronly /máytrənli/ *adj* **1** of or like a matron **2** mature and full-figured

matron of honour *n* a bride's married attendant

matt /mat/, **matte, mat** *adj* with a dull or nonglossy finish ■ *n* a matt finish

matter /máttər/ *n* **1** something to be considered or dealt with **2** a substance or material ○ *reading matter* **3** the material substance of the universe **4** the cause of a problem ○ *What's the matter?* **5** printed text **6** the subject of speech or writing ■ **matters** *npl* circumstances ○ *We were under a lot of stress, which didn't improve matters.* ■ *vi* **1** have importance **2** make a difference ◇ **for that matter** as far as that is concerned ◇ **no matter what** regardless of what happens ◊ See note at **subject**

Matterhorn /máttər hawrn/ mountain in the Pennine Alps, on the Italian-Swiss border. Height 4,478 m/14,690 ft.

matter of fact *n* something that is true and cannot be denied ◇ **as a matter of fact** really or actually

matter-of-fact *adj* **1** straightforward and not emotional **2** factual —**matter-of-factly** *adv*

Matthew /máthyoo/, **St** (*fl* AD 1C) one of the 12 apostles of Jesus Christ. By tradition he is considered to be the author of the first Gospel in the Bible.

Matthews /máthyooz/, **Sir Stanley** (1915–2000) British footballer

matting /mátting/ *n* **1** material woven from natural fibres. Use: mats, coverings. **2** mats

mattock /máttək/ *n* a tool like a pickaxe with a flattened blade at right angles to the handle

mattress /máttrəss/ *n* a pad containing springs or a soft material on which to sleep

mature /mə tyoŏr, -choŏr/ *adj* **1** showing characteristics typical of an adult **2** experienced **3** fully grown or fully developed **4** old and of good flavour **5** involving a period of serious thought ○ *on mature reflection* **6** due for payment or repayment ○ *mature bonds* ■ *vti* (**-turing, -tured**) make or become mature —**maturation** /máttyŏo ráysh'n, máchŏo-/ *n* —**maturely** *adv* —**matureness** *n* —**maturity** /-/ *n*

mature student *n* a student who has gone into higher education later than usual

maty *adj*, *n* = **matey**

matzo /mótsə/, **matzoh** *n* (*pl* **-zos** *or* **-zoth** /mótsŏt/; *pl* **-zohs** *or* **-zoth**) unleavened bread traditionally eaten during Passover ■ *adj* of or for matzo ○ *matzo meal*

Mauchly /máwkli/, **John W.** (1907–80) US physicist. He worked with John Eckert on the ENIAC project (1943–46) that developed the first general-purpose electronic digital computer.

maudlin /máwdlin/ *adj* tearfully or excessively sentimental

ORIGIN Maudlin represents a development of *Magdalen*, the name given to the woman Mary to whom Jesus Christ was said to have appeared after his resurrection (John 20:1–18). Mary Magdalen became identified with the sinner described in another of the gospels (Luke 8:37), and in art she was shown weeping in repentance. Initially the adjective **maudlin** referred specifically to the weepy stage of drunkenness, first recorded in *maudlin-drunk* in the early 16C. The more general use of tearfully or excessively sentimental developed in the mid-17C.

Maugham /mawm/, **W. Somerset** (1874–1965) British author

Maui /mów i/ second largest island of Hawaii. Pop. 105,336 (1995).

maul /mawl/ *vt* **1** batter or tear at ○ *was mauled by a tiger* **2** handle roughly **3** criticize fiercely ■ *n* **1** a crowd of people pushing and fighting **2** a pile-driving hammer, usually with a wooden head **3** a log-splitting hammer with one side of the head shaped like a wedge

maulvi /mówl wee/ (*pl* **-vis**) *n* an Islamic scholar or instructor in a religious school

maunder /máwndər/ *v* **1** *vti* speak or say in a vague or incoherent way **2** *vi* move or act aimlessly

Maundy Thursday /máwndi-/ *n* a Christian holy day marking the Last Supper. Date: Thursday before Easter Day.

Maupassant /mó pass oN, mó pass aáN/, **Guy de** (1850–93) French novelist and short-story writer

Mauriac /máw ri ak/, **François** (1885–1970) French poet, novelist, and playwright

Mauritania /mórri táyni ə/ country in NW Africa, on the Atlantic Ocean. Cap. Nouakchott. Pop. 2,747,312 (2001). —**Mauritanian** *n*, *adj*

Mauritius /mə ríshəss/ island country in the SW Indian Ocean, east of Madagascar. Cap. Port Louis. Pop. 1,189,825 (2001). —**Mauritian** *n*, *adj*

mausoleum /máwssə leé əm, máwzə-/ (*pl* **-ums** or **-a** /-ə/) *n* **1** a large grand tomb **2** an ornate building that contains tombs

ORIGIN The original **mausoleum** was built in the 4C BC for Mausolus, the king of Caria in Asia Minor, by his widow Artemisia. The word came from Greek through Latin.

mauve /mōv/ *n* a pale purplish colour —**mauve** *adj*

maven /máyvən/, **mavin** *n* an expert or enthusiast

maverick /mávvərik/ *n* **1** an independent person who refuses to conform **2** an unbranded animal

ORIGIN Mavericks are probably named after the

Texas cattle owner Samuel Augustus Maverick (1803–70), who did not brand some of his calves.

maw *n* an animal's mouth, throat, or stomach

mawkish /máwkish/ *adj* sentimental in a contrived way —**mawkishly** *adv* —**mawkishness** *n*

Mawlid al-Nabi /máwlid al naábi/ *n* in Islam, the celebrations marking the prophet Muhammad's birthday. Date: 12th day of Rabi I.

Mawson /máwss'n/, **Sir Douglas** (1882–1958) British-born Australian geologist and explorer

max *n* the maximum *(infml)*

max. *abbr* maximum

maxi /máksi/ *n* an ankle-length garment ■ *adj* **1** ankle-length **2** larger than standard

maxilla /mak síllə/ (*pl* **-lae** /-lee/) *n* **1** either of a fused pair of bones forming the upper jaw of vertebrates **2** a mouthpart of an insect or other arthropod —**maxillary** *adj*

maxim /máksim/ *n* **1** a pithy saying with some truth to it **2** a general rule

maximal /máksim'l/ *adj* **1** of a maximum **2** best possible —**maximally** *adv*

Maximilian /máksi mílli ən/ (1832–67) archduke of Austria and emperor of Mexico (1863–67)

maximize /máksi mīz/ (**-mizing**, **-mized**), **maximise** *vt* increase something to the maximum —**maximization** /máksi mī záysh'n/ *n*

maximum /máksiməm/ *n* **1** the greatest possible amount **2** the highest amount or level reached ■ *adj* of the greatest possible amount or value

Maxwell /máks wel, mákswəl/, **James Clerk** (1831–79) Scottish physicist known for his pioneering work on electromagnetics

may[1] *modal v* **1** an auxiliary verb indicating that something is possibly true ○ *That may be the best way.* **2** an auxiliary verb indicating that something could happen ○ *The crash may have been caused by faulty brakes.* **3** an auxiliary verb indicating permission *(fml)* ○ *You may go now.* **4** an auxiliary verb indicating a right to do something ○ *You may withdraw money from this account at any time.* **5** an auxiliary verb indicating polite requests or suggestions ○ *May I be of service?* **6** an auxiliary verb indicating a wish *(fml)* ○ *May you have a safe journey.* ◇ **be that as it may** nevertheless ◇ See note at **can**

may[2] *n* a hawthorn tree

May *n* the 5th month of the year in the Gregorian calendar

ORIGIN May is named after the Roman fertility goddess Maia.

Maya[1] /mí ə/ (*pl same* or **-yas**), **Mayan** /mí ən/ *n* **1** a member of a Native American people of Central America and S Mexico whose classical culture flourished from the 4C to the 8C AD **2** the language of the Maya people —**Maya** *adj* —**Mayan** *adj*

Maya² /mí ə/ n the mother of the Buddha

Mayakovsky /mí ə kófski/, **Vladimir** (1893–1930) Russian poet and propagandist

maybe /máybi, -bee/ adv perhaps ○ *Maybe he'll come later.* ○ *'Can I have a new bike?' 'Maybe'*.

May bug n a cockchafer

mayday /máy day/ n a distress call from a ship or aircraft

May Day n 1 a day for celebrating the coming of spring. Date: 1 May. 2 a holiday in honour of workers. Date: 1 May.

mayflower /máy flow ər/ (pl **-ers** or same) n 1 a plant that flowers in May 2 a hawthorn flower

mayfly /máy flī/ (pl **-flies**) n 1 a short-lived flying insect 2 a fishing fly resembling a mayfly

mayhem /máy hem/ n chaos or severe disruption

ORIGIN Mayhem is recorded from the late 15C. Another form of the French word from which it derives had been adopted earlier as a noun *maim* 'permanent injury or disfigurement', which is no longer used. The French noun was formed from the verb that gave us *maim*, which is therefore closely related to **mayhem**.

---

mayn't /maynt, máy ənt/ contr may not

Mayo /máy ō/ county in NW Republic of Ireland

~~mayonaise~~ incorrect spelling of **mayonnaise**

mayonnaise /máy ə náyz/ n a creamy sauce made from egg yolks and oil

---

ORIGIN There are several conflicting theories about the origin of **mayonnaise**, among them that it is an alteration of *bayonnaise*, as if the sauce originated in Bayonne, in SW France, and that it goes back to French *mayou* 'egg yolk'. But the early variant spelling *mahonnaise* suggests that it originally meant literally 'of Mahon', and that the sauce was so named to commemorate the taking of Port Mahon, the capital of the Balearic island of Menorca, by the duc de Richelieu in 1756.

---

mayor /mair/ n the head of a city or town government —**mayoral** adj —**mayorship** n

mayoralty /máirəlti/ (pl **-ties**) n a mayor's official position or period of office

maypole /máy pōl/ n a decorated pole for May Day celebrations

Mazarin /mázzərin/, **Jules, Cardinal** (1602–61) Italian-born French cardinal

maze n 1 an area of connecting paths designed to be difficult to find a way through 2 a confusing network of paths

MB abbr 1 Bachelor of Medicine 2 megabyte

MBA abbr Master of Business Administration

Mbabane /əm baa báani/ capital of Swaziland. Pop. 61,000 (1995).

MBE abbr Member of the Order of the British Empire

Mbeki /əm béki/, **Thabo** (b. 1942) South African president (1999–)

MBO abbr management buyout

Mbyte abbr megabyte

MC abbr 1 master of ceremonies 2 Military Cross

MCA abbr merchant certificate authority

McCarthy /mə kaárthi/, **Joseph R.** (1908–57) US politician

McCarthyism /mə kaárthi izəm/ n 1 the practice of publicly accusing somebody of having Communist sympathies 2 the practice of unfairly accusing or investigating people —**McCarthyist** n, adj —**McCarthyite** n, adj

McConnell /mə kónn'l/, **Jack** (b. 1960) First Minister of Scotland (2001–)

McCoy /mə kóy/ ◇ **the real McCoy** a genuine person or thing (infml)

McCubbin /mə kúbbin/, **Frederick** (1855–1917) Australian painter

McCullers /mə kúllərz/, **Carson** (1917–67) US writer

McEnroe /mákənrō/, **John** (b. 1959) US tennis player

McIndoe /mákindō/, **Sir Archibald Hector** (1900–60) New Zealand plastic surgeon

McKinley, Mt /mə kínnli/ highest mountain in North America, in the Alaska Range, in south-central Alaska. Height 6,194 m/20,320 ft. Also called **Denali**

McLaren /mə klárrən/, **Bruce Leslie** (1937–70) New Zealand motor racing driver

McLuhan /mə klóoən/, **Marshall** (1911–80) Canadian-born US critic and theorist

Md symbol mendelevium

MD abbr 1 Doctor of Medicine 2 managing director

me¹ /mee/ pron refers to the speaker or writer (as the object or complement of a verb or preposition) ○ *Listen to me.* ◇ See note at **I**¹

me² /mee/ n MUSIC = **mi**

ME /em eé/ n chronic fatigue syndrome (infml) Full form **myalgic encephalomyelitis**

mea culpa /máy ə kóolpə/ interj expresses an admission of guilt or fault (fml or humorous) —**mea culpa** n

mead /meed/ n an alcoholic drink made from honey

Mead /meed/, **Margaret** (1901–78) US anthropologist

meadow /méddō/ n a grassy field, sometimes used for producing hay or grazing livestock

meadowlark /méddō laark/ (pl **-larks** or same) n a brown songbird with a yellow breast

meager adj US = **meagre**

meagre /meégər/ adj 1 unsatisfactorily small 2 of bad quality —**meagrely** adv —**meagreness** n

meal¹ /meel/ n 1 a substantial amount of food eaten at one time 2 a time for eating a meal

meal² /meel/ n 1 a cereal ground to a powder 2 a ground-up substance

mealie /meéli/ n S Africa an ear of maize

meals on wheels n a service bringing hot meals to people who are unable to leave their homes (+ sing verb)

meal ticket n 1 a dependable source of money or support (infml) 2 a voucher for a meal

mealtime /meel tīm/ n the usual time of a meal

mealy-mouthed /meeli-/ adj lacking frankness or directness (disapproving)

mean[1] /meen/ (**meant** /ment/) vt 1 have a particular sense ○ What does this word mean? 2 intend to express a particular idea ○ That's not what I meant. 3 intend to do something ○ didn't mean to upset you 4 be serious in expressing an opinion or intention ○ I'm leaving you. And I mean it this time. 5 be a cause or sign of something ○ This means we'll have to go back.

mean[2] /meen/ adj 1 unkind or malicious 2 not generous 3 US, Can cruel 4 shabby 5 US excellent (infml) ○ He plays a mean sax. —**meanly** adv —**meanness** n

SYNONYMS mean, nasty, vile, low, base, ignoble CORE MEANING: below normal standards of accepted behaviour

mean[3] /meen/ n 1 a value intermediate between other values 2 an alternative in the middle of a range of possibilities ■ adj 1 medium 2 in an intermediate position

meander /mi ándər/ vi 1 follow a twisting route 2 wander slowly and aimlessly ■ n 1 a relaxed walk 2 a twist or bend in a route —**meanderingly** adv

ORIGIN The original meandering river was the Maeander in ancient Phrygia (now the Buyuk Menderes in Turkey).

meaning /meening/ n 1 what a word or symbol means 2 what somebody wants to express 3 what something signifies or indicates —**meaningless** adj —**meaninglessly** adv —**meaninglessness** n

meaningful /meeningf'l/ adj 1 with a discernible meaning 2 conveying a meaning that is not directly expressed ○ a meaningful look —**meaningfully** adv —**meaningfulness** n

means /meenz/ n something enabling somebody to do something (+ sing or pl verb) ■ npl available money and resources (+ pl verb) ◇ **by all means** certainly ◇ **by no means** not at all

means test n an examination of somebody's income to establish eligibility for financial aid —**means testing** n

meant past participle, past tense of **mean**[1]

meantime /meen tīm/ n the time between events

meanwhile /meen wīl/ adv 1 during the time between events 2 while something is happening

measles /meez'lz/ n a contagious viral disease producing a rash of red spots (+ sing or pl verb) ■ npl measles spots (+ pl verb)

measly /meezli/ (-slier, -sliest) adj 1 unsatisfactorily small (infml) 2 infected with measles

measure /mézhər/ n 1 the size of something 2 a system or standard for determining the size of something 3 a way of evaluating something 4 an action taken for a particular purpose (often pl) 5 a unit in a system for determining the size of something (often pl) 6 a standard amount of something such as alcohol 7 something such as a ruler or spoon used to determine size or quantity 8 a limited, appropriate, or particular extent or amount ○ contributed in no small measure to our success 9 a reasonable or appropriate limit ○ His rage had no measure. 10 a bill or law 11 the rhythm or metre of a piece of poetry ■ vt (-uring, -ured) 1 find the size, length, quantity, or rate of something using a suitable instrument or device 2 assess the effect or quality of something 3 be a particular size, length, quantity, or rate 4 determine the size of somebody for clothes 5 compare the size or quality of something with something else —**measurable** adj —**measurably** adv —**measureless** adj ◇ **beyond measure** very greatly ◇ **for good measure** beyond the amount required □ **measure up** vi be good enough

measured /mézhərd/ adj 1 unhurried or reasonable 2 determined by measuring

measurement /mézhərmənt/ n 1 the size of something measured 2 the measuring of something

meat /meet/ n 1 edible animal flesh 2 the edible part of something 3 the important part of something 4 material for stimulating thought

ORIGIN Originally meat just meant 'food' (as it still does in the phrase meat and drink). The restriction to animal flesh developed from the 13C. The word goes back to an ancient root meaning 'measure', through reference to a measured portion of food. Another early use, 'kind of food', survives in sweetmeat.

SPELLCHECK Do not confuse the spelling of meat and meet ('encounter'), which sound similar.

meatball /meet bawl/ n a small ball of minced meat

Meath /meeth, meeth/ county in E Republic of Ireland

meat loaf n a loaf-shaped minced meat mixture

meaty /meeti/ (-ier, -iest) adj 1 containing or tasting of meat 2 interesting and thought-provoking —**meatiness** n

mecca /mékə/ n an important or popular centre for something

Mecca /mékə/ city in W Saudi Arabia. The birthplace of the Prophet Muhammad, it is the holiest city of Islam. Pop. 770,000 (1995).

mechanic /mi kánnik/ n somebody who repairs or operates machinery or engines

mechanical /mi kánnik'l/ adj 1 machine-operated 2 involving or located in a machine or engine 3 done as if by machine —**mechanically** adv

mechanical engineering *n* the branch of engineering involving machines —**mechanical engineer** *n*

mechanics /mi kánniks/ *n* **1** the study of the effect of energy and forces on systems (+ *sing verb*) **2** the design, making, and running of machines (+ *sing or pl verb*) ■ *npl* the details of how something works or is done (+ *pl verb*)

mechanism /mékənizəm/ *n* **1** a machine or machine part that performs a particular task **2** something like a machine ○ *the fragile mechanism of the planet's ecology* **3** a method or means of doing something **4** the way that something works

mechanistic /mékə nístik/ *adj* **1** explaining natural phenomena by physical causes and processes **2** typical of a machine rather than a thinking feeling human being —**mechanistically** *adv*

mechanize /mékə nízz/ (-nizing, -nized), **mechanise** *vt* **1** use machinery to do something **2** equip somebody or something with machinery —**mechanization** /mékə nī záysh'n/ *n* —**mechanized** *adj*

Mechelen /mékələn, mékh-/ city in N Belgium. Pop. 75,689 (1991).

MEcon *abbr* Master of Economics

MEd /ém éd/ *abbr* Master of Education

med. *abbr* **1** medical **2** medieval

medal /médd'l/ *n* **1** a small flat piece of metal, usually inscribed, given as an award **2** a piece of metal with a religious image, worn as an accessory

> **ORIGIN** A **medal** is etymologically 'something made of metal', and goes back to the Latin and Greek words from which *metal* is derived. **Medal** came into English in the late 16C through French and Italian.

medallion /mə dálli ən/ *n* **1** a large medal **2** a large decorative metal disc worn on a neck chain **3** the microchip inside a smart card

medallist /médd'list/ *n* **1** somebody awarded a medal **2** somebody who designs, makes, or collects medals

Medan /máy daan/ city on N Sumatra, Indonesia. Pop. 1,974,300 (1997).

meddle /médd'l/ (-dling, -dled) *vi* interfere in somebody else's concerns —**meddler** *n* —**meddlesome** *adj*

~~medecine~~ incorrect spelling of **medicine**

~~medeival~~ incorrect spelling of **medieval**

Medellín /médda yeén/ city in northwest-central Colombia. Pop. 1,958,000 (1999).

medevac /méddi vak/ *n* the evacuation of injured people to a medical facility —**medevac** *vt*

media /meédi ə/ *n* television, newspapers, and radio collectively (+ *sing or pl verb*) ■ plural of **medium**

> **USAGE** When **media** means the broadcast and print press in general, it takes a singular verb: *The media has covered the story already.* If

media indicates separate journalistic outlets and their activities, it takes a plural verb: *The media have taken different approaches to coverage of war.* Use **medium**, not **media**, to refer to a single system or method of communication: *Cable television is a relatively inexpensive advertising medium.* Never use the false plural 'medias'.

mediaeval *adj* = **medieval**

medial /meédi əl/ *adj* at the middle —**medially** *adv*

median /meédi ən/ *n* **1** a middle point **2** the middle value of a set of ordered values **3** a midpoint in a frequency distribution **4** a line connecting the vertex of a triangle and the midpoint of the opposite side ■ *adj* **1** in, to, or through the middle **2** of or involving a statistical median

median strip *n* *Aus, US, Can* a central strip separating traffic lanes

media studies *n* the study of the mass media as an academic subject (+ *sing or pl verb*)

mediate /meédi ayt/ (-ating, -ated) *v* **1** *vi* intervene to resolve a conflict **2** *vt* achieve a solution to a dispute by bringing both sides to an agreement —**mediation** /meédi áysh'n/ *n* —**mediator** *n*

medic /méddik/ *n* a doctor or medical student (*infml*)

medical /méddik'l/ *adj* of medicine ■ *n* a physical examination by a doctor to determine somebody's state of health —**medically** *adv*

medical certificate *n* a document indicating a doctor's judgment of somebody's state of health

medical telematics *n* the use of computer networks for the international exchange and retrieval of medical data (+ *sing verb*)

medicament /mə díkəmənt/ *n* a substance used to treat an illness

Medicare /méddi kair/ *n* **1** a US health insurance programme under which medical expenses for senior citizens are partially paid by the government **2** the Australian health insurance scheme, funded by a tax levy

medicate /méddi kayt/ (-cating, -cated) *vt* **1** treat a patient with a drug **2** add a drug to —**medicated** *adj*

medication /méddi káysh'n/ *n* **1** a drug used to treat an illness **2** treatment of an illness using drugs

Medici /méddichi, mə deéchi/ family of Italian bankers and politicians including **Cosimo de'** (1389–1464), **Lorenzo de'** (1449–92), and **Cosimo I de'** (1519–74)

medicinal /mə díss'nəl/ *adj* **1** having properties that can be used to treat illness **2** intended to improve somebody's wellbeing —**medicinally** *adv*

medicine /médss'n, méddiss'n/ *n* **1** a drug or remedy used for treating illness, especially in liquid form **2** the diagnosis and treatment of illnesses and injuries

medicine man *n* a healer believed to use supernatural powers, especially among Native North American peoples

medieval /méddi eev'l/, **mediaeval** *adj* **1** of the Middle Ages **2** old-fashioned

Medina /me deéna/ city in west-central Saudi Arabia, site of the Prophet Muhammad's tomb and a holy city of Islam. Pop. 608,300 (1992).

mediocre /meèdi ókǝr/ *adj* adequate but not very good —**mediocrity** /meèdi ókrǝti/ *n*

meditate /méddi tayt/ (**-tating, -tated**) *vi* **1** empty or concentrate the mind for spiritual purposes or relaxation **2** think carefully —**meditation** /méddi táysh'n/ *n* —**meditative** /-tǝtiv/ *adj* —**meditator** *n*

Mediterranean /médditǝ ráyni ǝn/ *n* **1** the Mediterranean Sea or the surrounding area **2** somebody from around the Mediterranean Sea

Mediterranean Sea inland sea of Europe, Asia, and Africa, linked to the Atlantic Ocean at its western end by the Strait of Gibraltar

~~Mediterranean~~ incorrect spelling of **Mediterranean**

medium /meèdi ǝm/ *adj* **1** neither large nor small **2** neither dark nor light **3** cooked between rare and well-done ■ *n* (*pl* **-a** /-di ǝ/ *or* **-ums**) **1** an intermediate state between extremes **2** a means of mass communication **3** a means of conveying ideas or information **4** a substance that carries or transmits something **5** the means by which something is achieved **6** a material for storing or preserving something **7** somebody believed to transmit messages between the living and the dead **8** an artistic method or type of art

medium of exchange *n* something used like money

medium wave *n* a radio wave of intermediate length

medley /méddli/ (*pl* **-leys**) *n* **1** a mixture of things **2** a musical sequence of different tunes or songs **3** a swimming race with sections using different strokes

medulla /mi dúllǝ/ (*pl* **-lae** /-lee/ *or* **-las**) *n* the innermost part of an organ of a plant or animal —**medullar** *adj*

meek *adj* **1** mild or quiet by nature **2** submissive and lacking initiative or determination —**meekly** *adv* —**meekness** *n*

meerkat /meér kat/ *n* a South African mongoose

meet[1] /meet/ *v* (**met** /met/) **1** *vti* encounter or get together by chance or arrangement **2** *vti* encounter or be introduced for the first time **3** *vt* go and greet or fetch somebody **4** *vi* gather for a discussion **5** *vti* join or cross ◦ *where the two roads meet* **6** *vti* experience something such as a challenge or success ◦ *met with failure* **7** *vt* satisfy what is required ◦ *meet you on a price* ■ *n* **1** a sporting occasion for numbers of competitors and spectators **2** a gathering before a hunt for riders and hounds ◊ See note at **meat**

□ **meet up** *vi* encounter somebody or each other by chance or arrangement

meet[2] /meet/ *adj* appropriate (*archaic*) —**meetly** *adv*

meeting /meéting/ *n* **1** a gathering of people for a discussion or an event **2** the people at a meeting **3** an occasion when somebody meets somebody else

meeting house *n* a place where some religious groups, especially Quakers, meet for worship

mega /méggǝ/ *adj* very large, good, or impressive (*infml*)

mega- *prefix* **1** one million (10^6) ◦ *megavolt* **2** a binary million (2^{20}) ◦ *megabyte* **3** very large or great ◦ *megastar* **4** very (*slang*) ◦ *megarich*

megabit /méggǝ bit/ *n* **1** 1,048,576 bits **2** one million bits

megabyte /méggǝ bīt/ *n* **1** 1,048,576 bytes **2** one million bytes

megadeath /méggǝ deth/ *n* one million deaths

megadose /méggǝdóss/ *n* a very large dose of a medical drug or food supplement

megahertz /méggǝ hurts/ (*pl* same) *n* (*symbol* **MHz**) one million hertz

megalith /méggǝ lith/ *n* a large prehistoric standing stone —**megalithic** /méggǝ líthik/ *adj*

megalomania /méggǝlō máyni ǝ/ *n* **1** the enjoyment of or craving for power **2** a psychiatric disorder in which somebody has delusions of great power and importance —**megalomaniac** *n*, *adj* —**megalomaniacal** /-mǝ nī ǝk'l/ *adj*

megalopolis /méggǝ lóppǝliss/ *n* **1** an area consisting of several large cities **2** a very large city

megaphone /méggǝ fōn/ *n* a funnel-shaped device for amplifying the voice

megastar /méggǝ staar/ *n* a very well-known celebrity

megaton /méggǝ tun/ *n* **1** a unit of explosive power equivalent to one million tons of TNT **2** one million tons —**megatonnage** *n*

megawatt /méggǝ wot/ *n* one million watts

meiosis /mī óssiss/ *n* the process of cell division in which the nucleus divides into four nuclei, each containing half the usual number of chromosomes —**meiotic** /mī óttik/ *adj*

Golda Meir

Meir /may eér/, **Golda** (1898–1978) Russian-born Israeli prime minister (1969–74)

meitnerium /mīt neèri əm/ *n* (*symbol* **Mt**) an unstable radioactive chemical element

Mekong /mee kóng/ major river in Southeast Asia, flowing from SE China through the Indochinese peninsula and into the South China Sea in Vietnam. Length 4,200 km/2,610 mi.

melamine /méllə meen/ *n* **1** a white crystalline solid. Use: manufacture of synthetic resins, in leather tanning. **2** a type of resin or plastic made from melamine

melancholia /méllən kóli ə/ *n* depression as a form of psychiatric disorder (*dated*)

melancholic /méllən kóllik/ *adj* pensively sad (*literary*)

melancholy /méllənkəli/ *adj* feeling or causing pensive sadness ■ *n* pensive sadness

ORIGIN Medieval medical thought attributed physical and mental states to the balance of four bodily substances, of which one was 'black bile'. Excess of 'black bile' was considered to cause depression or **melancholy**, and 'black bile' is the literal meaning of the Greek word from which **melancholy** derives.

Melanesia /méllə neèzi ə, -neèzhə/ ethnographic grouping of islands of the W Pacific Ocean south of the equator, including New Guinea, the Solomon Islands, New Caledonia, Vanuatu, and Fiji —**Melanesian** *adj, n*

melange /may lóNzh, -laànzh/, **mélange** *n* a mixture of things (*literary or fml*)

melanin /méllənin/ *n* a brown skin pigment

melanoma /méllə nómə/ (*pl* -**mas** *or* -**mata** /-mətə/) *n* a malignant skin tumour

melatonin /méllə tónin/ *n* a hormone that causes changes in the colour of the skin

Library of Congress

Dame Nellie Melba

Melba /mélbə/, **Dame Nellie** (1859–1931) Australian opera singer

Melba toast *n* thin crisp curling toast

Melbourne /mélbərn/ capital of Victoria, Australia. Pop. 3,371,300 (1998).

Melbourne Cup *n* an important Australian horse race

meld[1] *vti* combine or blend —**meld** *n*

meld[2] *vti* show a hand of cards to score points —**meld** *n*

melee /méllay/, **mêlée** *n* **1** a confused fight **2** a confused mingling of people or things

mellifluous /mə líffloo əss/, **mellifluent** /-ənt/ *adj* pleasant to hear

mellow /méllō/ *adj* **1** soft and rich in colour or tone **2** smooth and rich in taste **3** fully ripe **4** easy-going —**mellow** *vti* —**mellowly** *adv* —**mellowness** *n*

melodic /mə lóddik/ *adj* of, consisting of, or characteristic of melody —**melodically** *adv*

melodious /mə lódi əss/ *adj* **1** having a pleasant melody **2** characterized by melody —**melodiously** *adv* —**melodiousness** *n*

melodrama /méllə draamə/ *n* **1** a dramatic or literary work with stereotyped characters, exaggerated emotions and language, and sensationalized events **2** an exaggerated or excessively dramatic situation or type of behaviour

melodramatic /méllədrə máttik/ *adj* **1** exaggeratedly theatrical **2** of melodrama —**melodramatically** *adv*

melody /méllədi/ (*pl* -**dies**) *n* **1** a series of musical notes forming a tune **2** the main tune in a piece of music

melon /méllən/ *n* **1** a round edible fruit with a tough rind and sweet juicy flesh **2** a plant that produces melons

ORIGIN Melon goes back to a Greek word that actually meant 'apple'. It formed a compound with another word meaning 'gourd', which passed into Latin. In late Latin this compound was shortened, but etymologically speaking the wrong element was dropped, and the part meaning literally 'apple' was left referring to a gourd.

melt *v* **1** *vti* change from a solid to a liquid state because of heat **2** *vti* disappear **3** *vi* disappear or merge gradually **4** *vti* move or be moved emotionally ■ *n* a grilled sandwich with melted cheese on top

☐ **melt down** *vti* liquefy by heating for reuse

meltdown /mélt down/ *n* **1** the melting of nuclear reactor fuel rods that results in a radiation leak **2** complete collapse (*infml*)

melting /mélting/ *adj* full of or causing sweet and tender emotions —**meltingly** *adv*

melting point *n* the temperature at which something changes from a solid to a liquid form

melting pot *n* a society composed of many different cultures

Melville /mélvil/, **Herman** (1819–91) US writer

Melville Island island in the Northern Territory, Australia, in the Timor Sea. Pop. 2,033 (1996).

member /mémbər/ *n* **1** somebody who belongs to a particular group or organization **2** *also* **Member** a representative elected to a legislative body **3** a limb **4** an individual part of a whole

Member of Parliament *n* somebody elected to a parliament

membership /mémbərship/ *n* **1** the state of belonging to a particular group or organization **2** the members of an organization (+ *sing or pl verb*)

membrane /mém brayn/ *n* **1** a thin layer of animal or plant tissue covering, lining, or separating organs **2** a thin pliable porous sheet of material —**membranous** /-brənəss/ *adj*

memento /mə méntō, mi-/ (*pl* **-tos** *or* **-toes**) *n* a souvenir

memo /mémmō/ (*pl* **-os**) *n* **1** a written communication circulated in an office **2** a note serving as a reminder

memoir /mém waar/ *n* a biography or historical account written from personal knowledge ■ **memoirs** *npl* **1** an autobiography **2** the proceedings of a learned society —**memoirist** *n*

memorabilia /mémmərə bílli ə/ *npl* **1** objects connected with a famous person **2** personal souvenirs

memorable /mémmərəb'l/ *adj* **1** worth remembering **2** easily remembered —**memorability** /mémmərə bílləti/ *n* —**memorably** *adv*

memorandum /mémmə rándəm/ (*pl* **-dums** *or* **-da** /-də/) *n* **1** an office memo **2** a note serving as a reminder

memorial /mə máwri əl/ *n* **1** a commemorative object or event **2** a statement of facts accompanying a petition ■ *adj* commemorative —**memorially** *adv*

memorize /mémmə rīz/ (**-rizing, -rized**), **memorise** *vt* learn and remember —**memorization** /mémmə rī záysh'n/ *n*

memory /mémməri/ (*pl* **-ries**) *n* **1** the ability to retain and retrieve knowledge of past events and experiences **2** somebody's stock of retained knowledge and experience **3** the retained impression of a particular person, event, or subject **4** the act of remembering **5** *also* **memory bank** the part of a computer where data is stored for quick retrieval **6** the data storage capacity of a computer

Memphis /mémfiss/ **1** ruined city and capital of ancient Egypt **2** city in SW Tennessee. Pop. 603,507 (1998). —**Memphian** *n, adj*

memsahib /mém saáb, mém saab/ *n* S Asia a former way of addressing a married European woman

menace /ménnəss/ *n* **1** a possible source of danger **2** a nuisance (*infml*) ■ *v* (**-acing, -aced**) **1** *vt* be dangerous to **2** *vti* threaten —**menacing** *adj* —**menacingly** *adv*

ménage /máy naazh/ *n* (*fml*) **1** a household **2** the management of a house

ménage à trois /máy naazh aa trwaá/ (*pl* **ménages à trois** /*pronunc. same*/) *n* a sexual arrangement involving three people

menagerie /mə nájjəri/ *n* **1** a collection of captive wild animals exhibited to the public **2** an enclosure for exhibited wild animals

mend *v* **1** *vti* restore something to a satisfactory condition **2** *vt* remove damage such as a hole **3** *vti* improve **4** *vi* recover or heal ■ *n* a repair —**mendable** *adj* —**mender** *n* ◊ **on the mend** recovering or healing after illness or injury

mendacious /men dáyshəss/ *adj* **1** having a tendency to tell lies **2** deliberately untrue —**mendacity** /men dássəti/ *n*

Mendel /ménd'l/, **Gregor Johann** (1822–84) Austrian monk and scientist. He developed the principles of heredity and laid the basis of modern genetics. —**Mendelian** /men deéli ən/ *adj*

mendelevium /méndə leévi əm/ *n* (*symbol* **Md**) a synthetic short-lived radioactive element

Mendeleyev /méndə láyef/, **Dmitry Ivanovich** (1834–1907) Russian chemist. He formulated the periodic law of elements and devised the periodic table (1869).

Mendelssohn /ménd'lssən/, **Felix** (1809–47) German composer

mendicant /méndikənt/ *adj* begging and living on charity ■ *n* **1** a beggar *(fml)* **2** a member of a religious order that lives by begging

Menelaus /ménni láyəss/ *n* in Greek mythology, the king of Sparta and husband of Helen of Troy

menfolk /mén fōk/ *npl* **1** the men associated with a family or group **2** men in general

menhir /mén heer/ *n* a single standing stone erected by prehistoric people

menial /meéni əl/ *adj* **1** of or involving unskilled work that confers low social status on those doing it **2** of servants ■ *n* a domestic servant —**menially** *adv*

meningitis /ménnin jítiss/ *n* a severe illness involving inflammation of the membranes around the brain and spinal cord —**meningitic** /-jíttik/ *adj*

Mennonite /ménnə nīt/ *n* a member of a Protestant group emphasizing adult baptism and pacifism —**Mennonitism** *n*

ORIGIN **Mennonite** was adopted from German in the mid-16C. It comes from the name of Menno Simons (1496–1561), an early leader of the group.

menopause /ménnō pawz/ *n* the time in a woman's life when she stops menstruating —**menopausal** /ménnō páwz'l/ *adj*

menorah /mə náwrə/ *n* **1** a six-branched ceremonial candlestick used in the Jewish Temple **2** an eight-branched candlestick lit during Hanukkah

Menorca /mi náwrkə/, **Minorca** island in the Balearic Islands, Spain. Pop. 66,900 (1989). Spanish **Menorca** —**Menorcan** *adj, n*

Menotti /mə nótti/, **Gian-Carlo** (*b.* 1911) Italian-born US composer

Mensa /ménssə/ *n* a constellation in the southern hemisphere that forms part of the larger Magellanic Cloud

menses /mén seez/ *n* (*technical; + sing or pl verb*) **1** menstruation **2** menstrual discharge

menstrual /ménstroo əl/ *adj* of menstruation

menstrual cycle *n* the month-long cycle during which a woman menstruates once

menstruate /ménstroo ayt/ (**-ating, -ated**) *vi* discharge blood and other matter from the

womb as part of the menstrual cycle
—**menstruation** /mén stroo áysh'n/ *n*

mental /mént'l/ *adj* **1** of the mind **2** carried out in the mind ○ *mental arithmetic* —**mentally** *adv*

mental age *n* a measure of intellectual development according to the norms of children of the same age

mentality /men tálləti/ (*pl* -**ties**) *n* **1** somebody's habitual way of thinking **2** somebody's intellectual ability

menthol /mén thol/ *n* a mint-tasting compound made from peppermint oil. Use: flavourings, perfumes, mild anaesthetic. —**mentholated** *adj*

mention /ménsh'n/ *n* **1** *vt* use a particular word or name when speaking or writing **2** *vt* acknowledge somebody for exceptional conduct —**mentionable** *adj* ◇ **not to mention** besides

mentor /mén tawr/ *n* **1** an experienced adviser and guide for somebody younger **2** somebody who trains and helps a junior colleague

ORIGIN In Greek mythology, Mentor was the teacher and protector of Odysseus' son Telemachus.

menu /ménnyoo/ *n* **1** a list of available dishes at a restaurant or formal meal **2** a list of options, e.g. program options on a computer

menu-driven *adj* operated using computer menus

Menuhin /ményoo in/, **Yehudi, Baron Menuhin of Stoke d'Abernon** (1916–99) US-born British violinist

Menzies /ménziz/, **Sir Robert** (1894–1978) Australian prime minister (1939–41, 1949–66)

meow *n, vi* = miaow

MEP *abbr* Member of the European Parliament

Mephistopheles /méffi stóffə leez/, **Mephisto** /mə fístó/ *n* in medieval mythology, a subordinate of Satan —**Mephistophelean** /méffistə feèli ən/ *adj*

mercantile /múrkən tíl/ *adj* of merchants or trading

Mercator /mur káytər/, **Gerardus** (1512–94) Flemish geographer, cartographer, and mathematician

mercenary /múrss'nəri/ (*pl* -**ies**) *n* **1** a professional soldier paid to fight in the army of another country **2** somebody motivated only by money —**mercenary** *adj*

merchandise /múrchən díz/ *n* goods for sale ■ *v* (-dising, -dised) **1** *vti* trade in goods commercially **2** *vt* promote a product for sale —**merchandiser** *n*

merchandising /múrchən dízing/ *n* **1** the promotion of products for sale **2** spin-off products from a film, TV programme, sports team, or event

merchant /múrchənt/ *n* **1** a dealer in wholesale goods **2** a retailer **3** somebody noted for a particular activity or quality (*infml; usually in combination*) ○ *a speed merchant in a souped-up*

car ■ *adj* **1** of trade or merchants **2** of a merchant navy

merchant account *n* a bank account for depositing payments made by credit card, used especially in Internet trading

merchant bank *n* a bank providing services for companies and large investors —**merchant banker** *n* —**merchant banking** *n*

merchant certificate authority *n* a certificate authority supplying certificates to merchants

merchantman /múrchəntmən/ (*pl* -**men** /-mən/), **merchant ship** *n* a seagoing cargo ship

merchant marine *n* US, Can a merchant navy

merchant navy *n* a country's seagoing cargo ships

Mercia /múrssi ə, múrshi ə/ ancient Anglo-Saxon kingdom of central England —**Mercian** *adj, n*

merciful /múrssif'l/ *adj* **1** showing mercy **2** welcome because of ending something unpleasant —**mercifully** *adv*

merciless /múrssiləss/ *adj* **1** showing no mercy **2** strict and intolerant —**mercilessly** *adv* —**mercilessness** *n*

Merckx /murks/, **Eddy** (b. 1945) Belgian bicycle racer

mercurial /mur kyoóri əi/ *adj* **1** lively and unpredictable **2** containing mercury

mercury /múrkyoóri/ *n* **1** (*symbol* **Hg**) a poisonous liquid metallic element. Use: in thermometers and barometers, dental fillings, lamps. **2** the mercury in a weather thermometer or barometer, or the temperature or pressure it indicates

Mercury /múrkyoóri/ *n* **1** in Roman mythology, the god of commerce who was the messenger of the gods. Greek equivalent **Hermes** **2** the planet in the solar system nearest the Sun

mercy /múrssi/ (*pl* -**cies**) *n* **1** compassion or forgiveness **2** a compassionate forgiving disposition **3** something to be thankful for ◇ **at the mercy of** completely unprotected against

mercy killing *n* euthanasia, or an act of euthanasia

mere[1] /meer/ (*superlative* **merest**) *adj* **1** just what is specified and nothing more ○ *She was no mere journalist.* **2** by itself and without anything more ○ *the mere mention of his name* —**merely** *adv*

mere[2] /mérri/ *n* a Maori club used as a weapon

meretricious /mérrə tríshəss/ *adj* **1** superficially attractive but without real value (*fml*) **2** misleadingly plausible or significant ○ *swayed by a meretricious argument*

merge (**merging, merged**) *vti* **1** combine into a single entity **2** blend together gradually —**merging** *n*

merger /múrjər/ *n* **1** a combining of two or more companies **2** a blend or combination

Mérida /mérridə/ **1** city in W Spain. Pop. 50,471 (1998). **2** capital of Yucatán State, SE Mexico. Pop. 649,770 (1995).

meridian /mə ríddi ən/ n 1 a line of longitude between the North and South poles 2 either half of the circle of the meridian, from pole to pole 3 a great circle of the celestial sphere passing through the celestial poles

meringue /mə ráng/ n 1 a cooked mixture of whipped egg whites and sugar 2 a meringue cake or shell

merit /mérrit/ n 1 value that deserves respect and acknowledgment 2 a good quality (often pl) ■ **merits** npl the facts of a matter considered objectively ■ vt be worthy of or deserve

meritocracy /mérri tókrəssi/ (pl -cies) n 1 a social system based on ability 2 an elite group of people who achieved their position on the basis of their ability —**meritocratic** /mérritō kráttik/ adj

meritorious /mérri táwri əss/ adj deserving honour and recognition —**meritoriously** adv

Merlin /múrlin/ n in Arthurian legend, a magician and adviser to King Arthur

mermaid /múr mayd/ n a mythical sea creature with the upper body of a woman and the tail of a fish instead of legs

ORIGIN The mer- of **mermaid** represents an old word mere 'sea'. Mere goes back to the same root as Latin mare 'sea', from which words like marine and mariner derive.

Merrick /mérrik/ hill in SW Scotland. Height 843 m/2,765 ft.

merry /mérri/ (-rier, -riest) adj 1 lively and cheerful ○ a merry laugh 2 tipsy (infml) 3 funny (dated) —**merrily** adv —**merriment** n —**merriness** n

merry-go-round n a fairground ride consisting of a rotating platform with moving seats shaped like animals

merrymaking /mérri mayking/ n lively celebration —**merrymaker** n

Mersey /múrzi/ river in NW England. Length 110 km/70 mi.

mesa /máyssə/ n a flat steep-sided elevated area in the SW United States

mescal /més kal/ (pl -cals or same) n 1 a Mexican spirit distilled from some species of agave 2 the peyote cactus

mescaline /méskəlin, -leen/, **mescalin** /-lin/ n a hallucinogenic drug extracted from the nodules of the peyote cactus

Mesdames 1 plural of **Madame** 2 plural of **Madam**

mesdemoiselles plural of **mademoiselle**

mesh n 1 material like net ○ wire mesh 2 one of the openings in the threads or wires of a net 3 the threads or wires of a net 4 something that traps or entangles (often pl) ■ vti 1 fit together 2 catch or entangle, or become caught or entangled 3 make gear teeth engage, or become engaged

Mesic /máysich/, **Stjepan** (b. 1934) president of Croatia (2000–)

mesmeric /mez mérrik/ adj fascinating or hypnotic —**mesmerically** adv

mesmerize /mézmə rīz/ (-izing, -ized), **mesmerise** vt 1 absorb the attention of 2 hypnotize —**mesmerization** /mézmə rī záysh'n/ n —**mesmerizingly** adv

ORIGIN The first person to be **mesmerized** were patients of the Austrian doctor Franz Anton Mesmer (1734–1815), who conducted experiments in which he induced trance-like states in his subjects.

meson /meé zon/ n an elementary particle that has a mass between that of an electron and proton and participates in the strong interaction —**mesonic** /mi zónnik/ adj

Mesopotamia /méssəpə táymi ə/ ancient region of W Asia, between the rivers Tigris and Euphrates in present-day Iraq. It was the site of several early civilizations, including Babylonia. —**Mesopotamian** n, adj

mesosphere /méssō sfeer/ n the atmospheric layer between the stratosphere and thermosphere —**mesospheric** /méssō sférrik/ adj

Mesozoic /méssō zō ik/ n an era of geological time 248–65 million years ago —**Mesozoic** adj

mesquite /me skeét/ (pl same or -quites) n 1 a hard wood often burned in a barbecue to flavour food 2 a small spiny tree that produces mesquite wood

mess n 1 an untidy condition or dirty state 2 a chaotic state 3 a place for communal meals 4 a group of people who eat communally (+ sing or pl verb) 5 a serving or quantity of food ■ v 1 vt make untidy or dirty 2 vi meddle 3 vi use something carelessly so as to cause a problem or damage ○ messing with his computer

□ **mess around** or **about** v (infml) 1 vi waste time 2 vti interfere in 3 vi behave in a joking or playful way

□ **mess up** vti spoil or bungle something (infml)

message /méssij/ n 1 a communication in speech, writing, or signals 2 a lesson or moral that somebody wants to communicate, e.g. in a work of art ■ **messages** npl Scotland shopping ■ vt (-saging, -saged) send a message to —**messaging** n

message board n an online bulletin board

message code authentication n the verification of the author of an e-mail message

messanger incorrect spelling of **messenger**

messenger /méss'njər/ n 1 somebody carrying a message 2 a paid courier

mess hall n a place for communal meals, especially in the armed forces

Messiaen /méssi oN, -ən/, **Olivier** (1908–92) French composer and organist

messiah /mə sí ə/ n 1 a saviour or liberator 2 **Messiah** in the Hebrew Bible, an anointed king who will lead the Jews back to the land of Israel and establish justice in the world 3 **Messiah** in Christianity, Jesus Christ regarded as the Messiah prophesied in the Hebrew Bible

messianic /méssi ánnik/ *adj* 1 *also* **Messianic** of the Messiah 2 involving great enthusiasm —**messianically** *adv*

Messieurs plural of **Monsieur**

Messina /me seena/ city in NE Sicily, Italy. Pop. 261,134 (1999).

Messrs plural of **Mr**

messy /méssi/ (**-ier, -iest**) *adj* 1 dirty or untidy 2 difficult to resolve or deal with —**messily** *adv* —**messiness** *n*

mestizo /mess teezō/ (*pl* **-zos** *or* **-zoes**) *n* a person of mixed ancestry, especially Native American and European

met /met/ past tense, past participle of **meet**[1]

Met /met/ *abbr* 1 Meteorological Office 2 Metropolitan Police

meta- *prefix* 1 later, behind ○ *metacarpus* ○ *metatarsus* 2 beyond, transcending, encompassing ○ *metalanguage*

metabolism /mə tábbəlìzəm/ *n* 1 the processes by which food is converted into the energy and products needed to sustain life 2 the biochemical activity of a particular substance in a living organism —**metabolic** /méttə bóllik/ *adj* —**metabolically** *adv*

metabolite /mə tábbə līt/ *n* a by-product of metabolism

metabolize /mə tábbə līz/ (**-lizing, -lized**), **metabolise** *vti* subject or be subjected to metabolism

metacarpus /méttə kaàrpəss/ (*pl* **-pi** /-pī/) *n* 1 a set of five long bones in the human hand between the wrist and fingers 2 the forefoot or hand of a vertebrate between the wrist and digits —**metacarpal** *adj, n*

metal /métt'l/ *n* 1 a solid shiny chemical element that is malleable, ductile, and able to conduct heat and electricity well 2 a mixture of one or more metals 3 heavy metal music *(slang)* ■ *vt* (**-alling, -alled**) 1 cover or provide with metal 2 make or mend a road with broken stones —**metalloid** /méttə loyd/ *n, adj*

metalanguage /méttə lang gwìj/ *n* language used to describe language

metal detector *n* 1 a device for detecting buried metal objects 2 a screening device for detecting weapons

metallic /mə tállik/ *adj* 1 of, containing, or typical of metal 2 shiny 3 tasting of metal —**metallically** *adv*

metallurgy /mə tállurji/ *n* the study of metals and the procedures for extracting, refining, and making things from them —**metallurgic** /méttə lúrjik/ *adj* —**metallurgical** *adj* —**metallurgist** *n*

metalwork /métt'l wurk/ *n* 1 the making of metal objects 2 metal objects —**metalworker** *n* —**metalworking** *n*

metamorphic /méttə máwrfik/, **metamorphous** /-máwrfəss/ *adj* 1 by or from metamorphism 2 of metamorphosis

metamorphism /méttə máwrfizəm/ *n* a change

in the structure of rock that results from long-term heat and pressure

metamorphose /méttə máwrfōz/ (**-phosing, -phosed**) *vti* change or cause to change by metamorphosis

metamorphosis /méttə máwrfəssiss/ (*pl* **-ses** /-seez/) *n* 1 change of physical form, appearance, or character 2 a supposed supernatural transformation

metaphor /méttəfər, -fawr/ *n* 1 the application of a word or phrase to somebody or something, meant not literally, but to make a comparison, e.g. saying that somebody is a snake 2 figurative language —**metaphorical** /méttə fórrik'l/ *adj* —**metaphorically** *adv*

metaphysical /méttə fízzik'l/ *adj* 1 of metaphysics 2 based on speculative reasoning 3 abstract or theoretical —**metaphysically** *adv*

metaphysics /méttə fízziks/, **metaphysic** /-fízzik/ *n* the branch of philosophy dealing with the nature of being (+ *sing verb*)

metastasis /me tástəssiss/ (*pl* **-ses** /-seez/) *n* 1 the spread of cancer through the body 2 a malignant tumour that has developed as a result of the spread of cancer cells —**metastatic** /méttə státtik/ *adj*

metatarsus /méttə társsəss/ (*pl* **-si** /-sī/) *n* 1 a set of five long bones in the human foot between the ankle and the toes 2 the hind foot of a vertebrate between the ankle and toes —**metatarsal** *adj, n*

mete /meet/ (**meting, meted**) □ **mete out** *vt* give out something such as punishment or justice, especially in a harsh or unfair way

meteor /meeti ə, -awr/ *n* 1 a mass of rock from space that burns up on entering the atmosphere 2 the light from a burning meteor

meteoric /meeti órrik/ *adj* 1 of meteors 2 very fast or brilliant —**meteorically** *adv*

meteorite /meeti ə rīt/ *n* a rock from outer space that has reached Earth

meteorology /meeti ə rólləji/ *n* the scientific study of the weather —**meteorological** /-ərə lójjik'l/ *adj* —**meteorologist** *n*

meter[1] /meetər/ *n* 1 a device for measuring the amount or flow of something 2 a parking meter —**meter** *vt*

meter[2] *n* US = **metre**

-meter *suffix* measuring device ○ *thermometer*

methadone /méthə dōn/, **methadon** /-don/ *n* a synthetic painkilling drug. Use: substitute for heroin in the treatment of addiction.

methane /mee thayn/ *n* a colourless odourless flammable gas that is the main constituent of natural gas. Use: fuel.

methanol /méthə nol/ *n* a colourless volatile poisonous liquid. Use: solvent, fuel, in antifreeze for motor vehicles.

methinks /mi thíngks/ (**-thought** /-tháwt/) *vi* it seems to me *(humorous or archaic)*

method /méthəd/ *n* 1 a planned way of doing something 2 orderliness

methodical /mə thóddik'l/, **methodic** /-ik/ adj systematic or painstaking —**methodically** adv —**methodicalness** n

Methodist /méthədist/ n an evangelical Protestant church founded in the 18C by John Wesley and his followers —**Methodism** n —**Methodist** adj —**Methodistic** /méthə dístik/ adj

methodology /méthə dólləji/ (pl **-gies**) n 1 the methods or organizing principles underlying an area of study 2 in philosophy, the study of organizing principles and underlying rules —**methodological** /méthədə lójjik'l/ adj —**methodologically** adv —**methodologist** n

meths /meths/ n UK methylated spirit (infml)

methuselah /mə thyoŏzələ/, **Methuselah** n a wine bottle holding the equivalent of 8 normal bottles

ORIGIN According to the Bible, Methuselah was an ancestor of Noah and lived 969 years (Gen 5: 21–27).

methyl alcohol /mee thīl-/ n methanol

methylated spirit /méthə laytid-/, **methylated spirits** n ethanol with methanol and a violet dye added. Use: fuel, solvents.

metical /méttik'l/ (pl **-cais** /-kīsh/ or **-cals**) n the main unit of Mozambican currency

meticulous /mə tíkyōŏləss/ adj precise and painstaking —**meticulously** adv —**meticulousness** n ◊ See note at **careful**

métier /métti ay/, **metier** n 1 somebody's occupation or trade 2 an activity that somebody is particularly good at

metonymy /me tónnəmi/ n a figure of speech in which an attribute of a thing stands for the thing itself

metre[1] /meetər/ n (symbol **m**) the basic SI unit of length, equivalent to 39.37 in

metre[2] /meetər/ n a rhythmic pattern in verse or music

metric /méttrik/ adj 1 of the metric system 2 also **metrical** of poetic metre —**metrically** adv

metric system n a decimal system of weights and measures based on units such as the kilogram and the metre

metric ton n (symbol **t**) a unit of weight equal to 1000 kg

metro /méttrō/ (pl **-ros**), **Metro** n an underground railway system in a city

metronome /méttrənōm/ n a device that indicates a given musical tempo, either aurally or visually —**metronomic** /méttrə nómmik/ adj

metropolis /mə tróppəliss/ n a large city ◊ See note at **city**

ORIGIN Metropolis goes back to a Greek word meaning literally 'mother city'. It entered English via Latin in the mid-16C.

metropolitan /méttrə póllitən/ adj 1 of or characteristic of a metropolis 2 forming a large city 3 of the home territory of a country rather than its territories elsewhere ■ n 1 an inhabitant of a metropolis 2 in Christianity, a high-ranking church official 3 the head of the Russian Orthodox Church

Metternich /méttə nikh/, **Klemens Wenzel Nepomuk Lothar von, Prince of Metternich-Winneburg-Beilstein** (1773–1859) German-born Austrian chancellor of the Hapsburg Empire (1821–48)

mettle /métt'l/ n 1 spirit or strength of character 2 somebody's temperament —**mettlesome** adj ◊ See note at **courage**

ORIGIN Mettle is actually a form of metal. Both spellings were formerly used for both words, even into the 19C, though 18C dictionaries had recognized the distinction. Although mettle is in origin a figurative or metaphorical use of metal, any conscious mental association between the two was lost long ago.

Meuse /mōz/ river flowing from NE France through Belgium and the Netherlands into the North Sea. Length 925 km/575 mi.

mew[1] /myoo/ n a seagull

mew[2] /myoo/ vi make a high-pitched cry (refers to cats and kittens) —**mew** n

mewl vi cry weakly

mews n a residential street converted from stables (+ sing or pl verb)

ORIGIN Mews were originally cages, and then buildings, for hawks kept for hunting. In the latter part of the 14C the Royal Mews were built in London on the site of what is now Trafalgar Square, to house the royal hawks. By Henry VII's time they were being used as stables, and from at least the early 17C the term mews was used for 'stabling around an open yard'. The modern application to a 'residential street converted from stables' dates from the early 19C.

Mexican American n an American of Mexican descent

Mexican wave n a rippling effect produced by a crowd in a stadium standing up, raising their arms, and sitting down again in sequence

ORIGIN The wave is 'Mexican' because it was first used at the football World Cup finals in Mexico City in 1986.

Mexico /méksikō/ country in S North America. Cap. Mexico City. Pop. 101,879,170 (2001). —**Mexican** /méksikən/ adj, n

Mexico, Gulf of arm of the Atlantic Ocean, east of Mexico and south of the United States

Mexico City capital of Mexico. Pop. 9,800,000 (1995).

mezzanine /mézzə neen/ n also **mezzanine floor** a low storey, especially one between the 1st and 2nd floors of a building ■ adj describes an intermediate range of investment

mezzo /métsō/ adv moderately (musical direction) ■ n (pl **-zos**) also **mezzo-soprano** a woman singer with a range between a soprano and a contralto

mezzotint /métsō tint/ *n* 1 an engraving process that involves scraping and burnishing a copper plate 2 a mezzotint print —**mezzotint** *vt*

mg *symbol* milligram

Mg *symbol* magnesium

MHz *symbol* megahertz

mi /mee/, **me** *n* a syllable used in singing the 3rd note of a scale

MI *abbr* Military Intelligence

mi. *abbr* mile

MI5 /ém ī fív/ *n* British Military Intelligence, section five, responsible for security and counterintelligence

MI6 /ém ī síks/ *n* British Military Intelligence, section six, responsible for secret intelligence and espionage

Miami /mī ámmi/ city in SE Florida. Pop. 368,624 (1998).

Miami Beach city in SE Florida, on an island opposite Miami. Pop. 97,053 (1998).

miaow /mi ów/, **meow** *n* a characteristic cry of a cat ■ *vi* utter miaows

miasma /mi ázmə, mī-/ (*pl* **-mata** /-mətə/ *or* **-mas**) *n* 1 a harmful or poisonous vapour 2 an unwholesome atmosphere

mica /míkə/ *n* a shiny mineral compound of aluminium and silicon. Use: electrical insulators, heating elements.

mice plural of **mouse**

Michael /mík'l/ (*b.* 1921) king of Romania (1927–30, 1940–47)

Michaelmas /mík'lməss/ (*pl* **-mases**) *n* a traditional Christian feast day. Date: 29 September.

Michelangelo /mík'l ánjəlō/ (1475–1564) Italian sculptor, painter, architect, and poet

Michigan /míshigən/ state in the N United States. Cap. Lansing. Pop. 9,938,444 (2000).

Michigan, Lake third largest of the Great Lakes, in the N United States

micro /míkrō/ *adj* very small

micro- *prefix* 1 small, minute ○ *microcosm* 2 using a microscope or requiring magnification ○ *microbiology* 3 one millionth (10 $^{-6}$) ○ *microgram* ○ *microsecond* 4 of a small area or on a small scale ○ *micromanage*

microbe /míkrōb/ *n* a microscopic organism that transmits disease —**microbial** /mī krōbi əl/ *adj*

ORIGIN Microbe is formed from Greek elements that mean literally 'small life'. It was coined in French in 1878, and adopted into English a few years later.

microbiology /míkrō bī ólləji/ *n* the scientific study of microscopic organisms —**microbiological** /míkrō bī ə lójjik'l/ *adj*

microbrewery /míkrō broo əri/ (*pl* **-ries**) *n* a small brewery —**microbrewer** *n* —**microbrewing** *n*

microchip /míkrō chip/ *n* a small wafer of semiconductor material on which an integrated circuit is laid out

microclimate /míkrō klīmət/ *n* the climate of a confined space or small geographical area —**microclimatic** /míkrō klī máttik/ *adj* —**microclimatologist** /míkrō klímə tólləjist/ *n* —**microclimatology** *n*

microcomputer /míkrō kəm pyootər/ *n* a small computer

microcosm /míkrō kozəm/ *n* a small version of something larger —**microcosmic** /míkrō kózmik/ *adj*

microdot /míkrō dot/ *n* a tiny photograph about the size of a dot

microelectronics /míkrō ilek trónniks, -elek-/ *n* the design, development, and construction of very small electronic circuits (*+ sing verb*) —**microelectronic** *adj* —**microelectronically** *adv*

microfibre /míkrō fībər/ *n* a very fine synthetic thread

microfiche /míkrō feesh/ *n* a sheet of microfilm containing pages of information

microfilm /míkrō film/ *n* a strip of film containing tiny photographs ■ *vti* photograph on microfilm

microform /míkrō fawrm/ *n* the miniaturized reproduction on film or paper of pages of information

microinstruction /míkrō in struksh'n/ *n* a single low-level programming instruction

microlight /míkrō līt/, **microlite** *n* a tiny aircraft

micromanage /míkrō manij/ (**-aging**, **-aged**) *vt* manage a business or organization by attending to small details —**micromanagement** *n* —**micromanager** *n*

micrometer /mī krómmitər/ *n* a device for measuring small distances accurately —**micrometric** /míkrō méttrik/ *adj* —**micrometry** /mī krómmətri/ *n*

micron /mī kron/ *n* one millionth of metre

Micronesia /míkrə neezi ə/ ethnographic grouping of islands of the W Pacific Ocean east of the Philippines and mainly north of the equator —**Micronesian** *adj*, *n*

Micronesia, Federated States of island nation in the W Pacific Ocean. Cap. Palikir. Pop. 134,597 (2001).

microorganism /míkrō áwrgənizəm/ *n* a microscopic organism

microphone /míkrə fōn/ *n* a device for converting sounds into electrical signals for amplification, transmission, or recording

microprocessor /míkrō prő sessər/ *n* a microcomputer's central processing unit consisting of a single chip

microprogram /míkrō prō gram/ *n* a computer program built into a microprocessor

microprogramming /míkrō prō gramming/ *n* a means of programming a computer's central processing unit by breaking down instructions into small steps

microscope /míkrə skōp/ *n* an instrument that uses a lens or system of lenses to produce a greatly magnified image of an object

microscopic /míkrə skóppik/ *adj* **1** very small **2** thorough and detailed **3** *also* **microscopical** invisible without the use of a microscope —**microscopically** *adv*

microsurgery /míkrō súrjəri/ *n* surgery using miniaturized instruments and a specially designed microscope —**microsurgical** *adj*

microwave /míkrə wayv/ *n* **1** a short electromagnetic wave. Use: radar, radio transmissions, cooking or heating devices. **2** an oven using microwaves to heat or cook food quickly —**microwavable** *adj* —**microwave** *vt*

mid *adj* occupying a middle or central position

'mid /mid/, **mid** *prep* amid

mid- *prefix* middle ○ *midfield*

midair /mid áir/ *n* a point in the air above a surface —**midair** *adj*

Midas /mídass/ *n* in Greek mythology, a king who turned objects to gold by touching them

mid-Atlantic *adj* North American and British in style

midday /mid dáy/ *n* the middle of the day

midden /mídd'n/ *n* a pile of dung or refuse

middle /mídd'l/ *n* **1** the part or position furthest from the sides, edges, or ends of something **2** the period halfway between the beginning and end of something **3** the inside or central part of something **4** the waist, stomach, or central part of the body (*infml*) ■ *adj* **1** equidistant from the sides, edges, or ends of something **2** halfway between the beginning and end of a period **3** occupying an intermediate position, e.g. in age or status

middle age *n* the period between youth and later life —**middle-aged** *adj*

middle-aged spread, middle-age spread *n* extra fat accumulated around the waist in middle age (*humorous*)

Middle Ages *n* the period in European history between antiquity and the Renaissance

Middle America *n* the socially traditional US middle class —**Middle American** *adj*, *n*

middlebrow /mídd'l brów/ *n* somebody with moderate and conventional cultural and intellectual interests (*infml*) —**middlebrow** *adj*

middle class *n* the social class between the poor and the wealthy —**middle-class** *adj*

middle distance *n* the area between the foreground and the background

middle-distance *adj* of medium-length foot races

middle ear *n* the central part of the ear containing the bones that transmit sound

Middle East *n* **1** the region from Egypt to Iran **2** the historical area from Iran to Myanmar —**Middle Eastern** *adj* —**Middle Easterner** *n*

Middle England *n* the socially traditional English middle class

Middle English *n* the English language from 1100 to 1500

middle finger *n* the finger between the forefinger and the third finger

middle ground *n* **1** the area between the foreground and the background **2** a position between extremes

middleman /mídd'l man/ (*pl* **-men** /-men/) *n* **1** somebody who buys goods from a producer and sells them to retailers or consumers **2** a go-between

middle management *n* the tier of managers below top executives —**middle manager** *n*

middle name *n* a name between somebody's first name and surname

middle-of-the-road *adj* **1** moderate and not extreme **2** intended to have broad music appeal ■ *n* music aiming for broad appeal —**middle-of-the-roader** *n*

middle school *n* **1** a British state school for children from 8 to 13 **2** a US school for children between the ages of about 11 and 14

middle-sized *adj* of average size

middleware /mídd'l wair/ *n* software that manages the connection between a client and a database

middleweight /mídd'l wayt/ *n* **1** a weight category for boxers between welterweight and light heavyweight **2** a boxer who competes at middleweight

middling /míddling/ *adj* **1** medium, moderate, or average **2** ordinary and unexceptional ■ *adv* moderately and unexceptionally (*infml*) —**middlingly** *adv*

middy /míddi/ (*pl* **-dies**) *n* **1** *also* **middy blouse** a blouse with a sailor collar **2** *Aus* a medium-sized beer glass

midfield /mid feeld/ *n* **1** the central area of a sports pitch **2** the players in the midfield (+ *sing or pl verb*) —**midfielder** *n*

midge *n* a biting insect that flies in swarms

midget /míjit/ *n* **1** an offensive term for an unusually short person **2** a very small version of something —**midget** *adj*

midi /míddi/ (*pl* **-is**) *n* a skirt or coat ending just below the knee

MIDI /míddi/ *n* the interface between an electronic musical instrument and a computer. Full form **musical instrument digital interface**

Midlands /mídləndz/ region of central England —**Midlander** *n*

Midlothian /mid lṓthi ən/ council area and former county in SE Scotland

midnight /mid nīt/ *n* twelve o'clock at night —**midnightly** *adj*, *adv*

midnight sun *n* the sun when visible at midnight in the Arctic or Antarctic circles in summer

midpoint /mid poynt/ *n* **1** the point on a line, journey, or distance halfway between the beginning and end **2** the point of time halfway through a period

midrange /mid raynj/ *adj* **1** occurring in the middle of a series **2** covering a medium distance

midriff /mídrif/ *n* the front area of the human body between the chest and the waist

midshipman /mídshipmən/ (*pl* **-men** /-mən/) *n*
1 a British naval officer of a rank above naval
cadet 2 *US* a student training to be a naval
officer

midst *n* the centre of something ■ *prep* amid
(*literary*)

midstream /mid streém/ *n* 1 the middle part of
a river or stream 2 a point halfway through
something —**midstream** *adv*

midsummer /mid súmmər/ *n* the middle period
of the summer

Midsummer Day, Midsummer's Day *n* the day
of the summer solstice in Europe. Date: 24
June.

midterm /mid túrm/ *n* 1 the midpoint of an
academic term or term of office 2 the period
midway through a pregnancy —**midterm** *adj*

midway /mid wáy/ *adv, adj* 1 halfway between
two points 2 halfway through a period

midweek /mid weék/ *n* the middle part of a
week —**midweek** *adj, adv* —**midweekly** *adj,
adv*

Midwest /mid wést/ *n* the northern part of the
central United States —**Midwestern** *adj*
—**Midwesterner** *n*

midwife /mid wíf/ (*pl* **-wives** /-wívz/) *n*
1 somebody trained to help deliver babies
2 somebody who helps to create something
—**midwifery** /mid wíffəri/ *n*

ORIGIN *Mid* is an obsolete preposition meaning
'with', and *wife* formerly meant simply
'woman'. A **midwife** is therefore literally a
woman who is with another woman giving birth.

midwinter /mid wíntər/ *n* the middle period of
the winter

mien /meen/ *n* somebody's manner or appearance taken as an indication of character
(*fml*)

Mies van der Rohe /meéz van dər rṓ ə/, **Ludwig**
(1886–1969) German-born US architect and
designer

might[1] /mīt/ *modal v* 1 indicates the possibility
that something is true or will happen o *might
still be alive* 2 prefaces advice or a suggestion
o *You might want to phone first.* 3 indicates
that somebody ought to do or have done
something o *You might have told me!*

SPELLCHECK Do not confuse the spelling of
might and **mite** ('a tiny eight-legged animal'),
which sound similar.

might[2] /mīt/ *n* great power or strength

might-have-been *n* something that might
have happened

mightn't /mī́tn't/ *contr* might not

mighty /mī́ti/ *adj* (**-ier, -iest**) 1 strong and
powerful 2 big and impressive ■ *adv US,
regional* extremely —**mightily** *adv*
—**mightiness** *n*

~~migrain~~ incorrect spelling of **migraine**

migraine /meé grayn, mī́-/ *n* a recurrent extremely bad headache, often affecting one
side of the head

ORIGIN **Migraine** goes back to Greek *hemi-*

kranion, literally 'half skull', the idea being of
a pain in one side of the head.

migrant /mígrənt/ *n* 1 somebody who moves
from place to place 2 a migratory animal
3 *Aus* a recent immigrant —**migrant** *adj*

migrate /mī́ gráyt/ (**-grating, -grated**) *vi* 1 move
from one region or country to another
2 move between habitats in response to seasonal changes 3 move within an organism
or substance —**migration** /mī gráysh'n/ *n*
—**migrational** *adj* —**migratory** /mígrətəri, mī
gráytəri/ *adj*

mihrab /meé rab, meérəb/ *n* 1 a niche in a
mosque pointing towards Mecca 2 a blank
rectangular space in the middle of a prayer
rug that faces Mecca during prayer

mike (*infml*) *n* a microphone ■ *vt* (**miking,
miked**) fit somebody or transmit something
with a microphone

Mike *n* a communications code word for the
letter 'M'

mil[1] *n* one thousandth of an inch

mil[2] *abbr* 1 military 2 military organization (*in
Internet addresses*)

milady /mi láydi/ (*pl* **-dies**), **miladi** *n* a British
gentlewoman or female aristocrat (*archaic or
humorous*)

Milan /mi lán/ city in N Italy. Pop. 1,307,785
(1999). —**Milanese** /míllə neéz/ *n, adj*

milch cow /mílch-/ *n* a source of easy income
(*infml*)

mild /mīld/ *adj* 1 not severe or harsh o *a mild
disagreement* 2 gentle and amiable 3 pleasant
and temperate o *a mild evening* 4 lightly flavoured 5 not dangerous o *a mild earthquake*
6 not containing chemicals that might harm
the skin or clothes ■ *n* a draught beer with
a light taste —**mildly** *adv* —**mildness** *n*

mildew /míl dyoo/ *n* 1 a fungal disease of plants
2 a grey or white fungus on damp walls or
materials ■ *vti* affect or be affected by
mildew —**mildewed** *adj* —**mildewy** *adj*

mild-mannered *adj* gentle and polite

mile *n* 1 a unit of distance equivalent to 5,280
ft or 1,760 yd or 1.6 km 2 a nautical mile ■
miles *npl* a long way (*infml*) ■ *adv* **miles**
emphasizes the degree or extent of something (*infml*)

ORIGIN The **mile** was originally a Roman unit of
distance equal to 1,000 paces. The word
comes ultimately from Latin *mille* 'thousand'.
The mile came to be associated with measurements that derived from agricultural rather
than military practices, and its length varied
greatly over history before it came to be standardized at 1,760 yards.

mileage /mílij/, **milage** *n* 1 a distance in miles
2 the number of miles a vehicle has travelled
3 the miles a vehicle can travel on a particular amount of fuel 4 a travel allowance
paid at a fixed rate per mile 5 the advantage
or usefulness of something (*infml*)

~~milennium~~ incorrect spelling of **millennium**

mileometer /mī lómmitər/, **milometer** n a device in a vehicle for recording the distance travelled

milepost /míl pōst/ n 1 a post on a racecourse one mile from the finish 2 US, Can a roadside post showing the distance to a place

miler /mílər/ n a competitor in a one-mile race

milestone /míl stōn/ n 1 a roadside stone showing the distance to a place 2 an important event in the course of something

Miletus /mə léétəss/ ruined ancient Ionian city in SW Asia Minor, in present-day Turkey

milieu /meêl yö, meel yö́/ (pl -lieus or -lieux /-yöz, -yö́/) n the surroundings that somebody lives in or is influenced by

militant /míllitənt/ adj 1 very actively or aggressively defending or supporting a cause 2 engaged in fighting or warfare —**militancy** n —**militant** n —**militantly** adv

militarism /míllitərizəm/ n 1 the pursuit of military aims 2 the strong influence of military personnel on a government —**militarist** n —**militaristic** /míllitə rístik/ adj

militarize /míllitə rīz/ (-rizing, -rized), **militarise** vt 1 equip or train for war 2 convert for military use —**militarization** /míllitə rī záysh'n/ n

military /míllitəri/ adj 1 of war or the armed forces 2 of the army or soldiers ■ n the armed forces, or its high-ranking officers —**militarily** adv

military academy n a training school for military officers

military police n a police force within the armed forces

militate /mílli tayt/ (-tating, -tated) vi have an influence, especially a negative one, on something

---

USAGE **militate** or **mitigate**? **Mitigate** means 'lessen the impact or degree of seriousness of something undesirable': *how to mitigate the worst effects of the recession There were mitigating circumstances.* **Militate**, usually followed by *against*, means 'have an influence, especially a negative one, on something': *Poor refereeing militated against a satisfactory outcome to the contest.*

---

militia /mə líshə/ n 1 an emergency army of soldiers who are civilians 2 an unauthorized quasi-military group —**militiaman** n

milk n 1 a nutritious white fluid produced by mammals to feed their young 2 a white liquid from a plant 3 a white liquid cosmetic or pharmaceutical product ■ v 1 vti take milk from a cow 2 vt exploit something (infml)

milk bar n a snack bar serving milkshakes

milk chocolate n chocolate made with milk

milk float n a small electric vehicle for door-to-door milk delivery

milking parlour, milking shed n a building for milking cows

milkmaid /mílk mayd/ n a woman who milks cows

milkman /mílkmən/ (pl -men /-mən/) n a man who delivers milk door-to-door

milk pudding n a cooked dessert of milk, sugar, and a grain such as rice

milk round n 1 a milkman's route 2 a recruitment tour of universities made by companies

milk shake n a cold whisked drink made from flavoured milk and usually ice cream

milksop /mílk sop/ n a man regarded as ineffectual (dated insult)

milkweed /mílk weed/ n a plant with a milky sap and seed pods that release silky tufted seeds

milky /mílki/ (-ier, -iest) adj 1 like milk in colour or consistency 2 containing milk 3 cloudy or opaque —**milkiness** n

Milky Way n the galaxy to which the Earth belongs

mill[1] n 1 a flour-making factory 2 a plant or machine for processing raw materials 3 a small device for grinding coffee, pepper, or salt ■ v 1 vt grind grain by machine 2 vt manufacture a product from raw materials by machine 3 vi move around in a confused or restless group —**milled** adj

mill[2] n a million in currency (infml)

mill[3] n a millilitre (infml)

Mill, James (1773–1836) British philosopher and economist

Mill, John Stuart (1806–73) British philosopher and economist

Millais /míl ay, mi láy/, **Sir John Everett** (1829–96) British painter

~~millenium~~ incorrect spelling of **millennium**

millennium /mi lénni əm/ (pl -ums or -a /-ə/) n 1 a period of 1,000 years 2 the thousand-year period of peace on earth prophesied in the Bible on the Second Coming of Jesus Christ 3 a hoped-for utopian age 4 a thousandth anniversary —**millennial** adj

millepede n INSECTS = millipede

miller /míllər/ n 1 a mill-operator 2 a milling machine

Arthur Miller

Miller /míllər/, **Arthur** (b. 1915) US playwright

Miller, Leszek (b. 1946) prime minister of Poland (2001–)

millet /míllit/ n 1 a pale shiny cereal grain. Use: flour, alcoholic drinks, birdseed, fodder. 2 a cereal plant that produces millet grain

Millet /meê ay/, **Jean-François** (1814–75) French painter

milli- *prefix* one thousandth (10 ⁻³) ○ *milligram* ○ *millisecond*

millibar /mílli baar/ *n* a unit of atmospheric pressure equal to one thousandth of a bar

milligram /mílli gram/ *n* a unit of mass and weight equal to one thousandth of a gram

millilitre /mílli leetər/ *n* a unit of volume equal to one thousandth of a litre

millimetre /mílli meetər/ *n* a unit of length equal to one thousandth of a metre

milliner /míllinər/ *n* a maker of women's hats —**millinery** *n*

ORIGIN Milliner originally meant somebody from the Italian city of Milan (a 'Milaner'). In the 16C it began to be used to refer to sellers of fancy goods and accessories of a type made in Milan, including *Milan bonnets*. Eventually **milliner** came to be restricted to makers of women's hats.

million /míllyən/ *n* **1** a thousand thousand **2** a large number *(infml; often pl)* **3** a million units of a currency ■ **millions** *npl* several million people or things —**million** *adj* —**millionth** *adj, n*

millionaire /míllyə náir/ *n* somebody worth more than one million units of currency

millionairess /míllyə náirəss, míllyə náir ess/ *n* a woman worth more than one million units of currency

~~millionnaire~~ incorrect spelling of **millionaire**

millipede /mílli peed/, **millepede** *n* an arthropod with a segmented tubular body on many pairs of legs

milliwatt /mílli wot/ *n* (*symbol* **mW**) an electrical unit

millpond /míl pond/ *n* a pond made by damming a stream in order to create a flow to drive a millwheel

millstone /míl stōn/ *n* **1** a grain-grinding stone **2** a burdensome responsibility

millwheel /míl weel/ *n* a wheel that powers a mill

Milne /miln/, **A. A.** (1882–1956) British writer

milometer *n* = mileometer

Milosevic /mi lóssəvich/, **Milošević, Slobodan** (*b.* 1941) Yugoslavian president of Serbia (1989–97) and the Federal Republic of Yugoslavia (1997–2000)

milt *n* fish semen

Milton /míltən/, **John** (1608–74) English poet —**Miltonian** /mil tóni ən/ *adj* —**Miltonic** /mil tónnik/ *adj*

Milwaukee /mil wáwki/ city in SE Wisconsin. Pop. 578,364 (1998). —**Milwaukeean** *adj, n*

mime *n* **1** acting using only gesture and action **2** *also* **mime artist** a performer who uses mime ■ *vti* (**miming, mimed**) **1** express something in mime **2** mouth words

mimetic /mi méttik, mī-/, **mimetical** /-méttik'l/ *adj* **1** of imitation **2** of mimicry in plants and animals —**mimetically** *adv*

mimic /mímmik/ *vt* (**-icking, -icked**) **1** mock somebody through imitation **2** copy some-

body or the mannerisms or appearance of somebody **3** resemble something, e.g. in style **4** take on the appearance of another plant or animal, e.g. to discourage predators ■ *n* somebody who imitates others, especially for comic effect ◊ See note at **imitate**

mimicry /mímmikri/ *n* **1** the imitation of others, often for comic effect **2** a plant's or animal's resemblance to another species or to its surroundings

mimosa /mi mṓzə, -mṓssə/ *n* a flowering tree whose leaves are sensitive to touch

min. *abbr* **1** minimum **2** minute¹

Min. *abbr* Minister

minaret /mínnə ret, mínnə rét/ *n* a tall slender tower attached to a mosque, from which the muezzin calls the faithful to prayer

minatory /mínnətəri/ *adj* menacing *(fml)*

mince *v* (**mincing, minced**) **1** *vt* chop food into tiny pieces **2** *vi* walk in an affectedly dainty way **3** *vt* use tact in choosing words ■ *n* minced meat —**mincer** *n*

mincemeat /mínss meet/ *n* **1** a chopped fruit and spice mixture **2** minced meat ◊ **make mincemeat of** defeat thoroughly *(infml)*

mince pie *n* an individual fruit pie filled with mincemeat

mind /mīnd/ *n* **1** the centre of consciousness that generates thoughts, feelings, and perceptions and stores knowledge and memories **2** the capacity to think and understand **3** a way of thinking ○ *changed my mind* **4** a state of thought or feeling regarded as usual ○ *out of my mind* **5** the desire to act in a particular way ○ *had a mind to go* ■ *v* **1** *vt* pay attention to ○ *Mind the traffic.* **2** *vt* control ○ *Mind your temper.* **3** *vti* object or object to **4** *vt* temporarily watch over

Mindanao /míndə nów/ island in S Philippines. Pop. 14,536,000 (1990).

mind-blowing *adj* extremely impressive, exciting, surprising, or shocking *(infml)* —**mind-blowingly** *adv*

mind-boggling *adj* mentally overwhelming *(infml)* —**mind-bogglingly** *adv*

minded /míndid/ *adj* inclined to do something

minder /míndər/ *n* **1** a child minder **2** a bodyguard *(infml)*

mindful /míndf'l/ *adj* aware and attentive —**mindfully** *adv* —**mindfulness** *n* ◊ See note at **aware**

mindless /míndləss/ *adj* **1** requiring little or no mental effort **2** purposeless or irrational —**mindlessly** *adv* —**mindlessness** *n*

mind-numbing *adj* exceedingly boring —**mind-numbingly** *adv*

Mindoro /min dóorō/ island in W Philippines. Pop. 282,593.

mind-reader *n* somebody who is able to sense other people's thoughts —**mind-reading** *n*

mindset /mínd set/ *n* a set of beliefs or thought processes that affect somebody's attitude or behaviour

mine[1] *n* **1** an excavated area in the earth from which minerals are extracted **2** the buildings, machinery, and people needed to work a mine **3** an area where there is a mineral deposit **4** a rich source of something o *a mine of information* **5** an underground or underwater explosive device ■ *v* (**mining, mined**) **1** *vti* remove minerals from the earth **2** *vt* lay explosive mines in an area **3** *vt* dig a tunnel beneath something

mine[2] *pron* indicates possession by the speaker or writer

minefield /mín feeld/ *n* **1** an area containing explosive mines **2** a hazardous situation

miner /mínər/ *n* **1** a worker in a mine **2** *Aus* a bird with a loud call that nests in colonies **3** somebody who lays explosive mines

SPELLCHECK Do not confuse the spelling of **miner** and **minor** ('small or insignificant', 'somebody not legally an adult'), which sound similar.

mineral /mínərəl/ *n* **1** an inorganic substance that occurs naturally in the ground **2** a mined substance **3** an inorganic nutritive substance in food —**mineral** *adj*

mineralogy /mínnə rálləji/ (*pl* -**gies**) *n* **1** the scientific study of minerals **2** a profile of an area's mineral deposits —**mineralogical** /mínnərə lójjik'l/ *adj* —**mineralogist** *n*

mineral water *n* drinkable water with a high mineral salt or gas content

Minerva /mi núrvə/ *n* in Roman mythology, the goddess of wisdom. Greek equivalent **Athena**

minestrone /mínni stróni/ *n* an Italian vegetable soup

minesweeper /mín sweepər/ *n* a ship that detects explosive mines

mingle /míng g'l/ (-**gling, -gled**) *v* **1** *vti* mix or be mixed gently or gradually **2** *vi* circulate among people at a party

mingy /mínji/ (-**gier, -giest**) *adj* stingy (*infml*)

mini /mínni/ *n* a smaller version of something (*infml*)

mini- *prefix* small, short, miniature o *minibus*

miniature /mínnichər/ *n* **1** a smaller-than-usual example or copy of something **2** a tiny detailed painting, especially a portrait ■ *adj* smaller than usual

ORIGIN It could easily be assumed that **miniature** is related to forms from the Latin words *minor* 'smaller, less' and *minimus* 'smallest, least'. In fact, **miniature** goes back to Latin *minium* 'red lead'. Red lead was used in ancient and medieval times to make a red ink used in decorating manuscripts. Italian *miniatura*, formed from a verb from Latin *minium*, meant 'painting, illumination', and was particularly used for the small paintings in manuscripts. English adopted this word in the late 16C, and it was immediately broadened to include any small image. The superficial resemblance to words such as *minor* and *minute* contributed to the development of the adjectival use 'smaller than usual', which is recorded from the early 18C.

miniature golf *n* a novelty version of golf with obstacles to avoid or hit the ball through

miniaturist /mínnichərist/ *n* a painter of miniatures

miniaturize /mínnichə rīz/ (-**izing, -ized**), **miniaturise** *vt* make a version of in a smaller size —**miniaturization** /mínnichə rī záysh'n/ *n*

minibar /mínni baar/ *n* a refrigerator in a hotel room stocked with alcoholic drinks

minibus /mínni buss/ *n* a small bus for short journeys

minicab /mínni kab/ *n* an ordinary car used as a taxi

minicomputer /mínni kəm pyootər/ *n* a computer intermediate in power between a personal computer and a mainframe

minim /mínnim/ *n* **1** a musical note equal to half a semibreve **2** a unit of fluid measure equal to approximately one drop

minimal /mínnim'l/ *adj* **1** very small **2** smallest possible in amount or extent —**minimally** *adv*

minimalism /mínniməlizəm/ *n* **1** simplicity of style in art, design, or literature **2** a trend in music towards simplicity of rhythm and tone —**minimalist** *adj*, *n*

minimize /mínni mīz/ (-**mizing, -mized**), **minimise** *vt* **1** reduce to a minimum **2** play down the extent or seriousness of —**minimization** /mínni mī záysh'n/ *n*

minimum /mínniməm/ (*pl* -**mums** or -**ma** /-mə/) *n* the lowest possible, recorded, or permissible amount or degree —**minimum** *adj*

minimum wage *n* the lowest rate of pay allowed by law

mining /mínîng/ *n* **1** the process of removing minerals from the earth **2** the process of laying explosives

minion /mínnyən/ *n* a servile or slavish follower of somebody

mini roundabout *n* a small traffic roundabout, often painted on the road

~~miniscule~~ incorrect spelling of **minuscule**

miniseries /mínni seeriz/ (*pl same*) *n* a short series of TV programmes

miniskirt /mínni skurt/ *n* a skirt with the hemline well above the knee

minister /mínnistər/ *n* **1** a member of the Christian, especially Protestant, clergy **2** a senior politician in a government department **3** a diplomat, especially of a rank below an ambassador ■ *vi* **1** give help to somebody in need (*fml*) **2** perform the duties of a member of the clergy —**ministerial** /mínni steèri əl/ *adj*

ORIGIN A **minister** was originally just a servant or agent of another, a relatively minor person as its origin in Latin *minus* 'less' would suggest. Early in its history, however, it came to refer especially to a functionary of the Christian Church, and in the 16C specifically to an ordained member of the clergy. **Minister** was not applied to a political appointee until the 17C.

Minister of State *n* an assistant government minister

ministry /mínnistri/ (*pl* **-tries**) *n* **1** *also* **Ministry** a government department **2** a government building **3** the work or period of service of a Christian minister **4** ministers collectively (+ *sing or pl verb*)

~~miniture~~ incorrect spelling of **miniature**

mink /mingk/ *n* **1** (*pl* **minks** *or* **same**) a web-toed member of the weasel family **2** the fur of a mink

Minneapolis /mínni áppəliss/ city in SE Minnesota. Pop. 351,731 (1998).

Minnesota /mínnə sṓtə/ state in the north-central United States. Cap. St Paul. Pop. 4,919,479 (2000). —**Minnesotan** *adj, n*

minnow /mínnō/ *n* **1** a small fish used as bait **2** any small fish

Minoan /mi nṓ ən/ *adj* of a Bronze Age civilization on Crete that lasted from around 3,000 to 1,100 BC

minor /mínər/ *adj* **1** relatively small in quantity, size, or degree **2** low in rank **3** low in severity or danger **4** describes a musical scale that has a semitone interval between the 2nd and 3rd, 5th and 6th, and sometimes 7th and 8th notes **5** describes a musical key based on a minor scale **6** not legally an adult ■ *n* **1** somebody who is not legally an adult **2** a musical key or harmony based on a minor scale ◊ See note at **miner**

Minorca ♦ **Menorca**

minority /mī nórrəti, mi-/ (*pl* **-ties**) *n* **1** a small group within a larger group **2** a group with insufficient votes to win **3** a group of people within a society whose ethnic, racial, national, religious, sexual, political, or linguistic characteristics differ from the rest of society **4** the period when somebody is a legal minor —**minority** *adj*

Minos /mín oss/ *n* in Greek mythology, a king of Crete who kept the Minotaur in a labyrinth

Minotaur /mínə tawr/ *n* in Greek mythology, a monster with the body of a man and the head of a bull

Minsk capital of Belarus. Pop. 1,680,000 (1999).

minster /mínstər/ *n* a large or important cathedral or church, usually one originally connected with a monastery

minstrel /mínstrəl/ *n* **1** a medieval travelling musician **2** a member of a troupe of entertainers who wore makeup to make themselves appear black and performed in variety shows (*a form of entertainment now usually considered racist and highly offensive*)

mint[1] *n* **1** a plant with aromatic leaves. Use: food flavouring. **2** a mint-flavoured sweet —**minty** *adj*

mint[2] *n* **1** a place where coins used as currency are made **2** a large amount of money (*infml*) ■ *vt* **1** make coins **2** invent something, especially a word or phrase ■ *adj* in perfect condition

mint julep *n* an alcoholic drink with a mint garnish

mint sauce *n* a sauce containing mint that is traditionally served with lamb

minuet /mínnyoo ét/ *n* **1** a stately 17C French court dance in triple time **2** the music for a minuet

ORIGIN The **minuet** takes its name from the 'small or dainty' (French *menuet*) steps taken in the dance.

minus /mínəss/ *prep* **1** reduced by subtracting a number **2** lacking ■ *adj* **1** showing subtraction **2** less than zero **3** having a detrimental effect ■ *n* **1** *also* **minus sign** a symbol (-) of subtraction or a negative quantity **2** a negative quantity **3** a disadvantage

minuscule /mínnəss kyool/ *adj* extremely small

minute[1] /mínnit/ *n* **1** a unit of time equal to 60 seconds or 1/60th of an hour **2** a very short time **3** a particular moment **4** (*symbol ′*) a unit of measurement of angles equivalent to 1/60th of a degree ■ **minutes** *npl* the official record of what was said at a meeting

minute[2] /mī nyoot/ (**-nuter, -nutest**) *adj* **1** very small **2** insignificant —**minutely** *adv* —**minuteness** *n*

minute hand /mínnit-/ *n* the longer hand on a clock, which indicates minutes

minutiae /mī nyṓoshi ee/ *npl* small details

Miocene /mī ə seen/ *n* an epoch of geological time 23.3–5.2 million years ago —**Miocene** *adj*

MIPS /mips/, **mips** *abbr* million instructions per second

miracle /mírrək'l/ *n* **1** an event regarded as an act of God **2** an amazing event

miraculous /mə rákyŏŏləss/ *adj* **1** regarded as caused by supernatural intervention **2** extraordinary —**miraculously** *adv* —**miraculousness** *n*

mirage /mírraazh, mə ráazh/ *n* **1** an optical illusion of water in the distance **2** something unreal or imagined

mire /mīr/ *n* **1** a bog **2** thick mud **3** a difficult situation ■ *v* (**miring, mired**) **1** *vti* sink or make sink into mud and become stuck **2** *vt* make muddy **3** *vt* involve or entangle in difficulties —**miry** *adj*

Miró /meerṓ, mee rṓ/, **Joan** (1893–1983) Spanish painter, sculptor, and printmaker

mirror /mírrər/ *n* **1** a highly reflective surface or piece of material that reflects an image **2** something that accurately reproduces or depicts something else **3** *also* **mirror site** a copy of a website maintained on a different file server so as to spread the distribution load or to protect data from loss ■ *vt* **1** reflect something in a surface **2** be similar to or reproduce something else **3** maintain an exact copy of a program, data, or a website, usually on another file server

mirror image *n* a reversed image

mirth /murth/ *n* enjoyment, especially accompanied by laughter —**mirthful** *adj*

—**mirthfully** *adv* —**mirthless** *adj*
—**mirthlessly** *adv*

mis- *prefix* **1** badly, wrongly ○ *mishandle* **2** bad, wrong ○ *misdeed*

misadventure /míssəd vénchər/ *n* **1** an unfortunate event **2** accidental death

misalign /míss ə lín/ *vt* position or arrange incorrectly —**misalignment** *n*

misalliance /míssə lí ənss/ *n* an alliance of mismatched partners

misanthrope /míss'n thrōp/, **misanthropist** /miss ánthrəpist/ *n* somebody who hates people —**misanthropic** /míss'n thróppik/ *adj* —**misanthropy** /miss ánthrəpi/ *n*

misapply /míssə plí/ *vt* (**-plies, -plied**) use incorrectly —**misapplication** /míss apli káysh'n/ *n*

misapprehension /míss apri hénsh'n/ *n* a false impression or incorrect understanding —**misapprehend** *vt* —**misapprehensive** *adj*

misappropriate /míssə próppri ayt/ *vt* (**-ating, -ated**) take or use dishonestly —**misappropriation** /míssə próppri áysh'n/ *n* ◊ See note at **steal**

misbegotten /míssbi gótt'n/ *adj* **1** ill-conceived and generally bad **2** dishonestly obtained **3** born illegitimately

misbehave /míssbi háyv/ *vi* (**-having, -haved**) be naughty and troublesome

misbehaviour /míssbi háyvyər/ *n* unacceptable behaviour

misc. *abbr* miscellaneous

miscalculate /miss kálkyoō layt/ *vti* **1** calculate something wrongly **2** make a wrong assessment about something or somebody —**miscalculation** /míss kalkyoō láysh'n/ *n*

miscarriage /miss kárrij, míss karij/ *n* **1** the premature expulsion of a foetus that is too immature to survive **2** the mishandling or failure of an undertaking (*fml*)

miscarriage of justice *n* a failure of the legal system to come to a just decision

miscarry /miss kárri/ (**-ries, -ried**) *vi* **1** lose a foetus through a miscarriage **2** be expelled from the womb at too early a stage to be able to survive **3** fail (*fml*)

miscast /miss káast/ *vt* (**-cast**) **1** give an actor an unsuitable part **2** choose the wrong actor for a part

miscegenation /míssijə náysh'n/ *n* sexual relations, marriage, or cohabitation between people of different races (*offensive when used disapprovingly, as often formerly*)

~~miscelaneous~~ incorrect spelling of **miscellaneous**

miscellaneous /míssə láyni əss/ *adj* **1** composed of varied things **2** each being different —**miscellaneously** *adv*

miscellany /mi sélləni/ (*pl* **-nies**) *n* **1** a miscellaneous collection **2** a collection of miscellaneous writings

mischance /míss cháanss/ *n* **1** misfortune **2** a piece of bad luck

~~mischeif~~ incorrect spelling of **mischief**

mischief /míschif/ *n* **1** naughty behaviour **2** the tendency to behave naughtily

mischief-maker *n* a troublemaker or spreader of gossip

~~mischievious~~ incorrect spelling of **mischievous**

mischievous /míschivəss/ *adj* **1** playfully naughty or troublesome **2** damaging (*fml*) —**mischievously** *adv* —**mischievousness** *n* ◊ See note at **bad**

misconceive /mísskən seev/ (**-ceiving, -ceived**) *vt* fail to understand

misconceived /mísskən seevd/ *adj* resulting from a wrong understanding

misconception /mísskən sépsh'n/ *n* a mistaken idea

misconduct *n* /míss kóndukt/ **1** immoral, unethical, or unprofessional behaviour **2** incompetence

misconstrue /mísskən stroō/ (**-struing, -strued**) *vt* misunderstand or misinterpret

miscount *vti* /míss kównt/ count things incorrectly ■ *n* /míss kownt/ an incorrect count

miscreant /mísskri ənt/ *n* a wrongdoer (*literary*)

miscue /míss kyoō/ *n* a faulty shot in billiards or snooker —**miscue** *vti*

misdeed /míss deéd/ *n* a wicked act

misdemeanour /míssdi meénər/ *n* a minor crime or misdeed

misdial /miss dī əl/ (**-alling, -alled**) *vti* dial a telephone number incorrectly —**misdial** /míss dī əl/ *n*

misdirect /míssdə rékt/ *vt* **1** give somebody wrong directions to a place **2** wrongly address mail

miser /mízər/ *n* **1** somebody who hoards money **2** an ungenerous or selfish person —**miserliness** *n* —**miserly** *adj*

miserable /mízzərəb'l/ *adj* **1** very unhappy **2** very unpleasant **3** contemptible **4** inadequate **5** dirty or squalid **6** *ANZ, Scotland* stingy —**miserably** *adv*

misery /mízzəri/ (*pl* **-ies**) *n* **1** great unhappiness **2** a source of great unhappiness **3** poverty **4** a gloomy person (*infml*)

misfire *vi* /miss fír/ (**-firing, -fired**) **1** fail to fire a bullet or shell properly **2** fail to ignite the fuel mixture in the cylinder properly (*refers to an internal-combustion engine*) **3** go wrong ■ *n* /míss fír/ a malfunction in firing

misfit /míss fit/ *n* **1** somebody who does not fit comfortably into a situation or environment **2** something that fits badly

misfortune /miss fáwrchən/ *n* **1** bad luck **2** an unhappy event

misgiving /miss gívving/ *n* a feeling of doubt or apprehension (*often pl*)

misguided /miss gídid/ *adj* mistaken or inappropriate —**misguidedly** *adv* —**misguidedness** *n*

mishandle /miss hánd'l/ (**-dling, -dled**) *vt* **1** deal with incompetently **2** treat roughly

mishap /míss hap/ *n* **1** an accident **2** bad luck (*fml*)

mishear /miss heer/ (**-heard** /-húrd/) *vti* not hear correctly

Mishima /míshimə/, **Yukio** (1925–70) Japanese novelist

mishit /miss hít/ (**-hitting, -hit**) *vt* hit in the wrong direction or with too little force

mishmash /mísh mash/ *n* a disorderly or confusing mixture

misinform /míssin fáwrm/ *vt* give wrong information to —**misinformation** /missinfər máysh'n/ *n*

misinterpret /míssin túrprit/ *vt* understand or explain incorrectly —**misinterpretation** /míssin túrpri táysh'n/ *n* —**misinterpreter** *n*

misjudge /miss júj/ (**-judging, -judged**) *vti* make a bad judgment about somebody or something —**misjudgment** *n*

mislay /miss láy/ (**-laid** /-láyd/) *vt* lose temporarily

mislead /miss leéd/ (**-led** /-léd/) *vt* **1** inform falsely **2** lead into bad actions **3** lead in the wrong direction —**misleading** *adj* —**misleadingly** *adv*

mismanage /miss mánnij/ (**-aging, -aged**) *vt* manage incompetently —**mismanagement** *n*

mismatch *n* /míss mach/ an unlikely or ill-suited pair ■ *vt* /míss mách/ match or pair unsuitably

misnomer /miss nómər/ *n* an unsuitable name

misogyny /mi sójjəni/ *n* hatred of women —**misogynist** *n* —**misogynistic** /mi sójjə nístik/ *adj*

~~mispelling~~ incorrect spelling of **misspelling**

misplace /miss pláyss/ (**-placing, -placed**) *vt* **1** mislay something **2** place trust or confidence in somebody or something unworthy or inappropriate —**misplacement** *n*

misprint *n* /miss print/ a mistake in printing ■ *vt* /miss print/ print incorrectly

mispronounce /mísspra nównss/ (**-nouncing, -nounced**) *vt* pronounce incorrectly —**mispronunciation** /mísspra núnssi áysh'n/ *n*

misquote /miss kwót/ (**-quoting, -quoted**) *vti* quote somebody or something inaccurately —**misquotation** /miss kwō táysh'n/ *n*

misread /miss reéd/ (**-read** /-réd/) *vt* **1** read inaccurately **2** misinterpret

misreport /míssri páwrt/ *vt* report in an inaccurate or distorted way —**misreport** *n*

misrepresent /míss repri zént/ *vt* **1** give a false account of **2** not represent truly —**misrepresentation** /míss repri zen táysh'n/ *n*

misrule /miss roól/ *vt* (**-ruling, -ruled**) rule a nation badly or unjustly ■ *n* **1** bad or unjust government **2** public disorder

miss[1] *v* **1** *vti* not hit a target **2** *vt* fail to be present at or on time for **3** *vt* not hear, see, or understand **4** *vt* not take advantage of **5** *vt* fail to achieve **6** *vt* manage to escape or avoid **7** *vt* feel sorry because of the absence of ■ *n* **1** a failure to hit a target **2** any failure —**missable** *adj*

☐ **miss out** *v* **1** *vt* omit **2** *vi* lose an opportunity

miss[2] *n* **1** a way of addressing a young woman *(dated)* **2** a young woman **3 Miss** a title given to a young or unmarried woman

missal /míss'l/ *n* a Roman Catholic prayer book

misshapen /miss sháypən/, **misshaped** /-sháypt/ *adj* having an undesirable shape —**misshapenness** *n*

missile /míssīl/ *n* **1** a rocket-propelled warhead **2** an object thrown or launched as a weapon

missing /míssing/ *adj* **1** absent **2** disappeared

missing link *n* **1** a theoretical animal that makes the evolutionary link between apes and humans **2** something required to complete something

mission /mísh'n/ *n* **1** an assigned task **2** a calling or vocation **3** a space vehicle's trip **4** a group of representatives or missionaries **5** a building used by missionaries

missionary /mísh'nəri/ (*pl* **-ies**) *n* **1** somebody sent to a foreign country by a church to spread its faith or do medical or social work **2** somebody who tries to persuade others to accept or join something —**missionary** *adj*

missionary position *n* a sexual position with the man on top facing the woman

mission creep *n* a tendency of military operations to increase gradually in scope and demand further commitment of personnel and resources

mission statement *n* a formal statement of the aims of an organization

Mississippi /míssi síppi/ **1** major river in the United States. It flows southward from N Minnesota to Louisiana, emptying into the Gulf of Mexico. Length 3,770 km/2,340 mi. **2** state in the SE United States. Cap. Jackson. Pop. 2,844,658 (2000). —**Mississippian** *n, adj*

missive /míssiv/ *n* a letter or written message

Missouri /mi zóori/ **1** major river in the United States. It flows from SW Montana southeastwards to join the Mississippi River in Missouri. Length 3,726 km/2,315 mi. **2** state in the central United States. Cap. Jefferson City. Pop. 5,595,211 (2000). —**Missourian** *n, adj*

misspell /miss spél/ (**-spelt** /-spélt/ *or* **-spelled**) *vt* spell incorrectly —**misspelling** *n*

misspend /miss spénd/ (**-spent** /-spént/) *vt* squander time or money

misstep /miss stép/ *n* **1** a wrong step **2** an error in judgment or conduct

mist *n* **1** thin fog **2** condensed water vapour on a surface **3** a fine spray ■ *vi* **1** become obscured by mist **2** become blurred by tears

mistake /mi stáyk/ *n* **1** an incorrect act or decision **2** an error ■ *vt* (**-taking, -took** /-toók/, **-taken** /-táykən/) **1** misunderstand **2** identify incorrectly —**mistakable** *adj*

SYNONYMS mistake, error, inaccuracy, slip, blunder, faux pas CORE MEANING: something incorrect or improper

mistaken /mi stáykən/ *adj* **1** wrong in your opinion **2** based on incorrect information —**mistakenly** *adv* —**mistakenness** *n*

mister /místər/ n 1 a way to address a man *(dated)* 2 **Mister** the full form of 'Mr'

Misti /meésti/ dormant volcano in the Andes, in S Peru. Height 5,822 m/19,101 ft.

mistime /miss tím/ vt fail to do at the correct time

mistletoe /míss'ltō/ n 1 an evergreen bush with white berries in winter 2 a Christmas decoration consisting of a sprig of mistletoe

---

ORIGIN *Mistle* in **mistletoe** is itself the ancient word for 'mistletoe'. The second element means 'twig'. The short and longer forms were used alongside each other in English until the late 17C, when **mistletoe** finally prevailed.

---

mistral /místrəl/ n a powerful wind in S France

mistreat /miss treét/ vt treat badly or roughly —**mistreatment** n ◊ See note at **misuse**

mistress /místrəss/ n 1 a woman with whom a man has a long extramarital affair 2 a woman who owns a pet 3 a highly skilled woman 4 a woman teacher 5 the woman who owns or controls something 6 **Mistress** Mrs *(archaic)*

mistrial /miss trí əl/ n a trial made invalid by a mistake such as an error in procedure

mistrust /miss trúst/ n suspicion or lack of trust ■ vt be suspicious or distrustful of —**mistrustful** adj

misty /místi/ (-ier, -iest) adj 1 covered in mist 2 like mist 3 dim and indistinct —**mistily** adv —**mistiness** n

misty-eyed adj 1 with tears in the eyes 2 sentimental

misunderstand /míss undər stánd/ (-stood /-stood/) vt fail to understand the true meaning, nature, or intentions of

misunderstanding /míss undər stánding/ n 1 a failure to understand or interpret something correctly 2 a minor dispute

misuse n /miss yóoss/ 1 the incorrect or improper use of something 2 cruel treatment ■ vt /miss yóoz/ (-using, -used) use incorrectly or improperly —**misused** adj

---

SYNONYMS misuse, abuse, ill-treat, maltreat, mistreat CORE MEANING: treat wrongly or badly or

---

Mitchell /míchəl/, **Margaret** (1900–49) US writer

Mitchell, Sir Thomas Livingstone (1792–1855) British-born Australian explorer and surveyor

mite[1] n a tiny eight-legged organism related to ticks ◊ See note at **might**

mite[2] n 1 a small child *(infml)* 2 a small amount

miter n, vt US = **mitre**

Mithras /míth rass/ n in Persian mythology, the god of light, truth, and goodness

mitigate /mítti gayt/ (-gating, -gated) vt 1 partly excuse a crime 2 make something less severe —**mitigating** adj —**mitigation** /mítti gáysh'n/ n ◊ See note at **militate**

mitochondrion /mítō kóndri ən/ (pl **-a** /-dri ə/) n a component of a cell that contains DNA and produces enzymes for the metabolic conversion of food to energy —**mitochondrial** adj

mitosis /mī tóssiss/ n the process by which a cell divides into two daughter cells, each having the same number of chromosomes as the original cell —**mitotic** /mī tóttik/ adj

mitre /mítər/ n 1 a Christian bishop's or abbot's ceremonial headdress 2 *also* **mitre joint** a corner joint in woodwork made by joining two pieces of wood that have been cut at 45° angles ■ vt join pieces of wood using a mitre joint

mitt n 1 a mitten *(infml)* 2 a hand covering similar to a mitten 3 a baseball player's padded glove

mitten /mítt'n/ n a glove with two sections, one for the thumb and one for the four fingers

mitzvah /mítsvə/ (pl **-vahs** or **-voth** /-vōt/) n 1 a Jewish religious duty 2 an act of kindness done by or for a Jewish person

mix v 1 vt combine ingredients 2 vi become combined, or be capable of combining ○ *Oil and water don't mix.* 3 vt make something by combining ingredients 4 vt add something ○ *Mix the flour into the water.* 5 vt closely associate one thing with another ○ *mix business with pleasure* 6 vi go well together 7 vi meet people socially 8 vt crossbreed plants or animals ■ n 1 an act of mixing 2 a combination ○ *an intriguing mix of styles* 3 a substance consisting of a number of ingredients from which something is prepared ○ *a cake mix* —**mixable** adj

□ **mix up** v 1 vt mistake the identity of people, or one person for another 2 vt change the order of things 3 vti involve or become involved in something

mixed adj 1 consisting of a mixture or combination 2 with good and bad elements

mixed bag n a diverse group or collection

mixed blessing n something that is both good and bad

mixed doubles n a tennis, table tennis, or badminton match played by two pairs, each consisting of a man and a woman *(+ sing verb)*

mixed economy n an economy with both state-owned and privately owned businesses and industries

mixed farming n the growing of crops and rearing of animals on the one farm

mixed grill n a dish of grilled meats

mixed marriage n a marriage between people of different ethnic origins or religions

mixed-race adj having or involving different racial backgrounds

mixer /míksər/ n 1 a mixing device or machine 2 a nonalcoholic drink such as fruit juice that is often mixed with alcohol 3 a sociable person

mixer tap n a tap mixing hot and cold water

mixture /míkschər/ n 1 a blend of ingredients 2 a number of different things existing or brought together **3** a medicine consisting of an insoluble solid suspended in a liquid **4** a substance formed by combining substances without a chemical reaction **5** the process of mixing things *(fml)*

SYNONYMS **mixture, blend, combination, compound, alloy, amalgam** CORE MEANING: something formed by mixing materials

mix-up *n* a state of confusion, or a mistake

mizzen /mízz'n/ *n* a mizzenmast or its sail ■ *adj* of or used on a mizzenmast

mizzenmast /mízz'n maast/ *n* the 3rd mast from the front on a ship with three or more masts

mk *abbr* mark

ml[1] *symbol* mile

ml[2] *abbr* millilitre

MLitt *abbr* Master of Letters

Mlle *abbr* Mademoiselle

mm *abbr* millimetre

Mme *abbr* Madame

MMR *n* a vaccine against measles, mumps, and rubella

Mn *symbol* manganese

mnemonic /ni mónnik/ *n* a short rhyme, phrase, or other mental technique that aids memory —**mnemonic** *adj* —**mnemonically** *adv*

Mo *symbol* molybdenum

MO, Mo. *abbr* Medical Officer

M.O., m.o. *abbr* modus operandi

Moab /mó ab/ *ancient kingdom situated to the east of the Dead Sea, in modern-day Jordan —**Moabite** /mó ə bīt/ *n, adj*

moan *v* **1** *vi* make a low sound expressing pain or misery, or a similar sound **2** *vti* complain *(infml)* ■ *n* **1** a sound of somebody moaning **2** a sound similar to a moan made by something such as the wind **3** a complaint *(infml)* —**moaner** *n*

moat *n* a ditch around a castle or fort dug for protection from attack

mob *n* **1** a large and unruly crowd **2** a group of people *(infml)* **3** ordinary people, especially regarded collectively as unintelligent or irrational *(infml)* **4 Mob** the Mafia or the world of organized crime *(infml)* ■ *vt* (**mobbing, mobbed**) **1** crowd round somebody or into a place **2** attack a person or animal in large numbers

ORIGIN **Mob** is a shortening of an archaic noun *mobile*, which was itself shortened from Latin *mobile vulgus* 'the fickle or excitable crowd'.

mobile /mó bīl/ *adj* **1** easy to move **2** operating from a vehicle **3** changing from one social or professional class to another ■ *n* **1** a mobile phone *(infml)* **2** a hanging sculpture or decoration that moves with air currents —**mobility** /mō bíllati/ *n*

-mobile *suffix* automobile, vehicle ○ *snowmobile*

mobile home *n* a large transportable caravan that is usually connected to utilities and left on one site

mobile phone *n* a portable wireless telephone

mobilize /móbə līz/ (**-lizing, -lized**), **mobilise** *vti* prepare forces for action —**mobilization** /móbə līzáysh'n/ *n*

mobster /móbstər/ *n US* a gangster *(infml)*

Mobutu Sese Seko /mə bootoo séss e sékô/ (1930–97) Congolese soldier and president of Zaïre (Democratic Republic of the Congo) (1965–97)

~~moccasin~~ incorrect spelling of **moccasin**

moccasin /mókəssin/ *n* a soft leather Native North American shoe

mocha /móka/ *n* **1** a dark-brown strong Arabian coffee **2** a coffee and cocoa flavouring used in baking

mock *v* **1** *vti* treat something or somebody with scorn **2** *vt* mimic as a way of making fun of somebody ■ *adj* **1** imitation ○ *mock leather* **2** done as an act, especially to be amusing ■ **mocks** *npl* practice examinations —**mocking** *adj* —**mockingly** *adv* ◊ See note at **ridicule**

mockery /mókəri/ *n* **1** scorn **2** something ridiculously inadequate

mock-heroic *adj* describes poetry that satirizes the heroic style ■ *n* a verse written in mock-heroic style

mockingbird /móking burd/ *n* a long-tailed greyish bird that imitates other birds' calls

mock-up *n* **1** a full-scale model **2** a preliminary layout of a newspaper or magazine

mod[1], **Mod** *n* a member of a 1960s youth group in Britain who dressed fashionably

mod[2], **Mod** *n* a Gaelic arts festival

MoD *abbr* Ministry of Defence

mod. *abbr* modern

modal /mód'l/ *adj* **1** describes a verb expressing a grammatical mood such as possibility or necessity **2** of musical modes —**modally** *adv*

mod cons /-kónz/ *npl* household facilities *(infml)*

mode *n* **1** a manner or form **2** a style or fashion **3** a machine setting **4** a musical scale that can be played over an octave using only the white keys of a piano **5** the most frequent value in a statistical range

model /módd'l/ *n* **1** a copy of an object, especially on a smaller scale **2** a particular version of a manufactured article **3** something used as a basis for a related idea, process, or system **4** somebody who is paid to display clothing or merchandise in shows or photographs **5** a simplified version of something used for analysis **6** a perfect example **7** somebody who poses for an artist ■ *v* (**-elling, -elled**) **1** *vti* display clothes as a fashion model **2** *vi* be an artist's model **3** *vt* base one thing on another **4** *vt* make something by shaping a material such as clay —**modeller** *n*

modem /mó dem/ *n* a device that connects computers via a phone line

ORIGIN **Modem** is a blend of *modulator* and *demodulator*.

moderate adj /móddərət/ **1** not large, great, or severe o *a moderate portion* **2** not excessive or unreasonable o *a moderate eater* **3** not extreme or radical o *moderate views* **4** neither particularly good nor particularly bad ■ *n* /móddərət/ somebody with moderate views ■ *vti* /móddə rayt/ (**-ating, -ated**) **1** make or become less extreme **2** preside over a meeting or discussion —**moderately** adv —**moderateness** *n*

moderation /móddə ráysh'n/ *n* **1** the state of being moderate **2** the limiting or controlling of something so that it becomes or remains moderate **3** the position or function of a moderator

moderator /móddə raytər/ *n* somebody who presides over an assembly or discussion

modern /móddərn/ adj **1** belonging to the present day **2** of or using the latest ideas, equipment, or techniques ■ *n* a modern person —**modernly** adv —**modernness** *n* ◊ See note at **new**

modern-day adj **1** resembling somebody or something from the past **2** existing in the present day

modernism /móddərnizəm/ *n* **1** the latest styles, tastes, attitudes, or practices **2** modern styles in art, architecture, and literature —**modernist** *n*, adj —**modernistic** /-ístik/ adj

modernize /móddərn īz/ (**-izing, -ized**), **modernise** vti make something more modern —**modernization** /móddərn ī záysh'n/ *n*

modest /móddist/ adj **1** not unduly proud of your own achievements or abilities **2** not extreme or excessive o *a modest income* **3** not showy or elaborate o *a modest dwelling* **4** not overtly sexual —**modestly** adv —**modesty** *n*

modicum /móddikəm/ *n* a small amount

modify /móddi fī/ (**-fies, -fied**) vt **1** make changes to something **2** make something less extensive, severe, or extreme **3** affect the meaning of a word, usually by describing or limiting it with an adjective, noun, or phrase —**modifiable** adj —**modification** /móddifi káy-sh'n/ *n* —**modifier** *n* ◊ See note at **change**

Modigliani /móddil yaáni/, **Amedeo** (1884–1920) Italian painter and sculptor

modish /módish/ adj fashionable —**modishly** adv —**modishness** *n*

Modred /módrid/, **Mordred** /máwdrid/ *n* in Arthurian legend, the knight who killed King Arthur

modular /móddyŏŏlər/ adj consisting of separate modules —**modularity** /móddyŏŏ lárrəti/ *n* —**modularly** adv

modulate /móddyŏŏ layt/ (**-lating, -lated**) vt **1** change the tone, pitch, or volume of a sound **2** alter something to make it less strong, forceful, or severe **3** vary the characteristics of a radio wave —**modulation** /móddyŏŏ láysh'n/ *n* —**modulator** *n*

module /móddyool/ *n* **1** an independent interchangeable unit of a structure or system **2** a self-contained part of a space vehicle

modus operandi /módəss óppə rán dee, -dī/ (*pl* **modi operandi** /mó dee óppə rán dee, mó dī óppə rán dī/) *n* a particular method of doing things

modus vivendi /módəss vi vén dee, -dī/ (*pl* **modi vivendi** /mó dee vi vén dee, mó dī vi vén dī/) *n* **1** a compromise that allows conflicting groups, parties, or ideas to coexist **2** a way of life for a particular group or person

Mogadishu /mogə díshŏŏ/ capital of Somalia. Pop. 982,000 (1995).

moggy /móggi/ (*pl* **-gies**), **moggie** *n* a cat (*infml*)

mogul[1] /mốg'l/ *n* a powerful person, especially in the media

mogul[2] /mốg'l/ *n* a skiing obstacle consisting of a mound of packed snow

Mogul *n*, adj = **Mughal**

mohair /mố hair/ *n* **1** the wool of an Angora goat **2** yarn made from mohair

ORIGIN **Mohair** comes from an Arabic word that means literally 'preferred, select, choice'. It was adopted into English in the late 16C, and began to be assimilated to *hair* during the 17C.

Mohenjo-daro /mə hénjō daarō/ ruined ancient city of a Bronze Age civilization, in modern-day S Pakistan

mohican /mō heekən, mó ikən/ *n* a hairstyle with the sides of the head shaved and a central strip of hair worn sticking up

ORIGIN The hairstyle is named after the deer-hair topknots of Native North American men in illustrations to the novel *The Last of the Mohicans* (1826) by James Fenimore Cooper.

moiety /móy əti/ (*pl* **-ties**) *n* **1** one of two parts (*fml*) **2** among Native South Americans and Aboriginal Australians, one of two divisions of society for ritual and marriage purposes

moiré /mwaá ray/ *n* **1** a wavy pattern on fabric created using engraved rollers **2** fabric with a wavy pattern and reflective finish —**moiré** adj

moist adj **1** slightly wet **2** pleasantly fresh, not dry or stale —**moisten** vt —**moistly** adv —**moistness** *n* ◊ See note at **wet**

moisture /móysschər/ *n* slight wetness

moisturize /móysschə rīz/ (**-izing, -ized**), **moisturise** v **1** vti apply cream or lotion to the skin of the face to keep it from drying out **2** vt make something moist —**moisturizer** *n*

Mojave Desert /mō haávi-/ dry region in S California

mol symbol **mole**[4]

molar[1] /mốlər/ *n* a back tooth

molar[2] /mốlər/ adj **1** of a mole of a substance **2** containing one mole per litre of solution —**molarity** /mə lárrəti/ *n*

molasses /mō lássiz/ *n* **1** the thick liquid residue of sugar refining **2** *US, Can* treacle

ORIGIN **Molasses** goes back to Latin *mel* 'honey'. It entered English in the 16C from Portuguese.

mold *n, vt* US = **mould**

Moldavia /mol dáyvi ə/ region and former principality of E Europe, in modern-day Romania and Moldova —**Moldavian** *n, adj*

molder *vi* US = **moulder**

Moldova /mol dôvə/ country in SE Europe. Cap. Chisinau. Pop. 4,431,570 (2001). —**Moldovan** *n, adj*

moldy *adj* US = **mouldy**

mole[1] /mōl/ *n* **1** a small burrowing mammal with large forelimbs, no external ears, minute eyes, and dense velvety fur **2** a spy within an organization who discloses secret information about the organization

mole[2] /mōl/ *n* a dark raised growth on the skin

mole[3] /mōl/ *n* **1** a massive sea wall **2** a harbour protected by a mole

mole[4] /mōl/ *n* (*symbol* **mol**) the SI unit of amount of substance equal to the same number of elementary units as the number of atoms in 12 grams of carbon-12

ORIGIN The name of the unit was adopted from German, and is a shortening of *Molekul* 'molecule'.

mole[5] /móli/ *n* a spicy Mexican chocolate sauce

molecular biology *n* the branch of biology concerned with the nature and function of biological phenomena at the molecular level

molecular weight *n* the total of all the atomic weights of the atoms in a molecule

molecule /mólli kyool/ *n* **1** the smallest physical unit of a substance that can exist independently **2** a tiny amount —**molecular** /mə lékyoolər/ *adj*

molehill /mōl hil/ *n* a small mound of earth dug up by a burrowing mole

moleskin /mōl skin/ *n* the fur of a mole

molest /mə lést/ *vt* **1** abuse somebody sexually, especially a child **2** bother, pester, or disturb a person or animal —**molestation** /mō le stáysh'n/ *n* —**molester** *n*

Molière /mólli air/ (1622–73) French dramatist

moll /mol/ *n* a gangster's woman companion (*slang*)

mollify /mólli fī/ (-fies, -fied) *vt* **1** pacify somebody who is angry or upset **2** make something less intense or severe —**mollification** /móllifi káysh'n/ *n*

mollusc /mólləsk/ *n* an invertebrate with a soft unsegmented body, usually protected by a shell —**molluscan** /mə lúskən/ *adj, n*

mollusk *n* US = **mollusc**

mollycoddle /mólli kod'l/ (-dling, -dled) *vt* treat in an overprotective and overindulgent way

Molotov cocktail /móllə tof-/ *n* a simple bomb made of a bottle filled with flammable liquid

ORIGIN Molotov cocktails are so called because Vyacheslav Mikhailovich Molotov (1890–1986), Soviet premier (1930–41) and foreign minister (1939–49), ordered their large-scale production after the Nazi invasion of Russia.

molt *vi, n* US = **moult**

molten /mólt'n/ *adj* melted and glowing with heat

molto /móltō/ *adv* very (*in musical directions*)

Moluccas /mə lúkəz/ group of islands in E Indonesia. Pop. 1,741,800 (1998). —**Moluccan** *n, adj*

molybdenum /mə líbdənəm/ *n* (*symbol* **Mo**) a very hard silvery metallic element. Use: strengthening steel alloys.

Mombasa /mom bássə/ port in SE Kenya, on the Indian Ocean. Pop. 465,000 (1989).

moment /mōmənt/ *n* **1** a short interval of time **2** a specific instant or time **3** the present time **4** a short period of excellence (*often pl*) ○ *It's not great opera, but it has its moments.* **5** importance (*fml*) ○ *a decision of great moment*

momentarily /mōməntərəli/ *adv* **1** briefly **2** US, Can very soon

momentary /mōməntəri/ *adj* **1** very brief **2** present or happening at every moment —**momentariness** *n*

~~momento~~ incorrect spelling of **memento**

momentous /mō méntəss/ *adj* highly significant —**momentously** *adv* —**momentousness** *n*

momentum /mō méntəm/ *n* **1** the power to increase or develop at an ever-growing pace ○ *in danger of losing momentum* **2** the speed or force of a forward moving object

MOMI /mōmi/ *abbr* Museum of the Moving Image (in London)

Mon. *abbr* Monday

mon- *prefix* = **mono-** (*before vowels*)

Monaco /mónnəkō, mə naàkō/ independent principality forming a coastal enclave in SE France. Cap. Monaco. Pop. 31,842 (2001). —**Monacan** *n, adj*

Monaghan /mónnəhən/ county in NE Republic of Ireland

monarch /mónnərk/ *n* **1** a king, queen, or other supreme ruler of a state **2** *also* **monarch butterfly** a large migrating orange and black butterfly —**monarchal** /mə naàrk'l/ *adj*

monarchic /mə naàrkik/, **monarchical** /-ik'l/ *adj* of a monarch or monarchy —**monarchically** *adv*

monarchist /mónnərkist/ *n* a supporter of monarchy —**monarchism** *n* —**monarchist** *adj*

monarchy /mónnərki/ (*pl* -chies) *n* **1** a political system in which a monarch rules **2** a royal family

monastery /mónnəstəri/ (*pl* -ies) *n* **1** the residence of a community of monks **2** a community of monks —**monasterial** /mónnə steèri əl/ *adj*

monastic /mə nástik/ *adj* **1** of monks, nuns, or monasteries **2** *also* **monastical** reclusive or austere ■ *n* a monk

~~monastry~~ incorrect spelling of **monastery**

Monck /mungk/, **George, 1st Duke of Albemarle** (1609–70) English soldier

Monday /mún day, -di/ *n* the first day of the traditional working week

ORIGIN Monday is literally the 'day of the moon'. The same name appears in other Germanic languages, and was translated from Latin *lunae dies*, from which Romance forms such as French *lundi* derive directly.

Mondrian /móndri aˈan, móndri aan/, **Piet** (1872–1944) Dutch painter

Monet /món ay/, **Claude** (1840–1926) French painter

monetarism /múnnitərizəm/ *n* 1 the theory that economic changes are caused by changes in the money supply 2 the policy of controlling an economy by making gradual changes in the money supply —**monetarist** *n, adj*

monetary /múnnitəri/ *adj* of money or a currency

monetary unit *n* a country's basic unit of currency

monetize /múnni tīz/ (**-tizing, -tized**), **monetise** *vt* make something the legal tender of a country —**monetization** /múnni tī záysh'n/ *n*

money /múnni/ *n* 1 the amount of coins and banknotes in somebody's possession or available to somebody 2 a national currency 3 an official or unofficial medium of exchange ■ **monies** *npl* sums of money *(fml)* ◇ **for somebody's money** in somebody's opinion ◇ **in the money** having a lot of money

money-back *adj* promising a refund

moneychanger /múnni chaynjər/ *n* a foreign currency exchanger

moneyed /múnnid/, **monied** *adj* 1 rich 2 consisting of or resulting from money

moneygrubber /múnni grubər/ *n* somebody intent on making money *(disapproving)* —**moneygrubbing** *adj, n*

moneylender /múnni lendər/ *n* somebody who lends money at interest —**moneylending** *n*

moneymaker /múnni maykər/ *n* 1 somebody who is good at making money 2 a project or business that makes a lot of money —**moneymaking** *n, adj*

money market *n* short-term trade in low-risk securities

money order *n* an order for a specific amount of money that can be used to make payments

money-spinner *n* a very profitable enterprise or business *(infml)*

money supply *n* the amount of money circulating in an economy

-monger *suffix* seller, dealer, promoter o *fishmonger*

Mongol /móng g'l/ *n* 1 somebody from Mongolia 2 **mongol** a former term, now offensive, for somebody affected by Down's syndrome *(dated)* —**Mongol** *adj*

Mongolia /mong góli ə/ country in Central Asia. Cap. Ulaanbaatar. Pop. 2,654,999 (2001). —**Mongolian** *n, adj*

mongoloid /móng gə loyd/ *adj* an offensive term meaning affected by Down's syndrome *(dated)*

Mongoloid /móng gə loyd/ *adj* 1 of an E Asian racial group in an obsolete classificatory system 2 **mongoloid** an offensive term meaning affected by Down's syndrome *(dated)* —**Mongoloid** *n*

mongoose /móng gooss/ *(pl* **-gooses)** *n* an animal that resembles a ferret and kills snakes

ORIGIN Mongoose was adopted from a South Asian language in the late 17C. It has no connection at all with geese.

mongrel /múng grəl/ *n* 1 a dog of mixed breed 2 any animal or plant of mixed breed ■ *adj* mixed in origin or character *(sometimes offensive)* —**mongrelism** *n*

monied *adj* = **moneyed**

monies plural of **money**

moniker /mónnikər/, **monicker** *n* a name or nickname *(slang)*

monitor /mónnitər/ *n* 1 a closed-circuit television set or viewing device 2 a computer screen 3 somebody who ensures proper conduct 4 a pupil who helps a teacher by being given a special duty 5 *also* **monitor lizard** a large tropical carnivorous lizard 6 a computer program that observes and controls other programs in a system ■ *vt* 1 check something regularly for developments 2 listen to broadcasts or telephone conversations 3 check the quality of transmitted signals 4 watch over somebody to ensure his or her proper conduct —**monitorial** /mónni táwri əl/ *adj*

monk /mungk/ *n* a man who lives in a religious community —**monkish** *adj*

AKG London

Thelonious Monk

Monk /mungk/, **Thelonious** (1920–82) US jazz pianist and composer

monkey /múngki/ *n (pl* **-keys)** 1 a medium-sized primate belonging to the group that includes baboons, marmosets, capuchins, and macaques 2 a mischievous child *(infml)* ■ *vt* (**-keying, -keyed**) mimic *(archaic)*

□ **monkey around** *or* **about** *vi* behave in a silly careless way

monkey business *n* illegal, dishonest, or dubious activity *(infml)*

monkey nut *n* a peanut in its shell *(infml)*

monkey wrench *n* a spanner with an adjustable jaw

Monmouthshire /mónməthshər/ county in SE Wales

mono /mónō/ n monophonic reproduction

mono- *prefix* **1** one, single, alone o *monoculture* **2** containing a single atom, radical, or group o *monoxide*

monochromatic /mónnōkrō máttik/ *adj* having only one colour —**monochromatically** *adv*

monochrome /mónnə krōm/ *adj* **1** created or displayed in shades of one colour or black and white **2** lacking interest or distinctiveness ■ *n* **1** a black-and-white photograph or transparency **2** a piece of artwork in shades of one colour **3** the artistic technique of using one colour —**monochromic** /mónnə krōmik/ *adj*

monocle /mónnək'l/ *n* a vision-correcting lens for one eye

monoclonal /mónnə klṓn'l/ *adj* describes cells or products of cells coming from a single clone

monocotyledon /mónnō kotə leéd'n/ *n* a plant belonging to the group that has a single seed leaf in the seed —**monocotyledonous** *adj*

monoculture /mónnō kulchər/ *n* the practice of growing only one crop in a field or larger area —**monocultural** /mónnō kúlchərəl/ *adj*

monogamy /mə nóggəmi/ *n* **1** the practice of only having one sexual partner or mate during a period of time **2** marriage to one person at a time —**monogamist** *n* —**monogamous** *adj*

monogram /mónnə gram/ *n* a set of decorative initials —**monogram** *vt* —**monogrammatic** /mónnəgrə máttik/ *adj* —**monogrammed** *adj*

monograph /mónnə graaf, -graf/ *n* a scholarly piece of writing on a particular topic —**monographer** /mə nóggrəfər/ *n* —**monographic** /mónnə gráffik/ *adj*

monolingual /mónnō líng gwəl/ *adj* **1** able to speak only one language **2** produced in only one language —**monolingualism** *n*

monolith /mónnə lith/ *n* **1** a pillar of rock standing by itself **2** a large block of building material **3** something large and immovable, especially a long-established organization —**monolithic** /mónnə líthik/ *adj*

monolithic technology *n* a technology used in electronics manufacture in which all circuit components are mounted on a single piece of material

monologue /mónnə log/ *n* **1** an actor's long speech **2** a long uninterrupted speech by anyone **3** a series of jokes or amusing stories told by a comedian —**monologist** /mónnə logist, mə nólləjist/ *n*

monomania /mónnō máyni ə/ *n* an obsessive preoccupation with a single thing —**monomaniac** *n*

monomer /mónnəmər/ *n* a simple molecule that can join in long chains with other molecules —**monomeric** /mónnə mérrik/ *adj*

mononucleosis /mónnō nyóokli óssiss/ *n* a condition marked by a significant rise in the number of atypical white blood cells

monophonic /mónnō fónnik/ *adj* using one channel to reproduce sound

monoplane /mónnō playn/ *n* an aeroplane with a single set of wings

monopolist /mə nóppə list/ *n* **1** a controller of a monopoly **2** a supporter of policies favouring monopolies —**monopolistic** /mə nóppə listik/ *adj*

monopolize /mə nóppə līz/ (**-lizing, -lized**), **monopolise** *vt* **1** have exclusive commercial control of **2** dominate selfishly —**monopolization** /mə nóppə līz áysh'n/ *n*

monopoly /mə nóppəli/ (*pl* **-lies**) *n* **1** a situation in which one company has exclusive control of the supply of a product or service **2** a company with a monopoly —**monopolism** *n*

monorail /mónnə ráyl/ *n* a railway in which the trains straddle or are suspended from a single beam

monosodium glutamate /mónnə sódi əm glóotə mayt/ *n* a flavour enhancer used in the food industry

monosyllabic /mónnō si lábbik/ *adj* **1** describes a statement or answer that is brief and unhelpful **2** containing only one syllable —**monosyllabically** *adv* —**monosyllabicity** /mónnō silə bíssəti/ *n*

monosyllable /mónnō siləb'l/ *n* a word consisting of one syllable

monotheism /mónnə thee izəm/ *n* belief in a single God —**monotheist** *n*, *adj* —**monotheistic** /mónnə thi ístik/ *adj*

monotone /mónnə tōn/ *n* **1** a sound that does not rise or fall in pitch **2** a series of sounds that stay at the same pitch ■ *adj* lacking variety in pitch, colour, or another quality —**monotonicity** /mónnə to níssəti/ *n*

monotonous /mə nóttənəss/ *adj* **1** repetitious and uninteresting **2** uttered in an unvaried tone —**monotonously** *adv* —**monotony** *n*

monounsaturated /mónnō un sáchə raytid/ *adj* describes a fatty acid with only one carbon double bond

monovalent /mónnō váylənt/ *adj* **1** describes a chemical element or isotope with a valency of one **2** containing only one type of antibody —**monovalence** *n* —**monovalency** *n*

monoxide /mo nók sīd/ *n* an oxide containing one oxygen atom

monozygotic /mónnō zī góttik/ *adj* describes twins derived from a single fertilized egg

Monroe /mən rṓ/, **Marilyn** (1926–62) US actor

Monrovia /mon rṓvi ə/ capital of Liberia. Pop. 421,058 (1984).

Monsieur /mə syúr/ (*pl* **Messieurs**) *n* **1** a French title equivalent to 'Mr' **2** a French word used to address a man

Monsignor /mon seényər, -nyawr/ (*pl* **-gnors** or **-gnori** /-nyáwri/) *n* a title for a high-ranking Roman Catholic cleric —**Monsignorial** /món see nyáwri əl/ *adj*

monsoon /mon soon/ *n* **1** a wind system that reverses direction seasonally **2** a period of heavy rainfall, especially during the summer in South Asia —**monsoonal** *adj*

monster /mónstər/ *n* **1** an imaginary or mythical being that is ugly and terrifying **2** somebody who is inhumane and vicious **3** something extraordinarily large *(infml)* ■ *vt* criticize or rebuke harshly *(infml)*

monstrosity /mon stróssəti/ (*pl* -**ties**) *n* **1** a very ugly thing **2** a monstrous quality

monstrous /mónstrəss/ *adj* **1** shocking and morally unacceptable **2** extremely large **3** resembling a mythical monster —**monstrously** *adv* —**monstrousness** *n*

Mont. *abbr* Montana

montage /mon taʼa<u>zh</u>/ *n* **1** an artwork created from a collection of materials and pieces of things **2** the technique of creating a montage **3** a sequence of overlapping film clips

Montaigne /mon táyn, mon tényə/, **Michel Eyquem de** (1533–92) French essayist

Montana /mon tánnə, -taʼanə/ state in the NW United States. Cap. Helena. Pop. 902,195 (2000). —**Montanan** *n, adj*

Mont Blanc /móN blaʼaN/ highest mountain in the Alps and W Europe, in E France, on the Italian border. Height 4,807 m/15,771 ft.

Montcalm /mont kaʼam, moN kálm/, **Louis-Joseph de, Marquis de Montcalm** (1712–59) French soldier

Monte Carlo /mónti kaʼarlō/ resort town in Monaco. Pop. 13,154 (1982).

Montélimar /món tay li maʼar/ town in central France. Pop. 31,344 (1999).

Montenegro /mónta neʼegrō/ constituent republic of the Federal Republic of Yugoslavia, in the southwest of the country. Cap. Podgorica. Pop. 673,981 (2001). —**Montenegrin** *n, adj*

Monterrey /mónta ráy/ capital of Nuevo Leon State, NE Mexico. Pop. 1,088,143 (1995).

Montesquieu /món təskyə, -təskyoo/, **Charles Louis de Secondat, Baron de la Brède et de** (1689–1755) French jurist and writer

Montessori /mónta sáwri/, **Maria** (1870 1952) Italian physician and educationalist

Monteverdi /mónti váirdi/, **Claudio** (1567–1643) Italian composer

Montevideo /mónti dáy ō/ capital of Uruguay. Pop. 1,378,707 (1996).

Montezuma II /mónti zoʼomə/ (1466–1520) Aztec emperor (1502–20)

Montfort /móntfərt/, **Simon de, Earl of Leicester** (1200?–65) English aristocrat and soldier

Montgolfier /mont gólfi ər, moN gólfyay/, **Joseph Michel** (1740–1810) and his brother **Jacques Etienne** (1745–99) French inventors who developed the hot-air balloon

Montgomery /mənt gómməri/ capital of Alabama. Pop. 197,014 (1998).

Montgomery, Bernard Law, 1st Viscount Montgomery of Alamein (1887–1976) British military commander

month /munth/ *n* **1** a major named division of the year in various calendar systems **2** a period of four weeks or 30 days **3** an interval between dates in consecutive months **4** one twelfth of a solar year **5** the time between one new moon and the next ■ **months** *npl* a long period of time

monthly /múnthli/ *adj* **1** happening or produced once a month **2** lasting a month ■ *adv* once a month ■ *n* (*pl* -**lies**) a magazine issued every month

Montpelier /mont peʼelyər/ capital of Vermont. Pop. 7,734 (1998).

Montpellier /mont pélli ər, moN pə lyáy/ city in S France. Pop. 225,392 (1999).

Montreal /móntri áwl/ city in S Quebec, Canada. Pop. 1,016,376 (1996).

Mont-Saint-Michel /móN saN mi shél/ granite islet off the coast of NW France, known for its Benedictine abbey

Montserrat /móntsə rát/ island in the E Caribbean Sea, a dependency of the United Kingdom. Pop. 12,771 (1996).

monument /mónnyŏomənt/ *n* **1** a large stone statue or carving serving as a tribute **2** a famous place or building **3** a carved headstone

monumental /mónnyŏo mént'l/ *adj* **1** huge in size, importance, or intensity **2** of or in the form of a monument —**monumentally** *adv*

moo (**moos, mooing, mooed**) *vi* make the deep drawn-out noise of a cow —**moo** *n*

MOO /moo/ *n* a virtual space in which participants can discuss a topic online. Full form **multi-user domain, object-oriented**

mood[1] *n* **1** a state of mind **2** the general feeling of a group

mood[2] *n* a set of verb forms expressing a particular attitude

moody /moʼodi/ (-**ier**, -**iest**) *adj* **1** tending to change mood unpredictably **2** displaying unhappiness or anger —**moodily** *adv* —**moodiness** *n*

moon *n* **1** *also* **Moon** the Earth's only natural satellite **2** any planet's natural satellite ■ *vi* **1** wander around in a dreamy or listless state **2** bend over and deliberately bare the buttocks *(infml)*

moonbeam /moʼon beem/ *n* a shaft of moonlight

moonlight /moʼon līt/ *n* light from the Moon ■ *vi* work at a second job in addition to a main job, often secretly *(infml)* —**moonlighter** *n* —**moonlighting** *n*

moonlit /moʼon lit/ *adj* brightened by moonlight

moonscape /moʼon skayp/ *n* **1** a view of the Moon's surface **2** a bare deserted landscape

moonshine /moʼon shīn/ *n* **1** illegally made alcohol *(infml dated or humorous)* **2** nonsense *(infml)* —**moonshiner** *n*

moonshot /moʼon shot/ *n* a launch of a spacecraft to the moon

moonstone /moʼon stōn/ *n* a semiprecious translucent variety of feldspar. Use: gems.

moonstruck /moʼon struk/ *adj* **1** in a daze, often because of love *(infml humorous)* **2** behaving in a wildly confused way *(dated literary)*

moor[1] /moor, mawr/ *n* a large wild area of treeless land, covered with bracken, heather, coarse grasses, or moss *(often pl)*

moor[2] /moor, mawr/ *vti* secure or be secured with ropes, cables, or an anchor

Moor /moor, mawr/ *n* a member of a nomadic people of Arab and Berber descent whose civilization flourished in North Africa from the 8C to the 15C —**Moorish** *adj*

Moore /moor, mawr/, **Michael Kenneth** (*b.* 1949) New Zealand prime minister (1990)

moorhen /moor hen, mawr-/ *n* a black water bird with a red bill

moorland /moorland, mawr-/ *n* an area of moor

moose (*pl same*) *n US, Can* an elk

moot *adj* 1 arguable 2 irrelevant 3 legally insignificant because of having already been decided or settled —**mootness** *n*

mop *n* 1 a long-handled tool for washing floors 2 a short-handled tool for washing dishes ■ *vt* (**mopping, mopped**) 1 wash with a mop 2 wipe to remove perspiration

□ **mop up** *v* 1 *vti* get rid of a liquid with a cloth 2 *vt* deal with remaining enemy forces to secure an area after a victory 3 *vt* clear up the final details of a task *(infml)*

MOP *n* somebody who has assets that are nominally worth a million pounds or dollars but that may never be realizable in cash. Full form **millionaire on paper**

mope /mōp/ (**moping, moped**) *vi* be miserable, listless, and full of self-pity —**moper** *n* —**mopy** *adj*

moped /mō ped/ *n* a motorized bicycle

moquette /mo két, mō-/ *n* a thick velvety fabric. Use: carpeting, upholstery.

MOR *abbr* middle-of-the-road *(in radio programming)*

moraine /mə ráyn/ *n* a mass of earth and rock debris left by a retreating glacier

moral /mórrəl/ *adj* 1 involving issues of right and wrong 2 based on personal conscience 3 regarded in terms of what is known to be right or just ○ *a moral victory.* 4 good or right by accepted standards ■ *n* a rule governing behaviour given as a conclusion of a story ■ **morals** *npl* standards of behaviour —**morally** *adv*

morale /mə raál/ *n* the general level of confidence or optimism in a group

moralist /mórrəlist/ *n* 1 a student, teacher, or critic of morals 2 somebody with high moral standards —**moralistic** /mórrə lístik/ *adj*

morality /mə rálləti/ *n* 1 accepted moral standards 2 the rightness or wrongness of something

moralize /mórrə līz/ (**-izing, -ized**), **moralise** *v* 1 *vi* criticize the morals of other people 2 *vt* analyse in terms of morality —**moralization** /mórrə līˈ záysh'n/ *n* —**moralizer** *n* —**moralizing** *n*

Morant /mə ránt/, **Breaker** (1864?–1902) British-born Australian soldier and poet

morass /mə ráss/ *n* 1 an area of soggy ground 2 an overwhelming or frustrating situation that slows progress

moratorium /mórrə táwri əm/ (*pl* **-ums** *or* **-a** /-ri ə/) *n* 1 an agreed halt or period of postponement 2 an authorized delay in meeting an obligation

Morauta /mə rówtə, maw-/, **Sir Mekere** (*b.* 1946) prime minister of Papua New Guinea (1999–)

Moray /múrri/ council area in NE Scotland

morbid /máwrbid/ *adj* 1 interested in gruesome or gloomy subjects 2 gruesome or gloomy 3 of or resulting in illness —**morbidly** *adv* —**morbidness** *n*

morbidity /mawr bíddəti/ *n* 1 the presence of illness or disease 2 the relative frequency of occurrence of a disease

more /mawr/ *adv* 1 to a greater extent, or in a larger number or amount *(forming the comparative of some adjectives and adverbs)* ○ *is more beautiful* ○ *behaved more sensibly* 2 the comparative of 'much' ○ *wanted it more* 3 for a longer time ○ *chatted a bit more* ■ *adv, pron* with greater frequency or intensity ○ *The more you listen, the more you hear.* ○ *are now going to the theatre more* ■ *det, pron* additional or further *(pronoun + sing or pl verb)* ○ *There aren't any more of these.* ○ *No more is expected.* ○ *needs more light* ◊ **more or less** 1 approximately 2 essentially or basically

More /mawr/, **Sir Thomas, St** (1478–1535) English politician and scholar

moreish /máwrish/, **morish** *adj* so enjoyable to eat or drink that you want more *(infml)*

moreover /mawr óvər/ *adv* furthermore or besides

mores /máwr ayz, -eez/ *npl* established customs and rules in a society or group

~~mortgage~~ incorrect spelling of **mortgage**

Morgan /máwrgən/, **John Pierpont** (1837–1913) US financier

Morgan, Rhodri (*b.* 1939) First Secretary of the Welsh Assembly (2000–)

Morgan le Fay /máwrgən lə fáy/ *n* in Arthurian legend, an evil sorceress who was the half-sister and enemy of King Arthur

morgue /mawrg/ *n* 1 a room or building run by a state or local government where dead bodies are kept for autopsy or identification 2 a file of information in a newspaper office, used for reference

ORIGIN The *Morgue* was a mortuary in Paris, where unidentified bodies were laid out. It was first used as an English word in the mid-19C.

MORI /máwri, mórri/, **Mori** *abbr* Market and Opinion Research Institute

moribund /mórri bund/ *adj* 1 nearly dead 2 becoming obsolete —**moribundity** /mórri búndəti/ *n*

morish *adj* = moreish

Morisot /mórri sō/, **Berthe** (1841–95) French painter

Mormon /máwrmən/ *n* a member of the Church of Jesus Christ of Latter-day Saints —**Mormon** *adj* —**Mormonism** *n*

morn *n* a morning *(literary)*

morning /máwrning/ *n* **1** the early part of the day, before noon **2** the period from midnight to midday **3** dawn

morning-after pill *n* a contraceptive pill taken after sexual intercourse

morning dress *n* a man's formal daytime suit

morning glory *n* a climbing plant with showy flowers

morning sickness *n* nausea in pregnant women

morning star *n* a planet seen clearly at dawn

morocco /mə rókō/, **morocco leather** *n* very soft goatskin leather

Morocco /mə rókō/ country in NW Africa. Cap. Rabat. Pop. 30,645,305 (2001). —**Moroccan** *n, adj*

moron /máwr on/ *n* **1** an offensive term for somebody regarded as unintelligent *(insult)* **2** an offensive term for somebody with learning difficulties —**moronic** /mə rónnik/ *adj* —**moronity** /mə rónnəti/ *n*

morose /mə róss/ *adj* having a withdrawn gloomy personality —**morosely** *adv* —**moroseness** *n*

morph[1] *n* one of two or more variant forms of an animal or plant

morph[2] *vti* **1** transform from one image to another by means of computer graphics, or be transformed in this way **2** transform in appearance completely and instantaneously

-morph *suffix* something that has a particular form, shape, or structure ○ *polymorph* —**-morphic** *suffix* —**-morphism** *suffix* —**-morphous** *suffix* —**-morphy** *suffix*

morpheme /máwr feem/ *n* the smallest meaningful unit of speech or writing —**morphemic** /mawr féemik/ *adj*

morphine /máwr feen/ *n* an opium-based pain-relieving drug

morphology /mawr fólləji/ *(pl* **-gies)** *n* **1** the form and structure of organisms, or the study of this **2** the structure of words in a language, or the study of this —**morphological** /máwrfə lójjik'l/ *adj* —**morphologist** *n*

Morris /mórriss/, **William** (1834–96) British artist, poet, and social activist

morris dance /mórriss-/ *n* an English folk dance, traditionally performed by men who wear white costumes and use small bells, sticks, and handkerchiefs —**morris dancer** *n* —**morris dancing** *n*

ORIGIN *Morris* is a contraction of *Moorish*, though the connection between the English **morris dance** and the Moors was probably entirely in the medieval imagination.

Toni Morrison

Morrison /mórriss'n/, **Toni** (*b.* 1931) US writer

morrow /mórrō/ *n* the next day *(literary)*

Morse /mawrss/, **Morse code** *n* a system for representing letters and numbers with short and long signals of sound or light that are printed out as dots and dashes

Morse /mawrss/, **Samuel F. B.** (1791–1872) US inventor and artist. He invented the electric telegraph (1837) and the Morse code.

morsel /máwrss'l/ *n* **1** a small piece of food **2** a small amount of anything

Mort /mawrt/, **Thomas Sutcliffe** (1816–78) British-born Australian merchant and ship-builder

mortal /máwrt'l/ *adj* **1** certain to die eventually **2** human **3** fatal **4** continuing until somebody dies ○ *mortal combat* **5** of death **6** hated ○ *a mortal enemy* **7** intense ■ *adj, adv* adds emphasis *(dated)* ■ *n* a human being —**mortally** *adv* ◊ See note at **deadly**

mortality /mawr tálləti/ *n* **1** the condition of being certain to die eventually **2** the number of deaths that occur at a given time, in a given group, or from a given cause

mortal sin *n* in the Roman Catholic Church, a sin that brings damnation

mortar /máwrtər/ *n* **1** a mixture of cement, sand, and water. Use: in building to hold bricks and stones together. **2** a cannon with a short wide barrel **3** a bowl in which a substance is ground with a pestle

mortarboard /máwrtər hawrd/ *n* **1** a hat with a square flat top and a tassel, worn on formal academic occasions **2** a board for carrying mortar

mortgage /máwrgij/ *n* **1** a loan to buy property that is security for the loan **2** the contract for a mortgage that exists between a borrower and a lender **3** the money borrowed in a mortgage ■ *vt* (**-gaging, -gaged**) give as security for a loan —**mortgageable** *adj*

ORIGIN Mortgage was adopted from French, and means literally 'dead pledge'. The idea is presumably that the property is 'dead' or lost to the mortgagor if the loan is not repaid.

mortgagee /máwrgi jeé/ *n* the lender in a mortgage agreement

mortgage rate *n* an interest rate on a mortgage loan

mortgagor /máwrgi jáwr, -jər/, **mortgager** /máwrgijər/ *n* the borrower in a mortgage agreement

mortician /mawr tísh'n/ *n US, Can* a funeral director

mortify /máwrti fī/ (**-fied**) *vt* 1 shame and humiliate 2 use self-inflicted hardship or pain to control desires and passions —**mortification** /máwrtifi káysh'n/ *n* —**mortifying** *adj* —**mortifyingly** *adv*

mortise /máwrtiss/, **mortice** *n* a hole cut to receive a projecting part to form a joint ■ *vt* (**-tising, -tised; -ticing, -ticed**) 1 cut a mortise in 2 join by means of a mortise and tenon

mortise lock *n* a lock fitted into the side of a door

mortuary /máwrchoŏ ǝri/ *n* (*pl* **-ies**) a room or building where dead bodies are kept until burial or cremation ■ *adj* of death

mosaic /mō záy ik/ *n* 1 a picture or design made with small pieces of coloured material stuck onto a surface 2 the art of making mosaics

Mosaic /mō záy ik/, **Mosaical** /-ik'l/ *adj* of Moses, the Hebrew prophet who, according to the Bible, led the Israelites out of captivity in Egypt

Moscow /móskō/ 1 capital of Russia. Pop. 10,666,935 (1995). 2 city in NW Idaho. Pop. 19,312 (1998).

Moselle /mō zél/ river in NE France and NW Germany. Length 550 km/342 mi.

Moses /mōziz/ (*fl* 14–13C BC) in the Bible, a Hebrew who led the Israelites out of slavery in Egypt

Moses basket *n* a wicker or straw cot

ORIGIN In the Bible, the prophet Moses was described as being placed in a similar basket as a baby (Exodus 29), hence the name.

mosey /mōzi/ (**-seys, -seying, -seyed**) *vi* walk unhurriedly (*infml*)

mosh *vt* dance in a frenzied way to rock music (*infml*)

Moslem /mózzlǝm, mǒzzlǝm/ *n* (*pl* **-lems** or *same*), *adj* ISLAM = **Muslim**

USAGE *Muslim* is to be preferred over **Moslem**.

Mosley /mōzli/, **Sir Oswald Ernald** (1896–1980) British politician

mosque /mosk/ *n* a Muslim place of worship

ORIGIN Mosque goes back to an Arabic word meaning literally 'place of bowing down'. It entered English through Italian and French.

mosquito /mǝ skeétō, mo-/ (*pl* **-toes** or **-tos**) *n* a small slender fly that feeds on the blood of mammals and transmits diseases such as yellow fever and malaria

mosquito net *n* a fine net curtain used as protection against mosquitoes

moss *n* a simple nonflowering plant that inhabits moist shady sites —**mossy** *adj*

Moss, Stirling (*b.* 1929) British racing driver

most /mōst/ *det, pron* greatest in number, amount, extent, or degree ○ *the candidate winning the most votes* ○ *The most I can lend you is £50.* ■ *adv* 1 to the greatest extent (*forming the superlative of some adjectives and adverbs*) ○ *the most expensive* 2 the superlative of 'much' ○ *He likes her most.* 3 very ○ *a most enjoyable day* ◊ **the most** the best of all (*slang dated*)

-most *suffix* 1 nearest to or towards ○ *topmost* 2 most ○ *southernmost*

mostly /mōstli/ *adv* 1 mainly 2 usually

MOT *n* 1 in the United Kingdom, an inspection of a vehicle to test its roadworthiness. Full form **Ministry of Transport** 2 *also* **MOT certificate** a roadworthiness certificate for a vehicle that has passed an MOT ■ *vt* carry out an MOT on a vehicle

mote *n* a speck or particle

motel /mō tél/ *n* a hotel for motorists

moter incorrect spelling of **motor**

motet /mō tét/ *n* a vocal composition based on a sacred text

moth /moth/ *n* a night-flying insect resembling a butterfly

mothball /móth bawl/ *n* a moth-repellent ball of a solid chemical substance ■ *vt* 1 put something off indefinitely 2 take a factory out of operation

moth-eaten *adj* 1 eaten by moth larvae 2 worn-out

mother /múthǝr/ *n* 1 a female parent 2 a woman acting as a parent 3 a woman who is the originator of something 4 the origin or stimulus of something ○ *Necessity is the mother of invention.* 5 **Mother** a title for a nun ■ *vt* 1 look after somebody with care, sometimes with excessive care 2 give birth to and bring up a baby —**motherhood** *n* —**motherless** *adj* —**motherliness** *n* —**motherly** *adj*

motherboard /múthǝr bawrd/ *n* the main circuit board of a computer

mother country *n* 1 the country that colonists have left 2 somebody's country of birth

mother hen *n* a woman who is regarded as overprotective and fussing

Mothering Sunday *n* Mother's Day

mother-in-law (*pl* **mothers-in-law**) *n* a spouse's mother

motherland /múthǝr land/ *n* somebody's country of birth

Mother Nature *n* the forces of nature regarded as a wilful being

Mother of God *n* a title given to the mother of Jesus Christ, especially by Roman Catholics

mother-of-pearl *n* the pearly inside layer of some shells. Use: decorative inlays.

Mother's Day *n* the 4th Sunday in Lent, when people give their mothers cards and presents

mother ship *n* a ship or spaceship that provides services and supplies for smaller ships

mother superior (*pl* **mother superiors** or **mothers superior**) *n* the head of a convent or community of Christian nuns

mother-to-be (*pl* **mothers-to-be**) *n* a pregnant woman

mother tongue *n* the first language somebody learns as a child at home

Motherwell /mútherwel, -wel/, **Robert** (1915–91) US artist

motif /mō teéf/ *n* 1 a repeated design 2 a sewn or printed decoration

motion /mósh'n/ *n* 1 the process or a way of moving 2 a movement or gesture 3 the power of movement 4 a formal proposal put forward for discussion or a vote 5 an item of solid waste emptied from the bowels *(dated; often pl)* ■ *vti* signal to somebody —**motionless** *adj* —**motionlessly** *adv* —**motionlessness** *n* ◇ **go through the motions** do something in a perfunctory or mechanical way

motion picture *n US, Can* a film *(technical)*

motion sickness *n* travel sickness

motivate /móti vayt/ (**-vating, -vated**) *vt* provide with an incentive —**motivated** *adj* —**motivation** /móti váysh'n/ *n* —**motivational** *adj* —**motivator** *n*

motive /mótiv/ *n* 1 a reason or incentive 2 a motif in literature, art, or music ■ *adj* 1 causing motion 2 driving somebody to do something —**motiveless** *adj*

SYNONYMS **motive, incentive, inducement, spur, goad** CORE MEANING: something that prompts action

mot juste /mō zhoóst/ (*pl* **mots justes** /*pronunc. same*/) *n* the right word or words to express something

motley /mótli/ *adj* (**-lier, -liest**) 1 made up of different types that do not combine well 2 of varied colours ■ *n* (*pl* **-lies**) a varied group

motocross /mótō kross/ *n* motorcycle racing over rough ground

motor /mótər/ *n* 1 a machine that creates motion 2 a car *(slang)* ■ *adj* 1 of vehicles 2 motor-driven 3 causing motion 4 of muscle activity ■ *vi* drive in a car *(fml)*

motorbike /mótər bīk/ *n* a motorcycle

motorboat /mótər bōt/ *n* a small boat with an engine —**motorboater** *n* —**motorboating** *n*

motorcade /mótər kayd/ *n* a procession of cars escorting somebody important

motor camp *n NZ* a campsite for motorists

motor car *n* a car *(dated or fml)*

motorcycle /mótər sīk'l/ *n* a two-wheeled motor-powered vehicle ■ *vi* (**-cling, -cled**) ride on a motorcycle —**motorcyclist** *n*

motor home *n US, Can* a large camper van

motorist /mótərist/ *n* a car driver

motorize /mótə rīz/ (**-izing, -ized**), **motorise** *vt* 1 fit something with a motor 2 equip troops with vehicles —**motorization** /mótə rī záysh'n/ *n*

motor neuron disease *n* a disease that causes muscle weakness and wasting

motor racing *n* the sport of racing in fast cars

motor scooter *n* a light motorcycle

motor vehicle *n* any road vehicle powered by an engine

motorway /mótər way/ *n UK* a multi-lane road for fast traffic

Motown /mó town/ *tdmk* a trademark for a music company based in Detroit whose music, consisting of elements of pop, soul, and gospel, was especially popular during the 1960s and 1970s

mottle /mótt'l/ *vt* (**-tling, -tled**) mark something with different colours ■ *n* 1 an irregular pattern of colours 2 a patch of colour

motto /móttō/ (*pl* **-toes** *or* **-tos**) *n* 1 a rule to live by 2 a saying on a coat of arms

moue /moo/ *n* a pout

mould[1] /mōld/ *n* 1 a container into which a molten or liquid substance is poured to make a shape 2 a frame on which something is formed 3 an object made in a mould 4 distinctive character or nature ◇ *a leader in the heroic mould* ■ *vt* 1 make in a mould 2 give a particular shape to 3 influence the character and development of ◇ **break the mould** to depart from established thinking

mould[2] /mōld/ *n* 1 a fungus that causes organic matter to decay 2 a growth of mould on something, or the discoloration it causes ■ *vi* become covered with mould

mould[3] /mōld/ *n* soil that is rich in humus

moulder /mōldər/ *vi* crumble and decay through natural processes

moulding /mōlding/ *n* 1 a decorative strip on a wall or a piece of furniture 2 something made in a mould

mouldy /mōldi/ (**-ier, -iest**) *adj* 1 with mould growing on it 2 stale or unpleasant from age or rot —**mouldiness** *n*

moult /mōlt/ *vi* shed feathers, fur, or skin periodically to allow for replacement with new growth ■ *n* 1 the shedding of feathers, fur, or skin 2 the feathers, fur, hair, or skin that are shed —**moulter** *n*

mound /mownd/ *n* 1 a small hill 2 a constructed pile of something 3 a pile of objects —**mound** *vt*

mount[1] /mownt/ *v* 1 *vt* climb something such as stairs or a hill 2 *vti* get onto a horse to ride 3 *vt* begin a course of action 4 *vt* organize an event or spectacle 5 *vi* increase 6 *vt* put somebody onto or sit on a form of transport 7 *vt* get onto something higher 8 *vi* go up into the air 9 *vt* secure something to something else 10 *vt* put something onto a support or into a position for use ■ *n* 1 a support or holder for fixing something in place 2 an animal used for riding

mount[2] /mownt/ *n* a mountain *(literary; often in placenames)*

mountain /mówntin/ *n* 1 a very high point of land 2 a large pile 3 a large amount *(infml; often pl)*

mountain ash *n* a rowan tree

mountain bike *n* a bicycle for rough terrain

mountain boarding *n* the sport of travelling down hillsides on a board similar to a skateboard but with bigger wheels

mountaineer /mównti neér/ *n* **1** a mountain climber **2** an inhabitant of mountains (*archaic*) ■ *vi* climb mountains —**mountaineering** *n*

mountain laurel *n* an evergreen North American shrub with pink or white flowers

mountain lion *n* a puma

mountainous /mówntənəss/ *adj* **1** having mountains **2** very large

mountain range *n* a connected series of mountains

mountainside /mówntən sīd/ *n* the sloping side of a mountain

mountaintop /mówntən top/ *n* the peak of a mountain

Mountbatten /mownt báttʼn/, **Louis, 1st Earl Mountbatten of Burma** (1900–79) British naval commander and diplomat

mountebank /mównti bangk/ *n* (*literary*) **1** somebody who deceives other people **2** a seller of fake medicines

mounted /mówntid/ *adj* **1** on horseback **2** fixed in place

Mountie /mównti/, **Mounty** (*pl* -ies) *n* a member of the Royal Canadian Mounted Police (*infml*)

mounting /mównting/ *n* a supporting device ■ *adj* becoming greater

mourn /mawrn/ *v* **1** *vti* express or feel sadness at somebody's death **2** *vi* express sadness at the loss of something —**mourner** *n*

mournful /máwrnfʼl/ *adj* **1** feeling sad, or expressing sadness **2** causing sadness —**mournfully** *adv* —**mournfulness** *n*

mourning /máwrning/ *n* a show of deep sadness following somebody's death

mouse /mowss/ *n* (*pl* **mice**) **1** a small rodent with a long mostly hairless tail **2** (*pl* **mouses** *or* **mice**) a hand-held input device for controlling a computer ■ *vi* (**mousing, moused**) hunt mice

mouse button *n* a push button on a computer mouse

mouse mat, mouse pad *n* a surface to move a computer mouse around on

mouser /mówssər/ *n* an animal that catches mice

mousetrap /mówss trap/ *n* a device used to catch mice

moussaka /moo saákə/ *n* a Greek dish of aubergine and minced meat

mousse /mooss/ *n* **1** a light sweet food with a base of whipped cream and egg **2** a foam for setting or styling hair ■ *vt* (**moussing, moussed**) style hair with mousse

moustache /mə staásh/ *n* **1** a line of hair above the upper lip **2** hair around an animal's mouth —**moustached** *adj*

mousy /mówssi/ (-ier, -iest), **mousey** *adj* **1** dull brown in colour **2** timid

mouth *n* /mowth/ (*pl* **mouths** /mowthz/) **1** the organ through which food is taken in and from which sound is emitted **2** the feature of the face that is the visible part of the mouth **3** the place where a river enters the sea **4** an opening in the earth **5** the opening of a container **6** an opening between parts of a tool ■ *vt* /mowth/ say loudly or insincerely ◇ **down in the mouth** looking sad or gloomy (*infml*)

mouthful /mówthfool/ *n* **1** a quantity of food or drink taken at one time **2** a small amount of food **3** a word or phrase that is hard to pronounce

mouth organ *n* a harmonica

mouthpart /mówth paart/ *n* a body part near the mouth of an insect or other arthropod that it uses to gather or chew food

mouthpiece /mówth peess/ *n* **1** a part of a musical instrument, telephone, or other device held to the mouth **2** a person or publication expressing the views of an organization (*sometimes disapproving*)

mouth-to-mouth, mouth-to-mouth resuscitation *n* a revival method in which the rescuer blows air into the victim's mouth and lungs

mouthwash /mówth wosh/ *n* a solution used for gargling

mouthwatering /mówth wawtəring/ *adj* whetting the appetite —**mouthwateringly** *adv*

mouthy /mówthi, mówthi/ (-ier, -iest) *adj* tending to talk loudly or too much (*infml*) —**mouthiness** *n*

movable /moóvəbʼl/, **moveable** *adj* **1** easily moved **2** changing date from year to year ○ *Easter is a movable holiday.* —**movability** /moóvə bílləti/ *n* —**movableness** *n*

movable feast *n* a festival that falls on a different day each year

move /moov/ *v* (**moving, moved**) **1** *vti* change or cause to change position **2** *vti* change your residence, job, or school, or make somebody change residence, job, or school **3** *vi* take action **4** *vi* change your view **5** *vti* improve or progress, or cause something to improve or progress **6** *vi* formally propose action **7** *vt* stir somebody's emotions **8** *vti* sell or be sold **9** *vti* empty the bowels, or be emptied ■ *n* **1** an instance of moving **2** a step in a series **3** somebody's turn to play in a board game **4** a manoeuvre ◇ **get a move on** start doing something right away, or do something more quickly (*infml*) ◇ **on the move 1** busy doing one thing after another **2** going forward, or making progress

☐ **move in** *vi* start living or working somewhere
☐ **move in on** *vt* attempt to take control of
☐ **move over** *vi* move to one side

movement /moóvmənt/ *n* **1** an act of moving **2** a way of moving **3** a collective effort to achieve a social or political goal **4** the moving parts of a clock or watch **5** a self-contained section of a long musical work **6** an act of emptying the bowels ■ **movements** *npl* somebody's activities and whereabouts

mover /moóvər/ *n* **1** somebody or something that causes motion **2** *US, Can* a company or person that moves people's property from one location to another **3** somebody who formally proposes something at a meeting

movie /moovi/ *US, Can n* a cinema film ■ **movies** *npl* **1** the film industry **2** the showing of a film

moving /mooving/ *adj* **1** making people feel emotion **2** able to move **3** in motion (*usually in combination*) ○ *slow-moving* —**movingly** *adv*

SYNONYMS moving, pathetic, pitiful, poignant, touching, heartwarming, heartrending
CORE MEANING: arousing emotion

moving staircase *n* an escalator

mow[1] /mō/ (**mowed**, **mown** /mōn/ *or* **mowed**) *vt* cut grass with a lawn mower or scythe □ **mow down** *vt* kill many people quickly

mow[2] /mō/ *n* **1** a storage place for hay **2** a pile of stored hay

Mozambique /mó̄ zam beék/ country in SE Africa. Cap. Maputo. Pop. 19,371,057 (2001). —**Mozambican** *n, adj*

Mozart /mó̄ts aart/, **Wolfgang Amadeus** (1756–91) Austrian composer —**Mozartian** /mō̄t saárti ən/ *n, adj*

mozzarella /mótsa rélla/ *n* a white cheese used in cooking, especially on pizza

MP *abbr* Member of Parliament

mp3 /ém pee threé/ *abbr* a file extension indicating a sound file that can be downloaded from the Internet

mpeg /ém peg/ *abbr* a file extension for an MPEG file

MPEG /ém peg/ *n* a computer file standard for storing and transmitting digital video and audio. Full form **Moving Pictures Experts Group**

mpg *abbr* **1** miles per gallon **2** a file extension for an MPEG file

mph *abbr* miles per hour

MPhil /ém fíl/ *abbr* Master of Philosophy

MPV *n* a car similar to a van, typically with three rows of seats. Full form **multipurpose vehicle**

Mr /místər/ *n* the customary courtesy title for a man, used before his name or job title ○ *Mr Lee* ○ *Mr President*

MR *abbr* Master of the Rolls

MRI *abbr* magnetic resonance imaging

Mrs /míssiz/ *n* the customary courtesy title for a married woman, used before her name

MRSA *n* a strain of bacteria that has become resistant to antibiotics. Full form **multiply resistant Staphylococcus aureus**

Ms /məz, miz/ *n* the customary courtesy title for a woman that makes no distinction between married and unmarried status

MS *abbr* multiple sclerosis

ms., MS. *abbr* manuscript

MSc *abbr* Master of Science

MS-DOS /ém ess dóss/ *tdmk* a trademark for a widely used computer operating system

MSG *abbr* monosodium glutamate

Msgr *abbr* Monsignor

MSP *abbr* Member of the Scottish Parliament

mss., MSS *abbr* manuscripts

Mt *abbr* **1** Mount **2** Mountain

MTBE *n* an antiknock additive in unleaded petrol. Full form **methyl tertiary-butyl ethyl**

M-theory *n* a theory describing the forces and matter that make up the universe that incorporates existing theories and suggests the existence of 11 dimensions

mu /myoo/ *n* the 12th letter of the Greek alphabet

Mubarak /moŏ baárək, moo-/, **Hosni** (b. 1928) Egyptian president (1981–)

much *adv* **1** to a great extent (*often in combination*) ○ *much-loved* **2** often ○ *don't go there much* ■ *pron, det* great in quantity or extent ○ *Much of the day was spent packing.* ○ *caused much joy* ◇ **as much** precisely that ◇ **(as) much as** although, or even though ◇ **much of a muchness** amounting to practically the same (*infml*)

mucilage /myoóssilij/ *n* **1** a thick water-based glue **2** a sticky plant product

mucilaginous /myoóssi lájjinəss/ *adj* **1** producing mucilage **2** moist and sticky

muck *n* **1** sticky dirt (*infml*) **2** manure **3** rubbish (*infml*) ■ *vt* make something dirty (*infml*) □ **muck about** *vi* waste time (*infml*) □ **muck in** *vi* share work with others (*infml*) □ **muck up** *vt* spoil (*infml*)

muckrake /múk rayk/ (**-raking**, **-raked**) *vi* seek out and expose scandal —**muckraker** *n* —**muckraking** *n*

mucky /múki/ (**-ier**, **-iest**) *adj* (*infml*) **1** filthy **2** rude or obscene —**muckily** *adv* —**muckiness** *n*

mucous /myoókəss/ *adj* of mucus

mucous membrane *n* a moist membrane that lines body cavities open to the exterior

mucus /myoókəss/ *n* a slimy secretion that lines mucous membranes —**mucoid** /myoŏ koyd/ *adj*

mud *n* **1** wet soil **2** defamatory material

MUD /mud/ *n* a virtual space for multiple users. Full form **multiuser domain**

mudbath /múd baathʹ/ (*pl* **-baths** /-baatnzʹ/) *n* a beauty treatment involving immersion in mud

muddle /múdd'l/ *v* (**-dling**, **-dled**) **1** *vt* mix things together in disorder **2** confuse things **3** make somebody confused ■ *n* **1** a confused state **2** a mix-up —**muddled** *adj* □ **muddle through** *vi* succeed despite a lack of organization

muddleheaded /múdd'l héddid/ *adj* **1** unable to think clearly **2** badly thought-out —**muddle-headedly** *adv* —**muddleheadedness** *n*

muddy /múddi/ *adj* (**-dier**, **-diest**) **1** made dirty with mud **2** resembling mud **3** lacking brightness or transparency **4** confused ■ *vt* (**-dies**, **-died**) make dirty or unclear —**muddily** *adv* —**muddiness** *n*

mud flap *n* a protective rubber flap behind a wheel of a vehicle

mudguard /múd gaard/ *n* an arch above a wheel of a vehicle

mudpack /múd pak/ *n* a cleansing facial treatment in which a preparation is smeared on the skin and allowed to dry

mud pie *n* a mass of mud shaped by a child

mudslide /múd slīd/ *n* a destructive flow of mud

mudslinging /múd slinging/ *n* defamation of an opponent —**mudslinger** *n*

MUD virtual *n* a virtual space for a collaborative project

Mueller /múllər, múllər/, **Sir Ferdinand Jakob Heinrich von, Baron** (1825–96) German-born Australian botanist and explorer

muesli /myo͝ozli/ *n* a breakfast food consisting of cereals, nuts, and dried fruits

muezzin /moo ézzin, myoo-/ *n* a man who calls Muslims to prayer

muff[1] *n* a furry cylinder used to put both hands in to keep them warm

muff[2] *vt* **1** fail to catch a ball **2** do something badly

muffin /múffin/ *n* **1** a small cake made on a griddle and usually eaten toasted **2** a small round cake for one person

muffle /múff'l/ *vt* (**-fling, -fled**) **1** wrap something to stifle sound **2** make something less loud **3** prevent something from being expressed ■ *n* a device that muffles sound —**muffled** *adj*

muffler /múfflər/ *n* **1** a scarf worn round the neck **2** *ANZ, US, Can* a silencer on a car exhaust

mufti /múfti, mo͝ofti/ *n* **1** civilian clothes when worn by somebody who usually wears a uniform **2** *also* **Mufti** an expert on Islamic law

mug[1] *n* **1** a large round straight-sided drinking cup **2** the contents of a mug —**mugful** *n*

mug[2] *n* (*slang*) **1** somebody's face **2** somebody regarded as unintelligent or easily duped ■ *v* (**mugging, mugged**) **1** *vt* rob somebody in the street **2** *vi* make faces **3** *vt US* photograph a suspected criminal —**mugger** *n* —**mugging** *n* □ **mug up** *vi* study hard at a particular subject (*infml*)

Mugabe /moo gaabi/, **Robert** (*b.* 1924) national leader and president (1987–) of Zimbabwe

muggins /múgginz/ *n* **1** somebody regarded as gullible (*humorous insult*) **2** a name that people use for themselves when they think they are being gullible (*infml humorous*)

muggy /múggi/ (**-gier, -giest**) *adj* very hot and humid —**mugginess** *n*

Mughal /mo͝og'l/, **Mogul** /mōg'l/ *n* a member of a Muslim dynasty ruling India from 1526–1857

mug shot *n* a photograph of a face, especially one taken by the police

Muhammad /mə hámmid/, **Mohammed** (570?–632) Arabian founder of Islam

Muharram /mə hárrəm/, **Moharram** /mō-/ *n* the 1st month of the Islamic calendar

mujaheddin /mo͝ojəhə deèn/, **mujahedeen, mujahidin** *npl* Islamic guerrillas

mukluk /múk luk/ *n* **1** *US* a large waterproof boot **2** an Inuit sealskin boot

mulatto /myoo láttō, moo-/ (*pl* **-tos** *or* **-toes**) *n* (*dated*) **1** an offensive term for somebody who has one Black and one white parent **2** an offensive term for somebody who has both Black and white parents or ancestors

mulberry /múlbəri/ (*pl* **-ries**) *n* **1** a small purple fruit **2** the tree that produces mulberries

mulch *n* a covering of organic material laid over the soil around plants to suppress weeds or retain moisture —**mulch** *vti*

Muldoon /mul do͝on/, **Sir Robert David** (*b.* 1921) prime minister of New Zealand (1975–84)

mule[1] /myool/ *n* a cross between a horse and a donkey

mule[2] /myool/ *n* a backless slipper or shoe

muleteer /myo͝olə teèr/ *n* a mule driver

mulga /múlgə/ *n* **1** an Australian acacia bush **2** *Aus* a dry area with mulgas as the dominant vegetation

mulish /myo͝olish/ *adj* stubborn —**mulishly** *adv* —**mulishness** *n*

mull[1] /mul/ □ **mull over** *vt* think about something carefully

mull[2] /mul/ *vt* heat and flavour wine, beer, or cider

mull[3] /mul/ *n Scotland* a promontory (*often in placenames*)

mullah /múllə, mo͝olə/ *n* **1** a Muslim scholar **2** a title of respect given to a learned Muslim man

mullet /múllit/ *n* **1** an orange-red Mediterranean fish **2** mullet as food

mulligatawny /múlligə táwni/ *n* a spicy meat and vegetable soup

mullion /múllyən/ *n* a vertical bar that divides the panes of a window —**mullioned** *adj*

multi- *prefix* many, multiple, more than one or two ○ *multimedia*

multiaccess /múlti ák sess/ *adj* allowing several users access at the same time

multicasting /múlti kaasting/ *n* the process of sending data to many network users simultaneously —**multicast** *vt*

multicolour /múlti kulər/, **multicoloured** /-kulərd/ *adj* of different colours

multicultural /múlti kúlchərəl/ *adj* **1** of more than one culture **2** supporting ethnic integration —**multiculturalism** *n*

multidisciplinary /múlti díssə plinəri/, **multidiscipline** /múlti díssəplin/ *adj* involving a range of subjects

multifaceted /múlti fássitid/ *adj* **1** with diverse qualities **2** describes a gemstone with many facets

multifarious /múlti fáiri əss/ *adj* diverse

multilateral /múlti láttərəl/ *adj* **1** involving several parties or nations **2** many-sided —**multilaterally** *adv*

multilingual /múlti ling gwəl/ *adj* of or speaking several languages —**multilingually** *adv*

multimedia /múlti meédi ə/ *n* **1** sound and video on computers **2** the use of various materials and media in art **3** in advertising, the use of all the communications media **4** in teaching, the use of video, film, and music in addition to other methods —**multimedia** *adj*

multimillion /múlti míllyən/ *adj* involving millions of a monetary unit

multimillionaire /múlti míllyə náir/ *n* a very rich person

multinational /múlti násh'nəl/ *adj* **1** operating in several countries **2** involving people from several countries ■ *n* a large company that operates in several countries —**multinationalism** *n*

multiple /múltip'l/ *adj* involving several things ■ *n* **1** a number that is divisible by another **2** a wiring system that gives access to communications lines at various points —**multiply** /-pli/ *adv*

multiple-choice *adj* offering several possible answers

multiple sclerosis *n* a serious progressive disease of the nervous system

multiplex /múlti pleks/ *n* **1** a cinema complex with several units **2** multiple transmission of signals along one communications line ■ *adj* complex ■ *vt* send signals by multiplex

multiplexer /múlti pleksər/, **multiplexor** *n* **1** a device for sending several data streams down a single communications line **2** a film-to-video system

multiplication /múltipli káysh'n/ *n* **1** an arithmetic operation in which a number is added to itself a stated number of times **2** a marked increase —**multiplicational** *adj* —**multiplicative** /múlti plíkətiv/ *adj*

multiplication sign *n* a symbol that indicates multiplication, e.g. x

multiplication table *n* a table giving the numbers from 1 to 12 or 10 and all their multiples

multiplicity /múlti plíssəti/ *n* **1** a great variety **2** complexity

multiply /múlti plī/ (**-plies, -plied**) *v* **1** *vti* combine numbers by multiplication **2** *vti* increase in amount **3** *vi* breed —**multiplicable** /-plikəb'l/ *adj*

multiport /múlti pawrt/ *adj* describes a computer network with several connection points

multiprocessing /múlti prṓ sessing/ *n* the use of several processing units in a single computer

multiprocessor /múlti prṓ sessər/ *n* a computer system for parallel processing

multipurpose /múlti púrpəss/ *adj* with several uses

multiracial /múlti ráysh'l/ *adj* of more than one race or ethnic group —**multiracially** *adv*

multistorey /múlti stáwri/ *adj* with several storeys

multitasking /múlti taasking/ *n* the simultaneous management of two or more tasks by a computer or a person

multitude /múlti tyood/ *n* **1** a crowd **2** a large number (*often pl*)

multitudinous /múlti tyōodinəss/ *adj* **1** very numerous **2** full of variety

multiuser /múltī yōozər/ *adj* used by several people

multivitamin /múlti vitəmin/ *n* a pill containing several vitamins —**multivitamin** *adj*

mum[1] *n* a mother (*infml*)

mum[2] *adj* silent (*infml*)

mum[3] (**mumming, mummed**), **mumm** *vi* **1** act in a masked play or mime **2** take part in masked festivities

mum[4] *n* a chrysanthemum (*infml*)

Mumbai /moõm bí/ port and capital of Maharashtra, west-central India. Pop. 9,925,891 (1991).

mumble /múmb'l/ *vti* (**-bling, -bled**) say something quietly and unclearly ■ *n* an indistinct way of speaking —**mumbling** *adj*

mumbo jumbo /múmbō júmbō/ *n* **1** confusing language, especially technical jargon (*infml*) **2** an offensive term for a religious belief or ritual regarded as meaningless

mummer /múmmər/ *n* **1** an actor taking part in a pantomime, folk play, or mime show **2** a masked partygoer **3** a mime artist

mummify /múmmi fī/ (**-fies, -fied**) *v* **1** *vt* preserve a corpse for burial by embalming and wrapping it in cloth **2** *vti* shrivel, or cause to shrivel —**mummification** /múmmifi káysh'n/ *n*

mummy[1] /múmmi/ (*pl* **-mies**) *n* **1** a body that has been embalmed and wrapped in cloth **2** a naturally preserved body

ORIGIN The name for an Egyptian **mummy** derived from an Arabic word that referred both to an embalmed body and to a substance like bitumen whose exact composition is not known, but which was reputed to have medicinal properties. These ideas seem to have blended to some extent as the word travelled through Latin and French, and **mummy** reached English as a medicinal substance that was supposed to be derived from mummified remains.

mummy[2] /múmmi/ (*pl* **-mies**) *n* a mother (*usually by or to children*)

mumps *n* a contagious disease that causes swelling of the salivary glands (*+ sing or pl verb*)

ORIGIN **Mumps** is in origin the plural of an obsolete noun meaning 'grimace'. The name presumably derives from the contortion of the face caused by swollen glands.

munch /munch/ *vti* chew noisily

Munch /moõngk/, **Edvard** (1863–1944) Norwegian painter

mundane /mun dáyn/ *adj* **1** commonplace **2** of this world —**mundanely** *adv* —**mundanity** /-dánniti/ *n*

mung bean *n* **1** a small green or yellow bean **2** the plant that produces mung beans

Munich /myoõnik/ capital of Bavaria, SE Germany. Pop. 1,244,676 (1997).

municipal /myoõ níssip'l/ *adj* of a municipality —**municipalism** *n* —**municipally** *adv*

municipality /myoŏ níssi pálləti/ *(pl* **-ties***) n* **1** a town or city with its own government **2** the members of a local government ◊ See note at **city**

munificent /myoŏ níffiss'nt/ *adj* very generous —**munificence** *n* —**munificently** *adv* ◊ See note at **generous**

munition /myoŏ nísh'n/ *vt* supply with weapons ■ **munitions** *npl* military supplies —**munitioner** *n*

munitionize /myoŏ nísh'n īz/ *(-izing, -ized),* **munitionise** *vt* process chemical, nuclear, or biological material so that it can be deployed as a weapon

Munro /mən rố/, **Alice** *(b.* 1931) Canadian writer

Munster /múnstər/ historic province in SW Republic of Ireland

Münster /moónstər/ inland port in NW Germany. Pop. 264,887 (1997).

muon /myoŏ on/ *n* an elementary particle with a mass about 200 times that of an electron —**muonic** /myoo ónnik/ *adj*

mural /myoŏrəl/ *n* a painting on a wall ■ *adj* of walls —**muralist** *n*

murder /múrdər/ *n* **1** the crime of killing somebody deliberately **2** something that is very difficult or unpleasant *(infml)* ■ *v* **1** kill somebody illegally and deliberately **2** *vt* destroy or completely spoil *(infml)* —**murderer** *n* —**murderess** *n* ◊ See note at **kill**

murderous /múrdərəss/ *adj* **1** likely to commit murder **2** difficult *(infml)* —**murderously** *adv*

Dame Iris Murdoch

Murdoch /múr dok/, **Dame Iris** (1919–99) Irish-born British novelist and philosopher

Murdoch, Rupert *(b.* 1931) Australian-born US media proprietor

Murillo /myoo rílló/, **Bartolomé Esteban** (1617–82) Spanish painter

murk, mirk *n* gloomy darkness

murky /múrki/ *(-ier, -iest),* **mirky** *adj* **1** dark and gloomy **2** hard to see through **3** difficult to understand —**murkily** *adv* —**murkiness** *n*

~~murmer~~ incorrect spelling of **murmur**

murmur /múrmər/ *n* **1** a continuous hum **2** something said quietly **3** a complaint **4** a sound usually heard via a stethoscope that indicates heart trouble ■ *v* **1** *vti* say something softly **2** *vi* complain discreetly —**murmuringly** *adv* —**murmurous** *adj*

Murphy's Law /múrfiz-/ *n* the principle that if anything can go wrong, it will *(infml)*

Murray /múrri/ river in SE Australia. Length 2,589 km/1,609 mi.

Murray, Sir James Augustus Henry (1837–1915) British philologist and lexicographer

Murray, Les *(b.* 1938) Australian poet and critic

Murrumbidgee /múrrəm bíjji/ river in New South Wales, Australia. Length 1,600 km/980 mi.

muscat /mús kat/ *n* a white grape. Use: wine making, raisins.

Muscat /mús kat/, **Masqat** capital of Oman. Pop. 635,000 (1995).

muscatel /múskə tél/, **muscadel** /-dél/ *n* a sweet white wine

muscle /múss'l/ *n* **1** body tissue that is specialized to undergo repeated contraction and relaxation, thereby producing movement of body parts **2** an organ composed of muscle tissue **3** power and influence **4** power and physical strength *(infml)* —**muscly** *adj*

ORIGIN Muscle goes back to Latin *musculus,* literally 'little mouse'. It seems that the shape and movement of some muscles under the skin reminded observers of a mouse. The same Latin word gave rise to **mussel.**

SPELLCHECK Do not confuse the spelling of **muscle** and **mussel** ('an edible marine organism'), which sound similar.

☐ **muscle in** *vi* get involved by force or against the wishes of others *(infml)*

muscle-bound *adj* **1** with overdeveloped muscles **2** rigid and inflexible

muscleman /múss'l man/ *(pl* **-men** /-men/*) n* a strong man with developed muscles

Muscovite /múskə vīt/ *n* somebody from Moscow, Russia ■ *adj* Russian *(archaic)*

muscular /múskyoŏlər/ *adj* **1** of the muscles **2** strong and with developed muscles —**muscularity** /múskyoŏ lárrəti/ *n*

muscular dystrophy *n* a muscle-wasting disease

musculature /múskoŏləchər/ *n* the arrangement of muscles in the body

muse[1] /myooz/ *vti* **1** think about something **2** say something thoughtfully —**musingly** *adv*

ORIGIN Muse 'think' is unrelated to **muse** 'inspiration' and the **Muses.** It came through French from a medieval Latin word meaning 'animal's muzzle or mouth', probably from the idea of staring open-mouthed.

muse[2] /myooz/ *n* **1** the source of an artist's inspiration **2** an artist's particular talent **3 Muse** in Greek mythology, one of the nine daughters of Zeus who presided over the creative arts

museum /myoo zeè əm/ *n* a place where objects of artistic, historical, or scientific importance are preserved, studied, and displayed

ORIGIN A **museum** is literally devoted to the Muses, who preside over the creative arts. The word first occurs in English in the early 17C as the name of a university building erected in Alexandria in Egypt in the 3C BC. The modern sense appears in the mid-17C.

museum piece n 1 a valuable and interesting object 2 somebody or something dismissed as old-fashioned (infml)

mush[1] /mush/ n 1 pulp 2 sentimental words or ideas 3 radio interference ■ vt US mash —**mushiness** n —**mushy** adj

mush[2] /mush/ interj US, Can a command to sled dogs to move forwards

Musharraf /moo shárraf/, **Pervez** (b. 1943) president of Pakistan (1999–)

mushroom /músh room, -room/ n 1 any of various types of umbrella-shaped fungus, many of which are edible 2 a fast-growing thing ■ vi 1 grow quickly 2 become mushroom-shaped

mushroom cloud n a mushroom-shaped cloud caused by a nuclear explosion

music /myoozik/ n 1 sounds that are made in order to create an effect 2 the art of producing and arranging sounds to create an effect 3 written notation for music ◊ **face the music** deal with a difficult or unpleasant consequence

musical /myoozik'l/ adj 1 of or for music 2 pleasant-sounding 3 good at music ■ n a film or play with songs —**musically** adv —**musicalness** n

musical box n a box containing a mechanical device that plays music

music hall n 1 a type of popular entertainment that consisted of a variety of performances 2 a theatre in which music hall shows were staged

musician /myoo zísh'n/ n somebody who plays a musical instrument —**musicianship** n

musicology /myoozi kólləji/ n the study of music —**musicological** /myoozikə lójjik'l/ adj —**musicologist** n

music stand n a stand for holding a player's sheets of music

musk n a glandular secretion of a deer. Use: perfume manufacture. —**muskiness** n —**musky** adj

musket /múskit/ n a long-barrelled gun of former times

ORIGIN **Musket** came via French from Italian moschetta 'crossbow bolt'. Early **muskets** could fire crossbow bolts as well as bullets. The Italian word was formed from mosca 'fly (the insect)', which also gave rise to moschetto 'sparrowhawk', because the bird's markings were thought to suggest a fly. This word may have reinforced the name for the weapon, as early guns were often named after birds of prey.

musketeer /múskə teér/ n 1 an infantryman who carried a musket 2 a royal bodyguard in 17C and 18C France

muskrat /músk rat/ (pl **-rats** or same) n 1 a large amphibious rodent 2 the fur of a muskrat

musle incorrect spelling of **muscle**

Muslim /moozlem/ n a follower of Islam ■ adj of Islam —**Muslimism** n

muslin /múzlin/ n a thin cotton fabric. Use: curtains, sheets, dresses.

ORIGIN **Muslin** is named after Mosul, a town in Iraq where such fabric was made. The word came into English in the early 17C through French from Italian.

mussel /múss'l/ n 1 an edible marine organism with a blue-black shell 2 a freshwater mollusc whose shell is a source of mother-of-pearl ◊ See note at **muscle**

Mussolini /moossə leéni/, **Benito** (1883–1945) Italian fascist leader

Mussorgsky /mə sáwrgski/, **Modest Petrovich** (1839–81) Russian composer

must[1] (stressed) /must/ (unstressed) /məst, məss/ modal v (**must**) 1 be compelled to do something o must vacate the building 2 be important or necessary to do or be something o must be simple to use 3 be certain that something is the case 4 indicates belief based on the available evidence o They must have left earlier. 5 intend o I must be going. 6 suggests or invites somebody to do something o You must see a doctor. ■ n something regarded as essential ■ prefix absolutely necessary (infml; added to a verb to form a noun or adjective) o a must-see

must[2] /must/ n grape juice before it is fermented into wine

must[3] /must/ n a musty condition

mustachio /mə staáshi ō/ (pl **-os**) n a thick or fancy moustache (archaic or humorous; often pl) —**mustachioed** adj

mustang /mús tang/ n a North American wild horse

mustard /mústərd/ n 1 a spicy condiment consisting of or made from powdered seeds 2 a plant with pungent seeds from which mustard is made 3 a dark yellow colour —**mustard** adj —**mustardy** adj ◊ **cut the mustard** be up to the desired standard (infml)

mustard gas n a poison gas that is an evaporated oily liquid

muster /mústər/ v 1 vti come together as a group, or order military personnel or a ship's crew to come together 2 vt summon up something such as strength or courage 3 vt ANZ round up livestock ■ n 1 a gathering of military personnel or a ship's crew for a particular reason 2 ANZ a round-up of animals ◊ **pass muster** measure up to set standards

must-have n something regarded as essential —**must-have** adj

mustn't /múss'nt/ contr must not

musty /músti/ (**-ier, -iest**) adj 1 with an old damp smell 2 stale —**mustiness** n

mutable /myootəb'l/ adj 1 tending to change 2 capable of change —**mutability** /myootə bílləti/ n —**mutably** adv

mutagen /myootəjən/ n something that in-

creases the rate of mutation of cells
—**mutagenic** /-jénnik/ *adj*

mutant /myoót'nt/ *n* something that has
mutated ■ *adj* resulting from mutation

mutate /myoo táyt/ (**-tating**, **-tated**) *vti* undergo
or cause to undergo mutation —**mutative**
/myoótativ, myoo táytiv/ *adj*

mutation /myoo táysh'n/ *n* 1 a random change
in a gene or chromosome resulting in a new
trait or characteristic that can be inherited
2 something that has mutated 3 the act or
process of changing —**mutational** *adj*

mutawaa /moo taã waa/ *n* in some Muslim countries, a police force whose duty is to ensure
that the population complies with the laws
of Islam

mute /myoot/ *adj* 1 unwilling or unable to speak
2 making no sound 3 not expressed in words
4 not pronounced ■ *n* 1 an offensive term
for somebody who is unable to speak (*dated*)
2 a silent letter 3 a device that reduces or
softens an instrument's tone ■ *vt* (**muting**,
muted) 1 moderate the volume of a sound
2 make something less bright 3 reduce or
soften an instrument's tone —**mutely** *adv*
—**muteness** *n*

muted /myóotid/ *adj* 1 not bright or intense 2 not
loud 3 understated —**mutedly** *adv*

muti /moóti/ *n S Africa* African medicine, especially herbal medicine

mutilate /myóoti layt/ (**-lating**, **-lated**) *vt* 1 injure
severely by damaging or removing body
parts 2 ruin by removing parts —**mutilation**
/myóoti láysh'n/ *n* —**mutilator** *n*

mutinous /myóotinǝss/ *adj* 1 involving mutiny
2 refusing to obey

mutiny /myóotǝni/ *n* (*pl* **-nies**) rebellion against
a legal authority, especially by soldiers or
sailors against their officers ■ *vi* (**-nies**, **-nied**)
participate in a mutiny —**mutineer** /myóoti
neér/ *n*

mutt *n* a mongrel dog (*slang*)

mutter /múttǝr/ *v* 1 *vti* say something quietly 2 *vi*
grumble —**mutter** *n* —**mutterer** *n*

mutton /mútt'n/ *n* meat from a mature sheep
—**muttony** *adj*

muttonchops /mútt'n chops/ *npl* elaborately
shaped whiskers that leave the chin bare

mutual /myoóchoo ǝl/ *adj* 1 felt and expressed
by each person ○ *mutual admiration* 2 with
the same feelings or relationship ○ *mutual
friendship* 3 shared by two people or groups
4 describes a financial company in which the
members constitute the shareholders
—**mutuality** /myoóchoo állǝti/ *n* —**mutually** *adv*

mutualize /myoóchoo ǝ līz/ (**-izing**, **-ized**), **mu-
tualise** *vti* make a business mutual, or
become mutual —**mutualization** /myoóchoo ǝ
lī záysh'n/ *n*

muumuu /moómoo/ (*pl* **-muus**), **mumu** (*pl* **-mus**) *n*
a loose Hawaiian dress

Muzak /myoó zak/ *tdmk* a trademark for recorded background music played in shops,
restaurants, lifts, and other public places

muzzle /múzz'l/ *n* 1 an animal's nose and jaws
2 a restraining device fitted on an animal's
muzzle 3 the end of a gun barrel ■ *vt* (**-zling**,
-zled) 1 put a muzzle on an animal 2 prevent
somebody's free expression

muzzy /múzzi/ (**-zier**, **-ziest**) *adj* 1 not thinking
clearly 2 vague

mW *abbr* milliwatt

MW *abbr* 1 medium wave 2 megawatt

my /mī/ *det* belonging to or associated with me
■ *interj* expresses sudden emotion

myalgia /mī álji ǝ/ *n* muscle pain —**myalgic** *adj*

Myanmar /mī ǝn maar, myán maar/ country in
Southeast Asia. Cap. Yangon. Pop.
41,994,678 (2001).

mycelium /mī seéli ǝm/ (*pl* **-a** /-li ǝ/) *n* the body
of a fungus —**mycelial** *adj*

Mycenae /mī seé nee/ ancient Greek city
—**Mycenaean** /míssǝ neé ǝn/ *n*, *adj*

mycology /mī kóllǝji/ *n* 1 the study of fungi 2 the
fungi of a particular area —**mycological**
/míkǝ lójjikl/ *adj* —**mycologist** *n*

mycotoxin /míkō tóksin/ *n* a fungal poison

myelin /mí ǝlin/ *n* the material that surrounds
nerve cells

myeloma /mí ǝ lōmǝ/ (*pl* **-mas** *or* **-mata** /-mǝtǝ/) *n*
a malignant tumour of the bone marrow

mynah /mínǝ/, **mynah bird**, **myna**, **myna bird** *n*
a bird of the starling family, some of which
are capable of imitating human speech

myopia /mī ōpi ǝ/ *n* 1 short-sightedness 2 lack
of foresight —**myopic** /mī óppik/ *adj*

myriad /mírri ǝd/ *adj* 1 too numerous to count
2 consisting of many different elements ■ *n*
a large number ○ *a myriad of stars*

myrrh /mur/ *n* an aromatic resinous gum. Use:
in perfume, incense, medicinal preparations.

myrtle /múrt'l/ *n* an evergreen tree with blue-
black berries

myself /mī sélf/ *pron* 1 refers to me as the subject
of the verb ○ *I hurt myself.* 2 emphasizes or
clarifies that I am being referred to ○ *I saw it
myself.* 3 shows that I am alone or unaided
○ *sitting by myself* 4 my normal self ○ *I'm not
myself today.*

Mysore /mī sáwr/ city in S India. Pop. 480,692
(1991).

mysterious /mi steéri ǝss/ *adj* involving or full
of mystery —**mysteriously** *adv* —**mys-
teriousness** *n*

~~mysterous~~ incorrect spelling of **mysterious**

mystery /místǝri/ (*pl* **-ies**) *n* 1 a puzzling event
or situation 2 an unknown person or thing
3 a story about a puzzling event, especially
an unsolved crime 4 something knowable
only by divine revelation 5 *also* **mystery play**
a medieval drama based on the life of Jesus
Christ

mystery tour *n* an excursion to an undisclosed
destination

mystic /místik/ *n* a follower of mysticism ■ *adj*
mystical

mystical /místik'l/ *adj* 1 with a divine meaning
2 of mysticism 3 with a supernatural sig-

nificance —**mystically** adv —**mysticalness** n

mysticism /místissizəm/ n 1 belief in intuitive spiritual revelation 2 a system of religious belief followed in order to achieve personal union with the divine

mystify /místi fì/ (**-fies, -fied**) vt 1 puzzle greatly 2 make mysterious —**mystification** /místifi káysh'n/ n —**mystifying** adj —**mystifyingly** adv

mystique /mi steék/ n a mysterious quality

myth /mith/ n 1 an ancient story about heroes or supernatural beings 2 myths collectively 3 a symbolic character or story 4 a fictitious person or thing

mythical /míthik'l/, **mythic** /míthik/ adj 1 of myths 2 imaginary —**mythically** adv

mythologize /mi thóllə jīz/ (**-gizing, -gized**), **mythologise** v 1 vt make into a myth 2 vi create myths —**mythologization** /mi thóllə jī záysh'n/ n

mythology /mi thóllə ji/ (pl **-gies**) n 1 the body of myths belonging to a particular culture 2 myths collectively —**mythological** /mithə lójjik'l/ adj —**mythologist** n

myxomatosis /míksəmə tóssiss/ n a highly infectious viral disease of rabbits

N

n[1] /en/ (pl **n's**), **N** (pl **N's** or **Ns**) n the 14th letter of the English alphabet

n[2] n an indefinite whole number

n[3] symbol neutron

N[1] symbol nitrogen

N[2] abbr 1 neutral (on gear sticks) 2 north 3 northern

Na symbol sodium

n/a abbr not applicable

NAAFI /náffi/, **Naafi** n 1 an organization supplying food and goods for forces personnel. Full form **Navy, Army, and Air Force Institutes** 2 (pl **NAAFIs** or **Naafis**) a canteen or shop provided by the NAAFI

naan n FOOD = **nan**

nab /nab/ (**nabbing, nabbed**) vt (infml) 1 grab something 2 catch and arrest a criminal or fugitive

nabob /náy bob/ n a European person who made a fortune in India

Nabokov /nə bók of, -bók-, nábbə kof/, **Vladimir** (1899–1977) Russian-born US writer

nachos /náchōz/ npl a hot dish of tortilla chips covered in cheese or salsa

nacre /náykər/ n mother-of-pearl

nadir /náy deer, nád eer/ n 1 the lowest point in something, e.g. somebody's life 2 a point on the celestial sphere that is directly opposite the zenith

ORIGIN **Nadir** derives from an Arabic word meaning 'opposite'. The full form from which it was shortened was an astronomical term, 'opposite the zenith'.

naevus /neévəss/ (pl **-i** /-ī, -ee/) n a birthmark

naff /naf/ adj unstylish (infml)

nag[1] v (**nagging, nagged**) 1 vti repeatedly ask somebody to do something 2 vti keep criticizing somebody 3 vi be persistently painful or bothersome ■ n a person regarded as somebody who nags (insult) —**nagging** n —**naggingly** adv ◊ See note at **complain**

nag[2] n an old horse

Nagasaki /nággə saáki/ city on W Kyushu, Japan. Pop. 423,021 (2000).

Nagoya /na góy ə/ city on S Honshu, Japan. Pop. 2,101,877 (2000).

Nagpur /nag poór/ city in central India. Pop. 1,624,752 (1991).

naiad /nī ad/ (pl **-ads** or **-ades** /nī ədeez/) n 1 in Greek mythology, a water nymph 2 an aquatic larva

nail /nayl/ n 1 a short pointed metal rod hammered into a surface to fix something 2 the horny covering on the end of a finger or toe 3 a claw ■ vt 1 fasten, attach, or secure something with nails 2 catch or convict a guilty person (infml) ○ nailed him for insider trading 3 expose an untruth (infml) 4 US establish or achieve something precisely or conclusively (infml) ○ nailed the jump —**nailer** n ◊ **hit the nail on the head** be absolutely correct

□ **nail down** v 1 vt to make somebody be definite about something 2 establish or agree something clearly and conclusively

nailbrush /náyl brush/ n a brush for cleaning fingernails

nail clippers npl a tool for trimming fingernails and toenails

nail file n a small file for fingernails and toenails

nail polish, nail varnish n lacquer to decorate fingernails and toenails

nail scissors npl small scissors for trimming fingernails

Naipaul /nī pawl/, **V. S.** (b. 1932) Trinidadianborn British novelist

naira /nírə/ n the main unit of Nigerian currency

Nairobi /nī róbi/ capital of Kenya. Pop. 1,810,000 (1995).

naive /nī eév/, **naïve** adj 1 with an extremely simple and trusting view of the world 2 not shrewd or sophisticated 3 in art, rejecting sophisticated techniques —**naively** adv

naked /náykid/ adj 1 without clothing 2 lacking the usual covering 3 not concealed ○ naked aggression 4 unadorned ○ the naked truth —**nakedly** adv —**nakedness** n

SYNONYMS **naked, bare, nude, undressed, unclothed** CORE MEANING: devoid of clothes or covering

naked eye *n* unaided vision

nakfa /nák fə/ *n* the main unit of Eritrean currency

N. Am. *abbr* **1** North America **2** North American

namaste /númmə stay/, **namaskar** /nummə skaàr/ *n* a Hindu gesture of greeting or farewell involving a bow with the palms of the hands together at chest height

Namatjira /námmət jeèrə/, **Albert** (1902–59) Australian Aboriginal painter

namby-pamby /námbi pámbi/ *adj* feeble and lacking strength of character (*infml; sometimes offensive*) **—namby-pamby** *n*

> **ORIGIN Namby-pamby** was an insulting nickname given to the English poet Ambrose Philips (1674–1749), playing on his first name. Philips was noted for feebly sentimental pastorals, which were ridiculed by the author Henry Carey in *Namby Pamby* (1726). The name was again publicly used by Alexander Pope in his poem *The Dunciad*. The generalized use first appears in the phrase 'namb-pamby style', attributed to Jonathan Swift, who died in 1745.

name *n* **1** what somebody or something is called **2** an uncomplimentary description ○ *called him names* **3** a reputation ○ *made a name for herself as a designer* **4** a famous person ■ *vt* (**naming, named**) **1** give a name to **2** identify by name **3** decide on and specify ○ *name the day* **—namable** *adj* ◇ **in the name of 1** by the authority of **2** for the sake of ◇ **name and shame** reveal the name of an offending person or organization in order to cause embarrassment and provoke an improvement ◇ **the name of the game** what something is all about (*infml*) ◇ **to somebody's name** credited or belonging to somebody

name-calling *n* calling somebody abusive names

name day *n* the feast day of the saint after whom somebody is named

name-dropping *n* the practice of mentioning the names of famous acquaintances **—name-drop** *vi* **—name-dropper** *n*

nameless /náymləss/ *adj* **1** lacking a name **2** anonymous **3** indescribable ○ *nameless fears* **4** too unpleasant or disgusting to describe **—namelessness** *n*

namely /náymli/ *adv* specifically

nameplate /náym playt/ *n* a plaque marked with somebody's name

namesake /náym sayk/ *n* somebody with the same name as another person

Namibia /nə míbbi ə/ country in SW Africa. Cap. Windhoek. Pop. 1,797,677 (2001). **—Namibian** *n, adj*

nan /naan, nan/, **naan** *n* a flat South Asian bread

Nanak /naànək/, **Guru Nanak** (1469–1539) Indian religious leader who founded Sikhism

Nanchang /nan chúng/ capital of **Jiangxi Province**, SE China. Pop. 1,410,000 (1995).

NAND /nand/, **NAND gate** *n* a type of logical operator used in computers. Full form **not and**

Nanga Parbat /núng gə paàr bat/ mountain in the W Himalaya range, in NW Kashmir. Height 8,125 m/26,657 ft.

Nanjing /nán jíng/ capital of **Jiangsu Province**, E China, on the River Yangtze. Pop. 2,960,000 (1995).

Nanning /nán níng/ capital of **Guangxi Zhuangzu Autonomous Region**, SE China. Pop. 1,370,000 (1995).

nanny /nánni/, **nannie** *n* (*pl* **-nies**) somebody employed to take care of a family's children ■ *vt* (**-nies, -nied**) be fussy and overprotective (*disapproving*)

nanny goat *n* a female goat

nanny state *n* a government regarded as interfering and patronizing

nano- *prefix* **1** extremely small ○ *nanotechnology* **2** one thousand millionth (10^{-9}) ○ *nanosecond*

nanosecond /nánnō sekənd/ *n* one billionth of a second

nanotechnology /nánnō tek nólləji/ (*pl* **-gies**) *n* the technology used to build microscopic devices

Nansen /nánss'n/, **Fridtjof** (1861–1930) Norwegian explorer

Nantes /naant, naaNt/ city in W France, on the Loire. Pop. 270,251 (1999).

Nantucket /nan túkət/ island in SE Massachusetts, on **Nantucket Sound**. Pop. 3,124 (1996).

nap[1] *n* a short sleep ■ *vi* (**napping, napped**) **1** sleep lightly **2** be off guard

nap[2] *n* the pile on a fabric ■ *vt* (**napping, napped**) raise the pile of a fabric by brushing it

nap[3] *n* **1** a card game similar to whist **2** a bid in nap **3** a good racing tip ■ *vt* (**napping, napped**) name the likely winner of a race

napalm /náy paam, ná-/ *n* **1** a highly flammable jelly. Use: in flame-throwers and fire bombs. **2** an aluminium-based thickening agent. Use: manufacture of jellied petrol. ■ *vt* attack with napalm

Napa Valley /náppə-/ region of west-central California, famous for its vineyards

nape /nayp/ *n* the back of the neck

Napier /náypi ər/, **John** (1550–1617) Scottish mathematician who invented logarithms

napkin /nápkin/ *n* **1** a piece of cloth for protecting clothes and wiping the mouth during eating **2** a baby's nappy (*fml*)

Naples /náyp'lz/ capital of Campania Region, S Italy, on the **Bay of Naples**. Pop. 1,020,120 (1999).

Napoleon I /nə pốli ən/ (1769–1821) emperor of

Napoleon I, emperor of the French: Portrait (1807)
by Andrea Appiani

the French (1804–14, 1815) —**Napoleonic** /nə póli ónnik/ *adj*

Napoleon III (1808–73) emperor of the French (1852–70)

nappy /náppi/ (*pl* **-pies**) *n* an absorbent towel worn around a baby's bottom to absorb urine and faeces

nappy rash *n* a rash on a baby's bottom

~~narative~~ incorrect spelling of **narrative**

Narayan /nə ríyən/, **R. K.** (1906–2001) Indian writer

narcissism /naárssissizəm/ *n* 1 excessive self-admiration 2 a personality disorder marked by an excessive need for admiration —**narcissist** *n* —**narcissistic** /nárssi sístik/ *adj*

narcissus /naar síssəss/ (*pl* **-suses** *or* **-si** /-sī/) *n* a spring plant with yellow or white flowers

narcolepsy /naárkō lepsi/ *n* a condition characterized by uncontrollable bouts of deep sleep —**narcoleptic** /naárkō léptik/ *adj, n*

narcosis /naar kóssiss/ *n* drug-induced stupor

narcotic /naar kóttik/ *n* 1 a drug that reduces pain and induces sleep or stupor 2 *US* an illegal drug ■ *adj* causing sleep, stupor, or altered mental states through chemical properties

nark /naark/ *v* 1 *vt* annoy (*infml*) 2 *vi* act as an informer (*slang*) ■ *n* a police informer (*slang*)

narrate /nə ráyt/ (**-rating**, **-rated**) *vt* 1 tell a story 2 give the commentary on a film or television programme —**narration** *n* —**narrational** *adj* —**narrator** *n*

narrative /nárrətiv/ *n* 1 a story 2 the process of narrating ■ *adj* 1 telling a story 2 of narration

narrow /nárrō/ *adj* 1 small in width 2 limited in size or scope ○ *a narrow range of options* 3 limited in outlook ○ *a narrow view of events* 4 just enough for success ○ *a narrow escape* 5 meagre ■ *n* a narrow passage ■ *vti also* **narrow down** make or become narrow in width, limit, or scope —**narrowly** *adv* —**narrowness** *n*

narrowband /nárrō band/ *adj* using a narrow band of broadcasting frequencies

narrowboat /nárrō bōt/ *n* a canal barge with a width under 2.1 m/7 ft

narrow gauge *n* 1 a distance between the two rails of a railway track under 143.5 cm/4 ft 8.5 in 2 a track or train with a narrow gauge —**narrow-gauge** *adj*

narrow-minded *adj* with a limited and often prejudiced outlook —**narrow-mindedly** *adv* —**narrow-mindedness** *n*

narrows /nárrōz/ *n* a narrow stretch of river or sea (+ *sing or pl verb*)

nartjie /naárchi/, **naartje** *n S Africa* a tangerine

NASA /nássə/ *n* the US space agency. Full form **National Aeronautics and Space Administration**

nasal /náyz'l/ *adj* 1 of the nose 2 pronounced through the nose —**nasality** /nay zálləti/ *n* —**nasally** *adv*

nasalize /náyzə līz/ (**-izing**, **-ized**), **nasalise** *vti* make a speech sound nasal —**nasalization** /náyzə līʼ záysh'n/ *n*

nascent /náss'nt, náyss-/ *adj* just beginning to develop —**nascence** *n* —**nascency** *n*

NASDAQ /náz dak/ *n* a US financial market for over-the-counter securities. Full form **National Association of Securities Dealers Automated Quotation System**

~~nash~~ incorrect spelling of **gnash**

Nash, John (1752–1835) British architect

Nash, Ogden (1902–71) US writer and lyricist

Nashville /násh vil/ capital of Tennessee. Pop. 510,274 (1998).

Nassau /nássaw/ capital of the Bahamas. Pop. 172,000 (1997).

Gamal Abdel Nasser

Nasser /nássər/, **Gamal Abdel** (1918–70) president of Egypt (1956–70)

nasturtium /nə stúrshəm/ *n* a plant with pungent round leaves and yellow to red flowers

nasty /naásti/ (**-tier**, **-tiest**) *adj* 1 spiteful 2 repugnant to the senses ○ *a nasty smell* 3 unpleasant or uncomfortable ○ *nasty weather* 4 likely to harm or be painful ○ *a nasty bruise* 5 morally offensive (*infml*) 6 difficult to solve or deal with (*infml*) —**nastily** *adv* —**nastiness** *n* ◊ See note at **mean**

natal /náyt'l/ *adj* of birth

Nathan /náyth'n/, **S. R.** (*b.* 1924) president of Singapore (1999–)

nation /náysh'n/ *n* 1 a community of people in a land under a single government 2 a community of people of the same ethnic origin, whether living together in one territory or not —**nationhood** *n*

national /násh'nəl/ *adj* 1 of a nation 2 for a whole nation 3 characteristic of the people of a particular nation 4 owned or controlled by central government ■ *n* 1 a citizen of a particular nation 2 a national newspaper —**nationally** *adv*

national anthem *n* the official song of a country

national assembly *n* a national legislative body

National Curriculum *n* the curriculum taught in state schools in England and Wales

national debt *n* the total debts of a government

national dress *n* the traditional clothes of a country

national grid *n* **1** a national network of power lines **2** the system of coordinates used by mapmakers

national guard *n* a military organization acting as a national defence or police force

National Health Service *n* the UK state health care provision

National Insurance *n* the UK compulsory state social security scheme

nationalism /násh'nəlizəm/ *n* **1** a desire for political independence **2** patriotism —**nationalist** *n, adj* —**nationalistic** /násh'nə lístik/ *adj*

nationality /náshə nálləti/ (*pl* **-ties**) *n* **1** citizenship of a particular nation **2** the people forming a nation-state **3** an ethnic group within a larger entity

nationalize /násh'nə līz/ (**-izing, -ized**), **nationalise** *vt* **1** transfer a private business to state ownership **2** give something a national character —**nationalization** /násh'nə līzáysh'n/ *n* —**nationalized** *adj*

national newspaper *n* a newspaper sold nationwide

national park *n* an area of public land protected by the government

national security *n* the protection of a nation from danger

national service *n* compulsory service in a country's armed forces

National Trust *n* **1** a UK charity that preserves historic sights **2** an Australian charity that preserves beautiful areas

Nation of Islam *n* a Black Islamic movement

nation-state *n* an independent state

nationwide /náysh'n wíd/ *adj, adv* everywhere in a nation

native /náytiv/ *adj* **1** inborn o *native intelligence* **2** born or originating in a particular place o *native to the Southwest* **3** of the indigenous inhabitants of a place (*dated; often considered offensive*) **4** occurring naturally ■ *n* **1** someone born in a particular place o *a native of Cardiff* **2** an original inhabitant (*dated; often considered offensive*) **3** a long-term local resident (*humorous*) **4** an indigenous plant or animal species —**natively** *adv* —**nativeness** *n*

SYNONYMS **native, aboriginal, indigenous, autochthonous** CORE MEANING: originating in a particular place

USAGE Avoid use of the lowercased noun and adjective **native** to mean 'an indigenous inhabitant of a place' and 'relating to the indigenous people of a place', as in *the natives of ...* and *the native people of ...*. Prefer *the indigenous* or *original* or *aboriginal people of ....*

Native American *n* a member of any of the indigenous peoples of North, Central, or South America —**Native American** *adj* ◊ See note at **Indian**

native speaker *n* a speaker of a language learned in infancy

native title *n* ANZ an Aboriginal right to land

nativity /nə tívvəti/ (*pl* **-ties**) *n* **1** birth or origin **2 Nativity** the birth of Jesus Christ

nativity play *n* a play that tells the story of Jesus Christ's birth, performed by children

NATO /náytō/, **Nato** *n* an international military alliance. Full form **North Atlantic Treaty Organization**

natter /náttər/ *vi* chat about unimportant things (*infml*) —**natter** *n*

natty /nátti/ (**-tier, -tiest**) *adj* neat and smart in appearance —**nattily** *adv* —**nattiness** *n*

natural /náchərəl/ *adj* **1** of nature **2** conforming with nature o *natural signs of ageing* **3** produced by nature o *a natural sapphire* **4** of the physical world o *striking natural features* **5** like human nature o *a natural desire for independence* **6** innate o *his natural charm* **7** behaving in a sincere unaffected way **8** not artificial o *all natural ingredients* **9** related by blood o *her natural mother* **10** describes a musical note that is not sharp or flat ■ *n* **1** somebody with innate skills or abilities **2** a musical sign cancelling a sharp or flat —**naturalness** *n*

natural childbirth *n* childbirth with little medical help

natural gas *n* a combustible mixture of hydrocarbon gases

natural history *n* the study and description of the natural world

naturalism /náchərəlizəm/ *n* in art or literature, a movement or school advocating realistic description

naturalist /náchərəlist/ *n* **1** somebody studying natural history **2** an advocate of naturalism —**naturalist** *adj*

naturalistic /náchərə lístik/ *adj* reproducing nature or reality in a faithful way —**naturalistically** *adv*

naturalize /náchərə līz/ (**-izing, -ized**), **naturalise** *v* **1** *vti* grant citizenship to somebody **2** *vt* introduce something foreign into general use **3** *vti* acclimatize a plant or animal —**naturalization** /náchərə līzáysh'n/ *n* —**naturalized** *adj*

natural language *n* a naturally evolved human language, especially as opposed to a computer language

natural language processing *n* the use of computers to process natural language

naturally /náchərəli/ *adv* **1** as expected **2** of course **3** by nature **4** in a normal way **5** without artificial aid or treatment

natural resource *n* a naturally occurring exploitable material

natural science *n* any of the sciences that deal with phenomena observable in nature —**natural scientist** *n*

natural selection *n* the Darwinian theory that the organisms that survive and pass on their genetic characteristics are those that adapt best to their natural environment

natural wastage *n* a reduction in a workforce achieved by not replacing staff who leave or retire

nature /náychər/ *n* 1 the physical world 2 *also* **Nature** the forces controlling the physical world 3 a type or sort of thing 4 the intrinsic character of a person or thing 5 a temperament 6 universal human behaviour

nature reserve *n* a protected area for animals or plants, especially rare ones

nature trail *n* a walking route designed to draw attention to interesting natural features

naturism /náychərizəm/ *n* 1 the practice of wearing no clothes, derived from the belief that nudity is a natural healthy state 2 nature worship —**naturist** *n* —**naturistic** /náychə rístik/ *adj*

naturopathy /náychə róppəthi/ *n* drug-free medical treatment —**naturopath** /náychərō path/ *n* —**naturopathic** /náychərō páthik/ *adj*

naught /nawt/ *n* 1 *US* a nought or zero 2 nothing *(literary)*

naughty /náwti/ (**-tier**, **-tiest**) *adj* 1 badly behaved 2 mildly indecent *(humorous)* —**naughtily** *adv* —**naughtiness** *n* ◊ See note at **bad**

Nauru /na róŏ, naa óoroo/ island country in the central Pacific Ocean, just south of the Equator. Cap. Yaren. Pop. 12,088 (2001). —**Nauruan** *n*, *adj*

nausea /náwzi ə, -si ə/ *n* 1 an unsettled feeling in the stomach 2 disgust *(literary)*

nauseate /náwzi ayt, -si ayt/ (**-ating**, **-ated**) *vti* 1 make somebody sick or nauseous 2 disgust somebody —**nauseating** *adj* —**nauseatingly** *adv*

nauseous /náwzi əss, -si əss/ *adj* 1 causing sickness in the stomach 2 having an unsettled feeling in the stomach

nautical /náwtik'l/ *adj* of sailors, ships, or seafaring —**nautically** *adv*

nautical mile *n* (*symbol* **M**) an international measure of distance at sea

Navajo /návvəhō/ (*pl same or* **-os** *or* **-oes**), **Navaho** *n* a member of a Native North American people who live mainly in N New Mexico and Arizona —**Navajo** *adj*

naval /náyv'l/ *adj* of navies or warships —**navally** *adv*

SPELLCHECK Do not confuse the spelling of **naval** and **navel** ('hollow on the stomach'), which sound similar.

Navarre /nə vaár/ autonomous region in NE Spain. Cap. Pamplona. Pop. 530,819 (1998).

nave /nayv/ *n* 1 the long central part of a cross-shaped church 2 a hub

navel /náyv'l/ *n* a hollow on the surface of the stomach where the umbilical cord was tied ◊ **examine** *or* **contemplate your navel** spend too much time in pointless self-analysis *(infml humorous)* ◊ See note at **naval**

navel-gazing *n* pointless self-analysis

navel orange *n* a seedless orange with a smaller secondary fruit

navigable /návvigəb'l/ *adj* 1 passable by ship 2 followable by links with related sections that users can move through

navigate /návvi gayt/ (**-gating**, **-gated**) *v* 1 *vti* find or follow a route through a place 2 *vi* give instructions to keep a car on the right route —**navigation** /návvi gáysh'n/ *n* —**navigational** *adj* —**navigator** *n*

Navratilova /na vrátti lóvə/, **Martina** (*b.* 1956) Czech-born US tennis player

navvy /návvi/ (*pl* **-vies**) *n* a labourer *(dated)* —**navvy** *vi*

navy /náyvi/ (*pl* **-vies**) *n* 1 a country's seagoing military force 2 a fleet of ships 3 *also* **navy blue** dark blue —**navy** *adj*

navy bean *n* a white variety of kidney bean

ORIGIN Navy beans are so called because they were formerly used as a staple food in the US Navy.

---

nawab /nə waàb/ *n* 1 an Indian nobleman during the Mughal empire 2 a distinguished Pakistani man

nay /nay/ *n* a no vote ■ *adv* introduces a correction *(literary)* ■ *interj* no *(archaic)*

Nazareth /názzərəth/ town in N Israel. Pop. 57,200 (1999).

Nazi /naátsi/ (*pl* **-zis**) *n* a member or supporter of the fascist German National Socialist Party under Adolf Hitler —**Nazi** *adj* —**Nazify** *vt* —**Nazism** *n*

Nb *symbol* niobium

N.B., NB, n.b., nb *interj* calls attention to something in writing. Full form **nota bene**

NBA *abbr* National Boxing Association

NC[1] *n* a UK vocational qualification. that is roughly equivalent to a GCSE. Full form **National Certificate**

NC[2] *abbr also* **N.C.** National Curriculum

NCO *abbr* noncommissioned officer

NCT *abbr* National Childbirth Trust

Nd *symbol* neodymium

ND *n* a UK vocational qualification that is roughly equivalent to two A levels. Full form **Ordinary National Diploma**

N'Djamena /ən ja máynə/ capital of Chad. Pop. 530,965 (1993).

né /nay/ *adj* born with a particular name *(for a man)*

Ne *symbol* neon

NE *abbr* 1 northeast 2 northeastern

Neandertal man /ni ándər taal-/, **Neanderthal man** *n* an extinct species of early Stone Age humans

---

ORIGIN Neandertal man is named after the valley (German *Tal*) of the River Neander in W Germany, where a skull providing the first evidence for the species was found in 1857.

Neapolitan /neeˈə póllitən/ *adj* of Naples, S Italy —**Neapolitan** *n*

neap tide /neèp-/ *n* a tide that shows the least range between high and low tides

near /neer/ *adv, prep, adj* **1** a short distance away **2** a short time away o *near the end of the week* o *the near future* ■ *adv, adj* **1** at a point not far away in state, resemblance, or number o *a sensation near to fear* o *the nearest thing to a champion* **2** almost o *near total failure* ■ *adj* **1** on a driver's or rider's left **2** closely related ■ *vti* approach a place, time, or state —**nearness** *n* ◊ **near the bone** *or* **knuckle** rather vulgar or indecent (*infml*)

ORIGIN Etymologically, **near** means 'nearer' and not 'near'. The ancient Germanic positive of which it is a comparative is represented by English **nigh**, and the superlative by **next**. The immediate source of **near** is an old Scandinavian word, which already simply meant 'close'.

NEAR /neer/ *n* a binary operator used in text searches that returns true if its operands occur within a specified proximity to each other, and false otherwise

nearby /neèr bíˈ/ *adj, adv* not far off

Near East *n* = Middle East 1 —**Near Eastern** *adj*

nearly /neèrli/ *adv* **1** almost but not quite the case **2** closely in time, proximity, or relationship

near miss *n* **1** a shot that comes close to a target but does not quite hit it **2** a near collision **3** a barely averted disaster (*infml*)

nearside /neèr síd/ *n* **1** the side of a vehicle that is opposite to the driver's side **2** the left side of a horse —**nearside** *adj*

nearsighted /neèr sítid/ *adj US, Can* shortsighted —**nearsightedly** *adv* —**nearsightedness** *n*

neat /neet/ *adj* **1** orderly in appearance **2** orderly by nature **3** simple and elegant o *a neat solution to a problem* **4** skilfully performed **5** undiluted **6** compact **7** *US* excellent (*infml*) —**neaten** *vt* —**neatly** *adv* —**neatness** *n*

neath /neeth/, **'neath** *prep* beneath (*literary*)

Nebraska /nə bráskə/ state in the central United States. Cap. Lincoln. Pop. 1,711,263 (2000). —**Nebraskan** *n, adj*

Nebuchadnezzar II /nébbyoŏkəd nézzər/ (fl 6C BC) Babylonian king (605–562 BC)

nebula /nébbyoŏlə/ (*pl* **-lae** /-lee/ *or* **-las**) *n* a region or cloud of interstellar dust and gas —**nebular** *adj*

nebulize /nébbyoŏ līz/ (-**lizing, -lized**), **nebulise** *vt* convert liquid to spray

nebulizer /nébbyoŏ līzər/, **nebuliser** *n* a device that releases a medicinal spray

nebulous /nébbyoŏləss/ *adj* **1** unclear **2** of nebulae —**nebulously** *adv* —**nebulousness** *n*

~~neccesary, neccessary~~ incorrect spelling of **necessary**

necessarily /néssəssərəli, nèssə sérrəli/ *adv* **1** inevitably **2** unavoidably

necessary /néssəssəri/ *adj* **1** essential or required **2** following inevitably ■ *n* (*pl* **necessaries**) something that is essential or required (*infml*)

SYNONYMS **necessary, essential, vital, indispensable, requisite, needed** CORE MEANING: describes something that is required

necessitate /nə séssi tayt/ (-**tating, -tated**) *vti* **1** make something necessary **2** oblige somebody to do something (*fml*) —**necessitation** /nə séssi táysh'n/ *n*

necessitous /nə séssitəss/ *adj* **1** in a state of poverty (*literary*) **2** necessary (*archaic*)

necessity /nə séssəti/ (*pl* **-ties**) *n* **1** something that is essential, especially a basic need o *food, shelter, and the other necessities* **2** requirement dictated by circumstances o *issuing replacements as necessity dictates*

neck *n* **1** the part of the body between the head and the torso **2** the part of a garment that fits round the neck **3** a cut of meat from an animal's neck **4** a long narrow opening o *the neck of a bottle* **5** a strip of land or water **6** a long narrow fingerboard on a stringed instrument **7** in horseracing, a narrow winning margin o *won the race by a neck* —**necked** *adj* ◊ **be breathing down somebody's neck 1** be close behind somebody **2** be putting pressure on somebody to do something more quickly ◊ **be in something up to your neck** be very much involved in something ◊ **break your neck** try very hard to achieve something (*infml*) ◊ **neck and neck** even in a competition (*infml*) ◊ **neck of the woods** a particular area (*infml*) ◊ **stick your neck out** take a risk (*infml*)

neckerchief /nékər chif, -cheef/ (*pl* -**chiefs** *or* -**chieves** /-cheevz/) *n* a square of cloth worn tied around the neck

necklace /nékləss/ *n* a decorative chain or string of jewels worn around the neck

necklet /néklət/ *n* a small necklace

neckline /nék līn/ *n* the line formed by the edge of a garment under the neck

necktie /nék tī/ *n US, Can* a tie for wearing with a shirt

necromancy /nékrō manssi/ *n* **1** the practice of supposedly predicting the future by communicating with the spirits of the dead **2** witchcraft (*literary*) —**necromancer** *n* —**necromantic** /nèkrō mántik/ *adj*

necrophilia /nékrō fílli ə/ *n* sexual desire for dead bodies —**necrophiliac** *n* —**necrophilic** *adj*

necropolis /nə króppəliss/ (*pl* **necropolises**) *n* a cemetery

necrosis /ne króssiss/ *n* the death of cells in tissue or organs —**necrotic** /ne króttik/ *adj*

nectar /néktər/ *n* **1** the liquid that plants produce to attract insects **2** in Greek and Roman mythology, the drink of the gods **3** any enjoyable drink (*infml*) —**nectary** *adj*

nectarine /néktə reen/ *n* **1** a smooth-skinned peach **2** the tree that produces nectarines

née /nay/, **nee** *adj* born with a particular name (of a woman)

need /need/ *vti* require something ■ *modal v* indicates that something is desirable or necessary ■ *n* a requirement ◊ See note at **knead, necessary**

needful /needf'l/ *adj (fml)* **1** required **2** requiring **—needfully** *adv* **—needfulness** *n*

needle /need'l/ *n* **1** a sharp metal tool used to carry the thread in sewing **2** a pointed rod used in knitting **3** a stylus on a record player **4** a pointer on a dial **5** a hypodermic syringe **6** a pointed leaf of a conifer ■ *vt* (**-dling, -dled**) provoke or annoy *(infml)* **—needler** *n*

needlecord /need'l kawrd/ *n* fine-ribbed corduroy

needle exchange *n* the provision of needles for drug users

needlepoint /need'l poynt/ *n* **1** embroidery on canvas **2** lace made with a needle and a paper pattern

needless /needless/ *adj* without reason or justification **—needlessly** *adv* **—needlessness** *n*

needlework /need'l wurk/ *n* **1** crafts involving sewing or knitting **2** a piece of sewing or embroidery **—needleworker** *n*

needn't /need'nt/ *contr* need not

needy /needi/ (**-ier, -iest**) *adj* **1** having a strong need for affection or emotional support **2** in a state of poverty *(dated)* **—needily** *adv* **—neediness** *n*

ne'er /nair/ *adv* never *(literary)*

ne'er-do-well *n* a person regarded as lazy and irresponsible *(dated)* **—ne'er-do-well** *adj*

nefarious /ni fáiri əss/ *adj* utterly immoral or wicked **—nefariously** *adv*

Nefertiti /néffər teeti/ ancient Egyptian queen

neg. *abbr* negative

negate /ni gáyt/ (**-gating, -gated**) *vt (fml)* **1** deny or prove false **2** invalidate **—negation** *n* **—negator** *n* ◊ See note at **nullify**

negative /néggətiv/ *adj* **1** indicating refusal, denial, or disagreement ○ *a negative response* **2** contributing to an unhappy situation ○ *negative feelings* **3** pessimistic **4** indicating the absence of something tested for **5** less than zero **6** of the same magnitude as, but opposite to, something positive **7** having the same electric charge as an electron ■ *n* **1** a photographic image with tones and colours reversed **2** an answer of 'no' **3** a word that implies 'no' **4** something or somebody undesirable or discouraging *(infml)* ■ *interj* no *(fml)* ■ *vt* (**-tiving, -tived**) say 'no' to something *(fml)* **—negatively** *adv* **—negativity** /néggə tívvəti/ *n*

negative equity *n* a situation in which property is worth less than the outstanding mortgage on it

Negev /néggev/, **Negeb** /néggeb/ desert region in Israel, comprising the southern half of the country

neglect /ni glékt/ *vt* **1** fail to care properly for **2** fail to do ○ *neglected to tell him* ■ *n* neglecting or being neglected **—neglectful** *adj* **—neglectfully** *adv*

SYNONYMS neglect, forget, omit, overlook
CORE MEANING: fail to do something

negligée /néggli zhay/, **negligé** *n* a woman's long dressing gown made of light fabric

negligence /négglijanss/ *n* **1** the condition of being negligent **2** a civil wrong causing injury or harm

negligent /négglijant/ *adj* **1** habitually careless or irresponsible **2** casual in appearance *(literary)* **—negligently** *adv*

negligible /négglijab'l/ *adj* insignificant

negotiable /ni gőshab'l, -gőshi ab'l/ *adj* **1** open to negotiation **2** exchangeable for money **—negotiable** *n*

negotiate /ni gőshi ayt/ (**-ating, -ated**) *v* **1** *vti* come to an agreement on something through discussion and compromise **2** *vt* exchange a cheque or security for money **3** *vt* get past or deal with something successfully **—negotiation** /ni gőshi áysh'n/ *n* **—negotiator** *n*

Negro[1] /neegrő/ (*pl* **-groes**) *n* a now usually offensive term for a Black person

Negro[2] /néggrő/ river in NW South America that rises in E Colombia and flows southeastwards to empty into the Amazon in N Brazil. Length 2,300 km/1,400 mi.

Negroid /nee groyd/ *adj* an offensive term, no longer in scientific use, describing a racial group that originated in Africa *(dated)*

Nehru /náir oo/, **Jawaharlal** (1889–1964) first prime minister of independent India (1947–64)

~~neice~~ incorrect spelling of **niece**

neigh /nay/ *n* the long high-pitched sound a horse makes **—neigh** *vi*

neighbour /náybər/ *n* **1** somebody living nearby **2** something or somebody located next to or very near another ■ *vti* be next to or very near something or somebody ○ *neighbouring countries*

neighbourhood /náybər hood/ *n* **1** a local community **2** an approximation *(infml)* ○ *in the neighbourhood of £175,000*

neighbourhood watch *n* crime prevention by residents

neighbourly /náybərli/ *adj* friendly or kind like a good neighbour

neither /níthər, neé-/ *det, pron, conj* not either ■ *adv* also not ○ *I don't tell tales, and neither should you.*

ORIGIN Neither was not formed directly from *either*, though the spelling has been changed under its influence. It was originally a compound formed from obsolete *na* 'not' and the ancestor of *whether* used in the sense 'which of two'.

Nelson /nélss'n/, **Horatio, Viscount** (1758–1805) British naval commander

nematode /némmə tőd/ *n* a tiny worm with an unsegmented body

nemesis /némməssiss/ (pl **-ses** /-seez/) n 1 an avenging person or force (literary) 2 deserved punishment resulting in downfall (literary) 3 **Nemesis** in Greek mythology, the goddess of retribution

neo- prefix new, recent ○ neoclassical ○ neo-Nazi

neoclassical /neè ō klássik'l/, **neoclassic** /-klássik/ adj of the revival of classical style or forms in the arts —**neoclassicism** n —**neoclassicist** n

neocolonialism /neè ō kə lóni əlizəm/ n economic domination of a weaker nation —**neocolonialist** n

neodymium /neè ō dímmi əm/ n (symbol **Nd**) a silvery-white or yellowish rare-earth metallic element. Use: lasers, glass manufacture.

Neolithic /neè ō líthik/ n the latest period of the Stone Age —**Neolithic** adj

neologism /ni óllǝjizəm/, **neology** /ni óllǝji/ (pl **-gies**) n 1 a new word or meaning 2 coinage of new words —**neologistic** /ni óllǝ jístik/ adj —**neologize** vi

neon /neè on, -ən/ n (symbol **Ne**) a gaseous chemical element that glows orange when electricity passes through it

neonate /neè ō nayt/ n a newborn child —**neonatal** /neè ō náyt'l/ adj

neo-Nazi n 1 a modern-day advocate of Nazism 2 a white racist —**neo-Nazism** n

neon light, neon lamp n a light filled with neon

neophyte /neè ō fīt/ n 1 a beginner 2 a recent convert

neoplasm /neè ō plazəm/ n a tumour or tissue containing a growth

neoprene /neè ō preen/ n a synthetic material resembling rubber. Use: in the manufacture of equipment for which waterproofing is important.

Nepal /nə páwl/ country in South Asia, on the NE border of India, in the Himalaya range. Cap. Katmandu. Pop. 25,284,463 (2001). —**Nepalese** /néppə leèz/ n, adj —**Nepali** n, adj

nephew /néffyoo, névvyoo/ n the son of a brother, sister, brother-in-law, or sister-in-law

nephritis /ni frítiss/ n kidney inflammation

nepotism /néppətizəm/ n favouritism shown to relatives —**nepotistic** /néppə tístik/ adj

Neptune /néptyoon/ n 1 the 8th planet from the Sun 2 in Roman mythology, the god of the sea. Greek equivalent **Poseidon**

neptunium /nep tyoóni əm/ n (symbol **Np**) a silvery radioactive chemical element. Use: neutron detection.

nerd n a single-minded enthusiast of highly technical things (often in combination; sometimes offensive) —**nerdish** adj —**nerdy** adj

Nero /neèrō/ (AD 37–68) Roman emperor (AD 54–68)

Neruda /ne roòdə, -roóthə/, **Pablo** (1904–73) Chilean poet and diplomat

nerve n 1 a fibre bundle transmitting impulses within the body 2 the sensitive tissue in a

tooth 3 courage 4 impudence ■ **nerves** npl 1 somebody's ability to tolerate stress 2 nervousness (infml) ◊ See note at **courage**

nerve centre n 1 a control centre 2 a group of nerve cells that performs a specific function

nerve gas n a gas that attacks the nervous system

nerveless /núrvləss/ adj 1 numb or weak 2 calm and fearless —**nervelessly** adv —**nervelessness** n

nerve-racking, nerve-wracking adj causing great anxiety or distress

nervous /núrvəss/ adj 1 apprehensive or uneasy 2 easily worried or frightened 3 of the nerves —**nervously** adv —**nervousness** n

nervous breakdown n a psychiatric disorder caused by stress or anxiety

nervous system n the network of nerves in the body

nervy /núrvi/ (**-ier**, **-iest**) adj nervous (infml)

Nesbit /nézbit/, **E.** (1858–1924) British novelist and poet

ness n a projecting section of coastline (often in placenames)

Ness, Loch lake in N Scotland. Length 37 km/23 mi.

-ness suffix state, condition, quality ○ sadness

nest n 1 a structure built by birds or other animals to live in 2 something shaped like a bird's nest 3 a place where something bad flourishes ■ v 1 vi build a nest 2 vti group together or one inside another

nest egg n a sum of money saved

nestle /néss'l/ v 1 vti settle or put into a comfortable position 2 vi be in a sheltered place ○ a village nestling in the foothills

nestling /néstling/ n a young bird

net[1] n 1 a mesh of loosely interwoven threads 2 a bag-shaped piece of net used to hold or catch something ○ a fishing net 3 a light openweave fabric 4 a system for selecting or restricting ○ slip through the net 5 a strip of net across a sports court 6 a piece of net forming part of the goal in some sports 7 a practice cricket pitch (often pl) 8 a broadcasting, telecommunications, or computer network 9 **Net** the Internet (infml) ■ vt (**netting, netted**) 1 catch in a net 2 get (infml) ○ netted several new clients 3 protect by covering with a net

net[2], **nett** adj 1 remaining after deductions ○ net pay 2 of the contents only, excluding packaging ○ net weight 3 overall ○ the net result ■ vt (**netting, netted**) earn or gain as profit after deductions ■ n a net amount

net[3] abbr networking organization (in Internet addresses)

Netanyahu /nétt'n yaàhool/, **Binyamin** (b. 1949) Israeli prime minister (1996–99)

netball /nét bawl/ n a women's team game played by passing a large ball and throwing it into a high net

nether /néthər/ adj lower —**nethermost** adj

Netherlands /néthərləndz/ country in NW Europe, on the North Sea. Cap. Amsterdam.

Pop. 15,981,472 (2001). —**Netherlander** *n* —**Netherlandish** *adj*

Netherlands Antilles two island groups in the Caribbean Sea, an overseas territory of the Netherlands. Cap. Willemstad. Pop. 212,226 (2001).

netiquette /nétti ket, -kət/ *n* rules for communication on the Internet *(infml)*

netphone /nét fōn/ *n* a phone that uses the Internet to make connections and carry voice messages

nett *adj* = **net²**

netting /nétting/ *n* mesh o *wire netting*

nettle /nétt'l/ *n* a plant with stinging leaves ■ *vt* (**-tling, -tled**) **1** irritate or annoy *(infml)* **2** sting with a nettle leaf

netwar /nét wawr/ *n* nontraditional warfare carried out by dispersed groups of activists without a central command, often communicating electronically

network /nét wurk/ *n* **1** a system of interconnected lines **2** a coordinated system of people or things **3** a group of broadcasting channels **4** a system of linked computers **5** netting ■ *v* **1** *vi* maintain relationships with useful contacts **2** *vt* link computers **3** *vt* broadcast a programme simultaneously within a network —**networker** *n* —**networking** *n*

neural /nyóorəl/ *adj* of nerves —**neurally** *adv*

neuralgia /nyoŏ ráljə/ *n* pain along the path of nerve —**neuralgic** *adj*

neural network *n* **1** an interconnecting system of nerve cells **2** *also* **neural net** a computer system that mimics the human brain

neuro- *prefix* nerve, neural o *neurosurgery*

neurocomputer /nyoŏrō kəm pyootər/, **neural computer** *n* a computer that mimics the human brain —**neurocomputing** *n*

neurology /nyoŏ róllɔji/ *n* the branch of medicine that deals with the nervous system —**neurologic** /nyoŏrō lójjik/ *adj* —**neurological** *adj* —**neurologist** *n*

neuron /nyoŏr on/, **neurone** /-ōn/ *n* a nerve cell —**neuronal** /nyoŏ rōn'l/ *adj*

neurosis /nyoŏ róssiss/ (*pl* **-ses** /-seez/) *n* a mild psychiatric disorder characterized by anxiety, depression, and hypochondria

neurosurgery /nyoŏrō súrjəri/ *n* surgery on the nervous system, including the brain —**neurosurgeon** *n* —**neurosurgical** *adj*

neurotic /nyoŏ róttik/ *adj* **1** affected by a neurosis **2** overanxious or obsessive *(often offensive)* —**neurotic** *n*

neurotransmitter /nyoŏrō tranz míttər/ *n* a chemical that carries communication between nerves

neuter /nyoŏtər/ *vt* remove the testicles or ovaries of ■ *adj* **1** without sex organs **2** grammatically neither masculine nor feminine in gender ■ *n* **1** a neutered animal **2** a grammatically neuter word

neutral /nyoŏtrəl/ *adj* **1** belonging to, supporting, or assisting no side **2** without distinctive qualities **3** neither acidic nor alkaline ■ *n* **1** a nonaligned person or country **2** a disengaged gear position —**neutrality** /nyoo trálləti/ *n* —**neutrally** *adv*

neutralize /nyoŏtrə līz/ (**-izing, -ized**), **neutralise** *vt* **1** make ineffective **2** make neutral —**neutralization** /nyoŏtrə līzáysh'n/ *n*

neutrino /nyoo treénō/ (*pl* **-nos**) *n* a neutral elementary particle with a zero rest mass and no charge

neutron /nyoŏ tron/ *n* an elementary particle with a zero electric charge —**neutronic** /nyoo trónnik/ *adj*

neutron bomb *n* a nuclear bomb with low radioactive contamination

neutron star *n* the remnant of a collapsed star, composed entirely of neutrons

Nevada /nə vaádə/ state in the W United States. Cap. Carson City. Pop. 1,998,257 (2000). —**Nevadan** *n, adj*

never /névvər/ *adv* **1** at no time **2** not in any circumstances ■ *interj* expresses great surprise

never-ending *adj* continuous and apparently unlikely ever to stop —**never-endingly** *adv*

nevermore /névvər máwr/ *adv* never again *(literary)*

never-never *n* **1** hire purchase *(infml dated)* **2** *Aus* the central Australian desert

never-never land *n* an imaginary place where wonderful things happen

ORIGIN *Never Never Land* was the fantasy land to which Peter Pan took the Darling children in J. M. Barrie's play *Peter Pan* (1904). The name was popularized through Barrie, but it has in fact been recorded earlier, in the subtitle of a one-act play by Israel Zangwill that was performed in 1900.

nevertheless /névvərthə léss/ *adv* in spite of that

Nevis, Ben ♦ Ben Nevis

new /nyoo/ *adj* **1** recently created or invented **2** not used or second-hand **3** introduced or acquired as a replacement o *new rules* o *our new home* **4** recently discovered **5** at the start of a period o *in the new year* **6** having recently acquired a particular status o *the new president* **7** unfamiliar —**newness** *n*

SYNONYMS new, fresh, modern, newfangled, novel, original CORE MEANING: never experienced before or having recently come into being

New Age *adj* of a modern cultural movement emphasizing spirituality ■ *n* a style of music intended to induce serenity —**New Ager** *n*

New Age traveller *n* a member of a group travelling to spiritually significant places

Newark /nyoŏ ərk/ **1** city in NE New Jersey. Pop. 267,823 (1998). **2** city in W California. Pop. 43,134 (1998). **3** city in N Delaware. Pop. 28,000 (1998).

New Australian *Aus* a recent immigrant to Australia

newbie /nyo͞obi/ *n* a new user of the Internet

newborn /nyo͞o bawrn/ *adj* **1** born very recently **2** newly discovered or recovered ○ *newborn faith* —**newborn** *n*

New Brunswick /-brúnzwik/ province in SE Canada. Cap. Fredericton. Pop. 756,598 (2000).

Newcastle upon Tyne /nyo͞o kaass'l ə pon tı́n/ port in NE England. Pop. 282,338 (1996).

Newcombe /nyo͞okəm/, **John** (*b.* 1944) Australian tennis player

Newcomen /nyo͞o kumən/, **Thomas** (1663–1729) English inventor

newcomer /nyo͞o kumər/ *n* a recent arrival

New Deal *n* **1** the reform policies introduced in the 1930s by the US president Franklin D. Roosevelt. **2** the period of Roosevelt reforms —**New Dealer** *n*

New Delhi capital of India. Pop. 301,000 (1991).

new economy *n* the economy of the information age

newel /nyo͞o əl/ *n* **1** a vertical pillar supporting a spiral staircase **2** *also* **newel post** a post supporting a handrail of a staircase on a landing

New England region of the NE United States, comprising the states of Maine, New Hampshire, Vermont, Massachusetts, Rhode Island, and Connecticut —**New Englander** *n*

newfangled /nyo͞o fáng g'ld/ *adj* puzzlingly or suspiciously new ◊ See note at **new**

ORIGIN The *-fangled* part of **newfangled** represents an ancient verb meaning 'capture, seize'. The original meaning of **newfangled** was 'easily carried away by new things'.

newfound /nyo͞o fownd/ *adj* recently discovered

Newfoundland, Island of /nyo͞ofəndlənd/ island in the Atlantic Ocean, part of the Canadian province of Newfoundland and Labrador. Pop. 538,099 (1991). —**Newfoundlander** *n*

Newfoundland and Labrador easternmost province in Canada, comprising the island of Newfoundland and part of Labrador. Cap. St John's. Pop. 538,823 (2000).

New Guinea island in the W Pacific Ocean, north of Australia, divided between Irian Jaya in the west and Papua New Guinea in the east. Pop. about 5,300,000 (1995). —**New Guinean** *n, adj*

New Hampshire state in the NE United States. Cap. Concord. Pop. 1,235,786 (2000).

Ne Win /náy wín/ (*b.* 1911) Burmese national leader (1962–81)

New Jersey state on the eastern coast of the United States. Cap. Trenton. Pop. 8,414,350 (2000). —**New Jerseyan** *n, adj* —**New Jerseyite** *n*

New Labour *n* the modern Labour Party, characterized by a shift away from the left

newly /nyo͞oli/ *adv* **1** recently or lately **2** again

newlywed /nyo͞oli wed/ *n* somebody recently married —**newlywed** *adj*

Newman /nyo͞omən/, **John Henry, Cardinal** (1801–90) British theologian

New Man *n* a modern sensitive man who shares domestic chores and parenting

New Mexico state in the SW United States. Cap. Santa Fe. Pop. 1,819,046 (2000). —**New Mexican** *n, adj*

new money *n* recently acquired wealth

new moon *n* the Moon, or the phase of the Moon, when it is invisible or seen as a narrow crescent

New Orleans /-awrli enz, -awr leénz/ port in SE Louisiana. Pop. 465,538 (1998).

Newport /nyo͞o pawrt/ city in SE Wales. Pop. 137,200 (1996).

news /nyooz/ *n* **1** information about recent events ○ *Any news from the hospital?* **2** information about current events provided by the media **3** a radio or television broadcast about the day's events **4** something previously unknown ○ *It's news to me.*

news agency *n* a news-gathering organization

newsagent /nyo͞oz ayjənt/ *n* a newspaper seller

newscast /nyo͞oz kaast/ *n* a broadcast of news —**newscaster** *n*

news conference *n* a press conference

news desk *n* an area where news is prepared for publication or broadcasting

news flash *n* a brief news item interrupting a programme

newsgroup /nyo͞oz groop/ *n* an Internet discussion group

newsletter /nyo͞oz letər/ *n* a printed report containing news of interest to a group

New South Wales state in SE Australia. Cap. Sydney. Pop. 6,384,300 (1998).

newspaper /nyo͞oss paypər, nyo͞oz-/ *n* **1** a daily or weekly publication containing news and advertisements **2** the pages of a newspaper used for some other purpose ○ *wrapped in newspaper* —**newspaperman** *n* —**newspaperwoman** *n*

newsprint /nyo͞oz print/ *n* inexpensive low-quality paper for newspapers

newsreader /nyo͞oz reedər/ *n* somebody who reads the news on radio or television

newsreel /nyo͞oz reel/ *n* a news film

newsroom /nyo͞oz room, -ro͞om/ *n* a room where news is prepared for publication or broadcasting

newssheet /nyo͞oz sheet/ *n* a newsletter

newsstand /nyo͞oz stand/ *n* a stall selling newspapers

newswire /nyo͞oz wír/ *n* an Internet news service

newsworthy /nyo͞oz wurthi/ (**-thier**, **-thiest**) *adj* interesting enough to be reported as news —**newsworthiness** *n*

newsy /nyo͞ozi/ (**-ier**, **-iest**) *adj* filled with news ○ *a newsy letter*

newt /nyoot/ *n* a small amphibian with short legs and a tail

ORIGIN 'A newt' was originally 'an ewt'. The initial *n* was gained when this common combination of words was misinterpreted. The origin of *ewt* itself is unknown.

New Territories area of Hong Kong situated mostly on the Chinese mainland north of Kowloon

New Testament *n* the second section of the Christian Bible, dealing with the life and teachings of Jesus Christ

newton /nyoŏt'n/ *n* (*symbol* **N**) an SI unit of force equivalent to the force that produces an acceleration of one metre per second on a mass of one kilogram

Newton /nyoŏt'n/, **Sir Isaac** (1642–1727) English scientist. He discovered gravitation and formulated the laws of motion. —**Newtonian** /nyoo tôni ən/ *adj*

new town *n* a self-sufficient planned town created with government funding

new wave *n* **1** an innovative arts movement **2** post-punk rock music

New World *n* the western hemisphere (*dated*)

New Year's Day *n* the first day of the year. Date: 1 January.

New Year's Eve *n* the last day of the year. Date: 31 December.

New York 1 *also* **New York City** city in SE New York State, at the mouth of the Hudson River. It comprises the boroughs of Manhattan, Queens, Brooklyn, the Bronx, and Staten Island. Pop. 7,420,166 (1998). **2** state in the NE United States. Cap. Albany. Pop. 18,976,457 (2000). —**New Yorker** *n*

New Zealand /-zeéland/ country in the SW Pacific Ocean, southeast of Australia, comprising mainly the North Island and the South Island. Cap. Wellington. Pop. 3,864,129 (2001). —**New Zealander** *n*

next /nekst/ *adj, adv* immediately following ■ *det* following this one ○ *getting married next week* ■ *adj* **1** adjoining ○ *in the next room* **2** closest ○ *several miles from the next village* ◇ **next to 1** adjacent to or beside **2** closest to, in comparison with something else **3** almost ○ *There was next to nothing left.*

next door *adv* **1** in or into the next house or room **2** very close ■ *adj* immediately adjacent

next of kin *n* somebody's nearest relative or relatives (+ *sing* or *pl verb*)

nexus /néksəss/ (*pl same* or **-uses**) *n* **1** a connection or link **2** a group of connected people or things **3** the centre or focus of something

Ngata /naàtə, əng gaàtə/, **Sir Apirana Turupa** (1874–1950) New Zealand Maori leader and politician

NGO *n* Nongovernment Organization

ngultrum /əng goóltrəm/ *n* the main unit of Bhutanese currency

NHS *abbr* National Health Service

Ni *symbol* nickel

NI *abbr* **1** National Insurance **2** Northern Ireland

niacin /nī əssin/ *n* a B complex vitamin found in meat and dairy products

Niagara /nī ággrə, nī ággərə/ river in NE North America, flowing from Lake Erie into Lake Ontario and forming part of the US-Canadian border. Length 56 km/35 mi.

Niagara Falls waterfall in the Niagara River, divided by Goat Island into American Falls and Horseshoe, or Canadian, Falls. Height 55–57 m/182–187 ft.

Niamey /ni aÀ may/ capital of Niger. Pop. 587,000 (1995).

niave incorrect spelling of **naive**

nib *n* a detachable metal writing tip for a pen

nibble /níbb'l/ *vti* (**-bling, -bled**) **1** take small quick or cautious bites of something **2** bite gently and playfully ■ *n* **1** an act of nibbling **2** a tiny amount of food (*infml*) ■ **nibbles** *npl* small things to eat, e.g. at a party

Nicaea /nī seé ə/ ancient Byzantine city of Asia Minor, on the site of present-day Iznik, NW Turkey

Nicaragua /níkə rággyoŏ ə/ largest country in Central America, situated between the North Pacific Ocean and the Caribbean Sea. Cap. Managua. Pop. 4,918,393 (2001). —**Nicaraguan** *n, adj*

nice /nīss/ (**nicer, nicest**) *adj* **1** pleasant **2** kind **3** respectable **4** attractive **5** subtle —**nicely** *adv* —**niceness** *n* ◇ **nice and** sufficiently or pleasingly

ORIGIN Nice has changed its meaning dramatically over the centuries. The original sense was 'foolish, stupid': it came through French from a Latin verb meaning 'not know'. In English it transformed through 'neat, dainty', 'shy', 'fastidious' and numerous other shades of meaning to reach its modern use as a general term of approval in the early 18C.

Nice /neess/ city in SE France. Pop. 342,738 (1999).

NICE /nīs/ *abbr* National Institute of Clinical Excellence

nicety /níssəti/ (*pl* **-ties**) *n* (*often pl*) **1** a fine distinction or detail **2** a refined feature

niche /neesh, nich/ *n* **1** a recess in a wall **2** a suitable place or activity for somebody ○ *She carved out her own niche in the industry.* **3** a specialized market —**niche** *vt*

Nicholas /níkələss/, **St** (*fl* 4C) prelate and saint from Asia Minor

Nicholas I (1796–1855) tsar of Russia (1825–55)

Nicholas II (1868–1918) tsar of Russia (1894–1917)

nick *n* **1** a small cut or notch **2** a police station or prison (*slang*) **3** a prison (*slang*) **4** the condition of something (*slang*) ○ *in good nick for it's age* ■ *vt* **1** make a nick in **2** steal (*slang*) **3** arrest (*slang*) ◇ **in the nick of time** at the last possible moment ◇ See note at **steal**

nickel /ník'l/ *n* **1** (*symbol* **Ni**) a silvery white metallic element. Use: alloys, batteries, electroplating, catalyst. **2** US, Can a five-cent coin

ORIGIN Nickel is a shortening of German *Kupfernickel* 'copper nickel' (an important ore of nickel). A *Nickel* was a dwarf or mischievous demon, and the ore was given that name because it yielded no copper. A similar reference to malicious supernatural thwarting of mining is seen in *cobalt* from German *Kobold*, literally a harmful goblin.

Nicklaus /ník lowss/, **Jack** (*b*. 1940) US golfer

~~nickle~~ incorrect spelling of **nickel**

nick-nack *n* HOUSEHOLD = **knick-knack**

nickname /ník naym/ *n* **1** a name used instead of somebody's or something's real name **2** a shortened form of a name —**nickname** *vt*

ORIGIN 'A **nickname**' was originally 'an ekename'. The initial *n* was gained when this common combination of words was misinterpreted. *Eke* itself is an obsolete word meaning 'addition' that is closely related to the verb *eke out*. A **nickname** is thus etymologically a name in addition to your proper name.

Nicobar Islands /níkə baar-/ island group in the Indian Ocean, east of Sri Lanka, part of the Indian union territory of the Andaman and Nicobar Islands. Pop. 39,022 (1991).

Nicosia /níkə seè ə/ capital of Cyprus. Pop. 194,000 (1997).

nicotine /níkə teen/ *n* a toxic alkaloid derived from tobacco. Use: insecticide. —**nicotinic** /níkə tínnik/ *adj*

ORIGIN **Nicotine** is named after the French courtier Jacques Nicot (1530–1604), who was ambassador to Lisbon in Portugal and introduced tobacco to France.

nicotine patch *n* a nicotine-impregnated patch worn on the skin by somebody trying to give up smoking

niece /neess/ *n* the daughter of a brother, sister, brother-in-law, or sister-in-law

~~nieghbour~~ incorrect spelling of **neighbour**

nielsbohrium /neelz báwri əm/ *n* an artificially produced radioactive chemical element

ORIGIN **Nielsbohrium** is named after the Danish physicist Niels Bohr.

Nielsen /neèlss'n/, **Carl August** (1865–1931) Danish composer

~~niether~~ incorrect spelling of **neither**

Nietzsche /neètsha/, **Friedrich Wilhelm** (1844–1900) German philosopher —**Nietzschean** *n*, *adj*

niff *n* an unpleasant smell (*slang*) —**niffy** *adj*

nifty /nífti/ (**-tier, -tiest**) *adj* very good or effective (*infml*) —**niftily** *adv* —**niftiness** *n*

Niger /níjər/ **1** country in West Africa, north of Nigeria. Cap. Niamey. Pop. 10,355,156 (2001). **2** river in W Africa, rising in S Guinea and flowing through Mali, Niger, and Nigeria into the Gulf of Guinea. Length 4,180 km/2,600 mi.

Nigeria /nī jeèri ə/ country in West Africa. Cap. Abuja. Pop. 126,635,630 (2001). —**Nigerian** *n*, *adj*

niggardly /níggərdli/ *adj* (**-lier, -liest**) **1** reluctant to give or spend anything **2** small or inadequate ■ *adv* in a miserly or stingy way —**niggard** *n*

nigger /níggər/ *n* a taboo term for a Black person (*offensive*)

niggle /nígg'l/ (**-gling, -gled**) *vi* **1** criticize in a petty way **2** be preoccupied with details —**niggle** *n* —**niggling** *adj* —**nigglingly** *adv*

nigh /nī/ *adv, adj* near (*literary*) ■ *adv* almost

night /nīt/ *n* **1** the daily period of darkness between sunset and sunrise **2** the time spent in bed **3** an evening spent in a particular way *o a night at the theatre* **4** nightfall —**night** *adj* ◊ See note at **knight**

nightcap /nít kap/ *n* **1** a drink before going to bed **2** a cap worn in bed

nightclothes /nít klōthz/ *npl* clothes for wearing in bed

nightclub /nít klub/ *n* a place of entertainment open late —**nightclubbing** *n*

nightdress /nít dress/ *n* a loose lightweight dress worn in bed

nightfall /nít fawl/ *n* the beginning of night

nightgown /nít gown/ *n* a nightdress or nightshirt

nighthawk /nít hawk/ *n* a nightjar with black, white, and buff plumage

nightie /níti/, **nighty** (*pl* **-ies**) *n* a nightdress (*infml*)

nightingale /níting gayl/ *n* a brownish songbird of the thrush family that sings at night

ORIGIN **Nightingale** means literally 'night singer' (*gale* is ultimately related to *yell*). There was originally no *n* in the middle of the word, but it began to be inserted in the 13C.

Florence Nightingale

Nightingale /níting gayl/, **Florence** (1820–1910) British nursing pioneer

nightjar /nít jaar/ *n* a nocturnal bird that feeds on insects caught in flight

nightlife /nít līf/ *n* evening entertainment

nightlight /nít līt/ *n* a small light left on at night

nightlong /nít lóng/ *adj, adv* throughout the entire night

nightly /nítli/ *adj* **1** occurring at night **2** happening every night ■ *adv* every night

nightmare /nít mair/ *n* **1** a very bad dream **2** a very upsetting or difficult experience —**nightmare** *adj* —**nightmarish** *adj*

ORIGIN The *mare* of **nightmare** is a spirit or monster that was supposed to settle on sleepers' chests and give them feelings of suffocation and bad dreams.

night owl *n* somebody who stays up late *(infml)*

night safe *n* a bank safe with access from outside

night school *n* a school with evening classes

night shift *n* **1** a nighttime work period **2** a group of people working at night *(+ sing or pl verb)*

nightshirt /nít shurt/ *n* a long loose shirt-like garment worn in bed

nightspot /nít spot/ *n* a nightclub

nightstick /nít stik/ *n* US a police officer's club

nighttime /nít tīm/ *n* the period of night

night watch *n* a guard or watch kept at night

night watchman *n* somebody who guards a place at night

nihilism /nī i lìzəm, níhi-/ *n* **1** the total rejection of morality and religion or political authority **2** the belief that nothing is worthwhile —**nihilist** *n* —**nihilistic** /nī i lístik, níhi-/ *adj*

Nijinsky /ni jínski/, **Vaslav** (1890–1950) Russian ballet dancer

Nike /níki/ *n* in Greek mythology, the goddess of victory

Nikkei Index /ní kay-/ *n* a Tokyo stock exchange index of shares

nil *n* zero

Nile /nīl/ river in NE Africa, rising in Lake Victoria, Uganda, and flowing northwards to empty into the Mediterranean Sea in Egypt. Length 6,695 km/4,160 mi.

nimble /nímb'l/ (**-bler, -blest**) *adj* **1** fast and agile **2** able to think quickly and cleverly —**nimbleness** *n* —**nimbly** *adv*

nimbus /nímbəss/ (*pl* **-buses** *or* **-bi** /-bī/) *n* **1** a dark rain-bearing cloud **2** a cloud of light or a halo around a representation of a deity or saint

NIMBY[1] /nímbi/ (*pl* **-BYs**), **Nimby** (*pl* **-bys**) *n* somebody who objects to the location of something undesirable near his or her home *(infml)* —**Nimbyism** *n*

NIMBY[2] *abbr* not in my backyard

nine /nīn/ *n* the number 9 —**nine** *adj, pron* —**ninth** *n, adj, adv* ◇ **dressed (up) to the nines** very elaborately or formally dressed

9–11 /nīn i lévv'n/ *n* US the coordinated terrorist attacks in the United States on 11 September 2001

nineteen /nín teen/ *n* the number 19 —**nineteen** *adj, pron* —**nineteenth** *n, adj, adv*

nineteenth man *n* a substitute in Australian Rules football

~~nineth~~ incorrect spelling of **ninth**

ninety /nínti/ *n* the number 90 ■ **nineties** *npl* **1** the numbers between 90 and 99, particularly as a range of temperatures **2** the years from 90 to 99 in a century or somebody's life —**ninetieth** *n, adj, adv* —**ninety** *adj, pron*

Nineveh /nínnəvə/ ancient capital of Assyria, in present-day N Iraq

ninja /nínjə/ (*pl* **-jas** *or* same) *n* a feudal Japanese mercenary trained in the martial arts

~~ninty~~ incorrect spelling of **ninety**

niobium /nī ṓbi əm/ *n* (*symbol* Nb) a lustrous light grey ductile metallic element that is a superconductor. Use: steel alloys.

nip[1] *v* (**nipping, nipped**) **1** *vt* pinch between two surfaces **2** *vt* sever by pinching, biting, or clipping **3** *vt* sting with cold **4** *vt* halt the growth of **5** *vi* go quickly *(infml)* ■ *n* **1** an act of nipping **2** a chill ◇ *a nip in the air* ◇ **nip and tuck** US, Can very closely and evenly contested *(infml)*

nip[2] *n* a small drink of something ■ *vti* (**nipping, nipped**) sip

ORIGIN Nip 'small drink' is probably a shortening of obsolete *nipperkin* 'small vessel for alcoholic drink', which was recorded in the early 17C. A nip was originally (late 18C) a half pint of ale, and only later a small drink.

nipper /níppər/ *n* **1** a large claw of a crustacean, especially a lobster or crab **2** a child *(infml dated)* ■ **nippers** *npl* pliers or clippers

nipple /nípp'l/ *n* the tip of a mammary gland

nippy /níppi/ (**-pier, -piest**) *adj* **1** chilly **2** small and fast —**nippiness** *n*

nirvana /neer vaánə, nur-/ *n* **1** *also* **Nirvana** in Hinduism, Buddhism, and Jainism, spiritual enlightenment **2** an ultimate experience of something pleasurable

Nisan /née saan/ *n* the 1st month of the Jewish calendar

Nissen hut /níss'n-/ *n* a curved metal shelter

ORIGIN The **Nissen hut** is named after the British military officer Lieutenant Colonel Peter Norman Nissen (1871–1930), who invented it.

nit /nit/ *n* the egg or larva of a louse —**nitty** *adj* ◇ See note at **knit**

nitpick /nít pik/ *vti* criticize insignificant details of something —**nitpicker** *n* —**nitpicking** *n* ◇ See note at **criticize**

nitrate /ní trayt/ *n* **1** a salt or ester of nitric acid **2** a fertilizer consisting of a nitrate —**nitrate** *vt* —**nitration** /nī tráysh'n/ *n*

nitre /nítər/ *n* potassium nitrate or sodium nitrate

nitric acid /nítrik-/ *n* a corrosive liquid. Use: manufacture of explosives, fertilizers, and rocket fuels.

nitrify /nítri fī/ (**-fies, -fied**) *vt* **1** treat or combine something with nitrogen **2** fertilize soil with nitrogen —**nitrification** /nítrifi káysh'n/ *n*

nitrogen /nítrəjən/ *n* (*symbol* N) a colourless odourless gaseous chemical element. Use: manufacture of ammonia, explosives, and fertilizers.

nitroglycerine /nítrō glíssərin, -reen/, **nitroglycerin** /-rin/ *n* a thick oily explosive liquid. Use: manufacture of explosives, treatment of angina pectoris.

nitrous oxide *n* a sweet-smelling gas. Use: anaesthetic.

nitty-gritty /nítti grítti/ n the basic, important, or practical details of something (infml) —**nitty-gritty** adj

nitwit /nít wit/ n a person regarded as unintelligent (insult)

Library of Congress

Richard Nixon

Nixon /níks'n/, **Richard Milhous** (1913–94) 37th president of the United States (1969–74)

Nizhniy Novgorod /nízhni nóvgərod/ port in W Russia. Pop. 1,840,212 (1995).

Nkomo /əng kṓmō/, **Joshua** (1917–99) Zimbabwean nationalist leader

Nkrumah /'n krooma, 'ng krooma/, **Kwame** (1909–72) first prime minister (1957–60) and president (1960–66) of Ghana

NLP abbr 1 natural language processing 2 neurolinguistic programming

NM abbr nautical mile

no[1] /nṓ/ adv, interj 1 indicates refusal, denial, or disagreement 2 indicates agreement with a negative statement ○ 'Nobody ever takes any notice'.'No, they don't'. 3 indicates shock or disbelief ■ n (pl **noes** or **nos**) 1 an answer or vote of 'no' 2 somebody who votes 'no' ◊ See note at **know**

no[2] /nṓ/ det 1 not any at all ○ no money 2 not at all ○ She's no fool.

No[1] /nṓ/, **Noh** n a highly stylized form of Japanese drama

No[2] symbol nobelium

no., No. abbr 1 north 2 northern

Noah /nṓ ə/ n in the Bible, a Hebrew patriarch who built an ark and saved human and animal life from the Flood

nob n a rich or important person (infml)

nobble /nóbb'l/ (-bling, -bled) vt (infml) 1 make contact with somebody in order to persuade him or her to do something 2 persuade somebody with threats or bribes 3 drug or disable a racehorse

Nobel /nṓ bél/, **Alfred** (1833–96) Swedish chemist and inventor of dynamite. He established the original Nobel Prizes.

nobelium /nṓ beeli əm/ n (symbol **No**) an artificially produced radioactive chemical element

Nobel Prize n an international award for achievement —**Nobel prizewinner** n

nobility /nṓ bílləti/ (pl -ties) n 1 the class of nobles 2 aristocratic rank 3 excellent moral character

noble /nṓb'l/ adj (-bler, -blest) 1 of the nobility 2 having or showing high moral principles 3 chemically inactive ■ n a titled aristocrat —**nobleman** n —**noblewoman** n —**nobly** adv

noblesse oblige /nṓ bléss ō bleézh/ n the idea that aristocrats must behave honourably and generously towards the lower classes

nobody /nṓbədi, -bodi/ pron not one single person ■ n (pl -ies) an unimportant person

no claims bonus, no claim bonus n a discount on insurance for somebody who has made no claim

nocturnal /nok túrn'l/ adj 1 occurring at night 2 describes animals that are active at night —**nocturnally** adv

nocturne /nók turn/ n 1 a piece of tranquil dreamy music 2 a painting of a night scene

nod (**nodding, nodded**) v 1 vti move the head up and down in agreement 2 vi also **nod off** doze 3 vi droop or sway in the wind —**nod** n

node /nṓd/ n 1 a lump or swelling 2 a point of leaf attachment on a plant stem 3 a point where lines meet or intersect in a diagram or graph 4 a point in a computer network where a message can be created or received —**nodal** adj

nodule /nóddyool/ n a small lump or protuberance —**nodular** adj

Noel /nṓ él/, **Noël** n Christmas

no-fly-zone n an area of the sky forbidden to aircraft

no-frills adj describes a service or establishment that is basic (infml)

no-go area n 1 a dangerous part of a town or city 2 an area forbidden to unauthorized people

noise /noyz/ n 1 a sound, especially a loud or unpleasant sound 2 a combination of sounds ○ too much noise in the room 3 electric disturbance that makes a signal unclear ■ vt (**noising, noised**) spread a rumour or gossip ○ a story being noised around in newsrooms —**noiseless** adj —**noiselessly** adv —**noiselessness** n —**noisily** adv —**noisiness** n —**noisy** adj ◊ **make noises** do or say something intended to attract attention or indicate an intention

ORIGIN Noise derives from the same Latin word as nausea. Nausea came directly from Latin, and specifically meant 'seasickness'. The fuss and commotion surrounding attacks of seasickness presumably led to its association with sound as the word reached English via French to become noise.

noise pollution n irritating noise from the environment

noisome /nóyssəm/ adj 1 foul or disgusting 2 dangerous —**noisomeness** n

Nolan /nṓlən/, **Sir Sidney Robert** (1917–92) Australian painter

nomad /nṓ mad/ n 1 a member of a people who move from place to place 2 a wanderer —**nomadic** adj

no-man's-land n 1 territory between opposing armed forces 2 unclaimed land 3 a situation in which rules or boundaries are uncertain

nom de guerre /nóm də gáir/ (*pl* **noms de guerre** /nóm-/) *n* a pseudonym

nom de plume /nóm də plóom/ (*pl* **noms de plume** /nóm-/) *n* a writer's pseudonym

nomenclature /nō méngkləchər, nốmən klaychər, -kláychər/ *n* **1** the assigning of names to organisms in a scientific classification system **2** a system of names

nominal /nómmin'l/ *adj* **1** in name only **2** very low in amount ○ *a nominal fee* **3** of a noun **—nominally** *adv*

nominal value *n* par value

nominate /nómmi nayt/ (**-nating, -nated**) *vt* **1** propose for election or for an award **2** appoint **—nomination** /nómmi náysh'n/ *n*

nominative /nómminətiv/ *n* **1** the grammatical case of the subject of a verb or sentence **2** a word in the nominative **—nominative** *adj*

nominee /nómmi neé/ *n* somebody nominated

non- *prefix* not, without, the opposite of ○ *nonrenewable* ○ *nonstick* ○ *nonviolence*

nonacceptance /nónnək séptənss/ *n* refusal or rejection

nonagenarian /nốnəjə náiri ən, nón-/ *n* somebody in his or her nineties **—nonagenarian** *adj*

nonagon /nónnə gon, nốn-/ *n* a nine-sided geometrical figure **—nonagonal** /no nággən'l, nō-/ *adj*

nonalcoholic /nón alkə hóllik/ *adj* containing no alcohol

nonaligned /nón ə línd/ *adj* not allied with another nation **—nonalignment** *n*

nonappearance /nónə peèrənss/ *n* a failure to turn up

nonattendance /nón ə téndənss/ *n* a failure to be present **—nonattender** *n*

nonbank /nón bángk/ *n* a financial enterprise that is not a bank but performs some bank functions **—nonbanking** *adj*

nonbusiness /nón bíznəss/ *adj* not relating to business

nonce /nonss/ *n* the present time (*archaic*) ○ *for the nonce*

nonce word *n* a word coined for a single occasion

nonchalant /nónshələnt/ *adj* calm and unconcerned **—nonchalance** *n* **—nonchalantly** *adv*

> **ORIGIN** Etymologically **nonchalant** means 'not hot'. The idea of being hot and bothered readily led the French verb 'be hot' to mean also 'be concerned'. **Nonchalant** was adopted into English from French in the mid-18C.

noncombatant /non kómbətənt/ *n* **1** a civilian in wartime **2** a nonfighting member of the armed forces

noncommissioned officer /nónkə mísh'nd-/ *n* an officer who has been appointed from the lower ranks

noncommittal /nónkə mítt'l/ *adj* not expressing an opinion **—noncommittally** *adv*

noncompliance /nónkəm plī́ ənss/ *n* failure to comply **—noncompliant** *adj*

non compos mentis /nón kómpəss méntiss/ *adj* in law, not mentally competent to understand what is happening and to make important decisions

nonconformist /nónkən fáwrmist/ *n* **1** an unconventional person **2** *also* **Nonconformist** a member of a Protestant church that is not the established church **—nonconformist** *adj*

nonconformity /nónkən fáwrməti/ *n* **1** unconventionality **2** lack of agreement with something

noncontributory /nónkən tríbbyŏŏtəri/ *adj* not requiring contributions from an employee or member ○ *a noncontributory pension scheme*

noncooperation /nónkō óppə ráysh'n/ *n* **1** refusal to cooperate **2** civil disobedience **—noncooperative** /nónkō óppərətiv/ *adj*

noncustodial /nón ku stódi əl/ *adj* not involving imprisonment ○ *a noncustodial sentence*

nondeductible /nóndi dúktəb'l/ *adj* not deductible from taxable income

nondelivery /nón di lívvəri/ *n* failure to deliver something

nondescript /nóndiskript/ *adj* unremarkable

nondigital /non díjjit'l/ *adj* **1** not involving computers or the Internet **2** not processing or representing data by numbers

nondisclosure agreement /nón diss klṓzhər-/ *n* an agreement of confidentiality, e.g. about a project or employer

none /nun/ *pron* **1** nobody **2** not any ◊ **have none of** refuse to tolerate (*infml*) ◊ **none the** in no degree (*with comparative adjectives*) ○ *none the wiser* ◊ **none too** not very ○ *none too pleased*

nonentity /no néntəti/ (*pl* **-ties**) *n* **1** an insignificant person **2** something nonexistent

nonessential /nón i sénsh'l/ *adj* **1** not absolutely necessary **2** not essential in the diet **—nonessential** *n*

nonetheless /núnthə léss/ *adv* nevertheless

nonevent /nón i vént/ *n* a disappointingly unexciting occasion

nonexecutive director /nón ig zékyŏŏtiv-/ *n* a director who advises other directors

nonexistent /nón ig zístənt/ *adj* not existing **—nonexistence** *n*

nonfat /nón fát/ *adj* without fat, or with the fat content removed

nonfiction /nón fíksh'n/ *n* prose that consists of factual information **—nonfictional** *adj*

nonflammable /nón flámməb'l/ *adj* difficult to burn

nongovernmental /nón gúvv'rn mént'l/ *adj* not run by a government

nonintervention /nón intər vénsh'n/ *n* lack of interference in other countries' affairs **—noninterventionist** *n, adj*

noninvasive /nón in váyssiv/ *adj* **1** not involving entering or cutting into the body **2** describes a medical condition that is not likely to spread to other parts of the body

nonmarketable /non maàrkitəb'l/ *adj* **1** not able to be marketed **2** not convertible into cash

nonmember /non mémbər/ *n* a person or group that is not a member

nonmetal /nón métt'l/ *n* a chemical element without the properties of a metal —**nonmetallic** /nón mə tállik/ *adj*

non-negotiable /nón ni góshəb'l, -shi əb'l/ *adj* **1** not open to negotiation **2** not legally transferable

nonnuclear /nón nyóokli ər/ *adj* not using nuclear power or weapons

no-no /nónó/ (*pl* **no-nos**) *n* something not allowed (*infml*)

nonobservance /nón əb zúrv'nss/ *n* failure to obey a rule or practice

no-nonsense *adj* **1** direct and practical **2** basic and unadorned

nonpareil /nónpə ráy'l/ *adj* peerless

nonpartisan /nón paàrti zán/ *adj* not supporting any political party —**nonpartisan** *n*

nonpayment /non páymənt/ *n* failure to pay

nonperson /nón púrss'n/ *n* **1** somebody ignored by a political regime **2** an insignificant person

nonplus /non plúss/ (**-plusses**, **-plussing**, **-plussed**) *vt* confuse or fluster —**nonplussed** *adj*

nonprinting /nón prínting/ *adj* describes a character used for formatting that does not appear on a printout

nonprofitmaking *adj* not run with the aim of making a profit ○ *a nonprofitmaking organization*

nonproliferation /nón prə líffə ráysh'n/ *n* limitation of the spread of something, especially nuclear weapons ○ *a nonproliferation agreement*

nonrefundable /nón ri fúndəb'l/ *adj* for which payment cannot be claimed back ○ *a nonrefundable deposit*

nonrenewable /nón ri nyóo əb'l/ *adj* **1** not replaceable once used **2** not renewable once expired

nonresident /nón rézzidənt/ *adj* **1** not living or staying in a place **2** not involving living at the workplace —**nonresident** *n*

nonrestrictive /nón ri stríktiv/ *adj* describes a relative clause giving nonessential additional information

nonsense /nónssənss/ *n* **1** meaningless language or behaviour **2** a pointless act or statement **3** irritating behaviour ○ *won't stand for any nonsense* ■ *interj* expresses emphatic contradiction —**nonsensical** /non sénssik'l/ *adj* —**nonsensicality** /non sénssi kálləti/ *n* —**nonsensically** *adv* —**nonsensicalness** *n*

non sequitur /nón sékwitər/ *n* a statement apparently unrelated to what preceded it

nonslip /nón slíp/ *adj* preventing slipping

nonsmoker /non smókər/ *n* **1** somebody who does not smoke **2** a railway carriage or compartment where smoking is forbidden

nonsmoking /nón smóking/ *adj* **1** restricted to nonsmokers **2** not smoking

nonspecific /nón spə síffik/ *adj* **1** general **2** without a particular medical cause

nonstandard /nón stándərd/ *adj* **1** not of an accepted standard **2** not used in standard language

nonstarter /nón staàrtər/ *n* **1** something or somebody unlikely to succeed (*infml*) **2** somebody or something that is entered for a race but does not take part

nonstate actor /nón stayt-/ *n* an individual or body acting independently of a state or government, e.g. a terrorist group

nonstick /nón stík/ *adj* preventing food from sticking during cooking

nonstop /nón stóp/ *adj*, *adv* **1** without a stop **2** without interruption

nontransferable /nón transs fúr əb'l/, **nontransferrable** *adj* for use only by the specified person

nonunion /nón yóonyən/ *adj* **1** not belonging to a trade union **2** not using trade-union members —**nonunionized** *adj*

nonverbal /nón vúrb'l/ *adj* not involving words —**nonverbally** *adv*

nonviolence /nón vî´ ələnss/ *n* the principle of refraining from using violence —**nonviolent** *adj*

nonvolatile /non vóllə tíl/ *adj* **1** not likely to evaporate **2** retaining data when the power is off

nonvoting /nón vóting/ *adj* describes a share that does not give the holder the right to vote

non-white, **non-White** *n* somebody from a dark-skinned ethnic group (*sometimes offensive*) —**non-white** *adj*

noodle /nóod'l/ *n* a long thin strip of pasta (*often pl*)

nook /nóok/ *n* **1** a quiet private place **2** a small corner or recess

noon /noon/ *n* 12 o'clock midday

> **ORIGIN Noon** derives from Latin *nona* 'ninth', as a shortening of a compound meaning 'ninth hour'. In ancient Rome the hours of the day were counted from sunrise, so the ninth hour fell at about three o'clock in the afternoon. This is what **noon** originally meant in English. Three o'clock was also an hour of prayer in the Roman Catholic Church, and the word **noon** was used for this office. It may be that the taking of a meal in preparation for this hour of prayer led **noon** to refer to an earlier part of the day. Obsolete *noonmeat* 'noon meal' is recorded from the 10C, followed by **noon** itself in the 12C for the midday meal, with the sense 'midday' following hard on its heels.

noonday /nóon day/ *adj* of or happening at midday (*literary*) —**noonday** *n*

no one *pron* nobody

noontime /nóon tîm/ *n* noon or the middle of the day

Noonuccal /noo núk'l/, **Oodgeroo** (1920–93) Australian poet

noose /nooss/ *n* a loop in a rope tied with a sliding knot

nope /nōp/ *adv, interj* no *(slang)*

nor /nawr/ *conj* and not either o *Neither he nor his brother was involved.* ■ *adv* also not o *She doesn't want to go, and nor do I.*

NOR /nawr/ *n* logical operator

ORIGIN NOR is a blend of *not* and *or*, and not a use of the conjunction *nor*.

Nor. *abbr* North

Nordic /náwrdik/ *adj* 1 Scandinavian 2 tall, fair, and blue-eyed —**Nordic** *n*

Norfolk /náwrfək/ county in E England, bordering on the North Sea

Norfolk Island island in the SW Pacific Ocean northeast of Sydney, a dependency of Australia. Pop. 1,912 (1991).

Norkay ♦ Tenzing Norkay

norm /nawrm/ *n* 1 a standard pattern of behaviour 2 the usual situation or circumstances

normal /náwrm'l/ *adj* 1 usual 2 healthy ■ *n* the usual standard or level —**normality** /nawr málləti/ *n* —**normally** *adv*

normalize /náwrmə līz/ (-izing, -ized), **normalise** *v* 1 *vti* make or become what is usual or regular 2 *vt* cause to conform —**normalization** /náwrmə līz záysh'n/ *n*

Norman /náwrmən/ *n* 1 a member of a Viking people who settled in Normandy and later invaded England 2 somebody from Normandy —**Norman** *adj*

Norman /náwrmən/, **Jessye** (b. 1945) US operatic soprano

Norman Conquest *n* the conquest of England by the Normans in 1066

Normandy /náwrmandi/ region of NW France, bordering on the English Channel. Cap. Rouen.

normative /náwrmətiv/ *adj (fml)* 1 of standards 2 creating or prescribing standards

Norse /nawrss/ *npl* 1 the Vikings 2 the people of Scandinavia ■ *n* early Norwegian, Danish, Icelandic, or a related language

north /nawrth/ *n* 1 the direction to the left of somebody facing the rising sun 2 the compass point that is opposite south 3 *also* **North** the part of an area or country that is in the north ■ *adj* 1 in the north 2 blowing from the north ■ *adv* towards the north —**northbound** *adj*

North Africa northern part of the African continent, comprising Morocco, Mauritania, Algeria, Tunisia, Libya, and Egypt —**North African** *adj, n*

North America continent in the western hemisphere, extending northwards from NW South America to the Arctic Ocean. It comprises Central America, Mexico, the United States, Canada, and Greenland. Pop. 405,000,000 (2000). —**North American** *adj, n*

Northamptonshire /nawr thámptənshər/ county in central England

North Ayrshire /-áirshər/ council area in west-central Scotland

North Carolina /-kár ə lí nə/ state on the coast of the E United States. Cap. Raleigh. Pop. 8,049,313 (2000). —**North Carolinian** *adj, n*

North Dakota state of the north-central United States. Cap. Bismarck. Pop. 642,200 (2000). —**North Dakotan** *adj, n*

northeast /náwrth eést/ *nautical usage* /náwr eést/ *n* 1 a direction or compass point between north and east 2 *also* **Northeast** the part of an area or country that is in the northeast ■ *adj* 1 *also* **Northeast** in the northeast 2 blowing from the northeast ■ *adv* towards the northeast

northeaster /náwrth eéstər/ *nautical usage* /náwr eéstər/ *n* a storm or wind from the northeast

northeasterly /náwrth eéstərli/ *nautical usage* /náwr eéstərli/ *adj* 1 in the northeast 2 blowing from the northeast ■ *n (pl* -**lies**) a wind from the northeast —**northeasterly** *adv*

northeastern /náwrth eéstərn/ *nautical usage* /náwr eéstərn/ *adj* 1 in the northeast 2 facing northeast 3 blowing from the northeast 4 *also* **Northeastern** of the northeast —**northeasterner** *n*

northeastward /náwrth eéstwərd/ *nautical usage* /náwr eéstwərd/ *adj* in the northeast ■ *n* a direction towards or point in the northeast ■ *adv also* **northeastwards** towards the northeast

northerly /náwrthərli/ *adj* 1 in the north 2 blowing from the north ■ *n (pl* -**lies**) a wind from the north —**northerly** *adv*

northern /náwrthərn/ *adj* 1 in the north 2 north of the equator 3 facing north 4 blowing from the north 5 *also* **Northern** of the north —**northernmost** *adj*

Northern Alliance *n* a loose coalition of Afghan military forces that ended Taliban rule in Afghanistan in 2001

northerner /náwrthərnər/, **Northerner** *n* somebody from the north of a country or region

northern hemisphere *n* the half of the Earth north of the equator

Northern Ireland province of the United Kingdom, in NE Ireland. Cap. Belfast. Pop. 1,689,000 (1998).

Northern Isles *npl* the Orkney and Shetland islands

northern lights *npl* the aurora borealis

Northern Mariana Islands /-márri ánnə-/ island group in the W Pacific Ocean, a self-governing commonwealth of the United States. Pop. 71,912 (2000).

Northern Territory territory of north-central Australia. Cap. Darwin. Pop. 191,400 (1998).

North Island northernmost principal island of New Zealand. Pop. 2,749,980 (1996).

North Korea /-kə reé ə/ country in East Asia, in the north of the Korean Peninsula. Cap.

Pyongyang. Pop. 21,968,228 (2001). —**North Korean** *n, adj*

North Lanarkshire /-lánnərkshər/ council area in S Scotland

north pole *n* **1** *also* **North Pole** the northern end of the Earth's axis **2** *also* **north magnetic pole** the point on the Earth's surface to which a compass needle is attracted

North Sea arm of the Atlantic Ocean lying between the NE United Kingdom and continental Europe

North Star *n* Polaris

Northumberland /nawr thúmbərlənd/ northernmost county of England

Northumbria /nawr thúmbri ə/ ancient Anglo-Saxon kingdom in N Great Britain —**Northumbrian** *adj, n*

northward /náwrthwərd/ *adj* moving in a direction towards the north ■ *n* a point in the north ■ *adv also* **northwards** towards the north —**northwardly** *adj, adv*

northwest /náwrth wést/ *nautical usage* /náwr wést/ *n* **1** a direction or compass point between north and west **2** *also* **Northwest** the part of an area or country that is in the northwest ■ *adj* **1** in the northwest **2** blowing from the northwest ■ *adv* towards the northwest

northwester /náwrth wéstər/ *nautical usage* /náwr wéstər/ *n* a storm or wind from the northwest

northwesterly /náwrth wéstərli/ *nautical usage* /náwr wéstərli/ *adj* **1** in the northwest **2** blowing from the northwest ■ *n* (*pl* **-lies**) a wind from the northwest —**northwesterly** *adv*

northwestern /náwrth wéstərn/ *nautical usage* /náwr wéstərn/ *adj* **1** in the northwest **2** facing northwest **3** blowing from the northwest **4** *also* **Northwestern** of the northwest —**northwesterner** *n*

Northwest Passage sea passage along the coast of N North America, connecting the Atlantic and Pacific oceans

Northwest Territories territory of NW Canada, extending north of the provinces between Yukon Territory and Hudson Bay. Cap. Yellowknife. Pop. 42,083 (2000).

Northwest Territory historic territory of the north-central United States, extending from the Ohio and Mississippi rivers northwards to the Great Lakes, and comprising present-day Ohio, Indiana, Illinois, Michigan, Wisconsin, and E Minnesota

northwestward /náwrth wéstwərd/ *nautical usage* /náwr wéstwərd/ *adj* in the northwest ■ *n* a direction towards or point in the northwest ■ *adv also* **northwestwards** towards the northwest

North Yorkshire county in N England

Norway /náwr way/ country in N Europe, in W Scandinavia. Cap. Oslo. Pop. 4,503,440 (2001).

Norwegian /nawr wéej'n/ *n* **1** somebody from Norway **2** the official language of Norway —**Norwegian** *adj*

nos., Nos. *abbr* numbers

nose /nōz/ *n* **1** the part of the face or head through which a person or animal breathes and smells **2** the sense of smell **3** an intuitive ability to detect or recognize something **4** a part resembling a nose, e.g. the projecting front part of an aircraft or vehicle ■ *v* (**nosing, nosed**) **1** *vi* pry or snoop (*infml*) **2** *vi* search for or discover something by or as if by scent ○ *nosed out my secret hoard of chocolate* **3** *vti* advance or cause to advance with caution ○ *nosed into the stream of traffic* ◊ **keep your nose clean** avoid getting into trouble (*infml*) ◊ **keep** *or* **have your nose to the grindstone** keep working hard without taking a break ◊ **look down your nose at** regard as inferior ◊ **put somebody's nose out of joint** make somebody feel thwarted or offended ◊ **thumb your nose at** express defiance or contempt of ◊ **turn up your nose at** refuse as unworthy of you (*infml*) ◊ **under somebody's nose** in full view of or very close to somebody

nosebag /nōz bag/ *n* a bag for a horse's food that can be hung around its head

nosebleed /nōz bleed/ *n* a flow of blood from the nose

nose dive *n* **1** a steep plunge through the air by an aircraft **2** a sharp decrease —**nose-dive** *vi*

nosegay /nōz gay/ *n* a posy of flowers

nosey *adj* = nosy

nosh /nosh/ (*infml*) *n* food ■ *vt* eat

no-show *n* somebody expected who does not arrive

nosh-up *n* a large meal (*infml*)

nostalgia /no stáljə, -ji ə/ *n* **1** sentimental recollection **2** things that arouse nostalgia —**nostalgic** *adj* —**nostalgically** *adv*

Nostradamus /nóstrə daàməss, -dáyməss/ (1503–66) French astrologer and physician

nostril /nóstrəl/ *n* a breathing hole in the nose

nostrum /nóstrəm/ *n* **1** an ineffective remedy for a social, political, or economic problem **2** a quack medicine

nosy /nōzi/ (**-ier, -iest**), **nosey** *adj* intrusively inquisitive (*infml*) —**nosily** *adv* —**nosiness** *n*

not *adv* **1** forms negatives (*often contracted in infml English to 'n't'*) **2** avoids repetition when indicating denial, refusal, or negation ○ *I don't think I'll be late, at least I hope not.* ■ indicates the opposite (*humorous*) ○ *You're really going to enjoy this – not!* ◊ See note at **knot**

NOT *n* a computer logic circuit

notable /nṓtəb'l/ *adj* **1** worthy of note **2** interesting or significant **3** distinguished or famous —**notable** *n* —**notably** *adv*

notary /nṓtəri/ (*pl* **-ries**) *n* somebody legally authorized to certify authenticity

notation /nō táysh'n/ *n* **1** a set of written symbols used to represent something **2** a set of symbols **3** noting or writing down **4** a note

notch /noch/ *n* **1** a small V-shaped cut **2** a degree on a scale, especially when measuring achievement ■ *vt* **1** make a notch in **2** achieve or score *(infml)* ○ *notched up another win* —**notchy** *adj*

note /nōt/ *n* **1** a jotted record or reminder **2** an informal letter **3** a comment or an item of supplementary information in a text **4** a banknote **5** a musical or vocal sound **6** a symbol in music **7** a key on a keyboard instrument **8** an indication of mood **9** distinction ■ **notes** *npl* a summary for future reference ■ *vt* (**noting, noted**) **1** notice or remember **2** mention **3** write down

~~noteable~~ incorrect spelling of **notable**

notebook /nōt book/ *n* **1** a small book of blank or lined paper **2** a small personal computer

noted /nōtid/ *adj* **1** well-known **2** marked or significant —**notedly** *adv*

notelet /nōtlət/ *n* a decorative card for a short letter

notepad /nōt pad/ *n* a small pad of blank or lined paper

notepaper /nōt paypər/ *n* paper for writing letters

noteworthy /nōt wurthi/ (**-thier, -thiest**) *adj* deserving attention —**noteworthily** *adv* —**noteworthiness** *n*

nothing /núthing/ *pron* **1** not anything **2** something of no importance **3** a quantity or number that when added to another does not change it ■ *n* a totally unimportant person or thing ◊ **there's nothing to it** it is very easy

nothingness /núthingnəss/ *n* **1** absence of everything **2** complete worthlessness or meaninglessness **3** nonexistence

~~noticable~~ incorrect spelling of **noticeable**

notice /nōtiss/ *n* **1** a public sign **2** a written announcement **3** warning **4** a period of warning **5** official notification of the end of employment **6** attention **7** a critical review ■ *v* (**-ticing, -ticed**) **1** *vti* observe or catch sight of something ○ *Did you notice what he had in his hand?* **2** *vti* perceive or become aware of something ○ *I noticed that he avoided mentioning her name.* **3** *vt* mention **4** *vt* write a critical review of

noticeable /nōtissəb'l/ *adj* **1** easily perceived **2** noteworthy —**noticeably** *adv*

noticeboard /nōtiss bawrd/ *n* a board on which notices can be temporarily displayed

notifiable /nōti fī əb'l/ *adj* describes an infectious disease that must be reported

notify /nōti fī/ (**-fies, -fied**) *vt* **1** tell officially **2** make known —**notification** /nōtifi káysh'n/ *n*

notion /nōsh'n/ *n* **1** an idea or concept **2** a vague impression

notional /nōsh'nəl/ *adj* abstract, imaginary, or hypothetical —**notionally** *adv*

notorious /nō táwri əss/ *adj* famous for something bad —**notoriety** /nōtə rī əti/ *n* —**notoriously** *adv*

Nottingham /nóttingəm/ city in central England. Pop. 283,969 (1996).

Nottinghamshire /nóttingəmshər/ county in central England

notwithstanding /nót with stánding/ *(fml) prep* despite *(often after nouns)* ○ *The lack of a catalogue notwithstanding, it was a very interesting exhibition.* ■ *adv* nevertheless ■ *conj* although

Nouakchott /nwak shót/ capital of Mauritania. Pop. 707,000 (1990).

nougat /noő gaa/ *n* a chewy sweet made with egg whites and honey and usually containing nuts

nought /nawt/ *n* the number zero

noughts and crosses *n* a game in which two players alternately mark '0' and 'X' on a grid to complete a line (+ *sing verb*)

noun /nown/ *n* a word used to name things, people, or places

nourish /núrrish/ *vt* **1** give food to **2** encourage or strengthen —**nourishing** *adj* —**nourishment** *n*

nous /nowss/ *n* **1** common sense *(infml)* **2** the capacity to reason and acquire knowledge

nouveau riche /noővō reésh/ (*pl* **nouveaux riches** /pronunc. same/) *n* somebody with newly acquired wealth —**nouveau riche** *adj*

nouvelle cuisine /noő vel kwi zeén/ *n* a lighter style of French cooking

Nov. *abbr* November

nova /nōvə/ (*pl* **-vas** *or* **-vae** /-vee/) *n* a star that has a temporary dramatic increase in brightness

Nova Scotia /nōvə skóshə/ province in E Canada. Cap. Halifax. Pop. 940,996 (2000). —**Nova Scotian** *n, adj*

novel[1] /nóvv'l/ *n* a relatively long fictional prose work

novel[2] /nóvv'l/ *adj* refreshingly new ◊ See note at **new**

novelette /nóvvə lét/ *n* a sentimental or short novel

novelist /nóvvəlist/ *n* a writer of novels

novella /nō véllə/ *n* a short novel

novelty /nóvvəlti/ (*pl* **-ties**) *n* **1** a new thing or experience **2** newness and originality **3** a small toy or trinket

November /nō vémbər/ *n* **1** the 11th month of the year in the Gregorian calendar **2** a communications code word for the letter 'N'

> **ORIGIN November** comes from a Latin word literally meaning 'ninth month'. In ancient Rome the calendar started the year in March.

novice /nóvviss/ *n* **1** a beginner **2** a member of a religious order who has not yet taken vows ◊ See note at **beginner**

novitiate /nō víshi ət/, **noviciate** *n* **1** the period of being a novice **2** religious novices' living quarters

Novosibirsk /nóvō si beérsk/ city in south-central Russia. Pop. 1,428,141 (1995).

now /now/ adv 1 at the present time 2 immediately 3 given the current situation ○ *It doesn't matter now.* 4 up to the present time ○ *for six months now* 5 prefaces a remark or calls for attention ○ *Now, what would you like to drink?* ■ conj since or in view of the fact that ■ n the present time ■ adj fashionable (infml)

nowadays /nów ə dayz/ adv in the present

~~nowdays~~ incorrect spelling of **nowadays**

nowhere /nó wair/ adv in or to no place ■ n a remote place ◇ **get** or **go nowhere** fail to make any progress

nowise /nó wīz/ adv in no manner at all

noxious /nókshəss/ adj 1 physically or morally harmful 2 disgusting —**noxiously** adv

nozzle /nózz'l/ n a projecting spout

nr abbr near

NSPCC abbr National Society for the Prevention of Cruelty to Children

NSW abbr New South Wales

NT abbr 1 National Trust 2 Aus Northern Territory

nth /enth/ adj indefinitely large numerically

nu /nyoo/ (pl **nus**) n the 13th letter of the Greek alphabet

nuance /nyoo aanss, noo oNss/ n a subtle difference —**nuanced** adj

nub n 1 the central issue 2 a small lump or projection —**nubby** adj

Nubia /nyoobi ə/ region of NE Africa, in S Egypt and N Sudan —**Nubian** n, adj

nubile /nyoo bīl/ adj ready for marriage (dated) —**nubility** /nyoo billəti/ n

nuclear /nyookli ər/ adj 1 of or forming a nucleus 2 of nuclear weapons or nuclear energy

nuclear energy n energy produced by combining or splitting atoms or atomic nuclei

nuclear family n a social unit of parents with their children

nuclear fission n the production of nuclear energy by splitting atoms or atomic nuclei

nuclear fusion n the process in which light atoms combine and form heavier atoms, releasing a great amount of energy

nuclear physics n the branch of physics in which nuclear structures and forces are studied (+ sing verb) —**nuclear physicist** n

nuclear power n power produced by combining or splitting atoms or atomic nuclei —**nuclear-powered** adj

nuclear reactor n a device producing nuclear energy

nuclear waste n unwanted material produced by nuclear reactors

nuclear weapon n an explosive nuclear device

nuclear winter n a cold dark period after a nuclear war

nucleic acid /nyoo kleè ik-, -kláy-/ n an acid, e.g. DNA or RNA, found in all living cells and conveying genetic information

nucleus /nyookli əss/ (pl **-i** /-kli ī/ or **-uses**) n 1 an important central element or part 2 the positively charged central region of an atom 3 the central part of a living cell

nuclide /nyoo klīd/ n one or more atomic nuclei identifiable as being of the same element by having the same number of protons and neutrons and the same energy content

~~nucular~~ incorrect spelling of **nuclear**

nude /nyood/ adj unclothed ■ n an unclothed figure —**nudity** n ◊ See note at **naked**

nudge (nudging, nudged) vt 1 push somebody or something gently 2 have nearly reached a level ○ *profits nudging the 100 million mark* —**nudge** n

nudist /nyoodist/ n somebody preferring to be nude, especially in designated public places —**nudism** n —**nudist** adj

nuevo sol /nwáyvō sól/ (pl **nuevos soles** /nwáyvōs sólays/) n MONEY = **sol²**

nugatory /nyoogətəri/ adj 1 trifling 2 not legally valid

nugget /núggit/ n 1 a lump of precious metal 2 a small precious thing

nuisance /nyooss'nss/ n 1 somebody or something irritating 2 something that causes harm or offence and is illegal

nuke /nyook/ (slang) vt (nuking, nuked) attack with nuclear weapons ■ n a nuclear weapon

~~nukular~~ incorrect spelling of **nuclear**

null adj 1 invalid 2 valueless 3 amounting to nothing ■ n zero (literary) —**nullity** n

nullah /núllə/ n S Asia a ditch

nullify /núlli fī/ (-fies, -fied) vt 1 make legally invalid 2 cancel out

---

SYNONYMS nullify, abrogate, annul, repeal, invalidate, negate CORE MEANING: put an end to the effective existence of something

---

numb /num/ adj 1 without sensation 2 unable to feel emotion ■ vt —**numbing** adj —**numbly** adv —**numbness** n

number /númbər/ n 1 counting 2 a figure used in counting 3 an identifying figure or group of figures ○ *a fax number* ○ *a number 6 shirt* 4 a countable quantity 5 an unspecified quantity ○ *taught me a number of things* 6 a single thing in a series 7 a piece of popular music 8 a thing (infml) 9 in grammar, quantity expressed by the form of a word ■ v 1 vt identify by a number 2 vt include in a group ○ *numbered among the best* 3 vti reach a particular total ◇ **somebody's days are numbered** somebody's life or career is about to end ◇ **have (got) somebody's number** understand somebody's true motives or character

---

USAGE Number is a collective noun that can take a singular or plural verb depending on how you use it. If you put the definite article *the* in front of **number** you must use a singular verb: *The number of styles available is limited.* If you put the indefinite article *a* before **number**, you must use a plural verb: *A number of styles are available.*

number-cruncher *n* (*slang*) **1** a computer that performs calculations **2** somebody whose job is to perform calculations —**number-crunching** *n*

numberless /númbərləss/ *adj* **1** countless **2** not numbered

number one *n* **1** the first in a series or hierarchy **2** somebody's own self and interests (*infml*) ■ *adj* **1** most important **2** excellent (*infml*)

number plate *n* a plate carrying a vehicle's registration number

numbskull /núm skul/ *n* a person regarded as unintelligent (*insult*)

numeracy /nyóomərəssi/ *n* mathematical competence

numeral /nyóomərəl/ *n* a symbol representing a number —**numeral** *adj*

numerate *adj* /nyóomərət/ mathematically competent

numerator /nyóomə raytər/ *n* in mathematics, a part of a common fraction appearing above the line and representing the number of parts of a whole

numerical /nyoo mérrik'l/, **numeric** /-mérrik/ *adj* **1** consisting of numbers **2** in terms of the numbers of things —**numerically** *adv*

numeric keypad *n* a part of a computer keyboard containing keys that are numbered like a calculator

numerology /nyóomə rólləji/ *n* the study of the supposed influence of numbers —**numerological** /nyóomərə lójjik'l/ *adj* —**numerologist** *n*

numerous /nyóomərəss/ *adj* many in number —**numerously** *adv* —**numerousness** *n*

numinous /nyóominəss/ *adj* mysteriously associated with a deity (*fml*)

numismatics /nyóomiz máttiks/ *n* the collecting of coins and medals (+ *sing verb*) —**numismatist** /nyoo mízmətist/ *n*

Num Lock *n* a keyboard feature that cancels the usual functions of the numeric keypad and allows it to be used to input numbers

nun *n* a woman who belongs to a religious order

ORIGIN Nun goes back to a Latin word that was used of anyone of advanced or advancing age. It came to be applied specifically to monks and nuns, although in English **nun** has always applied to a member of a women's community.

Nunavut /nóonə voot/ territory of N Canada. Cap. Iqaluit. Pop. 27,692 (2000).

nuncio /núnssi ō, nóón-, -shi ō/ (*pl* -**os**) *n* a representative of the pope in a country

nunnery /núnnəri/ (*pl* -**ies**) *n* a convent of nuns

nuptial /núpsh'l, -chəl/ *adj* of marriage or a wedding ■ **nuptials** *npl* a wedding (*fml*) —**nuptially** *adv*

Nuremberg /nyóorəm burg/ city in SE Germany. Pop. 495,845 (1997).

CORBIS/Bettmann
Rudolf Nureyev

Nureyev /nyoóri ef, nyoo ráy-/, **Rudolf** (1938–93) Russian-born ballet dancer and choreographer

nurse /nurss/ *n* **1** somebody trained to look after sick and injured people **2** a nanny (*dated*) **3** somebody who breast-feeds another woman's baby **4** somebody trained to look after young children ■ *v* (**nursing**, **nursed**) **1** *vt* look after a sick or injured person **2** *vi* work as a nurse **3** *vt* take care with a part of the body affected by illness or injury ○ *nursing a broken leg* **4** *vt* keep a negative feeling in the mind, often letting it develop ○ *nurses a grudge* **5** *vt* hold or manage somebody or something carefully and with devotion **6** *vt* consume something slowly ○ *nursing a drink* **7** *vti* breast-feed a baby

nursemaid /núrss mayd/ *n* a woman who looks after young children (*dated*)

nurse practitioner *n* a nurse trained in primary health care to assume some of the responsibilities of a doctor

nursery /núrssəri/ (*pl* -**ies**) *n* **1** a place that provides childcare **2** *also* **nursery school** a school for children under five **3** a small child's room in a house **4** a business that grows plants commercially

nurseryman /núrssərimən/ (*pl* -**men** /-mən/) *n* a commercial grower of plants

nursery rhyme *n* a song or poem for a child

nursing /núrssing/ *n* **1** caring for ill and injured people **2** breast-feeding

nursing home *n* a long-term residential health care facility

nursling /núrssling/ *n* (*literary*) **1** a baby who is being breast-fed **2** a child who is cared for by somebody other than the parents

nurture /núrchər/ *vt* (**-turing**, **-tured**) **1** care for a young child, animal, or plant during development **2** encourage somebody or something to flourish ■ *n* **1** care or encouragement given to a young child, animal, or plant **2** environmental influence, especially as opposed to genetic factors —**nurturer** *n*

nut *n* **1** a fruit with a hard outer shell that contains a seed **2** an edible kernel of a nut **3** a fastening screwed onto a bolt **4** a small piece of something hard ○ *a nut of coal* **5** a human head (*infml*) **6** an offensive term for somebody with a psychiatric disorder **7** an enthusiast (*infml*)

nutcase /nút kayss/ n an offensive term for somebody with a psychiatric disorder (infml)

nutcracker /nút krakər/ n 1 a tool for cracking nuts' shells 2 a bird that eats pine nuts

nutmeg /nút meg/ n 1 a spice produced by grating a hard nut, or the nut itself 2 a tropical evergreen tree that produces nutmegs

nutraceutical /nyoòtrə syoòtik'l/, **nutriceutical**, **neutraceutical** n a foodstuff that is promoted as having medical and health benefits

nutrient /nyoòtri ənt/ n a substance providing nourishment —**nutrient** adj

nutriment /nyoòtrimənt/ n nourishing food

nutrition /nyoo tríshʻn/ n 1 the processing of food by the body 2 the science of food —**nutritional** adj —**nutritionist** n

nutritious /nyoo tríshəss/ adj providing nutrition

nutritive /nyoòtritiv/ adj 1 containing nutrients 2 of nourishment —**nutritively** adv

nuts adj (slang) 1 an offensive term meaning affected by a psychiatric disorder 2 enthusiastic about something (sometimes offensive)

nutshell /nút shel/ n the hard outer shell of a nut ◊ **in a nutshell** in very few words

nutter /núttər/ n a person regarded as mentally disturbed or highly eccentric (slang offensive)

nutty /nútti/ (-**tier**, -**tiest**) adj 1 containing or tasting of nuts 2 an offensive term meaning affected by a psychiatric disorder (infml) —**nuttiness** n

Nuuk /nook/ capital of Greenland. Pop. 12,483 (1994).

nuzzle /núzz'l/ (-**zling**, -**zled**) vti rub something with the nose or face —**nuzzle** n

nvCJD abbr new variant CJD

NVQ n a UK work-related qualification proving competence. Full form **National Vocational Qualification**

NW abbr 1 northwest 2 northwestern

NY, N.Y. abbr New York

nybble /níbb'l/ n half of a byte

> ORIGIN **Nybble** is a humorous alteration of *nibble* with *y* from *byte* and a play on *bite*.

nylon /ní lon/ n a synthetic material. Use: clothing, food containers, brush bristles. ■ **nylons** npl women's stockings (dated)

> ORIGIN The word **nylon** was coined in 1938 by Du Pont, the inventors of the material. The ending -on was taken from other fabric names such as *cotton* and *rayon*, but *nyl*- has no particular significance.

nymph /nimf/ n 1 in mythology, a spirit of nature depicted as a beautiful young woman 2 an insect larva that develops directly into an adult without a pupa stage

nymphet /nímfit, nim fét/, **nymphette** /nim fét/ n a young woman regarded as sexually desirable

nymphomania /nímfə máyni ə/ n a supposed compulsive sexual desire in some women (often offensive) —**nymphomaniac** adj, n

O

o (pl **o's**), **O** (pl **O's** or **Os**) n the 15th letter of the English alphabet

o' contr of

O¹ n 1 a zero 2 a human blood type containing a specific antigen

O² interj 1 begins a strong plea or wish 2 expresses wonder (literary)

O³ symbol oxygen

-o suffix forms abbreviated or informal forms of words ○ *beano* ○ *demo*

-o- connects words and suffixes

oaf /ōf/ n a person regarded as clumsy or ignorant (insult) —**oafish** adj

Oahu /ō aáhoo/ island in central Hawaii. Pop. 870,761 (1995).

oak /ōk/ n 1 a tree that produces acorns and has leaves with several rounded or pointed lobes 2 the hard wood of an oak tree. Use: furniture-making, flooring. —**oaken** adj

oak apple n a rounded hollow growth on an oak tree caused by wasp infestation

Oakland /ōklənd/ city in W California. Pop. 365,874 (1998).

oakum /ōkəm/ n tar-soaked rope formerly used to seal gaps between planks in a boat's hull

OAP n a senior citizen. Full form **old-age pensioner**

oar /awr/ n 1 a pole with one broad flat end, used to propel a boat 2 also **oarsman**, **oarswoman** somebody rowing with an oar

> SPELLCHECK Do not confuse the spelling of **oar**, **or** (indicating an alternative), or **ore** ('a mineral from which metal is extracted'), which sound similar.

oarlock /áwr lok/ n US, Can ROWING = **rowlock**

oasis /ō áyssiss/ (pl -**ses** /-seez/) n an area of fertile land in a desert

oasthouse /ōst howss/ (pl -**houses** /-howziz/) n a building containing hop kilns

oat /ōt/ n a cereal plant with edible seeds ■ **oats** npl the edible seeds of an oat plant

oatcake /ōt kayk/ n 1 US a flat cake made of oatmeal 2 a hard unsweetened biscuit made of oatmeal

oath /ōth/ (pl **oaths** /ōthz/) n 1 a solemn promise 2 a swearword

oatmeal /ōt meel/ n 1 crushed oats 2 US, Can porridge made from oatmeal

Ob' /ob/ river in W Siberian Russia that flows northwards into the **Gulf of Ob'**. Length 3,680 km/2,290 mi.

oba /ōbə/ n a traditional ruler of the Yoruba people of West Africa

Obasanjo /óbbə saánjō/, **Olusegun** (b. 1937) president of Nigeria (1999–)

obbligato /óbbli gaátō/, **obligato** adj not to be

left out *(musical direction)* ■ *n* (*pl* **-tos** *or* **-ti** /-tee/) an obbligato part

obdurate /óbdyŏŏrət/ *adj* **1** stubborn **2** hard-hearted —**obduracy** *n* —**obdurately** *adv*

OBE *abbr* Officer of the (Order of the) British Empire

~~obedianee~~ incorrect spelling of **obedience**

obedient /ə beédi'nt/ *adj* following demands or orders —**obedience** *n* —**obediently** *adv*

obeisance /ō báyss'nss, ō bÉ-/ *n* a respectful gesture or attitude *(fml)*

obelisk /óbbə lisk/ *n* **1** a tall stone pillar with a square base and sides that taper to a pointed top **2** a dagger sign used in printing

obese /ō beéss/ *adj* unhealthily overweight —**obesity** *n*

obey /ə báy/ (**obeys, obeying, obeyed**) *vti* **1** follow instructions or comply with a rule or law **2** be controlled by somebody or something

obfuscate /ób fuss kayt, óbfəss-/ *v* **1** *vti* make something obscure or unclear **2** *vt* confuse somebody —**obfuscation** /ób fu skáysh'n, óbfə-/ *n* —**obfuscatory** /óbfə skáytəri/ *adj*

Ob'-Irtysh /ób eer tísh/ river system in W Siberian Russia, incorporating the rivers Irtysh and Ob'. Length 5,410 km/3,362 mi.

obituary /ə bíchoo əri/ (*pl* **-ies**) *n* an announcement of somebody's death, often with a short biography

object *n* /óbb jikt/ **1** something visible or tangible **2** a focus of attention or emotion **3** an aim or purpose **4** a noun or pronoun affected by the action of a verb or governed by a preposition **5** a block of information that can be selected and manipulated on a computer ■ *v* /əb jékt/ **1** *vi* be opposed or express opposition to something **2** *vt* state as an objection —**objector** *n* ◇ **be no object** not be a concern or difficulty

SYNONYMS object, protest, demur, remonstrate, expostulate CORE MEANING: indicate opposition to something

object code *n* the binary version of a computer program that is used by the computer to run the program

objectify /əb jékti fí/ (**-fies, -fied**) *vt* **1** think of or represent as actual **2** reduce to the status of an object

objection /əb jéksh'n/ *n* **1** a feeling or expression of opposition **2** a reason for a feeling or expression of opposition

objectionable /əb jéksh'nəb'l/ *adj* causing disapproval or offence —**objectionably** *adv*

objective /əb jéktiv/ *adj* **1** free of bias or prejudice **2** based on facts or observable evidence **3** of or being the case of a noun or pronoun that is the object of a verb or preposition ■ *n* **1** an aim or goal **2** the objective case, or a word in the objective case —**objectively** *adv* —**objectiveness** *n* —**objectivity** /ób jek tívvəti/ *n*

object language *n* the language that a computer interprets when it runs programs

object lesson *n* a concrete illustration of how to do something

object-oriented graphics *npl* graphic images present in a computer as instructions to draw objects

object-oriented programming *n* computer programming based on objects arranged in a branching hierarchy

objet d'art /ób zhay daár/ (*pl* **objets d'art** /pronunc. same/) *n* an object with artistic value

oblate /ób layt, o bláyt/ *adj* shaped like a flattened sphere —**oblately** *adv*

oblation /o bláysh'n/ *n* an offering of a gift to a deity —**oblational** *adj*

obligate /óbbli gayt/ (**-gating, -gated**) *vt* compel legally or morally

obligation /óbbli gáysh'n/ *n* **1** something that must be done because of legal or moral duty **2** the state of being morally or legally compelled to do something **3** a feeling of gratitude that makes somebody believe a favour must be returned —**obligational** *adj*

obligatory /ə blíggətəri/ *adj* **1** legally, morally, or religiously required **2** compulsory —**obligatorily** *adv*

oblige /ə blíj/ (**obliging, obliged**) *vt* **1** require somebody to do something for legal, moral, or religious reasons **2** force somebody to do something **3** cause somebody to feel indebted **4** do a favour for somebody

obliging /ə blíjing/ *adj* willing to be helpful —**obligingly** *adv* —**obligingness** *n*

oblique /ə bleék/ *adj* **1** sloping or slanting **2** indirect ○ *an oblique reference* **3** not parallel or perpendicular **4** not right-angled **5** of or being a grammatical case of a noun or pronoun other than the nominative or vocative ■ *adv* changing direction to or at an angle of 45° ■ *n* something oblique —**obliquely** *adv* —**obliqueness** *n*

obliterate /ə blíttə rayt/ (**-ating, -ated**) *vt* **1** destroy utterly **2** erase or obscure —**obliteration** /ə blíttə ráysh'n/ *n*

oblivion /ə blívvi ən/ *n* **1** the state of being completely forgotten **2** the state of forgetting everything completely

oblivious /ə blívvi əss/ *adj* **1** unaware **2** forgetting —**obliviously** *adv*

oblong /óbb long/ *adj* describes a shape that is longer than it is wide —**oblong** *n*

obloquy /óbbləkwi/ *n* (*fml or literary*) **1** severe criticism or defamation **2** disgrace

obnoxious /əb nókshəss/ *adj* thoroughly objectionable —**obnoxiously** *adv* —**obnoxiousness** *n*

oboe /óbō/ *n* a woodwind instrument with a double reed and keys —**oboist** *n*

ORIGIN The **oboe** was earlier called the *hautboy*, which came from the French name *hautbois*, literally 'high wood', referring to the instrument's high pitch. It is recorded from the mid-

16C. The French word also came into English via Italian as **oboe** and is recorded from the early 18C.

obscene /əb seén/ *adj* **1** indecent, especially by being sexually explicit **2** morally disgusting or outrageous —**obscenely** *adv* —**obscenity** /əb sénnəti/ *n*

obscure /əb skyoor/ *adj* **1** hard to understand **2** indistinct **3** unimportant or unknown **4** known to few people —**obscure** *vt* —**obscurely** *adv* —**obscurity** *n*

SYNONYMS **obscure, abstruse, recondite, arcane, cryptic, enigmatic** CORE MEANING: difficult to understand

~~obsene~~ incorrect spelling of **obscene**

obsequies /óbssi kwiz/ *npl* funeral rites

obsequious /əb seékwi əss/ *adj* too eager to please or obey —**obsequiously** *adv* —**obsequiousness** *n*

observance /əb zúrvənss/ *n* **1** compliance with laws, instructions, or customs **2** a ritual or ceremony

observant /əb zúrvənt/ *adj* **1** attentive and alert **2** complying with laws, instructions, or customs —**observantly** *adv*

observation /óbzər váysh'n/ *n* **1** attentive watching **2** a remark or comment **3** a record of something seen or noted **4** the observing of laws, instructions, or customs —**observational** *adj*

observation post *n* a military position from which soldiers can watch enemy movements

observatory /əb zúrvətəri/ (*pl* **-ries**) *n* **1** a place for scientific observations, especially of astronomical phenomena **2** a place for looking at a view

observe /əb zúrv/ (**-serving, -served**) *v* **1** *vt* see or notice **2** *vti* watch somebody or something attentively **3** *vti* be a formal witness to something **4** *vt* say as a comment on what has been seen or noted **5** *vt* comply with a law, instruction, or custom —**observable** *adj* —**observer** *n*

obsess /əb séss/ *vt* preoccupy to an unhealthy degree

obsession /əb sésh'n/ *n* **1** an unhealthy preoccupation **2** the state of being obsessed —**obsessional** *adj* —**obsessive** /əb séssiv/ *adj* —**obsessively** *adv* —**obsessiveness** *n*

obsessive-compulsive disorder *n* a psychiatric condition involving obsessive thoughts and compulsive behaviour

obsidian /ob síddi ən/ *n* jet-black volcanic glass

obsolescent /óbssə léss'nt/ *adj* becoming obsolete —**obsolescence** *n*

obsolete /óbssə leet, óbssə leét/ *adj* **1** no longer in use **2** out-of-date —**obsoletely** *adv*

obstacle /óbstək'l/ *n* **1** a hindrance to progress **2** something blocking the way

obstacle course *n* a course for an obstacle race

obstacle race *n* a race with obstacles that competitors must get past

obstetrics /ob stéttriks/ *n* the branch of medicine that deals with pregnancy and childbirth (+ *sing verb*) —**obstetric** *adj* —**obstetrician** /óbstə trish'n/ *n*

~~obsticle~~ incorrect spelling of **obstacle**

obstinate /óbstinət/ *adj* **1** stubborn **2** difficult to control or remove ○ *an obstinate stain* —**obstinacy** *n* —**obstinately** *adv*

obstreperous /əb stréppərəss/ *adj* noisily argumentative or unruly ◊ See note at **unruly**

obstruct /əb strúkt/ *vt* **1** prevent or hinder passage through **2** hinder the progress of **3** hide from sight by being in the way —**obstructor** *n* ◊ See note at **hinder**

obstruction /əb strúksh'n/ *n* **1** a block or hindrance **2** the obstructing of somebody or something **3** the state of being obstructed

obstructionist /əb strúksh'nist/ *adj* using delaying tactics —**obstructionist** *n*

obstructive /əb strúktiv/ *adj* **1** uncooperative **2** of or caused by obstruction —**obstructively** *adv*

obtain /əb táyn/ *v* **1** *vt* get possession of **2** *vi* be established or current ○ *the conditions that obtained at that time* —**obtainable** *adj* ◊ See note at **get**

obtrude /əb troód, ob-/ (**-truding, -truded**) *v* **1** *vti* impose yourself or your opinions on other people **2** *vt* push out —**obtrusion** /əb troózh'n/ *n* —**obtrusive** /əb troóssiv/ *adj* —**obtrusively** *adv*

obtuse /əb tyoóss/ *adj* **1** slow to understand something **2** describes an angle between 90° and 180° —**obtusely** *adv* —**obtuseness** *n*

obverse /ób vurss/ *n* **1** the main side of a coin or medal **2** a counterpart, complement, or opposite ■ *adj* **1** facing an observer **2** being a counterpart, complement, or opposite

obviate /óbvi ayt/ (**-ating, -ated**) *vt* **1** make something unnecessary (*fml*) **2** avoid or prevent an anticipated difficulty —**obviation** /óbvi áysh'n/ *n*

obvious /óbvi əss/ *adj* **1** easy to see **2** unsubtle —**obviously** *adv* —**obviousness** *n*

~~ocasionally~~ incorrect spelling of **occasionally**

occasion /ə káyzh'n/ *n* **1** a particular time, especially when something happens **2** a cause or reason **3** a chance or opportunity **4** need ○ *never had occasion to use it* **5** an important event ■ *vt* cause

occasional /ə káyzh'nəl/ *adj* **1** occurring from time to time **2** of or for a special event ◊ See note at **periodic**

occasionally /ə káyzh'nəli/ *adv* sometimes, but not regularly or frequently

occident /óksidənt/ *n* **1** the west (*fml*) **2** **Occident** the western hemisphere, especially the countries of Europe and the Americas (*dated*) —**occidental** /óksi dént'l/ *adj*

occluded /ə kloó dəd, o kloó did/ *adj* blocked or stopped up (*technical*) ○ *occluded arteries*

occult /ó kult, o kúlt/ *adj* **1** supposedly supernatural or magic **2** not understandable by ordinary human beings **3** describes symptoms not visible to the naked eye *(technical)* ■ *n* the realm of the supposed supernatural

occultism /ó kultizəm, ók'ltizəm, o kúltizəm/ *n* belief in the supposed supernatural —**occultist** *n*

occupant /ókyooʻopənt/ *n* a holder of a position, or the resident of a place —**occupancy** *n*

occupation /ókyoō páysh'n/ *n* **1** a job done for a living **2** an activity **3** an act of occupying or the state of being occupied **4** the invasion and control of a country or area by military forces —**occupational** *adj*

occupational hazard *n* a risk associated with a job

occupational pension *n* a pension from a scheme set up by an employer

occupational therapy *n* treatment of an illness or condition by periods of productive activity —**occupational therapist** *n*

occupy /ókyoō pĩ/ (**-pies, -pied**) *vt* **1** live in or be the regular occupant of a place **2** engage the attention of somebody **3** fill a space or an amount of time **4** invade and take control of a country or area —**occupier** *n*

occur /ə kúr/ (**-curring, -curred**) *vi* **1** take place **2** exist or be present **3** enter somebody's mind ○ *didn't occur to me to stop*

~~occurance, occurence~~ incorrect spelling of **occurrence**

~~occured~~ incorrect spelling of **occurred**

occurrence /ə kúrrənss/ *n* **1** something that happens **2** the fact of occurring

ocean /ósh'n/ *n* **1** a large sea **2** the whole body of the Earth's seas **3** a large amount or expanse —**oceanic** /óshi ánnik, óssi-/ *adj*

ORIGIN The ancient Greeks conceived of the world as surrounded by a great river or sea, to which they gave the name from which **ocean** ultimately derives. In early use in English, too, **ocean** presupposed a single body of water. The use of the word did not recognize individual **oceans** until the 14C.

Oceania /ōssi áaniə, ōshi-/ the smaller islands of the central and S Pacific Ocean, including Micronesia, Melanesia, and Polynesia, and sometimes Australasia —**Oceanian** *n, adj*

oceanography /óshə nóggrəfi, óshi ə-/ *n* the scientific study of oceans —**oceanographer** *n* —**oceanographic** /ósh'nə gráffik, óshi ənə-/ *adj*

ocelot /óssə lot/ (*pl* **-lots** or same) *n* a small wildcat resembling a leopard

ochre /ókər/ *n* a brownish-yellow colour —**ochre** *adj*

ocker /ókər/ *n Aus* an Australian regarded as boorish and chauvinistic *(slang insult)*

Ockham /ókəm/, **William of** (1285?–1349) English philosopher

o'clock /ə klók/ *adv* as a particular hour in telling the time ○ *arrive at 7 o'clock*

O'Connell /ō kónn'l/, **Daniel** (1775–1847) Irish politician, supporter of Irish independence

OCR *abbr* optical character recognition

Oct. *abbr* October

octagon /óktəgən/ *n* an eight-sided geometrical figure —**octagonal** /ok tággən'l/ *adj*

octal notation /ókt'l-/ *n* a computer-programming number system using the numerals 0 to 7, each unit being three bits

octane /ók tayn/ *n* C_8H_{18} a liquid hydrocarbon found in petroleum

octane number, octane rating *n* a measure of the ability of motor fuel to prevent misfiring or knocking

octave /óktiv/ *n* **1** an interval of eight notes on the diatonic musical scale **2** a group of eight lines of poetry

octet /ok tét/ *n* **1** a group of eight, especially musicians **2** a musical composition for a group of eight

October /ok tóbər/ *n* the 10th month of the year in the Gregorian calendar

ORIGIN October comes from a Latin word literally meaning 'eighth month'. In ancient Rome the calendar started the year in March.

octogenarian /óktō jə náiri ən/ *n* somebody in his or her eighties

octopus /óktəpəss/ *n* a sea animal with a soft oval body and eight arms with suckers

ocular /ókyoōlər/ *adj* of the eyes or eyesight ■ *n* an eyepiece of an optical instrument

oculist /ókyoōlist/ *n* an optometrist or ophthalmologist *(dated)*

~~ocupation~~ incorrect spelling of **occupation**

~~ocurr~~ incorrect spelling of **occur**

~~ocurred~~ incorrect spelling of **occurred**

~~ocurrence~~ incorrect spelling of **occurrence**

OD¹, O/D, o/d *abbr* overdraft

OD² /ō deeʻ/ (**OD'ing, OD'ed**) *vi* take an overdose of a drug *(infml)*

odd *adj* **1** unusual or strange **2** describes a number not divisible exactly by 2 **3** leftover ○ *a few odd coins* **4** separated or different from the rest of a pair or set ○ *wearing odd socks* **5** irregular or occasional ○ *gets the odd day off* **6** slightly greater than a particular number ○ *50-odd pounds* —**oddly** *adv* —**oddness** *n*

oddball /ód bawl/ *n* a person regarded as unconventional *(infml insult)*

oddity /óddəti/ (*pl* **-ties**) *n* somebody or something different from the rest

odd job *n* an occasional small job *(often pl)*

oddment /ódmənt/ *n* something left over *(usually pl)*

odds *npl* **1** the chances of something happening **2** the predicted chances in betting **3** a handicap or advantage used in competition ◇ **at odds (with)** in disagreement or conflict with ◇ **over the odds** more than is usual or necessary

odds and ends *npl* miscellaneous items

odds-on *adj* likeliest to win, succeed, or happen *(infml)*

ode /ōd/ *n* a lyric poem with a complex style and structure

Odense /őd'nssə/ port in south-central Denmark. Pop. 144,940 (1999).

Oder /ődər/ river in north-central Europe, flowing northwards from the Czech Republic into the Baltic Sea. Length 906 km/563 mi.

Odessa /ő déssə/, **Odesa** port in south-central Ukraine, on the Black Sea. Pop. 1,027,000 (1998).

Odin /ődin/ n in Norse mythology, the king of the gods

odious /ődi əss/ adj hateful —**odiously** adv —**odiousness** n

~~odissey~~ incorrect spelling of **odyssey**

odium /ődi əm/ n general hatred or disapproval directed at somebody

odometer /ő dómmitər, o-/ n US a mileometer

odontology /óddon tóllǝji/ n the study of teeth —**odontological** /o dóntǝ lójjik'l/ adj —**odontologist** n

odor n US = **odour**

odoriferous /ődǝ ríffǝrǝss/ adj having a strong odour (technical)

odorous /ődǝrǝss/ adj having a strong odour (literary)

odour /ődǝr/ n 1 a smell 2 a pervasive quality o the odour of sanctity —**odourless** adj

Odysseus /ő díssee ǝss/ n in Greek mythology, a hero of the Trojan War who spent ten years returning home. Roman equivalent **Ulysses**

odyssey /óddissi/ (pl -seys) n a long series of travels and adventures

OECD abbr Organization for Economic Co-operation and Development

oedema /i deemǝ/ (pl -mas or -mata /-mǝtǝ/) n 1 excess fluid in the tissues of the body 2 excess fluid in plants

Oedipus /eédipǝss/ n in Greek mythology, a man who unwittingly killed his father and married his mother

Oedipus complex n in psychoanalysis, a theorized unconscious sexual desire in a male child for his mother

OEIC /oyk/ n a limited company managing a portfolio of investments in which small investors can buy units. Full form **open-ended investment company**

o'er /ő ǝr, awr/ prep, adv over (literary)

oesophagus /i sóffǝgǝss/ (pl -gi /-gī/) n the passage for food between the throat and the stomach —**oesophageal** /i sóffǝ jeè ǝl/ adj

oestrogen /eéstrǝjǝn, és-/ n a hormone that regulates female reproductive functions and characteristics —**oestrogenic** /eéstrǝ jénnik, éstrǝ-/ adj

oeuvre /úrvrǝ, urvr/ n an artistic work, or an artist's works collectively

of (stressed) /ov/ (unstressed) /ǝv, ǝ/ prep 1 indicates the person or thing affected by or performing an action o the birth of their daughter 2 used after quantities to indicate what is being measured o millions of dollars 3 connected with o the president of France 4 containing o a mug of coffee 5 being part of o a slice of cake 6 made from o a rod of iron 7 indicates relationship or association o thinking of you 8 relating to as a feeling or quality o sure of himself o kind of you 9 indicates a particular type o something of an expert 10 having a particular quality o a musician of great talent o the gentleness of his manner 11 indicates amount o a limit of eight characters

off /of/ prep, adv 1 so as to get out of or leave o getting off the bus 2 so as to keep away from o Keep off the grass. 3 away from work o a day off 4 as a reduction on o 10 per cent off everything 5 so as to be removed from o washes off easily ■ adv 1 further away in space or time o two miles off o a week off 2 as a measurement or division o the distance marked off on the map 3 to completion o paid off 4 into a particular state o dozed off ■ prep 1 abstaining from o stay off caffeine 2 on a diet of o living off vegetables 3 not far away from, or leading away from o just off the main street ■ adv, adj 1 not in operation o switch off 2 cancelled o The deal's off. ■ adj 1 no longer fresh o The milk's off. 2 not on the menu 3 in a particular condition with regard to something o How are you off for cash? 4 in error or out of alignment ■ n the part of a cricket field facing the batsman taking strike ◊ **off and on** occasionally

USAGE In formal writing, avoid off plus of: The actors stepped off [not off of] the stage. Avoid also using off after verbs like buy or borrow: I bought the computer from [not off] my flatmate.

off-air adj happening during a recording but not broadcast —**off air** adv

offal /óff'l/ n 1 the edible internal organs of an animal 2 something thrown away

Offaly /óffǝli/ county in the central Republic of Ireland

off beat n an unaccented musical beat

offbeat /óf beet/ adj unconventional

off-Broadway n New York theatre productions away from the Broadway area

off-centre adj 1 not at the centre, especially when this causes a problem 2 slightly eccentric —**off centre** adv

off chance n a slight possibility ◊ **on the off chance** just in case something happens

off-colour adj 1 unwell 2 slightly sexually indecent or suggestive (infml)

offcut /óf kut/ n a remaining scrap of something that has been cut

off day n a day of not feeling or performing very well

Offenbach /óff'n baak/, **Jacques** (1819–80) German-born French composer

offence /ǝ fénss/ n 1 a legal or moral crime 2 an offensive 3 the attacking players on a team 4 anger or resentment felt at something

offend /ǝ fénd/ v 1 vti cause somebody anger, resentment, or hurt 2 vi break a law —**offender** n —**offending** adj

ORIGIN Offend goes back to a Latin verb

meaning 'strike against'. Some early uses retain the aspect of physical attack or contact, as do the related words **offence** and **offensive**, but during the 18C senses relating to feelings, morals, conduct, and society took over **offend** completely.

offense n US = **offence**

offensive /ə fénssiv/ adj **1** causing anger, resentment, or moral outrage **2** unpleasant to the senses **3** demonstrating aggression **4** designed for use in an attack ■ n an attack or assault —**offensively** adv —**offensiveness** n

offer /óffər/ vt **1** present something for acceptance or rejection **2** provide something for those who want it ○ *The town offers many attractions.* **3** volunteer to do something **4** have something for sale or hire **5** *also* **offer up** give something to God as part of worship **6** exhibit a quality ○ *offered little resistance* **7** make a bid or financial proposal ○ *offered £40 for it* ■ n a proposal

offering /óffəring/ n **1** the making of an offer, or an offer made **2** a gift for a deity

offer price, offering price n the price of something being sold

~~offerred~~ incorrect spelling of **offered**

offertory /óffərtəri/ (pl **-ries**) n **1** in Christianity, an offering of Communion bread and wine **2** a church collection

off-guard adj not anticipating a possible attack or approach

offhand /of hánd/ adv **1** casually **2** without preparation or research ■ adj *also* **offhanded** **1** unconcerned and uncaring **2** done casually or without planning —**offhandedly** adv

office /óffiss/ n **1** a room used for business activity **2** a place of business **3** a commercial or professional organization **4** the workers in an office **5** a government agency or department **6** a position of responsibility **7** a set form of a Christian service ■ **offices** npl something done on behalf of another *(fml)*

office block n a building housing offices

office holder n **1** an official in government **2** *also* **office-bearer** somebody who holds office in a society, club, or voluntary organization

office hours npl the times during which a business is open

office junior n an office worker given minor tasks

officer /óffissər/ n **1** somebody with a commission in the armed forces **2** a member of a police force **3** somebody licensed to be in authority on a ship **4** an elected or appointed official

official /ə físh'l/ n somebody holding office ■ adj **1** of a governmental body **2** approved by some authority **3** formal or ceremonial ○ *the building's official opening* —**officially** adv

officialdom /ə físh'ldəm/ n bureaucrats and bureaucracy *(infml)*

officialese /ə físhə léez/ n pompous, wordy language considered characteristic of official documents

Official Receiver n an official appointed to manage a bankrupt's property before the appointment of a trustee

officiate /ə físhi ayt/ vi act in an official capacity —**officiant** n

officious /ə físhəss/ adj meddlesome and interfering —**officiously** adv —**officiousness** n

offing /óffing/ ◇ **in the offing** expected or likely in the future

off-key adj **1** out of tune **2** inappropriate —**off-key** adv

off-licence n UK a place selling alcohol for consumption elsewhere

off-limits adj out of bounds

off-line adj **1** describes a computer or peripheral device disconnected or functioning separately from an associated computer or network **2** involved in preparing but not transmitting broadcast material —**off line** adv

offload /of lṓd, óf lōd/ v **1** vti unload goods **2** vt get rid of something unwanted by passing it on to somebody else

off-message adj departing from the party line

off-peak adj of the least busy time —**off peak** adv

off-piste adj not on regular ski-runs —**off piste** adv

offprint /óf print/ n a printed version of a single article from a periodical

off-putting adj irritating or disconcerting —**off-puttingly** adv

off-road adj taking place or for use away from public roads

off-road vehicle n a vehicle used on rough terrain

off-screen adj **1** not visible on a screen **2** occurring in ordinary life rather than on television or in a film ○ *their off-screen romance* —**off screen** adv

off-season n a time of year when an activity is stopped or at a low level ■ adv in the off-season

offset n /óf set/ **1** something counterbalancing or compensating for something else **2** something set apart **3** a printing process in which ink is transferred to paper from another surface **4** an abrupt bend in a straight line ■ v /of sét, óf set/ (**-setting, -set**) **1** vt counteract or compensate for **2** vti print by offset printing **3** vti form or be an offset in something

offshoot /óf shoot/ n **1** a shoot growing from the main stem of a plant **2** something that comes from something else

offshore adv /of sháwr/ **1** from water to land ○ *blowing offshore* **2** in water some way from a shore ○ *anchored offshore* ■ adj when attributive /óf shawr/ **1** blowing or positioned offshore **2** at sea some way from a shore **3** based in a foreign country

offside /adj when attributive/ /óf sīd/ in sports, illegally beyond the advance of the ball or puck during play ■ n /óf sīd/ the driver's side of a vehicle —**offside** /óf sīd/ adv

offsider /of sīdər/ n Aus an assistant

offsite /óff sīt/ adj not on the main site —**offsite** adv

offspring /óf spring/ (pl same or -**springs**) n 1 the child, children, young, or descendants of a person or animal 2 a result or product of something

offstage /óf stáyj/ adv 1 outside the area of a stage used for acting 2 in private life, as opposed to when performing in the theatre —**offstage** adj

off-street adj not in a street but in a car park or driveway

off-the-cuff adj said without preparation —**off the cuff** adv

off-the-peg adj ready-made and sold in standard sizes —**off the peg** adv

off-the-record adj said unofficially and not to be repeated or attributed to the speaker —**off the record** adv

off-the-shelf adj available from existing stock —**off the shelf** adv

off-the-wall adj bizarrely unusual (infml) —**off the wall** adv

off-white adj near-white in colour —**off-white** n

OFSTED /óff sted/, **Ofsted** n a government body that monitors the educational quality of schools and colleges in England and Wales. Full form **Office for Standards in Education**

oft adv often (literary; often in combination) ○ her oft-quoted remark

often /óff'n, óftən/ adv at short intervals or repeatedly ◇ **every so often** regularly but at fairly long intervals

ORIGIN The older word for 'often' is oft. Often is an extended form of this, perhaps formed on the analogy of selden, an earlier form of seldom.

oftentimes /óff'n tīmz, óftən-/, **ofttimes** /óft tīmz/ adv often (literary)

ogle /ốg'l/ (**ogling, ogled**) vti stare at somebody with sexual interest —**ogle** n ◇ See note at gaze

ogre /ốgər/ n 1 in fairy tales, a wicked giant or monster 2 a person regarded as frightening —**ogreish** adj

ogress /ốgriss/ n 1 in fairy tales, a wicked female monster 2 a woman regarded as frightening

oh /ố/ interj 1 expresses strong emotion 2 introduces a strong reaction ○ Oh what a fool I've been! 3 introduces a response 4 shows thought or hesitation

Ohio /ố hí ố/ state in the north-central United States. Cap. Columbus. Pop. 11,353,140 (2000). —**Ohioan** adj, n

ohm /ốm/ n (symbol Ω) the SI unit of electrical resistance

ORIGIN The **ohm** is named after the German physicist Georg Simon Ohm (1787–1854).

OHMS abbr On Her (or His) Majesty's Service

oho /ố hố/ interj expresses surprise or jubilation

OHP abbr overhead projector

oil n 1 a liquid fat that does not dissolve in water and will burn 2 petroleum, or a petroleum derivative used as a fuel or lubricant 3 a thick oily liquid 4 an oil paint (usually pl) ■ vt apply oil to —**oiled** adj

oil cake n livestock feed made from the solid residue remaining after extraction of the oil from some seeds

oilcan /óyl kan/ n a metal container for oil

oilcloth /óyl kloth/ n oil-treated cloth. Use: table coverings.

oil field n an oil-producing area

oil-fired adj using oil as fuel

oilman /óyl man, -mən/ (pl -**men** /-men, -mən/) n an executive or worker in the oil industry

oil paint n a paint containing oil that dries

oil painting n 1 a picture made using oil paints 2 the use of oil paints

oil rig n a platform and other equipment used in drilling for oil

oilskin /óyl skin/ n 1 fabric treated with oil to make it waterproof 2 a garment made of oilskin

oil slick n a film of oil, especially on water

oil well n a borehole for extracting oil

oily /óyli/ (-**ier**, -**iest**) adj 1 dirty with oil ○ don't want to get my hands oily 2 containing or like oil 3 ingratiating —**oiliness** n

oink /oyngk/ interj, n the characteristic sound made by a pig —**oink** vi

ointment /óyntmənt/ n a greasy soothing or softening substance used on the skin

OIRO abbr offers in the region of

Oise /waaz/ river in S Belgium and N France. Length 303 km/188 mi.

OK /ố káy/, **okay** (infml) interj indicates agreement ■ adj 1 rather good or pleasant 2 allowable ■ vt (**OK'ing, OK'ed; okaying, okayed**) give or obtain approval for ■ n (pl **OK's**; pl **okays**) somebody's approval or consent

ORIGIN Of the many competing theories about the origins of **OK**, the one now most widely accepted is that the letters stand for oll or orl korrect, a facetious early 19C American phonetic spelling of all correct. This was reinforced by the fact that they were also coincidentally the initial letters of Old Kinderhook, the nickname of US president Martin Van Buren (who was born in Kinderhook, New York State), which were used as a slogan in the presidential election of 1840 (a year after the first record of **OK** in print).

okapi /ố ka'api/ (pl -**pis** or same) n a plant-eating mammal resembling a small giraffe

Okeechobee, Lake /ˈōki chóbi/ lake in S Florida, in the N Everglades

Popperfoto

Georgia O'Keeffe

O'Keeffe /ō kéef/, **Georgia** (1887–1986) US artist

Okhotsk, Sea of /ō kótsk, ō khótsk/ arm of the NW Pacific Ocean, lying off the coast of E Siberia

Okinawa /óki naáwə/ **1** city on south-central Okinawa Island, Japan. Pop. 122,356 (2000). **2** largest of the Ryukyu Islands, SW Japan. Pop. 1,229,000 (1991).

Oklahoma /óklə hómə/ state in the south-central United States. Cap. Oklahoma City. Pop. 3,450,654 (2000). —**Oklahoman** *adj, n*

Oklahoma City capital of Oklahoma. Pop. 472,221 (1998).

okra /ókrə, ókrə/ *n* **1** a green finger-shaped pod used as a vegetable **2** the plant that produces okra

old /ōld/ *adj* (**older, oldest**) **1** having lived for a long time compared with others **2** originating years ago **3** showing characteristics sometimes associated with having lived long **4** wise or mature **5** having existed for a particular time (*usually in combination*) **6** of the remote past **7** former **8** familiar **9** existing or used over time **10** used for emphasis (*infml*) ○ *any old time* **11** expresses familiarity or affection (*infml*) ○ *Good old Charlie!* ■ *n* a person of a particular age (*in combination*) ○ *three-year-olds* ■ *npl* an offensive term for people who have lived a long time —**oldness** *n*

old age *n* the later years of a life lived out to its full term

old boy *n* **1** a male former student **2** used as a familiar form of address to a man (*infml dated*)

old-boy network *n* a system of informal contacts between men

old country *n* an immigrant's country of origin

olden /ṓldən/ *adj* of the distant past (*literary*)

Old English *n* the earliest form of the English language, used up to about AD 1150 —**Old English** *adj*

Old English sheepdog *n* a large shaggy dog with a white and grey coat

olde-worlde /ṓldi wúrldi/ *adj* quaintly historical

old-fashioned *adj* **1** out of date **2** maintaining the ways of an earlier time

SYNONYMS old-fashioned, outdated, antiquated, archaic, obsolete, passé, ante-

diluvian CORE MEANING: no longer in current use or no longer considered fashionable

old girl *n* a woman former student

old guard *n* the long-established and conservative members of a group (*+ sing or pl verb*)

old hand *n* a very experienced person

old hat *adj* boringly familiar (*infml*)

oldie /ṓldi/ *n* an old thing, especially a popular song (*infml*)

old master *n* **1** a great European painter between the Middle Ages and the 18C **2** a painting by an old master

old school *n* a group adhering to traditional values and practices —**old-school** *adj*

old school tie *n* **1** an identifying tie worn by former students of a particular school **2** loyalty between former students of the same school

Old Testament *n* the first section of the Christian Bible, corresponding to the Hebrew Bible

old-time *adj* **1** old-fashioned **2** long-established

old-timer *n* **1** a resident or worker who has been at a particular place for a long time **2** a senior citizen, especially a man (*sometimes offensive*)

Olduvai Gorge /ṓldə vī-/ ravine in N Tanzania, where fossil remains of early humans and hominids have been found. Length 50 km/30 mi. Depth 91 m/300 ft.

old wives' tale *n* a superstitious or erroneous belief

Old World *n* the eastern hemisphere

old-world *adj* typical of a former age

olé /ō láy/ *interj* expresses triumph, approval, or encouragement, especially at a bullfight ■ *n* a cry of 'olé'

oleaginous /óli ájjənəss/ *adj* **1** containing or like oil **2** ingratiating

oleander /óli ándər/ (*pl* **-ders** *or same*) *n* a poisonous evergreen shrub with leathery leaves and sweet-smelling flowers

olfactory /ol fáktəri/ *adj* of the sense of smell

oligarchy /ólli gaarki/ (*pl* **-chies**) *n* **1** a small governing group **2** a country or organization ruled by an oligarchy **3** government by an oligarchy —**oligarchic** /ólli gaàrkik/ *adj*

Oligocene /ólligō seen/ *n* an epoch of geological time 34–24 million years ago —**Oligocene** *adj*

Oliphant /ṓllifənt/, **Sir Mark** (1901–2000) Australian physicist who discovered tritium (1934)

olive /ólliv/ *n* **1** a small green or black fruit with a stone **2** the tree that produces olives

olive branch *n* **1** a conciliatory gesture **2** a branch of an olive tree used as a symbol of peace

olive drab *n* a greyish-green colour

olive oil *n* oil from olives. Use: salad dressings, cooking, manufacture of soap and cosmetics.

Olives, Mount of /óllivz/ ridge of hills in the West Bank, east of Jerusalem, the site of many events in early Christian history. Height 834 m/2,737 ft.

Olivier /ə lívvi ay/, **Laurence, 1st Baron Olivier of Brighton** (1907–89) British actor and director

Olympia /ə límpi ə/ plain in SW Greece, site of the ancient Olympic Games

Olympiad /ə límpi ad/ n **1** a single Olympic Games **2** a four-year period for calculating dates

Olympian /ə límpi ən/ adj **1** of Mount Olympus or the Greek gods **2** aloof or superior **3** enormous **4** of Olympia ■ n **1** in Greek mythology, a god **2** an Olympic athlete **3** a superior person **4** somebody from Olympia

Olympic /ə límpik/ adj of the Olympic Games

Olympic Games, Olympics npl **1** a large-scale international sports contest, held every four years **2** an ancient Greek festival of athletic, literary, and musical contests, held every four years

Olympus, Mt /ə límpəss/ highest mountain in Greece, the mythological home of the Greek gods. Height 2,917 m/9,570 ft.

Om /ōm, om/ n a sacred syllable chanted in Hindu and Buddhist mantras

OM abbr Order of Merit

Omaha /ómə haa/ city in E Nebraska, on the Missouri River. Pop. 371,291 (1998).

Oman /ō maán/ country on the SE Arabian Peninsula. Cap. Muscat. Pop. 2,622,198 (2001). —**Omani** adj, n

Oman, Gulf of arm of the Arabian Sea, situated between Oman and SE Iran

Omar Khayyam /ō maar kī aám, -ám/ (1050?–1122) Persian poet, mathematician, and astronomer

ombudsman /ómbŏodzmən/ (pl **-men** /-mən/) n an independent investigator of complaints against government, companies, or other organizations —**ombudsmanship** n

---

ORIGIN The word **ombudsman** was adopted from Swedish. Various official kinds of **ombudsmen** had existed in Sweden since the early 19C. The first **ombudsman** in an English-speaking country was appointed in New Zealand in 1962; the United Kingdom followed in 1966.

Omdurman /óm dur maán/ city in east-central Sudan. Pop. 1,267,077 (1993).

omega /ómigə/ n the 24th and final letter of the Greek alphabet

omelette /ómmlət/ n a dish of beaten eggs cooked in a thin layer

---

ORIGIN The **omelette** seems to take its name from its thin flat shape. It derives ultimately from Latin lamina 'thin plate'.

---

omen /ō men, ómən/ n a prophetic sign ■ vti indicate the future of somebody or something

omicron /ō mī kron/ n the 15th letter of the Greek alphabet

ominous /ómminəss/ adj threatening something bad —**ominously** adv —**ominousness** n

omission /ō míssh'n/ n **1** something omitted **2** the omitting of something

omit /ō mit/ (**omitting, omitted**) vt **1** leave somebody or something out **2** fail to do something —**omissible** /ō míssəb'l/ adj ◊ See note at **neglect**

~~omission~~ incorrect spelling of **omission**

~~ommited, ommitted~~ incorrect spelling of **omitted**

omni- prefix all ○ omnipresent

omnibus /ómnibəss/ n **1** a book collecting several related works **2** also **omnibus edition** a single continuous broadcast of programmes previously broadcast separately **3** a bus (archaic or fml) ■ adj bringing many different things together as a single unit

omnipotent /om níppətənt/ adj all-powerful ■ n **Omnipotent** God —**omnipotence** n

omnipresent /ómni prézz'nt/ adj **1** always present everywhere **2** found everywhere —**omnipresence** n

omniscient /om níssi ənt/ adj all-knowing —**omniscience** n

omnivore /ómni vawr/ n **1** an animal that eats any type of food **2** somebody with wide interests —**omnivorous** /om nívvərəss/ adj

Omsk /omsk/ city in SW Russia. Pop. 1,437,781 (1995).

on prep **1** above and in contact with ○ sitting on the bed **2** attached to or supported by ○ mounted on the wall **3** being carried by ○ no cash on me **4** located in or near ○ on the coast **5** at a time during ○ on Tuesday **6** relating to ○ a talk on international relations **7** by means of or using ○ on horseback **8** in a circumstance or position ○ on holiday ○ on equal terms **9** directed towards ○ shone a light on them ■ adv **1** in contact with something ○ an envelope with a stamp on **2** into a condition of attachment or suspension ○ sewing a button on **3** over part of the body ○ put gloves on **4** so as to continue ○ stayed on at college **5** in or into performance or operation ○ put a concert on ■ adj **1** taking place at the present time **2** arranged or planned ○ Is the game still on? ◊ **be on to** be aware of the real nature of (infml) ◊ **on and off** occasionally ◊ **on and on** in a continuous, persistent way

-on suffix **1** a subatomic particle ○ electron **2** a unit, quantum ○ photon

once /wunss/ adv **1** at a time in the past **2** on one occasion only **3** multiplied by one ○ Once three is three. **4** by one step or degree of relationship ○ a cousin once removed ■ conj as soon as ◊ **all at once 1** suddenly or unexpectedly **2** all at the same time ◊ **at once 1** immediately **2** all at the same time ◊ **for once** only on this particular occasion ◊ **once and for all** completely, finally, or definitively

once-over n a quick appraising look (infml)

oncology /ong kóllǝji/ n the branch of medicine

that deals with cancer **—oncological** /óngkə lójjik'l/ *adj* **—oncologist** *n*

oncoming /ón kuming/ *adj* heading directly towards somebody or something

oncost /ón kost/ *n* the ongoing expense of running a business

one /wun/ *det, pron* **1** a unique or separate person or thing ○ *the one exception* ○ *from one place to another* **2** a single person or thing ○ *one hour later* ○ *gave me only one* ■ *det* **1** definite but not identified ○ *one August afternoon* **2** a particular but unknown ○ *a letter from one Lee Smith* ■ *pron* **1** any person *(fml)* ○ *One can eat well here.* **2** refers to somebody or something previously mentioned ○ *an old vase, and a cracked one at that* ■ *n* the number 1 **—oneness** *n* ◇ **all one** not important enough to be of any consequence ◇ **at one** in harmony ◇ **one and all** everyone in a group ◇ **one by one** individually in sequence

one another *pron* each to the other or others

one-armed bandit *n* a gambling machine operated by a coin or token and a lever *(infml)*

one-horse *adj* **1** small, dull, and insignificant **2** with only one candidate or competitor who is likely to win

O'Neill /ō néel/, **Eugene** (1888–1953) US playwright

one-liner *n* a brief joke or witticism, usually in one sentence

one-man band *n* **1** a street musician who plays several instruments at once **2** an organization in which one person does everything

one-night stand *n* **1** a sexual or romantic encounter that occurs only once *(infml)* **2** a performance on one night only

one-off *adj* occurring only once **—one-off** *n*

onerous /ónərəss, ónnər-/ *adj* difficult **—onerously** *adv* **—onerousness** *n*

oneself /wun sélf/ *pron (fml)* **1** any person's own self **2** any person's normal self

one-sided *adj* **1** unfairly favouring one competitor **2** biased **—one-sidedness** *n*

one-stop *adj* providing a variety of goods or services in one place

onetime /wún tīm/ *adj* **1** former **2** *also* **one-time** happening only once

one-to-one *adj* **1** involving contact or communication between two people **2** with pairings between members of two mathematical sets that leave no remainder **—one-to-one** *adv*

one-track *adj* focused on or obsessed with one subject

one-two *n* **1** a combination of two successive punches **2** a combination of two quick sequential actions or events

one-upmanship /-úpmənship/ *n* the attempt to do better than or show up rivals

one-way *adj* **1** in one direction only **2** not allowing a return journey **3** involving only one of two people

ongoing /ón gō ing, -gó-/ *adj* continuing

onion /únnyən/ *n* **1** a pungent edible bulb used as a vegetable **2** a plant that produces onions **—oniony** *adj*

online /ón lín/ *adj* **1** attached to or available through a central computer or computer network **2** connected to a computer network via the Internet, or available via the Internet **—online** *adv*

online banking *n* a banking service accessed from a commercial online network

onliner /ón línər/ *n* a user of online services

onlooker /ón lóokər/ *n* an observer of an event **—onlooking** *adj*

only /ónli/ *adv* **1** solely or exclusively ○ *for members only* ○ *applying only to residents* **2** indicates the condition for something to happen or be true ○ *only if you come too* **3** merely ○ *could only stand and watch* **4** no more and no less ○ *only two people here* **5** as recently as ○ *only yesterday* **6** indicates an event that happens immediately after the one mentioned ○ *arrived only to find that they'd left* ■ *adj* indicates the single person or thing involved ○ *the only candidate* ○ *an only child* ■ *conj* except that ◇ **only too** very

on-message *adj* keeping to the official policy of a group

o.n.o. *abbr* or nearest offer *(in advertisements)*

onomatopoeia /ónnō matə pée ə/ *n* the formation of words that imitate a sound **—onomatopoeic** *adj*

onrush /ón rush/ *n* a forward rush **—onrushing** *adj*

on-screen *adj, adv* appearing on a TV or cinema screen

onset /ón set/ *n* **1** the beginning of something, especially something unpleasant **2** an initial military attack

onshore /ón sháwr/ *adj* **1** on land as opposed to the sea **2** in the direction of land **—onshore** *adv*

onside /ón síd/ *adj, adv* in sports, keeping a position that is allowed within the rules of the game

onslaught /ón slawt/ *n* an overwhelming assault or force

onstage /ón stáyj/ *adj, adv* performed or happening on the stage of a theatre

on-stream *adj, adv* in or into operation or production

Ontario /on táiri ō/ province of east-central Canada. Cap. Toronto. Pop. 11,669,344 (2000). **—Ontarian** *n, adj*

Ontario, Lake smallest and easternmost of the Great Lakes, on the border between NW New York State and SE Ontario, Canada

onto *(stressed)* /ón too/ *(unstressed)* /óntə, óntōō/ *prep* **1** so as to be on top of ○ *putting it onto the top shelf* **2** towards and into contact with ○ *splashed water onto her face* **3** making or about to make a discovery ○ *The police are onto them.*

ontogeny /on tójjəni/, **ontogenesis** /óntə jénnəsiss/ *n* development of an individual to maturity —**ontogenic** /óntə jénnik/ *adj*

ontology /on tólləji/ (*pl* -**gies**) *n* 1 the study of the nature of existence 2 a theory of existence —**ontological** /óntə lójjik'l/ *adj* —**ontologist** *n*

onus /ónəss/ *n* 1 a duty or responsibility 2 the blame for something

onward /ónwərd/ *adj* moving forward ■ *adv also* **onwards** at or to a point ahead

onyx /ónniks/ *n* a fine-grained mineral with coloured bands. Use: gems, cameo work.

oodles /ood'lz/ *npl* a large amount (*infml*)

OOG *abbr* object-oriented graphics

ooh /oo/ *vi* express surprise or pleasure

oomph /oomf/ *n* 1 energy 2 *US* sexual attractiveness (*slang*)

oops /oops, oops/ *interj* acknowledges clumsiness (*infml*)

ooze[1] *vti* (**oozing, oozed**) 1 flow or leak slowly 2 overflow with some quality or emotion ■ *n* a very slow flow —**oozy** *adj*

ooze[2] *n* thick mud or slime at the bottom of a river or lake

op *n* an operation (*infml*)

OP *abbr* out of print

opacity /ō pássəti/ *n* the state of being opaque

opal /óp'l/ *n* noncrystalline silica. Use: gems.

opalescent /ópə léss'nt/ *adj* shimmering with milky colours —**opalescence** *n*

opaque /ō páyk/ *adj* 1 not transparent or translucent 2 hard to understand —**opaquely** *adv*

op art *n* an abstract art movement using geometric shapes and colour —**op artist** *n*

OPEC /ó pek/ *abbr* full form **Organization of Petroleum Exporting Countries**

op-ed /óp éd/ *n* the page of a newspaper opposite the editorial page, containing contributed articles and personal views

open /ópən/ *adj* 1 not closed, enclosed, sealed, blocked, or locked 2 apart, wide, or unfolded 3 frank and honest 4 public or freely accessible ○ *open hearings* 5 receptive ○ *open to suggestions* 6 vulnerable ○ *open to criticism* 7 available to do business 8 vacant for applicants ○ *The position is still open.* 9 not predetermined or decided ○ *keeping my options open* ■ *v* 1 *vti* unfasten or unfold from a locked, closed, or sealed position or state 2 *vti* move apart, or part the lips or eyelids 3 *vti* start trading, or allow customers access to in order to trade 4 *vti* start or get something under way 5 *vi* start being shown to or performed for the general public for the first time 6 *vt* remove obstructions from something ○ *opened its borders* 7 *vi* give access to a place (*refers to part of a building*) ○ *opens onto a courtyard* ■ *n* 1 a competition anyone can enter 2 a large and unobstructed outdoor space 3 a public state ○ *get the facts into the open* —**openly** *adv* —**openness** *n*
□ **open up** *v* 1 *vi* unfold 2 *vti* make something accessible 3 *vt* make an opening in 4 *vi* speak freely

open-air *adj* outdoor

open-and-shut *adj* decisively clear

open bar *n* a bar where free drinks are served at a social function

open-cast *adj* describes mining from the surface

open day *n* a day when an institution opens to the public

open-ended *adj* 1 without a prearranged end or limit 2 easily modified —**open-endedly** *adv* —**open-endedness** *n*

opener /ópənər/ *n* a device for opening something ◊ **for openers** firstly (*infml*)

open-eyed *adj* 1 watchful 2 with eyes wide in wonder

openhanded /ópən hándid/ *adj* generous with money and material things —**openhandedly** *adv* —**openhandedness** *n*

openhearted /ópən haártid/ *adj* kindly and generous in spirit —**openheartedness** *n*

open-heart surgery *n* heart surgery during which the heart is exposed and blood is circulated outside the body by mechanical means

open house *n* a situation or occasion when visitors are welcome at any time

opening /ópəning/ *n* 1 a gap or hole in something 2 the first part or start of something 3 the occasion when something is formally opened 4 an opportunity 5 a job vacancy

opening night *n* the night of the first public performance of a play or other show

opening time *n* the time for a pub to open

open letter *n* a letter to somebody that is published

open market *n* trading without commercial restrictions

open-minded *adj* unprejudiced and receptive to new ideas —**open-mindedly** *adv* —**open-mindedness** *n*

open-mouthed *adj* with the mouth open in surprise or wonder

open-plan *adj* having a large space left open rather than divided up into smaller units

open prison *n* a prison with relatively relaxed security measures

open sandwich *n* a one-sided sandwich without a piece of bread on top

open season *n* a period when restrictions on hunting are lifted

open secret *n* something that is supposed to be secret but is widely known

open sesame /-séssəmi/ *n* a key to success

open system *n* a computer design system with uniform industry standards

open trading protocol *n* a standardized computer protocol for payments

Open University *n* a UK university offering courses mainly by correspondence and through broadcasts

open verdict *n* a decision of a coroner's court that the cause of death is not clear

open water *n* an expanse of unenclosed and unobstructed water

openwork /óppən wurk/ *n* 1 decorative work using patterns of holes 2 embroidery with decorated holes

opera[1] /óppərə/ *n* 1 a drama set to music 2 operas as a genre

opera[2] /óppərə/ plural of **opus**

operable /óppərəb'l/ *adj* 1 surgically treatable 2 able to be done

opera glasses *npl* small binoculars for the theatre

operand /óppə rand/ *n* 1 an entity that is to have a mathematical operation performed on it 2 a part of a computer instruction that specifies the location of the data to be manipulated

operate /óppə rayt/ (**-ating, -ated**) *v* 1 *vti* work or function, or make something work or function 2 *vi* perform surgery

~~operater~~ incorrect spelling of **operator**

operatic /óppə ráttik/ *adj* of opera —**operatically** *adv*

operating cycle *n* the time between selling and receiving payment

operating system *n* a master control program in a computer

operating table *n* a table used for surgical operations

operating theatre *n* a room in a hospital where surgical operations are performed

operation /óppə ráysh'n/ *n* 1 the controlling or operating of something 2 a functioning state 3 something carried out, especially something complex 4 a surgical procedure 5 an organized action or campaign 6 a mathematical process ■ **operations** *npl* the controlling of organized activities

operational /óppə ráysh'nəl/ *adj* 1 able to operate or be used 2 of the operating of something or the way something operates

operative /óppərətiv/ *adj* 1 in place and having an effect 2 significant 3 of surgery ■ *n* a skilled worker —**operatively** *adv*

operator /óppə raytər/ *n* 1 somebody operating machinery or equipment 2 an owner or manager of a business 3 a manipulative person (*infml*) 4 a symbol or other entity performing or describing a mathematical operation

operetta /óppə réttə/ *n* a comic opera with dancing —**operettist** *n*

ophthalmic /of thálmik/ *adj* of the eye

ophthalmology /óf thal mólləji/ *n* the medical study and treatment of eyes —**ophthalmological** /óf thálmə lójjik'l/ *adj* —**ophthalmologist** *n*

opiate /ópi ət/ *n* 1 an opium-containing drug 2 a sleep-inducing substance ■ *adj* containing opium

opine /ō pín/ (**opining, opined**) *vti* state an opinion (*fml*)

opinion /ə pínnyən/ *n* 1 a personal view about an issue 2 an estimation of worth 3 an expert view

opinionated /ə pínnyə naytid/ *adj* unwilling to change strongly held opinions

opinion poll *n* a survey of the public's views

opium /ópi əm/ *n* an addictive drug prepared from the seeds of a poppy

~~oponent~~ incorrect spelling of **opponent**

Oporto ♦ **Porto**

~~oportunity~~ incorrect spelling of **opportunity**

~~oposite~~ incorrect spelling of **opposite**

opossum /ə póssəm/ (*pl* **-sums** *or same*) *n* a small nocturnal marsupial

Oppenheimer /óppən hīmər/, **J. Robert** (1904–67) US nuclear physicist, leader of the team that developed the atomic bomb

~~opperation~~ incorrect spelling of **operation**

~~oppinion~~ incorrect spelling of **opinion**

opponent /ə pốnənt/ *n* 1 a rival in a contest 2 somebody opposing a course of action or a belief —**opponent** *adj*

opportune /óppər tyoon/ *adj* fitting or fortunate and well-timed —**opportunely** *adv* —**opportuneness** *n*

opportunist /óppər tyoónist/ *n* an unprincipled resourceful person ■ *adj* opportunistic —**opportunism** *n*

opportunistic /óppərtyoŏ nístik/ *adj* 1 taking advantage of opportunities, especially in an unprincipled way 2 usually minor but potentially life-threatening when immunity is low ○ *opportunistic infections*

opportunity /óppər tyoónəti/ (*pl* **-ties**) *n* 1 an advantageous chance 2 favourable conditions

opportunity cost *n* the cost of a business decision regarded as the value of the alternative that is forgone

opportunity shop *n* ANZ a charity-run second-hand shop

oppose /ə pốz/ (**-posing, -posed**) *v* 1 *vti* be actively against something 2 *vt* set in contrast to 3 *vi* put opposite to 4 *vt* compete with as opponents —**opposable** *adj* —**opposing** *adj*

opposed /ə pốzd/ *adj* actively against something

opposite /óppəzit/ *adj* 1 on the side that faces something or is at the farthest distance away 2 facing or moving away from each other 3 totally different ■ *n* 1 somebody or something different from another 2 an antonym ■ *adv* in the opposite position ■ *prep* 1 across from 2 in a complementing acting role to

opposite number *n* somebody's counterpart in another department or organization

opposite sex *n* men as a group as opposed to women, or women as a group as opposed to men

opposition /óppə zísh'n/ *n* 1 an actively hostile attitude 2 a sports opponent (+ *sing or pl verb*) 3 *also* **Opposition** an out-of-power political party (+ *sing or pl verb*) —**oppositional** *adj*

oppress /ə préss/ *vt* 1 dominate harshly 2 be

a source of stress or worry —**oppression** *n*
—**oppressor** *n*

oppressive /ə préssiv/ *adj* 1 dominating harshly 2 causing stress or discomfort —**oppressively** *adv* —**oppressiveness** *n*

opprobrium /ə próbri əm/ *n* 1 scorn 2 disgrace

~~opression~~ incorrect spelling of **oppression**

opt *vi* choose from alternatives

□ **opt out** *vi* choose not to do something *(infml)*

~~opthalmology~~ incorrect spelling of **ophthalmology**

optic /óptik/ *adj* of the eyes or vision ■ *n* an instrument's lens

optical /óptik'l/ *adj* 1 of visible light or optics 2 of vision —**optically** *adv*

optical character reader *n* a device for reading printed text into a computer by optical character recognition

optical character recognition *n* the use of light-sensing methods to convert an image or text into digital form

optical disk *n* a rigid computer disk read by a laser

optical fibre *n* a fibre used to transmit information in the form of pulses of laser light

optical illusion *n* 1 visual perception of something that is not actually there 2 a source of optical illusion

optical mouse *n* a computer mouse operated by light-emitting diodes

optical scanner *n* a device that converts an image or text into digital form

optician /op tísh'n/ *n* 1 a person qualified to examine eyes and prescribe lenses 2 a shop selling spectacles

optics /óptiks/ *n* the study of light *(+ sing verb)*

optimal /óptim'l/ *adj* most desirable or favourable —**optimally** *adv*

optimism /óptimizəm/ *n* 1 the tendency to expect or hope for the best 2 the philosophical doctrine that this is the best of all possible worlds —**optimist** *n* —**optimistic** /ópti místik/ *adj* —**optimistically** *adv*

ORIGIN Optimism was coined in French (as *optimisme*) in 1737 as a term for the doctrine of the German philosopher Leibniz that the actual world is the best of all possible worlds. The word is based on Latin *optimus* 'best'.

optimize /ópti mīz/ (**-mizing, -mized**), **optimise** *vt* 1 make something function at its best, or use something to its best advantage 2 solve a technical problem in the best way possible —**optimization** /ópti mī záysh'n/ *n*

optimum /óptiməm/ (*pl* **-ma** /-mə/ *or* **-mums**) *n* the best of several possible options or outcomes —**optimum** *adj*

option /ópsh'n/ *n* 1 a choice 2 freedom of choice 3 the right to buy or sell something at a fixed price within a given period

optional /ópsh'nəl/ *adj* not compulsory —**optionally** *adv*

optometrist /op tómmətrist/ *n* a qualified optician —**optometry** *n*

~~optimist~~ incorrect spelling of **optimist**

~~optimistic~~ incorrect spelling of **optimistic**

opt-out *n* a decision to choose not to do something

opulent /óppyŏŏlənt/ *adj* 1 characterized by a lavish display 2 in ample supply —**opulence** *n* —**opulently** *adv*

opus /ṓpəss/ (*pl* **opuses** *or* **opera** /óppərə/) *n* 1 one of a series of numbered musical works by the same composer 2 a creative work

or *(stressed)* /awr/ *(unstressed)* /ər/ *conj* 1 joins alternatives ○ *Either you typed the wrong name, or something is wrong with the equipment.* ○ *Do you prefer tea or coffee?* 2 indicates approximation ○ *one or two* 3 rephrases a statement ○ *German measles, or rubella* 4 otherwise ○ *You'd better leave or you'll be late.* ◇ **or other** not exactly identified or definite ○ *some play or other* ◇ **or so** approximately ◊ See note at **oar**

OR /awr/ *n* a Boolean operator whose result is true if one or both of its operands are true and false otherwise

-or *suffix* 1 somebody or something that does or performs ○ *sailor* 2 condition, state, activity ○ *horror*

oracle /órrək'l/ *n* 1 a source of wisdom or prophesy 2 a shrine of an ancient Greek or Roman prophetic deity 3 an ancient Greek or Roman prophetic deity —**oracular** /o rákyŏŏlər/ *adj*

oral /áwrəl/ *adj* 1 of the mouth 2 designed for use in the mouth 3 spoken 4 describes medicines that are taken by mouth ■ *n* a test requiring spoken answers —**orally** *adv* ◊ See note at **verbal, aural**

oral contraceptive *n* a pill taken to prevent pregnancy

oral history *n* 1 history recorded on tape by participants in events 2 a written work of history based on interviews with or recordings of participants —**oral historian** *n*

oral sex *n* stimulation of somebody's genitals with the mouth

orange /órrinj/ *n* 1 a round juicy citrus fruit with a skin between red and yellow in colour 2 a tree that produces oranges 3 a colour between red and yellow, like that of a ripe orange —**orange** *adj* —**orangey** *adj*

Orange /órrinj/ river in South Africa, flowing westwards from Lesotho into the Atlantic Ocean. Length 2,100 km/1,300 mi.

orangeade /órrinj áyd/ *n* an orange-flavoured drink

orange badge *n* a vehicle badge for drivers with disabilities

Orangeman /órrinjmən/ (*pl* **-men** /-mən/) *n* 1 a member of the Orange Order 2 a Protestant Northern Irishman

Orange Order *n* a Northern Irish Protestant organization

orangery /órrinjəri/ (*pl* **-ries**) *n* a large greenhouse where orange trees are grown

orange squash *n* a sweet orange-flavoured drink

orang-utan /aw rángə táng, -tán, ə rángə-/, **orang-utang** *n* a large reddish-brown ape

ORIGIN Orang-utan comes from the Malay name, meaning literally 'forest person' or 'wild man'. It is first recorded in English in the late 17C.

orate /aw ráyt/ (**orating, orated**) *vi* **1** make a formal public speech *(fml)* **2** speak pompously

oration /aw ráysh'n/ *n* **1** a formal public speech **2** a pompous speech

orator /órrətər/ *n* somebody skilled in making speeches

oratorio /órrə táwri ō/ *(pl* **-os**) *n* a piece of classical music for instruments and voices on a religious theme

oratory[1] /órrətəri/ *n* **1** the art of public speaking **2** skill at public speaking —**oratorical** /órrə tórrik'l/ *adj*

oratory[2] /órrətəri/ *(pl* **-ries**) *n* a small private room for prayer or worship

orb *n* **1** a jewelled sphere with a small cross on top that forms part of a king's or queen's regalia **2** a sphere **3** a spherical astronomical object **4** an eye or eyeball *(literary)* —**orbicular** /awr bíkyŏŏlər/ *adj*

orbit /áwrbit/ *n* **1** the path of a planet, satellite, or moon around another larger astronomical object **2** a revolution of one astronomical object around another larger one **3** an area of interest **4** an eye socket ■ *v* **1** *vti* move around an astronomical object **2** *vt* put into astronomical orbit

orbital /áwrbit'l/ *adj* of an orbit ■ *n* a road taking traffic around the outside of a city or town —**orbitally** *adv*

orbiter /áwrbitər/ *n* a spacecraft or satellite designed to orbit an astronomical object but not to land on it

orca /áwrkə/ *n* a killer whale

orchard /áwrchərd/ *n* an area of fruit or nut trees, or the trees planted in such an area

orchestra /áwrkistrə/ *n* a large group of musicians directed by a conductor —**orchestral** /awr késtrəl/ *adj*

ORIGIN In a theatre in ancient Greece, the **orchestra** was a semicircular area in front of the stage where the chorus (who commented in unison on the action of the play) danced and sang; in ancient Rome, it was an area in front of the stage with seats for senators and other important people. These are the contexts in which **orchestra** appeared in English during the 17C. In the early 18C, however, it began to refer to the place in a theatre or opera house where musicians sat (usually just in front of the stage), and then to the musicians themselves.

orchestra pit *n* the part of a theatre in front of the stage where the musicians sit

orchestrate /áwrki strayt/ (**-trating, -trated**) *vt* **1** arrange music for an orchestra **2** organize

unobtrusively o *carefully orchestrated the visit* —**orchestration** /áwrki stráysh'n/ *n* —**orchestrator** *n*

orchid /áwrkid/ *n* a plant prized for its beautiful fragrant flowers —**orchidaceous** /áwrki dáyshəss/ *adj*

ORIGIN The word **orchid** was introduced in 1845. It was taken from the modern Latin name of the family of plants to which the orchid belongs, where *orchid-* had wrongly been used as a form of *orchis*, the classical Latin name. Latin *orchis* came from a Greek word literally meaning 'testicle' and applied to the plant from the shape of the tubers.

ordain /awr dáyn/ *vt* **1** order something formally **2** make somebody officially a priest, minister, or rabbi —**ordainment** *n*

ordeal /awr deel, áwr deel/ *n* a difficult or harrowing experience

order /áwrdər/ *n* **1** a command or instruction to somebody to do something **2** an arrangement or sequence of items **3** neatness **4** the absence of crime **5** a properly functioning condition **6** an instruction to bring or supply something **7** something brought or supplied in response to an instruction **8** the arrangement of society into groups or classes and the relationship among them **9** a type of something o *a different order of intelligence* **10** *also* **Order** a religious community whose members live by a particular set of rules **11** *also* **Order** a group of people honoured for services to their country, or the decoration indicating such an honour o *the Order of the Garter* ■ **orders** *npl* holy orders ■ *v* **1** *vt* command somebody to do something **2** *vt* give an instruction for something to be done **3** *vti* give an instruction for something to be brought or supplied **4** *vt* arrange things in a neat or sensible order ◊ **a tall order** a request that is very difficult to fulfil *(infml)* ◊ **in order to** *or* **that** with the object or purpose of ◊ **on order** requested but not yet supplied or delivered

orderly /áwrdərli/ *adj* **1** well-behaved or peaceful **2** neatly arranged ■ *n* (*pl* **-lies**) **1** a hospital worker who does not provide medical care **2** a soldier who is a senior officer's personal assistant —**orderliness** *n*

order paper *n* a parliamentary agenda distributed daily to British MPs

ordinal /áwrdin'l/ *adj* showing position in a sequence of numbers ■ *n also* **ordinal number** a number such as first or tenth that shows position in a sequence

ordinance /áwrdinənss/ *n* a law or rule made by an authority, especially a municipal government

SPELLCHECK Do not confuse the spelling of **ordinance** and **ordnance** ('military weapons systems'), which sound similar.

~~ordinarly~~ incorrect spelling of **ordinarily**

ordinary /áwrd'nəri/ *adj* **1** of a common every-

day kind **2** unremarkable **3** usual
—**ordinarily** *adv* —**ordinariness** *n*
ordinary seaman *n* a Royal Navy sailor of the lowest rank
ordination /áwrdi náysh'n/ *n* the act or ceremony of making somebody officially a priest, minister, or rabbi
ordnance /áwrdnənss/ *n* **1** military weapons and equipment **2** the military department responsible for weapons and supplies ◊ See note at **ordinance**
Ordovician /áwrdō víshi ən/ *n* a period of geological time 495–443 million years ago —**Ordovician** *adj*
ordure /áwr dyoor/ *n* excrement *(fml)*
ore /awr/ *n* a mineral which metal is extracted ◊ See note at **oar**
oregano /órri gaánō/ *n* **1** the leaves of an aromatic herb used as a flavouring **2** an aromatic plant whose leaves are used as oregano
Oregon /órrigən/ state in the NW United States. Cap. Salem. Pop. 3,421,399 (2000). —**Oregonian** /órri gṓni ən/ *n, adj*
Orenburg /órrən burg/ city in SW Siberian Russia. Pop. 686,289 (1995).
Øresend /úrə sún, -sóond/, **Öresund** strait between SW Sweden and E Denmark. Length 100 km/65 mi.
Orff /awrf/, **Carl** (1895–1982) German composer
org /awrg/ *abbr* non-commercial organization *(in Internet addresses)*
organ /áwrgən/ *n* **1** a large musical keyboard instrument producing sound when air passes through its pipes **2** an instrument without pipes that makes a sound similar to an organ **3** an independent part of an animal or plant with a specific function **4** a newspaper or magazine regarded as a means of communication *(fml)*
organdie /áwrgəndi, awr gándi/ *n* a lightweight transparent cotton fabric. Use: dressmaking.
organelle /áwrgə nél/ *n* a specialized component of a cell that has its own particular function, e.g. a nucleus or mitochondrion
organ grinder *n* a street musician playing a barrel organ, traditionally accompanied by a small monkey for collecting money
organic /awr gánnik/ *adj* **1** of living things **2** occurring or developing naturally **3** consisting of efficiently combined elements in a seemingly natural relationship **4** produced without the use of synthetic agricultural chemicals **5** of the body's organs **6** describes chemical compounds based on carbon —**organically** *adv*
organic chemistry *n* the scientific study of carbon-based compounds
organism /áwrgənizəm/ *n* **1** a living thing **2** a functioning system of interdependent parts
organist /áwrgənist/ *n* an organ player
organization /áwrgə nī záysh'n/, **organisation** *n* **1** a group of people with a shared interest or purpose **2** coordination of separate elements into a unit or structure **3** the relationships between separate elements arranged into a whole —**organizational** *adj*
organize /áwrgə nīz/ (**-izing, -ized**), **organise** *v* **1** *vti* form or cause people to form a structured group **2** *vt* coordinate the various elements of something **3** *vt* arrange the elements of something so as to create a structure **4** *vt* make somebody or something become more effective —**organized** *adj*
organized crime *n* a large-scale network of professional criminals
organizer /áwrgə nīzər/, **organiser** *n* **1** somebody who organizes projects **2** a small portable diary in book or computer form
organophosphate /awr gánnō fóss fayt/ *n* an organic compound containing phosphate groups, which may be toxic. Use: pesticides, fertilizers.
organza /awr gánzə/ *n* a stiff transparent silk or synthetic fabric. Use: dressmaking.
orgasm /áwr gazəm/ *n* the climax of sexual excitement —**orgasm** *vi* —**orgasmic** /awr gázmik/ *adj*
orgy /áwrji/ *n* **1** a party where group sex occurs **2** a debauched party —**orgiastic** /áwrji ástik/ *adj*
orient /áwri ənt, órri-/ *v* **1** *vt* put in position facing a particular direction **2** *vr* find your position and the direction you need to travel in **3** *vt* direct something in a particular way ○ *advertising oriented towards teenage girls* **4** *vt* make somebody or yourself familiar with a new situation ■ *n also* **Orient** the countries of East Asia, especially China, Japan, and their neighbours *(dated)* ■ *adj* eastern *(archaic)* —**orientate** *vti* —**orientation** /áwri ən táysh'n, órri-/ *n*
Oriental /áwri ént'l, órri-/, **oriental** *adj* of East Asia *(dated)* ■ *n* a taboo term for somebody from East Asia
orienteering /áwri ən teéring, órri-/ *n* a sport that combines cross-country running and map-reading —**orienteer** *n, vi*
orifice /órrə fiss/ *n* an opening in the body
origami /órri gaámi/ *n* the Japanese art of paper-folding
origin /órrijin/ *n* (often pl) **1** the starting point or first cause of something **2** the source from which something comes or develops **3** somebody's ancestry, social class, or country

SYNONYMS origin, **source, derivation, provenance, root** CORE MEANING: the beginning of something

original /ə ríjj'nəl/ *adj* **1** first **2** completely new and not derivative **3** creative ■ *n* **1** the first version from which copies or alternative versions are made **2** an authentic piece of art —**originality** /ə ríjjə nálləti/ *n* —**originally** *adv* ◊ See note at **new**
original sin *n* the sinful state that Christians believe all people are born into

originate /ə ríjjə nayt/ (**-nating, -nated**) v **1** vi have an origin somewhere **2** vt invent or introduce —**originator** n

Orinoco /órri nṓkō/ river in Venezuela, flowing northwards into the Atlantic Ocean. Length 2,560 km/1,590 mi.

oriole /áwri ōl/ n a black-and-yellow songbird

Orkney Islands /áwrkni-/ island group in NE Scotland. Pop. 19,450 (1991).

Orlando /awr lándō/ city in N Florida. Pop. 181,175 (1998).

Orléans /awr leè ənz/ capital of Loire Department, north-central France. Pop. 113,126 (1999).

Orléans /awr leè ənz, awr lay aàN/, **Louis Philippe Joseph, Duc d'** (1747–93) French nobleman

ormolu /áwrməloo/ n a gold-coloured alloy of copper and zinc. Use: decorating furniture, jewellery, mouldings.

ornament n /áwrnəmənt/ **1** a decorative object put on display **2** decoration or decorative quality **3** something that decorates something else ■ vt /áwrnə ment/ add decorative elements or items to —**ornamentation** /áwrnə men táysh'n/ n

ornamental /áwrnə mént'l/ adj **1** decorative and with no practical purpose **2** describes a plant grown for its beauty ■ n an ornamental plant —**ornamentally** adv

ornate /awr náyt/ adj **1** elaborately or excessively decorative **2** using elaborate language —**ornately** adv

ornithology /áwrni thólləji/ n the study of birds —**ornithological** /áwrnithə lójjik'l/ adj —**ornithologist** n

OROM abbr optical read-only memory

orotund /órrō tund/ adj (fml) **1** loud, clear, and strong **2** pompous or bombastic

> **ORIGIN Orotund** was formed from Latin ore rotundo, literally 'with a round mouth'. The Latin phrase was used in English writing from the early 18C, and **orotund** itself appeared in the late 18C.

orphan /áwrf'n/ n **1** a child whose parents are dead **2** a young animal without a mother ■ vt make somebody an orphan —**orphanhood** n

orphanage /áwrfənij/ n a home for orphans

Orpheus /áwrfyooss, áwrfi əss/ n in Greek mythology, a poet and musician, who descended to the underworld to seek his wife, Eurydice, after her death but failed to bring her back

orthodontics /áwrthō dóntiks/, **orthodontia** /-dónti ə/ n the correction of teeth irregularities —**orthodontic** adj —**orthodontist** n

orthodox /áwrthə doks/ adj **1** following traditional doctrine **2 Orthodox** of the Eastern Orthodox Church **3 Orthodox** of the branch of Judaism that accepts the Torah as the literal work of God **4** customary —**orthodoxy** n

Orthodox Church n the Eastern Orthodox Church

orthogonal /awr thóggən'l/ adj of right angles —**orthogonally** adv

orthography /awr thóggrəfi/ (pl **-phies**) n **1** correct spelling **2** the study of how letters are arranged in words **3** the relationship between sounds and letters —**orthographical** /áwrthə gráffik'l/ adj

orthopaedic /áwrthə peédik/, **orthopedic** adj **1** of orthopaedics **2** of bone, joint, ligament, or muscle disorders —**orthopaedist** n

orthopaedics /áwrthə peédiks/, **orthopedics** n the branch of medicine dealing with bone, joint, ligament, or muscle disorders (+ sing verb)

orthotics /awr thóttiks/ n the science of the design and fitting of medical devices such as braces (+ sing verb) —**orthotic** adj —**orthotist** /áwrthətist/ n

George Orwell

Orwell /áwr wel/, **George** (1903–50) British writer —**Orwellian** /awr wélli ən/ adj

-ory suffix **1** of or relating to ○ compulsory ○ illusory **2** place or thing connected with or used for ○ refectory ○ oratory

oryx /órriks/ (pl same or **oryxes**) n an antelope with a black-and-white face and a hump

Os symbol osmium

OS abbr **1** operating system **2** also **o.s., O/s** out of stock **3** outsize

Osaka /ō saàka/ port on SE Honshu, Japan. Pop. 2,471,100 (2000).

Osborne /ózbən, óz bawrn/, **John** (1929–94) British playwright and screenwriter

Oscar /óskər/ n a communications code word for the letter 'O'

oscillate /óssi layt/ (**-lating, -lated**) vi **1** swing rhythmically between two points **2** be indecisive —**oscillation** /óssi láysh'n/ n —**oscillator** n

oscilloscope /ō sílllə skōp/ n a device for showing electrical current on a screen

osculate /óskyoō layt/ (**-lating, -lated**) v **1** vt kiss (fml or humorous) **2** vi make contact (technical) —**osculation** /óskyoō láysh'n/ n

-ose suffix full of, having the qualities of, resembling ○ verbose

O'Shane /ō sháyn/, **Pat** (b. 1941) Australian lawyer

osier /ózi ər/ n **1** a willow tree with long flexible stems used for making baskets **2** a willow branch

Osiris /ō síriss/ n the ancient Egyptian god of the underworld

Oslo /ózzlō/ capital of Norway. Pop. 499,693 (1998).

osmium /ózmi əm/ n (*symbol* **Os**) a hard white metallic element, the densest known. Use: catalyst, alloyed with iridium for pen nibs.

osmosis /oz móssiss/ n 1 the diffusion of solvent through a semipermeable membrane from a dilute to a more concentrated solution 2 the gradual absorption of knowledge through continued exposure rather than study —**osmotic** /oz móttik/ adj

osprey /óss pray, óspri/ (*pl* -**preys** *or same*) n a fish-eating hawk with long wings and a white head

ossify /óssi fī/ (-**fies**, -**fied**) vti 1 harden into bone 2 make or become rigidly conventional in attitude or behaviour —**ossification** /óssifi káysh'n/ n

ostensible /o sténssəb'l/, **ostensive** /o sténssiv/ adj seeming to be true, but open to doubt —**ostensibly** adv

ostentation /óss ten táysh'n/ n showiness —**ostentatious** adj —**ostentatiously** adv

osteo- prefix bone o osteoporosis

osteoarthritis /ósti ō aar thrítiss/ n a form of arthritis involving loss of cartilage in the joints

osteopathy /ósti óppəthi/ n the treatment of bodily misalignments through manipulation —**osteopath** /ósti ə path/ n —**osteopathic** /ósti ə páthik/ adj

osteoporosis /ósti ō pə róssiss/ n a disease in which the bones become very brittle

ostler /ósslər/, **hostler** /hósslər/ n formerly, somebody employed to look after horses at an inn

ostracize /óstrə sīz/ (-**cizing**, -**cized**), **ostracise** vt exclude from society or a group —**ostracism** n

---

ORIGIN Ostracize comes from a Greek verb based on *ostrakon* 'pottery fragment'. In ancient Athens, when it was proposed that a particular person should be sent into exile because he was becoming a danger to the state, a vote was taken on the matter. The method of voting was to inscribe the name of the prospective exile on a piece of broken pottery (*ostrakon*). If enough votes were cast against him, he was sent away for ten years.

Ostrava /óstrəvə/ city in NE Czech Republic. Pop. 322,111 (1999).

ostrich /óstrich/ (*pl* -**triches** *or same*) n a large long-necked flightless bird

OT abbr 1 occupational therapy 2 Old Testament

OTC abbr over-the-counter

other /úthər/ adj, pron 1 additional or further to somebody or something mentioned o *Let me make one other suggestion.* 2 different from somebody or something mentioned o *This issue, more than any other, has divided opinion.* 3 of the remaining people in a group o *She left earlier with the other kids.* 4 that is the second of two things when the first is known

o *Where's my other glove?* ■ pron **others** other people or things (+ *pl verb*) —**otherness** n ◊ **other than** apart from

otherwise /úthər wīz/ adv 1 or else o *I overslept; otherwise I would have called.* 2 differently o *Come at three unless you hear otherwise.* 3 in other ways o *It was noisy, but otherwise fun.* ■ adj different o *lots of information, digital and otherwise*

otherworldly /úthər wúrldli/ adj not being or seeming to be of this world

otiose /óti ōss, -ōz/ adj 1 not effective 2 worthless

OTT abbr over the top (*infml*)

Ottawa /óttəwə/ capital of Canada, in SE Ontario. Pop. 323,340 (1996).

otter /óttər/ (*pl same or* -**ters**) n 1 a fish-eating mammal with smooth brown fur and webbed feet 2 otter fur

Otto I /óttō/ (912–973) Holy Roman emperor (962–973) and king of Germany (936–973)

ottoman /óttəmən/ n 1 a long upholstered box used as a seat 2 a low upholstered stool 3 **Ottoman** a member of a Turkish people who conquered Asia Minor in the 13C —**Ottoman** adj

OU abbr Open University

Ouagadougou /waàgə dóogoo/ capital of Burkina Faso. Pop. 634,479 (1991).

oubliette /óobli ét/ n a dungeon with a trapdoor in the ceiling

ouch /owch/ interj expresses pain

ought[1] /awt/ modal v 1 indicates a duty or obligation or that it is morally right to do something o *You ought to be ashamed.* 2 indicates that something is important or a good idea o *You ought to see a doctor.* 3 indicates probability or expectation o *We ought to be there by now.* 4 indicates a desire or wish o *You ought to come to dinner sometime.*

ought[2] /awt/ n a zero

ouguiya /oo gée yə/ n the main unit of Mauritanian currency

ouma /ó maa/ n S Africa 1 a grandmother 2 an elderly woman

ounce[1] /ownss/ n 1 a unit of weight equal to one-sixteenth of a pound 2 a fluid ounce

---

ORIGIN The **ounce** in weight goes back through French to Latin *uncia* 'twelfth part', the same word that gave us *inch*.

---

ounce[2] /ownss/ (*pl same or* **ounces**) n a snow leopard

oupa /ó paa/ n S Africa 1 a grandfather 2 an elderly man

our /owr/ det 1 belonging to us 2 belonging to everyone ◊ See note at **hour**

Our Father n in Christianity, the Lord's Prayer

Our Lady n in Christianity, a title for Mary, the mother of Jesus Christ

ours /owrz/ pron that or those belonging to us o *Her house is OK, but I like ours better.* o *Ours are over there.*

ourselves /owr sélvz, aar-/ *pron* **1** refers to the speaker or writer and at least one other person *(as the object of a verb or preposition when the subject refers to the same people)* ○ *We didn't injure ourselves.* **2** refers to people in general ○ *secrets that we find difficult to admit even to ourselves* **3** refers emphatically to the speaker or writer and at least one other person ○ *We ourselves must bear the responsibility.* **4** our usual selves ○ *somewhere where we can really be ourselves*

-ous *suffix* **1** full of, having the qualities of ○ *virtuous* **2** having a lower valency than a corresponding compound or ion the name of which ends in *-ic* ○ *ferrous*

oust /owst/ *vt* **1** force somebody out of a place **2** remove somebody from office

out /owt/ *adv* **1** away from a place, especially the inside of something **2** so as to be removed from inside something ○ *took out her laptop* **3** outside ○ *It's cold out.* **4** in another place far away ○ *She's out in Australia.* **5** indicates a goal achieved in the action specified by the verb ○ *stuck it out to the end* **6** in or into existence ○ *one of the best albums out* ■ *adj, adv* **1** away from the home or workplace ○ *He's out at the moment.* **2** no longer alight or burning ○ *The fire's gone out.* **3** available to buy ○ *now out in paperback* ■ *adj* **1** no longer allowed to take part in a game **2** unacceptable or impossible ○ *Tomorrow's definitely out for me.* **3** unfashionable **4** intent on something ○ *out for what he can get* **5** unconscious **6** used up or finished **7** not working ○ *All the phones are out.* **8** open about being a homosexual man or woman ■ *vt* expose somebody as being a homosexual man or woman ■ *n US* a way of avoiding undesirable consequences *(infml)* —**outmost** *adj* ◊ **out of 1** so as to leave a place ○ *came out of the building* **2** so as to remove something from a place ○ *took a pen out of her bag* **3** towards the outside of ○ *looking out of the window* **4** no longer having ○ *We're out of butter.* **5** using as a source or material ○ *made out of scrap metal* **6** motivated by ○ *did it out of spite* **7** so as not or no longer to be in a situation ○ *stayed out of trouble* ◊ **out of it** very drunk, or under the influence of drugs *(infml)*

outage /ówtij/ *n* **1** an amount missing after delivery or storage **2** a temporary loss of electrical power

out-and-out *adj* thorough or utter

outback *n* /ówt bak/ a remote area, especially in Australia —**outback** *adj*

outbid /owt bíd/ (-**bidding**, -**bidded**) *vt* bid higher than somebody else

outboard /ówt bawrd/ *adj* **1** located on the outside of a boat **2** located away from the centre of a boat or aircraft —**outboard** *adv*

outbound /ówt bownd/ *adj* travelling away from a place

outbreak /ówt brayk/ *n* a sudden occurrence of something unpleasant

outbuilding /ówt bilding/ *n* a barn or shed situated away from the main building on a property

outburst /ówt burst/ *n* **1** a sudden display of emotion **2** a sudden intense period of activity

outcast /ówt kaast/ *n* somebody rejected by others —**outcast** *adj*

outcaste /ówt kaast/ *n* **1** somebody expelled from a Hindu caste **2** somebody who does not belong to a Hindu caste

outclass /owt klaáss/ *vt* be significantly better than

outcome /ówt kum/ *n* a result

outcrop /ówt krop/ *n* a part of a rock formation projecting from the ground —**outcrop** *vi*

outcry /ówt krī/ (*pl* -**cries**) *n* **1** a strong widespread reaction against something **2** a clamour from a group of people

outdated /ówt dáytid/ *adj* no longer in fashion or in use ◊ See note at **old-fashioned**

outdistance /owt dístanss/ (-**tancing**, -**tanced**) *vt* **1** go faster than other competitors in a race **2** be much better than others

outdo /owt doó/ (-**doing**, -**did** /-díd/, -**done** /-dún/) *vt* do more or better than

outdoor /ówt dáwr/ *adj* located in, belonging to, or suited to the open air

outdoors /owt dáwrz/ *adv* outside a building ■ *n* the open air, especially when away from populated areas

outdraw /owt dráw/ (-**drew** /-droó/, -**drawn** /-dráwn/) *vt* **1** draw a gun faster than **2** attract a larger audience than

outer /ówtər/ *adj* **1** on the outside of something **2** away from the centre of something —**outermost** *adj*

outer space *n* interplanetary and interstellar space

outerwear /ówtər wair/ *n* clothing for outdoors worn over other clothing

outface /owt fáyss/ (-**facing**, -**faced**) *vt* **1** stare somebody down **2** defy somebody

outfall /ówt fawl/ *n* the outlet of a sewer, drain, or stream that empties into a larger body of water

outfield /ówt feeld/ *n* **1** the outer part of a cricket pitch **2** the part of a baseball or softball field beyond the diamond —**outfielder** *n*

outfit /ówt fit/ *n* **1** a set of clothes worn together **2** a set of tools or equipment for a particular activity **3** a small team or organization *(infml)* ■ *vt* (-**fitting**, -**fitted**) **1** equip **2** provide with a set of clothes

outfitter /ówt fitər/ *n* a shop selling men's clothes

outflank /owt flángk/ *vt* **1** go around the main body of an enemy force and attack it from the side or behind **2** outwit or bypass somebody

outflow /ówtflō/ *n* **1** the process of flowing out or away **2** an amount of a liquid, gas, or money that moves away from a place

outfox /owt fóks/ *vt* outwit

outgo /owt gó/ (*pl* -**goes**) *n* an amount of money paid out

outgoing /ówt gō ing/ *adj* **1** departing or going out **2** leaving a job ○ *the outgoing president* **3** sociable —**outgoingness** *n*

outgoings /ówt gō ingz/ *npl* expenditure

outgrow /owt grṓ/ (**-grew** /-groó/, **-grown** /-grṓn/) *vt* **1** get too large for something **2** move beyond previous interests

outgrowth /ówt grṓth/ *n* **1** a natural development or result of something **2** an offshoot

outguess /owt géss/ *vt* gain an advantage over somebody by guessing that person's thoughts or intentions

outgun /owt gún/ (**-gunning**, **-gunned**) *vt* have more or better weapons than

outhouse /ówt howss/ (*pl* **-houses** /-howziz/) *n* **1** an outbuilding **2** *US, Can* an outdoor toilet

outing /ówting/ *n* **1** an excursion **2** the practice or an instance of revealing somebody to be homosexual or bisexual

outlandish /owt lándish/ *adj* strikingly peculiar —**outlandishly** *adv*

outlast /owt laàst/ *vt* exist or survive longer than

outlaw /ówt law/ *n* **1** a known criminal who is at liberty or a fugitive **2** somebody officially without legal rights ■ *vt* **1** make illegal **2** take away legal rights from —**outlaw** *adj* —**outlawry** *n*

outlay *n* /ówt lay/ **1** the spending of money or expending of resources **2** an amount of money spent ■ *vt* /owt láy/ (**-laid** /-láyd/) spend money

outlet /ówt let, -lǝt/ *n* **1** a vent **2** a release for the emotions **3** a place where something is sold **4** a market providing goods or services **5** *US, Can* an electric socket

outlier /ówt lī ǝr/ *n* **1** a separate part of a system, organization, or body that is at some distance from the main part **2** somebody living at a distance from work

outline /ówt līn/ *n* **1** the edge or outer shape of something **2** a line drawn round the outside of something **3** a rough plan or explanation of something ■ *vt* (**-lining**, **-lined**) **1** draw as an outline **2** describe the essential elements of

outlive /owt lív/ (**-living**, **-lived**) *vt* **1** live longer than **2** outlast

outlook /ówt loók/ *n* **1** an attitude **2** the likely future of something

outlying /ówt lī ing/ *adj* situated away from the central part of something

outmanoeuvre /ówt mǝ noóvǝr/ (**-vring**, **-vred**) *vt* outwit

outmoded /ówt mṓdid/ *adj* **1** old-fashioned **2** obsolete —**outmodedness** *n*

outnumber /owt númbǝr/ *vt* be more numerous than

out-of-court *adj* arranged without going to a court of law

out-of-date *adj* old-fashioned or not current

out-of-pocket *adj* **1** having lost money **2** requiring somebody to spend cash ○ *out-of-pocket travel expenses* **3** with no money

out-of-the-way *adj* **1** far from a populated area **2** unusual

out-of-town *adj* from or in another town

outpace /owt páyss/ (**-pacing**, **-paced**) *vt* be better or faster than

outpatient /ówt paysh'nt/ *n* a patient receiving treatment in a hospital without staying overnight

outperform /ówt pǝr fáwrm/ *vt* perform better than

outplacement /ówt playssmǝnt/ *n* a service provided by a company to help dismissed employees find new jobs

outplay /owt pláy/ *vt* play better than

outpost /ówt pōst/ *n* **1** a group of troops stationed away from the main force **2** a small remote military base **3** a remote or frontier settlement

outpouring /ówt pawring/ *n* something that floods out ○ *an outpouring of generosity* ○ *an outpouring of lava*

output /ówt poót/ *n* **1** an amount of something produced in a fixed period of time **2** energy or power produced by a system **3** information produced by a computer —**output** *vt*

outrage /ówt rayj/ *n* **1** a violent, cruel, or offensive act **2** anger or indignation provoked by an outrage ■ *vt* (**-raging**, **-raged**) **1** attack violently or cruelly **2** make angry or indignant

ORIGIN Outrage is not connected etymologically to either *out* or *rage*. It is an adoption of a French noun (with the noun suffix *-age*) formed from a verb *outrer* 'exceed, exaggerate', which goes back ultimately to Latin *ultra* 'beyond'.

outrageous /ówt ráyjǝss/ *adj* **1** extraordinary and unconventional **2** morally shocking **3** excessive —**outrageously** *adv* —**outrageousness** *n*

~~outragious, outragous~~ incorrect spelling of **outrageous**

~~outragous~~ incorrect spelling of **outrageous**

outrank /owt rángk/ *vt* have a higher rank or status than

outré /oó tray/ *adj* unconventional or bizarre

outreach *vt* /owt reéch/ **1** reach farther than somebody or something **2** exceed a limit ■ *n* /ówt reech/ **1** the provision of community services to particular social groups **2** the extent of the reach of somebody or something

outride /owt ríd/ (**-riding**, **-rode** /-rṓd/, **-ridden** /-rídd'n/) *vt* ride better or faster than somebody

outrider /ówt rīdǝr/ *n* a rider acting as an escort for a carriage, vehicle, or racehorse

outrigger /ówt rigǝr/ *n* **1** a stabilizing float on the side of a canoe **2** a boat or canoe fitted with an outrigger

outright *adv* /ówt rít/ **1** wholly and completely ○ *owns the business outright* **2** instantly ○ *refused our offer outright* ■ *adj* /ówt rít/ **1** absolute ○ *an outright lie* **2** without restrictions or limitations ○ *an outright gift*

outrival /owt rív'l/ (**-valling, -valled**) *vt* surpass

outrun /owt rún/ (**-running, -ran** /-rán/, **-run**) *vt* **1** run faster or farther than **2** escape by running away from

outsell /owt sél/ (**-sold** /-sóld/) *vt* **1** be sold more quickly or in greater quantities than **2** be a better salesperson than

outset /ówt set/ *n* the start of something

outshine /owt shín/ (**-shining, -shone** /-shón/) *vt* **1** shine brighter than **2** surpass in excellence or quality

outside /ówt síd/ *adv, prep, adj* **1** located on or beyond the outer surface or edge of something ○ *standing outside the circle* **2** out of doors ○ *went outside to sunbathe* **3** beyond the immediate environment ○ *in the world outside* ■ *adj* **1** slight or remote ○ *an outside chance* **2** the maximum possible or probable ○ *an outside estimate of three months* **3** farthest from the side of a road or the centre of a race track ○ *in the outside lane* ■ *prep* beyond the scope of ○ *outside my comprehension* ■ *n* **1** the outer surface or appearance of something ○ *The outside of the house needs painting.* **2** the part farthest from the side of a road or the centre of a race track ○ *coming up fast on the outside* ◇ **at the outside** at the most ◇ **outside of** other than

outside broadcast *n* a broadcast programme not made in a studio

outsider /owt sídər/ *n* **1** somebody who does not belong to a group **2** a competitor or candidate considered unlikely to win

outsize /ówt síz, ówt síz/ *n* an extra large size ■ *adj also* **outsized** extra large

outskirts /ówt skurts/ *npl* the outlying areas of a town or city

outsmart /owt smaárt/ *vt* outwit

outsold past participle, past tense of **outsell**

outsource /ówt sawrss/ (**-sourcing, -sourced**) *vt* buy goods or services normally produced or provided within a company from an outside source

outspoken /owt spókən/ *adj* fearlessly candid —**outspokenness** *n*

outspread *adj* /ówt spred/ extended or spread out flat —**outspread** *vt*

outstanding /owt stánding/ *adj* **1** unusually excellent **2** not yet resolved —**outstandingly** *adv*

outstare /owt staír/ (**-staring, -stared**) *vt* stare somebody down

outstay /owt stáy/ *vt* **1** stay longer than **2** show greater endurance than

outstretch /owt stréch/ *vt* extend or hold out

outstrip /owt stríp/ (**-stripping, -stripped**) *vt* **1** do better or go faster than **2** exceed

outtake /ówt tayk/ *n* a section cut from the final version of a film, television programme, or musical recording

out-tray *n* a tray for finished paperwork

outvote /owt vót/ (**-voting, -voted**) *vt* defeat by voting

outward /ówtwərd/ *adj* **1** located outside or on or towards the exterior of something **2** visible ○ *gave no outward indication that she was upset* **3** of the physical body ○ *His outward appearance belied his inner turmoil.* **4** apparent or superficial ○ *shouldn't judge by outward appearances* ■ *adv also* **outwards** towards the outside and away from the inside or middle —**outwardly** *adv*

outward-bound *adj* making an outgoing journey

outweigh /owt wáy/ *vt* **1** be more important or valuable than **2** weigh more than

outwit /owt wít/ (**-witting, -witted**) *vt* gain an advantage over somebody through cunning

outwork *n* /ówt wurk/ work done for a company at home

outworker /ówt wurkər/ *n* a company employee working at home

outworn /ówt wáwrn/ *adj* no longer current or useful

ouzo /óozō/ *n* a colourless Greek aniseed-flavoured alcoholic drink

ova plural of **ovum**

oval /óv'l/ *adj* egg-shaped or elliptical ■ *n* an egg shaped or elliptical form

ovary /óvəri/ (*pl* **-ries**) *n* **1** either of the two female reproductive organs that produce eggs **2** the part of a pistil that bears ovules and ripens into a fruit —**ovarian** /ō váiri ən/ *adj*

ovation /ō váysh'n/ *n* a loud and long round of applause

oven /úv'n/ *n* a heated compartment used for baking, roasting, or drying

ovenproof /úv'n proof/ *adj* capable of being used in an oven without being damaged by the heat

oven-ready *adj* already prepared and ready for cooking

ovenware /úv'n wair/ *n* dishes for baking and serving

over /óvər/ *prep, adv* **1** resting on the top of something or above the top of something with a space in between ○ *A cloud of smoke hung over the village.* ○ *wearing a shirt over his T-shirt* **2** on or to the other side of ○ *jumped over the fence* **3** throughout ○ *all over town* **4** more than ○ *people over thirty* ■ *adv* **1** across an intervening space ○ *reached over and turned off the TV* **2** so as to change position ○ *knocked over the vase* **3** remaining ○ *food left over from the party* **4** US, Can again or from the beginning again ○ *have to start over* ■ *prep* **1** by means of a communications device ○ *talking over the phone* **2** about or concerning ○ *grieving over the death of her husband* **3** as an effect or influence on somebody or something ○ *exercising more control over file access* **4** during ○ *discussed it over lunch* **5** recovered from an illness or something unpleasant ○ *was still getting over a cold* **6** in preference to somebody or something ○ *chose him over me* ■ *adj* **1** finished ○ *It's all over now.* **2** no longer fashionable (*infml*) ■ *interj* indicates that somebody speaking in a radio communication has finished talking ◇ **over again** once more ◇ **over against** in contrast with, or in opposition to ◇ **over and above** in addition to or in excess of ◇ **over and over** repeatedly

over- *prefix* **1** excessively ○ *overconfident* ○ *overeact* **2** extremely ○ *overjoyed* **3** going over something, extra ○ *overshoe* ○ *overtime* **4** above, over, on top ○ *overcast* ○ *overlap* **5** so as to turn over, completely ○ *overthrow*

overact /ốvər ákt/ *vti* act with exaggerated emphasis

overactive /ốvər áktiv/ *adj* too active —**overactivity** /ốvər ak tívvəti/ *n*

overage[1] /ốvər áyj/ *adj* **1** too old for something **2** no longer useful (*offensive of people*)

overage[2] /ốvəriij/ *n* a surplus

overall *adj* /ốvər awl/, *adv* /ốvər áwl/ **1** from one end to the other **2** in total ■ *adj* considered as a whole ■ *adv* on the whole ■ *n* /ốvər awl/ a loose-fitting lightweight coat worn to protect other clothes ■ **overalls** *npl* **1** a one-piece garment worn to protect a worker's clothes **2** loose-fitting work trousers with a bib and shoulder straps

overall majority *n* a majority of votes over all the combined votes of opponents

overarching /ốvər aárching/ *adj* including or overshadowing everything

overarm /ốvər aarm/ *adj*, *adv* with the arm or hand raised above the shoulder and rotating forwards

overate past tense of **overeat**

overawe /ốvər áw/ *vt* cause feelings of awe in

overbalance /ốvər bállənss/ (**-ancing**, **-anced**) *vti* lose or make lose balance

overbearing /ốvər baíring/ *adj* arrogant and bossy —**overbearingly** *adv*

overbite /ốvər bīt/ *n* a dental condition in which the upper front teeth project too far over the lower teeth

overblown /ốvər blốn/ *adj* **1** exaggerated **2** pretentious

overboard /ốvər bawrd, ốvər báwrd/ *adv* over the side of a ship ◇ **go overboard** behave with extreme enthusiasm

overbook /ốvər bóok/ *vti* take too many reservations for

overburden *vt* /ốvər búrd'n/ overload

overcame past tense of **overcome**

overcapacity /ốvər kə pássəti/ *n* an ability to produce more than demand requires

overcapitalize /ốvər káppit'l īz/ (**-izing**, **-ized**), **overcapitalise** *vt* **1** provide a business with too much capital **2** overvalue a business

overcast *adj* /ốvər kaast/ **1** cloudy **2** sewn along the edge with loose stitches to prevent rav-

elling ■ *v* /ốvər kaást/ **1** *vi* become cloudy **2** *vt* sew an edge with loose stitches

overcharge *v* /ốvər chaárj/ (**-charging**, **-charged**) **1** *vti* charge somebody too much **2** *vt* put excessive power into a battery or circuit ■ *n* /ốvər chaarj/ **1** an excessive charge for something **2** the act of charging too much for something

overcloud /ốvər klówd/ *vti* **1** cloud over **2** make or become dim and gloomy (*fml*)

overcoat /ốvər kốt/ *n* **1** a thick outer coat worn over other clothes **2** a top layer of paint or varnish, or the process of applying one

overcome /ốvər kúm/ (**-coming**, **-came** /-káym/, **-come**) *vt* **1** make somebody incapacitated or helpless ○ *completely overcome with emotion* **2** surmount a difficulty **3** defeat somebody or something (*fml*) ◇ See note at **defeat**

overcompensate /ốvər kómpən sayt/ (**-sating**, **-sated**) *v* **1** *vi* try too hard to make up for something **2** *vti* reward somebody too much —**overcompensation** /-kómpən sáysh'n/ *n*

overcook /ốvər kóok/ *vt* cook too long

overcrowd /ốvər krówd/ *vt* make too crowded —**overcrowded** *adj* —**overcrowding** *n*

overdo /ốvər dóo/ (**-did** /-díd/, **-done** /-dún/) *vt* **1** do to excess **2** spoil the effect of by exaggeration **3** overcook

overdose *n* /ốvər dóss/ a dangerously large amount of a drug ■ *vti* /ốvər dóss/ (**-dosing**, **-dosed**) take or give an overdose

overdraft /ốvər draaft/ *n* **1** a negative balance in a bank account **2** a borrowing limit for a negative balance in a bank account

overdrawn /ốvər dráwn/ *adj* having withdrawn more money than a bank account contains

overdrive *n* /ốvər drīv/ **1** an engine gear in a car that saves petrol at high speeds **2** an especially intense level of activity (*infml*) ○ *Production has gone into overdrive.* ■ *vt* /ốvər drīv/ (**-driving**, **-drove** /-drốv/, **-driven** /-drívv'n/) drive too hard

overdue /ốvər dyóo/ *adj* late or delayed

overeat /ốvər eét/ (**-ate** /-áyt, -ét/, **-eaten** /-eét'n/) *vi* consume too much food

overemphasis /ốvər émfəssiss/ *n* excessive emphasis —**overemphatic** /ốvər im fáttik/ *adj*

overemphasize /ốvər émfə sīz/ (**-sizing**, **-sized**), **overemphasise** *vt* give too much emphasis to

overestimate *vt* /ốvər ésti mayt/ (**-mating**, **-mated**) **1** calculate at too high a limit **2** give excessive merit or importance to ■ *n* /ốvər éstimət, -mayt/ an excessively high estimate —**overestimation** /-ésti máysh'n/ *n*

overexpose /ốvər ik spốz/ (**-posing**, **-posed**) *vt* **1** expose film to too much light **2** allow somebody, or expose somebody to, too much of something —**overexposure** /-ik spốzhər/ *n*

overextend /ốvər ik sténd/ *v* **1** *vt* force beyond a reasonable limit **2** *vt* prolong beyond the expected duration **3** *vr* risk financial ruin by borrowing or spending too much

overfill /ốvər fíl/ *vti* make or become too full

overflow v /óvər flṓ/ 1 vti pour out over the edge of a container 2 vt flood 3 vt spread beyond the limits of ■ n /óvər flṓ/ 1 the excess liquid contents of something 2 the excess quantity of people or things in a place 3 an outlet that allows liquid to escape before it runs over the top of its container 4 an amount in excess of a limit

overfly /óvər flí/ (-flies, -flew /-flṓo/, -flown /-flṓn/) vti 1 fly above an area 2 overshoot

overground /óvər grównd/ adj, adv on or above the ground

overgrown /óvər grṓn/ adj covered with unchecked vegetation

overhand /óvər hand/ adj with the hand raised above the shoulder and rotating forwards

overhang v /óvər háng/ (-hung /-húng/) 1 vti project over 2 vt loom over ■ n /óvər hang/ something that projects over the space beneath

overhaul vt /óvər háwl/ 1 look for mechanical defects in a machine 2 repair a machine extensively 3 revise something thoroughly ■ n /óvər hawl/ an extensive repair of something

overhead adv /óvər héd/ directly above ■ adj /óvər héd/ 1 positioned directly above 2 in racket games, describes a shot hit hard downwards with the racket above the head ■ **overheads** npl ongoing business costs

overhead projector n a piece of equipment for projecting an image on a transparency onto a wall or screen

overhear /óvər heér/ (-heard /-húrd/) vti hear words or a speaker without the speaker's knowledge

overheat /óvər heét/ vti 1 become or make too hot 2 grow or make an economy grow too quickly —**overheated** adj

overhung past tense, past participle of **overhang**

~~everide~~ incorrect spelling of **override**

overindulge /óvər in dúlj/ (-dulging, -dulged) v 1 vti give into a desire too much, especially in eating or drinking too much 2 vt be too indulgent with somebody —**overindulgence** n —**overindulgent** adj

overinvestment /óvər in véstmənt/ n the act of investing too much money in a company

overjoyed /óvər jóyd/ adj extremely delighted

overkill /óvər kil/ n 1 a response that far exceeds what is needed 2 a greater destructive capacity than is needed

overland /óvər land/ adv by or across land

overlap /óvər láp/ (-lapping, -lapped) v 1 vti place or be over the edge of something 2 vt extend beyond —**overlap** /óvər lap/ n

overlay /óvər láy/ (-laid /-láyd/) vt 1 place a covering or covering layer on top of something 2 be a covering on the surface of something —**overlay** /óvər lay/ n

overleaf /óvər leéf/ adv on the other side of the page

overload vt /óvər lṓd/ 1 put an excessive load on somebody or something or in something

2 use more current than an electrical system can handle 3 overburden somebody mentally or emotionally ■ n /óvər lōd/ 1 an excessive electrical load on a system 2 an excessive physical weight 3 an excessive mental or emotional burden

overlong /óvər lóng/ adj too long ■ adv for too long a time

overlook /óvər loók/ vt 1 fail to notice something 2 ignore a shortcoming or fault 3 provide a view of something from above 4 be located above something ◊ See note at **neglect**

overlord /óvər lawrd/ n 1 a ruler with power over other rulers 2 somebody powerful

overly /óvərli/ adv excessively

overmuch /óvər múch/ adv excessively ■ adj excessive

overnight /óvər nít/ adv 1 throughout or during the night 2 in the course of one night or very suddenly ■ adj 1 lasting one night 2 occurring at night 3 extremely quick

overnighter /óvər nítər/ n somebody on an overnight stay

overoptimistic /óvər opti místik/ adj excessively optimistic —**overoptimism** /óvər óptimizəm/ n —**overoptimistically** adv

overpass /óvər paass/ n ANZ, US, Can a road or bridge that crosses over another route

overpay /óvər páy/ (-paid /-páyd/) vti 1 pay more than a job warrants 2 pay too much by mistake —**overpaid** adj

overplay /óvər pláy/ v 1 vti overact a part 2 vt overstate something 3 vt hit or kick a ball too hard or far

overpower /óvər pów ər/ vt 1 subdue physically 2 overwhelm mentally —**overpowering** adj

overprint vti /óvər prínt/ print something additional on a printed surface ■ n /óvər print/ 1 an additional printing on a printed surface 2 an overprinted postage stamp

overproduce /óvər prə dyoóss/ (-ducing, -duced) vti produce too much of something —**overproduction** /-prə dúksh'n/ n

overqualified /óvər kwólli fīd/ adj with more academic qualifications or experience than is necessary for a particular job

overrate /óvər ráyt/ (-rating, -rated) vt overvalue —**overrated** adj

overreach /óvər reéch/ v 1 vr fail through excessive ambitiousness 2 vti extend too far or beyond something

overreact /óvər ri ákt/ vi react too strongly —**overreaction** n

override vt /óvər ríd/ (-riding, -rode /-rṓd/, -ridden /-ridd'n/) 1 cancel somebody's action or decision 2 outweigh something 3 take manual control of an automatic control system ■ n /óvər ríd/ 1 the act of overriding an automatic control system 2 a switch for overriding an automatic control system

overriding /óvər ríding/ adj most important —**overridingly** adv

overripe /óvər ríp/ adj too ripe

overrule /ōvər roōl/ (**-ruling, -ruled**) vt 1 reject somebody's argument as unsound 2 decide against somebody or something

overrun v /ōvər rún/ (**-running, -ran** /-rán/, **-run**) 1 vt spread rapidly over and crowd 2 vt conquer and take over the territory of 3 vti exceed a fixed limit 4 vt go farther than intended beyond 5 vti overflow or spill over something ■ n /ōvər run/ 1 the amount by which something overruns 2 the act of overrunning something

overscan /ōvər skán/ adj extending beyond the viewing boundary of a computer screen

overseas /ōvər seéz/ adv across a sea, especially in another country ■ adj also **oversea** 1 of or from a place across a sea ○ overseas visitors 2 involving travel across a sea ■ n a place or places across a sea (+ sing verb) ○ come from overseas

oversee /ōvər seé/ (**-saw** /-sáw/, **-seen** /-seén/) vt supervise

overseer /ōvər seer/ n a supervisor

oversell /ōvər séll/ (**-sold** /-sóld/) v 1 vt praise somebody or something to an implausible extent 2 vti sell something too aggressively 3 vti sell too much or too many of something

oversensitive /ōvər sénssətiv/ adj excessively sensitive —**oversensitivity** /-senssə tívvəti/ n

oversexed /ōvər sékst/ adj with excessive sex drive

overshadow /ōvər sháddō/ vt 1 take attention away from by appearing more important 2 cast a shadow over

overshoe /ōvər shoo/ n a protective shoe worn over an ordinary shoe

overshoot vti /ōvər shoót/ (**-shot** /-shót/) 1 send or go farther than intended 2 fail to take off or land before the end of a runway 3 exceed a fixed limit ■ n /ōvər shoót/ 1 the overshooting of a runway 2 the amount by which something exceeds a fixed limit

oversight /ōvər sīt/ n 1 a mistake resulting from a failure to do or notice something 2 supervision of something (fml)

oversimplify /ōvər símpli fī/ (**-fies, -fied**) vt distort by excessive simplification —**oversimplification** /-símplifi káysh'n/ n

oversize /ōvər sīz/, **oversized** /-sīzd/ adj larger than usual or necessary

oversleep /ōvər sleép/ (**-slept** /-slépt/) vi sleep longer than intended

oversold past participle, past tense of **oversell**

overspend vti /ōvər spénd/ (**-spent** /-spént/) spend too much ■ n /ōvər spend/ 1 an act of spending too much 2 an amount overspent

overspill n /ōvər spil/ 1 something that has spilt over 2 part of a population that has moved from within a city to its outskirts ■ vti /ōvər spil/ (**-spilt** /-spílt/ or **-spilled**) spill over

overstate /ōvər stáyt/ (**-stating, -stated**) vt exaggerate —**overstatement** n

overstay /ōvər stáy/ vti stay longer than the time intended for something

overstep /ōvər stép/ (**-stepping, -stepped**) vt exceed a limit or boundary

overstock /ōvər stók/ v 1 vti stock too much of something 2 vt keep too many animals on a piece of land

overstretch /ōvər strétch/ v 1 vti stretch too far so as to cause injury or damage 2 vt try to do too much with available resources

overt /ō vúrt/ adj open and unconcealed —**overtly** adv —**overtness** n

overtake /ōvər táyk/ (**-taking, -took** /-toók/, **-taken** /-táyk'n/) v 1 vti go past somebody or something travelling in the same direction 2 vt do better than somebody or something

overtax /ōvər táks/ vt 1 impose too great a strain on 2 levy excessive tax on

over-the-counter adj 1 buyable without a prescription 2 describes securities bought and sold electronically

over-the-top adj excessive and exaggerated (infml)

overthrow vt /ōvər thrō/ (**-threw** /-throó/, **-thrown** /-thrōn/) 1 remove somebody from power by force 2 throw a ball too far ■ n /ōvər thrō/ 1 the removal of somebody from power by force 2 a throw of a ball that goes too far

overtime /ōvər tīm/ n 1 time worked in addition to the normal hours of employment 2 pay for additional time worked 3 US, Can extra time in a game ■ adv beyond the normal length of time

overtook past tense of **overtake**

overtone /ōvər tōn/ n 1 a subtle supplementary meaning or nuance ○ an overtone of malice in his manner 2 a musical tone whose frequency is a multiple of a fundamental tone

overture /ōvər tyoor, -chər/ n 1 a single orchestral movement introducing a longer musical work such as an opera 2 a self-standing orchestral piece in one movement 3 an introductory proposal or initiative

overturn /ōvər túrn/ v 1 vti tip upside down 2 vt overthrow somebody or something 3 vt reverse a previous decision by using legal procedures

~~overun~~ incorrect spelling of **overrun**

overuse n /ōvər yoóss/ excessive use ■ vt /ōvər yoóz/ (**-using, -used**) use too much

overvalue /ōvər vállyoo/ (**-uing, -ued**) vt put too high a value on

overview /ōvər vyoo/ n 1 a broad survey 2 a summary

overweening /ōvər weéning/ adj 1 intolerably arrogant 2 excessive

overweight /ōvər wáyt/ adj 1 too heavy for good health 2 above an allowed weight limit ■ vt 1 overemphasize 2 overload

overwhelm /ōvər wélm/ vt 1 overpower somebody emotionally 2 overcome somebody physically 3 surge over and cover somebody or something 4 provide somebody with a huge amount of something —**overwhelming** adj —**overwhelmingly** adv

overwinter /óvər wíntər/ *v* **1** *vti* shelter livestock or plants throughout the winter, or be sheltered **2** *vi* live somewhere during the winter

overwork *v* /óvər wúrk/ **1** *vti* do or force to do too much work **2** *vt* overuse something, especially a word or expression ■ *n* /óvər wurk/ excessive work

overwrite /óvər rít/ (-writing, -wrote /-rót/, -written /-rítt'n/) *vti* **1** replace a computer file with another with the same name **2** write in too elaborate or polished a style

overwrought /óvər ráwt/ *adj* **1** very upset **2** too elaborate

Ovid /óvvid/ (43 BC–AD 17) Roman poet —**Ovidian** /o víddi ən/ *adj*

ovoid /ó voyd/ *adj* with the form of an egg —**ovoid** *n*

ovulate /óvvyŏo layt/ (-lating, -lated) *vi* release an egg from the ovary —**ovulation** /óvvyŏo láysh'n/ *n*

ovule /óvvyool/ *n* **1** the structure in a plant that develops into a seed after fertilization **2** an immature egg —**ovular** /óvvyŏolər/ *adj*

ovum /óvəm/ (*pl* **ova** /óvə/) *n* a female reproductive cell

ow /ow/ *interj* expresses pain

owe /ó/ (**owing, owed**) *v* **1** *vt* be obligated to pay somebody money o *owes the bank a lot of money* **2** *vti* be financially in debt to somebody o *doesn't owe anyone* **3** *vt* be indebted for something to somebody o *owed his success to her* **4** *vt* feel that a response is due somebody o *I owe you an explanation.*

Owen /ó in/, **Robert** (1771–1858) British social reformer

Owen, Wilfred (1893–1918) British poet

Jesse Owens: Photographed in the long jump competition at the Berlin Olympics (1936)

Owens /ó inz/, **Jesse** (1913–80) US athlete

owing /ó ing/ *adj* due to be paid ◇ **owing to** as a result of

owl /owl/ *n* **1** a nocturnal bird of prey with a large head, a flat face, and a hooting call **2** somebody with a quality or habit attributed to owls, e.g. wisdom or staying up late —**owlet** *n* —**owlish** *adj*

own /ōn/ *adj, pron* **1** emphasizes that somebody or something belongs to a particular person or thing o *has her own business* **2** indicates that somebody does something without help or interference o *makes his own clothes* ■ *v* **1** *vt* have as your property **2** *vti* acknowledge (*fml*) —**owner** *n* —**ownership** *n* ◇ **come into**

your own start to be really effective, useful, or successful ◇ **hold your own 1** put up effective resistance in an argument or contest **2** remain in a stable condition after an illness or injury ◇ **on your own 1** alone **2** without help or interference

own brand, own label *n* an item sold with the retailer's own label instead of the manufacturer's

owner-occupier *n* somebody who owns the home he or she lives in

own goal *n* **1** a goal scored accidentally for the opposing team **2** an action that backfires on the doer (*infml*)

ox /oks/ (*pl* **oxen** /óks'n/) *n* **1** an adult castrated bull, used as a draught animal **2** a cow or bull

oxbow /óks bō/ *n* a bend in a river, or a lake formed by one

Oxbridge /óksbrij/ *n* Oxford and Cambridge universities

oxeye /óks ī/ *n* **1** a daisy **2** a plant with flower heads like a daisy's

Oxfam /óks fam/ *n* an international relief agency

oxford /óksfərd/ *n* **1** *also* **Oxford** a sturdy leather lace-up shoe **2** a strong cotton used for making shirts, or a shirt made of this material

Oxford /óksfərd/ city in south-central England. Pop. 137,343 (1996).

Oxfordshire /óksfərdshər/ county in south-central England

oxidant /óksidənt/ *n* a substance that oxidizes other substances

oxidation /óksi dáysh'n/ *n* **1** addition of oxygen to a chemical or compound **2** loss of electrons from a chemical or compound

oxide /óks īd/ *n* a compound containing oxygen, especially in combination with a metal

oxidize /óksi dīz/ (-dizing, -dized), **oxidise** *vti* **1** react, or make a chemical react, with oxygen **2** lose, or make a chemical element or compound lose, electrons —**oxidization** /óksi dī záysh'n/ *n* —**oxidizer** *n*

Oxon. *abbr* Oxfordshire

oxtail /óks tayl/ *n* an ox's tail as food

oxyacetylene /óksi ə séttə leen, -lin/ *n* an oxygen and acetylene mixture that produces a hot flame. Use: cutting, welding metal.

oxygen /óksijən/ *n* (*symbol* **O**) a colourless odourless gaseous chemical element essential for breathing

ORIGIN Oxygen was coined in French in the late 18C by the chemist Lavoisier, originally as an adjective (in *principe oxygène* 'acidifying principle'), then as a noun. He gave the gas the name, from Greek words meaning 'acid forming', because it was at that time believed to be an essential component in the formation of acids.

oxygenate /óksijə nayt, ok síjjə nayt/ (-ating, -ated) *vti* combine with oxygen

oxygen mask *n* a device fitting over the nose and mouth for providing oxygen for breathing

oxygen tent *n* a transparent plastic structure into which oxygen is pumped for helping a patient in bed to breathe

oxymoron /óksi máw ron, -rən/ (*pl* **-ra** /-rə/) *n* a combination of two words with contradictory meanings that are used together for a special effect

oyez /ō yéz, -yéss, -yáy/, **oyes** *interj* calls for silence before an announcement or at the opening of a session in a court of law, usually spoken three times in succession ■ *n* a cry of 'oyez'

oyster /óystər/ *n* a shellfish with a rough irregularly shaped two-part shell

oystercatcher /óystər kachər/ *n* a shore bird with a long red bill and black-and-white plumage that lives on shellfish and worms

oz *abbr* **1** Australia (*in Internet addresses*) **2** ounce

Oz *n* Australia (*infml*)

Ozark Plateau /ő zaark-/, **Ozarks, Ozark Mountains** mountainous region of the south-central United States, extending from SW Missouri across NW Arkansas and E Oklahoma

ozone /ő zōn, ő zőn/ *n* **1** a form of oxygen produced by electrical discharge **2** fresh air, especially sea air (*infml*)

ozone-friendly *adj* not harming the ozone layer

ozone layer, ozonosphere /ō zŏnə sfeer, ō zónnə-/ *n* the layer of the upper atmosphere that absorbs harmful ultraviolet solar radiation

P

p[1] (*pl* **p's**), **P** (*pl* **P's** *or* **Ps**) *n* the 16th letter of the English alphabet ◇ **mind** *or* **watch your p's and q's** be careful to be polite and well-behaved

p[2] *symbol* **1** pence **2** penny **3** piano (*musical direction*)

p[3] *abbr* **1** page **2** part

P *symbol* **1** pataca **2** peseta **3** peso **4** phosphorus **5** pula

P2P /pee tə pee/ *adj* **1** describes payments or linkups made between two people via the Internet. Full form **person-to-person 2** describes software enabling Internet users to communicate without the use of intermediaries such as servers. Full form **peer-to-peer**

pa[1] /paa/ (*pl* **pa's** *or* **pas**) *n* a father (*infml*)

pa[2] /paa/ (*pl* **same**), **pah** *n* a Maori hilltop fort and settlement

Pa *symbol* **1** pascal **2** protactinium

PA[1] *abbr* personal assistant

PA[2] *n* an electronic sound-amplification system in a public place. Full form **public-address system**

pa'anga /paàng gə, paa áàng-/ *n* the main unit of Tongan currency

pace[1] /payss/ *n* **1** speed of movement or progress **2** a step in walking or running **3** the distance covered in a step **4** a way of walking ○ *an uneven pace* **5** the gait of a horse at different speeds ■ *v* (**pacing, paced**) **1** *vti* walk to and fro in an area **2** *vti* walk along with regular strides **3** *vti* measure by counting steps **4** *vt* set the speed at which somebody runs or does something **5** *vr* run or work at a controlled rate

pace[2] /páyssi, paà chay/ *prep* with all respect to

pacemaker /páyss maykər/ *n* **1** *also* **pacesetter** a competitor who sets the pace **2** *also* **pacesetter** a leader in a field of activity **3** an electrical device inserted into the body to regulate the heartbeat

pachisi /pə cheézi, paa-/ *n* an ancient South Asian board game similar to backgammon

pachyderm /páki durm/ *n* a large thick-skinned mammal such as an elephant, rhinoceros, or hippopotamus —**pachydermal** /páki dúrm'l/ *adj*

pacific /pə síffik/ *adj* **1** bringing peace **2** having a peaceful temperament

Pacific /pə síffik/, **Pacific Ocean** largest ocean in the world, stretching from the Arctic Ocean in the north to Antarctica in the south, and from North and South America in the east to East Asia, the Malay Archipelago, and Australia in the west —**Pacific** *adj*

Pacific Islands, Trust Territory of the former UN trust territory in the W Pacific Ocean administered by the United States, comprising 2,000 islands including the Caroline, Marshall, and Mariana islands

Pacific Northwest region of the NW United States that includes Washington and Oregon and sometimes SW British Columbia, Canada

Pacific Rim *n* the countries bordering the Pacific Ocean considered as an economic unit

pacifier /pássi fī ər/ *n* **1** somebody or something that pacifies **2** US, Can a baby's dummy

pacifism /pássi fizəm/ *n* **1** opposition to war or violence **2** refusal to participate in a war for moral or religious reasons —**pacifist** *n* —**pacifistic** /pássi fístik/ *adj*

pacify /pássi fī/ (**-fies, -fied**) *vt* **1** calm **2** bring peace to —**pacification** /pássifi káysh'n/ *n*

pack[1] *v* **1** *vti* put belongings into a container for transporting **2** *vti* put products into containers for sale, transport, or storage **3** *vt* create a parcel or bundle **4** *vt* fill something tightly ○ *a book packed with useful information* **5** *vti* crowd into or fill a place **6** *vt* compress a computer file **7** *vti* make or become compacted **8** *vt* press something round an object to hold or protect it ■ *n* **1** a commercial container **2** a collection of things in a package **3** the contents of a pack, or the amount contained in it **4** a large amount *(infml)* o *a pack of lies* **5** a bag carried on the back **6** a set of 52 playing cards **7** a group of animals living and hunting together **8** a large group of people acting together **9** a group of Brownies or Cubs **10** the main body of competitors in a race —**packed** *adj*

ORIGIN Pack 'container, put in a container' was adopted in the 12C from Dutch or German. **Pack** 'fill with supporters' is probably an alteration of *pact*, and dates from the early 16C.

☐ **pack in** *v* **1** *vt* attract in large numbers **2** *vti* stop doing something *(infml)*
☐ **pack off** *vt* send away unceremoniously *(infml)*
☐ **pack up** *vi* stop functioning *(infml)*

pack² *vt* fill a jury or committee with supporters

package /pákij/ *n* **1** a parcel **2** a number of different things constituting a single item or proposal o *a good severance package* **3** *also* **package holiday** a holiday or tour for which a travel company arranges transport, accommodation, and board ■ *vt* (**-aging, -aged**) **1** put into a package **2** present attractively —**packager** *n*

package deal *n* a set of proposals offered as a single item

packaging /pákijing/ *n* **1** the wrapping or container for something **2** the design or style of the wrapping or container for something

pack animal *n* **1** an animal that carries loads **2** an animal that lives and hunts in a pack

packed lunch *n* a lunch prepared and put into a container for eating later

packer /pákər/ *n* **1** somebody or something that packs goods **2** a person or company that processes and packages food

Packer /pákər/, **Kerry** (b. 1937) Australian media proprietor

packet /pákit/ *n* **1** a small container for goods **2** a small parcel **3** a data unit in a computer network **4** *also* **packet boat** a passenger or cargo boat on a regular short run

packet switching *n* the transmission of data as packets over a channel occupied only during transmission

packhorse /pák hawrss/ *n* a horse for carrying loads

pack ice *n* floating ice in a solid mass

packing /páking/ *n* **1** the act of putting things into containers for storage or transport **2** material for protecting a packed object

packing case *n* a wooden box for packing objects

pack rat *n* a woodland rat that collects and stores objects

packsaddle /pák sad'l/ *n* a saddle for carrying loads

pact /pakt/ *n* an agreement between two or more people or groups

pad¹ *n* **1** a piece of soft material for protecting, shaping, cleaning, or absorbing something **2** a protective covering for part of the body, especially when playing a sport **3** a block of sheets of paper **4** a piece of ink-filled material on which a rubber stamp is pressed **5** an area where a helicopter takes off and lands or a rocket is launched **6** a sanitary towel **7** a piece of backing material for something laid on a surface **8** a fleshy cushion on an animal's paw **9** the fleshy tip of a finger or toe **10** somebody's living quarters *(slang dated)* **11** a broad floating leaf of a water plant ■ *vt* (**padding, padded**) **1** use soft material to fill, protect, or shape something or make it more comfortable **2** add unnecessary material to a piece of writing

pad² *vti* (**padding, padded**) walk or walk along something quietly ■ *n* the sound of quiet footsteps

padded cell *n* a lockable room with padded walls and floor in a psychiatric hospital

padding /pádding/ *n* **1** thick soft material for filling, protecting, or shaping something **2** unnecessary additions to a piece of writing

paddle¹ /pádd'l/ *n* **1** a short flat-bladed oar for propelling a canoe or small boat **2** *US* a table tennis bat ■ *v* (**-dling, -dled**) **1** *vti* propel or carry in a canoe with a paddle **2** *vt* stir with a paddle

paddle² /pádd'l/ (**-dling, -dled**) *v* **1** *vi* walk about in shallow water **2** *vti* dabble the hands or feet in water —**paddle** *n*

paddleboat /pádd'l bōt/ *n* a boat propelled by one or more paddle wheels

paddle steamer *n* a steamship propelled by paddle wheels

paddle wheel *n* a bladed wheel attached to an engine and propelling a ship

paddock /páddək/ *n* **1** an enclosed field for horses **2** an area at a racecourse for mounting racehorses

paddy¹ /páddi/ (*pl* **-dies**), **paddy field** *n* a rice field kept under shallow water

paddy² /páddi/ (*pl* **-dies**) *n* a bad temper *(infml)*

Paderewski /páddə réfski/, **Ignace Jan** (1860–1941) Polish pianist, composer, and prime minister (1919)

padlock /pád lok/ *n* a small detachable lock with a semicircular bar at the top —**padlock** *vt*

padre /paádri, -dray/ *n* used to address a Roman Catholic priest in a Spanish, Portuguese, or Italian-speaking country

paean /pée ən/ *n* a written, spoken, or musical expression of joy or praise

paederast *n* = **pederast**

paediatrics /peedi áttriks/, **pediatrics** *n* the branch of medicine concerned with children's development and diseases (+ *sing verb*) —**paediatric** *adj* —**paediatrician** /peedi ə trísh'n/ *n*

paedophile /péedə fīl/, **pedophile** *n* an adult with sexual desire for children —**paedophilic** /peedə fíllik/ *adj*

paella /pī élla/ n 1 a Spanish dish of rice, chicken, and shellfish 2 a pan for making paella

pagan /páygən/ n 1 a follower of a religion that is not one of the main world religions (*sometimes offensive*) 2 a follower of an ancient polytheistic or pantheistic religion —**pagan** adj —**paganism** n

ORIGIN The Latin word *pagus*, from which **pagan** is derived, originally meant 'something stuck in the ground as a landmark'. It was extended metaphorically to 'rural district, village', and the noun *paganus* was derived from it, denoting 'country dweller, villager'. This shifted in meaning, first to 'civilian', and then (based on the early Christian notion that all members of the Church were 'soldiers' of Jesus Christ) to 'heathen'.

Paganini /pággə neéni/, **Niccolò** (1782–1840) Italian composer and violinist

page[1] n 1 one side of a sheet of paper 2 a single sheet in a book 3 the amount of writing on a page 4 the amount of computer data printing out as a page 5 the amount of data that can be seen on a computer screen at one time ■ v (**paging, paged**) 1 vi look through pages 2 vt number each page of

page[2] n 1 a boy attendant on a ceremonial occasion 2 a youth who runs errands or carries messages in a hotel or club ■ vt (**paging, paged**) 1 summon by calling out a name 2 contact on a pager

pageant /pájjənt/ n 1 a large-scale spectacle representing a historical event 2 an elaborate and colourful procession

pageantry /pájjəntri/ n magnificent ceremonial display

pageboy /páyj boy/ n a medium-length smooth hairstyle with the ends curled under

page break n an indication where a computer printer will start a new page

~~pagent~~ incorrect spelling of **pageant**

pager /páyjər/ n an electronic device for contacting somebody

paginate /pájji nayt/ (**-nating, -nated**) vt number each page of

pagination /pájji náysh'n/ n 1 the page numbers of a book or document 2 the process of numbering the pages of a book

paging[1] /páyjing/ n the transfer of computer data from main memory to auxiliary memory to speed up performance

paging[2] /páyjing/ n 1 the use of a pager 2 a facility that enables somebody to be contacted via a pager

pagoda /pə gódə/ n 1 a Buddhist temple with projecting roofs 2 a building designed like a Buddhist pagoda

Pahlavi /páaləvi/, **Muhammad Reza Shah** (1919–80) shah of Iran (1941–79)

paid past participle, past tense of **pay** ■ adj done to earn money o *paid employment*

paid-up adj 1 not owing anything 2 enthusiastic and committed 3 fully paid for

pail n a bucket

pain /payn/ n 1 an acutely unpleasant physical sensation resulting from being hit, injured, or ill 2 a feeling of pain in a particular part of the body (*often pl*) 3 severe emotional distress 4 somebody or something annoying (*infml*) ■ **pains** npl trouble taken to do something ■ v 1 vt sadden or distress 2 vti feel or cause to feel physical pain —**painless** adj —**painlessly** adv ◇ **on** or **under pain of** at the risk of the penalty of o *on pain of instant dismissal*

SPELLCHECK Do not confuse the spelling of **pain** and **pane** (of a window), which sound similar.

Paine /payn/, **Thomas** (1737–1809) British-born American writer, political philosopher, and revolutionary

pained adj expressing pain or wounded or disappointed feelings

painful /páynf'l/ adj 1 causing physical or mental pain 2 hurting as a result of an injury or disease —**painfully** adv

painkiller /páyn kilər/ n a pain-reducing drug —**painkilling** adj

painstaking /páynz tayking/ adj taking or showing great care and attention to detail —**painstakingly** adv ◇ See note at **careful**

paint n 1 a coloured liquid applied to a surface to decorate or protect it, or to create a painting 2 dried paint on a surface ■ v 1 vti cover something with paint 2 vti create a picture using paint 3 vt mark designs or words on a surface using paint 4 vt apply liquid to a surface with a brush 5 vt apply cosmetics to the face or nails 6 vt describe something vividly in words

paintball /páynt bawl/ n a combat game between teams with guns that fire a marking dye —**paintballer** n —**paintballing** n

paintbrush /páynt brush/ n a brush for applying paint

Painted Desert plateau region of north-central Arizona, noted for its vividly coloured rocks

painter[1] /páyntər/ n 1 an artist who paints pictures 2 a worker who paints houses

painter[2] /páyntər/ n a rope attached to the front of a boat for tying it up

painting /páynting/ n 1 a painted picture 2 the activity of applying paint

paintwork /páynt wurk/ n painted surfaces

pair /pair/ n 1 a set of two similar matching things used together o *a pair of socks* 2 something with two matching or identical joined parts o *a pair of binoculars* 3 two people or animals doing something together or connected in some way 4 one of two matching articles o *lost the pair to his cuff link* ■ v 1 vti form or cause to form a pair 2 vt match two things together

SPELLCHECK Do not confuse the spelling of **pair**, **pare** ('cut off'), or **pear** (the fruit), which sound similar.

paisley /páyzli/ *n* a bold pattern with curving shapes —**paisley** *adj*

pajamas *npl* US = pyjamas

pakeha /paàki haa/ (*pl same or* -has) *n NZ* a non-Maori New Zealander or other person

Pakistan /paàki staàn, páki-/ country in South Asia, bordering the Arabian Sea. Cap. Islamabad. Pop. 144,616,640 (2001). —**Pakistani** *n, adj*

pakora /pə káwrə/ *n* a South Asian vegetable, meat, or shellfish fritter

pal *n* a friend (*infml*) ■ *vi* (**palling, palled**) become friends, or spend time together as friends

☐ **pal up** *vi* become friends (*infml*)

PAL /pal/ *n* the British television broadcasting system. Full form **phase alternation line**

palace /pálləss/ *n* 1 the official residence of a sovereign 2 a large imposing building

> **ORIGIN** The original **palace** was the *Palatium* built on (and named after) the Palatine Hill in Rome by the emperor Augustus. The name came to be used for all grand and imposing residences. Latin *palatium* passed into English via French.

paladin /pállədin/ *n* a medieval champion or chivalric hero

palaeobiochemistry /páyli ō bīo kémmistri, pálli-/ *n* the study of the evolution of biochemical processes from evidence in fossils

Palaeocene /páyli ə seen, pálli-/ *n* the epoch of geological time when placental mammals first appeared, 65 to 55 million years ago —**Palaeocene** *adj*

palaeography /páyli óggrəfi, pálli-/ *n* the study of ancient handwriting and manuscripts —**palaeographer** *n* —**palaeographical** /páyli ə gráffik'l, pálli-/ *adj*

Palaeolithic /páyli ə líthik, pálli-/ *n* the early Stone Age —**Palaeolithic** *adj*

palaeontology /páyli on tóllaji, pálli-/ *n* the study of life in prehistoric times —**palaeontological** /páyli ontə lójjik'l, pálli-/ *adj* —**palaeontologist** *n*

Palaeozoic /páyli ə zō ik, pálli-/ *n* the era of geological time when fish, insects, amphibians, reptiles, and land plants first appeared, about 600 million to 230 million years ago —**Palaeozoic** *adj*

palanquin /pállən keén/ *n* a covered seat carried on poles on the shoulders of two or four people

palatable /pállətəb'l/ *adj* 1 having a good enough taste to be eaten or drunk 2 acceptable to somebody's sensibilities

palate /pállət/ *n* 1 the roof of the mouth 2 somebody's sense of taste —**palatal** *adj*

> **SPELLCHECK** Do not confuse the spelling of **palate**, **palette** ('a board for artist's paints'), or **pallet** ('a tray for stacking loads on'), which sound similar.

palatial /pə láysh'l/ *adj* 1 luxurious 2 suitable for a palace

palatinate /pə látti nayt, -nət/ *n* the territory or status of a palatine

palatine /pállə tīn/ *n* 1 a powerful feudal lord in central Europe 2 a court official in the late Roman and Byzantine empires ■ *adj* 1 of or suitable for a palace 2 being or of a palatine

Palau /pə lów/ country in the W Pacific Ocean comprising a group of islands that are part of the Caroline Islands. Cap. Koror. Pop. 19,092 (2001).

palaver /pə laávər/ *n* 1 inconvenient bother 2 empty talk

pale[1] *adj* (**paler, palest**) 1 lacking colour or intensity ○ *pale yellow* 2 with a whitish complexion, usually from illness or worry ■ *vi* (**paling, paled**) 1 become whiter or paler 2 become less important —**paleness** *n*

pale[2] *n* 1 a fence stake 2 a boundary fence ◇ **beyond the pale** outside the limits of what is considered to be acceptable

paleontology *n* US = palaeontology

Palermo /pə láirmō/ port on NW Sicily, Italy. Pop. 685,551 (1999).

Palestine /pállə stīn/ 1 historical region in SW Asia on the coast of the E Mediterranean Sea, the biblical land of Canaan 2 former country in SW Asia, between the Dead Sea and the Mediterranean Sea, divided in 1947 between Israel and Jordan. In 1993 Palestinians gained limited self-rule in Israeli-held territories in the Gaza Strip and on the West Bank of the River Jordan. —**Palestinian** /pállə stínni ən/ *n, adj*

palette /pállət/ *n* 1 a board on which an artist arranges and mixes paints 2 the range of colours used by an artist ◊ See note at **palate**

palette knife *n* 1 a blunt flexible knife for spreading, lifting, or turning food 2 a spatula for mixing paints

palfrey /páwlfri, pól-/ (*pl* -**freys**) *n* a woman's riding horse (*archaic*)

Pali /paáli/ *n* an ancient Indo-European language derived from Sanskrit —**Pali** *adj*

palimony /pállimoni/ (*pl* -**nies**) *n* US, Can alimony for an unmarried ex-lover

palimpsest /pállimp sest/ *n* a manuscript written over a partly erased older manuscript

palindrome /pállin drōm/ *n* a text reading the same backwards and forwards —**palindromic** /pállin drómmik/ *adj*

paling /páyling/ *n* 1 a fence of stakes 2 a stake in a fence

palisade /pálli sayd/ *n* a fence made of wooden stakes

pall[1] *n* 1 a covering that makes a place dark and gloomy 2 a gloomy atmosphere 3 a cloth covering for a coffin

pall[2] *vi* become boring or insipid

Palladio /pə laàdi ō, -laàdee-/, **Andrea** (1508–80) Italian architect

palladium /pə láydi əm/ *n* (*symbol* Pd) a soft, silvery-white metal. Use: catalyst, alloys.

> **ORIGIN Palladium** was named after *Pallas*, an

asteroid discovered in 1803, shortly before the element. *Pallas* itself is another name for Athena, the Greek goddess of wisdom and warfare.

pallbearer /páwl bairər/ *n* somebody who carries a coffin

pallet[1] /pállət/ *n* a platform on which cargo is stored or transported ◊ See note at **palate**

pallet[2] /pállət/ *n* **1** a straw mattress **2** a makeshift bed

palliate /pálli ayt/ (**-ating, -ated**) *vt* **1** alleviate a symptom of a medical condition **2** reduce the intensity or severity of something **3** make an offence seem less serious —**palliation** /pálli áysh'n/ *n*

pallid /pállid/ *adj* **1** unhealthily pale **2** lacklustre —**pallidity** /pə líddəti/ *n*

pallor /pállər/ *n* an unhealthy-looking paleness

pally /pálli/ (**-lier, -liest**) *adj* friendly (*infml*)

palm[1] /paam/ *n* the inner surface of the hand ■ *vt* **1** hide something in the hand **2** take something stealthily

ORIGIN The two English words **palm** go back to the same Latin word, which meant both 'palm of the hand' and 'palm tree'. The tree was so called because a cluster of palm leaves was thought to look like a hand and fingers. The two branches of Latin *palma* reached English by different routes: 'palm of the hand' through ancient Germanic forms, and 'palm tree' through early Romance words and French.

□ **palm off** *vt* **1** give something in a deceitful way **2** pass on something unwanted

palm[2] /paam/ *n* **1** a tropical tree or plant with fronds **2** a palm leaf used as a victory sign

Palma /pálmə/ port on SW Majorca, Spain, on the Bay of Palma. Pop. 319,181 (1998).

palmcorder /paám kawrdər/ *n* a small camcorder

Palmer /paámər/, **Arnold** (b. 1929) US golfer

Palmerston /paámərstən/, **Henry John Temple, 3rd Viscount** (1784–1865) prime minister of Great Britain (1855–58 and 1859–65)

palmistry /paámistri/ *n* examining the palms of the hands to predict a person's destiny —**palmist** *n*

palm oil *n* oil from the fruit of some palm trees. Use: lubricants, soap, cosmetics, foods.

Palm Springs city in S California. Pop. 43,942 (1998).

Palm Sunday *n* a Christian festival marking Jesus Christ's entry into Jerusalem. Date: Sunday before Easter.

palmtop /paám top/ *n* a computer that is small enough to hold in one hand

palmy /paámi/ (**-ier, -iest**) *adj* **1** of palm trees **2** prosperous or flourishing, especially formerly (*literary*)

palomino /pállə meenō/ (*pl* **-nos**) *n* a golden-coloured horse with a pale mane and tail

palpable /pálpəb'l/ *adj* **1** so intense as almost to produce a physical sensation **2** obvious or easily observed **3** able to be felt by the

hands, especially in a medical examination —**palpably** *adv*

palpate /pal páyt/ (**-pating, -pated**) *vt* examine medically by touching

palpitate /pálpi tayt/ (**-tating, -tated**) *vi* beat irregularly (*refers to the heart*) —**palpitant** *adj*

palsy /páwlzi/ *n* a muscular inability to move (*archaic*)

paltry /páwltri, pól-/ (**-trier, -triest**) *adj* **1** insignificant ◊ *a paltry sum of money* **2** despicable —**paltriness** *n*

~~pamflet~~ incorrect spelling of **pamphlet**

Pamirs /pə meérz/ mountainous region of central Asia, located mainly in Tajikistan and extending to NE Afghanistan and NW China. Highest peak Ismail Samani Peak, 7,495 m/24,590 ft.

pampas /pámpəss, -pəz/ *n* treeless grassland in South America (+ *sing* or *pl verb*) —**pampean** /pámpi ən, pam peé ən/ *adj*

pampas grass *n* a very tall ornamental grass

pamper /pámpər/ *vt* **1** treat lavishly and indulgently **2** indulge or gratify

pamphlet /pámflət/ *n* an informational or political leaflet

ORIGIN *Pamphilet* and *Pamflet* were popular names of a short anonymous 12C Latin love poem, *Pamphilus, seu de Amore*. The word came to be applied to any short text. **Pamphlet** began to establish itself as the standard form in the 16C.

pamphleteer /pámflə teér/ *n* a writer of political pamphlets —**pamphleteer** *vi*

Pamplona /pam plónə/ city in NE Spain. Pop. 171,150 (1998).

pan[1] /pan/ *n* a cooking pot, usually of metal ■ *v* (**panning, panned**) **1** *vt* criticize severely, especially in a review (*infml*) **2** *vi* wash or shake soil or gravel to separate precious metals

□ **pan out** *vi* turn out well or successfully (*infml*)

pan[2] /pan/ (**panning, panned**) *vti* move a camera horizontally from a fixed point —**pan** *n*

pan[3] /paan/, **paan** *n* **1** a betel leaf **2** a rolled betel leaf containing spices

Pan /pan/ *n* **1** in Greek mythology, the god of nature. Roman equivalent **Faunus 2** the innermost moon of Saturn

pan- *prefix* all, any, everyone ◦ *pantheism*

panacea /pánnə seé ə/ *n* a supposed cure for all diseases or problems —**panacean** *adj*

panache /pə násh/ *n* **1** dashing style **2** a plume of feathers on a helmet

panama /pánnə maa, -maá/, **Panama** *n* a man's lightweight hat made of plaited leaves or straw

Panama /pánnə maa, -maá/ country in Central America. Cap. Panama City. Pop. 2,845,647 (2001). —**Panamanian** /pánnə máyni ən/ *n, adj*

Panama, Isthmus of isthmus connecting North and South America

Panama Canal canal across the Isthmus of

Panama, connecting the Pacific Ocean and the Caribbean Sea. Length 64 km/40 mi.

Panama City capital of Panama. Pop. 668,927 (1996).

panatella /pánnə téllə/, **panatela** *n* a thin straight cigar

pancake /pán kayk/ *n* **1** a very thin fried cake **2** *Scotland* a drop scone

Panchen Lama /púnchən-/ *n* in Tibetan Buddhism, a lama of the second highest rank

pancreas /pángkri əss/ *n* a gland that produces insulin and digestive enzymes —**pancreatic** /pángkri áttik/ *adj*

panda /pándə/ *n* **1** a large black-and-white Chinese mammal **2** a red panda

pandemic /pan démmik/ *adj* having a widespread effect ■ *n* a very widespread disease or medical condition

pandemonium /pándə móni əm/ *n* chaos and uproar

ORIGIN The poet John Milton coined *Pandemonium* as the name of the capital of hell in his epic poem *Paradise Lost* (1667). It is formed from Greek words meaning 'of all the demons'. From the late 18C a **pandemonium** was applied to a place of vice, confusion, or uproar, and the sense 'chaos and uproar' developed in the mid-19C.

---

pander /pándər/ *vi* **1** indulge another person's weaknesses or questionable tastes ○ *tired of pandering to their children's demands* **2** procure sexual favours for somebody *(disapproving)* ■ *n also* **panderer** *(disapproving)* **1** somebody who indulges another person's weaknesses or questionable tastes **2** a go-between in a romantic or sexual relationship

pandit /pándit/ *n* a wise and learned Brahman

Pandora /pan dáwrə/ *n* in Greek mythology, the first woman, sent with a container of evils to avenge Prometheus's theft of fire

Pandora's box *n* **1** in Greek mythology, the container from which the evils of the world were released **2** a source of troubles

p & p *abbr* postage and packing

pane /payn/ *n* **1** a glazed section of a window or door **2** a piece of glass in a window or door ◊ See note at **pain**

paneer /pa neèr/, **panir** *n S Asia* curd cheese used in cooking

panegyric /pánnə jírrik/ *n* praise expressed in formal speech or writing —**panegyrist** *n* —**panegyrize** *vt*

panel /pánn'l/ *n* **1** a flat rectangular part of something such as a door or wall, often raised above or sunk in the surface **2** a strip of fabric in a garment **3** a wooden surface for painting **4** a surface on which measuring instruments are mounted **5** a group of people who discuss an issue or debate before an audience **6** a list of people for jury duty **7** a jury ■ *vt* (**-elling**, **-elled**) supply something with panels

panel beater *n* somebody who repairs car bodies

paneling *n US* = **panelling**

panelist *n US* = **panellist**

panelling /pánn'ling/ *n* **1** a decorative wooden wall covering **2** a panel-covered wall

panellist /pánn'list/ *n* a member of a panel

panel van *n ANZ* a small van

pang *n* **1** a sharp pain **2** an intense emotion

Pangaea /pan jeè ə/ *n* a hypothetical ancient supercontinent thought to have incorporated all the Earth's major landmasses before the beginning of continental drift

pangolin /páng gəlin, pang gólin/ *n* a scaly mammal with a long snout and a sticky tongue for catching ants and termites

panic /pánnik/ *n* overpowering fear or anxiety ■ *adj* of or caused by panic ○ *panic selling on the stock market* ■ *vti* (**-icking**, **-icked**) be or make extremely afraid —**panicky** *adj*

ORIGIN Panic is based on a Greek word meaning 'of Pan'. Pan, the god of nature in Greek mythology, was believed to frequent lonely spots and to frighten people by suddenly appearing or making noises. The earliest use of **panic** is as an adjective, in phrases such as *panic terror*, which came via French from modern Latin *panicus terror*. The adjective and noun are both recorded from the early 17C.

---

panic attack *n* a sudden overpowering feeling of fear or anxiety

panic button *n* an alarm for summoning help

panic-stricken, panic-struck *adj* affected by panic

~~**paniey**~~ incorrect spelling of **panicky**

Panjabi *n, adj* LANGUAGE, PEOPLES = **Punjabi**

AKG London

Emmeline Pankhurst

Pankhurst /pángk hurst/, **Emmeline** (1858–1928) British suffragette

pannier /pánni ər/ *n* a basket or bag on an animal, bicycle, or motorcycle, used for carrying things

panoply /pánnəpli/ *n* (*pl* **-plies**) **1** an impressive display or array **2** full armour **3** a protective covering

panorama /pánnə raàmə/ *n* **1** an all-round view **2** a comprehensive survey **3** a picture with a wide view —**panoramic** /-rámmik/ *adj*

ORIGIN Panorama is formed from Greek words meaning 'all' and 'view'. It was coined in the late 1780s by an Irish artist called Robert Barker for a method he had invented for painting a scene on the inside of a cylinder in such a way that its perspective would seem correct to somebody viewing it from inside the cylinder. In 1793 he opened his 'Panorama', a large building in Leicester Square, London, where the public could come and gaze at such all-encompassing scenes. The modern abstract meaning was in use by the early 19C.

panpipes /pán pīps/ *npl* a wind instrument consisting of a set of reeds of different lengths, bound together

pansy /pánzi/ (*pl* **-sies**) *n* **1** a flower with bright velvety petals **2** an offensive term for an effeminate man or boy (*dated*)

ORIGIN Pansy comes from a French word meaning literally 'thought'. The flower was so called because of its lowered head, thought to suggest a state of engrossed thoughtfulness.

pant *v* **1** *vi* take short fast shallow breaths **2** *vt* say breathlessly ■ *n* a shallow breath

pantaloons /pántə loõnz/ *npl* wide trousers gathered at the ankle

ORIGIN Pantaloons get their name from a stock character in a form of Italian popular comedy that developed during the 16C and 17C. Pantaloon (*Pantalone* in Italian) wore tight-fitting trousers in the style of the day, and these were the original **pantaloons**. The name was used again of a late 18C and early 19C fashion, and eventually became generic in application. In this general sense it was shortened to *pants*.

pantechnicon /pan téknikən/ *n* a large removal van

ORIGIN The original **Pantechnicon** was a huge complex of storage facilities in London. It seems originally to have been intended to be a bazaar, hence its name, literally 'everything artistic', but came to be used as a furniture repository. Removal vans taking furniture there came to be known as 'pantechnicon vans', and by the 1890s **pantechnicon** was a generic term.

pantheism /pánthi izəm/ *n* **1** the belief that God is present in everything **2** a belief in all or many deities —**pantheist** *n* —**pantheistic** /pánthi ístik/ *adj*

pantheon /pánthi ən, pan theé-/ *n* **1** a temple dedicated to all deities **2** of a specific religion **3** a memorial to dead heroes **4** the most important people in a particular field

panther /pánthər/ (*pl* **-thers** *or same*) *n* **1** a black leopard **2** *US, Can* a mountain lion

panties /pántiz/ *npl* women's or girls' underpants (*infml*)

pantomime /pántə mīm/ *n* **1** a humorous theatrical entertainment traditionally performed at Christmas **2** a mime artist **3** a theatrical performance in ancient Rome in which one masked actor played all the characters in mime —**pantomimist** *n*

~~pantomine~~ incorrect spelling of **pantomime**

pantry /pántri/ (*pl* **-tries**) *n* a large cupboard or small room for storing food

pants *npl* **1** an item of underwear that covers the buttocks and the genitals **2** *Aus, US, Can*

men's or women's trousers ■ *adj* no good (*slang*)

ORIGIN Pants is a shortening of *pantaloons* that originated in North America in the mid-19C.

pantyhose /pánti hōz/, **pantihose** *npl US* women's tights

pap *n* **1** semiliquid food **2** material lacking depth or substance —**pappy** *adj*

papa /pə paá/ *n* **1** a father (*dated*) **2** **Papa** /paápə/ a communications code word for the letter 'P'

papacy /páypəssi/ (*pl* **-cies**) *n* **1** papal power or status **2** a pope's period in power

Papa Doc /páppə dók/ ♦ Duvalier, François

papal /páyp'l/ *adj* of the pope

paparazzo /páppə rátsō/ (*pl* **-zi** /-rátsi/), **paparazzi** *n* a scandal-seeking photographer

papaya /pə pí ə/ *n* **1** a tropical fruit with orange pulp and numerous seeds **2** the tree that produces papayas

paper /páypər/ *n* **1** a thin flat material made from wood pulp. Use: for writing and printing on, for wrapping things in, for covering walls. **2** one or more sheets of paper **3** a newspaper **4** an academic article or talk **5** a student's essay **6** wallpaper (*infml*) **7** a government document **8** a commercial negotiable document ■ **papers** *npl* **1** personal identity documents **2** an assortment of documents ■ *adj* **1** made of or resembling paper **2** existing in documentary form ■ *vt* cover a wall with wallpaper —**paperer** *n* —**papery** *adj* ◊ **on paper 1** in theory, but not in fact **2** in writing

paperback /páypər bak/ *n* a book with a thin flexible cover —**paperback** *adj*

paperboy /páypər boy/ *n* a boy who delivers newspapers

paper chase *n* **1** a thorough search or collation of documents **2** a cross-country race following a trail of bits of scattered paper

paperclip /páypər klip/ *n* a clip for holding papers together

papergirl /páypər gurl/ *n* a girl who delivers newspapers

paperhanger /páypər hangər/ *n* somebody who hangs wallpaper

paperknife /páypər-/ (*pl* **-knives** /-nīvz/) *n* a knife for opening envelopes

paperless /páypərləss/ *adj* using electronic records or communications, rather than paper

paper money *n* banknotes

paper profit *n* an unrealized gain (*often pl*)

paper round *n* **1** a newspaper delivery job **2** the course followed by somebody delivering newspapers

paper-thin *adj* extremely thin —**paper-thin** *adv*

paper tiger *n* a person or thing that appears to be powerful but is not

paper trail *n* a sequence of documents from which a series of actions can be traced (*infml*)

paperweight /páypər wayl/ *n* an object used for keeping papers in place

paperwork /páypər wurk/ *n* routine clerical work

papier-mâché /páppi ay máshay, páypər-/ *n* sheets of paper pulp and glue stuck together in layers to form objects —**papier-mâché** *adj*

ORIGIN Papier-mâché is a French word meaning literally 'chewed paper', adopted into English in the mid-18C.

papist /páypist/ *n* an offensive term for a member of the Roman Catholic Church —**papistry** *n*

paprika /pápprikə, pə preékə/ *n* 1 a mild red spice made from sweet red peppers 2 a sweet red pepper

Papua New Guinea /páppoò ə nyoo gínni/ nation in the SW Pacific Ocean, comprising E New Guinea and several hundred smaller islands. Cap. Port Moresby. Pop. 5,049,055 (2001). —**Papua New Guinean** *n, adj*

papyrus /pə pírəss/ (*pl* **-ri** /-rī/ *or* **-ruses**) *n* 1 an ancient writing material resembling paper 2 a papyrus document 3 a tall marsh plant from which papyrus was made

par *n* 1 an average level or standard 2 the accepted value of a currency 3 the value of a security at issue 4 a standard score assigned to each hole on a golf course ■ *adj* average ■ *vt* (**parring, parred**) in golf, score a par on a hole

para- *prefix* 1 beside, near, along with ○ *parameter* 2 beyond ○ *paranormal* 3 resembling 4 assistant, auxiliary ○ *paramedic* 5 parachute ○ *parasailing*

parable /párrəb'l/ *n* 1 a moral or religious story 2 a story ascribed to Jesus Christ

parabola /pə rábbələ/ *n* a curve formed by the intersection of a cone with a plane parallel to its side

Paracelsus /párrə sélssəss/, **Philippus Aureolus** (1493?–1541) German physician and alchemist

paracetamol /párrə seétə mol, -séttə-/ *n* 1 a pain relieving drug 2 a paracetamol tablet

parachute /párrə shoot/ *n* a canopy for slowing somebody's fall from an aircraft ■ *vti* (**-chuting, -chuted**) drop by parachute —**parachutist** *n*

parade /pə ráyd/ *n* 1 a celebratory procession 2 a succession of people or things 3 a gathering of troops in formation 4 a flamboyant or flaunting exhibition of something ■ *vi* 1 march in a parade 2 assemble for a military parade

parade ground *n* an area where troops gather for inspection or training

paradice incorrect spelling of **paradise**

paradigm /párrə dīm/ *n* 1 an example that is typical or serves as a basis 2 a set of all possible inflections of a word, used as an example —**paradigmatic** /párrədig máttik/ *adj* —**paradigmatically** *adv*

paradigm shift *n* a radical change in somebody's basic assumptions or approach

paradise /párrə díss/ *n* 1 a place or state of perfect happiness 2 a place that is ideally suited to somebody (*infml*) 3 *also* **Paradise** heaven —**paradisaical** /párrədi sáy ik'l, -záy-/ *adj* —**paradisal** /párrə díss'l, -díz'l/ *adj* —**paradisiacal** /párrədi sí ək'l, -zī'-/ *adj*

paradox /párrə doks/ *n* 1 something that is absurd or contradictory 2 a self-contradictory statement —**paradoxical** /párrə dóksik'l/ *adj* —**paradoxically** *adv*

paraffin /párrəfin/ *n* 1 a mixture of liquid hydrocarbons obtained from petroleum. Use: fuel. 2 *also* **paraffin wax** a white waxy solid mixture of hydrocarbons. Use: in candles, pharmaceuticals, cosmetics, as a sealant. —**paraffinic** /párrə fínnik/ *adj*

paraffin incorrect spelling of **paraffin**

paragliding /párrə glíding/ *n* the sport of gliding with a parachute —**paraglider** *n*

paragon /párrəgən/ *n* an example of excellence

paragraph /párrə graaf, -graf/ *n* 1 a section of written matter that begins on a new or indented line and contains a distinct idea 2 a short news story

Paraguay /párrə gwī/ river in SW Brazil and Paraguay. Length 2,550 km/1,580 mi. ■ country in south-central South America. Cap. Asunción. Pop. 5,734,139 (2001). —**Paraguayan** /párrə gwī ən/ *n, adj*

parakeet /párrə keet/ *n* a small tropical parrot

paralel incorrect spelling of **parallel**

parallax /párrə laks/ *n* 1 the apparent change in the position of an object caused by a change in the observer's position 2 the angle used to measure an astronomical object's distance from the Earth —**parallactic** /párrə láktik/ *adj*

parallel /párrə lel/ *adj* 1 describes lines, planes, and curved surfaces that are always the same distance apart 2 having many characteristics in common 3 of a computer that processes several items of information simultaneously ■ *n* 1 each of a set of parallel lines or planes 2 somebody or something that shares many characteristics with another 3 a comparison 4 an imaginary line around the Earth that is parallel to the equator and represents a degree of latitude 5 a configuration of electrical components that distributes current evenly ■ *vt* 1 run parallel to 2 follow a similar course to ■ *adv* in a parallel manner or position —**parallelism** *n*

parallel bars *npl* two bars on upright supports used for gymnastic exercises (*+ pl verb*) ■ *n* the sports event in which gymnasts use the parallel bars (*+ sing verb*)

parallelogram /párrə lélə gram/ *n* a four-sided geometrical figure in which opposite sides are parallel and of equal length

parallel port *n* a computer connection point through which data can be sent and received simultaneously

parallel processing *n* the use of multiple processors to run different parts of the same computer program concurrently

paralyse /párrə līz/ (**-lysing, -lysed**) *vt* **1** cause somebody to lose the ability to move a part of the body **2** make temporarily unable to move, e.g. with fear **3** bring to a standstill

paralysis /pə rálləsiss/ *n* **1** the loss of voluntary movement as a result of damage to nerve or muscle function **2** failure to take action or make progress

paralytic /párrə líttik/ *adj* **1** drunk (*infml*) **2** relating to loss of voluntary movement

paralyze *vt* US = **paralyse**

paramedic /párrə méddik/ *n* somebody trained to give treatment in a medical emergency —**paramedical** *adj*

parameter /pə rámmitər/ *n* **1** a limiting factor or restriction ○ *working within the parameters of our budget* **2** a measurable variable quantity in a set that determines a system **3** a variable mathematical value —**parametric** /párrə méttrik/ *adj*

paramilitary /párrə míllitəri/ *adj* **1** using military tactics and weapons against the official ruling power **2** military in style **3** assisting official military forces ■ *n* (*pl* **-ies**) a member of a paramilitary organization

paramount /párrə mownt/ *adj* greatest in importance or significance —**paramountly** *adv*

paramour /párrə moor/ *n* a lover (*literary*)

Paraná /párrə naá/ river flowing southwards from SW Brazil through east-central South America into the Río de la Plata in Argentina. Length 2,800 km/1,740 mi.

paranoia /párrə nóy ə/ *n* **1** extreme suspicion or distrust **2** a psychiatric disorder involving delusion —**paranoid** /párrə noyd/ *adj, n*

paranormal /párrə náwrm'l/ *adj* not able to be explained scientifically ■ *n* paranormal events or phenomena —**paranormally** *adv*

parapet /párrəpət, -pet/ *n* **1** a low wall at the edge of a bridge or balcony **2** a protective wall of earth along the edge of a military trench

~~paraphanalia~~ incorrect spelling of **para-phernalia**

paraphernalia /párrəfər náyli ə/ *n* assorted objects or items of equipment

ORIGIN **Paraphernalia** was originally a legal term for property that remained a woman's own when she married, in contrast to her dowry, which belonged to her husband. It derives from a Greek word meaning literally 'beside the dowry'. **Paraphernalia** came to be used for any personal belongings and bits and pieces in the mid-18C.

paraphrase /párrə frayz/ *vt* (**-phrasing, -phrased**) rephrase and simplify ■ *n* a paraphrased version —**paraphrastic** /párrə frástik/ *adj*

paraplegia /párrə pleéjə/ *n* inability to move the lower body —**paraplegic** *adj, n*

parapsychology /párrə sī kólləji/ *n* the study of unexplained mental phenomena —**parapsychological** /párrə sīkə lójjik'l/ *adj* —**parapsychologist** *n*

paraquat /párrə kwot/ *n* a fast-acting weedkiller

parasailing /párrə sayling/ *n* the activity of hanging from a parachute behind a speedboat

parascending /párrə sending/ *n* the activity of parachuting to earth after rising into the air while being towed

parasite /párrə sīt/ *n* **1** an organism living on or in another without benefit to the host **2** a scrounger —**parasitic** /párrə síttik/ *adj*

parasol /párrə sol/ *n* an umbrella that provides shade from the sun

parastatal /párrə stáyt'l/ *adj* indirectly controlled by a state ■ *n* a parastatal organization

paratha /pə raátə/ *n* a flat South Asian bread

paratrooper /párrə troopər/ *n* a soldier trained to use a parachute —**paratroops** *npl*

parboil /paár boyl/ *vt* partly cook by boiling

Parcae /paàr see/ *npl* in Roman mythology, the Fates. Greek equivalent **Moirai**

parcel /paárss'l/ *n* **1** something wrapped up in paper or other packaging **2** a piece of land split off a larger piece ■ *vt* (**-celling, -celled**) wrap into a parcel

□ **parcel out** *vt* divide and distribute

parcel post *n* the postal service for parcels

parch *vt* make extremely dry by depriving of water

parched *adj* **1** very thirsty (*infml*) **2** dry from lack of rainfall ◊ See note at **dry**

parchment /paárchmənt/ *n* **1** a former writing material made from animal hide **2** a document written on parchment **3** thick high-quality paper

ORIGIN Ultimately **parchment** is named after two places: the city of Pergamum in Asia Minor, and the ancient kingdom of Parthia, in the northeast of present-day Iran. Pergamum was noted for its writing materials, and Parthia for a scarlet leather. Two Latin words became blended and resulted in the French word that English adopted as **parchment**.

pardon /paárd'n/ *vt* **1** forgive somebody for wrongdoing **2** excuse somebody for something impolite ■ *n* **1** the act of releasing somebody from punishment **2** a document authorizing freedom from punishment ■ *interj* **1** what did you say? **2** expresses apology —**pardonable** *adj* —**pardonably** *adv*

pare /pair/ (**paring, pared**) *vt* **1** trim fingernails or toenails **2** remove the skin of a vegetable or fruit ◊ See note at **pair**

parent /páirənt/ *n* **1** a mother, father, or legal guardian **2** the origin or source of something ■ *vt* act as a parent to a child —**parental** /pə rént'l/ *adj* —**parenthood** *n* —**parenting** *n*

parentage /páirəntij/ *n* **1** somebody's parents **2** the origin of something

parenthesis /pə rénthisiss/ (*pl* **-ses** /-seez/) *n* **1** a round bracket used in printing and writing **2** a word or phrase separated from a sentence by brackets or dashes —**parenthetical** /párrən théttik'l/ *adj*

Parent-Teacher Association *n* a school organization of parents and teachers

pareve /paˈarəvə/, **parveh** /paˈarvə/, **parve** *adj* describes food that, under Jewish law, is neither meat nor a dairy product

par excellence /paar éksə laaNss, -éksə laàNss, -éksələnss/ *adj* of the highest quality

parfait /paar fáy/ *n* a creamy frozen dessert

parhelion /paar heéli ən/ (*pl* **-a** /-li ə/) *n* a bright spot on either side of the Sun, caused by ice crystals in the atmosphere diffracting light

pariah /pə ríˈə/ *n* **1** an outcast **2** somebody of low caste in South Asia

paring knife /páiring-/ *n* a small kitchen knife for paring vegetables and fruit

Paris[1] /párriss/ *n* in Greek mythology, the Trojan prince whose abduction of Helen started the Trojan War

Paris[2] /párriss/ *French* /pa reé/ capital of France. Pop. 2,125,246 (1999). —**Parisian** /pə rízzi ən/ *adj, n*

parish /párrish/ *n* **1** a district with its own church **2** the people of a parish

parish council *n* the elected representatives of the government of an English parish

parishioner /pə rísh'nər/ *n* a member of a parish

parish pump *adj* of local interests only

parish register *n* an official church record of births, deaths, baptisms, and marriages

parity /párriti/ *n* **1** equality of status, pay, or value **2** equivalence in the exchange rate between currencies

park *n* **1** an area of land for public recreation **2** a protected area of countryside **3** a large area of land that is part of a private estate **4** an area of land developed for commercial enterprises ○ *an industrial park* ■ *v* **1** *vti* stop and leave a vehicle **2** *vti* manoeuvre a motor vehicle into a space **3** *vt* leave something somewhere *(infml)* —**parking** *n*

Park, Mungo (1771–1806) Scottish explorer

parka /paˈarkə/ *n* **1** a long, hooded jacket **2** an Arctic coat made of animal skin

park-and-ride *n* a traffic-reduction transport scheme in which buses take passengers from out-of-town car parks to the town centre

Parker /paˈarkər/, **Charlie** (1920–55) US jazz saxophonist and composer

Parker, Dorothy (1893–1967) US writer, critic, and humorist

Parkes, Sir Henry (1815–96) Australian politician

parkin /paˈarkin/ *n* NZ, N England, Scotland a ginger oatmeal cake

parking light *n* also called **sidelight** 1

parking meter *n* a coin-operated roadside meter for buying parking time

parking station *n* ANZ a multistorey car park

Parkinson's disease /paˈarkins'nz-/ *n* a progressive nervous disorder marked by trembling, a monotone voice, and a slow shuffling walk

ORIGIN **Parkinson's disease** is named after the

British physician James Parkinson (1755–1824), who described it.

Parkinson's law *n* the theory that work expands to fill the available time

ORIGIN **Parkinson's law** is named after the British historian C. Northcote Parkinson (1909–93), who formulated it.

park keeper *n* an official who looks after a public park

parkland /paˈark land/ *n* the land in a park

parkway /paˈark way/ *n* Aus, US, Can a wide road bordered by grass and trees

parky /paˈarki/ (**-ier, -iest**) *adj* describes cold or chilly weather *(infml)*

parlement *incorrect spelling of* **parliament**

parlance /paˈarlənss/ *n* **1** a style of speech or writing **2** speech

parley /paˈarli/ *vi* (**-leying, -leyed**) talk or negotiate ■ *n* (*pl* **-leys**) a round of talks or negotiations

parliament /paˈarləmənt/ *n* **1** a nation's legislative body **2** an assembly or conference **3 Parliament** the legislative body of the United Kingdom and other countries —**parliamentary** /paˈarlə méntəri/ *adj*

ORIGIN **Parliament** is adopted from French *parlement*, which was formed from *parler* 'speak'. The French word meant originally 'conversation, conference', and then 'consultative body'. Both these meanings passed into English, though only the second survives. The *-ia-* spelling derives from the form of the word in texts written in England using Latin.

parliamentarian /paˈarlə men táiri ən/ *n* **1** a member of a parliament **2** an expert in parliamentary procedures and history

parlour /paˈarlər/ *n* **1** a room equipped to provide particular goods or services *(often in combination)* ○ *a beauty parlour* **2** a living room for entertaining guests

parlous /paˈarləss/ *adj* unsafe or uncertain *(archaic or humorous)*

Parma /paˈarmə/ city in north-central Italy. Pop. 167,523 (1999).

Parmenides /paar ménni deez/ (*fl* 500 BC) Greek philosopher

Parmesan /paˈarmi zan, -zən, -zán/ *n* a pale hard strong-tasting cheese

ORIGIN **Parmesan** means literally 'of Parma', the Italian city where the cheese is traditionally made. The actual form of the word comes from French. *Parmesan cheese* is first recorded in English in the 16C.

Parnassus /paar nássəss/ mountain in central Greece. Height 2,457 m/8,061 ft.

Parnell /paar nél/, **Charles Stewart** (1846–91) Irish politician

parochial /pə rṓki əl/ *adj* **1** limited in interests and perspective **2** of a parish —**parochialism** *n* —**parochially** *adv*

parody /párrədi/ n (pl -dies) 1 a comic or satirical imitation of a literary or artistic work 2 parodies in general ■ vt (-dies, -died) write or perform a parody of —**parodical** /pə ród-dik'l/ adj —**parodist** n

parole /pə rṓl/ n the early release of a prisoner conditional on good behaviour ■ vt (-roling, -roled) release a prisoner on parole

parot incorrect spelling of **parrot**

paroxysm /párrək sizəm/ n 1 a sudden outburst of emotion 2 a sudden onset or intensification of a symptom

parquet /paár kay, paárki/ n flooring consisting of wooden blocks laid in a decorative pattern ■ vt cover a floor with parquet

Parr /paar/, **Catherine** (1512–48) queen of England (1543–47) as the sixth wife of Henry VIII

parrallel incorrect spelling of **parallel**

Parramatta /párrə máttə/ city in E New South Wales, Australia. Pop. 142,706 (1991).

parricide /párri síd/ n 1 the murder of a parent or close relative 2 somebody who commits parricide —**parricidal** /párri síd'l/ adj

parrot /párrət/ n 1 a brightly coloured tropical bird, some species of which can mimic speech 2 somebody who repeats the words of another by rote ■ vt repeat by rote —**parroter** n

parrot-fashion adv mechanically and without understanding (infml)

parrotfish /párrət fish/ (pl same or -fishes) n a tropical fish with a beak-like jaw

parry /párri/ (-ries, -ried) v 1 vti turn a blow aside 2 vt avoid answering a question —**parry** n

parse /paarz/ (parsing, parsed) v 1 vti describe the grammatical role of a word or structure of a sentence 2 vt analyse computer input in a specified language against the formal grammar of that language

Parsee /paár see, paar seé/, **Parsi** n a member of a Zoroastrian group living in South Asia —**Parsee** adj —**Parseeism** n

parser /paárzər/ n a computer program for analysing input

parsimonious /paárssi mṓni əss/ adj frugal —**parsimoniously** adv —**parsimony** /paárssiməni/ n

parsley /paárssli/ n a herb of the carrot family with compound leaves. Use: in cooking, as a garnish.

parsnip /paárssnip/ n 1 a whitish root vegetable shaped like a carrot 2 the plant that produces parsnips

parson /paárss'n/ n 1 an Anglican parish priest 2 a Protestant minister

ORIGIN Parson is in origin the same word as *person*, and in early texts both forms are used in both senses. How the meaning 'minister' developed is not clear: suggestions include that the minister was an 'important person', or that he was the 'person' legally responsible for the parish.

parsonage /paárss'nij/ n a parson's house

parson's nose n the tail end of a cooked bird

part n 1 a portion or section 2 a separable piece or component 3 an integral or essential feature or component o *be a part of the community* 4 an actor's role 5 somebody's involvement or influence o *his part in the crime* 6 somebody's side or viewpoint o *You always take her part.* 7 a separate musical role ■ **parts** npl a region (infml) o *unheard of in these parts* ■ v 1 vti move or be moved apart o *Part them to keep them from fighting.* 2 vti divide or be divided into parts 3 vt divide hair along a line 4 vi end a relationship ■ adj partial ■ adv partially ◇ **for the most part** in general, or mostly ◇ **in part** to an extent ◇ **on the part of** as far as somebody is concerned ◇ **part and parcel** an indivisible element ◇ **take part** be actively involved

□ **part with** vt give something up or away

partake /paar táyk/ (-taking, -took /-tóok/, -taken /-táykən/) vi 1 eat or drink something (fml) 2 participate —**partaker** n

part exchange n a system of giving goods as part payment

parthenogenesis /paáthənō jénnəssiss/ n reproduction without fertilization —**parthenogenetic** /paárthənō jə néttik/ adj

partial /paársh'l/ adj 1 not complete or total 2 affecting parts but not the whole 3 having a strong liking 4 biased —**partially** adv —**partialness** n

partiality /paárshi álləti/ n 1 fondness for something 2 a biased attitude or biased behaviour

participant /paar tíssipənt/ n somebody who takes part in something ■ adj participating

participate /paar tíssi payt/ (-pating, -pated) vi take part in something —**participation** /paar tíssi páysh'n/ n —**participatory** adj

participle /paárti sip'l, paar tíssip'l/ n a verb form that is used to form complex tenses —**participial** /paárti síppi əl/ adj

particlar incorrect spelling of **particular**

particle /paártik'l/ n 1 a tiny piece or speck o *airborne particles* 2 a tiny amount o *not a particle of truth in it* 3 a unit of matter smaller than the atom or its main components 4 an adverb or preposition that forms part of a phrasal verb

particle physics n the branch of physics that deals with the study of subatomic particles (+ sing verb)

parti-coloured /paárti-/, **party-coloured** adj multicoloured

particular /pər tíkyŏolər/ adj 1 that is one out of several 2 personal and different from others o *a particular dislike* 3 great or more than usual o *take particular care* 4 special and worth mentioning o *I have no particular objection.* 5 fussy or choosy ■ n an individual fact, detail, or item (often pl) —**particularly** adv ◇ **in particular** specifically or especially

particularity /pər tíkyŏŏ lárrəti/ (pl -ties) n (fml) 1 concern for accuracy 2 an individual fact, detail, or item

particularize /pər tíkyŏŏlə rīz/ (**-izing**, **-ized**), **particularise** *vt* **1** make particular to one person or thing **2** provide with specific examples

parting /paárting/ *n* **1** a leaving or departing **2** separation or division ■ *adj* done, made, or given while leaving

parting shot *n* a final hostile remark made on leaving

partisan /paárti zán/, **partizan** *n* **1** a strong supporter **2** a resistance fighter ■ *adj* showing strong and sometimes biased support —**partisanship** *n*

partition /paar tísh'n/ *n* **1** a structure that divides a space **2** the division of a country into separate countries **3** a division into parts *(fml)* ■ *vt* **1** divide a room with a partition **2** split a country into separate countries **3** divide something into parts —**partitionist** *n*

partitive /paártɔtiv/ *adj* **1** separating *(fml)* **2** describes a grammatical construction that expresses a part of something ■ *n* a partitive construction

partly /paártli/ *adv* not wholly

partner /paártnɔr/ *n* **1** somebody who shares in an activity **2** each member of a couple in a relationship **3** somebody joined in a dance or game with somebody else **4** a business associate ■ *vt* be the partner of

partnership /paártnɔr ship/ *n* **1** a relationship between partners **2** cooperation **3** a group of people working together **4** a company owned by partners

part of speech *n* a grammatical category of words with the same function in sentences

partook past tense of **partake**

partridge /paártrij/ *n* **1** a medium-sized game bird **2** the meat of a partridge

part-time *adj*, *adv* for less than the usual amount of time —**part-timer** *n*

parturition /paártyŏŏ rísh'n/ *n* the act of giving birth *(fml or technical)*

partway /paárt way/, **part way** *adv* some of the way

party /paárti/ *n* (*pl* **-ties**) **1** a social gathering for enjoyment **2** a group of people doing something together **3** a political organization that seeks office or power **4** one side in an agreement or dispute ■ *vi* (**-ties**, **-tied**) socialize or enjoy yourself at a party *(infml)* —**partyer** *n*

partygoer /paárti gō ɔr/ *n* an attender of a party

party line *n* **1** the official policy of a political party **2** a telephone line shared by more than one user

party piece *n* the usual thing that somebody does when called on to entertain people

party politics *n* party-oriented political activity (+ *sing or pl verb*) —**party-political** *adj*

party wall *n* a wall between separate but adjoining properties

par value *n* the value of a security at issue

parvenu /paárvɔ nyoo/ (*pl* **-nus**) *n* somebody who is newly rich or influential

pascal /pásk'l, pa skál/ *n* (*symbol* **Pa**) a unit of pressure or stress equal to one newton per square metre

ORIGIN The **pascal** is named after the 17C French philosopher and mathematician Blaise Pascal.

Pascal /pa skál, pásk'l/ *n* a high-level computer programming language

ORIGIN The name **Pascal** alludes to the 17C French philosopher and mathematician Blaise Pascal, but was also seen as an acronym from French *programme appliqué à la sélection et la compilation automatique de la littérature.*

Pascal /pa skaál/, **Blaise** (1623–62) French philosopher and mathematician

pas de deux /paá dɔ dő/ (*pl* **pas de deux** /pronunc. same/) *n* a ballet dance for two people

~~passenger~~ incorrect spelling of **passenger**

pashmina /pash meènɔ/ (*pl* **-nas**) *n* **1** a fine fabric made from goat's wool **2** a shawl made from pashmina

Pashto /púshtō/ (*pl* same or **-tos**) *n* **1** an official language of Afghanistan **2** somebody whose native language is Pashto —**Pashto** *adj*

Pashtun /push tŏon/ (*pl* **-tuns** or same) *n* a member of a people who live in E and S Afghanistan and NW Pakistan

pass *v* **1** *vti* move past a place or person **2** *vti* throw a ball, or hit a puck, to another player **3** *vt* hand something over **4** *vti* move or be moved in a particular way ○ *passed his hand along the banister* **5** *vi* extend past, through, or along something **6** *vi* undergo change **7** *vt* spend time **8** *vi* elapse **9** *vi* come to an end **10** *vti* be successful in an exam or subject **11** *vti* approve or get approval for something such as legislation **12** *vi* die *(fml)* **13** *vi* in card games, not raise a bid **14** *vt* excrete something from the body **15** *vt* give a judgment, opinion, or comment ■ *n* **1** a document granting something such as a privilege **2** an act of passing a ball or puck to another player **3** a successful grade in an exam or subject **4** a way through mountains *(often in placenames)* **5** an uninvited attempt to kiss or touch somebody sexually **6** in card games, a failure to bid —**passer** *n* ◇ **let something pass** make no comment or intervention ◇ See note at **past**

☐ **pass away** *vi* die

☐ **pass by** *vt* not affect

☐ **pass for** *vt* be easily mistaken for

☐ **pass off** *vt* **1** cause to be accepted under a false identity **2** *vi* happen *(refers to planned events)*

☐ **pass on** *vi* die

☐ **pass out** *v* **1** *vi* faint **2** *vt* distribute

☐ **pass over** *vt* **1** not consider for promotion **2** disregard

☐ **pass up** *vt* forgo

passable /paássɔb'l/ *adj* **1** acceptable **2** able to be crossed or travelled on —**passably** *adv*

passage /pássij/ n 1 a corridor or pathway 2 a way through an obstruction 3 a section of a piece of writing or music 4 the process of time passing 5 a journey 6 the right to travel as a passenger 7 the approval of a new law 8 a tube in the body

passageway /pássij way/ n a corridor or pathway

passbook /paàss bŏŏk/ n a customer's book containing a record of bank transactions

passé /pássay, paà-/ adj 1 out-of-date 2 no longer in prime condition

passenger /pássinjər/ n somebody travelling in a vehicle

passenger seat n the seat in the front of a vehicle next to the driver's seat

passer-by /pássər-/ (pl passers-by) n somebody who happens to be going past a place

passim /pássim/ adv indicates various occurrences in a book

passing /paàssing/ adj 1 going past 2 transitory 3 brief and without paying much attention ■ n 1 the fact of ceasing to exist 2 the elapsing of time 3 death (euphemistic) ◊ See note at **temporary**

passion /pásh'n/ n 1 intense emotion 2 strong sexual desire 3 intense enthusiasm 4 the object of somebody's enthusiasm 5 **Passion** in Christianity, the sufferings of Jesus Christ after the Last Supper ■ **passions** npl emotions —**passionless** adj ◊ See note at **love**

passionate /pásh'nət/ adj 1 showing sexual desire 2 showing intense emotion —**passionately** adv

passionflower /pásh'n flow ər/ n a climbing vine with large flowers

passion fruit n the edible fruit of the passionflower

Passion play n a play about Jesus Christ's sufferings

passive /pássiv/ adj 1 not actively taking part 2 obeying readily 3 affected or produced by something external o passive solar heat gain 4 describes a verb form or voice that expresses an action done to the subject of the verb ■ n the passive voice, or a verb in the passive voice —**passively** adv —**passiveness** n —**passivism** n —**passivity** /pa sívvəti/ n

passive resistance n nonviolent resistance —**passive resister** n

passive smoking n the breathing in of other people's tobacco smoke

passkey /paàss kee/ (pl -keys) n 1 a private key that gives access via a restricted entrance 2 a skeleton key

Passover /paàss ōvər/ n a Jewish festival marking the exodus of the Israelites from Egypt. Date: seven or eight days from the 14th day of Nisan.

passport /paàss pawrt/ n 1 an official identification document giving the bearer the right to travel 2 a means of access

~~passtime~~ incorrect spelling of **pastime**

password /paàss wurd/ n 1 a word that must be used to gain access 2 a sequence of keyed characters giving access to a computer system or program

past[1] prep, adv 1 moving beyond a person or thing o walked past without saying a word 2 later than a time o past his bedtime ■ prep 1 on the farther side of o the bakery past the school 2 beyond a number, amount, or point o Do what you like; I'm past caring. ◊ **not put it past somebody** believe that somebody is capable of doing something (infml)

past[2] adj 1 elapsed or gone by o the past few days 2 having existed or occurred at an earlier time 3 one-time or former 4 describes a verb tense that expresses an action that took place previously ■ n 1 the time before the present 2 the past tense, or verb on the past tense 3 somebody's previous history 4 a shameful personal history

USAGE **past** or **passed**? Do not confuse these two words. Consider these examples: He passed me at 80 mph; She is the past president of our student union. In the first example, the past tense of the verb pass, which is **passed**, is required: He passed me.... In the second sentence the adjective **past** ('one-time,' former') is required: She is the past president....

pasta /pástə/ n 1 a food made from flour, eggs, and water and formed into many shapes 2 a dish made with cooked pasta

paste /payst/ n 1 a soft adhesive mixture 2 a semisolid mixture 3 a soft food substance such as a spread or pastry dough 4 glass used to make imitation gems 5 porcelain clay ■ vt (**pasting, pasted**) 1 stick things together or on a surface using paste 2 place text, data, or an image in a document electronically

pasteboard /páyst bawrd/ n thick stiff paper ■ adj flimsy o pasteboard houses

pastel /pást'l, pa stél/ adj having a pale soft colour ■ n 1 a pale soft colour 2 a paste used for making artists' crayons 3 an artist's crayon 4 a drawing done with pastels —**pastellist** n

pastern /pástərn/ n the part of a horse's foot between the fetlock and the top of the hoof

Pasternak /pástər nak/, **Boris Leonidovich** (1890–1960) Soviet poet and author

paste-up n a number of sheets with printed pages pasted on them for checking

Pasteur /pa stúr/, **Louis** (1822–95) French scientist. He developed the process of pasteurization and vaccinations to induce immunity against certain viral diseases.

pasteurize /paàscha rīz, páschə-/ (-**izing, -ized**), **pasteurise** vt treat a liquid by heating it in order to destroy harmful bacteria —**pasteurization** /paàscha rī záysh'n, páschə-/ n

pastiche /pa steésh/ n a literary or artistic work that borrows from or imitates other works

pastille /pást'l/ n 1 a soft sweet 2 a substance burnt as an incense or fumigant

pastime /páass tīm/ n an agreeable activity

past master n an expert

pastor /páastər/ n 1 a religious minister 2 a spiritual adviser —**pastorship** n

pastoral /páastərəl/ adj 1 rural 2 idealizing rural life 3 of religious ministers or their duties —**pastorally** adv

past participle n a participle expressing completed action in the past

past perfect n the verb tense that uses 'had' plus a past participle —**past perfect** adj

pastrami /pə stráami/ n spicy smoked beef eaten cold in thin slices

pastry /páystri/ n 1 dough for pies 2 food, or an item of food, made from pastry

pasturage /páaschərij/ n 1 land for grazing 2 the grazing of livestock

pasture /páaschər/ n 1 land for grazing 2 plants that animals graze on ■ vti (-turing, -tured) graze, or put to graze ◊ **put out to pasture** impose early retirement on (infml)

pastureland /páaschər land/ n land used for pasture

~~pasturized~~ incorrect spelling of **pasteurized**

pasty[1] /pásti/ (pl **-ties**) n a type of pie made from a folded-over round of pastry

pasty[2] /páysti/ (**-ier, -iest**) adj 1 unhealthily pale 2 resembling paste —**pastiness** n

PA system n a sound-amplification system. Full form **public-address system**

pat[1] vt (**patting, patted**) 1 hit lightly with the palm of the hand 2 touch repeatedly with the palm of the hand to show affection 3 shape with the hands ■ n 1 a light blow or touch 2 a soft sound 3 a piece of a soft substance, especially butter

pat[2] adv 1 exactly or fluently ○ He has his lines off pat. 2 at the most appropriate time or place ■ adj glib ○ a pat answer

pataca /pə táakə/ n the main unit of currency of Macau

Patagonia /páttə gốni ə/ region of S Argentina, between the Andes Mountains and the South Atlantic Ocean —**Patagonian** n, adj

patch n 1 a piece of material that covers or mends a hole 2 a small area within a larger one 3 a small area of land where something is grown ○ a cabbage patch 4 a period of time ○ hit a bad patch 5 a pad or shield worn over a damaged eye 6 a cover for a wound 7 a sewn-on badge 8 a fix or update for a bug in software ■ vt 1 mend or repair with a patch 2 sew from cloth pieces ○ patched up their friendship 3 fix or update with a software patch

patchouli /páchōoli, pə chốoli/, **pachouli** n 1 an aromatic oil. Use: perfumes, aromatherapy. 2 a bush of the mint family whose leaves produce patchouli

patchwork /pách wurk/ n 1 needlework in which patches of cloth are sewn together 2 a collection of dissimilar parts

patchy /páchi/ (**-ier, -iest**) adj 1 occurring in patches 2 of varying quality —**patchily** adv —**patchiness** n

pate /payt/ n a head (archaic or humorous)

pâté /páttay, pátti/ n a spreadable food made from meat, fish, or vegetables

pâté de foie gras /páttay də fwáa gráa, pátti-/ n pâté made from the livers of fattened geese

patella /pə téllə/ (pl **-lae** /-lee/ or **-las**) n the kneecap (technical) —**patellar** adj

patent /páyt'nt, pátt'nt/ n 1 an exclusive right to make and sell an invention 2 an invention protected by a patent ■ adj 1 clear or obvious 2 protected by patent ■ vt protect by patent —**patently** adv

patent leather n leather with a glossy surface

patent medicine n a nonprescription medicine

pater /páytər/ n a father (slang or humorous dated)

paterfamilias /páytərfə mílli ass, páttər-/ (pl **-tres-familias** /paà trayz-/) n a man in the role of father or head of household

paternal /pə túrn'l/ adj 1 of fathers or fatherhood 2 related through or inherited from a father —**paternally** adv

paternalism /pə túrn'lizəm/ n an approach to relationships or management in which the desire to help and advise neglects personal choice and responsibility —**paternalistic** /pə túrnə lístik/ adj

paternity /pə túrnəti/ n 1 fatherhood 2 descent from a father

paternity leave n time off work granted to a new father

paternity suit n a lawsuit for financial support brought by a woman against a man who she claims is her child's father

paternity test n a genetic test to determine fatherhood

paternoster /páttər nóstər, -nostər/, **Paternoster** n in Roman Catholicism, the Lord's Prayer

Paterson /páttərss'n/, **A. B.** (1864–1941) Australian poet

path /paath/ n 1 a track made by people repeatedly walking on it 2 a surfaced track for walking or cycling 3 a route along which something moves 4 a course of action

-path suffix 1 somebody with a particular disorder ○ sociopath 2 somebody who practices a particular type of remedial treatment ○ osteopath

pathetic /pə théttik/ adj 1 arousing or expressing pity 2 contemptibly or laughably inadequate (infml) —**pathetically** adv ◊ See note at **moving**

pathfinder /páath fīndər/ n a discoverer of a way through uncharted territory or knowledge —**pathfinding** n

pathogen /páthəjən, -jen/ n an agent of disease such as a virus or bacterium —**pathogenic** /páthə jénnik/ adj

pathological /páthə lójjik'l/ adj 1 of pathology 2 of disease 3 uncontrolled or unreasonable ○ a pathological liar —**pathologically** adv

pathology /pə thóllɔji/ (*pl* **-gies**) *n* **1** the scientific study of disease **2** the processes of a particular disease **3** a condition that is not expected or usual —**pathologist** *n*

pathos /páy thoss/ *n* **1** a quality that arouses pity **2** the expression of pity

pathway /paáth way/ *n* **1** a path or route **2** a sequence of biochemical reactions in a metabolic process

patience /páysh'nss/ *n* **1** the capacity for waiting without becoming annoyed **2** a card game for one player

patient /páysh'nt/ *adj* capable of waiting without becoming annoyed ■ *n* somebody who is receiving medical treatment —**patiently** *adv*

patina /páttinə/ *n* **1** a thin green layer of corrosion on copper **2** a surface sheen —**patinated** /pátti naytid/ *adj*

patio /pátti ṓ/ (*pl* **-os**) *n* **1** a paved area outside a house, used for dining or recreation **2** a roofless courtyard

patio doors *npl* doors opening onto a patio

patisserie /pə teéssəri, -tíssəri/ *n* **1** a cake shop **2** pastries or cakes

Patna /pátnə/ capital of Bihar State, NE India. Pop. 917,243 (1991).

patois /pát waa/ (*pl* **-ois** /pát waaz/) *n* **1** a regional dialect **2** a jargon of a particular group **3** **Patois** a Creole language spoken on some islands of the Caribbean —**Patois** *adj*

Paton /páytn/, **Alan** (1903–88) South African writer and politician

~~patriachal~~ incorrect spelling of **patriarchal**

patrial /páytri əl, páttri əl/ *n* formerly, a person with the right to enter and stay in the United Kingdom

patriarch /páytri aark, páttri-/ *n* **1** the male head of a family or group **2** a respected elderly man **3** a senior bishop of the Eastern Orthodox Church or one of the Eastern Christian churches that recognize papal supremacy

patriarchal /páytri aárk'l, páttri-/ *adj* **1** of a patriarch **2** of or characteristic of a culture in which men dominate

patriarchy /páytri aarki, páttri-/ (*pl* **-chies**) *n* a social system or society in which men dominate

patrician /pə trísh'n/ *n* **1** a member of an aristocracy **2** somebody with qualities associated with the aristocracy —**patrician** *adj*

patricide /páttri sīd, páytri-/ *n* **1** the murder of a father by his child **2** somebody who commits patricide —**patricidal** /páttri síd'l, páytri-/ *adj*

Patrick /páttrik/, **St** (389?–461?) British-born Irish cleric and the patron saint of Ireland

patrilineal /páttrə línni əl/, **patrilinear** /-ər/ *adj* tracing descent through the male line

patrimony /páttriməni/ (*pl* **-nies**) *n* an inheritance from a male ancestor —**patrimonial** /páttri mṓni əl/ *adj*

patriot /páttri ət, páy-/ *n* somebody who proudly supports his or her own country

—**patriotic** /páttri óttik, páytri-/ *adj* —**patriotically** *adv* —**patriotism** *n*

patrol /pə trṓl/ *n* **1** a regular tour of a place made by a guard **2** somebody carrying out a patrol **3** a military unit on a mission ■ *vti* (**-trolling, -trolled**) go on a patrol of an area

patrol car *n* a police car

patrolman /pə trṓlmən/ (*pl* **-men** /-mən/) *n* **1** a mechanic providing a breakdown service **2** *US, Can* a patrolling police officer

patron /páytrən/ *n* **1** somebody who gives money or other support **2** a regular customer —**patronal** /pə trṓn'l/ *adj* —**patronly** *adj* ◊ See note at **backer**

patronage /páttrənij/ *n* **1** the support given by a patron **2** the business provided by a customer *(fml)* **3** condescending kindness **4** the power to make appointments **5** appointments given by a politician to loyal supporters

patronize /páttrə nīz/ (**-izing, -ized**), **patronise** *vt* **1** be condescending to **2** be a regular customer of *(fml)* —**patronizing** *adj* —**patronizingly** *adv*

patron saint *n* a saint believed to be a special guardian

patronymic /páttrə nímmik/ *adj* derived from a male ancestor's name —**patronymic** *n*

patsy /pátsi/ (*pl* **-sies**) *n* a person regarded as open to victimization or manipulation *(infml insult)*

patter /páttər/ *vi* **1** make a quick tapping sound **2** step lightly ■ *n* a light tapping noise

ORIGIN Although both English words **patter** contain an element of speed in their meaning, there is no etymological connection between them. **Patter** 'make a quick tapping sound' is a derivative of *pat* in the sense 'hit'. **Patter** 'fast talk' is a shortening of *paternoster* 'the Lord's Prayer'. The modern meaning evolved from 'mumble prayers quickly', the way the paternoster was said in church.

patter /páttər/ *n* **1** glib and rapid talk **2** jargon

pattern /páttərn/ *n* **1** a repeated decorative design **2** a regular or repetitive arrangement, occurrence, or way of behaving **3** a prototype **4** a plan or model used as a guide for making something **5** a good example ■ *vt* decorate or make using a pattern

Patterson /páttərss'n/, **Percival James** (*b.* 1935) prime minister of Jamaica (1992–)

USMA Archives, West Point

George S. Patton

Patton /pátt'n/, **George S.** (1885–1945) US general

patty /pátti/ (pl **-ties**) n **1** a flat individual portion of food **2** a small pie

paucity /páwssəti/ n **1** an inadequacy or lack of something **2** a small number of things

Paul /pawl/, **St** (AD 3?–62?) early Christian missionary —**Pauline** /páwl ĭn/ adj

Paul III (1468–1549) pope (1534–49)

Pauling /páwling/, **Linus** (1901–94) US chemist and peace activist

paunch /pawnch/ n a big stomach —**paunchy** adj

pauper /páwpər/ n **1** a very poor person **2** a recipient of public aid (archaic) —**pauperism** n

Pausa /páwzə/ n the 10th month of the Hindu calendar

pause /pawz/ vi (**pausing, paused**) **1** briefly stop doing something **2** stay briefly **3** hesitate ■ n **1** a brief stop **2** a short silence **3** a hesitation **4** a musical symbol indicating that a note is to be held longer —**pausal** adj ◊ **give somebody pause** make somebody hesitate or reconsider ◊ See note at **hesitate**

pave /payv/ (**paving, paved**) vt cover with a hard surface for walking or travelling on ◊ **pave the way** prepare for and facilitate

pavement /páyvmənt/ n **1** a path for pedestrians alongside a street **2** US the asphalt surface of a road

pavilion /pə vílli ən/ n **1** an open, often ornamental, building in a garden or park **2** a sports clubhouse **3** an exhibition tent **4** a large ornate tent **5** a detached building forming part of a building complex

~~pavillion~~ incorrect spelling of **pavilion**

paving /páyving/ n **1** the surface of a paved path **2** material for making a paved surface **3** the construction of a paved surface

paving stone n a slab used to make a pavement

Pavlov /páv lof/, **Ivan Petrovich** (1849–1936) Russian physiologist famous for his studies on conditioned reflexes with dogs

pavlova /pav lóvə/ n a meringue dessert

> **ORIGIN** The **pavlova** was created in honour of the ballerine Anna Pavlova when she visited Australia and New Zealand.

Pavlova /pav lóvə, pávləvə/, **Anna** (1882–1931) Russian ballet dancer

paw n **1** a mammal's foot with claws or nails **2** a human hand (infml) ■ vti **1** strike something repeatedly with a paw or hoof **2** touch clumsily

pawn[1] n **1** the chess piece of lowest value **2** a person manipulated by another

> **ORIGIN** The chess **pawn** came via French from a medieval Latin word meaning 'foot soldier'. Pawn 'deposit, pledge' was also adopted immediately from French, but it goes back to an ancient Germanic word.

pawn[2] vt **1** deposit something with a pawnbroker **2** pledge your honour, word, or life

■ n **1** an object deposited with a pawnbroker **2** a hostage

pawnbroker /páwn brōkər/ n a moneylender who accepts personal items as security

pawnshop /páwn shop/ n a place to pawn things

pawpaw /páwpaw/ n a papaya

pax n **1** a kiss of peace given during a Roman Catholic Mass **2** a tablet kissed during a Roman Catholic Mass

pay v (**paid**) **1** vti give somebody money in return for work, goods, or services **2** vti settle a debt **3** vti bring in money ○ How much does the job pay? **4** vti punish, or be punished **5** vt yield interest on an investment **6** vi be profitable or beneficial ○ Crime doesn't pay. **7** vt bestow a compliment or give attention **8** vt make a visit ■ n **1** money given in return for work, goods, or services **2** a reward of any kind ■ adj requiring payment to function ○ pay TV —**payee** /pay eé/ n ◊ **put paid to** put an end to or ruin (infml) ◊ See note at **wage**

□ **pay back** vt **1** repay **2** take revenge on

□ **pay off** v **1** vt repay in full **2** vt pay and lay off workers **3** vi prove successful

□ **pay out** v **1** vti pay money **2** vt unwind a rope

□ **pay up** vi pay the money that is due

payable /páy əb'l/ adj **1** requiring payment **2** granting payment to a particular person

pay and display n a parking system in which motorists display tickets purchased from a machine

pay-as-you-earn n full form of **PAYE**

pay-as-you-go n the practice of paying debts or costs as they arise

payback /páy bak/ n a return on an investment

pay bed n a private patient's hospital bed

pay cheque n **1** a salary or wage cheque **2** wages or a salary

payday /páy day/ n the day on which employees are paid

pay dirt n **1** US a potentially profitable discovery **2** a mineral deposit worth mining

PAYE n a system in which tax is deducted as wages are earned. Full form **pay-as-you-earn**

~~payed~~ incorrect spelling of **paid**

paying guest n a boarder in somebody's home

payload /páy lōd/ n **1** a quantity of cargo **2** the passengers and equipment carried by an aircraft or spacecraft **3** an explosive charge of a missile

paymaster /páy maastər/ n a person in charge of paying employees

payment /páymənt/ n **1** an amount paid **2** a reward or punishment **3** the act of paying

payment gateway n an Internet payments interface

payoff /páy of/ n **1** full payment of a debt **2** a final settlement or outcome **3** ultimate benefit or advantage

payola /pay ólə/ n US, Can a bribe for promoting a product

payout /páy owt/ n the act of paying money, or the sum paid

pay packet *n* **1** an envelope containing an employee's wages **2** wages

pay-per-view *n* a cable or satellite TV system in which individual programmes can be watched for a fee

payphone /páy fōn/ *n* a public telephone requiring coin or card payment

payroll /páy rōl/ *n* **1** a list of paid employees **2** the total wages paid to employees

payslip /páy slip/ *n* a statement of an employee's pay

pay television, pay TV *n* a system in which only viewers who have paid for unscrambling equipment can watch broadcasts

payware /páy wair/ *n* commercial software

Octavio Paz

Paz /pass, paz/, **Octavio** (1914–98) Mexican writer

Pb *symbol* lead

pc *abbr* per cent

PC[1] *abbr* **1** Police Constable **2** politically correct

PC[2] *n* **1** a personal computer **2** a computer compatible with IBM PCs and MS-DOS

PCI *n* a specification for extending a computer's internal circuitry by adding circuit boards. Full form **peripheral component interconnect**

pcm *abbr* per calendar month

Pd *symbol* palladium

PDA *abbr* personal digital assistant

pdf *n* a format or file extension for a computer document file that enables a document to be processed and printed on any computer using any printer or word-processing program. Full form **portable document format**

PE[1] *adv* used as a non-Christian equivalent of AD in dates. Full form **Present Era**

PE[2] *abbr* physical education

pea /pee/ *n* **1** a round green seed that grows in a pod, eaten as a vegetable **2** a leguminous plant with peas in pods

~~peaceable~~ incorrect spelling of **peaceable**

peace /peess/ *n* **1** freedom from war **2** mental calm **3** a peace treaty **4** law and order **5** a state of harmony ■ *interj* be calm or silent ◇ **at peace 1** dead *(euphemistic)* **2** in a state of calm and serenity ◇ **hold your peace** refrain from speaking *(dated)* ◇ **keep the peace** refrain from or prevent conflict

SPELLCHECK Do not confuse the spelling of **peace** and **piece** ('a part'), which sound similar.

peaceable /peéssəb'l/ *adj* **1** disposed towards peace **2** tranquil —**peaceably** *adv*

peaceful /peéssf'l/ *adj* **1** quiet and calm **2** mentally calm —**peacefully** *adv* —**peacefulness** *n*

peacekeeping /peéss keeping/ *n* the preservation of peace, especially between formerly warring groups —**peacekeeper** *n*

peacemaker /peéss maykər/ *n* somebody who establishes peace

peace offering *n* something given to an enemy to encourage reconciliation

peace pipe *n* a ceremonial Native North American pipe

peacetime /peéss tīm/ *n* a period without war

peach /peech/ *n* **1** a large orange-yellow fruit with a stone **2** a tree that produces peaches **3** an excellent person or thing *(infml)*

ORIGIN Etymologically the **peach** is 'from Persia'. The word goes back to Latin *malum persicum*, literally 'Persian apple'. The **peach** is actually from China, but only became familiar to western Europeans after its cultivation had spread to Persia.

peach melba *n* a dessert of peaches and vanilla ice cream with a raspberry sauce

ORIGIN The dish was created in honour of Dame Nellie Melba.

peachy /peéchi/ (**-ier**, **-iest**) *adj* resembling a peach in colour, taste, or texture —**peachily** *adv*

peacock /peé kok/ *n* **1** a male peafowl, whose long iridescent tail can be held up like an open fan **2** a peafowl of either sex

peafowl /peé fowl/ (*pl* **-fowls** *or* same) *n* a large Asian pheasant

peahen /peé hen/ *n* a female peafowl

peak /peek/ *n* **1** a pointed mountain top **2** a mountain with a pointed top **3** a pointed part **4** the point of greatest success, strength, or development ■ *vi* **1** reach the peak of success, strength, or development **2** form a peak ■ *adj* **1** maximum or highest ○ *peak efficiency* **2** during maximum use or demand ○ *peak viewing time*

SPELLCHECK Do not confuse the spelling of **peak**, **peek** ('look quickly'), or **pique** ('bad mood'), which sound similar.

Peak District region in central England forming the southern part of the Pennine Hills

peaked /peekt/ *adj* having a peak —**peakedness** *n*

peak season *n* the most popular time of the year for holidays

peaky /peéki/ (**-ier**, **-iest**) *adj* sickly

peal /peel/ *n* **1** a ringing of bells **2** a set of tuned bells **3** a noisy outburst or loud repetitive sound ○ *peals of laughter* ○ *a peal of thunder* ■ *vti* ring bells, or ring, loudly

SPELLCHECK Do not confuse the spelling of

peal and **peel** ('remove an outer layer'), which sound similar.

peanut /pée nut/ n an oily edible seed that grows underground ∎ **peanuts** npl a small amount of money (infml)

peanut butter n a spreadable food made from peanuts

pear /pair/ n 1 a fruit with a teardrop shape and white flesh 2 the tree that produces pears ◊ See note at **pair**

pearl /purl/ n 1 a small lustrous sphere formed in an oyster or other mollusc. Use: gems. 2 mother-of-pearl 3 a highly valued person or thing —**pearly** adj

pearl barley n polished barley grains

Pearl Harbor inlet of the Pacific Ocean on S Oahu, Hawaii. Japanese planes attacked the US naval base there on 7 December 1941, prompting the United States' entry into World War II.

Pearly Gates npl in Christianity, the entrance to heaven (infml)

Pearse /peerss/, **Patrick Henry** (1879–1916) Irish nationalist leader

Pearse, Richard William (1877–1953) New Zealand inventor who is said to have achieved a brief powered flight (1902) 20 months before the Wright Brothers

pear-shaped adj shaped like a pear ◊ **go pear-shaped** get out of control or go wrong (infml)

Pearson /peerss'n/, **Lester** (1897–1972) prime minister of Canada (1963–68)

Peary /peéri/, **Robert** (1856–1920) US explorer

peasant /pézz'nt/ n 1 an agricultural labourer or small farmer 2 a country-dweller

peasantry /pézz'ntri/ n peasants as a class

pease pudding /peéz-/ n a thick puree made from dried peas

peashooter /peé shootar/ n a toy pipe through which dried peas can be blown

peasouper /pee soópar/ n a thick fog (infml)

peat /peet/ n 1 a deposit of compacted organic debris 2 a piece of peat used for fuel —**peaty** adj

pebble /pébb'l/ n a small rounded smooth stone ∎ vt (-bling, -bled) give an irregular grainy surface to leather —**pebbly** adj

pebbledash /pébb'l dash/ n a finish for exterior walls consisting of small stones set in concrete

pecan /peékan, pi kán/ n 1 an edible nut resembling a long walnut 2 the tree that produces pecans

peccadillo /pékə díllō/ (pl -loes or -los) n a trifling offence

peck[1] v 1 vt pick up with the beak 2 vti strike with the beak 3 vi nibble at food, eating little ∎ n 1 a swift blow with the beak 2 a light kiss (infml)

peck[2] n a unit of dry measure equal to 9.09 litres/8 quarts

pecking order n a social hierarchy

peckish /pékish/ adj slightly hungry (infml)

pecs npl the pectoral muscles (infml)

pectin /péktin/ n a substance found in plant cell walls. Use: gelling agent. —**pectic** adj —**pectinous** adj

pectoral /péktərəl/ adj of the chest ∎ n a chest muscle

pectoral fin n a fin near a fish's gills

peculiar /pi kyoóli ər/ adj 1 unusual or strange ○ The situation was very peculiar. 2 unique —**peculiarity** /pi kyoóli árrəti/ n —**peculiarly** adv

~~peculier~~ incorrect spelling of **peculiar**

pecuniary /pi kyoóni əri/ adj of money

pedagogue /péddə gog/ n a teacher, often a dogmatic one

pedagogy /péddə goji/ n teaching —**pedagogical** /péddə gójjik'l/ adj

pedal /pédd'l/ n a foot-operated lever for a machine or musical instrument ∎ vti (-alling, -alled) 1 ride a bicycle 2 operate or play using a pedal ∎ adj of the foot

> **SPELLCHECK** Do not confuse the spelling of **pedal** and **peddle** ('sell goods'), which sound similar.

pedalo /péddəlō/ (pl -los or -loes) n a small pedal-operated pleasure boat

pedal pushers npl calf-length women's trousers

pedant /pédd'nt/ n 1 somebody who is too concerned with rules and details 2 somebody who shows off his or her knowledge —**pedantic** /pi dántik/ adj —**pedantry** n

~~pedastool~~ incorrect spelling of **pedestal**

peddle /pédd'l/ vt (-dling, -dled) vt 1 sell goods, especially while travelling from place to place 2 sell drugs —**peddler** n ◊ See note at **pedal**

pederast /péddə rast/, **paederast** n a man who has sexual relations with a boy (fml)

pedestal /péddist'l/ n 1 the base of a column 2 the supporting base of a piece of furniture 3 a position of being exalted or admired

pedestrian /pə déstri ən/ n somebody who is on foot ∎ adj ordinary or unexceptional —**pedestrianism** n

pedestrian crossing n a place for pedestrians to cross

pedestrianize /pə déstri ə nīz/ (-izing, -ized), **pedestrianise** vt make a street into a pedestrian area —**pedestrianization** /pə déstri ə nī záysh'n/ n

pediatrics n = **paediatrics**

pedicure /péddi kyoor/ n 1 medical care of the feet 2 a cosmetic treatment for the feet —**pedicurist** n

pedigree /péddi gree/ n 1 the line of ancestors of a pure-bred animal 2 a document listing an animal's ancestors 3 a family tree ∎ adj pure-bred —**pedigreed** adj

pediment /péddimənt/ n 1 a gable on a row of columns 2 a broad flat rock surface

pedlar /péddlər/ n a travelling seller of goods

pedometer /pi dómmitər/ n an instrument for measuring the distance walked

pedophile n = paedophile

pee (infml; sometimes offensive) vi (**peed**) urinate ■ n 1 urine 2 urination

peek /peek/ vi look quickly —**peek** n ◊ See note at **peak**

peekaboo /peekə boó, peekə boo/ n a children's game of hiding and uncovering the face and saying 'peekaboo'

peel /peel/ v 1 vt remove the skin or outer layer of 2 vt pull something away from a surface 3 vi lose an outer layer ○ Her nose was peeling. 4 vi come off in thin strips or pieces ■ n the skin of a fruit or vegetable —**peeler** n ◊ See note at **peal**

Peel /peel/, **Sir Robert** (1788–1850) prime minister of Great Britain (1834–35 and 1841–46)

peep[1] /peep/ v 1 vi look quickly or secretly 2 vti make or make become visible only briefly —**peep** n

peep[2] /peep/ vi 1 make a short high-pitched noise 2 make a quiet noise, or speak in quiet voice —**peep** n

peephole /peep hōl/ n a small opening to look through

peepshow /peep shō/, **peep show** n 1 an erotic show viewed from a private booth 2 in former times, a sequence of pictures viewed through a lens or hole

peer[1] /peer/ vi 1 look closely 2 be partially or briefly visible

---

SPELLCHECK Do not confuse the spelling of **peer** and **pier** ('a walkway jutting into the sea'), which sound similar.

---

peer[2] /peer/ n 1 a person of equal standing with another 2 a member of the nobility in Great Britain and Northern Ireland

peerage /peerij/ n 1 nobles considered as a group 2 the rank or title of a member of the nobility

peeress /peer ess/ n 1 a woman peer 2 the wife of a peer

peer group n a social group of equals

peerless /peerləss/ adj without equal —**peerlessly** adv

peer pressure n the social pressure on people to behave like their peers

peer review n evaluation of a piece of work by experts

peeve (infml) vt (**peeving, peeved**) annoy ■ n an annoying thing

peevish /peevish/ adj irritable —**peevishly** adv —**peevishness** n

peeform incorrect spelling of **perform**

peg n 1 a pin or bolt for fastening or marking something 2 a hook for hanging things on 3 a clip for fastening clothes on a washing line 4 a part for tuning a string on a musical instrument 5 a fast throw ■ vt (**pegging, pegged**) 1 secure or mark something with pegs 2 put a peg in something 3 fix a cost or value at a certain level ◊ **bring** or **take down a peg (or two)** make more humble ◊ **off the peg** ready to wear, not tailor-made

□ **peg away** vi continue working steadily

□ **peg out** vi die (infml)

pegboard /pég bawrd/ n a board with holes for playing games or keeping score

I. M. Pei

Pei /pay/, **I. M.** (b. 1917) Chinese-born US architect

peice incorrect spelling of **piece**

peir incorrect spelling of **pier**

Peirce /peerss/, **Charles Sanders** (1839–1914) US philosopher and physicist

pejorative /pi jórrətiv/ adj expressing disapproval (fml) —**pejorative** n —**pejoratively** adv

Peking /pee king/ former name for **Beijing**

Pekingese /peeki neez/, **Pekinese** n a small dog with a flat nose and long silky hair

pelagic /pə lájjik/ adj found in the open sea rather than near the shore

Pelé

Pelé /pél ay/ (b. 1940) Brazilian football player

pelican /péllikən/ n a large water bird that has a bill with a pouch

pelican crossing n a road crossing with pedestrian-operated traffic lights

pellagra /pə lággrə, pə láygrə/ n a disease caused by a dietary deficiency of niacin

pellet /péllət/ n 1 a small ball of compressed material 2 a small bullet or piece of shot —**pellet** vt

pell-mell /pél mél/ adv 1 in a disorderly rush 2 in a confused or untidy manner —**pell-mell** adj, n

pellucid /pə loóssid/ adj 1 transparent or translucent (literary) 2 clear in meaning (fml)

pelmet /pélmət/ n a decorative strip hiding a curtain rail

Peloponnese /péllapa neess, péllapa neess/ peninsula forming the southern part of mainland Greece —**Peloponnesian** /péllapa neézh'n, -neésh'n/ *n, adj*

pelota /pa lótta, -lóta/ *n* a game in which baskets are used to hit a ball against a wall and catch it

pelt[1] *n* an animal skin ■ *vt* remove the skin of an animal

pelt[2] *v* **1** *vt* bombard with blows or missiles **2** *vt* beat against **3** *vi* rain heavily **4** *vi* move quickly ■ *n* a strong blow —**pelter** *n*

pelvis /pélviss/ (*pl* **-vises** *or* **-ves** /-veez/) *n* the basin-shaped structure formed by the hip bones and sacrum —**pelvic** *adj*

Pembrokeshire /pémbroökshar/ county in SW Wales

pen[1] *n* **1** an instrument for writing in ink **2** a particular style of writing ■ *vt* (**penning, penned**) write *(fml)* —**penner** *n*

ORIGIN The **pen** for writing goes back to Latin *penna* 'feather', and was adopted from French. The origins of **pen** 'enclosure' and **pen** 'female swan' are unknown.

---

pen[2] *n* **1** a small enclosure for animals **2** an area where somebody or something is confined —**pen** *vt*

pen[3] *n* a female swan

penal /peén'l/ *adj* **1** of punishment **2** punishable by law

penal code *n* a body of laws relating to the punishment of crime

penalize /peéna līz/ (**-izing, -ized**), **penalise** *vt* **1** impose a penalty on **2** put at a disadvantage —**penalization** /peéna lī záysh'n/ *n*

penal servitude *n* confinement in a remote place of imprisonment and punishment

penalty /pénn'lti/ (*pl* **-ties**) *n* **1** a legal or official punishment for a crime or offence **2** a fine for breaking a contract **3** an unpleasant consequence ○ *paying the penalty of being too lenient* **4** in sport, a disadvantage imposed for breaking a rule

penalty area *n* an area in front of a football goal where the goalkeeper may handle the ball

penalty kick *n* in football, a free kick at an opposing team's goal

penalty rates *npl* ANZ the pay rate for extra hours worked

penalty shoot-out *n* in football, a tiebreaker involving a series of penalty kicks

penance /pénnanss/ *n* **1** self-imposed punishment for wrongdoing **2** a Christian sacrament of confession and forgiveness of sins —**penance** *vt*

penatrate incorrect spelling of **penetrate**

pence plural of **penny**

penchant /póN shoN/ *n* a liking or tendency

pencil /péns'l/ *n* **1** an instrument containing a stick of graphite used for drawing and writing **2** something resembling a pencil in shape or function ○ *an eyebrow pencil* ○ *a pencil of light* —**pencil** *vt*

pen computer *n* a computer that recognizes handwriting

pendant /péndant/ *n* **1** a hanging ornament or piece of jewellery **2** a necklace with a hanging ornament

pendent /péndant/ *adj (fml or literary)* **1** hanging or suspended **2** overhanging

pending /pénding/ *adj* **1** not yet dealt with or settled **2** about to happen ■ *prep* **1** until **2** during

pendulous /péndyoōlass/ *adj* hanging loosely —**pendulously** *adv*

pendulum /péndyoōlam/ *n* **1** a weight swinging freely from a fixed point **2** a swinging weighted rod controlling a clock mechanism —**pendular** *adj*

penecillin incorrect spelling of **penicillin**

penetrate /pénni trayt/ (**-trating, -trated**) *v* **1** *vti* enter or pass through something **2** *vt* permeate or spread through something **3** *vt* see into or through something dark or obscure —**penetrable** *adj* —**penetratingly** *adv* —**penetration** /pénni tráysh'n/ *n* —**penetrative** *adj*

penetrating /pénni trayting/ *adj* **1** able or tending to penetrate ○ *a penetrating odour* **2** piercing or probing ○ *a penetrating stare* **3** loud and shrill

pen friend *n* a friend made through letter-writing

penguin /péng gwin/ *n* an upright black-and-white seabird that cannot fly

---

ORIGIN The origin of **penguin** is somewhat mysterious. The word first appears in the late 16C, referring to both the penguin we know and a large flightless sea bird of N Atlantic coasts that is now extinct. A narrative of 1582 suggested that the word was Welsh, and *pen gwyn* 'white head' has been suggested. The familiar **penguin**, however, has a black head.

---

penicillin /pénni síllin/ *n* an antibiotic originally derived from mould

peninsula /pa nínsyoōla/ *n* a strip of land projecting into a body of water —**peninsular** *adj*

SPELLCHECK Do not confuse the spelling of **peninsula** (noun) and **peninsular** (adjective), which sound similar.

---

penis /peéniss/ (*pl* **-nises** *or* **-nes** /-neez/) *n* the male organ of copulation, in many mammals also used for urination —**penile** /peé nīl/ *adj*

penitent /pénnitant/ *adj* feeling regret for wrongdoing ■ *n* a penitent person —**penitence** *n* —**penitential** /pénni ténsh'l/ *adj* —**penitently** *adv*

penitentiary /pénni ténshari/ *n* (*pl* **-ries**) US, Can a prison ■ *adj* **1** of penance **2** of punishment or reform of offenders

penknife /pén nīf/ (*pl* **-knives** /-nīvz/) *n* a small knife with a folding blade

penmanship /pénman ship/ *n* the art or technique of writing by hand

Penn, William (1644–1718) English-born American Quaker reformer and colonialist

pen name n a false name used by a writer

pennant /pénnənt/ n 1 a triangular flag, especially displayed on a ship 2 Aus, US, Can a flag symbolizing a sports championship

penne /pénnay/ n short tube-shaped pasta cut diagonally at the ends

penniless /pénniləss/ adj without any money

Pennine Hills /pén īn-/ range of hills in N England, forming the 'spine' of the country. Highest peak Cross Fell 893 m/2,930 ft.

pennon /pénnən/ n 1 a long narrow flag carried on a lance 2 a pennant on a ship

Pennsylvania /pénss'l váyni ə/ state in the NE United States. Cap. Harrisburg. Pop. 12,281,054 (2000). —**Pennsylvanian** n, adj

penny /pénni/ (pl **pennies** or **pence** /penss/) n 1 (symbol **p**) a subunit of currency in the United Kingdom 2 a coin with a low value in some countries other than the United Kingdom, e.g. a US cent ◊ **cost a pretty penny** cost a great deal of money ◊ **the penny dropped** somebody suddenly understood or realized

penny dreadful n a cheap book or comic with sensational stories

penny-farthing n an early bicycle with a large front wheel carrying the pedals and a small back wheel

penny pincher n a mean person (infml) —**penny-pinching** adj

penny whistle n a high-pitched flute-like musical instrument

pennyworth /pénnee wurth, pénnərth/ n 1 (pl **pennyworths** or same) an amount that can be bought for a penny (dated) 2 a small amount (dated) 3 somebody's personal comment or opinion (infml) ○ always has to put in his pennyworth

pen pal n US, Can a pen friend

penpusher /pén pōōshər/ n somebody with a boring office job (infml) —**penpushing** adj, n

pension[1] /pénsh'n/ n money paid regularly to a retired person or as compensation ○ a widow's pension ■ vt pay a pension to —**pensionable** adj

□ **pension off** vt 1 force to retire 2 get rid of (infml)

pension[2] /póN syoN/ n a small hotel or boarding house in continental Europe

pensioner /pénsh'nər/ n somebody who receives a pension

pensive /pénssiv/ adj deeply thoughtful —**pensively** adv —**pensiveness** n

penta- prefix five ○ pentagon

pentagon /péntəgən/ n 1 a five-sided geometrical figure 2 **Pentagon** the US Department of Defense, or the building that houses it —**pentagonal** /pen tággən'l/ adj

pentagram /péntə gram/ n a five-pointed star

pentameter /pen támmitər/ n a line of poetry made up of five units of rhythm

pentathlon /pen táthlən/ n a sporting competition consisting of five events

Pentecost /pénti kost/ n a Christian festival marking the descent of the Holy Spirit upon the apostles. Date: 7th Sunday after Easter.

ORIGIN Pentecost goes back to the Greek word for 'fifty'. The Jewish festival to which the word originally referred is observed on the 50th day after the 2nd day of Passover.

Pentecostal /pénti kóst'l/ adj 1 of a Christian denomination that emphasizes the workings of the Holy Spirit 2 of Pentecost —**Pentecostal** n —**Pentecostalism** n —**Pentecostalist** n, adj

penthouse /pént howss/ (pl **-houses** /-howziz/) n 1 an expensive top-floor or rooftop flat 2 a sloping roof or shed attached to a building

ORIGIN A **penthouse** is not etymologically a type of house. It derives from a shortening of an old French word apentis meaning 'lean-to', which goes back to the Latin verb that is also the source of append. English adopted the word in the 14C, and it began to be linked to house in the 16C.

pent-up adj repressed or stifled ○ pent-up emotions

penultimate /pe núltimət/ adj second to last —**penultimately** adv

penumbra /pə númbrə/ (pl **-brae** /-bree/ or **-bras**) n a partial shadow, e.g. in an eclipse

penurious /pə nyóori əss/ adj (literary) 1 having little money 2 not generous with money

penury /pénnyŏori/ n extreme poverty

peon /peé ən/ n 1 a farm labourer, especially one working off a debt 2 a low-paid worker 3 a drudge

peony /peé əni/ (pl **-nies**), **paeony** n an ornamental plant with showy flowers

people /peép'l/ n a nation, community, or ethnic group ■ npl 1 human beings collectively 2 subordinates, e.g. subjects or employees 3 close relatives (infml) 4 ordinary men and women ■ vt (**-pling**, **-pled**) populate

people person n somebody who likes being with others

Peoria /pi áwri ə/ city in S Arizona. Pop. 87,048 (1998).

pep n liveliness (infml) —**peppily** adv —**peppy** adj

□ **pep up** vt make lively (infml)

pepper /péppər/ n 1 a hot seasoning made from ground dried berries 2 a plant that produces berries used to make pepper 3 a hollow fruit eaten as a vegetable 4 a plant that produces peppers ■ v 1 vt sprinkle or season with pepper 2 vt bombard with small missiles 3 sprinkle or scatter liberally ○ manuscripts peppered with typing errors

pepper-and-salt adj describes hair flecked with dark and light colours

peppercorn /péppər kawrn/ n a small dried berry that is ground to make pepper

peppercorn rent n a nominal rent

pepper mill n a pepper grinder

peppermint /péppər mint/ *n* **1** a flavouring made from the aromatic oil of a mint plant. Use: food industry, pharmaceuticals. **2** a sweet flavoured with peppermint **3** a plant with leaves that produce peppermint

pepperoni /péppə rṓni/ *n* a spicy sausage, often used on pizzas

peppery /péppəri/ *adj* **1** strongly flavoured with pepper **2** angry and critical

pepsin /pépsin/ *n* a stomach enzyme that digests protein

pep talk *n* an encouraging talk *(infml)*

peptic ulcer /péptik-/ *n* an ulcer in the upper digestive tract

peptide /pép tīd/ *n* a linear molecule made up of two or more linked amino acids —**peptidic** /pep tíddik/ *adj*

Pepys /peeps/, **Samuel** (1633–1703) English diarist

per /pər/ *prep* **1** for each ○ *50 miles per hour* **2** according to ○ *per instructions*

perambulate /pə rámbyōo layt/ (-lating, -lated) *vti* walk about a place *(fml)* —**perambulation** /pə rámbyōo láysh'n/ *n*

perambulator /pə rámbyōo laytər/ *n* a pram *(fml)*

per annum /pər ánnəm/ *adv* in every year, or by the year

percale /pər káyl/ *n* a smooth cotton or polyester fabric. Use: sheets, clothing.

per capita /pər káppitə/ *adv, adj* for each person

perceive /pər seév/ (-ceiving, -ceived) *vt* **1** become aware of using the senses **2** understand in a particular way ○ *the action was perceived as a conciliatory gesture* —**perceivable** *adj*

per cent, percent /pər sént/ *adv* (*symbol* %) expresses a proportion in hundredths ■ *n* (*pl same*) **1** one hundredth **2** a percentage

percentage /pər séntij/ *n* **1** a proportion expressed in hundredths **2** a part or proportion **3** a commission or share *(infml)*

> **USAGE** If you put the definite article *the* before **percentage**, you must use a singular verb after it: *The percentage of errors in the report is large.* If you put the indefinite article *a* before **percentage**, use a singular or plural verb, depending on whether what follows is regarded as a single unit or a plural: *A large percentage of the electorate remains undecided. A large percentage of the errors are found in this report.*

percentile /pər sén tīl/ *n* a statistical measure on a scale of 100

perceptible /pər séptəb'l/ *adj* detectable —**perceptibly** *adv*

perception /pər sépsh'n/ *n* **1** the process or result of perceiving **2** an attitude, impression, or understanding ○ *altered the public's perception of the issue* **3** the ability to be perceptive —**perceptional** *adj*

perceptive /pər séptiv/ *adj* **1** quick to understand or discern things **2** of perception —**perceptively** *adv* —**perceptiveness** *n*

perceptual /pər sépchoo əl/ *adj* of perception

perch¹ /pərch/ *n* **1** a place for a bird to sit **2** a temporary resting place **3** a unit of length equal to 5.03 m/5½ yd ■ *v* **1** *vti* sit precariously ○ *He was perched on a high stool.* **2** *vt* situate in a high place **3** *vi* land or sit on a perch *(refers to birds)*

perch² (*pl* **perches** *or same*) *n* **1** a freshwater fish with rough scales **2** perch as food

perchance /pər chaánss/ *adv* *(literary)* **1** perhaps **2** by chance

~~percieve~~ incorrect spelling of **perceive**

percipient /pər síppi ənt/ *adj* perceptive, observant, or discerning —**percipience** *n*

percolate /púrkə layt/ (-lating, -lated) *v* **1** *vti* pass through a filter **2** *vi* pass or spread slowly ○ *news percolating through to the hostages* **3** *vti* make coffee in a percolator, or be made in a percolator —**percolation** /púrkə láysh'n/ *n*

percolator /púrkə laytər/ *n* a coffeepot in which boiling water circulates through a basket of coffee grounds

percussion /pər kúsh'n/ *n* **1** the group of musical instruments that produce sound by being struck **2** impact, or the noise or shock of an impact *(fml)*

percussion cap *n* a detonator that explodes when struck, formerly used to fire some pistols

percussionist /pər kúsh'nist/ *n* a musician who plays a percussion instrument

percussive /pər kússiv/ *adj* having the effect of an impact

per diem /pər deé em, -dī em/ *adv, adj* by the day ■ *n* a daily payment or allowance

perdition /pər dísh'n/ *n* **1** everlasting punishment in Hell **2** Hell

peregrinate /pérrəgri nayt/ (-nating, -nated) *vti* travel *(literary)*

peregrination /pérrəgri náysh'n/ *n* a journey *(literary)*

peregrine falcon /pérrəgrin-/, **peregrine** *n* a large falcon with a blue-grey back and white underparts

> **ORIGIN** The **peregrine falcon** is literally a 'travelling falcon'. Falconers formerly captured them full-grown while migrating, and did not take them from their nests while young as with other birds.

peremptory /pə rémptəri/ *adj* **1** dictatorial **2** ending or closed to further discussion or action —**peremptorily** *adv*

~~perennial~~ incorrect spelling of **perennial**

perennial /pə rénni əl/ *adj* **1** describes a plant that lasts for more than two growing seasons **2** recurring or enduring —**perennial** *n* —**perennially** *adv*

Pérez de Cuéllar /pé ress də kwáy yaar/, **Javier** (*b.* 1920) Peruvian diplomat and secretary-general of the United Nations (1982–91)

perfect *adj* /púrfikt/ **1** without faults, flaws, or errors **2** complete and whole **3** excellent or ideal **4** especially suitable **5** utter or absolute o *perfect happiness* **6** describes a verb aspect or form expressing completed action ■ *vt* /pər fékt/ make perfect ■ *n* /púrfikt/ the perfect aspect, or a form of a verb in the perfect aspect —**perfectible** *adj* —**perfectly** *adv*

perfection /pər féksh'n/ *n* **1** the state or quality of being perfect **2** the process of perfecting

perfectionist /pər féksh'nist/ *n* somebody who strives for or demands perfection —**perfectionism** *n*

perfidy /púrfidi/ *n* deliberate treachery *(fml)* —**perfidious** /pər fíddi əss/ *adj*

perforate /púrfə rayt/ (-rating, -rated) *vt* **1** puncture **2** make a line of holes in for tearing —**perforated** *adj*

perforation /púrfə ráysh'n/ *n* **1** a hole **2** a line of holes for tearing **3** perforating or being perforated

perforce /pər fáwrss/ *adv* unavoidably *(literary)*

perform /pər fáwrm/ *v* **1** *vt* begin and bring an action to completion **2** *vt* fulfil what is required **3** *vti* present an artistic work such as a play or piece of music to an audience **4** *vi* function or behave in a particular way o *performs well under pressure* —**performer** *n*

SYNONYMS perform, do, carry out, fulfil, discharge, execute CORE MEANING: complete a task

performance /pər fáwrmənss/ *n* **1** a presentation of an artistic work to an audience **2** a manner of functioning o *a high-performance car* **3** an irritating procedure *(infml)* **4** the process of performing

performance art *n* art that combines static and dramatic artistic media —**performance artist** *n*

performing arts *npl* drama, dance, and music

perfume /púr fyoom/ *n* **1** a fragrant liquid **2** a pleasant smell —**perfume** *vt* ◊ See note at smell

perfumery /pər fyoomari/ (*pl* -ies) *n* **1** perfumes in general **2** a place where perfumes are made or sold

perfunctory /pər fúngktəri/ *adj* **1** done routinely o *a perfunctory kiss* **2** hasty and superficial o *a perfunctory search* —**perfunctorily** *adv*

Pergamum /púrgamam/ ancient Greek and Roman city in NW Asia Minor, in present-day W Turkey

pergola /púrgala/ *n* a structure of posts and latticework that supports climbing plants

perhaps /pər háps/ *informal* /praps/ *adv* **1** possibly **2** introduces a polite suggestion o *Perhaps we should leave.*

peri- *prefix* **1** around, surrounding o *perianth* **2** near o *perinatal*

perianth /pérri anth/ *n* the outer structure of a flower including the petals

Pericles /pérri kleez/ (495?–429? BC) Athenian political leader —**Periclean** /pérri klée ən/ *adj*

perigee /pérri jee/ *n* the point at which a satellite, moon, or planet comes nearest to the object it is orbiting

peril /pérrəl/ *n* **1** exposure to risk **2** a source of danger —**perilous** *adj* —**perilously** *adv*

perimeter /pə rímmitər/ *n* **1** a boundary enclosing an area **2** a curve enclosing an area, or the length of such a curve

perinatal /pérri náyt'l/ *adj* around the time of childbirth —**perinatally** *adv*

perineum /pérri née əm/ (*pl* -**a** /-née ə/) *n* the area of the body surrounding the genitals and anus —**perineal** *adj*

period /péeri əd/ *n* **1** an interval of time **2** a particular interval of time, e.g. in history o *the early Victorian period* **3** an occurrence of menstruation **4** a unit of geological time shorter than an era and longer than an epoch **5** *US, Can* a full stop in punctuation ■ *adj* of a particular historical time o *in period costume*

periodic /péeri óddik/ *adj* **1** recurring from time to time **2** occurring at regular intervals —**periodically** *adv* —**periodicity** /péeri ə díssəti/ *n*

SYNONYMS periodic, intermittent, occasional, sporadic CORE MEANING: recurring over a period of time

periodical /péeri óddik'l/ *n* a magazine or journal ■ *adj* **1** published at regular intervals **2** periodic

periodic table *n* a table of chemical elements arranged according to their atomic numbers

period piece *n* something such as a piece of furniture or work of art that dates from or evokes a particular historical period

peripatetic /pérripə téttik/ *adj* travelling from place to place ■ *n* a peripatetic worker

peripheral /pə ríffərəl/ *adj* **1** at the edge **2** minor or incidental ■ *n* a computer device external to but controlled by the central processing unit —**peripherally** *adv*

periphery /pə ríffəri/ (*pl* -ies) *n* the area around the edge

periphrasis /pə ríffrəssiss/ (*pl* -ses /-seez/) *n* **1** the use of more words than necessary to avoid saying something directly **2** an expression that states something indirectly

periscope /pérri skōp/ *n* a tubular optical instrument used to see something not in a direct line of sight

perish /pérrish/ *vi* **1** die *(literary)* **2** cease to exist *(fml)*

perishable /pérrishəb'l/ *adj* liable to rot or spoil ■ *n* something perishable, especially a food item

perished /pérrisht/ *adj* feeling very cold *(infml)*

perishing /pérrishing/ *adj* very cold o *a perishing easterly wind* —**perishingly** *adv*

peristalsis /pérri stálssiss/ (*pl* -ses /-seez/) *n* the involuntary contractions of the muscles of the intestine —**peristaltic** *adj*

peristyle /pérri stīl/ *n* a line of columns encircling a building or courtyard

peritonitis /pérritō nítiss/ *n* inflammation of the membrane lining the abdomen

periwig /pérri wig/ *n* a 17C and 18C man's wig

periwinkle /pérri wingk'l/ *n* a trailing plant with blue or white flowers

~~perjorative~~ incorrect spelling of **pejorative**

perjure /púrjər/ (**-juring, -jured**) *vr* tell lies under oath —**perjurer** *n* —**perjury** *n*

perk *n* an additional benefit o *one of the perks of the job*

□ **perk up** *vti* **1** make or become more cheerful, lively, or refreshed **2** stick up straight o *The dog's ears perked up.*

perky /púrki/ (**-ier, -iest**) *adj* **1** lively and cheerful **2** irritatingly self-confident —**perkily** *adv* —**perkiness** *n*

Perlman /púrlmən/**, Itzhak** (*b.* 1945) Israeli-born US violinist

perm *n* a hair treatment that gives long-lasting curls or waves —**perm** *vt*

Perm, Perm' city in E European Russia. Pop. 1,275,482 (1995).

permafrost /púrmə frost/ *n* permanently frozen subsoil

~~permanant~~ incorrect spelling of **permanent**

permanent /púrmənənt/ *adj* **1** lasting for ever **2** unchanging —**permanence** *n* —**permanently** *adv*

permanent press *n* a fabric treatment that gives shape and wrinkle resistance

permanent wave *n* a perm

permeable /púrmi əb'l/ *adj* allowing liquids or gases to pass through

permeate /púrmi ayt/ (**-ating, -ated**) *vti* **1** enter and spread through something **2** pass, or make pass, through tiny openings in a porous substance or membrane —**permeation** /púrmi áysh'n/ *n*

~~permenent~~ incorrect spelling of **permanent**

Permian /púrmi ən/ *n* a period of geological time 290–248 million years ago —**Permian** *adj*

~~permissable~~ incorrect spelling of **permissible**

permissible /pər míssəb'l/ *adj* allowable or permitted —**permissibility** /pər míssə bílləti/ *n* —**permissibly** *adv*

permission /pər mísh'n/ *n* agreement to allow something

permissive /pər míssiv/ *adj* **1** allowing freedom to behave in ways others might consider unacceptable **2** giving permission —**permissively** *adv* —**permissiveness** *n*

permit *vti* /pər mít/ (**-mitting, -mitted**) **1** agree to allow something **2** make something possible ■ *n* /púrmit/ a document giving permission

~~permited~~ incorrect spelling of **permitted**

permutation /púrmyŏŏ táysh'n/ *n* **1** an arrangement created by moving or reordering items **2** a transformation **3** an ordered arrangement of elements from a set

pernicious /pər níshəss/ *adj* **1** malicious **2** causing serious harm —**perniciously** *adv*

pernicious anaemia *n* a severe form of anaemia

pernickety /pər níkəti/ *adj* excessively concerned about details *(infml)*

~~perogative~~ incorrect spelling of **prerogative**

Eva Perón

Perón /pə rón/**, Eva** (1919–52) Argentine political figure. Married to President Juan Perón, she was extremely popular but never held public office.

Perón, Isabel de (*b.* 1931) president of Argentina (1974–76)

Perón, Juan (1895–1974) president of Argentina (1946–55 and 1973–74) —**Peronist** /pə rónnist/ *n, adj*

peroration /pérrə ráysh'n/ *n* **1** a conclusion summarizing the main points of a speech *(fml)* **2** a long-winded speech

peroxide /pə rók síd/ *n* **1** a chemical compound containing oxygen atoms **2** a substance used to lighten hair o *a peroxide blonde* —**peroxide** *vt*

perpendicular /púrpən díkyŏŏlər/ *adj* **1** vertical **2** very steep **3** at right angles **4** *also* **Perpendicular** of a late Gothic style of architecture —**perpendicular** *n*

perpetrate /púrpi trayt/ (**-trating, -trated**) *vt* do something illegal or morally wrong —**perpetration** /púrpi tráysh'n/ *n* —**perpetrator** *n*

perpetual /pər péchoo əl/ *adj* **1** lasting for ever or indefinitely **2** occurring repeatedly —**perpetually** *adv*

perpetuate /pər péchoo ayt/ (**-ating, -ated**) *vt* **1** cause to last for a long time **2** cause to be remembered —**perpetuation** /-péchoo áysh'n/ *n*

perpetuity /púrpi tyoo əti/ *n* **1** the condition of being perpetual **2** eternity

perplex /pər pléks/ *vt* puzzle or confuse —**perplexed** *adj* —**perplexing** *adj* —**perplexingly** *adv* —**perplexity** *n*

perquisite /púrkwizit/ *n* a perk *(fml)*

Perrault /pérrō, pə rố/**, Charles** (1628–1703) French writer and collector of fairy stories

~~perrenial~~ incorrect spelling of **perennial**

perry /pérri/ *n* a drink made from fermented pear juice

Perry /pérri/**, Fred** (1909–95) British tennis player

per se /pər sáy/ *adv* in itself

persecute /púrssi kyoot/ (**-cuting, -cuted**) *vt* **1** oppress or treat cruelly, e.g. because of ethnic origin or religious beliefs **2** pester or harass —**persecution** /púrssi kyoósh'n/ *n* —**persecutor** *n*

Persepolis /pər séppəlissa/ ruined ancient Persian city in present-day SW Iran

persevere /púrssi veér/ (**-vering, -vered**) *vi* persist determinedly despite difficulties —**perseverance** *n*

~~perseverence~~ incorrect spelling of **perseverance**

Persia /púrshə, púrzhə/ 1 former name for **Iran** 2 ancient empire in SW Asia that stretched eastwards from the E Mediterranean Sea to the River Indus in present-day Pakistan

Persian /púrsh'n, púrzhn/ *n* 1 somebody from Iran 2 a member of a people of ancient Persia 3 the language of the ancient Persians —**Persian** *adj*

Persian Gulf arm of the Arabian Sea, between the NE Arabian Peninsula and SW Iran

persimmon /pər símmən/ *n* 1 a smooth-skinned orange-red fruit 2 a tree that produces persimmons

persist /pər síst/ *vi* 1 continue steadily or obstinately 2 continue happening or existing —**persistence** *n* —**persistent** *adj* —**persistently** *adv*

~~persistant~~ incorrect spelling of **persistent**

person /púrss'n/ (*pl* **people** /peép'l/ *or* **persons** *formal*) *n* 1 a human being 2 somebody's body, including clothing ○ *objects found on her person* 3 a form of verbs and pronouns denoting the speaker, person addressed, or person referred to ○ *the third person singular* —**-person** *suffix* ◇ **in person** personally, rather than being represented by somebody else

persona /pər sṓnə/ (*pl* **-nae** /-neé/ *or* **-nas**) *n* 1 a character in literature (*often pl*) 2 an assumed identity or role 3 somebody's public image

personable /púrss'nəb'l/ *adj* having a pleasant personality and appearance

personage /púrss'nij/ *n* (*fml*) 1 an important person 2 a historical figure or fictional character

personal /púrss'nəl/ *adj* 1 of somebody's private life 2 of a particular person ○ *personal opinion* 3 done by a person himself or herself ○ *that personal touch* 4 intended for a specific person 5 referring offensively to somebody in particular ○ *making personal remarks about his appearance* 6 of the body ○ *personal hygiene*

personal allowance *n* a tax allowance for an individual person

personal assistant *n* an employee who performs secretarial and administrative tasks for somebody

personal column *n* a section of a magazine or newspaper containing advertisements or messages of a personal nature, e.g. from people seeking romance

personal computer *n* a computer intended for use by one person

personal digital assistant *n* a portable electronic notebook

personal identification number full form of **PIN**

personal information manager *n* a piece of software that organizes notes, contacts, and appointments

personality /púrssə nálləti/ (*pl* **-ties**) *n* 1 the totality of somebody's character and traits 2 distinctive or appealing personal characteristics ○ *lacking in personality* 3 a famous person

personality disorder *n* a psychiatric disorder that affects social interaction

personalize /púrss'nə līz/ (**-izing, -ized**), **personalise** *vt* 1 put somebody's initials or name on something 2 change something to reflect its owner's or occupier's personality —**personalization** /púrss'nə līz záysh'n/ *n*

personally /púrss'nəli/ *adv* 1 in your own opinion or experience ○ *Personally, I think they should be banned.* 2 as a person

personal organizer *n* 1 a diary with replaceable pages 2 a hand-held computer that can function as a diary, address book, and calculator

personal pronoun *n* a pronoun that refers to a person, e.g. 'I' or 'her'

personal stereo *n* a small audio cassette or CD player with earphones

personal watercraft *n* US, Can a water motorcycle

persona non grata /pər sṓnə non graátə/ (*pl* **personae non gratae** /-nee non graá teé/) *n* an unwelcome or unacceptable person —**persona non grata** *adj*

~~personel, personell~~ incorrect spelling of **personnel**

personify /pər sónni fī/ (**-fies, -fied**) *vt* 1 be an embodiment or perfect example of something 2 represent something abstract as human —**personification** /pər sónnifi káysh'n/ *n*

personnel /púrssə nél/ *n* the department of an organization that deals with employment and staffing issues ■ *npl* the people employed in an organization

person-to-person *adj* US describes a telephone call chargeable only when the recipient is reached

perspective /pər spéktiv/ *n* 1 a personal or subjective viewpoint ○ *a different perspective on the matter* 2 a measured or objective assessment ○ *keep things in perspective* 3 the way distant objects appear to an observer

Perspex /púr speks/ *tdmk* a trademark for a tough transparent acrylic plastic that can be used in place of glass

perspicacious /púrspi káyshəss/ *adj* perceptive —**perspicacity** /-kássəti/ *n*

perspicuous /pər spíkyoo əss/ *adj* clear and comprehensible —**perspicuity** /púrspi kyoó əti/ *n* —**perspicuously** *adv*

perspiration /púrspə ráysh'n/ *n* 1 sweat 2 the process or act of sweating

perspire /pər spír/ (**-spiring, -spired**) *vti* secrete sweat —**perspiringly** *adv*

Persson /páirss'n/, **Göran** (*b.* 1949) prime minister of Sweden (1996–)

persuade /pər swáyd/ (**-suading, -suaded**) *vt* **1** make somebody do something by reasoning, pleading, or coaxing **2** convince somebody of something —**persuadable** *adj*

persuasion /pər swáyzh'n/ *n* **1** the process of persuading **2** the ability to persuade **3** a set of beliefs

persuasive /pər swáyssiv/ *adj* persuading, or able to persuade —**persuasively** *adv* —**persuasiveness** *n*

~~**persue**~~ incorrect spelling of **pursue**

~~**persuit**~~ incorrect spelling of **pursuit**

~~**persumably**~~ incorrect spelling of **presumably**

pert *adj* **1** amusingly cheeky **2** jaunty and stylish —**pertly** *adv* —**pertness** *n*

PERT /purt/ *n* a method of prioritizing complex activities. Full form **programme evaluation and review technique**

pertain /pər táyn/ *vi* **1** relate or have relevance **2** be appropriate

Perth /purth/ **1** city in central Scotland. Pop. 41,453 (1991). **2** capital of Western Australia. Pop. 1,341,900 (1998).

Perth and Kinross council area in north-central Scotland

pertinacious /púrti náyshəss/ *adj* **1** resolute **2** persistent —**pertinacity** /-nássəti/ *n*

pertinent /púrtinənt/ *adj* relevant —**pertinence** *n* —**pertinently** *adv*

perturb /pər túrb/ *vt* disturb and trouble or worry —**perturbable** *adj* —**perturbation** /púrtər báysh'n/ *n*

pertussis /pər tússiss/ *n* whooping cough (*technical*) —**pertussal** *adj*

Peru /pə róō/ country in W South America. Cap. Lima. Pop. 27,483,864 (2001). —**Peruvian** /pə róővi ən/ *adj, n*

peruse /pə róōz/ (**-rusing, -rused**) *vt* read carefully —**perusal** *n*

Perutz /pə róōts/, **Max Ferdinand** (1914–2002) Austrian-born British biochemist

pervade /pər váyd/ (**-vading, -vaded**) *vt* spread throughout —**pervasion** /-váyzh'n/ *n* —**pervasive** /-váyssiv/ *adj* —**pervasively** *adv*

perverse /pər vúrss/ *adj* **1** purposely unreasonable, awkward, or stubborn **2** perverted —**perversely** *adv* —**perversity** *n*

perversion /pər vúrsh'n/ *n* **1** a sexual practice considered unusual or unacceptable **2** perverting or being perverted

pervert *vt* /pər vúrt/ **1** lead away from what is good, moral, or proper **2** misinterpret or distort **3** use improperly ■ *n* /púr vurt/ an offensive term for somebody whose sexual behaviour is considered unusual or unacceptable (*insult*) —**perverter** *n* —**pervertible** *adj*

pervious /púrvi əss/ *adj* able to be penetrated or permeated —**perviously** *adv*

peseta /pə sáytə/ *n* the main unit of the former Spanish currency

Peshawar /pə shaáwar/ city in N Pakistan, near the Khyber Pass. Pop. 988,055 (1998).

pesky /péski/ (**-kier, -kiest**) *adj US, Can* troublesome or irritating (*infml*) —**peskily** *adv*

peso /páyssō/ (*pl* **-sos**) *n* the main unit of currency in several South and Central American countries

pessary /péssəri/ (*pl* **-ries**) *n* a vaginal suppository

pessimist /péssə mist/ *n* somebody who always expects the worst to happen —**pessimism** *n* —**pessimistic** /péssə místik/ *adj* —**pessimistically** *adv*

pest *n* **1** a damaging organism **2** an annoying person or thing (*infml*)

> **ORIGIN Pest** originally referred to a fatal epidemic disease, especially bubonic plague. It was adopted in the late 15C from French.

Pestalozzi /péstə lótsi/, **Johann Heinrich** (1746–1827) Swiss educator

pester /péstər/ *vt* annoy constantly, especially by harassing with demands

pesticide /pésti sīd/ *n* a chemical substance used to kill pests —**pesticidal** /pésti sīd'l/ *adj*

pestilence /péstilənss/ *n* an epidemic of disease (*archaic*)

pestilent /péstilənt/ *adj* deadly —**pestilential** /pésti lénsh'l/ *adj*

pestle /péss'l/ *n* an object with a rounded end for crushing or grinding substances in a mortar —**pestle** *vt*

pesto /péstō/ *n* a sauce made of basil, pine nuts, oil, Parmesan cheese, and garlic

pet¹ *n* **1** an animal kept for companionship or amusement **2** a favourite person ■ *adj* **1** kept as a pet **2** special or favourite ○ *a pet topic* ■ *v* (**petting, petted**) **1** *vt* stroke **2** *vt* treat indulgently **3** *vi* touch each other for sexual pleasure —**petting** *n*

> **ORIGIN** The origin of neither English word **pet** is known. The use of an animal or person is of Scottish and N English origin. It is first recorded in the early 16C meaning 'indulged or spoilt child', and then applying to an animal in the mid-16C. The word referring to a 'sulky mood' also first appears in the mid-16C.

pet² *n* a sulky mood

peta- *prefix* one thousand million million ○ *petabyte*

petabyte /péttə bīt/ *n* one thousand million million bytes

Pétain /pe tán, pe táN/, **Henri Philippe** (1856–1951) French general and head of the Vichy government (1940–42)

petal /pétt'l/ *n* one of the coloured outer parts of a flower —**petalled** *adj*

petard /pe taárd/ *n* an explosive charge for breaching a door, wall, or fortification ◇ **be hoist with your own petard** be the victim of your own attempt to harm somebody else

peter /péetər/ *vi* become less

□ **peter out** *vi* dwindle and finally stop or disappear

Peter, **St** (*d.* AD 64?) one of the 12 apostles of Jesus Christ

Peter (the Great) (1672–1725) tsar of Russia (1682–1725)

Peter Principle *n* the theory that people are promoted until they reach their level of incompetence

ORIGIN The principle is named after the US author Laurence Johnston Peter (1919–90), who formulated it.

Peterson /péetərss'n/, **Oscar** (*b.* 1925) Canadian jazz pianist

pethidine /péthi deen/ *n* a painkilling or sedative drug

petiole /pétti ōl/ *n* the stalk of a leaf (*technical*) —**petiolate** /-ə layt/ *adj*

petit bourgeois /pétti boʻorzhwaa/ (*pl* **petits bourgeois** /*pronunc. same*/) *n* a member of the lower middle-class —**petite bourgeoisie** /pə teét boor zhwaa zeé/ *n*

petite /pə teét/ *adj* small and delicately built

petit four /pétti fáwr/ (*pl* **petits fours** /pétti fáwr, -fáwrz/) *n* a bite-size sweet biscuit or cake served after a meal

petition /pə tísh'n/ *n* 1 a demand for official action signed by many people 2 an appeal or request to a higher authority ■ *v* 1 *vt* give or address a petition to 2 *vi* make a demand or request using a petition ○ *petitioning for his release* —**petitioner** *n*

petit mal /pétti mál/ *n* a mild form of epilepsy

petit point /pétti póynt/ (*pl* **petits points** /*pronunc. same*/) *n* 1 a small stitch used in needlepoint for details 2 embroidery with small stitches

pet name *n* a name showing endearment

Petra /péttrə/ ancient ruined city in present-day SW Jordan

Petrarch /pét raark/ (1304–74) Italian poet and scholar —**Petrarchan** /pi traárkən/ *adj*

petrel /péttrəl/ *n* a seabird with a long hooked beak and tubular nostrils

ORIGIN The **petrel** is perhaps named after St Peter, who is described as walking on water (Matthew 14:29). The bird flies close to the sea, touching the water with its feet.

Petri dish /péttri-, peétri-/ *n* a flat-bottomed dish for growing bacterial cultures

ORIGIN The **Petri dish** is named after the German bacteriologist Julius Petri (1852–92), who invented it.

petrify /péttri fī/ (**-fies**, **-fied**) *v* 1 *vt* immobilize with fear 2 *vti* change into stone —**petrification** /péttrifi káysh'n/ *n*

petrochemical /péttrō kémmik'l/ *n* a derivative of petrol or natural gas —**petrochemical** *adj*

petrodollar /péttrō dolər/ *n* a unit of currency earned by an oil-exporting nation

petrol /péttrəl/ *n* a car fuel made from petroleum

petrol bomb *n* a bottle of petrol ignited and thrown as a bomb —**petrol bomb** *vt* —**petrol bomber** *n*

petroleum /pə trōli əm/ *n* crude oil found in sedimentary rocks

petroleum jelly *n* a greasy gelatinous substance derived from petroleum. Use: ointment base, lubricant, protective covering.

petrolhead /péttrəl hed/ *n* somebody interested in fast cars or motor racing (*slang*)

petrology /pə trólləji/ *n* the study of rocks —**petrological** /péttrə lójjik'l/ *adj* —**petrologist** *n*

petrol station *n* a place where drivers buy fuel

petticoat /pétti kōt/ *n* a woman's underskirt or slip

pettifogging /pétti foging/ *adj* 1 petty or trivial 2 quibbling (*insult*) —**pettifog** *vi* —**pettifogger** *n*

pettish /péttish/ *adj* peevish

petty /pétti/ (**-tier**, **-tiest**) *adj* 1 insignificant 2 narrow-minded 3 mean or spiteful —**pettily** *adv* —**pettiness** *n*

petty cash *n* money kept in an office for small business expenses

petty officer *n* a noncommissioned naval officer in the British Navy

petulant /péttyoʻolənt/ *adj* ill-tempered and sulky —**petulance** *n* —**petulantly** *adv*

petunia /pə tyoóni ə/ *n* a plant with bright funnel-shaped flowers

pew /pyoo/ *n* 1 a church or synagogue bench with a straight back 2 a seat (*infml humorous*) ○ *take a pew*

pewee /peé wee/, **peewee** *n* a drab medium-sized flycatcher

pewter /pyoótər/ *n* 1 a silver-grey alloy of tin and lead 2 objects made of pewter collectively

peyote /pay ōti/ *n* 1 a spineless globe-shaped cactus 2 *also* **peyote button** a nodule containing mescaline on the stem of a peyote

PG *tdmk* a rating indicating that a film may be seen by anyone, but parental guidance is suggested for children

PGCE *n* a UK postgraduate teaching qualification. Full form **Postgraduate Certificate of Education**

PGP *n* a computer encryption program. Full form **Pretty Good Privacy**

pH *n* a measure of acidity (low pH) or alkalinity (high pH). Full form **potential of hydrogen**

phaeton /fáytən/ *n* a light four-wheeled horse-drawn carriage

ORIGIN The **phaeton** was named in French in the mid-18C after a figure in Greek mythology. The god of the sun drove his golden chariot across the sky from east to west each day. His son Phaethon begged his father to let him drive it, but lost control of the horses, and threatened catastrophe to the earth. To prevent this, Zeus, the king of the gods, killed him with a thunderbolt.

phagocyte /fággə sīt/ *n* a cell that removes unwanted substances from the body —**phagocytic** /fággə síttik/ *adj*

phalanger /fə lánjər/ *n* an Australian tree marsupial with dense woolly fur and a long tail

phalanx /fállanks/ (*pl* -**lanxes** *or* -**langes** /fə lán jeez/) *n* 1 a tight group 2 a body of troops in close formation —**phalangeal** /fe lánji əl/ *adj*

Phalguna /fúl gōonə/ *n* the 12th month of the Hindu calendar

phallus /fálləss/ (*pl* -**luses** *or* -**li** /-lī/) *n* 1 a stylized representation of a penis 2 an erect penis —**phallic** *adj*

Phanerozoic /fánnərə zṓ ik/ *n* the present aeon of geological time, which began 570 million years ago —**Phanerozoic** *adj*

phantasm /fán tazəm/ *n* 1 a ghost or spirit 2 a delusion or illusion —**phantasmal** /fan tázm'l/ *adj*

phantasmagoria /fán tazmə gáwri ə/ *n* 1 a series of bizarre images 2 an ever-changing scene —**phantasmagorical** /-górrik'l/ *adj*

phantom /fántəm/ *n* 1 an unreal presence 2 an illusion —**phantom** *adj*

Pharaoh /fáirō/, **pharaoh** *n* a ruler of ancient Egypt —**Pharaonic** /fair rónnik/ *adj*

Pharisee /fárri see/ *n* 1 a member of an ancient Jewish religious group 2 *also* **pharisee** a person regarded as self-righteous or hypocritical *(disapproving)* —**Pharisaic** /fárri sáy ik/ *adj* —**Phariseeism** *n*

pharmaceutical /faármə syōotik'l/ *adj* of the preparation and sale of medicinal drugs ∎ *n* a medicinal drug *(usually pl)*

pharmacist /faárməsist/ *n* somebody who dispenses medicinal drugs

pharmacology /faármə kóllaji/ (*pl* -**gies**) *n* 1 the study of drugs 2 the effects of a drug —**pharmacological** /faárməkə lójjik'l/ *adj* —**pharmacologist** *n*

pharmacopoeia /faárməkə peé ə/, **pharmacopeia** *n* 1 a book describing drugs and their uses 2 a collection of drugs

pharmaceutieal incorrect spelling of **pharmaceutical**

pharmacy /faárməssi/ (*pl* -**cies**) *n* 1 the dispensing of medicinal drugs 2 a shop selling or dispensing medicinal drugs

pharyngitis /fárrin jítiss/ *n* a sore throat

pharynx /fárringks/ (*pl* **pharynges** /fə rín jeez/ *or* **pharynxes**) *n* the throat

phase /fayz/ *n* 1 a stage of development 2 a temporary pattern of behaviour 3 a part or aspect 4 a recurring visible form of the Moon or a planet ∎ *vt* (**phasing, phased**) 1 do something in stages ○ *a takeover that is being phased to minimize disruption* 2 synchronize two or more things —**phasic** *adj* ◊ See note at **faze**
□ **phase in** *vt* introduce gradually
□ **phase out** *vt* discontinue gradually

PhD *abbr* Doctor of Philosophy

pheasant /fézz'nt/ (*pl* -**ants** *or same*) *n* 1 a large long-tailed game bird 2 a pheasant as food

ORIGIN The **pheasant** is ultimately named after the Phasis, a river in the Caucasus (now the River Rioni in W Georgia) that was thought to be its original home. The name entered English via French and Latin from Greek.

phenobarbitone /feenō baárbitōn/ *n* a crystalline barbiturate. Use: sedative, hypnotic, anticonvulsant.

phenol /feé nol/ *n* a poisonous caustic compound. Use: manufacture of resins, dyes, and pharmaceuticals, antiseptic, disinfectant.

phenomenal /fə nómminəl/ *adj* remarkably impressive —**phenomenally** *adv*

phenomenom incorrect spelling of **phenomenon**

phenomenon /fə nómminən/ (*pl* -**na** /-nə/ *or* -**nons**) *n* 1 an observable occurrence 2 something extraordinary

USAGE The plural of **phenomenon**, which comes from Greek, is *phenomena*, not *phenomenas*. Never use the false singular *phenomena*.

phenotype /feénō tīp/ *n* the visible characteristics of an organism resulting from genetic and environmental interaction —**phenotypical** /-típpik'l/ *adj*

pheromone /férrəmōn/ *n* a chemical secreted by animals that has a developmental and behavioural influence on other members of the species —**pheromonal** /férrə mṓn'l/ *adj*

phew /fyoo/ *interj* expresses tiredness, relief, or disgust

phi /fī/ (*pl* **phis**) *n* the 21st letter of the Greek alphabet

phial /fī əl/ *n* a small medicine bottle

Phidias /fíddi ass/ (*fl* 490–430 BC) Greek sculptor

Philadelphia /fíllə délfi ə/ port in SE Pennsylvania. Pop. 1,436,287 (1998).

philander /fi lándər/ *vi* have casual affairs with women *(disapproving)* —**philanderer** *n*

philanthropy /fi lánthrəpi/ *n* a desire to improve the welfare of humanity —**philanthropic** /fíllən thróppik/ *adj* —**philanthropical** *adj* —**philanthropically** *adv* —**philanthropist** *n*

philately /fi láttəli/ *n* stamp collecting —**philatelic** /fíllə téllik/ *adj* —**philatelist** *n*

ORIGIN Monsieur Herpin, a French stamp collector, was looking for an impressive and learned-sounding term for his hobby. Because the Greeks and Romans did not have postage stamps, there was no classical term for them. So he went back a stage beyond stamps, to the days of franking with a postmark. In France, such letters were marked with the words *franc de port* 'carriage-free'. The nearest he could get to this in Greek was *ateleia*, and from it he created *philatélie*, the English form of which made its first recorded appearance in 1865.

-phile *suffix* somebody or something that loves

or has an affinity for ○ *bibliophile* —-**philic** *suffix* —-**philous** *suffix* —-**phily** *suffix*

philharmonic /fil haar mónnik, fillər-/ *adj* performing or promoting music ■ *n* a philharmonic orchestra, choir, or society

-**philia** *suffix* **1** intense or unusual attraction to **2** tendency towards ○ *haemophilia* —-**philiac** *suffix*

Philip /fillip/, **St** (*fl* AD 1stC) one of the 12 apostles of Jesus Christ

Philip II /fillip/ (1527–98) king of Spain (1556–98)

Philip II (382–336 BC) king of Macedonia (359–336 BC)

~~Philipines~~ incorrect spelling of **Philippines**

Philippi /fi líp ī, fílli pī/ ancient town of Macedonia, in present-day NE Greece

Philippines /fillə peenz/ country in Southeast Asia, comprising over 7,000 islands in the W Pacific Ocean. Cap. Manila. Pop. 82,841,518 (2001). —**Philippine** *adj*

Philippine Sea section of the W Pacific Ocean, between S Japan and NE Philippines

philistine /filli stīn/ *n* **1** a member of a people of ancient Palestine **2** somebody who does not appreciate artistic and intellectual achievements *(disapproving)* ■ *adj* **1 Philistine** of the Philistines **2** uncultured —**philistinism** /fillistinizəm/ *n*

Phillip /fillip/, **Arthur** (1738–1814) British naval officer and first governor of New South Wales (1788–92)

~~Phillipines~~ incorrect spelling of **Philippines**

philology /fi lólləji/ *n* **1** the study of the history and relationship of languages **2** the study of ancient texts —**philological** /fillə lójjik'l/ *adj* —**philologist** *n*

philosopher /fi lóssəfər/ *n* **1** somebody who studies the principles of existence and reality **2** somebody who thinks deeply about life in general

philosopher's stone, philosophers' stone *n* a substance that medieval alchemists believed could turn other metal into gold

philosophical /fillə sóffik'l, -zóffik'l/, **philosophic** /-sóffik, -zóffik/ *adj* **1** of philosophy **2** showing calmness and resignation —**philosophically** *adv*

philosophize /fi lóssə fīz/ (-phizing, -phized), **philosophise** *vi* **1** discuss the nature of reality **2** express opinions or moralize in a superficial or tedious way —**philosophizer** *n*

philosophy /fi lóssəfi/ (*pl* -phies) *n* **1** the study of basic concepts such as truth, existence, and reality **2** a school of thought **3** a set of guiding or underlying principles

philtre /filtər/ *n* a potion *(literary)*

~~phisical~~ incorrect spelling of **physical**

phlebitis /fli bítiss/ *n* inflammation of the wall of a vein

phlegm /flem/ *n* **1** thick mucus in the respiratory passages **2** unflappability —**phlegmy** *adj*

phlegmatic /fleg máttik/, **phlegmatical** /-máttik'l/ *adj* not easily excited or worried ◊ See note at **impassive**

~~phlem~~ incorrect spelling of **phlegm**

phloem /flō em/ *n* the nutrient-carrying tissue of vascular plants

phlox (*pl* same or **phloxes**) *n* a garden plant with clusters of scented flowers

Phnom Penh /nóm pén/ capital of Cambodia. Pop. 429,000 (1995).

-**phobe** *suffix* somebody fearing or disliking ○ *technophobe*

phobia /fṓbi ə/ *n* strong fear or dislike ○ *a phobia about travelling in lifts* —**phobic** *adj, n*

-**phobia** *suffix* an exaggerated or irrational fear of ○ *claustrophobia* —-**phobic** *suffix*

Phoenicia /fə níshə, fə neéshə/ ancient region of coastal city-states in the E Mediterranean —**Phoenician** *n, adj*

phoenix /feéniks/ *n* a mythological bird that burned itself, and from whose ashes another phoenix arose

Phoenix /feéniks/ capital of Arizona. Pop. 1,198,064 (1998).

phone /fōn/ *n* a telephone ■ *vti* (phoning, phoned) telephone

-**phone** *suffix* **1** a device that emits or receives sounds ○ *saxophone* ○ *microphone* **2** a telephone ○ *cellphone* **3** a speech sound ○ *homophone* —-**phonic** *suffix* —-**phony** *suffix*

phone book *n* a telephone directory

phone box *n* a telephone box

phonecard /fōn kaard/ *n* a plastic card used instead of money in a telephone box

phone-in *n* a programme broadcasting callers' comments

phoneme /fṓ neem/ *n* a speech sound that is the smallest unit that can distinguish one word from another —**phonemic** /fə neémik, fō-/ *adj*

phonetic /fə néttik, fō-/ *adj* **1** of speech sounds or phonetics **2** showing pronunciation —**phonetically** *adv*

phonetics /fə néttiks, fō-/ *n* (+ *sing verb*) **1** the study of speech sounds and how they are produced **2** the sound system of a language —**phonetician** /fṓnə tish'n, fónnə-/ *n*

phoney /fṓni/, **phony** (-nier, -niest) *adj* **1** not genuine **2** giving a false impression —**phoney** *n* —**phonily** *adv* —**phoniness** *n*

phoney war *n* a period of hostility without fighting

phonic /fónnik/ *adj* **1** of or using phonics **2** of sound **3** of speech sounds

phonics /fónniks/ *n* a reading method that involves associating letters with sounds *(+ sing verb)*

phonograph /fṓnə graaf, -graf/ *n US, Can* a record player

phonology /fə nólləji, fō-/ (*pl* -**gies**) *n* **1** the study of the pattern of speech sounds in language **2** the sound system of a language —**phonological** /fṓnə lójjik'l, fónnə-/ *adj*

phony *adj, n* – **phoney**

phosphate /fóss fayt/ *n* a salt or ester of phosphoric acid

phosphorescence /fóssfə réss'nss/ *n* the continued emission of light after exposure to and removal of a source of electromagnetic radiation —**phosphoresce** *vi* —**phosphorescent** *adj*

phosphoric acid *n* a transparent liquid or solid acid. Use: fertilizer, rust-proofing, in soft drinks, pharmaceuticals, and animal feeds.

phosphorus /fóssfərəss/ *n* **1** (*symbol* P) a poisonous nonmetallic chemical element that ignites in air and glows in the dark. Use: matches, fireworks, incendiary devices, fertilizers. **2** a phosphorescent substance —**phosphoric** /foss fórrik/ *adj* —**phosphorous** *adj*

ORIGIN **Phosphorus** goes back to a Greek word meaning literally 'light-bringer', which was also used as a name for the planet Venus as it appears in the morning (as the 'morning star'). It was applied from the early 17C to any substance or organism that glowed, and when the chemical element was isolated in the mid-17C it was adopted as its name, since **phosphorus** ignites when exposed to the air.

photo /fótō/ (*pl* **-tos**) *n* a photograph —**photo** *vt*

photo- *prefix* **1** light, radiant energy o *photosensitive* **2** photographic o *photocopy*

photocall /fótō kawl/ *n* a session for photographing celebrities

photo CD *n* a compact disc storing images from photographs

photocopy /fótə kopi/ (*pl* **-ies**) *n* a copy of a text or picture produced by a photographic process —**photocopier** *n* —**photocopy** *vti*

photoelectric cell /fótō i léktrik-/ *n* a photosensitive device controlling an electric current, e.g. in a burglar alarm or exposure meter

phntnes incorrect spelling of **photos**

photo finish *n* the end of a race so close that the result must be determined from a photograph

photogenic /fótə jénnik/ *adj* looking attractive in photographs

photograph /fótə graaf, -graf/ *n* a picture produced from an image recorded on light-sensitive film or a digitized array in a camera ■ *v* **1** *vti* take a photograph of somebody or something **2** *vi* be photographed with a particular result o *Scenes like this photograph best in bright sunlight.* —**photographer** /fə tóggrəfər/ *n*

photographic /fótə gráffik/ *adj* **1** of photography **2** like a photograph in accuracy or detail o *a photographic memory* —**photographically** *adv*

photography /fə tóggrəfi/ *n* the art, hobby, or profession of producing pictures with a camera

photojournalism /fótō júrnəlizəm/ *n* journalism using mainly photographs —**photojournalist** *n*

photometry /fō tómmətri/ *n* the measurement of the intensity of light —**photometer** *n* —**photometric** /fótō méttrik/ *adj*

photon /fó ton/ *n* a quantum of visible light or other form of electromagnetic radiation demonstrating both particle and wave properties —**photonic** /fō tónnik/ *adj*

photo opportunity *n* an opportunity for taking newsworthy photographs

photosensitive /fótō sénssətiv/ *adj* reacting to light —**photosensitivity** /fótō sénssə tívvəti/ *n*

photosynthesis /fótō sínthəssiss/ *n* the production by plants and some other organisms of carbohydrates and oxygen from carbon dioxide and water using light and chlorophyll —**photosynthesize** *vti* —**photosynthetic** /fótō sin théttik/ *adj*

photovoltaic cell /fótō vol táy ik-/ *n* a photoelectric cell that uses the potential difference between dissimilar materials exposed to electromagnetic radiation

phrasal verb *n* a verb combined with an adverb or preposition in an idiomatic way

phrase /frayz/ *n* **1** a string of words forming a grammatical unit that is not a complete sentence **2** a fixed expression ■ *vt* (**phrasing, phrased**) express in a particular way —**phrasal** *adj*

phrase book *n* a book of translated phrases for travellers abroad

phraseology /fráyzi ólləji/ *n* **1** the phrases used in a particular sphere of activity **2** the way words and phrases are chosen and put together —**phraseological** /fráyzi ə lójjik'l/ *adj*

phrasing /fráyzing/ *n* **1** the way words are chosen and put together **2** the way musical notes are grouped into phrases

phrenology /frə nóllǝji/ *n* the study of the bumps on the skull, formerly believed to indicate character —**phrenologist** *n*

Phrygia /fríjji ə/ ancient country in Asia Minor, in present-day west-central Turkey

phylactery /fi láktəri/ (*pl* **-ies**) *n* a Jewish aid to prayer consisting of each of two small leather boxes containing scriptures (often *pl*)

phylum /fíləm/ (*pl* **-la** /-lə/) *n* **1** a major taxonomic group in zoological classification **2** a large group of languages or language stocks thought to be historically related, e.g. Indo-European

physic /fízzik/ (*archaic*) *n* a medicine, especially a purgative ■ *vt* (**-icking, -icked**) treat with a medical remedy

physical /fízzik'l/ *adj* **1** of the body **2** real and touchable **3** needing bodily strength **4** involving bodily contact **5** describes sciences that deal with nonliving things —**physicality** /fízzi kállǝti/ *n* —**physically** *adv*

physical education *n* physical exercise as a school subject

physical examination *n* a general medical examination to check that somebody is fit and healthy

physical geography *n* the study of the natural features of the Earth's surface

physically challenged *adj* unable to perform some of the activities of daily life

physical science *n* a science that deals with nonliving things, e.g. physics or chemistry

physician /fi zísh'n/ *n* a doctor who diagnoses and treats diseases and injuries using methods other than surgery

physics /fízziks/ *n* the study of matter, energy, force, and motion (+ *sing verb*) ■ *npl* the physical properties or behaviour of something (+ *pl verb*) —**physicist** /fízzissist/ *n*

physio- *prefix* physical ○ *physiotherapy*

physiognomy /fízzi ónnəmi/ (*pl* -**mies**) *n* 1 somebody's facial features, especially viewed as a guide to character 2 the character or appearance of something —**physiognomist** *n*

physiology /fízzi óllǝji/ *n* 1 the study of the functioning of living things 2 the body's internal processes —**physiological** /fízzi ǝ lójik'l/ *adj* —**physiologically** *adv* —**physiologist** *n*

physiotherapy /fízzi ō thérrǝpi/ *n* the treatment of injuries by means such as exercise and massage —**physiotherapeutic** /fízzi ō therǝ pyoótik/ *adj* —**physiotherapist** *n*

physique /fi zeék/ *n* the shape and size of somebody's body

pi /pī/ *n* 1 the 16th letter of the Greek alphabet 2 a mathematical constant equal to the circumference of a circle divided by its diameter, approximately 3.142

Piaf /pee af/, **Édith** (1915–63) French singer

Piaget /pi ázh ay/, **Jean** (1896–1980) Swiss psychologist

pianissimo /pee ǝ níssimō/ *adv* very softly (*musical direction*) —**pianissimo** *adj*

pianist /pee ǝnist/ *n* a piano player

piano[1] /pi ánnō/ (*pl* -**os**) *n* a large musical instrument with a keyboard through which stretched wire strings are struck with hammers

ORIGIN Piano is a shortening of *pianoforte*, which in Italian (the language from which both terms derive) means literally 'soft loud'. The name referred to the ability of the instrument to vary volume using felt-covered blocks, a characteristic not shared by the harpsichord and other earlier keyboard instruments. **Piano** is recorded in English in the early 19C, and *pianoforte* in the mid-18C.

piano[2] /pyaánō/ *adv* softly (*musical direction*) —**piano** *adj*

pianoforte /pi ánnō fáwrti/ (*pl* -**tes**) *n* a piano (*fml*)

piazza /pi átsǝ/ (*pl* -**ze** /-átsay/) *n* (*pl* **piazze**) an Italian public square

picador /píkǝ dawr/ *n* a bullfighter on horseback

picaresque /píkǝ résk/ *adj* 1 of rogues 2 describes prose fiction about the adventures of a roguish hero

Pablo Picasso: Photographed in 1933 by Man Ray

Picasso /pikássō/, **Pablo** (1881–1973) Spanish painter and sculptor

piccalilli /píkǝ lílli/ *n* pickled vegetables in a mustard sauce

piccolo /píkǝlō/ (*pl* -**los**) *n* the smallest member of the flute family of musical instruments

pick[1] *vt* 1 remove fruit or flowers from a plant 2 choose somebody or something from a group 3 remove something in small pieces 4 open a lock without a proper key 5 start a fight or quarrel 6 play a stringed instrument by plucking the strings ■ *n* 1 a choice ○ *take your pick* 2 the best —**picker** *n* ◇ **pick and choose** select the best of several choices ◇ **pick your way** find a route and progress very carefully

☐ **pick at** *vt* 1 eat very little of a meal 2 scrape something with the fingernails

☐ **pick on** *vt* persistently criticize or bully

☐ **pick out** *vt* 1 choose 2 recognize or distinguish from a crowd or background 3 cause to stand out ○ *The design was picked out in green.*

☐ **pick over** *vt* go through a number of items to make a selection

☐ **pick up** *v* 1 *vt* lift or collect something or somebody 2 *vt* gather dropped things 3 *vti* take on a passenger or passengers 4 *vt* pay a bill 5 *vt* catch a disease 6 *vt* learn something in a casual or unsystematic way 7 *vi* become better (*infml*) 8 *vti* increase in strength, speed, or intensity 9 *vt* make the acquaintance of a prospective sexual partner (*infml*) 10 *vt* arrest (*infml*)

☐ **pick up on** *vt* notice and mention or question (*infml*)

pick[2] *n* 1 a tool for breaking up hard surfaces, consisting of a long handle and a curved metal head 2 a plectrum —**pick** *vi*

pickaxe /pík aks/ *n* a pick with a metal head that has one pointed and one flattened end

ORIGIN The **pickaxe** is etymologically not strictly an axe at all. The word came via French from Latin *picus* 'woodpecker'. It was altered by association with *axe* in the 15C.

picket /píkit/ *n* 1 a pointed post stuck in the ground 2 a soldier or group of soldiers on guard 3 a protester or group of protesters outside a place, e.g. during a strike ■ *v* 1 *vt* enclose or mark with pickets 2 *vt* guard with or as a picket 3 *vti* hold or take part in a protest outside a place —**picketer** *n*

picket fence *n* a simple fence of pointed stakes

picket line *n* a line of protesters picketing a place

pickings /pík!ŋz/ *npl* things available

pickle /pík'l/ *n* **1** a spicy savoury preserve containing chopped vegetables **2** a vegetable preserved in vinegar (*usually pl*) **3** liquid for pickling food **4** an awkward situation (*infml*) ■ *vt* (**-ling, -led**) preserve in vinegar or brine —**pickler** *n*

pickled /pík'ld/ *adj* **1** preserved in vinegar or brine **2** drunk (*infml*)

pick-me-up *n* an energizing drink (*infml*)

~~picknick~~ incorrect spelling of **picnic**

pick 'n' mix *n* a range of items, e.g. sweets, for personal selection

pickpocket /pík pokit/ *n* a thief who steals from people's pockets and bags —**pickpocketing** *n*

pick-up *n* **1** the collection of something to be taken somewhere else **2** somebody or something picked up **3** *also* **pick-up truck** a light open-backed truck with a hinged tailgate **4** an improvement or increase (*infml*)

picky /píki/ (**-ier, -iest**) *adj* hard to please or satisfy —**pickily** *adv* —**pickiness** *n*

picnic /píknik/ *n* **1** a meal taken on an outing and eaten outdoors **2** an easy or pleasant thing (*infml*) ○ *Moving house is no picnic.* ■ *vi* (**-nicking, -nicked**) eat a picnic —**picnicker** *n*

~~picnicing~~ incorrect spelling of **picnicking**

pictorial /pik táwri əl/ *adj* **1** of pictures **2** illustrated by pictures ■ *n* a highly illustrated periodical —**pictorially** *adv*

picture /píkchər/ *n* **1** a visual representation of something or somebody on a flat surface **2** a photograph **3** the image on a television screen **4** a film **5** a mental image **6** a description in writing or music **7** a situation in its context ○ *She was the picture of health.* ■ *vt* (**-turing, -tured**) **1** imagine **2** describe

picture book *n* a book with many illustrations, especially one for children

picture-postcard *adj* very scenic or beautiful

picture rail *n* a moulding on a wall for hanging pictures from

picturesque /píkchə résk/ *adj* **1** very attractive or scenic **2** vividly described —**picturesquely** *adv* —**picturesqueness** *n*

picture window *n* a large window, usually with a single pane of glass

PID *abbr* pelvic inflammatory disease

piddle /pídd'l/ (**-dling, -dled**) *vi* **1** urinate (*infml; usually used by children*) **2** spend time on unimportant things —**piddle** *n*

piddling /píddliŋ/ *adj* very small or trivial (*infml*) —**piddlingly** *adv*

pidgin /píjjin/ *n* a simplified language made up of elements of different languages and used as a common second language

ORIGIN Pidgin represents a Chinese alteration of *business*, and is itself an example of *pidgin*

English, the altered and simplified English used in trade and other communications in China and East Asia in the 19C.

pie /pī/ *n* **1** a baked dish consisting of a filling encased in pastry **2** a divisible whole ◊ **pie in the sky** a pipe dream

ORIGIN The origin of **pie** is not certain, but it may be named after the magpie (or *pie*, as it was earlier called). The fillings of early **pies** characteristically consisted of a mixture of ingredients (in contrast with *pasties*, which had one main ingredient), and may have been likened to the miscellaneous items collected by magpies.

piebald /pí bawld/ *adj* describes a horse with coloured patches —**piebald** *n*

piece /peess/ *n* **1** a part detached from a whole **2** an individual item or article ○ *a piece of equipment* **3** an interconnecting part ○ *a 500-piece jigsaw* **4** an example of something ○ *a piece of luck* **5** a statement of opinion ○ *I've said my piece.* **6** an artistic work **7** a published article **8** a coin **9** an object moved in a board game ■ *vt* (**piecing, pieced**) put together bit by bit ◊ *piece together the events of that night* **2** mend by adding a patch or piece ◊ **fall** *or* **go to pieces** become unable to cope ◊ **pull to pieces** criticize severely ◊ See note at **peace**

pièce de résistance /pi éss de re zís toNss/ (*pl* **pièces de résistance** /*pronunc. same*/) *n* **1** the most impressive thing **2** the most important dish of a meal (*fml*)

piecemeal /peéss meel/ *adv* **1** gradually **2** in separate parts ■ *adj* done bit by bit

piecework /peéss wurk/ *n* work paid by the amount done

piechart /pí chaart/ *n* a graphical representation in the form of a circle divided into sections

pied-à-terre /pi áyd aa taír, peè ed–/ (*pl* **pieds-à-terre** /-taír/) *n* a small secondary residence used for business purposes or holidays

pied piper /píd–/ *n* somebody who attracts supporters and followers

ORIGIN In German folklore, the Pied Piper was a visiting piper whose entrancing music rid the town of Hamelin of its rats. The story is the basis of a poem (1842) by Robert Browning.

pie-eyed *adj* very drunk (*infml*)

pier /peer/ *n* **1** a walkway on stilts jutting into the sea **2** a vertical structural support, e.g. for a bridge or wall ◊ See note at **peer**

pierce /peerss/ (**piercing, pierced**) *v* **1** *vti* bore into something with a pointed object **2** *vt* make a hole through something **3** *vti* penetrate a barrier **4** *vti* sound or shine suddenly and intensely through silence or darkness

piercing /peèrssiŋ/ *adj* **1** unpleasantly loud and shrill **2** acutely perceptive **3** intensely cold ■ *n* the practice of making holes in parts of the body so that ornamental rings can be inserted —**piercingly** *adv*

Piero della Francesca /pyáirō déllə fran chéskə/ (1420?–92) Italian painter

Pierre /peer/ capital of South Dakota. Pop. 13,267 (1998).

Pierrot /peêrō/ *n* a traditional French pantomime clown with a white face and costume

piety /pí ə ti/ (*pl* **-ties**) *n* **1** religious devotion **2** a devout act **3** a conventional or hypocritical statement or observance of a belief

piffle /pĭff'l/ *n* nonsense (*infml*)

piffling /pĭff'ling/ *adj* of little use or value (*infml*)

pig *n* **1** a short fat farm animal with a broad snout and a curly tail **2** pork **3** a person regarded as greedy or coarse (*infml insult*) **4** a rough block of cast metal **5** an offensive term for a police officer (*slang*) ■ *vi* (**pigging, pigged**) give birth to pigs ◇ **a pig in a poke** something that is bought or obtained without being inspected ◇ **make a pig's ear of** do something very badly (*infml*)
□ **pig out** *vi* eat greedily (*infml*)

pigeon /pĭjjən/ *n* a stocky medium-sized grey-and-white bird that is common in cities

pigeonhole /pĭjjən hōl/ *n* **1** one of a set of small compartments for putting messages in for different people **2** a category into which somebody or something is put without much thought ■ *vt* **1** put into a category without much thought **2** postpone

pigeon-toed *adj* walking with the toes turning in

piggery /pĭggəri/ (*pl* **-ies**) *n* **1** a place for raising pigs **2** greedy or coarse behaviour

piggish /pĭggish/, **piggy** /pĭggi/ (**-gier, -giest**) *adj* **1** greedy **2** obstinate —**piggishly** *adv*

piggy /pĭggi/ (*pl* **-gies**) *n* a pig or piglet (*baby talk*)

piggyback /pĭggi bak/ *n* **1** a ride on somebody's back **2** the transporting of one vehicle on another —**piggyback** *adj, adv, vt*

piggy bank *n* a child's money box, often in the shape of a pig

piggy in the middle *n* **1** a children's game in which one child stands in between two others throwing a ball to each other and tries to catch it **2** somebody caught up in an argument between two other people or groups

pigheaded /pĭg héddid/ *adj* obstinate —**pigheadedly** *adv* —**pigheadedness** *n*

pig iron *n* iron in rough blocks

piglet /pĭgglət/ *n* a young pig

pigment *n* /pĭgmənt/ **1** a substance added to give something such as paint or ink its colour **2** a natural colouring substance in plant or animal tissue ■ *vt* /pig mént/ give colour to —**pigmentary** *adj*

pigmentation /pĭg men táysh'n/ *n* the natural colour of plants and animals

pigpen /pĭg pen/ *n* **1** an enclosure for pigs on a modern farm **2** *US* a pigsty

pigsty /pĭg stī/ (*pl* **-sties**) *n* **1** an enclosure for pigs on a traditional farm **2** a dirty or untidy place

pigswill /pĭg swil/ *n* waste food for pigs

pigtail /pĭg tayl/ *n* a plait or bunch of hair gathered together —**pigtailed** *adj*

pika /píkə/ (*pl* **-kas** or same) *n* a small short-eared burrowing mammal related to the rabbit

pike[1] (*pl* **pikes** or same) *n* a large sharp-toothed freshwater fish

> **ORIGIN Pike** as a name for a fish comes from an earlier word meaning 'pointed object', from the shape of its jaws. The weapon name was adopted from French in the early 16C, and is formed from a verb meaning 'prick, irritate', which is also the source of *pique*. The diving and gymnastic **pike** is the most recent, dating from the early 20C, but its etymology has never been established.

pike[2] *n* formerly, a weapon consisting of a pole with a spike on top

pike[3] *n* a diving or gymnastic position in which the body is bent double

pikestaff /pík staaf/ *n* **1** the shaft of a pike **2** a walking stick with a metal point

pilaster /pi lástər/ *n* an ornamental column on a wall

Pilate /pílət/, **Pontius** (*fl* 1C) Roman administrator

pilau /peê low/, **pilaf** /-laf/ *n* a spiced rice dish

pilchard /pĭlchərd/ (*pl* **-chards** or same) *n* **1** a small sea fish **2** a pilchard as food

pile[1] *n* **1** a mound of things **2** a large quantity or amount (*infml; often pl*) **3** a large impressive building ■ *v* (**piling, piled**) **1** *vt* heap **2** *vt* place large amounts on **3** *vi* go as a crowd
□ **pile on** *vt* increase or intensify
□ **pile up** *vti* **1** accumulate **2** crash or collide with other vehicles

pile[2] *n* a support for a building that is driven into the ground

pile[3] *n* the surface of a carpet or a fabric such as velvet, formed of fibre loops

pile-driver *n* a machine that hammers piles into the ground

piles *npl* haemorrhoids (*infml*)

pile-up *n* **1** a collision involving several vehicles (*infml*) **2** an accumulation of things

pilfer /pĭlfər/ *vti* steal small things of little value —**pilferer** *n* —**pilfering** *n* ◇ See note at **steal**

pilgrim /pĭlgrim/ *n* **1** a traveller to a holy place for religious reasons **2** a traveller on a special journey (*literary*) —**pilgrimage** *n*

pilgrimmage incorrect spelling of **pilgrimage**

pill *n* **1** a round tablet of medicine taken orally **2** *also* **Pill** an oral contraceptive

pillage /pĭllij/ *vti* (**-laging, -laged**) **1** plunder a place **2** steal possessions as plunder ■ *n* **1** the plundering of somebody's possessions **2** possessions stolen as plunder —**pillager** *n*

pillar /pĭllər/ *n* **1** a column used for support or decoration **2** something tall and narrow ◇ **from pillar to post** from one place to another

pillar box *n* a tall red postbox

pillbox /píl bokss/ *n* 1 a small container for pills 2 *also* **pillbox hat** a woman's brimless flat-topped hat

pillion /pílli ən/ *n* a passenger seat behind the driver of a motorbike or the rider of a horse —**pillion** *adv*

pillock /píl lək/ *n* somebody regarded as unintelligent (*slang insult*)

pillory /pílləri/ *n* (*pl* **-ries**) a wooden frame with holes into which somebody's head and hands could be locked, formerly a method of public punishment ■ *vt* (**-ries**, **-ried**) 1 ridicule 2 punish in a pillory

pillow /píllō/ *n* 1 a cushion for the head in bed 2 a soft base for supporting the tools used in lace-making ■ *vt* 1 rest the head on a pillow 2 provide a soft and comfortable surface for something

pillowcase /píllō kayss/, **pillowslip** /-slip/ *n* a removable cover for a pillow

pillow talk *n* intimate talk in bed

pilot /pílət/ *n* 1 somebody who flies an aircraft or spacecraft 2 somebody who steers ships in ports or through difficult areas 3 a leader or guide 4 a television or radio programme intended to form the basis for a series ■ *vt* 1 fly an aircraft or spacecraft 2 navigate a ship 3 be in charge of running something

pilotage /pílətij/ *n* the piloting of an aircraft, spacecraft, or ship

pilot officer *n* a commissioned RAF officer of the lowest rank

Pilsner /pílznər/ *n* a Czech lager with a strong hops flavour

PIM *abbr* personal information manager

pimento /pi méntō/ *n* 1 *also* **pimiento** a large sweet red pepper. Use: paprika, olive stuffing, garnish. 2 a plant that produces pimentos

pimp *n* a man who solicits for prostitutes for money —**pimp** *vi*

pimpernel /pímpər nel/ (*pl* **-nels** *or same*) *n* a small flowering plant with trailing stems

pimple /pímp'l/ *n* an inflamed skin blemish —**pimply** *adj*

pin *n* 1 a small thin metal stick with a sharp point and a round head, used for holding pieces of fabric together 2 something resembling a pin in shape or function, e.g. a safety pin, hairpin, or the safety clip on a grenade 3 something decorative attached to clothing by means of a sharp metal point 4 a skittle 5 in golf, a pole with a flag on it, used to mark a hole ■ *vt* (**pinning**, **pinned**) 1 fasten with a pin 2 keep from moving

□ **pin down** *vt* 1 determine with certainty 2 force to keep a commitment or come to a decision

PIN /pin/, **PIN number** *n* a multidigit number used by a person to gain access to cash, a computer, or a telephone system. Full form **personal identification number**

~~pinacle~~ incorrect spelling of **pinnacle**

piña colada /peenə kō laádə, peenyə-/ *n* a cocktail made from pineapple juice, rum, and coconut

pinafore /pínnə fawr/ *n* 1 a sleeveless dress worn over a blouse or sweater 2 an apron with a bib (*dated*)

pinball /pínn bawl/ *n* an indoor game played on a sloping electronic table in which a player flicks a ball past obstacles to score points

pince-nez /pánss náy/ (*pl* **pince-nez** /-náyz/) *n* a pair of spectacles without legs that clip over the nose

pincer movement /pínssər-/ *n* a military manoeuvre in which two columns of troops converge on an enemy in a curving movement from opposite sides

pincers /pínssərz/ *npl* 1 the large front claws of some crustaceans and arachnids, e.g. the lobster 2 a tool for gripping things

pinch *v* 1 *vti* grip something between two objects, especially a finger and thumb 2 *vti* be too tight and painful for a part of the body 3 *vt* make somebody or something wither or shrink 4 *vti* steal (*infml*) ■ *n* 1 a painful squeeze, especially with the thumb and finger 2 a very small amount of something 3 a critical time ◊ **feel the pinch** have financial problems ◊ See note at **steal**

pincushion /pín kŏŏsh'n/ *n* a pad for storing pins on

Pindar /píndər/ (518–438 BC) Greek poet —**Pindaric** /pin dárrik/ *adj*

pine¹ *n* 1 wood from an evergreen tree. Use: furniture-making, construction, finishing material. 2 an evergreen coniferous tree grown for its wood

pine² (**pining**, **pined**) *vi* 1 yearn 2 waste away as a result of grief or longing

pineapple /pī nap'l/ *n* 1 a large fruit with juicy yellow flesh, a thick lumpy brown skin, and a tuft of leaves on the top 2 (*pl* **pineapples** *or same*) a plant that produces pineapples

ORIGIN The **pineapple** was given its name because it was thought to resemble a pine cone (the earlier and original sense of the word).

pine cone *n* the seed case of a pine tree

pine marten *n* a brown woodland animal similar to a weasel

pine needle *n* the needle-shaped leaf of a pine tree

pine nut *n* an edible pine seed

ping *n* a single light ringing sound —**ping** *vti*

Ping-Pong /píng pong/ *tdmk* a trademark for table tennis

pinhead /pín hed/ *n* the rounded end of a pin

pinhole /pín hōl/ *n* a tiny hole or puncture

pinion¹ /pínnyən/ *n* a bird's wing, especially the tip ■ *vt* 1 restrain somebody by holding or tying his or her arms 2 keep a bird from flying by removing or binding its wing feathers

pinion² /pínnyən/ *n* a small gear wheel that engages with a larger gear or a rack

pink[1] *n* **1** a pale reddish colour **2** a plant with fragrant pink, red, or white flowers **3** the highest degree or best example of something ■ *adj* of a pale reddish colour —**pinkness** *n*

ORIGIN The Dutch phrase *pinck oogen* meant literally 'small eyes'. It was adopted into English in the partially translated form *pink eyes*, which may have been used as the name of plants related to the **pink**. The abbreviated form **pink** emerged as a plant name in the 16C. Many of these plants have pale red flowers, and by the 18C **pink** was being used as a colour term.

pink[2] *vt* **1** cut with pinking shears **2** punch little holes in something such as leather as a decoration

pink[3] *vi* make knocking sounds through faulty combustion *(refers to engines)*

pink gin *n* gin with bitters

pinkie /píngki/, **pinky** (*pl* **-ies**) *n US, Can, Scotland* the little finger *(infml)*

pinking shears, pinking scissors *npl* scissors with a serrated blade for cutting cloth

pin money *n* **1** money for buying personal nonessential things **2** money that a man gives his wife for personal use *(dated)*

pinnacle /pínnək'l/ *n* **1** the highest point or level of something **2** a mountain peak

PIN number *n* BANKING, COMPUT = PIN

Pinochet /peenō shay/, **Augusto** (*b.* 1915) Chilean general and national leader (1973–90)

pinochle /peé nuk'l/, **pinocle** *n* a card game played with incomplete packs

piñon /pi nyón, pínnyən/ (*pl* **-ñons** *or* **-ñones** /pi nyṍ neez/), **pinyon** *n* **1** *also* **piñon nut** a small sweet nut **2** a pine tree that produces piñons

pinpoint /pín poynt/ *vt* identify or locate something correctly ■ *n* something small or trivial ■ *adj* exact

pinprick /pín prik/ *n* **1** a small hole made by a pin or something similar **2** a slight wound **3** a minor irritant

pins and needles *n* a tingling sensation in a body part (+ *sing or pl verb*)

pinstripe /pín strīp/ *n* **1** a narrow line in a fabric **2** fabric with very narrow lines. Use: business suits. —**pinstriped** *adj*

pint /pīnt/ *n* **1** a unit of liquid or dry measure equal to one eighth of a gallon **2** a container that can hold a pint **3** a pint of milk or beer *(infml)*

Pinter /píntər/, **Harold** (*b.* 1930) British playwright and director —**Pinteresque** /píntə résk/ *adj*

pinto /píntō/ *US, Can adj* piebald ■ *n* (*pl* **-tos**) a piebald horse

pinto bean *n* **1** an edible mottled brown and pink kidney-shaped bean **2** a plant that produces pinto beans

pint-size, pint-sized *adj* very small *(infml)*

pin-up *n* a posed picture of a sexually attractive person

pinwheel /pín weel/ *n US, Can* **1** a Catherine wheel **2** a child's windmill

pinyon *n* FOOD, TREES = piñon

pioneer /pí ə neér/ *n* the first person to do or develop something or to explore a territory ■ *vt* develop or explore something new

pious /pí əss/ *adj* **1** devoutly religious **2** acting in a falsely moralizing way **3** holy or sacred —**piously** *adv*

pip[1] *n* a small hard seed of a fruit such as an apple that usually has several seeds

pip[2] *n* **1** a spot on a die or domino **2** a symbol on a playing card **3** a short high-pitched sound used as a broadcasting time signal **4** a symbol indicating rank *(infml)*

pip[3] ◇ **give somebody the pip** annoy or irritate somebody *(infml dated)*

pip[4] (**pipping, pipped**) *vt* beat narrowly in a competition *(infml)*

pipe *n* **1** a tube for transporting liquid or gas **2** a tubular object, part, or organ **3** a small bowl with a hollow stem for smoking **4** the amount in a smoker's pipe **5** a tubular musical instrument played by blowing **6** a tubular part of a musical organ **7** a high-pitched noise ■ **pipes** *npl* bagpipes ■ *v* (**piping, piped**) **1** *vt* carry liquid or gas by pipe **2** *vti* install and connect pipes in something **3** *vt* play a tune on a pipe or bagpipes **4** *vt* send piped music through a place **5** *vt* decorate something with piping **6** *vti* sing, speak, or say something in a high-pitched voice —**pipeful** *n*

□ **pipe down** *vi* stop talking or become quieter *(infml)*

□ **pipe up** *vi* begin to speak in order to interrupt or explain

pipe band *n* a marching or military band with bagpipes and drums

pipe cleaner *n* a flexible wire covered with fluffy material for cleaning a tobacco pipe

piped music *n* background music in a public place

pipe dream *n* an unrealistic notion

pipeline /pīp līn/ *n* **1** a long pipe system for transporting oil or gas **2** a channel of communications —**pipeline** *vt* ◇ **in the pipeline** in preparation but not yet ready

piper /pípər/ *n* **1** a bagpiper **2** a pipe player

pipette /pi pét/ *n* a small glass tube for sucking up liquid to measure it before transferring it to another container

piping /píping/ *n* **1** a system of pipes **2** a fabric-covered cord. Use: decorating clothes, soft furnishings. **3** a decorative effect on food using something such as lines of icing **4** the art or skill of playing a pipe or bagpipes **5** the sound of a pipe or bagpipes **6** a shrill noise ■ *adj* shrill ◇ **piping hot** very hot

pipit /píppit/ *n* a small long-tailed songbird

pippin /píppin/ *n* a cultivated variety of apple

pipsqueak /píp skweek/ *n* a person or thing regarded as small or insignificant *(infml)*

piquant /peékənt, -kaant/ *adj* **1** spicy or savoury

2 stimulating or provocative —**piquancy** n —**piquantly** adv

pique /peek/ n a feeling of resentment caused by an insult ■ vt (**piquing, piqued**) **1** make resentful **2** arouse or provoke ○ *piqued my curiosity* ◊ See note at **peak**

piqué /pee kay/ n a closely woven ribbed fabric. Use: clothes.

piracy /pírəssi/ n the activity of a pirate

Piraeus /pī rée əss/ city in east-central Greece, the port of Athens. Pop. 182,671 (1991).

Pirandello /pírrən déllō/, **Luigi** (1867–1936) Italian playwright

piranha /pi raanə/ (*pl* -**nhas** *or same*), **piraña** (*pl* -**ñas** *or same*) n a small tropical fish with sharp teeth that attacks in large numbers

pirate /pírət/ n **1** a robber operating on the high seas **2** a ship used by sea robbers **3** somebody using copyright material without permission —**pirate** vt —**piratic** /pī ráttik/ adj

pirogue /pi rốg/ n a dugout canoe

pirouette /pírroo ét/ n a spin on one foot in ballet

Pisa /peezə/ city in west-central Italy. Pop. 93,303 (1997).

piscatorial /pískə táwri əl/, **piscatory** /pískətəri/ adj of fish or fishing (*fml*)

Pisces /pī seez/ n **1** a zodiacal constellation in the northern hemisphere **2** the 12th sign of the zodiac —**Piscean** /pīssi ən/ n —**Pisces** adj

piss (*slang*) vi an offensive term meaning to urinate ■ n an offensive term for urine ◊ **take the piss** an offensive phrase meaning ridicule or mock (*slang*)
□ **piss off** v (*slang*) **1** vt an offensive term meaning annoy or upset somebody **2** vi an offensive term meaning go away

Pissarro /pi saárō/, **Camille** (1830–1903) French painter

pissed adj an offensive term meaning drunk (*slang*)

pissoir /píss waar/ n a public urinal in a street

pistachio /pi staáshi ō, pi stásh-/ (*pl* -**os**) n **1** also **pistachio nut** a nut with an edible green kernel **2** (*pl* **pistachios** *or same*) a tree that produces pistachios

piste /peest/ n **1** a snow-covered slope for skiing **2** an area for a sports contest such as fencing

pistil /pístil/ n the female reproductive part of a plant

pistol /píst'l/ n a small gun designed to be held in one hand ■ vt (-**tolling, -tolled**) shoot with a pistol

pistol-whip vt hit with the butt or barrel of a pistol

piston /píst'n/ n **1** a metal cylinder that slides within a tube **2** a valve in a brass instrument used for altering the pitch

pit[1] n **1** a big hole in the ground **2** a hole or shaft in the ground for mining **3** a small circular scar left by a disease or skin disorder **4** a servicing area for racing cars (*often pl*)

5 in athletics, a sandy area where jumpers land **6** the very bottom of something ○ *in the pit of my stomach* **7** an orchestra pit in a theatre **8** a pitfall **9** *US, Can* the trading area on the floor of an exchange **10** an arena for cocks or dogs to fight in **11** Hell (*literary*) ■ **pits** npl the worst possible thing, person, or place (*infml*) ■ vt (**pitting, pitted**) **1** set up in opposition **2** mark with small holes or indentations

pit[2] (**pitting, pitted**) vt *US, Can* remove the kernel from a fruit

pita n FOOD = **pitta**

pitapat /pítta pát/ adv with a series of quick tapping sounds —**pitapat** n, vi

Pitcairn Island /pít kairn-/ island in the central South Pacific Ocean, the main island of a group forming a dependency of the United Kingdom. Pop. 61 (1991).

pitch[1] v **1** vti throw or hurl something **2** vt set up a tent, camp, or other temporary structure **3** vt secure something in the ground **4** vti fall, or make somebody or something fall down **5** vi slant in a particular way **6** vi move up and down (*refers especially to ships and aircraft*) **7** vt set something at a particular intellectual level **8** vti in baseball, throw a ball to the batter **9** vti in golf, hit a ball high in the air with some backspin **10** vt set a musical instrument to a particular key ■ n **1** a particular degree of something ○ *such a pitch of anxiety* **2** the degree of slope of something **3** a field for a team ball game **4** the area between the two sets of cricket stumps **5** in baseball, a throw of the ball **6** the level of a sound in a scale, according to its frequency **7** a place where a market stall is erected **8** an aggressive speech trying to sell or promote something (*infml*) **9** in golf, a high shot with some backspin
□ **pitch in** vi **1** help willingly **2** begin to do something enthusiastically
□ **pitch up** vi arrive (*infml*)

pitch[2] n **1** a dark sticky substance obtained from tar. Use: waterproofing roofs. **2** a natural tarry substance such as asphalt ■ vt spread pitch on

pitch-black, pitch-dark adj extremely dark

pitched battle n **1** a fierce battle at a pre-arranged location **2** a fierce conflict or argument

pitcher[1] /píchər/ n a large single-handled water jug

pitcher[2] /píchər/ n in baseball, the player who throws the ball to the batter

pitchfork /pích fawrk/ n a pronged long-handled farming tool for moving hay ■ vt **1** use a pitchfork to move hay **2** thrust somebody into a difficult situation

pitch pine n a pine tree that yields pitch or turpentine

piteous /pítti əss/ adj deserving or arousing pity —**piteously** adv

pitfall /pít fawl/ n **1** a potential difficulty or

disaster **2** a trap consisting of a disguised hole in the ground

pith /pith/ n **1** the white tissue under the rind of citrus fruits **2** the tissue inside the stem of a vascular plant **3** the central or most important part of something **4** vigour or stamina

pithead /pít hed/ n the top part of a mineshaft

pith helmet n a sun hat made from dried pith

pithy /píthi/ (-ier, -iest) adj **1** brief and to the point **2** of or resembling pith —**pithily** adv

pitiful /píttif'l/, **pitiable** /pítti əb'l/ adj **1** arousing pity **2** arousing contempt or derision —**pitiably** adv —**pitifully** adv

pitiless /píttiləss/ adj **1** lacking in pity **2** very severe —**pitilessly** adv

Pitlochry /pit lókhri, -lókri/ town in central Scotland. Pop. 2,541 (1991).

pitman /pítmən/ (pl -men /-mən/) n a miner

piton /pée ton/ n a spike for securing a rope when climbing

pit stop n **1** a refuelling stop for a car during a race **2** a brief stop during a road journey to rest, refuel, or eat (infml)

Pitt, William, 1st Earl of Chatham (1708–78) prime minister of Great Britain (1766–68)

Pitt, William (1759–1806) prime minister of Great Britain (1783–1801 and 1804–06)

pitta /pítta, peéta/, **pita, pitta bread, pita bread** n a flat round unleavened bread that can be opened to insert a filling

pittance /pítt'nss/ n a very small sum of money

pitter-patter /píttər patər/ n a rapid continuous tapping sound —**pitter-patter** adv, vi

~~pittiful~~ incorrect spelling of **pitiful**

Pittsburgh /píts burg/ city in SW Pennsylvania. Pop. 340,520 (1998).

pituitary gland /pi tyoó itəri-/, **pituitary** (pl -ies) n a gland at the base of the brain that produces growth hormones

pity /pítti/ n **1** a feeling of sympathy **2** something regrettable ■ vt (-ies, -ied) feel pity for —**pityingly** adv

~~pityful~~ incorrect spelling of **pitiful**

Pius XII /pí əss/ (1876–1958) pope (1939–58)

pivot /pívvət/ n **1** an object on which a larger object turns or swings **2** a turning movement on a pivot ■ vi turn on or as if on a pivot

pivotal /pívvət'l/ adj **1** vitally important **2** acting as a pivot —**pivotally** adv

pix n CHR = **pyx**

pixel /píks'l/ n a tiny dot of light that is the basic unit of a video screen image

ORIGIN Pixel is a compound of pix 'pictures' and a shortening of element.

pixie /píksi/, **pixy** (pl -ies) n a mischievous fairy or elf

pixilated /píksi laytid/ adj made up of pixels

ORIGIN Pixilated is formed from pixel in imitation of an earlier word that meant 'bewildered' or 'drunk' and was humorously

created from pixie and the ending of words like elated and titillated.

Pizarro /pi zaárō/, **Francisco** (1476?–1541) Spanish explorer

pizza /peétsə/ n a flat round piece of baked dough with a topping, usually of cheese, tomato sauce, and other ingredients

pizzazz /pə záz/, **pizzaz** n energy and style (infml)

pizzeria /peétsə reé ə/ (pl -as) n a pizza restaurant

pizzicato /pítsi kaátō/ adv by plucking the strings of a bowed instrument (musical direction) ■ n (pl -tos or -ti /-ti/) a piece of music played pizzicato —**pizzicato** adj

Pky, pky, Pkwy abbr parkway

pl abbr plural

Pl. abbr Place (in addresses)

placard /plá kaard/ n **1** a large piece of card or board with writing on it displayed or carried in public **2** a small card or metal plaque with a name on it ■ vt **1** put placards on **2** advertise or announce with placards

placate /plə káyt/ (-cating, -cated) vt make less angry —**placable** /plákəb'l/ adj —**placation** n

place /playss/ n **1** an area or portion of space **2** a geographical locality such as a town, country, or region **3** a relatively open area in a town **4** a home **5** an area where something in particular happens ○ his place of business **6** a particular point or position in something ○ lost my place **7** somebody's natural responsibility or right ○ not your place to tell me what to do **8** somewhere to sit ○ three places at the table **9** somebody's position in a ranking ○ finished in last place **10** the first, second, or third position in a horse race ■ vt (**placing, placed**) **1** put in a particular position or state **2** recognize or remember ○ can't place him **3** assign to a position or location **4** have accepted and dealt with ○ placed an order for a new car ◇ **all over the place** in a state of disorder or confusion (infml) ◇ **go places** become successful (infml) ◇ **in place of** instead of or as a replacement for ◇ **put somebody in his or her place** humble somebody who is behaving in an arrogant or insolent way (infml) ◇ **take place** happen

ORIGIN Place came into English via French from Latin platea 'broad way'. The 'broad' element is seen more clearly in piazza and plaza, words for an 'open square' that developed (through Italian and Spanish respectively) from the same Latin word.

SPELLCHECK Do not confuse the spelling of **place** and **plaice** (the fish), which sound similar.

placebo /plə seébō/ (pl -bos or -boes) n **1** something prescribed for a patient that has no physical effect but can produce a psychological improvement **2** an inactive substance given as a control to a participant in a clinical trial of a new drug

ORIGIN Placebo means 'I shall please' in Latin.

Its meaning of a medicine given more to please and have a psychological effect on the patient than for any physical benefit began in the late 18C.

placebo effect *n* a positive psychological effect felt simply from knowing that treatment has been given

place card *n* a card on a dining table showing where somebody is to sit

place kick *n* in American football or rugby, a kick in which the ball is propped or held up on the ground —**placekick** *vt*

place mat *n* a table mat for somebody's plate

placement /pláyssmənt/ *n* **1** the act of placing something, or the state of being placed **2** the process of matching somebody to a particular job or situation

placenta /plə séntə/ (*pl* **-tas** *or* **-tae** /-tee/) *n* **1** an organ that develops in the uterus of a pregnant mammal to feed the foetus **2** the part of the ovary of a flowering plant that bears ovules —**placental** *adj, n*

place setting *n* a set of cutlery, plates, and glasses for one person, arranged on a table

placid /plássid/ *adj* calm by nature —**placidity** /plə síddəti/ *n* —**placidly** *adv*

plagiarize /pláyjə rīz/ (**-rizing, -rized**), **plagiarise** *vti* copy somebody else's work and claim it is your own —**plagiarism** *n* —**plagiarist** *n* —**plagiaristic** /pláyjə rístik/ *adj*

plague /playg/ *n* **1** an epidemic disease that kills many people **2** bubonic plague **3** the appearance of something harmful or unpleasant in large numbers ■ *vt* (**plaguing, plagued**) **1** afflict **2** annoy or pester constantly

plaice /playss/ (*pl same*) *n* a large flatfish ◊ See note at **place**

plaid /plad/ *n* **1** a long piece of tartan cloth worn over the shoulder as part of traditional Scottish Highland dress **2** a tartan pattern —**plaid** *adj*

Plaid Cymru /plíd kúmri/ *n* the Welsh Nationalist Pa..y

plain /playn/ *adj* **1** simple and ordinary **2** clearly visible **3** clear in meaning **4** frank **5** not combined with another substance **6** uncoloured or unpatterned **7** not pretty **8** absolute ■ *adv* **1** absolutely **2** frankly ■ *n* **1** a flat expanse of land **2** the simplest knitting style or stitch —**plainly** *adv* —**plainness** *n* ◊ See note at **unattractive**

SPELLCHECK Do not confuse the spelling of **plain** and **plane** ('an aircraft', 'a flat surface'), which sound similar.

plain chocolate *n* **1** dark chocolate without added milk **2** a sweet coated with plain chocolate

plain clothes *npl* civilian clothes worn by a police officer on duty —**plain-clothes** *adj*

plain flour *n* flour without added baking powder

plain sailing *n* something that is easy to do

plainsong /pláyn song/ *n* church music consisting of unaccompanied singing in unison

plain-spoken *adj* honest and direct in speech —**plain-spokenness** *n*

plaint /playnt/ *n* an expression of grief (*literary*)

plain text *n* the form of a message that is in ordinary readable language, not in code

plaintiff /pláyntif/ *n* somebody who brings a civil action

plaintive /pláyntiv/ *adj* sad-sounding —**plaintively** *adv* —**plaintiveness** *n*

plait /plat/ *n* a length of something such as hair or dough consisting of strands woven over and under each other ■ *vt* form into a plait

plan *n* **1** a method worked out in order to achieve an objective **2** something that somebody intends or has arranged to do (*often pl*) **3** a diagram of the layout or structure of something ■ *vti* (**planning, planned**) **1** work out a plan for something **2** intend to do something

Planck /plangk/, **Max** (1858–1947) German physicist

plane[1] /playn/ *n* **1** an aeroplane **2** a flat or two-dimensional surface **3** a level of existence, mental activity, or achievement ■ *adj* flat or two-dimensional ◊ See note at **plain**

plane[2] /playn/ *n* **1** a tool with an adjustable metal blade at an angle, for smoothing wood **2** a tool with a flat metal blade, for smoothing clay or plaster —**plane** *vt*

plane[3] /playn/, **plane tree** *n* a tall deciduous tree that has leaves with pointed lobes and peeling bark

planet /plánnit/ *n* **1** an astronomical object that orbits a star **2** in astrology, the Sun, Moon, or any of the planets of the solar system, except the Earth, considered to influence people's lives —**planetary** *adj*

ORIGIN A **planet** goes back through French and Latin to a Greek word meaning literally 'wanderer'. The **planets** (in ancient and medieval astronomy including the Sun and Moon) were astronomical objects that moved in relation to the fixed stars. The modern use dates from the mid-17C.

planetarium /plánnə táiri əm/ (*pl* **-ums** *or* **-a** /-ri ə/) *n* **1** a building with a domed ceiling on which images of the night sky are projected **2** a projector used in a planetarium

plangent /plánjənt/ *adj* **1** expressing or suggesting sadness (*literary*) **2** resonant

plank *n* **1** a long flat piece of wood for use in building **2** a policy that is part of a political party's platform ■ *vt* cover with planks —**planking** *n*

plankton /plángktən/ *n* a mass of tiny floating organisms eaten by aquatic animals —**planktonic** /plangk tónnik/ *adj*

planned obsolescence *n* the policy of ensuring that something soon becomes obsolete, so that consumers will have to buy a replacement

planner /plánnər/ n 1 somebody who plans 2 a chart or book for planning future events

planning permission n official authorization from a local authority to build something

plant n 1 a vegetable organism that grows in earth or water and usually has green leaves 2 a smaller vegetable organism such as a flower or herb that does not have a permanent woody stem 3 a factory or other industrial complex 4 somebody secretly introduced into a group to spy on or influence it (infml) ■ v 1 vti put something into the ground to grow 2 vti place young plants or sow seeds in an area of ground ○ planted the bed with pansies 3 vt put something down firmly 4 vt put an idea in somebody's mind 5 vt place something in a concealed position 6 vt introduce somebody into a group to spy on or influence it (infml) —**plantable** adj —**plant-like** adj

ORIGIN There did exist a Latin noun planta that meant 'shoot, cutting', of uncertain origin, but the meaning of the English noun **plant** is not found. It is likely that this sense developed after the classical Latin period and is linked with the action of pressing on a shovel, or some other tool, with the planta 'sole of the foot' in order to work the soil for planting.

plantain[1] /plántin, -tayn/ n a small wild plant with leaves growing from its base and a greenish flower spike

plantain[2] /plántin, -tayn/ n 1 a green fruit like a banana, eaten cooked 2 a plant that produces plantains

plantar wart /plántər-/ n a wart on the sole of the foot

plantation /plaan táysh'n, plan-/ n 1 a large estate or farm for growing crops such as cotton, coffee, tea, or rubber 2 a group of cultivated crop plants

planter /plaántər/ n 1 an owner or manager of a plantation 2 a large decorative container for houseplants 3 a machine for planting seeds, tubers, or bulbs

plaque /plak, plaak/ n 1 an inscribed or decorated flat piece of metal or stone fixed to a surface, especially to commemorate somebody or something 2 a deposit that builds up on the surface of teeth and can lead to gum disease 3 a distinct raised patch or deposit, e.g. on the skin or an artery wall, as part of a medical condition

plasma /plázmə/ n 1 the clear yellowish fluid component of blood 2 a blood substitute prepared by removing the cells and corpuscles of sterile blood 3 a hot ionized gas found in the Sun, stars, and fusion reactors —**plasmatic** /plaz máttik/ adj

plaster /plaástər/ n 1 a mixture of lime, sand, and water for covering interior walls and ceilings 2 a strip of adhesive bandage 3 also **plaster of Paris** a white powder mixed with water to form a quick-hardening paste. Use: sculpting, casts for broken limbs. ■ vt 1 cover interior walls and ceilings with plaster

2 apply something thickly over a surface (infml) 3 stick a mass of things over a surface 4 make a name, story, or image appear in many locations —**plasterer** n —**plastery** adj

plasterboard /plaástər bawrd/ n plaster sandwiched between two layers of strong paper. Use: interior walls.

plaster cast n 1 a rigid plaster covering for a broken limb 2 a plaster copy of something

plastered /plaástərd/ adj very drunk (infml)

plasterwork /plaástər wurk/ n the plaster finish on surfaces or decorative plaster mouldings on interior walls and ceilings

plastic /plástik/ n 1 a mouldable synthetic material made from the polymerization of organic compounds 2 credit cards (infml) ■ adj 1 made of plastic 2 able to be moulded 3 of moulding, modelling, or sculpting 4 artificial and unnatural —**plasticity** /pla stíssəti/ n

plastic bullet n a large PVC bullet used for riot control

plastic explosive /pla steek-/, **plastique** n a soft mouldable explosive

Plasticine /plásti seen/ tdmk a trademark for a soft coloured modelling material used especially by children

plastic surgery n surgery to repair damaged tissue or improve somebody's appearance —**plastic surgeon** n

plastid /plástid/ n a component of a photosynthetic plant cell that contains DNA and is involved in food synthesis and storage

Plata, Río de la /plaátə/ marine inlet in SE South America between Uruguay and Argentina. Length 300 km/190 mi.

plat du jour /plaá doo zhoór/ (pl **plats du jour** /pronunc. same/) n the dish of the day on a restaurant menu

plate n 1 a flat or shallow dish, especially one from which food is eaten or served 2 the contents of a plate 3 a thin sheet of a substance 4 metal in thin sheets 5 a coating of gold or silver on a base metal 6 a prize of a gold or silver cup, especially for a horse race, or a competition for one 7 a flat piece of material with an inscription or engraving on it (often in combination) 8 a section of the Earth's crust that moves in relation to other segments 9 an artificial palate fitted with false teeth 10 a sensitized sheet of glass for receiving a photographic image 11 an engraved metal sheet or a typeset page from which to print 12 a print taken from an engraved surface 13 a full-page illustration in a book, especially on glossy paper ■ vt (**plating, plated**) 1 cover a base metal with a gold or silver coating 2 cover something with sheets of armour plating —**plated** adj —**plateful** n ◊ **have something on your plate** have something that requires your attention (infml)

plateau /plátto/ n (pl **-teaus** or **-teaux** /pláttoz/) 1 a raised area of land with a level top 2 a stable phase ■ vi level out

plate glass n strong thick glass in large sheets

platelayer /pláyt lay ər/ n somebody who lays and maintains railway track

platelet /pláytlət/ n a particle in the blood that is important in the clotting process

plate tectonics n the theory that continental drift and volcanic and seismic activity are due to movement of segments of the Earth's crust (+ sing verb)

~~plateu~~ incorrect spelling of **plateau**

platform /plát fawrm/ n 1 a raised floor or flat structure, higher than an adjacent area 2 a raised area providing access to trains 3 a particular policy of a party seeking election 4 also **platform shoe** a shoe with a thickened sole 5 a standard configuration of computer hardware or a particular operating system

CORBIS/Bettmann

Sylvia Plath

Plath /plath/, **Sylvia** (1932–63) US poet

plating /pláyting/ n 1 a thin covering of gold or silver applied to a base metal 2 a protective covering of metal plates on a ship or tank

platinum /pláttinəm/ n (symbol **Pt**) a precious silvery-white metallic element. Use: jewellery, catalyst, electroplating.

platitude /plátti tyood/ n 1 a pointless or un-original statement 2 the use of platitudes

Plato /pláytō/ (428?–347 BC) Greek philosopher

platonic /plə tónnik/ adj 1 involving friendship or affection without sexual relations 2 **Platonic** of Plato —**platonically** adv

platoon /plə tóon/ n 1 a subdivision of a company of soldiers 2 a group of people with a common aim

ORIGIN **Platoon** was adopted (in the mid-17C) from a French word meaning literally 'little ball'. Its meaning had been extended to a 'small group of people' and a tight unit such as a **platoon**.

platteland /plát land/ n remote rural areas in South Africa

platter /pláttər/ n 1 a large flat dish for serving food 2 a particular type of served food (often in combination) o a seafood platter

platypus /pláttipəss/ (pl **-puses** or **-pi** /-pī/) n an Australian egg-laying water-dwelling mammal with webbed feet and a snout like a duck's bill

plaudit /pláwdit/ n an expression of praise

~~plausable~~ incorrect spelling of **plausible**

plausible /pláwzəb'l/ adj 1 believable and ap-pearing likely to be true 2 persuasive —**plausibility** /pláwzə bílləti/ n —**plausibly** adv

Plautus /pláwtəss/, **Titus Maccius** (254?–184 BC) Roman comic dramatist

play v 1 vi engage in an enjoyable activity for amusement 2 vti take part in a game or sport 3 vt compete against somebody in a game or sport 4 vti assign or be assigned to a position on a sports field 5 vt use a ball, piece, or card in a game 6 vti deal with a situation in a particular way to achieve an aim o play it safe 7 vti act a part in a theatrical work, television show, or film 8 vt perform music on an in-strument 9 vti reproduce recorded music for listening, or be reproduced for listening 10 vti direct light or water somewhere, or be so directed ■ n 1 a dramatic composition for, e.g. the stage 2 enjoyable recreational activities 3 the action during a game 4 the amount of looseness in, e.g. a rope —**play-able** adj ◊ **play fast and loose** act ir-responsibly or recklessly ◊ **play hard to get** pretend not to be interested or available ◊ **play it by ear** improvise your response to a situation as it develops

☐ **play along** vi pretend to agree

☐ **play around** vi 1 engage in sexual activity outside of a marriage 2 also **play about** behave irresponsibly

☐ **play at** vt pretend to do or be something

☐ **play back** vti replay a recording

☐ **play down** vt minimize the importance of

☐ **play off** v 1 vi take part in a deciding game to find the winner of a tied contest 2 vt set one person against another to gain an advantage for yourself

☐ **play on** vt 1 take advantage of somebody's emotional weakness to achieve an aim 2 make a pun on a word

☐ **play up** vt emphasize

☐ **play up to** vi try insincerely to please

☐ **play with** vt 1 think about or deal with half-heartedly 2 treat carelessly

playback /pláy bak/ n 1 the replaying of a re-cording 2 a device or facility for replaying recordings

playbill /pláy bil/ n 1 a poster advertising a play (dated) 2 US a theatre programme

playboy /pláy boy/ n a wealthy pleasure-seeking man

Play-Doh /pláy dō/ tdmk a trademark for a soft coloured modelling material used especially by children

played out adj 1 exhausted 2 no longer popular or fashionable

player /pláy ər/ n 1 somebody who takes part in a sport or game (often in combination) 2 somebody who plays a musical instrument (usually in combination) o a trumpet player 3 a participant in an activity o a major player in the direct banking sector 4 a stage actor 5 a device for playing recorded sound o a CD player

playful /pláyf'l/ adj 1 enjoying fun and games 2 said or done in fun —**playfully** adv —**playfulness** n

playgoer /pláygō ər/ n somebody who attends the theatre

playground /pláy grownd/ *n* an enclosed outdoor play area for children

playgroup /pláy groop/ *n* a supervised meeting for preschool children to play together

playhouse /pláy howss/ (*pl* **-houses** /-howziz/) *n* a theatre *(often used in names)*

playing card *n* a card belonging to a set used for playing card games

playing field *n* a pitch for organized team games

playlist /pláy list/ *n* a list of recordings for playing on a radio programme or station

playmate /pláy mayt/ *n* somebody, especially a child, who plays with another

play-off *n* **1** a deciding match to find the winner of a tied contest **2** *US, Can* one of a series of matches that decides a championship

playpen /pláy pen/ *n* a structure for a baby to play in safely

playright incorrect spelling of **playwright**

playroom /pláy room, -rōom/ *n* a room for children to play in

playschool /pláy skool/ *n* a nursery school

plaything /pláy thing/ *n* **1** a toy **2** somebody or something treated as a toy

playtime /pláy tīm/ *n* a period for playing, especially as a break for children at school

playwright /pláy rīt/ *n* a writer of plays

playwrite incorrect spelling of **playwright**

plaza /plaázə/ *n* **1** an open square in a town or city, especially in a Spanish-speaking country *US, Can* a shopping centre

PLC *abbr also* **plc** public limited company

plea /plee/ *n* **1** an urgent emotional request **2** a defendant's answer to a charge **3** a statement of a defendant's or claimant's case **4** in Scotland, a court case **5** an excuse

plea bargaining *n* the practice of pleading guilty to a lesser charge to avoid being tried for a more serious charge —**plea bargain** *n* —**plea-bargain** *vi*

plead /pleed/ (**pleaded**) *v* **1** *vi* beg earnestly **2** *vt* offer something as an excuse **3** *vt* answer 'guilty' or 'not guilty' to a charge in a court —**pleadingly** *adv*

pleasant /plézz'nt/ *adj* **1** enjoyable **2** good-natured —**pleasantly** *adv* —**pleasantness** *n*

pleasantry /plézz'ntri/ (*pl* **-ries**) *n* a polite or witty remark

please /pleez/ *adv, interj* used in polite or urgent requests ○ *Please be quiet.* ■ *interj* expresses indignation ○ *Please! Do you expect me to believe that?* ■ *v* (**pleasing, pleased**) **1** *vti* give pleasure to somebody **2** *vt* be the wish or will of somebody *(fml or literary)* **3** *vi* like or wish to do something ○ *Do as you please.* —**pleased** *adj* —**pleasing** *adj* —**pleasingly** *adv*

pleasent incorrect spelling of **pleasant**

pleasurable /plézhərəb'l/ *adj* giving pleasure —**pleasurably** *adv*

pleasure /plézhər/ *n* **1** happiness or satisfaction **2** sensual or sexual gratification **3** recreation, relaxation, or amusement **4** a source of satisfaction ■ *vt* (**-uring, -ured**) give sexual pleasure to —**pleasureless** *adj*

pleat /pleet/ *n* a vertical fold sewn or pressed in a fabric ■ *vt* put pleats in

pleb *n* **1** somebody regarded as ill-educated *(insult)* **2** an ancient Roman plebeian —**plebby** *adj*

plebeian /plə beé ən/ *n* **1** an ordinary ancient Roman citizen **2** somebody from a lower social class *(insult)* —**plebeian** *adj*

plebian incorrect spelling of **plebeian**

plebiscite /plébbi sīt/ *n* a vote of all the electorate on a question of importance

plectrum /pléktrəm/ (*pl* **-tra** /-trə/ *or* **-trums**) *n* a small flat pointed piece of plastic for playing a guitar

pledge *n* **1** a solemn vow **2** something given as security or as a token **3** a promise to donate money, e.g. to a charity or a political cause **4** the state of being held as security ■ *vt* (**pledging, pledged**) **1** promise to do something **2** bind by a pledge **3** give something as security *(dated)* —**pledgable** *adj* —**pledger** *n*

Pleistocene /plístō seen/ *n* an epoch of geological time 1.8 million-10,000 years ago —**Pleistocene** *adj*

plenary /pleénəri/ *adj* **1** attended by every member or delegate **2** full or unlimited *(fml)* ■ *n* (*pl* **-ries**) a plenary meeting

plenipotentiary /plénnipə ténshəri/ *adj* having or conferring full power to act independently ■ *n* (*pl* **-ies**) an official with full powers

plenitude /plénni tyood/ *n* *(literary)* **1** abundance **2** completeness or fullness

plenteous /plénti əss/ *adj* *(literary)* **1** abundant **2** productive —**plenteously** *adv*

plentiful /pléntif'l/ *adj* **1** abundant or in good supply **2** productive —**plentifully** *adv*

plenty /plénti/ *pron* an adequate or abundant amount or quantity ■ *n* prosperity

pleonasm /pleé ə nazəm/ *n* **1** the use of superfluous words **2** an example of using superfluous words —**pleonastic** /pleé ə nástik/ *adj*

plesant incorrect spelling of **pleasant**

plesiosaur /pleéssi ə sawr/ *n* an extinct sea reptile of the Mesozoic era

plethora /pléthərə/ *n* a large or excessive amount or number of something

pleurisy /plóórəssi/ *n* an inflammation of the lung membrane —**pleuritic** /plōō ríttik/ *adj*

plexus /pléksəss/ (*pl* **-uses** *or* **same**) *n* **1** a network of nerves or blood vessels in the body **2** a complex network

pliable /plí əb'l/ *adj* **1** flexible **2** easily influenced —**pliability** /plí ə bílləti/ *n*

> **SYNONYMS** **pliable, ductile, malleable, elastic, pliant** CORE MEANING: able to be bent or moulded

pliant /plí ənt/ *adj* **1** supple **2** adaptable

—**pliancy** n —**pliantly** adv ◊ See note at pliable

pliers /plī ərz/ npl a tool with two hinged arms ending in jaws for gripping something

plight¹ /plīt/ n an unfortunate condition

plight² /plīt/ (**plighted** or **plight**) vt make a vow

plimsoll /plíms'l/, **plimsole** n UK a rubber-soled canvas shoe

---

ORIGIN Plimsolls are probably ultimately named after the British politician and reformer Samuel Plimsoll (1824–98). He introduced the Merchant Shipping Act of 1876, which advocated the use of marks on the side of merchant ships to show the limit to which they could be submerged when loaded. These came to be called *Plimsoll lines* or *Plimsoll marks*, and it is thought that a resemblance between these and the lines around the shoes led to the adoption of the name **plimsoll**.

---

plinth /plinth/ n a square supporting block for a column or statue

Pliny (the Elder) /plínni/ (AD 23–79) Roman scholar

Pliny (the Younger) (AD 62–113) Roman politician and writer

Pliocene /plī ō seen/, **Pleiocene** n an epoch of geological time 5.3–1.8 million years ago —**Pliocene** adj

PLO abbr Palestine Liberation Organization

plod vi (**plodding**, **plodded**) 1 walk heavily 2 work slowly but steadily ■ n 1 a walk with slow heavy steps 2 the sound of somebody walking with slow heavy steps 3 a laborious task —**plodding** adj —**ploddingly** adv

plonk vi 1 drop heavily or suddenly (infml) 2 play music inexpressively —**plonk** adv

plonker /plóngkər/ n a person regarded as unintelligent (slang insult)

plop n the sound of something dropping into water without a large splash ■ v (**plopping**, **plopped**) 1 vti fall or let fall with a plop 2 vi drop down quickly and heavily —**plop** adv

plosive /plóssiv/ adj describes a consonant that is pronounced with a suddenly released breath —**plosive** n

plot n 1 a secret plan to do something illegal or subversive 2 a story line 3 a small piece of ground ■ v (**plotting**, **plotted**) 1 vti make secret plans to do something illegal or subversive 2 vt mark the course of a ship or aircraft on a chart 3 vti mark points or a line on a graph, or be marked on a graph

plotter /plóttər/ n 1 somebody who secretly plans to do something illegal or subversive 2 a computer device for drawing graphs

plough /plow/ n 1 a farm implement for breaking up soil and making furrows 2 a heavy tool or machine for cutting or clearing a channel or route 3 ploughed land 4 **Plough** a group of the seven brightest stars in the constellation Ursa Major ■ v 1 vti make furrows in land 2 vti cut or force a way through something ○ *ploughed my way through the crowd* 3 vt make a channel or

cleared route in something 4 vt put something under the soil with a plough 5 vti work methodically at something

☐ **plough in** vt contribute
☐ **plough into** vt crash into
☐ **plough on** vi keep going
☐ **plough under** vt overwhelm

ploughman /plów mən/ (pl -**men** /-mən/) n somebody who operates a plough

ploughman's lunch n a lunch of bread, cheese, and pickle

ploughshare /plów shair/ n the part of a plough that cuts the soil

Plovdiv /plóv dif/ city in S Bulgaria. Pop. 344,326 (1996).

plover /plúvvər/ n a wading shore bird with a short bill and tail and long pointed wings

ploy n a deceptive tactic

pluck v 1 vt take away quickly 2 vt pull off the feathers or hair of 3 vt pull off or out of something else ○ *plucking flowers* 4 vti tug at 5 vt play by pulling and releasing the strings of ■ n 1 bravery 2 an act of plucking something ◊ See note at **courage**

plucky /plúki/ (-**ier**, -**iest**) adj brave —**pluckily** adv —**pluckiness** n

plug n 1 something used to fill and close a hole tightly 2 a stopper for a sink or bath 3 an electrical connection with prongs or pins that fit into a wall socket 4 an electrical wall socket (infml) 5 an unofficial favourable mention of something in order to publicize it (infml) 6 a cake of chewing tobacco ■ v (**plugging**, **plugged**) 1 vt fill and close up a hole 2 vt give something an unofficial favourable mention in order to publicize it (infml) 3 vt US shoot somebody (slang) 4 vi work steadily (infml) ◊ **pull the plug on** bring abruptly to an end

☐ **plug in** or **into** vti connect to a power source

plug and play n a technical standard that allows a peripheral device to connect to a computer and function immediately without the need for a further configuration of the system —**plug-and-play** adj

plughole /plúg hōl/ n an opening in a sink or bath for liquid to drain away when the plug is removed

plug-in adj connectible by a plug to a power source ■ n 1 a device that can be connected by a plug to a power source 2 a data file that alters an application

plum /plum/ n 1 a dark reddish-purple smooth-skinned fruit containing a flattened stone 2 a fruit tree that produces plums 3 a dark reddish-purple colour ■ adj 1 highly desirable (infml) 2 dark reddish-purple in colour

---

ORIGIN Plum goes back to a Latin word that is also the source of *prune* (the dried fruit). It was adopted into ancient Germanic languages, where the form with *l* rather than *r* developed. *Prune* came through French.

SPELLCHECK Do not confuse the spelling of

plum and **plumb** ('a weight attached to a line'), which sound similar.

---

plumage /plóomij/ n the feathers of a bird

plumb /plum/ n **1** a weight attached to a line, used for finding the depth of water or establishing a true vertical position **2** a true vertical position ■ *adv* **1** in true vertical position **2** exactly (*infml*) ■ *adj* vertical ■ *vt* **1** fully comprehend something mysterious **2** experience something unpleasant to an extreme degree **3** find the depth or true vertical position of something ◊ See note at **plumb**

plumber /plúmmər/ n somebody who installs and fixes pipes and water fixtures in buildings

plumbing /plúmming/ n **1** the work of a plumber **2** the pipes and water fixtures in a building

plumb line n a line with a weight attached, used for finding the depth of water or establishing a true vertical position

plume /ploom/ n **1** a large or ornamental feather **2** a feather or bunch of feathers used as a decorative crest **3** a rising column of something such as smoke or dust ■ *v* (**pluming, plumed**) **1** *vt* preen the feathers **2** *vr* pride yourself on something —**plumed** *adj*

plummet /plúmmit/ *vi* fall or drop steeply downwards —**plummet** n

plump[1] *adj* **1** slightly overweight (*sometimes offensive*) **2** having a satisfactory amount of flesh ○ *a plump chicken* ■ *vti* make or become fatter or rounder —**plumpness** n

plump[2] *vti* drop abruptly or heavily ■ n an abrupt or heavy fall, or the sound of one ■ *adv* **1** heavily **2** directly
□ **plump for** *vt* choose

plum pudding n a rich steamed suet pudding containing dried fruit

plum tomato n an elongated firm-textured tomato

plunder /plúndər/ *vti* rob a place or person or steal goods using violence and causing damage, especially in a war ■ n **1** goods stolen by force, especially in a war **2** the theft of goods by force or fraud —**plunderer** n

plunge *v* (**plunging, plunged**) **1** *vti* move suddenly downwards or forwards **2** *vt* put somebody or something suddenly in an unpleasant condition **3** *vt* thrust something quickly or firmly into a liquid or container **4** *vi* become involved enthusiastically in an activity **5** *vi* embark recklessly on a course of action **6** *vi* drop suddenly in value ■ n **1** a leap into something, especially water **2** a sudden sharp fall in value —**plunging** *adj*
◊ **take the plunge** commit to doing something

plunge pool n a small deep swimming pool used for cooling the body

plunger /plúnjər/ n **1** a tool for clearing clogged drains, consisting of a rubber suction cup on a handle **2** a part of a device with a plunging movement

plunk *vti* **1** twang the strings of a musical instrument **2** *US, Can* drop down suddenly and heavily —**plunk** n

pluperfect /ploo púrfikt/ n the past perfect tense of a verb —**pluperfect** *adj*

plural /plóorəl/ *adj* **1** referring grammatically to more than one person or thing **2** of more than one person or thing ■ n **1** the plural number category **2** the plural form of a word

pluralism /plóorəlizəm/ n the existence of different ethnic, religious, or political groups within a society —**pluralist** n —**pluralistic** /plóorə lístik/ *adj*

plurality /ploor rálləti/ (*pl* -**ties**) n **1** the condition of being plural **2** a great number or part of something

plus /pluss/ *prep* used for adding one number or amount to another (*often written as* '+') ○ *Two plus two equals four.* ■ *adj* **1** showing or involving addition **2** with a figure or value on the positive side of a scale (*often written as* '+') **3** advantageous ○ *on the plus side* **4** somewhat more than a particular number ■ n (*pl* **pluses** *or* **plusses**) **1** *also* **plus sign** the symbol '+', used to show addition or a positive quantity **2** a positive quantity **3** an advantageous factor (*infml*) ■ *conj* (*infml*) **1** △ and also **2** △ and furthermore

USAGE Avoid using **plus** to introduce an independent clause: *He is the head of the department, plus he has his own consulting firm.* Use instead: *As well as being the head of the department, he has his own consulting firm.* In formal writing avoid using **plus** in place of *and* as a conjunction joining two subjects in a sentence: *Lack of practice and* [not *plus*] *a knee injury have caused her to drop out.*

plus fours *npl* baggy trousers ending just below the knee

ORIGIN Plus fours were 'plus' four inches. They were about four inches (10.2 cm) longer than the standard knickerbockers worn by golfers at the time of their introduction, around 1920.

plush n a rich smooth fabric with a long soft nap ■ *adj also* **plushy** luxurious (*infml*) —**plushness** n

Plutarch /plóo taark/ (46–120) Greek historian, biographer, and philosopher

Pluto /plóotő/ n **1** in Roman mythology, the god of the underworld. Greek equivalent **Hades** **2** the smallest, and on average, the most distant planet in the solar system —**Plutonian** /ploo tőni ən/ *adj*

plutocracy /ploo tókrəssi/ (*pl* -**cies**) n **1** rule by the wealthy **2** a society ruled by the wealthy —**plutocrat** /plóotə krat/ n —**plutocratic** /plóotə kráttik/ *adj*

plutonium /ploo tőni əm/ n (*symbol* **Pu**) a silvery radioactive metallic element. Use: production of atomic energy and weapons.

ply[1] (**plies, plied**) *v* **1** *vti* work hard at an occupation **2** *vt* use a tool or weapon diligently or skilfully **3** *vt* offer goods or services for sale **4** *vt* supply somebody with or subject somebody to something in an insistent way **5** *vti* travel a route regularly

ply² *n* (*pl* **plies**) *(often in combination)* **1** a twisted strand of yarn or rope **2** a thin layer of something such as wood or a tyre ■ *vti* (**plies, plied**) twist or fold things together

Plymouth /plímməth/ **1** port in SW England. Pop. 260,000 (1996). **2** town in SE Massachusetts, settled by the Pilgrim Fathers. Pop. 7,258 (1996).

plywood /plí wòod/ *n* board made by gluing thin layers of wood together

pm, PM *adv* between twelve noon and midnight. Full form **post meridiem**

Pm *symbol* promethium

PM *abbr* Prime Minister

P-mail /peè mayl/, **pmail** *n* ordinary mail sent through the postal service

PMS *abbr* premenstrual syndrome

PMT *abbr* premenstrual tension

pneumatic /nyoo máttik/ *adj* **1** using or filled with compressed air **2** of air or other gases —**pneumatically** *adv*

pneumatic drill *n* a powerful drill operated by compressed air. Use: breaking up road surfaces.

pneumonia /nyoo mốni ə/ *n* an inflammation of one or both lungs

PNG *abbr* Papua New Guinea

~~pnuematic~~ incorrect spelling of **pneumatic**

~~pnuemonia~~ incorrect spelling of **pneumonia**

Po¹ *symbol* polonium

Po² /pṓ/ river in N Italy, flowing eastwards into the Adriatic Sea. Length 652 km/405 mi.

PO *abbr* **1** *also* **p.o.** postal order **2** post office

poach¹ *vti* **1** catch fish or game illegally **2** appropriate or remove somebody or something unfairly or secretly

poach² *vt* cook by simmering in liquid

poacher¹ /pốchər/ *n* somebody who poaches fish or game

poacher² /pốchər/ *n* a pan for poaching eggs

Pocahontas: Posthumous portrait (1666)

Pocahontas /pókə hóntəss/ (1595?–1617?) Powhatan princess

pocket /pókit/ *n* **1** a small pouch in a piece of clothing for holding small items **2** somebody's personal money ○ *paid for it out of his own pocket* **3** a small area differentiated from neighbouring areas in a particular way **4** a cavity or opening, or the contents of one ■ *vt* **1** put something in a pocket **2** take something dishonestly ■ *adj* **1** small enough

to carry in a pocket **2** small of its type —**pocketful** *n* ◇ **have deep pockets** have large financial resources ◇ **in pocket** making a profit from something ◇ **in somebody's pocket** fully under somebody's control ◇ **line your pocket(s)** profit at the expense of others ◇ **pick somebody's pocket** steal something from somebody's pocket without the person noticing

pocketbook /pókit bòok/ *n US, Can* **1** a small case for money and documents carried in a pocket **2** a handbag **3** somebody's financial resources

pocketknife /pókit nìf/ (*pl* **-knives** /-nîvz/) *n* a penknife

pocket money *n* **1** money given to a child by its parents to make small purchases **2** a small amount of personal money

pockmark /pók maark/ *n* (*often pl*) **1** a small circular scar on the skin left by smallpox, chickenpox, or acne **2** a small hollow disfiguring mark

pod¹ *n* **1** a long narrow seed case holding the seeds of plants such as peas and beans **2** a detachable compartment of a spacecraft **3** a streamlined housing for equipment on an aircraft or submarine

pod² *n* a small group of sea mammals

-pod, -pode *suffix* foot, part like a foot ○ *arthropod* —**-podous** *suffix*

Podgorica /pód gáwritsə/ capital of Montenegro, S Yugoslavia. Pop. 163,493 (1998).

podgy /pójji/ (**-ier, -iest**) *adj* short and overweight *(sometimes offensive)* —**podginess** *n*

podiatry /po dí ətri/ *n US, Can* MED = chiropody —**podiatric** /pódi áttrik/ *adj* —**podiatrist** *n*

podium /pốdɪ əm/ (*pl* **-ums** *or* **-a** /-di ə/) *n* a small raised platform for an orchestra conductor, lecturer, or speaker

Poe /pṓ/, **Edgar Allan** (1809–49) US writer and critic

poem /pố im/ *n* a piece of writing in verse, using rhythm, imagery, and often rhyme

~~poeple~~ incorrect spelling of **people**

poesy /pố əzi/ *n* poetry *(literary)*

poet /pố it/ *n* somebody who writes poems

poetaster /pố i tástər/ *n* a bad poet *(literary)*

poetic /po éttik/, **poetical** /-ik'l/ *adj* of or resembling poetry —**poetically** *adv*

poetic justice *n* just retribution for something

poetic licence *n* the freedom to disobey writing conventions to achieve a special effect

poet laureate (*pl* **poets laureate**) *n* a British court poet who writes poems celebrating great events

poetry /pố itri/ *n* **1** the work of a poet **2** poems collectively or as a genre **3** the writing of poems **4** a poetic quality

po-faced *adj* **1** humourless and disapproving **2** expressionless

pogo /pốgō/ (**-gos, -going, -goed**) *vi* dance by jumping up and down on the spot —**pogo** *n*

pogo stick *n* a pole with a spring and footrests at the bottom used for hopping around

pogrom /póggrəm/ *n* an organized campaign to kill a minority group

poignant /póynyənt/ *adj* causing sadness or pity —**poignance** *n* —**poignancy** *n* —**poignantly** *adv* ◊ See note at **moving**

poinsettia /poyn sétti ə/ (*pl* **-as** *or same*) *n* a bush with red leaves like petals

point *n* 1 an opinion, idea, or fact put forward 2 the essential idea 3 a purpose 4 an item in a list or plan 5 a distinguishing quality 6 a specific location 7 a moment in time 8 a particular stage, level, or degree 9 the sharp or tapering end of something 10 a prominent headland (*often in placenames*) 11 the act of pointing 12 a dot or punctuation mark, especially a full stop 13 a unit used in scoring, evaluating, or measuring something 14 a mark on a compass indicating bearing or direction ■ *v* 1 *vi* extend a finger to draw attention to somebody or something 2 *vt* aim the end of an object at a target 3 *vi* be turned towards or aimed in a particular direction 4 *vt* direct somebody towards a destination 5 *vi* suggest that something is the case ◊ *It all points to one conclusion.* 6 *vi* call attention to a fact or situation as being important ◊ **a sore point** a cause of annoyance ◊ **beside the point** irrelevant or unimportant ◊ **in point of fact** in reality ◊ **make a point of doing something** make a special effort to do something ◊ **stretch a point** exaggerate ◊ **to the point** relevant ◊ **(up) to a point** to a certain extent, but not completely

□ **point out** *vt* 1 indicate where somebody or something is 2 draw attention to something

□ **point up** *vt* emphasize

point-and-click *adj* describes a computer interface that allows a user to interact via a mouse click —**point-and-click** *vi*

point-blank *adv* 1 at close range 2 directly and bluntly —**point-blank** *adj*

point duty *n* the directing of traffic at a road junction by a police officer or traffic warden

pointed /póyntid/ *adj* 1 ending in a point 2 made with emphasis and implying criticism —**pointedly** *adv* —**pointedness** *n*

pointer /póyntər/ *n* 1 a stick or cane used for pointing 2 an indicator on a measuring device 3 a helpful piece of advice or information 4 a gun dog that indicates the position of game 5 an arrow on a computer screen showing the position of the mouse

pointillism /póyntilizəm/ *n* a style of 19C painting using dots of colour to create a picture —**pointillist** *n*, *adj*

pointing /póynting/ *n* mortar between bricks

pointless /póyntləss/ *adj* 1 without purpose or benefit 2 scoring no points —**pointlessly** *adv* —**pointlessness** *n*

point man *n* a lead soldier in a military formation

point of order *n* a question about procedure in a debate or meeting

point-of-sale *adj* located at the place where a product is sold —**point of sale** *n*

point of view *n* 1 a way of thinking about a subject 2 somebody's personal opinion on a subject

point-to-point *n* a cross-country steeplechase for amateurs ■ *adj* from one place to another

Point-to-Point Protocol *n* a protocol for dial-up access to the Internet

pointy /póynti/ (**-ier**, **-iest**) *adj* with a pointed end (*infml*) —**pointiness** *n*

poise /poyz/ *n* 1 composure 2 controlled grace in movement ■ *vti* (**poising**, **poised**) balance or suspend, or be balanced or suspended

poised /poyzd/ *adj* 1 ready to act ◊ *We are now poised to take over the company.* 2 ready to move 3 calm and composed

~~poisen~~ incorrect spelling of **poison**

poison /póyz'n/ *n* a toxic substance that causes illness or death if taken into the body ■ *vt* 1 harm or kill a person or animal with a toxic substance 2 add poison to something 3 pollute the environment 4 corrupt or undermine somebody or something —**poisoner** *n* —**poisonous** *adj*

ORIGIN A **poison** is etymologically simply a 'drink'. It goes back to the Latin word that also gave us **potion**, which was a derivative of the verb *potare* 'drink'. The application to toxic substances developed in Latin.

---

poisoned chalice *n* a task or decision that will harm the person who has to do or take it

poison gas *n* a toxic gas used as a weapon

poison ivy *n* 1 a vine that causes an itching rash 2 the rash produced by poison ivy

poison oak *n* 1 a plant related to poison ivy that causes an itching rash 2 the rash produced by poison oak

poison-pen letter *n* an anonymous abusive letter

poison pill *n* a company strategy intended to deter a hostile takeover

Poitier /pwaati ay/, **Sidney** (*b.* 1924) US actor and director

poke[1] *v* (**poking**, **poked**) 1 *vti* prod somebody or something with a finger, elbow, or stick 2 *vt* make a hole in something by pushing at it with a finger or sharp object 3 *vt* push something into a hole 4 *vti* protrude or make protrude from something 5 *vi* search haphazardly ◊ *poking around in a second-hand bookshop* 6 *vt* stir a fire with a poker ■ *n* a prod with a finger, elbow, or stick

poke[2] *n* regional a bag

poker[1] /pókər/ *n* a card game involving betting on combinations of cards

poker[2] /pókər/ *n* a metal rod for stirring a fire

pokie /póki/, **pokey** (*pl* **-eys**) *n* ANZ a slot machine (*infml*)

poky /póki/ (**-ier**, **-iest**), **pokey** *adj* small and cramped (*infml*) —**pokiness** *n*

Poland /pṓlənd/ country in E Europe, bordering on the Baltic Sea. Cap. Warsaw. Pop. 38,633,912 (2001).

polar /pṓlər/ *adj* 1 of or near either of the Earth's poles 2 of the pole of a rotating body, magnet, or electrically charged object

polar bear *n* a white Arctic bear

Polaris /pō laáriss/ *n* the brightest star of Ursa Minor, near the celestial north pole

polarity /pō lárrəti/ (*pl* **-ties**) *n* 1 an extreme difference between individuals or groups 2 the condition of having opposite characteristics at different points in a system, especially with regard to electric charge or magnetic properties

polarize /pṓlə rīz/ (**-izing**, **-ized**), **polarise** *vti* 1 make differences between groups or ideas even more extreme, or become even more extreme 2 acquire or cause something to acquire polarity —**polarization** /pṓlə rī záysh'n/ *n*

Polaroid /pṓlə royd/ *tdmk* 1 a trademark for a camera that produces instant pictures, or the film used in such a camera 2 a trademark for a transparent plastic that allows polarized light through and is used to reduce glare in sunglasses

pole[1] /pōl/ *n* 1 the North or South Pole 2 each of the two endpoints of the axis of a sphere 3 each of two opposites 4 each of the two ends of a magnet or an electric terminal ◇ **be poles apart** be as different as it is possible to be

---

SPELLCHECK Do not confuse the spelling of **pole** and **poll** ('an election or survey'), which sound similar.

---

pole[2] /pōl/ *n* a long straight piece of wood or metal with a round cross-section that can be held in the hand

Pole /pōl/ *n* somebody from Poland

poleaxe /pṓl aks/ *n* 1 an axe with a hammer face opposite the blade, formerly used for slaughtering animals 2 a battle-axe with a hammer or spike opposite the blade

polecat /pṓl kat/ *n* a small animal related to the weasel that emits a foul smell when disturbed

---

ORIGIN The first part of **polecat** may come from a French word meaning 'hen, fowl' (the source of *poultry* and *pullet*), because the animal was known to take hens from farmyards.

---

polemic /pə lémmik/ *n* a passionate argument against somebody or something —**polemic** *adj* —**polemical** *adj* —**polemicist** *n*

polemics /pə lémmiks/ *n* the art of making polemical arguments (+ *sing verb*)

polenta /pō léntə/ *n* Italian-style maize meal

pole position *n* the best starting position in a motor race

pole star, Pole Star *n* Polaris

pole vault *n* 1 a field event in which competitors attempt to clear a high crossbar using a pole to propel them into the air 2 a

jump in the pole vault —**pole-vault** *vti* —**pole-vaulter** *n*

police /pə léess/ *n* 1 a civil organization responsible for maintaining law and order 2 police officers collectively (+ *pl verb*) 3 a specialized force responsible for enforcing rules and procedures in a particular sphere of activity ■ *vt* (**-licing**, **-liced**) 1 maintain law and order in a place using the police 2 enforce rules and procedures in a particular sphere of activity

police constable *n* a police officer of the lowest rank

police dog *n* a dog trained to work with the police

police force *n* an organized body of police officers within a particular area

policeman /pə léessman/ (*pl* **-men** /-mən/) *n* a man who is a police officer

police officer *n* a member of a police force

police state *n* a country in which the government uses the police to exercise repressive control over the population

police station *n* the local headquarters of a police force

policewoman /pə léess woomən/ (*pl* **-women** /-wimin/) *n* a woman police officer

policy /póllassi/ (*pl* **-cies**) *n* 1 a course of action adopted by an individual or group 2 prudence in the pursuit of a course of action 3 an insurance contract

policyholder /póllassi hōldər/ *n* an insured person or organization

polio /pṓli ō/, **poliomyelitis** /pṓli ō mī ə lítiss/ *n* a disease that inflames the brain stem and spinal cord, sometimes leading to paralysis —**poliomyelitic** /-mī ə líttik/ *adj*

polish /póllish/ *v* 1 *vti* make or become smooth or glossy 2 *vt* remove the outer layers of brown rice 3 *vti* make or become more refined or elegant ■ *n* 1 a substance used for polishing 2 the smoothness or glossiness of something that has been polished 3 a rub given to something to make it smooth or glossy 4 refinement

☐ **polish off** *vt* finish quickly and completely

☐ **polish up** *vt* 1 make shiny 2 improve

Polish /pṓlish/ *npl* the people of Poland ■ *n* the official language of Poland —**Polish** *adj*

Politburo /póllit byoorō, pə lít-/ *n* the executive committee of a governing Communist Party

polite /pə lít/ (**-liter**, **-litest**) *adj* 1 well-mannered 2 elegant and refined —**politely** *adv* —**politeness** *n*

politic /póllətik/ *adj* prudent, shrewd, or cunning —**politicly** *adv*

political /pə líttik'l/ *adj* 1 of party politics 2 of government —**politically** *adv*

politically correct *adj* describes language or behaviour that deliberately avoids giving offence, e.g. in regard to ethnic origin or sexual orientation —**political correctness** *n*

politically incorrect *adj* describes language

or behaviour that could give offence, e.g. in regard to ethnic origin or sexual orientation

political prisoner n somebody imprisoned for his or her political beliefs

political science n the study of government —**political scientist** n

politician /pólla tísh'n/ n 1 somebody actively or professionally involved in politics 2 a member of a branch of government

politicize /pa lítti síz/ (-**cizing**, -**cized**), **politicise** v 1 vti introduce an issue into the political arena, or be introduced there 2 vt give political awareness to somebody or a political flavour to something

politicking /pólla tiking/ n political campaigning

politics /póllatiks/ n 1 the theory and practice of government (+ sing verb) 2 the activity within a political party that is concerned with debate and the creation and carrying out of policies (+ sing or pl verb) 3 the relationships in a particular field involving power, authority, or influence (+ sing or pl verb) o the politics of education 4 the use of tactics and strategy to gain advancement in a group (+ sing or pl verb) ■ npl (+ pl verb) 1 political activity 2 political beliefs

polity /póllati/ (pl -**ties**) n a particular form of government

polka /pólka, pól-/ n 1 a lively dance for couples involving three quick steps and a hop 2 the music for a polka —**polka** vi

polka dot n a dot repeated to form a regular pattern on fabric

poll /pōl/ n 1 an election 2 a survey of public opinion on an issue 3 the number of votes cast in an election ■ **polls** npl a place for voting in an election ■ vt 1 sample opinion methodically 2 receive a particular number of votes ◊ See note at **pole**

ORIGIN The original meaning of **poll**, underlying all its senses, is 'head'. The voting **poll** reflects the idea of counting heads.

pollack /póllak/ (pl -**lacks** or same), **pollock** (pl -**locks** or same) n 1 a N Atlantic fish of the cod family 2 a pollack as food

pollard /póllard, -aard/ n 1 a tree that has had its branches cut back to encourage growth 2 an animal whose horns have been removed or shed ■ vt cut branches or horns

pollen /póllan/ n a powdery substance containing male reproductive cells produced by flowering plants

pollen count n the amount of pollen in the air

pollinate /pólla nayt/ (-**nating**, -**nated**) vt transfer pollen from a male to a female part of a flower and so fertilize the plant —**pollination** /pólla náysh'n/ n

polling booth n a place for an individual voter to mark his or her ballot paper

polling station n an officially designated place for voting

polliwog /pólliwog/, **pollywog** n a tadpole

pollock /póllak/ n zool = **pollack**

Pollock /póllak/, **Jackson** (1912–56) US artist

pollster /pōlstar/ n somebody who conducts opinion polls

poll tax n a tax levied equally on all members of the population

pollutant /pa loot'nt/ n something that causes pollution

pollute /pa loot/ (-**luting**, -**luted**) vt 1 contaminate the natural environment 2 corrupt or defile —**pollution** n

Pollyanna /pólli ánna/ n an eternal optimist

ORIGIN The original **Pollyanna** was the central character in children's stories written by the US author Eleanor Hodgman Porter (1868–1920).

pollywog n zool = **polliwog**

polo /pōlō/ n a team game played on horseback and using mallets and a wooden ball to score goals

Polo /pōlō/, **Marco** (1254–1324) Venetian merchant and traveller

polonaise /pólla náyz/ n 1 a slow formal dance for couples in triple time 2 the music for a polonaise

polo neck n a high rollover collar —**polo-necked** adj

polonium /pa lōni am/ n (symbol Po) a rare radioactive metallic element. Use: removal of static electricity.

polo shirt n a casual cotton shirt with a buttoned opening at the neck

Pol Pot /pól pót/ (1928–98) Cambodian prime minister (1975–79) and leader of the Khmer Rouge

poltergeist /póltargīst/ n a supposed noisy and troublesome supernatural spirit

poltroon /pol troon/ n a person regarded as a contemptible coward (archaic insult)

~~polution~~ incorrect spelling of **pollution**

poly- prefix more than one o polygamy

polyandry /pólli andri/ n 1 the custom of having multiple husbands 2 in female animals, the practice of having multiple mates in a breeding season —**polyandrous** /pólli ándrass/ adj

polyanthus /pólli ánthass/ n a hybrid primrose

polycotton /pólli kot'n/ n a mixed cotton and polyester fabric

polyester /pólli éstar/ n 1 a synthetic polymer. Use: resins, plastics, textile fibres. 2 a strong synthetic fabric

polyethylene /pólli étha leen/ n US INDUST = **polythene**

polygamy /pa líggami/ n 1 the custom of having multiple spouses 2 in animals, the practice of having multiple mates in a breeding season —**polygamist** n —**polygamous** adj

polyglot /pólli glot/ adj 1 able to speak many languages 2 written in many languages —**polyglot** n

polygon /pólligan, -gon/ n a flat many-sided geometrical figure —**polygonal** /pa líggan'l/ adj

polygraph /pólli graaf, -graf/ *n* **1** a device that records pulse, perspiration, and other involuntary responses, often used as a lie detector **2** a test using a polygraph —**polygraph** *vt* —**polygraphic** /pólli gráffik/ *adj*

polyhedron /pólli heédrən/ (*pl* **-drons** *or* **-dra** /-drə/) *n* a many-sided solid geometrical figure —**polyhedral** *adj*

polymath /pólli math/ *n* somebody with wide-ranging knowledge —**polymathic** /pólli máthik/ *adj*

polymer /póllimər/ *n* a compound consisting of large molecules made up of smaller identical molecules —**polymeric** /pólli mérrik/ *adj* —**polymerization** /pə límmə rī záysh'n/ *n* —**polymerize** /póllimə rīz, pə límmə rīz/ *vt*

polymerase /póllimə rayz, pə límmə-/ *n* an enzyme that catalyses a polymer

polymorph /pólli mawrf/ *n* an organism, part of an organism, protein, or chemical compound that is found in different forms —**polymorphic** /pólli máwrfik/ *adj*

polymorphism /pólli máwrfizəm/ *n* **1** the characteristic of existing in different forms **2** a difference in DNA sequence between individuals

Polynesia /pólli neézi ə/ ethnographic grouping of islands in the central and S Pacific Ocean —**Polynesian** *n, adj*

polyp /póllip/ *n* **1** a marine invertebrate that remains attached to a rock **2** a usually benign growth on the skin or a mucous membrane —**polypoid** *adj*

polyphony /pə líffəni/ *n* music with several melodies sounded together —**polyphonous** *adj*

polypropylene /pólli própə leen/, **polypropene** /-prố peen/ *n* a versatile type of plastic. Use: pipes, industrial fibres, moulded objects.

polystyrene /pólli stī reen/ *n* a synthetic packing and insulating material

polysyllable /pólli siləb'l, pólli síllab'l/ *n* a word with many syllables —**polysyllabic** /pólli si lábbik/ *adj*

polytechnic /pólli téknik/ *n* a college offering mostly vocational courses

polytheism /pólli thi izəm, pólli theé izəm/ *n* belief in several or many deities —**polytheist** *n* —**polytheistic** /pólli thi ístik/ *adj*

polythene /pólli theen/ *n* a malleable thermoplastic. Use: containers, packaging, electrical insulation materials.

polyunsaturated /pólli un sáchə raytid/ *adj* describes a fat containing several double or triple bonds between carbon atoms, and less likely than some other fats to be converted into cholesterol in the body

polyurethane /pólli yoörə thayn/ *n* a thermoplastic polymer. Use: resins, coatings, insulation, adhesives, foams, fibres.

pom *n ANZ* a British person (*infml humorous or disapproving*)

pomade /pə máyd, -maåd/ *n* a perfumed oil or ointment for hair —**pomade** *vt*

pomander /pə mándər/ *n* **1** a mixture of aromatic substances kept in a container **2** a container for a pomander

Pomare /po maåri/, **Sir Maui Wiremu Pita Naera** (1876–1930) New Zealand Maori leader and politician

pomegranate /pómmi granit/ *n* **1** a round red fruit with numerous seeds within juicy red flesh **2** the tropical Asian tree that produces pomegranates

~~pomegranite~~ incorrect spelling of **pomegranate**

Pomeranian /pómmə ráyni ən/ *n* a small dog with a long silky coat

pommel /pómm'l, púmm'l/ *n* **1** the front part of a saddle that curves upwards **2** the knob on the hilt of a sword ■ *vt* beat or pummel

pommel horse *n* **1** a gymnastics apparatus consisting of a raised oblong pad with handles on top **2** a gymnastics event using a pommel horse

pommy /pómmi/ (*pl* **-mies**) *n ANZ* a British person (*infml humorous or disapproving*)

pomp *n* **1** ceremonial splendour **2** excessive self-importance

pompadour /pómpə door/ *n* a woman's hairstyle in which the hair is swept back high off the face

Pompadour /pómpə door/, **Marquise de** (1721–64) French mistress of Louis XV and patron of the arts

Pompeii: View of the Forum, with Vesuvius in the background

Pompeii /pom páy i/ ancient Roman city in present-day S Italy, buried by volcanic ash during the eruption of Mount Vesuvius in AD 79

Pompey /pómpi/ (106–48 BC) Roman general and leader

pompom /póm pom/ *n* **1** a small tufted wool ball used as a decoration on clothes **2** a cheerleader's tasselled paper ball on a handle

pompous /pómpəss/ *adj* **1** self-important **2** revealing self-importance —**pomposity** /pom póssəti/ *n* —**pompously** *adv*

ponce /ponss/ *n* a pimp (*slang*) —**poncy** *adj* □ **ponce about** *or* **ponce around** *vi* (*slang*) **1** behave affectedly (*sometimes offensive*) **2** waste time

Ponce (de León) /pónss də lay ón, pónth ay də lee ón/, **Juan** (1460–1521) Spanish explorer

poncho /póncho/ (*pl* **-chos**) *n* a simple cloak that fits over the head

pond *n* a small body of still water

ponder /póndər/ *vti* consider something carefully —**ponderable** *adj, n*

ponderous /póndərəss/ *adj* 1 moving heavily 2 lacking liveliness or wit —**ponderously** *adv* —**ponderousness** *n*

pondokkie /pon dóki/ *n S Africa* an improvised shelter or shack *(infml)*

pong *n* a stink *(infml)* —**pong** *vi* —**pongy** *adj*

poniard /pónnyərd, -yaard/ *n* a small dagger *(literary)*

Ponte ♦ Da Ponte, Lorenzo

pontiff /póntif/ *n* a pope

pontifical /pon tíffik'l/ *adj* 1 of a pontiff 2 pompous ■ **pontificals** *npl* a pontiff's vestments

pontificate *vi* /pon tíffi kayt/ (**-cating, -cated**) 1 speak pompously 2 officiate as a bishop ■ *n* /pon tíffikat, -kayt/ a pope's or bishop's term of office —**pontification** /pon tíffi káysh'n/ *n*

pontoon[1] /pon toón/ *n* 1 a floating support for a bridge 2 a float on a seaplane

pontoon[2] /pon toón/ *n* 1 a card game in which the winner has the hand with the value nearest to and not more than 21 2 a hand with 21 points

ORIGIN Pontoon is probably an alteration of the game's alternative name *vingt-et-un*, in French literally '21', the perfect score.

pony /póni/ (*pl* **-nies**) *n* 1 any breed of small horse 2 a horse used in polo

ponytail /póni tayl/ *n* a hairstyle with long hair tied together at the back —**ponytailed** *adj*

pony-trekking *n* the activity of riding ponies in open countryside

pooch *n* a dog *(infml)*

poodle /poód'l/ *n* a curly-haired dog

poof /poóf, poof/, **pouf** *n* an offensive term for an effeminate or gay man *(insult)*

pooh *interj* indicates disgust at an unpleasant smell *(infml)*

Pooh-Bah /poo baá/, **pooh-bah** *n* 1 a pompous but useless official 2 an important person

ORIGIN The original **Pooh-Bah** was a character in *The Mikado* (1885), an operetta by W. S. Gilbert and Sir Arthur Sullivan.

pooh-pooh *vt* show scorn for

pool[1] *n* 1 a small body of still water 2 a puddle 3 a swimming pool 4 a deep or still part of a river or stream 5 an arrangement of light that resembles a pool ○ *The floodlights bathed her in a pool of pink light.* —**pool** *vi*

pool[2] *n* 1 a game played on a table with a cue and a number of balls 2 a form of gambling in which stakes are placed in a common fund that is then shared by the winners 3 the total amount staked in a gambling game 4 any collective resource, e.g. of vehicles or typists 5 an agreement between businesses to control production and sales to guarantee profits ■ *vt* share resources

poolroom /poól room, -room/ *n* a place where pool is played

poolside /poól sīd/ *n* the area bordering a swimming pool

poop[1] *n* 1 a raised area at the rear of a ship 2 a poop deck

poop[2] *vt* tire out *(infml)* —**pooped** *adj*

poop deck *n* a raised deck at the stern of a ship, with cabins below

poor /pawr, poor/ *adj* 1 lacking money or possessions 2 inferior 3 lacking skill or ability 4 low or inadequate 5 weak 6 deficient *(often in combination)* 7 deserving pity ■ *npl* people who are poor —**poorness** *n*

poorhouse /páwr howss, poór-/ (*pl* **-houses** /-howziz/) *n* formerly, a publicly funded accommodation for poor people

poor law *n* a law for the support of poor people

poorly /páwrli, poórli/ *adv* 1 inadequately 2 unfavourably ■ *adj* physically unwell *(infml)*

poor relation *n* an inferior version of something or somebody

pootle /poót'l/ (**-tling, -tled**) *vi* proceed unhurriedly

pop[1] *n* 1 a sudden bursting sound 2 a fizzy soft drink *(infml)* 3 a gunshot ■ *v* (**popping, popped**) 1 *vti* make or cause to make a bursting sound 2 *vti* burst open, or cause to burst open 3 *vi* bulge *(refers to somebody's eyes)* 4 *vi* go briefly *(infml)* 5 *vt* move quickly into a particular position or place *(infml)*
□ **pop off** *vi* die *(infml)*
□ **pop up** *vi* appear suddenly

pop[2] *n* 1 *also* **Pop** a father *(infml)* 2 an offensive way of addressing an older man *(slang dated)*

pop[3] *n* 1 pop music 2 pop art ■ *adj* 1 musically commercial 2 popular *(infml)*

POP *abbr* persistent organic pollutant

pop. *abbr* population

pop art *n* a 1960s artistic movement that sought to incorporate popular culture into art

popcorn /póp kawrn/ *n* maize kernels heated until puffy and light

pope, Pope *n* the head of the Roman Catholic Church —**popedom** *n*

Pope, Alexander (1688–1744) English poet

pope's nose *n* the parson's nose of a cooked bird

popeyed /póp īd/ *adj* 1 with bulging eyes 2 wide-eyed

pop group *n* a band that plays pop music

popgun /póp gun/ *n* 1 a toy gun that makes a popping noise 2 a useless gun *(infml)*

poplar /pópplər/ *n* 1 a slender quick-growing tree of the willow family 2 the wood of a poplar

poplin /pópplin/ *n* a plain cotton fabric with fine ribbing. Use: clothes, upholstery.

pop music *n* modern commercial music aimed at the general public, especially young people

poppadom /póppədəm, -dom/, **poppadum** *n* a South Asian crispy bread

popper /póppər/ *n* a press stud

poppet /póppit/ *n* used as a term of endearment (infml)

poppy /póppi/ (*pl* **-pies**) *n* a plant with cup-shaped seed pods and red, orange, or white flowers

poppycock /póppi kok/ *n* nonsense (infml dated)

poppy seed *n* the seed of a poppy. Use: in baking.

populace /póppyŏŏləss/ *n* 1 the inhabitants of a place 2 the general public

SPELLCHECK Do not confuse the spelling of **populace** and **populous** ('highly populated'), which sound similar.

popular /póppyŏŏlər/ *adj* 1 appealing to the general public 2 well-liked 3 of the general public 4 believed by people in general —**popularity** /póppyŏŏ lárrəti/ *n* —**popularly** *adv*

popular front *n* a left-wing coalition

popularize /póppyŏŏlə rīz/ (**-izing**, **-ized**), **popularise** *vt* 1 make popular 2 make understandable to a general audience —**popularization** /póppyŏŏlə rī záysh'n/ *n*

populate /póppyŏŏ layt/ (**-lating**, **-lated**) *vt* 1 put people in a place 2 inhabit a place in numbers —**populated** *adj*

population /póppyŏŏ láysh'n/ *n* 1 all the people in a place 2 the total number of people in a place 3 all the plants or animals of a particular species in a place

populism /póppyŏŏlizəm/ *n* 1 politics based on principles considered unfavourable to a perceived elite 2 a focus on ordinary people, e.g. in the arts —**populist** *n, adj*

populous /póppyŏŏləss/ *adj* highly populated —**populousness** *n* ◊ See note at **populace**

pop-up *adj* 1 with a mechanism that makes something lift upwards quickly 2 presented on a computer screen temporarily 3 containing cut-out figures that rise up as a page is opened ○ *a pop-up book*

porcelain /páwrssəlin, -layn/ *n* 1 a hard translucent ceramic material 2 items or an object made of porcelain —**porcellaneous** /páwrssə láyni əss/ *adj*

porch *n* 1 a covered shelter at the entrance to a building 2 US, Can a roofed room on the outside of a building

porcine /páwr sīn/ *adj* of pigs

porcupine /páwrkyŏŏ pīn/ *n* a rodent with long protective quills

pore¹ *n* 1 a tiny opening in the skin 2 a tiny opening in a plant leaf or stem

pore² (**poring**, **pored**) *vi* 1 look at something concentratedly 2 think about something carefully ◊ See note at **pour**

pork *n* meat from a pig

porker /páwrkər/ *n* a fat young pig

pork pie *n* a pie containing minced pork

pork scratchings *npl* small pieces of fried pork rind eaten as a snack

porky /páwrki/ *adj* (**porkier**, **porkiest**) 1 of pork 2 regarded as overweight (infml disapproving) ■ *n* (*pl* **porkies**) a lie or untruth (slang; often pl)

ORIGIN As a noun, **porky** is a shortening of pork pie, rhyming slang for 'lie'.

porn /páwrn/, **porno** *n* pornography (infml)

pornography /pawr nóggrəfi/ *n* 1 the sex industry 2 sexually explicit material —**pornographer** *n* —**pornographic** /páwrnə gráffik/ *adj* —**pornographically** *adv*

porous /páwrəss/ *adj* 1 with pores or cavities 2 permeable —**porosity** /paw róssəti/ *n* —**porously** *adv*

porphyry /páwrfəri/ *n* 1 a reddish-purple rock 2 a rock with isolated large crystals

porpoise /páwrpəss/ (*pl same or* **-poises**) *n* a sea mammal like a dolphin with a blunt nose

porridge /pórrij/ *n* 1 a thick breakfast food made from oatmeal cooked in milk or water 2 imprisonment (slang)

port¹ *n* 1 a large harbour 2 a town with a large harbour 3 a waterfront

ORIGIN The six English words **port** are all ultimately related. **Port** 'harbour' is adopted from Latin portus in the same sense. The **port** side of a ship, recorded from the mid-16C, was probably originally the side turned towards the 'harbour', and so derived from that **port**. **Port** 'opening in a ship' came via French from Latin porta 'gate', which is closely related to portus. The drink **port** is named after the town of Porto or Oporto (literally 'the port') at the mouth of the river Douro in Portugal, from which the wine was shipped. Latin portus gave rise to a verb portare, which probably originally meant 'bring into port' but came to mean just 'carry', and it is from this verb that English **port** 'carry a weapon' derives: it came via French in the mid-16C. The most recent **port**, a verb used in computing, is either a specialized development of the 'carrying' word or from the computing sense of the noun **port²**.

port² *n* 1 an opening in the side of a boat for loading and unloading 2 a valve-operated opening 3 an external computer connection

port³ *n* the left side of a ship or plane —**port** *adj, adv*

port⁴ *n* a strong sweet fortified wine

port⁵ *vt* carry a weapon across the body

port⁶ *vt* convert software for a different computer system

portable /páwrtab'l/ *adj* 1 easily moved about 2 easy to convert to another computer operating system —**portable** *n* —**portably** *adv*

portable document format *n* full form of **pdf**

portage /páwrtij, pawr táàzh/ *n* the process of carrying boats overland ■ *vt* (**-aging**, **-aged**) carry a boat overland to a waterway

Portakabin /páwrtə kabin/ *tdmk* a trademark for a portable building that can be assembled quickly and used for a variety of purposes, e.g. as an office or a classroom

portal /páwrt'l/ *n* 1 a large gate or entrance *(literary)* 2 *also* **portal site** a home site for a web browser

Port-au-Prince /páwrt ō prínss/ capital of Haiti. Pop. 1,461,000 (1995).

portcullis /pawrt kúlliss/ *n* a heavy castle gate that can slide up and down

Port Elizabeth /-i lízzəbəth/ city in SE South Africa. Pop. 1,035,000 (1995).

portend /pawr ténd/ *vt* 1 be an omen of something unpleasant *(fml)* 2 indicate something

portent /páwr tent/ *n* 1 an omen 2 ominous significance

portentous /pawr téntəss/ *adj* 1 very significant for the future 2 pompous

porter[1] /páwrtər/ *n* 1 somebody who carries people's luggage 2 a hospital employee who moves patients

porter[2] /páwrtər/ *n* 1 a gatekeeper 2 an employee who supervises the entrance to a college

porter[3] /páwrtər/ *n* a type of dark beer

Porter /páwrtər/, **Cole** (1891–1964) US composer and lyricist

portfolio /pawrt fóli ō/ *(pl* **-os)** *n* 1 a large flat case used to carry documents or works of art 2 the contents of a portfolio, especially samples of somebody's creative work 3 a government minister's responsibilities 4 a group of investments

portfolio worker *n* an employee who acquires skills and experience in a number of different areas

porthole /páwrt hōl/ *n* a round window in a ship

portico /páwrtikō/ *(pl* **-coes** *or* **-cos)** *n* 1 a porch 2 a covered walkway

portion /páwrsh'n/ *n* 1 a part or section 2 a helping of food 3 somebody's fate *(literary)* ■ *vt* divide something into parts

Portland /páwrtlənd/ city in NW Oregon. Pop. 503,891 (1998).

Port Louis /-loō iss, -loō i/ capital of Mauritius. Pop. 147,131 (1998).

portly /páwrtli/ **(-lier, -liest)** *adj* regarded as slightly overweight —**portliness** *n*

portmanteau /páwrt mántō/ *n (pl* **-teaus** *or* **-teaux** /-tōz/) a large suitcase ■ *adj* multiple

---

ORIGIN Portmanteau was adopted in the mid-16C from a French word meaning literally 'carry a mantle or cloak'. In French the *portmanteau* was originally an official who carried the king's cloak, then the bag in which he carried it, and hence any large bag carrying items for a journey.

---

portmanteau word *n* a word that combines the sounds and meanings of two other words

Port Moresby /-máwrzbi/ capital of Papua New Guinea. Pop. 193,242 (1990).

Porto /páwrtō/, **Oporto** /ō-/ port in NW Portugal. Pop. 285,320 (1995).

Porto Alegre /páwrtoō ə léggri/ capital of Rio Grande do Sul State, SE Brazil. Pop. 1,288,879 (1996).

port of call *n* a foreign port visited by a ship

port of entry *n* an international border crossing

Port-of-Spain, Port of Spain capital of Trinidad and Tobago. Pop. 45,284 (1995).

Porto-Novo /páwrtō nōvō/ capital of Benin. Pop. 200,000 (1994).

Port Pirie /-peēri/ city in SE South Australia. Pop. 13,633 (1996).

portrait /páwrtrit, -trayt/ *n* 1 a picture of a person 2 a description of somebody or something —**portraitist** *n*

portraiture /páwrtrichər/ *n* 1 the making of portraits 2 portraits in general

portray /pawr tráy/ *vt* 1 depict somebody or something visually 2 describe somebody or something in words 3 play a role in a play or film —**portrayable** *adj* —**portrayal** *n*

Port Said /-síd/ city in NE Egypt. Pop. 469,000 (1998).

Portsmouth /páwrtsməth/ 1 city in S England. Pop. 192,000 (1996). 2 city in SE New Hampshire. Pop. 25,388 (1998).

Port Stanley ♦ Stanley

Port Sudan city in NE Sudan. Pop. 305,385 (1993).

Portugal /páwrchoōg'l/ country in SW Europe, in the W Iberian Peninsula. Cap. Lisbon. Pop. 10,066,253 (2001).

~~Portugese~~ incorrect spelling of **Portuguese**

Portuguese /páwrchoō geēz/ *n* 1 the language of Portugal and Brazil 2 somebody from Portugal —**Portuguese** *adj*

Portuguese man-of-war *n* a sea organism resembling a jellyfish

pose[1] /pōz/ *v* **(posing, posed)** 1 *vti* adopt a physical posture for a photograph or painting, or position somebody or something for this purpose 2 *vi* impersonate somebody 3 *vt* cause something to exist *o pose a threat to peace* 4 *vt* ask a question 5 *vi* behave in a pretentious way *(disapproving)* ■ *n* 1 a posture 2 a pretence *(disapproving)*

pose[2] /pōz/ **(posing, posed)** *vt* baffle *(archaic)*

Poseidon /pə síd'n/ *n* in Greek mythology, the god of the sea. Roman equivalent **Neptune**

poser[1] /pózər/ *n* somebody who poses for a photograph or painting

poser[2] /pózər/ *n* a challenging problem

~~posess~~ incorrect spelling of **possess**

~~posession~~ incorrect spelling of **possession**

poseur /pō zúr/ *n* a person regarded as pretentious *(disapproving)*

posh *adj (infml)* 1 elegant, fashionable, and expensive 2 upper-class —**posh** *adv* —**poshly** *adv* —**poshness** *n*

ORIGIN The legend has become widely circulated that **posh** is an acronym formed from the initial letters of 'port out, starboard home', an allusion to the fact that wealthy passengers could afford the more expensive cabins on the port side of the ships going out to India, and on the starboard side returning home, which kept them out of the heat of the sun. Pleasant as this story is, it has never been substantiated. Another possibility is that **posh** may be the same word as the now obsolete *posh* 'dandy, swell', a slang term current around the end of the 19C.

posit /pózzit/ *vt* put forward for consideration or as an assumption *(fml)*

position /pə zísh'n/ *n* **1** the place where somebody or something is **2** a bodily posture **3** the way in which something is placed or arranged **4** a particular set of circumstances **5** a rank or role **6** a job or post **7** a viewpoint or policy **8** the correct or usual place ■ *vt* **1** put in a particular position **2** determine the site or location of —**positional** *adj*

position paper *n* an in-depth report giving an official view

positive /pózzətiv/ *adj* **1** confident and optimistic **2** not in doubt **3** impossible to disprove **4** producing good results o *a very positive experience* **5** indicating agreement or approval o *positive feedback* **6** in test results, indicating the presence of a particular organism or component **7** adds emphasis *(infml)* o *a positive disaster* **8** (*symbol* +) more than zero **9** with an electrical charge like that of a proton **10** describes a photographic image with shading that matches the subject **11** not comparative or superlative in degree ■ *n* **1** a positive number or value **2** a positive photographic image **3** an adjective or adverb in the positive degree —**positively** *adv* —**positiveness** *n* —**positivity** /pózzə tívvəti/ *n*

positive discrimination *n* the deliberate favouring of traditionally disadvantaged groups

positivism /pózzətivizəm/ *n* the theory that knowledge can only be acquired through direct observation or experience —**positivist** *n*, *adj* —**positivistic** /pózzəti vístik/ *adj*

posse /póssi/ *n* **1** *US* a group of citizens called upon to help a sheriff **2** any assembled group *(infml)* **3** a street gang *(slang)*

ORIGIN Posse is a mid-17C shortening of *posse comitatus* (early 17C), in Latin literally 'force of the county', the body of men above the age of 15 in a county whom a sheriff could summon to quell a riot or for some other purpose. The briefer **posse** was always more common in the United States.

possess /pə zéss/ *vt* **1** have or own **2** have as an ability or quality **3** influence the behaviour or thinking of **4** have sex with *(dated; sometimes offensive)* —**possessor** *n*

possessed /pə zést/ *adj* **1** being the possessor of something o *possessed of wealth and beauty* **2** controlled by a supposed supernatural force or a strong feeling **3** calm and self-controlled

possession /pə zésh'n/ *n* **1** the fact of possessing something **2** something that somebody owns **3** a colony *(often pl)* **4** the state of being controlled by a supposed supernatural force or strong feeling **5** occupancy of property **6** the fact of having something illegal **7** control of the ball or puck in a team game ■ **possessions** *npl* personal property

possessive /pə zéssiv/ *adj* **1** demanding all of somebody's attention or love **2** selfish **3** of ownership **4** showing possession in grammatical terms ■ *n* the possessive form of words, or a possessive form —**possessively** *adv* —**possessiveness** *n*

possibility /póssə billəti/ *n* (*pl* **-ties**) **1** something that is possible **2** the state of being possible ■ **possibilities** *npl* potential

possible /póssəb'l/ *adj* **1** able or likely to happen, be done, exist, or be true **2** potential —**possibly** *adv*

possum /póssəm/ *n* **1** *US* an opossum *(infml)* **2** *ANZ* a phalanger ◊ **play possum** feign death, illness, or sleep

post /pōst/ *n* **1** an upright pole or stake **2** an upright part of a frame **3** a message on an Internet newsgroup **4** a system for sending and delivering items **5** letters and packages sent to people **6** the collection or delivery of items to be sent **7** a situation of employment **8** a workplace or assigned station **9** a military base **10** a bugle call ■ *v* **1** *vt* display information in a public place **2** *vt* publish text electronically **3** *vt* update a computer database **4** *vti* send a message to an Internet newsgroup **5** *vt* send a letter or package **6** *vt* send somebody to a particular place to work **7** *vt* transfer a soldier to a new unit **8** *vt* *US* pay bail to set somebody free

post- *prefix* after, later o *postwar* o *postdate*

postage /pōstij/ *n* the price paid for delivery of an item of post

postage stamp *n* a paper stamp stuck on an item to show that postage has been paid ■ *adj* tiny o *a postage-stamp bikini*

postal /pōst'l/ *adj* of a post office or post service

postal note *n* *ANZ* a postal order

postal vote *n* a vote sent through the post

postbag /pōst bag/ *n* **1** a bag for items of post **2** the post that somebody has received

post-bellum /pōst bélləm/, **postbellum** *adj* after a war

postbox /pōst boks/ *n* *UK* a box in a public place where letters can be posted

postcard /pōst kaard/ *n* a card for sending a short message on

postcode /pōst kōd/ *n* a code for addresses used to facilitate mail sorting

postcode lottery *n* an unequal or inconsistent distribution of a public service according to area

postdate /pōst dáyt/ (**-dating, -dated**) *vt* **1** put a later date on a cheque in order to delay payment **2** happen later than something

postdoctoral /pōst dóktərəl/ *adj* of academic work undertaken after a doctorate

poster /pṓstər/ n a printed picture used as a decoration or advertisement

poster child n a person or thing appearing as a representative or illustrative example *(sometimes offensive)*

poste restante /pṓst rést ont/ n a post office department where post is kept until people collect it

posterior /po steéri ər/ adj **1** situated at the rear of something **2** near the back of the body ■ n the buttocks *(humorous)*

posterity /po stérrəti/ n *(fml)* **1** all future generations **2** all of somebody's descendants

poster paint n children's paint made with water soluble gum

post-free adj postpaid

postgraduate /pṓst gráddyōō ət/, *(infml)* **postgrad** adj relating to graduates ■ n a student with a first degree who is studying for a higher degree

post-haste /pṓst háyst/ adv quickly

post hoc /pṓst hók/ n the error of arguing that a previous event necessarily caused a subsequent event

posthumous /póstyōōməss/ adj **1** after somebody's death **2** published after the writer's death —**posthumously** adv

postindustrial /pṓst in dústri əl/ adj after the decline of heavy industry

posting¹ /pṓsting/ n a message on an Internet newsgroup

posting² /pṓsting/ n an appointment to a job or unit

Post-it tdmk a trademark for a self-sticking slip of paper sold in pad form

postman /pṓstmən/ (pl **-men** /-mən/) n a man who delivers post

postmark /pṓst maark/ n an official stamp that shows when an item was posted —**postmark** vt

postmaster /pṓst maastər/ n an official in charge of a postal district

postmistress /pṓst mistrəss/ n a woman official in charge of a postal district *(dated)*

postmodernism /pṓst móddərnizəm/ n a style or trend in architecture, art, and literature that developed from modernism

postmortem /pṓst máwrtəm/ n **1** a medical examination of a corpse **2** a retrospective analysis ■ adj occurring after death

postnatal /pṓst náytˈl/ adj after birth —**postnatally** adv

postnatal depression n depression that affects some women after giving birth

post office n **1** a place where people can post items and buy stamps **2** a national postal system

post office box n a numbered box at a post office where post is kept until the addressee collects it

postoperative /pṓst ópprətiv/ adj occurring after surgery

postpaid /pṓst páyd/ adj with the postage paid in advance

postpone /pōst pṓn/ (**-poning, -poned**) vt put off until a later time —**postponement** n

postprandial /pṓst prándi əl/ adj after a meal *(fml or humorous)*

postscript /pṓst skript/ n a short message added to a letter below the signature

post-structuralism n an intellectual movement that developed from structuralism

post-traumatic stress disorder n a psychological condition that affects some people who have suffered a severe trauma

postulant /póstyŏŏlənt/ n somebody who applies to join a religious order *(fml)* —**postulancy** n

postulate vt /póstyŏŏ layt/ (**-lating, -lated**) **1** assume to be true **2** make a claim for ■ n /póstyŏŏlət/ **1** something postulated **2** a statement underpinning a theory —**postulation** /póstyŏŏ láysh'n/ n

posture /póschər/ n **1** a position that the body can assume **2** the way that somebody carries his or her body when standing or walking **3** an attitude or pose ■ vi (**-turing, -tured**) **1** assume a false attitude in order to impress people **2** put your body into a particular posture —**postural** adj

postviral syndrome /pṓst vírəl-/ n MED = **chronic fatigue syndrome**

postwar /pṓst wáwr/ adj after a war

posy /pṓzi/ (pl **-sies**) n a small bunch of flowers

pot¹ n **1** a watertight container for cooking or storage **2** a similar container, e.g. a flowerpot or teapot **3** a dish or container made from clay **4** the total money bet in one hand of a card game ■ vt (**potting, potted**) **1** put a plant in a pot **2** preserve food in a pot ◊ **go to pot** deteriorate *(infml)*

pot² n cannabis *(slang)*

potable /pṓtəb'l/ adj suitable for drinking

potash /pót ash/ n a potassium compound used in fertilizers

potassium /pə tássi əm/ n *(symbol* **K**) a highly reactive metallic element. Use: coolant in nuclear reactors, in fertilizers.

ORIGIN The name **potassium** was coined in 1807 by Sir Humphry Davy. The basis of the word is *potash*, in which potassium is found. French *potasse*, the equivalent of *potash*, was adopted into English as *potass*, a form now obsolete. Davy formed **potassium** from this obsolete English word or the original *potash*.

potassium bromide n a white crystalline compound. Use: in lithography, medicine, photography.

potassium nitrate n a white crystalline salt. Use: in fireworks, explosives, matches, as fertilizer, meat preservative.

potato /pə táytō/ (pl **-toes**) n **1** a rounded white tuber cooked in various ways as a vegetable **2** the plant that produces potatoes

potato chip n ANZ, US, Can a potato crisp

potato crisp n UK a thin piece of fried potato eaten as a snack

~~potatoe~~ incorrect spelling of **potato**

potbelly /pót beli/ (*pl* **-lies**) *n* a bulging stomach —**potbellied** *adj*

potboiler /pót boylər/ *n* a book or film of low quality *(infml)*

> **ORIGIN** The purpose of a **potboiler** is to 'keep the pot boiling', to provide an author with enough money to be able to continue to buy food and eat.

pot-bound *adj* describes a plant that is too big for its current container

poteen /po teen, -cheen/ *n* illegally distilled alcohol in Ireland

potent /pót'nt/ *adj* **1** strong and effective **2** capable of having an erection and sexual intercourse —**potency** *n* —**potently** *adv*

potentate /pót'n tayt/ *n* a powerful person, especially a ruler

potential /pə ténsh'l/ *adj* possible but not yet realized ■ *n* **1** the capacity to develop and be successful **2** the work required to bring a unit of positive electric charge from infinity to a specified point in an electric field —**potentially** *adv*

potential energy *n* (*symbol V or* E_p) the energy stored in a body or system

potholder /pót hōldər/ *n* a fabric pad used to handle hot cooking pots and utensils

pothole /pót hōl/ *n* **1** a hole in a road surface **2** a vertical hole in a limestone area

potholing /pót hōling/ *n* the activity of exploring limestone potholes —**potholer** *n*

potion /pōsh'n/ *n* a medicinal, magical, or poisonous drink

potluck /pot lúk/ *n* the food that is available to an unexpected guest

Potomac /pə tóm ak/ river of the E United States, flowing eastwards from West Virginia into Chesapeake Bay. Length 616 km/383 mi.

pot plant *n* a plant grown in a flowerpot

potpourri /pō poóri, pōpə reé/ (*pl* **-ris**) *n* **1** a collection of fragrant dried flowers **2** a miscellaneous mixture

~~potray~~ incorrect spelling of **portray**

pot roast *n* a piece of beef cooked in its own juices in a covered pot —**pot-roast** *vti*

Potsdam /póts dam/ city in NE Germany. Pop. 138,268 (1997).

potsherd /pót shurd/, **potshard** /-shard/ *n* a piece of broken pottery

potshot /pót shot/ *n* **1** an easy shot in sports **2** a criticism levelled at an easy target

potted /póttid/ *adj* **1** growing in a pot **2** preserved in a pot **3** superficially summarized *(infml)*

potter[1] /póttər/ *n* a maker of pottery

potter[2] /póttər/ *vi* **1** do something in an unhurried manner **2** proceed aimlessly

Popperfoto

Beatrix Potter

Potter /póttər/, **Beatrix** (1866–1943) British children's writer and illustrator

potter's wheel *n* a rotating device for making pottery by hand

pottery /póttəri/ *n* **1** objects made of baked clay **2** the activity of making pottery

potting compost *n* nutrient-enriched soil for pot plants

potting shed *n* a garden shed

potty[1] /pótti/ (**-tier, -tiest**) *adj (infml)* **1** irrational **2** keen or enthusiastic —**pottiness** *n*

potty[2] /pótti/ (*pl* **-ties**) *n* a bowl used as a toilet for a small child

POTUS /pótəss/ *n US* the US president. Full form **President of the United States**

pouch /powch/ *n* **1** a small soft bag **2** a pocket of skin in an animal

pouf /poof/, **pouffe** *n* a solid padded piece of furniture used as a seat or footrest

poultice /póltiss/ *n* a warm moist substance applied to an injury

poultry /póltri/ *n* **1** domestic fowl *(+ sing or pl verb)* **2** the meat from poultry

pounce /pownss/ (**pouncing, pounced**) *vi* **1** jump or swoop suddenly on somebody or something **2** move quickly in attacking or taking something —**pounce** *n*

pound[1] /pownd/ *n* **1** the main unit of currency in the United Kingdom and several other countries **2** the main unit of the former currency of the Republic of Ireland **3** an avoirdupois unit of weight divided into 16 ounces **4** a troy unit of weight divided into 12 ounces **5** a unit of force based on the pound weight

pound[2] /pownd/ *v* **1** *vti* strike something hard and repeatedly **2** *vt* beat something to a pulp or powder **3** *vi* throb **4** *vt* attack somebody continuously **5** *vi* run with heavy steps

□ **pound out** *vt* produce with heavy blows or loud thumping

pound[3] /pownd/ *n* **1** an enclosure for stray animals **2** an enclosure for vehicles or other goods being held by an authority

Pound /pownd/, **Ezra** (1885–1972) US writer

poundage /pówndij/ *n* **1** payment per pound of weight **2** weight in pounds

pound sign *n* **1** the symbol (£) that indicates pound sterling **2** *US* a hash sign on a keypad or keyboard.

pound sterling (*pl* **pounds sterling**) *n* the official name for the unit of currency used in the United Kingdom

pour /pawr/ v **1** vt make a substance flow **2** vti serve a drink from a container **3** vi flow in large quantities **4** vi rain heavily **5** vi come or go in large numbers **6** vt express feelings in an unrestrained way

USAGE **pour** or **pore**? You **pour** from the pot into a cup, **pore** over a text ('study it carefully'), and have **pores** in your skin.

pout /powt/ v **1** vti push the lips outwards in sulkiness or sexiness **2** vi sulk —**pout** n —**poutingly** adv —**pouty** adj

poverty /póvvərti/ n **1** the state of lacking money or possessions **2** a lack of something

poverty line, poverty level n an income below which somebody is thought to live in poverty

poverty-stricken adj lacking money or possessions to a problematic degree

poverty trap n a situation in which the income from working would not adequately replace the state benefits forfeited

POW abbr prisoner of war

powder /pówdər/ n **1** a substance in the form of tiny loose particles **2** gunpowder ■ v **1** vt put powder on the face **2** vti turn into powder —**powdery** adj

powder keg n **1** a keg for gunpowder **2** a tense situation

powder puff n a pad used for powdering the skin of the face

powder room n a women's toilet

Powell /pố əl/, **Sir Anthony** (1906–2000) British novelist

Department of Defense, Washington, D.C.

Colin Powell

Powell /pów əl/, **Colin** (b. 1937) US general and US Secretary of State (2001–)

power /pów ər/ n **1** the ability or capacity to do something **2** control and influence **3** the authority to act **4** political control of a country **5** a person or organization with power **6** an important country **7** physical strength **8** persuasiveness **9** a skill **10** the energy that drives machinery **11** electricity **12** (symbol P) a measure of the rate of doing work or transferring energy **13** the number of times a quantity is to be multiplied by itself **14** the magnifying ability of a lens ■ adj **1** run by electricity or fuel **2** intended for business success ○ a power tie ■ v **1** vt provide the operating energy for **2** vi move energetically —**powerless** adj —**powerlessly** adv —**powerlessness** n ◊ **the powers that be** the people in authority

□ **power down** vti switch a computer off

□ **power up** vti switch a computer on

power base n the foundation of somebody's political power

powerboat /pów ər bōt/ n a powerful motorboat —**powerboating** n

power broker n somebody with political or commercial influence

power cut n a loss of electrical power

powerful /pów ərf'l/ adj **1** influential **2** physically strong **3** effective —**powerfully** adv —**powerfulness** n

powerhouse /pów ər howss/ (pl **-houses** /-howziz/) n somebody or something very productive (infml)

power line n a cable carrying electricity

power of attorney n the legal authority to act for another person

power plant n **1** a power station **2** a unit that powers a self-propelled object

power point n a socket providing electricity

power politics n political relations based on power (+ sing verb)

power station n a station or plant for generating electricity

power steering n a vehicle steering system in which supplementary engine power makes steering easier

power walking n quick walking for exercise —**power walker** n

powwow /pów wow/ n **1** a meeting for discussion (infml) **2** a Native American ceremony during which a shaman performs rituals

Powys /pów iss/ county in central Wales

pox n **1** venereal disease (infml) **2** any disease that causes scarring spots on the skin

Poznań /póz nan/ city in west-central Poland. Pop. 580,000 (1997).

pp[1] abbr **1** past participle **2** pianissimo

pp[2], **pp.** abbr pages

PR[1] abbr public relations

PR[2] abbr proportional representation

practicable /práktikəb'l/ adj **1** capable of being done **2** usable

practical /práktik'l/ adj **1** concerned with facts and experience, not with theory **2** useful **3** good at solving problems **4** suitable for everyday use **5** virtual (infml) ○ a practical disaster —**practicality** /prákti kálləti/ n

practical joke n a trick played on somebody for amusement —**practical joker** n

practically /práktikli/ adv **1** almost **2** in a practical way

practice /práktiss/ n **1** repetition done in order to improve performance **2** the performance of a religion, profession, or custom **3** the process of carrying out an idea **4** the work of a professional person **5** a habit or custom ■ vti US = **practise** ◊ see note at **habit**

~~practicle~~ incorrect spelling of **practical**

~~practicly~~ incorrect spelling of **practically**

practise /práktiss/ (**-tising, -tised**) v **1** vti repeat something in order to improve performance

2 *vt* do something as a custom 3 *vti* work in law or medicine 4 *vt* follow a religion

practised /práktist/ *adj* expert

practising /práktissing/ *adj* pursuing a particular activity

practitioner /prak tísh'nər/ *n* somebody who practises a profession

praesidium *n* POL = **presidium**

pragmatic /prag máttik/ *adj* 1 concerned with practical results 2 of philosophical pragmatism —**pragmatically** *adv*

pragmatics /prag máttiks/ *n* the study of language in use (+ *sing verb*)

pragmatism /prágmətizəm/ *n* 1 the attitude of somebody who thinks about practical results rather than principles 2 the theory that something should be evaluated according to its practical success —**pragmatist** *n*

Prague /praag/ capital of the Czech Republic. Pop. 1,193,270 (1999).

Praia /prí ə/ capital of the Republic of Cape Verde, in SE São Tiago island. Pop. 95,000 (1998).

prairie /práiri/ *n* an area of North American grassland

prairie dog *n* a North American burrowing rodent

praise /prayz/ *n* 1 an expression of admiration 2 worship and thanks to God or a deity ■ *vt* (**praising, praised**) 1 express admiration for 2 worship and thank

praiseworthy /práyz wurthi/ *adj* admirable —**praiseworthiness** *n*

praline /práa leen/ *n* 1 a paste made from crushed caramelized nuts 2 a chocolate with a praline filling

ORIGIN Praline represents part of the name of the French military officer Marshal de Plessis-Praslin (1598–1675), whose cook invented it.

pram *n* a small wheeled vehicle for carrying babies

prance (**prancing, pranced**) *v* 1 *vi* move in a lively exaggerated way 2 *vti* jump, or make a horse jump, forwards on the back legs —**prance** *n* —**prancing** *adj*

prank[1] *n* a practical joke —**prankster** *n*

prank[2] *vti* decorate or display something, somebody, or yourself ostentatiously (*fml*)

prarie incorrect spelling of **prairie**

prasad /prə sáad/ *n* Hindu religious offerings

praseodymium /práyzi ō dímmi əm/ *n* (*symbol* Pr) a rare metallic element. Use: alloys, colouring for glass.

prat *n* a person regarded as foolish (*slang insult*) ■ *vi* (**pratting, pratted**) behave in a manner regarded as thoughtless or exasperating (*disapproving*)

prate (**prating, prated**) *vi* talk annoyingly or about trivial things —**prate** *n* —**pratingly** *adv*

prattle /prátt'l/ (**-tling, -tled**) *vi* talk idly or childishly —**prattle** *n* —**prattlingly** *adv*

prawn *n* an edible crustacean like a large shrimp ■ *vi* fish for prawns —**prawner** *n*

◊ **come the raw prawn** *Aus* try to deceive or mislead somebody, usually by acting or pleading innocent (*infml*)

prawn cocktail *n* a bowl of prawns in a sauce

praxis /práksiss/ *n* (*fml*) 1 the performance or practical application of a skill 2 an established practice

Praxiteles /prak síttə leez/ (390?–330? BC) Greek sculptor

pray /pray/ *vti* 1 speak to God, a deity, or a saint 2 hope for something strongly 3 make an earnest request

---

SPELLCHECK Do not confuse the spelling of **pray** and **prey** ('a hunted animal or person'), which sound similar.

---

prayer /prair/ *n* 1 a spoken or unspoken communication with God, a deity, or a saint 2 the act of praying 3 a religious service with prayers (*often pl*) 4 an earnest request or desire 5 a slight chance

prayer beads *npl* a string of beads for counting prayers

prayer book *n* a book of set prayers for religious services

praying mantis *n* an insect with raised forelegs

Pré ♦ du Pré, Jacqueline

pre- *prefix* before, earlier, in advance ○ *pre-school* ○ *predate* ○ *prerequisite*

preach /preech/ *v* 1 *vti* give a religious sermon 2 *vt* give advice in an irritating way 3 *vt* urge people to accept something —**preacher** *n* —**preachy** *adj*

preamble /pree ámb'l/ *n* 1 an introductory explanation 2 something that precedes something else

prearrange /pree ə ráynj/ (**-ranging, -ranged**) *vt* arrange in advance

Precambrian /pree kámbri ən/ *n* the earliest geological period —**Precambrian** *adj*

precarious /pri káiri əss/ *adj* 1 dangerously uncertain or insecure 2 not well founded (*fml*) —**precariously** *adv*

precast /pree kaàst/ *adj* allowed to harden in a mould before positioning ○ *precast concrete* —**precast** *vt*

precaution /pri káwsh'n/ *n* something done to give protection against a possible undesirable event —**precautionary** *adj*

precede /pri seéd/ (**-ceding, -ceded**) *vt* 1 come or go before something 2 say or do something before something else

---

SPELLCHECK Do not confuse the spelling of **precede** and **proceed** ('begin or continue with an action'), which sound similar.

---

precedence /préssidənss/, **precedency** /-dənssi/ *n* 1 priority 2 relative importance in status

precedent *n* /préssidənt/ 1 something used as an example for later action or as justification for a later decision 2 an established practice ■ *adj* /préssidənt, pri seéd'nt/ preceding (*fml*)

preceding /pri séeding/ *adj* coming before

~~preceed~~ incorrect spelling of **precede**

~~preceence~~ incorrect spelling of **presence**

precept /prée sept/ *n* a principle or instruction guiding conduct *(fml)*

precinct /prée singkt/ *n* **1** a part of a town built for a particular purpose **2** US a city area patrolled by a police unit **3** US, Can an electoral district ■ **precincts** *npl* the area around a place

preciosity /préshi óssəti/ (*pl* **-ties**) *n* ridiculous overrefinement

precious /préshəss/ *adj* **1** worth a lot of money **2** greatly valued **3** not to be wasted **4** fastidious or affected ■ *adv* very o *have precious little time* —**preciousness** *n*

precious metal *n* gold, silver, or platinum

precious stone *n* a gemstone

precipice /préssəpiss/ *n* **1** a high cliff or crag **2** a very dangerous situation —**precipiced** *adj*

precipitate *adj* /pri síppi tayt, -tət/ **1** done or acting rashly **2** hurried **3** sudden ■ *v* /pri síppi tayt/ (**-tating, -tated**) **1** *vt* make something happen quickly **2** *vt* send somebody or something rapidly **3** *vi* fall from the sky as rain, snow, or hail **4** *vti* separate a solid out of a solution, or be separated from a solution ■ *n* /pri síppi tət, -tayt/ a suspension of small particles formed in a solution —**precipitately** *adv* —**precipitative** *adj*

precipitation /pri síppi táysh'n/ *n* **1** rain, snow, or hail **2** the formation of rain, snow, or hail **3** the formation of a suspension in a solution **4** great haste *(fml)*

precipitous /pri síppitəss/ *adj* **1** done rashly **2** high and steep —**precipitously** *adv* —**precipitousness** *n*

précis /práy see/ (*pl* same) *n* a summary —**précis** *vt*

precise /pri síss/ *adj* **1** exact or detailed **2** able to deal with small details **3** indicates something specific o *at that precise moment* **4** careful about details **5** distinct and correct —**precisely** *adv* —**preciseness** *n*

precision /pri sízh'n/ *n* **1** exactness **2** mathematical accuracy ■ *adj* made with exactness or accuracy o *precision instruments*

preclude /pri klood/ (**-cluding, -cluded**) *vt* **1** prevent or make impossible *(fml)* **2** exclude in advance —**preclusion** *n* —**preclusive** /-kloóssiv/ *adj*

precocious /pri kṓshəss/ *adj* mentally advanced compared to other children of the same age, often irritatingly so —**precociously** *adv* —**precociousness** *n* —**precocity** /pri kóssəti/ *n*

precognition /prée kog nísh'n/ *n* **1** the supposed ability to foresee the future **2** a pretrial investigation in Scotland —**precognitive** /prée kógnitiv/ *adj*

preconceived /prée kən séevd/ *adj* formed in the mind in advance —**preconceive** *vt* —**preconception** /-sépsh'n/ *n*

precondition /prée kən dísh'n/ *n* something that must be done first ■ *vt* prepare for a particular event or state

precursor /pri kúrssər/ *n* somebody or something that comes earlier

predate /prée dáyt/ (**-dating, -dated**) *vt* exist earlier than

predator /préddətər/ *n* **1** a carnivorous animal or destructive organism **2** somebody who plunders or destroys —**predatory** *adj*

predecease /prée di séess/ (**-ceasing, -ceased**) *vt* die before —**predecease** *n*

predecessor /préedi sessər/ *n* **1** the previous holder of a job **2** something replaced

predefined /prée di fínd/ *adj* established in advance

predestination /pree désti náysh'n/ *n* the doctrine that God or fate has decided everything in advance

predetermine /prée di túrmin/ (**-mining, -mined**) *vt* decide, ordain, or arrange in advance

predicament /pri díkəmənt/ *n* a difficult situation

predicate *n* /préddikət/ **1** the part of a sentence that contains all elements except the subject **2** something affirmed or denied ■ *vt* /préddi kayt/ (**-cating, -cated**) *(fml)* **1** base an opinion, action, or result on something **2** state something about the subject of a statement —**predication** /préddi káysh'n/ *n*

predict /pri díkt/ *vt* say what will happen —**predictability** /pri díktə bílləti/ *n* —**predictable** *adj* —**predictably** *adv* —**prediction** *n* —**predictor** *n*

predictive /prə díktiv/ *adj* **1** relating to the forecasting of a likely result or outcome o *a predictive medical test* **2** using technology that anticipates the word a computer user is in the process of keying o *predictive indexing*

predilection /prée di léksh'n/ *n* a particular liking

predispose /prée di spṓz/ (**-posing, -posed**) *vt* *(fml)* **1** cause to be favourable to something **2** cause to be liable or inclined to do something —**predisposal** *n* —**predisposition** /prée dispə zísh'n/ *n*

predominant /pri dómminənt/ *adj* **1** most common **2** most important —**predominance** *n* —**predominantly** *adv*

predominate /pri dómmi nayt/ (**-nating, -nated**) *vi* **1** be in the majority **2** be more important

~~predominately~~ incorrect spelling of **predominantly**

pre-eminent /pri émminənt/ *adj* highly distinguished or outstanding —**pre-eminence** *n* —**pre-eminently** *adv*

pre-empt /pri émpt/ *vt* **1** act to prevent **2** take the place of —**pre-emption** *n* —**pre-emptory** *adj*

pre-emptive /pri émptiv/ *adj* **1** done before others can act **2** intended to prevent an attack —**pre-emptively** *adv*

~~preemptory~~ incorrect spelling of **peremptory**

preen v 1 vi groom the feathers with the beak 2 vti spend a long time grooming and dressing in a fussy way

prefab /prée fab/ n a prefabricated building (infml)

prefabricate /pree fábbri kayt/ (-cating, -cated) vt produce in standard sections for assembly elsewhere —**prefabrication** /pree fábbri káysh'n/ n

preface /préffəss/ n 1 an introductory part of a text 2 a preliminary action ■ vt (-acing, -aced) 1 introduce with a preface 2 serve as an introduction to

---

ORIGIN In spite of appearances, **preface** has no etymological connection with face. It derives through French from Latin praefatio, which is literally 'something said beforehand' and so an exact parallel with the more basically English formation foreword.

---

prefatory /préffətəri/ adj acting as a preface —**prefatorily** adv

prefect /prée fekt/ n 1 a pupil who assists a teacher with discipline 2 a high-ranking regional administrative official in France or Italy 3 a French chief of police 4 in ancient Rome, a senior administrative or military official —**prefectorial** /pree fek táwri əl/ adj

prefecture /prée fekchər/ n 1 the district over which a prefect has jurisdiction 2 the position of a prefect —**prefectural** /pree fékchərəl/ adj

prefer /pri fúr/ (-ferring, -ferred) vt 1 like better or want more than something else 2 lay before a court o preferred charges

preferable /préffərəb'l/ adj more desirable —**preferably** adv

~~preferance~~ incorrect spelling of **preference**

~~prefered~~ incorrect spelling of **preferred**

preference /préffərənss/ n 1 the view that one person or thing is better than another 2 somebody or something regarded as better than others 3 a right to express a choice o We exercised our preference.

preference shares npl shares the holders of which are the first to receive dividends

preferential /préffə rénsh'l/ adj showing favouritism o preferential treatment —**preferentialism** n —**preferentially** adv

preferment /pri fúrmənt/ n (fml) 1 promotion to a higher position 2 a high-ranking position

prefigure /pree fíggər/ (-uring, -ured) vt 1 represent or suggest something important that develops later 2 think about something beforehand —**prefigurative** adj —**prefigurement** n

prefix /preéfiks/ n a word element that is attached to the beginning of words to change their meaning ■ vt 1 put in front of something else 2 add a prefix to —**prefixal** /prée fiks'l, pree fíks'l/ adj —**prefixation** /pree fik sáysh'n/ n

prefrontal lobotomy /pree frúnt'l/ n a lobotomy

pregnant /prégnənt/ adj 1 carrying unborn offspring within the body 2 significant or full of meaning —**pregnancy** n —**pregnantly** adv

preheat /pree heet/ vt heat in advance

prehensile /pri hén sīl/ adj able to take hold of things, especially by wrapping round them o a prehensile tail —**prehensility** /pree hen síllǝti/ n

prehistoric /pree hi stórrik/ adj of the period before recorded history —**prehistorian** /-stáwri ən/ n —**prehistorically** adv —**prehistory** /pree hístəri/ n

prejudge /júj/ (-judging, -judged) vt judge prematurely —**prejudgment** n

prejudice /préjjŏodiss/ n 1 an opinion formed beforehand and based on irrational feelings, insufficient knowledge, or stereotyping 2 the holding of ill-informed opinions 3 disadvantage or harm ■ vt (-dicing, -diced) 1 cause to form an irrational opinion in advance 2 affect adversely —**prejudiced** adj —**prejudicial** /préjjŏo dísh'l/ adj —**prejudicially** adv ◊ **without prejudice** in law, without doing any harm to somebody's legal rights or any claim that somebody has (fml)

prelate /préllət/ n a high-ranking member of the clergy —**prelatic** /pri láttik/ adj

preliminary /pri límminəri/ adj coming before something and leading up to it ■ n (pl -ies) an introductory or preparatory activity (often pl) —**preliminarily** adv

preliterate /pree líttərət/ adj without written language

prelude /préllyood/ n 1 a piece of classical music that introduces or precedes another one 2 an introductory event or occurrence ■ vt (-uding, -uded) act as prelude to

premarital /pree márrit'l/ adj before marriage

premature /prémməchər/ adj 1 happening earlier than is usual or desirable 2 born before completing the usual gestation period —**prematurely** adv

premeditate /pri méddi tayt/ (-tating, -tated) v 1 vt plan beforehand 2 vti ponder something in advance —**premeditated** adj —**premeditatedly** adv

premeditation /pri méddi táysh'n/ n 1 in law, the act of planning and intending a crime beforehand 2 reflection before action

premenstrual /pree ménstruəl/ adj immediately before a menstrual period

premenstrual syndrome n symptoms such as irritability and headache experienced by some women immediately before a menstrual period

premier /prémmi ər/ adj 1 best or most important 2 coming first ■ n 1 a prime minister 2 the leader of the government of an Australian state —**premiership** n

premiere /prémmi air/ n the first public performance or showing of something ■ vti (-miering, -miered) present or be presented publicly for the first time

premise /prémmiss/ n 1 a statement given as the evidence for a conclusion 2 the basis of an argument ■ vti (-ising, -ised) propose something as a premise in an argument

premises /prémmissiz/ *npl* a piece of land and the buildings on it

premium /preèmi əm/ *n* **1** the regular sum of money paid for an insurance policy **2** an additional sum of money **3** a prize **4** the amount above its nominal value for which something sells ■ *adj* high-quality

Premium Bond, Premium Savings Bond *n* a UK savings bond with cash prizes

premolar /pree mólar/ *n* a grinding tooth between a canine and molar —**premolar** *adj*

premonition /prémmə nísh'n/ *n* **1** a strong but irrational feeling that something is going to happen **2** a warning about the future —**premonitory** *adj*

prenatal /pree náyt'l/ *adj* before childbirth —**prenatally** *adv*

prenominal /pree nómmin'l/ *adj* used before a noun

prenuptial agreement /pree núpsh'l-/, **prenup** /preè nup/ *n* a financial agreement between marriage partners made before the marriage

preoccupation /pri ókyoŏ páysh'n/, **pre-occupancy** /pri ókyoŏpánssi/ (*pl* -**cies**) *n* **1** the fact of constantly thinking about something **2** the focus of somebody's constant attention

preoccupied /pri ókyoŏ pïd/ *adj* **1** completely absorbed in thinking about something **2** already occupied —**preoccupy** *vt*

preowned /pree ónd/ *adj* ANZ, US second-hand

prep *n* homework or study time at a boarding school or private school *(infml)*

preparation /préppə ráysh'n/ *n* **1** the work involved in preparing something **2** the state of being prepared **3** a mixture made for a particular purpose **4** homework or study time at a boarding school or private school

preparatory /pri párrətəri/ *adj* **1** serving to make something ready **2** introductory

preparatory school *n* **1** a private junior school **2** US a secondary school

prepare /pri páir/ (-**paring**, -**pared**) *v* **1** *vti* make something ready for use or action **2** *vt* get ready, or make somebody ready, for something **3** *vt* make by putting things together **4** *vt* plan in advance —**prepared** *adj*

prepay /pree páy/ (-**paid** /-páyd/) *vt* pay for beforehand —**prepayable** *adj* —**prepayment** *n*

~~preperation~~ incorrect spelling of **preparation**

preponderate /pri póndə rayt/ (-**ating**, -**ated**) *vi* be greater or dominant —**preponderance** *n* —**preponderant** *adj* —**preponderantly** *adv*

preposition /préppə zísh'n/ *n* a word used before a noun or pronoun to express connections and relationships —**prepositional** *adj*

LANGUAGE NOTE In certain circumstances a preposition can go at the end of a sentence; for instance, in the case of the phrasal verbs *attend to* and *put up with*: *Are you being attended to? This noise is hard to put up with.* Some questions and clauses opening with *what, which*, or *who*, for example, typically have the preposition at the end, as in *What on earth*

---

were they thinking about? Some infinitive clauses also have prepositions at their ends, as in *I've been invited to the dance, but I need someone to go with*

---

prepossessing /preè pə zéssing/ *adj* giving a pleasing impression —**prepossessingly** *adv*

preposterous /pri póstərəss/ *adj* outrageous or absurd —**preposterously** *adv* —**preposterousness** *n*

ORIGIN Preposterous comes from a Latin word meaning 'inverted', and this sense was once used in English. The development to 'absurd, perverse' had already taken place in Latin, however, and this was also adopted. Both senses appeared in the mid-16C, but after the 18C 'inverted' was usually accompanied by a self-conscious reference to the literalness of the use.

---

preppy /préppi/, **preppie** *adj* US, Can of young well-educated affluent people *(infml)* —**preppily** *adv*

preprocess /pree próssess/ *vt* analyse and process something, e.g. computer data, beforehand

preprogram /pree pró gram/ (-**gramming**, -**grammed**) *vt* **1** program a computer in advance **2** prepare somebody in such a way that a desired response is later assured

prep school *n* a preparatory school *(infml)*

prepubescent /preèpyoŏ béss'nt/ *adj* of the period just before puberty ■ *n* a prepubescent child

prequel /preèkwəl/ *n* an earlier part of a story told in a previous book or film

Pre-Raphaelite /preè ráffə līt, -ráffi ə-/ *n* a member of a 19C group of painters who aimed to revive an early naturalistic style of Italian painting —**Pre-Raphaelite** *adj* —**Pre-Raphaelitism** *n*

ORIGIN The **Pre-Raphaelites** are so called because they aimed to revive the style of Italian painting before Raphael (1483–1520).

---

prerecord /preè ri káwrd/ *vt* record in advance

prerequisite /pree rékwəzit/ *n* something needed as a prior condition —**prerequisite** *adj*

prerogative /pri róggətiv/ *n* **1** a privilege restricted to people occupying a particular rank or position **2** an individual right or privilege

Pres. *abbr* President

presage /préssij/ *n* **1** a portent or omen **2** a feeling that a particular thing is going to happen ■ *vt* (**presaging, presaged**) be a warning that something will happen

presbyter /prézbitər/ *n* **1** an ordained member of the clergy in many Christian churches **2** a lay official in a Presbyterian church

presbyterian /prézbi teèri ən/ *adj* **1** of church administration by elected lay members **2 Presbyterian** of the Reformed churches ■ *n* **1** a supporter of church administration by elected lay officials **2 Presbyterian** a member of a Presbyterian church **—Presbyterianism** *n*

presbytery /prézbitəri/ (*pl* **-ies**) *n* 1 a group of presbyters 2 the governing body of a Presbyterian church 3 a part of a church for the use of the clergy only

preschool /preé skool/ *adj* 1 under school age 2 for preschool children ■ *n* a school for preschool children **—preschooler** *n* **—preschooling** *n*

prescient /préssi ənt/ *adj* knowing in advance **—prescience** *n*

prescribe /pri skríb/ (**-scribing, -scribed**) *v* 1 *vti* order the use of a particular medication 2 *vt* recommend a remedy 3 *vt* lay down a rule **—prescribable** *adj*

prescription /pri skrípsh'n/ *n* 1 a written order for medicine or corrective lenses 2 a prescribed medication 3 a proven formula for something 4 the establishing of regulations

prescription drug *n* a drug available only on prescription

prescriptive /pri skríptiv/ *adj* making or adhering to rules or regulations **—prescriptively** *adv* **—prescriptiveness** *n*

presence /prézz'nss/ *n* 1 the fact of being present 2 the area within sight or earshot of somebody 3 an impressive appearance or bearing 4 a person who is present 5 military or diplomatic personnel stationed in a place

presence of mind *n* the ability to stay calm in a crisis

present[1] *v* /pri zént/ 1 *vt* give something to 2 *vt* make somebody a gift or an award of 3 *vt* show or display something ○ *presented his best side to the camera* 4 *vt* pose or be the cause of ○ *presented a threat to national security* 5 *vt* bring a legal charge against 6 *vt* introduce formally 7 *vt* bring before the public 8 *vr* appear or arise ○ *when opportunity presents itself* ■ *n* /prézz'nt/ a gift **—presenter** *n* ◊ See note at **give**

present[2] /prézz'nt/ *adj* 1 currently happening or in existence 2 in a particular place ■ *n* 1 the current time 2 the verb tense used for indicating the current time, or a form in this tense

presentable /pri zéntəb'l/ *adj* 1 fit to appear in public 2 fit to be displayed or given **—presentably** *adv*

presentation /prézz'n táysh'n/ *n* 1 the act of presenting something 2 the way something appears when presented 3 a prepared talk or performance for an audience

present-day *adj* existing in modern times

presentiment /pri zéntimənt/ *n* a feeling that something will happen

presently /prézz'ntli/ *adv* 1 soon 2 at the present time *(sometimes objected to)*

present participle *n* the form of a verb that ends in '-ing' in English and suggests a progressive or active sense

present perfect *n* the form of a verb formed with 'has' or 'have' and a past participle

preservation /prézzər váysh'n/ *n* 1 protection from harm 2 the fact or process of keeping something unchanged **—preservationism** *n* **—preservationist** *n*

preservative /pri zúrvətiv/ *n* something that prevents spoilage or decay, especially a food additive **—preservative** *adj*

preserve /pri zúrv/ *vt* (**-serving, -served**) 1 make sure that something does not change or deteriorate 2 keep up or maintain something 3 make jam 4 protect somebody or something from danger or harm *(fml or literary)* ■ *n* 1 somebody's private place or particular area of activity 2 jam *(often pl)* 3 US an area where wildlife is protected **—preservable** *adj* **—preserver** *n*

preset /pree sét/ *vt* (**-setting, -set**) set a machine to switch on later ■ *n* a control that turns a machine on later

preside /pri zíd/ (**-siding, -sided**) *vi* be officially in charge or responsible

president /prézzidənt/, **President** *n* 1 the head of state of a republic 2 the highest-ranking member of an association 3 US, Can the head of a company 4 the head of some educational establishments **—presidency** *n* **—presidential** /prézzi dénsh'l/ *adj*

president-elect (*pl* **presidents-elect**) *n* a president who has been elected but has not yet taken office

presidium /pri síddi əm, -zíddi-/ (*pl* **-ums** or **-a** /-di ə/), **praesidium** (*pl* **-a**) *n* an executive committee in the former Soviet Union and other Communist countries

Elvis Presley

Presley /prézzli/, **Elvis** (1935–77) US singer and actor

press[1] *v* 1 *vti* push against something steadily 2 *vt* squeeze the juice out of 3 *vt* smooth using a hot iron 4 *vt* change the shape of by squeezing or applying a steady weight 5 *vt* hold tightly 6 *vt* force to do something 7 *vt* try to obtain something from ○ *pressed him for an apology* 8 *vti* pester *(dated or literary)* ■ *n* 1 the act of pressing something 2 a tightly-packed crowd, or the force they exert 3 a device for pressing something 4 a device for flattening clothes ○ *a trouser press* 5 newspapers or reporters in general 6 comments by journalists ○ *got a good press* 7 a machine for printing 8 a publishing company *(in names)* 9 the process of printing ○ *about to go to press* **—pressed** *adj* **—presser** *n* ◊ **pressed for** be short of something

□ **press for** *vti* emphatically demand something of somebody

□ **press on** *vi* carry on urgently or doggedly

press² *vt* force somebody into military service ■ *n* the forcing of people into military service

press agency *n* a news agency

press agent *n* somebody employed to get publicity for a client

press box *n* an area where journalists sit to report on an event

press conference *n* an arranged meeting with journalists

press gallery *n* a balcony for journalists to watch proceedings

press gang *n* formerly, a group with the job of forcing people into military service

press-gang *vt* force somebody to do something

pressing /préssing/ *adj* 1 urgent 2 very persistent —**pressingly** *adv* —**pressingness** *n*

press officer *n* somebody providing news to journalists about an organization's activities

press release *n* a statement or account of a news event supplied to journalists

press stud *n* a small fastener made up of two pieces that are snapped together

press-up *n UK, NZ* a keep-fit exercise in which the person lies face downwards and raises the upper body on the arms

pressure /préshər/ *n* 1 the process of applying a steady weight or force 2 a constant state of stress and urgency 3 an outside influence or requirement that affects behaviour or feelings 4 (*symbol p*) the force acting on a surface divided by the area over which it acts ■ *vt* (**-suring, -sured**) try to persuade somebody to do something

pressure cooker *n* a heavy cooking pot that steams food at high pressure and temperatures —**pressure-cook** *vt*

pressure group *n* a group working for social or political change

pressure point *n* a point on the body where an artery can be compressed

pressurize /préshə rīz/ (**-izing, -ized**), **pressurise** *vt* 1 increase the air pressure in an enclosed space or container 2 put somebody under pressure to do something —**pressurization** /préshə rī záysh'n/ *n*

prestige /pre stéezh, -stéej/ *n* 1 respect associated with high quality, success, or high rank 2 glamour —**prestigious** /pre stíjjəss/ *adj* —**prestigiously** *adv*

presto /préstó/ *adv* 1 very fast (*musical direction*) 2 suddenly (*infml*) —**presto** *adj*

Prestwich /préstwich/ town in NW England. Pop. 31,801 (1991).

presumably /pri zyóoməbli/ *adv* it is reasonable to suppose

presume /pri zyóom/ (**-suming, -sumed**) *v* 1 *vti* accept that something is true 2 *vi* behave arrogantly or overconfidently (*usually in negative statements*) —**presumable** *adj* —**presuming** *adj*

presumption /pri zúmpsh'n/ *n* 1 something believed without actual evidence 2 rudeness or arrogance 3 a legal inference

~~presumptious~~ incorrect spelling of **presumptuous**

presumptive /pri zúmptiv/ *adj* probable (*fml*) —**presumptively** *adv* —**presumptiveness** *n*

presumptuous /pri zúmptyŏŏ əss, -zúmpshəss/ *adj* rude or arrogant —**presumptuously** *adv*

presuppose /prèe sə póz/ (**-posing, -posed**) *vt* 1 assume in advance 2 require as a prior condition —**presupposition** /prèe supə zísh'n/ *n*

pretax /prée táks/ *adj* before the deduction of tax

preteen /prée téen/, **preteenager** /-téen ayjər/ *n* a child between 9 and 12 years old

pretence /pri ténss/ *n* 1 an insincere or feigned action or a false appearance 2 an unwarranted claim (*often in the negative*) ○ *makes no pretence of expertise* 3 make-believe

pretend /pri ténd/ *v* 1 *vti* act as if something were true 2 *vt* make an insincere claim about ○ *I don't pretend to be an expert.* 3 *vt* mislead somebody about ○ *pretending to be ill* 4 *vi* claim ownership of or a right to something (*fml*) ○ *pretends to the throne* —**pretended** *adj* —**pretender** *n*

pretense *n US* = **pretence**

pretension /pri ténsh'n/ *n* 1 a questionable claim to something (*often pl and with negatives*) 2 affected and usually ostentatious behaviour

pretentious /pri ténshəss/ *adj* 1 self-important and affected 2 made to look or sound important —**pretentiously** *adv* —**pretentiousness** *n*

preterite /préttərit/ *n* the past tense of a verb —**preterite** *adj*

preternatural /prèetər náchərəl/ *adj* 1 exceeding what is usual in nature (*fml or literary*) 2 supernatural or uncanny (*literary*) —**preternaturally** *adv*

pretext /prée tekst/ *n* a made-up excuse

Pretoria /pri táwri ə/ administrative capital of South Africa. Pop. 1,314,000 (1995).

prettify /prítti fī/ (**-fies, -fied**) *vt* make pretty, especially superficially —**prettification** /prìttifi káysh'n/ *n*

pretty /prítti/ *adj* (**-tier, -tiest**) 1 having a pleasant face 2 nice to look at or listen to 3 large in amount (*infml*) ○ *cost a pretty penny* 4 very bad (*infml*) ○ *got into a pretty mess* ■ *adv* to a fairly large extent (*infml*) ◇ **pretty well** nearly completely (*infml*)

pretzel /préts'l/ *n* a salted knot-shaped or stick-shaped snack biscuit (*often pl*)

prevail /pri váyl/ *vi* 1 be unbeaten and in control 2 be the most common or frequent 3 exist currently (*fml*) —**prevailing** *adj* —**prevailingly** *adv*

□ **prevail on** *or* **upon** *vt* persuade

prevalent /prévvələnt/ adj found commonly or widely —**prevalence** n —**prevalently** adv ◊ See note at **widespread**

prevaricate /pri várri kayt/ (-**cating**, -**cated**) vi avoid giving a direct or honest answer or opinion —**prevarication** /pri várri káysh'n/ n —**prevaricator** n

~~prevelant~~ incorrect spelling of **prevalent**

prevent /pri vént/ vt **1** stop from taking place **2** stop from doing something —**preventable** adj —**prevention** n

preventive /pri véntiv/, **preventative** /pri véntətiv/ adj done with or having the purpose of preventing something —**preventative** n —**preventive** n

preview /prée vyoo/ n **1** a showing of something, e.g. a film or exhibition, in advance **2** a description of a forthcoming broadcast ■ vt show or describe in advance

previous /préévi əss/ adj **1** coming before somebody or something of the same kind **2** already arranged ○ a previous engagement —**previously** adv

prewar /prée wáwr/ adj before the war

prey /pray/ (pl same or preys) n **1** animals hunted by other animals as food **2** somebody treated cruelly by others ◊ See note at **pray**
□ **prey on** or **upon** vt **1** hunt and kill other animals for food **2** victimize somebody

price n **1** the cost of something bought or sold **2** something sacrificed to get something else ■ vt (**pricing**, **priced**) decide, mark, or find out the price of ◊ **at a price** for a lot of money ◊ **at any price** no matter how much it costs ◊ **beyond price** priceless ◊ **have a price on your head** have had a reward offered for your capture or death ◊ **price out of the market** charge an extremely high price

Price, Leontyne (b. 1927) US operatic soprano

price-earnings ratio n the ratio of a share's price to its earnings

price fixing n the artificial setting of prices by producers or a government

priceless /príssləss/ adj **1** very valuable **2** hilarious (infml)

price tag n a label saying what something costs

pricey /príssi/ (-**ier**, -**iest**), **pricy** adj expensive (infml) —**priceyness** n

prick v **1** vt make a small hole through or in **2** vti hurt in a stinging way **3** vt cause to feel sudden unease ○ His conscience pricked him. **4** vt mark out on a surface with tiny holes ■ n **1** a quick sharp pain **2** a small puncture **3** a taboo term for a penis (offensive) **4** a taboo term for a man regarded as contemptible or unpleasant (insult) ◊ **prick up your ears** listen intently

prickle /prík'l/ n **1** a sharp pointed projection on a plant part **2** a tingling feeling ■ vti (-**ling**, -**led**) hurt in a stinging way

prickly /príkli/ (-**lier**, -**liest**) adj **1** with small sharp spikes **2** irritating to the skin **3** easily offended or annoyed (infml) —**prickliness** n

prickly heat n a rash caused by heat

prickly pear n a cactus with pear-shaped fruits

pricy adj = **pricey** (infml)

pride n **1** a feeling of personal superiority **2** a proper sense of your own value **3** satisfaction with something you have done or possess **4** a source of personal satisfaction **5** a group of lions —**prideful** adj —**pridefully** adv ◊ **pride of place** the most important position

priest /preest/ n **1** an ordained minister in some Christian denominations **2** a spiritual leader or teacher in a non-Christian religion —**priesthood** n —**priestly** adj

priestess /pree stéss, preést ess, preéstiss/ n a woman who is a spiritual leader of a pagan religion

Priestley /preestli/, **Joseph** (1733–1804) British chemist and religious radical

prig n a smug morally upright person (disapproving) —**priggery** n —**priggish** adj

prim (**primmer**, **primmest**) adj **1** prudish **2** formal and proper in manner or appearance —**primly** adv —**primness** n

prima ballerina /préemə-/ n a principal woman dancer in a ballet company

primacy /prímassi/ (pl -**cies**) n **1** the state of being first in importance ○ Speech is regarded as having primacy over writing. **2** the position or period of office of a church primate

prima donna /preémə dónnə/ (pl **prima donnas**) n **1** a leading woman opera singer **2** a person regarded as demanding and difficult to please (insult)

primaeval adj = **primeval**

prima facie /prímə fáyshi/ adv at first glance ■ adj **1** clear from a first impression **2** legally sufficient to establish a fact

primal /prím'l/ adj **1** first or original **2** primary or most significant

primarily /prímərəli, prī márrəli/ adv **1** mainly or mostly **2** originally or at first

primary /prímari/ adj **1** first in a sequence or development **2** most important ■ n (pl -**ies**) in the United States, a preliminary election of candidates for a government post

primary care n the level of professional health care given by a general practitioner or nurse

primary colour n any of the basic colours from which all other colours can be produced

primary school n a school for the first years of a child's compulsory education

primate[1] /prí mayt/ n **1** a member of an order of mammals including human beings, apes, and monkeys **2** also **Primate** an archbishop or high-ranking bishop —**primatial** /prī máysh'l/ adj

~~primative~~ incorrect spelling of **primitive**

prime[1] adj **1** of the best quality **2** first in importance or rank ■ n **1** the best stage of something ○ in the prime of life **2** the earliest period of something **3** also **prime number** a whole number that is not divisible without a remainder except by itself and one —**primeness** *n*

prime² *v* **1** *vti* make or become ready for use **2** *vt* prepare a surface for painting **3** *vt* put a charge in a gun **4** *vt* put liquid in a pump to get it started **5** *vt* brief somebody on how to behave or answer questions

prime cost *n* the cost of the material and labour necessary to make a product

prime minister *n* **1** the head of a cabinet and chief executive in a parliamentary democracy **2** a ruler's chief minister —**prime ministerial** *adj* —**prime ministership** *n*

prime mover *n* **1** the most important person or thing in initiating and continuing a process **2** God

primer¹ /prímər/ *n* **1** a book used to teach young children to read **2** an introductory text

primer² /prímər/ *n* an undercoat of paint or sealant

prime time *n* the hours of highest television viewing —**primetime** *adj*

primeval /prī meev'l/, **primaeval** *adj* ancient and original

primitive /prímmətiv/ *adj* **1** at or of the first stages of something **2** of or appearing in an early stage of biological development **3** very simple in design or construction **4** not relying on modern technology for comfort ○ *primitive camping facilities* ■ *n* **1** somebody or something from an original stage **2** somebody from a culture with simple technologies *(often offensive)* **3** an untrained artist, or a work by one —**primitively** *adv* —**primitiveness** *n*

primogenitor /prímō jénnitər, preèmō-/ *n (fml)* **1** the first ancestor of a people or group **2** any ancestor

primogeniture /prímō jénnichər, preèmō-/ *n (fml)* **1** status as a first-born child **2** a first-born child's right of inheritance

primordial /prī máwrdi əl/ *adj* **1** existing at the beginning of time or the development of something **2** basic or essential

primp *vti* groom in a fussy way

primrose /prím rōz/ *n* a plant with pale yellow flowers

primula /prímmyŏŏlə/ *(pl* **-las** *or same) n* a small perennial plant with colourful flowers

prince *n* **1** a son of a monarch or of a monarch's son **2** a man who rules a principality **3** a high-ranking nobleman in some European countries —**princedom** *n*

prince charming, Prince Charming *n* a charming man

ORIGIN The original **prince charming** is the prince whom the fairy-tale character Cinderella was able to meet at a ball with the help of her fairy godmother, after being left at home by her sisters. The story was popularized by a 1697 collection of traditional tales set down by the French writer Charles Perrault (1628–1703).

Prince Edward Island island province in SE Canada. Cap. Charlottetown. Pop. 138,928 (2000). —**Prince Edward Islander** *n*

princely /prínssli/ *(-lier, -liest) adj* **1** of a prince **2** very expensive or generous —**princeliness** *n*

princess /prin séss, prínsess/ *(pl* **-cesses**) *n* **1** a daughter of a monarch or of a monarch's daughter **2** a prince's wife **3** a woman who rules a principality **4** a high-ranking noblewoman in some European countries

princess royal *(pl* **princesses royal**) *n* a monarch's eldest daughter

principal /prínssip'l/ *adj* of primary importance ■ *n* **1** the leading or most highly ranked person **2** a significant participant **3** a head of a school **4** *also* **principal teacher** in Scotland, a head of a school department **5** a lead performer **6** the original amount invested or borrowed, or what remains of that **7** a person represented by another in a legal matter —**principally** *adv* —**principalship** *n*

USAGE principal or **principle**? **Principle** is a noun only, as in *the principles of a democratic system* and *a woman of principle*. **Principal**, as a noun, means 'a school administrator', 'an important participant', and 'a monetary amount invested'. As an adjective it means 'main': *our principal* [not *principle*] *reason for an appeal*.

principal boy *n* a lead male role in a pantomime, traditionally acted by a woman

principality /prínssə pálləti/ *n (pl* **-ties**) a territory ruled by a prince or princess ■ **principalities** *npl* one of the orders of angels in the traditional Christian hierarchy

principal parts *npl* **1** the basic verb forms from which other forms are derived in an inflected language **2** the infinitive, past tense, and participial forms of an English verb

principle /prínssip'l/ *n* **1** a basic law or assumption in a system of thought **2** an ethical standard **3** the basic way in which something works —**principled** *adj* ◇ **in principle** in theory, or in the essentials ◇ **on principle** because of belief in a particular ethical standard ◇ See note at **principal**

print *n* **1** a mark made by pressing something onto a surface **2** characters printed or written on a surface ○ *in small print* **3** status as a published text or author ○ *wants to get into print* **4** an artwork made by inking a raised design and pressing it onto paper or another surface **5** fabric with an inked or painted design ○ *a print dress* **6** a photograph made from a negative **7** a copy of a film ■ *vti* **1** make a document or publication using a printing press or computer printer **2** publish something on paper **3** mark something with lettering or a design using pressure ○ *prints the logo on T-shirts* **4** write something using separated letters rather than cursive script **5** make a copy of a photograph from a negative ■ *adj* of the published media ◇ **out of print** not currently available from a publisher

□ **print out** *vt* produce a printed copy of data from a computer

printable /príntəb'l/ *adj* **1** suitable for printing or publication **2** able to be printed

printed circuit *n* an electronic circuit in which components and connections are formed by etching a metallic coating on an insulating board

printed matter *n* published material such as books, magazines, and catalogues

printer /príntər/ *n* **1** a person or company in the printing trade **2** a machine for printing text or images

printing /prínting/ *n* **1** the production of copies of documents, publications, or images **2** printed characters **3** letters written separately rather than in cursive script, or the writing of such letters

printing press *n* a machine for pressing inked set type or etched plates onto paper or textiles

printout /print owt/ *n* a paper copy of data printed from a computer

print run *n* the production or output of one session of printing

prion /prí ən, preé ən/ *n* an infectious protein particle

prior[1] /prí ər/ *adj* **1** earlier **2** more important or basic

prior[2] /prí ər/ *n* **1** an officer in a monastery of a rank below abbot **2** a man who heads a religious community

prioress /prí ə réss/ *n* **1** an officer in a convent of a rank below abbess **2** a woman who heads a religious community

prioritize /prī órri tīz/ (-**tizing**, -**tized**), **prioritise** *v* **1** *vti* rank things according to importance or urgency **2** *vt* rank as the most important or urgent —**prioritization** /prī órri tī záysh'n/ *n*

priority /prī órriti/ (*pl* -**ties**) *n* **1** the state of having greater or the greatest importance or urgency **2** somebody or something ranked as having great importance or urgency **3** the state of having preceded something else

priory /prí əri/ (*pl* -**ies**) *n* a religious community headed by a prior or prioress, or the home of such a community

prise (**prising**, **prised**) *vt* **1** force something open with a lever **2** extract information

prism /prízzəm/ *n* a polygonal solid for separating white light into a spectrum of colours

prismatic /priz máttik/ *adj* **1** of a prism **2** describes light separated into the colours of the spectrum by a prism

prison /prízz'n/ *n* a place where criminals and people awaiting trial are confined

prison camp *n* a camp for prisoners of war

prisoner /prízz'nər/ *n* **1** somebody held in prison **2** somebody held against his or her will

prisoner of conscience *n* somebody imprisoned by a state because of his or her beliefs

prisoner of war *n* a soldier captured and imprisoned by the enemy

~~prisonner~~ incorrect spelling of **prisoner**

prissy /príssi/ (-**sier**, -**siest**) *adj* very prudish and proper —**prissily** *adv* —**prissiness** *n*

Priština /preéshtinə/ city in central Kosovo, Federal Republic of Yugoslavia. Pop. 155,496 (1991).

pristine /prís teen/ *adj* **1** immaculately clean and neat **2** in or of an original state

Pritchett /príchit/, **Sir V. S.** (1900–97) British writer

privacy /prívvəssi, prívvəssi/ *n* **1** the state of being apart from others **2** freedom from the observation, intrusion, and attention of others

private /prívvət/ *adj* **1** not for others to see or know about **2** secluded **3** not open to the public **4** acting in a personal rather than official capacity **5** not supported by government funding ○ *private enterprise* **6** requiring special knowledge to understand ○ *a private joke* ■ *n* a soldier of the lowest rank —**privately** *adv* —**privateness** *n*

private banking *n* management by a bank of a customer's wealth in its entirety

private detective, private investigator *n* a detective who is not a member of the police and is available for private hire

private enterprise *n* **1** business not owned or regulated by the government **2** a privately owned company

privateer /prívə teér/ *n* **1** a private ship authorized to engage in war **2** somebody sailing on a privateer

private eye *n* a private detective (*infml*)

private income *n* income not derived from working

private life *n* the part of somebody's life connected with personal relationships and activities rather than work or public duties

private member *n* a member of parliament who does not hold a ministerial post

private patient *n* a patient paying for medical treatment

private secretary *n* a secretary employed for somebody's personal or confidential affairs

privation /prī váysh'n/ *n* **1** the lack of life's necessities **2** depriving somebody of something

privatize /prívə tīz/ (-**tizing**, -**tized**), **privatise** *vt* take out of state ownership or control —**privatization** /prívə tī záysh'n/ *n*

~~privelage, privilage, priviledge~~ incorrect spelling of **privilege**

privet /prívvit/ *n* a common evergreen shrub used for hedges

privilege /prívvəlij/ *n* **1** a right or benefit that is not available to everyone **2** the advantages enjoyed by an elite group **3** a special honour ○ *a privilege to work with you* ■ *vt* (-**leging**, -**leged**) grant a privilege or privileges to —**privileged** *adj*

privy /prívvi/ *adj* **1** sharing secret knowledge ○ *privy to the planned surprise* **2** of somebody, especially the British monarch, as a private individual rather than in an official capacity ■ *n* (*pl* **-ies**) an outside toilet

privy council *n* a ruler's committee of advisers —**privy counsellor** *n*

Privy Purse *n* 1 the British monarch's personal allowance from public funds 2 an official who manages the British monarch's personal finances

prize[1] *n* 1 an award for a winner of a contest or competition 2 something highly valued, especially because it is hard to get ■ *vt* (**prizing, prized**) value very highly ■ *adj* worthy of or given a prize ◊ See note at **prise**

ORIGIN The two nouns **prize** are etymologically distinct. **Prize** 'award' is in fact a variant form of *price* and derives ultimately from Latin *pretium* 'price', which also gave us the verb *praise*. **Prize** 'captured ship' was adopted from French, where it meant literally 'something seized or taken'.

prize[2] *n* a captured ship or ship's cargo

prizefight /príz fìt/ *n* a boxing match for money —**prizefighter** *n* —**prizefighting** *n*

prize-giving *n* an occasion when prizes are given, especially for schoolwork

prizewinner /príz wìnər/ *n* somebody or something that wins a prize —**prizewinning** *adj*

pro[1] /prṓ/ *n* (*pl* **pros**) 1 an argument in favour of something 2 a person or side arguing in favour of something ■ *prep* in favour of ■ *adv* in favour

pro[2] /prṓ/ (*pl* **pros**) *n* 1 a professional, especially a sportsperson (*infml*) 2 a skilled person or expert —**pro** *adj, adv*

pro[3] /prṓ/ *abbr* professional practice (*in Internet addresses*)

pro- *prefix* 1 substituting for, acting in place of ◦ *pronoun* 2 in favour of ◦ *pro-life* 3 before, earlier than ◦ *prognosis* 4 in front of ◦ *prognathous*

proactive /prō áktiv/ *adj* taking the initiative rather than reacting to events —**proactively** *adv*

pro-am /prṓ ám/ *adj* combining professionals and amateurs ■ *n* a pro-am competition

probability /próbbə bílləti/ (*pl* **-ties**) *n* 1 the state of being probable 2 something likely to happen 3 the mathematical likelihood of an event

probable /próbbəb'l/ *adj* likely to exist, occur, or be true ■ *n* somebody or something likely to be chosen or to do something —**probably** *adv*

probate /prṓ bayt/ *n* legal certification of the validity of a will

probate court *n* a court that probates wills

probation /prə báysh'n/ *n* 1 the supervision of an offender in the community by a probation officer 2 a period of testing somebody's suitability for a job or other role —**probational** *adj* —**probationary** *adj*

probationer /prə báysh'nər/ *n* somebody on probation

probation officer *n* a supervisor of offenders released into the community under condition of good behaviour

probe *n* 1 a thorough investigation 2 an exploratory expedition or device ◦ *a space probe* 3 a long thin surgical instrument for exploring or examining ■ *vti* (**probing, probed**) 1 investigate thoroughly 2 explore or examine using a probe —**probingly** *adv*

probity /prṓbəti/ *n* moral integrity and honesty

problem /próbbləm/ *n* 1 a situation or person presenting a difficulty 2 a puzzle to be solved ■ *adj* hard to deal with

SYNONYMS **problem, mystery, puzzle, riddle, conundrum, enigma** CORE MEANING: something difficult to solve or understand

problematic /próbblə máttik/, **problematical** /-máttik'l/ *adj* presenting a problem or difficulty —**problematically** *adv*

~~probly~~ incorrect spelling of **probably**

pro bono /prō bṓnō/ *adj, adv* done for the public good without compensation

proboscis /prō bóssiss/ (*pl* **-cises** or **-ces** /-seez/ or **-cides** /-bóssi deez/) *n* a long flexible snout, especially an elephant's trunk

~~procede~~ incorrect spelling of **proceed**

procedure /prə seéjər/ *n* 1 an established or correct method of doing something 2 any means of doing something —**procedural** *adj*

proceed /prə seéd/ *vi* 1 go on to do something 2 continue with a course of action 3 progress 4 go in a particular direction, especially forwards 5 bring a legal action against somebody 6 arise or develop from something ◊ See note at **precede**

proceedings /prə seédingz/ *npl* 1 a series of events 2 an official record of a meeting

proceeds /prṓ seedz/ *npl* the money obtained from a transaction

process[1] /prṓ sess/ *n* 1 a series of actions directed towards a particular aim 2 a series of natural occurrences producing a change or development 3 a summons to appear in court 4 the entire proceedings in a lawsuit 5 a natural outgrowth on an organism ■ *vt* 1 prepare or treat something using a set procedure or a particular process 2 deal with somebody or something according to a set procedure 3 use a computer program to work on data

process[2] /prə séss/ *vi* move in a procession

procession /prə sésh'n/ *n* 1 a group of people or vehicles moving forwards in a line as part of a celebration, commemoration, or demonstration 2 forward movement in a procession

processional /prə sésh'nəl/ *adj* of or for a procession ■ *n* a piece of music for a procession

processor /prṓ sessər/ *n* 1 somebody or something that processes things 2 a central processing unit of a computer

pro-choice *adj* advocating access to legalized abortion

proclaim /prə kláym/ vt announce or declare publicly or formally —**proclamation** /próklə máysh'n/ n

proclivity /prə klívvəti/ (pl -ties) n a natural tendency

~~proclomation~~ incorrect spelling of **proclamation**

procrastinate /prō krásti nayt/ (-nating, -nated) vti postpone doing something, especially habitually —**procrastination** /prō krásti náysh'n/ n —**procrastinator** n

procreate /prókri ayt, -áyt/ (-ating, -ated) vti produce offspring —**procreation** /-áysh'n/ n —**procreative** /-aytiv/ adj

proctor /próktər/ n a university officer in charge of undergraduate discipline —**proctorial** /prok táwri əl/ adj —**proctorship** n

procurator fiscal /prókyoŏ raytər físk'l/ (pl procurators fiscal or procurator fiscals) n a public prosecutor and coroner in Scotland

procure /prə kyoŏr/ (-curing, -cured) v 1 vt acquire, especially by effort 2 vti provide somebody for prostitution —**procurable** adj —**procurement** n ◊ See note at **get**

prod vti (**prodding, prodded**) 1 jab or poke with a finger, elbow, or pointed object 2 incite somebody to action ■ n 1 a jab or poke 2 an incitement to action 3 an instrument used for prodding a person or animal

prodigal /próddig'l/ adj 1 spending money wastefully 2 extravagantly wasteful 3 giving or producing generous amounts —**prodigally** adv

prodigious /prə díjjəss/ adj 1 great in amount, size, or extent 2 marvellous or exceedingly impressive —**prodigiously** adv —**prodigiousness** n

prodigy /próddiji/ (pl -gies) n 1 somebody with exceptional talent at an early age 2 something marvellous or exceedingly impressive

prodrug /pró drug/ n a substance converted to an active drug in the body

produce v /prə dyooss/ (-ducing, -duced) 1 vti make or create something 2 vt cause something to happen or arise 3 vti yield or bring forth something 4 vt present or show something 5 vt organize and supervise the making of something ◊ produce a new album ■ n /próddyooss/ farm or garden products —**producer** n —**producible** adj

product /próddukt/ n 1 a commodity produced and offered for sale 2 a consequence 3 a result of multiplying quantities

production /prə dúksh'n/ n 1 the producing of something 2 something produced 3 the presentation of a play, opera, or musical ◊ appearing in a new production

productive /prə dúktiv/ adj 1 producing something in large quantities 2 producing worthwhile results —**productively** adv —**productivity** /pródduk tívvəti/ n

prof n a professor (infml)

profane /prə fáyn/ adj 1 showing disrespect for God or religion 2 not relating to religion ■ vt (-faning, -faned) treat irreverently

—**profanatory** /prə fánnətərl/ adj —**profanely** adv

ORIGIN Profane goes back to a Latin word meaning literally 'outside the temple'. Its root is also found in **fanatic**.

profanity /prə fánnəti/ (pl -ties) n 1 profane language or behaviour 2 a profane word or phrase

profess /prə féss/ (-fesses) v 1 vti acknowledge something publicly 2 vt claim something falsely 3 vt follow a particular religion —**professed** adj —**professedly** /prə féssidli/ adv

profession /prə fésh'n/ n 1 an occupation requiring extensive education 2 the people in a particular profession ◊ the legal profession 3 a declaration or public acknowledgment of something

professional /prə fésh'nəl/ adj 1 of a profession 2 engaged in an occupation or activity as a paid job rather than a hobby 3 highly competent —**professional** n —**professionally** adv

professionalism /prə fésh'nəlizəm/ n the skills and standards of a profession

professionalize /prə fésh'nə líz/ (-izing, -ized), **professionalise** vt cause to meet professional standards

professor /prə féssər/ n 1 the most senior grade of lecturer in a university department 2 a teacher, e.g. of music or dancing —**professorial** /próffə sáwri əl/ adj —**professorship** n

proffer /próffər/ vt 1 hold out for somebody to take 2 propose for consideration

~~proffesor~~ incorrect spelling of **professor**

proficient /prə físh'nt/ adj very skilled —**proficiency** n —**proficiently** adv

profile /pró fíl/ n 1 the side view of something, especially somebody's face 2 a short biographical article 3 a set of data that indicates the extent to which something conforms to a standard 4 a degree of attracting public attention ◊ kept a low profile ■ vt (-filing, -filed) 1 write a short biographical article on 2 show the facial profile of —**profiler** n

profit /próffit/ n 1 the excess of income over expenditure, especially in business 2 money made from an investment or transaction 3 an advantage or benefit derived from an activity ■ v 1 vi make a profit 2 vti benefit or cause to benefit from something (fml) —**profitless** adj

SPELLCHECK Do not confuse the spelling of **profit** and **prophet** ('a foreteller of the future'), which sound similar.

profitable /próffitəb'l/ adj 1 making a profit 2 useful to somebody —**profitability** /próffitə bílləti/ n —**profitably** adv

profiteer /próffi teèr/ vi make excessive profits from scarce or essential goods —**profiteering** n

profiterole /prə fíttərōl/ n a choux pastry ball

filled with cream and usually served with chocolate sauce

profitmaking /próffit mayking/ *adj* run for profit

profligate /próffligət/ *adj* 1 wasteful or extravagant 2 with low moral standards —**profligacy** *n* —**profligate** *n*

pro forma /prō fáwrmə/ *adj* done or existing only as a formality

profound /prə fównd/ *adj* 1 very great or intense 2 showing or requiring great understanding or knowledge —**profoundly** *adv* —**profundity** /prə fúndəti/ *n*

profuse /prə fyóoss/ *adj* 1 given or giving freely and extravagantly 2 existing in large amounts —**profusely** *adv* —**profusion** /prə fyoózh'n/ *n*

progenitor /prō jénnitər/ *n* 1 an ancestor 2 an originator or a prototype

progeny /prójjəni/ (*pl* -**nies**) *n* 1 the offspring of a person, animal, or plant 2 things developing as a result of something

progesterone /prō jéstərōn/ *n* a sex hormone produced in women that prepares the womb for a fertilized ovum and maintains pregnancy

prognathous /prógnəthəss, prog náythəss/, **prognathic** /prog náthik/ *adj* having a projecting jaw

prognosis /prog nốssiss/ (*pl* -**ses** /-seez/) *n* 1 an opinion on the likely course of a disease 2 a prediction of how something will develop

prognostic /prog nóstik/ *adj* of or acting as a prognosis or prediction ■ *n* a prediction

prognosticate /prog nósti kayt/ (-**cating**, -**cated**) *vti* predict or foretell future events —**prognostication** /prog nósti káysh'n/ *n* —**prognosticator** *n*

program /prố gram/ *n* 1 a list of instructions for a computer in a programming language 2 a set of coded operating instructions for a machine ■ *n*, *vti* (**programming**, **programmed**) US = **programme** ■ *v* 1 *vti* write a program for a computer 2 *vt* give coded operating instructions to a machine —**programmable** /prō grámməb'l/ *adj*

programmatic /prógrə máttik/ *adj* 1 of a programme 2 following a plan or programme

programme /prố gram/ *n* 1 a plan of action 2 a television or radio broadcast 3 a booklet giving details of a performance ■ *vt* 1 schedule as part of a programme 2 train to do something automatically —**programmability** /prố grəmə bílləti/ *n* —**programmable** /prō grámməb'l, prố gramab'l/ *adj*

programmed learning, programmed instruction *n* a learning method taking students through structured sequences at their own pace

programmer /prố gramər/ *n* somebody who programs computers

programming /prố graming/ *n* 1 creating of computer programs 2 selection and scheduling of broadcasts

programming language *n* a special vocabulary and set of rules for instructing a computer

progress *n* /prố gress/ 1 improvement or development ○ *making progress in the talks* 2 movement forwards or onwards ■ *vi* /prə gréss/ 1 improve or develop 2 move forwards or onwards

progress chaser *n* somebody who checks the progress of a process to ensure prompt completion or delivery

progression /prə grésh'n/ *n* 1 a gradual advance from one stage to another 2 movement forwards or onwards 3 a series of related things 4 a sequence of numbers related by a constant formula —**progressional** *adj*

progressive /prə gréssiv/ *adj* 1 developing gradually over a period of time 2 favouring social, economic, or political reform 3 describes taxation with higher rates for higher incomes 4 of an aspect of a verb expressing continuous action ■ *n* 1 a supporter of social, economic, or political reform 2 the progressive aspect of a verb, or a verb in the progressive aspect —**progressively** *adv* —**progressiveness** *n*

prohibit /prə híbbit/ *vt* 1 forbid by a law or rule 2 prevent

prohibition /prố i bísh'n/ *n* 1 the forbidding of something by a law or rule, or an order that forbids something 2 the outlawing of the production of and trade in alcoholic beverages

prohibitive /prə híbbitiv/ *adj* 1 too expensive for most people 2 forbidding something —**prohibitively** *adv*

prohibitory /prə híbbitəri/ *adj* (*fml*) 1 likely to prevent or forbid something 2 preventing or forbidding something

project *n* /prójjekt/ 1 a task or scheme requiring time and planning 2 an extensive organized unit of work ○ *a class project* ■ *v* /prə jékt/ 1 *vt* estimate something future using present data ○ *project a 3% growth rate* 2 *vti* stick out beyond something 3 *vt* communicate an impression of something or yourself ○ *projects himself as a confident speaker* 4 *vt* unconsciously attribute your own feelings to others 5 *vt* direct light or an image onto a surface 6 *vti* make the voice clearly heard at a distance —**projection** /prə jéksh'n/ *n*

projectile /prō jék tíl/ *n* a missile or shell ■ *adj* impelled forwards

projectionist /prə jéksh'nist/ *n* an operator of a film projector

projector /prə jéktər/ *n* a piece of equipment for projecting film or slides onto a screen

Prokofiev /prə kóffi ef/, **Sergey Sergeyevich** (1891–1953) Russian composer

prolapse /prố laps, prō láps/ *n* a slippage of an internal organ from its usual position —**prolapsed** *adj*

prole *n* a person regarded as inferior because he or she is a member of the working class (*infml insult*) —**prole** *adj*

proletarian /prōlə táiri ən/ *adj* of the working class —**proletarian** *n* —**proletarianism** *n*

proletariat /prōlə táiri ət/ *n* the working class (+ *sing* or *pl verb*)

ORIGIN The original **proletariat** was a social class in ancient Rome whose members owned no property and who were regarded as serving the state only in the production of offspring. The word was originally formed in French from Latin *proles* 'offspring', and first used in English in the mid-19C.

pro-life *adj* opposed to abortion or experimentation on the human embryo —**pro-lifer** *n*

proliferate /prə liffə rayt/ (**-ating**, **-ated**) *v* 1 *vi* increase greatly 2 *vti* reproduce rapidly —**proliferation** /prə liffə ráysh'n/ *n*

prolific /prə liffik/ *adj* 1 highly productive 2 producing a lot of fruit or many offspring —**prolifically** *adv*

prolix /prōliks, prō líks/ *adj* wordy —**prolixity** /prō líksəti/ *n* ◊ See note at **wordy**

prologue /prō log/ *n* an introductory passage or speech in a novel, play, or poem ■ *vt* (**-loguing**, **-logued**) preface with a prologue

prolong /prə lóng/ *vt* cause to go on longer —**prolongation** /prō long gáysh'n/ *n*

prom *n* (*infml*) 1 a seafront promenade 2 a promenade concert

promenade /prómmə naád/ *n* 1 a paved seafront path 2 a walk taken for pleasure or to be seen (*fml*) ■ *vti* (**-nading**, **-naded**) take a stroll in a public place

promenade concert *n* a concert of classical music at which part of the audience stands

promenade deck *n* a covered upper deck of a ship where passengers can walk

Prometheus /prə meéthi əss/ *n* in Greek mythology, a Titan who gave fire to humankind

promethium /prə meéthi əm/ *n* (*symbol* **Pm**) a radioactive metallic element. Use: phosphorescent paints, X-ray source.

ORIGIN Promethium is named after Prometheus. The element is the result of the ability to use the energy of nuclear fission, and this suggested a parallel with the Titan's original giving of fire.

prominence /prómminənss/ *n* 1 conspicuous importance 2 something that sticks out

prominent /prómminənt/ *adj* 1 sticking out 2 noticeable 3 eminent or well-known —**prominently** *adv*

~~promiscous~~ incorrect spelling of **promiscuous**

promiscuous /prə mískyoo əss/ *adj* (*disapproving*) 1 sexually indiscriminate 2 choosing without discriminating —**promiscuity** /prómmi skyoo əti/ *n* —**promiscuously** *adv*

promise /prómmiss/ *v* (**-ising**, **-ised**) 1 *vti* assure somebody that something will happen or be done ◊ *promised to come* ◊ *promised that the patient would recover* 2 *vt* pledge to give something to somebody ◊ *promised them a kitten* 3 *vti* make somebody expect something ◊ *The*

oley promised ruin. ■ *n* 1 a solemn assurance or undertaking 2 a good indication for the future ◊ *showed great promise*

promising /prómmissing/ *adj* likely to be successful or turn out well —**promisingly** *adv*

promissory /prómmissəri/ *adj* containing a promise

promissory note *n* a signed agreement to pay money

promontory /prómməntəri/ (*pl* **-ries**) *n* a projecting point of land

promote /prə mōt/ (**-moting**, **-moted**) *vt* 1 advance to a more senior position 2 support, encourage, or advocate 3 advertise —**promotable** *adj* —**promotion** *n* —**promotional** *adj*

promoter /prə mōtər/ *n* 1 an arranger of a public event such as an entertainment or sporting contest 2 a supporter or advocate of something

prompt *adj* 1 done immediately 2 quick to act ■ *v* 1 *vt* urge into action 2 *vt* bring about 3 *vti* provide an actor with lines that he or she has forgotten ■ *n* 1 a reminder of words to a performer who has forgotten them 2 a symbol or message informing a computer user that input is required —**prompter** *n* —**promptly** *adv* —**promptness** *n*

promulgate /prómm'l gayt/ (**-gating**, **-gated**) *vt* (*fml*) 1 announce or declare officially 2 make widely known —**promulgation** /prómm'l gáysh'n/ *n*

pron. *abbr* 1 pronoun 2 pronunciation

prone /prōn/ *adj* 1 inclined to do or be affected by something 2 lying face down —**proneness** *n*

prong *n* a sharp point at the end of something ■ *vt* pierce with something sharp —**pronged** *adj*

pronominal /prō nómmin'l/ *adj* acting as a pronoun —**pronominal** *n*

pronoun /prō nown/ *n* a member of a class of words replacing a noun or noun phrase

pronounce /prə nównss/ (**-nouncing**, **-nounced**) *vti* 1 articulate speech sounds or words 2 formally declare something —**pronounceable** *adj* —**pronouncement** *n*

pronounced /prə nównst/ *adj* 1 noticeable 2 voiced or spoken —**pronouncedly** /prə nównssidli/ *adv*

~~pronounciation~~ incorrect spelling of **pronunciation**

pronto /próntō/ *adv* immediately or fast (*infml*)

pronunciation /prə núnssi áysh'n/ *n* the way in which speech sounds or words are articulated

proof *n* 1 conclusive evidence 2 the relative strength of a drink's alcoholic content measured against a standard 3 a printed copy used for checking errors in something printed or reproduced 4 a sequence of steps to validate a solution 5 a photographic print from a negative ■ *adj* 1 impervious or resistant to something 2 having a particular relative alcoholic strength (*often in* *combination)* ■ *vt* make impervious or resistant

proofread /proof reed/ (**-read** /-red/) *vti* check a proof for errors in printing or reproduction —**proofreader** *n*

prop[1] *n* 1 a rigid support 2 a comforting person or thing 3 in rugby, a forward at each end of the front row of a scrum 4 *Aus* a sudden stop by a horse ■ *v* (**propping, propped**) 1 *vt* support with a prop 2 *vi Aus* stop abruptly *(refers to horses)*

□ **prop up** *vt* help to support or sustain

prop[2] *n* an object used in a theatrical performance or film

propaganda /próppə gándə/ *n* 1 publicity to promote an idea or cause 2 misleading information that is systematically spread —**propagandist** *n*, *adj* —**propagandize** *vti*

ORIGIN The first **propaganda**, etymologically, was sent out by the Congregation for the Propagation of the Faith (in Latin *Propaganda Fide*), a committee of Roman Catholic cardinals who supervised foreign missions and trained priests to serve in them. The modern sense of 'publicity' dates from the early 20C.

propagate /próppə gayt/ (**-gating, -gated**) *v* 1 *vti* reproduce, or cause an organism to reproduce 2 *vt* spread something widely —**propagation** /próppə gáysh'n/ *n* —**propagator** *n*

propane /pró payn/ *n* C_3H_8 a flammable hydrocarbon gas. Use: fuel, propellant, refrigerant.

propel /prə pél/ (**-pelling, -pelled**) *vt* 1 push forwards 2 cause to happen

propellant /prə péllənt/, **propellent** *n* 1 a substance burned to give upward thrust to a rocket 2 an explosive charge for projecting a bullet from a gun —**propellant** *adj*

propeller /prə péllər/ *n* a revolving shaft with spiral blades that causes a ship or aircraft to move

propelling pencil *n* a pencil with a lead that can be extended as it wears down

~~propeller~~ incorrect spelling of **propeller**

propensity /prə pénssəti/ (*pl* **-ties**) *n* a tendency to behave in a particular way

proper /próppər/ *adj* 1 appropriate or correct ○ *in its proper perspective* 2 fulfilling all requirements ○ *proper medical care* 3 with correct manners 4 as narrowly identified ○ *in the city proper* —**properly** *adv* —**properness** *n*

proper fraction *n* a fraction in which the numerator is less than the denominator

proper noun, proper name *n* a capitalized name of a specific person or thing

property /próppərti/ (*pl* **-ties**) *n* 1 something owned by a specific person 2 owned land or buildings 3 a trait, attribute, or quality *(often pl)* 4 a theatrical prop *(fml)*

prophecy /próffəssi/ (*pl* **-cies**) *n* 1 a prediction considered to reveal the will of a deity 2 a prediction

USAGE prophecy or prophesy? Prophecy, a

noun, means 'a prediction', as in *a dire economic prophecy*. The verb **prophesy** means 'predict', as in *had already prophesied a recession*.

prophesy /próffə sī/ (**-sies, -sied**) *v* 1 *vti* predict something 2 *vi* reveal the will of a deity with respect to the future ◊ See note at **prophecy**

prophet /próffit/ *n* 1 somebody who interprets and transmits the will of a deity 2 somebody who predicts the future 3 an inspired leader 4 **Prophet** Muhammad, the founder of Islam ◊ See note at **profit**

prophetess /próffi téss/ *n* a woman who is a prophet

prophetic /prə féttik/ *adj* 1 correctly predicting the future 2 of a prophet —**prophetical** *adj* —**prophetically** *adv*

prophylactic /próffi láktik/ *adj* protecting against disease ■ *n* 1 a condom *(fml)* 2 a drug that guards against disease

prophylaxis /próffi láksiss/ (*pl* **-es** /-seez/) *n* treatment that prevents disease

propinquity /prə píngkwəti/ *n* nearness *(fml)*

propitiate /prə píshi ayt/ (**-ating, -ated**) *vt* conciliate or win the favour of —**propitiation** /prə píshi áysh'n/ *n* —**propitiatory** *adj*

propitious /prə píshəss/ *adj* 1 favourable to success 2 kindly *(fml)* —**propitiously** *adv*

~~propoganda~~ incorrect spelling of **propaganda**

proponent /prə pónənt/ *n* an advocate of something

proportion /prə páwrsh'n/ *n* 1 a quantity that is part of a whole 2 the relationship between quantities 3 the correct or desirable relative size or importance ○ *in proportion* 4 a relationship between two variables that remains constant ■ **proportions** *npl* 1 the size or shape of something 2 the importance of something ■ *vt* 1 maintain a proportional relationship between 2 give pleasing proportions to

proportional /prə páwrsh'nəl/ *adj* 1 in the correct relationship of size, quantity, or degree 2 related by a constant ratio —**proportionally** *adv*

proportional representation *n* an electoral system in which a party's share of seats in government is in proportion to their share of the vote

proportionate /prə páwrsh'nət/ *adj* proportional in size, quantity, or degree —**proportionately** *adv*

proposal /prə póz'l/ *n* 1 an idea or plan put forward for consideration 2 the proposing of something

propose /prə póz/ (**-posing, -posed**) *v* 1 *vt* put forward as a suggestion 2 *vt* state as an intention 3 *vt* nominate for an elected position or for promotion 4 *vti* make an offer of marriage to 5 *vt* ask others to join in a toast —**proposer** *n*

proposition /próppə zísh'n/ *n* 1 a proposal for consideration 2 a statement of opinion or judgment 3 an invitation to have sexual intercourse 4 a private deal or agreement 5 somebody or something to be dealt with *(infml)* ■ *vt* **1** invite to have sexual intercourse **2** offer a deal to —**propositional** *adj*

propound /prə pównd/ *vt* suggest an idea or explanation —**propounder** *n*

proprietary /prə prí ətəri/ *adj* **1** manufactured or sold by somebody with an exclusive legal right to do so **2** of owners or ownership **3** privately owned

proprietor /prə prí ətər/ *n* the owner of something, especially a business —**proprietorial** /prə prí ə táwri əl/ *adj* —**proprietorship** *n*

propriety /prə prí əti/ *n* **1** socially correct or appropriate behaviour **2** the quality of being socially appropriate ■ **proprieties** *npl* the rules of etiquette

> **ORIGIN Propriety** derives from the same French word as *property*, and 'property' was one of its early senses. The better-developed strand of meaning, however, is based on 'appropriateness'. This emerged in the early 17C, though the modern sense of 'socially correct behaviour' is not recorded until the late 18C.

propulsion /prə púlsh'n/ *n* the process or force by which something is moved —**propulsive** *adj*

pro rata /-raátə/ *adv, adj* in a fixed proportion

prorate /prō ráyt/ *vti US, Can* calculate or divide something on a pro rata basis —**proration** *n*

prosaic /prō záy ik/ *adj* lacking imagination —**prosaically** *adv*

pros and cons *npl* advantages and disadvantages

proscenium /prə seéni əm/ *(pl* **-a** /-ə/ *or* **-ums)** *n* the part of a stage in front of the curtain

prosciutto /prō shoōtō/ *n* dried and smoked Italian ham

proscribe /prō skríb/ *(-scribing, -scribed)* *vt* **1** condemn or ban **2** banish —**proscriber** *n*

prose /prōz/ *n* ordinary writing or speech without the structure of poetry

prosecute /próssi kyoot/ *(-cuting, -cuted)* *vti* **1** take legal action against somebody **2** try to prove that somebody is guilty in a court of law —**prosecutable** *adj* —**prosecution** /próssi kyoŏsh'n/ *n* —**prosecutor** *n*

~~prosecuter~~ incorrect spelling of **prosecutor**

proselyte /próssə līt/ *n* somebody converted to a new belief —**proselytism** /próssələ tizəm/ *n*

proselytize /próssələ tīz/ *(-tizing, -tized)*, **proselytise** *vti* try to convert somebody to a new belief —**proselytization** /próssələ tī záysh'n/ *n* —**proselytizer** *n*

prosody /próssədi/ *n* the study of the structure of poetry —**prosodic** /prə sóddik/ *adj*

prospect *n* /próss pekt/ **1** a possibility of something happening soon **2** something that is expected to happen soon **3** an extensive view or scene **4** the direction in which something faces **5** a prospective customer **6** somebody or something with the potential to succeed ■ **prospects** *npl* expectations of success ■ *vti* /prə spékt, próss pekt/ search an area for mineral deposits

prospective /prə spéktiv/ *adj* likely to become or happen —**prospectively** *adv*

prospector /prə spéktər, próss pektər/ *n* somebody who looks for mineral deposits

prospectus /prə spéktəss/ *n* **1** a brochure giving information about an institution or organization **2** an official document giving advance information about something

prosper /próspər/ *vi* succeed and flourish, especially financially

prosperity /pro spérrəti/ *n* wealth or success

prosperous /próspərəss/ *adj* **1** successful and flourishing, especially financially **2** wealthy —**prosperously** *adv* —**prosperousness** *n*

prostate /pró stayt/, **prostate gland** *n* a gland surrounding the urethra below the bladder in male mammals that secretes a fluid into the semen —**prostatic** /pro státtik/ *adj*

prosthesis /pross theéssiss/ *n (pl* **-ses** /-seez/*)* **1** an artificial body part **2** the replacement of body parts with artificial devices —**prosthetic** /pross théttik/ *adj*

prostitute /prósti tyoot/ *n* **1** somebody paid for sexual intercourse **2** somebody who degrades his or her talent for money ■ *vt* *(-tuting, -tuted)* **1** misuse for gain **2** offer as a prostitute —**prostitution** /prósti tyoŏsh'n/ *n*

prostrate *v* /pro stráyt/ *(-trating, -trated)* **1** *vr* lie face downwards **2** *vt* lay or throw flat on the ground **3** *vt* make weak or helpless ■ *adj* /pró strayt/ **1** lying flat, facing downwards **2** lying down **3** drained of energy —**prostration** *n*

prosy /prózi/ *(-ier, -iest)* *adj* dull and unimaginative —**prosiness** *n*

protactinium /prō tak tínni əm/ *n (symbol* **Pa***)* a radioactive metallic chemical element

protagonist /prō tággənist/ *n* **1** the main character in a story **2** a leading figure in a contest or dispute

protean /prō teé ən, próti ən/ *adj* **1** variable in nature, appearance, or behaviour **2** versatile

> **ORIGIN** Being **protean** was originally an attribute of Proteus, a prophetic sea god in Greek mythology who could change his shape at will.

protect /prə tékt/ *vt* keep safe from harm or damage —**protective** *adj* —**protectively** *adv* —**protectiveness** *n* ◊ See note at **safeguard**

protected /prə téktid/ *adj* **1** classified as an endangered species **2** sheltered **3** locked against changes by unauthorized computer users

protection /prə téksh'n/ *n* **1** the protecting of somebody or something **2** something that protects **3** insurance cover **4** payment extorted by threatening harm or damage to property *(infml)* **5** *also* **protectionism** the imposition of duties on imports, designed to protect domestic industries against foreign competition

protector /prə téktər/ *n* **1** somebody or something that protects **2** *also* **Protector** somebody ruling in place of a monarch —**protectoral** *adj* —**protectorship** *n*

protectorate /prə téktərət/ *n* **1** a state dependent on another, or the relationship between such states **2** the position or term of office of a protector

protégé /prótti zhay, próti-/ *n* somebody under the patronage of another

protégée /próti zhay, próti-/ *n* a woman or girl under somebody's patronage

protein /prṓ teen/ *n* **1** a complex natural compound composed of linked amino acids **2** food rich in protein

ORIGIN The word **protein** was coined around 1838 (in a French form) by the Dutch chemist Gerardus Johannes Mulder (1802–80). He based it on Greek *prōteios* 'primary', a derivative of *protos* 'first'. It was originally applied to a substance regarded as the primary constituent of all animal and vegetable bodies, but when chemical advances proved the single substance not to exist, the word continued to appear appropriate for the group of substances that are now called **proteins**.

pro tem *adv, adj* for the time being

Proterozoic /prṓtərō zṓ ik/ *n* an aeon of geological time 2,500–570 million years ago —**Proterozoic** *adj*

protest *vti* /prə tést/ **1** complain or object strongly about something **2** say firmly that something is true ■ *n* /prṓ test/ **1** a strong complaint or objection **2** a demonstration of public opposition or disapproval —**protestant** /próttistənt/ *n, adj* —**protester** *n* ◊ See note at **complain, object**

Protestant /próttistənt/ *n* a member of a Western Christian church that rejects papal authority —**Protestant** *adj* —**Protestantism** *n*

protocol /prṓtə kol/ *n* **1** the etiquette of state occasions **2** a code of conduct **3** an international agreement **4** an amendment or addition to a treaty or similar document **5** a written record or draft of an agreement **6** a set of rules for exchanging information between computers

proton /prṓ ton/ *n* (*symbol* **p**) a stable positively charged nuclear particle —**protonic** /prō tónnik/ *adj*

protoplasm /prṓtə plazəm/ *n* the contents of a living cell including the nucleus and cytoplasm —**protoplasmic** /prṓtə plázmik/ *adj*

prototype /prṓtə tīp/ *n* **1** an original used as a model for later forms or stages **2** a standard example —**prototypal** /prṓtə tīp'l/ *adj* —**prototypical** /-típpik'l/ *adj* —**prototypically** *adv*

protozoan /prṓtə zṓ ən/ (*pl* **-ans** *or* **-a** /-ə/) *n* a single-celled organism such as an amoeba —**protozoan** *adj* —**protozoic** *adj*

protract /prə trákt/ *vt* make something last longer —**protraction** *n*

protracted /prə tráktid/ *adj* lasting a long time

protractor /prə tráktər/ *n* a flat semicircular instrument for measuring angles

~~protray~~ incorrect spelling of **portray**

protrude /prə troōd/ (**-truding, -truded**) *vti* stick or push out —**protrusion** *n* —**protrusive** *adj*

protuberance /prə tyoōbərənss/**, protuberancy** /-rənssi/ (*pl* **-cies**) *n* **1** something that sticks out **2** the fact of sticking out —**protuberant** *adj*

proud /prowd/ *adj* **1** pleased and satisfied **2** having self-respect **3** fostering feelings of pride ○ *the proudest moment* **4** arrogant **5** looking impressive **6** projecting slightly —**proudly** *adv* —**proudness** *n* ◊ **do somebody proud** bring honour or distinction to somebody

SYNONYMS proud, arrogant, conceited, egotistic, vain CORE MEANING: describing somebody who is pleased with himself or herself

AKG London

Marcel Proust

Proust /proost/**, Marcel** (1871–1922) French novelist —**Proustian** *adj*

prove /proov/ (**proving, proved, proved** *or* **proven** /proōv'n/, proov'n/) *v* **1** *vt* establish or demonstrate the truth of **2** *vt* subject something to scientific analysis to determine its worth or characteristics **3** *vti* turn out to be a particular thing or of a particular character ○ *It proved impossible to dislodge the rock.* —**provable** *adj*

proven /proōv'n, proov'n/ *adj* **1** tried and tested **2** proved true

provenance /próvənənss/ *n* **1** the place of origin of something **2** the source and ownership history of something such as an artwork ◊ See note at **origin**

Provence /pro vónss/ region of SE France

provender /próvvindər/ *n* **1** food for livestock (*archaic*) **2** food (*literary or humorous*)

proverb /próvvurb/ *n* a short well-known saying

proverbial /prə vúrbi əl/ *adj* **1** expressed as a proverb **2** used in a proverb

provide /prə víd/ (**-viding, -vided**) *v* **1** *vt* supply somebody with, or be a source of, something needed or wanted **2** *vt* require something as a condition (*fml*) **3** *vi* take precautions ○ *provide against disaster* **4** *vi* supply a means of support ○ *providing for her family* —**provider** *n*

provided /prə vídid/**, provided that** *conj* on condition that

providence /próvvid'nss/**, Providence** *n* **1** guidance and care believed to be provided by God **2** God perceived as a guiding and caring force

Providence /próvvid'nss/ capital of Rhode Island. Pop. 150,890 (1998).

provident /próvvid'nt/ *adj* **1** preparing for future needs **2** economical or frugal

providential /próvvi dénsh'l/ *adj* 1 of providence 2 very lucky ◊ See note at **lucky**

providing /prə víding/, **providing that** *conj* on condition that

province /próvinss/ *n* 1 an administrative division of a country 2 an area of knowledge ■ **provinces** *npl* the parts of a country outside the capital and main cities

provincial /prə vínsh'l/ *adj* 1 of a province or the provinces 2 unsophisticated and narrow-minded *(disapproving)* ■ *n* 1 somebody from the provinces 2 an unsophisticated person *(disapproving)* —**provincialism** *n* —**provincially** *adv*

proving ground *n* a place where something or somebody is tested

provision /prə vízh'n/ *n* 1 the supplying of something 2 an action taken to meet a possible or expected need 3 a legal clause stating a condition ■ **provisions** *npl* food and other supplies ■ *vt* provide with food and other supplies —**provisioner** *n*

provisional /prə vízh'nəl/ *adj* 1 temporary or conditional 2 **Provisional** of an unofficial faction of the Irish Republican Army ■ *n* **Provisional** a member of the Provisional IRA —**provisionally** *adv*

provisional licence *n* a learner's driving licence

proviso /prə vízō/ (*pl* -**sos** *or* -**soes**) *n* 1 a condition within an agreement 2 a clause added to a contract

provocation /próvvə káysh'n/ *n* 1 the provoking of somebody or something 2 a cause of anger

provocative /prə vókətiv/ *adj* 1 making people angry or excited 2 deliberately sexually arousing —**provocatively** *adv* —**provocativeness** *n*

provoke /prə vók/ (-**voking**, -**voked**) *vt* 1 make somebody feel angry 2 cause or stir somebody to an emotion or response —**provokingly** *adv*

provost /próvvəst/ *n* 1 a head of some educational establishments 2 a senior dignitary of a cathedral

prow /prow/ *n* 1 the front part of a ship 2 a projecting front part

prowess /prów ess/ *n* 1 superior skill 2 valour and ability in combat

prowl /prowl/ *vti* roam an area stealthily in search of prey, food, or opportunity ■ *n* an act of prowling —**prowler** *n*

proximate /próksimət/ *adj* 1 nearest 2 very close in space or time —**proximation** /próksi máysh'n/ *n*

proximity /prok símməti/ *n* closeness

proxy /próksi/ (*pl* -**ies**) *n* 1 the function or power of somebody authorized to act for another 2 somebody authorized to act for another

ORIGIN **Proxy** is a contraction of *procuracy*, a word that is now rare, meaning 'the managing of somebody else's affairs, acting on behalf of another'. It goes back to the same Latin verb as *procure*.

PRP *abbr* performance-related pay

prude *n* somebody easily shocked by matters relating to sex or nudity —**prudery** *n* —**prudish** *adj* —**prudishly** *adv* —**prudishness** *n*

prudent /prood'nt/ *adj* 1 having good sense in dealing with practical matters 2 carefully considering consequences —**prudence** *n* —**prudently** *adv* ◊ See note at **cautious**

prudential /prōō dénsh'l/ *adj* resulting from, depending on, or using prudence

prune[1] (**pruning**, **pruned**) *v* 1 *vti* cut branches from a plant to encourage fuller growth 2 *vt* reduce something by removing unwanted material

prune[2] *n* a dried plum

prurient /proori ənt/ *adj* marked by unwholesome sexual interest —**prurience** *n*

Prussia /prúshə/ historical region of Germany and former kingdom in north-central Europe —**Prussian** *adj, n*

prussic acid /prússik-/ *n* a colourless weak acid that smells of almonds

pry[1] (**pries**, **pried**) *vi* inquire nosily —**pryingly** *adv*

pry[2] (**pries**, **pried**) *vt US, Can* force open with a lever

PS, ps *abbr* postscript

psalm /saam/, **Psalm** *n* a sacred song or poem of praise —**psalmist** *n*

ORIGIN **Psalm** goes back to a Greek verb that originally meant 'pluck' but was extended to 'pluck harp strings'. The noun derived from it was used in the Greek translation of the Hebrew Bible, the Septuagint, and from there passed into Latin and the Germanic and Romance languages.

Psalter /sáwltər, sóltər/, **psalter** *n* a book containing psalms

psaltery /sáwltəri, sóltəri/ (*pl* -**ies**) *n* an ancient musical instrument with numerous strings

pseud /syood/ *n* somebody who pretends to be knowledgeable about culture

pseudo /syóōdō/ *adj* not genuine

pseudo- *prefix* false, spurious ○ *pseudoscience*

pseudonym /syóōdənim/ *n* a false name —**pseudonymous** /syoo dónniməss/ *adj*

pseudoscience /syóōdō sí ənss/ *n* a theory or method mistakenly held to be scientific

psi /psī/ *n* the 23rd letter of the Greek alphabet

psittacosis /sítta kóssiss/ *n* a bacterial disease of parrots and related birds that can be transmitted to humans

PSNI *abbr* Police Service of Northern Ireland

psoriasis /sə rí əssiss/ *n* a skin disease marked by red scaly patches

psuedonym incorrect spelling of **pseudonym**

psych /sīk/ □ **psych out** *vt (infml)* 1 intimidate 2 guess the thought processes of □ **psych up** *vt* prepare yourself or somebody else mentally *(infml)*

psyche /síki/ *n* 1 the human spirit or soul 2 the human mind

psychedelia /sīkə deèli ə/ *n* the subculture of psychedelic drugs

psychedelic /sīkə déllik/ *adj* 1 of hallucinogenic drugs 2 resembling images and sounds experienced under the influence of hallucinogenic drugs —**psychedelically** *adv*

psychiatry /sī kī ətri/ *n* the branch of medicine concerned with mental or behavioural disorders —**psychiatric** /sīki áttrik/ *adj* —**psychiatrist** *n*

psychic /sīkik/ *adj* 1 of the mind 2 supposedly sensitive to supernatural forces ■ *n* somebody supposedly sensitive to the supernatural —**psychically** *adv*

psycho- *prefix* 1 mind, mental ○ *psychoactive* 2 psychology, psychological ○ *psychobabble*

psychoactive /sīkō áktiv/ *adj* describes drugs that affect mood or behaviour

psychoanalysis /sīkō ə nálləssiss/ *n* 1 a method of psychiatric therapy based on the theory that mental life functions on both conscious and unconscious levels 2 treatment by psychoanalysis, involving the interpretation of dreams and the patient's free association of ideas —**psychoanalyse** /-ánnə līz/ *vt* —**psychoanalyst** /-ánnəlist/ *n* —**psychoanalytic** /-ánnə líttik/ *adj* —**psychoanalytical** *adj*

psychobabble /sīkō bab b'l/ *n* psychological jargon

psychedelic incorrect spelling of **psychedelic**

psychodrama /sīkō draamə/ *n* a form of psychotherapy in which patients perform roles in dramas that illustrate their problems —**psychodramatic** /sīkō drə máttik/ *adj*

psychogenic /sīkō jénnik/ *adj* arising from mental or emotional processes —**psychogenically** *adv*

psychokinesis /sīkō ki neéssiss, -kī-/ *n* the supposed moving of objects with the mind —**psychokinetic** /-ki néttik, -kī-/ *adj*

psychological /sīkə lójjik'l/ *adj* 1 of psychology 2 of the mind —**psychologically** *adv*

psychological warfare *n* 1 warfare by propaganda 2 the use of psychological tactics to disconcert or disadvantage somebody

psychology /sī kólləji/ (*pl* -**gies**) *n* 1 the study of the mind 2 the characteristic mental makeup of a person or group —**psychologist** *n*

psychopath /sīkō path/ *n* an offensive term for somebody with a personality disorder that leads to violent antisocial behaviour —**psychopathic** /sīkō páthik/ *adj*

psychopathology /sīkō pə thólləji/ *n* the study of psychiatric disorders —**psychopathological** /sīkō páthə lójjik'l/ *adj* —**psychopathologist** *n*

psychosexual /sīkō sékshoo əl/ *adj* of the mental and emotional aspects of sexuality

psychosis /sī kóssiss/ (*pl* -**ses** /-seez/) *n* a psychiatric disorder marked by loss of contact with reality —**psychotic** /sī kóttik/ *adj* —**psychotically** *adv*

psychosomatic /sīkō sə máttik/ *adj* 1 describes a physical illness that is mentally induced

2 of both the mind and body —**psychosomatically** *adv*

psychotherapy /sīkō thérrəpi/ *n* the treatment of mental disorders by psychological methods —**psychotherapeutic** /sīkō thérrə pyoótik/ *adj* —**psychotherapist** *n*

psycology incorrect spelling of **psychology**

pt *abbr* 1 part 2 pint 3 point

Pt *symbol* platinum

PT *n* physical exercise as a school subject. Full form **physical training**

p.t. *abbr* 1 part-time 2 past tense

PTA *abbr* Parent Teacher Association

ptarmigan /taármigən/ (*pl same or* -**gans**) *n* a grouse of cold regions that turns white in winter

pterodactyl /térrə dáktil/ *n* an extinct flying reptile with a rudimentary beak

pterosaur /térrə sawr/ *n* an extinct flying reptile with membranous wings

pto, PTO *abbr* please turn over

Ptolemy /tólləmi/ (AD 100?–170?) Greek astronomer, mathematician, and geographer

Ptolemy I (367?–283? BC) Macedonian king of Egypt (305–283? BC)

Pu *symbol* plutonium

pub *n* an establishment where alcohol is sold and drunk

pub-crawl *n* a session of drinking at several pubs in succession (*infml*) —**pub-crawl** *vi*

puberty /pyoóbərti/ *n* the stage of becoming physiologically mature —**pubertal** *adj*

pubescent /pyoo béss'nt/ *adj* 1 reaching or having reached puberty 2 covered with down or fine hair —**pubescence** *n*

pubic /pyoóbik/ *adj* of the pubis

pubis /pyoóbiss/ (*pl* -**bes** /-beez/) *n* the lower front of the hipbone

public /públik/ *adj* 1 of, for, or belonging to all members of the community ○ *public health* 2 open to all 3 of the state or state agencies 4 done openly 5 describes companies whose shares are available for anyone to buy ■ *n* 1 the community as a whole 2 a particular part of the community —**publicly** *adv*

public-address system *n* full form of **PA**

publically incorrect spelling of **publicly**

publican /públikən/ *n* 1 an owner or manager of a pub 2 a tax collector in the Roman Empire

publication /públi káysh'n/ *n* 1 the publishing of something 2 a published item, especially one in printed form, e.g. a book or magazine

public bar *n* a bar in a pub that is furnished more basically than a lounge bar

public company *n* a limited company whose shares can be bought and sold on the stock market

public convenience *n* a toilet for use by the public

public domain *n* the state of not being protected by a patent or copyright

public expenditure *n* government spending

public figure *n* a well-known person

public house *n* a pub *(fml)*

publicist /púbblissist/ *n* somebody who gets publicity for a client

publicity /pu blíssəti/ *n* **1** the stimulation of public interest in or awareness of something or somebody **2** interest or awareness created among the general public or media **3** the business of publicizing things

publicize /púbbli sīz/ (-cizing, -cized), **publicise** *vt* make generally known

public life *n* **1** a lifestyle attracting publicity or public scrutiny **2** public service, especially by a politician

public limited company *n* a company whose shares can be bought and sold on the stock market and whose shareholders have limited liability for debts or losses

public nuisance *n* an illegal action harming the community in general

public opinion *n* the general attitude of the public towards something

public ownership *n* state control of something regarded as a national asset

public prosecutor *n* a government prosecutor of criminal actions on behalf of the community

public relations *n* **1** the promotion of a favourable image and good relationship with the public (+ *sing verb*) **2** the particular image and relationship a person or organization has with the public (+ *sing or pl verb*)

public school *n* **1** an independent fee-paying secondary school **2** a state-funded school in the United States

public sector *n* the government-controlled part of the economy

public servant *n* **1** a holder of a government position **2** *ANZ* a civil servant

public service *n* **1** government employment **2** the provision of essential services **3** *ANZ* the departments implementing government policy **4** a service run for the benefit of the general public, e.g. a utility

public-spirited *adj* concerned for the community's welfare

public works *npl* civil-engineering projects undertaken or financed by the government

publish /púbblish/ *v* **1** *vti* prepare and produce material in printed or electronic form for distribution **2** *vt* make something public knowledge —**publishable** *adj* —**publisher** *n* —**publishing** *n*

Puccini /pooˈcheeni/, **Giacomo** (1858–1924) Italian composer

puce /pyooss/ *adj* purplish-red —**puce** *n*

puck *n* **1** a disc that the players hit in ice hockey **2** a stroke at the ball in hurling

Puck *n also* **puck** a mischievous spirit in English folklore

pucker /púkər/ *vti* gather into wrinkles ■ *n* a small wrinkle

puckish /púkish/ *adj* mischievous or naughty

pudding /pŏodding/ *n* **1** a sweet cooked dessert usually served hot *(often in combination)* **2** the dessert course of a meal **3** a cooked savoury dish usually covered with suet pastry *(often in combination)* —**puddingy** *adj*

ORIGIN A **pudding** was originally a sausage: an animal's stomach or intestine stuffed with minced meat and other ingredients and boiled. Other foods cooked in a bag came to be called **puddings**, then dishes made with flour or enclosed in a casing made with flour, until eventually neither the ingredients, nor the shape, nor the manner of cooking could determine what was and what was not a **pudding**. The sense 'dessert course of a meal' did not develop, however, until the 20C.

pudding basin *n* a deep bowl for making puddings, especially steamed puddings

puddle /púdd'l/ *n* a shallow pool of liquid, especially water

pudendum /pyoo déndəm/ (*pl* -**da** /déndə/) *n* the external genitals —**pudendal** *adj*

pueblo /pwébblō/ (*pl* -**los**) *n* **1** a Native North or Central American village with multistorey stone or adobe houses **2** a village in a Spanish-speaking country

puerile /pyoòr ī̄l/ *adj* silly and childish —**puerility** /pyoor rílləti/ *n*

puerperal /pyoo úrpərəl/ *adj* of childbirth

Puerto Rico /pwúrtō reèkō/ island in the N Caribbean Sea, east of Hispaniola, a self-governing commonwealth of the United States. Cap. San Juan. Pop. 3,937,316 (2001). —**Puerto Rican** *n, adj*

puff *n* **1** a short sudden rush of air, steam, or smoke **2** the sound made by a puff **3** a short exhalation of breath **4** an inhaling followed by exhaling when smoking **5** a light pastry snack or cake *(often in combination)* **6** a piece of exaggerated praise or publicity ■ *v* **1** *vi* breathe quickly and heavily **2** *vti* emit steam, smoke, or gas in short blasts **3** *vti* inhale and exhale smoke from a cigarette, cigar, or pipe **4** *vi* move while emitting puffs of smoke or steam **5** *vi* move while panting **6** *vti* swell, e.g. with air or pride

puffball /púf bawl/ *n* a round fungus that produces a cloud of dark spores if disturbed

puffed-up *adj* self-important

puffin /púffin/ (*pl* -**fins** *or same*) *n* a black-and-white diving bird with a short neck and a triangular colourful bill

puff pastry *n* light flaky multilayered pastry

puffy /púffi/ (-**ier**, -**iest**) *adj* **1** swollen **2** short of breath —**puffiness** *n*

pug /pug/ *n* a small dog with a wrinkled face, short coat, and curled tail

Puget Sound /pyoòjit-/ arm of the Pacific Ocean, in NW Washington State

pugilism /pyoòjilizəm/ *n* the sport of boxing —**pugilist** *n* —**pugilistic** /pyoòji lístik/ *adj*

pugnacious /pug náyshəss/ *adj* quarrelsome and aggressive —**pugnaciously** *adv*

—pugnaciousness *n* **—pugnacity** /pug nássǝti/ *n*

puissance /pweé soNs, pyoó iss'nss/ *n* a show-jumping competition with an obstacle that is raised higher for each round

puja /poójǝ/ *n* daily domestic worship in Hinduism

puke /pyook/ (**pukes, puking, puked**) *vti* vomit *(slang)* **—puke** *n*

pukka /púkǝ/, **pucka** *adj* **1** genuine *(infml)* **2** S Asia well done or made **3** excellent *(infml)*

pula /poólǝ/ (*pl* same) *n* the main unit of Botswanan currency

pulchritude /púlkri tyood/ *n* beauty *(literary or humorous)* **—pulchritudinous** /púlkri tyoódinǝss/ *adj*

pull /pool/ *v* **1** *vti* draw something or somebody nearer **2** *vt* remove something forcibly **3** *vt* draw a load along **4** *vti* tug at or jerk something or somebody **5** *vt* strain and damage a muscle **6** *vt* attract a crowd *(infml)* **7** *vt* take out a weapon in readiness to fight *(infml)* **8** *vt* apply force to a trigger **9** *vt* open or close curtains **10** *vti* tear or rip something **11** *vt* stretch something elastic **12** *vti* attract a sexual partner *(slang)* ■ *n* **1** a pulling or being pulled **2** a pulling force **3** the power to attract an audience or supporters *(infml)* **4** something such as a tab or handle used for pulling *(often in combination)* **—puller** *n*

SYNONYMS pull, drag, draw, haul, tow, tug, yank CORE MEANING: move something towards you or in the same direction as you

☐ **pull ahead** *vi* pass somebody or something moving in the same direction

☐ **pull away** *vi* **1** move away **2** draw back

☐ **pull back** *vti* withdraw

☐ **pull down** *vt* demolish

☐ **pull in** *v* **1** *vi* arrive and stop **2** *vti* stop a vehicle at the roadside **3** *vt* arrest or take to a police station for questioning *(slang)*

☐ **pull off** *vt* achieve despite difficulties *(infml)*

☐ **pull out** *vti* **1** depart from a stopping place and join the traffic **2** withdraw from an obligation or commitment

☐ **pull over** *vti* stop a vehicle at the roadside

☐ **pull through** *vti* recover from illness or difficulties

☐ **pull together** *v* **1** *vi* work together cooperatively **2** *vr* recover your composure *(infml)*

☐ **pull up** *vi* arrive and stop

pullback /pool bak/ *n* a withdrawal of troops

pull-down *adj* made to appear on a computer screen by clicking on a heading **—pull-down** *n*

pullet /poóllit/ *n* a young domestic hen

pulley /poólli/ (*pl* **-leys**) *n* a wheel with a grooved rim over which a belt or chain can run to change the direction of a pulling force

Pullman /poólmǝn/ *n* a comfortable train-carriage

pullout /pool owt/ *n* **1** a removable section of a publication **2** a withdrawal from an obligation or difficult circumstance **3** a retreat from a place or military involvement

pullover /poóll ōvǝr/ *n* a garment that is pulled on over the head, especially a jumper

pulmonary /púlmǝnǝri, poól-/ *adj* of the lungs

pulp /pulp/ *n* **1** the soft fleshy tissue inside a fruit or vegetable **2** the pith inside a plant stem **3** a soft or soggy mass of material **4** crushed wood for paper **5** cheap books and magazines **6** the sensitive tissue inside a tooth ■ *vti* crush or be crushed into pulp **—pulpy** *adj*

pulpit /poólpit/ *n* a raised platform in a church where the priest or minister stands

pulpwood /púlp wood/ *n* soft wood used to make paper

pulsar /púl saar/ *n* a small dense star that emits brief intense bursts of visible radiation, radio waves, and X-rays

pulsate /pul sáyt/ (**-sating, -sated**) *vi* **1** expand and contract with a regular beat *(refers to blood vessels)* **2** vibrate or throb **—pulsating** *adj* **—pulsation** *n*

pulse[1] /pulss/ *n* **1** the regular expansion and contraction of an artery, caused by the pumping of blood through the body **2** a rhythmical beat or throb **3** a sudden change in a constant quantity, or a repeating change in magnitude ■ *vi* (**pulsing, pulsed**) **1** beat rhythmically **2** undergo brief sudden changes in quantity, e.g. in voltage

pulse[2] /pulss/ *n* **1** an edible seed from a pod ○ *eats peas, beans, and other pulses* **2** a plant that has pods as fruit

pulverize /púlvǝ rīz/ (**-izing, -ized**), **pulverise** *vt* **1** crush to a powder **2** defeat convincingly *(infml)* **—pulverization** /púlvǝ rī záysh'n/ *n*

puma /pyoómǝ/ (*pl* **-mas** *or* same) *n* a large wild cat

pumice /púmmiss/ *n* a type of light rock full of air spaces

pummel /púmm'l/ (**-melling, -melled**), **pommel** /pómm'l, púmm'l/ *vt* hit repeatedly

pump[1] /pump/ *vt* **1** force a liquid or gas to flow in a particular direction **2** move something up and down energetically ○ *frantically pumping the brakes* **3** question somebody persistently ■ *n* a device for making a liquid or gas flow in a particular direction

☐ **pump out** *vt* **1** produce a great deal of **2** remove fluid from

☐ **pump up** *vt* inflate something

pump[2] /pump/ *n* **1** a canvas shoe with a rubber sole **2** a soft shoe for dancing

pumpernickel /púmpǝr nik'l, poóm-/ *n* dark rye bread

pumpkin /púmpkin/ *n* **1** a large orange fruit with a thick rind and many seeds **2** a plant that produces pumpkins

pump room *n* a room in a spa where water can be drunk

pun /pun/ *n* a play on words **—pun** *vi* **—punny** *adj*

Puncak Jaya /poón chaak jaȧ yaa/ highest mountain in Indonesia, in the Surdiman Range, in W New Guinea. Height 5,030 m/16,503 ft.

punch[1] *vt* **1** hit somebody with the fist **2** press a button or key ■ *n* **1** a blow with the fist **2** vigour ◊ **pack a punch** be very powerful (*infml*) ◊ **not pull any** *or* **your punches, pull no punches** be as forceful as necessary ◊ **roll with the punches** adapt easily to a difficult situation (*infml*)

ORIGIN Of the three English words **punch**, two are ultimately related. **Punch** 'hit' derives from a French verb meaning 'prick', which developed from Latin. The tool **punch** is probably an abbreviation of an earlier word *puncheon* 'wooden support', which is ultimately from the same Latin root. The odd one out, **punch** the drink, appears to go back to a Sanskrit word meaning 'five', because there were originally five essential ingredients. It was encountered in South Asia in the 17C.

punch[2] *n* **1** a tool for making holes **2** a stamping tool —**punch** *vt*

punch[3] *n* a drink of mixed fruit juices, spices, and alcohol

punchbag /púnch bag/ *n* a large heavy bag punched by boxers for training

punchball /púnch bawl/ *n* a large heavy ball punched by boxers as training

punchbowl /púnch bōl/ *n* **1** a bowl for serving punch **2** a hollow on a hill or mountain

punch-drunk *adj* disorientated by punches to the head

punchline /púnch līn/ *n* the funny ending of a joke

punch-up *n* a fight (*infml*)

punchy /púnchi/ (*-ier, -iest*) *adj* (*infml*) **1** forceful ◊ *a good punchy slogan* **2** punch-drunk

punctilious /pungk tilli əss/ *adj* **1** careful about correct behaviour **2** taking great care over details —**punctiliously** *adv* ◊ See note at **careful**

punctual /púngkchoo əl/ *adj* keeping to the arranged time —**punctuality** /púngkchoo álləti/ *n* —**punctually** *adv*

punctuate /púngktyoo ayt/ (*-ating, -ated*) *v* **1** *vti* add punctuation to a text **2** *vt* interrupt frequently

punctuation /púngkchoo áysh'n/ *n* **1** the marks used to organize writing into clauses, phrases, and sentences **2** the use of punctuation

punctuation mark *n* a sign used to punctuate text

puncture /púngkchər/ *n* a small hole ■ *v* (*-turing, -tured*) **1** *vti* make a hole in or get a hole **2** *vt* ruin somebody's confidence —**puncturable** *adj*

pundit /púndit/ *n* somebody who expresses an opinion, especially in the media

Pune /poónə/ city in west-central India. Pop. 1,566,651 (1991).

pungent /púnjənt/ *adj* **1** strong-smelling or strong-tasting **2** expressed in a witty and biting manner —**pungency** *n* —**pungently** *adv*

punish /púnnish/ *vt* **1** make somebody undergo a penalty **2** impose a penalty for an offence ◊ *crimes formerly punished by death* **3** treat somebody or something harshly —**punishable** *adj* —**punisher** *n* —**punishing** *adj* —**punishingly** *adv*

punishment /púnnishmənt/ *n* **1** the act of punishing **2** the penalty for doing something wrong **3** rough treatment or heavy use

punitive /pyoónətiv/ *adj* **1** of or as punishment ◊ *punitive air strikes* **2** causing hardship ◊ *punitive taxation* —**punitively** *adv*

Punjab /punjáab/ **1** state in NW India, bordering the province of Punjab in Pakistan. Cap. Chandigarh. Pop. 21,695,000 (1994). **2** province of NE Pakistan, bordering the Indian state of Punjab. Cap. Lahore. Pop. 72,585,000 (1998).

Punjabi /pun jáabi/ (*pl* **-bis**), **Panjabi** /ˈ/ **1** somebody from Punjab **2** the official language of Punjab —**Punjabi** *adj*

punk *n* **1** a 1970s youth movement marked by confrontational anti-establishment attitudes **2** a member of the punk movement **3** *also* **punk rock** the fast loud rock music of the punk movement ■ *adj* **1** no good (*infml*) **2** of the punk movement or punk rock

punka /púngkə/, **punkah** /ˈ/ *n S Asia* a large fan for ventilation, operated by a servant

punnet /púnnit/ *n* a small basket or container in which soft fruit is sold

punt[1] *n* a narrow flat-bottomed boat propelled using a long pole ■ *vti* propel or go in a punt —**punter** *n*

punt[2] *vti* drop a football and kick it before it hits the ground —**punt** *n* —**punter** *n*

punt[3] *n* a bet placed with a bookmaker (*infml*) ■ *vti* gamble

punt[4] *n* an indentation in the bottom of a bottle

punter /púntər/ *n* **1** a customer (*slang*) **2** a gambler (*infml*)

puny /pyoóni/ *adj* **1** small and weak **2** inadequate —**puniness** *n*

ORIGIN Puny is an alteration of a form *puisne* that more clearly reflects its origins. It is an adoption of a French word meaning literally 'born afterwards'. The original meaning of **puny** and *puisne* was 'junior'.

pup *n* **1** a young dog **2** a young seal or other animal ■ *vi* (**pupping, pupped**) give birth to pups

pupa /pyoópə/ (*pl* **-pae** /-pee/ *or* **-pas**) *n* a developing insect inside a cocoon —**pupal** *adj*

pupate /pyoo páyt/ (*-pating, -pated*) *vi* develop from a larva into a pupa

pupil[1] /pyoóp'l/ *n* a student

ORIGIN The two words **pupil** are closely related. **Pupil** 'student' goes back to Latin forms meaning 'orphan, ward', diminutives of *pupus* 'boy' and *pupa* 'girl'. 'Orphan' was in fact the original English meaning of **pupil**, with the need for orphan children to be cared for and taught leading to the 'student' sense in the mid-16C.

The connection with the **pupil** of the eye derives from the extension of Latin *pupa* to mean 'doll'. The small reflected images that people see in each other's eyes when they stand close prompted the part of the eye where the 'doll' was seen also to be called a *pupa*.

pupil[2] /pyoõp'l/ *n* the dark circular opening at the centre of the eye

puppet /púppit/ *n* **1** a doll with movable parts used in entertainment **2** somebody who can be manipulated

puppeteer /púppi teèr/ *n* somebody who operates puppets —**puppetry** /púppitri/ *n*

puppy /púppi/ (*pl* -**pies**) *n* a young dog —**puppyish** *adj*

ORIGIN Puppy was adopted in the late 15C from a French word meaning 'doll, toy', and originally referred to a small dog kept as a pet or plaything. The movement from 'toy dog' to 'young dog' took place in the late 16C. The French form goes back to a Latin word for 'girl' that is also the source of *puppet* and *pupil*.

puppy fat *n* childhood plumpness (*infml*)

puppy love *n* adolescent love or infatuation

purblind /púr blínd/ *adj* lacking understanding (*fml*)

Purcell /pər séll/, **Henry** (1659–95) English composer

purchase /púrchəss/ *vt* (-**chasing**, -**chased**) **1** get by paying money **2** obtain through effort or sacrifice ■ *n* **1** the act of buying something **2** an item bought **3** a firm grip or hold **4** influence, power, or other advantage —**purchasable** *adj* —**purchaser** *n*

purchasing power *n* **1** wealth regarded as the ability to spend **2** the value of currency

purdah /púrdə/ *n* the Hindu and Islamic practice of keeping women from public view

pure /pyoor, pyawr/ (**purer**, **purest**) *adj* **1** not mixed with another substance **2** free from contamination **3** complete or utter ○ *pure terror* **4** chaste (*literary*) **5** describes sound or colour that is clear and vivid **6** involving theory, not practice ○ *pure science* **7** of unmixed ancestry —**purely** *adv* —**pureness** *n* —**purity** *n*

purebred /pyoõr bred, pyáwr-/ *adj* with ancestors of the same breed —**purebred** *n*

purée /pyoõr ay, pyáwr-/, **puree** *n* food made into a thick paste ■ *vti* (-**réed**; -**reed**) make food into a purée

purgative /púrgətiv/ *n* a substance that causes evacuation of the bowels (*fml*) —**purgative** *adj*

purgatory /púrgətəri/ *n* **1** *also* **Purgatory** in Roman Catholic doctrine, a place where the souls of dead people go until they have made amends for their sins **2** a miserable situation —**purgatorial** /púrgə táwri əl/ *adj*

purge (**purging, purged**) *vt* **1** remove opponents from a place or organization **2** remove something undesirable or no longer wanted **3** free somebody from guilt or sin (*fml*) **4** delete

computer data from a storage device —**purge** *n*

purify /pyoõri fī, pyáwr-/ (-**fies, -fied**) *vt* **1** remove impurities from **2** make spiritually pure —**purification** /-fi káysh'n/ *n*

Purim /poõrim, pyoõrim, poo reém/ *n* a Jewish festival. Date: 14th day of Adar.

purist /pyoõrist, pyáwr-/ *n* an upholder of traditional standards —**purism** *n* —**puristic** /pyoor ístik, pyawr-/ *adj*

puritan /pyoõrit'n, pyáwrit'n/ *n* **1** somebody with a strict moral code who is suspicious of pleasure **2 Puritan** a member of a Protestant group of the 16C and 17C that advocated simple rites and a strict moral code —**puritan** *adj* —**puritanical** /pyoõri tánnik'l, pyáwr-/ *adj* —**puritanism** *n*

purl *n* a reverse plain knitting stitch —**purl** *vti*

purlieu /púrlyoo/ *n* an outlying district ■ **purlieus** *npl* environs or outskirts (*fml*)

purloin /pur lóyn/ *vt* steal (*fml or humorous*) —**purloiner** *n* ♢ See note at **steal**

purple /púrp'l/ *n* **1** a colour that combines red and blue **2** a purple robe, worn as a sign of high rank ■ *adj* **1** of a red-blue colour **2** elaborate or exaggerated in style ○ *purple prose* —**purpleness** *n*

purport *vt* /pur páwrt/ claim to be something or somebody ■ *n* /púr pawrt/ (*fml*) **1** meaning **2** intent —**purported** *adj* —**purportedly** *adv*

purpose /púrpəss/ *n* **1** the reason for which something exists, is done, or has been made **2** the desired effect of something **3** determination —**purposeless** *adj* —**purposelessly** *adv* ♢ **on purpose** deliberately

purpose-built *adj* specially made

purposeful /púrpəssf'l/ *adj* **1** determined **2** having a goal —**purposefully** *adv*

purposely /púrpəssli/ *adv* intentionally

purr *n* **1** a cat's low regular murmuring noise **2** any similar sound ■ *v* **1** *vi* emit a purr **2** *vti* say something in a soft throaty voice —**purringly** *adv*

purse *n* **1** a small bag for carrying personal money **2** *US, Can* a woman's handbag **3** an amount of prize money **4** an amount of available money ■ *vt* (**pursing, pursed**) draw your lips together at the sides

purser /púrssər/ *n* an officer on a ship or aircraft who manages money and, on a passenger ship, looks after passengers

purse strings *npl* control over finances

pursuance /pər syoõ ənss/ *n* the process of doing something as required (*fml*)

pursuant /pər syoõ ənt/ ♢ **pursuant to** in accordance with (*fml*)

pursue /pər syoõ/ (-**suing, -sued**) *v* **1** *vti* follow or chase somebody or something **2** *vt* be an ever-present problem for **3** *vt* continue or follow up on **4** *vt* try to accomplish —**pursuable** *adj* —**pursuer** *n*

pursuit /pər syoõt/ *n* **1** the act of pursuing somebody or something ○ *in pursuit of the stolen car* ○ *the pursuit of excellence* **2** a hobby

purvey /pər váy/ vt 1 supply goods (fml) 2 circulate gossip —**purveyor** n

purview /púr vyoo/ n 1 scope or range 2 the main enacting part of written legislation

pus /puss/ n a yellowish liquid formed at sites of infection

Pusan /poo sán/ city and port in SE South Korea. Pop. 3,813,814 (1995).

push /poosh/ v 1 vti press against somebody or something in order to move them 2 vti advance or cause to advance using pressure or force 3 vt encourage somebody strongly 4 vt exploit something to the limit o *Don't push your luck.* 5 vt force something to change o *push prices down* 6 vt try to sell something 7 vt sell drugs (slang) ■ n 1 an application of pressure 2 the process of advancing 3 an energetic effort 4 a military advance 5 a stimulus —**pushing** adj —**pushingly** adv ◊ **be pushing** . . . be approaching a particular age (infml) ◊ **give somebody the push** dismiss somebody (infml) ◊ **when** *or* **if push comes to shove** at the point when something must be done or a decision must be made

□ **push off** vi go away (infml)

□ **push on** vi continue a journey or task

push-bike n a bicycle (infml)

push-button adj 1 operated by pushing a button 2 equipped with automatic devices

pushchair /poosh chair/ n a lightweight wheeled chair for a baby or young child

pushdown /poosh down/ n a computer storage technique in which the last item stored is the first retrieved

pusher /pooshər/ n a seller of illegal drugs (slang)

Pushkin /pooshkin/, **Aleksandr Sergeyevich** (1799–1837) Russian writer

pushover /poosh ōvər/ n (infml) 1 something that is easy to do 2 an easy victim

push-start vt start a vehicle by pushing it and engaging the gear when it is moving —**push-start** n

push technology n Internet technology providing customized information

push-up n 1 Aus, US, Can = **press-up** 2 US a computer storage technique in which the first item stored is the first retrieved

pushy /pooshi/ (**-ier**, **-iest**) adj unpleasantly competitive or forceful (infml) —**pushily** adv —**pushiness** n

pusillanimous /pyooǒssi lánnimǝss/ adj cowardly —**pusillanimity** /pyooǒssilǝ nímmǝti/ n ◊ See note at **cowardly**

puss /pooss/ n a cat (dated infml)

pussy[1] /pooǒssi/ (pl **-ies**) n a cat (infml; often by or to children)

pussy[2] /pooǒssi/ (pl **-ies**) n a taboo term for a woman's genitals (offensive)

pussy[3] /pússi/ (**-ier**, **-siest**) adj containing pus

pussycat /pooǒssi kat/ n 1 a cat (often by or to children) 2 somebody who is gentle and amiable (infml)

pussyfoot /pooǒssi fooǒt/ vi behave hesitantly or speak vaguely (infml)

pussy willow n a willow tree with greyish catkins

pustule /púss tyool/ n a pimple or similar pus-filled inflammation —**pustular** /pústyooǒlǝr/ adj

put /poot/ vt (**putting**, **put**) 1 move something or somebody into a particular place or position 2 cause somebody or something to be in a particular place or situation 3 make somebody or something do something o *put her to work in the garden* 4 make somebody be affected by something o *put pressure on them* 5 use or apply something o *Put your mind to it.* 6 invest money in something 7 express something in a particular way 8 bring something up as a question or proposal 9 estimate something to be a particular amount o *put him in his late 30s* 10 throw the heavy metal ball in the shot put ■ n a throw of the heavy metal ball in the shot put

□ **put across** vt communicate clearly

□ **put back** vt make a clock show an earlier time

□ **put by** vt save money for the future

□ **put down** v 1 vt write something 2 vt suppress a rebellion 3 vt disparage or belittle somebody (infml) 4 vt pay a deposit 5 vt attribute something to something else 6 vt kill an animal humanely 7 vti land an aeroplane

□ **put forward** vt 1 submit or make known something such as a suggestion or an idea 2 suggest somebody as a candidate

□ **put in** vt 1 devote time or energy 2 install something 3 submit a claim

□ **put off** vt 1 postpone or delay 2 make disgusted 3 discourage 4 distract and cause to perform less well ◊ **put somebody off his** *or* **her stride** *or* **stroke** distract somebody and cause him or her to perform less well

□ **put on** vt 1 cover part of your body with something such as clothing 2 organize or stage an event 3 gain or add weight 4 adopt a false way of behaving

□ **put out** vt 1 extinguish a light or fire 2 annoy or upset somebody 3 cause somebody inconvenience

□ **put over** vt make understood ◊ **put one over (on)** trick somebody (infml)

□ **put through** vt 1 make somebody undergo something 2 connect somebody by telephone

□ **put up** v 1 vti give or find accommodation 2 vt engage in something defensive o *put up a fight* 3 vt provide money 4 vt arrange hair on top of the head

□ **put upon** vt treat somebody badly

□ **put up to** vt encourage somebody to do something bad

□ **put up with** vt tolerate

putative /pyooǒtǝtiv/ adj 1 generally accepted as being a particular thing o *the putative father of the child* 2 thought to exist —**putatively** adv

putdown /poot down/ n a crushing remark (infml)

Putin /poŏtin/, **Vladimir** (*b.* 1952) Russian president (2000–)

put-in *n* a throw of the ball into a rugby scrum

put out *adj* annoyed, upset, offended, or inconvenienced

putrefy /pyoŏtri fī/ (**-fies, -fied**) *vti* make or become putrid **—putrefaction** /pyoŏtri fáksh'n/ *n*

putrescent /pyoo tréss'nt/ *adj* **1** decaying **2** of decay **—putrescence** *n*

putrid /pyoŏtrid/ *adj* decaying with a foul smell **—putridity** /pyoo tríddəti/ *n* **—putridly** *adv*

putsch /poŏch/ *n* a sudden attempt by a group to overthrow a government

putt /put/ *vti* hit a golf ball with a gentle tapping stroke **—putt** *n*

putter /púttər/ *n* **1** a golf club for use on the green **2** a golfer who is putting

putto /poŏttō/ (*pl* **-ti** /poŏtti/) *n* in art, a cherub

putty /pútti/ *n* **1** a paste used to fill holes in wood or to fix glass in window frames **2** a paste used as a finishing coat on plaster

Putumayo /poŏta mīyo/ tributary of the Amazon in NW South America. Length 1,000 km/1,610 mi.

put-upon *adj* badly treated

puzzle /púzz'l/ *vt* (**-zling, -zled**) confuse somebody by being hard to understand ■ *n* **1** a game or toy involving skill or intelligence **2** somebody or something difficult to understand **—puzzlement** *n* **—puzzlingly** *adv* ◊ See note at **problem**

□ **puzzle out** *vt* solve or understand something by reasoning or logic

□ **puzzle over** *vt* think hard about something confusing or complicated

puzzler /púzzlər/ *n* something that is confusing or mystifying

PVC *n* a tough synthetic material. Use: flooring, piping, clothing. Full form **polyvinyl chloride**

p.w. *abbr* per week

PWA *abbr* person with Aids

pygmy /pígmi/, **pigmy** *n* (*pl* **-mies**) **1** an offensive term for somebody of shorter than average height **2 Pygmy, Pigmy** a member of an African or Asian people of small stature ■ *adj* of a small breed (*sometimes offensive*)

pyjama party *n* a party at which guests wear pyjamas

pyjamas /pə jáaməz/ *npl* light loose-fitting trousers and a matching shirt for wearing in bed

pylon /pílən/ *n* **1** a metal tower supporting high-voltage cables **2** a tower at an airfield that marks the course for pilots to follow **3** a monumental gateway or pillar

Pyongyang /pyóng yang/ capital of North Korea. Pop. 2,500,000 (1995).

pyorrhoea /pī ə reè ə/ *n* inflammation of the gums with a discharge of pus

pyramid /pírrəmid/ *n* **1** a huge ancient Egyptian stone tomb in the shape of a pyramid **2** a solid shape with a square base and sloping triangular sides **3** a system with a gradually expanding structure **—pyramidal** /pi rámmid'l/ *adj* **—pyramidic** /pírrə míddik/ *adj*

pyramid selling *n* the sale of goods to a number of distributors, each of whom sells the goods to a number of other distributors, and so on

pyre /pīr/ *n* a pile of burning material, especially one on which a body is cremated

Pyrenees /pírrə neèz/ mountain range forming a natural boundary between France and Spain. Highest peak Pic d'Aneto 3,404 m/11,168 ft.

Pyrex /pī́r eks/ *tdmk* a trademark for a type of glass that is resistant to heat and chemicals

pyrites /pī rī́ teez/, **pyrite** /pī́ rīt/ *n* a mineral with a metallic lustre. Use: a source of iron and sulphur.

pyromania /pī́rō máyni ə/ *n* an uncontrollable desire to burn things **—pyromaniac** *n*

pyrotechnics /pī́rō tékniks/ *n* (+ *sing* or *pl verb*) **1** a firework display **2** any showy display **—pyrotechnic** *adj* **—pyrotechnical** *adj*

Pyrrhic victory /pírrik-/ *n* a victory won at such great cost that it amounts to a defeat

---

ORIGIN The original **Pyrrhic victory** was won by Pyrrhus, king of the ancient Greek province of Epirus, who invaded Italy and defeated the Roman army at Heraclea (280 BC) and Asculum (279 BC), but sustained huge losses to his troops.

Pythagoras /pī thággərəss/ (582?–500? BC) Greek philosopher and mathematician **—Pythagorean** /pī thággə reè ən/ *adj*, *n*

python /pī́th'n/ *n* a large constricting snake

ORIGIN In Greek mythology, Python was a huge serpent or monster killed by the god Apollo near Delphi. The name **python** was adopted for a real snake in the mid-19C.

Pythonesque /pī́thə nésk/ *adj* amusing in a surreal way

ORIGIN **Pythonesque** draws a comparison with *Monty Python's Flying Circus*, a popular British television comedy series made in the 1970s.

---

pyx /piks/, **pix** *n* **1** a box for Communion wafers **2** a container for coins at a mint

Q

q¹ (*pl* **q's**), **Q** (*pl* **Q's** *or* **Qs**) *n* the 17th letter of the English alphabet

q² *abbr* **1** quarter **2** question

Q *abbr* **1** quarto **2** queen

Qaddafi ◊ **Gaddafi, Muammar al-**

Q & A /kyoo ənd ay/ *abbr* question and answer

Qatar /ka táar, káttaar/ country in E Arabia. Cap.

Doha. Pop. 769,152 (2001). —**Qatari** /kə taˈari/ adj, n

QC abbr **1** quality control **2** Queen's Counsel

QED adv indicates that a particular fact is proof of the theory that has just been advanced

> **ORIGIN QED** is an abbreviation of Latin quod erat demonstrandum 'which was to be proved'.

Q fever n an infectious bacterial disease

Qingdao /chíng dów/ city in E China, on the Yellow Sea. Pop. 3,140,000 (1995).

Qiqihar /chee chee haˈar/ port in NE China. Pop. 1,520,000 (1995).

Qom /kōˈom/, **Qum** city in west-central Iran. Pop. 777,677 (1996).

qt abbr quantity

q.t. ◊ **on the q.t.** quietly and secretly (infml)

qua /kway, kwaa/ prep as (fml)

quack[1] /kwak/ n the harsh sound made by a duck

quack[2] /kwak/ n **1** a fake doctor **2** a fraud —**quackery** n

> **ORIGIN Quack** is a shortening of the now obsolete quacksalver, a word that was adopted from Dutch in the late 16C. Its elements mean 'chatter, prattle' and 'remedy' (the second Dutch element is related to English salve), so that quacksalvers were people who constantly proclaimed the virtues of their remedies and medicines. The shortened form **quack** is recorded from the mid-17C.

quad[1] /kwod/ n a quadruplet (infml)

quad[2] /kwod/ n a quadrangle (infml)

quadrangle /kwód rang g'l/ n **1** a four-sided shape **2** an open area surrounded by buildings —**quadrangular** /kwod ráng gyóōlər/ adj

quadrant /kwóddrənt/ n **1** a quarter of the circumference of a circle **2** a quarter of the area of circle **3** a quarter of a surface **4** a device for measuring the angle of a star

quadraphonic /kwóddrə fónnik/ adj using a four-channel sound system —**quadraphonics** n

quadratic equation /kwo dráttik-/ n an equation containing squared terms

quadri- prefix four, fourth ○ quadrilateral

quadriceps /kwóddri seps/ (pl same or -cepses) n a large muscle at the front of the thigh

quadrilateral /kwóddri láttərəl/ n a four-sided figure ■ adj four-sided

quadrille /kwə dríl/ n **1** a square dance of French origin **2** the music for a quadrille

quadrillion /kwo drílli ən/ (pl -lions or same) n **1** the number written as one followed by 15 zeros **2** the number written as one followed by 24 zeros (dated) —**quadrillion** adj, pron —**quadrillionth** adj, n

quadriplegia /kwóddri pleéji ə/ n inability to move all four limbs or the entire body below the neck —**quadriplegic** n, adj

quadruped /kwóddrōo ped/ n a four-footed animal ■ adj four-footed —**quadrupedal** /kwo drōoˈpid'l, kwóddrōo pédd'l/ adj

quadruple /kwóddrōoˈp'l, kwo drōoˈp'l/ vti (-pling, -pled) increase fourfold ■ adj **1** multiplied by four **2** with four parts ■ n a quantity that is four times as great as another

quadruplet /kwóddrōoˈplət/ n one of four babies born to the same mother at the same time

quaff /kwof/ vti drink alcohol quickly or heartily (literary or humorous) —**quaff** n

quagmire /kwág mīr, kwóg-/ n **1** a bog or swamp **2** a difficult situation

quail[1] /kwayl/ (pl **quails** or same) n a small bird with mottled brown plumage

quail[2] /kwayl/ vi tremble or shrink with fear or apprehension ◊ See note at **recoil**

quaint /kwaynt/ adj **1** attractively old-fashioned **2** pleasantly strange —**quaintly** adv —**quaintness** n

quake /kwayk/ vi (**quaking**, **quaked**) **1** tremble with fear **2** shake ■ n an earthquake (infml) —**quaky** adj

Quaker /kwáykər/ n a member of a Christian group who believe in God's direct approach to each person, without formal sacraments, ministry, or creeds —**Quakerism** n —**Quakerly** adj

qualification /kwóllifi káysh'n/ n **1** an attribute or skill that makes somebody suitable for a specific job or activity **2** an official requirement for eligibility, e.g. passing an examination (often pl) **3** the meeting of requirements for eligibility **4** something that modifies or restricts something

qualifier /kwólli fī ər/ n **1** a person or team that qualifies for a later round in a tournament **2** an early round in a tournament

qualify /kwólli fī/ (-fies, -fied) v **1** vti be or make suitable **2** vti have or give eligibility **3** vt limit or change **4** vt moderate **5** vt modify or restrict the meaning of —**qualified** adj

qualitative /kwóllitətiv/ adj of quality —**qualitatively** adv

quality /kwólləti/ (pl -ties) n **1** a distinguishing characteristic **2** an essential property **3** the general standard of something **4** excellence

quality control n the process or job of controlling the quality of manufactured products

quality of life n the degree of somebody's contentment with everyday life

quality time n time devoted exclusively to somebody that strengthens mutual bonds

qualm /kwaam/ n a feeling of unease —**qualmish** adj

quandary /kwóndəri/ (pl -ries) n a dilemma

~~quandry~~ incorrect spelling of **quandary**

quango /kwáng gō/ (pl -gos) n an autonomous government-financed organization

quanta plural of **quantum**

quantifier /kwónti fī ər/ n a word such as 'all' or 'some' that indicates the range of things referred to

quantify /kwónti fī/ (-fies, -fied) vt determine the number, amount, degree, or extent of something —**quantifiable** /kwónti fī əb'l/ adj —**quantification** /kwóntifi káysh'n/ n

quantitative /kwóntitətiv/ adj 1 relating to quantity 2 measurable —**quantitatively** adv

quantity /kwóntəti/ (pl **-ties**) n 1 an amount or number of something 2 a large amount or number ○ imported in quantity 3 a mathematical entity with a numerical value

quantity surveyor n somebody who assesses the cost of building work

quantum /kwóntəm/ n (pl **-ta** /-tə/) the smallest quantity of energy ■ adj major —**quantal** adj

quantum leap n a sudden change or advance

quantum mechanics n the study and analysis of the interactions of atoms and elementary particles based on quantum theory (+ sing verb) —**quantum mechanical** adj

quantum physics n the branch of physics that uses quantum theory (+ sing verb)

quantum theory n a theory of elementary particles or energy states that assumes that energy is subdivided into discrete amounts and that matter possesses wave properties

quarantine /kwórrən teen/ n 1 isolation to prevent spread of disease 2 a place of isolation ■ vt (**-tining, -tined**) 1 isolate in order to avoid the spread of disease 2 detain for social or political reasons

ORIGIN A period of **quarantine** originally lasted for 40 days: the word goes back to the Latin word for 'forty'. The medical use entered English from Italian in the mid-17C, when ships with passengers or crew suspected of illness were prevented from entering Italian ports for 40 days.

~~quarentine~~ incorrect spelling of **quarantine**

quark /kwaark/ n an elementary particle with an electric charge that is believed to be a constituent of baryons and mesons

ORIGIN The **quark** was named by its discoverer, the US physicist Murray Gell-Mann. He associated his coinage with a nonsense word used in James Joyce's *Finnegan's Wake* (1939): 'Three quarks for Muster Mark'. The particle name **quark** first appeared in print in 1964.

quarrel /kwórrəl/ n 1 an angry dispute 2 a reason to argue ■ vi (**-relling, -relled**) 1 argue vehemently 2 disagree

quarrelsome /kwórrəlsəm/ adj argumentative —**quarrelsomeness** n

quarry[1] /kwórri/ n (pl **-ries**) an excavation from which stone or other material is extracted ■ vti (**-ries, -ried**) obtain stone or other material from a quarry

quarry[2] /kwórri/ n (pl **-ries**) n 1 a hunted animal or bird 2 an object of pursuit

quart /kwawrt/ n a unit of measurement equal to two pints

quarter /kwáwrtər/ n 1 one of four equal parts of something 2 a number equal to one divided by four 3 a period of three months 4 15 minutes before or after the hour 5 a unit

of weight equal to one quarter of a hundredweight 6 also **Quarter** a district of a town 7 an unspecified person or group (often pl) ○ help from any quarter 8 mercy 9 any of the four sections into which the body of an animal or bird may be divided ■ **quarters** npl accommodation, e.g. for military personnel or household employees ■ adj divided by four ■ vt 1 divide something into four 2 cut a human body into four following execution 3 give somebody lodgings ◊ **at close quarters** from very near

quarterback /kwáwrtər bak/ n in American football, the player who calls the signals for offensive plays

quarter day n a day when quarterly payments are due

quarterdeck /kwáwrtər dek/ n the rear part of the upper deck on a ship

quarterfinal /kwáwrtər fín'l/ n a match before a semifinal —**quarterfinalist** n

quarterly /kwáwrtərli/ adj happening every three months ■ adv every three months ■ n (pl **-lies**) a journal published every three months

quartermaster /kwáwrtər maastər/ n 1 an army officer with responsibility for food and equipment 2 a naval officer with duties including navigation and signals

quarter sessions npl a former English law court with limited powers

quartet /kwawr tét/, **quartette** n 1 a group of four singers or musicians (+ sing or pl verb) 2 a piece of music for a quartet

quartile /kwáwr tīl/ n any one of the four equal groups into which a statistical sample can be divided

quarto /kwáwrtō/ (pl **-tos**) n 1 a page size created by folding a standard sheet of printing paper in half twice, creating four leaves or eight pages 2 a book with quarto pages

quartz /kwawrts/ n a crystalline mineral. Use: electronics, gems.

quasar /kwáy zaar, -saar/ n a remote astronomical object that emits large amounts of energy

quash[1] /kwosh/ vt suppress

quash[2] /kwosh/ vt declare null and void

quasi- prefix as if, resembling ○ quasi-stellar object

quasi-stellar object n ASTRON = quasar

quatercentenary /kwáttər sen teénəri/ (pl **-ries**) n a 400th anniversary

Quaternary /kwə túrnəri/ n the present period of geological time, which began 1.8 million years ago —**Quaternary** adj

quatrain /kwó trayn/ n a four-line verse

quatrefoil /káttrə foyl/ n 1 a design or symbol in the shape of a flower with four petals or a leaf with four parts 2 an architectural ornament with four lobes

quaver /kwáyvər/ v 1 vi tremble slightly 2 vti say something in a trembling voice ■ n a musical note equal in length to one eighth of a semibreve —**quaveringly** adv

quay /kee/ *n* a waterside platform in a port or harbour

quayside /keé sīd/ *n* the edge of a quay

queasy /kweézi/ (**-sier**, **-siest**) *adj* 1 nauseous 2 causing nausea 3 easily made queasy 4 causing uneasiness —**queasily** *adv* —**queasiness** *n*

Quebec[1] /kwi bék, ki-/, **Québec** /kay-/ 1 *also* **Quebec City**, **Québec City** capital of Quebec Province, Canada. Pop. 167,264 (1996). 2 province in E Canada. Cap. Quebec. Pop. 7,372,448 (2000). —**Quebecker** *n*

Quebec[2] /kwi bék, ki-/ *n* a communications code word for the letter 'Q'

Québécois /kwi bé kwaa, kay-/, **Québecois**, **Quebecois** *adj* of Quebec ■ *n* (*pl same*) somebody from Quebec

Quechua /kéchwa/ (*pl same or* **-uas**) *n* 1 a member of a Native South American people living in the Andes 2 the language of the Quechua people —**Quechua** *adj*

queen /kween/ *n* 1 a female ruler 2 the wife or widow of a king 3 a woman, place, or thing admired above all others 4 the most powerful chess piece 5 a playing card with a picture of a queen on it 6 an egg-laying bee, ant, or termite 7 an offensive term for a homosexual man, especially one regarded as stereotypically effeminate *(insult)* —**queenliness** *n* —**queenly** *adj*

queen bee *n* a fertile female bee

queen mother *n* a monarch's widowed mother

Queens /kweenz/ borough of New York City, on W Long Island. Pop. 1,951,598 (1990).

Queen's Bench *n* a division of the English High Court

Queensberry rules /kweénzbəri-/ *npl* 1 the rules that govern boxing 2 fair play *(infml)*

Queen's Counsel *n* a senior barrister

Queen's English *n* standard British English

Queen's evidence *n* a criminal's evidence against an accomplice

Queensland /kweénzland, kweénz land/ state in NE Australia. Cap. Brisbane. Pop. 3,485,200 (1998). —**Queenslander** *n*

queer /kweer/ *adj* 1 strange or unusual *(dated)* 2 considered eccentric *(dated infml)* 3 an offensive term meaning gay ■ *n* an offensive term for a gay man *(insult)* ■ *vt* thwart or compromise *(dated infml)* —**queerly** *adv* —**queerness** *n*

quell /kwel/ *vt* 1 bring to an end, usually by force 2 allay a feeling

quench /kwench/ *vt* 1 satisfy a thirst or a desire 2 extinguish a fire 3 subdue a feeling —**quenchless** *adj*

querulous /kwérrŏŏləss, -ryŏŏ-/ *adj* 1 tending to complain 2 whining —**querulously** *adv*

query /kweéri/ *n* (*pl* **-ries**) 1 a question 2 a doubt ■ *vt* (**-ries**, **-ried**) 1 express doubts about something 2 ask a question

quest /kwest/ *n* 1 a search 2 an adventurous expedition ■ *vti* go in search of something *(literary)* —**questingly** *adv*

question /kwéschən/ *n* 1 a written or spoken inquiry 2 a doubt 3 a matter that is the subject of discussion 4 an examination problem ■ *vt* 1 interrogate somebody 2 raise doubts about something —**questioner** *n* —**questioning** *adj* —**questioningly** *adv* ◇ **beg the question** take for granted the very point that needs to be proved ◇ **be out of the question** be impossible or unacceptable ◇ **call into question** raise doubts about ◇ **in question** under discussion or being dealt with ◇ **pop the question** propose marriage *(infml)*

SYNONYMS question, quiz, interrogate, grill, give the third degree CORE MEANING: ask for information

questionable /kwéschənəb'l/ *adj* 1 open to doubt or disagreement 2 not respectable or morally acceptable ○ *questionable motives* —**questionably** *adv*

~~**questionaire**~~ incorrect spelling of **questionnaire**

question mark *n* the punctuation mark (?) used at the end of a direct question

questionnaire /kwéschə náir, késchə-/ *n* a list of questions used to gather information

question time *n* a parliamentary question-and-answer period

quetzal /kéts'l, kwéts'l/ (*pl* **-zals** *or* **-zales** /ket saa layss/) *n* 1 a bird with bright green and red plumage 2 the main unit of Guatemalan currency

queue /kyoo/ *n* 1 a line of people who are waiting for something 2 a set of computer tasks waiting to be performed ■ *v* (**queueing** *or* **queuing**, **queued**) 1 *vi* form a waiting line 2 *vt* add a job to a computer's list of tasks ◇ See note at **cue**

ORIGIN Queue goes back through French to Latin *cauda* 'tail'. In English it was in fact originally (late 16C) a term used in heraldry for an animal's tail. It was then (mid-18C) applied to a 'pigtail', and only in the mid-19C to a 'line of people'.

queue-jump *vi* push in or unfairly move ahead of others in a queue —**queue-jumper** *n*

quibble /kwíbb'l/ (**-bling**, **-bled**) *vi* make trivial objections —**quibble** *n* —**quibblingly** *adv*

quiche /keesh/ *n* a savoury tart filled with a mixture of eggs and various meat or vegetable ingredients

quick /kwik/ *adj* 1 acting fast 2 showing alertness or sharp perception 3 nimble 4 done without delay 5 brief ■ *n* 1 the flesh under a nail 2 somebody's deepest feelings or most private emotions ■ *adv* fast *(infml)* —**quickly** *adv* —**quickness** *n* ◇ **quick and dirty** hastily produced to meet an immediate or pressing need *(infml)* ◇ See note at **intelligent**

quicken /kwíkən/ *v* 1 *vti* make or become faster 2 *vti* stimulate or be stimulated 3 *vi* begin to come to life

quick-fire adj 1 firing shots rapidly 2 occurring in rapid succession (infml)

quickie /kwíki/ n an activity done hurriedly, especially an act of sex (infml)

quicklime /kwík līm/ n calcium oxide

quicksand /kwík sand/ n 1 a deep mass of wet sand that sucks down any heavy object on its surface 2 a dangerous situation

quicksilver /kwík silvər/ n mercury (literary) ■ adj changing unpredictably

quickstep /kwík step/ n 1 a fast marching step 2 a fast ballroom dance 3 the music for a quickstep

quick-tempered adj easily angered —**quick-temperedness** n

quick-witted adj able to think quickly —**quick-wittedly** adv —**quick-wittedness** n

quid[1] /kwid/ (pl same) n a pound sterling (infml)

quid[2] /kwid/ n a piece of chewing tobacco

quid pro quo /kwid prō kwó/ (pl quid pro quos) n 1 something done in exchange 2 the act of returning a favour

quiescent /kwi éss'nt/ adj inactive —**quiescence** n

quiet /kwí ət/ adj 1 making little noise 2 peaceful or relaxing 3 done in private 4 free from trouble 5 not showy ■ n the absence of noise —**quietly** adv —**quietness** n ◊ See note at **silent**

SPELLCHECK Do not confuse the spelling of **quiet** and **quite** ('somewhat'), which sound similar.

quieten /kwí ət'n/ v 1 vti make or become quiet 2 vt allay doubts or fears

quietism /kwí ətizəm/ n a form of Christian mysticism —**quietist** adj, n

quietude /kwí ə tyood/ n calmness or tranquillity (literary)

quietus /kwī eétəss, -áy-/ n (literary) 1 death 2 a release from a debt or duty

quiff /kwif/ n a man's hairstyle in which the front of the hair is brushed up and back

quill /kwil/ n 1 a large feather 2 a pen made from the shaft of a feather 3 a spine on the body of a porcupine or similar animal

quilt /kwilt/ n a thick bed cover made of two layers of fabric stitched together ■ vt make something by sewing two layers of fabric together with a filling in between —**quilting** n

quin /kwin/ n a quintuplet (infml)

quince /kwinss/ n 1 a pear-shaped fruit that is edible only when cooked. Use: preserves. 2 a tree that produces quinces

ORIGIN The **quince** takes its name from Cydonia (now Khania), a port in NW Crete from which the fruit was exported.

Quincey ♦ **de Quincey, Thomas**

Quine /kwīn/**, W. V.** (1908–2000) US philosopher

quinine /kwi neén, kwínneen/ n a drug made from cinchona bark. Use: treatment of malaria.

quintal /kwínt'l/ n 1 a metric unit of weight equal to 100 kg 2 a hundredweight

quintessence /kwin téss'nss/ n 1 the embodiment of something 2 the purest extract of a substance that contains all its properties —**quintessential** /kwínti sénsh'l/ adj

quintet /kwin tét/**, quintette** n 1 a group of five singers or musicians (+ sing or pl verb) 2 a piece of music for a quintet

quintuplet /kwín tyóoplət, kwin tyóop-/ n one of five babies born to the same mother at the same time

quip /kwip/ n a witticism ■ vti (**quipping, quipped**) say something wittily

quire /kwīr/ n a set of 24 or 25 sheets of paper, equal to one twentieth of a ream

quirk /kwurk/ n 1 an odd turn of events 2 an odd mannerism —**quirkily** adv —**quirkiness** n —**quirky** adj

quisling /kwízzling/ n a traitor

ORIGIN The original **quisling** was Vidkun Quisling, a Norwegian politician who from 1933 led the National Union Party, the Norwegian fascist party. (Quisling was not his real name – he was originally Abraham Lauritz Jonsson.) When the Germans invaded Norway in 1940 he gave them active support, urging his fellow Norwegians not to resist them, and in 1942 he was installed by Hitler as a puppet premier. In 1945 he was shot for treason.

quit /kwit/ (**quitting, quitted** or **quit**) v 1 vti resign or give up a job 2 vti stop doing something 3 vt leave a place (archaic)

quite /kwīt/ adv 1 to some degree, but not greatly ○ The film was quite good, but I wouldn't bother seeing it again. 2 entirely or altogether ○ not quite as bad as all that 3 adds emphasis ○ That was quite a party! 4 expresses agreement ◊ See note at **quiet**

Quito /keétō/ capital of Ecuador. Pop. 1,444,363 (1996).

quits /kwits/ adj on even terms, especially after repayment or retaliation (infml)

quittance /kwítt'nss/ n exemption

quitter /kwíttər/ n somebody who gives up easily (infml)

quiver[1] /kwívvər/ vi tremble —**quiver** n —**quivery** adj

quiver[2] /kwívvər/ n 1 a case for arrows 2 the arrows in a quiver

qui vive /keè veév/ ◊ **on the qui vive** alert and vigilant

quixotic /kwik sóttik/ adj romantic and impractical —**quixotically** adv

ORIGIN The original **quixotic** person was Don Quixote, the hero of a romance (1605–15) by the Spanish writer Miguel de Cervantes.

quiz /kwiz/ (**quizzing, quizzed**) vt interrogate ◊ See note at **question**

quizes incorrect spelling of **quizzes**

quizmaster /kwíz maastər/ n the presenter on a quiz show

quizzical /kwízzik'l/ adj questioning —**quizzically** adv

Qum ♦ **Qom**

quoits /koyts, kwoyts/ *n* a game in which rings are thrown over short posts (+ *sing verb*)

quondam /kwón dam, -dəm/ *adj* former *(literary)*

quorate /kwáw rayt, -rət/ *adj* with a quorum of members present

Quorn /kwawrn/ *tdmk* a trademark for a vegetable protein used in cooking as a meat substitute

quorum /kwáwrəm/ *n* the minimum number of people required to be present at a meeting for its business to be valid

quota /kwótə/ *n* **1** a proportional share **2** a maximum permitted number or amount

quotable /kwótəb'l/ *adj* **1** worth quoting **2** officially able to be quoted in a publication

quotation /kwō táysh'n/ *n* **1** a piece of quoted speech or writing **2** the act of quoting what somebody has said or written **3** an estimate of the cost of proposed work **4** the current price of a share —**quotational** *adj*

quotation mark *n* an inverted comma

quote /kwōt/ *vti* (**quoting, quoted**) **1** repeat somebody's exact words **2** refer to something in support of an argument **3** give an estimate of the cost of proposed work ■ *n* **1** a quotation *(infml)* **2** a quotation mark *(often pl)*

quoth /kwōth/ *vt* said *(literary)*

quotidian /kwō tíddi ən/ *adj (fml)* **1** commonplace **2** daily

quotient /kwósh'nt/ *n* **1** the number that results from the division of one number by another **2** a ratio

Qur'an *n* = Koran

QWERTY keyboard /kwúrti-/ *n* a standard computer keyboard

R

r[1] (*pl* **r's**), **R** (*pl* **R's** *or* **Rs**) *n* the 18th letter of the English alphabet ◇ **the three R's** the basic skills of reading, writing, and arithmetic

r[2] *symbol* **1** radius **2** resistance

r[3] *abbr* **1** right **2** river **3** road

R[1] *symbol* **1** radical **2** resistance

R[2] *abbr* **1** radius **2** Regina *(after the name of a queen)* **3** Rex *(after the name of a king)* **4** right **5** road

Ra *symbol* radium

Rabat /rə baát/ capital of Morocco. Pop. 1,385,872 (1994).

rabbi /rábbī/ *n* **1** the leader of a Jewish congregation or synagogue **2** a Jewish scholar —**rabbinical** /rə bínnik'l/ *adj*

rabbit /rábbit/ *n* (*pl* **-bits** *or* **same**) **1** a small burrowing mammal with long ears and a short tail **2** the fur of a rabbit **3** the flesh of a rabbit as food ■ *vi* chatter *(infml)*

rabbit punch *n* a blow to the back of the neck —**rabbit-punch** *vt*

rabble /rább'l/ *n* **1** an unruly crowd **2** an offensive term for ordinary people *(insult; + sing or pl verb)*

rabble-rouser *n* an agitator *(disapproving)* —**rabble-rousing** *n, adj*

Rabelais /rábbə lay/, **François** (1493?–1553) French humanist and writer —**Rabelaisian** /rábbə láyziən, rábbə láyzh'n/ *adj, n*

Rabi /raábi/, **Rabia** /rə beé ə/ *n* either the 3rd or the 4th month of the Islamic calendar

rabid /rábbid/ *adj* **1** having rabies **2** fanatical *(disapproving)* **3** extremely angry —**rabidity** /rə bíddəti/ *n* —**rabidly** *adv*

rabies /ráy beez/ *n* a severe viral disease that affects the nervous system and is transmitted in the saliva of an infected animal

Rabin /ra beén/, **Yitzhak** (1922–95) Israeli prime minister (1974–77 and 1992–95)

raccoon /rə koòn, ra-/ (*pl* **-coons** *or* **same**), **racoon** *n* **1** a small ring-tailed mammal **2** the fur of a raccoon

race[1] *n* **1** a contest of speed **2** any competitive effort between rivals ■ **races** *npl* horse races or horseracing ■ *v* (**racing, raced**) **1** *vti* compete against somebody in a race **2** *vi* move very fast **3** *vi* beat fast *(refers to the heart)* **4** *vti* run or make an engine run at high speed —**racer** *n* —**racing** *n*

race[2] *n* **1** any of the groups into which human beings are divided on the basis of physical characteristics **2** the fact of belonging to a particular race

race card ◇ **play the race card** use the issue of race, e.g. in legal argumentation or in a debate, to win an advantage or make a point *(infml)*

racecourse /ráyss kawrss/ *n* a track for horse races

racegoer /ráyss gō ər/ *n* somebody who frequents race meetings

racehorse /ráyss hawrss/ *n* a horse bred for participating in races

raceme /rásseem/ *n* a type of flower cluster that has flowers along a long main stem

race meeting *n* a series of races held at one course

racetrack /ráyss trak/ *n* a track around which cars or runners race

Sergei Rachmaninov

Rachmaninov /rak mánni nof/, **Sergei** (1873–1943) Russian-born composer and pianist

racial /ráysh'l/ adj 1 existing between races ○ *racial harmony* 2 of a particular race of people —**racially** adv

racialism /ráysh'lizəm/ n racism (dated) —**racialist** n, adj

racial profiling n the alleged tendency of some police officers to attribute criminal intentions to members of particular ethnic groups and to stop and question them in disproportionate numbers without proper cause

Racine /ra seén/, **Jean Baptiste** (1639–99) French playwright

racing car n a car used for participating in races

racism /ráyssizəm/ n 1 prejudice against or animosity towards people of other races 2 the belief that some races of people are inherently superior —**racist** adj, n

rack[1] n 1 a framework for holding things 2 a toothed bar that engages the teeth of a pinion or gear to turn rotary motion into linear motion 3 a former instrument of torture that stretched a person's body ■ vt 1 cause somebody great pain 2 stretch or strain something violently ○ *racked my brain* 3 torture somebody on a rack

ORIGIN Rack 'framework' was adopted from Dutch in the 14C (the cut of meat **rack** may represent a development of this). **Rack** 'ruin' is a late-16C variant of *wrack* in the same sense. *Wrack* originally meant 'vengeance', and is related to *wreak*.

□ **rack up** vt accumulate something such as points (infml)

rack[2] n a joint of meat consisting of one or both sides of the front ribs

rack[3] ◇ **go to rack and ruin** deteriorate into a state of neglect or ruin

racket[1] /rákit/, **racquet** n 1 a bat with a network of strings, used in sports such as tennis and badminton 2 a snowshoe in the shape of a racket

racket[2] /rákit/ n (infml) 1 a loud disturbing noise 2 an illegal scheme

racketeer /ráki teér/ n somebody who profits from illegal activities —**racketeer** vi —**racketeering** n

rackets n RACKET GAMES = **racquets**

Rackham /rákəm/, **Arthur** (1867–1939) British illustrator and watercolour painter

raconteur /rá kon túr/ n somebody who tells entertaining stories

racoon n ZOOL = **raccoon**

racquet n RACKET GAMES, LEISURE = **racket**[1]

racquetball /rákit bawl/ n an indoor sport similar to squash in which short-handled rackets are used

racquets /rákits/, **rackets** n an indoor sport similar to squash in which long-handled rackets are used (+ sing verb)

racy /ráyssi/ (-ier, -iest) adj mildly indecent —**racily** adv —**raciness** n

RADA /raّadə/ abbr Royal Academy of Dramatic Art

radar /ráy daar/ n 1 an object-locating system that uses reflected radio waves 2 a piece of object-locating equipment ◇ **be on somebody's radar screen** US be a focal point of interest (infml)

radar gun n a hand-held radar device for monitoring motorists' speed

radar trap n a police speed trap

raddled /rádd'ld/ adj haggard

radial /ráydi əl/ adj 1 running from the centre outwards 2 of a radius ■ n a tyre in which the foundation fabric cords run at right angles to the circumference —**radially** adv

radian /ráydi ən/ n (symbol **rad**) a unit of angular measurement equivalent to the angle between two radii that enclose a section of the circumference of a circle equal in length to the length of the radius

radiant /ráydi ənt/ adj 1 showing happiness, energy, or good health 2 shining with bright or glowing light 3 describes heat, light, or energy emitted in the form of waves or rays 4 emitting radiant energy —**radiance** n —**radiantly** adv

radiate vti /ráydi ayt/ (-ating, -ated) 1 send out energy, or be sent out, as rays or waves 2 show a feeling or quality clearly, or be shown clearly 3 spread or cause to spread from the centre ■ adj /ráydi ət, -ayt/ with parts radiating from the centre —**radiative** adj

radiation /ráydi áysh'n/ n 1 energy particles emitted by substances whose atoms are not stable and are spontaneously decaying 2 energy emitted in the form of rays or waves 3 the emission of energy in the form of waves 4 radiotherapy

radiation sickness n a medical condition caused by overexposure to radiation

radiator /ráydi aytər/ n 1 a room heater, especially one connected to a central boiler 2 an engine-cooling device

radical /ráddik'l/ adj 1 basic 2 far-reaching 3 favouring major changes ■ n 1 somebody with radical views 2 a mathematical root of another number or quantity —**radically** adv —**radicalness** n

radicalism /ráddik'lizəm/ n political policies or attitudes that advocate major changes —**radicalistic** /ráddikə lístik/ adj

radicalize /ráddikə līz/ (-izing, -ized), **radicalise** vti 1 change fundamentally 2 make or become politically radical —**radicalization** /ráddikə lī záysh'n/ n

radical sign n the mathematical symbol $\sqrt{}$ indicating a square root or higher root

radicchio /ra díki ō/ (pl -os), **radichio** n a reddish-purple variety of chicory

radio /ráydi ō/ n 1 the use of electromagnetic waves for communication 2 a device that receives sound broadcasts 3 sound broadcasts transmitted by means of radio waves ■ vti (-os, -oing, -oed) communicate with somebody by radio

radio- *prefix* **1** radiation o *radioactive* **2** radio o *radiotelephone*

radioactive /ráydi ō áktiv/ *adj* **1** emitting radiation **2** of or using radioactive substances —**radioactively** *adv*

radioactivity /ráydi ō ak tívvəti/ *n* **1** the radioactive nature of a substance **2** radiation

radio astronomy *n* the branch of astronomy dealing with radio waves from space —**radio astronomer** *n*

radio button *n* a symbol on a computer screen that represents one of a set of options from which a choice must be made

radiocarbon dating /ráydi ō kaárbən-/ *n* GEOL = **carbon dating**

radio-controlled *adj* remotely controlled using radio signals

radiogram /ráydi ō gram/ *n* **1** a telegram **2** a radio and record player combined *(dated)*

radiograph /ráydi ō graaf, -graf/ *n* a photograph taken using radiation other than visible light, especially X-rays ■ *vt* take a radiograph of —**radiographer** /ráydi ógrəfər/ *n* —**radiographic** /ráydi ō gráffik/ *adj* —**radiography** /ráydi ógrəfi/ *n*

radiology /ráydi ólləji/ *n* **1** the branch of medicine that uses X-rays **2** the science of radiation and radioactive substances —**radiological** /ráydi ə lójjik'l/ *adj* —**radiologist** *n*

radiotelephone /ráydi ō téllə fōn/ *n* a telephone that uses radio waves —**radiotelephony** /ráydi ō tə léffəni/ *n*

radio telescope *n* an instrument for studying radio waves emitted by astronomical objects

radiotherapy /ráydi ō thérrəpi/ *n* medical treatment using radiation —**radiotherapeutic** /ráydi ō thera pyóotik/ *adj* —**radiotherapist** *n*

radio wave *n* an electromagnetic wave of a frequency between 10 kHz and 300,000 MHz

radish /ráddish/ *n* **1** an edible red or white root, eaten raw **2** a plant that produces radishes

Radisic /ráddisich/, **Zivko** (b. 1936) Serb representative of the presidency of Bosnia and Herzegovina (1998–) which rotates between a Serb, a Bosnian Muslim and a Croat

radium /ráydi əm/ *n* (*symbol* **Ra**) a white radioactive chemical element. Use: luminous coatings, treatment of cancer.

radius /ráydi əss/ (*pl* **-i** /-di ī/ *or* **-uses**) *n* **1** (*symbol* **r**) a line from the centre of a circle to its edge **2** (*symbol* **r**) the length of a radius **3** the area of a circle with a particular radius o *all the houses within a radius of two miles* **4** the range of somebody's effectiveness or influence **5** the shorter and thicker of the two bones in the human forearm

radon /ráy don/ *n* (*symbol* **Rn**) a gaseous radioactive element. Use: radiotherapy.

Raeburn /ráybərn/, **Sir Henry** (1756–1823) Scottish painter

RAF *abbr* Royal Air Force

raffia /ráffi ə/ *n* **1** a fibre taken from the leaves of a palm tree. Use: mats, baskets. **2** *also* **raffia palm** a tree that produces raffia

raffish /ráffish/ *adj* **1** charmingly unconventional or disreputable **2** showy

raffle /ráff'l/ *n* a lottery with objects rather than money as prizes

raft¹ *n* **1** a flat floating structure used for transportation or as a platform **2** an inflatable boat or mat ■ *vi* travel on a raft —**rafting** *n*

raft² *n* a large number or amount *(infml)*

rafter /ráaftər/ *n* a sloping timber that supports a roof —**raftered** *adj*

rag¹ *n* **1** a small piece of scrap cloth **2** an inferior newspaper *(infml)* ■ **rags** *npl* worn-out clothes

rag² *v* (**ragging, ragged**) **1** *vti* tease or taunt somebody *(dated)* **2** *vt* scold persistently ■ *n* a charity fund-raising event at a university —**ragging** *n*

rag³ *n* a ragtime musical composition

raga /ráagə/ *n* a type of classical South Asian music

ragamuffin /rággə mufin/ *n* a neglected child dressed in tattered clothes *(dated)*

ORIGIN Ragamuffin is probably formed from *rag* and a second element that may just be fanciful or may be based on the Dutch word meaning 'mitten' that gave us *muff*.

---

rag-and-bone man *n* a travelling trader who buys unwanted household items

ragbag /rág bag/ *n* a miscellany *(infml)*

rag doll *n* a stuffed cloth doll

rage *n* **1** extreme anger **2** force or intensity **3** the object of a short-lived fashion or enthusiasm **4** ANZ a party ■ *vi* (**raging, raged**) **1** act with or feel rage **2** occur with violence **3** ANZ hold a party ◊ See note at **anger**

rageing incorrect spelling of **raging**

ragga /rággə/ *n* a type of reggae music

ragged /rággid/ *adj* **1** frayed or torn **2** wearing rags **3** with an uneven edge or surface **4** unkempt **5** of varying quality —**raggedly** *adv* —**raggedness** *n*

raging /ráyjing/ *adj* **1** very angry **2** very severe or painful

raglan /rágglən/ *adj* **1** describes a sleeve that extends to the collar **2** having raglan sleeves ■ *n* a garment with raglan sleeves

ragman /rág man/ (*pl* **-men** /-men/) *n* a dealer in rags

ragout /ra góo/ *n* stew

ragtag /rág tag/ *adj* **1** mixed and often of dubious quality **2** untidy

ragtime /rág tīm/ *n* a form of syncopated popular music of the early 20C

rag trade *n* the clothing industry *(infml)*

ragweed /rág weed/ *n* a wild plant with small green flowers that produce large amounts of pollen

ragwort /rág wurt/ *n* a wild plant with yellow flowers like daisies

rai /rī/ n a form of popular Algerian music

raid /rayd/ n a sudden attack made in an attempt to seize or destroy something ■ v 1 vti make a raid on a place 2 vt steal —**raider** n

ORIGIN Raid is actually a Scottish variant of road. The forms are related to ride, and 'riding with hostile intent' and 'raid' were early senses of road. The use had effectively died out when Sir Walter Scott revived raid in the early 19C, and its existence has never since looked in danger.

rail[1] n 1 a long piece of wood or metal 2 a fence or railing (often pl) 3 a steel bar that forms a railway track ◊ **go off the rails** begin to go wrong and lose direction

rail[2] vi complain bitterly

rail[3] (pl **rails** or same) n a wading bird with short wings and long toes

railcard /ráyl kaard/ n an identity card that entitles the holder to reduced rail fares

railing /ráyling/ n 1 a structure with rails and posts 2 a metal fence (usually pl)

raillery /ráyləri/ (pl **-ies**) n 1 good-humoured teasing 2 a joking remark

railroad /ráyl rṓd/ n US, Can a railway ■ vt 1 force a decision through quickly without discussion 2 force somebody to act hastily (infml) —**railroader** n

railway /ráyl way/ n 1 a track made of rails for trains to run on 2 a transport system that consists of trains —**railwayman** n

raiment /ráymənt/ n clothes (literary)

rain /rayn/ n condensed water falling from clouds ■ **rains** npl a period of rainy weather ■ v 1 vi drop rain 2 vti come or deliver in great numbers

SPELLCHECK Do not confuse the spelling of rain, reign ('of a monarch'), or rein ('strap for guiding a horse'), which sound similar.

rainbow /ráyn bṓ/ n an arc of light in the sky that has been separated into its constituent colours by moisture ■ adj 1 with varied colours 2 containing many different elements

rain check n US, Can a ticket for a rescheduled event

raincoat /ráyn kṓt/ n a waterproof coat

rainfall /ráyn fawl/ n 1 the amount of rain that falls in a particular period 2 the occurrence of rain

rainforest /ráyn forist/ n a thick tropical forest

rain gauge n a rain-measurement device

Rainier III /ráyni ay/ (b. 1923) prince of Monaco (1949–)

rainmaker /ráyn maykər/ n somebody who causes or is believed to cause rain —**rainmaking** n

rainstorm /ráyn stawrm/ n a storm with rain

rainwater /ráyn wawtər/ n water that has fallen as rain

rainy /ráyni/ (**-ier**, **-iest**) adj with a lot of rain —**raininess** n

raise /rayz/ v (**raising**, **raised**) 1 vt move something higher 2 vt erect something 3 vt make something larger or greater 4 vt improve something ○ raised his spirits 5 vt grow crops or breed animals 6 vt act as a parent or guardian to a child ○ raised by relatives 7 vt offer something for consideration ○ raised another point 8 vt collect something together ○ raising money for charity 9 vt cause something to appear, occur, or arise 10 vt contact somebody by radio or telephone 11 vti increase a bet or bid 12 vt end a siege ■ n 1 Aus, US, Can a pay increase 2 the act of increasing something —**raiser** n

raisin /ráyz'n/ n a dried grape

raison d'être /ráy zoN déttra/ (pl **raisons d'être** pronunc. same) n a reason for living or a justification for existing

Raj /raaj/ n the period of British rule in South Asia

Rajab /rə jáb/ n the 7th month of the year in the Islamic calendar

rajah /ráàjə/, **raja** n a Hindu ruler

Rajasthan /raajə staan/ state in NW India. Cap. Jaipur. Pop. 48,040,000 (1994).

rake[1] n 1 a long-handled gardening tool with a toothed head 2 a tool resembling a garden rake 3 an act of clearing, gathering, or smoothing something with a rake ■ v (**raking**, **raked**) 1 vt move, clear, or smooth with a rake 2 vti search through

ORIGIN Rake the tool is an old word of Germanic origin. Rake 'slope' is recorded from the early 17C, but its origins are unknown. The immoral rake was originally a rakehell. The longer form is recorded from the mid-16C, and rake itself from the mid-17C. The word meaning 'gully' was adopted from an old Scandinavian word meaning 'stripe, streak' in the 14C.

□ **rake in** vt gather in large quantities (infml)
□ **rake up** or **over** vt mention something from the past (infml)

rake[2] n 1 a slant or slope 2 the angle of a wing or propeller ■ vti (**raking**, **raked**) angle or be angled

rake[3] n an immoral seeker of pleasure

rake[4] n a gully on a rock face

rake-off n a share (infml)

rakish /ráykish/ adj 1 dashingly stylish 2 streamlined in a way that suggests speed —**rakishness** n

Raleigh /ráali, ráwli/ capital of North Carolina. Pop. 259,423 (1998).

Raleigh, Sir Walter (1554–1618) English navigator and writer

rally /rálli/ v (**-lies**, **-lied**) 1 vti gather together for a purpose 2 vti reorganize after a setback 3 vti revive after a setback or illness 4 vi increase in value 5 vi exchange shots in a racket sport ■ n (pl **-lies**) 1 a large gathering of people 2 a recovery or improvement 3 a renewed buying of stocks 4 an exchange of shots in a racket sport 5 a car race on public or rough roads —**rallier** n

☐ **rally round** *vt* come to somebody's aid

ram /ram/ *n* **1** a male sheep **2** a battering or crushing device **3 Ram** the zodiacal sign Aries ■ *v* (**ramming, rammed**) **1** *vti* strike horizontally with great force **2** *vt* collide with deliberately **3** *vt* force into place

RAM /ram/ *n* random-access memory

Rama /ráːmə/ *n* an incarnation of the Hindu god Vishnu

Rama IX /ráːmə/ (*b.* 1927) king of Thailand (1950–)

Ramadan /rámmə dáːn, -dan/ *n* the 9th month of the year in the Islamic calendar, during which Muslims fast between dawn and dusk

Rambert /raam báir/, **Dame Marie** (1888–1982) Polish-born British ballet dancer and teacher

ramble /rámb'l/ *vi* (**-bling, -bled**) **1** walk for pleasure, usually in the countryside **2** follow a changing course **3** grow in a random way **4** talk or write aimlessly and at length ■ *n* a walk for pleasure, usually in the countryside —**rambler** *n* —**rambling** *adj, n* —**ramblingly** *adv*

rambunctious /ram búngkshəss/ *adj* unruly —**rambunctiously** *adv*

ramekin /rámmikin/, **ramequin** *n* **1** a small baking dish for a single serving of food **2** a food served in a ramekin

Rameses II /rámmə seez/, **Ramses II** (*fl* 13C BC) Egyptian pharaoh

ramification /rámmifi káysh'n/ *n* **1** a complicating result **2** the process of dividing into branches or sections

ramify /rámmi fī/ (**-fies, -fied**) *vi* **1** divide into branches or sections **2** have complicating results

rammies /rámmiz/ *npl Aus, S Africa* trousers (*infml*)

ramp *n* **1** a sloping path or surface **2** a movable set of steps ■ *vt* build with a slope —**ramped** *adj*

☐ **ramp up** *vt* increase sharply

rampage *vi* /ram páyj/ (**-paging, -paged**) act violently or riotously ■ *n* /ram payj, ram páyj/ an outburst of violent or riotous behaviour —**rampaging** *adj*

rampant /rámpənt/ *adj* **1** occurring or growing unchecked **2** describes a heraldic animal on its hind legs —**rampancy** *n* —**rampantly** *adv*

rampart /rám paart/ *n* a fortified embankment, often with a low wall on top

ramrod /rám rod/ *n* **1** a rod for loading a charge into a gun or cannon **2** a cleaning rod for a gun ■ *adv* emphasizes rigidity or uprightness ○ *ramrod straight*

Ramsay /rámzi/, **Sir William** (1852–1916) British chemist. He discovered the noble gases.

ramshackle /rám shak'l/ *adj* badly built or rundown

ORIGIN **Ramshackle** ultimately derives from *ransack*. A derivative *ransackle* was formed from this, and in the late 17C its past participle *ransackled* was altered to *ramsackled* and used to mean 'disorderly'. **Ramshackle** appears in

dialect use with the same sense in the early 19C. The modern meaning developed in the mid-19C.

ran past tense of **run**

RAN *abbr Aus* Royal Australian Navy

ranch *n* **1** a livestock farm on open land **2** *also* **ranch house** a house on a ranch ■ *v* **1** *vi* work on a ranch **2** *vt* raise animals on a ranch —**ranching** *n*

rancher /ráanchər/ *n* a ranch owner

rancid /ránssid/ *adj* with the disagreeable taste or smell of decomposing fats or oils —**rancidity** /ran síddəti/ *n*

rancour /rángkər/ *n* deep-seated ill-will or resentment —**rancorous** *adj* —**rancorously** *adv*

rand (*pl same*) *n* the main unit of South African currency

R & B *abbr* rhythm and blues

R & D *abbr* research and development

random /rándəm/ *adj* **1** done or occurring without a pattern **2** not uniform or regular **3** of a set in which all the members have the same probability of occurrence ○ *a random sampling* —**randomly** *adv* —**randomness** *n* ◊ **at random** with no set plan, system, or connection

random-access *adj* retrieving data stored in an arbitrary sequence

random-access memory *n* the primary working memory of a computer

randomize /rándə mīz/ (**-izing, -ized**), **randomise** *vti* make or become random —**randomization** /rándə mī záysh'n/ *n*

R and R, R & R *abbr* **1** rest and recreation **2** rest and relaxation

ranee *n POL* = **rani**

rang past tense of **ring²**

rangatira /rángə teèrə/ *n NZ* a Maori chief

range /raynj/ *n* **1** a number or variety of different things ○ *dealing with a wide range of people* **2** a number of similar or related things, e.g. products for sale **3** an amount of variation **4** a category defined by its limits ○ *the age range 25 to 45* **5** an area of effective operation, or the limit of this area **6** a practice area ○ *a shooting range* **7** all the notes that a singer or a musical instrument can produce **8** a row of mountains **9** *US, Can* an area of open land for grazing farm animals **10** movement over an area **11** a stove for cooking ■ *v* **1** *vi* vary between limits **2** *vi* include or deal with a number of things ○ *Her interests range from parapsychology to parachuting.* **3** *vt* arrange in line ○ *ranged the chess pieces on the board* **4** *vt* align according to something, e.g. attributes ○ *The cadets were ranged into platoons by height.* **5** *vti* move freely and extensively over an area

ranger /ráynjər/ *n* **1** an official overseeing a state or national forest **2 Ranger** a member of the senior branch of the Guides **3** *also* **Ranger** *US* a member of an armed state law enforcement unit, especially in Texas

Rangoon /rang goón/ former name for **Yangon**

rangy /ráynji/ (**-ier, -iest**) *adj* slim and long-limbed

rani /raáni, raa neé/, **ranee** *n* an Indian queen or princess, or the wife of a rajah

rank¹ *n* 1 an official position within an organization, especially a military or police force 2 a degree of importance or excellence relative to others ○ *a political journalist of the first rank* 3 high status 4 a line of people or things side by side 5 a place where taxis wait ■ **ranks** *npl* 1 enlisted soldiers 2 people in a specific group or category ○ *joined the ranks of the unemployed* ■ *vti* 1 have or give a rating ○ *ranks high on my list of desirable improvements* 2 position or stand people or things in rows ◇ **pull rank (on)** assert authority over somebody in a hierarchy

rank² *adj* 1 describes vegetation that is growing too vigorously 2 utter or unmitigated 3 strong- or foul-smelling ○ *the rank odour of rotten eggs* —**rankly** *adv* —**rankness** *n*

rank and file *n* 1 enlisted troops 2 ordinary members ○ *the union's rank and file* —**rank-and-file** *adj* —**rank and filer** *n*

ranking /rángking/ *n* a position relative to others ■ *adj US, Can* holding the highest rank

rankle /rángk'l/ *vi* cause continuing bitter feelings

ORIGIN Nowadays feelings **rankle**, but originally the verb was used of parts of the body, wounds, and sores that festered. In the course of its history the word lost an initial *d-*. It goes back through a French verb to the Latin noun *draco* 'serpent' (from which *dragon* also derives). The original idea was therefore of an ulcer caused by the bite of a snake.

ransack /rán sak/ *vt* 1 search something very thoroughly 2 rob and despoil, e.g. a captured city

ORIGIN **Ransack** was adopted from an old Scandinavian compound formed from words meaning 'house' and 'search'. The second element *-sack* is related to *seek*.

ransom /ránsəm/ *n* 1 a sum of money demanded for releasing a captive 2 release of a captive in return for payment ■ *vt* pay money for the release of a captive ◇ **hold to ransom** use threats to try to make somebody do what you want

rant /rant/ *vti* speak or say in a loud or aggressive manner —**rant** *n*

rap¹ *v* (**rapping, rapped**) 1 *vti* hit something sharply 2 *vt* say sharply 3 *vt* criticize or rebuke ■ *n* 1 a sharp blow 2 a sound of knocking 3 *US* a criminal charge (*slang*) ◇ **take the rap (for)** take the blame or punishment for something (*slang*)

rap² *n* popular music with spoken rhyming vocals —**rap** *vi* —**rapper** *n*

rap³ *vt Aus* praise highly

rapacious /rə páyshəss/ *adj* greedy and de-structive —**rapaciously** *adv* —**rapacity** /rə pássəti/ *n*

rape¹ *n* 1 the crime of forcing somebody to have sexual intercourse 2 an instance of rape 3 violent destructive treatment ○ *the rape of the countryside* —**rape** *vt* —**rapist** *n*

rape² *n* a plant with bright yellow flowers grown commercially. Use: oil, fodder.

Raphael /ráffi el/ (1483–1520) Italian artist

rapid /ráppid/ *adj* quick or fast ■ **rapids** *npl* a fast-moving turbulent part of a river —**rapidity** /rə píddəti/ *n* —**rapidly** *adv* —**rapidness** *n*

rapier /ráypi ər/ *n* a sword with a long slender blade

rapine /ráppīn, -ppin/ *n* use of force to seize property (*literary*)

rapport /ra páwr/ *n* a friendly relationship or emotional bond

rapprochement /ra próshmoN/ *n* establishment or renewal of friendly relations

rapscallion /rap skálli ən/ *n* a rascal (*archaic or humorous*)

rapt *adj* 1 completely engrossed 2 blissfully happy —**raptly** *adv* —**raptness** *n*

rapture /rápchər/ *n* 1 bliss or ecstasy 2 mystical transportation ■ **raptures** *npl* a state of great happiness or enthusiasm ○ *went into raptures about the meal* —**rapturous** *adj*

rare¹ /rair/ (**rarer, rarest**) *adj* 1 not often happening or found 2 unusually great or excellent 3 describes air containing little oxygen —**rarely** *adv* —**rareness** *n* —**rarity** *n*

rare² /rair/ (**rarer, rarest**) *adj* describes lightly cooked meat that remains raw inside

rare-earth element *n* a metallic element of the lanthanide group

rarefied /ráiri fīd/ *adj* 1 describes an atmosphere with a low oxygen content 2 esoteric or elitist

raring /ráiring/ *adj* eager (*infml*) ○ *They are raring to go.*

~~rasberry~~ incorrect spelling of **raspberry**

rascal /raásk'l/ *n* 1 a mischievous person (*humorous*) 2 a dishonest person

rase *vt* = **raze** (*literary*)

rash¹ *adj* thoughtless and impetuous —**rashly** *adv* —**rashness** *n*

rash² *n* 1 a reddish itchy patch on the skin 2 a series of instances in a brief period ○ *a rash of robberies*

rasher /ráshər/ *n* a slice of bacon

Rasmussen /rássməss'n/, **Anders Fogh** (*b.* 1953) prime minister of Denmark (2001–)

rasp *n* 1 a file with large teeth 2 a harsh grating sound ■ *vt* 1 say in a harsh voice 2 smooth or scrape with a rasp —**raspy** *adj*

raspberry /raázbəri/ (*pl* **-ries**) *n* 1 a small red fruit made up of many tiny fleshy parts 2 a plant that produces raspberries 3 a rude noise imitating the sound of breaking wind (*infml*)

Grigory Yefimovich Rasputin

Rasputin /ra spyoótin/, **Grigory Yefimovich** (1869?–1916) Russian peasant and self-proclaimed holy man

Rasta /rástə/ n Rastafarian (infml) —**Rasta** adj

Rastafarian /rástə fáiri ən/ n a member of an Afro-Caribbean religious group that venerates the former emperor of Ethiopia, Haile Selassie —**Rastafarian** adj —**Rastafarianism** n

raster /rástər/ n the pattern of horizontal scanning lines that create the image on a television or computer screen

raster font n a bit-mapped font

rasterize /rástə rīz/ (-izing, -ized) vt convert a digitized image for display or printing

rat n 1 a long-tailed rodent resembling a large mouse 2 a person regarded as untrustworthy or disloyal (slang insult) ■ vi (ratting, ratted) hunt or catch rats ■ interj **rats** expresses annoyance —**ratter** n ◊ **smell a rat** be suspicious (infml)
□ **rat on** vt betray or inform on (infml)

ratatat-tat /rátta tat tát/, **rat-a-tat, rat-tat, rat-tat-tat** n the sound of sharp knocking

ratatouille /rátta too i/ n a dish of stewed tomatoes, onions, peppers, aubergines, and courgettes

ratchet /ráchit/ n 1 a turning mechanism allowing movement in one direction 2 also **ratchet wheel** a toothed wheel forming part of a ratchet ■ v 1 vti move with a ratchet 2 vt US force something to rise or fall in stages

rate /rayt/ n 1 a speed 2 an amount expressed in relation to something else o the mortality rate 3 an amount of money charged ■ **rates** npl a local tax on commercial properties ■ v (rating, rated) 1 vti have or regard as having a particular value or position relative to others 2 vt deserve 3 vt classify 4 vt think highly of (infml) —**ratable** adj —**rateable** adj ◊ **at any rate** whatever else may be true

rate of exchange n FIN = exchange rate

rate of return n an amount of income generated by an investment

rather /raáthər/ adv 1 to some extent or degree o rather tall o rather attractive 2 considerably 3 more willingly o I'd rather go to the mountains. 4 with more justification or precision o praise them rather than blame 5 on the contrary

ORIGIN Rather is in origin the comparative of an obsolete adjective rathe meaning 'quick'.

'More quickly' became 'more willingly' early in its history. The sense 'to some extent' did not develop until the late 16C.

ratify /rátti fī/ (-fies, -fied) vt formally approve —**ratification** /ráttifi káysh'n/ n

rating /ráyting/ n 1 an assessment or classification 2 an ordinary serving member of a navy ■ **ratings** npl a list showing the size of a television or radio audience

ratio /ráyshi ō/ (pl -tios) n 1 a proportional relationship 2 the relationship between two quantities arrived at by dividing one by another

ration /rásh'n/ n a fixed amount allocated to a person ■ **rations** npl an amount of food officially allocated ■ vt restrict the amount of something a person can have o Petrol was rationed during the crisis.
□ **ration out** vt distribute in limited quantities

rational /rásh'nəl/ adj 1 able to think clearly and sensibly 2 in accordance with logic or scientific knowledge o a rational explanation 3 able to reason 4 expressible as a ratio of two integers —**rationality** /ráshə nálləti/ n —**rationally** adv

rationale /ráshə naál/ n a set or statement of underlying reasons or principles

rationalism /rásh'nəlizəm/ n 1 reasoning as the basis of action 2 reason as the source of truth —**rationalist** n —**rationalistic** /rásh'nə lístik/ adj

rationalize /rásh'nə līz/ (-izing, -ized), **rationalise** v 1 vt make rational 2 vt interpret logically 3 vti offer a reasonable explanation for behaviour 4 vti make a business or operation more efficient and profitable, e.g. by reducing the workforce —**rationalization** /rásh'nə lī záysh'n/ n

rat race n a struggle to survive in the competitive environment of modern life (infml)

rattan /ra tán/ n the stems of a tropical Asian climbing plant. Use: wickerwork, furniture, canes.

rat-tat, rat-tat-tat n = ratatat-tat

rattle /rátt'l/ v (-tling, -tled) 1 vti make or cause to make short sharp knocking sounds 2 vt disconcert ■ n 1 a succession of short sharp knocking sounds 2 a baby's toy or other device that makes a rattling sound 3 the tip of rattlesnake's tail
□ **rattle off** vt say very quickly
□ **rattle on** vi talk quickly, inconsequentially, and at length
□ **rattle through** vt do quickly

rattlesnake /rátt'l snayk/ n a large venomous snake with vibrating horny segments in the tail

ratty /rátti/ (-tier, -tiest) adj 1 irritable (infml) 2 of or like a rat 3 infested with rats —**rattily** adv —**rattiness** n

raucous /ráwkəss/ adj unpleasantly loud or harsh —**raucously** adv —**raucousness** n

raunchy /ráwnchi/ (-chier, -chiest) adj sexually explicit or obscene (infml) —**raunchily** adv —**raunchiness** n

ravage /rávvij/ vt (-aging, -aged) 1 wreck or destroy 2 plunder ○ *a village ravaged of all its valuables by army deserters* ■ **ravages** npl damaging effects ○ *the ravages of time* —**ravager** n

rave /rayv/ vi (raving, raved) 1 offer enthusiastic praise about (infml) ○ *raving about her performance* 2 speak loudly and angrily 3 speak wildly and incoherently ■ n 1 an act of raving 2 a large-scale all-night party with pop music and dancing (slang) ■ adj very enthusiastic (infml) ○ *rave reviews* —**raving** n, adj

ravel /rávv'l/ (-elling, -elled) vti 1 tangle 2 fray

Ravel /rə vél/, **Maurice** (1875–1937) French composer

raven /ráyv'n/ n a large black bird of the crow family ■ adj black and shiny (literary)

ravenous /rávv'nəss/ adj extremely hungry —**ravenously** adv —**ravenousness** n

raver /ráyvər/ n somebody who has an active and uninhibited social life (infml)

ravine /rə veén/ n a deep narrow valley

ravioli /rávvi óli/ n filled square parcels of pasta

ravish /rávvish/ vt 1 overwhelm with deep and pleasurable emotion 2 sexually assault (literary) 3 carry off forcibly (literary) —**ravisher** n —**ravishing** adj —**ravishingly** adv

raw adj 1 not cooked 2 unprocessed or un-refined 3 inflamed and sore 4 inexperienced 5 unpleasantly cold ○ *a raw wind* 6 brutally realistic ○ *the raw facts* —**rawness** n

Rawalpindi /ráwl píndi/ city in NE Pakistan. Pop. 1,406,214 (1998).

rawhide /ráw hīd/ n 1 untanned hide 2 a whip or rope made of rawhide

ray[1] n 1 a beam of light or other radiant energy 2 a trace of something positive such as hope or comfort 3 a straight line that extends from a point infinitely in one direction —**rayed** adj

ray[2] n a fish with a flat body and broad fins

ray[3], **re** n a syllable used in singing the 2nd note of a scale

Ray, Man (1890–1976) US artist

Ray, Satyajit (1921–92) Indian film director

ray gun n in science fiction, a gun that fires energy rays that stun or destroy

rayon /ráy on/ n a synthetic textile fibre

raze /rayz/ (razing, razed), **rase** (rasing, rased) vt completely destroy a place

razoo /raa zóo, rə zóo/ (pl -zoos) n ANZ an im-aginary coin of little value (infml)

razor /ráyzər/ n an instrument for shaving —**razor** vt

razor blade n a disposable blade for a razor

razzle /rázz'l/ ◇ **on the razzle, on the razzle-dazzle** enjoying a spell of unrestrained partying or heavy drinking (infml dated)

razzmatazz /rázmə táz/ n exciting showiness

Rb symbol rubidium

RC abbr also **R.C.** Roman Catholic

Rd abbr Road (in addresses)

re[1] /ray/ n MUSIC = **ray**[3]

re[2] /ree, ray/ prep with reference to

're contr are

Re symbol 1 rhenium 2 rupee

RE abbr Religious Education

re- prefix 1 again, anew ○ *reinvest* 2 back, back-wards ○ *recall*

reach /reech/ v 1 vti stretch out or extend as far as a particular place 2 vi move the hand towards something to touch or grasp it 3 vt arrive at 4 vti influence or have an impact on people 5 vt communicate with ■ n 1 an act or extent of reaching 2 a range of pow-er ○ *beyond the reach of the law* ■ **reaches** npl an area or level of something ○ *the upper reaches of the Amazon*

react /ri ákt/ vi 1 say or do one thing as a result of another thing said or done to you 2 undergo physical or chemical change, e.g. as a result of contact with something —**reactive** adj

reaction /ri áksh'n/ n 1 one thing said or done as a result of another thing said or done to you 2 the process of reacting physically or chemically 3 an adverse response by the body to a substance 4 an equal but opposite force exerted by a body when a force acts upon it 5 strong conservatism (disapproving) 6 a nuclear process resulting in a structural change of atomic nuclei ■ **reactions** npl somebody's ability to react quickly

reactionary /ri áksh'nəri/ adj opposed to liberal or progressive change (disapproving) —**reactionary** n

reactivate /ri ákti vayt/ (-vating, -vated) vti make or become active again —**reactivation** /ri ákti váysh'n/ n

reactor /ri áktər/ n 1 somebody or something that reacts or takes part in a reaction 2 a device in which nuclear fission or fusion occurs, producing energy 3 a component in an electrical circuit

read /reed/ v (read /red/) 1 vti interpret written words 2 vti utter written words 3 vti learn something by reading ○ *I read it in a book.* 4 vt interpret nonverbal material, e.g. signs, symbols, or signals ○ *read a map* ○ *read music* 5 vt take a particular university course 6 vt understand something intuitively ○ *must have read my mind* 7 vti interpret something in a specific way ○ *However you read it, her idea is impractical.* 8 vi have a particular wording ○ *a sign reading KEEP OUT* 9 vti receive and understand a radio message 10 vt indicate or display data ○ *The therm-ometer reads zero.* 11 vti transfer data into com-puter memory ■ n 1 literary material of a particular quality for reading (slang) ○ *a novel that is an excellent read* 2 a spell of reading ◇ **take as read** assume to be the case

SPELLCHECK Do not confuse the spelling of **read** and **reed** (the plant), which sound similar.

□ **read into** vt detect unintended additional meanings in something

readable /reedəb'l/ *adj* **1** legible **2** enjoyable to read —**readably** *adv*

readdress /ree ə dréss/ *vt* **1** put a new address on **2** attend to again

reader /reedər/ *n* **1** somebody who reads **2** a reading device connected to a computer **3** an educational book **4** a high-ranking university lecturer

readership /reedər ship/ *n* **1** the people who read a specific publication **2** the position of a university reader

readily /réddili/ *adv* **1** without hesitation **2** with ease

reading /reeding/ *n* **1** an interpretation of written material **2** material that is read **3** an occasion when something is read ○ *a poetry reading* **4** a text read to an audience or congregation **5** a measurement or other information taken from a piece of equipment

reading age *n* a measure of a child's competence in reading

readjust /ree ə júst/ *vi* rearrange or make small changes to something —**readjustment** *n*

README file /reed mee-/ *n* a computer text file containing information about the installation or operation of software

readmit /ree əd mit/ (**-mitting, -mitted**) *vt* allow to enter, have access, or belong again —**readmission** *n*

read-only *adj* describes a computer file that cannot be changed or deleted

read-only memory *n* a small permanent computer memory for storing data that cannot be changed

read-out *n* **1** data retrieved by a computer **2** a display of information on a piece of equipment

readthrough /reed throo/ *n* the reading of a play before full rehearsals begin

read-write head *n* a device in a computer that reads and writes data

ready /réddi/ *adj* (**-ier, -iest**) **1** prepared for something **2** finished and available for use **3** on the point of doing something ○ *worked until I was ready to drop* **4** prepared in advance (*often in combination*) ○ *ready-sliced cheese* **5** willing or eager to do something ○ *ready to help* **6** quickly produced ○ *a ready answer* **7** intelligent or alert ○ *a ready wit* ■ *vt* (**-ies, -ied**) prepare —**readiness** *n* ◊ **at the ready** prepared for immediate use or action

ready-made *adj* **1** already prepared or made **2** thought out in advance ○ *ready-made excuses* ■ *n* a ready-to-wear garment

ready-to-wear *adj* describes clothing made in standard sizes and designs —**ready-to-wear** *n*

reaffirm /ree ə fúrm/ *vt* confirm that something is still true or right —**reaffirmation** /ree afər máysh'n/ *n*

Ronald Reagan

Reagan /ráygən/, **Ronald** (b. 1911) 40th president of the United States (1981–89)

reagent /ri áyjənt/ *n* a substance that takes part in a chemical reaction

real[1] /ree əl, reel/ *adj* **1** physically existing **2** verifiable as actual fact ○ *her real name* **3** not artificial or synthetic **4** traditional and authentic **5** sincere **6** adds emphasis ○ *a real professional* ○ *be in real trouble* ■ *adv US, Can* very (*infml*) ■ *n* real things or reality —**realness** *n*

SPELLCHECK Do not confuse the spelling of **real** and **reel** (of thread), which sound similar.

real[2] /ray aál/ (*pl* **-als** *or* **-ales** /-aáles/) *n* the main unit of Brazilian currency

real ale *n* cask-fermented beer without added carbon dioxide

real estate *n ANZ, US, Can* land and any immovable property on it

realign /ree ə lín/ *v* **1** *vt* put back into a straight line **2** *vti* change to fit a different situation —**realignment** *n*

realism /ree əlizəm/ *n* **1** the ability to view situations in a practical and objective way **2** the lifelike representation of people and objects in art and literature —**realist** *n*

realistic /ree ə lístik/ *adj* **1** practical and objective **2** reasonable ○ *a realistic price* **3** representing real life as it is —**realistically** *adv*

~~realisticly~~ incorrect spelling of **realistically**

reality /ri álləti/ (*pl* **-ties**) *n* **1** real existence **2** all that actually exists or happens **3** something that exists or happens ◊ **in reality** in actual fact

realize /ree ə líz/ (**-izing, -ized**), **realise** *v* **1** *vti* know and understand something **2** *vti* be or become aware of something **3** *vt* achieve something hoped or worked for **4** *vt* convert something into money, usually by selling it ○ *realize our assets* —**realizable** *adj* —**realization** /ree ə īɪ záysh'n/ *n* ◊ See note at **accomplish**

real-life *adj* real rather than fictional

reallocate /ree állə kayt/ (**-cating, -cated**) *vt* allocate differently —**reallocation** /ree allə káysh'n/ *n*

really /ree əli, reeli/ *adv* **1** in actual fact **2** in a genuine way ○ *felt really sorry* **3** adds emphasis ○ *really exciting* **4** properly ○ *You should really apply for the job in writing.* ■ *interj* expresses surprise, doubt, or exasperation

realm /relm/ n 1 an area or domain, e.g. of thought or knowledge ○ *within the realm of reason* 2 a kingdom

realpolitik /ray aál poli teek/ n politics based on practical considerations

real property /reé altí/, **realty** n land and immovable property on it

real time n 1 the time it takes for a computer system to process input data and no more 2 the actual time of occurrence —**real-time** adj

real-world adj relevant to everyday life

~~realy~~ incorrect spelling of **really**

ream[1] /reem/ n a quantity of paper, usually 500 sheets ■ **reams** npl a large quantity, especially of written material

ream[2] /reem/ vt form, enlarge, or shape a hole with a special tool —**reamer** n

reap /reep/ vt 1 cut and gather a crop 2 obtain something as a result —**reaper** n

reappear /reé ə peér/ vi appear again —**reappearance** n

reappraise /reé ə práyz/ (**-praising, -praised**) vt consider something again, often with a view to change —**reappraisal** n

rear[1] /reer/ v 1 vt raise animals or children 2 vi rise on the hind legs *(refers to animals)*

rear[2] /reer/ n 1 the back of something 2 the part of an army that is farthest from the front 3 somebody's buttocks, or the similar part of an animal *(infml)* ■ adj back —**rearmost** adj ○ **bring up the rear** be at the back

rear admiral n an officer of a rank above commodore in the British or Canadian navies, or above captain in the US Navy or Coast Guard

rearguard /reér gaard/ n 1 troops acting at the rear of a retreating army 2 members of an organization who oppose change or progress *(disapproving)* —**rearguard** adj

rearm /ree aárm/ vti equip a person, group, or nation with weapons again —**rearmament** n

rearrange /reé ə ráynj/ (**-ranging, -ranged**) vt 1 change the order or position of 2 change the appointed time of —**rearrangement** n

rearview mirror /reér vyoo-/ n a mirror providing a view of the road behind a vehicle

rearward /reérwərd/ adv also **rearwards** towards the rear ■ adj in or near the rear

reason /reéz'n/ n 1 a justification 2 a motive 3 a cause that explains something 4 the power of ordered or logical thought ■ vi 1 think logically 2 use rational argument to persuade somebody —**reasoned** adj —**reasoning** n ○ **it stands to reason** it seems obvious or logical ○ **within reason** within reasonable limits ◊ See note at **deduce**

USAGE The word **reason** is correctly followed by *that* rather than by *because* in sentences of the type *The reason I left is that* [not *because*] *I was bored.* Alternatively, simply use: *I left because I was bored.*

reasonable /reéz'nəb'l/ adj 1 capable of making rational judgments 2 being in accordance with common sense 3 not expecting or demanding more than is possible 4 fairly good 5 fairly large 6 not exorbitant —**reasonably** adv ◊ See note at **valid**

reassure /reé ə shoór, -sháwr/ (**-suring, -sured**) vt make somebody feel less worried —**reassurance** n —**reassuring** adj —**reassuringly** adv

reawaken /reé ə wáykən/ v 1 vti wake again 2 vt stimulate again

rebadge /ree báj/ (**-badging, -badged**) vt change the identifying marks of a product or business

rebarbative /ri baárbətiv/ adj repellent or objectionable *(fml)*

rebate[1] /reé bayt/ n a sum of money returned or deducted —**rebate** /ri báyt/ vt

rebate[2] /reé bayt/ n a groove cut for a wood joint ■ vt /ri báyt/ (**-bating, -bated**) 1 cut a rebate in something 2 join pieces with a rebate

rebel n /rébb'l/ 1 somebody who defies or protests against authority 2 an unconventional person 3 a soldier who opposes a ruling government ■ vi /ri bél/ (**rebelling, rebelled**) 1 fight to overthrow a government 2 protest by defying authority 3 refuse to conform 4 have or show intense dislike for something —**rebellious** /ri béllyəss/ adj

~~rebellion~~ incorrect spelling of **rebellion**

rebellion /ri béllyən/ n 1 an attempt to overthrow a government 2 defiance of authority

rebirth /ree búrth/ n 1 the regeneration of something dead or destroyed 2 the revival of ideas or forces

reboot /ree boót/ vti restart a computer —**reboot** /reé boot/ n

reborn /ree báwrn/ adj having been regenerated or renewed

rebound /ri bównd/ vi 1 spring back 2 recover from a setback —**rebound** /reé bownd/ n ◊ **on the rebound** starting something new after a disappointment or setback

rebuff /ri búf/ vt 1 reject or snub 2 repel or drive back —**rebuff** n

rebuild /ree bíld/ (**-built** /-bílt/) vt 1 build again 2 restore ○ *rebuilt her confidence*

rebuke /ri byoók/ (**-buking, -buked**) vt criticize or reprimand —**rebuke** n

rebus /reébəss/ (pl **-buses**) n a word puzzle made up of pictures, letters, or numbers

rebut /ri bút/ (**-butting, -butted**) vti refute —**rebuttal** n

recalcitrant /ri kálssitrənt/ adj resisting control —**recalcitrance** n —**recalcitrant** n ◊ See note at **unruly**

ORIGIN Recalcitrant derives ultimately from the Latin word for 'heel'. A **recalcitrant** person therefore literally 'kicks back' at the cause of restraint or offence. The word was adopted from French in the mid-19C.

recall /ri káwl/ v 1 vti remember 2 vt order to return o *recalled the ambassador to Washington* 3 vt request the return of, e.g. because of defects o *The manufacturer has recalled all models built in 2001.* 4 vt bring to mind o *a style that recalls the 1950s* ■ n 1 a manufacturer's request to return a defective product 2 the act of recalling 3 memory

recant /ri kánt/ vti deny a belief —**recantation** /reē kan táysh'n/ n

recap[1] /reē kap/ (**-capping, -capped**) vti restate the main points of something —**recap** n

recap[2] *ANZ, US* n /reē kap/ a remould ■ vt /ree káp/ (**-capping, -capped**) remould a tyre

recapitulate /reēkə pícho̅o̅ layt/ (**-lating, -lated**) vti restate the essence of something *(fml)* —**recapitulation** /reēkə pícho̅o̅ láysh'n/ n

recapture /ree kápchər/ (**-turing, -tured**) vt 1 capture again 2 experience again o *an attempt to recapture their youth* —**recapture** n

recast /ree kaást/ (**-cast**) vt change the form of

recce /réki/ n a reconnaissance *(slang)*

~~**recommend**~~ incorrect spelling of **recommend**

recd, rec'd abbr received

recede /ri seéd/ (**-ceding, -ceded**) vi 1 go back or down o *waiting for the flood waters to recede* 2 become more distant 3 slope backwards

receipt /ri seét/ n 1 an acknowledgment of receiving something 2 an act of receiving ■ **receipts** npl the amount received, especially in business ■ v 1 vt acknowledge payment of a bill with a signature 2 vti give a receipt for money or goods

receivable /ri seévəb'l/ adj 1 suitable to be received 2 due to be paid ■ **receivables** npl money owed

receive /ri seév/ (**-ceiving, -ceived**) v 1 vti get or take something given or sent 2 vti pick up and convert electronic signals 3 vt meet with, experience, or be subjected to 4 vt catch or hold o *a barrel that receives rainwater* 5 vti greet or entertain visitors 6 vt allow to enter o *was received into the scholarly community* 7 vt react to o *The proposals were not well received.* 8 vti accept or deal in stolen goods

received /ri seévd/ adj generally accepted o *received opinion*

Received Pronunciation n the educated pronunciation of S Britain

receiver /ri seévər/ n 1 somebody who receives 2 the part of a telephone that contains the mouthpiece and earpiece 3 a device for picking up signals 4 somebody appointed by a court to manage a bankrupt business

receivership /ri seévərship/ n being in the hands of a receiver o *The company is now in receivership.*

recent /reéss'nt/ adj 1 having happened not long ago 2 modern —**recency** n —**recently** adv —**recentness** n

receptacle /ri séptək'l/ n a container

reception /ri sépsh'n/ n 1 the act of receiving 2 the way somebody or something is received 3 a formal party 4 the place where

visitors to a hotel, business, or public building are first received 5 the quality of a radio or television signal received 6 the first class at an infant school

reception centre n 1 a place providing temporary accommodation 2 a local authority children's home

receptionist /ri sépsh'nist/ n an employee who greets visitors, customers, or patients

reception room n 1 a room for entertaining guests in a house 2 a room for parties in a hotel

receptive /ri séptiv/ adj 1 willing to accept something o *receptive to new ideas* 2 able to receive something 3 quick to learn —**receptively** adv —**receptiveness** n —**receptivity** /reē sep tívvəti/ n

receptor /ri séptər/ n a nerve ending that converts stimuli into nerve impulses

recess /ri séss, reè sess/ n 1 an indentation or hollowed-out space, e.g. a niche or alcove 2 a remote place *(often pl)* o *the recesses of her mind* 3 a break from work, business, or other activity ■ vt 1 put in a niche 2 make a niche in

recession /ri sésh'n/ n 1 a decline in economic activity 2 a ceremonial withdrawal from a building at the conclusion of a formal ceremony, e.g. a wedding 3 the process of receding —**recessionary** adj

recessive /ri séssiv/ adj 1 engaged in receding o *recessive tides* 2 describes a gene that produces an effect in some conditions only 3 describes a characteristic determined by a recessive gene

recharge /ree chaárj/ (**-charging, -charged**) vt replenish the electricity in a battery —**rechargeable** adj —**recharger** n

recherché /rə sháir shay/ adj rare or obscure

recidivism /ri síddivizəm/ n relapsing into crime —**recidivist** n, adj

~~**receipt**~~ incorrect spelling of **receipt**

~~**recieve**~~ incorrect spelling of **receive**

Recife /re seéfa/ capital of Pernambuco State, NE Brazil. Pop. 1,346,045 (1996).

recipe /réssəpi/ n 1 a set of instructions for preparing food 2 something likely to have a particular result o *the recipe for success* o *a recipe for disaster*

ORIGIN Recipe was originally an instruction at the beginning of medical prescriptions (rather like *take* in 'Take three pills daily'). It is the imperative form of Latin *recipere* 'receive, take'. **Recipe** came first to be used as a noun in the sense 'prescription, remedy' in the late 16C. The modern cookery sense did not appear until the early 18C. The earlier word in both these noun senses was *receipt*.

recipient /ri síppi ənt/ n somebody who receives something ■ adj in the process of receiving

reciprocal /ri sípprək'l/ adj 1 given or shown by each side 2 given or done in return 3 describes a number or quality that is related to another by the fact that when multiplied together the product is one —**reciprocal** *n* —**reciprocality** /ri sípprə kálləti/ *n* —**reciprocally** *adv*

reciprocate /ri sípprə kayt/ (**-cating, -cated**) *vti* **1** give something mutually or in return for something similar **2** move backwards and forwards —**reciprocation** /ri sípprə káysh'n/ *n*

reciprocity /réssi próssəti/ (*pl* **-ties**) *n* a reciprocal relationship or act

recital /ri sīt'l/ *n* **1** a solo performance of music or dance **2** the reciting of something in public —**recitalist** *n*

recitation /réssi táysh'n/ *n* the reciting of something, e.g. a poem

recite /ri sīt/ (**-citing, -cited**) *vt* **1** repeat from memory or read aloud **2** give a detailed account or list of

reckless /rékləss/ *adj* showing a lack of thought about danger —**recklessly** *adv* —**reckless-ness** *n*

reckon /rékən/ *v* **1** *vti* count or calculate **2** *vt* regard or consider ○ *reckoned to be the best in her field* **3** *vt* include ○ *reckon him among my friends* **4** *vt* think or believe
□ **reckon with** *vt* face or deal with ○ *If he lets you down he'll have me to reckon with.*

reckoning /rékəning/ *n* **1** a calculation **2** the settlement of an account **3** a time to account for wrongs

reclaim /ri kláym/ *vt* **1** claim something back **2** convert wasteland for cultivation **3** extract a useful substance for reuse —**reclaimable** *adj* —**reclamation** /réklə máysh'n/ *n*

recline /ri klīn/ (**-clining, -clined**) *v* **1** *vi* lie back or down **2** *vti* tilt back ○ *Do these seats recline?* —**recliner** *n*

recluse /ri klóoss/ *n* **1** somebody who lives alone and avoids social contact **2** somebody who lives a solitary life of prayer —**reclusive** *adj* —**reclusiveness** *n*

recognition /rékəg nísh'n/ *n* **1** an act of recognizing, or the fact of being recognized **2** appreciation for an achievement **3** acknowledgment of validity or truth

recognizance /ri kógnizənss/, **recognisance** *n* a formal agreement to do something, e.g. appear in court, or the sum of money pledged for this ○ *was released on her own recognizance* —**recognizant** *adj*

recognize /rékəg nīz/ (**-nizing, -nized**), **recognise** *vt* **1** identify somebody or something seen before **2** acknowledge or show appreciation of somebody else's achievement **3** accept the validity or truth of something —**recognizable** *adj* —**recognizably** *adv* —**recognized** *adj*

recoil /ri kóyl/ *vi* **1** move back suddenly and violently **2** draw back in horror or disgust —**recoil** /ri kóyl, rée koyl/ *n*

SYNONYMS **recoil, flinch, quail, shrink, wince** CORE MEANING: draw back in fear or distaste

recollect /rékə lékt/ *vti* remember —**recollection** *n*

recombination /rée kombi náysh'n/ *n* any process that produces offspring with genes different from those of either parent

~~recomend~~ incorrect spelling of **recommend**

recommend /rékə ménd/ *vt* **1** suggest as being most suitable **2** endorse as worthy or pleasing **3** make appealing or attractive ○ *The film has little to recommend it.* —**recommendable** *adj* —**recommendation** /rékə men dáysh'n/ *n*

SYNONYMS **recommend, advise, advocate, counsel, suggest** CORE MEANING: put forward ideas to somebody deciding on a course of action

recompense /rékəm penss/ *vt* (**-pensing, -pensed**) **1** pay or reward ○ *was recompensed for her heroism* **2** give compensation to or for ■ *n* **1** remuneration **2** compensation

reconcile /rékən sīl/ (**-ciling, -ciled**) *vt* **1** make disputing people friendly again **2** make somebody accept something unpleasant ○ *reconciled herself to the fact that her career was over* **3** make conflicting things consistent or compatible —**reconcilable** *adj* —**reconcilement** *n* —**reconciliation** /rékən sili áysh'n/ *n* —**reconciliatory** /rékən sílli ətəri/ *adj*

recondite /rékən dīt, ri kón-/ *adj* understood only by experts —**reconditeness** *n* ◊ See note at **obscure**

recondition /réekən dísh'n/ *vt* repair and replace the worn-out parts of ◊ See note at **renew**

~~reconize~~ incorrect spelling of **recognize**

~~reconnaissance~~ incorrect spelling of **reconnaissance**

reconnaissance /ri kónniss'nss/ *n* exploration of an area to gather information

reconnoiter *vti* US = **reconnoitre**

reconnoitre /rékə nóytər/ (**-tring, -tred**) *vti* explore an area to gather information

reconsider /réekən síddər/ *vti* think about something again, usually with a view to changing a decision —**reconsideration** /réekən sidə ráysh'n/ *n*

reconstitute /rée kónsti tyoot/ (**-tuting, -tuted**) *vt* **1** bring something back to its original state, e.g. by adding water to a concentrated form **2** alter the form of something —**reconstitution** /rée konsti tyóosh'n/ *n*

reconstruct /réekən strúkt/ *vt* **1** put something back together **2** replicate something from the past on the basis of evidence **3** restore government and the rule of law to a destroyed nation —**reconstruction** *n* —**reconstructive** *adj*

record *n* /ré kawrd/ **1** a lasting account, usually in writing **2** a written account of proceedings **3** a document containing history **4** a body of information or statistics (*often pl*) ○ *the hottest summer on the meteorological record* **5** the greatest accomplishment so far ○ *broke the record for the high jump* ○ *in record time* **6** a disc of recorded music for a gramophone (*dated*) **7** a list of past accomplishments or crimes **8** a collection of related data items in a computer database ■ *v* /ri káwrd/ **1** *vt* make a lasting account of **2** *vt* make a note of **3** *vti* indicate a measurement **4** *vti* make a copy of sounds or images on a tape or disc —**recordable** *adj* ◇ **off the record** not intended to be made public ◇ **set the record straight** put right a mistake or misunderstanding

ORIGIN Record goes back to Latin *cor* 'heart', and so to **record** something is etymologically to put it to your heart.

recorded delivery *n* a method of postage with an official record of sending and delivery

recorder /ri káwrdər/ *n* **1** a machine for recording **2** a person who makes a written record **3** a wind instrument with a whistle-shaped mouthpiece and finger holes —**recordership** *n*

recording /ri káwrding/ *n* **1** the making of a tape or CD, especially of music **2** a copy of sounds or images **3** a broadcast that is not live

record player *n* a machine for playing records

recount /ri kównt/ *vt* tell a story

re-count /ree kównt/ *vti* count again —**re-count** /reé kownt/ *n*

recoup /ri koóp/ *vt* **1** regain something lost or obtain an equivalent **2** reimburse somebody —**recoupable** *adj*

~~recouperate~~ incorrect spelling of **recuperate**

recourse /ri káwrss/ *n* **1** the seeking of assistance ○ *without recourse to further borrowing* **2** a source of help or a solution ○ *our only recourse*

recover /ri kúvvər/ *v* **1** *vt* regain **2** *vi* return to a previous or usual state, e.g. of health **3** *vi* return to the right position ○ *The goalkeeper recovered and blocked the incoming puck.* **4** *vt* compensate for ○ *working hard to recover their losses* **5** *vt* reclaim from waste —**recoverable** *adj* —**recovery** *n*

re-cover /ree kúvvər/ *vt* **1** put a new cover on **2** cover again

recreant /rékri ənt/ *adj (fml)* **1** disloyal **2** cowardly —**recreant** *n*

re-create /reé kri áyt/ (**re-creating**, **re-created**) *vt* create again —**re-creation** *n* ◊ See note at **copy**

recreation /rékri áysh'n/ *n* **1** engagement in enjoyable activities, especially after work **2** an activity engaged in for pleasure or relaxation —**recreate** /-áyt/ *vi* —**recreational** *adj*

recreational vehicle *n US* a large motor vehicle used for recreational activities such as camping

recreation ground *n* an outdoor public recreation area

recreation room *n* **1** a room in a public building for games and social events **2** *US, Can* a room in a house used for relaxation and recreation

recrimination /ri krímmi náysh'n/ *n* an accusation made against somebody who has made a previous accusation —**recriminatory** /ri krímminətəri/ *adj*

recruit /ri kroót/ *v* **1** *vti* engage a person or people for military service or work **2** *vt* raise an armed force ■ *n* a new member, especially of a military force —**recruiter** *n* —**recruitment** *n*

recta plural of **rectum**

rectangle /rék tang g'l/ *n* a four-sided figure with four right angles —**rectangular** /rek táng gyoōlər/ *adj*

rectifier /rékti fī ər/ *n* an electronic device that converts alternating current to direct current

rectify /rékti fī/ (**-fies, -fied**) *vt* **1** correct errors in **2** purify, especially by distillation —**rectifiable** *adj* —**rectification** /réktifi káysh'n/ *n*

rectilinear /rékti línni ər/, **rectilineal** /-ni əl/ *adj* **1** having straight lines **2** moving in a straight line

rectitude /rékti tyood/ *n* **1** moral integrity **2** correctness of judgment *(fml)*

recto /réktō/ (*pl* **-tos**) *n* **1** the front of a printed sheet **2** a right-hand page

rector /réktər/ *n* **1** a cleric in charge of an Episcopal parish **2** a cleric in charge of a Roman Catholic congregation or community **3** the head of some educational institutions **4** an officer elected by students at some Scottish universities —**rectorship** *n*

rectory /réktəri/ (*pl* **-ries**) *n* a religious rector's house

rectum /réktəm/ (*pl* **-tums** *or* **-ta** /-tə/) *n* the lower part of the large intestine —**rectal** *adj* —**rectally** *adv*

ORIGIN Rectum is a form of Latin *rectus* 'straight'. It is short for *intestinum rectum* 'straight intestine' ('straight' in contrast with the twisting shape of the rest of the intestine).

recumbent /ri kúmbənt/ *adj* lying down flat *(literary)* ○ *a recumbent statue of the general*

recuperate /ri koópə rayt/ (**-ating, -ated**) *v* **1** *vi* recover from an illness or injury **2** *vt* get back something lost ○ *recuperate investment losses* —**recuperation** /ri koópə ráysh'n/ *n* —**recuperative** *adj*

recur /ri kúr/ (**-curring, -curred**) *vi* **1** occur again **2** occur as an infinitely repeated digit or series of digits at the end of a decimal fraction —**recurrence** /ri kúrrənss/ *n* —**recurrent** /ri kúrrənt/ *adj*

recycle /ree sík'l/ (**-cling, -cled**) *v* **1** *vti* process used material for later re-use **2** *vti* save something for later reprocessing or re-use **3** *vt* use again unimaginatively ○ *recycling the same old ideas* —**recyclable** *adj* —**recycling** *n*

red *adj* (**redder, reddest**) **1** of the colour of blood **2** describes hair that is reddish-brown **3** blushing or flushed **4** *also* **Red** Socialist or Communist *(infml disapproving)* ■ *n* **1** the colour of blood **2** *also* **Red** a Socialist or Communist *(infml disapproving)* —**reddish** *adj* —**redness** *n* ◇ **in the red** in debt ◇ **see red** become very angry *(infml)*

red alert *n* a warning of or state of heightened readiness for an emergency

Red Army *n* the former Soviet Army

red blood cell *n* a blood cell carrying oxygen

red-blooded *adj* strong, vigorous, determined, and high-spirited

redbreast /réd brest/ (*pl* **-breasts** *or same*) *n* a robin or other bird with a red chest

redbrick /rédbrik/ *adj* **1** of British universities founded in the late 19C and early 20C **2** built of red bricks

red card *n* in football, a referee's card displayed when dismissing a player

red carpet *n* **1** a strip of carpet laid down for important visitors **2** VIP treatment

redcoat /réd kōt/ *n* **1** a British soldier, especially during the American War of Independence **2** a holiday camp attendant

Red Crescent *n* the Red Cross in Islamic countries

Red Cross *n* an international organization that provides medical care

redcurrant /red kúrrənt/ *n* **1** a sharp-tasting red berry. Use: jam or jelly. **2** a bush that produces redcurrants

redden /rédd'n/ *vti* make or become red

redecorate /ree déka rayt/ (**-rating, -rated**) *vti* renew the interior decoration of a house or room —**redecoration** /reè deka ráysh'n/ *n*

redeem /ri deém/ *vt* **1** make something acceptable in spite of negative qualities **2** restore a good opinion of somebody **3** buy something back **4** exchange a voucher or coupon for money or goods **5** pay off a debt **6** atone for human sin (*refers to Jesus Christ*) —**redeemable** *adj* —**redeemer** *n* —**redeeming** *adj* —**redemption** /ri démpsh'n/ *n* —**redemptive** /ri démptiv/ *adj*

redeploy /reèdi plóy/ *vti* move people or equipment to a different area or activity —**redeployment** *n*

redevelop /reèdi véllap/ *vt* improve a rundown area —**redevelopment** *n*

red-faced *adj* blushing, especially with embarrassment

red flag *n* **1** a flag symbolizing Communism or Socialism **2** a warning signal

red-handed *adj* in the act of committing an offence o *caught red-handed*

redhead /réd hed/ *n* somebody with reddish-brown hair —**red-headed** *adj*

red herring *n* something introduced to divert attention or mislead

red-hot *adj* **1** glowing red with heat **2** very hot **3** very exciting (*infml*) o *red-hot news*

redial /ree dī al/ (**-alling, -alled**) *vti* dial a telephone number again

~~rediculous~~ incorrect spelling of **ridiculous**

redid past tense of **redo**

redirect /reèdi rékt, -dī-/ *vt* **1** send something received to another place o *redirecting the previous tenant's mail* **2** reroute traffic —**redirection** *n*

redistribute /reèdi strí byoot/ (**-uting, -uted**) *vt* **1** distribute again **2** apportion differently —**redistribution** /reèdistri byoósh'n/ *n*

red-letter day *n* a very special day

red light *n* a warning signal

red-light *adj* describes a district where commercial sex-based activities are concentrated

redline /réd līn/ (**-lining, -lined**) *vti* refuse financial services to people or businesses in a supposedly high-risk area

red meat *n* meat that is red when raw

red mullet *n* **1** an orange-red Mediterranean fish **2** red mullet as food

redo /ree doó/ (**-does** /-dúz/, **-doing, -did** /-díd/, **-done** /-dún/) *vt* do again or differently

redolent /rédd'lant/ *adj* **1** suggestive or reminiscent of something o *redolent of corruption* **2** aromatic (*literary*) **3** having a particular smell o *redolent of beeswax* —**redolence** *n*

Redon /rə dón, rə dóN/, **Odilon** (1840–1916) French painter and lithographer

redouble /ri dúbb'l/ (**-bling, -bled**) *vti* increase considerably o *redoubled our efforts*

redoubt /ri dówt/ *n* **1** a stronghold (*literary*) **2** a temporary fortification

redoubtable /ri dówtəb'l/ *adj* with formidable personal qualities —**redoubtably** *adv*

redound /ri dównd/ *vi* **1** have a particular result o *a decision that redounded to her credit* **2** return as a consequence to a person or group (*fml*) o *His attempts at revenge redounded upon his own head.*

red panda *n* a reddish animal resembling a raccoon

red pepper *n* a hollow red fruit eaten as a vegetable

redraw /ree dráw/ (**-drew** /-droó/, **-drawn** /-dráwn/) *vt* **1** draw something again or differently **2** reposition a boundary

redress /ri dréss/ *n* compensation or reparation ■ *vt* **1** make up for a loss or wrong **2** impose fairness or equality on a situation

Red River 1 river in Southeast Asia, rising in S China and emptying into the Gulf of Tonkin. Length 800 km/500 mi. **2** river in the north-central United States and south-central Canada, flowing northwards from Minnesota and emptying into Lake Winnipeg. Length 877 km/545 mi.

Red Sea inland sea between Arabia and NE Africa

red tape *n* bureaucracy (*infml*)

reduce /ri dyoóss/ (**-ducing, -duced**) *v* **1** *vti* decrease **2** *vt* bring to an undesirable state o *reduce to tears* **3** *vt* make cheaper **4** *vt* simplify **5** *vt* analyse systematically **6** *vt* demote **7** *vti* thicken by the evaporation of water **8** *vti* undergo or cause to undergo a chemical reaction in which there is a loss of oxygen or a gain of hydrogen —**reducible** *adj*

reduction /ri dúksh'n/ *n* **1** a reducing or a being reduced **2** the amount by which something is reduced —**reductive** *adj*

redundancy /ri dúndənssi/ (pl **-cies**) n 1 dismissal from work because the employee is no longer needed 2 the state of being superfluous 3 duplication as a safety measure 4 use of superfluous words —**redundant** adj —**redundantly** adv

redwood /réd wõod/ n a tall sequoia with reddish bark

re-echo v 1 vi echo back 2 vt repeat something

reed /reed/ n 1 a tall water plant 2 the stalk of a reed. Use: thatching, basketry. 3 a vibrating part in a musical instrument that produces sound when air passes it ◊ See note at **read**

re-educate /ree éddyoo kayt, -éddyə-/ vt teach or train again to change or update knowledge, skills, or behaviour

reedy /reédi/ (**-ier**, **-iest**) adj 1 full of reeds 2 high-pitched —**reediness** n

reef[1] n a ridge of rock or coral in a body of water

reef[2] vt gather in part of a sail ■ n the part of a reefed sail that is gathered in

reefer n a marijuana cigarette (slang)

reefer jacket n a double-breasted woollen jacket or coat

reef knot n a symmetrical knot that will not slip

reek /reek/ vi 1 have a very strong unpleasant smell 2 give clear evidence of something unpleasant ○ The document reeks of the double standard. ■ n a strong unpleasant smell ○ the reek of disinfectant ◊ See note at **smell**

SPELLCHECK Do not confuse the spelling of **reek** and **wreak** ('cause havoc or destruction'), which sound similar.

reel[1] /reel/ n 1 a cylindrical or wheel-shaped device on which something such as thread or tape is wound 2 a section of a cinema film 3 a winder on a fishing rod ■ vt wind onto or off a reel ◊ See note at **real**
□ **reel off** vt list quickly and easily

reel[2] /reel/ vi 1 stagger backwards 2 move unsteadily 3 feel giddy or confused ○ still reeling from the shock —**reel** n

reel[3] /reel/ n a lively dance for sets of couples

re-enter /ree éntər/ v 1 vti go into a place again 2 vt enter data again

re-entry /ree éntri/ n 1 the act of re-entering 2 a return to Earth's atmosphere from space

re-establish vt establish something again —**re-establishment** n

re-examine /reè ig zámmin/ vt 1 examine again 2 question again after cross-examination —**re-examination** /reè ig zami náysh'n/ n

ref n a referee (infml)

refectory /ri féktəri/ (pl **-ries**) n a dining hall

refer /ri fúr/ (**-ferring**, **-ferred**) v 1 vi make or have reference to somebody or something ○ referred to him by name ○ This clause refers to you as the tenant. 2 vi consult somebody or something for information ○ refer to the manual 3 vt direct to a source of help —**referral** n

referee /réffə reé/ n 1 an official overseeing a sporting contest or a team game 2 somebody asked to settle a dispute or make a judgment —**referee** vti

reference /réffərənss/ n 1 a spoken or written mention 2 the process of referring 3 relevance or connection 4 a source of information ○ a reference book 5 a note directing a reader to a source of information ■ prep with reference to

referendum /réffə réndəm/ (pl **-dums** or **-da** /-də/) n a vote by an whole population on an issue

~~reference~~ incorrect spelling of **reference**

refill vti /ree fíl/ fill again ■ n /ree fíl/ a replacement for the contents of a container —**refillable** adj

refine /ri fín/ (**-fining**, **-fined**) vti 1 make or become purer 2 make or become more cultured or elegant 3 make or become more effective or sophisticated ○ refining my technique —**refined** adj —**refiner** n

refinement /ri fínmənt/ n 1 elegance, politeness, and good taste 2 an improvement 3 the process of refining 4 superior quality and sophistication ○ a dish of great refinement

refinery /ri fínəri/ (pl **-ies**) n a place for processing and purifying substances such as oil or sugar

refit /ree fit/ (**-fitting**, **-fitted**) vti repair and equip again —**refit** /ree fit/ n

reflation /ree fláysh'n/ n the process of bringing an economy out of recession

reflect /ri flékt/ v 1 vt send light, sound, or heat back from a surface 2 vti show a mirror image of something 3 vt show or indicate something ○ The election results reflect discontent among voters. 4 vi think seriously 5 vt have or express a particular thought ○ reflected that withdrawal might be the safest option 6 vti bring credit or discredit to somebody or something ○ an action that reflects badly on the school

reflection /ri fléksh'n/ n 1 the act of reflecting or being reflected 2 a reflected image 3 careful thought 4 a considered idea 5 an indication or result ○ a reflection of your hard work

reflective /ri fléktiv/ adj 1 thoughtful 2 able to reflect —**reflectiveness** n

reflector /ri fléktər/ n something that reflects light

reflex /reé fleks/ adj 1 automatic and involuntary 2 without thought or preparation 3 describes an angle of between 180° and 360° 4 also **reflexed** bent or folded back ○ reflex leaves ■ n an involuntary physiological reaction, such as a sneeze

reflexive /ri fléksiv/ adj 1 describes a pronoun ending in '-self', used to refer back to the subject of a sentence or clause 2 describes a verb denoting self-directed action —**reflexive** n —**reflexively** adv

reflexology /reè flek sólləji/ n massage of the feet or hands to relax or heal other parts of the body —**reflexologist** n

reform /ri fáwrm/ v 1 vt improve by removing faults 2 vti adopt or cause to adopt a more acceptable way of behaving ■ n 1 political or social reorganization and improvement 2 an improving change —**reformer** n —**reformism** n —**reformist** adj, n

re-form /ree fáwrm/ vti form again

reformat /ree fáwr mat/ (**-matting, -matted**) vt format computer data again or differently

reformation /réffər máysh'n/ n 1 a process of reforming 2 **Reformation** the 16C religious movement that established Protestantism —**reformational** adj

reformatory /ri fáwrmətəri/ n (pl -**ries**) formerly, an institution for young offenders ■ adj intended to reform (fml)

Reform Judaism n a branch of Judaism that seeks to adapt religious practice to modern times

refract /ri frákt/ vt alter the course of a wave of energy, as water does to light —**refraction** n —**refractive** adj —**refractivity** /ree frak tívvəti/ n

refractory /ri fráktəri/ adj 1 stubborn, rebellious, and uncontrollable 2 highly heat-resistant ■ n a material that is able to withstand high temperatures without melting —**refractorily** adv

refrain[1] /ri fráyn/ vi hold yourself back from doing something —**refrainment** n

ORIGIN The two English words **refrain** are unrelated, though both were adopted from French in the 14C. **Refrain** 'hold back' goes back to Latin frenum 'bridle'. **Refrain** 'chorus' comes ultimately from Latin frangere 'break', the idea being of a chorus breaking off and then resuming.

refrain[2] /ri fráyn/ n 1 a recurring piece of verse in a poem 2 the chorus in a song

~~refrence~~ incorrect spelling of **reference**

refresh /ri frésh/ vt 1 renew the energy of somebody with rest, food, or drink 2 make somebody feel cool or clean 3 prompt the memory 4 make something fresh or bright again 5 replenish something 6 update a visual display or electronic device with data —**refresher** adj —**refreshing** adj —**refreshingly** adv

refresher course n a course of study updating previous training

refreshment /ri fréshmənt/ n 1 something that refreshes 2 an act of refreshing or being refreshed ■ **refreshments** npl food and drink

~~refridgerator~~ incorrect spelling of **refrigerator**

refrigerant /ri fríjjərənt/ n a substance used to cool or freeze something

refrigerate /ri fríjjə rayt/ (**-ating, -ated**) vt make or keep something cool —**refrigeration** /ri fríjjə ráysh'n/ n

refrigerator /ri fríjjə raytər/ n an artificially cooled appliance for storage

refuel /ree fyóo əl, -fyóol/ (**-elling, -elled**) v 1 vti refill with fuel 2 vt provide new material or impetus for something such as a debate

refuge /réff yooj/ n 1 shelter or protection 2 a place providing refuge

refugee /réffyoo jeé/ n somebody who seeks refuge in a foreign country

refund vt /ri fúnd/ return money to somebody ■ n /ree fund/ 1 an amount of money refunded 2 an act of refunding —**refundable** adj

refurbish /ree fúrbish/ vt restore something to good condition —**refurbishment** n

refusal /ri fyóoz'l/ n 1 an act of refusing 2 the chance to accept or reject something before others ○ gave us right of first refusal

refuse[1] /ri fyóoz/ (**-fusing, -fused**) v 1 vti indicate that you will not do something 2 vt not accept something —**refusable** adj

refuse[2] /réffyooss/ n things thrown away as rubbish

refute /ri fyoót/ (**-futing, -futed**) vt 1 prove false or wrong by providing evidence to the contrary 2 deny —**refutable** /réffyóotəb'l, ri fyóotəb'l/ adj —**refutably** adv —**refutation** /réffyoo táysh'n/ n

regain /ri gáyn/ vt 1 get something back 2 reach a place again

regal /reeg'l/ adj characteristic of or suitable for a monarch —**regally** adv

regale /ri gáyl/ (**-galing, -galed**) vt 1 entertain somebody, e.g. by storytelling 2 give somebody plenty to eat and drink

regalia /ri gáyli ə/ n (+ sing or pl verb) 1 the ceremonial objects and clothing of royalty or other holders of high office 2 the distinctive clothing or symbols of a particular group of people

regard /ri gaárd/ vt 1 consider ○ regards her as a friend 2 have a particular feeling about ○ regarded the prospect with horror 3 judge the quality or worth of ○ is highly regarded in the community 4 look at attentively ■ n 1 attention or concern ○ little regard for their safety 2 favourable opinion ■ **regards** npl friendly greetings —**regardful** adj ◊ **in this** or **that regard** as far as this or that is concerned (fml)

SYNONYMS **regard, admiration, esteem, favour, respect, reverence, veneration** CORE MEANING: appreciation of the worth of somebody or something

regarding /ri gaárding/ prep about or on the subject of

regardless /ri gaárdləss/ adv in spite of everything ■ adj heedless —**regardlessly** adv ◊ See note at **irregardless**

regatta /ri gáttə/ n a series of boat races

ORIGIN The original **regattas** were gondola races on the Grand Canal in Venice. The word means a 'fight, struggle' in the Venetian dialect of Italian. The first recorded use for a boat race in England was in 1775, when a **regatta** was held on the Thames in London.

regd abbr registered

regency /reejənssi/ (pl -**cies**) n 1 a group of people ruling on behalf of a monarch 2 the authority or rule of a regent

regenerate v /ri jénnə raytʹ (**-ating, ated**) 1 vti recover or cause to recover from decline 2 vti form again 3 vt restore somebody spiritually ■ adj /ri jénnərət/ 1 spiritually reborn or renewed 2 newly formed or grown —**regeneration** /ri jénnə ráysh'n/ n —**regenerative** /-rətiv/ adj

regenerative medicine n the branch of medicine that deals with repairing or replacing tissues and organs by using advanced materials and methodologies, e.g. cloning

regent /reejənt/ n somebody ruling on behalf of a monarch —**regent** adj

reggae /réggay/ n popular music of Jamaican origin combining rock, calypso, and soul

regicide /réjji sīd/ n 1 the killing of a king 2 somebody who kills a king —**regicidal** /réjji sīd'l/ adj

regime /ray zheèm, re-/, **régime** n 1 a form of government 2 a specific government, especially an oppressive one 3 an established way of doing things

regimen /réjjimən, -men/ n a programme of diet, exercise, and other measures to improve health

regiment n /réjjimənt/ 1 a military unit made up of two or more battalions 2 a large number of people or things ■ vt /réjji ment/ 1 control strictly 2 group systematically —**regimental** /réjji mént'l/ adj —**regimentation** /réjji men táysh'n/ n

Regina¹ /ri jīnə/ n 1 the reigning queen 2 the Crown as a legal entity when the monarch is female

Regina² /ri jīnə/ capital of Saskatchewan, Canada. Pop. 180,400 (1996).

region /reejən/ n 1 a geographical, political, cultural, or ecological area 2 an administrative unit 3 a large indefinite area 4 the range within which a particular figure falls ○ in the region of £1,000 ■ **regions** npl the provinces

regional /reejən'l/ adj 1 of a region 2 characteristic of or limited to a specific area of a country ○ a regional accent —**regionalization** /reejənə lī záysh'n/ n —**regionalize** vt —**regionally** adv

regionalism /reejənəlizəm/ n 1 division into administrative areas 2 a regional linguistic feature

register /réjjistər/ n 1 an official list 2 a book for official records, e.g. of attendance 3 a device that automatically records numbers or quantities 4 a grate in a heating system 5 a computer memory location 6 a musical range ■ v 1 vti record something, or cause something to be recorded, in a register 2 vti enrol 3 vt show something as a measurement 4 vt display or express a feeling ○ registered her disapproval 5 vti note or be noted mentally —**registrant** n

registered nurse n ANZ, US, Can a qualified licensed nurse

registered post n a secure mail service

registered trademark n an official trademark

register office n a registry office (technical)

registrar /réjji straār, réjji straar/ n 1 an official who keeps student records in a college or university 2 somebody who keeps official records 3 a recorder of births, marriages, and deaths 4 a senior hospital doctor 5 a law court official —**registrarship** n

registration /réjji stráysh'n/ n 1 the act of registering, or the state of being registered 2 an entry in a register, or a document certifying its making 3 the time for recording the presence or absence of school students 4 the number of people registering together

registration document n a vehicle identification document

registration number n an identifying sequence of letters and numbers displayed on a vehicle

registry /réjjistri/ (pl -tries) n 1 a records office 2 registration

registry office n an office where civil marriages are performed

regress /ri gréss/ v 1 vi return to an earlier worse condition 2 vi go back or move backwards 3 vti cause to go back to an earlier psychological period or state —**regress** /reè gress/ n —**regression** n

regressive /ri gréssiv/ adj 1 regressing 2 describes a tax system in which less well-off people pay proportionally more in taxes —**regressively** adv

regret /ri grét/ vt (**-gretting, -gretted**) 1 wish you had not done or said something 2 be sorry to say ○ We regret to tell you that the hotel is full. ■ n a feeling of regretting something —**regretful** adj —**regretfully** adv —**regretfulness** n —**regrettable** adj —**regrettably** adv

regroup /ree groόp/ v 1 vti form into an organized body again 2 vi recover and prepare for further effort 3 vt arrange in new groups

regular /réggyoolər/ adj 1 separated by equal times or spaces 2 happening frequently 3 usual 4 following a routine or pattern 5 of a standard or medium size ○ a regular coffee 6 symmetrical 7 proper or qualified ○ not a regular doctor 8 belonging to a professional force ○ a regular army officer 9 thorough and absolute (infml) ○ a regular tyrant in the office ■ n 1 a frequent visitor or customer (infml) 2 a professional soldier (often pl) —**regularity** /réggyoõb lárrəti/ n —**regularization** /réggyoõlə rī záysh'n/ n —**regularize** vt —**regularly** adv

regulate /réggyoõb layt/ (**-lating, -lated**) vt 1 control something 2 adjust machinery so that it works correctly 3 make something regular —**regulative** adj —**regulatory** adj

regulation /réggyoõb láysh'n/ n 1 an official rule or law (often pl) 2 an act of regulating, or the state of being regulated ■ adj 1 officially approved for use 2 standard

regulator /réggyoõb laytər/ n (often in combination) 1 a control mechanism 2 a controlling official ○ the industry regulator

regurgitate /ri gúrji tayt/ (**-tating**, **-tated**) *vt*
1 bring food back up from the stomach
2 repeat information mechanically
—**regurgitation** /ri gúrji táysh'n/ *n*

rehab /reé hab/ *n* US rehabilitation (*infml*)

rehabilitate /reé ə billi tayt, reé hə-/ (**-tating**, **-tated**) *vt* 1 help somebody return to good health or to life away from a hospital or prison 2 restore somebody to a rank or rights —**rehabilitative** *adj*

rehabilitation /reé ə billi táysh'n, reé hə-/ *n* the process of rehabilitating somebody, especially after confinement in a hospital or prison

rehash /ree hásh/ *vt* repeat or reuse old material or ideas —**rehash** /reé hash/ *n*

rehearse /ri húrss/ (**-hearsing**, **-hearsed**) *v* 1 *vti* practise something before performing it 2 *vt* train somebody for a performance —**rehearsal** *n*

ORIGIN **Rehearse** goes back to a French word meaning 'large agricultural rake' (from which *hearse* also derives). Its etymological meaning is therefore 'rake over', and saying something over again was what **rehearsing** originally implied. The sense of practising for a performance developed in the late 16C.

reheat /ree heét/ *v* 1 *vti* heat something again 2 *vt* inject fuel into a jet engine

rehoboam /reé ə bố əm/ *n* a large wine bottle, six times the size of a normal bottle

ORIGIN In the Bible, Rehoboam was the son of Solomon and king of ancient Judah (922?–915? BC), who 'fortified the strongholds, and put captains in them... and stores of oil and wine' (2 Chronicles 11:11).

rehouse /ree hówz/ (**-housing**, **-housed**) *vt* move somebody to better housing

Reich /rīk, rīkh/ *n* the German state or empire in any of its various historical manifestations

reign /rayn/ *n* 1 a period of royal rule 2 control or influence ■ *vi* 1 rule a nation, especially as a monarch 2 be the overarching influence ○ *After he spoke, silence reigned.* ◊ See note at **rain**

reign of terror *n* a time of systematic violence or intimidation

reimburse /reé im búrss/ (**-bursing**, **-bursed**) *vt* pay back money spent by somebody —**reimbursable** *adj* —**reimbursement** *n*

Reims /reemz/, **Rheims** city in NE France. Pop. 187,206 (1999).

rein /rayn/ *n* 1 a strap for controlling a horse (*often pl*) 2 a means of exercising power (*often pl*) ■ **reins** *npl* straps for guiding and controlling a young child ■ *vt* tightly restrain or control ○ *had to rein back inflation* ◊ **give (free) rein to** impose no restraints or limitations on ◊ **have** *or* **keep a (tight) rein on** maintain strict control over ◊ See note at **rain**

□ **rein in** *v* 1 *vti* stop or slow a horse 2 *vt* restrain or control ○ *Let's rein in the rhetoric.*

reincarnation /reé in kaar náysh'n/ *n* 1 in some religions, rebirth of the soul in a new body 2 in some religions, a body in which somebody is reborn —**reincarnate** /ree ín kaar nayt, reé in kaàr-/ *vt* —**reincarnate** /reé in kaàrnət, -nayt/ *adj*

reindeer /ráyn deer/ (*pl same or* **-deers**) *n* a large deer with branched antlers

reinforce /reé in fáwrss/ (**-forcing**, **-forced**) *vt* 1 strengthen or support something with something additional 2 provide a military force with more troops or weapons 3 influence behaviour by reward or punishment —**reinforcer** *n*

reinforced concrete *n* concrete strengthened with metal

reinforcement /reé in fáwrssmənt/ *n* 1 the addition of strength or support 2 material added to reinforce something ■ **reinforcements** *npl* additional troops, weapons, or resources

reinstate /reé in stáyt/ (**-stating**, **-stated**) *vt* 1 restore to a former job or position 2 bring back into use or force —**reinstatement** *n*

reintroduce /reé in intra dyoóss/ (**-ducing**, **-duced**) *vt* 1 bring or take back to a place ○ *a plan to reintroduce wild boar to the forests* 2 bring back into effect —**reintroduction** /-dúksh'n/ *n*

reinvent /reé in vént/ *vt* 1 invent again 2 create a new version of —**reinvention** *n*

reinvest /reé in vést/ *vti* 1 invest income made on a previous investment 2 invest profits in improving the business that produced them —**reinvestment** *n*

reiterate /ree ítti rayt/ (**-ating**, **-ated**) *vt* repeat —**reiteration** /ree ittə ráysh'n/ *n* —**reiterative** /-ətiv, -raytiv/ *adj*

Reith /reeth/**, John, 1st Baron** (1889–1971) British broadcasting executive

reject *vt* /ri jékt/ 1 not accept, believe, or make use of 2 deny love, kindness, or friendship to ■ *n* /reé jekt/ something or somebody rejected as unsuitable —**rejection** *n*

rejig /ree jíg/ (**-jigging**, **-jigged**) *vt* alter, rearrange, or readjust (*infml*)

rejoice /ri jóyss/ (**-joicing**, **-joiced**) *vi* feel or express great happiness (*literary*) —**rejoicing** *n*

□ **rejoice in** *vt* have and enjoy something desirable ○ *They rejoice in their good health.*

rejoin[1] /ree jóyn/ *v* 1 *vt* return to somebody after being apart 2 *vti* become a member of something again

rejoin[2] /ri jóyn/ *vti* reply immediately and orally (*fml*)

rejoinder /ri jóyndər/ *n* a reply or retort (*fml*) ◊ See note at **answer**

rejuvenate /ri joóvi nayt/ (**-nating**, **-nated**) *vt* 1 make somebody feel or look young again 2 restore something to its original condition —**rejuvenation** /ri joóvi náysh'n/ *n*

rekindle /ree kínd'l/ (**-dling**, **-dled**) *vt* 1 make a fire burn again 2 revive a feeling

relapse /ri láps/ (**-lapsing**, **-lapsed**) *vi* go back to a former undesirable state —**relapse** /ri láps, reè laps/ n

relate /ri láyt/ (-lating, -lated) v 1 vi have a connection with something else 2 vt find or show a connection between 3 vi involve or apply to somebody or something else 4 vi respond favourably, or form a friendly relationship based on understanding (infml) ○ I just can't relate to him. 5 vt tell or describe ○ related a tale of sorrow —**relatable** adj

related /ri láytid/ adj 1 connected by similarity or a common origin 2 belonging to the same family —**relatedness** n

relation /ri láysh'n/ n 1 a connection based on similarity or relevance 2 a member of the same family ■ **relations** npl 1 contacts between groups or people 2 sexual intercourse (euphemistic)

relational /ri láysh'nəl/ adj 1 involving a relationship 2 describes a computer database organized or presented as a set of tables

relationship /ri láysh'nship/ n 1 a connection or similarity 2 feelings for or behaviour towards somebody else 3 a close friendship, especially one involving sex

relative /réllətiv/ adj 1 in comparison with each other or another ○ discussed the relative merits of commuting by car pool or by public transport 2 changing with circumstances or context 3 dependent on or in proportion to something else ■ n a member of the same family —**relatively** adv

relative clause n a clause that provides additional information about a preceding noun or pronoun

relative density n (symbol d) the ratio of the density of a substance to the density of a standard substance at the same temperature and pressure

relative humidity n the ratio of the amount of water vapour in the air at a given temperature to the maximum amount air can hold at the same temperature, expressed as a percentage

relative pronoun n a pronoun, e.g. 'that' or 'which', that introduces a relative clause

relativism /réllətivizəm/ n the belief that concepts such as right and wrong are not absolute —**relativistic** /rélləti vístik/ adj

relativity /réllə tívvəti/ n 1 a theory showing that mass, length, and time change with velocity, or a similar theory relating to gravitation and acceleration 2 dependence on a variable factor

relax /ri láks/ v 1 vti make or become less tense or tight 2 vi to spend time resting or doing something enjoyable 3 vti make or become less anxious or hostile 4 vti make or become less formal or strict —**relaxant** n, adj —**relaxation** /reè lak sáysh'n/ n —**relaxed** adj —**relaxing** adj

relay n /reè lay/ 1 the passing of something to somebody else 2 also **relay race** a race for teams in which each member covers part of the total distance (infml) 3 a replacement

team of people or animals 4 a switching device that regulates another device or a system 5 an apparatus that receives and retransmits signals. ■ vt /ri láy/ 1 pass something on to somebody or something else ○ relay a message 2 receive and retransmit a signal

re-lay /ree láy/ (**re-laid** /-láyd/) vt lay again

release /ri leèss/ vt (-leasing, -leased) 1 set somebody or something free 2 stop holding something 3 let something out ○ released a plume of smoke 4 free somebody from an obligation 5 make something available, e.g. for sale or publication 6 operate a mechanism to let something work ○ released the clutch ■ n 1 an act of releasing or being released 2 something made available to the public 3 the deliberate or accidental introduction of an industrial product into the environment 4 a control mechanism 5 a document confirming the surrender or relinquishment of something —**releasable** adj —**releaser** n

relegate /rélli gayt/ (-gating, -gated) vt move somebody or something to a lower or less important position or category than before —**relegation** /rélli gáysh'n/ n

~~releive~~ incorrect spelling of **relieve**

relent /ri lént/ vi 1 become less strict and stop refusing to permit or do something 2 become less intense

relentless /ri léntləss/ adj 1 ceaseless and intense 2 persistently hostile and merciless —**relentlessly** adv —**relentlessness** n

relevant /rélləvənt/ adj 1 having a logical connection 2 having current significance —**relevance** n —**relevantly** adv

~~relevent~~ incorrect spelling of **relevant**

reliable /ri lí əb'l/ adj 1 able to be trusted or relied on 2 likely to be accurate —**reliability** /ri lí ə bílləti/ n —**reliably** adv

reliance /ri lí ənss/ n 1 dependence ○ a reliance on painkillers 2 trust or confidence —**reliant** adj

relic /réllik/ n 1 something old surviving from the past 2 a keepsake 3 something from a dead holy person

relief /ri leéf/ n 1 a freeing from suffering, anxiety, or boredom 2 a source of relief 3 aid provided to those in need 4 a tax reduction 5 somebody who replaces another 6 extra transport 7 the freeing of a besieged place 8 prominence caused by contrast 9 the projection of figures or shapes from a surface, e.g. in sculpture 10 the variations in the height of land

relief map n a map showing variations in the height of land

relief road n a road bypassing a town

relieve /ri leèv/ (-lieving, -lieved) v 1 vt stop something unpleasant 2 vt make less anxious (usually passive) 3 vt replace another person in a job or position 4 vt remove a burden from somebody 5 vt free a besieged place 6 vr urinate

religion /ri líjjən/ n **1** people's beliefs about and worship of deities **2** a particular system of such beliefs **3** a set of strongly held personal beliefs or values —**religionless** adj

religious /ri líjjəss/ adj **1** of religion **2** believing in a higher being **3** thorough or conscientious —**religiously** adv —**religiousness** n

~~religous~~ incorrect spelling of **religious**

relinquish /ri língkwish/ vt **1** renounce or surrender **2** abandon or let go of —**relinquishment** n

reliquary /réllikwəri/ (pl -**ies**) n a container or shrine for relics

relish /réllish/ vt **1** take great pleasure in **2** enjoy the taste of ■ n **1** enjoyment **2** a spicy sauce or accompaniment to food **3** interest or excitement ○ added relish to an otherwise dull weekend

---

ORIGIN Relish is an adoption of a French noun formed from the verb that is the source of release. The idea is of a taste or smell being released to or left on the senses.

---

relive /rêe lív/ (-**living**, -**lived**) vt experience again

~~rellevant~~ incorrect spelling of **relevant**

rellie /rélli/ n ANZ A relative (infml)

reload /rêe lốd/ vti load something into something again

relocate /rêe lō káyt/ (-**cating**, -**cated**) vti move to a new place —**relocation** /rêe lō káysh'n/ n

reluctant /ri lúktənt/ adj **1** not willing or enthusiastic **2** uncooperative —**reluctance** n —**reluctantly** adv ◊ See note at **unwilling**

rely /ri lî/ (-**lies**, -**lied**) vi **1** depend on somebody or something **2** trust somebody or something

remain /ri máyn/ vi **1** stay or wait somewhere **2** continue in a particular state **3** be left **4** be left to be dealt with ○ The question still remains. —**remaining** adj

remainder /ri máyndər/ n **1** the part of something that is left over **2** the amount left over when a number or quantity cannot be divided exactly by another **3** an unsold copy of a book ■ vt sell unsold copies of a book at a reduced price

remains /ri máynz/ npl **1** all that is left of something **2** a corpse **3** ancient ruins

remake n /rêe mayk/ a new version of something, especially a film ■ vt /rêe máyk/ (-**making**, -**made** /-máyd/) produce again

remand /ri maánd/ vt return a prisoner or accused person to custody ■ n the return of a prisoner or accused person to custody pending trial —**remandment** n

remand centre n a place of detention for accused people awaiting trial

remark /ri maárk/ n **1** a casual comment **2** the making of a remark ■ v **1** vti comment on something **2** vt observe or notice (fml)

remarkable /ri maárkəb'l/ adj **1** worth commenting on **2** unusual or exceptional —**remarkably** adv

Remarque /ri maárk/, **Erich Maria** (1898–1970) German-born US writer

remarry /rêe márri/ (-**ries**, -**ried**) vi marry a second or subsequent time —**remarriage** n

remaster /rêe maástər/ vt make an improved master recording or film of

rematch /rêe mach/ n a second match between opponents —**rematch** vt

Rembrandt van Rijn /rém brant vaan rîn/ (1606–69) Dutch artist

remedial /ri mêedi əl/ adj **1** acting as a remedy **2** helping to improve skills

remediation /ri mêedi áysh'n/ n the use of remedial methods, especially to improve skills or reverse environmental damage

remedy /rémmədi/ n (pl -**dies**) **1** a treatment for disease **2** a way of putting something right ■ vt (-**dies**, -**died**) **1** cure a disease **2** put something right —**remediable** /ri mêedi ab'l/ adj

remember /ri mémbər/ v **1** vti recall something forgotten **2** vti keep something in your memory **3** vt keep somebody in mind **4** vt give greetings to somebody from somebody else ○ Remember me to your parents.

remembrance /ri mémbrənss/ n **1** remembering or being remembered **2** the process of honouring the memory of a person or event **3** something remembered **4** a memento

Remembrance Day n **1** a day for the commemoration of war dead. Date: 11 November. **2** also **Remembrance Sunday** in the UK, a day for the commemoration of war dead on the Sunday nearest 11 November

remind /ri mînd/ vt cause to remember or think of ○ Remind me to collect the dry-cleaning. ○ He reminds me of his father. —**reminder** n

~~reminice~~ incorrect spelling of **reminisce**

reminisce /rémmi níss/ (-**niscing**, -**nisced**) vi talk or think about the past

reminiscence /rémmi níss'nss/ n **1** recollection of the past **2** something remembered from the past

reminiscent /rémmi níss'nt/ adj **1** suggestive of somebody or something else **2** suggestive of the past —**reminiscently** adv

remiss /ri míss/ adj careless or negligent

remission /ri mísh'n/ n **1** the easing or disappearance of the symptoms of disease **2** a reduction in a prison term **3** release from a debt or obligation

remit v /ri mít/ (-**mitting**, -**mitted**) **1** vt send a payment **2** vt cancel or not enforce something **3** vti reduce in intensity **4** vt pardon or forgive something ■ n /rêemit, ri mít/ somebody's area of responsibility —**remittal** n

remittance /ri mítt'nss/ n **1** the sending of payment **2** money sent as payment

remix vt /rêe míks/ produce a new version of a piece of recorded music by adding or altering tracks ■ n /rêemiks/ a remixed recording

remnant /rémnənt/ n **1** a small part left over **2** a trace of something

remodel /ree módd'l/ (**-elling, -elled**) *vt* renovate or alter the structure or style of

remonstrance /ri mónstranss/ *n* **1** a forceful argument **2** a formal protest

remonstrate /rémmən strayt/ (**-strating, -strated**) *vi* argue strongly —**remonstration** /rémmən stráysh'n/ *n* —**remonstrative** /ri mónstrətiv/ *adj* ◊ See note at **object**

remorse /ri máwrss/ *n* a strong feeling of guilt and regret —**remorseful** *adj* —**remorsefully** *adv*

remorseless /ri máwrssləss/ *adj* **1** showing no compassion **2** continuing unabated —**remorselessly** *adv* —**remorselessness** *n*

remortgage /ree máwrgij/ (**-gaging, -gaged**) *vt* change the terms of a mortgage on a property —**remortgage** *n*

remote /ri mót/ *adj* (**-moter, -motest**) **1** far away **2** away from populated areas **3** distantly related **4** distant in time **5** slight ○ *a remote possibility* **6** aloof **7** operated from a distance ■ *n* **1** a remote control (*infml*) **2** a computer situated far from a central computer —**remotely** *adv* —**remoteness** *n*

remote access *n* access to a computer from a separate terminal

remote control *n* **1** a hand-held control that operates something from a distance **2** operation from a distance —**remote-controlled** *adj*

remould *n* /rèe mōld/ a tyre with a new tread bonded to it ■ *vt* /ree mōld/ fit a tyre with a new tread

remount /ree mównt/ *v* **1** *vt* mount again or differently **2** *vti* get back onto a horse

removalist /ri moóvəlist/ *n* ANZ a company that transports the belongings of people moving house

removal van *n* a van for transporting the belongings of people moving house

remove /ri moóv/ *v* (**-moving, -moved**) **1** *vt* take away from somebody or something **2** *vti* go or take to a new place **3** *vt* take off ○ *removed his hat* **4** *vt* got rid of ○ *removed the stain* **5** *vt* dismiss from office ■ *n* the degree of distance between people or things —**removable** *adj* —**removal** *n*

removed /ri moóvd/ *adj* **1** distant **2** distantly related —**removedness** /ri moóvidnəss, ri moóvdnəss/ *n*

REM sleep /rém-/ *n* a stage of sleep marked by dreaming and rapid eye movements

remunerate /ri myoónə rayt/ (**-ating, -ated**) *vt* give payment to —**remunerable** *adj* —**remuneration** /ri myoónə ráysh'n/ *n* —**remunerative** *adj*

Remus /reémass/ *n* in Roman mythology, the son of Mars and twin brother of Romulus, the founder of the city of Rome

renaissance /ri náys'nss/, **renascence** /ri náss'nss, -náy-/ *n* **1** a rebirth or revival **2** **Renaissance** the period of European history that followed the Middle Ages and was characterized by cultural revival and scientific development —**Renaissance** *adj*

Renaissance man *n* a man with wide-ranging interests and talents

renal /reén'l/ *adj* of the kidneys

rename /ree náym/ (**-naming, -named**) *vt* give a new name to

renascent /ri náss'nt, ri náyss'nt/ *adj* newly active

rend (**rent**) *v* **1** *vti* tear apart violently **2** *vt* disturb or pierce with a loud sound ○ *A scream rent the air.* **3** *vt* cause pain or distress to ◊ See note at **tear**

Rendell /rénd'l, ren dél/, **Ruth** (*b*. 1930) British novelist

render /réndər/ *vt* (*fml*) **1** give help or provide a service **2** translate something **3** portray something artistically **4** submit something for action **5** give what is due **6** put somebody into a particular state ○ *were rendered powerless* —**renderable** *adj* —**rendering** *n*

rendezvous /róndi voo, -day-/ *n* (*pl* **-vous** /-voóz/) **1** a meeting **2** the location of an arranged meeting ■ *vti* (**-vouses** /-vooz/, **-vousing** /-voo ing/, **-voused** /-vood/) meet

rendition /ren dísh'n/ *n* **1** a version of a musical or theatrical piece **2** a translation

renegade /rénni gayd/ *n* **1** a traitor **2** a rebel

renege /ri neég, ri náyg/ (**-neging, -neged**) *vi* **1** break a promise **2** in cards, not follow suit when able to

renew /ri nyoó/ *vt* **1** begin again **2** make effective or available for a longer period of time ○ *renewed the contract* **3** repair or replace **4** revitalize —**renewal** *n*

SYNONYMS renew, recondition, renovate, restore, revamp CORE MEANING: improve the condition of something

renewable /ri nyoó əb'l/ *adj* able to be sustained or renewed ○ *renewable resources* —**renewably** *adv*

Renfrewshire /rén frooshər/ council area in SW Scotland

rennet /rénnit/ *n* **1** a preparation made from the stomach lining of calves. Use: cheese making. **2** a substance containing rennet, used in cheese-making

Reno /reénō/ city in W Nevada. Pop. 163,334 (1998).

AKG London

Pierre Auguste Renoir

Renoir /rén waar, rən waár/, **Pierre Auguste** (1841–1919) French painter and sculptor

renounce /ri nównss/ (**-nouncing, -nounced**) *vt* **1** give up a claim to something **2** reject or disavow a belief —**renouncement** *n*

renovate /rénnə vaytɪ/ (**-vating, -vated**) vt restore to good condition —**renovation** /rénnə váy-sh'n/ n —**renovator** n◊ See note at **renew**

renown /ri nównʲ/ n widespread acclaim —**renowned** adj

rent[1] n 1 regular payment by a tenant for the use of property 2 payment for the use of equipment ■ vti 1 pay to use somebody's property 2 allow the use of property for payment —**rentable** adj —**renter** n

rent[2] past tense, past participle of **rend** ■ n 1 a hole made by tearing 2 a rift in a relationship

rental /rént'l/ n 1 the amount of money paid or received in rent 2 the renting of something 3 US something rented

rent boy n an offensive term for a young man working as a prostitute (slang)

rent-free adj free of charge ■ adv at no cost

renunciation /ri núnssi áysh'n/ n 1 the denial or rejection of something 2 a formal declaration giving something up —**renunciatory** /ri núnssi ətəri/ adj

reopen /ree ṓpən/ vti 1 open again 2 start again ◊ reopen the discussion

reorganize /ree áwrgə nīzʲ/ (**-izing, -ized**), **reorganise** vti 1 organize again after being disturbed 2 organize differently —**reorganization** /ree áwrgə nī záysh'n/ n

rep[1] /rep/, **repp** n a ribbed fabric

rep[2] n a sales representative (infml)

rep[3] n a reputation (infml)

rep[4] n a repetition of a fitness exercise (infml)

Rep. abbr 1 US Representative 2 Republic

repaid past tense, past participle of **repay**

repair[1] /ri páirʲ/ vt 1 restore something damaged or broken to good condition ◊ in need of repair 2 put something right ■ n 1 the act of repairing something 2 the condition of something ◊ no longer in good repair —**repairable** adj —**repairer** n

repair[2] /ri páirʲ/ vi go somewhere (fml)

reparable /réppərəb'l/ adj able to be repaired —**reparably** adv

reparation /réppə ráysh'n/ n 1 amends 2 the repairing of something (fml) ■ **reparations** npl compensation for damage requested by the victorious side in a war —**reparatory** /ri párrətəri/ adj

repartee /réppaar teéʲ/ n 1 witty talk 2 a witty remark

repast /ri paást/ n a meal (literary)

repatriate vt /ree páttri aytʲ/ (**-ating, -ated**) send somebody back to his or her country of birth, citizenship, or origin ■ n /ree páttri ət/ somebody who has been repatriated —**repatriation** /ree páttri aysh'n/ n

repay /ri páyʲ/ (**-paid** /-páyd/) vt 1 pay back money to somebody 2 return a favour —**repayable** adj —**repayment** n

repeal /ri peélʲ/ vt revoke a law ■ n the repealing of a law —**repealable** adj

repeat /ri peétʲ/ v 1 vti say, do, or experience something again 2 vti echo somebody's words 3 vt tell what you have heard 4 vt say

something memorized 5 vr say something again or happen again as before ■ n something such as a broadcast, pattern, or customer order that is repeated or recurs —**repeatable** adj —**repeated** adj —**repeatedly** adv

repel /ri pélʲ/ (**-pelling, -pelled**) vt 1 disgust somebody 2 resist an attack 3 keep something away 4 exert a force that tends to push something away 5 spurn somebody

~~repellant~~ incorrect spelling of **repellent**

repellent /ri péllənt/ adj 1 causing disgust 2 resistant or impervious to something (often in combination) 3 pushing or driving away ■ n 1 a substance that drives away insects 2 a substance that makes a surface resistant to something —**repellence** n —**repellently** adv

repent /ri péntʲ/ v 1 vti be sorry for something 2 vi abandon bad habits or ways —**repentance** n —**repentant** adj —**repentantly** adv

~~repentence~~ incorrect spelling of **repentance**

repercussion /reépər kúsh'n/ n 1 an indirect or undesirable result of an action (often pl) 2 the rebounding of a force after impact —**repercussive** adj

repertoire /réppər twaarʲ/ n 1 a stock of artistic material that somebody can perform 2 a range of resources that somebody has

repertory /réppərtəri/ (pl **-ries**) n 1 a system in which a theatre company presents a set of plays during a single season 2 a performer's repertoire —**repertorial** /réppər táwri əl/ adj

repetition /réppə tísh'n/ n 1 the process of repeating something 2 something that is the same as something that happened before

repetitious /réppə tíshəss/ adj full of repeated material

repetitive /ri péttətiv/ adj involving repetition, especially to a boring degree —**repetitively** adv —**repetitiveness** n

repetitive strain injury, repetitive stress injury n full form of **RSI**

rephrase /ree fráyz/ (**-phrasing, -phrased**) vt say or write in different words

~~repitition~~ incorrect spelling of **repetition**

replace /ri pláyss/ (**-placing, -placed**) vt 1 take or fill the place of 2 put back in its place —**replaceable** adj

USAGE replace or substitute? These words take different constructions, although the resulting meaning is the same. You **replace** item B with (or less often by) item A, but **substitute** item A for item B.

replacement /ri pláyssmənt/ n 1 the process of replacing something or somebody 2 a person or thing that takes another's place

replay vt /ree pláy/ 1 play a match or contest again 2 play a recording again ■ n /reé play/ 1 a match or contest played again 2 a second playing of recorded material

replenish /ri plénnish/ vt replace used items in a stock —**replenishment** n

replete /ri pleétʲ/ adj 1 amply or fully equipped 2 having eaten enough —**repleteness** n

replica /répplikə/ n an accurate reproduction

replicate /réppli kayt/ (**-cating, -cated**) vt 1 repeat, copy, or reproduce something 2 reproduce by copying cellular or genetic material —**replication** /réppli káysh'n/ n ◊ See note at **copy**

reply /ri plí/ v (**-plies, -plied**) 1 vti respond to what somebody says or writes 2 vi respond to an action or gesture with an action or gesture ■ n (pl **-plies**) 1 a spoken or written answer 2 an action performed as a response —**replier** n ◊ See note at **answer**

reply-paid adj with postage for a reply paid by the sender

report /ri páwrt/ v 1 vti tell somebody about something that happened 2 vti tell people news using the media 3 vt inform the authorities about something 4 vti give details about research results or an investigation 5 vi inform somebody of your arrival 6 vi be under somebody's authority ■ n 1 an account of something 2 a news item or broadcast 3 a document giving information about something 4 an unconfirmed account of something 5 a written account of a child's academic performance 6 a sharp loud noise —**reportable** adj

reportage /ri páwr tij, réppawr taazh/ n 1 the reporting of news by the media 2 a body of reported news

reportedly /ri páwrtidli/ adv according to unconfirmed reports

reported speech n LING = **indirect speech**

reporter /ri páwrtər/ n somebody who gathers and reports the news —**reportorial** /réppawr táwri əl/ adj

repose[1] /ri póz/ n 1 rest 2 tranquillity, calmness, or peace of mind ■ v (**-posing, -posed**) (fml) 1 vti lie somewhere resting 2 vi be dead (euphemistic) —**reposal** n

repose[2] /ri póz/ (**-posing, -posed**) vt put faith or confidence in somebody or something (fml)

repository /ri pózzitəri/ (pl **-ries**) n 1 a place or receptacle for storage 2 somebody with extensive knowledge

repossess /reé pə zéss/ vt reclaim goods or property that a buyer has not paid for —**repossession** n

reprehensible /réppri hénssəb'l/ adj deserving to be censured —**reprehensibly** adv

represent /réppri zént/ vt 1 act or speak on behalf of 2 go somewhere on behalf of 3 be the equivalent of 4 symbolize 5 depict as being something in particular —**representable** adj

representation /réppri zen táysh'n/ n 1 the fact of being represented by somebody else 2 an electoral system of representatives, or the representatives elected 3 a depiction of something 4 action or speech on behalf of somebody else

representational /réppri zen táysh'nəl/ adj 1 of or characterized by representation 2 describes art that portrays recognizable objects

representative /réppri zéntətiv/ n 1 somebody who speaks or acts for another 2 a member of a legislature 3 also **Representative** US a member of the US House of Representatives or of a state legislature 4 a commercial agent or salesperson ■ adj 1 characteristic of something 2 involving or made up of elected representatives 3 made up of all types —**representatively** adv —**representativeness** n

~~representitive~~ incorrect spelling of **representative**

repress /ri préss/ vt 1 curb an action that would show feelings 2 use authority to control people's freedom 3 block something from the conscious mind —**repressed** adj —**repressible** adj —**repression** n —**repressive** adj —**repressively** adv

reprieve /ri preev/ vt (**-prieving, -prieved**) 1 halt or delay somebody's punishment 2 offer respite to somebody ■ n a halt to or delay of punishment —**reprievable** adj

reprimand /réppri maand/ vt rebuke for wrongdoing ■ n a rebuke

reprint vt /ree prínt/ print again ■ n /reé print/ a reissue of a printed work

reprisal /ri príz'l/ n 1 a retaliation in war 2 any strong or violent retaliation

reprise /ri preez/ n 1 a repeat of a musical passage 2 the chorus of a song ■ vt (**-prising, -prised**) repeat a passage of music or a showing of a film

reproach /ri próch/ v 1 vt criticize somebody for wrongdoing 2 vt feel blameworthy ■ n 1 adverse criticism 2 discredit —**reproachable** adj

reproachful /ri próchf'l/ adj disapproving —**reproachfully** adv —**reproachfulness** n

reprobate /répprō bayt/ n somebody who lives an immoral life

reprocess /ree pró sess/ vt process something again in order to reuse it

reproduce /reépro dyubss/ (**-ducing, -duced**) v 1 vti duplicate or be duplicated by a process such as photography or scanning 2 vt repeat 3 vi produce offspring 4 vt remember or imagine again —**reproducible** adj ◊ See note at **copy**

reproduction /reépro dúksh'n/ n 1 a copy of an object in an earlier style 2 the process of reproducing 3 a printed, electronic, or photographic duplicate 4 the recording of sound 5 the production of offspring by sexual or asexual means

reproductive /reépro dúktiv/ adj involving the production of offspring —**reproductiveness** n

reprogram /ree pró gram/ (**-gramming** or **-graming, -grammed** or **-gramed**) vt program a computer system differently —**reprogrammable** adj

reproof /ri proóf/, **reproval** /ri proóv'l/ n severe criticism

reprove /ri proóv/ (**-proving, -proved**) vt criticize severely —**reprovingly** adv

reptile /rép tīl/ *n* a cold-blooded scaly vertebrate —**reptile** *adj* —**reptilian** /rep tílli ən/ *adj, n*

republic /ri púbblik/ *n* **1** a political system with elect representatives to exercise power and an elected representative, not a monarch, at its head **2** *also* **Republic** a country whose political system is a republic

ORIGIN Republic came through French from Latin *res publica*, literally 'public matter'. It was adopted into English in the late 16C, and in early use could mean 'the state, the general good' as well as 'a state in which the people hold supreme power'.

republican /ri púbblikən/ *n* **1** a supporter of republics as a form of government **2** **Republican** somebody who wants or works for a united Ireland **3** **Republican** a member of the US Republican Party —**republican** *adj*

Republican Party *n* one of the two main US political parties

repudiate /ri pyóodi ayt/ (**-ating, -ated**) *vt* **1** disapprove of and refuse to be associated with **2** deny the truth or validity of **3** refuse to acknowledge or pay ○ *repudiate a debt* —**repudiation** /ri pyóodi áysh'n/ *n*

repugnant /ri púgnənt/ *adj* **1** offensive and unacceptable **2** revolting —**repugnance** *n* —**repugnantly** *adv*

repulse /ri púlss/ *vt* (**-pulsing, -pulsed**) repel an attacking force ■ *n* **1** a rejection **2** the process of repelling an attacking force

repulsion /ri púlsh'n/ *n* **1** disgust **2** a repelling force between two bodies of like electric charge or magnetic polarity

repulsive /ri púlssiv/ *adj* **1** disgusting **2** tending to repel —**repulsively** *adv* —**repulsiveness** *n*

reputable /réppyŏotəb'l/ *adj* known to be honest, reliable, or respectable

reputation /réppyŏo táysh'n/ *n* the views that are generally held about somebody or something

repute /ri pyóot/ *n (fml)* **1** estimation of character **2** good reputation

reputed /ri pyóotid/ *adj* generally believed —**reputedly** *adv*

request /ri kwést/ *vt* **1** ask politely for something **2** ask somebody to do something ■ *n* **1** the polite expression of a wish **2** something asked for

requiem /rékwi əm, -wi em/, **Requiem** *n* **1** a Roman Catholic service for somebody who has died **2** the music for a requiem

require /ri kwīr/ (**-quiring, -quired**) *vt* **1** need for a particular purpose or as a precondition **2** demand by law **3** insist on —**required** *adj* —**requirement** *n*

requisite /rékwizit/ *adj* essential *(fml)* ■ *n* something that is essential ◊ See note at **necessary**

requisition /rékwi zísh'n/ *n* **1** a formal demand or request for something **2** the process of making a formal demand or request ■ *vt* demand and take officially

requite /ri kwít/ (**-quiting, -quited**) *vt* return a kindness or hurt in kind —**requital** *n*

rerelease /ree ri leéss/ *vt* (**-leasing, -leased**) distribute a music recording or film again ■ *n* a rereleased recording or film

reroute /ree róot/ (**-routing, -routed**) *vt* direct vehicles or people another way

rerun /ree rún/ (**-running, -ran /-rán/, -run**) *vt* **1** show a broadcast again **2** repeat a race —**rerun** /ree run/ *n*

resale /ree sayl/ *n* **1** the selling of something again **2** the selling of something second-hand —**resalable** /ree sáylab'l/ *adj*

reschedule /ree shéddyool, -skédd-/ (**-uling, -uled**) *vt* **1** change the time fixed for something **2** extend the repayment period of a loan

rescind /ri sínd/ *vt* cancel or abolish something —**rescindable** *adj*

rescue /réskyoo/ *v* (**-cuing, -cued**) **1** *vt* save from danger or harm **2** save from being discarded ■ *n* **1** removal from danger or harm **2** an instance of providing help to somebody in a difficult situation —**rescuable** *adj* —**rescuer** *n*

research /ri súrch, ree surch/ *n* methodical study or investigation to discover facts or establish a theory ■ *vti* study something methodically —**researcher** *n*

research and development *n* investigation and development of new or improved products

resell /ree sél/ (**-sold /-sóld/**) *vt* sell something on to a new buyer

resemblance /ri zémblənss/ *n* similarity, especially in appearance, to somebody or something else

resemble /ri zémb'əl/ (**-bling, -bled**) *vt* be similar to

~~resemblence~~ incorrect spelling of **resemblance**

resent /ri zént/ *vt* be annoyed about or towards for a perceived unfairness —**resentment** *n* ◊ See note at **anger**

resentful /ri zéntf'l/ *adj* annoyed about something regarded as unfair —**resentfully** *adv* —**resentfulness** *n*

reservation /rézzər váysh'n/ *n* **1** an arrangement by which something such as a room or seat is booked in advance **2** the process of arranging something in advance **3** an area of land set aside for a particular purpose **4** a limiting condition ■ **reservations** *npl* doubts or misgivings

reserve /ri zúrv/ *vt* (**-serving, -served**) **1** set something aside for future use or a specific purpose **2** book a place beforehand **3** retain something such as a right for your own benefit **4** postpone a decision ○ *reserve judgment* ■ *n* **1** a wildlife conservation area **2** coolness of manner **3** a substitute player **4** a part or member of the armed services not on active duty at a given time **5** a supply of something kept for future or emergency use *(often pl)* **6** a country's supply of gold and foreign currency kept as a contingency **7** a supply of a natural resource not yet utilized **8** *also* **reserve price** the lowest price acceptable to a seller ■ **reserves** *npl* inner strengths drawn on in an emergency —**reservable** *adj*

reserve bank *n* **1** one of 12 banks in the US Federal Reserve system **2** the central bank of Australia

reserve currency *n* a foreign currency held by a central bank for settling international transactions

reserved /ri zúrvd/ *adj* **1** booked in advance **2** set aside for a specific use **3** reticent or emotionally restrained —**reservedly** /-idli/ *adv* —**reservedness** *n*

reservist /ri zúrvist/ *n* a member of a military reserve force

reservoir /rézzər vwaar/ *n* **1** a lake or tank for storing water **2** a part of a machine or device where liquid is stored

reset /ree sét/ (**-setting, -set**) *vt* **1** set something again **2** put a dial or counter back to its original setting

resettle /ree sétt'l/ (**-tling, -tled**) *vt* relocate a population —**resettlement** *n*

~~resevoir~~ incorrect spelling of **reservoir**

reshape /ree sháyp/ (**-shaping, -shaped**) *vt* **1** change or restore the shape of **2** change the organization of

reshuffle /rèe shúff'l/ *n* **1** a redistribution of jobs **2** a shuffling of cards again —**reshuffle** /ree shúff'l/ *vti*

reside /ri zíd/ (**-siding, -sided**) *vi* **1** live somewhere **2** be present

residence /rézzidənss/ *n* **1** a place where somebody lives **2** the fact or time of living somewhere

residency /rézzidənssi/ (*pl* **-cies**) *n* **1** a period of being a creative or performing artist in residence **2** the fact or time of living somewhere

resident /rézzidənt/ *n* **1** somebody who is living in a place **2** a junior doctor who lives in the hospital where he or she is working ■ *adj* **1** living in a particular place **2** living somewhere as part of a job **3** belonging to a group **4** permanently retained in a computer's random-access memory for quick access —**residentship** *n*

residential /rèzzi dénsh'l/ *adj* **1** consisting of private housing rather than offices or factories **2** providing living accommodation o *a residential post*

residential care *n* a supervised environment for people who cannot care for themselves at home

residents' association *n* an association of neighbours

residual /ri zíddyoō əl/ *adj* left over ■ *n* **1** something left over **2** a fee paid to writers, performers, and directors when their work is broadcast again —**residually** *adv*

residual unemployment *n* unemployment arising from ill health rather than lack of work

residue /rézzi dyoo/ *n* something left over after another part has been removed

resign /ri zín/ *v* **1** *vti* give up a job or position **2** *vr* accept something reluctantly —**resigned** *adj* —**resignedly** /-idli/ *adv*

re-sign /ree sín/ *vti* sign or have a player sign another contract

resignation /rézzig náysh'n/ *n* **1** the act of resigning, or a formal notification of this **2** reluctant acceptance of something

resilient /ri zílli ənt/ *adj* **1** recovering quickly from setbacks **2** elastic —**resilience** *n* —**resiliency** *n* —**resiliently** *adv*

resin /rézzin/ *n* **1** a semisolid substance secreted in the sap of some plants **2** a synthetic compound resembling natural resin. Use: manufacture of petrochemicals and plastics. —**resinous** *adj*

resist /ri zíst/ *v* **1** *vti* oppose or stand firm against **2** *vt* refuse to accept or comply with **3** *vt* be unaffected by o *ability to resist infection* **4** *vti* say no to something tempting —**resister** *n* —**resistible** *adj*

resistance /ri zístənss/ *n* **1** opposition **2** refusal to accept or comply with something **3** the ability to remain undamaged by something **4** (*symbol R*) a force that opposes or slows another force **5** (*symbol R*) the opposition that a device or substance presents to the flow of electricity **6** **Resistance** a secret organization that fights for freedom against an occupying power —**resistant** *adj*

~~resistence~~ incorrect spelling of **resistance**

resistor /ri zístər/ *n* a component that controls the flow of electricity

resit *vt* /ree sít/ (**-sitting, -sat** /-sát/) take an examination again ■ *n* /rèe sit/ an examination taken again

resold past tense, past participle of **resell**

resolute /rézzə loot/ *adj* determined and purposeful —**resolutely** *adv* —**resoluteness** *n*

resolution /rèzzə loŏsh'n/ *n* **1** the process of resolving something such as a dispute **2** a firm decision **3** determination **4** a solution to a problem **5** a formal expression of the consensus of a group, usually as the result of a vote **6** the quality of the detail on a screen or in a photographic image

resolve /ri zólv/ *v* **1** (**-solving, -solved**) **1** *vt* come to a firm decision about **2** *vt* find a solution to **3** *vt* dispel o *resolved all doubts* **4** *vt* bring to a satisfactory conclusion **5** *vt* express formally as the consensus of a group **6** *vti* split into constituent parts ■ *n* **1** determination **2** a firm decision —**resolvable** *adj* —**resolved** *adj*

resonance /rézzənənss/ *n* **1** the resonant quality of something **2** an underlying meaning of an event or work of art **3** an intense and prolonged sound produced by sympathetic vibration

resonant /rézzənənt/ *adj* **1** deep and rich in sound **2** continuing to sound for some time —**resonantly** *adv*

resonate /rézzə nayt/ (**-nating, -nated**) v 1 vti resound or echo, or cause to resound or echo 2 vi have an impact beyond that which is apparent

resonator /rézzə naytər/ n a resonating device or part that produces sound or microwaves

resort /ri záwrt/ n 1 a place popular with people on holiday 2 a source of help 3 the act of turning to somebody or something for help ◊ **resort to** have recourse to something, often an extreme measure, in order to achieve something ○ *had to resort to blackmail*

re-sort /ree sáwrt/ vt sort again

resound /ri zównd/ vi 1 be filled with a reverberating sound 2 sound loudly and clearly 3 make a reverberating sound

resounding /ri zównding/ adj 1 clear and emphatic 2 echoing loudly —**resoundingly** adv

resource /ri záwrss, -sáwrss/ n 1 a source of help 2 a supply of something needed 3 the ability to find solutions to problems ■ **resources** npl 1 inner abilities drawn on when necessary 2 natural, economic, or military assets ■ vt (**-sourcing, -sourced**) provide with resources

resourceful /ri záwrsf'l, -sáwrs-/ adj ingenious and enterprising —**resourcefully** adv —**resourcefulness** n

respect /ri spékt/ n 1 an attitude of admiration and deference 2 the state of being respected 3 consideration or thoughtfulness 4 an individual characteristic ○ *satisfactory in all respects* ■ **respects** npl polite greetings ■ vt 1 feel or show admiration and deference towards 2 pay attention to or not violate ○ *respect the law* 3 be considerate of or towards —**respected** adj —**respecter** n ◊ See note at **regard**

respectable /ri spéktəb'l/ adj 1 reflecting accepted standards of correctness or decency 2 satisfactory 3 of a presentable appearance (*infml*) —**respectability** /ri spéktə bílləti/ n —**respectably** adv

respectful /ri spéktf'l/ adj showing respect —**respectfully** adv —**respectfulness** n

respective /ri spéktiv/ adj relating to each one considered separately ○ *returning to their respective homes* —**respectively** adv

respiration /réspə ráysh'n/ n 1 breathing 2 the process in living organisms that produces energy by the exchange of gases with the environment —**respiratory** /ri spírrətəri, réspərətəri/ adj

respirator /réspə raytər/ n 1 a machine that artificially maintains breathing 2 a protective mask through which somebody breathes

respire /ri spír/ v 1 vti breathe 2 vi undergo the process of respiration

respite /ré spīt, réspit/ n 1 a brief period of rest or relief 2 a temporary delay or reprieve

respite care n temporary residential care to provide relief for permanent carers

~~resplendant~~ incorrect spelling of **resplendent**

resplendent /ri spléndənt/ adj dazzlingly impressive —**resplendence** n —**resplendently** adv

respond /ri spónd/ v 1 vti provide an answer 2 vi react

~~respondant~~ incorrect spelling of **respondent**

respondent /ri spóndənt/ n 1 the defendant in a divorce case or an appeal 2 somebody who replies to something —**respondent** adj

~~responsability~~ incorrect spelling of **responsibility**

response /ri spónss/ n 1 a reply to a question 2 a reaction 3 a reply made by the church choir or congregation during some services ◊ See note at **answer**

response time n 1 a reaction time 2 a time from issuing an instruction to action

responsibility /ri spónssə bílləti/ (*pl* **-ties**) n 1 the state of being responsible 2 something for which somebody is responsible 3 blame for something ○ *take full responsibility* 4 the authority to act

responsible /ri spónssəb'l/ adj 1 accountable to somebody for something 2 in charge of somebody or something 3 being to blame for something 4 requiring trustworthiness and conscientiousness ○ *a responsible position* 5 reliable 6 rational and accountable for your actions 7 authorized to act —**responsibly** adv

responsive /ri spónssiv/ adj 1 done in response to something 2 showing a positive response 3 reacting to a stimulus —**responsively** adv —**responsiveness** n

rest[1] n 1 a state or period of refreshing freedom from exertion 2 the repose of sleep 3 a stopping of movement 4 the repose of death 5 freedom from anxiety ○ *put her mind at rest* 6 a pause in music 7 a place to stop and relax 8 a support, especially on a piece of furniture ■ v 1 vti regain or cause to regain energy by means of relaxation or sleep 2 vi be tranquil 3 vi be dead 4 vti stop moving or working temporarily 5 vi be subject to no further attention ○ *Let the matter rest.* 6 vti support or be supported 7 vi depend on somebody or something —**rested** adj

rest[2] n the remainder (+ *sing* or *pl verb*) ■ vi continue to be (*usually a command*)

~~restaraunt~~ incorrect spelling of **restaurant**

rest area n ANZ, US, Can a stopping place for drivers

restart /ree staárt/ vti start again —**restart** /reé staart/ n

restaurant /résta ront, -roN, -rənt/ n a place where meals are sold and served to customers

ORIGIN A **restaurant** is literally a place where people are 'restored' or refreshed. The word was adopted from French in the early 19C.

restaurant car n a railway carriage where passengers eat

~~restauranteur~~ incorrect spelling of **restaurateur**

restaurateur /réstərə túr/ n a restaurant owner or manager

restful /réstf'l/ *adj* 1 providing rest 2 calm or tranquil —**restfully** *adv* —**restfulness** *n*

rest home *n* a supervised home for infirm senior citizens and chronically ill people

restitution /résti työósh'n/ *n* 1 the return of something to its owner 2 compensation for loss, damage, or injury

restive /réstiv/ *adj* impatient and on the verge of resisting control —**restively** *adv* —**restiveness** *n*

restless /réstləss/ *adj* 1 constantly moving, or unable to be still 2 seeking change because of discontent 3 unable to rest or sleep —**restlessly** *adv* —**restlessness** *n*

restock /ree stók/ *vti* replenish a stock of something

restoration /réstə ráysh'n/ *n* 1 the returning of something to its former condition or state 2 **Restoration** the return to monarchy in England in 1660

restorative /ri stáwrətiv/ *adj* restoring strength or vigour —**restorative** *n*

restore /ri stáwr/ (**-storing, -stored**) *vt* 1 give or put back 2 return to an earlier or better condition or position —**restorer** *n* ◊ See note at **renew**

restrain /ri stráyn/ *vt* 1 prevent from doing something 2 control or keep within limits —**restrainable** *adj* —**restrained** *adj*

restraint /ri stráynt/ *n* 1 moderate or controlled behaviour ○ *showing admirable restraint* 2 something that restrains, controls, or limits ○ *impose trade restraints* 3 a device for limiting somebody's freedom of movement

~~**restraunt**~~ incorrect spelling of **restaurant**

restrict /ri stríkt/ *vt* keep within limits —**restricted** *adj* —**restrictedness** *n* —**restriction** *n*

restrictive /ri stríktiv/ *adj* 1 tending to restrict 2 limiting the range of reference or application of a word, phrase, or clause —**restrictively** *adv* —**restrictiveness** *n*

rest room *n* US, Can a public toilet

restructure /ree strúkchər/ (**-turing, -tured**) *v* 1 *vti* change the basic structure of something 2 *vt* alter the terms of a loan

result /ri zúlt/ *n* 1 something that is caused by another action, condition, or event 2 a score, e.g. in a sports match or an exam 3 a successful outcome *(infml)* ■ **results** *npl* the desired outcome ■ *vi* 1 cause a particular outcome 2 follow as a consequence —**resultant** *adj*

resume /ri zyoóm/ (**-suming, -sumed**) *v* 1 *vti* continue after a pause 2 *vt* take, assume, or occupy again —**resumption** /ri zúmpsh'n/ *n*

résumé /rézzyoò may, ráy-/ *n* 1 a summary 2 ANZ, US, Can a CV

resurface /ree súrfiss/ (**-facing, -faced**) *v* 1 *vi* come to the surface again 2 *vi* appear again 3 *vt* put a new surface on

resurgence /ri súrjənss/ *n* a rising or strengthening again ○ *a resurgence of patriotism* —**resurgent** *adj*

resurrect /rézzə rékt/ *vt* 1 raise from the dead 2 bring back into use

resurrection /rézzə réksh'n/ *n* 1 in some belief systems, a rising from or raising of somebody from the dead 2 **Resurrection** in Christian belief, Jesus Christ's rising from the dead 3 the revival of something

resuscitate /ri sússi tayt/ (**-tating, -tated**) *vti* revive, or be revived, from unconsciousness —**resuscitation** /-táysh'n/ *n* —**resuscitative** *adj*

retail /ree tayl/ *n* the sale of goods to consumers ■ *adv* from a shop in small quantities at the consumer price ■ *vti* sell goods to consumers —**retailer** *n* —**retailing** *n*

retail price index *n* a guide to inflation that lists the prices of essential consumer goods

retain /ri táyn/ *vt* 1 keep possession of 2 remember 3 keep in a particular place or position 4 pay a fee in order to reserve the professional services of —**retainable** *adj* —**retainment** *n*

retainer /ri táynər/ *n* 1 a device for holding something in place 2 a paid servant in a household 3 a fee paid to reserve professional services 4 a fee that reserves accommodation while the tenant is away ◊ **on (a) retainer** paid regularly in order to be consulted whenever necessary

retaining wall *n* a wall built to keep earth or water in place

retake /ree táyk/ (**-taking, -took** /-toók/, **-taken** /-táykən/) *vt* 1 recapture from an enemy 2 record, photograph, or film again —**retake** /ree tayk/ *n*

retaliate /ri tálli ayt/ (**-ating, -ated**) *vi* deliberately harm somebody in revenge —**retaliation** /ri tálli áysh'n/ *n* —**retaliatory** /-ətəri/ *adj*

retard /ri taárd/ *vt* slow or delay the progress of —**retardation** /ree taar dáysh'n/ *n*

retarded /ri taárdid/ *adj* 1 underdeveloped 2 an offensive term meaning intellectually or emotionally challenged

retch /rech/ *vi* 1 experience a vomiting spasm 2 vomit ■ *n* a vomiting spasm

SPELLCHECK Do not confuse the spelling of **retch** and **wretch** ('somebody who is pitied'), which sound similar.

retention /ri ténsh'n/ *n* 1 the process of retaining something or the condition of being retained 2 memory

retentive /ri téntiv/ *adj* 1 able to retain something 2 with a good memory —**retentiveness** *n*

rethink *vti* /ree thíngk/ (**-thought** /-tháwt/) think about something again with a view to changing opinions or plans ■ *n* /ree thingk/ a reconsideration

reticent /réttis'nt/ *adj* 1 tending not to talk openly or much 2 reluctant —**reticence** *n* —**reticently** *adv* ◊ See note at **silent**

retina /réttinə/ (*pl* **-nas** *or* **-nae** /-nee/) *n* the light-sensitive membrane at the back of the eye —**retinal** *adj*

retinue /rétti nyoo/ *n* a group of followers or attendants

retire /ri tír/ (-**tiring**, -**tired**) *v* 1 *vi* stop working permanently and voluntarily 2 *vi* go to bed 3 *vi* leave a place or position ○ *has retired from public life* 4 *vt* take out of service 5 *vti* withdraw from a sports contest —**retirement** *n*

retired /ri tírd/ *adj* 1 no longer working 2 having withdrawn

retiree /ri tí rée/ *n* somebody who has retired from work

retiring /ri tíring/ *adj* 1 shy and reserved 2 involving or undergoing retirement —**retiringly** *adv*

retort[1] /ri táwrt/ *vt* 1 respond sharply or wittily 2 put forward as an argument in reply to ■ *n* a sharp or witty answer ◊ See note at **answer**

retort[2] /ri táwrt/ *n* 1 a glass container with a long spout used in distillation 2 a closed container for heating substances ■ *vt* heat in a retort

retouch /ree túch/ *vt* remove imperfections from, or make small finishing changes to —**retouch** /reé tuch/ *n*

retrace /ri tráyss/ (-**tracing**, -**traced**) *vt* go back over a path or route again

retract /ri trákt/ *v* 1 *vti* move or draw in from an extended position 2 *vt* withdraw a statement or promise —**retractable** *adj* —**retraction** *n*

retrain /ree tráyn/ *vti* teach or learn a new skill

retreat /ri treét/ *n* 1 a movement away from danger or confrontation 2 a withdrawal of military forces, or a signal for this 3 a withdrawal from a previously held point of view 4 a place or period of time for rest, meditation, or privacy ■ *vi* 1 move away, especially from danger or confrontation 2 make a military withdrawal

retrench /ri trénch/ *vi* economize —**retrenchment** *n*

retrial /ree trí əl, ree trí əl/ *n* a second trial following a flawed or inconclusive trial

retribution /rétti byoósh'n/ *n* punishment or vengeance —**retributive** /ri tríbbyoótiv/ *adj* —**retributory** /ri tríbbyoótəri/ *adj*

retrieve /ri treév/ (-**trieving**, -**trieved**) *vt* 1 get something back 2 save something from being lost or damaged 3 remedy a situation 4 get data from a computer storage device —**retrievable** *adj* —**retrieval** *n*

retriever /ri treévər/ *n* 1 a large dog belonging to a breed originally used to fetch game shot by a hunter 2 somebody or something that retrieves

retro /réttrō/ *adj* modelled on something from the past ■ *n* (*pl* -**ros**) 1 the use of past styles 2 a retrorocket

retro- *prefix* back, backwards, after ○ *retrorocket* ○ *retrofit*

retroactive /réttrō áktiv/ *adj* applying to the past and continuing into the present ○ *retroactive pay increases*

retrofit /réttrō fit/ *vt* modify something old with a newly available part —**retrofit** *n*

retroflex /réttrō fleks/, **retroflexed** /-flekst/ *adj* bent backwards

retrograde /réttrō grayd/ *adj* 1 moving backwards 2 returning to an earlier worse state

retrogress /réttrō gréss/ *vi* 1 return to an earlier worse condition 2 go backwards —**retrogression** *n* —**retrogressive** *adj* —**retrogressively** *adv*

retrorocket /réttrō rokit/ *n* a small rocket engine that produces thrust to act against the main engines

retrospect /réttrō spekt/ ◊ **in retrospect** when reviewing the past, especially from a new perspective or with new information

retrospection /réttrō spéksh'n/ *n* the act of looking back over the past

retrospective /réttrō spéktiv/ *adj* 1 reviewing the past 2 containing an artist's past works ■ *n* an exhibition of an artist's past work

retry *v* /ree trí/ (-**tries**, -**tried**) 1 *vt* try again in a court of law 2 *vti* attempt again ■ *n* /reé trí/ (*pl* -**tries**) a second attempt

retsina /ret seénə/ *n* a resin-flavoured wine from Greece

return /ri túrn/ *v* 1 *vi* come or go back to a place or former condition 2 *vi* mention or consider something again 3 *vi* appear or happen again 4 *vt* put, give, send, or bring something back 5 *vt* yield a profit 6 *vt* re-elect somebody to office 7 *vt* give a verdict in court 8 *vti* in racket sports, hit a ball back ■ *n* 1 a going or coming back to a place or previous condition 2 the act of returning something 3 something returned 4 the reappearance of something 5 a response to something done or given ○ *give love in return* 6 a profit (*often pl*) 7 *also* **return ticket** a two-way travel ticket 8 *also* **return key** a key on a keyboard used to create a new line or execute an instruction ■ **returns** *npl* election results ■ *n* 1 of going or coming back to a place 2 happening again —**returnable** *adj*, *n* —**returnee** /ri túr neé/ *n*

returning officer *n UK, Aus, Can* an election official responsible for overseeing the count

reunify /ree yoóni fī/ (-**fies**, -**fied**) *vti* reunite after being divided —**reunification** /ree yoónifi káysh'n/ *n*

reunion /ree yoónyən/ *n* 1 a gathering of relatives, old friends, or former colleagues 2 the act of reuniting or being reunited

reunite /reé yoo nít/ (-**niting**, -**nited**) *vti* come or bring back together after separation

reuse *vt* /ree yooz/ (-**using**, -**used**) use again ■ *n* /ree yoóss/ the reusing of something —**reusable** *adj*

Reuters /róytərz/ *n* a London-based news agency providing international news reports

reutilize /ree yoóti līz/ (-**izing**, -**ized**), **reutilise** *vt* utilize something again —**reutilization** /ree yoóti līz záysh'n/ *n*

rev *vti* (**revving, revved**) increase the speed of an engine ■ *n* a single engine revolution (*infml; usually pl*)

rev. *abbr* 1 revenue 2 revolution

Rev., Revd *abbr* Reverend

revalue /ree vállyoo/ (**-uing, -ued**), **revaluate** /-ayt/ (**-ating, -ated**) *vt* 1 raise the value of a currency 2 reassess the value of something

revamp /ree vámp/ *vt* alter for the better —**revamp** /rée vamp/ *n* ◊ See note at **renew**

reveal /ri veel/ *vt* 1 make known 2 expose to view

revealing /ri veeling/ *adj* 1 showing parts of the body that are normally covered 2 disclosing new or surprising information —**revealingly** *adv*

reveille /ri válli/ *n* a bugle call to awaken military personnel

revel /révv'l/ *vi* (**-elling, -elled**) 1 take pleasure in something 2 enjoy a party ■ *n* a noisy celebration (*often pl*) —**reveller** *n*

~~revelant~~ incorrect spelling of **relevant**

revelation /révvə láysh'n/ *n* 1 a piece of new or surprising information that is disclosed 2 an unexpectedly good or valuable new experience 3 a demonstration of divine will —**revelatory** /révvə láytəri/ *adj*

revelry /révvəlri/ (*pl* **-ries**) *n* noisy celebrating (*often pl*)

revenge /ri vénj/ *n* 1 punishment administered in retaliation for harm done 2 the desire to punish somebody in revenge ■ *vt* (**-venging, -venged**) administer punishment in retaliation for something —**revengeful** *adj* —**revenger** *n*

revenue /révvə nyoo/ *n* the income of a business or government

reverb /rée vurb/ *n* 1 an electronically produced echo in music 2 an echo-producing device —**reverb** /ri vúrb/ *vi*

reverberate /ri vúrbə rayt/ (**-ating, -ated**) *v* 1 *vti* echo or cause to echo 2 *vi* have a continuing or far reaching effect —**reverberant** *adj* —**reverberation** /ri vúrbə ráysh'n/ *n*

ORIGIN **Reverberate** derives from a Latin verb meaning 'beat back', which was formed from *verbera* 'whips, rods'. 'Beat or drive back' was the original English sense, lasting from the late 15C to the late 18C. Figurative senses such as 'echo' developed from the late 16C.

revere /ri veer/ (**-vering, -vered**) *vt* treat or regard with admiring respect

reverence /révvərənss/ *n* 1 feelings of deep respect 2 *also* **Reverence** a form of address for a member of the Christian clergy ■ *vt* (**-encing, -enced**) show deep respect for (*fml*) ◊ See note at **regard**

reverend /révvrənd/ *adj* 1 of the Christian clergy 2 respected (*fml*) ■ *n* 1 a member of the Christian clergy (*infml*) 2 **Reverend** a form of address for a member of the Christian clergy

Reverend Mother *n* a form of address for a Mother Superior

reverential /révvə rénsh'l/ *adj* 1 *also* **reverent** /révvərənt/ deeply respectful 2 deserving respect —**reverentially** *adv*

reverie /révvəri/ (*pl* **-ies**) *n* a daydream

reversal /ri vúrss'l/ *n* 1 a change to the opposite direction 2 a setback 3 the reversing of something

reverse /ri vúrss/ *v* (**-versing, -versed**) 1 *vt* change something to the opposite direction or position 2 *vti* go or cause to go backwards 3 *vt* turn something inside out 4 *vt* revoke an earlier ruling ■ *n* 1 the opposite of something 2 the back side of something 3 a change to the opposite direction or position 4 a setback 5 the gear in a vehicle for backward movement ■ *adj* 1 opposite to the usual or previous arrangement 2 on the back side 3 for backward movement

reverse engineering *n* piracy of a competitor's technology by dismantling and reproducing its product —**reverse-engineer** *vt*

reverse takeover *n* a sale of a company to avoid a hostile takeover

reverse video *n* the reversal of the usual colour combination on a computer screen

reversible /ri vúrssəb'l/ *adj* able to be changed or undone —**reversibility** /ri vúrssə billəti/ *n*

reversing light *n* a rear light that is illuminated when a vehicle is reversing

reversion /ri vúrsh'n/ *n* 1 a return to a former condition or point of view 2 restoration of an organism's original genetic characteristics, by a second mutation 3 the return of property to the former owner, or property so returned

revert /ri vúrt/ *vi* 1 return to a previous state 2 return to an earlier topic in a discussion 3 return to old habits 4 become the property of the former owner

review /ri vyóo/ *vt* 1 look at something critically 2 give an opinion on the quality of something 3 consider something again 4 look back on something 5 reconsider an earlier judicial decision 6 subject troops to military inspection ■ *n* 1 a survey of past actions, performance, or events 2 a journalistic article giving an assessment of something 3 a publication featuring reviews 4 a re-examination 5 a military inspection —**reviewer** *n*

SPELLCHECK Do not confuse the spelling of **review** and **revue** ('musical variety show'), which sound similar.

revile /ri víl/ (**-viling, -viled**) *v* 1 *vt* attack verbally 2 *vi* use abusive language —**revilement** *n*

revise /ri víz/ (**-vising, -vised**) *v* 1 *vt* change something such as an opinion or estimate after reconsideration 2 *vt* prepare a new version of text 3 *vti* study for an exam by looking over course materials —**revision** /ri vízh'n/ *n*

Revised Version *n* a 19C British edition of the Authorized Version of the Bible

revisionism /ri vízh'nizəm/ *n* 1 the reconsidering of accepted truths 2 an anti-

Marxist socialist movement that advocates gradual reform —**revisionist** *adj, n*

revisit /ree vízzit/ *vt* **1** go to a place again **2** reconsider something ■ *n* a subsequent visit

revitalize /ree víta līz/ (**-izing, -ized**), **revitalise** *vt* give new life or energy to —**revitalization** /ree víta līz záysh'n/ *n*

revival /ri vív'l/ *n* **1** a renewal of interest in something **2** a new production of a play **3** the reviving of something or somebody **4** an evangelical Christian meeting

revivalism /ri vívalìzam/ *n* **1** the desire to foster new interest in something **2** an evangelical religious movement —**revivalist** *adj*

revive /ri vív/ (**-viving, -vived**) *v* **1** *vti* recover or cause to recover consciousness **2** *vti* make or become active, accepted, or popular again **3** *vt* cause an experience or feeling to return **4** *vt* stage a play again —**revivable** *adj*

revivify /ree vívvi fī/ (**-fies, -fied**) *vt* give new life or energy to —**revivification** /ree vívvifi káysh'n/ *n*

revoke /ri vók/ (**-voking, -voked**) *vt* formally cancel or withdraw —**revocation** /révva káysh'n/ *n*

revolt /ri vólt/ *v* **1** *vi* rebel against the state or authority **2** *vt* cause to feel disgust ■ *n* **1** an uprising against a government **2** a defiance of authority —**revolting** *adj* —**revoltingly** *adv*

revolution /révva loósh'n/ *n* **1** an overthrow of a political system, or an attempt to do so **2** a major change **3** a complete circular turn

revolutionary /révva loósh'nari/ *adj* **1** of or advocating political revolution **2** new and different ■ *n* (*pl* **-ies**) somebody committed to political revolution

revolutionize /révva loósha nīz/ (**-izing, -ized**), **revolutionise** *vt* cause radical change in

revolve /ri vólv/ (**-volving, -volved**) *v* **1** *vti* move in a circle on an axis or around a point **2** *vi* be focused on something or somebody —**revolvable** *adj*

revolver /ri vólvar/ *n* a pistol with a revolving cylinder of chambers

revolving credit *n* a credit plan that imposes regular repayments

revolving door *n* **1** a door with sections that turn round a central pivot **2** a system in which people are constantly entering and leaving, e.g. by being hired and fired

revolving fund *n* a fund that can be drawn upon and repaid as desired

revue /ri vyoó/ (*pl* **-vues**) *n* a musical variety show ◊ See note at **review**

revulsion /ri vúlsh'n/ *n* **1** a feeling of disgust **2** a pulling or turning back (*fml*)

reward /ri wáwrd/ *n* **1** something good given or received in return for something done **2** an amount of money offered for information about a criminal or the return of lost property ■ *vt* **1** give somebody something as a reward **2** repay somebody's efforts —**rewardable** *adj* —**rewarding** *adj* —**rewardingly** *adv*

rewind *vt* /ree wínd/ (**-wound** /-wównd/) wind back to an earlier point or onto the original spool ■ *n* /rée wìnd/ the rewinding process or function

rewire /ree wír/ (**-wiring, -wired**) *vt* provide with new electrical wiring

reword /ree wúrd/ *vt* revise the wording of

rework /ree wúrk/ *vt* **1** make changes or improvements to **2** amend for reuse in a different context

reworking /ree wúrking/ *n* a revised version

rewritable /ree rítab'l/ *adj* describes magnetic media that can be written on repeatedly

rewrite *vt* /ree rít/ (**-writing, -wrote** /-rót/, **-written** /-rítt'n/) **1** change the wording or structure of text **2** change the way that history is perceived ■ *n* /rée rìt/ a rewritten text —**rewriter** *n*

Rex /reks/ *n* the title of a reigning king

Reykjavik /ráykya vik/ capital of Iceland. Pop. 108,351 (1998).

Reynolds /rénn'ldz/, **Sir Joshua** (1723–92) British painter

Rf *symbol* rutherfordium

RGB *abbr* red, green, blue (*describes a colour monitor or colour value*)

Rh *symbol* rhodium

rhapsodize /rápsa dīz/ (**-dizing, -dized**), **rhapsodise** *vi* express great enthusiasm

rhapsody /rápsadi/ (*pl* **-dies**) *n* **1** a free-form musical composition **2** an expression of intense enthusiasm (*often pl*) —**rhapsodic** /rap sóddik/ *adj*

Rheims ♦ **Reims**

rhenium /reéni am/ *n* (*symbol* **Re**) a rare heavy metallic element. Use: catalyst, alloyed with tungsten in thermocouples.

rhesus monkey /reéssass-/ *n* a brown monkey of the macaque family

rhetoric /réttarik/ *n* **1** persuasive speech or writing **2** pretentious or empty language **3** the art or study of using language effectively —**rhetorical** /ri tórrik'l/ *adj* —**rhetorically** *adv* —**rhetorician** /rétta rísh'n/ *n*

rhetorical question *n* a question asked for effect and requiring no answer

rheumatic /roo máttik/ *adj* of or affected by rheumatism

rheumatic fever *n* a childhood disease that causes fever and joint swelling and often damage to the heart valves

rheumatism /roómatizam/ *n* **1** pain and stiffness in the joints or muscles **2** rheumatoid arthritis

ORIGIN Rheumatism was once thought to be caused by the flow of watery discharges within the body, and the name is based on Latin and Greek *rheuma* 'bodily fluid'. It was adopted into English from French in the 17C.

rheumatoid arthritis /roóma toyd-/ *n* a chronic disease of the joints that causes painful stiffness and swelling

rheumatology /roomǝ tóllǝji/ n the branch of medicine that deals with rheumatic diseases —**rheumatologist** n

Rh factor n an antibody-producing substance in red blood cells

ORIGIN **Rh factor** is short for *Rhesus factor.* The antigen was given this name because it was first discovered in the blood of rhesus monkeys.

Rhine /rīn/ river in W Europe, flowing north-westwards from SE Switzerland through Germany and the Netherlands, emptying into the North Sea. Length 1,320 km/820 mi.

rhinestone /rín stōn/ n a small fake gem

rhinitis /rī nítiss/ n inflammation of the mucous membrane of the nose

rhino /rínō/ (pl **-nos** or same) n a rhinoceros (infml)

rhinoceros /rī nóssǝrǝss/ (pl **-oses** or same) n a massive thick-skinned mammal with a horn or horns on its nose

ORIGIN **Rhinoceros** is formed from Greek words meaning literally 'nose horn'.

~~rhinocerous~~ incorrect spelling of **rhinoceros**

rhizome /rízōm/ n a horizontal underground stem

rho /rō/ (pl **rhos**) n the 17th letter of the Greek alphabet

Rhode Island /rōd-/ state in the NE United States. Cap. Providence. Pop. 1,048,319 (2000). —**Rhode Islander** n

Rhodes /rōdz/ **1** largest island of the Dodecanese, Greece. Pop. 87,831 (1981). **2** capital of Rhodes, Greece. Pop. 43,619 (1991).

Rhodes, Cecil (1853–1902) British financier and colonial administrator

Rhodesia /rō deeshǝ, -zhǝ/ former name for **Zimbabwe** —**Rhodesian** adj, n

rhodium /ródi ǝm/ n (symbol **Rh**) a hard corrosion-resistant metallic element. Use: alloys, in plating other metals.

rhododendron /rōdǝ déndrǝn/ n an ornamental evergreen flowering tree

rhomboid /róm boyd/ n a parallelogram with unequal adjacent sides ■ adj **1** rhomboid-shaped **2** of a rhombus

rhombus /rómbǝss/ (pl **-buses** or **-bi** /-bī/) n an oblique-angled parallelogram —**rhombic** adj

Rhône /rōn/ river in Switzerland and France, flowing south-westwards from the Alps into the Mediterranean Sea. Length 813 km/505 mi.

rhubarb /roo baarb/ n **1** the pink stalks of a perennial plant, cooked as a fruit **2** the plant whose stalks are rhubarb

ORIGIN The Greeks had two words for **rhubarb:** *rhēon* (which evolved into Latin *rheum,* now the plant's scientific name) and *rha,* which is said to have come from *Rha,* an ancient name of the river Volga, in allusion to the fact that **rhubarb** was grown on its banks. **Rhubarb** is native to China, and was once imported to

Europe via Russia, and in medieval Latin became known as *rha barbarum* 'barbarian rhubarb, foreign rhubarb'. In due course association with Latin *rheum* altered this to *rheubarbarum.*

rhyme /rīm/ n **1** similarity in the sound of word endings **2** a word whose ending sounds similar to another **3** a short poem ■ v (**rhyming**, **rhymed**) **1** vi have a word ending that sounds similar **2** vt match a word with another as a rhyme ◇ **without rhyme or reason** without any rational explanation

rhyming slang n slang that uses rhyming expressions as substitutes for words

rhythm /rí<u>th</u>ǝm/ n **1** the pattern of beats in music, or a particular pattern of beats **2** the pattern of stress in poetry, or a particular stress pattern **3** any regular or characteristic pattern —**rhythmic** /rí<u>th</u>mik/ adj —**rhythmical** adj —**rhythmically** adv

rhythm and blues n a style of music that combines elements of blues and jazz

rhythm method n a method of contraception that relies on knowing a woman's fertile period

rhythm section n the instruments in a band that provide the basic rhythm

RI abbr religious instruction

rial /ri aál/ n the main unit of currency in Iran and Oman

rib n **1** any of the curved bones of the chest **2** a cut of meat that contains a rib or ribs **3** a ridged pattern in knitting **4** a raised vein on a leaf ■ v (**ribbing**, **ribbed**) **1** vti tease somebody (infml) **2** vt shape, support, or fit with ribs —**ribbing** n

ribald /ríbb'ld/ adj coarse and funny —**ribaldry** n

Ribbentrop /ríbbǝn trop/, **Joachim von** (1893–1946) German Nazi official

ribbon /ríbbǝn/ n **1** a decorative strip of fabric **2** a strip of inked material in a typewriter or printer **3** a long narrow strip of anything ■ **ribbons** npl tatters

ribbon development n housing built along the sides of a main road

rib cage n the ribs as a unit

riboflavin /ríbō fláyvin/, **riboflavine** n a vitamin that is the yellow component of the B complex group

ribonucleic acid /ríbō nyoo kleeʹik-/ n full form of **RNA**

Ricardo /ri kaárdō/, **David** (1772–1823) British economist

rice /riss/ n **1** the edible seeds of a cereal plant **2** a cereal plant that grows in warm countries and produces rice grains

rice paper n **1** thin edible paper made from plants, used to prevent some foods sticking during baking **2** artists' paper made from the pith of a Chinese tree

rich /rich/ adj **1** having a lot of money or property **2** expensive and fine **3** with a good supply of a resource ◇ *a city rich in culture* o *cotton-rich fabric* **4** plentiful **5** productive or fertile **6** with a high proportion of fatty ingredients **7** deeply and fully saturated with colour **8** having a deep full sound ■ *npl* rich people o *the rich and famous* —**richly** *adv* —**richness** *n*

Richard I /ríchərd/ (1157–99) king of England (1189–99)

Richard II (1367–1400) king of England (1377–99)

Richard III (1452–85) king of England (1483–85)

Richards /ríchərdz/, **Viv** (b. 1952) Jamaican cricketer

Richardson /ríchərdss'n/, **Henry Handel** (1870–1946) Australian novelist

Richardson, Samuel (1689–1761) British novelist

Richelieu /reesh lyó/, **Armand Jean du Plessis, Duc de** (1585–1642) French religious and political leader

rich e-mail *n* an e-mail with a voice message attached

riches /ríchiz/ *npl* **1** great wealth **2** plentiful natural resources

Richmond /ríchmənd/ **1** town in NE England. Pop. 7,862 (1991). **2** capital of Virginia. Pop. 194,173 (1998). **3** town in E New South Wales, Australia. Pop. 3,099 (1991).

Richter scale /ríktər-, ríkhtər-/ *n* a scale for measuring the magnitude of earthquakes

ORIGIN The scale is named after the US seismologist Charles Francis Richter (1900–85), who devised it.

rich text *n* computer text that includes formatting codes

rick[1] *n* a stack of hay or straw

rick[2] *vt* wrench or sprain part of the body slightly ■ *n* a slight injury

rickets /ríkits/ *n* a bone-softening disease

rickety /ríkiti/ (**-ier, -iest**) *adj* **1** unstable **2** infirm **3** affected by rickets

rickshaw /rík shaw/, **ricksha** *n* **1** a two-wheeled passenger vehicle pulled by a person **2** a three-wheeled passenger vehicle pedalled by a driver

ricochet /ríkə shay/ *vi* (**-cheting** or **-chetting**, **-chetted**, **-cheted** or **-chetted**) rebound ■ *n* a rebounding action

ricotta /ri kóttə/ *n* soft cheese used mostly in cooking

rid (**ridding, rid**) *vt* free a place, thing, or person of something undesirable

riddance /rídd'nss/ *n* the removal or destruction of something undesirable

riddle[1] /rídd'l/ *n* **1** a word puzzle **2** a puzzling thing ■ *vi* (**-dling, -dled**) talk in riddles —**riddler** *n*

riddle[2] /rídd'l/ *vt* (**-dling, -dled**) **1** make holes in something **2** affect every part of something —**riddler** *n* ◊ See note at **problem**

ride *v* (**riding, rode** or **ridden** /rídd'n/) **1** *vti* sit on and control a horse or other animal **2** *vti*

travel on a bike or motorbike **3** *vt* use a surfboard, skateboard, or similar piece of sports equipment **4** *vti* travel as a passenger in a vehicle **5** *vt* travel over an area o *ride the range* **6** *vi S Africa* drive a car **7** *vti* move on or as if on water o *riding the air currents* **8** *vi* do something effortlessly **9** *vi* depend on something o *Her future rides on this interview.* **10** *vi* be allowed to continue o *Let it ride for now.* ■ *n* **1** a journey by vehicle or animal, especially one taken for pleasure **2** the quality of travel in a vehicle **3** an entertainment at a fairground or amusement park **4** a path on which to ride horses ◊ **be riding high** be enjoying a period or feeling of success ◊ **ride roughshod over 1** treat somebody very inconsiderately **2** disregard a rule, law, or agreement ◊ **take somebody for a ride** cheat or deceive somebody

□ **ride out** *vt* deal with a problem and survive

rider /rídər/ *n* **1** somebody riding a horse, bike, skateboard, or snowboard **2** an additional clause to a bill or contract

ridge *n* **1** a long narrow raised area **2** a raised land formation **3** the line formed where the sloping sides of a roof meet ■ *vti* (**ridging, ridged**) form ridges or make ridges in

ridicule /ríddi kyool/ *vt* (**-culing, -culed**) mock ■ *n* mocking laughter, behaviour, or comments

SYNONYMS ridicule, deride, laugh at, mock, send up CORE MEANING: belittle by making fun of

ridiculous /ri díkyoÓləss/ *adj* **1** unreasonable **2** completely silly —**ridiculously** *adv* —**ridiculousness** *n*

riding[1] /ríding/ *n* the activity of sitting on and controlling a moving horse ■ *adj* used while on horseback

riding[2] /ríding/ *n* **1** *also* **Riding** a district of Yorkshire **2** *Can* a Canadian constituency **3** *NZ* a rural local government electorate

ORIGIN Riding comes from an old Scandinavian word meaning 'third part'.

Riefenstahl /reéf'n shtaal/, **Leni** (b. 1902) German film director and photographer

riel /ree əl/ *n* the main unit of Cambodian currency

~~rien~~ incorrect spelling of **rein**

rife /rīf/ *adj* **1** widespread and plentiful **2** full of something undesirable ◊ See note at **widespread**

riff /rif/ *n* a short distinctive series of notes in rock music or jazz

riffle /ríff'l/ (**-fling, -fled**) *v* **1** *vti* flick through the pages of something **2** *vt* shuffle cards by making two piles, raising the corners, and letting them fall and overlap —**riffle** *n*

riffraff /rif raf/ *n* an offensive term for people regarded as socially inferior (*insult*)

rifle[1] /ríf'l/ *n* a gun with a long barrel that is fired from the shoulder ■ *vt* (**-fling, -fled**) cut a gun barrel with spiral grooves

rifle[2] /rîf'l/ (-fling, -fled) v 1 vti search vigorously 2 vt rob —**rifler** n

rifleman /rîf'lmən/ (pl -men /-mən/) n 1 a soldier with a rifle 2 somebody skilled in the use of a rifle

rifle range n an area for shooting practice

rift n 1 a gap or break 2 a disagreement 3 a displacement of rock layers caused by stress ■ vti split

rift valley n a valley formed by a geological rift

rig[1] vt (rigging, rigged) 1 equip a ship with rigging 2 provide somebody or something with equipment 3 construct something hastily and without proper materials ■ n 1 a drilling structure for oil 2 an arrangement of sails and masts 3 a large truck (infml) □ **rig out** vt put special clothes on (infml)

rig[2] vt (rigging, rigged) arrange the outcome of dishonestly ■ n a trick

Riga /reegə/ capital of Latvia. Pop. 796,732 (1999).

rigatoni /riggə tóni/ n pasta in the form of thick tubes

rigging /rigging/ n a system of ropes, wires, and pulleys

right /rît/ adj 1 consistent with facts or belief o the right answer 2 socially approved 3 conforming to what is usual or expected 4 proper with regard to use 5 most suitable or desirable o waiting for the right offer 6 on or towards the east when somebody is facing north 7 main or most prominent o right side up 8 perpendicular ■ adv 1 properly o did it right 2 just or exactly o right at that moment 3 straight 4 correctly 5 morally and appropriately 6 on or towards the right side 7 used as part of a title ■ n 1 the morally appropriate thing 2 something correct or true 3 an entitlement or freedom (often pl) 4 a legal entitlement 5 a claim to property (often pl) 6 also **Right** political conservatives as a group 7 the right side of somebody or something 8 a right-hand turn ■ v 1 vti put something into an upright position 2 vt correct a mistake 3 vt make amends for a wrong —**rightable** adj —**rightly** adv —**rightness** n ◇ **have** or **catch somebody bang to rights** catch a criminal in the act of committing a crime (infml) ◇ **in your own right** because of your birth, ability, or other entitlement ◇ **set** or **put something to rights** put something into the correct or ordered state

right angle n a 90° angle —**right-angled** adj

right-angled triangle n a triangle with one right angle

right-click vi press the right-hand mouse button

righteous /ríchəss/ adj 1 always observing a religious or moral code 2 justifiable —**righteously** adv —**righteousness** n

rightful /rît'l/ adj having or owned by somebody with a legal or moral claim —**rightfully** adv —**rightfulness** n

right-hand adj 1 on or to the right 2 for the right hand 3 most important and trusted

right-handed adj 1 preferring to use the right hand 2 done with or designed for the right hand ■ adv with the right hand —**right-handedly** adv —**right-handedness** n

right-hander n somebody who is right-handed

Right Honourable n 1 in Britain, a form of address for an MP 2 in Britain, the title of a Privy Counsellor or judge

rightist /rítist/ adj of or favouring political conservatism ■ n a political conservative —**rightism** n

right-minded adj sensible and fair —**right-mindedness** n

right of way n 1 a vehicle's right to proceed ahead of another 2 a lawful route across somebody's property, or the right to use it

rights issue n an offering of shares to existing shareholders on favourable terms

right-size (right-sizing, right-sized) vi make redundancies to achieve a company's supposed appropriate size

right-thinking adj sensible and fair

rightward /rîtward/ adj directed to the right ■ adv also **rightwards** towards the right

right wing n the conservative membership of a group —**right-wing** adj —**right-winger** n

rigid /rîjjid/ adj 1 firm and stiff 2 applied strictly 3 refusing to change —**rigidity** /ri jíddəti/ n —**rigidly** adv —**rigidness** n

rigmarole /rîgməröl/ n 1 an overelaborate explanation or account 2 a ridiculously complicated process

ORIGIN **Rigmarole** is first recorded in the mid-18C, and appears to be a contraction of ragman roll. A ragman roll was a parchment scroll used in a medieval gambling game. The roll had things such as names written on it, with pieces of string attached to them, and participants had to select a string at random. The word ragman may have been a contraction of ragged man, perhaps in allusion to the appearance of the scroll, with all its bits of string hanging from it. Ragman roll eventually came to be used for any list or catalogue, and ragman itself denoted a 'long rambling discourse' in 16C Scottish English – a meaning that seems to have transferred itself eventually to **rigmarole**.

rigor mortis /rîggər máwrtiss/ n the progressive stiffening of the body after death

rigorous /riggərəss/ adj 1 strict or difficult o rigorous training 2 precise and exacting o rigorous standards —**rigorously** adv

rigour /riggər/ n 1 severity in dealings with people 2 the application of demanding standards 3 harshness or hardship

rile (riling, riled) vt make somebody angry (infml)

Riley /rîli/ ◇ **the life of Riley** a comfortable life with no worries

Rilke /rilkə/, **Rainer Maria** (1875–1926) Bohemian-born German poet

rim *n* the outer edge of something circular or rounded ■ *vt* (**rimming, rimmed**) form a rim around —**rimmed** *adj*

Rimbaud /rámb ó/, **Arthur** (1854–91) French poet

rime[1] /rīm/ *n* a coating of frost —**rimy** *adj*

rime[2] /rīm/ *(archaic) n* a rhyme ■ *vti* (**riming, rimed**) rhyme

Rimsky-Korsakov /rímski káwssə kof/, **Nikolay** (1844–1908) Russian composer

rind /rīnd/ *n* **1** the tough outer layer of a fruit or other food **2** the bark of a tree

ring[1] *n* **1** a hard circular band of something **2** a circular piece of jewellery worn on a finger **3** a circular mark, arrangement, or device **4** a circular motion **5** a group of people operating dishonestly **6** a circular area for a performance, exhibition, or contest **7** a platform for boxing or wrestling ■ *vt* **1** draw a circle round something **2** form a circle round something **3** identify an animal with a tag

SPELLCHECK Do not confuse the spelling of **ring** and **wring** ('twist forcefully'), which sound similar.

ring[2] *v* (**rang, rung**) **1** *vti* make or cause to make the sound of a bell **2** *vti* telephone somebody **3** *vi* echo loudly **4** *vi* call somebody by sounding a bell or buzzer **5** *vi* make a particular impression on somebody ○ *His excuse didn't ring true.* **6** *vi* hear continuous high-pitched sounds ○ *My ears are ringing.* ■ *n* **1** the sound of a bell **2** a sound like a bell **3** a telephone call *(infml)* **4** a general impression **5** a loud repeated sound —**ringer** *n*

□ **ring in** *vt* **1** celebrate the beginning of something **2** *Aus* fraudulently substitute

□ **ring out** *v* **1** *vi* sound loudly **2** *vt* celebrate the end of

□ **ring up** *vti* telephone somebody

ring binder *n* a stiff cover with metal rings inside for holding papers

ring-fence *vt* (**ring-fencing, ring-fenced**) specify the use of money ■ *n* **1** an agreement restricting the use of money **2** a fence enclosing an area

ring finger *n* the finger next to the little finger, especially on the left hand

ringgit /ríng git/ *n* the main unit of currency of Malaysia

ringing /rínging/ *n* a continuing sound like a bell ■ *adj* stated loudly and unmistakably

ringleader /ríng leedər/ *n* the chief troublemaker in a group

ringlet /rínglət/ *n* a curly lock of hair

ringmaster /ríng maastər/ *n* a member of a circus who announces events

ring-pull *n* a ring pulled to open a drinks can

ring road *n* a road that circles an urban area

ringside /ríng sīd/ *n* the area next to a boxing or wrestling ring

ringworm /ríng wurm/ *n* a fungal skin disease

rink *n* **1** an area of ice used for sports **2** a surface used for roller-skating

rinse /rinss/ *vt* (**rinsing, rinsed**) **1** lightly wash or clean in liquid **2** flush with water after washing or cleaning ■ *n* **1** an act of rinsing something **2** a cosmetic treatment for colouring hair

Rio de Janeiro /reè ō də zhə neèr ō, -day-, -di-/ city in SE Brazil, the capital of **Rio de Janeiro State**. Pop. 5,551,538 (1996).

Rio Grande /reè ō gránd, -grándi/ river of SW North America, flowing from SW Colorado into the Gulf of Mexico and forming part of the Texas-Mexico border. Length 3,100 km/1,900 mi.

riot /rí ət/ *n* **1** a violent public disturbance **2** an extremely entertaining event or person *(infml)* ■ *vi* take part in a violent public disturbance —**rioter** *n* ◊ **run riot** behave in a wild and uncontrolled way

riotous /rí ətəss/ *adj* **1** unrestrained **2** rioting or likely to riot *(fml)* —**riotously** *adv*

riot police *n* police officers equipped for controlling a riot

rip *v* (**ripping, ripped**) **1** *vti* tear or be torn roughly **2** *vt* use force to remove something that is firmly attached **3** *vi* move with extreme speed ■ *n* a place where something has been torn ◊ **let rip** speak without restraint *(infml)* ◊ See note at **tear**

□ **rip off** *vt* *(infml)* **1** treat unfairly over money **2** steal

RIP *abbr* rest in peace

ripcord /ríp kawrd/ *n* **1** a cord pulled to open a parachute **2** a cord that releases some of the gas in a hot-air balloon

ripe (**riper, ripest**) *adj* **1** mature and ready to harvest or eat **2** mature and full of flavour ○ *ripe cheese* **3** at the most suitable stage for something to happen ○ *The time is ripe for asking for a pay rise.* —**ripeness** *n*

ripen /rípən/ *vti* **1** make or become ripe **2** reach or cause to reach the right stage of development —**ripening** *adj, n*

rip-off *n* something not worth the price asked or paid for it *(infml)*

riposte /ri póst/ *n* **1** a quick and clever response **2** a quick fencing thrust made after parrying an attack ◊ See note at **answer**

ripper *n* a program for copying digital music from a CD to a computer —**ripping** *n*

ripple /rípp'l/ *v* (**-pling, -pled**) **1** *vti* have or cause to have tiny gentle waves **2** *vti* have or cause to have a gentle wavy pattern **3** *vi* make a lapping sound ■ *n* **1** a tiny wave or a series of tiny waves **2** a gentle wavy shape or mark **3** a sound that passes through a group or place, increasing and decreasing in loudness ■ **ripples** *npl* repercussions or consequences

ripple effect *n* a spreading series of repercussions or consequences

rip-roaring *adj* exciting and energetic *(infml)* —**rip-roaringly** *adv*

riptide /ríp tīd/ *n* a strong turbulent current that opposes other currents

RISC /risk/ *abbr* reduced-instruction-set computer

rise *vi* (**rising, rose, risen** /rízz'n/) **1** stand up **2** ascend **3** increase in height or level **4** increase in amount, degree, or intensity **5** achieve greater status **6** extend upwards ○ *The tower rose above the village.* **7** swell in size ○ *allow the bread to rise* **8** engage in a revolt **9** have a beginning or source ○ *a stream rising in the hills* **10** spring up or grow **11** get up after sleeping **12** appear over the horizon **13** become resurrected ■ *n* **1** an increase **2** a salary increase **3** a process of coming to public notice and acclaim **4** an upward slope **5** higher ground **6** an ascent ◇ **get a rise out of** provoke an angry reaction from by teasing *(infml)* ◇ **give rise to** cause or produce

□ **rise above** *vt* cope well in spite of

riser /rízər/ *n* **1** somebody who gets out of bed at a particular time ○ *an early riser* **2** the vertical part of a step

risible /rízzəb'l/ *adj* **1** causing laughter **2** inclined to laugh *(fml)* —**risibly** *adv*

rising /rízing/ *adj* **1** getting more important **2** becoming powerful ■ *adv* almost a particular age *(dated infml)* ○ *rising 60* ■ *n* **1** a revolt **2** something getting higher **3** an upward movement **4** the action of standing up

risk *n* **1** the chance or possibility of danger or harm **2** a factor, state, or course that poses a possible danger ■ *vt* **1** endanger **2** do something despite a possible danger —**riskily** *adv* —**riskiness** *n* —**risky** *adj* ◇ **at risk** in danger of injury, damage, or loss

risotto /ri zóttō/ *n* a dish of rice and other in-· gredients cooked in stock

risqué /rísk ay, ree skáy/ *adj* sexually suggestive

rissole /ríssōl/ *n* a small fried cake of meat coated in breadcrumbs

rite *n* **1** a ceremonial or formal procedure *(often pl)* **2** a system of ceremonial procedures

rite of passage *n* **1** a significant transitional event in human life **2** a ceremony marking somebody's passage from one stage of life to another

ritual /ríchōō əl/ *n* **1** an established and prescribed pattern of observance, e.g. in a religion **2** the performance of actions in a set, ordered, and ceremonial way ■ *adj* of a rite —**ritualistic** /ríchōō ə lístik/ *adj* —**ritually** *adv*

ritzy /rítsi/ (**-ier, -iest**) *adj* expensively stylish *(infml)*

rival /rív'l/ *n* **1** a person or group competing with another for something or somebody **2** a person or thing that can equal or surpass another in a specific respect ■ *v* (**-valling, -valled**) **1** *vt* equal or surpass **2** *vti* compete with ■ *adj* competing —**rivalry** *n*

> **ORIGIN** A **rival** is etymologically 'somebody using the same stream as another', and therefore a competitor for the same resources. The word was adopted from Latin in the late 16C, and goes back to Latin *rivus* 'stream'.

riven /rívv'n/ *adj* torn apart *(literary)*

river /rívvər/ *n* **1** a large natural channel of flowing fresh water **2** a large flow of something *(often pl)* ◇ **sell down the river** betray or desert *(infml)*

Rivera /ree vérraa/, **Diego** (1886–1957) Mexican artist

riverbank /rívvər bangk/ *n* the ground rising up beside a river's edge

riverbed /rívvər bed/ *n* the ground over which a river flows

riverfront /rívvər frunt/ *n* the area of a town or property facing a river

riverside /rívvər sīd/ *n* the area of land by a river —**riverside** *adj*

rivet /rívvit/ *n* a short metal fastener for two metal sheets ■ *vt* **1** firmly fix the attention *(infml)* **2** fasten something with a rivet

riveting /rívviting/ *adj* fascinating *(infml)* —**rivetingly** *adv*

~~rivetting~~ incorrect spelling of **riveting**

Riviera /rívvi áirə/ coastal region of SE France and NW Italy

rivulet /rívvyōōlət/ *n* **1** a little stream *(literary)* **2** a small flow of something

Riyadh /reè ad, ree aàd/ capital of Saudi Arabia. Pop. 2,620,000 (1995).

riyal /ri aàl/ *n* the main unit of currency in Qatar, Saudi Arabia, and Yemen

RL *abbr* Rugby League

Rn *symbol* radon

RNA *n* a nucleic acid containing ribose, a five-carbon sugar, and found in all living cells. Full form **ribonucleic acid**

RNLI *abbr* Royal National Lifeboat Institution

ro *abbr* recto

roach (*pl* **same** or **roaches**) *n* **1** a European freshwater fish **2** a small North American sunfish

road *n* **1** a long surfaced route for vehicles **2** a course of action leading to a particular outcome ◇ **down the road** in the future

roadblock /rṓd blok/ *n* **1** a barrier across a road to stop traffic **2** an obstacle

road hog *n* a motorist regarded as selfish and inconsiderate *(infml)*

roadhouse /rṓd howss/ (*pl* **-houses** /-howziz/) *n* a hotel or pub located beside a road *(dated)*

roadie /rṓdi/ *n* somebody whose job is to look after and set up equipment for a band of musicians when travelling

road map *n* a map for motorists showing roads and distances

road pricing *n* a toll system to control road use

road rage *n* uncontrollable anger experienced by a driver in difficult road conditions

roadrunner /rṓd runər/ *n* a fast-running desert bird

roadshow /rṓd shṓ/ *n* **1** a group travelling from place to place to publicize or promote something **2** a performance by a touring company of entertainers or broadcasters

roadside /rṓd sīd/ *n* an area at a road's edge

road sign n a sign by the side of a road providing directions for road users

roadster /ró̄dstər/ n US an open-top sports car (dated)

road test n a test of a vehicle or tyre under actual operating conditions —**road-test** vt

road-train n Aus a long-distance truck with trailers

roadway /ró̄d way/ n the driving area of a road

roadwork /ró̄d wurk/ n a form of exercise consisting of running on roads

roadworks /ró̄d wurks/ n repairs to a road

roadworthy /ró̄d wurthi/ adj fit to be driven safely —**roadworthiness** n

roam vti wander aimlessly —**roamer** n

roaming /ró̄ming/ n the use of a mobile phone outside your home country

roan adj describes an animal with a reddish-brown, brown, or black coat speckled with white ■ n a roan horse

roar v 1 vi growl loudly 2 vti shout loudly 3 vi laugh loudly 4 vi make a continuous deep sound ○ A fire roared in the grate. ■ n 1 a loud shout 2 a loud laugh 3 a loud growl 4 a continuous deep sound ○ the roar of the tempest

roaring /ráwring/ adj very great ■ adv exceedingly —**roaringly** adv ◇ **do a roaring trade** sell a product easily and rapidly (infml)

Roaring Twenties npl the 1920s, when thought of as a time of exuberance and prosperity

roast /ró̄st/ vti 1 cook in an oven using fat 2 prepare coffee beans or nuts by drying or browning, or be prepared in this way 3 overheat ■ n an oven-cooked piece of meat ■ adj oven-cooked

roasting /ró̄sting/ (infml) adj very hot ■ n harsh criticism

rob (**robbing**, **robbed**) vt 1 steal from a person or place 2 deprive somebody unfairly —**robber** n

robber baron n 1 an unscrupulous 19C US industrialist 2 a medieval nobleman who stole from travellers passing through his lands

robbery /róbbəri/ (pl -**ies**) n a theft of property

robe n 1 a long loose ceremonial garment (often pl) 2 a dressing gown or bathrobe ■ vti (**robing**, **robed**) dress in a robe

Robert I /róbbərt/, **'Robert the Bruce'** /-brooss/ (1274–1329) king of Scotland (1306–29)

Roberts /róbbərts/, **Tom** (1856–1931) British-born Australian painter

AKG London

Paul Robeson

Robeson /ró̄bsən/, **Paul** (1898–1976) US singer and actor

Robespierre /ró̄bz pyair/, **Maximilien** (1758–94) French lawyer and revolutionary

robin /róbbin/ n 1 a small brown European thrush, the male of which has a red chest 2 a large North American thrush with a rust-coloured breast

Robin Hood /róbbin hoŏd/ n in English legend, a 12C outlaw, famous for his practice of stealing from the rich to give to the poor

Robinson /róbbinss'n/, **Arthur** (b. 1926) prime minister (1986–91) and president (1997–) of Trinidad and Tobago

Express Newspapers

Mary Robinson

Robinson, Mary (b. 1944) president of the Republic of Ireland (1990–97) and UN High Commissioner for Human Rights (1997–)

robot /ró̄ bot/ n 1 a machine programmed to perform tasks normally done by people 2 an imaginary machine functioning like a human 3 somebody who behaves like a machine 4 S Africa a set of traffic lights (infml) —**robotic** /ró̄ bóttik/ adj

ORIGIN The first **robots** appeared in the play *R. U. R.* (*Rossum's Universal Robots*) (1920) by the Czech dramatist Karel Čapek. Čapek coined the name from Czech *robota* 'forced labour', and it entered English via German. The first English use is recorded in 1923.

robotics /ró̄ bóttiks/ n the design and use of robots (+ sing verb)

Rob Roy /rób róy/ (1671–1734) Scottish brigand

robust /ró̄ búst/ adj 1 strong and healthy 2 full-flavoured —**robustly** adv —**robustness** n

Rochester /róchistər/ city in SE England. Pop. 145,000 (1994).

rock[1] n 1 a hard aggregate of more than one mineral 2 a boulder 3 somebody dependable 4 a hard boiled sweet in the shape of a cylindrical stick 5 a diamond (infml) ◇ **between a rock and a hard place** faced with two equally undesirable choices ◇ **on the rocks** 1 ruined or in great difficulties (infml) 2 served with ice cubes

rock[2] v 1 vti sway to and fro 2 vti shake violently 3 vt shock (infml) 4 vi play or dance to rock music (infml) ■ n 1 an act of rocking 2 a type of pop music derived from rock and roll

rockabilly /rókə bili/ n a type of pop music combining rock and roll with country music

rock and roll /rókən ró̄l/, **rock'n'roll** n 1 pop music with a heavy beat, played on electric instruments 2 dancing done to rock and roll —**rock and roll** vi —**rock and roller** n

rock bottom *n* the lowest possible level or price —**rock-bottom** *adj*

rock cake, rock bun *n* a hard individual fruit-cake

Rockefeller /rókə fellər/ family of US industrialists and philanthropists including **John D.** (1839–1937) and his son **John D., Jr.** (1874–1960) and grandson **Nelson A.** (1908–79), vice president of the United States (1974–77).

rocker /rókər/ *n* 1 a rocking device 2 a curved piece of wood or metal that allows a rocking chair or cradle to rock 3 a rocking chair 4 a rock musician or fan (*infml*)

rockery /rókəri/ (*pl* -**ies**), **rock garden** a garden containing large stones with small plants between them

rocket[1] /rókit/ *n* 1 a device that burns fuel and oxidizer, producing thrust by expelling the hot gases 2 a space vehicle 3 a rocket-propelled weapon 4 a firework or flare containing combustible propellants 5 a severe rebuke (*infml*) ■ *vi* 1 move fast 2 increase quickly (*infml*)

ORIGIN The earliest sense of **rocket**, 'self-propelled flare', is recorded from the early 17C. The word was adopted from Italian *rocchetta*, literally 'small distaff' (a rod for thread used in spinning by hand), and **rockets** were so called because of their shape. The name for the salad leaf is unrelated. It came from French in the late 15C.

rocket[2] /rókit/ *n* a plant with peppery leaves used in salads

rocket science *n* any complex and intellectually demanding activity (*infml*)

Rockies /rókiz/ ♦ **Rocky Mountains**

rocking chair *n* a chair on rockers for rocking backwards and forwards in

rocking horse *n* a child's model horse on rockers for rocking backwards and forwards on

rock melon *n ANZ* a cantaloupe

rock'n'roll *n*, *vi* MUSIC, DANCE = **rock and roll**

rock salt *n* common salt found in mineral deposits, usually sold as small chunks

rock-solid *adj* 1 firm and unshakable 2 hard and unlikely to break

rock steady *n* a type of Jamaican reggae

Rockwell /rókwəl/, **Norman** (1894–1978) US illustrator

rocky[1] /róki/ (-**ier**, -**iest**) *adj* 1 consisting of or covered with rocks 2 hard like rock —**rockiness** *n*

rocky[2] /róki/ (-**ier**, -**iest**) *adj* 1 full of difficulties 2 unsteady —**rockiness** *n*

Rocky Mountains major mountain system of W North America, extending more than 4,800 km/3,000 mi. from N Alaska to New Mexico. Highest peak Mt Elbert 4,399 m/14,433 ft.

~~rococco~~ incorrect spelling of **rococo**

Rococo: Detail of stucco at Wies church, Bavaria, Germany (1745–54)

rococo /rə kókō/, **Rococo** *n* an ornate 18C style of art or music —**rococo** *adj*

rod *n* 1 a narrow cylindrical length of a material such as wood, metal, or plastic 2 a pole for fishing 3 a stick or bundle of sticks for beating somebody 4 a surveying pole 5 a staff of office 6 oppressive power 7 a receptor cell in the eye that is sensitive to dim light but not colour 8 an obsolete unit of length equal to 5.03 m/5.5 yd 9 an obsolete unit of area equal to 25.3 sq. m/30.25 sq. yd

rode past tense of **ride**

rodent /ród'nt/ *n* a small mammal such as a rat or a mouse with large gnawing incisor teeth

rodeo /rō dáy ō, ródi-/ (*pl* -**os**) *n* 1 a competition involving cowboy skills 2 a cattle round-up

Rodin /rō dáN/, **Auguste** (1840–1917) French sculptor

roe[1] /rō/ *n* fish eggs or sperm

roe[2] /rō/ (*pl* **roes** *or* **same**) *n* a reddish-brown woodland deer

Roentgen /róntgən/, **Wilhelm Conrad** (1845–1923) German physicist. He discovered X-rays, originally known also as 'Roentgen rays'.

roger /rójjər/ *interj* 1 indicates that a message has been received and understood (*in telecommunications*) 2 OK (*infml*)

Rogers, Ginger (1911–95) US dancer and actor

Roget /rō zhay, rō zháy/, **Peter Mark** (1779–1869) British doctor and compiler of *Roget's Thesaurus of English Words and Phrases* (1852)

rogue /rōg/ *n* 1 somebody dishonest, especially somebody who is also likable 2 somebody mischievous 3 a plant inferior to others of the same type ■ *adj* 1 describes an animal that is solitary and dangerous 2 unorthodox and unpredictable —**roguery** /rōgəri/ *n* —**roguish** *adj* —**roguishly** *adv*

rogue site *n* a website that acquires visitors by having a domain name similar to that of a popular site

rogue state *n* a nation believed by Western countries to sabotage international political stability, sponsor terrorists, and develop weapons of mass destruction

Rohe ♦ Mies van der Rohe, Ludwig

roister /róystər/ *vi* celebrate rowdily (*dated*)

role, rôle *n* 1 a part played by somebody in a play, film, opera, or other performance 2 the function that somebody or something performs in an action or event **3** a part played by somebody in a social context that demands a particular pattern of behaviour

role model *n* somebody who is a good example for others to copy

role-play, role-playing *n* the acting out of a part, especially that of somebody with a particular social role, in order to understand it better —**role-play** *vti*

Rolfing /rólfing/ a proprietary name for a therapy using vigorous massage to alleviate physical or psychological tension

roll /rōl/ *v* **1** *vti* turn over and over **2** *vti* move on wheels or rollers **3** *vti* form into a round or cylindrical shape **4** *vti* move in a steady flowing motion **5** *vi* extend in a series of gentle slopes **6** *vt* flatten something with a roller or rolling pin **7** *vi* reverberate loudly **8** *vt* trill a sound, especially an 'r' **9** *vti* move while rocking from side to side **10** *vti* start to operate, e.g. a movie camera **11** *vti* throw dice, or score a number by throwing dice ■ *n* **1** a tube, cylinder, or coil **2** a small individual bread product, or a sandwich made with one **3** an official list of people in a group **4** a rumbling noise **5** a series of drum beats **6** an act of rolling **7** a rolling movement **8** a trilling sound **9** a toss of a die or dice ◇ **be rolling in it** be very rich *(infml)* ◇ **on a roll** enjoying a period of success *(infml)*

☐ **roll back** *vt* reduce the influence or effectiveness of something

☐ **roll in** *vi* **1** arrive in a casual way **2** appear in large numbers

☐ **roll off** *vi* flow easily or in large numbers

☐ **roll out** *vt* **1** flatten something with a rolling pin **2** introduce a product into a market

☐ **roll over** *v* **1** *vt* extend a loan **2** *vt* reinvest funds **3** *vti* add prize money not won on one occasion to the amount for the next occasion

☐ **roll up** *vi* arrive, especially late or unexpectedly

rollback /rôl bak/ *n* a reduction of the influence or effectiveness of something

rollbar /rôl baar/ *n* a bar across the top of an open-top or rally car providing protection if the vehicle overturns

roll call *n* **1** an attendance check **2** a time for a roll call

rolled gold *n* a base metal covered with a thin layer of gold

roller /rôlər/ *n* **1** a rolling tube for applying paint or ink **2** a large heavy revolving cylinder with a handle for flattening lawns **3** a hair curler **4** a long heavy wave that only breaks on reaching the shore **5** a small solid wheel with no spokes

rollerball /rôlər bawl/ *n* **1** a pen with a tip in the form of a movable ball **2** a device containing a ball that is used instead of a computer mouse

Rollerblade /rôlər blayd/ *tdmk* a trademark for a type of roller skate on which the wheels are arranged in one straight line

roller blind *n* a window blind consisting of a length of fabric wrapped around a pole

roller coaster *n* **1** a fairground ride consisting of open cars on a narrow rail track with extreme peaks and troughs and sharp bends **2** a situation with sudden extreme changes

roller skate *n* **1** a frame with wheels that attaches to a shoe **2** a special shoe fitted with wheels —**roller-skate** *vi* —**roller-skater** *n* —**roller-skating** *n*

rollicking¹ /rólliking/ *adj* boisterous

rollicking² /rólliking/ *n* a scolding *(infml)*

rolling /rôling/ *adj* **1** having gentle slopes **2** developing gradually in stages ○ *a rolling program of reform* **3** constantly updated

rolling pin *n* a cylindrical kitchen utensil for flattening dough or pastry

rolling stock *n* railway vehicles

roll of honour *n* **1** a list of distinguished names **2** a list of war dead

roll-on *adj* applied to the skin with a rotating ball in the top of the container ■ *n* a deodorant with a rotating ball applicator

roll-on roll-off *adj* describes a ferry designed for vehicles to be driven on at one end and off at the other on reaching their destination —**roll-on roll-off** *n*

roll-out /rôl owt/ *n* the launch of a product into a market

rollover /rôl ōvər/ *n* a transfer of funds from one investment to another

roll-top desk, roll-top *n* a writing desk with a rounded flexible cover that can be pulled down over the writing area

roll-up *n* a hand-rolled cigarette *(infml)*

Rolodex /rôlə deks/ *tdmk* a trademark for a desktop filing system in which cards containing names, addresses, and telephone numbers are attached to a central cylinder

roly-poly /róli póli/ *adj* overweight *(sometimes offensive)* ■ *n (pl* **roly-polies)** *also* **roly-poly pudding** a jam suet pudding in a roll

Rom /rom/ (*pl* **Roma** /rómmə/) *n* a group of nomadic people who migrated from India in the 15C *(+ pl verb)*

ROM /rom/ *abbr* read-only memory

rom., rom *abbr* roman

Roman /rômən/ *adj* **1** of modern or ancient Rome **2** of the Roman Catholic church **3** *roman* in or of the upright type used as the standard type in printing ■ *n* **1** somebody from modern or ancient Rome **2** **roman** roman type

Roman alphabet *n* the Western writing system of 26 letters

Roman candle *n* a short cylindrical free-standing firework

Roman Catholic *adj* of the Catholic Church headed by the Pope in Rome ■ *n* a member of the Roman Catholic Church —**Roman Catholicism** *n*

romance /rō mánss, rô manss/ *n* **1** a love affair **2** exciting or intense love **3** a feeling of adventure and excitement **4** a love story **5** a medieval story of chivalry **6** a fictitious narrative of exciting or mysterious adventures

7 Romance the group of Indo-European languages that are descended from Latin ■ *vt* (**-mancing, -manced**) treat somebody romantically —**Romance** *adj* —**romancer** *n*

ORIGIN The original **romances** were written in *Romance*, then a name for the vernacular language of France as opposed to Latin. They were medieval tales of chivalry or extraordinary adventures. The French word from which **romance** derives means literally 'of Rome'.

Roman Empire *n* **1** the territories ruled by Roman emperors **2** the rule of Roman emperors

Romanesque: Carved stone capital (1127–45) from Pamplona Cathedral, Spain

Romanesque /rṓmə nésk/ *adj* of an early European architectural or artistic style of the 11C and 12C —**Romanesque** *n*

Romania /roō máyni ə, rō-/ country in SE Europe, bordering the Black Sea. Cap. Bucharest. Pop. 22,364,022 (2001). —**Romanian** *n, adj*

Roman nose *n* a high-bridged nose

Roman numeral *n* a letter or letters representing a number used by the ancient Romans

Romansch /rō mánsh/, **Romansh** *n* a Romance language that is one of the official languages of Switzerland —**Romansch** *adj*

romantic /rō mántik/ *adj* **1** involving exciting or intense sexual love **2** suitable for lovemaking or tender emotions **3** idealistic and impractical **4 Romantic** of a musical, literary, and artistic movement of the late 18C and early 19C that emphasized feelings, nature, and interest in other cultures ■ *n* **1** a romantic person **2 Romantic** a composer, writer, or artist involved in the Romantic movement —**romantically** *adv* —**romanticism** /-sizəm/ *n* —**romanticist** *n*

romanticize /rō mánti sīz/ (**-cizing, -cized**), **romanticise** *v* **1** *vt* make something appear glamorous **2** *vi* think romantically

Romany /rṓməni, rómməni/ (*pl* **-nies**), **Romani** *n* **1** the language of the Roma people **2** a member of the Roma people (*dated*) —**Romany** *adj*

Rome /rōm/ capital of Italy. Pop. 2,646,408 (1999).

Romeo /rṓmi ō/ (*pl* **-os**) *n* **1** an amorous man **2** a communications code word for the letter 'R'

ORIGIN The original **Romeo** was the young lover

of Juliet in Shakespeare's play *Romeo and Juliet* (1594).

Rommel /rómməl/, **Erwin** (1891–1944) German general

romp *vi* **1** play boisterously **2** make easy progress towards ■ *n* boisterous activity

Romulus /rómyōōləss/ *n* in Roman mythology, the founder of the city of Rome

ROMvelope /rómvelōp/, **romvelope** *n* a protective cardboard cover for a CD-ROM

rondavel /ron daával/ *n S Africa* a thatched circular building

roo bar *n Aus* a bar on the front of a vehicle to protect it in a collision with an animal

rood *n* **1** a crucifix **2** a unit of area equal to a quarter of an acre

rood screen *n* a partition in a church separating off the choir or chancel

roof *n* **1** the outer covering of the top of a building **2** the top covering of something **3** the top of the inside of a cavity ■ *vt* build a roof on ◇ **hit the roof** become extremely angry ◇ **go through the roof** rise to an extremely high level

roofer /roófər/ *n* somebody who builds or repairs roofs

roof garden *n* a garden on top of a building

roofing /roófing/ *n* material for making a roof

roof rack *n* a frame attached to the top of a car for carrying things

rooftop /roóf top/ *n* the outer surface of the roof of a building

rooibos /róy boss/ *n also* **rooibos tea** *S Africa* a tea made from the leaves of a wild bush

rook[1] /roōk/ *n* a large black bird that nests in colonies in treetops

rook[2] /roōk/ *n* a chess piece that can be moved any distance in a straight line

rookery /roókəri/ (*pl* **-les**) *n* **1** a colony of rooks **2** a breeding place for rooks

rookie /roóki/ *n* somebody inexperienced in an activity or job (*infml*)

room /room, roōm/ *n* **1** available space that may or may not be filled with something or where something can happen ○ *need more room* **2** a part of a building consisting of four walls and a ceiling **3** the people in a room **4** scope or opportunity for something to exist or happen ○ *there's room for improvement* ■ **rooms** *npl* accommodation for rent —**roomful** *n*

roommate /roóm mayt, roōm-/ *n* somebody sharing a room

room service *n* a hotel service providing guests with food and drink in their rooms

roomy /roómi, roō-/ (**-ier, -iest**) *adj* spacious —**roominess** *n*

Roosevelt /rṓzə velt/, **Eleanor** (1884–1962) US first lady (1933–45), social activist, and writer

Franklin D. Roosevelt

Roosevelt, Franklin D. (1882–1945) 32nd president of the United States (1933–45)

Roosevelt, Theodore (1858–1919) 26th president of the United States (1901–09)

roost /roost/ n a place where birds sleep ■ vi go to sleep in a roost ◊ **rule the roost** be in charge

rooster /roóstər/ n an adult male domestic fowl

root[1] n 1 the underground base of a plant that gets water from the soil 2 the underground edible part of a plant 3 the portion of a body part such as a tooth or hair embedded in tissue 4 the base of something ○ the root of the tongue 5 the fundamental cause of something 6 a number multiplied by itself a particular number of times 7 the core part of a word left when any affixes are removed ■ **roots** npl somebody's cultural or family origins ■ vti 1 grow or cause to grow roots 2 become or cause to become fixed or embedded ◊ **root and branch** completely ◊ **take root** become established ◊ See note at **origin**

SPELLCHECK Do not confuse the spelling of **root** and **route** ('a direction of travel'), which sound similar.

□ **root up** vt dig up a plant

root[2] v 1 vti dig in the ground with the snout 2 vi rummage

□ **root out** vt remove completely

root[3] vi 1 cheer or shout in support 2 provide with support

root beer n a soft drink made from root extracts

root directory n the top-level directory in a computer's filing system

rooted /roótid/ adj 1 fixed in the ground by roots 2 well established 3 seemingly unable to move —**rootedness** n

rootstock /root stok/ n 1 a rhizome 2 a root used in grafting

root vegetable n a vegetable grown for its edible root

rope n 1 a strong cord made by twisting fibres together 2 a row of things strung or twisted together ■ **ropes** npl the usual procedures (infml) ■ vt (**roping, roped**) 1 secure somebody or something with rope 2 enclose an area with ropes ◊ **on the ropes** in a hopeless position and likely to fail (infml)

□ **rope in** vt involve

Rosario /rō saári ō/ city in east-central Argentina. Pop. 1,157,372 (1991).

rosary /rõzəri/ (pl **-ries**) n 1 a series of Roman

Catholic prayers 2 a string of beads used in counting the prayers said in a rosary

---

ORIGIN Rosary comes from a Latin word meaning 'rose garden', and this is one of its early senses in English. In the early 16C it came also to refer to a series of Roman Catholic prayers. It was a common stylistic device at the time to name collections of verse or similar short pieces after bunches of flowers (anthology comes from the Greek word for 'flower').

Roscommon /ross kómmən/ county in west-central Republic of Ireland. Pop. 51,897 (1997).

rose[1] n 1 a prickly bush with ornamental flowers 2 a flower of the rose 3 a reddish-pink colour ■ adj of, having, or resembling roses

rose[2] past tense of **rise**

rosé /rõ zay/ n a pink wine

roseate /rõzi ət/ adj 1 rose-coloured 2 optimistic

Roseau /rō sõ/ capital of Dominica. Pop. 15,853 (1991).

rosebud /rõz bud/ n the unopened flower of a rose

rosehip /rõz hip/ n the fruit of the rose plant. Use: jelly, herbal tea, medicinal syrups.

rosemary /rõzməri/ n 1 aromatic grey-green needle-shaped leaves. Use: food flavouring, perfume. 2 a bush that produces rosemary

---

ORIGIN The earlier form of **rosemary** was ros-marine, which gives a clearer clue to its etymology. It originally had no connection with roses or the name Mary, but derived from a Latin word meaning 'dew of the sea' (because it grew near sea coasts and its blossoms were thought to resemble dew). The earlier form was altered during the 14C by association with rose and Mary, probably referring to the mother of Jesus Christ.

---

rosette /rō zét/ n a decoration resembling a rose

Rosewall /rõz wawl/, **Ken** (b. 1934) Australian tennis player

rose water n water scented with rose petals

rose window n a round window with tracery in a pattern resembling a rose

rosewood /rõz wood/ n 1 the dark rose-scented wood of various tropical trees. Use: furniture. 2 a tree from which rosewood is obtained

Rosh Hashanah /rósh hə shaánə/, **Rosh Hashana** n Jewish New Year Festival. Date: 1st and 2nd of Tishri in the autumn.

Ross /ross/, **Sir James Clark** (1800–62) British explorer

Christina Rossetti

Rossetti /rə zétti/, **Christina** (1830–94) British poet

Rossetti, Dante Gabriel (1828–82) British painter and poet

Rossini /ro seeni/, **Gioacchino Antonio** (1792–1868) Italian composer

Ross Sea arm of the S Pacific Ocean, extending into E Antarctica between Victoria Land and Marie Byrd Land, and incorporating the **Ross Ice Shelf**

roster /róstər/ n 1 a list of names of employees, athletes, or members of the armed forces, usually detailing their periods of duty 2 the people on a roster ■ vt put on a roster

Rostock /rós tok/ city and port in NE Germany. Pop. 232,634 (1997).

Rostov /rós tov/ city in SW European Russia, on the River Don. Pop. 1,127,339 (1995).

rostrum /róstrəm/ (pl **-trums** or **-tra** /-trə/) n 1 a platform for public speaking 2 an orchestra conductor's platform

rosy /rózi/ (**-ier, -iest**) adj 1 pinkish-red 2 having a pinkish complexion 3 promising 4 optimistic ○ takes a rosy view of things —**rosily** adv —**rosiness** n

rot v (**rotting, rotted**) 1 vti break down organically or decompose 2 vi deteriorate badly ■ n 1 the process of decaying 2 nonsense (infml)

rota /rótə/ n a list of people's names and the order in which they are to perform duties

rotary /rótəri/ (pl **-ries**) n a rotating part or machine

Rotary Club n a local branch of an organization of business and professional people that encourages service to the community —**Rotarian** /rō táiri ən/ n —**Rotarianism** n

rotate /rō táyt/ (**-tating, -tated**) vti 1 turn around an axis 2 alternate or vary —**rotation** n

rote n mechanical repetition in order to remember something

Roth, Philip (b. 1933) US writer

Rothermere /róthər meer/, **Harold Sydney, 1st Viscount Harmsworth** (1868–1940) British newspaper magnate

Rothko /róth kō/, **Mark** (1903–70) Russian-born US artist

Rothschild /róth chīld, róths-/ family of German and British financiers including **Mayer Amschel** (1743–1812), his sons **Salomon** (1774–1855) and **Nathan Mayer** (1777–1836), and grandson **Lionel Nathan** (1808–79)

roti /róti/ (pl **-tis**) n a South Asian unleavened bread

rotisserie /rō tíssəri/ n 1 a roasting spit 2 a shop or restaurant where meat is roasted and sold

rotten /rótt'n/ adj 1 decayed 2 of a low standard or quality (infml) 3 very bad or unwell (infml) —**rottenly** adv —**rottenness** n

rotter /róttər/ n somebody nasty (infml dated)

Rotterdam /róttər dam/ port in SW Netherlands. Pop. 593,321 (2000).

Rottweiler /rót vīlər, -wīlər/ n a large powerful black dog with tan markings

rotund /rō túnd/ adj 1 overweight 2 rich in sound —**rotundity** n

rotunda /rō túndə/ n a round domed building or room

Rouault /roo ó/, **Georges Henri** (1871–1958) French painter and engraver

rouble /roob'l/, **ruble** n the main unit of currency in Russia, Belarus, and Tajikistan

Rouen /roo aaN/ city in N France. Pop. 106,592 (1999).

rouge /roozh/ n 1 reddish makeup for the cheeks (dated) 2 a reddish polish in powder form —**rouge** vt

rough /ruf/ adj 1 not having a smooth or flat surface 2 coarse in texture 3 windy or turbulent 4 not gentle 5 not refined or polite 6 harsh in sound or taste 7 general and approximate 8 makeshift ○ a rough shelter made from branches 9 crude ○ a rough wooden carving 10 severe or unpleasant (infml) 11 rowdy ■ n 1 the part of a golf course where the grass is left long 2 a preliminary version 3 a violent person ■ vt roughen —**roughly** adv —**roughness** n ◇ **in the rough** in a crude, unfinished, or uncultivated state ◇ **rough it** live in a less comfortable way than usual (infml)

SPELLCHECK Do not confuse the spelling of **rough** and **ruff** ('a stiff pleated collar'), which sound similar.

☐ **rough out** vt outline in broad terms
☐ **rough up** vt beat somebody violently (infml)

roughage /rúffij/ n fibre in food

rough-and-ready adj 1 crude but serviceable 2 not refined or polite but friendly and kind

rough-and-tumble n a situation that lacks rules or order —**rough-and-tumble** adj

rough diamond n 1 an uncut and unpolished diamond 2 somebody unrefined but likable

roughen /rúff'n/ vti make or become rough

rough-hewn adj 1 cut without precision and not smoothed 2 crudely made

roughneck /rúf nek/ n somebody rough and bad-mannered (infml)

roulette /roo lét/ n a gambling game in which a ball is rolled onto a spinning horizontal wheel divided into compartments

round[1] adj 1 circular or spherical 2 curved 3 not less or more than ○ a round dozen 4 expressed by an integer ○ a round number 5 considerable ○ a round sum —**roundish** adj —**roundness** n

round[2] n 1 a round shape or object 2 a session of a particular event ○ the first round of talks 3 a stage of a competition 4 a game of golf in which all the holes are played 5 a turn of play, as in a card game 6 a charge of ammunition 7 a gun discharge 8 a series of regular visits (often pl) 9 a set of drinks bought, one for each person in a group 10 an outburst of applause 11 a song for several voices, each starting at a different time 12 a circular dance 13 a cut of beef from between the rump and the shank ◇ **in the round** 1 visible or viewed from all sides 2 in perspective from all sides

round[3] *v* **1** *vt* move in a curve past something **2** *vti* express a number as the nearest significant number above or below it

□ **round down** *vt* express a number as the nearest significant number below it

□ **round off** *vt* **1** make more rounded **2** finish in a pleasing way

□ **round out** *vti* make or become more complete

□ **round up** *vt* **1** gather people or animals together **2** express a number as the nearest significant number above it

round[4] *prep, adv* **1** surrounding or enclosing somebody or something ○ *clasped her hands round her knees* ○ *A crowd gathered round.* **2** in different parts of something ○ *scattered round the room* **3** in all directions ○ *drove round for hours* **4** in a partial circuit of something ○ *coming round the corner* **5** turning on an axis ○ *cylinders going round at 1,000 revolutions per second* ■ *adv* in the opposite direction ○ *turned round when he called her name* ■ *prep, adv* in circumference ○ *30 inches round the waist* ■ *adv* to visit somebody or something ○ *went round to tell them* ◊ **round about** approximately

roundabout /równdə bowt/ *n* **1** a revolving ride in a playground **2** a circular road junction ■ *adj* indirect and not straightforward

rounders /równdərz/ *n* a ball game resembling baseball (+ *sing verb*)

roundly /równdli/ *adv* severely ○ *was roundly criticized*

round robin *n* a tournament in which everyone plays everyone else

round table *n* a discussion in which all the participants are on equal terms —**round-table** *adj*

Round Table *n* **1** the legendary circular table at which King Arthur and his knights sat **2** King Arthur's knights as a whole

round-the-clock *adj* 24 hours a day

round trip *n* a journey to a place and back

round-up *n* **1** a gathering of people or animals **2** a summary

roundworm /równd wurm/ *n* a parasitic worm found in the human intestine

rouse /rowz/ (**rousing, roused**) *v* **1** *vti* wake **2** *vt* shake somebody out of apathy **3** *vt* provoke a feeling in somebody

rousing /rówzing/ *adj* **1** inciting emotion **2** lively —**rousingly** *adv*

Rousseau /roo só/, **Henri** (1844–1910) French painter

Rousseau, Jean Jacques (1712–78) French philosopher and writer

roust /rowst/ *vt* force to get up

roustabout /rówstə bowt/ *n* **1** *US, Can* an unskilled labourer **2** *also* **rouseabout** *ANZ* an unskilled worker on a sheep or cattle station (*dated*)

rout /rowt/ *n* **1** a disorderly retreat by a defeated army **2** a crushing defeat ■ *vt* **1** force to retreat **2** defeat thoroughly

route /root/ *in military usage also* /rowt/ *n* **1** a way to travel from one place to another **2** the

course that something follows or the way it progresses **3** a regular journey usually consisting of a series of stops ■ *vt* (**routeing, routed**) send along a particular route ◊ See note at **root**

router /rootər/ *n* a computer switching program for transferring messages

routine /roo teen/ *n* **1** the usual sequence for a set of activities **2** something boringly repetitive **3** a rehearsed set of actions or speeches making up a performance **4** a part of a computer program that performs a particular task ■ *adj* **1** usual or standard **2** boringly repetitive —**routinely** *adv* —**routineness** *n* ◊ See note at **habit, usual**

roux /roo/ *n* a base of flour and fat for a sauce

rove /rōv/ (**roving, roved**) *v* **1** *vti* wander or travel over an area aimlessly **2** *vi* move in changing directions ○ *as his gaze roved around the room*

rover /rōvər/ *n* **1** a wanderer **2** a small vehicle for exploring the surface of a planet

roving /rōving/ *adj* **1** moving about **2** erratic or fickle

row[1] /rō/ *n* **1** a line of people or things placed next to each other **2** a narrow street lined by houses ◊ **in a row** one after the other ◊ **a hard row to hoe** something difficult to do

row[2] /rō/ *vti* propel a boat with oars —**rower** *n* —**rowing** *n*

row[3] /row/ *n* **1** a noisy argument **2** an unpleasant loud noise ■ *vi* argue noisily

rowan /ró ən, rów ən/ *n* **1** a tree that produces red berries **2** *also* **rowanberry** /-berri/ (*pl* **-ries**) a red berry produced by a rowan tree

rowdy /rówdi/ *adj* (**-dier, -diest**) unruly ■ *n* (*pl* **-dies**) hooligan —**rowdily** *adv* —**rowdiness** *n* —**rowdyism** *n*

rowing boat *n* a small boat propelled by somebody rowing

Rowling / róling/, **J. K.** (*b.* 1965) British author of children's books

rowlock /róllək, rúllək/ *n* a metal rest for an oar on the side of a boat

Rowntree /równ tree/, **Benjamin Seebohm** (1871–1954) British manufacturer and philanthropist

royal /róy əl/ *adj* **1** of kings and queens **2** enjoying royal patronage **3** excellent ○ *given a royal welcome* **4** extremely bad (*infml*) ○ *a right royal pain in the neck* ■ *n* a monarch or a member of the monarch's family (*infml*)

royal blue *adj* of a deep bright blue colour —**royal blue** *n*

Royal Commission *n* a committee of inquiry set up by the British monarch on the prime minister's advice

royal flush *n* in poker, a hand consisting of the top five cards of a suit

Royal Highness *n* a title used for a member of a royal family other than a king or queen

royalist /róy əlist/ *n* **1** somebody in favour of a monarchy **2** **Royalist** a Cavalier in the English Civil War —**royalism** *n* —**royalist** *adj*

royally /róy əlli/ *adv* generously or splendidly

royalty /róy əlti/ (*pl* **-ties**) *n* **1** a royal person or royal people collectively **2** a royal person's status **3** a percentage of the income from a book, piece of music, or invention paid to its creator (*often pl*)

RP *abbr* Received Pronunciation

RPI *abbr* retail price index

rpm *abbr* revolutions per minute

Rs *symbol* rupees

RSC *abbr* Royal Shakespeare Company

RSI *n* a painful muscle condition caused by a repetitive activity such as using a keyboard. Full form **repetitive strain injury**

RSL *n* an Australian organization for ex-service personnel. Full form **Returned Services League**

RSPCA *abbr* Royal Society for the Prevention of Cruelty to Animals

RSVP used on an invitation to request a response to it

ORIGIN RSVP is an abbreviation of French *repondez s'il vous plaît* 'please reply'.

RT *abbr* real time (*in e-mails*)

RTDS *abbr* real-time data system

rtf[1] *n* a computer document file that contains formatting codes. Full form **rich text format**

rtf[2] *abbr* a file extension for a rich text format file

Rt Hon. *abbr* Right Honourable

Ru *symbol* ruthenium

RU *abbr* **1** Rugby Union **2** are you (*in e-mails*)

Ruapehu /roo ə páy hoo/ active volcano in the centre of the North Island, New Zealand. Height 2,797 m/9,177 ft.

rub *v* (**rubbing**, **rubbed**) **1** *vt* move the hand or an object over the surface of something, pressing down with repeated circular or backwards and forwards movements **2** *vi* make dragging contact with a surface **3** *vti* cause soreness on the skin as a result of repeated friction ■ *n* **1** a rubbing action **2** a massage **3** a difficulty

□ **rub down** *vt* **1** dry a person's or animal's body after exercise by rubbing with a towel or cloth **2** massage somebody

□ **rub in** *vt* mention an error or failure repeatedly to annoy somebody (*infml*)

□ **rub off** *vi* be passed on

□ **rub out** *vti* remove or be removed with a rubber

Rub al-Khali /roob al kaáli/ desert region in SE Arabia

rubber[1] /rúbbər/ *n* **1** a natural elastic substance made from the dried sap of various tropical trees **2** an elastic synthetic substance using or resembling natural rubber **3** a piece of rubber used for erasing writing —**rubbery** *adj*

rubber[2] /rúbbər/ *n* **1** in card games, a deciding game **2** in card games, a match or session of play (*infml*)

rubber band *n* a rubber loop for holding things together

rubberize /rúbbə rīz/ (**-izing**, **-ized**), **rubberise** *vt* treat with rubber

rubberneck /rúbbər nek/ (*infml*) *n* somebody who gawks at people or things ■ *vi* gawk ◊ See note at **gaze**

rubber plant *n* a plant with thick glossy leaves and a rubbery sap, often grown as houseplant

rubber stamp *n* **1** a stamping device consisting of an embossed rubber pad that is inked **2** an automatic authorization or approval —**rubber-stamp** *vt*

rubbing /rúbbing/ *n* an impression of a surface made by covering it with paper and rubbing it with a drawing implement

rubbish /rúbbish/ *n* **1** waste material **2** worthless things **3** nonsense ■ *vt* dismiss as worthless (*infml*) —**rubbish** *adj* —**rubbishy** *adj*

rubble /rúbb'l/ *n* **1** fragments of broken buildings **2** rough stones used as filler or bulk between walls

rubdown /rúb down/ *n* a massage or vigorous drying after exercise

rubella /roo béllə/ *n* a contagious childhood disease that causes swelling of the lymph glands and a reddish rash (*technical*)

Rubens /roobənz/, **Peter Paul** (1577–1640) Flemish painter

Rubicon /roobikən, -kon/, **rubicon** *n* a point of no return

---

ORIGIN The **Rubicon** was a stream in N Italy (now called the Rubicone) that formerly constituted part of the boundary between Gaul and Italy. By crossing it with his army en route to Rome in 49 BC, Julius Caesar broke a law forbidding a general to lead an army out of his own province, and so committed himself to civil war against the Roman Senate and his rival Pompey.

---

rubicund /roobikənd/ *adj* having a healthy reddish skin colour (*literary*)

rubidium /roo biddi əm/ *n* (*symbol* **Rb**) a silvery-white radioactive chemical element. Use: photocells.

Rubinstein /roobin stīn/, **Artur** (1887–1982) Polish-born US pianist

ruble *n* MONEY = **rouble**

rubric /roobrik/ *n* **1** a printed title or heading **2** a category

ruby /roobi/ (*pl* **-bies**) *n* a red precious stone. Use: jewellery, manufacture of watches, precision instruments.

RUC *abbr* Royal Ulster Constabulary

ruck *n* **1** in rugby, a loose scrum **2** in Australian Rules football, a group of three roving players —**ruck** *vi*

rucksack /rúk sak, rook-/ *n* a bag carried on the back

ruckus /rúkəss/ *n* a noisy disturbance

rudder /rúddər/ *n* **1** a pivoting blade under the water at the stern of a ship for steering it **2** an aerofoil on the tail of an aircraft for steering it

ruddy /rúddi/ *adj* (**-dier, -diest**) **1** having a healthy reddish skin colour **2** reddish ■ *adj, adv* emphasizes how good or bad something is *(slang; sometimes offensive)* —**ruddiness** *n*

rude /rood/ (**ruder, rudest**) *adj* **1** ill-mannered or discourteous **2** sudden and unpleasant ○ *a rude awakening* **3** roughly made —**rudely** *adv* —**rudeness** *n*

rudiment /róodimənt/ *n* **1** something basic to a subject *(often pl)* **2** an undeveloped body part

rudimentary /róodi méntəri/ *adj* **1** basic **2** still developing

rue[1] /roo/ (**ruing, rued**) *vti* feel regret for something

rue[2] /roo/ (*pl* **rues** *or* **same**) *n* a flowering plant once used medicinally

rueful /róof'l/ *adj* regretful —**ruefully** *adv* —**ruefulness** *n*

ruff[1] /ruf/ *n* **1** a fancy pleated collar worn in the 16C and 17C **2** a growth of long bushy neck hair or feathers on an animal or bird —**ruffed** *adj* ◊ See note at **rough**

ruff[2] /ruf/ *n* in bridge or whist, the act of playing a trump card

ruffian /rúffi ən/ *n* somebody rough or violent *(dated)* —**ruffian** *adj* —**ruffianly** *adj*

ruffle /rúff'l/ *v* (**-fling, -fled**) **1** *vt* disorder somebody's hair **2** *vti* disturb or ripple a surface, or become disturbed or rippled **3** *vt* annoy somebody **4** *vt* make the feathers erect **5** *vt* gather or pleat material to use as trim ■ *n* **1** something uneven or disordered in a surface **2** something irritating **3** a trim of gathered or pleated fabric **4** a ruff on an animal or bird —**ruffled** *adj*

rufiyaa /roo fee yaa/ (*pl* **same**) *n* the main unit of currency in the Maldives

rug *n* **1** a fabric covering for an area of floor **2** a mat of animal skin

rugby /rúgbi/, **rugby football** *n* a team sport played with an oval ball that is passed by hand or kicked

ORIGIN The game was named after Rugby School, a public school in Warwickshire, where it was reputedly invented. Legend has it that a boy called William Webb Ellis picked up the ball and ran with it during an ordinary game of football in 1823. The name itself is first recorded in the 1860s.

rugged /rúggid/ *adj* **1** with a rough, irregular surface **2** strong-featured **3** physically resilient **4** strongly built —**ruggedly** *adv* —**ruggedness** *n*

rugger /rúggər/ *n* rugby *(infml)*

Ruhr /roor/ river in W Germany. Length 235 km/146 mi.

ruin /róo in/ *n* **1** the physical remains of a destroyed building or city *(often pl)* **2** a state of complete loss or destruction **3** a cause of destruction ■ *vt* **1** destroy something completely **2** destroy somebody financially **3** damage something beyond repair —**ruination** /róo i náysh'n/ *n* —**ruined** *adj*

ruinous /róo inəss/ *adj* **1** causing destruction **2** decayed or deteriorated beyond repair

rule /rool/ *n* **1** a principle governing conduct **2** a norm **3** a prevailing condition or quality **4** a governing or reigning power **5** a reign or period of government ■ *v* (**ruling, ruled**) **1** *vti* govern **2** *vti* dominate **3** *vt* make a straight line **4** *vt* control or restrain **5** *vti* issue a legal decision or order

□ **rule out** *vt* **1** exclude **2** prevent

rulebook /rool book/ *n* **1** a publication containing the rules of an activity **2** the approved way of doing something

ruler /róolər/ *n* **1** somebody who rules **2** a straight calibrated plastic, wood, or metal strip for measuring and for drawing straight lines

ruling /róoling/ *adj* **1** governing **2** most powerful ■ *n* an official or binding decision by an authority

rum[1] *n* an alcoholic spirit made from sugar cane

rum[2] (**rummer, rummest**) *adj* bizarre *(infml dated)*

rumba /rúmbə, room-/, **rhumba** *n* **1** a rhythmically complex Cuban dance **2** a ballroom dance based on the Cuban rumba **3** the music for a rumba ■ *vi* (**-bas, -baing, -baed**) dance a rumba

rumble /rúmb'l/ *v* (**-bling, -bled**) **1** *vi* make a deep rolling sound **2** *vt* say something with a deep rolling voice **3** *vi* NZ, US, Can take part in a street fight *(slang)* ■ *n* **1** a deep rolling sound **2** NZ, US, Can a street fight *(slang)*

rumbling /rúmbling/ *n* **1** a deep rolling sound **2** a first indication of discontent or an unpleasant event *(often pl)*

rumbustious /rum búschəss/ *adj* noisy and exuberant

rumen /róo men, róomən/ (*pl* **-mens** *or* **-mina** /róominə/) *n* the first stomach of a ruminant animal

ruminant /róominənt/ *n* any cud-chewing hoofed mammal with an even number of toes and a stomach with multiple chambers ■ *adj* **1** of ruminants **2** thoughtful and reflective

ruminate /róomi nayt/ *v* (**-nating, -nated**) **1** *vi* chew partially digested food *(refers to ruminants)* **2** *vi* think carefully about something —**rumination** /róomi náysh'n/ *n* —**ruminative** *adj*

rummage /rúmmij/ *v* (**-maging, -maged**) **1** *vti* search through things in an untidy way **2** *vt* find by rummaging ■ *n* an untidy search through things

rummage sale *n* US, Can a jumble sale

rummy /rúmmi/ *n* a card game in which players try to get cards of the same value or a run of cards of one suit

rumour /róomər/ *n* **1** an unverified report **2** idle speculation ■ *vt* pass on as a rumour

rumourmonger /róomər mung gər/ *n* somebody who habitually spreads rumours ■ *vi* spread rumours habitually

rump *n* **1** an animal's hindquarters **2** beef from an animal's hindquarters **3** somebody's buttocks *(infml)*

rumple /rúmp'l/ *vti* (**-pling**, **-pled**) make or become creased or unkempt ■ *n* a crease

rumpus /rúmpəss/ *n* a noisy disturbance

rumpus room *n* ANZ, US, Can a room in a house for parties and play

run *v* (**running**, **ran**, **run**) **1** *vi* go on foot fast **2** *vt* travel a particular distance by running **3** *vti* participate in a race **4** *vti* US, Can be or make somebody be a candidate in an election **5** *vti* perform something ○ *run a test* **6** *vti* leave or cause to leave quickly ○ *take the money and run* **7** *vt* speed across, over, or through something ○ *running the rapids* **8** *vt* transport ○ *ran me into town* **9** *vi* turn to somebody for help ○ *ran to his brother for money* **10** *vi* visit a place briefly ○ *ran out to the mountains for the weekend* **11** *vti* move smoothly over or through something ○ *ropes running easily through the pulleys* **12** *vi* enter a state or condition ○ *Supplies were running low.* **13** *vti* operate ○ *Let the engine run.* **14** *vt* direct the activities, affairs, or operation of something ○ *runs the whole department* **15** *vti* flow or cause to flow ○ *run a tap* **16** *vi* spread or leak undesirably ○ *The colours have run.* **17** *vi* range between particular limits ○ *The work ran from difficult to impossible.* **18** *vti* extend along a route or for a particular distance ○ *ran the cable under the road* **19** *vi* continue for a particular length or time ○ *a report running to ten pages* **20** *vt* experience something ○ *running a high temperature* **21** *vti* total a particular amount ○ *The bill runs to four figures.* **22** *vi* recur ○ *Stubbornness runs in the family.* **23** *vi* unravel (*refers to stitches*) ■ *n* **1** a fast pace on foot **2** a gallop **3** an act of running **4** a foot race **5** a regular trip **6** a distance or period covered **7** a brief trip **8** free use of a place ○ *the run of the house* **9** a period when a condition or circumstance prevails ○ *a run of bad luck* **10** an operating period of, e.g. a machine **11** a series of continuous performances **12** an urgent demand for something ○ *a run on coffee* **13** the general tendency of things ○ *the usual run of events* **14** an average or typical kind ○ *the general run of merchandise* **15** a place in a knitted garment with unravelled stitches **16** an animal enclosure **17** a baseball score made by travelling round all the bases ◇ **be on the run** be fleeing from somebody or something ◇ **give somebody a run for his** *or* **her money** provide somebody with serious competition

☐ **run across** *vt* encounter unexpectedly

☐ **run after** *vt* pursue

☐ **run along** *vi* leave (*usually a command*)

☐ **run away** *vi* flee or escape

☐ **run by** *or* **past** *vt* consult somebody about something

☐ **run down** *v* **1** *vti* stop or cause to stop functioning through loss of power **2** *vt* hit with a vehicle **3** *vt* belittle **4** *vt* catch eventually

☐ **run in** *vt* treat a vehicle carefully while it is still new

☐ **run into** *v* **1** *vt* encounter somebody or something by chance **2** *vti* collide or cause to collide with somebody or something

☐ **run off** *v* **1** *vi* leave in haste **2** *vt* make copies on a photocopier

☐ **run on** *vi* talk at length

☐ **run out** *vi* **1** come to an end **2** exhaust supplies

☐ **run over** *v* **1** *vt* knock down with a vehicle **2** *vti* go beyond a set limit **3** *vt* review

☐ **run through** *vt* **1** use up quickly **2** rehearse quickly

☐ **run up** *vt* **1** incur as an expense **2** make by sewing fast

☐ **run up against** *vt* encounter a problem unexpectedly

runabout /rúnnə bowt/ *n* **1** a small vehicle for short journeys **2** a wanderer

runaround /rún ə rownd/ *n* delaying or misleading tactics (*infml*)

runaway /rúnnə way/ *n* somebody who escapes ■ *adj* **1** escaped from captivity or harm **2** out of control **3** easily won (*infml*)

rundown /rún down/ *n* **1** a summary of the main points of something **2** a controlled reduction in something

run-down *adj* **1** tired and not in normal good health **2** shabby and neglected

rune /roon/ *n* **1** a character in an ancient Germanic alphabet **2** a magical symbol or spell —**runic** *adj*

rung[1] *n* **1** a step of a ladder **2** a crosspiece of a chair

rung[2] past participle of **ring**[2]

run-in *n* an argument (*infml*)

~~runing~~ incorrect spelling of **running**

runnel /rúnn'l/ *n* **1** a small stream **2** a narrow water channel

runner /rúnnər/ *n* **1** an athlete or horse in a race **2** a candidate in an election **3** a blade on a sledge or ice skate **4** a long narrow strip of carpet **5** a door or drawer slide **6** a messenger **7** a thin horizontal plant stem that grows roots **8** a smuggler (*often in combination*) ○ *gun runner* **9** a manager or operator of a business or machine **10** in American football, a player who carries the ball

runner bean *n* **1** a long flat green seed pod, cooked and eaten as a vegetable **2** a plant that produces runner beans

runner-up (*pl* **runners-up**) *n* **1** somebody in second place **2** a contestant or competitor who performs well

running /rúnning/ *n* the sport or exercise of running ■ *adj* **1** used or worn by runners ○ *running shoes* **2** long-standing ○ *a running joke* ■ *adv* consecutively ○ *for five days running* ◇ **be in** *or* **out of the running** have or not have a chance of success

running board *n* a narrow step beneath the doors of some early vehicles

running mate *n* US a nominee for a lesser office

runny /rúnni/ (**-nier**, **-niest**) *adj* **1** of a liquid consistency **2** releasing mucus —**runniness** *n*

runoff /rún of/ *n* **1** rainfall not absorbed by the soil **2** waste products carried by rainfall into surface waters **3** a tie-breaking contest

run-of-the-mill *adj* unexceptional

run-on *adj* added to a line of text without a line break ■ *n* **1** a section of text added without a line break **2** an undefined word appearing at the end of a dictionary entry

runs /runz/ *n* diarrhoea (*infml*; + *sing or pl verb*)

runt *n* **1** the smallest and weakest animal in a litter **2** somebody regarded as small and weak (*insult*) —**runty** *adj*

run-through *n* **1** a rehearsal **2** a brief review

runway /rún way/ *n* **1** a strip for aircraft landings and takeoffs **2** an extension of a stage into the audience

rupee /roo pée/ *n* the main unit of currency in India, Mauritius, Nepal, Pakistan, the Seychelles, and Sri Lanka

rupiah /roo pée ə/ (*pl* **-ahs** *or same*) *n* the main unit of Indonesian currency

rupture /rúpchər/ *n* **1** a break in or breaking apart of something **2** a tear in or tearing of bodily tissue ■ *vti* (**-turing, -tured**) **1** break, burst, or tear **2** cause or undergo a rift in a relationship **3** cause or undergo a tearing of bodily tissue

rural /roórəl/ *adj* **1** outside the city **2** characteristic of the countryside —**rurally** *adv*

ruse /rooz/ *n* something done to deceive others

rush[1] *v* **1** *vi* move fast **2** *vt* hurry somebody or something along **3** *vt* take or send somebody or something to a place urgently **4** *vt* do something hastily **5** *vt* attack suddenly ■ *n* **1** a hurry, or a need for hurry **2** a sudden fast movement by somebody towards a place **3** a busy time **4** a sudden great demand for something **5** a sudden attack **6** a sudden quick flow **7** a sudden surge of feeling ■ **rushes** *npl* the first unedited prints of film scenes ■ *adj* done or needing to be done quickly —**rushed** *adj*

rush[2] *n* **1** the stem of a plant that grows in wet areas. Use: weaving baskets and mats. **2** the plant from which rushes are obtained

rush hour *n* the peak period of travel to or from work

Rushmore, Mt /rúsh mawr/ mountain in the Black Hills, SW South Dakota, carved with the heads of US presidents Washington, Jefferson, Lincoln, and Theodore Roosevelt, a national memorial. Height 1,745 m/5,725 ft.

rusk *n* a sweet biscuit for babies and young children

Ruskin /rússkin/**, John** (1819–1900) British art and social critic

Russell /rúss'l/**, Bertrand, 3rd Earl Russell** (1872–1970) British philosopher and mathematician

russet /rússit/ *n* a reddish-brown colour —**russet** *adj*

Russia /rúshə/ country in E Europe and N Asia, extending from the Baltic Sea to the Pacific Ocean, and from the Arctic Ocean to the Caucasus. Cap. Moscow. Pop. 145,470,200 (2001).

Russian /rúsh'n/ *n* **1** somebody from Russia **2** the official language of Russia ■ *adj* **1** of Russia **2** of the former Soviet Union (*dated*)

Russian roulette *n* **1** a game in which people take turns aiming a revolver containing one bullet at their own heads **2** a dangerous action or activity

ORIGIN The game is 'Russian' because it was reportedly played by Russian officers in Romania in 1917, though their version of the game was even more deadly in that only one bullet was removed from the revolver.

rust *n* **1** a reddish-brown coating of iron oxide on iron or steel **2** a plant disease caused by a fungus ■ *vti* corrode with rust

rustic /rústik/ *adj* **1** of a country lifestyle **2** plain and simple ■ *n* somebody who lives in the country (*sometimes offensive*) —**rustically** *adv* —**rusticity** /ru stíssəti/ *n*

rustle[1] /rúss'l/ (**-tling, -tled**) *v* **1** *vti* make or cause to make a swishing or soft crackling sound **2** *vi* move with a rustling sound —**rustle** *n* —**rustlingly** *adv*

☐ **rustle up** *vt* prepare food quickly (*infml*)

rustle[2] /rúss'l/ (**-tling, -tled**) *vti US, Can* steal livestock —**rustler** *n*

rustproof /rúst proof/ *adj* not susceptible to rust ■ *vt* make metal rustproof —**rustproofing** *n*

rusty /rústi/ (**-ier, -iest**) *adj* **1** corroded **2** out of practice **3** old or old-fashioned —**rustily** *adv* —**rustiness** *n*

rut[1] *n* **1** a narrow groove made by a vehicle wheel **2** a boring situation ■ *vt* (**rutting, rutted**) make ruts in

rut[2] *n* an annual period of sexual excitement in male ruminants —**rut** *vi* —**ruttish** *adj*

ruthenium /roo theeni əm/ *n* (*symbol* **Ru**) a white metallic element. Use: hardening of platinum and palladium alloys.

Rutherford /rúthər furd/**, Ernest, 1st Baron Rutherford of Nelson and Cambridge** (1871–1937) New Zealand-born British physicist. He discovered the nuclear structure of the atom (1909).

rutherfordium /rúthər fáwrdi əm/ *n* (*symbol* **Rf**) a radioactive chemical element produced artificially in atomic collisions

ruthless /roóthləss/ *adj* having or showing no pity —**ruthlessly** *adv* —**ruthlessness** *n*

Rutland /rúttlənd/ county in central England

Rwanda /roō ándə/ country in east-central Africa. Cap. Kigali. Pop. 7,312,756 (2001). —**Rwandan** *n, adj*—**Rwandese** /roō ən déez/ *n, adj*

rye /rī/ *n* **1** the edible seeds of a cereal plant, also used to produce whisky **2** a cereal plant that produces rye grains **3** *also* **rye whisky** a whisky distilled from fermented rye

ryme incorrect spelling of **rhyme**

rythm incorrect spelling of **rhythm**

Ryukyu Islands /ri oókoo-/ archipelago in SW Japan. Pop. 1,222,458 (1990).

S

s[1] (*pl* **s's**), **S** (*pl* **S's** *or* **Ss**) *n* the 19th letter of the English alphabet

s[2] *symbol* second

S[1] *symbol* **1** entropy **2** sulphur

S[2] *abbr* **1** small (*in clothes sizes*) **2** south

-'s *suffix* forms the possessive of nouns ○ *school's* ○ *men's*

-s, -es *suffix* **1** forms the plural of many regular nouns ○ *dogs* ○ *bananas* **2** forms the 3rd person present singular of regular verbs and most irregular verbs ○ *speaks*

SA *abbr* **1** South Africa **2** South America **3** South Australia

SAA *abbr* systems application architecture

saag *n* S *Asia* spinach

Sabbath /sábbəth/ *n* **1** Sunday as a day of Christian religious worship and rest **2** in Judaism and some Christian groups, Saturday as a day of worship and rest

sabbatical /sə báttik'l/, **sabbatic** /-báttik/ *n* a period of leave from work for research, study, or travel —**sabbatical** *adj*

saber *n* US = sabre

sable /sáyb'l/ *n* **1** a marten with soft dark fur **2** sable fur

sabotage /sábbə taazh/ *n* **1** deliberate damaging or destroying of property or equipment, e.g. by enemy agents or disgruntled workers **2** an action taken to hinder somebody's efforts —**sabotage** *vt*

ORIGIN **Sabotage** derives ultimately from a French word meaning 'clog'. The underlying idea was of clattering along in clogs. Through the implication of clumsiness, this came to mean 'do work badly', and then 'destroy deliberately'.

saboteur /sábbə túr/ *n* somebody who sabotages property or equipment

sabre /sáybər/ *n* **1** a heavy sword with a curved blade **2** a fencing sword with a tapering blade

sabre-rattling *n* an aggressive show of force

sabre-toothed tiger, sabre-toothed cat *n* an extinct member of the cat family with long curving upper canine teeth

sac /sak/ *n* a small bag or pouch formed by a membrane in an animal or plant

SPELLCHECK Do not confuse the spelling of **sac** and **sack** ('a large bag'), which sound similar.

saccharin /sákərin/ *n* $C_7H_5NO_3S$ a white crystalline compound. Use: sugar substitute.

saccharine /sákə reen, -rīn, -rin/ *adj* **1** of or like sugar **2** too sweet and insincere

sacerdotal /sássər dốt'l, sákər-/ *adj* of a priest or the priesthood

sachet /sásh ay/ *n* **1** a small envelope of powder, cream, or liquid **2** a bag containing perfumed powder or potpourri for scenting clothes

sack[1] /sak/ *n* **1** a large bag made of coarse cloth or heavy paper **2** dismissal from a job (*infml*) **3** a bed (*infml*) ■ *vt* **1** dismiss from employment (*infml*) **2** put in a sack —**sacker** *n* ◇ **hit the sack** go to bed (*infml*) ◊ See note at **sac**

ORIGIN The two words **sack** entered English by different routes, but are ultimately related. **Sack** 'bag' is derived from Latin *saccus*, which is of Semitic origin. **Sack** 'destroy and plunder' goes back to the same Latin word, probably through the idea of carrying off plunder in bags, but came through Italian and French.

sack[2] /sak/ *vt* destroy and plunder —**sack** *n*

sack[3] /sak/ *n* dry white wine from Spain, Portugal, or the Canary Islands (*archaic*)

sackcloth /sák kloth/ *n* **1** coarse cloth for sacks **2** clothes made from sackcloth worn in mourning or penitence ◇ **sackcloth and ashes** a show of mourning or repentance

sacking /sáking/ *n* coarse cloth made from hemp or jute. Use: sacks.

sack race *n* a race in which competitors jump along in a sack

sacra plural of **sacrum**

~~sacrafice~~ incorrect spelling of **sacrifice**

sacrament /sákrəmənt/ *n* **1** a Christian religious rite or ceremony considered to bring divine grace **2** *also* **Sacrament** the consecrated elements of the Christian Communion

Sacramento /sákrə méntō/ capital of California, on the **Sacramento River**. Pop. 404,168 (1998).

sacred /sáykrid/ *adj* **1** dedicated to a deity or a religious purpose **2** of religion **3** worthy of worship or respect **4** dedicated to or in honour of somebody —**sacredness** *n*

sacred cow *n* somebody or something exempt from criticism

~~sacreligious~~ incorrect spelling of **sacrilegious**

sacrifice /sákri fiss/ *n* **1** the giving up of somebody or something valuable in exchange for something or something considered more worthwhile **2** something valued and given up **3** something or somebody offered to a god ■ *v* (**-ficing, -ficed**) **1** *vt* give up as a sacrifice **2** *vti* make an offering of an animal or person to a god —**sacrificeable** *adj* —**sacrificial** /sákri fish'l/ *adj*

sacrilege /sákrilij/ *n* **1** theft or desecration of something considered holy **2** disrespect towards something others consider worthy of respect —**sacrilegious** /sákri líjjəss/ *adj*

sacristan /sákristən/, **sacrist** /sákrist, sáy-/ *n* **1** somebody responsible for objects kept in a Christian church **2** a sexton (*dated*)

sacristy /sákristi/ *n* (*pl* **-ties**) *n* a room for sacred objects in a Christian church

sacroiliac /sáykrō ílli ak, sák-/ *adj* of the bones joining the back and the hip

sacrosanct /sákrŏ sangkt/ *adj* **1** sacred **2** not to be criticized or tampered with

sacrum /sáykrəm, sák-/ (*pl* **-crums** *or* **-cra** /-krə/) *n* a triangular bone in the lower back

sad (**sadder**, **saddest**) *adj* **1** feeling or showing unhappiness **2** causing or containing unhappiness ○ *sad news* **3** regrettable ○ *the sad fact is* **4** pitiable or contemptible (*slang*) —**sadly** *adv* —**sadness** *n*

ORIGIN Sad originally meant 'satisfied' or 'sated' and is related to Latin *satis* 'enough'. The modern senses developed through 'weary' and 'dignified, grave, solemn'.

SAD *abbr* seasonal affective disorder

AKG London

Anwar al-Sadat

Sadat /sə dát/**, Anwar al-** (1918–81) president of Egypt (1970–81)

sadden /sádd'n/ *vti* make or become sad

saddhu *n* HINDUISM = sadhu

saddle /sádd'l/ *n* **1** a seat for riding an animal **2** a seat on a bicycle or motorcycle **3** a cut of meat including part of the backbone and both loins ■ *vt* (**-dling**, **-dled**) strap a saddle onto ◇ **in the saddle** in control

□ **saddle with** *vt* burden somebody with something

saddlebag /sádd'l bag/ *n* a bag attached to a saddle on a horse, bicycle, or motorcycle

saddler /sáddlər/ *n* a maker, repairer, or seller of saddlery

saddlery /sáddləri/ (*pl* **-ies**) *n* **1** saddles and other equipment for horses **2** the job of a saddler **3** a saddler's shop

saddle sore *n* a sore on a rider's buttocks or leg caused by the rubbing of a saddle —**saddle-sore** *adj*

Sadducee /sáddyŏŏ see/ *n* a member of an ancient Jewish group of priests and aristocrats —**Sadducean** /sáddyŏŏ sée ən/ *adj* —**Sadduceeism** *n*

Sade /saad/**, Marquis de** (1740–1814) French philosopher and novelist

sadhu /sáadoo/**, saddhu** *n* in Hinduism, a holy beggar

sadism /sáydizəm/ *n* the deriving of pleasure, especially sexual pleasure, from inflicting pain on others —**sadist** *n* —**sadistic** /sə dístik/ *adj* —**sadistically** *adv*

ORIGIN Sadism is named after the French writer and philosopher the Marquis de Sade.

sadomasochism /sáydō mássəkizəm/ *n* sexual practices involving sadism and masochism

—**sadomasochist** *n* —**sadomasochistic** /sáydō mássə kístik/ *adj*

s.a.e., SAE *abbr* **1** self-addressed envelope **2** stamped addressed envelope

Safar /sə faár/ *n* the 2nd month of the year in the Islamic calendar

safari /sə faári/ *n* a cross-country expedition, especially in Africa, to hunt or observe wild animals

safari park *n* a zoo where animals roam relatively freely in large enclosed spaces and are observed from vehicles

safe *adj* (**safer**, **safest**) **1** not dangerous **2** not in danger **3** unharmed or undamaged **4** sure to be successful ○ *a safe bet* **5** probably correct ○ *safe to assume that* **6** cautious and conservative ■ *n* a strong metal container for valuables —**safely** *adv* —**safeness** *n*

safe-conduct *n* **1** the official guaranteeing of a traveller's safety **2** a document or escort guaranteeing a traveller's safety

safe-deposit box *n* a strong metal box for storing valuables at a bank

safeguard /sáyf gaard/ *n* a protective measure ■ *vt* keep safe

SYNONYMS **safeguard, protect, defend, guard, shield** CORE MEANING: keep safe from actual or potential damage or attack

safe house *n* a house used as a hiding-place from enemies or pursuers

safekeeping /sáyf keéping/ *n* protection from harm, damage, loss, or theft

safe seat *n* a parliamentary seat that is unlikely to be lost to another party

safe sex *n* sexual activity in which precautions are taken to prevent the spread of sexually transmitted disease

safety /sáyfti/ *n* **1** freedom from danger **2** lack of danger **3** a safe place or situation **4** the fact of being unharmed or undamaged ○ *She led them to safety.*

safety belt *n* **1** a seat belt in a car **2** a strap to prevent somebody from falling

safety catch *n* a device preventing the unintentional operation of a mechanism

safety curtain *n* a fireproof curtain in a theatre at the front of the stage

safety glass *n* shatterproof glass

safety match *n* a match that has to be struck against a special surface in order to be lit

safety net *n* **1** a net below a high place to catch somebody falling **2** something intended to help people in the event of difficulty or hardship

safety pin *n* a loop-shaped pin that fastens into itself with its point under a cover

safety razor *n* a razor with a partially covered blade to minimize the risk of accidental injury

safety valve *n* **1** a valve that releases fluid when pressure reaches a dangerous level **2** a means of releasing emotion or energy

safflower /sá flow ər/ n 1 a plant with orange or red flowers. Use: dye, cooking oil, paints, medicines. 2 dried flowers of the safflower, or a red dye made from them

saffron /sáffrən/ n 1 a spice made from the stigmas of a crocus. Use: food colourant or flavouring. 2 a bright orange-yellow colour —**saffron** adj

~~saftey, safty~~ incorrect spelling of **safety**

sag (**sagging**, **sagged**) v 1 vti bend under weight 2 vi become weaker or lose enthusiasm —**saggy** adj

saga /saágə/ n 1 an epic tale in Norse literature 2 a long novel or series of novels 3 a long and complicated series of events (infml)

sagacious /sə gáyshəss/ adj wise or shrewd —**sagacity** /sə gássəti/ n

sage[1] (literary) n a wise person ■ adj wise —**sagely** adv —**sageness** n

sage[2] (pl **sages** or same) n 1 a plant with aromatic greyish-green leaves. Use: flavouring food. 2 a sagebrush

sagebrush /sáyj brush/ (pl -**brushes** or same) n a bush with silvery wedge-shaped leaves and large flower clusters

Sagittarius /sájji táiri əss/ n 1 a zodiacal constellation in the southern hemisphere 2 the 9th sign of the zodiac —**Sagittarian** adj, n

sago /sáygō/ n a starchy substance obtained from the pith of a palm. Use: cookery, stiffening fabric.

Sahara /sə haárə/ largest desert in the world, covering much of North Africa —**Saharan** adj, n

Sahel /sə hél/ dry zone in North Africa, extending from Sudan westwards to Senegal

sahib /saab, saá hib, -ib/, **saheb** /saab, saá heb/ n S Asia a polite form of address for European men used in South Asia in colonial times

said /sed/ v past tense, past participle of **say** ■ adj previously mentioned o discovered the said car

Saigon /sī gón/ former name for **Ho Chi Minh City**

sail /sayl/ n 1 a large piece of fabric for catching the wind to propel a boat 2 a trip or voyage in a boat or ship, especially one with a sail or sails 3 the sails of a vessel collectively o under full sail 4 something resembling a sail in form or function ■ v 1 vti travel by boat or ship across a stretch of water 2 vti move across water driven by wind or engine power o ships that sailed the seas 3 vt control the movements of a boat or ship, especially using sails 4 vi begin a sea journey o We sail at noon. 5 vi move smoothly or swiftly —**sailing** n ◇ **set sail** depart in a boat or ship ◇ **under sail** with sails hoisted, and not propelled by an engine

> **SPELLCHECK** Do not confuse the spelling of **sail** and **sale** (of goods), which sound similar.

□ **sail through** vti do something with ease

sailboard /sáyl bawrd/ n a surfboard with a sail —**sailboard** vi —**sailboarder** n

sailcloth /sáyl kloth/ n 1 strong fabric for sails 2 a lightweight cotton fabric with a texture like canvas. Use: clothes.

sailing boat n a boat with a sail or sails

sailing ship n a ship with sails

sailor /sáylər/ n 1 somebody who serves in the navy or works on a ship 2 somebody on a boat or ship, especially in relation to sport or seasickness o a weekend sailor o a poor sailor

sailplane /sáyl playn/ n a light glider —**sailplane** vi —**sailplaner** n

saint stressed /saynt/ unstressed /sənt, sən/ n 1 in Christianity, somebody formally recognized after death as having led a holy life 2 a virtuous person ■ vt in Christianity, declare officially to be a saint —**sainted** adj —**sainthood** n —**saintliness** n —**saintly** adj

St Bernard /-búrnərd/ n a large dog bred to rescue lost mountain travellers

St Catharines /sənt káth'rinz/ city in SE Ontario, Canada. Pop. 130,926 (1996).

Saint-Exupéry /sánt eg zoópe ree/, **Antoine Marie Roger de** (1900–44) French aviator and writer

St Helena /-hə leénə/ British island in the S Atlantic Ocean, off the coast of West Africa, the site of Napoleon's death in exile in 1821. Pop. 7,266 (2001).

St Helens, Mt /-héllənz/ active volcano in SW Washington State. Height 2,550 m/8,365 ft.

St John's /-jónz/ 1 capital of Newfoundland, Canada. Pop. 101,936 (1996). 2 capital of Antigua and Barbuda. Pop. 23,000 (1990).

St Kitts and Nevis /-kits ənd neéviss/ independent state in the Caribbean, comprising two islands of the Leeward Islands group. Cap. Basseterre. Pop. 38,756 (2001).

St Lawrence /-lórrənss/ river in SE Canada, flowing northeastwards from Lake Ontario into the Gulf of St Lawrence. Length 1,300 km/800 mi.

St Lawrence, Gulf of deep inlet of the Atlantic Ocean between Newfoundland and the Canadian mainland

St Lawrence Seaway waterway in SE Canada and the NE United States that permits oceangoing vessels to navigate between the Atlantic Ocean and the Great Lakes

St Louis /-loŏ iss, -loŏ i/ city in E Missouri, on the Mississippi River. Pop. 339,316 (1998).

St-Louis /sáN loo eé/ port in NW Senegal. Pop. 132,499 (1994).

St Lucia /-loŏshə/ independent island state in the Caribbean, one of the Windward Islands. Cap. Castries. Pop. 158,178 (2001).

St Martin /-maártin/ one of the Leeward Islands, divided between a dependency of Guadeloupe in the north and part of the Netherlands Antilles in the south. Pop. 65,774 (1994).

St Paul /-páwl/ capital of Minnesota. Pop. 257,284 (1998).

St Petersburg /-peétərz burg/ second-largest city in Russia. Pop. 5,149,689 (1995).

Saint-Saëns /sáN sóNss, -sóN/, **Camille** (1835–1921) French composer

saint's day n a day commemorating a specific saint

St Valentine's Day /-vállontīnz-/ n the day on which valentines are traditionally sent. Date: 14 February

St Vincent and the Grenadines /-vínsant ənd thə grénnə deenz/ independent state in the Caribbean comprising the island of St Vincent and 32 of the islands of the Grenadine group. Cap. Kingstown. Pop. 115,942 (2001).

sake[1] /sayk/ n **1** somebody's or something's good, benefit, or welfare o *for my sake* **2** the motive for or objective of something o *for the sake of arriving early*

sake[2] /saáki/, **saki, saké** n a Japanese alcoholic drink made from fermented rice

Sakhalin /sákə leēn/ island of E Russia, in the Sea of Okhotsk. Pop. 660,000 (1983).

Sakharov /sákərov/, **Andrei Dmitriyevich** (1921–89) Soviet physicist and political dissident

salaam /sə laàm/ n a deep bow with the palm of the right hand on the forehead —**salaam** vti

salable adj = saleable

salacious /sə láyshəss/ adj explicitly sexual or lewd —**salaciously** adv —**salacity** /sə lássəti/ n

salad /sálləd/ n **1** a dish made of a mixture of raw vegetables **2** a cold dish of a particular food or type of food o *fruit salad* o *potato salad* **3** a dish of a particular food accompanied by salad o *chicken salad*

salad bar n a counter in a shop or restaurant serving or selling salads

salad cream n a creamy dressing for eating with salad

salad dressing n a sauce for putting on salad

Saladin /sálpədin/ (1138–93) sultan of Egypt and Syria (1174–93)

Salamanca /sállə mángkə/ city in west-central Spain. Pop. 158,457 (1998).

salamander /sállə mandər/ n a small amphibious animal resembling a lizard

salami /sə laàmi/ n a spicy sausage, usually served cold in thin slices

salary /sálləri/ (pl -ries) n a fixed sum of money paid at regular intervals to an employee —**salaried** adj ◊ See note at **wage**

ORIGIN The first **salary** was money paid to soldiers in the army of ancient Rome for the purchase of salt (Latin *sal*). Salt was then a valued and valuable commodity.

salaryman /sálləri man/ (pl -men /-men/) n in Japan, a loyal and unambitious employee of a large company

sale /sayl/ n **1** the selling of goods or services **2** a period of time when a shop sells goods at a discount **3** an event at which second-hand goods are sold **4** an auction **5** an

amount sold (often pl) ◊ **for sale** available for purchase ◊ See note at **sail**

saleable /sáylab'l/, **salable** adj suitable for selling —**saleability** /sáylə bílləti/ n

Salem /sáyləm/ **1** city in NE Massachusetts, site of witchcraft trials in 1692. Pop. 38,351 (1998). **2** capital of Oregon. Pop. 126,702 (1998).

sale of work n a sale of handicrafts

Salerno /sə lúrnō/ capital of **Salerno Province**, Italy. Pop. 142,458 (1999).

saleroom /sáyl room, -rōōm/ n a place where goods are sold by auction

~~salery~~ incorrect spelling of **salary**

sales assistant n a shop assistant

sales force n a body of salespeople employed by a company

salesman /sáylzmən/ (pl -men /-mən/) n a man employed to sell goods or services

salesperson /sáylz purss'n/ (pl -people /-peep'l/ or -persons) n somebody employed to sell goods or services

sales pitch n the statements, arguments, or assurances made by somebody trying to sell something

sales representative n somebody who visits prospective customers to sell a company's products

sales resistance n buyers' opposition to a seller's tactics

sales tax n a government tax on retail merchandise collected at the point of sale by the retailer

sales team n the body of salespeople employed by a company

saleswoman /sáylz wōōmən/ (pl -en /-wimin/) n a woman employed to sell goods or services

salicylic acid /sálli síllik-/ n a white crystalline acid. Use: preservative, manufacture of aspirin and dyes.

salient adj **1** particularly noticeable, striking, or relevant **2** projecting from a surface —**salience** n —**saliency** n

saline /sáy līn/ adj containing salt —**salinity** /sə línnəti/ n

Salinger /sállinjər/, **J. D.** (b. 1919) US writer

Salisbury Plain /sáwlzbəri-, -bri-/ area of rolling, chalky downs in SW England, site of Stonehenge

saliva /sə līvə/ n the liquid secreted by glands into the mouth in mammals

salivary gland /sə līvəri-, sállivəri-/ n a saliva-producing gland

salivate /sálli vayt/ (-vating, -vated) vi produce saliva, especially in expectation of food —**salivation** /sálli váysh'n/ n

Salk /sawk/, **Jonas** (1914–95) US physician and epidemiologist. He developed the first vaccine against polio.

sallow[1] /sállō/ adj unnaturally pale and yellowish —**sallowness** n

sallow[2] /sállō/ (pl -lows or same) n a willow tree

sally /sálli/ *n* (*pl* -**lies**) **1** an attack from a defensive position **2** a sudden rush forward **3** a witty remark ■ *vi* (-**lies**, -**lied**) **1** make a sally from a defensive position **2** set out from indoors or on an excursion

salmon /sámmən/ (*pl same or* -**ons**) *n* **1** a large fish that migrates up freshwater rivers to spawn **2** the pinkish flesh of the salmon as food

salmonella /sálmə néllə/ (*pl* -**lae** /-lee/) *n* a bacterium that can cause food poisoning

salon /sállon/ *n* **1** an elegant sitting room in a large house **2** a social gathering of intellectuals **3** a place for hairdressing or beauty treatments

Salonika /sə lónnikə/ ♦ **Thessaloníki**

saloon /sə loón/ *n* **1** *also* **saloon car** *UK* a car with a fixed roof, four to six seats, and a separate boot **2** *also* **saloon bar** a comfortable bar in a pub **3** in North America, a place where alcohol can be bought and drunk **4** a large room on a ship for passengers to sit in **5** *S Asia* a barber's shop

salsa /sálssə/ *n* **1** a spicy sauce of chopped vegetables eaten with Mexican foods **2** Latin American dance music combining jazz and rock elements with Cuban melodies

salt /sawlt, solt/ *n* **1** small white crystals consisting largely of sodium chloride. Use: food seasoning and preservative. **2** a crystalline chemical compound formed from the neutralization of an acid by a base containing a metal or group acting like a metal **3** something that adds zest **4** dry wit **5** a sailor with long experience ■ **salts** *npl* a chemical or crystalline solution used for a particular purpose ○ *smelling salts* ■ *adj* **1** preserved with salt ○ *salt cod* **2** containing salt ○ *salt tears* **3** containing or associated with salt water ○ *a salt marsh* ■ *vt* season, preserve, or treat with salt ◇ **take with a grain** *or* **pinch of salt** listen to without fully believing ◇ **the salt of the earth** a very good, worthy person or group ◇ **worth your salt** productive
☐ **salt away** *vt* put money aside for future use

SALT /sawlt, solt/ *abbr* Strategic Arms Limitation Talks (or Treaty)

saltbox /sáwlt boks, sólt-/ *n* a box for storing salt, usually with a sloping lid

saltcellar /sáwlt selər, sólt-/ *n* a small container for salt, especially one for use at table

---

ORIGIN Saltcellars are not etymologically cellars. The second part represents *saler*, an old word that itself meant 'saltcellar'. The strictly redundant *salt* had been added, and the spelling changed to *cellar*, before *saler* finally fell into disuse in the early 16C. It had come into English from French, and goes back to Latin *sal* 'salt'.

Salt Lake City capital of Utah. Pop. 174,348 (1998).

salt marsh *n* a marsh that regularly floods with salt water

saltpeter *n US* = **saltpetre**

saltpetre /sawlt peetər, solt-/ *n* **1** sodium nitrate **2** potassium nitrate

salt water *n* **1** water containing a lot of salt **2** seawater

saltwater /sáwlt wawtər, sólt-/ *adj* **1** consisting of or containing salt water **2** living in salt water

salty /sáwlti, sólti/ (-**ier**, -**iest**) *adj* **1** tasting of salt **2** lively and amusing and sometimes mildly indecent —**saltiness** *n*

salubrious /sə loóbri əss/ *adj* good for the health —**salubrity** *n*

salutary /sállyōotəri/ *adj* **1** useful or valuable **2** healthful *(fml)*

salutation /sállyōo táysh'n/ *n* **1** an expression or act of greeting **2** the opening phrase of a letter or speech

salute /sə loót/ *v* (-**luting**, -**luted**) **1** *vti* give a formal gesture of respect to another member of the armed forces or to a flag **2** *vt* greet **3** *vt* formally praise or honour ■ *n* **1** an act of saluting somebody or something **2** a firing of guns as a military honour

Salvador /sálvə dawr/ capital of Bahia State, E Brazil. Pop. 2,211,539 (1996).

Salvador, El ♦ **El Salvador**

Salvadoran /sálvə dáwrən/, **Salvadorian** /-dáwri ən/, **Salvadorean** *n* somebody from El Salvador ■ *adj* of El Salvador

salvage /sálvij/ *vt* (-**vaging**, -**vaged**) save something from destruction or loss ■ *n* **1** the rescue of property from destruction or loss **2** the rescue of a ship or its cargo or crew from the sea **3** rescued goods —**salvageable** *adj*

salvation /sal váysh'n/ *n* **1** the saving of somebody or something from harm or loss **2** a means of salvation **3** in Christian doctrine, deliverance from sin through Jesus Christ —**salvational** *adj*

Salvation Army *n* a worldwide evangelical Christian organization that provides help to those in need

salve[1] /salv/ *n* **1** a soothing ointment **2** something that eases worry or distress ■ *vt* (**salving, salved**) ease pain, worry, or distress

salve[2] (**salving, salved**) *vt* salvage

salver /sálvər/ *n* a serving tray

ORIGIN A **salver** is etymologically for making something safe, and in actuality was used for presenting food that had been tested for poison to the Spanish king. It came through French *salve* from Spanish *salva* in the mid-17C, but on entering English was altered on the model of *platter* or some similar word.

---

salvo /sálvō/ (*pl* -**vos** *or* -**voes**) *n* **1** a simultaneous discharge of weapons **2** a heavy burst of bombing, or the bombs so released **3** an outburst of applause or cheering

sal volatile /sál və láttəli/ *n* a solution of ammonium carbonate used as smelling salts

salwar /shál vaar/, **shalwar** *n* South Asian women's loose trousers

Salween /sál ween/ river in Southeast Asia, flowing through SW China and Myanmar into the Gulf of Martaban. Length 2,800 km/1,740 mi.

Salzburg /sálts burg/ capital of **Salzburg Province**, W Austria. Pop. 143,991 (1999).

SAM /sam/ *abbr* surface-to-air missile

Samaria /sə máiri ə/ city and state in ancient Palestine, in present-day NW Jordan —**Samarian** *n, adj*

Samaritan /sə márritən/ *n* 1 somebody from Samaria 2 a helper of somebody in trouble ■ **Samaritans** *npl* an organization that runs a telephone helpline for people in crisis —**Samaritanism** *n*

samarium /sə máiri əm/ *n* (*symbol* **Sm**) silvery-grey metallic element. Use: strong magnets, carbon-arc lighting, laser materials, neutron absorber.

Samarkand /sámmaar kánd, sámmər kand/, **Samarqand** city in S Uzbekistan. Pop. 368,000 (1994).

samba /sámbə/ *n* 1 a Brazilian dance with strong African influences 2 the music for a samba —**samba** *vi*

same *adj, pron, adv* 1 alike in every significant respect ○ *the same age* ○ *thinks much the same* ○ *look the same* 2 not changed or changing ○ *wore the same hat as yesterday* ■ *adj, pron* previously mentioned or described ○ *went because he was bored and I left for the same reason* —**sameness** *n*

same-sex *adj* of homosexual men or women

samey /sáymi/ *adj* boringly unchanging (*infml*)

Sami /saámi/ (*pl* **same** *or* **-mis**) *n* a member of an indigenous people of Lapland

Samoa /sə mó ə/ island country in the S Pacific Ocean. Cap. Apia. Pop. 179,058 (2001). —**Samoan** *n, adj*

samosa /sə mósə, -mózə/ (*pl* **-sas** *or* **same**) *n* a spicy South Asian pastry

samovar /sámə vaar/ *n* a large Russian tea urn

sampan /sám pan/ *n* a small Southeast Asian boat with a flat bottom

sample /saámp'l/ *n* 1 a small amount used as an example of something 2 a piece of recorded sound taken from an existing recording ■ *vti* (**-pling, -pled**) take a sample of something

sampler /saámplər/ *n* 1 somebody who tests samples for quality 2 a representative selection 3 an embroidered cloth containing rows of different stitches 4 an electronic equipment for sampling musical phrases

Samson /sámss'n/ *n* a very strong man —**Samsonian** /sam sóni ən/ *adj*

ORIGIN In the Bible, Samson was an Israelite judge and warrior who used his enormous strength to fight the Philistines.

samurai /sámmoŏ rī, sámmyoŏ-/ (*pl* **same** *or* **-rais**) *n* a member of the former aristocratic Japanese warrior class

San[1] *n* used as a title, usually in placenames, before the name of a male saint

San[2] (*pl* **same** *or* **Sans**) *n* a member of a southern African people

San Andreas Fault /-an dráy əss-/ *n* a geological fault zone in California

San Antonio /-an tóni ō/ city in south-central Texas. Pop. 1,114,130 (1998).

sanatorium /sánnə táwri əm/ (*pl* **-ums** *or* **-a** /-táwri ə/) *n* 1 a medical facility for long-term illness 2 a health resort (*dated*)

sanctify /sángkti fī/ (**-fies, -fied**) *vt* 1 make holy 2 free from sin 3 give a religious blessing to ○ *sanctified the marriage* —**sanctification** /sángktifi káysh'n/ *n*

sanctimonious /sángkti mốni əss/ *adj* making an exaggerated show of holiness or moral superiority (*disapproving*) —**sanctimoniously** *adv* —**sanctimony** /sángktiməni/ *n*

sanction /sángksh'n/ *n* 1 official authorization 2 a penalty imposed for breaking a rule 3 a punitive measure to pressure a country to conform to international law or opinion (*often pl*) ○ *imposed trade sanctions* ■ *vt* 1 authorize 2 approve of —**sanctionable** *adj*

sanctity /sángktəti/ *n* sacredness or holiness

sanctuary /sángkchoo əri/ (*pl* **-ies**) *n* 1 a place of refuge 2 the safety provided by a refuge 3 a place where wildlife is protected 4 a holy place such as a church, temple, or mosque

sanctum /sángktəm/ (*pl* **-tums** *or* **-ta** /-tə/) *n* 1 a sacred inner place 2 a quiet private place

sand /sand/ *n* 1 material made of tiny grains of rock and minerals, found especially on beaches and in deserts 2 an area of sand ■ *vt* 1 smooth using sandpaper 2 sprinkle or fill with sand

Sand /saan, saaN/, **George** (1804–76) French writer

sandal /sánd'l/ *n* a light open shoe with straps —**sandalled** *adj*

ORIGIN Sandals have no etymological connection with *sandalwood*, though they were in fact originally made of wood. **Sandal** derives through Latin from Greek, though its exact origins are unknown they are probably in an Asian language. *Sandal* in *sandalwood* goes back through Greek, Persian, and Arabic to a known Sanskrit word.

sandalwood /sánd'l woŏd/ *n* 1 the fragrant wood of a tropical evergreen tree. Use: furniture-making, incense. 2 an aromatic oil extracted from sandalwood. Use: perfumes, incense, aromatherapy oil.

sandbag /sánd bag/ *n* 1 a sealed sack of sand. Use: building defences, as ballast. 2 a small bag of sand used as a weapon ■ *vt* (**-bagging, -bagged**) protect with sandbags —**sandbagger** *n*

sandbank /sánd bangk/ *n* a mound of sand that is usually submerged

sandbar /sánd baar/ *n* a long ridge of sand caused by currents or the tide

sandcastle /sánd kaass'l/ *n* a small model of a castle made of damp sand

sander /sándər/ n a power tool for smoothing surfaces

sandfly /sánd flī/ n a tropical biting fly resembling a moth

San Diego /-di áygō/ city in SW California, on San Diego Bay. Pop. 1,220,666 (1998).

sandman /sánd man/ n in folklore, a character who makes children sleep by sprinkling sand in their eyes

sandpaper /sánd paypər/ n strong paper coated on one side with sand or another abrasive material ■ vt smooth using sandpaper

sandpiper /sánd pīpər/ (pl **-pers** or same) n a long-billed shore bird

sandpit /sánd pit/ n 1 a contained area of sand for children to play in 2 a pit for excavating sand

sandshoe /sánd shoo/ n a light canvas shoe

sandstone /sánd stōn/ n a type of rock made of sand bound together with a mineral cement

sandstorm /sánd stawrm/ n a strong wind carrying sand

sandwich /sánwij, -wich/ n 1 a snack consisting of slices of bread with a filling in between 2 something arranged in layers or made up of things squashed together ■ vt fit tightly between two other things or people in space or time

ORIGIN The **sandwich** was named after John Montague, 4th earl of Sandwich (1718–92). He is said to have been so addicted to the gambling table that in order to sustain him through an entire 24-hour session uninterrupted, he had a portable meal of cold beef between slices of toast brought to him. The idea was not new, but the earl's patronage ensured that it became a vogue.

sandwich board n 1 a pair of boards carrying notices hanging from the shoulders 2 one board of a sandwich board

sandwich course n an educational course alternating study with work experience

~~sandwitch~~ incorrect spelling of **sandwich**

sandy /sándi/ (**-ier**, **-iest**) adj 1 made up of, covered with, or full of sand 2 resembling sand in texture or colour —**sandiness** n

sane (**saner**, **sanest**) adj 1 mentally healthy 2 based on rational thinking —**sanely** adv —**saneness** n

San Fernando Valley /-fər nándō-/ residential and industrial region in S California. Pop. 1,300,000 (1998).

San Francisco /-frən sískō/ city in W California. Pop. 745,774 (1998). —**San Franciscan** n, adj

San Francisco Bay inlet of the Pacific Ocean in W California. Length 100 km/60 mi.

sang past tense of **sing**

Sanger /sángər/, **Frederick** (b. 1918) British biochemist, noted for his work on insulin, the structure of proteins, and the nucleotide sequence of nucleic acids

Sanger, Margaret (1883–1966) US social reformer

sang-froid /song frwaä, sang-/ n calmness under pressure

sangoma /sang gómə/ n S Africa in South Africa, a traditional healer

sangria /sang greé ə, sáng gri ə/ n a drink made with red wine, brandy, lemonade or soda, and fruit juice, served chilled

sanguinary /sáng gwinəri/ adj (fml) 1 involving bloodshed 2 bloodthirsty

sanguine /sáng gwin/ adj 1 cheerfully optimistic 2 having a healthy rosy colour o a sanguine complexion —**sanguinity** /sang gwínnəti/ n

sanitary /sánnitəri/ adj 1 of public health, especially general hygiene 2 clean and hygienic

sanitary protection n sanitary towels and tampons

sanitary towel, sanitary pad, sanitary napkin n a pad for absorbing menstrual blood

sanitation /sánni táysh'n/ n 1 the study and maintenance of public health, especially through water and sewage systems 2 sewage and refuse collection and disposal

sanitize /sánni tīz/ (**-tizing**, **-tized**), **sanitise** vt 1 clean by disinfecting or sterilizing 2 make less likely to offend o a sanitized version of the article —**sanitization** /sánni tī záysh'n/ n

~~sanitorium~~ incorrect spelling of **sanatorium**

sanity /sánnəti/ n 1 the condition of being mentally healthy 2 good sense

San Jose /-hō záy/ city in W California. Pop. 861,284 (1998).

San José /-hō záy/ capital of Costa Rica. Pop. 329,154 (1997).

San Juan /-waän/ 1 river in S Colorado, NW New Mexico, and SE Utah. Length 580 km/360 mi. 2 capital of Puerto Rico. Pop. 426,832 (1990).

sank past tense of **sink**

San Marino /-mə reénō/ small independent enclave in NE Italy. Cap. San Marino. Pop. 27,336 (2001).

San Martín /-maar teén/, **José Francisco de** (1778–1850) Argentine revolutionary leader

San Salvador /-sálvə dawr/ 1 capital of El Salvador. Pop. 415,346 (1992). 2 island of the central Bahamas. Pop. 465 (1990).

Sanskrit /sánskrit/ n an ancient South Asian language that is the language of classical Hindu texts —**Sanskrit** adj —**Sanskritist** n

sans serif /sán sérrif/, **sanserif** n a style of typeface with no small horizontal lines at the ends of the main strokes

Santa Claus /sántə klawz, -kláwz/ n Father Christmas

Santa Cruz /sántə kroŏz/ 1 river in S Argentina. Length 400 km/250 mi. 2 city in central Bolivia. Pop. 914,795 (1997). 3 city in W California. Pop. 52,853 (1998).

Santa Fe /-fáy/ 1 capital of **Santa Fe Province**, NE Argentina. Pop. 353,063 (1991). 2 capital of New Mexico. Pop. 67,879 (1998).

Santamaria /sántə mə reè ə/, **B. A.** (1915–98) Australian writer and political activist

Santiago /sánti áàgō/ capital of Chile. Pop. 4,703,954 (1998).

Santiago de Cuba /-day koóbə/ second largest city in Cuba. Pop. 432,396 (1996).

Santo Domingo /sántō də míng gō/ capital of the Dominican Republic. Pop. 3,166 (1995).

Saône /sōn/ river in east-central France. Length 480 km/298 mi.

São Paulo /sow pówlō/ capital of **São Paulo State**, SE Brazil. Pop. 9,839,436 (1996).

São Tomé and Príncipe /-tō máy ənd prínssi pay/ island country off the coast of Gabon, in the Gulf of Guinea. Cap. São Tomé. Pop. 165,034 (2001).

sap[1] *n* **1** a watery fluid containing nutrients that circulates through the tissues of plants **2** energy or vitality —**sappy** *adj*

sap[2] *n* a covered trench leading to enemy territory ■ *v* (**sapping, sapped**) **1** *vti* dig a sap or a tunnel that undermines enemy fortifications **2** *vt* gradually take away somebody's energy o *sapping his strength*

~~saphire~~ incorrect spelling of **sapphire**

sapient /sáypi ənt/ *adj* wise —**sapience** *n*

sapling /sáppling/ *n* a young tree

saponify /sə pónni ft/ (**-fies, -fied**) *vti* make or be made into soap —**saponification** /sə pónni káysh'n/ *n*

sapper /sáppər/ *n* **1** a military engineer specializing in trenches and tunnels **2** a private in the Royal Engineers

sapphire /sáff ɪr/ *n* **1** a deep blue variety of corundum. Use: gems. **2** a brilliant blue colour —**sapphire** *adj*

Sappho /sáffō/ (*fl* 7C BC) Greek poet

Sapporo /sə pórō/ city on W Hokkaido Island, Japan. Pop. 1,801,327 (2000).

saprophyte /sápprō ftt/ *n* an organism that lives on decaying organic matter —**saprophytic** /sápprō fíttik/ *adj*

Saracen /sárrəss'n/ *n* **1** a Muslim who fought the Christian Crusaders in the Middle Ages **2** a member of an ancient desert people of Syria and Arabia —**Saracen** *adj*

Saragossa /sárrə góssə/ ◆ **Zaragoza**

Sarajevo /sárrə yáyvō/ capital of Bosnia-Herzegovina. Pop. 360,000 (1997).

sarcasm /saár kazəm/ *n* language meaning the opposite of what it says and intended to mock or deride

sarcastic /saar kástik/ *adj* using or characterized by sarcasm —**sarcastically** *adv*

SYNONYMS **sarcastic, ironic, sardonic, satirical, caustic** CORE MEANING: describes remarks that are designed to hurt or mock

sarcoma /saar kṓmə/ (*pl* **-mas** *or* **-mata** /-mətə/) *n* a malignant tumour that begins growing in connective tissue

sarcophagus /saar kóffəgəss/ (*pl* **-gi** /-gī/ *or* **-guses**) *n* a stone coffin

ORIGIN **Sarcophagus** came through Latin from a Greek word meaning literally 'flesh eater'. The Greek word originally referred to a stone that was fabled to consume the flesh of dead bodies and that was used for coffins.

sardine /saar deén/ *n* **1** a tiny ocean fish related to the herring **2** a sardine as food

Sardinia /saar dínni ə/ Italian island in the W Mediterranean Sea. Cap. Cagliari. Pop. 1,659,466 (1995). —**Sardinian** *adj, n*

Sardis /saárdiss/ ancient city of W Asia Minor, near present-day Izmir, Turkey, the capital of the ancient kingdom of Lydia

sardonic /saar dónnik/ *adj* disdainfully or ironically mocking —**sardonically** *adv* ◊ See note at **sarcastic**

Sargasso Sea /saar gássō-/ section of the North Atlantic Ocean between the Greater Antilles and the Azores, noted for its predominantly still waters

sarge /saarj/ *n* a sergeant (*infml*)

Sargeson /saárjəss'n/, **Frank** (1903–82) New Zealand writer

Sargon II /saárgon/ (?763–705 BC) king of Assyria (721–705 BC)

sari /saári/, **saree** *n* a South Asian woman's garment consisting of a long rectangle of fabric wrapped around the body and over the shoulder

sarin /saárin, sárrin/ *n* a toxic gas that attacks the central nervous system, causing convulsions and death

sarky /saárki/ (**sarkier, sarkiest**) *adj* sarcastic (*infml*)

sarnie /saárni/ *n* a sandwich (*infml*)

sarong /sə róng/ *n* a traditional garment of Malaysia and Java consisting of a length of fabric wrapped around the body

sarsaparilla /saárspə ríllə/ (*pl* **-las** *or same*) *n* **1** the dried root of a tropical creeper or temperate plant. Use: traditional or herbal medicine, flavouring in soft drinks. **2** a tropical vine or similar plant whose roots are dried as sarsaparilla **3** a soft drink flavoured with sarsaparilla

Sarto ◆ **Andrea del Sarto**

sartorial /saar táwri əl/ *adj* of tailoring or tailored clothing

AKG London

Jean-Paul Sartre

Sartre /saártrə/, **Jean-Paul** (1905–80) French philosopher, playwright, and novelist

SAS *n* á UK military force trained for dangerous clandestine operations. Full form **Special Air Service**

SASE *abbr* self-addressed stamped envelope

sash *n* 1 a fabric belt 2 a wide ribbon worn across the chest

sashay /sásh ay/ *vi* 1 walk with an exaggerated sway to attract attention *(humorous)* 2 perform a sequence of steps in square dancing

sashimi /sáshimi/ *n* a Japanese dish of sliced raw fish, usually served with a dip

sash window *n* a window consisting of two frames, one above the other, that are able to overlap in vertical grooves

Saskatchewan /sa skáchəwən/ 1 river in central Canada, rising in central Saskatchewan and flowing into Lake Winnipeg in Manitoba. Length 550 km/340 mi. 2 province in central Canada. Cap. Regina. Pop. 1,023,636 (2000). —**Saskatchewanian** /sa skáchə wáyni ən/ *n, adj*

sassafras /sássə frass/ (*pl* same) *n* 1 the aromatic dried root bark of a tree. Use: flavouring, perfumes, medicines. 2 a deciduous tree whose root bark is dried as sassafras

~~sassafrass~~ incorrect spelling of **sassafras**

Sassenach /sássə nak, -nakh/ (*pl* -**nachs**) *n Ireland, Scotland* an offensive term for an English person

Sassoon /sásə soốn/**, Siegfried** (1886–1967) British poet and novelist

sassy[1] /sássi/ (-**sier**, -**siest**) *adj US, Can* 1 impudent or disrespectful 2 high-spirited —**sassily** *adv* —**sassiness** *n*

sassy[2] /sássi/ (*pl* -**sies**) *n* an African tree with poisonous bark

sat past tense, past participle of **sit**

Sat. *abbr* Saturday

~~satalite~~ incorrect spelling of **satellite**

Satan /sáyt'n/ *n* in Christianity, the devil

satanic /sə tánnik/ *adj* 1 of Satan or the worship of Satan 2 extremely evil —**satanically** *adv*

Satanism /sáyt'nizəm/ *n* Satan worship

satay /sáttay/ *n* a Southeast Asian kebab served with peanut sauce

satchel /sáchəl/ *n* a small bag for carrying things such as books, often with a shoulder strap

sate (**sating, sated**) *vt* 1 fully gratify the hunger or desire of 2 provide with too much

~~satelite~~ incorrect spelling of **satellite**

satellite /sáttə lít/ *n* 1 an object sent into space that orbits a planet and relays information to Earth 2 a moon orbiting another astronomical object 3 a country dependent on another more powerful country 4 a suburb or town near a large city

satellite dish *n* a dish-shaped aerial for receiving television signals broadcast via satellite

satellite television *n* television broadcast via satellite

~~Saterday~~ incorrect spelling of **Saturday**

satiate /sáyshi ayt/ (-**ating**, -**ated**) *vt* 1 provide somebody with too much of something desirable 2 fully gratify hunger or desire

Satie /saáti/**, Erik** (1866–1925) French composer

satiety /sə tí əti/ *n* the state of having been satiated

satin /sáttin/ *n* a glossy silk or rayon fabric ■ *adj* 1 made of satin 2 glossy like satin —**satiny** *adj*

> **ORIGIN Satin** is ultimately named after the port of Tseutung (now Tsinkiang) in S China, from where it was exported. It came to English via French from an Arabic form of the name.

satinwood /sáttin woŏd/ *n* 1 a smooth hard yellow-brown wood. Use: furniture making. 2 a tree that produces satinwood

satire /sáttīr/ *n* 1 use of wit to attack vice and folly 2 a literary work using satire —**satirical** /sə tírrik'l/ *adj* —**satirically** *adv* —**satirist** /sáttərist/ *n*

satirize /sáttə rīz/ (-**rizing**, -**rized**), **satirise** *vt* use satire against —**satirization** /sáttə rī záysh'n/ *n*

satisfaction /sáttiss fáksh'n/ *n* 1 the feeling of pleasure that comes when a need or desire is fulfilled 2 fulfilment of a need or desire 3 contentment with something such as an arrangement or performance

satisfactory /sáttiss fáktəri/ *adj* good enough to meet a requirement or expectation —**satisfactorily** *adv*

satisfy /sáttiss fī/ (-**fies**, -**fied**) *v* 1 *vt* make somebody feel pleased or content 2 *vti* fulfil a need or desire 3 *vt* resolve the doubts of somebody 4 *vt* meet a requirement or condition —**satisfied** *adj* —**satisfyingly** *adv*

satori /sə táwri/ *n* in Zen Buddhism, a state of spiritual enlightenment

satsuma /sat soŏma/ *n* 1 a cultivated variety of mandarin orange 2 a citrus tree that produces satsumas

~~sattellite~~ incorrect spelling of **satellite**

saturate /sáchə rayt/ (-**rating**, -**rated**) *vt* 1 soak something with liquid 2 fill something completely 3 supply a market fully —**saturated** *adj* —**saturation** /sáchə ráysh'n/ *adj*

saturated fat *n* fat from animal products in which the carbon atoms are fully combined with hydrogen

saturation point *n* a limit to the scope for expansion or absorption

Saturday /sáttər day, -di/ *n* the 6th day of the week

> **ORIGIN Saturday** is named after the Roman god Saturn.

Saturn /sáttərn/ *n* 1 in Roman mythology, the god of agriculture and ruler of the universe until deposed by his son Zeus. Greek equivalent **Cronus** 2 the 6th planet from the Sun —**Saturnian** /sa túrni ən/ *adj*

saturnalia /sáttər náyli ə/ *n* (*pl* -**as** or same) 1 a wild celebration 2 **Saturnalia** *n* the ancient

Roman festival in celebration of Saturn. Date: mid-December.

saturnine /sáttər nīn/ *adj* gloomy and morose

satyr /sáttər/ *n* 1 in Greek mythology, a woodland creature that is half-man, half-goat 2 a man displaying inappropriate or excessive sexual behaviour

sauce /sawss/ *n* 1 a thick liquid added to or served with food 2 something that adds zest or excitement ■ *vt* (**saucing, sauced**) add a sauce to food

sauce boat *n* a low jug for sauce or gravy

saucepan /sáwspən/ *n* a deep cooking pan with a handle

saucer /sáwssər/ *n* 1 a small circular dish for holding a cup 2 a round flat object

saucy /sáwssi/ (**-ier, -iest**) *adj* 1 cheeky 2 pert —**saucily** *adv* —**sauciness** *n*

Saud ♦ Ibn Saud, Abdul Aziz

Saud (1902–69) king of Saudi Arabia (1953–64)

Saudi Arabia /sówdi ə ráybi ə/ country in SW Asia, on the Arabian Peninsula. Cap. Riyadh. Pop. 22,757,092 (2001). —**Saudi Arabian** *n, adj*

sauerkraut /sów ər krowt/ *n* shredded cabbage fermented in its own juice with salt

Saul /sawl/ (*fl* 11C BC) first king of ancient Israel (about 1020–00 BC)

sauna /sáwnə/ *n* 1 a steam bath followed by a plunge in cold water or a light brushing with birch or cedar boughs 2 a room for a sauna

saunter /sáwntər/ *vi* walk at an easy pace ■ *n* 1 an easy walking pace 2 a walk at an easy pace

~~saurkraut~~ incorrect spelling of **sauerkraut**

sausage /sóssij/ *n* spicy chopped meat and other ingredients in a casing

sausage dog *n* a dachshund (*infml*)

sausagemeat /sóssij meet/ *n* seasoned minced pork, usually mixed with fat and bread or cereal

sausage roll *n* a length of sausagemeat baked in pastry

Saussure /sō syoór, -soór/, **Ferdinand de** (1857–1913) Swiss linguist

sauté /sō tay/ *vt* fry lightly in a little fat ■ *n a* sautéed dish

savage /sávvij/ *adj* 1 vicious or violent 2 severe in effect o *savage job cuts* 3 an offensive term meaning belonging or relating to a culture perceived as uncivilized ■ *n* 1 a vicious or violent person 2 an offensive term for a member of a people considered to be uncivilized ■ *vt* (**-aging, -aged**) 1 attack violently 2 criticize cruelly —**savagely** *adv* —**savageness** *n* —**savagery** *n*

ORIGIN A *savage* is etymologically somebody from the woods or forest, regarded as the opposite of civilization. The word goes back to Latin *silva* 'wood, forest', and was adopted into French.

Savage /sávvij/, **Michael Joseph** (1872–1940) Australian-born prime minister of New Zealand (1935–40)

savanna /sə vánnə/, **savannah** *n* a grassy plain

Savannah /sə vánnə/ 1 river rising in NW South Carolina and flowing along the South Carolina-Georgia border into the Atlantic Ocean. Length 505 km/314 mi. 2 city in SE Georgia, United States, at the mouth of the Savannah River. Pop. 131,674 (1998).

savant /sávvənt/ *n* a learned person

save[1] /sayv/ *v* (**saving, saved**) 1 *vt* rescue somebody or something from harm or danger 2 *vti* set aside and accumulate money for later use 3 *vt* avoid wasting or using something o *save time* o *switched it off to save the batteries* 4 *vti* reduce expense o *saving on fuel* 5 *vti* store a copy of computer data on a storage medium 6 *vt* redeem somebody from the consequences of sin ■ *n* an action that prevents an opponent from scoring a goal —**saver** *n*

save[2] /sayv/ *prep, conj* except o *everybody save me*

save as you earn *n* in the United Kingdom, a tax-free savings plan involving monthly deposits over five years

saving /sáyving/ *n* 1 an amount kept from being spent, wasted, or used 2 the rescuing of somebody or something from harm or danger ■ **savings** *npl* money set aside ■ *prep, conj* except (*literary*)

saving grace *n* a redeeming quality or feature

savings account *n* a bank or building society account for saving money

savings bank *n* a bank that invests savings and pays interest

saviour /sáyyər/ *n* 1 somebody who saves another from harm or danger 2 **Saviour** in Christianity, Jesus Christ

savoir-faire /sáv waar fáir/ *n* social adeptness

Savonarola /sàvvənə rôlə/, **Girolamo** (1452–98) Italian religious leader and martyr

savory[1] *adj*, *n* US = **savoury**

savory[2] /sáyvəri/ *n* a herb with aromatic leaves. Use: flavouring food.

savour /sáyvər/ *vt* 1 enjoy unhurriedly 2 enjoy the taste or smell of ■ *n* 1 the taste or smell that something has 2 a distinctive quality

savoury /sáyvəri/ *adj* 1 salty or sharp-tasting rather than sweet 2 appetizing ■ *n* (*pl* **savouries**) a light savoury dish

savvy /sávvi/ (*infml*) *adj* shrewd and well informed ■ *n* shrewdness and practical knowledge

saw[1] /saw/ *n* a tool with a toothed metal blade for cutting ■ *vti* (**sawed** or **sawn** /sawn/) cut something using a saw

SPELLCHECK Do not confuse the spelling of **saw**, **soar** ('fly high'), and **sore** ('painful'), which may sound similar.

saw[2] /saw/ *n* a trite old saying

saw[3] /saw/ past tense of **see**[1]

SAW *abbr* surface acoustic wave

sawdust /sáw dust/ n fine particles of wood produced during sawing

sawfish /sáw fish/ (pl **same** or **-fishes**) n a fish with a long toothed snout

sawmill /sáw mil/ n a factory where wood is sawn

sawn past participle of **saw**[1]

sawyer /sáw yər/ n somebody who saws wood for a living

sax n a saxophone (infml)

saxifrage /sáksi frayj/ (pl **-frages** or **same**) n a plant with small flowers that grows on rocky ground

Saxon /sáks'n/ n 1 a member of an ancient Germanic people who established kingdoms in S Britain 2 the language of the ancient Saxons 3 somebody from Saxony —**Saxon** adj

Saxony /sáksəni/ state in east-central Germany. Cap. Dresden. Pop. 4,489,415 (1998).

saxophone /sáksə fōn/ n a metal wind instrument with keys and a reed —**saxophonist** /sak sóffənist/ n

---

ORIGIN The **saxophone** is named after the Belgian instrument-maker Antoine Joseph ('Adolphe') Sax (1814–94), who devised it. The name first appears in English in 1851 in the catalogue of the Great Exhibition of that year held in London.

---

say v (**said** /sed/) 1 vt utter in a normal voice 2 vti express something verbally 3 vt indicate in numbers or symbols ○ *The clock said midnight.* 4 vt suppose ○ *Let's say we can't afford it.* 5 vt recite ○ *says his prayers* ■ n 1 a chance to speak ○ *have your say* 2 the right to give an opinion and have it considered ○ *had no say in the decision* ■ adv approximately ○ *if we get, say, three gallons* —**sayer** n ◇ **it goes without saying** it is obvious or self-evident

SAYE abbr save as you earn

Sayers /sáy ərz/, **Dorothy L.** (1893–1957) British writer

saying /sáy ing/ n a proverbial expression

say-so n permission or authorization from somebody (infml)

Sb symbol antimony

SBA n a radio navigation system that signals aircraft during the approach to landing. Full form **standard beam approach**

S-bend n an S-shaped bend

SBS abbr 1 sick building syndrome 2 Special Boat Service

SBU abbr strategic business unit

sc, s.c. abbr small capital

Sc symbol scandium

SC abbr Security Council

s/c abbr self-contained (in advertisements)

scab n 1 a crust over a healing wound 2 a strikebreaker (disapproving) ■ vi (**scabbing, scabbed**) 1 become covered with a scab 2 work during a strike (disapproving)

scabbard /skábbərd/ n a sheath for a sword or dagger

scabby /skábbi/ (**-bier, -biest**) adj having or covered with scabs —**scabbiness** n

scabies /skáy beez/ n a contagious skin disease caused by a mite, with itching, inflammation, and small red lumps

scabious /skáybi əss/ (pl **-ouses** or **same**) n a plant with dome-shaped flowers

scabrous /skáybrəss, skább-/ adj with a rough scaly or hairy surface

scads npl large quantities (infml)

scaffold /skáffōld, -f'ld/ n 1 a framework of poles and planks erected against or around a building to support workers 2 a platform for executions by hanging or beheading 3 death by hanging —**scaffolder** n

scaffolding /skáffōlding, -f'lding/ n 1 a system of scaffolds 2 the materials for building a scaffold

scalable /skáyləb'l/ adj 1 climbable 2 describes computer graphics fonts whose size can be altered

scalar /skáylər/ n a quantity with magnitude but no direction

scalawag n = scallywag

scald vt 1 burn with hot liquid or steam 2 heat to near boiling point ■ n a burn caused by hot liquid or steam

scalding /skáwlding/ adj 1 extremely hot 2 scathing

scale[1] n 1 any of the small flat bony or horny overlapping plates on fish and some reptiles and mammals 2 a thin flat piece or flake 3 a deposit formed, e.g. inside a kettle, when hard water boils or evaporates ■ v (**scaling, scaled**) 1 vt clean scales or scale from ○ *scaling the fish* 2 vi flake off

scale[2] n 1 a measuring system based on a series of marks at regular intervals representing numerical values 2 a classification system based on differing quantity or value ○ *a pay scale* 3 the extent or relative size of something ○ *the scale of the devastation* 4 a measuring instrument with graduated markings 5 a series of musical notes arranged according to pitch ■ **Scales** npl the zodiacal sign Libra ■ vt (**scaling, scaled**) 1 climb up or over 2 make or draw to scale ◇ **to scale** with the same proportion of reduction or enlargement throughout

☐ **scale down** vt reduce

☐ **scale up** vt increase

scale[3] n a weighing machine (often pl)

scale insect, scale n a destructive plant-sucking insect that covers itself with a waxy secretion resembling scales

scalene /skáyl een/ adj describes a triangle in which each side is a different length

scallion /skálli ən/ n a small onion with long leaves, e.g. a spring onion

scallop /skóllap, skáll-/, **scollop** n 1 a sea mollusc with a wavy fan-shaped shell 2 the flesh of a scallop as food 3 a wavy ornamental fabric edging 4 Aus a fried potato cake ■ v 1 vt make a series of curves along the edge of fabric **2** *vi* collect scallops —**scalloped** *adj* —**scalloping** *n*

scallywag /skálli wag/**, scalawag** /skálla-/ *n* a mischievous or rascally person *(dated infml)*

scalp *n* **1** the skin and underlying tissue on top of the head **2** the scalp of an enemy cut off as a trophy ■ *vt* cut off the scalp of —**scalper** *n*

scalpel /skálp'l/ *n* a surgical knife with a short blade

scaly /skáyli/ (**-ier, -iest**) *adj* covered in scales —**scaliness** *n*

scam *n* a dishonest scheme for making money *(slang)*

scamp *n* a mischievous child *(infml)* —**scampish** *adj*

scamper /skámpər/ *vi* run quickly or playfully —**scamper** *n*

scampi /skámpi/ *n* fried prawn tails (+ *sing or pl verb)*

scan *vt* (**scanning, scanned**) **1** examine something thoroughly or intently *o scanning the horizon* **2** look through or read something quickly **3** analyse verse in terms of its metre **4** direct a light-sensitive device over a surface in order to convert an image into digital or electronic form ■ *n* **1** the scanning of something **2** an image produced by scanning something —**scannable** *adj*

scandal /skánd'l/ *n* **1** something causing public outrage or censure **2** an outburst of public outrage or censure **3** malicious talk or gossip

scandalize /skándə līz/ (**-izing, -ized**), **scandalise** *vt* offend by shocking behaviour —**scandalization** /skándə līzáysh'n/ *n*

scandalmonger /skánd'l mung gər/ *n* a spreader of malicious gossip —**scandalmongering** *n*

scandalous /skándələss/ *adj* **1** causing or deserving public outrage or censure **2** defamatory —**scandalously** *adv*

Scandinavia /skán di náyvi ə/ region in N Europe comprising Norway, Sweden, Denmark, Finland, Iceland, and the Faroe Islands —**Scandinavian** *n, adj*

scandium /skándi əm/ *n* (*symbol* **Sc**) a rare silvery-white metallic element. Use: tracer.

~~scandle~~ incorrect spelling of **scandal**

scanner /skánnər/ *n* **1** a device for scanning the internal organs or structure of the body **2** a device for scanning written or recorded data **3** a device for converting an image or text into digital form

scansion /skánsh'n/ *n* **1** the analysis of verse in terms of the rules of poetic metre **2** the metre of a line, poem, or verse

scant *adj* **1** not enough **2** only or not quite a particular amount *o a scant twenty votes* —**scantly** *adv*

scanty /skánti/ (**-ier, -iest**) *adj* **1** not much and less than is needed **2** only just enough **3** hardly covering the body —**scantily** *adv* —**scantiness** *n*

-scape *suffix* a scene or view *o landscape*

scapegoat /skáyp gōt/ *n* **1** somebody made to take the blame for others **2** somebody wrongly blamed ■ *vt* make a scapegoat of

scapula /skáppyoōlə/ (*pl* **-lae** /-lee/ *or* **-las**) either of two flat triangular bones forming the back of the shoulder

scar[1] *n* **1** a mark left on the skin after a wound heals **2** a lasting mental effect of a distressing experience ■ *vt* (**scarring, scarred**) mark with scars

scar[2] *n* **1** a steep craggy rock formation **2** a rock submerged in the sea

scarab /skárrəb/ *n* **1** a large black beetle sacred to the ancient Egyptians **2** a representation of a scarab

scarce /skairss/ (**scarcer, scarcest**) *adj* **1** in insufficient supply **2** rarely found —**scarceness** *n* ◇ **make yourself scarce** go or stay away *(infml)*

scarcely /skáirssli/ *adv* **1** only just *o scarcely arrived when she was put to work* **2** hardly at all *o scarcely slept all night* **3** almost certainly not *o scarcely a good reason*

scarcity /skáirssəti/ (*pl* **-ties**) *n* **1** an insufficient supply **2** a rarity

scare /skair/ *v* (**scaring, scared**) **1** *vt* frighten **2** *vi* be or become frightened ■ *n* **1** a sudden fright **2** a situation causing general alarm *o another food scare*

scarecrow /skáir krō/ *n* an object in the shape of a person set up for scaring birds away

scared /skaird/ *adj* frightened

scarf[1] (*pl* **scarfs** *or* **scarves**) *n* a cloth worn round the neck, head, or shoulders

scarf[2] *n* **1** *also* **scarf joint** a joint made between corresponding notched ends of boards **2** either of the notched ends of a scarf joint —**scarf** *vt*

scarify /skárri fī, skáiri-/ (**-fies, -fied**) *vt* **1** make scratches on the skin **2** loosen soil **3** scratch the cover of hard seeds to help germination —**scarification** /skárrifi káysh'n/ *n*

scarlatina /skaárlə teénə/ *n* scarlet fever *(technical)*

Scarlatti /skaar látti/**, Alessandro** (1659–1725) and his son **Domenico** (1685–1757) Italian composers

scarlet /skaárlət/ *n* a bright red colour —**scarlet** *adj*

scarlet fever *n* a contagious disease with fever, sore throat, and a red rash, mainly affecting children

scarlet pimpernel *n* a plant with small scarlet, purple, or white flowers that close in cloudy weather

scarp *n* a steep slope or cliff

scarper /skaárpər/ *vi* leave quickly *(slang)*

scarves plural of **scarf**[1]

scary /skáiri/ (**-ier, -iest**) *adj* frightening *(infml)* —**scarily** *adv* —**scariness** *n*

scat *n* a jazz vocal style using nonsense syllables —**scat** *vi*

scathing /skáything/ *adj* highly critical and scornful —**scathingly** *adv*

scatology /skə tóllɔji/ n a preoccupation with excrement or obscene language —**scatological** /skáttə lójjik'l/ adj —**scatologist** n

scatter /skáttər/ v 1 vt throw things about over a wide area 2 vt cover by scattering something 3 vti disperse in different directions

SYNONYMS scatter, broadcast, distribute, disseminate CORE MEANING: spread around

scatterbrain /skáttər brayn/ n a person regarded as incapable of organized thought —**scatterbrained** adj

scatter cushion n a small cushion for a sofa or armchair (often pl)

scattered /skáttərd/ adj 1 dispersed 2 infrequent or isolated

scattering /skáttəring/ n a small amount or number spread irregularly

scattershot /skáttər shot/ adj unsystematic

scatty /skátti/ (-tier, -tiest) adj UK, Can forgetful or eccentric (infml) —**scattily** adv —**scattiness** n

scavenge /skávvinj/ (-enging, -enged) vti 1 look for something usable among discarded material 2 feed on carrion or scraps —**scavenger** n

SCE n a Scottish school examination taken in the last three years of secondary school. Full form **Scottish Certificate of Education**

~~seedule~~ incorrect spelling of **schedule**

~~seeince~~ incorrect spelling of **science**

~~seeme~~ incorrect spelling of **scheme**

scenario /si naári ō/ (pl -os) n 1 a possible situation or sequence of events 2 an outline of the plot of a play or opera

scene /seen/ n 1 a division of an act of a play or opera, presenting continuous action in one place 2 a short section of a play, opera, film, or work of literature, presenting a single event o the love scene 3 a place where something happens o the scene of the crime 4 the scenery for a dramatic work o a quick scene change 5 a view or picture 6 an embarrassing public display of emotion 7 the setting or environment of a particular activity o the fashion scene ◊ **behind the scenes** in private and away from public view

scenery /seenəri/ n 1 the set or backdrop for a piece of theatre or film 2 landscape or natural surroundings, especially when picturesque

scenic /seenik/ adj 1 picturesque 2 of natural scenery

scent /sent/ n 1 a characteristic pleasant smell 2 a smell left behind by a person or animal and used as a trail 3 cosmetic fragrances or perfume ■ v 1 vti perceive by smelling 2 vt detect as imminent 3 vt fill with a pleasant smell ◊ See note at **smell**

scepter n US = **sceptre**

sceptic /sképtik/ n 1 a doubter of accepted beliefs 2 a doubter of religious teachings —**sceptical** adj —**sceptically** adv ◊ See note at **doubtful**

scepticism /sképtisizəm/ n a doubting attitude towards accepted beliefs or religious teachings

sceptre /séptər/ n 1 a staff used as a royal emblem 2 royal authority

schadenfreude /shaád'n froydə/, **Schadenfreude** n malicious or smug pleasure at somebody else's misfortune

schedule /shéddyool, skéd-/ n 1 a plan of work to be done 2 a list of meetings, commitments, or appointments 3 a timetable ■ vt (-uling, -uled) 1 plan for a particular time 2 make a list of, or include in a list —**scheduler** n

Scheduled Castes npl castes in India officially considered disadvantaged and granted special treatment

scheduled territories npl the group of countries that use British currency or link their currency to it

Schelling /shélling/, **Friedrich Wilhelm Joseph von** (1775–1854) German philosopher

schema /skeemə/ (pl -mata /skeemətə, skee maátə/) n a diagram or plan showing the basic outline of something

schematic /skee máttik, ski-/ adj showing the basic form or layout of something —**schematically** adv

schematize /skeemə tīz/ (-tizing, -tized), **schematise** vt arrange systematically or in schematic form —**schematization** /skeemə tī záysh'n/ n

scheme /skeem/ n 1 a secret plot or plan 2 a systematic plan of action or arrangement of parts ■ v (scheming, schemed) 1 vi make a secret plan 2 vt plan systematically —**schemer** n

Schengen Agreement /shéngən-/ n an agreement between some European countries abolishing internal border controls

ORIGIN Schengen is a village on the borders of Luxembourg, France, and Germany, where the agreement was signed.

scherzo /skáirtsō/ (pl -zos or -zi /-tsi/) n a fast and lighthearted musical movement or piece

Schiele /sheelə/, **Egon** (1890–1918) Austrian painter

Schiller /shíllər/, **Friedrich von** (1759–1805) German poet, dramatist, historian, and philosopher

schilling /shílling/ n the main unit of the former Austrian currency

schism /skízzəm, sízzəm/ n a division into factions, especially within a religion or religious denomination

schismatic /skiz máttik, siz-/ adj of a schism ■ n a participant in or promoter of a schism

schist /shist/ n a rock that splits into layers

schizoid /skít soyd/ adj 1 tending towards schizophrenia 2 an offensive term describing a personality that suggests violent inner conflicts

schizophrenia /skítsō freeni ə/ n 1 a severe psychiatric disorder with symptoms of withdrawal into the self **2** an offensive term for contradictory attitudes or behaviour —**schizophrenic** /-frénnik/ *adj, n*

schlep /shlep/ (**schlepping, schlepped**) *vt* carry clumsily or with difficulty *(infml)*

Schliemann /shleémən/, **Heinrich** (1822–90) German archaeologist

schmaltz /shmawlts, shmolts/, **schmalz** *n* cloying or exaggerated sentimentality *(infml)* —**schmaltzy** *adj*

schmooze /shmooz/ (**schmoozing, schmoozed**) *vt* be ingratiating towards

schnapps /shnaps/, **schnaps** *n* a strong alcoholic spirit made in N Europe

~~schnaps~~ incorrect spelling of **schnapps**

schnitzel /shníts'l/ *n* a fried thin slice of meat

Schoenberg /shúrn burg, shön boörk/, **Arnold** (1874–1951) Austrian composer

scholar /skóllər/ *n* **1** a learned person **2** a student with a scholarship —**scholarliness** *n* —**scholarly** *adj*

scholarship /skóllər ship/ *n* **1** a sum of money granted to a student on the basis of academic merit for expenses such as tuition fees **2** academic learning

scholastic /skə lástik/ *adj* **1** of schools, scholarship, or studying **2** of scholasticism

scholasticism /skə lástissizəm/ *n* medieval theology and philosophy based on the writings of Aristotle

school[1] /skool/ *n* **1** a building or institution where children are taught **2** a university department specializing in a particular subject ○ *business school* **3** an institution teaching a nonacademic skill ○ *a riding school* **4** the staff and students of a school **5** time spent at school **6** a group of artists or writers sharing the same approach ■ *vt* **1** instruct in a particular skill **2** educate in school **3** discipline

---

ORIGIN The **school** for children and the **school** for fish are unrelated. The first was adopted into the ancient Germanic languages from Latin; the second came around 1400 from a Dutch word meaning 'troop, multitude', and is related to *shoal*.

---

school[2] /skool/ *n* a large group of fish or sea mammals swimming together ■ *vi* form or swim in a school

school age *n* the age at which children are legally required to attend school —**school-age** *adj*

schoolboy /skóol boy/ *n* a boy attending school ■ *adj* appropriate to schoolboys

School Certificate *n* in New Zealand, a school exam taken at 16

schoolchild /skóol chíld/ (*pl* **-children** /-children/) *n* a child attending school

school day *n* **1** a day on which school is conducted **2** the part of the day spent at school ■ **school days** *npl* the years spent at school

schoolfellow /skóol feló/ *n* a pupil attending the same school *(fml)*

schoolgirl /skóol gurl/ *n* a girl attending school

schoolhouse /skóol howss/ (*pl* **-houses** /-howziz/) *n* **1** a building used as a school **2** a teacher's house attached to a school

schooling /skóoling/ *n* **1** education at school **2** systematic instruction or training

school-leaver *n* a young person who is about to leave school or who has just left school

schoolmarm /skóol maarm/ *n* an offensive term for a woman schoolteacher, especially one regarded as prim or old-fashioned *(dated insult)*

schoolmaster /skóol maastər/ *n* a man schoolteacher ■ *vi* be a schoolmaster *(dated)*

schoolmate /skóol mayt/ *n* a friend or another pupil attending the same school

schoolmistress /skóol mistrəss/ *n* a woman schoolteacher

school of thought *n* a shared way of thinking about something

schoolroom /skóol room, -rōōm/ *n* a school classroom

schoolteacher /skóol teechər/ *n* a teacher in a school —**schoolteaching** *n*

schoolwork /skóol wurk/ *n* work done by a pupil in or after school

school year *n* **1** a 12-month period during which pupils are assigned to the same class **2** the months when schools are open

schooner /skoónər/ *n* **1** a sailing vessel with two or more masts **2** a large sherry glass **3** *Aus, US, Can* a beer glass

Schopenhauer /shốpən hówər/, **Arthur** (1788–1860) German philosopher

Schröder /shrúrdər/, **Gerhard** (*b.* 1944) chancellor of Germany (1998–)

Schrödinger /shrúrdingər, shród-, shród-/, **Erwin** (1887–1961) Austrian physicist. He made a major contribution to quantum theory.

Schubert /shoóbərt/, **Franz** (1797–1828) Austrian composer

Schulz /shoólts/, **Charles** (1922–2000) US cartoonist

Schumacher /shoó maakər, -maakher/, **Michael** (*b.* 1969) German racing driver

Schumann /shoómən/, **Robert** (1810–56) German composer

Schüssel /shoóss'l/, **Wolfgang** (*b.* 1945) chancellor of Austria (2000–)

schwa /shwaa/ *n* an unstressed vowel sound, e.g. the 'a' in 'above', or the symbol 'ə' used to represent it

Schwarzkopf /shvaárts kopf, swaárts kopf/, **Dame Elisabeth** (*b.* 1915) German soprano

Schweitzer /shwítsər/, **Albert** (1875–1965)

Albert Schweitzer

German-born theologian, musicologist, and missionary

sciatica /sī áttikə/ n pain in the hip and leg caused by pressure on a nerve

science /sī ənss/ n 1 the study of the physical world by systematic observation and experiment 2 a branch of science o *the life sciences* 3 knowledge gained from science 4 a systematic body of knowledge

science fiction n fiction based on futuristic science and technology

science park n a place for commercial scientific research

scientific /sī ən tíffik/ adj 1 of science 2 systematic or methodical —**scientifically** adv

scientist /sī əntist/ n an expert in or student of science

sci-fi /sī fī/ n science fiction (infml)

scimitar /símmitər, -taar/ n a sword with a curved blade that broadens towards the point

scintilla /sin tíllə/ n a small amount

scintillate /sínti layt/ (-**lating**, -**lated**) vi 1 sparkle 2 be dazzlingly lively or clever —**scintillating** adj —**scintillation** /sínti láysh'n/ n

scion /sī ən/ n 1 a living shoot or twig of a plant used for grafting 2 a descendant

Scipio /skíppi ō, síppi ō/, **Publius Cornelius** (d. 211 BC) Roman general

Scipio Africanus (the Elder) /-áffri kaánəss/ (234?–183 BC) Roman general

scissors /sízzərz/ npl a cutting instrument consisting of two crossed blades with ring-shaped handles ■ n (pl same) a movement of the legs resembling the opening and closing of scissors o *a scissors kick* —**scissor** vti

sclerosis /sklə rṓssiss, skleer-/ (pl -**ses** /-rṓ seez/) n the hardening and thickening of body tissue —**sclerotic** /sklə róttik, skleer-/ adj

scoff[1] /skof/ vi express derision or scorn —**scoff** n —**scoffer** n

scoff[2] vti eat hungrily (infml)

scold /skōld/ vti criticize somebody sharply ■ n somebody who scolds —**scolding** adj, n

sconce /skonss/ n a wall bracket for candles or light bulbs

scone /skon, skōn/ n a sweet or savoury cake usually served split and buttered

ORIGIN Scone is probably a shortening of early Dutch *schoonbroot* 'fine bread'. For the first three hundred years of its life, from the early 16C, the word was largely confined to Scotland.

scoop n 1 a tool or utensil used for shovelling or ladling 2 a utensil with a bowl-shaped head used to serve soft food in round portions 3 the digging part of a machine 4 an exclusive news story (infml) ■ vt 1 make a hollow with a scoop or similar object o *scooped a hole in the ground* 2 remove something with a scoop or cupped hand o *scooped up a handful of sand* 3 lift somebody or some-

thing swiftly 4 publish or broadcast a news item before rivals

scoot vi (infml) 1 go away quickly (usually a command) 2 move quickly —**scoot** n

scooter /skṓotər/ n 1 a wheeled toy with a footboard and handlebars 2 a light motor-cycle

scope n 1 freedom or space to act 2 the range covered by an activity or topic

-scope suffix an instrument for viewing or observing o *telescope* —**-scopic** suffix —**-scopy** suffix

scorch vti 1 burn on the surface 2 dry out with intense heat ■ n a surface burn

scorched earth policy n 1 the policy of destroying everything of use to an advancing enemy 2 a company strategy of avoiding a hostile takeover by appearing financially unattractive

scorcher /skáwrchər/ n 1 a very hot day (infml) 2 a severely critical remark

score n 1 in a game or match, the number of points gained by a team or a player 2 a record of points gained o *Who's keeping the score?* 3 (pl same or **scores**) a group of 20 4 a written or printed copy of a musical composition 5 a superficial cut 6 a grudge o *settling old scores* ■ **scores** npl a great many ■ v (**scoring**, **scored**) 1 vti gain a point or points 2 vti record or award the points in a game or competition 3 vt cut notches or lines in the surface of something 4 vt orchestrate or arrange a piece of music —**scoreless** adj —**scorer** n ◊ **on this** or **that score** as far as this or that is concerned

ORIGIN Score can be traced to an ancient root meaning 'cut', from which *shear* and *short* also derive. It was adopted from an old Scandinavian word meaning both 'notch' and '20'. Senses connected with counting derive from making notches on a surface to keep a tally or count. The **score** of a game is an 18C development of meaning. The musical **score** may refer to the bar line linking together related staffs.

scoreboard /skáwr bawrd/ n a board at a sports place where the score is displayed

scorecard /skáwr kaard/ n 1 a card for recording a player's score 2 a card listing players in a match

scoresheet /skáwr sheet/ n a record of scoring

scorn n contempt and lack of respect ■ vt 1 disdain or hold in contempt 2 reject contemptuously o *scorned our offer of help* —**scornful** adj —**scornfully** adv

Scorpio /skáwrpi ō/ n 1 also **Scorpius** a zodiacal constellation in the southern hemisphere 2 the 8th sign of the zodiac —**Scorpio** adj

scorpion /skáwrpi ən/ n an arachnid with a poisonous sting at the tip of its upturned tail

Scot n 1 somebody from Scotland 2 a member of an ancient people of Ireland and N Britain

scotch vt put a stop to o *scotch a rumour*

Scotch *n* whisky produced in Scotland ■ *adj* of or from Scotland

Scotch broth *n* soup made from meat, vegetables, and barley

Scotch egg *n* an egg in a sausagemeat covering

Scotch mist *n* drizzly mist

Scotch terrier *n* DOGS = Scottish terrier

scot-free *adv* without punishment or penalty

ORIGIN The Scots do not lend their name to **scot-free**. It comes from a completely unrelated word meaning 'payment, tax'.

Scotland /skótlənd/ country forming the northernmost part of Great Britain and of the United Kingdom. Cap. Edinburgh. Pop. 5,120,000 (1998).

Scots *adj* of Scotland ■ *n* a form of English spoken in parts of Scotland —**Scotsman** *n* —**Scotswoman** *n*

Scott, Robert Falcon (1868–1912) British naval officer and explorer

Scott, Sir Walter (1771–1832) Scottish novelist and poet

Scottish /skóttish/ *adj* of Scotland ■ *npl* the people of Scotland ■ *n* Scots —**Scottishness** *n*

Scottish National Party *n* a nationalist political party of Scotland

Scottish terrier, Scotch terrier *n* a small dog with pointed ears and wiry black hair

scoundrel /skówndrəl/ *n* a dishonourable or unprincipled person

scour[1] /skowr/ *vt* clean or remove by rubbing with something abrasive —**scour** *n* —**scourer** *n*

scour[2] /skowr/ *vti* 1 search something carefully 2 move quickly over or through an area

scourge /skurj/ *n* 1 somebody or something that torments or punishes 2 a whip —**scourge** *vt*

Scouse /skowss/ *n* (*infml*) 1 = Scouser 2 the dialect of Liverpool —**Scouse** *adj*

Scouser /skówssər/ *n* somebody who comes from Liverpool (*infml*)

scout /skowt/ *n* 1 a soldier sent to gather information 2 somebody sent to find talented new people 3 **Scout** a member of the Scout Association, an international organization for boys 4 a search ○ *have a scout around for somewhere to camp* ■ *vi* 1 search an area 2 gather information

---

ORIGIN A **scout** may be thought of as looking out for things, but etymologically a **scout** listens. The word is shortened from early French *escouter* 'listen' (*écouter* in modern French).

Scouting /skówting/ *n* the activities of the Scout Association

scoutmaster /skówt maastər/ *n* the adult leader of a troop of Scouts

scowl /skowl/ *n* a frown of anger or displeasure —**scowl** *vi*

scrabble /skrább'l/ (**-bling, -bled**) *vi* 1 scratch or grope with hurried movements of the fingers or claws 2 climb hastily or clumsily 3 struggle to get something —**scrabble** *n*

Scrabble /skrább'l/ *tdmk* a trademark for a word-based board game

scraggly /skrággli/ (**-glier, -gliest**) *adj* untidy in appearance

scraggy /skrággi/ (**-gier, -giest**) *adj* scrawny ◊ See note at **thin**

scram (**scramming, scrammed**) *vi* leave quickly (*infml; usually a command*)

scramble /skrámb'l/ (**-bling, -bled**) *v* 1 *vi* climb hastily using the hands and feet 2 *vi* hurry urgently 3 *vi* compete frantically 4 *vt* jumble things together 5 *vt* beat and cook eggs 6 *vt* make a transmitted signal unintelligible 7 *vti* take off quickly or cause aircraft to take off quickly in an military emergency —**scramble** *n*

scrambled eggs *n* cooked beaten eggs (+ *sing or pl verb*)

scrap[1] *n* 1 a small piece 2 waste material to be reprocessed or reused ■ **scraps** *npl* leftovers ■ *vt* (**scrapping, scrapped**) 1 get rid of 2 convert to scrap

scrap[2] *n* a minor fight (*infml*) ■ *vi* (**scrapping, scrapped**) fight or disagree

scrapbook /skráp bŏŏk/ *n* an album used to collect pictures, cuttings, and other material

scrape *v* (**scraping, scraped**) 1 *vti* move something hard, sharp, or rough across the surface of something 2 *vt* remove by scraping 3 *vt* damage or injure by scraping 4 *vti* make or cause to make a grating noise ■ *n* 1 an act of scraping 2 a light scratch 3 a grating sound 4 a dangerous or awkward situation (*infml*) —**scraper** *n*

□ **scrape together** *or* **up** *vt* gather with difficulty

scrapheap /skráp heep/ *n* a place for discarded things or people (*infml*)

scrapie /skráypi/ *n* a disease of the nervous system in sheep and goats

scrappy[1] /skráppi/ (**-pier, -piest**) *adj* 1 consisting of fragments 2 disjointed or disconnected —**scrappiness** *n*

scrappy[2] /skráppi/ (**-pier, -piest**) *adj* (*infml*) 1 plucky, determined, and willing to fight or argue 2 belligerent or quarrelsome

scrapyard /skráp yaard/ *n* a place where scrap is stored

scratch *vti* 1 mark the surface of something with something sharp or rough 2 tear the skin of a person or animal 3 make or cause to make a scraping movement or noise 4 rub the nails or claws over an itchy part of the body 5 withdraw from a competition ■ *n* 1 a mark or wound caused by scratching 2 an act or sound of scratching ■ *adj* 1 done randomly 2 assembled hastily —**scratcher** *n* ◊ **from scratch** right from the beginning, or with nothing having been done previously (*infml*) ◊ **up to scratch** of a satisfactory standard (*infml*)

scratch card *n* a card with one or more sections that can be scratched to reveal a possible prize

scratch file *n* a temporary computer file

scratchpad /skrách pad/ *n* **1** *US* a pad of paper for making rough notes **2** a temporary storage area in a computer memory

scratchy /skráchi/ (-ier, -iest) *adj* **1** causing itchiness **2** making a scratching sound —**scratchily** *adv* —**scratchiness** *n*

scrawl *vti* write or draw something untidily or hastily —**scrawl** *n* —**scrawly** *adj*

scrawny /skráwni/ (-nier, -niest) *adj* very thin and bony —**scrawniness** *n* ◊ See note at **thin**

scream /skreem/ *n* **1** a piercing cry **2** a high-pitched noise **3** somebody or something highly amusing (*infml*) ■ *v* **1** *vi* utter a scream **2** *vt* shout in a piercing voice **3** *vi* laugh loudly and shrilly **4** *vi* make a high-pitched noise —**screamingly** *adv*

scree *n* **1** rock debris at the base of a hill **2** a scree-covered slope

screech *n* **1** a shrill scream **2** a loud high-pitched grating sound ◦ *the screech of brakes* —**screech** *vi* —**screechy** *adj*

screed *n* a lengthy piece of writing (*often pl*)

screen *n* **1** a flat vertical structure used for concealment, partitioning, protection, or decoration **2** something that conceals or shelters ◦ *protected by a screen of leaves* **3** a surface on which images such as films or data are displayed or projected **4** the cinema industry **5** a sieve ■ *v* **1** *vt* conceal, protect, or partition with a screen **2** *vt* protect from something unpleasant or dangerous **3** *vt* show in a cinema or on television ◦ *The programme will be screened next month.* **4** *vt* test or examine people for a disease or for suitability **5** *vt* sieve —**screenful** *n* —**screening** *n*

screen dump *n* the printing or saving of data on a computer screen

screen font *n* a font used on a computer screen

screenplay /skreen play/ *n* a film script

screen saver *n* a utility that provides a moving display for a computer screen during periods of inactivity

screen test *n* a filmed audition for a part in a film —**screen-test** *vti*

screenwriter /skreen ritar/ *n* a writer of screenplays —**screenwriting** *n*

screw *n* **1** a tapering threaded piece of metal used to fasten parts together **2** a propeller **3** an offensive term for an act of sexual intercourse (*slang*) **4** a prison warder (*slang*) ■ *v* **1** *vti* fasten with screws **2** *vti* rotate along a thread to attach or tighten ◦ *screw the bulb into the socket* **3** *vt* crumple into a tight ball ◦ *screwed up the letter and threw it away* **4** *vti* contort or be contorted ◦ *screwed up her eyes against the glare* **5** *vti* an offensive term meaning to have sexual intercourse with somebody (*slang*) **6** *vt* extort (*infml*) —**screwable** *adj*

□ **screw up** *v* **1** *vti* an offensive term meaning make a mess of something (*slang*) **2** *vt* muster courage or nerve

screwdriver /skroo drivar/ *n* **1** a tool for turning screws **2** a vodka and orange juice cocktail

screw top *n* a lid or cap that screws onto a container

scribble /skribb'l/ (-bling, -bled) *vti* **1** write hastily or untidily **2** make meaningless markings —**scribble** *n* —**scribbly** *adj*

scribe *n* **1** somebody who copies documents or manuscripts **2** a clerk —**scribal** *adj*

scrimmage /skrimmij/ *n* a confused struggle —**scrimmage** *vti*

scrimp *vi* economize drastically or excessively

scrip *n* *US* temporary paper currency

script *n* **1** the text of a play, film, or broadcast **2** a system of writing **3** handwriting **4** a sequence of automated computer commands that tells a program to execute a specific procedure ■ *vt* write the script for

scripture /skripchar/, **Scripture** *n* **1** biblical or other sacred writings **2** a biblical or other sacred text —**scriptural** *adj*

scriptwriter /skript ritar/ *n* a writer of film, radio, or television scripts —**scriptwriting** *n*

scrofula /skróffyoolə/ *n* tuberculosis of the lymph glands of the neck

scroll /skrōl/ *n* **1** a roll of parchment or paper for writing a document **2** an ornamental design resembling a scroll ■ *vti* move text or graphics up, down, or across a computer screen

scroll bar *n* a bar on a computer screen for moving through a display

scrooge /skrooj/, **Scrooge** *n* a miser (*infml*)

ORIGIN The original **scrooge** was Ebenezer Scrooge, a character in *A Christmas Carol* (1843) by Charles Dickens.

scrotum /skrótəm/ (*pl* -tums *or* -ta /-tə/) *n* the pouch containing the testicles —**scrotal** *adj*

scrounge /skrownj/ *vti* beg or borrow (*infml*) —**scrounger** *n*

scrub[1] (**scrubbing, scrubbed**) *v* **1** *vti* clean something by rubbing hard, e.g. with a brush **2** *vt* remove dirt by scrubbing **3** *vt* cancel (*infml*) —**scrub** *n*

scrub[2] *n* **1** low straggly vegetation, or an area covered with this **2** a stunted tree or bush —**scrubby** *adj*

scrubber /skrúbbər/ *n* an offensive term for a woman considered to be sexually promiscuous or slovenly (*slang*)

scruff[1] *n* the back of the neck

scruff[2] *n* a scruffy person (*infml*)

scruffy /skrúffi/ (-ier, -iest) *adj* untidy or shabby —**scruffily** *adv* —**scruffiness** *n*

scrum *n* **1** *also* **scrummage** /skrúmmij/ a rugby formation with heads down and linked arms **2** a crowd of jostling people ■ *vi* (**scrumming, scrummed**) form a rugby scrum

scrum half *n* a rugby halfback

scrumptious /skrúmpshəss/ *adj* delightful or delicious (*infml*) —**scrumptiousness** *n*

scrumpy /skrúmpi/ *n SW England* rough cider *(infml)*

scrunch *vt* crumple, crush, or squeeze

scrunchie /skrúnchi/ *n* a fabric-covered elasticated band for fastening hair

scruple /skroõp'l/ *n* 1 a moral or ethical consideration 2 a unit of weight equal to about 1.3 g ■ *vi* (**-pling, -pled**) hesitate because of scruples ○ *wouldn't scruple to cheat*

scrupulous /skroõpyŏŏləss/ *adj* 1 having or showing moral integrity 2 very precise —**scrupulosity** /skroõpyŏŏ lóssəti/ *n* —**scrupulously** *adv* —**scrupulousness** *n* ◊ See note at **careful**

scrutineer /skroõti neér/ *n* an inspector or examiner, e.g. of votes at an election

scrutinize /skroõti nīz/ (**-nizing, -nized**), **scrutinise** *vt* examine closely and carefully

scrutiny /skroõti ni/ *n* 1 careful inspection 2 observation

SCSI /skúzzi/ *n* a high-speed computer interface specification. Full form **small computer systems interface**

scuba /skoõbə/ *n* an underwater breathing apparatus consisting of a portable canister of compressed air and a mouthpiece

scud *vi* (**scudding, scudded**) move swiftly and smoothly ○ *clouds scudding across the sky* ■ *n* 1 a swift smooth movement 2 clouds driven by the wind

Scud missile *n* a surface-to-surface missile

scuff *vti* 1 lightly scrape the surface of something, or become scraped superficially 2 scrape the feet while walking ■ *n* 1 the act or sound of scuffing 2 a mark made by scuffing 3 a flat backless shoe

scuffle /skúff'l/ *n* a disorderly fight at close quarters ■ *vi* (**-fling, -fled**) 1 engage in a scuffle 2 shuffle quickly

scull *n* 1 a single oar at the back of a boat 2 each of a pair of short oars used by a single rower 3 a light racing boat —**scull** *vti* —**sculler** *n*

scullery /skúlləri/ (*pl* **-ies**) *n* a room for kitchen chores

scullion /skúlli ən/ *n* a kitchen servant *(archaic)*

sculpt *v* 1 *vti* make a sculpture 2 *vti* carve or model material 3 *vi* be a sculptor

~~sculpter~~ incorrect spelling of **sculptor**

sculptor /skúlptər/ *n* an artist who makes sculptures

~~sculptur~~ incorrect spelling of **sculpture**

sculpture /skúlpchər/ *n* 1 the creation of three-dimensional art 2 a three-dimensional work of art ■ *vti* (**-turing, -tured**) 1 make a sculpture 2 carve or model material —**sculptural** *adj*

scum *n* 1 a filmy layer on the surface of liquid 2 an offensive term for a person or group of people regarded as disreputable or worthless *(slang insult)* —**scummy** *adj*

scungy /skúnji/ (**-gier, -giest**) *adj ANZ* messy or dirty *(slang)*

scupper¹ /skúppər/ *n* an opening for draining water, e.g. from a ship's deck

scupper² /skúppər/ *vt* 1 sink a ship 2 wreck or ruin a plan or chance

scurrilous /skúrriləss/ *adj* 1 abusive or defamatory 2 foul-mouthed or vulgar —**scurrility** /skə rílləti/ *n* —**scurrilously** *adv*

scurry /skúrri/ (**-ries, -ried**) *vi* 1 move briskly with small steps 2 move about agitatedly or with a swirling motion —**scurry** *n*

scurvy /skúrvi/ *n* a disease caused by a deficiency of vitamin C ■ *adj* (**-vier, -viest**) despicable —**scurviness** *n*

scuttle¹ /skútt'l/ *n* a small covered hatch in a ship's deck or hull ■ *vt* (**-tling, -tled**) 1 sink a ship by letting water into the hull 2 destroy or end something

scuttle² /skútt'l/ *n* a coal container used indoors

scuttle³ /skútt'l/ *vi* (**-tling, -tled**) move with short fast steps —**scuttle** *n*

Scylla /sílla/ *n* a mythological sea monster

scythe /sīth/ *n* a tool with a curved blade for mowing or reaping —**scythe** *vti*

SD *abbr* standard deviation

SDI *abbr* Strategic Defense Initiative

SDLP *abbr* Social Democratic and Labour Party

SDP *abbr* Social Democratic Party

Se *symbol* selenium

SE *abbr* 1 southeast 2 southeastern 3 stock exchange

sea /see/ *n* 1 the salt waters of the Earth 2 a body of salt water 3 a large lake 4 the state of the sea's surface ○ *big seas* 5 a large number or quantity ○ *a sea of faces* ◊ **at sea** bewildered and confused

> **SPELLCHECK** Do not confuse the spelling of **sea** and **see** ('look at'), which sound similar.

sea anemone *n* a small sea animal with tentacles that is usually attached to a rock

seabed /see bed/ *n* the floor of the sea

seabird /see burd/ *n* a bird that lives near the sea

seaboard /see bawrd/ *n* land near the sea

seaborgium /see báwrgi əm/ *n* (*symbol* **Sg**) an unstable radioactive chemical element

sea breeze *n* a breeze blowing from the sea

sea change *n* a great change

seafaring /see fairing/ *adj* 1 regularly going to sea 2 of sea travel or transport ■ *n* a sailor's way of life —**seafarer** *n*

seafood /see food/ *n* edible fish and shellfish

seafront /see frunt/ *n* a seaside waterfront

seagoing /see gō ing/ *adj* 1 for sailing on the open sea 2 regularly going to sea

seagull /see gul/ *n* a common white-and-grey sea bird

sea horse *n* a bony fish that has a head like a horse's and swims upright

seal¹ /seel/ *n* 1 a tight or perfect closure 2 a closure that must be broken to open something 3 an authenticating stamp, or a piece of wax marked with one 4 an ornamental adhesive stamp ■ *vt* 1 close tightly or securely 2 make watertight or airtight

3 authenticate with a seal —**sealable** *adj* —**sealer** *n*

□ **seal off** *vt* make an area inaccessible

seal² /seel/ *n* **1** a fish-eating sea mammal with flippers **2** sealskin ■ *vi* hunt seals —**sealer** *n*

sea-lane *n* an established route for large ships at sea

sealant /seélənt/ *n* a substance used to make something watertight or airtight

sea level *n* the level of the surface of the sea relative to the land

sea lion *n* a large seal with external ears

sealskin /seél skin/ *n* **1** a seal's pelt **2** leather made from a seal's skin

seam /seem/ *n* **1** a line or ridge where pieces are joined, especially by sewing **2** a linear indentation, such as a wrinkle ■ *vt* **1** join pieces along their edges **2** mark with lines

SPELLCHECK Do not confuse the spelling of **seam** and **seem** ('appear to be'), which sound similar.

seaman /seémən/ (*pl* **-men** /-mən/) *n* a sailor —**seamanship** *n*

seamless /seémləss/ *adj* **1** without seams **2** smoothly continuous —**seamlessly** *adv*

seamstress /sémstrəss, seém-/ *n* a woman who sews

seamy /seémi/ (**-ier**, **-iest**) *adj* having unpleasant qualities associated with a degraded way of living —**seaminess** *n*

seance /sáy oNss, -onss, -aanss/ *n* a meeting at which a spiritualist attempts to communicate with the dead

seaplane /seé playn/ *n* an aircraft that can land on water

seaport /seé pawrt/ *n* a town or city's harbour where seagoing ships can berth

sea power *n* **1** a nation with naval strength **2** naval strength

sear /seer/ *v* **1** *vt* burn or scorch **2** *vti* wither or dry up —**sear** *n*

search /surch/ *v* **1** *vti* examine something thoroughly in order to find somebody or something **2** *vt* examine the clothing or body of somebody for concealed items **3** *vt* discover something by investigation ○ *searched out the relevant file* —**search** *n* —**searchable** *adj*

search engine *n* a computer program that searches for specific words, especially on the Internet

searching /súrching/ *adj* penetrating or probing —**searchingly** *adv*

searchlight /súrch līt/ *n* **1** an apparatus for projecting a powerful beam of light **2** the light from a searchlight

search party *n* a group that is looking for a missing person

search warrant *n* a court order authorizing a search of somebody's property

sea salt *n* coarse salt produced from seawater

seascape /seé skayp/ *n* a sea view, or a picture of the sea

sea serpent *n* **1** a legendary giant snake reportedly seen at sea **2** *also* **sea snake** a venomous snake that swims

seashell /seé shel/ *n* the empty shell of a sea mollusc

seashore /seé shawr/ *n* land lying next to the sea, especially a beach

seasick /seé sik/ *adj* feeling sick from the rocking of a ship or boat —**seasickness** *n*

seaside /seé sīd/ *n* land bordering the sea —**seaside** *adj*

season /seéz'n/ *n* **1** a traditional division of the year based on weather conditions **2** a period of the year marked by something such as a particular activity or the availability of a particular food ○ *mating season* ○ *the cricket season* ○ *the asparagus season* **3** a connected series of performances **4** the time when a female animal is sexually receptive **5** a period of time of unspecified length ■ *v* **1** *vti* add salt, pepper, herbs, or spices to food **2** *vt* enliven by adding something ○ *a speech seasoned with wit* **3** *vti* dry out before use *(refers to timber)* **4** *vt* cause to gain experience or toughness ○ *seasoned troops* —**seasoning** *n* ◇ **in season 1** plentifully available and at a peak of quality **2** allowed to be hunted, caught, or killed

ORIGIN **Season** goes back to a Latin verb meaning 'sow, plant', and so is etymologically the 'time for sowing seeds'. In French, the immediate source of **season**, it developed the sense 'suitable time for doing something', and from there it began to refer to divisions of the year characterized by distinctive conditions that made the **season** suitable for particular activities.

seasonable /seéz'nəb'l/ *adj* **1** typical of the season **2** opportune —**seasonably** *adv*

seasonal /seéz'nəl/ *adj* **1** dependent on season **2** limited to particular times —**seasonally** *adv*

seasonal affective disorder *n* depression related to winter

season ticket *n* a ticket valid for multiple use during a specific period of time

seat /seet/ *n* **1** a place to sit **2** something to sit on **3** the part of a garment covering the buttocks **4** a position as member of an official group ○ *a seat on the council* **5** a parliamentary constituency **6** a place where something is located *(fml)* ○ *the seat of emotions* **7** a large or inherited residence ■ *vt* **1** place in a seat **2** provide seats for ◇ **by the seat of your pants** using intuition and guesswork

seat belt *n* a strap designed to keep somebody in a vehicle or aircraft seat

seating /seéting/ *n* **1** seats provided **2** the arrangement of seats or sitters

Seattle /si átt'l/ city in west-central Washington State. Pop. 536,978 (1998).

sea urchin *n* a sea animal with a spiny spherical shell

sea wall *n* a wall built to hold back the sea

seaward /séewərd/, **seawards** /-wərdz/ *adv* towards the sea ■ *adj* situated or directed towards the sea

seawater /sée wawtər/ *n* salt water from the sea

seaway /sée way/ *n* **1** an inland waterway for seagoing ships **2** a route across the sea

seaweed /sée weed/ *n* plants that grow in the sea

seaworthy /sée wurthi/ *adj* fit to sail safely on the sea —**seaworthiness** *n*

sebaceous /sə báyshəss/ *adj* of or producing a waxy substance that lubricates the hair and skin

Sebastian /sə básti ən/, **St** (*fl* 3C) Roman Christian martyr

Sebastopol /sə bástə pol/, **Sevastopol** city in S Ukraine. Pop. 356,000 (1998).

sec[1] *n* a second (*infml*)

sec[2] *adj* describes wine that is dry in taste

sec[3] *abbr* secant

secant /séekənt/ *n* **1** a straight line that intersects with a curve in two or more places **2** the ratio of the hypotenuse to the side adjacent to a given angle in a right-angled triangle

secateurs /sékə turz, -túrz/ *npl* a tool resembling scissors for pruning plants

secede /si séed/ (**-ceding, -ceded**) *vi* withdraw formally from an alliance

~~seceed~~ incorrect spelling of **secede**

secession /si sésh'n/ *n* **1** formal withdrawal from an alliance **2 Secession** the withdrawal of 11 American States from the Union in 1860–61 —**secessionist** *n, adj*

seclude /si klóod/ (**-cluding, -cluded**) *vt* **1** isolate somebody **2** make a place private —**secluded** *adj* —**secludedness** *n* —**seclusion** *n*

second[1] /sékənd/ *adj* **1** coming immediately after the first **2** another **3** additional and less important ■ *n* **1** the one after the first in a series **2** another person or thing **3** a boxer's or duellist's assistant **4** an imperfect article sold cheap **5** in a car, the forward gear between first and third ■ **seconds** *npl* another helping or serving (*infml*) ■ *vt* **1** state support for a motion or nomination proposed by another **2** express agreement with something (*infml*) ○ *I second that.* ■ *adv* **1** except for one ○ *the second-highest mountain in the world* **2** secondly ◇ **second to none** better than anyone or anything else

second[2] /sékənd/ *n* **1** (*symbol* **s**) a unit of time equal to 1/60th of a minute **2** (*symbol* **˝**) a unit of measurement of angles equal to 1/360th of a degree **3** a very short time

second[3] /si kónd/ *vt* transfer somebody temporarily to other duties —**secondment** *n*

secondary /sékəndəri/ *adj* **1** less important than something else **2** happening as a result of something else ○ *secondary tumours* **3** for students aged between 11 and 18 ○ *a secondary school* —**secondarily** *adv* —**secondary** *n*

second best *adj* **1** surpassed only by the best ○ *my second-best suit* **2** inferior to the best —**second best** *n*

second chamber *n* the upper house of a legislative assembly

second class *n* **1** the category immediately below the best **2** a slower and cheaper mail service ■ *adj* **1** of the second class ○ *second-class mail* **2** inferior ○ *treated as second-class citizens* —**second-class** *adv*

Second Coming *n* the prophesied return of Jesus Christ at the end of the world

second cousin *n* a child of a parent's first cousin

second generation *n* **1** the children of immigrants **2** a later stage in the development of something —**second-generation** *adj*

second-guess *vti* predict what will happen or what somebody will do

second hand *n* a hand on a clock or watch that shows the time in seconds

second-hand *adj* **1** previously owned by somebody else **2** selling second-hand goods ■ *adv* **1** in second-hand condition ○ *bought it second-hand* **2** through an intermediary ○ *acquires the information second-hand*

second-in-command *n* a deputy

second lieutenant *n* an officer of the lowest commissioned rank

secondly /sékəndli/ *adv* as the second point in an argument or discussion

second mortgage *n* an additional mortgage on a mortgaged property

second nature *n* an ingrained habit

second opinion *n* an opinion or assessment by another expert

second person *n* the form of a verb or pronoun used when addressing somebody

second sight *n* clairvoyance —**second-sighted** *adj*

second string *n* an alternative plan —**second-string** *adj*

second thought *n* a reconsideration (*often pl*) ○ *having second thoughts about going*

second wind /-wínd/ *n* renewed energy

Second World War *n* = **World War II**

~~secretary~~ incorrect spelling of **secretary**

secrecy /séekrəssi/ *n* **1** the state of being secret ○ *talks held in secrecy* **2** the keeping of a secret or secrets ○ *sworn to secrecy*

secret /séekrət/ *adj* **1** withheld from general knowledge **2** undercover **3** not confessed or admitted ○ *a secret admirer* **4** private and secluded ■ *n* **1** a piece of secret information **2** a mystery —**secretly** *adv*

SYNONYMS **secret, clandestine, covert, furtive, stealthy, surreptitious** CORE MEANING: conveying a desire or need for concealment

secret agent *n* a spy

secretariat /sékrə táiri ət/ *n* **1** an administrative department **2** the secretarial staff of a secretary-general

secretary /sékritəri/ (*pl* **-ies**) *n* **1** somebody who does clerical or administrative work for a person or organization **2** a government minister in charge of a major department **3** a senior civil servant —**secretarial** /sékri táiri əl/ *adj*

secretary-general (*pl* **secretaries-general**) *n* the chief executive officer of an organization such as the United Nations

Secretary of State *n* the US cabinet-level official in charge of foreign affairs

secrete[1] /si kreet/ (**-creting, -creted**) *vti* produce and discharge a substance from a gland or organ —**secretion** *n* —**secretory** *adj*

secrete[2] /si kreet/ (**-creting, -creted**) *vt* put in a hidden place

secretive /seekrətiv/ *adj* unwilling to reveal information —**secretively** *adv* —**secretiveness** *n*

secret service *n* **1** an undercover government organization **2 Secret Service** a US president's security officers

sect *n* **1** a religious group with beliefs at variance with an established group **2** a denomination of a larger religious group

ORIGIN Sect goes back to the past participle of Latin *sequi* 'follow'. In spite of appearances it is not related to *section* or *sector*, but to *sequence* and *second*. The immediate source of **sect** was French.

sectarian /sek táiri ən/ *adj* **1** of relations between religious groups **2** of a single religious group —**sectarian** *n* —**sectarianism** *n*

section /séksh'n/ *n* **1** a distinct part or subdivision **2** a view of something cut through ■ *vt* **1** divide **2** confine to a psychiatric hospital

sectional /séksh'nəl/ *adj* **1** of a particular section **2** involving different sections —**sectionally** *adv*

sectionalism /séksh'nəlizəm/ *n* excessive concern for the interests of a particular group —**sectionalist** *n, adj*

sector /séktər/ *n* **1** a component of an integrated system, e.g. an economy or society **2** a part of an area of military operations **3** a part of a circle bounded by two radii —**sector** *vt* —**sectorial** /sek táwri əl/ *adj*

secular /sékyoolər/ *adj* **1** not concerned with religion **2** not religious or spiritual **3** not belonging to a monastic order ○ *secular clergy* ■ *n* **1** a member of the secular clergy **2** a lay person —**secularity** /sékyoo lárrəti/ *n* —**secularly** *adv*

secularism /sékyoolərizəm/ *n* **1** the exclusion of religion from public affairs **2** rejection of religion —**secularistic** /sékyoolə rístik/ *adj*

secularize /sékyoolə rīz/ (**-izing, -ized**), **secularise** *vt* **1** transfer from religious to state control **2** make secular —**secularization** /sékyoolə rī záysh'n/ *n*

secure /si kyoor, -kyáwr/ *adj* **1** not troubled by fear or doubt **2** firmly fixed or attached

3 unlikely to fail or be lost ○ *a secure investment* **4** safe from attack or theft ■ *vt* (**-curing, -cured**) **1** fix or attach firmly **2** make safe **3** acquire —**securely** *adv* —**securement** *n* ◊ See note at **get**

secure server *n* an Internet server suitable for confidential communications, e.g. e-commerce payments

security /si kyoorəti, -kyáwr-/ (*pl* **-ties**) *n* **1** the state or feeling of safety **2** freedom from worry about loss **3** something giving assurance **4** protection against attack, crime, espionage, or other danger **5** people entrusted to guard a building or organization **6** an asset deposited to guarantee repayment **7** a guarantor **8** a financial instrument such as a share certificate or bond

security blanket *n* **1** a familiar object, e.g. a blanket, that a child carries around **2** a policy of withholding information in the interests of security

security guard *n* a guard employed to protect a building or site

security risk *n* somebody or something considered likely to compromise security

sedan /si dán/ *n* **1** *ANZ, US, Can* a car with a permanent roof, front and rear seats, and a separate boot **2** *also* **sedan chair** an enclosed chair carried on poles

sedate /si dáyt/ *adj* dignified and unhurried ■ *vt* give a sedative to —**sedately** *adv* —**sedateness** *n* —**sedation** *n*

sedative /séddətiv/ *n* a drug that induces a state of calm or drowsiness —**sedative** *adj*

Seddon /sédd'n/, **Richard John** (1845–1906) British-born prime minister of New Zealand (1893–1906)

sedentary /sédd'ntəri/ *adj* **1** involving a lot of sitting **2** taking little exercise

Seder /sáydər/ *n* a Jewish feast on either of the first two nights of Passover, commemorating the exodus of the Jews from Egypt

sedge *n* a plant resembling grass

sediment /séddimənt/ *n* **1** settled matter at the bottom of a liquid **2** eroded material transported and deposited elsewhere

sedimentary /séddi méntəri/ *adj* **1** of or forming sediment **2** describes rock formed from eroded material

sedimentation /séddi men táysh'n/ *n* the formation of sedimentary rocks or sediment

sedition /si dísh'n/ *n* rebellion against government authority, or incitement to rebel —**seditious** *adj* —**seditiously** *adv*

seduce /si dyooss/ (**-ducing, -duced**) *vt* **1** induce to have sexual relations **2** tempt or win over —**seducer** *n* —**seduction** /si dúksh'n/ *n* —**seductive** /si dúktiv/ *adj* —**seductively** *adv* —**seductress** /si dúktrəss/ *n*

sedulous /séddyooləss/ *adj* painstaking (*literary*) —**sedulity** /si dyooləti/ *n*

see[1] /see/ (**saw, seen**) *v* **1** *vti* perceive with the eyes **2** *vi* have vision **3** *vti* view or watch something **4** *vti* understand something **5** *vt* meet, visit, consult, or have an interview with somebody **6** *vt* have a romantic relationship with somebody **7** *vt* imagine something in a particular way ○ *see her as a potential rival* **9** *vt* undergo or experience something ○ *saw active service* **10** *vt* escort somebody **11** *vt* make sure that something happens ○ *See that they wash their hands.* **12** *vt* find out ○ *see what he wants* ◊ See note at **sea**

□ **see about** *vt* attend to or deal with
□ **see off** *vt* attend the departure of
□ **see out** *vt* escort to the exit
□ **see over** *or* **round** *vt* make a tour of a building
□ **see through** *vt* **1** help somebody through a difficulty **2** finish something **3** perceive the truth beneath the exterior ○ *I saw through his bravado.*
□ **see to** *vt* attend to or take care of

see[2] /see/ *n* **1** a bishop's diocese **2** a bishop's authority

seed /seed/ *n* **1** a plant part produced by sexual reproduction containing the embryo of a new plant **2** plant parts used for propagation, as a whole **3** a source or beginning ○ *the seeds of doubt* **4** descendants *(literary)* **5** a graded competitor ■ *vt* **1** plant seeds in **2** remove seeds from **3** rank a player —**seedless** *adj* ◊ **go** *or* **run to seed** become shabby or unhealthy

seedbed /seed bed/ *n* **1** a plot of ground for growing seedlings **2** a place where something develops

seed capital *n* initial funding for a business venture

seedling /seedling/ *n* a young plant grown from a seed

seedy /seedi/ (-**ier**, -**iest**) *adj* **1** shabby or disreputable **2** having many seeds

seeing /see ing/ *conj* in view of the fact ○ *Seeing that you're an old friend, I'll give you a special price.*

seek (**sought** /sawt/, **sought**) *v* **1** *vti* try to find **2** *vt* try to obtain or reach **3** *vt* attempt ○ *seeking to exploit the rift between them* —**seeker** *n*

seem /seem/ *vti* give an impression of being or doing something ○ *It's not as easy as it seems.* ○ *We seem to have a misunderstanding.* ◊ See note at **seam**

seeming /seeming/ *adj* apparent but not necessarily true or real —**seemingly** *adv*

seemly /seemli/ (-**lier**, -**liest**) *adj* suitable and correct —**seemliness** *n*

seen past participle of **see**[1]

seep *vi* **1** pass slowly through a small opening *(refers to liquids or gases)* **2** enter or depart gradually —**seep** *n* —**seepage** *n*

seer /seer, see ər/ *n* **1** somebody believed to be able to predict the future **2** somebody with supposed supernatural powers

seersucker /seer sukər/ *n* a lightweight fabric with alternate puckered and smooth stripes

ORIGIN Seersucker derives via Hindi from a Persian phrase meaning literally 'milk and honey', which came to refer to a striped linen

garment. The word is first recorded in English in the early 18C.

seesaw /see saw/ *n* **1** a playground toy on which people go up and down at opposite ends of a bar **2** an up-and-down or other alternating movement ■ *vi* **1** ride on a seesaw **2** move like a seesaw

seethe /seeth/ (**seething, seethed**) *vi* **1** boil or appear to boil **2** be angry **3** be full of bustling activity —**seething** *adj*

see-through *adj* made of transparent material

segment *n* /segmənt/ a component or section ■ *vt* /seg mént/ split into segments —**segmental** /seg mént'l/ *adj* —**segmentation** /ség men táysh'n/ *n*

Segovia /si gṓvi ə/, **Andrés** (1893–1987) Spanish guitarist

segregate /séggri gayt/ (-**gating**, -**gated**) *v* **1** *vt* separate people or groups **2** *vti* keep different groups within a population separate —**segregation** /séggri gáysh'n/ *n* —**segregational** *adj*

ORIGIN Segregate comes from a Latin word meaning literally 'separate from the flock'. It was adopted into English in the mid-16C.

segue /sé gway/ (-**gues**, -**gueing**, -**gued**) *vi* **1** in music, continue by playing another piece or passage without a pause **2** make a smooth transition —**segue** *n*

~~seige~~ incorrect spelling of **siege**

Seine /sayn, sen/ river rising in E France and flowing northwestwards through Paris into the English Channel. Length 776 km/482 mi.

seismic /síɀmik/ *adj* **1** of earthquakes **2** extremely large or great *(infml)* ○ *had a seismic impact* —**seismically** *adv*

seismograph /síɀmə graaf, -graf/ *n* a device for detecting and measuring earthquakes —**seismographer** /síɀ mógrəfər/ *n* —**seismographic** /síɀmə gráffik/ *adj* —**seismography** /síɀ mógrəfi/ *n*

seismology /síɀ mólləji/ *n* the study of earthquakes —**seismological** /síɀmə lójjik'l/ *adj* —**seismologist** *n*

~~seive~~ incorrect spelling of **sieve**

seize /seez/ (**seizing, seized**) *vt* **1** take hold of quickly and firmly **2** take advantage of eagerly and immediately **3** affect suddenly **4** appropriate or confiscate **5** take into custody

seizure /sée zhər/ *n* **1** the act of seizing, or the state of being seized **2** an attack of an illness or condition, e.g. of epilepsy

seldom /séldəm/ *adv* rarely —**seldomness** *n*

select /si lékt/ *vti* choose from among others ■ *adj* **1** of particularly good quality **2** having limited membership **3** specially chosen —**selectee** /si lék tee/ *n* —**selectness** *n*

select committee *n* a parliamentary investigative group

selection /si léksh'n/ *n* **1** the act of choosing, or the state of being chosen **2** the available choice **3** somebody or something chosen

selective /si léktiv/ adj 1 not universal 2 discerning —**selectively** adv —**selectiveness** n —**selectivity** /si lék tívvəti/ n

selenium /si leèni əm/ n (symbol Se) a nonmetallic chemical element. Use: photocells, photocopiers.

self n (pl **selves**) 1 somebody's perceived personality o *not his usual self* 2 somebody's individual personality o *develop a sense of self* 3 self-interest ■ pron myself, yourself, himself, or herself (infml) o *not enough to sustain self and family* ■ adj 1 self-coloured 2 of the same fabric

self- prefix of, by, for, or in itself o *self-assured* o *self-control*

self-absorbed adj preoccupied with yourself —**self-absorption** n

self-addressed adj addressed to the sender o *enclose a self-addressed envelope*

self-adhesive adj having a sticky surface

self-analysis n analysis of your own personality

self-appointed adj assuming a particular role personally o *a self-appointed arbiter of good taste*

self-assembly n construction from a kit of parts

self-assured adj relaxed and self-confident —**self-assurance** n

self-catering adj describes accommodation with cooking facilities but no food provided —**self-catering** n

self-centred adj thinking only of yourself —**self-centredness** n

self-coloured adj all of one colour

self-confessed adj according to your own admission

self-confidence n confidence in yourself and your abilities —**self-confident** adj —**self-confidently** adv

self-congratulation n smugness —**self-congratulatory** adj

self-conscious adj 1 ill at ease in the company of others 2 highly conscious of the impression you make on others —**self-consciously** adv —**self-consciousness** n

self-contained adj 1 having everything required 2 keeping feelings and opinions private 3 not needing the company or support of others —**self-containment** n

self-control n the ability to control your own reactions or impulses —**self-controlled** adj

self-defeating adj thwarting its own aims

self-defence n 1 the use of force to defend yourself, or the legal right to do this 2 martial arts or other unarmed combat techniques

self-denial n denial of your own desires —**self-denying** adj

self-deprecating, self-deprecatory adj belittling yourself or your achievements

self-destruct /-di strúkt/ vi 1 destroy itself automatically 2 ruin your own life —**self-destruct** adj

self-destruction n 1 an act of self-destructing 2 suicide —**self-destructive** adj

self-determination n 1 the right of a people to choose their own government 2 the right to decide for yourself

self-discipline n the ability to motivate or control yourself —**self-disciplined** adj

self-discovery n learning about yourself

self-doubt n lack of self-confidence

self-drive adj describes a hired vehicle driven by the hirer

self-effacing adj modest and reserved —**self-effacingly** adv

self-employed adj working independently or running your own business —**self-employment** n

self-esteem n self-respect

self-evident adj obvious without explanation or proof —**self-evidently** adv

self-examination n 1 reflection on your own thoughts and behaviour 2 the regular examination of parts of your own body for signs of disease

self-explanatory adj easy to understand by itself

self-expression n expression of your personality and feelings, e.g. through art

self-financing adj financed without outside support

self-fulfilling adj 1 happening because expected 2 satisfying —**self-fulfilment** n

self-governing, self-governed adj governed or run by its own inhabitants or employees

self-government n democracy or political independence

self-help n the solving of problems without outside professional or government help

selfhood /sélf hòod/ n 1 individuality 2 a sense of self 3 somebody's character or personality

self-image n your opinion of your own worth or attractiveness

self-importance n excessively high evaluation of your own importance —**self-important** adj —**self-importantly** adv

self-imposed adj taken on by choice o *a self-imposed deadline*

self-improvement n improvement of yourself by your own effort

self-induced adj resulting from your own actions

self-indulgence n excessive pursuit of your own pleasure or satisfaction —**self-indulgent** adj —**self-indulgently** adv

self-inflicted adj done to yourself o *a self-inflicted wound*

self-interest n 1 selfishness 2 your own advantage —**self-interested** adj

selfish /sélfish/ adj looking after your own interests, needs, and desires —**selfishly** adv —**selfishness** n

self-knowledge n understanding of yourself

selfless /sélfləss/ adj putting others' needs

ahead of your own —**selflessly** adv —**selflessness** n

self-made adj 1 successful as a result of your own efforts 2 made without others' help

self-opinionated adj 1 certain of being right 2 very conceited

self-perpetuating adj having the power to preserve or renew itself indefinitely

self-pity n feeling sorry for yourself —**self-pitying** adj —**self-pityingly** adv

self-portrait n a portrait or written description of the artist or writer who made it

self-possessed adj in control of emotions —**self-possession** n

self-preservation n the instinct to keep yourself safe

self-proclaimed adj claiming to be a particular thing

self-promotion n action to attract attention to yourself or your abilities

self-regard n 1 concern or admiration only for yourself 2 self-respect

self-reproach n criticizing or blaming yourself —**self-reproachful** adj

self-respect n belief in your own worth and dignity —**self-respecting** adj

self-restraint n control over what you say and do

self-righteous adj sure of your moral superiority (disapproving) —**self-righteously** adv —**self-righteousness** n

self-rule n the right of a people to choose their own government

self-sacrifice n the giving up of personal needs for the sake of others —**self-sacrificing** adj

selfsame /sélf saym/ adj identical

self-seeking adj selfish —**self-seeking** n

self-service adj describes a shop, restaurant, or machine where people help themselves —**self-service** n

self-serving adj putting personal considerations first

self-styled adj claiming to be as stated ◊ See note at **so-called**

self-sufficient adj 1 able to provide everything you need without buying from others 2 able to manage alone —**self-sufficiency** n

self-supporting adj 1 getting along financially without outside help 2 standing without being held —**self-support** n

self-taught adj having learned something without formal instruction

self-tender n an offer made by a company to buy back its own shares

self-worth n a belief in your own value

Seljuk /sel jóok/ n a member of a Turkish ruling family before the Ottoman Empire —**Seljuk** adj

Selkirk /sél kurk/, **Alexander** (1676–1721) Scottish sailor

sell (**sold**) v 1 vti exchange something for money 2 vt offer something for sale 3 vi be bought in quantity 4 vt make people want to buy a product 5 vt persuade somebody to accept an idea ○ need to sell the proposal to shareholders —**seller** n ◊ **sell yourself** emphasize your positive qualities as a candidate for a particular job ◊ **sold on** enthusiastic about something (infml)

☐ **sell off** vt sell cheaply

☐ **sell out** vti 1 sell all of something 2 betray your own principles (infml)

sell-by date n the date something perishable should be sold by ◊ **past its** or **your sell-by date** thought to be too advanced in years or old-fashioned to be taken seriously any longer (infml; sometimes offensive)

seller's market n a time when demand is greater than supply, resulting in higher prices

selling point n a feature of a product or idea that makes people want to buy or accept it

sell-off n a cheap quick sale of goods

Sellotape /séllō tayp/ tdmk a trademark for a type of transparent adhesive tape

sellout /sél owt/ n 1 an event for which no more tickets are available 2 a betrayal (infml)

selves plural of **self**

semantic /sə mántik/ adj 1 of the meanings of words 2 of semantics —**semantically** adv

semantics /sə mántiks/ n (+ sing verb) 1 the study of meaning in language 2 the study of symbols —**semanticist** /-tissist/ n

semaphore /sémmə fawr/ n 1 a system of signalling using hand-held flags 2 a mechanical signalling device —**semaphore** vti

Semarang /sémmə ráng/ port on the island of Java, Indonesia. Pop. 812,979 (1997).

semblance /sémblənss/ n 1 a trace of a quality 2 an outward appearance

semen /seémən/ n fluid containing sperm ejaculated by a male

semester /sə méstər/ n a division of the academic year lasting 15 to 18 weeks or 6 months

semi /sémmi/ n (infml) 1 a semidetached house 2 a semifinal

semi- prefix 1 partial, partially, somewhat ○ semiconductor 2 half ○ semibreve 3 resembling, having some characteristics of ○ semitropical 4 occurring twice during a particular period ○ semiweekly

semiautomatic /sémmi awtə máttik/ adj 1 describes a weapon that reloads automatically 2 partially automated —**semiautomatic** n

semibreve /sémmi breev/ n the longest musical note in common use, with a duration equivalent to four crotchets

semicircle /sémmi surk'l/ n a half circle —**semicircular** /sémmi súrkyŏŏlər/ adj

semicolon /sémmi kõlən, -lon/ n a punctuation mark separating parts of a sentence or list

USAGE A **semicolon** is used to separate two related parts of a sentence when each part could stand alone as a sentence: The building is chiefly a tourist attraction; it is rarely used *as a church these days.* Semicolons may also be used instead of commas to separate parts of a list: *We invited Jack and Kate, who live next door; Maria, my sister-in-law; and some of our colleagues from work.* See also **colon**.

semiconductor /sémmi kən dúktər/ *n* a solid material that has partial electrical conductivity —**semiconductive** *adj*

semiconscious /sémmi kónshəss/ *adj* partially conscious —**semiconsciousness** *n*

semidetached /sémmi di tácht/ *adj* sharing a wall with a neighbouring house —**semidetached** *n*

semifinal /sémmi fín'l/ *n* a round of a competition immediately before the final —**semifinal** *adj* —**semifinalist** *n*

seminal /sémmin'l/ *adj* **1** influential, especially in stimulating further thought or research **2** capable of development

seminar /sémmi naar/ *n* **1** a meeting for the presentation or discussion of a specialized subject **2** a meeting of students for study or discussion with a tutor

seminary /sémminəri/ (*pl* **-ies**) *n* a college for training the clergy —**seminarian** /sémmi naíri ən/ *n*

semiotics /sémmi óttiks, seèmi-/ *n* (+ *sing verb*) **1** the study of signs and symbols **2** the study of symptoms of diseases —**semiotic** *adj* —**semiotician** /ə tísh'n, seèmi-/ *n*

semipermanent /sémmi púrmənent/ *adj* lasting for a long time

semipermeable /sémmi púrmi əb'l/ *adj* filtering selectively

semiprecious /sémmi préshəss/ *adj* describes moderately valuable stones and minerals

semiprofessional /sémmi prə fésh'nəl/ *adj* **1** participating in a sport or artistic activity for pay but not as a full-time professional **2** for semiprofessional athletes or players —**semiprofessional** *n* —**semiprofessionally** *adv*

semiquaver /sémmi kwáyvər/ *n* a musical note equivalent to 1/16th of a semibreve

semiskilled /sémmi skíld/ *adj* with or requiring some skill or training

semi-skimmed *adj* describes milk with some cream removed

semisolid /sémmi sóllid/ *adj* half solid, half liquid

Semite /seè mīt, sémm-/ *n* a member of a Semitic-speaking people

Semitic /sə míttik/ *n* a group of languages spoken in North Africa and SW Asia, including Hebrew and Arabic ■ *adj* **1** of Semitic **2** speaking a Semitic language

semitone /sémmi tōn/ *n* the smallest interval in a musical scale —**semitonic** /-tónnik/ *adj*

semitropical /sémmi tróppik'l/ *adj* subtropical

semiweekly /sémmi weèkli/ *adj* happening or published twice a week —**semiweekly** *adv*

semolina /sémmə leènə/ *n* small particles of ground-up wheat. Use: pasta, couscous, other foods.

senate /sénnət/ *n* **1** *also* **Senate** the upper legislative body of government, e.g. in the United States **2** the highest council of ancient Rome **3** the building where a senate meets

ORIGIN The original Roman **senate** was literally an 'assembly of elders'. The word is formed from Latin *senex* 'man of advanced years, elder'.

senator /sénnətər/ *n* a member of a senate —**senatorial** /sénnə táwri əl/ *adj*

send (**sent**) *vt* **1** cause somebody or something to go **2** communicate a message **3** tell or command somebody to go somewhere **4** cause something to happen or be received **5** propel something ○ *A gust of wind sent the papers swirling round the room.* **6** drive somebody into a particular state ○ *The delay is sending her into fits of frustration.* —**sender** *n* ◇ **send packing** send away in a brusque way (*infml*)

□ **send away for** *vt* order by post

□ **send down** *vt* **1** expel from a university **2** sentence to imprisonment (*infml*)

□ **send for** *vt* request the delivery or appearance of

□ **send in** *vt* submit by post

□ **send off** *vt* dismiss a player from a game for rule-breaking

□ **send up** *vt* mock by imitation (*infml*)

Sendai /sen dí/ city on NE Honshu Island, Japan. Pop. 975,723 (2000).

sendoff /sénd of/ *n* a farewell

sendup /sénd up/ *n* a parody (*infml*)

Seneca /sénnəkə/ (4? BC–AD 65) Spanish-born Roman philosopher and writer

Senegal /sénni gáwl, -gaàl/ country in West Africa, on the Atlantic Ocean. Cap. Dakar. Pop. 10,284,929 (2001). —**Senegalese** /sénni gə leèz/ *n, adj*

~~senery~~ incorrect spelling of **scenery**

senescent /si néss'nt/ *adj* ageing —**senescence** *n*

senile /seè nīl/ *adj* **1** mentally less acute in later life **2** of later life ○ *senile dementia* —**senilely** *adv* —**senility** /sə níllət/ *n*

senior /seèni ər/ *adj* **1** more advanced in age **2** higher in rank —**senior** *n*

senior citizen *n* somebody of retirement age or older

seniority /seèni órrəti/ (*pl* **-ties**) *n* **1** status accorded to greater age or higher rank **2** the state of being senior to somebody else

senna /sénnə/ *n* **1** dried plant leaves or pods. Use: purgative, laxative. **2** the plant from which senna is obtained

Ayrton Senna

Senna /sénnə/, **Ayrton** (1960–94) Brazilian racing driver

señor /se nyáw/ (*pl* **-ñors** *or* **-ñores** /-nyáw ress/) *n* the Spanish equivalent of Mr

señora /se nyáwrə/ *n* the Spanish equivalent of Mrs

señorita /sénnyaw réetə/ *n* the Spanish equivalent of Miss

sensation /sen sáysh'n/ *n* **1** a physical feeling **2** the power to perceive through the sense organs **3** a mental impression **4** a state or cause of avid public interest

sensational /sen sáysh'nəl/ *adj* **1** extraordinary ○ *a sensational defeat* **2** exceptionally good (*infml*) **3** involving sensationalism —**sensationally** *adv*

sensationalism /sen sáysh'nəlizəm/ *n* emphasis on the most shocking, lurid, or emotive aspects of something —**sensationalist** *n, adj* —**sensationalize** *vt*

sense *n* **1** a physical faculty for acquiring information about the world, e.g. sight or smell **2** a feeling derived from the senses or intuition ○ *a sense of security* **3** the ability to perceive or appreciate a particular quality ○ *a sense of humour* **4** intelligence or sound judgment **5** a useful purpose or good reason **6** a meaning ■ **senses** *npl* a rational state of mind ■ *vt* (**sensing, sensed**) **1** perceive **2** understand intuitively —**sensate** /sén sayt/ *adj* ◇ **in a sense 1** considered from one point of view **2** as a partial description ◇ **make sense** be understandable and consistent with reason ◇ **make sense of** understand

senseless /sénssləss/ *adj* **1** having lost consciousness **2** with no apparent purpose ○ *a senseless crime* —**senselessly** *adv* —**senselessness** *n*

sense organ *n* an organ such as the eye or ear that receives stimuli from the physical world and transmits them to the brain

sensibility /sénn sə bílləti/ *n* the capacity to respond emotionally ■ **sensibilities** *npl* sensitivity about moral or ethical issues

sensible /sénssəb'l/ *adj* **1** showing intelligence and sound judgment **2** able to be perceived **3** aware of something (*fml*) —**sensibleness** *n* —**sensibly** *adv* ◇ See note at **aware**

sensitive /sénssətiv/ *adj* **1** acutely perceptive **2** easily damaged or irritated ○ *sensitive teeth* **3** affected by an external stimulus (*often in combination*) ○ *sensitive to light* ○ *a touch-sensitive screen* **4** thoughtful and sympathetic **5** easily offended, annoyed, or upset —**sensitively** *adv* —**sensitivity** /sénssə tívvəti/ *n*

sensitize /sénssə tīz/ (**-tizing, -tized**), **sensitise** *vt* **1** make sensitive **2** induce sensitivity to a particular substance —**sensitization** /sénssə tī záysh'n/ *n*

sensor /sénssər/ *n* a detecting device

sensory /sénssəri/ *adj* of sensation and the senses

sensual /sénssyoo əl, -shoo əl/ *adj* **1** of the senses rather than the intellect **2** of physical or sexual pleasure —**sensually** *adv* —**sensualness** *n*

sensuous /sénssyoo əss, -shoo əss/ *adj* **1** of sense stimulation **2** causing or appreciating pleasurable sense stimulation —**sensuously** *adv* —**sensuousness** *n*

sent past tense, past participle of **send**

~~sentance~~ incorrect spelling of **sentence**

sentence /séntənss/ *n* **1** a complete meaningful linguistic unit **2** a judgment specifying punishment for a crime ■ *vt* (**-tencing, -tenced**) allocate a punishment to a criminal

sentence adverb *n* an adverb modifying a whole sentence

sententious /sen ténshəss/ *adj* **1** full of aphorisms **2** excessively moralizing —**sententiously** *adv*

sentient /sénsh'nt, -shi ənt/ *adj* **1** capable of feeling and perception **2** capable of responding with feeling —**sentience** *n*

sentiment /séntimənt/ *n* **1** an idea based on a feeling or emotion **2** a general feeling or opinion ■ **sentiments** *npl* a view or opinion

sentimental /sénti mént'l/ *adj* **1** affected acutely by emotional matters **2** displaying too much emotion **3** appealing to tender feelings —**sentimentalist** *n* —**sentimentality** /sénti men tálləti/ *n* —**sentimentalize** *vti* —**sentimentally** *adv*

sentinel /séntinəl/ *n* a lookout or guard —**sentinel** *vt*

sentry /séntri/ (*pl* **-tries**) *n* a member of the armed services posted as a lookout or guard

sentry box *n* a shelter for a sentry

Seoul /sōl/ capital and largest city of South Korea. Pop. 10,229,262 (1995).

Sep. *abbr* September

sepal /sépp'l/ *n* a modified leaf that encloses the petals of a flower

separate *adj* /sépparət/ **1** not touching or connected **2** distinct or unrelated ■ *v* /séppə rayt/ (**-rating, -rated**) **1** *vt* move or keep apart **2** *vt* be positioned between **3** *vt* be the factor that distinguishes **4** *vi* come apart or become detached **5** *vi* part company **6** *vi* cease living as a couple **7** *vt* categorize or sort **8** *vti* divide —**separable** *adj* —**separately** *adv* —**separateness** *n* —**separation** /séppə ráysh'n/ *n* —**separator** *n*

☐ **separate out** *vti* come or cause to come out of a mixture

separated /séppə raytid/ *adj* no longer living together but still married

separatist /sépparətist/ *n* **1** an advocate of breaking away from a group or country **2** a supporter of the separation of different groups —**separatism** *n* —**separatist** *adj*

~~seperate~~ incorrect spelling of **separate**

sepia /séè pi ə/ *n* **1** a reddish-brown pigment or colour **2** a sepia-tinted drawing or photograph —**sepia** *adj*

sepsis /sépsiss/ *n* the condition caused by the presence of microorganisms or their toxins in body tissue or blood

Sept. *abbr* September

September /sep témbər, səp-/ *n* the 9th month of the year in the Gregorian calendar

ORIGIN September comes from a Latin word literally meaning 'seventh month'. In ancient Rome the calendar started the year in March.

septet /sep tét/, **septette** *n* 1 a group of seven musical performers 2 a piece of music for seven performers

septic /séptik/ *adj* 1 affected by sepsis and full of pus 2 of sepsis —**septicity** /sep tíssəti/ *n*

septicaemia /sépti seémi ə/ *n* the presence of microorganisms in the bloodstream —**septicaemic** *adj*

septic tank *n* a container in which human waste is decomposed by bacteria

septuagenarian /séptyoo əjə náiri ən/ *n* somebody who is between 70 and 79 years old —**septuagenarian** *adj*

Septuagint /séptyoo əjint/ *n* a Greek version of the Hebrew Bible made in the 3C and 2C BC

sepulcher *n*, *vt* US = sepulchre

sepulchral /si púlkrəl/ *adj* 1 dismal or gloomy 2 of sepulchres *(fml)*

sepulchre /sépp'lkər/ *n* a burial vault —**sepulchre** *vt*

sequel /seékwəl/ *n* 1 a film, book, or television programme that continues the story of an earlier one 2 something that follows something else

sequence /seékwənss/ *n* 1 a series of things arranged or connected in a particular way, or happening one after another 2 the order in which things happen or are arranged ■ *vt* (-quencing, -quenced) put or do things in order —**sequential** /si kwénsh'l/ *adj* —**sequentially** *adv*

sequential access *n* a method of accessing and reading a computer file by starting at the beginning

sequester /si kwéstər/ *vt* 1 put somebody into isolation *(fml)* 2 take somebody's property temporarily until an obligation is discharged

sequestrate /seékwə strayt, si kwé-/ (-trating, -trated) *vt* take somebody's property temporarily —**sequestration** /seé kwe stráysh'n, sék-/ *n* —**sequestrator** /seékwi straytər/ *n*

sequin /seékwin/ *n* 1 a small shiny decoration on clothing or accessories 2 a former gold coin used in Venice and Turkey —**sequinned** *adj*

sequoia /si kwóy ə/ (*pl same or* -as) *n* a very tall Californian redwood tree

sera plural of serum

seraglio /sə raáli ō/ (*pl* -glios) *n* 1 a Muslim harem 2 a Turkish palace

seraph /sérrəf/ (*pl* -aphs *or* -aphim /-əfim/) *n* an angel of the highest rank —**seraphic** /sə ráffik/ *adj*

Serbia /súrbi ə/ republic in SE Europe that, together with Montenegro, makes up the Federal Republic of Yugoslavia. Cap. Bel-

grade. Pop. 10,003,309 (2001). —**Serbian** *n*, *adj*

Serbo-Croatian /súrbō krō áysh'n/, **Serbo-Croat** /-krố at/ *n* 1 the Slavic languages spoken by the Serbians and Croatians 2 a speaker of Serbo-Croatian ■ *adj* of Serbo-Croatian

sere /seer/, **sear** *adj* dry and withered *(literary)*

serenade /sérrə náyd/ *n* 1 a love song performed for the loved one, traditionally in the evening outside a window 2 an instrumental composition for a small ensemble —**serenade** *vt* —**serenader** *n*

ORIGIN Serenades are traditionally sung in the evening, but this was not originally part of the meaning. The word came through French from Italian *serenata*, which was formed from *sereno* 'serene' but came to be associated with *sera* 'evening'.

serendipity /sérrən díppəti/ *n* a talent for making useful discoveries by chance —**serendipitous** *adj* —**serendipitously** *adv* ◊ See note at **lucky**

ORIGIN Serendipity was coined by the writer Horace Walpole, who introduced it in a letter to a friend dated 28 January 1754. He formed it from the title of a fairy tale, *The Three Princes of Serendip*, whose heroes possessed the talent. *Serendip* is said to be an old name for Sri Lanka.

serene /sə reén/ *adj* 1 calm and untroubled 2 cloudless —**serenely** *adv* —**serenity** /sə rénnəti/ *n*

serf *n* 1 a medieval farmworker treated as the landowner's property 2 any enslaved labourer —**serfdom** *n*

~~sergant~~ incorrect spelling of sergeant

serge *n* a type of strong cloth

ORIGIN Serge is etymologically related to *silk*. It came via French from Latin *sericus* in its feminine form *lana serica*, literally 'wool of the Seres'. *Seres* was the name given to the people of China and other countries from where silk was obtained, and *sericus* gave rise to the word *silk*.

sergeant /saárjənt/ *n* 1 in various armed forces, a noncommissioned officer of a rank above corporal 2 a police officer of a rank above constable —**sergeancy** *n*

sergeant at arms (*pl* sergeants at arms), **serjeant at arms** (*pl* serjeants at arms) *n* a court official responsible for keeping order

sergeant major (*pl* sergeants major *or* sergeant majors) *n* in various armed forces, a noncommissioned officer of the highest rank

serial /seéri əl/ *n* 1 a story that is published or broadcast in parts 2 a regular newspaper or magazine ■ *adj* 1 happening or doing something repeatedly 2 produced in parts —**serially** *adv* ◊ See note at **cereal**

serialize /seéri ə līz/ (-izing, -ized), **serialise** *vt* produce a story in parts —**serialization** /seéri ə līz záysh'n/ *n*

serial killer *n* somebody who murders many people over a period of time —**serial killing** *n*

serial number *n* an identification number

serial port *n* a computer socket for peripherals

series /seer eez/ (*pl same*) *n* 1 a number of things that come one after another 2 a set of broadcast programmes 3 a set of matches between the same teams 4 an arrangement of electric elements

USAGE If you use **series** to mean 'a single set of things', use a singular verb even if **series** is followed by the preposition *of* and a plural noun: *A series of meetings is planned for next year.* If you use **series** to mean 'two or more sets of things', use a plural verb: *Three series of meetings are planned for next year.*

serif /sérrif/ *n* a decorative line finishing a stroke of a printed letter

serious /seeri əss/ *adj* 1 very bad or great 2 important and grave 3 likely to succeed 4 thoughtful or thought-provoking 5 needing careful thought or attention 6 not lighthearted —**seriously** *adv* —**seriousness** *n*

serjeant at arms *n* = sergeant at arms

sermon /súrmən/ *n* 1 a religious talk that forms part of a church service 2 a long lecture on behaviour

sermonize /súrmə nīz/ (**-izing, -ized**), **sermonise** *vti* lecture somebody about his or her behaviour

serotonin /sérrə tónin/ *n* a chemical in the body that acts as a transmitter of nerve impulses

serpent /súrpənt/ *n* 1 a snake *(literary)* 2 a treacherous person 3 **Serpent** Satan

serpentine /súrpən tīn/ *adj* 1 winding or curving 2 resembling a snake *(literary)* ■ *n* a green or brown mineral. Use: ornamental stone.

SERPS /surps/, **Serps** *n* a government pension for people who have been employees. Full form **state earnings-related pension scheme**

serrated /sə ráytid/ *adj* with notches or projections

serration /sə ráysh'n/ *n* 1 a series of notches like the teeth of a saw 2 a tooth or notch

serried /sérrid/ *adj* close together *(literary)*

serum /seerəm/ (*pl* -**rums** *or* -**ra** /-rə/) *n* 1 the liquid part of blood without clotting agents 2 MED = **antiserum**

servant /súrvənt/ *n* 1 somebody employed to do household jobs 2 somebody who works for the public

serve *v* (**serving, served**) 1 *vti* prepare and supply food or drink 2 *vti* give food or drink to somebody 3 *vt* provide goods or services for a customer 4 *vi* be of use 5 *vti* have a particular effect 6 *vt* spend a particular length of time in prison 7 *vi* be in the armed forces 8 *vi* in racket games, put the ball or shuttlecock into play 9 *vt* deliver a legal document to somebody *(fml)* 10 *vti* work for somebody as a servant ■ *n* in racket games,

a hit that starts a point ◊ **serve somebody right** be a deserved punishment

server /súrvər/ *n* 1 somebody who serves customers 2 in racket sports, somebody who starts a point 3 a tray or utensil for serving food or drinks 4 the central computer in a network

~~serviceable~~ incorrect spelling of **serviceable**

service /súrviss/ *n* 1 work done for somebody else 2 a system that meets a public need, e.g. for transport 3 a government agency 4 a branch of the armed forces 5 the act or job of serving somebody 6 a maintenance operation for machinery 7 current use or operation o *not in service* 8 a religious ceremony 9 in racket sports, the act of serving a ball or shuttlecock 10 a set of dishes ■ **services** *npl* armed forces ■ *vt* (**servicing, serviced**) 1 clean and adjust machinery 2 provide a service to the community ■ *adj* 1 used by employees or for deliveries 2 providing a service, not goods —**servicer** *n* ◊ **press into service** use for an unusual purpose

serviceable /súrvissəb'l/ *adj* 1 likely to withstand hard wear 2 in working condition —**serviceably** *adv*

service area *n* 1 a complex of facilities for motorway travellers 2 an area over which a broadcasting company can achieve a satisfactory signal

service centre *n* 1 a garage that repairs vehicles 2 a retail store that repairs its products

service charge *n* 1 an amount of money added to a bill for service 2 a charge for paying in instalments

service contract *n* 1 a contract with a senior executive 2 a repair contract

service industry *n* an industry that provides services

serviceman /súrvissmən/ (*pl* -**men** /-mən/) *n* 1 a soldier 2 *also* **service man** a repairman

service mark *n* the logo used by the providers of a particular service

serviceperson /súrviss purss'n/ (*pl* -**people** /-peep'l/ *or* -**persons**) *n* 1 a soldier 2 *also* **service person** a person who undertakes repairs

service provider *n* 1 a business that connects people to the Internet 2 a company that provides services

service road *n* a minor road beside a main road

service station *n* a place that sells petrol to motorists

servicewoman /súrviss woobmən/ (*pl* -**en** /-wimin/) *n* 1 a woman soldier 2 *also* **service woman** a woman who undertakes repairs

serviette /súrvi étt/ *n* a table napkin

servile /súr vīl/ *adj* 1 too obedient 2 menial —**servilely** *adv* —**servility** /sur vílləti/ *n*

serving /súrving/ *n* a quantity of food served to one person

servitor /súrvitər/ *n* a servant *(archaic)*

servitude /súrvi tyood/ *n* **1** the state of being a slave **2** work imposed as a punishment

sesame /séssəmi/ (*pl* **-mes** *or* **same**) *n* **1** the seeds of a tropical plant. Use: cooking, oil extraction. **2** the tropical plant that produces sesame seeds

session /sésh'n/ *n* **1** a meeting of an official body **2** a series of official meetings **3** a time when classes are held in a school or university **4** a period during which a specific thing is done ■ **sessions** *npl* the sittings of a justice of the peace —**sessional** *adj*

set[1] *v* (**setting, set**) **1** *vt* put something somewhere **2** *vt* put somebody into a particular condition **3** *vt* make something happen **4** *vt* focus on something **5** *vt* prepare something to be used **6** *vti* become or make solid **7** *vt* adjust a measuring device **8** *vt* decide on or impose something, e.g. a price **9** *vt* be an example **10** *vt* establish a record **11** *vt* arrange hair using styling products or clips **12** *vt* put a gem into a setting **13** *vt* put a broken bone back into position **14** *vi* heal after being broken (*refers to bones*) **15** *vt* provide the music for something **16** *vt* portray something in a particular setting **17** *vt* position the sails on a boat **18** *vi* go below the horizon (*refers to the Sun*) **19** *vi* get ready to start a race **20** *vi* become permanent (*refers to a dyes or colours*) ■ *n* **1** the condition of being solid **2** an arrangement of theatrical scenery **3** a hairstyle created using styling products or clips **4** INDUST, ZOOL = **sett** ■ *adj* **1** established **2** inflexible **3** ready **4** determined

☐ **set about** *vt* **1** begin **2** attack somebody

☐ **set apart** *vt* **1** reserve for a specific use **2** make conspicuous or different

☐ **set aside** *vt* reserve

☐ **set back** *vt* delay something

☐ **set down** *vt* **1** write down **2** judge as being a particular thing **3** attribute to a cause

☐ **set forth** *v* **1** *vi* leave (*literary*) **2** *vt* state (*fml*)

☐ **set in** *vi* begin and become established

☐ **set off** *v* **1** *vi* start out on a trip **2** *vt* make something operate **3** *vt* make somebody start doing something **4** *vt* make something start to happen **5** *vt* make something look attractive

☐ **set on** *vt* **1** *also* **set upon** attack somebody **2** incite

☐ **set out** *v* **1** *vi* begin a journey **2** *vt* display or lay out **3** *vt* present

☐ **set up** *v* **1** *vt* erect something **2** *vti* prepare the equipment for an event **3** *vt* organize something **4** *vti* start a business **5** *vt* cause somebody to be blamed (*infml*)

set[2] *n* **1** a collection considered as or forming a unit **2** a social group **3** a device that receives radio or television signals **4** a main division of a tennis match ■ *vi* (**setting, set**) dance facing a partner

set-aside *n* an EU agricultural scheme in which farmers are paid not to produce crops

setback /sét bak/ *n* **1** something that delays progress **2** a shelf or recess in a wall

set piece *n* **1** a carefully planned action **2** a formal work of art **3** a piece of scenery

set square *n* a drawing instrument in the shape of a triangle

sett *n* **1** a rectangular paving stone **2** a badger's burrow

settee /se teé, sə-/ *n* a comfortable seat for two people

setter /séttər/ *n* a long-haired dog belonging to various breeds trained as gun dogs

setting /sétting/ *n* **1** a set of surroundings **2** the period or place in which a story takes place **3** the metal fixture of a jewel **4** a chosen point or level in the operation of a machine **5** the cutlery for one person at a table

settle /sétt'l/ *v* (**-tling, -tled**) **1** *vti* make somebody or yourself comfortable in a particular position **2** *vi* move downwards and come to rest **3** *vt* solve a problem or end a dispute **4** *vti* decide on something **5** *vt* pay a debt **6** *vt* put something in order **7** *vti* make or become calm **8** *vti* make or become resident in a particular place **9** *vti* cause a cloudy liquid to become clear, or become clear by forming a sediment **10** *vti* end a legal dispute ■ *n* a long wooden seat with a high back

☐ **settle down** *v* **1** *vti* make or become calm **2** *vi* start to live in an orderly life

☐ **settle for** *vt* agree to accept

☐ **settle in** *v* **1** *vti* adapt or cause to adapt to new circumstances **2** *vi* make yourself comfortable for a long stay o *decided to settle in for the night*

settlement /sétt'lmənt/ *n* **1** an agreement reached after discussion **2** a colony **3** a small community **4** an arrangement transferring property to somebody

settler /séttlər/ *n* an early resident in a new place

set-to (*pl* **set-tos**) *n* an argument or fight (*infml*)

set-top box *n* a decoding device that enables a traditional television to receive satellite, cable, or digital programmes

setup /sét up/ *n* **1** the organization of something **2** a set of prepared objects for a particular task **3** a dishonest plan or trick (*infml*)

Seurat /súr aa, sör a/, **Georges** (1859–91) French painter

seven /sévv'n/ *n* the number 7 —**seven** *adj, pron*

sevens /sévv'nz/ *n* seven-a-side rugby (+ *sing verb*)

seventeen /sévv'n teén/ *n* the number 17 —**seventeen** *adj, pron* —**seventeenth** *adj, adv, n*

seventh /sévv'nth/ *n* **1** one of seven parts of something **2** in music, an interval of seven notes —**seventh** *adj, adv* —**seventhly** *adv*

Seventh-Day Adventist /-ádvəntist/ *n* a member of a Protestant Christian denomination that observes the Sabbath on Saturday

seventh heaven *n* **1** a state of perfect happiness **2** in Islamic and Talmudic belief, the highest heaven

seventy /sévv'nti/ n the number 70 ■ **seventies** npl 1 the numbers 70 to 79, particularly as a range of Fahrenheit temperatures 2 the years from 70 to 79 in a century or somebody's life —**seventieth** adj, adv, n —**seventy** adj, pron

seventy-eight, 78 n a gramophone record played at 78 revolutions per minute

sever /sévvər/ vti 1 cut through something, or cut something off 2 separate something 3 break off a tie

several /sévvərəl/ det, pron a small number, though more than two or three ○ several days ago ○ several of them ■ adj 1 various or different ○ went their several ways 2 separate or individual ○ joint and several liability

severally /sévvrəli/ adv (fml or literary) 1 separately or individually 2 in turn or respectively

severance /sévvərənss/ n 1 the act of severing something 2 US loss of employment because of lack of available work 3 also **severance pay** compensation for the loss of a job

severe /si véer/ adj 1 strict or harsh 2 looking stern or serious 3 extremely bad or dangerous ○ severe injuries 4 extremely unpleasant or difficult 5 exacting 6 plain or austere in style —**severely** adv —**severeness** n —**severity** /si vérrəti/ n

Severn /sévvərn/ longest river in Britain, rising in Wales and flowing through W England to the Bristol Channel. Length 354 km/220 mi.

Seville /sə víl/ capital of **Sevilla Province** and the autonomous region of Andalusia, SW Spain. Pop. 701,927 (1998).

~~sevral~~ incorrect spelling of **several**

sew /sō/ (**sewn** /sōn/ or **sewed**) vti make or repair things with a needle and thread —**sewer** n

SPELLCHECK Do not confuse the spelling of sew, so ('in order that'), and sow ('plant seed'), which sound similar.

□ **sew up** vt finish successfully

sewage /soó ij, syoó-/ n waste matter from homes carried off in drains

sewage farm n a place where sewage is treated

Sewell /soó əl/, **Henry** (1807–79) British-born first premier of New Zealand (1856)

sewer /soó ər, syoó-/ n an underground drain for waste

sewerage /soó ərij, syoó-/ n 1 a system of sewers 2 the removal of toilet waste from homes

sewing /só ing/ n 1 the activity of using a needle and thread 2 material being sewn

sewing machine n a machine for sewing

sewn past participle of **sew**

sex n 1 the male or female gender 2 sexual activity or sexual intercourse ■ adj of sex ■ vt determine the sex of an animal

sex- prefix six ○ sextet

sexagenarian /séksəjə náiri ən/ n somebody aged between 60 and 69 —**sexagenarian** adj

sex appeal n sexual attractiveness

sex change n a surgical change from one sex to the other

sexism /séksizəm/ n 1 discrimination on the grounds of sex 2 sexual stereotyping —**sexist** adj, n

sexless /séksləss/ adj 1 without sexual activity 2 without sexual characteristics —**sexlessness** n

sex offender n somebody who commits a crime involving sex

sexology /sek sólləji/ n the study of human sexuality —**sexological** /séksə lójjik'l/ adj —**sexologist** n

sex symbol n a sexually attractive celebrity

sextant /sékstənt/ n a navigational instrument incorporating a telescope and an angular scale

sextet /sek stét/, **sextette** n 1 a group of six musicians or singers 2 any group of six people or things

sexton /sékstən/ n 1 a church caretaker 2 also **sexton beetle** a beetle that eats dead animals

sextuplet /sékstyōōplət, seks tyōōplət/ n 1 one of six offspring born together 2 a group of six musical notes

sexual /sékshoo əl/ adj 1 of sexual activity 2 of both sexes or either sex —**sexually** adv

sexual harassment n unwanted sexual advances

sexual intercourse n sex involving penetration

sexuality /sékshoo álləti/ n 1 sexual appeal 2 the state or fact of being sexual 3 involvement in sexual activity

sexually transmitted infection, sexually transmitted disease n a disease caught through sexual activity

sexual orientation n the direction of somebody's sexual desire towards people of the opposite sex, the same sex, or both sexes

sexy /séksi/ (**-ier, -iest**) adj 1 arousing sexual desire 2 sexually aroused 3 appealing (infml) ○ a sexy new slogan —**sexily** adv —**sexiness** n

Seychelles /say shélz/ island country in the W Indian Ocean. Cap. Victoria. Pop. 79,715 (2001). —**Seychellois** /sáy shel waá/ adj, n

Seymour /seém awr/, **Jane** (1509?–37) queen of England (1536–37) as the 3rd wife of Henry VIII

Sezer /sé zair/, **Ahmet Necdet** (b. 1941) president of Turkey (2000–)

sf, SF abbr science fiction

Sg symbol seaborgium

SGML n a method of representing text electronically by defining the relationship between form and structure. Full form **Standard Generalized Markup Language**

Sgt abbr Sergeant

sh, shh interj be silent

Sha'ban /sha baan, shaa-/, **Shaban, Shaaban** n the 8th month of the year in the Islamic calendar

Shabbat /shaa baát/ n the Jewish Sabbath, celebrated on Saturday

shabby /shábbi/ (**-bier, -biest**) *adj* **1** worn and threadbare **2** wearing worn clothes **3** unfair or inconsiderate **4** inferior in quality —**shabbily** *adv* —**shabbiness** *n*

shack *n* a small flimsy building
□ **shack up** *vi* live with a lover (*infml disapproving*)

shackle /shák'l/ *n* a metal locking band fastened round the wrists or ankles of prisoners (*often pl*) ■ *vt* (**-ling, -led**) **1** restrict the freedom of ○ *felt shackled by the rules* **2** restrain or secure with shackles

Shackleton /shák'ltən/, **Sir Ernest Henry** (1874–1922) Irish explorer

shade *n* **1** an area out of direct sunlight **2** a variation on a basic colour **3** something that blocks out light **4** *US* a window blind **5** a small amount **6** a variation or nuance ■ **shades** *npl* sunglasses (*infml*) ■ *v* (**shading, shaded**) *vt* protect something from sunlight **2** *vt* darken a part of a picture **3** *vi* change slightly or gradually

shading /sháyding/ *n* **1** a dark area in a picture **2** a slight difference

shadow /sháddō/ *n* **1** a darkened shape of somebody or something blocking the light **2** darkness in a place or painting **3** a hint of something **4** ominous gloom **5** a dark area under the eyes **6** an opposition minister with a particular job **7** a ghost ■ *vt* **1** protect something from light **2** follow somebody secretly ■ *adj* in the capacity of counterpart in the opposition political party ◊ See note at **follow**

shadowy /sháddō i/ (**-ier, -iest**) *adj* **1** full of shadows **2** not clearly seen

shady /sháydi/ (**-ier, -iest**) *adj* **1** having little natural light **2** dishonest —**shadily** *adv* —**shadiness** *n*

shaft *n* **1** a long handle **2** a vertical passage **3** a passage for ventilation in a building **4** a rotating rod that provides motion or power for a machine **5** a beam of light **6** a pole on a cart to which a horse is harnessed **7** an arrow or spear (*literary*) **8** the long thin body of a spear or similar weapon **9** the main part of an architectural column ■ *vt* treat unfairly (*slang*)

Shaftesbury /sháaftsbəri/, **Anthony Ashley Cooper, 7th Earl of** (1801–85) British philanthropist

shag[1] *n* long pile on a textile

shag[2] *n* a small cormorant

shagged, shagged out *adj* exhausted (*slang*)

shaggy /shággi/ (**-gier, -giest**) *adj* **1** long and untidy **2** having coarse long hair or wool —**shagginess** *n*

shaggy dog story *n* a long story with a weak ending

shah /shaa/ *n* a former hereditary monarch of Iran

Shah Jahan /shaà jə haàn/ (1592–1666) emperor of India (1628–58)

shaitan /shī taàn/ *n* **1** in Islamic countries, an evil spirit or person **2 Shaitan** in Islamic belief, the devil

Shaka /shaàkə/ (1787?–1828) South African Zulu ruler

shake *v* (**shaking, shook** /shŏŏk/, **shaken** /sháykən/) **1** *vti* move or cause to move back and forth in short quick movements **2** *vi* tremble or quaver **3** *vti* get or put into a particular state by shaking **4** *vt* shock and upset somebody **5** *vti* clasp hands as a greeting, farewell, or sign of agreement **6** *vt* move your head to express 'No' ■ *n* **1** an act of shaking **2** a vibration **3** a milk shake **4** a handshake ■ **shakes** *npl* uncontrollable trembling ◊ **no great shakes** not very good or important (*infml*)
□ **shake down** *vi* become accustomed to new circumstances (*infml*)
□ **shake off** *vt* **1** get rid of something unwanted **2** escape from a pursuer
□ **shake up** *vt* **1** make major changes to or in **2** shock or upset

shakedown /sháyk down/ *n* a makeshift bed

shake-out *n* a change resulting in losses

shaker /sháykər/ *n* **1** a container for dispersing the contents in fine particles **2** a container for mixing drinks **3 Shaker** a member of an ascetic Christian denomination

~~Shakespear, Shakspeare~~ incorrect spelling of **Shakespeare**

Barnaby's

William Shakespeare

Shakespeare /sháyks peer/, **William** (1564–1616) English poet and playwright —**Shakespearean** /shayk spéeri ən/ *adj, n* —**Shakespearian** *adj, n*

shake-up *n* a major change

shaky /sháyki/ (**-ier, -iest**) *adj* **1** trembling **2** likely to collapse **3** weak and not likely to last —**shakily** *adv* —**shakiness** *n*

shale *n* a dark rock composed of layers of dark sediment and clay —**shaly** *adj*

shall stressed /shal/ unstressed /sh'l/ *modal v* **1** indicates that something will or ought to happen in the future **2** indicates determination **3** indicates that something must happen because of a rule **4** makes offers and suggestions (*in questions*) ○ *Shall we go now?*

LANGUAGE NOTE shall or **will**? The traditional rule, often stated in grammars and usage books, is that to express a simple future tense **shall** is used after *I* and *we* (*I shall leave promptly at noon*) and **will** in other cases (*They/you will leave at noon*). To express intention, command, or wish their roles are reversed: *I will do this right or die trying*; *Passengers shall present two photo IDs prior to* *ticketing*. It is unlikely that this rule has ever been regularly observed, however, and many examples in the printed works of the best writers contradict it.

shallot /shə lót/ *n* **1** a vegetable like a small onion **2** the plant that produces shallots

shallow /shállō/ *adj* **1** not physically deep **2** not thinking or feeling deeply ■ **shallows** *npl* an area of shallow water —**shallowly** *adv* —**shallowness** *n*

shalom /sha lóm/ *interj* used as a Jewish greeting or farewell

sham *n* **1** a fake **2** an impostor ■ *adj* not genuine ■ *vti* (**shamming, shammed**) feign

shaman /shámmən, sháymən, shaámən/ *n* a spiritual leader with healing powers —**shamanic** /shə mánnik/ *adj* —**shamanism** *n*

shamble /shámb'l/ *vi* (-bling, -bled) shuffle along clumsily ■ *n* a shuffling walk

ORIGIN The verb **shamble** is probably from a dialect adjective meaning 'ungainly'. This may be related to *shambles*, through the phrase *shamble legs*, referring to the legs of trestle tables set up for a meat market or 'shambles'.

shambles /shámb'lz/ *n* **1** a disorganized failure **2** a state of disorder or chaos

ORIGIN A *shamble* was originally a stool or table. The word gradually acquired the specialized meaning 'meat table', being applied to meat sellers' stalls at markets (a street in the old butchers' quarter of York is still known as the Shambles). The plural form **shambles** came to denote a slaughterhouse, and hence metaphorically any place of carnage. The milder modern sense 'state of disorder' did not emerge until the early 20C.

shambolic /sham bóllik/ *adj* disorderly or chaotic (*infml*)

shame *n* **1** a feeling that combines dishonour, unworthiness, and embarrassment **2** the capacity to feel unworthy **3** a state of disgrace **4** a cause for regret ■ *vt* (**shaming, shamed**) **1** cause to feel ashamed **2** force to do something through shame ◇ **put to shame** cause to seem inferior by comparison

shamefaced /sháym fáyst/ *adj* **1** showing shame **2** timid —**shamefacedly** /sháym fáyssidli, -fáystli/ *adv*

ORIGIN **Shamefaced** originally had no connection with the face. The word was *shamefast*, and the literal meaning 'held fast by shame'. It was altered under the influence of *face* in the mid-16C.

shameful /sháymf'l/ *adj* disgraceful or scandalous —**shamefully** *adv* —**shamefulness** *n*

shameless /sháymləss/ *adj* feeling or showing no shame —**shamelessly** *adv* —**shamelessness** *n*

Shamir /sha meèr/, **Yitzhak** (*b.* 1914) Polish-born Israeli prime minister (1983–84, 1986–92)

shammy /shámmi/ (*pl* -mies) *n* a chamois cloth used for household cleaning

shampoo /sham poó/ *n* **1** a liquid soap for cleaning the hair **2** a sudsy detergent for cleaning upholstery and carpets ■ *vt* (-poos, -pooing, -pooed) clean with shampoo

shamrock /shám rok/ *n* a three-leafed clover

shandy /shándi/ *n* a mixture of beer and lemonade

Shanghai /sháng hí/ port in E China. Pop. 13,580,000 (1995). —**Shanghainese** /sháng hī neèz/ *npl*

Shangri-la /sháng gri laà/ *n* an imaginary utopia

ORIGIN The original **Shangri-la** was an imaginary land in *The Lost Horizon* (1933) by the British novelist James Hilton.

shank *n* **1** a long, narrow part of something **2** a cut of meat from an animal's leg **3** the lower part of an animal's leg **4** the lower part of the human leg

Ravi Shankar

Shankar /shángk aar/, **Ravi** (*b.* 1920) Indian sitarist, composer, and teacher

Shannon /shánnən/ longest river in the British Isles, rising in north-central Republic of Ireland and flowing southwestwards to the Atlantic Ocean. Length 370 km/230 mi.

shan't /shaant/ *contr* shall not

shanty[1] /shánti/ (*pl* -ties) *n* a crude shack

shanty[2] /shánti/ (*pl* -ties) *n* a sailors' rhythmical work song

shantytown /shánti town/ *n* a settlement consisting of crudely made shacks

shape *n* **1** the outline of something or somebody **2** something that is not clearly seen **3** a geometric form such as a square or cone **4** general health or condition **5** a mould or form ■ *vt* (**shaping, shaped**) **1** influence greatly **2** decide on the character of **3** give a particular shape to
□ **shape up** *vi* **1** improve (*infml*) **2** reach an acceptable standard

SHAPE /shayp/ *abbr* Supreme Headquarters Allied Powers Europe

shapeless /sháypləss/ *adj* lacking precise shape or structure —**shapelessly** *adv* —**shapelessness** *n*

shapely /sháypli/ (-lier, -liest) *adj* having a pleasing shape —**shapeliness** *n*

shard, sherd *n* a fragment of glass, metal, or pottery

share /shair/ *v* (**sharing, shared**) **1** *vti* use something along with other people **2** *vti* take responsibility for something together **3** *vti* let somebody use or have part of something **4** *vt* divide something equally between people **5** *vti* have a similar feeling or experience ■ *n* **1** the part of something that somebody has been allotted **2** a part of a company's stock —**sharer** *n*

share certificate *n* a document that certifies share ownership

sharecropper /sháir kropər/ *n US* a tenant farmer working for a share in the value of the crop

shared ownership *n* home ownership in which a purchaser part-buys and part-rents the property

shareholder /sháir hōldər/ *n* an owner of company stock

share index *n* an index of share prices

share option *n* a benefit by which an employee of a company can buy its shares at a special price

shareware /sháir wair/ *n* software that is available free for a trial period and is paid for voluntarily afterwards

sharia /shə reé ə/, **shari'a**, **shari'ah** *n* Islamic religious law, based on the Koran

shark *n* **1** a large carnivorous fish **2** a ruthless or dishonest person *(infml)*

Sharman /shaármən/, **Helen** (*b.* 1963) British astronaut

Sharon /sha rón/, **Ariel** (*b.* 1928) Israeli soldier, politician, and prime minister (2001–)

sharp *adj* **1** able to cut and puncture things **2** pointed **3** quick-witted **4** critical and unsympathetic **5** sudden and significant **6** distinct o *in sharp contrast* **7** clearly detailed **8** piercing in sound **9** strong and bitter or acidic in taste **10** describes a musical note that is higher by a semitone **11** describes a musical note that has too high a pitch **12** stylish ■ *adv* **1** precisely **2** at slightly too high a pitch ■ *n* **1** (*symbol* ♯) a note that is higher by a semitone, or a printed symbol for this **2** a sharp medical instrument *(usually pl)* **3** *also* **sharper** /shaárpər/ a skilful cheat *(infml)* —**sharpen** *vti* —**sharpener** *n* —**sharply** *adv* —**sharpness** *n*

sharp-eyed *adj* **1** alert to detail **2** having good eyesight

sharpish /shaárpish/ *adv* soon or rapidly *(infml)*

sharpshooter /shaárp shootər/ *n* somebody who shoots firearms precisely

sharp-tongued *adj* critical or sarcastic

sharp-witted *adj* mentally keen —**sharp-wittedly** *adv*

shat past tense, past participle of **shit** *(taboo offensive)*

Shatt al-Arab /shát al árrəb/ river channel in SE Iraq forming part of the border between Iran and Iraq. Length 170 km/110 mi.

Shatten /shátt'n/, **Gerald P.** (*b.* 1949) US developmental biologist. He led the research team that produced the first genetically modified monkey.

shatter /sháttər/ *v* **1** *vti* smash into pieces **2** *vt* destroy hope or belief **3** *vt* shock somebody ■ **shatters** *npl* fragments

shattered /sháttərd/ *adj* exhausted *(infml)*

shatterproof /sháttər proof/ *adj* resistant to shattering

shave /shayv/ *v* (**shaving, shaved, shaved** *or* **shaven** /sháyvən/) **1** *vti* remove hair with a razor **2** *vt* reduce an amount slightly **3** *vt* barely touch something in passing **4** *vt* remove a thin layer ■ *n* an act of shaving hair off, especially off the face

shaven /sháyvən/ *v* past participle of **shave** ■ *adj* (*often in combination*) **1** without any beard or other facial hair **2** trimmed

shaver /sháyvər/ *n* a device for shaving facial hair

Shavuoth /shə voo ōth/, **Shavuot** /-ōt/ *n* a Jewish festival marking the giving of the Law to Moses. Date: 6th of Sivan, in May or June.

Shaw, George Bernard (1856–1950) Irish playwright

shawl *n* a fabric square for the head and shoulders or to wrap a baby in

Shawwal /shə wól/ *n* the 10th month of the year in the Islamic calendar

she *stressed* /shee/ *unstressed* /shi/ *pron* refers to a female person or animal, or an object perceived as female, that has been previously mentioned or whose identity is known (*as the subject of a verb*) ■ *n* a female person or animal, especially a new baby

s/he /shee awr heé/ *pron* she or he (*intended to avoid sexism in writing*)

sheaf /sheef/ (*pl* **sheaves** /sheevz/) *n* **1** a bundle of harvested grain stalks **2** any bundle

shear /sheer/ *vt* (**sheared** *or* **shorn**) **1** cut something off **2** cut hair, wool, or foliage from something ■ *n* **1** the removal of an animal's fleece **2** the wool cut off an animal ■ **shears** *npl* a cutting tool with blades like scissors —**shearer** *n*

SPELLCHECK Do not confuse the spelling of **shear** and **sheer** ('complete and utter'), which sound similar.

---

sheath /sheeth/ *n* (*pl* **sheaths** /sheethz, sheeths/) **1** a case for a blade **2** a close-fitting covering **3** a closely fitting dress **4** a condom ■ *vt* sheathe

sheathe /sheeth/ (**sheathing, sheathed**) *vt* **1** put into a sheath **2** enclose something with a covering or case

sheathing /sheéthing/ *n* a protective covering

sheath knife *n* a knife carried in a sheath

sheaves plural of **sheaf**

Sheba /sheébə/ ancient kingdom of SW Arabia, in present-day Yemen

shebang /shi báng/ ◇ **the whole shebang** everything *(infml)*

shebeen /shi beén/ *n* an illegal drinking establishment

shed[1] (**shedding, shed**) *v* **1** *vt* cause tears or blood to flow **2** *vt* radiate light **3** *vti* lose something such as hair or fur naturally **4** *vt* get rid of something **5** *vt* lose something accidentally

shed² *n* **1** a small building used for storage or shelter **2** a large open building used for storage or shelter or as a work area

she'd /sheed/ *contr* **1** she had **2** she would

sheen *n* a glossy appearance

sheep (*pl same*) *n* **1** a domesticated hooved mammal kept for its wool and meat **2** a submissive person

sheep-dip *n* **1** a disinfectant for sheep **2** a bath containing sheep-dip

sheepdog /sheep dog/ *n* a breed of dog used to herd sheep

sheepfold /sheep fold/ *n* a pen for sheep

sheepish /sheepish/ *adj* **1** embarrassed **2** timid —**sheepishly** *adv* —**sheepishness** *n*

sheepskin /sheep skin/ *n* sheep leather with or without wool

sheer¹ /sheer/ *adj* **1** complete and utter **2** pure or unadulterated **3** nearly vertical or perpendicular ■ *n* a nearly transparent fabric —**sheer** *adv* —**sheerness** *n* ◊ See note at shear

sheer² /sheer/ *vi* swerve from a course —**sheer** *n*

sheet¹ /sheet/ *n* **1** a cloth used on a bed **2** a flat thin rectangular piece **3** a broad thin expanse

sheet² /sheet/ *n* a rope for changing a sail's position ■ **sheets** *npl* spaces at the bow and stern of a ship

sheeting /sheeting/ *n* thin material for covering

sheet lightning *n* lightning that appears in a broad sheet

sheet metal *n* metal in sheet form

sheet music *n* printed music on unbound sheets

Sheffield /sheffeeld/ city in N England. Pop. 530,375 (1996).

sheik /shayk, sheek/, **sheikh** *n* **1** the leader of an Arab family or village **2** an Islamic religious leader —**sheikdom** *n*

sheika /sháy kaa/, **sheikha** *n* a sheik's wife

sheila /sheelə/ *n ANZ* a woman (*infml*)

~~sheild~~ incorrect spelling of **shield**

shekel /shék'l/ *n* **1** the main unit of Israeli currency **2** an ancient Jewish unit of weight

shelduck /shél duk/ (*pl* -**ducks** or same) *n* a large European duck with a thick bill

ORIGIN The first element of **shelduck** probably represents a dialect word *sheld* meaning 'variegated, patchy in colour'. The earlier name for the bird, from the beginning of the 14C, was *sheldrake*; *duck* was substituted for *drake* in the early 18C.

shelf (*pl* **shelves**) *n* **1** a flat surface on which to put objects **2** the contents of a shelf **3** a ledge of rock or ice —**shelfful** *n* ◊ **on the shelf** no longer wanted, used, or taken account of

shelf life *n* a period of time during which a product remains fresh

shell *n* **1** the hard protective covering of a turtle, crab, other mollusc or crustacean, or of an insect **2** the covering of an egg or nut **3** a protective casing **4** the framework of a building **5** a pastry case **6** a hollow or empty thing **7** a large explosive projectile **8** a gun cartridge **9** a narrow racing boat **10** a group of electrons with similar energy in similar orbits around the nucleus of an atom ■ *v* **1** *vt* take something out of a shell **2** *vti* bombard a target

□ **shell out** *vti* pay out money (*infml*)

she'll /sheel/ *contr* **1** she shall **2** she will

shellac /shə lák, shéllak/ *n* **1** purified resin from a tropical insect **2** a varnish made from shellac dissolved in alcohol ■ *vt* (-**lacking**, -**lacked**) apply shellac to

shell company *n* a company that exists largely in name only and has no independent assets

Popperfoto

Mary Shelley

Shelley /shélli/, **Mary** (1797–1851) British writer

Shelley, Percy Bysshe (1792–1822) British poet

shellfire /shél fīr/ *n* **1** fired artillery shells **2** the act or noise of firing artillery shells

shellfish /shél fish/ (*pl same* or -**fishes**) *n* an edible water animal with a shell

shell shock *n* a psychiatric disorder caused by the stress of warfare (*dated*) —**shell-shocked** *adj*

shell suit *n* a bright lightweight tracksuit

shelter /shéltər/ *n* **1** a structure providing protection or covering **2** an establishment for people who need to leave a violent or otherwise dangerous situation **3** protection or cover **4** a place in which to live ■ *vti* provide with or find shelter

sheltered /shéltərd/ *adj* **1** protected from the elements **2** not exposed to the rigours or unpleasantness of life

shelve¹ (**shelving**, **shelved**) *vt* **1** put on a shelf **2** set aside

shelve² (**shelving**, **shelved**) *vi* slope gradually

shelves plural of **shelf**

shelving /shélving/ *n* **1** shelves **2** material used for making shelves

Shenyang /shən yúng/ city in NE China. Pop. 5,120,000 (1995).

~~shepard, sheppard~~ incorrect spelling of **shepherd**

Shepard /shéppərd/, **Alan, Jr.** (1923–98) US astronaut

shepherd /shéppərd/ n somebody who tends sheep ■ v 1 vti tend sheep 2 vt guide a group of people somewhere

shepherd's pie n a dish of minced meat topped with mashed potato

Sheppard /shéppərd/, **Kate** (1848–1934) British-born New Zealand suffragist

Sheraton /shérrətən/, **Thomas** (1751–1806) British cabinetmaker

sherbet /shúrbət/ n a fizzy powder eaten as a sweet or mixed with water

> **ORIGIN Sherbet** goes back to an Arabic verb meaning 'drink', from which *syrup* also derives. The noun formed from this verb made its way through Persian and Turkish to enter English as *sherbet*, a cooling drink, in the early 17C. By a diversion through Italian and French the Arabic noun also made an appearance as *sorbet*.

sherd n = shard

Sheridan /shérridən/, **Richard Brinsley** (1751–1816) Irish-born British playwright

sheriff /shérrif/ n 1 the senior representative of the Crown in a county in England and Wales 2 a Scottish judge in one of the lower courts 3 the chief law enforcement officer in a US county 4 an Australian or Canadian court official

> **ORIGIN** A **sheriff** is etymologically a *shire reeve*, the representative of royal authority in an English shire.

sheriff court n a Scottish local court

Sherlock Holmes /shúr lok hốmz/ n somebody with exceptional powers of deduction and perception (humorous)

> **ORIGIN** The original **Sherlock Holmes** was a detective in stories by Sir Arthur Conan Doyle (1859–1930).

Sherman /shúrmən/, **William T.** (1820–91) US Union general

Sherpa /shúrpa/ (pl **-pas** or same) n a member of a Himalayan people

~~sherrif~~ incorrect spelling of **sheriff**

sherry /shérri/ n a fortified Spanish wine

Sherwood Forest /shúr wŏod-/ n ancient forest in central England

she's /sheez/ contr 1 she has 2 she is

Shetland Islands /shétlənd-/ island group of N Scotland, comprising about 150 islands in the Atlantic Ocean. Cap. Lerwick. Pop. 23,232 (1996). —**Shetlander** n

Shetland pony n a small sturdy pony with a long shaggy mane and tail

Shevat /shə vót/, **Shebat** /-bót, -vót/ n the 11th month of the year in the Jewish calendar

shh interj = sh

Shia /shee ə/, **Shi'a**, **Shi'ah** n one of the major branches of Islam

shiatsu /shi aåt soo/, **shiatzu** n a form of massage applying pressure to acupuncture points

shibboleth /shíbbə leth/ n 1 a catchword or slogan 2 an identifying pronunciation, word, or custom

> **ORIGIN Shibboleth** derives from a Hebrew word meaning 'stream'. According to the Bible, the people of Gilead, east of the River Jordan, used the word *šibbōleṯ* as a password, for they knew their enemies the Ephraimites, from west of the Jordan, could not pronounce the initial /sh/ properly (Judges 12:5–6).

~~shiek~~ incorrect spelling of **sheik**

Shiel, Loch /sheel/ long narrow lake in W Scotland. Length 27 km/17 mi.

shield /sheeld/ n 1 a flat or convex piece of armour carried on the arm 2 something that provides protection or a defence 3 something resembling a shield in shape ■ vti protect with or act as a shield ◊ See note at **safeguard**

shift v 1 vti move to a different position 2 vti change or exchange something for something else 3 vti remove a stain, or be removed 4 vti change gears 5 vi provide for your own needs 6 vi press the shift key on a computer keyboard ■ n 1 a change made 2 any of the periods into which a 24-hour working day is divided, or the people working during one 3 also **shift key** a keyboard key that makes letters capitals 4 a loose-fitting dress 5 a woman's undergarment resembling a shirt ◊ See note at **change**

shiftless /shíftləss/ adj lacking ambition —**shiftlessness** n

shiftwork /shíft wurk/ n a system of working in shifts

shifty /shífti/ (**-ier, -iest**) adj untrustworthy or evasive —**shiftily** adv —**shiftiness** n

Shiite /shee īt/, **Shi'ite** n a follower of the Shia branch of Islam —**Shiite** adj —**Shiitic** /shee íttik/ adj

Shijiazhuang /shə jyaa joo úng/ capital of Hebei Province, east-central China. Pop. 1,600,000 (1995).

shikari /shi kaári/ n S Asia a big-game hunter or guide

shilling /shílling/ n 1 a former British coin and subunit of currency 2 the main unit of currency in several East-African countries

shilly-shally /shílli shali/ (**shilly-shallies, shilly-shallied**) vi 1 hesitate or vacillate 2 waste time

shimmer /shímmər/ vti 1 shine with a wavering light 2 be or make visible as a wavering image ■ n 1 a wavering light or glow 2 a wavering image or appearance —**shimmery** adj

shimmy /shímmi/ n 1 a popular dance of the 1920s involving shaking of the body from the shoulders down 2 a quick movement of the body to the side ■ vi (**-mies, -mied**) 1 dance the shimmy 2 move quickly to the side

shin n 1 the front of the lower leg 2 also **shinbone** the bone at the front of the lower leg **3** a cut of beef used for stew ■ *vti* (**shinning, shinned**) climb using the arms and legs

shindig /shíndig/ *n* a noisy party *(infml)*

shine /shīn/ *v* (**shining, shone** /shon/) **1** *vi* emit light **2** *vi* be bright **3** *vt* direct light somewhere **4** *vi* excel **5** *vt* polish ■ *n* **1** brightness from a light source **2** a bright surface **3** an act of polishing something

shiner /shínər/ *n* a black eye *(infml)*

shingle[1] /shíng g'l/ *n* a small flat roof or wall tile ■ *vt* (**-gling, -gled**) **1** cover a roof or wall with shingles **2** cut hair to taper at the back —**shingler** *n*

shingle[2] /shíng g'l/ *n* **1** pebbles on a beach **2** a beach covered in shingle

shingles /shíng g'lz/ *n* a viral disease related to chickenpox causing inflammation and pain along a nerve path

shining /shíning/ *adj* **1** bright **2** excellent —**shiningly** *adv*

shinny /shínni/ (**-nies, -nied**) *vi* climb quickly

Shinto /shíntō/ *n* a Japanese religion with numerous gods and spirits of the natural world —**Shintoism** *n* —**Shintoist** *n, adj*

shiny /shíni/ (**-ier, -iest**) *adj* **1** bright and polished **2** worn smooth and glossy —**shininess** *n*

ship *n* a large boat designed to carry passengers or cargo ■ *vt* (**shipping, shipped**) **1** transport something in a ship or by a common carrier **2** send something or somebody somewhere **3** take in water over the sides of a ship or boat

-ship *suffix* **1** condition, state, or quality ○ *companionship* **2** skill, art, craft ○ *musicianship* **3** office, title, position, profession ○ *governorship* **4** a group of people collectively ○ *membership* **5** a person holding a particular title ○ *ladyship* **6** something showing a particular quality or condition ○ *township*

shipboard /shíp bawrd/ *adj* occurring on board a ship

shipbuilder /shíp bildər/ *n* a person or business that makes ships —**shipbuilding** *n*

Shipley /shíppli/, **Jenny** (*b.* 1952) prime minister of New Zealand (1997–99)

shipload /shíp lōd/ *n* the amount carried in a ship

shipmate /shíp mayt/ *n* a sailor or passenger on the same ship as another

shipment /shípmənt/ *n* **1** a quantity of goods shipped together **2** the act of shipping goods

shipper /shíppər/ *n* a transporter of goods

shipping /shípping/ *n* **1** the act of transporting goods **2** ships generally

shipshape /shíp shayp/ *adj* in good order —**shipshape** *adv*

shipwreck /shíp rek/ *n* **1** the sinking or destruction of a ship **2** a sunken ship ■ *vt* **1** involve somebody in a shipwreck **2** destroy a ship

shipwright /shíp rīt/ *n* a shipbuilder

shipyard /shíp yaard/ *n* a place where ships are built

shire *n* **1** a county in England or Wales **2** *also* **Shire, shire horse** a heavy cart horse with long hair growing from its fetlocks

shirk *v* **1** *vt* avoid an obligation, task, or responsibility **2** *vi* avoid work or duty

shirt *n* **1** a garment for the upper body, usually with sleeves, a collar, and a front opening **2** a man's undergarment with sleeves ◇ **keep your shirt on** control your temper *(infml; usually a command)* ◇ **lose your shirt** lose everything you have

ORIGIN Shirt derives from the ancient Germanic root that gave us *short*, and also, through a Scandinavian language, *skirt*.

shirtwaister /shúrt waystər/ *n* a woman's shirt-style dress, buttoning down the front

shirty /shúrti/ (**-ier, -iest**) *adj* annoyed and bad-tempered *(infml)* —**shirtiness** *n*

shish kebab /shísh-/ *n* a dish of grilled meat and vegetables on a skewer

shit *n* **1** a taboo term for human or animal excrement *(offensive)* **2** a taboo term for somebody regarded as unpleasant or malicious *(insult)* **3** a taboo term for something of no value or of inferior quality *(offensive)* ■ *interj* a taboo term expressing strong anger or surprise *(offensive)* —**shittiness** *n* —**shitty** *adj*

Shiva /sheeva/, **Siva** /seeva/ *n* an important Hindu god, called the Destroyer

shiver[1] /shívvər/ *vi* tremble because of cold, fear, or illness ■ *n* a body tremor —**shivery** *adj*

shiver[2] /shívvər/ *n* a fragment ■ *vti* shatter into fragments

Shoah /shō ə/ *n* the Holocaust

shoal[1] /shōl/ *n* **1** a large school of fish **2** a large group of people

shoal[2] /shōl/ *n* **1** an area of shallow water **2** an underwater sandbank ■ *adj* *also* **shoaly** /shōli/ shallow

shock[1] *n* **1** something surprising and upsetting **2** the feelings of distress or numbness experienced after a shock **3** a state of physiological collapse **4** a forceful physical impact **5** an electric shock ■ *v* **1** *vt* surprise and upset **2** *vti* offend or disgust, or be offended or disgusted —**shockable** *adj* —**shockproof** *adj*

shock[2] *n* a group of sheaves of drying corn

shock[3] *n* a mass of shaggy hair

shock absorber *n* a device on a vehicle for absorbing shocks

shocker /shókər/ *n* *(infml)* **1** something unpleasant **2** a shocking story, play, or film

shocking /shóking/ *adj* **1** outrageous **2** distressing **3** very bad *(infml)* ■ *adj, adv* very bright in colour —**shockingly** *adv* —**shockingness** *n*

shock jock *n* a provocative host of a radio programme *(slang)*

Shockley /shókli/, **William B.** (1910–89) US physicist

shock tactics *npl* methods that are likely to shock people, used to achieve a goal

shock therapy, shock treatment *n* electric shock treatment for psychiatric disorders

shock troops *npl* soldiers trained to lead an assault

shock wave *n* **1** a wave of heat and air pressure produced by an explosion, earthquake, or movement of a supersonic body **2** a surprised reaction *(often pl)*

shod past participle, past tense of **shoe**

shoddy /shóddi/ *adj* (**-dier, -diest**) **1** poorly made **2** of inferior material ■ *n* (*pl* **-dies**) something inferior —**shoddily** *adv* —**shoddiness** *n*

shoe /shoo/ *n* **1** a stiff outer covering for the human foot **2** a horseshoe **3** a part of a machine that protects against wear **4** a device on an electric train that connects to the electrified rail ■ *vt* (**shod**) **1** fit a horse with horseshoes **2** supply a person with shoes ◇ **be in somebody's shoes** be in somebody else's position *(infml)*

shoebox /shoo boks/ *n* a box for a pair of shoes

shoehorn /shoo hawrn/ *n* a device to help a person's heel into a shoe ■ *vt* squeeze somebody or something into a space

shoelace /shoo layss/ *n* a cord for fastening a shoe

shoemaker /shoo maykər/ *n* somebody who makes or repairs shoes —**shoemaking** *n*

shoeshine /shoo shīn/ *n* an instance of polishing shoes

shoestring /shoo string/ *adj* consisting of little money ◇ **on a shoestring** using very little money

shoetree /shoo tree/ *n* a device inserted into a boot or shoe to keep it in shape

shofar /shó faar/ (*pl* **-fars** *or* **-froth** /-frót/) *n* a ram's horn blown in a synagogue on Rosh Hashanah and Yom Kippur

shogun /shó gun/ *n* a military commander in feudal Japan —**shogunal** *adj*

~~sholder~~ incorrect spelling of **shoulder**

shone past tense, past participle of **shine**

shoo /shoo/ *interj* used to get an animal to leave ■ *vt* (**shoos, shooing, shooed**) wave an animal away

shook past tense of **shake**

shoot /shoot/ *v* (**shot**) **1** *vti* fire a weapon or projectile **2** *vt* hit somebody or something with a bullet **3** *vti* move or cause to move fast **4** *vt* travel over a stretch of water fast **5** *vti* record something on film **6** *vti* kick or throw a ball in an attempt to get a point **7** *vt* move a bolt into place **8** *vi* begin to grow or germinate ■ *n* **1** a newly grown aerial part of a plant, e.g. a leaf bud or branch **2** an occasion for photographing or filming **3** a hunting event, party, or area ◇ See note at **chute**

□ **shoot down** *vt* kill by shooting

□ **shoot through** *vi* Aus leave suddenly *(infml)*

□ **shoot up** *v* **1** *vi* increase suddenly **2** *vi* get taller **3** *vti* inject an illegal drug *(slang)*

shoot-'em-up /shoo təm up/ *n* a computer game with shooting

shooter /shoo tər/ *n* **1** a gun *(infml)* **2** somebody or something that shoots

shooting gallery *n* a place to practise shooting

shooting star *n* a meteor

shooting stick *n* a walking stick with a handle that folds out to make a seat

shoot-out *n* a decisive fight with guns

shop *n* **1** a retail business **2** a workshop ■ *v* (**shopping, shopped**) **1** *vi* buy goods **2** *vt* inform on somebody *(slang)* —**shopper** *n* ◇ **talk shop** talk about your work

□ **shop around** *vi* look around for the best deal

shop assistant *n* somebody who serves in a shop

shop floor *n* **1** the manufacturing area in a factory **2** workers as distinct from managers

shopfront /shóp frunt/ *n* the façade of a shop

shopkeeper /shóp keepər/ *n* the owner or manager of a shop

shoplift /shóp lift/ *vti* steal goods from a shop —**shoplifter** *n* —**shoplifting** *n*

shopping /shópping/ *n* **1** the activity of going to shops **2** goods purchased in shops

shopping agent *n* a computer program used to browse websites for products and services

shopping bag *n* a strong bag with handles in which to carry shopping

shopping centre *n* an enclosed area with shops

shopping list *n* **1** a list of items to shop for **2** a list of things wanted

shopping mall *n* a large shopping centre

shopping precinct *n* UK a pedestrianized shopping area

shopping trolley *n* a small trolley for carrying shopping

shopsoiled /shóp soyld/ *adj* damaged in a shop

shop steward *n* a union official who represents workers in talks with management

shopwalker /shóp wawkər/ *n* a supervisor in a department store

shore[1] *n* the strip of land at the edge of water

shore[2] *vt* (**shoring, shored**) **1** prop up a structure **2** help to stop something from failing ■ *n* a prop to support something

shore leave *n* **1** permission for a sailor to go ashore **2** the time a sailor spends ashore

shoreline /sháwr līn/ *n* the line where water meets land

shorn past participle of **shear** ■ *adj* **1** having short hair **2** deprived of something

short *adj* **1** not long or tall **2** lasting briefly **3** concise **4** having less than needed **5** recalling only recent events ○ *a short memory* **6** curtly discourteous **7** full of fat and so flaky ○ *short pastry* ■ *adv* **1** in an abrupt way **2** before reaching a target ■ *n* **1** a film of less than full length **2** a short circuit **3** a small drink of alcoholic spirits *(infml)* ■ **shorts** *npl*

1 short trousers above the knee 2 *US, Can* men's underpants ■ *vti* short-circuit —**shortness** *n* ◊ **short of** 1 not having something, or not having enough of something 2 less than 3 without actually doing something

shortage /sháwrtij/ *n* a lack of something needed or wanted ◊ See note at **lack**

short back and sides *n* a short hairstyle for men

shortbread /sháwrt bred/, **shortcake** /sháwrt kayk/ *n* a rich crumbly biscuit made with butter

shortchange /sháwrt cháynj/ (**-changing, -changed**) *vt* 1 give a customer too little change 2 treat somebody unfairly

short-circuit *v* 1 *vti* have or cause a failure in an electrical circuit 2 *vt* use a quicker and more direct method of achieving something —**short circuit** *n*

shortcoming /sháwrt kuming/ *n* a defect or deficiency (*often pl*)

shortcrust pastry /sháwrt krust-/ *n* crumbly pastry

short cut *n* 1 a shorter route 2 a more direct method that saves time or trouble —**short-cut** *vti*

shorten /sháwrt'n/ *v* 1 *vti* become or make something shorter 2 *vti* reduce the odds on a bet, or be reduced 3 *vt* reduce the area of a sail

shortening /sháwrtning/ *n US* fat added to pastry dough

shortfall /sháwrt fawl/ *n* an amount that is lacking

shorthand /sháwrt hand/ *n* 1 a quick way of writing by using symbols 2 a shorter way of saying something

short-handed *adj* short of workers

shorthand typist *n* somebody who is skilled at shorthand and typing

short-haul *adj* for short distances

short head *n* in horseracing, a distance that is less than a head's length

short list *n* a final list from which to make a selection

short-lived *adj* lasting only a short time ◊ See note at **temporary**

shortly /sháwrtli/ *adv* 1 in a short time 2 curtly

short-range *adj* 1 operating over a short distance 2 concerning the near future

short shrift *n* unsympathetic treatment

short-sighted *adj* 1 unable to see distant objects clearly 2 failing to consider potential difficulties in the long term —**shortsightedly** *adv* —**short-sightedness** *n*

short-staffed *adj* with fewer workers than are needed

short story *n* a short work of prose fiction

short-tempered *adj* quick to become angry

short-term *adj* 1 not lasting long 2 payable or maturing relatively soon

short-termism /-túrmizəm/ *n* the practice of considering only the short term

short ton *n* MEASURE = **ton** 2

short wave *n* a radio wave that is shorter than 100 metres

Shostakovich /shóstə kóvich/, **Dmitri** (1906–75) Russian composer

shot¹ *n* 1 a single occasion of shooting a gun 2 somebody who shoots a gun with a particular level of skill 3 a bullet or cannonball 4 small metal pellets 5 in sports, an attempt to score 6 in sports, an act of hitting a ball 7 the shot put 8 a particular view from a film camera 9 a continuous uninterrupted film sequence 10 an attempt 11 a guess (*infml*) 12 a hypodermic injection (*infml*) 13 a small amount of alcohol (*infml*) ◊ **deliver** *or* **fire a shot across somebody's bows** warn somebody of what might happen ◊ **like a shot** very eagerly and quickly

shot² past tense, past participle of **shoot** ■ *adj* 1 two-tone in colour 2 streaked with a different colour 3 filled with a particular quality

shotgun /shót gun/ *n* a gun that shoots a load of small pellets

shotgun wedding, shotgun marriage *n* a marriage arranged hastily owing to pregnancy

shot put *n* 1 an athletics competition in which a heavy ball is thrown from the shoulder 2 the ball used in the shot put —**shot-putter** *n*

should stressed /shŏŏd/ unstressed /shəd/ *modal v* 1 expresses desirability or rightness ○ *You should work less.* 2 expresses likelihood or probability ○ *I should hear next week.* 3 expresses conditions or consequences ○ *If anything should happen, let me know.* 4 would ○ *I should love to meet her.* 5 reports a past viewpoint about the future ○ *He was keen that I should meet his publisher friend.* ◊ See note at **would**

shoulder /shōldər/ *n* 1 either part of a human body where an arm attaches to the trunk 2 in vertebrate animals, a joint that attaches a forelimb to the trunk 3 meat from an animal's shoulder 4 something that is sloped like a shoulder ■ **shoulders** *npl* 1 the upper area of the back 2 the capacity to handle responsibility ■ *vt* 1 carry or place something on your shoulders 2 accept responsibility ◊ **rub shoulders with** associate with ◊ **shoulder to shoulder** side by side ◊ **stand shoulder to shoulder** act with or support somebody in a common aim

shoulder bag *n* a bag carried by means of a shoulder strap

shoulder blade *n* a flat triangular bone in the back of the shoulder

shoulder strap *n* a strap that goes over a shoulder to carry a bag or support clothing

shouldn't /shŏŏd'nt/ *contr* should not

shout *vti* call out something loudly ■ *n* 1 a loud cry 2 a turn to pay (*infml*) —**shouter** *n* ◊ **nothing to shout about** not very good (*infml*)

□ **shout down** *vt* drown a speaker out by shouting

shove /shuv/ (**shoving, shoved**) v 1 vt move something with force 2 vti push somebody or something roughly —**shove** n
□ **shove off** vi leave (infml)

shovel /shúvv'l/ n 1 a scooping tool with a long or short handle 2 a machine for digging earth ■ v (-**elling, -elled**) 1 vti dig with a shovel for something 2 vt put or throw large amounts of something carelessly —**shovelful** n

show /shó/ v (**shown** /shón/) 1 vt make or be visible 2 vti exhibit or display publicly, or be exhibited or displayed 3 vt guide somewhere 4 vt point out 5 vt demonstrate as a quality or attitude 6 vt establish, demonstrate, or present as an argument or information 7 vi arrive or put in an appearance (infml) ■ n 1 an expression or demonstration of something 2 a public entertainment, performance, or exhibition 3 an appearance or outward display 4 an impressive display —**showing** n ◇ **get the** or **this show on the road** begin an activity or start an event (infml) ◇ **steal the show** attract the most attention
□ **show off** v 1 vi try to impress others 2 vt present for approval
□ **show up** v 1 vi arrive (infml) 2 vt expose or reveal something 3 vt be easily seen

show-and-tell n a classroom activity in which each child says something about an object

show biz n show business (infml)

showboat /shó bót/ n a riverboat theatre

show business n the entertainment industry

showcase /shó kayss/ n 1 a glass case for displaying objects 2 the most favourable setting for something ■ vt (-**casing, -cased**) present to advantage

showdown /shó down/ n a confrontation

shower /shów ər/ n 1 a wash under a spray of water 2 a place or the equipment for a shower 3 a brief period of rain, snow, sleet, or hail 4 a sudden fall of something from the sky ○ a meteor shower 5 a large amount 6 ANZ, US, Can a party at which gifts are given to somebody 7 UK a disagreeable group (infml) ■ v 1 vi wash under a shower 2 vti fall or make things fall like a spray —**showery** adj

shower gel n gel soap for washing with in a shower

showerproof /shów ər proof/ adj resistant to light, but not heavy, rain —**showerproofing** n

showgirl /shó gurl/ n a young woman performing in a stage show

showground /shó grownd/ n an area of land for an open-air event

showjumping /shó jumping/ n a competition in which people on horseback jump over obstacles —**showjump** vi —**showjumper** n

showman /shómən/ (pl **-men** /-mən/) n 1 a gifted entertainer 2 the producer of a show —**showmanship** n

shown past participle of **show**

show-off n somebody who tries to impress others (infml)

show of hands n a vote in which opinions are expressed by raised hands

showpiece /shó peess/ n an excellent example

showplace /shó playss/ n 1 a place visited for its beauty or historical importance 2 something that is exceptionally beautiful

showroom /shó room, -room/ n a room where retail products are displayed

showstopper /shó stopər/ n 1 a performance that receives prolonged applause from an audience 2 something so striking that it stops action

show trial n a trial held for political reasons

showy /shó i/ (**-ier, -iest**) adj 1 making an impressive display 2 ostentatious —**showily** adv —**showiness** n

shrank past participle of **shrink**

shrapnel /shrápnəl/ n 1 fragments from an explosive device 2 a shell that scatters metal fragments

ORIGIN Shrapnel is named after General Henry Shrapnel (1761–1842), a British artillery officer who invented an exploding shell.

shred n 1 a long torn strip 2 a small part ■ vt (**shredding, shredded**) 1 tear something into shreds 2 put something through a shredder

shredder /shréddər/ n a machine for destroying documents or cutting wood into chips

shrew n 1 a small insect-eating nocturnal mammal with a pointed nose 2 an offensive term for a woman regarded as quarrelsome or ill-tempered

shrewd adj good at judging people or situations —**shrewdly** adv —**shrewdness** n

ORIGIN Shrewd is formed from shrew, in the obsolete uses 'wicked person' and as a verb meaning curse. The animal was formerly believed to have a poisonous bite and was considered by the superstitious to be evil. The original meaning of **shrewd** was 'evil, vile'. The modern sense 'clever, good at judging people' did not develop until the early 16C.

shrewish /shróo ish/ adj quarrelsome or ill-tempered —**shrewishly** adv —**shrewishness** n

shriek /shreek/ v 1 vi make a loud shrill sound 2 vt say something in a loud shrill voice —**shriek** n

shrift n (archaic) 1 confession to a priest 2 absolution

shrill adj 1 penetratingly high-pitched 2 tending to talk in a shrill voice 3 insistent ■ v 1 vi make a shrill sound (literary) 2 vt say something in a piercing voice —**shrillness** n —**shrilly** /shril li/ adv

shrimp n 1 a small sea crustacean with ten legs 2 something undersized (infml) ■ vi fish for shrimps —**shrimper** n

shrine /shrīn/ n 1 a holy place of worship 2 a container for holy relics 3 the tomb of a holy person 4 an alcove in a church for a religious icon

shrink v (**shrank** or **shrunk, shrunk** or **shrunken** /shrúngkən/) 1 vti make or become smaller or less 2 vi move away in disgust or fear ■ n a

psychiatrist *(slang; sometimes offensive)*
—**shrinkable** *adj* ◊ See note at **recoil**

shrinkage /shríngkij/ *n* **1** the amount lost when something shrinks **2** the act of shrinking

shrinking violet *n* a meek person *(infml)*

shrive /shrīv/ (**shriving, shrove** /shrōv/ *or* **shrived, shriven** /shrívv'n/ *or* **shrived**) *vt* **1** absolve somebody of sins **2** impose penance

shrivel /shrívv'l/ (**-elling, -elled**) *vti* **1** make or become shrunken and wrinkled **2** weaken

shroff /shrof/ *n* a South Asian banker or money-changer

Shropshire /shrópshər/ county in W England, on the Welsh border

shroud *n* **1** a burial cloth **2** a covering, especially one designed for protection **3** a piece of wire that supports a mast **4** a supporting cable that stops a tall structure from swaying ■ *vt* **1** wrap a corpse in a shroud **2** cover or conceal something

Shrove Tuesday /shrōv-/ *n* the day of the Christian calendar that comes before Ash Wednesday

ORIGIN **Shrove** is an irregular use of the past tense of *shrive*, a verb used in the Christian Church and meaning 'hear the confession of and give absolution to'. *Shrive* itself derives from Latin *scribere* 'write'.

shrub[1] *n* a woody plant with several stems growing from the base

shrub[2] *n* an alcoholic fruit juice drink

shrubbery /shrúbbəri/ (*pl* **-ies**) *n* **1** a part of a garden with shrubs **2** shrubs collectively

shrubby /shrúbbi/ (**-bier, -biest**) *adj* **1** with shrubs **2** like a shrub

shrug (**shrugging, shrugged**) *vti* raise and drop your shoulders briefly to indicate lack of interest or knowledge —**shrug** *n*
□ **shrug off** *vt* dismiss as unimportant

shrunk past tense, past participle of **shrink**

shrunken past participle of **shrink**

shuck *n* **1** US, Can the husk or shell of something **2** an oyster or clam shell

shudder /shúddər/ *vi* **1** shiver violently **2** vibrate rapidly —**shudder** *n*

shuffle /shúff'l/ (**-fling, -fled**) *v* **1** *vi* walk or dance without lifting your feet **2** *vt* change where things are located **3** *vt* mix things up **4** *vti* rearrange the order of playing cards in a random way —**shuffle** *n* —**shuffler** *n*

shuffleboard /shúff'l bawrd/ *n* **1** a game of guiding discs into numbered scoring areas **2** a surface for shuffleboard

shun (**shunning, shunned**) *vt* deliberately avoid —**shunner** *n*

shunt *v* **1** *vt* move somebody or something elsewhere **2** *vti* change or cause a train to change tracks **3** *vt* get rid of a responsibility **4** *vt* divert an electric current ■ *n* **1** a minor car crash *(infml)* **2** a device for diverting electric current

shush /shoŏsh, shush/ *interj* be quiet ■ *vt* silence *(infml)*

shut *v* (**shutting, shut**) **1** *vti* close an opening, or be closed **2** *vt* stop access to or exit from a place **3** *vt* close something by bringing its covering parts together **4** *vti* stop operations in a place ■ *adj* secured
□ **shut down** *vti* stop operations in a place
□ **shut in** *vt* confine or enclose
□ **shut off** *v* **1** *vti* stop operating, or cause to stop operating **2** *vt* cut off the flow of something **3** *vt* block off
□ **shut out** *vt* **1** exclude **2** stop from entering
□ **shut up** *v* **1** *vi* stop talking *(infml)* **2** *vt* confine somebody somewhere

shutdown /shút down/ *n* the permanent closing of a business

shuteye /shút ī/ *n* sleep *(infml)*

shut-off *n* **1** a valve or other device that shuts something off **2** an interruption or temporary stoppage

shutout /shút owt/ *n* an occasion when management prevent workers from entering the workplace

shutter /shúttər/ *n* **1** a hinged door or window cover **2** the part of a camera that opens the lens aperture to let light in ■ *vt* **1** close a door or window using shutters **2** fit something with shutters

shuttle /shútt'l/ *n* **1** the part of a loom that holds the weft and passes it between the warp threads **2** a spindle or bobbin for holding thread **3** a passenger vehicle that makes frequent trips between places **4** a space shuttle **5** the act of going back and forth ■ *vti* (**-tling, -tled**) travel or take something frequently between two places

shuttlecock /shútt'l kok/ *n* in badminton, a cone-shaped object of feathers or plastic in a rounded base that is hit over the net

shuttle diplomacy *n* diplomatic negotiations in which the mediator travels back and forth between countries

Shwe /shə wáy/**, Than** (*b.* 1933) national leader of Myanmar (1992–)

shy[1] *adj* (**shier, shiest**) **1** reserved and uncomfortable in the company of others **2** cautious **3** reluctant **4** showing a dislike of something ○ *workshy* **5** short of a desired amount ■ *vi* (**shies, shied**) **1** move suddenly in fright **2** behave evasively ■ *n* (*pl* **shies**) a sudden move —**shyly** *adv* —**shyness** *n*

shy[2] (**shies, shied**) *vti* throw something quickly —**shy** *n*

shylock /shī lok/ *n* a heartless creditor

ORIGIN **Shylock** is a character in Shakespeare's *Merchant of Venice*.

shyster /shístər/ *n* a person regarded as unscrupulous *(slang insult)*

ORIGIN **Shyster** first appeared in the United States in the 1840s, but its precise origin is not certain. It may be from German *Scheisser*, an offensive term of abuse.

Si *symbol* silicon

SI *abbr* **1** International System of Units Full form: **Système international (d'unités) 2** *NZ* South Island

Siam /sī ám/ former name for **Thailand** —**Siamese** /sī ə meéz/ *n, adj*

Siamese cat /sī ə meez-/ *n* a short-haired domestic cat with a cream-coloured body and dark ears, paws, face, and tail

Siamese twins *npl* twins born physically joined together

> **ORIGIN** The two most famous such twins, Chang and Eng (1811–74), were born in Siam (modern Thailand).

SIB *abbr* Securities and Investments Board

Sibelius /si báyli əss/, **Jean** (1865–1957) Finnish composer

Siberia /sī beéri ə/ vast region of E Russia, extending from the Ural Mountains to the Pacific Ocean —**Siberian** *n, adj*

sibilant /síbbilənt/ *adj* pronounced with a hissing sound ■ *n* a sibilant consonant —**sibilance** *n*

sibling /síbbling/ *n* a brother or sister

sibyl /síbbil, síbb'l/ *n* **1** in ancient Greece or Rome, a woman prophet **2** a woman fortune teller —**sibyllic** /si bíllik/ *adj*

sic[1] /sik/ *adv* thus or so

sic[2] /sik/ (**siccing** *or* **sicking, sicced** *or* **sicked**), **sick** *vt* **1** attack or chase somebody **2** incite a person or animal to attack or chase somebody

Sichuan /si chwaán/, **Szechwan** /se-/ province of S China. Cap. Chengdu. Pop. 114,300,000 (1997).

Sicily /síssəli/ island of S Italy, the largest in the Mediterranean Sea. Pop. 5,082,697 (1995). —**Sicilian** /si sílli ən/ *n, adj*

sick *adj* **1** affected by an illness **2** of or for illness **3** likely to vomit **4** an offensive term meaning thought to have a psychiatric disorder **5** in bad taste *(infml)* **6** distraught **7** very bored ○ *I'm sick of listening to you.* **8** yearning **9** disgusted or repelled **10** impaired ○ *a sick economy* ■ *npl* sick people ■ *n* vomit *(infml)*

sickbay /sík bay/ *n* **1** a ship's hospital **2** a treatment facility in a large building

sickbed /sík bed/ *n* a sick person's bed

sick building syndrome *n* a set of symptoms associated with working in buildings that have poor ventilation or contain toxic building materials

sicken /síkən/ *vti* **1** make or become nauseous **2** make or feel disgusted —**sickening** *adj* —**sickeningly** *adv*

sickie /síki/ *n* a day of sick leave from work, especially one taken for reasons other than genuine illness *(infml)*

sickle /sík'l/ *n* a tool with a curved blade and a handle, used for cutting tall grass or grain crops

sick leave *n* absence from work owing to illness

sickle-cell anaemia *n* a hereditary form of anaemia

sickly /síkli/ (**-lier, -liest**) *adj* **1** often ill ○ *a sickly child* **2** produced by illness **3** causing illness or nausea **4** feeble —**sickliness** *n*

sickness /síknəss/ *n* **1** an illness **2** nausea

sickness benefit *n* a government payment made to somebody who is absent from work because of illness

sick note *n* an employee's certificate given to an employer to show that absence from work was due to illness

sick pay *n* the salary given to an employee who is absent from work because of illness

sickroom /sík room, -ròom/ *n* a room to which a sick person is confined

side *n* **1** a line forming part of the edge of something **2** a surface of something, especially a vertical surface **3** either of the surfaces of something flat **4** the left or right part of something **5** a place or direction relative to a central point or to the observer ○ *the east side of the city* **6** either of the areas separated by a barrier ○ *the south side of the river* **7** an area at the edge of something ○ *the side of the road* **8** either half of the body, especially the area from shoulder to hip **9** the place next to somebody or something ○ *standing at my side* **10** a person or group opposing another person or group **11** an opinion in a dispute **12** an aspect or view of an issue or event ○ *saw the funny side* **13** a line of descent ○ *on his father's side* ■ *adj* **1** at or on a side **2** from the side **3** incidental or of subsidiary importance ○ *a side issue* ■ *vi* (**siding, sided**) align with or against one of the people or groups in a dispute ◊ **let the side down** disappoint associates or supporters by not doing as well as expected or by behaving in an embarrassing way ◊ **on the side 1** illegally or secretly **2** in addition to a main job or activity ◊ **side by side** close beside each other ◊ **take sides** support one person or group against another ◊ **the other side of the coin** the contrasting or contrary aspect of something ◊ **the wrong side of the tracks** the less affluent part of a town *(infml)*

sideboard /síd bawrd/ *n* a piece of dining room furniture for storing tableware and linen

sideboards /síd bawrdz/ *npl* HAIR = **sideburns**

sideburns /síd burnz/ *npl* hair in front of the ears

> **ORIGIN** Sideburns were originally *burnsides*, and named after the US general Ambrose Burnside (1824–81), who wore them.

sidecar /síd kaar/ *n* a passenger vehicle attached to a motorcycle

side dish *n* food served with a main dish

side effect *n* an undesirable secondary effect, especially of a drug or medical treatment

sidekick /síd kik/ *n* a companion *(infml)*

sidelight /síd līt/ *n* **1** either of two small lights on a vehicle, used instead of headlights in some conditions **2** a piece of incidental information

sideline /síd līn/ *n* **1** either of two lines marking the side boundaries of a sports field **2** a supplementary source of income ■ **sidelines** *npl* **1** the area of a sports field outside its boundaries **2** the position of being uninvolved in something ■ *vt* (**-lining, -lined**) exclude somebody from participation

sidelong /síd long/ *adj* directed to the side —**sidelong** *adv*

side order *n* a portion of food ordered to accompany a main dish

sidereal /sī déeri əl/ *adj* of the stars

sideroad /síd rōd/ *n* a secondary road off the main road

sidesaddle /síd sad'l/ *n* a saddle designed for women in long skirts ■ *adv* with both legs on the same side of the horse

sideshow /síd shō/ *n* a minor attraction at a circus or fair

sidesplitting /síd spliting/ *adj* hilarious

sidestep /síd step/ *vti* (**-stepping, -stepped**) **1** step aside to avoid somebody or something **2** avoid saying or discussing something ■ *n* a sideways movement

side street *n* a small street off a main street

sideswipe /síd swīp/ *n* **1** a glancing blow **2** a jibe made in passing (*infml*) ■ *vt* (**-swiping, -swiped**) strike with a glancing blow

sidetrack /síd trak/ *vt* divert from the original subject or activity

sidewalk /síd wawk/ *n US, Can* a pavement along a street

sideward /sídwərd/ *adj* towards or at one side ■ *adv also* **sidewards** towards one side

sideways /síd wayz/, **sidewise** /-wīz/ *adj, adv* **1** to or towards one side **2** from the side **3** with the side facing the front

siding /síding/ *n* a short railway track leading off the main line

sidle /síd'l/ (**-dling, -dled**) *v* **1** *vi* edge along furtively **2** *vti* move sideways —**sidle** *n*

Sidney /sídni/, **Sir Philip** (1554–86) English soldier, courtier, and poet

Sidon /síd'n/ city in SW Lebanon. Pop. 38,000 (1998).

SIDS *abbr* sudden infant death syndrome

siege /seej/ *n* **1** a military or police operation in which a place is surrounded until the people inside surrender **2** a prolonged effort or period ■ *vt* (**sieging, sieged**) subject a place to a siege

Siena /si énnə/ capital of **Siena Province**, Tuscany Region, in north-central Italy. Pop. 54,769 (1997). —**Sienese** /seè ə neèz/ *n, adj*

~~sience~~ incorrect spelling of **science**

~~siene~~ incorrect spelling of **scene**

sienna /si énnə/ *n* artists' paint made with iron-rich soil —**sienna** *adj*

ORIGIN Sienna is named after the town of Siena in Italy, where the pigment was originally produced.

sierra /si érrə/ *n* **1** a range of mountains with jagged peaks **2 Sierra** a communications code word for the letter 'S' —**sierran** *adj*

Sierra Leone /si érrə li ṓn/ country in West Africa. Cap. Freetown. Pop. 5,426,618 (2001). —**Sierra Leonean** /-lee ṓnee ən/ *n, adj*

Sierra Madre /-ma̍a dray/ mountain system in Mexico, extending from the US border in the north to the border with Guatemala in the south. Length 1,100 km/680 mi. Highest peak Orizaba 5,610 m/18,406 ft.

Sierra Nevada /si érrə nə va̍adə/ **1** mountain range in SE Spain. Highest peak Cerro de Mulhacén 3,480 m/11,411 ft. **2** mountain range in E California. Highest peak Mt Whitney 4,417 m/14,491 ft.

siesta /si éstə/ *n* an early afternoon rest or nap

ORIGIN Siesta came through Spanish from Latin *sexta* '6th' in *sexta hora* '6th hour (of the day)'.

sieve /siv/ *n* a meshed utensil used for straining or sifting ■ *vt* (**sieving, sieved**) put something through a sieve

~~sieze~~ incorrect spelling of **seize**

sift *v* **1** *vti* pass a substance through a sieve to separate out the larger particles **2** *vt* separate out with a sieve or by selection **3** *vti* sort or examine minutely —**sifter** *n*

SIG *abbr* special interest group

sigh /sī/ *vi* **1** breathe deeply and audibly in relief or tiredness **2** make a sound like somebody sighing ○ *The wind sighed in the trees.* **3** yearn ■ *n* the act or sound of sighing

sight /sīt/ *n* **1** the ability to see **2** the perception of something or somebody with the eyes **3** the range or field of vision **4** something seen **5** something worth seeing (*often pl*) **6** somebody or something unpleasant to look at (*infml*) **7** an alignment device on a gun or surveying instrument ■ *v* **1** *vt* see or notice **2** *vti* observe or measure something using an optical device **3** *vti* aim at something with a gun —**sighted** *adj* —**sightedness** *n* ◊ **at** *or* **on sight** as soon as something or somebody is seen ◊ **out of sight** no longer able to be seen ◊ **set** *or* **have your sights on something** decide to try to get something ◊ **sight unseen** without seeing or inspecting first ◊ See note at **cite**

sighting /síting/ *n* an occasion of seeing something

sightless /sítləss/ *adj* unable to see —**sightlessness** *n*

sight-read *vti* read or perform something such as music without preparation or seeing it beforehand —**sight-reader** *n*

sightseeing /sít see ing/ *n* the visiting of places of interest

sigint /síggint/, **SIGINT** *n* intelligence data acquired electronically. Full form **signals intelligence**

sigma /sígmə/ *n* the 18th letter of the Greek alphabet

sign /sīn/ *n* **1** an indication of the existence or presence of something ○ *a sign of wealth* ○ *a* *sign of illness* **2** an act or gesture that conveys an idea or information **3** a public notice bearing advertising, directions, instructions, or a warning **4** an omen **5** one of the 12 divisions of the zodiac, each represented by a symbol **6** a symbol used in maths, logic, or music ■ *vti* **1** write your name in a characteristic way on something **2** approve a document by signing it **3** employ or become employed by a signed agreement **4** communicate in sign language —**signer** *n*

SPELLCHECK Do not confuse the spelling of **sign** and **sine** ('a trigonometric function'), which sound similar.

□ **sign away** *vt* give up rights or property with a signed document

□ **sign in** *v* **1** *vi* write your name in a register on arrival **2** *vt* allow somebody to be admitted by writing your name in a register

□ **sign off** *v* **1** *vi* end a form of communication **2** *vt* certify somebody as too ill or injured to work **3** *vt* approve something *(infml)*

□ **sign on** *v* **1** *vi* register as unemployed **2** *vt* employ

□ **sign over** *vt* transfer ownership of something with a signed document

□ **sign up** *vti* **1** agree or make somebody agree to participate in something **2** enlist for military service

signal /sígnəl/ *n* **1** an action, gesture, or sign used as a means of communication **2** a piece of information communicated by a signal **3** a piece of information transmitted by electrical current or electromagnetic wave ■ *adj* notable ○ *a signal accomplishment* ■ *v* (**-nalling, -nalled**) **1** *vti* communicate by sending a signal **2** *vt* indicate ○ *The event signalled the end of the conflict.* —**signaller** *n* —**signally** *adv*

signal box *n* a building from which a section of railway track is controlled

signalman /sígnəlmən/ (*pl* **-men** /-mən/) *n* **1** somebody in the armed forces who sends and receives signals **2** a railway employee in charge of operating signals

signatory /sígnətəri/ *n* (*pl* **-ries**) a party to a treaty or contract ■ *adj* bound by a treaty or contract

signature /sígnəchər/ *n* **1** somebody's signed name **2** a distinctive identifying characteristic **3** a key signature

signature file *n* a text file containing the user's name and address serving as a signature at the end of an e-mail

signature tune *n* a piece of music used to introduce a performer or a television or radio programme

signboard /sín bawrd/ *n* a board bearing a notice or advertisement

signet /sígnət/ *n* **1** a small seal, especially one engraved on a ring **2** a seal for stamping official documents

signet ring *n* a finger ring with an engraved seal

significance /sig níffikənss/ *n* **1** importance or value **2** implied or intended meaning

significant /sig níffikənt/ *adj* **1** having or expressing a meaning **2** having a hidden or implied meaning **3** momentous and influential **4** substantial —**significantly** *adv*

significant other *n* somebody's spouse or long-term sexual partner

signification /sígnifi káysh'n/ *n* **1** the meaning of something **2** the act of signifying

~~significent~~ incorrect spelling of **significant**

signify /sígni fī/ (**-fies, -fied**) *v* **1** *vt* mean **2** *vt* be a sign of **3** *vi* be important

signing /síning/, **sign language** *n* communication by gestures, especially a system used by or to people who are hearing-impaired

signor /see nyawr/ (*pl* **-gnors** *or* **-gnori** /-nyáwri/) *n* the Italian equivalent of Mr

signpost /sín pōst/ *n* **1** a pole with a sign on it giving directions or information **2** something that gives a clue or indication ■ *vt* give an indication of

Sihanouk /see ə nook/, **Norodom** (*b.* 1922) king of Cambodia (1993–)

Sikh /seek/ *n* a member of a monotheistic religion founded in Punjab in the 16C —**Sikh** *adj* —**Sikhism** *n*

Sikkim /síkim/ state in NE India. Cap. Gangtok. Pop. 444,000 (1994). —**Sikkimese** /síki meez/ *n, adj*

Sikorsky /si káwrski/, **Igor** (1889–1972) Russian-born US aeronautical engineer and corporate executive

silage /sílij/ *n* animal fodder consisting of partly fermented green plant material

silence /sílənss/ *n* **1** the absence or lack of noise **2** a refusal, failure, or inability to speak ■ *vt* (**-lencing, -lenced**) **1** stop from speaking or making a noise **2** suppress the expression of ○ *silence criticism*

silencer /sílənssər/ *n* **1** the part of a vehicle's exhaust system designed to lessen noise **2** a device for muffling the noise of a gun

silent /sílənt/ *adj* **1** without noise or sound **2** not speaking **3** inclined to say little **4** unspoken **5** unable or forbidden to speak **6** describes a letter that is not pronounced —**silently** *adv* —**silentness** *n*

SYNONYMS silent, quiet, reticent, taciturn, uncommunicative CORE MEANING: not speaking or not saying much

silent majority *n* the greater part of a population who do not express their opinions

Silesia /sī leeshə/ historic region in east-central Europe, lying mostly within present-day SW Poland —**Silesian** *n, adj*

silhouette /sílloo ét/ *n* **1** a picture of somebody or something as a black shape against a lighter background **2** something dark against a light background ■ *vt* (**-etting, -etted**) cause to appear as a silhouette

ORIGIN The **silhouette** was named in French

after the author and politician Etienne de Silhouette (1709–67). As French finance minister in the late 1750s, he gained a reputation for stinginess, and **silhouette** came to be used for anything skimped. One account of the application of the word to a simple picture showing a dark shape against a light background is that it carries on this notion of 'simplicity' or 'lack of finish', but an alternative theory is that Silhouette himself was in the habit of making such pictures.

silica /síllikə/ n a naturally occurring colourless transparent solid with a high melting point. Use: manufacture of glass, abrasives, concrete.

silicate /síllikət, -kayt/ n a common rock-forming mineral containing silicon and oxygen

silicon /síllikən/ n (symbol Si) a brittle non-metallic chemical element. Use: alloys, semiconductors, building materials.

silicon chip n a wafer of silicon on which an integrated circuit is laid out

silicone /sílli kōn/ n a silicon-based synthetic substance in the form of a grease, oil, or plastic. Use: lubricants, insulators, water-repellents, adhesives, coatings, prosthetics.

Silicon Valley region in W California, an important centre for the electronics and computer industries

silicosis /sílli kóssiss/ n a chronic lung disease caused by inhalation of silica dust

silk n 1 the fine fibre secreted by silkworms to make their cocoons. Use: threads, fabrics. 2 silk thread or fabric 3 the fine fibre secreted by spiders to make their webs 4 a King's or Queen's Counsel (infml)

silken /sílkən/ adj 1 made of silk 2 like silk in texture or appearance

silk-screen vti print a design on paper or fabric by forcing ink through areas of a silk screen that are not blocked out with an impermeable substance ■ n 1 a print produced by silk-screening 2 also **silk-screen printing** a method of printing designs by silk-screening

silkworm /sílk wurm/ n a moth larva that produces silk

silky /sílki/ (-ier, -iest) adj 1 looking or feeling like silk 2 made of silk 3 smooth or unctuous in manner —**silkily** adv —**silkiness** n

sill n 1 a window ledge 2 the bottom of a window or door frame

silly /sílli/ (-lier, -liest) adj 1 lacking common sense 2 trivial 3 dazed or light-headed —**sillily** adv —**silliness** n

ORIGIN The meaning of **silly** has undergone one of the most astonishing changes in the history of English word development. In a thousand years it has gone from 'blessed, happy' to 'foolish'. The transformation began with 'blessed' becoming 'pious'. This led on via 'innocent, harmless', 'pitiable', and 'feeble' to 'feeble in mind, foolish'.

silly season n a period in summer when newspapers, lacking political news, print frivolous articles

silo /sílō/ n (pl **-los**) 1 a cylindrical tower for storing grain or animal feed or for making silage 2 a chamber for storing and launching missiles ■ vt store in a silo

~~silouette~~ incorrect spelling of **silhouette**

silt n sediment in a river or lake ■ vti clog up with silt —**siltation** /sil táysh'n/ n —**silty** adj

Silurian /sí lyóori ən/ n a period of geological time 443–417 million years ago —**Silurian** adj

silvan adj = **sylvan**

silver /sílvər/ n 1 (symbol Ag) a shiny greyish-white metallic element. Use: ornaments, solders, photographic chemicals, conductors. 2 tableware or other household goods made of or covered with silver 3 coins made of silver or a silver-coloured metal 4 a lustrous greyish-white colour ■ adj 1 made of silver 2 of the colour or lustre of silver 3 25th 4 resonant and clear ■ v 1 vt coat with silver 2 vti make or become silver in colour

silver birch n a tree with silvery-white bark

silverfish /sílvər fish/ (pl same or **-fishes**) n a small silvery wingless insect that feeds on starch in household materials

silver medal n a silver disc awarded for coming second in a race or competition —**silver medallist** n

silver plate n 1 a thin coating of silver on a base metal 2 items coated in silver

silver screen n films or the cinema

silver service n a formal way of serving restaurant food using a silver spoon and fork in one hand

silversmith /sílvər smith/ n somebody who makes or repairs silver objects

silver-tongued adj eloquent or persuasive

silverware /sílvər wair/ n silver items, especially tableware

silvery /sílvəri/ adj 1 like silver in colour or lustre 2 containing or coated with silver

~~simbol~~ incorrect spelling of **symbol**

Simenon /seemə náwN/, **Georges** (1903–89) Belgian-born French writer

Simferopol /símfə rópp'l/, **Simferopol'** city in S Ukraine, on the Crimean Peninsula. Pop. 341,000 (1998).

simian /símmi ən/ adj of or like monkeys and apes ■ n a monkey or ape

similar /símmilər/ adj 1 sharing some qualities 2 describes geometric figures that differ in size or proportion but not in shape or angular measurements —**similarly** adv

USAGE In its meaning 'sharing some qualities', **similar** is followed by to, not as: I had a similar experience to [not as] yours.

similarity /símmi lárrəti/ (pl **-ties**) n 1 the quality of being similar 2 a shared characteristic

simile /símmili/ *n* a figure of speech drawing a comparison between two things

~~similer, simlar~~ incorrect spelling of **similar**

~~similie~~ incorrect spelling of **simile**

Simitis /símtis/**, Kostas** (*b.* 1936) prime minister of Greece (1996–)

SIMM /sim/ *n* a module plugged into a computer's motherboard to add memory. Full form **single inline memory module**

simmer /símmər/ *v* **1** *vti* cook or remain just below the boiling point **2** *vi* be filled with unexpressed emotion, especially anger —**simmer** *n*

□ **simmer down** *vi* become calm

simnel cake /símnəl-/ *n* a fruitcake with marzipan eaten during Lent or at Easter

Simon /símən/ *n* (*fl* AD 1C) one of the 12 apostles of Jesus Christ

simpatico /sim páttikō/ *adj* compatible in temperament or interests

simper /símpər/ *v* **1** *vi* smile in an affectedly coy manner **2** *vt* say something with a simpering smile —**simper** *n* —**simpering** *adj*, *n* —**simperingly** *adv*

simple /símp'l/ (**-pler, -plest**) *adj* **1** easy **2** lacking decoration or embellishment **3** consisting of only one part **4** uncomplicated **5** ordinary or straightforward **6** an offensive term meaning having limited intellectual ability **7** naive or guileless **8** humble and unsophisticated —**simpleness** *n* —**simply** *adv* ◊ See note at **simplistic**

simple fraction *n* a fraction that consists of two whole numbers separated by a horizontal or slanting line, as opposed to a decimal fraction

simple interest *n* interest on an investment that is not compounded

simple-minded *adj* **1** showing a lack of due thought or consideration **2** an offensive term meaning having limited intellectual ability —**simple-mindedly** *adv* —**simple-mindedness** *n*

simpleton /símp'ltən/ *n* an offensive term for somebody regarded as lacking intelligence or judgment

~~simpley~~ incorrect spelling of **simply**

simplicity /sim plíssəti/ (*pl* **-ties**) *n* **1** lack of complexity, embellishment, or difficulty **2** a simple quality or thing

simplify /símpli fī/ (**-fies, -fied**) *vt* make less complicated or easier to understand —**simplification** /símplifi káysh'n/ *n* —**simplifier** *n*

simplistic /sim plístik/ *adj* **1** naively simple **2** tending to oversimplify something —**simplistically** *adv*

USAGE simple or **simplistic**? **Simplistic** implies that something is oversimplified and shows disapproval: *far too simplistic an approach to the problem.* It should not be used as an alternative or stronger word for **simple**: *I recommended a simple* [not *simplistic*] *solution to the problem.*

simulacrum /símmyōō láykrəm/ (*pl* **-cra** /-krə/) *n* **1** a representation or image **2** something vaguely similar to something else

simulate /símmyōō layt/ (**-lating, -lated**) *vt* **1** reproduce a feature or features of something, especially by computer **2** fake, feign, or imitate something —**simulation** /símmyōō láysh'n/ *n* —**simulator** *n*

simulcast /símm'l kaast/ *n* **1** a simultaneous television and radio broadcast **2** a live broadcast of an event on closed-circuit television —**simulcast** *vt*

simultaneous /símm'l táyni əss/ *adj* happening at the same time —**simultaneity** /símm'ltə née əti/ *n* —**simultaneously** *adv*

~~simultanious~~ incorrect spelling of **simultaneous**

sin¹ *n* **1** a transgression of a religious law **2** in Christianity, being denied God's grace because of having committed a sin **3** an offence against a moral or ethical principle —**sin** *vi* —**sinner** *n*

sin² *abbr* sine

Sinai /sī nī/ peninsula of NE Egypt, bounded on the east by the Gulf of Aqaba and on the west by the Gulf of Suez

Sinai, Mt mountain in NE Egypt on the south-central Sinai Peninsula. Height 2,888 m/7,500 ft.

Sinatra /si naátrə/**, Frank** (1915–98) US singer and actor

since *prep, conj* happening after the time mentioned ■ *adv* subsequently ■ *conj* because

sincere /sin seér/ (**-cerer, -cerest**) *adj* **1** honest and open **2** not feigned —**sincerely** *adv* —**sincerity** /sin sérrəti/ *n*

~~sincerly~~ incorrect spelling of **sincerely**

sine /sīn/ *n* for an angle in a right-angled triangle, a trigonometric function equal to the length of the side opposite the angle divided by the hypotenuse ◊ See note at **sign**

sinecuro /sínni kyʊ̄oor, sínī-, -kyáwr/ *n* **1** a paid job requiring little work **2** a paid church office without duties

sine die /sīni dí ee, sínni deé ay/ *adv* without a day being fixed for a further meeting

sine qua non /sīni kway nón, sínnay kwaa nón/ *n* an essential condition

sinew /sínnyoo/ *n* **1** a tendon **2** strength or power (*literary*)

sinewy /sínnyoo i/ *adj* **1** thin and strong **2** consisting of or containing tendons or stringy parts resembling tendons

sinful /sínf'l/ *adj* **1** committing or characterized by sin **2** morally or ethically wrong —**sinfully** *adv* —**sinfulness** *n*

sing (**sang, sung**) *v* **1** *vti* use the voice to produce musical sounds **2** *vti* perform songs professionally **3** *vti* make a characteristic tuneful sound (*refers to animals*) **4** *vi* make a whistling, humming, or ringing sound ○ *The wind made the wires sing.* **5** *vt* put in a particular state by singing ○ *sang the baby to sleep* —**singer** *n*

□ **sing along** *vi* join in a song with others

Singapore /síngə páwr/ city-state in Southeast Asia, comprising one major island and several islets south of the Malay Peninsula. Cap. Singapore. Pop. 4,300,419 (2001). —**Singaporean** n, adj

singe v 1 vti burn slightly on the surface or edge 2 vt remove feathers or hair from a carcass with flame —**singe** n

Singer /síngər/, **Isaac Bashevis** (1904–91) Polish-born US writer

Singhalese n, adj PEOPLES, LANG = Sinhalese

single /síng g'l/ adj 1 one ○ didn't get a single reply 2 considered individually ○ every single time 3 unmarried 4 for one person 5 consisting of one thing or part ■ n 1 a room or bed for one person 2 a recording consisting of one song with a secondary song on the other side 3 a ticket for a journey in one direction only —**singleness** n —**singly** /síng gli/ adv

□ **single out** vt choose from a group for a particular purpose

single-breasted adj with a slight overlap at the front and a single row of buttons

single cream n UK cream that is relatively low in butterfat and is not suitable for whipping

single currency n a monetary unit shared by several countries

single-decker n a bus with only one deck

single file n a single line of people, animals, or vehicles ■ adv moving in a single line

single-handed adj 1 unaided 2 using or requiring only one hand ■ adv without help —**single-handedly** adv

single-minded adj 1 with a single aim 2 preoccupied with one task —**single-mindedness** n

single parent n somebody who brings up a child alone —**single-parenting** n

singles /síng g'lz/ n (pl same) a racket game between two players ■ npl unmarried people

singlet /síng glət/ n a light sleeveless shirt worn by a sports player

singsong /síng song/ n 1 a rising and falling intonation in speech 2 an occasion when people sing together ■ adj with rising and falling intonation

singular /síng gyōōlər/ adj 1 referring to one person or thing 2 exceptional or unusual ■ n a singular word or form —**singularity** /síng gyōō lárrəti/ n —**singularly** adv

Sinhalese /sínhə leéz/ (pl same), **Singhalese** /síngə-, síng gə-/ n 1 a member of a Sri Lankan people 2 the language of the Sinhalese —**Sinhalese** adj

sinister /sínnistər/ adj 1 suggesting evil or trouble 2 in heraldry, the left part of a shield —**sinisterly** adv

sink /singk/ v (**sank** /sangk/ or **sunk** /sungk/, **sunk** or **sunken** /súngkən/) 1 vti go beneath the surface of a liquid 2 vi appear to descend to or below the horizon 3 vi become lower 4 vi fall or collapse gently ○ sank to his knees 5 vt drill a well, tunnel, or shaft in the ground 6 vti penetrate or cause to penetrate a surface or an object ○ sank its fangs into her leg 7 vi become quieter 8 vi diminish or decline 9 vt invest money in a business or project 10 vt bring somebody or something to ruin 11 vt make a successful shot or hit (infml) ■ n 1 a basin fixed to a wall with a piped water supply and drainage 2 also **sinkhole** a natural depression in the ground —**sinkable** adj

SPELLCHECK Do not confuse the spelling of **sink** and **sync** ('synchronization'), which sound similar.

□ **sink in** vi 1 become absorbed 2 finally become understood

sinker /síngkər/ n a weight on a fishing line

sinking fund n a fund reserved to pay debt

sinuous /sínnyoo əss/ adj 1 moving in graceful curves 2 full of bends and curves —**sinuously** adv —**sinuousness** n

sinus /sínəss/ n 1 a cavity filled with air in the bones of the skull, especially in the nasal passages 2 a widened channel in the body containing blood, especially venous blood

sinusitis /sínə sítiss/ n inflammation of the sinus lining

Sioux /soo/ (pl same) n a member of a group of Native North American peoples who lived throughout the Great Plains, and now live mainly in North and South Dakota —**Sioux** adj

sip vti (**sipping**, **sipped**) drink slowly in very small amounts ■ n a small amount of drink taken into the mouth

siphon /síf'n/, **syphon** v 1 vt draw liquid through a tube from one container to another using atmospheric pressure 2 vti illegally tap funds or resources ■ n a bent tube for siphoning liquids

sir (stressed) /sur/ (unstressed) /sər/ n 1 a polite form of address for a man 2 **Sir** a title used before the name of a knight or baronet

sire n 1 also **Sire** a respectful form of address for a king or lord (archaic) 2 the male parent of a four-legged animal ■ vt (**siring**, **sired**) father offspring

siren /síərən/ n 1 a warning device that produces a loud wailing sound 2 in Greek mythology, a woman believed to lure sailors onto rocks with her singing

sirloin /súr loyn/ n a prime cut of beef from the lower ribs or upper loin

ORIGIN One of the most persistent of etymological fictions is that the **sirloin** got its name because a particular English king found the joint of beef so excellent that he knighted it. The monarch has been variously identified as Henry VIII, James I, and Charles II, but none of these is chronologically possible, and the story has no truth in it at all. **Sirloin** actually comes from an Old French word meaning 'above the loin'. The spelling sir-, which began to replace the original sur- 'above' in the 18C, no doubt owes something to the 'knighting' story.

sirocco /si rókō/ (*pl* **-cos**), **scirocco** *n* an oppressive hot Mediterranean wind

sis /siss/ *n* a way of addressing a sister (*infml*)

sisal /síss'l, síz'l/, **sisal hemp** *n* **1** a strong fibre obtained from the leaves of the agave plant. Use: rope, rugs. **2** a plant from which sisal is obtained

Sisley /sízzli, síssli/, **Alfred** (1839–99) French painter

~~sissors~~ incorrect spelling of **scissors**

sissy /síssi/ (*pl* **-sies**) *n* an offensive term for a boy or man regarded as lacking in strength or courage (*infml*) —**sissyish** *adj*

sister /sístər/ *n* **1** a female sibling **2** a stepsister or half-sister **3** *also* **Sister** a nun **4** a woman of the most senior grade of hospital nurse **5** a woman who belongs to the same organization as another **6** a woman who supports feminism ■ *adj* closely associated —**sisterliness** *n* —**sisterly** *adj, adv*

sisterhood /sístər hồod/ *n* **1** solidarity among women **2** a group of women with a shared aim or interest (+ *sing or pl verb*) **3** the status of a sister

sister-in-law (*pl* **sisters-in-law**) *n* **1** a spouse's sister **2** a brother's wife

sit (**sitting, sat**) *v* **1** *vi* rest on a surface with the weight on the buttocks **2** *vt* place somebody or yourself in a seat **3** *vi* rest the body on the lowered hindquarters (*refers to four-legged animals*) **4** *vi* perch, roost, or cover eggs (*refers to birds*) **5** *vi* pose for a portrait **6** *vti* take an exam **7** *vi* be or remain idle ○ *sat around all day* **8** *vi* be placed or situated somewhere ○ *The dishes were still sitting on the table.* **9** *vi* rest, weigh, hang, or lie in a particular way ○ *The responsibility sat heavily on his shoulders.* **10** *vt* have seating space for a particular number of people ◊ **sit tight** refrain from moving or acting (*infml*) ◊ **sitting pretty** in a favourable position (*infml*)

□ **sit back** *vi* take no action

□ **sit down** *vti* seat or become seated

□ **sit in** *vi* attend something without taking an active part

□ **sit on** *vt* **1** be a member of a decision-making group **2** suppress or delay dealing with something (*infml*)

□ **sit out** *vt* **1** stay until the end of **2** not participate in

□ **sit up** *vi* **1** sit upright or rise to a sitting position **2** stay up late

Sita /seé taa/ *n* an incarnation of the Hindu goddess Lakshmi

sitar /si taár, síttaar/ *n* a South Asian stringed instrument —**sitarist** *n*

sitcom /sít kom/ *n* a situation comedy (*infml*)

sit-down *n* **1** *also* **sit-down strike** a strike in which workers sit down in their place of work and refuse to work or leave **2** *also* **sit-in** the occupation of a building by a group of people as a protest ■ *adj* served to people sitting at a table

site /sīt/ *n* **1** a place where something stands **2** a place where a significant event happened ■ *vt* (**siting, sited**) position or locate somewhere ◊ See note at **cite**

sitter /síttər/ *n* **1** somebody hired to look after something or somebody (*often in combination*) **2** an artist's or photographer's model **3** a broody hen

sitting /sítting/ *n* **1** one of the periods when a meal is served in a place not large enough to seat everyone simultaneously **2** a period spent seated, e.g. while posing for a portrait **3** a session of a public body ■ *adj* **1** seated or for being seated **2** currently in office

Sitting Bull (1831?–90) Sioux leader

sitting duck *n* an easy target (*infml*)

sitting room *n* a room in a home used for relaxing or entertaining guests

sitting tenant *n* a tenant with a legal right to remain in a property when it changes ownership

situate /síttyoo ayt/ *vt* place in a location or context —**situated** *adj*

situation /síttyoo áysh'n/ *n* **1** a set of conditions or circumstances, e.g. in a place or in somebody's life **2** the location of a property **3** a job or position of employment (*fml*) —**situational** *adj*

situation comedy *n* a TV or radio comedy series based on everyday situations

sit-up *n* an abdominal exercise done by lying on the back with the legs bent and raising the upper body

sitz bath /sits-/ *n* **1** a bath shaped like a chair **2** an act of bathing in a sitz bath

SI unit *n* an internationally accepted unit of measurement

Sivan /sívv'n, see vaán/ *n* the 3rd month of the Jewish calendar

six *n* **1** the number 6 **2** a group of Cubs or Brownies —**six** *adj, pron* —**sixth** *n, adj, adv* ◊ **at sixes and sevens** (*infml*) **1** disorganized or in disarray **2** in disagreement ◊ **knock** *or* **hit for six** surprise somebody completely (*infml*)

sixfold /síks fõld/ *adj* **1** six times greater **2** with six parts ■ *adv* by six times as much or as many

six-pack *n* six cans or bottles sold together as a unit

sixteen /síks teén/ *n* the number 16 —**sixteen** *adj, pron* —**sixteenth** *n, adj, adv*

sixth form *n* the final two years in an English or Welsh secondary school —**sixth-former** *n*

sixth-form college *n* a separate educational institution for sixth-form students

sixth sense *n* a supposed extra sense allowing somebody to perceive things not detectable by the other senses

sixty /síksti/ *n* (*pl* **-ties**) the number 60 ■ **sixties** *npl* **1** the numbers 60 to 69, particularly as a range of temperatures **2** the years from 60 to 69 in a century or somebody's life —**sixtieth** n, adj, adv —**sixty** adj, pron

sizable /síz əb'l/, **sizeable** adj fairly large —**sizably** adv

size¹ n 1 the amount, extent, or degree of something in terms of how large or small it is 2 the largeness of something 3 a standard measurement of a manufactured item ■ vt (**sizing, sized**) 1 sort according to size 2 make to a particular size —**sized** adj ◊ **cut down to size** cause to be less self-important and arrogant

□ **size up** vt assess

size² n a gelatinous mixture made from glue, starch, or varnish. Use: filling pores in the surface of paper, textiles, or plaster. —**size** vt

sizzle /síz'l/ (**-zling, -zled**) vi 1 make the noise of food frying 2 be hot (infml) —**sizzle** n —**sizzling** adj

SJ abbr Society of Jesus

Sjælland /syélland/ main island of Denmark, on which Copenhagen, the country's capital, is situated. Pop. 2,159,260 (1994).

ska /skaa/ n a type of popular Jamaican dance music

skate¹ n 1 an ice skate 2 a roller skate ■ vi (**skating, skated**) move on skates —**skater** n —**skating** n

□ **skate over** vt treat in cursory way (infml)

skate² (pl same or **skates**) n 1 a bottom-dwelling sea fish 2 skate as food

skateboard /skáyt bawrd/ n a wheeled board on which to ride standing up or to perform stunts —**skateboard** vi —**skateboarder** n —**skateboarding** n

skedaddle /ski dádd'l/ (**-dling, -dled**) vi run away quickly (slang) —**skedaddle** n

skein /skayn/ n 1 a length of yarn wound loosely and coiled together 2 a flock of geese in flight

skeletal /skéllit'l/ adj 1 of a skeleton 2 very thin

skeleton /skéllitən/ n 1 the framework of bones of a person or animal 2 the supportive protective structure of an invertebrate 3 the basic frame something is built around 4 something with only the essential parts left 5 an outline description of something ◊ **a skeleton in the cupboard** a closely kept secret that is a source of shame or embarrassment

skeleton key n a key that can unlock many doors

skeptic n US = sceptic

sketch n 1 a picture drawn quickly and roughly 2 a rough description or explanation 3 a short piece of writing 4 a short comic performance ■ vti make a sketch of something —**sketcher** n

sketchbook /skéch bòok/, **sketchpad** /-pad/ n a book of plain paper in which to make sketches

sketchy /skéchi/ (**-ier, -iest**) adj 1 giving only the main points 2 superficial —**sketchily** adv —**sketchiness** n

skew /skyoo/ v 1 vti make or become slanted or unsymmetrical 2 vt misrepresent or distort ■ adj 1 slanted or unsymmetrical 2 distorting the truth ■ n a slanted position

skewer /skyoo ər/ n 1 a thin pointed rod pushed through pieces of food to hold them during cooking 2 a thin pointed object used to pierce something and hold it in place ■ vt pierce with or as if with a skewer

skewwhiff /skyoo wif/ adj not level or straight (infml)

ski /skee/ n (pl **skis** or same) either of a pair of long thin boards used to slide across snow or in waterskiing ■ vti (**skis, skiing, skied** or **ski'd**) move across snow or water on skis —**skier** n —**skiing** n

skid n 1 an uncontrolled slide in a wheeled vehicle 2 a runner on an aircraft 3 a block used to prevent a wheel from turning ■ v (**skidding, skidded**) 1 vti slide or cause to slide dangerously across a surface 2 vi slide over a surface without turning and gripping it (refers to wheels) ◊ **on the skids** heading for failure (infml)

skiff n a small flat-bottomed boat

skiffle /skiff'l/ n a type of 1950s pop music played by a small group with guitars and improvised instruments

ski jump n 1 a steep artificial slope from which skiers jump 2 a jump made from a ski jump —**ski jumper** n —**ski jumping** n

skilful /skílf'l/ adj 1 particularly adept at something 2 requiring or done with a special skill —**skilfully** adv —**skilfulness** n

skillfull incorrect spelling of **skilful**

ski lift n an apparatus for transporting skiers up a mountainside

skill n 1 the ability to do something well 2 something requiring experience or training to do well —**skilled** adj ◊ See note at ability

skillet /skíllit/ n a small shallow long-handled frying pan

skillful adj US = **skilful**

skim (**skimming, skimmed**) v 1 vt scoop a substance such as fat from the top of a liquid 2 vt rid a liquid of material accumulating on its surface 3 vti pass closely over a surface 4 vti glance quickly through a book or paper 5 vt send something bouncing lightly along the surface of water —**skim** n

skimmed milk n milk with the fat removed

skimp v 1 vti use or provide too little of something 2 vt do something inadequately

skimpy /skímpi/ (**-ier, -iest**) adj 1 done using barely enough of the necessary materials 2 stingy —**skimpiness** n

skin n 1 the external protective membrane or covering of an animal's body 2 a thin outer layer, especially of a fruit or vegetable 3 a hide or pelt of an animal 4 a thin pliant layer that forms on a liquid 5 the outer covering of a structure such as an aircraft 6 a piece of software for changing the appearance of images produced by existing software without changing their function ■ *vt* (**skinning, skinned**) **1** remove the skin or outer layer of something **2** scrape the skin accidentally from a part of the body **3** change the appearance of software images without changing their function ◊ **be no skin off somebody's nose** not matter to somebody (*infml*) ◊ **by the skin of your teeth** by a very narrow margin (*infml*) ◊ **get under somebody's skin** (*infml*) **1** annoy or irritate somebody **2** interest or attract somebody ◊ **save somebody's skin** prevent somebody from suffering hurt, loss, or punishment (*infml*)

skin-deep *adj* superficial and without depth ■ *adv* superficially

skin diving *n* the sport of underwater diving with a snorkel, mask, and flippers —**skin-dive** *vi* —**skin diver** *n*

skinflint /skín flint/ *n* a miser

skinful /skín fool/ *n* a large quantity of alcoholic drink (*infml*)

~~skiing~~ incorrect spelling of **skiing**

skin graft *n* a piece of skin taken from part of the body to replace damaged skin

skinhead /skín hed/ *n* (*slang*) **1** somebody with a shaved head **2** a young person with a shaved head and extreme right-wing views

Skinner /skínnər/, **B. F.** (1904–90) US psychologist —**Skinnerian** /ski néeri ən/ *adj*, *n*

skinny /skínni/ (**-nier, -niest**) *adj* very thin ◊ See note at **thin**

skint *adj* penniless (*infml*)

skintight /skín tít/ *adj* fitting close to the body

skip[1] *v* (**skipping, skipped**) **1** *vi* move with small hopping steps **2** *vti* jump repeatedly over a rope swung over the head and under the feet **3** *vti* omit or pass over something **4** *vt* not attend an event or activity (*infml*) **5** *vti* move or cause to move in a series of small bounces ■ *n* **1** a small hopping step **2** an omission

skip[2] *n* a large container for rubbish or rubble

skipper /skíppər/ *n* **1** somebody in charge of a boat or ship **2** the leader of a team (*infml*) ■ *vt* be the skipper of (*infml*)

skipping rope *n* a rope used for skipping

skirl /skurl/ *Scotland n* the wailing noise of bagpipes ■ *vti* produce a wailing noise on the bagpipes

skirmish /skúrmish/ *n* **1** a small brief battle in a war **2** a short fight or argument —**skirmish** *vi* —**skirmisher** *n* ◊ See note at **fight**

skirt *n* **1** a garment that hangs from the waist and does not divide into separate legs **2** the section from the waist to the hem on a dress, coat, or robe **3** something that hangs down like a skirt ■ *v* **1** *vti* form a border around the outside of an area or object **2** *vti* move around the outside of an area or object **3** *vt* avoid giving proper attention to

skirting /skúrting/, **skirting board** *n* a narrow board covering the joint between the base of a wall and a floor

skit *n* a short comic dramatic performance or piece of writing, especially a satirical one

skitter /skíttər/ *vi* **1** scamper **2** skid lightly across a surface

skittish /skíttish/ *adj* **1** silly and irresponsible **2** nervous —**skittishly** *adv* —**skittishness** *n*

skittle /skítt'l/ *n* one of a set of bottle-shaped pins used as a target for knocking over in the game of skittles

skittles /skítt'lz/ *n* a game of bowling at upright bottle-shaped targets (+ *sing verb*)

skive /skīv/ (**skiving, skived**) *vti* avoid work or studies (*infml*) —**skive** *n*

skivvy /skívvi/ (*pl* **-vies**) *n* a woman servant who performs menial work (*infml insult*)

Skopje /skóp yi/ capital of the Former Yugoslav Republic of Macedonia, in the north-central part of the country. Pop. 440,577 (1994).

SKU /éss kay yoō, skyoo/, **Sku** *n* a unique code assigned to a stock item for identification and stock control. Full form **stockkeeping unit**

skulduggery /skul dúggəri/, **skullduggery** *n* unfair or dishonest tricks carried out secretively against somebody (*humorous*)

skulk *vi* **1** move furtively for a sinister purpose **2** hide for a reason

skull /skul/ *n* the bony part of the head encasing the brain

skull and crossbones *n* **1** a representation of a skull above two crossed bones, used as a symbol of danger or death **2** a black flag bearing a white skull and crossbones, used by pirates

skullcap /skúl kap/ *n* a small round brimless hat fitting over the crown of the head

skunk (*pl same or* **skunks**) *n* a black-and-white mammal that defends itself by ejecting a foul-smelling liquid from an anal gland

sky (*pl* **skies**) *n* **1** the region above the Earth **2** the way the sky appears in a particular place or at a particular time (*often pl*) ◊ **the sky's the limit** there is no upper limit (*infml*)

skydive /skī dīv/ (**-diving, -dived**) *vi* jump from an aeroplane and free-fall before opening a parachute —**sky diver** *n* —**skydiving** *n*

Skye /skī/ largest island in the Inner Hebrides, W Scotland. Pop. 8,843 (1991).

sky-high *adj* extremely high ■ *adv* high into the air or in all directions, and often in pieces

skyjack /skī jak/ *vt* hijack an aeroplane —**skyjacker** *n* —**skyjacking** *n*

skylark /skī laark/ *n* a lark that sings melodiously while high in the air

skylight /skī līt/ *n* a window in a roof

skyline /skī līn/ *n* **1** the outline of buildings or landscape features against the sky **2** the horizon

sky marshal *n US* an armed guard who provides in-flight security on commercial passenger aircraft

skyrocket /skī rokit/ *n* a brilliant firework that explodes high in the air ■ *vti* increase dramatically and quickly (*infml*)

skyscraper /skí skraypər/ *n* a very tall building

skysurfing /skí surfing/ *n* the sport of jumping from an aircraft and performing various manoeuvres before parachuting to the ground —**skysurf** *vi* —**skysurfer** *n*

skyward /skíword/, **skywards** /-wərdz/ *adv* towards the sky

skywriting /skí rîting/ *n* writing with coloured smoke released from an aircraft, or the resulting message —**skywrite** *vti*

slab *n* 1 a thick flat broad piece of something 2 a large outer section of a log sawn off before it is made into planks 3 *Aus* a pack of 24 cans or bottles of beer *(infml)* ■ *adj ANZ* made of coarse wooden planks ■ *vt* (**slabbing**, **slabbed**) make or saw into slabs

slack *adj* 1 not taut 2 not showing enough care 3 not busy ■ *adv* loosely ■ *n* 1 looseness or give in something 2 unused productive potential in an organization or system 3 time that is not busy ■ **slacks** *npl* casual trousers ■ *v* 1 *vi* avoid work or not work hard 2 *vti* make or become slower or less intense —**slacker** *n* —**slackly** *adj* —**slackness** *n*

slacken /slákən/ *vti* 1 make or become slower or less intense 2 loosen or relax

slag *n* 1 waste material from smelting 2 coal waste produced in mining ■ *vt* (**slagging**, **slagged**) insult or criticize *(slang)*

slag heap *n* a mound of waste from a coal mine or factory

slain past participle of **slay**

slake (**slaking**, **slaked**) *v* 1 *vt* satisfy a need, especially a thirst 2 *vti* treat lime with water to make calcium hydroxide, or undergo this process

Popperfoto

Slalom

slalom /slaálom/ *n* 1 a downhill zigzag ski race 2 a zigzag race ■ *vi* follow a zigzag course

slam[1] *v* (**slamming**, **slammed**) 1 *vti* close forcefully and noisily 2 *vti* put down violently or land heavily 3 *vti* hit suddenly or violently 4 *vt* criticize forcefully *(infml)* ■ *n* 1 a loud forceful blow or impact 2 a forceful criticism

slam[2] *n* the winning of all the tricks in a hand of bridge or whist

slam dunk *n* in basketball, a shot thrown forcefully into the basket from above —**slam-dunk** *vt*

slammer /slámmər/ *n* a jail *(slang)*

slander /slaándər/ *n* a false statement that is damaging to somebody's reputation, or the making of such a statement ■ *vt* utter a slander against —**slanderer** *n* —**slanderous**

adj —**slanderously** *adv* ◊ See note at **malign**

slang *n* 1 very casual speech or writing 2 a form of language used by a particular group —**slang** *adj* —**slangy** *adj*

slanging match *n UK, Can* an exchange of insults

slant *v* 1 *vti* be or set at an angle 2 *vt* make appealing to a particular group of people ○ *a magazine slanted towards the youth market* 3 *vt* present in a biased way ■ *n* 1 a slope 2 a particular point of view or perspective ○ *a new slant on the events* —**slanted** *adj* —**slanting** *adj*

slap *n* 1 a blow with the open hand or a flat object 2 the noise of a slap 3 a rebuke or insult 4 make-up *(slang)* ■ *v* (**slapping**, **slapped**) 1 *vt* hit with the open hand or a flat object 2 *vi* strike sharply and noisily ○ *water slapping against the hull* 3 *vt* put down sharply 4 *vt* apply quickly and carelessly ○ *slapped on a coat of paint* ■ *adv* forcefully *(infml)* ○ *landed slap on the floor*

slap-bang *adv* in a sudden, violent way *(infml)*

slapdash /sláp dash/ *adj* careless —**slapdash** *adv*

slapstick /sláp stik/ *n* comedy that depends on physical action

slap-up *adj* consisting of large amounts of good food *(infml)*

slash *vt* 1 make long cuts in 2 attack with sweeping strokes of a sharp object 3 reduce or shorten greatly ○ *slash prices* ■ *n* 1 a sweeping stroke made with a sharp object 2 a long cut 3 a keyboard character or punctuation mark in the form of a leaning diagonal line —**slasher** *n*

slash-and-burn *adj* describes a form of agriculture in which trees and vegetation are cut down and burnt in order to plant crops

slat *n* a thin narrow wooden or metal strip —**slatted** *adj*

slate[1] *n* 1 a fine-grained rock that splits easily into layers 2 something such as a roofing tile or writing tablet made of slate 3 a dark grey colour ■ *vt* (**slating**, **slated**) cover with slate —**slate** *adj* —**slaty** *adj*

slate[2] (**slating**, **slated**) *vt* criticize harshly *(infml)*

slattern /sláttərn/ *n* an offensive term for a woman regarded as having poor standards of hygiene or grooming *(dated)* —**slatternly** *adj*

slaughter /sláwtər/ *n* 1 the killing of animals for their meat 2 the brutal killing of a person or large numbers of people ■ *vt* 1 kill an animal for its meat 2 kill a person or large numbers of people brutally 3 defeat somebody overwhelmingly *(slang)* —**slaughterer** *n* —**slaughterous** *adj* ◊ See note at **kill**

slaughterhouse /sláwtər howss/ *(pl* **-houses** /-howziz/) *n* a place where animals are killed for their meat

slave /slayv/ *n* 1 formerly, a person forced to work for another for no payment and regarded as that person's property 2 a person dominated by somebody or something **3** somebody who works very hard, in bad conditions, and for low pay ∎ *vi* (**slaving, slaved**) work very hard

ORIGIN Slave is etymologically the same word as the root of *Slavic*, the Slavic-speaking peoples having been reduced to a state of captivity by conquest in the 9C. The immediate source of **slave** was French.

slave-driver *n* **1** somebody who makes people work unduly hard **2** formerly, an overseer of enslaved labourers

slaver[1] /sláyvər/ *n* **1** a slave owner or dealer **2** *also* **slave ship** a ship used to carry captured and enslaved people

slaver[2] /slávvər, sláyvər/ *vi* **1** dribble saliva from the mouth **2** behave obsequiously ∎ *n* saliva dribbling from somebody's mouth

slavery /sláyvəri/ *n* **1** being an enslaved labourer **2** a system based on the use of enslaved labour **3** very hard work in bad conditions and for low pay

Slavic /slaávik, **Slavonic** /slə vónnik/ *n* an Eastern European language group that includes Bulgarian, Russian, and Polish —**Slavic** *adj*

slavish /sláyvish/ *adj* (*sometimes offensive*) **1** servile **2** unoriginal —**slavishly** *adv*

slay /slay/ (**slew** /sloo/, **slain** /slayn/) *vt* kill (*fml or literary*) —**slayer** *n*

SPELLCHECK Do not confuse the spelling of **slay** and **sleigh** ('a horse-drawn carriage used on snow'), which sound similar.

sleaze /sleez/ *n* dishonesty or corruption, especially among public figures

sleazy /sleezi/ (**-zier, -ziest**) *adj* **1** sordid **2** dishonest or immoral —**sleazily** *adv* —**sleaziness** *n*

sledge /slej/ *n* **1** a small vehicle with runners for travelling or transporting goods over snow **2** a child's toy vehicle on runners for sliding down snowy hills ∎ *vti* (**sledging, sledged; sledding, sledded**) travel or transport using a sledge

sledgehammer /sléj hamər/ *n* a large heavy hammer ∎ *adj* very forceful

sleek *adj* **1** smooth and shiny **2** well-groomed and healthy-looking ∎ *vt* make sleek —**sleekly** *adv* —**sleekness** *n*

sleep *n* **1** the state of resting while not being awake **2** an inactive or dormant state resembling sleep ∎ *v* (**slept**) **1** *vi* go into or be in a state of sleep **2** *vi* be inactive or dormant **3** *vt* provide beds for a particular number of people ◇ **in your sleep** with extreme ease (*infml*) ◇ **not lose (any) sleep over** not worry unnecessarily about ◇ **put to sleep** kill an animal in a humane way ◇ **sleep on it** postpone a decision ◇ **sleep rough** sleep outdoors, usually because of being homeless

□ **sleep around** *vi* have casual sex with many people (*infml*)

□ **sleep in** *vi* sleep longer than usual

□ **sleep off** *vt* sleep until you recover from

□ **sleep with** *vt* have sex with (*infml; euphemistic*)

sleeper /sleepər/ *n* **1** somebody who sleeps in a particular way **2** a railway carriage with beds or a train with such carriages **3** a beam supporting rails on a railway track **4** somebody or something that is belatedly successful (*infml*)

sleeping bag *n* a padded or lined fabric bag for sleeping in, especially while camping

sleeping car *n* a railway carriage where passengers sleep

sleeping partner *n* an investor in a business who is not involved in running it

sleeping pill, sleeping tablet *n* a pill containing a sleep-inducing drug

sleeping policeman *n* a bump in the road made to slow down motorists

sleeping sickness *n* **1** a tropical disease spread by tsetse flies **2** a form of encephalitis causing lethargy

sleepless /sleepləss/ *adj* **1** without sleep, or unable to sleep **2** always awake or active —**sleeplessly** *adv* —**sleeplessness** *n*

sleep-out *n* ANZ an outdoor sleeping area

sleepover /sleep ōvər/ *n* an overnight stay for children at somebody else's house (*infml*)

sleepwalk /sleep wawk/ *vi* walk while asleep —**sleepwalker** *n* —**sleepwalking** *n*

sleepwear /sleep wair/ *n* nightclothes

sleepy /sleepi/ (**-ier, -iest**) *adj* **1** drowsy **2** quiet and without much activity —**sleepily** *adv* —**sleepiness** *n*

sleepyhead /sleepi hed/ *n* a drowsy person (*infml*) —**sleepyheaded** *adj*

sleet *n* rain mixed with snow ∎ *vi* fall as sleet

sleeve *n* **1** either of the parts of a garment that cover the arms **2** a tubular piece fitting in or over a cylinder **3** a protective cover, e.g. for a record —**sleeved** *adj* —**sleeveless** *adj* ◇ **up your sleeve** kept hidden or secret but available for use

sleigh /slay/ *n* an open horse-drawn vehicle with runners for use on snow ∎ *vi* travel in a sleigh ◇ See note at **slay**

sleight of hand /slīt-/ *n* **1** skill with the hands in conjuring or card tricks **2** skill in doing something without revealing how

slender /sléndər/ *adj* **1** small in circumference or width in proportion to height or length **2** slim **3** limited in degree, extent, or size ◇ *win by a slender margin* —**slenderness** *n* ◇ See note at **thin**

slept past tense, past participle of **sleep**

sleuth /slooth/ *n* a detective (*infml*) ∎ *vi* investigate as or like a detective

S level *n* in England and Wales, a post-A-level secondary school qualification. Full form **special level**

slew[1] past tense of **slay**

slew[2] *vti* turn around suddenly, forcefully, or uncontrollably —**slew** *n*

slice *n* **1** a thin broad piece cut from something **2** a share of something **3** in golf, a shot in which the ball curves away to the side **4** in tennis, a shot that makes the ball spin and stay low ■ *v* (**slicing, sliced**) **1** *vti* cut into slices **2** *vti* cut cleanly **3** *vi* move swiftly and cleanly, especially through air or water **4** *vt* cut something off something else **5** *vt* in golf or tennis, hit the ball with a slice —**slicer** *n*

slick *adj* **1** crafty (*infml*) **2** superficially impressive or persuasive **3** smooth or slippery ■ *n* a slippery patch of something ■ *vt* make smooth —**slickly** *adv* —**slickness** *n*

slicker /slíkər/ *n* somebody sophisticated but untrustworthy (*infml*)

slide *v* (**sliding, slid**) **1** *vti* move smoothly across a surface **2** *vti* move or pass unobtrusively **3** *vi* lose your grip or secure footing on a surface **4** *vi* change to a worse condition ■ *n* **1** a sliding movement **2** a structure with a smooth slope for children to slide down **3** a small positive photograph viewed by projection on a screen **4** a downhill displacement of rock, mud, or earth **5** a glass holder for viewing a specimen under a microscope **6** a hair slide **7** a sliding part ◊ **let things** *or* **something slide** let a situation gradually deteriorate

slide rule *n* a calculating device consisting of two rulers marked with graduated logarithmic scales

sliding scale *n* a scale that varies according to changes in another factor

~~slieght of hand~~ incorrect spelling of **sleight of hand**

slight /slīt/ *adj* **1** very small in size or degree **2** thin ■ *vt* **1** ignore or treat disrespectfully **2** treat as unimportant ■ *n* a disrespectful act —**slightly** *adv* —**slightness** *n* ◊ **not in the slightest** not at all (*infml*)

Sligo /slígō/ county in Connacht Province, NW Ireland

slim *adj* (**slimmer, slimmest**) **1** smaller in width, thickness, or girth than height or length **2** pleasingly thin ■ *v* (**slimming, slimmed**) **1** *vi* lose weight, especially by dieting **2** *vt* reduce in size or scope —**slimmer** *n* —**slimming** *n, adj* —**slimness** *n* ◊ See note at **thin**

Slim, William Joseph, 1st Viscount (1891–1970) British general

slime *n* **1** an unpleasantly thick slippery liquid **2** a mucous secretion of some organisms such as snails —**sliminess** *n* —**slimy** *adj*

slimline /slím līn/ *adj* **1** thinner than the standard type **2** low-calorie

sling¹ *n* **1** a wide bandage tied around the neck for supporting an injured arm or hand **2** a carrying strap for something such as a rifle **3** a loop or net for moving something heavy **4** a weapon consisting of a leather loop used for launching stones ■ *v* (**slung**) **1** *vt* throw with force **2** carry or move in a sling —**slinger** *n*

sling² *n* a drink containing spirits, sugar, lemon or lime juice, and water

slingback /slíng bak/ *n* a woman's shoe with an open back and a strap for the heel

slingshot /slíng shot/ *n* US, Can a catapult for firing stones

slink (**slunk**) *vi* **1** move furtively **2** move sexily

slinky /slíngki/ (**-ier, -iest**) *adj* **1** seductive in appearance or movement **2** attractively close-fitting —**slinkily** *adv* —**slinkiness** *n*

slip¹ *v* (**slipping, slipped**) **1** *vi* lose your footing or grip on a surface **2** *vi* move accidentally out of place **3** *vti* move smoothly **4** *vi* go quietly or unobtrusively **5** *vt* put or give secretly **6** *vti* put on or take off something quickly and easily **7** *vi* do something wrong **8** *vi* get worse ■ *n* **1** a loss of footing or grip on a surface **2** an error **3** a decline **4** a light sleeveless woman's undergarment **5** in cricket, a fielding position behind and near the wicketkeeper **6** a landslide ◊ **give somebody the slip** escape from somebody ◊ **let slip 1** reveal without meaning to **2** allow somebody or something to escape ◊ **slip one over on** trick or deceive (*infml*) ◊ See note at **mistake**

☐ **slip up** *vi* err (*infml*)

slip² *n* **1** a small piece of paper such as a receipt **2** a stem or branch of a plant cut off and used to start a new plant **3** a slightly built young person

SLIP /slip/ *n* a protocol for dial-up access to the Internet. Full form **serial line Internet protocol**

slipknot /slíp not/ *n* **1** a knot that slips easily along the rope around which it is tied **2** a knot that can be unfastened by pulling

slip-on *n* a shoe without a fastening —**slip-on** *adj*

slippage /slíppij/ *n* **1** an act or the process of slipping **2** the amount that something slips

slipper /slíppər/ *n* an indoor shoe

slippery /slíppəri/ (**-ier, -iest**) *adj* **1** causing sliding **2** hard to hold firmly **3** untrustworthy —**slipperily** *adv* —**slipperiness** *n*

slippery slope *n* a dangerous situation that can lead to disaster

slippy /slíppi/ (**-pier, -piest**) *adj* causing sliding (*infml*)

slip road *n* a short road for leaving or joining a motorway

slipshod /slíp shod/ *adj* **1** carelessly done **2** untidy

slipstream /slíp streem/ *n* **1** the air behind a propeller **2** the area of reduced air pressure behind a fast-moving vehicle

slip-up *n* an error (*infml*)

slipway /slíp way/ *n* a ramp used to launch, land, build, or repair boats

slit (**slitting, slit**) *vt* make a long straight cut in —**slit** *n* ◊ See note at **tear**

slither /slíthər/ *v* **1** *vti* slide without control **2** *vi* move with a sliding snake-like motion —**slither** *n*

sliver /slívvər/ *n* **1** a thin piece of something that has been split, cut, or broken off **2** a small portion or slice of something —**sliver** vti

slivovitz /slívvəvits/ n an E European plum brandy

slob n an offensive term for a person regarded as lazy, untidy, or bad-mannered —**slobbish** adj

slobber /slóbbər/ v **1** vti dribble saliva **2** vi be excessively sentimental or emotional ■ n **1** dribbled saliva **2** excessively sentimental or emotional writing or talk

sloe /slō/ (pl **sloes** or same) n **1** a sour blue-black fruit of the blackthorn **2** a blackthorn

sloe gin n a liqueur made of gin flavoured with sloes

slog (**slogging**, **slogged**) vi **1** walk slowly and with effort **2** work long and hard —**slog** n

slogan /slṓgən/ n **1** a motto **2** a catchy advertising phrase

sloop n a single-masted sailing boat

slop n **1** something spilled **2** mud or slush **3** unappealing watery food (often pl) ■ **slops** npl kitchen waste used as pig food ■ v (**slopping**, **slopped**) **1** vti spill a liquid or be spilled **2** vt serve food messily

slope n **1** a piece of ground that inclines **2** the side of a hill or mountain **3** a slant or something slanted ■ vti (**sloping**, **sloped**) go or cause to go up or down at an angle —**sloping** adj

□ **slope off** vi leave unobtrusively or furtively (infml)

sloppy /slóppi/ (**-pier, -piest**) adj **1** untidy or in disorder **2** slushy, muddy, or wet **3** not done well (infml) **4** baggy

slosh v **1** vt spill or splash a liquid over something **2** vti move or splash in a liquid (infml) —**sloshy** adj

sloshed adj drunk (infml)

slot n **1** a narrow opening into which something can be inserted **2** a place and time scheduled for somebody or something **3** a job in an organization **4** a receptacle for an expansion card in a computer ■ v (**slotting, slotted**) **1** vti put or be put in a slot **2** vt cut a slot in

sloth /slōth/ n **1** laziness **2** a slow-moving tree-dwelling mammal

slothful /slṓthf'l/ adj lazy —**slothfully** adv

slot machine n a coin-operated gambling or vending machine

slouch vti walk, stand, or sit in a lazy drooping way, or make a part of the body sag lazily ■ n a lazy or inept person (infml; usually in negative statements)

slough[1] /slow/ n **1** a muddy hole **2** US a swampy area **3** a spiritual low point —**sloughy** adj

slough[2] /sluf/ n **1** the dead outer skin shed by a reptile or amphibian **2** a layer of dead skin shed after an infection ■ v **1** vti shed or be shed **2** vt ignore

Slovakia /slō vaáki ə/ country in east-central Europe. Cap. Bratislava. Pop. 5,414,937

(2001). —**Slovak** /slṓ vak/ n, adj —**Slovakian** n, adj

Slovenia /slō veéni ə/ country in E Europe, on the Balkan Peninsula. Cap. Ljubljana. Pop. 1,930,132 (2001). —**Slovene** /slṓ veen/ n, adj —**Slovenian** n, adj

slovenly /slúvv'nli/ (**-lier, -liest**) adj an offensive term meaning dirty and untidy —**slovenliness** n

slow /slō/ adj **1** not moving quickly **2** taking a long time **3** taking too much time **4** describes a clock or watch showing a time that is earlier than the correct time **5** hesitant **6** lacking the usual volume of sales or customers **7** regarded as unintelligent (infml insult) **8** dull and boring ■ adv **1** behind the correct time or pace **2** slowly (nonstandard) ■ vti **1** make or become slow **2** delay or be delayed —**slowly** adv —**slowness** n

slowcoach /slṓ kōch/ n somebody who is too slow (infml)

slow motion n a method or effect in films or videos that shows action happening more slowly than in reality —**slow-motion** adj

slowworm /slṓ wurm/ n a lizard without legs

sludge n **1** watery mud or slush **2** the solids in sewage that separate out during treatment —**sludgy** adj

slug[1] n **1** a bullet **2** a single shot of strong alcoholic drink (infml)

slug[2] n a slow-moving land mollusc without a shell

slug[3] (**slugging, slugged**) vt hit hard —**slug** n

sluggard /slúggərd/ n a lazy person (archaic) —**sluggardly** adv

sluggish /slúggish/ adj **1** moving slowly or very little **2** not very responsive **3** lacking alertness and energy —**sluggishly** adv —**sluggishness** n

sluice /slooss/ n **1** an artificial water channel controlled by a valve or floodgate **2** a valve or floodgate controlling the water in a sluice **3** a drainage channel **4** a trough for separating gold from sand or gravel ■ v (**sluicing, sluiced**) **1** vt flush something with water **2** vt wash gold in a sluice **3** vti release or be released from a sluice

slum n a poor area of a city (often pl) ■ v (**slumming, slummed**) **1** vti accept lower living standards than usual (often humorous) **2** vi visit a slum out of curiosity

slumber /slúmbər/ vi **1** sleep **2** be inactive or resting ■ n **1** an act or period of sleeping **2** inactivity —**slumberless** adj

slump vi **1** collapse **2** slouch **3** decrease sharply ■ n **1** a slouched posture **2** an economic decline

slung past tense, past participle of **sling**[1]

slunk past tense, past participle of **slink**

slur v (**slurring, slurred**) **1** vti speak or say indistinctly **2** vt insult or disparage somebody **3** vt gloss over something **4** vt play musical notes in a smooth uninterrupted way ■ n **1** an insulting or disparaging remark **2** an indistinct pronunciation or sound **3** a curved line connecting musical notes to show that they are to be played in a smooth uninterrupted way

slurp *vti* drink noisily ■ *n* the sound of something being slurped —**slurpingly** *adv*

slurry /slúrri/ *n* a mixture of water and an indissoluble solid

slush *n* 1 melting snow or ice 2 a semiliquid substance 3 excessively sentimental speech or writing —**slushiness** *n* —**slushy** *adj*

slush fund *n* an amount of money set aside for illegal activities

slut *n* an offensive term for a woman regarded as sexually promiscuous or having poor standards of hygiene —**sluttish** *adj* —**slutty** *adj*

sly (**slier, sliest**) *adj* 1 crafty 2 evasive —**slyly** *adv* —**slyness** *n* ◊ **on the sly** without the knowledge or permission of others

Sm *symbol* samarium

smack¹ *v* 1 *vti* slap somebody 2 *vi* hit an object or surface noisily 3 *vt* press the lips together and then open them with a short loud noise ■ *n* 1 a slap 2 a noisy smacking sound 3 a loud kiss ■ *adv* 1 with a loud noise 2 exactly or directly

smack² *n* 1 a distinctive taste of something 2 a hint of something ■ *vi* 1 be distinctively flavoured 2 suggest or hint at something ○ *an appointment that smacks of nepotism*

smack³ *n* a fishing vessel

smacker /smákər/ *n* (*infml*) 1 a loud kiss 2 a pound sterling

small *adj* 1 little in size 2 little in quantity or value 3 insignificant 4 limited in scale 5 young 6 petty and mean-spirited 7 printed in lower-case letters 8 humiliated ■ *adv* 1 in or into little pieces 2 in a moderate or limited way ■ *n* a narrow or small part of something ○ *the small of the back* ■ **smalls** *npl UK* undergarments (*infml or humorous*) —**smallish** *adj* —**smallness** *n*

small beer *n* something trivial (*infml*)

small change *n* 1 low-denomination coins 2 something trivial

small claims court *n* a local court for claims involving small amounts of money

Smalley /smáwli/, **Richard E.** (*b*. 1943) US chemical physicist. He jointly discovered the molecular family of carbon called fullerenes.

small fry *npl* 1 unimportant people or things 2 young fish 3 young children (*infml*)

smallholding /smáwl hōlding/ *n* a small farm —**smallholder** *n*

small hours *n* the early morning hours after midnight

small intestine *n* the part of the digestive tract where digestion of food and most absorption of nutrients takes place

small-minded *adj* petty —**small-mindedly** *adv* —**small-mindedness** *n*

smallpox /smáwl poks/ *n* a highly contagious viral disease that leaves distinctive scars

small print *n* important information in small type in a legal document

small-scale *adj* 1 limited in scope or size 2 made in a smaller version

small talk *n* casual conversation

small-time *adj* unimportant (*infml*)

smarmy /smaármi/ (**-ier, -iest**) *adj* excessively ingratiating (*infml*) —**smarmily** *adv* —**smarminess** *n*

smart *adj* 1 neat and orderly in appearance 2 clever 3 insolent 4 witty and amusing 5 shrewd 6 fashionable 7 lively and vigorous 8 fitted with a microprocessor ■ *vi* 1 cause or have a stinging pain 2 feel embarrassed ■ *adv* in a smart manner ■ *n* a stinging pain —**smartly** *adv* —**smartness** *n* ◊ See note at **intelligent**

smart aleck /-álik/, **smart alec** *n* somebody who likes to show how clever he or she is (*infml*) —**smart-aleck** *adj*

smart bomb *n* a missile guided by laser or radio beams

smart card *n* an electronic card storing personal data and used for identification and financial transactions

smarten /smaárt'n/ *vt* 1 improve the appearance of 2 speed up

smart money *n* 1 an investment or bet that is likely to succeed 2 people who know what to invest in or bet on to make a profit

smart terminal *n* a network terminal that carries out processing but uses another computer for data storage

smash *v* 1 *vti* break with force 2 *vti* break into pieces 3 *vti* hit against an object or surface 4 *vt* defeat or destroy 5 *vt* in racket games, hit downwards with force over with an overhead stroke ■ *n* 1 a loud noise of something hitting something else and breaking into pieces 2 a heavy blow 3 a collision 4 in racket games, an overhead stroke hit downwards with force 5 a great success ■ *adv* with the sound of a smash —**smasher** *n*

smash-and-grab *adj* a crime committed by breaking a shop window and stealing the goods on display —**smash-and-grab** *n*

smashed *adj* intoxicated (*infml*)

smashing /smáshing/ *adj* very good (*dated infml*)

smash-up *n* a serious car crash

smattering /smáttəring/ *n* 1 a slight knowledge of something 2 a small amount of something

SME *abbr* small and medium-sized enterprise

smear /smeer/ *v* 1 *vti* spread a greasy, sticky, or liquid substance over something, or be spread in this way 2 *vt* spread damaging rumours about ■ *n* 1 an act of smearing or a smeared patch of something 2 a cell sample smeared on a microscope slide for examination 3 *also* **smear test** a test for cervical cancer (*infml*) 4 a harmful rumour —**smeary** *adj*

smear campaign *n* a deliberate sustained attempt to harm somebody's reputation

smell v (**smelt** or **smelled**) **1** vti detect, recognise, or assess something by means of the nose **2** vi have a particular smell ○ *Something smells good.* **3** vi have an unpleasant smell ○ *That really smells!* **4** vt detect the presence of something undesirable ■ n **1** the sense based on the nerves in the nose that distinguish odours **2** the quality of something detected by the nose **3** an act of smelling something in order to judge or identify it —**smeller** n

SYNONYMS smell, odour, aroma, bouquet, scent, perfume, fragrance, stink, stench, reek CORE MEANING: the way something smells

smelling salts npl a mixture of ammonium carbonate and perfume. Use: formerly, to revive somebody who felt faint or had become unconscious.

smelly /smélli/ (**-ier, -iest**) adj with a strong or unpleasant smell —**smelliness** n

smelt[1] vti melt ore in order to get metal, or undergo this process

smelt[2] (pl **smelts** or same) n **1** a small silvery fish of northern waters **2** smelt as food

smelt[3] past tense, past participle of **smell**

smelter /méltər/ n **1** somebody who smelts ore **2** a smelting apparatus or factory

Smetana /métsənə/, **Bedřich** (1824–84) Czech composer

smidgen /smíjjən/, **smidgin, smidgeon, smidge** n a small amount (infml)

smile v (**smiling, smiled**) **1** vti raise the corners of the mouth in an expression of amusement or pleasure **2** vi look happy or pleased **3** vi show favour to somebody ■ n **1** an expression of amusement or pleasure made by smiling **2** an appearance of pleasure or approval (often pl) —**smilingly** adv

smiley /smíli/ adj (**-ier, -iest**) smiling ■ n (pl **-eys**) a symbol :-) used in e-mails to express pleasure, approval, or humour

smirk n an insolent smile ■ vi smile insolently

smite (**smiting, smote** or **smit, smitten** /smítt'n/) v **1** vti hit hard (literary) **2** vt affect somebody strongly or disastrously (literary) **3** vt fill somebody with love (literary; often passive)

smith /smith/ n **1** somebody who makes or repairs metal objects **2** a blacksmith

Smith /smith/, **Adam** (1723–90) British philosopher and economist

Smith, Bessie (1894–1937) US blues singer

Smith, Joseph (1805–44) US founder of the Church of Jesus Christ of Latter-Day Saints

Smith, Stevie (1902–71) British poet and novelist

smithereens /smíthə reénz/ npl very small broken pieces (infml)

smithy /smíthi/ (pl **-ies**) n a blacksmith's workplace

smitten past participle of **smite**

smock n **1** a loose dress with gathers at the chest **2** a loose garment worn to protect the clothes ■ vt sew with decorative gathering stitches

smocking /smóking/ n decorative stitching used to gather fabric

smog n a mixture of fog and smoke or exhaust fumes —**smoggy** adj

smoke n **1** a cloud of tiny particles rising from something burning **2** minute particles suspended in a gas **3** an act of smoking a cigarette, cigar, or pipe **4** a cigarette (infml) ■ v (**smoking, smoked**) **1** vti inhale smoke from burning tobacco or another substance in a cigarette, cigar, or pipe **2** vi give off smoke **3** vt cure food with smoke **4** vt fumigate something with smoke **5** vt darken something to give it the colour of smoke ◇ **go up in smoke** fail to happen as planned or hoped □ **smoke out** vt drive from hiding with smoke

smoke alarm n a device that sounds an alarm when it detects smoke

smoke bomb n a weapon producing irritating chemical smoke, used for forcing people or animals out of a place

smoke hood n a plastic head covering with a breathing apparatus

smokeless /smókləss/ adj **1** producing no smoke **2** allowing no smoke-producing fires

smoker /smókər/ n **1** somebody who smokes tobacco **2** a railway carriage designated for smoking **3** an apparatus for smoking food

smoke screen n **1** a mass of smoke used for hiding ship or troop movements **2** an action intended to mislead somebody or obscure something

smoke signal n a signal made with a column of smoke

smokestack /smók stak/ n a tall industrial chimney

smokestack industry n an industry using large factories or heavy equipment and causing pollution

smoking gun n a piece of conclusive evidence or proof of wrongdoing

smoking room n a room for smokers

smoky /smóki/ (**-ier, -iest**) adj **1** filled with smoke **2** coloured like smoke **3** tasting of smoke **4** giving off excessive smoke —**smokily** adv —**smokiness** n

smolder vi, n US = **smoulder**

Smolensk /smo lénsk/ city in W Russia. Pop. 398,405 (1995).

Smollett /smóllət/, **Tobias George** (1721–71) British novelist

smooch (infml) v **1** vti kiss and caress **2** vi dance slowly and closely ■ n an act or period of smooching

smooth /smooth/ adj **1** not having a rough or bumpy surface **2** without lumps **3** proceeding without upheaval or difficulties **4** without jerks or jolts **5** not harsh, sharp, or sour **6** insincerely pleasant or flattering ■ vt **1** remove roughness or bumps from something **2** remove lines and creases from something **3** remove obstacles or difficulties from something ■ n **1** an act or the process of smoothing **2** a smooth part of something —**smoothly** adv —**smoothness** n

□ **smooth over** *vt* lessen difficulties or tensions

smoothie /smóothi/ *n* 1 *also* **smoothy** (*pl* **-ies**) an insincerely charming man (*infml*) 2 a puréed fruit drink, often with milk, yoghurt, or ice cream

smorgasbord /smáwrgəss bawrd/ *n* a buffet meal with a large variety of dishes

smote past tense of **smite**

smother /smúthər/ *v* 1 *vti* deprive or be deprived of air 2 *vti* kill or die by suffocation 3 *vt* overwhelm somebody with affection 4 *vt* put out a fire 5 *vt* suppress or hide a feeling —**smotheringly** *adv*

smoulder /smóldər/ *vi* 1 burn slowly without a flame 2 have or exist as a suppressed emotion ■ *n* 1 thick smoke from a slow-burning fire 2 a slow-burning fire

SMS *n* a service for sending short textual messages, e.g. between mobile phones and pagers. Full form **short message service**

smudge *n* 1 a patch of smeared ink or paint 2 a dirty mark 3 a blurred or indistinct area ■ *vti* (**smudging**, **smudged**) 1 smear or be smeared 2 make or become dirty —**smudgy** *adj*

smug (**smugger**, **smuggest**) *adj* self-satisfied —**smugly** *adv* —**smugness** *n*

smuggle /smúgg'l/ (**-gling**, **-gled**) *v* 1 *vti* bring goods into a country illegally 2 *vt* bring or take away secretly —**smuggler** *n*

smut *n* 1 obscene jokes, stories, or pictures 2 a small piece of soot or dirt 3 a fungal plant disease characterized by sooty spores on leaves —**smuttiness** *n* —**smutty** *adj*

Smuts /smutss, smótss/, **Jan** (1870–1950) South African general and prime minister (1919–24, 1939–48)

Sn *symbol* tin

SNA *abbr* systems network architecture

snack *n* 1 a small quick meal 2 food eaten between meals —**snack** *vi*

snack bar *n* a restaurant selling snacks

snaffle /snáff'l/ *n also* **snaffle bit** a jointed bit with rings at either side for attaching a horse's reins ■ *vt* (**-fling**, **-fled**) 1 steal something (*infml*) 2 fit a horse with a snaffle

SNAFU *abbr* situation normal all fouled up (*in e-mails*)

snag *n* 1 a small problem that impedes progress 2 a sharp point on which something may catch and tear 3 a small hole or loose thread in a fabric 4 *ANZ* a sausage (*slang*) ■ *vti* (**snagging**, **snagged**) catch on a snag —**snaggy** *adj*

snail *n* a small animal with a coiled shell and a retractable muscular foot on which it crawls

snail mail *n* postal mail (*infml*)

snake *n* 1 a legless reptile with a scaly tubular body 2 an offensive term for somebody regarded as untrustworthy ■ *vi* (**snaking**, **snaked**) move or extend in curves like a snake

snakebite /snáyk bīt/ *n* 1 the bite of a poisonous snake 2 an alcoholic drink of cider mixed with lager

snake charmer *n* an entertainer who elicits a swaying movement from snakes with music

snake oil *n* worthless medicine

snakes and ladders *n* a board game in which players can advance rapidly up ladders or go backwards down snakes (+ *sing verb*)

snakeskin /snáyk skin/ *n* 1 a snake's skin 2 leather made of snakes' skins

snaky /snáyki/ (**-ier**, **-iest**) *adj* 1 bending or twisting 2 treacherous —**snakily** *adv*

snap *vti* (**snapping**, **snapped**) 1 break with a sharp noise 2 move or operate with a sharp noise 3 say something angrily 4 bite or grasp somebody or something suddenly 5 move sharply ■ *n* 1 a sharp sound 2 a short period of cold weather 3 an informal photograph 4 liveliness ○ *His campaign needs more snap.* ■ *adj* decided without reflection ○ *a snap decision* ■ *interj* acknowledges two identical things

□ **snap up** *vt* take hastily or eagerly

snapdragon /snáp dragən/ *n* a garden plant with spikes of flowers

snapper /snáppər/ *n* 1 (*pl* **snappers** *or same*) a carnivorous tropical fish 2 (*pl* **snappers** *or same*) a red Australian food fish with blue spots 3 snapper as food

snappish /snáppish/ *adj* showing irritation or impatience —**snappishly** *adv*

snappy /snáppi/ (**-pier**, **-piest**) *adj* 1 showing irritation or impatience 2 interesting and to the point (*infml*) 3 hasty 4 stylish (*infml*) —**snappily** *adv*

snapshot /snáp shot/ *n* a photograph taken quickly and casually

snare[1] *n* 1 an animal trap 2 something designed to trap an unwary person ■ *vt* (**snaring**, **snared**) 1 catch in a trap 2 entrap by alluring deception

snare[2] *n* a set of metal cords on the underside of a drum (*often pl*)

snare drum *n* a drum with a snare on its underside that makes a harsh metallic sound when the drum is hit

snarl[1] *v* 1 *vi* growl 2 *vti* say something angrily —**snarl** *n* —**snarlingly** *adv*

snarl[2] *n* 1 a tangled mass of something 2 a knot in wood ■ *vti* tangle or become tangled

□ **snarl up** *vti* make or become confused or congested

snarl-up *n* 1 a tangled situation 2 a traffic jam

snatch *vt* 1 grab or take quickly 2 move or remove quickly 3 take or get when the opportunity arises 4 *US, Can* kidnap somebody (*infml*) ■ *n* 1 an act of snatching something 2 a small amount 3 a theft (*infml*) —**snatcher** *n*

snazzy /snázzi/ (**-zier**, **-ziest**) *adj* attractively new, bright, or fashionable (*infml*) —**snazzily** *adv*

sneak /sneek/ *v* 1 *vi* go or move stealthily 2 *vt* do without being noticed 3 *vt* bring or take stealthily 4 *vi* report acts of wrongdoing to somebody in authority ■ *n* 1 a person regarded as untrustworthy (*insult*) 2 somebody who tells tales on others **3** a stealthy departure ■ *adj* stealthily done

sneaker /sneekar/ *n* ANZ, US, Can a sports shoe with a rubber sole *(often pl)*

sneaking /sneeking/ *adj* slight but persistent ○ *a sneaking suspicion*

sneaky /sneeki/ (**-ier, -iest**) *adj* underhanded —**sneakily** *adv* —**sneakiness** *n*

sneer *n* an expression of scorn in which the upper lip is raised ■ *v* **1** *vi* feel or show scorn **2** *vt* say with scorn —**sneering** *adj* —**sneeringly** *adv*

sneeze *n* an involuntary explosive expulsion of air through the nose and mouth —**sneeze** *vi*

Snell, Peter George (*b.* 1938) New Zealand runner

snick *n* **1** a small cut **2** a glancing blow from a cricket bat —**snick** *vi*

snicker /sníkar/ *vi* neigh —**snicker** *n*

snide (**snider, snidest**) *adj* derisively sarcastic —**snidely** *adv*

sniff *v* **1** *vti* breathe in through the nose, e.g. in smelling something **2** *vt* have a suspicion of ○ *began to sniff trouble* ■ *n* **1** an act or sound of sniffing **2** a suspicion

□ **sniff out** *vt* find out *(infml)*

sniffer /sníffar/ *n* **1** a device that monitors data transmission **2** a program on a computer system designed legitimately or illegitimately to capture data being transmitted on a network

sniffer dog *n* a dog trained to detect things by scent

sniffle /sníff'l/ *vi* (**-fling, -fled**) **1** inhale mucus **2** weep quietly ■ *n* an act or sound of sniffling ■ **sniffles** *npl* a slight cold that causes sniffling *(infml)*

sniffy /sníffi/ (**-ier, -iest**) *adj* haughty or disdainful *(infml)* —**sniffily** *adv* —**sniffiness** *n*

snifter /sníftar/ *n* **1** a glass for serving brandy **2** a small alcoholic drink *(infml)*

snigger /sníggar/ *vi* laugh disrespectfully —**snigger** *n*

snip *vti* (**snipping, snipped**) cut using small strokes ■ *n* **1** a small cut **2** a small piece that has been snipped off **3** a bargain *(infml)* **4** an act or sound of snipping

snipe *n* (*pl* **snipes** or **same**) a wading bird with a long straight bill ■ *vi* (**sniping, sniped**) a shot fired from a concealed position —**sniper** *n*

snippet /sníppat/ *n* a small piece of something such as information or music

snippy /sníppi/ (**-pier, -piest**) *adj* sharp-tongued *(infml)* —**snippily** *adv* —**snippiness** *n*

snitch *(slang)* *v* **1** *vt* pilfer **2** *vi* inform on somebody ■ *n* an informer

snivel /snívv'l/ (**-elled, -elling**) *vi* **1** sniff audibly **2** behave in a tearful or self-pitying way —**snivel** *n* —**sniveller** *n* —**snivelling** *n, adj*

snob *n* **1** somebody who looks down on people who are not cultivated or not from a high social class **2** somebody who disdains things that he or she considers inferior

—**snobbery** *n* —**snobbish** *adj* —**snobbishly** *adv* —**snobbism** *n* —**snobby** *adj*

ORIGIN Snob originally meant 'shoemaker' (a sense that survives in places). In England, Cambridge University students of the late 18C adopted it as a slang term for a 'townsman, somebody not a member of the university', and it seems to have been this usage that formed the basis in the 1830s for a new general sense 'member of the lower classes'. The modern senses began as 'somebody who admires and cultivates social superiors', and this use received a considerable boost when Thackeray used it in his *Book of Snobs* (1848). The suggestion that the word itself comes from *s.nob.*, short for Latin *sine nobilitate* 'without nobility', is ingenious but ignores the word's early history.

snog UK *(slang)* *vti* (**snogging, snogged**) kiss and cuddle ■ *n* a prolonged kiss or kissing session

snook[1] (*pl* **same** or **snooks**) *n* a large fish of warm seas and rivers

snook[2] *n* a rude gesture made with the thumb on the nose and the fingers outstretched

snooker /snóokar/ *n* **1** a cue game played with fifteen red balls and six balls of other colours **2** in snooker, a position from which the target ball cannot be hit directly ■ *vt* **1** in snooker, put an opponent in a snooker **2** thwart somebody or something *(infml)*

ORIGIN Snooker is probably an adaptation of late 19C British army slang *snooker* 'new recruit'. The game was invented by British army officers serving in India in the 1870s.

snoop *vi* pry in a furtive way *(infml)* —**snooper** *n* —**snoopy** *adj*

snoot *n* a nose *(infml)*

snooty /snooti/ (**-ier, -iest**) *adj* showing haughty condescension *(infml)* —**snootily** *adv*

snooze (**snoozing, snoozed**) *vi* sleep lightly *(infml)* —**snooze** *n* —**snoozy** *adj*

snore (**snoring, snored**) *vi* breathe noisily while asleep —**snore** *n* —**snorer** *n*

snorkel /snáwrk'l/ *n* **1** an underwater breathing apparatus consisting of a U-shaped tube **2** a ventilator on a submarine ■ *vi* (**snorkelling, snorkelled, snorkelled**) swim with a snorkel —**snorkeller** *n* —**snorkelling** *n*

snort *v* **1** *vi* force air through the nose explosively **2** *vi* show contempt by snorting **3** *vti* inhale an illegal drug, especially cocaine *(infml)* ■ *n* **1** a harsh sound made by snorting **2** a gulp of alcohol *(infml)* —**snorting** *n, adj*

snot *n* **1** an offensive term for the mucus produced in the nose *(slang)* **2** an offensive term for somebody regarded as arrogant *(slang insult)* —**snottily** *adv* —**snotty** *adj*

snout *n* an animal's nose —**snouted** *adj*

snow /snō/ *n* **1** water vapour in the form of falling flakes of ice crystals **2** snow on the ground **3** cocaine or heroin in the form of a white powder *(slang)* **4** a fall of snow ○ *had a* *heavy snow last night* ■ *vi* fall as snow *(refers to rain and snow)* ○ *It's snowing!*

Snow /snō/, **C. P., Baron Snow of Leicester** (1905–80) British novelist and critic

snowball /snō bawl/ *n* **1** a ball of compacted snow that is thrown, especially by children ■ *v* **1** *vi* increase rapidly **2** *vti* throw snowballs at somebody

snowblower /snō blō ər/ *n* a machine for clearing snow from roads

snowboard /snō bawrd/ *n* a board for sliding downhill on snow ■ *vi* use a snowboard —**snowboarder** *n* —**snowboarding** *n*

snowbound /snō bownd/ *adj* prevented by snow from leaving or travelling

Snowdon, Mt /snōd'n/ highest peak in Wales, in the northwest of the country. Height 1,085 m/3,560 ft.

Snowdonia National Park /snō dṓni ə-/ national park in NW Wales, incorporating Mt Snowdon

snowdrift /snō drift/ *n* a bank of snow blown together by the wind

snowdrop /snō drop/ *n* a plant that bears white flowers in early spring

snowfall /snō fawl/ *n* **1** a fall of snow **2** the amount of fallen snow in a particular place or a given period

snowfield /snō feeld/ *n* a large permanently snow-covered area

snowflake /snō flayk/ *n* an individual mass of ice crystals falling as snow

snow leopard *n* a large mountain cat with a thick pale-grey or brown coat marked with dark splotches

snow line *n* the boundary of a snowfield or the line of altitude above which there is permanent snow

snowman /snō man/ (*pl* **-men** /-men/) *n* a roughly human figure made out of compacted snow

snowmobile /snṓmə beel, -mō beel/ *n* a small vehicle for travelling over snow

snow pea *n* ANZ, US, Can a variety of pea with a thin flat edible pod

snowplough /snō plow/ *n* **1** a vehicle for clearing snow **2** a turning or braking technique in skiing in which the skis are pointed towards each other ■ *vi* ski in the snowplough position

snowshoe /snō shoo/ *n* a framework attached to a boot for walking over snow

snowstorm /snō stawrm/ *n* a storm with heavy snow

snow-white *adj* very white or clean

snowy /snō i/ *adj* **1** covered in snow **2** like snow —**snowiness** *n*

Snowy Mountains mountain range in SE New South Wales, Australia. Highest peak Mt Kosciuszko 2,228 m/7,310 ft.

Snr, snr *abbr* Senior

snub *vt* (**snubbing, snubbed**) treat somebody rudely, especially by excluding or ignoring them ■ *n* an action intended to humiliate somebody

snub-nosed *adj* **1** with a short turned-up nose **2** with a short barrel or blunt end

snuff[1] *v* **1** *vt* inhale through the nose **2** *vti* sniff ■ *n* a sniffing sound

snuff[2] *vt* **1** extinguish a flame **2** trim off the burnt end of a candle wick **3** put an end to somebody or something *(infml)*

snuff[3] *n* powdered tobacco for inhaling through the nostrils ■ *vi* take snuff

snuffbox /snúf boks/ *n* a box for storing snuff

snuffer /snúffər/ *n* a long-handled candle extinguisher

snuffle /snúff'l/ *v* (**-fling, -fled**) **1** *vi* breathe noisily **2** *vti* say something nasally ■ *n* a sound of snuffling ■ **snuffles** *npl* a runny nose —**snuffly** *adj*

snuff movie *n* a pornographic film in which one of the participants is actually and deliberately killed

snug *adj* (**snugger, snuggest**) **1** cosy **2** small but comfortable **3** sheltered **4** close-fitting ■ *n* **1** a small room in a pub **2** a peg for holding a bolt —**snugly** *adv* —**snugness** *n*

snuggle /snúgg'l/ *v* (**-gling, -gled**) *vi* **1** cuddle up to somebody **2** settle into a warm and comfortable position

so[1] /sō/ *conj* **1** in order that ○ *held her tight so she wouldn't fall* **2** introduces a result ○ *Everything is done on a shoestring, so their prices are very low.* **3** indicates similarity ○ *Just as my circumstances have changed, so too have my aims in life.* ■ *adv* **1** indicates that what is true of one person or thing is also true of another *(followed by an auxiliary or modal verb, or by the main verb 'do', 'have', or 'be')* ○ *If you can keep a secret, so can I.* **2** as described ○ *The company has the potential to be very successful, and will soon be so.* **3** refers back to something mentioned earlier ○ *for those who would like to do so* **4** to such an extent **5** emphasizes a quality ○ *I was so scared.* **6** therefore or in consequence ○ *She said that she would like to see me again so I gave her my phone number.* **7** introduces a comment or question ○ *So I see you've changed your mind.* **8** indicates something using actions or gestures ○ *Hold onto the boat like so.* **9** indeed *(nonstandard)* ○ *'You never explained what to do'.'I did so!'* ◇ **and so on** *or* **forth** and other similar things ◇ **so much, so many** a limited or unspecified degree or amount ◇ **so much for** indicates a particular person or thing has not been useful or helpful *(infml)* ◇ **so what?** asks rather rudely why something is important, implying that it is not ◊ See note at **sew**

so[2] /sō/ *n* MUSIC = **soh**

SO *abbr* **1** significant other *(in e-mails)* **2** standing order

soak *v* **1** *vti* immerse or be immersed in liquid for a time **2** *vt* make very wet **3** *vti* absorb or be absorbed **4** *vi* permeate ■ *n* **1** an act of soaking **2** a habitual drinker *(slang)*

soaking /sṓking/ *n* an act or the process of immersing something in liquid ■ *adj* very wet *(infml)*

so-and-so (*pl* **so-and-sos**) *n* **1** an unnamed person or thing (*infml*) **2** a person regarded as unpleasant or annoying (*infml insult*)

Soane /sōn/, **Sir John** (1753–1837) British architect

soap *n* **1** a solid, liquid, or powdered preparation used for washing or cleaning **2** a metallic salt combined with a fatty acid. Use: bases for waterproofing agents, ointments, greases. **3** a soap opera (*infml*) ■ *vt* put soap on

soapbox /sōp boks/ *n* a platform for impromptu public speaking

soap opera *n* a serial drama on television or radio

ORIGIN In the early days of radio and television in the United States, serials were often sponsored by soap manufacturers, hence the name **soap opera**.

soap powder *n* a powdered detergent for use in washing machines

soapstone /sōp stōn/ *n* a soft variety of the mineral talc. Use: decorative carving.

soapsuds /sōp sudz/ *npl* water with a soapy lather

soapy /sōpi/ (**-ier**, **-iest**) *adj* **1** full of or covered with soap **2** like soap —**soapiness** *adv*

soar /sawr/ *vi* **1** fly, glide, or rise high in the air **2** increase rapidly —**soar** *n* ◊ See note at **saw**

sob (**sobbing**, **sobbed**) *v* **1** *vi* cry with gasping sounds **2** *vt* say while sobbing —**sob** *n* —**sobbingly** *adv*

sober /sōbər/ *adj* **1** not drunk **2** tending not to drink alcohol **3** serious in demeanour **4** lacking vitality or brightness in appearance **5** based on rational thinking ■ *vti* lessen intoxication —**sobering** *adj* —**soberingly** *adv* —**soberly** *adv* —**soberness** *n* ◊ **sober up** make or become sober after being drunk

sobriety /sə brī əti/ *n* **1** the state of not being drunk **2** seriousness **3** a lack of vitality or brightness

sobriquet /sóbri kay/, **soubriquet** *n* a nickname

sob story *n* a story that is intended to provoke pity (*infml*)

so-called *adj* **1** popularly known as **2** incorrectly known as

USAGE Do not put quotation marks around expressions following **so-called** and *self-styled*, which already convey the ideas 'popularly called or known' and 'incorrectly or falsely called or known', respectively: *a so-called generalissimo of capitalism*, not *a so-called 'generalissimo of capitalism'*.

soccer /sókər/ *n* the sport of football

ORIGIN Soccer was formed in the 1870s from *Assoc.*, an abbreviation of *Association*. The game is played under the rules of the Football Association (hence the alternative name, *association football*). The ending *-er* was fashionable in public-school slang of the day.

soceity incorrect spelling of **society**

sociable /sōshəb'l/ *adj* **1** enjoying the company of other people **2** friendly —**sociability** /sōshə billəti/ *n* —**sociably** *adv*

social /sōsh'l/ *adj* **1** of society **2** of the way people interact **3** describes animals that live in communities ○ *social insects such as ants* **4** offering opportunities for interaction ○ *a social club* **5** of human welfare ○ *social services* ■ *n* an informal get-together —**socially** *adv*

social climber *n* somebody who seeks social advancement (*disapproving*) —**social climbing** *n*

social democracy *n* the principle of a gradual shift from capitalism to socialism —**social democrat** *n* —**social democratic** *adj*

social engineering *n* the practical application of a social science in solving social problems

socialism /sōshəlizəm/ *n* **1** a political system of communal ownership **2** *also* **Socialism** a political movement based on socialism —**socialist** *n* —**socialistic** /sōshə lístik/ *adj*

socialite /sōshə līt/ *n* somebody who is well known in fashionable society

socialize /sōshə līz/ (**-izing**, **-ized**), **socialise** *v* **1** *vi* take part in social activities **2** *vt* train to be a fit member of society ○ *socialize a child* **3** *vt* place under public ownership or control —**socialization** /sōshə līzáysh'n/ *n* —**socializer** *n*

social mobility *n* the ability of people to change their social status

social science *n* **1** the study of societies **2** a discipline in which a specific area of society is studied, e.g. sociology, economics, or anthropology —**social scientist** *n*

social security *n* **1** *also* **Social Security** a government scheme that provides economic security to people who are retired, unemployed, or unable to work **2** money paid to somebody under the Social Security scheme

social service *n* any of the public services provided for the welfare of a person or community (*often pl*) ■ **social services** *npl* the agencies of local government that provide social services

social studies *n* a school subject involving the study of society (+ *sing verb*)

social welfare *n* the social services provided by a state or private organization

society /sə sí əti/ (*pl* **-ties**) *n* **1** the sum of the social relationships among groups of people or animals **2** a structured community of people **3** the customs of a community and the way it is organized **4** a subset of a society **5** the prominent or fashionable people in a community **6** companionship **7** a group of people who share a common interest —**societal** *adj*

Society of Friends *n* the Christian group also known as the Quakers

Society of Jesus *n* a Roman Catholic order engaged in missionary and educational work worldwide

socio- *prefix* society, social ○ *sociopath* ○ *socioeconomic*

socioeconomic /sóssi ō ékkə nómmik, sṓshi ō-, -eékə-/ *adj* involving economic and social factors —**socioeconomically** *adv*

sociology /sóssi ólləji, sṓshi-/ *n* **1** the study of human societies **2** the study of an individual social institution —**sociological** /sóssi ə lójjik'l, sṓshi ə-/ *adj*—**sociologist** *n*

sociopath /sóssi ō path, sṓshi ō-/ *n* an offensive term for somebody whose personality disorder leads to violent antisocial behaviour —**sociopathic** /sóssi ō páthik, sṓshi ō-/ *adj* —**sociopathy** /sóssi óppəthi, sṓshi-/ *n*

sociopolitical /sóssi ō pə líttik'l, sṓshi ō-/ *adj* involving social and political factors

sock[1] *n* a soft covering for the foot and lower leg

sock[2] *vt* hit hard, especially with the fist *(infml)*

socket /sókit/ *n* **1** a shaped hole that receives a part to make a connection, e.g. a receptacle for an electric plug **2** a hollow in the body into which a joint or other part fits ■ *vt* put in a socket

Socrates /sókrə teez/ (469–399 BC) Greek philosopher

sod[1] *n* a layer or piece of earth with growing grass

sod[2] *n* an offensive term for somebody regarded as annoying or objectionable *(slang insult)*

soda /sṓdə/ *n* **1** soda water **2** sodium that is chemically combined with other elements

soda siphon *n* a bottle for dispensing soda water

soda water *n* water made effervescent by the addition of carbon dioxide

sodden /sódd'n/ *adj* **1** thoroughly wet **2** drunk —**soddenly** *adv*—**soddenness** *n*

sodium /sṓdi əm/ *n* (*symbol* **Na**) an abundantly occurring chemical element. Use: catalyst, tracer, in chemical processes.

sodium bicarbonate *n* a white crystalline powder. Use: leavening agent, antacid, in effervescent drinks and fire extinguishers.

sodium chloride *n* a colourless crystalline compound, commonly known as salt. Use: food seasoning, preservative.

sodium nitrate *n* a white crystalline salt. Use: curing of meats, rocket propellant, fertilizer, manufacture of explosives and glass.

sodomize /sóddə mīz/ (**-izing**, **-ized**), **sodomise** *vt* an offensive term meaning to have anal intercourse with somebody

sodomy /sóddəmi/ *n* an offensive term for anal intercourse

Sod's Law *n* the principle that if anything can go wrong, it will *(infml)*

sofa /sṓfə/ *n* an upholstered seat for more than one person

sofa bed *n* a sofa that converts to a bed

Sofia /sṓfi ə/ capital of Bulgaria. Pop. 1,141,712 (1996).

soft *adj* **1** easily shaped or cut **2** yielding to physical pressure ○ *a soft cushion* **3** with a smooth texture ○ *soft fur* **4** quiet **5** without glare or intensity of light or colour **6** gentle **7** lenient **8** undemanding *(infml)* ○ *a soft job* **9** incapable of enduring hardship **10** describes water in which soap lathers easily **11** US based on negotiation, flexibility, and good will ○ *a soft sell* **12** not politically extreme **13** of a currency or system not backed by gold **14** describes the consonant sounds 'c' and 'g' as in 'dance' and 'age' ■ *adv* softly —**softly** *adv*—**softness** *n*

softback /sóft bak/ *n* a paperback —**softback** *adj*

softball /sóft bawl/ *n* **1** baseball played with a larger softer ball **2** the ball used for softball

soft-boiled *adj* describes a boiled egg with a liquid yolk

soft copy *n* data stored on a computer, not printed on paper

soft-core *adj* sexually suggestive without being explicit

soft drink *n* a nonalcoholic drink

soft drug *n* an illegal drug regarded as less dangerous or addictive than heroin and cocaine

soften /sóff'n/ *vti* **1** make or become less hard **2** make or become kinder **3** make or become less resilient or determined —**softener** *n*

soft focus *n* the deliberate blurring of a photographic image

soft fruit *n* any small fruit without a stone

soft furnishings *npl* home furnishings made from fabric

soft-hearted *adj* kind —**soft-heartedly** *adv* —**soft-heartedness** *n*

softie *n* = softy

soft landing *n* **1** the safe landing of a spacecraft **2** an uncomplicated solution

softly-softly *adj* cautious

soft palate *n* the soft upper back part of the mouth

soft pedal *n* a piano pedal that reduces volume

soft-pedal (**soft-pedalling**, **soft-pedalled**) *vti* **1** play a piano's soft pedal **2** play something down *(infml)*

soft sell *n* a subtle selling approach *(infml)*

soft soap *n* persuasive flattery *(infml)*

soft-soap *vt* persuade by flattery *(infml)*

soft-spoken *adj* with a quiet gentle voice

soft spot *n* a weak spot ◇ **have a soft spot for** have especially tender feelings or affection for

soft top *n* a car with a fabric roof that can be folded back

software /sóft wair/ *n* programs and applications for computers

software engineering *n* the design and implementation of computer programs

softwood /sóft wŏod/ *n* the wood of any coniferous tree

softy /sófti/ (pl **-ies**), **softie** n a weak, timid, or sentimental person (infml)

soggy /sóggi/ (**-gier, -giest**) adj 1 thoroughly wet 2 with too much liquid —**sogginess** n

soh /sō/, **so** n a syllable used in singing the 5th note of a scale

soil[1] n 1 the top layer of the ground 2 a particular type of earth o sandy soil 3 a country (literary) o their native soil

soil[2] vt 1 make dirty 2 bring dishonour on ■ n 1 dirt 2 faeces

soiree /swaà ray/, **soirée** n an evening party

sojourn /sójjurn/ (literary) n a brief visit ■ vi stay for a time —**sojourner** n

sol[1] n MUSIC = **soh** ⵑ

sol[2] (pl **soles** /sólays/) n the main unit of currency in Peru

Sol n in Roman mythology, the sun god. Greek equivalent **Helios**

solace /sólləss/ n 1 comfort or relief from emotional distress 2 a source of solace ■ vt (**-acing, -aced**) provide with solace

solar /sólər/ adj 1 of or from the Sun 2 operating using energy from the Sun

solar cell n an electric cell that converts solar radiation directly into electricity

solar energy n energy from the Sun

solarium /sə láiri əm/ (pl **-a** /-ri ə/ or **-ums**) n 1 a room built for enjoying sunlight 2 a place fitted with sunlamps or sunbeds

solar panel n a panel that collects solar energy

solar plexus n 1 a mass of nerve cells in the upper abdomen 2 a point on the upper abdomen just below where the ribs separate

ORIGIN The nerves form a radial network and so were likened to the sun's rays and called 'solar'.

solar system n the Sun and the bodies orbiting it

sold past participle, past tense of **sell**

solder /sóldər/ n 1 an alloy for joining metal 2 something that unites people or things ■ vti 1 join or be joined with solder 2 unite to form a whole —**solderer** n

soldering iron n a tool for melting and applying solder

~~soldiar~~ incorrect spelling of **soldier**

soldier /sóljər/ n 1 somebody who serves in an army 2 an army member below officer rank 3 a dedicated worker for a cause 4 a sterile ant or termite that protects a colony ■ vi serve in an army —**soldierly** adj

ORIGIN **Soldier** goes back to Latin solidus, an ancient Roman gold coin (literally a 'solid' coin), and so a **soldier** is etymologically one who fights for pay. It was adopted into English from French.

□ **soldier on** vi continue determinedly

soldier of fortune n a soldier who enlists or serves for money or adventure

soldiery /sóljəri/ n 1 soldiers collectively 2 a soldier's work or skill

sold-out adj with no tickets left

sole[1] /sōl/ n 1 the underside of a foot 2 the bottom of a shoe ■ vt (**soling, soled**) put a sole on a shoe

SPELLCHECK Do not confuse the spelling of **sole** and **soul** ('a person's spirit'), which sound similar.

sole[2] /sōl/ adj 1 of which there is only one o the sole reason 2 belonging to one person or group o has sole responsibility for the department —**soleness** n

sole[3] /sōl/ (pl **soles** or same) n 1 a fish with a flat body 2 sole as food

solecism /sólləssizəm/ n 1 a grammatical mistake 2 something incorrect or inappropriate, e.g. a breach of etiquette —**solecistical** /sóllə sístik'l/ adj

solely /sól li/ adv 1 only o sold the company solely for commercial reasons 2 exclusively o He is solely to blame.

~~solemly~~ incorrect spelling of **solemnly**

solemn /sólləm/ adj 1 serious or earnest 2 humourless 3 formal —**solemnly** adv —**solemnness** n

solemnity /sə lémnəti/ (pl **-ties**) n 1 the solemn quality of something 2 a solemn ceremony (often pl)

solemnize /sólləm nīz/ (**-nizing, -nized**), **solemnise** vt 1 celebrate or observe with a ceremony or formality 2 make dignified —**solemnization** /sólləm nī záysh'n/ n

sol-fa n a system of using syllables to denote degrees of a musical scale

solicit /sə líssit/ v 1 vti try to get something by making repeated pleas 2 vt ask somebody for something 3 vti offer people sex for money —**solicitation** /sə líssi táysh'n/ n

solicitor /sə líssitər/ n a lawyer who draws up legal documents and does preparatory work for barristers

Solicitor General (pl **Solicitors General**) n 1 in England and Wales, the law officer ranking below the Attorney General 2 in Scotland, the law officer ranking below the Lord Advocate 3 in New Zealand, the chief law officer

solicitous /sə líssitəss/ adj 1 expressing an attitude of concern 2 ready and willing —**solicitously** adv —**solicitousness** n

solicitude /sə líssi tyood/ n concern and consideration, especially when expressed

solid /sóllid/ adj 1 not soft or yielding 2 not hollow 3 unadulterated or unmixed 4 of strong and secure construction 5 unanimous o Support for the proposal was solid. 6 uninterrupted o worked for a solid two hours 7 reliable 8 financially secure 9 three-dimensional 10 without spaces between words or lines of type ■ n 1 a solid thing 2 a three-dimensional figure 3 a substance that retains its shape, unlike a liquid or gas —**solidity** /sə líddəti/ n —**solidly** adv —**solidness** n

solidarity /sólli dárrəti/ *n* mutual agreement and support

solidify /sə líddi fī/ (**-fies, -fied**) *vti* **1** make or become solid **2** make or become strong and united —**solidification** /sə líddifi káysh'n/ *n*

soliloquy /sə lílləkwi/ (*pl* **-quies**) *n* **1** the act of talking when alone **2** a speech made by an actor alone on stage

solipsism /sóllipsizəm/ *n* a belief in the self as the only reality —**solipsist** —**solipsistic** /sóllip sístik/ *adj*

solitaire /sólli tair, sólli táir/ *n* **1** a game for one person in which pegs are gradually eliminated from a board **2** a single gemstone that is set in a ring

solitary /sóllitəri/ *adj* **1** done alone **2** preferring to be or live alone **3** remote or apart from others **4** single ○ *a solitary boat on the river* **5** describes animals that live alone or in pairs rather than in colonies or social groups ■ *n* (*pl* **-ies**) **1** a recluse **2** *also* **solitary confinement** imprisonment in an isolated cell —**solitarily** *adv* —**solitariness** *n*

solitude /sólli tyood/ *n* **1** the state of being alone **2** remoteness

solo /sólō/ *n* (*pl* **-li** /-li/) **1** a musical piece or passage performed by one person **2** any performance by one person ■ *adj* **1** for a single performer **2** done by one person **3** ANZ having no partner ■ *adv* alone ■ *vi* (**-loing, -loed**) do something without help or accompaniment

soloist /sólō ist/ *n* somebody who performs a musical solo

Solomon Islands /sólləmən-/ country comprising over 35 islands and atolls in the South Pacific Ocean. Cap. Honiara. Pop. 480,442 (2001). —**Solomon Islander** *n*

solstice /sólstiss/ *n* **1** the longest or shortest day of the year **2** either of the points on the ecliptic when the Sun reaches its northernmost or southernmost point —**solstitial** /sol stísh'l/ *adj*

Solti /shólti/, **Sir Georg** (1912–97) Hungarian conductor

soluble /sóllyoōb'l/ *adj* **1** able to be dissolved in liquid **2** able to be solved —**solubility** /sóllyoō bíllǝti/ *n* —**solubly** *adv*

solution /sə loōsh'n/ *n* **1** a way of resolving a problem or difficulty **2** the answer to a puzzle or question **3** the act of finding a solution **4** a fluid with a substance dissolved in it **5** the process of forming a solution

solve /solv/ (**solving, solved**) *vt* **1** deal with a problem successfully **2** find the answer to a puzzle **3** work out the solution to an equation or other mathematical problem —**solvability** /sólvə bílləti/ *n* —**solvable** *adj*

solvent /sólvənt/ *adj* **1** having enough money to cover expenses and debts **2** able to dissolve substances ■ *n* a substance that dissolves other substances —**solvency** *n*

Solway Firth /sól way-/ arm of the Irish Sea on the border between NW England and SW Scotland. Length 64 km/40 mi.

Solzhenitsyn /sólzhə nee̅tsin, səlzhə nyee̅tsin/, **Aleksandr Isayevich** (*b*. 1918) Russian writer

som (*pl* **same**) *n* the main unit of currency of Kyrgyzstan

Somalia /sə maáli ə/ country in E Africa. Cap. Mogadishu. Pop. 7,488,773 (2001). —**Somalian** *n, adj*

Somaliland /sə maáli land/ region of NE Africa, comprising Somalia, Djibouti, and part of Ethiopia

somatic /sə máttik/ *adj* affecting the body

somatic cell *n* any body cell except a reproductive cell

somber *adj* US = **sombre**

sombre /sómbər/ *adj* **1** dark and gloomy **2** dark in colour **3** serious and melancholy —**sombrely** *adv* —**sombreness** *n*

sombrero /som bráirō/ (*pl* **-ros**) *n* a wide-brimmed hat

some /(stressed) sum, (unstressed) səm/ *det, pron* indicates an unspecified number, quantity, or proportion ○ *I agree with you to some extent.* ○ *Some of you will not agree with me.* ■ *det* **1** quite a few ○ *We have been debating this problem for some months now.* **2** particular but unspecified ○ *some medical book* **3** adds emphasis (*infml*) ○ *That was some performance!* ■ *adv* approximately ○ *for some 30 years*

-some *suffix* **1** characterized by a particular quality, condition, or thing ○ *troublesome* **2** a group containing a particular number of members ○ *threesome*

somebody /súmbədi/, **someone** /súm wun/ *pron* some unspecified person ■ *pron, n* (*pl* **-ies**; *pl* **someones**) an important or well-known person

someday /súm day/ *adv* at an unspecified time in the future

somehow /súm how/ *adv* **1** in some way, often with great effort or difficulty ○ *He somehow managed to climb back up.* **2** for an unknown reason ○ *She somehow forgot to tell anyone where she was going.*

somersault /súmmər solt, -sawlt/ *n* an acrobatic rolling of the body in a complete circle ■ *vi* perform a somersault

ORIGIN **Somersault** came from a French word deriving ultimately from Latin *super* 'above' and *saltus* 'leap'. It is recorded in English from the mid-16C.

Somerset /súmmər sèt/ county in SW England

something /súm thing/ *pron* **1** an unspecified thing ○ *I knew there was something wrong.* **2** an unspecified amount ○ *something over 50%* **3** suggesting a resemblance ○ *something of the athlete about him* **4** rather ○ *something of a disappointment* ■ *adv* **1** to some extent ○ *Your voice sounds something like hers.* **2** to an extreme degree (*infml*) ○ *It hurts something awful.* ◇ **something else** somebody or something really special or remarkable (*infml*) ◇ **have something to do with** be connected with or involve

sometime /súm tīm/ *adv* at an unspecified time in the future o *They intend to marry sometime soon.* ■ *adj* former o *a sometime student of this university*

sometimes /súm tīmz/ *adv* on some occasions or from time to time o *We go to the theatre sometimes.*

someway /súm way/ *adv* using some means that is not yet known or stated o *We'll figure it out someway.*

somewhat /súm wot/ *adv* to some extent

somewhere /súm wair/ *adv* 1 in some unspecified place o *He lives somewhere in Scotland.* 2 expresses approximation o *somewhere between three and four hundred* ◇ **get somewhere** make progress towards achieving something

Somme /som/ river in N France, flowing into the English Channel. Length 241 km/150 mi.

somnambulate /som námbyŏŏ layt/ (**-lating, -lated**) *vi* sleepwalk (*technical*) —**somnambulation** /som námbyŏŏ láysh'n/ *n* —**somnambulator** *n*

somnambulism /som námbyŏŏlizəm/ *n* sleepwalking (*technical*) —**somnambulist** *n*

somnolent /sómnələnt/ *adj* 1 sleepy 2 lacking activity —**somnolence** *n* —**somnolently** *adv*

~~something~~ incorrect spelling of **something**

son /sun/ *n* 1 somebody's male child 2 a male descendant 3 a man or boy connected with a particular place or period o *the achievements of the sons of the Industrial Revolution* 4 **Son** in Christianity, Jesus Christ —**sonless** *adj*

SPELLCHECK Do not confuse the spelling of **son** and **sun** ('a star'), which sound similar.

sonar /só naar/ *n* 1 a system for detecting underwater objects by means of sound waves 2 a device that uses sonar

sonata /sə naátə/ *n* a classical composition for one or more solo instruments

son et lumière /són ay lóomi air/ *n* an outdoor spectacle with music and lights

song /song/ *n* 1 a set of words that are sung 2 singing as an activity or form of expression 3 an instrumental work in the style of a song 4 the characteristic sound of a bird or insect ◇ **for a song** very cheaply (*infml*)

songbird /sóng burd/ *n* a bird with a musical call

songbook /sóng bŏŏk/ *n* a book of songs

songster /sóngstər/ *n* 1 a singer 2 a songbird

songwriter /sóng rītər/ *n* a writer of songs

sonic /sónnik/ *adj* 1 of sound or sound waves 2 of the speed of sound in air

sonic boom *n* a loud boom produced when an aircraft flies faster than the speed of sound

son-in-law (*pl* **sons-in-law**) *n* a daughter's husband

sonnet /sónnət/ *n* a fourteen-line rhyming poem with a set structure

Sonoran Desert /sə náwrən-/ desert in SW Arizona, S California, and NW Mexico

sonorous /sónnərəss/ *adj* 1 producing sound 2 sounding with loud deep tones —**sonorously** *adv*

soon *adv* 1 after a short time o *She soon realized that she had made a mistake.* 2 quickly o *How soon will you be ready?* 3 early o *It's a bit soon to be thinking of leaving, isn't it?* ◇ **as soon as** immediately after ◇ **no sooner...than** immediately after one thing had happened, another took place ◇ **sooner or later** at some as yet unspecifiable time in the future

soot /sŏŏt/ *n* the black dust given off by a fire —**sooty** *adj*

soothe /sŏŏth/ (**soothing, soothed**) *vt* 1 ease pain 2 calm somebody down —**soothing** *adj* —**soothingly** *adv*

soothsayer /sŏŏth say ər/ *n* somebody who predicts the future —**soothsay** *vi*

sop *n* 1 something given to satisfy a discontented person 2 a piece of food dipped in liquid ■ *vti* (**sopping, sopped**) soak in liquid □ **sop up** *vt* soak up liquid

SOP *abbr* standard operating procedure

sophism /sóffizəm/ *n* an apparently clever but flawed argument —**sophist** *n* —**sophistic** /sə fístik/ *adj* —**sophistically** *adv*

sophisticate /sə físti kayt/ *vt* (**-cating, -cated**) 1 make somebody more cultured or worldly 2 make something more complex ■ *n* a cultured or worldly person

sophisticated /sə físti kaytid/ *adj* 1 knowledgeable and cultured 2 suitable for sophisticated people —**sophisticatedly** *adv* —**sophistication** /sə fístə káysh'n/ *n*

ORIGIN Sophisticated originally meant 'adulterated, impure', and later 'falsified, dishonest'. It did not acquire positive associations until the late 19C. Like *sophistry*, **sophisticated** ultimately refers to the Sophists, a group of Greek philosophers in the 5C BC who became discredited because of their specious reasoning and moral scepticism.

sophistry /sóffistri/ *n* apparently clever but flawed reasoning

Sophocles /sóffə kleez/ (496?–406? BC) Greek dramatist

sophomore /sóffə mawr/ *n* US, Can a second-year student in a high school, college, or university

soporific /sóppə ríffik/ *adj* 1 causing sleep or drowsiness 2 feeling sleepy ■ *n* a sleep-inducing drug

sopping /sópping/, **sopping wet** *adj* thoroughly wet

soppy /sóppi/ (**-pier, -piest**) *adj* 1 excessively sentimental or affectionate (*infml*) 2 very wet —**soppily** *adv* —**soppiness** *n*

soprano /sə praánō/ (*pl* **-os** or **-i** /-ni/) *n* 1 a woman or boy with the highest singing voice 2 the highest singing voice, or a part written for this voice

sorbet /sáwr bay, sáwrbit/ *n* a frozen dessert made with fruit syrup

sorcery /sáwrssəri/ n the supposed supernatural use of magic —**sorcerer** n —**sorceress** n —**sorcerous** adj

sordid /sáwrdid/ adj 1 demonstrating the worst aspects of humanity 2 dirty and depressing —**sordidly** adv —**sordidness** n

sore /sawr/ adj (**sorer**, **sorest**) 1 painful 2 causing anger, embarrassment, or distress ○ His dismissal has always been a sore point. 3 urgent ○ in sore need of help ■ n a painful open skin infection —**soreness** n ◊ See note at **saw**

sorely /sáwrli/ adv very ○ I was sorely tempted to give her the money.

sorghum /sáwrgəm/ (pl -**ghums** or same) n a cereal crop grown in warm areas of the world

Soroptimist /sə róptəmist/ n a member of a professional women's club that promotes public service

sorority /sə rórrəti/ (pl -**ties**) n a social society for women students

sorrel[1] /sórrəl/ (pl -**rels** or same) n a plant with sharp-tasting leaves. Use: salad greens, medicines.

sorrel[2] /sórrəl/ adj reddish-brown ■ n 1 a reddish-brown colour 2 a reddish-brown horse

sorrow /sórrō/ n 1 a feeling of deep sadness 2 a cause of sorrow ■ vi grieve (literary) ◊ **drown your sorrows** drink alcohol in order to try to forget a source of sadness or disappointment

ORIGIN **Sorrow** and sorry look as though they should be closely related, but in fact they are not. **Sorrow** comes from an ancient Germanic root meaning 'care'. Sorry also represents a Germanic word, but is related to sore.

sorrowful /sórrəf'l/ adj sad —**sorrowfully** adv

sorry /sórri/ adj (-**rier**, -**riest**) 1 apologetic 2 sympathetic 3 pitiful ■ interj 1 expresses apology 2 asks somebody to repeat something (infml) —**sorriness** n

sort n 1 a category 2 a person of a particular type (infml) 3 something similar to a particular thing ○ It's a sort of play with dancing. 4 the process of arranging electronic data in a set order ■ vt 1 put in categories 2 put in a set order —**sorter** n ◊ **of a sort, of sorts** of a mediocre kind ◊ **out of sorts** 1 slightly unwell 2 not in a very good mood ◊ **sort of** rather (infml) ◊ See note at **type**

□ **sort out** vt 1 resolve effectively 2 put into a state of order 3 punish (infml)

sortation /sawr táysh'n/ n the process of sorting things, especially when done by a machine or computer

sort code n a number that identifies a particular branch of a bank

sorted /sáwrtid/ adj put right or dealt with satisfactorily (infml)

sortie /sáwrti/ n 1 an attack on an enemy 2 a combat aircraft mission ■ vi (-**tied**) make a sortie

sorting office n an office where mail is sorted

SOS /éss ō éss/ n 1 a distress signal 2 a call for help

so-so adj neither good nor bad (infml)

sot n an offensive term for somebody who habitually drinks a lot of alcohol (literary)

Soto ♦ de Soto, Hernando

sotto voce /sóttō vṓchi/ adv in a quiet voice —**sotto voce** adj

soubriquet n = sobriquet

~~souce~~ incorrect spelling of **source**

soufflé /sŏof lay/ n a light dish containing whisked egg whites —**soufflé** adj

Soufriere Hills Volcano /soŏfri áir-/ volcano on the island of Montserrat, in the Caribbean Sea. Height 914 m/2,999 ft.

sought past tense, past participle of **seek**

sought-after /sáwt aaftər/ adj in demand

souk /soŏk/, **suq** n an outdoor Arab market

soul /sōl/ n 1 the nonphysical aspect of a person 2 a person's spirit regarded as surviving after death 3 somebody's feelings ○ Her soul was in turmoil. 4 spiritual depth ○ The work lacked soul. 5 the essence of a people or nation ○ discover the soul of the Russian people 6 a type of person 7 an individual person (usually pl) ○ a country of some 10 million souls 8 a perfect example or personification of something ○ the soul of discretion ◊ **sell your soul** abandon your principles in order to obtain wealth or success ◊ See note at **sole**

soul-destroying adj unfulfilling

soulful /sōlf'l/ adj deeply or sincerely emotional —**soulfully** adv —**soulfulness** n

soulless /sōl ləss/ adj 1 lacking warmth or feeling 2 lacking interesting or engaging qualities

soul mate n a friend with whom somebody shares deep feelings and attitudes

soul music n a kind of African American music that developed out of blues and gospel music

soul-searching n thorough examination of personal thoughts and feelings

sound[1] /sownd/ n 1 something that can be heard 2 vibrations sensed by the ear 3 the sensation produced in the ear by vibrations 4 reproduced music or speech 5 the activity of recording music or speech 6 an impression formed from available information ○ From the sound of it she's finally found a job she likes. 7 earshot ○ within the sound of the church bells 8 a basic element of speech formed by the vocal tract and interpreted through the ear ■ v 1 vi seem from what is reported ○ The meal sounded awful. 2 vi indicate a particular condition by means of speech ○ He sounded exhausted. 3 vi have a particular quality when heard 4 vti make or cause to make a noise ○ An alarm sounded. 5 vt articulate an element of speech 6 vt make a bodily organ emit a sound as a test of its physical condition —**soundless** adj —**soundlessly** adv

□ **sound off** vi speak forcefully (infml)

□ **sound out** *vt* probe somebody's opinion

sound² /sownd/ *adj* **1** not damaged **2** healthy **3** sensible **4** completely acceptable **5** deep and peaceful **6** complete or thorough **7** with little financial risk **8** logically or legally valid ■ *adv* deeply ◇ *sound asleep* —**soundly** *adv* —**soundness** *n* ◇ See note at **valid**

sound³ /sownd/ *v* ◇ *vti* measure the depth of water **2** *vi* dive suddenly and swiftly *(refers to whales)* **3** *vt* examine with a probe ■ *n* a surgical probe

sound⁴ /sownd/ *n* **1** a wide channel **2** a long wide arm of the sea

sound barrier *n* a sudden increase in the force of air opposing a moving body as it approaches the speed of sound, producing a sonic boom

sound bite *n* a brief broadcast remark, especially one by a politician

sound card *n* a circuit board for computer sound

sound effect *n* a recording or imitation of a sound used in a broadcast or performance ■ **sound effects** *npl* film sounds other than dialogue and music

sounding /sównding/ *n* **1** a measurement of the depth of water **2** a measurement of atmospheric conditions at a particular altitude ■ **soundings** *npl* a preliminary inquiry into people's opinions

sounding board *n* **1** somebody asked for a preliminary opinion **2** a structure that reflects sound

soundproof /sównd proof/ *adj* impenetrable to noise ■ *vt* make soundproof

sound system *n* a set of electronic equipment for amplifying sound

soundtrack /sównd trak/ *n* **1** the sound recorded for a film **2** a strip on film that carries the sound

sound wave *n* an audible pressure wave caused by a disturbance in air or water

soup /soop/ *n* **1** a liquid food made by cooking ingredients such as meat, fish, or vegetables in water, milk, or stock **2** something thick and swirling ◇ *the primordial soup of hydrogen, oxygen, and other gases* ◇ **in the soup** in difficulties or trouble *(infml)*

ORIGIN Soup was adopted from French *soupe*, which meant 'soup' but also 'broth poured on slices of bread'. This gives a better clue to the origin of the word, which goes back to a Latin verb meaning 'soak'.

□ **soup up** *vt* modify a car to make it more powerful *(infml)*

soupçon /soóp son, -soN/ *n* a tiny amount

soup kitchen *n* a place that serves free meals to needy people

soupy /soópi/ (**-ier, -iest**) *adj* like soup

sour /sowr/ *adj* **1** with a naturally sharp acidic taste **2** with a bad taste because of unwanted fermentation **3** characterized by bitter feelings **4** unfriendly or unpleasant ■ *vti* **1** make

or become sour **2** make or become dissatisfied —**sourly** *adv* —**sourness** *n*

source /sawrss/ *n* **1** the place where something begins or the thing that something derives from **2** a provider of information ◇ *a reliable source* **3** the beginning of a river ■ *vt* (**sourcing, sourced**) locate something for use ◇ See note at **origin**

source code *n* a computer code that can be converted into machine code

sour cream *n* cream that has been artificially soured

sourdough /sówr dō/ *n* **1** fermenting dough reserved for use as a leavening **2** bread made with sourdough

sour grapes *n* an affected scorn for something secretly desired

---

ORIGIN Sour grapes alludes to the fable *The Fox and the Grapes* by Aesop, in which the fox calls some grapes sour when he cannot reach them.

---

sourpuss /sówr pŏoss/ *n* a bad-tempered person *(infml)*

souse /sowss/ *v* (**sousing, soused**) **1** *vt* steep food in vinegar or brine to preserve it **2** *vti* drench or soak something, or become drenched or soaked **3** *vt* make somebody intoxicated *(slang)* ■ *n* **1** a liquid used in pickling **2** pickled food

south /sowth/ *n* **1** the direction to the right of somebody facing the rising sun **2** the compass point that is opposite north **3** *also* **South** the part of an area or country that is in the south ■ *adj* **1** *also* **South** in the south **2** blowing from the south ■ *adv* towards the south —**southbound** *adj*

South Africa country in southern Africa. Cap. Pretoria. Pop. 43,586,097 (2001). —**South African** *n, adj*

South America fourth largest continent in the world, lying between the Atlantic and Pacific oceans southeast of North America and stretching from the isthmus of Panama southwards to Cape Horn. Pop. 317,846,000 (1996). —**South American** *adj, n*

Southampton /sow thámptən, sowth hámptən/ port in S England. Pop. 214,859 (1996).

South Asia region comprising Bangladesh, Bhutan, India, the Maldives, Nepal, Pakistan, and Sri Lanka —**South Asian** *n, adj*

South Australia state in south-central Australia. Cap. Adelaide. Pop. 1,490,400 (1998). —**South Australian** *n, adj*

South Ayrshire council area in the former Strathclyde Region of west central Scotland. The administrative centre is Ayr. Pop. 14,247 (1997).

South Carolina state of the SE United States. Cap. Columbia. Pop. 4,012,012 (2000). —**South Carolinian** *n, adj*

South China Sea part of the China Sea, bounded by SE China, Vietnam, Malaysia, and the Philippines

South Dakota state of the north-central United States. Cap. Pierre. Pop. 754,844 (2000). —**South Dakotan** n, adj

southeast /sówth eèst/ n **1** the compass point between south and east **2** also **Southeast** the part of an area or country that is in the southeast ■ adj **1** also **Southeast** in the southeast **2** blowing from the southeast ■ adv towards the southeast —**southeastward** adj —**southeastwards** adv

Southeast Asia region comprising Brunei, Cambodia, Indonesia, Laos, Malaysia, Myanmar, the Philippines, Singapore, Thailand, and Vietnam —**Southeast Asian** n, adj

southeasterly /sowth eèstərli/ adj **1** in the southeast **2** blowing from the southeast ■ n (pl -lies) also **southeaster** /sowth eèstər/ a wind from the southeast

southeastern /sowth eèstərn/ adj **1** in the southeast **2** facing southeast **3** also **Southeastern** of the southeast

southerly /súthərli/ adj **1** in or towards the south **2** blowing from the south ■ n (pl -lies) a wind from the south

southern /súthərn/ adj **1** in the south **2** south of the equator **3** facing south **4** also **Southern** of the south of a country —**southernmost** adj

Southern Alps /súthərn-/ mountain range on the South Island, New Zealand. Highest peak Mt Cook 3,754 m/12,316 ft.

Southern Cross n a constellation in the southern hemisphere

southerner /súthərnər/ n somebody from the south of a country

southern hemisphere n the half of the Earth south of the equator

South Island largest island of New Zealand. Pop. 931,566 (1996).

South Korea /-kə reè ə/ country in East Asia, occupying the **S Korean Peninsula**. Cap. Seoul. Pop. 47,904,370 (2001). —**South Korean** n, adj

southpaw /sówth paw/ n somebody who is left-handed, especially a boxer (infml)

South Pole n the southern end of the Earth's axis

South Seas npl **1** the South Pacific **2** the seas of the southern hemisphere

southward /sówthwərd/ adj in or towards the south ■ n a point in the south ■ adv also **southwards** towards the south —**southwardly** adv, adj

southwest /sówth wèst/ n **1** the compass point between south and west **2** also **Southwest** the part of an area or country that is in the southwest ■ adj **1** also **Southwest** in the southwest **2** blowing from the southwest ■ adv towards the southwest —**southwestward** adj —**southwestwards** adv

southwesterly /sówth wèstərli/ adj **1** in or towards the southwest **2** blowing from the southwest ■ n (pl -lies) a wind from the southwest

southwestern /sówth wèstərn/ adj **1** in the southwest **2** facing southwest **3** also **Southwestern** of the southwest

South Yorkshire metropolitan county in N England

~~souvenier~~ incorrect spelling of **souvenir**

souvenir /sóova neèr/ n an object that reminds you of the place where you got it

sou'wester /sow wèstər/ n a broad-brimmed waterproof hat

sovereign /sóvrin/ n **1** a monarch **2** an old British gold coin worth one pound ■ adj **1** politically independent **2** with complete power **3** outstanding or excellent (dated)

sovereignty /sóvvrinti/ n **1** supreme authority over a state **2** political independence

~~sovereighn~~ incorrect spelling of **sovereign**

~~soverign~~ incorrect spelling of **sovereign**

soviet /sóv i ət, sóv-/ n **1** a Communist council in the former Soviet Union **2** an early Russian revolutionary council **3 Soviet** somebody from the former Soviet Union ■ adj **Soviet** of the former Soviet Union —**sovietism** n

Soviet Union /sóvi ət yoonyən/ former federation of Communist states in E Europe and northern and central Asia from 1922 until 1991

sow /sō/ (**sown** /sōn/ or **sowed**) v **1** vti plant seeds **2** vt cause a feeling or idea to arise or become widespread —**sower** n ◊ See note at **sew**

Soweto /sə wáytō, sə wéttō/ township in NE South Africa. Pop. 596,632 (1991).

soya /sóy ə/, **soy** /soy/ n **1** a soya bean plant **2** also **soy sauce** a dark salty liquid made from soya beans. Use: flavouring foods. ■ adj made or derived from soya beans

soya bean n **1** the edible seed of a South Asian plant. Use: soy sauce, soya milk, tofu, textured vegetable protein. **2** the plant that produces soya beans

Soyinka /so yíngkə/, **Wole** (b. 1934) Nigerian writer and political activist

sozzled /sózz'ld/ adj intoxicated (infml)

spa /spaa/ n **1** a resort with mineral springs (often in placenames) **2** a whirlpool bath

space n **1** the region beyond the Earth's atmosphere **2** the region that exists between all astronomical objects **3** the three-dimensional expanse where matter exists **4** an interval of time ○ In the space of two hours the situation was resolved. **5** an area set apart for a particular purpose **6** a blank area between printed words or lines **7** an empty or available area ■ vt (**spacing**, **spaced**) set things apart from each other

space age n the era of space exploration —**space-age** adj

space-bar n a keyboard bar pressed to introduce a space

space capsule n the part of a spacecraft where the crew and passengers travel

spacecraft /spáyss kraaft/, **spaceship** /spáyss ship/ n a vehicle for space travel

spaced-out adj inattentive or dazed (slang)

space heater *n* a portable appliance used to heat a small area

spaceman /spáyss man/ (*pl* **-men** /-men/) *n* **1** an astronaut **2** an extraterrestrial

space probe *n* a spacecraft with no crew that is used to explore distant regions of space and send data back to Earth

space shuttle *n* a reusable spacecraft

space station, space platform *n* a satellite used as a base in space

Spacesuit: Astronaut Buzz Aldrin on the Moon

spacesuit /spáyss soot, -syoot/ *n* an astronaut's suit

spacewalk /spáyss wawk/ *n* an astronaut's excursion out of a spacecraft ■ *vi* go out of a spacecraft in space

spacewoman /spáyss woomən/ (*pl* **-women** /-wimin/) *n* **1** a woman astronaut **2** a female extraterrestrial

spacial *adj* = spatial

spacing /spáyssing/ *n* **1** the space between things, e.g. between printed words or lines **2** the arranging of things in spaces

spacious /spáyshəss/ *adj* containing ample space —**spaciously** *adv* —**spaciousness** *n*

spade[1] *n* a digging tool with a long handle and a wide flat blade ■ *vt* (**spading, spaded**) dig or remove with a spade ◊ **call a spade a spade** speak plainly and bluntly

spade[2] *n* a playing card of the suit with black spear-shaped symbols ◊ **in spades** to a very great degree (*infml*)

spadework /spáyd wurk/ *n* **1** digging **2** preliminary work

~~spagetti~~ incorrect spelling of **spaghetti**

spaghetti /spə gétti/ *n* **1** string-shaped pasta **2** a dish of cooked spaghetti

spaghetti junction *n* a complex motorway interchange

spaghetti western *n* a western made in Europe by an Italian film company

Spain /spayn/ country in SW Europe on the Iberian Peninsula. Cap. Madrid. Pop. 40,037,995 (2001).

spake past tense of **speak** (*archaic*)

spam *n* electronic junk mail ■ *vti* (**spamming, spammed**) send unwanted electronic messages

Spam *tdmk* a trademark for tinned chopped meat, mainly pork, that is pressed into a loaf

span[1] *n* **1** the distance between two limits or extremities, e.g. the wing tips of an aeroplane **2** the distance between two supports of a bridge or other structure **3** a period of time ■ *vt* (**spanning, spanned**) **1** extend over or across **2** measure with the hand

span[2] *n* a pair of horses or other animals driven together

spangle /spáng g'l/ *n* **1** a small shiny decoration **2** a small sparkling spot or object ■ *v* (**-gling, -gled**) **1** *vt* sprinkle or decorate with spangles **2** *vi* glitter with spangles —**spangly** *adj*

Spanglish /spáng glish/ *n* a variety of Spanish with many English borrowings

Spaniard /spánnyərd/ *n* **1** somebody from Spain **2** a New Zealand rock plant

spaniel /spánnyəl/ *n* a medium-sized dog with a wavy coat and large drooping ears

Spanish /spánnish/ *n* a Romance language spoken in most of Spain and much of Central and South America ■ *npl* the people of Spain ■ *adj* **1** of Spain **2** of the Spanish language

Spanish America the part of America that was colonized by the Spanish from the 16C and where Spanish is still widely spoken, including much of Central and South America and some Caribbean islands —**Spanish-American** *n, adj*

Spanish Main 1 in the 16C and 17C, the region of Spanish America from the isthmus of Panama to the mouth of the Orinoco River, in present-day Venezuela **2** the part of the Caribbean Sea crossed by Spanish ships in colonial times

Spanish omelette *n* a deep flat omelette containing vegetables

Spanish Sahara former name for **Western Sahara**

spank[1] *vt* slap the buttocks of —**spank** *n*

spank[2] *vi* move briskly or spiritedly

spanking /spángking/ *n* a beating on the buttocks with the open hand ■ *adj* **1** exceptional (*infml*) **2** brisk ■ *adv* very ○ *a spanking new car*

spanner /spánnər/ *n* a tool used to grasp and turn a nut ◊ **put** *or* **throw a spanner in the works** ruin or impede a plan or system

spar[1] *n* a thick strong pole that supports the rigging on a ship

spar[2] *vi* (**sparring, sparred**) **1** box, especially for practice **2** argue ■ *n* a practice bout of boxing

spar[3] *n* any light-coloured mineral that splits easily

spare *vt* (**sparing, spared**) **1** refrain from harming **2** treat leniently **3** save from doing something **4** withhold or avoid **5** use frugally **6** afford ○ *I can't spare any time to exercise.* ■ *adj* **1** kept in reserve **2** superfluous **3** lean **4** scanty ■ *n* **1** something extra **2** in tenpin bowling, an instance of knocking down all the pins with two balls —**sparely** *adv* —**spareness** *n* ◊ **to spare** more than what is needed

spare part *n* a replacement component

spare-part surgery *n* transplant surgery

spare time *n* leisure time

spare tyre n 1 an extra tyre carried in case of a puncture 2 a band of extra flesh around the waist (humorous)

sparing /spáiring/ adj 1 frugal 2 scanty —**sparingly** adv

spark n 1 a fiery particle thrown from something that is burning or rubbing 2 an electric discharge 3 something that activates or initiates something o a spark of interest ■ v 1 vi throw off sparks 2 vt stimulate or incite

Spark, Dame Muriel (b. 1918) British writer

sparkle /spaárk'l/ vi (-**kling**, -**kled**) 1 throw off sparks 2 shine with a flickering reflected light 3 perform in an impressive or lively way ■ n 1 a shining particle 2 animation —**sparkly** adj

sparkler /spaárklər/ n a hand-held firework that throws off sparks

sparkling /spaárkling/ adj 1 reflecting glittering light 2 describes drinks that are effervescent 3 vivacious

spark plug n a device that ignites the fuel in an engine

sparks n (infml; + sing verb) 1 an electrician 2 a radio operator

sparky /spaárki/ (-**ier**, -**iest**) adj lively

sparring partner n 1 somebody who spars with a boxer 2 a debating partner

sparrow /spárrō/ n a small brownish songbird

sparrowhawk /spárr ō hawk/ n 1 a small European and Asian hawk 2 a small North American falcon

sparse /spaarss/ (**sparser**, **sparsest**) adj thinly distributed —**sparsely** adv —**sparseness** n

Sparta /spaárta/ town in the S Peloponnese, Greece, the site of an ancient city-state that was an important military power between the 6C and 4C BC. Pop. 14,084 (1991).

Spartacus /spaártəkəss/ (d. 71 BC) Roman enslaved labourer and rebel leader

Spartan /spaárt'n/ n 1 a native of ancient Sparta 2 a person with a strong character ■ adj 1 of ancient Sparta 2 **spartan** marked by discipline and austerity —**Spartanism** n —**spartanly** adv

spasm /spázzəm/ n 1 an involuntary muscle contraction 2 a sudden burst of activity

spasmodic /spaz móddik/ adj 1 affected by spasms 2 intermittent —**spasmodically** adv

spastic /spástik/ adj 1 affected by spasms 2 an offensive term describing somebody who lacks physical coordination (dated) ■ n an offensive term for somebody with a disability that affects physical coordination (dated) —**spastically** adv

spat¹ n a petty quarrel ■ vi (**spatting**, **spatted**) quarrel pettily

spat² past tense, past participle of **spit¹**

spat³ n a fabric covering for the upper part of a shoe

spate n 1 a flood or a state of flooding 2 an outburst

spatial /spáysh'l/, **spacial** adj of space —**spatially** adv

spatter /spáttər/ v 1 vti come or force out in scattered drops 2 vt splash with a liquid ■ n 1 a droplet of something spattered 2 a small amount

spatula /spáttyoōlə/ n a flat utensil used to lift or mix food and other substances

spawn n 1 a mass of eggs produced by a water animal 2 offspring ■ v 1 vi deposit eggs 2 vi produce young 3 vt give rise to

spay vt remove a female animal's ovaries

spaza /spaázə/ n S Africa a South African shop

~~speech~~ incorrect spelling of **speech**

speak /speek/ (**spoke** or **spake** (archaic), **spoken** /spōkən/) v 1 vti utter words with the voice 2 vi converse or communicate 3 vt be able to use a particular language 4 vi be on good terms o They're not speaking any more. 5 vi deliver a speech ◇ **so to speak** in one way of expressing it ◇ **to speak of** worth mentioning

□ **speak out** or **up** vi 1 speak frankly 2 talk loudly

□ **speak up for** vt speak in support of

-speak suffix the way of speaking or vocabulary characteristic of a particular group or field o adspeak

speaker /speekər/ n 1 somebody who speaks 2 somebody who makes a speech 3 a loudspeaker 4 **Speaker** the presiding officer of a legislative body

speaking clock n a telephone service providing the time

spear¹ /speer/ n 1 a long-handled weapon with a blade that is thrown from the shoulder 2 a weapon with a sharp point and barbs for catching fish ■ vt pierce or stab with a spear or a pointed utensil —**spearman** n

spear² /speer/ n a young shoot of some plants

spearhead /speér hed/ n 1 the pointed head of a spear 2 the leading forces in a military attack ■ vt act as the leader of an undertaking

spearmint /speér mint/ (pl same or -**mints**) n a common mint plant. Use: flavouring.

spec n a detailed description, especially one providing information needed to make or build something (infml) ◇ **on spec** with a chance of achieving something but no certainty of it (infml)

special /spésh'l/ adj 1 unusual or superior in comparison to others 2 held in esteem 3 reserved o It's my special chair. 4 made or arranged for a particular purpose ■ n 1 something designed or reserved for a particular purpose 2 a television programme that is not part of a schedule 3 a dish that is not on the usual menu —**specialness** n

Special Branch n a branch of the UK police force that deals with matters of political security

special constable n a UK police volunteer deployed when a large force is necessary

special delivery n the delivery of mail with priority treatment or outside normal times

special education *n* teaching for students with special needs

special interest group *n* a group trying to influence government policy on a particular issue

specialist /spéshəlist/ *n* 1 somebody specializing in a particular interest, activity, or field 2 a doctor who practises in a particular field only

speciality /spéshi álləti/ (*pl* **-ties**) *n* 1 something that somebody specializes in 2 a product or service that somebody is specialized in producing

specialize /spéshə līz/ (**-izing, -ized**), **specialise** *v* 1 *vi* devote time to a particular activity, skill, or field of study 2 *vt* adapt to suit a specific purpose —**specialization** /spéshə lī záysh'n/ *n*

~~speciall~~ incorrect spelling of **special**

specially /spésh'li/ *adv* for a particular purpose or occasion ◊ See note at **especially**

special needs *npl* the particular educational requirements that some people have because of physical or mental disabilities

Special Olympics *n* a competition for athletes with disabilities (+ *sing* or *pl verb*)

special operations, special ops *n* a branch of a military force engaged in covert operations (+ *sing* or *pl verb*)

special pleading *n* 1 a request for a court to consider new evidence 2 an argument presenting only one aspect of an issue

special school *n* a school for students with special needs

specialty /spésh'lti/ (*pl* **-ties**) *n* 1 a medical specialization 2 *US, Can* = **speciality**

specie /speéshi/ *n* money in the form of coins

~~speciel~~ incorrect spelling of **special**

species /speé sheez/ (*pl same*) *n* 1 a biological classification that is a subdivision of a genus 2 the organisms in a species 3 a type, sort, or variety of something ◊ See note at **type**

specific /spə siffik/ *adj* 1 precise 2 of a particular thing 3 of a biological species 4 describes a treatment that is effective for a particular medical condition ■ *n* 1 a detail 2 a medication that is effective against a particular disease —**specifically** *adv* —**specificity** /spéssi físsəti/ *n*

specification /spéssifi káysh'n/ *n* 1 a detailed description, especially one providing information needed to make or build something 2 something specified 3 the act of specifying something

specific gravity *n* PHYS = **relative density**

~~specificly~~ incorrect spelling of **specifically**

specify /spéssi fī/ (**-fies, -fied**) *vt* 1 state explicitly 2 state as a condition ◊ *The rules specify that pets cannot be kept here.* 3 include something in a specification —**specifiable** *adj*

~~speciman~~ incorrect spelling of **specimen**

specimen /spéssimin/ *n* 1 something that is representative because it is typical of its kind or of a whole ◊ *a specimen of his handwriting* 2 a type of person (*infml*) ◊ *a loathsome specimen* 3 a sample, e.g. of urine or blood, for testing and diagnosis

specious /speéshəss/ *adj* 1 apparently true but actually false 2 deceptively attractive —**speciously** *adv* —**speciousness** *n*

speck *n* 1 a small spot 2 a particle ■ *vt* mark with specks

speckle /spék'l/ *n* a small coloured spot, e.g. on plumage or an eggshell ■ *vt* (**-ling, -led**) mark with speckles —**speckled** *adj*

specs *npl* spectacles (*infml*)

spectacle /spéktək'l/ *n* 1 something remarkable that is seen 2 a lavish performance or display

spectacles /spéktək'lz/ *npl* glasses worn to correct vision

spectacular /spek tákyŏólər/ *adj* 1 visually impressive 2 remarkable ■ *n* a lavish artistic production —**spectacularly** *adv*

spectator /spek táytər/ *n* somebody who watches an event —**spectate** *vi*

spectator sport *n* a sport that is interesting to watch

specter *n* US = **spectre**

spectral /spéktrəl/ *adj* 1 ghostly 2 of or produced by a spectrum

spectre /spéktər/ *n* 1 a ghost 2 an unpleasant prospect ◊ *the spectre of nuclear war*

spectrum /spéktrəm/ (*pl* **-tra** /-trə/ or **-trums**) *n* 1 the distribution of coloured light produced when white light is dispersed 2 a radiation frequency range with a particular property 3 any range, especially between two extremes

speculate /spékyŏó layt/ (**-lating, -lated**) *v* 1 *vti* form an opinion based on incomplete or available facts 2 *vi* consider possibilities 3 *vi* make risky deals for profit —**speculation** /spékyŏó láysh'n/ *n* —**speculative** /spékyŏólətiv/ *adj* —**speculatively** *adv* —**speculativeness** *n* —**speculator** *n*

sped past tense, past participle of **speed**

speech *n* 1 the ability to speak 2 communication by speaking 3 spoken language ◊ *recordings of human speech* 4 a talk given to an audience 5 a particular way of speaking

speech community *n* a group that includes all the speakers of a particular language

speech day *n* a school prize-giving occasion

speechless /speéchləss/ *adj* 1 temporarily unable to speak 2 permanently unable to speak 3 remaining silent 4 unspoken —**speechlessly** *adv* —**speechlessness** *n*

speech recognition *n* a computer's ability to understand human speech

speech synthesis *n* a computer's ability to imitate human speech

speech therapy *n* the treatment of speech disorders —**speech therapist** *n*

speechwriter /speéch rítər/ *n* somebody who writes speeches that other people deliver

speed *n* 1 the rate at which something moves or happens 2 rapidity 3 an amphetamine drug (*slang*) **4** a gear ratio ○ *operates at three different speeds* ■ v (**sped** or **speeded**) **1** *vti* go or move quickly, or cause to go or move quickly **2** *vi* drive faster than the speed limit **3** *vi* pass or happen quickly —**speeder** n —**speeding** *adj* ◊ **be** or **get up to speed** be or become fully informed about the latest developments

□ **speed up** *vti* increase or cause to increase in rate or speed

speedboat /spéed bòt/ n a fast motorboat

speed bump n a bump in the road made to slow down motorists

speed limit n the maximum permitted speed on a stretch of road

speedometer /spi dómmitər/ n an instrument in a vehicle that shows its speed

speed skating n the sport of racing on ice with skates

speed trap n an area monitored by traffic police, usually with radar equipment

speedway /spéed way/ n **1** a motor sport involving motorbikes on a short dirt track **2** a speedway track

speedy /spéedi/ (**-ier**, **-iest**) *adj* **1** fast **2** capable of moving fast —**speedily** *adv* —**speediness** n

~~speek~~ incorrect spelling of **speak**

Speke /speek/, **John Hanning** (1827–64) British explorer

speleology /spèeli ólləji/, **spelaeology** n **1** the study of caves **2** the exploration of caves —**speleological** /-ə lójjik'l/ *adj* —**speleologist** n

spell[1] (**spelt** or **spelled**) v **1** *vti* name or write the letters of a word **2** *vt* form a particular word **3** *vt* signify something ○ *conditions that could spell disaster*

□ **spell out** *vt* **1** state explicitly **2** read slowly or letter by letter

spell[2] n **1** a word or set of words believed to have magical power **2** the influence of a spell **3** a fascination or attraction

spell[3] n **1** a short period (*infml*) **2** a period of particular weather **3** a bout of illness **4** a period of work or duty **5** *ANZ*, *Scotland* a rest period ■ v (**spelt** or **spelled**) **1** *vt* ANZ, US, Scotland relieve somebody who is working **2** *vi* ANZ take turns working

spellbinding /spél bìnding/ *adj* captivating —**spellbind** *vt* —**spellbindingly** *adv* —**spellbound** /spél bòwnd/ *adj*

spellchecker /spél chèkər/ n a computer program that corrects spelling errors —**spellcheck** n, *vt*

speller /spéllər/ n **1** somebody with a particular level of skill at spelling ○ *an excellent speller* **2** a book for teaching or improving spelling

spelling /spélling/ n **1** the ability to spell **2** the act of forming words by ordering letters **3** the way a word is actually spelt

spelt past tense, past participle of **spell**

Spencer /spénssər/, **Sir Stanley** (1891–1959) British painter

spend v (**spent**) **1** *vti* pay money in exchange for goods or services **2** *vt* devote time or effort to something ○ *spent a lot of time thinking about it* **3** *vt* pass a particular amount of time in a particular place or way ○ *spent two weeks in Japan* **4** *vt* use something up ■ n an amount of money spent or set aside for spending —**spender** n

spending money n cash for personal expenses

spendthrift /spénd thrìft/ n an extravagant spender ■ *adj* wasteful with money

ORIGIN Thrift is used in **spendthrift** in the old sense 'savings, earnings'.

Spenser /spénssər/, **Edmund** (1552?–99) English poet —**Spenserian** /spen séeri ən/ *adj*

spent past tense, past participle of **spend** ■ *adj* **1** used ○ *tossed the spent match into the fire* **2** exhausted ○ *felt totally spent by the end of the day*

sperm (*pl* same or **sperms**) n **1** semen **2** *also* **spermatozoon** /spur mátto zō on, spúrmətō-/ (*pl* **-a** /-zó ə/) a male reproductive cell —**spermatic** /spur máttik/ *adj*

spermaceti /spúrmə sétti, -séeti/ n a white waxy solid from sperm whales. Use: formerly, in cosmetics, candles, and ointments.

sperm bank n a place where semen is stored

sperm count n the concentration of sperm in somebody's semen, or a test to determine this

spermicide /spúrmi sìd/ n a sperm-killing agent used as a contraceptive —**spermicidal** /spúrmi síd'l/ *adj*

sperm oil n a pale yellow oil from the head of a sperm whale. Use: formerly, industrial lubricant.

sperm whale n a whale whose massive square head has a cavity filled with a mixture of sperm oil and spermaceti

ORIGIN Sperm here is short for *spermaceti*.

spew *vti* **1** vomit **2** pour or flow out forcefully ■ n vomit

Speyer /spí ər, shpí ər/ city in SW Germany, scene in 1529 of a protest by supporters of Martin Luther. Pop. 45,100 (1989).

SPF n a cream's sun protection rating. Full form **sun protection factor**

sphagnum /sfágnəm/ n a type of moss that forms peat

sphere /sfeer/ n **1** a ball-shaped object **2** a perfectly round solid figure **3** a field of knowledge or activity **4** an area of control or influence **5** a group within a society —**spheral** *adj* —**spherical** /sférrik'l/ *adj* —**spherically** *adv* —**sphericalness** n —**sphericity** /sfe ríssəti/ n

spheroid /sférroyd, sféer oyd/ n something that is like a sphere but is not perfectly round —**spheroidal** /sfi róyd'l/ *adj*

sphincter /sfíngktər/ n a circular band of muscle around the opening of a body passage —**sphincteral** *adj*

Sphinx, Giza, Egypt

sphinx /sfingks/ (*pl* **sphinxes** *or* **sphinges** /sfín jeez/) *n* 1 in Greek mythology, a winged creature with a lion's head and woman's body 2 in Egyptian mythology, a creature with a lion's body and the head of a man, ram, or bird 3 a statue of a sphinx

spice /spīss/ *n* 1 an aromatic substance derived from the nonleafy parts of plants and used as a flavouring 2 a source of excitement or interest ■ *vt* (**spicing, spiced**) 1 season with spice 2 make more exciting

~~spicey~~ incorrect spelling of **spicy**

spick-and-span /spĭk-/, **spic-and-span** *adj* 1 tidy 2 in perfect condition

spicy /spīssi/ (**-ier, -iest**) *adj* 1 seasoned with spice 2 arousing interest because of its sexual impropriety (*infml*) —**spiciness** *n*

spider /spīdər/ *n* 1 an eight-legged invertebrate animal that spins webs 2 a computer program that searches for information to be added to a search engine's index

spiderweb /spīdər web/ *n* a web spun by a spider

spidery /spīdəri/ *adj* 1 thin and irregular 2 spider-infested

spiel /shpeel, speel/ *n* a speech designed to convince somebody, especially a salesperson's patter (*infml*) —**spiel** *vi*

Steven Spielberg

Spielberg /speel burg/, **Steven** (*b.* 1947) US film director and producer

spigot /spĭggət/ *n* 1 *US* an outdoor tap 2 a tap fitted to a cask 3 a plug for a cask hole

spike[1] *n* 1 a pointed metal or wooden piece, especially one along the top of a railing or wall 2 a large nail 3 a metal point on the sole of a running shoe (*often pl*) 4 a sharp point 5 a sudden surge in voltage 6 a graphic image of a sudden peak and fall 7 a sudden brief increase ■ **spikes** *npl* a pair of running shoes with spikes on the soles ■ *v* (**spiking, spiked**) 1 *vt* render something useless or ineffective (*infml*) 2 *vt* sneakily add some-

thing, e.g. a drug or alcohol, to a drink 3 *vt* injure or disable somebody or something with a spike or spikes 4 *vi* rise abruptly —**spiked** *adj*

spike[2] *n* 1 a long cluster of flowers attached directly to a stem with the newest flowers at the tip 2 an ear of corn

spiky /spīki/ (**-ier, -iest**) *adj* with one or several spikes —**spikiness** *n*

spill[1] *v* (**spilt** *or* **spilled**) 1 *vti* flow or cause to flow accidentally from a container 2 *vi* come out of a confined space in large numbers or quantities ○ *The fans spilled onto the pitch.* 3 *vti* fall or cause to fall off a horse or bike (*infml*) ■ *n* 1 a fall from a horse or bike (*infml*) 2 something that flows accidentally from a container ○ *working to contain the spill* —**spiller** *n*

spill[2] *n* a splinter or twist of paper used to light something

spillage /spĭllij/ *n* 1 the spilling of something 2 a quantity spilled

spin *v* (**spinning, spun**) 1 *vti* rotate or turn around quickly 2 *vti* create thread or yarn from raw materials 3 *vti* make a web or cocoon 4 *vt* tell an improbable story as though it were true 5 *vti* present information in the best possible light 6 *vti* go or cause to go into a deep spiral dive (*refers to aircraft*) 7 *vi* become dizzy ○ *My head was spinning.* 8 *vti* remove water, especially from washed clothes, by spinning in a machine ■ *n* 1 a quick rotating movement 2 a spiralling dive by an aircraft 3 a dizzy state 4 favourable bias or distortion in presenting information 5 a short journey taken for pleasure in a vehicle (*infml*) —**spinner** *n*

□ **spin out** *vt* 1 prolong something 2 make supplies last by careful management

spina bifida /spīnə bĭfidə, -bīfidə/ *n* a condition in which part of the spinal cord or surrounding membrane protrudes through a cleft in the spinal column

spinach /spĭnich/ *n* a plant with edible leaves. Use: cooked vegetable, raw in salads.

spinal /spīn'l/ *adj* of the spinal column

spinal column *n* the interconnected bones of a vertebrate animal's back

spinal cord *n* a thick cord of nerve tissue extending from the bottom of the brain and down the spinal column

spindle /spĭnd'l/ *n* 1 a handheld rod for spinning thread 2 a mechanical thread-spinning device 3 a rotating rod for operating a device

spindly /spĭndli/ (**-dlier, -dliest**), **spindling** /spĭndling/ *adj* long or tall and thin

spin doctor *n* somebody who imparts a favourable bias to information given to the public or media (*infml*)

spindrift /spĭn drift/ *n* spray from waves

spin-dryer, spin-drier *n* a machine for removing water from wet laundry by spinning it

spine n 1 the spinal column 2 the vertical back of a book's cover 3 a hard sharp projection on an animal or a plant

spineless /spínləss/ adj 1 weak and cowardly 2 without a spine —**spinelessly** adv —**spinelessness** n ◊ See note at **cowardly**

spinet /spi nét/ n a small harpsichord with strings set at a slant to the keyboard

spine-tingling adj frightening or exciting —**spine-tinglingly** adv

spinnaker /spínnəkər/ n a large triangular sail at the front of a yacht

spinneret /spínnə ret/ n a spider's silk-producing organ

spinney /spínni/ (pl **-neys**) n a small thicket

spinning jenny /-jénni/ n an early spinning machine with more than one spindle

spinning wheel n a domestic device for spinning yarn by means of a large wheel driven by hand or a treadle

spin-off n 1 a product, material, or service derived incidentally from something else 2 a subsidiary that is divested by distributing shares to shareholders of the parent company

Spinoza /spi nṓzə/, **Baruch** (1632–77) Dutch philosopher

spinster /spínstər/ n an offensive term for a woman who has remained unmarried beyond the usual age (dated)

ORIGIN A **spinster** was originally a woman who made her livelihood by spinning yarn.

---

spiny /spíni/ (**-ier**, **-iest**) adj with spines or thorns —**spininess** n

spiracle /spírək'l/ n 1 a blowhole of a whale, dolphin, or similar sea mammal (technical) 2 a small aperture for breathing, e.g. in an insect's side

spiral /spírəl/ n 1 a flat curve or series of curves that constantly increase or decrease in size in circling around a central point 2 a helix 3 something with the shape of a spiral or helix ■ adj of or with the shape of a spiral or helix ■ v (**-ralling**, **-ralled**) 1 vti shape or be shaped like a spiral 2 vti move in a spiral 3 vi change with ever increasing speed —**spiroid** adj

spiral staircase n a staircase that winds round a central axis

spire[1] n 1 a narrow tapering structure topping a roof, tower, or steeple, or a tower or steeple with one 2 a slender, upward-pointing part of a plant

spire[2] n 1 a spiral or coil 2 a convolution of a spiral or coil

spirit /spírrit/ n 1 a vital force that characterizes a human being 2 a person's will or sense of self 3 enthusiasm and energy for living 4 a person's disposition 5 the attitude or state of mind of a person or group 6 the intention behind something rather than its literal meaning 7 a supernatural being without a physical body 8 **Spirit** in Christianity, the Holy Spirit 9 a strong alcoholic drink made by distillation (often pl) ■ **spirits** npl mood ■ vt remove secretly or mysteriously ◊ **in high spirits** happy

spirited /spírritid/ adj 1 lively 2 behaving in a particular way (usually in combination) ○ mean-spirited —**spiritedly** adv —**spiritedness** n

spirit lamp n a lamp that burns alcohol

spiritless /spírritləss/ adj lacking in courage or energy

spirit level n an instrument placed on a surface to determine if it is level

spiritual /spírrichoo əl/ adj 1 of the soul or spirit 2 of religion or sacred things ■ n a religious song arising from African American culture —**spirituality** /spírrityoo álləti/ n —**spiritually** adv —**spiritualness** n

spiritualism /spírrichoo ə lizəm/ n belief in the possibility of communication with dead people, especially through a medium —**spiritualist** /spírrichoò ə list/ n

spit[1] v (**spitting**, **spat** or **spit**) 1 vi eject saliva from the mouth 2 vt expel from the mouth 3 vi make a sputtering or hissing sound 4 vi rain lightly ■ n 1 saliva ejected from the mouth 2 an expulsion of something from the mouth ◊ **spit it out** say something at once (infml; usually a command)

spit[2] n 1 a thin rod on which meat is impaled for roasting 2 an elongated point of land projecting from a shore ■ vt (**spitting**, **spitted**) impale on a spit

spite n petty ill will ■ vt (**spiting**, **spited**) act maliciously towards ◊ **in spite of** notwithstanding, or without taking account of

spiteful /spítf'l/ adj vindictive in a petty way —**spitefully** adv —**spitefulness** n

spitfire /spít fīr/ n somebody excitable and quick-tempered

spitting image n an exact likeness of somebody (infml)

spittle /spítt'l/ n 1 saliva ejected from the mouth 2 something resembling frothy saliva

spittoon /spi toón/ n a receptacle for spittle

spiv n UK an offensive term for a smartly dressed man whose honesty is suspect (slang insult)

splash v 1 vti scatter liquid on something 2 vi be scattered or fly up in drops or larger amounts (refers to liquid) 3 vti move through water, scattering it about 4 vt display prominently ○ splashed it across the front page ■ n 1 a noise of liquid splashing 2 a drop or larger amount of liquid splashed 3 a small patch of colour 4 a tiny amount of liquid (infml) 5 a prominent display ◊ **make a splash** attract a great deal of attention or publicity (infml)

splashback /splásh bak/ n a sheet on a wall to protect it against splashes

splashy /spláshi/ (**-ier**, **-iest**) adj 1 colourful 2 making splashes —**splashiness** n

splat n a wet smacking sound —**splat** adv

splatter /splátter/ vti spatter or splash —**splatter** n

splay vti 1 spread wide and outwards, especially awkwardly 2 have or give slanting sides ■ adj also **splayed** spread flat and outwards

spleen n 1 an organ in the abdomen that helps to destroy old red blood cells, form cells for the immune system, and store blood 2 bad temper —**spleenful** adj

splendid /spléndid/ adj 1 magnificent 2 reflecting light brilliantly 3 excellent —**splendidly** adv —**splendidness** n

splendiferous /splen díffərəss/ adj magnificent (humorous) —**splendiferously** adv

splendour /spléndər/ n 1 magnificence 2 something splendid ○ the splendours of Egypt —**splendorous** adj

splenetic /spli néttik/ adj bad-tempered (literary)

splice /spliss/ vt (**splicing**, **spliced**) join different strands or pieces of a material ■ n a connection made by splicing

spliff n a marijuana cigarette (slang)

splint n 1 a rigid device to immobilize a broken bone 2 a strip of wood used in basketry —**splint** vt

splinter /splíntər/ n a thin sharp fragment ■ vti 1 break into sharp fragments 2 divide into factions —**splintery** adj

splinter group n a group split from another because of a disagreement

split v (**splitting**, **split**) 1 vti divide lengthwise 2 vti burst or rip apart 3 vti separate into parts or factions 4 vt share among a group ○ split the proceeds ■ n 1 a splitting of something 2 a crack or lengthwise break in something 3 a division or separation caused by disagreement 4 a share, especially a share of money (infml) ■ adj 1 broken, cracked, or separated into parts 2 divided because of a disagreement —**splitter** n ◊ See note at **tear**
□ **split up** vi end a relationship

Split port in S Croatia, on the Adriatic Sea. Pop. 189,388 (1991).

split infinitive n a phrase in which 'to' and its verb are separated by another word or words

split-level adj 1 with the floor of a storey on different levels ○ a split-level house 2 describes a cooker with a separate oven and hob —**split-level** n

split pea n a dried pea used in soup

split personality n 1 a psychological disorder in which somebody appears to have two or more different personalities 2 a tendency to mood swings

split screen n a television or cinema screen divided into more than one image

split second n a very short time

split shift n a single work period divided into two or more sessions with a long break between them

splitting /splítting/ adj very painful ○ a splitting headache

split-up n a separation and ending of a relationship

splodge, splotch n a large irregular patch —**splodge** vt

splosh vi make or move with a splashing sound —**splosh** n

splurge (**splurging**, **splurged**) v 1 vi indulge in something extravagant or expensive (infml) 2 vt spend money extravagantly

splutter /splútter/ v 1 vi make a spitting or choking sound 2 vti say something incoherently —**splutter** n —**spluttering** n, adj

Dr Spock

Spock, Dr (1903–98) US paediatrician and political activist

spoil v (**spoiled** or **spoilt**) 1 vt impair, damage, or ruin 2 vt harm the character of by overindulgence 3 vt treat indulgently 4 vi become rotten ■ **spoils** npl property seized by a victor ◊ **be spoiling for** be eager for

spoilage /spóylij/ n 1 the process of decaying or becoming damaged, or the resulting condition 2 waste arising from decay or damage

spoiled, spoilt adj 1 ruined by decay or damage 2 wilful or selfish because of having been overindulged

spoiler /spóylər/ n 1 a device on the back of an car to deflect air and keep its wheels on the ground 2 somebody or something that can ruin another's success

spoilsport /spóyl spawrt/ n somebody who spoils others' fun

Spokane /spō kán/ city in E Washington State, on the Spokane River. Pop. 184,058 (1998).

spoke[1] n 1 a supporting rod extending from the hub of a wheel to its rim 2 a rung of a ladder

spoke[2] past tense of **speak**

spoken /spṓkən/ past participle of **speak** ■ adj 1 expressed with the voice 2 speaking in a particular way (in combination) ◊ **spoken for** 1 already owned or reserved by somebody 2 already married, engaged, or romantically committed (dated) ◊ See note at **verbal**

spokesman /spṓksmən/ (pl **-men** /-mən/) n somebody speaking on behalf of another or others

spokesperson /spṓks purss'n/ n somebody speaking on behalf of another or others

spokeswoman /spṓks wŏŏmən/ (pl **-women** /-wimin/) n a woman speaking on behalf of another or others

spoliation /spṓli áysh'n/ n the seizing or plundering of things by force

sponge /spunj/ n 1 an invertebrate sea animal with a porous fibrous skeleton 2 a lightweight absorbent piece of a sponge's skeleton, or a piece of synthetic material resembling this. Use: washing, cleaning. ■ v (**sponging**, **sponged**) 1 vt clean or remove with a sponge 2 vi live off the generosity of others (infml) —**sponger** n

sponge bag n a bag for toiletries

sponge cake n a light open-textured cake made with flour, eggs, and sugar, and usually without fat

sponge pudding n a light steamed or baked pudding made from a sponge-cake mixture

spongy /spúnji/ (**-ier**, **-iest**) adj 1 open-textured 2 absorbent and elastic —**sponginess** n

~~sponser~~ incorrect spelling of **sponsor**

sponsor /spónssər/ n 1 a contributor to an event's funding 2 a legislator who proposes and supports a bill 3 a person who pledges money to charity on the basis of somebody's performance in a fundraising event 4 a godparent (fml) 5 a radio or television advertiser who pays for programming ■ vt act as a sponsor to ◊ See note at **backer**

ORIGIN A **sponsor** is etymologically, in Latin, 'somebody who makes a solemn promise'. The word was adopted into English in the mid-17C in the sense 'godparent', which had developed during the Christian era.

spontaneous /spon táyni əss/ adj 1 arising from an internal or natural cause 2 arising from impulse or inclination —**spontaneity** /spóntə neé əti, -náy-/ n —**spontaneously** adv

spontaneous combustion n ignition caused by internal heat generation

~~spontanious~~ incorrect spelling of **spontaneous**

spoof n 1 a good-humoured hoax 2 an amusing satire —**spoof** vt

ORIGIN Spoof was invented by the British comedian Arthur Roberts (1852–1933) as the name of a game of his creation that involved hoaxing. It was first mentioned in print in 1884.

spook n a ghost (infml) ■ vt 1 haunt as a ghost 2 US, Can startle

spooky /spooki/ (**-ier**, **-iest**) adj (infml) 1 scarily suggestive of the supernatural 2 strange or amazing —**spookily** adv —**spookiness** n

spool n 1 a cylinder on which something is wound 2 an amount on a spool ■ v 1 vti wind something on a spool 2 vi transfer computer data to a memory store for printing later

spoon n 1 an eating utensil consisting of a shallow oval bowl attached to a handle 2 a shiny fishing lure ■ vt eat or transfer using a spoon —**spoonful** n

spoonbill /spoon bil/ n a tropical wading bird with a long flat bill

spoonerism /spoonərizəm/ n an accidental verbal error in which the initial sounds of words are transposed

ORIGIN The **spoonerism** is named after the

British educationalist Rev. William Spooner (1844–1930), who was known for such slips.

spoon-feed (**spoon-fed**) vt 1 feed with a spoon 2 provide with everything, so that no independent thought or effort is required

spoor /spoor, spawr/ n an animal's track or trail

Sporades /spórrə deez/ group of Greek islands in the Aegean Sea

sporadic /spə ráddik/ adj occurring at irregular intervals ◊ See note at **periodic**

spore n an asexual reproductive cell in seedless plants, algae, fungi, and some protozoans ■ vi (**sporing**, **spored**) produce spores

sporran /spórrən/ n a pouch worn at the front of a kilt

sport n 1 a competitive physical activity governed by rules, or such activities as a group 2 an active pastime 3 somebody who remains cheerful in losing circumstances (infml) 4 ANZ a form of address used especially between men or boys (infml) ■ v 1 vt wear proudly or flamboyantly (infml) 2 vi play happily (fml) —**sportful** adj

sporting /spáwrting/ adj 1 used in sports 2 in keeping with the principles of fair competition —**sportingly** adv

sporting chance n a fair chance of success

sportive /spáwrtiv/ adj 1 playful 2 done as a joke —**sportively** adv —**sportiveness** n

sports car n a small fast car

sportscast /spáwrts kaast/ n a sports broadcast —**sportscaster** n

sports day n UK, Can a day when schoolchildren have sports events

sports drink n a thirst-quenching drink for use during or after physical exercise

sports jacket n a man's casual jacket worn with nonmatching trousers

sportsman /spáwrtsmən/ (pl **-men** /-mən/) n 1 a man engaging in sport 2 somebody fair and honourable —**sportsmanlike** adj

sportsmanship /spáwrtsmən ship/ n 1 fair and honourable conduct 2 participation in sports

sportsperson /spáwrts purss'n/ n a person engaging in sport

sports supplement n a dietary supplement to enhance physical performance

sportswear /spáwrts wair/ n clothes for sport

sportswoman /spáwrts woomən/ (pl **-en** /-wimin/) n 1 a woman engaging in sport 2 a fair and honourable woman

sporty /spáwrti/ (**-ier**, **-iest**) adj 1 for sport 2 enthusiastic about sport 3 similar to a sports car

spot n 1 a distinct small round area on a surface 2 a mark or pimple on the skin 3 a particular place, point, position, or location 4 a small amount 5 an awkward situation (infml) ■ adj made or available immediately ■ v (**spotting**, **spotted**) 1 vt see or detect suddenly 2 vti make or become stained 3 vt mark with dots —**spotted** adj ◊ **hit the spot** be absolutely what is required for total satisfaction (infml) ◊ **in a spot** in a difficult or embarrassing position *(infml)* ◊ **on the spot 1** in the exact place where something is happening **2** immediately **3** in a difficult situation or under pressure

spot check *n* a random inspection —**spot-check** *vt*

spotless /spótləss/ *adj* **1** immaculately clean **2** beyond reproach —**spotlessly** *adv* —**spotlessness** *n*

spotlight /spót līt/ *n* **1** a strong beam of light illuminating a small area, or a lamp producing such a light **2** the focus of attention ■ *vt* (-**lit** /-lit/ *or* -**lighted**) **1** illuminate with a spotlight **2** focus attention on

spot-on *adj* correct or accurate *(infml)*

spot price *n* a current market price

spotted dick *n* a suet pudding containing dried fruit

spotter /spóttər/ *n* **1** somebody watching out for something *(often in combination)* **2** a locater of enemy positions **3** a talent scout

spotty /spótti/ (-**tier**, -**tiest**) *adj* **1** pimply **2** marked with spots —**spottily** *adv* —**spottiness** *n*

spouse /spowss, spowz/ *n* a husband or wife —**spousal** /spówz'l/ *adj* —**spousally** *adv*

spout *vti* **1** discharge or be discharged in a jet or stream **2** talk about something at great length ■ *n* **1** a tube or opening for pouring liquid **2** a stream of liquid

sprain *n* an injury to ligaments ■ *vt* injure the ligaments of

sprang past tense of **spring**

sprat *n* **1** (*pl* **sprats** *or* same) a small edible fish of the herring family **2** a sprat as food

sprawl *vi* **1** sit or lie with arms and legs spread awkwardly **2** extend in a disordered way ■ *n* **1** a sprawling position **2** the unchecked growth of an urban area —**sprawling** *adj*

spray[1] *n* **1** a moving cloud or mist of water or other liquid particles **2** a jet of liquid from an atomizer or pressurized container **3** a container for releasing liquid in a spray ■ *vt* **1** disperse or discharge as a spray **2** apply a spray, e.g. of paint or insecticide, to —**sprayer** *n*

spray[2] *n* **1** a shoot or branch of a plant, with flowers, leaves, or berries on it **2** a flower arrangement

spray can *n* a container of liquid under pressure

spray gun *n* a device with a trigger for applying liquid under pressure

spread /spred/ *v* (**spread**) **1** *vt* open or extend something fully **2** *vti* extend or disperse over a large area **3** *vti* extend over a period of time **4** *vti* extend over a wider range than before **5** *vt* separate things by stretching or pulling **6** *vti* make or become widely known **7** *vt* coat something with a layer of a substance **8** *vti* send or go out in all directions ■ *n* **1** the extension or distribution of something over an area **2** a wide variety of things **3** the limit of extension of something **4** the distance or range between two points or things **5** a bed

or table cover **6** a food for spreading on bread or crackers **7** a pair of facing pages of a newspaper, magazine, or book **8** a large meal laid out on a table *(infml)* —**spreadable** *adj* —**spreader** *n*

spread betting *n* betting on the movement of a stock price in relation to a given range of high and low values

spread eagle *n* **1** the image of an eagle with its wings and legs outstretched **2** a way of standing or lying that resembles this —**spread-eagle** *v*, *vti* —**spread-eagled** *adj*

spreadsheet /spréd sheet/ *n* **1** a computer program for numerical or other data in cells forming rows and columns **2** a display or printout of a spreadsheet

spree *n* a period of extravagant or self-indulgent activity

sprig *n* a small shoot or twig from a plant

sprightly /sprítli/ (-**tier**, -**tiest**) *adj* light and vigorous —**sprightliness**, *n*

spring *v* (**sprang**, **sprung**) **1** *vi* move suddenly, especially upwards or forwards, in a single movement **2** *vt* leap over **3** *vi* rapidly resume an original position ◊ *branches springing back* **4** *vi* appear or emerge rapidly or suddenly **5** *vi* originate from a particular source **6** *vt* operate by releasing a mechanism **7** *vi* Aus, US, Can pay for *(slang)* ◊ *I'll spring for lunch.* ■ *n* **1** a coil of metal that can regain its shape after pressure **2** the ability to regain an original position or shape **3** an onward or upward leap **4** a stream of water emerging from underground **5** the season of the year between winter and summer

springboard /spríng bawrd/ *n* **1** a flexible diving board **2** a flexible board on which gymnasts jump before vaulting

springbok /spríng bok/ *n* **1** (*pl* same *or* **springboks**) a small gazelle that can leap high in the air **2** a member of the South African national rugby team

spring-clean *vti* clean a house or room thoroughly at the end of winter —**spring-clean** *n* —**spring-cleaning** *n*

springer /spríngər/, **springer spaniel** *n* a small spaniel with a long wavy coat and floppy ears

spring fever *n* feelings of restlessness or longing aroused by springtime

Springfield /spríng feeld/ capital of Illinois. Pop. 117,098 (1998).

spring-loaded *adj* fixed in place or controlled by a spring

spring onion *n* a young onion with a small white bulb and a long green shoot

spring roll *n* a snack or starter consisting of minced vegetables and meat wrapped in a pancake and fried

spring tide *n* a tide with a greater than average range that occurs near the times of the new moon and full moon

springtime /spríng tīm/ *n* the season of spring

springy /spríngi/ (-**ier**, -**iest**) *adj* returning

readily to shape after pressure —**springily** *adv* —**springiness** *n*

sprinkle /spríngk'l/ (-**kling**, -**kled**) *vt* **1** scatter small drops or particles over a surface **2** scatter or be scattered randomly among other things ○ *hedgerows sprinkled with poppies*

sprinkler /spríngklər/ *n* **1** a device for sending out a spray of water **2** a perforated nozzle for fitting onto a watering can or hose

sprinkling /spríngkling/ *n* a small amount scattered or distributed thinly

sprint *n* **1** a short race at high speed **2** a fast finishing run at the end of a longer race ■ *vi* go at top speed —**sprinter** *n*

sprite *n* **1** a supernatural being like an elf or fairy **2** a ghost or spirit

spritz *vt* spray through a nozzle —**spritz** *n*

spritzer /sprítsər/ *n* a drink of wine and effervescent water or lemonade

sprocket /sprókit/ *n* **1** a tooth on a wheel **2** *also* **sprocket wheel** a wheel with sprockets that engage with perforations on film or the links of a chain

sprout *n* **1** *vti* develop buds or shoots **2** *vi* begin to grow from a seed ■ *n* **1** a new growth on a plant **2** a Brussels sprout

spruce[1] (*pl* **spruces** *or* **same**) *n* **1** an evergreen tree of the pine family **2** the soft light wood of a spruce tree

---

ORIGIN No connection is now perceived between **spruce** the tree and **spruce** 'neat and trim', but they may have the same ultimate origin. *Spruce* was an old name for Prussia, and the tree is literally a 'Prussian fir'. **Spruce** 'neat and trim' may be shortened from obsolete *spruce leather*, a leather from Prussia formerly used especially for jerkins.

---

spruce[2] *adj* looking neat and trim ■ *vti* (**sprucing**, **spruced**) make neater or smarter in appearance —**sprucely** *adv*

spruik *vi ANZ* promote in public (*humorous*)

sprung past participle of **spring**

spry /sprī/ (**spryer** *or* **sprier**, **spryest** *or* **spriest**) *adj* agile and energetic —**spryly** *adv* —**spryness** *n*

spud *n* **1** a potato (*infml*) **2** a spade with a sharp narrow blade

spume *n* foam on the surface of a liquid, especially the sea (*literary*) —**spumous** *adj* —**spumy** *adj*

spun past tense, past participle of **spin**

spunk *n* pluckiness (*infml*) —**spunkily** *adv* —**spunky** *adj*

spur *n* **1** a device attached to a rider's heel, used to encourage a horse to go faster **2** an inducement to take action **3** a mountain ridge that projects outwards **4** a short section of railway track off a main line **5** a short road off a major road ■ *vt* (**spurring**, **spurred**) **1** encourage somebody to take action or try harder **2** use spurs on a horse —**spurred** *adj* ◊ **on the spur of the moment** without thinking or making preparations ◊ **win or**

gain your spurs gain recognition and respect for the first time ◊ See note at **motive**

spurious /spyoóri əs/ *adj* not genuine or valid —**spuriously** *adv* —**spuriousness** *n*

spurn *vt* reject with disdain —**spurner** *n*

spur-of-the-moment *adj* done or occurring on impulse

spurt *n* **1** a jet of liquid or gas **2** a sudden increase, e.g. of energy ■ *vti* expel or gush out in a jet

sputnik /spoótnik, spút-/ *n* an Earth-orbiting satellite launched by the former Soviet Union

sputter /spúttər/ *vi* **1** make a popping and spitting sound **2** spit out food and saliva —**sputter** *n*

sputum /spyoótəm/ (*pl* -**ta** /-tə/) *n* a substance that is coughed up, such as phlegm

spy /spī/ *n* (*pl* **spies**) **1** somebody employed by a government to obtain secret information about other countries **2** an employee who obtains information about rival organizations ■ *v* (**spies**, **spied**) **1** *vi* act as a spy **2** *vt* catch sight of

□ **spy out** *vt* discover or examine covertly

spyglass /spī glaass/ *n* a small telescope

spyhole /spī hōl/ *n* a small peephole in a door

spyware /spī wair/ *n* software surreptitiously installed on a hard disk to relay encoded information via an Internet connection

sq. *abbr* square *adj* 3

Sq. *abbr* square *n* 3 (*in addresses*)

SQL *n* a computer language for obtaining information from databases. Full form **structured query language**

squabble /skwóbb'l/ *n* a petty argument —**squabble** *vi*

squad /skwod/ *n* **1** a group of players from which a team is selected **2** a group of police officers **3** a team of people

squad car *n* a police car

squaddie /skwóddi/ *n* an ordinary soldier (*slang*)

squadron /skwóddrən/ *n* **1** a naval unit containing two or more divisions of a fleet **2** an air force unit containing two or more flights

squadron leader *n* in the RAF, a commander of a squadron of military aircraft

squalid /skwóllid/ *adj* **1** neglected and dirty **2** lacking in dignity, honesty, or morals —**squalidly** *adv* —**squalidness** *n* ◊ See note at **dirty**

squall[1] /skwawl/ *n* **1** a sudden windstorm, often with heavy rain or snow **2** a brief but noisy disturbance ■ *vi* blow strongly and suddenly (*refers to winds*) —**squally** *adj*

squall[2] /skwawl/ *vi* yell or cry noisily —**squall** *n*

squalor /skwóllər/ *n* **1** shabbiness and dirtiness **2** moral degradation

squander /skwóndər/ *vt* use wastefully or extravagantly

square /skwair/ *n* **1** a geometric figure with four right angles and four equal sides **2** an object shaped like a square **3** an open space in an urban area where two streets meet **4** the result of multiplying a number or term by

itself ■ *adj* **1** shaped like a square or cube **2** forming a right angle **3** describes a measurement of surface area according to the length of each side of a square ○ *100 square feet* **4** describes a square with sides of a particular length ○ *a room ten feet square* **5** completely fair **6** boring and old-fashioned *(slang dated)* ■ *v* (**squaring, squared**) **1** *vt* make something square **2** *vt* multiply a number by itself **3** *vt* divide something into squares **4** *vt* move something so that it is straight or level **5** *vti* concur or make something agree ○ *does not square with what we know* ■ *adv* **1** at right angles **2** directly *(infml)* —**squareness** *n*
◇ **all square** with all debts and obligations to each other cleared
□ **square off** *vi* take up the position for a fight with fists
□ **square up** *vi* settle debts

square-bashing *n* military drill *(slang)*

square bracket *n* either of the symbols [and], used in pairs for enclosing and separating text

USAGE **Square brackets** are used around text that is added by somebody other than the original writer or speaker, especially to explain or comment on a word or phrase used in a quotation: *He wrote 'As we travelled across Rhodesia [now Zimbabwe] the weather changed for the worse'.* They are also used to provide information needed when a quotation is taken out of its original context: *She said 'I have never seen him [the accused] before'.* The word *sic* (Latin for 'thus'), enclosed in square brackets, indicates that the preceding word, although wrong, is the one actually used: *The notice read 'In case of fire please excite [sic] the building by the nearest door'.*

square dance *n* a country dance in which sets of four couples form squares —**square dancing** *n*

squarely /skwáirli/ *adv* **1** directly and forcefully **2** honestly

square meal *n* a filling and nourishing meal

square-rigged *adj* describes a ship with its principal sails at right angles to its length

square root *n* a number that when multiplied by itself produces the given number

squash[1] /skwosh/ *v* **1** *vt* flatten or crush something with pressure **2** *vti* force your way into or put something into a small space **3** *vt* put down a rebellion ■ *n* **1** a juice-based soft drink **2** the action or noise of squashing **3** a racket game played in a walled court with a hard rubber ball

squash[2] /skwosh/ (*pl same or* **squashes**) *n* **1** a vegetable of the gourd family **2** a plant that produces squashes

squashy /skwóshi/ (**-ier, -iest**) *adj* easily squashed

squat /skwot/ *vi* (**squatting, squatted**) **1** crouch down with the knees bent and the thighs resting on the calves **2** occupy property without a legal claim ■ *adj* (**squatter, squattest**) **1** short and solid **2** in a crouched

posture ■ *n* **1** the action of squatting **2** a squatting position **3** a property occupied by illegal squatters —**squatness** *n*

squatter /skwóttər/ *n* **1** an illegal occupant of property, especially somebody's empty house, or land **2** *Aus* an early Australian settler on grazing land for which a government lease was subsequently granted **3** *Aus* a wealthy landowner **4** *NZ* an early settler in New Zealand who leased government land

squaw *n* an offensive term for a Native North American woman or wife *(dated)*

squawk *vi* utter a loud harsh cry —**squawk** *n*

squeak /skweek/ *v* **1** *vi* make a high-pitched sound or cry **2** *vt* say shrilly **3** *vi* manage something with only a narrow margin *(infml)* —**squeak** *n*

squeaky /skweeki/ (**-ier, -iest**) *adj* **1** tending to squeak **2** designed to make a squeaking noise when pressed —**squeakily** *adv* —**squeakiness** *n*

squeaky-clean *adj* extremely clean

squeal /skweel/ *n* **1** a short shrill cry **2** a loud high sound made by tyres when a vehicle brakes suddenly ■ *v* **1** *vti* give a short high cry, or say in a shrill voice **2** *vi* become an informer *(slang disapproving)* —**squealer** *n*

squeamish /skweémish/ *adj* **1** easily made to feel sick **2** easily offended or disgusted —**squeamishly** *adv* —**squeamishness** *n*

squeegee /skweé jee/ *n* a T-shaped implement edged with plastic or rubber, used in cleaning windows to remove water from the surface

squeeze *v* (**squeezing, squeezed**) **1** *vt* press something from two sides **2** *vt* press somebody's hand or other part of the body affectionately or reassuringly **3** *vti* exert pressure on something **4** *vt* push a person or object into a gap **5** *vi* push into or through a small space **6** *vt* press fruit to obtain juice **7** *vt* find time for somebody or something in a busy schedule **8** *vi* just manage to do something ○ *squeezed through the exam* ■ *n* **1** a squeezing action **2** something squeezed out **3** a government-imposed restriction on credit and investment in a financial crisis —**squeezable** *adj*

squelch *v* **1** *vi* make a sucking or gurgling sound like that of trampling on muddy ground **2** *vt* crush something by trampling **3** *vt* silence something such as a rumour or an unwanted remark *(slang)* —**squelch** *n* —**squelchy** *adj*

squib *n* **1** a small firework **2** a faulty firework that burns without exploding **3** a short satirical piece

squid (*pl same or* **squids**) *n* **1** an invertebrate sea animal with ten arms and a long tapered body **2** squid as food

squidgy /skwíjji/ (**-gier, -giest**) *adj* **1** soft and damp **2** feeling squashy *(infml)*

squiffy /skwíffi/ (**squiffier, squiffiest**) *adj* slightly drunk *(infml)*

squiggle /skwíggʼl/ n 1 a wavy line or mark 2 an illegible word —**squiggly** adj

squint vi 1 partly close the eyes to see better 2 have eyes that do not look in parallel 3 glance at something sideways ■ n 1 a condition in which the eyes do not look in parallel 2 a quick glimpse (infml) 3 a narrowing of the eyes to see better —**squinty** adj

squire n 1 a rural landowner, especially the main local landowner 2 an attendant to a knight in the Middle Ages 3 a form of address used by one man to another (infml)

squirearchy /skwír aarki/ n the class of landed gentry

squirm /skwurm/ vi 1 wriggle from discomfort 2 feel or show signs of emotional distress and embarrassment —**squirm** n —**squirmer** n —**squirmy** adj

squirrel /skwírrəl/ n a small bushy-tailed rodent that lives in trees ■ vt (-relling, -relled) hoard ◦ squirrelled away some money

squirt /skwurt/ v 1 vti force or spurt out from a narrow opening 2 vt squirt liquid at or over ■ n 1 a small stream of squirted liquid 2 an offensive term for a young or small person (infml insult)

squish v 1 vt squeeze or crush 2 vi make a soft splashing noise ■ n a soft splashing noise —**squishy** adj

Sr[1] symbol strontium

Sr[2] abbr 1 senior 2 señor 3 signor 4 sister

SRAM abbr static random access memory

Sravana /sráavənə/ n the 5th month of the year in the Hindu calendar

Srebrenica /srébbrə neétsə/ town in E Bosnia-Herzegovina. Pop. 37,211 (1991).

Sri /sree/ n 1 S Asia a title for a man, equivalent to 'Mr' 2 in Hinduism, a title for a god or holy man

Sri Lanka /sri lángkə/ island country in South Asia, off the tip of SE India. Cap. Colombo. Pop. 19,408,635 (2001). —**Sri Lankan** n, adj

SS[1] abbr 1 Saints 2 Social Security 3 steamship

SS[2] n a Nazi paramilitary force acting as Hitler's bodyguard

SSSI /tríp'l ess í/ abbr site of special scientific interest

St for saints, see under first name ■ abbr 1 Saint. See also under **Saint** 2 Strait 3 Street (in addresses)

stab v (stabbing, stabbed) 1 vt thrust a knife or other sharp pointed instrument into 2 vti jab a finger or object at something or somebody 3 vi hurt suddenly and sharply ■ n 1 an act of stabbing ◦ a stab wound 2 a sudden brief painful feeling 3 an attempt (infml) —**stabbing** adj

~~stabalize~~ incorrect spelling of **stabilize**

stability /stə bílləti/ n the state or quality of being stable

stabilize /stáybi līz/ (-lizing, -lized), **stabilise** v 1 vti make or become stable 2 vt maintain the level of something —**stabilization** /stàybi līz áysh'n/ n

stabilizer /stáybi līzər/, **stabiliser** n 1 an aerofoil that keeps an aircraft aligned with the direction of flight 2 a pair or set of fins to control a ship's rolling 3 a chemical compound added to another substance to make it resistant to change ■ **stabilizers** npl extra wheels to balance a bicycle while somebody is learning to ride

stable[1] /stáyb'l/ adj 1 steady and not liable to change or move 2 not excitable or liable to mental illness 3 not subject to changes in chemical or physical properties —**stableness** n —**stably** adv

stable[2] /stáyb'l/ n 1 a building in which horses are kept 2 a group of horses owned by one person or kept or trained together ■ vti (stabling, stabled) put, keep, or live in a stable

stable boy n a youth or man working in a racing stable

stable door n a door with separate upper and lower sections

stable girl n a girl or woman working in a racing stable

stablemate /stáyb'l mayt/ n 1 a horse from the same racing stable as another 2 a person associated with another

~~stablize~~ incorrect spelling of **stabilize**

staccato /stə kaatō/ adv in quick separate notes (musical direction) —**staccato** adj, n

stack n 1 a pile of things arranged one on top of another 2 a large pile of hay, straw, or grain stored outdoors 3 a tall chimney or group of chimneys 4 a large number or amount (infml) ◦ stacks of money 5 a number of aircraft waiting a turn to land ■ **stacks** npl an area of book storage in a library that is not usually open to the public ■ v 1 vti put or be arranged in a stack 2 vt load or heap with objects —**stackable** adj ◇ **be stacked against** amount to an unfair disadvantage for

☐ **stack up** vi 1 make sense (usually with negatives) 2 Aus, US add up to a total

stacked adj dishonestly arranged

stadium /stáydi əm/ (pl **-ums** or **-a** /-di ə/) n an arena, usually open, with tiered seats for spectators of sports or other activities

Staël /staal/, **Madame de** (1766–1817) French writer

staff n 1 the people who work for an employer or in a particular section of an organization 2 the teachers in a school or other educational institution as opposed to the students 3 a group of officers assisting a military commander 4 Malaysia, Singapore a member of staff 5 (pl **staffs** or **staves**) a large heavy stick 6 (pl **staffs** or **staves**) a pole on which a flag is flown 7 a set of five horizontal lines for writing music ■ vt provide with employees

staff nurse n a fully qualified hospital nurse

staff officer n a military officer aiding a commander or working as a planner or adviser at headquarters

Staffordshire /stáffərdshər/ county in central England

staff sergeant *n* a noncommissioned officer of a rank above a sergeant

stag *n* a mature male deer

stage *n* **1** a period or step during a process **2** the area in a theatre where the action takes place **3** a platform where speeches are made or ceremonies performed **4** the profession of actors **5** a division of a journey or route ■ *vt* (**staging, staged**) **1** organize or carry out something, e.g. a show or a protest **2** set a play in a particular place or time —**stageable** *adj* ◇ **take centre stage** draw people's attention

stagecoach /stáyj kōch/ *n* a large horse-drawn coach

stagecraft /stáyj kraaft/ *n* the technique or art of putting on plays

stage direction *n* an instruction directing an actor in the script of a play

stage door *n* an outside door into the backstage part of a theatre

stage fright *n* fear of performing for an audience

stagehand /stáyj hand/ *n* a helper on a stage set

stage left *n* the side of a stage on the actor's left

stage-manage *v* **1** *vt* tightly control every aspect of an event **2** *vti* serve as stage manager for a play —**stage-management** *n*

stage manager *n* somebody who manages backstage activities in a theatre

stage right *n* the side of a stage on the actor's right

stage-struck *adj* loving the theatre and desperately wanting to be involved in it, especially as a performer

stage whisper *n* a loud whisper

stagey *adj* = stagy

stagflation /stag fláysh'n/ *n* a period of inflation and little growth in an economy —**stagflationary** *adj*

stagger /stággər/ *v* **1** *vi* move unsteadily, nearly falling **2** *vt* make a person or animal stumble **3** *vt* astonish or shock somebody **4** *vt* arrange activities for separate or partly overlapping times **5** *vt* arrange things so that they do not form a straight line *(often passive)* —**stagger** *n* —**staggered** *adj* —**staggerer** *n*

staggering /stággəring/ *adj* amazing —**staggeringly** *adv*

staging /stáyjing/ *n* **1** the process or technique of presenting a stage play **2** a structure of scaffolding for a building

staging area *n* a place for assembling a military force

staging post *n* a place where travellers stop briefly

stagnant /stágnənt/ *adj* **1** still and not flowing **2** foul or stale from lack of motion **3** not developing or making progress —**stagnancy** *n* —**stagnantly** *adv*

stagnate /stag náyt/ (**-nating, -nated**) *vi* **1** stop flowing or moving **2** become foul or stale from lack of motion **3** fail to develop or make progress —**stagnation** *n*

stag night, stag party *n* a men-only social occasion, especially for a man about to be married *(infml)*

stagy /stáyji/ (**-ier, -iest**), **stagey** *adj* exaggerated or artificial in manner, as if in a play *(disapproving)* —**staginess** *n*

staid /stayd/ *adj* sedate and settled in habits or temperament —**staidly** *adv* —**staidness** *n*

stain *n* **1** a discoloured patch **2** a colour finish for wood **3** a dye used to colour microscopic specimens **4** something that detracts from a person's good reputation ■ *v* **1** *vti* leave a discoloured mark on something **2** *vt* finish or dye with a stain **3** *vt* disgrace or detract from —**stainless** *adj*

stained glass *n* coloured glass often used in windows

stainless steel *n* corrosion-resistant steel containing chromium

stair /stair/ *n* **1** a single step in a series leading from one floor or level to another **2** a series of stairs ■ **stairs** *npl* a set or several sets of stairs

> **SPELLCHECK** Do not confuse the spelling of **stair** and **stare** ('look fixedly'), which sound similar.

staircase /stáir kayss/ *n* a flight of stairs inside a building

stairway /stáir way/ *n* a passageway between floors or levels that contains stairs

stairwell /stáir wel/ *n* a vertical shaft for a staircase

stake[1] /stayk/ *n* **1** a thin pointed post driven into the ground **2** a former method of execution in which somebody was tied to a post and burnt ■ *vt* (**staking, staked**) **1** support or strengthen with a stake **2** tie or tether to a stake **3** mark or fence with stakes **4** assert rights over

> **SPELLCHECK** Do not confuse the spelling of **stake** and **steak** ('a thick cut of meat or fish'), which sound similar.

☐ **stake out** *vt* **1** watch continuously from a hiding place *(infml)* **2** establish the boundaries of

stake[2] /stayk/ *n* **1** an amount of money risked in gambling **2** a share or interest in something ■ **stakes** *npl* **1** the degree of risk in a situation **2** the prize or winnings available ■ *vt* (**staking, staked**) **1** wager **2** put down as an investment in something ◇ **at stake** at risk of being lost

ORIGIN The origin of **stake** 'money risked' is not certain, but it may be a use of **stake** 'post', deriving from a supposed former custom of putting whatever was wagered (for example your shirt) on a post before the start of the contest being bet on. It is first recorded in the mid-16C. **Stake** meaning 'post' is from an ancient Germanic root.

stakeholder /stáyk hōldər/ n a person or group with a direct interest or investment in something —**stakeholding** n

stakeholder pension n a UK pension administered by the private sector but regulated by government

stakeout /stáyk owt/ n hidden surveillance, especially by the police (infml)

stalactite /stállək tīt/ n a conical limestone pillar hanging in a cave —**stalactitic** /stállək títtik/ adj

ORIGIN Stalactite is formed from a Greek word meaning 'dripping'. Its companion stalagmite is based on a related Greek word meaning 'dropping'. Both were taken from modern Latin in the late 17C.

stalagmite /stálləg mīt/ n a conical limestone pillar rising from a cave floor —**stalagmitic** /stálləg míttik/ adj

stale (**staler, stalest**) adj 1 no longer fresh 2 frequently heard and boring —**stale** vti

stalemate /stáyl mayt/ n 1 a situation in which no side can take any further effective action 2 a chess situation with no winner because neither player can move without being in check —**stalemate** vt

Joseph Stalin

Stalin /stáalin/, **Joseph** (1879–1953) Georgian-born general secretary of the Communist Party of the USSR (1922–53)

Stalingrad /stáalin grad/ former name for **Volgograd**

Stalinism /stáalinizəm/ n the political and economic theories of Stalin, developed from Marxism-Leninism —**Stalinist** n, adj

stalk[1] /stawk/ n 1 a fleshy main stem of a plant, or a part that supports a leaf or flower 2 a slender supporting part of an object

stalk[2] /stawk/ v 1 vt follow stealthily 2 vi walk stiffly and angrily 3 vi proceed steadily and malevolently 4 vt harass with persistent and inappropriate attention —**stalk** n —**stalker** n

stalking horse n 1 a means to disguise an objective 2 a candidate whose motive is to conceal somebody else's candidacy or to divide or assess the opposition

stall[1] /stawl/ n 1 a booth, counter, or other small structure set up to sell goods or dispense information 2 a compartment in a building for a large animal 3 a situation in which an engine stops abruptly in an undesired way 4 a small room or partitioned space for a shower or toilet 5 a sudden dive by an aircraft 6 a pew or enclosed seat in a church 7 a protective sheath for a finger or thumb ■ **stalls** npl the seats closest to the stage in a theatre ■ vti 1 stop suddenly, or make an engine stop suddenly, in an undesired way 2 go into a dive, or cause an aircraft to go into a dive

stall[2] /stawl/ vti delay somebody with hesitation, evasion, or obstruction, or use delaying tactics —**stall** n

stallholder /stáwl hōldər/ n a person who has a stall at a market or fair

stallion /stállyən/ n an uncastrated male horse

stalwart /stáwlwərt/ adj 1 dependable and loyal 2 sturdy and strong ■ n a hard-working loyal supporter —**stalwartly** adv —**stalwartness** n

stamen /stáy men, -mən/ (pl -**mens** or -**mina** /stámminə/) n the male reproductive organ of a flower —**staminal** /stámmin'l/ adj

Stamford /stámfərd/ market town in E England. Pop. 17,492 (1991).

stamina /stámminə/ n resilient energy and strength —**staminal** adj

stammer /stámmər/ vti speak or say with hesitations and repetitions ■ n a speech condition that makes somebody stammer —**stammerer** n

stamp n 1 a small piece of gummed paper showing payment for postage or official acknowledgment 2 a small block for printing a design 3 a design printed onto paper with a stamp 4 a characteristic or distinguishing sign 5 the banging down of a foot ■ v 1 vt stick or press a stamp on something 2 vti bang a foot down 3 vi walk forcefully 4 vt have a lasting effect on somebody —**stamped** adj

□ **stamp out** vt 1 eradicate 2 extinguish 3 cut out using a sharp tool

Stamp Act n a British law of 1765 taxing legal documents and some printed material in the North American colonies

stamp collecting n the collecting of postage stamps as a hobby —**stamp collector** n

stamp duty n a duty on some legal documents

stampede /stam peéd/ n 1 a headlong rush, especially of animals 2 a sudden rush of people to do something ■ v(-peding, -peded) 1 vti rush forwards in a frightened headlong surge, or make animals or people do this 2 vt force somebody into doing something prematurely or ill-advisedly

stamping ground n a habitual haunt or gathering place (infml)

stance /stanss, staanss/ n 1 an attitude towards something 2 a way of standing

stanch vt = **staunch**[1]

stanchion /stáanchən/ n an upright supporting pole

stand v (**stood** /stood/) 1 vti be or set upright 2 vi get up onto the feet from a sitting or lying posture 3 vi be situated in a particular place

4 *vi* be in a particular state ○ *stands in need of renovation* **5** *vi* remain motionless or unused **6** *vi* remain valid or in existence **7** *vt* tolerate **8** *vt* undergo without harm or damage **9** *vt* submit or be subjected to ○ *stand trial* **10** *vi* be a candidate **11** *vt* pay for something for somebody else ○ *stood them all a drink* ■ *n* **1** the action or a period of standing **2** an attitude towards something **3** a supporting structure **4** a piece of furniture on which things are hung or in which things are held upright *(often in combination)* ○ *an umbrella stand* **5** a large seating area for spectators **6** a booth or stall where something is sold, distributed, or exhibited *(often in combination)* ○ *a refreshment stand* —**standee** /stan deé/ *n*

□ **stand by** *v* **1** *vi* remain ready to act **2** *vi* be present without taking part **3** *vt* support or remain faithful to

□ **stand down** *vi* **1** resign **2** end your testimony in court

□ **stand for** *vt* **1** mean or represent **2** believe in and fight for **3** put up with

□ **stand in** *vi* act as a substitute

□ **stand out** *vi* **1** be conspicuous **2** project or protrude

□ **stand up** *v* **1** *vti* rise to or put in an upright position **2** *vi* resist scrutiny ○ *evidence that won't stand up in court*

□ **stand up for** *vt* defend the interests of

□ **stand up to** *vt* **1** resist or refuse to be cowed by **2** endure without being badly affected ○ *won't stand up to that kind of treatment*

stand-alone *adj* operating independently of a computer network or system

standard /stándərd/ *n* **1** a level of quality, excellence, or achievement **2** a flag with an emblematic design **3** an authorized model or specification by which things are measured or judged **4** an upright pole or post ■ *adj* **1** constituting or not differing from the norm **2** widely used and respected **3** regarded as linguistically correct ■ **standards** *npl* principles governing behaviour —**standardly** *adv*

standard assessment task *n* a progress test for UK schoolchildren

standard-bearer *n* **1** somebody who carries a standard or flag **2** a leader or inspiring representative or advocate of something

standard deviation *n* a statistical measure of the amount by which a set of values differs from the arithmetical mean

standardize /stándər dīz/ (**-izing**, **-ized**), **standardise** *v* **1** *vti* conform or cause to conform to a standard **2** *vt* assess by comparison with a standard —**standardization** /stándər dī záysh'n/ *n*

standard lamp *n* a tall lamp that stands on the floor

standard of living *n* a level of material comfort experienced by a person or group

stand-by *n* **1** a person or thing that can be relied on or is available as a substitute or in an emergency **2** an unreserved travel ticket,

or a passenger having no prior reservation ■ *adj* **1** able to be used as a substitute or in an emergency **2** describes a ticket that is unreserved and subject to availability, or a person using such a ticket ■ *adv* on a stand-by basis

stand-down *n* a return to normal after an alert or a military presence

stand-in *n* **1** a temporary replacement **2** a film actor's double —**stand-in** *adj*

standing /stánding/ *n* **1** somebody's status and reputation **2** the duration of something ■ *adj* **1** performed while upright **2** permanently in existence or effect **3** not flowing

standing army *n* a professional military force maintained in times of peace as well as war

standing committee *n* a permanent committee for dealing with a particular issue

standing order *n* **1** an instruction to a bank to make a regular payment from an account **2** an order or rule that remains in force on all relevant occasions until it is specifically revoked

standing room *n* space for people to stand but not sit

standing stone *n* a large stone set upright in the ground in prehistoric times

standoff /stánd of/ *n* a deadlock

standoffish /stand óffish/ *adj* aloof or uncommunicative —**standoffishly** *adv* —**standoffishness** *n*

standpipe /stánd pīp/ *n* **1** a pipe with a tap in the street, for emergency water supply **2** a vertical open-ended pipe attached to a pipeline to regulate pressure

standpoint /stánd poynt/ *n* a point of view

standstill /stánd stil/ *n* a complete halt

standup /stánd up/ *adj* **1** erect and not folded down **2** at which people stand, especially to eat or drink ○ *a standup buffet* **3** noisy and intense ○ *a standup fight* **4** performing or performed by standing alone on stage and telling jokes ○ *standup comedy* ■ *n* standup comedy or a standup comedian

stank past tense of **stink**

Stanley[1] /stánli/ town in N England. Pop. 18,905 (1991).

Stanley[2] capital of the Falkland Islands. Pop. 1,232 (1986).

Stanley, Sir H. M. (1841–1904) British journalist and explorer

Stanley knife *tdmk* a trademark for a knife with a sharp retractable blade

stanza /stánzə/ *n* a group of lines forming a division of a poem —**stanzaic** /stan záy ik/ *adj*

stapes /stáy peez/ (*pl same or* **-pedes** /-peédeez/) *n* a stirrup-shaped bone in the middle ear —**stapedial** /stə peédi əl/ *adj*

staple[1] /stáyp'l/ *n* **1** a small thin piece of bent wire used to fasten papers and sheets of other thin materials together **2** a U-shaped piece of strong metal wire with two sharp points, driven into wood or masonry to fasten something ■ *vt* fasten with a staple or staples

staple[2] /stáyp'l/ *n* **1** the most important article of trade **2** a basic ingredient of a diet **3** a principal or recurring element or feature **4** wool, cotton, or flax fibre graded according to length and fineness —**staple** *adj*

staple gun *n* a powerful device used to drive staples into wood or masonry

stapler /stáyplər/ *n* a device for stapling papers together

star *n* **1** an astronomical object visible as a point of light in the night sky **2** a shape with four or more triangular points radiating from a centre **3** an asterisk **4** a very famous or successful performer **5** an especially important or proficient person ■ *v* (**starring, starred**) **1** *vt* have as a leading actor **2** *vi* be a leading performer in something such as a film or show **3** *vt* mark with an asterisk ■ *adj* very important or successful ◊ **see stars** see flashes of light after receiving a hard blow to the head

starboard /staárbərd/ *n* the right-hand side of somebody facing the front of a ship or aircraft —**starboard** *adj, adv*

ORIGIN **Starboard** has no connection with the stars. *Star-* represents a form related to *steer* and meaning 'paddle'. The name derives from the ancient custom of steering boats by means of a paddle on the right-hand side.

starburst /staár burst/ *n* a radiating pattern of lines or light

starch *n* **1** a natural carbohydrate substance made by plants. Use: food, production of alcohol. **2** a white powder extracted from potatoes and grain. Use: stiffening fabric. ■ *vt* stiffen fabric with starch

star chamber *n* a harsh and arbitrary tribunal

starchy /staárchi/ (**-ier, -iest**) *adj* **1** of or containing starch **2** formal and appearing to lack warmth and humour —**starchiness** *n*

star-crossed *adj* believed to be destined to be unhappy

stardom /staárdəm/ *n* star status in sport or entertainment

stardust /staár dust/ *n* a magical or dreamy quality or feeling, or the imaginary substance supposed to induce this

stare /stair/ *vi* (**staring, stared**) **1** look directly and fixedly **2** be wide open with shock or amazement (*refers to eyes*) ■ *n* **1** a long concentrated look **2** a facial expression with the eyes wide open ◊ See note at **stair, gaze**

starfish /staár fish/ (*pl same or* **-fishes**) *n* a star-shaped invertebrate sea animal

star fruit *n* a yellow tropical fruit with a star-shaped cross section

stargazer /staár gayzər/ *n* a daydreamer

stark *adj* **1** forbiddingly bare and plain **2** presented in unambiguous and harsh terms **3** complete or utter ■ *adv* utterly —**starkly** *adv* —**starkness** *n*

Dame Freya Stark

Stark, Dame Freya (1893–1993) British writer

starkers /staárkərz/ *adj* completely unclothed (*infml*)

starlet /staárlət/ *n* a young woman actor seen as a possible future star

starlight /staár līt/ *n* light from the stars

starling /staárling/ *n* a common bird with glossy greenish-black plumage

starlit /staár lit/ *adj* lit by starlight

Star of David *n* a six-pointed star formed by two equilateral triangles superimposed on each other, used as a symbol of Judaism and the state of Israel

starry /staári/ (**-rier, -riest**) *adj* **1** with many stars shining **2** covered or decorated with stars

starry-eyed *adj* naively idealistic

Stars and Stripes *n* the national flag of the United States (*+ sing or pl verb*)

star sign *n* a sign of the zodiac

Star-Spangled Banner *n* **1** the national anthem of the United States **2** the Stars and Stripes

starstruck /staár struk/, **star-struck** *adj* fascinated by stars of the entertainment world and by stardom

star-studded *adj* with many film or stage stars

start *v* **1** *vti* do something that was not being done before ○ *started work* ○ *started to laugh* **2** *vti* come or bring into being, or get under way ○ *starts at one o'clock* ○ *starting a new business* **3** *vti* begin working, or make an engine begin to work **4** *vi* make a sudden or involuntary movement **5** *vi* begin at a particular level ○ *Prices start at £15.* ■ *n* **1** the first part of something that proceeds through time **2** the place or time at which something starts **3** a quick sudden or involuntary movement **4** a position ahead of others **5** a set of conditions at the beginning of something ○ *a good start in life*
□ **start off** *v* **1** *vti* begin or cause to begin doing something **2** *vi* begin a journey
□ **start out** *vi* **1** begin a journey or process **2** do or be something at the beginning ○ *started out being friendly*
□ **start up** *vti* begin to operate

START /staart/ *abbr* Strategic Arms Reduction Talks

starter /staártər/ *n* **1** a starting device for an engine **2** somebody signalling the start of a race **3** a competitor who starts in a race **4** a first course of a meal

starter home *n* a small property suitable for a first-time buyer

starting block *n* a support for a runner's feet at the start of a race

starting gate *n* 1 a line of stalls from which horses start a race 2 a set of tapes across the track raised at the start of a horse race

starting grid *n* a pattern of lines marking starting positions on an motor racing track

starting gun *n* a gun fired to start a race

starting line *n* a line on a racetrack behind which runners start

starting price *n* the odds being offered by a bookmaker just before a race

startle /staárt'l/ (**-tling, -tled**) *vt* disconcert or frighten into making an involuntary movement —**startling** *adj* —**startlingly** *adv*

startup /staárt up/ *n* 1 something such as a company that is just beginning operations 2 the beginning of an activity or project —**startup** *adj*

star turn *n* the main item or performer in an entertainment

starvation /staar váysh'n/ *n* severe lack of food or the physical condition caused by this

starve (**starving, starved**) *v* 1 *vti* weaken or die because of hunger, or cause somebody to do this 2 *vi* be very hungry (*infml*) 3 *vt* deprive of something vitally needed 4 *vi Ireland, N England, Scotland* be very cold

starveling /staárvling/ *n* a very thin person (*archaic*)

stash *n* a hidden store or supply (*infml*) —**stash** *vt*

stasis /stáyssiss/ *n* 1 a motionless or unchanging state 2 a stoppage of the flow of body fluids

state *n* 1 a condition that somebody or something is in 2 any form that a physical substance can be in 3 a developmental stage of an animal or plant 4 a country with its own independent government 5 a mostly autonomous region of a federal country 6 a country's government and government-controlled institutions 7 a ceremonious way of doing something 8 a nervous, upset, or excited condition ■ **States** *npl* the United States (*infml*) ■ *adj* 1 of a country's government 2 done with full ceremony ■ *vt* (**stating, stated**) express or announce in words

state benefit *n* money given by government to those with not enough to live on

statecraft /stáyt kraaft/ *n* the art of governing well

statehood /stáyt hood/ *n* the status of a state in a federal union

statehouse /stáyt howss/ (*pl* **-houses** /-howziz/) *n* in the United States, a building in which a state legislature convenes

stateless /stáytləss/ *adj* having no official nationality

stately /stáytli/ (**-lier, -liest**) *adj* 1 impressively weighty and dignified 2 grand and imposing

stately home *n* a large and impressive country house

statement /stáytmənt/ *n* 1 an expression in words of something definite 2 an account of facts relating to a crime or legal case 3 an expression of an idea through a medium other than words 4 a printed record of the transactions relating to an account

Staten Island /státt'n-/ one of the five boroughs of New York City. Pop. 378,977 (1990).

state of affairs *n* a particular set of circumstances

state of concern *n* a rogue state (*fml*)

state of the art *n* the most advanced level of technology —**state-of-the-art** *adj*

stateroom /stáyt room, -rōōm/ *n* 1 a luxurious private cabin or compartment on a ship 2 a large room used on state occasions

state school *n* a school run by a public authority and providing free education

state secret *n* a secret important to national security and revealed only to authorized people

stateside /stáyt sīd/ *US, Can adv* in or towards the United States ■ *adj* of the United States

statesman /stáytsmən/ (*pl* **-men** /-mən/) *n* a leading or senior man politician —**statesmanlike** *adj* —**statesmanship** *n*

stateswoman /stáyts wōōmən/ (*pl* **-men** /-wimin/) *n* a leading or senior woman politician

static /státtik/ *adj* 1 motionless or unchanging 2 of forces or pressures that act without causing movement 3 of stationary electric charges 4 of or caused by electrical interference in a radio or television broadcast ■ *n* 1 electrical interference in a radio or television broadcast 2 *also* **static electricity** a stationary electric charge that builds up on an insulated object —**statically** *adv*

statin /státtin/ *n* a drug belonging to a group that reduces cholesterol in the blood

station /stáysh'n/ *n* 1 a stop on a railway route 2 a local branch or headquarters of an organization such as the police force, fire brigade, or ambulance service 3 a building specially equipped to perform a function ○ *a pumping station* 4 a building equipped to make and transmit radio or television broadcasts 5 a broadcasting channel 6 a place where somebody is assigned to be 7 a rank or social position 8 *ANZ* a sheep or cattle farm ■ *vt* assign to a place

stationary /stáysh'nəri/ *adj* 1 not moving or at a standstill 2 fixed and not able to be moved 3 unchanging

> **SPELLCHECK** Do not confuse the spelling of **stationary** and **stationery** ('paper and envelopes'), which sound similar.

stationer /stáysh'nər/ *n* a seller of stationery

> **ORIGIN** In medieval Latin a *stationarius* was originally a 'trader who kept a permanent stall'. The word's Latin source meant literally 'stand-

ing, keeping still'. Of the comparatively rare permanent shops that existed in the Middle Ages, the commonest were bookshops, licensed by the universities, and so English adopted the Latin term. It has since come down in the world somewhat to 'seller of paper, pens, etc' (a sense first recorded in the mid-17C), but the earlier application is preserved in the name of the 'Stationers' Company', a London livery company to which booksellers and publishers belong.

stationery /stáysh'nəri/ *n* paper, envelopes, pens, and other things used for writing ◊ See note at **stationary**

stationmaster /stáysh'n maastər/, **station manager** *n* a railway official in charge of a station

station wagon *n* ANZ, US, Can a large car with an extended area behind the rear seats and a tailgate

statistic /stə tístik/ *n* **1** an element of data from a collection **2** a numerical value or function used to describe a sample —**statistical** *adj* —**statistically** *adv*

statistics /stə tístiks/ *n* the branch of mathematics that deals with numerical data in terms of samples and populations (+ *sing verb*) ■ *npl* a collection of numerical data (+ *pl verb*) ○ this *month's sales statistics* —**statistician** /státti stísh'n/ *n*

stative /stáytiv/ *adj* describes a verb expressing a state, not an action —**stative** *n*

~~statment~~ incorrect spelling of **statement**

statuary /státtyoo əri/ *n* **1** statues considered collectively **2** the art of making statues

statue /státtyoo/ *n* a carved or cast three-dimensional image of a human or animal

statuesque /státtyoo ésk/ *adj* attractive in a stately way

statuette /státtyoo ét/ *n* a small statue

stature /stáchər/ *n* **1** the height of a person or animal in a standing position **2** a person's social or professional standing

status /stáytəss/ *n* **1** rank in society or a group **2** prestige or high standing **3** somebody's legal standing

status bar *n* a bar on a computer screen that displays information about an application being used

status quo /–kwṓ/ *n* the way things are now

status symbol *n* a sign of wealth or prestige

statute /státtyoot/ *n* **1** a law enacted by a legislature **2** an established rule or law

statute book *n* a record of acts passed by a legislature and remaining in force

statute law *n* law enacted by a legislature

statutory /státtyōōtəri/ *adj* of a statute

staunch[1] /stawnch/, **stanch** /staanch/ *v* **1** *vti* stop the flow of a liquid, or stop flowing **2** *vt* stop a wound bleeding —**stauncher** *n*

staunch[2] /stawnch/ *adj* **1** loyal **2** sturdy —**staunchly** *adv* —**staunchness** *n*

stave /stayv/ *n* **1** a band of wood used in making the hull of a boat or the body of a barrel **2** a rung or bar of wood or other material **3** a wooden staff or stick **4** a musical staff ■ *v* (**staving**, **staved** *or* **stove**, **staved**) **1** *vt* break the staves of a boat or barrel **2** *vti* cause something to break inwards

□ **stave off** *vt* avoid or prevent something unpleasant, often only temporarily

stay[1] *v* **1** *vi* continue to be in the same position or state **2** *vi* live temporarily or permanently in a place **3** *vti* pass a particular length of time in a place or in doing something **4** *vt* persevere in doing or supporting something ○ *stay the course* **5** *vi* linger or pause ○ *Stay a moment.* **6** *vt* put a stop to something **7** *vt* postpone or hinder something ■ *n* **1** a short period spent away from home **2** a curb or check **3** a temporary halt in legal proceedings ◊ **stay put** remain in a place or position

stay[2] *n* **1** a support such as a brace, prop, or buttress **2** a small piece of hard material used to stiffen a corset or girdle ■ **stays** *npl* a stiffened corset ■ *vt* support or prop up (*archaic*)

stay[3] *n* **1** a rope or cable supporting a mast **2** a rope used to steady or guide something

stay-at-home *adj* not leaving home much by choice —**stay-at-home** *n*

staying power *n* the ability to keep doing something or to keep trying

STD *abbr* **1** sexually transmitted disease **2** subscriber trunk dialling

stead /sted/ *n* the position or role of another ◊ **stand somebody in good stead** be useful to somebody

Stead /sted/, **Christina Ellen** (1902–83) Australian writer

steadfast /stéd faast/ *adj* **1** firm in purpose, loyalty, or resolve **2** firmly fixed or constant —**steadfastly** *adv* —**steadfastness** *n*

steady /stéddi/ *adj* (**-ier, -iest**) **1** stable or not easily moved **2** staying the same **3** constant or continuous **4** reliable but dull or routine **5** not easily upset or excited **6** staid or serious ■ *vti* (**-ies, -ied**) make or become steady —**steadily** *adv* —**steadiness** *n* ◊ **go steady** go out together regularly as a couple (*infml*)

steak /stayk/ *n* **1** a thick cut of lean beef **2** a thick piece of other meat or of fish ◊ See note at **stake**

steakhouse /stáyk howss/ (*pl* **-houses** /-howziz/) *n* a restaurant serving steaks

steak tartare /–taar táar/ *n* a dish of uncooked minced beef with raw egg and chopped onions

steal /steel/ *v* (**stole** /stōl/, **stolen** /stṓlən/) **1** *vti* take another's property unlawfully **2** *vt* take something furtively or through trickery **3** *vi* go quietly or unobtrusively **4** *vt* take and use another's ideas ■ *n* an act of stealing

SPELLCHECK Do not confuse the spelling of **steal** and **steel** (the metal), which sound similar.

SYNONYMS steal, pinch, nick, filch, purloin,

pilfer, embezzle, misappropriate CORE MEANING: the taking of property unlawfully

stealth /stelth/ n 1 the doing of something slowly, quietly, and covertly to avoid detection 2 furtiveness ■ adj virtually undetectable by radar —**stealthful** adj

stealthy /stélthi/ (-ier, -iest) adj 1 done in a deliberately slow, careful, and quiet way 2 furtive or cunning —**stealthily** adv —**stealthiness** n ◊ See note at **secret**

steam /steem/ n 1 the vapour that is formed when water is boiled 2 the visible mist of condensed water vapour ■ adj driven by or using steam ■ v 1 vi produce steam 2 vi move by steam 3 vti cook in the steam of boiling water 4 vi move fast and energetically (infml) ◊ **get up steam** gather together enough energy to do something (infml)
□ **steam up** vti become or make clouded with condensed water vapour

steamboat /steem bōt/ n a boat powered by steam

steam engine n an engine powered by steam

steamer /steemər/ n 1 a steamboat or steamship 2 a covered pan for steaming food

steaming /steeming/ adj very angry (infml)

steam iron n an iron with a chamber for water that produces steam to dampen the laundry

steamroller /steem rōlər/ n 1 a vehicle with large heavy rollers as wheels for flattening roads 2 a crushing force that eliminates resistance ■ vt also **steamroll** 1 flatten with a steamroller 2 ruthlessly crush

steamship /steem ship/ n a ship powered by steam

steamy /steemi/ (-ier, -iest) adj 1 full of steam 2 overtly sexual (infml) —**steamily** adv

steatite /steeə tīt/ n soapstone

steed /steed/ n a spirited horse (literary)

steel /steel/ n 1 a strong alloy of iron and carbon 2 something made of steel ■ vt 1 coat or edge with steel 2 prepare or brace for a setback or trial —**steel** adj ◊ See note at **steal**

steel band n a musical group playing steel drums

steel drum, steel pan n a Caribbean percussion instrument made from an oil drum

Steele /steel/, **Sir Richard** (1672–1729) English playwright and essayist

steel guitar n a guitar played on a horizontal stand with a plectrum and metal slide

steel wool n a clump of abrasive steel strands. Use: cleaning, polishing.

steelworks /steel wurks/ n a steel-making factory

steely /steeli/ adj 1 like steel 2 determined and tough —**steeliness** n

steep¹ adj 1 sloping sharply 2 excessively high, especially in cost (infml) 3 very large ○ a steep decline in demand —**steepen** vti —**steeply** adv —**steepness** n

steep² v 1 vti immerse or soak in liquid 2 vt permeate —**steep** n

steeple /steep'l/ n 1 a church tower 2 a spire

steeplechase /steep'l chayss/ n 1 a horse race with jumps on the track 2 a track event with hurdles and a water jump ■ vi (-chasing, -chased) run a steeplechase —**steeplechaser** n

steeplejack /steep'l jak/ n a builder or repairer of steeples and other tall structures

steer¹ v 1 vti guide a vehicle or ship by a device such as a wheel or rudder 2 vt influence somebody to go in a particular direction or take a particular course —**steerable** adj ◊ See note at **guide**

steer² n a young castrated ox

steerage /steerij/ n 1 the cheapest accommodation on a passenger ship, usually near the rudder and steering gear 2 the process of steering a boat

steering column n a part of a motor vehicle connecting the steering wheel with the main steering mechanism

steering committee n a group of people selected to set agendas, decide topics for discussion, and prioritize business

steering wheel n a wheel in a vehicle or ship that is turned to change its direction

steersman /steerzmən/ (pl -men /-mən/) n somebody who steers a boat or ship

stein /stīn/ n 1 an earthenware or pewter beer mug, often with a lid 2 the quantity of beer held by a stein

Stein /stīn/, **Gertrude** (1874–1946) US writer

Viking Press

John Steinbeck

Steinbeck /stín bek/, **John Ernst** (1902–68) US writer

Steiner /shtínər, stínər/, **Rudolf** (1861–1925) Austrian philosopher

stellar /stéllər/ adj of or like a star or stars

stem¹ n 1 the main stalk of a plant 2 a secondary stalk of a plant, bearing a leaf, bud, or flower 3 a narrow part of an object, e.g. a wine glass or tobacco pipe 4 the main part of a word, to which inflections and affixes are added ■ v (stemming, stemmed) 1 vi originate 2 vt remove the stem of 3 vt provide with a stem —**stemmed** adj

stem² (stemming, stemmed) vt prevent from flowing

stench n a horrible smell ◊ See note at **smell**

stencil /sténss'l/ n 1 a plate with a cut-out design that is marked on a surface when paint or ink is applied 2 a pattern or lettering marked using a stencil ■ vt (-cilling, -cilled) 1 apply a design or lettering using a stencil

2 decorate a surface using a stencil —**stenciller** n

Stendhal /stén daal/ (1783–1842) French novelist

stenography /stə nóggrəfi/ (pl **-phies**) n 1 shorthand writing or typing 2 something written or typed in shorthand —**stenographer** n —**stenographic** /sténnə gráffik/ adj —**stenographically** adv

stentorian /sten táwri ən/ adj loud or declamatory

ORIGIN The original **stentorian** voice belonged to Stentor, a Greek herald in the stories of the Trojan War in Greek mythology.

step /step/ n 1 a short movement made by raising one foot and putting it down ahead of the other 2 the distance of a step 3 the sound of a footfall 4 a way of walking 5 a very short distance 6 a raised surface for the foot, especially one of a series going up or down 7 a stage in progress 8 a degree, grade, or interval ■ **steps** npl 1 outdoor stairs 2 a path or course made by somebody else ■ v (**stepping, stepped**) 1 vi move a foot onto something or in a particular direction 2 vi walk a short distance 3 vi move forward by taking steps 4 vt arrange in or provide with steps —**stepped** adj ◊ **be in** or **out of step** agree or disagree with somebody or something ◊ **step by step** gradually ◊ **step on it** hurry (infml; usually a command) ◊ **take steps** take action ◊ **watch your step** 1 be careful and cautious 2 tread carefully (usually a command)

SPELLCHECK Do not confuse the spelling of **step** and **steppe** ('a wide grassy plain'), which sound similar.

☐ **step down** vi resign, retire, or withdraw from a position
☐ **step in** vi intervene or become involved
☐ **step out** vi leave briefly
☐ **step up** vt raise in stages

step- prefix related because of remarriage, not by blood o stepson o stepmother

stepbrother /stép brúthər/ n a son of a stepparent

step change n a significant change

stepchild /stép chīld/ (pl **-children** /-childrən/) n a stepson or stepdaughter

stepdaughter /stép dawtər/ n a daughter of somebody's spouse from a previous marriage

step-down adj 1 decreasing in stages 2 lowering voltage —**step-down** n

stepfamily /stép famli/ (pl **-lies**) n a family with a stepparent

stepfather /stép faathər/ n a mother's subsequent husband

Stephen /steev'n/, **St** (d. AD 36) Christian martyr

Stephenson /steevənss'n/, **George** (1781–1848) British railway engineer

stepladder /stép ladər/ n a folding ladder with steps and a supporting frame

stepmother /stép muthər/ n a father's subsequent wife

stepparent /stép pairənt/ n a stepfather or stepmother

steppe /step/ n a vast dry and grass-covered plain ■ **Steppes** npl the plains of Russia and Ukraine ◊ See note at **step**

stepping stone n 1 a stone to put a foot on to cross a stream or wet area 2 a step towards a goal

stepsister /stép sistər/ n a daughter of a stepparent

stepson /stép sun/ n a son of somebody's spouse from a previous marriage

step-up adj 1 increasing in stages 2 raising voltage —**step-up** n

stere /steer/ n a cubic metre

stereo /stérri ō, steer-/ (pl **-os**) n 1 a device producing stereophonic sound 2 stereophonic reproduction —**stereo** adj

stereophonic /stérri ə fónnik, steeree-/ adj using two soundtracks and transmission channels for recorded sound —**stereophonically** adv

stereoscopic /stérri ə skóppik, steeri ə-/ adj producing a three-dimensional effect when seen —**stereoscopically** adv

stereotype /stérri ə tīp, steeri ə-/ n 1 a conventional oversimplified or standardized conception of a person or group 2 a metal printing plate cast from a mould ■ vt (**-typing, -typed**) 1 reduce to a stereotype 2 print using a stereotype —**stereotypical** /stérri ə típpik'l, steeri ə-/ adj —**stereotypically** adv

sterile /stérrīl/ adj 1 incapable of producing offspring 2 incapable of supporting vegetation 3 free of bacteria and other organisms —**sterility** /stə rílləti, ste-/ n

sterilize /stérri līz/ (**-izing, -ized**), **sterilise** vt make sterile —**sterilization** /stérri lī záysh'n/ n

~~sterio~~ incorrect spelling of **stereo**

sterling /stúrling/ n 1 British currency 2 also **sterling silver** an alloy containing at least 92.5% silver ■ adj 1 of sterling silver 2 admirable o sterling efforts

ORIGIN A **sterling** was originally an English penny of Norman times. The name probably literally means 'little star': some early Norman coins bore a small star on them. The pound sterling is altered from pound of sterlings, the weight of 240 of the silver coins, which became a recognized unit of weight and then a name for 240 pennies as a money of account.

stern[1] adj 1 strict and uncompromising 2 showing disapproval or anger —**sternly** adv —**sternness** n

stern[2] n the rear of a ship or boat —**stern** adj

Sternberg ♦ von Sternberg, Josef

Sterne /sturn/, **Laurence** (1713–68) Irish novelist

sternum /stúrnəm/ (pl **-na** /-nə/ or **-nums**) n the breastbone (technical) —**sternal** adj

steroid /steer oyd, stérroyd/ n any of a group of organic compounds including the sex hormones —**steroidal** /ste róyd'l/ adj

stethoscope /stéthə skóp/ n a medical instrument for listening to breathing and heartbeats —**stethoscopic** /stéthə skóppik/ adj

stevedore /steevə dawr/ n a docker who loads and unloads ships —**stevedore** vti

Stevens /steev'nz/, **Wallace** (1879–1955) US poet

Stevenson /steevənss'n/, **Robert Louis** (1850–94) Scottish writer

stew /styoo/ n a simmered dish, usually of meat and vegetables ■ v 1 vti cook by simmering 2 vi be troubled or agitated ◇ **in a stew** agitated, anxious, or in a difficult situation (infml)

steward /styoo ərd/ n 1 a passenger attendant on an aircraft or ship 2 a property or household manager 3 somebody in charge of meals on a ship or at a hotel or club 4 an official at a public event —**steward** vti —**stewardship** n

Stewart /styoo ərt/, **Jimmy** (1908–97) US film actor

Sth abbr South

STI abbr sexually transmitted infection

stick[1] n 1 a thin branch 2 a long often cylindrical piece of wood or other material used for a particular purpose ◦ a hockey stick ◦ a walking stick 3 a stick-like part or piece ◦ a stick of celery 4 criticism (infml) ■ **sticks** npl a remote place (infml) ◇ **in a cleft stick** in a situation where no possible course of action will bring a good result

stick[2] v (**stuck**) 1 vti fasten or be fixed on contact, usually by means of a viscous substance 2 vt fasten with a pointed object 3 vt pierce or stab 4 vti protrude 5 vt put somewhere (infml) 6 vi be or become unable to move 7 vt puzzle ◦ was stuck for an answer 8 vi stay in the mind 9 vt impose something unpleasant on ◦ I always get stuck with the boring jobs. ■ n ability to adhere ◇ **stick in your craw** or **throat** go against your sense of what is right (infml) ◇ **stick it out** persist with something to the end

□ **stick around** or **about** vi remain or wait (infml)

□ **stick by** or **with** vt stay loyal to

□ **stick out** v 1 vti extend or protrude 2 vt endure something disagreeable

□ **stick to** vt be loyal to

□ **stick together** vi stay close or remain unified

□ **stick up** vti point upwards

□ **stick up for** vt defend a person or belief

sticker /stíkər/ n 1 a small piece of adhesive paper or plastic, e.g. a label 2 something that sticks

sticking plaster n an adhesive dressing

sticking point n a point likely to cause deadlock

stick insect n an insect resembling a twig

stick-in-the-mud n somebody determinedly old-fashioned (infml)

stickleback /stík'l bak/ (pl **-backs** or same) n a small spiny fish

stickler /stíklər/ n somebody insistent about details and correctness

sticky /stíki/ (**-ier**, **-iest**) adj 1 covered in something gluey 2 able to stick to a surface 3 humid and hot 4 difficult (infml) 5 describes a website that attracts and retains visitors (infml) —**stickily** adv —**stickiness** n

stiff adj 1 rigid or hard to move 2 painful and not supple 3 severe 4 difficult 5 forceful ◦ a stiff breeze 6 potent ◦ a stiff drink 7 very formal in manner ■ adv 1 totally ◦ bored stiff 2 in a stiff way ■ n a corpse (slang) —**stiffen** vti —**stiffly** adv —**stiffness** n

stiff-necked adj obstinately proud

stifle /stíf'l/ (**-fling**, **-fled**) v 1 vti suffocate 2 vt check or repress ◦ stifle opposition ◦ stifle a yawn

stifling /stífling/ adj 1 uncomfortably hot and stuffy 2 repressive —**stiflingly** adv

stigma /stígmə/ n 1 a sign of social unacceptability 2 the part of a flower's female reproductive organ that receives the male pollen grains —**stigmatic** /stig máttik/ adj

stigmata /stígmətə, stig maátə/ npl marks resembling crucifixion wounds on the hands and feet

stigmatize /stígmə tīz/ (**-tizing**, **-tized**), **stigmatise** v 1 vt label as socially undesirable 2 vti mark with a stigma or stigmata —**stigmatization** /stígmə tī záysh'n/ n

stile /stīl/ n a step or steps for climbing over a fence

SPELLCHECK Do not confuse the spelling of **stile** and **style** ('a way of doing something'), which sound similar.

stiletto /sti léttō/ (pl **stilettos** or **stilettoes**) n 1 a small dagger 2 a woman's shoe with a high pointed heel

still[1] adj 1 not moving 2 describes a drink that is not carbonated 3 calm or quiet ■ adv silently or without motion ■ n 1 silence or peace (literary) ◦ the still of the night 2 a photograph of a scene from a film ■ v 1 vti make or become still 2 vt relieve ◦ stilled our fears —**stillness** n

still[2] adv 1 now as before ◦ It's still my favourite. 2 even at this time ◦ He may still be around. 3 even more (often with a comparative) ◦ better still

still[3] n an apparatus for distilling

stillborn /stíl bawrn/ adj 1 dead at birth 2 useless from the start —**stillbirth** n

~~stilleto, stilletto~~ incorrect spelling of **stiletto**

still life (pl **still lifes**) n a picture of something inanimate

stilt n 1 each of a pair of poles with footrests on which somebody balances and walks 2 a supporting post

stilted /stíltid/ adj 1 describes speech or writing that does not flow naturally 2 unduly formal —**stiltedly** adv

Stilton /stíltən/ n a strong British cheese usually with blue veins

stimulant /stímmyŏŏlənt/ n 1 a source of a stimulus 2 a drug producing an increase in functional activity —**stimulant** adj

stimulate /stímmyŏŏ layt/ (-lating, -lated) vt 1 cause to begin or develop ○ stimulate discussion 2 make interested or excited 3 cause physical activity in something such as a nerve or an organ —**stimulating** adj —**stimulation** /stímmyŏŏ láysh'n/ n —**stimulative** adj

stimulus /stímmyŏŏləss/ (pl -li /-lī/) n 1 something that encourages something to begin, increase, or develop 2 something that causes a physical response in an organism

sting v (stung) 1 vti prick the skin of a person or animal and inject a poisonous or irritant substance (usually refers to insects and plants) 2 vti feel or cause to feel a sharp pain 3 vt upset 4 vt goad ■ n 1 a wound caused by stinging 2 an organ used for stinging 3 a sharp pain —**stinger** n —**stinging** adj

stingray /stíng ray/ (pl -rays or same) n a ray with a flexible tail that has poisonous spines

stingy /stínji/ (-gier, -giest) adj not giving or spending much (infml) —**stingily** adv —**stinginess** n

stink vi (stank or stunk, stunk) 1 smell horrible 2 be very bad or worthless (infml) ■ n 1 a foul smell 2 a scandal (infml) —**stinky** adj ◊ See note at **smell**

stink bomb n a practical joker's device emitting a foul smell

stinker /stíngkər/ n 1 something very difficult or unpleasant (infml) 2 an offensive term for somebody regarded as obnoxious (slang insult) 3 US something of very poor quality (slang)

stinking /stíngking/ adj very smelly ■ adv adds emphasis (infml) ○ stinking rich —**stinkingly** adv

stint v 1 vi be miserly or too sparing ○ Don't stint on the cream. 2 vt deny somebody something ■ n 1 a fixed period of work or duty 2 a limitation —**stinter** n

stipend /stí pend/ n a fixed allowance or salary, especially one paid to a cleric ◊ See note at **wage**

stipendiary /stī péndi əri/ adj receiving or paying a stipend —**stipendiary** n

stipple /stípp'l/ (-pling, -pled) vt paint, mark, or apply with dabbing strokes —**stipple** n —**stippling** n

stipulate /stíppyŏŏ layt/ (-lating, -lated) vt state or demand as a condition —**stipulation** /stíppyŏŏ láysh'n/ n

stir[1] v (stirring, stirred) 1 vt mix ingredients with a spoon or similar implement 2 vti move slightly 3 vi get up after resting 4 vt goad somebody into action 5 vt arouse a feeling or memory (fml) 6 vti arouse strong emotions in somebody ■ n 1 an act of stirring 2 a commotion 3 a slight movement

□ **stir up** vt cause trouble

stir[2] n prison (slang)

stir-crazy adj made unsettled by confinement (infml or humorous)

stir-fry vt fry food rapidly over a high heat, stirring continuously ■ n a stir-fried dish

Stirling /stúrling/ 1 city in central Scotland. Pop. 30,515 (1991). 2 town in S South Australia. Pop. 4,698 (1991).

stirring /stúring/ adj 1 causing an emotional reaction 2 lively —**stirringly** adv

stirrup /stírrəp/ n a foot support hanging from a horse's saddle

stitch n 1 a length of thread passed through material in sewing or skin in surgery 2 a loop of yarn made in knitting or crochet 3 a style of sewing or knitting 4 a sudden pain in the side of the abdomen ■ vt 1 sew something 2 close a wound with stitches —**stitcher** n —**stitchery** n ◊ **in stitches** laughing a great deal

□ **stitch up** vt cause to appear guilty (slang)

stoat (pl **stoats** or same) n a small long-bodied mammal with a sleek brown coat

stock n 1 a supply of goods for sale 2 a supply held in reserve 3 the shares issued by a company, or the money raised by selling them 4 an individual investor's share (often pl) 5 farm animals 6 ancestry or descent 7 the original variety from which others are descended 8 a related group of animals or plants 9 broth used as a base for soups, stews, and sauces 10 a supporting part or frame ■ adj unoriginal ■ vt 1 have or keep a product in stock 2 fill something with a supply of goods ○ a well-stocked larder ◊ **take stock** think carefully about a situation

□ **stock up** vi collect a large supply ○ stock up on wine

stockade /sto káyd/ n 1 a defensive barrier 2 the area inside a stockade —**stockade** vt

stockbreeder /stók breedər/ n a breeder of farm animals —**stockbreeding** n

stockbroker /stók brōkər/ n somebody who deals in the stock market for clients —**stockbrokerage** n

stockbroker belt n an affluent commuter district

stock car n a car modified for racing

stock cube n a cube of concentrated stock for use in cooking

stock exchange n a stock market, or the building in which it is sited

Stockhausen /shtók howz'n/, **Karlheinz** (b. 1928) German composer

stockholder /stók hōldər/ n 1 US a shareholder 2 Aus a livestock farmer —**stockholding** n

Stockholm /stók hōm/ capital of Sweden. Pop. 736,113 (1998).

stockinette /stóki nét/, **stockinet** n a stretchy knitted fabric. Use: bandages, dishcloths.

stocking /stóking/ n a thin close-fitting knitted covering for a woman's foot and leg (often pl) —**stockinged** adj

stocking filler *n* a small Christmas present

stock-in-trade *n* 1 a basic resource 2 goods and equipment

stockist /stókist/ *n* a seller of a particular product

stockman /stókmən/ (*pl* **-men** /-mən/) *n* somebody who owns, breeds, or looks after farm animals

stock market *n* 1 a financial market for trading in stocks and shares 2 trading in stocks and shares

stockpile /stók pīl/ (**-piling, -piled**) *vti* amass large quantities of something —**stockpile** *n* ◊ See note at **collect**

stockroom /stók room, -room/ *n* a storeroom in a shop, office, or factory

stocks *n* a wooden frame with holes for the hands and feet or head and hands, formerly used for public punishment (*+ sing or pl verb*)

stock-still *adv* completely still

stocktaking /stók tayking/ *n* 1 evaluation of a situation 2 counting and listing the stock in a shop or business

stocky /stóki/ (**-ier, -iest**) *adj* short, broad, and strong-looking —**stockily** *adv* —**stockiness** *n*

stockyard /stók yaard/ *n* a temporary animal enclosure

stodge *n* 1 heavy filling food (*infml*) 2 dull or unimaginative writing —**stodgily** *adv* —**stodginess** *n* —**stodgy** *adj*

stoep /stoop/ *n S Africa* a veranda

stoic /stó ik/ *n* 1 somebody who endures adversity patiently and impassively 2 **Stoic** a member of an ancient Greek school of philosophy that accepted life's ups and downs with equanimity —**stoic** *adj* —**Stoic** *adj* —**stoical** *adj* —**stoically** *adv* —**stoicism** *n* —**Stoicism** *n* ◊ See note at **impassive**

stoke (**stoking, stoked**) *vti* 1 add fuel to a fire and stir it up 2 tend a boiler or furnace —**stoker** *n*

stole[1] past tense of **steal**

stole[2] *n* 1 a woman's scarf or shawl 2 a long narrow ecclesiastical scarf

stolen past participle of **steal**

stolid /stóllid/ *adj* solemn and impassive —**stolidity** /stə líddəti/ *n* —**stolidly** *adv* ◊ See note at **impassive**

stoma /stṓmə/ (*pl* **-mata** /-mətə/) *n* a plant pore —**stomatal** *adj*

stomach /stúmmək/ *n* 1 a sac-like digestive organ in vertebrates 2 the abdomen (*infml*) 3 an appetite or desire o *no stomach for a fight* ■ *vt* 1 tolerate something 2 eat a particular food without ill effects

stomachache /stúmmək ayk/ *n* a pain in the abdomen

stomp *vi* walk with heavy steps ■ *n* 1 a jazz dance with stamping foot movements 2 the music for a stomp —**stompingly** *adv*

stone /stōn/ *n* 1 the hard substance that rocks are made of 2 a rock fragment 3 a shaped piece of stone, e.g. a gravestone (*often in combination*) 4 a small hard mass (*usually in combination*) 5 a gem 6 a hard central part containing the seed of a fruit 7 (*pl same or* **stones**) a unit of weight equivalent to 6.35 kg/14lb 8 a small hard mineral mass that forms in an organ ■ *adv* adds emphasis o *stone sober* ■ *vt* (**stoning, stoned**) 1 throw stones at somebody or something 2 remove the stone from a fruit ◊ **be carved** *or* **set** *or* **cast in (tablets of) stone** be firmly established and impossible to alter ◊ **leave no stone unturned** make every possible effort

Stone Age *n* the earliest period of human history

stone-cold *adj* completely cold

stoned /stōnd/ *adj* 1 under the influence of drugs (*slang*) 2 intoxicated (*infml*)

stoneground /stṓn grownd/ *adj* ground with millstones

Stonehenge

Stonehenge /stōn hénj/ prehistoric monument on Salisbury Plain, S England, consisting of two concentric circles of large standing stones

stonemason /stṓn mayss'n/ *n* somebody who works with stone as a building material —**stonemasonry** *n*

stonewall /stōn wáwl/ *vi* deliberately create a delay —**stonewaller** *n*

stoneware /stṓn wair/ *n* dense opaque pottery

stonewashed /stṓn wosht/ *adj* given a worn faded look by washing with small pumice pebbles

stonework /stṓn wurk/ *n* 1 the stone parts of a building 2 the process of building with stone —**stoneworker** *n*

stony /stṓni/ (**-ier, -iest**), **stoney** *adj* 1 of or like stone 2 covered with stones 3 emotionless —**stonily** *adv* —**stoniness** *n*

stood past tense, past participle of **stand**

stooge /stooj/ *n* 1 a comedian's partner who is the butt of the jokes 2 a person regarded as being easily exploited by others (*slang insult*)

stool *n* 1 a simple backless seat 2 a piece of excrement

stool pigeon *n* 1 a police informer (*slang*) 2 a pigeon used as a hunter's decoy

ORIGIN Pigeons used as decoys were originally tied to stools or wooden platforms. The term **stool pigeon** is first recorded in 1830 in the United States.

stoop *v* 1 *vti* bend the head and upper body forwards and downwards while walking or standing **2** *vi* behave in a degrading way **3** *vi* condescend ■ *n* **1** a stooping posture **2** a bird's downward swoop —**stooping** *adj*

stop *v* (**stopping, stopped**) **1** *vti* cease or cause to cease doing something or moving **2** *vti* end **3** *vt* prevent something **4** *vi* pause or interrupt a journey before continuing **5** *vti* stay for a short time *(infml)* ○ *The children's friends like to stop the night.* **6** *vt* fill, block, or plug something **7** *vt* instruct a bank not to honour a cheque **8** *vt* deduct something from pay ■ *n* **1** an end of movement or action **2** a break in a journey, or a place visited on the way **3** a place where a bus or train pauses for passengers **4** a plug that blocks something **5** a device preventing movement *(often in combination)* ○ *a doorstop* **6** an instruction not to honour a cheque **7** a subset of organ pipes, or a knob controlling them ◇ **pull out all the stops** make every possible effort

stopcock /stóp kok/ *n* a valve for controlling flow

~~stoped~~ incorrect spelling of **stopped**

Popperfoto

Marie Stopes

Stopes /stōps/, **Marie** (1880–1958) Scottish pioneer advocate of birth control

stopgap /stóp gap/ *n* a temporary substitute —**stopgap** *adj*

stop-go *adj* alternating between discouragement and encouragement of economic demand

stop light *n* **1** a red traffic light **2** a brake light

stopover /stóp ōvər/ *n* **1** a halt made during a journey **2** a place where a stopover is made

stoppage /stóppij/ *n* **1** a brief industrial strike **2** a deduction from pay **3** a time during a game when play is halted

stopper /stóppər/ *n* a cork or plug —**stopper** *vt*

stop press *n* **1** late news inserted into a newspaper after printing has begun **2** a space for late news

stopstreet /stóp street/ *n S Africa* a street with a stop sign

stopwatch /stóp woch/ *n* a watch that can be started and stopped instantly to time somebody or something

storage /stáwrij/ *n* **1** storing or being stored **2** space for storing things **3** the price charged for storing something **4** a device or medium for storing computer data

storage dump *n* a printout of all stored computer data

storage heater *n* a device accumulating off-peak energy for heat

store *vt* (**storing, stored**) **1** put away for future use **2** put into safekeeping, e.g. in a warehouse **3** fill or provide ■ *n* **1** a place that sells goods at retail **2** a quantity saved for future use **3** a place where goods are kept in quantity ■ **stores** *npl* supplies ◇ **in store** about to happen ◇ **set great store by** consider to be important or valuable —**storable** *adj*

storefront /stáwr frunt/ *n* **1** *US, Can* a shopfront **2** a virtual shop on the Internet

storehouse /stáwr howss/ (*pl* -**houses** /-howziz/) *n* **1** a building where things are stored **2** an abundant source or collection

storekeeper /stáwr keepər/ *n* **1** somebody in charge of supplies **2** *US* a shopkeeper

storeroom /stáwr room, -rōōm/ *n* a room used for storage

storey /stáwri/ *n* a floor or level in a building —**storeyed** *adj*

SPELLCHECK Do not confuse the spelling of **storey** and **story** ('a factual or fictional narrative'), which sound similar.

storied /stáwrid/ *adj* interesting, famous, or celebrated in stories *(literary)*

stork (*pl* **storks** or **same**) *n* a large black-and-white wading bird with long legs and a long neck

storm *n* **1** a spell of violent weather **2** a heavy bombardment of objects **3** a sudden outburst of strong feeling **4** a sudden strong attack on a defended position ■ *v* **1** *vt* attack a place violently **2** *vi* be violently and noisily angry **3** *vi* rush with violence or anger ○ *stormed out of the room* **4** *vi* blow strongly with or without precipitation —**stormily** *adv* —**storminess** *n* —**stormy** *adj* ◇ **a storm in a teacup** a fuss or row over something trivial ◇ **take by storm 1** capture or overwhelm suddenly and with great force **2** make a great and immediate impression on

storm cloud *n* **1** a cloud indicating bad weather **2** a sign of impending trouble, especially war

storm trooper *n* **1** a member of the Nazi militia **2** a member of a military attack force

story[1] /stáwri/ (*pl* -**ries**) *n* **1** a factual or fictional narrative **2** a short piece of prose fiction **3** *also* **story line** the plot of a novel, play, or film **4** an account of facts ○ *changed her story several times* **5** a falsehood *(infml)* ◇ See note at **storey**

story[2] /stáwri/ *n US* = **storey**

storybook /stáwri bŏŏk/ *n* a book of children's stories ■ *adj* typical of children's stories

storyteller /stáwri telər/ *n* a teller or writer of stories —**storytelling** *n*

stoup /stoop/ *n* a basin for holy water

stout /stowt/ *adj* **1** thickset or heavy **2** courageous and determined **3** strong and substantial ○ *stout footwear* ■ *n* a dark strong beer —**stoutly** *adv* —**stoutness** *n*

stouthearted /stówt haártid/ *adj* courageous or

unyielding —**stoutheartedly** adv —**stoutheartedness** n

stove[1] /stōv/ n an appliance for cooking or heating

stove[2] /stōv/ past tense, past participle of **stave**

stovepipe hat /stōv pīp-/ n a man's tall silk hat

stow /stō/ vt 1 put away 2 fill with tightly packed things 3 store for later use
☐ **stow away** vi hide on a ship or aircraft to travel free

stowage /stō ij/ n 1 stowing or being stowed 2 a place or space for stowing something

stowaway /stō ə way/ n somebody who stows away on a ship or aircraft

Library of Congress
Harriet Beecher Stowe

Stowe /stō/, **Harriet Beecher** (1811–96) US writer and abolitionist

straddle /stráddʼl/ (-**dling**, -**dled**) vt 1 sit or stand with legs astride something 2 be on both sides of something ○ The city straddles the river. 3 belong or apply to more than one category or situation —**straddle** n —**straddler** n

Stradivari /stráddi vaári/, **Antonio** (1644–1737)

Stradivari /stráddi vaári/, **Antonio** (1644–1737) Italian violin maker

Stradivarius /stráddi váiri əss/ n a violin made by Stradivari

strafe /straaf, strayf/ (**strafing, strafed**) vt attack with gunfire from a low-flying aircraft —**strafe** n

straggle /strágg'l/ (-**gling**, -**gled**) vi 1 stray from a path, or fall behind a group 2 be or become spread out —**straggle** n —**straggler** n —**straggly** adj

straight /strayt/ adj 1 not curved or bent 2 candid or direct ○ a straight answer 3 level 4 correct or accurate 5 honest and fair ○ straight dealings 6 consecutive 7 not diluted 8 neat and tidy 9 not comic ○ a straight actor 10 heterosexual (slang) 11 conventional (slang) ■ adv in a straight manner or course ■ n 1 something straight, e.g. part of a racing track 2 a poker hand containing five cards in sequence 3 a heterosexual person (slang) 4 a conventional person (slang) —**straightly** adv —**straightness** n

SPELLCHECK Do not confuse the spelling of **straight** and **strait** ('a sea channel'), which sound similar.

straightaway /stráyt ə wáy/, **straight away** adv immediately

straighten /stráyt'n/ vti make or become straight
☐ **straighten out** vti make or become clear or satisfactory
☐ **straighten up** vti make something neat and orderly

straightforward /stráyt fáwrwərd/ adj 1 frank or honest 2 not difficult or complicated —**straightforwardly** adv —**straightforwardness** n

straightjacket n, vt = straitjacket

straight man n a comedian's partner who sets up or responds to a joke

straight-to-video adj describes a film released only in video format

strain[1] v 1 vti pull or stretch tight, or be pulled or stretched tight 2 vi make the utmost effort 3 vt use to the utmost 4 vt injure by twisting, stretching, or overexertion 5 vti be or make tense or stressed 6 vti pass through a strainer 7 vt remove using a strainer ■ n 1 straining or being strained 2 a pulling or stretching force 3 mental or physical stress 4 a cause of stress 5 a great exertion 6 an injury caused by twisting, stretching, or overexertion

strain[2] n 1 a line of ancestry 2 a subgroup of a species of organism distinguished by specific characteristics 3 an inherited quality or trait 4 a trace 5 the character, mood, or theme of something

strainer /stráynər/ n a device for removing solids from liquids

strait /strayt/ n (often pl) 1 a channel joining two seas 2 a difficult situation ■ adj (archaic) 1 narrow or confined 2 strict or rigid ◊ See note at **straight**

straitened /stráyt'nd/ adj made difficult or restricted ○ living in straitened circumstances

straitjacket /stráyt jakit/, **straightjacket** n 1 a jacket-shaped garment with sleeves that can be tied to restrain somebody 2 something that limits or restricts —**straitjacket** vt

strait-laced adj excessively strict in morals

strand[1] n a strip of land at the water's edge ■ v 1 vti go or leave ashore or aground 2 vt leave somebody in difficulty, especially in a strange or remote place —**stranded** adj

strand[2] n 1 a single fibre or filament, often twisted with others 2 a length of something such as wire or string 3 a string of beads

strange /straynj/ (**stranger, strangest**) adj 1 unexpected or unusual 2 unfamiliar 3 hard to explain 4 from a different place, or of a different kind —**strangely** adv —**strangeness** n

stranger /stráynjər/ n 1 an unfamiliar person 2 a newcomer 3 an outsider

strangle /stráng g'l/ (-**gling**, -**gled**) vti 1 kill by squeezing the throat 2 suppress the utterance of ○ strangled a sob —**strangler** n

stranglehold /stráng g'l hōld/ n 1 a choking wrestling hold 2 a state of complete power

strangulate /stráng gyōō layt/ (-**lating**, -**lated**) v 1 vt strangle 2 vti constrict a part of the body, or become constricted, until the natural flow of blood or air is prevented —**strangulation** /stráng gyŏŏ láysh'n/ n

strap n 1 a flexible strip, e.g. of leather, used to bind or secure something 2 a loop of flexible material used as a handle, e.g. for a bag 3 a thin strip of material that forms part of a garment and passes over the shoulder ■ vt (**strapping, strapped**) 1 secure with a strap 2 also **strap up** bandage tightly 3 beat with a strap —**strapless** adj

strapped adj short of something (infml) ○ strapped for cash

strapping /strápping/ adj robust (infml) ■ n 1 straps 2 material for straps

Strasbourg /stráz burg/ city in NE France. Pop. 264,115 (1999).

strata plural of **stratum**

stratagem /stráttəjəm/ n 1 a military tactic or manoeuvre for deceiving an enemy 2 a clever ruse

~~stratagy~~ incorrect spelling of **strategy**

strategic /strə teéjik/, **strategical** /-ik'l/ adj 1 of or involving strategy 2 done for reasons of strategy —**strategically** adv

strategist /stráttəjist/ n somebody skilled in strategy

strategy /stráttəji/ (pl **-gies**) n 1 the planning and conducting of a military campaign 2 a plan of action in any field, or the development and execution of such a plan ○ business strategy

Stratford-upon-Avon /strátfərd ə pon áyvən/ town in west-central England, birthplace of William Shakespeare. Pop. 111,211 (1996).

stratify /strátti fī/ (**-fies, -fied**) vti 1 form into layers 2 separate into groups based on social status —**stratification** /stráttifi káysh'n/ n

stratosphere /strátta sfeer/ n 1 the region of the Earth's atmosphere between the troposphere and mesosphere 2 a very high level or position —**stratospheric** /strátta sférrik/ adj

stratum /straátəm, stráy-/ (pl **-ta** /-tə/ or **-tums**) n 1 a layer, especially of sedimentary rock (fml) 2 a level of society —**stratal** adj

> **USAGE** The plural of **stratum** is strata, reflecting the word's Latin history. Do not use the false plural stratas or the incorrect false Latin plural stratae: in all strata [not stratas or stratae] of society. A variant plural stratums exists but is relatively infrequent.

stratus /stráytəss, straá-/ (pl **-ti** /-tī/) n a flat grey cloud formation

Strauss /strowss/ family of Austrian composers including **Johann, the Elder** (1804–49) and his son **Johann, the Younger** (1825–99)

Strauss, Richard (1864–1949) German conductor and composer

Igor Stravinsky

Stravinsky /strə vínski/, **Igor** (1882–1971) Russian-born US composer

straw n 1 the stalks of threshed cereal crops 2 a dried grass stalk 3 a thin tube for sucking up a drink 4 something worthless ◇ **clutch** or **grasp at straws** be willing to try anything that may help in a desperate situation ◇ **draw the short straw** be chosen to do a difficult or unpleasant task

strawberry /stráwbəri/ (pl **-ries**) n 1 a small soft red fruit 2 a plant that produces strawberries

strawberry blonde adj describes hair that is blonde with a reddish tinge —**strawberry blonde** n

strawberry mark n a red birthmark

straw poll, straw vote n an unofficial poll or vote

stray vi 1 wander away from a place or group 2 wander about aimlessly 3 digress from a subject ■ adj 1 lost or homeless ○ a stray dog 2 scattered or separated ■ n somebody or something lost or homeless, especially a domestic animal

streak /streek/ n 1 a thin stripe of contrasting colour 2 a layer or strip of something 3 a contrasting characteristic 4 a short period or unbroken run ○ a winning streak 5 a lightning flash ■ v 1 vti mark with or form streaks 2 vi dash or rush 3 vi run naked through a public place (infml) —**streaked** adj —**streaker** n —**streaky** adj

streaky bacon n bacon with alternate layers of meat and fat

stream /streem/ n 1 a small river 2 a constant flow 3 an air or water current 4 a continuous series 5 a beam of light ■ v 1 vi flow in large quantities 2 vi move in the same direction 3 vti produce a flow of liquid ○ His nose streamed blood. 4 vi float freely ○ with her hair streaming behind 5 vi pour out in a trail or beam 6 vti put pupils in ability groups 7 vt broadcast on the Internet —**streaming** n

streamer /streémər/ n 1 a narrow flag 2 a decorative paper strip

streamline /streém līn/ (**-lining, -lined**) vt 1 design or build with an aerodynamic shape 2 make more efficient —**streamlined** adj —**streamlining** n

stream of consciousness n 1 a literary style that presents a flow of thoughts 2 a flow of thoughts

~~streech~~ incorrect spelling of **stretch**

street *n* **1** a public road in a town or city **2** the buildings or inhabitants of a street ■ *adj* of modern urban society ◊ **right up somebody's street** exactly suitable for somebody ◊ **streets ahead (of)** much better than somebody or something else ◊ **the man** *or* **person** *or* **woman in the street** the average person

streetcar /street kaar/ *n US, Can* a passenger tram

street credibility, street cred *n* popularity and acceptance, especially among the young

streetlight /street līt/, **streetlamp** /-lamp/ *n* a light on a post that illuminates a street

street value *n* the price obtainable for something illegal, especially drugs

streetwalker /street wawkər/ *n* a prostitute (*infml*) —**streetwalking** *n*

streetwise /street wīz/, **street-smart** *adj* able to survive in difficult and dangerous situations in a modern city (*infml*)

strength *n* **1** physical power **2** emotional toughness ○ *strength of mind* **3** the ability to withstand force or pressure **4** defensive ability **5** degree of intensity, e.g. of light or sound **6** persuasive power ○ *the strength of her argument* **7** potency, e.g. of alcohol or drugs **8** the number of people needed for something ◊ **in strength** in large numbers ◊ **on the strength of** on the basis of

strengthen /strength'n/ *vti* make or become stronger

~~strenous~~ incorrect spelling of **strenuous**

~~strenth~~ incorrect spelling of **strength**

strenuous /strénnyoo əss/ *adj* **1** requiring great effort or strength **2** energetic or determined —**strenuously** *adv* —**strenuousness** *n* ◊ See note at **hard**

streptococcus /stréptə kókəss/ (*pl* -**ci** /-kók sī/) *n* a round bacterium that can cause disease —**streptococcal** *adj*

streptomycin /stréptə mīssin/ *n* an antibiotic. Use: treatment of bacterial infections.

stress *n* **1** a feeling of anxiety and tiredness, often caused by personal problems or overwork **2** a cause of stress **3** special importance or emphasis **4** a more forceful pronunciation of a syllable or playing of a note ■ *vt* **1** emphasize **2** pronounce or play forcefully **3** subject to stress —**stressed** *adj* —**stressful** *adj* —**stressor** *n* ◊ See note at **worry**

stress fracture *n* a small bone fracture caused by repeated physical strain

stress mark *n* a mark showing a syllable to be stressed

stretch *v* **1** *vti* make or become longer or wider **2** *vi* be capable of expanding and regaining its original shape **3** *vti* extend the body or part of it to full length **4** *vti* make or become taut **5** *vt* suspend something between two points **6** *vti* extend in space or time **7** *vt* make a small amount go further **8** *vi* be enough **9** *vt* exceed a limit or break a rule ■ *n* **1** an act of stretching **2** a length or expanse **3** a period of time **4** a prison term (*infml*) **5** elasticity ■ *adj* **1** elastic **2** extended to provide

extra space ○ *a stretch limousine* —**stretchable** *adj* —**stretchy** *adj* ◊ **at a stretch** continuously ◊ **at full stretch** using all the energy or resources available

stretcher /stréchər/ *n* **1** a device for carrying somebody in a lying position **2** *ANZ* a camp bed —**stretcher** *vt*

stretch mark *n* a mark on skin that has been stretched, especially during pregnancy (*often pl*)

strew /stroo/ (**strewn** *or* **strewed**) *vt* **1** scatter untidily or over a large area **2** cover with strewn things

striated /strī áytid/ *adj* marked with parallel grooves, ridges, or narrow bands —**striation** *n*

stricken /stríkən/ *adj* **1** deeply or badly affected (*often in combination*) ○ *grief-stricken* **2** affected by illness

~~strickly, striely~~ incorrect spelling of **strictly**

strict *adj* **1** severe in maintaining discipline **2** enforced rigorously **3** precise **4** closely observing rules or practices —**strictly** *adv* —**strictness** *n*

stricture /stríkchər/ *n* (*fml*) **1** a severe criticism **2** a limit or restriction

stride *v* (**striding**, **strode**, **stridden** /strídd'n/) **1** *vi* walk with long regular steps **2** *vti* take a long step over something ■ *n* **1** a long step or the distance covered by it **2** an advance towards improving or developing something ■ **strides** *npl Aus* trousers (*infml*) ◊ **take something in your stride** accept something without being unduly upset

strident /strīd'nt/ *adj* **1** loud or harsh **2** strongly expressed —**stridency** *n* —**stridently** *adv*

strife *n* bitter conflict or rivalry

strike *v* (**striking**, **struck**) **1** *vti* hit a person or thing **2** *vti* deliver a blow **3** *vti* collide with a person or thing **4** *vt* produce fire by friction, or light a match **5** *vt* press a key on a keyboard or musical instrument **6** *vti* indicate the time by making a sound (*refers to clocks*) **7** *vt* make something, e.g. a coin, by stamping **8** *vt* make an impression on somebody **9** *vti* discover something suddenly, e.g. oil **10** *vti* attack an opponent **11** *vti* **struck, stricken** *or* **struck** affect somebody suddenly ○ *was stricken with a heart attack* **12** *vi* stop working as a protest **13** *vt* cross something out **14** *vt* lower a flag or sail ■ *n* **1** a hit or blow **2** a sound of striking **3** a work stoppage as a protest **4** a refusal to do something as a protest ○ *a hunger strike* **5** a military attack **6** a sudden discovery of something **7** in bowling, the knocking down of all the pins with a single ball ◊ **strike it rich** become extremely wealthy or successful

☐ **strike down** *vt* cause to become very ill

☐ **strike out** *vi* set out energetically

☐ **strike up** *v* **1** *vti* begin to play a piece of music, or cause to begin playing **2** *vt* begin ○ *struck up a friendship*

strikebreaker /strīk braykər/ *n* **1** somebody who works while colleagues strike **2** somebody hired to replace a striker

striker /strĩkər/ n 1 somebody who is on strike 2 an attacking player in a football team

striking /strĩkĩg/ adj 1 conspicuous 2 attractive or impressive —**strikingly** adv

Strindberg /strĩnd burg/, **August** (1849–1912) Swedish dramatist —**Strindbergian** /strĩnd búrgi ən/ adj

Strine, strine n Australian English (humorous)

string n 1 a strong thin cord used for fastening, hanging, or tying 2 something resembling string 3 a succession of items 4 a line of things 5 a sequence of similar elements, e.g. letter or numbers 6 a set of objects threaded together 7 a cord stretched across a musical instrument, a sports racket, or an archer's bow ■ **strings** npl the stringed instruments of an orchestra, or the musicians playing them ■ vt (**strung**) 1 thread onto a string 2 hang between two points 3 arrange or extend in a line 4 provide with a string or strings —**string** adj —**stringed** adj —**stringiness** n —**stringy** adj ◇ **pull strings** use influence to try to gain an advantage ◇ **with no strings (attached)** unconditionally

□ **string along** vi accompany another person or group (infml)

string bean n 1 a runner bean 2 US a French bean

stringed instrument, string instrument n a musical instrument with strings that are bowed or plucked

stringent /strĩnjənt/ adj rigorous or severe —**stringency** n —**stringently** adv

stringer /strĩngər/ n 1 a freelance or part-time journalist 2 a horizontal structural timber

string quartet n 1 a group of four musicians playing stringed instruments 2 a piece of music for a string quartet

strip[1] v (**stripping, stripped**) 1 also **strip off** vi undress 2 vi do a striptease 3 vt remove something covering a surface o strip the walls of paper o strip the paper from the walls 4 vt remove the entire contents of a place 5 vt deprive somebody of his or her status 6 vt take something apart in order to clean or repair it ■ n a striptease —**stripper** n

strip[2] n 1 a long narrow flat piece 2 an airstrip 3 a series of cartoons that tell a story or joke

stripe[1] n 1 a long narrow band of a different colour or texture 2 a pattern of stripes 3 a symbol of rank sewn onto a uniform —**stripe** vt —**striped** adj —**stripy** adj

stripe[2] n a blow from a whip or cane

striplight /strĩp lĩt/ n 1 a long tubular fluorescent light 2 a row of lamps used to light a stage

stripling /strĩpplĩg/ n an adolescent boy

strip poker n a card game in which losing players gradually remove their clothes

strip-search vti search the clothing and body of a suspect —**strip search** n

striptease /strĩp teez, strĩp teĕz/ n an erotic entertainment in which somebody slowly undresses

strive /strĩv/ (**striving, strove** /strōv/, **striven** /strĩv'n/) vi 1 try hard 2 fight or compete

strobe light, strobe n a high-intensity flashing light

stroboscope /strōbə skōp/ n a flashing device that makes moving objects appear stationary —**stroboscopic** /strōbə skóppik, strōbbə-/ adj

strode past tense of **stride**

Stroheim ♦ **von Stroheim, Erich**

stroke n 1 a blockage or rupture of a blood vessel in the brain 2 a sudden occurrence o a stroke of luck 3 a sound made by a striking clock 4 an act or way of hitting a ball 5 a swimming style or movement 6 a single movement in a series, e.g. of an oar, wing, or piston 7 a hit or blow 8 a single mark or movement of a pen or brush 9 a caressing movement ■ vt (**stroking, stroked**) 1 move the hand gently over 2 push gently

stroll /strōl/ vi 1 walk unhurriedly 2 do something effortlessly ■ n a leisurely walk

stroller /strōlər/ n 1 somebody who is strolling 2 Aus, US, Can a lightweight pushchair

Stromboli /strómbəli/ volcanic island in the Lipari Islands in the Tyrrhenian Sea, north of Sicily

strong adj 1 physically powerful 2 forceful 3 not easily damaged or broken 4 healthy and well 5 thriving o a strong economy 6 convincing o a strong argument 7 skilful or knowledgeable 8 exerting influence or authority 9 felt or expressed powerfully or forcefully 10 bold, clearly defined, and prominent o strong features 11 extreme o strong measures 12 having an intense effect on the senses 13 containing a lot of the main ingredient o strong black coffee 14 containing a lot of alcohol 15 well defended —**strongly** adv ◇ **come on strong** behave or express something aggressively (slang) ◇ **going strong** thriving and doing well

strong-arm adj using force or coercion (infml)

strongbox /stróng boks/ n a secure container for valuables

stronghold /stróng hōld/ n 1 a fortified place 2 a place where a particular group or activity is concentrated

strongman /stróng man/ (pl -**men** /-men/) n 1 a performer of feats of strength 2 a powerful leader

strongroom /stróng room, -rŏŏm/ n a reinforced room for safe storage

strontium /strónti əm, -shi-/ n (symbol Sr) a silvery-white metallic chemical element. Use: fireworks, flares, alloys.

strop n a leather strap for sharpening a razor —**strop** vt

stroppy /stróppi/ (-**pier, -piest**) adj bad-tempered (infml) —**stroppily** adv —**stroppiness** n

strove past tense of **strive**

struck past tense, past participle of **strike**

structuralism /strúkchərə lizzəm/ n the study of literature, language, and society as a network of interrelated elements —**structuralist** n, adj

structure /strúkchər/ n 1 something built or assembled from parts 2 an orderly system of interrelated parts 3 the way that parts link or work together ■ vt (-turing, -tured) organize or arrange into a system —**structural** adj —**structurally** adv

structured query language n full form of **SQL**

strudel /stroōd'l/ n a filled rolled pastry

struggle /strúgg'l/ vi (-gling, -gled) 1 make a great physical or mental effort to do something difficult 2 fight by grappling 3 wriggle forcefully to escape 4 move with difficulty ■ n 1 a great effort 2 a hard task 3 a fight —**struggler** n

strum (strumming, strummed) vti play a musical instrument by brushing the strings —**strum** n

strumpet /strúmpit/ n an offensive term for a prostitute or a woman regarded as sexually promiscuous (archaic)

strung past tense, past participle of **string**

strung out adj weakened by long-term drug use (slang)

strut vi (strutting, strutted) walk in an arrogant or pompous way ■ n 1 a long rigid supporting structural member 2 a strutting walk

strychnine /strík neen, -nin/ n a poisonous plant product. Use: rodent control, stimulant.

Stuart /styoō ərt/, **Charles Edward** (1720–88) grandson of James II of England, Scotland, and Ireland and claimant to the British throne

Stuart, James Francis Edward (1688–1766) son of James II of England, Scotland, and Ireland and claimant to the British throne

Stuart, John McDouall (1815–66) British-born Australian explorer

stub n 1 a short remaining part 2 a detachable part, e.g. of a ticket or cheque, retained as a record ■ vt (stubbing, stubbed) bang the toe against something

□ **stub out** vt extinguish a cigarette or cigar

stubble /stúbb'l/ n 1 short stalks left in the ground after harvesting 2 a short growth of beard —**stubbly** adj

stubborn /stúbbərn/ adj 1 dogged 2 unreasonably and obstructively determined 3 hard to remove or deal with —**stubbornly** adv —**stubbornness** n

stubborness incorrect spelling of **stubbornness**

Stubbs, George (1724–1806) British painter and engraver

stubby /stúbbi/ adj short and thick or thick-set

stucco /stúkō/ n 1 wall plaster 2 decorative plaster work —**stucco** vt

stuck past tense, past participle of **stick** ■ adj 1 jammed, caught, or unable to move o The drawer's stuck. o We were stuck in traffic. 2 unable to find a solution

stuck-up adj snobbish and conceited (infml)

stud[1] n 1 a decorative metal knob 2 a simple earring 3 a collar fastener 4 a knob on a boot or tyre to prevent sliding 5 a vertical support

for a wall ■ vt (studding, studded) 1 fit or decorate with studs 2 be present or visible throughout o a star studded sky

stud[2] n 1 a stallion or other male animal used for breeding 2 a sexually attractive or skilful man (infml)

studbook /stúd boŏk/ n a record book of horse or dog pedigrees

student /styoōd'nt/ n 1 somebody who studies at a school, college, or university 2 somebody knowledgeable about or interested in a particular thing o a student of human foibles ■ adj in training for a profession o a student teacher

students' union n 1 an organization of students that represents their interests 2 a building with social facilities for students

studied /stúddid/ adj not spontaneous

studing incorrect spelling of **studying**

studio /styoōdi ō/ n 1 an artist's workplace 2 a room or building for the production of films, broadcasts, or musical recordings 3 also **studio flat** US a small one-roomed flat 4 a dance school 5 a film production company

studious /styoōdi əss/ adj 1 inclined to study 2 careful and painstaking —**studiously** adv —**studiousness** n

study /stúddi/ v (-ies, -ied) 1 vti learn about a subject 2 vti take an educational course 3 vt investigate by research 4 vt look at or read carefully ■ n (pl -ies) 1 the process of studying 2 an investigation 3 a report on research 4 a room for studying, reading, or writing 5 a preparatory work of art

stuff vt 1 fill something with stuffing 2 push things into a container 3 put something somewhere hurriedly 4 eat or feed somebody a lot of food ■ n 1 miscellaneous or unspecified things or material 2 personal possessions 3 personal qualities o the stuff that heroes are made of 4 special skill or knowledge o She knows her stuff. 5 foolish words or action 6 woollen fabric —**stuffed** adj —**stuffer** n ◊ **do your stuff** do what is required or expected

stuffed shirt n a pompous person (infml)

stuffing /stúffing/ n 1 a well-flavoured filling for meat or vegetables 2 a soft filling for cushions, pillows, or toys

stuffy /stúffi/ (-ier, -iest) adj 1 airless 2 straitlaced —**stuffiness** n

stultify /stúlti fī/ (-fies, -fied) vt 1 diminish interest by being tedious or boring 2 make somebody seem stupid —**stultification** /stúltifi káysh'n/ n

stumble /stúmb'l/ (-bling, -bled) vi 1 trip when walking or running 2 walk unsteadily 3 speak or act hesitatingly 4 make a minor mistake 5 find something by chance o stumbled across a vital piece of evidence —**stumble** n —**stumblingly** adv ◊ See note at **hesitate**

stumbling block n an obstacle

stump n 1 the remaining base of a felled tree 2 a small part remaining after the rest has been removed **3** in cricket, any of the three upright posts of the wicket ■ *v* **1** *vt* baffle **2** *vt* in cricket, dismiss a batsman by hitting the wicket **3** *vi* walk heavily —**stumper** *n*

stumpy /stúmpi/ (**-ier, -iest**) *adj* short and thick

stun (**stunning, stunned**) *vt* **1** make unconscious **2** shock

stung past tense, past participle of **sting**

stunk past tense, past participle of **stink**

stunner /stúnnər/ *n* an impressive or beautiful person or thing (*infml*)

stunning /stúnning/ *adj* outstandingly impressive or attractive —**stunningly** *adv*

stunt[1] *vt* restrict the growth of something

stunt[2] *n* **1** a dangerous feat done for entertainment **2** something unusual done for attention *o a publicity stunt* —**stunt** *vi*

stuntman /stúnt man/ (*pl* **-men** /-men/) *n* somebody who replaces an actor in a dangerous scene

stuntwoman /stúnt woʻomən/ (*pl* **-en** /-wimin/) *n* a woman who replaces an actor in a dangerous scene

stupefy /styoʻopi fí/ (**-fies, -fied**) *vt* **1** amaze **2** make unable to think clearly —**stupefaction** /styoʻopi fáksh'n/ *n* —**stupefyingly** *adv*

stupendous /styoo péndəss/ *adj* impressively great —**stupendously** *adv*

stupid /styoʻopid/ *adj* **1** regarded as unintelligent **2** silly —**stupidity** /styoo píddəti/ *n* —**stupidly** *adv*

~~stupify~~ incorrect spelling of **stupefy**

stupor /styoʻopər/ *n* **1** a dazed state **2** a state of near-unconsciousness —**stuporous** *adj*

sturdy /stúrdi/ (**-dier, -diest**) *adj* **1** solidly made **2** with a strong build —**sturdily** *adv* —**sturdiness** *n*

sturgeon /stúrjən/ (*pl* **-geons** or same) *n* **1** a large fish that is a source of caviar **2** sturgeon as food

Sturt, Charles (1795–1869) British explorer and administrator in Australia

stutter /stúttər/ *vti* say or speak with a stammer —**stutter** *n* —**stutterer** *n* —**stuttering** *adj*

Stuttgart /stoʻot gaart/ capital of Baden-Württemberg State, SW Germany. Pop. 588,482 (1997).

sty[1] (*pl* **sties**) *n* an enclosure for pigs —**sty** *vt*

sty[2] (*pl* **sties**), **stye** *n* a swelling on an eyelid

style /stíl/ *n* **1** a distinctive form **2** a way of doing something (*often in combination*) *o a hands-on management style* **3** the way something is written or performed *o Style is more important than content.* **4** flair or good taste **5** fashionable status **6** a way in which clothes or hair are cut or shaped **7** luxuriousness *o dining in style* ■ *vt* (**styling, styled**) **1** give a style to **2** cause to conform to a style —**style** *n* —**stylistic** /stī lístik/ *adj* ◇ **cramp somebody's style** restrict what somebody is able to do (*infml*) ◊ See note at **stile**

stylish /stílish/ *adj* sophisticated, elegant, and fashionable —**stylishly** *adv* —**stylishness** *n*

stylist /stílist/ *n* **1** a hairdresser **2** somebody whose creative work shows an accomplished style

stylize /stí líz/ (**-izing, -ized**), **stylise** *vt* give a distinctive or artificial style to —**stylization** /stí lī záysh'n/ *n*

stylus /stíləss/ (*pl* **-li** /-lī/) *n* **1** a record-player needle **2** an engraving or writing tool **3** a pointed device for use on a computer screen that responds to pressure

stymie /stími/, **stymy** (**-mies, -mied**) *vt* hinder the progress of —**stymie** *n*

styptic /stíptik/ *adj* able to stop bleeding

suave /swaav/ (**suaver, suavest**) *adj* charming, especially in an insincere way —**suavely** *adv* —**suaveness** *n* —**suavity** *n*

sub *n* a submarine

sub- *prefix* **1** under, below, beneath *o subconscious* **2** subordinate, secondary *o sublet* **3** less than completely *o subhuman* **4** subdivision *o subcontinent*

subaltern /súbb'ltərn/ *n* **1** a British army officer of a rank below captain **2** a subordinate person ■ *adj* subordinate

subaqua /súb ákwə/ *adj* of underwater sports

subarctic /súb áarktik/ *adj* of or like the area south of the Arctic Circle

subatomic /súb ə tómmik/ *adj* **1** smaller than or part of an atom *o a subatomic particle* **2** on a scale smaller than the atom, or involving phenomena at this level

subcommittee /súbkəmiti/ *n* a special-purpose group within a committee

subconscious /sub kónshəss/ *adj* existing unknown in the mind ■ *n* the part of the mind not consciously perceived —**subconsciously** *adv* —**subconsciousness** *n*

subcontinent /sub kóntinənt/ *n* a separate part of a continent, e.g. the area of Asia containing India, Pakistan, and Bangladesh —**subcontinental** /súb konti nént'l/ *adj*, *n*

subcontract /súb kon trakt/ *n* a secondary contract in which a person or company hired to do something passes on some or all of the work to another —**subcontract** /súbkən trákt/ *vti* —**subcontractor** *n*

subculture /súb kulchər/ *n* a separate social group within a larger culture

subcutaneous /súbkyoʻo táyni əss/ *adj* under the skin —**subcutaneously** *adv*

subdirectory /súbdi rektəri, -dī-/ (*pl* **-ries**) *n* a directory within another directory on a storage device such as a hard drive

subdivide /súbdi víd/ (**-viding, -vided**) *vti* divide further —**subdivider** *n* —**subdivision** /súb di vizh'n/ *n*

subdomain name /sub də máyn-, -dō-/, **subdomain** *n* a subdivision or second level of an Internet domain name

subdue /səb dyoʻo/ (**-duing, -dued**) *vt* **1** bring under control, often using force **2** make less intense —**subdued** *adj*

subeditor /súb édditər/ n 1 an assistant editor 2 somebody who reads and corrects material for a newspaper or magazine

subgroup /súb groop/ n a distinct group within a larger group

subhuman /sub hyóomən/ adj of or displaying behaviour inferior to that expected of human beings

subject n /súb jikt/ 1 a matter being discussed, examined, or otherwise dealt with 2 a course of study 3 a person ruled by a monarch or other authority 4 somebody who is the focus of an activity o *not an appropriate subject for hypnosis* 5 somebody or something represented in a picture or written about in a book o *the subject of her latest biography* 6 in grammar, the performer of a verb's action, e.g. 'she' in 'Where does she live?' ■ adj /súbjikt/ 1 prone or susceptible o *areas subject to flooding* 2 ruled or controlled o *not subject to the laws of this country* ■ adv /súbjikt/, adv depending o *subject to your approval* ■ vt /səb jékt/ 1 cause to undergo something, especially an unpleasant experience o *were subjected to rigorous training* 2 bring under the power of another person or group —**subjection** /səb jéksh'n/ n

SYNONYMS subject, topic, subject matter, matter, theme, burden CORE MEANING: what is under discussion

subjective /səb jéktiv/ adj 1 based on personal feelings or opinions 2 existing only in the mind 3 of the subject of a verb —**subjectively** adv —**subjectivity** /súb jek tívvəti/ n

subject line n an e-mail line indicating the subject of the message

subject matter n the material dealt with, e.g. in a book, documentary, or discussion ◊ See note at **subject**

sub judice /súb joodəssi/ adj being examined in court and therefore not for public comment

subjugate /súbjòo gayt/ (-gating, -gated) vt conquer or force into submission —**subjugation** /súbjòo gáysh'n/ n —**subjugator** n

subjunctive /səb júngktiv/ n a grammatical mood expressing doubts, wishes, and possibilities, or a verb in this mood —**subjunctive** adj

sublease /sub leéss/ n an arrangement to rent a property from a tenant —**sublease** vt

sublet /sub lét/ vti (-letting, -let) rent property under a sublease ■ n a property rented under a sublease

sublimate v /súbbli mayt/ (-mating, -mated) 1 vt redirect impulses or energies towards a more acceptable activity 2 vti change directly from a solid to a gas or vice versa ■ n /súbbli mayt, -mət/ a sublimated solid or gas —**sublimation** /súbbli máysh'n/ n

sublime /sə blím/ adj (-limer, -limest) 1 awe-inspiringly beautiful 2 of the highest moral or spiritual value ■ vti (-liming, -limed) change directly from a solid to a gas or vice versa —**sublime** n —**sublimely** adv —**sublimity** /sə blímməti/ n

subliminal /sub límmin'l/ adj below the threshold of conscious awareness —**subliminally** adv

submachine gun /súbmə sheén-/ n a hand-held machine gun

submarine /súbmə reen, súbmə reén/ n an underwater boat that can travel long distances ■ adj underwater —**submariner** /sub márrinər/ n

submerge /səb múrj/ (-merging, -merged) v 1 vti put or go under the surface of water or other liquid 2 vt suppress —**submerged** adj —**submergence** n

submersible /səb múrssəb'l/ adj for underwater use ■ n an underwater boat

submission /səb mísh'n/ n 1 yielding, or readiness to yield 2 something submitted for consideration

submissive /səb missiv/ adj ready to submit to others —**submissively** adv

submit /səb mit/ (-mitting, -mitted) v 1 vt propose or hand in 2 vi yield 3 vi agree to undergo something 4 vi defer to somebody —**submittal** n ◊ See note at **yield**

subnormal /sub náwrm'l/ adj lower than usual or average —**subnormality** /súb nawr málləti/ n

subnotebook /sub nòt bóok/ n a portable computer smaller than a notebook

suborbital /sub áwrbit'l/ adj 1 below the eye socket 2 not making a full orbit of a planet

subordinate adj /sə báwrdinət/ 1 lower in rank 2 of secondary importance ■ n /sə báwrdinət/ somebody of lower rank than another ■ vt /sə báwrdi nayt/ (-ating, -ated) 1 treat as less important than something else 2 place in a lower rank —**subordinately** adv —**subordination** /sə báwrdi náysh'n/ n

suborn /sə báwrn/ vt persuade to do wrong —**subornation** /súbbawr náysh'n/ n

subplot /súb plot/ n 1 a story secondary to the main story 2 a smaller section of a plot of land

subpoena /sə peénə, səb-/ n a legal order summoning a witness or demanding evidence —**subpoena** vt

sub-post office n a small post office inside a shop

subroutine /súb roo teen/ n an independent sequence of computer programming instructions

subscribe /səb skríb/ (-scribing, -scribed) v 1 vi make advance payment for something 2 vti promise to give money regularly or invest in something 3 vi support a theory or view —**subscriber** n

subscript /súb skript/ n a character printed slightly below another character

subscription /səb skrípsh'n/ n 1 advance payment for something, or an agreement to pay for something to be received over a period of time 2 a membership fee

subsection /súb seksh'n/ n a division of a section, e.g. in a document

subsequent /súbssikwənt/ *adj* later in time or order —**subsequently** *adv*

subservient /səb súrvi ənt/ *adj* **1** too eager to obey **2** secondary in importance —**subservience** *n* —**subserviently** *adv*

subset /súb set/ *n* a mathematical set whose elements are contained in another set

subside /səb síd/ (**-siding, -sided**) *vi* **1** diminish in intensity **2** drop to a lower level

subsidence /səb síd'nss, súbssidənss/ *n* **1** the sinking of land **2** the decreasing of something

subsidiarity /səb síddi árrəti/ *n* **1** the assignment of power to the smallest possible political units **2** being subsidiary

subsidiary /səb síddi əri/ *adj* secondary in importance ■ *n* (*pl* **-aries**) **1** a subsidiary person or thing **2** a company controlled by a larger one —**subsidiarily** *adv*

subsidize /súbssi dīz/ (**-dizing, -dized**), **subsidise** *vt* give a subsidy to —**subsidization** /súbssi dī záysh'n/ *n*

subsidy /súbssidi/ (*pl* **-dies**) *n* **1** a grant of money given by a government to a private organization **2** a contribution to help with expenses

subsist /səb síst/ *vi* manage to live on only just enough food or money —**subsistent** *adj*

subsistence /səb sístənss/ *n* **1** subsisting **2** existence

subsistence farming *n* farming that feeds the farmer's family alone —**subsistence farmer** *n*

subsistence level *n* a barely adequate standard of living

subsoil /súb soyl/ *n* the soil beneath the topsoil

subsonic /sub sónnik/ *adj* **1** slower than the speed of sound **2** flying at subsonic speed —**subsonically** *adv*

subspecies /súb spee sheez/ (*pl* same) *n* a distinct plant or animal category within a species

substance /súbstənss/ *n* **1** a kind of matter or material **2** tangible physical matter **3** real or practical value **4** material wealth **5** the gist or actual meaning of something

substance abuse *n* excessive consumption or misuse of any substance, especially drugs or alcohol

~~substancial~~ incorrect spelling of **substantial**

substandard /sub stándərd/ *adj* below the expected or required standard

substantial /səb stánsh'l/ *adj* **1** considerable **2** solid or sturdy **3** filling and satisfying **4** wealthy **5** real and tangible —**substantially** *adv*

substantiate /səb stánshi ayt/ (**-ating, -ated**) *vt* **1** prove or support **2** make real or actual —**substantiation** /səb stánshi áysh'n/ *n*

substantive *adj* /səb stántiv, súbstəntiv/ **1** with practical importance **2** basic or essential **3** of or used like a noun ■ *n* /súbstəntiv/ a noun —**substantively** *adv*

substation /súb staysh'n/ *n* **1** a branch of power station where electrical power is modified or redistributed **2** a subsidiary office or station

substitute /súbsti tyoot/ *vti* (**-tuting, -tuted**) put in or take the place of another ■ *n* **1** something used in place of something else **2** somebody who replaces another, especially during a sports game —**substitution** /súbsti tyoo sh'n/ *n* ◊ See note at **replace**

substratum /sub straátəm, -stráytəm/ (*pl* **-ta** /-tə/) *n* an underlying base or layer, e.g. subsoil or bedrock —**substratal** *adj*

substructure /súb strukchər/ *n* **1** the foundation of a building **2** an underlying structure —**substructural** /sub strúkchərəl/ *adj*

subsume /səb syoom/ (**-suming, -sumed**) *vt* **1** include in a larger category **2** make subject to a rule

subtenant /súb tenənt/ *n* somebody renting property from a tenant —**subtenancy** *n*

subtend /səb ténd/ *vt* **1** extend from one side to the other, opposite an angle or side of a geometric figure **2** lie underneath and enclose

subterfuge /súbtər fyooj/ *n* something designed to hide a real objective

subterranean /súbtə ráyni ən/, **subterraneous** /-ni əss/ *adj* **1** underground **2** secret

subtext /súb tekst/ *n* an underlying meaning —**subtextual** /sub tékschoo əl/ *adj*

subtitle /súb tīt'l/ *n* **1** a printed text or translation of what is being said on television or in a film **2** a subsidiary and often explanatory title —**subtitle** *vt*

subtle /sútt'l/ *adj* **1** slight and not obvious **2** pleasantly understated **3** able to make refined judgments —**subtleness** *n* —**subtlety** *n* —**subtly** *adv*

~~subtley~~ incorrect spelling of **subtly**

subtotal /súb tōt'l/ *n* the total of part of a set of figures —**subtotal** *vt*

subtract /səb trákt/ *v* **1** *vti* perform the arithmetical calculation of deducting one number or quantity from another **2** *vt* remove something from something larger —**subtraction** *n*

subtropical /sub tróppik'l/ *adj* located between tropical and temperate areas —**subtropics** *npl*

subunit /súb yoonit/ *n* a unit that forms part of a larger unit

suburb /súbburb/ *n* a residential area on the edge of a city —**suburban** /sə búrbən/ *adj*

suburbanite /sə búrbə nīt/ *n* an inhabitant of a suburb

suburbia /sə búrbi ə/ *n* suburbs or suburbanites in general

subvention /səb vénsh'n/ *n* a grant or subsidy

subversive /səb vúrssiv/ *adj* intended or likely to subvert ■ *n* somebody involved in subversive activities —**subversively** *adv* —**subversiveness** *n*

subvert /səb vúrt/ *vt* undermine or overthrow a government or other institution —**subversion** *n*

subway /súb way/ n **1** an underground passage for pedestrians **2** *US, Can, Scotland* an underground railway

subzero /sub zeerō/ adj below zero degrees

~~succede~~ incorrect spelling of **succeed**

succeed /sək seéd/ v **1** *vi* achieve what is planned or attempted **2** *vi* gain fame, wealth, or power **3** *vti* follow after in a position or role o *succeed to a title* **4** *vt* come after in time

~~succesful~~ incorrect spelling of **successful**

~~succesive~~ incorrect spelling of **successive**

success /sək séss/ n **1** the achievement of an objective **2** the attainment of fame, wealth, or power

successful /sək séssf'l/ adj **1** achieving what is planned or attempted **2** popular and making a lot of money o *a successful play* **3** prosperous or well known —**successfully** adv

succession /sək sésh'n/ n **1** a series of people or things coming one after another o *a succession of blows* **2** the taking over of a title or position —**successional** adj

successive /sək séssiv/ adj following in sequence —**successively** adv

successor /sək séssər/ n somebody who succeeds another to a position

success story n a successful person or thing

succinct /sək síngkt/ adj brief and to the point —**succinctly** adv —**succinctness** n

succour /súkər/ n help or relief *(literary)*

succulent /súkyoōlənt/ adj **1** juicy and tasty **2** describes a plant with fleshy water-storing parts ■ n a succulent plant —**succulence** n —**succulently** adv

succumb /sə kúm/ vi **1** yield **2** die from an illness or injury ◊ See note at **yield**

~~succed~~ incorrect spelling of **succeed**

~~succesful~~ incorrect spelling of **successful**

~~succesive~~ incorrect spelling of **successive**

such adj **1** of the kind mentioned o *beware of such offers* **2** so great o *Don't be such a fool.* ■ adv very o *such lovely flowers* ■ n this or something of this kind o *Such was his fate.* ◊ **such as** introduces an example ◊ **such as it is** being what it is and no more

such and such adj unspecified ■ pron something unspecified

suchlike /súch līk/ pron others of the same kind *(infml)* ■ adj similar to those just mentioned

suck v **1** *vti* draw liquid out of something with the mouth **2** *vti* make something dissolve in the mouth **3** *vt* draw something in or out o *Fuel is sucked into the cylinder.* **4** *vt* pull with a powerful force **5** *vi US, Can* be very bad *(slang)* —**suck** n

sucker /súkər/ n **1** somebody regarded as easily fooled, influenced, or exploited *(infml)* **2** a concave disc of plastic or rubber that clings by suction **3** an organ, e.g. of a sea animal, that clings by suction **4** an organ for sucking in food **5** a shoot growing from an underground stem or root **6** a freshwater fish with a sucking mouth

suckle /súk'l/ (**-ling, -led**) v **1** *vti* feed from a breast, teat, or udder **2** *vt* nourish *(literary)*

suckling /súkling/ n a baby or young animal

sucrose /soō krōss, syoō-/ n a sugar found naturally in many plants

suction /súksh'n/ n **1** a force created by a difference in pressure **2** the process of sucking

suction pump n a pump that works by suction

Sudan /soo dán/ **1** country in NE Africa. Cap. Khartoum. Pop. 36,080,373 (2001). **2** region of savanna and dry grassland in north-central Africa, south of the Sahara —**Sudanese** /soōdə neéz/ n, adj

sudden /súdd'n/ adj happening quickly and unexpectedly —**suddenly** adv —**suddenness** n ◊ **all of a sudden** in a sudden, unexpected way

sudden death n in sport, the continuation of play until a deciding goal or point is scored

sudden infant death syndrome n cot death *(technical)*

suds npl bubbles on soapy water —**sudsy** adj

sue /syoo, soo/ (**suing, sued**) v **1** *vti* undertake legal proceedings against somebody **2** *vi* make a formal request *(fml)* o *sued for peace after the long siege* —**suer** n

suede /swayd/ n **1** leather with a velvety surface **2** fabric resembling suede

suet /soō it/ n hard fat from sheep and cattle kidneys. Use: cooking, tallow.

Suetonius /swee tṓni əss/, **Gaius Tranquillus** (69?–140) Roman biographer and historian

Suez /soō iz/ port in NE Egypt, at the head of the Gulf of Suez. Pop. 417,000 (1998).

Suez Canal canal in NE Egypt, connecting the Mediterranean and the Red Sea. Length 195 km/121 mi.

suffer /súffər/ v **1** *vti* feel pain or great discomfort in body or mind **2** *vti* undergo something unpleasant **3** *vti* tolerate something **4** *vi* have an illness o *suffers from asthma* **5** *vi* appear to be less good o *suffers in comparison* **6** *vi* be adversely affected —**sufferable** adj —**sufferer** n

~~sufferage~~ incorrect spelling of **suffrage**

sufferance /súffərənss/ n **1** tolerance of something prohibited **2** endurance of difficulty or pain

suffering /súffəring/ n mental or physical pain

suffice /sə físs/ (**-ficing, -ficed**) vi be enough

~~sufficiant~~ incorrect spelling of **sufficient**

sufficient /sə físh'nt/ adj enough —**sufficiency** n —**sufficiently** adv

suffix n /súffiks/ an element added at the end of a word ■ vt /súffiks, sə fíks/ add as suffix —**suffixation** /súffik sáysh'n/ n

suffocate /súffə kayt/ (**-cating, -cated**) vti **1** stop or cause to stop breathing **2** die from a lack of air, or kill by cutting off air **3** not allow or be allowed to develop —**suffocating** adj —**suffocation** /súffə káysh'n/ n

Suffolk /súffək/ county in E England

suffragan /súffrəgən/ n **1** an assistant bishop

2 a bishop working as an assistant to an archbishop —**suffragan** *adj*

suffrage /súffrij/ *n* 1 the right to vote 2 the act of voting *(archaic)*

suffragette /súffrə jét/ *n* a woman who campaigned for women's voting rights

suffragist /súffrəjist/ *n* an advocate of extending voting rights —**suffragism** *n*

suffuse /sə fyoóz/ (**-fusing, -fused**) *vt* spread throughout and over —**suffusion** *n* —**suffusive** /sə fyoóssiv/ *adj*

Sufi /soófi/ (*pl* **-fis**) *n* a Muslim mystic —**Sufi** *adj* —**Sufic** *adj* —**Sufism** *n* —**Sufistic** /soo fístik/ *adj*

~~sufficient~~ incorrect spelling of **sufficient**

sugar /shoóggər/ *n* 1 a sweet-tasting substance in the form of tiny white or brown grains. Use: food sweetener, drinks. 2 a portion of sugar 3 any simple carbohydrate that is sweet-tasting, crystalline, and soluble in water 4 used as a term of endearment *(infml)* ■ *vt* 1 add sugar to something 2 try to make something more agreeable ■ *interj* expresses annoyance —**sugared** *adj*

sugar beet *n* a variety of beet grown for the sugar in its root

sugar cane *n* a tall plant whose sap is a source of sugar

sugar daddy *n* a rich older man who spends money lavishly on a much younger partner *(infml)*

sugary /shoóggəri/ *adj* 1 containing sugar 2 like sugar in taste or appearance 3 exaggeratedly and often insincerely pleasant

suggest /sə jést/ *vt* 1 propose for consideration as a possible choice or course of action 2 remind somebody of 3 express indirectly ◊ See note at **recommend**

suggestible /sə jéstəb'l/ *adj* easily influenced —**suggestibility** /sə jéstə bílləti/ *n*

suggestion /sə jéschən/ *n* 1 an idea or proposal put forward for consideration 2 a slight trace 3 the act of suggesting something 4 the ability to conjure up associations

suggestive /sə jéstiv/ *adj* 1 conjuring up ideas or images 2 implying something improper —**suggestively** *adv* —**suggestiveness** *n*

Suharto /soo haártō/ (b. 1921) president of Indonesia (1967–98)

suicidal /soò i síd'l/ *adj* 1 wanting to commit suicide 2 of suicide 3 extremely dangerous —**suicidally** *adv*

suicide /soò i síd/ *n* 1 the act of killing yourself 2 somebody who commits suicide

suicide bombing *n* a bomb attack in which the bomber dies —**suicide bomber** *n*

suicide pact *n* an agreement between people to kill themselves together

suicide watch *n* a regular check by prison guards on inmates suspected of having suicidal impulses

suit /soot, syoot/ *n* 1 a set of clothes for wearing together, usually made of the same material 2 a set of clothes for a particular purpose

(often in combination) 3 a set of playing cards bearing the same symbols 4 a case brought to a law court 5 the wooing of a woman *(archaic)* ■ *v* 1 *vti* be right or appropriate for somebody or something 2 *vt* look good on somebody 3 *vt* be pleasing or satisfying to somebody 4 *vt* make something suitable 5 *vr* please yourself ◊ **be somebody's strong suit** be something at which somebody is particularly good ◊ **follow suit** 1 do the same as somebody else has done 2 play a card of the same suit as the previous player

suitable /soótəb'l, syoo-/ *adj* right for a particular purpose —**suitability** /soótə bílləti, syoót-/ *n* —**suitably** *adv*

suitcase /soot kayss, syoot-/ *n* a rectangular container for carrying belongings while travelling

suite /sweet/ *n* 1 a set of matching furniture 2 a set of rooms 3 a set of instrumental works performed together 4 the people accompanying an important person 5 an integrated software package

---

SPELLCHECK Do not confuse the spelling of **suite** and **sweet** ('sugary'), which sound similar.

---

suitor /soótər, syoótər/ *n* 1 a man who is wooing a woman *(fml)* 2 somebody seeking to take over a business

Sukarno /soo kaárnō/ (1901–70) president of Indonesia (1945–68)

Sukarnoputri /soo kaárnə pootri/, **Megawati** (b. 1947) Indonesian president (2001–)

Sukkoth /soókəss, -kōt, -kōth, -kōss/, **Succoth**, **Sukkot** *n* a Jewish harvest festival. Date: from the eve of the 15th of Tishri.

Sulawesi /soolə wáyssi/ island in Indonesia, in the Malay Archipelago east of Borneo. Pop. 13,732,500 (1995).

Suleiman I (**the Magnificent**) /soólli maán, soóli maán, soól ay maán/, **Sulayman I** (1494–1566) Ottoman sultan

sulfur *n* (US or technical) CHEM ELEM = **sulphur**

sulk *vi* be angrily silent or aloof ■ *n* 1 a period or state of sulking 2 somebody who sulks —**sulker** *n*

sulky /súlki/ *adj* (**-ier, -iest**) angrily silent or aloof ■ *n* (*pl* **-ies**) a horse-drawn vehicle for one person —**sulkily** *adv* —**sulkiness** *n*

sullen /súllən/ *adj* maintaining a hostile silence —**sullenly** *adv* —**sullenness** *n*

Sullivan /súllivən/, **Sir Arthur** (1842–1900) British composer

sully /súlli/ (**-lies, -lied**) *vt* 1 spoil or tarnish ○ *a reputation sullied by scandal* 2 make dirty —**sullied** *adj*

sulpha drug /súlfə-/ *n* an antibacterial drug

sulphate /súl fayt/ *n* a salt or ester of sulphuric acid ■ *vt* (**-phating, -phated**) treat with sulphur or a sulphate

sulphide /súl fíd/ *n* a compound in which sulphur is typically combined with one or more elements or groups with a positive electric charge

sulphite /súl fīt/ *n* a salt or ester of sulphurous acid

sulphur /súlfər/ *n* (*symbol* S) a yellow nonmetallic chemical element. Use: manufacture of sulphuric acid, matches, fungicides, and gunpowder.

sulphur dioxide *n* a strong-smelling toxic gas. Use: food preservative, fumigant, bleaching agent, manufacture of sulphuric acid.

sulphureous *adj* = sulphurous

sulphuric /sul fyóorik/ *adj* containing sulphur, especially with a valency of six

sulphuric acid *n* a strong corrosive acid. Use: batteries, manufacture of fertilizers, explosives, detergents and dyes.

sulphurize /súlfyoŏ rīz/ (**-izing, -ized**), **sulphurise** *vt* treat or combine something with sulphur or a sulphur compound

sulphurous /súlfərəss/, **sulphureous** /sul fyŏōri əss/ *adj* 1 containing sulphur, especially with a valency of four 2 similar to burning sulphur, especially in colour or smell

sulphurous acid *n* a weak colourless acid. Use: food preservative, disinfectant, bleaching agent.

sultan /súltən/ *n* especially formerly, a Muslim ruler —**sultanship** *n*

sultana /sul taánə/ *n* 1 a dried grape 2 a sultan's woman relative

sultanate /súltənət/ *n* 1 a country ruled by a sultan 2 the rank of sultan

sultry /súltri/ *adj* 1 hot and damp 2 sensual —**sultriness** *n*

Sulu Sea /soŏloo-/ arm of the Pacific Ocean west of the Philippines and northeast of Borneo

sum[1] /sum/ *n* 1 an amount of money 2 an arithmetical calculation 3 a total 4 the gist of something (*literary*) ■ *vt* (**summing, summed**) add up (*fml*)

ORIGIN **Sum** came through French from a Latin word literally meaning 'highest thing'. The development in meaning from 'highest' to 'sum total' results from the Roman practice of counting columns of figures from the bottom upwards, the total being written at the top.

☐ **sum up** *vti* 1 summarize something 2 review evidence for a jury (*refers to a judge*)

sum[2] /soom/, **som** *n* the main unit of currency in Uzbekistan

sumach /soŏ mak, shoŏ-/ *n* 1 a tree of the cashew family 2 ground and dried leaves from one kind of sumach tree. Use: tanning, dyeing.

~~sumary~~ incorrect spelling of **summary**

Sumatra /soŏ maátrə/ island in W Indonesia, separated from the Malay Peninsula by the Strait of Malacca. Pop. 40,830,400 (1995). —**Sumatran** *n, adj*

Sumer /soŏmər/ ancient country of S Mesopotamia, in present-day Iraq

Sumerian /soo meéri ən/ *n* 1 a member of a people of ancient Babylonia 2 the language of ancient Sumer —**Sumerian** *adj*

summarize /súmmə rīz/ (**-rizing, -rized**), **summarise** *vt* make a summary of —**summarist** *n* —**summarization** /súmmə rī záysh'n/ *n*

summary /súmməri/ *n* (*pl* **summaries**) a short version of something, containing the main points ■ *adj* 1 done immediately and with little discussion or attention to formalities 2 giving only the main points —**summarily** /súmmərəli/ *adv* —**summariness** *n*

summation /su máysh'n/ *n* 1 arithmetical addition 2 a total 3 a summary of something said —**summative** /súmmətiv/ *adj*

summer /súmmər/ *n* 1 the warmest season of the year 2 the warm weather associated with summer ■ *vi* spend the summer somewhere —**summery** *adj*

summer camp *n* a place of summer recreation for children, usually in the country

summerhouse /súmmər howss/ (*pl* **-houses** /-howziz/) *n* a light shelter in a garden or park

summer pudding *n* a pudding of soft fruits encased in bread

summer school *n* a course of study attended in the summer

summer time *n* the time set one hour ahead of standard time during the summer

summertime /súmmər tīm/ *n* the season of summer

summit /súmmit/ *n* 1 the highest point of a mountain 2 the highest point of anything 3 a conference between heads of government on a matter of great importance

summon /súmmən/ *v* 1 *vt* order somebody to appear in court 2 *vt* send for somebody 3 *vt* convene a group 4 *vi* gather resources such as courage or strength

summons /súmmənz/ *n* an official order to appear in a specific place, especially in court, at a specific time ■ *vt* serve somebody with a summons

sumo /soŏmō/ *n* a Japanese style of wrestling

sump *n* 1 a low area into which a liquid drains 2 the oil reservoir at the bottom of an engine's crankcase 3 a cesspool for waste

~~sumptious~~ incorrect spelling of **sumptuous**

sumptuous /súmptyoo əss/ *adj* 1 splendid in appearance 2 lavish or extravagant —**sumptuously** *adv* —**sumptuousness** *n*

sum total *n* 1 everything put together 2 a final total

sun /sun/ *n* 1 *also* **Sun** the star around which the Earth revolves 2 any star 3 light or heat from the Sun ■ *v* (**sunning, sunned**) 1 *vr* bask in the sun 2 *vt* warm or dry in the sun —**sunless** *adj* ◊ **under the sun** in the whole world ◊ See note at **son**

Sun. *abbr* Sunday

sunbaked /sún baykt/ *adj* hardened, dried, or baked by the sun

sunbathe /sún bayth/ *vi* expose the body to the rays of the sun —**sunbather** *n* —**sunbathing** *n*

sunbeam /sún beem/ *n* a ray of sunlight

sunbed /sún bed/ *n* an apparatus that tans by means of ultraviolet light

sun blind *n* a shade that gives protection from the sun

sunblock /sún blok/ *n* a cream or lotion applied to the skin to block out ultraviolet rays

sunburn /sún burn/ *n* a painful inflammation or blistering of the skin as the result of over-exposure to the sun ■ *vti* (**-burnt** /-burnt/ *or* **-burned**) suffer or cause to suffer sunburn —**sunburnt** *adj*

sunburst /sún burst/ *n* **1** a sudden burst of sunshine **2** a design consisting of rays extending from a central circle

sundae /sún day, -di/ *n* an ice-cream dessert with toppings

Sunda Islands /súndə-/ island group of the Malay Archipelago comprising the Greater Sunda Islands, which include Sumatra, Java, and Borneo, and the Lesser Sunda Islands, which include Bali and Timor

Sunday /sún day, -di/ *n* **1** the 7th day of the week **2** the Christian Sabbath day ■ *adj* **1** of Sunday **2** for special occasions

ORIGIN The origin of **Sunday** is exactly what it appears to be, the 'day of the sun'.

Sunday best *n* somebody's best clothes

Sunday school *n* a class offering religious education on Sundays

sun deck *n* ANZ, US a balcony or terrace used for sunbathing

sunder /súndər/ *vti* break or be broken apart (*literary*)

sundial /sún dī əl/ *n* an instrument that shows the time by a sun-generated shadow

sundown /sún down/ *n* sunset

sundrenched /sún drencht/ *adj* describes a place that enjoys much hot sunshine

sundress /sún dress/ *n* a sleeveless dress worn in hot weather

sun-dried *adj* dried in the sun

sundry /súndri/ *adj* various ■ **sundries** *npl* various miscellaneous items or goods

sunfish /sún fish/ (*pl same or* **-fishes**) *n* **1** a large sea fish **2** a North American spiny-finned freshwater fish, often with iridescent colours

sunflower /sún flow ər/ *n* a tall plant with large yellow-rayed flowers

sung past participle of **sing**

sunglasses /sún glaassiz/ *npl* tinted glasses that protect the eyes against strong sunlight

sunk past participle, past tense of **sink**

sunken /súngkən/ *adj* **1** submerged **2** appearing hollow o *sunken cheeks* **3** situated at a lower level than the surrounding area o *a sunken garden*

sunlamp /sún lamp/ *n* an ultraviolet lamp used for tanning or therapeutic purposes

sunlight /sún līt/ *n* light from the sun —**sunlit** /súnlit/ *adj*

Sunni /sóoni, súnni/ (*pl same or* **-nis**) *n* **1** one of the main branches of Islam **2** a member of the Sunni branch of Islam

sunnies /súnniz/ *npl* ANZ sunglasses (*infml*)

sunny /súnni/ (**-nier, -niest**) *adj* **1** full of sunshine **2** full of sunlight **3** cheerful —**sunniness** *n*

sunny-side up *adj* describes an egg that is fried on one side only

sunrise /sún rīz/ *n* the coming up of the sun, or the time when this occurs

sunroof /sún roof/ *n* a window in the roof of a car

sunscreen /sún skreen/ *n* a substance applied to the skin to prevent sunburn when tanning

sunset /sún set/ *n* the going down of the sun, or the time when this occurs

sunshade /sún shayd/ *n* an awning, parasol, or similar object that gives shade from the sun

sunshine /sún shīn/ *n* **1** direct sunlight **2** a place where the sun's rays can be felt **3** a source of good feelings —**sunshiny** *adj*

sunspot /sún spot/ *n* **1** a dark patch on the sun **2** a warm and sunny place (*infml*)

sunstroke /sún strōk/ *n* an illness caused by overexposure to the sun

suntan /sún tan/ *n* a darkening of the skin from exposure to the sun —**suntanned** *adj*

suntrap /sún trap/ *n* a sunny spot without wind

sunup /sún up/ *n* US sunrise

Sun Yat-sen /soón yát sén/ (1866–1925) Chinese revolutionary leader

sup[1] *vt* (**supping, supped**) **1** sip liquid **2** eat something by the spoonful ■ *n* a sip of liquid

sup[2] (**supping, supped**) *vi* have supper (*fml or literary*)

super /sóopər/ (*infml*) *adj* **1** excellent **2** very great ■ *adv* especially ■ *n* **1** a superintendent **2** ANZ superannuation ■ *interj* expresses great enthusiasm or approval

super- *prefix* **1** something larger, stronger, or faster than others of its kind o *superstore* **2** over, above, on o *superstructure* **3** exceeding the usual limits o *superheat* **4** in addition to, over and above o *supernumerary*

superannuated /sóopər ánnyoo aytid/ *adj* **1** retired **2** worn out **3** out-of-date

superannuation /sóopər anyoo aysh'n/ *n* **1** a regular deduction from wages as a contribution to a pension scheme **2** a retirement pension

superb /soo púrb, syoo-/ *adj* **1** excellent **2** grand —**superbly** *adv*

superbug /sóopər bug/, **supergerm** /-jurm/ *n* an antibiotic-resistant bacterium

~~supercede~~ incorrect spelling of **supersede**

supercharger /sóopər chaarjər/ *n* a device used to increase an engine's power

supercilious /sóopər sílli əss/ *adj* contemptuously indifferent —**superciliously** *adv*

ORIGIN **Supercilious** comes from a Latin adjective formed from *supercilium* 'eyebrow' (from *super* 'above' and *cilium* 'eyelid'). It refers to raised eyebrows as a sign of haughty disdain.

supercomputer /sóopər kəm pyóotər/ n a high-speed computer

superconductivity /sóopər kon duk tívvəti/ n the ability to conduct electricity without resistance —**superconductive** /-kən dúktiv/ adj —**superconductor** /-kən dúktər/ n

superficial /sóopər físh'l/ adj **1** concerned only with the obvious or main parts of something **2** of or on the surface **3** without depth of character **4** only apparent **5** insignificant —**superficiality** /-fishi álləti/ n —**superficially** adv

superfine /sóopər fín/ adj **1** of extremely fine grain or texture **2** of the highest quality

superfluity /sóopər flóo əti/ (pl **-ties**) n **1** an excessive quantity **2** something inessential

superfluous /soo púr floo əss/ adj **1** more than necessary **2** not essential —**superfluously** adv

supergerm n = superbug

superglue /sóopər gloo/ n a fast-acting strong glue

supergroup /sóopər groop/ n a world-famous rock music band

superheat /sóopər heét/ vt heat something to an extremely high degree or beyond its boiling point

superheavyweight /sóopər hévvi wayt/ n **1** the heaviest weight category for boxers **2** a boxer who competes at superheavyweight

superhero /sóopər heeró/ (pl **-roes**) n a superhuman cartoon character who fights crime

superhighway /sóopər hí way/ n US a major motorway

superhuman /sóopər hyóomən/ adj **1** beyond human capability, or having more-than-human capabilities **2** supernatural —**superhumanly** adv

superimpose /sóopərim póz/ (**-posing**, **-posed**) vt lay something over something else —**superimposition** /sóopər impə zísh'n/ n

superintend /sóopərin ténd/ vt be in charge of superintendant incorrect spelling of **superintendent**

superintendent /sóopərin téndənt/ n **1** somebody in charge **2** a high-ranking police officer ■ adj in charge —**superintendence** n —**superintendency** n

superior /soo peéri ər/ adj **1** higher in quality, degree, rank, or position **2** above average **3** condescending **4** above being affected by something ○ regarded herself as superior to spurious gossip **5** written or printed higher than the main characters ■ n **1** somebody or something higher or better than others **2** somebody in charge of a religious order —**superiority** /soo peéri órrəti/ n —**superiorly** adv

Superior, Lake /soo peéri ər/ westernmost of the Great Lakes, between the north-central United States and S Ontario, Canada. Depth 406 m/1,333 ft. Length 560 km/350 mi.

superlative /soo púrlətiv/ adj **1** excellent **2** highest in degree of grammatical comparison ■ n **1** the form of an adjective or adverb that expresses the highest degree of grammatical comparison **2** a superlative adjective or adverb **3** somebody or something of the highest degree of excellence —**superlatively** adv

superman /sóopər man/ (pl **-men** /-men/) n **1** a man who is a high achiever **2** Nietzsche's ideal man

ORIGIN **Superman** was introduced by George Bernard Shaw as a translation of German Übermensch, a coinage by Friedrich Nietzsche. Shaw used it in the title of his play Man and Superman (1903).

supermarket /sóopər maarkit/ n a large self-service shop selling groceries and household goods

supermodel /sóopər mod'l/ n a famous and highly paid fashion model

supernatural /sóopər náchərəl/ adj **1** not of the natural world **2** of a deity ■ n **1** supernatural things **2** the realm of supernatural things —**supernaturally** adv

supernova /sóopər nóvə/ (pl **-vae** /-vee/ or **-vas**) n an exploding star

supernumerary /sóopər nyóomərəri/ adj **1** exceeding the usual number **2** employed as a substitute or extra worker ■ n (pl **-ies**) **1** somebody or something extra **2** an actor without a speaking part

superordinate /sóopər áwrdinət/ n **1** a word whose meaning includes another more specific word **2** somebody or something superior —**superordinate** adj

superpower /sóopər pow ər/ n **1** a powerful nation **2** extremely high electrical or mechanical power —**superpowered** adj

superscript /sóopər skript/ n a letter, number, or symbol written or printed higher than the main characters —**superscript** adj

supersede /sóopər seéd/ (**-seding**, **-seded**) vt **1** replace something less efficient, modern, or appropriate **2** succeed somebody or something else, e.g. in a position (fml) —**supersedence** n

superserver /sóopər survər/ n a powerful computer that controls a network

supersonic /sóopər sónnik/ adj capable of exceeding the speed of sound —**supersonically** adv

superstar /sóopər staar/ n a very famous person in sports or entertainment

superstition /sóopər stísh'n/ n **1** an irrational belief that something bad or good will happen if a specific thing is done **2** irrational beliefs in general

superstitious /sóopər stíshəss/ adj **1** believing in superstitions **2** based on an irrational belief

superstore /sóopər stawr/ n a very large supermarket or specialist retailer

superstructure /sóopər strukchər/ n **1** a ship's upper structure **2** the visible part of a building **3** the part of something that has developed from a base —**superstructural** /sóopər strúkchərəl/ adj

supertanker /sōōpər tangkər/ *n* a big tanker ship

supervise /sōōpər vīz/ (**-vising**, **-vised**) *vti* oversee an activity or a group of people —**supervision** /sōōpər vízh'n/ *n*

~~superviser~~ incorrect spelling of **supervisor**

supervision order *n* an order that gives a named social worker the job of supervising the welfare of a specific child

supervisor /sōōpər vīzər/ *n* **1** somebody who supervises a group of workers **2** a tutor for a graduate student —**supervisory** /-vīzəri, -vízəri/ *adj*

superwoman /sōōpər wŏmən/ (*pl* **-en** /-wimin/) *n* a woman regarded as superhuman

supine /sōō pīn, syōō-/ *adj* **1** lying on the back **2** passive or lethargic

~~supose~~ incorrect spelling of **suppose**

supper /súppər/ *n* **1** a snack or small meal eaten before bedtime **2** the main evening meal

suppertime /súppər tīm/ *n* the time when supper is eaten

supplant /sə plaánt/ *vt* **1** take somebody's place by force **2** take the place of something outmoded or irrelevant —**supplantation** /súpplaan táysh'n/ *n*

supple /súpp'l/ (**-pler**, **-plest**) *adj* **1** flexible **2** moving with ease and grace —**supplely** *adv* —**suppleness** *n*

supplement *n* /súpplimənt/ **1** an addition **2** a publication that enlarges on or corrects something previously published **3** an additional section in a newspaper or magazine **4** a food substance taken to improve the diet **5** an extra charge ■ *vt* /súppli ment/ **1** make an addition to **2** be an additional part of —**supplemental** /súppli mént'l/ *adj* —**supplementation** /súppli men táysh'n/ *n* —**supplementer** *n*

supplementary /súppli méntəri/ *adj* **1** additional **2** making up for something lacking

supplementary benefit *n* a former state allowance given to low-income families

suppliant /súppli ənt/ *adj* making a humble appeal (*fml*) —**suppliance** *n*

supplicant /súpplikənt/ *n* somebody who makes a supplication (*fml*)

supplication /súppli káysh'n/ *n* (*fml*) **1** a humble appeal made to somebody in authority **2** the addressing of wishes to somebody able to grant them —**supplicate** /súppli kayt/ *vti* —**supplicatory** /súpplikətəri, -kaytəri/ *adj*

~~suppliment~~ incorrect spelling of **supplement**

supply /sə plī/ *vt* (**-plies**, **-plied**) **1** provide something wanted or needed by somebody **2** satisfy a need (*fml*) ■ *n* (*pl* **-plies**) **1** the available amount of something **2** the act of providing something **3** the quantity of something that is available in a market ■ **supplies** *npl* basic things needed to survive or operate —**supplier** *n*

supply-side economics *n* the economics of production (+ *sing or pl verb*)

supply teacher *n* a temporary replacement for a teacher

support /sə páwrt/ *vt* **1** keep from falling **2** bear the weight of **3** sustain financially **4** give help or encouragement to **5** be in favour of **6** give comfort to **7** corroborate **8** play a subsidiary role alongside ■ *n* **1** something that supports **2** assistance, encouragement, or approval **3** a supportive person **4** a group of supporters, e.g. of a team —**supportable** *adj* —**supporter** *n* —**supportive** *adj*

support group *n* a group of people who meet to discuss their problems and help one another

support stockings *npl* stockings that support the veins in the lower legs

suppose /sə pốz/ (**-posing**, **-posed**) *vt* **1** believe or imagine to be true **2** consider or imagine as possible **3** take or require as a precondition **4** require or expect to do something (*usually passive*) ○ *You're supposed to be in school.*

supposed /sə pốzd, -pốzid/ *adj* accepted as true but doubtful —**supposedly** /-idli/ *adv*

supposing /sə pốzing/ *conj* if it is assumed that (*infml*)

supposition /súppə zísh'n/ *n* **1** a hypothesis **2** the mental act of supposing —**suppositional** *adj*

suppository /sə pózzitəri/ (*pl* **-ries**) *n* a small medicated solid designed to dissolve in the rectum or vagina

suppress /sə préss/ *vt* **1** put an end to something by force ○ *swiftly suppressed the student protest* **2** prevent or restrain something **3** stop the spread or publication of information **4** resist feelings or memories consciously —**suppressant** *n* —**suppressible** *adj* —**suppression** *n*

supra /sōōprə/ *adv* above

supra- *prefix* transcending ○ *supranational*

supranational /sōōprə násh'nəl/ *adj* multinational —**supranationalism** *n*

supremacist /sōō prémməssist, syōō-/ *n* a believer in the superiority of a particular racial group (*usually in combination*)

supremacy /sōō prémməssi, syōō-/ *n* a position of superiority or authority

supreme /sōō preém, syōō-/ *adj* **1** above all others in power or status **2** highest in degree —**supremely** *adv*

suprême /sōō preém, syōō-, -prém/ *adj* describes food served with a rich cream sauce

Supreme Being *n* God

supremo /sōō preémō, syōō-/ (*pl* **-mos**) *n* somebody with overriding authority (*infml*)

~~supress~~ incorrect spelling of **suppress**

~~suprise~~ incorrect spelling of **surprise**

Surabaya /sōōrə bī ə/ city on NE Java Island, Indonesia. Pop. 2,351,303 (1997).

Surat /sōō rát, sōōrət/ port in W India. Pop. 1,498,817 (1991).

surcharge /súr chaarj/ *vti* (**-charging**, **-charged**) **1** charge a customer an additional amount **2** overcharge a customer ■ *n* an extra charge

sure /shoor, shawr/ *adj* (**surer**, **surest**) **1** definitely true **2** firmly believing something **3** certain to happen **4** certain to be obtained **5** very confident **6** always effective **7** firm and secure ■ *adv US (infml)* **1** undoubtedly **2** yes —**sureness** *n* ◊ **for sure** without a doubt *(infml)* ◊ **make sure (that) 1** take the necessary action to or make something happen **2** check that something is the case, or that something has been done properly ◊ **sure enough** as was expected o *Sure enough, the cat came back.*

sure-fire *adj* certain to succeed *(infml)*

sure-footed *adj* unlikely to stumble or fall —**sure-footedly** *adv*—**sure-footedness** *n*

surely /shoórli, sháwr-/ *adv* **1** invites a response, e.g. of confirmation or denial o *Surely you don't mean that!* **2** without fail **3** *US* without doubt

surety /shoórəti, sháwr-/ *(pl* **-ties)** *n* **1** a guarantee against loss or damage **2** a guarantor —**suretyship** *n*

surf *n* foamy waves ■ *v* **1** *vi* ride waves on a surfboard **2** *vt* visit various sites on the Internet in search of something, often casually —**surfer** *n*—**surfing** *n*

surface /súrfiss/ *n* (*pl* **-faces**) **1** the outermost or uppermost part of something **2** a solid flat area **3** a thin layer applied to the outside of something **4** a superficial part ■ *adj* **1** used on or applied to a surface **2** superficial ■ *v* (**-facing, -faced**) **1** *vi* come up to the surface of water **2** *vi* appear **3** *vi* become known **4** *vt* give a surface to ◊ **on the surface** as an outward appearance or when examined superficially ◊ **scratch the surface** deal with only a very small or relatively unimportant part of something

surface mail *n* the ordinary mail service, as opposed to air mail

surface tension *n* (*symbol* γ *or* σ) the naturally elastic quality of the surface of a liquid

surface-to-air *adj* describes a missile launched from the ground or a ship against an air target

surfboard /súrf bawrd/ *n* a board on which to ride ocean waves —**surfboarder** *n* —**surfboarding** *n*

surfeit /súrfit/ *n* **1** an excessive number or amount **2** overindulgence in food or drink ■ *vt* give somebody a surfeit of something

surge *vi* (**surging, surged**) **1** move like a wave **2** make a concerted rush **3** increase suddenly ■ *n* **1** a surging movement **2** a sudden increase in an emotion or feeling **3** a sudden power increase

surgeon /súrjən/ *n* **1** a doctor who specializes in performing operations **2** a medical officer in the armed forces

ORIGIN Surgeon goes back ultimately to the Greek words for 'hand' and 'work', so a **surgeon** is one who performs manual operations.

surge protector *n* a device that protects electrical equipment against power surges

surgery /súrjəri/ (*pl* **-ies**) *n* **1** medical treatment involving operations **2** the branch of medicine that deals with operations **3** a doctor's or dentist's place of work **4** the time when a doctor, politician, or other professional person is available for consultation

surgical /súrjik'l/ *adj* **1** of surgery **2** resulting from surgery —**surgically** *adv*

surgical spirit *n* methylated spirit mixed with oil. Use: cleaning the skin before medical procedures

Suriname /soóri nám, -naàmə/ country in NE South America. Cap. Paramaribo. Pop. 433,998 (2001). —**Surinamese** /soóri nə meéz/ *n, adj*

surly /súrli/ (**-lier, -liest**) *adj* bad-tempered and rude —**surliness** *n*

ORIGIN Surly means etymologically 'like a lord or sir'. It is a mid-16C alteration of obsolete *sirly* 'lordly, haughty, imperious'. **Surly** shared these early meanings, but they did not survive far into the 18C, and from the late 16C the modern sense of 'bad-tempered' dominated.

surmise /sur míz/ *vti* make a guess about something ■ *n* guesswork or conjecture —**surmisable** *adj*

surmount /sur mównt/ *vt* **1** overcome a difficulty **2** get to the top of something *(fml)* **3** be placed on top of something *(fml)* —**surmountable** *adj*

surname /súr naym/ *n* somebody's family name —**surname** *vt*

~~surround~~ incorrect spelling of **surround**

surpass /sur paáss/ *vt* **1** go beyond or be greater or better than **2** do better than

surpassing /sur paássing/ *adj* outstanding *(literary)* —**surpassingly** *adv*

surplice /súrpliss/ *n* a white ecclesiastical outer garment

surplus /súrpləss/ *n* an excess amount ■ *adj* additional to requirements

surprise /sər príz/ *vt* (**-prising, -prised**) **1** make somebody amazed **2** catch somebody or something unawares **3** give somebody something unexpectedly ■ *n* **1** something surprising or unexpected **2** amazement —**surprising** *adj*—**surprisingly** *adv* ◊ **take by surprise** happen unexpectedly to

~~surprize~~ incorrect spelling of **surprise**

surreal /sə reé el/ *adj* **1** bizarrely unreal or dreamlike **2** of surrealism —**surreal** *n* —**surreally** *adv*

surrealism /sə reé əlizəm/ *n* **1** an early 20C artistic and literary movement that represented the subconscious with fantastic imagery and the juxtaposition of contradictory elements **2** surreal art or literature —**surrealist** *n, adj*—**surrealistic** /sə reé ə lístik/ *adj*—**surrealistically** *adv*

surrender /sə réndər/ *v* **1** *vi* stop fighting because you are unable to win **2** *vt* give up possession or control of **3** *vt* give up or abandon **4** *vi* give yourself up to something such as an emotion ■ *n* the act of surrendering ◊ See note at **yield**

surreptitious /súrrəp tíshəss/ *adj* secret and stealthy —**surreptitiously** *adv* ◊ See note at **secret**

surrey /súrri/ (*pl* -**reys**) *n* a 19C horse-drawn carriage with two or four seats

Surrey /súrri/ county in SE England

surrogate *adj* /súrrəgat, -gayt/ taking the place of somebody or something else ■ *n* /súrrəgət, -gayt/ 1 a substitute 2 a woman who bears a child for another 3 a substitute authority figure ■ *vt* /súrrə gayt/ (-**gating**, -**gated**) appoint as a stand-in —**surrogacy** *n* —**surrogateship** *n* —**surrogation** /súrrə gáysh'n/ *n*

surround /sə równd/ *vt* 1 occupy the space all around 2 encircle in order to close off all means of escape ■ *n* 1 an outside border 2 an area around something

surroundings /sə równdingz/ *npl* the landscape, events, circumstances, or objects around somebody or something

surtax /súr taks/ *n* 1 an additional tax 2 a higher tax that applies above a specific level

Surtees /súrt eez/, **John** (*b.* 1934) British motorcyclist and motor racing driver

~~surveilance~~ incorrect spelling of **surveillance**

surveillance /sur váylənss/ *n* continual close observation

survey /sur váy, súr vay/ (-**veys**, -**veying**, -**veyed**) 1 look at or consider something generally 2 look at or consider something carefully 3 plot a map of an area 4 inspect a building 5 question people in a poll ■ *n* /súr vay/ (*pl* -**veys**) 1 an opinion poll, or an analysis of the results 2 an act or the process of surveying 3 a result of surveying, e.g. a report or map 4 a general view —**surveyable** *adj*

~~surveyer~~ incorrect spelling of **surveyor**

surveyor /sur váy ər/ *n* 1 somebody who surveys land 2 a building inspector

survival /sur vív'l/ *n* 1 the fact of surviving 2 the act or process of surviving in adverse conditions

survive /sər vív/ (-**viving**, -**vived**) *v* 1 *vi* remain alive or in existence 2 *vt* stay alive longer than somebody 3 *vt* live through something difficult or unpleasant —**survivable** *adj*

~~surviver~~ incorrect spelling of **survivor**

survivor /sə vívər/ *n* 1 somebody who survives a difficult or dangerous experience 2 a close relative who outlives another

~~susceptable, suseptible~~ incorrect spelling of **susceptible**

susceptible /sə séptəb'l/ *adj* 1 easily affected 2 likely to be affected —**susceptibility** /sə séptə bílləti/ *n* —**susceptibly** *adv*

sushi /soo shee/ *n* small cakes of rice mixed with fish or vegetables and wrapped in seaweed

~~suspecious~~ incorrect spelling of **suspicious**

suspect *vt* /sə spékt/ 1 think that somebody may be guilty 2 doubt the truth or validity of something 3 believe something to be so ■ *n* /súss pekt/ a person suspected of wrongdoing ■ *adj* /súss pekt/ 1 likely to be false or

untrustworthy 2 likely to contain something illegal or dangerous ○ *inspected the suspect luggage* ◊ **the usual suspects** the people or organizations frequently mentioned in the context of a specific activity *(slang)*

~~suspence~~ incorrect spelling of **suspense**

suspend /sə spénd/ *vt* 1 hang something from above 2 stop something for a period of time 3 bar somebody for a period of time 4 postpone something 5 disperse particles in a liquid or gas

suspended animation *n* 1 the temporary slowing of biological functions 2 an unconscious state resembling death

suspended sentence *n* a penal sentence that will be served only if the offender commits a similar offence within the stated period

suspender /sə spéndər/ *n* 1 a strap for holding up a woman's stockings 2 *US* a strap for holding up trousers *(usually pl)*

suspender belt *n* a belt with suspenders to hold a woman's stockings up

suspense /sə spénss/ *n* 1 uncertainty 2 enjoyable tension —**suspenseful** *adj*

suspension /sə spénsh'n/ *n* 1 a temporary stopping or postponement of something 2 the temporary removal of somebody, e.g. from a job, school, or team, usually as a punishment 3 a system that reduces the effects of vibration in a vehicle 4 a dispersion of particles in a liquid or gas

suspension bridge *n* a bridge suspended from cables

suspicion /sə spísh'n/ *n* 1 the feeling that somebody has done something wrong 2 mistrust 3 the condition of being suspected

suspicious /sə spíshəss/ *adj* 1 arousing suspicion 2 tending to suspect 3 indicating suspicion —**suspiciously** *adv* —**suspiciousness** *n*

suss □ **suss out** *vt* understand all about *(infml)*

sustain /sə stáyn/ *vt* 1 continue something in spite of difficulties 2 experience something such as injury or loss 3 make something continue to exist 4 nourish somebody 5 support something from below 6 provide somebody with moral support 7 decide that something, e.g. an objection, is valid 8 confirm something ○ *sustained the lower court's ruling*

sustainable /sə stáynəb'l/ *adj* 1 able to be maintained 2 exploiting natural resources without destroying ecological balance ○ *sustainable agriculture* —**sustainably** *adv*

sustenance /sússtənənss/ *n* 1 nourishment 2 the condition of being sustained 3 livelihood

Sutherland /súthərlənd/, **Dame Joan** (*b.* 1926) Australian operatic soprano

~~sutle~~ incorrect spelling of **subtle**

Sutlej /súttlij/ river in South Asia, flowing through SW Tibet, N India, and E Pakistan. Length 1,450 km/901 mi.

sutra /soo trə/ *n* 1 a summary of Hindu teachings 2 *also* **sutta** /soóttə/ a Buddhist religious text

Sutton /súttʹn/, **Henry** (1856–1912) Australian inventor

suture /soóchər/ n 1 material used for surgical stitching 2 the line of a seam or join, e.g. between the edges of a wound 3 an immovable joint between bones ■ vt (-**turing**, -**tured**) close a wound with sutures —**sutural** adj

Suva /soóvə/ capital of Fiji. Pop. 77,366 (2000).

~~suvivor~~ incorrect spelling of **survivor**

svelte /svelt/ adj graceful and slender

Svengali /sven gaáli/ n an evil manipulator

> **ORIGIN** The original **Svengali** was a villainous hypnotist in the novel *Trilby* (1894) by the French-born novelist and illustrator George du Maurier (1834–96).

SVGA n a video screen specification. Full form **super video graphics array**

SW abbr 1 short wave 2 southwest 3 southwestern

swab /swob/ n 1 a piece of soft material for soaking up blood 2 a small ball of cotton wool attached to a short stick 3 a specimen of mucus or other secretion taken using a swab 4 a mop ■ vt (**swabbing, swabbed**) 1 clean or treat with a swab 2 mop

swaddle /swódd'l/ (-**dling, -dled**) vt 1 wrap somebody in something 2 wrap a baby up tightly

swag n 1 a curtain that hangs in a curve 2 a festoon 3 loot (slang) 4 Aus the personal belongings of an itinerant person ■ vi (**swagging, swagged**) move with a lurch

swagger /swággər/ vi 1 walk in an arrogant way 2 speak boastfully —**swagger** n —**swaggerer** n —**swaggeringly** adv

Swahili /swə heéli, swaa-/ (pl same or -**lis**) n 1 a member of an E African people 2 the Bantu language of the Swahili people —**Swahili** adj

swain n a woman's male admirer or lover (literary)

SWALK /swawlk, swolk/ abbr sealed with a loving kiss

swallow¹ /swóllō/ v 1 vti take in something through the mouth and down the throat 2 vi make the movement of swallowing food or drink with the throat 3 vt engulf or destroy something 4 vt suppress feelings 5 vt believe something (infml) 6 vt endure something ■ n 1 the act of swallowing food or drink 2 an amount of food or drink swallowed

swallow² /swóllō/ n a small songbird with pointed wings and a forked tail

swam past tense of **swim**

swami /swaámi/ n a respected Hindu religious teacher

swamp /swomp/ n an area of wetland ■ v 1 vt inundate an area 2 vti become, or cause a boat to become, full of water and sink 3 vt overburden somebody or something —**swampy** adj

swampland /swómp land/ n an area of wetland

swan /swon/ n a large long-necked water bird ■ vi (**swanning, swanned**) wander about idly (infml)

swank /swangk/ vi show off (infml) —**swankiness** n —**swanky** adj

swansdown /swónz down/, **swan's-down** n swan feathers

Swansea /swónzi/ port in S Wales. Pop. 230,180 (1996). Welsh **Abertawe**

swansong /swón song/ n a final public performance or act

swap /swop/, **swop** (infml) vti (**swapping, swapped; swopping, swopped**) exchange things ■ n an exchange —**swappable** adj

> **ORIGIN** **Swap** originally meant 'hit'. The sense 'exchange' emerged in the 16C from the idea of striking hands to seal a bargain.

sward /swawrd/ n an area of grass

swarf /swawrf/ n 1 space debris that orbits the Earth (infml) 2 metal shavings

swarm¹ /swawrm/ n 1 a group of insects 2 a large mass of people ■ vi 1 form a flying group 2 move in a mass 3 be overrun

> **ORIGIN** The two English words **swarm** are etymologically distinct. The **swarm** of bees goes back to an ancient root that was an imitation of the sound of buzzing. The origin of **swarm** 'climb', which appeared in the mid-16C, is unknown.

swarm² vi climb using the arms and legs

swarthy /swáwrthi/ (-**ier, -iest**) adj having a dark complexion —**swarthiness** n

swashbuckler /swósh buklər/ n 1 an adventurer 2 a novel or film about an adventurer —**swashbuckling** adj

swastika /swóstikə/ n 1 a Nazi symbol consisting of a cross with four arms of the same length bent clockwise 2 an ancient religious symbol consisting of a cross with four arms of the same length bent clockwise or anticlockwise

swat /swot/, **swot** vti (**swatting, swatted; swotting, swotted**) strike or slap somebody or something ■ n 1 a sharp blow 2 a device used for swatting insects —**swatter** n

swatch /swoch/ n a fabric sample

swath /swoth/, **swathe** /swayth/ n 1 the width cut by a mowing machine 2 a path cut through a growing crop

swathe /swayth/ vt (**swathing, swathed**) 1 wrap completely 2 enfold ■ n a wrapping

sway v 1 vti swing or move back and forth 2 vi lean to one side or from side to side in turn 3 vti waver, or cause somebody to waver, between opinions 4 vt persuade or influence ■ n 1 a swaying motion 2 control over a person or area —**swayable** adj ◊ **hold sway** have control or influence

Swaziland /swaázi land/ landlocked country in southern Africa. Cap. Mbabane. Pop. 1,104,343 (2001).

swear /swair/ (**swore**, **sworn**) v 1 vti affirm the truth of something 2 vti solemnly promise something 3 vi use blasphemous or obscene language 4 vti take an oath 5 vti declare something under oath

□ **swear by** vt have great faith or complete confidence in

□ **swear in** vt make somebody take an oath when taking up an office

□ **swear off** vt renounce a bad habit

swearword /swáir wurd/ n an offensive or taboo word

sweat /swet/ n 1 moisture exuded on the skin, e.g. as a result of heat or anxiety 2 the state of having sweat on the skin 3 moisture condensed or exuded on a surface 4 hard or boring work ■ v 1 vti produce or cause to produce sweat 2 vt wet or mark with sweat 3 vti cook in its own juices 4 vi work hard (infml) ◊ **no sweat** it can be done with ease (infml)

□ **sweat out** vt endure something to the end (infml)

sweatband /swét band/ n 1 a strip of cloth worn around the head or wrist to absorb sweat 2 a band inside a hat that protects it from sweat

sweater /swéttər/ n a knitted garment with sleeves for the upper body, pulled over the head

sweat gland n a small tubular organ in the skin from which sweat is released

sweatshop /swét shop/ n a workplace staffed with overworked, underpaid employees

sweaty /swétti/ (-ier, -iest) adj 1 damp with sweat 2 causing sweating —**sweatiness** n

Swede /sweed/ n 1 somebody from Sweden 2 **swede** a large round root with yellowish flesh eaten as a vegetable 3 **swede** the plant that produces swedes

Sweden /sweed'n/ country in NW Europe. Cap. Stockholm. Pop. 8,875,053 (2001).

Swedenborg /sweed'n bawrg/, **Emanuel** (1688–1772) Swedish scientist and theologian —**Swedenborgian** /sweed'n báwrji ən, -gi ən/ n, adj

Swedish /sweedish/ n the official language of Sweden ■ adj of Sweden or Swedish

sweep v (**swept**) 1 vti clean a place with a broom or brush 2 vt move something with a horizontal stroke 3 vti brush against the ground when moving 4 vti move with speed, force, or dignity 5 vti spread through a place 6 vt carry somebody or something along 7 vti win something overwhelmingly 8 vti stretch out in an arc, or extend broadly ■ n 1 an instance of cleaning with a broom or brush 2 a brushing stroke 3 a long smooth movement 4 a long smooth curve 5 a wide expanse 6 a curved or broad range 7 an overwhelming victory ◊ **make a clean sweep (of)** get rid of everything or everyone unwanted or unnecessary

sweepback /sweep bak/ n an aircraft wing that is angled backwards

sweeper /sweepər/ n 1 somebody who sweeps 2 a machine that sweeps floors or carpets 3 in football, a roving defensive player

sweeping /sweeping/ adj 1 on a large scale 2 too general o *sweeping statements* 3 overwhelming o *a sweeping victory* —**sweepingly** adv

sweepings /sweepingz/ npl things swept up

sweepstake /sweep stayk/ n a lottery in which the payout depends on the amount paid in

sweet /sweet/ adj 1 tasting or smelling of sugar 2 containing sugar 3 not bitter or sour 4 fresh 5 not salty or savoury 6 pleasing to the senses 7 satisfying o *a sweet victory* 8 kind 9 charming or endearing ■ adv in a pleasant way ■ n 1 something that is pleasing to the emotions or feelings o *had to take the bitter with the sweet* 2 a term of endearment 3 a dessert 4 a shaped item of confectionery ■ **sweets** npl confectionery —**sweetly** adv —**sweetness** n ◊ See note at **suite**

sweet-and-sour adj containing sugar and vinegar

sweetbread /sweet bred/ n an animal's pancreas or thymus gland eaten as food

sweetcorn /sweet kawrn/ n 1 a type of maize with sweet kernels 2 maize kernels eaten as food

sweeten /sweet'n/ v 1 vti increase in sweetness 2 vt improve the taste or smell of 3 vt make more desirable o *sweeten a deal* 4 vt soften or persuade

sweetener /sweet'nər/ n 1 a substance added to make something sweet or sweeter 2 an extra payment or gift (infml)

sweetening /sweet'ning/ n 1 a substance making something sweet or sweeter 2 the act of making something sweet or sweeter

sweetheart /sweet haart/ n 1 a boyfriend or girlfriend (dated) 2 used as an affectionate term of address 3 a kind person

sweetie /sweeti/ n (infml) 1 a piece of confectionery 2 a term of endearment 3 an endearing person

sweetmeat /sweet meet/ n a sweet delicacy (archaic)

sweet nothings npl romantic words

sweet pea n a climbing plant with pastel-coloured flowers

sweet pepper n 1 a bell-shaped pepper eaten as a vegetable 2 the plant that produces sweet peppers

sweet potato n the fleshy orange root of a tropical plant, eaten as a vegetable

sweetshop /sweet shop/ n a shop that sells sweets

sweet-talk vti use flattering and persuasive language to somebody (infml)

sweet tooth n a fondness for sweet food

sweet william /-willyəm/ (pl **sweet williams** or **same**) n a plant with variously coloured flowers

swell v (**swollen** /swólən/ or **swelled**) 1 vti increase in size, quantity, or degree 2 vi become temporarily larger than usual **3** *vti* increase and decrease in loudness **4** *vti* fill with emotion ■ *n* **1** the undulation of the sea surface **2** a rounded part that sticks out **3** an increase in size or number **4** in music, a crescendo followed by a diminuendo **5** a fashionable person *(dated infml)* ■ *adj US* good *(slang)* ○ did a swell job

swelling /swélling/ *n* **1** an enlargement of something such as tissue **2** a lump or protuberance

swelter /swéltər/ *vi* be oppressed by heat ■ *n* unpleasant heat or an unpleasant sensation of hotness —**sweltering** *adj*

swept past tense, past participle of **sweep**

sweptback /swépt bák/ *adj* describes an aircraft wing that is angled backwards

swerve *vti* (**swerving, swerved**) turn suddenly away from a direct course ■ *n* an abrupt change in direction

swift *adj* **1** happening or done fast **2** moving or acting fast ■ *adv* quickly ■ *n* (*pl same or* **swifts**) a small bird that resembles a swallow —**swiftly** *adv* —**swiftness** *n*

Swift, Jonathan (1667–1745) Anglo-Irish author and cleric —**Swiftian** *adj*

swig *(infml)* *vti* (**swigging, swigged**) drink something in large gulps ■ *n* a large gulp of a drink

swill *v* **1** *vt* wash or rinse with water **2** *vti* move, or cause liquid to move, around in a container **3** *vt* drink greedily or in large amounts *(disapproving)* ■ *n* **1** watery feed for pigs **2** kitchen waste **3** a wash or rinse with water **4** any sloppy liquid mixture

swim *v* (**swimming, swam, swum**) **1** *vi* move unsupported through water by moving parts of the body **2** *vt* travel a particular distance or cross a particular stretch of water by swimming **3** *vt* swim with a particular stroke **4** *vi* be dizzy **5** *vi* seem to move or spin **6** *vi* be covered in liquid ○ meat swimming in gravy ■ *n* **1** a period of time spent swimming **2** dizziness —**swimmer** *n* **swimming** *n* ◇ be in the swim be involved with the latest fashions or trends *(dated infml)*

~~swiming~~ incorrect spelling of **swimming**

swimming costume *n* an outfit worn for swimming

swimmingly /swímmingli/ *adv* smoothly and successfully

swimming pool *n* an artificial body of water in which to swim

swimming trunks *npl* men's or boys' shorts worn for swimming

swimsuit /swím soot, -syoot/ *n* an outfit worn for swimming

swimwear /swím wair/ *n* clothing worn for swimming

swindle /swind'l/ *vt* (**-dling, -dled**) obtain something from somebody by fraud ■ *n* a fraudulent transaction —**swindler** *n*

swine (*pl same*) *n* **1** (*pl same or* **swines**) a person regarded as extremely unpleasant *(insult)* **2** a pig raised domestically —**swinish** *adj*

swing *v* (**swung**) **1** *vti* move to and fro **2** *vti* pivot or rotate **3** *vti* move in a curve **4** *vi* walk with a swaying motion **5** *vti* strike or attempt to strike somebody or something with a sweeping blow **6** *vi* ride on a swinging seat **7** *vi* fluctuate or vacillate **8** *vt* arrange or manipulate *(infml)* ○ swing a deal **9** *vi* be hanged as a punishment *(infml)* **10** *vi* swap sexual partners *(dated slang)* ■ *n* **1** a hanging seat that moves backwards and forwards **2** a swinging movement **3** the range of movement of something that swings **4** a sweeping stroke or blow **5** a shift or fluctuation **6** *also* **swing music** a style of jazz music suitable for dancing —**swinger** *n* —**swinging** *adj* ◇ in full swing in vigorous progress ◇ get into the swing of things get into the established routine ◇ swings and roundabouts indicates that a situation has both advantages and disadvantages, or is sometimes good and sometimes bad

swing bridge *n* a movable bridge that pivots horizontally

swing-by *n* a deliberate change in a space vehicle's course to accommodate the gravitational pull of a nearby object

swing door *n* a door that opens both ways

swingeing /swínjing/ *adj* severe or extreme ○ swingeing cuts in spending

swingometer /swing ómmitər/ *n* a television device for showing projected shifts in voting

swipe *v* (**swiping, swiped**) **1** *vti* hit somebody or something hard with a sweeping blow **2** *vt* steal something *(infml)* ■ *n* **1** a sweeping blow **2** a critical attack *(infml)*

swipe card *n* a card containing coded information that can be passed through and read by an electronic device

swirl *v* **1** *vti* turn or cause to turn with a circular motion **2** *vi* be dizzy ■ *n* **1** a circular motion **2** a spiral —**swirly** *adj*

swish *vti* make or move with a smooth whistling or rustling sound ■ *n* a swishing sound or movement ■ *adj* elegant *(infml)* ○ a swish restaurant —**swishy** *adj*

Swiss *n* (*pl same*) **1** somebody from Switzerland **2** the dialect of German, French, or Italian that is spoken in Switzerland ■ *adj* of Switzerland

Swiss chard *n* a leafy vegetable similar to spinach

swiss roll *n* a light sponge cake spread with jam or cream and rolled into a cylinder

switch *n* **1** a button or lever that controls an electrical circuit **2** a sudden change **3** a substitution **4** a thin rod or cane **5** the tip of an animal's tail **6** a routing device used within telephone exchanges ■ *v* **1** *vti* change from one thing to another **2** *vti* exchange or be exchanged **3** *vti* flick or swing to and fro **4** *vt* beat somebody with a switch —**switchable** *adj* —**switcher** *n*

☐ **switch off** *vti* turn off a piece of electrical equipment *(infml)*

☐ **switch on** *vt* turn on a piece of electrical equipment

switchback /swích bak/ *n* **1** a twisty road with many hills **2** a sharp bend on a steep slope **3** a roller coaster

switchblade /swích blayd/ *n US* = **flick knife**

switchboard /swích bawrd/ *n* **1** a manual device for connecting telephone lines **2** a control panel containing electrical devices

Swithin /swíthin, swíthin, swíth'n, swíth'n/, **Swithun, St** *(d. 862)* English bishop

Switzerland /swítsərlənd/ country in west-central Europe. Cap. Bern. Pop. 7,283,274 (2001).

swivel /swívv'l/ *vti* (**-elling, -elled**) pivot or rotate ■ *n* a device that allows a mechanical part to turn

swivel chair *n* a chair that can rotate

swizzle stick /swízz'l-/ *n* a small rod used to stir an alcoholic drink

swollen past participle of **swell**

swoon *vi* **1** feel faint with joy **2** fall in a faint ■ *n* a loss of consciousness

swoop *vi* **1** make a sweeping descent **2** pounce ■ *n* **1** a sudden descent **2** a sudden attack ◇ **at** *or* **in one fell swoop** in a single fast action

swoosh /swoosh, swōōsh/ *vti* make or move with a rushing sound —**swoosh** *n*

swop *vti, n* = **swap**

sword /sawrd/ *n* a hand-held weapon with a long blade

sword dance *n* a dance performed over crossed swords laid on the floor

swordfish /sáwrd fish/ (*pl* same *or* **-fishes**) *n* **1** a large sea fish with a sword-shaped jaw **2** swordfish as food

swordplay /sáwrd play/ *n* sword fighting

swordsman /sáwrdzmən/ (*pl* **-men** /-mən/) *n* somebody who fights with a sword —**swordsmanship** *n*

swore past tense of **swear**

sworn past participle of **swear** ■ *adj* **1** legally binding **2** unwavering in resolve

swot[1] *vi* (**swotting, swotted**) study very hard *(infml)* ■ *n* a hard-working student *(infml disapproving)*

swot[2] *vti, n* = **swat**

swum past participle of **swim**

swung past tense, past participle of **swing**

sycamore /síkə mawr/ (*pl* **-mores** *or* same) *n* a maple tree with winged seeds

sycophant /síkəfənt, -fant/ *n* a fawning flatterer —**sycophancy** *n* —**sycophantic** /síkə fántik/ *adj* —**sycophantically** *adv*

Sydney /sídni/ capital of New South Wales, SE Australia. Pop. 3,986,700 (1998).

Sydney Opera House

Sydney Opera House *n* an arts centre in Sydney Harbour, Australia

~~sylable~~ incorrect spelling of **syllable**

~~sylabus~~ incorrect spelling of **syllabus**

syllabic /si lábbik/ *adj* **1** of syllables **2** describes a consonant that forms a syllable without a vowel, such as the 'l' in 'bottle' **3** marked by clear enunciation

syllable /sílləb'l/ *n* **1** a unit of spoken language containing a single vowel sound or syllabic consonant **2** a letter or group of letters that corresponds to a spoken syllable

syllabub /síllə bub/, **sillabub** *n* a dessert of cream whipped with brandy or wine

syllabus /sílləbəss/ (*pl* **-bi** /-bī/ *or* **-buses**) *n* **1** an outline of a course of study **2** a list of subjects offered by an educational institution

ORIGIN *Syllabus* has its origins in a misprint. In an early edition of some of Cicero's letters, the Latin word *sittybas* 'labels, tables of contents' was printed as *syllabos*. This was then wrongly referred to a nonexistent Greek noun (supposed to be from the verb *sullambanein* 'gather together', from which *syllable* derives), and a Latin equivalent *syllabus* was formed.

syllogism /síllə jizəm/ *n* **1** a logical argument involving three propositions **2** deductive reasoning

sylph /silf/ *n* **1** a slim and graceful girl or woman **2** an imaginary female being inhabiting the air —**sylph-like** *adj*

sylvan /sílvən/, **silvan** *adj (literary)* **1** of a forest **2** wooded ■ *n* an inhabitant of a forest

symbiosis /sím bī ṓssiss, -bi-/ (*pl* **-ses** /-seez/) *n* **1** a close association of animals or plants that is usually mutually beneficial **2** any mutually beneficial relationship —**symbiotic** /sím bī óttik, -bi-/ *adj* —**symbiotical** *adj* —**symbiotically** *adv*

~~symble~~ incorrect spelling of **symbol**

symbol /símb'l/ *n* **1** something that represents something else **2** a sign with a specific meaning ◊ See note at **cymbal**

symbolic /sim bóllik/, **symbolical** /-ik'l/ *adj* **1** of or using symbols **2** representing something else —**symbolically** *adv*

symbolic language *n* **1** an artificial language that uses symbols extensively **2** a computer programming language that uses symbols

symbolism /símbəlizəm/ *n* **1** the use of symbols **2** a system of symbols **3** symbolic meaning **4** *also* **Symbolism** a 19C literary and artistic movement using symbolic images to evoke ideas or feelings —**symbolist** *n, adj*

symbolize /símbə līz/ (**-izing, -ized**), **symbolise** *vt* **1** be a symbol of **2** represent by means of a symbol —**symbolization** /símbə līˈzáyshˈn/ *n*

~~symetrical~~ incorrect spelling of **symmetrical**

~~symetry~~ incorrect spelling of **symmetry**

symmetrical /si méttrik'l/, **symmetric** /-méttrik/ *adj* **1** exhibiting symmetry **2** equally or evenly balanced **3** describes body parts that have the same function but are situated on opposite sides of an organ or the body —**symmetrically** *adv*

symmetry /símmətri/ (*pl* **-tries**) *n* **1** the property of sameness on both sides of a dividing line **2** the beauty that derives from balanced proportions

sympathetic /símpə théttik/ *adj* **1** feeling or showing sympathy **2** showing agreement or approval **3** provoking sympathy **4** suited to something —**sympathetically** *adv*

sympathize /símpə thīz/ (**-thizing, -thized**), **sympathise** *vi* **1** feel or show sympathy **2** be of the same opinion —**sympathizer** *n*

sympathy /símpəthi/ (*pl* **-thies**) *n* **1** the capacity to understand and share somebody else's feelings **2** sorrow for another person's pain or trouble **3** the inclination to think or feel the same as somebody else **4** agreement or harmony ○ *a plan in sympathy with our wishes* **5** allegiance or loyalty (*often pl*) ○ *nationalist sympathies*

sympathy strike *n* a labour strike to support other strikers

symphony /símfəni/ (*pl* **-nies**) *n* **1** a complex musical composition **2** a symphony orchestra **3** a harmonious composition or arrangement —**symphonic** /sim fónnik/ *adj* —**symphonically** *adv*

symphony orchestra *n* a large orchestra that includes wind, string, and percussion instruments

symposium /sim pốzi əm/ (*pl* **-ums** *or* **-a** /-zi ə/) *n* **1** a formal meeting for the discussion of a subject **2** a published collection of opinions —**symposiac** *adj*

ORIGIN A **symposium** was originally a convivial affair with drinking. The word is ultimately formed from Greek *sym-* 'together' and *potēs* 'drinker'. When first adopted into English from Latin in the late 16C, it especially applied to meetings held in ancient Greece for drinking and conversation. The modern, drier sense of 'formal meeting for discussion' emerged in the late 18C.

symptom /símptəm/ *n* **1** an indication of illness felt by a patient **2** a sign of something to come ○ *early symptoms of a recession*

symptomatic /símptə máttik/ *adj* **1** indicating illness **2** typical or indicative of something —**symptomatically** *adv*

synagogue /sínnə gog/ *n* **1** a place of worship for a Jewish congregation **2** a Jewish congregation —**synagogal** /sínnə gógg'l/ *adj*

sync /singk/, **synch** *n* synchronization *(infml)* ◊ See note at **sink**

synchromesh /síngkrō mesh/ *n* a gear system with synchronized parts —**synchromesh** *adj*

synchronic /sin krónnik/ *adj* studying something at a point in time rather than over its history —**synchronically** *adv*

synchronicity /síngkrə níssəti/ *n* the coincidence of events that seem related

synchronize /síngkrə nīz/ (**-nizing, -nized**), **synchronise** *v* **1** *vi* happen together **2** *vi* go or work together or in unison **3** *vt* make things happen or work at the same time or rate **4** *vt* align the sound with the image of a film —**synchronization** /síngkrə nī záysh'n/ *n*

synchronized swimming *n* stylized group swimming in which swimmers perform choreographed movements

synchronous /síngkrənəss/ *adj* **1** occurring simultaneously **2** working at the same rate —**synchronously** *adv* —**synchrony** *n*

syncopation /síngkə páysh'n/ *n* the modifying of a musical rhythm by placing the accent on a weak beat —**syncopate** /síngkə payt/ *vti* —**syncopated** *adj*

~~syncronous~~ incorrect spelling of **synchronous**

syndic /síndik/ *n* **1** a business agent **2** a government official in some European countries —**syndical** *adj*

syndicalism /síndikəlizəm/ *n* **1** a revolutionary political doctrine that advocates workers' seizure of the means of production **2** a system of government in which unionized workers control the means of production —**syndicalist** *adj, n*

syndicate *n* /síndikət/ **1** a group of businesses **2** a business that sells news to the media **3** a group of newspapers under a single owner **4** a group of people who combine for a common purpose ■ *vt* /síndi kayt/ (**-cating, -cated**) **1** sell something for multiple publication **2** *US* sell TV programmes to independent stations **3** control something as a syndicate

syndrome /síndrōm/ *n* **1** a group of identifying signs and symptoms **2** a set of things that form a pattern

synergy /sínnərji/ (*pl* **-gies**) *n* the combined effort or action of two or more things, people, or organizations that is greater than the sum of its parts —**synergetic** /sínnər jéttik/ *adj* —**synergic** /si núrjik/ *adj*

Synge /sing/, **J. M.** (1871–1909) Irish dramatist

J. M. Synge: Portrait by John B. Yeats

synod /sínnəd, sínnod/ *n* **1** a church council **2** a Presbyterian church court —**synodal** *adj*

~~synonim~~ incorrect spelling of **synonym**

~~synonomous~~ incorrect spelling of **synonymous**

synonym /sínnənim/ *n* a word that means the same as another —**synonymity** /-nímməti/ *n* —**synonymous** /si nónniməss/ *adj*

synonymy /si nónnimi/ (*pl* -**mies**) *n* **1** equivalence of meaning **2** the study of synonyms **3** an annotated list of synonyms

synopsis /si nópsiss/ (*pl* -**ses** /-seez/) *n* **1** a summary of a text **2** a summary of a subject

syntactic /sin táktik/, **syntactical** /-ik'l/ *adj* **1** of syntax **2** conforming to the rules of syntax —**syntactically** *adv*

syntax /sín taks/ *n* **1** the organization of words in sentences **2** the branch of grammar that deals with syntax **3** the rules of syntax **4** the rules governing the structure of computer programs

synthesis /sínthəssiss/ (*pl* -**ses** /-seez/) *n* **1** a unified whole resulting from the combining of different elements **2** the combining of different elements into a new whole *(fml)* **3** the formation of compounds through one or more chemical reactions involving simpler substances **4** the producing of sound with a synthesizer —**synthesist** *n*

synthesize /sínthə sīz/ (-**sizing**, -**sized**), **synthesise**, **synthetize** /sínthə tīz/, **synthetise** *v* **1** *vti* combine different elements into a new whole, or be combined in this way **2** *vt* produce a substance or material by chemical or biological synthesis —**synthesization** /sínthə sī záysh'n/ *n*

synthesizer /sínthə sīzər/, **synthesiser** *n* an electronic musical instrument with a keyboard

synthespian /sin théspi ən/ *n* **1** a computer simulation of a well-known actor **2** an actor used in animation

synthetic /sin théttik/ *adj* **1** made artificially by chemical synthesis, especially so as to resemble a natural product **2** insincere ■ *n* a chemically produced substance or material —**synthetical** *adj* —**synthetically** *adv*

syphilis /síffəliss/ *n* a sexually transmitted disease that affects many parts of the body —**syphilitic** /síffə líttik/ *adj*

syphon *n*, *vt* = **siphon**

Syracuse /sírrə kyooz/ capital of **Syracuse Province**, SE Sicily, Italy. Pop. 126,721 (1999).

Syria /sírri ə/ country in SW Asia. Cap. Damascus. Pop. 16,728,808 (2001). —**Syrian** *n, adj*

syringe /si rínj/ *n* **1** an instrument for injecting or withdrawing fluids **2** a device for pumping and spraying fluids ■ *vt* (-**ringing**, -**ringed**) use a syringe on

syrup /sírrəp/ *n* **1** a sweet liquid consisting of sugar dissolved in water **2** a thick flavoured sweet liquid **3** medicine in the form of a thick liquid **4** golden syrup —**syrupy** *adj*

ORIGIN Syrup goes back to an Arabic verb meaning 'drink', from which *sherbet* also derives. Since many Arabic drinks are sweet-

ened, the words tended to be adopted into Western languages with the association 'sweet drink'.

system /sístəm/ *n* **1** a number of parts organized into a complex whole **2** a set of principles **3** a way of proceeding **4** a transport network **5** a set of organs or structures in the body that have a common function **6** the whole human body **7** an assembly of components **8** a set of computer hardware, software, and peripherals functioning together **9** the state of being orderly **10** a group of astronomical objects **11** the established order in society

systematic /sístə máttik/, **systematical** /-ik'l/ *adj* **1** done methodically **2** well organized **3** of, constituting, or based on a system —**systematically** *adv*

systematize /sístəmə tīz/ (-**tizing**, -**tized**), **systematise**, **systemize** /sístə mīz/, **systemise** *vti* make or become systematic —**systematization** /sístəmə tī záysh'n/ *n* —**systematizer** *n*

systemic /si stémmik, si steémik/ *adj* **1** of a system or affecting all elements in a system **2** affecting the whole body **3** affecting all the tissues of a plant ○ *a systemic herbicide* —**systemically** *adv*

system operator *n* the operator of an electronic bulletin board

systems analysis *n* analysis of an organization's data-processing requirements —**systems analyst** *n*

Szczecin /shtshéchin/ capital of **Szczecin Province**, NW Poland. Pop. 419,000 (1997).

Szechwan = **Sichuan**

T

t¹ (*pl* **t's**), **T** (*pl* **T's** *or* **Ts**) *n* the 20th letter of the English alphabet ◊ **to a T** exactly

t² *symbol* **1** time **2** troy

t³ *abbr* **1** tare **2** teaspoon **3** tenor **4** tense **5** ton **6** transitive

T *symbol* **1** absolute temperature **2** kinetic energy **3** period **4** surface tension **5** temperature **6** tritium

T1 line, **T-1 line** *n* a dedicated Internet phone line

ta /taa/ *interj* thank you *(infml)*

Ta *symbol* tantalum

TA *abbr* Territorial Army

tab¹ *n* **1** an attachment for holding, lifting, or opening something **2** a tag or label **3** a bill in a bar or restaurant *(infml)* ◊ **keep tabs on** keep a close watch on *(infml)*

tab² *n* a key on a computer keyboard that moves the cursor several spaces or from one field to the next

TAB n ANZ a New Zealand betting agency. Full form **Totalizator Agency Board**

tabard /tábbaard/ n a sleeveless tunic

Tabasco /tə báskō/ tdmk a trademark for a hot-tasting sauce made from peppers, vinegar, and spices

tabby /tábbi/ n (pl **-bies**) **1** a striped cat **2** a pet female cat **3** silk with a striped or wavy pattern ■ adj striped or brindled

ORIGIN The fabric **tabby** is ultimately named after a quarter in Baghdad, where it was made. It was originally striped, and this feature led to its application to **tabby** cats. The name for the fabric entered English through Arabic and French in the late 16C. The first recorded use of 'tabby' cat' occurs a century later.

tabernacle /tábbər nak'l/ n **1** also **Tabernacle** a portable tent used by the Israelites as a sanctuary for the Ark of the Covenant **2** a nonconformist place of worship **3** a container for holy bread and wine —**tabernacular** /tábbər nákyoolər/ adj

tabla /tábbla/ n a South Asian percussion instrument

table /táyb'l/ n **1** an item of furniture with legs and a flat top on which to put things **2** a flat surface used for working on **3** the quality or quantity of food served **4** the people eating at a table **5** an arrangement of information in columns or a condensed list **6** a slab on which an inscription is engraved ■ vt(-**bling, -bled**) **1** propose something for discussion **2** US, Can postpone discussion of something ◇ **on the table** presented for discussion at a meeting ◇ **turn the tables (on)** gain the advantage from somebody who previously held it

tableau /tábblō/ (pl **-leaux** /-lōz/ or **-leaus**) n **1** a picturesque display **2** also **tableau vivant** /-vee vaaN/ a group of costumed people posing silent and motionless to recreate a famous scene **3** any striking visual scene

tablecloth /táyb'l kloth/ n a cloth cover for a dining table

table d'hôte /taab'l dôt/ n a fixed-price meal from a limited menu

tableland /táyb'l land/ n an elevated flat region

table mat n a mat placed under a plate or dish to protect a table

table salt n fine salt for use at the table

tablespoon /táyb'l spoon/ n **1** a serving spoon **2** also **tablespoonful** a measure based on the capacity of a tablespoon

tablet /tábblət/ n **1** a compressed powdered drug to be swallowed **2** a small flat cake of a substance such as soap **3** an inscribed stone or wooden slab **4** a number of sheets of paper fastened together

table tennis n a game similar to tennis played with small paddles and light hollow balls on a table

tableware /táyb'l wair/ n plates, glasses, and other items used at meals

table wine n inexpensive wine served with everyday meals

tabloid /tábbloyd/ n also **tabloid newspaper** a small-format popular newspaper with short, often sensationalist articles ■ adj sensationalist

ORIGIN **Tabloid** was registered as a proprietary name for a brand of tablet in 1884 by Burroughs, Wellcome, and Company. It was the underlying notion of 'compression' or 'condensation' that led to its application to newspapers of small page size and 'condensed' versions of news stories, which emerged at the beginning of the 20C.

taboo /tə boo/, **tabu** adj **1** socially or culturally forbidden **2** sacred and prohibited ■ n (pl **-boos**; pl **-bus**) **1** a social or cultural prohibition **2** a subject or type of behaviour that is forbidden or deeply disapproved of —**taboo** vt

tabor /táybər/, **tabour** n a small drum —**taborer** n

tabular /tábbyŏolər/ adj **1** arranged in a table **2** having a flat surface **3** broad and flat —**tabularly** adv

tabula rasa /tábbyŏolə ráazə/ (pl **tabulae rasae** /-lee ráazee/) n **1** the supposed state of the mind prior to experiences **2** a chance to start afresh

tabulate /tábbyŏo layt/ (**-lating, -lated**) vt **1** arrange information in a table **2** make something flat —**tabulation** /tábbyŏo láysh'n/ n

tabulator /tábbyŏo laytər/ n **1** somebody or something that tabulates data **2** a tab key on a computer keyboard, or a similar device on a typewriter

tachograph /táka graaf, -graf/ n a device in a commercial vehicle that records speeds and distances travelled

tachometer /ta kómmitər/ n a device in a motor vehicle for measuring rotation speed —**tachometric** adj —**tachometry** /ta kómmətri/ n

tacit /tássit/ adj implied but not expressed —**tacitly** adv —**tacitness** n

taciturn /tássi turn/ adj uncommunicative —**taciturnity** /tássi túrnəti/ n —**taciturnly** adv ◇ See note at **silent**

Tacitus /tássitəss/ (AD 55?–117?) Roman historian

tack[1] n **1** a small sharp broad-headed nail **2** a loose temporary stitch **3** a course of action or method of approach ■ v **1** vt fasten something with or as if with a tack or tacks **2** vt sew something loosely and temporarily **3** vti change the direction of a sailing vessel so that the wind is blowing on the opposite side —**tacker** n

☐ **tack on** vt add as an extra

tack[2] n saddles, bridles, and harnesses

tackle /ták'l/ n **1** in some ball games, an attempt to stop an opposing player's progress **2** equipment for a particular activity **3** ropes and pulleys used for lifting ■ *vt* (**-ling, -led**) **1** deal with something difficult **2** confront somebody **3** make a tackle on an opposing player

tacky[1] /táki/ (**-ier, -iest**) *adj* slightly sticky —**tackily** *adv* —**tackiness** *n*

tacky[2] /táki/ (**-ier, -iest**) *adj* in bad taste —**tackily** *adv* —**tackiness** *n*

taco /tákō/ (*pl* **-cos**) *n* a filled crisp tortilla shell

Tacoma /tə kốmə/ city in W Washington State. Pop. 179,814 (1998).

tact *n* **1** the ability to avoid giving offence **2** discretion —**tactful** *adj* —**tactfully** *adv* —**tactfulness** *n* —**tactless** *adj* —**tactlessly** *adv* —**tactlessness** *n*

tactic /táktik/ *n* a means to achieve a goal

tactical /táktik'l/ *adj* **1** of tactics **2** serving as a means to an end **3** showing skilful planning **4** done or used to support a military objective —**tactically** *adv*

tactical voting *n* the practice of voting for the second strongest candidate in order to prevent the strongest candidate from winning

tactics /táktiks/ *n* (+ *sing verb*) **1** the science of directing forces in battle to achieve an objective **2** the art of finding and implementing means to achieve immediate aims —**tactician** /tak tísh'n/ *n*

tactile /ták tīl/ *adj* **1** of the sense of touch **2** tangible —**tactilely** *adv* —**tactility** /tak tíllɔti/ *n*

tad *n* a small amount (*infml*) ◊ **a tad** somewhat (*infml*)

tadpole /tád pōl/ *n* a frog or toad larva

Tadzhikistan ♦ Tajikistan

tae kwon do /tī kwon dố/ *n* a Korean martial art including kicking moves

taffeta /táffitə/ *n* a stiff shiny silk or similar fabric. Use: women's clothes.

tag[1] *n* **1** a label **2** an electronic monitoring device **3** a classifying label for a piece of data to facilitate retrieval **4** a plastic or metal tip at the end of a shoelace **5** a descriptive word or phrase used about somebody or something **6** a graffiti artist's signature ■ *v* (**tagging, tagged**) **1** *vt* label something with a tag **2** *vt* add something on at the end **3** *vt* give somebody a nickname **4** *vt* attach an electronic monitoring tag to an offender **5** *vti* follow somebody closely

☐ **tag along** *vi* accompany or follow somebody

tag[2] *n* **1** a children's chasing game **2** *also* **tag wrestling** a form of team wrestling in which one wrestler replaces a partner after touching hands ■ *vt* (**tagging, tagged**) **1** catch and touch a player in a game of tag **2** *Aus* in Australian Rules football, mark an opponent

tagliatelle /tállyə télli/ *n* pasta in long narrow ribbons

Rabindranath Tagore

Tagore /tə gáwr/, **Rabindranath** (1861–1941) Indian writer

Tagus /táygəss/ river flowing through central Spain and central Portugal to the Atlantic Ocean. Length 1,007 km/626 mi. Portuguese **Tejo**. Spanish **Tajo**

tahini /tə héeni, -nə/, **tahina** /-nə/ *n* a paste made from crushed sesame seeds. Use: seasoning.

Tahiti /tə héeti/ island of French Polynesia, in the S Pacific Ocean. Pop. 115,820 (1998). —**Tahitian** /tə héesh'n/ *n, adj*

Tahoe, Lake /taáhố/ lake in the W United States, on the border of Nevada and California

tai chi /tí cheế/, **t'ai chi ch'uan** /-chwaàn/ *n* a Chinese system of exercise characterized by very slow and deliberate balletic body movements

tail /tayl/ *n* **1** the rearmost part of an animal's body, or the movable extension to it **2** the rear, last, or lowest part of something **3** the rearmost part of an aircraft, missile, or bomb **4** the luminous stream of gas behind a comet **5** somebody following another person secretly (*infml*) ■ **tails** *npl* **1** a tail coat **2** a man's formal evening clothes **3** the reverse of a coin ■ *vt* follow secretly (*infml*)—**tailless** *adj* ◊ **turn tail** run away ◊ **with your tail between your legs** in an abject manner (*infml*)

SPELLCHECK Do not confuse the spelling of **tail** and **tale** ('a factual or fictional narrative'), which sound similar.

---

tailback /táyl bak/ *n* a queue of traffic

tail coat *n* a man's formal short-fronted coat with two long tapering parts at the back

tail end *n* the last or rear part of something

tailgate /táyl gayt/ *n* **1** *also* **tailboard** a gate at the back of a lorry that drops down for loading or unloading ■ *vti* (**-gating, -gated**) drive close behind another vehicle —**tailgater** *n*

tailor /táylər/ *n* **1** a maker of clothes, especially men's clothes **2** *Aus* a fish with sharp teeth ■ *v* **1** *vti* make clothes **2** *vt* adapt something to a particular purpose

tailored /táylərd/ *adj* **1** made to fit neatly **2** made for a particular purpose

tailor-made *adj* **1** ideal for somebody or something **2** made by a tailor

tailpiece /táyl peess/ *n* **1** something forming an end or added at the end **2** a decoration at the bottom of a page

tailpipe /táyl pīp/ n US the rear part of an exhaust pipe

tailplane /táyl playn/ n the horizontal part of an aircraft tail

tailspin /táyl spin/ n a rapid spiral descent by an aircraft

tailwind /táyl wind/ n a wind blowing in the direction in which something is travelling

taint vt 1 pollute 2 corrupt morally ■ n 1 an imperfection detracting from the quality of something 2 something that pollutes

taipan /tí pan/ n a large brown venomous Australian snake

Taipei /tí páy/, **T'aipei** capital and largest city of Taiwan. Pop. 2,639,939 (1999).

Taiwan /tí waán/ island country of Southeast Asia, administered independently since 1949 by the Chinese Nationalist government. It is claimed as a province by the People's Republic of China. Cap. Taipei. Pop. 22,370,461 (2001). —**Taiwanese** /tí waa neéz/ n, adj

Taiyuan /tí ywán, tí yoo án/ capital of **Shanxi Province**, east-central China. Pop. 2,100,000 (1995).

Tajikistan /tə jeéki staán/, **Tadzhikistan** country in SE Central Asia. Cap. Dushanbe. Pop. 6,578,681 (2001).

taka /taáka/ n the main unit of Bangladeshi currency

take /tayk/ v (**taking**, **took** /toŏk/, **taken** /táykən/) 1 vt remove or steal something belonging to somebody else 2 vt convey somebody or something somewhere 3 vt capture or win something ○ took the city 4 vt get hold of somebody or something 5 vt perform or do something 6 vt get into or onto something ○ Please take a seat. 7 vt claim or assume something such as credit, glory, or blame 8 vt enable somebody to go somewhere, or go along a course leading somewhere ○ Will this road take us to the beach? ○ Take the first road on the left. 9 vt agree to perform or assume the duties associated with something ○ decided to take the job 10 vt be willing to accept something ○ wouldn't take my credit card 11 vt be able to bear something ○ can't take criticism 12 vt react to something ○ took the news badly 13 vt travel by a particular means 14 vt be able to contain a particular amount 15 vt write something ○ took notes 16 vt make a photograph 17 vt study something ○ taking Spanish 18 vt start to perform or occupy something ○ took office last month 19 vt carry something out ○ take action 20 vt consider or discuss something ○ Let's take your last point first. 21 vt require a particular thing ○ took courage to speak out 22 vt experience an emotion or have a particular view ○ taking pity on us 23 vt interpret or understand somebody or something in a particular way ○ took that to mean he agreed 24 vt consume or ingest something ○ take medicine 25 vi work or be successful ○ The perm didn't take. 26 vt measure something with a device or procedure ○ took his temperature 27 vi become

ill ○ took sick 28 vt subtract a number from something 29 vt assume charge of something ■ n 1 an uninterrupted recording by a camera or sound equipment 2 a personal impression (infml) ○ her take on his presentation —**taker** n ◇ **be taken with** consider pleasing or attractive ◇ **on the take** taking or willing to take bribes (infml) ◇ **take it** 1 be able to tolerate a difficult situation 2 assume that something is true ◇ **take it or leave it** either accept a thing the way it is or refuse it (usually spoken)

□ **take after** vt resemble

□ **take back** vt withdraw something said or written

□ **take for** vt believe somebody to be, often mistakenly ○ took you for your sister

□ **take in** vt 1 understand and remember something 2 include something 3 deceive somebody 4 give somebody shelter in your home 5 make a garment narrower 6 US go and see a performance or sports event

□ **take off** v 1 vt remove a garment 2 vt deduct an amount from a price or sum 3 vt imitate somebody or something for comic effect (infml) 4 vi begin flying 5 vi jump ○ took off from the diving board 6 vi depart hurriedly or suddenly (infml) 7 vi succeed suddenly (infml)

□ **take on** vt 1 undertake something 2 hire somebody 3 adopt a characteristic ○ Her voice took on a kindlier tone. 4 oppose somebody or something in a competition or fight

□ **take out** vt 1 remove something 2 obtain something such as a permit, mortgage, or insurance by applying for it 3 take somebody as a companion to a social event 4 direct something such as anger at something or somebody not the cause of it ○ took his annoyance out on me

□ **take over** vti take control of something from somebody else

□ **take to** vt 1 form a liking for somebody or something 2 start doing something habitually

□ **take up** vt 1 begin doing something regularly as an occupation or hobby 2 accept an offer 3 raise the hem to shorten a garment 4 use or consume something wastefully ○ trivial tasks that took up my entire afternoon

□ **take up on** vt 1 accept an offer or wager from somebody 2 argue with somebody on a point

□ **take up with** vt begin associating with somebody

takeaway /táykə way/ adj 1 bought readycooked for eating elsewhere 2 selling readycooked food for eating elsewhere ■ n 1 a restaurant selling takeaway food 2 a takeaway meal

take-home pay n pay left after deductions

takeoff /táyk of/ n 1 the process of leaving the ground at the beginning of a flight 2 the beginning of a jump 3 a point of rapid growth

takeover /táyk ōvər/ n the act of assuming control of something, especially a business

take-up *n* **1** the level of acceptance of an offer **2** the part of a mechanism onto which something passing through it is wound

takings /táykingz/ *npl* money received through sales by a business

takkie /táki/ *n S Africa* a sports shoe (*infml*)

tala /taálə/ (*pl same or* **-las**) *n* the main unit of Samoan currency

Talbot /táwlbət, tól-/, **William Henry Fox** (1800–77) British photographic pioneer

talc /talk/ *n* **1** a soft mineral consisting of hydrated magnesium silicate **2** *also* **talcum powder** a powder for the skin made from talc

tale /tayl/ *n* **1** a narrative or account of events **2** a short piece of fiction **3** an untrue story or report ◊ See note at **tail**

talent /tállənt/ *n* **1** a natural ability to do something well **2** a person or people with an exceptional ability **3** an ancient unit of weight and money —**talented** *adj*

SYNONYMS talent, gift, aptitude, flair, bent, knack, genius CORE MEANING: the natural ability to do something well

talent scout *n* a discoverer and recruiter of talented people

talent show *n* a performance by amateur entertainers competing for a prize

Taliban /tálli ban/, **Taleban** *npl* a strict Islamic group that controlled Afghanistan from 1996 to 2001

talisman /tállizmən/ *n* **1** an object believed to give protection, magical powers, or good fortune to somebody carrying or wearing it **2** something believed to have magical power —**talismanic** /tálliz mánnik/ *adj*

ORIGIN Talisman is not a compound of *man* (and so forms its plural as -*mans* not -*men*). It was adopted in the mid-17C from French or Spanish, and appears to be ultimately from Greek.

TALISMAN /tállizmən/ *n* a computer system for securities trading on the London Stock Exchange. Full form **Transfer Accounting Lodgement for Investors and Stock Management**

talk /tawk/ *v* **1** *vti* speak or express something by speaking **2** *vi* have a conversation ◊ *talked for an hour* **3** *vti* discuss a subject ◊ *talk business* **4** *vi* communicate or negotiate **5** *vti* speak a language ◊ *talks Italian* **6** *vi* reveal information when interrogated **7** *vi* gossip **8** *vt* persuade somebody ◊ *talked her out of going* ■ *n* **1** a conversation **2** the things said in a conversation **3** a speech or lecture **4** gossip **5** empty speech ◊ *He's all talk.* **6** a subject of discussion or gossip ◊ *the talk of the town* ■ **talks** *npl* negotiations ■ *adj* made up of informal interviews or telephone calls ◊ *talk radio* —**talker** *n*
□ **talk back** *vi* reply impudently
□ **talk down to** *vt* speak patronizingly to
□ **talk over** *vt* discuss

talkative /táwkətiv/ *adj* inclined to talk readily and at length —**talkativeness** *n*

SYNONYMS talkative, chatty, gossipy, garrulous, loquacious CORE MEANING: talking a lot

talking book *n* a book recorded on an audio cassette

talking point *n* an item for provoking discussion

talking-to *n* a scolding (*infml*)

tall *adj* **1** reaching or having grown to a considerable or above-average height **2** having grown to a particular height ◊ *five foot tall* **3** substantial, demanding, or difficult ◊ *a tall order* **4** improbable or exaggerated ◊ *a tall story* ■ *adv* proudly ◊ *walking tall* —**tallish** *adj* —**tallness** *n*

Tallahassee /tállə hássi/ capital of Florida. Pop. 136,628 (1998).

tallboy /táwl boy/ *n* a high chest of drawers

Talleyrand /tálli ránd/, **Charles Maurice de** (1754–1838) French politician and diplomat

Tallinn /tállin, ta lín, -leèn/ capital of Estonia. Pop. 420,470 (1997).

Tallis /tálliss/, **Thomas** (1510?–85) English composer

tallith /tállith/ (*pl* **-lithim** /tálli theèm/ *or* **-liths**) *n* a Jewish prayer shawl

tallow /tállō/ *n* a fatty substance extracted from the fat of sheep or cattle. Use: candles, soap. —**tallowy** *adj*

tall poppy syndrome *n Aus* a tendency to denigrate somebody prominent

tall ship *n* a square-rigged sailing ship

tally /tálli/ *vti* (**-lies**, **-lied**) **1** agree, correspond, or come to the same amount, or cause to do so **2** count or keep a record of something such as a score ■ *n* (*pl* **-lies**) **1** a record of items ◊ *kept a tally of what I had bought* **2** the score achieved by somebody

Talmud /tálmŏŏd, -məd/ *n* the collection of ancient Jewish writings used as the basis for Jewish law —**Talmudic** /tal mŏŏddik, -myŏŏdik/ *adj* —**Talmudical** *adj* —**Talmudist** *n*

talon /tállən/ *n* **1** a hooked claw of a bird of prey **2** something resembling a claw —**taloned** *adj*

tamale /tə maáli/ *n* a Mexican dish of meat and peppers rolled in cornmeal dough and wrapped in maize husks

tamarind /támmərind/ *n* **1** a pod containing many seeds in an acidic pulp. Use: preserves, drinks, medicines. **2** a tree that produces tamarinds

tamarisk /támmərisk/ *n* a tree with leaves resembling scales

Tambo /támbō/, **Oliver** (1917–93) South African political leader

tamboura /tam boŏrə, -báwrə/ *n* an Asian stringed instrument resembling a lute

tambourine /támbə reèn/ *n* a circular lid-shaped percussion instrument with jingling metallic discs —**tambourinist** *n*

tame *adj* (**tamer, tamest**) **1** no longer wild **2** describes an animal that is unafraid of human

contact **3** bland o *a tame rendition of the anthem*
■ *vt* (**taming, tamed**) **1** domesticate a wild
animal or make land cultivable **2** bring
somebody or something under control
3 moderate something —**tamable** *adj*
—**tamely** *adv*—**tameness** *n*—**tamer** *n*

Tamerlane /támmər layn/, **Tamburlaine** /támbər-
/ (1336–1405) Turkic ruler and conqueror

Tamil /támmil/ (*pl* -ils *or same*) *n* **1** a member
of a people who live in S India and N Sri
Lanka **2** the language of the Tamil people
—**Tamil** *adj*

Tammuz /támmōöz/ *n* the 4th month of the year
in the Jewish calendar

tam-o'-shanter /támmə shántər/ *n* a brimless
Scottish woollen hat with a bobble in the
centre

tamp *vt* **1** pack something down by tapping
2 pack sand or earth into a drill hole above
an explosive

Tampa /támpa/ seaport in west-central Florida,
on **Tampa Bay**, an arm of the Gulf of Mexico.
Pop. 289,156 (1998).

tamper /támpər/ *vi* **1** interfere with something
in a way that causes harm or damage **2** influence a person or process corruptly o *tamp-
ering with the jury*

Tampere /támpər ray/ city in SW Finland. Pop.
193,174 (2000).

Tampico /tam peèkō/ seaport in E Mexico. Pop.
278,933 (1995).

tampon /tám pon/ *n* **1** a plug of soft material
used during menstruation **2** an absorbent
pad used to control bleeding, especially
during surgery

tan¹ *n* **1** a light-brown colour **2** a suntan ■ *v*
(**tanning, tanned**) **1** *vti* get or give a suntan **2** *vt*
convert hide to leather ■ *adj* (**tanner, tannest**)
of a light brown colour

tan² *abbr* tangent

Tanami Desert /ta naàmi-/ desert in central
Australia

tandem /tándəm/ *n* **1** a bicycle for two riders,
one behind the other **2** a team of two horses
harnessed one behind the other, or a carriage
drawn by such a team ■ *adv* with one behind
the other ◊ **in tandem 1** in partnership or
cooperation **2** with one behind the other

tandoori /tan doòri/ *adj* cooked in a clay oven
after marination in yoghurt and spices
—**tandoori** *vt*

tang *n* **1** a strong sharp taste or smell **2** a slight
suggestion of something o *a tang of lemon*
—**tangy** *adj*

~~tangable~~ incorrect spelling of **tangible**

Tanganyika /táng gən yeèka/ former country in
East Africa, constituting the mainland part
of what is now Tanzania —**Tanganyikan** *n*,
adj

Tanganyika, Lake lake in east-central Africa,
with shorelines in Burundi, Tanzania,
Zambia, and the Democratic Republic of the
Congo. Length 680 km/420 mi.

tangata whenua /tánguttə fénnoo ə/ *npl NZ*
Maori people

tangelo /tánjəlō/ (*pl* -los) *n* **1** a citrus fruit with
smooth skin and orange flesh **2** a hybrid
between a tangerine tree and a grapefruit
tree that produces tangelos

tangent /tánjənt/ *n* **1** a line, curve, or surface
that touches another but does not cross or
intersect it **2** for a given angle in a right-
angled triangle, a trigonometric function
equal to the length of the side opposite the
angle divided by the length of the adjacent
side ■ *adj* **1** *also* **tangential** /tan jénsh'l/ of a
tangent **2** touching but not crossing or intersecting **3** *also* **tangential** straying away from
the current subject —**tangency** *n* —**tan-
gentially** *adv* ◊ **go off at** *or* **on a tangent**
change to a different subject or line of
thought

tangerine /tánjə reèn/ *n* **1** a small orange citrus
fruit **2** a tree that produces tangerines **3** a
bright orange colour —**tangerine** *adj*

ORIGIN The fruit is named after Tangier in
Morocco, from where it was exported to Britain
in the 1840s. The colour name dates from the
late 19C.

tangi /túng ee/ (*pl* -gis) *n NZ* a Maori funeral
ceremony

tangible /tánjəb'l/ *adj* **1** able to be touched
2 actual or real ■ *n* something with a physical form, especially a financial asset (*often
pl*) —**tangibility** /tánjə bílləti/ *n*

Tangier /tan jeèr/ city in N Morocco. Pop.
526,215 (1994).

tangle /táng g'l/ (-**gling, -gled**) *v* **1** *vti* make or
become twisted into a jumbled mass **2** *vt*
catch and entwine **3** *vi* become involved in
a conflict or disagreement with somebody
o *Don't tangle with those people.* —**tangle** *n*
—**tanglement** *n*

tango /táng gō/ (*pl* tangos) *n* **1** a Latin American
ballroom dance with gliding steps and
sudden pauses **2** the music for a tango
3 Tango a communications code word for
the letter 'T' —**tango** *vi* —**tangoist** *n*

Tangshan /táng shán/ city in NE China. Pop.
1,540,000 (1995).

tank *n* **1** a large container for liquids or gases
2 the amount held by a tank **3** a large
armoured combat vehicle with tracks, a
rotating turret, and a heavy gun ■ *vi* go fast
—**tankful** *n*

ORIGIN Tank 'container for liquids' originated
in a South Asian word for 'pond, cistern' and
was first used in English in the early 17C. It
was a code name for an armoured vehicle used
for secrecy during its development in 1915,
supposedly because the new machine re-
sembled a tank for benzene.

□ **tank up** *vi* get drunk (*slang*)

tankard /tángkərd/ *n* a big beer mug

tanked, tanked-up *adj* very drunk (*slang*)

tanker /tángkər/ n a ship, lorry, or aircraft transporting large quantities of liquid or gas

tanned adj with a suntan

tanner /tánnər/ n somebody who tans hides

tannery /tánnəri/ (pl -ies) n a place for tanning hides

tannin /tánnin/ n a brownish or yellowish plant compound. Use: tanning, dyes, astringents.

tanning /tánning/ n 1 the conversion of animal skin into leather 2 the browning of skin in sunlight or ultraviolet light 3 a sound thrashing

Tannoy /tánnoy/ tdmk UK a trademark for a public-address system

tansy /tánzi/ (pl -sies) n a plant with yellow flowers and divided leaves

tantalize /tántə līz/ (-lizing, -lized), **tantalise** vt tease or torment by showing but not giving something desired —**tantalization** /tántə līzáysh'n/ n —**tantalizing** adj —**tantalizingly** adv

---

ORIGIN To **tantalize** a person is to subject him or her to the same torments as Tantalus in Greek mythology.

---

tantalum /tántələm/ n (symbol Ta) a blue-grey metallic element. Use: electronic components, alloys, plates and pins for orthopaedic surgery.

Tantalus /tántələss/ n in Greek mythology, a king who was tormented by having fruit and water kept just beyond his reach

tantamount /tántə mownt/ adj equivalent

tantrum /tántrəm/ n a childish fit of temper

Tanzania /tánzə neè ə/ country in E Africa. Cap. Dodoma. Pop. 36,232,074 (2001).

Tao /tow, dow/ n in Taoist philosophy, the ultimate reality or energy, and a person's relationship to it

Taoiseach /teèshək/ n the prime minister of the Republic of Ireland

Taoism /tów izəm, dów-/ n 1 a Chinese philosophy advocating a simple life and non-interference with the natural course of things 2 a Chinese religion based on Taoism —**Taoist** n, adj —**Taoistic** /tow ístik, dow-/ adj

tap[1] v (**tapping, tapped**) 1 vti hit somebody or something lightly 2 vt hit an object lightly against something else 3 vt make a sound by tapping 4 vi move making a series of light sounds ■ n 1 a light blow 2 the sound of a light blow 3 a metal part on a tap-dancing shoe —**tapper** n

tap[2] n 1 a valve on a pipe, operated by a handle and used for drawing off water 2 a stopper in a cask or barrel 3 beer from a cask 4 a listening device secretly fitted in telecommunications equipment ■ vt (**tapping, tapped**) 1 attach a tap to something 2 draw liquid from something 3 get into a power supply and divert energy from it 4 fit a secret listening device in telecommunications equipment 5 secretly listen to or record a telephone conversation using a tap 6 make an internal screw thread in something ◊ **on**

tap (infml) 1 available for immediate use 2 available to be drawn from a container ◊ local beers on tap

tapas /táppəss/ npl Spanish snacks served as appetizers with alcoholic drinks

tap dance n a dance performed wearing shoes with metal tips to make a rhythmic sound —**tap-dance** vi —**tap-dancer** n —**tap-dancing** n

tape n 1 a long narrow strip of material used to secure or tie something 2 a strip of adhesive material on a roll 3 magnetic tape 4 also **tape recording** a recording on magnetic tape 5 a video or audio cassette 6 a long strip of material marking the finishing line in a race ■ v (**taping, taped**) 1 vti record on magnetic tape 2 vt secure or tie with tape

tape deck n an electrical device for playing and recording audio tapes

tape measure n a calibrated strip for measuring length

taper /táypər/ vti 1 become or make gradually narrower at one end 2 reduce gradually ■ n 1 a slim candle narrowing at the top 2 a strip of wood or wax paper for taking a flame to light something else —**tapering** adj —**taperingly** adv

tape recorder n a machine for recording or playing audio tapes —**tape-record** vt

tapestry /táppistri/ (pl -tries) n 1 a heavy fabric or wall hanging with a woven or embroidered design 2 needlepoint 3 something varied and intricate

tapeworm /táyp wurm/ n a parasitic worm found in the gut of vertebrates

tapioca /táppi ốkə/ n 1 a starch obtained from the root of a cassava plant. Use: puddings, thickener for sauces. 2 a pudding made from tapioca

tapir /táypər, táy peer/ (pl -pirs or same) n a nocturnal hoofed mammal with a fleshy snout

taproot /táp root/ n the large main root of some plants

tapu /taà poo/ adj NZ taboo

tap water n water from a domestic or commercial water supply, as opposed to mineral water or rainwater

tar n 1 a thick black liquid distilled from wood or coal 2 the residue from tobacco smoke ■ vt (**tarring, tarred**) cover with tar —**tarry** adj

taramasalata /tárrəməssə laàtə/ n a fish roe paste

tarantella /tárrən téllə/ n 1 an Italian whirling dance 2 the music for a tarantella

---

ORIGIN The **tarantella** is ultimately named after Taranto, which also gave its name to the tarantula (since the spider was found near there). Between the 15C and 17C, S Italy saw many cases of a nervous disorder characterized by uncontrollable body movements and popularly attributed to the tarantula's bite. The most effective cure for the condition was thought to be a whirling dance that mimicked its symptoms, which was consequently called the **tarantella**.

Taranto /ta rántŏ/ port in **Taranto Province,** Apulia Region, S Italy. Pop. 209,297 (1999).

tarantula /tə rántyŏŏlə/ (pl **-las** or **-lae** /-lee/) n 1 a large hairy tropical or subtropical American spider 2 a European wolf spider

tardy /táárdi/ (**-dier, -diest**) adj late —**tardily** adv —**tardiness** n

tare[1] /tair/ n a vetch plant or seed

tare[2] /tair/ n 1 the weight of the packaging on goods, or an allowance made for this 2 a vehicle's unladen weight

target /táárgit/ n 1 a round object marked with concentric circles, aimed at in shooting sports 2 somebody or something aimed at 3 an objective 4 the focus or object of an action ○ *the target of her anger* ■ vt 1 make the focus or object of something ○ *a campaign that targets under-35s* 2 aim at or direct towards a person, thing, or place ○ *missiles targeted on the capital*

targetcast /táárgit kaast/ (**-cast** or **-casted**) vi broadcast a website to a selected audience

tariff /tárrif/ n 1 a duty levied on imported or exported goods 2 a list of tariffs 3 a list of fees, fares, or prices

Tarmac /táár mak/ tdmk a trademark for a material used for surfacing roads

tarn n a small mountain lake formed by glacier action

tarnish /táárnish/ v 1 vti become or make dull and discoloured from oxidation or rust 2 vt damage somebody's reputation ■ n dullness and discoloration caused by oxidation or rust —**tarnishable** adj

tarot /tárrŏ/ n 1 a system of fortune-telling with cards 2 also **tarot card** a card used for fortune-telling

tarpaulin /taar páwlin/ n 1 a heavy waterproof canvas material. Use: covering. 2 a sheet of tarpaulin

Tarquinius Superbus /taar kwínni əss soo púrbəss/, **Lucius** (fl 6C BC) king of Rome (534–510 BC)

tarragon /tárrəgən/ n a herb with aromatic leaves. Use: flavouring food.

Tarragona /tárrə gŏnə/ port in **Tarragona Province,** NE Spain. Pop. 112,795 (1998).

tarrif incorrect spelling of **tariff**

tarry /tárri/ (**-ries, -ried**) vi 1 remain temporarily 2 linger 3 wait

tarsus /táárssəss/ (pl **-si** /-sī/) n the ankle bones of a vertebrate —**tarsal** adj

tart[1] adj 1 sour or sharp-tasting 2 sharply critical —**tartly** adv —**tartness** n
□ **tart up** vt try to improve the appearance of (infml)

tart[2] n a pie without a top crust

tart[3] n an offensive term for a prostitute or a woman regarded as sexually provocative (slang insult)

tartan /táárt'n/ n a multicoloured checked pattern associated with a Scottish clan or regiment, or fabric in this pattern

tartar /táártər/ n 1 a hard deposit on teeth 2 a deposit that forms in wine casks —**tartarous** adj

Tartar /táártər/ n 1 a member of the Tartar people 2 also **tartar** somebody fearsome (sometimes offensive) —**Tartar** adj

tartare sauce /táár taar-/, **tartar sauce** n a cold sauce for fish made from mayonnaise with chopped capers and pickles

Tarzan /táárz'n/ n a strong man with a rugged appearance (infml)

Tashkent /tásh ként/ capital of Uzbekistan. Pop. 2,282,000 (1995).

task n 1 an assigned job 2 an important or difficult piece of work ■ vt 1 assign a task to ○ *tasked me with writing the letter* 2 burden with work ◇ **take to task** scold or criticize

taskbar /táask baar/ n a bar on a computer screen with buttons showing which programs are running

task force n 1 a temporary group for performing a task 2 a temporary military group for a mission

taskmaster /táask maastər/ n 1 somebody who supervises work demandingly 2 a demanding discipline or responsibility

Tasmania /taz máyni ə/ Australian island state off SE Australia. Cap. Hobart. Pop. 471,100 (1998). —**Tasmanian** n, adj

Tasman Sea /tázmən-/ region of the South Pacific Ocean between Australia and New Zealand

tassel /táss'l/ n 1 a bunch of loose threads tied together at one end and used as a decoration 2 a tuft at the top of a maize stem ■ v (**-selling, -selled**) 1 vt decorate with tassels 2 vi produce a tassel (refers to maize)

taste n 1 the sense that perceives flavours through the sensory organs of the tongue 2 the sensation stimulated in the taste buds on contact with food or drink 3 an act of perceiving the flavour of something 4 a small quantity of something eaten or drunk to perceive its taste 5 a brief or first experience of something 6 a liking for something ○ *a taste for expensive clothes* 7 the ability to make good aesthetic judgments 8 a sense of what is socially acceptable ○ *a remark in poor taste* ■ v (**tasting, tasted**) 1 vt discern the flavour of something with the taste buds 2 vi have a particular flavour ○ *tastes fishy* 3 vt test something for its flavour 4 vti experience something briefly or for the first time —**tastable** adj

taste bud n one of the sensory receptors on the tongue that is involved in the sense of taste

tasteful /táystf'l/ adj showing good aesthetic taste —**tastefully** adv —**tastefulness** n

tasteless /táystləss/ adj 1 without flavour 2 showing a lack of good aesthetic taste —**tastelessly** adv —**tastelessness** n

taster /táystər/ n 1 a judge of the quality of food or drink 2 a short preview of something 3 somebody testing an important person's food or drink for poison by tasting it first

tasty /táysti/ (**-ier, -iest**) adj having a pleasant flavour —**tastily** adv —**tastiness** n

tat[1] n things in poor condition or of very low quality (infml)

tat[2] (**tatting, tatted**) vti work at or produce tatting

Tatar /táatər/ n a member of a people of Central Asia —**Tatar** adj

~~tatoo~~ incorrect spelling of **tattoo**

tattered /táttərd/ adj 1 ragged or in shreds 2 dressed in rags —**tatters** npl

tatting /tátting/ n 1 lace made with a shuttle 2 the process of making tatting —**tatter** n

tattle /tátt'l/ v (**-tling, -tled**) 1 vi engage in gossiping 2 vti disclose a secret ■ n 1 somebody who gossips 2 gossip and tale-telling —**tattler** n

tattletale /tátt'l tayl/ n US, Can a telltale

tattoo[1] /ta tóo, tə-/ n (pl **-toos**) a permanent picture or design made on the skin ■ vt (**-toos, -tooed**) make a tattoo on —**tattooer** n —**tattooist** n

ORIGIN Tattoo 'design on the skin' was adopted from a Polynesian language in the mid-18C. Tattoo 'military signal or display' is a century older. It came from Dutch taptoe, literally 'tap to', an instruction to shut off the tap of beer barrels at closing time in taverns. The earliest use in English was 'a call summoning soldiers back to their quarters'.

tattoo[2] /ta tóo, tə-/ n (pl **-toos**) 1 a bugle or drum call telling soldiers to return to their quarters in the evening 2 an evening military display performed as entertainment ■ vti beat with a steady rhythm

tatty /tátti/ (**-tier, -tiest**) adj in poor condition —**tattiness** n

tau /taw, tow/ n the 19th letter of the Greek alphabet

tau cross n a cross shaped like T

taught past tense, past participle of **teach**

taunt /tawnt/ vt 1 provoke or mock hurtfully 2 tantalize ■ n a hurtfully mocking or provocative remark —**tauntingly** adv

taupe /tōp/ n a brownish-grey colour —**taupe** adj

Taurus /táwrəss/ (pl **-ruses** or **-ri** /-rī/) n 1 a zodiacal constellation in the northern hemisphere 2 the 2nd sign of the zodiac 3 somebody born under Taurus —**Taurean** /táwri ən, taw reé ən/ n —**Taurus** adj

TAURUS /táwrəss/ n a computerized system for trading in securities on the International Stock Exchange. Full form **Transfer of Automated Registration of Uncertified Stock**

Taurus Mountains /táwrəss-/ mountain range in S Turkey. Highest peak Aladag 3,734 m/12,251 ft.

taut /tawt/ adj 1 stretched tightly 2 firm and flexed 3 stressed or anxious 4 concise ○ taut prose —**tautly** adv —**tautness** n

tautology /taw tólləji/ (pl **-gies**) n 1 the redundant repetition of meaning in different words 2 an instance of tautology —**tautological** /táwtə lójjik'l/ adj

Tavener /távvənər/, **John** (b. 1944) British composer

tavern /távvərn/ n a pub or inn (archaic)

Taverner /távvərnər/, **John** (1490?–1545) English composer

tawdry /táwdri/ (**-drier, -driest**) adj 1 gaudy and of poor quality 2 shabby and worthless —**tawdrily** adv —**tawdriness** n

ORIGIN Tawdry is a 17C shortening of tawdry lace, itself an alteration of St Audrey's lace. The name Audrey is a contracted form of Etheldreda, and the Etheldreda in question was a 7C Anglo-Saxon queen of Northumbria. She was very fond in her youth of fine lace neckerchiefs, and when she later developed a fatal tumour of the neck, she regarded it as divine retribution for her former extravagance. After her death in 679 she was canonized and made patron saint of Ely. In the Middle Ages fairs were held in her memory, known as 'St Audrey's fairs', at which lace neckties were sold. These were often made from cheap gaudy material, and by the 17C the eroded form tawdry was being used generally for 'cheap and gaudy'.

tawny /táwni/ (**-nier, -niest**) adj 1 of an orangey-brown colour 2 describes port wine that has matured for more than ten years in the barrel —**tawniness** n

tax n 1 an amount of money paid to a government by its citizens, used to run the country 2 a strain or heavy demand ■ vt 1 make somebody pay a tax on something 2 pay the road tax for a vehicle 3 strain or make heavy demands on somebody or something 4 accuse or charge somebody ○ She was taxed for failure to appear in court. —**taxable** adj —**taxably** adv

taxation /tak sáysh'n/ n 1 the levying of taxes, or a system of doing this 2 money collected in taxes —**taxational** adj

tax avoidance n the paying of the minimum amount of tax possible by claiming all allowable deductions

tax-deductible adj able to be deducted as an expense from taxable income

tax-deferred adj not taxable until a later time

tax disc n a small circular document displayed on a vehicle showing that its road tax has been paid

tax evasion n illegal failure to pay taxes

tax-exempt adj legally exempt from taxation

tax exile n somebody who moves abroad to avoid paying high taxes

tax file number n in Australia, a number assigned to an individual registering with the Tax Office and required by an employer

tax-free *adj* not subject to taxation

tax haven *n* a country with favourable tax rates

taxi /táksi/ *n* (*pl* **-is** *or* **-ies**) *also* **taxicab** /-kab/ a car that carries paying passengers ∎ *vti* (**-is**, **-iing** *or* **-ying**, **-ied**) **1** make an aircraft move along the ground before take-off or after landing, or move in this way **2** transport or travel in a taxi

taxidermy /táksi durmi/ *n* the art of stuffing dead animals for display —**taxidermist** *n*

taxing /táksing/ *adj* demanding —**taxingly** *adv*

taxi rank *n* a place for taxis to wait for customers

tax loss *n* a transaction resulting in a reduced tax liability

taxonomy /tak sónnəmi/ (*pl* **-mies**) *n* **1** the classification of organisms **2** the principles of classification —**taxonomic** /táksə nómmik/ *adj* —**taxonomist** *n*

taxpayer /táks pər/ *n* somebody who pays a tax or taxes, especially income tax —**taxpaying** *adj*

tax relief *n* a reduction in the tax payable by somebody

tax return *n* a government form for recording income and expenses in order to calculate tax liability

tax shelter *n* an investment intended to reduce income tax liability —**tax-sheltered** *adj*

Tay longest river in Scotland, flowing through **Loch Tay** and the **Firth of Tay** into the North Sea. Length 190 km/120 mi.

Taylor /táylər/, **Elizabeth** (*b.* 1932) British-born US film actor

Tb *symbol* terbium

TB, T.B. *abbr* tuberculosis

t.b.a. *abbr* **1** to be agreed **2** to be announced

Tbilisi /təbi leéssi/ capital of the Republic of Georgia. Pop. 1,268,000 (1990 estimate).

T-bone steak *n* a large sirloin steak containing a T-shaped bone

tbs., tbsp. *abbr* tablespoon

Tc *symbol* technetium

T-cell *n* a white blood cell from the thymus, important to the immune system

AKG London

Peter Ilich Tchaikovsky

Tchaikovsky /chī kófski/, **Peter Ilich** (1840–93) Russian composer

TCP/IP *abbr* transmission control protocol/Internet protocol

Te *symbol* tellurium

tea /tee/ *n* **1** the dried shredded leaves of an Asian plant, used for making a drink by adding boiling water **2** a tea drink **3** a drink made by the infusion of plant leaves or flowers **4** an Asian evergreen bush whose leaves are used to make tea **5** an early-evening meal **6** a snack or light meal of cakes, sandwiches, and tea

SPELLCHECK Do not confuse the spelling of **tea** and **tee** ('a golf peg'), which sound similar.

tea bag *n* a small bag containing tea leaves that is placed in boiling water to make a tea drink

tea break *n* a break from work to have a drink of tea or coffee

teacake /teé kayk/ *n* a large flat currant bun

teach /teech/ (**taught** /tawt/) *v* **1** *vt* impart knowledge or skill to somebody by instruction **2** *vt* give lessons to a person or animal **3** *vt* make somebody understand through experience **4** *vti* be a teacher in an institution ○ *teaches college* —**teachable** *adj*

SYNONYMS teach, educate, train, instruct, coach, tutor, school, drill CORE MEANING: impart knowledge or skill in something

teacher /teéchər/ *n* **1** somebody who teaches, especially professionally **2** something that teaches ○ *Experience is a great teacher.* —**teacherly** *adj*

tea chest *n* a large light wooden box for transporting tea

teach-in *n* an extended period of speeches and lectures as part of a protest

teaching /teéching/ *n* **1** the practice or profession of being a teacher **2** something taught (*often pl*) ∎ *adj* **1** used for teaching **2** involved in teaching

teaching hospital *n* a hospital that trains medical students

tea cosy *n* a soft cover for keeping a teapot warm

tea dance *n* an afternoon social event with dancing at which tea is served

teak /teek/ *n* **1** a durable red-brown wood. Use: furniture, shipbuilding. **2** a tree from which teak is obtained

teal /teel/ (*pl* **teals** *or* same) *n* **1** a small duck with iridescent blue or green wing patches **2** a greenish-blue colour —**teal** *adj*

team /teem/ *n* **1** a group of people forming one side in a sports competition **2** a number of people functioning cooperatively as a group **3** a group of animals made to work together ∎ *vti* form into a team

SPELLCHECK Do not confuse the spelling of **team** and **teem** ('be full of'), which sound similar.

team-mate *n* a member of the same team

team player *n* somebody who works co-operatively

team spirit *n* enthusiasm about working as a team

teamwork /téem wurk/ n 1 cooperative work by a group 2 the results produced by group work

teapot /tee pot/ n a container with a spout and handle for infusing and serving tea

tear¹ /tair/ v (**tore**, **torn**) 1 vti pull something such as paper or fabric apart, or come apart in this way 2 vt make a hole in something by tearing 3 vt cut something such as flesh leaving jagged edges 4 vt injure a muscle or ligament so that some of the tissue is pulled apart and separated 5 vt separate something using force 6 vt cause something to become divided or fragmented 7 vi move or act very quickly (infml) ○ *tearing down the road* ■ n 1 a split caused by tearing 2 an act of tearing

SYNONYMS **tear**, **rend**, **rip**, **split** CORE MEANING: pull apart forcibly

☐ **tear apart** vt 1 divide or separate by tearing 2 distress somebody

☐ **tear down** vt demolish or dismantle

☐ **tear into** vt attack physically or verbally

☐ **tear up** vt tear into small pieces

tear² /teer/ n a drop of salty fluid from the eye ■ **tears** npl 1 weeping, e.g. from grief or pain 2 the salty liquid that moistens and protects the eyes —**tearily** adv —**teariness** n —**teary** adj

SPELLCHECK Do not confuse the spelling of **tear** and **tier** ('a row of seats'), which sound similar.

tearaway /táirə way/ n somebody reckless

teardrop /teer drop/ n 1 a drop of salty fluid from the eye 2 a shape resembling a teardrop, or something having this shape

tearful /teerf'l/ adj 1 crying or about to cry 2 sad enough to cause tears —**tearfully** adv

tear gas /teer-/ n a chemical agent that incapacitates people by irritating their eyes —**tear-gas** vt

tear-jerker /teer-/ n an excessively sentimental story, play, or film (infml) —**tear-jerking** adj

tear-off /táir-/ adj produced so that individual sheets can be removed easily

tearoom /tee room, -rōom/, **teashop** /-shop/ n a restaurant serving tea and light refreshments

tease /teez/ v (**teasing**, **teased**) 1 vti make fun of somebody 2 vti annoy a person or animal on purpose 3 vt urge somebody by coaxing 4 vt arouse physical desire in somebody without intending to give satisfaction 5 vt pull fibres apart by combing or carding 6 vt raise a nap on cloth by combing ■ n 1 a provocative opening remark 2 an act of teasing —**teasing** adj —**teasingly** adv

☐ **tease out** vt extract information or the truth gradually

teasel /teez'l/ n 1 a plant that produces flowers covered with hooked leaves 2 an implement used to raise fabric nap

teaser /teezar/ n 1 a tricky problem 2 somebody

who teases somebody else 3 an advertisement offering a gift

tea service, **tea set** n a set of matching articles for serving tea

teaspoon /tee spoon/ n 1 a small spoon for stirring tea 2 *also* **teaspoonful** the amount held by a teaspoon

teat /teet/ n 1 a protuberance on the breast or udder of a female mammal through which milk is excreted 2 the teat-shaped mouthpiece of a baby's or animal's feeding bottle

tea towel n a cloth for drying dishes

tea tree n a tree with leaves that yield an antiseptic oil. Use: in cosmetics, lotions.

Tebet n JUDAISM, CALENDAR = **Tevet**

tech /tek/ n a technical college or university (infml)

techie /téki/, **tekkie** n somebody competent in technology (infml)

technetium /tek neeshi əm/ n (symbol Tc) a silvery-grey radioactive metallic element. Use: tracer, corrosion-resistant materials.

technical /téknik'l/ adj 1 of industrial techniques or applied science 2 specializing or skilled in practical or scientific subjects 3 belonging to a specific subject or profession ○ *a technical glossary* 4 strictly interpreted 5 exhibiting or deriving from technique —**technically** adv

technicality /tékni kálləti/ (pl -ties) n 1 a detail or term understood only by a specialist 2 a trivial point arising from the strict application of rules ○ *a legal technicality* 3 the quality of being technical

technical support n a repair or advice service offered by computer or software manufacturers

technician /tek nísh'n/ n 1 a specialist in industrial techniques 2 a laboratory employee

Technicolor /tékni kulər/ tdmk a trademark for an early colour process for making films

~~technique~~ incorrect spelling of **technique**

technique /tek neek/ n 1 the procedure or skill required for a specific task 2 treatment of the basics of something such as an artistic work or a sport 3 skill or expertise in doing a specific thing

techno /téknō/ n fast electronic dance music using digitally synthesized instruments

techno- prefix technology, technological ○ *technocrat*

technocracy /tek nókrəssi/ (pl -cies) n 1 a government or social system in which scientists, engineers, and technicians are politically powerful 2 a philosophy promoting technocracy

technocrat /téknə krat/ n 1 a bureaucrat who is a technical expert 2 a proponent of technocracy —**technocratic** /téknə kráttik/ adj

technology /tek nóllǝji/ (pl -gies) n 1 the development and application of tools, machines, and methods for manufacturing and other processes 2 a method of applying technical knowledge or tools —**technological**

/téknə lójjik'l/ *adj* —**technologically** *adv*
—**technologist** *n*

technophile /téknō fīl/ *n* somebody who likes or is interested in new technology or computerization

technophobe /téknə fōb/ *n* somebody who dislikes or is intimidated by new technology or computerization —**technophobia** /téknō fóbi ə/ *n*

techy *adj* = **tetchy**

~~teenical~~ incorrect spelling of **technical**

~~tecnique~~ incorrect spelling of **technique**

tectonic /tek tónnik/ *adj* 1 of the forces that produce movement or deformation of the Earth's crust 2 of construction and architecture —**tectonics** *n*

teddy[1] /téddi/ (*pl* **-dies**), **teddy bear** *n* a soft furry toy bear

> **ORIGIN Teddies** are named after US president Theodore Roosevelt, who was fond of bear hunting. His nickname, 'Teddy', was used in a humorous poem in the *New York Times* about the adventures of two bears. Their names (Teddy B and Teddy G) were then appropriated to two bears in the Bronx Zoo whose popularity caused toy manufacturers to market toy bears as *teddy bears*.

teddy[2] /téddi/ (*pl* **-dies**) *n* a woman's one-piece short undergarment

teddy boy *n* in the United Kingdom in the 1950s and 1960s a youth with tight narrow trousers, pointed shoes, and long sideboards

> **ORIGIN** 1950s **teddy boys** adopted styles resembling those of the Edwardian period, and took their name from *Teddy*, the pet form of *Edward*, in allusion to Edward VII. The name is first recorded in 1954.

tedious /teedi əss/ *adj* boringly long or repetitive —**tediously** *adv* —**tediousness** *n*

tedium /teedi əm/ *n* the quality of being tedious

tee /tee/ *n* 1 a peg with a cupped end placed in the ground to hold a golf ball 2 an area on a golf course where play for a new hole starts ■ *vti* (**teed**) put a golf ball on a tee ◊ See note at **tea**

□ **tee off** *vi* in golf, hit a ball from a tee at the start of a hole

TEE *abbr* Trans-Europe Express (train)

tee-hee /tee hee/, **te-hee** *interj* expresses laughter —**tee-hee** *vi*

teem *vi* be full of people or animals —**teemingly** *adv* ◊ See note at **team**

teen (*infml*) *adj* teenage ■ *n* a teenager

teenage /teen ayj/, **teenaged** /-ayjd/ *adj* 1 aged between 13 and 19 2 of teenagers

teenager /teen ayjər/ *n* a young person aged between 13 and 19 ◊ See note at **youth**

teens *npl* 1 the years between 13 and 19 in somebody's life 2 the numbers ending in '-teen'

teensy-weensy /teenzi weenzi/, **teeny-weeny** /teeni weeni/ *adj* very tiny (*infml*)

teeny /teeni/ (**-nier**, **-niest**) *adj* very tiny (*infml*)

teepee *n* CULTL ANTHROP = **tepee**

tee shirt *n* CLOTHING = **T-shirt**

teeter /teetər/ *vi* move totteringly

teeth plural of **tooth**

teethe /teeth/ (**teething**, **teethed**) *vi* grow your first teeth

teething troubles *npl* difficulties early on in an activity

teetotal /tee tōt'l/ *adj* abstaining from alcohol —**teetotalism** *n* —**teetotaller** *n*

> **ORIGIN** The *tee* of **teetotal** represents an emphatic repetition of the initial consonant of *total*. The adjective 'abstaining from alcohol' is attributed to a Richard Turner of Preston, Lancashire, who is said to have used it in a speech to a temperance society in September 1833.

teetotaler *n* US = **teetotaller**

TEFL *abbr* teaching (of) English as a foreign language

Teflon /téf lon/ *tdmk* a trademark for a plastic with nonstick properties that is used as a coating, e.g. for cookware

Tegucigalpa /te goóssi gálpə/ capital of Honduras. Pop. 813,900 (1995).

te-hee *interj, vi* = **tee-hee**

Tehran /te raán/ capital of Iran. Pop. 6,758,845 (1996).

Te Kanawa /tə kaánəwə, tay-/, **Dame Kiri** (*b.* 1944) New Zealand opera singer

tekkie *n* = **techie** (*infml*)

tel. *abbr* 1 telegram 2 telegraph 3 telegraphic 4 telephone

Tel Aviv /tél ə veev/, **Tel Aviv-Jaffa** /-jáffə/ city in west-central Israel. Pop. 348,100 (1999).

telco hotel /télkō-/ *n* an Internet hotel

tele- *prefix* 1 distant, operating at a distance ○ *telecommute* 2 television ○ *telegenic* 3 telegraph, telephone ○ *telebanking*

telebanking /télli bangking/ *n* a system of banking carried out by telephone

telecast /télli kaast/ *n* a TV broadcast ■ *vti* (**-cast** *or* **-casted**) broadcast a TV programme —**telecaster** *n*

telecommunication /télli kə myoóni káysh'n/ *n* electronic communication using wires or radio signals

telecommunications /télli kə myoóni káysh'nz/ *n* the science of transmitting information electronically by wires or radio signals (+ *sing or pl verb*)

telecommute /télli kə myoot/ (**-muting**, **-muted**) *vi* work from home on a computer linked to the workplace via a modem —**telecommuter** *n* —**telecommuting** *n*

teleconferencing /télli konfərənssing/ *n* video conferencing using telephone lines —**teleconference** *n, vi*

telecottage /télli kotij/ *n* a place in a rural area where people can use computers to telecommute —**telecottaging** *n*

telegenic /télli jénnik/ adj looking good on TV

telegram /télli gram/ n a telegraph message
—**telegrammatic** /télli grə máttik/ adj

telegraph /télli graaf, -graf/ n 1 a method of long-distance communication by coded electrical impulses transmitted through wires 2 a telegram ■ v 1 vti send a message to somebody by telegraph 2 vt communicate something indirectly or without words ○ telegraphed her annoyance with a frown —**telegrapher** /ti léggrəfər/ n —**telegraphist** /ti léggrəfist/ n —**telegraphy** /ti léggrəfi/ n

telegraphic /télli gráffik/ adj 1 of telegraphy or telegrams 2 concise or elliptical —**telegraphically** adv

telegraph pole, telegraph post n a pole for supporting telephone wires

telekinesis /télli ki neéssiss, -kī-/ n the supposed power to move an object without using any physical means —**telekinetic** /-néttik/ adj

Telemann /táylə man, téllə-/, **Georg Philipp** (1681–1767) German composer

telemarketing /télli maarkiting/ n selling or promoting goods and services by telephone —**telemarketer** n

telematics /telli máttiks/ n the science of data transmission (+ sing verb) —**telematic** adj

telepathy /tə léppəthi/ n supposed communication directly from one person's mind to another —**telepath** /télli path/ n —**telepathic** /télli páthik/ adj —**telepathically** adv

telephone /télli fōn/ n 1 an electronic device containing a receiver and transmitter and linked to a telecommunications system 2 a system of communication using telephones ■ vti (-phoning, -phoned) 1 speak to somebody using the telephone 2 send a message by telephone —**telephonic** /télli fónnik/ adj

telephone book, telephone directory n an alphabetical listing of names, addresses, and telephone numbers of people or businesses

telephone box n a structure with a pay phone in it

telephone exchange n a centre housing equipment for interconnecting telephone lines

telephonist /tə léffənist/ n a telephone switchboard operator

telephony /tə léffəni/ n the science or a system of communication by telephone

telephoto lens /télli fōtō-/ n a camera lens that makes distant objects seem nearer or larger

teleport /télli pawrt/ v 1 vt move something supposedly using mental power 2 vi in science fiction, move somewhere instantly without travelling —**teleportation** /télli pawr táysh'n/ n

teleprinter /télli printər/ n a piece of equipment for telegraphic communication that uses a device like a typewriter for data input and output

teleprocessing /télli prő sessing/ n use of remote computer terminals to process data

telesales /télli saylz/ n telemarketing (+ sing verb)

telescope /télli skōp/ n 1 a device using compound lenses or concave mirrors for looking at distant objects 2 a radio telescope ■ v (-scoping, -scoped) 1 vi slide concentric parts neatly inside each other 2 vt condense

telescopic /télli skóppik/ adj 1 of telescopes 2 able to make distant objects seem nearer or larger 3 with concentric parts that slide neatly inside each other —**telescopically** adv

teleshopping /télli shoping/ n the purchase of goods advertised on TV by telephone or computer —**teleshop** vi —**teleshopper** n

teletext /télli tekst/ n a system of broadcasting written information on TV over or instead of the picture

telethon /téllə thon/ n a lengthy TV broadcast combining entertainment with appeals for donations to a charity

televangelist /télli vánjəlist/ n a Christian evangelist whose services are broadcast on TV —**televangelism** n

televise /télli vīz/ (-vising, -vised) vt broadcast on TV

television /télli vizh'n, -vízh'n/ n 1 a system of capturing images and sounds, broadcasting them electronically, and reproducing them for viewing and listening 2 also **television set** an electronic device for receiving and reproducing the images and sounds of a television signal 3 the television broadcasting industry —**televisual** /télli vízhyoo əl, téllə-, -víz-/ adj —**televisually** adv

ORIGIN The word **television** is first recorded in English in 1907. Its literal meaning is 'far vision'. During its early history it was criticized for being a hybrid of elements of Greek (tēle 'far off') and Latin origin, but nothing now could sound more familiar.

teleworking /télli wurking/ n telecommuting

telex /télleks/ n 1 a communications system using teleprinters 2 a message sent or received by telex ■ vti send a message to somebody by telex

Telford /télfərd/, **Thomas** (1757–1834) British civil engineer

tell (**told** /tōld/) v 1 vt inform somebody of something 2 vt relate events or facts 3 vti express thoughts or feelings to somebody in words 4 vt express a particular thing in speech ○ tell a lie 5 vt order somebody to do something 6 vt distinguish two or more things ○ couldn't tell one pup from the other 7 vt ascertain or perceive something ○ couldn't tell whether she was pleased or not 8 vt purport to reveal the future ○ tell fortunes 9 vi reveal a secret ○ Don't worry, I won't tell. ◇ **all told** altogether ◇ **tell it like it is** give an accurate account of something (infml)
□ **tell off** vt scold (infml)

Tell, William n legendary Swiss patriot

teller /téllər/ n 1 a bank employee who receives

and pays out money **2** somebody who tells something o *a teller of tall tales*

Teller /téllər/, **Edward** (*b.* 1908) Hungarian-born US physicist. He helped construct the first atomic bomb and was the principal architect of the hydrogen bomb.

telling /télling/ *adj* **1** inadvertently revealing something o *a telling look* **2** highly effective o *written in telling detail* —**tellingly** *adv*

telling-off (*pl* **tellings-off**) *n* a scolding (*infml*)

telltale /tél tayl/ *adj* clearly showing or indicating something secret ■ *n* somebody who reveals somebody else's secrets or wrongdoing

tellurium /te loŏri əm/ *n* (*symbol* **Te**) a semimetallic chemical element. Use: alloys, various manufacturing processes.

telly /télli/ (*pl* **-lies**) *n* television, or a television set (*infml*)

temerity /tə mérrəti/ *n* reckless boldness

temp *n* a temporary worker, especially one hired from an agency ■ *vi* work as a temp o *She's temping with a bank.*

temper /témpər/ *n* **1** a tendency to get angry easily **2** an angry state **3** an emotional condition of a particular kind o *an even temper* **4** a calm state o *lost his temper* **5** the hardness of a metal ■ *vt* **1** make something less harsh or more acceptable by adding something else o *temper criticism with kindness* **2** harden metal by heating and cooling it **3** make somebody stronger through exposure to hardship

tempera /témpərə/ *n* **1** a painting technique using colours made from pigment mixed with water and egg yolk **2** a painting done in tempera

temperament /témprəmənt/ *n* **1** a quality of mind that characterizes somebody **2** the state of being excessively excitable and irritable

temperamental /témprə mént'l/ *adj* **1** easily upset and irritated **2** unpredictable o *a temperamental car* **3** of temperament —**temperamentally** *adv*

temperance /témpərənss/ *n* **1** abstinence from alcohol **2** self-restraint

~~temperary~~ incorrect spelling of **temporary**

temperate /témpərət/ *adj* **1** mild or restrained in behaviour or attitude **2** describes a climate without temperature extremes —**temperately** *adv* —**temperateness** *n*

Temperate Zone *n* the parts of the Earth that have hot summers, cold winters, and intermediate autumns and springs

temperature /témprichər/ *n* **1** the degree of heat of an object or place **2** the degree of heat of a person's body **3** an unusually high body temperature in excess of 37.0° C/98.6° F o *running a temperature*

~~temperment~~ incorrect spelling of **temperament**

~~temperture~~ incorrect spelling of **temperature**

tempest /témpist/ *n* a severe storm (*literary*)

tempestuous /tem péstyoo əss/ *adj* **1** with severe storms **2** emotionally turbulent —**tempestuously** *adv* —**tempestuousness** *n*

template /tém playt, -plət/ *n* a pattern from which other similar things can be made

temple[1] /témp'l/ *n* **1** a building for worship **2** an institution or building regarded as a guardian of, or place set aside for, a particular activity **3** a meeting place for a fraternal order **4** a place of worship for the Church of Jesus Christ of Latter-Day Saints

temple[2] /témp'l/ *n* the part of each side of the head between the eye and the ear

Temple /témp'l/, **Shirley** ♦ **Black, Shirley Temple**

tempo /témpō/ (*pl* **-pos** *or* **-pi** /-pee/) *n* **1** the speed of a piece of music **2** the pace or rate of an activity

temporal[1] /témpərəl/ *adj* **1** of time **2** in the Christian church, of the laity rather than the clergy **3** of worldly life rather than spiritual life —**temporally** *adv*

temporal[2] /témpərəl/ *adj* of the temples of the head

temporary /témpərəri/ *adj* having a limited duration ■ *n* (*pl* **-ies**) a worker hired for a limited time —**temporarily** *adv*

SYNONYMS temporary, fleeting, passing, transitory, ephemeral, evanescent, short-lived CORE MEANING: lasting only a short time

---

temporize /témpə rīz/ (**-rizing, -rized**), **temporise** *vi* use delaying tactics to gain time o *temporized before answering the question* —**temporization** /témpə rī záysh'n/ *n*

~~temprature~~ incorrect spelling of **temperature**

tempt *vt* **1** incite desire in **2** incite to wrongdoing **3** invite or attract o *brochures tempted us to go* **4** risk the possible destructive powers of o *tempt fate* —**temptable** *adj* —**tempting** *adj* —**temptingly** *adv*

temptation /temp táysh'n/ *n* **1** a desire for something considered wrong **2** the incitement of desire in somebody **3** a person or thing that tempts somebody

temptress /témptriss/ *n* a woman regarded as sexually alluring (*dated; sometimes offensive*)

tempura /témpoorə/ *n* a Japanese dish of vegetables or seafood coated in light batter and deep-fried

ten *n* the number 10 —**ten** *adj*, *pron* —**tenth** *n*, *adj*, *adv*

tenable /ténnəb'l/ *adj* **1** justifiable with reasoned arguments **2** fit to be occupied (*fml*) —**tenability** /ténnə billəti/ *n* —**tenably** *adv*

tenacious /tə náyshəss/ *adj* **1** very determined or stubborn **2** difficult to loosen or shake off o *a tenacious head cold* **3** able to remember many things —**tenaciously** *adv* —**tenaciousness** *n* —**tenacity** /tə nássəti/ *n*

tenancy /ténnənssi/ (*pl* **-cies**) *n* **1** possession or occupancy of property or land owned by somebody else for a fixed period in return for rent **2** the period of somebody's tenancy

tenant /ténnənt/ n 1 a renter of property 2 the occupier of a place (dated literary) ■ vti occupy somebody else's property as a tenant —**tenanted** adj

tenant farmer n somebody who rents and farms a piece of land

Ten Commandments npl the ten laws given by God to Moses, according to the Bible

tend[1] vi 1 be generally inclined or likely to do something, or be in the habit of doing something 2 move gradually or slightly in a particular direction

tend[2] vt look after —**tendance** n

~~tendancy~~ incorrect spelling of **tendency**

tendency /téndənssi/ (pl -cies) n 1 a way that somebody or something typically behaves or is likely to behave 2 a gradual movement or development in a given direction (dated or fml)

tendentious /ten dénsshəs/ adj promoting a specific cause or supporting a specific view

tender[1] /téndər/ adj 1 painful when touched or pressed 2 showing care, gentleness, and feeling 3 kind and sympathetic o a tender disposition 4 pleasantly soft for eating 5 young, vulnerable, or delicate o children at the tender age of five —**tenderly** adv —**tenderness** n

tender[2] /téndər/ v 1 vt offer something formally in writing o tendered her resignation 2 vi offer to undertake a job or supply goods o tender for a contract 3 vt offer something as payment ■ n 1 a formal offer to undertake a job or supply goods 2 money o legal tender —**tenderable** adj

tender[3] /téndər/ n 1 a small boat used to go to and from a larger boat 2 the rear part of a steam locomotive that carries its coal and water 3 an emergency vehicle carrying tools, equipment, and personnel (usually in combination)

tenderfoot /téndər fŏŏt/ (pl -foots or -feet /-feet/), **Tenderfoot** n a new member of a Scout troop or Guide company

tenderhearted /téndər haártid/ adj kindly and caring —**tenderheartedly** adv —**tenderheartedness** n

tenderize /téndə rīz/ (-izing, -ized), **tenderise** vt make meat tender —**tenderization** /téndə rī záysh'n/ n —**tenderizer** n

tenderloin /téndər loyn/ n a prime cut of meat from the curve of the ribs at the backbone

tendinitis /téndə nítiss/, **tendonitis** n inflammation of a tendon

tendon /téndən/ n a tough band of tissue connecting a muscle to a bone —**tendinous** /-dinəss/ adj

tendril /téndrəl/ n 1 a thin plant part that coils around and attaches the plant to a support 2 a delicate twist or coil (literary)

tenement /ténnəmənt/ n a large multiple-occupancy residential building

~~tenent~~ incorrect spelling of **tenant**

~~Tenessee~~ incorrect spelling of **Tennessee**

tenet /ténnit/ n an established fundamental belief

tenfold /tén fōld/ adj 1 multiplied by ten 2 made up of ten parts ■ adv ten times over

ten-gallon hat n a cowboy hat with a large round crown

tenge /téngay/ (pl same) n the main unit of Kazakh currency

tenner /ténnər/ n ten pounds sterling, or a ten-pound note (infml)

~~Tennesee~~ incorrect spelling of **Tennessee**

Tennessee /ténnə see/ state in the east-central United States. Cap. Nashville. Pop. 5,689,283 (2000). —**Tennessean** n, adj

Tenniel /ténni əl/, **Sir John** (1820–1914) British illustrator

tennis /ténniss/ n a racket game played by two or four players who hit a ball over a net across a rectangular court

tennis elbow n painful inflammation of the tendon in the outer elbow caused by repetitive strain

Tennyson /ténniss'n/, **Alfred, 1st Baron Tennyson of Freshwater and Aldworth** (1809–92) British poet —**Tennysonian** /ténni sóni ən/ n, adj

tenon /ténnən/ n a projection on a piece of wood for fitting into a mortise on another piece to make a joint

tenor /ténnər/ n 1 the highest natural adult male singing voice, or a man with this voice 2 the way something is progressing (fml) 3 overall nature, pattern, or meaning (fml) o the positive tenor of the reply

tenpin /tén pin/ n a bottle-shaped bowling pin

tenpin bowling n an indoor bowling game in which players try to knock down ten bottle-shaped pins by rolling a heavy ball at them

tense[1] adj (**tenser, tensest**) 1 worried and nervous 2 causing anxiety or nervousness o a tense wait 3 stretched tight or held stiffly o tense muscles ■ vti (**tensing, tensed**) make or become tense —**tensely** adv —**tenseness** n

tense[2] n the form of a verb that expresses the time at which action takes place in relation to the speaker or writer o in the future tense

tensile /tén sīl/ adj 1 of tension 2 capable of stretching or being stretched —**tensility** /ten sílləti/ n

tensile strength n the maximum stretching force that a material can withstand

tension /ténsh'n/ n 1 anxious feelings 2 an uneasy or hostile feeling in a relationship (often pl) 3 the buildup of suspense in a fictional work 4 the tautness of something 5 a pulling or stretching force 6 voltage or electromotive force (often in combination) o high-tension wires —**tensional** adj

tensor /ténssər, -sawr/ n a muscle that tenses or stretches a part of the body

tent n a collapsible movable fabric shelter held up by poles and kept in place by ropes and pegs

tentacle /téntək'l/ *n* a long flexible organ used by some animals for holding, feeling, or moving —**tentacled** *adj* —**tentacular** /ten tákyōōlər/ *adj*

tentative /téntətiv/ *adj* 1 hesitant or uncertain 2 rough or provisional ○ *tentative plans* —**tentatively** *adv* —**tentativeness** *n*

tenterhook /téntər hŏŏk/ ◇ **on tenterhooks** anxious or in great suspense

tenuous /ténnyōō əss/ *adj* weak and unconvincing —**tenuity** /te nyōŏ əti/ *n* —**tenuously** *adv* —**tenuousness** *n*

tenure /ténnyər, ténnyoor/ *n* 1 occupation of an official position, or the period of occupation (*fml*) 2 the rights of a tenant to hold property —**tenured** *adj*

Tenzing Norkay /ténssing náwrkay/ (1914?–86) Nepalese mountaineer who was one of the first two climbers to reach the summit of Mount Everest (1953)

Tenzin Gyatso /ténssin gyátsō/ (*b.* 1935) 14th Dalai Lama (1940–)

tepee /tée pee/, **teepee** *n* a Native North American conical tent dwelling

tepid /téppid/ *adj* 1 lukewarm ○ *tepid water* 2 unenthusiastic ○ *tepid applause* —**tepidity** /te píddəti/ *n* —**tepidly** *adv* —**tepidness** *n*

Te Puea Herangi /te pŏŏ i ə hérrungi/ (1884–1952) New Zealand Maori leader

tequila /ti kéelə, te-/ *n* a Mexican alcoholic drink made from the agave plant

terabyte /térrə bīt/ *n* in computing, an information unit of one million million bytes

teraflop /térrə flop/ *n* a measure of computer speed that is one million million floating-point operations per second

terbium /túrbi əm/ *n* (*symbol* **Tb**) a silvery-grey metallic chemical element. Use: lasers, X-rays, television tubes. —**terbic** *adj*

tercentenary /túr sen téenəri, -ténnəri/ (*pl* **-ries**) *n* a 300th anniversary —**tercentenary** *adj*

Terence /térrənss/ (185–159 BC) Roman playwright

Express Newspapers

Mother Teresa

Teresa (of Calcutta) /tə réessə-, -ráyzə-/, **Mother** (1910–97) Albanian-born nun

Tereshkova /térrish kŏvə/, **Valentina** (*b.* 1937) Soviet cosmonaut and the first woman in space (1963)

~~terestrial~~ incorrect spelling of **terrestrial**

teriyaki /térri yáki/ *n* a Japanese dish of marinated and grilled shellfish or meat

term *n* 1 a specific name or word for something 2 the period of time something lasts, with a fixed beginning and end (*fml*) ○ *during her term of office* 3 a period of time that a political or legal body continues meeting 4 a division of an academic year 5 a specific time, especially for making a payment 6 the expected time for the birth of a child ○ *a pregnancy that came to term* 7 a mathematical expression forming part of a fraction, proportion, or series ■ **terms** *npl* 1 the way people get on together ○ *parted on good terms* 2 the conditions that make up an agreement or contract ○ *the terms of the lease* 3 the words used or chosen when speaking or writing ○ *overly technical terms* ■ *vt* describe with a specific word ○ *termed the situation precarious* ◇ **come to terms (with)** reach a state of acceptance about something ◇ **in terms of** in relation to

termagant /túrməgənt/ *n* a woman regarded as quarrelsome and fault-finding (*insult*)

ORIGIN A non-Christian deity *Termagant* was represented in medieval mystery plays as a violent overbearing person. By the 16C the name had become a term of abuse for people regarded as having similar characteristics.

terminal /túrminəl/ *adj* 1 causing death ○ *a terminal illness* 2 dying of a fatal illness, or relating to patients so affected ○ *terminal care* 3 of or at the very end of something ■ *n* 1 a place at the end of a transport route 2 a conductor attached at the point where electricity enters or leaves a circuit ○ *a battery terminal* 3 a remote input or output device linked to computer, or a combination of such devices —**terminally** *adv* ◇ See note at **deadly**

terminate /túrmi nayt/ (**-nating, -nated**) *vti* finish ○ *terminate a broadcast* —**termination** /túrmi náysh'n/ *n* —**terminator** *n*

terminology /túrmi nólləji/ (*pl* **-gies**) *n* 1 specialized vocabulary, or an example of this 2 the study of names and terms —**terminological** /túrminə lójjik'l/ *adj* —**terminologist** *n*

terminus /túrminəss/ (*pl* **-ni** /-nī/ *or* **-nuses**) *n* 1 a station, town, or city where a public transport route ends 2 a point where something ends (*literary or fml*)

termite /túr mīt/ *n* an insect that lives in large colonies and destroys wood

tern (*pl* **terns** *or* **same**) *n* a black-and-white seabird related to the gull

terrace /térrəss/ *n* 1 a porch or walkway with pillars at the side 2 one of a series of flat strips of land constructed in steps on a hillside for growing crops 3 a row of identical houses joined together at the sides 4 an artificially constructed bank of ground 5 a flat area beside a building used for sitting or eating outdoors ■ **terraces** *npl* the broad shallow open-air steps providing standing areas in a football stadium ■ *vt* (**-racing, -raced**) convert land into a terrace or terraces

terraced house, terrace house *n* a house in a row of identical houses joined at the sides —**terraced housing** *n*

terracotta /térrə kóttə/ *n* **1** a reddish-brown pottery clay **2** something made of terracotta

terra firma /térrə fúrmə/ *n* dry land *(literary or humorous)*

terrain /tə ráyn/ *(pl* **-rains** *or same) n* **1** a specific area of land o *surveyed the local terrain* **2** topography o *mountainous terrain*

terra incognita /-in kógnitə/ *(pl* **terrae incognitae** /térree in kógni tee/) *n* **1** an unexplored region **2** an unexplored subject

terra nullius /térrə noólli əss/ *n* the concept that when the first Europeans arrived in Australia the land was owned by no one and therefore open to settlement

terrapin /térrəpin/ *(pl* **-pins** *or same) n* **1** a moderate-sized turtle that lives in brackish water **2** a small freshwater turtle

terrarium /tə ráiri əm/ *(pl* **-ums** *or* **-a** /-ri ə/) *n* an enclosure for keeping plants or small animals indoors in a simulated natural environment

~~terrestial~~ incorrect spelling of **terrestrial**

terrestrial /tə réstri əl/ *adj* **1** of the Earth **2** belonging to the land **3** living or growing on land **4** broadcast by a land-based transmitter ■ *n* in science fiction, a person or animal that lives on Earth

terrestrial link *n* a telecommunications connection running on or under the ground

terrible /térrəb'l/ *adj* **1** very serious or severe **2** very unpleasant **3** extremely low in quality o *a terrible film* **4** very ill or unhappy **5** very troubling —**terribly** *adv*

terrier /térri ər/ *n* a breed of small dog originally bred for hunting animals in burrows

terrific /tə ríffik/ *adj* **1** very good *(infml)* **2** very great in size, force, or degree o *a terrific crash* —**terrifically** *adv*

~~terrifically~~ incorrect spelling of **terrifically**

terrify /térri fī/ *(***-fies, -fied***) vt* **1** make very frightened **2** coerce or intimidate —**terrifying** *adj* —**terrifyingly** *adv*

terrine /te réen/ *n* **1** a small tight-lidded dish for cooking pâté **2** a coarse pâté cooked in a terrine

territorial /térrə táwri əl/ *adj* **1** of land or water owned by a country **2** asserting ownership of an area and protecting it against intruders —**territorially** *adv*

Territorial Army *n* a British reserve army

territorial waters *npl* the area of sea around a country's coast recognized as being under that country's jurisdiction

Territorian /térrə táwri ən/ *n Aus* somebody from the Northern Territory

territory /térrətəri/ *(pl* **-ries***) n* **1** land, or an area of land **2** a geographical area owned and controlled by a country **3** *also* **Territory** an area of a country that is not a state or province but has a separate government **4** a field of knowledge, inquiry, or experience **5** an area that an animal considers its own and defends against intruders **6** the district that an agent covers ◊ **come** *or* **go with the** *or* **somebody's territory** be an inseparable part of or accompaniment to something else *(infml)* o *Danger goes with a firefighter's territory.*

terror /térrər/ *n* **1** intense fear **2** terrorism **3** a cause or source of fear **4** a young person regarded as highly annoying *(infml offensive)*

terrorism /térrərizəm/ *n* the unlawful use or threat of violence to intimidate or coerce, usually for political or ideological reasons —**terrorist** *n*

terrorize /térrə rīz/ *(***-izing, -ized***),* **terrorise** *vt* **1** intimidate or coerce with violence or the threat of violence **2** make very fearful over a period of time —**terrorization** /térrə rī záysh'n/ *n*

terry /térri/, **terry towelling** *n* a fabric with uncut loops of thread on both sides. Use: towels, bath mats, bathrobes.

Terry /térri/, **Dame Ellen** (1847–1928) British actor

terse (**terser, tersest**) *adj* **1** brief and unfriendly o *a terse reply* **2** concise —**tersely** *adv* —**terseness** *n*

tertiary /túrshəri/ *adj* third *(fml)* ■ *n* **Tertiary** a period of geological time 65–1.64 million years ago —**Tertiary** *adj*

tertiary education *n* education at college or university level

TESL /téss'l/ *abbr* teaching (of) English as a second language

TESSA /téssə/, **Tessa** *abbr* Tax-Exempt Special Savings Account

test *n* **1** a series of questions, problems, or tasks to gauge somebody's knowledge, ability, or experience **2** a trial use of a process or equipment to find out whether it works **3** a basis for the evaluation of somebody or something **4** a difficult situation or event that will provide information about somebody or something **5** a medical examination of a part of the body **6** a procedure to detect the presence or properties of a substance **7** in cricket or rugby, a test match ■ *v* **1** *vt* use something on a trial basis in order to evaluate it **2** *vt* ask somebody questions or set somebody a task in order to gauge knowledge, ability, or experience **3** *vt* carry out a medical or scientific test on something **4** *vi* achieve a particular test result o *tested positive for the virus* —**testable** *adj* —**testing** *adj*

ORIGIN **Test** came via French from a Latin word meaning 'earthenware pot'. The original English application was "pot in which metals were heated', and the use of this means of investigating the properties of metals gave rise in the late 16C to the sense 'investigative or trial procedure'.

testament /téstəmənt/ *n* **1** a proof of something **2** a will o *the decedent's last will and testament* **3** **Testament** each half of the Christian Bible

4 Testament a copy of the New Testament —**testamentary** /téstə méntəri/ adj

test ban n an international agreement banning nuclear weapons testing

test card n a pattern transmitted to help in tuning a television set

test case n an important legal case that establishes a precedent

test drive n a short drive to try out a car before buying it

tester /téstər/ n 1 somebody who tests new products 2 a sample of a product, especially a cosmetic 3 a piece of equipment for checking the proper functioning of something

testes plural of **testis**

testicle /téstik'l/ n either of the male sperm-producing glands with their surrounding membranes —**testicular** /te stíkyŏolər/ adj

testify /tésti fī/ (-fies, -fied) vi 1 make a declaration under oath in court 2 make a factual statement based on personal experience 3 be proof or evidence (fml) —**testifier** n

testimonial /tésti mōni əl/ n 1 a statement backing up a claim 2 a favourable report on somebody or something —**testimonial** adj

testimony /téstiməni/ (pl -nies) n 1 evidence given by a witness in court 2 proof of something

testis /téstiss/ (pl -tes /-teez/) n either of the male sperm-producing glands

test match n a cricket or rugby match in a series between two international teams

testosterone /te stóstərōn/ n a male hormone produced in the testicles and responsible for the development of secondary sex characteristics

test pilot n a pilot who flies new aircraft to test their performance

test tube n a glass tube closed and rounded at one end and open at the other, used in a laboratory

test-tube adj made in a test tube or by other artificial means

test-tube baby n a baby conceived from an egg fertilized in a laboratory and then inserted into the womb (infml)

testy /tésti/ (-tier, -tiest) adj impatient or irritable —**testily** adv —**testiness** n

tetanus /téttənəss/ n an infectious disease causing severe muscular spasms —**tetanal** adj

tetchy /téchi/ (-ier, -iest), **techy** adj easily upset or annoyed (infml) —**tetchily** adv —**tetchiness** n

tête-à-tête /tét ə tét/ n a private conversation between two people ■ adj, adv in private between two people

tether /téthər/ n a rope attached to an animal and fixed at the other end to restrict its movement ■ vt tie an animal with a tether ◇ **at the end of your tether** having reached the limit of your patience, strength, or endurance

Teton /teeton, teet'n/ range of the Rocky Mountains in NW Wyoming and SW Idaho. Highest peak Grand Teton 4,197 m/13,770 ft.

tetra /téttrə/ (pl -ras or same) n a brightly coloured freshwater fish popular as an aquarium fish

tetra- prefix four o tetrahedron

tetrahedron /téttrə heédrən/ (pl -drons or -dra /-drə/) n a solid figure with four faces

Teutonic /tyoo tónnik/ adj of German-speaking peoples (infml or humorous)

Tevet /te vét/, **Tebet** n the 10th month of the year in the Jewish calendar

Te Whiti /te fítti/ (1830–1907) New Zealand Maori leader and prophet

Texas /téksəss/ state of the SW United States. Cap. Austin. Pop. 20,851,820 (2000). —**Texan** n, adj

Tex-Mex /téks méks/ adj with a blend of Texan and Mexican cultures or cuisines

text n 1 written, typed, or printed words 2 the main body of text, e.g. in a book or article, as distinct from illustrations, headings, and other material 3 a textbook 4 a Bible passage used as the basis of a sermon ■ vt send a text message to somebody, or somebody's mobile phone —**textual** adj

textbook /tékst bŏok/ n a book containing essential information for a course of study ■ adj typical and thus a suitable example for study

text editor n a computer program allowing the creation and editing of text

text file n a computer file of alphanumeric characters

textile /tékst tīl/ n a fabric

text message n a message sent in textual form, especially to a mobile phone or pager —**text-messaging** n

text processing n the use of computers to manipulate text

texture /tékschər/ n 1 the feel of a surface 2 the structure of a substance or material ■ vt (-turing, -tured) give a rough or grainy feel to —**textural** adj —**textured** adj

textured vegetable protein n full form of **TVP**

TGWU abbr Transport and General Workers' Union

Th symbol thorium

Thackeray /tháckə ray/, **William Makepeace** (1811–63) British novelist

Thaddaeus /tháddi əss/ n one of the 12 apostles of Jesus Christ

Thai /tī/ (pl Thais or same) n 1 somebody from Thailand 2 the official language of Thailand —**Thai** adj

Thailand /tí land, -lənd/ country in Southeast Asia. Cap. Bangkok. Pop. 61,797,751 (2001).

Thailand, Gulf of wide inlet of the South China Sea in S Thailand. Length 800 km/500 mi.

thalidomide /thə líddə mīd/ n a synthetic drug formerly used as a sedative but found to damage foetuses

thallium /thálli əm/ *n* (*symbol* **TI**) a toxic metallic chemical element. Use: manufacture of low-melting glass, photocells, infrared detectors.

Thames /temz/ major river of S England, flowing through London and emptying into the North Sea. Length 338 km/210 mi.

than *stressed* /than/ *unstressed* /thən/ *conj* introduces the second element of a comparison ○ *We're older than he is.* ■ *prep* in contrast with or in preference to (*infml*) ○ *I'm older than him.*

USAGE than he or **than him?** Because **than** is a preposition as well as a conjunction, either construction is possible, as is the fuller form *than he is.* The form *than him* is common in conversation and other spoken contexts (*We're older than him*) but is still frowned upon in formal writing, where *We're older than he is* is preferred.

thane *n* **1** an Anglo-Saxon nobleman who held lands in return for military service to a lord **2** a feudal baron in Scotland —**thaneship** *n*

thank *vt* **1** express gratitude to **2** blame or hold responsible for something

thankful /thángkf'l/ *adj* **1** feeling gratitude **2** glad about something —**thankfulness** *n*

thankfully /thángkf'li/ *adv* **1** expresses relief (*infml*) ○ *Thankfully, they were all safe.* **2** with gratitude

thankless /thángkləss/ *adj* **1** unappreciated **2** ungrateful —**thanklessly** *adv* —**thanklessness** *n*

thanks *interj* expresses gratitude (*infml*) ■ *npl* **1** an expression of gratitude **2** gratitude or appreciation ◇ **no thanks to** despite or without the assistance of ◇ **thanks to** because of

thanksgiving /thángks giving/ *n* **1** a prayer of thanks **2** a giving of thanks **3 Thanksgiving, Thanksgiving Day** a legal holiday in the United States. Date: 4th Thursday in November. **4 Thanksgiving, Thanksgiving Day** a legal holiday in Canada. Date: 2nd Monday in October.

thank-you *n* an expression of gratitude ■ *adj* expressing gratitude

Thant /thant/, **U** (1909–74) Burmese politician and secretary-general of the United Nations (1961–71)

that *stressed* /that/ *unstressed* /thət/ *det, pron* **1** indicates somebody or something already mentioned or identified, or something understood by both speaker and hearer ○ *later that week* ○ *Do you remember that?* **2** indicates distance from the speaker ○ *that girl over there* ■ *pron* introduces a clause identifying the noun it follows ○ *The committee that deals with such matters.* ■ *conj* **1** introduces a comment or fact ○ *said that he would* **2** introduces a result ○ *so loud that I jumped* **3** introduces a cause ○ *felt hurt that she said so* **4** introduces a purpose ○ *gave his life that others could live* ■ *adv* **1** to the indicated degree ○ *came that close to crashing* **2** so very (*infml*) ○ *didn't think they'd be that annoyed*

◇ **that is** in other words ◇ **that's that** that is finished

USAGE For centuries **that** has been used to refer to people as well as things. Though occasionally clumsy, this usage is correct: *He's the one that did it.*; *Anything or anyone that helps me is my friend.*

USAGE that or **which?** The relative pronoun **that** introduces a restrictive clause, i.e. a clause providing essential information: *A car that has bald tyres is not roadworthy.* When the relative clause is nonrestrictive, i.e. it gives information that is additional rather than necessary for identifying the noun it follows, **which** is used and is preceded by a comma: *The largest house, which stands on the corner, is up for sale.*

thatch *n* **1** plant material such as straw or rushes used for a roof **2** a roof of thatch ■ *vti* roof a building with thatch —**thatched** *adj* —**thatcher** *n*

British Information Services

Margaret Thatcher

Thatcher /tháchər/, **Margaret, Baroness Thatcher of Kesteven** (*b.* 1925) first woman prime minister of Great Britain (1979–90)

thaw *v* **1** *vti* change from a solid to a liquid state **2** *vti* change from a frozen to an unfrozen state **3** *vi* become less cold or numb **4** *vi* be warm enough for snow or ice to melt ■ *n* **1** the process of thawing **2** a period of weather warm enough to melt snow and ice

the (*stressed/emphatic*) /thee/ (*unstressed; before a vowel*) /thi/ (*unstressed; before a consonant*) /thə/ *det* **1** indicates somebody or something already mentioned or identified, or something understood by both speaker and hearer ○ *the state you're in* ○ *the clock on the wall* ○ *Put them in the small bag.* ○ *the president of the United States* **2** indicates a generic class ○ *the rich* ○ *good for the heart* ■ *adv* **1** to that extent (*before comparatives*) ○ *the worse for wear* **2** by how much or by that much (*before each of two comparative adjectives or adverbs*) ○ *The more you exercise, the better you'll feel.*

theater *n* US = **theatre**

theatre /theeŕtər/ *n* **1** a place where plays and other entertainments are performed **2** a room with tiers of seats **3** plays and other dramatic literature **4** drama as an art or profession **5** a place of significant events ○ *the theatre of war*

theatregoer /theeŕtər gō ər/ *n* somebody who goes to the theatre —**theatregoing** *n, adj*

theatrical /thi áttrik'l/ adj 1 of the theatre 2 marked by exaggerated or artificial emotion ■ n an actor ■ **theatricals, theatrics** npl 1 the performance of plays 2 dramatic behaviour —**theatricality** /thi àttri kállǝti/ n —**theatrically** adv

Thebes /theebz/ 1 city of ancient Greece, north-west of present-day Athens 2 capital of ancient Egypt, south of present-day Cairo —**Theban** n, adj

thee pron the objective form of 'thou' (archaic)

theft n the stealing of property

~~theif~~ incorrect spelling of **thief**

their /thair/ det 1 belonging to or associated with them 2 △ belonging to or associated with him or her ○ Everyone should have their own copy ◊ See note at **they**

USAGE their, there, or they're? Their is used before a noun: Their [not They're or There] attitudes have changed. There can be an adverb or a pronoun: Look over there [not their or they're]. There [not They're or Their] are several unanswered questions. They're is a contraction of 'they are', as in They're [not There or Their] sitting in the front row.

theirs /thairz/ pron 1 that or those belonging to them 2 that or those belonging to him or her

theism /theé izǝm/ n 1 belief in one God 2 belief in a god or gods —**theist** n —**theistic** /thee ístik/ adj —**theistical** adj

them stressed /them/ unstressed /thǝm/ pron 1 the objective form of 'they' 2 him or her

thematic /thi máttik/ adj of or being a theme —**thematically** adv

theme n 1 a subject of something spoken or written 2 a distinct and unifying idea 3 a repeated melody in a piece of music 4 a piece of music identified with a film or programme —**themed** adj ◊ See note at **subject**

theme park n an amusement park designed around a particular subject or idea

~~themometer~~ incorrect spelling of **thermometer**

themself /them sélf/ pron himself or herself (nonstandard) ○ as anybody can see for themself

themselves /them sélvz/ pron 1 the reflexive form of 'they' or 'them' ○ hurt themselves 2 their normal selves ○ not feeling themselves today 3 the emphatic form of 'they' or 'them' ○ did it themselves 4 himself or herself (infml) ○ Everyone should do it themselves.

then adv 1 indicates a specific time in the past or future ○ We were much happier then. 2 after that 3 therefore 4 in addition ■ adj being at that time ○ my then teacher

thence adv from that place or time (fml or literary)

thenceforth /thénss fáwrth/ adv from then on (fml or literary)

thenceforward /thénss fáwrwǝrd/ adv from there or then on (fml or literary)

theo- prefix god ○ theology

theocracy /thi ókrǝssi/ (pl -cies) n 1 government by a god or by priests 2 a community governed by a god or by priests —**theocrat** /theé ǝ krat/ n —**theocratic** /theé ǝ kráttik/ adj —**theocratically** adv

theodolite /thi óddǝ līt/ n a surveyor's instrument for measuring angles —**theodolitic** /thi óddǝ líttik/ adj

theology /thi óllǝji/ (pl -gies) n 1 the study of religion, especially God's relation to the world 2 a religious theory or system of belief —**theologian** /theé ǝ lójǝn/ n —**theological** /theé ǝ lójjik'l/ adj —**theologist** n

theorem /theérǝm/ n 1 a proposition or formula that is provable from a set of axioms and basic assumptions 2 an idea accepted as true —**theorematic** /theérǝ máttik/ adj

theoretical /theer réttik'l/, **theoretic** /-réttik/ adj 1 based on theory 2 dealing with theory rather than practical applications 3 hypothetical

theoretically /theer réttikli/ adv 1 in theory but not in reality 2 under hypothetical or ideal circumstances but perhaps not in reality

theoretician /theerǝ tísh'n/ n somebody skilled in theorizing

theorist /theé ǝ ríst, theérist/ n a holder or expounder of a theory

theorize /theé ǝ rīz, theér īz/ (-rizing, -rized), **theorise** v 1 vi speculate or form a theory about something 2 vt conceive of theoretically —**theorization** /theé ǝ rī záysh'n, theér ī-/ n

theory /theéri/ (pl -ries) n 1 the body of rules, principles, and techniques used in a subject 2 abstract thought or speculation 3 an idea formed by speculation 4 a set of hypothetical circumstances 5 a scientific principle used to explain phenomena

~~theorys~~ incorrect spelling of **theories**

theosophy /thi óssǝfi/ (pl -phies) n a religious system based on intuitive insight —**theosophic** /theé ǝ sóffik/ adj —**theosophical** adj

therapeutic /thérrǝ pyóotik/ adj of the treatment or prevention of disease —**therapeutically** adv

therapeutic cloning n the use of cloning to produce new body tissues

therapy /thérrǝpi/ (pl -pies) n treatment that is meant to cure a physical or mental disorder (often in combination) —**therapist** n

there stressed /thair/ unstressed /thǝr/ adv 1 at or to that place or point ○ stop there ○ go there 2 on that matter ○ I can agree with you there. 3 identifies somebody or something ○ that house there ■ pron introduces a sentence stating that something or somebody exists ○ There's a hole in it. ○ Once upon a time there was a prince. ■ interj expresses strong feelings or reassurance ◊ **be there for** be ready to give your support or sympathy to ◊ **not all there** not fully conscious, rational, or aware ◊ See note at **their**

USAGE When there is followed by a verb like be, appear, or seem, the verb must agree with the grammatical subject coming after it: There are [not is] beaches and hotels nearby. There *appear* [not *appears*] *to be mistakes in your essay. There's* stands for 'there is' and should be used only with a singular grammatical subject: *There's a lot still to be done. There's a car in the garage.* Don't say: *There's three cars in the garage. There's a lot of children in the hall.*

thereabouts /tháirə bowts, -bówts/ *adv* near that place or number

thereafter /tháir áaftər/ *adv* after that time

thereby /tháir bī, -bī/ *adv* **1** by means of or because of that **2** in connection with that

~~therefor~~ incorrect spelling of **therefore**

therefore /tháir fawr/ *adv* **1** and so, or because of that **2** accordingly, or to that purpose

therefrom /tháir fróm/ *adv* from there *(archaic or fml)*

therein /tháir ín/ *adv* **1** in or into that place *(fml)* **2** in that matter or detail

thereinafter /tháirin áaftər/ *adv* from then on *(fml)*

thereof /tháir óv/ *adv (fml)* **1** of or about that **2** from that cause or for that reason

thereon /tháir ón/ *adv* on that place or surface *(fml)*

Theresa of Lisieux /tə reézə əv lee zyố/ (1873–97) French nun

thereto /tháir toó/ *adv* to that thing just mentioned *(fml)*

thereupon /tháirə pón/ *adv* **1** immediately after or in consequence of that **2** upon or concerning that point *(fml)*

therewith /tháir with, -wíth/, **therewithal** /tháir with áwl/ *adv* **1** with that, or as well as that *(fml)* **2** at that point, or immediately

~~therfore~~ incorrect spelling of **therefore**

therm *n* a unit of heat equal to 1.055 x 10⁸ joules

thermal /thúrm'l/ *adj* **1** involving heat **2** hot or warm ○ *thermal baths* **3** describes clothing designed to retain body heat ■ *n* a current of warm air rising through cooler surrounding air —**thermally** *adv*

thermal imaging *n* the use of a device that detects areas of different temperatures and displays them on a screen

thermal printer *n* a device that produces visible characters by moving heated wires over special paper

thermo- *prefix* heat ○ *thermometer*

thermobaric /thúrmō bárrik/ *adj* describes a bomb containing explosive gas that is released and detonated

thermocouple /thúrmō kup'l/ *n* a temperature-measuring device in which two wires of different metals are joined

thermodynamics /thúrmō dī námmiks/ *n* the branch of physics that deals with the conversions of forms of energy from one to another *(+ sing verb)* ■ *npl* the processes of thermodynamics *(+ pl verb)* —**thermodynamic** *adj* —**thermodynamicist** *n*

thermometer /thər mómmitər/ *n* an instrument for measuring temperature

thermonuclear /thúrmō nyoókli ər/ *adj* of nuclear fusion

thermoplastic /thúrmo plástik/ *n* a material that softens when heated, without a change in its intrinsic properties —**thermoplastic** *adj* —**thermoplasticity** /thúrmō pla stíssəti/ *n*

Thermopylae /thər móppəli/ pass in ancient Greece, northwest of Athens, site of a major battle between the Greeks and Persians in 480 BC

Thermos /thúrməss/ *tdmk* a trademark for a vacuum flask

thermosphere /thúrmə sfeer/ *n* an atmospheric region beginning about 85 km/53 mi. above the Earth's surface

thermostat /thúrmə stat/ *n* **1** a device that regulates temperature by means of a sensor **2** a device that activates something, e.g. a fire alarm, in response to a temperature change —**thermostatic** /thúrmə státtik/ *adj* —**thermostatically** *adv*

~~thesarus~~ incorrect spelling of **thesaurus**

thesaurus /thə sáwrəss/ *(pl* **-ri** /-rī/ *or* **-ruses**) *n* **1** a book listing groups of words related in meaning **2** a book of specialist vocabulary

ORIGIN **Thesaurus** was adopted from a Latin word meaning 'storehouse, treasury' that is also the source of *treasure.*

these /theez/ *pron, det* the plural of 'this'

thesis /théesiss/ *(pl* **-ses** /-seez/) *n* **1** a lengthy academic dissertation based on original research **2** a proposition advanced as an argument

thespian /théspi ən/ *n* an actor

ORIGIN **Thespians** are named after Thespis, a Greek poet of the 6C BC who was regarded as the founder of Greek tragedy.

Thessaloníki /théssələ neéki/ city in NE Greece. Pop. 383,967 (1991).

Thessaly /théssəli/ region of north-central Greece —**Thessalian** /the sáyli ən/ *n, adj*

theta /théetə/ *n* the 8th letter of the Greek alphabet

they *pron* **1** the people or things already mentioned or identified, or understood by both the speaker and hearer **2** people in general **3** he or she *(infml)*

USAGE Because English does not have a gender-neutral third person singular pronoun that can be used to refer to people, **they**, together with associated words such as *their*, is often used in this role: *Everyone we approached gave their permission.* In more formal contexts it is necessary to use *he or she*, which can be cumbersome. Avoid the problem in writing by recasting the sentence: *All the people we approached gave their permission*, or *We got permission from everyone we approached.*

they'd *contr* **1** they had **2** they would

they'll *contr* **1** they shall **2** they will

they're /tháir/ *contr* they are ◊ See note at **their**

they've *contr* they have

thiamine /thí ə meen, -əmin/, **thiamin** /-min/ *n* a B vitamin that plays a role in carbohydrate metabolism

thick *adj* 1 deep or broad 2 large in diameter 3 having a particular depth or breadth 4 having a liquid consistency that is not free-flowing 5 composed of many densely packed things ○ *a thick forest* 6 made of a heavy material 7 densely filled or covered ○ *thick with dust* 8 hard to see through 9 very pronounced or noticeable ○ *a thick accent* 10 regarded as slow to learn or understand *(infml insult)* 11 on very friendly terms *(infml)* ■ *n* 1 the most active part ○ *the thick of the battle* 2 the densest part —**thickly** *adv* ◇ **through thick and thin** in both good times and bad times

thicken /thíkən/ *v* 1 *vti* make or become thick or thicker 2 *vi* become more complex ○ *The plot thickens.* —**thickener** *n* —**thickening** *n*

thicket /thíkit/ *n* a thick growth of small trees or bushes

thickness /thíknəss/ *n* 1 the quality of being thick 2 a dimension between two surfaces of an object, especially the shortest dimension 3 a single layer

thickset /thík sét/ *adj* 1 with a stocky build 2 growing closely together

thick-skinned *adj* 1 unsympathetic to others' feelings 2 not easily offended by criticism

thief /theef/ *(pl* **thieves** /theevz/*) n* somebody who steals —**thievish** /theevish/ *adj*

~~thier~~ incorrect spelling of **their**

thigh /thī/ *n* the top part of the leg between the knee and the hip

thimble /thímb'l/ *n* a cover for the finger to protect it when sewing —**thimbleful** *n*

Thimphu /thímfoo/, **Thimbu** /-boo/ capital of Bhutan. Pop. 22,000 (1999).

thin *adj* (**thinner, thinnest**) 1 shallow or narrow 2 having a small diameter ○ *thin wire* 3 with little body fat 4 sparsely distributed ○ *thin hair* 5 watery 6 made of lightweight material 7 easy to see through 8 lacking volume or resonance ○ *a thin sound* ■ *vti* (**thinning, thinned**) make or become thin or thinner —**thinly** *adv* —**thinness** *n*

SYNONYMS thin, lean, slim, slender, emaciated, scraggy, scrawny, skinny CORE MEANING: without much flesh, the opposite of fat

thine *pron, det* yours or your *(archaic; before vowels)*

thing *n* 1 an inanimate object 2 an unspecified item 3 an occurrence ○ *The fire was a terrible thing.* 4 a word or thought ○ *Don't say another thing.* 5 a detail or piece of information ○ *forgot one important thing* 6 an aim or objective ○ *The thing is to win.* 7 a responsibility or concern ○ *several things to finish* 8 an act or deed ○ *do great things* 9 a living being 10 a preferred activity *(infml)* ○ *not my thing* 11 a fashion *(infml)* ○ *the latest thing* ■ **things** *npl* 1 personal belongings 2 equipment for a particular purpose ○ *our camping things*

ORIGIN The long-lost ancestral meaning of **thing** is 'time'. Its prehistoric Germanic precursor evolved semantically via 'appointed time' to 'judicial or legislative assembly'. This was the meaning it originally had in English, and it survives in other Germanic languages (the Icelandic parliament is known as the *Althing*, literally 'general assembly'). In English, however, the word moved on through 'subject for discussion in such an assembly' to 'subject in general, affair, matter' and finally 'entity, object'.

thingamajig /thíngəməjig/, **thingumajig**, **thingamabob** /-bob/, **thingumabob**, **thingummy** /thíngəmi/ *(pl* **-mies**), **thingy** /thíngi/ *(pl* **-ies**) *n* somebody or something whose name is temporarily forgotten or not known

think *v* (**thought** /thawt/) 1 *vti* use the mind to form thoughts, consider ideas, and make judgments 2 *vt* have as an opinion 3 *vti* bring something to mind 4 *vti* imagine or understand something or the possibility of something ○ *I can't think of leaving without you.* 5 *vt* view in a particular way ○ *thought her most generous* 6 *vti* intend or decide to do something ○ *He thought he'd stay after all.* 7 *vt* expect ○ *didn't think you'd be early* ■ *n* a spell of thinking *(infml)* —**thinkable** *adj* —**thinker** *n* —**thinking** *n, adj* ◇ **not think much of** regard as not being very good ◇ **think better of** change your mind about ◇ **think nothing of** regard as easy or ordinary ◇ **think twice** reconsider very carefully

☐ **think over** *vt* reflect on

☐ **think through** *vt* consider all aspects and possible consequences of

☐ **think up** *vt* invent or devise

thinking cap ◇ **put your thinking cap on** think carefully about something, especially to find a solution to a problem

think-tank *n* a committee of experts who give advice, especially to a government

thinner /thínnər/ *n* a liquid that dilutes paint or varnish

thin-skinned *adj* 1 sensitive to criticism 2 with a thin peel

third *n* 1 one of three parts into which something is or could be divided 2 the one after the second in a series —**third** *adj, adv*

third class *n* the category two below the best —**third-class** *adj, adv*

third degree *n* intensive interrogation *(infml)*

third-degree burn *n* the most severe class of burn, with serious damage to the skin and tissues beneath

thirdly /thúrdli/ *adv* as a third point

third party *n* somebody involved in a legal matter but not as a principal party

third person *n* the form of a verb or pronoun that refers to somebody or something being spoken about

third-rate *adj* of a low or the lowest quality

Third Reich *n* the Nazi regime in Germany between 1933 and 1945

Third World, third world *n* the developing nations —**Third Worlder** *n*

thirst *n* 1 the desire or need for liquid to drink 2 a craving ○ *a thirst for knowledge* —**thirst** *vi*

thirsty /thúrsti/ (**-ier, -iest**) *adj* 1 wanting or needing liquid to drink 2 having a craving 3 causing thirst (*infml*) —**thirstily** *adv* —**thirstiness** *n*

thirteen /thúr teén/ *n* the number 13 —**thirteen** *adj, pron* —**thirteenth** *n, adj, adv*

thirty /thúrti/ *n* (*pl* **-ties**) the number 30 ■ **thirties** *npl* 1 the numbers 30 to 39, particularly as a range of temperatures 2 the years from 30 to 39 in a century or somebody's life —**thirty** *adj, pron* —**thirtieth** *n, adj, adv*

Thirty-nine Articles *npl* the principles of the Church of England

this /thiss/ *det, pron* 1 indicates somebody or something present or close by ○ *This book is brilliant.* ○ *Is this what you're looking for?* 2 indicates somebody or something just mentioned ○ *This holiday – how much is it going to cost?* ○ *Is this why you've been happy lately?* 3 indicates words to follow ○ *All I can say is this – I didn't know about it.* 4 indicates a particular time in the present or past ○ *I expected him back before this.* ■ *adv* emphasizes the degree of a feeling or quality ○ *was this close to leaving* ◊ **this and that** miscellaneous unimportant things

thistle /thíss'l/ *n* a plant with prickly stems and leaves and rounded, usually purple, flowers

thistledown /thíss'l down/ *n* 1 the fluffy mass of hairs attached to the seeds of a thistle 2 a fine silky substance

thither /thíthər/ *adv* in that direction (*archaic fml*)

~~thoght~~ incorrect spelling of **thought**

Thomas /tómməss/ *n*, **St** (*fl* AD 1C) one of the 12 apostles of Jesus Christ

Dylan Thomas

Thomas /tómməss/, **Dylan** (1914–53) Welsh poet

thong *n* 1 a long thin piece of leather 2 a whip 3 a light sandal held on by a strip between the toes 4 a narrow strip of fabric with a waistband, used as underwear or beachwear

Thor *n* in Norse mythology, the god of thunder

thorax /tháw raks/ *n* (*pl* **-raxes** or **-races** /tháwrə seez/) *n* 1 the upper part of the body, enclosed by the ribs 2 the part between the head and abdomen of an insect, crustacean, or arachnid —**thoracic** /thaw rássik/ *adj*

thorium /tháwri əm/ *n* (*symbol* **Th**) a soft radioactive element. Use: alloys, source of nuclear energy. —**thoric** *adj*

thorn *n* 1 a sharp point on a plant stem 2 a plant with thorns

thorny /tháwrni/ (**-ier, -iest**) *adj* 1 problematic 2 prickly with thorns —**thorniness** *n*

thorough /thúrrə/ *adj* 1 extremely careful and accurate 2 done fully —**thoroughly** *adv* —**thoroughness** *n* ◊ See note at **careful**

ORIGIN **Thorough** was originally a form of *through*, and used to be used as a preposition and adverb in the same way. The adjective sense that survives developed from 'through so as to affect every part'.

thoroughbred /thúrrə bred/ *n* 1 a purebred animal 2 an aristocrat 3 **Thoroughbred** a breed of racehorse descended from English mares and Arabian stallions —**thoroughbred** *adj*

thoroughfare /thúrrə fair/ *n* 1 a public road 2 a route or passage from one place to another

thoroughgoing /thúrrə gó ing/ *adj* 1 thoroughly done 2 in every respect ○ *a thoroughgoing pragmatist*

those /thōz/ *pron, det* the plural of 'that'

thou[1] /thow/ (*pl* **thous** or **same**) *n* a thousandth of an inch

thou[2] /thow/, **Thou** *pron* you (*when addressing God*)

though /thō/ *conj* although ■ *adv* 1 and yet 2 nevertheless

thought /thawt/ *n* 1 the process of thinking or considering 2 an idea produced by mental activity 3 a set of ideas ○ *medieval religious thought* 4 reasoning power 5 an intention, expectation, or hope ○ *entertains no thoughts of failing* 6 compassionate consideration ○ *no thought for other* ■ past participle, past tense of **think**

thoughtful /tháwtf'l/ *adj* 1 considerate 2 appearing to be in deep thought —**thoughtfully** *adv* —**thoughtfulness** *n*

thoughtless /tháwtləss/ *adj* 1 inconsiderate 2 done without thought —**thoughtlessly** *adv* —**thoughtlessness** *n*

thought police *n* a group that tries to monitor or regulate people's thoughts

thought-provoking *adj* making somebody reflect deeply

~~thourough~~ incorrect spelling of **thorough**

thousand /thówz'nd/ *n* (*pl* **same** or **-sands**) 1 the number 1,000 2 a large number (*infml*) ■ **thousands** *npl* very many —**thousandth** *adj, adv, n*

~~thousend~~ incorrect spelling of **thousand**

Thrace region in SE Europe, including parts of present-day Greece, Bulgaria, and Turkey —**Thracian** *adj, n*

thrall /thrawl/ *n* the state of being dominated (*literary*) ○ *in the thrall of greed* —**thraldom** *n*

thrash v 1 vt beat a person or animal with a whip or stick 2 vt defeat an opponent or team decisively 3 vti toss the body and limbs about ∎ n a beating with a whip or stick —**thrashing** n

□ **thrash out** vt discuss fully

thread /thred/ n 1 fine twisted cord. Use: sewing, weaving. 2 a piece of thread 3 a very thin strand, trickle, or wisp 4 the helical or spiral ridge on a screw 5 something connecting elements of a story, discussion, or series of events 6 a set of related messages in an Internet discussion group ∎ v 1 vt pass thread, tape, or film through something 2 vt string beads on a thread 3 vti make your way through something, following a winding route —**thread-like** adj

threadbare /thréd bair/ adj 1 worn away to reveal threads 2 overused so no longer convincing 3 meagre ○ a threadbare existence

threat /thret/ n 1 a declaration of an intent to cause harm 2 an indication of something bad ○ a threat of rain 3 somebody or something likely to cause harm

threaten /thrétt'n/ vti 1 express a threat against somebody 2 be a threat to the wellbeing of somebody or something 3 be a sign of something bad —**threatening** adj —**threateningly** adv

three n the number 3 —**three** adj, pron

three-D, 3-D n a three-dimensional effect

three-day event n an equestrian competition held over three days, consisting of dressage, cross-country, and show-jumping events

three-dimensional adj 1 having the dimensions of height, width, and depth 2 appearing to have depth behind a flat surface —**three-dimensionality** n

threefold /thrée fóld/ adj 1 consisting of three 2 three times as many or much ∎ adv by three times

three-legged race n a race between pairs of runners who have their adjacent legs tied together

three-line whip n a notice to MPs to attend Parliament and vote in a specific way, underlined three times for emphasis

Three Mile Island island in the Susquehanna River in SE Pennsylvania, site of a major nuclear reactor accident in 1979

three-piece suite n a sofa and two matching armchairs

three-ply adj with three layers or strands

three-point turn n a turn to change the direction of a motor vehicle involving two forward movements and one reverse movement

three-quarter adj being three quarters of something measurable or countable ○ a three-quarter coat ∎ n a rugby player in a position between the forwards and fullback

three Rs /-aárz/, **3 Rs** npl reading, writing, and arithmetic

threescore /thrée skáwr/ adj, n sixty (archaic)

threesome /thrée'ssəm/ n 1 a group of three 2 an activity for three

three-wheeler n a vehicle with three wheels

Three Wise Men n in Christianity, the three Magi

threnody /thrénnədi/ (pl -dies) n a lament for the dead —**threnodic** /thri nóddik/ adj —**threnodist** n

thresh v 1 vti separate the seeds from harvested plants with a machine or flail 2 vi move about violently —**thresh** n —**thresher** n

~~threshhold~~ incorrect spelling of **threshold**

threshold /thrésh hōld, -old/ n 1 a piece of wood or stone that forms the bottom of a doorway 2 an entrance 3 the point at which something starts

threw past tense of **throw**

thrice adv three times (literary)

thrift n the prudent use of money and goods

thrifty /thrífti/ (-ier, -iest) adj careful with money and resources —**thriftily** adv —**thriftiness** n

thrill vti 1 make or be very excited or pleased 2 vibrate or cause to vibrate ∎ n 1 a cause of great excitement 2 a feeling of great excitement —**thrilling** adj —**thrillingly** adv

thriller /thríllər/ n a book, play, or film with an exciting plot

thrive (**thriving, thrived** or **throve, thrived** or **thriven** /thrívv'n/) vi 1 grow well 2 be successful

throat n 1 the part of the digestive and breathing passage between the rear of the mouth and the oesophagus 2 the front of the neck 3 a narrow part or passage

throaty /thróti/ (-ier, -iest) adj deep or rough in sound or tone —**throatily** adv —**throatiness** n

throb (**throbbing, throbbed**) vi 1 beat or pulsate rapidly and forcefully 2 have a regular or rhythmic beat —**throb** n —**throbbingly** adv

throe n a spasm of pain ◇ **in the throes of** in the process of doing something

thrombosis /throm bóssis/ (pl -ses /-seez/) n the formation or presence of blood clots in an artery —**thrombotic** /throm bóttik/ adj

throne /thrōn/ n 1 a ceremonial chair for a monarch or bishop 2 the power of a monarch

throng n a large crowd (literary) ∎ v 1 vt crowd into or around 2 vi move in a crowd

throttle /thrótt'l/ n 1 a valve controlling the flow of a fluid, especially fuel and air entering an engine 2 a control for a throttle ∎ vt (-tling, -tled) 1 regulate fuel flow or engine speed using a throttle 2 kill a person or animal by choking 3 silence or suppress somebody or something

through /throo/ prep, adv 1 passing from one side or end of something to the other 2 travelling across or to various places in a town, country, or area 3 among or in the midst of people or things ○ wandering through the crowds 4 past the limitations or difficulties of a barrier or problem 5 to a successful conclusion ∎ prep 1 by means of 2 happening or existing over the extent of **3** because of ■ *adv* completely and in every part ■ *prep US, Can* up to and including ■ *adj* going directly without stopping or requiring a change ○ *a through road* ◇ **be through with** have finished with, or have no further connections with *(infml)* ◇ **through and through** completely

throughout /throo ówt/ *prep, adv* through the whole of

throughput /throó poot/ *n* the volume of data or material processed over a given period

throve past tense of **thrive**

throw /thrō/ *vt* (**threw** /throo/, **thrown** /thrōn/) **1** propel something from the hand and through the air **2** put or drop something carelessly **3** force somebody or something into a particular place or condition ○ *was thrown into confusion* **4** hurl somebody to the ground **5** project light, or cast a shadow by blocking light **6** cast doubt or suspicion **7** take somebody by surprise *(infml)* **8** move an operating switch or lever **9** show an extreme reaction ○ *throw a tantrum* **10** direct or deliver something such as a punch **11** make an object on a potter's wheel **12** host a party ■ *n* **1** an act or way of throwing **2** a distance or score thrown —**thrower** *n* ◇ **throw yourself into** start doing something with great energy

SYNONYMS throw, chuck, fling, heave, hurl, toss, cast CORE MEANING: send something through the air

☐ **throw away** *vt* **1** discard something **2** waste an opportunity

☐ **throw in** *vt* add as an extra ◇ **throw in the towel** *or* **sponge** admit defeat *(infml)*

☐ **throw off** *vt* **1** free yourself from something troublesome or oppressive **2** escape from a pursuer

☐ **throw out** *vt* **1** discard something **2** eject or expel somebody **3** reject a bill or lawsuit **4** confuse somebody by doing something unexpected

☐ **throw up** *vti* vomit *(infml)*

throwaway /thrō ə way/ *adj* **1** designed to be thrown away after use **2** wasteful and tending to discard things too readily ○ *a throwaway society* **3** said or written in an offhand manner

throwback /thrō bak/ *n* **1** an organism with the characteristics of an earlier type or ancestor **2** reversion to an earlier type **3** a contemporary person or thing that seems to belong to the past

thru /throo/ *prep, adv, adj US, Can* through *(infml)*

thrum (**thrumming, thrummed**) *v* **1** *vti* strum on a stringed instrument **2** *vi* tap or beat steadily or monotonously —**thrum** *n*

~~thruogh~~ incorrect spelling of **through**

thrush[1] (*pl* **thrushes** *or* **same**) *n* a songbird with a speckled breast

thrush[2] *n* a fungal infection of the mouth or vagina

thrust *v* (**thrust**) **1** *vti* push forcefully **2** *vti* stretch or extend ○ *spires thrusting into the sky* **3** *vt* force to go somewhere or do something ○ *was thrust into the limelight* ■ *n* **1** a forceful push **2** forward movement **3** a stabbing action **4** the gist or main purpose ○ *the thrust of her argument* **5** the propulsive force of a rotating propeller **6** the reactive force of expelled gases generated by a rocket or jet engine **7** the force exerted by one structure on another —**thrusting** *adj*

Thucydides /thyoo síddi deez/ (460?–400? BC) Athenian historian

thud *n* a dull heavy sound or blow —**thud** *vi*

thug *n* a brutal and violent person, especially a criminal —**thuggery** *n* —**thuggish** *adj*

ORIGIN The original **thugs** were members of a group of robbers and murderers in India, worshippers of the goddess Kali, who usually strangled their victims. The first English references to them appear in the early 19C, and by the 1830s the name **thug** was being given to any violent robber.

thulium /thyoóli əm/ *n* (*symbol* **Tm**) a grey metallic chemical element. Use: X-ray source.

thumb /thum/ *n* **1** the shortest thickest digit on the human hand located next to the forefinger, or a corresponding digit on an animal's hand **2** a section of a glove or mitten for the thumb ■ *v* **1** *vti* hitch a lift by signalling with the thumb to passing drivers **2** *vt* make dirty by handling **3** *vti* flip through printed matter ◇ **all thumbs** extremely awkward or clumsy ◇ **stick out like a sore thumb** be obvious, or conspicuously out of place ◇ **twiddle your thumbs** be idle ◇ **under somebody's thumb** under somebody's influence and control

thumb index *n* a series of labelled indentations in the edge of a book, to help find a place —**thumb-index** *vt*

thumbnail /thúm nayl/ *n* **1** a nail of a thumb **2** a miniature graphic image on a computer monitor ■ *adj* concise ○ *a thumbnail sketch*

thumbscrew /thúm skroo/ *n* **1** an instrument of torture that crushes people's thumbs **2** a flatheaded screw to be turned with the thumb and forefinger

thumbtack /thúm tak/ *n US, Can* a drawing pin

thump *v* **1** *vti* strike somebody or something heavily with the fist or an object **2** *vi* beat fast or loudly *(refers to the heart)* **3** *vi* make a dull heavy sound —**thump** *n*

thumping /thúmping/ *adj* **1** large or impressive *(infml)* ○ *won by a thumping majority* **2** painful and throbbing ○ *a thumping headache* —**thumpingly** *adv*

thunder /thúndər/ *n* **1** a loud rumbling noise following lightning **2** a noise resembling thunder ■ *v* **1** *vi* make a loud rumbling noise **2** *vti* shout something loudly and angrily ◇ **steal somebody's thunder** present somebody else's idea as if it were your own

thunderbolt /thúndər bōlt/ *n* **1** a flash of lightning accompanied by thunder **2** a sudden shocking occurrence

thunderclap /thúndər klap/ n a crash of thunder

thundercloud /thúndər klowd/ n a dark cloud that produces thunder and lightning

thunderous /thúndərəss/ adj **1** very loud **2** angry and threatening —**thunderously** adv

thunderstorm /thúndər stawrm/ n a storm with thunder and lightning

thunderstruck /thúndər struk/ adj extremely surprised or incredulous

Thurber /thúrbər/, **James** (1894–1961) US writer and cartoonist

Thurs., Thur. abbr Thursday

Thursday /thúrz day, -di/ n the 4th day of the week

ORIGIN **Thursday** meant literally 'day of thunder'. It was a translation of Latin *Jovi dies* 'day of Jove (Jupiter)'.

thus /thuss/ adv (fml) **1** consequently **2** like this ◊ **thus far** up to this point

thwack vt hit hard with a flat object —**thwack** n

thwart /thwawrt/ vt prevent from being successful ■ n a crosswise seat in a boat

thy det your (archaic)

thyme /tīm/ n a small low-growing plant with aromatic leaves used in cooking ◊ See note at **time**

thymus /thíməss/ (pl **-muses** or **-mi**) n an organ of the immune system, located at the base of the neck

thyroid /thī royd/ n **1** the thyroid gland **2** a preparation obtained from an animal's thyroid gland. Use: treating conditions of the thyroid gland. ■ adj also **thyroidal** /thī róyd'l/ of the thyroid gland

thyroid gland n a ductless gland in the base of the neck that secretes hormones responsible for controlling metabolism and growth

thyself /thī sélf/ pron yourself (archaic)

Ti symbol titanium

Tian Shan ▶ Tien Shan

tiara /ti aárə/ n **1** a woman's jewelled head ornament **2** a crown consisting of three coronets with an orb on top, worn by popes

Tiber /tíbər/ river of central Italy, emptying into the Tyrrhenian Sea. Length 406 km/252 mi.

Tiberius /tī beéri əss-/ (42 BC–AD 37) Roman emperor (AD 14–37)

Tibet /ti bét/ former independent state and provincial-level administrative area of SW China. Cap. Lhasa. Pop. 2,440,000 (1997). —**Tibetan** adj, n

tibia /tíbbi ə/ (pl **-ae** /-bi ee/ or **-as**) n the inner and larger bone of the lower leg —**tibial** adj

tic n **1** a sudden involuntary twitch of a muscle **2** a quirk of behaviour

tick[1] n **1** a recurring click, especially one made by a clock or watch **2** a very short time (infml) **3** a mark put against an item, e.g. to indicate that it is correct ■ v **1** vi make a recurring clicking sound **2** vt mark with a tick something checked or dealt with ◊ **what makes**

somebody tick what causes somebody to behave and think in a particular way (infml)

☐ **tick away** vi elapse steadily (refers to time)

☐ **tick off** vt scold somebody (infml)

☐ **tick over** vi continue to function at a low level

tick[2] n a tiny bloodsucking parasitic insect

tick[3] n a cloth covering of a pillow or mattress

ticker /tíkər/ n somebody's heart (infml)

ticket /tíkit/ n **1** a printed piece of paper or cardboard entitling the holder to go somewhere or do something **2** a notification of a traffic offence **3** a label or tag showing the price of an article **4** US, Can a group of candidates running for office together ■ vt attach or issue a ticket to

ticket tout n somebody who buys tickets for entertainments and sports events and offers them for sale at a profit

ticking /tíking/ n strong cotton fabric. Use: mattress and pillow covers.

ticking-off (pl **tickings-off**) n a scolding (infml)

tickle /tík'l/ (**-ling**, **-led**) v **1** vt make somebody laugh and twitch by lightly touching a sensitive part of the body **2** vti cause itchiness in a part of the body **3** vt please or amuse (often passive) —**tickle** n ◊ **tickled pink** or **silly** or **to death** extremely pleased (infml)

ticklish /tík'lish/ adj **1** sensitive to tickling **2** problematic —**ticklishness** n

tidal /tíd'l/ adj of or affected by tides

tidal wave n **1** a huge ocean wave **2** an overwhelming surge ◊ a *tidal wave of emotion*

tiddler /tídd'lər/ n (infml) **1** a tiny fish **2** a small person or thing

tiddly[1] /tídd'li/ (**-dlier**, **-dliest**) adj slightly drunk (infml)

tiddly[2] /tídd'li/ (**-dlier**, **-dliest**) adj tiny (infml)

tiddlywinks /tídd'li wingks/ n a game in which players flip plastic counters into a cup (+ sing verb)

tide /tīd/ n **1** the cyclical rise and fall of the sea and other open waters produced by the attraction of the Moon and Sun **2** an inflow or outflow of water as the sea rises or falls **3** a general trend **4** a crucial point **5** a period of time (archaic; usually in combination) ◊ *harvest tide* —**tideless** adj ◊ **swim against the tide** oppose a popular idea or trend ◊ **turn the tide** reverse the course of events

ORIGIN **Tide** originally meant 'time'. The sense 'rise and fall of the sea' arose in the 14C, probably under the influence of related Dutch and German words that had developed the meaning 'fixed time'. The original sense 'time' has been longest preserved in compounds such as *eventide*, *Christmastide*, *noontide*, *Whitsuntide*, and *Yuletide*, all of which are now archaic or literary.

SPELLCHECK Do not confuse the spelling of **tide** and **tied** (past tense and past participle of *tie*), which sound similar.

☐ **tide over** vt help through a difficult time

tidemark /tíd maark/ n 1 *also* **tideline** a mark left by the highest or lowest point of a tide 2 a marker indicating the levels of tides 3 a grimy ring round a bath where the level of water was (*infml*)

tidings /tídingz/ npl news (*literary*)

tidy /tídi/ adj (**-dier, -diest**) 1 neat in appearance 2 methodical 3 considerable (*infml*) ○ *a tidy sum* ■ vti (**-dies, -died**) make somebody or something neat ■ n (pl **-dies**) 1 *also* **tidy-up** a process or session of tidying (*infml*) 2 a box for holding small objects 3 a small receptacle for waste scraps —**tidily** adv —**tidiness** n

tie /tī/ v (**tying** /tí ing/, **tied** /tīd/) 1 vt fasten things together with rope, string, or something similar 2 vt fasten something with a knot or bow 3 vt make a knot or bow 4 vt connect or link people or things 5 vt restrict somebody to particular conditions 6 vi have an equal score in a game or competition ■ n 1 a strip of fabric worn round the neck under a shirt collar 2 a long thin piece of material for attaching or fastening something 3 a connection or link 4 a restriction 5 an equal outcome in a game or competition 6 a match in a knockout competition 7 a strengthening beam

□ **tie up** v 1 vt bind using rope, string, or cord 2 vti moor a boat or ship by securing lines 3 vt occupy or keep busy 4 vt use for one purpose that precludes others ○ *money tied up in a savings account*

tiebreaker /tí braykər/, **tie-break** n a method of deciding the winner of a game or competition when there is a tie —**tiebreaking** adj

tie clip, tie clasp n a clasp for holding a necktie in place

tied /tīd/ adj 1 owned by a producer and selling only the owner's products 2 owned by the occupant's employer ◊ See note at **tide**

tie-dye vt dye designs on cloth by tying portions of it with waxed thread so that only exposed areas take the dye —**tie-dyeing** n

tie-in n 1 a link or relationship 2 a product that is sold or marketed through its connection with another

~~tieing~~ incorrect spelling of **tying**

Tien Shan /tyén shaàn/, **Tian Shan** mountain range in Central Asia, stretching from Kyrgyzstan through NW China to Mongolia. Highest peak Victory Peak 7,439 m/24,406 ft. Length 2,400 km/1,500 mi.

tiepin /tí pin/ n a decorative pin for holding a necktie in place

Tiepolo /tyéppəlō/, **Giovanni Battista** (1696–1770) Italian artist

tier /teer/ n 1 a row of seats in a rising series 2 a layer (*often in combination*) ■ vt arrange in rising rows —**tiered** adj ◊ See note at **tear**

Tierra del Fuego /ti érrə del fwáygō/ archipelago off the tip of S South America, belonging partly to Argentina and partly to Chile

tie-up n a connection

tiff n 1 a minor quarrel 2 a brief period of bad temper —**tiff** vi

TIFF /tif/ abbr tagged image file format

TIFF file, TIF file n a graphic file in a format often used for storing bit-mapped images

tiffin /tíffin/ n S Asia 1 a light midday meal or snack 2 *also* **tiffin-carrier** a carrier for prepared food consisting of several stacked metal containers

tiger /tígər/ (pl **-gers** or same) n 1 a large wild cat with a tawny coat and black stripes 2 a fierce person —**tigerish** adj

tiger lily n a lily with dark-spotted red or orange flowers

tight /tīt/ adj 1 fitting closely or too closely ○ *a tight sweater* 2 stretched so that there is no slack 3 firmly secured or held 4 sealed against leaks or exposure to air 5 strictly controlled ○ *tight security* 6 cramped and preventing free movement 7 allowing no extra time or money 8 miserly 9 closely contested 10 drunk (*slang*) —**tight** adv —**tighten** vti —**tightly** adv —**tightness** n ◊ **in a tight spot** *or* **corner** in a difficult or dangerous situation

tightfisted /tīt fístid/ adj disinclined to spend money —**tightfistedness** n

tightknit /tīt nít/ adj 1 closely united by affection or loyalty 2 well-organized to function as a unit

tight-lipped /-lípt/ adj 1 unwilling to talk 2 having the lips firmly closed

tightrope /tīt rōp/ n a rope stretched taut above the ground for somebody to perform a balancing act on ◊ **walk a tightrope** have to deal cautiously with a precarious situation

tights npl a one-piece close-fitting garment stretching from the toes to the waist or neck

tigress /tígrəss/ n 1 a female tiger 2 a fierce woman

Tigris /tígriss/ river in SW Asia, rising in SE Turkey and flowing through Iraq to the River Euphrates. Length 1,900 km/1,180 mi.

Tijuana /ti waàna/ city in NW Mexico, near the US border. Pop. 991,592 (1995).

tike n = **tyke**

tikka /téekə/ adj a South Asian dish of pieces of meat that are marinated and then roasted

tilde /tíldə/ n a mark (~) placed over a letter to indicate a specific pronunciation

tile n 1 a thin piece of baked clay or synthetic material used with others as a covering for floors, roofs, or walls 2 a short pipe in a drain 3 a playing piece in some board games ■ vt (**tiling, tiled**) 1 lay tiles on 2 fit with drainage tiles —**tiler** n —**tiling** n

till[1], **'til, 'till** conj, prep until

USAGE till or until? Till is an older form of until, not a shortening as the forms *'til* or *'till* would suggest. It is more likely to be heard in speech: *Just wait till we get home!* Until is more usual at the beginning of a sentence: *Until last week no decision had been taken.*

till[2] n 1 a container for money taken from customers 2 a supermarket checkout

till[3] *vt* prepare land for crops —**tiller** *n*

tillage /tíllij/ *n* **1** the tilling of land **2** tilled land

tiller /tíllər/ *n* a handle for steering a boat

tilt *v* **1** *vti* move so as to slope or slant **2** *vi* make a spoken or written attack on somebody or something **3** *vti* charge an opponent with a lance **4** *vi* joust ■ *n* **1** an act of tilting **2** a slope or incline **3** a joust ◇ **(at) full tilt** at full speed

timber /tímbər/ *n* **1** wood or logs that can be used as a building material **2** growing trees **3** wooded land **4** a large piece of wood used as a support or as part of a framework —**timbered** *adj*

timberyard /tímbər yaard/ *n* an establishment selling timber

timbre /támbər, tímbər, táNbrə/ *n* the distinctive quality of a sound other than its pitch or volume

Timbuktu ♦ **Tombouctou**

time /tīm/ *n* **1** (*symbol t*) a dimension that distinguishes events taking place at the same point in space **2** a period during which something exists or happens **3** a system for measuring intervals of time **4** the minute or hour as indicated on a clock **5** a moment or period when something occurs or is designated to occur **6** a suitable moment **7** a period with a particular quality (*often pl*) ○ *rough times* **8** a limited but unspecified period ○ *stayed for a time* **9** a period in history (*often pl*) ○ *in Shakespeare's time* **10** the present (*often pl*) ○ *technology that is ahead of the times* **11** a prison term (*infml*) ○ *doing time* **12** an instance ○ *told you three times* **13** the tempo or rhythm of music ■ *vt* (*timing, timed*) **1** measure how long something takes **2** plan the moment or occasion for ○ *time an entrance* ◇ **at one time 1** at a time in the past **2** simultaneously ◇ **at the same time 1** simultaneously **2** nevertheless ◇ **at times** sometimes ◇ **behind the times** out of touch with modern fashions, methods, or attitudes ◇ **bide your time** wait patiently for the right opportunity ◇ **for the time being** for a short time starting from now ◇ **from time to time** occasionally ◇ **have no time for** regard with dislike or contempt ◇ **have the time of your life** have a very enjoyable experience ◇ **in good time 1** early enough **2** quickly ◇ **in (less than) no time** in a very short period of time ◇ **in time 1** early enough **2** after some time has passed **3** in the correct rhythm ◇ **in your own time** at a speed or pace that feels comfortable ◇ **keep time 1** show the time accurately **2** do something in the correct rhythm, or in the same rhythm as somebody or something else ◇ **mark time 1** march in rhythm without moving forwards **2** do nothing while waiting for something to happen ◇ **on time** at the scheduled time ◇ **pass the time of day (with)** engage in casual conversation with somebody ◇ **play for time** delay action or a decision in the hope that conditions will improve ◇ **take your time 1** take whatever time is necessary **2** do something unacceptably slowly ◇ **time after time, time and (time) again** repeatedly

time and motion study *n* an analysis of working practices aimed at increasing efficiency

time bomb *n* **1** a bomb that is set to explode at a fixed time **2** a future danger though not a current one

time capsule *n* a container with items representative of the present, buried for a future generation to find

timecard /tím kaard/ *n* an employee's record of working hours to be stamped by a time clock

time clock *n* a clock with a mechanism for stamping a card when an employee starts and finishes work

time-consuming *adj* taking up a great deal of time

time frame *n* a period during which something takes place or is planned to take place

time-honoured *adj* respected because of being traditional

timekeeper /tím keepər/ *n* **1** somebody recording the time, e.g. during a sporting event **2** somebody considered in terms of punctuality ○ *a good timekeeper* **3** a watch or clock —**timekeeping** *n*

time lag *n* a delay between two connected events

timeless /tímləss/ *adj* **1** unchanged and unchanging **2** eternal —**timelessly** *adv* —**timelessness** *n*

time limit *n* a maximum time allowed

time line *n* a chronology of significant events shown pictorially

timely /tímli/ (*-lier, -liest*) *adj* occurring at an appropriate time —**timeliness** *n* —**timely** *adv*

time machine *n* a fictional or hypothetical machine for travelling through time

time-off *n* time not spent at work

timeout /tím owt/ *n* **1** a time during which a game temporarily stops **2** an interruption in the operation of a computer when a command is not responded to in a predetermined time

timepiece /tím peess/ *n* an instrument such as a watch or clock for indicating the time

timer /tímər/ *n* **1** a device that can be set to do something at a given time **2** somebody or something that records or measures time

times *prep* multiplied by

timesaving /tím sayving/ *adj* designed to reduce the time taken to do something

timescale /tím skayl/ *n* **1** a period of time scheduled for the completion of something **2** a measurement of time relative to the time in which a typical event occurs

timeserver /tím survər/ *n* an opportunist whose opinions and behaviour change to suit the times —**timeserving** *n, adj*

timeshare /tím shair/ n **1** the joint ownership of property by people who use it at different times **2** a house or apartment owned and used in this way

time sharing n **1** the joint ownership of property by people who use it at different times **2** a technique for simultaneous use of central computer resources by remote terminals —**time-share** vti —**time-sharer** n

time sheet n a record of the hours somebody has worked

time signature n a symbol showing musical metre

time switch n an electrical switch that can be set to switch a device on or off at given times

timetable /tím tayb'l/ n a schedule of the times at which events are to occur —**timetable** vi

time trial n a race in which competitors compete individually against the clock

time warp n a hypothetical distortion in space-time

timeworn /tím wawrn/ adj **1** having deteriorated through long use **2** overused and no longer effective

time zone n any of the areas of the world in which the same standard time is used

timid /tímmid/ adj lacking courage or assertiveness —**timidity** /ti míddəti/ n —**timidly** adv

timing /tíming/ n **1** the ability to choose, or the choice of, the best moment to do or say something **2** the recording of the time taken to do something

Timişoara /timmi shwaárə/ city in W Romania. Pop. 332,277 (1997).

Timor /tée mawr/ largest and easternmost of the Lesser Sunda Islands, in the Malay Archipelago. Pop. 3,900,000 (1990).

timorous /tímmərəss/ adj fearful and hesitant —**timorously** adv —**timorousness** n

Timor Sea arm of the Indian Ocean separating the island of Timor from N Australia

Timothy, St /tímməthi/ disciple of St Paul

timpani /tímpəni/, **tympani** n a set of kettledrums used in an orchestra (+ sing or pl verb) —**timpanist** n

tin n **1** (symbol **Sn**) a silvery metallic chemical element. Use: alloys such as solder, bronze, and pewter, protective coating for steel. **2** a sealed container for food or drink made of sheet metal **3** a container with a lid, made of sheet metal ■ adj made of tin ■ vt (**tinning, tinned**) **1** put in tins **2** coat with tin

tin can n a container made of tin or aluminium

tincture /tíngkchər/ n **1** a solution of a plant extract or chemical in alcohol **2** a tint or slight coloration **3** a tiny amount of something ■ vt (-**turing, -tured**) **1** add a tint to **2** suffuse with a quality ◊ praise tinctured with criticism

tinder /tíndər/ n material such as dry sticks for starting a fire

tinderbox /tíndər boks/ n **1** a box containing tinder **2** somebody or something potentially violent

tine n a prong of an implement or utensil such as a fork —**tined** adj

tinfoil /tín foyl/ n aluminium or tin in a very thin sheet

ting n a light high-pitched ringing sound —**ting** vti

tinge (**tingeing** or **tinging, tinged**) vt **1** add a slight amount of colour to **2** mix a slight amount of something with ◊ a celebration tinged with sadness —**tinge** n

tingle /tíng g'l/ (-**gling, -gled**) vti feel or cause a stinging, prickling, or vibrating sensation —**tingle** n —**tinglingly** adv —**tingly** adj

tin god n **1** somebody self-important and overbearing **2** somebody or something unjustifiably esteemed

tinker /tíngkər/ n **1** a travelling mender of pots and pans and other household utensils **2** an unskilful worker **3** an act of tinkering with something **4** Ireland, Scotland a person who travels from place to place as a way of life ■ vi **1** fiddle or meddle with something in an attempt to repair or improve it **2** work as a tinker —**tinkerer** n

tinkle /tíngk'l/ vti (-**kling, -kled**) make or cause to make light metallic ringing sounds ■ n a tinkling sound —**tinkly** adj

tinned adj packed in a sealed tin

tinnie /tínni/, **tinny** (pl -**nies**) n Aus a can of beer (infml)

tinnitus /tínnitəss/ n a persistent ringing or roaring noise in the ear

tinny /tínni/ (-**nier, -niest**) adj **1** having a thin metallic sound **2** of tin **3** tasting of metal **4** inferior in quality —**tinniness** n

tin-opener n a tool for opening tins of food

tin plate n iron or steel in thin sheets coated with tin —**tin-plate** vt

tinpot /tín pot/ adj regarded as inferior (infml)

tinsel /tínss'l/ n **1** glittering material in thin strips, used for decoration **2** something glamorous but worthless —**tinsel** adj

Tinseltown /tíns'l town/ n Hollywood (infml disapproving)

tint n **1** a shade of a colour, especially a pale one **2** a trace of colour **3** a hair dye —**tint** vti —**tinter** n

tintinnabulation /tínti nábbyōō láysh'n/ n a pealing of bells

Tintoretto /tíntə réttō/ (1518?–94) Italian painter

tiny /tíni/ (-**nier, -niest**) adj very small —**tininess** n

-tion suffix an action or process, or the result of it ◊ pollution

tip[1] n **1** a narrow or pointed end **2** a part fitted on an end ■ vt (**tipping, tipped**) **1** provide or be the end of **2** cover the end of ◊ **on the tip of somebody's tongue** nearly, but not quite, brought to mind ◊ **the tip of the iceberg** the small visible or obvious part of a largely unseen problem or difficulty

tip[2] vti (**tipping, tipped**) **1** tilt or slant **2** knock or be knocked over **3** dump rubbish ■ n

1 an act of tipping 2 a tilt or slant 3 a rubbish dump 4 a thoroughly untidy place (infml)

tip³ /tĭp/ n 1 a gift of money for a service 2 a piece of useful information or advice ■ vti (tipping, tipped) give somebody a tip

□ **tip off** vt give a warning or advance notice to

tip⁴ n a light glancing blow

~~tipical~~ incorrect spelling of **typical**

tip-off n a warning or piece of advance information (infml)

Tipperary /típpə ráiri/ former county in Munster Province, S Republic of Ireland

tippet /típpit/ n a stole or cape with ends that hang in front

Tippett /típpit/, **Sir Michael** (1905–98) British composer

tipple /típp'l/ vi (-pling, -pled) drink alcohol habitually or repeatedly ■ n an alcoholic drink (infml) —**tippler** n

tipster /típstər/ n somebody who sells information to horseracing betters and speculators

tipsy /típsi/ (-sier, -siest) adj slightly drunk —**tipsily** adv —**tipsiness** n

tiptoe /típ tō/ (-toed) vi 1 walk on the toes and balls of the feet with the heels raised 2 move or proceed very cautiously —**tiptoe** n, adj, adv

tiptop /típ tóp/ adj of the highest quality (infml)

tirade /tī ráyd, ti-/ n a long angry speech

tiramisu /tírrə mee soò, -meè soo/ n an Italian dessert made with layers of sponge cake soaked in espresso coffee, Marsala, mascarpone cheese, and chocolate

Tirana /ti ráànə/ capital of Albania, in the central part of the country. Pop. 244,200 (1990).

tire¹ (tiring, tired) vti 1 make or become tired 2 lose interest or cause to lose interest in something —**tiring** adj

tire² n US = **tyre**

tired adj 1 needing rest 2 having lost patience or interest —**tiredly** adv —**tiredness** n

tireless /tírləss/ adj apparently immune to fatigue —**tirelessly** adv —**tirelessness** n

tiresome /tírssəm/ adj causing annoyance or fatigue —**tiresomely** adv —**tiresomeness** n

Tirol /ti rōl/, **Tyrol** province in W Austria. Cap. Innsbruck. Pop. 663,603 (1998). —**Tirolean** /tírrə leè ən/ n, adj —**Tirolese** /tírrə leèz/ n, adj

'tis /tiz/ contr it is (literary)

Tishri /tíshri/ (pl -ris) n the 7th month of the year in the Jewish calendar

tissue /tíshoo, tíssyoo/ n 1 a piece of soft absorbent paper 2 a group of cells in an organism that are similar in form or function 3 an intricate series ○ a tissue of lies

tissue paper n thin soft paper. Use: wrapping and protecting delicate items.

tit¹ n 1 a teat 2 an offensive term for a woman's breast (slang)

tit² n a small songbird with a short bill

Titan /tít'n/ n 1 in Greek mythology, each of 12 rulers of the universe who were overthrown by Zeus 2 the largest moon of Saturn 3 **titan** a powerful or impressive person

titanic /tī tánnik/ adj enormous in size or power —**titanically** adv

titanium /tī táyni əm, ti-/ n (symbol **Ti**) a silvery metallic chemical element. Use: alloys for aerospace industry.

titbit /tít bit/ n 1 a small morsel 2 a piece of gossip

titch, tich n somebody very small (infml) —**titchy** adj

tit for tat n the repaying of a wrong or injury by inflicting equivalent harm on the doer

tithe /tīth/ n 1 one tenth of somebody's income or produce given to support a church or its clergy 2 a voluntary contribution or tax ■ v (tithing, tithed) 1 vti give something as a tithe 2 vt collect a tithe from —**tither** n

Titian /tísh'n/ (1485?–1576) Italian painter

Titicaca, Lake /títti kaà kaa/ largest lake in South America, extending from SE Peru to W Bolivia

titillate /títti layt/ (-lating, -lated) vti excite somebody pleasurably, usually in a slightly sexual way —**titillatingly** adv —**titillation** /títti láysh'n/ n

titivate /títti vayt/ (-vating, -vated) vti spruce up —**titivation** /títti váysh'n/ n

title /tít'l/ n 1 a name that identifies a literary, artistic, or musical work 2 a descriptive heading 3 a published work 4 a designation added to a name to indicate rank or status 5 a name describing a job position in an organization 6 the status of champion in a sport or competition 7 the legal right to possession of property, or a document giving this right ■ **titles** npl credits or subtitles on a screen —**titled** adj

title deed n a document that is evidence of somebody's legal right to property

titleholder /tít'l hōldər/ n a holder of a championship title —**titleholding** n

title page n a page of a book showing the title and author

title role n a role in a play or film that gives the work its name

titmouse /tít mowss/ (pl -mice /-mīss/) n a small songbird with a short bill

ORIGIN Titmouse is a 16C alteration, under the influence of *mouse*, of the earlier form *titmose*. *Tit* formed compounds meaning 'small', and probably came from a Scandinavian language. *Mose* represents an ancient Germanic root itself meaning 'titmouse'.

AKG London

Tito

Tito /teetō/ (1892–1980) Yugoslav patriot and president of Yugoslavia (1942–77)

titter /títtər/ *vi* laugh lightly and nervously —**titteringly** *adv*

tittle-tattle /títt'l tat'l/ *n* gossip —**tittle-tattle** *vi*

titular /títtyŏŏlər/ *adj* 1 in name only 2 holding a title of rank —**titularly** *adv* —**titulary** *n*

Tizard /tiz aard/, **Dame Cath** (*b*. 1931) governor general of New Zealand (1990–96)

tizzy /tízzi/, **tizz**, **tiz-woz** *n* a state of nervous agitation (*infml*)

T-junction *n* a junction where a road joins another at right angles but does not cross it

Tl *symbol* thallium

TLA *abbr* three-letter acronym

TLC *abbr* tender loving care (*infml*)

Tm *symbol* thulium

TM *abbr* 1 trademark 2 transcendental meditation

TMT *abbr* technology, media, and telecommunications

TNT *n* a yellow flammable compound. Use: explosive. Full form **trinitrotoluene**

to *stressed* /tool/ *unstressed* /tŏŏ, tə/ *prep* 1 indicates direction, destination, or position 2 forms the infinitive of verbs 3 indicates purpose ○ *used to chop vegetables with* 4 indicates a recipient (*with a noun phrase to form the indirect object*) ○ *gave it to me* 5 indicates who or what a feeling or action is directed towards ○ *grateful to them* 6 indicates attachment 7 until ○ *from Tuesday to Saturday* 8 indicates a range ○ *everything from pollution to pesticides* 9 indicates the result of a change ○ *excitement turned to gloom* 10 indicates equality ○ *12 inches to the foot* 11 as compared with ○ *5 to 3 in our favour* ■ *adv* /tool/ 1 so as to be shut or almost shut ○ *pushed the door to* 2 so as to be conscious again ○ *came to*

SPELLCHECK Do not confuse the spelling of **to**, **too** ('as well'), or **two** ('number 2'), which sound similar.

toad *n* a terrestrial amphibian similar to a frog but with dry warty skin

toad-in-the-hole *n* sausages in batter

toadstool /tŏd stool/ *n* a poisonous fungus with a round flat cap on a stalk

toady /tŏdi/ (*pl* **-ies**) *n* a servile and ingratiating person —**toady** *vi* —**toadyism** *n*

ORIGIN Toady is an early 19C shortening of *toadeater*, a name that originated in the dubious selling methods of itinerant doctors. They employed an assistant who pretended to eat a toad (toads were thought to be poisonous), so that the doctor could appear to effect a miraculous cure with his medicine.

to and fro /-frō/ *adv* 1 back and forth 2 here and there —**to-and-fro** *adj*, *n* —**toing and froing** *n*

toast /tōst/ *n* 1 bread browned with dry heat, or a piece of this 2 a call to honour somebody or something by raising a glass and drinking 3 a raising of glasses and drinking in response to a toast ■ *v* 1 *vti* brown food with dry heat, or become browned 2 *vt* warm the body or part of the body near a source of heat 3 *vti* drink a toast in somebody's honour

toaster /tōstər/ *n* a small appliance for making toast

toastmaster /tōst maastər/ *n* somebody who proposes toasts and introduces speakers at a banquet or reception

toastmistress /tōst mistrəss/ *n* a woman who proposes toasts and introduces speakers at a banquet or reception

toasty /tōsti/ (**-ier**, **-iest**) *adj* pleasantly warm

tobacco /tə bákō/ (*pl* **-cos** *or* **-coes** *or* same) *n* 1 dried leaves processed for smoking in cigarettes, cigars, and pipes 2 the plant that produces tobacco

tobacconist /tə bákənist/ *n* a seller of tobacco products and supplies

~~tobacco~~ incorrect spelling of **tobacco**

Tobago /tə báygō/ island in the Caribbean, part of Trinidad and Tobago. Pop. 50,282 (1990).

toboggan /tə bóggən/ *n* a long narrow sledge without runners ■ *vi* ride on a toboggan —**tobogganer** *n* —**tobogganist** *n*

toby jug /tōbi-/ *n* a beer mug or jug in the shape of a rotund man

toccata /tə kaátə/ (*pl* **-tas**) *n* a keyboard composition written in a free style that includes full chords and elaborate runs

tocsin /tóksin/ *n* 1 an alarm sounded by means of a bell 2 a bell that sounds a tocsin

tod ◇ **on your tod** alone (*infml*)

today /tə dáy/ *n* 1 this day, as distinct from yesterday or tomorrow 2 the present age or period in history —**today** *adv*

toddle /tódd'l/ (**-dling**, **-dled**) *vi* 1 take short unsteady steps, as a child does when learning to walk 2 walk unhurriedly (*infml*) —**toddle** *n*

toddler /tódd'lər/ *n* a young child who is learning to walk

toddy /tóddi/ (*pl* **-dies**) *n* a drink of an alcoholic spirit mixed with hot water and sugar

to-do /tə dóo/ *n* a commotion (*infml*)

toe *n* 1 each of the digits of the foot of human beings and some vertebrates 2 the part of something such as a shoe or sock that covers the toes ■ *vt* (**toed**) touch with the toes —**toed** *adj* ◇ **on your toes** alert and ready for action ◇ **tread on somebody's toes** interfere with something considered to be that person's responsibility

toecap /tó kap/ *n* a reinforcement for the toe of a shoe or boot

toehold /tó hóld/ *n* **1** a small recess in rock that can support a climber's toe **2** a small advantage or gain

toenail /tó nayl/ *n* a nail on a toe

toerag /tó rag/ *n* an offensive term for a person regarded as worthless *(insult)*

toff *n* an upper-class person *(infml)*

toffee /tóffi/ *n* a sweet made by boiling brown sugar or treacle with butter

toffee apple *n* a caramel-coated apple

toffee-nosed *adj* snobbish *(infml)*

tofu /tó foo/ *n* soya bean curd pressed into a cake

tog *n* a measure of the thermal insulation properties of fabrics, quilts, and clothes ■ **togs** *npl* clothes *(infml)*

toga /tógə/ *n* a garment worn by citizens of ancient Rome, consisting of a piece of cloth draped round the body —**togaed** *adj*

together /tə géthər/ *adv* **1** in company with others **2** interacting or in a relationship with one another **3** by joint effort **4** into contact, or into a unified whole ○ *sewn together* **5** collectively **6** uninterruptedly ○ *raining for 10 days together* **7** in agreement **8** simultaneously ■ *adj* stable and self-confident *(infml)*

togetherness /tə géthərnəss/ *n* a feeling of closeness with others

toggle /tógg'l/ *n* **1** a peg or rod inserted into a loop to hold or fasten something **2** a key for switching between two computer operations ■ *v* (**-gling, -gled**) **1** *vti* switch between two computer operations with one key **2** *vt* supply or fasten with toggles

toggle switch *n* **1** a small spring-loaded switch for opening and closing an electrical circuit manually **2** a toggle for switching between computer operations

Togo /tógō/ country in West Africa, on the Gulf of Guinea. Cap. Lomé. Pop. 5,153,088 (2001).

toil[1] *n* hard work ■ *vi* **1** work hard **2** progress with difficulty —**toiler** *n*

toil[2] *n* a net, snare, or other trap *(literary)*

toilet /tóylət/ *n* **1** a fixture with a waste drain and a flush for disposing of faeces and urine **2** a room with a toilet **3** *also* **toilette** /twaa lét/ washing, dressing, and attending to your personal appearance *(fml)*

toilet paper *n* paper for cleaning the body after urinating or defecating

toilet roll *n* a roll of toilet paper

toiletry /tóylətri/ (**-ries**) *n* an article used in washing or grooming *(usually pl)*

toilet training *n* the process of teaching a young child to control bladder and bowel movements and to use a toilet

toilet water *n* light perfume

Tojo Hideki /tójō hee déki/ (1884–1948) Japanese general and prime minister (1941–44)

token /tókən/ *n* **1** something representing something else **2** a disc used like money **3** a keepsake ■ *adj* existing or done as a gesture only

tokenism /tókənizəm/ *n* the making of only a symbolic or minimal effort to do something —**tokenistic** /tókə nístik/ *adj*

Tokyo /tóki ō/ capital of Japan, on Tokyo Bay, on the coast of E Honshu Island. Pop. 7,919,771 (2000).

tolar /tólaar/ *n* the main unit of Slovenian currency

told past tense, past participle of **tell**

Toledo /to láydō/ historic city and administrative centre of **Toledo Province**, central Spain. Pop. 63,561 (1991).

Toledo, Alejandro (*b.* 1946) president of Peru (2001–)

tolerable /tóllərəb'l/ *adj* **1** capable of being tolerated **2** fairly good —**tolerably** *adv*

tolerance /tóllərənss/ *n* **1** the acceptance of the different views of others **2** the ability to endure hardship or annoyance **3** an allowance made for deviation from a standard, or the limit within which deviation is allowed **4** the loss of response to a drug after prolonged use or exposure

tolerant /tóllərənt/ *adj* **1** accepting the different views of others **2** able to withstand harsh treatment or annoyance **3** no longer responding to a drug —**tolerantly** *adv*

tolerate /tóllə rayt/ (**-ating, -ated**) *vt* **1** be willing to allow something to happen or exist **2** endure the unpleasant effect of something **3** accept the existence of different views —**toleration** /tóllə ráysh'n/ *n* —**tolerationist** *n*, *adj*

Tolkien /tól keen/, **J. R. R.** (1892–1973) South African-born British scholar and writer

toll[1] /tōl/ *n* **1** a fee for using a road or crossing a bridge **2** deaths or damage sustained in an accident or disaster **3** a charge for a long-distance telephone call **4** a fee for a service

toll[2] /tōl/ *v* **1** *vti* ring a bell slowly and repeatedly **2** *vt* announce with the tolling of a bell —**toll** *n*

tollbooth /tól booth, -booth/, **tolbooth** *n* a booth on a road or bridge for collecting tolls

toll bridge *n* a bridge where a toll is payable

tollgate /tól gayt/ *n* a barrier where a toll must be paid to proceed

Count Leo Tolstoy

Tolstoy /tólstoy/, **Leo** (1828–1910) Russian writer

tom *n* the male of various animals, especially a domestic cat

Tom, Dick, and Harry /-hárri/, **Tom, Dick, or Harry** *n* anyone and everyone

tomahawk /tómmə hawk/ *n* **1** a Native North American weapon in the form of a small axe **2** *ANZ* a small axe —**tomahawk** *vt*

tomato /tə máàtō/ (*pl* **-toes**) *n* **1** a round red vegetable with pulpy flesh **2** a plant that produces tomatoes

tomb /toom/ *n* **1** a grave **2** a burial chamber

tombola /tom bṓlə/ *n* a small-scale lottery with tickets drawn from a revolving drum

Tombouctou /tóN book toó/, **Timbuktu** /tím buk toó/ city in central Mali, on the southern edge of the Sahara Desert. Pop. 36,000 (1998).

tomboy /tóm boy/ *n* a girl who enjoys boys' activities —**tomboyish** *adj*

tombstone /toóm stōn/ *n* an ornamental stone that marks a grave

tomcat /tóm kat/ *n* a male domestic cat

tome *n* a large or serious book *(fml or humorous)*

tomfoolery /tom foóləri/ *n* silliness *(infml)*

~~tommorrow~~ incorrect spelling of **tomorrow**

tomography /tō móggrəfi/ *n* the use of ultrasound, gamma rays, or X-rays to produce a focused image of the structures across a specific depth within the body

tomorrow /tə mórrō/ *n* **1** the day after today **2** the future ■ *adv* **1** on the day after today **2** in the future ◊ **like** *or* **as if there was** *or* **were no tomorrow** with great speed, intensity, or carelessness *(infml)*

tom-tom *n* **1** a drum hit with the hands **2** a deep-sided drum in a modern drum kit

ton /tun/ *n* **1** a UK unit of weight equal to 1016 kilograms **2** a US unit of weight equal to 907 kilograms **3** a metric ton **4** a unit measuring a ship's displacement equal to 0.85 cubic metres/35 cubic feet of water **5** a large amount *(infml; often pl)* **6** a figure of a hundred *(slang)* ■ *adv* **tons** a great deal

tonal /tōn'l/ *adj* **1** of tone **2** of harmonic music —**tonally** *adv*

tonality /tō nálləti/ *n* **1** the quality of tone of an instrument or voice **2** a system or arrangement of musical tones in relation to a tonic

tone /tōn/ *n* **1** a particular kind of sound **2** a way of saying something, or the general quality of something, that indicates an attitude o *the optimistic tone of the report* **3** the prevailing character or style of something o *Neon signs lower the tone of the place.* **4** a shade of a colour **5** the natural firmness of somebody's muscles **6** the timbre of a voice or instrument **7** the largest musical interval in the diatonic scale ■ *v* (**toning, toned**) **1** *vi* blend in with something **2** make muscles firmer and stronger —**toneless** *adj*

□ **tone down** *vt* make less intense or extreme

□ **tone up** *vt* make muscles firmer and stronger

Tone /tōn/, **Wolfe** (1763–98) Irish revolutionary

tone-deaf *adj* unable to differentiate between musical notes —**tone-deafness** *n*

tone language *n* a language in which the pitch of sounds affects meaning

tone poem *n* an orchestral piece of music based on a literary or artistic theme

toner /tōnər/ *n* **1** a cosmetic that firms the skin **2** ink for laser printers and photocopiers

Tonga /tóngə, tóng gə/ independent island nation consisting of more than 150 islands in the S Pacific Ocean. Cap. Nukualofa. Pop. 104,227 (2001). —**Tongan** *n, adj*

tongs *npl* **1** a utensil with two arms for grabbing and lifting things **2** curling tongs

tongue /tung/ *n* **1** a fleshy organ inside the mouth that is used for tasting and licking **2** an animal's tongue as food **3** a language **4** a way of speaking *(fml)* **5** the flap over the instep of a shoe ■ **tongues** *npl* speech in no known language that results from religious ecstasy ■ *vt* (**tonguing, tongued**) touch with the tongue —**tongued** *adj* ◊ **hold your tongue** keep silent ◊ See note at **language**

tongue-in-cheek *adj* joking

tongue-lashing *n* a severe scolding

tongue-tied *adj* speechless through nervousness

tongue twister *n* a word or phrase that is difficult to say

tonic /tónnik/ *n* **1** something that lifts the spirits **2** a medicine that purports to produce a sense of well-being **3** *also* **tonic water** a carbonated drink flavoured with quinine **4** the first note of a musical scale ■ *adj* **1** lifting the spirits **2** boosting energy **3** of muscle tone **4** of the first note of a musical scale —**tonically** *adv*

tonic sol-fa *n* a musical scale system using syllables that are movable depending on the key of the piece

tonight /tə nít/ *n* the night of the present day —**tonight** *adv*

Tonkin, Gulf of /tón kin, tóng-/ arm of the South China Sea, on the coast of NE Vietnam and SE China

tonnage /túnnij/ *n* **1** weight in tons **2** the size or capacity of a ship **3** the weight of the cargo of a ship **4** a duty charged on the cargo of a ship

tonne /tun/ *n* a metric ton

tonsil /tónss'l, -sil/ *n* an oval mass of tissue, especially each of the two at the back of the mouth —**tonsillar** *adj*

~~tonsilitis~~ incorrect spelling of **tonsillitis**

tonsillectomy /tónssi léktəmi/ (*pl* **-mies**) *n* the surgical removal of inflamed tonsils

tonsillitis /tónssi lítiss/ *n* inflammation of the tonsils —**tonsillitic** /-líttik/ *adj*

tonsorial /ton sáwri əl/ *adj* of barbers *(fml or humorous)*

tonsure /tónshər, -syər/ *n* a partially shaved head —**tonsure** *vt*

too /toó/ *adv* **1** as well o *caught the virus too* **2** more than is desirable o *too flamboyant for* *my taste* **3** adds emphasis ○ *too kind* **4** very *(in negative statements)* ○ *didn't look too happy* ◊ See note at **to**

took past tense of **take**

tool *n* **1** a device for doing a particular kind of work **2** the cutting part of a machine **3** a bookbinder's implement for making a design on leather **4** a means to an end **5** something used for a job ○ *Words are the poet's tool.* **6** somebody who is manipulated by somebody else ■ *vt* **1** cut or shape using hand tools **2** provide with tools

toolbar /tóol baa/ *n* a row of icons on a computer screen that are clicked on to perform functions

toolkit /tóol kit/ *n* a set of tools

tool shed *n* a shed for storing tools

toot *n* the sound of a vehicle's horn ■ *vti* make a short hooting sound

tooth /tooth/ *n* (*pl* **teeth** /teeth/) **1** a whitish bony object in the mouth that is used for biting and chewing **2** a part resembling a tooth **3** an indentation ■ **teeth** *npl* effective power ○ *sanctions without teeth* —**toothed** *adj* ◊ **cut your teeth (on)** learn how to do something and gain experience from it ◊ **get** *or* **sink your teeth into** start doing something that will be challenging ◊ **in the teeth of** against opposition or contradiction from ◊ **set somebody's teeth on edge** irritate somebody ◊ **show your teeth** indicate that you have power and intend to use it

toothache /tooth ayk/ *n* pain in a tooth

toothbrush /tooth brush/ *n* a brush for cleaning teeth

tooth fairy *n* in children's folklore, a fairy that replaces a child's lost milk tooth with money

toothless /toothlass/ *adj* **1** lacking teeth **2** lacking power

toothpaste /tooth payst/ *n* a paste for cleaning teeth

toothpick /tooth pik/ *n* a stick used for removing food from between the teeth

tooth powder *n* a tooth-cleansing powder that is mixed with water

toothsome /toothsam/ *adj* delicious —**toothsomely** *adv* —**toothsomeness** *n*

toothy /toothi/ (**-ier, -iest**) *adj* having many or large teeth —**toothily** *adv* —**toothiness** *n*

tootle /tóot'l/ (**-tling, -tled**) *vti* make or cause to make a tooting sound

top[1] *n* **1** the highest part or point **2** an upper surface **3** a lid or cover **4** a garment for the upper body **5** the most important one **6** the best part **7** the most excellent or intense level ○ *at the top of her voice* **8** the beginning or earliest part ○ *the top of the news* ■ *adj* **1** uppermost or highest **2** leading or most successful **3** of the best quality **4** maximum ■ *vt* (**topping, topped**) **1** add a topping to food **2** cut the top off something **3** be at the head of a list or ranking **4** exceed somebody or something **5** reach the apex of something **6** kill somebody *(slang)* —**topmost** *adj* ◊ **blow your top** lose your temper *(infml)* ◊ **off the**

top of your head without thinking deeply or planning

□ **top out** *vi* add the final level to a building

top[2] *n* a spinning toy

topaz /tó paz/ *n* **1** a transparent brown gemstone. Use: gems. **2** a yellowish gemstone

top brass *n* the highest-ranking officers *(infml)*

topcoat /tóp kōt/ *n* **1** a final coat of paint **2** a lightweight outdoor coat *(dated)*

top dog *n* the most powerful person in a group or organization *(infml)*

top-down *adj* **1** controlled by the most senior people **2** working from the general to the specific

top drawer *n* **1** the highest level of excellence **2** the upper class —**top-drawer** *adj*

topee *n* ACCESSORIES = **topi**[2]

Topeka /tō peéka/ capital of Kansas. Pop. 118,977 (1998).

top-flight *adj* outstanding

top gear *n* the highest gear in a motor vehicle

top hat *n* a man's formal tall hat

top-heavy *adj* **1** unbalanced because of being too heavy at the top **2** describes an organization that has too many executives —**top-heaviness** *n*

topi[1] /tó pee/ (*pl* **-pis** *or* **same**) *n* an antelope with curved horns

topi[2] /tó pee/ (*pl* **-pis**), **topee** *n* a pith helmet

topiary /tópi əri/ *n* **1** the art of trimming bushes into decorative shapes **2** decoratively shaped bushes —**topiarist** *n*

topic /tóppik/ *n* a subject that is written or spoken about ◊ See note at **subject**

TOPIC /tóppik/ *abbr* Teletext Output of Price Information by Computer

topical /tóppik'l/ *adj* **1** of current interest **2** describes medication applied externally —**topicality** /tóppi kálləti/ *n* —**topically** *adv*

topknot /tóp not/ *n* a ribbon or an arrangement of hair worn on the top of the head

topless /tópləss/ *adj* **1** with nothing covering the breasts **2** permitting women to show their breasts in public ○ *topless beaches* **3** with no top part —**toplessness** *n*

top-level *adj* **1** involving important people **2** at the most senior level

top-level domain *n* the part of an Internet address that comes after the dot

topnotch /tóp nóch/ *adj* excellent *(infml)* —**topnotcher** *n*

topography /tə póggrəfi/ *n* **1** the mapping of the surface features of the Earth **2** the physical features of an area —**topographer** *n* —**topographic** /tóppə gráffik/ *adj* —**topographical** *adj*

topper /tóppər/ *n* **1** a person or machine that removes or adds tops **2** a top hat *(infml)*

topping /tópping/ *n* a garnish for food

topple /tópp'l/ (**-pling, -pled**) *vti* **1** fall or make something fall over **2** overthrow somebody

top-rated *adj* highly rated

tops n (pl same) the best person or thing (infml)

top-secret adj highly secret

topside /tóp sīd/ n 1 an upper side 2 a lean cut of beef from the outer thigh 3 the part of a ship's hull above the water —**topside** adj

topsoil /tóp soyl/ n the top layer of soil

topspin /tópspin/ n forward spin given to a ball

topsy-turvy /tópsi túrvi/ adj, adv 1 upside down 2 in or into confusion ■ n utter disorder or confusion —**topsy-turvily** adv —**topsy-turviness** n

top-up n 1 an extra serving of a drink 2 an additional sum of money

Torah /táwrə/ n 1 the first five books of the Hebrew Bible, or a scroll containing these 2 the body of teachings in the Hebrew Bible and the Talmud

torch n 1 a small hand-held lamp, usually powered by batteries 2 a burning stick used as a light source 3 a device that emits a flame, used especially in welding ■ vt deliberately set on fire (infml)

torchlight /táwrch līt/ n 1 the light of a torch 2 a burning torch

tore past tense of **tear**[1]

toreador /tórri ə dawr/ n a bullfighter on horseback

torment vt /tawr mént/ 1 inflict torture, pain, or anguish on 2 tease ■ n /táwr ment/ 1 torture 2 a cause of annoyance or anguish —**tormented** adj —**tormentedly** adv —**tormentor** n

torn past participle of **tear**[1]

tornado /tawr náydō/ (pl -**dos** or -**does**) n a destructive column of swirling wind —**tornadic** /-náddik/ adj

> **ORIGIN Tornado** looks like a genuine Spanish word, but in fact it was formed in English. It is probably an alteration of Spanish tronada 'thunderstorm', associated with the verb tornar 'turn'. It was first used in the mid-16C for any violent thunderstorm in the tropical Atlantic, but by the early 17C had come to suggest swirling winds.

tornament incorrect spelling of **tournament**

Toronto /tə róntō/ capital of Ontario Province, Canada. Pop. 653,734 (1996). —**Torontonian** /tə ron tṓnee ən/ n, adj

torpedo /tawr peédō/ n (pl -**does**) a self-propelled underwater missile ■ vt (-**does**, -**doing**, -**doed**) 1 hit with a torpedo 2 destroy (infml)

torpid /táwrpid/ adj 1 sluggish 2 dormant —**torpidity** /tawr píddəti/ n

torpor /táwrpər/ n 1 lack of energy 2 dormancy —**torporific** /táwrpə ríffik/ adj

torque /tawrk/ n 1 a force that causes a rotating or twisting movement 2 a measurement of the ability of a rotating mechanism to overcome resistance

Torquemada /táwrkwi maádə/, **Tomás de** (1420–98) Spanish monk and grand inquisitor

torrent /tórrənt/ n 1 a fast and powerful rush of liquid 2 a forceful outpouring

torrential /tə rénsh'l/ adj flowing or falling fast and powerfully —**torrentially** adv

torrid /tórrid/ adj 1 full of passion 2 scorching hot —**torridity** /to ríddəti/ n —**torridly** adv —**torridness** n

torsion /táwrsh'n/ n 1 the twisting of an object by applying equal and opposite torques 2 mechanical stress on a twisted object —**torsional** adj

torso /táwrssō/ (pl -**sos** or -**si** /-see/) n 1 the upper part of the human body, excluding the head and arms 2 a sculpture of somebody's torso

tort n a civil wrongdoing for which damages can be sought

Tortelier /tawr télli ay/, **Paul** (1914–90) French cellist

tortilla /tawr teè ə/ n 1 a flat Mexican bread cooked on a hot griddle 2 a Spanish omelette

tortilla chip n a maize crisp

tortoise /táwrtəss/ n 1 a slow-moving land-dwelling reptile with a shell 2 somebody or something that moves slowly

> **ORIGIN** The word for the **tortoise** originally had a wide variety of forms, derived from French tortue, Spanish tortuga, and their source medieval Latin tortuca, a word whose ultimate origin is unknown. The modern form emerged in the mid-16C. The name for the reptile the turtle is thought to be an alteration of French tortue 'tortoise'.

tortoiseshell /táwrtəss shel/ n 1 the outer part of the shell of a turtle. Use: combs, ornaments, jewellery. 2 a synthetic substance that resembles tortoiseshell 3 a cat with black and brown markings ■ adj mottled yellow and brown

tortuous /táwrtyoo əss/ adj with many turns or bends —**tortuously** adv —**tortuousness** n

torture /táwrchər/ vt (-**turing**, -**tured**) 1 deliberately inflict pain on somebody 2 cause somebody anguish 3 distort something ■ n 1 the deliberate inflicting of pain 2 a method of inflicting pain 3 anguish —**torturer** n —**torturous** adj —**torturously** adv

Tory /táwri/ (pl -**ries**) n 1 a member or supporter of the Conservative Party in the United Kingdom or Canada 2 a member or supporter of an English political party from the 17C to the 19C that supported the established order —**Tory** adj —**Toryism** n

> **ORIGIN Tory** was adopted in the mid-17C from an Irish word meaning 'highwayman', and originally referred to a group of Irishmen who in the 1640s were thrown off their property by the British occupiers and took to a life of harrying and plundering. In the 1670s it was applied as a term of abuse to Irish Catholic royalists, and then more generally to supporters of the Catholic James II, and after 1689 it came to be used for the members of the British political party that had at first opposed the removal of

James and his replacement with the Protestants William and Mary.

Toscanini /tóskə neeni/, **Arturo** (1867–1957) Italian-born US conductor

tosh *n* nonsense *(infml)*

toss *v* 1 *vt* lightly throw something 2 *vti* throw or be thrown up and down or to and fro 3 *vti* throw a coin to decide something 4 *vt* mix a salad with a dressing 5 *vt* throw somebody or something upwards 6 *vt* jerk the head upwards 7 *vi* move restlessly, especially in sleep ■ *n* 1 an act of lightly throwing something 2 a jerk of the head ◊ See note at **throw**
□ **toss off** *vt* do quickly

toss-up *n* 1 a deciding throw of a coin 2 an even chance

tot[1] *n* 1 a little child *(infml)* 2 a small amount

tot[2] (**totting, totted**) □ **tot up** *v* 1 *vi* mount up to a large total 2 *vt* add amounts together

total /tót'l/ *n* a sum of amounts added or considered together ■ *adj* 1 complete or utter 2 with all amounts or elements considered together ■ *vt* (**-talling, -talled**) 1 add things together 2 amount to a particular total —**totally** *adv*

total eclipse *n* an eclipse of the entire surface of the sun or another astronomical object

totalitarian /tō tálli táiri ən/ *adj* of a centralized system of government in which a single party or leader exercises dictatorial control —**totalitarian** *n* —**totalitarianism** *n*

totality /tō tálləti/ *(pl* **-ties***)* *n* 1 completeness 2 a total amount

tote[1] *vt* (**toting, toted**) carry something heavy *(infml)* ■ *n* 1 a heavy load 2 *also* **tote bag** a large soft bag with handles

tote[2] *n* an electronic betting system that totals all bets, makes deductions, and determines the final odds and payout *(infml)*

totem /tótəm/ *n* 1 an object, animal, plant, or other natural phenomenon revered as a symbol of a people 2 a carving or other representation of a totem —**totemic** /tō témmik/ *adj*

totem pole *n* a Native North American pole carved with totems

totter /tóttər/ *vi* 1 walk unsteadily 2 wobble ■ *n* a wobbling gait —**tottering** *adj* —**totteringly** *adv* —**tottery** *adj*

tottie, totty /tótti/ *(pl* **-ties***)* *n* an offensive term for women collectively regarded as sexually available or desirable *(slang)*

toucan /tóokən/ *(pl* **-cans** *or same)* *n* a tropical bird with a large curved beak

touch /tuch/ *n* 1 the sense by which objects are felt through contact with the body 2 the qualities of something as perceived by feeling it 3 an instance of coming into contact with something 4 a light stroke 5 a small amount 6 a distinctive style ○ *a sure touch* 7 a detail 8 the fact of being in communication ■ *v* 1 *vti* be, or put a part of the body, in contact with something so as to feel it 2 *vti* be, or put something, in contact with something

else 3 *vt* disturb something by handling 4 *vt* affect somebody emotionally 5 *vt* consume even a small amount of food or drink *(usually in negatives)* ○ *never touches meat* 6 *vt* deal or become involved with something or somebody ○ *won't touch that issue* 7 *vt* match something or somebody in excellence —**touchable** *adj* —**toucher** *n* ◊ **a touch** somewhat
□ **touch down** *vi* land in an aircraft or spacecraft
□ **touch off** *vt* 1 make explode 2 initiate
□ **touch on** *or* **upon** *vt* 1 mention briefly 2 verge on
□ **touch up** *vt* make small improvements or changes to ○ *touched up the photograph*

touch-and-go *adj* uncertain or risky

touchdown /túch down/ *n* 1 a landing made by an aircraft or spacecraft 2 in American football, a score achieved by being in possession of the ball behind an opponent's goal line

touché /too shay/ *interj* 1 acknowledges a telling remark 2 in fencing, acknowledges a scoring hit

touched /tucht/ *adj* affected emotionally

touching /túching/ *adj* causing feelings of tenderness or pity —**touchingly** *adv* ◊ See note at **moving**

touchline /túch līn/ *n* a side boundary of a sports pitch

touch pad *n* 1 an electronic input device operated by touch 2 on a laptop computer, a surface that is touched to move the cursor

touchpaper /túch paypər/ *n* a piece of paper that is lit to set off an explosive

touch screen *n* a computer screen operated by touch

touchstone /túch stōn/ *n* 1 an excellent example regarded as a standard 2 a hard black stone formerly used to test the quality of gold rubbed against it

touch-type *vi* type without looking at the keyboard —**touch-typist** *n*

touchy /túchi/ (**-ier, -iest**) *adj* 1 easily upset 2 tricky —**touchily** *adv* —**touchiness** *n*

touchy-feely /-feeli/ *adj* physically demonstrative *(infml; disapproving)*

tough /tuf/ *adj* 1 durable 2 hard to chew or cut 3 physically or mentally very strong 4 characterized by antisocial behaviour 5 strong-minded 6 difficult to deal with 7 severe or strict ○ *tough on crime* 8 unfortunate or hard to endure *(infml)* ○ *a tough break* ■ *n* somebody who is aggressive or antisocial ■ *interj* expresses a lack of sympathy when something unfortunate happens —**toughly** *adv* —**toughness** *n* ◊ **tough it out** endure through a time of difficulty *(infml)* ◊ See note at **hard**

toughen /túff'n/ *vti* 1 make or become tougher or more durable 2 make or become stronger

tough love *n* a caring but strict attitude

tough-minded *adj* determined and realistic in attitude —**tough-mindedly** *adv* —**tough-mindedness** *n*

Toulouse /too looz/ city in SW France. Pop. 390,350 (1999).

Toulouse-Lautrec /too looz lō trék/, **Henri de** (1864–1901) French artist

toupee /too pay/ n a partial wig worn to cover a bald area

tour /toor, tawr/ n 1 a pleasure trip 2 a trip to several places to play or perform 3 a brief trip for the purpose of viewing something ■ vti take part in a tour of a place

tour de force /toor də fáwrss, tawr-/ (pl **tours de force** /toor də fáwrss, tawr də fáwrss/) n a skilful feat

tourism /toorizəm, táw-/ n 1 travel undertaken for pleasure 2 the travel business 3 travel to benefit from a service or activity, especially when it is unobtainable at home ○ health tourism

tourist /toorist, táw-/ n 1 somebody who travels for pleasure 2 a member of a touring team ■ adj for or of tourists

tourist class n the cheapest class of travel on an aircraft or ship

tourist trap n a place where prices are inflated to take advantage of its popularity with tourists

touristy /tooristi, táw-/ adj catering expressly for tourists or popular with tourists (infml disapproving)

tournament /toornəmənt, táwr-/ n 1 an event made up of a series of games or contests 2 a medieval contest involving mock fighting

~~tournement~~ incorrect spelling of **tournament**

tourniquet /toorni kay, táwr-/ n a band tightened around an arm or leg to stop bleeding

tour operator n a company that organizes holidays

Tours /toor, toorz/ city in west-central France. Pop. 132,820 (1999).

tousle /tówz'l/ vt (**-sling, -sled**) ruffle or tangle hair ■ n a tangled mass —**tousled** adj

Toussaint L'Ouverture /too saN loov air chóor, -tür/, **François Dominique** (1743–1803) Haitian general and independence leader

tout /towt/ v 1 vi try aggressively to attract customers or support 2 vt advertise or offer for sale 3 vt praise ○ being touted as the best novel in years 4 vi spy on racehorses to gain betting information ■ n 1 somebody who sells information about racehorses 2 an aggressive seller —**touter** n

tow[1] /tō/ vt pull something heavy by a rope or chain ■ n an act of towing something, or the state of being towed ◊ See note at **pull**

tow[2] /tow/ n fibres that are ready for spinning

towards /tə wáwrdz/, **toward** /tə wáwrd/ prep 1 in a particular direction 2 shortly before ○ towards midnight 3 with a particular audience intended ○ geared towards teenagers 4 regarding

towbar /tō baar/ n a metal bar fitted to a vehicle to allow it to tow others

towel /tów əl/ n 1 an absorbent cloth used for drying the body 2 a cloth for drying dishes ■ vt dry somebody with a towel

towelling /tów əling/ n an absorbent looped fabric. Use: towels, bathrobes.

tower /tów ər/ n 1 a tall building or structure 2 a fortress 3 a tall stand for storing CDs 4 a tall slim case for the CPU and drives of a computer ■ vi 1 be tall or much taller than somebody or something else 2 be much superior

tower block n a tall building containing homes or offices

towering /tów əring/ adj 1 high or tall 2 outstanding —**toweringly** adv

towhead /tó hed/ n 1 somebody with light blond hair 2 a head of light blond hair —**towheaded** adj

towline /tó līn/ n a towrope

town /town/ n 1 a populated area that is larger than a village and smaller than a city 2 a large urban area 3 US, Can a unit of local government that is smaller than a county or city 4 the nearest town, or the town centre ○ going into town 5 the population of a settled area ○ The whole town's talking about it. 6 the nonacademic population of a university town —**townsman** n —**townswoman** n ◊ **go to town (on)** do something with great enthusiasm or thoroughness (infml) ◊ **on the town** enjoying the entertainment available in a town or city (infml) ◊ **paint the town red** go out and celebrate (infml) ◊ See note at **city**

town-and-gown adj of students and local residents of a university town

town clerk n 1 formerly, the chief administrative officer of a town 2 US a town official who keeps records

town council n a group of people who govern a town

town crier n somebody who makes public announcements

town hall n the building that houses the offices of a local administration

town house n 1 a terraced house in a town 2 a house in a town owned by somebody who also has a country house 3 ANZ a modern town dwelling

townie /tówni/, **towny** (pl **-ies**), **townee** /tow née/ n 1 a town dweller (infml) 2 a nonacademic resident of a university town

town meeting n a public meeting of a town's inhabitants

town planning n the organized planning of the building work done in a town —**town planner** n

townscape /tówn skayp/ n 1 the visible area of a town 2 a picture of a town

township /tówn ship/ n 1 a small town 2 US, Can a subdivision of a county 3 in South Africa, an urban settlement for Black people under apartheid 4 ANZ a village

townspeople /tównz peep'l/, **townsfolk** /-fōk/ npl the inhabitants of a town

towpath /tó paath/ (pl **-paths** /-paathz/) n a path beside a canal

towrope /tó rōp/ n a rope for towing

toxaemia /tok seémi ə/ n the presence of bacterial toxins in the blood —**toxaemic** adj

toxic /tóksik/ adj 1 poisonous, or involving something poisonous 2 deadly —**toxically** adv —**toxicity** /tok sissəti/ n

toxicology /tóksi kóləji/ n the scientific study of poisons, their effects, and their antidotes —**toxicological** /tóksikə lójjik'l/ adj —**toxicologically** adv —**toxicologist** n

toxic shock syndrome n a serious circulatory failure caused by toxin-producing bacteria

toxin /tóksin/ n 1 a poison produced by a living organism 2 any substance that accumulates in the body and causes it harm

toy n 1 a thing to play with 2 a replica 3 an animal belonging to a miniature breed □ **toy with** vt 1 play or fiddle with 2 think about

toy boy n an offensive term for a young man who is the lover of an older person

toyi-toyi /tóy toyi/ n S Africa a militant dance

tr. abbr 1 transitive 2 transpose 3 transposition

trace[1] n 1 an indication of the former presence of something 2 a tiny quantity 3 a footprint 4 a line made by a recording instrument 5 a drawing made using tracing paper ■ v (tracing, traced) 1 vt search and find somebody or something 2 vti follow something's course of development, or be able to be followed along a course 3 vti copy something using tracing paper 4 vt draw something carefully 5 vt give an outline of something —**traceable** adj —**traceless** adj

ORIGIN The Latin word tractus 'drawing', from which trace is derived, passed into early French as trait 'pulling, draught', hence 'harnessstrap'. English trait derives from this. The French plural trais was borrowed into English in the 14C as trace 'harness strap'. It also formed the basis of a Latin verb that evolved into French tracier, from which English in the 14C got the verb trace. A noun trace was also derived from tracier, and this too was acquired by English as trace, in the 13C. At first it denoted a 'path' or 'track'; the modern sense 'indication of the former presence of something' did not develop until the 17C.

trace[2] n a strap or chain attached to a horse's harness by which it pulls something along (often pl)

tracer /tráyssər/ n 1 also **tracer bullet** a chemically treated bullet that leaves a glowing trail 2 also **tracer element** a substance used in biological or medical experiments or tests so that its movements can be monitored from its colour, radioactivity, or other property 3 an investigation or investigator 4 somebody or something that makes tracings

tracery /tráyssəri/ (pl **-ies**) n an interlaced pattern —**traceried** adj

trachea /trə keé ə/ (pl **-ae** /-eé/ or **-as**) n 1 the human windpipe (technical) 2 a breathing tube in insects and related air-breathing invertebrate animals —**tracheal** adj

tracheotomy /tráki óttəmi/ (pl **-mies**) n a cut through the trachea to assist breathing in medical emergencies

trachoma /trə kőmə/ n a contagious bacterial eye disease —**trachomatous** /trə kómmətəss, -kőmə-/ adj

tracing /tráyssing/ n 1 a traced copy 2 a graphic record made by an instrument such as a seismograph

tracing paper n translucent paper for copying something showing through it

track n 1 a mark left by something that passes 2 a path or trail 3 the metal structure that trains run on 4 the course followed by somebody who is travelling 5 a line of action or thought 6 a course for running or racing 7 a separate item on or section of a recording or storage medium 8 the treads of a tank or bulldozer 9 a supporting rail for a curtain or something similar ■ v 1 vti follow a path or trail 2 vt follow the flight path of an aircraft or spacecraft 3 vt follow the progress of somebody or something 4 vt follow a path through a place 5 vt follow a moving object with a camera 6 vi be in alignment 7 vi follow the groove on a record —**trackable** adj ◊ **in your tracks** immediately (infml) ◊ **make tracks** leave (infml)

□ **track down** vt find by searching

track and field n athletics

trackball /trák bawl/ n a rotating ball in a socket used instead of a computer mouse

tracker /trákər/ n somebody who follows a trail

tracker dog n a dog that hunts people

tracker fund n an investment fund that follows market performance

track event n a competition on a running track

tracking /tráking/ n 1 the following of a trail 2 a mechanism in video recorders that finds the best picture

tracking station n a site for monitoring the movement of something such as a missile or space vehicle

track record n 1 a record of past performance (infml) 2 a record for a particular sports arena

tracksuit /trák soot, -syoot/ n a loose top and trousers worn before and after exercise

tract[1] n 1 an area of land or water 2 a group of bodily organs that provide for the passage of something

tract[2] n a religious or moralistic pamphlet

tractable /tráktəb'l/ adj 1 easy to persuade or control 2 easy to bend or shape —**tractably** adv

traction /tráksh'n/ n 1 the application of a pulling force for medical purposes 2 adhesive friction between a moving object and a surface 3 the act or process of pulling 4 a means of moving vehicles —**tractional** adj

traction engine *n* a steam-powered road loco-motive for pulling heavy loads

tractor /tráktər/ *n* **1** a farm vehicle used in fields **2** the front part of an articulated lorry

Tracy /tráyssi/, **Spencer** (1900–67) US actor

trad *abbr* traditional

trade *n* **1** an area of business or industry **2** a skilled occupation, usually one requiring manual labour **3** people in a particular industry ○ *a reception for the trade only* **4** the activity of buying and selling **5** work in commerce, not in a profession **6** customers or sales ○ *losing trade to the competition* **7** *US, Can* an exchange **8** a trade wind *(often pl)* ■ *v* **(trading, traded) 1** *vi* buy and sell goods **2** *vt* exchange **3** *vt* deal in —**tradable** *adj* —**tradeless** *adj* —**trader** *n*

☐ **trade down** *vi* buy something cheaper

☐ **trade in** *vt* give an old item in partial payment for a new one

☐ **trade on** *vt* exploit

☐ **trade up** *vi* buy something more costly

trade gap *n* the difference between the value of imports and exports

~~tradegy~~ incorrect spelling of **tragedy**

trade-in *n* **1** an item used in partial payment **2** the act of trading something in

trademark /tráyd maark/ *n* **1** a company's identifying name or symbol for a product, legally registered so that no other manufacturer can use it **2** a distinctive characteristic ■ *vt* **1** register a name or symbol as a trademark **2** label a product with a trademark

trade name *n* a product name

trade-off *n* an exchange involving compromise

trade route *n* a route used by traders

Tradescant /trə déskant, tráddə skant/, **John** (1570–1638?) English naturalist. As head gardener to Charles I, he introduced many foreign plants into England.

trade secret *n* a company secret concerning a product

tradesman /tráydzmən/ *(pl* **-men** /-mən/*) n* **1** a skilled worker **2** a shopkeeper *(dated)*

tradespeople /tráydz peep'l/ *npl* **1** skilled workers **2** shopkeepers *(dated)*

Trades Union Congress *n* an association of British trade unions

trade union, trades union *n* an association of workers in a particular trade or profession, formed to represent their interests —**trade unionism** *n* —**trade unionist** *n*

trade wind *n* a prevailing tropical wind blowing towards the equator

~~tradgedy~~ incorrect spelling of **tragedy**

trading card *n* a card with a picture or information that is one of a set designed to be collected

trading estate *n* an industrial estate

trading post *n* **1** a shop in a remote area **2** a location in a stock exchange

tradition /trə dísh'n/ *n* **1** a long-established custom or belief **2** a body of long-established customs or beliefs that serve as precedents **3** the handing down of customs and beliefs ◊ See note at **habit**

traditional /trə dísh'nəl/ *adj* **1** based on or done according to tradition **2** describes older styles of jazz —**traditionally** *adv*

traditionalism /trə dísh'nəlizəm/ *n* respect for tradition —**traditionalist** *n* —**traditionalistic** /trə dísh'nə lístik/ *adj*

traduce /trə dyoóss/ *(-ducing, -duced) vt* disparage or defame —**traducement** *n*

Trafalgar, Cape /trə fálgər/ cape in SW Spain between Cádiz and the Strait of Gibraltar

traffic /tráffik/ *n* **1** the movement of vehicles on roads in a particular area **2** the movement of ships, trains, or aircraft, or the volume of people or goods transported by sea, rail, or air **3** the business of transporting goods or people **4** illegal trade **5** the flow or volume of communications ■ *vi* **(-ficking, -ficked) 1** trade illegally **2** have dealings

traffic calming *n* the use of obstructions to slow traffic down

traffic cone *n* a movable cone-shaped marker used on roads

traffic island *n* a pedestrian area in the middle of a road

traffic jam *n* a line of vehicles at a standstill —**traffic-jammed** *adj*

traffic light *n* a signal using red, green, and amber lights to control traffic

traffic officer *n NZ* an official concerned with road traffic

traffic warden *n UK* an official who enforces parking regulations

tragedian /trə jéedi ən/ *n* **1** somebody who writes tragedies **2** an actor in tragedies

tragedy /trájjədi/ *(pl* **-dies***) n* **1** a very sad event **2** an event that causes great suffering **3** a tragic play or other piece of literature

ORIGIN Tragedy goes back through French to a Greek word meaning literally 'goat's song'. The name may derive from a type of ancient Greek drama in which the chorus, who commented on the action of the play, were dressed as satyrs, mythological woodland creatures who were half man, half goat.

tragic /trájjik/, **tragical** /-ik'l/ *adj* **1** very sad or upsetting, especially because of involving death or loss ○ *a tragic accident* **2** of dramatic or literary tragedy ○ *a tragic hero* —**tragically** *adv*

tragicomedy /trájji kómmədi/ *(pl* **-dies***) n* **1** a work that combines tragedy and comedy **2** tragicomedies as a genre —**tragicomic** *adj* —**tragicomical** *adj*

trail *v* **1** *vti* drag something, or be dragged **2** *vi* to hang or float loosely **3** *vi* lag behind **4** *vt* follow a person or animal by using marks or signs left behind **5** *vti* fall behind somebody in a competition **6** *vt* show an excerpt of a film or television programme in advance ■ *n* **1** a route through countryside **2** marks or

a scent left where somebody or something moved **3** a path
☐ **trail away** *or* **off** *vi* grow fainter

trail bike *n* a motorcycle for off-road use

trailblazer /tráyl blayzər/ *n* **1** a pioneer or innovator in a specific field **2** somebody who makes a new route through wilderness —**trailblazing** *adj, n*

trailer /tráylər/ *n* **1** a vehicle for towing behind another vehicle **2** the rear part of an articulated lorry **3** *US, Can* a caravan for living in **4** an advertisement for a film or television programme, containing extracts from it **5** somebody or something that lags behind

train *n* **1** a number of linked railway carriages **2** a trailing part of a gown **3** a long moving line **4** the people and vehicles supporting an army **5** a sequence of events, actions, or things **6** an entourage ■ *v* **1** *vti* learn or teach skills **2** *vt* domesticate an animal **3** *vti* prepare for a sporting competition **4** *vt* make a plant or hair grow as wanted **5** *vt* focus or aim a device ○ *trained her binoculars on the nest* —**training** *n* ◊ See note at **teach**

trainee /tray neé/ *n* somebody who is undergoing training —**traineeship** *n*

trainer /tráynər/ *n* **1** somebody who trains animals or people **2** a training apparatus **3** a sports shoe with a thick cushioned sole, often worn as leisurewear

training college *n* a college where teachers are trained

trainspotting /tráyn spoting/ *n* the hobby of collecting railway locomotive numbers

traipse *vi* **(traipsing, traipsed)** walk ploddingly *(infml)* ■ *n* a tiring walk

trait /trayt, tray/ *n* **1** an individual characteristic **2** an inherited characteristic

traitor /tráytər/ *n* a disloyal person, especially one who commits treason —**traitorous** *adj*

Trajan /tráyjən/ (53?–117) Roman emperor (AD98–117)

trajectory /trə jéktəri/ (*pl* **-ries**) *n* the path of a flying object

Trajkovski /trī kófski/, **Boris** (*b.* 1956) president of the Former Yugoslav Republic of Macedonia (1999–)

tram *n* **1** a passenger vehicle that runs on rails in the road **2** a vehicle on rails used in a coal mine

~~tramatic~~ incorrect spelling of **traumatic**

trammel /trámm'l/ *n* something that limits freedom ■ *vt* **(-melling, -melled) 1** restrain or confine **2** ensnare

tramp *n* **1** a homeless person who moves from place to place **2** *UK* a long journey on foot **3** the sound of walking feet **4** a heavy step **5** a cargo ship without a regular route **6** an offensive term for a woman regarded as sexually promiscuous ■ *v* **1** *vi* tread heavily **2** *vi* walk a long way **3** *vt* cover a particular distance wearily on foot **4** *vt* crush something underfoot **5** *vi* *NZ* hike in the bush —**tramper** *n* —**trampish** *adj*

trample /trámp'l/ **(-pling, -pled)** *vti* **1** tread heavily on something **2** treat somebody arrogantly

trampoline /trámpə leen/ *n* a stretched canvas for gymnastic tumbling and jumping —**trampoline** *vi* —**trampoliner** *n* —**trampolinist** *n*

tramway /trám way/ *n* **1** the lines that trams run on **2** a transport system that uses trams

trance *n* **1** a dazed state **2** a hypnotic or cataleptic state **3** a rapturous state

tranche /traansh/ *n* a portion or section of something, especially an amount of money

tranquil /trángkwil/ *adj* **1** free from commotion **2** free from anxiety or agitation —**tranquillity** /trang kwílləti/ *n* —**tranquilly** *adv*

tranquilize *vti* US = **tranquillize**

tranquillize /trángkwi līz/ **(-lizing, -lized), tranquillise** *vti* make or become calm, especially using medication —**tranquillization** /trángkwi līzáysh'n/ *n*

tranquillizer /trángkwi līzər/, **tranquilliser** *n* **1** a calming drug. Use: treatment of anxiety, neuroses, psychoses. **2** something that makes a person or animal calm

trans. *abbr* **1** transaction **2** transferred **3** transitive **4** translated **5** translation **6** transport **7** transpose **8** transverse

trans- *prefix* **1** across, on the other side of, beyond ○ *transcontinental* **2** through ○ *transfusion* **3** indicating change, transfer, or conversion ○ *transliterate*

transact /tran zákt, -sákt/ *vt* conduct business

transaction /tran záksh'n, -sák-/ *n* **1** a business deal **2** the act of negotiating **3** an interaction *(fml)* **4** an addition to a database —**transactional** *adj*

transatlantic /tránzət lántik/ *adj* **1** beyond the Atlantic **2** crossing the Atlantic

Transcaucasia /tránz kaw káyzhə, -káyzi ə/ region of SE Europe, between the Black and Caspian seas. It consists of the republics of Georgia, Armenia, and Azerbaijan. —**Transcaucasian** *adj, n*

transceiver /tran seévər/ *n* **1** a combined radio transmitter and receiver **2** a data transmitter and receiver

transcend /tran sénd/ *vt* **1** go beyond a limit **2** surpass something in quality or achievement

transcendent /tran séndənt/ *adj* **1** superior in quality or achievement **2** beyond the limits of experience **3** beyond all known categories **4** independent of the material world —**transcendence** *n* —**transcendent** *n* —**transcendentness** *n*

transcendental /trán sen dént'l/ *adj* **1** not experienced but knowable **2** mystical —**transcendentally** *adv*

transcendental meditation *n* a form of meditation in which a mantra is repeated

transcontinental /tránz konti nént'l/ *adj* **1** extending across a continent **2** from or on the other side of a continent

transcribe /tran skríb/ (**-scribing, -scribed**) vt
1 write a copy of something 2 write something out in full form from notes 3 write sounds phonetically 4 arrange a piece of music for a different instrument 5 record something for later broadcasting

transcript /trán skript/ n a written record

transcription /tran skrípsh'n/ n 1 the process of transcribing something 2 something transcribed —**transcriptional** adj

transducer /tranz dyoóssər/ n a device that transforms one type of energy into another

transept /trán sept/ n 1 the crosswise part of a church 2 an arm of a transept

transfer v /transs fúr/ (**-ferring, -ferred**) 1 vti move from one place or thing to another 2 vti pass from one person to another 3 vti start working, playing a game, or studying elsewhere, or send or tell somebody to do so 4 vti change vehicles or aircraft 5 vt give ownership of something to somebody 6 vt copy an image onto another surface ■ n /tránss fur/ 1 a change of place 2 a design applied to a surface 3 a player or worker who is transferred 4 the passing of property to a new owner —**transferable** adj —**transferral** /transs fúrəl/ n

~~transfered~~ incorrect spelling of **transferred**

transference /tránssfərənss/ n 1 the act of transferring something from one place or person to another 2 the process of being transferred

transfer fee n a fee for a professional player moving from one club to another before the first contract has expired

transfer list n a list of players who are eligible for transfer

transfigure /transs fíggər/ (**-uring, -ured**) vt change the appearance of to reveal great beauty or spirituality —**transfiguration** /transs figgə ráysh'n/ n —**transfigurement** n

transfix /transs fíks/ vt 1 pierce somebody or something through with a weapon 2 make somebody immobile with shock —**transfixion** n

transform /transs fáwrm/ vti change completely or dramatically —**transformable** adj —**transformation** /tránsfər máysh'n/ n —**transformational** adj —**transformationally** adv—**transformative** adj◊ See note at **change**

transformer /transs fáwrmər/ n 1 a device that changes electrical voltage, current, phase, or impedance 2 somebody or something that transforms

transfuse /transs fyoóz/ (**-fusing, -fused**) vt 1 spread throughout something and affect every part of it 2 give a blood transfusion to

transfusion /transs fyoózh'n/ n the process of transferring blood or blood products into somebody's bloodstream

transgender /trans jéndər, tranz-/ adj of transgendered people

transgendered /trans géndərd, tranz-/ adj adopting the dress, behaviour, or physiology of a member of the opposite sex

transgenic /tranz jénnik/ adj 1 with genes from a different species 2 involving the transfer of genetic material

transgress /tranz gréss/ v 1 vi do something wrong 2 vt break a law —**transgression** n —**transgressive** adj —**transgressor** n

transient /tránzi ənt/ adj 1 short in duration 2 not permanently settled in a place ■ n somebody who stays in a place only briefly —**transience** n —**transiently** adv

transistor /tran zístər/ n 1 a small solid-state electronic device used as an amplifier and rectifier 2 also **transistor radio** a small portable radio

transistorize /tran zístə ríz/ (**-izing, -ized**), **transistorise** vt equip with transistors

transit /tránzit/ n 1 the act of travelling across or through a place 2 US, Can a system of public transport 3 the passage of a planet across the Sun ■ vti pass or cause to pass through a place

transit camp n a camp set up for people such as refugees or soldiers who are temporarily in a region

transition /tran zísh'n/ n the process of change from one state, form, style, or activity to another —**transitional** adj

transitive /tránssətiv/ adj describes a verb that requires a direct object —**transitively** adv —**transitivity** /tránssə tívvəti/ n

transit lounge n an airport waiting room for passengers who are making a connecting flight

transitory /tránssətəri/ adj not permanent or lasting —**transitorily** adv —**transitoriness** n ◊ See note at **temporary**

translate /transs láyt/ (**-lating, -lated**) v 1 vti turn words into a different language 2 vi be capable of being translated 3 vt convert computer data to a different form 4 vt rephrase something in simpler terms 5 vt interpret the meaning of something 6 vti change the form of something, or undergo a change in form —**translatable** adj —**translator** n

translation /transs láysh'n/ n 1 a version of a word, phrase, or text in another language 2 the act of translating something into a different language —**translational** adj

transliterate /transs líttə rayt, tranz-/ (**-ating, -ated**) vt transcribe something into another alphabet —**transliteration** /transs líttə ráysh'n, tranz-/ n

translucent /transs loóss'nt/ adj letting only some light through —**translucence** n —**translucency** n

transmigration /tránz mī gráysh'n/ n 1 movement from or to another region or country 2 in some religions, the passing of the soul after death into another body —**transmigrate** vi —**transmigrational** adj

transmission /tranz mísh'n/ n 1 the act of transmitting something 2 something that is transmitted 3 a radio or TV broadcast 4 a mechanism in a motor vehicle that transfers power from the engine to the wheels **5** *US* a set of gears in a vehicle

transmit /tranz mít/ (**-mitting, -mitted**) *v* **1** *vt* send something or pass something on to another place or person **2** *vt* communicate information **3** *vti* send a signal **4** *vti* broadcast a programme —**transmissible** *adj* —**transmissive** *adj* —**transmittable** *adj* —**transmittal** *n*

transmitter /tranz mítter/ *n* **1** an agent or means of transmission **2** a piece of broadcasting equipment that generates and sends out radio waves

transmogrify /tranz móggri fí/ (**-fies, -fied**) *vt* change the form or appearance of, especially grotesquely —**transmogrification** /tranz móggrifi káysh'n/ *n*

transmute /tranz myoót/ (**-muting, -muted**) *vti* **1** change from one form, substance, or state to another **2** change from one chemical element to another, or undergo this change —**transmutable** *adj* —**transmutation** /tránz myoo táysh'n/ *n* ◊ See note at **change**

transnational /tranz násh'nəl/ *adj* including, extending over, or operating in several nations

transom /tránssəm/ *n* **1** a crosspiece above a window or door or in a window **2** the planking at a ship's stern —**transomed** *adj*

transparency /transs párrənssi/ (*pl* **-cies**) *n* **1** the state of being transparent **2** a positive photographic image on transparent material

transparent /transs párrənt/ *adj* **1** easily seen through **2** fine enough to see through **3** obvious and easy to recognize **4** frank and open —**transparently** *adv*

transpire /tran spír/ (**-spiring, -spired**) *v* **1** *vt* come to light **2** *vi* happen **3** *vti* give off a vapour through the pores —**transpiration** /tránsspi ráysh'n/ *n*

transplant *vt* /transs plaánt/ **1** relocate a plant **2** move somebody to another place **3** transfer a body organ from one place or body to another ■ *n* /tránss plaánt/ **1** a surgical procedure in which an organ is transplanted **2** a transplanted organ or tissue —**transplantation** /tránss plaan táysh'n/ *n*

transpolar /tranz pólər/ *adj* crossing a polar region

transponder /tran spóndər/, **transpondor** *n* **1** a radio or radar transceiver **2** a satellite receiver and transmitter

transport *vt* /transs páwrt/ **1** carry or take something somewhere **2** make somebody imagine being elsewhere **3** affect somebody with strong emotion ■ *n* /tráns pawrt/ **1** the transporting of people or goods from one place to another **2** a means of transporting people or goods **3** a vehicle that carries people or goods **4** an experience or display of intense emotion (*often pl*) —**transportability** /tránss pawrtə bílləti/ *n* —**transportable** *adj*

transportation /tránsspawr táysh'n/ *n US, Can* transport of people or goods, or a means of transport

transporter /transs páwrtər/ *n* **1** somebody or something that transports something **2** a large vehicle for heavy loads

transpose /trans póz/ (**-posing, -posed**) *v* **1** *vt* reverse the order of things **2** *vt* move something to a different position **3** *vt* change the setting of something ◊ *transposing the action from Shakespeare's time to the present* **4** *vti* change a piece of music to a different key —**transposal** *n* —**transposition** /tránsspə zísh'n/ *n*

transputer /tranz pyoótər/ *n* a powerful microchip with the capability of a microprocessor

transsexual /tranz sékshoo əl/ *n* **1** somebody who has undergone treatment to change his or her anatomical sex **2** somebody who identifies himself or herself as a member of the opposite sex —**transsexual** *adj* —**transsexualism** *n*

transubstantiation /tránssəb stanshi áysh'n/ *n* **1** the doctrine of the Roman Catholic and Eastern Orthodox Christian churches that the bread and wine in Communion become the body and blood of Christ **2** the process in which one substance changes into another (*fml*) —**transubstantiationalist** *n*

Transvaal /tránz vaal/ former province of South Africa, in the northeast of the country

transverse /tranz vúrss/ *adj* going across something ■ *n* a crosswise part —**transversely** *adv*

transvestite /tranz vés tīt/ *n* somebody who dresses like the opposite sex —**transvestism** *n*

Transylvania /tránssil váyni ə/ historic region in E Europe that now forms the central and northwestern parts of Romania —**Transylvanian** *adj*, *n*

Transylvanian Alps mountain range in the Carpathian Mountains, extending through south-central Romania. Highest peak Mt Moldoveanu, 2,544 m/8,395 ft.

trap *n* **1** a device designed to catch animals **2** a scheme to catch somebody out **3** a confining situation **4** a device such as a curved section of a drainpipe that prevents the passage of gas **5** a trapdoor **6** the mouth (*infml*) **7** a starting stall for a greyhound ■ *v* (**trapping, trapped**) **1** *vt* catch something in a trap **2** *vi* set traps for animals **3** *vt* hold something in a tight grip or narrow space **4** *vt* place somebody in a confining situation **5** *vt* take somebody by surprise **6** *vt* prevent air from escaping —**trapper** *n*

trapdoor /tráp dawr/ *n* a movable panel in a floor or ceiling

trapeze /trə peéz/ *n* a bar attached to suspended ropes, used by acrobats

ORIGIN Trapeze came through French from the Latin word that was separately adopted as *trapezium* 'four-sided figure'. The reference was to the shape made by the trapeze's ropes and crossbar and the roof or other supporting structure. **Trapeze** is first recorded in English in the mid-19C.

trapezium /trə peézi əm/ (pl **-ums** or **-a** /-zi ə/) n a quadrilateral with two parallel sides —**trapezial** adj

trapezoid /tráppi zoyd/ n a quadrilateral with no parallel sides —**trapezoidal** /tráppi zóyd'l/ adj

trappings /tráppingz/ npl 1 accessories and outward signs 2 an ornamental harness for a horse

Trappist /tráppist/ n a member of a silent austere Christian order of monks

trapshooting /tráp shooting/ n shooting at clay pigeons —**trapshooter** n

trash n 1 nonsense 2 poor quality literature or art 3 US, Can discarded material 4 US an offensive term for somebody regarded as socially or morally inferior ■ vt destroy something (infml)

trashy /tráshi/ (**-ier, -iest**) adj of little worth or merit —**trashily** adv —**trashiness** n

trattoria /tráttə reé ə/ (pl **-as** or **-e** /-ay/) n a simple Italian restaurant

trauma /tráwmə/ (pl **-mas** or **-mata** /-mətə/) n 1 a deep emotional shock, often having long-lasting psychological effects 2 a physical injury —**traumatic** /traw máttik/ adj —**traumatize** vt

travail /trávvayl/ n 1 hard work 2 childbirth (archaic) —**travail** vi

travel /trávv'l/ v (**travelling, travelled**) 1 vi go on a journey 2 vt journey through an area 3 vt cover a particular distance 4 vi go at a particular speed 5 vi tolerate being transported o Some products do not travel well. 6 vi be transmitted o News travels fast. 7 vi move in a path while operating ■ n 1 the activity of travelling 2 the total distance a mechanical part moves ■ **travels** npl a series of journeys ■ adj for travellers

travel agency n a business that arranges travel —**travel agent** n

travelator n = travolator

travelcard /trávv'l kaard/ n a multi-journey public transport ticket

traveler n US = traveller

traveller /trávv'lər/ n 1 somebody on a journey 2 somebody who has travelled 3 a travelling salesperson 4 a member of a group of people who live an itinerant lifestyle

traveller's cheque n an internationally accepted cheque

travelogue /trávvə log/ n a film or lecture on travel

travel sickness n a sick feeling caused by movement —**travel-sick** adj

traverse /trávvurss, trə vúrss/ v (**-versing, -versed**) 1 vt move across an area 2 vti move back and forth across something 3 vt extend across something 4 vti move at an angle across a rock face while ascending or descending 5 vti follow a zigzag course down a ski slope ■ n 1 a journey or route across, over, or through something 2 a crosswise beam, barrier, or other element ■ adj crosswise —**traversable** adj —**traversal** n

travesty /trávvəsti/ (pl **-ties**) n 1 false representation 2 a grotesque imitation of something —**travesty** vt

ORIGIN Travesty was taken in the mid-17C from French travesti 'dressed in disguise'. The Latin elements from which the French derived were also used to form transvestite.

travolator /trávvə laytər/, **travelator** n a moving walkway for pedestrians

trawl n 1 a commercial fishing net dragged along the sea bottom 2 a suspended fishing line with smaller lines attached to it ■ vti 1 fish with a trawl 2 search through a large amount of information

trawler /tráwlər/ n 1 a fishing boat used in trawling 2 somebody who trawls —**trawlerman** n

tray n 1 a flat carrier for small objects 2 the objects carried on a tray

treacherous /tréchərəss/ adj 1 betraying trust or confidence 2 involving hidden dangers —**treacherously** adv —**treacherousness** n

treachery /tréchəri/ n betrayal

treacle /treek'l/ n 1 syrup from sugar refining. Use: cakes, sweets, puddings. 2 something cloying —**treacly** adj

ORIGIN Etymologically, **treacle** is an 'antidote to the bite of wild animals'. It came through French and Latin from Greek. **Treacle** retained its meaning of 'antidote' when it came into English, but later broadened out into 'medicine'. The practice of disguising the unpleasant taste of medicine with sugar syrup led in the 17C to its application to 'syrup'.

tread /tred/ v (**trod, trodden** /tródd'n/ or **trod**) 1 vi put a foot on something, especially heavily 2 vti walk or step on, across, or along something 3 vt spread something dirty by walking 4 vt form a path by walking a particular course 5 vi act in a particular way ■ n 1 a way or act of treading 2 the horizontal part of a step 3 the width of a step 4 the grooved outer surface of a tyre —**treadless** adj

treadle /trédd'l/ n a foot-operated pedal ■ vti (**-ling, -led**) power a machine with a treadle

treadmill /tréd mil/ n 1 a device that is turned by people or animals walking on it, providing power 2 an exercise machine on which you can walk or run

treason /treéz'n/ n betrayal of your country

treasonable /treéz'nəb'l/, **treasonous** /treéz'nəss/ adj of treason, or punishable as treason

treasure /trézhər/ n 1 jewels and precious objects 2 somebody or something considered valuable ■ vt (**-uring, -ured**) 1 regard as valuable 2 accumulate and store as something valuable

treasure hunt n a game in which players solve a series of clues leading to a hidden prize

treasurer /trézhərər/ n 1 a manager of the finances of an organization 2 **Treasurer** Aus the federal government's finance minister —**treasurership** n

treasure trove /-trōv/ n **1** money found buried in the earth **2** anything of value that is discovered

treasury /tréžhəri/ (pl **-ies**) n **1** a place for things of value **2** a store of money **3** a collection of valuable things **4 Treasury** in many countries, the government department responsible for managing revenue

treat /treet/ v **1** vt regard or deal with somebody or something in a particular way **2** vt give medical aid to cure an illness or patient **3** vt subject something to a process or agent **4** vt pay for somebody else's food, drink, or entertainment **5** vt provide somebody with something pleasurable **6** vi discuss a topic ■ n **1** an entertainment paid for by somebody else **2** the act of paying for somebody else **3** something enjoyable —**treatable** adj

treatise /treétiss, -iz/ n a detailed written account of a subject

treatment /treétmənt/ n **1** the provision of medical care **2** a particular remedy or medical procedure **3** a way of handling something **4** the presentation of a subject **5** an act of subjecting something to a physical, chemical, or biological process or agent

treaty /treéti/ (pl **-ties**) n **1** an agreement between countries **2** a pact

treble /trébb'l/ adj **1** three times as many or as much **2** of the highest musical range ■ n **1** a high-pitched instrument, voice, or sound **2** the higher audio frequency range in sound reproduction **3** a control for high-frequency audio responses **4** something that is tripled **5** a set of three wins ■ vti (**-ling, -led**) make or become three times as many or as much —**trebly** adv

treble clef n a clef that puts G above middle C on the second line

~~trecherous~~ incorrect spelling of **treacherous**

tree n **1** a large perennial woody plant, usually with a single main stem **2** a large plant resembling a tree **3** something that is branched like a tree **4** a wooden support **5** a diagram of a branching hierarchical structure **6** a hierarchical data structure ■ vt (**treed**) force up a tree —**treeless** adj

tree fern n a large tropical fern that grows to tree height

tree house n a platform or house in a tree

tree line n **1** the boundary of tree growth on a hillside or mountainside **2** the edge of a forest

tree surgeon n somebody who treats diseased or damaged trees —**tree surgery** n

treetop /treé top/ n the top of a tree

treeware /teé wair/ n books and other material printed on paper made from wood pulp

trek vi (**trekking, trekked**) **1** make a long difficult journey **2** go slowly or laboriously **3** S Africa go by ox wagon ■ n **1** a long difficult journey **2** S Africa a stage of a journey —**trekker** n

trellis /trélliss/ n **1** a lattice for supporting a plant **2** any latticework structure

tremble /trémb'l/ (**-bling, -bled**) vi **1** shake slightly but uncontrollably **2** vibrate **3** be afraid —**tremble** n —**trembling** adj

tremendous /trə méndəss/ adj **1** very large, powerful, or great **2** very good, successful, or impressive —**tremendously** adv

tremolo /trémmələ̄/ (pl **-los**) n **1** a quavering sound in music produced by rapid repetition of a tone or rapid alternation between two tones **2** a device for producing a tremolo

tremor /trémmər/ n **1** a minor earthquake **2** a trembling, e.g. from fear or illness —**tremorous** adj

tremulous /trémmyŏŏləss/ adj **1** trembling **2** fearful —**tremulously** adv

trench n **1** a deep ditch with steep sides **2** a long excavation, used as protection against enemy fire —**trench** vt

trenchant /trénchənt/ adj **1** direct and deliberately hurtful **2** effective and incisive —**trenchancy** n

trench coat n a long double-breasted raincoat with a belt

trencher /trénchər/ n a wooden platter (archaic)

trench warfare n **1** warfare between armies in trenches **2** long-standing and bitter conflict

trend n **1** a tendency **2** a prevailing style ■ vi tend or move

trendsetter /trénd setər/ n somebody or something starting a trend —**trendsetting** adj

trendy /tréndi/ (**-ier, -iest**) adj adopting the latest fad (infml) —**trendily** adv —**trendiness** n

Trenton /tréntən/ capital of New Jersey. Pop. 84,494 (1998).

trepan /tri pán/ n an early type of surgical instrument used to cut a hole in the skull ■ vt (**-panning, -panned**) remove a circle of bone with a trepan —**trepanation** /tréppə náysh'n/ n

trepidation /tréppi dáysh'n/ n apprehension

trespass /tréspəss/ vi **1** enter somebody else's land unlawfully **2** encroach on somebody's privacy or time **3** break a moral or social law (archaic) ■ n **1** unlawful entry onto somebody else's land **2** a sin (archaic) —**trespasser** n

tress n a lock of hair

trestle /tréss'l/ n **1** a supporting framework consisting of a horizontal beam with a pair of splayed legs at each end **2** a tower for supporting a bridge

trestle table n a table with a top supported on trestles

trews /trooz/ npl close-fitting tartan trousers

tri- prefix three, third o **trilateral**

triad /trí ad, -əd/ n **1** a set of three **2** a musical chord consisting of three notes **3 Triad** a secret Chinese criminal organization —**triadic** /trí áddik/ adj

triage /treé aazh, trí ij/ n the process of prioritizing patients for medical treatment

trial /trí əl/ n **1** a formal legal process to determine an issue **2** a difficult test **3** a painful experience **4** a troublesome person or thing **5** an effort (fml) ■ **trials** npl competitions for animals ■ *adj* 1 experimental 2 of a court trial ■ *vt* (**-alling, -alled**) test something

trial balloon *n* a proposal put forward to test opinion

trial run *n* a test of something new

triangle /trī ang g'l/ *n* 1 a three-sided geometrical figure 2 an object with three sides 3 a percussion instrument consisting of a metal bar bent into a triangle shape —**triangular** /trī áng gyōolər/ *adj* —**triangularity** /trī áng gyōo lárrəti/ *n*

Triassic /trī ássik/ *n* a period of geological time 248–206 million years ago —**Triassic** *adj*

triathlon /trī áthlən, -lon/ *n* an athletic contest with three long-distance events —**triathlete** *n*

tribalism /tríbəlizəm/ *n* 1 the customs and social organization of a tribe 2 allegiance to a group —**tribalistic** /tríbə lístik/ *adj*

tribe *n* 1 a society whose members have common ancestors, customs, and leadership 2 a group with something in common —**tribal** *adj* —**tribally** *adv*

tribesman /tríbzmən/ (*pl* -**men** /-mən/) *n* a man tribe member

tribespeople /tríbz peep'l/ *npl* members of a tribe

tribeswoman /tríbz wōomən/ (*pl* -**women** /-wimin/) *n* a woman tribe member

tribulation /tríbbyōo láysh'n/ *n* 1 great hardship or distress 2 a cause of suffering

tribunal /trī byōon'l, tri-/ *n* 1 a law court 2 a body appointed to make a judgment or carry out an inquiry

tribune /tríbbyoon/ *n* 1 a representative elected by the Roman common people 2 a defender of public rights —**tribuneship** *n*

tributary /tríbbyōōtəri/ *n* (*pl* -**ies**) 1 a stream that feeds a larger body of water 2 somebody who pays a monetary tribute ■ *adj* 1 flowing into a larger body of water 2 paid as a tribute

tribute /tríbbyoot/ *n* 1 an expression of gratitude or praise 2 evidence of the value of something 3 payment made by one ruler to another

trice *n* a brief moment

tricentennial /trí sen ténni əl, trís'n-/ *adj* a 300th anniversary

triceps /trí seps/ (*pl* -**cepses** *or* same) *n* a muscle attached at three points, especially the muscle at the back of the upper arm

triceratops /trī sérrə tops/ *n* a three-horned plant-eating dinosaur

trick /trik/ *n* 1 a cunning deception 2 a prank 3 a special skill ○ *taught me the tricks of the trade* 4 a skilful act designed to entertain people 5 a deceptive effect of light 6 a peculiar habit 7 an unforeseen event ○ *a cruel trick of fate* 8 the cards won by a player in a round ■ *vt* cheat or deceive ■ *adj* 1 of tricks 2 made as an imitation so that it can be used to play a joke on somebody ◇ **do the trick** be effective and do what is needed (*infml*) ◇ **not miss**

a **trick** notice everything that is happening (*infml*)

□ **trick out** *or* **trick up** *vt* decorate or dress up

trickery /tríkəri/ (*pl* -**ies**) *n* the use of tricks or deception

trickle /trik'l/ (-**ling**, -**led**) *v* 1 *vti* flow, or cause to flow, slowly in a thin stream 2 *vi* move slowly or gradually —**trickle** *n* —**trickling** *adj*

trickle-down theory *n* the economic theory that financial benefits received by big businesses and wealthy people will spread to the rest of society

trick or treat *n* a Halloween custom in which children playfully threaten to play tricks on neighbours unless they are given sweets ■ *interj* a greeting used when trick-or-treating

trick-or-treat *vi* ask for sweets at Halloween

trickster /tríkstər/ *n* somebody who plays tricks

tricksy /tríksi/ *adj* 1 mischievous 2 not straightforward —**tricksiness** *n*

tricky /tríki/ (-**ier**, -**iest**) *adj* 1 difficult to do or deal with 2 crafty or sly —**trickily** *adv* —**trickiness** *n*

tricolour /tríkələr, trí kulər/ *n* 1 a three-coloured flag 2 *also* **Tricolour** the French national flag ■ *adj also* **tricoloured** 1 three-coloured 2 piebald

tricycle /tríssik'l/ *n* a three-wheeled vehicle, usually driven by pedals —**tricycle** *vi* —**tricyclist** *n*

trident /tríd'nt/ *n* 1 a three-pronged spear 2 in classical mythology, the three-pronged spear of Poseidon or Neptune

tried past tense, past participle of **try** ■ *adj* (*often in combination*) 1 proved to be good 2 subjected to stress or worry

triennial /trī énni əl/ *adj* 1 happening every three years 2 lasting three years ■ *n* 1 a 3rd anniversary 2 a three-yearly event —**triennially** *adv*

Trieste /tri ést/ seaport of Friuli-Venezia Region, NE Italy. Pop. 217,865 (1999).

Trieste, Gulf of inlet of the N Adriatic Sea, bordered by Italy, Slovenia, and Croatia

trifecta /trī féktə/ *n* Aus, US, Can a bet on the first three winners in a race

trifle /trīf'l/ *n* 1 something trivial 2 a small quantity 3 a cold dessert made with sponge cake topped with custard or cream —**trifler** *n* ◇ **a trifle** slightly or somewhat (*fml or humorous*)

□ **trifle with** *vt* treat thoughtlessly

trifling /trífling/ *adj* 1 insignificant 2 frivolous —**triflingly** *adv*

trigger /tríggər/ *n* 1 a small lever that fires a gun 2 a lever that operates a mechanism 3 a stimulus for something ■ *vt* 1 set something off, or make something happen 2 fire a weapon by pulling a trigger

trigger-happy *adj* (*infml*) 1 overeager to fire a gun 2 rash

trigonometry /tríggə nómmətri/ *n* the branch of mathematics that deals with functions of angles and arcs —**trigonometric** /tríggənə méttrik/ adj —**trigonometrical** adj

trike n a tricycle (infml)

trilateral /trī láttərəl/ adj **1** three-sided **2** involving three countries or parties ■ n a three-sided geometrical figure —**trilaterally** adv

trilby /trílbi/ (pl -**bies**) n a soft felt hat with a deep crease in the crown and a narrow brim

---

ORIGIN The **trilby** derives from the name of Trilby O'Ferrall, heroine of the novel Trilby (1894) by the French-born novelist and illustrator George du Maurier (1834–96). Trilby was an artist's model who fell under the spell of the hypnotist Svengali. In the stage version of the book, the character Trilby wore a soft felt hat with an indented top, and the style soon became fashionable.

---

trilingual /trī líng gwəl/ adj **1** knowing three languages **2** written in three languages —**trilingual** n —**trilingualism** n —**trilingually** adv

trill n **1** a warbling sound **2** a melodic ornament consisting of a rapid alternation between two notes —**trill** vti

trillion /tríllyən/ (pl same or -**lions**) n **1** the number 1 followed by 12 zeros **2** the number 1 followed by 18 zeros (dated) —**trillion** adj

trilobite /trílə bīt/ n an extinct sea arthropod of the Palaeozoic era with a flat oval body in three sections

trilogy /tríllaji/ (pl -**gies**) n a set of three related artistic works

trim v (**trimming**, **trimmed**) **1** vt make something tidy by cutting **2** vt cut something to the required size **3** vt remove an excess by cutting **4** vt decorate something **5** vti change the arrangement of sails on a boat **6** vt make adjustments to improve an aircraft's stability in flight ■ adj (**trimmer**, **trimmest**) **1** slim and fit-looking **2** neat and tidy ■ n **1** an act of cutting something, e.g. hair, to neaten it **2** a decoration **3** decorative parts of a motor vehicle **4** decorative additions to a building **5** something trimmed off, e.g. film cut during editing **6** adjustment of an aircraft for stability **7** the appearance of a vessel ready to sail —**trim** adv —**trimly** adv —**trimming** n —**trimness** n

trimaran /trímə ran, trímə rán/ n a sailing boat with three hulls

Trimble /trímb'l/, **David** (b. 1944) first minister of the Northern Ireland Assembly (1998–)

trimester /trī méstər/ n a period of three months —**trimestral** adj

trimmer /trímmər/ n **1** a device used for trimming **2** somebody who alters an opinion according to circumstances (disapproving)

Trinidad /trínni dad/ island in the Caribbean, part of Trinidad and Tobago. Pop. 1,065,245 (1998). —**Trinidadian** /trínni dáddi ən/ n, adj

Trinidad and Tobago country in the Caribbean, comprising two islands off the NE

coast of Venezuela. Cap. Port-of-Spain. Pop. 1,169,682 (2001).

trinity /trínnəti/ (pl -**ties**) n **1** a group of three **2** **Trinity** in Christianity, the union of the Father, Son, and Holy Spirit in a single God

trinket /tríngkit/ n **1** an ornament or piece of jewellery of little value **2** something trivial

trio /tree ō/ (pl -**os**) n **1** a group of three related people or things **2** a group of three musicians playing together **3** a musical composition for three players

trip n **1** a journey or outing **2** a fall or stumble **3** a light or nimble step **4** an error **5** a switch that activates a mechanism **6** a drug-induced hallucination (infml) ■ v (**tripping**, **tripped**) **1** vti stumble or fall, or cause to stumble or fall, by catching the foot **2** vti make or cause to make a mistake **3** vi move with rapid light steps **4** vt cause a device to operate **5** vi experience hallucinatory drug effects (infml) **6** vi go on a trip —**tripper** n

tripartite /trī paár tīt/ adj **1** involving three parties or groups **2** having or divided into three parts

tripe n **1** the stomach lining of a cow or sheep as food **2** rubbish or nonsense (infml)

trip hop n a rhythmic dance music

triple /trípp'l/ adj **1** having three parts **2** three times as much **3** done three times ■ vti (-**pling**, -**pled**) make or become three times as much ■ n **1** something three times greater than usual or another, e.g. a measure of spirits **2** a set of three —**triply** adv

triple crown, Triple Crown n victory in a set of three sports events

triple jump n an athletic event involving three jumps, landing on one foot, then the other, then both feet, in continuous motion

triplet /trípplət/ n **1** a group of three related things **2** any of three offspring born together **3** a group of three musical notes played in the time of two

triplicate n /trípplikət/ the state of having three identical parts or copies ○ in triplicate ■ adj /trípplikət/ threefold ■ vt /tríppli kayt/ (-**cating**, -**cated**) make three copies of —**triplication** /tríppli káysh'n/ n

tripod /trī pod/ n **1** a three-legged support, e.g. for a camera **2** a three-legged object, e.g. a cauldron or stool —**tripodal** /tríppəd'l/ adj

Tripoli /tríppəli/ capital of Libya. Pop. 1,682,000 (1995).

triptych /tríptik/ n a work of art in three panels

tripwire /tríp wīr/ n a wire that activates a trap, alarm, or other device

Triratna /tree rátnə/ n the three principal components of Buddhism, namely the Buddha or teacher, the teaching, and the priesthood

trisect /trī sékt/ vt divide into three parts —**trisection** n

trite (**triter**, **tritest**) adj overused and lacking originality —**tritely** adv —**triteness** n

tritium /trítti əm/ n (symbol **T**) a radioactive isotope of hydrogen

triumph /trí umf/ *n* **1** a success or victory **2** great joy or pride about success or victory ■ *vi* **1** win or succeed **2** be exultant —**triumphal** /trī úmf'l/ *adj* —**triumphant** /trī úmfənt/ *adj* —**triumphantly** *adv*

triumvirate /trī úmvərət/ *n* **1** a group of three rulers of ancient Rome **2** a group of three people sharing authority **3** the term of office of a triumvirate —**triumvir** *n* —**triumviral** *adj*

trivet /trívvit/ *n* a three-legged stand or support, e.g. for a hot dish

trivia /trívvi ə/ *n* unimportant things (+ *sing* or *pl verb*)

trivial /trívvi əl/ *adj* **1** having little importance or value **2** commonplace —**triviality** /trívvi álləti/ *n* —**trivially** *adv*

ORIGIN Medieval teachers and scholars recognized seven liberal arts: the lower three, grammar, logic, and rhetoric, were known as the *trivium*, and the upper four, arithmetic, astronomy, geometry, and music, were known as the *quadrivium*. The notion of 'less important subjects' led in the 16C to the use of the derived adjective **trivial** for 'commonplace, of little importance'.

trivialize /trívvi ə līz/ (**-izing, -ized**), **trivialise** *vt* treat something as less important or valuable than it really is —**trivialization** /trívvi ə īt záysh'n/ *n*

trochee /trốki/ *n* a metrical foot consisting of a stressed syllable followed by an unstressed syllable —**trochaic** /trō káy ik/ *adj*

trod past tense, past participle of **tread**

trodden past participle of **tread**

troglodyte /trógglə dīt/ *n* **1** a cave dweller **2** somebody living in seclusion —**troglodytic** /trógglə dittik/ *adj*

troika /tróykə/ *n* a Russian carriage drawn by three horses harnessed abreast

Trojan /trójən/ *n* **1** a citizen of ancient Troy **2** a determined or courageous person —**Trojan** *adj*

Trojan Horse *n* **1** in Greek mythology, a hollow horse containing Greek soldiers, left at the gates of Troy **2** a treacherous or subversive element concealed within an organization **3** a destructive computer program

Trojan War *n* the ten-year siege of Troy by the Greeks to recover Helen, the abducted wife of King Menelaus

troll[1] /trōl/ *vti* fish by dragging a baited line through water behind a boat —**troll** *n* —**troller** *n*

troll[2] /trōl, trol/ *n* in Scandinavian folklore, an imaginary being depicted as a giant or a dwarf that lives in caves or under bridges

trolley /trólli/ *n* (*pl* **-leys**) **1** a wheeled cart, e.g. for luggage or shopping, pushed by hand **2** a wheeled hospital bed **3** a wheeled table for food and drink **4** *also* **trolleybus** an electric bus powered by overhead wires **5** a device that collects power from an overhead

wire **6** a cart on rails or suspended from a rail ■ *vti* (**-leys, -leying, -leyed**) move by trolley

trollop /trólləp/ *n* an offensive term for a woman regarded as promiscuous or untidy (*dated*)

Trollope /trólləp/, **Anthony** (1815–82) British novelist —**Trollopian** /trólla peé ən/ *adj*

trombone /trom bốn/ *n* a brass musical instrument with a U-shaped sliding part —**trombonist** *n*

trompe l'oeil /tromp lőyə/ (*pl* **trompe l'oeils** /*pronunc. same*/) *n* **1** a painting technique that creates an illusion of three-dimensionality **2** an artistic work that uses trompe l'oeil

Trondheim /trónd hīm/ city in central Norway, on **Trondheim Fjord**. Pop. 145,778 (1998).

troop /troop/ *n* **1** a large group **2** a unit of soldiers ■ **troops** *npl* soldiers ■ *vi* **1** go as a large orderly group **2** go as if marching

SPELLCHECK Do not confuse the spelling of **troop** and **troupe** ('group of travelling performers'), which sound similar.

trooper /troopər/ *n* **1** a member of a cavalry unit **2** a cavalry horse

troopship /troop ship/ *n* a ship for transporting military personnel

trope *n* a word or expression used figuratively

trophy /trốfi/ (*pl* **-phies**) *n* **1** a token of victory, especially a cup or other award given to the winner of a sporting contest **2** a symbol of personal success

tropic /tróppik/ *n* each of the lines of latitude at 23° 26′ north and south of the equator ■ **tropics** *npl* the area between the two tropics —**tropic** *adj*

tropical /tróppik'l/ *adj* **1** of or typical of the tropics **2** hot and sultry —**tropically** *adv*

tropism /trốpizəm/ *n* involuntary movement in response to a stimulus such as heat or light

tropopause /tróppə pawz/ *n* the boundary between the troposphere and the stratosphere

troposphere /tróppə sfeer/ *n* the lowest and most dense layer of the atmosphere —**tropospheric** /tróppə sférrik/ *adj*

trot *vi* (**trotting, trotted**) **1** move at a pace between walking and cantering (*refers to horses*) **2** move at a jogging pace ■ *n* **1** a trotting pace **2** a ride on a trotting horse ■ **trots** *npl* a prolonged bout of diarrhoea (*infml*) ◊ **on the trot** in succession

□ **trot out** *vt* come up with something repeatedly (*infml*) ○ *trotting out the same old excuses*

troth /trōth/ *n* a solemn vow, especially between an engaged or married couple (*fml*)

AKG London

Leon Trotsky

Trotsky /trótski/, **Leon** (1879–1940) Russian revolutionary leader —**Trotskyite** n, adj

trotter /tróttər/ n 1 the foot of a pig or sheep used as food 2 a trotting person or animal

troubadour /troóbə dawr, -door/ n a writer or singer of love poems or songs, especially in medieval Europe

trouble /trúbb'l/ n 1 a condition of distress, worry, difficulty, or danger 2 a cause of trouble 3 a failing or drawback 4 a problematic medical condition ○ *back trouble* 5 effort ○ *went to a lot of trouble* 6 disorder or unrest ■ vt (-bling, -bled) 1 worry or upset 2 cause pain to 3 disturb, inconvenience, or impose on —**troubled** adj —**troubling** adj ◊ See note at **bother**

troublemaker /trúbb'l maykər/ n somebody who constantly causes trouble —**trouble-making** n, adj

troubleshooter /trúbb'l shootər/ n 1 somebody who finds and solves problems 2 a mediator —**troubleshooting** n

troublesome /trúbb'lssəm/ adj causing or involving trouble

trouble spot n a place where trouble, especially political unrest, occurs

trough /trof/ n 1 a long narrow open container, e.g. for animal food or water 2 a channel for liquid 3 an area of low atmospheric pressure 4 a sunken area 5 a low point, e.g. in an economic cycle

trounce /trownss/ (**trouncing, trounced**) vt defeat decisively ◊ See note at **defeat**

troupe /troop/ n a group of travelling performers ■ vi (**trouping, trouped**) travel or perform with a troupe ◊ See note at **troop**

trouper /troópər/ n 1 a member of a troupe 2 somebody reliable and dedicated

trousers /trówzərz/ npl a garment for the lower body with separate sections covering the legs —**trouser** adj —**trousered** adj ◊ **wear the trousers** UK be the member of a household who makes the important decisions (infml)

trouser suit n a woman's suit with trousers

trousseau /troóssō/ (pl **-seaus** or **-seaux** /-sōz/) n a set of clothes and linen collected by a bride

trout /trowt/ (pl **trouts** or same) n 1 a freshwater fish related to the salmon 2 trout as food

trove /trōv/ n 1 a collection of valuables 2 a valuable discovery

trowel /trów əl/ n 1 a flat-bladed hand tool used for spreading and smoothing 2 a short-handled digging tool with a curved blade —**trowel** vt

troy adj in troy weight

Troy ancient Greek city in present-day NW Turkey, on the Aegean Sea

troy weight n a system of weights based on a 12-ounce pound

truant /troó ənt/ n somebody absent from school without permission or good reason —**truancy** n —**truant** adj, vi

truce n 1 an agreed break in fighting or arguing 2 an agreement to stop fighting or arguing

truck[1] n 1 a large road vehicle for transporting goods 2 a wheeled unit used for moving heavy objects 3 a railway goods wagon ■ vti transport goods by truck —**trucker** n —**trucking** n

truck[2] n dealings (infml) ○ *have no truck with that kind of behaviour*

truckle /trúk'l/ (**-ling, -led**) vi be submissive

truculent /trúkyŏŏlənt/ adj aggressively defiant or uncooperative —**truculence** n

Trudeau /troódō/, **Pierre** (1919–2000) prime minister of Canada (1968–79 and 1980–84)

trudge vti (**trudging, trudged**) walk wearily ■ n a long walk

true /troo/ adj (**truer, truest**) 1 real, factual, or correct 2 genuine 3 personally faithful 4 committed, e.g. to a cause or belief 5 conforming to a standard or measure 6 rightful or legitimate 7 in relation to the Earth's poles rather than to points of magnetic attraction ○ *true north* 8 meeting criteria for inclusion in a category ○ *A shooting star is not a true star.* ■ adv 1 so as to correspond with reality or fact ○ *didn't ring true* 2 accurately 3 honestly ■ vt (**truing, trued**) make straight or level ■ n 1 correct alignment ○ *out of true* 2 absolute truth —**trueness** n

true-life adj presenting real events

~~truely~~ incorrect spelling of **truly**

Trueman /troómən/, **Fred** (b. 1931) British cricketer

Truffaut /troó fō/, **François** (1932–84) French film director and critic

truffle /trúff'l/ n 1 a fleshy fungus eaten as a delicacy 2 a soft rich chocolate sweet

trug n a gardener's shallow wooden basket

truism /troó izəm/ n an obvious statement —**truistic** /troo ístik/ adj

Trujillo /troo heé yō, -heél yō/ city in NW Peru. Pop. 627,553 (1995).

~~truley~~ incorrect spelling of **truly**

truly /troóli/ adv 1 sincerely 2 adds emphasis ○ *truly remarkable* ◊ **yours truly** I or me (humorous)

Harry S. Truman

Truman /troomən/, **Harry S.** (1884–1972) 33rd president of the United States (1945–53)

trump n also **trump card** 1 in a card game, a card from a suit declared to be highest in value 2 a highly valuable resource or advantage ■ vt 1 defeat by playing a trump 2 outdo ◇ **turn up trumps** prove unexpectedly to be a valuable asset
□ **trump up** vt invent in order to deceive or cheat ○ a trumped-up charge

trumpery /trúmpəri/ (pl -ies) n (literary) 1 something showy but worthless 2 nonsense

trumpet /trúmpit/ n 1 a brass instrument with a flared bell 2 something shaped like a trumpet ■ vt 1 announce loudly or proudly 2 speak in praise of —**trumpeter** n ◇ **blow your own trumpet** speak confidently, proudly, or boastfully about yourself (infml)

trumps n the suit in a card game with the highest value (+ sing or pl verb)

truncate /trung káyt/ vt (-cating, -cated) shorten by removing a part ■ adj truncated —**truncated** adj —**truncation** n

truncheon /trúnchən/ n a police officer's short heavy stick —**truncheon** vt

trundle /trúnd'l/ vti (-dling, -dled) move slowly and heavily on wheels ■ n 1 a trundling movement 2 a trolley or cart

trundler /trúndlər/ n NZ 1 a golf cart 2 a shopping trolley 3 a pushchair

trunk n 1 the main stem of a tree 2 a large travelling case 3 the body excluding the head and limbs 4 the long muscular flexible snout of an elephant 5 the main part of something that branches 6 US, Can the boot of a car ■ **trunks** npl men's shorts worn as swimwear

trunk call n a long-distance telephone call (dated)

trunk road n a long-distance road for heavy traffic

truss vt 1 bind somebody or something tightly 2 tie meat for cooking 3 support a structure with a framework of beams 4 support a hernia ■ n 1 a support for a hernia 2 a supporting framework of beams

trust n 1 confidence in and reliance on good qualities 2 care ○ children in the trust of a child-minder 3 a position of obligation or responsibility 4 hope for the future 5 the holding and managing of another's property, or a legal arrangement for this ■ v 1 vti rely on somebody or something 2 vt place

confidence in the decisions and behaviour of 3 vt place in the care of somebody —**trustable** adj

trustee /tru steé/ n 1 somebody holding and managing another's property 2 a member of a board of financial managers —**trusteeship** n

trustful /trústf'l/ adj willing to trust people —**trustfully** adv —**trustfulness** n

trust fund n a fund managed on behalf of another

trusting /trústing/ adj tending to trust people —**trustingly** adv —**trustingness** n

trustworthy /trúst wurthi/ adj honest or reliable —**trustworthiness** n

trusty /trústi/ adj (-ier, -iest) reliable (dated or humorous) ■ n (pl -ies) a trusted person, especially a prisoner —**trustily** adv —**trustiness** n

truth /trooth/ n 1 correspondence to fact or reality 2 something that corresponds to fact or reality 3 a true statement 4 an obvious fact 5 something generally believed 6 honesty 7 descriptive accuracy

truthful /troothf'l/ adj 1 honest 2 accurate in description —**truthfully** adv —**truthfulness** n

try v (tries, tried) 1 vti make an effort to do something 2 vt test or sample something for the purpose of assessment 3 vt strain or vex somebody or something ○ trying my patience 4 vt subject somebody to a legal trial 5 vt conduct a case in court ■ n (pl **tries**) 1 an effort ○ a good try 2 in rugby, a score achieved by touching the ball down behind the opponent's goal line
□ **try on** vt put on clothing to test its suitability

~~tryed~~ incorrect spelling of **tried**

trying /trí ing/ adj stressful —**tryingly** adv

try-out n a test of an applicant's suitability or skills

tryst /trist/ n a secret meeting, especially between lovers (literary) —**tryst** vi

tsar /zaar/, **czar, tzar** n 1 formerly, a Russian emperor 2 a person given authority in a particular area (infml) ○ a drugs tsar —**tsardom** n —**tsarist** n, adj

tsarina /zaa reénə/, **tsaritsa** /-reétsə/ n formerly, a Russian empress, or a tsar's wife or widow

tsetse fly /tétsi-, tsétsi-/ n a fly that transmits sleeping sickness

T-shirt, tee shirt n a collarless short-sleeved shirt without fastenings

tsotsi /tsótsi/ n S Africa a member of a Black criminal gang (infml)

tsp. abbr teaspoon

T-square, tee-square n a T-shaped drawing-board ruler

tsunami /tsoō naámi/ (pl -mis) n a large ocean wave caused by movement of the Earth's surface —**tsunamic** adj

tub n 1 a low round open container 2 a tub-shaped container with a lid for soft foods 3 a bath (infml) —**tub** vti

tuba /tyooˊbə/ n a low-pitched brass instrument played with the open end pointing upwards

tubby /túbbi/ (-bier, -biest) adj 1 overweight (infml; sometimes offensive) 2 tub-shaped —**tubbiness** n

tube /tyoob/ n 1 a long hollow cylinder for transporting liquids or gases 2 a collapsible tube-shaped container with a cap 3 London's underground railway, or a train that runs on it (infml) 4 a cathode ray tube in a television 5 US, Can television (infml)

tuber /tyooˊbər/ n 1 a fleshy underground plant part, from which new growth sprouts 2 a small swelling on the body —**tuberous** adj

tubercle /tyoobˊbark'l/ n 1 a nodule 2 a small rounded swelling in the lungs characteristic of tuberculosis

tuberculin /tyoo búrkyooˊlin/ n a liquid obtained from the tubercle-causing bacillus, used to test for tuberculosis

tuberculosis /tyoo búrkyoo lṓssiss/ n an infectious disease in which small rounded swellings form in the lungs —**tubercular** /tyoo búrkyooˊlər/ adj —**tuberculoid** /tyoo búrkyoo loyd/ adj —**tuberculous** /tyoo búrkyooˊləs/ adj

tubing /tyooˊbing/ n 1 a system of tubes 2 material used for tubes

tubular /tyooˊbyooˊlər/ adj tube-shaped

TUC abbr Trades Union Congress

tuck v 1 push or fold into position 2 vti draw or be drawn in 3 vt sew a fold in ■ n 1 a fold sewn into something to reduce its size or for decoration 2 food, especially sweets and cakes o a tuck shop 3 in cosmetic surgery, a removal of loose skin

☐ **tuck away** vt put somewhere safe or concealed

☐ **tuck in** v 1 also **tuck up** vt make comfortable in bed by securing the bedclothes 2 vi eat hungrily (infml)

tucker /túkər/ n ANZ food (infml)

Tucson /tooˊson/ city in S Arizona. Pop. 460,466 (1998).

Tudor /tyooˊdər/ adj 1 of the English royal family that ruled between 1485 and 1603, or of this period 2 describes an architectural style with exterior timber frameworks

Tuesday /tyooˊz day, -di/ n the 2nd day of the week

ORIGIN Tuesday is named after Tiu, a Germanic god of war identified with Mars (the Latin equivalent meant 'Mars' day'). The Germanic first element is related to Latin deus 'god'.

tuft n a bunch of fibres, hair, feathers, or grass held or growing together —**tuft** vti —**tufted** adj

tug v (tugging, tugged) 1 vti pull sharply 2 vt tow or haul with effort ■ n 1 a sharp or strong pull 2 a struggle between opposing forces 3 also **tugboat** a small powerful boat used for towing ◊ See note at **pull**

Tugela Falls /too gáylə-/ series of waterfalls on the **River Tugela**, E South Africa. Height 948 m/3,110 ft.

tug of war n 1 a contest in which two teams pull at opposite ends of a rope 2 a struggle between evenly-matched parties or influences

tugrik /tooˊg reek/ (pl same or tugriks or togrog or togrogs) n the main unit of Mongolian currency

tuition /tyoo ísh'n/ n 1 instruction given individually or in a small group 2 a fee for instruction —**tuitional** adj

tularaemia /tooˊlə reeˊmi ə/ n a bacterial disease of rabbits and rodents that can spread to human beings —**tularaemic** adj

tulip /tyooˊlip/ n a spring-flowering plant with cup-shaped flowers

ORIGIN Tulip is ultimately the same word as turban. Both came through Turkish from Persian dulband 'turban'. The immediate source of English **tulip** was French tulipe, where the final consonant of tulipan 'turban, tulip' had been lost. The name was given to the plant because of the shape of the expanded flower.

tulle /tyool/ n a thin netted fabric. Use: evening or ballet dresses, veils.

Tulsa /túlsə/ city in NE Oklahoma. Pop. 381,393 (1998).

tum n the stomach (infml)

tumble /túmb'l/ (-bling, -bled) vi 1 fall suddenly, often rolling over 2 roll about 3 reduce steeply o Prices have tumbled. 4 cascade 5 perform gymnastic or acrobatic leaps or rolls —**tumble** n

tumbledown /túmbl down/ adj dilapidated

tumble dryer, tumble drier n a machine for drying laundry in a rotating metal drum

tumbler /túmblər/ n 1 a drinking glass with no stem or handle 2 an acrobat 3 the part of a lock that is engaged by a key 4 a tumble dryer or its drum

tumbleweed /túmb'l weed/ (pl -weeds or same) n a plant of dry regions that withers and is blown about by the wind

tumescent /tyoo méss'nt/ adj swollen or swelling —**tumescence** n

tummy /túmmi/ (pl -mies) n the stomach (infml)

tumour /tyooˊmər/ n 1 an uncontrolled growth of tissue 2 a swelling in or on the body

tumult /tyoo mult/ n 1 noisy commotion 2 emotional upheaval

tumultuous /tyoo múlchoo əss/ adj 1 noisy and unrestrained 2 confused and agitated —**tumultuousness** n

tumulus /tyooˊmyooˊləss/ (pl -li /-līˊ/) n an ancient burial mound

tun n a large beer or wine cask

tuna /tyooˊnə/ (pl same or -nas) n 1 a large sea fish 2 tuna as food

tundra /túndrə/ n the plain with permanently frozen subsoil that stretches across Arctic North America, Europe, and Asia

tune /tyoon/ *n* **1** a simple melody **2** a song ■ *vt* (**tuning, tuned**) **1** adjust a musical instrument for pitch **2** adjust an engine to make it run better **3** adjust a radio or television to a station or channel —**tunable** *adj* —**tuneable** *adj* —**tuneless** *adj* —**tunelessly** *adv* —**tunelessness** *n* ◊ **call the tune** be in charge ◊ **change your tune** change your attitude or opinion ◊ **in tune 1** played or sung at the appropriate pitch **2** in accord or agreement **3** adjusted to the correct frequency ◊ **to the tune of** to the amount of ○ *in debt to the tune of £10,000*
□ **tune in** *vi* watch or listen to a television or radio programme
□ **tune up** *vti* adjust a musical instrument to the correct pitch

tuneful /tyoonf'l/ *adj* having a pleasant melody or sound —**tunefully** *adv* —**tunefulness** *n*

tuner /tyoonər/ *n* **1** somebody who tunes musical instruments **2** a device that accepts signals, e.g. in a hi-fi system

tune-up *n* an act of tuning an engine

tungsten /túngstən/ *n* (*symbol* **W**) a hard grey metallic chemical element. Use: high-temperature alloys, lamp filaments, high-speed cutting tools.

tunic /tyoonik/ *n* **1** a loose garment that usually extends to the hip or knee **2** a knee-length garment with sleeves, worn in ancient or medieval times

tuning fork *n* a two-pronged metal fork that produces a sound, used in tuning musical instruments

Tunis /tyooniss/ capital of Tunisia. Pop. 674,100 (1995).

Tunisia /tyoo nízzi ə/ country in North Africa. Cap. Tunis. Pop. 9,705,102 (2001). —**Tunisian** *n, adj*

tunnel /túnn'l/ *n* **1** a passageway under or through an obstruction, such as road or mountain **2** an underground passage ■ *v* (**-nelling, -nelled**) **1** *vti* make a tunnel through or under something **2** *vt* dig something resembling a tunnel

tunnel vision *n* **1** a condition in which peripheral vision is lost **2** narrow-minded thinking

tunny /túnni/ (*pl same or* **-nies**) *n* a tuna

tuppence /túppənss/ *n* MONEY = **twopence**

tuppenny *adj* MONEY = **twopenny**

turban /túrbən/ *n* a headdress that consists of a long piece of fabric wrapped around the head —**turbaned** *adj*

turbid /túrbid/ *adj* **1** opaque and muddy **2** dense and cloudy —**turbidity** /tur bíddəti/ *n* —**turbidly** *adv*

turbine /túrb Īn, -bin/ *n* a machine powered by rotating blades

turbo /túrbō/ (*pl* **-bos**) *n* **1** a turbine **2** a turbocharger

turbocharger /túrbō chaarjər/ *n* a turbine that increases the power of an internal-combustion engine —**turbocharged** *adj*

turbot /túrbət/ (*pl same or* **-bots**) *n* **1** a nearly circular flatfish **2** turbot as food

turbulent /túrbyŏólənt/ *adj* **1** moving violently **2** marked by change and unrest ○ *a turbulent year in politics* **3** atmospherically unstable —**turbulence** *n* —**turbulently** *adv*

turd *n* **1** a taboo term for a piece of excrement (*offensive*) **2** a taboo term for somebody who is seen as contemptible (*insult*)

tureen /tyŏŏ réen/ *n* a large serving bowl for soups and stews

turf (*pl* **turfs** *or* **turves**) *n* **1** grass and the dense layer of underlying soil and roots **2** artificial grass **3** a piece of soil with grass growing in it **4** peat for fuel **5** horseracing, or a horseracing track **6** somebody's territory (*infml*)
□ **turf out** *vt* eject (*infml*)

turf accountant *n* a bookmaker

Popperfoto

Ivan Turgenev

Turgenev /tur gáy nyef/, **Ivan** (1818–83) Russian writer

turgid /túrjid/ *adj* **1** pompous and over-complicated **2** swollen or distended by a build-up of fluid —**turgidity** /tur jíddəti/ *n* —**turgidness** *n*

Turin /tyoor rín/ capital of **Turin Province**, Piedmont Region, NW Italy. Pop. 909,717 (1999).

Turing /tyŏŏring/, **Alan** (1912–54) British mathematician. He was a major figure in the theoretical development of the computer.

Turing machine *n* a mathematical model of a hypothetical computer

Turk *n* **1** somebody from Turkey **2** a member of a Turkish-speaking ethnic group

turkey /túrki/ (*pl* **-keys**) *n* **1** a large bird with a bare wattled head **2** turkey as food **3** *US, Can* a failure (*slang*)

ORIGIN Although North American, the bird is indeed named after the country of Turkey. The Europeans who first encountered it saw a resemblance to the guinea fowl. *Turkeycock* and *turkeyhen* were 16C names for guinea fowl, which were imported through Turkish territory. Shortenings of these forms were adopted in the mid-16C for the **turkey** itself.

Turkey /túrki/ country in SE Europe and SW Asia. Cap. Ankara. Pop. 66,493,970 (2001).

Turkish /túrkish/ *adj* **1** of Turkey **2** of the Turkish language ■ *n* the official language of Turkey —**Turkishness** *n*

Turkish bath *n* a steam bath followed by a shower and massage

Turkish coffee *n* strong coffee served with the grounds

Turkish delight *n* a soft sweet made with flavoured gelatin

Turkmenistan /turk ménni staán/ country in SW Central Asia, on the Caspian Sea. Cap. Ashgabat. Pop. 4,603,244 (2001). —**Turkmen** /túrk men/ *n, adj*

Turks and Caicos Islands /túrks ənd káykoss-/ British dependency consisting of two island groups in the Caribbean. Cap. Cockburn Town. Pop. 18,122 (2001).

turmeric /túrmərik/ *n* 1 a bright yellow spice. Use: cooking, yellow dye. 2 a plant with rhizomes that are dried to produce turmeric

turmoil /túr moyl/ *n* confused disturbance or commotion

turn *v* 1 *vti* move to face a different direction 2 *vti* move round an axis 3 *vt* move a control on a machine 4 *vti* go or cause to go in a different direction 5 *vt* go round a corner 6 *vt* move something to expose the other side ○ *turned the pages* 7 *vti* change into a different form ○ *turned into a butterfly* 8 *vti* change colour 9 *vti* redirect, or be redirected ○ *Her thoughts turned to the past.* 10 *vi* appeal to somebody or something for help 11 *vti* upset or become upset ○ *violence that turned my stomach* 12 *vt* twist an ankle 13 *vt* pass a particular time or age 14 *vi* become sour *(refers to milk)* 15 *vti* change or cause to change allegiance ■ *n* 1 a time when somebody may or must do something 2 a change of direction 3 a rotation 4 a winding of something such as wire around something else 5 a sudden fright 6 the end of a period ○ *at the turn of the century* —**turner** *n* ◇ **at every turn** everywhere ◇ **in turn** one after the other ◇ **out of turn** 1 not in a regular or correct order 2 in an inappropriate way, or at an inappropriate time

☐ **turn against** *vt* no longer support or like

☐ **turn away** *vt* refuse admission to

☐ **turn back** *vti* stop going forward and return, or cause to do this

☐ **turn down** *vt* 1 reject 2 reduce the volume or intensity of

☐ **turn in** *v* 1 *vt* submit something 2 *vt* take somebody to the police 3 *vi* go to bed *(infml)* 4 *vt* produce a particular result ○ *turned in a creditable performance*

☐ **turn off** *v* 1 *vt* operate a control to stop 2 *vti* make or become uninterested or unresponsive *(infml)*

☐ **turn on** *vt* 1 operate a control to start 2 attack 3 make excited or aroused *(infml)*

☐ **turn out** *v* 1 *vt* switch off 2 *vi* come to an event 3 *vt* force to leave 4 *vi* end up 5 *vt* create or produce ○ *turning out 400 cars a week*

☐ **turn over** *v* 1 *vt* think about 2 *vt* give to somebody else 3 *vti* sell and restock goods, or be sold and restocked

☐ **turn round** *or* **around** *vt* improve something significantly

☐ **turn up** *v* 1 *vt* increase the volume or intensity of something 2 *vt* shorten a garment 3 *vi* be

found 4 *vt* find something by searching 5 *vi* arrive

turnabout /túrn ə bowt/ *n* a complete shift in something such as policy or attitude

turnaround *n* = **turnround**

turncoat /túrn kōt/ *n* a traitor

Turner /túrnər/, **J. M. W.** (1775–1851) British painter and watercolourist

turning /túrning/ *n* 1 a junction 2 a deviation

turning circle *n* the smallest circle a vehicle can turn in

turning point *n* an important moment of change

turnip /túrnip/ *n* 1 a white rounded root eaten as a vegetable 2 a plant that produces turnips

turnkey /túrn kee/ *adj* ready to use on delivery or installation ■ *n (pl* -**keys**) a keeper of keys, especially a jailer *(archaic)*

turn-off *n* 1 a road branching off a main road 2 something disgusting or off-putting *(infml)*

turn of phrase *n* a particular way of expressing yourself

turn-on *n* somebody or something causing sexual arousal *(infml)*

turnout /túrn owt/ *n* total attendance or participation

turnover /túrn övər/ *n* 1 the amount of business transacted over a given period 2 a throughput of stock 3 the number of employees who leave and are replaced 4 a filled pastry made by folding one half of a piece of dough over the other half

turnpike /túrn pīk/ *n* 1 a toll road, especially a US motorway 2 a tollgate

turnround /túrn rownd/, **turnaround** /-ə rownd/ *n* the time it takes to complete an order or task or to prepare an aircraft, ship, or vehicle between journeys

turnstile /túrn stīl/ *n* a revolving barrier

turntable /túrn tayb'l/ *n* 1 a revolving platform on a record player 2 a rotating platform for turning a locomotive

turn-up *n* 1 *UK* a fold at the bottom of a trouser leg 2 something surprising *(infml)* ○ *That's a turn-up for the books!* —**turn-up** *adj*

turpentine /túrpən tīn/ *n* 1 a substance obtained from pine trees, or an oil distilled from it. Use: paint solvent, in medicine. 2 a petroleum-based paint thinner —**turpentine** *vt*

turpitude /túrpi tyood/ *n* immorality *(fml)*

turps *n* turpentine *(infml)*

turquoise /túr kwoyz, -kwaaz/ *n* 1 a semiprecious stone. Use: gems. 2 a greenish-blue colour —**turquoise** *adj*

turret /túrrit/ *n* 1 a small tower projecting from a building 2 a dome or rotating structure containing a gun

turtle /túrt'l/ *n* 1 a sea reptile resembling a tortoise with paddle-shaped limbs 2 *US* a tortoise or related animal 3 turtle as food

turtledove /túrt'l duv/ *n* a dove with a purring call

ORIGIN The *turtledove* was earlier simply the

turtle. The name derives from Latin *turtur*, an imitation of the bird's cooing sound. It is unrelated to *turtle* the reptile, which is probably an alteration of French *tortue* 'tortoise'.

turtleneck /túrt'l nek/ *n* **1** a high round collar on a garment such as a sweater **2** *US, Can* a polo neck

Tuscany /túskəni/ region in N Italy. Cap. Florence. Pop. 3,528,563 (1998).

tusk *n* an enlarged projecting tooth —**tusked** *adj*

tussle /túss'l/ (**-sling, -sled**) *vi* have a vigorous fight or struggle —**tussle** *n*

tussock /tússək/ *n* a small thick clump of grass

tut, tut-tut *interj* expresses disapproval ■ *vi* (**tutting, tutted; tut-tutting, tut-tutted**) make a clicking sound with the tongue to express disapproval

Tutankhamen /tōōtən kaámən/, **Tutankhamun** /-kaa moòn/ (1343–1325 BC) Egyptian pharaoh

tutelage /tyōōtəlij/ *n* **1** instruction and guidance **2** the state of being a tutor or guardian **3** supervision by a tutor or guardian

tutor /tyōōtər/ *n* a teacher of an individual pupil or a small group —**tutor** *vti* —**tutorage** *n* —**tutorship** *n* ◊ See note at **teach**

tutorial /tyoo táwri əl/ *n* **1** a lesson with a tutor **2** a lesson forming part of a manual or computer program ■ *adj* of a tutor

tutti-frutti /tōōti frōōti/ (*pl* **tutti-fruttis**) *n* ice cream containing mixed fruit

tutu /tóōtoo/ *n* a ballet dancer's short skirt that stands out from the body

Desmond Tutu

Tutu /tóōtoo/, **Desmond** (*b.* 1931) South African archbishop and political activist

Tuvalu /too vaáloo/ country consisting of coral islands in the W Pacific Ocean. Cap. Funafuti. Pop. 10,991 (2001). —**Tuvaluan** *n, adj*

tuxedo /tuk seédō/ (*pl* **-dos**) *n US, Can* a dinner jacket or dinner suit

ORIGIN The **tuxedo** is named after the town of Tuxedo Park, New York, in the United States, where the jacket was first worn at a country club in 1886. The first printed record of the name is from 1889.

TV *n* television (*infml*)

TV dinner *n* a precooked meal that can be reheated and eaten from the tray it comes in

TVP *n* a soya food product that is flavoured to taste like meat. Full form **textured vegetable protein**

twaddle /twódd'l/ *n* nonsense (*infml*) —**twaddle** *vi* —**twaddler** *n*

twain *npl* two (*literary*)

Mark Twain

Twain, Mark (1835–1910) US writer

twang *n* **1** the sound of a tight string vibrating **2** a nasal sound in various accents —**twang** *vti* —**twangy** *adj*

twat *n* **1** a taboo term for a woman's genitals (*offensive*) **2** a taboo term for somebody regarded as unintelligent or contemptible (*insult*)

tweak /tweek/ *vt* **1** pinch and twist sharply **2** adjust slightly (*infml*) —**tweak** *n*

twee *adj* too sweet or pretty —**tweely** *adv* —**tweeness** *n*

tweed *n* a woollen cloth with a flecked appearance ■ **tweeds** *npl* clothes made of tweed

ORIGIN Tweed is an alteration of *tweel*, a Scottish form of *twill*, influenced by the name of the Tweed, a river in S Scotland and NE England. Early accounts date the coinage of **tweed** to 1831, and ascribe it to the London cloth merchant James Locke (although Locke himself in his book *Tweed and Don* (1860) does not make any such claim). The term was in general use by 1850, and it was for a time registered as a trademark.

tweedy /tweédi/ (**-ier, -iest**) *adj* of or like tweed —**tweediness** *n*

tweet *n* a high-pitched sound made by a bird —**tweet** *vi*

tweeter /tweétər/ *n* a high-frequency loudspeaker

tweezers /tweézərz/ *npl* a tool with two narrow pivoted arms used for plucking or holding small things

~~twelfth~~ incorrect spelling of **twelfth**

twelve *n* the number 12 —**twelfth** *n, adj, adv* —**twelve** *adj, pron*

twelvemonth /twélv munth/ *n* a year (*archaic*)

~~twelveth~~ incorrect spelling of **twelfth**

twenty /twénti/ *n* the number 20 ■ **twenties** *npl* **1** the numbers 20 to 29, particularly as a range of temperatures **2** the years from 20 to 29 in a century or somebody's life —**twentieth** *n, adj, adv* —**twenty** *adj, pron*

twenty-first *n* somebody's 21st birthday

24/7 /twéntee fawr séw'n/ *adv, adj* 24 hours a day, 7 days a week

twerp /twurp/ *n* an offensive term for somebody regarded as foolish (*infml insult*)

twice *adv* **1** two times **2** double

twiddle /twídd'l/ (**-dling, -dled**) *vti* **1** turn a knob or dial back and forth **2** keep twisting or turning something in a bored or absent-minded way —**twiddler** *n*

twig[1] *n* a small branch —**twiglet** *n*

twig[2] (**twigging, twigged**) *vti* realize or understand (*infml*)

twilight /twí līt/ *n* **1** the time just after sunset or just before sunrise **2** the faint light of twilight **3** a closing or declining period ○ *the twilight of the empire* —**twilit** *adj*

twilight war *n* a period of ominous inactivity that occurs during a war or leads up to a war

twilight zone *n* **1** an uncertain area between two opposing conditions **2** a run-down area

twill *n* a strong fabric with diagonal ribs

twin *n* **1** each of two offspring born together **2** somebody or something similar or identical to another ■ *adj* double ○ *the twin hulls of a catamaran* ■ *vt* (**twinning, twinned**) link as a twin town

twin bed *n* each of a pair of matching single beds

twine *n* **1** strong string **2** something made by twisting strands ■ *v* (**twining, twined**) **1** *vti* twist around or together **2** *vi* follow a winding course (*literary*)

twinge *n* **1** a brief pain **2** a brief uncomfortable emotion —**twinge** *vti*

twinkle /twíngk'l/ *vi* (**-kling, -kled**) **1** shine with flickering light **2** shine with amusement or mischief (*refers to people's eyes*) ■ *n* **1** a bright unsteady light **2** a brightness in somebody's eyes —**twinkly** *adj*

twinkling /twíngkling/ *n* a moment ■ *adj* flickering ◊ **in the twinkling of an eye** very quickly or very soon

twinset /twín set/ *n* a matching jumper and cardigan

twin town *n* a town linked with another town in a different country for cultural or administrative purposes

twirl /twurl/ *v* **1** *vti* spin round quickly **2** *vt* fiddle with something by turning or twisting it **3** *vi* turn suddenly and face the other way ■ *n* **1** a quick spinning movement **2** a spiral —**twirly** *adj*

twist *v* **1** *vti* make the ends of something turn in opposite directions **2** *vti* distort the shape or position of something **3** *vti* wind round something or together **4** *vt* injure part of the body by moving awkwardly **5** *vti* rotate **6** *vt* distort the meaning of something **7** *vt* distort the mind or outlook of somebody **8** *vi* constantly change direction ■ *n* **1** a twisting movement **2** something shaped by being twisted **3** an unexpected development **4** a bend **5** a 1960s dance with rotation of the hips **6** a painful wrench —**twistable** *adj* —**twisted** *adj* —**twisting** *adj* —**twistingly** *adv* —**twisty** *adj*

twister /twístər/ *n* **1** *US, Can* a tornado (*infml*) **2** somebody or something that twists

twit *n* an offensive term for somebody regarded as unthinking (*infml insult*) ■ *vt* (**twitting, twitted**) tease somebody playfully (*dated*) —**twitter** *n*

twitch *v* **1** *vi* jerk slightly **2** *vt* pull lightly and quickly ■ *n* **1** a jerky movement **2** a rapid involuntary muscle contraction

twitcher /twíchər/ *n* **1** somebody or something that twitches **2** an obsessive birdwatcher (*infml*)

twitchy /twíchi/ (**-ier, -iest**) *adj* **1** nervous (*infml*) **2** twitching —**twitchily** *adv* —**twitchiness** *n*

twitter /twíttər/ *vi* **1** make a succession of chirping sounds (*refers to birds*) **2** chatter ■ *n* **1** a twittering sound **2** excitement or agitation —**twittery** *adj*

two /too/ (*pl* **twos**) *n* the number 2 —**two** *adj, pron* ◊ See note at **to**

two-dimensional *adj* **1** having the dimensions of length and width **2** lacking depth of character —**two-dimensionality** /too di ménshə nálləti, too dī-/ *n* —**two-dimensionally** *adv*

two-edged *adj* **1** having two sharp edges **2** having two opposite effects

two-faced *adj* **1** hypocritical **2** having two surfaces —**two-facedly** /-fáyssidli, -fáystli/ *adv* —**two-facedness** /-fáyssidnəss/ *n*

twofold /too fold/ *adj* **1** having two parts or elements **2** double ■ *adv* doubly

two-handed *adj* **1** using two hands **2** designed for two people —**two-handedly** *adv*

twopence /túppənss/, **tuppence** *n* **1** the sum of two pence **2** anything at all ○ *don't care twopence*

twopenny /túppəni/, **tuppenny** *adj* **1** costing twopence **2** cheap and inferior

two-piece *adj* having two parts or pieces

two-ply *adj* having two layers or strands

two-seater *n* **1** a vehicle with two seats **2** a seat for two people

two-sided *adj* **1** having two surfaces **2** having two contesting sides

twosome /toossəm/ *n* a pair of people

two-step *n* **1** a ballroom dance in 2/4 time **2** the music for a two-step —**two-step** *vi*

two-stroke *adj* describes an engine that has two piston movements per cycle

two-time (**two-timing, two-timed**) *vt* be unfaithful to a romantic or sexual partner (*infml*) —**two-timer** *n*

two-tone *adj* **1** having two colours or shades **2** consisting of two sounds

two-way *adj* **1** moving in both directions **2** involving two participants **3** able to transmit and receive

two-way mirror *n* an observation device that is a window on one side and a mirror on the other

txt *abbr* a computer file extension for a basic text file

tycoon /tī koon/ *n* somebody powerful and wealthy in business

ORIGIN Tycoon was originally a title applied by

non-Japanese people to the shogun of Japan who was in power between 1857 and 1868. The Japanese word from which it was adopted was formed from Chinese elements meaning 'great' and 'lord'. In the US it was used as a nickname for Abraham Lincoln, and then extended to any powerful person, in particular (from the 1920s) one in business.

tyke /tike/, **tike** *n* **1** a naughty child *(infml)* **2** a mongrel

Tyler /tílər/, **Wat** (*d.* 1381) English revolutionary leader

Tyndale /tínd'l/, **Tindal, William** (1492?–1536) English religious reformer

Tyne /tin/ river in NE England, flowing through Newcastle upon Tyne to the North Sea. Length 48 km/30 mi.

type /tip/ *n* **1** a kind or sort **2** a representative member of a category **3** a particular kind of person *(infml)* ○ *an outdoor type* **4** a small block with a raised character on one side, used in printing **5** blocks of type collectively **6** printed letters on a page ■ *v* (**typing, typed**) **1** *vti* produce words or characters using a typewriter or computer keyboard **2** *vt* classify

---

SYNONYMS **type, kind, sort, category, class, species, genre** CORE MEANING: a group having a common quality or qualities

---

typecast /típ kaast/ (-**cast**) *vt* **1** cast repeatedly in similar acting roles **2** cast in a suitable role

typeface /típ fayss/ *n* **1** a style of printed characters **2** the surface of a block of type

typescript /típ skript/ *n* a typed document

typesetter /típ setər/ *n* a person or machine that prepares text for printing —**typeset** *vt* —**typesetting** *n*

typewriter /típ rítər/ *n* a machine with keys that are pressed to print words on paper —**typewrite** *vt* —**typewritten** *adj*

typhoid /tí foyd/ *n* a serious bacterial disease of the digestive system ■ *adj* of typhoid or typhus —**typhoidal** /tí fóyd'l/ *adj*

typhoon /tí fóon/ *n* a violent tropical storm in the W Pacific and Indian oceans —**typhonic** /tí fónnik/ *adj*

typhus /tífəss/, **typhus fever** *n* an infectious disease that causes fever —**typhous** *adj*

typical /típpik'l/ *adj* **1** having the characteristics of a particular type **2** usual, or conforming to expectation —**typicality** /típpi kálləti/ *n* —**typically** *adv* —**typicalness** *n*

typify /tippi fí/ (-**fies, -fied**) *vt* **1** be typical of **2** epitomize or embody —**typification** /típpifi káysh'n/ *n*

typist /típist/ *n* an operator of a typewriter or keyboard

typo /típó/ (*pl* -**pos**) *n* an error in typing or printing *(infml)*

typography /tí póggrəfi/ *n* **1** the preparation of texts for printing **2** the appearance of printed matter —**typographer** *n* —**typographical** /típə gráffik'l/ *adj*

typology /tí póllǝji/ *n* the study or classification of types —**typological** /típə lójji-k'l/ *adj* —**typologically** *adv* —**typologist** *n*

tyrannical /ti ránnik'l/, **tyrannic** /ti ránnik/ *adj* **1** ruling absolutely and oppressively **2** authoritarian —**tyrannically** *adv*

tyrannize /tírrə nīz/ (-**nizing, -nized**), **tyrannise** *vti* **1** govern cruelly **2** treat harshly

tyrannosaur /ti ránnə sawr/, **tyrannosaurus** /-əss/, **tyrannosaurus rex** /-réks/ *n* a large flesh-eating dinosaur that walked on powerful hind legs and had small front legs

tyranny /tírrəni/ (*pl* -**nies**) *n* **1** cruelty and injustice in the use of power **2** oppressive government **3** a cruel act —**tyrannous** *adj*

tyrant /tírənt/ *n* **1** an absolute and oppressive ruler **2** an authoritarian person

~~tyrany~~ incorrect spelling of **tyranny**

tyre /tir/ *n* a rubber or metal edging for a wheel

Tyre /tir/ town in S Lebanon. It was the most important city of ancient Phoenicia. Pop. 120,000 (1988). —**Tyrian** /tírri ən/ *adj*

tyro /tíró/ (*pl* -**ros**) *n* a beginner —**tyronic** /tí rónnik/ *adj* ◊ See note at **beginner**

Tyrol = **Tirol**

~~tyrany~~ incorrect spelling of **tyranny**

Tyrrhenian Sea /ti reéni ən-/ arm of the Mediterranean Sea between W Italy and the islands of Corsica, Sardinia, and Sicily

tzar *n* = **tsar**

tzatziki /sat seéki, tsat-/ *n* a dip made from yoghurt, cucumber, mint, and garlic

U

u (*pl* **u's**), **U** (*pl* **U's** *or* **Us**) *n* the 21st letter of the English alphabet

U[1] (*pl* **U's** *or* **Us**) *n* a film classified as suitable for everybody. Full form **universal**

U[2] *n* the Myanmar equivalent of Mr

U[3] *symbol* uranium

U[4] *abbr* **1** united **2** university

u. *abbr* upper

UAE *abbr* United Arab Emirates

ubiquitous /yoo bíkwitəss/ *adj* present everywhere —**ubiquitously** *adv* —**ubiquitousness** *n* —**ubiquity** *n*

U-boat *n* a German submarine

ORIGIN **U-boat** is a partial translation of German *U-Boot*, a shortening of *Unterseeboot*, literally 'under sea boat'. A **U-boat** was first mentioned in English in 1916.

---

ubuntu /ŏŏ bŏŏntoo/ *n S Africa* kindness and goodness

UCAS *abbr* Universities and Colleges Admissions Service

Ucayali /oó kaa ya'áli/ river in E Peru. Length 1,900 km/1,200 mi.

UDA *abbr* Ulster Defence Association

udder /úddər/ *n* a bag-shaped milk-secreting organ of a cow, sheep, or goat

Udjung Pandang /oòjoöng pan dáng/ capital of Sulawesi Selantan Province, on S Sulawesi, Indonesia. Pop. 944,372 (1990).

UDR *abbr* Ulster Defence Regiment

UEFA /yoo áyfə/ *abbr* Union of European Football Associations

UFO /yoò ef ō, yoofó/ (*pl* **UFOs**) *n* an unidentified flying object

Uganda /yoo gándə/ country in E Africa. Cap. Kampala. Pop. 23,985,712 (2001). —**Ugandan** *n, adj*

ugly /úggli/ (**-lier, -liest**) *adj* **1** unattractive to look at **2** angry **3** threatening —**uglily** *adv* —**ugliness** *n* ◊ See note at **unattractive**

ugly duckling *n* an unattractive or undervalued person or thing

ORIGIN The original **ugly duckling** appears in a children's story by Hans Christian Andersen, in which a cygnet raised by a duck is considered ugly until it grows into a beautiful swan.

UHF *n* a frequency range between 300 and 3000 megahertz. Full form **ultrahigh frequency**

UI *abbr* user interface

UK *abbr* United Kingdom

Ukraine /yoo kráyn/ country in E Europe. Cap. Kiev. Pop. 48,760,474 (2001).

Ukrainian /yoo kráyni ən/ *n* **1** somebody from Ukraine **2** the official language of Ukraine —**Ukrainian** *adj*

ukulele /yoòka láyli/, **ukelele** *n* a small stringed instrument resembling a guitar

ORIGIN Ukulele was adopted in the late 19C from a Hawaiian word meaning literally 'jumping flea'. The reason for the name is not known for certain, but it may have been the Hawaiian nickname of Edward Purvis, a British army officer who popularized the instrument.

Ulaanbaatar /oò laan baátər/ capital of the Republic of Mongolia. Pop. 600,900 (1992).

ulama /oolimə/, **ulema** *npl* a body of Islamic scholars who have jurisdiction over legal and social matters for the people of Islam

Ulan-Ude /oo laàn oo dáy/ port in S Siberian Russia. Pop. 410,359 (1995).

ulcer /úlssər/ *n* **1** a sore on the skin or on a mucous membrane, especially the stomach lining **2** a corrupting or debilitating influence —**ulcerous** *adj*

ulcerate /úlssə rayt/ (**-ating, -ated**) *vti* develop, or undergo the development of, an ulcer or ulcers — **ulceration** /úlssə ráysh'n/ *n*

Ulm /oolm/, **Charles** (1898–1934) Australian aviator

ulna /úlnə/ (*pl* **-nae** /-nee/ *or* **-nas**) *n* **1** the longer bone of the human forearm **2** a bone of the lower forelimb of an animal —**ulnar** *adj*

ulster /úlstər/ *n* a man's long heavy double-breasted overcoat

Ulster /úlstər/ **1** historic province in the north of Ireland, comprising nine counties, including the six that make up Northern Ireland **2** Northern Ireland (*infml*) —**Ulsterman** *n* —**Ulsterwoman** *n*

ulterior /ul teèri ər/ *adj* **1** underlying or existing in addition ○ *an ulterior motive* **2** lying outside

ultimate /últimət/ *adj* **1** final **2** fundamental **3** greatest (*infml*) **4** farthest away —**ultimate** *n* —**ultimately** *adv*

ultimatum /últi máytəm/ (*pl* **-tums** *or* **-ta** /-tə/) *n* a final demand accompanied by a threat

ultra /últrə/ *adj* **1** extreme **2** holding extremist views —**ultra** *n*

ultra- *prefix* **1** more than normal, excessively, completely ○ *ultracautious* **2** outside the range of ○ *ultrasound*

ultramarine /últrəmə reèn/ *n* a deep blue pigment or colour —**ultramarine** *adj*

ultrasonic /últrə sónnik/ *adj* of or having frequencies above the range of human hearing

ultrasound /últrə sownd/ *n* **1** ultrasonic sound **2** an imaging technique that uses high-frequency sound for medical examinations

ultraviolet /últrə vī ələt/ *adj* of or producing light beyond the violet end of the visible spectrum —**ultraviolet** *n*

ululate /yoólyoò layt/ (**-lating, -lated**) *vi* howl or wail, in grief or in jubilation —**ululation** /yoólyoò láysh'n/ *n*

Uluru /oóolə roó/ largest rock mass in the world, in S Northern Territory, Australia. Height 868 m/2,848 ft.

Ulverstone /úlvərstən/ coastal town in N Tasmania, Australia. Pop. 9,935 (1991).

Ulysses /yoo lísseez, yoóli seez/ *n* the Roman name for Odysseus

umber /úmbər/ *n* **1** a brown pigment or dye made from soil **2** soil used for umber

umbilical /um bíllik'l/ *adj* **1** of the umbilical cord **2** resembling a navel ■ *n* an umbilical cord

umbilical cord *n* **1** the tube connecting a foetus to the placenta **2** a cable or pipe providing an essential link or supply of something

umbilicus /um bíllikəss, úmbi líkəss/ (*pl* **-ci** /-sī/) *n* a navel (*technical*)

umbra /úmbrə/ (*pl* **-brae** /-bree/ *or* **-bras**) *n* **1** a shadow caused by the complete blockage of all light **2** the darkest part of the shadow cast by an astronomical object during an eclipse —**umbral** *adj*

umbrage /úmbrij/ *n* offence ○ *take umbrage*

umbrella /um bréllə/ *n* **1** a round collapsible canopy that protects somebody from rain or sun **2** something resembling an umbrella in shape or function ■ *adj* **1** coordinating or protecting member organizations **2** including a number of things ○ *an umbrella term*

Umbria /úmbri ə/ region in central Italy. Pop. 832,675 (1998).

umlaut /óóm lowt/ *n* **1** a change in a vowel sound under the influence of a vowel in the next syllable **2** two dots above a vowel indicating an umlaut —**umlaut** *vti*

umpire /úm pīr/ *n* **1** an official who supervises and enforces the rules of a game **2** somebody who settles a dispute —**umpire** *vti*

ORIGIN 'An umpire' was originally 'a noumpere'. The *n* was lost when this common combination of words was misinterpreted. *Noumpere* came from a French word meaning literally 'not an equal'.

umpteen /úmp teén/ *det* very many (*infml*) —**umpteenth** *det*

UN *abbr* United Nations

un- *prefix* **1** not o *unavoidable* **2** opposite of, lack of o *unrest* **3** do the opposite of, reverse o *uninstall* **4** deprive of, remove something from o *unburden* **5** release from o *uncork* **6** completely o *unloose*

unabashed /únnə básht/ *adj* not ashamed or embarrassed —**unabashedly** /-báshədli/ *adv*

unabated /únnə báytid/ *adj* just as forceful as before

unable /un áyb'l/ *adj* not able

unacceptable /únnək séptəb'l/ *adj* **1** below the required standard **2** unable to be accepted —**unacceptability** /-séptə bílləti/ *n* —**unacceptably** *adv*

unaccompanied /únnə kúmpənid/ *adj, adv* **1** alone **2** without other musical instruments or voices

unaccountable /únnə kówntəb'l/ *adj* **1** inexplicable **2** not answerable to anyone —**unaccountability** /-kówntə bílləti/ *n* —**unaccountably** *adv*

unaccustomed /únnə kústəmd/ *adj* **1** not accustomed to something **2** unfamiliar —**unaccustomedness** *n*

unacquainted /únnə kwáyntid/ *adj* **1** unfamiliar with something **2** unknown to somebody —**unacquaintedness** *n*

unadopted /únnə dóptid/ *adj* **1** not adopted **2** describes a road that is not maintained by local government

unadulterated /únnə dúltə raytid/ *adj* **1** not mixed or diluted with anything else **2** absolute o *unadulterated joy*

unadventurous /únnəd vénchərəss/ *adj* **1** cautious **2** unexciting —**unadventurously** *adv*

unaffected /únnə féktid/ *adj* **1** sincere, genuine, and natural **2** not affected by something —**unaffectedly** *adv*

unafraid /únnə fráyd/ *adj* not afraid

unaided /un áydid/ *adj* alone and without help

Unaipon /oo ní pon/, **David** (1873–1967) Australian writer and inventor of agricultural machinery

unalloyed /únnə lóyd/ *adj* **1** containing no impurities, and mixed with no other metals **2** absolute o *unalloyed pleasure*

unalterable /un áwltərəb'l/ *adj* unable to be changed —**unalterably** *adv*

unambiguous /ún am bíggyoo əss/ *adj* clear and unable to be misunderstood —**unambiguously** *adv*

un-American *adj* **1** at odds with US ways and traditions **2** not loyal to the United States

unanimous /yoo nánniməss/ *adj* **1** agreed on by everyone **2** in complete agreement —**unanimity** /yoŏnə nímməti/ *n* —**unanimously** *adv*

unanswerable /un áanssərəb'l/ *adj* **1** impossible to answer or solve **2** impossible to contradict or deny

unappetizing /un áppi tīzing/, **unappetising** *adj* **1** not stimulating the appetite **2** not appealing —**unappetizingly** *adv*

unapproachable /únnə próchəb'l/ *adj* **1** too unfriendly to approach or contact **2** inaccessible —**unapproachability** /-próchə bílləti/ *n* —**unapproachably** *adv*

unarchive /un áar kīv/ (**-chiving, -chived**) *vt* retrieve a computer file from archive storage

unarguable /un áargyoo əb'l/ *adj* **1** undeniably true or correct **2** not fit to use as an argument —**unarguably** *adv*

unarmed /un áarmd/ *adj* **1** without weapons **2** with the firing mechanism disabled

unashamed /únnə sháymd/ *adj* **1** not ashamed or apologetic **2** unrestrained —**unashamedly** /-sháymidli/ *adv*

unasked /un áaskt/ *adj* **1** not having been asked **2** coming to a gathering without being invited

unassailable /únnə sáyləb'l/ *adj* **1** impossible to challenge o *an unassailable lead* **2** impossible to attack —**unassailably** *adv*

unassuming /únnə syoóming/ *adj* modest —**unassumingly** *adv* —**unassumingness** *n*

unattached /únnə tácht/ *adj* **1** without a spouse or partner **2** not attached to something

unattended /únnə téndid/ *adj* **1** with no one present to listen, watch, or participate **2** not looked after or dealt with **3** not escorted (*fml*)

unattractive /únnə tráktiv/ *adj* **1** not having a pleasing appearance **2** not having obvious advantages or interesting aspects —**unattractively** *adv* —**unattractiveness** *n*

SYNONYMS unattractive, unsightly, ugly, hideous, homely, plain CORE MEANING: not pleasant to look at

unattributed /únnə tríbbyətid/ *adj* not credited to any source or creator

~~unatural~~ incorrect spelling of **unnatural**

unavailable /únnə váyləb'l/ *adj* **1** not obtainable or able to be used **2** unable to undertake something —**unavailability** /únnə vaylə bílləti/ *n*

unavailing /únnə váyling/ *adj* useless or futile —**unavailingly** *adv*

unavoidable /únnə vóydəb'l/ *adj* impossible to avoid —**unavoidably** *adv*

unaware /únnə wáir/ *adj* **1** not aware **2** not knowledgeable ■ *adv* unawares —**unawareness** *n*

unawares /únnə wáirz/ *adv* **1** unexpectedly ○ *caught me unawares* **2** without intending to

unbalanced /un bállənst/ *adj* **1** lacking a balanced distribution of weight **2** psychologically unstable **3** done or provided from only one perspective

unbearable /un báirəb'l/ *adj* too unpleasant to tolerate —**unbearably** *adv*

unbeatable /un beétəb'l/ *adj* too good to surpass

unbeaten /un beét'n/ *adj* **1** undefeated **2** not whipped or pounded ○ *unbeaten eggs* **3** not travelled on ○ *an unbeaten path*

unbecoming /únbi kúmming/ *adj* **1** not making somebody look attractive **2** not right or proper —**unbecomingly** *adv*

unbeknown /únbi nón/, **unbeknownst** /-nónst/ *adj* **1** happening without somebody knowing **2** not known to somebody ■ *adv* without being noticed

unbelief /únbi leéf/ *n* lack of religious or political belief —**unbeliever** *n* —**unbelieving** *adj*

unbelievable /únbi leévəb'l/ *adj* **1** impossible to believe **2** extraordinary —**unbelievably** *adv*

unbend /un bénd/ *vti* **1** make or become more relaxed or informal **2** make or become straight —**unbendable** *adj*

unbending /un bénding/ *adj* **1** inflexible in opinions or attitudes **2** strictly applied or observed —**unbendingly** *adv*

unbiased /un bí əst/, **unbiassed** *adj* fair, impartial, or objective

unbidden /un bídd'n/ *adj, adv (literary)* **1** spontaneous **2** unsolicited

unblemished /un blémmisht/ *adj* **1** not marked with imperfections **2** not spoilt by errors

unblinking /un blíngking/ *adj* **1** without hesitation **2** without blinking —**unblinkingly** *adv*

unblock /un blók/ *vt* remove a blockage from

unborn /un báwrn/ *adj* not yet born

unbosom /un boózzəm/ *vr* say what is on your mind *(literary)* ○ *unbosomed himself to us*

unbounded /un bówndid/ *adj* **1** not restrained **2** without restrictions

unbowed /un bówd/ *adj* **1** not defeated or subdued **2** remaining erect, not bent

unbridgeable /un bríjjəb'l/ *adj* **1** impossible to span with a bridge **2** impossible to reduce ○ *an unbridgeable gulf between the two parties*

unbridled /un bríd'ld/ *adj* **1** openly expressed **2** without a bridle

unbroken /un brókən/ *adj* **1** without gaps or pauses **2** undefeated **3** untamed **4** intact **5** viable or in force

unburden /un búrd'n/ *vr* get something off your mind by telling somebody *(fml)*

unbutton /un bútt'n/ *vt* undo the buttons of

uncalled-for /un káwld-/ *adj* unjustified

uncanny /un kánni/ (**-nier, -niest**) *adj* **1** very strange or eerie **2** unexpectedly accurate —**uncannily** *adv* —**uncanniness** *n*

uncared-for /un káird-/ *adj* neglected

uncaring /un káiring/ *adj* **1** unsympathetic **2** unconcerned ○ *uncaring of what others might think* —**uncaringly** *adv*

unceasing /un seéssing/ *adj* never stopping —**unceasingly** *adv* —**unceasingness** *n*

unceremonious /ún seri móni əss/ *adj* **1** abrupt and rude **2** informal —**unceremoniously** *adv*

uncertain /un súrt'n/ *adj* **1** lacking clear knowledge or a definite opinion **2** not yet known or settled **3** changeable —**uncertainly** *adv* —**uncertainty** *n* ◊ See note at **doubtful**

uncharacteristic /ún karəktə rístik/ *adj* not typical or usual —**uncharacteristically** *adv*

uncharitable /un chárritəb'l/ *adj* lacking in kindness or mercy —**uncharitably** *adv*

uncharted /un cháartid/ *adj* **1** not mapped **2** unknown

unchecked /un chékt/ *adj* **1** not limited or controlled **2** not verified or tested

uncivil /un sívv'l/ *adj* rude —**uncivilly** *adv*

uncivilized /un sívvə lízd/, **uncivilised** *adj* **1** not culturally advanced **2** far from settled areas

unclad /un klád/ *adj* naked

unclassified /un klássi fïd/ *adj* **1** not arranged systematically **2** available for examination by anyone

uncle /úngk'l/ *n* **1** a parent's brother or brother-in-law **2** a parent's male friend

unclean /un kleén/ *adj* **1** dirty **2** sinful, especially involving a sexual sin —**uncleanness** *n* ◊ See note at **dirty**

unclear /un kleér/ *adj* **1** not obvious **2** not sure

Uncle Sam *n* **1** a personification of the United States **2** the United States, its government, or its people

ORIGIN **Uncle Sam** was invented from *US*, an abbreviation for the United States. It is first recorded in 1813.

unclothed /un klóthd/ *adj* having no clothes or covering on

uncoil /un kóyl/ *vti* unwind, or release from being coiled

uncomfortable /un kúmftəb'l/ *adj* **1** not physically comfortable **2** awkward or uneasy —**uncomfortably** *adv*

uncommon /un kómmən/ *adj* **1** rare **2** very great —**uncommonly** *adv* —**uncommonness** *n*

uncommunicative /únkə myoónikətiv/ *adj* not willing or tending to say much —**uncommunicativeness** *n* ◊ See note at **silent**

uncomprehending /ún kompri hénding/ *adj* unable to understand —**uncomprehendingly** *adv*

uncompromising /un kómprə mīzing/ *adj* not willing to compromise or give in —**uncompromisingly** *adv*

unconcerned /únkən súrnd/ *adj* 1 not anxious 2 uninterested, or unwilling to become involved —**unconcernedly** /-súrnidli/ *adv*

unconditional /únkən dísh'nəl/ *adj* with no conditions or limitations —**unconditionally** *adv*

uncongenial /únkən jeényəl/ *adj* 1 unfriendly 2 unsuitable or unappealing o *finds the job uncongenial* —**uncongenially** *adv*

unconscionable /un kónsh'nəb'l/ *adj* 1 morally unacceptable 2 unreasonable —**unconscionably** *adv*

unconscious /un kónshəss/ *adj* 1 experiencing temporary loss of all senses 2 unaware ■ *n* the part of the mind containing things the person is unaware of —**unconsciously** *adv* —**unconsciousness** *n*

~~unconsious~~ incorrect spelling of **unconscious**

unconstitutional /ún konsti tyoosh'nəl/ *adj* contrary to a constitution —**unconstitutionality** /ún konsti tyoosh'n álləti/ *n* —**unconstitutionally** *adv*

uncontrollable /únkən trólləb'l/ *adj* 1 too strongly felt to be suppressed 2 too unruly or wild to control —**uncontrollably** *adv*

unconventional /únkən vénsh'nəl/ *adj* different from what is usual or standard —**unconventionality** /-vénshə nálləti/ *n* —**unconventionally** *adv*

unconvincing /únkən vínssing/ *adj* 1 not able to persuade people to believe or accept something as real 2 not impressive —**unconvincingly** *adv*

uncooked /un kookt/ *adj* not having been cooked

uncooperative /ún kō óppərətiv/ *adj* unwilling to cooperate —**uncooperatively** *adv*

uncoordinated /ún kō áwrdi naytid/ *adj* 1 clumsy in movement or action 2 not organized

uncork /un káwrk/ *vt* 1 remove the cork from a bottle 2 release something repressed

uncouple /un kúpp'l/ (**-pling, -pled**) *v* 1 *vti* unfasten 2 *vt* release from restraint

uncouth /un kooth/ *adj* 1 ill-mannered 2 awkward —**uncouthly** *adv* —**uncouthness** *n*

uncover /un kúvvər/ *vt* 1 take the cover off something 2 expose or reveal something secret or previously hidden

uncrewed /un krood/ *adj* having no personnel, especially no pilot or crew

uncritical /un kríttik'l/ *adj* not critical or discriminating —**uncritically** *adv*

uncross /un króss/ *vt* straighten out from a crossed position

unction /úngksh'n/ *n* 1 the anointing of somebody with oil 2 an oil, ointment, or salve used in a rite 3 real or pretended earnestness 4 flattering efforts to charm

unctuous /úngkchoo əss/ *adj* 1 excessively ingratiating 2 oily, fatty, or greasy —**unctuously** *adv* —**unctuousness** *n*

uncurl /un kúrl/ *vti* unwind from a curl, coil, or spiral

uncut /ún kút/ *adj* 1 not cut with a sharp implement 2 complete and unabridged 3 describes a gemstone before facets have been cut o *uncut diamonds*

undaunted /un dáwntid/ *adj* not frightened or deterred —**undauntedly** *adv* —**undauntedness** *n*

undecided /úndi sídid/ *adj* 1 not yet having made a choice or decision 2 not yet finalized —**undecidedness** *n*

undelete /úndi leet/ (**-leting, -leted**) *vt* reinstate an electronic file or text that has been deleted

undemonstrative /úndi mónstrətiv/ *adj* tending not to show emotion openly —**undemonstrativeness** *n*

undeniable /úndi ní əb'l/ *adj* 1 unquestionably true or real 2 unable to be refused —**undeniably** *adv*

under /úndər/ *prep* 1 below the top or base of 2 beneath a layer of 3 less than 4 subordinate to 5 subject to the control or authority of o *under existing legislation* 6 during the rule of 7 in view of o *impossible under these conditions* 8 undergoing o *under scrutiny* 9 using as a protective pretence or pretext o *travelling under a false name* 10 classified as or in o *filed under 'Miscellaneous'* 11 powered by o *under sail* ■ *adv* 1 below a surface or point 2 fewer or less ■ *adv, adj* in a subservient position (*infml*) o *keeping the masses under*

under- *prefix* 1 too little, less than usual o *underachiever* o *underpay* 2 below, underneath o *underpants* o *underscore* 3 subordinate, of lower rank o *undersecretary*

underachiever /úndər ə cheevər/ *n* somebody who does less well than expected —**underachieve** *vi*

underage /úndər áyj/ *adj* 1 below the legal or required age for something 2 done by underage people o *underage driving*

underarm /úndər aarm/ *adj* 1 done with the arm below shoulder height o *an underarm throw* 2 on the underside of the arm, or used in the armpit ■ *n* 1 the underside of the arm on the body or a garment 2 the armpit —**underarm** *adv*

underbelly /úndər belli/ (*pl* **-lies**) *n* 1 the lowest part of an animal's belly 2 a weak or vulnerable point

underbite /úndər bīt/ *n* a dental condition in which the lower incisor teeth overlap the upper

underbooked /úndər bookt/ *adj* not having attracted enough bookings

undercarriage /úndər karij/ *n* 1 the framework of struts and wheels supporting an aircraft on the ground 2 the supporting structure underneath a vehicle

undercharge *vti* /úndər chaarj/ (**-charging, -charged**) not charge enough ■ *n* /úndər chaarj/ an excessively low price

underclass /úndər klaass/ *n* a social class so poor and deprived as to be outside mainstream society

underclothes /ún̲dər klō̲t͟hz/ *npl* underwear

undercoat /ún̲dər kōt/ *n* **1** a coat of paint beneath the final coat **2** paint for use as an undercoat **3** a dense layer of short hair under an animal's outer coat ■ *vt* paint with an undercoat

undercover /ún̲dər kúvvər/ *adj* secretly gathering information —**undercover** *adv*

undercurrent /ún̲dər kurrənt/ *n* **1** an underlying current of water or air **2** a hidden feeling or force ○ *an undercurrent of resentment*

undercut /ún̲dər kút/ *v* **1** *vt* charge a lower amount than **2** *vt* reduce the force of **3** *vt* cut the lower part of **4** *vti* hit a ball so as to give it backspin —**undercut** /ún̲dər kut/ *n*

underdeveloped /ún̲dər di vélləpt/ *adj* **1** not grown to the full or usual extent **2** without the means for economic growth —**underdevelopment** *n*

underdog /ún̲dər dog/ *n* **1** the expected loser of a contest **2** somebody at a disadvantage

underdone /ún̲dər dún/ *adj* **1** inadequately cooked **2** cooked only lightly

underemployed /ún̲dər im plóyd/ *adj* not being used fully —**underemployment** *n*

underestimate *v* /ún̲dər ésti mayt/ (**-mating, -mated**) **1** *vti* make too low an estimate of something **2** *vt* make too low a judgment of the worth of ■ *n* /ún̲dər éstimət/ an estimate that is too low —**underestimation** /ún̲dər ésti máysh'n/ *n*

underfelt /ún̲dər felt/ *n* a layer of felt or other material put down below a carpet

underfinanced /ún̲dər fi nánst, -fí nanst/ *adj* without sufficient money or funding

underfloor /ún̲dər fláwr/ *adj* beneath the flooring

underfoot /ún̲dər fŏŏt/ *adv* **1** beneath the feet **2** in the way

underfund /ún̲dər fúnd/ *vt* not provide enough funding for

undergarment /ún̲dər gaarmənt/ *n* a garment worn as underwear

undergo /ún̲dər gṓ/ (**-goes, -going, -went** /-wént/, **-gone** /-gón/) *vt* experience or endure

undergraduate /ún̲dər grájjoo ət/ *n* a student studying for a first degree

underground *adj* /ún̲dər grownd/ **1** beneath the Earth's surface **2** covert **3** contrary to the prevailing culture ■ *n* /ún̲dər grownd/ **1** a railway running below ground (*often before nouns*) **2** a secret resistance movement **3** a movement contrary to the prevailing culture ■ *adv* /ún̲dər grównd/ **1** below ground **2** secretly

undergrowth /ún̲dər grṓth/ *n* vegetation growing under the trees in a forest

underhand /ún̲dər hánd, ún̲dər hand/ *adj* secret and dishonest —**underhand** *adv* —**underhanded** *adj, adv* —**underhandedly** *adv* —**underhandedness** *n*

underlay *vt* /ún̲dər láy/ (**-laid** /-láyd/) lay something underneath something else ■ *n* /ún̲dər lay/ **1** a layer of cushioning under a carpet **2** a base, support, or foundation underneath something —**underlaid** *adj*

underlie /ún̲dər lī́/ (**-lying, -lay** /-láy/, **-lain** /-láyn/) *vt* **1** lie or be put underneath **2** be the basis or cause of

underline *vt* /ún̲dər lī́n/ (**-lining, -lined**) **1** draw or type a line below **2** emphasize ■ *n* /ún̲dər līn/ a line drawn or typed below something

underling /ún̲dərling/ *n* a servant or subordinate, especially one regarded as of little importance

underlying /ún̲dər lī́ ing/ *adj* **1** lying underneath **2** hidden and significant **3** basic or essential

undermentioned /ún̲dər mensh'nd/ *adj* named later (*fml*)

undermine /ún̲dər mī́n/ (**-mining, -mined**) *vt* **1** weaken by removing material from below **2** weaken gradually or imperceptibly ○ *begin to undermine her confidence*

underneath /ún̲dər néeth/ *prep, adv* **1** below or beneath something, and perhaps covered by it **2** underlying something shown on the surface or openly expressed ■ *adv, adj* on the lower part or the part that faces the ground ■ *n* the lower part, or the part that faces the ground

undernourished /ún̲dər núrrisht/ *adj* not having had enough food or nutrients for health

underpants /ún̲dər pants/ *npl* briefs or shorts used as underwear

underparts /ún̲dər paarts/ *npl* the sides and belly of an animal

underpass /ún̲dər paass/ *n* **1** a road under another road or a railway **2** a tunnel for pedestrians under a road or railway

underpay /ún̲dər páy/ (**-paid** /-páyd/) *vt* not pay enough —**underpayment** *n*

underpin /ún̲dər pín/ (**-pinning, -pinned**) *vt* **1** support by propping from below **2** act as a support or foundation for ○ *the facts that underpin these assumptions*

underpinning /ún̲dər pining/ *n* **1** a support for a weakened structure **2** a foundation or basis (*usually pl*)

underplay /ún̲dər pláy/ *v* **1** *vti* act a role subtly or with restraint **2** *vt* present or deal with in a subtle or restrained way

underpopulated /ún̲dər póppyŏŏ laytid/ *adj* having a population smaller than desirable or expected —**underpopulation** /ún̲dər popyŏŏ láysh'n/ *n*

underprivileged /ún̲dər prívvəlijd/ *adj* denied social privileges and rights, usually as a result of poverty (*euphemistic*)

underrate /ún̲dər ráyt/ (**-rating, -rated**) *vt* give or have too low an assessment of

underrun *vt* /ún̲dər rún/ (**-running, -ran** /-rán/, **-run**) pass or move under ■ *n* /ún̲dər run/ **1** a lower-than-estimated cost **2** a lower-than-required production run

underscore *vt* /ún̲dər skáwr/ (**-scoring, -scored**) **1** draw a line under **2** emphasize ■ *n* /ún̲dər skawr/ a line drawn under something

undersea /úndər see/ *adj* of the area below the surface of the sea ■ *adv also* **underseas** to the area below the surface of the sea

undersecretary /úndər sékritəri/ (*pl* **-ies**) *n* 1 an assistant secretary in a government department 2 a subordinate of a secretary of state —**undersecretariat** /úndər sékri táiri ət/ *n*

undersell /úndər sél/ (**-sold** /-sóld/) *vt* 1 sell something below the proper value 2 sell goods more cheaply than a competitor 3 present or advertise the merits of something or somebody with too little enthusiasm

underside /úndər síd/ *n* 1 the lower side, or the side facing the ground 2 an undesirable, and usually hidden, aspect

undersigned /úndər sínd/ *n* the person whose signature appears below (*fml*) —**undersigned** *adj*

undersized /úndər sízd/ *adj* smaller than the usual or preferred size

underskirt /úndər skurt/ *n* a skirt worn underneath another one

undersold past tense, past participle of **undersell**

underspend /úndər spénd/ (**-spent** /-spént/) *vi* spend less than usual or expected

understand /úndər stánd/ (**-stood** /-stóod/) *v* 1 *vti* grasp the meaning of something 2 *vti* realize or be aware of something 3 *vt* know and be able to use ○ *understands Spanish* 4 *vti* know the character or situation of and sympathize with somebody 5 *vt* interpret in a particular way ○ *understood it as a peaceful gesture* 6 *vt* take as settled or agreed 7 *vt* gather or assume by learning or hearing ○ *He is, I understand, expected later.* —**understandable** *adj* —**understandably** *adv*

understanding /úndər stánding/ *n* 1 the ability to understand something or somebody 2 somebody's interpretation of something 3 a state of mutual comprehension or agreement ○ *came to an understanding* 4 knowledge of and sympathy with another's character or situation ■ *adj* sympathetically aware of another's character or situation —**understandingly** *adv*

understate /úndər stáyt/ (**-stating, -stated**) *vt* 1 express with restraint 2 describe as being less than its true amount ○ *understate the cost*

understated /úndər stáytid/ *adj* subtly restrained

understatement /úndər stáytmənt, úndər stáytmənt/ *n* 1 a deliberately restrained or muted statement or way of expressing yourself 2 a statement that reports something as less large or significant than it is

understood /úndər stóod/ past tense, past participle of **understand** ■ *adj* agreed, assumed, or implied

understudy /úndər studi/ (*pl* **-ies**) *n* 1 an actor who learns the role of another actor so as to be able to act as a replacement 2 a trained substitute —**understudy** *vti*

undertake /úndər táyk/ (**-taking, -took** /-tóok/,

-taken /-táykən/) *v* 1 *vti* make a commitment to do something 2 *vt* set about doing

undertaker /úndər taykər/ *n* somebody whose business is to arrange burials and cremations

undertaking /úndər táyking/ *n* 1 a task or project 2 a commitment to do something

under-the-counter *adj* sold secretly or illegally

undertone /úndər tón/ *n* 1 a low or quiet tone 2 something suggested or implied rather than stated openly

undertow /úndər tó/ *n* 1 the pull of water away from a shore after a wave has broken 2 an underlying feeling or force that is opposite to the apparent one ○ *an undertow of dissatisfaction*

underused /úndər yóozd/ *adj* insufficiently used —**underuse** /-yóoss/ *n*

undervalue /úndər vállyoo/ (**-uing, -ued**) *vt* 1 estimate or set at too low a value 2 hold in lower esteem than is deserved or appropriate —**undervaluation** /úndər vállyoo áysh'n/ *n*

underwater /úndər wawtər/ *adj* below the surface of water —**underwater** /úndər wáwtər/ *adv*

under way, underway /úndər wáy/ *adj* in motion or progress

underwear /úndər wair/ *n* clothes worn underneath other clothes and usually not meant to be visible

underweight /úndər wáyt/ *adj* not heavy enough

underwent past tense of **undergo**

underwhelm /úndər wélm/ *vt* fail to impress (*humorous*) —**underwhelming** *adj*

underwire /úndər wír/ *n* a wire under each cup of a bra to provide support —**underwired** *adj*

underworld /úndər wurld/ *n* 1 criminal society ○ *an underworld shooting* 2 in Greek and Roman mythology, the abode of the dead

underwrite /úndər rít, úndər rít/ (**-writing, -wrote** /-rót, -rōt/, **-written** /-ritt'n, -ritt'n/) *vti* 1 issue insurance for somebody or something 2 agree to buy unsold securities at a fixed price and time 3 agree to cover the losses of somebody or something

underwriter /úndər rítər/ *n* 1 somebody who underwrites 2 somebody whose job is to assess risks and fix insurance premiums

undeserved /úndi zúrvd/ *adj* not deserved —**undeservedly** /-zúrvidli/ *adv*

undesirable /úndi zírəb'l/ *adj* not wanted, liked, or approved of ■ *n* somebody regarded as undesirable —**undesirability** /úndi zírə bíllati/ *n*

undeveloped /únndi vélləpt/ *adj* 1 not exploited or used in a productive way 2 without the means for economic growth (*sometimes offensive*) 3 not processed to produce a photographic negative or print 4 not grown to maturity

undid past tense of **undo**

undies /úndiz/ *npl* underwear, especially for women and girls (*infml*)

undisputed /ún di spyoótid/ *adj* accepted as true, valid, or rightfully deserving the description

undivided /ún di vídid/ *adj* **1** not separated or split **2** concentrated on one thing

undo /un doó/ (**-does** /-dúz/, **-doing**, **-did** /-díd/, **-done** /-dún/) *v* **1** *vti* unfasten, untie, or unwrap, or become unfastened, untied, or unwrapped **2** *vt* cancel or reverse the effect of an action **3** *vt* bring somebody or something to ruin or disaster *(literary)*

undoing /un doó ing/ *n* the act of bringing somebody or something to ruin or disaster, or the cause of this o *Pride was our undoing.*

undone /un dún/ past participle of **undo** ■ *adj* **1** not yet done or completed **2** unfastened, untied, or unwrapped **3** brought to ruin or disaster *(fml or humorous)*

undoubted /un dówtid/ *adj* not subject to doubt or dispute —**undoubtedly** *adv*

~~undoubtly~~ incorrect spelling of **undoubtedly**

undreamed-of /un dreémd ov/, **undreamt-of** /-drémt-/ *adj* impossible to imagine in advance

undress /un dréss/ *vti* remove the clothes from somebody's or your own body ■ *n* **1** the state of having no clothes on **2** informal clothing or an everyday uniform

undressed /un drést/ *adj* **1** naked, or scantily clothed **2** not processed or treated **3** without a sauce or salad dressing **4** without a bandage or sterile dressing ◊ See note at **naked**

undue /ún dyoó/ *adj* **1** excessive, inappropriate, or unjustified **2** not payable now

undulate /úndyoó layt/ (**-lating**, **-lated**) *v* **1** *vti* have or give a movement or appearance resembling waves **2** *vi* go up and down gracefully —**undulation** /úndyoó láysh'n/ *n*

unduly /un dyoólí/ *adv* excessively

undying /un dí ing/ *adj* not diminishing over time

unearned /un úrnd/ *adj* **1** not gained by work **2** undeserved

unearth /un úrth/ *vt* **1** dig out of the ground **2** discover or disclose

unearthly /un úrthli/ *adj* **1** not being or seeming to be from this world **2** inappropriate or unreasonable *(fml)* o *at this unearthly hour* —**unearthliness** *n*

uneasy /un eézi/ (**-ier**, **-iest**) *adj* **1** anxious or afraid **2** uncertain and not easing anxiety —**unease** *n* —**uneasily** *adv* —**uneasiness** *n* ◊ See note at **worry**

~~unecessary~~ incorrect spelling of **unnecessary**

uneconomic /ún eekə nómmik, -ekə-/ *adj* **1** not making a profit **2** *also* **uneconomical** not efficient

uneducated /un éddyoó kaytid/ *adj* not educated, or not well educated

unemotional /únni mósh'nəl/ *adj* **1** showing little or no feeling **2** reasoned and objective —**unemotionally** *adv*

unemployable /únnim plóy əb'l/ *adj* lacking the skills, education, or ability to get a job

unemployed /únnim plóyd/ *adj* **1** without a paid job **2** not in use

unemployment /únnim plóymənt/ *n* **1** the condition of having no job **2** the number of unemployed people

unending /un énding/ *adj* continuing or seeming to continue forever

unenviable /un énvee əb'l/ *adj* unpleasant or difficult o *had the unenviable task of breaking the bad news* —**unenviably** *adv*

unequal /un eékwəl/ *adj* **1** not measurably the same **2** variable **3** not evenly balanced or matched **4** without the necessary ability to do something o *unequal to the task* —**unequally** *adv*

unequalled /un eékwəld/ *adj* unparalleled or unprecedented

unequivocal /únni kwívvək'l/ *adj* allowing for no doubt or misinterpretation —**unequivocally** *adv* ·

unerring /un úr ing/ *adj* consistently accurate —**unerringly** *adv*

UNESCO /yoo néskō/, **Unesco** *n* a UN agency that promotes international collaboration on culture, education, and science. Full form **United Nations Educational, Scientific, and Cultural Organization**

unethical /un éthik'l/ *adj* not conforming to agreed standards of moral conduct o *unethical business practices* —**unethically** *adv*

uneven /un eév'n/ *adj* **1** not level or flat **2** varying **3** not straight or parallel **4** not equal **5** not divisible by two —**unevenly** *adv* —**unevenness** *n*

uneventful /únni véntf'l/ *adj* with nothing remarkable happening —**uneventfully** *adv* —**uneventfulness** *n*

unexceptionable /únnik sépsh'nəb'l/ *adj* providing no grounds for criticism

unexceptional /únnik sépsh'nəl/ *adj* not special or unusual —**unexceptionally** *adv*

unexpected /únnik spéktid/ *adj* coming as a surprise —**unexpectedly** *adv* —**unexpectedness** *n*

unfailing /un fáyling/ *adj* **1** always reliable or constant **2** always accurate or faultless —**unfailingly** *adv*

unfair /un fáir/ *adj* **1** not equal or just **2** not ethical in business dealings —**unfairly** *adv* —**unfairness** *n*

unfaithful /un fáythf'l/ *adj* **1** untrue to commitments or beliefs **2** not faithful to your spouse or partner —**unfaithfully** *adv* —**unfaithfulness** *n*

unfamiliar /únfə mílli ər/ *adj* **1** not previously known or experienced, or not recognized **2** with no previous knowledge or experience o *unfamiliar with the software* —**unfamiliarity** /únfə mílli árrəti/ *n* —**unfamiliarly** *adv*

unfashionable /un fásh'nəb'l/ *adj* **1** not in the current style **2** not socially approved of —**unfashionably** *adv*

unfasten /un faáss'n/ *vt* separate the parts of something so as to release a fastening

unfathomable /un fáthəməb'l/ *adj* impossible to understand —**unfathomably** *adv*

unfavourable /un fáyvərəb'l/ *adj* 1 expressing disapproval or opposition 2 unlikely to be beneficial —**unfavourably** *adv*

unfeeling /un feeling/ *adj* 1 not sympathetic 2 numb —**unfeelingly** *adv*

unfettered /un féttərd/ *adj* free of or freed from restrictions

unfinished /un fínnisht/ *adj* 1 not completed 2 not finally treated with something such as dye, paint, or varnish

unfit /un fít/ *adj* 1 unsuitable 2 unqualified 3 not fit and healthy —**unfitly** *adv* —**unfitness** *n*

unflagging /un flágging/ *adj* remaining strong and unchanging —**unflaggingly** *adv*

unflappable /un fláppəb'l/ *adj* remaining composed under all circumstances

unflinching /un flínching/ *adj* strong and un-hesitating —**unflinchingly** *adv*

unfold /un fóld/ *vti* 1 open and spread out 2 make or be understood by gradual exposure

unforeseen /ún fawr seén/ *adj* not expected beforehand

unforgettable /únfər géttəb'l/ *adj* remarkable and never to be forgotten —**unforgettably** *adv*

unforgivable /únfər gívvəb'l/ *adj* so bad that it can never be forgiven —**unforgivably** *adv*

unforgiving /únfər gívving/ *adj* 1 unwilling to forgive 2 providing no margin for mistakes

unformed /un fáwrmd/ *adj* 1 with no real shape 2 not yet fully developed

unfortunate /un fáwrchənət/ *adj* 1 never experiencing good luck 2 accompanied by or bringing bad luck 3 inappropriate o *an unfortunate choice of words* ■ *n* somebody unlucky or lacking adequate resources —**unfortunately** *adv*

unfounded /un fówndid/ *adj* not supported by evidence

unfrequented /únfri kwéntid/ *adj* not often visited

unfriendly /un fréndli/ *adj* 1 hostile or cold in manner 2 unfavourable —**unfriendliness** *n*

unfurl /un fúrl/ *vti* unroll or spread out

unfurnished /un fúrnisht/ *adj* without furniture

ungainly /un gáynli/ *adj* 1 lacking grace while moving 2 awkward to handle

ungodly /un góddli/ *adj* 1 not revering God 2 wicked 3 inappropriate or unreasonable *(infml)* —**ungodliness** *n*

ungovernable /un gúvvərnəb'l/ *adj* incapable of being controlled

ungracious /un gráyshəss/ *adj* ill-mannered —**ungraciously** *adv*

ungrammatical /ún grə máttik'l/ *adj* not using correct grammar —**ungrammatically** *adv*

ungrateful /un gráytf'l/ *adj* not thankful or appreciative —**ungratefully** *adv* —**ungratefulness** *n*

unguarded /un gaárdid/ *adj* 1 with no protection 2 not wary —**unguardedly** *adv*

unguent /úng gwənt/ *n* a healing or soothing ointment

unhand /un hánd/ *vt* let go of somebody by releasing a grasp *(archaic or humorous)*

unhappy /un háppi/ *(-pier, -piest)* *adj* 1 not cheerful or joyful 2 unfortunate —**unhappily** *adv* —**unhappiness** *n*

UNHCR *abbr* United Nations High Commission for Refugees

unhealthy /un hélthi/ *(-ier, -iest)* *adj* 1 affected by ill health 2 bad for the health 3 symptomatic of ill health 4 harmful to the character 5 morally corrupt —**unhealthily** *adv* —**unhealthiness** *n*

unheard /un húrd/ *adj* 1 not perceived by the ear 2 not given a hearing

unheard-of *adj* 1 unknown 2 unprecedented

unhelpful /un hélpf'l/ *adj* not providing or willing to provide help —**unhelpfully** *adv* —**unhelpfulness** *n*

unhinge /un hínj/ *(-hinging, -hinged)* *vt* 1 remove something from its hinges 2 make somebody mentally unstable

unholy /un hóli/ *(-lier, -liest)* *adj* 1 not blessed or consecrated 2 defying religious laws 3 extremely bad or awful *(for emphasis)*

unhook /un hoók/ *vt* 1 remove from a hook 2 undo the hooks of

unhoped-for /un hópt-/ *adj* not expected but very welcome

unhurried /un húrrid/ *adj* done in a relaxed and deliberate way —**unhurriedly** *adv*

unhygienic /ún hī jeénik/ *adj* not clean, sanitary, or healthy

uni /yoóni/ *n* a university *(infml)*

uni- *prefix* one, single o *unicellular*

unicameral /yoóni kámmərəl/ *adj* with one legislative chamber —**unicameralism** *n*

unicast /yoóni kast/ *n* a transmission from one computing terminal to one other

UNICEF /yoóni sef/, **Unicef** *n* a UN agency that works for the protection and survival of children around the world. Full form **United Nations Children's Fund**

unicellular /yoóni séllyoōlər/ *adj* single-celled

unicorn /yoóni kawrn/ *n* a mythical one-horned horse

unicycle /yoóni sík'l/ *n* a pedal-powered vehicle with a single wheel and a seat on a frame above it —**unicyclist** *n*

unidentified /ún ī dénti fīd/ *adj* 1 unable to be recognized or named 2 wanting to remain anonymous

Unification Church *n* a religious denomination founded in 1954 by Sun Myung Moon

uniform /yoóni fawrm/ *n* 1 a distinctive set of clothes indicating somebody's occupation or membership of a particular group 2 **Uniform** a communications code word for the letter 'U' ■ *adj* 1 unchanging or unvarying 2 conforming to one standard 3 like another or others —**uniformed** adj —**uniformity** /yóoni fáwrmɒti/ n —**uniformly** adv

Uniform Resource Locator n full form of **URL**

unify /yóoni fī/ (-**fies**, -**fied**) vt make into a single unit or entity —**unification** /yóonifi káysh'n/ n —**unified** adj —**unifying** adj

unilateral /yóoni láttərəl/ adj decided by, done by, or affecting one party only —**unilaterally** adv

unilateralism /yóoni láttərəlizəm/ n the exercise of a foreign policy that pays little or no regard to the views of allies

unimaginable /únni májjinəb'l/ adj beyond imagination —**unimaginably** adv

unimpeachable /únnim peéchəb'l/ adj 1 impossible to discredit or challenge 2 faultless —**unimpeachably** adv

unimportant /únnim páwrt'nt/ adj of little or no significance —**unimportance** n

unincorporated /únnin káwrpə raytid/ adj US not designated as part of a specific country or municipality

uninhabitable /únnin hábbitəb'l/ adj not fit to be lived in

uninhabited /únnin hábbitid/ adj with no one living there

uninhibited /únnin híbbitid/ adj not subject to social or other constraints —**uninhibitedly** adv

uninitiated /únni níshi aytid/ adj without knowledge or experience of a subject or activity ■ npl uninitiated people

uninspired /únnin spírd/ adj lacking originality

uninspiring /únnin spíring/ adj not inspiring

uninstall /únnin stáwl/ vt remove software from a computer

unintelligible /únnin téllijəb'l/ adj impossible to understand —**unintelligibly** adv

unintentional /únnin ténsh'nəl/ adj not done on purpose —**unintentionally** adv

uninterested /un íntrəstid/ adj lacking interest or concern —**uninterestedly** adv ◊ See note at **disinterested**

uninteresting /un íntrəsting/ adj without interesting qualities —**uninterestingly** adv

uninterrupted /únnintə rúptid/ adj 1 without interruption or break 2 without obstructions

union /yóonyən/ n 1 the joining of people or things together, or the result of this 2 agreement 3 a marriage 4 sexual intercourse 5 a political alliance 6 a trade union 7 also **Union** an organization or building providing recreational facilities for students 8 **Union** the union of Great Britain and Northern Ireland 9 **Union** the United States of America

unionism /yóonyənizəm/ n 1 the principles of trade unions 2 advocacy of trade unions 3 **Unionism** support for the union of Great Britain with Northern Ireland —**unionist** n, adj

unionize /yóonyə nīz/ (-**izing**, -**ized**), **unionise** vti organize workers into or join a trade union —**unionization** /yóonyə nī záysh'n/ n

Union Jack, Union flag n the flag of the United Kingdom

union territory, Union Territory n a territory in India ruled directly by the central government

~~uniqe~~ incorrect spelling of **unique**

unique /yoo neék/ adj 1 being the only one 2 very unusual and worthy of note 3 limited to somebody or something —**uniquely** adv —**uniqueness** n

USAGE The use of **unique** in its sense 'worthy of note' is common in marketing and advertising (*Don't miss this unique offer*), as well as in conversation. Many dictionaries and usage guides argue that **unique** is an absolute concept and so cannot be used with qualifying words such as *very* and *rather*, but this stricture seems pedantic. It is, however, best avoided in formal writing.

unisex /yóoni seks/ adj 1 suitable for either sex 2 not distinctly male or female

unison /yóoniss'n/ n 1 musical notes at the same pitch 2 the performance of musical parts at the same pitch or an octave apart ◊ **in unison** 1 in perfect agreement 2 at the same time

UNISON /yóoniss'n/ n a UK trade union for public service employees

unit /yóonit/ n 1 one person, thing, or group 2 a discrete part 3 a group with a particular function 4 a component, or an assembly of components 5 *Aus, NZ, US, Can* one of a number of similar residences in a building or development 6 a number less than ten

ORIGIN The term **unit** was introduced in the 1570s by the English mathematician, astrologer, and magician John Dee. It is formed from Latin *unus* 'one', probably on the model of *digit*.

Unitarian /yóoni táiri ən/ n a member of a Christian Church that rejects the doctrine of the Trinity and stresses individual conscience —**Unitarian** adj —**Unitarianism** n

unitary /yóonitəri/ adj 1 of a unit 2 characterized by unity 3 undivided and existing as a unit —**unitarily** adv

unite /yoo nít/ (**uniting**, **united**) vti 1 come or bring together to form a unit 2 join in marriage

united /yoo nítid/ adj 1 combined into one 2 in agreement or harmony

United Arab Emirates federation of seven independent states on the E Arabian Peninsula, including Abu Dhabi and Dubai. Cap. Abu Dhabi. Pop. 2,407,460 (2001).

United Kingdom country in NW Europe, comprising the historic kingdoms of England and Scotland, the principality of Wales, and the province of Northern Ireland. Cap. London. Pop. 59,647,790 (2001).

United Nations n an organization of nations formed in 1945 to promote peace, security, and international cooperation (+ sing or pl verb)

United States, United States of America country in central North America, comprising 50 states. Cap. Washington, D.C. Pop. 278,058,880 (2001).

unitize /yoʻoni tīz/ (**-izing, -ized**), **unitise** v **1** vti make or become one **2** vt divide into units

unit of account n the function of money in accounting

unit price n a price per item or measure

unit trust n a trust company that manages investments in the form of units representing a fraction of the total value handled

unity /yoʻonəti/ (pl **-ties**) n **1** the state of being one **2** the combining of separate entities into one **3** a whole formed by combining separate entities **4** harmony of opinion, interests, or feeling **5** the arrangement of artistic elements to create an overall aesthetic impression **6** in mathematics, the number 1

univ. abbr university

universal /yoʻoni vúrss'l/ adj **1** of or affecting the whole world or everybody in it **2** of the universe or cosmos **3** of or affecting all those in a particular group or category **4** applicable to all situations or purposes ■ n a characteristic common to everybody or to all people or things in a particular group or category —**universality** /yoʻoni vur sállati/ n —**universally** adv ◊ See note at **widespread**

Universal Product Code n US a bar code

Universal Time, Universal Time Coordinated n **1** the time in the zone that includes the prime meridian. Also called **Greenwich Mean Time 2** an international time standard based on International Atomic Time

universe /yoʻoni vurss/ n **1** the totality of all the matter and energy in space **2** humanity and its history

university /yoʻoni vúrssəti/ (pl **-ties**) n an educational institution for undergraduates and postgraduates

UNIX /yoʻoniks/ tdmk a trademark for a widely used computer operating system that can support multitasking in a multiuser environment

unjust /un júst/ adj not just or fair —**unjustly** adv —**unjustness** n

unjustifiable /un jústi fī əb'l/ adj wrong and impossible to justify —**unjustifiably** adv

unkempt /un kémpt/ adj **1** needing combing or grooming **2** untidy and neglected

ORIGIN **Unkempt** literally means 'uncombed'.

unkind /un kínd/ adj **1** lacking kindness **2** severe, harsh, or inclement —**unkindly** adv —**unkindness** n

unknowing /un nó ing/ adj **1** unaware **2** unintentional —**unknowingly** adv

unknown /ún nón/ adj **1** not known or identified ○ an unknown assailant **2** without somebody's knowledge ○ Unknown to her family, she left town. **3** not famous ■ n **1** somebody or something unknown **2** somebody or something not widely known

unlawful /un láwf'l/ adj not in accordance with or recognized by the law —**unlawfully** adv

SYNONYMS **unlawful, illegal, illicit, wrongful**
CORE MEANING: not in accordance with laws or rules

unleaded /un léddid/ adj not containing lead or a compound of lead as an additive ■ n unleaded petrol

unlearn /un lúrn/ (**-learnt** /un lúrnt/ or **-learned** /un lúrnd/) vt **1** rid the mind of **2** break the habit or end the practice of

unleash /un léesh/ vt **1** free from a leash **2** allow to have its full effect

unleavened /un lév'nd/ adj made without a raising agent

unless /un léss/ conj except under the circumstances that

unlettered /un léttərd/ adj **1** not well-educated **2** unable to read and write

unlighted /un lítid/, **unlit** /-lít/ adj **1** not having lighting **2** not alight

unlike /un lík/ prep **1** dissimilar to or different from **2** in contrast with **3** untypical of —**unlikeness** n

unlikely /un líkli/ (**-lier, -liest**) adj **1** improbable **2** not believable —**unlikelihood** n —**unlikeliness** n

unlimited /un límmitid/ adj **1** without restrictions or controls **2** lacking or appearing to lack a boundary or end

unlisted /un lístid/ adj **1** not on a list **2** not listed on a stock exchange and so not traded there **3** ANZ, US, Can not included in a telephone directory available to the public

unlit adj = **unlighted**

unload /un lód/ vti **1** remove a cargo or load from a carrier **2** discharge passengers or cargo **3** remove the charge from a gun **4** take the film out of a camera **5** pass on or sell something unwanted **6** get relief from troubles by sharing them with somebody else

unlock /un lók/ v **1** vti open after being locked **2** vt give access to for the first time **3** vt release a pent-up emotion **4** vt reveal or explain

unlooked-for /un loʻokt-/ adj unexpected

unloose /un loʻoss/ (**-loosing, -loosed**), **unloosen** /-loʻoss'n/ vt **1** unfasten **2** set free by untying **3** release from restraint or confinement

unlovely /un lúvvli/ (**-lier, -liest**) adj **1** not beautiful **2** not pleasurable —**unloveliness** n

unlucky /un lúki/ (**-ier, -iest**) adj **1** having bad luck **2** full of misfortune or failure **3** bringing misfortune —**unluckily** adv —**unluckiness** n

unmade /un máyd/ adj **1** not made neat and tidy after being slept in ○ an unmade bed **2** not covered with a durable road surfacing material

unmanned /ún mánd/ adj uncrewed (often offensive)

unmannerly /un mánnərli/ adj lacking good manners —**unmanneriness** n

unmask /un maʼask/ v **1** vti remove a mask from

somebody's face 2 *vt* expose the true nature of

unmatched /ún mácht/ *adj* 1 not belonging to a matching pair 2 having no equal or rival

unmentionable /un ménsh'nəb'l/ *adj* not to be mentioned, especially in polite conversation —**unmentionable** *n* —**unmentionableness** *n* —**unmentionably** *adv*

unmistakable /únmi stáykəb'l/, **unmistakeable** *adj* easily recognized or understood —**unmistakably** *adv*

unmitigated /un mítti gaytid/ *adj* 1 not lessened or eased in any way 2 complete and utter —**unmitigatedly** *adv*

unmoved /un moóvd/ *adj* not affected emotionally ◊ See note at **impassive**

unnamed /ún náymd/ *adj* 1 not mentioned by name 2 having no name

unnatural /un náchərəl/ *adj* 1 contrary to the laws of nature 2 contrary to natural feelings or expected standards of behaviour 3 artificial —**unnaturally** *adv* —**unnaturalness** *n*

unnecessary /un néssəssəri/ *adj* 1 not essential or required 2 unjustified and hurtful —**unnecessarily** *adv*

unnerve /un núrv/ (-**nerving**, -**nerved**) *vt* 1 deprive of resolve or courage 2 make nervous —**unnerving** *adj* —**unnervingly** *adv*

unnumbered /un númbərd/ *adj* 1 too many to be counted 2 lacking an identifying number

UNO *abbr* United Nations Organization

unobtrusive /únnəb troóssiv/ *adj* not conspicuous or assertive —**unobtrusively** *adv*

unofficial /únnə físh'l/ *adj* 1 not authorized or approved 2 not acting or done officially —**unofficially** *adv*

unopposed /únnə pózd/ *adj*, *adv* 1 meeting with no opposition 2 having no opponent

unorganized /un áwrgə nízd/, **unorganised** *adj* 1 not done or acting in an organized way 2 not unionized

unpack /un pák/ *v* 1 *vti* remove the contents from something such as a box or luggage 2 *vt* remove from a container or packaging

unpaid /ún páyd/ *adj* 1 awaiting payment 2 working or worked for no pay ○ *unpaid volunteers* ○ *unpaid overtime*

unpalatable /un pállətəb'l/ *adj* 1 having an unpleasant taste 2 hard or disagreeable to accept —**unpalatably** *adv*

unparalleled /un párrə leld/ *adj* having no equal or parallel in kind or quality

unparliamentary /ún paarlə méntəri/ *adj* not acceptable according to the practice of a parliament

unperson /ún purss'n/ *n* somebody whose existence is not acknowledged

ORIGIN Unperson was introduced by George Orwell in his novel *Nineteen Eighty-Four* (1949).

unpick /un pík/ *vt* undo by pulling out the threads or stitches of

unplaced /un pláyst/ *adj* not among the first three finishers in a race

unplanned /un plánd/ *adj* not happening according to a plan

unpleasant /un plézz'nt/ *adj* 1 not pleasing 2 unfriendly or unkind —**unpleasantly** *adv* —**unpleasantness** *n*

unplug /un plúg/ (-**plugging**, -**plugged**) *vt* 1 disconnect by pulling a plug out of a socket 2 disconnect from a supply of electricity

unplugged /ún plúgd/ *adv*, *adj* without amplified musical instruments

unpopular /un póppyoŏlər/ *adj* not liked —**unpopularity** /ún popyoŏ lárrəti/ *n* —**unpopularly** *adv*

unpractised /un práktist/ *adj* 1 untrained or inexperienced 2 not done frequently

unprecedented /un préssi dentid/ *adj* having no earlier parallel or equivalent

unpredictable /únpri díktəb'l/ *adj* difficult to predict —**unpredictably** *adv*

unprepared /únpri páird/ *adj* 1 not ready for something or not expecting something to happen 2 not made ready as required or expected 3 improvised —**unpreparedly** /únpri páiridli/ *adv* —**unpreparedness** /-páiridnəss/ *n*

unprepossessing /ún preepə zéssing/ *adj* not producing a favourable impression —**unprepossessingly** *adv*

unpretentious /únpri ténshəss/ *adj* natural and modest —**unpretentiously** *adv*

unprincipled /un prínssip'ld/ *adj* not moral or ethical

unprintable /un príntəb'l/ *adj* not fit for publication

unproductive /únprə dúktiv/ *adj* 1 fruitless 2 producing little —**unproductively** *adv* —**unproductiveness** *n*

unprofessional /únprə fésh'nəl/ *adj* 1 contrary to professional standards 2 amateurish —**unprofessionalism** *n* —**unprofessionally** *adv*

unprofitable /un próffitəb'l/ *adj* 1 making no profit 2 not helpful or useful —**unprofitability** /un próffitə bílləti/ *n* —**unprofitably** *adv*

unpromising /un prómmissing/ *adj* 1 unlikely to succeed 2 unfavourable —**unpromisingly** *adv*

unprompted /un prómptid/ *adj* spontaneous

unpronounceable /únprə nównssəb'l/ *adj* difficult to pronounce

unprotected /únprə téktid/ *adj* 1 having no protection from harm 2 lacking safety precautions

unproven /un próv'n, -proóv'n/ *adj* 1 not tried and tested 2 not proved

unputdownable /ún poŏt dównəb'l/ *adj* too interesting to stop reading (*infml*)

unqualified /un kwólli fīd/ *adj* 1 lacking qualifications or the qualifications required 2 not limited by any condition or reservation 3 complete and absolute ○ *an unqualified success*

unquenchable /un kwénchəb'l/ *adj* **1** impossible to satisfy **2** inextinguishable

unquestionable /un kwéschənəb'l/ *adj* **1** impossible to doubt **2** universally recognized and acknowledged —**unquestionably** *adv*

unquestioned /un kwéschənd/ *adj* **1** undisputed **2** not asked questions

unquestioning /un kwéschəning/ *adj* not asking questions or expressing doubt —**unquestioningly** *adv*

unquote /un kwót/ *adv* indicates the end of a quotation

unravel /un rávv'l/ (**-elling, -elled**) *vti* **1** separate the strands of or undo the stitches of, or become unravelled **2** disentangle or become disentangled **3** make or become less complex and more understandable

unreadable /un reédəb'l/ *adj* **1** illegible **2** not enjoyable to read —**unreadably** *adv*

unreal /un reél, un reé əl/ *adj* **1** not real or existing **2** not true or genuine **3** excellent (*infml*) —**unreality** /únri álləti/ *n* —**unreally** *adv*

unrealistic /ún ree ə lístik/ *adj* not taking into account the way the world actually is and how events are likely to happen —**unrealistically** *adv*

unreasonable /un reéz'nəb'l/ *adj* **1** not acting with or subject to reason **2** excessive —**unreasonably** *adv*

unreasoning /un reéz'ning/ *adj* not having sound judgment or reasoning —**unreasoningly** *adv*

unrecognizable /un rékəg nīzəb'l/, **unrecognisable** *adj* not able to be recognized —**unrecognizably** *adv*

unrecognized /un rékəgnīzd/ *adj* not formally given legal or independent status

unreconstructed /ún reekən strúktid/ *adj* **1** clinging to outdated beliefs **2** not rebuilt

unredeemed /únri deémd/ *adj* **1** not made acceptable **2** not paid off or cashed in

unrefined /únri fínd/ *adj* **1** not processed **2** vulgar

unregenerate /únri jénnərət/ *adj* **1** not reformed spiritually and not repentant **2** clinging to outdated beliefs **3** stubborn —**unregenerately** *adv*

unrelated /ún ri láytid/ *adj* not connected by similarities, source, or family

unrelenting /únri lénting/ *adj* **1** determined and unyielding **2** not lessening or easing up —**unrelentingly** *adv*

unreliable /únri lī əb'l/ *adj* not able to be relied on or trusted —**unreliability** /únri lī ə bílləti/ *n* —**unreliably** *adv*

unrelieved /únri leévd/ *adj* unvaried and monotonous

unremarkable /únri maárkəb'l/ *adj* not noteworthy —**unremarkably** *adv*

unremarked /únri maárkt/ *adj* unnoticed

unremitting /únri mítting/ *adj* continuing without slackening or easing —**unremittingly** *adv*

unrepeatable /únri peétəb'l/ *adj* **1** not able to be repeated **2** too shocking to repeat

unrepentant /únri péntənt/, **unrepenting** /-ing/ *adj* feeling no regret for wrongdoing

unrequited /únri kwítid/ *adj* not reciprocated

unreserved /únri zúrvd/ *adj* **1** not reserved for a particular use **2** given without qualification —**unreservedly** /-zúrvidli/ *adv*

unrest /un rést/ *n* **1** social or political discontent that disrupts the established order **2** anxiety

unrestrained /únri stráynd/ *adj* **1** not controlled or restricted **2** spontaneous —**unrestrainedly** /-stráynidli/ *adv*

unrivalled /un rív'ld/ *adj* without a rival or equal

unroll /un ról/ *vti* **1** unwind or uncoil **2** disclose or become disclosed gradually

unruffled /un rúff'ld/ *adj* calm and poised, especially in a crisis

unruly /un roóli/ (**-lier, -liest**) *adj* difficult to control —**unruliness** *n*

> **SYNONYMS** unruly, intractable, recalcitrant, obstreperous, wilful, wild, wayward CORE MEANING: not submitting to control

unsafe /un sáyf/ (**-safer, -safest**) *adj* **1** dangerous **2** in danger

unsaid /un séd/ *adj* not mentioned

unsatisfactory /ún satiss fáktəri/ *adj* not adequate, acceptable, or satisfying —**unsatisfactorily** *adv*

unsaturated /un sáchə raytid/ *adj* **1** describes a solution that is able to dissolve more of a substance **2** describes fats with a high proportion of fatty acid molecules with double bonds, regarded as healthy in the diet

unsavoury /un sáyvəri/ *adj* **1** distasteful **2** immoral **3** tasting or smelling unappetizing —**unsavouriness** *n*

unscathed /un skáythd/ *adj* unhurt or undamaged

unscientific /ún sī ən tíffik/ *adj* **1** not scientific in method or principle **2** not informed about science —**unscientifically** *adv*

unscramble /un skrámb'l/ (**-bling, -bled**) *vt* **1** restore order to something jumbled or confused **2** make a message understandable by undoing the effects of scrambling —**unscrambler** *n*

unscrew /un skroó/ *vti* **1** remove or loosen the screws holding something, or have the screws removed **2** remove or adjust something by rotating, or be removed or adjusted by rotating **3** open something by removing a threaded lid or cap, or be opened in this way

unscrupulous /un skroópyoóləss/ *adj* not restrained by moral or ethical principles —**unscrupulously** *adv*—**unscrupulousness** *n*

unseasonable /un seéz'nəb'l/ *adj* **1** unusual for the time of year **2** not timely —**unseasonably** *adv*

unseat /un seét/ *vt* **1** eject from a saddle **2** remove from office

unsecured /únssi kyoórd, -kyáwrd/ *adj* **1** not made secure **2** not protected against financial loss

unseeded /un seédid/ *adj* in sports, not ranked as a seed

unseemly /un seémli/ *adj* contrary to good taste or appropriate behaviour —**unseemliness** *n*

unseen /ún seén/ *adj* **1** not seen or observed **2** done without previous study, practice, or preparation

unselfish /un sélfish/ *adj* not selfish —**unselfishly** *adv* —**unselfishness** *n*

unsettle /un sétt'l/ (**-tling, -tled**) *vt* **1** disrupt **2** make upset or insecure —**unsettling** *adj*

unsettled /un sétt'ld/ *adj* **1** lacking order or stability **2** changeable ○ *unsettled weather* **3** not resolved or decided ○ *an unsettled issue* **4** not inhabited or colonized **5** unpaid ○ *unsettled debts* **6** not regular or fixed ○ *an unsettled lifestyle*

unshakable /un sháykəb'l/, **unshakeable** *adj* firm and certain whatever happens —**unshakably** *adv*

unshaken /un sháykən/ *adj* firm and certain in spite of something that has happened

unshift /un shíft/ *vi* release the depressed shift key on a computer keyboard or typewriter

unsightly /un sítli/ *adj* unappealing to look at —**unsightliness** *n* ◊ See note at **unattractive**

unskilful /un skílf'l/ *adj* not skilled or skilful —**unskilfully** *adv*

unskilled /ún skíld/ *adj* **1** lacking skill or training **2** not requiring special skills

unsmiling /un smíling/ *adj* showing no signs of pleasure, amusement, or approval ○ *his grim unsmiling manner* —**unsmilingly** *adv*

unsociable /un sṓshəb'l/ *adj* **1** not liking or seeking the company of other people **2** not encouraging social interaction —**unsociability** /ún sṓshə bílləti/ *n* —**unsociably** *adv*

unsocial /un sṓsh'l/ *adj* **1** not liking or seeking the company of other people **2** inconsiderate or indifferent to the needs of others **3** describes working hours that fall outside the usual working day

unsophisticated /únssə físti kaytid/ *adj* **1** not worldly or sophisticated **2** simple and lacking in refinements

unsound /un sównd/ *adj* **1** unhealthy **2** not solid or firm structurally **3** based on unreliable information or reasoning ○ *an unsound conclusion* **4** not safe or secure financially ○ *unsound investments* —**unsoundly** *adv* —**unsoundness** *n*

unsparing /un spáiring/ *adj* **1** merciless **2** generous in giving —**unsparingly** *adv*

unspeakable /un speékəb'l/ *adj* **1** not describable in words **2** extremely bad or awful —**unspeakably** *adv*

unspecified /un spéssi fíd/ *adj* not stated explicitly

unspoiled /ún spóyld/, **unspoilt** /-spóylt/ *adj* **1** unchanged by development **2** not damaged

unspoken /un spṓkən/ *adj* not mentioned

unsporting /un spáwrting/ *adj* not fair or sporting —**unsportingly** *adv*

unstable /un stáyb'l/ *adj* **1** not firm, solid, or fixed **2** likely to fall or collapse **3** subject to change **4** lacking mental stability —**unstableness** *n* —**unstably** *adv*

unsteady /un stéddi/ *adj* **1** not firmly fixed **2** likely to fall **3** changeable —**unsteadily** *adv* —**unsteadiness** *n* —**unsteady** *vt*

unstick /un stík/ (**-stuck**) *vt* cause to stop sticking

unstinting /un stínting/ *adj* given or giving generously —**unstintingly** *adv*

unstop /un stóp/ (**-stopping, -stopped**) *vt* **1** remove a stopper from **2** unblock

unstoppable /un stóppəb'l/ *adj* impossible to stop —**unstoppably** *adv*

unsubscribe /únsəb scríb/ *vi* end a subscription to something, especially an e-mail mailing list

unsuccessful /únssək sésf'l/ *adj* not resulting in or achieving success —**unsuccessfully** *adv*

unsuitable /un soótəb'l/ *adj* not appropriate —**unsuitability** /un soótə bílləti/ *n* —**unsuitably** *adv*

unsuited /un soótid, -syoót-/ *adj* **1** lacking the right qualities **2** incompatible

unsung /un súng/ *adj* not praised or honoured

unsure /un shoór, -sháwr/ *adj* **1** uncertain **2** not confident ◊ See note at **doubtful**

unsuspecting /únssə spékting/ *adj* not suspicious or aware —**unsuspectingly** *adv*

unsustainable /únssə stáynəb'l/ *adj* **1** unable to be maintained **2** not maintaining the ecological balance of an area

unswerving /un swúrving/ *adj* steady and unchanging —**unswervingly** *adv*

unsympathetic /ún simpə théttik/ *adj* showing no sympathy or approval —**unsympathetically** *adv*

untangle /un táng g'l/ (**-gling, -gled**) *vt* **1** free from tangles **2** clarify or resolve the complexities of

untapped /ún tápt/ *adj* **1** not yet in use, but available **2** not opened

untenable /un ténnəb'l/ *adj* impossible to defend in an argument —**untenably** *adv*

unthinkable /un thíngkəb'l/ *adj* **1** too strange or extreme to be considered **2** impossible even to conceive of

unthinking /un thíngking/ *adj* done without thinking of the consequences —**unthinkingly** *adv*

untidy /un tídi/ (**-dier, -diest**) *adj* **1** not neat or tidy **2** not properly organized or ordered —**untidily** *adv* —**untidiness** *n* —**untidy** *vt*

untie /un tí/ (**-tying, -tied**) *v* **1** *vti* undo a knot or similar fastening in something, or become undone **2** *vt* free somebody or something that is tied up

until /ən tíl, un tíl/ *conj, prep* **1** up to a time or event but not afterwards ○ *lived at home until she left school* ○ *from 1999 until 2002* **2** before

○ *agrees not to speak until the verdict is announced* ○ *did not go until Monday* ◊ See note at **till**

~~untill~~ incorrect spelling of **until**

untimely /un tīmli/ *adj* **1** occurring at a bad or inappropriate time **2** occurring prematurely —**untimeliness** *n* —**untimely** *adv*

untiring /un tīring/ *adj* **1** not becoming tired **2** continuing in spite of difficulties —**untiringly** *adv*

untitled /un tīt'ld/ *adj* **1** unnamed **2** not belonging to the nobility

unto *(stressed)* /úntoo/ *(unstressed)* /úntŏŏ, únta/ *prep (archaic)* **1** to ○ *the elders of Gilead said unto Jephthah* ○ *and they said unto God* **2** until ○ *faithful unto death*

untold /un tṓld/ *adj* **1** not revealed or related **2** unable to be described or counted

untouchable /un túchab'l/ *adj* **1** not to be touched **2** out of reach **3** above criticism ■ *n also* **Untouchable** an offensive term for a member of a hereditary Hindu class regarded as unclean by the four castes

untouched /un túcht/ *adj* **1** not touched or handled **2** not eaten or drunk **3** not injured, damaged, or harmed **4** not changed or altered **5** emotionally unaffected

untoward /únta wáwrd/ *adj* **1** inappropriate ○ *untoward rudeness* **2** unexpected **3** causing misfortune ○ *several untoward events* —**untowardly** *adv*

untrained /un tráynd/ *adj* lacking any training in a specific skill

untrammelled /un trámm'ld/ *adj* not restricted or restrained

untreated /un treétid/ *adj* **1** not subjected to a physical process **2** not given medical attention

untried /ún tríd/ *adj* **1** not tested or proved **2** not tried in court

untroubled /un trúbb'ld/ *adj* not anxious or disturbed

untrue /un troŏ/ *adj* **1** wrong or false **2** unfaithful —**untruly** *adv*

untruth /un troŏth/ *n* **1** something that is untrue **2** lack of truth ◊ See note at **lie**

untruthful /un troŏthf'l/ *adj* **1** untrue **2** not telling the truth —**untruthfully** *adv* —**untruthfulness** *n*

untutored /un tyoŏtard/ *adj* **1** not formally taught **2** unsophisticated

untypical /un típpik'l/ *adj* lacking the characteristics shared by others of a particular type —**untypically** *adv*

ununbium /ún un beé am/ *n (symbol* **Uub***)* an artificially produced, highly unstable radioactive chemical element with an atomic number of 112

ununhexium /ún un héksi am/ *n (symbol* **Uuh***)* an artificially produced, highly unstable radioactive chemical element with an atomic number of 116

ununnilium /ún un ílli am/ *n (symbol* **Uun***)* an artificially produced, highly unstable radio-

active chemical element with an atomic number of 110

ununquadium /ún un kwáydi am/ *n (symbol* **Uuq***)* an artificially produced, highly unstable radioactive chemical element with an atomic number of 114

unununium /ún un únni am/ *n (symbol* **Uuu***)* an artificially produced, highly unstable radioactive chemical element with an atomic number of 111

unused /un yoŏzd, -yoŏst/ *adj* **1** never having been used **2** not in use **3** not familiar with or accustomed to something

unusual /un yoŏzhoo al/ *adj* **1** not common or familiar **2** remarkable or out of the ordinary —**unusually** *adv* —**unusualness** *n*

unutterable /un úttarab'l/ *adj* unable to be expressed or described because of emotional intensity —**unutterably** *adv*

unvarnished /un vaárnisht/ *adj* **1** without a coat of varnish **2** presented with no attempt to disguise the truth ○ *the unvarnished facts*

unveil /un váyl/ *vt* **1** remove a veil or covering from **2** reveal for the first time —**unveiling** *n*

unvoiced /un vóyst/ *adj* **1** not spoken **2** pronounced without vibration of the vocal cords

unwaged /ún wáyjd/ *adj* not in paid employment

unwanted /un wóntid/ not welcome or needed

unwarranted /un wórrantid/ *adj* **1** not authorized **2** not justified or deserved

unwary /un wáiri/ *adj* failing to be alert and cautious

unwavering /un wáyvaring/ *adj* steady and firm in purpose —**unwaveringly** *adv*

unwelcome /un wélkam/ *adj* **1** not welcome **2** causing distress —**unwelcomely** *adv*

unwell /un wél/ *adj* not in good health

unwholesome /un hōlsam/ *adj* **1** harmful to health **2** regarded as harmful to character or morals —**unwholesomeness** *n*

~~unwieldly~~ incorrect spelling of **unwieldy**

unwieldy /un weéldi/ *adj* not easy to handle because of being large, heavy, or awkward —**unwieldiness** *n*

unwilling /un willing/ *adj* **1** not willing to do something **2** given reluctantly or grudgingly —**unwillingly** *adv* —**unwillingness** *n*

SYNONYMS unwilling, reluctant, disinclined, averse, hesitant, loath CORE MEANING: lacking the desire to do something

---

unwind /un wínd/ (**-wound** /un wównd/) *vti* **1** undo from being wound **2** relax after a time of stress or worry

unwise /un wíz/ (**-wiser, -wisest**) *adj* lacking wisdom —**unwisely** *adv*

unwitting /un witting/ *adj* **1** unaware of what is happening **2** said or done unintentionally —**unwittingly** *adv*

unwonted /un wōntid/ *adj* unusual or unexpected —**unwontedly** *adv*

unworkable /un wúrkab'l/ *adj* **1** too complicated or ambitious to be practical **2** not able to be cut, shaped, or otherwise worked —**unworkably** adv

unworldly /un wúrldli/ adj 1 not materialistic 2 inexperienced —**unworldliness** n

unworthy /un wúrthi/ adj 1 not deserving a particular benefit, privilege, or compliment 2 beneath somebody's usual standards of behaviour ○ conduct unworthy of them 3 without value or merit —**unworthily** adv —**unworthiness** n

unwound past tense, past participle of **unwind**

unwrap /un ráp/ (-**wrapping**, -**wrapped**) vt remove the wrapping from

unwritten /un rítt'n/ adj 1 not written down 2 generally accepted though not formally recorded ○ an unwritten law

unyielding /un yéelding/ adj 1 stubborn 2 inflexible —**unyieldingly** adv

unzip /un zíp/ (-**zipping**, -**zipped**) v 1 vti undo the zip of something such as clothing or luggage, or be opened by this means 2 vt decompress a computer file

up prep, adv 1 in, at, or to a higher level or position 2 along ○ went up the road ■ adv 1 thoroughly or completely ○ tore up the photograph 2 upright ○ sitting up in bed 3 so as to detach or remove something ○ pulling up weeds 4 into consideration ○ The subject didn't come up. 5 in or towards a northerly position ○ up in Scotland 6 to a higher value 7 to a greater intensity 8 so as to move near ○ ran up to me ■ adj 1 increased ○ Her grades are up. 2 out of bed 3 facing or raised upwards 4 going higher or north 5 cheerful 6 over or finished 7 nominated or in the running ○ up for promotion 8 having knowledge ○ well up on the subject ■ n an upward slope ■ vt (**upping**, **upped**) raise or increase ◇ **up against it** facing difficulty or danger ◇ **up to 1** occupied with or involved in 2 able to undertake or endure 3 as many as, or as long as 4 until

up-and-coming adj already successful and becoming more so

upbeat /úp beet/ n an unaccented beat in music, especially one that ends a bar ■ adj optimistic (infml)

upbraid /up bráyd/ vt speak harshly and critically to

upbringing /úp bringing/ n the manner and circumstances in which somebody is brought up

upcoming /úp kumming/ adj forthcoming

upcountry adj /úp kuntri/ coming from or located in the interior of a country ■ n /úp kuntri/ an inland region ■ adv /up kúntri/ towards the interior of a country

update vt /up dáyt/ (-**dating**, -**dated**) provide with the most recent information ■ n /úp dayt/ a communication of the latest information —**updatable** adj

Popperfoto

John Updike

Updike /úp dīk/, **John** (b. 1932) US writer

upend /up énd/ vti place, stand, or turn on one end

up-front, upfront /up frúnt/ adj (infml) 1 frank or straightforward 2 in advance —**up front** adv —**up-frontness** n

upgrade v /up gráyd/ (-**grading**, -**graded**) 1 vt promote somebody or increase the status of somebody's job or position 2 vti improve the quality or performance of something 3 vti exchange something for another of better quality ■ n /úp grayd/ 1 an improvement in the quality or performance of something 2 something that improves quality or performance —**upgradable** adj

Upham /úppəm/, **Charles Hazlitt** (1908–94) New Zealand soldier

upheaval /up héev'l/ n 1 a sudden change in political or social conditions or personal circumstances 2 a sudden rising of part of the Earth's crust

uphill adv /up híl/ 1 up a slope 2 against resistance or in spite of difficulty ■ adj /úp híl/ 1 sloping up 2 on higher ground 3 requiring a lot of effort

uphold /up hóld/ (-**held** /up héld/) vt maintain or support —**upholder** n

upholster /up hólstər/ vt fit furniture with padding and coverings —**upholsterer** n

upholstery /up hólstəri/ n 1 materials used for upholstering furniture 2 the work of upholstering

~~upholstry~~ incorrect spelling of **upholstery**

upkeep /úp keep/ n 1 maintenance in proper condition or operation 2 the cost of providing maintenance

upland /úpplənd, úp land/ n high land —**upland** adj

uplift vt /up líft/ 1 physically lift 2 improve the spiritual level or living conditions of 3 NZ, S Africa, Scotland collect passengers or baggage ■ n /úp lift/ 1 something uplifting to the spirit 2 a lifting up —**uplifting** adj

uplifting /up lífting/ adj raising people's moral or spiritual level or emotions

uplighter /úp lītər/ n a lamp casting light upwards

uplink /úp lingk/ n a transmitter on the ground sending messages to aircraft or satellites ■ vti transmit a message via an uplink

upload /úp lōd/ vti transfer data or programs,

usually from a peripheral to a central computer

upmarket /up maárkit/ *adj* intended for wealthy consumers ■ *adv* towards more expensive tastes

upon /ə pón/ *prep* on *(fml)*

upper /úppər/ *adj* **1** higher in position or rank ○ *the upper deck* ○ *upper management* **2** more distant or inland ○ *the upper reaches of the river* ■ *n* **1** the higher of two people or objects **2** the part of a boot or shoe covering the upper surface of the foot **3** a stimulant drug *(slang)*

uppercase /úppər kayss, úppər káyss/ *n* capital letters —**uppercase** *adj* —**uppercase** *vt*

upper class *n* the highest social class, or its members *(often pl)* —**upper-class** *adj*

upper crust *n* the highest social class *(infml)*

uppercut /úppər kut/ *n* a swinging upward blow to an opponent's chin —**uppercut** *vt*

upper hand *n* the dominant position

upper house *n* the smaller and less representative house in a two-house legislature, e.g. the House of Lords

uppermost /úppər mōst/ *adj, adv* in the highest position or rank

upper school *n* the senior students in a secondary school

Upper Volta /úppər vóltə/ former name for **Burkina Faso**

uppity /úppəti/ *adj* presumptuous *(infml)* —**uppityness** *n*

upright /úp rīt/ *adj* **1** standing vertically or erect **2** righteous or moral ■ *adv* vertically ■ *n* **1** a vertical support **2** *also* **upright piano** a piano with an upright rectangular case and strings mounted vertically —**uprightly** *adv* —**uprightness** *n*

uprising /úp rīzing/ *n* a rebellion

upriver /up rívvər/ *adv, adj* towards or closer to the source of a river

uproar /úp rawr/ *n* a noisy disturbance

ORIGIN Uproar is not etymologically connected to *roar*. It came from Dutch *oproer* (or a closely related early German form), literally 'stirring up', formed from *roer* 'motion'. The original meaning in English (early 16C) was 'tumult, popular uprising', but the word was early associated with *roar* and developed (mid-16C) into 'noisy disturbance'.

---

uproarious /up ráwri əss/ *adj* **1** involving an uproar **2** hilarious —**uproariously** *adv* —**uproariousness** *n*

uproot /up root/ *vt* **1** pull up from soil by the roots **2** displace from a home or habitual environment —**uprootedness** *n*

uprush /úp rush/ *n* an upward rush

upsadaisy *interj* = **upsy-daisy**

upset *adj* /up sét/ **1** distressed or sad **2** overturned or spilled **3** affected by indigestion or nausea ■ *v*/up sét/ (**-setting, -set**) **1** *vt* cause emotional distress to **2** *vti* turn or tip over accidentally, usually spilling the contents

3 *vt* disturb the usual order or course of **4** *vt* defeat unexpectedly ■ *n* /úp set/ **1** an unexpected problem causing distress or a change of plans **2** an unexpected result or defeat **3** a mild illness of the stomach

upshot /úp shot/ *n* the result or outcome

upside /úp sīd/ *n* the positive side or aspect of a situation or event

upside down *adv* **1** so that the side that should be higher is lower **2** in complete confusion or disorder —**upside-down** *adj*

upsilon /up sílən, úpsi lon/ *n* the 20th letter of the Greek alphabet

upstage /up stáyj/ *vt* (**-staging, -staged**) **1** outdo and divert attention from somebody else **2** make another actor turn away from the audience by moving towards the back of the stage ■ *adv, adj* towards or at the back of the stage ■ *n* the back of the stage

upstairs /úp stáirz/ *adv* on, to, or towards an upper floor ■ *n* an upper floor

upstanding /up stánding/ *adj* honest and socially responsible —**upstandingness** *n*

upstart /úp staart/ *n* somebody with newly acquired status who is regarded as arrogant

upstream /up streém, úp streem/ *adv* **1** in or towards the source of a river or stream **2** in an early stage of an industrial or commercial operation

upsurge /úp surj/ *n* a sudden increase

upswing /úp swing/ *n* an increase or improvement

upsy-daisy /úpsi-/, **upsadaisy** /úpsə-/ *interj* reassures a child being lifted or who has just fallen *(baby talk)*

uptake /úp tayk/ *n* **1** a vent for smoke or air **2** physical absorption ◊ **be quick** *or* **slow on the uptake** be quick or slow to understand things *(infml)*

uptempo *n* /úp tempō/ a fast tempo ■ *adj* /up témpō/ fast-paced and exciting

uptight /úp tīt/ *adj* *(infml)* **1** tense and anxious **2** emotionally repressed —**uptightness** *n*

uptime /úp tīm/ *n* the time during which a computer or machine is in operation

up-to-date *adj* **1** familiar with or reflecting current knowledge or fashions **2** of the current time

up-to-the-minute *adj* familiar with or reflecting the most recent knowledge or fashions

uptrend /úp trend/ *n* an improving trend

upturn *v* /up túrn/ **1** *vti* turn over or upside down **2** *vt* turn upwards ■ *n* /úp turn/ an improvement in the economy or business conditions

upward /úppwərd/ *adj* going or directed towards a higher level —**upwardly** *adv*

upwardly mobile *adj* aspiring to a higher social class

upwards /úppwərdz/, **upward** /-wərd/ *adv* towards a higher level

upwind /úp wind/ *adv, adj* **1** against the wind **2** on the windward side

Ur /ur/ ancient city of Mesopotamia, in present-day SE Iraq

uraemia /yoŏ reĕmi ə/ *n* a form of blood poisoning caused by the accumulation of products that are usually eliminated in urine

Ural /yoŏrəl/ river of S Russia and NW Kazakhstan, flowing southwards into the Caspian Sea. Length 2,428 km/1,509 mi.

Ural Mountains mountain system in W Russia, the traditional dividing line between Asia and Europe. Highest peak Mt Narodnaya, 1,894 m/6,214 ft. Length 2,400 km/1,490 mi.

uranium /yoŏ ráyni əm/ *n* (*symbol* U) a radioactive chemical element. Use: in one isotope, as fuel in nuclear reactors and weapons.

Uranus /yoŏrənəss, yoŏ ráynəss/ *n* **1** in Greek mythology, the god ruling the heavens, husband of Gaia and father of the Titans **2** the 7th planet from the Sun

urban /úrbən/ *adj* of a city

urbane /ur báyn/ (**-baner, -banest**) *adj* sophisticated, refined, or courteous —**urbanely** *adv* —**urbanity** /ur bánnəti/ *n*

urbanite /úrbə nīt/ *n* a city dweller

urbanize /úrbə nīz/ (**-izing, -ized**), **urbanise** *vt* **1** make into a town or city **2** cause to migrate to a town or city —**urbanization** /úrbə nī záysh'n/ *n*

urban myth, **urban legend** *n* a bizarre and untrue story circulating in a society

urban renewal *n* redevelopment of urban areas

urban sprawl *n* expansion of an urban area into the surrounding countryside

urchin /úrchin/ *n* a mischievous child, especially one of unkempt appearance

Urdu /oórdoo, úrdoo/ *n* the official language of Pakistan, spoken also in Bangladesh and parts of India —**Urdu** *adj*

urea /yoo reé ə, yoŏri ə/ *n* a constituent of the urine of mammals. Uses: fertilizers, animal feed, manufacture of resins. —**ureal** *adj*

ureter /yoŏ reétər, yoŏritər/ *n* each of a pair of ducts that carry urine from the kidneys to the bladder

urethra /yoŏ reéthrə/ (*pl* **-thras** *or* **-thrae** /-ree/) *n* a tube for discharging urine from the body —**urethral** *adj*

urge *vt* (**urging, urged**) **1** advise or encourage strongly to do something **2** advocate earnestly ■ *n* a strong need or impulse

urgent /úrjənt/ *adj* **1** requiring immediate action **2** showing earnestness —**urgency** *n* —**urgently** *adv*

urinal /yoŏ rín'l, yoŏrin'l/ *n* **1** a receptacle attached to a wall for men to urinate into **2** a place with urinals

urinary /yoŏrinəri/ *adj* of urine or the organs that form and excrete urine

urinate /yoŏri nayt/ (**-nating, -nated**) *vi* expel urine —**urination** /yoŏri náysh'n/ *n*

urine /yoŏrin/ *n* a yellowish liquid containing waste products that is excreted by the

kidneys and discharged through the urethra —**urinous** *adj*

URL *n* an address identifying the location of a file on the Internet. Full form **Uniform Resource Locator**

urn *n* **1** an ornamental vase with a pedestal **2** a vase for the ashes of somebody cremated **3** a large vessel with a tap, for hot drinks

urogenital /yoŏrō jénnit'l/, **urinogenital** /yoŏrinō jénnit'l/ *adj* of the urinary and reproductive organs

urology /yoŏ rólləji/ *n* the branch of medicine that deals with the urinary and urogenital system —**urologic** /yoŏrō lójjik/ *adj* —**urologist** *n*

ursine /úr sīn/ *adj* of or like bears

urticaria /úrti káiri ə/ *n* a skin rash marked by itching and small pale or red swellings (*technical*)

Uruguay /yoŏrə gwī/ **1** river in SE South America, rising in S Brazil and entering the Atlantic Ocean through the Río de la Plata. Length 1,600 km/990 mi. **2** country in SE South America. Cap. Montevideo. Pop. 3,360,105 (2001). —**Uruguayan** /yoŏrə gwī ən/ *n, adj*

Urumqi /oŏ roŏmchi/ capital of Xinjiang Uygur Autonomous Region, NW China. Pop. 1,310,000 (1995).

us /uss, əss/ *pron* me and another person or other people (*after a verb or preposition*)

US, U.S. *abbr* United States

USA, U.S.A. *abbr* United States of America

usability engineer *n* somebody employed to observe people learning to use new products prior to their release in the marketplace —**usability engineering** *n*

usable /yoŏzəb'l/, **useable** *adj* fit for use —**usability** /yoŏzə bílləti/ *n* —**usably** *adv*

USAF, U.S.A.F. *abbr* United States Air Force

usage /yoŏssij, yoŏz-/ *n* **1** the using of something, or the way in which or degree to which something is used **2** an accepted practice or procedure **3** the way language is actually used

~~usally~~ incorrect spelling of **usually**

use *v* /yooz/ (**using, used**) **1** *vt* put into action or service for some purpose **2** *vt* expend or consume **3** *vt* manipulate or exploit ○ *the type who uses people* **4** *vti* consume drugs or alcohol regularly **5** *vt* behave in a particular way towards ○ *uses his employees poorly* ■ *n* /yooss/ **1** the using of something **2** the state of being used for something **3** a way of using something **4** the right or ability to use something **5** the purpose for which something is used **6** usefulness **7** the occasion or need to use something —**user** *n* ◇ **make use of** use ◇ **use** *or* **used to** used as a modal verb to indicate habitual or customary past action ○ *Did you use to go?* ○ *We used to eat out more often.*

SYNONYMS use, employ, make use of, utilize
CORE MEANING: put something to use

USAGE used to or **use to**? The spelling **used to,**

with a final *-d*, indicates habitual or customary past actions, as in *On Saturdays we used* [not *use*] *to go to football matches*. People tend to drop the *-d* because it is often inaudible in speech, but this is unacceptable in writing. When *did* precedes **use(d) to**, the correct form is *use to*, as in *Did you use to go to football matches every Saturday?*

□ **use up** *vt* expend or consume, often until none is left

useage incorrect spelling of **usage**

used[1] /yoozd/ *adj* **1** previously owned **2** having been put to a purpose or expended

used[2] /yoost/ *adj* accustomed to or familiar with something ○ *We're not used to this weather.*

useful /yoóssl'l/ *adj* **1** serving a purpose **2** having value or benefit —**usefully** *adv* —**usefulness** *n*

usefull incorrect spelling of **useful**

useing incorrect spelling of **using**

useless /yoósslass/ *adj* **1** not fit for use **2** unsuccessful, or unlikely to be worthwhile **3** not able to do something properly *(infml)* —**uselessly** *adv* —**uselessness** *n*

Usenet /yoóz net/ *n* a worldwide system for distributing newsgroup messages over the Internet or other networks

user-friendly (**user-friendlier**, **user-friendliest**) *adj* easy to operate or understand ○ *user-friendly software* —**user-friendliness** *n*

user group *n* a group of computer users who exchange and provide information about hardware or software

user interface *n* the part of the design of a computer, peripheral device, or program that accepts commands from and returns information to the user

usful incorrect spelling of **useful**

usher /úshər/ *n* **1** somebody who shows people to their seats **2** a doorkeeper **3** an official in English courts who keeps order ■ *vt* escort to or from a place or seat

□ **usher in** *vt* herald or introduce

USM *abbr* unlisted securities market

USP *n* a product's differentiating characteristic *(in advertisements and marketing)* Full form **unique selling proposition, unique selling point**

USS *abbr* United States Ship

USSR *abbr* Union of Soviet Socialist Republics

usual /yoózhoo əl/ *adj* customary or characteristic ■ *n* the ordinary way of things **2** what somebody customarily has, especially food or a drink *(infml)* —**usually** *adv* —**usualness** *n*

SYNONYMS usual, customary, habitual, routine, wonted CORE MEANING: often done, used, bought, or consumed

usualy incorrect spelling of **usually**

usurp /yoo zúrp/ *vti* seize something without the right to do so —**usurpation** /yoò zur páysh'n/ *n* —**usurper** *n*

usury /yoózhəri/ (*pl* **-ries**) *n* the lending of money at an exorbitant rate of interest —**usurer** *n*

—**usurious** /yoo zhoòri əss/ *adj* —**usuriously** *adv*

UT *abbr* Universal Time

Utah /yoöt aa, -aw/ state in the W United States. Cap. Salt Lake City. Pop. 2,233,169 (2000). —**Utahan** *n, adj*

UTC *abbr* Universal Time Coordinated

utensil /yoo ténss'l/ *n* a tool or container, especially one for use in a kitchen

uterus /yoötərəss/ (*pl* **-uses** or **-i** /-rī/) *n* a hollow organ in the pelvic cavity of female animals, in which the embryo develops *(technical)* —**uterine** /yoöta rīn/ *adj*

utilitarian /yoo tílli táiri ən/ *adj* **1** of or advocating utilitarianism **2** designed to be practical rather than beautiful ■ *n* a believer in utilitarianism

utilitarianism /yoo tílli táiri ənizəm/ *n* **1** the ethical doctrine that the greatest happiness of the greatest number should be the criterion of the virtue of an action **2** the doctrine that value lies in usefulness

utility /yoo tíllati/ *n* (*pl* **-ties**) **1** usefulness **2** something useful **3** a company that provides an essential public service such as gas or water, or a service so supplied **4** *also* **utility truck** *Aus* a pick-up truck **5** *also* **utility program** a computer program that performs routine tasks and supports operations ■ *adj* **1** designed for practical use **2** able to perform several functions **3** *ANZ, US* designed for strength and versatility ○ *a utility vehicle*

utility room *n* a room in a house containing large domestic appliances

utilize /yoóti līz/ (**-izing, -ized**), **utilise** *vt* make use of —**utilizable** *adj* —**utilization** /yoòti ī záysh'n/ *n* —**utilizer** *n* ○ See note at **use**

utmost /útmōst/, **uttermost** /úttərmōst/ *adj* **1** of the greatest degree **2** located at an extremity ■ *n* the greatest degree or amount

utopia /yoo tōpi ə/, **Utopia** *n* an ideal and perfect state —**utopian** *adj, n*

ORIGIN The original **utopia** was the ideal state in *Utopia* (1516), a work written in Latin by Sir Thomas More. He coined the name from Greek *ou* 'not' and *topos* 'place', literally meaning 'the land of nowhere'.

Utrecht /yoòt rekt, -rekht, yoo trékt, -trékht/ city in the central Netherlands. Pop. 234,323 (2000).

utter[1] /úttər/ *vt* **1** say **2** emit as a vocal sound —**utterable** *adj*

utter[2] /úttər/ *adj* absolute or total

utterance /úttərənss/ *n* **1** something said **2** a way of speaking **3** an act or power of speaking

utterly /úttərli/ *adv* completely or absolutely

uttermost *adj, n* = **utmost**

U-turn *n* **1** a turn made to face the opposite direction **2** a reversal of action or policy

UV *abbr* ultraviolet

UVF *abbr* Ulster Volunteer Force

uvula /yoóvyoòlə/ (*pl* **-las** or **-lae** /-lee/) *n* a fleshy flap hanging at the back of the throat —**uvular** *adj*

Uzbekistan /ŏŏz béki staǎn, uz-/ country in Central Asia. Cap. Tashkent. Pop. 25,155,064 (2001).

Uzi /ŏŏzi/ *n* a 9 mm compact submachine gun

ORIGIN The **Uzi** is unusual in being named after the first name of Uzi el-Gal, a 20C Israeli army officer and weapons designer, rather than his surname.

V

v[1] (*pl* **v's**), **V** (*pl* **V's** *or* **Vs**) *n* the 22nd letter of the English alphabet

v[2] *abbr* 1 velocity 2 verb 3 versus

V[1] *symbol* 1 electromotive force 2 potential 3 potential energy 4 vanadium 5 volt 6 volume

V[2] *abbr* 1 verb 2 versus

v. *abbr* volume

vacancy /váykənsi/ (*pl* **-cies**) *n* 1 a vacant position or hotel room 2 the state of being vacant

vacant /váykənt/ *adj* 1 having no occupant or contents 2 not filled by an incumbent or employee ○ *The post remains vacant.* 3 lacking any sign of mental activity or expression ○ *a vacant stare* —**vacantly** *adv*

SYNONYMS **vacant, empty, void** CORE MEANING: lacking contents or occupants

vacate /və káyt, vay-/ (**-cating, -cated**) *vt* 1 give up occupancy of 2 resign from

vacation /və káysh'n/ *n* 1 a period when the activities of a university or law court are suspended 2 *US, Can* a holiday ■ *vi US, Can* take a holiday —**vacationer** *n*

vaccinate /váksi nayt/ (**-nating, -nated**) *vt* administer a vaccine to —**vaccination** /váksi náysh'n/ *n*

vaccine /vák seen/ *n* 1 a preparation administered to protect the body against a specific disease 2 a piece of software that protects a computer against viruses

ORIGIN Vaccine derives from a Latin adjective meaning 'of a cow'. It was used by the British physician Edward Jenner at the end of the 18C in the terms *vaccine disease*, meaning 'cowpox', and hence *vaccine inoculation*, meaning the technique he developed for preventing smallpox by injecting people with cowpox virus. There is no evidence of the use of **vaccine** as a noun to denote the inoculated material until the 1840s.

~~vaccum, vaccuum, vacum~~ incorrect spelling of **vacuum**

vacillate /vássi layt/ (**-lating, -lated**) *vi* 1 be indecisive or irresolute 2 sway from side to side —**vacillation** /vássi láysh'n/ *n* ◊ See note at **hesitate**

vacuity /va kyóŏ əti/ (*pl* **-ties**) *n* a lack of intelligent or serious content

vacuole /vákyoo ōl/ *n* a membrane-bound compartment containing fluid in the cytoplasm of a cell —**vacuolar** /vákyoo ōlər/ *adj*

vacuous /vákyoo əss/ *adj* 1 lacking or showing a lack of ideas or intelligence 2 empty (*archaic*) —**vacuously** *adv* —**vacuousness** *n*

vacuum /vákyoo əm, vákyóŏm/ *n* (*pl* **-ums** *or* **-a** /-ə/) 1 a space that is completely empty of matter 2 a space from which all the gas has been removed 3 emptiness caused by the absence of something 4 *also* **vacuum cleaner** an electrical cleaning appliance that uses suction ■ *vti* clean something using a vacuum cleaner

vacuum flask *n* an insulated container for keeping drinks hot or cold

vacuum-packed *adj* packed in a container from which most of the air has been removed

vacuum pump *n* a device for removing air

vade mecum /vaˈadi máykəm/ *n* a useful book or object that you take along with you

Vadodara /və dṓdərə/ city in W India. Pop. 1,031,346 (1991).

Vaduz /fa dŏŏts/ capital of Liechtenstein. Pop. 5,106 (1999).

vagabond /vággə bond/ *n* 1 a homeless wanderer 2 a beggar —**vagabond** *adj, vi* —**vagabondage** *n*

vagina /və jīnə/ (*pl* **-nas** *or* **-nae** /-nee/) *n* the part of the female reproductive tract that connects the vulva to the cervix —**vaginal** *adj*

vagrant /váygrənt/ *n* 1 somebody who wanders from place to place 2 somebody who is illegally living on the streets ■ *adj* 1 homeless 2 wandering from place to place —**vagrancy** *n*

vague /vayg/ (**vaguer, vaguest**) *adj* 1 not explicit 2 not distinctly seen 3 not clearly perceived in the mind —**vaguely** *adv* —**vagueness** *n*

vain /vayn/ *adj* 1 excessively proud 2 unsuccessful ○ *a vain attempt to escape* 3 lacking substance or real meaning —**vainly** *adv* ◊ **in vain** fruitlessly, pointlessly, or unsuccessfully

SPELLCHECK Do not confuse the spelling of **vain**, **vane** ('a rotating blade'), and **vein** ('a blood vessel'), which sound similar.

SYNONYMS **vain, empty, hollow, idle** CORE MEANING: without substance or unlikely to be carried though

vainglorious /vayn gláwri əss/ *adj* excessively proud or ostentatious (*literary*) —**vainglory** *n*

Vaisakha /víss aakə/ *n* the 2nd month of the year in the Hindu calendar

Vajpayee /vaj páyee/, **Atal Bihari** (*b.* 1924) Indian prime minister (1996 and 1998–)

val. *abbr* 1 valley 2 value

valance /vállənss/, **valence** *n* **1** a fabric cover for a bed base **2** a cover for a curtain rod

vale /vayl/ *n* a valley *(often in placenames)*

SPELLCHECK Do not confuse the spelling of **vale** and **veil** ('a face covering'), which sound similar.

valediction /válli díksh'n/ *n (fml)* **1** the act of saying goodbye **2** a farewell speech

valedictory /válli díktəri/ *(fml) n (pl* **-ries)** a farewell speech ■ *adj* saying goodbye

Valencia /və lénshi ə, -si ə/ **1** capital of the autonomous region of **Valencia** in E Spain. Pop. 739,412 (1998). **2** city in N Venezuela. Pop. 1,034,033 (1992 estimate).

valency /váylənssi/ *(pl* **-cies)**, **valence** /-lənss/ *n* **1** the combining power of atoms measured by the number of electrons the atom or group will receive, give up, or share in forming a compound **2** a measure of an atom's combining power

valentine /vállən tīn/ *n* **1** a Valentine's Day card **2** somebody who receives a valentine

Valentine's Day *n* a day when romantic messages are traditionally sent. Date: 14 February.

Valentino /vállən teenō/, **Rudolph** (1895–1926) Italian-born US actor

Valerian /və leéri ən/ *(d.* 260?) Roman emperor (253–260?)

valet /vállit, vállay/ *n* **1** a personal male servant who looks after a man's clothes and prepares his meals **2** a male employee who cleans the clothes of hotel guests **3** somebody who performs a car parking or car cleaning service —**valet** *vti*

ORIGIN Valet is essentially the same word as *varlet*, and both go back through French to the Latin word from which *vassal* derives. The forms diverged in French. In early English use a **valet** was an attendant for a horseman or knight, and *varlet* was similarly used, but in the 16C it developed derogatory associations that **valet** avoided.

~~valey~~ incorrect spelling of **valley**

Valhalla /val hállə/ *n* in Norse mythology, a hall where slain heroes live

valiant /válli ənt/ *adj* courageous —**valiantly** *adv*

valid /vállid/ *adj* **1** able to be justified or believed **2** legally binding or effective —**validity** /və líddəti/ *n* —**validly** *adv* —**validness** *n*

SYNONYMS valid, cogent, convincing, reasonable, sound CORE MEANING: worthy of acceptance or credence

validate /válli dayt/ *(-dating, -dated) vt* **1** confirm the truthfulness of something **2** make something legal —**validation** /válli dáysh'n/ *n*

Valkyrie /válkəri, val keéri/ *n* in Norse mythology, a woman attendant escorting the dead to Valhalla —**Valkyrian** /val keéri ən/ *adj*

Valladolid /vállədə líd/ capital of **Valladolid Province**, N Spain. Pop. 319,946 (1998).

Valletta /və léttə/ capital and chief port of Malta. Pop. 7,100 (1999).

valley /válli/ *(pl* **-leys)** *n* **1** a low-lying area between mountains or hills **2** low-lying land around a river —**valleyed** *adj*

Valley Forge village in SE Pennsylvania that served as the winter headquarters in 1777–78 for George Washington during the War of American Independence

valor *n* US = **valour**

valour /vállər/ *n* courage —**valorous** *adj*

Valparaiso /válpə rízō/ capital of **Valparaiso Region** in central Chile. Pop. 293,800 (1998).

valuable /vállyōob'l, -yōo əb'l/ *adj* **1** worth a great deal of money **2** very important because of usefulness, scarcity, or personal attachment ■ *n* a valuable item *(often pl)* —**valuably** *adv*

valuation /vállyoo áysh'n/ *n* **1** an appraisal of the monetary value of something **2** the price of something —**valuational** *adj*

~~valuble~~ incorrect spelling of **valuable**

value /vállyoo/ *n* **1** monetary worth **2** an adequate return on something o *value for money* **3** worth or importance **4** a numerical quantity assigned to a mathematical symbol **5** the length of a musical note **6** the lightness or darkness of a colour ■ **values** *npl* principles or standards ■ *vt* **(-uing, -ued) 1** estimate the value of **2** regard highly

value-added network *n* full form of **VAN**

value-added tax *n* full form of **VAT**

valve *n* **1** a device that controls the flow of a liquid **2** a part on a brass instrument that is pressed to make a note **3** a device in which electrons flow in one direction. Use: control of current, amplification. **4** a flap in a bodily organ, e.g. the heart **5** either of the hinged parts of a shell

vamp[1] *n* a woman who is regarded as seductive *(sometimes offensive)* —**vamp** *vt* —**vampish** *adj* —**vampy** *adj*

vamp[2] *n* **1** the upper part of a shoe **2** an improvised musical introduction ■ *v* **1** *vt* put a vamp on a shoe **2** *vti* improvise a musical introduction or accompaniment

vampire /vám pīr/ *n* **1** in folklore, a corpse that is believed to rise each night from the grave to suck blood from living people **2** *also* **vampire bat** a bat of tropical America that sucks blood —**vampiric** /vam pírrik/ *adj*

van[1] *n* **1** an enclosed motor vehicle with rear or side doors **2** a railway wagon for luggage or mail —**van** *vti*

van[2] *n* **1** the leading position *(infml)* **2** the divisions of an army that lead an advance

van[3], **Van** see also under surname

VAN /van/ *n* a private computer network. Full form **value-added network**

vanadium /və náydi əm/ *n (symbol* **V)** a silvery-white metallic chemical element. Use: catalyst, alloyed with steel.

ORIGIN Vanadium was named in 1830 after the Scandinavian goddess Vanadis (Freya) by a Swedish chemist who found some of the element in iron. It had earlier been discovered in Mexican lead ores in 1810 and called *erythronium*, but **vanadium** is the name that stood the test of time.

Van Allen /van állən/, **James** (*b.* 1914) US physicist and discoverer of two radiation belts encircling Earth

Van Buren /van byoorən/, **Martin** (1782–1862) 8th president of the United States (1837–41)

Vancouver /van koovər/ city in SW British Columbia, Canada. Pop. 514,008 (1996).

Vancouver, Mt peak of the St Elias Range in SW Yukon Territory, Canada. Height 4,828 m/15,840 ft.

Vancouver Island island of SW Canada, off SW British Columbia in the Pacific Ocean. Pop. 702,000.

V and A, V & A *abbr* Victoria and Albert Museum

vandal /vánd'l/ *n* **1** somebody who illegally damages or destroys property **2** **Vandal** a member of an ancient Germanic people who conquered much of the Mediterranean region between AD 300 and 500 —**Vandalic** /van dállik/ *adj* —**vandalism** *n*

ORIGIN The reputation of the **Vandals** for wanton destruction was the impetus for the English adaptation of their name in the 17C to describe a person who wantonly and wilfully damages or destroys another person's property.

vandalize /vándə līz/ (**-izing**, **-ized**), **vandalise** *vt* illegally damage or destroy property —**vandalization** /vándə līz záysh'n/ *n*

vane /vayn/ *n* **1** a rotating blade, e.g. on a propeller **2** a weather vane **3** a stabilizer on a missile **4** a blade of a feather ◊ See note at **vain**

van Gogh /van gókh, -góf/, **Vincent** (1853–90) Dutch painter

vanguard /ván gaard/ *n* **1** the divisions of an army that lead an advance **2** the leading position or people in any action or movement —**vanguardism** *n*

vanilla /və níllə/ *n* **1** a long pod of a tropical climbing orchid. Use: flavouring. **2** a substance extracted from vanilla. Use: flavouring, perfumes. ■ *adj* **1** flavoured with vanilla **2** plain or dull (*slang*)

vanish /vánnish/ *vi* **1** disappear suddenly **2** stop existing —**vanishment** *n*

vanishing point *n* **1** an apparent meeting point of parallel lines **2** a point where something disappears

vanity /vánnəti/ (*pl* **-ties**) *n* **1** excessive pride **2** something that somebody is vain about **3** futility

vanity case *n* a small cosmetics case

vanity unit *n* a cabinet in which a hand basin is fitted

vanquish /vángkwish/ *vt* **1** defeat opponents in battle or competition **2** overcome an emotion —**vanquisher** *n* —**vanquishment** *n* ◊ See note at **defeat**

vantage point /vaántij-/ *n* **1** a position that gives a good view **2** a personal standpoint

Vanuatu /vánnoo aátoo/ country in the SW Pacific Ocean, comprising approximately 80 islands. Cap. Port-Vila. Pop. 192,910 (2001).

vapid /váppid/ *adj* lacking interest or liveliness —**vapidity** /və píddəti/ *n* —**vapidly** *adv*

vapor *n*, *vti* US = **vapour**

vaporize /váypə rīz/ (**-izing**, **-ized**), **vaporise** *vti* **1** change into, or cause something to change into, vapour **2** vanish or cause to vanish —**vaporization** /váypə rī záysh'n/ *n*

vapour /váypər/ *n* **1** moisture particles visible in the air as mist **2** the gaseous state of a liquid or solid at a temperature below its boiling point ■ **vapours** *npl* low spirits or hysteria (*literary or ironic*) —**vapoury** *adj*

vapour trail *n* a trail of condensed vapour left in the air by an aircraft

vapourware /váypər wair/ *n* software that has been advertised but not developed

Varanasi /və raánəssi/ city in N India, on the River Ganges. Pop. 929,270 (1991).

~~vareity~~ incorrect spelling of **variety**

Mario Vargas Llosa

Vargas Llosa /vaárgəss lóssə/, **Mario** (*b.* 1936) Peruvian writer and critic

variable /váiri əb'l/ *adj* **1** likely to vary or change **2** capricious in nature **3** not having a fixed numerical value ■ *n* **1** something that can vary or change **2** a symbol that represents an unspecified or unknown mathematical quantity —**variability** /váiri ə bílləti/ *n* —**variableness** *n* —**variably** *adv*

variance /váiri ənss/ *n* **1** a change in something **2** a difference between things **3** disagreement ◊ *a witness's testimony at variance with the facts*

variant /váiri ənt/ *adj* **1** differing slightly **2** changeable ■ *n* a slightly different form

variation /váiri áysh'n/ *n* **1** the act of varying **2** the state of being different **3** degree of difference **4** something that differs slightly from something else **5** an altered version of a musical theme —**variational** *adj*

~~variaty~~ incorrect spelling of **variety**

varicoloured /váiri kulərd/ *adj* multicoloured

varied /váirid/ *adj* **1** diverse **2** having been changed —**variedness** *n*

variegate /váiri gayt/ (**-gating**, **-gated**) *vt* **1** change the look of, especially by adding different colours **2** add variety to —**variegation** /váiri gáysh'n/ *n*

variegated /váiri gaytid/ *adj* **1** with patches of different colours **2** diverse

variety /və rí əti/ (*pl* **-ties**) *n* **1** the quality of being varied **2** a specific type **3** a collection of varied things **4** entertainment made up of different acts

~~varigated~~ incorrect spelling of **variegated**

various /váiri əss/ *det* many different ○ *after various attempts* ■ *adj* of different kinds —**variously** *adv*

varlet /váarlət/ *n* (*archaic*) **1** a rascal **2** a servant or page

varmint /váarmint/ *n* a troublesome person or animal (*regional*)

varnish /váarnish/ *n* **1** a transparent resin solution that gives a surface a protective gloss **2** a smooth coating of varnish ■ *vt* **1** apply varnish to **2** make superficially attractive —**varnisher** *n*

varsity /váarssati/ (*pl* **-ties**) *n* university (*dated*)

vary /váiri/ (**-ies, -ied**) *v* **1** *vti* undergo or cause to undergo change **2** *vi* be different **3** *vt* give variety to —**varying** *adj* —**varyingly** *adv* ◊ See note at **change**

vascular /váskyŏŏlər/ *adj* of fluid-carrying vessels in animals and plants

vase /vaaz/ *n* a container for cut flowers

vasectomy /və séktəmi/ (*pl* **-mies**) *n* the surgical cutting of the sperm duct to make a male sterile

Vaseline /vássə leen/ *tdmk* a trademark for medical petroleum jelly

vassal /váss'l/ *n* a dependent holder of land in a feudal society —**vassal** *adj*

vast *adj* very great in size or amount

vat *n* a large container for liquid

VAT /vee ay tee, vat/ *n* a tax added to the value of a product. Full form **value-added tax**

Vatican City /váttikən-/ papal state, an enclave within Rome, Italy. Pop. 850 (1997).

vatu /váa too/ (*pl* **same**) *n* a unit of currency in Vanuatu

vaudeville /váwdəvil/ *n* US music hall entertainment —**vaudevillian** /váwdə villi ən/ *adj, n*

ORIGIN Vaudeville comes from a French word that was earlier *vau de vire* and in full *chanson du Vau de Vire* 'song of the Valley of Vire'. In 15C France there was a fashion for songs from this valley, in the Calvados region of Normandy (particularly popular, apparently, were the satirical songs composed by a local man, Olivier Basselin). The geographical connection had been lost by the time English acquired the word, and the element *-vire* had been replaced with *-ville* 'town'. The semantic transition from 'popular song' to 'theatrical entertainment' is not recorded until the early 19C.

Vaughan Williams /vawn wílly əmz/, **Ralph** (1872–1958) British composer

vault[1] /vawlt, volt/ *n* **1** an arched ceiling **2** a room with an arched ceiling **3** a strengthened room for valuables **4** a burial chamber **5** something that arches overhead (*literary*) ○ *the great vault of the sky* ■ *v* **1** *vt* put an arched structure over **2** *vi* form a vault —**vaulted** *adj*

vault[2] /vawlt, volt/ *vti* spring over an object, often using the hands or a pole —**vault** *n* —**vaulter** *n*

vaunted /váwntid/ *adj* boasted about (*disapproving*) ○ *their vaunted home and car*

VC *abbr* **1** vice chancellor **2** Victoria Cross

V-chip *n* an electronic chip in a television that enables parents to block programmes with sexual or violent content

vCJD *n* a form of Creutzfeldt-Jakob disease with a shorter incubation period. Full form **variant Creutzfeldt-Jakob disease**

VCR *n* a video recorder. Full form **video cassette recorder**

VD *abbr* venereal disease

VDR *abbr* **1** videodisk recorder **2** videodisk recording

VDU *abbr* visual display unit

've /əv, v/ *contr* have

veal /veel/ *n* meat from a young calf

vector /véktər/ *n* **1** a quantity with direction and magnitude **2** the course of an aircraft or missile **3** a disease-transmitting organism ■ *vt* direct an aircraft by radio —**vectorial** /vek táwri əl/ *adj*

vector graphics *npl* COMPUT = **object-oriented graphics**

Veda /váydə, veedə/ *n* a Hindu sacred text —**Vedaic** /vi dáy ik/ *adj*

vee-jay /vee jáy/ *n* a video jockey ■ *vi* work or act as a video jockey

veer *vti* change or cause to change direction, opinion, or purpose ■ *n* a change in direction

veg[1] /vej/ (*pl* **same**) *n* a vegetable or vegetables (*infml*)

veg[2] /vej/, **veg out** *vi* relax or loaf (*slang*)

vegan /véegən/ *n* a person who never eats animal products —**vegan** *adj* —**veganism** *n*

vegetable /véjtəb'l/ *n* **1** an edible plant **2** any plant **3** an offensive term for somebody whose brain functions have been severely reduced by injury ■ *adj* consisting of vegetables

vegetal /véjjit'l/ *adj* **1** relating to plants **2** involving growth rather than sexual reproduction

vegetarian /véjjə táiri ən/ *n* somebody who does not eat meat or fish —**vegetarian** *adj* —**vegetarianism** *n*

vegetate /véjjə tayt/ (**-tating, -tated**) *vi* **1** live or behave in a dull or inactive way (*sometimes disapproving*) **2** grow or sprout like a plant

vegetation /véjjə táysh'n/ *n* **1** plants in general **2** the process of vegetating —**vegetational** *adj*

vegetative /véjjətətiv/ *adj* **1** of or typical of plants **2** involving growth rather than sexual reproduction **3** describes reproduction from the body cells of a parent rather than from specialized sex cells

~~vegtable~~ incorrect spelling of **vegetable**

vehement /vée əmənt/ adj 1 full of strong feeling or conviction 2 strong or energetic —**vehemence** n —**vehemently** adv

~~vehical~~ incorrect spelling of **vehicle**

vehicle /vée ik'l/ n 1 a means of transport for moving people or things 2 a medium for communicating or expressing something —**vehicular** /vi hík yoolər/ adj

veil /vayl/ n 1 a covering of netting or fabric worn by women over their heads or faces 2 something that obscures like a curtain ■ vt 1 cover with a veil 2 hide or disguise —**veiled** adj ◊ See note at **vale**

Veil /vīl/, **Simone** (b. 1927) French government official and politician

vein /vayn/ n 1 a vessel that carries blood to the heart 2 a sap-conducting bundle of vessels visible on a leaf 3 a layer of mineral in the ground 4 a particular quality or mood 5 a streak of different colour ■ vt 1 streak o *green marble veined with white* 2 form veins in —**veined** adj ◊ See note at **vain**

vela plural of **velum**

Velázquez /vi láskwez, ve láthketh/, **Diego** (1599–1660) Spanish painter

Velcro /vélkrō/ tdmk a trademark for a fastener consisting of two strips, one with a dense layer of hooks and the other of loops that interlock with them

vellum /vélləm/ n 1 high quality parchment made of animal skin 2 off-white heavy paper resembling vellum —**vellum** adj

velociraptor /və lóssi raptər/ n a small two-legged carnivorous dinosaur

velocity /və lóssəti/ (pl **-ties**) n 1 speed 2 the rate of change over time in the position of an object as it moves in space

velodrome /vélladrōm/ n a stadium for bicycle races

velour /və loŏr/, **velours**)) a thick-piled fabric like velvet. Use: upholstery, clothing.

velum /véeləm/ (pl **-la** /-lə/) n the soft palate —**velar** adj

velvet /vélvit/ n 1 a fabric with a soft lustrous pile. Use: clothing, curtains, upholstery. 2 something smooth and soft like velvet ■ adj 1 made of velvet 2 like velvet —**velvety** adj

velveteen /vélvə teen/ n a fabric resembling velvet. Use: clothing, upholstery.

venal /veen'l/ adj 1 open to bribery 2 corrupt —**venality** /vee nálləti/ n —**venally** adv

vend /vend/ v 1 vt sell goods from a vending machine 2 vti sell goods on the street

vendetta /ven déttə/ n 1 a blood feud between families 2 any prolonged feud or hostile campaign

vending machine n a machine that dispenses goods when you insert money

vendor /véndər/, **vender** n a seller of goods or property

veneer /və neer/ n 1 a thin layer of a superior material fixed to the surface of something inferior 2 a deceptive appearance ■ vt cover with a veneer

venerable /vénnərəb'l/ adj 1 worthy of respect because of age or status 2 revered because of religious associations —**venerably** adv

venerate /vénnə rayt/ (-ating, -ated) vt respect or honour —**veneration** /vénnə ráysh'n/ n

venereal /və neéri əl/ adj associated with or passed on through sex

venereal disease n a sexually transmitted infection (dated)

Venetian /və neésh'n/ adj of Venice —**Venetian** n

Venetian blind, venetian blind n a blind made of thin slats

Venezuela /vénnə zwáylə/ country in NE South America, on the Caribbean Sea and the Atlantic Ocean. Cap. Caracas. Pop. 23,916,810 (2001). —**Venezuelan** n, adj

~~vengeance, vengence~~ incorrect spelling of **vengeance**

vengeance /vénjənss/ n revenge ◊ **with a vengeance** in an extreme or intense manner

vengeful /vénjf'l/ adj 1 wanting revenge 2 done in order to get revenge —**vengefully** adv —**vengefulness** n

venial /veéni əl/ adj forgivable —**veniality** /veéni álləti/ n

Venice /vénniss/ seaport in NE Italy, built on islands in a lagoon in the **Gulf of Venice**, an arm of the N Adriatic Sea. Pop. 291,531 (1999).

venison /vénniss'n, -z'n/ n meat from a deer

Venn diagram n a representation of mathematical sets that uses overlapping circles

ORIGIN The diagram is named after the British specialist in logic John Venn (1834–1923).

venom /vénnəm/ n 1 a poisonous fluid injected by an animal 2 malice —**venomous** adj —**venomously** adv

venous /veénəss/ adj 1 of veins 2 having veins

vent[1] n an opening that allows air, gas, smoke, or steam to enter or escape ■ v 1 vt release emotions o *She vented her frustration on her family.* 2 vti let something out through a vent 3 vti make a vent in something ◊ **give vent to** express a strong feeling or emotion freely

vent[2] n a vertical slit in the seam of a jacket or other garment —**vented** adj

ventilate /vénti layt/ (-lating, -lated) vt 1 admit fresh air into a room 2 put a vent for air in something 3 expose something to moving fresh air 4 examine issues publicly 5 supply oxygen to the blood through the blood vessels of the lungs —**ventilation** /vénti láysh'n/ n

ventilator /vénti laytər/ n 1 a device for circulating fresh air 2 a machine that helps somebody to breathe

ventral /véntrəl/ adj 1 of the lower surface of an animal's body, or the front of the human

body ○ *ventral fin* **2** of the abdomen
—**ventrally** *adv*

ventricle /véntrik'l/ *n* a hollow in a body part, especially a chamber in the heart or a brain cavity

ventriloquist /ven tríllǝkwist/ *n* somebody who throws his or her voice, especially a performer who makes a puppet appear to speak —**ventriloquism** *n*

venture /vénchǝr/ *n* **1** a risky project **2** a new business enterprise ■ *v* (**-turing, -tured**) **1** *vi* make a dangerous trip **2** *vt* express tentatively ○ *ventured a suggestion* **3** *vti* dare to do something **4** *vt* put at risk

venture capital *n* money for high-risk investment —**venture capitalist** *n*

Venture Scout, Venturer /vénchǝrǝr/ *n* a senior Scout

venturesome /vénchǝrssǝm/ *adj* (*fml*) **1** adventurous **2** involving risk —**venturesomeness** *n*

venue /vénnyoo/ *n* the place where an event is held

Venus /véenǝss/ *n* **1** in Roman mythology, the goddess of love. Greek equivalent **Aphrodite** **2** the planet that is 2nd from the Sun —**Venusian** /vǝ nyóòzi ǝn/ *adj*, *n*

Venus flytrap /-flī' trap/ *n* a plant that traps and consumes insects

veracity /vǝ rássǝti/ *n* (*pl* **-ties**) *n* **1** truth or accuracy **2** a true statement —**veracious** /vǝ ráyshǝss/ *adj* —**veraciousness** *n*

Veracruz /veérǝ króòz, vérrǝ-/ city in E Mexico, on the Gulf of Mexico. Pop. 425,140 (1995).

veranda /vǝ rándǝ/, **verandah** *n* **1** a porch extending along an outside wall of a building **2** *ANZ* a canopy sheltering a walkway —**verandaed** *adj*

verb *n* a word that indicates an action, existence, or possession

verbal /vúrb'l/ *adj* **1** using words rather than pictures or action **2** oral rather than written **3** using words without conveying meaning **4** involving skill with words **5** of or forming verbs ■ *n* a word formed from a verb —**verbally** *adv*

SYNONYMS verbal, spoken, oral CORE MEANING: expressed in words

verbalize /vúrbǝ līz/ (**-izing, -ized**), **verbalise** *vt* **1** express something in words **2** make a word into a verb —**verbalization** /vúrbǝ lī záysh'n/ *n*

verbal noun *n* a noun ending in '-ing' that is formed from a verb, e.g. 'hiking'

verbatim /vur báytim/ *adj*, *adv* using identical words

verbiage /vúrbi ij/ *n* an excess of words

verbose /vur bóss/ *adj* using too many words —**verbosely** *adv* —**verboseness** *n* —**verbosity** /vur bóssǝti/ *n* ◊ See note at **wordy**

verboten /fǝr bốt'n, vǝr-/ *adj* not allowed

verdant /vúrd'nt/ *adj* **1** with lush green growth **2** green —**verdancy** *n*

Verde, Cape /vurd/ ♦ **Cape Verde**

Verdi /váirdi/, **Giuseppe** (1813–1901) Italian composer

verdict /vúrdikt/ *n* **1** a jury's decision **2** any decision or opinion

verdigris /vúrdi gree, -greess/ *n* **1** a green deposit on copper **2** a greenish powder formed by the action of acetic acid on copper. Use: paint pigment, fungicide.

ORIGIN **Verdigris** came from a French word meaning literally 'green of Greece'. The reason for the Greek association is not known.

Verdun /vur dún/ town in NE France, site of one of the longest and bloodiest battles of World War I. Pop. 19,624 (1999).

verdure /vúrjǝr/ *n* **1** the vivid green colour of plants **2** vegetation

verge *n* **1** the point beyond which something happens **2** a boundary or edge **3** a narrow border, usually of grass, alongside a road
□ **verge on** *or* **upon** *vt* **1** border on an area **2** come close to a particular quality or condition

verger /vúrjǝr/ *n* **1** a church caretaker **2** a church official with ceremonial duties

Verhofstadt /vǝr hóf stat/, **Guy** (*b.* 1953) prime minister of Belgium (1999–)

verify /vérri fī/ (**-fies, -fied**) *vt* **1** prove something **2** check whether something is true —**verifiable** *adj* —**verifiably** *adv* —**verification** /vérrifi káysh'n/ *n*

verily /vérrili/ *adv* to be sure (*archaic*)

verisimilitude /vérrissi mílli tyood/ *n* (*fml*) **1** the appearance of being true **2** something that seems true but is not

veritable /vérritǝb'l/ *adj* absolute —**veritably** *adv*

verity /vérrǝti/ (*pl* **-ties**) *n* (*fml*) **1** truth or reality **2** something that is true

Verlaine /vair lén/, **Paul** (1844–96) French poet

Vermeer /vǝr meér, -máir/, **Jan** (1632–75) Dutch artist

vermicelli /vúrmi chélli/ *n* **1** pasta in long thin threads **2** small chocolate strands

vermiculite /vur míkyoŏ līt/ *n* a compound of aluminium, magnesium, or iron. Use: insulation, lubricant, horticulture.

vermiform /vúrmi fawrm/ *adj* shaped like a worm

vermilion /vǝr mílli ǝn/, **vermillion** *n* **1** a red pigment **2** a bright red colour —**vermilion** *adj*

vermin /vúrmin/ *n* harmful or destructive small animals or insects such as rats or cockroaches —**verminous** *adj*

Vermont /vǝr mónt/ state in the NE United States. Cap. Montpelier. Pop. 608,827 (2000). —**Vermonter** *n*

vermouth /vúrmǝth, vǝr moŏth/ *n* wine flavoured with herbs

vernacular /vǝr nákyoŏlǝr/ *n* **1** the ordinary language spoken by a specific people **2** the language of a specific profession or class —**vernacular** adj

vernal /vúrn'l/ adj of the spring

Verne /vurn/, **Jules** (1828–1905) French writer

Verona /və rốnə/ capital of **Verona Province**, Veneto Region, N Italy. Pop. 254,712 (1999). —**Veronese** /vérrõ neéz/ n, adj

Veronese /vérrõ náyzi/, **Paolo** (1528–88) Italian artist

verruca /və rόʊkə/ (pl -**cas** or -**cae** /-see, -kee/) n a wart on the foot

Versailles /vair sí/ n a 17C palace near Paris

versatile /vúrssə tíl/ adj 1 having many uses 2 having many skills —**versatilely** adv —**versatility** /vúrssə tíllətí/ n

verse n 1 a section of a song or poem 2 a numbered division of a chapter of the Bible 3 poetry 4 a particular form of poetry o in blank verse

versed /vurst/ adj skilled or knowledgeable

versify /vúrssi fí/ (-**fies**, -**fied**) v 1 vt change prose into poetry 2 vi write poetry —**versification** /vúrssifi káysh'n/ n

version /vúrsh'n, vúrzh'n/ n 1 an account of something 2 a specific form or variety of something o a later version of the text 3 an adaptation 4 a translation —**versional** adj

verso /vúrssõ/ (pl -**sos**) n 1 the back of a printed page 2 a left-hand page in a book

versus /vúrssəss/ prep 1 against 2 as opposed to

vertebra /vúrtibrə/ (pl -**brae** /-bray, -bree/ or -**bras**) n a bone in the spinal column —**vertebral** adj

vertebrate /vúrtibrət/ n an animal with a backbone —**vertebrate** adj

~~**verternarian**~~ incorrect spelling of **veterinarian**

vertex /vúrt eks/ (pl -**texes** or -**tices** /-ti seez/) n 1 the highest point 2 the point of a geometrical figure that is opposite the base 3 a point where the two sides of a figure or angle intersect

vertical /vúrtik'l/ adj 1 at right angles to the horizon or to the base of something 2 directly overhead ■ n 1 something vertical 2 an upright position —**vertically** adv

vertiginous /vur tíjjinəss/ adj 1 so high as to cause dizziness 2 suffering from vertigo 3 rotating around an axis —**vertiginously** adv

vertigo /vúrtigõ/ n a condition marked by a whirling sensation that causes a loss of balance

verve n 1 creative enthusiasm 2 vitality

very /vérri/ adv adds emphasis o very cold ■ adj 1 indicates an extreme o at the very back of the hall 2 right or suitable o the very person I wanted to see o the very thing I need 3 adds emphasis o shook the industry to its very foundation o trembled at the very mention of her name

vespers /véspərz/, **Vespers** n an evening church service (+ sing or pl verb)

Vespucci /ve spóochi/, **Amerigo** (1454–1512) Italian explorer

vessel /véss'l/ n 1 a container 2 a ship or boat 3 a tubular structure that conducts fluid around the body or through a plant

vest n 1 UK, NZ a sleeveless undergarment 2 a waistcoat ■ v 1 vt confer power or rights on somebody 2 vti dress in vestments

Vesta /véstə/ n in Roman mythology, the goddess of the hearth. Greek equivalent **Hestia**

vestal virgin /vést'l-/ n in ancient Rome, a celibate woman consecrated to the goddess Vesta

vested interest n 1 a right to possess property in the future 2 a special interest in something for reasons of private gain

vestibule /vésti byool/ n 1 an entrance hall 2 a cavity or space in the body that serves as the entrance to another cavity or canal

vestige /véstij/ n 1 a trace of something gone 2 the slightest amount

vestigial /ve stíjjī əl/ adj remaining after the rest has disappeared or dwindled —**vestigially** adv

vestment /véstmənt/ n 1 a robe worn to show rank 2 a ceremonial robe worn by members of the clergy

vestry /véstri/ (pl -**tries**) n 1 a room in a church where vestments and sacred objects are stored 2 a meeting room in a church

Vesuvius, Mt /və soóvi əss/ active volcano overlooking the Bay of Naples, S Italy. An eruption in AD 79 destroyed the Roman cities of Pompeii and Herculaneum. Height 1,277 m/4,190 ft.

vet n a veterinary surgeon ■ vt (**vetting, vetted**) examine somebody or something in order to determine suitability

vet. abbr 1 veteran 2 veterinarian 3 veterinary

vetch n a climbing or twining plant with small flowers. Use: silage, fodder.

veteran /véttərən/ n 1 somebody with a lot of experience 2 a member or former member of the armed forces who has seen active service —**veteran** adj

veteran car n a car made before 1919

veterinarian /véttəri náiri ən/ n US, Can a veterinary surgeon

veterinary /véttərinəri/ adj of animal diseases

veterinary surgeon n UK, Aus a medical practitioner who treats animals

~~**vetinary**~~ incorrect spelling of **veterinary**

veto /veétõ/ n (pl -**toes**) 1 the right to reject something, especially a piece of legislation 2 an exercise of the right to reject something 3 a prohibition ■ vt (-**toes**, -**toing**, -**toed**) 1 reject 2 prohibit —**vetoer** n

vex vt 1 annoy 2 agitate or confuse —**vexingly** adv

vexation /vek sáysh'n/ n 1 the state of being vexed 2 the act of vexing 3 something that vexes

vexatious /vek sáyshəss/ adj troublesome or annoying —**vexatiously** adv

vexed /vekst/ *adj* **1** irritated **2** much debated ○ *a vexed issue such as global warming* —**vexedly** /véksidli/ *adv*

vg *abbr* very good

VGA *n* a specification for computer screens. Full form **video graphics array**

VHF, vhf *abbr* very high frequency

VHS *n* a video recording system. Full form **Video Home System**

via /ví ə, vee ə/ *prep* **1** by way of **2** by means of

viable /ví əb'l/ *adj* **1** practicable or worthwhile **2** able to survive, grow, or develop **3** describes a foetus that is able to survive outside the womb —**viability** /ví ə bílləti/ *n* —**viably** *adv*

viaduct /ví ə dukt/ *n* a bridge consisting of a series of arches that spans a valley

Viagra /vi ággrə/ *tdmk* a trademark for sildenafil citrate, an enzyme-inhibiting drug. Use: treatment of male impotence.

vial /ví əl/ *n* a small glass bottle for medicine

viand /ví ənd, vee-/ *(fml)* *n* an article of food ■ **viands** *npl* food provisions

vibe /víb/ *n* an atmosphere or feeling *(slang; often pl)*

vibrant /víbrənt/ *adj* **1** pulsating with energy **2** having a full rich sound that resonates **3** dazzlingly bright —**vibrancy** *n* —**vibrantly** *adv*

vibraphone /víbrə fōn/ *n* a percussion instrument with metal bars —**vibraphonist** *n*

vibrate /ví bráyt/ (**-brating, -brated**) *v* **1** *vti* make or cause to make small movements back and forth rapidly **2** *vi* resonate —**vibratory** /ví bráytəri, víbrətəri/ *adj*

vibration /ví bráysh'n/ *n* **1** the process or an instance of shaking or moving to and fro very rapidly **2** the atmosphere given off by a place or situation, or the feeling conveyed *(infml; often pl)* —**vibrational** *adj*

vibrato /vi bráátō/ (*pl* **-tos**) *n* a throbbing effect produced in playing a musical instrument or singing

vibrator /ví bráytər/ *n* **1** a device that vibrates, especially one used for massage or sexual stimulation **2** a device converting direct to alternating current

vicar /víkər/ *n* **1** an Anglican priest in charge of a parish **2** a Roman Catholic priest who represents or deputizes for a bishop —**vicarage** /víkərij/ *n*

vicarious /vi káiri əss, vī-/ *adj* **1** experienced through another person by sympathy or in imagination **2** endured for somebody else —**vicariously** *adv* —**vicariousness** *n*

vice[1] *n* a tool with jaws for keeping an object immobile while it is worked on —**vice-like** *adj*

vice[2] *n* **1** an immoral habit **2** immoral conduct **3** a mild character flaw

vice admiral *n* a naval officer of a rank above rear admiral —**vice-admiralty** *n*

vice chancellor *n* **1** an assistant chancellor of a university **2** a deputy chancellor of a state —**vice-chancellorship** *n*

vice president *n* a president's deputy —**vice-presidency** *n* —**vice-presidential** *adj*

viceregal /víss reeg'l/ *adj* **1** of viceroys **2** *ANZ* of a governor or governor general

viceroy /víss roy/ *n* a governor who represents a sovereign in a colony —**viceroyship** *n*

vice squad *n* a police division enforcing laws relating to gambling, drug abuse, and prostitution

vice versa /víss vúrssə, víssi-/ *adv* the other way round

Vichy /veeshi/ city in central France. It was the seat of a French government that collaborated with the Germans during World War II. Pop. 26,528 (1999).

vicinity /vi sínnəti/ (*pl* **-ties**) *n* **1** the area surrounding or near a place **2** proximity **3** an approximate amount or number ○ *something in the vicinity of 1,000 jobs*

vicious /víshəss/ *adj* **1** ferocious and violent **2** dangerous and aggressive **3** intended to cause harm —**viciously** *adv* —**viciousness** *n*

vicious circle, vicious cycle *n* a situation that is worsened by attempts to solve it

vicissitude /vi síssə tyood, -tyōōd/ *n* variability *(literary)* ■ **vicissitudes** *npl* unexpected and often unwelcome changes

victim /víktim/ *n* **1** somebody hurt or killed **2** somebody or something harmed or adversely affected **3** a living being used for a sacrifice

victimize /víkti mīz/ (**-izing, -ized**), **victimise** *vt* **1** treat unfairly **2** make into a victim —**victimization** /víkti mī záysh'n/ *n*

victor /víktər/ *n* **1** a winner **2 Victor** a communications code word for the letter 'V'

Victor Emmanuel II /víktər i mánnyoo əl/ (1820–78) king of Sardinia (1849–78) and first king of Italy (1861–78)

Victoria /vik táwri ə/ **1** river in NW Northern Territory, Australia. Length 640 km/398 mi. **2** state in SE Australia. Cap. Melbourne. Pop. 4,689,800 (1998). **3** capital of British Columbia, Canada. Pop. 73,504 (1996). **4** capital of the Republic of Seychelles. Pop. 60,000 (1994).

Victoria (1819–1901) queen of the United Kingdom (1837–1901)

Victoria, Lake largest lake in Africa, with shorelines in Tanzania, Uganda, and Kenya

Victoria Cross *n* a military decoration given for bravery

Victoria Falls waterfall in south-central Africa on the River Zambezi, on the border between Zambia and Zimbabwe. Height 108 m/355 ft.

Victoria Land region of Antarctica, west of the Ross Sea

Victorian /vik táwri ən/ *adj* **1** of the time of Queen Victoria **2** viewed as conventional, hypocritical, or prudish ■ *n* somebody who lived in Queen Victoria's reign —**Victorianism** *n*

Victoriana /vik táwri a'ənə/ *npl* objects from the time of Queen Victoria

victorious /vik táwri əss/ *adj* **1** having won **2** of victory —**victoriously** *adv* —**victoriousness** *n*

victory /víktəri/ (*pl* -**ries**) *n* **1** the defeat of an opponent or enemy **2** success in a difficult situation

victuals /vítt'lz/ *npl* food or other provisions (*often humorous*)

ORIGIN **Victuals** retains a pronunciation appropriate to the French word from which it was adopted, but the spelling has been altered to conform to the original source, Latin *victualia*. This was formed from *victus* 'livelihood, food', a derivative of the verb *vivere* 'live'. **Victuals** are thus etymologically what you need to live on.

vicuña /vi kyóönə, -koónyə/ *n* **1** a South American mammal related to the llama **2** a fine cloth made from vicuña wool

video /víddi ő/ *n* (*pl* -**os**) **1** the visual part of a television broadcast **2** a video recorder (*infml*) **3** a video cassette (*infml*) **4** something recorded onto videotape o *a video of my brother's wedding* ■ *adj* of television, especially the reproduction of images ■ *vt* (-**os**, -**oing**, -**oed**) record on videotape

video adapter *n* COMPUT = **graphics card**

video arcade *n* a place where people pay to play video games

video camera *n* a camera that uses videotape

video card *n* a circuit board that enables a computer to display screen information

video cassette *n* a cassette that contains videotape

video cassette recorder *n* a video recorder

video conferencing *n* the holding of a meeting in which participants in different places communicate via video —**video conference** *n*

videodisk /víddi ő disk/, **videodisc** *n* a disk on which video and audio information is recorded digitally

video game *n* an electronic game played on a computer or television screen or on a handheld device with a screen

video jockey *n* a presenter of music videos on television

videophone /víddi ő fōn/ *n* a communication device that simultaneously transmits the speech and a video image of the caller

video recorder *n* a tape recorder that uses video cassettes

videotape /víddi ő tayp/ *n* magnetic tape on which pictures and sound can be recorded ■ *vt* (-**taping**, -**taped**) record on videotape

videotext /víddi ő tekst/ *n* a video communications service that gives access to pages of information

~~vidio~~ incorrect spelling of **video**

vie /vī/ (**vying**, **vied**) *vi* compete

~~viel~~ incorrect spelling of **veil**

Vienna /vi énnə/ capital of Austria. Pop. 1,606,843 (1999). —**Viennese** /vee ə neéz/ *n, adj*

Vientiane /vyén tyaán/ capital of Laos. Pop. 528,109 (1995).

Vietnam /vyet nám/ country in Southeast Asia, on the South China Sea. Cap. Hanoi. Pop. 79,939,014 (2001). —**Vietnamese** /vyétnə meéz/ *n, adj*

Vietnam War *n* a conflict in Vietnam (1954–75) that involved US forces

view /vyoo/ *n* **1** an act of looking at something **2** a range of vision **3** a scene **4** a pictorial representation **5** a perspective **6** an opinion ■ *vt* **1** observe or watch **2** inspect **3** consider or think of a range of things —**viewable** *adj* —**viewer** *n* —**viewing** *n* ◇ **in view of** because of or bearing in mind ◇ **on view** put somewhere so as to be seen ◇ **take a dim view of** disapprove of ◇ **with a view to** with the aim, intention, or hope of

viewdata /vyoö daytə/ *n* an interactive information system accessed via a home television

viewfinder /vyoö fíndər/ *n* a device on a camera that shows what will appear in the picture

viewpoint /vyoö poynt/ *n* **1** a point of view **2** a viewing location

vigil /víjil/ *n* **1** a period of keeping watch during the night **2** the eve of a festival or holy day ■ **vigils** *npl* religious services at night

vigilant /víjilənt/ *adj* watchful, especially for danger —**vigilance** *n* —**vigilantly** *adv* ◇ See note at **cautious**

vigilante /víjji lánti/ *n* somebody who seeks to punish lawbreakers personally and unofficially

vignette /vin yét/ *n* **1** a small design printed on a book page **2** a short essay **3** a picture without a border that gradually fades into the background at the edges **4** a brief scene —**vignettist** *n*

vigorous /víggərəss/ *adj* **1** very strong and healthy **2** energetic —**vigorously** *adv* —**vigorousness** *n*

vigour /víggər/ *n* **1** great strength and energy **2** intensity **3** the ability to grow

Viking /víking/ *n* a member of an ancient Scandinavian seafaring people

~~vilage~~ incorrect spelling of **village**

vile (**viler**, **vilest**) *adj* **1** disgusting **2** wicked **3** very unpleasant —**vilely** *adv* —**vileness** *n* ◇ See note at **mean**

vilify /vílli fī/ (-**fies**, -**fied**) *vt* make malicious and abusive statements about —**vilification** /víllifi káysh'n/ *n* —**vilifier** *n* ◇ See note at **malign**

villa /víllə/ *n* **1** a large expensive country house **2** a holiday home, especially one rented abroad

village /víllij/ *n* **1** a small rural community **2** the inhabitants of a village —**villager** *n*

villa home n Aus a type of modern suburban house

villain /víllən/ n 1 an evil character, e.g. in a film 2 a person regarded as wicked or contemptible 3 HIST = villein

villainous /víllənəss/ adj 1 wicked 2 unpleasant or undesirable —**villainously** adv

villainy /víllani/ n 1 evil conduct 2 the state of being evil

Villa-Lobos /víllə lób oss/, **Heitor** (1887–1959) Brazilian composer

~~villan~~ incorrect spelling of **villain**

~~villege~~ incorrect spelling of **village**

villein /víllən, villayn/, **villain** n a feudal serf

Villon /vee yóN/, **François** (1431?–63?) French poet

Vilnius /vílni əss/ capital of Lithuania. Pop. 577,970 (2000).

vim n exuberant vitality and energy (infml)

~~vinagrette~~ incorrect spelling of **vinaigrette**

vinaigrette /vínnay grét, vínni-/ n a salad dressing with a base of vinegar and oil

vindaloo /víndə lóō/ n a very hot curry

vindicate /víndi kayt/ (-cating, -cated) vt 1 show to be blameless 2 justify or substantiate —**vindicable** adj —**vindication** /víndi káysh'n/ n —**vindicator** n

vindictive /vin díktiv/ adj 1 desiring revenge or done for revenge 2 spiteful

vine n 1 a climbing plant 2 the stem of a climbing plant 3 a grapevine —**viny** adj

vinegar /vínnigər/ n a sour-tasting liquid made by fermenting wine, cider, or beer —**vinegary** adj

> **ORIGIN** Vinegar came from French, and means literally 'sour wine'.

~~vinegarette~~ incorrect spelling of **vinaigrette**

vineyard /vínnyərd, -yaard/ n a place where grapes are grown

vingt-et-un /vánt ay úN/ n the card game pontoon

viniculture n = viticulture

Vinland /vínnlənd/ coastal area of NE North America, now N Newfoundland, visited by Norse voyagers in about AD 986

vino /veénō/ n wine (infml)

Vinson Massif /vínss'n máss eef/ highest mountain in Antarctica, in the central Ellsworth Mountains. Height 4,897 m/16,066 ft.

vintage /víntij/ n 1 the year in which a wine was produced 2 a wine from a particular year or place 3 the harvesting of grapes 4 the period when something originated or flourished ■ adj 1 describing a high-quality wine from a single year 2 representing what is best or most typical 3 of high quality and lasting appeal ■ vt (-taging, -taged) 1 gather grapes 2 make wine —**vintager** n

vintage car n an old car built between 1919 and 1930

vintner /víntnər/ n a wine merchant

vinyl /vín'l/ n a synthetic plastic or resin. Use: wallpaper, coverings. —**vinyl** adj

viol /ví əl/ n a stringed instrument of the 16C and 17C

viola[1] /vi ólə/ n a stringed instrument like a violin but slightly larger

> **ORIGIN** The two English words **viola** are unrelated. The instrument name was adopted from Spanish and Italian, and probably derives from a word in the old language of Provence that was related to fiddle. The flower name represents the Latin word for 'violet'.

viola[2] /ví ələ/ n a small plant with flowers of various colours

~~violance~~ incorrect spelling of **violence**

violate /ví ə layt/ (-lating, -lated) vt 1 act contrary to a law or rule 2 disturb something in a violent way 3 defile something sacred —**violable** adj —**violation** /ví ə láysh'n/ n —**violative** adj —**violator** n

violence /ví ələnss/ n 1 physical force designed to cause injury or damage ○ threats of violence 2 the illegal use of unjustified force 3 extreme or destructive force ○ the violence of the storm 4 intensity of feeling or expression

violent /ví ələnt/ adj 1 using or showing violence 2 intense ○ a violent headache ○ violent passion 3 caused by force —**violently** adv

violet /ví ələt/ n 1 a low-growing flowering plant with typically mauve or purple flowers 2 a purplish-blue colour —**violet** adj

violin /ví ə lín/ n a stringed instrument held under the chin and played with a bow —**violinist** n

VIP abbr very important person

viper /vípər/ n 1 any of a family of poisonous snakes 2 an adder 3 an offensive term for somebody regarded as treacherous (offensive literary) —**viperous** adj

> **ORIGIN** Viper came via French from Latin vipera 'snake'. There was an ancient belief that the snake bore live young, and vipera was probably earlier vivipera, literally 'live-bearing'.

virago /vi raágō/ (pl -goes or -gos) n an offensive term for a woman regarded as overbearing and aggressive

viral /vírəl/ adj 1 caused by a virus 2 of or using unsolicited emails that are forwarded spontaneously from one user to another —**viral** n —**virally** adv

virement /veér moN/ n a fund transfer

Virgil /vúrjil/, **Vergil** (70–19 BC) Roman poet —**Virgilian** /vur jílli ən/ adj

virgin /vúrjin/ n 1 somebody who has never had sex 2 a woman who has taken a religious vow of chastity 3 **Virgin, Virgin Mary** the mother of Jesus Christ ■ adj 1 of a virgin 2 pure or untouched ○ virgin snow 3 describes a natural area that has never been explored or exploited by human beings —**virginity** /vər jínnəti/ n

virginal[1] /vúrjin'l/ adj 1 of a virgin 2 not corrupted or spoiled

virginal[2] /vúrjin'l/ *n* an old keyboard instrument like a small harpsichord —**virginalist** *n*

Virginia /və jínni ə/ state of the east-central United States. Cap. Richmond. Pop. 7,078,515 (2000). —**Virginian** *n, adj*

Virginia creeper *n* a woody vine with bluish-black berries

Virgo /vúrgō/ (*pl* **-gos**) *n* 1 a zodiacal constellation on the celestial equator 2 the 6th sign of the zodiac 3 somebody born under Virgo —**Virgo** *adj* —**Virgoan** /vur gṓ ən/ *n, adj*

viridescent /vírri déss'nt/ *adj* greenish —**viridescence** *n*

viridian /vi ríddi ən/ *n* 1 a green pigment 2 a bluish-green colour —**viridian** *adj*

virile /vírrīl/ *adj* 1 having the characteristics of an adult male 2 forceful or energetic —**virility** /və rílləti/ *n*

virology /vī róllaji/ *n* the study of viruses —**virologic** /vírə lójjik/ *adj* —**virological** *adj* —**virologist** *n*

virtual /vúrchoo əl/ *adj* 1 being something in effect, if not in reality or name 2 generated by computer —**virtuality** /vúrchoo álləti/ *n* —**virtually** *adv*

virtual reality *n* a computer simulation of three-dimensional space that the user can interact with

~~virtualy~~ incorrect spelling of **virtually**

virtue /vúrchoo/ *n* 1 the quality of being morally good 2 a good or admirable quality 3 chastity ◊ **by** *or* **in virtue of** because of or through the power of

virtuoso /vúrchoo ṓssō/ (*pl* **-sos** *or* **-si** /-ṓssi/) *n* 1 an exceptional performer 2 a highly talented person —**virtuosic** /-ṓssik/ *adj* —**virtuosity** /vúrchoo ṓssəti/ *n*

virtuous /vúrchoo əss/ *adj* 1 having or showing moral goodness 2 chaste —**virtuously** *adv*

virulent /vírrōlənt, vírryōō-/ *adj* 1 poisonous or damaging 2 malicious or bitter —**virulence** *n* —**virulently** *adv*

virus /vírəss/ *n* 1 a minute parasitic particle that multiplies in the cells of another organism 2 a disease caused by a virus 3 a disruptive computer program ◊ **Trojan Horse, worm** 7

visa /veézə/ *n* a passport insertion that allows the bearer to enter or leave a specific country

~~visable~~ incorrect spelling of **visible**

visage /vízzij/ *n* the human face (*literary*)

vis-à-vis /veèzə veé/ *prep* 1 regarding 2 opposite ■ *adv* face to face

viscera /víssərə/ *npl* the internal organs of the body

visceral /víssərəl/ *adj* 1 instinctual 2 emotional 3 of the viscera —**viscerally** *adv*

viscid /víssid/ *adj* thick and sticky —**viscidity** /vi síddəti/ *n* —**viscidly** *adv*

viscose /vískōss/ *n* 1 soft rayon made from a thick cellulose solution 2 the cellulose used in making viscose

viscosity /vi skóssəti/ (*pl* **-ties**) *n* 1 a thick sticky quality 2 the property of a fluid that resists flowing

viscount /ví kownt/ *n* 1 a British nobleman of a rank above baron 2 a European count's son or younger brother —**viscountcy** *n* —**viscounty** *n*

viscountess /ví kowntəss/ *n* 1 a woman with the rank of viscount 2 a viscount's wife or widow

viscous /vískəss/ *adj* 1 thick and sticky 2 describes a fluid that has a relatively high resistance to flow —**viscously** *adv* —**viscousness** *n*

Vishnu /víshnoo/ *n* the Hindu god called the Preserver

visibility /vízzə bílləti/ *n* 1 the ability to be seen 2 the distance within which it is possible to see things 3 a clear view

visible /vízzəb'l/ *adj* 1 able to be seen 2 in sight 3 obvious or apparent 4 often in the public eye —**visibly** *adv*

vision /vízh'n/ *n* 1 eyesight 2 a mental picture 3 something seen in a dream or trance 4 the ability to anticipate possible future developments 5 a beautiful person or thing —**visional** *adj* —**visionless** *adj*

visionary /vízh'nəri/ *adj* 1 full of foresight 2 imaginary 3 idealistic and impracticable 4 given to dreaminess 5 of mystical visions ■ *n* (*pl* **-ies**) 1 somebody with great foresight 2 somebody who has visions

visit /vízzit/ *v* 1 *vti* go to see somebody or something 2 *vti* stay with somebody as a guest, or in a place as a tourist 3 *vt* go to inspect a place 4 *vt* inflict something on somebody (*archaic literary or fml*) ◊ *an administration upon which many trials were visited* ■ *n* 1 a social or official call 2 a stay in a place 3 an official call paid for the purpose of inspection ◊ *a visit to the ship by the admiral* —**visitable** *adj*

visitation /vízzi táysh'n/ *n* 1 an official visit 2 a divine punishment 3 a supposed appearance from the spirit world 4 **Visitation** the Virgin Mary's visit to Elizabeth after the Annunciation 5 **Visitation** the Christian festival that celebrates the Visitation. Date: 2 July. —**visitational** *adj*

visiting card *n* a name card presented by a visitor

visitor /vízzitər/ *n* somebody who is visiting

visor /vízər/, **vizor** *n* 1 a transparent front part of a helmet 2 the front of a medieval helmet, with slits for the eyes 3 a shade for the eyes like the peak of a cap 4 a flap fitted over a windscreen to shield the eyes from the sun's glare —**visored** *adj*

vista /vístə/ *n* 1 a scenic view 2 a view through a narrow opening

Vistula /vístyoōlə/ longest river in Poland, emptying into the Baltic Sea at the Gulf of Gdansk. Length 1,090 km/675 mi.

visual /vízhoo əl, vízzyoo-/ *adj* 1 of vision 2 visible 3 done by sight only —**visually** *adv*

visual display unit *n* a device used to display data from a computer

visualize /vízhoo ə līz, vízzyoo-/ (**-izing**, **-ized**),

visualise /vti/ imagine —**visualization** /vízhoo ə lī záysh'n, vízzyoo-/ n

visually impaired adj having reduced vision or no vision

vital /vít'l/ adj 1 crucial 2 of or needed for life ○ *vital bodily organs* 3 lively —**vitally** adv ◊ See note at **necessary**

vitality /vī tállǝti/ n 1 the quality of being lively 2 the ability to live and grow or to continue in existence

vitals /vít'lz/ npl 1 the internal organs of the body that are essential to life 2 essentials

vital statistics npl 1 data about the human population, including births and deaths 2 a woman's bust, waist, and hip measurements (dated infml)

vitamin /víttǝmin, vítǝ-/ n an organic substance essential to nutrition —**vitaminic** /víttǝ mínnik, vítǝ-/ adj

ORIGIN Vitamins were originally *vitamines*: the German biochemist Casimir Funk who introduced them to the world in 1912 believed that they were amino acids and so formed the name from Latin *vita* 'life' and *amine*. It was soon discovered that Funk's belief was mistaken, and alternative names were suggested, but in 1920 it was successfully proposed that the *-e* be dropped to avoid confusion, and the form **vitamin** was born.

vitamin A, vitamin A₁ n a fat-soluble vitamin found in some vegetables, fish, milk, and eggs, important for normal vision

vitamin B n BIOCHEM = **vitamin B complex**

vitamin B₁₂ n a water-soluble vitamin obtained only from animal products and fish, important for normal blood formation

vitamin B₂ n riboflavin

vitamin B complex n a group of water-soluble vitamins found in many foods

vitamin C n a water-soluble vitamin found in fruits and leafy vegetables

vitamin D n a fat-soluble vitamin that occurs in fish-liver oils and eggs, essential for the formation of bones and teeth

vitamin E n a mixture of fat-soluble vitamins found in seed oils, essential for normal reproduction

vitamin K n a fat-soluble vitamin essential for blood clotting

vitiate /víshi ayt/ (-ating, -ated) vt (fml) 1 make ineffective 2 make defective 3 debase —**vitiation** /víshi áysh'n/ n

viticulture /vítti kulchǝr/, **viniculture** /vínni kulchǝr/ n the science or practice of growing grapes —**viticultural** /vítti kúlchǝrǝl/ adj —**viticulturist** /vítti kúlchǝrist/ n

vitreous /víttri ǝss/ adj 1 similar to glass 2 of glass —**vitreosity** /víttri óssǝti/ n

vitreous humour n the fluid component of the gel that fills the main cavity of the eye

vitrify /víttri fī/ (-fies, -fied) vti change into glass —**vitrification** /víttrifi káysh'n/ n

vitriol /víttri ǝl/ n 1 bitterly expressed antipathy 2 sulphuric acid (literary)

vitriolic /víttri óllik/ adj expressing bitter hatred —**vitriolically** adv

vituperation /vī tyoópǝ ráysh'n, vi-/ n 1 an outburst of abuse 2 the use of violent abuse —**vituperate** /vī tyoópǝ rayt, vi-/ vt —**vituperative** /vī tyoópǝrǝtiv, vi-/ adj

viva¹ /veévǝ/ interj long live

viva² /vīvǝ/ n a university examination in which questions are asked and answered orally —**viva** vt

vivace /vi vaáchi/ adv in a lively way (musical direction) —**vivace** adj, n

vivacious /vi váyshǝss/ adj lively and full of high spirits —**vivaciously** adv —**vivaciousness** n —**vivacity** /vi vássǝti/ n

Vivaldi /vi váldi/, **Antonio** (1678–1741) Italian composer

vivarium /vī váiri ǝm/ (pl -a /-ri ǝ/ or -ums) n a place for keeping and watching small animals

viva voce /vīvǝ vōchi/ n a university viva ■ adv orally

vivid /vívvid/ adj 1 very bright 2 extremely clear or true to life 3 producing strong mental images 4 inventive ○ *a vivid imagination* —**vividly** adv —**vividness** n

viviparous /vi víppǝrǝss/ adj bearing live young —**viviparously** adv

vivisect /vívvi sekt/ vti operate on a live animal to gain knowledge of pathological or physiological processes —**vivisection** /vívvi séksh'n/ n

vixen /víks'n/ n 1 a female fox 2 an offensive term for a woman regarded as vindictive or bad-tempered —**vixenish** adj —**vixenly** adj, adv

viz adv namely

ORIGIN Viz is a shortening of *videlicet*, which was formed from Latin *vide* 'see' and *licet* 'it is permissible'.

vizier /vi zeér/ n a high-ranking diplomat in the former Turkish empire

vizor n = **visor**

VJ abbr video jockey

Vladivostok /vláddi vóstok/ major port in SE Russia. Pop. 640,672 (1995).

vlei /flay, vlay/ (pl vleis) n S Africa an area of low-lying ground

VLSI adj having thousands of components on a single microchip. Full form **very large-scale integration**

V neck n a V-shaped neckline —**V-necked** adj

VOC abbr volatile organic compound

vocabulary /vō kábbyōōlǝri/ (pl -ies) n 1 all the words known by a person or used in a language or profession 2 a list of words ◊ See note at **language**

vocal /vōk'l/ adj 1 uttered 2 of the voice 3 having the power of speech 4 outspoken ○ *vocal objections* 5 of or for singing ■ n 1 the sung part of a song 2 a pop or jazz song

—**vocality** /vō kálləti/ n —**vocally** adv —**vocalness** n

vocal cords, vocal chords npl membranes in the larynx that produce sounds by vibrating

vocalise vti = vocalize

vocalist /vókəlist/ n a singer of pop songs

vocalize /vókə līz/ (-izing, -ized), **vocalise** vti 1 express something with the voice 2 transform a consonant into a vowel, or be transformed into a vowel —**vocalization** /vókə īī záysh'n/ n

vocation /vō káysh'n/ n 1 a profession 2 an urge to follow a specific career —**vocational** adj —**vocationally** adv

vocative /vókətiv/ adj describes a word or grammatical case that indicates the person or thing addressed by the speaker —**vocative** n

vociferate /vō síffə rayt/ (-ating, -ated) vti shout out —**vociferation** /-siffə ráysh'n/ n

vociferous /vō sífferəss/ adj 1 shouting noisily 2 full of noisy shouting —**vociferously** adv —**vociferousness** n

vocoder /vō kṓdər/ n a speech synthesizer

vodka /vódkə/ n a colourless distilled spirit made from a grain or from potatoes

Vogel /vṓg'l/, **Sir Julius** (1835–99) British-born premier of New Zealand (1873–75, 1876)

vogue /vōg/ n 1 the prevailing fashion 2 popularity ■ adj fashionable

voice n 1 the sound made using the vocal organs 2 the sound of singing 3 the ability to use the voice for speaking or singing 4 a sound like the human voice 5 the right to state an opinion 6 an expressed opinion 7 a medium of communication or expression ○ *the voice of reason* 8 a singer or singing part 9 a form of a verb that indicates the relationship between subject and verb ■ vt (**voicing, voiced**) 1 express orally 2 pronounce with a vibration of the vocal cords —**voicer** n ◇ **with one voice** simultaneously or unanimously

voice box n the larynx

voiced adj pronounced with a vibration of the vocal cords —**voicedness** n

voiceless /vóyssləss/ adj 1 saying nothing 2 unable to speak 3 pronounced without a vibration of the vocal cords —**voicelessly** adv —**voicelessness** n

voice mail n a computerized system for storing telephone messages

voiceover /vóyss ōvər/ n the spoken words of an unseen commentator

voiceprint /vóyss print/ n a representation of a voice in graph form

void /voyd/ adj 1 not legally valid 2 totally lacking in something (fml) 3 empty or vacant ■ n 1 a vacuum 2 a state of loss or a feeling of emptiness ■ v 1 vt make legally invalid 2 vt empty the contents of 3 vti empty the bowels or bladder —**voidable** adj —**voidness** n ◇ See note at **vacant**

voilà /vwa laá/ interj acknowledges or expresses satisfaction that something has been done

voile /voyl/ n a lightweight translucent fabric

VoIP n a technology that enables voice messages to be sent via the Internet. Full form **voice over Internet protocol**

vol. abbr 1 volume 2 volunteer

volatile /vóllə tīl/ adj 1 prone to sudden change 2 unstable and potentially dangerous 3 unpredictable or fickle 4 evaporating at a relatively low temperature 5 short-lived —**volatility** /vóllə tílləti/ n

volcanic /vol kánnik/ adj 1 of volcanoes 2 sudden and violent

volcano /vol káynō/ (pl -noes or -nos) n 1 an opening in the Earth's crust through which molten material is ejected 2 a mountain formed from the deposited material from a vent in the Earth's surface

---

ORIGIN **Volcanoes** are named after Vulcan, the Roman god of fire. The word was adopted from Italian in the early 17C.

---

vole (pl **voles** or same) n a small rodent like a mouse with a short tail

Volga /vólgə/ longest river in Europe, in W Russia. It rises northwest of Moscow and flows southeast and south before emptying into the Caspian Sea. Length 3,700 km/2,300 mi.

Volgograd /vólgə grad/ city in SW Russia. Pop. 1,260,171 (1995).

volition /vō lísh'n/ n 1 the exercise of the will 2 the ability to choose or decide —**volitional** adj —**volitionally** adv

volk /folk/ n S Africa a people or nation

volley /vólli/ n 1 a simultaneous firing of several weapons 2 a discharge of missiles fired simultaneously 3 a simultaneous expression of things, e.g. protests or questions 4 a kick or hit of a ball before it bounces ■ vti (-leys, -leying, -leyed) 1 strike a ball before it lands 2 fire weapons simultaneously —**volleyer** n

volleyball /vólli bawl/ n 1 a team sport in which the hands are used to hit a ball over a high net 2 the large inflated ball used in volleyball —**volleyballer** n

volt[1] /volt/ n (symbol V) a unit of electric potential difference

---

ORIGIN The **volt** is named after Count Alessandro Volta (1745–1827), an Italian physicist who developed the first electric battery in 1800.

---

volt[2] /volt/, **volte** n a circular motion by a horse in dressage

Volta /vólta/ river in SE Ghana, emptying into the Atlantic Ocean. Length 1,500 km/930 mi.

voltage /vóltij/ n electric potential expressed in volts

Voltaire /vol táir/ (1694–1778) French writer and philosopher

volte-face /vólt faáss/ n 1 a sudden reversal of opinion 2 a change in position to face the opposite direction

voltmeter /vōlt meetər/ n an instrument that measures voltage

voluble /vóllyŏob'l/ *adj* talking a great deal —**volubility** /vóllyŏo bílləti/ *n* —**volubly** *adv*

volume /vóllyoom/ *n* **1** (*symbol* V) the three-dimensional space inside or occupied by an object **2** a total amount **3** loudness of sound **4** a sound control on something such as a television **5** a book **6** one of a set of books **7** a set of consecutive magazine issues spanning one year ■ *adj* involving large quantities

voluminous /və lŏominəss/ *adj* **1** having great size, capacity, or fullness **2** taking up many pages or books —**voluminously** *adv* —**voluminousness** *n*

voluntary /vólləntəri/ *adj* **1** acting or resulting from free will **2** done without pay or reward **3** partly or largely funded by charitable donations ○ *Many organizations in the voluntary sector receive some state funding.* **4** controlled through conscious choices ■ *n* (*pl* -**ies**) **1** a short composition for a solo instrument **2** a short piece of church music —**voluntarily** /vólləntərəli, -térrəli/ *adv*

volunteer /vóllən teĕr/ *n* **1** somebody who works without pay **2** somebody who does something voluntarily ■ *v* **1** *vti* offer free help **2** *vti* do something by choice **3** *vt* give something such as information or an opinion without being asked **4** *vi* offer to do military service

~~voluptius~~ incorrect spelling of **voluptuous**

voluptuary /və lúpchoo əri/ (*pl* -**ies**) *n* somebody who enjoys the pleasures of the senses

voluptuous /və lúpchoo əss/ *adj* **1** sensual **2** devoted to a life of sensual pleasure —**voluptuously** *adv* —**voluptuousness** *n*

vomit /vómmit/ *vti* **1** expel stomach contents through the mouth **2** gush or cause to gush forth ■ *n* **1** expelled stomach contents **2** an act of vomiting

von, Von see also under surname

von Braun /von brówn/**, Wernher** (1912–77) German rocket engineer

von Sternberg /von stúrn burg/**, Josef** (1894–1969) Austrian-born US film director

von Stroheim /von strŏ hĩm/**, Erich** (1885–1957) Austrian-born US actor and film director

voodoo /vóodoo/ *n* (*pl* **voodoos**) **1** a Caribbean religion that involves supposed communication with ancestors **2** a practitioner of voodoo **3** a supposedly magic charm or spell used in voodoo ■ *vt* (**voodoos, voodooing, voodooed**) cast a spell on

voorkamer /fóor kaamər/ *n S Africa* a front room

voracious /və ráyshəss/ *adj* **1** very hungry **2** especially eager or insatiable —**voraciously** *adv* —**voraciousness** *n* —**voracity** /və rássəti/ *n*

Voronezh /və rónnezh/ city in W Russia. Pop. 1,084,734 (1995).

vortex /váwr teks/ (*pl* -**texes** *or* -**tices** /-ti seez/) *n* **1** a whirling mass of water or air **2** a situation or feeling that engulfs everything else

Vosges /vŏzh/ mountain range in NE France. Length 190 km/120 mi. Highest peak Grand Ballon 1,424 m/4,672 ft.

votary /vótəri/ (*pl* -**ries**), **votarist** /-rist/ *n* **1** a monk or nun **2** a devotee

vote *n* **1** a formal choice for or against, e.g. in an election or referendum **2** the act of casting a vote **3** the number of votes cast in an election **4** the right to cast a vote **5** the outcome of an election **6** the opinion expressed by a particular group ■ *v* (**voting, voted**) **1** *vti* indicate a formal preference **2** *vt* cast a vote for or against somebody ○ *was voted out of office* **3** *vt* make something available or create something by vote ○ *refused to vote additional funds for the new building* **4** *vt* indicate an opinion (*infml*) —**voter** *n*

□ **vote down** *vt* defeat somebody or something in a vote

vote of no confidence *n* a vote to bring down a government

votive /vótiv/ *adj* **1** symbolizing a wish **2** fulfilling a vow —**votively** *adv*

vouch for *vt* guarantee somebody's good behaviour

voucher /vówchər/ *n* **1** a substitute for money used for making purchases **2** a piece of documentary evidence **3** somebody or something that guarantees or provides proof

vouchsafe /vówch sáyf/ (-**safing, -safed**) *vt* (*fml*) **1** condescend to give something, e.g. a reply **2** promise, agree, or allow something

vow *n* a solemn pledge, e.g. one of the promises made by a bride and groom or by somebody joining a religious order ■ *v* **1** *vt* promise solemnly **2** *vti* dedicate somebody to something

vowel /vów əl/ *n* a speech sound in which the air passes through the oral tract relatively unobstructed

voxel /vóksəl/ *n* a three-dimensional pixel

vox pop /vóks póp/ *n* public opinions gathered in interviews

voyage /vóy ij/ *n* a long journey, especially by sea or through space ■ *vti* (-**aging, -aged**) go on a voyage —**voyager** *n*

voyeur /vwī yúr/ *n* **1** somebody who watches others for sexual pleasure **2** a fascinated observer of misery or scandal —**voyeurism** *n* —**voyeuristic** /vwī yur rístik/ *adj*

VP *abbr* **1** verb phrase **2** vice president

VR *abbr* **1** Victoria Regina **2** virtual reality

VRML *n* a computer-graphics programming language. Full form **Virtual Reality Modelling Language**

vs *abbr* versus

V-sign *n* a V-shaped sign made with the index and middle fingers, indicating contempt or anger when the palm faces inwards and victory or solidarity when the palm faces outwards

VSO *n* an organization for volunteers working abroad in developing countries. Full form **Voluntary Service Overseas**

Vulcan /vúlkən/ *n* in Roman mythology, the god of fire. Greek equivalent **Hephaestus** —**Vulcanian** /vul káyni ən/ *adj*

vulgar /vúlgər/ *adj* 1 crude or indecent 2 tastelessly showy 3 lacking courtesy and manners 4 spoken by ordinary people —**vulgarly** *adv*

vulgarian /vul gáiri ən/ *n* a wealthy but tasteless or ostentatious person

vulgarism /vúlgərizəm/ *n* 1 a crude term 2 a term in ordinary people's language

vulgarity /vul gárrəti/ (*pl* **-ties**) *n* 1 the quality of being vulgar 2 a crude or indecent remark or act

vulgarize /vúlgə rīz/ (**-izing**, **-ized**), **vulgarise** *vt* 1 make less refined or of lower quality 2 present in a more accessible way —**vulgarization** /vúlgə rī záysh'n/ *n*

vulgate /vúl gayt/ *n* 1 ordinary speech 2 **Vulgate** a Latin version of the Bible authorized for use by Roman Catholics

vulnerable /vúlnərəb'l/ *adj* 1 open to physical or emotional danger or harm 2 exposed to attack or damage 3 easily persuaded or tempted 4 physically or psychologically weak —**vulnerability** /vúlnərə bílləti/ *n* —**vulnerably** *adv*

vulpine /vúl pīn/ *adj* 1 of or like a fox 2 having a trait attributed to foxes, especially cunning

vulture /vúlchər/ *n* 1 a large bird of prey that feeds on carrion 2 a person who waits to exploit somebody vulnerable

vulva /vúlvə/ (*pl* **-vae** /-vee/ or **-vas**) *n* the external female genitals —**vulval** *adj* —**vulvar** *adj*

vying present participle of **vie**

W

W[1] (*pl* **w's**), **W** (*pl* **W's** or **Ws**) *n* the 23rd letter of the English alphabet

W[2] *abbr* 1 week 2 wicket(s) 3 width 4 with

W[1] *symbol* 1 tungsten 2 watt 3 weight 4 work

W[2] *abbr* 1 Wales 2 Welsh 3 West 4 Western

w/ *abbr* with

W3 *abbr* World Wide Web

WA *abbr* Western Australia

wacky /wáki/ (**-ier**, **-iest**), **whacky** *adj* 1 an offensive term meaning unconventional or unpredictable *(slang)* 2 entertainingly silly *(infml)* —**wackily** *adv* —**wackiness** *n*

Waco /wáykō/ city in central Texas. Pop. 108,272 (1998).

wad /wod/ *n* 1 a small rounded mass of soft material used for packing or stuffing 2 a roll or small bundle of paper money 3 a rounded compressed lump of soft material, especially tobacco or gum 4 a plug or disc holding the powder or shot in a gun or cartridge ■ *v* (**wadding**, **wadded**) 1 *vti* compress or be compressed tightly 2 *vt* stuff or plug with wadding

wadding /wódding/ *n* 1 a soft protective material used in packaging 2 material for holding powder or shot in a gun or cartridge

waddle /wódd'l/ (**-dling**, **-dled**) *vi* walk with short steps and a side-to-side gait —**waddle** *n* —**waddly** *adj*

wade (**wading**, **waded**) *v* 1 *vti* walk in or through deep water or mud 2 *vi* get through something with difficulty ○ *wading through the paperwork that had accumulated in her absence* —**wadable** *adj* —**wade** *n*

□ **wade in** *vti* 1 interrupt forcefully 2 intervene in a situation

wader /wáydər/ *n* also **wading bird** a long-legged bird that stands in water to hunt for food ■ **waders** *npl* high waterproof boots or combined boots and trousers worn for fishing

wadi /wóddi/ (*pl* **wadis** or **wadies**), **wady** (*pl* **-dies**) *n* 1 a steep-sided watercourse through which water flows only after heavy rain 2 an oasis

wafer /wáyfər/ *n* 1 a thin crisp biscuit 2 a thin disc of unleavened bread used in the Christian Communion service 3 a slice of semiconducting material used as a base for an integrated circuit

wafer-thin *adj* extremely thin

waffle[1] /wóff'l/ (*infml*) *vi* (**-fling**, **-fled**) speak irrelevantly at length ■ *n* pointless speech or writing —**waffly** *adj*

waffle[2] /wóff'l/ *n* a thick light crisp pancake with a pattern of indentations on both sides

waft /woft, waaft/ *vti* move gently through the air ■ *n* 1 something such as a scent carried on the air 2 a light breeze

wag[1] (**wagging**, **wagged**) *vti* move a body part rapidly to and fro, or be moved in this way —**wag** *n*

wag[2] *n* somebody witty *(dated)* —**waggish** *adj*

wage *n* a payment for work done on an hourly, daily, weekly, or piece-rate basis *(often pl)* ■ *vt* (**waging**, **waged**) engage in a war or fight —**wageless** *adj*

SYNONYMS wage, salary, pay, fee, remuneration, emolument, honorarium, stipend
CORE MEANING: money given for work done

---

wage earner *n* 1 somebody who supports a household by earning wages 2 somebody who is paid wages

wage incentive *n* an additional amount of money paid for improved productivity

wage packet *n* an income earned by work

wager /wáyjər/ *n* 1 a bet on an outcome in which the loser pays the winner a specific amount 2 an amount bet in a wager ■ *vt* bet money on an outcome

waggle /wágg'l/ (**-gling**, **-gled**) *vti* move rapidly back and forth —**waggle** *n* —**waggly** *adj*

AKG London

Richard Wagner

Wagner /vaàgnər/, **Richard** (1813–83) German composer —**Wagnerian** /vaag neèri ən/ *adj*, *n*

wagon /wággən/, **waggon** *n* **1** a rectangular wheeled vehicle for carrying heavy loads, often pulled by an animal or tractor **2** a railway goods truck —**wagoner** *n*

wagtail /wág tayl/ *n* a long-tailed songbird

Wahhabi /wə haàbi/ (*pl* **-bis**), **Wahabi** *n* a member of a very conservative Islamic group that rejects any innovation that occurred after the 3C of Islam —**Wahhabism** *n*

wahine /waa heèni/ *n NZ, Hawaii* a Hawaiian or Maori woman

waiata /wî aatə/ *n NZ* a Maori song

waif /wayf/ *n* **1** somebody homeless or friendless, especially an abandoned child **2** a stray animal

Waikato /wî kaatō/ region in the north of the North Island, New Zealand. Pop. 357,290 (1996).

Waikiki /wî kee keè/ beach resort on S Oahu Island, Hawaii

wail /wayl/ *v* **1** *vti* make a mournful cry, or utter something in this way **2** *vi* make a long high-pitched noise —**wail** *n* —**wailer** *n*

SPELLCHECK Do not confuse the spelling of **wail** and **whale** ('marine mammal'), which sound similar.

wainscot /wáynskət, wáyn skot/ *n* **1** a set of wooden panels lining the walls of a room **2** the lower part of an interior wall, especially when panelled in wood ■ *vt* (**-scoting** *or* **-scotting**, **-scoted** *or* **-scotted**) cover a wall with panelling

waist /wayst/ *n* **1** the part of the body between the ribs and the hips **2** the part of a garment covering the waist **3** the middle part of something —**waisted** *adj*

SPELLCHECK Do not confuse the spelling of **waist** and **waste** ('use carelessly'), which sound similar.

waistband /wáyst band/ *n* a band of fabric circling the waist of a garment

waistcoat /wáyss kōt, wáyst-/ *n* a sleeveless waist-length garment worn over a shirt and sometimes under a suit jacket —**waistcoated** *adj*

waistline /wáyst līn/ *n* **1** the measurement of somebody's waist **2** the point at the waist where the bodice and skirt of a dress meet

wait /wayt/ *vi* **1** do nothing for a period of time, expecting something to happen **2** stop so that somebody can catch up **3** be postponed ○ *Fame would just have to wait.* **4** be ready or available for somebody ■ *n* a time spent waiting ◇ **lie in wait for** be waiting to catch or attack

SPELLCHECK Do not confuse the spelling of **wait** and **weight** ('heaviness'), which sound similar.

□ **wait on** *vt* **1** serve somebody by bringing requested items **2** serve somebody with food and drink at a table

□ **wait out** *vt* wait for something to end

□ **wait up** *vi* delay going to bed because somebody or something is expected

waiter /wáytər/ *n* somebody who brings food and drink to people at tables

waiting game *n* a tactic whereby somebody waits for a situation to improve in his or her favour

waiting list *n* a list of people waiting for something that is not immediately available

waiting room *n* a room for people to wait in

waitress /wáytrəss/ *n* a woman who brings food and drink to people at tables

wait state *n* a period of time during which a CPU sits idle while a slower component functions

waive /wayv/ (**waiving**, **waived**) *vt* **1** surrender a right or claim voluntarily **2** not enforce or apply something

SPELLCHECK Do not confuse the spelling of **waive** and **wave** ('of the sea, of a hand'), which sound similar.

waiver /wáyvər/ *n* a formal statement relinquishing a right or claim

wake[1] *v* (**waking**, **woke**, **woken** /wōkən/) **1** *vti* come or bring out of a state of sleep **2** *vti* become or make aware of something **3** *vi* hold a vigil over a corpse **4** *vi* be or stay awake ■ *n* **1** a watch kept over a corpse **2** a social gathering held after a funeral

□ **wake up** *v* **1** *vti* rouse or be roused from sleep, daydreaming, or inertia **2** *vt* make more interesting or attractive

wake[2] *n* **1** the track left in water by a vessel moving through it **2** the stream of turbulence in the air behind a moving aircraft or land vehicle **3** a position or the area behind somebody or something moving ◇ **in the wake of** immediately after

wakeboarding /wáyk bawrding/ *n* a sport in which somebody standing on a board is pulled behind a boat to perform jumps in its wake —**wakeboard** *vi* —**wakeboarder** *n*

Wakefield /wáyk feeld/, **Edward Gibbon** (1796–1862) British-born New Zealand social theorist

wakeful /wáykf'l/ *adj* **1** not sleeping **2** passed without sleep ○ *a wakeful night* —**wakefully** *adv* —**wakefulness** *n*

waken /wáykən/ vti rouse or be roused from sleep or inertia

wake-up call n 1 a telephone call to awaken a hotel guest 2 a frightening experience taken as a sign that a major change is needed

Walachia /wo láyki ə/ former region in SE Europe, in present-day S Romania —**Walachian** n, adj

Walcott /wáwlkət/, **Derek** (b. 1930) St Lucian writer

Waldorf salad /wáwl dawrf-, wól-/ n a salad made with apples, celery, walnuts, and mayonnaise

Wales /waylz/ principality in Great Britain, part of the United Kingdom. Cap. Cardiff. Pop. 2,933,000 (1998).

walk /wawk/ v 1 vi move on foot at a moderate pace 2 vt travel along a path or through a place on foot 3 vt take an animal for exercise by walking 4 vt accompany somebody on foot to a particular place 5 vt help or force somebody to walk 6 vi in cricket, acknowledge being out by leaving the wicket ■ n 1 a journey made on foot, especially for pleasure or exercise 2 the distance or time of a journey on foot 3 the slowest gait of a horse 4 a particular way of walking 5 a place or route for people walking —**walkable** adj —**walker** n ◇ **walk all over** 1 ignore the rights or feelings of 2 defeat easily ◇ **walk tall** feel and display self-confidence and pride

□ **walk away** vi not become involved in a situation or problem

□ **walk off with** vt 1 steal 2 win easily

□ **walk out** vi go on strike

walkabout /wáwkə bowt/ n 1 Aus an extended journey on foot through a remote area by an Australian Aborigine wishing to experience a traditional way of life 2 an informal walk among ordinary people by royalty or a celebrity ◇ **go walkabout** Aus (infml) 1 go on a walkabout 2 leave your normal surroundings

Walker /wáwkər/, **Alice** (b. 1944) US writer

walkie-talkie /wáwki táwki/, **walky-talky** (pl **walky-talkies**) n a hand-held radio transmitter and receiver

walk-in adj large enough to enter ○ a walk-in cupboard

walking /wáwking/ adj 1 able to walk 2 used or designed for walking

walking stick n a stick that assists in walking

walking wounded npl 1 casualties who can walk 2 people who continue to be affected by emotional trauma

Walkman /wáwkmən/ tdmk a trademark for a small portable cassette player with earphones

walk-on n 1 a small non-speaking part in a play or film 2 somebody with a walk-on part

walkout /wáwk owt/ n 1 an organized strike in which workers leave the premises 2 a departure in protest or anger

walkover /wáwk ōvər/ n an easy victory (infml)

walk-through n a rehearsal of a play without costumes or props, or of a television programme without cameras

walkway /wáwk way/ n 1 a specially built path for pedestrians 2 a passage above ground level designed for pedestrian use

wall /wawl/ n 1 a flat side of a building or room 2 a narrow upright structure, usually of stone or brick, that acts as a boundary or keeps something in or out 3 a physical or psychological obstacle 4 in football, a line of defensive players trying to block a shot on goal 5 a lining or covering for something such as a body cavity, organ, or cell ■ vt surround, separate, or close with a wall —**walled** adj ◇ **be climbing the wall** or **walls** be extremely bored or frustrated (infml) ◇ **drive somebody up the wall** annoy or irritate somebody to an extreme degree (infml) ◇ **go to the wall** be destroyed or ruined, especially financially ◇ **hit a brick wall** encounter an insurmountable difficulty

wallaby /wóllabi/ (pl -**bies**) n an Australian marsupial like a small kangaroo

Wallace /wólliss/, **Alfred Russel** (1823–1913) British naturalist

Sir William Wallace: Commemorative statue near Melrose, Scotland

Wallace, Sir William (1272?–1305) Scottish patriot

wallaroo /wóllə róó/ (pl -**roos** or same) n a large kangaroo of the rocky uplands of Australia

wallchart /wáwl chaart/ n a chart designed to be displayed on a wall to provide information or help in teaching

wallet /wóllit/ n 1 a small flat folding leather or plastic case for paper money and credit cards 2 a software program for making online purchases

wallflower /wáwl flow ər/ n 1 a spring-flowering garden plant 2 somebody shy who remains unnoticed at a social event (infml)

Walloon /wo lóón/ n a member of a French-speaking people of S Belgium, or their dialect

Wallis and Futuna Islands /wólliss ənd fə tyóónə-/ island group in the SW Pacific Ocean, an overseas territory of France. Cap. Mata Utu. Pop. 15,435 (2001).

wallop /wólləp/ (infml) vt strike very hard ■ n a hard hit

wallow /wóllō/ vi 1 roll in mud or water 2 indulge yourself ■ n 1 an act of wallowing

2 a place where animals roll in mud or water

wallpaper /wáwl paypər/ *n* **1** decorative paper pasted on walls **2** the background pattern for a computer screen —**wallpaper** *vti*

Wall Street *n* the street in New York City where many major US financial institutions are located, or the US financial markets

wall-to-wall *adj* **1** completely covering a floor **2** completely filling, covering, or pervading something *(infml)*

walnut /wáwl nut/ *n* **1** a wrinkled edible nut in a hard shell **2** a light ornamental wood. Use: cabinetmaking, panelling, veneers. **3** a tree that produces walnuts and walnut wood

ORIGIN Walnut means etymologically 'foreign nut'. The prehistoric Germanic peoples regarded the **walnut** as 'foreign' because it did not originally grow in N Europe but was introduced from France and Italy.

Walpole /wáwlpōl/, **Horace** (1717–97) British writer

Walpole, Robert, 1st Earl of Orford (1676–1745) English political leader

walrus /wáwlrəss, wóll-/ (*pl* **-ruses** *or same*) *n* an Arctic sea mammal like a seal with large tusks and bristly whiskers

walrus moustache *n* a thick drooping moustache resembling a walrus's whiskers

Walton /wáwltən/, **Izaak** (1593–1683) English writer

waltz /wawlss, wolss, wawlts/ *n* (*pl* **waltzes**) **1** a ballroom dance in triple time for couples **2** the music for a waltz ■ *v* (**waltzes**) **1** *vti* dance or lead somebody in a waltz **2** *vi* move in a relaxed confident manner *(infml)*

wampum /wómpəm/ *n* decorative beads formerly used as money by some Native North Americans

wan /won/ (**wanner, wannest**) *adj* **1** unhealthily pale **2** indicative of ill health or low spirits —**wanly** *adv* —**wanness** *n*

WAN *abbr* wide area network

wand /wond/ *n* **1** a thin rod with supposed magical powers **2** a thin staff carried as a symbol of office

wander /wóndər/ *v* **1** *vti* travel around without a purpose or destination **2** *vi* follow a winding course **3** *vi* stroll somewhere **4** *vi* stray from a path or course **5** *vi* lose the ability to concentrate or pay attention ○ *My mind was wandering.* **6** *vi* fail to think or speak coherently ■ *n* an aimless or leisurely act of moving from place to place —**wanderer** *n* —**wandering** *adj* —**wanderingly** *adv*

SPELLCHECK Do not confuse the spelling of **wander** and **wonder** ('speculate about something', 'be amazed by something'), which may sound similar.

wanderlust /wóndər lust/ *n* a desire to travel

wane /wayn/ *vi* (**waning, waned**) **1** show a decreasing illuminated surface *(refers to the Moon or a planet)* **2** decrease gradually in intensity or power ■ *n* **1** a gradual decrease in intensity

or power **2** the time during which the Moon is waning

wangle /wáng g'l/ (*infml*) *vt* (**-gling, -gled**) **1** get something deviously **2** falsify accounts or records ■ *n* a devious method of getting something —**wangler** *n*

wank /wank/ *vi* a taboo term meaning masturbate *(offensive)*

wanker /wángkər/ *n* a taboo term for somebody considered unpleasant, pretentious, or arrogant *(insult)*

wannabe /wónnə bee/ *n* somebody emulating somebody else *(infml disapproving)*

want /wont/ *vt* **1** desire something ○ *wants a new car* **2** desire to do something or that something be done ○ *wants his steak well done* **3** wish to see or speak to somebody ○ *You're wanted on the phone.* **4** seek somebody as a suspect in a crime ○ *want them for murder* **5** indicates that something is desirable or advisable *(infml)* ○ *You want to see a doctor about that.* **6** need something *(infml)* ○ *The cupboards want cleaning.* ■ *n* **1** something desired or needed *(usually pl)* **2** a lack of something **3** poverty ◊ See note at **lack**

SYNONYMS want, desire, wish, long, yearn, covet, crave CORE MEANING: seek to have, do, or achieve

□ **want for** *vt* lack

wanted /wóntid/ *adj* sought as a suspect in a crime

wanting /wónting/ *adj* **1** lacking **2** unsatisfactory ○ *found their writing skills wanting* ■ *prep* missing something necessary ○ *a chair wanting one leg*

wanton /wóntən/ *adj* **1** sexually unrestrained **2** done without reason or provocation **3** done out of a desire to cause harm **4** excessive ■ *n* somebody without sexual restraint —**wantonly** *adv* —**wantonness** *n*

WAP /wap/, **Wap** *n* a standard protocol for data transmission between hand-held wireless devices such as mobile phones and the Internet or other networks. Full form **wireless application protocol**

wapiti /wóppiti/ (*pl* **-tis** *or same*) *n* a large North American deer with long antlers

war /wawr/ *n* **1** an armed conflict between countries or groups **2** a period of armed conflict **3** the techniques of armed conflict **4** a serious struggle, argument, or conflict **5** a sustained effort to end something harmful ○ *the war on crime* ■ *vi* (**warring, warred**) engage in war ◊ See note at **fight**

~~waranty~~ incorrect spelling of **warranty**

warble /wáwrb'l/ *vti* (**-bling, -bled**) sing a song or note with trills or modulations ■ *n* **1** the act of warbling **2** a warbling sound

warbler /wáwrblər/ *n* **1** a dull-coloured songbird of Europe and Asia **2** a brightly coloured American songbird **3** somebody who warbles

war bride *n* a woman who marries a serviceman in wartime, especially one from another country

war chest *n* funds set aside for a war or campaign

war crime *n* a crime committed during a war in violation of international agreements on the conduct of warfare *(often pl)* —**war criminal** *n*

war cry *n* a battle cry

ward /wawrd/ *n* 1 an administrative or electoral division of an area 2 a room for patients in hospital 3 a prison division 4 a child or young person under the care of a guardian or court

□ **ward off** *vt* 1 repel a blow or attack 2 avert something bad

-ward, -wards *suffix* 1 in a particular direction, or towards a particular place ○ *homeward* 2 lying or occurring in a particular direction ○ *windward*

war dance *n* a ceremonial dance performed before or after a battle

warden /wáwrd'n/ *n* 1 somebody in charge of a building 2 somebody in charge of an institution such as a college or school 3 an official responsible for enforcing regulations 4 a churchwarden —**wardenship** *n*

warder /wáwrdər/ *n* 1 a prison officer 2 a guard

wardrobe /wáwrdrōb/ *n* 1 a large cupboard with a rail or shelves for clothes 2 all of somebody's clothes 3 a collection of clothes for a particular season or purpose 4 the costumes used by a theatre company

wardrobe mistress *n* a woman in charge of costumes in a theatre or on a film set

wardroom /wáwrd room, -rōōm/ *n* a room on a warship used by all the officers except the captain

ware /wair/ *n* 1 similar things or things made of the same material ○ *glassware* 2 ceramics of a particular kind or made by a particular manufacturer ■ **wares** *npl* 1 things for sale 2 marketable skills

SPELLCHECK Do not confuse the spelling of **ware**, **wear** (clothing), and **where** ('in or to a place'), which sound similar.

warehouse /wáir howss/ *(pl* **-houses** /-howziz/*)* a large building for storing goods or raw materials ■ *vt* /wáir howz, -howss/ *(***-houses** /-howziz/, **-housing** /-howzing/, **-housed** /-howzd/*)* store in a warehouse —**warehouseman** /-howssmən/ *n*

warehousing /wáir howzing/ *n* the stockpiling of a security in order to force the price up as a result of the reduced supply

~~**warf**~~ incorrect spelling of **wharf**

warfare /wáwr fair/ *n* 1 the waging of a war 2 conflict or struggle

warfarin /wáwrfərin/ *n* a colourless crystalline compound. Use: rat poison, anticoagulant in medicine.

warfighting /wáwr fíting/ *n* US the conducting of war —**warfighter** *n*

war game *n* 1 a military exercise 2 a game using model soldiers and equipment to re-enact a battle —**war gaming** *n*

warhead /wáwr hed/ *n* the destructive material carried by a bomb, missile, rocket, or torpedo

AKG London

Andy Warhol

Warhol /wáwrhōl/, **Andy** (1928–87) US artist

warhorse /wáwr hawrss/ *n* 1 a horse ridden in battle 2 a survivor of many conflicts *(infml)*

warlike /wáwr līk/ *adj* 1 hostile 2 of war

warlock /wáwr lok/ *n* a male sorcerer

warlord /wáwr lawrd/ *n* a powerful military leader not controlled by a government —**warlordism** *n*

ORIGIN One of the first uses of **warlord** was by the US poet Ralph Waldo Emerson in 1856. The term began to appear in the US and UK press with frequency during the late 1800s, referring to Kaiser Wilhelm II, emperor of Germany and king of Prussia (1888–1918). One of his many titles was the German word *Kriegsherr*, translated literally as 'war man'. English-speaking writers decided to translate this as 'warlord', thereby causing it to become a household word.

warm /wawrm/ *adj* 1 moderately hot 2 providing heat or protection against cold 3 having or feeling adequate heat 4 friendly 5 passionate 6 enthusiastic 7 describes a colour suggesting warmth 8 describes a scent in hunting that is fresh and strong ■ *v* 1 *vti* make or become warm 2 *vt* make cheerful or happy 3 *vi* become enthusiastic ○ *warming to the idea* ■ *n* a warm place *(infml)* —**warmish** *adj* —**warmly** *adv* —**warmness** *n*

□ **warm up** *vi* 1 prepare for strenuous exercise by performing gentle exercise 2 prepare for something

war machine *n* the military resources with which a country can fight a war

warm-blooded *adj* with a constant body temperature independent of the environment —**warm-bloodedness** *n*

warmboot /wáwrm boot/ *vt* restart a computer without switching it off

warm-hearted *adj* having or showing a kind nature —**warm-heartedly** *adv* —**warm-heartedness** *n*

warmonger /wáwr mung gər/ *n* somebody eager for war —**warmongering** *n*

warmth /wawrmth/ *n* 1 a warm state, quality, or feeling 2 affection 3 a moderate amount of heat 4 strong emotion, especially anger or zeal

warm-up *n* an act or period of warming up before strenuous exercise

warn /wawrn/ *v* 1 *vti* tell somebody about something that might cause injury or harm 2 *vt* tell somebody about something in advance 3 *vt* advise somebody against something potentially risky ○ *were warned against complacency*

SPELLCHECK Do not confuse the spelling of **warn** and **worn** (past participle of *wear*), which sound similar.

□ **warn off** *vt* 1 tell to keep away 2 advise against

warning /wáwrning/ *n* 1 a threat or a sign that something bad is going to happen 2 advice to be careful or stop doing something ■ *adj* meant to warn —**warningly** *adv*

war of nerves *n* a psychological conflict

warp /wawrp/ *vti* 1 twist out of shape ○ *warped wood* 2 turn or be turned from a usual or correct course or condition ○ *warped judgment* ■ *n* 1 a distortion of the shape of something 2 a perversion of mind or character 3 the threads running lengthwise on a loom or a piece of fabric —**warpage** *n*

war paint *n* 1 paint for decorating warriors before a battle 2 make-up (*infml*)

warpath /wáwr paath/ *n* formerly, a route taken by Native North Americans on the way to war ◊ **on the warpath** angry and in the mood for a confrontation (*infml*)

warrant /wórrənt/ *n* 1 an authorization 2 a certifying document 3 a document authorizing the police to do something 4 an option to buy shares at a later date and at a fixed price ■ *vt* 1 serve as a reason to do, believe, or think something 2 guarantee something such as the truth, accuracy, or dependability of something or somebody 3 authorize somebody —**warranter** *n*

warrant officer *n* an officer in the armed forces of a rank above noncommissioned officer

warranty /wórrənti/ (*pl* **-ties**) *n* 1 a guarantee on purchased goods 2 a condition in an insurance contract in which the insured person guarantees that something is the case 3 a justification or authorization

warren /wórrən/ *n* 1 a group of connected rabbit burrows 2 a building or area that is crowded or has a complicated layout

~~warrent~~ incorrect spelling of **warrant**

warring /wáwring/ *adj* in conflict

warrior /wórri ər/ *n* somebody who fights or is experienced in warfare

Warsaw /wáwr saw/ capital of Poland. Pop. 1,632,500 (1997).

warship /wáwr ship/ *n* an armoured ship for use in war

wart /wawrt/ *n* a small growth on the skin caused by a virus —**warty** *adj* ◊ **warts and all** including any flaws or disadvantages

wart hog *n* a wild pig with tusks and warty growths on its face

wartime /wáwr tīm/ *n* a period when a war is being fought

war-torn *adj* disrupted by war

Warwick 1 /wórrik/ town in central England. Pop. 22,476 (1991). 2 /wáwr wik/ town in SE Queensland, Australia. Pop. 10,371 (1991).

Warwickshire /wórrikshər/ county in central England

wary /wáiri/ (**-ier**, **-iest**) *adj* cautious —**warily** *adv* —**wariness** *n* ◊ See note at **cautious**

was past tense of **be** (*with I, he, she, it, and sing nouns*)

wasabi /wə saabi/ (*pl* **-bis** or *same*) *n* 1 a strong-tasting green powder or paste made from a plant root. Use: condiment in Japanese cooking. 2 a plant from which wasabi is obtained

wash /wosh/ *v* 1 *vt* clean something, e.g. clothes, with water and usually soap 2 *vti* remove or be removed by washing 3 *vi* clean yourself by washing 4 *vi* be washable 5 *vt* flow over something 6 *vt* move something along on water 7 *vi* be convincing (*infml*) ○ *That story won't wash with her.* ■ *n* 1 an act of washing 2 a quantity of clothes washed or to be washed 3 a lotion, antiseptic, or cosmetic applied to the skin 4 a flow of water against a surface 5 a thin layer of colour applied with a brush 6 a surge of disturbed water or air from an oar, propeller, or jet engine 7 alluvial material carried and left by water 8 land periodically covered by water

□ **wash down** *vt* follow something drunk or eaten with another drink

□ **wash out** *v* 1 *vt* clean the inside of something 2 *vti* remove or be removed by washing 3 *vt* cause an event to be cancelled because of rain

□ **wash up** *vti* wash the dishes

washable /wóshəb'l/ *adj* capable of being washed without being damaged

washbasin /wósh bayss'n/ *n* a basin for washing the face and hands or small articles

washboard /wósh bawrd/ *n* 1 a ridged board for rubbing clothes on when washing them 2 a ridged board used as a musical instrument to produce a scratching sound

washday /wósh day/ *n* a day for washing clothes

washed-out *adj* 1 faded 2 exhausted

washed-up *adj* not likely to be successful again (*infml*)

washer /wóshər/ *n* 1 a small ring for keeping a screw secure or preventing leakage at a joint 2 a washing machine or dishwasher 3 somebody who washes 4 *Aus* a facecloth (*infml*)

washer-dryer *n* a washing machine and tumble dryer in one

washerwoman /wóshər wŏoman/ (*pl* **-women** /-wimin/) *n* a woman paid to wash clothes

washing /wóshing/ *n* 1 clothes that have been or are to be washed 2 the process of washing clothes

washing machine *n* a machine for washing clothes

washing soda *n* sodium carbonate crystals. Use: washing and cleaning.

Washington /wóshingtən/ **1** state of the NW United States. Cap. Olympia. Pop. 5,894,121 (2000). **2** *also* **Washington, D.C.** capital of the United States. The city of Washington has the same boundaries as the District of Columbia, a federal territory. Pop. 523,124 (1998). **3** town in NE England. Pop. 61,500 (1996). —**Washingtonian** /wóshing tŏni ən/ *n, adj*

Library of Congress

George Washington

Washington, George (1732–99) 1st president of the United States (1789–97)

washing-up *n* **1** the washing of dishes **2** the items needing washing after a meal

washing-up liquid *n* a liquid detergent for washing dishes

washout /wósh owt/ *n* **1** a complete failure (*infml*) **2** erosion caused by running water

washroom /wósh room, -rŏom/ *n* a room in a public place with a toilet and washing facilities

washstand /wósh stand/ *n* a stand for a basin and jug for washing the face and hands

wash-up *n Aus* the outcome of something

wasn't /wózz'nt/ *contr* was not

wasp /wosp/ *n* a black-and-yellow striped stinging winged insect

Wasp /wosp/, **WASP** *n US, Can* an offensive term for a white person from an Anglo-Saxon Protestant background (*infml*)

waspish /wóspish/, **waspy** /wóspi/ (**-ier, -iest**) *adj* **1** of wasps **2** easily irritated —**waspishness** *n*

wassail /wóssayl/ (*archaic*) *n* **1** a festive occasion at which people drink a great deal **2** mulled wine or ale drunk on a festive occasion ■ *vi* drink in celebration —**wassailer** *n*

wastage /wáystij/ *n* **1** an amount wasted **2** loss caused through use, wear, decay, or leakage

waste /wayst/ *v* (**wasting, wasted**) **1** *vt* use carelessly or ineffectively **2** *vt* fail to make use of **3** *vti* become or make weaker or more ill **4** *vt* destroy ■ *n* **1** the careless or ineffective use of something **2** unwanted or unusable by-products **3** liquid or solid matter excreted from the body after digestion **4** a wild area (*often pl*) **5** a destroyed area **6** rubbish or refuse ■ *adj* **1** useless or not needed **2** unproductive or uncultivated **3** excreted from the body after digestion —**waster** *n* ◊ See note at **waist**

wasted /wáystid/ *adj* **1** not used **2** useless **3** withered

waste disposal, waste disposal unit *n* an electrical device in a kitchen sink for grinding up food so that it can go into the waste pipe

wasteful /wáystf'l/ *adj* **1** extravagant **2** causing waste or devastation —**wastefully** *adv* —**wastefulness** *n*

wasteland /wáyst land, -lənd/ *n* **1** a desolate area **2** an intellectually or spiritually barren place or time

wastepaper /wáyst páypər/ *n* paper that is not needed and has been thrown away

wastepaper basket, wastepaper bin *n* a small container for rubbish, especially paper

waste pipe *n* a pipe carrying waste liquid from a sink or bath

wastrel /wáystrəl/ *n* a person regarded as wasteful, extravagant, or lazy (*insult*)

watch /woch/ *n* **1** a small clock worn on the wrist or kept in a pocket **2** the act or a period of observing or guarding something **3** a fixed period of a day spent on duty on a ship **4** the members of a ship's crew on duty at one time ■ *v* **1** *vti* look carefully at something **2** *vi* keep a lookout **3** *vti* monitor something or somebody —**watcher** *n* ◊ **watch it** be careful (*infml; usually a command*)

□ **watch out** *vi* **1** be careful **2** look and wait

□ **watch over** *vt* look after or guard

watchable /wóchəb'l/ *adj* **1** observable **2** enjoyable to watch

watchband /wóch band/ *n Aus, US, Can* a wristwatch strap

watchdog /wóch dog/ *n* **1** a dog for guarding property or people **2** a person or organization guarding against undesirable practices ■ *vti* (**-dogging, -dogged**) be a watchdog over something

watchful /wóchf'l/ *adj* observing closely —**watchfully** *adv* —**watchfulness** *n*

watchmaker /wóch maykər/ *n* somebody who makes or repairs watches

watchman /wóchmən/ (*pl* **-men** /-mən/) *n* somebody employed to guard a building or area

watchstrap /wóch strap/ *n UK, NZ* a wristwatch strap

watchtower /wóch tow ər/ *n* a lookout tower for guards

watchword /wóch wurd/ *n* **1** a slogan **2** a password

water /wáwtər/ *n* **1** the liquid that falls as rain and forms lakes, rivers, and seas **2** an area of water **3** the surface of an area of water **4** a solution of a particular chemical or substance in water ○ *lavender water* **5** a watery body fluid such as tears or urine **6** a lustrous wavy pattern on a fabric such as silk ■ **waters** *npl* **1** the fluid surrounding the foetus in the womb (*sometimes sing*) **2** a particular area of sea **3** a naturally occurring water containing minerals ■ *v* **1** *vt* sprinkle or soak something with water **2** *vt* irrigate crops or land **3** *vti* give an animal water for drinking, or get water for drinking **4** *vi* fill with tears when irritated (*refers to eyes*) **5** *vi* produce saliva (*refers to the mouth*) **6** *vt* give a lustrous wavy pattern to a fabric such as silk —**water-less** *adj* ◇ **be dead in the water** have no chance of success or survival ◇ **be water under the bridge** be in the past and impossible to alter ◇ **hold water** be well-founded ◇ **in deep water** in a difficult or complicated situation ◇ **in hot water** in trouble ◇ **muddy the waters** cause confusion ◇ **pour** *or* **throw cold water on** *or* **onto** discourage a plan or idea ◇ **tread water** maintain the status quo, but make no progress □ **water down** *vt* **1** dilute **2** reduce the difficulty or offensiveness of —**watered-down** *adj*

Water Bearer *n* the zodiacal sign Aquarius

water bed *n* a bed with a water-filled mattress

water bird *n* a bird living near water

water biscuit *n* a thin plain biscuit

waterborne /wáwtər bawrn/ *adj* transported or transmitted by water

water buffalo *n* a large buffalo used for haulage and milk in Southeast Asia

water butt *n* a barrel for collecting rainwater from a drainpipe

water cannon *n* an apparatus producing a high-pressure jet of water, used for controlling crowds

Water Carrier *n* the zodiacal sign Aquarius

water chestnut *n* **1** a round white crunchy underground stem. Use: in Asian cooking. **2** a Chinese sedge plant that is the source of water chestnuts

water closet *n* a toilet

watercolour /wáwtər kulər/ *n* **1** a painting made with pigments mixed with water **2** a pigment or pigments mixed with water *(often pl)* —**watercolourist** *n*

water cooler *n* a drinking-water dispenser

watercourse /wáwtər kawrss/ *n* **1** a natural or artificial channel for flowing water **2** the water flowing along a watercourse

watercress /wáwtər kress/ *n* a water plant with peppery leaves and stems. Use: salads, soups, garnish.

waterfall /wáwtər fawl/ *n* a vertical flow of water falling over the edge of a steep place

Waterford /wáwtərfərd/ **1** county in Munster Province, in the south of the Republic of Ireland **2** city in the southeast of the Republic of Ireland. Pop. 44,000 (1996).

waterfowl /wáwtər fowl/ *n (pl same or* **-fowls**) any bird that swims on water ■ *npl* swimming game birds considered collectively

waterfront /wáwtər frunt/ *n* **1** the part of a town lying alongside a body of water **2** the land beside a body of water

Watergate /wáwtər gayt/ *n* **1** a 1972 US political scandal that led to President Nixon's resignation **2** a political scandal and attempted cover-up

ORIGIN The 1972 scandal began with a break-in at the US Democratic National Committee headquarters in the Watergate complex in Washington, D.C. **Watergate** has lent its second syllable *-gate* to the formation of numerous names for other subsequent scandals, domestic and foreign.

water hole *n* a water-filled hollow where animals drink

water ice *n* a frozen dessert of sweet-flavoured ice

watering can *n* a container with a handle and a spout for watering plants

watering hole *n* **1** a water hole **2** a pub *(infml)*

watering place *n* **1** a water hole **2** a spa

water level *n* the height of the surface of a body of water

water lily *n* a water plant with floating leaves

water line *n* **1** a line on the hull of a ship indicating the level to which it can sink in the water **2** the line to which a body of water rises

waterlogged /wáwtər logd/ *adj* saturated with water —**waterlog** *vt*

Waterloo /wáwtər lóò/ town in central Belgium, site of Napoleon's defeat by British and Prussian forces on 18 June 1815. Pop. 28,111 (1995).

water main *n* a large underground pipe bringing water

watermark /wáwtər maark/ *n* **1** a hidden mark in paper visible when the paper is held up to the light **2** a line left by water **3** an embedded pattern of bits in a data file used in detecting unauthorized copies ■ *vt* **1** put a watermark in paper **2** embed a watermark in a data file

water meadow *n* a meadow that is often flooded

watermelon /wáwtər melən/ *n* **1** a large round green fruit with sweet juicy pink flesh and black seeds **2** a plant that produces watermelons

water meter *n* a device for recording the amount of water passing through pipes

water mill *n* a mill with water-powered machinery

water pipe *n* **1** a pipe for conveying water **2** a pipe for smoking something such as cannabis in which the smoke is cooled by being drawn through water

water pistol *n* a toy gun that shoots water

water polo *n* a game played in a swimming pool by two teams trying to score points by sending a large ball into the opposing team's goal

water power *n* electric power generated by the force of water

waterproof /wáwtər proof/ *adj* impervious to water ■ *n* an item of waterproof clothing —**waterproof** *vt*

Waters /wáwtərz/, **Muddy** (1915–83) US blues guitarist and singer

watershed /wáwtər shed/ *n* **1** the boundary between the catchment basins of different rivers **2** the region draining into a particular river, lake, or sea **3** a major turning point

waterside /wáwtər síd/ *n* the land beside an area

of water ■ *adj* living, working, or located beside an area of water

waterski /wáwtər skee/ (-skis, -skiing, -skied) *vi* ski over water while being towed by a boat —**water ski** *n*—**waterskier** *n*—**waterskiing** *n*

water slide *n* a chute for sliding down into a swimming pool

water softener *n* an apparatus or a chemical for reducing the hardness of water

water-soluble *adj* dissolvable in water

water sports *npl* sports played on or in water

water table *n* the upper surface of ground water, below which pores in the rocks are filled with water

watertight /wáwtər tīt/ *adj* 1 keeping water in or out 2 standing up to scrutiny ○ *a watertight argument* —**watertightness** *n*

water tower *n* 1 a water storage tower 2 a firefighting apparatus for lifting hoses

water vapour *n* water in vapour form, but below boiling point

water vole *n* an amphibious vole living near water

waterway /wáwtər way/ *n* a river or canal used by boats

water wings *npl* inflatable arm supports for somebody learning to swim

waterworks /wáwtər wurks/ *n* 1 the system for supplying water to a community or area (+ *sing or pl verb*) 2 tears (*infml*; + *pl verb*)

watery /wáwtəri/ *adj* 1 of or containing water 2 having excessive water 3 filled with tears 4 lacking force or intensity —**wateriness** *n*

Watson /wóts'n/, **James D.** (*b.* 1928) US biochemist. With Francis H. Crick and Maurice Wilkins he discovered the structure of DNA (1953).

watt /wot/ *n* (*symbol* **W**) the SI unit of electrical power equal to the power produced by a current of one ampere acting across a potential difference of one volt

Watt /wot/, **James** (1736–1819) British inventor

wattage /wóttij/ *n* electrical power measured in watts

Watteau /wóttō/, **Jean-Antoine** (1684–1721) French painter

wattle /wótt'l/ *n* 1 stakes interwoven with branches, used for walls, fences, and roofs 2 a loose fold of skin hanging from the throat or cheek of a bird or lizard —**wattled** *adj*

Waugh /waw/, **Evelyn** (1903–66) British novelist

wav /wav/ *abbr* a file extension indicating a sound file

wave /wayv/ *v* (**waving, waved**) 1 *vti* move the hand repeatedly from side to side or up and down as a greeting, farewell, or signal 2 *vti* move repeatedly in the air from side to side or up and down 3 *vt* direct somebody or something by waving 4 *vti* curl slightly ■ *n* 1 a moving ripple on a liquid or sea 2 a waving of the hand 3 a line curving in alternating directions 4 an undulating motion 5 a sudden occurrence of repeated events ○ *a heat wave* 6 a sudden overwhelming feeling

7 an advancing or incoming group of people 8 a loose curve in the hair 9 an oscillation of energy travelling through a medium ○ *sound waves* ◊ **make waves** cause a disturbance or trouble ◊ See note at **waive**

waveband /wáyv band/ *n* a range of radio transmission frequencies

wave file *n* a computer file containing digitized sound waves

waveform /wáyv fawrm/ *n* a representation of the shape of a wave

wavelength /wáyv length/ *n* 1 (*symbol* **λ**) in physics, the distance between two points on adjacent waves that have the same phase, e.g. the distance between two consecutive peaks or troughs 2 the wavelength of the radio wave used by a broadcasting station ◊ **be on the same wavelength** have the same opinions, attitudes, or tastes

waveoff /wáyv of/ *n* an instruction to an aircraft not to land

waver /wáyvər/ *vi* 1 fluctuate between possibilities or be indecisive 2 begin to change your opinion 3 move in one way and then another in an irregular pattern 4 tremble or flicker —**waver** *n* —**waveringly** *adv* ◊ See note at **hesitate**

wavy /wáyvi/ (-ier, -iest) *adj* 1 forming a series of wave shapes 2 moving like a wave 3 describes hair with soft curves —**wavily** *adv* —**waviness** *n*

wax¹ *n* 1 a naturally occurring greasy substance 2 a wax preparation for polishing ■ *vt* 1 polish something with wax 2 remove unwanted hair from part of the body with wax —**waxer** *n*

wax² *vi* 1 appear with a larger illuminated surface each night (*refers to the Moon or a planet*) 2 increase (*literary*) 3 talk about something in a particular way (*literary*) ○ *waxed lyrical*

waxen /wáks'n/ *adj* 1 like wax 2 made of wax 3 pale and unhealthy-looking

waxwork /wáks wurk/ *n* 1 a wax model of somebody 2 a wax object or ornament 3 the art of using wax for modelling

waxworks /wáks wurks/ (*pl same*) *n* a museum containing an exhibition of wax figures

waxy /wáksi/ (-ier, -iest) *adj* 1 like wax 2 covered with or full of wax —**waxiness** *n*

way /way/ *n* 1 a means, manner, or method of doing something ○ *I'll do it my way.* 2 a feature, aspect, or example ○ *In some ways, they're very similar.* 3 a particular state or condition ○ *He's in a bad way.* 4 something somebody wants to happen or to do ○ *always wants his own way* 5 a tradition, custom, or habit 6 a path or route from one place to another 7 a door or opening ○ *came in the front way* 8 a journey ○ *on my way home* 9 progress 10 a direction or position 11 space for action ○ *got out of the way* 12 a particular area or district (*infml*) ○ *out our way* 13 a distance away in space or time ○ *a long way off* 14 an extent or amount ■ *adv* 1 to a considerable degree or at a considerable distance *(infml)* ○ *way out of our price range* **2** very *(slang)* ◇ **by the way** incidentally ◇ **by way of** as a means of or for the purpose of ◇ **give way 1** give in or give precedence to somebody else **2** become useless, break, or otherwise fail ◇ **give way to** be overcome by ○ *gave way to grief* ◇ **go out of your way** do more than is usual or necessary ○ *went out of his way to welcome us* ◇ **have a way with** be good at dealing with ◇ **have it both ways** have the benefits of opposing situations or actions ◇ **in a big way** to a great degree or with great enthusiasm *(infml)* ◇ **in a way** from a certain point of view ◇ **make your way 1** go somewhere **2** become successful ◇ **pay your way** pay your share of expenses

SPELLCHECK Do not confuse the spelling of **way**, **weigh** ('find the weight of'), and **whey** ('watery part of milk'), which sound similar.

wayfarer /wáy fairər/ *n* a traveller on foot *(literary)* —**wayfaring** *n*, *adj*

waylay /way láy/ (-**laid** /-láyd/) *vt* **1** lie in wait or ambush for **2** stop or accost

waymark /wáy maark/ *n* *also* **waymarker** /-maarkər/ a signpost for walkers or other travellers ■ *vt* mark a route with waymarks

John Wayne

Wayne, John (1907–79) US actor

way of life *n* a lifestyle

-ways *suffix* in a particular direction or position ○ *sideways*

wayside /wáy sīd/ *n* the side of a road ■ *adj* situated at the side of a road ◇ **fall by the wayside** fail to continue or complete something

wayward /wáywərd/ *adj* **1** wilful or disobedient **2** erratic or unpredictable —**waywardly** *adv* —**waywardness** *n* ◊ See note at **unruly**

WBC *abbr* **1** white blood cell **2** World Boxing Council

WC *n* a toilet. Full form **water closet**

we *(stressed)* /wee/ *(unstressed)* /wi/ *pron* **1** refers to the speaker or writer and one or more others *(1st person pl personal pronoun, used as the subject of a verb)* ○ *We're going on holiday.* **2** refers to all people or people in general ○ *We're getting closer to the election.* **3** used instead of 'I' by a speaker or writer to include the listener or reader ○ *We will now consider the causes of the war.*

USAGE we or **us**? When **we** or **us** accompanies a noun, use **we** if the pronoun is the subject,

us if the pronoun is the object of a verb or preposition: *We* [not *us*] *trainees have to stick together; For us* [not *we*] *trainees, there are many opportunities.*

WEA *abbr* Workers' Educational Association

weak /week/ *adj* **1** not physically or mentally strong **2** easily defeated **3** lacking strength of character **4** not powerful or intense **5** lacking particular skills or abilities ○ *weak in maths* **6** watery or tasteless ○ *weak tea* **7** unconvincing ○ *a weak argument* **8** describes a syllable or word that is not stressed or accented —**weaken** *vti*

SPELLCHECK Do not confuse the spelling of **weak** and **week** ('a period of seven days'), which sound similar.

SYNONYMS weak, feeble, frail, infirm, debilitated, decrepit, enervated CORE MEANING: lacking physical strength or energy

weak-kneed /-née'd/ *adj* easily persuaded or intimidated *(infml)*

weakling /wée'kling/ *n* a person regarded as weak

weakly /wée'kli/ *adj* (-**lier**, -**liest**) sickly ■ *adv* without strength or force —**weakliness** *n*

weak-minded *adj* easily persuaded *(disapproving)* —**weak-mindedly** *adv* —**weak-mindedness** *n*

weakness /wée'knəss/ *n* **1** a lack of strength or determination **2** a weak point or flaw in something **3** a character flaw **4** a fondness for something

weak-willed *adj* lacking strong will

weal[1] /weel/ *n* **1** a reddened area on the skin from a blow **2** an itchy swelling on the skin

weal[2] /weel/ *n* a general state of wellbeing *(literary)*

wealth /welth/ *n* **1** a large amount of money or possessions **2** the state of having wealth **3** an abundance of something

wealth tax *n* a tax on financial assets above a fixed level

wealthy /wélthi/ (-**ier**, -**iest**) *adj* **1** having a large amount of money or possessions **2** enjoying an abundance of something —**wealthily** *adv* —**wealthiness** *n*

wean /ween/ *v* **1** *vti* start to give a baby or young animal food other than its mother's milk **2** *vt* stop somebody having or doing something habitual or pleasurable

weapon /wéppən/ *n* **1** a device designed to injure or kill somebody **2** something used to gain an advantage —**weaponed** *adj*

weaponize /wéppə nīz/ (-**izing**, -**ized**), **weaponise** *vt* process chemical, nuclear, or biological material so that it can be deployed as a weapon —**weaponization** /wéppənī záysh'n/ *n*

weapon of mass destruction *n* a weapon, typically nuclear, biological, or chemical, that causes overwhelming devastation and loss of life

weaponry /wéppənri/ n weapons considered collectively

weapons-grade adj describes plutonium, uranium, or other material in a form suitable for manufacturing weapons

wear /wair/ v (**wore**, **worn**) 1 vt have something on the body, e.g. as clothing, jewellery, or protection 2 vt display an expression on the face o *wearing a smile* 3 vti damage by using or rubbing, or be damaged in this way 4 vt produce a hole by using or rubbing 5 vti rub off or away 6 vti tire out 7 vi last in the same condition despite much use o *The carpet's wearing well.* 8 vti pass slowly o *as the evening wore on* ■ n 1 the act of wearing something 2 damage from being used or rubbed 3 the ability to last despite much use 4 clothing of a particular kind (often in combination) —**wearer** n ◊ **the worse for wear** 1 in a poor condition because of much use 2 looking unwell ◊ **wear thin** become unacceptable or implausible because of excessive use o *That excuse is beginning to wear a bit thin.* ◊ See note at **ware**

□ **wear down** vti overcome or be overcome gradually

□ **wear off** vi lose effectiveness gradually

□ **wear out** v 1 vti use something until it is no longer usable, or become useless through long use 2 vt exhaust somebody

wearable computer /wáirəb'l-/ n a small computer worn on the body

wear and tear /-táir/ n damage caused by use over a period of time

wearing /wáiring/ adj tiring —**wearingly** adv

wearisome /weérissəm/ adj tiring and tedious —**wearisomely** adv —**wearisomeness** n

weary /weéri/ adj (**-rier**, **-riest**) 1 tired 2 tiring ■ vti (**-ries**, **-ried**) become or make tired, bored, or impatient —**wearily** adv —**weariness** n —**wearying** adj

weasel /weéz'l/ (pl **-sels** or same) n 1 a small brown furry mammal with a long body 2 somebody regarded as sly or underhand (infml insult) —**weaselly** adj

weather /wéthər/ n 1 the state of the atmosphere with regard to conditions such as temperature, wind, or precipitation 2 bad weather ■ adj used in weather forecasting ■ v 1 vti expose or be exposed to the weather 2 vti change in colour or texture because of exposure to the weather 3 vi endure the damaging effects of the weather 4 vt come safely through a crisis ◊ **make heavy weather of** make a fairly easy task seem more difficult ◊ **under the weather** slightly unwell

---

SPELLCHECK Do not confuse the spelling of **weather** and **whether** (indicating an alternative), which may sound similar.

---

weather-beaten adj damaged or worn by exposure to the weather

weatherboard /wéthər bawrd/ n 1 a sloping piece of wood fitted on the bottom of a door to allow rain to run off 2 one of a series of overlapping horizontal boards for cladding a wall or roof ■ vt cover a building with weatherboards

weatherbound /wéthər bownd/ adj delayed or stopped by bad weather

weather centre n an agency collecting meteorological data and providing weather forecasts

weathercock /wéthər kòk/ n 1 a weather vane shaped like a farmyard cock 2 somebody changeable or fickle

weather forecast n a broadcast announcing weather conditions —**weather forecaster** n —**weather forecasting** n

weatherproof /wéthər proof/ adj able to withstand bad weather —**weatherproof** vt

weather ship n a ship collecting meteorological data

weather station n a meteorological observation post

weather strip n a strip of protective material fitted around a door or window to keep out wind, rain, and cold —**weatherstrip** vt

weather vane n a device mounted on a roof that turns to show the direction of the wind

weatherworn /wéthər wawrn/ adj worn by exposure to the weather

weave¹ /weev/ v (**weaving**, **wove** /wōv/ or **weaved**, **woven** /wōv'n/ or **weaved**) 1 vti make cloth by interlacing vertical and horizontal threads 2 vt make something by interlacing strands 3 vti spin a web 4 vt construct a story by combining separate parts ■ n the way in which something is woven —**weaver** n

weave² /weev/ (**weaving**, **weaved**) vi move forwards in a zigzag course

web n 1 a structure woven by a spider to catch its prey 2 a membrane of skin between the toes of a bird or amphibian 3 a complex network o *a web of interconnecting wires* o *web of deceit* 4 a piece of woven fabric 5 also **Web** the World Wide Web (infml) —**webbed** adj

webbing /wébbing/ n 1 a strong coarse fabric. Use: belts, harnesses, upholstery support. 2 the membrane of skin between a bird's or amphibian's toes

web browser n a program for displaying and using pages on the World Wide Web

web bug n a minute inclusion in a webpage or e-mail message designed to record information about the person reading it

webcam /wéb kam/ n a video camera recording pictures that are broadcast live on the Internet

webcast /wéb kaast/ n a broadcast on the World Wide Web —**webcasting** n

web crawler n a program for searching through pages on the World Wide Web for documents containing a particular topic or set of words

web-enable vt make a device such as a mobile phone capable of accessing the Internet —**web-enabled** adj

Weber /váybər/, **Carl Maria von** (1786–1826) German composer

Weber, Max (1864–1920) German economist and sociologist

Webern /váybərn/, **Anton Friedrich Wilhelm von** (1883–1945) Austrian composer

webliography /wébbli óggrəfi/ (*pl* **-phies**) *n* 1 a list of specific documents available on the World Wide Web 2 a list or catalogue of all the web-based material relating to a specific subject

weblish /wébblish/ *n* the form of English used online

weblog /wéb log/ *n* a frequently updated personal journal on a website, intended for public viewing

webmaster /wéb maastər/ *n* a creator or maintainer of a website

webpage /wéb payj/ *n* a computer file encoded in HTML and providing text and graphics, accessible through the World Wide Web

webphone /wéb fōn/ *n* a phone that uses the Internet to make connections and carry voice messages

web ring *n* a series of interlinked websites visited one after the other until the first is reached again

web server *n* a program that provides webpages when requested by a client

website /wéb sīt/ *n* a group of related webpages, or a program providing access to them

Webster /wébstər/, **John** (1578?–1632?) English playwright

webzine /wéb zeen/ *n* a website with magazine-style content and layout

wed (**wedding, wedded** *or* **wed**) *v* 1 *vt* get married to somebody *(fml or literary)* ○ *wanted to wed a princess* 2 *vi* get married ○ *They wed in April.* 3 *vt* join a couple in marriage 4 *vt* unite two things

we'd /weed/ *contr* 1 we had 2 we would

Wed. *abbr* Wednesday

wedded /wéddid/ *adj* 1 married 2 of marriage 3 committed to something ○ *wedded to the idea of reform*

Weddell Sea /wédd'l-/ *arm* of the South Atlantic Ocean, south of Cape Horn and the Falkland Islands

wedding /wédding/ *n* 1 a marriage ceremony 2 the anniversary of a wedding *(in combination)*

wedding breakfast *n* a celebratory meal served after a wedding

wedding dress *n* the dress worn by a bride at her wedding

wedding march *n* a piece of music played at a wedding when the bride enters the church

~~Wednesday~~ incorrect spelling of **Wednesday**

wedge /wej/ *n* 1 a tapering solid block used to secure or separate two objects 2 a wedge-shaped object ○ *a wedge of cake* 3 something that acts like a wedge, e.g. by causing division ○ *drove a wedge between the two families* 4 **wedge heel**

a shoe heel shaped like a wedge, or a shoe with this type of heel ■ *v* (**wedging, wedged**) 1 *vt* force apart with a wedge 2 *vt* secure with a wedge 3 *vti* squeeze into a small space —**wedgy** *adj*

Wedgwood /wéj wŏŏd/, **Josiah** (1730–95) British potter

wedlock /wéd lok/ *n* the married state

ORIGIN **Wedlock** is not etymologically something people are 'locked' into. The original form was *wedlac*, formed from *wed* 'pledge' and a suffix meaning 'action, proceedings'.

Wednesday /wénz day, -di/ *n* the 3rd day of the week

ORIGIN **Wednesday** is named after Woden (Odin), the chief Germanic god. The Latin equivalent meant 'Mercury's day'.

~~Wednsday~~ incorrect spelling of **Wednesday**

wee[1] *adj* small ■ *n Scotland* a short time

wee[2] *n* (*infml or baby talk*) 1 urine 2 an act of urinating ■ *vi* (**weed**) urinate

weed[1] *n* 1 a wild plant growing where it is not wanted 2 a plant growing in water, especially seaweed 3 cannabis for smoking as a drug *(slang)* ■ *vti* remove weeds from the ground —**weeder** *n*
□ **weed out** *vt* separate out undesirable elements

weed[2] *n* something worn as a sign of mourning ■ **weeds** *npl* a widow's black clothes *(literary)*

weedkiller /weed kilər/ *n* a chemical used to destroy weeds

weedy /weedi/ (**-ier, -iest**) *adj* 1 full of weeds 2 like a weed 3 considered thin and weak-looking —**weediness** *n*

week /week/ *n* 1 a period of seven consecutive days 2 a calendar week of seven days beginning on a specific day, usually Sunday 3 the days of the week spent working ○ *goes to bed early during the week* ■ *adv* one week after or before a particular day ○ *arranged to meet on Thursday week* ◊ See note at **weak**

weekday /week day/ *n* a day other than Saturday or Sunday

weekend /week énd/ *n* the period from Friday evening until Sunday evening ■ *vi* spend the weekend somewhere —**weekender** *n*

weeklong /week lóng/ *adj* lasting a week

weekly /weekli/ *adj* 1 happening once a week 2 calculated by the week ○ *weekly pay* ■ *adv* 1 once a week 2 every week 3 by the week ■ *n* (*pl* **-lies**) a newspaper or magazine published once a week

weeknight /week nīt/ *n* the evening or night of a weekday

weeny /weeni/ (**-nier, -niest**) *adj* very tiny *(infml)*

weep *v* (**wept**) 1 *vi* shed tears 2 *vti* leak fluid ■ *n* a period of shedding tears

weepie /weepi/, **weepy** (*pl* **-ies**) *n* a sentimental film, play, or book *(infml)*

weeping /weepíng/ adj 1 with drooping branches 2 shedding tears —**weepingly** adv

weeping willow n a willow tree with drooping branches

weepy /weepi/ (-ier, -iest) adj 1 inclined to weep (infml) 2 moving people to tears —**weepily** adv

weevil /weev'l/ n 1 a destructive beetle with a snout 2 a beetle whose larvae live in the seeds of peas and beans —**weevily** adj

weft n 1 the horizontal threads on a loom or piece of fabric 2 yarn used for the weft

weigh /way/ v 1 vt find out the weight of somebody or something 2 vi be a particular weight 3 vt measure or distribute something by weight 4 vt evaluate something ○ weighing my options 5 vi have importance ○ Her advice weighs heavily with him. 6 vi be burdensome ○ weighs on his mind 7 vti raise the anchor of a vessel ◊ See note at **way**

□ **weigh down** vt 1 oppress 2 burden or press down

□ **weigh in** vi 1 be weighed for a race or contest 2 have baggage weighed before a flight 3 contribute a comment (infml)

□ **weigh up** vt consider carefully

weighbridge /wáy brij/ n a weighing machine for vehicles that consists of a metal plate set into a road

weigh-in n the weighing of a competitor before or after a race or contest

weight /wayt/ n 1 the heaviness of somebody or something 2 a system of standard measures for establishing the heaviness of somebody or something 3 (symbol W) the vertical force experienced by a mass because of gravity 4 a unit used as a measure of weight 5 a heavy object used to hold something down 6 a mental or moral burden 7 a heavy load to carry 8 importance or significance 9 the greater part of something 10 a heavy object used in weightlifting (often pl) 11 the thickness of cloth ■ vt 1 add weight or weights to 2 bias —**weighted** adj ◊ **pull your weight** do your fair share ◊ **throw your weight around** or **about** be domineering ◊ See note at **wait**

weighting /wáyting/ n additional pay given in special cases, e.g. to somebody in a place with a high cost of living

weightless /wáytləss/ adj weighing nothing, especially because of being in a gravity-free environment —**weightlessly** adv —**weightlessness** n

weightlifting /wáyt lifting/ n the sport of lifting heavy objects such as dumbbells for exercise or in competition —**weightlifter** n

weight training n physical training using weights to strengthen muscles

weight watcher /wáyt wochər/ n a person who diets to control body weight —**weight-watching** n

weighty /wáyti/ (-ier, -iest) adj 1 heavy 2 important 3 influential —**weightily** adv —**weightiness** n

weild incorrect spelling of **wield**

weir /weer/ n 1 a dam across a river to regulate or change the flow of water 2 a barricade in a stream for catching fish

weird /weerd/ adj strange or unusual —**weirdly** adv —**weirdness** n

weirdo /weerdō/ n an offensive term for a person regarded as strange or unconventional (slang)

Weizmann /vítsmən/, **Chaim** (1874–1952) Russian-born chemist and first president of modern Israel (1949–52)

welch vi = **welsh**

Welch, Jack (b. 1936) US business executive

welcome /wélkəm/ adj 1 received or accepted gladly ○ a welcome gift 2 freely invited or permitted ○ You're welcome to stay for dinner. 3 having no obligation in return ○ You're welcome, it was no trouble. ■ n 1 a greeting or reception given to somebody on arrival 2 a particular reaction to something ○ received the proposal with a cautious welcome ■ vt (-coming, -comed) 1 greet or receive somebody in a polite or friendly way 2 accept something with pleasure ■ interj expresses a friendly or polite greeting —**welcomely** adv —**welcomeness** n —**welcomer** n ◊ **wear out** or **overstay your welcome** stay longer than is polite

welcome page n a website's opening page

welcoming /wélkəming/ adj providing a warm and friendly greeting —**welcomingly** adv

weld vti join pieces of metal or other material by heating, hammering, or pressure, or be joined in this way ■ n a joint formed by the fusion of pieces —**welder** n

welfare /wél fair/ n 1 physical, social, or financial wellbeing 2 US, Can government financial aid and other benefits given to people in need ■ adj aiding people in need

welfare state n a political system or nation in which the government assumes responsibility for the welfare of citizens

welfarism /wél fairizəm/ n the policies and practices characterizing the welfare state (disapproving)

well[1] n 1 a hole made in the ground to draw up water, petroleum, or natural gas 2 a spring of water 3 a source of a free and abundant supply of something 4 a container or sunken area for holding ink or another liquid 5 a vertical passage in a building, often used for stairs or lifts ■ v 1 vti rise or bring to the surface 2 vi surge from within ○ Fear welled up inside me. 3 vi become filled with liquid ○ My eyes welled with tears.

well[2] adv 1 efficiently, satisfactorily, or desirably ○ The presentation went very well. 2 ethically, properly, or courteously ○ treated us very well 3 skilfully or expertly ○ plays tennis really well 4 with justice and good reason ○ couldn't very well refuse 5 in ease and comfort ○ lives well 6 advantageously ○ married well 7 in a way that promotes good health and physical well-being ○ Mother and *baby are doing well.* **8** considerably ○ *well past midnight* **9** fully and thoroughly ○ *stirring the mixture well* **10** familiarly and intimately ○ *knew him well* **11** very *(slang)* ○ *was well angry* ■ *adj* (**better** /béttər/, **best**) **1** mentally and physically healthy ○ *I hope you're well.* **2** proper or appropriate **3** satisfactory ○ *Is everything well with you?* ○ *I had the impression that all was not well.* ■ *interj* **1** expresses an emotion such as surprise, indignation, or approval ○ *Well! Here you are at last!* **2** introduces a comment or resumes a conversation ○ *Well, it looks as if we'll be waiting a while.* ◇ **as well** in addition ◇ **as well as** to an equal degree or extent ◇ **be as well to do something** be advisable or sensible to do something ◇ **be well out of** be fortunate in having escaped from a situation *(infml)* ◇ **that's** *or* **it's (just) as well** it is fortunate

we'll /weel, wil/ *contr* **1** we shall **2** we will

well-adjusted *adj* **1** successfully adapted to prevailing conditions **2** content with your own self and life and therefore emotionally stable

well-advised *adj* acting prudently

well-appointed *adj* fully furnished or equipped

well-balanced *adj* **1** sensible and rational **2** organized with all the parts in proportion

well-behaved *adj* behaving properly

wellbeing /wél bée ing/ *n* the state of being healthy, happy, and comfortable

wellborn /wél báwrn/ *adj* belonging to an aristocratic, respected, or wealthy family

well-bred *adj* **1** having or showing good manners **2** describes an animal with a desirable pedigree

well-built *adj* **1** physically big and strong **2** soundly constructed

well-chosen *adj* carefully selected

well-connected *adj* with influential relatives or friends

well-defined *adj* **1** stated precisely and clearly **2** with a distinct outline or form

well-disposed *adj* sympathetic and likely to be helpful

well-done *adj* **1** performed correctly and well **2** cooked through

well-dressed *adj* wearing smart clothes

well-earned *adj* fully deserved as a result of hard work

Orson Welles

Welles /welz/, **Orson** (1915–85) US actor and director

well-established *adj* having been in existence long enough to become generally respected or successful

~~welfare~~ incorrect spelling of **welfare**

well-fed *adj* **1** with a good diet **2** overweight

well-founded *adj* supported by good reasons or solid evidence

well-groomed *adj* **1** taking care of your appearance **2** carefully cleaned, brushed, or tended

well-grounded *adj* familiar with all the essential details of a subject

well-heeled *adj* wealthy *(infml)*

wellie /wélli/, **welly** (*pl* -**ies**) *n* a wellington boot *(infml)*

well-informed *adj* having broad and detailed knowledge, especially of current affairs

wellington /wéllingtən/, **wellington boot** *n* a loose waterproof knee-length rubber boot

Wellington /wéllingtən/ **1** capital of New Zealand, at the southern end of the North Island. Pop. 165,200 (1998). **2** administrative region of New Zealand, occupying the southern tip of the North Island and including the city of Wellington. Pop. 416,019 (1996).

Wellington, Arthur Wellesley, 1st Duke of (1769–1852) British general and prime minister (1828–30)

well-intentioned *adj* intended or trying to help, but often producing a negative effect

well-kept *adj* **1** carefully looked after **2** revealed to no one or to only a few people ○ *a well-kept secret*

well-known *adj* **1** widely known **2** fully known or understood

well-mannered *adj* polite and courteous

well-meaning *adj* intended or trying to help, but often producing a negative effect

well-nigh *adv* very nearly

well-off (**better-off**, **best-off**) *adj* **1** fairly wealthy **2** in a favourable situation or circumstances

well-oiled *adj* functioning smoothly

well-preserved *adj* in good condition despite advanced age

well-read /-réd/ *adj* knowing much from reading widely

well-rounded *adj* **1** with skills, experience, or achievements in many areas **2** comprehensive and varied

Wells, H. G. (1866–1946) British writer

well-spoken *adj* **1** articulate and refined in speech **2** expressed appropriately

wellspring /wél spring/ *n* **1** the source of a spring or stream **2** a plentiful source of something

well-thought-of *adj* highly regarded

well-thought-out *adj* carefully planned

well-thumbed *adj* with worn pages from much use

well-timed *adj* done at the right moment

well-to-do *adj* fairly wealthy

well-tried *adj* thoroughly tested and known to be reliable

well-turned *adj* 1 having a naturally graceful or attractive shape 2 skilfully expressed ○ *a well-turned phrase*

well-wisher *n* somebody expressing good wishes to somebody else —**well-wishing** *adj, n*

well-woman *adj* providing women with health advice

well-worn *adj* 1 showing signs of much wear 2 trite or hackneyed

welly *n* CLOTHING = **wellie** *(infml)*

welsh, welch *vi* an offensive term meaning fail to fulfil or honour an obligation —**welsher** *n*

Welsh *npl* the people of Wales ■ *n* a Celtic language spoken in Wales —**Welsh** *adj* —**Welshman** *n* —**Welshwoman** *n*

Welsh dresser *n* a sideboard with open shelves in the top part and cupboards and drawers in the bottom part

Welsh rarebit /-ráir bit/, **Welsh rabbit** *n* a dish of melted cheese on toast

welt *n* 1 a ridge on the skin caused by a lash from a whip, scratch, or something similar 2 a strip sewn into a shoe between the upper and the sole to strengthen the seam 3 a reinforcement or decoration for a seam in a garment or pillow ■ *vt* beat somebody severely, especially with a whip

welter /wéltər/ *n* 1 a confused mass of something 2 a confused condition 3 a surging motion of water ■ *vi* 1 wallow in something 2 lie soaked in liquid 3 be completely involved, absorbed, or entangled in something

welterweight /wéltər wayt/ *n* 1 the weight category for boxers between lightweight and middleweight 2 a boxer who competes at welterweight

wench *n* 1 a servant girl or young woman *(archaic)* 2 an offensive term for a young woman

wend *vti* travel or make one's way

Wendy house /wéndi-/ *n* a small model house for children to go inside and play in

Wensleydale /wénzli dayl/ *n* 1 a white crumbly English cheese 2 a sheep with a blue-grey head and dark mottled legs

went past tense of **go**[1]

wept past tense, past participle of **weep**

were past tense of **be**

we're /weer/ *contr* we are

weren't /wurnt/ *contr* were not

werewolf /wáir woólf, weér-/ (*pl* -**wolves** /-woólvz/), **werwolf** (*pl* -**wolves**) *n* in folklore, a person who has been transformed into a wolf, or is capable of changing into a wolf

Wesley /wézzli/, **John** (1703–91) British religious leader —**Wesleyan** *adj* —**Wesleyanism** *n*

Wessex /wéssiks/ ancient Anglo-Saxon kingdom in S England

west *n* 1 the direction in which the sun sets 2 the compass point opposite east 3 *also*

West the part of an area or country that is in the west 4 *also* **West** the part of the United States west of the Mississippi River or west of the Allegheny Mountains 5 *also* **West** the countries of Europe and North and South America ■ *adj* 1 in the west 2 blowing from the west ■ *adv* towards the west —**west-bound** *adj*

West Africa region in sub-Saharan W Africa, including Ghana and Nigeria

West Bank disputed territory in SW Asia, on the western bank of the River Jordan, bordered by Israel and Jordan. Pop. 2,090,713 (2001).

West Dunbartonshire /-dun baárt'nshər/ council area in west-central Scotland

westerly /wéstərli/ *adj* 1 in the west 2 blowing from the west ■ *n* (*pl* -**lies**) a wind from the west —**westerly** *adv*

western /wéstərn/ *adj* 1 in the west 2 facing west 3 *also* **Western** of the west of a region or country 4 **Western** of or typical of Europe and the Americas, or their culture and society 5 **Western** characteristic of the US West in the early history of that nation ■ *n* **Western** a film or novel set in the W United States, usually during the late 19C —**westernmost** *adj*

Western Australia state occupying the western part of Australia. Cap. Perth. Pop. 1,847,800 (1998).

westerner /wéstərnər/ *n* somebody from the west of a region or country

Western Front *n* a World War I battle line in W Europe

westernize /wéstər nīz/ (-**izing**, -**ized**), **westernise** *v* 1 *vti* adopt or cause to adopt Western customs 2 *vt* change to resemble Western practices —**westernization** /wéstər nī záysh'n/ *n*

Western Sahara disputed region in NW Africa

Western Samoa former name for **Samoa**

West Germany former republic of W Europe, now the western part of Germany —**West German** *n, adj*

West Indies /-in deez/ former name for the islands of the Caribbean, now used only for its cricket team —**West Indian** *adj, n*

West Lothian /-lṓthi ən/ council area and historic county in central Scotland

Westmeath /wést meéth/ county in the SE Republic of Ireland

Westphalia /west fáyli ə/ former province in NE Germany —**Westphalian** *n, adj*

West Sussex county in SE England

West Virginia state of the east-central United States. Cap. Charleston. Pop. 1,808,344 (2000). —**West Virginian** *n, adj*

westward /wéstwərd/ *adj* in the west ■ *n* a direction towards or point in the west ■ *adv* *also* **westwards** towards the west —**westwardly** *adv, adj*

wet *adj* 1 soaked or dampened with water or another liquid 2 not yet dry 3 not yet set ○ *wet* *concrete* **4** rainy, showery, misty, or foggy **5** lacking assertiveness or decisiveness *(infml insult)* ■ *n* **1** liquid or moisture **2** rainy or damp weather **3** wet ground **4** *Aus* the N Australian wet season ■ *v* **(wetting, wet** *or* **wetted)** **1** *vti* make or become wet **2** *vt* make clothes or a bed wet by urinating accidentally —**wetly** *adv*—**wetness** *n*—**wettish** *adj*

WET *abbr* Western European Time

wet blanket *n* a killjoy *(infml)*

wet dream *n* an erotic dream that results in ejaculation *(sometimes offensive)*

wet fish *n* fresh fish, as distinct from fish sold frozen or cooked

wetland /wétlənd/ *n* a swamp or marsh

wet look *n* a glossy sheen on material or the hair —**wet-look** *adj*

wet nurse *n* a woman who breast-feeds another person's baby

wet suit *n* a diver's tight-fitting rubber suit

we've *contr* we have

Wexford /wéksfərd/ **1** county in the SE Republic of Ireland **2** port in the SE Republic of Ireland. Pop. 16,000 (1996).

wf, w.f. *abbr* wrong font

whack *v* **1** *vti* hit somebody or something with a loud sharp blow **2** *vt* place something somewhere casually and quickly *(infml)* ■ *n* **1** a sharp blow **2** the sound of a sharp blow **3** an attempt *(infml)* **4** a share of something *(infml)*

whacked *adj* *UK, US, Can* extremely tired *(infml)*

whacky /wáki/ *adj* = **wacky**

whale¹ *n* **1** a large sea mammal with a blow-hole on the top of its head, front flippers, and a flat horizontal tail **2** an impressive example *(infml)* ○ *a whale of a party* ■ *vi* **(whaling, whaled)** hunt whales —**whaling** *n* ◊ See note at **wail**

whale² **(whaling, whaled)** *vt* beat somebody physically

whalebone /wáyl bōn/ *n* the bony plates in the mouths of some whales

whaler /wáylər/ *n* **1** somebody who works in the whaling industry **2** a ship used to hunt or process whales

wham *(infml)* *interj* represents the sound of a blow ■ *adv* suddenly and forcefully

whap *n, vt* = **whop**

whare /wáwrri/ *n* *NZ* a traditional Maori home

wharf /wawrf/ *n* *(pl* **wharves** /wawrvz/ *or* **wharfs)** a landing place for ships ■ *vt* unload or store cargo on a wharf

Wharton /wáwrt'n/**, Edith** (1862–1937) US writer

AKG London

Edith Wharton

what /wot/ *det, pron* **1** requests information, e.g. about the identity or nature of something or somebody ○ *What time is it?* ○ *What are they doing?* **2** that which *o used what money they had o in what remains of the house* ■ *det* adds emphasis ○ *What miserable weather!* ■ *adv* **1** in what respect or to what degree ○ *What does it matter?* **2** at a guess ○ *We've known each other for, what, ten years.* ■ *interj* expresses surprise, anger, or disappointment ◊ **what have you** other things similar to those just mentioned ◊ **what's what** the true facts or actual situation *(infml)* ◊ **what with** because of

whatchamacallit /wóchəmə kawlit/ *n* something whose name has been forgotten or is not known *(infml)*

whatever /wot évvər/ *pron, adj* no matter what ■ *pron also* **what ever** an emphatic form of 'what' ○ *Whatever is the matter now?* ■ *adv* of any kind

whatnot /wót not/ *n* **1** something of the same or a similar kind **2** a small lightweight set of shelves

whatsit /wótsit/ *n* a thing whose name is not known or has been forgotten *(infml)*

whatsoever /wót sō évvər/ *adv* at all ○ *no water whatsoever* ■ *pron, det* whatever *(fml)*

wheat /weet/ *n* **1** the edible seeds of a cereal plant, which are ground into flour **2** a cereal plant that produces wheat grains

wheaten /weét'n/ *adj* made from wheat

wheat germ *n* the vitamin-rich centre of a grain of wheat

wheatgrass /weét graass/ *n* a health drink made from pulped wheat shoots

wheatish /weétish/ *adj* *S Asia* light creamy brown, or with a light brown complexion

wheatmeal /weét meel/ *n* wheat flour that contains some bran

wheedle /weéd'l/ *(-dling, -dled)* *v* **1** *vti* try to persuade somebody gently but persistently **2** *vt* obtain something by wheedling —**wheedler** *n* —**wheedlingly** *adv*

wheel *n* **1** a rotating round part or device *(often in combination)* **2** a round machine part that turns another **3** a steering wheel **4** a castor **5** something that resembles a wheel in shape or function **6** a turn or revolution **7** a movement in a circle ■ **wheels** *npl* **1** a car *(slang)* **2** the driving force or workings of something ■ *v* **1** *vti* move on wheels **2** *vt* transport somebody or something in a wheeled object **3** *vt* provide something with wheels **4** *vi* turn quickly **5** *vi* make a circular movement —**wheeled** *adj* ◊ **reinvent the wheel** waste time recreating something that already exists *(disapproving)* ◊ **wheel and deal** use complex and skilful, but sometimes slightly dishonest, negotiating techniques *(infml)*

wheelbarrow /weél barō/ *n* a container with a wheel and handles that you push

wheelbase /weél bayss/ *n* the distance between the front and rear axles of a vehicle

wheelchair /weel chair/ *n* a chair on wheels that somebody who cannot walk uses to move around

wheel clamp *n* a device fitted to a wheel of a car or other vehicle to immobilize it —**wheel-clamp** *vt*

wheeler-dealer *n* a skilled but possibly dishonest negotiator *(infml)* —**wheeler-dealing** *n*

wheelhouse /weel howss/ *(pl* -**houses** /-howziz/) *n* the enclosure on a ship where the wheel or other steering device is housed

wheelie /weeli/ *n* a bike rider's stunt on one wheel

wheelie bin *n* a large rubbish bin fitted with wheels

wheelwright /weel rīt/ *n* somebody who makes or repairs wheels

wheeze *v* (**wheezing, wheezed**) 1 *vi* breathe with a hoarse whistling sound 2 *vt* say something with a wheezing sound ■ *n* 1 a noisy breathing sound 2 a clever idea *(dated infml)* —**wheezily** *adv* —**wheeziness** *n* —**wheezy** *adj*

whelk *(pl* same *or* **whelks**) *n* a small sea invertebrate animal with a conical shell

whelp *n* 1 a young animal 2 a young man regarded as high-handedly rude *(insult)* ■ *vti* bear young *(refers to animals, especially carnivores)*

when *conj* 1 while ○ *When I was a child, I lived in the country.* 2 as soon as ○ *I'll do it when I can.* 3 at a specific point ○ *We got him when he was still a puppy.* 4 each time ○ *When a train goes by, the whole house shakes.* 5 if ○ *Why walk when you can ride?* 6 although ○ *They think I'm smart when I'm really not.* ■ *adv* at or during which time ○ *When did it happen?* ■ *n* an unspecified time period *(often pl)* ○ *We need to determine the whens and hows of this project.*

whence *adv (literary)* 1 from where ○ *She returned whence she came.* 2 from the place previously mentioned

whenever /wen évvər/ *conj* 1 at any time 2 at every time

whensoever /wén sō évvər/ *adv, conj* whenever *(fml)*

where /wair/ *adv* 1 in or to a place ○ *Stay where you are.* 2 asks about location, destination, origin, or purpose ○ *Where will that attitude get you?* ○ *Where do they live?* 3 in any situation in which ○ *Where there's life, there's hope.* ■ *n* an unknown place *(usually pl)* ○ *Let us know the wheres and whens of your itinerary.* ◊ See note at **ware**

whereabouts /wáir ə bowts/ *adv* in what place ■ *n* the location of somebody or something *(+ sing or pl verb)*

whereas /wair áz/ *conj* 1 while on the other hand 2 because *(fml)* 3 connects a series of statements in legal documents *(fml)*

whereby /wair bī/ *rel adv* by means of which

~~**whereever**~~ incorrect spelling of **wherever**

wherefore /wáir fawr/ *n* a reason ○ *the whys and wherefores of the issue* ■ *adv* 1 therefore *(fml)* 2 for what reason *(archaic)*

wherein /wair ín/ *adv* in what specific way *(fml)*

whereof /wair óv/ *rel adv* of what thing or person *(fml)*

wheresoever /wáir sō évvər/ *adv, conj* wherever *(fml)*

whereto /wair toó/, **whereunto** /-ún too/ *adv* to which *(fml)*

whereupon /wáir ə pón/ *conj* at which point ○ *The door opened, whereupon the guests entered the dining room.*

wherever /wair évvər/ *conj* 1 in, at, or to any place 2 every time or place that ■ *adv* 1 no matter where 2 at an unknown place 3 *also* **where ever** where indeed 4 *also* **where ever** an emphatic form of 'where' ○ *Wherever can it be?*

wherewithal /wáir with awl/ *n* the money or resources required for a purpose

whet (**whetting, whetted**) *vt* 1 sharpen a tool or weapon 2 stimulate something, especially the appetite

whether /wéthər/ *conj* 1 introduces alternatives 2 introduces an indirect question ○ *I wonder whether it's worth the effort.* ◊ **whether or no** whatever the circumstances might be ◊ See note at **weather**

whetstone /wét stōn/ *n* a stone for sharpening a tool or weapon

whey /way/ *n* the watery part of curdled milk ◊ See note at **way**

which /wich/ *det, pron, adj* asks for something to be identified from a known group or range ○ *Which hat should I wear?* ■ *pron* 1 introduces a relative clause that provides additional information ○ *We like the food, which is always delicious.* 2 introduces a relative clause that provides identifying information ○ *the money with which the project was funded* 3 refers to a previous phrase or sentence ○ *We had to leave early, which was a pity.* ■ *det, pron* 1 one from a known set ○ *can't decide which activity would be best* 2 indicates choice ○ *Take which one you want.* ◊ See note at **that**

SPELLCHECK Do not confuse the spelling of **which** and **witch** ('somebody with supposed magic powers'), which may sound similar.

---

whichever /wich évvər/ *det, pron* no matter which

whiff *n* 1 a slight or brief odour 2 a bad smell 3 a trace of something ○ *a whiff of corruption* 4 a gentle gust or puff 5 a sniff, smell, or brief inhalation of something ■ *v* 1 *vti* come or send in light gusts 2 *vt* sniff, smell, or inhale

whiffy /wíffi/ (-**ier**, -**iest**) *adj* bad-smelling *(infml)*

Whig *n* 1 a member of a former British political party that became the core of the Liberal Party 2 a supporter of free enterprise 3 *Scotland* a Scottish Presbyterian

—**Whiggery** n —**Whiggish** adj —**Whiggism** n

ORIGIN Whig was originally a Scots word, a shortening (mid-17C) of *whiggamaire* (probably from *whig* 'drive briskly' and *mare* 'female horse'). It seems originally to have been a contemptuous term for a country dweller, and was then applied to Presbyterian supporters in Scotland. It was later adopted as a name for those who opposed the succession of the Catholic King James II, and by 1689 was the title of a political party.

while /wīl/ *conj* **1** at or during the same time **2** even though ○ *While we support your tenacity, we cannot agree with your methods.* **3** but on the other hand ■ *n* a fairly long period of time ○ *This may take a while.* ◊ **once in a while** very occasionally ◊ **worth (somebody's) while** deserving somebody's time, money, or support

SPELLCHECK Do not confuse the spelling of **while** and **wile** ('a cunning strategy'), which may sound similar.

USAGE while or **whilst?** In all the main meanings **while** and **whilst** are interchangeable, but **whilst** is used more in the north of Britain than in the south.

□ **while away** *vt* pass time idly

whilst /wīlst/ *conj* while ◊ See note at **while**

whim *n* a passing impulse

~~whimp~~ incorrect spelling of **wimp**

whimper /wímpər/ *vi* **1** sob or whine softly **2** complain peevishly —**whimper** *n* —**whimperingly** *adv*

whimsical /wímzik'l/ *adj* **1** fanciful **2** odd in an endearing way **3** erratic or unpredictable —**whimsicality** /wímzi kálləti/ *n* —**whimsically** *adv*

whimsy /wímzi/ (*pl* **-sies**) *n* **1** endearing quaintness or oddity **2** an impulsive notion

whine /wīn/ *v* (**whining, whined**) **1** *vi* make a long high-pitched plaintive sound **2** *vi* grumble peevishly **3** *vt* say something in an annoyingly plaintive voice ■ *n* **1** a whining cry or sound **2** a peevish complaint —**whiner** *n* —**whiningly** *adv* —**whiny** *adj* ◊ See note at **complain**

SPELLCHECK Do not confuse the spelling of **whine** and **wine** ('alcohol fermented from grapes'), which may sound similar.

whinge (**whingeing, whinged**) *vi* grumble peevishly *(infml)* —**whinge** *n* —**whinger** *n* —**whingy** *adj*

whinny /wínni/ (**-nies, -nied**) *vi* emit a soft neigh or a neighing sound —**whinny** *n*

whip *v* (**whipping, whipped**) **1** *vt* hit a person or animal with a whip or something similar **2** *vti* strike against something sharply **3** *vti* flick rapidly to and fro with a lashing motion **4** *vti* move, remove, or produce rapidly **5** *vt* beat a liquid such as cream until it is stiff or frothy **6** *vt* bind the end of a rope **7** *vt* steal something *(infml)* ■ *n* **1** a flexible rod, a strip

of leather attached to a handle, or a similar instrument for inflicting pain **2** a lashing stroke or blow **3** something that resembles a whip in form, motion, or flexibility **4 Whip** somebody in charge of discipline in a political party **5** a call for party solidarity **6** a weekly legislative agenda sent to members of a political party indicating for which items it is important to be present **7** a light creamy dessert —**whipping** *n* ◊ **crack the whip** enforce discipline

□ **whip up** *vt* **1** provoke strong feelings in a group **2** prepare something rapidly, especially an impromptu meal *(infml)*

whipcord /wíp kawrd/ *n* strong fabric with a pattern of diagonal ribs

whiplash /wíp lash/ *n* **1** the flexible part of a whip **2** a lashing blow **3** an injury to the neck caused by jerking

whippersnapper /wíppər snapər/ *n* an insignificant and outspoken person *(dated)*

whippet /wíppit/ *n* a fast slender dog bred for racing

whipping boy *n* somebody who is blamed for somebody else's faults

whipping cream *n* cream that stiffens when whipped

whip-round *n* an impromptu collection of money within a group of people for a particular person or cause *(infml)*

whipstitch /wíp stich/ *n* a small stitch passing over the edge of a piece of fabric —**whipstitch** *vt*

whirl /wurl/ *v* **1** *vti* turn or spin rapidly **2** *vti* move along while turning quickly **3** *vti* feel dizzy or confused **4** *vti* move very fast ■ *n* **1** a spinning motion **2** something that moves with a rapid circular or spiral motion **3** a sensation of spinning **4** a series of things that happen in quick succession —**whirly** *adj* ◊ **give something a whirl** try something *(infml)*

whirligig /wúrligig/ *n* **1** a spinning toy **2** a merry-go-round

whirlpool /wúrl pool/ *n* a spiralling current of water

whirlwind /wúrl wind/ *n* **1** a spinning column of air **2** something that happens or changes swiftly *(often before nouns)*

whirr /wur/, **whir** (**whirring, whirred**) *vti* make a whirling or vibrating sound —**whirr** *n*

whisk *n* **1** a kitchen utensil used with short quick movements to make soft substances thick and frothy **2** a brushing movement ■ *v* **1** *vt* beat with a whisk or something similar **2** *vt* brush away lightly **3** *vti* move quickly

whisker /wískər/ *n* **1** a hair near an animal's mouth **2** a hair on somebody's face **3** a small margin ■ **whiskers** *npl* facial hair —**whiskered** *adj* —**whiskery** *adj*

whiskey /wíski/ *n US, Ireland* whisky

whisky /wíski/ *n* **1** an alcoholic beverage made from fermented grain such as barley or rye **2 Whisky** a communications code word for the letter 'W'

whisper /wɪspər/ v 1 vti utter words voicelessly 2 vti speak or suggest something secretly, e.g. in conspiring or spreading gossip 3 vi rustle softly ■ n 1 a very low voice 2 something said quietly 3 a rumour 4 a rustling sound —**whisperer** n

whispering campaign n a deliberate attempt to defame somebody or something by circulating rumours

whist n a card game for pairs of players

whist drive n a card party for playing whist

whistle /wɪssˈl/ v (-tling, -tled) 1 vti make a shrill or musical sound through pursed lips 2 vi produce a shrill sound by forcing air or steam through a narrow opening 3 vi move at great speed with a shrill sound ■ n 1 a device that produces a shrill sound when air passes through it 2 a whistling sound ◊ **blow the whistle** report somebody for doing something wrong or illegal (infml)

whistle-blower n an informant, especially somebody who reports wrongdoing within an organization (infml) —**whistle-blowing** n

Whistler /wɪsslər/, **James Abbott McNeill** (1834–1903) US artist

whit n the smallest amount

Whit n, adj = Whitsun

white /wɪt/ adj (**whiter**, **whitest**) 1 of the colour of fresh snow 2 lacking colour 3 also **White** belonging to a race of people with naturally pale skin 4 comparatively light in colour 5 describes wine made from light-green grapes 6 lacking pigment 7 having a very pale complexion 8 having white parts or colourings 9 describes flour without bran or germ 10 made from white flour 11 describes hot beverages served with milk ■ n 1 the colour of snow 2 white clothing (usually pl) 3 also **White** a pale-skinned person 4 the part of an egg that surrounds the yolk 5 the part of the eye that surrounds the eyeball 6 a light-coloured game piece or player 7 a butterfly that is predominantly white —**whiteness** n —**whitish** adj

□ **white out** v 1 vt cover a written mistake with white correction fluid 2 vi lose visibility because of snow or fog

Patrick White

White /wɪt/, **Patrick** (1912–90) British-born Australian writer

white ant n a termite

White Australia Policy n an early 20C policy of limiting the numbers of non-white people settling in Australia

whitebait /wɪt bayt/ (pl same) n 1 a small young fish eaten whole, especially a herring 2 a small Australian sea fish

white blood cell n a blood cell that protects the body against infection

whiteboard /wɪt bawrd/ n a board with a white surface on which to write with erasable pens

white bread n bread made from white flour

white-collar adj of office workers

white elephant n 1 something very costly to maintain 2 a conspicuous failed venture 3 an unwanted object

whitefish /wɪt fish/ (pl -**fishes** or same) n 1 a freshwater fish with white or silvery skin 2 whitefish as food

white flag n a sign of truce or surrender

white flight n the departure of white people from areas where non-whites are settling

white flour n flour with the bran removed

white goods npl 1 household linen 2 large household appliances such as washing machines

white hat hacker n a benevolent computer hacker, especially one employed to counter malicious hacking

white heat n 1 a very high temperature 2 intense excitement

Whitehorse /wɪt hawrss/ capital of the Yukon Territory, Canada. Pop. 19,157 (1996).

white-hot adj 1 extremely hot 2 extremely excited

White House n 1 the official residence of the US President 2 the executive branch of the US government

white knight n 1 a rescuing hero 2 a financial saviour

white lie n a harmless lie ◊ See note at **lie**

white magic n magic supposedly practised for good purposes

white meat n light-coloured meat such as pork and chicken

whiten /wɪtˈn/ vti make or become white

whitener /wɪtˈnər/ n 1 a white colouring substance 2 a milk substitute added to hot beverages

White Nile section of the River Nile from near the Sudan-Uganda border to its junction with the Blue Nile at Khartoum. Length 2,084 km / 1,295 mi.

white noise n low-volume electrical or radio interference

whiteout /wɪt owt/ n loss of visibility due to heavy snow, or when low cloud merges with snow-covered land

white paper n 1 an official government report 2 an authoritative report

white pepper n pepper made from husked peppercorns

white sale n a sale of linens

white sauce n a thick milk-based sauce

white spirit n a clear liquid used like turpentine

white supremacy *n* the discredited view that white people are genetically and culturally superior to people of all other races —**white supremacist** *n*

white tie *n* **1** a white bow tie **2** a man's evening clothes, including a tail coat and white bow tie

white-tie *adj* describes an event that requires formal evening clothes

whitewall /wít wawl/, **whitewall tyre** *n* a car tyre with a band of white around the side

whitewash /wít wosh/ *n* **1** a solution of lime in water used for painting walls **2** a cover-up (*infml*) ■ *v* **1** *vt* paint with whitewash **2** *vti* hide the truth about something

white water *n* **1** fast-flowing foamy water **2** light-coloured sea water visible in shallow water

whitewater rafting /wít wawtər-/ *n* rafting on a fast-flowing river

white wedding *n* a wedding for which the bride wears a traditional white dress

white whale *n* a small fish-eating whale

whither /wíthər/ (*literary*) *adv*, *rel adv* to what place ■ *adv* into what state

whiting /wíting/ (*pl same*) *n* **1** a small silvery European fish **2** a Pacific and Atlantic fish **3** whiting as food

Whitlam /wíttləm/, **Gough** (*b.* 1916) prime minister of Australia (1972–75)

Library of Congress

Walt Whitman

Whitman /wítmən/, **Walt** (1819–92) US poet and essayist

Whitsun /wíts'n/, **Whitsuntide** /wíts'n tīd/ *n* the Christian festival of Pentecost —**Whitsun** *adj*

whittle /wítt'l/ (**-tling, -tled**) *vti* carve with small cuts

□ **whittle away** *vt* use up gradually

□ **whittle down** *vt* reduce gradually

Whittle /wítt'l/, **Sir Frank** (1907–96) British engineer who invented and developed the turbojet engine (1936)

whiz, whizz *vi* (**whizzes, whizzing, whizzed**) **1** move swiftly with a humming or buzzing noise **2** go or move quickly ■ *n* (*pl* **whizzes**) **1** a whizzing sound **2** a fast movement **3** *also* **wiz** an expert (*infml*)

whiz kid, whizz kid, wiz kid *n* somebody who is young and exceptionally talented (*infml*)

who /hoo/ *pron* **1** what person ○ *Who did that?* **2** introduces a relative clause ○ *The person who did that has left.*

USAGE who or **whom**? **Whom** as the form of

who used as the object of a verb or preposition has fallen into disuse in many contexts. In speech, *Do you remember whom you saw?* may be expressed as *Do you remember who you saw?*, and *The man to whom I was talking* as *The man I was talking to.* In formal contexts, **whom** is still preferred by careful writers.

WHO *abbr* World Health Organization

whoa /wō/ *interj* expresses a command to stop

who'd /hood/ *contr* **1** who had **2** who would

whodunit /hoo dúnnit/, **whodunnit** *n* a novel, film, or play that centres on the solving of a crime.

whoever /hoo évvər/ *pron* **1** an emphatic form of 'who' ○ *Whoever could have dared to do that?* **2** any person who ○ *Whoever takes over will have to work hard.* ○ *You can bring whoever you like.*

whole /hōl/ *adj* **1** including all parts or aspects **2** not divided into parts **3** of full duration or extent ○ *the whole night* **4** unbroken or unimpaired **5** healed or healthy ■ *adv* **1** as a single piece ○ *swallowed the fish whole* **2** completely and in every way (*infml*) ○ *a whole new angle* ■ *n* **1** something complete **2** a single entity or unit —**wholeness** *n* ◊ **on the whole 1** as a rule or in general **2** taking all relevant factors into account ◊ See note at **hole**

wholefood /hōl food/ *n* food that has undergone very little processing

wholegrain /hōl grayn/ *adj* containing or made with whole unprocessed cereal grains

wholehearted /hōl haártid/ *adj* enthusiastic and unreserved —**wholeheartedly** *adv* —**wholeheartedness** *n*

~~wholely~~ incorrect spelling of **wholly**

wholemeal /hōl meel/ *adj* **1** describes flour that has not had the bran removed **2** made from wholemeal flour

whole number *n* a number that does not contain a fraction

wholesale /hōl sayl/ *n* the business of buying and selling goods in large quantities to businesses that sell them on ■ *adj* **1** of trade in large quantities **2** done on a large scale ■ *adv* **1** in bulk **2** in an indiscriminate manner ■ *vti* (**-saling, -saled**) buy or sell goods wholesale —**wholesaler** *n*

wholesome /hōlssəm/ *adj* **1** beneficial to health **2** promoting moral wellbeing —**wholesomely** *adv* —**wholesomeness** *n*

who'll /hool/ *contr* **1** who shall **2** who will

wholly /hōl li/ *adv* **1** completely and entirely **2** solely and exclusively

whom /hoom/ *pron* the form of 'who' used as the object of a verb or preposition (*fml*) ○ *Whom did they choose?* ○ *the person to whom the letter is addressed* ◊ See note at **who**

whomever /hoom évvər/ *pron* a form of 'whoever' used as the object of a verb or preposition (*fml*)

whomsoever /hoŏm sō évvər/ *pron* whomever (*fml*)

whoop /woop, hoop/ *v* **1** *vi* cry out in excitement or joy **2** *vt* exclaim loudly and excitedly **3** *vt* urge or drive forward with a whooping cry ◼ *n* **1** a loud cry **2** the sharp shrill inhalation associated with whooping cough ◇ **whoop it up** have fun or celebrate in an extravagant or noisy way (*infml*)

whoopee /woŏ peé/ *interj* expresses exultation (*infml; often ironic*)

whoopee cushion /woŏppi-/ *n* an inflatable joke cushion that makes a flatulent noise when sat upon

whooping cough /hoŏping-/ *n* an infectious bacterial disease accompanied by spasms of coughing followed by a sharp shrill inhalation

whoops /woops/, **whoops-a-daisy** *interj* indicates that a mistake has been made (*infml*)

whoosh /woŏsh/, **woosh** *n* **1** a noise of rushing air or water **2** a swift motion or rush ◼ *vi* **1** make a rushing sound **2** move fast

whop /wop/, **whap** *vt* (**whopping, whopped; whapping, whapped**) hit forcefully (*infml*) ◼ *n* a blow or the noise of a blow

whopper /wóppər/ *n* (*infml*) **1** something very big of its kind **2** an outrageous lie

whopping /wópping/ *adj* very big (*infml*)

whore /hawr/ *n* (*insult*) **1** an offensive term for a prostitute **2** an offensive term for somebody regarded as sexually indiscriminate —**whoredom** *n*

whorl /wurl/ *n* **1** something spiral-shaped **2** a pattern of concentric ridges on a fingerprint **3** a circular arrangement of leaves or petals —**whorled** *adj*

who's /hooz/ *contr* **1** who has **2** who is ◊ See note at **whose**

whose /hooz/ *pron, det* belonging to who or which ○ *Whose boots are these?* ○ *a theatre whose doors will always be open to talented performers*

USAGE **whose** or **who's**? **Whose** means 'of whom' or 'of which' and denotes possession or association: *the children whose* [not *who's*] *father we met, a car whose* [not *who's*] *paintwork had been damaged.* (Some people dislike the use of **whose** to mean 'of which', but it is a well-established use.) **Who's** is a contraction of *who is* or *who has*: *the friend who's* [not *whose*] *coming to dinner next week; Who's* [not *Whose*] *got my pen?*

whosoever /hoŏ sō évvər/ *pron* whoever (*fml*)

why /wī/ *adv* **1** for what reason ○ *Why didn't you call?* **2** because of what or which ○ *I don't know why he came.* ◼ *interj* expresses surprise

WI *abbr* Women's Institute

wick *n* a string or strip of fabric that draws the fuel to the flame in candles and lamps ◼ *vti* move liquid by capillary action

wicked /wíkid/ *adj* **1** very bad **2** playfully mischievous **3** tending to say unpleasant things **4** very good (*slang*) —**wickedly** *adv* —**wickedness** *n*

wicker /wíkər/, **wickerwork** /wíkər wurk/ *n* **1** woven twigs, canes, or reeds **2** things made of wicker

wicket /wíkit/ *n* **1** a small door or gate **2** in cricket, the set of sticks defended by a batsman **3** in cricket, the ending of somebody's turn at batting

wicketkeeper /wíkit keepər/ *n* in cricket, a player who stands behind the wicket to catch the ball

Wicklow /wíklō/ **1** county in the SE Republic of Ireland **2** town in the E Republic of Ireland. Pop. 6,215 (1991).

wide *adj* **1** having sides or edges far apart **2** having a particular distance between sides or edges **3** opened to a great extent **4** involving many types or choices **5** involving many people **6** large in scope **7** not hitting a target ◼ *adv* (**wider, widest**) **1** to a great extent **2** over a large area **3** to the side of a target ◼ *n* in cricket, a ball bowled beyond the batsman's reach —**widely** *adv* —**widen** *vti* —**wideness** *n* —**widish** *adj*

-wide *suffix* effective throughout a particular place ○ *statewide*

wide area network *n* a network of computers connecting users over a wide area

wide-awake *adj* fully awake

widebody /wíd bóddi/ *n* a commercial jet aircraft with a fuselage wide enough to accommodate three rows of seats and two aisles

wide boy *n* a clever unscrupulous man (*infml*)

wide-eyed *adj* **1** with eyes wide open **2** easily fooled

wide-ranging *adj* affecting or dealing with many people or things

wide-screen *adj* **1** describes a film or television programme in which the image is much wider than standard **2** describes a television with a screen designed to accommodate wide-screen broadcasts —**wide screen** *n*

widespread /wíd spred/ *adj* **1** commonly seen or occurring **2** spread far apart

SYNONYMS **widespread, prevalent, rife, epidemic, universal** CORE MEANING: occurring over a wide area

widget /wíjjit/ *n* any useful little device or mechanism, especially one whose name is unknown or forgotten (*humorous*)

widow /wíddō/ *n* **1** a woman whose husband has died **2** a woman left behind by a partner who is frequently away (*only in combination*) ○ *a golf widow* **3** in printing, a short final line of a paragraph at the top or bottom of text ◼ *vt* make somebody a widow or widower —**widowhood** *n*

widower /wíddō ər/ *n* a man whose wife has died

width *n* 1 the distance across something 2 the state of being wide

widthwise /width wīz, witth-/, **widthways** /-wayz/ *adv* across the width

~~wiegh~~ incorrect spelling of **weigh**

~~wieght~~ incorrect spelling of **weight**

wield /weeld/ *vt* 1 have and exercise something such as power 2 use or hold a weapon or tool —**wielder** *n*

wiener /weenər/ *n* a frankfurter

~~wier~~ incorrect spelling of **weir**

~~wierd~~ incorrect spelling of **weird**

Wiesbaden /veess baad'n/ capital of Hesse State in west-central Germany. Pop. 266,081 (1997).

wife /wīf/ (*pl* **wives** /wīvz/) *n* a woman to whom a man is married —**wifehood** *n* —**wifely** *adj*

> **ORIGIN** A **wife** was originally a 'woman' (as still dialectally in parts of the United Kingdom), but the specialization as 'married woman' began as early as the written records.

wig *n* a covering of false hair worn on the head, e.g. to conceal baldness —**wigged** *adj*

wiggle /wigg'l/ *vti* (**-gling, -gled**) make or cause to make small back- and-forth movements ■ *n* 1 an instance of wiggling 2 a wavy line —**wiggly** *adj*

Wight, Isle of ⟶ **Isle of Wight**

wigwam /wig wam/ *n* a Native North American conical hut

Wilberforce /wilbər fawrss/, **William** (1759–1833) British politician and political reformer

wild /wīld/ *adj* 1 not tame or domesticated 2 not cultivated 3 rough, desolate, and barren 4 an offensive term meaning supposedly culturally or socially inferior 5 stormy ○ *wild winds and seas* 6 enthusiastic or eager 7 unruly or unrestrained 8 overwhelmed by strong emotion ○ *wild with grief* 9 not carefully thought out ○ *What a wild idea!* 10 poorly aimed ■ *adv* in a wild state or manner ■ *n* 1 an undomesticated or uncultivated state 2 = **wilds** *npl* ■ **wilds** *npl* an uninhabited area —**wildly** *adv* —**wildness** *n* ◊ See note at **unruly**

wild boar *n* a wild pig with grey or black bristles and small tusks

wild card *n* 1 an unpredictable person or thing (*infml*) 2 a computer symbol that represents any character 3 in card games, a card of no fixed value

wildcat /wīld kat/ *n* (*pl* **-cats** or same) 1 a wild European or Asian cat 2 *US, Can* a medium-sized wild feline animal such as a lynx or ocelot 3 a person regarded as quick-tempered (*sometimes offensive*) 4 an exploratory oil or gas well in a new area ■ *vti* (**-catting, -catted**) *US* drill an exploratory well —**wildcatting** *n, adj*

wildcat strike *n* a sudden unofficial strike

AKG London

Oscar Wilde

Wilde /wīld/, **Oscar** (1854–1900) Irish writer

wildebeest /wíldə beest, wildə-/ (*pl* **-beests** or same) *n* a gnu

Wilder /wíldər/, **Thornton** (1897–1975) US writer

wilderness /wildərnəss/ *n* 1 natural uncultivated land 2 a barren area 3 an uncomfortable or isolated situation

wild-eyed *adj* 1 having eyes wide with fear, anger, or other emotion 2 marked by extreme and impracticable ideas

wildfire /wíld fīr/ *n* 1 a fire that spreads uncontrollably and rapidly 2 a phosphorescent light sometimes seen over marshy ground at night ◊ **like wildfire** very rapidly

wild flower *n* an uncultivated flower

wildfowl /wíld fowl/ (*pl* same) *n* a bird hunted for sport —**wildfowling** *n*

wild-goose chase *n* a pointless search

wildlife /wíld līf/ *n* wild animals and other living things in their natural environment

wild oat *n* a weedy annual grass similar to cultivated oats

wild rice *n* 1 the dark edible grain of a grass that grows in water 2 a perennial North American grass that grows in water and produces wild rice grains

Wild West *n* the lawless W United States in the late 19C

wile /wīl/ *n* a trick or ruse ■ **wiles** *npl* trickery used to persuade somebody to do something ◊ See note at **while**

wilful /wilf'l/ *adj* 1 deliberate 2 stubborn —**wilfully** *adv* —**wilfulness** *n*

Wilkes /wilks/, **John** (1725–97) British political leader and reformer

Wilkins /wilkinz/, **Maurice** (*b.* 1916) New Zealand-born British biophysicist. With Francis H. Crick and James D. Watson he discovered the structure of DNA (1953).

will[1] *vi* 1 indicates future time ■ *modal v* 1 indicates intent, purpose, or determination 2 expresses polite offers or suggestions ○ *Will you join us?* 3 expresses requests or commands ○ *Will you please set the table?* 4 indicates customary behaviour ○ *When they get together, they will talk all night.* 5 indicates willingness ○ *I will gladly join you.* 6 indicates ability or capacity ○ *This car will seat six.* 7 indicates expectation ○ *She will be married by now.*

will[2] *n* 1 the part of the mind that makes decisions 2 the power or process of making decisions **3** determination **4** a desire or an inclination **5** an attitude towards somebody else **6** a statement of the way a deceased person's property should be distributed ■ *vt* **1** try to cause something by thinking or wishing strongly **2** leave somebody something in a will ◊ **at will** when somebody wishes *(fml)*

Willemstad /wíllam staat/ capital and port of the Netherlands Antilles, on S Curaçao. Pop. 125,000 (1985).

willful *adj* US = wilful

William I /wíllyam/ (1028?–87) king of England (1066–87)

William III (1650–1702) king of England, Scotland, and Ireland (1689–1702)

William IV (1765–1837) king of the United Kingdom (1830–37)

Williams /wíllyamz/, **Fred** (1927–82) Australian painter

Williams, John (*b.* 1941) Australian-born British classical guitarist

Williams, Tennessee (1911–83) US playwright

Williams, William Carlos (1883–1963) US writer

Williamsburg /wíllyamz burg/ city in SE Virginia, site of a restored colonial-era town. Pop. 11,971 (1998).

willies /wílliz/ *npl* an anxious or fearful feeling *(infml)*

willing /wílling/ *adj* **1** ready to do something voluntarily **2** offered voluntarily —**willingly** *adv* —**willingness** *n*

will-o'-the-wisp /wíll a tha wísp/ *n* **1** a phosphorescent light sometimes seen at night above a marshy area **2** an elusive person or thing

willow /wíllō/ *n* **1** a tree with long flexible branches **2** the wood from a willow tree. Use: furniture.

willowy /wíllō i/ (**-ier, -iest**) *adj* **1** tall, slim, and graceful **2** flexible

willpower /wíl pow ar/ *n* determination and self-discipline

Wills, Helen Newington (1906–98) US tennis player

Wills, William John (1834–61) British-born Australian surveyor and explorer

willy /wílli/ (*pl* **-lies**), **willie** *n* an offensive term for a penis *(infml)*

willy-nilly /wílli nílli/ *adv* **1** whether somebody wants it or not **2** haphazardly ■ *adj* **1** happening without choice **2** haphazard

Wilmut /wílmat/, **Ian** (*b.* 1944) Scottish embryologist, with Keith Campbell responsible for the first successful cloning of a mammal from adult cells

AKG London

Harold Wilson

Wilson /wílss'n/, **Harold, Baron Wilson of Rievaulx** (1916–95) British prime minister (1964–70 and 1974–76)

Wilson, Woodrow (1856–1924) 28th president of the United States (1913–21) —**Wilsonian** /wil sóni an/ *adj*

wilt *v* **1** *vti* droop or shrivel, or cause to droop or shrivel **2** *vi* become weak ■ *n* **1** the process of wilting **2** a plant disease that causes stems to droop and leaves to shrivel

Wiltshire /wíltshar/ county in SW England

wily /wíli/ (**-ier, -liest**) *adj* cunningly crafty —**wilily** *adv* —**wiliness** *n*

wimp *n* an offensive term for somebody regarded as timid, cowardly, or unassertive *(infml insult)* —**wimpish** *adj* —**wimpy** *adj*

WIMP /wimp/ *n* a computer user interface system. Full form **windows, icons, mice, and pull-down menus**

win *v* (**winning, won** /wun/) **1** *vti* achieve a victory in a competition, contest, or fight **2** *vt* get something for defeating others **3** *vt* cause somebody to win something ○ *a shot that could win her the match* **4** *vt* gain something ○ *has won the hearts of the voters* ○ *an attitude that has won him few friends* ■ *n* **1** a victory **2** an amount of money won —**winnable** *adj*

☐ **win over** *vt* persuade somebody to agree

wince (**wincing, winced**) *vi* **1** recoil involuntarily from pain or fear **2** make a pained expression   **winoo** *n* ◊ See note at **recoil**

winch *n* **1** a lifting machine with a rotating cylinder **2** a crank or handle used for turning ■ *vt* move with a winch

wind[1] /wind/ *n* **1** air moving through the atmosphere **2** a current of air created artificially **3** a social or economic force *(literary)* ○ *the winds of change* **4** breath or the power to breathe **5** musical instruments that you blow through **6** stomach gas **7** idle talk **8** news that hints at something **9** air carrying a scent ■ *v* **1** *vt* make somebody short of breath **2** *vt* make a baby release painful stomach gas **3** *vt* let a horse rest **4** *vti* get a scent of somebody or something in the air —**winded** *adj* ◊ **be in the wind** be about to happen ◊ **break wind** pass intestinal gas through the anus ◊ **get your** *or* **a second wind** recover your natural breathing pattern after a period of breathlessness and great effort ◊ **see which way** *or* **how the wind is blowing** find out the nature of a situation before making a decision ◇ **take the wind out of somebody's sails** make somebody feel deflated

wind² /wind/ v (**wound** /wownd/) **1** vti go along a twisting or spiral course **2** vti coil round something **3** vti move by the operation of a turning mechanism ○ *wound the window up* ○ *wind the film back* **4** vt cause something to revolve **5** vt make the mechanism of a clockwork device work ■ n **1** a curve or bend **2** an act of winding something —**winder** n

☐ **wind down** v **1** vi relax **2** vti steadily reduce work **3** vi go more slowly

☐ **wind up** v **1** vt close a business down **2** vt finish an activity **3** vi end up (infml) **4** vt lie to somebody as a joke (infml)

wind³ /wind/ (**winded** or **wound** /wownd/) v **1** vti blow a horn or bugle **2** vt make a signal by blowing a horn or bugle

windbag /wind bag/ n a person regarded as a pompous, boring, incessant talker (infml insult)

windblown /wind blōn/ adj **1** blown into disarray by the wind **2** growing in a shape caused by the wind

windbreak /wind brayk/ n an object or screen erected to lessen the force of the wind

windburn /wind burn/ n a skin inflammation caused by exposure to harsh winds —**windburnt** adj

windcheater /wind cheetər/ n a jacket that protects against the wind

wind-chill factor /wind-/, **wind-chill** n the cooling effect of wind on air temperature, or a measurement of this effect

windfall /wind fawl/ n **1** an amount of money obtained unexpectedly **2** a fruit blown down by the wind

wind farm /wind-/ n an area on which a number of wind turbines are sited for electricity generation

Windhoek /wind hook, wint-, vint-/ capital of Namibia. Pop. 169,000 (1997).

winding /winding/ adj **1** twisting and curving **2** coiling or spiralling ■ n **1** a winding course **2** a wire coil that carries electricity

winding sheet n a sheet wrapped around a body for burial

wind instrument /wind-/ n a musical instrument played by blowing

windjammer /wind jamər/ n a large sailing ship

windlass /windləss/ n a revolving lifting device —**windlass** vt

windmill /wind mil/ n **1** a building or device with revolving blades that harness wind power for grinding grain, pumping water, or generating electricity **2** a child's toy with spinning blades

window /windō/ n **1** a glass-covered opening designed to let light or air into a building or vehicle **2** a windowpane **3** a display in a shop window **4** an opening above a counter where customers are dealt with **5** an opening similar to a window, e.g. in an envelope **6** a

period of available time or opportunity **7** a rectangular section on a computer screen ◇ **go out of the window** be lost for good (infml)

window box n a box for plants on a window ledge

window dressing n **1** the art of arranging a display in a shop window **2** a deceptively appealing presentation

windowpane /windō payn/ n a sheet of glass in a window

window seat n **1** an indoor seat under a window **2** a seat by a window, e.g. in a plane

window-shop vi look at things in shops without buying anything —**window-shopper** n

windowsill /windō sil/ n a shelf along the bottom edge of a window

windpipe /wind pīp/ n the tube in the body that takes air from the mouth into the lungs

wind scale /wind-/ n a scale for measuring the force of wind

windscreen /wind skreen/ n the piece of glass that forms the front window of a vehicle

wind shear /wind-/ n a sudden change in wind direction at different altitudes, causing dangerous downdraughts

windshield /wind sheeld/ n **1** a screen that provides protection from the wind **2** US, Can a vehicle's windscreen

windsock /wind sok/ n a fabric tube that blows to show the wind direction

Windsor /winzər/ **1** town in S England, on the River Thames, the site of **Windsor Castle**. Pop. 30,832 (1991). **2** town in SE New South Wales, Australia. Pop. 5,364 (1991).

windstorm /wind stawrm/ n a storm with wind but no rain

Windsurfing

windsurf /wind surf/ vi ride and steer a sailboard on water —**windsurfing** n

windswept /wind swept/ adj **1** exposed to much wind **2** dishevelled as a result of exposure to the wind

wind tunnel /wind-/ n a tunnel for testing aerodynamic properties

wind-up /wind up/ n **1** a tease (infml) **2** the ending of something ■ adj operated by turning a handle

windward /windwərd/ adj facing the wind ■ adv into the wind ■ n the side of something that faces the wind

Windward Islands group of islands in the E Caribbean Sea, including Martinique and the independent island states of Barbados, Dominica, St Lucia, Grenada, and St Vincent and the Grenadines

windy /windi/ (**-ier, -iest**) adj 1 with the wind blowing 2 describes a place where much wind blows 3 full of empty words (infml) —**windily** adv —**windiness** n

wine /wīn/ n 1 alcohol fermented from grapes 2 alcohol fermented from a flower, another fruit, or a vegetable o *dandelion wine* 3 a dark purplish-red colour —**wine** adj ◊ See note at **whine**

wine bar n a bar that specializes in wine

wine cooler n 1 a container for keeping wine chilled 2 a wine cocktail

wineglass /wīn glaass/ n a glass with a stem

winery /wínəri/ (pl **-ies**) n ANZ, US, Can a place for making wine

wing n 1 a bird's, insect's, or bat's limb used for flying 2 a flat surface projecting from the side of an aircraft 3 any flat projecting part 4 the fact of being in flight o *birds on the wing* 5 a part of a building that projects from the middle 6 either of the longer sides of a sports field 7 in some team sports, an attacking player on the side of the field 8 a subsidiary group, especially a subdivision of a political group 9 a corner of the body of a car 10 an air force unit that is larger than a squadron but smaller than a group 11 one side of a military formation ■ **wings** npl 1 the sides of a theatre stage that are not visible to the audience 2 a qualified pilot's badge ■ v 1 vti move swiftly 2 vt wound a bird by hitting its wing 3 vt wound somebody or damage something superficially —**winged** adj —**wingless** adj ◊ **be (waiting) in the wings** be ready and prepared to do something ◊ **take under your wing** look after or protect somebody ◊ **wing it** improvise (infml)

wing chair n an armchair with high side panels

wing collar n a stiff upturned collar with projecting points

wing commander n an officer in the RAF of a rank above squadron leader

winger /wíngər/ n in soccer, a player who plays on a wing

wing nut n a nut with projections that allow it to be tightened by hand

wingspan /wíng span/, **wingspread** /-spred/ n the distance between wing tips, e.g. of a bird

wing tip n the point of a wing that is farthest from the body

wink vi 1 gesture by closing one eye briefly 2 shine intermittently ■ n 1 a brief closing of one eye 2 a twinkling light 3 a short time ◊ **not sleep a wink, not get a wink of sleep** be unable to sleep

winkle /wíngk'l/ n an edible shellfish of coastal waters

□ **winkle out** vt extract information with difficulty

winner /wínnər/ n 1 somebody or something that wins a competition or contest 2 somebody or something successful

winning /wínning/ adj 1 victorious 2 charming ■ **winnings** npl money won —**winningness** n

winning post n the post that marks the finish line on a racecourse

Winnipeg /wínni peg/ capital of Manitoba, Canada. Pop. 618,477 (1996).

Winnipeg, Lake freshwater lake in central Manitoba, Canada. Depth 18m/60 ft.

winnitude /wínni tyood/ n success or the fact of being successful

winnow /wínnō/ v 1 vti separate grain from chaff by tossing it in the air or blowing air through it 2 vt examine something to remove bad parts —**winnow** n

wino /wínō/ (pl **-os**) n an offensive term for a homeless person addicted to alcohol (infml insult)

winsome /wínssəm/ adj charming in manner —**winsomely** adv —**winsomeness** n

winter /wíntər/ n the coldest season of the year ■ v 1 vi spend the winter somewhere 2 vt keep somewhere in winter

winter sport n a sport performed on snow or ice

wintertime /wíntər tīm/ n the winter season

wintry /wíntri/ (**-trier, -triest**), **wintery** (**-terier, -teriest**) adj 1 of or typical of winter 2 cheerless or unfriendly —**wintriness** n

wipe v (**wiping, wiped**) 1 vt rub something with or on soft material to clean or dry it 2 vti remove or be removed by rubbing 3 vt remove a recording from a tape 4 vt remove something as if by wiping ■ n 1 a light rubbing stroke 2 a disposable cleaning cloth

□ **wipe out** vt destroy in large numbers (infml)

wiper /wípər/ n a device for cleaning a windscreen

wire n 1 a strand of metal 2 a metal strand encased in insulating material that carries an electric current 3 a cable that provides a telecommunications link ■ vt (**wiring, wired**) 1 fasten something with wire 2 connect electrical equipment ◊ **have** or **get your wires crossed** have a misunderstanding

wired adj 1 equipped for accessing the Internet (infml) 2 nervy and overstimulated (slang)

wirehaired /wír haird/ adj describes a dog with a rough coat

wireless /wírləss/ n a radio (dated) ■ adj 1 not having or using wires 2 describes communications systems and devices that make use of mobile phone technology o *wireless telephone technology* —**wirelessly** adv

wireless markup language n a system for tagging computer text files that specifies the interfaces of narrowband wireless devices

wire netting n mesh made of wire

wiretap /wír tap/ (**-tapping**, **-tapped**) *vti* fit a secret connection to a telephone line to allow covert monitoring of conversations —**wiretap** *n*

wire wool *n* steel wool

wiring /wíring/ *n* a system or layout of electrical wires

wiry /wíri/ (**-ier**, **-iest**) *adj* 1 slim but strong 2 coarse in texture ○ *a dog with wiry hair* —**wirily** *adv* —**wiriness** *n*

Wisconsin /wi skónssin/ state of the north-central United States. Cap. Madison. Pop. 5,363,675 (2000). —**Wisconsinite** *n*

wisdom /wízdəm/ *n* 1 the good sense and judgment that come from experience 2 accumulated learning 3 a widely held opinion

wisdom tooth *n* one of the four backmost teeth

wise /wíz/ (**wiser**, **wisest**) *adj* 1 having acquired good sense and judgment from experience 2 sensible 3 having been well educated 4 shrewd —**wisely** *adv* ◊ **be** *or* **get wise (to)** be or become aware of *(infml)* ◊ **put wise (to)** inform somebody about something *(infml)*

□ **wise up** *vti* make or become informed *(infml)*

-wise *suffix* 1 in a particular manner or direction ○ *clockwise* 2 with regard to *(infml)* ○ *salary-wise*

wisecrack /wíz krak/ *(infml)* *n* a flippant remark ■ *vi* make wisecracks —**wisecracker** *n*

wish *v* 1 *vti* desire something 2 *vt* demand something 3 *vti* express a desire for ○ *wished us a safe journey* 4 *vt* want something to be otherwise 5 *vt* greet somebody in a particular way ○ *wished me good afternoon* ■ *n* 1 a yearning 2 an expression of a desire 3 something desired or demanded 4 a hope for somebody's welfare *(usually pl)* —**wisher** *n* ◊ See note at **want**

wishbone /wísh bōn/ *n* a V-shaped bone in a bird's breast

wishful thinking /wíshf'l-/ *n* the belief that wishes correspond with reality

wish list *n* a list of things you would like to have

wishy-washy /wíshi woshi, wíshi wóshi/ *adj (infml)* 1 incapable of making firm decisions 2 lacking strength or colour —**wishy-washiness** *n*

wisp *n* 1 something thin and delicate, e.g. a piece of straw or a streak of smoke 2 a slender, delicate person 3 something insubstantial —**wispiness** *n* —**wispy** *adj*

wisteria /wi steéri ə/ (*pl* **-as** *or same*) *n* a deciduous climbing flowering plant

wistful /wístf'l/ *adj* sadly pensive —**wistfully** *adv* —**wistfulness** *n*

wit *n* 1 ingenious humour 2 witty speech or writing 3 a witty person 4 intelligence ■ **wits** *npl* shrewdness or reasoning power ◊ **be at your wits' end** be in despair as to how to cope with something

witblits /vitblits/ *n* S Africa illegally distilled alcohol

witch /wich/ *n* 1 a woman deemed to have magic powers 2 a follower of a pre-Christian religion based on nature 3 an offensive term for a woman regarded as unattractive or malicious *(insult)* ◊ See note at **which**

witchcraft /wich kraaft/ *n* 1 the exercise of supposed magical powers 2 the effect of supposed magical powers

witch doctor *n* 1 a tribal healer or magician 2 in some African cultures, somebody who hunts witches

witch hazel, wych hazel *n* 1 a soothing lotion that contains extracts from specific bark and flowers. Use: astringent, relieving bruises and sprains. 2 a tree or bush from which witch hazel is obtained

witch-hunt *n* 1 an intensive campaign against dissenters or those suspected of wrongdoing 2 a persecution of witches —**witch-hunter** *n*

witching hour /wíching-/ *n* midnight

with /with/ *prep* 1 in the company of ○ *sit with the other children* 2 used or done together ○ *It doesn't go with roast beef.* 3 involving ○ *a meeting with department heads* 4 against ○ *competing with each other* 5 by means of ○ *treated with the drug* 6 carrying ○ *came in with a box of files* 7 having ○ *with English subtitles* 8 because of ○ *faint with anxiety* 9 on or in ○ *walls covered with photographs* 10 concerning ○ *not happy with the service* 11 in a particular way ○ *sitting with her hands on her lap* ○ *walking with a limp* 12 in view of ○ *with the problems in the economy* 13 in spite of ○ *With all his charm, I still wouldn't trust him.* 14 at the same time as or immediately after ○ *With that, he stormed out.* 15 following the direction of ○ *sail with the tide* 16 according to or in proportion to ○ *The risk increases with age.* ◊ **be with it** 1 be fashionable *(infml dated)* 2 understand a situation *(infml)*

withal /with áwl/ *adv (archaic)* 1 moreover 2 nevertheless

withdraw /with dráw/ (**-drew** /-drōó/, **-drawn** /-dráwn/) *v* 1 *vt* remove something or somebody from a place 2 *vt* retract an earlier statement 3 *vi* leave or retreat 4 *vt* take money from an account —**withdrawable** *adj*

withdrawal /with dráw əl/ *n* 1 an instance of taking money from an account 2 a period of fighting an addiction, or the physical effects of fighting it 3 the act of withdrawing 4 the retreat of an army from an area

withdrawn /with dráwn/ past participle of **withdraw** ■ *adj* 1 not sociable or outgoing 2 removed from the market

wither /wíthər/ *v* 1 *vti* shrivel 2 *vi* fade away 3 *vti* make somebody feel embarrassed or foolish as the object of scorn —**withered** *adj* —**withering** *adj* —**witheringly** *adv*

withers /wíthərz/ *npl* the ridge between the shoulder bones of a horse, or similar four-legged animal

withhold /with hōld/ (**-held** /-héld/) *vt* refuse to give something

within /wɪθ ín/ prep, adv **1** inside a place **2** inside a group or organization **3** inside yourself ■ prep not beyond the limits, range, time, or extent of ○ trying to keep within our budget ○ finish the job within a week ■ adv indoors (literary)

~~withhold~~ incorrect spelling of **withhold**

without /wɪθ ówt/ prep **1** not having ○ was left without food **2** not accompanied by **3** not feeling ○ without remorse **4** not happening ○ passed without objection ■ prep, adv outside (literary) ○ without the city walls ■ conj unless (nonstandard)

withstand /wɪθ stánd/ (**-stood** /-stoód/) vti be resistant to something

witless /wítləss/ adj unintelligent ○ a witless comment —**witlessly** adv —**witlessness** n

witness /wítnəss/ n **1** somebody who sees a specific incident happen **2** somebody who countersigns a document **3** somebody who testifies to Christian beliefs ■ vt **1** see something happen **2** countersign a document **3** experience or be the time of important events or changes **4** be a sign or proof of —**witnessable** adj

witness box n a place in court where a witness gives evidence

Wittenberg /vítt'n burg/ city in east-central Germany where Martin Luther began his campaign for the reform of the Roman Catholic Church in 1517. Pop. 53,400 (1989).

witter /wíttər/ vi say unimportant things at length (infml)

Wittgenstein /vítgən stīn/, **Ludwig** (1889–1951) Austrian-born British philosopher

witticism /wíttɪsɪzəm/ n a witty remark

witty /wítti/ (**-tier**, **-tiest**) adj using words with ingenious humour —**wittily** adv —**wittiness** n

Witwatersrand /wɪt wáwtərz rand/ rocky ridge in NE South Africa, the most productive goldmining area in the world. Length 100 km/60 mi.

wivoo plural of **wife**

wiz (pl **wizzes**) n an expert (infml)

wizard /wízzərd/ n **1** a man with supposed magic powers **2** somebody who excels at something (infml) —**wizardly** adj

wizardry /wízzərdri/ n **1** the art of wizards **2** impressive skill

wizened /wízz'nd/ adj dried up or wrinkled

wiz kid n = **whiz kid** (infml)

wk abbr **1** week **2** work

WML abbr wireless markup language

woad n **1** a blue dye obtained from the leaves of a plant. Use: formerly, body paint. **2** the European plant whose leaves yield woad

wobble /wóbb'l/ (**-bling**, **-bled**) v **1** vti move from side to side **2** vi quaver —**wobble** n —**wobblingly** adv

wobbly /wóbbli/ (**-blier**, **-bliest**) adj **1** unsteady **2** feeling weak (infml) —**wobbliness** n

Wodehouse /woŏd howss/, **P. G.** (1881–1975) British writer

wodge n a large lump (infml)

woe n **1** a serious misfortune **2** grief

woebegone /wó bi gon/ adj sorrowful

woeful /wóf'l/ adj **1** unhappy **2** causing grief **3** pathetically bad —**woefully** adv —**woefulness** n

wok n a large curved Chinese cooking pan

woke past tense of **wake**[1]

woken past participle of **wake**[1]

wold /wōld/ n upland

wolf /woōlf/ n (pl **wolves** /woŏlvz/) **1** any of various carnivorous mammals, related to the dog, that hunt in packs **2** a greedy, cruel person **3** a sexually predatory man (infml) ■ vt eat quickly and greedily —**wolfish** adj —**wolfishly** adv ◇ **cry wolf** give a false alarm too many times, so that when help is really needed, no one will give it ◇ **throw to the wolves** abandon somebody to take blame or to be ruined

Wolfe /woōlf/, **James** (1727–59) British general

Wolfe, Thomas (1900–38) US writer

Wolfe, Tom (b. 1930) US journalist and writer

wolfhound /woŏlf hownd/ n a large breed of dog

wolfram /woŏlfrəm/ n tungsten (archaic)

wolf whistle n a whistle that signifies sexual interest —**wolf-whistle** vti

Mary Wollstonecraft: Portrait (1790) by John Opie

Wollstonecraft /woŏlstən kraaft/, **Mary** (1759–97) British feminist

Wolsey /woŏlzi/, **Thomas** (1475–1530) English cleric and politician

wolverine /woŏlvə reen/ (pl **-ines** or same) n a strong dark-furred carnivore of the weasel family

woman /woŏmmən/ (pl **-en** /wímmin/) n **1** a female adult **2** women as a group **3** a female domestic employee **4** a wife or girlfriend (infml; sometimes offensive) —**woman-like** adj

womanhood /woŏmmənhoŏd/ n **1** the condition of being a woman **2** women in general

womanize /woŏmmə nīz/ (**-izing**, **-ized**), **womanise** vi be constantly seeking casual sex with women (disapproving; refers to men) —**womanizer** n

womankind /woŏmmən kínd/, **womenkind** /wímmən-/ n women as a group

womanly /woŏmmənli/ adj characteristic of mature women —**womanliness** n

womb /woom/ n **1** a uterus **2** a place of origin

wombat /wóm bat/ n a small Australian marsupial

women plural of **woman**

womenfolk /wímmin fōk/ *npl* women collectively, or the women in a family or group (*dated*)

Women's Institute *n* an organization for rural women

women's lib *n* women's liberation (*infml*) —**women's libber** *n*

women's liberation *n* a political movement to free women from social oppression

women's movement *n* a movement to improve the position of women in society

women's refuge *n* a safe place for women who have left home to escape domestic abuse

women's studies *n* a course of study examining the roles and achievements of women (+ *sing or pl verb*)

won[1] /won/ (*pl same*) *n* the main unit of currency in North and South Korea

won[2] /wun/ past tense, past participle of **win**

wonder /wúndər/ *n* **1** amazed admiration **2** something marvellous ■ *adj* extraordinarily good ■ *v* **1** *vti* speculate about something **2** *vi* be amazed ◇ **no** *or* **small** *or* **little wonder** it is not surprising ◊ See note at **wander**

wonderful /wúndərf'l/ *adj* **1** exciting admiration **2** very good or suitable —**wonderfully** *adv* —**wonderfulness** *n*

wonderland /wúndər land/ *n* a land of wonderful things

wonderment /wúndərmənt/ *n* **1** amazed admiration **2** puzzlement

wondrous /wúndrəss/ (*literary*) *adj* exciting wonder ■ *adv* to an amazing degree —**wondrously** *adv* —**wondrousness** *n*

wonky /wóngki/ (-**kier**, -**kiest**) *adj*, *adv* (*infml*) **1** unreliable in use **2** askew —**wonkily** *adv* —**wonkiness** *n*

wont /wōnt/ (*fml*) *adj* accustomed or likely to do something ○ *He is wont to ask hard questions.* ■ *n* something that somebody often does ○ *She arrived late and left early, as is her wont.* ◊ See note at **habit**

won't /wōnt/ *contr* will not

wonted /wóntid/ *adj* usual (*literary*) —**wontedly** *adv* ◊ See note at **usual**

woo (**woos**, **wooing**, **wooed**) *vti* **1** seek the love of a woman (*literary*) **2** try to please or attract somebody —**wooer** *n* —**wooingly** *adv*

wood /wood/ *n* **1** the hard fibrous substance that trees are chiefly composed of **2** wood used as a fuel or building material **3** an area with trees **4** a golf club with a thick head ■ *adj* **1** made of wood **2** found or located among trees ■ *vt* cover an area with trees —**wooded** *adj* ◇ **cannot see the wood for the trees** too concerned with the details to appreciate the general nature of a situation or problem ◇ **out of the woods** out of danger or difficulty (*infml*)

ORIGIN The ancestral meaning of **wood** is probably 'collection of trees, forest'. The meanings 'tree' (now obsolete) and 'substance from which trees are made' are secondary developments. It has been suggested that **wood** may go back to an ancient source meaning 'separate', in which case it would originally have denoted a 'separated' or 'remote' piece of territory. Since such remote, uninhabited areas were usually wooded, the word came to mean 'forest'.

SPELLCHECK Do not confuse the spelling of **wood** and **would** (indicating a conditional statement), which sound similar.

Wood /wood/, **Sir Henry** (1869–1944) British conductor

woodblock /wood blok/ *n* **1** a block of wood for making prints **2** a small piece of wood laid with others to surface a floor

woodcarving /wood kaarving/ *n* **1** the art of carving wood **2** an object carved from wood

woodchuck /wood chuk/ (*pl* -**chucks** *or same*) *n* a heavy-set North American rodent

woodcock /wood kok/ (*pl* -**cocks** *or same*) *n* a small stocky game bird with a long beak

woodcraft /wood kraaft/ *n* skill in things concerning woods and forests —**woodcrafter** *n*

woodcut /wood kut/ *n* **1** a block of wood for making prints **2** a print made with a woodcut

woodcutter /wood kutər/ *n* **1** a lumberjack **2** somebody who makes woodcut prints

wooden /wood'n/ *adj* **1** made of wood **2** lacking flexibility or grace ○ *a ballet dancer with wooden movements* **3** inexpressive —**woodenly** *adv* —**woodenness** *n*

wooden spoon *n* a booby prize

woodland /woodlənd/ *n* an area of land that is covered with trees

woodlouse /wood lowss/ (*pl* -**lice** /-līss/) *n* a small land crustacean

woodpecker /wood pekər/ *n* a woodland bird that hammers trees with its beak to extract insects

wood pigeon *n* a large pigeon that lives in the woods

woodpile /wood pīl/ *n* a stack of firewood

wood pulp *n* wood broken down for use in paper-making

Tiger Woods

Woods /woodz/, **Tiger** (b. 1975) US golfer

woodshed /wood shed/ *n* a room or building for storing firewood

woodsman /woodzmən/ (*pl* -**men** /-mən/) *n* somebody who is skilled at living in the woods

woodwind /woŏd wind/ *n* **1** the family of musical instruments that includes the flute and the clarinet (+ *sing* or *pl verb*) **2** a musical instrument of the woodwind family —**woodwind** *adj*

woodwork /woŏd wurk/ *n* **1** the manufacture of wooden items **2** items or parts made from wood —**woodworker** *n* ◇ **crawl** *or* **come out of the woodwork** appear suddenly and unexpectedly (*slang*)

woodworm /woŏd wurm/ *n* **1** a wood-boring larva **2** damage to wood caused by wood-boring insects, especially larvae

woody /woŏdi/ (*-ier*, *-iest*) *adj* **1** having many trees **2** made of wood **3** resembling wood

woof[1] /woŏf/ *n*, *interj* the sound of a dog's bark —**woof** *vi*

woof[2] /woof/ *n* **1** the weft on a loom **2** a woven fabric or its texture

woofer /woŏffər, woŏfər/ *n* a loudspeaker for low frequencies

wool /woŏl/ *n* **1** the curly hair of sheep and some other mammals **2** yarn made from wool. Use: knitting, weaving. **3** material made of wool yarn **4** a mass of soft hairs that grows on some plants

woolen *adj*, *n* US = **woollen**

Corbis/Bettmann
Virginia Woolf

Woolf /woŏlf/, **Virginia** (1882–1941) British novelist and critic

woolgathering /woŏl gathəring/ *n* daydreaming —**woolgatherer** *n*

woollen /woŏllən/ *adj* **1** made of wool **2** producing wool or woollen items ■ *n* a woollen garment

woolly /woŏlli/ *adj* (*-ier*, *-liest*) **1** made of wool **2** covered in furry hair **3** vague or lacking focus ■ *n* (*pl* **-lies**) a woollen garment (*infml*) —**woollily** *adv* —**woolliness** *n*

Woolworth /woŏlwərth/, **Frank W.** (1852–1919) US retailer

woozy /woŏzi/ (*-ier*, *-iest*) *adj* **1** weak and dizzy **2** confused —**woozily** *adv* —**wooziness** *n*

Worcester /woŏstər/ city in west-central England. Pop. 89,500 (1994).

Worcester sauce *n* a pungent dark-brown sauce sold in bottles

Worcestershire /woŏstərshər/ county of west-central England

word /wurd/ *n* **1** a meaningful combination of sounds or letters that forms a unit of language **2** a brief comment or discussion ○ *Could I have a word with you in my office, please?* **3** information or news ○ *Is there any*

word on your daughter? **4** a rumour ○ *The word is that she's leaving the company.* **5** a promise ○ *I give you my word.* **6** a command or verbal signal ○ *He gave the word to attack.* **7** a fixed number of bits processed by a computer as a unit **8 Word, Word of God** holy Christian scriptures ■ **words** *npl* **1** an angry exchange **2** the text of a song ■ *vt* express in words —**worded** *adj* ◇ **be as good as your word** do as promised ◇ **eat your words** admit humbly that you were wrong or mistaken (*infml*)

wording /wúrding/ *n* the choice of words made by a writer or speaker

wordless /wúrdləss/ *adj* **1** not using words **2** unable to speak —**wordlessly** *adv* —**wordlessness** *n*

word of honour *n* a promise

word-perfect *adj* **1** knowing or performing something such as a song or speech perfectly **2** absolutely correct and accurate

wordplay /wúrd play/ *n* clever use of words

word processing *n* the creation or manipulation of text using computers

word processor *n* **1** a piece of equipment with a keyboard and screen for creating or manipulating text **2** a computer program for creating or manipulating text

Wordsworth /wúrdz wurth/, **Dorothy** (1771–1855) British writer

Wordsworth, William (1770–1850) British poet —**Wordsworthian** /wúrdz wúrthi ən/ *adj*

word wrap, word wrapping *n* a word-processing feature that automatically takes a word over to the next line if it will not fit

wordy /wúrdi/ (*-ier*, *-iest*) *adj* using too many words —**wordily** *adv* —**wordiness** *n*

SYNONYMS **wordy, verbose, long-winded, rambling, prolix, diffuse** CORE MEANING: too long or not concisely expressed

wore past tense of **wear**

work /wurk/ *n* **1** a paid job or its duties **2** a place of employment **3** purposeful effort **4** something made or done ○ *Your work is not satisfactory.* **5** an artistic or intellectual creation (*often pl*) **6** (*symbol* **W**) the transfer of energy, measured as the product of the force applied to a body and the distance moved by that body in the direction of the force ■ *v* (**worked** *or* **wrought** *archaic* /rawt/) **1** *vi* have a job **2** *vti* make or cause to make a physical or mental effort **3** *vti* function or cause to function **4** *vi* be successful ○ *This relationship isn't working.* **5** *vti* shape a material, or be shaped **6** *vt* cultivate land **7** *vti* attain or cause to attain a particular condition ○ *The screw worked itself loose.* **8** *vti* move slowly and with effort ○ *worked his way through the crowd* **9** *vti* exercise a muscle or part of the body **10** *vt* provoke an emotional response in somebody **11** *vt* solve, e.g. a crossword puzzle ◇ **have your work cut out (for you)** be faced with a difficult task ◇ See note at **wrought**

☐ **work off** *vt* **1** pay a debt by working **2** use

something up by exercising ○ *worked off the extra fat*

☐ **work out** v **1** vt solve or calculate something **2** vt resolve a difficulty **3** vt think something up **4** vi end satisfactorily **5** vi end in a particular way **6** vi exercise your body **7** vi make a total

☐ **work through** vt come to terms with or gradually solve a problem

☐ **work up** v **1** vt excite emotions in **2** vi become more intense

☐ **work up to** vt gradually reach a particular level

workable /wúrkəb'l/ adj **1** able to be done **2** able to be handled or shaped —**workably** adv

workaday /wúrkə day/ adj **1** routine and commonplace **2** appropriate for work

workaholic /wúrkə hóllik/ n a compulsively hard worker

workaround /wúrkə rownd/ n a technique that enables somebody to overcome a fault or defect in a computer program or system without actually correcting or eliminating it

workbench /wúrk bench/ n a carpenter's or mechanic's table

workbook /wúrk bŏŏk/ n **1** a student's exercise book **2** an instruction book

worked up adj in a state of heightened emotion, especially anger or nervousness (infml)

worker /wúrkər/ n **1** a person who works **2** an employee **3** a member of the working class **4** an insect belonging to a group that does the work in a colony

work ethic n a belief in the moral value of work

workfare /wúrk fair/ n a government scheme that obliges unemployed people to do community work in return for benefit payments

workforce /wúrk fawrss/ n **1** all the workers in a company **2** all the people in a specific place who are employed or employable

workhorse /wúrk hawrss/ n **1** a horse used for heavy work **2** a hard-working person (infml) **3** a reliable tool or machine

workhouse /wúrk howss/ (pl -**houses** /-howziz/) n formerly, an institution in which poor people were given food and accommodation in return for unpaid work

work-in n an occasion when workers occupy their workplace as a protest

working /wúrking/ adj **1** functioning **2** worn at work **3** having a paid job **4** spent at work ○ *all his working life* **5** only adequate ○ *a working knowledge of Italian* **6** providing a basis for further work ○ *a working theory* ■ n **1** the process of shaping something **2** a jerking motion (fml) ■ **workings** npl **1** the way that something functions ○ *the workings of the government* **2** the internal mechanism of a device

working capital n **1** the money that a company has available to use **2** the value of a company's current assets minus its liabilities

working class n the part of society made up

of people who do manual or unskilled work (often pl) —**working-class** adj

working day n **1** a day on which somebody works **2** the number of hours somebody spends at work

working party n a group appointed to study something and report on it

working storage n temporary computer memory storage

working week n the number of hours or days that somebody works in a week

work in progress n an incomplete ongoing piece of work, especially an artistic work

workload /wúrk lōd/ n **1** the amount of work given to one person or group **2** the amount of work that a machine does

workman /wúrkmən/ (pl -**men** /-mən/) n **1** a man who does manual work, e.g. building or repairs **2** a man judged on his working ability

workmanlike /wúrkmən līk/, **workmanly** /-li/ adj thorough and satisfactory but not imaginative or original

workmanship /wúrkmənship/ n **1** the skill of a worker or artisan **2** the quality or result of somebody's skill

workmate /wúrk mayt/ n a fellow worker

work of art n **1** a piece of fine art, e.g. a painting or sculpture **2** something made or done well

workout /wúrk owt/ n **1** a strenuous exercise session **2** a rigorous test

workplace /wúrk playss/ n a place of employment

workroom /wúrk room, -rŏŏm/ n a room in which work, especially manual work, is done

works /wurks/ n (pl same) a place for industrial production ■ npl **1** everything (infml) **2** the interior driving mechanisms of a device **3** acts ◇ **in the works** being prepared or worked on

worksheet /wúrk sheet/ n **1** a sheet of questions for students **2** a written record of work done or scheduled

workshop /wúrk shop/ n **1** a place where manual work is done **2** a group of people studying, discussing, or working on a creative project together

workshy /wúrk shī/ adj unwilling to work

workspace /wúrk spayss/ n an area in which to work

workstation /wúrk staysh'n/ n **1** an area of an office where a single person works **2** a single terminal of a computer network or mainframe **3** a powerful specialized computer

work-study n an investigation into an organization's efficiency

work surface n a flat area for working on, especially in a kitchen

worktable /wúrk tayb'l/ n a table at which work, e.g. writing or sewing, is done

worktop /wúrk top/ n a flat surface for food preparation

work-to-rule n UK, Can a protest in which

workers adhere to rules strictly in order to slow production down

workup /wúrk up/ *n* a complete diagnostic medical examination

world /wurld/ *n* **1** the planet Earth **2** the Earth and everything on it **3** the human race or human society **4** a particular part of the Earth ○ *the western world* **5** an area of activity ○ *the world of fashion* **6** the universe **7** a realm or domain ○ *the world of reptiles* **8** an astronomical object supposedly inhabited ○ *the alien worlds of science fiction* **9** everything in somebody's life ○ *Her entire world collapsed.* **10** a great deal or amount ○ *a world of difference* ■ *adj* **1** of the entire world **2** exerting an influence globally ◇ **out of this world** extraordinarily good (*infml*) ◇ **think the world of** be extremely fond of somebody

World Bank *n* an agency of the United Nations that guarantees loans to member nations for reconstruction and development

world-beating *adj* surpassing all others

world-class *adj* ranked among the best in the world

World Council of Churches *n* an international church organization that promotes co-operation among churches

World Cup *n* a major international sports tournament

World English *n* the English language in all its varieties

world-famous *adj* internationally known

World Health Organization *n* a UN medical organization that helps countries develop health services

World Heritage Site *n* a globally significant site or structure given special protection

worldly /wúrldli/ *adj* **1** belonging to the physical world **2** materialistic **3** *also* **worldly-wise** experienced in life —**worldliness** *n*

world music *n* music from countries outside the western world

world power *n* an internationally powerful country

world-shaking, world-shattering *adj* with an extremely powerful effect or significance

World Trade Organization *n* an organization that promotes international trade

world-view *n* a comprehensive interpretation or image of the universe and humanity

world war *n* a war involving many countries

World War I *n* a war fought in Europe from 1914 to 1918

World War II *n* a war fought in Europe, Africa, and Asia from 1939 to 1945

world-weary *adj* bored with life —**world-weariness** *n*

worldwide /wúrld wíd/ *adj* of the whole world ■ *adv* throughout the world

World Wide Web *n* all the computer files located on computers that can be accessed via the Internet

worm /wurm/ *n* **1** a long cylindrical invertebrate (*often in combination*) **2** an insect larva

3 something that resembles a worm in form or movement **4** an offensive term for somebody regarded as contemptible (*insult*) **5** an invasive computer program ■ *v* **1** *vt* proceed deviously ○ *wormed her way out of trouble* **2** *vt* obtain something deviously ○ *They wormed his secret out of him.* **3** *vt* treat a person or animal for parasitic worms **4** *vi* move like a worm

WORM /wurm/ *n* a storage medium for computer data. Full form **write once read many (times)**

wormcast /wúrm kaast/ *n* a small mound of debris excreted by a worm

worm-eaten *adj* **1** eaten into by worms **2** in a state of decay

wormhole /wúrm hōl/ *n* **1** a hole made by a worm **2** a hypothetical passage between widely separate parts of the universe

wormwood /wúrm wŏŏd/ *n* a plant that yields a bitter-tasting extract. Use: flavouring for absinthe, formerly, medicine for intestinal worms.

wormy /wúrmi/ *adj* **1** infested by worms **2** resembling a worm —**worminess** *n*

worn /wawrn/ *past participle of* **wear** ■ *adj* **1** showing the effects of wear **2** showing the effects of fatigue —**wornness** *n* ◊ See note at **warn**

worn-out *adj* **1** damaged or weakened by prolonged use **2** exhausted

worrisome /wúrrissəm/ *adj* **1** causing worry **2** tending to worry —**worrisomely** *adv*

worry /wúrri/ *v* (**-ries, -ried**) **1** *vti* be or make anxious **2** *vt* bother or annoy somebody **3** *vt* try to bite an animal ○ *a dog suspected of worrying sheep* **4** *vt* tear at something with the teeth ○ *a dog worrying a bone* ■ *n* (*pl* **-ries**) **1** anxiety **2** a cause of anxiety —**worried** *adj* —**worriedly** *adv* —**worriedness** *n* —**worrier** *n* —**worrying** *adj* —**worryingly** *adv* ◊ See note at **bother**

SYNONYMS worry, unease, care, anxiety, angst, stress CORE MEANING: a troubled mind

worry beads *npl* beads to finger when feeling tense

worse /wurss/ *comparative of* **bad, badly, ill** ■ *adj* **1** less good **2** more severe ○ *Her fever is worse this morning.* **3** more ill ○ *The patient is worse today.* ■ *adv* to a worse degree ■ *n* something that is worse than something else —**worsen** *vti* ◇ **be none the worse for** experience no harm or ill effects from ◇ **if (the) worse comes to (the) worst** if the situation reaches an intolerable state

worship /wúrship/ *v* (**-shipping, -shipped**) **1** *vti* regard and show respect to somebody or something as a deity **2** *vt* love somebody or something deeply **3** *vi* take part in a religious service ■ *n* **1** religious adoration **2** religious services **3** great devotion **4** **Worship** *UK, Can* a title of respect for a mayor, magistrate, or similar dignitary —**worshipper** *n*

~~worshiped~~ incorrect spelling of **worshipped**

worshipful /wúrshipf'l/ *adj* **1** showing worship **2** *also* **Worshipful** distinguished —**worshipfully** *adv*

worst /wurst/ superlative of **bad, badly, ill** ■ *adj* least good or most unfavourable ■ *adv* least well or most unfavourably ■ *n* the worst thing ■ *vt* defeat somebody ○ *We were worsted by the visiting team.*

worsted /wóostid/ *n* **1** a smooth woven woollen cloth **2** the yarn from which worsted is made

worth /wurth/ *n* **1** the monetary value of something **2** the amount of something that can be bought for a particular sum of money **3** the goodness, usefulness, or importance of something or somebody ■ *adj* **1** equal in value to a particular amount ○ *a painting worth thousands* **2** important or good enough to justify something ○ *His friendship is not worth having.*

worthless /wúrthləss/ *adj* **1** having no value **2** lacking good, attractive, or admirable qualities —**worthlessly** *adv* —**worthlessness** *n*

worthwhile /wúrth wíl/ *adj* sufficiently rewarding or beneficial to justify time or effort

worthy /wúrthi/ *adj* (**-thier, -thiest**) **1** deserving ○ *worthy of respect* ○ *a worthy cause* **2** respectable ○ *a worthy person* ■ *n* (*pl* **-thies**) somebody regarded as good or moral (*often ironic*) ○ *colonial governors and other worthies* —**worthily** *adv* —**worthiness** *n*

would /wood/ *modal v* **1** a form of 'will' used in reported speech or to state what might happen ○ *You would know him if you saw him.* **2** expresses polite requests ○ *Would you mind closing the window?* **3** indicates habitual action in the past ○ *Every Sunday we would drive to the coast.* ◊ See note at **wood**

USAGE **would have** or **would of**? Although the nonstandard form *would of* sounds similar to the contracted form *would've*, it is incorrect to use it for *would have: It would have/would've* [not *would of*] *been nice if you'd told me this before.* The same confusion arises with *could have* and *should have.*

would-be *adj* hoping to do or be ○ *a would-be poet*

wouldn't /woodd'nt/ *contr* would not

would've /woodd*ə*v/ *contr* would have (*infml*)

wound[1] /woond/ *n* **1** an injury to the body in which the skin or other tissue is cut or torn **2** an emotional injury ■ *vti* cause a wound to somebody or something ○ *was wounded in the leg* ○ *wounding her pride* —**wounded** *adj* —**wounding** *adj*

wound[2] **1** past participle, past tense of **wind**[2] **2** past participle, past tense of **wind**[3]

Wounded Knee /woondid nee/ village in SW South Dakota, site of a massacre of mostly unarmed Native North Americans in 1890

wound up /wównd úp/ *adj* nervously agitated (*infml*)

wove past tense of **weave**[1]

woven /wóv'n/ past participle of **weave**[1] ■ *adj* created by weaving

wow[1] (*infml*) *interj* expresses surprise ■ *vt* impress greatly

wow[2] *n* a pitch fluctuation in recorded sound

wowser /wówzər/ *n* ANZ a killjoy (*infml*)

WP *abbr* **1** without prejudice **2** word processing **3** word processor

WPC *abbr* woman police constable

wpm *abbr* words per minute

wrack[1] /rak/ *n* seaweed in general, or brown seaweed in particular

wrack[2] /rak/ *n* **1** destruction **2** a remnant of something destroyed (*literary*)

wraith /rayth/ *n* **1** a ghost **2** a supposed apparition of somebody who is soon to die —**wraith-like** *adj*

Wrangel Island /ráng g'l-/ island of NE Russia, in the Arctic Ocean

wrangle /ráng g'l/ *v* (**-gling, -gled**) **1** *vi* argue noisily **2** *vt* US, Can herd animals ■ *n* a long argument —**wrangler** *n*

wrap /rap/ *v* (**wrapping, wrapped**) **1** *vt* cover something by winding or folding paper, cloth, or a similar material around it **2** *vti* coil around something ○ *wrapped his arms around the pole* **3** *vt* envelop something ○ *hilltops wrapped in mist* **4** *vt* give something an aura ○ *The whole affair was wrapped in secrecy.* **5** *vt* engross somebody ○ *wrapped in thought* **6** *vti* take a word that is too long over to the next line, or be taken over for this reason **7** *also* **rap** *vt* Aus praise somebody ■ *n* **1** a shawl, cloak, or similar outer garment **2** material used for wrapping things **3** the completion of filming **4** a filled tortilla sandwich ○ *a ham and cheese wrap* ◊ **keep something under wraps** keep something secret

☐ **wrap up** *vt* complete (*infml*)

wraparound /ráp *ə* rownd/, **wraparound** /ráp rownd/ *adj* curving around the sides of the thing it is fitted to ■ *n* **1** a garment worn wrapped around the body **2** a wraparound fitment **3** a computer function that automatically starts a new line

wrapped *adj* Aus thrilled (*infml*)

wrapper /ráppər/ *n* **1** the paper, plastic, or other material wrapped around merchandise **2** a tobacco leaf that forms the outside of a cigar

wrapping /rápping/ *n* the paper, plastic, or other material used to wrap things

wrath /roth/ *n* **1** great anger (*fml*) **2** divine retribution —**wrathful** *adj* —**wrathfully** *adv* ◊ See note at **anger**

wreak /reek/ *vt* **1** cause havoc or destruction **2** inflict revenge on somebody ◊ See note at **reek, wrought**

wreath /reeth/ (*pl* **wreaths** /reethz, reeths/) *n* **1** a circular arrangement of flowers or greenery **2** a hollow circular shape

wreathe /reeth/ (**wreathing, wreathed**) *vt* **1** put a wreath on or around something **2** make things into a wreath by intertwining them

◇ **be wreathed in** be covered in or surrounded by ○ *was wreathed in smiles*

wreck /rek/ *vt* **1** destroy, damage, or ruin something **2** cause a ship to sink or run aground and be destroyed ■ *n* **1** destruction **2** the remains of something wrecked, e.g. a sunken ship **3** somebody who looks or feels terrible

wreckage /rékij/ *n* **1** the remains of something destroyed **2** the process of wrecking something *(fml)*

wrecked /rekt/ *adj* **1** exhausted *(infml)* **2** intoxicated *(slang)*

wrecker /rékər/ *n* **1** somebody or something that destroys or ruins things **2** *US, Can* somebody who demolishes buildings or dismantles old cars and ships

wren /ren/ *n* **1** a small brown songbird **2 Wren** a member of the WRNS

Wren /ren/, **Sir Christopher** (1632–1723) English architect, scientist, and mathematician

wrench /rench/ *v* **1** *vti* pull and twist something away **2** *vt* injure a part of your body by twisting it ■ *n* **1** a forceful twisting pull **2** an adjustable spanner **3** a feeling of sadness and loss ○ *Leaving Liverpool was a terrible wrench after having lived there for 20 years.* **4** a sprain caused by twisting

wrest /rest/ *vt* **1** take control or power from somebody **2** pull something away forcibly **3** get something with effort ■ *n* a forceful pull

wrestle /réss'l/ (**-tling, -tled**) *v* **1** *vti* fight or participate in the sport of wrestling **2** *vti* have a struggling fight with somebody **3** *vi* struggle to do or deal with something ○ *spent the evening wrestling with his accounts* —**wrestle** *n* —**wrestler** *n*

wrestling /réssling/ *n* a sport in which contestants fight by gripping and throwing

wretch /rech/ *n* **1** somebody who is pitied **2** an annoying person *(humorous)* ◇ See note at **retch**

wretched /réchid/ *adj* **1** unhappy or ill **2** appearing miserable or deprived **3** inadequate or of low quality **4** causing annoyance ○ *The wretched car won't start.* —**wretchedly** *adv* —**wretchedness** *n*

Wrexham /réksəm/ town in NE Wales. Pop. 40,614 (1991).

wriggle /rigg'l/ (**-gling, -gled**) *v* **1** *vti* twist and turn **2** *vi* move while twisting and turning —**wriggle** *n* —**wriggly** *adj*

□ **wriggle out of** *vt* avoid doing or suffering the consequences of something

Wright /rīt/, **Frank Lloyd** (1867–1959) US architect

Wright, Judith Arundell (*b.* 1915) Australian poet

Wilbur (right) and Orville Wright

Wright Brothers, Wilbur (1867–1912) and his brother **Orville** (1871–1948) US inventors and aviation pioneers who made the first successful flight of a powered aircraft (1903)

wring /ring/ *vt* (**wrung** /rung/, **wrung**) **1** twist and compress something in order to force liquid out **2** force liquid out of something by wringing it **3** extract something with difficulty ○ *finally managed to wring an answer out of him* **4** twist something forcibly and painfully ■ *n* an act of wringing something wet ◇ See note at **ring**

wringer /ríngər/ *n* a device used to squeeze water out of wet washing ◇ **put through the wringer** subject to a very stressful experience *(infml)*

wrinkle /ríngk'l/ *n* **1** a facial line caused by ageing **2** a small fold in material **3** a problem **4** an ingenious new feature *(infml)* ○ *We've added a couple of new wrinkles to the policy.* ■ *vti* (**-kling, -kled**) make wrinkles in something, or develop wrinkles —**wrinkled** *adj* —**wrinkly** *adj*

wrist /rist/ *n* the joint that connects the hand to the arm

wristband /ríst band/ *n* **1** a band worn round the wrist, e.g. for identification or to absorb sweat **2** a watch strap **3** the part of a garment that fits round the wrist

wrist support, wrist rest *n* a rest for a keyboarder's wrists

wristwatch /ríst woch/ *n* a watch worn on the wrist

writ /rit/ *n* a written court order

write /rīt/ (**writing** /ríting/, **wrote** /rōt/, **written** /ritt'n/) *v* **1** *vti* put letters or numbers on a surface using a pen, pencil, or similar implement **2** *vti* create a book, poem, play, or piece of music, or other material for publication or performance **3** *vti* compose and send a letter **4** *vt* fill in a cheque or other official form **5** *vt* say something in writing ○ *wrote that she would be back next week* **6** *vt* spell something ○ *two words that are written the same but mean different things* **7** *vi* work as a writing tool ○ *This pen won't write.* **8** *vt* display a quality ○ *guilt written all over his face* **9** *vt* store computer data

ORIGIN The notion underlying **write** is of 'cutting' or 'scratching'. The earliest form of writing involved cutting marks on hard materials such as stone and wood, and the same word was carried over when the technique of writing moved on to pen and ink.

□ **write in** v **1** vt write details on a form **2** vi write to an organization

□ **write off** v **1** vi write to an organization **2** vt decide that somebody or something is worthless (infml) **3** vt damage a vehicle so badly that it is uneconomic to repair it **4** vt reduce the value of an asset for accounting purposes **5** vt remove a bad debt or valueless asset

□ **write out** vt **1** write something in its complete form **2** remove a character from a television or radio series

□ **write up** vt **1** write something in a complete form from earlier notes **2** write a review of something

write-down n a reduction in the value of an asset for accounting purposes

~~writeing~~ incorrect spelling of **writing**

~~writen~~ incorrect spelling of **written**

write-off n **1** a vehicle that is damaged beyond repair **2** a reduction in the value of a business asset

write-protected adj describes a computer disk that cannot be altered or erased

writer /rítər/ n **1** somebody who writes books, articles, or similar material as a profession **2** the person who wrote a specific text or document **3** somebody with a particular style of handwriting or use of language

writer's block n a situation in which a writer lacks inspiration and cannot write

writer's cramp n a muscular spasm in the wrist

write-up n a review of a performance, book, or recording

writhe /ríth/ (**writhing, writhed**) vi **1** twist or squirm **2** experience a strong emotion such as embarrassment

writing /ríting/ n **1** words or symbols that have been written down **2** written material such as books and poems **3** the activity or profession of a writer **4** handwriting ■ **writings** npl somebody's written output ○ Churchill's writings on the war ◇ **the writing on the wall** an omen that signals an unpleasant outcome

writing desk n a desk for writing at

writing paper n paper for writing on

written past participle of **write**

~~writting~~ incorrect spelling of **writing**

Wrocław /vrót slaaf, -swaaf/ city in SW Poland. Pop. 639,400 (1997).

wrong /rong/ adj **1** incorrect ○ the wrong answer **2** having a mistaken opinion ○ I thought it would be fun, but I was wrong. **3** not the intended or desired one ○ sent to the wrong address **4** not in a normal state ○ What's wrong with you today? **5** not conforming to accepted moral standards ○ Stealing is wrong. **6** unsuitable ○ the wrong time of year to be planting seeds **7** not functioning properly ○ Something's wrong with the TV. **8** describes the side of a fabric that is not intended to be seen ■ adv **1** incorrectly **2** in the wrong direction or a wrong manner ■ n **1** an action or situation that is not considered moral or just **2** unacceptable behaviour ■ vt **1** treat somebody unjustly ○ felt he had been wronged **2** discredit somebody —**wrongly** adv —**wrongness** n

wrongdoing /róng doo ing/ n behaviour that is considered wrong —**wrongdoer** n

wrong-foot vt **1** catch somebody unawares **2** catch an opponent off balance

wrongful /róngf'l/ adj **1** unlawful **2** unjust —**wrongfully** adv —**wrongfulness** n ◊ See note at **unlawful**

wrong-headed adj **1** irrational ○ a wrong-headed notion **2** obstinately unreasonable —**wrong-headedly** adv —**wrong-headedness** n

wrote past tense of **write**

wrought /rawt/ past tense, past participle of **work** (archaic) ■ adj **1** made carefully or decoratively (often in combination) **2** describes decorative metalwork shaped by hammering

---

USAGE Wrought is a rare past tense and past participle not of wreak (for which the past tense is wreaked) but of work, though worked is the common, modern past tense of this verb. **Wrought** is seen only in specialized contexts such as wrought iron. Wrought havoc is not correct; it should be wreaked havoc.

---

wrought iron n a refined form of iron that is strong but easy to shape. Use: decorative metalwork. —**wrought-iron** adj

wrought-up, wrought up adj in a nervous state

wrung past tense, past participle of **wring**

WRVS abbr Women's Royal Voluntary Service

wry /rī/ (**wrier** or **wryer, wriest** or **wryest**) adj **1** amusing and ironic **2** expressing ironic acceptance of something unpleasant ○ a wry grin **3** twisted out of shape —**wryly** adv —**wryness** n

wt abbr weight

WTO abbr World Trade Organization

Wuhan /woo hán/ capital of **Hubei Province**, in central China. Pop. 4,250,000 (1995).

wunderkind /wúndər kind, vo'ondər-/ (pl **-kinds** or **-kinder** /-kindər/) n **1** a young successful person **2** a child prodigy

Wuppertal /voʻoppər taal/ city in NW Germany. Pop. 383,776 (1997).

wuss /woʻoss/ n an offensive term for somebody regarded as weak or ineffectual (slang insult) —**wussy** adj

WWF abbr **1** World Wide Fund for Nature **2** World Wrestling Federation

WWW abbr World Wide Web

Wycliffe /wíklif/, **John** (1330?–84) English philosopher and religious reformer —**Wycliffite** n, adj

Wyoming /wī óming/ state of the NW United States. Cap. Cheyenne. Pop. 493,782 (2000). —**Wyomingite** n

WYSIWYG /wízzi wig/ adj printing out as shown on a computer screen. Full form **what you see is what you get**

X

x[1] (*pl* **x's**), **X** (*pl* **X's** *or* **Xs**) *n* **1** the 24th letter of the English alphabet **2** an X-shaped mark used for indicating a vote, showing that something is incorrect, representing a kiss, or representing a signature by somebody who cannot write **3** the Roman numeral for 10

x[2] *symbol* **1** used to represent an unknown **2** by *(used when giving dimensions)* **3** multiplied by

X *adj* describing a film with adult content in a former classification system. Now called **18**

Xavier /závvi ər, záyvi ər/, **St Francis** (1506–52) Spanish missionary in India, Japan, and parts of Southeast Asia

X-certificate *adj* containing explicitly sexual or violent material

X chromosome *n* a chromosome that is present in both sexes and is paired with another X chromosome in females

xenon /zée'n on, zén-/ *n* (*symbol* **Xe**) a colourless gaseous chemical element. Use: electronic tubes, specialized lamps.

xenophobe /zénnəfōb/ *n* somebody who fears or dislikes foreigners —**xenophobia** /zénnə fóbi ə/ *n* —**xenophobic** /-fóbik/ *adj*

Xenophon /zénnəfən/ (430?–355? BC) Greek historian and soldier

Xerox /zeer roks/ *tdmk* a trademark for a photocopying process

Xerxes I /zúrk seez/ (519?–465 BC) king of Persia (486–465 BC)

Xhosa /kóssə, káwssə/ (*pl same or* -**sas**), **Xosa** *n* **1** a member of a South African people **2** the language of the Xhosa people —**Xhosa** *adj*

xi /zī, sī, ksī, ksee/ (*pl* **xis**) *n* the 14th letter of the Greek alphabet

Xiamen /shyaá mén/ seaport in SE China, on **Xiamen Island** in the Taiwan Strait. Pop. 357,290 (1991).

Xi'an /shyaan/ capital of **Shaanxi Province**, N China. Pop. 2,970,000 (1995).

Xi Jiang /sheé jyáng/ river in S China, rising in Yunnan Province and flowing eastward to the South China Sea. Length 2,100 km/1,300 mi.

Xizang /sheé dzáng/ Chinese name for **Tibet**

XL *abbr* extra large *(clothing size)*

Xmas /kríssməss, éksməss/ *n* Christmas *(infml)*

XML *n* a programming language designed for web documents. Full form **Extensible Markup Language**

Xmodem /éks mō dem/ *n* a computer file transfer protocol for asynchronous communications

Xosa *n*, *adj* PEOPLES, LANG = **Xhosa**

X-rated *adj* containing explicitly sexual or violent material

X-ray, x-ray *n* **1** a high-energy electromagnetic radiation **2** a photographic image made using X-rays **3** a communications code word for the letter 'X' ■ *vt* photograph or examine with X-rays —**X-radiation** *n*

xylem /zílǝm, -lem/ *n* plant tissue that carries water and dissolved minerals

xylophone /zílǝfōn/ *n* a percussion instrument consisting of a row of wooden bars that are struck with soft hammers —**xylophonist** /zī lóffǝnist/ *n*

Y

y[1] (*pl* **y's**), **Y** (*pl* **Y's** *or* **Ys**) *n* the 25th letter of the English alphabet

y[2] *abbr* year

Y[1] *symbol* yttrium

Y[2] *abbr* **1** yen **2** yuan

-y *suffix* **1** consisting of or characterized by o *muddy* **2** somewhat, like o *chilly* **3** a condition, state, or quality o *infamy* **4** an activity, or a place for an activity o *cannery* **5** = **-ie**

yacht /yot/ *n* **1** a sailing boat with living quarters **2** a motorboat for cruising ■ *vi* sail in a yacht —**yachting** *n* —**yachtsman** *n* —**yachtswoman** *n*

yahoo /yaa hoó, yə-, yaá hoo/ (*pl* -**hoos**) *n* somebody regarded as loud or unruly *(infml insult)* —**yahooism** *n*

ORIGIN The original **yahoos** were brutish creatures resembling human beings in Jonathan Swift's *Gulliver's Travels* (1726).

Yahweh /yaá way/, **Yahveh** /-vay/ *n* a Hebrew name for God

yak[1] (*pl* **yaks** *or same*) *n* a large long-haired ox

yak[2] *(infml)* *vi* (**yakking**, **yakked**) chatter continuously ■ *n* continuous chatter

yakka /yákə/, **yakker** /yákər/, **yacker** *n ANZ* work *(infml)*

Yalta /yáltə, yóltə/ resort city in S Ukraine, on the Black Sea, site of an Allied conference in 1945 between Joseph Stalin, Franklin Roosevelt, and Winston Churchill. Pop. 115,548 (1993).

Yalu /yaá loo/ river in East Asia, forming most of the boundary between North Korea and China. Length 790 km/490 mi.

yam *n* **1** a root vegetable that looks like a potato **2** the tropical plant that produces yams

ORIGIN Yam 'sweet potato' came, most immediately, from the Portuguese word *inhame* or the obsolete Spanish term *iñame*, from Portuguese and English Creole *nyam* 'to eat', of West African origin.

yammer /yámmər/ *vi* talk loudly and at length *(infml)*

Yamoussoukro /yámmoo soókrō/ capital of Côte d'Ivoire. Pop. 120,000 (1990).

Yamuna /júmnə/, **Jumna** river in N India flowing south into the River Ganges. Length 1,400 km/870 mi.

yang /yang/, **Yang** n the masculine element in Chinese philosophy

Yangon /yang gón/ capital of Myanmar. Pop. 3,873,000 (1995).

Yangtze /yáng tsee, -see/, **Yangzi** longest river in China, rising in the Kunlun Mountains and flowing southwards and then eastwards to the East China Sea. Length 6,300 km/3,900 mi.

yank v 1 vti pull sharply 2 vt remove somebody or something swiftly ■ n a sharp pull ◊ See note at **pull**

Yank n somebody from the United States (infml; sometimes offensive)

Yankee /yángki/ n 1 somebody from the United States (infml) 2 a communications code word for the letter 'Y' —**Yankeedom** n

ORIGIN Yankee is recorded in North America in the late 17C as a nickname for a Dutchman, and probably represents the Dutch *Janke*, a form of the common name *Jan*. In the mid-18C it began to be used for an inhabitant of New England (where there were many Dutch settlers), and later for people from any of the northern states. Outside the United States, it was adopted from the late 18C as a general term for an American.

Yaoundé /yaa oõnd ay/ capital of Cameroon. Pop. 1,000,000 (1997).

yap vi (**yapping**, **yapped**) 1 make a high barking sound 2 chatter annoyingly (infml) ■ n a short high-pitched bark —**yapper** n —**yappy** adj

yard¹ n 1 an imperial unit of length equal to 0.9144 m/3 ft 2 a spar that supports a sail

yard² n 1 an enclosed paved piece of land 2 US, Can the land around a house 3 an area used for a particular business or activity (often in combination) 4 a railway storage area 5 a livestock enclosure

yardage /yaárdij/ n measurement in yards, or an amount measured in yards

yardarm /yaárd aarm/ n an end of a yard used to support a sail

Yardie /yaárdi/ n a member of a Jamaican criminal group

yardstick /yaárd stik/ n 1 a yard-long measuring stick 2 a standard of comparison

yarmulke /yaármoõlkə/ n a skullcap for Jewish men and boys

yarn n 1 a continuous twisted strand of wool, cotton, or synthetic fibre. Use: knitting, weaving. 2 a long story (infml)

yarrow /yárrō/ (pl **-rows** or same) n a plant with flat heads of small flowers

yashmak /yásh mak/ n a veil covering the face except for the eyes worn by some Muslim women in public

yaw vti 1 go or cause to go off course 2 turn around a vertical axis 3 zigzag or cause to zigzag —**yaw** n

yawl n 1 a sailing ship with a large mainmast and a smaller mizzenmast towards the stern 2 a ship's rowing boat

yawn vi 1 open the mouth wide to take a deep breath because of tiredness 2 be a wide open space in front of somebody or something ■ n an act of yawning —**yawningly** adv

yaws n an infectious tropical disease that causes red sores and joint swelling (+ sing or pl verb)

Yb symbol ytterbium

Y chromosome n a sex chromosome that is present in males only

yd abbr yard

ye pron plural of **thou** (archaic or regional)

yea /yay/ (archaic) adv, n yes ■ adv indeed

Yeager /yáygər/, **Chuck** (b. 1923) US aviator. He was the first person to fly faster than the speed of sound.

yeah /yaa, yair/ adv, interj 1 yes (infml) 2 expresses scepticism (infml)

year /yeer, yur/ n 1 a 12-month period from January 1 to December 31 2 a 12-month period from any date 3 the time taken for the Earth or another planet to orbit the Sun 4 the time occupied by a particular activity within a twelve-month period ○ the academic year ■ **years** npl 1 a long time (infml) 2 age ○ too much activity for a man of his years 3 time in general ○ in years to come ◊ **year in, year out** over a long period of time (infml)

yearbook /yeĕr boŏk, yúr-/ n 1 an annual record of events within a specific field of activity 2 a book that commemorates a school year

yearling /yeérling, yúr-/ n 1 an animal between the ages of one and two 2 a one-year-old racehorse

yearlong /yeĕr lóng, yúr-/ adj lasting a whole year

yearly /yeérli, yúrli/ adj 1 annual 2 of one year ■ adv 1 once a year 2 per year

yearn /yurn/ vi 1 have a longing 2 feel affection or compassion —**yearningly** adv ◊ See note at **want**

yearning /yúrning/ n a longing

year-round adj existing or lasting throughout the year ■ adv throughout the year

yeast /yeest/ n 1 a small single-celled fungus 2 a commercial preparation of yeast cells. Use: brewing, baking, food supplement. —**yeasty** adj

yeast extract n a sticky brown food eaten as a spread

Barnaby's

William Butler Yeats

Yeats /yayts/, **William Butler** (1865–1939) Irish poet and dramatist yeild incorrect spelling of **yield**

Yekaterinburg /ye kátta reen burg/ city in central Russia. Pop. 1,398,774 (1995).

yell *vti* shout loudly ■ *n* a loud cry

yellow /yéllō/ *adj* 1 of the colour of butter 2 cowardly (insult) ■ *n* the colour of butter ■ *vti* make or become yellow —**yellowish** *adj* —**yellowness** *n* —**yellowy** *adj*

yellow card *n* in football, a card that a referee shows when cautioning a player

yellow fever *n* an infectious viral disease transmitted by mosquitoes

yellowhammer /yéllō hamər/ *n* a songbird, the male of which has a bright yellow head, neck, and breast

Yellowknife /yéllō nīf/ capital of the Northwest Territories, Canada. Pop. 17,275 (1996).

yellow line *n* a road marking that indicates parking restrictions

Yellow Pages *tdmk* a trademark for a telephone directory printed on yellow paper and containing the telephone numbers of businesses and other organizations arranged by category

Yellow River ♦ Huang He

Yellow Sea arm of the Pacific Ocean between NE China and the Korean Peninsula. It merges with the East China Sea to the south. Chinese **Huang Hai**

Yellowstone National Park /yéllō stōn-/ the world's first national park, established in 1872 in parts of Wyoming, Montana, and Idaho

yelp *v* 1 *vi* bark or cry sharply 2 *vt* say something with a yelping sound ■ *n* a short bark or cry

Yeltsin /yéltsin/, **Boris** (*b*. 1931) Russian president (1991–99)

Yemen /yémmən/ country on the S Arabian Peninsula, bordering the Red Sea and the Gulf of Aden. Cap. Sana'a. Pop. 18,078,035 (2001). —**Yemeni** *n*, *adj*

yen[1] (*pl same*) *n* the main unit of Japanese currency

yen[2] *n* a yearning ■ *vi* (**yenning, yenned**) have a yearning

Yenisey /yénni sáy/ river in central Siberian Russia, rising in S Siberia and flowing northwards into the Kara Sea. Length 4,090 km/2,540 mi.

yeoman /yṓmən/ *n* (*pl* -**men** /-mən/) 1 a signals officer in the Royal Navy or the Marines 2 a farmer with a small freehold, especially a member of a former class of such farmers in England 3 an attendant to a member of the nobility or royalty 4 *also* **yeoman of the guard** a member of a British royal guard who perform ceremonial duties ■ *adj* performed diligently

yeomanry /yṓmənri/ *n* 1 a former social class consisting of small freeholder farmers 2 a former British cavalry force

Yerevan /yérrə vaán/ capital of Armenia. Pop. 1,305,000 (1995).

yes *adv*, *interj* 1 indicates assent or agreement o *'Are we agreed on the plan?' 'Yes'.* 2 indicates contradiction o *Oh yes you will!* 3 indicates a readiness to pay attention o *'Doctor?' 'Yes?'* ■ *n* (*pl* **yeses** or **yesses**) 1 an affirmative response o *if we get a yes from the planning committee* 2 somebody who votes in the affirmative

yeshiva /yə sheévə/, **yeshivah** *n* a school at which Jewish students study the Talmud

yes-man *n* somebody who unquestioningly agrees with a superior

yesterday /yéstərday, -di/ *n* 1 the day before today 2 the past ■ *adv* 1 on the day before today 2 in the past

yesteryear /yéstər yeer, -yur/ *n* 1 the past 2 last year (*literary*)

yet *adv* 1 so far (*often with a negative or interrogative*) o *The information has not yet been analysed.* 2 now (*often with a negative*) o *I can't come just yet.* 3 even or still (*often with a comparative*) o *yet greater efforts* 4 in spite of everything o *We'll solve this problem yet.* 5 up to now o *the largest study yet* 6 indicates a time in the future o *It won't be finished for hours yet.* o *They have yet to give us their decision.* ■ *conj* nevertheless o *Her problems are increasing, yet she keeps smiling.*

yeti /yétti/ (*pl* -**tis**) *n* a humanoid said to live in the Himalaya range

Yevtushenko /yévtə shéngkō/, **Yevgeny Aleksandrovich** (*b*. 1933) Russian poet

yew *n* 1 a poisonous evergreen tree 2 the fine-grained wood of a yew

YHA *abbr* Youth Hostels Association

Yiddish /yíddish/ *n* a language based on German and written in Hebrew —**Yiddish** *adj*

yield /yeeld/ *v* 1 *vt* produce something naturally 2 *vt* produce something as a result 3 *vt* give a profit or a return on an investment 4 *vi* stop resisting or opposing something or somebody 5 *vt* give something up to somebody else o *yielded control of the company to his daughter* 6 *vi* move, bend, or collapse under pressure 7 *vi* be replaced by something else o *Old homes in the area finally yielded to modern purpose-built flats.* ■ *n* 1 an amount, e.g. of a crop, that is produced 2 a return on an investment —**yielding** *adj* —**yieldingly** *adv*

SYNONYMS yield, capitulate, submit, succumb, surrender CORE MEANING: give in

yikes *interj* expresses surprise (*infml*)

yin, Yin *n* the feminine element in Chinese philosophy

YMCA *abbr* Young Men's Christian Association

Ymodem /wí mō dem/ *n* a variation of the Xmodem computer file transfer protocol

yo *interj* used as a greeting (*slang*)

yob, yobbo /yóbbō/ *n* a hooligan (*infml*) —**yobbery** *n* —**yobbish** *adj*

yodel /yṓd'l/ *vi* (-**delling, -delled**) sing in a high voice that rapidly switches in and out of falsetto ■ *n* a yodelling song —**yodeller** *n*

yoga /yṓgə/ *n* **1** in Hinduism, a discipline that promotes spiritual unity with the divine **2** a system of physical exercises based on those used in the Hindu yoga

yoghurt /yóggərt, yṓgərt/, **yogurt** *n* a thick fermented milk product

yogi /yṓgi/ (*pl* **-gis**) *n* **1** a yoga practitioner **2** a student of a Hindu guru

yoke /yṓk/ *n* **1** a wooden frame for harnessing two draught animals together, or a pair of animals so harnessed **2** a frame placed on the shoulders for carrying loads **3** something oppressive or restrictive **4** a fitted part of a garment around the shoulders or waist **5** something that bonds people together **6** *Ireland, N Ireland* a whatsit or thingumabob ■ *vt* (**yoking, yoked**) **1** fit animals with a yoke **2** link things together

> **SPELLCHECK** Do not confuse the spelling of **yoke** and **yolk** ('yellow part of an egg'), which sound similar.

yokel /yṓk'l/ *n* an offensive term for somebody from a rural area who is regarded as unsophisticated (*insult*) —**yokelish** *adj*

Yokohama /yṓkō haámə/ port of SE Honshu Island, Japan. Pop. 3,375,772 (2000).

yolk /yṓk/ *n* the yellow part of an egg —**yolky** *adj* ◊ See note at **yoke**

Yom Arafat /yom árrə fat/ *n* an Islamic festival of prayer. Date: 9th day of Dhu al-Hijjah.

Yom Kippur /yom kíppər, -ki pòŏr/ *n* the holiest day of the Jewish calendar, marked by fasting and prayer. Date: 10th day of Tishri.

yon *adv* yonder ○ *wandered hither and yon* ■ *det N England, Scotland* that or those

yonder /yóndər/ (*regional*) *adv* over there ■ *det* that

Yonkers /yóngkərz/ city in SE New York State. Pop. 190,153 (1998).

yonks *n* a long time (*infml*)

yoo-hoo /yoŏ hoo/ *interj* hello

yore *n* bygone days (*literary*)

York /yawrk/ historic city in N England. Pop. 175,095 (1996).

Yorkshire /yáwrkshər/ former county in N England

Yorkshire pudding *n* a batter pudding served with roast meat

Yoruba /yórrŏŏbə/ (*pl same or* **-bas**) *n* **1** a member of a West African people **2** a West African language —**Yoruba** *adj* —**Yoruban** *adj*

Yosemite Falls /yə sémməti-, yō-/ waterfall in the Yosemite National Park. Height 739 m/2,245 ft.

Yosemite National Park national park in central California

you (*stressed*) /yoo/ (*unstressed*) /yoŏ, yə/ *pron* **1** the person or people being addressed **2** an unspecified person, or people in general ○ *then you mix them all together*

you'd *contr* **1** you had **2** you would

you'll *contr* **1** you shall **2** you will

young /yung/ *adj* **1** not very old **2** of somebody's youth ○ *my younger days* **3** youthful ○ *very young for her age* **4** for young people ○ *young fashions* **5** recently begun ○ *The night is still young.* ■ *npl* **1** offspring ○ *watching her young* **2** young people ○ *a club for the young* —**youngish** *adj*

Young /yung/, **Brigham** (1801–77) US religious leader, 2nd president of the Church of Jesus Christ of Latter-Day Saints (1844–77)

young offender *n* a juvenile criminal

youngster /yúngstər/ *n* a child or young person ◊ See note at **youth**

your (*stressed*) /yawr, yoor/ (*unstressed*) /yər/ *det* **1** belonging to the person or people spoken to ○ *What's your phone number?* **2** belonging or relating to an unspecified person ○ *the house on your left* **3** indicates somebody or something as an example or topic (*infml*) ○ *Take your Queen, for example.* ○ *your typical local park*

> **USAGE your** or **you're**? The word **your** is a possessive adjective, used before a noun (*Your* [not *You're*] *e-mail password must be protected*), whereas **you're** is a contraction of 'you are' (*You're* [not *Your*] *responsible for protecting your e-mail password*).

you're (*stressed*) /yoor, yawr/ (*unstressed*) /yər/ *contr* you are ◊ See note at **your**

yours /yawrz, yoorz/ *pron* **1** refers to something belonging to the person or people addressed **2** *also* **Yours** a letter ending ○ *Yours, John Smith*

yourself /yawr sélf, yoor-, yər-/ *pron* **1** refers to the person or people being addressed ○ *Don't hurt yourself.* **2** adds emphasis when addressing somebody or a group of people ○ *How would you yourself deal with that?* **3** your normal self ○ *You're just not yourself tonight.*

youth /yooth/ *n* **1** the time when somebody is young **2** the state of being young **3** a young man ■ *npl* young people

> **SYNONYMS youth, child, kid, teenager, youngster** CORE MEANING: somebody who is young

youth club *n* an activity centre for young people

youthful /yoŏthf'l/ *adj* **1** of or typical of young people **2** vigorous and energetic **3** not fully developed —**youthfully** *adv* —**youthfulness** *n*

youth hostel *n* an establishment offering inexpensive accommodation for young people

you've /yoov/ *contr* you have

yowl /yowl/ *vi* cry out mournfully or in pain —**yowl** *n*

yo-yo /yṓ yō/ *n* (*pl* **yo-yos**) **1** a toy consisting of a spool that can be dropped and raised again using the string wound round it **2** something that is constantly fluctuating ■ *vi* (**yo-yos, yo-yoing, yo-yoed**) fluctuate

yo-yo dieting *n* the repeated losing and regaining of weight

Ypres /eèprə/ town in SW Belgium, site of several major battles of World War I. Pop. 35,409 (1995).

yr *abbr* year

ytterbium /i túrbi əm/ *n* (*symbol* **Yb**) a rare metallic chemical element. Use: strengthening steel, in laser devices and portable X-ray machines. —**ytterbic** *adj*

> **ORIGIN Ytterbium** is named after Ytterby, a quarry in Sweden where *ytterbite*, a mineral containing the element, was found.

yttrium /íttri əm/ *n* (*symbol* **Y**) a rare metallic chemical element. Use: superconductive alloys, permanent magnets. —**yttric** *adj*

yuan /yoo án/ (*pl same*) *n* the main unit of Chinese currency

Yucatán /yóokə taán/ peninsula in E Central America, comprising three Mexican states, Belize, and part of N Guatemala

yucca /yúkə/ *n* an evergreen flowering plant with sharp lance-shaped leaves

yuck, yuk *interj* expresses disgust (*infml*)

yucky /yúki/ (**-ier, -iest**) *adj* unpleasant (*infml*) —**yuckiness** *n*

Yugoslavia /yóogō slaávi ə/ country in SE Europe, consisting of Serbia and Montenegro. Cap. Belgrade. Pop. 11,206,039 (1998). —**Yugoslav** /yóogō slaav/ *n, adj* —**Yugoslavian** *adj, n*

Yukon /yóok on/ river in NW North America, rising in S Yukon Territory, Canada, and flowing through Alaska to the Bering Sea. Length 3,190 km/1,980 mi.

Yukon Territory territory in NW Canada. Cap. Whitehorse. Pop. 30,663 (2000).

Yule /yool/, **yule** *n* Christmas (*literary*)

yule log *n* a log traditionally burned on Christmas Eve

Yuletide /yóol tīd/ *n* the Christmas season

yummy /yúmmi/ (**-mier, -miest**) *adj* delicious (*infml*) —**yumminess** *n*

Yupik /yóopik/ (*pl same or* **-piks**) *n* a member of an aboriginal people of W Alaska and parts of coastal Siberia —**Yupik** *adj*

yuppie /yúppi/ *n* a young professional citydweller regarded as materialistic (*disapproving*)

> **ORIGIN Yuppie** was formed from the initial letters of 'young urban professional', extended on the model of *hippie*. It first appeared in print in 1984 in the title of *The Yuppie Handbook*.

yuppify /yúppi fī/ (**-fies, -fied**) *vt* populate with yuppies (*disapproving*) —**yuppification** /yúppifi káysh'n/ *n*

yurt *n* a circular Asian tent made of animal skins

YWCA *abbr* Young Women's Christian Association

Z

z (*pl* **z's**), **Z** (*pl* **Z's** *or* **Zs**) *n* the 26th and final letter of the English alphabet

Z *symbol* impedance

Zagreb /záa greb/ capital of Croatia. Pop. 706,770 (1991).

zaibatsu /zī bátsoo/ (*pl same*) *n* a large Japanese industrial combine

Zaire /zī éer, zaa-/ **1** former name for **Congo, Democratic Republic of the 2** former name for **Congo, Republic of the** —**Zairean** *adj*

zakat /zə kaát/ *n* an Islamic tax for charity

Zambezi /zam beézi/ river in southern Africa, flowing through Zambia, Angola, Botswana, Zimbabwe, and Mozambique to the Indian Ocean. Length 2,650 km/1,650 mi.

Zambia /zámbi ə/ country in south-central Africa. Cap. Lusaka. Pop. 9,770,199 (2001). —**Zambian** *n, adj*

zany /záyni/ *adj* (**-nier, -niest**) amusingly unconventional ■ *n* (*pl* **-nies**) a clown —**zanily** *adv* —**zaniness** *n*

> **ORIGIN Zany** came via French from the name of a character in traditional Italian comedy who tried to imitate the antics of the clown. It derives from a dialect form of the Italian man's name *Gianni*, a form of *Giovanni*. The earliest uses in English are as a noun, referring to a comic performer, a mimic, or a buffoon. An adjectival use is recorded from the early 17C, but the modern sense 'amusingly unconventional' does not appear until the 19C.

Zanzibar /zánzi baar/ island of Tanzania, in the Indian Ocean. Pop. 456,934 (1995).

zap (**zapping, zapped**) *v* (*infml*) **1** *vt* destroy **2** *vi* change television channels using a remote control **3** *vt* cook in a microwave

Zaragoza /sárrə góssə/ capital of **Zaragoza Province** in the autonomous region of Aragon, NE Spain. Pop. 603,367 (1998).

Zarathustra ♦ **Zoroaster**

zeal /zeel/ *n* enthusiasm, especially for a cause

zealot /zéllət/ *n* a zealous follower, especially of a religious movement —**zealotry** *n*

zealous /zélləss/ *adj* full of zeal —**zealously** *adv* —**zealousness** *n*

zebra /zébbrə, zeébrə/ *n* a striped mammal that resembles a horse —**zebrine** /zéb rīn, zeéb-/ *adj*

zebra crossing *n* a pedestrian crossing marked by white stripes in the road

zed *n* the letter 'Z'

Zeitgeist /zīt gīst, tsīt-/ *n* the ideas and spirit of a specific time and place

Zeman /zémmən/, **Milos** (*b.* 1944) prime minister of the Czech Republic (1998–)

Zen, Zen Buddhism *n* a form of Buddhism that developed in China

zenith /zénnith/ n 1 the highest point reached by an astronomical object 2 the most successful or exciting point —**zenithal** adj

Zeno of Citium /zeenō uv síshee əm/ (fl late 4C–early 3C BC) Greek philosopher

Zeno of Elea /-eéli ə/ (fl 5C BC) Greek mathematician and philosopher

zephyr /zéffər/ n 1 a mild wind 2 a delicate fabric or garment

zeppelin /zéppəlin/ n a cylindrical airship

zero /zeérō/ n (pl -ros or -roes) 1 the numerical symbol 0 2 the number 0 3 the starting point for values on a gauge 4 the temperature indicated by 0 5 the lowest possible point o *Her spirits are at zero.* ■ vt (-roing, -roed) set a gauge or other instrument to zero ■ adj 1 amounting to zero o *zero growth* 2 minimal (infml) o *had zero confidence*
□ **zero in** vi 1 locate a target and aim at it 2 identify something and concentrate on it o *The report zeroed in on the weaknesses in the current policy.*

zero hour n 1 the scheduled starting time of a military operation 2 the time when something important will occur

zero option n the offer to limit the number of nuclear weapons held if another nation makes the same offer

zero-rate vt UK, Can charge no value added tax on —**zero-rated** adj —**zero rating** n

zero tolerance n the complete absence of leniency, especially in dealing with antisocial behaviour

zest n 1 hearty enjoyment 2 an exciting element that adds to enjoyment 3 citrus peel used as a flavouring —**zestful** adj —**zestfully** adv —**zesty** adj

zeta /zeétə/ n the 6th letter of the Greek alphabet

Zeus /zyooss/ n in Greek mythology, the king of the gods

Zhengzhou /júng jố/ capital of Henan Province, E China, on the Huang He. Pop. 1,990,000 (1995).

Zhou Enlai /jố ən líˈ/ (1898–1976) premier of the People's Republic of China (1949–75)

Zia /zeè ə/, **Khaleda** (b. 1945) prime minister of Bangladesh (1991–96 and 2001–)

zigzag /zíg zag/ n 1 a line that takes alternating turns 2 something that repeatedly switches direction sharply ■ adv in sharply alternating directions ■ v (-zagging, -zagged) 1 vi proceed in a path with alternating sharp turns 2 vt make the pattern of a zigzag on

zilch pron nothing (infml) o *took all the money and left us with zilch*

ORIGIN The origin of **zilch** is not known. It first appeared as a generalized surname in the early 1930s ('Mr Zilch', etc.). The earliest recorded use in the sense 'nothing' dates from 1966.

zillion /zíllyən/ n a huge number of people or things (infml) —**zillion** det

Zimbabwe /zim baábwi, -way/ country in southern Africa. Cap. Harare. Pop. 11,365,366 (2001). —**Zimbabwean** n, adj

zinc n (symbol Zn) a bluish metallic chemical element. Use: in alloys, protective corrosion-resistant metal coatings. ■ vt (**zincing** or **zincking**, **zinced** or **zincked**) coat with zinc

zindabad /zíndə bad/ S Asia interj expresses loud enthusiasm ■ n a loud shout of enthusiasm

zine /zeen/ n a paper, Internet magazine, or other periodical for a specialist readership, published by the author (infml)

zing n 1 a short high-pitched humming sound 2 a lively and exciting quality (infml) —**zingy** adj

~~**zink**~~ incorrect spelling of **zinc**

Zionism /zí ənizəm/ n the worldwide movement that seeks to maintain and further develop the Jewish state of Israel —**Zionist** adj, n

zip[1] n 1 a fastener with interlocking teeth 2 a lively, exciting quality (infml) 3 a brief whizzing sound ■ v (**zipping**, **zipped**) 1 vti fasten with a zip 2 vti go or move very fast (infml) 3 vt compress a computer file

zip[2] abbr a file extension indicating a compressed file

ZIP Code tdmk US a trademark for a mail delivery system using a set of numbers to identify a postal district

zip file n a compressed computer file

zippy /zíppi/ (-pier, -piest) adj (infml) 1 energetic 2 accelerating quickly

zip-up adj closing with a zip

zircon /zúr kon/ n a hard mineral containing zirconium. Use: source of zirconium, gems.

zirconium /zur kốni əm/ n (symbol Zr) a greyish-white metallic chemical element. Use: coating nuclear reactor fuel rods. —**zirconic** /-kónnik/ adj

zit n a pimple on the skin (slang) —**zitty** adj

zither /zíthər/ n a flat box-shaped stringed instrument —**zitherist** n

zloty /zlótti/ (pl -ties or same) n the main unit of currency in Poland

Zn symbol zinc

zodiac /zṓdi ak/ n 1 an astrologically significant part of the sky, divided into 12 sections 2 an astrologer's chart linking the zodiac to 12 divisions of the year —**zodiacal** /zō dí ək'l/ adj

Zola /zṓlə/, **Émile** (1840–1902) French novelist

zombie /zómbi/ n 1 an offensive term for somebody regarded as lacking energy or responsiveness (infml insult) 2 a corpse supposedly given life by voodoo 3 a voodoo spirit that supposedly revives a corpse —**zombify** vt

zonal /zṓn'l/, **zonary** /zṓnəri/ adj 1 of zones 2 split into zones —**zonally** adv

zone /zōn/ n 1 a separate area with a specific function 2 a subsection of an area 3 a horizontal climatic band around the Earth 4 an area distinguished from others, e.g. by its plants and animals or by a standard time

■ *vti* (**zoning**, **zoned**) **1** split something into zones **2** designate an area for a particular purpose —**zoning** *n*

□ **zone out** *vi US* lose your concentration or fall asleep *(slang)*

zonked /zongkt/, **zonked out** *adj* not conscious, alert, or energetic *(slang)*

zoo (*pl* **zoos**) *n* **1** *also* **zoological garden** a park that displays live animals in enclosures **2** a chaotic place *(infml)*

zookeeper /zoo keepər/ *n* somebody who looks after zoo animals

zoology /zō óllǝji, zoo-/ (*pl* -**gies**) *n* **1** the scientific study of animals **2** the animal life of a specific region —**zoological** /zō ǝ lójjik'l, zoó-/ *adj* —**zoologist** *n*

zoom *v* **1** *vi* make a loud buzzing noise **2** *vi* move speedily **3** *vi* increase suddenly **4** *vti* climb steeply through the air, or make an aircraft climb steeply **5** *vi* simulate movement towards or away from an object with a camera lens that allows various focal lengths ■ *n* **1** a loud buzzing noise **2** *also* **zoom lens** a camera lens assembly that allows various focal lengths

Zoroaster /zórrō ástǝr/, **Zarathustra** /zárrǝ thoóstrǝ/ (630?–550? BC) Persian prophet

Zoroastrianism /zórrō ástri ǝnizǝm/ *n* an ancient Persian religion centred on belief in a supreme deity and the struggle between good and evil —**Zoroastrian** *n*, *adj*

Zr *symbol* zirconium

zucchini /zoo keéni/ (*pl same or* -**nis**) *n Aus, US, Can* **1** a courgette **2** the plant that produces courgettes

~~zuchini~~ incorrect spelling of **zucchini**

Zulu /zoóloo/ (*pl same or* -**lus**) *n* **1** a member of a South African people **2** the Bantu language of the Zulu people **3** a communications code word for the letter 'Z' —**Zulu** *adj*

Zululand /zoóloo land/ historic region in South Africa

Zurich /zyoórik, zoórik/ largest city in Switzerland, in the north of the country. Pop. 336,821 (1998).

Zurich, Lake lake in N Switzerland

zwieback /zweè bak/ *n* a type of rich sweet bread baked hard

Zwingli /zwínglee/, **Huldreich** (1484–1531) Swiss religious reformer

zydeco /zídikō/ *n* popular music of S Louisiana, a mix of Caribbean tunes, French dance music, and blues

zygote /zígōt/ *n* a fertilized ovum —**zygotic** /zī góttik/ *adj*